In celebration of the diverse cultures represented in Kirszner & Mandell's third edition of *Literature: Reading, Reacting, Writing*, textile artist Greta Vaught designed this quilt.

1 *Indian Twilight*	5 *Oriental Wave*
2 *South American Sunset*	6 *African Ravine*
3 *European Fan*	7 *Canadian Wind*
4 *American Blossom*	8 *Asian Fields*

LITERATURE

READING ◆ REACTING ◆ WRITING

Third Edition

LITERATURE
READING ◆ REACTING ◆ WRITING

Third Edition

Laurie G. Kirszner

Philadelphia College of Pharmacy and Science

Stephen R. Mandell

Drexel University

Harcourt Brace College Publishers

Fort Worth   Philadelphia   San Diego   New York   Orlando   Austin   San Antonio
Toronto   Montreal   London   Sydney   Tokyo

Publisher	Christopher P. Klein
Executive Editor	Michael Rosenberg
Senior Developmental Editor	Camille Adkins
Project Editor	Barbara Moreland
Project Manager	Publications Development Company
Senior Production Manager	Kathleen Ferguson
Art Director	Melinda Welch
Cover Artwork by	Greta Vaught

ISBN 0-15-503622-X

Library of Congress Catalog Card Number 96-75432

Address editorial correspondence to: 301 Commerce St., Suite 3700, Fort Worth, TX 76102

Address orders to: 6277 Sea Harbor Dr., Orlando, FL 32887. 1-800-782-4479 (outside Florida) or 1-800-433-0001 (inside Florida)

Acknowledgments begin on page 2065.

Printed in the United States of America

6 7 8 9 0 1 2 3 4 5   069   9 8 7 6 5 4 3 2 1

Harcourt Brace College Publishers may provide complimentary instructional aids and supplements or supplement packages to those adopters qualified under our adoption policy. Please contact your sales representative for more information. If as an adopter or potential user you receive supplements you do not need, please return them to your sales representative or send them to:

Attn: Returns Department
Troy Warehouse
465 South Lincoln Drive
Troy, MO 63379

Preface

When we began the process of choosing readings for the first edition of *Literature: Reading, Reacting, Writing,* our goal was to move away from the predictability of traditional literature anthologies. During our work on the second and third editions, we became even more committed to the belief that a literature anthology should take chances. Today, although we continue to recognize the value of including many established favorite writers and works—students and teachers like and expect to see them, and their familiarity makes them good starting points for introducing students to literature—we also include works that represent a varied assortment of cultures and viewpoints. We believe that all of us have been enriched by this expansion. Accordingly, we continue to showcase these diverse voices from many regions and ethnic backgrounds as well as the voices of younger writers whose reputations are still developing.

As we write this preface to the third edition in mid-1996, "expanding the canon" has become something of a cliché; even the most traditional literary anthologies are careful to acknowledge the trend toward inclusiveness. However, many anthologies are still reluctant to look too different; therefore, they tend to include works that are new only to their text, not to the canon, choosing only "safe" writers whose works have been anthologized frequently. Alternatively, editors may limit the number of new works to a sprinkling, or even relegate "nontraditional" or "contemporary" works to separate sections of the text. Our practice is to place such works where they belong, alongside the "classics": to integrate new with old, familiar with unfamiliar, inviting students simultaneously to discover new works and to see familiar works in new contexts. Thus, our goal in this anthology remains what it has been from the start: not just to expand the literary canon, but also to expand the personal canons of both students and instructors.

In order to further this purpose in the third edition, we have fine-tuned the reading selections in response to thoughtful comments from users of the second edition. In fiction, we have added stories ranging from perennial favorites ("Miss Brill," "Eveline," "The Story of an Hour") to provocative stories by established minority writers (Ann Petry's "Like a Winding Sheet," Richard Wright's "Big Black Good Man") to works anthologized for the first time (Sherman Alexie's "This Is What It Means to Say Phoenix, Arizona," Sandra Cisneros's "Mericans"). In the poetry section as well we have deleted some selections and added others, with additions ranging from works by classic poets like Robert Frost, Emily Dickinson, and Matthew Arnold to song lyrics by Jerry Garcia and Bob Marley. The third edition also includes a new section, *Poets' Corner*, which offers biographies and photographs of seventy-five of the poets represented in the text. (Author photographs now also accompany many stories and all plays.) Finally, the third edition offers four new plays: William Shakespeare's *Much Ado about Nothing*, Sam Shepard's *True West*, Beth Henley's *Crimes of the Heart*, and August Wilson's *Fences*.

We feel confident that the changes we have made reflect our own vision of what we want this book to be as well as what instructors have told us they want it to be. To meet their needs, and the needs of their students, we have worked hard to achieve a compatible mix of ideas and literary styles, and we have continued to offer students many opportunities to write about literature and to see its relevance to their own experiences.

To introduce students to some of the complex issues involved in the study of literature, we begin our text with a chapter called "Understanding Literature." After surveying traditional literary themes, we summarize the reasons why many students of literature believe that the traditional canon needs to be revised. We then discuss the processes of interpreting and evaluating literature, placing special emphasis on how readers' personal experiences affect meaning. Finally, we examine the role of literary criticism and consider how it can offer students perspectives that can help them to expand their literary horizons.

Fulfilling its commitment to emphasizing writing about literature, the text now includes eight student papers, five of which are source-based (the other three are accompanied by drafts). To help students to see writing about literature as a process of exploring and testing ideas, of growing into a point of view or critical stance, and of participating in an ongoing critical debate, we include writing instruction not as an afterthought, tucked away in an appendix or scattered in a few polished sample student papers, but in four full chapters that examine the writing process as it applies to literature.

In Chapter 2 we discuss concepts familiar to composition teachers and students of writing—gathering and arranging ideas, drafting, and so on—and explain and illustrate how to apply these concepts to writing about literature. Then, within each of the text's three major sections, we narrow our focus to follow the progress of a student as he or she moves through the process of writing in response to literary works: Alberto Alvaro Ríos's story "The Secret Lion" (p. 43); two poems, Robert Hayden's "Those Winter Sundays" and Seamus Heaney's "Digging" (p. 646); and Susan Glaspell's play *Trifles* (p. 1171). We believe that these chapters will encourage students to explore the literary works in this anthology with confidence and creativity.

Although the student essays-in-progress do not make use of critical sources, we recognize that many literary essays, including those assigned in introductory literature courses, do. For this reason, we have assembled three separate casebooks, one each for fiction, poetry, and drama. In these three casebooks we include articles by literary critics as well as biographical and critical material from a variety of sources. The casebooks are designed to supplement students' reading of Joyce Carol Oates's story "Where Are You Going, Where Have You Been?", of a selection of poems by Gwendolyn Brooks, and Tennessee Williams's play *The Glass Menagerie* (new to this edition). Students can use the material in these casebooks to supplement their reading or to do a complete research project. To illustrate to students how they can use the casebooks in their own writing, we include a source-based student paper at the end of each casebook. By collecting research materials in a convenient format, these casebooks offer students a controlled, self-contained introduction to source-based writing, encouraging them to write thoughtful critical essays on works by the writers represented—and, eventually, on other works as well.

Other features in this anthology are designed to enhance and strengthen the text's emphasis on reading and writing about literary works. Each of the eighteen chapters based on an element of literature (plot, setting, point of view, etc.) contains a checklist of questions designed to help students generate, explore, focus, and organize ideas for writing about works of literature in relation to one or more literary elements. In addition, a glossary of literary terms, with definitions cross-referenced to fuller explanations and examples in the text, provides the student writer with an accessible reference tool. The text also includes three appendices. Appendix A, "Documenting Sources," explains and illustrates the most up-to-date information on MLA documentation style (including how to document electronic sources) and contains two new source-based student papers. One, on Eudora Welty's "A Worn Path," uses conventional print sources; the other, on John Updike's "A&P," uses a variety of electronic sources, including an E-mail communication and a newspaper article accessed through the Internet. In addition, each paper cites a filmed interview with the story's author. These original films ("A Worn Path" and "A&P") are available through your local Harcourt Brace representative. Appendix B, "Literary History: Aristotle to the Twentieth Century," and Appendix C, "Twentieth-Century Literary Theories," provide a context for the articles in the casebooks as well as useful information for students' own critical writing.

Throughout the text, reading and reacting questions, including suggestions for journal entries, follow many selections, and writing suggestions are included at the end of each chapter. The reading and reacting questions ask students to interpret and evaluate what they have read, with many of the journal entries encouraging students to make connections—between two works, between two genres, between two themes, or between a given work and their own lives and experiences.

New to the third edition are two features designed to introduce students to the voices of literary critics. Most chapters now open with a collection of quotations pertaining to the chapter's focus—point of view, imagery, staging, and so on. These provocative quotations offer an accessible introduction to literary criticism, inviting students to begin each chapter by actively engaging in an informal dialogue with critics from a variety of backgrounds and historical periods. In addition, a critical perspective question is now included in most sets of reading and reacting questions. This feature asks students to respond to an analytical, interpretative, or evaluative comment a critic has made about the work being considered, thus encouraging students to apply their own critical thinking skills not just to a particular literary work but also to literary criticism of that work.

Each of the features described above is designed to serve the text's dual goals: to encourage students both to appreciate works representing diverse literary subjects, styles, and perspectives and to recognize their own roles in bringing these diverse works into their personal literary canons by reading, reacting to, and writing about them. If this anthology can encourage students to respond spontaneously and enthusiastically to what they read and to see their responses as involving them in an ongoing and stimulating (if sometimes unpredictable) dialogue—with their peers, with critics, with their instructors, with themselves, and with the work itself—then we will have accomplished our purpose.

To assist users of *Literature: Reading, Reacting, Writing,* Third Edition, the following ancillary materials are available from Harcourt Brace:

Instructor's Resource Guide (print version)—discussion and activities for every story, poem, and play in the anthology; thematic table of contents; semester and quarter syllabi; articles on evolution of the literary canon and reader-response theory.

Instructor's Resource Guide (electronic version)—available in Macintosh, Windows, and DOS. This electronic version of the Instructor's Resource Guide provides all the information in the print version with the additional feature of allowing instructors to add their own material.

The Harcourt Brace Casebook Series in Literature—seven additional casebooks, including John Updike's "A&P," Eudora Welty's "A Worn Path," Charlotte Perkins Gilman's "The Yellow Wall-Paper," ten poems by Emily Dickinson, five poems by Langston Hughes, Athol Fugard's *"Master Harold"* . . . *and the Boys,* and William Shakespeare's *Hamlet.* Each casebook presents literary text(s), a variety of source material, an extensive bibliography of print and electronic references, an introduction to MLA documentation, and a sample student paper.

Student Writing Supplement—a collection of student writing from users of *Literature: Reading, Reacting, Writing* to be used as model papers and/or revision exercises.

The Harcourt Brace Original Film Series in Literature—film adaptations of Eudora Welty's "A Worn Path" and John Updike's "A&P."

Each film lasts 30 minutes or less and includes an interview with the author.

Additional Videos—thirteen videos, including eleven adaptations of plays in the Third Edition and videos for all the casebooks.

From start to finish, this text has been a true collaboration for us, not only with each other, but also with our students and colleagues. We have worked hard on the book, and many people at Harcourt Brace have worked along with us. As always, the credit for the endless day-to-day coordination of people and pages goes to our smart, funny, and incredibly patient development editor, Camille Adkins. Michael Rosenberg, Executive Editor, has (as usual) worked hard to make good things happen, and Nancy Land of Publications Development Company has again brought her team's skill to the book's production. In addition, we have been fortunate to work once again with Mark Gallaher, who contributed his creativity, his research skills, and his first-rate instincts to helping us develop the new critical features of the text. We are also grateful to users of the Second Edition who contributed biographies for Poets' Corner—Ellen Arl, University of South Carolina–Sumter; Scott Douglass, Chattanooga State Technical Community College; Joan Reeves, Northeast Alabama State Junior College; and David Zucker, Quinnipiac College—and to Laura Zaidman, University of South Carolina–Sumter, not only for contributing biographies to this section but also for coordinating and unifying all 75 entries. We also thank Odeana Kramer and Abby Bardi of St. George's Community College for their work on the revision of the Instructor's Resource Guide.

We would like to thank all the reviewers who made valuable contributions through several drafts of the text: Ben Accardi, University of Kansas; Thomas Bailey, Western Michigan University; John Bails, University of Sioux Falls, Leigh Boyd, Temple Junior College; Cathy Cowan, Cabrillo College; Pat Cowart, Frostburg State University; Kitty Dean, Nassau Community College; Jo Devine, University of Alaska–Southeast; Jack Doyle, University of South Carolina at Sumter; Lynn Fauth, Oxnard College; David Fear, Valencia Community College; Mary Fleming, Jackson State Community College; Ann Fogg, University of Maine; Wayne Gilbert, Community College of Aurora; Shain Graham, Orange Coast College; Linda Gruber, Kishwaukee College; Chris Hacskaylo, University of Alaska–Ketchikan; Richard Hascal, Contra Costa College; Gwen Hauk, Temple Junior College; Michael Herzog, Gonzaga University; Andrew Kelly, Jackson State Community College; Benna Kime, Jackson State Community College; Amy Sparks Kolker, University of Kansas; Michael Kraus, Marian College of Fond du Lac; Heidi Ledett, Ulster County Community College; Teri Maddox, Jackson State Community College; Jeanne Mauzy, Valencia Community College; Fred Milley, Anderson University; Robert Milliken, University of Southern Maine; Andrew Moody, University of Kansas; Paul Perry, Palo Alto Community College; Angela Rapkin, Manatee Community College; Jean Reynolds, Polk Community College; Ellen Robbins, Ulster

County Community College; Paul Rogalus, Plymouth State College, Neil Sebacher, Valencia Community College; Larry Severeid, College of Eastern Utah; Sharon Small, Des Moines Area Community College; Virginia Streamer, Dundalk Community College; Robert Temple, Manatee Community College; Margie Whelan, Mt. San Antonio College; Mike White, Odessa College; Rebecca Yancey, Jackson State Community College; Donnie Yielding, Central Texas College; and Martha Zamorano, Miami Dade–Kendall Campus.

Reviewers of the second edition were Deborah Barberbousse, Horry-Georgetown Technical College; Bob Mayberry, University of Nevada Las Vegas; Shireen Carroll, University of Miami; Stephen Wright, Seminole Community College; Robert Dees, Orange Coast College; Larry Gray, Southeastern Louisiana University; Nancy Rayl, Cypress College; James Clemmer, Austin Peay State University; Roberta Kramer, Nassau Community College.

Reviewers of the first edition included Anne Agee, Anne Arundel Community College; Lucien Agosta, California State University, Sacramento; Diana Austin, University of New Brunswick; Judith Bechtel, Northern Kentucky University; Laureen Belmont, North Idaho College; Vivian Brown, Laredo Junior College; Rebecca Butler, Dalton Junior College; Susan Coffey, Central Virginia Community College; Douglas Crowell, Texas Tech University; Shirley Ann Curtis, Polk Community College; Kitty Dean, Nassau Community College; Robert Dees, Orange Coast College; Joyce Dempsey, Arkansas Tech University; Mindy Doyle, Orange County Community College; James Egan, University of Akron; Susan Fenyves, University of North Carolina, Charlotte; Marvin Garrett, University of Cincinnati; Ann Gebhard, State University of New York, Cortland; Emma Givaltney, Arkansas Tech University; Corrinne Hales, California State University, Fresno; Gary Hall, North Harris County College; Iris Hart, Santa Fe Community College; James Helvey, Davidson County Community College; Chris Henson, California State University, Fresno; Gloria Hochstein, University of Wisconsin, Eau Claire; Angela Ingram, Southwest Texas State University; John Iorio, University of South Florida; George Ives, North Idaho College; Lavinia Jennings, University of North Carolina, Chapel Hill; Judy Kidd, North Carolina State University; Leonard Leff, Oklahoma State University; Michael Matthews, Tarrant County Junior College, Northeast; Craig McLuckie, Okanagan College; Candy Meier, Des Moines Area Community College; Judith Michna, DeKalb College, North; Christopher O'Hearn, Los Angeles Harbor College; James O'Neil, Edison Community College; Melissa Pennell, University of Lowell; Sam Phillips, Gaston College; Robbie Pinter, Belmont College; Joseph Sternberg, Harper College; Kathleen Tickner, Brevard Community College; Betty Wells, Central Virginia Community College; Susan Yaeger, Monroe Business Institute.

We would also like to thank our families—Mark, Adam, and Rebecca Kirszner and Demi, David, and Sarah Mandell—for being there when we needed them. And finally, we each thank the person on the other side of the ampersand for making our collaboration work one more time.

Brief Contents

Detailed Contents

Fiction

Chapter 8   Style, Tone, and Language 241

Chapter 9   Symbol and Allegory 291

CHAPTER 10   THEME 336

Interpreting Themes 338

Identifying Themes 339

STORIES FOR FURTHER READING

FICTION CASEBOOK 577

Poetry

CHAPTER 11   UNDERSTANDING POETRY 628

CHAPTER 14   WORD CHOICE, WORD ORDER 706

POEMS FOR FURTHER READING

POETS' CORNER 1034

POETRY CASEBOOK 1071

Drama

CHAPTER 24   STAGING 1569

CHAPTER 25   THEME 1702

CHAPTER 1

Understanding Literature

What Is Literature?

IMAGINATIVE LITERATURE

Imaginative literature begins with a writer's need to convey a personal vision to readers. Even when writers use factual material—historical documents, newspaper stories, personal experience—their primary purpose is to give a unique view of experience, one that has significance beyond the moment. (As the poet Ezra Pound said, "Literature is the news that *stays* news.") To convey their views of experience, writers of imaginative literature often manipulate facts—change dates, invent characters, and create dialogue. For example, when the nineteenth-century American author Herman Melville wrote his novella *Benito Cereno,* he drew many of his facts from an eighteenth-century account of an actual slave revolt. In his story he reproduces court records and plot details from this primary source, but he leaves out many incidents, and he adds material of his own. The result is an original work of literature that serves the author's purpose. Wanting to do more than tell the original story, Melville used the factual material as "a skeleton of actual reality" upon which to build a story that attacks the institution of slavery and examines the nature of truth.

Imaginative literature is more likely than other types of writing to include words chosen not only because they communicate the writer's ideas, but also because they are memorable. Using vivid imagery and evocative comparisons, writers of imaginative literature can strive to stretch language to its limits. By relying on the multiple connotations of words and images, a work of imaginative literature can suggest many possible interpretations. Thus, imaginative literature encourages readers to see the possibilities of language and to move beyond the factual details of an event. Consider, for example, how William Wordsworth uses language in the following lines from his poem "Composed upon Westminster Bridge, September 3, 1802" (p. 1026).

> This City now doth, like a garment, wear
> The beauty of the morning; silent, bare,
> Ships, towers, domes, theatres, and temples lie
> Open unto the fields, and to the sky;
> 5   All bright and glittering in the smokeless air.

Notice that Wordsworth does not try to present a picture of London that is topographically or sociologically accurate. Instead, by comparing the city at dawn to a person wearing a beautiful garment, Wordsworth creates a striking picture that has its own kind of truth, one that enables readers to participate in the speaker's imaginative experience. The city, traditionally the antithesis of nature, is "open unto the fields, and to the sky" and is therefore a part of nature. By using a vivid, original comparison, the poet is able to suggest the unity of the city, nature, and himself—an idea that is not easily communicated.

Even though imaginative literature can be divided into types called **genres**—fiction, poetry, and drama—the nature of literary genres varies from culture to culture. In fact, some literary forms that Western readers take for granted are alien to other literary traditions. For example, the poetic forms of non-Western literature are quite different from those of Western Europe and North America. The sonnet, although fairly common in the West, is not a conventional literary form in Chinese or Arabic poetry. Similarly, the most popular theatrical entertainment in Japan since the mid-seventeenth century, the kabuki play, has no exact counterpart in the West. In a kabuki play, which includes stories, scenes, dances, music, acrobatics, and elaborate costumes and stage settings, all of the actors are men, some of whom play the parts of females. Many of the kabuki plays have little plot and seem to be primarily concerned with spectacle. One feature of this form of drama is a walkway that extends from the stage through the audience to the back of the theater.

Finally, conventions of narrative organization and character development can vary considerably, especially in literature descended from an oral tradition. For example, narrative organization in some Native American stories (and, even more commonly, in some African stories) can be very different from what contemporary Western readers are accustomed to. Events may be arranged spatially instead of chronologically: First a story presents all the events that happened in one place, then it presents everything that happened in another location, and so on. Character development is also much less important in some traditional African and Native American stories than in modern short fiction. In fact, a character's name, description, and personality can change dramatically (and without warning) during the course of a story.

Despite such differences, the imaginative literature of all cultures can have similar effects on readers. A short story, a play, or a poem can arrest readers' attention and cause them to marvel. Memorable characters, vivid descriptions, imaginative use of language, and intricately developed plots can fascinate and delight readers. Finally, literature can take readers where they have never been before and, in so doing, can create a sense of wonder and adventure.

At another level, however, readers can find more than just pleasure or escape in literature. Beyond transporting readers out of their lives and times, literature can enable readers to see their lives and times more clearly. Whether a work of imaginative literature depicts a young girl as she experiences the disillusionment of adulthood for the first time, as in David Michael Kaplan's "Doe Season" (p. 342), or examines the effect of discrimination on a black African who is looking for an apartment, as in Wole Soyinka's "Telephone Conversation" (p. 7), it can enlighten readers and help them to understand their own experiences and the experiences of others. In this sense, literature offers readers increased insight and awareness. As the Chilean poet Pablo Neruda said, works of imaginative literature fulfill "the most ancient rites of our conscience in the awareness of being human and of believing in a common destiny."

CONVENTIONAL THEMES

The **theme** of a work of literature is its central or dominant idea. This idea is seldom stated explicitly; rather, it is conveyed through the selection and arrangement of details, through the emphasis of certain words, events, or images, and through the actions and reactions of the characters.

Although one central theme may dominate a literary work, most works explore a number of different themes or ideas. For example, the central theme of Mark Twain's *The Adventures of Huckleberry Finn* might be the idea that an individual's innate sense of right and wrong is superior to society's artificial and sometimes unnatural values. The main character, Huck, gains a growing awareness of this idea by witnessing feuds, duels, and all manner of human folly. As a result he makes a decision to help his friend Jim escape from slavery despite the fact that society, as well as his own conscience, condemns this action. However, *The Adventures of Huckleberry Finn* also examines other themes. Throughout his novel Twain criticizes many of the ideas that prevailed in the pre–Civil War South, such as the racism and religious hypocrisy that pervaded the towns along the Mississippi.

A literary work can explore any theme, but certain themes have recurred so frequently that they have become conventions. These themes express ideas that have meaning to many individuals, regardless of the time or place in which they live. One theme frequently explored in literature, a character's loss of innocence, appears in the biblical story of Adam and Eve and later finds its way into works such as Nathaniel Hawthorne's 1835 short story "Young Goodman Brown" (p. 298) and James Joyce's 1914 short story "Araby" (p. 249). Another conventional theme—the conflict between an individual's values and the values of society—is examined in the ancient Greek play *Antigone*, by Sophocles (p. 1708). Almost two thousand years later Norwegian playwright Henrik Ibsen deals with the same theme in *A Doll House* (p. 1185).

Other themes frequently examined in literary works include the individual's quest for spiritual enlightenment, the *carpe diem* ("seize the day") theme, the making of the artist, the nostalgia for a vanished past, the disillusionment of adulthood, the pain of love, the struggle of women for equality, the conflict between parents and children, the clash between civilization and the wilderness, the evils of unchecked ambition, the inevitability of fate, the impact of the past on the present, the conflict between human beings and machines, and the tension between the ideal and the actual realms of experience. Modern works of literature sometimes treat such traditional themes in new ways. For example, in *1984* George Orwell explores the negative consequences of unchecked power by creating a nightmare world in which technology controls and dehumanizes a population. Even though Orwell's novel is set in an imaginary future (it was written in 1948), its theme echoes ideas frequently examined in the plays of both Sophocles and Shakespeare.

Nearly every culture explores themes similar to those just mentioned, but writers from different cultures may develop these themes differently. A culture's history, a particular region's geography, or a country's social structure can suggest unique ways of developing conventional themes. In addition, the assumptions, concerns, values, ideals, and beliefs of a particular country or society—or of a particular group within that society—can help to determine the themes writers choose to explore and the manner in which they do so.

Themes occurring repeatedly in American literature include the loss of innocence, rites of passage, childhood epiphanies, and the ability (or inability) to form relationships. American writers of color, in addition to exploring these themes, also develop themes that reflect their unique perspectives. African-American and Latino writers, for example, may express their frustration with racism in the dominant society or celebrate their cultural identities. Even when they explore conventional themes, writers of color in America may choose to do so in the context of their own experience. For example, the theme of loss of innocence may be presented as a first encounter with racial prejudice; a conflict between the individual and society may be presented as a conflict between a minority view and the values of the dominant group; and the theme of failure or aborted relationships may be explored in a work about language difficulties or cultural misunderstandings.

THE LITERARY CANON

Originally the term *canon* referred to the authoritative or accepted list of books that made up the Christian Bible. Recently, the term **literary canon** has come to denote a group of works generally agreed upon by writers, teachers, and critics to be worth reading and studying. Over the years, as standards have changed, the definition of what is "good" literature has also changed, and the literary canon has been modified accordingly. For example, at various times, critics have characterized Shakespeare's plays as either mundane, immoral, commonplace, or brilliant. The eighteenth-century critic Samuel Johnson said of Shakespeare that "in his comick scenes he is seldom very successful" and in tragedy "his performance seems constantly to be worse, as his labor is more." Many people find it difficult to believe that a writer whose name today is synonymous with great literature could ever have been judged so harshly. But like all aesthetic works, the plays of Shakespeare affect individuals in different periods of history or in different societies in different ways.

Lately, educators and literary scholars have charged that the traditional literary canon, like a restricted club, admits some authors and excludes all others. This fact is borne out, they say, by an examination of the literature curriculum that until recently was found at many North American colleges and universities. This curriculum typically began with Homer, Plato, Dante, and Chaucer, progressed to Shakespeare, Milton, the eighteenth-century novel, the Romantics, and the Victorians, and ended with some of the classics of modern British and American literature. Most of the authors of these works are white and male, and their writing reflects only Western values. In educational institutions in other countries, the situation has been much the same: Students have typically studied works that reflect and reinforce their society's or their country's values.

For many years, literature courses in North American universities overlooked South American, African, and Asian writers. Students of literature were not encouraged to consider the perspectives of women or of Latinos, Native Americans, or other ethnic or racial groups. Now this situation has begun to change. In the United States during the past decade, some universities have sought to expand the traditional canon by including more works by women, people of color, and writers from a variety of cultures. These additions are meant to open up the curriculum and redefine the standards by which literature is judged. By revising and updating the list of works to be studied, critics of the traditional canon believe that we convey the diversity of both American and world cultures as well as expanding the definition of great literature.

Consider the following brief story, "All about Suicide" by Luisa Valenzuela, an Argentinean writer. Not only is it experimental, moving freely in time, bending the facts, and speaking directly to readers, but it also focuses on the political realities of contemporary Argentina. Although ten years ago such a story probably would not have been included in a traditional syllabus at many American universities, today many critics would recognize it as part of a large and growing category of writing that purposely violates standard literary expectations to make its point.

L U I S A   V A L E N Z U E L A

(1938-   )

All about Suicide

(1967)

Translated by Helen Lane

Ismael grabbed the gun and slowly rubbed it across his face. Then he pulled the trigger and there was a shot. Bang. One more person dead in the city. It's getting to be a vice. First he grabbed the revolver that was in a desk drawer, rubbed it gently across his face, put it to his temple, and pulled the trigger. Without saying a word. Bang. Dead.

Let's recapitulate: the office is grand, fit for a minister. The desk is ministerial too, and covered with a glass that must have reflected the scene, the shock. Ismael knew where the gun was, he'd hidden it there himself. So he didn't lose any time, all he had to do was open the right-hand drawer and stick his hand in. Then he got a good hold on it and rubbed it over his face with a certain pleasure before putting it to his temple and pulling the trigger. It was something almost sensual and quite unexpected. He hadn't even had time to think about it. A trivial gesture, and the gun had fired.

There's something missing: Ismael in the bar with a glass in his hand thinking over his future act and its possible consequences.

We must go back farther if we want to get at the truth: Ismael in the cradle crying because his diapers are dirty and nobody is changing him.

5   Not that far.

Ismael in the first grade fighting with a classmate who'll one day become a minister, his friend, a traitor.

No, Ismael in the ministry without being able to tell what he knew, forced to be silent. Ismael in the bar with the glass (his third) in his hand, and the irrevocable decision: better death.

Ismael pushing the revolving door at the entrance to the building, pushing the swinging door leading to the office section, saying good morning to the guard, opening the door of his office. Once in his office, seven steps to his desk. Terror, the act of opening the drawer, taking out the revolver, and rubbing it across his face, almost a single gesture and very quick. The act of putting it to his temple and pulling the trigger—another act, immediately following the previous one. Bang. Dead. And Ismael coming out of his office (the other man's office, the minister's) almost relieved, even though he can predict what awaits him.

The Nigerian poet and playwright Wole Soyinka is another writer whose works have only recently become part of the expanding literary canon. The subject of the following poem, which is rooted in the context of a society that openly discriminates on the basis of shades of skin color, may not seem "relevant" to European audiences, and the language ("pillar-box," "omnibus") may not be clear to Americans. Still, as a reading of the poem demonstrates, Soyinka's work makes a moving plea for individual rights and self-determination—a theme that transcends limits of time and place.

WOLE SOYINKA

(1934–   )

Telephone Conversation

(1962)

The price seemed reasonable, location
Indifferent. The landlady swore she lived
Off premises. Nothing remained
But self-confession. "Madam," I warned
5 "I hate a wasted journey—I am—African."
Silence. Silenced transmission of
Pressurized good-breeding. Voice, when it came,
Lip-stick coated, long gold-rolled
Cigarette-holder pipped. Caught I was, foully.
10 "HOW DARK?" . . . I had not misheard . . .
    "ARE YOU LIGHT
OR VERY DARK?" Button B. Button A. Stench
Of rancid breath of public-hide-and-speak.
Red booth. Red pillar-box. Red double-tiered
15 Omnibus squelching tar. It *was* real! Shamed
By ill-mannered silence, surrender
Pushed dumbfoundment to beg simplification.
Considerate she was, varying the emphasis—
"ARE YOU DARK? OR VERY LIGHT?" Revelation came.
20 "You mean—like plain or milk chocolate?"
Her assent was clinical, crushing in its light,
Impersonality. Rapidly, wave-length adjusted,
I chose, "West African sepia"—and as an afterthought,
"Down in my passport." Silence for spectroscopic
25 Flight of fancy, till truthfulness clanged her accent
Hard on the mouthpiece. "WHAT'S THAT?" conceding
"DON'T KNOW WHAT THAT IS." "Like brunette."
"THAT'S DARK, ISN'T IT?" "Not altogether.
"Facially, I am brunette, but madam, you should see
30 The rest of me. Palm of my hand, soles of my feet

Are a peroxide blond. Friction, caused—
Foolishly madam—by sitting down, has turned
My bottom raven black—One moment madam!"—sensing
Her receiver rearing on the thunder clap
35   About my ears—"Madam," I pleaded, "Wouldn't you rather
See for yourself?"

Certainly canon revision is not without problems—for example, the possibility of including a work more for political or sociological reasons than for literary merit. Nevertheless, if the debate about the literary canon has accomplished anything, it has revealed that the canon is not fixed and that many works formerly excluded—African-American slave narratives and eighteenth-century women's diaries, for example—deserve to be considered.

This is an exciting time in literary study, and as the debate about the canon continues, new questions will continue to arise. Reflecting the on-going debate, this anthology includes works that are considered part of the traditional canon, as well as others that reflect the diversity of the expanding literary canon.

Thinking Critically

INTERPRETING LITERATURE

When you *interpret* a literary work, you attempt to determine its possible meanings. One commonly held idea about reading a literary work is that its meaning lies buried somewhere within it, waiting to be unearthed. This reasoning suggests that a clever reader has only to discover the author's intent to find out what a story or poem means. The one actual meaning of a work is, therefore, hidden between the lines, unaffected by a reader's experiences or interpretations. More recently, however, a different model of the reading process—one that takes into consideration the reader as well as the work he or she is interpreting—has emerged.

Many contemporary critics recognize that the reading process is *interactive:* Meaning is created through the reader's interaction with a text. The meaning of a particular work comes alive in the imagination of an individual reader, and no reader can determine a work's meaning without considering his or her reaction to the text. Meaning, therefore, is created partly by what is supplied by a work and partly by what is supplied by the reader.

The most obvious kind of meaning a work supplies is factual, the information that enables a reader to follow the plot of a story, the action of a play, or the development of a poem. For instance, the work itself will provide some factual details about the setting; the characters' names, ages, and appearances; the sequence of events; and the emotions and attitudes of a poem's speaker, a story's narrator, or the characters in a play or story. This factual information cannot be ignored: If a play's stage directions identify its setting as nineteenth-century Norway or the forest of Arden, that is where it is set.

In addition to facts, however, a work also conveys the social, political, class, and gender attitudes of the writer. Thus, a work may have an overt feminist or working-class bias or a subtle political agenda; it may confirm or challenge contemporary attitudes; it may communicate a writer's nostalgia for a vanished past or his or her outrage at a corrupt present; it may take an elitist, distant view of characters and events or present a sympathetic, involved perspective. A reader's understanding of these attitudes will contribute to his or her interpretation of the work.

Finally, a work also contains assumptions about literary conventions. A poet, for example, may have definite ideas about whether a poem should be rhymed or unrhymed or about whether a particular subject is appropriate or inappropriate for poetic treatment. Therefore, a knowledge of the literary conventions of a particular period or the preferences of a particular writer may provide a starting point for your interpretation of literature.

As a reader you also bring to a work your own personal perspectives. Your experiences, your ideas about the issues discussed in the work, and your assumptions about literature color your interpretations; so do your religious, social, and cultural beliefs. In fact, virtually every literary work has a somewhat different meaning to different people, depending on their age, gender, nationality, political and religious beliefs, ethnic background, social and economic class, education, knowledge, and experiences. Depending on your religious beliefs, for instance, you can react to a passage from the Old Testament as literal truth, symbolic truth, or fiction. Depending on your race, where you live, your biases, and the nature of your experience, a story about racial discrimination can strike you as accurate and realistic, exaggerated and unrealistic, or understated and restrained.

In a sense, then, the process of determining meaning is like a conversation, one in which both you and the text have a voice. Sometimes, by clearly dictating the terms of the discussion, the text determines the direction of the conversation; at other times, by using your knowledge and experience to interpret the text, you dominate. Thus, because every reading of a literary work is actually an interpretation, it is a mistake to look for a single "correct" reading.

The 1923 poem "Stopping by Woods on a Snowy Evening" (p. 936) by the American poet Robert Frost illustrates how a single work can have more than one interpretation. Readers may interpret the poem as being about the inevitability of death; as suggesting that the poet is tired or world weary; or as making a comment about duty and the need to persevere, or about the conflicting pulls of life and art. Beyond these possibilities, readers' own associations of snow with quiet and sadness could lead them to define the mood of the poem as sorrowful or melancholy. Information about Robert Frost's life or his ideas about poetry could add to readers' appreciation of the poem, and they might even develop ideas about the poem that are quite different from the poet's. In fact, on several occasions when he spoke about "Stopping by Woods on a Snowy Evening," Frost himself gave strikingly different, even contradictory, interpretations of the poem, sometimes insisting the poem had no hidden meaning and at other times saying that it required a good deal of explication. Literary critics also disagree about its meaning. When reading a work of literature, then, keep in mind that the meaning of the text is not fixed. Your best strategy is to open yourself up to the text's many possibilities and to explore the full range of your responses.

Although no single reading of a literary work is "correct," some readings are more plausible than others. Like a scientific theory, a literary interpretation must have a basis in fact, and the text supplies the facts against which your interpretations should be judged. For example, after you read Shirley Jackson's "The Lottery" (p. 309), a 1948 short story in which a randomly chosen victim is stoned to death by her neighbors, it would be reasonable for you to conclude that the ceremonial aspects of the lottery suggest a contemporary pagan ritual. Your understanding of what a pagan ritual is, combined with your observation that a number of specific details in the text suggest ancient fertility ceremonies, might lead you to this conclusion. Another possibility is that "The Lottery" provides a commentary on mob psychology. The way characters reinforce one another's violent tendencies lends support to this interpretation. However, the interpretation that the ritual of the lottery is a thinly veiled attack on the death penalty would be difficult to support. Certainly a character in the story is killed, but she is not accused of a crime, nor is she tried or convicted. The killing is random and seemingly without motivation. Still, although seeing the "The Lottery" as a comment on the death penalty may be far-fetched, this interpretation is a good beginning. A second, closer reading of the story will most likely lead you in different directions, allowing you to explore other, more plausible, interpretations.

As you read, do not be afraid to take chances and develop unusual or creative interpretations of a work. A "safe" reading of a work is likely to result in a dull paper that simply states the obvious. An aggressive or "strong" reading of a work—one that challenges generally held assumptions—can raise issues that lead to interesting and intellectually challenging conclusions. Even if your reading differs from established interpretations, you should not assume it has no merit. Your special knowledge of the material discussed in the text—a regional practice, an ethnic custom, an attitude toward gender—may give you a unique perspective from which to view the work. Whatever interpretation you make, be sure that you support it with specific references to the text. If your interpretation is based on your own experiences, explain those experiences and relate them clearly to the work you are discussing. As long as you can make a reasonable case, you have the right (and perhaps the obligation) to present your ideas. By doing so you may provide your fellow students and your instructor with a reading that gives them new insight into the work.

It is important to keep in mind, however, that some interpretations are *not* reasonable. Readers may contribute ideas based on their own perspectives, but they cannot ignore or contradict evidence in the text to suit their own biases. As you read and reread a text, continue to question and reexamine your judgments. The conversation between you and the text should be a dialogue, not a monologue or a shouting match.

EVALUATING LITERATURE

When you *evaluate* a work of literature, you do more than interpret it; you make a judgment about it. You reach conclusions—not simply about whether the work is good or bad, but also about how effectively the work presents itself to you, the reader. To evaluate a work, you *analyze* it, breaking it apart and considering its individual elements. As you evaluate a work of literature, remember that different works are designed to fulfill different needs—for entertainment, education, or enlightenment, for example. Before you begin to evaluate a work, be sure you understand its purpose; then, apply the following guidelines:

Begin your evaluation by considering how various elements function individually within a work.   For instance, fiction may be divided into chapters and use flashbacks and foreshadowing. Plays are divided into scenes and acts and include dialogue and special staging techniques. Poems may be arranged in regularly ordered groups of lines and use poetic devices such as rhyme and meter. Understanding the choices writers make can lead you to insights that can help you make judgments about the work. For example, why does Alberto Alvaro Rios use a first-person narrator (*I* and *we*) in his story "The Secret Lion" (p. 43)? Would the story have been different had it been told in the third person (*they*) by a narrator who was not a participant in the action? How does unusual staging contribute to the effect Edward Albee achieves in his play *The Sandbox* (p. 1695)? How would a realistic setting change the play? Naturally, you cannot focus on every aspect of a particular story, poem, or play. But you can and should focus on those that play a major role in determining your responses to a work. For this reason the unusual stanzaic form in E. E. Cummings's poem "Buffalo Bill's" (p. 911), or the stage directions in Arthur Miller's *Death of a Salesman* (p. 1458) should be of special interest to you.

As you read, then, you should ask questions. Do the characters in a short story seem real, or do they seem like cardboard cutouts? Are the images in a poem original and thought-provoking, or are they clichéd? Are the stage directions of a play sketchy or very detailed? The answers to these questions will help you to shape your response to the work.

As you continue your evaluation, decide whether or not the literary elements of a work interact to achieve a common goal.   Well-crafted literary works are aesthetically pleasing, fitting together in a way that conceals the craft of the writer. Good writers are like master cabinetmakers; their skill disguises the actual work that goes into the process of creation. Consider the following stanza from the 1862 poem "Echo" by Christina Rossetti:

> Come to me in the silence of the night;
>   Come to me in the speaking silence of a dream;
> Come with soft round cheeks and eyes as bright
>   As sunlight on a stream;
> 5   Come back in tears,
> O memory, hope, love of finished years.

Throughout this stanza Rossetti repeats words (<u>Come</u> to me. . . ./<u>Come</u> with soft. . . ./<u>Come</u> back. . . .) and initial consonants (<u>s</u>peaking <u>s</u>ilence/<u>s</u>unlight on a <u>s</u>tream) to create an almost hypnotic mood. The rhyme scheme (*night/bright, dream/stream,* and *tears/years*) reinforces the mood by creating a musical undercurrent that extends throughout the poem. This stanza is effective because its repeated words and sounds work together to create a single lyrical effect.

The chorus in *Antigone* by Sophocles (p. 1708) also illustrates how the elements of a well-crafted work of literature function together. In ancient Greece plays were performed by masked male actors who played both male and female roles. A chorus of fifteen men would remain in a central circle called the *orchestra* and comment on and react to the action taking place around them, thereby contributing to the total effect of *Antigone.* The chorus expresses the moral judgment of the community and acts as a guide for the audience. Once modern audiences grow accustomed to the presence of the chorus, it becomes an integral part of the play. It neither distracts the audience nor intrudes upon the action. In fact, eliminating the chorus would diminish the impact of the play.

Next, consider whether a work reinforces or calls into question your ideas about the world.   The 1985 short story "Gryphon" by Charles Baxter (p. 125) is one that may lead readers to question their assumptions. It presents a boy in a rural town whose sick teacher is replaced by an eccentric substitute. In her idiosyncratic, even exotic, way, the substitute introduces the boy to a whole new range of intellectual possibilities. Because we, like the children in the story, have learned to expect substitute teachers to be dull and conventional, the story challenges our basic assumptions about substitute teachers and, by extension, about education itself.

Works of popular fiction—those aimed at a mass audience—usually do little more than reassure readers that what they believe is correct. Catering to people's prejudices, or to their desires (for wealth or success, for example), or to their fears, these works serve as escapes from life. Serious fiction, however, often goes against the grain, challenging cherished beliefs and leading readers to reexamine long-held assumptions. For instance, in the 1957 short story "Big Black Good Man" (p. 197) Richard Wright's protagonist, a night porter at a hotel, struggles with his consuming yet irrational fear of a "big black" sailor and his inability to see beyond the man's size and color. Only at the end of the story do readers see that they, like the night porter, have stereotyped and dehumanized the sailor.

Then, consider whether or not a work is intellectually challenging. The extended comparison between a draftperson's compass and two people in love in "A Valediction: Forbidding Mourning" by the seventeenth-century English poet John Donne (p. 777) illustrates how an intellectually challenging image can communicate ideas to a reader. Compressed into this comparison are ideas about the perfection of love, the pain of enforced separation, and the difference between sexual and spiritual love. As complex as the extended comparison is, it is nonetheless accessible to the careful reader. After all, many people have used a compass to draw a circle and, therefore, are able to understand the relationship between the two points of the compass and the two lovers.

A fine line exists, however, between works that are intellectually challenging and those that are intellectually obscure. An *intellectually challenging* work makes readers think; it requires some effort on the part of readers to unlock ideas that enrich and expand their understanding of themselves and the world. Although complex, the work gives readers a sense that they have gained something by putting forth the effort to read and interpret it. An *intellectually obscure* work, however, seems to exist solely to display a writer's erudition or intellectual idiosyncrasies. In such works allusions to other works and events are so numerous and confusing that the work seems more like a private code than an effort to communicate with or enlighten readers. Consider the following excerpt from "Canto LXXVI" by the twentieth-century American poet Ezra Pound:

> Le Paradis n'est pas artificiel
> > States of mind are inexplicable to us.
> > δακρύων   δακρύων   δακρύων
> L.   P.   gli onesti
> 5   J'ai eu pitié des autres
> probablement pas assez, and at moments that suited my own
> > convenience
> > > Le paradis n'est pas artificiel,
> > > > l'enfer non plus.
> > Came Eurus as comforter
> 10 and at sunset la pastorella dei suini
> > driving the pigs home, benecomata dea
> > > under the two-winged cloud
> > > as of less and more than a day

This segment contains lines in French, Greek, and Italian; a reference to Eurus, the ancient Greek personification of the east wind; and the initials L.P. (Loomis Pound?). Admittedly this passage demands a lot from readers; the question is whether the reward is worth the effort.

No hard and fast rule exists for determining whether a work is intellectually challenging or simply obscure. Just as a poem has no fixed meaning, it also has no fixed value. Some readers would say that the passage is good, even great, poetry. Others would argue that these lines do not yield enough pleasure and insight to justify the work needed to analyze them. As a careful reader, you must draw your own conclusions and justify them in a clear and reasonable way. Do not assume that just because a work is difficult, it is obscure. (Nor should you assume that all difficult works are great literature or that all accessible literature is trivial.) Some of the most beautiful and inspiring literary works demand a great deal of effort from readers. Most readers would agree, however, that the time spent exploring such works yields tremendous rewards.

Finally, consider whether a work gives you pleasure.   One of the primary reasons that literature endures is that it gives readers enjoyment. As subjective as this assessment is, it is a starting point for critical judgment. When readers ask themselves what they liked about a work, why they liked it, or what they learned, they begin the process of evaluation. Although this process is largely uncritical, it can lead to an involvement with the work and to a critical response. When you encounter great literature, with all its complexities, you may lose sight of the idea of literature as a source of pleasure. But literature should touch you on a deep emotional or intellectual level, and if it does not—despite its technical perfection—it fails to achieve one of its primary aims.

The Function of Literary Criticism

Sometimes your personal reactions and knowledge cannot give you enough insight into a literary work. For example, archaic language, obscure references, historical allusions, and textual inconsistencies can make reading a work particularly difficult. Similarly, an intellectual or philosophical movement such as Darwinism, Marxism, naturalism, structuralism, or feminism may influence a work, and if this is the case, you will need some knowledge of the movement before you can interpret the work (see Appendix C, Twentieth-Century Literary Theories). In addition, you may not have the background to appreciate the technical or historical dimension of a work. To widen the context of your reading, you may choose to read **literary criticism**—books and journal articles written by experts who describe, analyze, interpret, or evaluate a work of literature. Reading literary criticism enables you not only to expand your knowledge of a particular work, but also to participate in the public dialogue about literature. In a sense, you become part of a community of scholars who share their ideas and who are connected to one another through their writing.

Just because literary criticism is written by experts, do not assume you must always automatically accept it. You have to evaluate literary criticism just as you do any new opinion that you encounter. Not all criticism is valid, timely, or responsible (and not all literary criticism is pertinent to your assignment or useful for your purposes). Some critical comments will strike you as plausible, while others will seem unfounded or biased. Quite often two critics will reach strikingly different conclusions about the quality or significance of the same work or writer, or interpret a character, a symbol, or even the entire work quite differently.

The Fiction Casebook that closes this section of the text contains articles in which critics disagree in just this fashion. In "In Fairyland, without a Map: Connie's Exploration Inward in Joyce Carol Oates' 'Where Are You Going, Where Have You Been?'" Gretchen Schulz and R. J. R. Rockwood examine the parallels between a character, Arnold Friend, and a real-life psychopathic killer. They see Arnold in mythological terms and conclude that he is the "exact transpositional counterpart of the real-life Pied Piper of Tucson." In Mike Tierce and John Michael Crafton's "Connie's Tambourine Man: A New Reading of Arnold Friend," however, the authors explicitly reject this suggestion as well as other critical interpretations, concluding instead that "The key question . . . is who is this musical messiah, and the key to the answer is the dedication 'For Bob Dylan.' "

As you can see, critics may disagree, but even conflicting ideas can help you to reach your own conclusions about a work. It is up to you to sort out the various opinions and decide which have merit and which do not. The following questions can help you to evaluate literary criticism:

◆ What is the main point of the critical article you are reading?

◆ Does the critic supply enough examples to support his or her conclusions?

◆ Does the critic acknowledge and refute the most obvious arguments against his or her position?

◆ Does the critic ignore any information in the text that might call his or her conclusions into question?

◆ Does the critic present historical information? Biographical information? Literary information? How does this information shed light on significant aspects of the work or works being discussed?

◆ Does the critic demonstrate any beliefs or prejudices that might interfere with his or her critical judgment?

◆ Does the critic seem to slant the facts, or does he or she offer a fair and objective reading of the text?

◆ Does the critical book or article support its conclusions with documentation? Does it contain a list of works cited? Are these works current?

◆ Do other critics mention the critical book or article you are reading? Do they support or challenge its conclusions?

With your instructor's help, you might also try to answer these questions:

- Does the critic identify with a particular critical school of thought—deconstruction, Marxism, or feminism, for example? What unique perspective does this school of thought provide?

- Is the critic well known and respected or unknown?

- Does the critic take into consideration the most important critical books and articles on his or her subject? Are there works that should have been mentioned that were not? Do these gaps cast doubts on the critic's conclusions?

- Is the critical work's publication date of any significance?

CHAPTER 2

Reading and Writing
about Literature

Reading Literature

The process of writing about literature actually starts the moment you begin to read. At that point you begin interacting with a work and start to discover ideas about it. This process of interacting with the text—**active reading**—helps you to interpret what you read and, eventually, to organize your ideas into a clear and logical paper.

Three strategies in particular will help you to become a more effective reader: *previewing, highlighting,* and *annotating.* As you engage in these activities, remember that reading and responding to what you read is not an orderly process—or even a sequential one. You will most likely find yourself engaging in more than one of the strategies simultaneously—annotating at the same time you highlight, for example. For the sake of clarity, however, we discuss each active reading strategy separately in the pages that follow.

PREVIEWING

The first time you encounter a work you should **preview** it to get a general idea of what to look for later, when you read it more carefully. At the previewing stage you simply want to glance through the work, getting a sense of what it looks like on the page.

Begin with the work's most obvious physical features. For example, how long is a short story? How many acts and scenes does a play have? Is a poem divided into stanzas? The answers to these and similar questions will help you begin to notice more subtle aspects of the work's form. For example, previewing may reveal that a contemporary short story is presented entirely in a question-and-answer format; that it is organized as diary entries, as is Lorrie Moore's "How to Talk to Your Mother (Notes)" (p. 89); or that it is divided into sections by headings. Previewing may identify poems that seem to lack formal structure, such as E. E. Cummings's unconventional "l(a" (p. 634); those written in traditional forms

17

(such as sonnets) or in experimental forms, such as the numbered list of questions and answers in Denise Levertov's "What Were They Like?" (p. 966); or concrete poems such as George Herbert's "Easter Wings" (p. 859). Your awareness of these and other distinctive features may help you gain insight into a work.

Perhaps the most physically distinctive element of a work is its title. Not only can the title give you a general idea of what the work is about, as straightforward titles like "Miss Brill" and "The Lottery" do, but it can also isolate and highlight a word or phrase that is central to the work. For example, the title of Amy Tan's short story "Two Kinds" (p. 553) emphasizes the mother-daughter conflict that is central to the plot, and the title of David Henry Hwang's play *F.O.B.* calls attention to the "fresh off the boat" status of a key character. A title can also be an allusion to another work. Thus, *The Sound and the Fury,* the title of a novel by William Faulkner, alludes to a speech from Shakespeare's *Macbeth* that reinforces the major theme of the novel. Finally, a title can introduce a symbol that will gain meaning in the course of a work—as the concept of a shroud does in Ann Petry's story "Like a Winding Sheet" (p. 117).

Other physical elements—such as paragraphing, capitalization, italics, and punctuation—can also provide clues about how to read a work. In William Faulkner's short story "Barn Burning" (p. 216), for instance, previewing would reveal passages in italic type, indicating the protagonist's thoughts, which occasionally interrupt the narrator's story.

Finally, previewing can identify some of the more obvious stylistic and structural features of a work—the point of view used in a story, how many characters a play has and where it is set, or the repetition of certain words or lines in a poem, for example. Such features may or may not be important; at this stage, your goal is to observe, not to analyze or evaluate.

Previewing is a useful strategy not because it provides answers but because it suggests questions to ask later, as you read more closely. For instance, *why* does Faulkner use italics in "Barn Burning," and *why* does Herbert shape his poem on the page as he does? Remember, while elements such as those described above may be noticeable as you preview, they will gain significance only as you read more carefully and review your notes.

HIGHLIGHTING

When you go on to read a work closely, you will notice additional, sometimes more subtle, elements that you may want to examine further. At this point, you should begin **highlighting**—physically marking the text to identify key details and to note relationships among ideas.

What should you highlight? As you read, ask yourself whether repeated words or phrases form a pattern, as they do in Ernest Hemingway's short story "A Clean, Well-Lighted Place" (p. 256), in which the Spanish word *nada* ("nothing") appears again and again. Because this unusual word appears so frequently, and because it appears at key points in the story, it helps to reinforce the story's theme—that all human experience amounts to *nada,* or nothingness. Repeated words and phrases are particularly important in poetry. In Dylan Thomas's "Do Not Go Gentle into That Good Night" (p. 642), for example, the repetition of two of the poem's nineteen lines four times each enhances the effect of the poem's rhythmic, almost monotonous, cadence. As you read, then, you should highlight your text to identify such repeated words and phrases. Later on, you can consider *why* they are repeated.

During the highlighting stage, you should also pay particular attention to images that occur repeatedly in a work; such repeated images may form patterns that can help you to interpret the work, and for this reason they should be highlighted. When you reread the work, you can begin to determine what pattern the images form and perhaps try to decide how this pattern enhances the work's ideas. When highlighting Robert Frost's "Stopping by Woods on a Snowy Evening" (p. 936), for instance, you might simply identify the poem's related images of silence, cold, and darkness. Later, you can go on to consider their significance.

When you highlight, you call attention to portions of the text with a system of marks and symbols. As you become experienced with the techniques of active reading, you will develop the system of shorthand that works best for you. For the time being, however, you can experiment with some of the following:

- ◆ Underline important ideas that you should read again.
- ◆ Box or circle repeated words, phrases, or images.
- ◆ Put question marks beside confusing passages, unfamiliar references, or words that need to be defined.
- ◆ Draw lines or arrows to connect related ideas or images.
- ◆ Number incidents that occur in sequence.
- ◆ Set off a long portion of the text with a vertical line in the margin.
- ◆ Place stars beside particularly important ideas.

The following poem by Maya Angelou has been highlighted by a student preparing to write about it. Notice how the student uses the marks and symbols described above to help him identify stylistic features, key points, and patterns of repetition that he may want to examine later.

MAYA ANGELOU

(1928–   )

My Arkansas

(1978)

There is a deep brooding
in Arkansas.
Old crimes like moss pend ?
from poplar trees.
5 The sullen earth
is much too
red for comfort.

Sunrise seems to hesitate
and in that second
10 lose its
incandescent aim, and
dusk no more shadows
than the noon.
❋ The past is brighter yet.

15 Old hates and
ante-bellum lace are rent ?
but not discarded.
❋ Today is yet to come
in Arkansas.
20 It writhes. It writhes in awful
waves of brooding.

This student identifies repeated words and phases ("brooding"; "it writhes") and places question marks beside the two words ("pend" and "rent") he plans to look up in a dictionary. He also questions the possible meanings of "old crimes" and "ante-bellum lace," two references he needs to think more about. Finally, he stars what he tentatively identifies as the poem's key ideas. When he rereads the poem, his highlighting will make it easier for him to react to and interpret the writer's ideas.

ANNOTATING

At the same time you highlight a text, you also **annotate** it, making marginal notes on the page. By engaging in this activity, you record your reactions and perhaps begin to map out a preliminary plan for your paper. Your notes may define new words, identify allusions, identify patterns of language or imagery, summarize plot relationships, list a work's possible themes, suggest a character's motivation, or examine the possible significance of particular images or symbols. You may also use annotations to record questions that occur to you as you read.

Many works explore issues that are purposely left unresolved and that you must try to explain. For example, what motivates Sammy to quit his job at the end of John Updike's 1961 short story "A&P" (p. 105)? The following paragraph from "A&P" was highlighted and annotated by a student in an introduction to literature course who was writing an essay in response to this question:

> Lengel sighs and begins to look very patient and old and gray. He's been a friend of my parents for years. "Sammy, you don't want to do this to your Mom and Dad," he tells me. It's true, I don't. But it seems to me that once you begin a gesture it's fatal not to go through with it. I fold the apron, "Sammy" stitched in red on the pocket, and put it on the counter, and drop the bow tie on top of it. The bow tie is theirs, if you've ever wondered. "You'll feel this for the rest of your life," Lengel says, and I know that's true, too, but remembering how he made the pretty girl blush makes me so scrunchy inside I punch the No Sale tab and the machine whirs "pee-pul" and the drawer splats out. One advantage to this scene taking place in summer, I can follow this up with a clean exit, there's no fumbling around getting your coat and galoshes, I just saunter into the electric eye in my white shirt that my mother ironed the night before, and the door heaves itself open, and outside the sunshine is skating around on the asphalt.

[Left margin annotation:] ction es not em to the sult of ought. mmy acts to e girls' barrass ent.

[Annotation above "galoshes":] cowboy-John Wayne

[Annotation below last line:] Romantic cowboy, but his mother irons his shirt. Irony.

[Right margin annotation:] * need for a clean exit—reinforces immature romantic ideas

Because the student's instructor had discussed the story in class and because the student had a specific assignment—to explain Sammy's actions at the end of the story—her annotations are quite focused. In addition to highlighting important information, she notes her reactions to the story and tries to interpret Sammy's actions. You may, however, annotate before you have decided on a topic—in fact, the process of reading and responding to your text can help you to focus on a topic. In the absence of a topic, your annotations are likely to be less focused; therefore, you will need to highlight and annotate again when your paper's direction is more firmly fixed in your mind.

Writing about Literature

Writing about literature—or about anything else, for that matter—is an idiosyncratic process during which many activities occur at once: As you write, you think of ideas; as you think of ideas, you clarify the focus of your essay; and as you clarify your focus, you reshape your paragraphs and sentences and refine your word choice. Even though this process sounds chaotic, it has three stages: *planning, drafting,* and *revising and editing.* Remember, however, that although for the sake of clarity we discuss these stages separately, they actually overlap.

PLANNING AN ESSAY

Considering Your Audience

Sometimes—for example, in a journal entry—you write primarily for yourself. At other times, however, you write for others. As you write an essay, you should consider the special requirements of that **audience.** Is your audience your classmates or your instructor? Can you assume your readers are familiar with your paper's topic and with any technical terms you will use, or will they need brief plot summaries or definitions of key terms? If your audience is your instructor, remember that he or she is a representative of a larger academic audience and therefore expects accurate information; standard English; correct grammar, mechanics, and spelling; logical arguments; and a certain degree of stylistic fluency. In addition, your instructor expects you to support your statements with specific information, to express yourself clearly and explicitly, and to document your sources. In short, your instructor wants to see how clearly you think and whether you are able to arrange your ideas into a well-organized, coherent essay.

In addition to being a member of a general academic audience, your instructor is also a member of a particular community of scholars—in this case, those who study literature. By writing about literature, you engage in a dialogue with this community. For this reason, you should adhere to the specific conventions—procedures that by habitual use have become accepted practice—its members follow. Many of the conventions that apply specifically to writing about literature—matters of style, format, and the like—will be discussed in this book.

Understanding Your Purpose

In addition to considering your audience, you need to consider your **purpose** (or purposes) for writing. Sometimes you write with a single purpose in mind; at other times a single assignment or writing task may suggest more than one purpose. In general terms, you may write for any of the following reasons:

Writing to Respond   When you write to *respond,* your goal is to discover and express your reactions to a work. To record your responses you engage in relatively informal activities, such as brainstorming, listing, and journal writing (see pp. 24–26). As you write you explore your own ideas, forming and reforming your impressions of the work.

Writing to Interpret   When you write to *interpret,* you explain a work's possible meanings. To do so, you may summarize, identify examples, or compare and contrast the work to other works or to your own experiences. Then, you may go on to analyze the work, studying each of its elements in turn, putting complex statements in your own words, defining difficult concepts, or placing ideas in context.

Writing to Evaluate   When you write to *evaluate,* your purpose is to assess a work's literary merits. You may consider not only its aesthetic appeal, but also its ability to retain that appeal over time and across national or cultural boundaries. As you write, you use your own critical sense and the opinions of experts in the field to help you make judgments about the work.

Choosing a Topic

When you write an essay about literature, you develop and support an idea about a literary work or works. Before you begin your writing, you should make certain that you understand your assignment. Do you know how much time you have to complete your essay? Are you expected to rely on your own ideas, or are you able to consult journal articles in the library? Is your essay to focus on a specific work or on a particular element of literature? Do you have to write on an assigned topic, or are you free to choose a topic? About how long should your essay be? Do you understand exactly what the assignment is asking you to do?

Sometimes your assignment limits your options by telling you what you should discuss:

♦ Write an essay in which you analyze Robert Frost's use of the color white in his poem "Design."

♦ Discuss Hawthorne's use of allegory in his short story "Young Goodman Brown."

♦ Write a short essay in which you explain Nora's actions at the end of Ibsen's *A Doll House.*

At other times, however, your instructor will give you no specific guidelines other than a paper's length and format. In such situations, where you must choose a topic on your own, you can find a topic by brainstorming or by writing journal entries. As you engage in these activities, however, keep in mind that you have many options for writing papers about literature. Some of these options are listed below:

♦ Compare two works of literature.

♦ Compare two characters, or discuss some trait those characters share.

- Trace a common theme—jealousy, revenge, repression, coming of age—in several works.

- Consider how a common subject—war, love, nature—is treated in several works.

- Examine a single element in one or more works—for instance, plot, point of view, or character development.

- Focus on a single aspect of that element, such as the role of flashbacks, the effect of a shifting narrative perspective, or a character's motivation.

- Apply a critical theory to a work of literature—for instance, apply a feminist perspective to Tillie Olsen's "I Stand Here Ironing."

- Examine connections between an issue treated in a work of literature—for instance, spousal abuse in Ann Petry's "Like a Winding Sheet"—and that same issue as it is treated in sociological or psychological journals or in the popular press.

- Examine some aspect of history or biography and consider its impact on a literary work—for instance, the influence of World War I on Wilfred Owen's poems.

- Explore a problem within a work and propose a possible solution—for example, consider the narrator's actual reason for killing the old man in Edgar Allan Poe's "The Tell-Tale Heart."

Any of the options above may lead you to an interesting topic. Remember, however, that you will still have to narrow the scope of your topic so that it fits within the limits of your assignment.

Finding Something to Say

Once you have a topic, you have to find something to say about it. The information you collected when you highlighted and annotated will help you formulate the statement that will be the central idea of your essay and find ideas that can support that statement.

You can use a variety of different strategies to find supporting material.

- You can discuss ideas with others—friends, classmates, instructors, or parents, for example.

- You can ask questions.

- You can do research.

- You can **freewrite**—that is, keep writing on your topic for a given period of time without pausing to consider style, structure, or content.

Three additional strategies—*brainstorming, keeping a journal,* and *listing*—are especially helpful.

Brainstorming When you **brainstorm**, you jot down ideas—single words, phrases, or sentences; statements or questions; quotations, paraphrases, summaries, or your own ideas—as they occur to you, moving as quickly as possible. Your starting point may be a general assignment, a particular work (or works) of literature, a specific topic, or even a thesis statement; in fact, you can brainstorm at any stage of the writing process, and you can repeat this activity as often as you like.

The brainstorming notes that follow were made by a student preparing to write a paper on the relationships between children and parents in four poems. She began by brainstorming about each poem and went on to consider thematic relationships among the poems. These notes are her preliminary reactions to one of the four poems she planned to study, Adrienne Rich's "A Woman Mourned by Daughters" (p. 638).

> (Memory:) then and now
> Then: leaf, straw, dead insect (= light); ignored
> Now: swollen, puffed up, weight (= heavy); focus of attention.
>   controls their movements.
> *Kitchen = a "universe"
> (Teaspoons, goblets, etc.) = concrete representations of mother;
>   also = obligations, responsibilities (like plants and father)
>   (weigh on them, keep
> them under her spell)
> Milestones of past: weddings, being fed as children
> "You breathe upon us now"
>   PARADOX? (Dead, she breathes, has weight, fills house and
> sky. Alive, she was a dead insect, no one paid attention to her.)

Keeping a Journal   You can use a journal to find ideas—and, later, to help you to find a topic or a thesis. In a **journal** you expand your marginal annotations, recording your responses to works you have read, noting questions, exploring emerging ideas, experimenting with possible paper topics, trying to paraphrase or summarize difficult concepts, or speculating about a work's ambiguities. A journal is the place to take chances, to try out ideas that may initially seem frivolous or irrelevant; here you can think on paper until connections become clear or ideas crystallize. You can also use your journal as a convenient place to collect your brainstorming notes and, later, your lists of related ideas.

As he prepared to write a paper analyzing the role of Jim, the "gentleman caller" in Tennessee Williams's play *The Glass Menagerie* (p. 1898), a student explored ideas in the following journal entry.

> When he tells Laura that being disappointed is not the same
> as being discouraged, and that he's disappointed but not
> discouraged, Jim reveals his role as a symbol of the power of
> newness and change—a "bulldozer" that will clear out whatever
> is in its path, even delicate people like Laura. But the fact that
> he is disappointed shows Jim's human side. He has run into

problems since high school, and these problems have blocked his progress toward a successful future. Working at the warehouse, Jim needs Tom's friendship to remind him of what he used to be (and what he still can be?), and this shows his insecurity. He isn't as sure of himself as he seems to be.

This journal entry presents the student's initial response to a character; it is personal and subjective. Even so, these preliminary explorations can help him to decide on a specific direction for his essay.

Listing After you have actively read a work, you should have a good many underlinings and marginal notes. Some of this material will be useful, and some will be irrelevant. **Listing** is the process of reviewing the notes you collected through brainstorming, keeping a journal, and annotating your text; deciding what material is pertinent; and arranging that material into categories so that you can determine a direction for your essay. As you prepare to list, reread your information and try to determine what categories this information suggests. Then, after writing down these categories, list specific bits of information under each heading. Listing enables you to discover patterns: to see repeated images, similar characters, recurring words and phrases, and interrelated themes or ideas. Identifying these patterns helps you to decide which points to make in your paper and what information you will use to support these points. Remember that the lists you make do not yet reflect the order or emphasis of the ideas you will develop in your paper. As your ideas become more focused, you will add, delete, and rearrange material.

After reading Lorrie Moore's "How to Talk to Your Mother (Notes)" (p. 89), a student decided to write a paper about the relationship between the narrator's personal history and the events of the larger world. She arranged the related points from her annotations, brainstorming notes, and journal entries into categories, as reflected on the lists below:

PERSONAL/COMMONPLACE
  Details of day-to-day life
      Laundromat
      Apple crisp
      Dishwasher
      Meals
      Party
      Funeral
  Babies
      Abortions
      Kids on public transportation
      Stretch marks
      Doll ("the Sue")
      Brother's children

WORLD
  Songs
   "You'll Never Walk Alone"
   "Oklahoma!"
   "Three Little Fishies"
   "Shoofly Pie"
  Historical Events
   Dead Sea Scrolls discovered
   Elections
   Germany invades Poland
   Bicentennial
   Grandma Moses dies
   Kennedy is shot
  Scientific/Medical Events
   Polyurethane heart
   Temporary artificial heart
   Moon landing

Deciding on a Thesis

After you finish listing, you should try to express the direction of your thinking in a tentative **thesis statement**—an idea, often expressed in a single sentence, that the rest of your essay supports. This idea, which you will develop as you write, should emerge out of your highlighting, annotations, brainstorming notes, journal entries, and lists of related points. (In many cases, in fact, you will decide on a tentative thesis at an earlier stage of the writing process.)

An effective thesis statement tells readers what your essay will discuss and how you will approach your material. Consequently, it should be precisely worded, making its point clear to your readers. It should contain no vague words or inexact diction that will make it difficult for readers to follow your discussion. Although the statement "The use of sound in Tennyson's poem 'The Eagle' is interesting" is accurate, it does not convey a precise idea to your readers because the words *sound* and *interesting* are not specific enough. An effective thesis statement might be "Unity in 'The Eagle' is achieved by Tennyson's use of alliteration, assonance, and rhyme throughout the poem." In addition to being specific, your thesis statement should give your readers an accurate sense of the scope and direction of your essay. It should not make promises that you do not intend to fulfill or contain extraneous details that might confuse your readers. If, for example, you are going to write a paper about the dominant image in a poem, your thesis should not imply that you will focus on setting or tone.

Remember that as you organize your ideas and as you write, you will probably modify and sharpen your tentative thesis. Sometimes you will even begin your essay with one thesis in mind and end it with an entirely different idea. If this happens, be sure to revise your support paragraphs so that they are consistent with your changes and so that the points you include support your new thesis. If you find that your thoughts about your topic are changing, remember that this is how the writing process works. As you write, you will discover new ideas, and your essay will become stronger.

Preparing an Outline

Once you have decided on a tentative thesis and have some idea of how you will support it, you can begin to plan your essay's structure. Quite often, an outline can help you to shape your essay. Not all writers outline, but many do at some point in the writing process because it helps them to clarify their ideas and the relationship of these ideas to one another. Realizing, however, that they will discover many new ideas as they write, even these writers seldom take the time to prepare a detailed formal outline, preferring instead a scratch outline that lists just the major points they plan to make.

A **scratch outline,** perhaps the most useful kind of outline for a short paper, is an informal list of the main points you will discuss in your essay in the order in which they will be introduced. As its name implies, a scratch outline is rough, lacking the detail and the degree of organization of a more formal outline. The main purpose of a scratch outline is to give you a sense of the shape and order of your paper and thus enable you to begin writing. A student writing a short essay on American poet Edwin Arlington Robinson's use of irony in his poem "Miniver Cheevy" (p. 989) used the following scratch outline as a guide:

Speaker's Attitude
    Ironic
    Cynical
    Critical
Use of Diction
    Formal
    Detached
Use of Allusions
    Thebes
    Camelot
    Priam
    Medici
Use of Repetition
    "Miniver"
    "thought"
    repetitious rhyme

Once this outline was complete, the student was ready to write a first draft.

DRAFTING

Your first draft is a preliminary version of your paper, something to react to and revise. Still, before you begin to write, you should be familiar with one of the most common ways of arranging information: thesis and support. In a **thesis and support** paper you state your thesis in your introduction, support your thesis in the body paragraphs of your essay, and restate your thesis or summarize your points in your conclusion. Knowing this basic method of organizing information will not only help you to write your first draft, but also help you with the revisions that you do later.

Before you draft your paper, you should review the material you have collected to support your thesis.

First, make sure you have collected enough information to support your thesis.   The points you make are only as convincing as the evidence you present to support them. As you read and took notes, you collected examples from the work or works about which you are writing—summaries, paraphrases, or quoted lines of narrative, verse, or dialogue—to back up your statements. Just how many of these examples you need to use in your draft depends on the nature of your thesis and how skeptical you believe your audience to be. In general, the more inclusive your thesis, the more material you need to support it. For example, if you were supporting the rather narrow thesis that the speech of a certain character in the second scene of a play was wooden or awkward, only a few examples would be enough. However, if you wanted to support the inclusive thesis that Nora and Torvald Helmer in Henrik Ibsen's 1879 play *A Doll House* (p. 1185) are trapped in their roles, you would need to present a wide range of examples.

Second, see if the work includes any details that contradict your thesis. Before you can determine the validity of your thesis, you should test it by looking for details that contradict it. For example, if you plan to support the thesis that in *A Doll House* Ibsen makes a strong case for the rights of women, you should look for counterexamples. Can you find subtle hints in the play that suggest women should remain locked in their traditional roles and continue to defer to their fathers and husbands? If so, you will want to modify your thesis accordingly.

Finally, consider whether you need to use literary criticism to help you support your thesis.   You could, for example, strengthen the thesis that *A Doll House* challenged contemporary attitudes about marriage by including the fact that when the play first opened, Ibsen was convinced by an apprehensive theater manager to write another ending. In the new ending, Ibsen had Nora decide, after she stopped briefly to look in at her sleeping children, that she could not leave her family. Sometimes information from another source can even lead you to change your thesis. For example, after reading *A Doll House,* you might have decided that Ibsen's purpose was to make a strong case for the rights of women. In class, however, you might learn that Ibsen repeatedly said that his play was about the rights of all human beings, not just women. This information could lead you to a thesis that suggests Torvald is just as trapped in his role as Nora is in hers. Naturally, Ibsen's interpretation of his work does not invalidate your first judgment, but it does suggest another conclusion that is worth investigating.

After you have carefully evaluated the completeness, relevance, and validity of your supporting material, you can begin drafting your essay, using your scratch outline as your guide. Your goal is to get your ideas down on paper, so you should write quickly. Once you have a draft, you will be able to examine the connections among ideas and to evaluate preliminary versions of your paragraphs and sentences. Your focus in this draft should be on the body of your essay; this is not the time to worry about constructing the "perfect" introduction and conclusion. In fact, many writers, knowing that their ideas will change as they write, postpone writing these paragraphs until a later draft, preferring instead to begin with just their tentative thesis. As you write, remember that your first draft is naturally going to be rough and will probably not be as clear as you would like it to be; still, it will enable you to see the ideas you have outlined begin to take shape.

REVISING AND EDITING

As soon as you begin to draft your essay, you begin the process of revision. When you **revise,** you literally "re-see" your draft and, in many cases, you go on to reorder and rewrite substantial portions of your essay. Before you are satisfied with your essay, you will probably write several drafts, each more closely focused and more coherent than the previous one.

Strategies for Revision

Two strategies can help you to revise your drafts: *peer review* and a *dialogue with your instructor.*

Peer review is a process in which students assess each other's work. This activity may be carried out in informal sessions, during which one student comments on another's draft, or it may be a formal process in which a student responds to specific questions on a form supplied by the instructor. In either case, one student's reactions can help another student revise. Peer review can be carried out on any draft, and questions can focus on style, essay structure, or any other issue.

A **dialogue with your instructor**—in conference or in writing— can give you a sense of how to proceed with your revision. Establishing such an oral or written dialogue can help you learn how to respond critically to your own writing, and your reactions to your instructor's comments on any draft can help you to clarify your essay's goals. (If your instructor is not available, you may be able to schedule a conference with a writing center tutor, if your school offers this service.) Using your own responses as well as those of your classmates and your instructor, you can write drafts that are increasingly more consistent with these goals.

The Revision Process

As you move through successive drafts, the task of revising your essay will be easier if you follow a systematic process. As you read and react to your essay, begin by assessing the effectiveness of the larger elements—thesis and support, for instance—and proceed to examine increasingly smaller details.

Thesis Statement   First, reconsider your **thesis statement.** Is it carefully and precisely worded? Does it provide a realistic idea of what your essay will cover? Does it make a point that is worth supporting? It is not enough, for instance, to base an essay about literature on a vague thesis like one of the following.

> <u>Vague:</u>   Many important reasons exist to explain why Margot Macomber's shooting of her husband was probably intentional.

> <u>Vague:</u>   Dickens's characters are a lot like those of Addison and Steele.

To give focus and direction to your essay a thesis statement must be more pointed and more specific, as the following revisions are.

> <u>Revised:</u>   Although Hemingway's text states that Margot Macomber "shot at the buffalo," a careful analysis of her relationship with her husband suggests that in fact she intended to kill him.

> <u>Revised:</u>   With their extremely familiar, almost caricature-like physical and moral traits, many of Charles Dickens's minor characters reveal that he owes a debt to the "characters" created by the seventeenth-century essayists Joseph Addison and Richard Steele for the newspaper <u>The Spectator.</u>

Support   Next, assess the appropriateness of your **supporting ideas** and consider whether you present enough support for your thesis and whether all the details you include are relevant to that thesis. Make sure you have supported all points with specific, concrete examples from the work or works you are discussing, briefly summarizing key events, quoting dialogue or description, describing characters or settings, or paraphrasing key ideas. Make certain, however, that your own ideas control the essay and that you have not substituted plot summary for analysis and interpretation. Your goal is to draw a conclusion about one or more works and to support that conclusion with pertinent details. If a plot detail supports a point you wish to make, include a *brief* summary of the event or series of events, showing its relevance by explicitly connecting the summary to the point you are making. In the following excerpt from a paper on a short story by James Joyce, the first sentence summarizes a key event and the second sentence explains its significance.

> At the end of "Counterparts," when Farrington returns home after a day of frustration and abuse at work, his reaction is to strike out at his son Tom. This act shows that while he and his son are similarly victimized, Farrington is also the counterpart of his tyrannical boss.

Topic Sentences   Now, turn your attention to the **topic sentences** that present the main idea of each body paragraph, making sure that they are clearly worded and that they communicate the direction of your ideas, and the precise relationships of ideas to one another.

Be especially careful to avoid abstractions and vague generalities in topic sentences.

> <u>Vague:</u>   One similarity revolves around the dominance of the men by women. (*What exactly is the similarity?*)
>
> <u>Revised:</u>   In both stories, a man is dominated by a woman.
>
> <u>Vague:</u>   There is one reason for the fact that Jay Gatsby remains a mystery. (*What is the reason?*)
>
> <u>Revised:</u>   Because <u>The Great Gatsby</u> is narrated by the outsider Nick Carraway, Jay Gatsby himself remains a mystery.

When revising topic sentences that are intended to move readers from one point (or section of your paper) to another, be sure the relationship between the ideas they link is clear.

> <u>Relationship between ideas unclear:</u>   Now the poem's imagery will be discussed.
>
> <u>Revised:</u>   Another reason for the poem's effectiveness is its unusual imagery.
>
> <u>Relationship between ideas unclear:</u>   The sheriff's wife is another interesting character.
>
> <u>Revised:</u>   Like her friend Mrs. Hale, the sheriff's wife also has mixed feelings about what Mrs. Wright has done.

When you are satisfied with the body of your essay, you can go on to examine your paper's introduction and conclusion.

Introduction   The **introduction** of an essay about literature should specifically identify the works to be discussed and indicate the emphasis of the paper to follow. Depending on your purpose and on your paper's topic, you may want to provide some historical background or biographical information or to discuss the work in relation to other, similar works. Like all introductions, the one you write for an essay about literature should create interest in your topic and include a clear statement of the essay's thesis. The following introduction, while more than adequate for a first draft, is in need of revision:

> Revenge, which is defined as "the chance to retaliate, get satisfaction, take vengeance, or inflict damage or injury in return for an injury, insult, etc.," is a major component in many of the stories we have read. The stories that will be discussed here deal with a variety of ways to seek revenge. In my essay, I will show some of these differences.

Although the student clearly identifies her paper's topic, she does not identify the works she will discuss or the particular point she will make about revenge. Her tired opening strategy, a dictionary definition, is not likely to arouse interest in her topic, and her announcement of her intention in the last sentence is awkward and unnecessary. The following revision is much more effective:

> In Edgar Allan Poe's "The Cask of Amontillado" Montresor vows revenge on Fortunato for an unspecified "insult"; in Ring Lardner's "Haircut" Paul, a young retarded man, gets even with a cruel practical joker who has taunted him for years. Both of these stories present characters who seek revenge, and both stories end in murder. However, the murderers' motivations are presented very differently. In "Haircut" the unreliable narrator is unaware of the significance of many events, and his ignorance helps to create sympathy for the murderer. In "The Cask of Amontillado," where the untrustworthy narrator is the murderer himself, Montresor's inability to offer a convincing motive turns the reader against him.

Conclusion   In your conclusion you restate your thesis or sum up your essay's main points; then, you make a graceful exit. The concluding paragraph below represents an acceptable effort for a first draft, but it communicates little information:

> Although the characters of Montresor and Paul were created by different authors at different times, they do have similar motives and goals. However, they are portrayed very differently.

The following revision reinforces the essay's main point, effectively incorporating a brief quotation from the introductory paragraph of the Poe story (p. 208):

> In fact, then, what is significant is not whether or not each murderer's acts are justified, but rather how each murderer, and each victim, is portrayed by the narrator. Montresor—driven by a thirst to avenge "a thousand injuries" as well as a final insult—is shown to be sadistic and unrepentant; in "Haircut" it is Jim, the victim, whose sadism and lack of remorse are revealed to the reader.

Sentences and Words Now, focus on the individual sentences and words of your essay. Begin be evaluating your **transitions,** the words and phrases that link sentences and paragraphs. Be sure that every necessary transitional element has been supplied, and that each word or phrase you have selected accurately conveys the exact relationship (sequence, contradiction, and so on) between ideas. When you are satisfied with the clarity and appropriateness of your paper's transitions, consider word choice and sentence variety.

First, be sure you have varied your sentence structure. You will bore your readers if all your sentences begin the same way ("The story. . . ."; "The story. . . ."), or if they are all about the same length. In addition, make sure all the words you select accurately communicate your ideas and that you have not used vague, inexact diction where precision is called for. For example, saying that a character is bad is a lot less effective than characterizing him or her as ruthless, conniving, or malicious.

Next, focus on the specific conventions that govern essays about works of literature. For instance, use present tense verbs when discussing literary works (Jake Barnes *is* a major character in Ernest Hemingway's novel *The Sun Also Rises*). Use past tense verbs only when discussing historical events (Stephen Crane's *The Red Badge of Courage* deals with a battle that *took* place during the American Civil War), presenting biographical data (Samuel Taylor Coleridge *was* a close friend of William Wordsworth's), or referring to events that took place before the time of the work's main action (Hamlet's father *was* murdered by Claudius, his mother's new husband). In addition, eliminate subjective expressions, such as *I think, in my opinion, I believe, it seems to me,* and *I feel.* These phrases weaken your essay by suggesting that its ideas are "only" opinions and have no objective validity.

Using and Documenting Sources Make certain that all references to sources are integrated smoothly and documented appropriately (see Appendix A, Documenting Sources).

- Acknowledge all sources, including the work or works under discussion, using the documentation style of the Modern Language Association (MLA).

◆ Combine paraphrases, summaries, and quotations with your own interpretations, weaving quotations smoothly into your paper. Introduce the words or ideas of others with a phrase that identifies their source ("According to Richard Wright's biographer, . . ."), and end with appropriate parenthetical documentation.

◆ Use quotations *only* when something vital would be lost if you did not reproduce the author's exact words.

◆ Integrate short quotations (four lines or less) smoothly into your paper. Make sure that you set off quotations with quotation marks.

◆ Set off quotations of more than four lines by indenting ten spaces (approximately one inch) from the left-hand margin. Double-space, and do not use quotation marks. If you are quoting a single paragraph, do not indent the first line.

◆ Use the correct reference formats for fiction, poetry, and drama. When citing a part of a short story or novel, supply the page number (143); for a poem, give the line numbers (3–5); for a play, include the act, scene, and line numbers (2.2.17–22).

Editing

Once you have finished revising, you **edit**—that is, you make certain that your paper's grammar, punctuation, spelling, and mechanics are correct. As you edit, pay particular attention to the mechanical conventions of literary essays. For instance, titles of short works and titles of parts of long works—short stories, short poems, and magazine or journal articles—should be in quotation marks ("A Rose for Emily"); titles of long works—books, long poems, plays, and newspapers and journals, for example—should be underlined or italicized (*Invisible Man;* the *Washington Post*).

In addition, refer to authors of literary works by their full names in your first reference to them and by their last names in subsequent references. Never refer to them by their first names, and never use titles that indicate marital status (*Willa Cather* or *Cather,* never Willa or Miss Cather). Also, make sure you have used literary terms accurately. For example, be careful to avoid confusing **narrator** or **speaker** with author; feelings or opinions expressed by a narrator or character do not necessarily represent those of the author. Do not say, "In the poem 'Patterns' Amy Lowell expresses her anger" when you mean that the **persona**—the speaker in the poem, who may or may not be the poet—expresses anger.

When your editing is complete, give your essay a descriptive title; before you retype or reprint it, make sure that its format conforms to your instructor's requirements.

Fiction

CHAPTER 3

Reading and Writing about Fiction

Understanding Fiction

A **narrative** tells a story by presenting events in some logical or orderly way. Works of narrative fiction originate in the imagination of the author, not in history or fact. Certainly some fiction—historical or autobiographical fiction, for example—focuses on real people and actual events, but the way the characters interact and how the plot unfolds are the author's invention.

Even before they know how to read, most people have learned how narratives are structured. Once children can tell a story, they also know how to exaggerate, how to add or delete details, how to rearrange events, and how to bend facts—in other words, how to fictionalize a narrative to achieve a desired effect. This kind of informal, personal narrative is similar in many ways to the more structured literary narratives included in this anthology.

Our earliest examples of narrative fiction are stories and songs that came out of a prehistoric oral tradition. These stories, embellished with each telling, were often quite long, embodying the history, the central myths, and the religious beliefs of the cultures in which they originated. Eventually transcribed, these extended narratives became **epics**—long narrative poems about heroic figures whose actions determine the fate of a nation or an entire race. Homer's *Iliad* and *Odyssey*, the ancient Babylonian *Epic of Gilgamesh*, the Hindu *Bhagavad Gita*, and the Anglo-Saxon *Beowulf* are examples. Many of the tales of the Old Testament also came out of this tradition. The setting of an epic is vast—sometimes worldwide or cosmic, including heaven and hell—and the action commonly involves a battle or a perilous journey. Quite often divine beings participate in the action and influence the outcome of events, as they do in the Trojan War in the *Iliad* and in the founding of Rome in Vergil's *Aeneid*.

Folktales and **fairy tales** also come out of the oral tradition. These tales, which developed along with other narrative forms, have influenced works as diverse as Chaucer's *The Canterbury Tales* and D. H. Lawrence's "The Rocking-Horse Winner" (p. 512). The folktales and fairy tales that survive (such as "Cinderella" and Aesop's *Fables*) are contemporary versions of old, even ancient, tales that can be traced back centuries through many different cultures. Despite their variety, these narrative forms have several elements in common. First, they feature simple characters who illustrate a quality or trait that can be summed up in a few words. Much of the appeal of "Cinderella," for example, depends on the contrast between the selfish, sadistic stepsisters and poor, gentle, victimized Cinderella. In addition, the folktale or fairy tale has an obvious theme or moral—good triumphing over evil, for instance. The stories move directly to their conclusions, never interrupted by ingenious or unexpected twists of plot. (Love is temporarily thwarted, but the prince eventually finds Cinderella and marries her.) Finally, these tales are anchored not in specific times or places but in "Once upon a time" settings, green worlds of prehistory filled with royalty, talking animals, and magic.

During the Middle Ages, the **romance** supplanted the epic. Written initially in verse but later in prose, the romance replaced the epic's gods and central heroic figures with knights, kings, and damsels in distress. Events were controlled by enchantments rather than by the will of divine beings. *Sir Gawain and the Green Knight* and other tales of King Arthur and the Knights of the Round Table are examples of romances. Eventually the romance gave way to other types of narratives. Short prose tales, such as those collected in Giovanni Boccaccio's *The Decameron,* originated in fourteenth-century Italy, and the **picaresque,** an episodic, often satirical work about a rogue or rascal, such as Miguel de Cervantes's *Don Quixote,* emerged in seventeenth-century Spain. The **pastoral romance,** a prose tale set in an idealized rural world, and the **character,** a brief satirical sketch illustrating a type of personality, both became popular in Renaissance England.

From these diverse sources emerged the **novel.** The English writer Daniel Defoe is commonly given credit for writing the first novel in 1719. His *Robinson Crusoe* is an episodic narrative similar to the picaresque but unified not only by a central character but also by a single setting. By the nineteenth century the novel reached a high point in its development, supplanting other kinds of extended narratives. Because of its ability to present a wide range of characters in realistic settings and to develop them in depth, the novel appealed to members of the rising middle class who seemed to have an insatiable desire to see themselves portrayed. Writers such as George Eliot, Charles Dickens, William Thackeray, and Charlotte and Emily Brontë appealed to this desire by creating large fictional worlds populated by many different characters who reflected the complexity—and at times the melodrama—of Victorian society. From these roots, the novel as a literary form has continued to develop in the twentieth century.

The Short Story

Like the novel, the short story evolved from the various forms of narrative discussed above. Because the short story comes from so many different sources from all over the world, it is difficult to determine where it originated. We can say with certainty, however, that in the United States during the nineteenth century a group of writers—in particular Nathaniel Hawthorne and Edgar Allan Poe—took it seriously and exploited its fictional possibilities. Because the short story was embraced so readily and developed so quickly in the United States, it is commonly, although not quite accurately, thought of as an American art form.

Whereas the novel is an extended piece of narrative fiction, the **short story** is limited in length and scope. These limitations account for the characteristics that distinguish the short story from longer prose forms. Unlike the novelist, the short story writer cannot devote a great deal of space to developing a highly complex plot or a large number of characters. As a result, the short story begins close to or at the height of action and develops one character in depth. Usually concentrating on a single incident, the writer develops a character by showing his or her responses to events. (This attention to character development, as well as its detailed description of setting, is what distinguishes the short story from earlier short narrative forms, such as folktales and fairy tales.) In many contemporary stories, a character experiences an **epiphany,** a moment of illumination in which something hidden or not understood becomes immediately clear. Examples of epiphany are found in this anthology in James Joyce's "Araby," John Updike's "A&P," and David Michael Kaplan's "Doe Season."

Today the term *short story* is applied to a wide variety of prose narratives: short stories such as Charles Baxter's "Gryphon" (p. 125), which runs about twelve pages; **short short stories,** such as Luisa Valenzuela's "All About Suicide" (p. 6), which are under five pages in length; and long stories, such as Franz Kafka's "The Metamorphosis" (p. 476), which may more accurately be called short novels or **novellas.**

The possibilities of the short story are infinite. A short story may be comic or tragic; its subject may be growing up, marriage, crime and punishment, war, sexual awakening, death, or any number of other human concerns. The setting can be an imaginary world, the old West, rural America, the jungles of Uruguay, nineteenth-century Russia, pre-communist China, or modern Egypt. The story's form may be conventional, with a definite beginning, middle, and end, or it may be structured as a letter, as a diary entry, or even as a collection of random notes. The narrator of a story may be trustworthy or unreliable, involved in the action or a disinterested observer, sympathetic or deserving of scorn, extremely ignorant or highly insightful, limited in vision or able to see inside the minds of all the characters. And, as the stories in this anthology show, the conventions of short fiction are constantly changing.

Reading Fiction

As you read more works of short fiction, you will begin paying careful attention to elements such as plot; character; setting; point of view; style, tone, and language; symbol and allegory; and theme. The following guidelines, designed to help you explore works of fiction, focus on issues that will be examined in depth in chapters to come.

- Look at the **plot** of the story. How do the events in the story relate to one another, and how do they relate to the story as a whole? What conflicts occur in the story, and how are these conflicts developed or resolved? Does the story include any noteworthy plot devices, such as flashbacks or foreshadowing? (See Chapter 4.)

- Analyze the **characters** of a story. What are their most striking traits? How do these individuals interact with one another? Are the characters fully developed, or are they stereotypes whose sole purpose is to express a single trait (good, evil, generosity) or to move the plot along? (See Chapter 5.)

- Identify the **setting** of the story. At what time period and in what geographic location does the action of the story occur? How does the setting affect the characters of the story? How does it determine the relationships among the characters? How does the setting affect the plot? Does the setting create a mood for the story? In what way does the setting reinforce the central ideas that the story examines? (See Chapter 6.)

- Examine the narrative **point of view** of the story. What person or persons are telling the story? Is the story told in the first person (*I* or *we*) or in the third person (*he, she,* or *they*)? Is the narrator all-knowing, or is the story restricted to the perspective of one person—a major character, a minor character, or just an observer? How much does the narrator know about the events in the story? Does the narrator present an accurate or inaccurate picture of events? Does the narrator understand the full significance of the story he or she is telling? (See Chapter 7.)

- Analyze the **style, tone,** and **language** of the story. Does the writer make any unusual use of diction or syntax? Does the writer use figures of speech? Patterns of imagery? What styles or levels of speech are associated with particular characters? What words or phrases are repeated throughout the work? Is the narrative style of the story plain or elaborate? Does the narrator's tone reveal his or her attitude toward characters or events? Are there any discrepancies between the narrator's attitude and the attitude of the author? Is the tone of the story playful, humorous, ironic, satirical, serious, somber, solemn, bitter, condescending, formal, informal—or does the tone suggest some other attitude? (See Chapter 8.)

◆ Focus on **symbolism** and **allegory.** Does the author use any objects or ideas symbolically? What characters or objects in the story are part of an **allegorical framework?** How does an object establish its symbolic or allegorical significance in the story? Does the same object have different meanings at different places in the story? Are the symbols or **allegorical figures** conventional or unusual? At what points in the story do symbols or allegorical figures appear? (See Chapter 9.)

◆ Identify the **themes** of the story. What is the central theme? How is this idea or concept expressed in the work? What elements of the story develop the central theme? How do character, plot, setting, point of view, and symbols reinforce the central theme? How does the title of the story contribute to readers' understanding of the central theme? What other themes are explored? (See Chapter 10.)

Active Reading

John Frei, a student in an introduction to literature course, was assigned to write a two- to three-page essay on a topic of his choice, focusing on any short story in this literature anthology. After considering a number of possible choices, John selected Alberto Alvaro Ríos's "The Secret Lion," which appears on the pages that follow.

ALBERTO ALVARO RÍOS (1952–   ) was born and raised in the border town of Nogales, Arizona, the son of a Mexican father and an English mother. He has published many poems and short stories, including the poetry collections *Teodora Luna's Two Kisses* (1990); *The Warring Poems* (1989); *The Lime Orchard Woman* (1988); and *Whispering to Fool the Wind* (1982), which won the American Academy of Poets Walt Whitman Award; and the short story collections *Pig Cookies and Other Stories* (1995) and *The Iguana Killer: Twelve Stories of the Heart* (1984), from which "The Secret Lion" is drawn. Ríos lives in Chandler, Arizona, and teaches at Arizona State University in Tempe.

Reviewer Mary Logue, writing in the October 1982 *Village Voice Literary Supplement,* says that Ríos's writings "carry the feel of another world. . . . Ríos's tongue is both foreign and familiar," reflecting an upbringing "where one is neither in this country nor the other." In many of his stories, Ríos expresses the seeming "other-ness" of Anglo culture as seen through the eyes of Chicano children: a little boy frightened by the sight of his first snowfall, or (as in "The Secret Lion") boys amazed by the otherworldly sight of "heaven." Through Ríos's children, we see our own world with new eyes.

ALBERTO ALVARO RÍOS

The Secret Lion

(1984)

I was twelve and in junior high school and something happened that we didn't have a name for, but it was there nonetheless like a lion, and roaring, roaring that way the biggest things do. Everything changed. Just that. Like the rug, the one that gets pulled—or better, like the tablecloth those magicians pull where the stuff on the table stays the same but the gasp! from the audience makes the staying-the-same part not matter. Like that.

What happened was there were teachers now, not just one teacher, teach-erz, and we felt personally abandoned somehow. When a person had all these teachers now, he didn't get taken care of the same way, even though six was more than one. Arithmetic went out the door when we walked in. And we saw girls now, but they weren't the same girls we used to know because we couldn't talk to them anymore, not the same way we used to, certainly not to Sandy, even though she was my neighbor, too. Not even to her. She just played the piano all the time. And there were words, oh there were words in junior high school, and we wanted to know what they were, and how a person did them—that's what school was supposed to be for. Only, in junior high school, school wasn't school, everything was backward-like. If you went up to a teacher and said the word to try and find out what it meant you got in trouble for saying it. So we didn't. And we figured it must have been that way about other stuff, too, so we never said anything about anything—we weren't stupid.

But my friend Sergio and I, we solved junior high school. We would come home from school on the bus, put our books away, change shoes, and go across the highway to the arroyo. It was the one place we were not supposed to go. So we did. This was, after all, what junior high had at least shown us. It was our river, though, our personal Mississippi, our friend from long back, and it was full of stories and all the branch forts we had built in it when we were still the Vikings of America, with our own symbol, which we had carved everywhere, even in the sand, which let the water take it. That was good, we had decided; whoever was at the end of this river would know about us.

At the very very top of our growing lungs, what we would do down there was shout every dirty word we could think of, in every combination we could come up with, and we would yell about girls, and all the things we wanted to do with them, as loud as we could—we didn't know what we wanted to do with them, just things—and we would yell about teachers, and how we loved some of them, like Miss Crevelone, and how we wanted to dissect some of them, making signs of the cross, like priests, and we would yell this stuff over and over because it felt good, we couldn't explain why, it just felt good and for the first time in our lives there was nobody to tell us we couldn't. So we did.

5   One Thursday we were walking along shouting this way, and the railroad, the Southern Pacific, which ran above and along the far side of the arroyo, had dropped a grinding ball down there, which was, we found out later, a cannonball thing used in mining. A bunch of them were put in a big vat which turned around and crushed the ore. One had been dropped, or thrown—what do caboose men do when they get bored—but it got down there regardless and as we were walking along yelling about one girl or another, a particular Claudia, we found it, one of these things, looked at it, picked it up, and got very very excited, and held it and passed it back and forth, and we were saying "Guythisis, this is, geeGuythis . . . ": we had this perception about nature then, that nature is imperfect and that round things are perfect: we said "GuyGodthis is perfect, thisisthis is perfect, it's round, round and heavy, it'sit's the best thing we'veeverseen. Whatisit?" We didn't know. We just knew it was great. We just, whatever, we played with it, held it some more.

And then we had to decide what to do with it. We knew, because of a lot of things, that if we were going to take this and show it to anybody, this discovery, this best thing, was going to be taken away from us. That's the way it works with little kids, like all the polished quartz, the tons of it we had collected piece by piece over the years. Junior high kids too. If we took it home, my mother, we knew, was going to look at it and say "throw that dirty thing in the, get rid of it." Simple like, like that. "But ma it's the best thing I" "Getridofit." Simple.

So we didn't. Take it home. Instead, we came up with the answer. We dug a hole and buried it. And we marked it secretly. Lots of secret signs. And came back the next week to dig it up and, we didn't know, pass it around some more or something, but we didn't find it. We dug up that whole bank, and we never found it again. We tried.

Sergio and I talked about that ball or whatever it was when we couldn't find it. All we used were small words, neat, good. Kid words. What we were really saying, but didn't know the words, was how much that ball was like that place, that whole arroyo: couldn't tell anybody about it, didn't understand what it was, didn't have a name for it. It just felt good. It was just perfect in the way it was that place, that whole going to that place, that whole junior high school lion. It was just iron-heavy, it had no name, it felt good or not, we couldn't take it home to show our mothers, and once we buried it, it was gone forever.

The ball was gone, like the first reasons we had come to that arroyo years earlier, like the first time we had seen the arroyo, it was gone like everything else that had been taken away. This was not our first lesson.

We stopped going to the arroyo after not finding the thing, the same way
we had stopped going there years earlier and headed for the mountains.
Nature seemed to keep pushing us around one way or another, teaching us
the same thing every place we ended up. Nature's gang was tough that
way, teaching us stuff.

10   When we were young we moved away from town, me and my family.
Sergio's was already out there. Out in the wilds. Or at least the new place
seemed like the wilds since everything looks bigger the smaller a man is. I
was five, I guess, and we had moved three miles north of Nogales where we
had lived, three miles north of the Mexican border. We looked across the
highway in one direction and there was the arroyo; hills stood up in the
other direction. Mountains, for a small man.

When the first summer came the very first place we went to was of
course the one place we weren't supposed to go, the arroyo. We went down
in there and found water running, summer rain water mostly, and we went
swimming. But every third or fourth or fifth day, the sewage treatment
plant that was, we found out, upstream, would release whatever it was that
it released, and we would never know exactly what day that was, and a person really couldn't tell right off by looking at the water, not every time,
not so a person could get out in time. So, we went swimming that summer
and some days we had a lot of fun. Some days we didn't. We found a thousand ways to explain what happened on those other days, constructing
elaborate stories about the neighborhood dogs, and hadn't she, my
mother, miscalculated her step before, too? But she knew something was
up because we'd come running into the house those days, wanting to take
a shower, even—if this can be imagined—in the middle of the day.

That was the first time we stopped going to the arroyo. It taught us to
look the other way. We decided, as the second side of summer came, we
wanted to go into the mountains. They were still mountains then. We
went running in one summer Thursday morning, my friend Sergio and
I, into my mother's kitchen, and said, well, what'zin, what'zin those hills
over there—we used her word so she'd understand us—and she said
nothingdon'tworryaboutit. So we went out, and we weren't dumb, we
thought with our eyes to each other, ohhoshe'stryingtokeepsomething-
fromus. We knew adults.

We had read the books, after all; we knew about bridges and castles
and wildtreacherousraging alligatormouth rivers. We wanted them. So we
were going to go out and get them. We went back that morning into that
kitchen and we said, "We're going out there, we're going into the hills,
we're going away for three days, don't worry." She said, "All right."

"You know," I said to Sergio, "if we're going to go away for three days,
well, we ought to at least pack a lunch."

15   But we were two young boys with no patience for what we thought at
the time was mom-stuff: making sa-and-wiches. My mother didn't offer.
So we got out little kid knapsacks that my mother had sewn for us, and
into them we put the jar of mustard. A loaf of bread. Knivesforksplates,

bottles of Coke, a can opener. This was lunch for the two of us. And we were weighed down, humped over to be strong enough to carry this stuff. But we started walking anyway, into the hills. We were going to eat berries and stuff otherwise. "Goodbye." My mom said that.

After the first hill we were dead. But we walked. My mother could still see us. And we kept walking. We walked until we got to where the sun is straight overhead, noon. That place. Where that is doesn't matter; it's time to eat. The truth is we weren't anywhere close to that place. We just agreed that the sun was overhead and that it was time to eat, and by tilting our heads a little we could make that the truth.

"We really ought to start looking for a place to eat."

"Yeah. Let's look for a good place to eat." We went back and forth saying that for fifteen minutes, making it lunchtime because that's what we always said back and forth before lunchtimes at home. "Yeah, I'm hungry all right." I nodded my head. "Yeah, I'm hungry all right too. I'm hungry." He nodded his head. I nodded my head back. After a good deal more nodding, we were ready, just as we came over a little hill. We hadn't found the mountains yet. This was a little hill.

And on the other side of this hill we found heaven.

20   It was just what we thought it would be.

Perfect. Heaven was green, like nothing else in Arizona. And it wasn't a cemetery or like that because we had seen cemeteries and they had gravestones and stuff and this didn't. This was perfect, had trees, lots of trees, had birds, like we had never seen before. It was like "The Wizard of Oz," like when they got to Oz and everything was so green, so emerald, they had to wear those glasses, and we ran just like them, laughing, laughing that way we did that moment, and we went running down to this clearing in it all, hitting each other that good way we did.

We got down there, we kept laughing, we kept hitting each other, we unpacked our stuff, and we started acting "rich." We knew all about how to do that, like blowing on our nails, then rubbing them on our chests for the shine. We made our sandwiches, opened our Cokes, got out the rest of the stuff, the salt and pepper shakers. I found this particular hole and I put my Coke right into it, a perfect fit, and I called it my Coke-holder. I got down next to it on my back, because everyone knows that rich people eat lying down, and I got my sandwich in one hand and put my other arm around the Coke in its holder. When I wanted a drink, I lifted my neck a little, put out my lips, and tipped my Coke a little with the crook of my elbow. Ah.

We were there, lying down, eating our sandwiches, laughing, throwing bread at each other and out for the birds. This was heaven. We were laughing and we couldn't believe it. My mother was keeping something from us, ah ha, but we had found her out. We even found water over at the side of the clearing to wash our plates with—we had brought plates. Sergio started washing his plates when he was done, and I was being rich with my Coke, and this day in summer was right.

When suddenly these two men came, from around a corner of trees and the tallest grass we had ever seen. They had bags on their backs, leather bags, bags and sticks.

25   We didn't know what clubs were, but I learned later, like I learned about the grinding balls. The two men yelled at us. Most specifically, one wanted me to take my Coke out of my Coke-holder so he could sink his golf ball into it.

Something got taken away from us that moment. Heaven. We grew up a little bit, and couldn't go backward. We learned. No one had ever told us about golf. They had told us about heaven. And it went away. We got golf in exchange.

We went back to the arroyo for the rest of that summer, and tried to have fun the best we could. We learned to be ready for finding the grinding ball. We loved it, and when we buried it we knew what would happen. The truth is, we didn't look so hard for it. We were two boys and twelve summers then, and not stupid. Things get taken away.

We buried it because it was perfect. We didn't tell my mother, but together it was all we talked about, till we forgot. It was the lion.

Previewing

John Frei began the reading process by previewing his text. A quick glance at the story showed him that it was quite short (under five pages), that it was written in the first person ("I was twelve"), that it included dialogue as well as narrative, and that it had a provocative title.

Previewing "The Secret Lion" prepared John to read it more closely and, eventually, to write about it. In preparation for writing, he read and reread the story, highlighting and annotating it as he went along.

Highlighting and Annotating

As he reread the story, John highlighted words and ideas that he thought might be useful to him, indicated possible connections among ideas, and noted questions and comments as they occurred to him. During this process, he tried to interpret the meaning of the term *secret lion,* and he paid close attention to the narrator's voice. The highlighted and annotated passage below illustrates his responses to the last five paragraphs of the story.

When suddenly these two men came, from around a corner of trees
and the tallest grass we had ever seen. They had bags on their backs,
leather bags, bags and sticks.
    We didn't know what clubs were, <u>but I learned later, like I learned
about the grinding balls.</u> The two men yelled at us. Most specifically,   **pt. of
view**
one wanted me to take my Coke out of my Coke-holder so he could sink
his golf ball into it.

Something got taken away from us that moment. Heaven.   *Heaven=*
We grew up a little bit, and couldn't go backward. We   *innocence*
learned. No one had ever told us about golf. They had   *Golf:*
told us about heaven. And it went away. We got golf in   *adulthood*
exchange.

We went back to the arroyo for the rest of that summer, and tried to   *Lose the*
have fun the best we could. We learned to be ready for finding the   *magic &*
grinding ball. We loved it, and when we buried it we knew what would   *specialness*
happen. The truth is, we didn't look so hard for it. We were two boys and *Also- loss*
twelve summers then, and not stupid. Things get taken away.   *innocence*
                                                                        trust, belief
                                                                        in things
                                                                        being
                                                                        perfect.

5   We buried it because it was perfect. We didn't tell my mother, but
together it was all we talked about, till we forgot. It was the lion.   *Lion= Knowledge*
ball?   *that growing up*
                                                                        loss? or is lion
                                                                        growing up itself

John's highlighting and annotations suggested a number of interesting possibilities for his paper. First, John noticed that the story reveals
both the narrator's childhood innocence and his adult knowledge. John's
highlighting also identified some unusual stylistic features, such as words
run together ("Getridofit") and repetition of words like *neat* and *perfect*.
Finally, John noticed that four items—the arroyo, the grinding ball, the
golf course, and the lion—were mentioned again and again. This emphasis led him to suspect that one or more of these items—particularly the
secret lion, prominently mentioned in the story's title—had some symbolic significance.

Writing about Fiction

PLANNING AN ESSAY

At this stage, John had not yet thought of a topic; he knew only that he
would be writing a paper on "The Secret Lion." However, his previewing,
highlighting, and annotations had helped him to move toward a topic,
revealing some interesting ideas about style and point of view—and, possibly, about symbolism. Now, because his paper was to be no more
than three pages long, he decided to select just one element on which to
concentrate.

Choosing a Topic   To help him settle on a direction for his paper, John
decided to explore possible topics in his journal. His journal entry on the
story's style and point of view appears below:

Style--Style is informal, with lots of contractions and
slang terms like "neat." Words are run together. Most of the
time, the boys combine words to indicate something unimportant

to them. When they're packing the lunch, they include "knivesforksplates." They're not interested in packing the lunch-- they just want to get to the "mountains." Packing lunches is very important to the mother, so she does the opposite of combining words: She breaks them down ("sa-and-wiches"). Maybe the words running together are supposed to suggest the days of a child, especially in the summer, when days just blend together. This style gets pretty annoying after a while, though--it's too cute.

Point of view--We see the story through the eyes of the narrator, who is a participant in the story. Sergio is developed along with the narrator as part of a "we." It's unusual that the characters are not really individuals--they function as "we" for most of the story, and nothing is done to give them separate voices. We don't see into the minds of the boys to any extent greater than what the narrator tells us, but the narrator has a double perspective: He takes the reader back to childhood, and this helps us understand the boys' excitement and disappointment, but he also shows us how much more he knows now, so we know that too.

John had no trouble writing paragraphs on style and point of view in his journal, but he ran out of ideas quickly; he knew that he did not have enough material to write a paper about either of these two possible topics. When he started to write a journal entry about the symbolic significance of certain items, however, he immediately found himself becoming involved. As a result, he chose "Symbols in 'The Secret Lion' " as his paper's topic. His journal entry on symbolism appears below:

Symbolism--The arroyo, the grinding ball, the golf course, and of course the secret lion all seem to mean something beyond their literal meanings as objects and places. (Maybe the "mountains" do too.) For one thing, they're all repeated over and over again. Also, they all seem to be related somehow to magic and perfection and surprise and expectation and idealism (and later, to disillusionment and disappointment). If this is a story about growing up, these things could be related somehow to that theme.

Finding Something to Say

Brainstorming   Once he had decided to write about symbolism, John moved on to brainstorm about his topic, focusing on what he considered the story's most important—and most obvious—symbol: the secret lion itself.

(Lion) = "roaring, roaring that way the biggest things do"
EVERYTHING CHANGED   (= secret because it's
                                something they have to find
                                out on their own, not from
                                adults?)
(Tablecloth)-rug (= magic).   "Staying-the-same part" is
                                most important--why?
(Arroyo:) not supposed to go (= rebellion)--Mississippi, "friend
from long back"; freedom. Place that doesn't change.
(Grinding ball)-Perfection in imperfect world, innocence in adult
world. "Nature is imperfect," but "round things are perfect"--"the
best thing." ("That ball was like that place, that whole arroyo")
      Buried and "gone forever"--"taken away" (like arroyo)
(Mountains:) "everything looks bigger the smaller a man is";
hills = "Mountains for a small man." (Mother calls them hills)
(Arroyo) = polluted with sewage (never know when it's
      coming)--went to mts.
On other side of hills = (golf course) (= heaven)--perfect   "perfect" x3
                          *Like Oz--green, emerald
                          *Place to act "rich"
                          *Men with clubs = reality,
                          future--they go back to arroyo
                          (= end of innocence)
"Things get taken away" (heaven, ball--something buried and
lost--arroyo)
"We buried it because it was perfect. . . . It was the lion."
Lion = secret place inside us that still craves childhood (as
adults, we learn we have to keep it buried, like ball).
How can a roaring lion be secret?

Listing   When he looked over his brainstorming notes in search of an organizing scheme for his paper, John saw that most of his information was
about four items: the secret lion, the arroyo, the grinding ball, and the golf
course. His most obvious option was to discuss one item at a time. But he
knew that he needed to find a common element among the four separate
items, a thematic connection that would relate them to one another.
When he noticed that each item seemed to have different meanings at different periods of the boys' lives, he realized that his essay could trace the
changes in meaning that occurred as the boys move from childhood to
adolescence to adulthood. He experimented with this possibility in the
following lists of related details:

The secret lion
Beginning: "raging beast" inside of them (6th grade
class) = frustration, puberty
Beginning: "roaring, roaring that way the biggest things do"
Middle: "that whole junior high school lion"
End: Lion = greatness, something important (also = puberty?)
Also = great discoveries they expect to make in their lives.
End: "It was the lion."

Arroyo
Place that doesn't change (= childhood); constant in changing
lives. (But it changes, too)
Mississippi--horizons
Freedom of childhood
Waste dump

Grinding ball
Perfection (in imperfect world)
Childhood innocence (in adult world)
Undiscovered knowledge?
Secrets of childhood (buried)
Something lost: "Things get taken away"

Golf course
Heaven--knowledge that there is no heaven, that it's a fraud, like
the Wizard of Oz.
Adulthood--men with clubs
Scene of remembered humiliation
End of innocence (realization that it's just a golf course)

John's lists confirmed what he had suspected—the meanings of the four items did seem to change as the boys grew up. To the boys, the arroyo, the grinding ball, and the golf course were magical, but when the boys grew up, all three lost their magic and became ordinary. The secret lion, however, seemed more complex than the other three, and John knew that he would have to develop his ideas further before he could show how the lion's meaning changes and how these changes affect the story as a whole.

Deciding on a Thesis

With his key ideas organized into lists that clarified some possible relationships among them, John began to see a tentative thesis emerging. Although he still was not sure he would limit his essay to the four items on his lists, he now felt certain that these items were symbols: Prominently and repeatedly mentioned, they helped to convey the story's theme. As a result, he was able to decide on the main idea he wanted his essay to communicate, and he expressed this idea in his tentative thesis statement, the main idea he wanted to support in his essay's first draft:

> The meanings of the story's key symbols change as the boys move from childhood to adolescence to adulthood; these changes reveal corresponding changes in the boys' view of the world from idealism to frustration to resignation.

Preparing an Outline

Even though his essay was to be short, John prepared an outline that mapped out a simple arrangement for his ideas. He decided that discussing the four key symbols one by one and drawing conclusions about their common purpose in his essay's opening and closing paragraphs would be the most effective strategy. This arrangement would allow him to group his information into the four by-now-familiar categories. He also decided to discuss the lion last because he saw it as the story's pivotal symbol, the one he believed to be the most important.

Looking back over all his notes, and paying close attention to his thesis statement, John constructed the following scratch outline:

Arroyo
    Mississippi
    Rebellion
    Waste dump
Grinding ball
    [Not yet discovered]
    Lost perfection
    "Things get taken away."
Golf course
    Heaven
    Humiliation
    Golf course
Lion
    [Not yet discovered]
    "roaring"; "raging beast"
    Just the lion

Drafting

Guided by his scratch outline, his thesis statement, and his notes, John Frei wrote the following first draft. Because his notes included many ideas not included on his scratch outline, and because he discovered new ideas and connections among ideas as he wrote, the draft does not follow the scratch outline exactly.

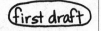

Symbols in "The Secret Lion"

"The Secret Lion" is a story that is rich in symbols. It is also a story about change. The meanings of the story's key symbols change as the boys move from childhood to adolescence to adulthood; these changes reveal corresponding changes in the boys' view of the world from idealism to frustration to resignation.

The arroyo, or river, is special to the narrator and his friend Sergio when they are boys. Literally, it is a place to play. Symbolically, it is a place to rebel (they're not supposed to be there; they yell forbidden words). It could also symbolize the continuum of discoveries they will make before they are completely grown up. To the young boys, the arroyo symbolizes a retreat from the disappointment of the golf course; it is their second choice. Later, it represented adventure, the uncertainty and unpredictability of adolescence, as illustrated by the fact that they could not tell just by looking at it from the riverside whether the river was going to be tainted with sewage. When they are children, it is their Mississippi. When they are adolescents, it is a place to hang out and a symbol of adolescent rebellion; as an adult, the narrator looks back at it for what it was: an ordinary river polluted by sewage. The arroyo doesn't change, but the boys' view of it changes as they change.

At first, when they find the grinding ball, it stands for everything that is perfect and fascinating (and therefore forbidden and unattainable) in life. Like a child's life, it is perfect. They knew they couldn't keep it forever, just as they couldn't be children forever, so they buried it. When they tried to look for it again, they couldn't find it. They admit later that they don't look very hard. (People always wish they can find youth again, but they can't.) The ball represents perfection in an imperfect world, childhood innocence in an adult world. They hide it from their mother because they know she won't see it as perfect; she'll make them "getridofit" (44). They hide it because they want to retain the excitement of the undiscovered, but once they've used it and seen it and buried it, it's not new anymore. Even if they'd been able to find it, it would still be lost. To the adult narrator, it's just an ordinary object used in mining.

The golf course, which they wander into at age five, is, for a short period of time, "heaven" (46). It is lush and green and carefully cared for, and it is the opposite of the polluted arroyo. It is also another world, as mysterious as the Land of Oz. With the realization that it is not heaven to the golfers, the boys see what outsiders they really are. They may start "acting 'rich'" (46), but it will be just an act. There are no Coke-holders, no Oz, no heaven. The adolescents see the golf course as a scene of defeat and embarrassment, the setting for the confrontation that sent them back to the arroyo. To the adult, the golf course is just a golf course.

5   The secret lion is the most complex symbol in the story. In a sense it stands for the innocence of childhood, something we lose when we learn more. The lion symbolizes a great "roaring" disturbance (43). It is a change that unsettles everything for a brief time and then passes, leaving everything changed in irrevocable, indescribable ways. It symbolizes the boys' growing up: they are changed, but still the same people. The "secret lion" is that thing that changes

little boys into men. It is secret because no one notices it happening; before it is noticed, the change has occurred, and the little boy is gone forever. It is a lion because it "roars" through the boy like a storm, and makes all of the growing up changes which can be "the biggest things" (43). In a more specific sense, the lion stands for puberty, reflected in their rage and frustration when they shout profanity. In the beginning of the story, the lion is rage (puberty, adolescence); in the middle, it suggests greatness (passing through adolescence into manhood); at the end it's just the lion--("It was the lion" [47])--without any symbolic significance.

By the time they bury the ball, they have already learned one lesson, and the force of adulthood is pushing childhood aside. The golf course changes from heaven to shame to golf course; the ball changes from a special, perfect thing to something ordinary; the arroyo changes from grand river to polluted stream. Maybe it is the knowledge that life is not perfect, the knowledge that comes with growing up, that is the secret lion.

First Draft: Commentary

As John reviewed his first draft, he made a number of changes in content, style, and organization. He decided to delete wordiness and repetition; add more specific references, including quotations, from the story; sharpen transitions and add clearer topic sentences; and reorganize paragraphs to make logical and causal connections more obvious. He also planned to revise his introduction and conclusion.

Discussions with classmates in a peer review group and with his instructor gave him some additional insights. The students' major criticism was that John's thesis seemed to make a claim he could not support: that the development of all four symbols follows the three stages of the boys' lives. One student pointed out that two of the four symbols (the grinding ball and the secret lion) do not even enter the boys' lives until adolescence, and John's treatment of the story's most prominent symbol—the lion—does not show it to change in any significant way. The group decided that he should simplify his thesis and focus on the way the four symbols all reflect the story's theme about the inevitability of change.

John also discussed his draft with his instructor, who agreed with the students' suggestions and supported John's own assessment of his essay's strengths and weaknesses. In addition, he helped John with the arrangement of his essay, suggesting that he discuss the golf course first because it is the setting for the event that occurred first in time, and because the disillusionment associated with it influences the subsequent events.

John and his instructor also discussed ideas for his introduction and conclusion, deciding to use these paragraphs to stress the common theme that all four symbols convey instead of focusing on the different ways in which each of the four separate symbols changes.

Finally, John's instructor was concerned about John's tendency in this draft to engage in "symbol hunting." He suggested that rather than focusing on finding equivalents for each of the four items ("the ball represents perfection," "the lion stands for puberty," and so on), John should consider how the use of these symbols opens up the story, how they work together to communicate the story's theme. His instructor pointed out that in looking for neat equivalent values for each symbol, John was oversimplifying very complex, suggestive symbols. And, as John's own draft indicates, the symbols seem to suggest different things at different stages in the boys' lives.

Revising and Editing

The revisions John decided to make are reflected in his second draft.

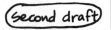

Symbols in "The Secret Lion"

"The Secret Lion" is a story about change. The first paragraph of the story gives a twelve-year-old's view of growing up: Everything changes. When the child watches the magician, he is amazed at the "staying-the-same part" (43); adults focus on the tablecloth. As adults, we lose the ability to see the world through innocent eyes. We have the benefit of experience, confident the trick will work as long as the magician pulls the tablecloth in the proper way. The "staying-the-same part" is less important than the technique. In a story full of prominent symbols, the magician's trick does not seem very important, but all the key symbols, like the sleight of hand, are about change. In fact, each of the story's key symbols highlights the theme of the inevitability of change that permeates the lives of the narrator and his friend Sergio.

The golf course is one such symbol. When the boys first see it, it is "heaven" (46). Lush and green and carefully cared for, it is completely different from the dry brown Arizona countryside and the polluted arroyo. In fact, to the boys it is another world, as mysterious as Oz--and just as unreal. Almost at once, the Emerald City becomes black and white again, the "Coke-holders" disappear, and the boys stop "acting 'rich'" (46). Heaven becomes a golf course, and the boys are changed forever.

The arroyo, or river, is another symbol that reinforces the theme of the inevitability of change. It is a special place for the boys--a place to rebel, to shout forbidden words, to swim in waters polluted by a sewage treatment plant. Although it represents a retreat from the disillusionment of the golf course, clearly second choice, it is the boys' "personal Mississippi" (43), full of possibilities. Eventually, though, the arroyo too disappoints the boys, and they stop going there. "Nature seemed to keep pushing us around one way or another, teaching us the same thing every place we ended up" (45). The lesson they keep learning is that nothing is permanent.

The grinding ball, round and perfect, seems to suggest permanence and stability. But when the boys find it, they realize at once that they cannot keep it forever, just as they cannot remain children forever. Like a child's life, it is perfect--but temporary. Burying it is their futile attempt to make time stand still, to preserve perfection in an imperfect world, innocence in an adult world, and they have already learned Nature's lesson well enough to know that this is not possible. They do not look very hard for the ball, but even if they'd been able to find it, the perfection and the innocence it represents would still be unattainable.

5   The secret lion, the most complex symbol, suggests the most profound kind of change: moving from innocence to experience, from childhood to adulthood. When the narrator is twelve, he says, "something happened that we didn't have a name for, but it was there nonetheless like a lion, and roaring, roaring that way the biggest things do. Everything changed" (43). School is different, girls are different, language is different. Innocence was lost. The lion is associated with a great "roaring" disturbance, a change that unsettles everything for a brief time and then passes, leaving everything changed in irrevocable, indescribable ways. The secret lion is the thing that changes little boys into men. It is a

lion because it "roars" through the boy like a storm; every-thing changes.

In an attempt to make things stay the same, to make time stand still, the boys bury the grinding ball "because it was perfect. . . . It was the lion" (47). The grinding ball is "like that place, that whole arroyo" (44): secret and perfect. In other words, the ball and the arroyo and the lion are all tightly connected. By the time the boys bury the ball, they have already learned one sad lesson and are already on their way to adulthood. Heaven is just a golf course; the round, perfect object is only "a cannonball thing used in mining" (44); the arroyo is no Mississippi but a polluted stream; and childhood does not last forever. "Things get taken away" (47), and this knowledge that things do not last is the secret lion.

Second Draft: Commentary

John felt fairly satisfied with his second draft. His revised thesis statement seemed more reasonable than the one in his first draft; it was also convincingly supported, with clearly worded topic sentences that introduced support paragraphs and connected them to the thesis statement. The second draft was also a good deal less wordy and more focused than the first, notably in the paragraphs about the arroyo and the grinding ball, and the introduction and conclusion were more fully developed. Moreover, he had given up his search for the one true "meaning" of each symbol, focusing instead on the many possibilities of each.

Now that John felt comfortable with the larger concerns of his essay, he was ready to turn his attention to smaller items, such as style, grammar, mechanics, punctuation, and format. For instance, he planned to eliminate contractions, to check all verb tenses carefully, to review documentation and work quotations into his text more smoothly, to make his thesis statement more precise and his title more interesting, and to revise the language of his introduction and conclusion further. As he made his revisions, he planned to scrutinize this draft carefully, aiming to make his final paper more concise.

John Frei

Professor Nyysola

English 102

15 April 1996

"The Secret Lion": Everything Changes

     The first paragraph of Alberto Alvaro Ríos's "The Se-
cret Lion" presents a twelve-year-old's view of growing up:
Everything changes. When the magician pulls a tablecloth
out from under a pile of dishes, the child is amazed at the
"staying-the-same part" (43); adults focus on the tablecloth. As adults, we have the benefit of experience; we know
the trick will work as long as the technique is correct. We
gain confidence, but we lose our innocence, and we lose our
sense of wonder. The price we pay for knowledge is a permanent sense of loss, and this tradeoff is central to "The
Secret Lion," a story whose key symbols reinforce its central theme: that change is inevitable, and that change is always accompanied by loss.

     The golf course is one symbol that helps to convey this
theme. When the boys first see the golf course, it is
"heaven" (46). Lush and green and carefully tended, it is
the antithesis of the dry, brown Arizona landscape and the
polluted arroyo. In fact, to the boys it is another world, as
exotic as Oz and ultimately as unreal. Before long the Emerald City becomes black and white again. They learn that
there is no such thing as a "Coke-holder," that their "acting
'rich'" is just an act, and that their heaven is only a golf
course (46). As the narrator acknowledges, "Something got
taken away from us that moment. Heaven" (46).

Frei 2

Topic
sentence
identifies
another key
symbol
The arroyo, or river, is another symbol that reflects the idea of the inevitability of change, and of the loss that accompanies change. It is a special, Eden-like place for the boys--a place where they can rebel by shouting forbidden words and by swimming in forbidden waters. Although it is a retreat from the disillusionment of the golf course, it is still their "personal Mississippi" (43), full of possibilities. Eventually, though, the arroyo too disappoints the boys, and they stop going there. As the narrator says, "Nature seemed to keep pushing us around one way or another, teaching us the same thing every place we ended up" (45). The lesson they keep learning is that nothing is permanent.

Topic
sentence
identifies
another key
symbol
The grinding ball, round and perfect, suggests permanence and stability. But when the boys find it, they realize at once that they cannot keep it forever, just as they cannot remain balanced forever between childhood and adulthood. Like a child's life, the ball is perfect--but temporary. Burying it is their desperate attempt to stop time, to preserve perfection in an imperfect world, innocence in an adult world. But the boys are already twelve years old, and they have learned nature's lesson well enough to know that this action will not work. Even if they had been able to find the ball, the perfection and the innocence it suggests to them would still be unattainable. Perhaps that is why they do not try very hard to find it.

Topic
sentence
identifies
final (and
most
important)
symbol
to be
discussed
5   Like the story's other symbols, the secret lion itself suggests the most profound kind of change: the movement from innocence to experience, from childhood to adulthood, from expectation to disappointment to resignation. The narrator

explains that when he was twelve, "something happened that we didn't have a name for, but it was there nonetheless like a lion, and roaring, roaring that way the biggest things do. Everything changed" (43). School was different, girls were different, language was different. Despite its loud roar, the lion remained paradoxically "secret," unnoticed until it passed. Like adolescence, the secret lion is a roaring disturbance that unsettles everything for a brief time and then passes, leaving everything changed.

Conclusion In an attempt to make things stay the same, to make time stand still, the boys bury the grinding ball "because it was perfect. . . . It was the lion" (47). The grinding ball is "like that place, that whole arroyo" (44): secret and perfect. The ball and the arroyo and the lion are all perfect, but all, ironically, are temporary. The first paragraph of "The Secret Lion" tells us "Everything changed" (43); by the last paragraph we learn what this change means: "Things get taken away" (47). In other words, change implies loss. Heaven turns out to be just a golf course; the round, perfect object only "a cannonball thing used in mining" (44); the arroyo just a polluted stream; and childhood just a phase. "Things get taken away," and this knowledge that things do not last is the lion, secret yet roaring.

Final Draft: Commentary

As he revised and edited his second draft, John made many changes in word choice and sentence structure. He also changed his title, edited to eliminate errors in mechanics and punctuation, and ran a spell check. In this final draft he made his thesis statement even more precise than it was in the previous draft, to communicate the idea of the relationship between change and loss that is central to the essay. In addition, he worked all quoted material smoothly into his essay, taking care to use quotations only when the author's words added something vital to the paper. Finally, John checked all his references to page numbers in the story, so readers would be able to return to his source if necessary to check the accuracy and appropriateness of his quotations.

CHAPTER 4

Plot

It's a truism that there are only two basic plots in fiction: one, somebody takes a trip; two, a stranger comes to town.

LEE SMITH, NEW YORK TIMES BOOK REVIEW

Plot *is very imperfectly understood, and has never been rightly defined. Many persons regard it as mere complexity of incident. In its most rigorous acceptation, it is* that from which no component atom can be removed, and in which none of the component atoms can be displaced, without ruin to the whole; *and although a sufficiently good plot may be constructed, without attention to the whole rigor of this definition, still it is the definition which the true artist should always keep in view, and always endeavor to consummate in his works.*

EDGAR ALLAN POE

The beginning of an action always presents us with a situation in which there is some element of instability, some conflict; in the middle of an action there is a period of readjustment of forces in the process of seeking a new kind of stability; in the end of an action, some point of stability is reached, the forces that have been brought into play have been resolved.

CLEANTH BROOKS AND ROBERT PENN WARREN, UNDERSTANDING FICTION

The simplest way to tell a story, equally favoured by tribal bards and parents at bedtime, is to begin at the beginning, and go on until you reach the end, or your audience falls asleep. But even in antiquity, storytellers perceived the interesting effects that could be obtained by deviating from chronological order. The classical epic began *in medias res, in the midst of the story. For example, the narrative of the* Odyssey *begins halfway through the hero's hazardous voyage home from the Trojan War, loops back to describe his earlier adventures, then follows the story to its conclusion in Ithaca.*

Through time-shift, narrative avoids presenting life as just one damn thing after another, and allows us to make connections of causality and irony between widely separated events. A shift of narrative focus back in time may change our interpretation of something which happened much later in the chronology of the story, but which we have already experienced as readers of the text. This is a familiar device of cinema, the flashback. Film has more difficulty accommodating the effect of "flashforward"—the anticipatory glimpse of what is going to happen in the future of the narrative, known to classical rhetoricians as "prolepsis." This is because such information implies the existence of a narrator who knows the whole story and films do not normally have narrators.

DAVID LODGE, *THE ART OF FICTION*

Why do we read fiction? The answer is simple. We read it because we like it. And we like it because fiction, as an image of life, stimulates and gratifies our interest in life. But whatever interests may be appealed to by fiction, the special and immediate interest that takes us to fiction is always our interest in a story.

A story is not merely an image of life, but life in motion—specifically, the presentation of individual characters moving through their particular experiences to some end that we may accept as meaningful. And the experience that is characteristically presented in a story is that of facing a problem, a conflict. To put it bluntly: no conflict, no story.

ROBERT PENN WARREN, *NEW & SELECTED ESSAYS*

Alfred Hitchcock's 1951 film *Strangers on a Train,* based on a suspense novel by Patricia Highsmith, offers an intriguing premise: Two men, strangers, can each murder someone the other wishes dead; because they have no apparent connection to their victims, both can escape suspicion. Many people would describe this ingenious scheme as the film's "plot," but in fact it is simply the gimmick around which the complex plot revolves. Certainly a clever twist can be an important ingredient of a story's plot, but plot is more than "what happens"; it is how what happens is presented. **Plot** is the way in which a story's events are arranged; it is shaped by causal connections—historical, social, and personal—by the interaction between characters, and by the juxtaposition of events. In *Strangers on a Train,* as in many well-developed works of fiction, the plot that unfolds is complex, with one character directing the events and determining their order while the other character is drawn into the action against his will. The same elements that enrich the plot of the film—unexpected events, conflict, suspense, flashbacks, foreshadowing—can also enrich the plot of a work of short fiction.

CONFLICT

Readers' interest and involvement are heightened by a story's **conflict,** the struggle between opposing forces that emerges as the action develops. This conflict is a clash between the **protagonist,** a story's principal character, and an **antagonist,** someone or something presented in opposition to the protagonist. Sometimes the antagonist is clearly a villain; more often, he or she simply represents a conflicting point of view or advocates a course of action different from the one the protagonist follows. Sometimes the antagonist is not a character at all but a situation (war, poverty) or an event (a natural disaster, such as a flood or a storm) that challenges the protagonist. In other stories, the protagonist may struggle against a supernatural force, or the conflict may be internal, occurring within a character's mind. It may, for example, be a struggle between two moral choices, such as whether to stay at home and care for an aging parent or to leave and make a new life. In such a case, the parent is not the antagonist; rather, the conflict occurs within the protagonist's mind.

STAGES OF PLOT

A work's plot explores one or more conflicts, moving from *exposition* through a series of *complications* to a *climax,* and, finally, to a *resolution.*

In a story's **exposition** the writer presents the basic information readers need to understand the events that follow. Typically, the exposition sets the story's scene, introduces the major characters, and perhaps suggests the major events or conflicts that will follow. In a very brief story, a single sentence like "Knowing that Mrs. Mallard was afflicted with a heart trouble, great care was taken to break to her as gently as possible the news of her husband's death" can present exposition clearly and economically. This sentence, which opens Kate Chopin's classic "The Story of an Hour" (p. 70), gives readers two pieces of information vital to their understanding of the plot that will unfold: Mrs. Mallard is physically delicate, and she is about to hear news of her husband's death. In a longer story, John Updike's "A&P" (p. 105), a more fully developed exposition section establishes the story's setting, introduces the main characters, and suggests possible conflicts. In some experimental stories a distinct exposition component may be absent, as it is in Lorrie Moore's "How to Talk to Your Mother (Notes)" (p. 89).

As the plot progresses, the story's conflict unfolds through a series of complications that will eventually lead readers to the story's climax. The action may include several crises. A **crisis** is a peak in the story's action, a moment of considerable tension or importance; the **climax** is the point of greatest tension or importance, the scene that presents a story's decisive action.

The final stage of plot, the **resolution,** or **denouement** (French for "untying of the knot"), draws the action to a close and ties up all remaining loose ends. Sometimes this resolution is achieved by virtue of a **deus ex machina** (Latin for "a god from a machine"), an intervention of some force or agent previously extraneous to the story—the appearance of a long-lost relative or a fortuitous inheritance, the discovery of a character's true identity, a last-minute rescue by a character not previously introduced. Usually, however, the resolution is more plausible: All the events lead logically and convincingly (although not necessarily predictably) to the resolution.

Sometimes the ending of a story is indefinite—that is, readers are not quite sure what the protagonist will do, or what will happen next. This kind of resolution, although it may leave some readers feeling cheated, has its advantages: It mirrors the complexity of life, where closure rarely occurs, and it can draw readers into the action as they try to understand the significance of the story's ending or to decide how conflicts should have been resolved.

ORDER AND SEQUENCE

A writer may present a story's events in strict chronological order, with each event presented in the sequence in which it actually took place. More often, however, especially in relatively modern fiction, writers do not present events chronologically. Instead, they present incidents out of expected order, or in no apparent order. For example, a writer may choose to begin **in medias res** (Latin for "in the midst of things"), starting with a key event and later going back in time to explain events that preceded it, as Tillie Olsen does in "I Stand Here Ironing" (p. 152). Or, a writer can decide to begin a work of fiction at the end and then move back to reconstruct events that led up to the final outcome, as William Faulkner does in "A Rose for Emily" (p. 80). Many sequences are possible as the writer manipulates events to create interest, suspense, confusion, wonder, or some other effect.

Writers commonly use established techniques such as flashbacks and foreshadowing to vary chronological order. A **flashback** moves out of sequence to examine an event or situation that occurred before the time in which the story's action takes place. A character can remember an earlier event, or a story's narrator can recreate an earlier situation. For example, in Alberto Alvaro Rios's "The Secret Lion" (p. 43) the adult narrator looks back at events that occurred when he was twelve years old—and then moves back further in time to consider related events that occurred when he was five. In Edgar Allan Poe's "The Cask of Amontillado" (p. 209) the entire story is recounted as a flashback. Flashbacks are valuable because they can substitute for or supplement formal exposition by presenting background vital to the readers' understanding of a story's events. One disadvantage of flashbacks is that, because they interrupt the natural flow of events, they may be intrusive or distracting. Such distractions, however, can be an advantage if the writer wishes to reveal events gradually and subtly or to obscure causal links.

Foreshadowing is the introduction early in a story of situations, events, characters, or objects that hint at things to come. Eventually, a chance remark, a natural occurrence, or a seemingly trivial event is revealed to have great significance. For example, a dark cloud passing across the sky can foreshadow future troubles. In this way, foreshadowing allows a writer to hint provocatively at what is to come, so that readers only gradually become aware of a particular detail's role in a story. Thus, foreshadowing helps to create suspense as readers begin to sense what will occur and grow increasingly involved as they see the likelihood (or even the inevitability) of a particular outcome.

In addition to employing conventional techniques like flashbacks and foreshadowing, writers may experiment with sequence by substantially tampering with—or even dispensing with—chronological order. Two examples are the scrambled chronology of "A Rose for Emily" and the reverse chronology of "How to Talk to Your Mother (Notes)." In such instances the experimental form enhances interest and encourages readers to become involved with the story as they work to untangle or reorder the events and determine their logical and causal connections.

A FINAL NOTE

In some popular forms of fiction, plot is likely to be the dominant element. For example, in mystery or adventure stories, which may lack fully developed characters, complex themes, and elaborately described settings, the plot line will be clear and easy to follow. In richer, more complicated works of fiction, however, plot, like other elements, may be more complex and less obvious.

▼▼

CHECKLIST FOR WRITING ABOUT PLOT

- ◆ What happens in the story?
- ◆ Where does the story's formal exposition section end? What do readers learn about characters in this section? What do readers learn about setting? What possible conflicts are suggested here?
- ◆ What is the story's central conflict? What other conflicts are presented? Who is the protagonist? Who (or what) serves as the antagonist?
- ◆ Identify the story's crisis or crises.
- ◆ Identify the story's climax.
- ◆ How is the story's central conflict resolved? Is this resolution plausible? Satisfying? Logical?
- ◆ Which portion of the story constitutes the resolution? Do any problems remain unresolved? Does any uncertainty remain? If so, does this uncertainty strengthen or weaken the story? Would another ending be more effective?
- ◆ How are the story's events arranged? Are they presented in chronological order? What events are presented out of logical sequence? Does the story use foreshadowing? Flashbacks? Are the causal connections between events clear? Logical? If not, can you explain why?

▲▲

KATE CHOPIN (1851–1904)   must, in a sense, be considered a contemporary writer. Her honest, sexually frank stories (many of which were out of print for more than half a century) were rediscovered in the 1960s and 1970s, influencing a new generation of writers. Though she was a popular contributor of stories and sketches to the magazines of her day, Chopin scandalized many critics with her outspoken novel *The Awakening* (1899), in which a woman seeks sexual and emotional fulfillment with a man who is not her husband. The book was removed from the shelves of the public library in St. Louis, where Chopin was born.

Chopin was born Katherine O'Flaherty, the daughter of a wealthy Irish-born merchant and his aristocratic Creole wife. Educated at convent schools, she was married at nineteen to Oscar Chopin, a Louisiana cotton broker who took her to live first in New Orleans and later on a plantation at Cloutierville, near Natchitoches, in central Louisiana, where it is said that she offended members of polite society by drinking beer and crossing her legs—at the knees. Chopin's representations of the Cane River region and its people in two volumes of short stories—*Bayou Folk* (1894) and *A Night in Arcadie* (1897)—are the foundation of her reputation as a local colorist. Resemblances have been noted between these stories and certain works of Guy de Maupassant, which Chopin had translated from French to English.

A busy wife and mother, Chopin seems to have begun writing only after she returned to St. Louis following her husband's sudden death in 1883. "The Story of an Hour" depicts a brief event in a woman's life, but in this single hour, Chopin reveals both a lifetime's emotional torment and the momentary joy of freedom.

KATE CHOPIN

The Story of an Hour

(1894)

Knowing that Mrs. Mallard was afflicted with a heart trouble, great care was taken to break to her as gently as possible the news of her husband's death.

It was her sister Josephine who told her, in broken sentences, veiled hints that revealed in half concealing. Her husband's friend Richards was there, too, near her. It was he who had been in the newspaper office when intelligence of the railroad disaster was received, with Brently Mallard's name leading the list of "killed." He had only taken the time to assure himself of its truth by a second telegram, and had hastened to forestall any less careful, less tender friend in bearing the sad message.

She did not hear the story as many women have heard the same, with a paralyzed inability to accept its significance. She wept at once, with sudden, wild abandonment, in her sister's arms. When the storm of grief had spent itself she went away to her room alone. She would have no one follow her.

There stood, facing the open window, a comfortable, roomy armchair. Into this she sank, pressed down by a physical exhaustion that haunted her body and seemed to reach into her soul.

5   She could see in the open square before her house the tops of trees that were all aquiver with the new spring life. The delicious breath of rain was in the air. In the street below a peddler was crying his wares. The notes of a distant song which some one was singing reached her faintly, and countless sparrows were twittering in the eaves.

There were patches of blue sky showing here and there through the clouds that had met and piled one above the other in the west facing her window.

She sat with her head thrown back upon the cushion of the chair, quite motionless, except when a sob came up into her throat and shook her, as a child who has cried itself to sleep continues to sob in its dreams.

She was young, with a fair, calm face, whose lines bespoke repression and even a certain strength. But now there was a dull stare in her eyes, whose gaze was fixed away off yonder on one of those patches of blue sky. It was not a glance of reflection, but rather indicated a suspension of intelligent thought.

There was something coming to her and she was waiting for it, fearfully. What was it? She did not know; it was too subtle and elusive to name. But she felt it, creeping out of the sky, reaching toward her through the sounds, the scents, the color that filled the air.

10   Now her bosom rose and fell tumultuously. She was beginning to recognize this thing that was approaching to possess her, and she was striving to beat it back with her will—as powerless as her two white slender hands would have been.

When she abandoned herself a little whispered word escaped her slightly parted lips. She said it over and over under her breath: "Free, free, free!" The vacant stare and the look of terror that had followed it went from her eyes. They stayed keen and bright. Her pulses beat fast, and the coursing blood warmed and relaxed every inch of her body.

She did not stop to ask if it were not a monstrous joy that held her. A clear and exalted perception enabled her to dismiss the suggestion as trivial.

She knew that she would weep again when she saw the kind, tender hands folded in death; the face that had never looked save with love upon her, fixed and gray and dead. But she saw beyond that bitter moment a long procession of years to come that would belong to her absolutely. And she opened and spread her arms out to them in welcome.

There would be no one to live for during those coming years; she would live for herself. There would be no powerful will bending her in that blind persistence with which men and women believe they have a right to impose a private will upon a fellow creature. A kind intention or a cruel intention made the act seem no less a crime as she looked upon it in that brief moment of illumination.

15 And yet she had loved him—sometimes. Often she had not. What did it matter! What could love, the unsolved mystery, count for in face of this possession of self-assertion which she suddenly recognized as the strongest impulse of her being.

"Free! Body and soul free!" she kept whispering.

Josephine was kneeling before the closed door with her lips to the key-hole, imploring for admission. "Louise, open the door! I beg; open the door—you will make yourself ill. What are you doing, Louise? For heaven's sake open the door."

"Go away. I am not making myself ill." No; she was drinking in a very elixir of life through that open window.

Her fancy was running riot along those days ahead of her. Spring days, and summer days, and all sorts of days that would be her own. She breathed a quick prayer that life might be long. It was only yesterday she had thought with a shudder that life might be long.

20 She arose at length and opened the door to her sister's importunities. There was a feverish triumph in her eyes, and she carried herself unwittingly like a goddess of Victory. She clasped her sister's waist, and together they descended the stairs. Richards stood waiting for them at the bottom.

Some one was opening the front door with a latchkey. It was Brently Mallard who entered, a little travel-stained, composedly carrying his grip-sack and umbrella. He had been far from the scene of the accident, and did not even know there had been one. He stood amazed at Josephine's piercing cry; at Richards' quick motion to screen him from the view of his wife.

But Richards was too late.

When the doctors came they said she had died of heart disease—of joy that kills.

READING AND REACTING

1. The story's basic exposition is presented in its first two paragraphs. What additional information about character or setting would you like to know? Why do you suppose the writer does not supply this information?

2. "The Story of an Hour" is a very economical story, with little action or dialogue. Is this a strength or a weakness? Explain.

3. When it was first published in *Vogue* magazine in 1894, the magazine's editors titled this story "The Dream of an Hour." A film version of "The Story of an Hour," echoing the last words of the story, is called *The Joy That Kills.* Which of the three titles do you believe most accurately represents what happens in the story?

4. Did Brently Mallard abuse his wife? Did he love her? Did she love him? Exactly why was she so relieved to be rid of him? Can readers answer any of these questions with certainty?

5. What is the nature of the conflict in this story? Who, or what, is Mrs. Mallard's antagonist?

6. What emotions does Mrs. Mallard experience during the hour she spends alone in her room? What events do you imagine take place during this same period outside her room? Outside her house?

7. Do you find the story's ending satisfying? Believable? Contrived?

8. Was the story's ending unexpected or were you prepared for it? What elements foreshadowed this ending?

9. **JOURNAL ENTRY**   Rewrite the story's ending, substituting a few paragraphs of your own for the last three paragraphs of the story.

10. **CRITICAL PERSPECTIVE**   Writing in the *Southern Literary Journal,* Cynthia Griffin Wolff observes that before the 1960s, many critics had a "tendency to dismiss Chopin's fiction as little more than local color," viewing her as essentially a regional writer. Accordingly, they saw her major contribution to literature as the accurate depiction of setting, customs, and manners in the Louisiana bayou. Other critics, according to Wolff, believe Chopin's major contribution is her surprise or "trick" conclusions, endings that are not what readers expect. Which do you see as more important to "The Story of an Hour," the setting or the ending? Do you believe that the story has something to offer beyond these two elements, or do you agree with those critics who would see Chopin as "only" a local colorist or the creator of clever plot twists?

NADINE GORDIMER (1923–   ), winner of the 1991 Nobel Prize in literature, has been publishing short stories, essays, and novels about South Africa, her native country, since she was fifteen. Gordimer once explained that after growing up as a middle-class child of Jewish immigrants, becoming a politically aware writer in South Africa was like "peeling an onion. You're sloughing off all the conditioning that you've had since you were a child." The prevailing attitude of her extensive work has evolved from cautious optimism to pessimism in accord with the changing nature of Africa in her lifetime. Michiko Kakutani of the *New York Times* suggests that in the attempt to illustrate that apartheid debases the lives of both blacks and whites, "she has mapped out the social, political and emotional geography of that troubled land with extraordinary passion and precision." Though her work was often banned in her own country because of its condemnation of apartheid, Gordimer continues to live in Johannesburg.

Gordimer's novels include *The Lying Days* (1953), *A Guest of Honor* (1970), *Burger's Daughter* (1979), *July's People* (1981), and *None to Accompany Me* (1994). Her short stories have been collected in such volumes as *Face to Face* (1949), *Jump and Other Stories* (1991), and *Why Haven't You Written?* (1992).

N A D I N E   G O R D I M E R

Once Upon a Time

(1991)

Someone has written to ask me to contribute to an anthology of stories for children. I reply that I don't write children's stories; and he writes back that at a recent congress/book fair/seminar a certain novelist said every writer ought to write at least one story for children. I think of sending a postcard saying I don't accept that I 'ought' to write anything.

And then last night I woke up—or rather was wakened without knowing what had roused me.

A voice in the echo-chamber of the subconscious?

A sound.

5   A creaking of the kind made by the weight carried by one foot after another along a wooden floor. I listened. I felt the apertures of my ears distend with concentration. Again: the creaking. I was waiting for it; waiting to hear if it indicated that feet were moving from room to room, coming up the passage—to my door. I have no burglar bars, no gun under the pillow, but I have the same fears as people who do take these precautions, and my windowpanes are thin as rime, could shatter like a wineglass. A woman was murdered (how do they put it) in broad daylight in a house two blocks away, last year, and the fierce dogs who guarded an old widower and his collection of antique clocks were strangled before he was knifed by a casual labourer he had dismissed without pay.

I was staring at the door, making it out in my mind rather than seeing it, in the dark. I lay quite still—a victim already—but the arrhythmia of my heart was fleeing, knocking this way and that against its body-cage. How finely tuned the senses are, just out of rest, sleep! I could never listen intently as that in the distractions of the day; I was reading every faintest sound, identifying and classifying its possible threat.

But I learned that I was to be neither threatened nor spared. There was no human weight pressing on the boards, the creaking was a buckling, an epicentre of stress. I was in it. The house that surrounds me while I sleep is built on undermined ground; far beneath my bed, the floor, the house's foundations, the stopes and passages of gold mines have hollowed the rock, and when some face trembles, detaches and falls, three thousand feet below, the whole house shifts slightly, bringing uneasy strain to the balance and counterbalance of brick, cement, wood and glass that hold it as a structure around me. The misbeats of my heart tailed off like the last muffled flourishes on one of the wooden xylophones made by the Chopi and Tsonga migrant miners who might have been down there, under me in the earth at that moment. The stope where the fall was could have been disused, dripping water from its ruptured veins; or men might now be interred there in the most profound of tombs.

I couldn't find a position in which my mind would let go of my body—release me to sleep again. So I began to tell myself a story; a bedtime story.

In a house, in a suburb, in a city, there were a man and his wife who loved each other very much and were living happily ever after. They had a little boy, and they loved him very much. They had a cat and a dog that the little boy loved very much. They had a car and a caravan trailer for holidays, and a swimming-pool which was fenced so that the little boy and his playmates would not fall in and drown. They had a housemaid who was absolutely trustworthy and an itinerant gardener who was highly recommended by the neighbours. For when they began to live happily ever after they were warned, by that wise old witch, the husband's mother, not to take on anyone off the street. They were inscribed in a medical benefit society, their pet dog was licensed, they were insured against fire, flood damage and theft, and subscribed to the local Neighbourhood Watch, which supplied them with a plaque for their gates lettered YOU HAVE BEEN WARNED over the silhouette of a would-be intruder. He was masked; it could not be said if he was black or white, and therefore proved the property owner was no racist.

10   It was not possible to insure the house, the swimming pool or the car against riot damage. There were riots, but these were outside the city, where people of another colour were quartered. These people were not allowed into the suburb except as reliable housemaids and gardeners, so there was nothing to fear, the husband told the wife. Yet she was afraid that some day such people might come up the street and tear off the plaque YOU HAVE BEEN WARNED and open the gates and stream in . . . Nonsense, my dear, said the husband, there are police and soldiers and tear-gas and guns to keep them away. But to please her—for he loved her very much and buses were being burned, cars stoned, and schoolchildren shot by the police in those quarters out of sight and hearing of the suburb—he had electronically-controlled gates fitted. Anyone who pulled off the sign YOU HAVE BEEN WARNED and tried to open the gates would have to announce his intentions by pressing a button and speaking into a receiver relayed to the house. The little boy was fascinated by the device and used it as a walkie-talkie in cops and robbers play with his small friends.

The riots were suppressed, but there were many burglaries in the sub-urb and somebody's trusted housemaid was tied up and shut in a cup-board by thieves while she was in charge of her employers' house. The trusted housemaid of the man and wife and little boy was so upset by this misfortune befalling a friend left, as she herself often was, with responsi-bility for the possessions of the man and his wife and the little boy that she implored her employers to have burglar bars attached to the doors and windows of the house, and an alarm system installed. The wife said, She is right, let us take heed to her advice. So from every window and door in the house where they were living happily ever after they now saw the trees and sky through bars, and when the little boy's pet cat tried to climb in by the fanlight to keep him company in his little bed at night, as it customarily had done, it set off the alarm keening through the house.

The alarm was often answered—it seemed—by other burglar alarms, in other houses, that had been triggered by pet cats or nibbling mice. The alarms called to one another across the gardens in shrills and bleats and wails that everyone soon became accustomed to, so that the din roused the inhabitants of the suburb no more than the croak of frogs and musical grat-ing of cicadas' legs. Under cover of the electronic harpies' discourse intrud-ers sawed the iron bars and broke into homes, taking away hi-fi equipment, television sets, cassette players, cameras and radios, jewellery and clothing, and sometimes were hungry enough to devour everything in the refrigera-tor or paused audaciously to drink the whisky in the cabinets or patio bars. Insurance companies paid no compensation for single malt, a loss made keener by the property owner's knowledge that the thieves wouldn't even have been able to appreciate what it was they were drinking.

Then the time came when many of the people who were not trusted housemaids and gardeners hung about the suburb because they were un-employed. Some importuned for a job: weeding or painting a roof; any-thing, *baas*, madam. But the man and his wife remembered the warning about taking on anyone off the street. Some drank liquor and fouled the street with discarded bottles. Some begged, waiting for the man or his wife to drive the car out of the electronically-operated gates. They sat about with their feet in the gutters, under the jacaranda trees that made a green tunnel of the street—for it was a beautiful suburb, spoilt only by their presence—and sometimes they fell asleep lying right before the gates in the midday sun. The wife could never see anyone go hungry. She sent the trusted housemaid out with bread and tea, but the trusted housemaid said these were loafers and *tsotsis*, who would come and tie her up and shut her in a cupboard. The husband said, She's right. Take heed of her advice. You only encourage them with your bread and tea. They are looking for their chance . . . And he brought the little boy's tricycle from the garden into the house every night, because if the house was surely secure, once locked and with the alarm set, someone might still be able to climb over the wall or the electronically-closed gates into the garden.

You are right, said the wife, then the wall should be higher. And the wise old witch, the husband's mother, paid for the extra bricks as her

Christmas present to her son and his wife—the little boy got a Space Man outfit and a book of fairy tales.

15   But every week there were more reports of intrusion: in broad daylight and the dead of night, in the early hours of the morning, and even in the lovely summer twilight—a certain family was at dinner while the bedrooms were being ransacked upstairs. The man and his wife, talking of the latest armed robbery in the suburb, were distracted by the sight of the little boy's pet cat effortlessly arriving over the seven-foot wall, descending first with a rapid bracing of extended forepaws down on the sheer vertical surface, and then a graceful launch, landing with swishing tail within the property. The whitewashed wall was marked with the cat's comings and goings; and on the street side of the wall there were larger red-earth smudges that could have been made by the kind of broken running shoes, seen on the feet of unemployed loiterers, that had no innocent destination.

When the man and wife and little boy took the pet dog for its walk round the neighbourhood streets they no longer paused to admire this show of roses or that perfect lawn; these were hidden behind an array of different varieties of security fences, walls and devices. The man, wife, little boy and dog passed a remarkable choice: there was the low-cost option of pieces of broken glass embedded in cement along the top of walls, there were iron grilles ending in lance-points, there were attempts at reconciling the aesthetics of prison architecture with the Spanish Villa style (spikes painted pink) and with the plaster urns of neoclassical façades (twelve-inch pikes finned like zigzags of lightning and painted pure white). Some walls had a small board affixed, giving the name and telephone number of the firm responsible for the installation of the devices. While the little boy and the pet dog raced ahead, the husband and wife found themselves comparing the possible effectiveness of each style against its appearance; and after several weeks when they paused before this barricade or that without needing to speak, both came out with the conclusion that only one was worth considering. It was the ugliest but the most honest in its suggestion of the pure concentration-camp style, no frills, all evident efficacy. Placed the length of walls, it consisted of a continuous coil of stiff and shining metal serrated into jagged blades, so that there would be no way of climbing over it and no way through its tunnel without getting entangled in its fangs. There would be no way out, only a struggle getting bloodier and bloodier, a deeper and sharper hooking and tearing of flesh. The wife shuddered to look at it. You're right, said the husband, anyone would think twice . . . And they took heed of the advice on a small board fixed to the wall: Consult DRAGON'S TEETH The People for Total Security.

Next day a gang of workmen came and stretched the razor-bladed coils all round the walls of the house where the husband and wife and little boy and pet dog and cat were living happily ever after. The sunlight flashed and slashed, off the serrations, the cornice of razor thorns encircled the home, shining. The husband said, Never mind. It will weather. The wife said, You're wrong. They guarantee it's rust-proof. And she waited until the little boy had run off to play before she said, I hope the cat will take heed . . . The husband said, Don't worry, my dear, cats always look before they leap. And it was true that from that day on the cat slept in the little boy's bed and kept to the garden, never risking a try at breaching security.

One evening, the mother read the little boy to sleep with a fairy story from the book the wise old witch had given him at Christmas. Next day he pretended to be the Prince who braves the terrible thicket of thorns to enter the palace and kiss the Sleeping Beauty back to life: he dragged a ladder to the wall, the shining coiled tunnel was just wide enough for his little body to creep in, and with the first fixing of its razor-teeth in his knees and hands and head he screamed and struggled deeper into its tangle. The trusted housemaid and the itinerant gardener, whose 'day' it was, came running, the first to see and to scream with him, and the itinerant gardener tore his hands trying to get at the little boy. Then the man and his wife burst wildly into the garden and for some reason (the cat, probably) the alarm set up wailing against the screams while the bleeding mass of the little boy was hacked out of the security coil with saws, wire-cutters, choppers, and they carried it—the man, the wife, the hysterical trusted housemaid and the weeping gardener—into the house.

Reading and Reacting

1. How is the introduction—paragraphs 1 through 8—related thematically to the fairy tale the narrator tells? What specific plot elements do they share?

2. In what respects is the story that begins with paragraph 9 of "Once Upon a Time" like a fairy tale? In what respects is it different? Would the story be more or less effective without the narrator's introduction?

3. In paragraph 8, the narrator characterizes the paragraphs that follow as a "bedtime story." How does her tale differ from your idea of a bedtime story?

4. The story's events are presented in strict chronological order. Give some examples of phrases that move readers from one time period to another. Why is chronological order so important?

5. Imagine Gordimer's fairy tale dramatized, perhaps as a television documentary. Where would you interrupt the story to provide commercial breaks or station identification? How would you present the introduction? Explain your decisions.

6. Throughout the fairy tale, various objects and events (and even specific warnings) foreshadow the grim ending. Give several examples of such hints, and explain how each anticipates the ending.

7. Which characters are set in opposition in the fairy tale? Does it have a hero? A villain? What larger forces are in conflict? Are the conflicts between these forces resolved at the end? Explain.

8. What tendencies in her society do you think the author of "Once Upon a Time" means to criticize? Do you agree that these tendencies are dangerous?

9. **JOURNAL ENTRY**   "Once Upon a Time" is set in South Africa. Could it have been set in the United States?

10. **CRITICAL PERSPECTIVE**   In an interview conducted in the early 1980s, Gordimer spoke about her education and about the town in which she lived:

> *When I got to university, it was through mixing with other people who were writing or painting that I got to know black people as equals. In a general and inclusive, nonracial way, I met people who lived in the world of ideas, in the world that interested me passionately.*
>
> *In the town where I lived, there was no mental food of this kind at all. I'm often amazed to think how they live, those people, and what an oppressed life it must be, because human beings must live in the world of ideas. This dimension in the human psyche is very important. It was there, but they didn't know how to express it. Conversation consisted of trivialities. For women, household matters, problems with children. The men would talk about golf or business or horseracing or whatever their practical interests were. Nobody ever talked about, or even around, the big things—life and death.*

Focusing on Gordimer's characterization of the conversation in her town as consisting of "trivialities" rather than of "the big things," consider how her description of that town might apply to "Once Upon a Time." How, for example, might the family's self-exclusion from what Gordimer calls "the world of ideas" have contributed to the story's tragic outcome?

WILLIAM FAULKNER (1897–1962),   winner of the 1949 Nobel Prize for literature and the 1955 and 1963 Pulitzer prizes for fiction, was an unabashedly "Southern" writer whose work continues to transcend the regional label. His nineteen novels, notably *The Sound and the Fury* (1929), *As I Lay Dying* (1930), *Light in August* (1932), *Absalom, Absalom!* (1936), and *The Reivers* (1962), explore a wide range of human experience—from high comedy to tragedy—as seen in the life of one community, Faulkner's fictional "Yoknapatawpha County" (modeled on the area around Faulkner's own hometown of Oxford, Mississippi). Faulkner's Yoknapatawpha stories—a fascinating blend of complex Latinate prose and primitive Southern dialect— paint an extraordinary portrait of a community bound together by ties of blood, by a shared belief in moral "verities," and by an old grief (the Civil War). Faulkner's grandfather raised "Billy" on Civil War tales and local legends, including many about the "Old Colonel," the writer's great-grandfather, who was a colorful Confederate officer. But Faulkner was no Margaret Mitchell. Like Mitchell's *Gone With the Wind*, his stories elegize the agrarian virtues of the Old South, but his look unflinchingly at that world's tragic flaw: the "peculiar institution" of slavery.

Local legends and gossip frequently served as the spark for Faulkner's stories. As John B. Cullen, writing in *Old Times in Faulkner Country*, notes, "A Rose for Emily," Faulkner's first nationally published short story, was based on the tale of Oxford's aristocratic "Miss Mary" Neilson, who married Captain Jack Hume, the charming Yankee foreman of a street-paving crew, over her family's shocked protests. But Hume didn't meet the fate of "Miss Emily's" lover. He lived on to a ripe old age and lovingly cared for his wife during her final illness. According to Cullen, one of Faulkner's neighbors said he created his story "out of fears and rumors"—the dire predictions of what *might* happen if Mary Neilson married her Yankee.

W I L L I A M   F A U L K N E R

A Rose for Emily

(1930)

I

When Miss Emily Grierson died, our whole town went to her funeral: the men through a sort of respectful affection for a fallen monument, the women mostly out of curiosity to see the inside of her house, which no one save an old manservant—a combined gardener and cook—had seen in at least ten years.

It was a big, squarish frame house that had once been white, decorated with cupolas and spires and scrolled balconies in the heavily lightsome style of the seventies, set on what had once been our most select street. But garages and cotton gins had encroached and obliterated even the august names of that neighborhood; only Miss Emily's house was left, lifting its stubborn and coquettish decay above the cotton wagons and the gasoline pumps—an eyesore among eyesores. And now Miss Emily had gone to join the representatives of those august names where they lay in the cedar-bemused cemetery among the ranked and anonymous graves of Union and Confederate soldiers who fell at the battle of Jefferson.

Alive, Miss Emily had been a tradition, a duty, and a care; a sort of hereditary obligation upon the town, dating from that day in 1894 when Colonel Sartoris, the mayor—he who fathered the edict that no Negro woman should appear on the streets without an apron—remitted her taxes, the dispensation dating from the death of her father on into perpetuity. Not that Miss Emily would have accepted charity. Colonel Sartoris invented an involved tale to the effect that Miss Emily's father had loaned money to the town, which the town, as a matter of business, preferred this way of repaying. Only a man of Colonel Sartoris' generation and thought could have invented it, and only a woman could have believed it.

When the next generation, with its more modern ideas, became mayors and aldermen, this arrangement created some little dissatisfaction. On the first of the year they mailed her a tax notice. February came, and there was no reply. They wrote her a formal letter, asking her to call at the sheriff's office at her convenience. A week later the mayor wrote her himself, offering to call or to send his car for her, and received in reply a note on paper of an archaic shape, in a thin, flowing calligraphy in faded ink, to the effect that she no longer went out at all. The tax notice was also enclosed, without comment.

5   They called a special meeting of the Board of Aldermen. A deputation waited upon her, knocked at the door through which no visitor had passed since she ceased giving china-painting lessons eight or ten years earlier. They were admitted by the old Negro into a dim hall from which a stairway mounted into still more shadow. It smelled of dust and disuse—a close, dank smell. The Negro led them into the parlor. It was furnished in heavy, leather-covered furniture. When the Negro opened the blinds of one window, they could see that the leather was cracked; and when they sat down, a faint dust rose sluggishly about their thighs, spinning with slow motes in the single sun-ray. On a tarnished gilt easel before the fireplace stood a crayon portrait of Miss Emily's father.

They rose when she entered—a small, fat woman in black, with a thin gold chain descending to her waist and vanishing into her belt, leaning on an ebony cane with a tarnished gold head. Her skeleton was small and spare; perhaps that was why what would have been merely plumpness in another was obesity in her. She looked bloated, like a body long submerged in motionless water, and of that pallid hue. Her eyes, lost in the fatty ridges of her face, looked like two small pieces of coal pressed into a lump of dough as they moved from one face to another while the visitors stated their errand.

She did not ask them to sit. She just stood in the door and listened quietly until the spokesman came to a stumbling halt. Then they could hear the invisible watch ticking at the end of the gold chain.

Her voice was dry and cold. "I have no taxes in Jefferson. Colonel Sartoris explained it to me. Perhaps one of you can gain access to the city records and satisfy yourselves."

"But we have. We are the city authorities, Miss Emily. Didn't you get a notice from the sheriff, signed by him?"

10   "I received a paper, yes," Miss Emily said. "Perhaps he considers himself the sheriff . . . I have no taxes in Jefferson."

"But there is nothing on the books to show that, you see. We must go by the—"

"See Colonel Sartoris. I have no taxes in Jefferson."

"But, Miss Emily—"

"See Colonel Sartoris." (Colonel Sartoris had been dead almost ten years.) "I have no taxes in Jefferson. Tobe!" The Negro appeared. "Show these gentlemen out."

II

15 So she vanquished them, horse and foot, just as she had vanquished their fathers thirty years before about the smell. That was two years after her father's death and a short time after her sweetheart—the one we believed would marry her—had deserted her. After her father's death she went out very little; after her sweetheart went away, people hardly saw her at all. A few of the ladies had the temerity to call, but were not received, and the only sign of life about the place was the Negro man—a young man then—going in and out with a market basket.

"Just as if a man—any man—could keep a kitchen properly," the ladies said; so they were not surprised when the smell developed. It was another link between the gross, teeming world and the high and mighty Griersons.

A neighbor, a woman, complained to the mayor, Judge Stevens, eighty years old.

"But what will you have me do about it, madam?" he said.

"Why, send her word to stop it," the woman said. "Isn't there a law?"

20 "I'm sure that won't be necessary," Judge Stevens said. "It's probably just a snake or a rat that nigger of hers killed in the yard. I'll speak to him about it."

The next day he received two more complaints, one from a man who came in diffident deprecation. "We really must do something about it, Judge. I'd be the last one in the world to bother Miss Emily, but we've got to do something." That night the Board of Aldermen met—three graybeards and one younger man, a member of the rising generation.

"It's simple enough," he said. "Send her word to have her place cleaned up. Give her a certain time to do it in, and if she don't . . ."

"Dammit, sir," Judge Stevens said, "will you accuse a lady to her face of smelling bad?"

So the next night, after midnight, four men crossed Miss Emily's lawn and slunk about the house like burglars, sniffing along the base of the brickwork and at the cellar openings while one of them performed a regular sowing motion with his hand out of a sack slung from his shoulder. They broke open the cellar door and sprinkled lime there, and in all the outbuildings. As they recrossed the lawn, a window that had been dark was lighted and Miss Emily sat in it, the light behind her, and her upright torso motionless as that of an idol. They crept quietly across the lawn and into the shadow of the locusts that lined the street. After a week or two the smell went away.

25 That was when people had begun to feel really sorry for her. People in our town, remembering how old lady Wyatt, her great-aunt, had gone completely crazy at last, believed that the Griersons held themselves a little too high for what they really were. None of the young men were quite good enough for Miss Emily and such. We had long thought of them as a tableau, Miss Emily a slender figure in white in the background, her father a spraddled silhouette in the foreground, his back to her and clutching a

horsewhip, the two of them framed by the back-flung front door. So when she got to be thirty and was still single, we were not pleased exactly, but vindicated; even with insanity in the family she wouldn't have turned down all of her chances if they had really materialized.

When her father died, it got about that the house was all that was left to her; and in a way, people were glad. At last they could pity Miss Emily. Being left alone, and a pauper, she had become humanized. Now she too would know the old thrill and the old despair of a penny more or less.

The day after his death all the ladies prepared to call at the house and offer condolence and aid, as is our custom. Miss Emily met them at the door, dressed as usual and with no trace of grief on her face. She told them that her father was not dead. She did that for three days, with the ministers calling on her, and the doctors, trying to persuade her to let them dispose of the body. Just as they were about to resort to law and force, she broke down, and they buried her father quickly.

We did not say she was crazy then. We believed she had to do that. We remembered all the young men her father had driven away, and we knew that with nothing left, she would have to cling to that which had robbed her, as people will.

III

She was sick for a long time. When we saw her again, her hair was cut short, making her look like a girl, with a vague resemblance to those angels in colored church windows—sort of tragic and serene.

30   The town had just let the contracts for paving the sidewalks, and in the summer after her father's death they began the work. The construction company came with niggers and mules and machinery, and a foreman named Homer Barron, a Yankee—a big, dark, ready man, with a big voice and eyes lighter than his face. The little boys would follow in groups to hear him cuss the niggers, and the niggers singing in time to the rise and fall of picks. Pretty soon he knew everybody in town. Whenever you heard a lot of laughing anywhere about the square, Homer Barron would be in the center of the group. Presently we began to see him and Miss Emily on Sunday afternoons driving in the yellow-wheeled buggy and the matched team of bays from the livery stable.

At first we were glad that Miss Emily would have an interest, because the ladies all said, "Of course a Grierson would not think seriously of a Northerner, a day laborer." But there were still others, older people, who said that even grief could not cause a real lady to forget *noblesse oblige*[1]— without calling it *noblesse oblige*. They just said, "Poor Emily. Her kinsfolk should come to her." She had some kin in Alabama; but years ago her father had fallen out with them over the estate of old lady Wyatt, the crazy

---

[1] The obligation of those of high birth or rank to behave in an honorable fashion.

woman, and there was no communication between the two families. They had not even been represented at the funeral.

And as soon as the old people said, "Poor Emily," the whispering began. "Do you suppose it's really so?" they said to one another. "Of course it is. What else could . . ." This behind their hands; rustling of craned silk and satin behind jalousies closed upon the sun of Sunday afternoon as the thin, swift clop-clop-clop of the matched team passed: "Poor Emily."

She carried her head high enough—even when we believed that she was fallen. It was as if she demanded more than ever the recognition of her dignity as the last Grierson; as if it had wanted that touch of earthiness to reaffirm her imperviousness. Like when she bought the rat poison, the arsenic. That was over a year after they had begun to say "Poor Emily," and while the two female cousins were visiting her.

"I want some poison," she said to the druggist. She was over thirty then, still a slight woman, though thinner than usual, with cold, haughty black eyes in a face the flesh of which was strained across the temples and about the eye-sockets as you imagine a lighthouse-keeper's face ought to look. "I want some poison," she said.

35   "Yes, Miss Emily. What kind? For rats and such? I'd recom—"

"I want the best you have. I don't care what kind."

The druggist named several. "They'll kill anything up to an elephant. But what you want is—"

"Arsenic," Miss Emily said. "Is that a good one?"

"Is . . . arsenic? Yes, ma'am. But what you want—"

40   "I want arsenic."

The druggist looked down at her. She looked back at him, erect, her face like a strained flag. "Why, of course," the druggist said. "If that's what you want. But the law requires you to tell what you are going to use it for."

Miss Emily just stared at him, her head tilted back in order to look him eye for eye, until he looked away and went and got the arsenic and wrapped it up. The Negro delivery boy brought her the package; the druggist didn't come back. When she opened the package at home there was written on the box, under the skull and bones: "For rats."

IV

So the next day we all said, "She will kill herself"; and we said it would be the best thing. When she had first begun to be seen with Homer Barron, we had said, "She will marry him." Then we said, "She will persuade him yet," because Homer himself had remarked—he liked men, and it was known that he drank with the younger men in the Elks' Club—that he was not a marrying man. Later we said, "Poor Emily" behind the jalousies as they passed on Sunday afternoon in the glittering buggy, Miss Emily with her head high and Homer Barron with his hat cocked and a cigar in his teeth, reins and whip in a yellow glove.

Then some of the ladies began to say that it was a disgrace to the town and a bad example to the young people. The men did not want to interfere, but at last the ladies forced the Baptist minister—Miss Emily's people were Episcopal—to call upon her. He would never divulge what happened during that interview, but he refused to go back again. The next Sunday they again drove about the streets, and the following day the minister's wife wrote to Miss Emily's relations in Alabama.

45   So she had blood-kin under her roof again and we sat back to watch developments. At first nothing happened. Then we were sure that they were to be married. We learned that Miss Emily had been to the jeweler's and ordered a man's toilet set in silver, with the letters H. B. on each piece. Two days later we learned that she had bought a complete outfit of men's clothing, including a nightshirt, and we said, "They are married." We were really glad. We were glad because the two female cousins were even more Grierson than Miss Emily had ever been.

So we were not surprised when Homer Barron—the streets had been finished some time since—was gone. We were a little disappointed that there was not a public blowing-off, but we believed that he had gone on to prepare for Miss Emily's coming, or to give her a chance to get rid of the cousins. (By that time it was a cabal, and we were all Miss Emily's allies to help circumvent the cousins.) Sure enough, after another week they departed. And, as we had expected all along, within three days Homer Barron was back in town. A neighbor saw the Negro man admit him at the kitchen door at dusk one evening.

And that was the last we saw of Homer Barron. And of Miss Emily for some time. The Negro man went in and out with the market basket, but the front door remained closed. Now and then we would see her at a window for a moment, as the men did that night when they sprinkled the lime, but for almost six months she did not appear on the streets. Then we knew that this was to be expected too; as if that quality of her father which had thwarted her woman's life so many times had been too virulent and too furious to die.

When we next saw Miss Emily, she had grown fat and her hair was turning gray. During the next few years it grew grayer and grayer until it attained an even pepper-and-salt iron-gray, when it ceased turning. Up to the day of her death at seventy-four it was still that vigorous iron-gray, like the hair of an active man.

From that time on her front door remained closed, save for a period of six or seven years, when she was about forty, during which she gave lessons in china-painting. She fitted up a studio in one of the downstairs rooms, where the daughters and granddaughters of Colonel Sartoris' contemporaries were sent to her with the same regularity and in the same spirit that they were sent to church on Sundays with a twenty-five-cent piece for the collection plate. Meanwhile her taxes had been remitted.

50   Then the newer generation became the backbone and the spirit of the town, and the painting pupils grew up and fell away and did not send their

children to her with boxes of color and tedious brushes and pictures cut from the ladies' magazines. The front door closed upon the last one and remained closed for good. When the town got free postal delivery, Miss Emily alone refused to let them fasten the metal numbers above her door and attach a mailbox to it. She would not listen to them.

Daily, monthly, yearly we watched the Negro grow grayer and more stooped, going in and out with the market basket. Each December we sent her a tax notice, which would be returned by the post office a week later, unclaimed. Now and then we would see her in one of the downstairs windows—she had evidently shut up the top floor of the house—like the carven torso of an idol in a niche, looking or not looking at us, we could never tell which. Thus she passed from generation to generation—dear, inescapable, impervious, tranquil, and perverse.

And so she died. Fell ill in the house filled with dust and shadows, with only a doddering Negro man to wait on her. We did not even know she was sick; we had long since given up trying to get any information from the Negro. He talked to no one, probably not even to her, for his voice had grown harsh and rusty, as if from disuse.

She died in one of the downstairs rooms, in a heavy walnut bed with a curtain, her gray head propped on a pillow yellow and moldy with age and lack of sunlight.

V

The Negro met the first of the ladies at the front door and let them in, with their hushed, sibilant voices and their quick, curious glances, and then he disappeared. He walked right through the house and out the back and was not seen again.

55   The two female cousins came at once. They held the funeral on the second day, with the town coming to look at Miss Emily beneath a mass of bought flowers, with the crayon face of her father musing profoundly above the bier and the ladies sibilant and macabre; and the very old men— some in their brushed Confederate uniforms—on the porch and the lawn, talking of Miss Emily as if she had been a contemporary of theirs, believing that they had danced with her and courted her perhaps, confusing time with its mathematical progression, as the old do, to whom all the past is not a diminishing road but, instead, a huge meadow which no winter ever quite touches, divided from them now by the narrow bottle-neck of the most recent decade of years.

Already we knew that there was one room in that region above stairs which no one had seen in forty years, and which would have to be forced. They waited until Miss Emily was decently in the ground before they opened it.

The violence of breaking down the door seemed to fill this room with pervading dust. A thin, acrid pall as of the tomb seemed to lie everywhere upon this room decked and furnished as for a bridal: upon the valance curtains of faded rose color, upon the rose-shaded lights, upon the dressing table, upon the delicate array of crystal and the man's toilet things backed with tarnished silver, silver so tarnished that the monogram was obscured. Among them lay collar and tie, as if they had just been removed, which, lifted, left upon the surface a pale crescent in the dust. Upon a chair hung the suit, carefully folded; beneath it the two mute shoes and the discarded socks.

The man himself lay in the bed.

For a long while we just stood there, looking down at the profound and fleshless grin. The body had apparently once lain in the attitude of an embrace, but now the long sleep that outlasts love, that conquers even the grimace of love, had cuckolded him. What was left of him, rotted beneath what was left of the nightshirt, had become inextricable from the bed in which he lay; and upon him and upon the pillow beside him lay that even coating of the patient and biding dust.

60   Then we noticed that in the second pillow was the indentation of a head. One of us lifted something from it, and leaning forward, that faint and invisible dust dry and acrid in the nostrils, we saw a long strand of iron-gray hair.

READING AND REACTING

1. Arrange these events in the sequence in which they actually occur: Homer's arrival in town, the aldermen's visit, Emily's purchase of poison, Colonel Sartoris's decision to remit Emily's taxes, the development of the odor around Emily's house, Emily's father's death, the arrival of Emily's relatives, Homer's disappearance. Then, list the events in the sequence in which they are presented in the story. Why do you suppose Faulkner presents events out of their actual chronological order?

2. Despite the story's confusing sequence, many events are foreshadowed. Give some examples of this technique. How does foreshadowing enrich the story?

3. Where does the exposition end and the movement toward the story's climax begin? Where does the resolution stage begin?

4. Emily is clearly the story's protagonist. In the sense that he opposes her wishes, Homer is the antagonist. What other characters—or what larger forces—are set in opposition to Emily?

5. Explain how each of these phrases moves the story's plot along: "So she vanquished them, horse and foot . . ." (15); "After a week or two the smell went away" (24); "And that was the last we saw of Homer Barron" (47); "And so she died" (52); "The man himself lay in the bed" (58).

6. The narrator of the story is an observer, not a participant. Who might this narrator be? How do you suppose the narrator might know so much about Emily? Why do you think the narrator uses *we* instead of *I?*

7. The original version of "A Rose for Emily" had a two-page death bed scene in which Emily tells a servant that Homer's body lies upstairs. Why do you think Faulkner deleted this scene? Do you think he made the right decision?

8. Some critics have suggested that Miss Emily Grierson is a kind of symbol of the Old South, the last defender of its outdated ideas of chivalry, formal manners, and tradition. Do you think this interpretation is justified? Would you characterize Miss Emily as a victim of the values her town tries to preserve?

9. **JOURNAL ENTRY**   When asked at a seminar at the University of Virginia about the meaning of the title "A Rose for Emily," Faulkner replied, "Oh, it's simply the poor woman had no life at all. Her father had kept her more or less locked up and then she had a lover who was about to quit her, she had to murder him. It was just 'A Rose for Emily'—that's all." In another interview, asked the same question, he replied, "I pitied her and this was a salute, just as if you were to make a gesture, a salute, to anyone; to a woman you would hand a rose, as you would lift a cup of *sake* to a man." What do you make of Faulkner's responses? Can you offer other possible interpretations of the title's significance?

10. **CRITICAL PERSPECTIVE**   In his essay "William Faulkner: An American Dickens," literary critic Leslie A. Fiedler characterizes Faulkner as "primarily . . . a sentimental writer; not a writer with the occasional vice of sentimentality, but one whose basic mode of experience is sentimental." He continues, "In a writer whose very method is self-indulgence, that sentimentality becomes sometimes downright embarrassing." Fiedler also notes Faulkner's "excesses of maudlin feelings and absurd indulgences in overripe rhetoric."

Do you think these criticisms apply to "A Rose for Emily"? If so, does the "vice of sentimentality" diminish the story, or do you agree with Fiedler—who calls Faulkner a "supereminently good 'bad' writer"—that the author is able to surmount these excesses?

LORRIE MOORE* (1957–   ) gives this advice in her story "How to Become a Writer": "First, try to become something, anything, else. A movie star/astronaut. A movie star/missionary. A movie star/kindergarten teacher. President of the World. Fail miserably." Born in Glens Falls, New York, Moore was educated at St. Lawrence University and at Cornell University. Her first book was *Self-Help* (1985), a collection of short stories—including "How to Talk to Your Mother (Notes)," which rated an enthusiastic front-page review in the *New York Times Book Review*. More recent works include *Anagrams* (1986), *The Forgotten Helper* (1987), *Like Life* (1990), and *Who Will Run the Frog Hospital?* (1994). Moore divides her time

---

* No photograph available for this author.

between New York City and her teaching position at the University of Wisconsin, Madison.

Of the origins of her writing career, Moore is typically humorous. In a 1985 interview printed in the magazine *Vanity Fair* she explains, "I signed up for a course called 'The Romance and Reality of Words' in high school and got put in the creative writing class by mistake." Her voice is what *New York Times* reviewer Michiko Kakutani describes as the "wry, crackly" and vulnerable voice of the women in her stories: women who fend off anxiety with irreverent, self-bolstering humor. The stories of *Self-Help* are, according to Moore's comments in *Contemporary Authors,* "second person, mock-imperative narratives . . . what happens when one appropriates the 'how-to' form for a fiction, for an irony, for a 'how-not-to.' "

LORRIE MOORE

How to Talk to Your Mother (Notes)

(1985)

1982.   Without her, for years now, murmur at the defrosting refrigerator, "What?" "Huh?" "Shush now," as it creaks, aches, groans, until the final ice block drops from the ceiling of the freezer like something vanquished.

Dream, and in your dreams babies with the personalities of dachshunds, fat as Macy balloons, float by the treetops.

The first permanent polyurethane heart is surgically implanted.[1]

Someone upstairs is playing "You'll Never Walk Alone" on the recorder. Now it's "Oklahoma!" They must have a Rodgers and Hammerstein book.[2]

5 *1981.*   On public transportation, mothers with soft, soapy, corduroyed seraphs glance at you, their faces dominoes of compassion. Their seraphs are small and quiet or else restlessly counting bus-seat colors: "Blue-blue-blue, red-red-red, lullow-lullow-lullow." The mothers see you eyeing their children. They smile sympathetically. They believe you envy them. They believe you are childless. They believe they know why. Look quickly away, out the smudge of the window.

---

[1] The Jarvik-7, created by Robert K. Jarvik, was implanted in Barney Clark by Dr. William C. DeVries on December 2, 1982.

[2] The American songwriting team of composer Richard Rodgers (1902–1979) and lyricist Oscar Hammerstein II (1895–1960) created many modern classics, including "You'll Never Walk Alone" (from *Carousel*) and "Oklahoma!" (from the musical of the same name).

1980.   The hum, rush, clack of things in the kitchen. These are some of the sounds that organize your life. The clink of the silverware inside the drawer, piled like bones in a mass grave. Your similes grow grim, grow tired.

Reagan is elected President, though you distributed donuts and brochures for Carter.

Date an Italian. He rubs your stomach and says, "These are marks of stretch, no? Marks of stretch?" and in your dizzy mind you think: Marks of Harpo, Ideas of Marx, Ides of March, Beware.[3] He plants kisses on the sloping ramp of your neck, and you fall asleep against him, your underpants peeled and rolled around one thigh like a bride's garter.

1979.   Once in a while take evening trips past the old unsold house you grew up in, that haunted rural crossroads two hours from where you now live. It is like Halloween: the raked, moonlit lawn, the mammoth, tumid trees, arms and fingers raised into the starless wipe of sky like burns, cracks, map rivers. Their black shadows rock against the side of the east porch. There are dream shadows, other lives here. Turn the corner slowly but continue to stare from the car window. This house is embedded in you deep, something still here you know, you think you know, a voice at the top of those stairs, perhaps, a figure on the porch, an odd apron caught high in the twigs, in the too-warm-for-a-fall-night breeze, something not right, that turret window you can still see from here, from outside, but which can't be reached from within. (The ghostly brag of your childhood: "We have a mystery room. The window shows from the front, but you can't go in, there's no door. A doctor lived there years ago and gave secret operations, and now it's blocked off.") The window sits like a dead eye in the turret.

10   You see a ghost, something like a spinning statue by a shrub.

1978.   Bury her in the cold south sideyard of that Halloweenish house. Your brother and his kids are there. Hug. The minister in a tweed sportscoat, the neighborless fields, the crossroads, are all like some stark Kansas. There is praying, then someone shoveling. People walk toward the cars and hug again. Get inside your car with your niece. Wait. Look up through the windshield. In the November sky a wedge of wrens moves south, the lines of their formation, the very sides and vertices mysteriously choreographed, shifting, flowing, crossing like a skater's legs. "They'll descend instinctively upon a tree somewhere," you say, "but not for miles yet." You marvel, watch, until, amoeba-slow, they are dark, faraway stitches in the horizon. You do not start the car. The quiet niece next to you finally speaks: "Aunt Ginnie, are we going to the restaurant with the others?" Look at her. Recognize her: nine in a pile parka. Smile and start the car.

---

[3] The narrator's "free association," prompted by "marks of stretch" (stretch marks) alludes to comedian Arthur 'Harpo' Marx (1893–1964), philosopher Karl Marx (1818–1883), and the warning the soothsayer issues ("Beware the Ides of March") in Shakespeare's *Julius Caesar.*

1977. She ages, rocks in your rocker, noiseless as wind. The front strands of her white hair dangle yellow at her eyes from too many cigarettes. She smokes even now, her voice husky with phlegm. Sometimes at dinner in your tiny kitchen she will simply stare, rheumy-eyed, at you, then burst into a fit of coughing that racks her small old man's body like a storm.

Stop eating your baked potato. Ask if she is all right.

She will croak: "Do you remember, Ginnie, your father used to say that one day, with these cigarettes, I was going to have to 'face the mucus'?" At this she chuckles, chokes, gasps again.

15   Make her stand up.

Lean her against you.

Slap her lightly on the curved mound of her back.

. Ask her for chrissakes to stop smoking.

She will smile and say: "For chrissakes? Is that any way to talk to your mother?"

20   At night go in and check on her. She lies there awake, her lips apart, open and drying. Bring her some juice. She murmurs, "Thank you, honey." Her mouth smells, swells like a grave.

1976. The Bicentennial. In the laundromat, you wait for the time on your coins to run out. Through the porthole of the dryer, you watch your bedeviled towels and sheets leap and fall. The radio station piped in from the ceiling plays slow, sad Motown; it encircles you with the desperate hopefulness of a boy at a dance, and it makes you cry. When you get back to your apartment, dump everything on your bed. Your mother is knitting crookedly: red, white, and blue. Kiss her hello. Say: "Sure was warm in that place." She will seem not to hear you.

1975. Attend poetry readings alone at the local library. Find you don't really listen well. Stare at your crossed thighs. Think about your mother. Sometimes you confuse her with the first man you ever loved, who ever loved you, who buried his head in the pills of your sweater and said magnificent things like "Oh god, oh god," who loved you unconditionally, terrifically, like a mother.

The poet loses his nerve for a second, a red flush through his neck and ears, but he regains his composure. When he is finished, people clap. There is wine and cheese.

Leave alone, walk home alone. The downtown streets are corridors of light holding you, holding you, past the church, past the community center. March, like Stella Dallas,[4] spine straight, through the melodrama of

---

[4] Originally introduced in Olive Higgins Prouty's novel *Stella Dallas;* also the main character in the radio show of the same name, which the announcer introduced as a "world famous drama of mother love and sacrifice." *Stella Dallas* was filmed three times, in 1926 (with Belle Bennett), 1937 (with Barbara Stanwyck), and 1990 (with Bette Midler).

street lamps, phone posts, toward the green house past Borealis Avenue, toward the rear apartment with the tilt and the squash on the stove.

25   Your horoscope says: Be kind, be brief.

You are pregnant again. Decide what you must do.

1974.   She will have bouts with a mad sort of senility. She calls you at work. "There's no food here! Help me! I'm starving!" although you just bought forty dollars' worth of groceries yesterday. "Mom, there is too food there!"

When you get home the refrigerator is mostly empty. "Mom, where did you put all the milk and cheese and stuff?" Your mother stares at you from where she is sitting in front of the TV set. She has tears leaking out of her eyes. "There's no food here, Ginnie."

There is a rustling, scratching noise in the dishwasher. You open it up, and the eyes of a small rodent glint back at you. It scrambles out, off to the baseboards behind the refrigerator. Your mother, apparently, has put all the groceries inside the dishwasher. The milk is spilled, a white pool against blue, and things like cheese and bologna and apples have been nibbled at.

30   *1973.*   At a party when a woman tells you where she bought some wonderful pair of shoes, say that you believe shopping for clothes is like masturbation—everyone does it, but it isn't very interesting and therefore should be done alone, in an embarrassed fashion, and never be the topic of party conversation. The woman will tighten her lips and eyebrows and say, "Oh, I suppose you have something more fascinating to talk about." Grow clumsy and uneasy. Say, "No," and head for the ginger ale. Tell the person next to you that your insides feel sort of sinking and vinyl like a Claes Oldenburg toilet.[5] They will say, "Oh?" and point out that the print on your dress is one of paisleys impregnating paisleys. Pour yourself more ginger ale.

1972.   Nixon wins by a landslide.

Sometimes your mother calls you by her sister's name. Say, "No, Mom, it's me. Virginia." Learn to repeat things. Learn that you have a way of knowing each other which somehow slips out and beyond the ways you have of not knowing each other at all.

Make apple crisp for the first time.

1971.   Go for long walks to get away from her. Walk through wooded areas; there is a life there you have forgotten. The smells and sounds seem sudden, unchanged, exact, the papery crunch of the leaves, the mouldering sachet of the mud. The trees are crooked as backs, the fence posts splintered, trusting and precarious in their solid grasp of arms, the asters

---

5   Claes Oldenburg (1929–   )—American artist noted for his oversized soft sculptures of everyday objects, made from such materials as canvas and vinyl.

spindly, dry, white, havishammed (Havishammed!)[6] by frost. Find a beautiful reddish stone and bring it home for your mother. Kiss her. Say: "This is for you." She grasps it and smiles. "You were always such a sensitive child," she says.

35   Say: "Yeah, I know."

1970.   You are pregnant again. Try to decide what you should do.
Get your hair chopped, short as a boy's.

1969.   Mankind leaps upon the moon.
Disposable diapers are first sold in supermarkets.

40   Have occasional affairs with absurd, silly men who tell you to grow your hair to your waist and who, when you are sad, tickle your ribs to cheer you up. Moonlight through the blinds stripes you like zebras. You laugh. You never marry.

1968.   Do not resent her. Think about the situation, for instance, when you take the last trash bag from its box: you must throw out the box by putting it in that very trash bag. What was once contained, now must contain. The container, then, becomes the contained, the enveloped, the held. Find more and more that you like to muse over things like this.

1967.   Your mother is sick and comes to live with you. There is no place else for her to go. You feel many different emptinesses.
The first successful heart transplant is performed in South Africa.[7]

1966.   You confuse lovers, mix up who had what scar, what car, what mother.

45 *1965.*   Smoke marijuana. Try to figure out what has made your life go wrong. It is like trying to figure out what is stinking up the refrigerator. It could be anything. The lid off the mayonnaise, Uncle Ron's honey wine four years in the left corner. Broccoli yellowing, flowering fast. They are all metaphors. They are all problems. Your horoscope says: Speak gently to a loved one.

1964.   Your mother calls long distance and asks whether you are coming home for Thanksgiving, your brother and the baby will be there. Make excuses.
"As a mother gets older," your mother says, "these sorts of holidays become increasingly important."
Say: "I'm sorry, Mom."

1963.   Wake up one morning with a man you had thought you'd spend your life with, and realize, a rock in your gut, that you don't even like

---

[6] Miss Havisham, in Charles Dickens's *Great Expectations,* is an elderly recluse who lives surrounded by the decaying remnants of her aborted wedding, called off years earlier by her fiancé.

[7] By Dr. Christiaan Barnard (1923–   ).

him. Spend a weepy afternoon in his bathroom, not coming out when he knocks. You can no longer trust your affections. People and places you think you love may be people and places you hate.

50   Kennedy is shot.

Someone invents a temporary artificial heart, for use during operations.

1962.   Eat Chinese food for the first time, with a lawyer from California. He will show you how to hold the chopsticks. He will pat your leg. Attack his profession. Ask him whether he feels the law makes large spokes out of the short stakes of men.

1961.   Grandma Moses dies.[8]

You are a zoo of insecurities. You take to putting brandy in your morning coffee and to falling in love too easily. You have an abortion.

55   *1960.*   There is money from your father's will and his life insurance. You buy a car and a green velvet dress you don't need. You drive two hours to meet your mother for lunch on Saturdays. She suggests things for you to write about, things she's heard on the radio: a woman with telepathic twins, a woman with no feet.

1959.   At the funeral she says: "He had his problems, but he was a generous man," though you know he was tight as a scout knot, couldn't listen to anyone, the only time you remember loving him being that once when he got the punchline of one of your jokes before your mom did and looked up from his science journal and guffawed loud as a giant, the two of you, for one split moment, communing like angels in the middle of that room, in that warm, shared light of mind.

Say: "He was okay."

"You shouldn't be bitter," your mother snaps. "He financed you and your brother's college educations." She buttons her coat. "He was also the first man to isolate a particular isotope of helium, I forget the name, but he should have won the Nobel Prize." She dabs at her nose.

Say: "Yeah, Mom."

60   *1958.*   At your brother's wedding, your father is taken away in an ambulance. A tiny cousin whispers loudly to her mother, "Did Uncle Will have a hard attack?" For seven straight days say things to your mother like: "I'm sure it'll be okay," and "I'll stay here, why don't you go home and get some sleep."

1957.   Dance the calypso with boys from a different college. Get looped on New York State burgundy, lose your virginity, and buy one of the first portable electric typewriters.

1956.   Tell your mother about all the books you are reading at college. This will please her.

---

8   Grandma Moses (Anna Mary Robertson Moses, 1860–1961)—American artist, famous for her "primitive" paintings depicting rural life. Completely self-taught, she did not begin painting seriously until the age of 67.

1955.   Do a paint-by-numbers of Elvis Presley. Tell your mother you are in love with him. She will shake her head.

1954.   Shoplift a cashmere sweater.

65 *1953.*   Smoke a cigarette with Hillary Swedelson. Tell each other your crushes. Become blood sisters.

1952.   When your mother asks you if there are any nice boys in junior high, ask her how on earth would you ever know, having to come in at nine! every night. Her eyebrows will lift like theater curtains. "You poor, abused thing," she will say.

Say, "Don't I know it," and slam the door.

1951.   Your mother tells you about menstruation. The following day you promptly menstruate, your body only waiting for permission, for a signal. You wake up in the morning and feel embarrassed.

1949.   You learn how to blow gum bubbles and to add negative numbers.

70 *1947.*   The Dead Sea Scrolls are discovered.[9]

You have seen too many Hollywood musicals. You have seen too many people singing in public places and you assume you can do it, too. Practice. Your teacher asks you a question. You warble back: "The answer to number two is twelve." Most of the class laughs at you, though some stare, eyes jewel-still, fascinated. At home your mother asks you to dust your dresser. Work up a vibrato you could drive a truck through. Sing: "Why do I have to do it now?" and tap your way through the dining room. Your mother requests that you calm down and go take a nap. Shout: "You don't care about me! You don't care about me at all!"

1946.   Your brother plays "Shoofly Pie" all day long on the Victrola.

Ask your mother if you can go to Ellen's for supper. She will say, "Go ask your father," and you, pulling at your fingers, walk out to the living room and whimper by his chair. He is reading. Tap his arm. "Dad? Daddy? Dad?" He continues reading his science journal. Pull harder on your fingers and run back to the kitchen to tell your mother, who storms into the living room, saying, "Why don't you ever listen to your children when they try to talk to you?" You hear them arguing. Press your face into a kitchen towel, ashamed, the hum of the refrigerator motor, the drip in the sink scaring you.

1945.   Your father comes home from his war work. He gives you a piggyback ride around the broad yellow thatch of your yard, the dead window in the turret, dark as a wound, watching you. He gives you wordless pushes on the swing.

75   Your brother has new friends, acts older and distant, even while you wait for the school bus together.

---

9   Parchment scrolls containing Hebrew and Aramaic scriptural texts, as well as communal writings. Generally dated from 100 B.C. to A.D. 100, they were discovered in a cave near the Dead Sea, between Israel and Jordan.

You spend too much time alone. You tell your mother that when you grow up you will bring your babies to Australia to see the kangaroos.

Forty thousand people are killed in Nagasaki.

1944.   Dress and cuddle a tiny babydoll you have named "the Sue." Bring her everywhere. Get lost in the Wilson Creek fruit market, and call softly, "Mom, where are you?" Watch other children picking grapes, but never dare yourself. Your eyes are small, dark throats, your hand clutches the Sue.

1943.   Ask your mother about babies. Have her read to you only the stories about babies. Ask her if she is going to have a baby. Ask her about the baby that died. Cry into her arm.

80 *1940.*   Clutch her hair in your fist. Rub it against your cheek.

1939.   As through a helix, as through an ear, it is here you are nearer the dream flashes, the other lives.

There is a tent of legs, a sundering of selves, as you both gasp blindly for breath. Across the bright and cold, she knows it when you try to talk to her, though this is something you never really manage to understand.

Germany invades Poland.

The year's big song is "Three Little Fishies" and someone, somewhere, is playing it.

Reading and Reacting

1. What do you think the word *notes* in the story's title means?

2. Who is the story's protagonist? With whom (or what) is the protagonist in conflict? Explain the nature of this conflict.

3. What does the writer gain by arranging the story's events in reverse chronological order? What, if anything, does she lose?

4. What do the dates and the references to historical events contribute to the story?

5. Despite its unconventional sequence of events, does the story contain any foreshadowing? Explain.

6. A student, encountering this story for the first time, commented, "It's hard to follow because it has no plot." Do you agree with this student's assessment? Does this story include any of the conventional stages of plot (exposition, resolution, and so on)? If so, where? Identify several crises (peaks of tension). Does the story have a climax? Explain.

7. Moore says that in the stories in *Self-Help* she is "telling a how-to that is, of course, a how-not-to." What do you think she means? What does the narrator in this story want to teach her readers?

8. What is the effect of the narrator's use of the second person, as in the title and in phrases like "The mothers see you eyeing their children"? Explain the impact of the imperative mood, as in "Date an Italian."

9. **JOURNAL ENTRY**   Although the story's title is "How to Talk to Your Mother (Notes)," the narrator actually does *not* talk to her mother. What do you think she wants to tell her mother? What stops her?

10. **CRITICAL PERSPECTIVE**   When *Self-Help,* the collection in which "How to Talk to Your Mother (Notes)" appeared, was published in 1985, reviews were mixed. For example, the *Kirkus Reviews* called the book a "flimsy, strained collection" that relied on "a single gimmick and two limited situations. The gimmick? Stories in the form of self-help/instruction manuals. . . . The situations: a young woman caught in an unhappy no-win romantic relationship; and a young woman's recollections of her unhappy, unstable mother. . . ." The reviewer concluded by characterizing the book as "maudlin/juvenile work overall: boutique fiction at its most cutesy-poo." Other critics disagreed. Jay McInerney, writing in the *New York Times Book Review,* called "How to Talk to Your Mother (Notes)" a "splendid" story and saw the "complex puzzle of maternal love" as "haunting the quests" of many of Moore's narrators. Ray Olson's review in *Booklist,* although it expressed disappointment with the way the distant narrative voice robbed the stories of emotion, nevertheless called the book "absorbing," and the critic commented that it contained "many funny and sharp lines and effects."

    How can you account for such different opinions of Moore's work? With which evaluation do you agree?

WRITING SUGGESTIONS: PLOT

1. Write your own life story, imitating the style and structure of "How to Talk to Your Mother (Notes)." That is, use reverse chronology, use *you* instead of *I,* and divide your story into sections according to year. Be sure to include mentions of world events, song titles, and the like, as well as recurring themes in your life, to provide continuity and to unify your "notes" into a story.

2. Find a newspaper story that disturbs you. Then, write a "once upon a time" story like Gordimer's in which you retell the story's events in a detached tone without adding analysis or commentary.

3. "The Story of an Hour" includes a **deus ex machina,** an outside force or agent that suddenly appears to change the course of events. Consider the possible effects of a *deus ex machina* on the three other stories in this chapter. What might this outside force be in each story? How might it change the story's action? How plausible would such a dramatic turn of events be in each case?

4. Like Emily in "A Rose for Emily," the narrator of "The Yellow Wall-Paper" (Chapter 6) is a privileged, protected woman driven to the edge of madness by events she cannot control. Despite similarities in the two women's situations, however, their tragic stories are resolved in very different ways. What factors account for the two stories' different outcomes?

5. Read the following article from the January 30, 1987, *Philadelphia Inquirer*. After listing some similarities and differences between the events in the article's story and those in "A Rose for Emily," write an essay in which you discuss how the presentation of events differs. Can you draw any conclusions about journalistic and fictional treatments of similar incidents?

A Woman's Wintry Death Leads to a Long-Dead Friend

DICK POTHIER AND THOMAS J. GIBBONS, JR.

For more than two years, Frances Dawson Hamilton lived with the body of her long-time companion, draping his skeletonized remains with palm fronds and rosary beads.

Yesterday, the 70-year-old woman was found frozen to death in the home in the 4500 block of Higbee Street where she had lived all her life—the last year without heat or hot water. Her body was found by police accompanying a city social worker who came bearing an order to have her taken to a hospital.

Police investigators said the body of Bernard J. Kelly, 84, was found in an upstairs bedroom of the two-story brick home in the Wissinoming section, on the twin bed where he apparently died at least two years ago.

Two beds had been pushed together, and Hamilton apparently had been sleeping beside Kelly's remains since he died of unknown causes, police said.

Kelly's remains were clothed in long johns and socks, investigators said. The body was draped with rosary beads and palm fronds, and on the bed near his body were two boxes of Valentine's Day candy.

"It was basically a funeral—we've seen it before in such cases," said

one investigator who was at the scene but declined to be identified.

Neighbors and investigators said Hamilton and Kelly had lived together in the house for at least 15 years. Several neighbors said Hamilton came from an affluent family, was educated in Europe, and lived on a trust fund until a year or so ago.

Last winter, said John Wasniewski, Hamilton's next-door neighbor, the basement of the home was flooded and the heater destroyed. "There was no heat in that house last winter or this winter," he said.

An autopsy will be performed on Hamilton today, but she apparently froze to death sometime since Monday, when a friend spoke to her on the telephone, investigators said.

Over the last two years, neighbors said, Hamilton had become increasingly reclusive and irrational. Just last week, a city social worker summoned by a friend arranged for a Philadelphia Gas Works team to visit the home and try to repair the furnace—but she refused to let them in.

The friend was James Phillips, 44, of Horsham, a salesman for Apex Electric in Souderton.

In October 1985, he said, Hamilton visited the Frankford Avenue electrical shop where he was then working, told him that she had an electrical problem in her house and had no lights, and asked whether he could help.

Phillips said he visited the house, fixed the problem and gave her some light bulbs.

"She was really paranoid," Phillips said. "She believed that all her problems were from people doing things to her. For some reason or other, she took to me."

Phillips said that he began visiting her, taking her shopping and doing some shopping for her. But, he said, he never saw the body on the second floor.

Hamilton told him there was a man up there. "I thought it was a story she was telling to protect herself," Phillips said.

He provided her with electric heaters and also contacted a caseworker with the city's Department of Human Services whom Phillips identified as Albert Zbik.

Between the two of them, he said, "we got her through last winter." Phillips said Zbik helped her obtain food stamps and Social Security assistance.

When the snowstorm hit last week, Phillips became concerned because he knew Hamilton would have trouble getting food. On Saturday, he took her a plate of hot food and bought more food from a local store.

On Monday, she telephoned him. "I didn't like the way she sounded," he said. He called Zbik and told him he felt it was time that they forced her to go to a hospital.

Phillips said Zbik went to her home yesterday, carrying a form authorizing an involuntary admission to a hospital for observation or required medical treatment.

Phillips told police that he was never allowed above the first floor and was often told by Hamilton that "Bernie is not feeling well today."

Neighbors and police investigators said Kelly was last seen alive about two years ago, and appeared to be quite ill at the time.

"As recently as last month, I asked Frances how Bernard was and whether she should get a doctor, and she said it wasn't necessary. She said 'He's sick, but I'm taking care of him—I'm feeding him with an eyedropper,'" Wasniewski said.

"I told her in December that if he was that sick, she should call a doctor, but she'd say she was taking care of him very well." Wasniewski said.

CHAPTER 5

Character

An editor heard I had told my students that the dirtiest four-letter word a writer can use is plot. He slashed out at me in his magazine. So often when something is quoted, it is out of context and therefore misunderstood. I never denied there are such things as plots. Heaven knows, life is full of plots. But new writers think the way to begin a piece of fiction is to invent the most original plot possible. It is the way I myself was taught in college and too many classes still use that approach. Think up a plot, think up some characters, think up a conflict and suspense, pigeon-hole them into the plot. Voilà, a story! Baloney. Every real writer I ever knew, and I have known many both in Europe and in this country, starts with people and their emotions and actions and lets them make their own stories. A woman once applied for one of my classes when I was teaching at Columbia University. "I want to be a writer," she told me, "so I can be like God and make people do what I want them to do." I had to tell her it was just the opposite. Characters make the author do what they want him to do.

MARTHA FOLEY, *BEST AMERICAN SHORT STORIES* (FOREWORD)

Making false biography, false history, concocting a half-imaginary existence out of the actual drama of my life is my life. There has to be some pleasure in this job, and that's it. To go around in disguise. To act a character. To pass oneself off as what one is not. To pretend. The sly and cunning masquerade. Think of the ventriloquist. He speaks so that his voice appears to proceed from someone at a distance from himself. But if he weren't in your line of vision you'd get no pleasure from his art at all. His art consists of being present and absent; he's most himself by simultaneously being someone else, neither of whom he "is" once the curtain is down. You don't necessarily, as a writer, have to abandon your biography completely to engage in an act of impersonation. It may be more intriguing when you don't. You distort it, caricature it, parody it, you torture and subvert it, you exploit it—all to give the biography that dimension that will excite your verbal life. Millions of people do this all the time, of course, and not with the justification of making literature. They mean it. It's amazing what lies people can sustain behind the mask of their real faces.

PHILIP ROTH, *WRITERS AT WORK*, 7TH. ED.

Much of what a writer learns he learns simply by imitation. Making up a scene, he asks himself at every step. "Would she really say that?" or "Would he really throw

100

the shoe?" He plays the scene through in his imagination, taking all the parts, being absolutely fair to everyone involved (mimicking each in turn, as Aristotle pointed out, and never sinking to stereotype for even the most minor characters), and when he finishes the scene he understands by sympathetic imitation what each character has done throughout and why the fight, or accident, or whatever, developed as it did.

JOHN GARDNER, *ON MORAL FICTION*

A **character** is a fictional representation of a person—usually (but not necessarily) a psychologically realistic depiction. **Characterization** is the way writers develop characters and reveal those characters' traits to readers. Writers may portray characters through their actions, through their reactions to situations or to other characters, through their physical appearance, through their speech and gestures and expressions, and even through their names.

Generally speaking, characters are developed in two ways. First, readers can be *told* about characters. Third-person narrators can give us information about what characters are doing and thinking, what experiences they have had, what they look like, how they are dressed, and so on. They can even provide analysis of and judgments about a character's behavior. Similarly, first-person narrators can tell us about themselves or about other characters. Thus, Sammy in John Updike's "A&P" (p. 105) tells us that he lives with his parents and that he disapproves of the supermarket's customers. He also tells us what various characters are wearing and describes their actions, attitudes, and gestures.

Alternatively, a character's personality traits and motivation may be revealed through actions, dialogue, or thoughts. For instance, Sammy's vivid fantasies and his rejection of his customers' lives suggest to readers that he is not suited for conventional supermarket society, that he is something of a nonconformist; however, Sammy himself does not actually tell us this information.

ROUND AND FLAT CHARACTERS

In his influential 1927 work *Aspects of the Novel,* English novelist E. M. Forster classifies characters as **round** (well developed, closely involved in and responsive to the action) or **flat** (barely developed or stereotypical). In an effective story the major characters will usually be complex and fully developed; if they are not, readers will not care what happens to them. In much modern fiction, readers are encouraged to become involved with the characters, even to identify with them. This empathy is possible only when we know something about the characters—their strengths and weaknesses, for example, or their likes and dislikes. We must know at least enough to understand why characters act the way they do. In some cases, of course, a story can be effective even when its central characters are not well developed. Sometimes, in fact, a story's effectiveness is enhanced by an *absence* of character development, as in Shirley Jackson's "The Lottery" (p. 309).

Readers often expect characters to behave as "real people" in their situation might behave. Real people are not perfect, and realistic characters cannot be perfect either. The flaws that are revealed as round characters are developed—greed, gullibility, naïveté, shyness, a quick temper, or a lack of insight or judgment or tolerance or even intelligence—make them believable. In modern fiction, the protagonist is seldom if ever the noble "hero"; more often, he or she is at least partly a victim, someone to whom some unpleasant things happen, and someone who is sometimes ill-equipped to cope with events.

Unlike a story's major characters, its minor characters are frequently not well developed. Often they are flat, perhaps acting as foils for the protagonist. A **foil** is a supporting character whose role in the story is to highlight a major character by presenting a contrast with him or her. For instance, in "A&P," Stokesie, another young checkout clerk, is a foil for Sammy. Because he is a little older than Sammy and shows none of Sammy's imagination, restlessness, or nonconformity, Stokesie suggests what Sammy might become if he were to continue to work at the A&P. Some flat characters are **stock characters,** easily identifiable types who behave so consistently that readers can readily recognize them. The kindly old priest, the tough young bully, the ruthless business executive, and the reckless adventurer are all stock characters. Some flat characters can even be **caricatures,** characterized by a single dominant trait, such as miserliness, or even by one physical trait, such as nearsightedness.

Dynamic and Static Characters

Characters may also be classified as either dynamic or static. **Dynamic** characters grow and change in the course of a story, developing as they react to events and to other characters. In "A&P," for instance, Sammy's decision to speak out in defense of the girls—as well as the events that lead him to do so—changes him. His view of the world is different at the end of the story, and as a result his position in that world will be different too. A **static** character may face the same challenges a dynamic character might encounter but will remain essentially unchanged: A static character who was selfish and arrogant will remain selfish and arrogant, regardless of the nature of the story's conflict. In the fairy tale "Cinderella," for example, the title character is as sweet and good-natured at the end of the story—despite her mistreatment by her family—as she is at the beginning. Her situation may have changed, but her character has not.

Whereas round characters tend to be dynamic, flat characters tend to be static. But even a very complex, well-developed major character may be static; sometimes, in fact, the point of a story may hinge on a character's inability to change. A familiar example is the title character in William Faulkner's "A Rose for Emily" (p. 80), who lives a wasted, empty life, at least in part because she is unwilling or unable to accept that the world around her and the people in it have changed.

A story's minor characters are often static; their growth is not usually relevant to the story's development. Moreover, we usually do not learn enough about a minor character's traits, thoughts, actions, or motivation to determine whether or not the character changes significantly.

MOTIVATION

Because round characters are complex, they are not always easy to understand. They may act differently in similar situations, just as real people do. They wrestle with decisions, resist or succumb to temptation, make mistakes, ask questions, search for answers, hope and dream, rejoice and despair. What is important is not whether we approve of a character's actions but whether those actions are *plausible*—whether the actions make sense in light of what we know about the character. We need to see a character's **motivation**—the reasons behind his or her behavior—or we will not believe or accept that behavior. For instance, given Sammy's age, his dissatisfaction with his job, and his desire to impress the young woman he calls Queenie, his sudden resignation is perfectly plausible. Without having established his motivation, Updike could not have expected readers to accept Sammy's actions.

Even when readers get to know a character, they still are not able to predict how a complex, round character will behave in a given situation; only a flat character is predictable. The tension that develops as readers wait to see how a character will act or react, and thus how a story's conflict will be resolved, is what holds readers' interest and keeps them involved as a story's action unfolds.

▼▼

CHECKLIST FOR WRITING ABOUT CHARACTER

- Who is the story's protagonist? Who is the antagonist? Who are the other major characters?
- Who are the minor characters? What role does each play in the story?
- What do the major characters look like? Is their physical appearance important?
- What are the major characters' most noticeable traits?

- ◆ What are the major characters' likes and dislikes? Their strengths and weaknesses?

- ◆ What are we told about the major characters' backgrounds and prior experiences? What can we infer?

- ◆ Are characters developed for the most part directly (through the narrator's comments and descriptions) or indirectly (through the characters' actions and dialogue)?

- ◆ Are the characters round or flat?

- ◆ Are the characters dynamic or static?

- ◆ Does the story include any stock characters? Any caricatures? Does any character serve as a foil?

- ◆ Do the characters act in a way that is consistent with how readers expect them to act?

- ◆ With which characters are readers likely to be most (and least) sympathetic?

JOHN UPDIKE (1932–   ) is a prolific writer of novels, short stories, essays, poems, plays, and children's tales. Updike's earliest ambition was to be a cartoonist for *The New Yorker*. He attended Harvard hoping to draw cartoons for *The Lampoon*, studied drawing and fine art at Oxford, and in 1955 went to work for *The New Yorker*—not as a cartoonist, but as a "Talk of the Town" reporter. Updike left *The New Yorker* after three years to write full-time, but (over thirty years later) is still contributing stories, reviews, and essays to the magazine. Among his novels are *Rabbit, Run* (1960), *The Centaur* (1963), *Rabbit Redux* (1971), *Rabbit Is Rich* (1981), *The Witches of Eastwick* (1985), *Rabbit at Rest* (1990), *Memories of the Ford Administration* (1992), and *Brazil* (1994). Updike has also published *Collected Poems 1953–1993* (1993), and a collection of essays titled *The Afterlife and Other Stories* (1994). His most recent novel is *In the Beauty of the Lilies* (1996).

In early stories such as "A&P" (1961), Updike draws on memories of his childhood and teenage years for the sort of "small" scenes and stories for which he quickly became famous. "There is a great deal to be said about almost anything," Updike comments in an interview in *Contemporary Authors*. "All people can be equally interesting. . . . Now either nobody is a hero or everybody is. I vote for everybody. My subject is the American Protestant small-town middle class. I like middles. It is in middles that extremes clash. . . ."

"What John Updike does for a living," writes John Romano in the *New York Times Book Review*, "is remind us of the human costliness of an everyday situation." In "A&P" there is cost, and a small triumph—and a young man's growing awareness of the "hard" world ahead.

J O H N   U P D I K E

A & P

(1961)

In walks these three girls in nothing but bathing suits. I'm in the third check-out slot, with my back to the door, so I don't see them until they're over by the bread. The one that caught my eye first was the one in the plaid green two-piece. She was a chunky kid, with a good tan and a sweet broad soft-looking can with those two crescents of white just under it, where the sun never seems to hit, at the top of the backs of her legs. I stood there with my hand on a box of HiHo crackers trying to remember if I rang it up or not. I ring it up again and the customer starts giving me hell. She's one of these cash-register-watchers, a witch about fifty with rouge on her cheekbones and no eyebrows, and I know it made her day to trip me up. She'd been watching cash registers for fifty years and probably never seen a mistake before.

By the time I got her feathers smoothed and her goodies into a bag— she gives me a little snort in passing, if she'd been born at the right time they would have burned her over in Salem—by the time I get her on her way the girls had circled around the bread and were coming back, without a push-cart, back my way along the counters, in the aisle between the check-outs and the Special bins. They didn't even have shoes on. There was this chunky one, with the two-piece—it was bright green and the seams on the bra were still sharp and her belly was still pretty pale so I guessed she just got it (the suit)—there was this one, with one of those chubby berry-faces, the lips all bunched together under her nose, this one, and a tall one, with black hair that hadn't quite frizzed right, and one of these sunburns right across under the eyes, and a chin that was too long—you know, the kind of girl other girls think is very "striking" and "attractive" but never quite makes it, as they very well know, which is why they like her so much—and then the third one, that wasn't quite so tall. She was the queen. She kind of led them, the other two peeking around and making their shoulders round. She didn't look around, not this queen, she just walked straight on slowly, on these long white prima-donna legs. She came down a little hard on her heels, as if she didn't walk in her bare feet that much, putting down her heels and then letting the weight move along to her toes as if she was testing the floor with every step, putting a little deliberate extra action into it. You never know for sure how girls' minds work (do you really think it's a mind in there or just a little buzz like a bee in a glass jar?) but you got the idea she had talked the other two into coming in here with her, and now she was showing them how to do it, walk slow and hold yourself straight.

She had on a kind of dirty-pink—beige maybe, I don't know—bathing suit with a little nubble all over it and, what got me, the straps were down. They were off her shoulders looped loose around the cool tops of her arms, and I guess as a result the suit had slipped a little on her, so all around the top of the cloth there was this shining rim. If it hadn't been there you wouldn't have known there could have been anything whiter than those shoulders. With the straps pushed off, there was nothing between the top of the suit and the top of her head except just *her,* this clean bare plane of the top of her chest down from the shoulder bones like a dented sheet of metal tilted in the light. I mean, it was more than pretty.

She had sort of oaky hair that the sun and salt had bleached, done up in a bun that was unravelling, and a kind of prim face. Walking into the A&P with your straps down, I suppose it's the only kind of face you *can* have. She held her head so high her neck, coming up out of those white shoulders, looked kind of stretched, but I didn't mind. The longer her neck was, the more of her there was.

5   She must have felt in the corner of her eye me and over my shoulder Stokesie in the second slot watching, but she didn't tip. Not this queen. She kept her eyes moving across the racks, and stopped, and turned so slow it made my stomach rub the inside of my apron, and buzzed to the other two, who kind of huddled against her for relief, and they all three of them went up the cat-and-dog-food-breakfast-cereal-macaroni-rice-raisins-seasonings-spreads-spaghetti-soft-drinks-crackers-and-cookies aisle. From the third slot I look straight up this aisle to the meat counter, and I watched them all the way. The fat one with the tan sort of fumbled with the cookies, but on second thought she put the packages back. The sheep pushing their carts down the aisle—the girls were walking against the usual traffic (not that we have one-way signs or anything)—were pretty hilarious. You could see them, when Queenie's white shoulders dawned on them, kind of jerk, or hop, or hiccup, but their eyes snapped back to their own baskets and on they pushed. I bet you could set off dynamite in an A&P and the people would by and large keep reaching and checking oatmeal off their lists and muttering "Let me see, there was a third thing, began with A, asparagus, no, ah, yes, applesauce!" or whatever it is they do mutter. But there was no doubt, this jiggled them. A few houseslaves in pin curlers even looked around after pushing their carts past to make sure what they had seen was correct.

You know, it's one thing to have a girl in a bathing suit down on the beach, where what with the glare nobody can look at each other much anyway, and another thing in the cool of the A&P, under the fluorescent lights, against all those stacked packages, with her feet paddling along naked over our checkerboard green-and-cream rubber-tile floor.

"Oh Daddy," Stokesie said beside me. "I feel so faint."

"Darling," I said. "Hold me tight." Stokesie's married, with two babies chalked up on his fuselage already, but as far as I can tell that's the only difference. He's twenty-two, and I was nineteen this April.

"Is it done?" he asks, the responsible married man finding his voice. I forgot to say he thinks he's going to be manager some sunny day, maybe in 1990 when it's called the Great Alexandrov and Petrooshki Tea Company or something.

10   What he meant was, our town is five miles from a beach, with a big summer colony out on the Point, but we're right in the middle of town, and the women generally put on a shirt or shorts or something before they get out of the car into the street. And anyway these are usually women with six children and varicose veins mapping their legs and nobody, including them, could care less. As I say, we're right in the middle of town, and if you stand at our front doors you can see two banks and the Congregational church and the newspaper store and three real-estate offices and about twenty-seven old freeloaders tearing up Central Street because the sewer broke again. It's not as if we're on the Cape; we're north of Boston and there's people in this town haven't seen the ocean for twenty years.

The girls had reached the meat counter and were asking McMahon something. He pointed, they pointed, and they shuffled out of sight behind a pyramid of Diet Delight peaches. All that was left for us to see was old McMahon patting his mouth and looking after them sizing up their joints. Poor kids, I began to feel sorry for them, they couldn't help it.

Now here comes the sad part of the story, at least my family says it's sad but I don't think it's sad myself. The store's pretty empty, it being Thursday afternoon, so there was nothing much to do except lean on the register and wait for the girls to show up again. The whole store was like a pinball machine and I didn't know which tunnel they'd come out of. After a while they come around out of the far aisle, around the light bulbs, records at discount of the Caribbean Six or Tony Martin Sings or some such gunk you wonder they waste the wax on, sixpacks of candy bars, and plastic toys done up in cellophane that fall apart when a kid looks at them anyway. Around they come, Queenie still leading the way, and holding a little gray jar in her hand. Slots Three through Seven are unmanned and I could see her wondering between Stokes and me, but Stokesie with his usual luck draws an old party in baggy gray pants who stumbles up with four giant cans of pineapple juice (what do these bums *do* with all that pineapple juice? I've often asked myself) so the girls come to me. Queenie puts down the jar and I take it into my fingers icy cold. Kingfish Fancy Herring Snacks in Pure Sour Cream: 49. Now her hands are empty, not a ring or a bracelet, bare as God made them, and I wonder where the money's coming from. Still with that prim look she lifts a folded dollar bill out of the hollow at the center of her nubbled pink top. The jar went heavy in my hand. Really, I thought that was so cute.

Then everybody's luck begins to run out. Lengel comes in from haggling with a truck full of cabbages on the lot and is about to scuttle into that door marked MANAGER behind which he hides all day when the girls touch his eye. Lengel's pretty dreary, teaches Sunday school and the rest, but he doesn't miss that much. He comes over and says, "Girls, this isn't the beach."

Queenie blushes, though maybe it's just a brush of sunburn I was noticing for the first time, now that she was so close. "My mother asked me to pick up a jar of herring snacks." Her voice kind of startled me, the way voices do when you see the people first, coming out so flat and dumb yet kind of tony, too, the way it ticked over "pick up" and "snacks." All of a sudden I slid right down her voice into her living room. Her father and the other men were standing around in ice-cream coats and bow ties and the women were in sandals picking up herring snacks on toothpicks off a big plate and they were all holding drinks the color of water with olives and sprigs of mint in them. When my parents have somebody over they get lemonade and if it's a real racy affair Schlitz in tall glasses with "They'll Do It Every Time" cartoons stencilled on.

15   "That's all right," Lengel said. "But this isn't the beach." His repeating this struck me as funny, as if it had just occurred to him, and he had been thinking all these years the A&P was a great big dune and he was the head lifeguard. He didn't like my smiling—as I say he doesn't miss much—but he concentrates on giving the girls that sad Sunday-school-superintendent stare.

Queenie's blush is no sunburn now, and the plump one in plaid, that I liked better from the back—a really sweet can—pipes up, "We weren't doing any shopping. We just came in for the one thing."

"That makes no difference," Lengel tells her, and I could see from the way his eyes went that he hadn't noticed she was wearing a two-piece before. "We want you decently dressed when you come in here."

"We *are* decent," Queenie says suddenly, her lower lip pushing, getting sore now that she remembers her place, a place from which the crowd that runs the A&P must look pretty crummy. Fancy Herring Snacks flashed in her very blue eyes.

"Girls, I don't want to argue with you. After this come in here with your shoulders covered. It's our policy." He turns his back. That's policy for you. Policy is what the kingpins want. What the others want is juvenile delinquency.

20   All this while, the customers had been showing up with their carts but, you know, sheep, seeing a scene, they had all bunched up on Stokesie, who shook open a paper bag as gently as peeling a peach, not wanting to miss a word. I could feel in the silence everybody getting nervous, most of all Lengel, who asks me, "Sammy, have you rung up this purchase?"

I thought and said "No" but it wasn't about that I was thinking. I go through the punches, 4, 9, GROC, TOT—it's more complicated than you think, and after you do it often enough, it begins to make a little song, that you hear words to, in my case "Hello (*bing*) there, you (*gung*) hap-py *pee*-pul (*splat*)!"—the *splat* being the drawer flying out. I uncrease the bill, tenderly as you may imagine, it just having come from between the two smoothest scoops of vanilla I had ever known were there, and pass a half and a penny into her narrow pink palm, and nestle the herrings in a bag and twist its neck and hand it over, all the time thinking.

The girls, and who'd blame them, are in a hurry to get out, so I say "I quit" to Lengel quick enough for them to hear, hoping they'll stop and watch me, their unsuspected hero. They keep right on going, into the electric eye; the door flies open and they flicker across the lot to their car, Queenie and Plaid and Big Tall Goony-Goony (not that as raw material she was so bad), leaving me with Lengel and a kink in his eyebrow.

"Did you say something, Sammy?"

"I said I quit."

25   "I thought you did."

"You didn't have to embarrass them."

"It was they who were embarrassing us."

I started to say something that came out "Fiddle-de-doo." It's a saying of my grandmother's, and I know she would have been pleased.

"I don't think you know what you're saying," Lengel said.

30   "I know you don't," I said. "But I do." I pull the bow at the back of my apron and start shrugging it off my shoulders. A couple customers that had been heading for my slot begin to knock against each other, like scared pigs in a chute.

Lengel sighs and begins to look very patient and old and gray. He's been a friend of my parents for years. "Sammy, you don't want to do this to your Mom and Dad," he tells me. It's true, I don't. But it seems to me that once you begin a gesture it's fatal not to go through with it. I fold the apron, "Sammy" stitched in red on the pocket, and put it on the counter, and drop the bow tie on top of it. The bow tie is theirs, if you've ever wondered. "You'll feel this for the rest of your life," Lengel says, and I know that's true, too, but remembering how he made that pretty girl blush makes me so scrunchy inside I punch the No Sale tab and the machine whirs "pee-pul" and the drawer splats out. One advantage to this scene taking place in summer, I can follow this up with a clean exit, there's no fumbling around getting your coat and galoshes, I just saunter into the electric eye in my white shirt that my mother ironed the night before, and the door heaves itself open, and outside the sunshine is skating around the asphalt.

I look around for my girls, but they're gone, of course. There wasn't anybody but some young married screaming with her children about some candy they didn't get by the door of a powder-blue Falcon station wagon. Looking back in the big windows, over the bags of peat moss and aluminum lawn furniture stacked on the pavement, I could see Lengel in my place in the slot, checking the sheep through. His face was dark gray and his back stiff, as if he'd just had an injection of iron, and my stomach kind of fell as I felt how hard the world was going to be to me hereafter.

READING AND REACTING

1. Summarize the information Sammy gives readers about his tastes and background. Why is this exposition vital to the story's development?

2. List some of the most obvious physical characteristics of the A&P's customers. How do these characteristics make them foils for Queenie and her friends?

3. What is it about Queenie and her friends that appeals to Sammy?

4. Is Queenie a stock character? Explain.

5. What rules and conventions are customers expected to follow in a supermarket? How does the behavior of Queenie and her friends violate these conventions?

6. Is the supermarket setting vital to the story? Could the story have been set in a car wash? In a fast-food restaurant?

7. How accurate are Sammy's judgments about the other characters? How might the characters be portrayed if the story were told by Lengel?

8. Given what you learn about Sammy during the course of the story, what do you see as his *primary* motivation for quitting his job? What other factors motivate him?

9. **JOURNAL ENTRY** Where do you think Sammy will find himself in ten years? Why?

10. **CRITICAL PERSPECTIVE** In her 1976 book *The Necessary Blackness* critic Mary Allen observes, "Updike's most tender reverence is reserved for women's bodies. The elegant style with which he describes female anatomy often becomes overwrought, as his descriptions do generally. But it always conveys wonder."

    In what passages in "A&P" does Updike (through Sammy) convey this sense of wonder? Do you think today's audience, reading the story more than thirty years after Updike wrote it, and more than twenty years after Allen's essay was published, would still see such passages as conveying "tender reverence?" Or do you think readers might now see Sammy (and, indeed, Updike) as sexist? How do you see these passages?

KATHERINE MANSFIELD (1888–1923),   one of the pioneers of the modern short story, was born in New Zealand and educated in England. Very much a "modern young woman," she began living on her own in London at the age of nineteen, soon publishing stories and book reviews in many of the most influential literary magazines of the day. One of these she edited with critic John Middleton Murry, whom she married in 1918.

A short story writer of great versatility, Mansfield produced sparkling social comedies for popular consumption as well as more intellectually and technically complex works intended for "perceptive readers." According to one critic, her best works "[w]ith delicate plainness . . . present elusive moments of decision, defeat, and small triumph." Her last two story collections—*Bliss and Other Stories* (1920) and *The Garden Party and Other Stories* (1922)—were met with immediate critical acclaim, but Mansfield's career was cut short in 1923 when she died of complications from tuberculosis at the age of thirty-five.

One notable theme in Mansfield's work is the *dame seule*, the "woman alone," which provides the basis for the poignant "Miss Brill."

KATHERINE MANSFIELD

Miss Brill

(1922)

Although it was so brilliantly fine—the blue sky powdered with gold and great spots of light like white wine splashed over the Jardins Publiques[1]— Miss Brill was glad that she had decided on her fur. The air was motionless, but when you opened your mouth there was just a faint chill, like a chill from a glass of iced water before you sip, and now and again a leaf came drifting—from nowhere, from the sky. Miss Brill put up her hand and touched her fur. Dear little thing! It was nice to feel it again. She had taken it out of its box that afternoon, shaken out the moth-powder, given it a good brush, and rubbed the life back into the dim little eyes. "What has been happening to me?" said the sad little eyes. Oh, how sweet it was to see them snap at her again from the red eiderdown! . . . But the nose, which was of some black composition, wasn't at all firm. It must have had a knock, somehow. Never mind—a little dab of black sealing-wax when the time came—when it was absolutely necessary. . . . Little rogue! Yes, she really felt like that about it. Little rogue biting its tail just by her left ear.

---

[1] Public Gardens (French).

She could have taken it off and laid in on her lap and stroked it. She felt a tingling in her hands and arms, but that came from walking, she supposed. And when she breathed, something light and sad—no, not sad, exactly—something gentle seemed to move in her bosom.

There were a number of people out this afternoon, far more than last Sunday. And the band sounded louder and gayer. That was because the Season had begun. For although the band played all year round on Sundays, out of season it was never the same. It was like some one playing with only the family to listen; it didn't care how it played if there weren't any strangers present. Wasn't the conductor wearing a new coat, too? She was sure it was new. He scraped with his foot and flapped his arms like a rooster about to crow, and the bandsmen sitting in the green rotunda blew out their cheeks and glared at the music. Now there came a little "flutey" bit—very pretty!—a little chain of bright drops. She was sure it would be repeated. It was; she lifted her head and smiled.

Only two people shared her "special" seat: a fine old man in a velvet coat, his hands clasped over a huge carved walking-stick, and a big old woman, sitting upright, with a roll of knitting on her embroidered apron. They did not speak. This was disappointing, for Miss Brill always looked forward to the conversation. She had become really quite expert, she thought, at listening as though she didn't listen, at sitting in other people's lives just for a minute while they talked round her.

She glanced, sideways, at the old couple. Perhaps they would go soon. Last Sunday, too, hadn't been as interesting as usual. An Englishman and his wife, he wearing a dreadful Panama hat and she button boots. And she'd gone on the whole time about how she ought to wear spectacles; she knew she needed them; but that it was no good getting any; they'd be sure to break and they'd never keep on. And he'd been so patient. He'd suggested everything—gold rims, the kind that curved round your ears, little pads inside the bridge. No, nothing would please her. "They'll always be sliding down my nose!" Miss Brill wanted to shake her.

5   The old people sat on the bench, still as statues. Never mind, there was always the crowd to watch. To and fro, in front of the flower-beds and the band rotunda, the couples and groups paraded, stopped to talk, to greet, to buy a handful of flowers from the old beggar who had his tray fixed to the railings. Little children ran among them, swooping and laughing; little boys with big white silk bows under their chins, little girls, little French dolls, dressed up in velvet and lace. And sometimes a tiny staggerer came suddenly rocking into the open from under the trees, stopped, stared, as suddenly sat down "flop," until its small high-stepping mother, like a young hen, rushed scolding to its rescue. Other people sat on the benches and green chairs, but they were nearly always the same, Sunday after Sunday, and—Miss Brill had often noticed—there was something funny about nearly all of them. They were odd, silent, nearly all old, and from the way they stared they looked as though they'd just come from dark little rooms or even—even cupboards!

Behind the rotunda the slender trees with yellow leaves down drooping, and through them just a line of sea, and beyond the blue sky with gold-veined clouds.

Tum-tum-tum tiddle-um! tiddle-um! tum tiddley-um tum ta! blew the band.

Two young girls in red came by and two young soldiers in blue met them, and they laughed and paired and went off arm-in-arm. Two peasant women with funny straw hats passed, gravely, leading beautiful smoke-colored donkeys. A cold, pale nun hurried by. A beautiful woman came along and dropped her bunch of violets, and a little boy ran after to hand them to her, and she took them and threw them away as if they'd been poisoned. Dear me! Miss Brill didn't know whether to admire that or not! And now an ermine toque and a gentleman in grey met just in front of her. He was tall, stiff, dignified, and she was wearing the ermine toque she'd bought when her hair was yellow. Now everything, her hair, her face, even her eyes, was the same color as the shabby ermine, and her hand, in its cleaned glove, lifted to dab her lips, was a tiny yellowish paw. Oh, she was so pleased to see him—delighted! She rather thought they were going to meet that afternoon. She described where she'd been—everywhere, here, there, along by the sea. The day was so charming—didn't he agree? And wouldn't he, perhaps? . . . But he shook his head, lighted a cigarette, slowly breathed a great deep puff into her face, and, even while she was still talking and laughing, flicked the match away and walked on. The ermine toque[2] was alone; she smiled more brightly than ever. But even the band seemed to know what she was feeling and played more softly, played tenderly, and the drum beat, "The Brute! The Brute!" over and over. What would she do? What was going to happen now? But as Miss Brill wondered, the ermine toque turned, raised her hand as though she'd seen some one else, much nicer, just over there, and pattered away. And the band changed again and played more quickly, more gaily than ever, and the old couple on Miss Brill's seat got up and marched away, and such a funny old man with long whiskers hobbled along in time to the music and was nearly knocked over by four girls walking abreast.

Oh, how fascinating it was! How she enjoyed it! How she loved sitting here, watching it all! It was like a play. It was exactly like a play. Who could believe the sky at the back wasn't painted? But it wasn't till a little brown dog trotted on solemn and then slowly trotted off, like a little "theatre" dog, a little dog that had been drugged, that Miss Brill discovered what it was that made it so exciting. They were all on the stage. They weren't only the audience, not only looking on; they were acting. Even she had a part and came every Sunday. No doubt somebody would have noticed if she hadn't been there; she was part of the performance after all. How strange she'd never thought of it like that before! And yet it explained

---

[2] Small, close-fitting woman's hat.

why she made such a point of starting from home at just the same time each week—so as not to be late for the performance—and it also explained why she had quite a queer, shy feeling at telling her English pupils how she spent her Sunday afternoons. No wonder! Miss Brill nearly laughed out loud. She was on the stage. She thought of the old invalid gentleman to whom she read the newspaper four afternoons a week while he slept in the garden. She had got quite used to the frail head on the cotton pillow, the hollowed eyes, the open mouth and the high pinched nose. If he'd been dead she mightn't have noticed for weeks; she wouldn't have minded. But suddenly he knew he was having the paper read to him by an actress! "An actress!" The old head lifted; two points of light quivered in the old eyes. "An actress—are ye?" And Miss Brill smoothed the newspaper as though it were the manuscript of her part and said gently: "Yes, I have been an actress for a long time."

10   The band had been having a rest. Now they started again. And what they played was warm, sunny, yet there was just a faint chill—a something, what was it?—not sadness—no, not sadness—a something that made you want to sing. The tune lifted, lifted, the light shone; and it seemed to Miss Brill that in another moment all of them, all the whole company, would begin singing. The young ones, the laughing ones who were moving together, they would begin, and the men's voices, very resolute and brave, would join them. And then she too, she too, and the others on the benches—they would come in with a kind of accompaniment—something low, that scarcely rose or fell, something so beautiful—moving. . . . And Miss Brill's eyes filled with tears and she looked smiling at all the other members of the company. Yes, we understand, we understand, she thought—though what they understood she didn't know.

Just at that moment a boy and a girl came and sat down where the old couple had been. They were beautifully dressed; they were in love. The hero and heroine, of course, just arrived from his father's yacht. And still soundlessly singing, still with that trembling smile, Miss Brill prepared to listen.

"No, not now," said the girl. "Not here, I can't."

"Buy why? Because of that stupid old thing at the end there?" asked the boy. "Why does she come here at all—who wants her? Why doesn't she keep her silly old mug at home?"

"It's her fu-fur which is so funny," giggled the girl. "It's exactly like a fried whiting."[3]

15   "Ah, be off with you!" said the boy in an angry whisper. Then: "Tell me, my petite chérie—"[4]

"No, not here," said the girl. "Not *yet*."

---

[3] Food fish related to the cod.

[4] Little darling (French).

On her way home she usually bought a slice of honeycake at the baker's. It was her Sunday treat. Sometimes there was an almond in her slice, sometimes not. It made a great difference. If there was an almond it was like carrying home a tiny present—a surprise—something that might very well not have been there. She hurried on the almond Sundays and struck the match for the kettle in quite a dashing way.

But to-day she passed the baker's boy, climbed the stairs, went into the little dark room—her room like a cupboard—and sat down on the red eiderdown. She sat there for a long time. The box that the fur came out of was on the bed. She unclasped the necklet quickly; quickly, without looking, laid it inside. But when she put the lid on she thought she heard something crying.

READING AND REACTING

1. What specific details can you infer about Miss Brill's character (and, perhaps, about her life) from this statement: "She had become really quite expert, she thought, at listening as though she didn't listen, at sitting in other people's lives just for a minute while they talked round her" (3)?

2. How do Miss Brill's observations of the people around her give us insight into her own character? Why do you suppose she doesn't interact with any of the people she observes?

3. In paragraph 9 Miss Brill realizes that the scene she observes is "exactly like a play" and that "even she had a part and came every Sunday." What part does Miss Brill play? Is she a stock character in this play, or is she a three-dimensional character? Does she play a lead or a supporting role?

4. What do you think Miss Brill means when she says, "I have been an actress for a long time" (9)? What does this comment reveal about how Miss Brill sees herself? Is her view of herself similar to or different from the view the other characters have of her?

5. What role does Miss Brill's fur piece play in the story? In what sense, if any, does it function as a character?

6. What happens in paragraphs 11–16 to break Miss Brill's mood? Why is the scene she observes so upsetting to her?

7. At the end of the story, has Miss Brill changed in response to what she overhears, or is she the same person she was at the beginning? Do you think she will return to the park the following Sunday?

8. The story's last paragraph describes Miss Brill's room as being "like a cupboard." Where else has this image appeared in the story? What does its repetition in the conclusion tell us?

9. **JOURNAL ENTRY**   Write a character sketch of Miss Brill, inventing a plausible family and personal history that might help to explain the character you see in the story.

10. **CRITICAL PERSPECTIVE**   Critic Gillian Boddy, in *Katherine Mansfield: The Woman, The Writer,* offers the following analysis of Mansfield's fiction:

The story evolves through the characters' minds. The external narrator is almost eliminated. As so often in her work, the reader is dropped into the story and simply confronted by a particular situation. There is no preliminary establishing and identification of time and place. The reader is immediately involved; it is assumed that he or she has any necessary prerequisite knowledge and is, in a sense, part of the story too.

Do you see this absence of conventional exposition as a problem in "Miss Brill"? Do you think the story would be more effective if Mansfield had supplied more preliminary information about setting and character? Or do you believe that what Boddy calls Mansfield's "concentration on a moment or episode" is a satisfactory substitute for the missing exposition, effectively shifting interest from "what *happens*" to "*why* it happens"?

ANN PETRY (1908–   ) was born in Old Saybrook, Connecticut, the daughter of a pharmacist and a businesswoman. She later studied pharmacy herself and between 1931 and 1938 worked as a pharmacist in her hometown. In 1938 she moved to New York City to pursue a writing career, attending Columbia University and working for the *Amsterdam News,* a newspaper geared to the city's African-American residents. She also worked as a teacher and as an actress with the American Negro Theatre.

Petry's early short stories appeared in various magazines, but it was with the publication of her first novel, *The Street* (1946), that she was recognized as an important talent. The first novel by an African-American woman to focus on the prejudice and economic difficulties facing poor urban blacks, *The Street* was also the first best-seller by an African-American woman. It is still in print today. Petry has published just two other novels—*Country Place* (1947) and *The Narrows* (1953)—in addition to a number of books aimed at young people, including a biography of Harriet Tubman.

"Like a Winding Sheet" appears in her 1945 collection *Miss Muriel and Other Stories.* It is a grim reminder of how the insult of injustice can fester into anger and blind violence.

ANN PETRY

Like a Winding Sheet

(Circa 1945)

He had planned to get up before Mae did and surprise her by fixing breakfast. Instead he went back to sleep and she got out of bed so quietly he didn't know she wasn't there beside him until he woke up and heard the queer soft gurgle of water running out of the sink in the bathroom.

He knew he ought to get up but instead he put his arms across his forehead to shut the afternoon sunlight out of his eyes, pulled his legs up close to his body, testing them to see if the ache was still in them.

Mae had finished in the bathroom. He could tell because she never closed the door when she was in there and now the sweet smell of talcum powder was drifting down the hall and into the bedroom. Then he heard her coming down the hall.

"Hi, babe," she said affectionately.

5   "Hum," he grunted, and moved his arms away from his head, opened one eye.

"It's a nice morning."

"Yeah." He rolled over and the sheet twisted around him, outlining his thighs, his chest. "You mean afternoon, don't ya?"

Mae looked at the twisted sheet and giggled. "Looks like a winding sheet," she said. "A shroud—"[1] Laughter tangled with her words and she had to pause for a moment before she could continue. "You look like a huckleberry—in a winding sheet—"

"That's no way to talk. Early in the day like this," he protested.

10   He looked at his arms silhouetted against the white of the sheets. They were inky black by contrast and he had to smile in spite of himself and he lay there smiling and savoring the sweet sound of Mae's giggling.

"Early?" She pointed a finger at the alarm clock on the table near the bed and giggled again. "It's almost four o'clock. And if you don't spring up out of there, you're going to be late again."

"What do you mean 'again'?"

"Twice last week. Three times the week before. And once the week before and—"

"I can't get used to sleeping in the daytime," he said fretfully. He pushed his legs out from under the covers experimentally. Some of the ache had gone out of them but they weren't really rested yet. "It's too light for good sleeping. And all that standing beats the hell out of my legs."

15   "After two years you oughta be used to it," Mae said.

---

[1] Cloth wrapped around a corpse; a winding sheet.

He watched her as she fixed her hair, powdered her face, slipped into a pair of blue denim overalls. She moved quickly and yet she didn't seem to hurry.

"You look like you'd had plenty of sleep," he said lazily. He had to get up but he kept putting the moment off, not wanting to move, yet he didn't dare let his legs go completely limp because if he did he'd go back to sleep. It was getting later and later but the thought of putting his weight on his legs kept him lying there.

When he finally got up he had to hurry, and he gulped his breakfast so fast that he wondered if his stomach could possibly use food thrown at it at such a rate of speed. He was still wondering about it as he and Mae were putting their coats on in the hall.

Mae paused to look at the calendar. "It's the thirteenth," she said. Then a faint excitement in her voice. "Why, it's Friday the thirteenth." She had one arm in her coat sleeve and she held it there while she stared at the calendar. "I oughta stay home," she said. "I shouldn't go outa the house."

20   "Aw, don't be a fool," he said. "Today's payday. And payday is a good luck day everywhere, any way you look at it." And as she stood hesitating he said, "Aw, come on."

And he was late for work again because they spent fifteen minutes arguing before he could convince her she ought to go to work just the same. He had to talk persuasively, urging her gently, and it took time. But he couldn't bring himself to talk to her roughly or threaten to strike her like a lot of men might have done. He wasn't made that way.

So when he reached the plant he was late and he had to wait to punch the time clock because the day-shift workers were streaming out in long lines, in groups and bunches that impeded his progress.

Even now just starting his workday his legs ached. He had to force himself to struggle past the outgoing workers, punch the time clock, and get the little cart he pushed around all night, because he kept toying with the idea of going home and getting back in bed.

He pushed the cart out on the concrete floor, thinking that if this was his plant he'd make a lot of changes in it. There were too many standing-up jobs for one thing. He'd figure out some way most of 'em could be done sitting down and he'd put a lot more benches around. And this job he had—this job that forced him to walk ten hours a night, pushing this little cart, well, he'd turn it into a sitting-down job. One of those little trucks they used around railroad stations would be good for a job like this. Guys sat on a seat and the thing moved easily, taking up little room and turning in hardly any space at all like on a dime.

25   He pushed the car near the foreman. He never could remember to refer to her as the forelady even in his mind. It was funny to have a white woman for a boss in a plant like this one.

She was sore about something. He could tell by the way her face was red and her eyes were half-shut until they were slits. Probably been out late and didn't get enough sleep. He avoided looking at her and hurried a little, head down, as he passed her though he couldn't resist stealing a glance at her out of the corner of his eye. He saw the edge of the light-colored slacks she wore and the tip end of a big tan shoe.

"Hey, Johnson!" the woman said.

The machines had started full blast. The whirr and the grinding made the building shake, made it impossible to hear conversations. The men and women at the machines talked to each other but looking at them from just a little distance away, they appeared to be simply moving their lips because you couldn't hear what they were saying. Yet the woman's voice cut across the machine sounds—harsh, angry.

He turned his head slowly. "Good evenin', Mrs. Scott," he said, and waited.

30   "You're late again."

"That's right. My legs were bothering me."

The woman's face grew redder, angrier looking. "Half this shift comes in late," she said. "And you're the worst one of all. You're always late. Whatsa matter with ya?"

"It's my legs," he said. "Somehow they don't ever get rested. I don't seem to get used to sleeping days. And I just can't get started."

"Excuses. You guys always got excuses," her anger grew and spread. "Every guy comes in here late always has an excuse. His wife's sick or his grandmother died or somebody in the family had to go to the hospital," she paused, drew a deep breath. "And the niggers is the worse. I don't care what's wrong with your legs. You get in here on time. I'm sick of you niggers—"

35   "You got the right to get mad," he interrupted softly. "You got the right to cuss me four ways to Sunday but I ain't letting nobody call me a nigger."

He stepped closer to her. His fists were doubled. His lips were drawn back in a thin narrow line. A vein in his forehead stood out swollen, thick.

And the woman backed away from him, not hurriedly but slowly— two, three steps back.

"Aw, forget it," she said. "I didn't mean nothing by it. It slipped out. It was an accident." The red of her face deepened until the small blood vessels in her cheeks were purple. "Go on and get to work," she urged. And she took three more slow backward steps.

He stood motionless for a moment and then turned away from the sight of the red lipstick on her mouth that made him remember that the foreman was a woman. And he couldn't bring himself to hit a woman. He felt a curious tingling in his fingers and he looked down at his hands. They were clenched tight, hard, ready to smash some of those small purple veins in her face.

40   He pushed the cart ahead of him, walking slowly. When he turned his head, she was staring in his direction, mopping her forehead with a dark blue handkerchief. Their eyes met and then they both looked away.

He didn't glance in her direction again but moved past the long work benches, carefully collecting the finished parts, going slowly and steadily up and down, and back and forth the length of the building, and as he walked he forced himself to swallow his anger, get rid of it.

And he succeeded so that he was able to think about what had happened without getting upset about it. An hour went by but the tension stayed in his hands. They were clenched and knotted on the handles of the cart as though ready to aim a blow.

And he thought he should have hit her anyway, smacked her hard in the face, felt the soft flesh of her face give under the hardness of his hands. He tried to make his hands relax by offering them a description of what it would have been like to strike her because he had the queer feeling that his hands were not exactly a part of him anymore—they had developed a separate life of their own over which he had no control. So he dwelt on the pleasure his hands would have felt—both of them cracking at her, first one and then the other. If he had done that his hands would have felt good now—relaxed, rested.

And he decided that even if he'd lost his job for it, he should have let her have it and it would have been a long time, maybe the rest of her life, before she called anybody else a nigger.

45   The only trouble was he couldn't hit a woman. A woman couldn't hit back the same way a man did. But it would have been a deeply satisfying thing to have cracked her narrow lips wide open with just one blow, beautifully timed and with all his weight in back of it. That way he would have gotten rid of all the energy and tension his anger had created in him. He kept remembering how his heart had started pumping blood so fast he had felt it tingle even in the tips of his fingers.

With the approach of night, fatigue nibbled at him. The corners of his mouth drooped, the frown between his eyes deepened, his shoulders sagged; but his hands stayed tight and tense. As the hours dragged by he noticed that the women workers had started to snap and snarl at each other. He couldn't hear what they said because of the sound of machines but he could see the quick lip movements that sent words tumbling from the sides of their mouths. They gestured irritably with their hands and scowled as their mouths moved.

Their violent jerky motions told him that it was getting close on to quitting time but somehow he felt that the night still stretched ahead of him, composed of endless hours of steady walking on his aching legs. When the whistle finally blew he went on pushing the cart, unable to believe that it had sounded. The whirring of the machines died away to a murmur and he knew then that he'd really heard the whistle. He stood still for a moment, filled with a relief that made him sigh.

Then he moved briskly, putting the cart in the storeroom, hurrying to take his place in the line forming before the paymaster. That was another thing he'd change, he thought. He'd have the pay envelopes handed to the people right at their benches so there wouldn't be ten or fifteen minutes lost waiting for the pay. He always got home about fifteen minutes late on payday. They did it better in the plant where Mae worked, brought the money right to them at their benches.

He stuck his pay envelope in his pants' pocket and followed the line of workers heading for the subway in a slow-moving stream. He glanced up at the sky. It was a nice night, the sky looked packed full to running over with stars. And he thought if he and Mae would go right to bed when they got home from work they'd catch a few hours of darkness for sleeping. But they never did. They fooled around—cooking and eating and listening to the radio and he always stayed in a big chair in the living room and went almost but not quite to sleep and when they finally got to bed it was five or six in the morning and daylight was already seeping around the edges of the sky.

50   He walked slowly, putting off the moment when he would have to plunge into the crowd hurrying toward the subway. It was a long ride to Harlem and tonight the thought of it appalled him. He paused outside an all-night restaurant to kill time, so that some of the first rush of workers would be gone when he reached the subway.

The lights in the restaurant were brilliant, enticing. There was life and motion inside. And as he looked through the window he thought that everything within range of his eyes gleamed—the long imitation marble counter, the tall stools, the white porcelain-topped tables and especially the big metal coffee urn right near the window. Steam issued from its top and a gas flame flickered under it—a lively, dancing, blue flame.

A lot of the workers from his shift—men and women—were lining up near the coffee urn. He watched them walk to the porcelain-topped tables carrying steaming cups of coffee and he saw that just the smell of the coffee lessened the fatigue lines in their faces. After the first sip their faces softened, they smiled, they began to talk and laugh.

On a sudden impulse he shoved the door open and joined the line in front of the coffee urn. The line moved slowly. And as he stood there the smell of the coffee, the sound of the laughter and the voices, helped dull the sharp ache in his legs.

He didn't pay any attention to the white girl who was serving the coffee at the urn. He kept looking at the cups in the hands of the men who had been ahead of him. Each time a man stepped out of the line with one of the thick white cups the fragrant steam got in his nostrils. He saw that they walked carefully so as not to spill a single drop. There was a froth of bubbles at the top of each cup and he thought about how he would let the bubbles break against his lips before he actually took a big deep swallow.

55   Then it was his turn. "A cup of coffee," he said, just as he had heard the others say.

The white girl looked past him, put her hands up to her head and gently lifted her hair away from the back of her neck, tossing her head back a little. "No more coffee for a while," she said.

He wasn't certain he'd heard her correctly and he said "What?" blankly.

"No more coffee for a while," she repeated.

There was silence behind him and then uneasy movement. He thought someone would say something, ask why or protest, but there was only silence and then a faint shuffling sound as though the men standing behind him had simultaneously shifted their weight from one foot to the other.

60   He looked at the girl without saying anything. He felt his hands begin to tingle and the tingling went all the way down to his finger tips so that he glanced down at them. They were clenched tight, hard, into fists. Then he looked at the girl again. What he wanted to do was hit her so hard that the scarlet lipstick on her mouth would smear and spread over her nose, her chin, out toward her cheeks, so hard that she would never toss her head again and refuse a man a cup of coffee because he was black.

He estimated the distance across the counter and reached forward, balancing his weight on the balls of his feet, ready to let the blow go. And then his hands fell back down to his sides because he forced himself to lower them, to unclench them and make them dangle loose. The effort took his breath away because his hands fought against him. But he couldn't hit her. He couldn't even now bring himself to hit a woman, not even this one, who had refused him a cup of coffee with a toss of her head. He kept seeing the gesture with which she had lifted the length of her blond hair from the back of her neck as expressive of her contempt for him.

When he went out the door he didn't look back. If he had he would have seen the flickering blue flame under the shiny coffee urn being extinguished. The line of men who had stood behind him lingered a moment to watch the people drinking coffee at the tables and then they left just as he had without having had the coffee they wanted so badly. The girl behind the counter poured water in the urn and swabbed it out and as she waited for the water to run out, she lifted her hair gently from the back of her neck and tossed her head before she began making a fresh lot of coffee.

But he had walked away without a backward look, his head down, his hands in his pockets, raging at himself and whatever it was inside of him that had forced him to stand quiet and still when he wanted to strike out.

The subway was crowded and he had to stand. He tried grasping an overhead strap and his hands were too tense to grip it. So he moved near the train door and stood there swaying back and forth with the rocking of the train. The roar of the train beat inside his head, making it ache and throb, and the pain in his legs clawed up into his groin so that he seemed to be bursting with pain and he told himself that it was due to all that anger-born energy that had piled up in him and not been used and so it had spread through him like a poison—from his feet and legs all the way up to his head.

65   Mae was in the house before he was. He knew she was home before he put the key in the door of the apartment. The radio was going. She had it turned up loud and she was singing along with it.

"Hello, babe," she called out, as soon as he opened the door.

He tried to say "hello" and it came out half grunt and half sigh.

"You sure sound cheerful," she said.

She was in the bedroom and he went and leaned against the doorjamb. The denim overalls she wore to work were carefully draped over the back of a chair by the bed. She was standing in front of the dresser, tying the sash of a yellow housecoat around her waist and chewing gum vigorously as she admired her reflection in the mirror over the dresser.

"Whatsa matter?" she said. "You get bawled out by the boss or somep'n?"

"Just tired," he said slowly. "For God's sake, do you have to crack that gum like that?"

"You don't have to lissen to me," she said complacently. She patted a curl in place near the side of her head and then lifted her hair away from the back of her neck, ducking her head forward and then back.

He winced away from the gesture. "What you got to be always fooling with your hair for?" he protested.

"Say, what's the matter with you anyway?" She turned away from the mirror to face him, put her hands on her hips. "You ain't been in the house two minutes and you're picking on me."

He didn't answer her because her eyes were angry and he didn't want to quarrel with her. They'd been married too long and got along too well and so he walked all the way into the room and sat down in the chair by the bed and stretched his legs out in front of him, putting his weight on the heels of his shoes, leaning way back in the chair, not saying anything.

"Lissen," she said sharply. "I've got to wear those overalls again tomorrow. You're going to get them all wrinkled up leaning against them like that."

He didn't move. He was too tired and his legs were throbbing now that he had sat down. Besides the overalls were already wrinkled and dirty, he thought. They couldn't help but be for she'd worn them all week. He leaned farther back in the chair.

"Come on, get up," she ordered.

"Oh, what the hell," he said wearily, and got up from the chair. "I'd just as soon live in a subway. There'd be just as much place to sit down."

He saw that her sense of humor was struggling with her anger. But her sense of humor won because she giggled.

"Aw, come on and eat," she said. There was a coaxing note in her voice. "You're nothing but an old hungry nigger trying to act tough and—" she paused to giggle and then continued, "You—"

He had always found her giggling pleasant and deliberately said things that might amuse her and then waited, listening for the delicate sound to emerge from her throat. This time he didn't even hear the giggle. He didn't let her finish what she was saying. She was standing close to him and that funny tingling started in his finger tips, went fast up his arms and sent his fist shooting straight for her face.

There was the smacking sound of soft flesh being struck by a hard object and it wasn't until she screamed that he realized he had hit her in the mouth—so hard that the dark red lipstick had blurred and spread over her full lips, reaching up toward the tip of her nose, down toward her chin, out toward her cheeks.

The knowledge that he had struck her seeped through him slowly and he was appalled but he couldn't drag his hands away from her face. He kept striking her and he thought with horror that something inside him was holding him, binding him to this act, wrapping and twisting about him so that he had to continue it. He had lost all control over his hands. And he groped for a phrase, a word, something to describe what this thing was like that was happening to him and he thought it was like being enmeshed in a winding sheet—that was it—like a winding sheet. And even as the thought formed in his mind, his hands reached for her face again and yet again.

READING AND REACTING

1. This story appeared in a 1945 collection of Petry's stories. What information does this date suggest about the characters' experiences prior to the beginning of the story? Does the date help in any way to explain Johnson's character? His motivation?

2. Johnson is portrayed as exhausted, frustrated, and tense with rage. How are these character traits communicated to readers?

3. When the forelady calls Johnson a nigger, he speaks up to her quietly yet firmly, and she backs off. Given what we know about Johnson, is his action plausible? Is it consistent with his other actions?

4. How do Johnson's physical ailments help to develop his character? How do they help to explain his motivation? Do you think they in any way mitigate his final act?

5. What do readers really know about Mae besides the facts that she wears overalls to work, sings along with the radio, wears red lipstick, and chews gum? Do we really *need* to know anything else? Would the story have a different impact if Mae's character were as fully developed as Johnson's?

6. What function is served by each of the story's two minor characters—Johnson's boss, Mrs. Scott, and the woman at the coffee urn? Are both characters necessary to the story? Is it vital or incidental that both are women?

7. What finally causes Johnson the snap? Why does he lose his temper at this point? Why do you think he doesn't lose it earlier?

8. Do you see the story's outcome as inevitable? How is this outcome foreshadowed?

9. **JOURNAL ENTRY** Whom do you blame for Johnson's violent act? Is he alone to blame, or should someone—or something—else also be held responsible? Could you argue that Johnson is as much a victim as Mae is?

10. **CRITICAL PERSPECTIVE**   In *From the Dark Tower: Afro-American Writers 1900–1960*, Arthur P. Davis focuses on Petry's short fiction:

> The short stories of Ann Petry show a great sensitivity. They tend to deal with those subtle aspects of racial hurt which are not always understood by non-blacks. . . . Petry's voice is low when she speaks of the tragedy of ghetto living in these stories—the broken homes, the deserted children, the faithless wives, the young girls going on the street—and it is more effective than shouting.

In his discussion, Davis uses "Like a Winding Sheet" as one example to support his assertions. Do you agree with him that the muted voice Petry uses in this story is "more effective than shouting," or do you believe that "shouting" would have conveyed Petry's point more effectively? How might she have "shouted" in this story?

CHARLES BAXTER (1947–   ) was born in Minneapolis and educated at Macalester College and at the State University of New York, Buffalo. He is currently a professor of English at the University of Michigan. Baxter is the author of three much-praised collections of short stories, *Harmony of the World* (1984), *Through the Safety Net* (1985), and *A Relative Stranger: Stories* (1990); two novels, *First Light* (1987) and *Shadow Play* (1993); and one book of poetry, *Imaginary Paintings and Other Poems* (1989).

Baxter's critics often mention the compassion he shows in writing about his fictional characters: a couple who lose their child, a hospital worker who wants to be famous, a tired businessman who really wants to paint. In many of the short stories in *Through the Safety Net* (from which "Gryphon" is taken), unexpected events jar Baxter's characters out of their routines—forcing them to consider different choices, to call on inner strength, or to swim against the tide of "middle America's" conventions.

CHARLES   BAXTER

Gryphon

(1985)

On Wednesday afternoon, between the geography lesson on ancient Egypt's hand-operated irrigation system and an art project that involved drawing a model city next to a mountain, our fourth-grade teacher, Mr. Hibler, developed a cough. This cough began with a series of muffled throat clearings and progressed to propulsive noises contained within Mr. Hibler's closed mouth. "Listen to him," Carol Peterson whispered to me. "He's gonna blow up." Mr. Hibler's laughter—dazed and infrequent—sounded a bit like his cough, but as we worked on our model cities we would look up, thinking he was enjoying a joke, and see Mr. Hibler's face turning red, his cheeks puffed out. This was not laughter. Twice he bent over, and his loose tie, like a plumb line, hung down straight from his neck as he exploded himself into a Kleenex. He would excuse himself, then go on coughing. "I'll bet you a dime," Carol Peterson whispered, "we get a substitute tomorrow."

Carol sat at the desk in front of mine and was a bad person—when she thought no one was looking she would blow her nose on notebook paper, then crumble it up and throw it into the wastebasket—but at times of crisis she spoke the truth. I knew I'd lose the dime.

"No deal," I said.

When Mr. Hibler stood us up in formation at the door just prior to the final bell, he was almost incapable of speech. "I'm sorry, boys and girls," he said. "I seem to be coming down with something."

5 "I hope you feel better tomorrow, Mr. Hibler," Bobby Kryzanowicz, the faultless brown-noser said, and I heard Carol Peterson's evil giggle. Then Mr. Hibler opened the door and we walked out to the buses, a clique of us starting noisily to hawk and cough as soon as we thought we were a few feet beyond Mr. Hibler's earshot.

Five Oaks being a rural community, and in Michigan, the supply of substitute teachers was limited to the town's unemployed community college graduates, a pool of about four mothers. These ladies fluttered, provided easeful class days, and nervously covered material we had mastered weeks earlier. Therefore it was a surprise when a woman we had never seen came into the class the next day, carrying a purple purse, a checkerboard lunchbox, and a few books. She put the books on one side of Mr. Hibler's desk and the lunchbox on the other, next to the Voice of Music phonograph. Three of us in the back of the room were playing with Heever, the chameleon that lived in the terrarium and on one of the plastic drapes, when she walked in.

She clapped her hands at us. "Little boys," she said, "why are you bent over together like that?" She didn't wait for us to answer. "Are you tormenting an animal? Put it back. Please sit down at your desks. I want no cabals this time of the day." We just stared at her. "Boys," she repeated, "I asked you to sit down."

I put the chameleon in his terrarium and felt my way to my desk, never taking my eyes off the woman. With white and green chalk, she had started to draw a tree on the left side of the blackboard. She didn't look usual. Furthermore, her tree was outsized, disproportionate, for some reason.

"This room needs a tree," she said, with one line drawing the suggestion of a leaf. "A large, leafy, shady, deciduous . . . oak."

10 Her fine, light hair had been done up in what I would learn years later was called a chignon, and she wore gold-rimmed glasses whose lenses seemed to have the faintest blue tint. Harold Knardahl, who sat across

from me, whispered "Mars," and I nodded slowly, savoring the imminent weirdness of the day. The substitute drew another branch with an extravagant arm gesture, then turned around and said, "Good morning. I don't believe I said good morning to all you yet."

Facing us, she was no special age—an adult is an adult—but her face had two prominent lines, descending vertically from the sides of her mouth to her chin. I knew where I had seen those lines before: *Pinocchio.* They were marionette lines. "You may stare at me," she said to us, as a few more kids from the last bus came into the room, their eyes fixed on her, "for a few more seconds, until the bell rings. Then I will permit no more staring. Looking I will permit. Staring, no. It is impolite to stare, and a sign of bad breeding. You cannot make a social effort while staring."

Harold Knardahl did not glance at me, or nudge, but I heard him whisper "Mars" again, trying to get more mileage out of his single joke with the kids who had just come in.

When everyone was seated, the substitute teacher finished her tree, put down her chalk fastidiously on the phonograph, brushed her hands, and faced us. "Good morning," she said. "I am Miss Ferenczi, your teacher for the day. I am fairly new to your community, and I don't believe any of you know me. I will therefore start by telling you a story about myself."

While we settled back, she launched into her tale. She said her grandfather had been a Hungarian prince; her mother had been born in some place called Flanders, had been a pianist, and had played concerts for people Miss Ferenczi referred to as "crowned heads." She gave us a knowing look. "Grieg," she said, "the Norwegian master, wrote a concerto for piano that was," she paused, "my mother's triumph at her debut concert in London." Her eyes searched the ceiling. Our eyes followed. Nothing up there but ceiling tile. "For reasons that I shall not go into, my family's fortunes took us to Detroit, then north to dreadful Saginaw, and now here I am in Five Oaks, as your substitute teacher, for today, Thursday, October the eleventh. I believe it will be a good day: All the forecasts coincide. We shall start with your reading lesson. Take out your reading book. I believe it is called *Broad Horizons,* or something along those lines."

15   Jeannie Vermeesch raised her hand. Miss Ferenczi nodded at her. "Mr. Hibler always starts the day with the Pledge of Allegiance," Jeannie whined.

"Oh, does he? In that case," Miss Ferenczi said, "you must know it *very* well by now, and we certainly need not spend our time on it. No, no allegiance pledging on the premises today, by my reckoning. Not with so much sunlight coming into the room. A pledge does not suit my mood." She glanced at her watch. "Time *is* flying. Take out *Broad Horizons.*"

She disappointed us by giving us an ordinary lesson, complete with vocabulary word drills, comprehension questions, and recitation. She didn't seem to care for the material, however. She sighed every few minutes and rubbed her glasses with a frilly perfumed handkerchief that she withdrew, magician style, from her left sleeve.

After reading we moved on to arithmetic. It was my favorite time of the morning, when the lazy autumn sunlight dazzled its way through ribbons of clouds past the windows on the east side of the classroom, and crept across the linoleum floor. On the playground the first group of children, the kindergartners, were running on the quack grass just beyond the monkey bars. We were doing multiplication tables. Miss Ferenczi had made John Wazny stand up at his desk in the front row. He was supposed to go through the tables of six. From where I was sitting, I could smell the Vitalis soaked into John's plastered hair. He was doing fine until he came to six times eleven and six times twelve. "Six times eleven," he said, "is sixty-eight. Six times twelve is . . ." He put his fingers to his head, quickly and secretly sniffed his fingertips, and said, "seventy-two." Then he sat down.

"Fine," Miss Ferenczi said. "Well now. That was very good."

20 "Miss Ferenczi!" One of the Eddy twins was waving her hand desperately in the air. "Miss Ferenczi! Miss Ferenczi!"

"Yes?"

"John said that six times eleven is sixty-eight and you said he was right!"

"*Did* I?" She gazed at the class with a jolly look breaking across her marionette's face. "Did I say that? Well, what *is* six times eleven?"

"It's sixty-six!"

25 She nodded. "Yes. So it is. But, and I know some people will not entirely agree with me, at some times it is sixty-eight."

"When? When is it sixty-eight?"

We were all waiting.

"In higher mathematics, which you children do not yet understand, six times eleven can be considered to be sixty-eight." She laughed through her nose. "In higher mathematics numbers are . . . more fluid. The only thing a number does is contain a certain amount of something. Think of water. A cup is not the only way to measure a certain amount of water, is it?" We were staring, shaking our heads. "You could use saucepans or thimbles. In either case, the water *would be the same*. Perhaps," she started again, "it would be better for you to think that six times eleven is sixty-eight only when I am in the room."

"Why is it sixty-eight," Mark Poole asked, "when you're in the room?"

30 "Because it's more interesting that way," she said, smiling very rapidly behind her blue-tinted glasses. "Besides, I'm your substitute teacher, am I not?" We all nodded. "Well, then, think of six times eleven equals sixty-eight as a substitute fact."

"A substitute fact?"

"Yes." Then she looked at us carefully. "Do you think," she asked, "that anyone is going to be hurt by a substitute fact?"

We looked back at her.

"Will the plants on the windowsill be hurt?" We glanced at them. There were sensitive plants thriving in a green plastic tray, and several wilted ferns in small clay pots. "Your dogs and cats, or your moms and dads?" She waited. "So," she concluded, "what's the problem?"

35   "But it's wrong," Janice Weber said, "isn't it?"

"What's your name, young lady?"

"Janice Weber."

"And you think it's wrong, Janice?"

"I was just asking."

40   "Well, all right. You were just asking. I think we've spent enough time on this matter by now, don't you, class? You are free to think what you like. When your teacher, Mr. Hibler, returns, six times eleven will be sixty-six again, you can rest assured. And it will be that for the rest of your lives in Five Oaks. Too bad, eh?" She raised her eyebrows and glinted herself at us. "But for now, it wasn't. So much for that. Let us go to your assigned problems for today, as painstakingly outlined, I see, in Mr. Hibler's lesson plan. Take out a sheet of paper and write your names in the upper left-hand corner."

For the next half hour we did the rest of our arithmetic problems. We handed them in and went on to spelling, my worst subject. Spelling always came before lunch. We were taking spelling dictation and looking at the clock. "Thorough," Miss Ferenczi said. "Boundary." She walked in the aisles between the desks, holding the spelling book open and looking down at our papers. "Balcony." I clutched my pencil. Somehow, the way she said those words, they seemed foreign, Hungarian, mis-voweled and mis-consonanted. I stared down at what I had spelled. *Balconie.* I turned my pencil upside down and erased my mistake. *Balconey.* That looked better, but still incorrect. I cursed the world of spelling and tried erasing it again and saw the paper beginning to wear away. *Balkony.* Suddenly I felt a hand on my shoulder.

"I don't like that word either," Miss Ferenczi whispered, bent over, her mouth near my ear. "It's ugly. My feeling is, if you don't like a word, you don't have to use it." She straightened up, leaving behind a slight odor of Clorets.

At lunchtime we went out to get our trays of sloppy joes, peaches in heavy syrup, coconut cookies, and milk, and brought them back to the classroom, where Miss Ferenczi was sitting at the desk, eating a brown sticky thing she had unwrapped from tightly rubber-banded wax paper. "Miss Ferenczi," I said, raising my hand. "You don't have to eat with us. You can eat with the other teachers. There's a teachers' lounge," I ended up, "next to the principal's office."

"No, thank you," she said. "I prefer it here."

45   "We've got a room monitor," I said. "Mrs. Eddy." I pointed to where Mrs. Eddy, Joyce and Judy's mother, sat silently at the back of the room, doing her knitting.

"That's fine," Miss Ferenczi said. "But I shall continue to eat here, with you children. I prefer it," she repeated.

"How come?" Wayne Razmer asked without raising his hand.

"I talked with the other teachers before class this morning," Miss Ferenczi said, biting into her brown food. "There was a great rattling of the words for the fewness of ideas. I didn't care for their brand of hilarity. I don't like ditto machine jokes."

"Oh," Wayne said.

50   "What's that you're eating?" Maxine Sylvester asked, twitching her nose. "Is it food?"

"It most certainly *is* food. It's a stuffed fig. I had to drive almost down to Detroit to get it. I also bought some smoked sturgeon. And this," she said, lifting some green leaves out of her lunchbox, "is raw spinach, cleaned this morning before I came out here to the Garfield-Murry school."

"Why're you eating raw spinach?" Maxine asked.

"It's good for you," Miss Ferenczi said. "More stimulating than soda pop or smelling salts." I bit into my sloppy joe and stared blankly out the window. An almost invisible moon was faintly silvered in the daytime autumn sky. "As far as food is concerned," Miss Ferenczi was saying, "you have to shuffle the pack. Mix it up. Too many people eat . . . well, never mind."

"Miss Ferenczi," Carol Peterson said, "what are we going to do this afternoon?"

55   "Well," she said, looking down at Mr. Hibler's lesson plan, "I see that your teacher, Mr. Hibler, has you scheduled for a unit on the Egyptians." Carol groaned. "Yessss," Miss Ferenczi continued, "that is what we will do: the Egyptians. A remarkable people. Almost as remarkable as the Americans. But not quite." She lowered her head, did her quick smile, and went back to eating her spinach.

After noon recess we came back into the classroom and saw that Miss Ferenczi had drawn a pyramid on the blackboard, close to her oak tree. Some of us who had been playing baseball were messing around in the back of the room, dropping the bats and the gloves into the playground box, and I think that Ray Schontzeler had just slugged me when I heard Miss Ferenczi's high-pitched voice quavering with emotion. "Boys," she said, "come to order right this minute and take your seats. I do not wish to waste a minute of class time. Take out your geography books." We trudged to our desks and, still sweating, pulled out *Distant Lands and Their People*. "Turn to page forty-two." She waited for thirty seconds, then looked over at Kelly Munger. "Young man," she said, "why are you still fossicking in your desk?"

Kelly looked as if his foot had been stepped on. "Why am I what?"

"Why are you . . . burrowing in your desk like that?"

"I'm lookin' for the book, Miss Ferenczi."

60   Bobby Kryzanowicz, the faultless brown-noser who sat in the first row by choice, softly said, "His name is Kelly Munger. He can't ever find his stuff. He always does that."

"I don't care what his name is, especially after lunch," Miss Ferenczi said. *"Where is your book?"*

"I just found it." Kelly was peering into his desk and with both hands pulled at the book, shoveling along in front of it several pencils and crayons, which fell into his lap and then to the floor.

"I hate a mess," Miss Ferenczi said. "I hate a mess in a desk or a mind. It's . . . unsanitary. You wouldn't want your house at home to look like your desk at school, now, would you?" She didn't wait for an answer. "I should think not. A house at home should be as neat as human hands can make it. What were we talking about? Egypt. Page forty-two. I note from Mr. Hibler's lesson plan that you have been discussing the modes of Egyptian irrigation. Interesting, in my view, but not so interesting as what we are about to cover. The pyramids and Egyptian slave labor. A plus on one side, a minus on the other." We had our books open to page forty-two, where there was a picture of a pyramid, but Miss Ferenczi wasn't looking at the book. Instead, she was staring at some object just outside the window.

"Pyramids," Miss Ferenczi said, still looking past the window. "I want you to think about the pyramids. And what was inside. The bodies of the pharaohs, of course, and their attendant treasures. Scrolls. Perhaps," Miss Ferenczi said, with something gleeful but unsmiling in her face, "these scrolls were novels for the pharaohs, helping them to pass the time in their long voyage through the centuries. But then, I am joking." I was looking at the lines on Miss Ferenczi's face. "Pyramids," Miss Ferenczi went on, "were the repositories of special cosmic powers. The nature of a pyramid is to guide cosmic energy forces into a concentrated point. The Egyptians knew that; we have generally forgotten it. Did you know," she asked, walking to the side of the room so that she was standing by the coat closet, "that George Washington had Egyptian blood, from his grandmother? Certain features of the Constitution of the United States are notable for their Egyptian ideas."

65   Without glancing down at the book, she began to talk about the movement of souls in Egyptian religion. She said that when people die, their souls return to Earth in the form of carpenter ants or walnut trees, depending on how they behaved—"well or ill"—in life. She said that the Egyptians believed that people act the way they do because of magnetism produced by tidal forces in the solar system, forces produced by the sun and by its "planetary ally," Jupiter. Jupiter, she said, was a planet, as we had been told, but had "certain properties of stars." She was speaking very fast. She said that the Egyptians were great explorers and conquerors. She said that the greatest of all the conquerors, Genghis Khan, had had forty horses and forty young women killed on the site of his grave. We listened. No one tried to stop her. "I myself have been in Egypt," she said, "and have witnessed much dust and many brutalities." She said that an old man in Egypt who worked for a circus had personally shown her an animal in a cage, a monster, half bird and half lion. She said that this monster was

called a gryphon and that she had heard about them but never seen them until she traveled to the outskirts of Cairo. She said that Egyptian astronomers had discovered the planet Saturn, but had not seen its rings. She said that the Egyptians were the first to discover that dogs, when they are ill, will not drink from rivers, but wait for rain, and hold their jaws open to catch it.

"She lies."

We were on the school bus home. I was sitting next to Carl Whiteside, who had bad breath and a huge collection of marbles. We were arguing. Carl thought she was lying. I said she wasn't, probably.

"I didn't believe that stuff about the bird," Carl said, "and what she told us about the pyramids? I didn't believe that either. She didn't know what she was talking about."

"Oh yeah?" I had liked her. She was strange. I thought I could nail him. "If she was lying," I said, "what'd she say that was a lie?"

70   "Six times eleven isn't sixty-eight. It isn't ever. It's sixty-six, I know for a fact."

"She said so. She admitted it. What else did she lie about?"

"I don't know," he said. "Stuff."

"What stuff?"

"Well." He swung his legs back and forth. "You ever see an animal that was half lion and half bird?" He crossed his arms. "It sounded real fakey to me."

75   "It could happen," I said. I had to improvise, to outrage him. "I read in this newspaper my mom bought in the IGA about this scientist, this mad scientist in the Swiss Alps, and he's been putting genes and chromosomes and stuff together in test tubes, and he combined a human being and a hamster." I waited, for effect. "It's called a humster."

"You never." Carl was staring at me, his mouth open, his terrible bad breath making its way toward me. "What newspaper was it?"

"The *National Enquirer*," I said, "that they sell next to the cash registers." When I saw his look of recognition, I knew I had bested him. "And this mad scientist," I said, "his name was, um, Dr. Frankenbush." I realized belatedly that this name was a mistake and waited for Carl to notice its resemblance to the name of the other famous mad master of permutations, but he only sat there.

"A man and a hamster?" He was staring at me, squinting, his mouth opening in distaste. "Jeez. What'd it look like?"

When the bus reached my stop, I took off down our dirt road and ran up through the back yard, kicking the tire swing for good luck. I dropped my books on the back steps so I could hug and kiss our dog, Mr. Selby. Then I hurried inside. I could smell Brussels sprouts cooking, my unfavorite vegetable. My mother was washing other vegetables in the kitchen sink, and my baby brother was hollering in his yellow playpen on the kitchen floor.

80   "Hi, Mom," I said, hopping around the playpen to kiss her, "Guess what?"

"I have no idea."

"We had this substitute today, Miss Ferenczi, and I'd never seen her before, and she had all these stories and ideas and stuff."

"Well. That's good." My mother looked out the window behind the sink, her eyes on the pine woods west of our house. Her face and hairstyle always reminded other people of Betty Crocker, whose picture was framed inside a gigantic spoon on the side of the Bisquick box; to me, though, my mother's face just looked white. "Listen, Tommy," she said, "go upstairs and pick your clothes off the bathroom floor, then go outside to the shed and put the shovel and ax away that your father left outside this morning."

"She said that six times eleven was sometimes sixty-eight!" I said. "And she said she once saw a monster that was half lion and half bird." I waited. "In Egypt, she said."

85   "Did you hear me?" my mother asked, raising her arm to wipe her forehead with the back of her hand. "You have chores to do."

"I know," I said. "I was just telling you about the substitute."

"It's very interesting," my mother said, quickly glancing down at me, "and we can talk about it later when your father gets home. But right now you have some work to do."

"Okay, Mom." I took a cookie out of the jar on the counter and was about to go outside when I had a thought. I ran into the living room, pulled out a dictionary next to the TV stand, and opened it to the G's. *Gryphon:* "variant of griffin." *Griffin:* "a fabulous beast with the head and wings of an eagle and the body of a lion." Fabulous was right. I shouted with triumph and ran outside to put my father's tools back in their place.

Miss Ferenczi was back the next day, slightly altered. She had pulled her hair down and twisted it into pigtails, with red rubber bands holding them tight one inch from the ends. She was wearing a green blouse and pink scarf, making her difficult to look at for a full class day. This time there was no pretense of doing a reading lesson or moving on to arithmetic. As soon as the bell rang, she simply began to talk.

90   She talked for forty minutes straight. There seemed to be less connection between her ideas, but the ideas themselves were, as the dictionary would say, fabulous. She said she had heard of a huge jewel, in what she called the Antipodes, that was so brilliant that when the light shone into it at a certain angle it would blind whoever was looking at its center. She said that the biggest diamond in the world was cursed and had killed everyone who owned it, and that by a trick of fate it was called the Hope diamond. Diamonds are magic, she said, and this is why women wear them on their fingers, as a sign of the magic of womanhood. Men have strength, Miss Ferenczi said, but no true magic. That is why men fall in love with women but women do not fall in love with men; they just love being loved. George Washington had died because of a mistake he made about a

diamond. Washington was not the first *true* President, but she did not say who was. In some places in the world, she said, men and women still live in the trees and eat monkeys for breakfast. Their doctors are magicians. At the bottom of the sea are creatures thin as pancakes which have never been studied by scientists because when you take them up to the air, the fish explode.

There was not a sound in the classroom, except for Miss Ferenczi's voice, and Donna DeShano's coughing. No one even went to the bathroom.

Beethoven, she said, had not been deaf; it was a trick to make himself famous, and it worked. As she talked, Miss Ferenczi's pigtails swung back and forth. There are trees in the world, she said, that eat meat: their leaves are sticky and close up on bugs like hands. She lifted her hands and brought them together, palm to palm. Venus, which most people think is the next closest planet to the sun, is not always closer, and, besides, it is the planet of greatest mystery because of its thick cloud cover. "I know what lies underneath those clouds," Miss Ferenczi said, and waited. After the silence, she said, "Angels. Angels live under those clouds." She said that angels were not invisible to everyone and were in fact smarter than most people. They did not dress in robes as was often claimed but instead wore formal evening clothes, as if they were about to attend a concert. Often angels *do* attend concerts and sit in the aisles where, she said, most people pay no attention to them. She said the most terrible angel had the shape of the Sphinx. "There is no running away from that one," she said. She said that unquenchable fires burn just under the surface of the earth in Ohio, and that the baby Mozart fainted dead away in his cradle when he first heard the sound of a trumpet. She said that someone named Narzim al Harrardim was the greatest writer who ever lived. She said that planets control behavior, and anyone conceived during a solar eclipse would be born with webbed feet.

"I know you children like to hear these things," she said, "these secrets, and that is why I am telling you all this." We nodded. It was better than doing comprehension questions for the readings in *Broad Horizons*.

"I will tell you one more story," she said, "and then we will have to do arithmetic." She leaned over, and her voice grew soft. "There is no death," she said. "You must never be afraid. Never. That which is, cannot die. It will change into different earthly and unearthly elements, but I know this as sure as I stand here in front of you, and I swear it: you must not be afraid. I have seen this truth with these eyes. I know it because in a dream God kissed me. Here." And she pointed with her right index finger to the side of her head, below the mouth, where the vertical lines were carved into her skin.

95 Absent-mindedly we all did our arithmetic problems. At recess the class was out on the playground, but no one was playing. We were all standing in small groups, talking about Miss Ferenczi. We didn't know if she was crazy, or what. I looked out beyond the playground, at the rusted cars

piled in a small heap behind a clump of sumac, and I wanted to see shapes there, approaching me.

On the way home, Carl sat next to me again. He didn't say much, and I didn't either. At last he turned to me. "You know what she said about the leaves that close up on bugs?"

"Huh?"

"The leaves," Carl insisted. "The meat-eating plants. I know it's true. I saw it on television. The leaves have this icky glue that the plants have got smeared all over them and the insects can't get off 'cause they're stuck. I saw it." He seemed demoralized. "She's tellin' the truth."

"Yeah."

100   "You think she's seen all those angels?"

I shrugged.

"I don't think she has," Carl informed me. "I think she made that part up."

"There's a tree," I suddenly said. I was looking out the window at the farms along County Road H. I knew every barn, every broken windmill, every fence, every anhydrous ammonia tank, by heart. "There's a tree that's . . . that I've seen . . ."

"Don't you try to do it," Carl said. "You'll just sound like a jerk."

105   I kissed my mother. She was standing in front of the stove. "How was your day?" she asked.

"Fine."

"Did you have Miss Ferenczi again?"

"Yeah."

"Well?"

110   "She was fine. Mom," I asked, "can I go to my room?"

"No," she said, "not until you've gone out to the vegetable garden and picked me a few tomatoes." She glanced at the sky. "I think it's going to rain. Skedaddle and do it now. Then you come back inside and watch your brother for a few minutes while I go upstairs. I need to clean up before dinner." She looked down at me. "You're looking a little pale, Tommy." She touched the back of her hand to my forehead and I felt her diamond ring against my skin. "Do you feel all right?"

"I'm fine," I said, and went out to pick the tomatoes.

Coughing mutedly, Mr. Hibler was back the next day, slipping lozenges into his mouth when his back was turned at forty-five minute intervals and asking us how much of the prepared lesson plan Miss Ferenczi had followed. Edith Atwater took the responsibility for the class of explaining to Mr. Hibler that the substitute hadn't always done exactly what he would have done, but we had worked hard even though she talked a lot. About what? he asked. All kinds of things, Edith said. I sort of forgot. To our relief, Mr. Hibler seemed not at all interested in what Miss Ferenczi had said to fill the day. He probably thought it was woman's talk; unserious and not suited for school. It was enough that he had a pile of arithmetic problems from us to correct.

For the next month, the sumac turned a distracting red in the field, and the sun traveled toward the southern sky, so that its rays reached Mr. Hibler's Halloween display on the bulletin board in the back of the room, fading the scarecrow with a pumpkin head from orange to tan. Every three days I measured how much farther the sun had moved toward the southern horizon by making small marks with my black Crayola on the north wall, ant-sized marks only I knew were there, inching west.

115　　And then in early December, four days after the first permanent snowfall, she appeared again in our classroom. The minute she came in the door, I felt my heart begin to pound. Once again, she was different: this time, her hair hung straight down and seemed hardly to have been combed. She hadn't brought her lunchbox with her, but she was carrying what seemed to be a small box. She greeted all of us and talked about the weather. Donna DeShano had to remind her to take her overcoat off.

When the bell to start the day finally rang, Miss Ferenczi looked out at all of us and said, "Children, I have enjoyed your company in the past, and today I am going to reward you." She held up the small box. "Do you know what this is?" She waited. "Of course you don't. It is a tarot pack."

Edith Atwater raised her hand. "What's a tarot pack, Miss Ferenczi?"

"It is used to tell fortunes," she said. "And that is what I shall do this morning. I shall tell your fortunes, as I have been taught to do."

"What's fortune?" Bobby Kryzanowicz asked.

120　　"The future, young man. I shall tell you what your future will be. I can't do your whole future, of course. I shall have to limit myself to the five-card system, the wands, cups, swords, pentacles, and the higher arcanes. Now who wants to be first?"

There was a long silence. Then Carol Peterson raised her hand.

"All right," Miss Ferenczi said. She divided the pack into five smaller packs and walked back to Carol's desk, in front of mine. "Pick one card from each of these packs," she said. I saw that Carol had a four of cups, a six of swords, but I couldn't see the other cards. Miss Ferenczi studied the cards on Carol's desk for a minute. "Not bad," she said. "I do not see much higher education. Probably an early marriage. Many children. There's something bleak and dreary here, but I can't tell what. Perhaps just the tasks of a housewife life. I think you'll do very well, for the most part." She smiled at Carol, a smile with a certain lack of interest. "Who wants to be next?"

Carl Whiteside raised his hand slowly.

"Yes," Miss Ferenczi said, "let's do a boy." She walked over to where Carl sat. After he picked his five cards, she gazed at them for a long time. "Travel," she said. "Much distant travel. You might go into the Army. Not too much romantic interest here. A late marriage, if at all. Squabbles. But the Sun is in your major arcana, here, yes, that's a very good card." She giggled. "Maybe a good life."

125   Next I raised my hand, and she told me my future. She did the same with Bobby Kryzanowicz. Kelly Munger, Edith Atwater, and Kim Foor. Then she came to Wayne Razmer. He picked his five cards, and I could see that the Death card was one of them.

"What's your name?" Miss Ferenczi asked.

"Wayne."

"Well, Wayne," she said, you will undergo a *great* metamorphosis, the greatest, before you become an adult. Your earthly element will leap away, into thin air, you sweet boy. This card, this nine of swords here, tells of suffering and desolation. And this ten of wands, well, that's certainly a heavy load."

"What about this one?" Wayne pointed to the Death card.

130   "That one? That one means you will die soon, my dear." She gathered up the cards. We were all looking at Wayne. "But do not fear," she said. "It's not really death, so much as change." She put the cards on Mr. Hibler's desk. "And now, let's do some arithmetic."

At lunchtime Wayne went to Mr. Faegre, the principal, and told him what Miss Ferenczi had done. During the noon recess, we saw Miss Ferenczi drive out of the parking lot in her green Rambler. I stood under the slide, listening to the other kids coasting down and landing in the little depressive bowl at the bottom. I was kicking stones and tugging at my hair right up to the moment when I saw Wayne come out to the playground. He smiled, the dead fool, and with the fingers of his right hand he was showing everyone how he had told on Miss Ferenczi.

I made my way toward Wayne, pushing myself past two girls from another class. He was watching me with his little pinhead eyes.

"You told," I shouted at him. "She was just kidding."

"She shouldn't have," he shouted back. "We were supposed to be doing arithmetic."

135   "She just scared you," I said. "You're a chicken. You're a chicken, Wayne. You are. Scared of a little card," I singsonged.

Wayne fell at me, his two fists hammering down on my nose. I gave him a good one in the stomach and then I tried for his head. Aiming my fist, I saw that he was crying. I slugged him.

"She was right," I yelled. "She was always right! She told the truth!" Other kids were whooping. "You were just scared, that's all!"

And then large hands pulled at us, and it was my turn to speak to Mr. Faegre.

In the afternoon Miss Ferenczi was gone, and my nose was stuffed with cotton clotted with blood, and my lip had swelled, and our class had been combined with Mrs. Mantei's sixth-grade class for a crowded afternoon science unit on insect life in ditches and swamps. I knew where Mrs. Mantei lived: she had a new house trailer just down the road from us, at the Clearwater Park. She was no mystery. Somehow she and Mr. Bodine, the other fourth-grade teacher, had managed to fit forty-five desks into the room. Kelly Munger asked if Miss Ferenczi had been arrested, and Mrs. Mantei said no, of course not. All that afternoon, until the buses came to pick us up, we learned about field crickets and two-striped grasshoppers, water bugs, cicadas, mosquitoes, flies, and moths. We learned about insects' hard outer shell, the exoskeleton, and the usual parts of the mouth, including the labrum, mandible, maxilla, and glossa. We learned about compound eyes and the four-stage metamorphosis from egg to larva to pupa to adult. We learned something, but not much, about mating. Mrs. Mantei drew, very skillfully, the internal anatomy of the grasshopper on the blackboard. We learned about the dance of the honeybee, directing other bees in the hive to pollen. We found out about which insects were pests to man, and which were not. On lined white pieces of paper we made lists of insects we might actually see, then a list of insects too small to be clearly visible, such as fleas; Mrs. Mantei said that our assignment would be to memorize these lists for the next day, when Mr. Hibler would certainly return and test us on our knowledge.

READING AND REACTING

1. In classical mythology a gryphon (also spelled *griffin*) is a monster that has the head and wings of an eagle and the body of a lion. Why is this story called "Gryphon"?

2. Describe Miss Ferenczi's physical appearance, including her personal belongings. Why is her appearance important to the story? How does it change as the story progresses?

3. How is Miss Ferenczi different from other teachers? From other substitute teachers? From other people in general? How is her differentness communicated to her pupils? To the story's readers?

4. What is the significance of the narrator's comment, in paragraph 11, that the lines on Miss Ferenczi's face remind him of Pinocchio?

5. Is Miss Ferenczi a round or a flat character? Explain.

6. In what sense is the narrator's mother a foil for Miss Ferenczi?

7. Why does the narrator defend Miss Ferenczi, first in his argument with Carl Whiteside and later on the playground? What does his attitude toward Miss Ferenczi reveal about his character?

8. Are all of Miss Ferenczi's "substitute facts" lies, or is there some truth in what she says? Is she correct when she says that substitute facts cannot hurt anyone? Could it be argued that much of what is taught in schools today could be viewed as "substitute facts"? Explain.

9. **JOURNAL ENTRY**   Is Miss Ferenczi a good teacher? Why or why not?

10. **CRITICAL PERSPECTIVE**   Writing in the *New York Times Book Review*, critic William Ferguson characterizes *A Relative Stranger*, a more recent

collection of Baxter's short stories than the one in which "Gryphon" appeared, as follows:

The thirteen stories in A Relative Stranger, *all quietly accomplished, suggest a mysterious yet fundamental marriage of despair and joy. Though in one way or another each story ends in disillusionment, the road that leads to that dismal state is so richly peopled, so finely drawn, that the effect is oddly reassuring.*

Do you think this characterization of Baxter's work in *A Relative Stranger* applies to "Gryphon" as well? For example, how are despair and joy joined? Do you find the story reassuring in any way, or does it convey only the sense of disillusionment?

Writing Suggestions: Character

1. Focusing on an unconventional character in a conventional setting, "Gryphon" explores the question of what constitutes a good education. Taking into account your own school experiences as well as those of the students in the story, write an essay in which you discuss what you believe the purpose of education should (and should not) be.

2. In "A&P," "Like a Winding Street," and "Gryphon," characters struggle against rules, authority figures, and inflexible social systems. Choose two of these stories, and compare and contrast the nature of the struggle in which the characters are engaged.

3. Write an essay in which you contrast the character of Miss Brill with the character of Phoenix Jackson in "A Worn Path" (Chapter 10). Focus on how each character interacts with those around her as well as how each seems to see her role or mission in the world.

4. Write a letter from Mae to Johnson in which you reveal information about her character that does not appear in "Like a Winding Sheet." What is her typical day like? What frustrations does *she* experience? Does she too feel a sense of rage? Conclude the letter by explaining what she plans to do now, as she recovers physically and emotionally. Will she leave Johnson or stay with him?

5. Sammy, Miss Brill, and Miss Ferenczi all use their active imaginations to create scenarios that help get them through the day. None of them is able to sustain the illusion, however. As a result, all three eventually find out how harsh reality can be. What steps could these three characters take to fit more comfortably into the worlds they inhabit? *Should* they take such steps?

CHAPTER 6

Setting

Many authors find it hard to write about new environments that they did not know in childhood. The voices reheard from childhood have a truer pitch. And the foliage—the trees of childhood—are remembered more exactly. When I work from within a different locale from the South, I have to wonder what time the flowers are in bloom—and what flowers? I hardly let characters speak unless they are Southern. Wolfe wrote brilliantly of Brooklyn, but more brilliantly of the Southern cadence and ways of speech. This is particularly true of Southern writers because it is not only their speech and the foliage, but their entire culture—which makes it a homeland within a homeland. No matter what the politics, the degree or non-degree of liberalism in a Southern writer, he is still bound to this particular regionalism of language and voices and foliage and memory.

CARSON MCCULLERS, "THE FLOWERING DREAM"

I don't think you transcend region, anymore than a plant transcends earth. I think that you come out of something, and you can then branch out in all kinds of different directions, but that doesn't mean cutting yourself off from your roots and from your earth. To me an effective writer is one who can make what he or she is writing about understandable and moving to someone who has never been there. All good writing has that kind of transcendence.

MARGARET ATWOOD, "USING WHAT YOU'RE GIVEN" (INTERVIEW)

I write about South Africa because it is the only place I know to write about. But I write about it because I must write about it. What I have written about South Africa appears to have the property of being able to move people who know nothing about it. I know of course that there are things about life in South Africa which are common to life anywhere, that fears and hopes and griefs and joys are common to all men. But what astonishes me is that people, disregarding, yet not altogether disregarding, the South African shades and tones and colours, find that these fears and hopes and griefs and joys are their own. This encourages me, and makes me feel a strong desire to write again.

ALAN PATON, "WHY I WRITE"

I think that the sense of place is extremely important to most writers. Certainly it is to me. I identify very strongly with places where I have lived, where I have been, where I have invested some part of my being. . . . The earth was here before I was. When I came, I simply identified place by living in it or looking at it. One does create place in the same way that the storyteller creates himself, creates his listener. The writer creates a place.

N. SCOTT MOMADAY, *ANCESTRAL VOICES*

We all know that the weather affects our moods. The [writer] is in the happy position of being able to invent whatever weather is appropriate to the mood he or she wants to evoke.

Weather is therefore frequently a trigger for the effect John Ruskin called the pathetic fallacy, the projection of human emotions onto phenomena in the natural world. "All violent feelings . . . produce in us a falseness in our impressions of external things, which I would generally characterize as the pathetic fallacy," he wrote. As the name implies, Ruskin thought it was a bad thing, a symptom of the decadence of modern (as compared to classical) art and literature, and it is indeed often the occasion of overblown, self-indulgent writing. But used with intelligence and discretion it is a rhetorical device capable of moving and powerful effects, without which fiction would be much the poorer.

DAVID LODGE, *THE ART OF FICTION*

The **setting** of a work of fiction establishes its historical, geographical, and physical location. *Where* a work is set—on a tropical island, in a dungeon, at a crowded party, in a tent in the woods—influences our interpretation of the story's events and characters. *When* a work takes place—during the French Revolution, during the Vietnam War, today, or in the future—is equally important. Setting, however, is more than just the approximate time and place in which the work is set; setting also encompasses a wide variety of physical and cultural features.

Clearly, setting is more important in some works than in others. In some stories no particular time or place is specified, or even suggested, perhaps because the writer does not consider a specific setting to be important or because the writer wishes the story's events to seem timeless and universal. In Nadine Gordimer's "Once Upon a Time" (p. 74), for example, the writer follows the conventions of fairy tales, which are set in unidentified, faraway places. In other stories a writer may provide only minimal information about setting, telling readers little more than where and when the action takes place. In still other instances setting may be of obvious importance, helping to define the action as well as to explain characters' behavior, as it does in Charlotte Perkins Gilman's "The Yellow Wall-Paper" (p. 160). In fact, setting may be so important that it is the key factor influencing the characters or the plot development. In such cases setting is clearly identified and fully described.

One function of setting is its ability to highlight some aspect of a character's behavior or some feature of plot development. This emphasis is frequently achieved when a character is set in opposition to the setting. Alice in Wonderland; a northerner in the South; a naive, unsophisticated American tourist in an old European city; a sane person in a mental hospital; a moral person in a corrupt environment; an immigrant in a new world; a city dweller in the country—all these characters are set in opposition to the setting in which they find themselves, and this opposition helps to define the characters and to create the central conflict of the story.

In much the same way, a contrast between situation and setting can create interest—for example, the intrusion of nuclear war into a typical suburban neighborhood; the intrusion of modern social ideas into an old-fashioned world; or the intrusion of a brutal, senseless murder into a peaceful English village. In each of these cases, the setting enhances the plot.

HISTORICAL CONTEXT

A particular historical period, and the events associated with it, can be important in a story; therefore, some familiarity with a period can be useful (or even essential) to readers who wish to understand a story fully. Historical context establishes a social, cultural, economic, and political environment. Knowing, for instance, that "The Yellow Wall-Paper," written in 1892, is set in a period in which doctors treated women as delicate and dependent creatures, helps to explain the narrator's emotional state. Likewise, it may be important to know that a story is set during a particularly volatile (or static) political era, during a time of permissive (or repressive) attitudes toward sex, during a war, or during a period of economic prosperity or recession. Any one of these factors may determine—or help to explain—characters' actions: Historical events or cultural norms may, for instance, limit or multiply a character's options, and our knowledge of history may reveal to us a character's incompatibility with his or her milieu. In F. Scott Fitzgerald's "Bernice Bobs Her Hair," set in the 1920s in a midwestern town, a young girl is goaded into cutting her long hair. To understand the significance of Bernice's act—and to understand the reactions of others to that act—readers must know that during that era only racy "society vampires," not nice girls from good families, bobbed their hair.

Knowing the approximate year or historical period during which a story takes place can explain forces that act on characters, help to account for their behavior, clarify circumstances that influence the story's action, and help to justify a writer's use of plot devices that might otherwise seem improbable. For instance, stories set before the development of modern transportation and communication systems may hinge on plot devices readers would not accept in a modern story. Thus, in "Paul's Case," a 1904 story by Willa Cather, a young man who steals a large sum of money in Pittsburgh is able to spend several days enjoying it before the news of the theft reaches New York, where he has fled. In other stories we see such out-dated plot devices as characters threatened by diseases that have now been eradicated (and subjected to outdated medical or psychiatric treatment). In addition, characters may be constrained by social conventions different from those that operate in our own society.

GEOGRAPHICAL CONTEXT

In addition to knowing when a work takes place, readers need to know *where* it takes place. A story's geographical context can also help readers to understand characters' behavior. For instance, knowing whether a story is set in the United States, in Europe, or in a developing nation can help to explain anything from why language and customs are unfamiliar to us to why characters act in ways we find improbable. Even in stories set in our own country, regional differences may account for differences in plot de-velopment and characters' motivation. For example, knowing that William Faulkner's "A Rose for Emily" (p. 80) is set in the post–Civil War American South helps to explain why the townspeople are so chivalrously protective of Miss Emily. Similarly, the fact that Bret Harte's "The Outcasts of Poker Flat" is set in the American West accounts for its unusual cast of charac-ters—including a gambler, a prostitute, and a traveling salesman.

The size of the town or city in which a story takes place may also be important. In a small town, for example, a character's problems are more likely to be subject to intense scrutiny by other characters, as they are in stories of small-town life such as those in Sherwood Anderson's *Winesburg, Ohio*. In a large city, characters may be more likely to be isolated and anonymous, like Mrs. Miller in Truman Capote's "Miriam," who is so lonely that she creates an imaginary companion. Characters may also be alienated by their big-city surroundings, as Gregor Samsa is in Franz Kafka's "The Metamorphosis" (p. 476).

Of course, a story may not have a recognizable geographical context; its location may not be specified, and it may even be set in a fantasy world. Such settings may free writers from the constraints placed on them by familiar environments, allowing them to experiment with situations and characters, unaffected by readers' expectations or associations with familiar settings.

PHYSICAL CONTEXT

The *time of day* can clearly influence a story's mood as well as its develop-ment. The gruesome murder described in Edgar Allan Poe's "The Cask of

Amontillado" (p. 209) takes place in an appropriate setting: not just underground, but in the darkness of night. Conversely, the horrifying events of Shirley Jackson's "The Lottery" (p. 309) take place in broad daylight, contrasting dramatically with the darkness of the society that permits—and even participates in—such events. Many stories, of course, move through several time periods as the action unfolds, and changes in time may also be important. For instance, the approach of evening, or of dawn, can signal the end of a crisis in the plot.

Whether a story is set primarily *inside* or *out-of-doors* may also be significant. The characters may be physically constrained by a closed-in setting or liberated by an expansive landscape. Some interior settings may be psychologically limiting. For instance, the narrator in "The Yellow Wall-Paper" feels suffocated by her room, whose ugly wallpaper comes to haunt her. In many of Poe's stories the central character is trapped, physically or psychologically, in a confined, suffocating space. In other stories an interior setting may serve a symbolic function. For instance, in "A Rose for Emily" the house is for Miss Emily a symbol of the South's past glory as well as a refuge, a fortress, and a hiding place. Similarly, a building or house may represent society, with its rules and norms and limitations. In John Updike's "A&P" (p. 105), for instance, the supermarket establishes social as well as physical limits. This is also the case in Katherine Mansfield's "Her First Ball," where a ballroom serves as the setting for a young girl's initiation into the rules and realities of adult society.

Conversely, an outdoor setting can free a character from social norms of behavior, as it does for Ernest Hemingway's Nick Adams, a war veteran who, in "Big Two-Hearted River," finds order, comfort, and peace only when he is away from civilization. Of course, an outdoor setting can also expose characters to physical dangers, such as untamed wilderness, uncharted seas, and frighteningly empty open spaces, as in Stephen Crane's story "The Open Boat" (p. 420).

Weather can be another important aspect of setting. A storm can threaten a character's life or just make the character—and readers—*think* danger is present, distracting us from other, more subtle threats. Extreme weather conditions can make characters act irrationally or uncharacteristically, as in Doris Lessing's "A Woman on the Roof" (p. 524), where the intense heat encourages desperate flirtation, or in Kate Chopin's "The Storm" (p. 146), where a storm provides the complication and determines the characters' actions. In numerous stories set in hostile landscapes, where extremes of heat and cold influence the action, weather may pose a test for characters, as in Jack London's "To Build a Fire," in which the main character struggles unsuccessfully against a brutally cold, hostile environment.

The various physical attributes of setting combine to create an **atmosphere,** or **mood,** that may be critical to a story. This atmosphere may emphasize a story's theme, helping to explain a character's reactions or state of mind, advancing or impeding the action. Characters may react one way in a crowded, busy, hectic atmosphere but behave very differently in a peaceful rural environment. Darkness and isolation can cause (or reflect) behavior disturbances, while an idyllic, peaceful setting can change or reinforce a character's positive mood—or serve an ironic purpose, as it does in a story of horror such as "The Lottery." In "The Cask of Amontillado" several factors work together to create the eerie, intense atmosphere appropriate to the story's events: It is nighttime; it is the hectic carnival season; and the catacombs are dark, damp, and filled with the bones of the narrator's ancestors.

▼▼

CHECKLIST FOR WRITING ABOUT SETTING

◆ Is the setting specified or unidentified? Is it fully described or just sketched in?

◆ Is the setting just background, or is it a key force in the story?

◆ How does the setting influence the characters? Does it affect (or reflect) their emotional state? Does it help to explain their motivation?

◆ Are any characters set in opposition to their environment?

◆ Are any situations set in sharp contrast to the setting?

◆ How does the setting influence the story's plot? Does it cause characters to act?

◆ Does the setting add irony to the story?

◆ In what time period does the story take place? How can you tell? What social, political, or economic characteristics of the historical period might influence the story?

◆ In what geographical location is the story set? Is this location important to the story?

◆ At what time of day is the story set? Is time important to the development of the story?

◆ Is the story set primarily indoors or out-of-doors? What role does this aspect of the setting play in the story?

◆ What role do weather conditions play in the story?

◆ Is the story's general atmosphere dark or bright? Clear or murky? Tumultuous or calm? Gloomy or cheerful?

◆ Does the atmosphere change as the story progresses? Is this change significant?

▲▲

KATE CHOPIN (1851–1904)   (picture and biography on page 70)

Chopin's style is realistic yet infused with a dense, sensual texture that is perhaps, in part, Chopin's artistic response to her memories of the exotic Louisiana bayou country. Like her contemporary Gustave Flaubert (*The Awakening* has often been called a "Creole *Bovary*"), Chopin used the physical world—as in the charged atmosphere of "The Storm"—to symbolize the inner truths of her characters' minds and hearts. Unlike Flaubert, however, she depicts sex not as a frantic and destructive force, but as a joyous, elemental part of life. Apparently Kate Chopin knew how daring "The Storm" was: She never submitted it for publication.

KATE CHOPIN

The Storm

(c. 1899)

I

The leaves were so still that even Bibi thought it was going to rain. Bobinôt, who was accustomed to converse on terms of perfect equality with his little son, called the child's attention to certain sombre clouds that were rolling with sinister intention from the west, accompanied by a sullen, threatening roar. They were at Friedheimer's store and decided to remain there till the storm had passed. They sat within the door on two empty kegs. Bibi was four years old and looked very wise.

"Mama'll be 'fraid, yes," he suggested with blinking eyes.

"She'll shut the house. Maybe she got Sylvie helpin' her this evenin'," Bobinôt responded reassuringly.

"No; she ent got Sylvie. Sylvie was helpin' her yistiday," piped Bibi.

5   Bobinôt arose and going across to the counter purchased a can of shrimps, of which Calixta was very fond. Then he returned to his perch on the keg and sat stolidly holding the can of shrimps while the storm burst. It shook the wooden store and seemed to be ripping great furrows in the distant field. Bibi laid his little hand on his father's knee and was not afraid.

II

Calixta, at home, felt no uneasiness for their safety. She sat at a side window sewing furiously on a sewing machine. She was greatly occupied and did not notice the approaching storm. But she felt very warm and often stopped to mop her face on which the perspiration gathered in beads. She unfastened her white sacque at the throat. It began to grow dark, and suddenly realizing the situation she got up hurriedly and went about closing windows and doors.

Out on the small front gallery she had hung Bobinôt's Sunday clothes to air and she hastened out to gather them before the rain fell. As she stepped outside, Alcée Laballière rode in at the gate. She had not seen him very often since her marriage, and never alone. She stood there with Bobinôt's coat in her hands, and the big rain drops began to fall. Alcée rode his horse under the shelter of a side projection where the chickens had huddled and there were plows and a harrow piled up in the corner.

"May I come and wait on your gallery till the storm is over, Calixta?" he asked.

"Come 'long in, M'sieur Alcée."

His voice and her own startled her as if from a trance, and she seized Bobinôt's vest. Alcée, mounting to the porch, grabbed the trousers and snatched Bibi's braided jacket that was about to be carried away by a sudden gust of wind. He expressed an intention to remain outside, but it was soon apparent that he might as well have been out in the open: the water beat in upon the boards in driving sheets, and he went inside, closing the door after him. It was even necessary to put something beneath the door to keep the water out.

"My! what a rain! It's good two years since it rain' like that," exclaimed Calixta as she rolled up a piece of bagging and Alcée helped her to thrust it beneath the crack.

She was a little fuller of figure than five years before when she married; but she had lost nothing of her vivacity. Her blue eyes still retained their melting quality; and her yellow hair, dishevelled by the wind and rain, kinked more stubbornly than ever about her ears and temples.

The rain beat upon the low, shingled roof with a force and clatter that threatened to break an entrance and deluge them there. They were in the dining room—the sitting room—the general utility room. Adjoining was her bed room, with Bibi's couch along side her own. The door stood open, and the room with its white, monumental bed, its closed shutters, looked dim and mysterious.

Alcée flung himself into a rocker and Calixta nervously began to gather up from the floor the lengths of a cotton sheet which she had been sewing.

"If this keeps up, *Dieu sait*[1] if the levees goin' to stan' it!" she exclaimed.

"What have you got to do with the levees?"

"I got enough to do! An' there's Bobinôt with Bibi out in that storm— if he only didn't left Friedheimer's!"

"Let us hope, Calixta, that Bobinôt's got sense enough to come in out of a cyclone."

She went and stood at the window with a greatly disturbed look on her face. She wiped the frame that was clouded with moisture. It was stiflingly

---

[1] God knows.

hot. Alcée got up and joined her at the window, looking over her shoulder. The rain was coming down in sheets obscuring the view of far-off cabins and enveloping the distant wood in a gray mist. The playing of the lightning was incessant. A bolt struck a tall chinaberry tree at the edge of the field. It filled all visible space with a blinding glare and the crash seemed to invade the very boards they stood upon.

20   Calixta put her hands to her eyes, and with a cry, staggered backward. Alcée's arm encircled her, and for an instant he drew her close and spasmodically to him.

"*Bonté!*"[2] she cried, releasing herself from his encircling arm and retreating from the window, "the house'll go next! If I only knew w'ere Bibi was!" She would not compose herself; she would not be seated. Alcée clasped her shoulders and looked into her face. The contact of her warm, palpitating body when he had unthinkingly drawn her into his arms, had aroused all the old-time infatuation and desire for her flesh.

"Calixta," he said, "don't be frightened. Nothing can happen. The house is too low to be struck, with so many tall trees standing about. There! aren't you going to be quiet? say, aren't you?" He pushed her hair back from her face that was warm and steaming. Her lips were as red and moist as pomegranate seed. Her white neck and a glimpse of her full, firm bosom disturbed him powerfully. As she glanced up at him the fear in her liquid blue eyes had given place to a drowsy gleam that unconsciously betrayed a sensuous desire. He looked down into her eyes and there was nothing for him to do but to gather her lips in a kiss. It reminded him of Assumption.

"Do you remember—in Assumption, Calixta?" he asked in a low voice broken by passion. Oh! she remembered; for in Assumption he had kissed her and kissed and kissed her; until his senses would well nigh fail, and to save her he would resort to a desperate flight. If she was not an immaculate dove in those days, she was still inviolate; a passionate creature whose very defenselessness had made her defense, against which his honor forbade him to prevail. Now—well, now—her lips seemed in a manner free to be tasted, as well as her round, white throat and her whiter breasts.

They did not heed the crashing torrents, and the roar of the elements made her laugh as she lay in his arms. She was a revelation in that dim, mysterious chamber; as white as the couch she lay upon. Her firm, elastic flesh that was knowing for the first time its birthright, was like a creamy lily that the sun invites to contribute its breath and perfume to the undying life of the world.

25   The generous abundance of her passion, without guile or trickery, was like a white flame which penetrated and found response in depths of his own sensuous nature that had never yet been reached.

When he touched her breasts they gave themselves up in quivering ecstasy, inviting his lips. Her mouth was a fountain of delight. And when

---

[2] "Goodness!"

he possessed her, they seemed to swoon together at the very borderland of life's mystery.

He stayed cushioned upon her, breathless, dazed, enervated, with his heart beating like a hammer upon her. With one hand she clasped his head, her lips lightly touching his forehead. The other hand stroked with a soothing rhythm his muscular shoulders.

The growl of the thunder was distant and passing away. The rain beat softly upon the shingles, inviting them to drowsiness and sleep. But they dared not yield.

The rain was over; and the sun was turning the glistening green world into a palace of gems. Calixta, on the gallery, watched Alcée ride away. He turned and smiled at her with a beaming face; and she lifted her pretty chin in the air and laughed aloud.

III

30 Bobinôt and Bibi, trudging home, stopped without at the cistern to make themselves presentable.

"My! Bibi, w'at will yo' mama say! You ought to be ashame'. You oughtn' put on those good pants. Look at 'em! An' that mud on yo' collar! How you got that mud on yo' collar, Bibi? I never saw such a boy!" Bibi was the picture of pathetic resignation. Bobinôt was the embodiment of serious solicitude as he strove to remove from his own person and his son's the signs of their tramp over heavy roads and through wet fields. He scraped the mud off Bibi's bare legs and feet with a stick and carefully removed all traces from his heavy brogans. Then, prepared for the worst— the meeting with an over-scrupulous housewife, they entered cautiously at the back door.

Calixta was preparing supper. She had set the table and was dripping coffee at the hearth. She sprang up as they came in.

"Oh, Bobinôt! You back! My! but I was uneasy. W'ere you been during the rain? An' Bibi? he ain't wet? he ain't hurt?" She had clasped Bibi and was kissing him effusively. Bobinôt's explanations and apologies which he had been composing all along the way, died on his lips as Calixta felt him to see if he were dry, and seemed to express nothing but satisfaction at their safe return.

"I brought you some shrimps, Calixta," offered Bobinôt, hauling the can from his ample side pocket and laying it on the table.

35 "Shrimps! Oh, Bobinôt! you too good fo' anything!" and she gave him a smacking kiss on the cheek that resounded. "*J'vous réponds,*[3] we'll have a feas' tonight! umph-umph!"

Bobinôt and Bibi began to relax and enjoy themselves, and when the three seated themselves at table they laughed much and so loud that anyone might have heard them as far away as Laballière's.

---

3 "I tell you."

IV

Alcée Laballière wrote to his wife, Clarisse, that night. It was a loving letter, full of tender solicitude. He told her not to hurry back, but if she and the babies liked it at Biloxi, to stay a month longer. He was getting on nicely; and though he missed them, he was willing to bear the separation a while longer—realizing that their health and pleasure were the first things to be considered.

V

As for Clarisse, she was charmed upon receiving her husband's letter. She and the babies were doing well. The society was agreeable; many of her old friends and acquaintances were at the bay. And the first free breath since her marriage seemed to restore the pleasant liberty of her maiden days. Devoted as she was to her husband, their intimate conjugal life was something which she was more than willing to forego for a while.

So the storm passed and everyone was happy.

Reading and Reacting

1. Trace the progress of the weather through the five parts of the story. Then, trace the stages of the story's plot. How does the progress of the storm parallel the developing plot?

2. How does the storm help to create the story's atmosphere? How would you characterize this atmosphere?

3. In Part I the "sombre clouds . . . rolling with sinister intention" introduce the storm. In what sense does this description introduce the story's action as well?

4. In what ways does the storm force the action of the story? List specific events that occur because of the storm.

5. Is the presence of the storm essential to the story? Explain.

6. The weather is the most obvious element of the story's setting. What other aspects of setting are important to the story?

7. After Part II the storm is not mentioned again until the last line of the story. What signs of the storm remain in Parts III, IV, and V?

8. Besides denoting the weather, what else might the title suggest?

9. **Journal Entry**   The storm sets in motion the chain of events that leads to the characters' adultery. Do you think the storm excuses the characters in any way from responsibility for their actions?

10. **Critical Perspective**   In his discussion of "The Storm," Donald F. Larsson focuses on the story's ending:

    While the storm mirrors the physical passion of the couple, neither it nor the passion itself is destructive. Where one would expect some retribution

for this infidelity in a story, the results are only beneficial: Calixta,
physically fulfilled, happily welcomes back her returning husband and son;
Alcée writes to Clarisse, off visiting relatives, that he does not need her
back right away; and Clarisse, enjoying "the first free breath since her
marriage," is content to stay where she is for the time. Even today, Chopin's
ending seems audacious: "So the storm passed and every one was happy."

Do you agree that the ending is "audacious"? What do you think
should have happened at the end of the story?

TILLIE OLSEN (1912 or 1913–   ) is known for
her works of fiction about working-class Americans.
Her short stories and one novel are inhabited by
those she called the "despised people"—coal miners, farm laborers, packinghouse butchers, and
housewives. Olsen was born in Nebraska into a
working-class family. Though she has been described as a Depression-era dropout, Olsen has observed that she educated herself, with libraries as
her college. According to an account in her nonfic-
tion work *Silences* (1978), Olsen was at age fifteen inspired to write about
working-class people when she read Rebecca Harding Davis's *Life in the
Iron Mills,* a tale of the effects of industrialization upon workers, in an
1861 issue of *Atlantic Monthly* bought for ten cents in a junk shop.

Shortly after she left high school, she was jailed for helping to organize
packinghouse workers. Motivated by her experiences, she began to write a
novel, *Yonnondio.* Under her maiden name, Tillie Lerner, she published two
poems, a short story, and part of her novel in the 1930s. After her marriage
she did not publish again for twenty-two years, spending her time raising
four children and working at a variety of jobs. The collection of short stories *Tell Me a Riddle* (1961), which includes "I Stand Here Ironing" (originally titled "Help Her to Believe"), was published when she was fifty. Her
only other work of fiction is *Yonnondio* (1974), which she pieced together
from drafts she wrote in the 1930s and edited for publication in 1974.

Because she believed her own career was "ruined" by the passage of
time when she could not write because of other responsibilities, she focuses on encouraging young writers by lecturing or reading her own works
to writers' groups and holding writer-in-residency or visiting professorships at several major universities. She is also known for her efforts to re-
discover long-forgotten works by other working-class women. In 1984, she
edited *Mother to Daughter, Daughter to Mother: Mothers on Mothering,* a collection of poems, letters, short fiction, and diary excerpts written by famous and not-so-famous women. Olsen lives in San Francisco.

T I L L I E   O L S E N

I Stand Here Ironing

(1961)

I stand here ironing, and what you asked me moves tormented back and forth with the iron.

"I wish you would manage the time to come and talk with me about your daughter. I'm sure you can help me understand her. She's a youngster who needs help and whom I'm deeply interested in helping."

"Who needs help." . . . Even if I came, what good would it do? You think because I am her mother I have a key, or that in some way you could use me as a key? She has lived for nineteen years. There is all that life that has happened outside of me, beyond me.

And when is there time to remember, to sift, to weigh, to estimate, to total? I will start and there will be an interruption and I will have to gather it all together again. Or I will become engulfed with all I did or did not do, with what should have been and what cannot be helped.

5   She was a beautiful baby. The first and only one of our five that was beautiful at birth. You do not guess how new and uneasy her tenancy in her now-loveliness. You did not know her all those years she was thought homely, or see her poring over her baby pictures, making me tell her over and over how beautiful she had been—and would be, I would tell her—and was now, to the seeing eye. But the seeing eyes were few or nonexistent. Including mine.

I nursed her. They feel that's important nowadays. I nursed all the children, but with her, with all the fierce rigidity of first motherhood, I did like the books then said. Though her cries battered me to trembling and my breasts ached with swollenness, I waited till the clock decreed.

Why do I put that first? I do not even know if it matters, or if it explains anything.

She was a beautiful baby. She blew shining bubbles of sound. She loved motion, loved light, loved color and music and textures. She would lie on the floor in her blue overalls patting the surface so hard in ecstasy her hands and feet would blur. She was a miracle to me, but when she was eight months old I had to leave her daytimes with the woman downstairs to whom she was no miracle at all, for I worked or looked for work and for Emily's father, who "could no longer endure" (he wrote in his good-bye note) "sharing want with us."

I was nineteen. It was the pre-relief, pre-WPA[1] world of the depression. I would start running as soon as I got off the streetcar, running up the

---

[1] Works Progress Administration, created in 1935 as part of President Franklin D. Roosevelt's New Deal program. The purpose of the WPA (renamed the Works Projects Administration in 1939) was to provide jobs for the unemployed during the Great Depression.

stairs, the place smelling sour, and awake or asleep to startle awake, when she saw me she would break into a clogged weeping that could not be comforted, a weeping I can hear yet.

10   After a while I found a job hashing at night so I could be with her days, and it was better. But it came to where I had to bring her to his family and leave her.

It took a long time to raise the money for her fare back. Then she got chicken pox and I had to wait longer. When she finally came, I hardly knew her, walking quick and nervous like her father, looking like her father, thin, and dressed in a shoddy red that yellowed her skin and glared at the pockmarks. All the baby loveliness gone.

She was two. Old enough for nursery school they said, and I did not know then what I know now—the fatigue of the long day, and the lacerations of group life in the kinds of nurseries that are only parking places for children.

Except that it would have made no difference if I had known. It was the only place there was. It was the only way we could be together, the only way I could hold a job.

And even without knowing, I knew. I knew the teacher that was evil because all these years it has curdled into my memory, the little boy hunched in the corner, her rasp, "why aren't you outside, because Alvin hits you? that's no reason, go out, scaredy." I knew Emily hated it even if she did not clutch and implore "don't go Mommy" like the other children, mornings.

15   She always had a reason why we should stay home. Momma, you look sick. Momma, I feel sick. Momma, the teachers aren't there today, they're sick. Momma, we can't go, there was a fire there last night. Momma, it's a holiday today, no school, they told me.

But never a direct protest, never rebellion. I think of our others in their three-, four-year-oldness—the explosions, the tempers, the denunciations, the demands—and I feel suddenly ill. I put the iron down. What in me demanded that goodness in her? And what was the cost, the cost to her of such goodness?

The old man living in the back once said in his gentle way: "You should smile at Emily more when you look at her." What *was* in my face when I looked at her? I loved her. There were all the acts of love.

It was only with the others I remembered what he said, and it was the face of joy, and not of care or tightness or worry I turned to them—too late for Emily. She does not smile easily, let alone almost always as her brothers and sisters do. Her face is closed and sombre, but when she wants, how fluid. You must have seen it in her pantomimes, you spoke of her rare gift for comedy on the stage that rouses laughter out of the audience so dear they applaud and applaud and do not want to let her go.

Where does it come from, that comedy? There was none of it in her when she came back to me that second time, after I had had to send her away again. She had a new daddy now to learn to love, and I think perhaps it was a better time.

20   Except when we left her alone nights, telling ourselves she was old enough.

"Can't you go some other time, Mommy, like tomorrow?" she would ask. "Will it be just a little while you'll be gone? Do you promise?"

The time we came back, the front door open, the clock on the floor in the hall. She rigid awake. "It wasn't just a little while. I didn't cry. Three times I called you, just three times, and then I ran downstairs to open the door so you could come faster. The clock talked loud. I threw it away, it scared me what it talked."

She said the clock talked loud again that night I went to the hospital to have Susan. She was delirious with the fever that comes before red measles, but she was fully conscious all the week I was gone and the week after we were home when she could not come near the new baby or me.

She did not get well. She stayed skeleton thin, not wanting to eat, and night after night she had nightmares. She would call for me, and I would rouse from exhaustion to sleepily call back: "You're all right, darling, go to sleep, it's just a dream," and if she still called, in a sterner voice, "now go to sleep, Emily, there's nothing to hurt you." Twice, only twice, when I had to get up for Susan anyhow, I went in to sit with her.

25   Now when it is too late (as if she would let me hold and comfort her like I do the others) I get up and go to her at once at her moan or restless stirring. "Are you awake, Emily? Can I get you something?" And the answer is always the same: "No, I'm all right, go back to sleep, Mother."

They persuaded me at the clinic to send her away to a convalescent home in the country where "she can have the kind of food and care you can't manage for her, and you'll be free to concentrate on the new baby." They still send children to that place. I see pictures on the society page of sleek young women planning affairs to raise money for it, or dancing at the affairs, or decorating Easter eggs or filling Christmas stockings for the children.

They never have a picture of the children so I do not know if the girls still wear those gigantic red bows and the ravaged looks on the every other Sunday when parents can come to visit "unless otherwise notified"—as we were notified the first six weeks.

Oh it is a handsome place, green lawns and tall trees and fluted flower beds. High up on the balconies of each cottage the children stand, the girls in their red bows and white dresses, the boys in white suits and giant red ties. The parents stand below shrieking up to be heard and the children shriek down to be heard, and between them the invisible wall: "Not to Be Contaminated by Parental Germs or Physical Affection."

There was a tiny girl who always stood hand in hand with Emily. Her parents never came. One visit she was gone. "They moved her to Rose Cottage," Emily shouted in explanation. "They don't like you to love anybody here."

30   She wrote once a week, the labored writing of a seven-year-old. "I am fine. How is the baby. If I write my leter nicly I will have a star. Love."

There never was a star. We wrote every other day, letters she could never hold or keep but only hear read—once. "We simply do not have room for children to keep any personal possessions," they patiently explained when we pieced one Sunday's shrieking together to plead how much it would mean to Emily, who loved so to keep things, to be allowed to keep her letters and cards.

Each visit she looked frailer. "She isn't eating," they told us.

(They had runny eggs for breakfast or mush with lumps, Emily said later, I'd hold it in my mouth and not swallow. Nothing ever tasted good, just when they had chicken.)

It took us eight months to get her released home, and only the fact that she gained back so little of her seven lost pounds convinced the social worker.

I used to try to hold and love her after she came back, but her body would stay stiff, and after a while she'd push away. She ate little. Food sickened her, and I think much of life too. Oh she had physical lightness and brightness, twinkling by on skates, bouncing like a ball up and down up and down over the jump rope, skimming over the hill; but these were momentary.

35   She fretted about her appearance, thin and dark and foreign-looking at a time when every little girl was supposed to look or thought she should look a chubby blonde replica of Shirley Temple. The doorbell sometimes rang for her, but no one seemed to come and play in the house or be a best friend. Maybe because we moved so much.

There was a boy she loved painfully through two school semesters. Months later she told me how she had taken pennies from my purse to buy him candy. "Licorice was his favorite and I brought him some every day, but he still liked Jennifer better'n me. Why, Mommy?" The kind of question for which there is no answer.

School was a worry to her. She was not glib or quick in a world where glibness and quickness were easily confused with ability to learn. To her overworked and exasperated teachers she was an overconscientious "slow learner" who kept trying to catch up and was absent entirely too often.

I let her be absent, though sometimes the illness was imaginary. How different from my now-strictness about attendance with the others. I wasn't working. We had a new baby, I was home anyhow. Sometimes, after Susan grew old enough, I would keep her home from school, too, to have them all together.

Mostly Emily had asthma, and her breathing, harsh and labored, would fill the house with a curiously tranquil sound. I would bring the two old dresser mirrors and her boxes of collections to her bed. She would select beads and single earrings, bottle tops and shells, dried flowers and pebbles, old postcards and scraps, all sorts of oddments; then she and Susan would play Kingdom, setting up landscapes and furniture, peopling them with action.

40 Those were the only times of peaceful companionship between her and Susan. I have edged away from it, that poisonous feeling between them, that terrible balancing of hurts and needs I had to do between the two, and did so badly, those earlier years.

Oh there are conflicts between the others too, each one human, needing, demanding, hurting, taking—but only between Emily and Susan, no, Emily toward Susan that corroding resentment. It seems so obvious on the surface, yet it is not obvious. Susan, the second child, Susan, golden- and curly-haired and chubby, quick and articulate and assured, everything in appearance and manner Emily was not; Susan, not able to resist Emily's precious things, losing or sometimes clumsily breaking them; Susan telling jokes and riddles to company for applause while Emily sat silent (to say to me later: that was *my* riddle, Mother, I told it to Susan); Susan, who for all the five years' difference in age was just a year behind Emily in developing physically.

I am glad for that slow physical development that widened the difference between her and her contemporaries, though she suffered over it. She was too vulnerable for that terrible world of youthful competition, of preening and parading, of constant measuring of yourself against every other, of envy, "If I had that copper hair," "If I had that skin. . . ." She tormented herself enough about not looking like the others, there was enough of the unsureness, the having to be conscious of words before you speak, the constant caring—what are they thinking of me? without having it all magnified by the merciless physical drives.

Ronnie is calling. He is wet and I change him. It is rare there is such a cry now. That time of motherhood is almost behind me when the ear is not one's own but must always be racked and listening for the child cry, the child call. We sit for a while and I hold him, looking out over the city spread in charcoal with its soft aisles of light. "*Shoogily,*" he breathes and curls closer. I carry him back to bed, asleep. *Shoogily.* A funny word, a family word, inherited from Emily, invented by her to say: *comfort.*

In this and other ways she leaves her seal, I say aloud. And startle at my saying it. What do I mean? What did I start to gather together, to try and make coherent? I was at the terrible, growing years. War years. I do not remember them well. I was working, there were four smaller ones now, there was not time for her. She had to help be a mother, and housekeeper, and shopper. She had to set her seal. Mornings of crisis and near hysteria trying to get lunches packed, hair combed, coats and shoes found, everyone to school or Child Care on time, the baby ready for transportation. And always the paper scribbled on by a smaller one, the book looked at by Susan then mislaid, the homework not done. Running out to that huge school where she was one, she was lost, she was a drop; suffering over the unpreparedness, stammering and unsure in her classes.

45 There was so little time left at night after the kids were bedded down. She would struggle over books, always eating (it was in those years she

developed her enormous appetite that is legendary in our family) and I would be ironing, or preparing food for the next day, or writing V-mail to Bill, or tending the baby. Sometimes, to make me laugh, or out of her despair, she would imitate happenings or types at school.

I think I said once: "Why don't you do something like this in the school amateur show?" One morning she phoned me at work, hardly understandable through the weeping: "Mother, I did it. I won, I won; they gave me first prize; they clapped and clapped and wouldn't let me go."

Now suddenly she was Somebody, and as imprisoned in her difference as she had been in anonymity.

She began to be asked to perform at other high schools, even in colleges, then at city and statewide affairs. The first one we went to, I only recognized her that first moment when thin, shy, she almost drowned herself into the curtains. Then: Was this Emily? The control, the command, the convulsing and deadly clowning, the spell, then the roaring, stamping audience, unwilling to let this rare and precious laughter out of their lives.

Afterwards: You ought to do something about her with a gift like that—but without money or knowing how, what does one do? We have left it all to her, and the gift has as often eddied inside, clogged and clotted, as been used and growing.

50   She is coming. She runs up the stairs two at a time with her light graceful step, and I know she is happy tonight. Whatever it was that occasioned your call did not happen today.

"Aren't you ever going to finish the ironing, Mother? Whistler painted his mother in a rocker. I'd have to paint mine standing over an ironing board." This is one of her communicative nights and she tells me everything and nothing as she fixes herself a plate of food out of the icebox.

She is so lovely. Why did you want me to come in at all? Why were you concerned? She will find her way.

She starts up the stairs to bed. "Don't get me up with the rest in the morning." "But I thought you were having midterms." "Oh, those," she comes back in, kisses me, and says quite lightly, "in a couple of years when we'll all be atom-dead they won't matter a bit."

She has said it before. She *believes* it. But because I have been dredging the past, and all that compounds a human being is so heavy and meaningful in me, I cannot endure it tonight.

55   I will never total it all. I will never come in to say: She was a child seldom smiled at. Her father left me before she was a year old. I had to work her first six years when there was work, or I sent her home and to his relatives. There were years she had care she hated. She was dark and thin and foreign-looking in a world where the prestige went to blondeness and curly hair and dimples, she was slow where glibness was prized. She was a child of anxious, not proud, love. We were poor and could not afford for her the soil of easy growth. I was a young mother, I was a distracted

mother. There were other children pushing up, demanding. Her younger sister seemed all that she was not. There were years she did not want me to touch her. She kept too much in herself, her life was such she had to keep too much in herself. My wisdom came too late. She has much to her and probably little will come of it. She is a child of her age, of depression, of war, of fear.

Let her be. So all that is in her will not bloom—but in how many does it? There is still enough left to live by. Only help her to know—help make it so there is cause for her to know—that she is more than this dress on the ironing board, helpless before the iron.

READING AND REACTING

1. "I Stand Here Ironing" focuses on incidents that took place in the "pre-relief, pre-WPA world of the depression." In light of social, political, and economic changes that have occurred since the 1930s, do you think the events the story presents could occur today? Explain.

2. In what sense is the image of a mother at an ironing board appropriate for this story?

3. The narrator is overwhelmed by guilt. What does she believe she has done wrong? What, if anything, do *you* think she has done wrong? Do you think she has been a good mother? Why or why not?

4. Who, or what, do you blame for the narrator's problems? For example, do you blame Emily's father? The Depression? The social institutions and "experts" to which the narrator turns?

5. Do you see the narrator as a victim limited by the times in which she lives? Do you agree with the narrator that Emily is "a child of her age, of depression, of war, of fear"? Or do you believe both women have some control over their own destinies, regardless of the story's historical setting?

6. What do you think the narrator wants for her daughter? Do you think her goals for Emily are realistic ones?

7. Paragraph 28 describes the physical setting of the convalescent home to which Emily was sent. What does this description add to the story? Why do you suppose there is no physical description of the apartment in which Emily lived as a child? How do you picture this apartment?

8. To whom do you think the mother is speaking in this story?

9. **JOURNAL ENTRY**   Put yourself in Emily's position. What do you think she would like to tell her mother?

10. **CRITICAL PERSPECTIVE**   Writing in *The Red Wheelbarrow*, psychologist Robert Coles discusses the complex family relationships depicted in "I Stand Here Ironing" and reaches an optimistic conclusion:

But the child did not grow to be a mere victim of the kind so many of us these days are rather eager to recognize—a hopeless tangle of psychopathology. The growing child, even in her troubled moments, revealed herself to be persistent, demanding, and observant. In the complaints we make, in the "symptoms" we develop, we reveal our strengths as well as our weaknesses. The hurt child could summon her intelligence, exercise her will, smile and make others smile.

Do you agree with Coles's psychological evaluation of Emily? Do you find the story's ending as essentially uplifting as he seems to? Why or why not?

 **CHARLOTTE PERKINS GILMAN** (1860–1935)   was a prominent feminist and social thinker at the turn of the century. Her essays, lectures, and nonfiction works—such as *Women and Economics* (1898), *Concerning Children* (1900), and *The Man-Made World* (1911)—are forceful statements of Gilman's opinions on women's need for economic independence and social equality. In the main, Gilman's fiction is a didactic expression of her social views. She is probably best known for three utopian feminist novels: *Moving the Mountain* (1911), *Herland* (1915; unpublished until 1978), and *With Her in Ourland* (1916). Gilman's fictional works are full of humor and satire: In *Herland,* for instance, a male sociologist (wandering in by accident from the outside world) is chagrined to find that the women of "Herland" want him for a friend, not a lover.

Although "The Yellow Wall-Paper" (1899) is not typical of Gilman's other fiction, it is considered her artistic masterpiece. The terse, clinical precision of the writing, conveying the tightly wound and distraught mental state of the narrator, is particularly chilling when it is read with a knowledge of Gilman's personal history. In the 1880s, she met and married a young artist, Charles Walter Stetson. Following the birth of their daughter, she grew increasingly depressed and turned to a noted Philadelphia neurologist for help. Following the traditions of the time, he prescribed complete bed rest and mental inactivity—a treatment that, Gilman said later, drove her "so near the borderline of utter mental ruin that I could see over." "The Yellow Wall-Paper" is not simply a psychological study. Like most of Gilman's work, it makes a point—this time about the dangers of women's utter dependence on a male interpretation of their needs.

CHARLOTTE PERKINS GILMAN

The Yellow Wall-Paper

(1899)

It is very seldom that mere ordinary people like John and myself secure ancestral halls for the summer.

A colonial mansion, a hereditary estate, I would say a haunted house, and reach the height of romantic felicity—but that would be asking too much of fate!

Still I will proudly declare that there is something queer about it.

Else, why should it be let so cheaply? And why have stood so long untenanted?

5   John laughs at me, of course, but one expects that in marriage.

John is practical in the extreme. He has no patience with faith, an intense horror of superstition, and he scoffs openly at any talk of things not to be felt and seen and put down in figures.

John is a physician, and *perhaps*—(I would not say it to a living soul, of course, but this is dead paper and a great relief to my mind—) *perhaps* that is one reason I do not get well faster.

You see he does not believe I am sick!

And what can one do?

10   If a physician of high standing, and one's own husband, assures friends and relatives that there is really nothing the matter with one but temporary nervous depression—a slight hysterical tendency—what is one to do?

My brother is also a physician, and also of high standing, and he says the same thing.

So I take phosphates or phosphites[1]—whichever it is, and tonics, and journeys, and air, and exercise, and am absolutely forbidden to "work" until I am well again.

Personally, I disagree with their ideas.

Personally, I believe that congenial work, with excitement and change, would do me good.

15   But what is one to do?

I did write for a while in spite of them; but it *does* exhaust me a good deal—having to be so sly about it, or else meet with heavy opposition.

I sometimes fancy that in my condition if I had less opposition and more society and stimulus—but John says the very worst thing I can do is to think about my condition, and I confess it always makes me feel bad.

---

[1] Both terms refer to salts of phosphorous acid. The narrator, however, means "phosphate," a carbonated beverage of water, flavoring, and a small amount of phosphoric acid.

So I will let it alone and talk about the house.

The most beautiful place! It is quite alone, standing well back from the road, quite three miles from the village. It makes me think of English places that you read about, for there are hedges and walls and gates that lock, and lots of separate little houses for the gardeners and people.

20 There is a *delicious* garden! I never saw such a garden—large and shady, full of box-bordered paths, and lined with long grape-covered arbors with seats under them.

There were greenhouses, too, but they are all broken now.

There was some legal trouble, I believe, something about the heirs and co-heirs; anyhow, the place has been empty for years.

That spoils my ghostliness, I am afraid, but I don't care—there is something strange about the house—I can feel it.

I even said so to John one moonlight evening, but he said what I felt was a *draught,* and shut the window.

25 I get unreasonably angry with John sometimes. I'm sure I never used to be so sensitive. I think it is due to this nervous condition.

But John says if I feel so, I shall neglect proper self-control; so I take pains to control myself—before him, at least, and that makes me very tired.

I don't like our room a bit. I wanted one downstairs that opened on the piazza and had roses all over the window, and such pretty old-fashioned chintz hangings! But John would not hear of it.

He said there was only one window and not room for two beds, and no near room for him if he took another.

He is very careful and loving, and hardly lets me stir without special direction.

30 I have a schedule prescription for each hour in the day; he takes all care from me, and so I feel basely ungrateful not to value it more.

He said we came here solely on my account, that I was to have perfect rest and all the air I could get. "Your exercise depends on your strength, my dear," said he, "and your food somewhat on your appetite; but air you can absorb all the time." So we took the nursery at the top of the house.

It is a big, airy room, the whole floor nearly, with windows that look all ways, and air and sunshine galore. It was nursery first and then play-room and gymnasium, I should judge; for the windows are barred for little children, and there are rings and things in the walls.

The paint and paper look as if a boys' school had used it. It is stripped off—the paper—in great patches all around the head of my bed, about as far as I can reach, and in a great place on the other side of the room low down. I never saw a worse paper in my life.

One of those sprawling flamboyant patterns committing every artistic sin.

35 It is dull enough to confuse the eye in following, pronounced enough to constantly irritate and provoke study, and when you follow the lame un-certain curves for a little distance they suddenly commit suicide—plunge off at outrageous angles, destroy themselves in unheard of contradictions.

The color is repellent, almost revolting; a smouldering unclean yellow, strangely faded by the slow-turning sunlight.

It is a dull yet lurid orange in some places, a sickly sulphur tint in others.

No wonder the children hated it! I should hate it myself if I had to live in this room long.

There comes John, and I must put this away,—he hates to have me write a word.

40 We have been here two weeks, and I haven't felt like writing before, since that first day.

I am sitting by the window now, up in this atrocious nursery, and there is nothing to hinder my writing as much as I please, save lack of strength.

John is away all day, and even some nights when his cases are serious.

I am glad my case is not serious!

But these nervous troubles are dreadfully depressing.

45 John does not know how much I really suffer. He knows there is no *reason* to suffer, and that satisfies him.

Of course it is only nervousness. It does weigh on me so not to do my duty in any way!

I meant to be such a help to John, such a real rest and comfort, and here I am a comparative burden already!

Nobody would believe what an effort it is to do what little I am able,— to dress and entertain, and order things.

It is fortunate Mary is so good with the baby. Such a dear baby!

50 And yet I *cannot* be with him, it makes me so nervous.

I suppose John never was nervous in his life. He laughs at me so about this wall-paper!

At first he meant to repaper the room, but afterwards he said that I was letting it get the better of me, and that nothing was worse for a nervous patient than to give way to such fancies.

He said that after the wall-paper was changed it would be the heavy bedstead, and then the barred windows, and then that gate at the head of the stairs, and so on.

"You know the place is doing you good," he said, "and really, dear, I don't care to renovate the house just for a three months' rental."

55 "Then do let us go downstairs," I said, "there are such pretty rooms there."

Then he took me in his arms and called me a blessed little goose, and said he would go down cellar, if I wished, and have it whitewashed into the bargain.

But he is right enough about the beds and windows and things.

It is an airy and comfortable room as any one need wish, and, of course, I would not be so silly as to make him uncomfortable just for a whim.

I'm really getting quite fond of the big room, all but that horrid paper.

Out of one window I can see the garden, those mysterious deep-shaded arbors, the riotous old-fashioned flowers, and bushes and gnarly trees.

Out of another I get a lovely view of the bay and a little private wharf belonging to the estate. There is a beautiful shaded lane that runs down there from the house. I always fancy I see people walking in these numerous paths and arbors, but John has cautioned me not to give way to fancy in the least. He says that with my imaginative power and habit of story-making, a nervous weakness like mine is sure to lead to all manner of excited fancies, and that I ought to use my will and good sense to check the tendency. So I try.

I think sometimes that if I were only well enough to write a little it would relieve the press of ideas and rest me.

But I find I get pretty tired when I try.

It is so discouraging not to have any advice and companionship about my work. When I get really well, John says we will ask Cousin Henry and Julia down for a long visit; but he says he would as soon put fireworks in my pillow-case as to let me have those stimulating people about now.

I wish I could get well faster.

But I must not think about that. This paper looks to me as if it *knew* what a vicious influence it had!

There is a recurrent spot where the pattern lolls like a broken neck and two bulbous eyes stare at you upside down.

I get positively angry with the impertinence of it and the everlastingness. Up and down and sideways they crawl, and those absurd, unblinking eyes are everywhere. There is one place where two breadths didn't match, and the eyes go all up and down the line, one a little higher than the other.

I never saw so much expression in an inanimate thing before, and we all know how much expression they have! I used to lie awake as a child and get more entertainment and terror out of blank walls and plain furniture than most children could find in a toy-store.

I remember what a kindly wink the knobs of our big, old bureau used to have, and there was one chair that always seemed like a strong friend.

I used to feel that if any of the other things looked too fierce I could always hop into that chair and be safe.

The furniture in this room is no worse than inharmonious, however, for we had to bring it all from downstairs. I suppose when this was used as a playroom they had to take the nursery things out, and no wonder! I never saw such ravages as the children have made here.

The wall-paper, as I said before, is torn off in spots, and it sticketh closer than a brother—they must have had perseverance as well as hatred.

Then the floor is scratched and gouged and splintered, the plaster itself is dug out here and there, and this great heavy bed which is all we found in the room, looks as if it had been through the wars.

But I don't mind it a bit—only the paper.

There comes John's sister. Such a dear girl as she is, and so careful of me! I must not let her find me writing.

She is a perfect and enthusiastic housekeeper, and hopes for no better profession. I verily believe she thinks it is the writing which made me sick!

But I can write when she is out, and see her a long way off from these windows.

There is one that commands the road, a lovely shaded winding road, and one that just looks off over the country. A lovely country, too, full of great elms and velvet meadows.

80 This wall-paper has a kind of sub-pattern in a different shade, a particularly irritating one, for you can only see it in certain lights, and not clearly then.

But in the places where it isn't faded and where the sun is just so—I can see a strange, provoking, formless sort of figure, that seems to skulk about behind that silly and conspicuous front design.

There's sister on the stairs!

Well, the Fourth of July is over! The people are all gone and I am tired out. John thought it might do me good to see a little company, so we just had mother and Nellie and the children down for a week.

Of course I didn't do a thing. Jennie sees to everything now.

85 But it tired me all the same.

John says if I don't pick up faster he shall send me to Weir Mitchell[2] in the fall.

But I don't want to go there at all. I had a friend who was in his hands once, and she says he is just like John and my brother, only more so!

Besides, it is such an undertaking to go so far.

I don't feel as if it was worth while to turn my hand over for anything, and I'm getting dreadfully fretful and querulous.

90 I cry at nothing, and cry most of the time.

Of course I don't when John is here, or anybody else, but when I am alone.

And I am alone a good deal just now. John is kept in town very often by serious cases, and Jennie is good and lets me alone when I want her to.

So I walk a little in the garden or down that lovely lane, sit on the porch under the roses, and lie down up here a good deal.

I'm getting really fond of the room in spite of the wall-paper. Perhaps *because* of the wall-paper.

95 It dwells in my mind so!

I lie here on this great immovable bed—it is nailed down, I believe—and follow that pattern about by the hour. It is as good as gymnastics, I assure you. I start, we'll say, at the bottom, down in the corner over there

---

2 Silas Weir Mitchell (1829–1914)—a Philadelphia neurologist-psychologist who introduced the "rest cure" for nervous diseases.

where it has not been touched, and I determine for the thousandth time that I *will* follow that pointless pattern to some sort of a conclusion.

I know a little of the principle of design, and I know this thing was not arranged on any laws of radiation, or alternation, or repetition, or symmetry, or anything else that I ever heard of.

It is repeated, of course, by the breadths, but not otherwise.

Looked at in one way each breadth stands alone, the bloated curves and flourishes—a kind of "debased Romanesque" with *delirium tremens*[3] go waddling up and down in isolated columns of fatuity.

100   But, on the other hand, they connect diagonally, and the sprawling outlines run off in great slanting waves of optic horror, like a lot of wallowing seaweeds in full chase.

The whole thing goes horizontally, too, at least it seems so, and I exhaust myself in trying to distinguish the order of its going in that direction.

They have used a horizontal breadth for a frieze, and that adds wonderfully to the confusion.

There is one end of the room where it is almost intact, and there, when the crosslights fade and the low sun shines directly upon it, I can almost fancy radiation after all,—the interminable grotesques seems to form around a common center and rush off in headlong plunges of equal distraction.

It makes me tired to follow it. I will take a nap I guess.

105   I don't know why I should write this.

I don't want to.

I don't feel able.

And I know John would think it absurd. But I *must* say what I feel and think in some way—it is such a relief!

But the effort is getting to be greater than the relief.

110   Half the time now I am awfully lazy, and lie down ever so much.

John says I mustn't lose my strength, and has me take cod liver oil and lots of tonics and things, to say nothing of ale and wine and rare meat.

Dear John! He loves me very dearly, and hates to have me sick. I tried to have a real earnest reasonable talk with him the other day, and tell him how I wish he would let me go and make a visit to Cousin Henry and Julia.

But he said I wasn't able to go, nor able to stand it after I got there; and I did not make out a very good case for myself, for I was crying before I had finished.

It is getting to be a great effort for me to think straight. Just this nervous weakness I suppose.

115   And dear John gathered me up in his arms, and just carried me upstairs and laid me on the bed, and sat by me and read to me till it tired my head.

---

[3] Mental confusion caused by alcohol poisoning and characterized by physical tremors and hallucinations.

He said I was his darling and his comfort and all he had, and that I must take care of myself for his sake, and keep well.

He says no one but myself can help me out of it, that I must use my will and self-control and not let any silly fancies run away with me.

There's one comfort, the baby is well and happy, and does not have to occupy this nursery with the horrid wall-paper.

If we had not used it, that blessed child would have! What a fortunate escape! Why, I wouldn't have a child of mine, an impressionable little thing, live in such a room for worlds.

120   I never thought of it before, but it is lucky that John kept me here after all, I can stand it so much easier than a baby, you see.

Of course I never mention it to them any more—I am too wise,—but I keep watch of it all the same.

There are things in that paper that nobody knows but me, or ever will.

Behind that outside pattern the dim shapes get clearer every day.

It is always the same shape, only very numerous.

125   And it is like a woman stooping down and creeping about behind that pattern. I don't like it a bit. I wonder—I begin to think—I wish John would take me away from here!

It is so hard to talk with John about my case, because he is so wise, and because he loves me so.

But I tried it last night.

It was moonlight. The moon shines in all around just as the sun does.

I hate to see it sometimes, it creeps so slowly, and always comes in by one window or another.

130   John was asleep and I hated to waken him, so I kept still and watched the moonlight on that undulating wall-paper till I felt creepy.

The faint figure behind seemed to shake the pattern, just as if she wanted to get out.

I got up softly and went to feel and see if the paper *did* move, and when I came back John was awake.

"What is it, little girl?" he said. "Don't go walking about like that— you'll get cold."

I thought it was a good time to talk, so I told him that I really was not gaining here, and that I wished he would take me away.

135   "Why, darling!" said he, "our lease will be up in three weeks, and I can't see how to leave before.

"The repairs are not done at home, and I cannot possibly leave town just now. Of course if you were in any danger, I could and would, but you really are better, dear, whether you can see it or not. I am a doctor, dear, and I know. You are gaining flesh and color, your appetite is better, I feel really much easier about you."

"I don't weigh a bit more," said I, "nor as much; and my appetite may be better in the evening when you are here, but it is worse in the morning when you are away!"

"Bless her little heart!" said he with a big hug, "she shall be as sick as she pleases! But now let's improve the shining hours by going to sleep, and talk about it in the morning!"

"And you won't go away?" I asked gloomily.

140   "Why, how can I, dear? It is only three weeks more and then we will take a nice little trip of a few days while Jennie is getting the house ready. Really dear you are better!"

"Better in body perhaps—" I began, and stopped short, for he sat up straight and looked at me with such a stern, reproachful look that I could not say another word.

"My darling," said he, "I beg of you, for my sake and for our child's sake, as well as for your own, that you will never for one instant let that idea enter your mind! There is nothing so dangerous, so fascinating, to a temperament like yours. It is a false and foolish fancy. Can you not trust me as a physician when I tell you so?"

So of course I said no more on that score, and we went to sleep before long. He thought I was asleep first, but I wasn't, and lay there for hours trying to decide whether that front pattern and the back pattern really did move together or separately.

On a pattern like this, by daylight, there is a lack of sequence, a defiance of law, that is a constant irritant to a normal mind.

145   The color is hideous enough, and unreliable enough, and infuriating enough, but the pattern is torturing.

You think you have mastered it, but just as you get well underway in following, it turns back-somersault and there you are. It slaps you in the face, knocks you down, and tramples upon you. It is like a bad dream.

The outside pattern is a florid arabesque, reminding one of a fungus. If you can imagine a toadstool in joints, an interminable string of toadstools, budding and sprouting in endless convolutions—why, that is something like it.

That is, sometimes!

There is one marked peculiarity about this paper, a thing nobody seems to notice but myself, and that is that it changes as the light changes.

150   When the sun shoots in through the east window—I always watch for that first long, straight ray—it changes so quickly that I never can quite believe it.

That is why I watch it always.

By moonlight—the moon shines in all night when there is a moon—I wouldn't know it was the same paper.

At night in any kind of light, in twilight, candlelight, lamplight, and worst of all by moonlight, it becomes bars! The outside pattern I mean, and the woman behind it is as plain as can be.

I didn't realize for a long time what the thing was that showed behind, that dim sub-pattern, but now I am quite sure it is a woman.

155   By daylight she is subdued, quiet. I fancy it is the pattern that keeps her so still. It is so puzzling. It keeps me quiet by the hour.

I lie down ever so much now. John says it is good for me, and to sleep all I can.

Indeed he started the habit by making me lie down for an hour after each meal.

It is a very bad habit I am convinced, for you see I don't sleep.

And that cultivates deceit, for I don't tell them I'm awake—O no!

160 The fact is I am getting a little afraid of John.

He seems very queer sometimes, and even Jennie has an inexplicable look.

It strikes me occasionally, just as a scientific hypothesis,—that perhaps it is the paper!

I have watched John when he did not know I was looking, and come into the room suddenly on the most innocent excuses, and I've caught him several times *looking at the paper!* And Jennie too. I caught Jennie with her hand on it once.

She didn't know I was in the room, and when I asked her in a quiet, a very quiet voice, with the most restrained manner possible, what she was doing with the paper—she turned around as if she had been caught stealing, and looked quite angry—asked me why I should frighten her so!

165 Then she said that the paper stained everything it touched, that she had found yellow smooches on all my clothes and John's, and she wished we would be more careful!

Did not that sound innocent? But I know she was studying that pattern, and I am determined that nobody shall find it out but myself!

Life is very much more exciting now than it used to be. You see I have something more to expect, to look forward to, to watch. I really do eat better, and am more quiet than I was.

John is so pleased to see me improve! He laughed a little the other day, and said I seemed to be flourishing in spite of my wall-paper.

I turned it off with a laugh. I had no intention of telling him it was *because* of the wall-paper—he would make fun of me. He might even want to take me away.

170 I don't want to leave now until I have found it out. There is a week more, and I think that will be enough.

I'm feeling ever so much better! I don't sleep much at night, for it is so interesting to watch developments; but I sleep a good deal in the daytime.

In the daytime it is tiresome and perplexing.

There are always new shoots on the fungus, and new shades of yellow all over it. I cannot keep count of them, though I have tried conscientiously.

It is the strangest yellow, that wall-paper! It makes me think of all the yellow things I ever saw—not beautiful ones like buttercups, but old foul, bad yellow things.

175 But there is something else about that paper—the smell! I noticed it the moment we came into the room, but with so much air and sun it was

not bad. Now we have had a week of fog and rain, and whether the windows are open or not, the smell is here.

It creeps all over the house.

I find it hovering in the dining-room, skulking in the parlor, hiding in the hall, lying in wait for me on the stairs.

It gets into my hair.

Even when I go to ride, if I turn my head suddenly and surprise it—there is that smell!

180   Such a peculiar odor, too! I have spent hours in trying to analyze it, to find what it smelled like.

It is not bad—at first, and very gentle, but quite the subtlest, most enduring odor I ever met.

In this damp weather it is awful, I wake up in the night and find it hanging over me.

It used to disturb me at first. I thought seriously of burning the house—to reach the smell.

But now I am used to it. The only thing I can think of that it is like is the *color* of the paper! A yellow smell.

185   There is a very funny mark on this wall, low down, near the mopboard. A streak that runs round the room. It goes behind every piece of furniture, except the bed, a long, straight, even *smooch,* as if it had been rubbed over and over.

I wonder how it was done and who did it, and what they did it for. Round and round and round—round and round and round!—it makes me dizzy!

I really have discovered something at last.

Through watching so much at night, when it changes so, I have finally found out.

The front pattern *does* move—and no wonder! The woman behind shakes it!

190   Sometimes I think there are a great many women behind, and sometimes only one, and she crawls around fast, and her crawling shakes it all over.

Then in the very bright spots she keeps still, and in the very shady spots she just takes hold of the bars and shakes them hard.

And she is all the time trying to climb through. But nobody could climb through that pattern—it strangles so; I think that is why it has so many heads.

They get through, and then the pattern strangles them off and turns them upside down, and makes their eyes white!

If those heads were covered or taken off it would not be half so bad.

195   I think that woman gets out in the daytime!

And I'll tell you why—privately—I've seen her!

I can see her out of every one of my windows!

It is the same woman, I know, for she is always creeping, and most women do not creep by daylight.

I see her in that long shaded lane, creeping up and down. I see her in those dark grape arbors, creeping all around the garden.

200 I see her on that long road under the trees, creeping along, and when a carriage comes she hides under the blackberry vines.

I don't blame her a bit. It must be very humiliating to be caught creeping by daylight!

I always lock the door when I creep by daylight. I can't do it at night, for I know John would suspect something at once.

And John is so queer now, that I don't want to irritate him. I wish he would take another room! Besides, I don't want anybody to get that woman out at night but myself.

I often wonder if I could see her out of all the windows at once.

205 But, turn as fast as I can, I can only see out of one at one time.

And though I always see her, she *may* be able to creep faster than I can turn!

I have watched her sometimes away off in the open country, creeping as fast as a cloud shadow in a high wind.

If only that top pattern could be gotten off from the under one! I mean to try it, little by little.

I have found out another funny thing, but I shan't tell it this time! It does not do to trust people too much.

210 There are only two more days to get this paper off, and I believe John is beginning to notice. I don't like the look in his eyes.

And I heard him ask Jennie a lot of professional questions about me. She had a very good report to give.

She said I slept a good deal in the daytime.

John knows I don't sleep very well at night, for all I'm so quiet!

He asked me all sorts of questions, too, and pretended to be very loving and kind.

215 As if I couldn't see through him!

Still, I don't wonder he acts so, sleeping under this paper for three months.

It only interests me, but I feel sure John and Jennie are secretly affected by it.

Hurrah! This is the last day, but it is enough. John to stay in town over night, and won't be out until this evening.

Jennie wanted to sleep with me—the sly thing! But I told her I should undoubtedly rest better for a night all alone.

220 That was clever, for really I wasn't alone a bit! As soon as it was moonlight and that poor thing began to crawl and shake the pattern, I got up and ran to help her.

I pulled and she shook, I shook and she pulled, and before morning we had peeled off yards of that paper.

A strip about as high as my head and half around the room.

And then when the sun came and that awful pattern began to laugh at me, I declared I would finish it to-day!

We go away to-morrow, and they are moving all my furniture down again to leave things as they were before.

225   Jennie looked at the wall in amazement, but I told her merrily that I did it out of pure spite at the vicious thing.

She laughed and said she wouldn't mind doing it herself, but I must not get tired.

How she betrayed herself that time!

But I am here, and no person touches this paper but me,—not *alive!*

She tried to get me out of the room—it was too patent! But I said it was so quiet and empty and clean now that I believed I would lie down again and sleep all I could; and not to wake me even for dinner—I would call when I woke.

230   So now she is gone, and the servants are gone, and the things are gone, and there is nothing left but that great bedstead nailed down, with the canvas mattress we found on it.

We shall sleep downstairs to-night, and take the boat home tomorrow.

I quite enjoy the room, now it is bare again.

How those children did tear about here!

This bedstead is fairly gnawed!

235   But I must get to work.

I have locked the door and thrown the key down into the front path.

I don't want to go out, and I don't want to have anybody come in, till John comes.

I want to astonish him.

I've got a rope up here that even Jennie did not find. If that woman does get out, and tries to get away, I can tie her!

240   But I forgot I could not reach far without anything to stand on!

This bed will *not* move!

I tried to lift and push it until I was lame, and then I got so angry I bit off a little piece at one corner—but it hurt my teeth.

Then I peeled off all the paper I could reach standing on the floor. It sticks horribly and the pattern just enjoys it! All those strangled heads and bulbous eyes and waddling fungus growths just shriek with derision!

I am getting angry enough to do something desperate. To jump out of the window would be admirable exercise, but the bars are too strong even to try.

245   Besides I wouldn't do it. Of course not. I know well enough that a step like that is improper and might be misconstrued.

I don't like to *look* out of the windows even—there are so many of those creeping women, and they creep so fast.

I wonder if they all come out of that wall-paper as I did?

But I am securely fastened now by my well-hidden rope—you don't get *me* out in the road there!

I suppose I shall have to get back behind the pattern when it comes night, and that is hard!

250   It is so pleasant to be out in this great room and creep around as I please!

I don't want to go outside. I won't, even if Jennie asks me to.

For outside you have to creep on the ground, and everything is green instead of yellow.

But here I can creep smoothly on the floor, and my shoulder just fits in that long smooch around the wall, so I cannot lose my way.

Why there's John at the door!

255   It is no use, young man, you can't open it!

How he does call and pound!

Now he's crying for an axe.

It would be a shame to break down that beautiful door!

"John dear!" said I in the gentlest voice, "the key is down by the front steps, under a plantain leaf!"

260   That silenced him for a few moments.

Then he said—very quietly indeed. "Open the door, my darling!"

"I can't," said I. "The key is down by the front door under a plantain leaf!"

And then I said it again, several times, very gently and slowly, and said it so often that he had to go and see, and he got it of course, and came in. He stopped short by the door.

"What is the matter?" he cried. "For God's sake, what are you doing!"

265   I kept on creeping just the same, but I looked at him over my shoulder.

"I've got out at last," said I, "in spite of you and Jane. And I've pulled off most of the paper, so you can't put me back!"

Now why should that man have fainted? But he did, and right across my path by the wall, so that I had to creep over him every time!

READING AND REACTING

1. The story's narrator, who has recently given birth, is suffering from what her husband, a doctor, calls "temporary nervous depression—a slight hysterical tendency" (10). What is the relationship between this depression and the story's setting?

2. Describe the house and grounds. How do they affect the narrator's mood?

3. What aspects of the room in which the narrator lives upset her? Why?

4. Describe the wallpaper. What does the narrator actually see in it, and what does she imagine? How can you tell the difference?

5. What do the following comments reveal about the narrator's situation: "John laughs at me, of course, but one expects that in marriage" (5); "I must put this away,—he hates to have me write a word" (39); "He laughs at me so about this wall-paper" (51); "Then he took me in his arms and called me a blessed little goose" (56)?

6. What has probably caused the narrator's depression? What factors aggravate it? How much insight does the narrator seem to have into her situation?

7. How does the narrator's mood change as the story progresses? How do her descriptions of her setting change?

8. Aside from the physical setting—the room, the house, and the garden—what other aspects of the story's setting play an important role?

9. **Journal Entry**   Do you think a present-day physician or psychiatrist would give the narrator different advice? Do you think a present-day woman would respond differently to advice from her husband or doctor? Explain.

10. **CRITICAL PERSPECTIVE**   "The Yellow Wall-Paper" was originally seen as a horror story, and even anthologized as such. More recently, critics have tended to interpret the story from a feminist perspective, focusing on the way in which the nameless narrator is victimized by the men around her and by the values of the Victorian society which they uphold. In the essay "An Unnecessary Maze of Sign-Reading," Mary Jacobus concludes that the overwhelmingly feminist perspective of recent criticism, while certainly valuable and enlightening, has overlooked other promising critical possibilities. For example, she says:

    The "feminist" reading contradicts the tendency to see women as basically unstable or hysterical, simultaneously (and contradictorily) claiming that women are not mad and that their madness is not their fault. But a thematic reading cannot account for the Gothic and uncanny elements present in the text.

    If you were teaching "The Yellow Wall-Paper," would you present it as a feminist story or as a chilling Gothic ghost story? Do you think interpreting the story as a Gothic horror tale precludes a feminist reading, or do you see the two interpretations as compatible?

SHERMAN ALEXIE (1966–   ),   a highly praised young Native American writer, was born in Spokane, Washington, of Spokane and Coeur d'Alene heritage. He attended Pullman State University with plans to become a doctor but changed his mind after attending a poetry workshop; by the time he left school, he had already written over two hundred poems. Since then his work has appeared in various magazines and journals, and he has published three poetry collections—*The Business of Fancydancing* (1992), *I Would Steal Anything* (1992), and *Old Shirts and New Skins* (1993)—as well as a collection of short stories, *The Lone Ranger and Tonto Fistfight in Heaven* (1993), and a well-received novel, *Reservation Blues* (1995).

Of Native American culture Alexie has said, "One of the biggest misconceptions about Indians is that we're stoic, but humor is an essential part of our culture." "This Is What It Means to Say Phoenix, Arizona" demonstrates this unique use of humor to transcend the harsh realities of life on the reservation and the struggle to adapt to contemporary American life.

SHERMAN ALEXIE

This Is What It Means to Say Phoenix, Arizona

(1993)

Just after Victor lost his job at the Bureau of Indian Affairs,[1] he also found out that his father had died of a heart attack in Phoenix, Arizona. Victor hadn't seen his father in a few years, had only talked to him on the telephone once or twice, but there still was a genetic pain, which was as real and immediate as a broken bone. Victor didn't have any money. Who does have money on a reservation, except the cigarette and fireworks salespeople? His father had a savings account waiting to be claimed, but Victor needed to find a way to get from Spokane to Phoenix. Victor's mother was just as poor as he was, and the rest of his family didn't have any use at all for him. So Victor called the tribal council.

"Listen," Victor said. "My father just died. I need some money to get to Phoenix to make arrangements."

"Now Victor," the council said, "you know we're having a difficult time financially."

---

[1] Division of the U.S. Department of the Interior that manages Native American matters; operated by government officials, not tribal leaders.

"But I thought the council had special funds set aside for stuff like this."

"Now, Victor, we do have some money available for the proper return of tribal members' bodies. But I don't think we have enough to bring your father all the way back from Phoenix."

"Well," Victor said. "It ain't going to cost all that much. He had to be cremated. Things were kind of ugly. He died of a heart attack in his trailer and nobody found him for a week. It was really hot, too. You get the picture."

"Now, Victor, we're sorry for your loss and the circumstances. But we can really only afford to give you one hundred dollars."

"That's not even enough for a plane ticket."

"Well, you might consider driving down to Phoenix."

"I don't have a car. Besides, I was going to drive my father's pickup back up here."

"Now, Victor," the council said, "we're sure there is somebody who could drive you to Phoenix. Or could anybody lend you the rest of the money?"

"You know there ain't nobody around with that kind of money."

"Well, we're sorry, Victor, but that's the best we can do."

Victor accepted the tribal council's offer. What else could he do? So he signed the proper papers, picked up his check, and walked over to the Trading Post to cash it.

While Victor stood in line, he watched Thomas Builds-the-Fire standing near the magazine rack talking to himself. Like he always did. Thomas was a storyteller whom nobody wanted to listen to. That's like being a dentist in a town where everybody has false teeth.

Victor and Thomas Builds-the-Fire were the same age, had grown up and played in the dirt together. Ever since Victor could remember, it was Thomas who had always had something to say.

Once, when they were seven years old, when Victor's father still lived with the family, Thomas closed his eyes and told Victor this story: "Your father's heart is weak. He is afraid of his own family. He is afraid of you. Late at night, he sits in the dark. Watches the television until there's nothing but that white noise. Sometimes he feels like he wants to buy a motorcycle and ride away. He wants to run and hide. He doesn't want to be found."

Thomas Builds-the-Fire had known that Victor's father was going to leave, known it before anyone. Now Victor stood in the Trading Post with a one-hundred-dollar check in his hand, wondering if Thomas knew that Victor's father was dead, if he knew what was going to happen next.

Just then, Thomas looked at Victor, smiled, and walked over to him.

"Victor, I'm sorry about your father," Thomas said.

"How did you know about it?" Victor asked.

"I heard it on the wind. I heard it from the birds. I felt it in the sunlight. Also, your mother was just in here crying."

"Oh," Victor said and looked around the Trading Post. All the other Indians stared, surprised that Victor was even talking to Thomas. Nobody talked to Thomas anymore because he told the same damn stories over and over again. Victor was embarrassed, but he thought that Thomas might be able to help him. Victor felt a sudden need for tradition.

"I can lend you the money you need," Thomas said suddenly. "But you have to take me with you."

25   "I can't take your money," Victor said. "I mean, I haven't hardly talked to you in years. We're not really friends anymore."

"I didn't say we were friends. I said you had to take me with you."

"Let me think about it."

Victor went home with his one hundred dollars and sat at the kitchen table. He held his head in his hands and thought about Thomas Builds-the-Fire, remembered little details, tears and scars, the bicycle they shared for a summer, so many stories.

Thomas Builds-the-Fire sat on the bicycle, waiting in Victor's yard. He was ten years old and skinny. His hair was dirty because it was the Fourth of July.

30   "Victor," Thomas yelled. "Hurry up. We're going to miss the fireworks."

After a few minutes, Victor ran out of his family's house, vaulted over the porch railing, and landed gracefully on the sidewalk.

Thomas gave him the bike and they headed for the fireworks. It was nearly dark and the fireworks were about to start.

"You know," Thomas said, "it's strange how us Indians celebrate the Fourth of July. It ain't like it was our independence everybody was fighting for."

"You think about things too much," Victor said. "It's just supposed to be fun. Maybe Junior will be there."

35   "Which Junior? Everybody on this reservation is named Junior."

The fireworks were small, hardly more than a few bottle rockets and a fountain. But it was enough for two Indian boys. Years later, they would need much more.

Afterward, sitting in the dark, fighting off mosquitoes, Victor turned to Thomas Builds-the-Fire.

"Hey," Victor said. "Tell me a story."

Thomas closed his eyes and told this story: "There were these two Indian boys who wanted to be warriors. But it was too late to be warriors in the old way. All the horses were gone. So the two Indian boys stole a car and drove to the city. They parked the stolen car in the front of the police station and then hitchhiked back home to the reservation. When they got back, all their friends cheered and their parents' eyes shone with pride. 'You were very brave,' everybody said to the two Indian boys. 'Very brave.'"

40   "Ya-hey," Victor said. "That's a good one. I wish I could be a warrior."

"Me too," Thomas said.

Victor sat at his kitchen table. He counted his one hundred dollars again and again. He knew he needed more to make it to Phoenix and back. He knew he needed Thomas Builds-the-Fire. So he put his money in his wallet and opened the front door to find Thomas on the porch.

"Ya-hey, Victor," Thomas said. "I knew you'd call me."

Thomas walked into the living room and sat down in Victor's favorite chair.

45   "I've got some money saved up," Thomas said. "It's enough to get us down there, but you have to get us back."

"I've got this hundred dollars," Victor said. "And my dad had a savings account I'm going to claim."

"How much in your dad's account?"

"Enough. A few hundred."

"Sounds good. When we leaving?"

50 When they were fifteen and had long since stopped being friends, Victor and Thomas got into a fistfight. That is, Victor was really drunk and beat Thomas up for no reason at all. All the other Indian boys stood around and watched it happen. Junior was there and so were Lester, Seymour, and a lot of others.

The beating might have gone on until Thomas was dead if Norma Many Horses hadn't come along and stopped it.

"Hey, you boys," Norma yelled and jumped out of her car. "Leave him alone."

If it had been someone else, even another man, the Indian boys would've just ignored the warnings. But Norma was a warrior. She was powerful. She could have picked up any two of the boys and smashed their skulls together. But worse than that, she would have dragged them all over to some tepee and made them listen to some elder tell a dusty old story.

The Indian boys scattered, and Norma walked over to Thomas and picked him up.

55   "Hey, little man, are you O.K.?" she asked.

Thomas gave her a thumbs-up.

"Why they always picking on you?"

Thomas shook his head, closed his eyes, but no stories came to him, no words or music. He just wanted to go home, to lie in his bed and let his dreams tell the stories for him.

Thomas Builds-the-Fire and Victor sat next to each other in the airplane, coach section. A tiny white woman had the window seat. She was busy twisting her body into pretzels. She was flexible.

60   "I have to ask," Thomas said, and Victor closed his eyes in embarrassment.

"Don't," Victor said.

"Excuse me, miss," Thomas asked. "Are you a gymnast or something?"

"There's no something about it," she said. "I was first alternate on the 1980 Olympic team."

"Really?" Thomas asked.

65   "Really."

"I mean, you used to be a world-class athlete?" Thomas asked.

"My husband thinks I still am."

Thomas Builds-the-Fire smiled. She was a mental gymnast too. She pulled her leg straight up against her body so that she could've kissed her kneecap.

"I wish I could do that," Thomas said.

70   Victor was ready to jump out of the plane. Thomas, that crazy Indian storyteller with ratty old braids and broken teeth, was flirting with a beautiful Olympic gymnast. Nobody back home on the reservation would ever believe it.

"Well," the gymnast said. "It's easy. Try it."

Thomas grabbed at his leg and tried to pull it up into the same position as the gymnast's. He couldn't even come close, which made Victor and the gymnast laugh.

"Hey," she asked. "You two are Indian, right?"

"Full-blood," Victor said.

75   "Not me," Thomas said. "I'm half magician on my mother's side and half clown on my father's."

They all laughed.

"What are your names?" she asked.

"Victor and Thomas."

"Mine is Cathy. Pleased to meet you all."

80   The three of them talked for the duration of the flight. Cathy the gymnast complained about the government, how they screwed the 1980 Olympic team by boycotting the games.

"Sounds like you all got a lot in common with Indians," Thomas said.

Nobody laughed.

After the plane landed in Phoenix and they had all found their way to the terminal, Cathy the gymnast smiled and waved goodbye.

"She was really nice," Thomas said.

85   "Yeah, but everybody talks to everybody on airplanes," Victor said.

"You always used to tell me I think too much," Thomas said. "Now it sounds like you do."

"Maybe I caught it from you."

"Yeah."

Thomas and Victor rode in a taxi to the trailer where Victor's father had died.

90   "Listen," Victor said as they stopped in front of the trailer. "I never told you I was sorry for beating you up that time."

"Oh, it was nothing. We were just kids and you were drunk."

"Yeah, but I'm still sorry."

"That's all right."

Victor paid for the taxi, and the two of them stood in the hot Phoenix summer. They could smell the trailer.

95   "This ain't going to be nice," Victor said. "You don't have to go in."

"You're going to need help."

Victor walked to the front door and opened it. The stink rolled out and made them both gag. Victor's father had lain in that trailer for a week in hundred-degree temperatures before anyone had found him. And the only reason anyone found him was the smell. They needed dental records to identify him. That's exactly what the coroner said. They needed dental records.

"Oh, man," Victor said. "I don't know if I can do this."

"Well, then don't."

100   "But there might be something valuable in there."

"I thought his money was in the bank."

"It is: I was talking about pictures and letters and stuff like that."

"Oh," Thomas said as he held his breath and followed Victor into the trailer.

When Victor was twelve, he stepped into an underground wasps' nest. His foot was caught in the hole and no matter how hard he struggled, Victor couldn't pull free. He might have died there, stung a thousand times, if Thomas Builds-the-Fire had not come by.

105   "Run," Thomas yelled and pulled Victor's foot from the hole. They ran then, hard as they ever had, faster than Billy Mills, faster than Jim Thorpe, faster than the wasps could fly.

Victor and Thomas ran until they couldn't breathe, ran until it was cold and dark outside, ran until they were lost and it took hours to find their way home. All the way back, Victor counted his stings.

"Seven," Victor said. "My lucky number."

Victor didn't find much to keep in the trailer. Only a photo album and a stereo. Everything else had that smell stuck in it or was useless anyway. "I guess this is all," Victor said. "It ain't much."

"Better than nothing," Thomas said.

110   "Yeah, and I do have the pickup."

"Yeah," Thomas said. "It's in good shape."

"Dad was good about that stuff."

"Yeah, I remember your dad."

"Really?" Victor asked. "What do you remember?"

115   Thomas Builds-the-Fire closed his eyes and told this story: "I remember when I had this dream that told me to go to Spokane, to stand by the falls in the middle of the city and wait for a sign. I knew I had to go there but I didn't have a car. Didn't have a license. I was only thirteen. So I walked all the way, took me all day, and I finally made it to the falls. I stood there for an hour waiting. Then your dad came walking up. 'What the hell are you doing here?' he asked me. I said, 'Waiting for a vision.'

Then your father said, 'All you're going to get here is mugged.' So he drove me over to Denny's, bought me dinner, and then drove me home to the reservation. For a long time, I was mad because I thought my dreams had lied to me. But they hadn't. Your dad was my vision. *Take care of each other* is what my dreams were saying. *Take care of each other.*"

Victor was quiet for a long time. He searched his mind for memories of his father, found the good ones, found a few bad ones, added it all up, and smiled.

"My father never told me about finding you in Spokane," Victor said.

"He said he wouldn't tell anybody. Didn't want me to get in trouble. But he said I had to watch out for you as part of the deal."

"Really?"

120   "Really. Your father said you would need the help. He was right."

"That's why you came down here with me, isn't it?" Victor asked.

"I came because of your father."

Victor and Thomas climbed into the pickup, drove over to the bank, and claimed the three hundred dollars in the savings account.

Thomas Builds-the-Fire could fly.

125   Once, he jumped off the roof of the tribal school and flapped his arms like a crazy eagle. And he flew. For a second he hovered, suspended above all the other Indian boys, who were too smart or too scared to jump too.

"He's flying," Junior yelled, and Seymour was busy looking for the trick wires or mirrors. But it was real. As real as the dirt when Thomas lost altitude and crashed to the ground.

He broke his arm in two places.

"He broke his wing, he broke his wing, he broke his wing," all the Indian boys chanted as they ran off, flapping their wings, wishing they could fly too. They hated Thomas for his courage, his brief moment as a bird. Everybody has dreams about flying. Thomas flew.

One of his dreams came true for just a second, just enough to make it real.

130 Victor's father, his ashes, fit in one wooden box with enough left over to fill a cardboard box.

"He always was a big man," Thomas said.

Victor carried part of his father out to the pickup, and Thomas carried the rest. They set him down carefully behind the seats, put a cowboy hat on the wooden box and a Dodgers cap on the cardboard box. That was the way it was supposed to be.

"Ready to head back home?" Victor asked.

"It's going to be a long drive."

135   "Yeah, take a couple days, maybe."

"We can take turns," Thomas said.

"O.K.," Victor said, but they didn't take turns. Victor drove for sixteen hours straight north, made it halfway up Nevada toward home before he finally pulled over.

"Hey, Thomas," Victor said. "You got to drive for a while."

"O.K."

140 Thomas Builds-the-Fire slid behind the wheel and started off down the road. All through Nevada, Thomas and Victor had been amazed at the lack of animal life, at the absence of water, of movement.

"Where is everything?" Victor had asked more than once.

Now, when Thomas was finally driving, they saw the first animal, maybe the only animal in Nevada. It was a long-eared jackrabbit.

"Look," Victor yelled. "It's alive."

Thomas and Victor were busy congratulating themselves on their discovery when the jackrabbit darted out into the road and under the wheels of the pickup.

145 "Stop the goddamn car," Victor yelled, and Thomas did stop and backed the pickup to the dead jackrabbit.

"Oh, man, he's dead," Victor said as he looked at the squashed animal. "Really dead."

"The only thing alive in this whole state and we just killed it."

"I don't know," Thomas said. "I think it was suicide."

150 Victor looked around the desert, sniffed the air, felt the emptiness and loneliness, and nodded his head.

"Yeah," Victor said. "It had to be suicide."

"I can't believe this," Thomas said. "You drive for a thousand miles and there ain't even any bugs smashed on the windshield. I drive for ten seconds and kill the only living thing in Nevada."

"Yeah," Victor said. "Maybe I should drive."

"Maybe you should."

155 Thomas Builds-the-Fire walked through the corridors of the tribal school by himself. Nobody wanted to be anywhere near him because of all those stories. Story after story.

Thomas closed his eyes and this story came to him: "We are all given one thing by which our lives are measured, one determination. Mine are the stories that can change or not change the world. It doesn't matter which, as long as I continue to tell the stories. My father, he died on Okinawa[2] in World War II, died fighting for this country, which had tried to kill him for years. My mother, she died giving birth to me, died while I was still inside her. She pushed me out into the world with her last breath. I have no brothers or sisters. I have only my stories, which came to me before I even had the words to speak. I learned a thousand stories before I took my first thousand steps. They are all I have. It's all I can do."

Thomas Builds-the-Fire told his stories to all those who would stop and listen. He kept telling them long after people had stopped listening.

---

[2] Largest island of the Ryukus, a chain of Japanese islands in the Western Pacific Ocean.

Victor and Thomas made it back to the reservation just as the sun was rising. It was the beginning of a new day on earth, but the same old shit on the reservation.

"Good morning," Thomas said.

160   "Good morning."

The tribe was waking up, ready for work, eating breakfast, reading the newspaper, just like everybody else does. Willene LeBret was out in her garden, wearing a bathrobe. She waved when Thomas and Victor drove by.

"Crazy Indians made it," she said to herself and went back to her roses.

Victor stopped the pickup in front of Thomas Builds-the-Fire's HUD[3] house. They both yawned, stretched a little, shook dust from their bodies.

"I'm tired," Victor said.

165   "Of everything," Thomas added.

They both searched for words to end the journey. Victor needed to thank Thomas for his help and for the money, and to make the promise to pay it all back.

"Don't worry about the money," Thomas said. "It don't make any difference anyhow."

"Probably not, enit?"

"Nope."

170   Victor knew that Thomas would remain the crazy storyteller who talked to dogs and cars, who listened to the wind and pine trees. Victor knew that he couldn't really be friends with Thomas, even after all that had happened. It was cruel but it was real. As real as the ash, as Victor's father, sitting behind the seats.

"I know how it is," Thomas said. "I know you ain't going to treat me any better than you did before. I know your friends would give you too much shit about it."

Victor was ashamed of himself. Whatever happened to the tribal ties, the sense of community? The only real thing he shared with anybody was a bottle and broken dreams. He owed Thomas something, anything.

"Listen," Victor said and handed Thomas the cardboard box that contained half of his father. "I want you to have this."

Thomas took the ashes and smiled, closed his eyes, and told this story: "I'm going to travel to Spokane Falls one last time and toss these ashes into the water. And your father will rise like a salmon, leap over the bridge, over me, and find his way home. It will be beautiful. His teeth will shine like silver, like a rainbow. He will rise, Victor, he will rise."

175   Victor smiled.

"I was planning on doing the same thing with my half," Victor said. "But I didn't imagine my father looking anything like a salmon. I thought it'd be like cleaning the attic or something. Like letting things go after they've stopped having any use."

---

[3] The U.S. Department of Housing and Urban Development.

"Nothing stops, cousin," Thomas said. "Nothing stops."

Thomas Builds-the-Fire got out of the pickup and walked up his drive-way. Victor started the pickup and began the drive home.

"Wait," Thomas yelled suddenly from his porch. "I just got to ask one favor."

180 Victor stopped the pickup, leaned out the window, and shouted back.

"What do you want?" he asked.

"Just one time when I'm telling a story somewhere, why don't you stop and listen?" Thomas asked.

"Just once?"

"Just once."

185 Victor waved his arms to let Thomas know that the deal was good. It was a fair trade. That's all Thomas had ever wanted from his whole life. So Victor drove his father's pickup toward home while Thomas went into his house, closed the door behind him, and heard a new story come to him in the silence afterward.

READING AND REACTING

1. In paragraph 1 readers are told that Victor lives on an Indian reservation. What details elsewhere in the story establish this setting? What associations does this setting have for you? Do you think the story could take place anywhere else?

2. In addition to various locations on the reservation, the story's settings include an airplane, a trailer in Phoenix, and a road through Nevada. What does each of these settings contribute to the story's plot?

3. Is the scene on the plane necessary? Intrusive? Distracting? Farfetched?

4. How would you characterize the story's mood or atmosphere? How do Thomas's stories help to create this mood? How do they help to establish his character? Do you think Alexie should have included more of these stories?

5. Why do you suppose Victor and Thomas cannot be friends when they get back to the reservation? Why can they be friends when they are traveling to Phoenix?

6. Do the flashbacks to the two men's childhood add something vital to the story? What purpose do these flashbacks serve?

7. In Native American culture the storyteller holds an important position, telling tales that transmit and preserve the tribe's basic beliefs. Do you think Thomas's stories serve such a function? Or is he, as Victor characterizes him near the end of the story, simply "the crazy storyteller who talked to dogs and cars, who listened to the wind and pine trees" (170)?

8. What do you think the story's title means?

9. **JOURNAL ENTRY**   At the end of the story, when Thomas returns home, he hears "a new story come to him in the silence" after he closes the door. What kind of story do you think comes to him at this point? Why do you think so?

10. **CRITICAL PERSPECTIVE**   In the introduction to a collection of Native American literature, Clifford E. Trafzer, the collection's editor, discusses the unique characteristics of Native American writers:

> *Due to their grounding in the oral tradition of their people, Native American writers do not follow the literary canon of the dominant society in their approach to short stories. Rather than focusing on one theme or character in a brief time frame, or using one geographical area, they often use multiple themes and characters with few boundaries of time or place. Their stories do not always follow a linear and clear path, and frequently the past and present, real and mythic, and conscious and unconscious are not distinguishable. Multidimensional characters are common, and involved stories usually lack absolute conclusions. Native American writers may also play tricks with language, deliberately misusing grammar, syntax, and spelling—sometimes in defiance of the dominant culture—in order to make English reflect the language of their peoples.*

Do you think "This Is What It Means to Say Phoenix, Arizona" has the characteristics Trafzer associates with Native American writers?

WRITING SUGGESTIONS: SETTING

1. Write the story of the trip to Phoenix as Thomas-Builds-the-Fire ("This Is What It Means to Say Phoenix, Arizona") might tell it.

2. In the first three of the four stories in this chapter, social constraints determined by the story's historical context limit a woman's options. Explore the options each woman might reasonably exercise in order to break free of the limits that social institutions impose on her.

3. In stories in which setting is a strong presence, the danger always exists that the writer will neglect character development in favor of atmosphere. Does this problem occur in any of the stories in this chapter? Explain your answer.

4. Write an essay in which you consider how any one of the four stories in this chapter would be different if a major aspect of its historical, geographical, or physical setting were changed to settings of your choice. In your essay, examine the changes (in plot development as well as in the characters' conflicts, reactions, and motivation) that might be caused by the change in setting.

5. Select a story from another chapter, and write an essay in which you consider how setting affects its plot—for example, how it creates conflict or crisis, how it forces characters to act, or how it determines how the plot is resolved.

CHAPTER 7

Point of View

It is not surprising to hear practicing [writers] report that they have never had help from critics about point-of-view. In dealing with point-of-view the [writer] must always deal with the individual work: which particular character shall tell this particular story, or part of a story, with what precise degree of reliability, privilege, freedom to comment, and so on. Shall he be given dramatic vividness? Even if the [writer] has decided on a narrator who will fit one of the critic's classifications "omniscient," "first-person," "limited omniscient," "objective," . . . and so on—his troubles have just begun. He simply cannot find answers to his immediate, precise, practical problems by referring to statements that the "omniscient is the most flexible method," or "the objective the most rapid or vivid," or whatever. Even the soundest of generalizations at this level will be of little use to him.

WAYNE C. BOOTH, "DISTANCE AND POINT OF VIEW"

For reasons that should not need explanation here, until very recently, and regardless of the race of the author, the readers of virtually all of American fiction have been positioned as white. I am interested to know what that assumption has meant to the literary imagination. When does racial "unconsciousness" or awareness of race enrich interpretive language, and when does it impoverish it? What does positing one's writerly self, in the wholly racialized society that is the United States, as unraced and all others as raced entail? What happens to the writerly imagination of a black author who is at some level always *conscious of representing one's own race to, or in spite of, a race of readers that understands itself to be "universal" or race-free? In other words, how is "literary whiteness" and "literary blackness" made, and what is the consequence of that construction?*

TONI MORRISON, *PLAYING IN THE DARK*

Tied to issues of gender, social stratification, racial oppression, and the need to restore the foundations of our history and culture, the most recurrent theme in our writing is what I call claiming America for Asian Americans. That does not mean disappearing like raindrops in the ocean of white America, fighting to become "normal," losing ourselves in the process. It means inventing a new identity, defining ourselves according to the truth instead of a racial fantasy, so that we can be reconciled with one another in order to celebrate our marginality. It is this seeming paradox, the Asian American claim on America, that is the oppositional quality of our discourse.

ELAINE H. KIM, "DEFINING ASIAN AMERICAN
REALITIES THROUGH LITERATURE"

All stories are told, or narrated, by someone, and one of the first choices writers make is who tells the story. This choice determines the story's **point of view**—the angle or vantage point from which events are presented. The implications of this choice are far reaching. Consider for a moment the following scenario. Five people witness a crime and are questioned by law enforcement officials. Their stories agree on certain points: A crime was committed, a body was found, and the crime occurred at noon. But in other ways their stories are very different. The man who fled the scene was either tall or of average height; his hair was either dark or light; he was either carrying an object or was empty handed. The events that led up to the crime and even the description of the crime itself are markedly different depending on who tells the story. Thus, the perspective from which a story is told determines what details are included in the story and how they are arranged—in short, the plot. In addition, the perspective of the narrator affects the story's style, language, and themes.

The narrator's voice in a work of fiction is not the same as the author's voice. Even when an author uses the first-person *I* to narrate a story, do not assume that the narrator is the author. Authors create characters, often with personalities and opinions far different from theirs, to tell their stories. Critics use the technical term **persona**—which literally means "mask"—to describe the narrator created by authors to tell a story. By assuming this mask, authors enhance the creative possibilities of their writing.

When deciding on a point of view for a work of fiction, a writer can choose to tell the story in the first person or in the third person.

First-Person Narrator

Sometimes the narrator is a character who uses the **first person** *I* (or sometimes *we*) to tell the story. This narrator may be a major character telling his or her own story or a minor character who plays only a small part (or no part at all) in the story's events. Both Sammy in John Updike's "A&P" (p. 105) and the boy in James Joyce's "Araby" (p. 249) are major characters who tell their own stories and are the focus of those stories. Sometimes, however, a first-person narrator may tell a story that is primarily about someone else. Such a narrator may be a minor character who plays a relatively small part in the story or simply an observer who reports events experienced or related by others. The narrator of William Faulkner's "A Rose for Emily" (p. 80), for example, is an unidentified witness to the story's events. By using *we* instead of the more commonly used *I*, this narrator seems to be speaking on behalf of all the residents of the town, expressing their shared views of their neighbor, Emily Grierson.

> *We did not say she was crazy then. We believed she had to do that. We remembered all the young men her father had driven away, and we knew that with nothing left, she would have to cling to that which had robbed her, as people will.*

Writers gain a number of advantages when they use a first-person narrator. First, they are able to present incidents very convincingly. Readers are more willing to accept a statement such as "My sister changed a lot after that day" as personal testimony than as the impersonal observation of a third-person narrator. The first-person narrator also simplifies a writer's task of selecting details. Only the events and details that the narrator could actually have seen or experienced can reasonably be introduced into the story.

Another major advantage of first-person narrators is that their restricted view, as well as their unique perspectives, can create **irony**—a discrepancy between what a narrator says and what readers believe to be true. Irony may be *dramatic, situational,* or *verbal.* **Dramatic irony** occurs when the narrator perceives less about the events he or she describes than the audience does. Dramatic irony occurs in the story "Greasy Lake" by T. Coraghessan Boyle (p. 397). Although readers are shocked by an attempted rape, the narrator and his friends never acknowledge the significance of their actions, and they do not seem to understand the tragic consequences that might have resulted. **Situational irony** occurs when what happens is at odds with what the story leads readers to expect will happen; **verbal irony** occurs when the narrator says one thing but actually means another. "Gryphon" by Charles Baxter (p. 125) illustrates both situational and verbal irony. The setting of the story—a conventional school—creates irony because it contrasts sharply with the unexpected events that unfold there. In addition, many of the narrator's comments have more meaning than they seem to have. At the end of the story, for example, after the substitute, Miss Ferenczi, has been dismissed, the narrator relates another teacher's comment that life will now return to "normal" and their regular teacher will soon return to test them on their "knowledge." These comments are extremely ironic in light of all Miss Ferenczi has done to redefine the narrator's ideas about "normal" education.

Unreliable Narrators Sometimes first-person narrators may be self-serving, mistaken, confused, unstable, or even mad. These *unreliable narrators,* whether intentionally or unintentionally, misrepresent events and misdirect readers. In Edgar Allan Poe's "The Cask of Amontillado" (p. 209), for example, the narrator, Montresor, tells his story to justify a crime he committed fifty years before. Montresor's version of what happened and why is not accurate, and perceptive readers know it: His obvious self-deception, his sadistic manipulation of Fortunato, his detached description of the cold-blooded murder, and his lack of remorse lead readers to question his sanity (and, therefore, to distrust his version of events). This distrust creates an ironic distance between readers and narrator.

The narrator of Charlotte Perkins Gilman's "The Yellow Wall-Paper" (p. 160) is also an unreliable narrator. Suffering from "nervous depression," she unintentionally distorts the facts when she says that the shapes in the wallpaper of her bedroom are changing and moving. Moreover, she does not realize what is wrong with her or why, or how her husband's "good intentions" are hurting her. Readers, however, see the disparity between the narrator's interpretation of events and their own, and this irony enriches their understanding of the story.

Some narrators are unreliable simply because they are naive. Because they are immature, sheltered, or innocent of evil, these narrators may not be aware of the full significance of the events they are relating. Readers, having the benefit of experience, interpret events differently from the way these narrators do. When we read a passage by a child narrator—such as the following from J. D. Salinger's novel *The Catcher in the Rye*—we are aware of the narrator's innocence, and we know the child's interpretation of events is flawed.

> *Anyway, I keep picturing all these little kids playing some game in this big field of rye and all. Thousands of little kids, and nobody's around—nobody big, I mean—except me. And I'm standing on the edge of some crazy cliff. What I have to do, I have to catch everybody if they start to go over the cliff— I mean if they're running and they don't look where they're going I have to come out from somewhere and catch them. I'd just be the catcher in the rye. . . .*

The irony in the preceding passage comes from our knowledge that the naive narrator, Holden Caulfield, cannot stop children from growing up. Ultimately, they all fall off the "crazy cliff" and mature into adults. Although he is not aware of the futility of his efforts to protect his sister and the other children from the dangers of adulthood, readers know that they are doomed from the start.

A naive narrator's background can also limit his or her ability to understand a situation. The narrator in Sherwood Anderson's "I'm a Fool," for example, lies to impress a rich girl he meets at a race track. At the end of the story the boy laments the fact that he lied, believing that if he had not, he could have seen the girl again. The reader knows, however, that the narrator is deceiving himself, and that the social gap that separates the narrator and the girl could never have been bridged.

Keep in mind that there is a difference between an unreliable narrator and a narrator whose perspective is limited. All first-person narrators are, by definition, limited because they present a situation as only one person sees it. "In a Grove," by the Japanese writer Ryūnosuke Akutagawa (p. 232), illustrates this idea. In this story, seven characters give different accounts of a murder. Some of the characters seem to be lying or bending the facts to suit their own needs, but others simply have an incomplete or incorrect understanding of the event. No character, of course, has all the information the story's author has.

As a reader focusing on a story's point of view, you should look for discrepancies between a narrator's view of events and your own sense of what has happened. Discovering that a story has an unreliable narrator enables you not only to question the truth of the narrative but also to recognize the irony inherent in the narrator's version of events. By doing so, you are able to gain a better sense of the story and to learn something about the writer's purpose.

THIRD-PERSON NARRATOR

Writers can also use **third-person** narrators, who are not characters in the story. These narrators fall into three categories.

Omniscient   Some third-person narrators are **omniscient** (all-knowing) narrators, moving at will from one character's mind to another. By doing so they not only reveal the thoughts of the individual characters, but also present a body of information that no single character could possibly know. One advantage of omniscient narrators is that they are objective; they have none of the naïveté, dishonesty, gullibility, or mental instability that can characterize first-person narrators. In addition, because omniscient narrators are not characters in the story, their perception is not limited to what any one character can observe or comprehend. As a result, they can present a more inclusive overview of events and characters than first-person narrators can. Notice how the narrator of Nadine Gordimer's "Once Upon a Time" (p. 74) is able to give such an overview:

> In a house, in a suburb, in a city, there were a man and his wife who loved each other very much and were living happily ever after. They had a little boy, and they loved him very much. They had a cat and a dog that the little boy loved very much. They had a car and a caravan trailer for holidays, and a swimming-pool which was fenced so that the little boy and his playmates would not fall in and drown. They had a housemaid who was absolutely trustworthy and an itinerant gardener who was highly recommended by the neighbours. For when they began to live happily ever after they were warned, by that wise old witch, the husband's mother, not to take anyone off the street.

Occasionally, omniscient narrators not only move in and out of the minds of the characters but also in and out of a persona that speaks in the first person, directly addressing readers. This experimental narrative technique was popular with writers such as Laurence Sterne and Henry Fielding during the eighteenth century, when the novel was a new literary form. It permitted writers to present themselves as masters of artifice, able to know and control all aspects of experience. Few contemporary writers would give themselves the license that Henry Fielding does in the following passage from *Tom Jones:*

> And true it was that [Mr. Alworthy] did many of these things; but had he done nothing more I should have left him to have recorded his own merit on some fair freestone over the door of that hospital. Matters of a much more extraordinary kind are to be the subject of this history, or I should grossly misspend my time in writing so voluminous a work; and you my sagacious friend, might with equal profit and pleasure travel through some pages which certain droll authors have been facetiously pleased to call The History of England.

A contemporary example of this type of omniscient point of view occurs in Ursula K. LeGuin's "The Ones Who Walk Away from Omelas." This story presents a description of a city that in the narrator's words is "like a city in a fairy tale." As the story proceeds, however, the description of Omelas changes, and the narrator's perspective changes as well: "Do you believe? Do you accept the festival, the city, the joy? No? Then let me describe one more thing." In this way the narrator underscores the ironic theme of the story, which suggests the impossibility of ideal societies and the inability of human beings to achieve happiness.

Limited Omniscient   Third-person narrators can have **limited omniscience,** focusing on only what a single character experiences. In other words, events are limited to one character's perspective, and nothing is revealed that the character does not see, hear, feel, or think. Andy in David Michael Kaplan's "Doe Season" (p. 342) is just such a limited-focus character. Limited omniscient narrators, like all third-person narrators, have certain advantages over first-person narrators—for example, greater flexibility. When a writer uses a first-person narrator, the narrator's personality and speech color the story, creating a personal or even idiosyncratic narrative. Also, the narrator's character flaws or lack of knowledge may limit his or her awareness of the significance of events. Limited omniscient narrators take readers into a particular character's mind just as a first-person narrator does, but without the limitations of the first-person narrator's subjectivity, self-deception, or naïveté. In short, because limited omniscient narrators speak from outside a character, they are reliable; they maintain an objective distance from events, giving readers an accurate version of what happened. In the following example from Anne Tyler's "Teenage Wasteland" (p. 569), the limited omniscient narrator presents the story from the point of view of a single character, Daisy:

> Daisy and Matt sat silent, shocked. Matt rubbed his forehead with his
> fingertips. Imagine, Daisy thought, how they must look to Mr. Lanham: an

overweight housewife in a cotton dress and a too-tall, too-thin insurance agent in a baggy, frayed suit. Failures, both of them—the kind of people who are hurrying to catch up, missing the point of things that everyone else grasps at once. She wished she'd worn nylons instead of knee socks.

Notice how the narrative point of view in the above example gives readers the impression that they are standing off to the side watching Daisy and her husband Matt. At the same time we get this objective view of the scene, however, we are able to see into the mind of a major character.

Objective   Finally, third-person narrators can tell a story from an **objective** (or dramatic) point of view, remaining entirely outside the characters' minds, recording the action as a camera would. With objective narrators, events unfold the way they would in a play or a movie. Narrators tell the story only by reproducing dialogue and recounting events. They do not present the characters' thoughts or explain their motivations. Thus, they allow readers to interpret the actions of the characters without any interference. Ernest Hemingway uses the objective point of view in his short story "A Clean, Well-Lighted Place" (p. 256):

> *The waiter took the brandy bottle and another saucer from the counter inside the café and marched out to the old man's table. He put down the saucer and poured the glass full of brandy.*
> *"You should have killed yourself last week," he said to the deaf man. The old man motioned with his finger. "A little more," he said. The waiter poured on into the glass so that the brandy slopped over and ran down the stem into the top saucer of the pile. "Thank you," the old man said. The waiter took the bottle back inside the café. He sat down at the table with his colleague again.*

The story's narrator is distant, seemingly emotionless, and this perspective is consistent with the author's purpose: For Hemingway the attitude of the narrator reflects the stunned, almost anesthetized condition of people in the modern world.

SELECTING AN APPROPRIATE POINT OF VIEW

Writers of short stories often maintain a consistent point of view, but there is no rule that says they must. Although one point of view may be dominant, writers of fiction frequently introduce additional points of view to achieve complexity and depth. The main criterion writers use when they decide on a point of view is how the distance they maintain from their material will enhance the effect of their narrative. For example, consider the following passage from "Doe Season."

Limited Omniscient Point of View

> *They were always the same woods, she thought sleepily as they drove through the early morning darkness—deep and immense, covered with yesterday's*

snowfall, which had frozen overnight. They were the same woods that lay behind her house, and they stretch all the way to here, *she thought,* for miles and miles, longer than I could walk in a day, or a week even, but they are still the same woods. *The thought made her feel good: it was like thinking of God; it was like thinking of the space between here and the moon; it was like thinking of all the foreign countries from her geography book where even now, Andy knew, people were going to bed, while they—she and her father and Charlie Spoon and Mac, Charlie's eleven-year-old son—were driving deeper into the Pennsylvania countryside, to go hunting.*

They had risen before dawn. Her mother, yawning and not trying to hide her sleepiness, cooked them eggs and French toast. Her father smoked a cigarette and flicked ashes into his saucer while Andy listened, wondering Why doesn't he come? *and* Won't he ever come? *until at last a car pulled into the graveled drive and honked. "That will be Charlie Spoon," her father said; he always said "Charlie Spoon," even though his real name was Spreun, because Charlie was, in a sense, shaped like a spoon, with a large head and a narrow waist and chest.*

In the preceding passage, David Michael Kaplan uses a third-person limited omniscient narrator to tell the story of Andy, a nine-year-old girl who is going hunting with her father for the first time. This point of view has the advantage of allowing the narrator to focus on the thoughts, motivations, and reactions of the child while at the same time giving readers information about Andy that she herself is too immature or unsophisticated to know. Rather than simply presenting the thoughts of the child (represented in the original story by italics), the third-person narrator makes connections between ideas and offers a level of language and a degree of insight that readers would not accept from Andy as a first-person narrator. In addition, the limited omniscient perspective enables the narrator to maintain some distance. Consider how different the passage would be if it were narrated by nine-year-old Andy.

First-Person Point of View (Child)

"I like the woods," I thought. "They're big and scary. I wonder if they're the same woods that are behind my house. They go on for miles. They're bigger than I could walk in a day, or a week even." It was neat to think that while we were driving into the woods people were going to bed in other countries.

When I woke up this morning, I couldn't wait to go hunting. My mother was cooking breakfast, but all I could think of was, "When will he come?" and "Won't he ever come?" Finally, I heard a car honk. "That will be Charlie Spoon," my father said. I think he called him "Charlie Spoon" because he thought Charlie was shaped like a big spoon.

Notice that as a first-person narrator, nine-year-old Andy must have the voice of a child; moreover, she is restricted to only those observations that a nine-year-old could reasonably make. Because of these limitations, the passage lacks the level of vocabulary, syntax, and insight necessary to develop the central character and the themes of the story. This point of view could succeed only if Andy's words established an ironic contrast between her naive sensibility and the reality of the situation.

Kaplan could have avoided these problems and still gained the advantages of using a first-person narrator by having Andy tell her story as an adult looking back on a childhood experience. (This technique is used by James Joyce in "Araby," p. 249; Charles Baxter in "Gryphon," p. 125; and Alberto Alvaro Ríos in "The Secret Lion," p. 43.)

First-Person Point of View (Adult)

"They are always the same woods," I thought sleepily as we drove through the early morning darkness—deep and immense, covered with yesterday's snowfall, which had frozen overnight. "They're the same woods that lie behind my house, and they stretch all the way to here," I thought. I knew that they stretched for miles and miles, longer than I could walk in a day, or even in a week but that they were still the same woods. Knowing this made me feel good: I thought it was like thinking of God; it was like thinking of the space between that place and the moon; it was like thinking of all the foreign countries from my geography book where even then, I knew, people were going to bed, while we—my father and I and Charlie Spoon and Mac, Charlie's eleven-year-old son—were driving deeper into the Pennsylvania countryside, to go hunting.

We had risen before dawn. My mother, who was yawning and not trying to hide her sleepiness, cooked us eggs and French toast. My father smoked a cigarette and flicked ashes into his saucer while I listened, wondering, "Why doesn't he come?" and "Won't he ever come?" until at last a car pulled into our driveway and honked. "That will be Charlie Spoon," my father said. He always said "Charlie Spoon," even though his real name was Spreun, because Charlie was, in a sense, shaped like a spoon, with a large head and a narrow waist and chest.

Although this passage presents the child's point of view, it does not use a child's voice; obviously the language and scope of the passage are too sophisticated for a child. By using a mature style, the adult narrator is able to consider ideas that a child could not possibly understand, such as the symbolic significance of the woods. In this passage the first-person adult narrator closes the distance between Andy and the narrator. By doing so, however, he sacrifices the detachment that characterizes the narrator of the original story.

Kaplan had other options as well. For example, he could have used an omniscient narrator to tell his story. In this case, the narrator would be free to reveal and comment not only on Andy's thoughts but also on those of her father, and possibly even on the thoughts of her mother and Charlie Spoon. Notice in the following passage how the omniscient narrator interprets the behavior of the characters and tells what each one is thinking.

Omniscient Point of View

They were always the same woods, she thought sleepily as they drove through the early morning darkness—deep and immense, covered with yesterday's snowfall, which had frozen overnight. They were the same woods that lay behind her house, and they stretch all the way to here, she thought, for miles and miles, longer than I could walk in a day, or a week even, but they are still the same woods.

They had risen before dawn. The mother, yawning and not trying to hide her sleepiness, cooked them eggs and French toast. She looked at her husband and her daughter and wondered if she was doing the right thing by allowing them to go hunting together. "After all," she thought, "he's not the most careful person. Will he watch her? Make sure that no harm comes to her?"

The father smoked a cigarette and flicked ashes into his saucer. He was listening to the sounds of the early morning. "I know everything will be all right," he thought. "It's about time Andy went hunting. When I was her age. . . ." Andy listened, wondering Why doesn't he come? and Won't he ever come? until at last a car pulled into the graveled drive and honked. Suddenly the father cocked his head and said, "That will be Charlie Spoon."

Andy thought it was funny that her father called Charlie "Spoon" even though his real name was Spreun, because Charlie was, in a sense, shaped like a spoon, with a large head and a narrow waist and chest.

Certainly this point of view has its advantages; for example, the wide scope of this point of view provides a great deal of information about the characters. However, the use of an omniscient point of view deprives the story of its focus on Andy.

Finally, Kaplan could have used an objective narrator. This point of view would eliminate all interpretation by the narrator and force readers to make judgments solely on the basis of what the characters say and do. Here is an example of the passage from "Doe Season" presented from this point of view.

Objective Point of View

Andy sat sleepily staring into her cereal. She played with the dry flakes of bran as they floated in the surface of the milk.

Andy's mother, yawning, cooked them eggs and French toast. She looked at her husband and her daughter, paused for a second, and then went about what she was doing.

Andy's father smoked a cigarette and flicked ashes into his saucer. He looked out the window and said, "I wonder where Charlie Spoon is?"

Andy squirmed restlessly and repeatedly looked up at the clock that hung above the stove.

The disadvantage of this point of view is that it creates a great deal of distance between the characters and the readers. Instead of gaining the intimate knowledge of Andy that the limited omniscient point of view provides—knowledge even greater than she herself has—the reader must infer what she thinks and feels without any help from the narrator.

Although other choices were possible, the point of view Kaplan uses in "Doe Season" is well suited to his purpose. Ideally, writers choose the point of view that best enables them to achieve their objectives. If they want to create an intimate, subjective portrait of a character, they will employ a first-person narrator. If they want to have a great deal of freedom in telling their story, they will use an omniscient narrator. A limited omniscient narrator enables writers to maintain the focus on a single individual while commenting on the action. And finally, the objective point of view allows writers to remove the narrator from the story and present events in a distant, emotionless way.

▼▼▼

FIRST-PERSON NARRATOR (I OR WE)

◆ *Major character telling his or her own story* "Every morning I lay on the floor in the front parlour watching her door." (James Joyce, "Araby")

◆ *Minor character as witness or nonparticipant* "And so she died. . . . We did not even know she was sick; we had long since given up trying to get information. . . ." (William Faulkner, "A Rose for Emily")

THIRD-PERSON NARRATOR (HE, SHE, IT, OR THEY)

◆ *Omniscient—able to move at will from character to character and comment about them* "In a house, in a suburb, in a city, there were a man and his wife who loved each other very much. . . . " (Nadine Gordimer, "Once Upon a Time")

◆ *Limited Omniscient—restricts focus to a single character* "The wagon went on. He did not know where they were going." (William Faulkner, "Barn Burning")

◆ *Objective (Dramatic)—simply reports the dialogue and the actions of characters* " 'You'll be drunk,' the waiter said. The old man looked at him. The waiter went away." (Ernest Hemingway, "A Clean, Well-Lighted Place")

▲▲▲

A FINAL NOTE

One other option for writers is the **second-person** point of view, the consistent use of *you* and the imperative mood (commands) throughout the story. This unusual technique is used by Lorrie Moore in "How to Talk to Your Mother (Notes)" (p. 89).

You have seen too many Hollywood musicals. You have seen too many people singing in public places and you assume you can do it, too. Practice. Your teacher asks you a question. You warble back: "The answer to number two is twelve." Most of the class laughs at you. . . .

Here Moore uses the second person to address an unspecified audience. The "real" narrator hides behind the protective *you* and gives the appearance of not talking about herself. By using this technique, the narrator attempts to distance herself psychologically from the action and perhaps to abdicate responsibility for what she is saying.

▼▼▼

CHECKLIST FOR WRITING ABOUT POINT OF VIEW

- ◆ What is the dominant point of view from which the story is told?
- ◆ Is the narrator of the story a participant in the story or just a witness?
- ◆ Does the story's point of view create irony?
- ◆ If the story has a first-person narrator, is the narrator reliable or unreliable? Are there any inconsistencies in the narrator's presentation of the story?
- ◆ How do you explain any distortions of fact that you detect? Are these distortions intentional or unintentional?
- ◆ If the story has a third-person narrator, is he or she omniscient? Does he or she have limited omniscience? Is the narrator objective?
- ◆ What are the advantages of the story's point of view? How does the point of view accomplish the author's purpose?
- ◆ Is there anything unusual about the point of view?
- ◆ Does the point of view remain consistent throughout the story, or does it shift?
- ◆ How might a different point of view change the story?

▲▲▲

RICHARD WRIGHT (1908–1960) was born near Natchez, Mississippi, the son of sharecroppers. He had little formal schooling but as a young man was a voracious reader, attracted particularly to naturalistic fiction. Relocating to Chicago in the late 1920s, Wright worked as a postal clerk before joining the Federal Writers' Project in 1935, an association that took him to New York City soon after. Deeply troubled by the economic and social oppression suffered by fellow African-Americans, Wright joined the Communist Party in 1932, and his early poems and stories reflect a distinctly Marxist perspective. However, he broke with the party in 1944 because of its stifling effect on "new ideas, new facts, . . . new hints at ways to live."

In 1938 Wright began to reach a mainstream audience when a group of four long stories on the theme of racial oppression and violence were judged best manuscript in a contest sponsored by *Story* magazine; these were published as *Uncle Tom's Children* in 1938. Two year later Wright published his most famous work, *Native Son,* an angry and brutal novel exploring the moral devastation wrought by a racist society. The autobiographical *Black Boy* was published in 1945. In later years Wright abandoned the United States for Paris in protest against the treatment of blacks in his native country and focused his work on reports about national independence movements in Africa and elsewhere in the third world.

The following story, published in the posthumous collection *Eight Men* (1961), is uncharacteristic of Wright's work in a number of ways—not least of which is that it is told through the eyes of a white protagonist.

RICHARD WRIGHT

Big Black Good Man

(1957)

Through the open window Olaf Jenson could smell the sea and hear the occasional foghorn of a freighter; outside, rain pelted down through an August night, drumming softly upon the pavements of Copenhagen,[1] inducing drowsiness, bringing dreamy memory, relaxing the tired muscles of his work-wracked body. He sat slumped in a swivel chair with his legs outstretched and his feet propped atop an edge of his desk. An inch of white ash tipped the end of his brown cigar and now and then he inserted the end of the stogie[2] into his mouth and drew gently upon it, letting wisps of blue smoke eddy from the corners of his wide, thin lips. The watery gray irises behind the thick lenses of his eyeglasses gave him a look of abstraction, of absentmindedness, of an almost genial idiocy. He sighed, reached for his half-empty bottle of beer, and drained it into his glass and downed it with a long slow gulp, then licked his lips. Replacing the cigar, he slapped his right palm against his thigh and said half aloud:

"Well, I'll be sixty tomorrow. I'm not rich, but I'm not poor either . . . Really, I can't complain. Got good health. Traveled all over the world and had my share of girls when I was young . . . And my Karen's a good wife. I own my home. Got no debts. And I love digging in my garden in the spring

---

[1] The capital of Denmark.

[2] Cheap cigar.

. . . Grew the biggest carrots of anybody last year. Ain't saved much money, but what the hell . . . Money ain't everything. Got a good job. Night portering ain't too bad." He shook his head and yawned. "Karen and I could of had some children, though. Would of been good company . . . 'Specially for Karen. And I could of taught 'em languages . . . English, French, German, Danish, Dutch, Swedish, Norwegian, and Spanish . . ." He took the cigar out of his mouth and eyed the white ash critically. "Hell of a lot of good language learning did me . . . Never got anything out of it. But those ten years in New York were fun . . . Maybe I could of got rich if I'd stayed in America . . . Maybe. But I'm satisfied. You can't have everything."

Behind him the office door opened and a young man, a medical student occupying room number nine, entered.

"Good evening," the student said.

5   "Good evening," Olaf said, turning.

The student went to the keyboard and took hold of the round, brown knob that anchored his key.

"Rain, rain, rain," the student said.

"That's Denmark for you," Olaf smiled at him.

"This dampness keeps me clogged up like a drainpipe," the student complained.

10   "That's Denmark for you," Olaf repeated with a smile.

"Good night," the student said.

"Good night, son," Olaf sighed, watching the door close.

Well, my tenants are my children, Olaf told himself. Almost all of his children were in their rooms now . . . Only seventy-two and forty-four were missing . . . Seventy-two might've gone to Sweden . . . And forty-four was maybe staying at his girl's place tonight, like he sometimes did . . . He studied the pear-shaped blobs of hard rubber, reddish brown like ripe fruit, that hung from the keyboard, then glanced at his watch. Only room thirty, eighty-one, and one hundred and one were empty . . . And it was almost midnight. In a few moments he could take a nap. Nobody hardly ever came looking for accommodations after midnight, unless a stray freighter came in, bringing thirsty, women-hungry sailors. Olaf chuckled softly. Why in hell was I ever a sailor? The whole time I was at sea I was thinking and dreaming about women. Then why didn't I stay on land where women could be had? Hunh? Sailors are crazy . . .

But he liked sailors. They reminded him of his youth, and there was something so direct, simple, and childlike about them. They always said straight out what they wanted, and what they wanted was almost always women and whisky . . . "Well, there's no harm in that . . . Nothing could be more natural," Olaf sighed, looking thirstily at his empty beer bottle. No; he'd not drink any more tonight; he'd had enough; he'd go to sleep . . .

15   He was bending forward and loosening his shoelaces when he heard the office door crack open. He lifted his eyes, then sucked in his breath. He did not straighten; he just stared up and around at the huge black thing that filled the doorway. His reflexes refused to function; it was not fear; it

was just simple astonishment. He was staring at the biggest, strangest, and blackest man he'd ever seen in all his life.

"Good evening," the black giant said in a voice that filled the small office. "Say, you got a room?"

Olaf sat up slowly, not to answer but to look at this brooding black vision; it towered darkly some six and a half feet into the air, almost touching the ceiling, and its skin was so black that it had a bluish tint. And the sheer bulk of the man! . . . His chest bulged like a barrel; his rocklike and humped shoulders hinted of mountain ridges; the stomach ballooned like a threatening stone; and the legs were like telephone poles . . . The big black cloud of a man now lumbered into the office, bending to get its buffalolike head under the door frame, then advanced slowly upon Olaf, like a stormy sky descending.

"You got a room?" the big black man asked again in a resounding voice.

Olaf now noticed that the ebony giant was well dressed, carried a wonderful new suitcase, and wore black shoes that gleamed despite the raindrops that peppered their toes.

20   "You're American?" Olaf asked him.

"Yeah, man; sure," the black giant answered.

"Sailor?"

"Yeah. American Continental Lines."

Olaf had not answered the black man's question. It was not that the hotel did not admit men of color; Olaf took in all comers—blacks, yellows, whites, and browns . . . To Olaf, men were men, and, in his day, he'd worked and eaten and slept and fought with all kinds of men. But this particular black man . . . Well, he didn't seem human. Too big, too black, too loud, too direct, and probably too violent to boot . . . Olaf's five feet seven inches scarcely reached the black giant's shoulder and his frail body weighed less, perhaps, than one of the man's gigantic legs . . . There was something about the man's intense blackness and ungainly bigness that frightened and insulted Olaf; he felt as though this man had come here expressly to remind him how puny, how tiny, and how weak and how white he was. Olaf knew, while registering his reactions, that he was being irrational and foolish; yet, for the first time in his life, he was emotionally determined to refuse a man a room solely on the basis of the man's size and color . . . Olaf's lips parted as he groped for the right words in which to couch his refusal, but the black giant bent forward and boomed:

25   "I asked you if you got a room. I got to put up somewhere tonight, man."

"Yes, we got a room," Olaf murmured.

And at once he was ashamed and confused. Sheer fear had made him yield. And he seethed against himself for his involuntary weakness. Well, he'd look over his book and pretend that he'd made a mistake; he'd tell this hunk of blackness that there was really no free room in the hotel, and that he was so sorry . . . Then, just as he took out the hotel register to make believe that he was pouring over it, a thick roll of American bank notes, crisp and green, was thrust under his nose.

"Keep this for me, will you?" the black giant commanded. "Cause I'm gonna get drunk tonight and I don't wanna lose it."

Olaf stared at the roll; it was huge, in denominations of fifties and hundreds. Olaf's eyes widened.

30   "How much is there?" he asked.

"Two thousand six hundred," the giant said. "Just put it into an envelope and write 'Jim' on it and lock it in your safe, hunh?"

The black mass of man has spoken in a manner that indicated that it was taking it for granted that Olaf would obey. Olaf was licked. Resentment clogged the pores of his wrinkled white skin. His hands trembled as he picked up the money. No; he couldn't refuse this man . . . The impulse to deny him was strong, but each time he was about to act upon it something thwarted him, made him shy off. He clutched about desperately for an idea. Oh yes, he could say that if he planned to stay for only one night, then he could not have the room, for it was against the policy of the hotel to rent rooms for only one night . . .

"How long are you staying? Just tonight?" Olaf asked.

"Naw. I'll be here for five or six days, I reckon," the giant answered offhandedly.

35   "You take room number thirty," Olaf heard himself saying. "It's forty kroner a day."

"That's all right with me," the giant said.

With slow, stiff movements, Olaf put the money in the safe and then turned and stared helplessly up into the living, breathing blackness looming above him. Suddenly he became conscious of the outstretched palm of the black giant; he was silently demanding the key to the room. His eyes downcast, Olaf surrendered the key, marveling at the black man's tremendous hands . . . He could kill me with one blow, Olaf told himself in fear.

Feeling himself beaten, Olaf reached for the suitcase, but the black hand of the giant whisked it out of his grasp.

"That's too heavy for you, big boy; I'll take it," the giant said.

40   Olaf let him, He thinks I'm nothing . . . He led the way down the corridor, sensing the giant's lumbering presence behind him. Olaf opened the door of number thirty and stood politely to one side, allowing the black giant to enter. At once the room seemed like a doll's house, so dwarfed and filled and tiny it was with a great living blackness . . . Flinging his suitcase upon a chair, the giant turned. The two men looked directly at each other now. Olaf saw that the giant's eyes were tiny and red, buried, it seemed, in muscle and fat. Black cheeks spread, flat and broad, topping the wide and flaring nostrils. The mouth was the biggest that Olaf had ever seen on a human face; the lips were thick, pursed, parted, showing snow-white teeth. The black neck was like a bull's . . . The giant advanced upon Olaf and stood over him.

"I want a bottle of whisky and a woman," he said. "Can you fix me up?"

"Yes," Olaf whispered, wild with anger and insult.

But what was he angry about? He'd had requests like this every night from all sorts of men and he was used to fulfilling them; he was a night porter in a cheap, water-front Copenhagen hotel that catered to sailors and students. Yes, men needed women, but this man, Olaf felt, ought to have a special sort of woman. He felt a deep and strange reluctance to phone any of the women whom he habitually sent to men. Yet he had promised. Could he lie and say that none was available? No. That sounded too fishy. The black giant sat upon the bed, staring straight before him. Olaf moved about quickly, pulling down the window shades, taking the pink coverlet off the bed, nudging the giant with his elbow to make him move as he did so . . . That's the way to treat 'im . . . Show 'im I ain't scared of 'im . . . But he was still seeking for an excuse to refuse. And he could think of nothing. He felt hypnotized, mentally immobilized. He stood hesitantly at the door.

"You send the whisky and the woman quick, pal?" the black giant asked, rousing himself from a brooding stare.

45   "Yes," Olaf grunted, shutting the door.

Goddamn, Olaf sighed. He sat in his office at his desk before the phone. Why did *he* have to come here? . . . I'm not prejudiced . . . No, not at all . . . But . . . He couldn't think any more. God oughtn't make men as big and black as that . . . But what the hell was he worrying about? He'd sent women of all races to men of all colors . . . So why not a woman to the black giant? Oh, only if the man were small, brown, and intelligent-looking . . . Olaf felt trapped.

With a reflex movement of his hand, he picked up the phone and dialed Lena. She was big and strong and always cut him in for fifteen per cent instead of the usual ten per cent. Lena had four small children to feed and clothe. Lena was willing; she was, she said, coming over right now. She didn't give a good goddamn about how big and black the man was . . .

"Why you ask me that?" Lena wanted to know over the phone. "You never asked that before . . ."

"But this one is *big*," Olaf found himself saying.

50   "He's just a man," Lena told him, her voice singing stridently, laughingly over the wire. "You just leave that to me. You don't have to do anything. *I'll* handle 'im."

Lena had a key to the hotel door downstairs, but tonight Olaf stayed awake. He wanted to see her. Why? He didn't know. He stretched out on the sofa in his office, but sleep was far from him. When Lena arrived, he told her again how big and black the man was.

"You told me that over the phone," Lena reminded him.

Olaf said nothing. Lena flounced off on her errand of mercy. Olaf shut the office door, then opened it and left it ajar. But why? He didn't know. He lay upon the sofa and stared at the ceiling. He glanced at his watch; it was almost two o'clock . . . She's staying in there a long time . . . Ah, God, but he could do with a drink . . . Why was he so damned worked up and nervous about a nigger and a white whore? . . . He'd never been so upset in all his life. Before he knew it, he had drifted off to sleep. Then he heard the office door swinging creakingly open on its rusty hinges. Lena stood in it, grim and businesslike, her face scrubbed free of powder and rouge. Olaf scrambled to his feet, adjusting his eyeglasses, blinking.

"How was it?" he asked her in a confidential whisper.

55   Lena's eyes blazed.

"What the hell's that to you?" she snapped. "There's your cut," she said, flinging him his money, tossing it upon the covers of the sofa. "You're sure nosy tonight. You wanna take over my work?"

Olaf's pasty cheeks burned red.

"You go to hell," he said, slamming the door.

"I'll meet you there!" Lena's shouting voice reached him dimly.

60   He was being a fool; there was no doubt about it. But, try as he might, he could not shake off a primitive hate for that black mountain of energy, of muscle, of bone; he envied the easy manner in which it moved with such a creeping and powerful motion; he winced at the booming and commanding voice that came to him when the tiny little eyes were not even looking at him; he shivered at the sight of those vast and clawlike hands that seemed always to hint of death . . .

Olaf kept his counsel. He never spoke to Karen about the sordid doings at the hotel. Such things were not for women like Karen. He knew instinctively that Karen would have been amazed had he told her that he was worried sick about a nigger and a blonde whore . . . No; he couldn't talk to anybody about it, not even the hard-bitten[3] old bitch who owned the hotel. She was concerned only about money; she didn't give a damn about how big and how black a client was as long as he paid his room rent.

Next evening, when Olaf arrived for duty, there was no sight or sound of the black giant. A little later after one o'clock in the morning he appeared, left his key, and went out wordlessly. A few moments past two the giant returned, took his key from the board, and paused.

"I want that Lena again tonight. And another bottle of whiskey," he said boomingly.

"I'll call her and see if she's in," Olaf said.

65   "Do that," the black giant said and was gone.

He thinks he's God, Olaf fumed. He picked up the phone and ordered Lena and a bottle of whiskey, and there was a taste of ashes in his mouth. On the third night came the same request: Lena and whiskey. When the black giant appeared on the fifth night, Olaf was about to make a sarcastic remark to the effect that maybe he ought to marry Lena, but he checked it in time . . . After all, he could kill me with one hand, he told himself.

---

[3] Stubborn, tough.

Olaf was nervous and angry with himself for being nervous. Other black sailors came and asked for girls and Olaf sent them, but with none of the fear and loathing that he sent Lena and a bottle of whiskey to the giant . . . All right, the black giant's stay was almost up. He'd said that he was staying for five or six nights; tomorrow night was the sixth night and that ought to be the end of this nameless terror.

On the sixth night Olaf sat in his swivel chair with his bottle of beer and waited, his teeth on edge, his fingers drumming the desk. But what the hell am I fretting for? . . . The hell with 'im . . . Olaf sat and dozed. Occasionally he'd awaken and listen to the foghorns of freighters sounding as ships came and went in the misty Copenhagen harbor. He was half asleep when he felt a rough hand on his shoulder. He blinked his eyes open. The giant, black and vast and powerful, all but blotted out his vision.

"What I owe you, man?" the giant demanded. "And I want my money."

70   "Sure," Olaf said, relieved, but filled as always with fear of this living wall of black flesh.

With fumbling hands, he made out the bill and received payment, then gave the giant his roll of money, laying it on the desk so as not to let his hands touch the flesh of the black mountain. Well, his ordeal was over. It was past two o'clock in the morning. Olaf even managed a wry smile and muttered a guttural "Thanks" for the generous tip that the giant tossed him.

Then a strange tension entered the office. The office door was shut and Olaf was alone with the black mass of power, yearning for it to leave. But the black mass of power stood still, immobile, looking down at Olaf. And Olaf could not, for the life of him, guess at what was transpiring in that mysterious black mind. The two of them simply stared at each other for a full two minutes, the giant's tiny little beady eyes blinking slowly as they seemed to measure and search Olaf's face. Olaf's vision dimmed for a second as terror seized him and he could feel a flush of heat overspread his body. Then Olaf sucked in his breath as the devil of blackness commanded:

"Stand up!"

Olaf was paralyzed. Sweat broke on his face. His worst premonitions about this black beast were coming true. This evil blackness was about to attack him, maybe kill him . . . Slowly Olaf shook his head, his terror permitting him to breathe:

75   "What're you talking about?"

"Stand up, I say!" the black giant bellowed.

As though hypnotized, Olaf tried to rise; then he felt the black paw of the beast helping him roughly to his feet.

They stood an inch apart. Olaf's pasty-white features were glued to the giant's swollen black face. The ebony ensemble of eyes and nose and mouth and cheeks looked down at Olaf, silently; then, with a slow and deliberate movement of his gorillalike arms, he lifted his mammoth[4] hands

---

[4] Huge, enormous.

to Olaf's throat. Olaf had long known and felt that this dreadful moment was coming; he felt trapped in a nightmare. He could not move. He wanted to scream, but could find no words. His lips refused to open; his tongue felt icy and inert. Then he knew that his end had come when the giant's black fingers slowly, softly encircled his throat while a horrible grin of delight broke out on the sooty face . . . Olaf lost control of the reflexes of his body and he felt a hot stickiness flooding his underwear . . . He stared without breathing, gazing into the grinning blackness of the face that was bent over him, feeling the black fingers caressing his throat and waiting to feel the sharp, stinging ache and pain of the bones in his neck being snapped, crushed . . . He knew all along that I hated 'im . . . Yes, and now he's going to kill me for it, Olaf told himself with despair.

The black fingers still circled Olaf's neck, not closing, but gently massaging it, as it were, moving to and fro, while the obscene face grinned into his. Olaf could feel the giant's warm breath blowing on his eyelashes and he felt like a chicken about to have its neck wrung and its body tossed to flip and flap dyingly in the dust of the barnyard . . . Then suddenly the black giant withdrew his fingers from Olaf's neck and stepped back a pace, still grinning. Olaf sighed, trembling, his body seeming to shrink; he waited. Shame sheeted him for the hot wetness that was in his trousers. Oh, God, he's teasing me . . . He's showing me how easily he can kill me . . . He swallowed, waiting, his eyes stones of gray.

80   The giant's barrel-like chest gave forth a low, rumbling chuckle of delight.

"You laugh?" Olaf asked whimperingly.

"Sure I laugh," the giant shouted.

"Please don't hurt me," Olaf managed to say.

"I wouldn't hurt you, boy," the giant said in a tone of mockery. "So long."

85   And he was gone. Olaf fell limply into the swivel chair and fought off losing consciousness. Then he wept. He was showing me how easily he could kill me . . . He made me shake with terror and then laughed and left . . . Slowly, Olaf recovered, stood, then gave vent to a string of curses:

"Goddamn 'im! My gun's right there in the desk drawer; I should of shot 'im. Jesus, I hope the ship he's on sinks . . . I hope he drowns and the sharks eat 'im . . ."

Later, he thought of going to the police, but sheer shame kept him back; and, anyway, the giant was probably on board his ship by now. And he had to get home and clean himself. Oh, Lord, what could he tell Karen? Yes, he would say that his stomach had been upset . . . He'd change clothes and return to work. He phoned the hotel owner that he was ill and wanted an hour off; the old bitch said that she was coming right over and that poor Olaf could have the evening off.

Olaf went home and lied to Karen. Then he lay awake the rest of the night dreaming of revenge. He saw that freighter on which the giant was sailing; he saw it springing a dangerous leak and saw a torrent of sea water flooding, gushing into all the compartments of the ship until it found the bunk in which the black giant slept. Ah, yes, the foamy, surging waters would surprise that sleeping black bastard of a giant and he would drown, gasping and choking like a trapped rat, his tiny eyes bulging until they glittered red, the bitter water of the sea pounding his lungs until they ached and finally burst . . . The ship would sink slowly to the bottom of the cold, black, silent depths of the sea and a shark, a *white* one, would glide aimlessly about the shut portholes until it found an open one and it would slither inside and nose about until it found that swollen, rotting, stinking carcass of the black beast and it would then begin to nibble at the decomposing mass of tarlike flesh, eating the bones clean . . . Olaf always pictured the giant's bones as being jet black and shining.

Once or twice, during these fantasies of cannibalistic revenge, Olaf felt a little guilty about all the many innocent people, women and children, all white and blonde, who would have to go down into watery graves in order that that white shark could devour the evil giant's black flesh . . . But, despite feelings of remorse, the fantasy lived persistently on, and when Olaf found himself alone, it would crowd and cloud his mind to the exclusion of all else, affording him the only revenge he knew. To make me suffer just for the pleasure of it, he fumed. Just to show me how strong he was . . . Olaf learned how to hate, and got pleasure out of it.

90   Summer fled on wings of rain. Autumn flooded Denmark with color. Winter made rain and snow fall on Copenhagen. Finally spring came, bringing violets and roses. Olaf kept to his job. For many months he feared the return of the black giant. But when a year had passed and the giant had not put in an appearance, Olaf allowed his revenge fantasy to peter out, indulging in it only when recalling the shame that the black monster had made him feel.

Then one rainy August night, a year later, Olaf sat drowsing at his desk, his bottle of beer before him, tilting back in his swivel chair, his feet resting atop a corner of his desk, his mind mulling over the more pleasant aspects of his life. The office door cracked open. Olaf glanced boredly up and around. His heart jumped and skipped a beat. The black nightmare of terror and shame that he had hoped that he had lost forever was again upon him . . . Resplendently dressed, suitcase in hand, the black looming mountain filled the doorway. Olaf's thin lips parted and a silent moan, half a curse, escaped them.

"Hi," the black giant boomed from the doorway.

Olaf could not reply. But a sudden resolve swept him: this time he would even the score. If this black beast came within so much as three feet of him, he would snatch his gun out of the drawer and shoot him dead, so help him God . . .

"No rooms tonight," Olaf heard himself announcing in a determined voice.

95   The black giant grinned; it was the same infernal grimace of delight and triumph that he had had when his damnable black fingers had been around his throat . . .

"Don't want no room tonight," the giant announced.

"Then what are you doing here?" Olaf asked in a loud but tremulous voice.

The giant swept toward Olaf and stood over him; and Olaf could not move, despite his oath to kill him . . .

"What do you want then?" Olaf demanded once more, ashamed that he could not lift his voice above a whisper.

100   The giant still grinned, then tossed what seemed the same suitcase upon Olaf's sofa and bent over it; he zippered it open with a sweep of his clawlike hand and rummaged in it, drawing forth a flat, gleaming white object done up in glowing cellophane. Olaf watched with lowered lids, wondering what trick was now being played on him. Then, before he could defend himself, the giant had whirled and again long, black, snakelike fingers were encircling Olaf's throat . . . Olaf stiffened, his right hand clawing blindly for the drawer where the gun was kept. But the giant was quick.

"Wait," he bellowed, pushing Olaf back from the desk.

The giant turned quickly to the sofa and, still holding his fingers in a wide circle that seemed a noose for Olaf's neck, he inserted the rounded fingers into the top of the flat, gleaming object. Olaf had the drawer open and his sweaty fingers were now touching the gun, but something made him freeze. The flat, gleaming object was a shirt and the black giant's circled fingers were fitting themselves into its neck . . .

"A perfect fit!" the giant shouted.

Olaf stared, trying to understand. His fingers loosened about the gun. A mixture of a laugh and a curse struggled in him. He watched the giant plunge his hands into the suitcase and pull out other flat, gleaming shirts.

105   "One, two, three, four, five, six," the black giant intoned, his voice crisp and businesslike. "Six nylon shirts. And they're all yours. One shirt for each time Lena came . . . See, Daddy-O?"

The black, cupped hands, filled with billowing nylon whiteness, were extended under Olaf's nose. Olaf eased his damp fingers from his gun and pushed the drawer closed, staring at the shirts and then at the black giant's grinning face.

"Don't you like 'em?" the giant asked.

Olaf began to laugh hysterically, then suddenly he was crying, his eyes so flooded with tears that the pile of dazzling nylon looked like snow in the dead of winter. Was this true? Could he believe it? Maybe this too was a trick? But, no. There were six shirts, all nylon, and the black giant had had Lena six nights.

"What's the matter with you, Daddy-O?" the giant asked. "You blowing your top? Laughing and crying . . ."

110   Olaf swallowed, dabbed his withered fists at his dimmed eyes; then he realized that he had his glasses on. He took them off and dried his eyes and sat up. He sighed, the tension and shame and fear and haunting dread of his fantasy went from him, and he leaned limply back in his chair . . .

"Try one on," the giant ordered.

Olaf fumbled with the buttons of his shirt, let down his suspenders, and pulled the shirt off. He donned a gleaming nylon one and the giant began buttoning it for him.

"Perfect, Daddy-O," the giant said.

His spectacled face framed in sparkling nylon, Olaf sat with trembling lips. So he'd not been trying to kill me after all.

115 "You want Lena, don't you?" he asked the giant in a soft whisper. "But I don't know where she is. She never came back here after you left—"

"I know where Lena is," the giant told him. "We been writing to each other. I'm going to her house. And, Daddy-O, I'm late." The giant zippered the suitcase shut and stood a moment gazing down at Olaf, his tiny little red eyes blinking slowly. Then Olaf realized that there was a compassion in that stare that he had never seen before.

"And I thought you wanted to kill me," Olaf told him. "I was scared of you . . ."

"Me? Kill you?" the giant blinked. "When?"

"That night when you put your fingers around my throat—"

120 "What?" the giant asked, then roared with laughter. "Daddy-O, you're a funny little man. I wouldn't hurt you. I like you. You a *good* man. You helped me."

Olaf smiled, clutching the pile of nylon shirts in his arms.

"You're a good man too," Olaf murmured. Then loudly, "You're a big black good man."

"Daddy-O, you're crazy," the giant said.

He swept his suitcase from the sofa, spun on his heel, and was at the door in one stride.

125 "Thanks!" Olaf cried after him.

The black giant paused, turned his vast black head, and flashed a grin.

"Daddy-O, drop dead," he said and was gone.

READING AND REACTING

1. Why do you suppose Wright has his third-person narrator see events through Olaf's eyes? How would the story be different if the black man told it?

2. Why do you think the story, which takes place in 1957, is set in Copenhagen? Could it have been set in the United States in 1957?

3. Why does Olaf dislike the sailor? What does Olaf mean in paragraph 23 when he says that the sailor's "intense blackness and ungainly bigness . . . frightened and insulted" him?

4. In what ways do the sailor's words and actions contribute to Olaf's fears? Do you think Olaf's reactions are reasonable, or do you believe he is overreacting?

5. How are Lena's reactions to the sailor different from Olaf's? How do you account for the differences in their responses?

6. Do you think the story's title is ironic? How many different kinds of irony can you find in the story? In other words, can you identify examples of dramatic, verbal, and situational irony?

7. Is it important for readers to know that Richard Wright is African-American? Would your response to the story be different if you believed "Big Black Good Man" to be written by a white author?

8. List the figures of speech Wright uses to characterize the sailor. What connotations do they have? Do they encourage readers to identify with the sailor or with Olaf? Explain.

9. **JOURNAL ENTRY** What do you think the black man thinks of Olaf? Do you suppose he realizes the effect he has on him? How do you explain his last comment?

10. **CRITICAL PERSPECTIVE** In his 1982 article "The Short Stories: *Uncle Tom's Children, Eight Men*," Edward Margolies notes that "Big Black Good Man" was somewhat of a departure for Wright:

> "Big Black Good Man," which first appeared in Esquire in 1957, is the last short story Wright published in his lifetime. Possibly it is the last he ever wrote. In any event it represents a more traditional approach to storytelling in that Wright here avoids confining himself exclusively to dialogue. On the other hand, "Big Black Good Man" deviates from the usual Wright short story. For one thing, the narrative, by Wright's standards at least, is practically pointless. Scarcely anything "happens." There is no violence, practically no external narrative action, and no change of milieu.

How would the addition of some or all of these missing elements change the story?

EDGAR ALLAN POE (1809–1849) profoundly influenced many corners of the literary world. His tales of psychological terror and the macabre, his hauntingly musical lyric poems, and his writings on the craft of poetry and short-story writing affected the development of symbolic fiction, the modern detective story, and the Gothic horror tale. In most of Poe's horror tales (as in "The Cask of Amontillado"), readers vicariously "live" the story through the first-person narrator who tells the tale.

Poe was born in 1809, the son of a talented English-born actress who, deserted by her actor husband, died of tuberculosis before her son's third birthday. Though raised in material comfort by foster parents in Richmond, Virginia, Poe's life was increasingly uncertain: His foster mother loved him, but her husband became antagonistic. He kept the young Poe so short of money at the University of Virginia (and later at West Point) that Poe resorted to gambling to raise money for food and clothing. Finally, debt-ridden, he left school altogether.

Poe found work as a magazine editor, gaining recognition as a perceptive (if sometimes vitriolic) literary critic. In 1836, he married his frail thirteen-year-old cousin, Virginia Clemm. Poe produced many of his most famous stories and poems in the next few years, working feverishly to support his tubercular wife; but although his stories were widely admired, financial success never came. His wife died in 1847. Less than two years later, Poe was found barely conscious in a Baltimore street after a mysterious disappearance; three days later, he was dead at age forty.

EDGAR ALLAN POE

The Cask of Amontillado

(1846)

The thousand injuries of Fortunato I had borne as I best could, but when he ventured upon insult I vowed revenge. You, who so well know the nature of my soul, will not suppose, however, that I gave utterance to a threat. *At length* I would be avenged; this was a point definitely settled— but the very definitiveness with which it was resolved precluded the idea of risk. I must not only punish but punish with impunity. A wrong is unredressed when retribution overtakes its redresser. It is equally unredressed when the avenger fails to make himself felt as such to him who has done the wrong.

It must be understood that neither by word nor deed had I given Fortunato cause to doubt my good will. I continued, as was my wont, to smile in his face, and he did not perceive that my smile *now* was at the thought of his immolation.

He had a weak point—this Fortunato—although in other regards he was a man to be respected and even feared. He prided himself on his connoisseurship in wine. Few Italians have the true virtuoso spirit. For the most part their enthusiasm is adopted to suit the time and opportunity, to practise imposture upon the British and Austrian *millionaires*. In painting and gemmary, Fortunato, like his countrymen, was a quack, but in the matter of old wines he was sincere. In this respect I did not differ from him materially;—I was skillful in the Italian vintages myself, and bought largely whenever I could.

It was about dusk, one evening during the supreme madness of the carnival season, that I encountered my friend. He accosted me with excessive warmth, for he had been drinking much. The man wore motley.[1] He had on a tight-fitting parti-striped dress, and his head was surmounted by the conical cap and bells. I was so pleased to see him that I thought I should never have done wringing his hand.

---

[1] The many-colored attire of a court jester.

5   I said to him—"My dear Fortunato, you are luckily met. How remarkably well you are looking to-day. But I have received a pipe[2] of what passes
for Amontillado,[3] and I have my doubts."

"How?" said he. "Amontillado? A pipe? Impossible! And in the middle
of the carnival!"

"I have my doubts," I replied; "and I was silly enough to pay the full
Amontillado price without consulting you in the matter. You were not to
be found, and I was fearful of losing a bargain."

"Amontillado!"

"I have my doubts."

10   "Amontillado!"

"And I must satisfy them."

"Amontillado!"

"As you are engaged, I am on my way to Luchresi. If any one has a critical turn it is he. He will tell me—"

"Luchresi cannot tell Amontillado from Sherry."

15   "And yet some fools will have it that his taste is a match for your
own."

"Come, let us go."

"Whither?"

"To your vaults."

"My friend, no; I will not impose upon your good nature. I perceive
you have an engagement. Luchresi—"

20   "I have no engagement;—come."

"My friend, no. It is not the engagement, but the severe cold with
which I perceive you are afflicted. The vaults are insufferably damp. They
are encrusted with nitre."[4]

"Let us go, nevertheless. The cold is merely nothing. Amontillado! You
have been imposed upon. And as for Luchresi, he cannot distinguish
Sherry from Amontillado."

Thus speaking, Fortunato possessed himself of my arm; and putting
on a mask of black silk and drawing a *roquelaire*[5] closely about my person,
I suffered him to hurry me to my palazzo.

There were no attendants at home; they had absconded to make merry
in honor of the time. I had told them that I should not return until the
morning, and had given them explicit orders not to stir from the house.
These orders were sufficient, I well knew, to insure their immediate disappearance, one and all, as soon as my back was turned.

---

[2] In the United States and England, a cask containing a volume equal to 126 gallons.

[3] A pale, dry sherry; literally, a wine "from Montilla" (Spain).

[4] Mineral deposits.

[5] A short cloak.

25   I took from their sconces two flambeaux, and giving one to Fortunato, bowed him through several suites of rooms to the archway that led into the vaults. I passed down a long and winding staircase, requesting him to be cautious as he followed. We came at length to the foot of the descent, and stood together upon the damp ground of the catacombs of the Montresors.

The gait of my friend was unsteady, and the bells upon his cap jingled as he strode.

"The pipe," he said.

"It is farther on," said I; "but observe the white web-work which gleams from these cavern walls."

He turned towards me, and looked into my eyes with two filmy orbs that distilled the rheum of intoxication.

30   "Nitre?" he asked at length.

"Nitre," I replied. "How long have you had that cough?"

"Ugh! ugh! ugh!—ugh! ugh! ugh!—ugh! ugh! ugh!—ugh! ugh! ugh!— ugh! ugh! ugh!"

My poor friend found it impossible to reply for many minutes.

"It is nothing," he said at last.

35   "Come," I said, with decision, "we will go back; your health is precious. You are rich, respected, admired, beloved; you are happy, as once I was. You are a man to be missed. For me it is no matter. We will go back; you will be ill, and I cannot be responsible. Besides, there is Luchresi—"

"Enough," he said; "the cough is a mere nothing; it will not kill me. I shall not die of a cough."

"True—true," I replied; "and, indeed, I had no intention of alarming you unnecessarily—but you should use all proper caution. A draught of this Médoc[6] will defend us from the damps."

Here I knocked off the neck of a bottle which I drew from a long row of its fellows that lay upon the mould.

"Drink," I said, presenting him the wine.

40   He raised it to his lips with a leer. He paused and nodded to me familiarly, while his bells jingled.

"I drink," he said, "to the buried that repose around us."

"And I to your long life."

He again took my arm, and we proceeded.

"These vaults," he said, "are extensive."

45   "The Montresors," I replied, "were a great and numerous family."

"I forget your arms."

"A huge human foot d'or, in a field azure; the foot crushes a serpent rampant whose fangs are imbedded in the heel."

"And the motto?"

"*Nemo me impune lacessit.*"[7]

---

6   A claret from the Médoc, near Bordeaux, France.

7   "No one insults me with impunity"; this is the legend of the royal arms of Scotland.

50   "Good!" he said.

The wine sparkled in his eyes and the bells jingled. My own fancy grew warm with the Médoc. We had passed through long walls of piled skeletons, with casks and puncheons[8] intermingling, into the inmost recesses of the catacombs. I paused again, and this time I made bold to seize Fortunato by an arm above the elbow.

"The nitre!" I said; "see, it increases. It hangs like moss upon the vaults. We are below the river's bed. The drops of moisture trickle among the bones. Come, we will go back ere it is too late. Your cough—"

"It is nothing," he said; "let us go on. But first, another draught of the Médoc."

I broke and reached him a flagon of De Grâve.[9] He emptied it at a breath. His eyes flashed with a fierce light. He laughed and threw the bottle upwards with a gesticulation I did not understand.

55   I looked at him in surprise. He repeated the movement—a grotesque one.

"You do not comprehend?" he said.

"Not I," I replied.

"Then you are not of the brotherhood."

"How?"

60   "You are not of the masons."[10]

"Yes, yes," I said; "yes, yes."

"You? Impossible! A mason?"

"A mason," I replied.

"A sign," he said, "a sign."

65   "It is this," I answered, producing from beneath the folds of my *roquelaire* a trowel.

"You jest," he exclaimed, recoiling a few paces. "But let us proceed to the Amontillado."

"Be it so," I said, replacing the tool beneath the cloak and again offering him my arm. He leaned upon it heavily. We continued our route in search of the Amontillado. We passed through a range of low arches, descended, passed on, and descending again, arrived at a deep crypt, in which the foulness of the air caused our flambeaux rather to glow than flame.

At the most remote end of the crypt there appeared another less spacious. Its walls had been lined with human remains, piled to the vault overhead, in the fashion of the great catacombs of Paris. Three sides of this interior crypt were still ornamented in this manner. From the fourth side the bones had been thrown down, and lay promiscuously upon the earth,

---

8   Barrel.

9   Correctly, "Gráves," a light wine from the Bordeaux area.

10   Freemasons (members of a secret fraternity). The trowel is a symbol of their alleged origin as a guild of stonemasons.

forming at one point a mound of some size. Within the wall thus exposed by the displacing of the bones, we perceived a still interior crypt or recess, in depth about four feet, in width three, in height six or seven. It seemed to have been constructed for no especial use within itself, but formed merely the interval between two of the colossal supports of the roof of the catacombs, and was backed by one of their circumscribing walls of solid granite.

It was in vain that Fortunato, uplifting his dull torch, endeavored to pry into the depth of the recess. Its termination the feeble light did not enable us to see.

70 "Proceed," I said; "herein is the Amontillado. As for Luchresi—"

"He is an ignoramus," interrupted my friend, as he stepped unsteadily forward, while I followed immediately at his heels. In an instant he had reached the extremity of the niche, and finding his progress arrested by the rock, stood stupidly bewildered. A moment more and I had fettered him to the granite. In its surface were two iron staples, distant from each other about two feet, horizontally. From one of these depended a short chain, from the other a padlock. Throwing the links about his waist, it was but the work of a few seconds to secure it. He was too much astounded to resist. Withdrawing the key I stepped back from the recess.

"Pass your hand," I said, "over the wall; you cannot help feeling the nitre. Indeed, it is *very* damp. Once more let me *implore* you to return. No? Then I must positively leave you. But I must first render you all the little attentions in my power."

"The Amontillado!" ejaculated my friend, not yet recovered from his astonishment.

"True," I replied; "the Amontillado."

75 As I said these words I busied myself among the pile of bones of which I have before spoken. Throwing them aside, I soon uncovered a quantity of building stone and mortar. With these materials and with the aid of my trowel, I began vigorously to wall up the entrance of the niche.

I had scarcely laid the first tier of the masonry when I discovered that the intoxication of Fortunato had in a great measure worn off. The earliest indication I had of this was a low moaning cry from the depth of the recess. It was *not* the cry of a drunken man. There was a long and obstinate silence. I laid the second tier, and the third, and the fourth; and then I heard the furious vibrations of the chain. The noise lasted for several minutes, during which, that I might hearken to it with the more satisfaction, I ceased my labors and sat down upon the bones. When at last the clanking subsided, I resumed the trowel, and finished without interruption the fifth, the sixth, and the seventh tier. The wall was now nearly upon a level with my breast. I again paused, and holding the flambeaux over the mason-work, threw a few feeble rays upon the figure within.

A succession of loud and shrill screams, bursting suddenly from the throat of the chained form, seemed to thrust me violently back. For a brief moment I hesitated, I trembled. Unsheathing my rapier, I began to grope with it about the recess; but the thought of an instant reassured me. I placed my hand upon the solid fabric of the catacombs, and felt satisfied. I reapproached the wall; I replied to the yells of him who clamoured. I re-echoed, I aided, I surpassed them in volume and in strength. I did this, and the clamourer grew still.

It was now midnight, and my task was drawing to a close. I had completed the eighth, the ninth and the tenth tier. I had finished a portion of the last and the eleventh; there remained but a single stone to be fitted and plastered in. I struggled with its weight; I placed it partially in its destined position. But now there came from out the niche a low laugh that erected the hairs upon my head. It was succeeded by a sad voice, which I had difficulty in recognizing as that of the noble Fortunato. The voice said—

"Ha! ha! ha!—he! he! he!—a very good joke, indeed—an excellent jest. We will have many a rich laugh about it at the palazzo—he! he! he!—over our wine—he! he! he!"

80   "The Amontillado!" I said.

"He! he! he!—he! he! he!—yes, the Amontillado. But is it not getting late? Will not they be awaiting us at the palazzo, the Lady Fortunato and the rest? Let us be gone."

"Yes," I said, "let us be gone."

"For the love of God, Montresor!"

"Yes," I said, "for the love of God."

85   But to these words I hearkened in vain for a reply. I grew impatient. I called aloud—

"Fortunato!"

No answer. I called again—

"Fortunato!"

No answer still. I thrust a torch through the remaining aperture and let it fall within. There came forth in return only a jingling of the bells. My heart grew sick; it was the dampness of the catacombs that made it so. I hastened to make an end of my labour. I forced the last stone into its position; I plastered it up. Against the new masonry I re-erected the old rampart of bones. For the half of a century no mortal has disturbed them. *In pace requiescat!*[11]

READING AND REACTING

1. Montresor cites a "thousand injuries" and an "insult" as his motivation for murdering Fortunato. Given what you learn about the two men during the course of the story, what do you suppose the "injuries" and "insult" might be?

2. Do you find Montresor to be a reliable narrator? If not, what makes you distrust his version of events?

---

[11] "May he rest in peace."

3. What is Montresor's concept of personal honor? Is it consistent or inconsistent with the values of contemporary American society? How relevant are the story's ideas about revenge and guilt to present-day society? Explain.

4. Does Fortunato ever understand why Montresor hates him? What is Fortunato's attitude toward Montresor?

5. What is the significance of Montresor's family coat of arms and motto? What is the significance of Fortunato's costume?

6. In what ways does Montresor manipulate Fortunato? What weaknesses of Fortunato does Montresor exploit?

7. Why does Montresor wait fifty years to tell his story? How would the story be different if he had told it the next morning?

8. Why does Montresor wait for a reply before he puts the last stone in position? What do you think he wants Fortunato to say?

9. **JOURNAL ENTRY**   Do you think the use of a first-person point of view makes you more sympathetic toward Montresor than you would be if his story were told by a third-person narrator? Why or why not?

10. **CRITICAL PERSPECTIVE**   In his discussion of this story in *Edgar Allan Poe: A Study of the Short Fiction*, Charles E. May says that a reader's primary concern should not be Montresor's reason for killing Fortunato, but his reason for telling about it.

    If we go back to the first paragraph and ask who would know the nature of Montresor's soul, we cannot say it is the reader, for at that point in the story the reader knows nothing about Montresor's soul. We can legitimately hypothesize that the listener is a priest and that Montresor is an old man who is dying and making final confession. . . . One final irony, however, is that even if our hypothesis that Montresor tells the story as a final confession to cleanse his soul before death is correct, the tone and manner of his telling makes it clear that he has not atoned, for he enjoys himself in the telling too much—as much, in fact, as he did when he committed the crime itself. Thus, Montresor's plot to murder Fortunato so delights him by its perfection that in the very telling of it he undercuts its nature as repentant confession and condemns himself in gleeful boast.

    Explain why you agree or disagree with May's interpretation of the story. Does Montresor seem to "[enjoy] . . . the telling too much," or do you think he has atoned for his sin?

WILLIAM FAULKNER (1897–1962)   (pictured and biography on p. 79)
"Barn Burning" (1939) marks the first appearance of the Snopes clan in Faulkner's fiction. These crafty and unappealing tenant farmers and traders run roughshod over the aristocratic families of Yoknapatawpha County in three Faulkner novels: *The Hamlet* (1940), *The Town* (1957), and

The Mansion (1959). According to Ben Wasson in *Count No 'Count*, Faulkner once told a friend that "somebody said I was a genius writer. The only thing I'd claim genius for is thinking up that name *Snopes*." In Southern literary circles, at least, the name "Snopes" still serves as a shorthand term for the graceless and greedy (but frequently successful) opportunists of the "New South."

W I L L I A M   F A U L K N E R

Barn Burning

(1939)

The store in which the Justice of the Peace's court was sitting smelled of cheese. The boy, crouched on his nail keg at the back of the crowded room, knew he smelled cheese, and more: from where he sat he could see the ranked shelves close-packed with the solid, squat, dynamic shapes of tin cans whose labels his stomach read, not from the lettering which meant nothing to his mind but from the scarlet devils and the silver curve of fish—this, the cheese which he knew he smelled and the hermetic meat[1] which his intestines believed he smelled coming in intermittent gusts momentary and brief between the other constant one, the smell and sense just a little of fear because mostly of despair and grief, the old fierce pull of blood. He could not see the table where the Justice sat and before which his father and his father's enemy (*our enemy* he thought in that despair; *ourn! mine and hisn both! He's my father!*) stood, but he could hear them, the two of them that is, because his father had said no word yet:

"But what proof have you, Mr. Harris?"

"I told you. The hog got into my corn. I caught it up and sent it back to him. He had no fence that would hold it. I told him so, warned him. The next time I put the hog in my pen. When he came to get it I gave him enough wire to patch up his pen. The next time I put the hog up and kept it. I rode down to his house and saw the wire I gave him still rolled on to the spool in his yard. I told him he could have the hog when he paid me a dollar pound fee. That evening a nigger came with the dollar and got the hog. He was a strange nigger. He said, 'He say to tell you wood and hay kin burn.' I said, 'What?' 'That whut he say to tell you,' the nigger said. 'Wood and hay kin burn.' That night my barn burned. I got the stock out but I lost the barn."

"Where is the nigger? Have you got him?"

5   "He was a strange nigger, I tell you. I don't know what became of him."

---

[1] Canned meat.

"But that's not proof. Don't you see that's not proof?"

"Get that boy up here. He knows." For a moment the boy thought too that the man meant his older brother until Harris said, "Not him. The little one. The boy," and, crouching, small for his age, small and wiry like his father, in patched and faded jeans even too small for him, with straight, uncombed, brown hair and eyes gray and wild as storm scud, he saw the men between himself and the table part and become a lane of grim faces, at the end of which he saw the Justice, a shabby, collarless, graying man in spectacles, beckoning him. He felt no floor under his bare feet; he seemed to walk beneath the palpable weight of the grim turning faces. His father, stiff in his black Sunday coat donned not for the trial but for the moving, did not even look at him. *He aims for me to lie,* he thought, again with that frantic grief and despair. *And I will have to do hit.*

"What's your name, boy?" the Justice said.

"Colonel Sartoris Snopes," the boy whispered.

10   "Hey?" the Justice said. "Talk louder. Colonel Sartoris? I reckon anybody named for Colonel Sartoris in this country can't help but tell the truth, can they?" The boy said nothing. *Enemy! Enemy!* he thought; for a moment he could not even see, could not see that the Justice's face was kindly nor discern that his voice was troubled when he spoke to the man named Harris: "Do you want me to question this boy?" But he could hear, and during those subsequent long seconds while there was absolutely no sound in the crowded little room save that of quiet and intent breathing it was as if he had swung outward at the end of a grape vine, over a ravine, and at the top of the swing had been caught in a prolonged instant of mesmerized gravity, weightless in time.

"No!" Harris said violently, explosively. "Damnation! Send him out of here!" Now time, the fluid world, rushed beneath him again, the voices coming to him again through the smell of cheese and sealed meat, the fear and despair and the old grief of blood:

"This case is closed. I can't find against you, Snopes, but I can give you advice. Leave this country and don't come back to it."

His father spoke for the first time, his voice cold and harsh, level, without emphasis: "I aim to. I don't figure to stay in a country among people who . . ." he said something unprintable and vile, addressed to no one.

"That'll do," the Justice said. "Take your wagon and get out of this country before dark. Case dismissed."

15   His father turned, and he followed the stiff black coat, the wiry figure walking a little stiffly from where a Confederate provost's man's[2] musket ball had taken him in the heel on a stolen horse thirty years ago, followed the two backs now, since his older brother had appeared from somewhere in the crowd, no taller than the father but thicker, chewing tobacco

---

[2] Military policeman.

steadily, between the two lines of grim-faced men and out of the store and across the worn gallery and down the sagging steps and among the dogs and half-grown boys in the mild May dust, where as he passed a voice hissed:

"Barn burner!"

Again he could not see, whirling; there was a face in a red haze, moon-like, bigger than the full moon, the owner of it half again his size, he leaping in the red haze toward the face, feeling no blow, feeling no shock when his head struck the earth, scrabbling up and leaping again, feeling no blow this time either and tasting no blood, scrabbling up to see the other boy in full flight and himself already leaping into pursuit as his father's hand jerked him back, the harsh, cold voice speaking above him: "Go get in the wagon."

It stood in a grove of locusts and mulberries across the road. His two hulking sisters in their Sunday dresses and his mother and her sister in calico and sunbonnets were already in it, sitting on and among the sorry residue of the dozen and more movings which even the boy could remember—the battered stove, the broken beds and chairs, the clock inlaid with mother-of-pearl, which would not run, stopped at some fourteen minutes past two o'clock of a dead and forgotten day and time, which had been his mother's dowry. She was crying, though when she saw him she drew her sleeve across her face and began to descend from the wagon. "Get back," the father said.

"He's hurt. I got to get some water and wash his . . ."

20   "Get back in the wagon," his father said. He got in too, over the tail-gate. His father mounted to the seat where the older brother already sat and struck the gaunt mules two savage blows with the peeled willow, but without heat. It was not even sadistic; it was exactly that same quality which in later years would cause his descendants to overrun the engine before putting a motor car into motion, striking and reining back in the same movement. The wagon went on, the store with its quiet crowd of grimly watching men dropped behind; a curve in the road hid it. *Forever* he thought. *Maybe he's done satisfied now, now that he has . . .* stopping himself, not to say it aloud even to himself. His mother's hand touched his shoulder.

"Does hit hurt?" she said.

"Naw," he said. "Hit don't hurt. Lemme be."

"Can't you wipe some of the blood off before hit dries?"

"I'll wash to-night," he said. "Lemme be, I tell you."

25   The wagon went on. He did not know where they were going. None of them ever did or ever asked, because it was always somewhere, always a house of sorts waiting for them a day or two days or even three days away. Likely his father had already arranged to make a crop on another farm before he . . . Again he had to stop himself. He (the father) always did. There was something about his wolf-like independence and even courage when the advantage was at least neutral which impressed strangers, as if they got

from his latent ravening ferocity not so much a sense of dependability as a feeling that his ferocious conviction in the rightness of his own actions would be of advantage to all whose interest lay with his.

That night they camped, in a grove of oaks and beeches where a spring ran. The nights were still cool and they had a fire against it, of a rail lifted from a nearby fence and cut into lengths—a small fire, neat, niggard almost, a shrewd fire; such fires were his father's habit and custom always, even in freezing weather. Older, the boy might have remarked this and wondered why not a big one; why should not a man who had not only seen the waste and extravagance of war, but who had in his blood an inherent voracious prodigality with material not his own, have burned everything in sight? Then he might have gone a step farther and thought that that was the reason: that niggard blaze was the living fruit of nights passed during those four years in the woods hiding from all men, blue or gray, with his strings of horses (captured horses, he called them). And older still, he might have divined the true reason: that the element of fire spoke to some deep mainspring of his father's being, as the element of steel or of powder spoke to other men, as the one weapon for the preservation of integrity, else breath were not worth the breathing, and hence to be regarded with respect and used with discretion.

But he did not think this now and he had seen those same niggard blazes all his life. He merely ate his supper beside it and was already half asleep over his iron plate when his father called him, and once more he followed the stiff back, the stiff and ruthless limp, up the slope and on to the starlit road where, turning, he could see his father against the stars but without face or depth—a shape black, flat, and bloodless as though cut from tin in the iron folds of the frockcoat which had not been made for him, the voice harsh like tin and without heat like tin:

"You were fixing to tell them. You would have told him." He didn't answer. His father struck him with the flat of his hand on the side of the head, hard but without heat, exactly as he had struck the two mules at the store, exactly as he would strike either of them with any stick in order to kill a horse fly, his voice still without fear or anger: "You're getting to be a man. You got to learn. You got to learn to stick to your own blood or you ain't going to have any blood to stick to you. Do you think either of them, any man there this morning, would? Don't you know all they wanted was a chance to get at me because they knew I had them beat? Eh?" Later, twenty years later, he was to tell himself, "If I had said they wanted only truth, justice, he would have hit me again." But now he said nothing. He was not crying. He just stood there. "Answer me," his father said.

"Yes," he whispered. His father turned.

30   "Get on to bed. We'll be there tomorrow."

Tomorrow they were there. In the early afternoon the wagon stopped before a paintless two-room house identical almost with the dozen others it had stopped before even in the boy's ten years, and again, as on the other dozen occasions, his mother and aunt got down and began to unload the wagon, although his two sisters and his father and brother had not moved.

"Likely hit ain't fitten for hawgs," one of the sisters said.

"Nevertheless, fit it will and you'll hog it and like it," his father said. "Get out of them chairs and help your Ma unload."

The two sisters got down, big, bovine, in a flutter of cheap ribbons; one of them drew from the jumbled wagon bed a battered lantern, the other a worn broom. His father handed the reins to the older son and began to climb stiffly over the wheel. "When they get unloaded, take the team to the barn and feed them." Then he said, and at first the boy thought he was still speaking to his brother: "Come with me."

35   "Me?" he said.

"Yes," his father said. "You."

"Abner," his mother said. His father paused and looked back—the harsh level stare beneath the shaggy, graying, irascible brows.

"I reckon I'll have a word with the man that aims to begin tomorrow owning me body and soul for the next eight months."

They went back up the road. A week ago—or before last night, that is— he would have asked where they were going, but not now. His father had struck him before last night but never before had he paused afterward to explain why; it was as if the blow and the following calm, outrageous voice still rang, repercussed, divulging nothing to him save the terrible handicap of being young, the light weight of his few years, just heavy enough to prevent his soaring free of the world as it seemed to be ordered but not heavy enough to keep him footed solid in it, to resist it and try to change the course of its events.

40   Presently he could see the grove of oaks and cedars and the other flowering trees and shrubs, where the house would be, though not the house yet. They walked beside a fence massed with honeysuckle and Cherokee roses and came to a gate swinging open between two brick pillars, and now, beyond a sweep of drive, he saw the house for the first time and at that instant he forgot his father and the terror and despair both, and even when he remembered his father again (who had not stopped) the terror and despair did not return. Because, for all the twelve movings, they had sojourned until now in a poor country, a land of small farms and fields and houses, and he had never seen a house like this before. *Hit's big as a courthouse* he thought quietly, with a surge of peace and joy whose reason he could not have thought into words, being too young for that: *They are safe from him. People whose lives are a part of this peace and dignity are beyond his touch, he no more to them than a buzzing wasp: capable of stinging for a little moment but that's all; the spell of this peace and dignity rendering even the barns and stable and cribs which belong to it impervious to the puny flames he might contrive* . . . this, the peace and joy, ebbing for an instant as he looked again at the stiff black back, the stiff and implacable limp of the figure which was not dwarfed by the house, for the reason that it had never looked big anywhere and which now, against the serene columned

backdrop, had more than ever that impervious quality of something cut ruthlessly from tin, depthless, as though, sidewise to the sun, it would cast no shadow. Watching him, the boy remarked the absolutely undeviating course which his father held and saw the stiff foot come squarely down in a pile of fresh droppings where a horse had stood in the drive and which his father could have avoided by a simple change of stride. But it ebbed only for a moment, though he could not have thought this into words either, walking on in the spell of the house, which he could even want but without envy, without sorrow, certainly never with that ravening and jealous rage which unknown to him walked in the ironlike black coat before him: *Maybe he will feel it too. Maybe it will even change him now from what maybe he couldn't help but be.*

They crossed the portico. Now he could hear his father's stiff foot as it came down on the boards with clocklike finality, a sound out of all proportion to the displacement of the body it bore and which was not dwarfed either by the white door before it, as though it had attained to a sort of vicious and ravening minimum not to be dwarfed by anything— the flat, wide, black hat, the formal coat of broadcloth which had once been black but which had now that friction-glazed greenish cast of the bodies of old house flies, the lifted sleeve which was too large, the lifted hand like a curled claw. The door opened so promptly that the boy knew the Negro must have been watching them all the time, an old man with neat grizzled hair, in a linen jacket, who stood barring the door with his body, saying, "Wipe yo foots, white man, fo you come in here. Major ain't home nohow."

"Get out of my way, nigger," his father said, without heat too, flinging the door back and the Negro also and entering, his hat still on his head. And now the boy saw the prints of the stiff foot on the doorjamb and saw them appear on the pale rug behind the machinelike deliberation of the foot which seemed to bear (or transmit) twice the weight which the body compassed. The Negro was shouting "Miss Lula! Miss Lula!" somewhere behind them, then the boy, deluged as though by a warm wave by a suave turn of carpeted stair and a pendant glitter of chandeliers and a mute gleam of gold frames, heard the swift feet and saw her too, a lady—perhaps he had never seen her like before either—in a gray, smooth gown with lace at the throat and an apron tied at the waist and the sleeves turned back, wiping cake or biscuit dough from her hands with a towel as she came up the hall, looking not at his father at all but at the tracks on the blond rug with an expression of incredulous amazement.

"I tried," the Negro cried, "I tole him to . . ."

"Will you please go away?" she said in a shaking voice. "Major de Spain is not at home. Will you please go away?"

45   His father had not spoken again. He did not speak again. He did not even look at her. He just stood stiff in the center of the rug, in his hat, the shaggy iron-gray brows twitching slightly above the pebble-colored eyes as he appeared to examine the house with brief deliberation. Then with the

same deliberation he turned; the boy watched him pivot on the good leg and saw the stiff foot drag round the arc of the turning, leaving a final long and fading smear. His father never looked at it, he never once looked down at the rug. The Negro held the door. It closed behind them, upon the hysteric and indistinguishable woman-wail. His father stopped at the top of the steps and scraped his boot clean on the edge of it. At the gate he stopped again. He stood for a moment, planted stiffly on the stiff foot, looking back at the house. "Pretty and white, ain't it?" he said. "That's sweat. Nigger sweat. Maybe it ain't white enough yet to suit him. Maybe he wants to mix some white sweat with it."

Two hours later the boy was chopping wood behind the house within which his mother and aunt and the two sisters (the mother and aunt, not the two girls, he knew that; even at this distance and muffled by walls the flat loud voices of the two girls emanated an incorrigible idle inertia) were setting up the stove to prepare a meal, when he heard the hooves and saw the linen-clad man on a fine sorrel mare, whom he recognized even before he saw the rolled rug in front of the Negro youth following on a fat bay carriage horse—a suffused, angry face vanishing, still at full gallop, beyond the corner of the house where his father and brother were sitting in the two tilted chairs; and a moment later, almost before he could have put the axe down, he heard the hooves again and watched the sorrel mare go back out of the yard, already galloping again. Then his father began to shout one of the sisters' names, who presently emerged backward from the kitchen door dragging the rolled rug along the ground by one end while the other sister walked behind it.

"If you ain't going to tote, go on and set up the wash pot," the first said.

"You, Sarty!" the second shouted. "Set up the wash pot!" His father appeared at the door, framed against that shabbiness, as he had been against that other bland perfection, impervious to either, the mother's anxious face at his shoulder.

"Go on," the father said. "Pick it up." The two sisters stooped, broad, lethargic; stooping, they presented an incredible expanse of pale cloth and a flutter of tawdry ribbons.

50   "If I thought enough of a rug to have to git hit all the way from France I wouldn't keep hit where folks coming in would have to tromp on hit," the first said. They raised the rug.

"Abner," the mother said. "Let me do it."

"You go back and git dinner," his father said. "I'll tend to this."

From the woodpile through the rest of the afternoon the boy watched them, the rug spread flat in the dust beside the bubbling wash-pot, the two sisters stooping over it with that profound and lethargic reluctance, while the father stood over them in turn, implacable and grim, driving them though never raising his voice again. He could smell the harsh homemade lye[3]

---

[3] A soap made from wood ashes and water, unsuitable for washing fine fabrics.

they were using; he saw his mother come to the door once and look toward them with an expression not anxious now but very like despair; he saw his father turn, and he fell to with the axe and saw from the corner of his eye his father raise from the ground a flattish fragment of field stone and examine it and return to the pot, and this time his mother actually spoke: "Abner. Abner. Please don't. Please, Abner."

Then he was done too. It was dusk; the whippoorwills had already begun. He could smell coffee from the room where they would presently eat the cold food remaining from the mid-afternoon meal, though when he entered the house he realized they were having coffee again probably because there was a fire on the hearth, before which the rug now lay spread over the backs of the two chairs. The tracks of his father's foot were gone. Where they had been were now long, water-cloudy scoriations resembling the sporadic course of a Lilliputian mowing machine.

55   It still hung there while they ate the cold food and then went to bed, scattered without order or claim up and down the two rooms, his mother in one bed, where his father would later lie, the older brother in the other, himself, the aunt, and the two sisters on pallets on the floor. But his father was not in bed yet. The last thing the boy remembered was the depthless, harsh silhouette of the hat and coat bending over the rug and it seemed to him that he had not even closed his eyes when the silhouette was standing over him, the fire almost dead behind it, the stiff foot prodding him awake. "Catch up the mule," his father said.

When he returned with the mule his father was standing in the black door, the rolled rug over his shoulder. "Ain't you going to ride?" he said.

"No. Give me your foot."

He bent his knee into his father's hand, the wiry, surprising power flowed smoothly, rising, he rising with it, on to the mule's bare back (they had owned a saddle once; the boy could remember it though not when or where) and with the same effortlessness his father swung the rug up in front of him. Now in the starlight they retraced the afternoon's path, up the dusty road rife with honeysuckle, through the gate and up the black tunnel to the drive to the lightless house, where he sat on the mule and felt the rough warp of the rug drag across his thighs and vanish.

"Don't you want me to help?" he whispered. His father did not answer and now he heard again that stiff foot striking the hollow portico with that wooden and clocklike deliberation, that outrageous overstatement of the weight it carried. The rug, hunched, not flung (the boy could tell that even in the darkness) from his father's shoulder struck the angle of wall and floor with a sound unbelievably loud, thunderous, then the foot again, unhurried and enormous; a light came on in the house and the boy sat, tense, breathing steadily and quietly and just a little fast, though the foot itself did not increase its beat at all, descending the steps now; now the boy could see him.

60   "Don't you want to ride now?" he whispered. "We kin both ride now," the light within the house altering now, flaring up and sinking. *He's coming down the stairs now,* he thought. He had already ridden the mule up beside the horse block; presently his father was up behind him and he

doubled the reins over and slashed the mule across the neck, but before the animal could begin to trot the hard, thin arm came round him, the hard, knotted hand jerking the mule back to a walk.

In the first red rays of the sun they were in the lot, putting plow gear on the mules. This time the sorrel mare was in the lot before he heard it at all, the rider collarless and even bareheaded, trembling, speaking in a shaking voice as the woman in the house had done, his father merely looking up once before stooping again to the hame[4] he was buckling, so that the man on the mare spoke to his stooping back:

"You must realize you have ruined that rug. Wasn't there anybody here, any of your women . . ." he ceased, shaking, the boy watching him, the older brother leaning now in the stable door, chewing, blinking slowly and steadily at nothing apparently. "It cost a hundred dollars. But you never had a hundred dollars. You never will. So I'm going to charge you twenty bushels of corn against your crop. I'll add it in your contract and when you come to the commissary you can sign it. That won't keep Mrs. de Spain quiet but maybe it will teach you to wipe your feet off before you enter her house again."

Then he was gone. The boy looked at his father, who still had not spoken or even looked up again, who was now adjusting the loggerhead in the hame.

"Pap," he said. His father looked at him—the inscrutable face, the shaggy brows beneath which the gray eyes glinted coldly. Suddenly the boy went toward him, fast, stopping as suddenly. "You done the best you could!" he cried. "If he wanted hit done different why didn't he wait and tell you how? He won't git no twenty bushels! He won't git none! We'll gether hit and hide hit! I kin watch . . ."

65   "Did you put the cutter back in that straight stock like I told you?"

"No, sir," he said.

"Then go do it."

That was Wednesday. During the rest of that week he worked steadily, at what was within his scope and some which was beyond it, with an industry that did not need to be driven nor even commanded twice; he had this from his mother, with the difference that some at least of what he did he liked to do, such as splitting wood with the half-size axe which his mother and aunt had earned, or saved money somehow, to present him with at Christmas. In company with the two older women (and on one afternoon, even one of the sisters), he built pens for the shoat and the cow which were a part of his father's contract with the landlord, and one afternoon, his father being absent, gone somewhere on one of the mules, he went to the field.

They were running a middle buster now, his brother holding the plow straight while he handled the reins, and walking beside the straining

---

[4] Harness.

mule, the rich black soil shearing cool and damp against his bare ankles, he thought *Maybe this is the end of it. Maybe even that twenty bushels that seems hard to have to pay for just a rug will be a cheap price for him to stop forever and always from being what he used to be;* thinking, dreaming now, so that his brother had to speak sharply to him to mind the mule: *Maybe he even won't collect the twenty bushels. Maybe it will all add up and balance and vanish—corn, rug, fire; the terror and grief, the being pulled two ways like between two teams of horses—gone, done with for ever and ever.*

70   Then it was Saturday; he looked up from beneath the mule he was harnessing and saw his father in the black coat and hat. "Not that," his father said. "The wagon gear." And then, two hours later, sitting in the wagon bed behind his father and brother on the seat, the wagon accomplished a final curve, and he saw the weathered paintless store with its tattered tobacco- and patent-medicine posters and the tethered wagons and saddle animals below the gallery. He mounted the gnawed steps behind his father and brother, and there again was the lane of quiet, watching faces for the three of them to walk through. He saw the man in spectacles sitting at the plank table and he did not need to be told this was a Justice of the Peace; he sent one glare of fierce, exultant, partisan defiance at the man in collar and cravat now, whom he had seen but twice before in his life, and that on a galloping horse, who now wore on his face an expression not of rage but of amazed unbelief which the boy could not have known was at the incredible circumstance of being sued by one of his own tenants, and came and stood against his father and cried at the Justice: "He ain't done it! He ain't burnt . . ."

"Go back to the wagon," his father said.

"Burnt?" the Justice said. "Do I understand this rug was burned too?"

"Does anybody here claim it was?" his father said. "Go back to the wagon." But he did not, he merely retreated to the rear of the room, crowded as that other had been, but not to sit down this time, instead, to stand pressing among the motionless bodies, listening to the voices:

"And you claim twenty bushels of corn is too high for the damage you did to the rug?"

75   "He brought the rug to me and said he wanted the tracks washed out of it. I washed the tracks out and took the rug back to him."

"But you didn't carry the rug back to him in the same condition it was in before you made the tracks on it."

His father did not answer, and now for perhaps half a minute there was no sound at all save that of breathing, the faint, steady suspiration of complete and intent listening.

"You decline to answer that, Mr. Snopes?" Again his father did not answer. "I'm going to find against you, Mr. Snopes. I'm going to find that you were responsible for the injury to Major de Spain's rug and hold you liable for it. But twenty bushels of corn seems a little high for a man in your circumstances to have to pay. Major de Spain claims it cost a hundred dollars. October corn will be worth about fifty cents. I figure that if Major de Spain can stand a ninety-five dollar loss on something he paid cash for, you can stand a five-dollar loss you haven't earned yet. I hold you in damages to Major de Spain to the amount of ten bushels of corn over and above your contract with him, to be paid to him out of your crop at gathering time. Court adjourned."

It had taken no time hardly, the morning was but half begun. He thought they would return home and perhaps back to the field, since they were late, far behind all other farmers. But instead his father passed on behind the wagon, merely indicating with his hand for the older brother to follow with it, and crossed the road toward the blacksmith shop opposite, pressing on after his father, overtaking him, speaking, whispering up at the harsh, calm face beneath the weathered hat: "He won't git no ten bushels neither. He won't git one. We'll . . ." until his father glanced for an instant down at him, the face absolutely calm, the grizzled eyebrows tangled above the cold eyes, the voice almost pleasant, almost gentle:

80   "You think so? Well, we'll wait till October anyway."

The matter of the wagon—the setting of a spoke or two and the tightening of the tires—did not take long either, the business of the tires accomplished by driving the wagon into the spring branch behind the shop and letting it stand there, the mules nuzzling into the water from time to time, and the boy on the seat with the idle reins, looking up the slope and through the sooty tunnel of the shed where the slow hammer rang and where his father sat on an upended cypress bolt, easily, either talking or listening, still sitting there when the boy brought the dripping wagon up out of the branch and halted it before the door.

"Take them on to the shade and hitch," his father said. He did so and returned. His father and the smith and a third man squatting on his heels inside the door were talking, about crops and animals; the boy, squatting too in the ammoniac dust and hoof-parings and scales of rust, heard his father tell a long and unhurried story out of the time before the birth of the older brother even when he had been a professional horsetrader. And then his father came up beside him where he stood before a tattered last year's circus poster on the other side of the store, gazing rapt and quiet at the scarlet horses, the incredible poisings and convolutions of tulle and tights and the painted leers of comedians, and said, "It's time to eat."

But not at home. Squatting beside his brother against the front wall, he watched his father emerge from the store and produce from a paper sack a segment of cheese and divide it carefully and deliberately into three with his pocket knife and produce crackers from the same sack. They all three squatted on the gallery and ate, slowly, without talking; then in the store again, they drank from a tin dipper tepid water smelling of the cedar bucket and of living beech trees. And still they did not go home. It was a horse lot this time, a tall rail fence upon and along which men stood and sat and out of which one by one horses were led, to be walked and trotted and then cantered back and forth along the road while the slow swapping and buying went on and the sun began to slant westward, they—the three of them—watching and listening, the older brother with his muddy eyes and his steady, inevitable tobacco, the father commenting now and then on certain of the animals, to no one in particular.

It was after sundown when they reached home. They ate supper by lamplight, then, sitting on the doorstep, the boy watched the night fully accomplish, listening to the whippoorwills and the frogs, when he heard his mother's voice: "Abner! No! No! Oh, God. Oh, God. Abner!" and he rose, whirled, and saw the altered light through the door where a candle stub now burned in a bottle neck on the table and his father, still in the hat and coat, at once formal and burlesque as though dressed carefully for some shabby and ceremonial violence, emptying the reservoir of the lamp back into the five-gallon kerosene can from which it had been filled, while the mother tugged at his arm until he shifted the lamp to the other hand and flung her back, not savagely or viciously, just hard, into the wall, her hands flung out against the wall for balance, her mouth open and in her face the same quality of hopeless despair as had been in her voice. Then his father saw him standing in the door.

85 "Go to the barn and get that can of oil we were oiling the wagon with," he said. The boy did not move. Then he could speak.

"What . . ." he cried. "What are you . . ."

"Go get that oil," his father said. "Go."

Then he was moving, running, outside the house, toward the stable: this the old habit, the old blood which he had not been permitted to choose for himself, which had been bequeathed him willy nilly and which had run for so long (and who knew where, battening on what of outrage and savagery and lust) before it came to him. *I could keep on,* he thought. *I could run on and on and never look back, never need to see his face again. Only I can't. I can't,* the rusted can in his hand now, the liquid sploshing in it as he ran back to the house and into it, into the sound of his mother's weeping in the next room, and handed the can to his father.

"Ain't you going to even send a nigger?" he cried. "At least you sent a nigger before!"

90 This time his father didn't strike him. The hand came even faster than the blow had, the same hand which had set the can on the table with almost excruciating care flashing from the can toward him too quick for him to follow it, gripping him by the back of his shirt and on to tiptoe before he had seen it quit the can, the face stooping at him in breathless and frozen ferocity, the cold, dead voice speaking over him to the older brother who leaned against the table, chewing with that steady, curious, sidewise motion of cows:

"Empty the can into the big one and go on. I'll catch up with you."

"Better tie him to the bedpost," the brother said.

"Do like I told you," the father said. Then the boy was moving, his bunched shirt and the hard, bony hand between his shoulderblades, his toes just touching the floor, across the room and into the other one, past the sisters sitting with spread heavy thighs in the two chairs over the cold hearth, and to where his mother and aunt sat side by side on the bed, the aunt's arms about his mother's shoulders.

"Hold him," the father said. The aunt made a startled movement. "Not you," the father said. "Lennie. Take hold of him. I want to see you do it." His mother took him by the wrist. "You'll hold him better than that. If he gets loose don't you know what he is going to do? He will go up yonder." He jerked his head toward the road. "Maybe I'd better tie him."

95   "I'll hold him," his mother whispered.

"See you do then." Then his father was gone, the stiff foot heavy and measured upon the boards, ceasing at last.

Then he began to struggle. His mother caught him in both arms, he jerking and wrenching at them. He would be stronger in the end, he knew that. But he had no time to wait for it. "Lemme go!" he cried. "I don't want to have to hit you!"

"Let him go!" the aunt said. "If he don't go, before God, I am going up there myself!"

"Don't you see I can't?" his mother cried. "Sarty! Sarty! No! No! Help me, Lizzie!"

100   Then he was free. His aunt grasped at him but it was too late. He whirled, running, his mother stumbled forward on to her knees behind him, crying to the nearer sister: "Catch him, Net! Catch him!" But that was too late too, the sister (the sisters were twins, born at the same time, yet either of them now gave the impression of being, encompassing as much living meat and volume and weight as any other two of the family) not yet having begun to rise from the chair, her head, face, alone merely turned, presenting to him in the flying instant an astonishing expanse of young female features untroubled by any surprise even, wearing only an expression of bovine interest. Then he was out of the room, out of the house, in the mild dust of the starlit road and the heavy rifeness of honey-suckle, the pale ribbon unspooling with terrific slowness under his run-ning feet, reaching the gate at last and turning in, running, his heart and lungs drumming, on up the drive toward the lighted house, the lighted door. He did not knock, he burst in, sobbing for breath, incapable for the moment of speech; he saw the astonished face of the Negro in the linen jacket without knowing when the Negro had appeared.

"De Spain!" he cried, panted. "Where's . . ." then he saw the white man too emerging from a white door down the hall. "Barn!" he cried. "Barn!"

"What?" the white man said. "Barn?"

"Yes!" the boy cried. "Barn!"

"Catch him!" the white man shouted.

105   But it was too late this time too. The Negro grasped his shirt, but the entire sleeve, rotten with washing, carried away, and he was out that door too and in the drive again, and had actually never ceased to run even while he was screaming into the white man's face.

Behind him the white man was shouting, "My horse! Fetch my horse!" and he thought for an instant of cutting across the park and climbing the fence into the road, but he did not know the park nor how high the vine-massed fence might be and he dared not risk it. So he ran on down the drive, blood and breath roaring; presently he was in the road again though he could not see it. He could not hear either: the galloping mare was almost upon him before he heard her, and even then he held his course, as if the very urgency of his wild grief and need must in a moment more find him wings, waiting until the ultimate instant to hurl himself aside and into the weed-choked roadside ditch as the horse thundered past and on, for an instant in furious silhouette against the stars, the tranquil early summer night sky which, even before the shape of the horse and rider vanished, stained abruptly and violently upward: a long, swirling roar incredible and soundless, blotting the stars, and he springing up and into the road again, running again, knowing it was too late yet still running even after he heard the shot and, an instant later, two shots, pausing now without knowing he had ceased to run, crying "Pap! Pap!", running again before he knew he had begun to run, stumbling, tripping over something and scrabbling up again without ceasing to run, looking backward over his shoulder at the glare as he got up, running on among the invisible trees, panting, sobbing, "Father! Father!"

At midnight he was sitting on the crest of a hill. He did not know it was midnight and he did not know how far he had come. But there was no glare behind him now and he sat now, his back toward what he had called home for four days anyhow, his face toward the dark woods which he would enter when breath was strong again, small, shaking steadily in the chill darkness, hugging himself into the remainder of his thin, rotten shirt, the grief and despair now no longer terror and fear but just grief and despair. *Father. My father,* he thought. "He was brave!" he cried suddenly, aloud but not loud, no more than a whisper: "He was! He was in the war! He was in Colonel Sartoris' cav'ry!" not knowing that his father had gone to that war a private in the fine old European sense, wearing no uniform, admitting the authority of and giving fidelity to no man or army or flag, going to war as Malbrouck[5] himself did: for booty—it meant nothing and less than nothing to him if it were enemy booty or his own.

The slow constellations wheeled on. It would be dawn and then sunup after a while and he would be hungry. But that would be tomorrow and now he was only cold, and walking would cure that. His breathing was easier now and he decided to get up and go on, and then he found that he had been asleep because he knew it was almost dawn, the night almost over. He could tell that from the whippoorwills. They were everywhere now among the dark trees below him, constant and inflected and ceaseless,

---

[5] A character in a popular eighteenth-century nursery rhyme about a famous warrior.

so that, as the instant for giving over to the day birds drew nearer and nearer, there was no interval at all between them. He got up. He was a little stiff, but walking would cure that too as it would the cold, and soon there would be the sun. He went on down the hill, toward the dark woods within which the liquid silver voices of the birds called unceasing—the rapid and urgent beating of the urgent and quiring heart of the late spring night. He did not look back.

READING AND REACTING

1. Is the third-person narrator of "Barn Burning" omniscient, or does he have limited omniscience? Explain.

2. What is the point of view of the italicized passages? What do we learn from them? Do they create irony? How would the story have been different without these passages?

3. "Barn Burning" includes a great deal of dialogue. How would you characterize its tone? What information about the characters does the dialogue provide?

4. What are the major conflicts of "Barn Burning"? Which, if any, are resolved in the story? Are the conflicts avoidable? Explain.

5. Why does Ab Snopes burn barns? Do you think his actions are justified? Explain your reasoning.

6. What role does the Civil War play in "Barn Burning"? What does Abner Snopes's behavior during the war tell readers about his character?

7. In Books 1 and 2 of Samuel in the Old Testament, Abner was a relative of King Saul and commander in chief of his armies. Abner supported King Saul against David and was killed as a result of his own jealousy and rage. What, if any, significance is there in the fact that Faulkner names Ab Snopes, loyal to no man, fighter "for booty, and father of the Snopes clan," after this mighty biblical leader?

8. Why does Sarty Snopes insist that his father was brave? How does your knowledge of events unknown to the boy affect your reactions to this statement?

9. **JOURNAL ENTRY**   How would the story be different if it were told from Ab's point of view? From Sarty's? From the point of view of Ab's wife? From the point of view of a member of a community in which the Snopeses have lived?

10. **CRITICAL PERSPECTIVE**   Critic Edmond L. Volpe argues in his article " 'Barn Burning': A Definition of Evil" that "Barn Burning" is not really about the class conflict between the sharecropping Snopeses and landowners like the de Spains.

The story is centered upon Sarty's emotional dilemma. His conflict would not have been altered in any way if the person whose barn Ab burns had been a simple poor farmer, rather than an aristocratic plantation owner. The child's tension, in fact, begins to surface during the hearing in which a simple farmer accuses Ab of burning his barn. The moral antagonists mirrored in Sarty's conflict are not sharecropper and farmer. . . . Sarty's struggle is against the repressive and divisive force his father represents. The boy's anxiety is created by his awakening sense of his own individuality. Torn between strong emotional attachment to the parent and his growing need to assert his own identity, Sarty's crisis is psychological and his battle is being waged far below the level of his intellectual and moral awareness.

Do you think "Barn Burning" is, as Volpe suggests, a coming-of-age story, or do you believe it is essentially a story of class conflict?

RYŪNOSUKE AKUTAGAWA* (1892–1927)   was one of modern Japan's first internationally famous writers. Today, Akutagawa is best-known in the West for his short stories, among them "Rashomon," "The Hell Screen," "The Nose," and "In a Grove." Akutagawa, a popular haiku poet, was known also for his collected aphorisms, *Maxims of a Midget,* and for his works of literary philosophy, including "Ten Rules for Writing a Novel," and the polemical "Literary, Too Literary."

A highly analytical artist, Akutagawa agonized endlessly about the role of writers and fiction. Writing, he believed, should do more than chronicle the activities of life; it should illuminate *seimei* (literally translated, "the source of life"), the wellspring of energy and vitality that drives people to go on living. With growing conviction, however, Akutagawa came to see this life force as a monstrous kind of "animal energy" capable of driving men and women to dreadful acts.

"In a Grove" is the best-known of Akutagawa's multiple-narrator stories—stories in which the same event, described in contradictory ways by different voices, leaves the reader incapable of judging the truth.

"Akutagawa liked to create deliberate ambiguity in his stories," says his biographer Makoto Ueda, "because he did not believe in simple truths." In 1927, plagued by deteriorating physical and mental health, Akutagawa chose to end his own life rather than face a diminished intellectual life. At the end of his published suicide note he placed himself squarely in the world of his all-too-human fictional characters: "I too, am one of the human animals."

---

* No photograph available for this author.

RYŪNOSUKE AKUTAGAWA

In a Grove

(1952)

THE TESTIMONY OF A WOODCUTTER
QUESTIONED BY A HIGH POLICE COMMISSIONER

Yes, sir. Certainly, it was I who found the body. This morning, as usual, I went to cut my daily quota of cedars, when I found the body in a grove in a hollow in the mountains. The exact location? About 150 meters off the Yamashina[1] state road. It's an out-of-the-way grove of bamboo and cedars.

The body was lying flat on its back dressed in a bluish silk kimono[2] and a wrinkled head-dress of the Kyoto style. A single sword-stroke had pierced the breast. The fallen bamboo-blades[3] around it were stained with bloody blossoms. No, the blood was no longer running. The wound had dried up, I believe. And also, a gad-fly[4] was stuck fast there, hardly noticing my footsteps.

You ask me if I saw a sword or any such thing?

No, nothing, sir. I found only a rope at the root of a cedar near by. And . . . well, in addition to a rope, I found a comb. That was all. Apparently he must have made a battle of it before he was murdered, because the grass and fallen bamboo-blades had been trampled down all around.

5   "A horse was near by?"

No, sir. It's hard enough for a man to enter, let alone a horse.

THE TESTIMONY OF A TRAVELING BUDDHIST PRIEST
QUESTIONED BY A HIGH POLICE COMMISSIONER

The time? Certainly, it was about noon yesterday, sir. The unfortunate man was on the road from Sekiyama to Yamashina. He was walking toward Sekiyama with a woman accompanying him on horseback, who I have since learned was his wife. A scarf hanging from her head hid her face from view. All I saw was the color of her clothes, a lilac-colored suit. Her horse was a sorrel[5] with a fine mane. The lady's height? Oh, about four

---

[1] City near Kyoto; the capital of Japan until 1868.

[2] Wide-sleeved garment that is the traditional ceremonial dress of Japan.

[3] Foliage stemming from bamboo shoots.

[4] Large fly that bites livestock, i.e., a horsefly.

[5] Reddish-brown horse.

feet five inches. Since I am a Buddhist[6] priest, I took little notice about her details. Well, the man was armed with a sword as well as a bow and arrows. And I remember that he carried some twenty odd arrows in his quiver.

Little did I expect that he would meet such a fate. Truly human life is an evanescent as the morning dew or a flash of lightning. My words are inadequate to express my sympathy for him.

THE TESTIMONY OF A POLICEMAN
QUESTIONED BY A HIGH POLICE COMMISSIONER

The man that I arrested? He is a notorious brigand[7] called Tajomaru. When I arrested him, he had fallen off his horse. He was groaning on the bridge at Awataguchi. The time? It was in the early hours of last night. For the record, I might say that the other day I tried to arrest him, but unfortunately he escaped. He was wearing a dark blue silk kimono and a large plain sword. And, as you see, he got a bow and arrows somewhere. You say that this bow and these arrows look like the ones owned by the dead man? Then Tajomaru must be the murderer. The bow wound with leather strips, the black lacquered quiver, the seventeen arrows with hawk feathers—these were all in his possession I believe. Yes, sir, the horse is, as you say, a sorrel with a fine mane. A little beyond the stone bridge I found the horse grazing by the roadside, with his long rein dangling. Surely there is some providence in his having been thrown by the horse.

10   Of all the robbers prowling around Kyoto, this Tajomaru has given the most grief to the women in town. Last autumn a wife who came to the mountain back of the Pindora of the Toribe Temple, presumably to pay a visit, was murdered, along with a girl. It has been suspected that it was his doing. If this criminal murdered the man, you cannot tell what he may have done with the man's wife. May it please your honor to look into this problem as well.

THE TESTIMONY OF AN OLD WOMAN
QUESTIONED BY A HIGH POLICE COMMISSIONER

Yes, sir, that corpse is the man who married my daughter. He does not come from Kyoto. He was a samurai in the town of Kokufu in the province of Wakasa. His name was Kanazawa no Takehiko, and his age was twenty-six. He was of a gentle disposition, so I am sure he did nothing to provoke the anger of others.

My daughter? Her name is Masago, and her age is nineteen. She is a spirited, fun-loving girl, but I am sure she has never known any man

---

[6] Buddhism, a religious and philosophical system, teaches that self-denial and proper thinking lead to the divine state of Nirvana.

[7] Bandit, criminal.

except Takehiko. She has a small, oval, dark-complected face with a mole at the corner of her left eye.

15   Yesterday Takehiko left for Wakasa with my daughter. What bad luck it is that things should have come to such a sad end! What has become of my daughter? I am resigned to giving up my son-in-law as lost, but the fate of my daughter worries me sick. For heaven's sake leave no stone unturned to find her. I hate that robber Tajomaru, or whatever his name is. Not only my son-in-law, but my daughter . . . (Her later words were drowned in tears.)

TAJOMARU'S CONFESSION

I killed him, but not her. Where's she gone? I can't tell. Oh, wait a minute. No torture can make me confess what I don't know. Now things have come to such a head, I won't keep anything from you.

Yesterday a little past noon I met that couple. Just then a puff of wind blew, and raised her hanging scarf, so that I caught a glimpse of her face. Instantly it was again covered from my view. That may have been one reason; she looked like a Bodhisattva.[8] At that moment I made up my mind to capture her even if I had to kill her man.

Why? To me killing isn't a matter of such great consequence as you might think. When a woman is captured, her man has to be killed anyway. In killing, I use the sword I wear at my side. Am I the only one who kills people? You, you don't use your swords. You kill people with your power, with your money. Sometimes you kill them on the pretext of working for their good. It's true they don't bleed. They are in the best of health, but all the same you've killed them. It's hard to say who is a greater sinner, you or me. (An ironical smile.)

But it would be good if I could capture a woman without killing her man. So, I made up my mind to capture her, and do my best not to kill him. But it's out of the question on the Yamashina stage road. So I managed to lure the couple into the mountains.

It was quite easy. I became their traveling companion, and I told them there was an old mound in the mountain over there, and that I had dug it open and found many mirrors and swords. I went on to tell them I'd buried the things in a grove behind the mountain, and that I'd like to sell them at a low price to anyone who would care to have them. Then . . . you see, isn't greed terrible? He was beginning to be moved by my talk before he knew it. In less than half an hour they were driving their horse toward the mountain with me.

When he came in front of the grove, I told them that the treasures were buried in it, and I asked them to come and see. The man had no

---

[8] In Buddhist tradition, a person who has achieved great morality and spiritual wisdom; a potential Buddha.

objection—he was blinded by greed. The woman said she would wait on horseback. It was natural for her to say so, at the sight of a thick grove. To tell you the truth, my plan worked just as I wished, so I went into the grove with him, leaving her behind alone.

20   The grove is only bamboo for some distance. About fifty yards ahead there's a rather open clump of cedars. It was a convenient spot for my purpose. Pushing my way through the grove, I told him a plausible lie that the treasures were buried under the cedars. When I told him this, he pushed his laborious way toward the slender cedar visible through the grove. After a while the bamboo thinned out, and we came to where a number of cedars grew in a row. As soon as we got there, I seized him from behind. Because he was a trained, sword-bearing warrior, he was quite strong, but he was taken by surprise, so there was no help for him. I soon tied him up to the root of a cedar. Where did I get a rope? Thank heaven, being a robber, I had a rope with me, since I might have to scale a wall at any moment. Of course it was easy to stop him from calling out by gagging his mouth with fallen bamboo leaves.

When I disposed of him, I went to his woman and asked her to come and see him, because he seemed to have been suddenly taken sick. It's needless to say that this plan also worked well. The woman, her sedge[9] hat off, came into the depths of the grove, where I led her by the hand. The instant she caught sight of her husband, she drew a small sword. I've never seen a woman of such violent temper. If I'd been off guard, I'd have got a thrust in my side. I dodged, but she kept on slashing at me. She might have wounded me deeply or killed me. But I'm Tajomaru. I managed to strike down her small sword without drawing my own. The most spirited woman is defenseless without a weapon. At least I could satisfy my desire for her without taking her husband's life.

Yes, . . . without taking his life. I had no wish to kill him. I was about to run away from the grove, leaving the woman behind in tears, when she frantically clung to my arm. In broken fragments of words, she asked that either her husband or I die. She said it was more trying than death to have her shame known to two men. She gasped out that she wanted to be the wife of whichever survived. Then a furious desire to kill him seized me. (Gloomy excitement.)

Telling you in this way, no doubt I seem a crueler man than you. But that's because you didn't see her face. Especially her burning eyes at that moment. As I saw her eye to eye, I wanted to make her my wife even if I were to be struck by lightning. I wanted to make her my wife . . . this single desire filled my mind. This was not only lust, as you might think. At that time if I'd had no other desire than lust, I'd surely not have minded knocking her down and running away. Then I wouldn't have stained my sword with his blood. But the moment I gazed at her face in the dark grove, I decided not to leave there without killing him.

---

[9] Greyish-brown colored.

But I didn't like to resort to unfair means to kill him. I untied him and told him to cross swords with me. (The rope that was found at the root of the cedar is the rope I dropped at the time.) Furious with anger, he drew his thick sword. And quick as thought, he sprang at me ferociously, without speaking a word. I needn't tell you how our fight turned out. The twenty-third stroke . . . please remember this. I'm impressed with this fact still. Nobody under the sun has ever clashed swords with me twenty strokes. (A cheerful smile.)

25   When he fell, I turned toward her, lowering my blood-stained sword. But to my great astonishment she was gone. I wondered to where she had run away. I looked for her in the clump of cedars. I listened, but heard only a groaning sound from the throat of the dying man.

As soon as we started to cross swords, she may have run away through the grove to call for help. When I thought of that, I decided it was a matter of life and death to me. So, robbing him of his sword, and bow and arrows, I ran out to the mountain road. There I found her horse still grazing quietly. It would be a mere waste of words to tell you the later details, but before I entered town I had already parted with the sword. That's all my confession. I know that my head will be hung in chains anyway, so put me down for the maximum penalty. (A defiant attitude.)

The Confession of a Woman Who Has Come to the *Shimizu* Temple

That man in the blue silk kimono, after forcing me to yield to him, laughed mockingly as he looked at my bound husband. How horrified my husband must have been! But no matter how hard he struggled in agony, the rope cut into him all the more tightly. In spite of myself I ran stumblingly toward his side. Or rather I tried to run toward him, but the man instantly knocked me down. Just at that moment I saw an indescribable light in my husband's eyes. Something beyond expression . . . his eyes make me shudder even now. That instantaneous look of my husband, who couldn't speak a word, told me all his heart. The flash in his eyes was neither anger nor sorrow . . . only a cold light, a look of loathing. More struck by the look in his eyes than by the blow of the thief, I called out in spite of myself and fell unconscious.

In the course of time I came to, and found that the man in blue silk was gone. I saw only my husband still bound to the root of the cedar. I raised myself from the bamboo-blades with difficulty, and looked into his face; but the expression in his eyes was just the same as before.

Beneath the cold contempt in his eyes, there was hatred. Shame, grief, and anger . . . I didn't known how to express my heart at that time. Reeling to my feet, I went up to my husband.

30   "Takejiro," I said to him, "since things have come to this pass, I cannot live with you. I'm determined to die, . . . but you must die, too. You saw my shame. I can't leave you alive as you are."

This was all I could say. Still he went on gazing at me with loathing and contempt. My heart breaking, I looked for his sword. It must have been taken by the robber. Neither his sword nor his bow and arrows were to be seen in the grove. But fortunately my small sword was lying at my feet. Raising it over head, once more I said, "Now give me your life. I'll follow you right away."

When he heard these words, he moved his lips with difficulty. Since his mouth was stuffed with leaves, of course his voice could not be heard at all. But at a glance I understood his words. Despising me, his look said only, "Kill me." Neither conscious nor unconscious, I stabbed the small sword through the lilac-colored kimono into his breast.

Again at this time I must have fainted. By the time I managed to look up, he had already breathed his last—still in bonds. A streak of sinking sunlight streamed through the clump of cedars and bamboos, and shone on his pale face. Gulping down my sobs, I untied the rope from his dead body. And . . . and what has become of me since I have no more strength to tell you. Anyway I hadn't the strength to die. I stabbed my own throat with the small sword, I threw myself into a pond at the foot of the mountain, and I tried to kill myself in many ways. Unable to end my life, I am still living in dishonor. (A lonely smile.) Worthless as I am, I must have been forsaken even by the most merciful Kwannon.[10] I killed my own husband. I was violated by the robber. Whatever can I do? Whatever can I . . . I . . . (Gradually, violent sobbing.)

THE STORY OF THE MURDERED MAN,
as TOLD THROUGH A MEDIUM

After violating my wife, the robber, sitting there, began to speak comforting words to her. Of course I couldn't speak. My whole body was tied fast to the root of a cedar. But meanwhile I winked at her many times, as much as to say "Don't believe the robber." I wanted to convey some such meaning to her. But my wife, sitting dejectedly on the bamboo leaves, was looking hard at her lap. To all appearances, she was listening to his words. I was agonized by jealousy. In the meantime the robber went on with his clever talk, from one subject to another. The robber finally made his bold, brazen proposal. "Once your virtue is stained, you won't get along well with your husband, so won't you be my wife instead? It's my love for you that made me be violent toward you."

35   While the criminal talked, my wife raised her face as if in a trance. She had never looked so beautiful as at that moment. What did my beautiful wife say in answer to him while I was sitting bound there? I am lost in space, but I have never thought of her answer without burning with anger

---

[10] A Bodhisattva often regarded as female; known in the West as the Buddhist goddess of mercy.

and jealousy. Truly she said, . . . "Then take me away with you wherever you go."

This is not the whole of her sin. If that were all, I would not be tormented so much in the dark. When she was going out of the grove as if in a dream, her hand in the robber's, she suddenly turned pale, and pointed at me tied to the root of the cedar, and said, "Kill him! I cannot marry you as long as he lives." "Kill him!" she cried many times, as if she had gone crazy. Even now these words threaten to blow me headlong into the bottomless abyss of darkness. Has such a hateful thing come out of a human mouth ever before? Have such cursed words ever struck a human ear, even once? Even once such a . . . (A sudden cry of scorn.) At these words the robber himself turned pale. "Kill him," she cried, clinging to his arms. Looking hard at her, he answered neither yes or no . . . but hardly had I thought about his answer before she had been knocked down into the bamboo leaves. (Again a cry of scorn.) Quietly folding his arms, he looked at me and said, "What will you do with her? Kill her or save her? You have only to nod. Kill her?" For these words alone I would like to pardon his crime.

While I hesitated, she shrieked and ran into the depths of the grove. The robber instantly snatched at her, but he failed even to grasp her sleeve.

After she ran away, he took up my sword, and my bow and arrows. With a single stroke he cut one of my bonds. I remember his mumbling, "My fate is next." Then he disappeared from the grove. All was silent after that. No, I heard someone crying. Untying the rest of my bonds, I listened carefully, and I noticed that it was my own crying. (Long silence.)

I raised my exhausted body from the root of the cedar. In front of me there was shining the small sword which my wife had dropped. I took it up and stabbed it into my breast. A bloody lump rose to my mouth, but I didn't feel any pain. When my breast grew cold, everything was as silent as the dead in their graves. What profound silence! Not a single bird-note was heard in the sky over this grave in the hollow of the mountains. Only a lonely light lingered on the cedars and mountains. By and by the light gradually grew fainter, till the cedars and bamboo were lost to view. Lying there, I was enveloped in deep silence.

40   Then someone crept up to me. I tried to see who it was. But darkness had already been gathering round me. Someone . . . that someone drew the small sword softly out of my breast in its invisible hand. At the same time once more blood flowed into my mouth. And once and for all I sank down into the darkness of space.

READING AND REACTING

1. What is the effect on readers of the shifting point of view of "In a Grove"? How would the story be different if it were told from the point of view of a single person?

2. On which points do the witnesses agree? On which do they differ? How can you account for these differences?

3. Which witnesses are telling the truth, and which are lying? How do you know?

4. Do you think any single character's point of view is more accurate than the others'? Explain.

5. In what order does the author arrange the testimony of the witnesses? How does this order affect the way readers respond to the story?

6. How do the characters' assumptions about gender affect the way they act? What comment does "In a Grove" make about the nature of the relationship between men and women? Do your own ideas about sex roles affect the way you respond to "In a Grove"?

7. Who creeps up to the murdered man and pulls the knife out of his chest? Why do you think that the narrator does not clarify this detail?

8. The characters in "In a Grove" represent a cross section of Japanese society. What insights—if any—do the various characters give readers about the relationships that exist among the various classes?

9. **JOURNAL ENTRY**   What comment does "In a Grove" make about people's ability to tell the whole truth? To what aspects of our own contemporary society is this comment relevant? In what sense is the story as relevant today as it was when it was written?

10. **CRITICAL PERSPECTIVE**   According to Noriko Mizuta Lippit's "Tale to Short Story: Akutagawa's 'Toshishun' and Its Chinese Origins," most of Akutagawa's stories are based on other stories, usually classical tales or the works or older writers. This does not mean, however, that Akutagawa was not concerned with contemporary problems.

    By borrowing stories and taking the reader away from immediate reality, Akutagawa sought to present symbolic situations relevant to all human reality. A self-avowed literary cosmopolitan, Akutagawa was confident of the universal validity of his works, confident that his works transcended the particular time and place in which they were set. Most of Akutagawa's works deal with complex psychological situations that exist in human relations, and they often reveal his fundamental skepticism about human life and belief in the relativity of human relations. In other words, Akutagawa's borrowing of the stories was a device for dealing with the modern human situation and psychology. The borrowed story provided the distance of time and space which helped give universality to the situation with which he was dealing. In this sense, the story provided only a convenient framework.

    Do you think Akutagawa succeeded in presenting "situations relevant to all human reality" in "In a Grove"? Is this story so universal that it is relevant to recent events in the United States?

WRITING SUGGESTIONS: POINT OF VIEW

1. How would Poe's "The Cask of Amontillado" be different if it were told by a minor character who observed the events? Rewrite the story from this point of view—or tell the story that precedes the story, explaining the thousand injuries and the insult.

2. You are a police officer who has been given the job of solving the murder described in "In a Grove." Cross-examine each of the suspects, and identify the one you think has committed the crime. Then, write a report to your superior presenting the reasons you think your suspect is guilty. Remember, you must provide enough evidence from the story to convince your superior that the person you have identified should be arrested and charged with murder.

3. Assume that you are the sailor in "Big Black Good Man" and that you are keeping a journal of your travels. Write the journal entries for the time you spent in Copenhagen. Include your perceptions of Olaf, Lena, the hotel, and anything else that caught your attention. Make sure you present your interpretation of the events described in the story—especially Olaf's reaction to you.

4. Both "The Cask of Amontillado" and "Barn Burning" deal with crimes that essentially go unpunished and with the emotions that accompany these crimes. In what sense does each story's use of point of view shape its treatment of the crime in question? For instance, how does point of view determine how much readers know about the motives for the crime, the crime's basic circumstances, and the extent to which the crime is justified?

5. Write an essay in which you compare the information about the crime given by the characters in "In a Grove" with the information given by the characters in "A Jury of Her Peers" (p. 455). What comment do both stories make about telling the truth? What light do these stories shed on recent high-profile court cases such as the O. J. Simpson murder trial?

CHAPTER 8

Style, Tone, and Language

A word is intrinsically powerful. If you believe in the power of words, you can bring about physical change in the universe. This is a notion of language that is ancient and it is valid to me. For example, the words of a charm or a spell are formulaic. They are meant to bring about physical change. The person who utters such a formula believes beyond any shadow of doubt that his utterance is going to have this or that actual effect. Because he believes in it and because words are what they are, it is true. It is true. . . . Every day we produce magical results with words.

N. SCOTT MOMADAY, *ANCESTRAL VOICES*

INTERVIEWER: You describe seemingly fantastic events in such minute detail that it gives them their own reality. Is this something you have picked up from journalism?

GARCÍA MÁRQUEZ: That's a journalistic trick which you can also apply to literature. For example, if you say that there are elephants flying in the sky, people are not going to believe you. But if you say that there are four hundred and twenty-five elephants in the sky, people will probably believe you. . . . I remember particularly the story about the character who is surrounded by yellow butterflies. . . . I discovered that if I didn't say the butterflies were yellow, people would not believe it. . . . The problem for every writer is credibility. Anybody can write anything so long as it's believed.

GABRIEL GARCÍA MÁRQUEZ, *WRITERS AT WORK*, 6TH ED.

When a writer starts in very young, his problems apart from his story are those of technique, of words, of rhythms, of story methods, of transition, of characterization, of ways of creating effects. But after years of trial and error most of these things are solved and one gets what is called a style. It is then that a story conceived falls into place neatly and is written down having the indelible personal hallmark of the writer. This is thought to be an ideal situation. And the writer who is able to achieve this is thought to be very fortunate.

I have only just arrived at a sense of horror about this technique. If I think of a story, it is bound automatically to fall into my own personal long struggle for technique. But the penalty is terrible. The tail of the kite is designed to hold and in many cases drags it to the earth. Having a technique, is it not possible that the technique not only dictates how a story is to be written but also what story is to be written? In other words, style or technique may be a straitjacket which is the destroyer of the writer. It does seem to be true that when it becomes easy to write the writing is not likely to be any good. Facility can be the greatest danger in the world. But is there any alternative? Suppose I want to change my themes and my approach. Will not my technique, which has become almost unconscious, warp and drag me around the old attitudes and subtly force the new work to the old?

JOHN STEINBECK, LETTER

Way back there when Hell wasn't no bigger than Maitland, man found out something about the laws of sound. He had found out something before he even stood erect to think. He found out that sounds could be assembled and manipulated and that such a collection of sound forms could become as definite and concrete as a war-axe or a food-tool. So he had language and song. Perhaps by some happy accident he found out about percussion sounds and spacing the intervals for tempo and rhythm. Anyway, it is evident that the sound-arts were the first inventions and that music and literature grew from the same root. Somewhere songs for sound-singing branched off from songs for story-telling until we arrived at prose.

ZORA NEALE HURSTON, "FOLKLORE AND MUSIC"

One of the qualities that gives a work of literature its individual personality is its **style,** the way in which a writer selects and arranges words to say what he or she wants to say. Style encompasses elements such as word choice; syntax; sentence length and structure; and the presence, frequency, and prominence of imagery and figures of speech. Closely related to style is **tone,** the attitude of the speaker or author of a work toward the subject matter, characters, or audience. Word choice and word order help to create a work's tone, which may be intimate or distant, bitter or affectionate, straightforward or cautious, supportive or critical, respectful or condescending. (Tone may also be ironic; see Chapter 7, Point of View, for a discussion of irony.)

Style offers almost limitless possibilities to a writer. Creative use of language (unusual word choice, word order, or sentence structure, for instance) can enrich a story and add to its overall effect. Sometimes style can reveal a narrator's attitude toward a character or a character's mental state. In other cases, it can help to create an atmosphere that enhances setting or theme. For instance, the breathless, disjointed style of Edgar Allan Poe's "The Tell-Tale Heart" (p. 542) suggests the narrator's increasing emotional instability: "Was it possible they heard not? Almighty God!—no, no! They heard!—they suspected!—they *knew!*—they were making a mockery of my horror!" In his short story "Big Two-Hearted River," Ernest Hemingway strings sentences together without transitions to create a flat, emotionless prose style that reveals his character's alienation and fragility as he struggles to maintain control: "Now things were done. There had been this to do. Now it was done. It had been a hard trip. He was very tired. That was done. He had made his camp. He was settled. Nothing could touch him." Finally, James Joyce's well-known **stream-of-consciousness** style mimics thought, allowing ideas to run into one another as random associations are made, so that readers may follow and participate in the thought processes of the narrator. Here, for example, is a stream-of-consciousness passage from Joyce's experimental novel *Ulysses*:

> *frseeeeeeeefronnnng train somewhere whistling the strength those engines have in them like big giants and the water rolling all over and out of them all sides like the end of Loves old sweet sonnnng the poor men that have to be out all the night from their wives and families in those roasting engines stifling it was today. . . .*

Use of stylistic devices that place emphasis on the sounds and rhythm of words and sentences also enriches works of fiction. Consider the use of such techniques in the following sentence from James Joyce's "Araby" (p. 249):

> *The light from the lamp opposite our door caught the white curve of her neck, lit up her hair that rested there and, falling, lit up the hand upon the railing.*

The narrator is describing his first conversation with a girl who fascinates him, and the lush, lyrical, almost musical language reflects his enchantment. Note in particular the **alliteration** (light/lamp; caught/curve; hair/hand), the repetition (lit up/lit up), and the rhyme (lit up her *hair*/that rested *there*) and **near rhyme** (falling/railing); these poetic devices connect the words of the sentence into a smooth, rhythmic whole. Another example of this emphasis on sound may be found in the measured **parallelism** of this sentence from Nathaniel Hawthorne's "The Birthmark":

> *He had left his laboratory to the care of an assistant, cleared his fine countenance from the furnace smoke, washed the stain of acids from his fingers, and persuaded a beautiful woman to become his wife.*

The style of the preceding sentence, conveying methodical precision and order, reflects the compulsive personality of the character being described.

Although many stylistic options are available to writers, style must be consistent with the writer's purpose and with the effect he or she hopes to create. Just as writers may experiment with point of view or manipulate events to create a complex plot, so they can adjust style to suit particular narrators, characters, settings, or themes. Two elements with which writers frequently experiment are level of diction, and imagery and figurative language.

LEVEL OF DICTION

The level of diction—how formal or informal a story's language is—can suggest a good deal about those who use the language, thus providing insights into the story's theme.

Formal Diction   Formal diction is characterized by elaborate, complex sentences; a learned vocabulary, which may include **allusions** and **figurative language;** and a serious, objective, detached tone. The speaker avoids contractions, shortened word forms (like *phone*), regional expressions, and slang, and he or she may use *one* or *we* in place of *I*. At its most extreme, formal language may be stiff and stilted, far removed from everyday speech.

Formal diction, whether used by a narrator or by a character, may indicate erudition, a high educational level, a superior social or professional position, or emotional detachment. When one character's language is significantly more formal than others', he or she may seem old-fashioned or stuffy; when language is inappropriately elevated or complex, it may reveal the character to be pompous or ridiculous; when a narrator's language is noticeably more formal than that of the characters, the narrator may seem superior or even condescending. Thus, style reveals a good deal about characters and about the narrator's attitude toward them.

The following passage from "The Birthmark" illustrates formal style:

> *In the latter part of the last century there lived a man of science, an eminent proficient in every branch of natural philosophy, who not long before our story opens had made experience of a spiritual affinity more attractive than any chemical one. He had left his laboratory to the care of an assistant, cleared his fine countenance from the furnace smoke, washed the stain of acids from his fingers, and persuaded a beautiful woman to become his wife. In those days when the comparatively recent discovery of electricity and other kindred mysteries of Nature seemed to open paths into the region of miracle, it was not unusual for the love of science to rival the love of woman in its depth and absorbing energy. The higher intellect, the imagination, the spirit, and even the heart might all find their congenial aliment in pursuits which, as some of their ardent votaries believed, would ascend from one step of powerful intelligence to another, until the philosopher should lay his hand on the secret of creative force and perhaps make new worlds for himself.*

The long, complex sentences, learned vocabulary ("countenance," "aliment," "votaries"), and absence of colloquialisms suit Hawthorne's purpose well, recreating the formal language of the earlier era in which his story is set. The omniscient narrator, despite his use of the first person in "our story," is appropriately aloof and controlled.

Informal Diction   Informal diction, consistent with everyday speech, is characterized by slang, contractions, colloquial expressions like *you know* and *I mean*, shortened word forms, incomplete sentences, and a casual, conversational tone. A first-person narrator may use informal style, or characters may speak informally; in either case, informal style tends to narrow the distance between readers and text.

Informal language can range from the straightforward contemporary style of Cal's dialogue in "Teenage Wasteland" ("'I think this kid is hurting. You know?'") to the regionalisms and dialect employed in Flannery O'Connor's "A Good Man Is Hard to Find" ("aloose"; "you all"; "britches"). In "Teenage Wasteland" (p. 569) Cal's self-consciously slangy, conversational style tells readers a good deal about his motives and his method of operating; in "A Good Man Is Hard to Find" (p. 261) the characters' speech patterns and diction reveal their geographic origin and social class. In other stories, a character's use of obscenities may suggest his or her crudeness or adolescent bravado, and use of racial or ethnic slurs suggests that a character is insensitive and bigoted.

The following passage from John Updike's "A&P" (p. 105) illustrates informal style:

> She had sort of oaky hair that the sun and salt had bleached, done up in a bun that was unravelling, and a kind of prim face. Walking into the A&P with your straps down, I suppose it's the only kind of face you can have. She held her head so high her neck, coming out of those white shoulders, looked kind of stretched, but I didn't mind. The longer her neck was, the more of her there was.

In the preceding passage, the first-person narrator uses a conversational style, including colloquialisms ("sort of," "I suppose," "kind of"), contractions ("it's," "didn't"), and the imprecise, informal *you* ("Walking into the A&P with *your* straps down. . . ."). No elaborate sentences or learned diction are used.

IMAGERY AND FIGURATIVE LANGUAGE

Imagery   **Imagery**—words and phrases that describe what is seen, heard, smelled, tasted, or touched—can have a significant impact in a story. A pattern of repeated imagery can help to convey a particular impression about a character or situation, or a writer may use such a pattern to communicate or reinforce a story's theme. For example, the theme of newly discovered sexuality can be conveyed through repeated use of words and phrases suggesting blooming or ripening.

In T. Coraghessan Boyle's "Greasy Lake" (p. 397) the narrator's vivid description of Greasy Lake itself uses rich visual imagery to evoke a scene. By characterizing a natural setting with surprising words like "fetid," "murky," and "greasy" and unpleasant images such as the "glittering of broken glass," the "ravaged island," and the "charred remains of bonfires," Boyle creates a picture that is completely at odds with the traditional pastoral view of nature. The incongruous images are nevertheless perfectly consistent with the sordid events that unfold at Greasy Lake.

Through the center of town, up the strip, past the housing developments and shopping malls, street lights giving way to the thin streaming illumination of the headlights, trees crowding the asphalt in a black unbroken wall: that was the way out to Greasy Lake. The Indians had called it Wakan, a reference to the clarity of its waters. Now it was fetid and murky, the mud banks glittering with broken glass and strewn with beer cans and the charred remains of bonfires. There was a single ravaged island a hundred yards from shore, so stripped of vegetation it looked as if the air force had strafed it. We went up to the lake because everyone went there, because we wanted to snuff the rich scent of possibility on the breeze, watch a girl take off her clothes and plunge into the festering murk, drink beer, smoke pot, howl at the stars, savor the incongruous full-throated roar of rock and roll against the primeval susurrus of frogs and crickets. This was nature.

Figurative Language   **Figures of speech**—such as *similes, metaphors,* and *personification*—can enrich a story, subtly revealing information about characters, conveying or reinforcing themes, or creating a mood that enhances setting.

Metaphors and **similes**—imaginative comparisons—can convey a writer's or narrator's attitude toward characters and events. Thus, Flannery O'Connor's many grotesque similes in "A Good Man Is Hard to Find" help to dehumanize her characters; the children's mother, for instance, has a face "as broad and innocent as a cabbage." In Tillie Olson's "I Stand Here Ironing" (p. 152) an extended metaphor in which a mother compares her daughter to a dress waiting to be ironed expresses the mother's attitude toward her daughter, effectively suggesting to readers the daughter's vulnerability. Similes and metaphors are used freely in Kate Chopin's "The Storm" (p. 146). In a scene of sexual awakening Calixta's skin is "like a creamy lily," her passion is "like a white flame," and her mouth is "a fountain of delight"; these figures of speech add a lushness and sensuality to the story.

Personification—endowing inanimate objects or abstract ideas with life or with human characteristics—is used in "Araby," where houses, "conscious of decent lives within them, gazed at one another with brown imperturbable faces." This use of figurative language expands readers' vision of the story's setting and gives a dreamlike quality to the passage. (Other figures of speech, such as **hyperbole** and **understatement,** can also enrich works of fiction. See Chapter 16, Figures of Speech, for further information.)

Allusions—references to familiar historical or literary personages or events—may also expand readers' understanding of a work. An allusion widens a work's context by bringing it into the context of a related subject or idea. For instance, Lorrie Moore's frequent references to historical events and popular songs in "How to Talk to Your Mother (Notes)" (p. 89) enhance readers' appreciation of the story's unusual movement backward through time. In addition, readers who recognize the references may gain a deeper understanding of the narrator's position on various political or social issues. Literary or biblical allusions may be used in much the same way.

The following passage from Alberto Alvaro Ríos's story "The Secret Lion" (p. 43) includes many of the stylistic devices discussed above, thus illustrating the power of language to communicate valuable information about a story's characters, setting, and theme:

> We had read the books, after all; we knew about bridges and castles and wildtreacherousraging alligatormouth rivers. We wanted them. So we were going to go out and get them. We went back that morning into that kitchen and we said, "We're going out there, we're going into the hills, we're going away for three days, don't worry." She said, "All right."
>
> "You know," I said to Sergio, "if we're going to go away for three days, well, we ought to at least pack a lunch."
>
> But we were two young boys with no patience for what we thought at the time was mom-stuff: making sa-and-wiches. My mother didn't offer. So we got out little kid knapsacks that my mother had sewn for us, and into them we put the jar of mustard. A loaf of bread. Knivesforksplates, bottles of Coke, a can opener. This was lunch for the two of us. And we were weighed down, humped over to be strong enough to carry this stuff. But we started walking anyway, into the hills. We were going to eat berries and stuff otherwise. "Goodbye." My mom said that.

The preceding paragraphs are written in an informal, conversational style. Through language, the adult narrator recaptures the bravado of the boys in search of "wildtreacherousraging alligatormouth rivers" even as he suggests to readers that the boys are not going far. The story's use of language is original and inventive: Words are blended together ("getridofit," "knivesforksplates"), linked to form new language ("mom-stuff"), and drawn out ("sa-and-wiches"). These experiments with language show the narrator's willingness to move back into a child's personality and frame of reference while maintaining the advantage of distance. Style is informal: The adult narrator uses sentence fragments ("A loaf of bread."), colloquialisms ("kid," "mom," "stuff"), and contractions. He also includes conversational elements such as *you know* and *well* in the dialogue, accurately recreating the childhood scene at the same time he sees its folly and remains aware of the disillusionment that awaits him. Thus, the unique style permits the narrator to bring readers with him into the child's world even as he maintains his adult stance: "But we were two young boys with no patience for what we thought at the time was mom-stuff. . . ."

A FINAL NOTE

In analyzing the use of language in a work of fiction, you may occasionally encounter obscure allusions, foreign words and phrases, unusual comparisons, and unfamiliar regional expressions—particularly in works treating cultures and historical periods other than your own. Frequently such language will be clarified by the context, or by explanatory notes in your text; when it is not, you should consult a dictionary, encyclopedia, or other reference work to discover the significance of the unfamiliar words or expressions.

▼▼

CHECKLIST FOR WRITING ABOUT STYLE, TONE, AND LANGUAGE

- ◆ Is the story's tone intimate? Distant? Ironic? How does the tone advance the writer's purpose?

- ◆ Does the writer make any unusual creative use of diction, word order, or sentence structure?

- ◆ Does the style emphasize the sound and rhythm of language? For example, does the writer use alliteration and assonance? Repetition and parallelism? What do such techniques add to the story?

- ◆ Is the level of diction generally formal, informal, or somewhere in between?

- ◆ Is there a difference between the style of the narrator and the style of the characters' speech? If so, what is the effect of this difference?

- ◆ Do any of the story's characters use regionalisms, colloquial language, or nonstandard speech? If so, what effect does this language have?

- ◆ What do different characters' levels of diction reveal about them?

- ◆ What kind of imagery predominates? Where, and why, is imagery used?

- ◆ Does the story develop a pattern of imagery? How does this pattern of imagery relate to the story's themes?

- ◆ Does the story use simile and metaphor? Personification? What is the effect of these figures of speech?

- ◆ Do figures of speech reinforce the story's themes? Reveal details about characters? Create a mood that enhances setting?

- ◆ Does the story make any historical, literary, or biblical allusions? Why are these allusions appropriate? What do they contribute to the story?

- ◆ What unfamiliar, obscure, or foreign words, phrases, or images are used in the story? What is the effect of these words or expressions?

▲▲

JAMES JOYCE (1884–1941) was born in Dublin but lived his entire adult life in self-imposed exile from his native Ireland. Though his parents sent him to schools that trained young men for the priesthood, Joyce saw himself as a religious and artistic rebel, and he fled to Paris soon after graduation in 1902. Recalled briefly to Dublin by his mother's fatal illness, Joyce returned to the Continent in 1904, taking with him an uneducated Irish country girl named Nora Barnacle, who became his wife in 1931. In dreary quarters in Trieste, Zurich, and Paris, Joyce struggled to support a growing family, sometimes teaching classes in Berlitz language schools.

Though Joyce never again lived in Ireland, he continued to write about Dublin. Publication of *Dubliners* (1914), a collection of short stories including "Araby," was delayed for seven years because the Irish publisher feared libel suits from local citizens who were thinly disguised as characters in the stories. Joyce's autobiographical *Portrait of the Artist as a Young Man* (1916) tells of a young writer's rejection of family, church, and country. *Ulysses* (1922), the comic tale of eighteen hours in the life of a wandering Dublin advertising salesman, was banned when the U.S. Post Office brought charges of obscenity against the book, and it remained banned in the United States and England for more than a decade. In *Ulysses* Joyce begins a revolutionary journey away from traditional techniques of plot and characterization to the interior monologues and stream-of-consciousness style that mark his last great novel, *Finnegans Wake* (1939).

JAMES JOYCE

Araby

(1914)

North Richmond Street, being blind,[1] was a quiet street except at the hour when the Christian Brothers' School set the boys free. An uninhabited house of two storeys stood at the blind end, detached from its neighbours in a square ground. The other houses of the street, conscious of decent lives within them, gazed at one another with brown imperturbable faces.

The former tenant of our house, a priest, had died in the back drawing-room. Air, musty from having been long enclosed, hung in all the rooms, and the waste room behind the kitchen was littered with old useless papers. Among these I found a few paper-covered books, the pages of which

---

[1] A dead-end street.

were curled and damp: *The Abbot,* by Walter Scott, *The Devout Communicant* and *The Memoirs of Vidocq.*[2] I liked the last best because its leaves were yellow. The wild garden behind the house contained a central apple-tree and a few straggling bushes under one of which I found the late tenant's rusty bicycle-pump. He had been a very charitable priest; in his will he had left all his money to institutions and the furniture of his house to his sister.

When the short days of winter came dusk fell before we had well eaten our dinners. When we met in the street the houses had grown sombre. The space of sky above us was the colour of ever-changing violet and towards it the lamps of the street lifted their feeble lanterns. The cold air stung us and we played till our bodies glowed. Our shouts echoed in the silent street. The career of our play brought us through the dark muddy lanes behind the houses where we ran the gauntlet of the rough tribes from the cottages, to the back doors of the dark dripping gardens where odours arose from the ashpits, to the dark odorous stables where a coachman smoothed and combed the horse or shook music from the buckled harness. When we returned to the street light from the kitchen windows had filled the areas. If my uncle was seen turning the corner we hid in the shadow until we had seen him safely housed. Or if Mangan's sister came out on the doorstep to call her brother in to his tea we watched her from our shadow peer up and down the street. We waited to see whether she would remain or go in and, if she remained, we left our shadow and walked up to Mangan's steps resignedly. She was waiting for us, her figure defined by the light from the half-opened door. Her brother always teased her before he obeyed and I stood by the railings looking at her. Her dress swung as she moved her body and the soft rope of her hair tossed from side to side.

Every morning I lay on the floor in the front parlour watching her door. The blind was pulled down to within an inch of the sash so that I could not be seen. When she came out on the doorstep my heart leaped. I ran to the hall, seized my books and followed her. I kept her brown figure always in my eye and, when we came near the point at which our ways diverged, I quickened my pace and passed her. This happened morning after morning. I had never spoken to her, except for a few casual words, and yet her name was like a summons to all my foolish blood.

5   Her image accompanied me even in places the most hostile to romance. On Saturday evenings when my aunt went marketing I had to go to carry some of the parcels. We walked through the flaring streets, jostled by drunken men and bargaining women, amid the curses of labourers, the shrill litanies of shop-boys who stood on guard by the barrels of pigs' cheeks, the nasal chanting of street-singers, who sang a *come-all-you* about

---

[2] Sir Walter Scott (1771–1832)—an English Romantic novelist; *The Devout Communicant* is a variant title for *Pious Meditations,* written by an eighteenth-century English Franciscan friar, Pacifus Baker; *The Memoirs of Vidocq*—an autobiography of François–Jules Vidocq (1775–1857), a French soldier of fortune turned police agent.

O'Donovan Rossa,[3] or a ballad about the troubles in our native land. These noises converged in a single sensation of life for me: I imagined that I bore my chalice safely through a throng of foes. Her name sprang to my lips at moments in strange prayers and praises which I myself did not understand. My eyes were often full of tears (I could not tell why) and at times a flood from my heart seemed to pour itself out into my bosom. I thought little of the future. I did not know whether I would ever speak to her or not or, if I spoke to her, how I could tell her of my confused adoration. But my body was like a harp and her words and gestures were like fingers running upon the wires.

One evening I went into the back drawing-room in which the priest had died. It was a dark rainy evening and there was no sound in the house. Through one of the broken panes I heard the rain impinge upon the earth, the fine incessant needles of water playing in the sodden beds. Some distant lamp or lighted window gleamed below me. I was thankful that I could see so little. All my senses seemed to desire to veil themselves and, feeling that I was about to slip from them, I pressed the palms of my hands together until they trembled, murmuring: *"O love! O love!"* many times.

At last she spoke to me. When she addressed the first words to me I was so confused that I did not know what to answer. She asked me was I going to *Araby*. I forgot whether I answered yes or no. It would be a splendid bazaar, she said she would love to go.

"And why can't you?" I asked.

While she spoke she turned a silver bracelet round and round her wrist. She could not go, she said, because there would be a retreat that week in her convent.[4] Her brother and two other boys were fighting for their caps and I was alone at the railings. She held one of the spikes, bowing her head towards me. The light from the lamp opposite our door caught the white curve of her neck, lit up her hair that rested there and, falling, lit up the hand upon the railing. It fell over one side of her dress and caught the white border of a petticoat, just visible as she stood at ease.

10 "It's well for you," she said.

"If I go," I said, "I will bring you something."

What innumerable follies laid waste my waking and sleeping thoughts after that evening! I wished to annihilate the tedious intervening days. I chafed against the work of school. At night in my bedroom and by day in the classroom her image came between me and the page I strove to read. The syllables of the word *Araby* were called to me through the silence in which my soul luxuriated and cast an Eastern enchantment over me. I asked for leave to go to the bazaar on Saturday night. My aunt was surprised and

---

[3] Any popular song beginning "Come all you gallant Irishmen . . ."; O'Donovan Rossa was an Irish nationalist who was banished in 1870 for advocating violent rebellion against the British.

[4] A week devoted to prayer and meditation in her convent school.

hoped it was not some Freemason[5] affair. I answered few questions in class. I watched my master's face pass from amiability to sternness; he hoped I was not beginning to idle. I could not call my wandering thoughts together. I had hardly any patience with the serious work of life which, now that it stood between me and my desire, seemed to me child's play, ugly monotonous child's play.

On Saturday morning I reminded my uncle that I wished to go to the bazaar in the evening. He was fussing at the hallstand, looking for the hat-brush, and answered me curtly:

"Yes, boy, I know."

15   As he was in the hall I could not go into the front parlour and lie at the window. I left the house in bad humour and walked slowly towards the school. The air was pitilessly raw and already my heart misgave me.

When I came home to dinner my uncle had not yet been home. Still it was early. I sat staring at the clock for some time and, when its ticking began to irritate me, I left the room. I mounted the staircase and gained the upper part of the house. The high cold empty gloomy rooms liberated me and I went from room to room singing. From the front window I saw my companions playing below in the street. Their cries reached me weakened and indistinct and, leaning my forehead against the cool glass, I looked over at the dark house where she lived. I may have stood there for an hour, seeing nothing but the brown-clad figure cast by my imagination, touched discreetly by the lamplight at the curved neck, at the hand upon the railings and at the border below the dress.

When I came downstairs again I found Mrs. Mercer sitting at the fire. She was an old garrulous woman, a pawnbroker's widow, who collected used stamps for some pious purpose. I had to endure the gossip of the tea-table. The meal was prolonged beyond an hour and still my uncle did not come. Mrs. Mercer stood up to go: she was sorry she couldn't wait any longer, but it was after eight o'clock and she did not like to be out late, as the night air was bad for her. When she had gone I began to walk up and down the room, clenching my fists. My aunt said:

"I'm afraid you may put off your bazaar for this night of Our Lord."

At nine o'clock I heard my uncle's latchkey in the halldoor. I heard him talking to himself and heard the hallstand rocking when it had received the weight of his overcoat. I could interpret these signs. When he was midway through his dinner I asked him to give me the money to go to the bazaar. He had forgotten.

20   "The people are in bed and after their first sleep now," he said.

I did not smile. My aunt said to him energetically:

"Can't you give him the money and let him go? You've kept him late enough as it is."

My uncle said he was very sorry he had forgotten. He said he believed in the old saying: "All work and no play makes Jack a dull boy." He asked

---

[5] At the time the story takes place, Catholics in Ireland thought the Masonic Order was a threat to the church.

me where I was going and, when I had told him a second time he asked me did I know *The Arab's Farewell to his Steed*.[6] When I left the kitchen he was about to recite the opening lines of the piece to my aunt.

I held a florin tightly in my hand as I strode down Buckingham Street towards the station. The sight of the streets thronged with buyers and glaring with gas recalled to me the purpose of my journey. I took my seat in a third-class carriage of a deserted train. After an intolerable delay the train moved out of the station slowly. It crept onward among ruinous houses and over the twinkling river. At Westland Row Station a crowd of people pressed to the carriage doors; but the porters moved them back, saying that it was a special train for the bazaar. I remained alone in the bare carriage. In a few minutes the train drew up beside an improvised wooden platform. I passed out on to the road and saw by the lighted dial of a clock that it was ten minutes to ten. In front of me was a large building which displayed the magical name.

25 I could not find any sixpenny entrance and, fearing that the bazaar would be closed, I passed in quickly through a turnstile, handing a shilling to a weary-looking man. I found myself in a big hall girdled at half its height by a gallery. Nearly all the stalls were closed and the greater part of the hall was in darkness. I recognised a silence like that which pervades a church after a service. I walked into the centre of the bazaar timidly. A few people were gathered about the stalls which were still open. Before a curtain, over which the words *Café Chantant*[7] were written in coloured lamps, two men were counting money on a salver. I listened to the fall of the coins.

Remembering with difficulty why I had come I went over to one of the stalls and examined porcelain vases and flowered tea-sets. At the door of the stall a young lady was talking and laughing with two young gentlemen. I remarked their English accents and listened vaguely to their conversation.

"O, I never said such a thing!"

"O, but you did!"

"O, but I didn't!"

30 "Didn't she say that?"

"Yes. I heard her."

"O, there's a . . . fib!"

Observing me the young lady came over and asked me did I wish to buy anything. The tone of her voice was not encouraging; she seemed to have spoken to me out of a sense of duty. I looked humbly at the great jars that stood like eastern guards at either side of the dark entrance to the stall and murmured:

"No, thank you."

---

[6] A sentimental poem by Caroline Norton (1808–1877) that tells the story of a nomad's heartbreak after selling his much-loved horse.

[7] A Paris café featuring musical entertainment.

35   The young lady changed the position of one of the vases and went back to the two young men. They began to talk of the same subject. Once or twice the young lady glanced at me over her shoulder.

I lingered before her stall, though I knew my stay was useless, to make my interest in her wares seem the more real. Then I turned away slowly and walked down the middle of the bazaar. I allowed the two pennies to fall against the sixpence in my pocket. I heard a voice call from one end of the gallery that the light was out. The upper part of the hall was now completely dark.

Gazing up into the darkness I saw myself as a creature driven and derided by vanity; and my eyes burned with anguish and anger.

READING AND REACTING

1. How would you characterize the story's level of diction? Is this level appropriate for a story about a young boy's experiences? Explain.

2. In what particular situations or contexts is Joyce most likely to use figurative language? Why?

3. What words, phrases, and figures of speech express the boy's extreme idealism and romantic view of the world? In what way does such language express the story's major theme?

4. In paragraph 4 the narrator says, "her name was like a summons to all my foolish blood." In the story's last sentence he sees himself as "a creature driven and derided by vanity." What other expressions does he use to describe his feelings? How would you characterize these feelings?

5. How is language used to emphasize the contrast between the narrator's day-to-day life and the exotic promise of the bazaar?

6. What does each of the italicized words suggest: "We walked through the *flaring* streets" (5); "I heard the rain *impinge* upon the earth" (6); "I *chafed* against the work of school" (11); "I found myself in a big hall *girdled* at half its height by a gallery" (25)? What other examples of unusual word choice can you identify in the story?

7. What is it about the events in this story that causes the narrator to remember them years later?

8. Identify words and phrases in the story that are associated with religion. What purpose do these references to religion serve?

9. **JOURNAL ENTRY** Rewrite a brief passage from this story in the voice of the young boy. Use informal style, simple figures of speech, and vocabulary appropriate for a child.

10. **CRITICAL PERSPECTIVE** In *Notes on the American Short Story Today*, Richard Kostelanetz defines the epiphany, one of Joyce's most significant contributions to literature:

    In Joyce's pervasively influential theory of the short story we remember, the fiction turned upon an epiphany, a moment of revelation in which, in [critic] Harry Levin's words, "amid the most encumbered circumstances it suddenly happens that the veil is lifted, the . . . mystery laid bare, and the ultimate secret of things made manifest." The epiphany, then, became a technique for jelling the narrative and locking the story's import into place. . . . What made this method revolutionary was the shifting of the focal point of the story from its end . . . to a spot within the body of the text, usually near (but not at) the end.

Where in "Araby" does the story's epiphany occur? Does it do all that Kostelanetz's definition says an epiphany should do? Or do you believe that, at least in the case of "Araby," the epiphany may not be as significant a force as Kostelanetz suggests?

ERNEST HEMINGWAY (1898–1961) grew up in Oak Park, Illinois, and after high school graduation began his writing career as a cub reporter on the *Kansas City Star.* As a volunteer ambulance driver in World War I, eighteen-year-old Hemingway was wounded by machine-gun fire while carrying an Italian soldier to safety. In 1922, Hemingway and his first wife (he married four times) moved to Paris, where he taught Ezra Pound how to box, let Gertrude Stein mind the baby, and talked literary shop with expatriate writers F. Scott Fitzgerald and James Joyce. He was, said Joyce, "a big, powerful peasant, as strong as a buffalo . . . and ready to live the life he writes about." In fact, this public image of the "man's man"—the war correspondent, the deep-sea fisherman, the hunter on safari—was one Hemingway carefully created for himself.

Success came early, with publication of the short story collection *In Our Time* (1925) and his first and most acclaimed novel, *The Sun Also Rises* (1926), a portrait of a postwar "lost generation" of Americans adrift in Europe. Hemingway's novels make fiction and art out of the reality of his own life. *A Farewell to Arms* (1929) harks back to his war experiences; *For Whom the Bell Tolls* (1940) emerged out of his experiences as a journalist in Spain during the Spanish Civil War. Late in life, he made his home in Key West, Florida, and then in Cuba, where he wrote *The Old Man and the Sea* (1952). Hemingway's heroes embody the writer's own belief that while life may be followed by *nada,* or nothingness, strong individuals can embrace life and live it with dignity and honor. In 1961, plagued by poor health and mental illness—and perhaps by the difficulty of living up to his own image—Hemingway took his own life.

According to novelist and critic Anthony Burgess, Hemingway changed the sound of English prose by struggling to write a "true simple declarative sentence." His spare, unadorned style "sounds easy now, chiefly because Hemingway has shown us how to do it, but it was not easy at a time when 'literature' still meant fine writing in the Victorian sense. . . ." Hemingway was awarded the 1954 Nobel Prize in literature.

ERNEST HEMINGWAY

A Clean, Well-Lighted Place
(1933)

It was late and every one had left the café except an old man who sat in the shadow the leaves of the tree made against the electric light. In the day time the street was dusty, but at night the dew settled the dust and the old man liked to sit late because he was deaf and now at night it was quiet and he felt the difference. The two waiters inside the café knew that the old man was a little drunk, and while he was a good client they knew that if he became too drunk he would leave without paying, so they kept watch on him.

"Last week he tried to commit suicide," one waiter said.

"Why?"

"He was in despair."

5   "What about?"

"Nothing."

"How do you know it was nothing?"

"He has plenty of money."

They sat together at a table that was close against the wall near the door of the café and looked at the terrace where the tables were all empty except where the old man sat in the shadow of the leaves of the tree that moved slightly in the wind. A girl and a soldier went by in the street. The street light shone on the brass number on his collar. The girl wore no head covering and hurried beside him.

10   "The guard will pick him up," one waiter said.

"What does it matter if he gets what he's after?"

"He had better get off the street now. The guard will get him. They went by five minutes ago."

The old man sitting in the shadow rapped on his saucer with his glass. The younger waiter went over to him.

"What do you want?"

15   The old man looked at him. "Another brandy," he said.

"You'll be drunk," the waiter said. The old man looked at him. The waiter went away.

"He'll stay all night," he said to his colleague. "I'm sleepy now. I never get into bed before three o'clock. He should have killed himself last week."

The waiter took the brandy bottle and another saucer from the counter inside the café and marched out to the old man's table. He put down the saucer and poured the glass full of brandy.

"You should have killed yourself last week," he said to the deaf man. The old man motioned with his finger. "A little more," he said. The waiter poured on into the glass so that the brandy slopped over and ran down the stem into the top saucer of the pile. "Thank you," the old man said. The waiter took the bottle back inside the café. He sat down at the table with his colleague again.

20   "He's drunk now," he said.

"He's drunk every night."

"What did he want to kill himself for?"

"How should I know."

"How did he do it?"

25   "He hung himself with a rope."

"Who cut him down?"

"His niece."

"Why did they do it?"

"Fear for his soul."

30   "How much money has he got?"

"He's got plenty."

"He must be eighty years old."

"Anyway I should say he was eighty."

"I wish he would go home. I never get to bed before three o'clock. What kind of hour is that to go to bed?"

35   "He stays up because he likes it."

"He's lonely. I'm not lonely. I have a wife waiting in bed for me."

"He had a wife once too."

"A wife would be no good to him now."

"You can't tell. He might be better with a wife."

40   "His niece looks after him. You said she cut him down."

"I know."

"I wouldn't want to be that old. An old man is a nasty thing."

"Not always. This old man is clean. He drinks without spilling. Even now, drunk. Look at him."

"I don't want to look at him. I wish he would go home. He has no regard for those who must work."

45   The old man looked from his glass across the square, then over at the waiters.

"Another brandy," he said, pointing to his glass. The waiter who was in a hurry came over.

"Finished," he said, speaking with that omission of syntax stupid people employ when talking to drunken people or foreigners. "No more tonight. Close now."

"Another," said the old man.

"No. Finished." The waiter wiped the edge of the table with a towel and shook his head.

50   The old man stood up, slowly counted the saucers, took a leather coin purse from his pocket and paid for the drinks, leaving half a peseta tip.

The waiter watched him go down the street, a very old man walking unsteadily but with dignity.

"Why didn't you let him stay and drink?" the unhurried waiter asked. They were putting up the shutters. "It is not half-past two."

"I want to go home to bed."

"What is an hour?"

55   "More to me than to him."

"An hour is the same."

"You talk like an old man yourself. He can buy a bottle and drink at home."

"It's not the same."

"No, it is not," agreed the waiter with a wife. He did not wish to be unjust. He was only in a hurry.

60   "And you? You have no fear of going home before your usual hour?"

"Are you trying to insult me?"

"No, hombre, only to make a joke."

"No," the waiter who was in a hurry said, rising from pulling down the metal shutters. "I have confidence. I am all confidence."

"You have youth, confidence, and a job," the older waiter said. "You have everything."

65   "And what do you lack?"

"Everything but work."

"You have everything I have."

"No. I have never had confidence and I am not young."

"Come on. Stop talking nonsense and lock up."

70   "I am of those who like to stay late at the café," the older waiter said. "With all those who do not want to go to bed. With all those who need a light for the night."

"I want to go home and into bed."

"We are of two different kinds," the older waiter said. He was now dressed to go home. "It is not only a question of youth and confidence although those things are very beautiful. Each night I am reluctant to close up because there may be some one who needs the café."

"Hombre, there are bodegas[1] open all night long."

"You do not understand. This is a clean and pleasant café. It is well lighted. The light is very good and also, now, there are shadows of the leaves."

75   "Good night," said the younger waiter.

"Good night," the other said. Turning off the electric light he continued the conversation with himself. It is the light of course but it is necessary that the place be clean and pleasant. You do not want music. Certainly you do not want music. Nor can you stand before a bar with dignity although that is all that is provided for these hours. What did he fear? It was not fear or dread. It was a nothing that he knew too well. It was all a nothing and a man was nothing too. It was only that and light was all it needed and a certain cleanness and order. Some lived in it and never felt it but he knew it all was nada y pues nada y nada y pues nada.[2]

---

[1]   Wineshops, sometimes combined with grocery stores.

[2]   Nothing and then nothing and nothing and then nothing.

Our nada who art in nada, nada be thy name thy kingdom nada thy will be nada in nada as it is in nada. Give us this nada our daily nada and nada us our nada as we nada our nadas and nada us not into nada but deliver us from nada; pues nada. Hail nothing full of nothing, nothing is with thee. He smiled and stood before a bar with a shining steam pressure coffee machine.

"What's yours?" asked the barman.

"Nada."

"Otro loco más[3]," said the barman and turned away.

80　"A little cup," said the waiter.

The barman poured it for him.

"The light is very bright and pleasant but the bar is unpolished," the waiter said.

The barman looked at him but did not answer. It was too late at night for conversation.

"You want another copita[4]?" the barman asked.

85　"No, thank you," said the waiter and went out. He disliked bars and bodegas. A clean, well-lighted café was a very different thing. Now, without thinking further, he would go home to his room. He would lie in the bed and finally, with daylight, he would go to sleep. After all, he said to himself, it is probably only insomnia. Many must have it.

Reading and Reacting

1. Throughout the story certain words—*nada,* for example—are repeated. Identify as many of these repeated words as you can. What do you think such repetition achieves?

2. The story's dialogue is presented in alternating exchanges of very brief sentences. What is the effect of these clipped exchanges?

3. Characterize the tone of the story.

4. Does the story present the human condition in optimistic or pessimistic terms? In what sense are the story's style and tone well suited to this worldview?

5. Why does Hemingway use Spanish in the story? Would the impact of the prayer be different if it had been spoken in English? Explain.

6. The café is described as "clean" and "pleasant." Why is this description a key element of the story? In what sense is this description ironic?

7. The story's primary point of view is objective. At times, however, a limited omniscient point of view is used. Identify such instances, and try to explain the reason for each shift in point of view.

---

[3] Another lunatic.

[4] Little cup.

8. Identify examples of figurative language used in the story. How does the presence (or absence) of such language help to convey the story's theme?

9. **JOURNAL ENTRY**   Rewrite about half a page of the story, supplying logical transitions between sentences. How does your editing change the passage? Do your changes improve the style or take something away?

10. **CRITICAL PERSPECTIVE**   In *The Writer's Art of Self-Defense,* Jackson J. Benson states, "Blindness versus awareness is Hemingway's most pervasive theme, and it is borne on a rippling wave of irony into almost everything he writes." How do the contrasting perspectives of the two waiters in "A Clean, Well-Lighted Place" express this theme? Which one is "blind," and which one is "aware"? How do their words reveal their knowledge or lack of knowledge?

(MARY) FLANNERY O'CONNOR (1925–1964)   was born to a prosperous Catholic family in Savannah, Georgia, and spent most of her adult life on a farm near the town of Milledgeville. She left the South to study writing at the University of Iowa, moving to New York to work on her first novel, *Wise Blood* (1952). On a train going south for Christmas, O'Connor fell desperately ill; she was diagnosed as having lupus, the immune system disease that killed her father and would cause O'Connor's death when she was only thirty-nine years old.

While her mother ran the farm, O'Connor spent mornings writing and afternoons wandering the fields with cane or crutches. Her short story collection *A Good Man Is Hard to Find* (1955) and an excellent French translation of *Wise Blood* established her international reputation, which was solidified with publication of a second novel, *The Violent Bear It Away* (1960), and a posthumously published book of short stories, *Everything That Rises Must Converge* (1965).

O'Connor delighted in local reaction to her grotesque, often grisly stories: "Ask her," the men at the hardware store prodded her uncle, "why she don't write about some nice people." O'Connor, said a friend, believed that an artist "should face all the truth down to the worst of it." Yet however dark, O'Connor's stories are infused with grim humor and a fierce belief in the possibility of spiritual redemption, even for her most tortured characters. A line from her short story "A Good Man Is Hard to Find" says much about what O'Connor perceived about both natural things and her characters: "The trees were full of silver-white sunlight and the meanest of them sparkled." In O'Connor's work, the "meanest" things and people can sparkle, touched by a kind of holy madness and beauty.

FLANNERY O'CONNOR

A Good Man Is Hard to Find

(1955)

The grandmother didn't want to go to Florida. She wanted to visit some of her connections in east Tennessee and she was seizing at every chance to change Bailey's mind. Bailey was the son she lived with, her only boy. He was sitting on the edge of his chair at the table, bent over the orange sports section of the *Journal*. "Now look here, Bailey," she said, "see here, read this," and she stood with one hand on her thin hip and the other rattling the newspaper at his bald head. "Here this fellow that calls himself The Misfit is aloose from the Federal Pen and headed toward Florida and you read here what it says he did to these people. Just you read it. I wouldn't take my children in any direction with a criminal like that aloose in it. I couldn't answer to my conscience if I did."

Bailey didn't look up from his reading so she wheeled around then and faced the children's mother, a young woman in slacks, whose face was as broad and innocent as a cabbage and was tied around with a green head-kerchief that had two points on the top like a rabbit's ears. She was sitting on the sofa, feeding the baby his apricots out of a jar. "The children have been to Florida before," the old lady said. "You all ought to take them somewhere else for a change so they would see different parts of the world and be broad. They never have been to east Tennessee."

The children's mother didn't seem to hear her but the eight-year-old boy, John Wesley, a stocky child with glasses, said, "If you don't want to go to Florida, why dontcha stay at home?" He and the little girl, June Star, were reading the funny papers on the floor.

"She wouldn't stay at home to be queen for a day," June Star said without raising her yellow head.

5   "Yes and what would you do if this fellow, the Misfit, caught you?" the grandmother asked.

"I'd smack his face," John Wesley said.

"She wouldn't stay at home for a million bucks," June Star said. "Afraid she'd miss something. She has to go everywhere we go."

"All right, Miss," the grandmother said. "Just remember that the next time you want me to curl your hair."

June Star said her hair was naturally curly.

10   The next morning the grandmother was the first one in the car, ready to go. She had her big black valise that looked like the head of a hippopotamus in one corner, and underneath it she was hiding a basket with Pitty Sing, the cat, in it. She didn't intend for the cat to be left alone in the house for three days because he would miss her too much and she was afraid he might brush against one of the gas burners and accidentally asphyxiate himself. Her son, Bailey, didn't like to arrive at a motel with a cat.

She sat in the middle of the back seat with John Wesley and June Star on either side of her. Bailey and the children's mother and the baby sat in front and they left Atlanta at eight forty-five with the mileage on the car at 55890. The grandmother wrote this down because she thought it would be interesting to say how many miles they had been when they got back. It took them twenty minutes to reach the outskirts of the city.

The old lady settled herself comfortably, removing her white cotton gloves and putting them up with her purse on the shelf in front of the back window. The children's mother still had on slacks and still had her head tied up in a green kerchief, but the grandmother had on a navy blue straw sailor hat with a bunch of white violets on the brim and a navy blue dress with a small white dot in the print. Her collars and cuffs were white organdy trimmed with lace and at her neckline she had pinned a purple spray of cloth violets containing a sachet. In case of an accident, anyone seeing her dead on the highway would know at once that she was a lady.

She said she thought it was going to be a good day for driving, neither too hot nor too cold, and she cautioned Bailey that the speed limit was fifty-five miles an hour and that the patrolmen hid themselves behind billboards and small clumps of trees and sped out after you before you had a chance to slow down. She pointed out interesting details of the scenery: Stone Mountain; the blue granite that in some places came up to both sides of the highway; the brilliant red clay banks slightly streaked with purple; and the various crops that made rows of green lace-work on the ground. The trees were full of silver-white sunlight and the meanest of them sparkled. The children were reading comic magazines and their mother had gone back to sleep.

"Let's go through Georgia fast so we won't have to look at it much," John Wesley said.

15   "If I were a little boy," said the grandmother, "I wouldn't talk about my native state that way. Tennessee has the mountains and Georgia has the hills."

"Tennessee is just a hillbilly dumping ground," John Wesley said, "and Georgia is a lousy state too."

"You said it," June Star said.

"In my time," said the grandmother, folding her thin veined fingers, "children were more respectful of their native states and their parents and everything else. People did right then. Oh look at the cute little pickaninny!" she said and pointed to a Negro child standing in the door of a shack. "Wouldn't that make a picture, now?" she asked and they all turned and looked at the little Negro out of the back window. He waved.

"He didn't have any britches on," June Star said.

20   "He probably didn't have any," the grandmother explained. "Little niggers in the country don't have things like we do. If I could paint, I'd paint that picture," she said.

The children exchanged comic books.

The grandmother offered to hold the baby and the children's mother passed him over the front seat to her. She set him on her knee and bounced him and told him about the things they were passing. She rolled her eyes and screwed up her mouth and stuck her leathery thin face into his smooth bland one. Occasionally he gave her a faraway smile. They passed a large cotton field with five or six graves fenced in the middle of it, like a small island. "Look at the graveyard!" the grandmother said, pointing it out. "That was the old family burying ground. That belonged to the plantation."

"Where's the plantation?" John Wesley asked.

"Gone With the Wind," said the grandmother. "Ha. Ha."

25   When the children finished all the comic books they had brought, they opened the lunch and ate it. The grandmother ate a peanut butter sandwich and an olive and would not let the children throw the box and the paper napkins out the window. When there was nothing else to do they played a game by choosing a cloud and making the other two guess what shape it suggested. John Wesley took one the shape of a cow and June Star guessed a cow and John Wesley said, no, an automobile, and June Star said he didn't play fair, and they began to slap each other over the grandmother.

The grandmother said she would tell them a story if they would keep quiet. When she told a story, she rolled her eyes and waved her head and was very dramatic. She said once when she was a maiden lady she had been courted by a Mr. Edgar Atkins Teagarden from Jasper, Georgia. She said he was a very good-looking man and a gentleman and that he brought her a watermelon every Saturday afternoon with his initials cut in it, E. A. T. Well, one Saturday, she said, Mr. Teagarden brought the watermelon and there was nobody at home and he left it on the front porch and returned in his buggy to Jasper, but she never got the watermelon, she said, because a nigger boy ate it when he saw the initials, E. A. T.! This story tickled John Wesley's funny bone and he giggled and giggled but June Star didn't think it was any good. She said she wouldn't marry a man that just brought her a watermelon on Saturday. The grandmother said she would have done well to marry Mr. Teagarden because he was a gentleman and had bought Coca-Cola stock when it first came out and that he died only a few years ago, a very wealthy man.

They stopped at The Tower for barbecued sandwiches. The Tower was a part stucco and part wood filling station and dance hall set in a clearing outside of Timothy. A fat man named Red Sammy Butts ran it and there were signs stuck here and there on the building and for miles up and down the highway saying, TRY RED SAMMY'S FAMOUS BARBECUE. NONE LIKE FAMOUS RED SAMMY'S! RED SAM! THE FAT BOY WITH THE HAPPY LAUGH. A VETERAN! RED SAMMY'S YOUR MAN!

Red Sammy was lying on the bare ground outside The Tower with his head under a truck while a gray monkey about a foot high, chained to a small chinaberry tree, chattered nearby. The monkey sprang back into the tree and got on the highest limb as soon as he saw the children jump out of the car and run toward him.

Inside, The Tower was a long dark room with a counter at one end and tables at the other and dancing space in the middle. They all sat down at a board table next to the nickelodeon and Red Sam's wife, a tall burnt-brown woman with hair and eyes lighter than her skin, came and took their order. The children's mother put a dime in the machine and played "The Tennessee Waltz," and the grandmother said that tune always made her want to dance. She asked Bailey if he would like to dance but he only glared at her. He didn't have a naturally sweet disposition like she did and trips made him nervous. The grandmother's brown eyes were very bright. She swayed her head from side to side and pretended she was dancing in her chair. June Star said play something she could tap to so the children's mother put in another dime and played a fast number and June Star stepped out onto the dance floor and did her tap routine.

30   "Ain't she cute?" Red Sam's wife said, leaning over the counter. "Would you like to come be my little girl?"

"No I certainly wouldn't," June Star said. "I wouldn't live in a broken-down place like this for a million bucks!" and she ran back to the table.

"Ain't she cute?" the woman repeated, stretching her mouth politely.

"Aren't you ashamed?" hissed the grandmother.

Red Sam came in and told his wife to quit lounging on the counter and hurry up with these people's order. His khaki trousers reached just to his hip bones and his stomach hung over them like a sack of meal swaying under his shirt. He came over and sat down at a table nearby and let out a combination sigh and yodel. "You can't win," he said. "You can't win," and he wiped his sweating red face off with a gray handkerchief. "These days you don't know who to trust," he said. "Ain't that the truth?"

35   "People are certainly not nice like they used to be," said the grandmother.

"Two fellers come in here last week," Red Sammy said, "driving a Chrysler. It was a old beat-up car but it was a good one and these boys looked all right to me. Said they worked at the mill and you know I let them fellers charge the gas they bought? Now why did I do that?"

"Because you're a good man!" the grandmother said at once.

"Yes'm, I suppose so," Red Sam said as if he were struck with this answer.

His wife brought the orders, carrying the five plates all at once without a tray, two in each hand and one balanced on her arm. "It isn't a soul in this green world of God's that you can trust," she said. "And I don't count nobody out of that, not nobody," she repeated, looking at Red Sammy.

40   "Did you read about that criminal, The Misfit, that's escaped?" asked the grandmother.

"I wouldn't be a bit surprised if he didn't attact this place right here," said the woman. "If he hears about it being here, I wouldn't be none surprised to see him. If he hears it's two cent in the cash register, I wouldn't be at all surprised if he . . ."

"That'll do," Red Sam said. "Go bring these people their Co'-Colas," and the woman went off to get the rest of the order.

"A good man is hard to find," Red Sammy said. "Everything is getting terrible. I remember the day you could go off and leave your screen door unlatched. Not no more."

He and the grandmother discussed better times. The old lady said that in her opinion Europe was entirely to blame for the way things were now. She said the way Europe acted you would think we were made of money and Red Sam said it was no use talking about it, she was exactly right. The children ran outside into the white sunlight and looked at the monkey in the lacy chinaberry tree. He was busy catching fleas on himself and biting each one carefully between his teeth as if it were a delicacy.

45   They drove off again into the hot afternoon. The grandmother took cat naps and woke up every few minutes with her own snoring. Outside of Toombsboro she woke up and recalled an old plantation that she had visited in this neighborhood once when she was a young lady. She said the house had six white columns across the front and that there was an avenue of oaks leading up to it and two little wooden trellis arbors on either side in front where you sat down with your suitor after a stroll in the garden. She recalled exactly which road to turn off to get to it. She knew that Bailey would not be willing to lose any time looking at an old house, but the more she talked about it, the more she wanted to see it once again and find out if the little twin arbors were still standing. "There was a secret panel in this house," she said craftily, not telling the truth but wishing that she were, "and the story went that all the family silver was hidden in it when Sherman came through but it was never found . . ."

"Hey!" John Wesley said. "Let's go see it! We'll find it! We'll poke all the woodwork and find it! Who lives there? Where do you turn off at? Hey Pop, can't we turn off there?"

"We never have seen a house with a secret panel!" June Star shrieked. "Let's go to the house with the secret panel! Hey Pop, can't we go see the house with the secret panel!"

"It's not far from here, I know," the grandmother said. "It wouldn't take over twenty minutes."

Bailey was looking straight ahead. His jaw was as rigid as a horseshoe. "No," he said.

50   The children began to yell and scream that they wanted to see the house with the secret panel. John Wesley kicked the back of the front seat and June Star hung over her mother's shoulder and whined desperately into her ear that they never had any fun even on their vacation, that they could never do what THEY wanted to do. The baby began to scream and John Wesley kicked the back of the seat so hard that his father could feel the blows in his kidney.

"All right!" he shouted and drew the car to a stop at the side of the road. "Will you all shut up? Will you all just shut up for one second? If you don't shut up, we won't go anywhere."

"It would be very educational for them," the grandmother murmured.

"All right," Bailey said, "but get this: this is the only time we're going to stop for anything like this. This is the one and only time."

"The dirt road that you have to turn down is about a mile back," the grandmother directed. "I marked it when we passed."

55   "A dirt road," Bailey groaned.

After they had turned around and were headed toward the dirt road, the grandmother recalled other points about the house, the beautiful glass over the front doorway and the candle-lamp in the hall. John Wesley said that the secret panel was probably in the fireplace.

"You can't go inside this house," Bailey said. "You don't know who lives there."

"While you all talk to the people in front, I'll run around behind and get in a window," John Wesley suggested.

"We'll all stay in the car," his mother said.

60   They turned onto the dirt road and the car raced roughly along in a swirl of pink dust. The grandmother recalled the times when there were no paved roads and thirty miles was a day's journey. The dirt road was hilly and there were sudden washes in it and sharp curves on dangerous embankments. All at once they would be on a hill, looking down over the blue tops of trees for miles around, then the next minute, they would be in a red depression with the dust-coated trees looking down on them.

"This place had better turn up in a minute," Bailey said, "or I'm going to turn around."

The road looked as if no one had traveled on it in months.

"It's not much farther," the grandmother said and just as she said it, a horrible thought came to her. The thought was so embarrassing that she turned red in the face and her eyes dilated and her feet jumped up, upsetting her valise in the corner. The instant the valise moved, the newspaper top she had over the basket under it rose with a snarl and Pitty Sing, the cat, sprang onto Bailey's shoulder.

The children were thrown to the floor and their mother, clutching the baby, was thrown out the door onto the ground; the old lady was thrown into the front seat. The car turned over once and landed right-side-up in a gulch off the side of the road. Bailey remained in the driver's seat with the cat—gray-striped with a broad white face and an orange nose—clinging to his neck like a caterpillar.

65   As soon as the children saw they could move their arms and legs, they scrambled out of the car, shouting, "We've had an ACCIDENT!" The grandmother was curled up under the dashboard, hoping she was injured so that Bailey's wrath would not come down on her all at once. The horrible thought she had had before the accident was that the house she had remembered so vividly was not in Georgia but in Tennessee.

Bailey removed the cat from his neck with both hands and flung it out the window against the side of a pine tree. Then he got out of the car and started looking for the children's mother. She was sitting against the side of the red gutted ditch, holding the screaming baby, but she only had a cut down her face and a broken shoulder. "We've had an ACCIDENT!" the children screamed in a frenzy of delight.

"But nobody's killed," June Star said with disappointment as the grandmother limped out of the car, her hat still pinned to her head but the broken front brim standing up at a jaunty angle and the violet spray hanging off the side. They all sat down in the ditch, except the children, to recover from the shock. They were all shaking.

"Maybe a car will come along," said the children's mother hoarsely.

"I believe I have injured an organ," said the grandmother, pressing her side, but no one answered her. Bailey's teeth were clattering. He had on a yellow sport shirt with bright blue parrots designed in it and his face was as yellow as the shirt. The grandmother decided that she would not mention that the house was in Tennessee.

70   The road was about ten feet above and they could see only the tops of the trees on the other side of it. Behind the ditch they were sitting in there were more woods, tall and dark and deep. In a few minutes they saw a car some distance away on top of a hill, coming slowly as if the occupants were watching them. The grandmother stood up and waved both arms dramatically to attract their attention. The car continued to come on slowly, disappeared around a bend and appeared again, moving even slower, on top of the hill they had gone over. It was a big black battered hearse-like automobile. There were three men in it.

It came to a stop just over them and for some minutes, the driver looked down with a steady expressionless gaze to where they were sitting, and didn't speak. Then he turned his head and muttered something to the other two and they got out. One was a fat boy in black trousers and a red sweat shirt with a silver stallion embossed on the front of it. He moved around on the right side of them and stood staring, his mouth partly open in a kind of loose grin. The other had on khaki pants and a blue striped coat and a gray hat pulled down very low, hiding most of his face. He came around slowly on the left side. Neither spoke.

The driver got out of the car and stood by the side of it, looking down at them. He was an older man than the other two. His hair was just beginning to gray and he wore silver-rimmed spectacles that gave him a scholarly look. He had a long creased face and didn't have on any shirt or undershirt. He had on blue jeans that were too tight for him and was holding a black hat and a gun. The two boys also had guns.

"We've had an ACCIDENT!" the children screamed.

The grandmother had the peculiar feeling that the bespectacled man was someone she knew. His face was as familiar to her as if she had known him all her life but she could not recall who he was. He moved away from the car and began to come down the embankment, placing his feet carefully so that he wouldn't slip. He had on tan and white shoes and no socks, and his ankles were red and thin. "Good afternoon," he said. "I see you all had you a little spill."

75   "We turned over twice!" said the grandmother.

"Oncet," he corrected. "We seen it happen. Try their car and see will it run, Hiram," he said quietly to the boy with the gray hat.

"What you got that gun for?" John Wesley asked. "Watcha gonna do with that gun?"

"Lady," the man said to the children's mother, "would you mind calling them children to sit down by you? Children make me nervous. I want all you all to sit down right together there where you're at."

"What are you telling US what to do for?" June Star asked.

80   Behind them the line of woods gaped like a dark open mouth. "Come here," said their mother.

"Look here now," Bailey began suddenly, "we're in a predicament! We're in . . ."

The grandmother shrieked. She scrambled to her feet and stood staring. "You're The Misfit!" she said. "I recognized you at once!"

"Yes'm," the man said, smiling slightly as if he were pleased in spite of himself to be known, "but it would have been better for all of you, lady, if you hadn't of reckernized me."

Bailey turned his head sharply and said something to his mother that shocked even the children. The old lady began to cry and The Misfit reddened.

85   "Lady," he said, "don't you get upset. Sometimes a man says things he don't mean. I don't reckon he meant to talk to you thataway."

"You wouldn't shoot a lady, would you?" the grandmother said and removed a clean handkerchief from her cuff and began to slap at her eyes with it.

The Misfit pointed the toe of his shoe into the ground and made a little hole and then covered it up again. "I would hate to have to," he said.

"Listen," the grandmother almost screamed, "I know you're a good man. You don't look a bit like you have common blood. I know you must come from nice people!"

"Yes mam," he said, "finest people in the world." When he smiled he showed a row of strong white teeth. "God never made a finer woman than my mother and my daddy's heart was pure gold," he said. The boy with the red sweat shirt had come around behind them and was standing with his gun at his hip. The Misfit squatted down on the ground. "Watch them children, Bobby Lee," he said. "You know they make me nervous." He looked at the six of them huddled together in front of him and he seemed to be embarrassed as if he couldn't think of anything to say. "Ain't a cloud in the sky," he remarked, looking up at it. "Don't see no sun but don't see no cloud neither."

90   "Yes, it's a beautiful day," said the grandmother. "Listen," she said, "you shouldn't call yourself The Misfit because I know you're a good man at heart. I can just look at you and tell."

"Hush!" Bailey yelled. "Hush! Everybody shut up and let me handle this!" He was squatting in the position of a runner about to sprint forward but he didn't move.

"I pre-chate that, lady," The Misfit said and drew a little circle in the ground with the butt of his gun.

"It'll take a half a hour to fix this here car," Hiram called, looking over the raised hood of it.

"Well, first you and Bobby Lee get him and that little boy to step over yonder with you," The Misfit said, pointing to Bailey and John Wesley. "The boys want to ast you something," he said to Bailey. "Would you mind stepping back in them woods there with them?"

95   "Listen," Bailey began, "we're in a terrible predicament! Nobody realizes what this is," and his voice cracked. His eyes were as blue and intense as the parrots in his shirt and he remained perfectly still.

The grandmother reached up to adjust her hat brim as if she were going to the woods with him but it came off in her hand. She stood staring at it and after a second she let it fall on the ground. Hiram pulled Bailey up by the arm as if he were assisting an old man. John Wesley caught hold of his father's hand and Bobby Lee followed. They went off toward the woods and just as they reached the dark edge, Bailey turned and supporting himself against a gray naked pine trunk, he shouted, "I'll be back in a minute, Mamma, wait on me!"

"Come back this instant!" his mother shrilled but they all disappeared into the woods.

"Bailey Boy!" the grandmother called in a tragic voice but she found she was looking at The Misfit squatting on the ground in front of her. "I just know you're a good man," she said desperately. "You're not a bit common!"

"Nome, I ain't a good man," The Misfit said after a second as if he had considered her statement carefully, "but I ain't the worst in the world neither. My daddy said I was a different breed of dog from my brothers and sisters. 'You know,' Daddy said, 'it's some that can live their whole life out without asking about it and it's others has to know why it is, and this boy is one of the latters. He's going to be into everything!'" He put on his black hat and looked up suddenly and then away deep into the woods as if he were embarrassed again. "I'm sorry I don't have on a shirt before you ladies," he said, hunching his shoulders slightly. "We buried our clothes that we had on when we escaped and we're just making do until we can get better. We borrowed these from some folks we met," he explained.

100   "That's perfectly all right," the grandmother said. "Maybe Bailey has an extra shirt in his suitcase."

"I'll look and see terrectly," The Misfit said.

"Where are they taking him?" the children's mother screamed.

"Daddy was a card himself," The Misfit said. "You couldn't put anything over on him. He never got in trouble with the Authorities though. Just had the knack of handling them."

"You could be honest too if you'd only try," said the grandmother. "Think how wonderful it would be to settle down and live a comfortable life and not have to think about somebody chasing you all the time."

105   The Misfit kept scratching in the ground with the butt of his gun as if he were thinking about it. "Yes'm, somebody is always after you," he murmured.

The grandmother noticed how thin his shoulder blades were just behind his hat because she was standing up looking down on him. "Do you ever pray?" she asked.

He shook his head. All she saw was the black hat wiggle between his shoulder blades. "Nome," he said.

There was a pistol shot from the woods, followed closely by another. Then silence. The old lady's head jerked around. She could hear the wind move through the tree tops like a long satisfied insuck of breath. "Bailey Boy!" she called.

"I was a gospel singer for a while," The Misfit said. "I been most everything. Been in the arm service, both land and sea, at home and abroad, been twict married, been an undertaker, been with the railroads, plowed Mother Earth, been in a tornado, seen a man burnt alive oncet," and he looked up at the children's mother and the little girl who were sitting close together, their faces white and their eyes glassy; "I even seen a woman flogged," he said.

110   "Pray, pray," the grandmother began, "pray, pray . . ."

"I never was a bad boy that I remember of," The Misfit said in an almost dreamy voice, "but somewheres along the line I done something wrong and got sent to the penitentiary. I was buried alive," and he looked up and held her attention to him by a steady stare.

"That's when you should have started to pray," she said. "What did you do to get sent to the penitentiary that first time?"

"Turn to the right, it was a wall," The Misfit said, looking up again at the cloudless sky. "Turn to the left, it was a wall. Look up it was a ceiling, look down it was a floor. I forget what I done, lady. I set there and set there, trying to remember what it was I done and I ain't recalled it to this day. Oncet in a while, I would think it was coming to me, but it never come."

"Maybe they put you in by mistake," the old lady said vaguely.

115   "Nome," he said. "It wasn't no mistake. They had the papers on me."

"You must have stolen something," she said.

The Misfit sneered slightly. "Nobody had nothing I wanted," he said. "It was a head-doctor at the penitentiary said what I had done was kill my daddy but I known that for a lie. My daddy died in nineteen ought nineteen of the epidemic flu and I never had a thing to do with it. He was buried in the Mount Hopewell Baptist churchyard and you can go there and see for yourself."

"If you would pray," the old lady said, "Jesus would help you."

"That's right," The Misfit said.

120   "Well then, why don't you pray?" she asked trembling with delight suddenly.

"I don't want no hep," he said. "I'm doing all right by myself."

Bobby Lee and Hiram came ambling back from the woods. Bobby Lee was dragging a yellow shirt with bright blue parrots in it.

"Thow me that shirt, Bobby Lee," The Misfit said. The shirt came flying at him and landed on his shoulder and he put it on. The grandmother couldn't name what the shirt reminded her of. "No, lady," The Misfit said while he was buttoning it up, "I found out the crime don't matter. You can do one thing or you can do another, kill a man or take a tire off his car, because sooner or later you're going to forget what it was you done and just be punished for it."

The children's mother had begun to make heaving noises as if she couldn't get her breath. "Lady," he asked, "would you and that little girl like to step off yonder with Bobby Lee and Hiram and join your husband?"

125   "Yes, thank you," the mother said faintly. Her left arm dangled helplessly and she was holding the baby, who had gone to sleep, in the other. "Hep that lady up, Hiram," The Misfit said as she struggled to climb out of the ditch, "and Bobby Lee, you hold onto that little girl's hand."

"I don't want to hold hands with him," June Star said. "He reminds me of a pig."

The fat boy blushed and laughed and caught her by the arm and pulled her off into the woods after Hiram and her mother.

Alone with The Misfit, the grandmother found that she had lost her voice. There was not a cloud in the sky nor any sun. There was nothing around her but woods. She wanted to tell him that he must pray. She opened and closed her mouth several times before anything came out. Finally she found herself saying, "Jesus, Jesus," meaning, Jesus will help you, but the way she was saying it, it sounded as if she might be cursing.

"Yes'm," The Misfit said as if he agreed. "Jesus thown everything off balance. It was the same case with Him as with me except He hadn't committed any crime and they could prove I had committed one because they had the papers on me. Of course," he said, "they never shown me my papers. That's why I sign myself now. I said long ago, you get you a signature and sign everything you do and keep a copy of it. Then you'll know what you done and you can hold up the crime to the punishment and see do they match and in the end you'll have something to prove you ain't been treated right. I call myself The Misfit," he said, "because I can't make what all I done wrong fit what all I gone through in punishment."

130   There was a piercing scream from the woods, followed closely by a pistol report. "Does it seem right to you, lady, that one is punished a heap and another ain't punished at all?"

"Jesus!" the old lady cried. "You've got good blood! I know you wouldn't shoot a lady! I know you come from nice people! Pray! Jesus, you ought not to shoot a lady. I'll give you all the money I've got!"

"Lady," The Misfit said, looking beyond her far into the woods, "there never was a body that give the undertaker a tip."

There were two more pistol reports and the grandmother raised her head like a parched old turkey hen crying for water and called, "Bailey Boy, Bailey Boy!" as if her heart would break.

"Jesus was the only One that ever raised the dead," The Misfit continued, "and He shouldn't have done it. He thown everything off balance. If He did what He said, then it's nothing for you to do but thow away everything and follow Him, and if He didn't, then it's nothing for you to do but enjoy the few minutes you got left the best way you can—by killing somebody or burning down his house or doing some other meanness to him. No pleasure but meanness," he said and his voice became almost a snarl.

135   "Maybe He didn't raise the dead," the old lady mumbled, not knowing what she was saying and feeling so dizzy that she sank down in the ditch with her legs twisted under her.

"I wasn't there so I can't say He didn't," The Misfit said. "I wisht I had of been there," he said, hitting the ground with his fist. "It ain't right I wasn't there because if I had of been there I would of known. Listen, lady," he said in a high voice, "if I had of been there I would of known and I wouldn't be like I am now." His voice seemed about to crack and the grandmother's head cleared for an instant. She saw the man's face twisted close to her own as if he were going to cry and she murmured, "Why you're one of my babies. You're one of my own children!" She reached out and touched him on the shoulder. The Misfit sprang back as if a snake had bitten him and shot her three times through the chest. Then he put his gun down on the ground and took off his glasses and began to clean them.

Hiram and Bobby Lee returned from the woods and stood over the ditch, looking down at the grandmother who half sat and half lay in a puddle of blood with her legs crossed under her like a child's and her face smiling up at the cloudless sky.

Without his glasses, The Misfit's eyes were red-rimmed and pale and defenseless-looking. "Take her off and thow her where you thown the others," he said, picking up the cat that was rubbing itself against his leg.

"She was a talker, wasn't she?" Bobby Lee said, sliding down the ditch with a yodel.

140   "She would of been a good woman," The Misfit said, "if it had been somebody there to shoot her every minute of her life."

"Some fun!" Bobby Lee said.

"Shut up, Bobby Lee," The Misfit said. "It's no real pleasure in life."

READING AND REACTING

1. How are the style and tone of the narrator's voice different from those of the characters? What, if anything, is the significance of this difference?

2. Figurative language in this story sometimes creates unflattering, even grotesque, pictures of the characters. Find several examples of such negative figures of speech. Why do you think the author uses them?

3. What does the grandmother's use of the words *pickaninny* and *nigger* reveal about her? How are readers expected to reconcile this language with her very proper appearance and her preoccupation with manners? How does her use of these words affect your reaction to her?

4. Explain the irony in this statement: "In case of an accident, anyone seeing her dead on the highway would know at once that she was a lady" (12).

5. How does The Misfit's dialect characterize him?

6. What does the allusion to *Gone With the Wind* (24) contribute to the story?

7. How do the style and tone of the two-paragraph description of the three men in the car (71–72) help to prepare readers for the events that follow?

8. When The Misfit tells the grandmother about his life, his language takes on a measured, rhythmic quality: "Been in the arm service, both land and sea, at home and abroad, been twict married, been an undertaker, been with the railroads, plowed Mother Earth, been in a tornado, seen a man burnt alive oncet, . . ." (109). Find other examples of parallelism and rhythmic repetition in this character's speech. How is this style consistent with The Misfit's character?

9. **JOURNAL ENTRY**   Why do you think the grandmother tells The Misfit she recognizes him? Why does she fail to realize the danger of her remark?

10. **CRITICAL PERSPECTIVE**   In a discussion of "A Good Man Is Hard To Find," Martha Stephens is critical of the story's ending, commenting that "the failure of the final scene—and hence of the story—seems to result from the fact that a tonal shift that occurs midway through the story finally runs out of control." The "tonal shift" to which she refers is the abrupt movement from grotesque comedy to senseless, shocking tragedy. Stephens asks:

What is the reader to think or feel about anything in the massacre scene? There is pain and shock but much that mocks that pain and shock—the heavy comedy, for instance, indeed one might say the almost burlesque treatment, of the three killers. There is the feeling that though we cannot help but pity the tormented family, the story continues to demand our contempt for them. One feels that somehow the central experience of the story—in spite of the affecting, the chilling details surrounding these deaths, in spite even of the not altogether abusive treatment of the grandmother in Part One—will elude anyone who gives way to these feelings of pain and pity. If the writer's task is, as Conrad said, to make us "see," what is here to be seen? Surely not that life is wholly senseless and contemptible and that our fitting end is in senseless pain.

Do you agree that the story's ending is unsatisfactory? Does the violence "make us 'see,'" or is it just gratuitous? Explain.

TIM O'BRIEN (1946–   ) is sometimes described as a writer whose books are on the shortlist of essential fiction about the Vietnam War. His plots focus on danger, violence, courage, endurance, despair, and other topics often associated with war fiction, but O'Brien treats these topics with an emphasis on the contemporary dilemmas faced by those who may be unwilling participants in an unpopular war. O'Brien calls *If I Die in a Combat Zone, Box Me Up and Ship Me Home* (1979) a memoir because it relates his war experiences as a naive young college graduate who suddenly finds himself facing bullets and land mines rather than sitting behind a desk. *Northern Lights* (1975) concentrates on the wilderness survival experiences of two brothers, one of whom has just returned from the Vietnam War. A fantastic daydream of an American soldier, *Going After Cacciato* (1978), which has been compared to *Catch 22*, won a National Book Award. *The Things They Carried* (1990) is a quasi-fictional collection of interrelated stories that deal with a single platoon; some stories involve a young soldier named Tim O'Brien, and some a forty-three-year-old writer named Tim O'Brien who writes about his memories. *The Vietnam in Me* (1994) emphasizes the destructive effects of war upon a soldier, even after he has returned home. *In the Lake of the Woods* (1994) tells a dramatic story of a couple missing in Minnesota.

After graduating summa cum laude from Macalester College in 1968, O'Brien was immediately drafted into the U.S. Army and sent to Vietnam, where he served with the 198th Infantry Brigade. He was promoted to sergeant and awarded a Purple Heart after receiving a shrapnel wound in a battle near My Lai. In 1970, after discharge from the army, he attended Harvard graduate school to study government. He worked as a reporter for the *Washington Post* before pursuing a full-time career as a writer. Currently, O'Brien lives in Cambridge, Massachusetts.

TIM O'BRIEN

The Things They Carried

(1986)

First Lieutenant Jimmy Cross carried letters from a girl named Martha, a junior at Mount Sebastian College in New Jersey. They were not love letters, but Lieutenant Cross was hoping, so he kept them folded in plastic at the bottom of his rucksack. In the late afternoon, after a day's march, he would dig his foxhole, wash his hands under a canteen, unwrap the letters, hold them with the tips of his fingers, and spend the last hour of light pretending. He would imagine romantic camping trips into the White Mountains in New Hampshire. He would sometimes taste the envelope flaps, knowing her tongue had been there. More than anything, he wanted Martha to love him as he loved her, but the letters were mostly chatty, elusive on the matter of love. She was a virgin, he was almost sure. She was an English major at Mount Sebastian, and she wrote beautifully about her professors and roommates and midterm exams, about her respect for Chaucer and her great affection for Virginia Woolf. She often quoted lines of poetry; she never mentioned the war, except to say, Jimmy, take care of yourself. The letters weighed ten ounces. They were signed "Love, Martha," but Lieutenant Cross understood that "Love" was only a way of signing and did not mean what he sometimes pretended it meant. At dusk, he would carefully return the letters to his rucksack. Slowly, a bit distracted, he would get up and move among his men, checking the perimeter, then at full dark he would return to his hole and watch the night and wonder if Martha was a virgin.

The things they carried were largely determined by necessity. Among the necessities or near necessities were P-38 can openers, pocket knives, heat tabs, wrist watches, dog tags, mosquito repellent, chewing gum, candy, cigarettes, salt tablets, packets of Kool-Aid, lighters, matches, sewing kits, Military Payment Certificates, C rations, and two or three canteens of water. Together, these items weighed between fifteen and twenty pounds, depending upon a man's habits or rate of metabolism. Henry Dobbins, who was a big man, carried extra rations; he was especially fond of canned peaches in heavy syrup over pound cake. Dave Jensen, who practiced field hygiene, carried a toothbrush, dental floss, and several hotel-size bars of soap he'd stolen on R&R in Sydney, Australia. Ted Lavender, who was scared, carried tranquilizers until he was shot in the head outside the village of Than Khe in mid-April. By necessity, and because it was SOP, they all carried steel helmets that weighed five pounds including the liner and camouflage cover. They carried the standard fatigue jackets and trousers. Very few carried underwear. On their feet they carried jungle boots—2.1 pounds—and Dave Jensen carried three pairs of socks and a can of Dr. Scholl's foot powder as a precaution against trench foot. Until he was shot, Ted Lavender carried six or seven ounces of premium dope, which for him was a necessity. Mitchell Sanders, the RTO, carried condoms. Norman Bowker carried a diary. Rat Kiley carried comic books. Kiowa, a devout Baptist, carried an illustrated New Testament that had been presented to him by his father, who taught Sunday school in Oklahoma City, Oklahoma. As a hedge against bad times, however, Kiowa also carried his grandmother's distrust of the white man, his grandfather's old hunting hatchet. Necessity dictated. Because the land was mined and booby-trapped, it was SOP for each man to carry a steel-centered, nylon-covered flak jacket, which weighed 6.7 pounds, but which on hot days seemed much heavier. Because you could die so quickly, each man carried at least one large compress bandage, usually in the helmet band for easy access. Because the nights were cold, and because the monsoons were wet, each carried a green plastic poncho that could be used as a raincoat or ground sheet or makeshift tent. With its quilted liner, the poncho weighed almost two pounds, but it was worth every ounce. In April, for instance, when Ted Lavender was shot, they used his poncho to wrap him up, then to carry him across the paddy, then to lift him into the chopper that took him away.

They were called legs or grunts.

To carry something was to "hump" it, as when Lieutenant Jimmy Cross humped his love for Martha up the hills and through the swamps. In its intransitive form, "to hump" meant "to walk," or "to march," but it implied burdens far beyond the intransitive.

5   Almost everyone humped photographs. In his wallet, Lieutenant Cross carried two photographs of Martha. The first was a Kodachrome snapshot signed "Love," though he knew better. She stood against a brick wall. Her eyes were gray and neutral, her lips slightly open as she stared straight-on at the camera. At night, sometimes, Lieutenant Cross wondered who had taken the picture, because he knew she had boyfriends, because he loved her so much, and because he could see the shadow of the picture taker spreading out against the brick wall. The second photograph had been clipped from the 1968 Mount Sebastian yearbook. It was an action shot— women's volleyball—and Martha was bent horizontal to the floor, reaching, the palms of her hands in sharp focus, the tongue taut, the expression frank and competitive. There was no visible sweat. She wore white gym shorts. Her legs, he thought, were almost certainly the legs of a virgin, dry and without hair, the left·knee cocked and carrying her entire weight, which was just over one hundred pounds. Lieutenant Cross remembered touching that left knee. A dark theater, he remembered, and the movie was *Bonnie and Clyde,* and Martha wore a tweed skirt, and during the final scene, when he touched her knee, she turned and looked at him in a sad, sober way that made him pull his hand back, but he would always remember the feel of the tweed skirt and the knee beneath it and the sound of the gunfire that killed Bonnie and Clyde, how embarrassing it was, how slow

and oppressive. He remembered kissing her good night at the dorm door. Right then, he thought, he should've done something brave. He should've carried her up the stairs to her room and tied her to the bed and touched that left knee all night long. He should've risked it. Whenever he looked at the photographs, he thought of new things he should've done.

What they carried was partly a function of rank, partly of field specialty.

As a first lieutenant and platoon leader, Jimmy Cross carried a compass, maps, code books, binoculars, and a .45-caliber pistol that weighed 2.9 pounds fully loaded. He carried a strobe light and the responsibility for the lives of his men.

As an RTO, Mitchell Sanders carried the PRC-25 radio, a killer, twenty-six pounds with its battery.

As a medic, Rat Kiley carried a canvas satchel filled with morphine and plasma and malaria tablets and surgical tape and comic books and all the things a medic must carry, including M&M's for especially bad wounds, for a total weight of nearly twenty pounds.

10 As a big man, therefore a machine gunner, Henry Dobbins carried the M-60, which weighed twenty-three pounds unloaded, but which was almost always loaded. In addition, Dobbins carried between ten and fifteen pounds of ammunition draped in belts across his chest and shoulders.

As PFCs or Spec 4s, most of them were common grunts and carried the standard M-16 gas-operated assault rifle. The weapon weighed 7.5 pounds unloaded, 8.2 pounds with its full twenty-round magazine. Depending on numerous factors, such as topography and psychology, the riflemen carried anywhere from twelve to twenty magazines, usually in cloth bandoliers, adding on another 8.4 pounds at minimum, fourteen pounds at maximum. When it was available, they also carried M-16 maintenance gear—rods and steel brushes and swabs and tubes of LSA oil—all of which weighed about a pound. Among the grunts, some carried the M-79 grenade launcher, 5.9 pounds unloaded, a reasonably light weapon except for the ammunition, which was heavy. A single round weighed ten ounces. The typical load was twenty-five rounds. But Ted Lavender, who was scared, carried thirty-four rounds when he was shot and killed outside Than Khe, and he went down under an exceptional burden, more than twenty pounds of ammunition, plus the flak jacket and helmet and rations and water and toilet paper and tranquilizers and all the rest, plus the unweighed fear. He was dead weight. There was no twitching or flopping. Kiowa, who saw it happen, said it was like watching a rock fall, or a big sandbag or something—just boom, then down—not like the movies where the dead guy rolls around and does fancy spins and goes ass over teakettle—not like that, Kiowa said, the poor bastard just flat-fuck fell. Boom. Down. Nothing else. It was a bright morning in mid-April. Lieutenant Cross felt the pain. He blamed himself. They stripped off Lavender's canteens and ammo, all the heavy things, and Rat Kiley said the obvious, the guy's dead, and Mitchell Sanders used his radio to report one U.S. KIA and to request a chopper. Then they wrapped Lavender in his poncho. They carried him out to a dry paddy, established security, and sat smoking the dead man's dope until the chopper came. Lieutenant Cross kept to himself. He pictured Martha's smooth young face, thinking he loved her more than anything, more than his men, and now Ted Lavender was dead because he loved her so much and could not stop thinking about her. When the dust-off arrived, they carried Lavender aboard. Afterward they burned Than Khe. They marched until dusk, then dug their holes, and that night Kiowa kept explaining how you had to be there, how fast it was, how the poor guy just dropped like so much concrete. Boom-down, he said. Like cement.

In addition to the three standard weapons—the M-60, M-16, and M-79— they carried whatever presented itself, or whatever seemed appropriate as a means of killing or staying alive. They carried catch-as-catch-can. At various times, in various situations, they carried M-14s and CAR-15s and Swedish Ks and grease guns and captured AK-47s and Chi-Coms and RPGs and Simonov carbines and black-market Uzis and .38-caliber Smith & Wesson handguns and 66 mm LAWs and shotguns and silencers and blackjacks and bayonets and C-4 plastic explosives. Lee Strunk carried a slingshot; a weapon of last resort, he called it. Mitchell Sanders carried brass knuckles. Kiowa carried his grandfather's feathered hatchet. Every third or fourth man carried a Claymore antipersonnel mine—3.5 pounds with its firing device. They all carried fragmentation grenades—fourteen ounces each. They all carried at least one M-18 colored smoke grenade— twenty-four ounces. Some carried CS or tear-gas grenades. Some carried white-phosphorus grenades. They carried all they could bear, and then some, including a silent awe for the terrible power of the things they carried.

In the first week of April, before Lavender died, Lieutenant Jimmy Cross received a good-luck charm from Martha. It was a simple pebble, an ounce at most. Smooth to the touch, it was a milky-white color with flecks of orange and violet, oval-shaped, like a miniature egg. In the accompanying letter, Martha wrote that she had found the pebble on the Jersey shoreline, precisely where the land touched water at high tide, where things came together but also separated. It was this separate-but-together quality, she wrote, that had inspired her to pick up the pebble and to carry it in her breast pocket for several days, where it seemed weightless, and then to send it through the mail, by air, as a token of her truest feelings for him. Lieutenant Cross found this romantic. But he wondered what her truest feelings were, exactly, and what she meant by separate-but-together. He wondered how the tides and waves had come into play on that afternoon along the Jersey shoreline when Martha saw the pebble and bent down to rescue it from geology. He imagined bare feet. Martha was a poet, with the poet's sensibilities, and her feet would be brown and bare, the toenails unpainted, the eyes chilly and somber like the ocean in March, and though it was painful, he wondered who had been with her that afternoon. He imagined a pair of shadows moving along the strip of sand where things came together but also separated. It was phantom jealousy, he knew, but he couldn't help himself. He loved her so much. On the march, through the hot days of early April, he carried the pebble in his mouth, turning it with his tongue, tasting sea salts and moisture. His mind wandered. He had difficulty keeping his attention on the war. On occasion he would yell at his men to spread out the column, to keep their eyes open, but then he would slip away into daydreams, just pretending, walking barefoot along the Jersey shore, with Martha, carrying nothing. He would feel himself rising. Sun and waves and gentle winds, all love and lightness.

What they carried varied by mission.

15   When a mission took them to the mountains, they carried mosquito netting, machetes, canvas tarps, and extra bug juice.

If a mission seemed especially hazardous, or if it involved a place they knew to be bad, they carried everything they could. In certain heavily mined AOs, where the land was dense with Toe Poppers and Bouncing Betties, they took turns humping a twenty-eight-pound mine detector. With its headphones and big sensing plate, the equipment was a stress on the lower back and shoulders, awkward to handle, often useless because of the shrapnel in the earth, but they carried it anyway, partly for safety, partly for the illusion of safety.

On ambush, or other night missions, they carried peculiar little odds and ends. Kiowa always took along his New Testament and a pair of moccasins for silence. Dave Jensen carried night-sight vitamins high in carotin. Lee Strunk carried his slingshot; ammo, he claimed, would never be a problem. Rat Kiley carried brandy and M&M's. Until he was shot, Ted Lavender carried the starlight scope, which weighed 6.3 pounds with its aluminum carrying case. Henry Dobbins carried his girlfriend's pantyhose wrapped around his neck as a comforter. They all carried ghosts. When dark came, they would move out single file across the meadows and paddies to their ambush coordinates, where they would quietly set up the Claymores and lie down and spend the night waiting.

Other missions were more complicated and required special equipment. In mid-April, it was their mission to search out and destroy the elaborate tunnel complexes in the Than Khe area south of Chu Lai. To blow the tunnels, they carried one-pound blocks of pentrite high explosives, four blocks to a man, sixty-eight pounds in all. They carried wiring, detonators, and battery-powered clackers. Dave Jensen carried earplugs. Most often, before blowing the tunnels, they were ordered by higher command to search them, which was considered bad news, but by and large they just shrugged and carried out orders. Because he was a big man, Henry Dobbins was excused from tunnel duty. The others would draw numbers. Before Lavender died there were seventeen men in the platoon, and whoever drew the number seventeen would strip off his gear and crawl in head first with a flashlight and Lieutenant Cross's .45-caliber pistol. The rest of them would fan out as security. They would sit down or kneel, not facing the hole, listening to the ground beneath them, imagining cobwebs and ghosts, whatever was down there—the tunnel walls squeezing in—how the flashlight seemed impossibly heavy in the hand and how it was tunnel vision in the very strictest sense, compression in all ways, even time, and how you had to wiggle in—ass and elbows—a swallowed-up feeling—and how you found yourself worrying about odd things—will your flashlight go dead? Do rats carry rabies? If you screamed, how far would the sound carry? Would your buddies hear it? Would they have the courage to drag you out? In some respects, though not many, the waiting was worse than the tunnel itself. Imagination was a killer.

On April 16, when Lee Strunk drew the number seventeen, he laughed and muttered something and went down quickly. The morning was hot and very still. Not good, Kiowa said. He looked at the tunnel opening, then out across a dry paddy toward the village of Than Khe. Nothing moved. No clouds or birds or people. As they waited, the men smoked and drank Kool-Aid, not talking much, feeling sympathy for Lee Strunk but also feeling the luck of the draw. You win some, you lose some, said Mitchell Sanders, and sometimes you settle for a rain check. It was a tired line and no one laughed.

20   Henry Dobbins ate a tropical chocolate bar. Ted Lavender popped a tranquilizer and went off to pee.

After five minutes, Lieutenant Jimmy Cross moved to the tunnel, leaned down, and examined the darkness. Trouble, he thought—a cave-in maybe. And then suddenly, without willing it, he was thinking about Martha. The stresses and fractures, the quick collapse, the two of them buried alive under all that weight. Dense, crushing love. Kneeling, watching the hole, he tried to concentrate on Lee Strunk and the war, all the dangers, but his love was too much for him, he felt paralyzed, he wanted to sleep inside her lungs and breathe her blood and be smothered. He wanted her to be a virgin and not a virgin, all at once. He wanted to know her. Intimate secrets—why poetry? Why so sad? Why that grayness in her eyes? Why so alone? Not lonely, just alone—riding her bike across campus or sitting off by herself in the cafeteria. Even dancing, she danced alone—and it was the aloneness that filled him with love. He remembered telling her that one evening. How she nodded and looked away. And how, later, when he kissed her, she received the kiss without returning it, her eyes wide open, not afraid, not a virgin's eyes, just flat and uninvolved.

Lieutenant Cross gazed at the tunnel. But he was not there. He was buried with Martha under the white sand at the Jersey shore. They were pressed together, and the pebble in his mouth was her tongue. He was smiling. Vaguely, he was aware of how quiet the day was, the sullen paddies, yet he could not bring himself to worry about matters of security. He was beyond that. He was just a kid at war, in love. He was twenty-two years old. He couldn't help it.

A few moments later Lee Strunk crawled out of the tunnel. He came up grinning, filthy but alive. Lieutenant Cross nodded and closed his eyes while the others clapped Strunk on the back and made jokes about rising from the dead.

Worms, Rat Kiley said. Right out of the grave. Fuckin' zombie.

25   The men laughed. They all felt great relief.

Spook City, said Mitchell Sanders.

Lee Strunk made a funny ghost sound, a kind of moaning, yet very happy, and right then, when Strunk made that high happy moaning sound, when he went *Ahhooooo,* right then Ted Lavender was shot in the head on his way back from peeing. He lay with his mouth open. The teeth were broken. There was a swollen black bruise under his left eye. The cheekbone was gone. Oh shit, Rat Kiley said, the guy's dead. The guy's dead, he kept saying, which seemed profound—the guy's dead. I mean really.

The things they carried were determined to some extent by superstition. Lieutenant Cross carried his good-luck pebble. Dave Jensen carried a rabbit's foot. Norman Bowker, otherwise a very gentle person, carried a thumb that had been presented to him as a gift by Mitchell Sanders. The thumb was dark brown, rubbery to the touch, and weighed four ounces at most. It had been cut from a VC corpse, a boy of fifteen or sixteen. They'd found him at the bottom of an irrigation ditch, badly burned, flies in his mouth and eyes. The boy wore black shorts and sandals. At the time of his death he had been carrying a pouch of rice, a rifle, and three magazines of ammunition.

You want my opinion, Mitchell Sanders said, there's a definite moral here.

30   He put his hand on the dead boy's wrist. He was quiet for a time, as if counting a pulse, then he patted the stomach, almost affectionately, and used Kiowa's hunting hatchet to remove the thumb.

Henry Dobbins asked what the moral was.

Moral?

You know. *Moral.*

Sanders wrapped the thumb in toilet paper and handed it across to Norman Bowker. There was no blood. Smiling, he kicked the boy's head, watched the flies scatter, and said, It's like with that old TV show—Paladin. Have gun, will travel.

35   Henry Dobbins thought about it.

Yeah, well, he finally said. I don't see no moral.

There it *is,* man.

Fuck off.

They carried USO stationery and pencils and pens. They carried Sterno, safety pins, trip flares, signal flares, spools of wire, razor blades, chewing tobacco, liberated joss sticks and statuettes of the smiling Buddha, candles, grease pencils, *The Stars and Stripes,* fingernail clippers, Psy Ops leaflets, bush hats, bolos, and much more. Twice a week, when the resupply choppers came in, they carried hot chow in green Mermite cans and large canvas bags filled with iced beer and soda pop. They carried plastic water containers, each with a two-gallon capacity. Mitchell Sanders carried a set of starched tiger fatigues for special occasions. Henry Dobbins carried Black Flag insecticide. Dave Jensen carried empty sandbags that could be filled at night for added protection. Lee Strunk carried tanning lotion. Some things they carried in common. Taking turns, they carried the big PRC-77 scrambler radio, which weighed thirty pounds with its battery. They shared the weight of memory. They took up what others could no longer bear. Often, they carried each other, the wounded or weak. They carried infections. They carried chess sets, basketballs, Vietnamese-English dictionaries, insignia of rank, Bronze Stars and Purple Hearts, plastic cards imprinted with the Code of Conduct. They carried diseases, among them malaria and dysentery. They carried lice and ringworm and leeches and paddy algae and various rots and molds. They carried the land itself—Vietnam, the place, the soil—a powdery orange-red dust that covered their boots and fatigues and faces. They carried the sky. The whole atmosphere, they carried it, the humidity, the monsoons, the stink of fungus and decay, all of it, they carried gravity. They moved like mules. By daylight they took sniper fire, at night they were mortared, but it was not battle, it was just the endless march, village to village, without purpose, nothing won or lost. They marched for the sake of the march. They plodded along slowly, dumbly, leaning forward against the heat, unthinking, all blood and bone, simple grunts, soldiering with their legs, toiling up the hills and down into the paddies and across the rivers and up again and down, just humping, one step and then the next and then another, but no volition, no will, because it was automatic, it was anatomy, and the war was entirely a matter of posture and carriage, the hump was everything, a kind of inertia, a kind of emptiness, a dullness of desire and intellect and conscience and hope and human sensibility. Their principles were in their feet. Their calculations were biological. They had no sense of strategy or mission. They searched the villages without knowing what to look for, not caring, kicking over jars of rice, frisking children and old men, blowing tunnels, sometimes setting fires and sometimes not, then forming up and moving on to the next village, then other villages, where it would always be the same. They carried their own lives. The pressures were enormous. In the heat of early afternoon, they would remove their helmets and flak jackets, walking bare, which was dangerous but which helped ease the strain. They would often discard things along the route of march. Purely for comfort, they would throw away rations, blow their Claymores and grenades, no matter, because by nightfall the resupply choppers would arrive with more of the same, then a day or two later still more, fresh watermelons and crates of ammunition and sunglasses and woolen sweaters—the resources were stunning—sparklers for the Fourth of July, colored eggs for Easter. It was the great American war chest—the fruits of science, the smokestacks, the canneries, the arsenals at Hartford, the Minnesota forests, the machine shops, the vast fields of corn and wheat—they carried like freight trains; they carried it on their backs and shoulders—and for all the ambiguities of Vietnam, all the mysteries and unknowns, there was at least the single abiding certainty that they would never be at a loss for things to carry.

40   After the chopper took Lavender away, Lieutenant Jimmy Cross led his men into the village of Than Khe. They burned everything. They shot chickens and dogs, they trashed the village well, they called in artillery and watched the wreckage, then they marched for several hours through the hot afternoon, and then at dusk, while Kiowa explained how Lavender died, Lieutenant Cross found himself trembling.

He tried not to cry. With his entrenching tool, which weighed five pounds, he began digging a hole in the earth.

He felt shame. He hated himself. He had loved Martha more than his men, and as a consequence Lavender was now dead, and this was something he would have to carry like a stone in his stomach for the rest of the war.

All he could do was dig. He used his entrenching tool like an ax, slashing, feeling both love and hate, and then later, when it was full dark, he sat at the bottom of his foxhole and wept. It went on for a long while. In part, he was grieving for Ted Lavender, but mostly it was for Martha, and for himself, because she belonged to another world, which was not quite real, and because she was a junior at Mount Sebastian College in New Jersey, a poet and a virgin and uninvolved, and because he realized she did not love him and never would.

Like cement, Kiowa whispered in the dark. I swear to God—boom-down. Not a word.

45   I've heard this, said Norman Bowker.

A pisser, you know? Still zipping himself up. Zapped while zipping.

All right, fine. That's enough.

Yeah, but you had to see it, the guy just—

I *heard,* man. Cement. So why not shut the fuck *up?*

50   Kiowa shook his head sadly and glanced over at the hole where Lieutenant Jimmy Cross sat watching the night. The air was thick and wet. A warm, dense fog had settled over the paddies and there was the stillness that precedes rain.

After a time Kiowa sighed.

One thing for sure, he said. The Lieutenant's in some deep hurt. I mean that crying jag—the way he was carrying on—it wasn't fake or anything, it was real heavy-duty hurt. The man cares.

Sure, Norman Bowker said.

Say what you want, the man does care.

55   We all got problems.

Not Lavender.

No, I guess not, Bowker said. Do me a favor, though.

Shut up?

That's a smart Indian. Shut up.

60   Shrugging, Kiowa pulled off his boots. He wanted to say more, just to lighten up his sleep, but instead he opened his New Testament and arranged it beneath his head as a pillow. The fog made things seem hollow and unattached. He tried not to think about Ted Lavender, but then he was thinking how fast it was, no drama, down and dead, and how it was hard to feel anything except surprise. It seemed un-Christian. He wished he could find some great sadness, or even anger, but the emotion wasn't there and he couldn't make it happen. Mostly he felt pleased to be alive. He liked the smell of the New Testament under his cheek, the leather and ink and paper and glue, whatever the chemicals were. He liked hearing the sounds of night. Even his fatigue, it felt fine, the stiff muscles and the prickly awareness of his own body, a floating feeling. He enjoyed not being dead. Lying there, Kiowa admired Lieutenant Jimmy Cross's capacity for grief. He wanted to share the man's pain, he wanted to care as Jimmy Cross cared. And yet when he closed his eyes, all he could think was Boom-down, and all he could feel was the pleasure of having his boots off and the fog curling in around him and the damp soil and the Bible smells and the plush comfort of night.

After a moment Norman Bowker sat up in the dark.

What the hell, he said. You want to talk, *talk*. Tell it to me.

Forget it.

No, man, go on. One thing I hate, it's a silent Indian.

65   For the most part they carried themselves with poise, a kind of dignity. Now and then, however, there were times of panic, when they squealed or wanted to squeal but couldn't, when they twitched and made moaning sounds and covered their heads and said Dear Jesus and flopped around on the earth and fired their weapons blindly and cringed and sobbed and begged for the noise to stop and went wild and made stupid promises to themselves and to God and to their mothers and fathers, hoping not to die. In different ways, it happened to all of them. Afterward, when the firing ended, they would blink and peek up. They would touch their bodies, feeling shame, then quickly hiding it. They would force themselves to stand. As if in slow motion, frame by frame, the world would take on the old logic—absolute silence, then the wind, then sunlight, then voices. It was the burden of being alive. Awkwardly, the men would reassemble themselves, first in private, then in groups, becoming soldiers again. They would repair the leaks in their eyes. They would check for casualties, call in dust-offs, light cigarettes, try to smile, clear their throats and spit and begin cleaning their weapons. After a time someone would shake his head and say, No lie, I almost shit my pants, and someone else would laugh, which meant it was bad, yes, but the guy had obviously not shit his pants,

it wasn't that bad, and in any case nobody would ever do such a thing and then go ahead and talk about it. They would squint into the dense, oppressive sunlight. For a few moments, perhaps, they would fall silent, lighting a joint and tracking its passage from man to man, inhaling, holding in the humiliation. Scary stuff, one of them might say. But then someone else would grin or flick his eyebrows and say, Roger-dodger, almost cut me a new asshole, *almost.*

There were numerous such poses. Some carried themselves with a sort of wistful resignation, others with pride or stiff soldierly discipline or good humor or macho zeal. They were afraid of dying but they were even more afraid to show it.

They found jokes to tell.

They used a hard vocabulary to contain the terrible softness. *Greased,* they'd say. *Offed, lit up, zapped while zipping.*[1] It wasn't cruelty, just stage presence. They were actors and the war came at them in 3-D. When someone died, it wasn't quite dying, because in a curious way it seemed scripted, and because they had their lines mostly memorized, irony mixed with tragedy, and because they called it by other names, as if to encyst and destroy the reality of death itself. They kicked corpses. They cut off thumbs. They talked grunt lingo. They told stories about Ted Lavender's supply of tranquilizers, how the poor guy didn't feel a thing, how incredibly tranquil he was.

There's a moral here, said Mitchell Sanders.

70   They were waiting for Lavender's chopper, smoking the dead man's dope.

The moral's pretty obvious. Sanders said, and winked. Stay away from drugs. No joke, they'll ruin your day every time.

Cute, said Henry Dobbins.

Mind-blower, get it? Talk about wiggy—nothing left, just blood and brains.

They made themselves laugh.

75   There it is, they'd say, over and over, as if the repetition itself were an act of poise, a balance between crazy and almost crazy, knowing without going. There it is, which meant be cool, let it ride, because oh yeah, man, you can't change what can't be changed, there it is, there it absolutely and positively and fucking well *is.*

They were tough.

They carried all the emotional baggage of men who might die. Grief, terror, love, longing—these were intangibles, but the intangibles had their own mass and specific gravity, they had tangible weight. They carried shameful memories. They carried the common secret of cowardice barely restrained, the instinct to run or freeze or hide, and in many respects this was the heaviest burden of all, for it could never be put down, it required

---

[1] Offed, lit up—killed; zapped while zipping—killed while urinating.

perfect balance and perfect posture. They carried their reputations. They carried the soldier's greatest fear, which was the fear of blushing. Men killed, and died, because they were embarrassed not to. It was what had brought them to the war in the first place, nothing positive, no dreams of glory or honor, just to avoid the blush of dishonor. They died so as not to die of embarrassment. They crawled into tunnels and walked point and advanced under fire. Each morning, despite the unknowns, they made their legs move. They endured. They kept humping. They did not submit to the obvious alternative, which was simply to close the eyes and fall. So easy, really. Go limp and tumble to the ground and let the muscles unwind and not speak and not budge until your buddies picked you up and lifted you into the chopper that would roar and dip its nose and carry you off to the world. A mere matter of falling, yet no one ever fell. It was not courage, exactly; the object was not valor. Rather, they were too frightened to be cowards.

By and large they carried these things inside, maintaining the masks of composure. They sneered at sick call. They spoke bitterly about guys who had found release by shooting off their own toes or fingers. Pussies, they'd say. Candyasses. It was fierce, mocking talk, with only a trace of envy or awe, but even so, the image played itself out behind their eyes.

They imagined the muzzle against flesh. They imagined the quick, sweet pain, then the evacuation to Japan, then a hospital with warm beds and cute geisha nurses.

80   They dreamed of freedom birds.

At night, on guard, staring into the dark, they were carried away by jumbo jets. They felt the rush of takeoff. *Gone!* they yelled. And then velocity, wings and engines, a smiling stewardess—but it was more than a plane, it was a real bird, a big sleek silver bird with feathers and talons and high screeching. They were flying. The weights fell off, there was nothing to bear. They laughed and held on tight, feeling the cold slap of wind and altitude, soaring, thinking *It's over, I'm gone!*—they were naked, they were light and free—it was all lightness, bright and fast and buoyant, light as light, a helium buzz in the brain, a giddy bubbling in the lungs as they were taken up over the clouds and the war, beyond duty, beyond gravity and mortification and global entanglements—*Sin loi!* they yelled, *I'm sorry, motherfuckers, but I'm out of it, I'm goofed, I'm on a space cruise, I'm gone!*—and it was a restful, disencumbered sensation, just riding the light waves, sailing that big silver freedom bird over the mountains and oceans, over America, over the farms and great sleeping cities and cemeteries and highways and the golden arches of McDonald's. It was flight, a kind of fleeing, a kind of falling, falling higher and higher, spinning off the edge of the earth and beyond the sun and through the vast, silent vacuum where there were no burdens and where everything weighed exactly nothing. *Gone!* they screamed, *I'm sorry but I'm gone!* And so at night, not quite dreaming, they gave themselves over to lightness, they were carried, they were purely borne.

On the morning after Ted Lavender died, First Lieutenant Jimmy Cross crouched at the bottom of his foxhole and burned Martha's letters. Then he burned the two photographs. There was a steady rain falling, which made it difficult, but he used heat tabs and Sterno to build a small fire, screening it with his body, holding the photographs over the tight blue flame with the tips of his fingers.

He realized it was only a gesture. Stupid, he thought. Sentimental, too, but mostly just stupid.

Lavender was dead. You couldn't burn the blame.

85   Besides, the letters were in his head. And even now, without photographs, Lieutenant Cross could see Martha playing volleyball in her white gym shorts and yellow T-shirt. He could see her moving in the rain.

When the fire died out, Lieutenant Cross pulled his poncho over his shoulders and ate breakfast from a can.

There was no great mystery, he decided.

In those burned letters Martha had never mentioned the war, except to say, Jimmy, take care of yourself. She wasn't involved. She signed the letters "Love," but it wasn't love, and all the fine lines and technicalities did not matter.

The morning came up wet and blurry. Everything seemed part of everything else, the fog and Martha and the deepening rain.

90   It was a war, after all.

Half smiling, Lieutenant Jimmy Cross took out his maps. He shook his head hard, as if to clear it, then bent forward and began planning the day's march. In ten minutes, or maybe twenty, he would rouse the men and they would pack up and head west, where the maps showed the country to be green and inviting. They would do what they had always done. The rain might add some weight, but otherwise it would be one more day layered upon all the other days.

He was realistic about it. There was that new hardness in his stomach.

No more fantasies, he told himself.

Henceforth, when he thought about Martha, it would be only to think that she belonged elsewhere. He would shut down the daydreams. This was not Mount Sebastian, it was another world, where there were no pretty poems or midterm exams, a place where men died because of carelessness and gross stupidity. Kiowa was right. Boom-down, and you were dead, never partly dead.

95   Briefly, in the rain, Lieutenant Cross saw Martha's gray eyes gazing back at him.

He understood.

It was very sad, he thought. The things men carried inside. The things men did or felt they had to do.

He almost nodded at her, but didn't.

Instead he went back to his maps. He was now determined to perform his duties firmly and without negligence. It wouldn't help Lavender, he knew that, but from this point on he would comport himself as a soldier.

He would dispose of his good-luck pebble. Swallow it, maybe, or use Lee Strunk's slingshot, or just drop it along the trail. On the march he would impose strict field discipline. He would be careful to send out flank security, to prevent straggling or bunching up, to keep his troops moving at the proper pace and at the proper interval. He would insist on clean weapons. He would confiscate the remainder of Lavender's dope. Later in the day, perhaps, he would call the men together and speak to them plainly. He would accept the blame for what had happened to Ted Lavender. He would be a man about it. He would look them in the eyes, keeping his chin level, and he would issue the new SOPs in a calm, impersonal tone of voice, an officer's voice, leaving no room for argument or discussion. Commencing immediately, he'd tell them, they would no longer abandon equipment along the route of march. They would police up their acts. They would get their shit together, and keep it together, and maintain it neatly and in good working order.

100   He would not tolerate laxity. He would show strength, distancing himself.

Among the men there would be grumbling, of course, and maybe worse, because their days would seem longer and their loads heavier, but Lieutenant Cross reminded himself that his obligation was not to be loved but to lead. He would dispense with love; it was not now a factor. And if anyone quarreled or complained, he would simply tighten his lips and arrange his shoulders in the correct command posture. He might give a curt little nod. Or he might not. He might just shrug and say Carry on, then they would saddle up and form into a column and move out toward the villages west of Than Khe.

READING AND REACTING

1. Although the setting and the events described in "The Things They Carried" are dramatic and moving, its tone is often flat and emotionless. How is this tone created? Why do you think the narrator adopts this kind of tone?

2. Consider the different meanings of the word *carry*, which can refer to burdens abstract or concrete and to things carried physically or emotionally, actively or passively. Give several examples of the different senses in which O'Brien uses the word. How does his use of the word enhance the story?

3. A striking characteristic of the story's style is its thorough catalogs of the concrete, tangible "things" the soldiers carry. Why do you suppose such detailed lists are included? What does what each man carries tell you about him? In a less literal, more abstract sense, what else do these men "carry"?

4. One stylistic technique O'Brien uses is intentional repetition—of phrases ("they carried"); people's names and identifying details

(Martha's virginity, for example); and pieces of equipment. What effect do you think O'Brien hopes to achieve through such repetition? Is he successful?

5. Interspersed among long paragraphs crammed with detail are short one- or two-sentence paragraphs. What function do these brief paragraphs serve?

6. What function does Martha serve in the story? Why does Lieutenant Cross burn her letters?

7. In paragraph 68 the narrator says of the soldiers, "They used a hard vocabulary to contain the terrible softness." What do you think he means by this? Do you think this "hard vocabulary" is necessary? How does it affect your reaction to the story?

8. Describing Lieutenant Cross's new sense of purpose in the story's final paragraph, the narrator uses the phrase "Carry on." Do you think this phrase is linked in any way to the story's other uses of the word *carry,* or do you believe it is unrelated? Explain.

9. **JOURNAL ENTRY**   "The Things They Carried" is a story about war. Do you think it is an antiwar story? Why or why not?

10. **CRITICAL PERSPECTIVE**   In an essay about war memoirs, Clayton W. Lewis questions O'Brien's decision to present "the nightmare [he] faced in a Vietnam rice paddy" as fiction. Lewis believes that some of O'Brien's stories "dissolve into clever artifice" and, therefore, are not as effective as actual memoirs of the Vietnam experience would be. He concludes that "for all its brilliance and emotional grounding, [the stories do not] satisfy one's appetite to hear what happened rendered as it was experienced and remembered."

Do you think Lewis has a point? Or do you think O'Brien's "artifice" communicates his emotions and experiences more effectively than a straightforward memoir could? Explain your position.

WRITING SUGGESTIONS: STYLE, TONE, AND LANGUAGE

1. "A Clean, Well-Lighted Place" does not have a conventional plot in which characters grow and change and conflicts are resolved. For this reason, it might be argued that in this story language takes on more of a central role than it plays in other stories. Write an essay in which you examine this idea as it applies to "A Clean, Well-Lighted Place" and to any other story in this text.

2. Both "Araby" and "The Things They Carried" deal, at least in part, with infatuation. Compare and contrast the infatuations described in the two stories. How do the kinds of language used by the narrators in the two stories communicate the two men's fascination and subsequent disillusionment?

3. Several of the stories in this chapter present characters who are outsiders or misfits in their social milieus. Choose two or three characters, and explain why each is estranged from others and what efforts, if any, each makes to reconcile himself with society. Be sure to show how language helps to convey each character's alienation.

4. In each of this chapter's stories careful word choice is instrumental in creating a mood or atmosphere. Explain how the use of language creates an appropriate mood in any one of the stories; then explain how that mood helps to communicate the story's central theme.

5. In each of the chapter's four stories, the title communicates a good deal of information in a very few words. Write an essay in which you explain what each title communicates about the story's theme.

CHAPTER 9

Symbol and Allegory

*Symbols and metaphors share several qualities, but they are far from being syn-
onymous. Both are figurative expressions that transcend literal language. Both
rely heavily on implication and suggestion. Both present the abstract in concrete
terms, and both can be interpreted with varying degrees of openness or specificity.
They differ, however, in important ways. A symbol expands language by substitution, a metaphor by comparison and interaction. A symbol does not ask a reader
to merge two concepts but rather to let one thing suggest another. A symbol derives its meaning through development and consensus, a metaphor through invention and originality. A symbol is strengthened by repetition, but a metaphor is
destroyed by it.*

ROLAND BARTEL, *METAPHORS AND SYMBOLS*

*Symbols have to spring from the work direct, and stay alive. Symbols for the sake of
symbols are counterfeit, and were they all stamped on the page in red they couldn't
any more quickly give themselves away. So are symbols failing their purpose when
they don't keep to proportion in the book. However alive they are, they should never
call for an emphasis greater than the emotional reality they serve, in their moment,
to illuminate.*

EUDORA WELTY, "WORDS INTO FICTION"

*When dealing with a vigorously living author we must also not be too timid to ana-
lyze symbolically what we, as critics, may see in the text—that which the author
may not consciously have intended. We know that there are many levels of symbolic
discourse that we may not be aware of at any given moment. When the text is published, when the author gives it up to the public domain, it is released and opened up
to interpretation by the reader. It exists on its own, separate from the author. The
textual interpretation, therefore, is one of integration between the authorial intent,
and the text itself,* and *the third (and separate) interpretation or grasping of those
two aspects by the reader.*

TEY DIANA REBOLLEDO, *THE POLITICS OF POETICS*

Moby-Dick . . . *is a work of which certain basic elements, such as the whale, the
sea, and the quest, have both symbolic and direct representational value. There is no*

consensus among commentators as to what the symbolic value of those elements comes to in specific, exact terms; and it is proof of the merit of this work that no such consensus is in fact possible. The narrative, not being an allegory, has no meanings that can be mentally tabulated and neatly accounted for. Its symbols are integrally a part of its fictive reality, and it is precisely their organic character that renders them immune to purely intellectual specification.

PHILIP RAHV, *FICTION AND THE CRITICISM OF FICTION*

If it were asked why allegory is so conscientiously mistrusted while speculations about symbolisms abound as never before, one might say that in a scientific age allegory suggests something obvious and old-fashioned, like Sunday-school religion, but symbolism suggests something esoteric and up-to-date, like higher mathematics. It is a glib answer but not too far from the sources of the modern prejudice. Allegory is of course uncongenial to readers who find in it only an occasion for loquacious moralizing. But no one has yet shown that allegory is inherently of that crude type or why symbolism, for which critics always claim large potencies denied to allegory, is a superior literary practice.

EDWIN HONING, *THE DARK CONCEIT: THE MAKING OF ALLEGORY*

A **symbol** is a person, object, action, place, or event that, in addition to its literal meaning, suggests a more complex meaning or range of meanings. **Universal** or **archetypal symbols,** such as the Old Man, the Mother, or the Grim Reaper, are so much a part of human experience that they suggest much the same thing to most people. **Conventional symbols** are also likely to suggest the same thing to most people, provided they share common cultural and social assumptions (a rose suggests love, a skull and crossbones denotes poison). Such symbols are often used as a kind of shorthand in films, popular literature, and advertising, where they encourage automatic responses.

Conventional symbols such as the stars and stripes of the American flag can evoke powerful feelings of pride and patriotism in a group of people who share the same orientation toward it, just as the maple leaf and the Union Jack can. Symbols used in works of literature can function in much the same way, enabling writers to convey particular emotions or messages with a high degree of predictability. Thus, spring can be expected to suggest rebirth and promise; autumn, declining years and powers; summer, youth and beauty. Because a writer expects a dark forest to evoke fear, or a rainbow to communicate hope, he or she can be quite confident in using such an image to convey a particular idea or mood (provided the audience shares the writer's frame of reference).

Many symbols, however, have the power to suggest different things to different people. (For one thing, different cultures may react differently to the same symbols. In the United States, for example, an owl suggests wisdom; in India it suggests just the opposite.) Thus, symbols enrich meaning, expanding the possibilities for interpretation and for reader interaction with the text. It is precisely because they are so potentially rich that symbols have the power to open up a work of literature.

LITERARY SYMBOLS

Both universal and conventional symbols can function as **literary symbols** that derive additional meanings through their use in a particular work. For instance, a watch or clock denotes time; as a literary symbol in a particular work, it might seem to suggest just the passing of time, or it might convey anything from a character's inability to recapture the past to the idea of time running out—or, it might suggest more than one of these ideas.

Thinking about an object's possible meanings can suggest a variety of ways to interpret a text. For instance, William Faulkner focuses attention on an unseen watch in a pivotal scene in "A Rose for Emily" (p. 80). The reader's first view of Miss Emily Grierson reveals her as "a small, fat woman in black, with a thin gold chain descending to her waist and vanishing into her belt." Several sentences later the narrator returns to the watch, noting that Miss Emily's visitors "could hear the invisible watch ticking at the end of the gold chain." Like these visitors, readers are drawn to the unseen watch as it ticks away. Because Miss Emily is portrayed as a woman living in the past, readers can assume that the presence of the watch is intended to reinforce the impression that she cannot see that time (the watch) has moved on. The vivid picture of the pale, plump woman in the musty room with the watch invisibly ticking does indeed suggest both that she has been left back in time and that she remains unaware of the progress around her. Thus, the symbol enriches both the depiction of character and the story's theme.

In "Barn Burning" (p. 216), another Faulkner story, the clock is a somewhat more complex symbol. The itinerant Snopes family is without financial security and apparently without a future. The clock the mother carries from shack to shack—"The clock inlaid with mother-of-pearl, which would not run, stopped at some fourteen minutes past two o'clock of a dead and forgotten day and time, which had been [Sarty's] mother's dowry"—is their only possession of value. The fact that the clock no longer works seems at first to suggest that time has run out for the family, and to reflect their impotence and paralysis. On another level, the clock stands in pathetic contrast to Major de Spain's grand home, with its gold and glitter and Oriental rugs. Knowing that the clock was part of the mother's dowry, and that a dowry suggests a promise, readers may decide that the broken clock symbolizes lost hope; the fact that the mother still clings to the clock, however, could suggest just the opposite.

As you read, you should not concentrate on finding the one exact equivalent for each symbol; in fact, this kind of search is very limiting and not very productive. Instead, consider the possibilities, the different meanings a symbol might suggest. Then consider how various interpretations enrich other elements of the story and the work as a whole.

Recognizing Symbols   When is a clock just a clock, and when is it also a symbol with a meaning or meanings beyond its literal significance? If a character waiting for a friend glances once at his or her watch to verify the time, there is probably nothing symbolic about the watch or about the act of looking at it. If, however, the watch keeps appearing again and again in the story, at key moments; if the narrator devotes a good deal of time to describing it; if it is placed in a conspicuous physical location; if characters keep noticing it and commenting on its presence; if it is lost (or found) at a critical moment; if its function in some way parallels the development of plot or character (for instance, if it stops as a relationship ends or as a character dies); if the story's opening or closing paragraph focuses on the timepiece; or if the story is called "The Watch"—the watch probably has symbolic significance. In other words, considering how an image is used, how often it is used, and when it appears will help you to determine whether or not it functions as a symbol.

The Purpose of Symbols   Symbols expand the possible meanings of a story, thereby heightening interest and actively involving readers in the text. In "The Lottery" (p. 309), for example, the mysterious black box has symbolic significance. It is mentioned prominently and repeatedly, and it plays a pivotal role in the story's action. Of course, the black box is important on a purely literal level: It functions as a key component of the lottery. But the box has other associations as well, and it is these associations that suggest what its symbolic significance might be.

The black wooden box is very old, a relic of many past lotteries; the narrator observes that it represents tradition. It is also closed and closely guarded, suggesting mystery and uncertainty. It is shabby, "splintered badly along one side . . . and in places faded or stained." This state of disrepair could suggest that the ritual it is part of has also deteriorated, or that tradition itself has deteriorated. The box is also simple in construction and design, suggesting the primitive (and therefore perhaps outdated) nature of the ritual. This symbol encourages readers to probe the story for values and ideas, to consider and weigh the suitability of a variety of interpretations. It serves as a "hot spot" that invites questions and exploration. The answers to these questions reinforce and enrich the story's theme.

ALLEGORY

An **allegory** communicates a doctrine, message, or moral principle by making it into a narrative in which the characters personify ideas, concepts, qualities, or other abstractions. Thus, an allegory is a story with two parallel and consistent levels of meaning—one literal and one figurative. The figurative level, which offers some moral or political lesson, is the story's main concern. The allegorical figures are significant only because they represent something beyond their literal meaning in a fixed system.

Whereas a symbol has multiple symbolic associations as well as a literal meaning, an **allegorical figure**—a character, object, place, or event in the allegory—has just one meaning within an **allegorical framework,** the set of ideas that conveys the allegory's message. (At the simplest level, for instance, one character can stand for good and another can stand for evil.) For this reason, allegorical figures do not open up a text to various interpretations by readers the way symbols do. Because the purpose of allegory is to communicate a particular lesson, readers are not encouraged to speculate about the allegory's possible meanings as they are with other fictional forms; each element has only one equivalent, which readers must discover if they are to make sense of the allegorical framework.

Naturally, the better a reader understands the political, religious, and literary assumptions of a writer, the easier it will be to recognize the allegorical significance of his or her work. John Bunyan's *The Pilgrim's Progress,* for example, is a famous seventeenth-century allegory based on the Christian doctrine of salvation. In order to appreciate the complexity of Bunyan's work, you would have to familiarize yourself with this doctrine—possibly by consulting an encyclopedia or a reference work such as *The Oxford Companion to English Literature.*

One type of allegory, called a **beast fable,** is a short tale, usually including a moral, in which animals assume human characteristics. Aesop's Fables are the best-known examples of beast fables. More recently, contemporary writers have used beast fables to satirize the political and social conditions of our time. In one such tale, "The Gentlemen of the Jungle" by the Kenyan writer Jomo Kenyatta, an elephant is allowed to put his trunk inside a man's hut during a rainstorm. Not content with keeping his trunk dry, the elephant pushes his entire body inside the hut, displacing the man. When the man protests, the elephant takes the matter to the lion, who appoints a Commission of Enquiry to settle the matter. Eventually the man is forced not only to abandon his hut to the elephant, but also to build new huts for all the animals in the Commission. Even so, the jealous animals occupy the man's new hut and begin fighting for space; while they are arguing, the man burns down the hut, animals and all. Like the tales told by Aesop, "The Gentlemen of the Jungle" has a moral: "Peace is costly," says the man as he walks away happily, "but it's worth the expense." The following passage from "The Gentlemen of the Jungle" reveals how the allegorical figures work within the framework of the allegory:

> The elephant, obeying the command of his master (the lion), got busy with the other ministers to appoint a Commission of Enquiry. The following elders of the jungle were appointed to sit in the Commission: (1) Mr. Rhinoceros; (2) Mr. Buffalo; (3) Mr. Alligator; (4) The Rt. Hon. Mr. Fox to act as chairman; and (5) Mr. Leopard to act as Secretary of the Commission. On

> *seeing the personnel, the man protested and asked if it was not necessary to*
> *include in this Commission a member from his side. But he was told that it*
> *was impossible, since no one from his side was well enough educated to*
> *understand the intricacy of jungle law.*

From this excerpt we can see how each character represents a particular idea. For example, the members of the Commission stand for bureaucratic smugness and inequity, and the man stands for the citizens who are victimized by the government. In order to fully understand the allegorical significance of each figure in this story, of course, readers would have to know something about government bureaucracies, colonialism in Africa, and possibly a specific historical event in Kenya.

Some works contain both symbolic elements *and* allegorical elements, as Nathaniel Hawthorne's "Young Goodman Brown" (p. 298) does. The names of the story's two main characters, "Goodman" and "Faith," suggest that they fit within an allegorical system of some sort: Young Goodman Brown represents a good person who, despite his best efforts, strays from the path of righteousness; his wife, Faith, represents the quality he must hold on to in order to avoid temptation. As characters, they have no significance outside of their allegorical functions. Other elements of the story, however, are not so clear-cut. The older man whom Young Goodman Brown meets in the woods carries a staff that has carved on it "the likeness of a great black snake, so curiously wrought, that it might almost be seen to twist and wriggle itself like a living serpent." This staff, carried by a Satanic figure who represents evil and temptation, suggests the snake in the Garden of Eden, an association that neatly fits into the allegorical context of the story. Alternately, however, the staff could suggest the "slippery," ever-changing nature of sin, the difficulty people have in perceiving sin, or sexuality (which may explain Young Goodman Brown's susceptibility to temptation). This range of possible meanings opens the staff to interpretation and thus suggests it functions as a symbol through which Hawthorne creates a complex image of sin and enriches his allegory.

Other stories work entirely on a symbolic level and contain no allegorical figures. "The Lottery," despite its moral overtones, is not an allegory. For one thing, as has been demonstrated, its symbols do not have easily assignable equivalents. Moreover, the story is not the sum total of a neat system of fixed value, interlocking characters, events, and objects arranged to serve one rigid, didactic purpose. In fact, many different interpretations have been suggested for this story. When it was first published in June 1948 in *The New Yorker,* some readers believed it to be nonfiction, a report of an actual custom or ritual. As Shirley Jackson reports in her essay "Biography of a Story," even those who recognized it as fiction speculated about its meaning, seeing it as (among other things) an attack on prejudice, a criticism of society's need for a scapegoat, or a treatise on witchcraft, Christian martyrdom, or village gossip. Various critics have argued that "The Lottery" is a story about the evils of violence, mob psychology, or Nazi Germany. The fact is, no single allegorical interpretation will account for every major character, object, and event in the story.

▼▼

CHECKLIST FOR WRITING ABOUT SYMBOL AND ALLEGORY

♦ Are any universal symbols used in the work? Any conventional symbols? What is their function?

♦ Is any character, place, action, event, or object given unusual prominence or emphasis in the story? If so, does this element seem to have symbolic as well as literal value?

♦ What possible meanings does each symbol suggest?

♦ How do symbols help to depict the story's characters?

♦ How do symbols help to characterize the story's setting?

♦ How do symbols help to advance the story's plot?

♦ Are any of the symbols related? Taken together, do they seem to support a common theme?

♦ Does the story have a moral or didactic purpose? What is the message, idea, or moral principle the story seeks to convey?

♦ What equivalent may be assigned to each allegorical figure in the story?

♦ Does the story combine allegorical figures and symbols? What is their function in the story?

▲▲

NATHANIEL HAWTHORNE (1804–1864) was born in Salem, Massachusetts, the great-great-grandson of a judge who presided over the infamous Salem witch trials. After his sea captain father was killed on a voyage when Hawthorne was four years old, his childhood was one of genteel poverty. An uncle paid for his education at Bowdoin College in Maine, where Hawthorne's friends included a future president of the United States, Franklin Pierce, who in 1853 would appoint him U.S. consul in Liverpool, England. Hawthorne published four novels—*The Scarlet Letter* (1850), *The House of the Seven Gables* (1851), *The Blithedale Romance* (1852), and *The Marble Faun* (1860)—and more than one hundred short stories and sketches.

Hawthorne referred to his own work as *romance*. He used this term to mean not an escape from reality, but a method of confronting "the depths of our common nature" and "the truth of the heart." His stories probe the dark side of human nature and frequently paint a world that is virtuous on the surface but (as Young Goodman Brown comes to believe) "one stain of guilt, one mighty blood spot" beneath. Hawthorne's stories often emphasize the ambiguity of human experience. For example, the reader is left to wonder whether Goodman Brown actually saw a witch's coven or dreamed a dream. For Hawthorne, what is important is Brown's recognition that evil may be found everywhere. "Young Goodman Brown," as Hawthorne's neighbor and friend Herman Melville once said, is a tale "as deep as Dante."

NATHANIEL HAWTHORNE

Young Goodman Brown

(1835)

Young Goodman Brown came forth at sunset, into the street of Salem village, but put his head back, after crossing the threshold, to exchange a parting kiss with his young wife. And Faith, as the wife was aptly named, thrust her own pretty head into the street, letting the wind play with the pink ribbons of her cap, while she called to Goodman Brown.

"Dearest heart," whispered she, softly and rather sadly, when her lips were close to his ear, "prithee, put off your journey until sunrise, and sleep in your own bed to-night. A lone woman is troubled with such dreams and such thoughts, that she's afeard of herself, sometimes. Pray, tarry with me this night, dear husband, of all nights in the year!"

"My love and my Faith," replied young Goodman Brown, "of all nights in the year, this one night must I tarry away from thee. My journey, as thou callest it, forth and back again, must needs be done 'twixt now and sunrise. What, my sweet, pretty wife, dost thou doubt me already, and we but three months married!"

"Then God bless you!" said Faith with the pink ribbons, "and may you find all well, when you come back."

5   "Amen!" cried Goodman Brown. "Say thy prayers, dear Faith, and go to bed at dusk, and no harm will come to thee."

So they parted; and the young man pursued his way, until, being about to turn the corner by the meeting-house, he looked back and saw the head of Faith still peeping after him, with a melancholy air, in spite of her pink ribbons.

"Poor little Faith!" thought he, for his heart smote him. "What a wretch am I, to leave her on such an errand! She talks of dreams, too. Methought, as she spoke, there was trouble in her face, as if a dream had warned her what work is to be done to-night. But no, no! 't would kill her to think it. Well; she's a blessed angel on earth; and after this one night, I'll cling to her skirts and follow her to Heaven."

With this excellent resolve for the future, Goodman Brown felt himself justified in making more haste on his present evil purpose. He had taken a dreary road, darkened by all the gloomiest trees of the forest, which barely stood aside to let the narrow path creep through, and closed immediately behind. It was as lonely as could be; and there is this peculiarity in such a solitude, that the traveller knows not who may be concealed by the innumerable trunks and the thick boughs overhead; so that, with lonely footsteps, he may yet be passing through an unseen multitude.

"There may be a devilish Indian behind every tree," said Goodman Brown to himself; and he glanced fearfully behind him, as he added, "What if the devil himself should be at my very elbow!"

10   His head being turned back, he passed a crook of the road, and looking forward again, beheld the figure of a man, in grave and decent attire, seated at the foot of an old tree. He arose at Goodman Brown's approach, and walked onward, side by side with him.

"You are late, Goodman Brown," said he. "The clock of the Old South[1] was striking, as I came through Boston; and that is full fifteen minutes agone."

"Faith kept me back awhile," replied the young man, with a tremor in his voice, caused by the sudden appearance of his companion, though not wholly unexpected.

It was now deep dusk in the forest, and deepest in that part of it where these two were journeying. As nearly as could be discerned, the second traveller was about fifty years old, apparently in the same rank of life as Goodman Brown, and bearing a considerable resemblance to him, though perhaps more in expression than features. Still, they might have been taken for father and son. And yet, though the elder person was as simply clad as the younger, and as simple in manner too, he had an indescribable air of one who knew the world, and would not have felt abashed at the governor's dinner-table, or in King William's court,[2] were it possible that his affairs should call him thither. But the only thing about him that could be fixed upon as remarkable, was his staff, which bore the likeness of a great black snake, so curiously wrought, that it might almost be seen to twist and wriggle itself like a living serpent. This, of course, must have been an ocular deception, assisted by the uncertain light.

"Come, Goodman Brown!" cried his fellow-traveller, "this is a dull pace for the beginning of a journey. Take my staff, if you are so soon weary."

15   "Friend," said the other, exchanging his slow pace for a full stop, "having kept covenant by meeting thee here, it is my purpose now to return whence I came. I have scruples, touching the matter thou wot'st of."

---

[1] Old South Church, Boston, renowned meeting place for American patriots during the Revolution.

[2] William III, king of England from 1689 to 1702.

"Sayest thou so?" replied he of the serpent, smiling apart. "Let us walk on, nevertheless, reasoning as we go, and if I convince thee not, thou shalt turn back. We are but a little way in the forest, yet."

"Too far, too far!" exclaimed the goodman, unconsciously resuming his walk. "My father never went into the woods on such an errand, nor his father before him. We have been a race of honest men and good Christians, since the days of the martyrs. And shall I be the first of the name of Brown that ever took this path and kept—"

"Such company, thou wouldst say," observed the elder person, interrupting his pause. "Well said, Goodman Brown! I have been as well acquainted with your family as with ever a one among the Puritans; and that's no trifle to say. I helped your grandfather, the constable, when he lashed the Quaker woman so smartly through the streets of Salem. And it was I that brought your father a pitch-pine knot, kindled at my own hearth, to set fire to an Indian village, in King Philip's war.[3] They were my good friends, both; and many a pleasant walk have we had along this path, and returned merrily after midnight. I would fain be friends with you, for their sake."

"If it be as thou sayest," replied Goodman Brown, "I marvel they never spoke of these matters. Or, verily, I marvel not, seeing that the least rumor of the sort would have driven them from New England. We are a people of prayer, and good works to boot, and abide no such wickedness."

20   "Wickedness or not," said the traveller with the twisted staff, "I have a very general acquaintance here in New England. The deacons of many a church have drunk the communion wine with me; the selectmen, of divers towns, make me their chairman; and a majority of the Great and General Court are firm supporters of my interest. The governor and I, too—but these are state secrets."

"Can this be so!" cried Goodman Brown, with a stare of amazement at his undisturbed companion. "Howbeit, I have nothing to do with the governor and council; they have their own ways, and are no rule for a simple husbandman like me. But, were I to go on with thee, how should I meet the eye of that good old man, our minister, at Salem village? Oh, his voice would make me tremble, both Sabbath-day and lecture-day!"[4]

Thus far, the elder traveller had listened with due gravity, but now burst into a fit of irrepressible mirth, shaking himself so violently, that his snakelike staff actually seemed to wriggle in sympathy.

"Ha, ha, ha!" shouted he, again and again; then composing himself, "Well, go on, Goodman Brown, go on; but, prithee, don't kill me with laughing!"

---

[3] A war of Indian resistance, led by King Philip, or Metacomet, of the Wampanoags. The war, intended to halt expansion of English settlers in Massachusetts, collapsed after King Philip's death in August 1676.

[4] The day of the midweek sermon, usually Thursday.

"Well, then, to end the matter at once," said Goodman Brown, considerably nettled, "there is my wife, Faith. It would break her dear little heart; and I'd rather break my own!"

25   "Nay, if that be the case," answered the other, "e'en go thy ways, Goodman Brown. I would not, for twenty old women like the one hobbling before us, that Faith should come to any harm."

As he spoke, he pointed his staff at a female figure on the path, in whom Goodman Brown recognized a very pious and exemplary dame, who had taught him his catechism in youth, and was still his moral and spiritual adviser, jointly with the minister and Deacon Gookin.

"A marvel, truly, that Goody[5] Cloyse should be so far in the wilderness, at nightfall!" said he. "But, with your leave, friend, I shall take a cut through the woods, until we have left this Christian woman behind. Being a stranger to you, she might ask whom I was consorting with, and whither I was going."

"Be it so," said his fellow-traveller. "Betake you to the woods, and let me keep the path."

Accordingly, the young man turned aside, but took care to watch his companion, who advanced softly along the road, until he had come within a staff's length of the old dame. She, meanwhile, was making the best of her way, with singular speed for so aged a woman, and mumbling some indistinct words, a prayer, doubtless, as she went. The traveller put forth his staff, and touched her withered neck with what seemed the serpent's tail.

30   "The devil!" screamed the pious old lady.

"Then Goody Cloyse knows her old friend?" observed the traveller, confronting her, and leaning on his writhing stick.

"Ah, forsooth, and is it your worship, indeed?" cried the good dame. "Yea, truly is it, and in the very image of my old gossip, Goodman Brown, the grandfather of the silly fellow that now is. But, would your worship believe it? my broomstick hath strangely disappeared, stolen, as I suspect, by that unhanged witch, Goody Cory, and that, too, when I was all anointed with the juice of smallage and cinque-foil and wolf's bane—"[6]

"Mingled with fine wheat and the fat of a new-born babe," said the shape of old Goodman Brown.

"Ah, your worship knows the recipe," cried the old lady, cackling aloud. "So, as I was saying, being all ready for the meeting, and no horse to ride on, I made up my mind to foot it; for they tell me there is a nice young man to be taken into communion to-night. But now your good worship will lend me your arm, and we shall be there in a twinkling."

---

5 A contraction of "Goodwife," a term of politeness used in addressing a woman of humble station. Goody Cloyse, like Goody Cory and Martha Carrier, who appear later in the story, was one of the Salem "witches" sentenced in 1692.

6 All plants believed to have magical powers. "Smallage" is wild celery.

35   "That can hardly be," answered her friend. "I may not spare you my arm, Goody Cloyse, but here is my staff, if you will."

So saying, he threw it down at her feet, where, perhaps, it assumed life, being one of the rods which its owner had formerly lent to the Egyptian Magi. Of this fact, however, Goodman Brown could not take cognizance. He had cast his eyes in astonishment, and looking down again, beheld neither Goody Cloyse nor the serpentine staff, but his fellow-traveller alone, who waited for him as calmly as if nothing had happened.

"That old woman taught me my catechism!" said the young man; and there was a world of meaning in this simple comment.

They continued to walk onward, while the elder traveller exhorted his companion to make good speed and persevere in the path, discoursing so aptly, that his arguments seemed rather to spring up in the bosom of his auditor, than to be suggested by himself. As they went he plucked a branch of maple, to serve for a walking-stick, and began to strip it of the twigs and little boughs, which were wet with evening dew. The moment his fingers touched them, they became strangely withered and dried up, as with a week's sunshine. Thus the pair proceeded, at a good free pace, until suddenly, in a gloomy hollow of the road, Goodman Brown sat himself down on the stump of a tree, and refused to go any farther.

"Friend," said he, stubbornly, "my mind is made up. Not another step will I budge on this errand. What if a wretched old woman do choose to go to the devil, when I thought she was going to Heaven! Is that any reason why I should quit my dear Faith, and go after her?"

40   "You will think better of this by and by," said his acquaintance, composedly. "Sit here and rest yourself awhile; and when you feel like moving again, there is my staff to help you along."

Without more words, he threw his companion the maple stick, and was as speedily out of sight as if he had vanished into the deepening gloom. The young man sat a few moments by the roadside, applauding himself greatly, and thinking with how clear a conscience he should meet the minister, in his morning walk, nor shrink from the eye of good old Deacon Gookin. And what calm sleep would be his, that very night, which was to have been spent so wickedly, but purely and sweetly now, in the arms of Faith! Amidst these pleasant and praiseworthy meditations, Goodman Brown heard the tramp of horses along the road, and deemed it advisable to conceal himself within the verge of the forest, conscious of the guilty purpose that had brought him thither, though now so happily turned from it.

On came the hoof-tramps and the voices of the riders, two grave old voices, conversing soberly as they drew near. These mingled sounds appeared to pass along the road, within a few yards of the young man's hiding-place; but owing, doubtless, to the depth of the gloom, at that particular spot, neither the travellers nor their steeds were visible. Though their figures brushed the small boughs by the wayside, it could not be seen that they intercepted, even for a moment, the faint gleam from the strip of bright sky, athwart which they must have passed. Goodman

Brown alternately crouched and stood on tiptoe, pulling aside the branches, and thrusting forth his head as far as he durst, without discerning so much as a shadow. It vexed him the more, because he could have sworn, were such a thing possible, that he recognized the voices of the minister and Deacon Gookin, jogging along quietly, as they were wont to do, when bound to some ordination or ecclesiastical council. While yet within hearing, one of the riders stopped to pluck a switch.

"Of the two, reverend Sir," said the voice like the deacon's, "I had rather miss an ordination dinner than to-night's meeting. They tell me that some of our community are to be here from Falmouth and beyond, and others from Connecticut and Rhode Island; besides several of the Indian powwows, who, after their fashion, know almost as much deviltry as the best of us. Moreover, there is a goodly young woman to be taken into communion."

"Mighty well, Deacon Gookin!" replied the solemn old tones of the minister. "Spur up, or we shall be late. Nothing can be done, you know, until I get on the ground."

45   The hoofs clattered again, and the voices, talking so strangely in the empty air, passed on through the forest, where no church had ever been gathered, nor solitary Christian prayed. Whither, then, could these holy men be journeying, so deep into the heathen wilderness? Young Goodman Brown caught hold of a tree, for support, being ready to sink down on the ground, faint and over-burthened with the heavy sickness of his heart. He looked up to the sky, doubting whether there really was a Heaven above him. Yet, there was the blue arch, and the stars brightening in it.

"With Heaven above, and Faith below, I will yet stand firm against the devil!" cried Goodman Brown.

While he still gazed upward, into the deep arch of the firmament, and had lifted his hands to pray, a cloud, though no wind was stirring, hurried across the zenith, and hid the brightening stars. The blue sky was still visible, except directly overhead, where this black mass of cloud was sweeping swiftly northward. Aloft in the air, as if from the depths of the cloud, came a confused and doubtful sound of voices. Once, the listener fancied that he could distinguish the accents of townspeople of his own, men and women, both pious and ungodly, many of whom he had met at the communion-table, and had seen others rioting at the tavern. The next moment, so indistinct were the sounds, he doubted whether he had heard aught but the murmur of the old forest, whispering without a wind. Then came a stronger swell of those familiar tones, heard daily in the sunshine, at Salem village, but never, until now, from a cloud at night. There was one voice, of a young woman, uttering lamentations, yet with an uncertain sorrow, and entreating for some favor, which, perhaps, it would grieve her to obtain. And all the unseen multitude, both saints and sinners, seemed to encourage her onward.

"Faith!" shouted Goodman Brown, in a voice of agony and desperation; and the echoes of the forest mocked him, crying—"Faith! Faith!" as if bewildered wretches were seeking her, all through the wilderness.

The cry of grief, rage, and terror was yet piercing the night, when the unhappy husband held his breath for a response. There was a scream, drowned immediately in a louder murmur of voices fading into far-off laughter, as the dark cloud swept away, leaving the clear and silent sky above Goodman Brown. But something fluttered lightly down through the air, and caught on the branch of a tree. The young man seized it and beheld a pink ribbon.

50 "My Faith is gone!" cried he, after one stupefied moment. "There is no good on earth, and sin is but a name. Come, devil! for to thee is this world given."

And maddened with despair, so that he laughed loud and long, did Goodman Brown grasp his staff and set forth again, at such a rate, that he seemed to fly along the forest path, rather than to walk or run. The road grew wilder and drearier, and more faintly traced, and vanished at length, leaving him in the heart of the dark wilderness, still rushing onward, with the instinct that guides mortal man to evil. The whole forest was peopled with frightful sounds: the creaking of the trees, the howling of wild beasts, and the yell of Indians; while, sometimes, the wind tolled like a distant church bell, and sometimes gave a broad roar around the traveller, as if all Nature was laughing him to scorn. But he was himself the chief horror of the scene, and shrank not from its other horrors.

"Ha! ha! ha!" roared Goodman Brown, when the wind laughed at him. "Let us hear which will laugh loudest! Think not to frighten me with your deviltry! Come witch, come wizard, come Indian powwow, come devil himself! and here comes Goodman Brown. You may as well fear him as he fear you!"

In truth, all through the haunted forest, there could be nothing more frightful than the figure of Goodman Brown. On he flew, among the black pines, brandishing his staff with frenzied gestures, now giving vent to an inspiration of horrid blasphemy, and now shouting forth such laughter, as set all the echoes of the forest laughing like demons around him. The fiend in his own shape is less hideous, than when he rages in the breast of man. Thus sped the demoniac on his course, until, quivering among the trees, he saw a red light before him, as when the felled trunks and branches of a clearing have been set on fire, and throw up their lurid blaze against the sky, at the hour of midnight. He paused, in a lull of the tempest that had driven him onward, and heard the swell of what seemed a hymn, rolling solemnly from a distance, with the weight of many voices. He knew the tune. It was a familiar one in the choir of the village meeting-house. The verse died heavily away, and was lengthened by a chorus, not of human voices, but of all the sounds of the benighted wilderness, pealing in awful harmony together. Goodman Brown cried out; and his cry was lost to his own ear, by its unison with the cry of the desert.

In the interval of silence, he stole forward, until the light glared full upon his eyes. At one extremity of an open space, hemmed in by the dark wall of the forest, arose a rock, bearing some rude, natural resemblance either to an altar or a pulpit, and surrounded by four blazing pines, their tops aflame, their stems untouched, like candles at an evening meeting. The mass of foliage, that had overgrown the summit of the rock, was all on fire, blazing high into the night, and fitfully illuminating the whole field. Each pendent twig and leafy festoon was in a blaze. As the red light arose and fell, a numerous congregation alternately shone forth, then disappeared in shadow, and again grew, as it were, out of the darkness, peopling the heart of the solitary woods at once.

55   "A grave and dark-clad company!" quoth Goodman Brown.

In truth, they were such. Among them, quivering to-and-fro, between gloom and splendor, appeared faces that would be seen, next day, at the council-board of the province, and others which, Sabbath after Sabbath, looked devoutly heavenward, and benignantly over the crowded pews, from the holiest pulpits in the land. Some affirm, that the lady of the governor was there. At least, there were high dames well known to her, and wives of honored husbands, and widows a great multitude, and ancient maidens, all of excellent repute, and fair young girls, who trembled lest their mothers should espy them. Either the sudden gleams of light, flashing over the obscure field, bedazzled Goodman Brown, or he recognized a score of the church members of Salem village, famous for their especial sanctity. Good old Deacon Gookin had arrived, and waited at the skirts of that venerable saint, his reverend pastor. But, irreverently consorting with these grave, reputable, and pious people, these elders of the church, these chaste dames and dewy virgins, there were men of dissolute lives and women of spotted fame, wretches given over to all mean and filthy vice, and suspected even of horrid crimes. It was strange to see, that the good shrank not from the wicked, nor were the sinners abashed by the saints. Scattered, also, among their pale-faced enemies, were the Indian priests, or powwows, who had often scared their native forest with more hideous incantations than any known to English witchcraft.

"But, where is Faith?" thought Goodman Brown; and, as hope came into his heart, he trembled.

Another verse of the hymn arose, a slow and mournful strain, such as the pious love, but joined to words which expressed all that our nature can conceive of sin, and darkly hinted at far more. Unfathomable to mere mortals is the lore of fiends. Verse after verse was sung, and still the chorus of the desert swelled between, like the deepest tone of a mighty organ. And, with the final peal of that dreadful anthem, there came a sound, as if the roaring wind, the rushing streams, the howling beasts, and every other voice of the unconverted wilderness were mingling and according with the voice of guilty man, in homage to the prince of all. The four blazing pines threw up a loftier flame, and obscurely discovered shapes and visages of horror on the smoke-wreaths, above the impious assembly. At the same moment, the fire on the rock shot redly forth, and formed a glowing arch above its base, where now appeared a figure. With reverence be it spoken, the apparition bore no slight similitude, both in garb and manner, to some grave divine of the New England churches.

"Bring forth the converts!" cried a voice, that echoed through the field and rolled into the forest.

60   At the word, Goodman Brown stepped forth from the shadow of the trees, and approached the congregation, with whom he felt a loathful brotherhood, by the sympathy of all that was wicked in his heart. He could have well-nigh sworn, that the shape of his own dead father beckoned him to advance, looking downward from a smoke-wreath, while a woman, with dim features of despair, threw out her hand to warn him back. Was it his mother? But he had no power to retreat one step, nor to resist, even in thought, when the minister and good old Deacon Gookin seized his arms, and led him to the blazing rock. Thither came also the slender form of a veiled female, led between Goody Cloyse, that pious teacher of the cate- chism, and Martha Carrier, who had received the devil's promise to be queen of hell. A rampant hag was she! And there stood the proselytes, be- neath the canopy of fire.

"Welcome, my children," said the dark figure, "to the communion of your race! Ye have found, thus young, your nature and your destiny. My children, look behind you!"

They turned; and flashing forth, as it were, in a sheet of flame, the fiend-worshippers were seen; the smile of welcome gleamed darkly on every visage.

"There," resumed the sable form, "are all whom ye have reverenced from youth. Ye deemed them holier than yourselves, and shrank from your own sin, contrasting it with their lives of righteousness and prayerful as- pirations heavenward. Yet, here are they all, in my worshipping assembly! This night it shall be granted you to know their secret deeds; how hoary- bearded elders of the church have whispered wanton words to the young maids of their households; how many a woman, eager for widow's weeds, has given her husband a drink at bedtime, and let him sleep his last sleep in her bosom; how beardless youths have made haste to inherit their fa- ther's wealth; and how fair damsels—blush not, sweet ones!—have dug lit- tle graves in the garden, and bidden me, the sole guest, to an infant's funeral. By the sympathy of your human hearts for sin, ye shall scent out all the places—whether in church, bedchamber, street, field, or forest— where crime has been committed, and shall exult to behold the whole earth one stain of guilt, one mighty blood-spot. Far more than this! It shall be yours to penetrate, in every bosom, the deep mystery of sin, the fountain of all wicked arts, and which inexhaustibly supplies more evil impulses than human power—than my power, at its utmost!—can make manifest in deeds. And now, my children, look upon each other."

They did so; and, by the blaze of the hell-kindled torches, the wretched man beheld his Faith, and the wife her husband, trembling before that un- hallowed altar.

65   "Lo! there ye stand, my children," said the figure, in a deep and solemn tone, almost sad, with its despairing awfulness, as if his once an- gelic nature could yet mourn for our miserable race. "Depending upon one

another's hearts, ye had still hoped that virtue were not all a dream! Now are ye undeceived!—Evil is the nature of mankind. Evil must be your only happiness. Welcome, again, my children, to the communion of your race!"

"Welcome!" repeated the fiend-worshippers, in one cry of despair and triumph.

And there they stood, the only pair, as it seemed, who were yet hesitating on the verge of wickedness, in this dark world. A basin was hollowed, naturally, in the rock. Did it contain water, reddened by the lurid light? or was it blood? or, perchance, a liquid flame? Herein did the Shape of Evil dip his hand, and prepare to lay the mark of baptism upon their foreheads, that they might be partakers of the mystery of sin, more conscious of the secret guilt of others, both in deed and thought, than they could now be of their own. The husband cast one look at his pale wife, and Faith at him. What polluted wretches would the next glance show them to each other, shuddering alike at what they disclosed and what they saw!

"Faith! Faith!" cried the husband. "Look up to Heaven, and resist the Wicked One!"

Whether Faith obeyed, he knew not. Hardly had he spoken, when he found himself amid calm night and solitude, listening to a roar of the wind, which died heavily away through the forest. He staggered against the rock, and felt it chill and damp, while a hanging twig, that had been all on fire, besprinkled his cheek with the coldest dew.

70   The next morning, young Goodman Brown came slowly into the street of Salem village staring around him like a bewildered man. The good old minister was taking a walk along the grave-yard, to get an appetite for breakfast and meditate his sermon, and bestowed a blessing, as he passed, on Goodman Brown. He shrank from the venerable saint, as if to avoid an anathema. Old Deacon Gookin was at domestic worship, and the holy words of his prayer were heard through the open window. "What God doth the wizard pray to?" quoth Goodman Brown. Goody Cloyse, that excellent old Christian, stood in the early sunshine, at her own lattice, catechising a little girl, who had brought her a pint of morning's milk. Goodman Brown snatched away the child, as from the grasp of the fiend himself. Turning the corner by the meeting-house, he spied the head of Faith, with the pink ribbons, gazing anxiously forth, and bursting into such joy at sight of him that she skipt along the street, and almost kissed her husband before the whole village. But Goodman Brown looked sternly and sadly into her face, and passed on without a greeting.

Had Goodman Brown fallen asleep in the forest, and only dreamed a wild dream of a witch-meeting?

Be it so, if you will. But, alas! it was a dream of evil omen for young Goodman Brown. A stern, a sad, a darkly meditative, a distrustful, if not a desperate man did he become, from the night of that fearful dream. On the Sabbath day, when the congregation were singing a holy psalm, he could not listen, because an anthem of sin rushed loudly upon his ear, and drowned all the blessed strain. When the minister spoke from the pulpit, with power and fervid eloquence, and with his hand on the open Bible, of the sacred truths of our religion, and of saint-like lives and triumphant deaths, and of future bliss or misery unutterable, then did Goodman Brown turn pale, dreading lest the roof should thunder down upon the gray blasphemer and his hearers. Often, awaking suddenly at midnight, he shrank from the bosom of Faith, and at morning or eventide, when the family knelt down at prayer, he scowled, and muttered to himself, and gazed sternly at his wife, and turned away. And when he had lived long, and was borne to his grave, a hoary corpse, followed by Faith, an aged woman, and children and grand-children, a goodly procession, besides neighbors not a few, they carved no hopeful verse upon his tombstone; for his dying hour was gloom.

READING AND REACTING

1. Who is the narrator of "Young Goodman Brown"? What advantages does the narrative point of view give the author?

2. What does Young Goodman Brown mean when he says "of all nights in the year, this one must I tarry away from thee" (3)? What is important about *this* night, and why does Young Goodman Brown believe he must journey "twixt now and sunrise"?

3. Is Young Goodman Brown surprised to encounter the second traveler on the road, or does he seem to expect him? What is the significance of their encounter? What do you make of the fact that the stranger bears a strong resemblance to young Goodman Brown?

4. What sins are the various characters Young Goodman Brown meets in the woods guilty of committing?

5. "Young Goodman Brown" has two distinct settings: Salem and the woods. What are the differences between these settings? What does each contribute to the story?

6. Which figures in the story are allegorical, and which have symbolic significance? On what evidence do you base your conclusions?

7. Why do the people gather in the woods? Why do they attend the ceremony?

8. Explain the change that takes place in Young Goodman Brown at the end of the story. Why can he not listen to the singing of holy psalms or to the minister's sermons? What causes him to turn away from Faith and die in gloom?

9. **JOURNAL ENTRY** At the end of the story the narrator suggests that Goodman Brown might have fallen asleep and imagined his encounter with the witches. Do you think the events are all a dream?

10. **CRITICAL PERSPECTIVE** In *The Power of Blackness,* his classic study of nineteenth-century American writers, Harry Levin observes that Hawthorne had doubts about conventional religion. This, Levin

believes, is why all efforts to read an enlightening theological message into Hawthorne's works are "doomed to failure." What comment do you think Hawthorne is making in "Young Goodman Brown" about the redeeming power of religious faith?

SHIRLEY JACKSON (1916–1965)   is best known for her restrained tales of horror and the supernatural, most notably her novel *The Haunting of Hill House* (1959) and the short story "The Lottery" (1948). Among her other works are two novels dealing with divided personalities—*The Bird's Nest* (1954) and *We Have Always Lived in the Castle* (1962)—and two collections of comic tales about her children and family life, *Life Among the Savages* (1953) and *Raising Demons* (1957).

Jackson was an intense, self-destructive, contradictory personality: a witty hostess to crowds of literary friends; a self-described witch, clairvoyant, and student of magic; a cookie-baking "Mom" who wrote chilling tales between loads of laundry. With her husband, literary critic Stanley Edgar Hyman, she settled in the small town of Bennington, Vermont, but was never accepted by the townspeople. "The Lottery" is set in much the same kind of small, hidebound town. The story's publication in *The New Yorker* magazine provoked a torrent of letters from enraged and horrified readers. Americans of the post–World War II era saw themselves as "good guys" defending the world against foreign evils. Jackson's story, written scarcely three years after the liberation of Auschwitz, told Americans something they did not want to hear—that the face of human evil could look just like their next-door neighbor. Horror master Stephen King dedicates his book *Firestarter* "to Shirley Jackson, who never had to raise her voice."

S H I R L E Y   J A C K S O N

The Lottery

(1948)

The morning of June 27th was clear and sunny, with the fresh warmth of a full-summer day; the flowers were blossoming profusely and the grass was richly green. The people of the village began to gather in the square, between the post office and the bank, around ten o'clock; in some towns there were so many people that the lottery took two days and had to be started on June 26th, but in this village, where there were only about three hundred people, the whole lottery took less than two hours, so it could begin at ten o'clock in the morning and still be through in time to allow the villagers to get home for noon dinner.

The children assembled first, of course. School was recently over for the summer, and the feeling of liberty sat uneasily on most of them; they tended to gather together quietly for a while before they broke into boisterous play, and their talk was still of the classroom and the teacher, of books and reprimands. Bobby Martin had already stuffed his pockets full of stones, and the other boys soon followed his example, selecting the smoothest and roundest stones; Bobby and Harry Jones and Dickie Delacroix—the villagers pronounced this name "Dellacroy"—eventually made a great pile of stones in one corner of the square and guarded it against the raids of the other boys. The girls stood aside, talking among themselves, looking over their shoulders at the boys, and the very small children rolled in the dust or clung to the hands of their older brothers or sisters.

Soon the men began to gather, surveying their own children, speaking of planting and rain, tractors and taxes. They stood together, away from the pile of stones in the corner, and their jokes were quiet and they smiled rather than laughed. The women, wearing faded house dresses and sweaters, came shortly after their menfolk. They greeted one another and exchanged bits of gossip as they went to join their husbands. Soon the women, standing by their husbands, began to call to their children, and the children came reluctantly, having to be called four or five times. Bobby Martin ducked under his mother's grasping hand and ran, laughing, back to the pile of stones. His father spoke up sharply, and Bobby came quickly and took his place between his father and his oldest brother.

The lottery was conducted—as were the square dances, the teen-age club, the Halloween program—by Mr. Summers, who had time and energy to devote to civic activities. He was a round-faced, jovial man and he ran the coal business, and people were sorry for him, because he had no children and his wife was a scold. When he arrived in the square, carrying the black wooden box, there was a murmur of conversation among the villagers, and he waved and called, "Little late today, folks." The postmaster, Mr. Graves, followed him, carrying a three-legged stool, and the stool was put in the center of the square and Mr. Summers set the black box down on it. The villagers kept their distance, leaving a space between themselves and the stool, and when Mr. Summers said, "Some of you fellows want to give me a hand?" there was a hesitation before two men, Mr. Martin and his oldest son, Baxter, came forward to hold the box steady on the stool while Mr. Summers stirred up the papers inside it.

5   The original paraphernalia for the lottery had been lost long ago, and the black box now resting on the stool had been put into use even before Old Man Warner, the oldest man in town, was born. Mr. Summers spoke frequently to the villagers about making a new box, but no one liked to upset even as much tradition as was represented by the black box. There was a story that the present box had been made with some pieces of the

box that had preceded it, the one that had been constructed when the first people settled down to make a village here. Every year, after the lottery, Mr. Summers began talking again about a new box, but every year the subject was allowed to fade off without anything's being done. The black box grew shabbier each year; by now it was no longer completely black but splintered badly along one side to show the original wood color, and in some places faded or stained.

Mr. Martin and his oldest son, Baxter, held the black box securely on the stool until Mr. Summers had stirred the papers thoroughly with his hand. Because so much of the ritual had been forgotten or discarded, Mr. Summers had been successful in having slips of paper substituted for the chips of wood that had been used for generations. Chips of wood, Mr. Summers had argued, had been all very well when the village was tiny, but now that the population was more than three hundred and likely to keep on growing, it was necessary to use something that would fit more easily into the black box. The night before the lottery, Mr. Summers and Mr. Graves made up the slips of paper and put them in the box, and it was then taken to the safe of Mr. Summers' coal company and locked up until Mr. Summers was ready to take it to the square next morning. The rest of the year, the box was put away, sometimes one place, sometimes another; it had spent one year in Mr. Graves's barn and another year underfoot in the post office, and sometimes it was set on a shelf in the Martin grocery and left there.

There was a great deal of fussing to be done before Mr. Summers declared the lottery open. There were the lists to make up—of heads of families, heads of households in each family, members of each household in each family. There was the proper swearing-in of Mr. Summers by the postmaster, as the official of the lottery; at one time, some people remembered, there had been a recital of some sort, performed by the official of the lottery, a perfunctory, tuneless chant that had been rattled off duly each year; some people believed that the official of the lottery used to stand just so when he said or sang it, others believed that he was supposed to walk among the people, but years and years ago this part of the ritual had been allowed to lapse. There had been, also, a ritual salute, which the official of the lottery had had to use in addressing each person who came up to draw from the box, but this also had changed with time, until now it was felt necessary only for the official to speak to each person approaching. Mr. Summers was very good at all this; in his clean white shirt and blue jeans, with one hand resting carelessly on the black box, he seemed very proper and important as he talked interminably to Mr. Graves and the Martins.

Just as Mr. Summers finally left off talking and turned to the assembled villagers, Mrs. Hutchinson came hurriedly along the path to the square, her sweater thrown over her shoulders, and slid into place in the back of the crowd. "Clean forgot what day it was," she said to Mrs. Delacroix, who stood next to her, and they both laughed softly. "Thought my old man was out back stacking wood," Mrs. Hutchinson went on, "and

then I looked out the window and the kids was gone, and then I remembered it was the twenty-seventh and came a-running." She dried her hands
on her apron, and Mrs. Delacroix said, "You're in time, though. They're
still talking away up there."

Mrs. Hutchinson craned her neck to see through the crowd and found
her husband and children standing near the front. She tapped Mrs.
Delacroix on the arm as a farewell and began to make her way through the
crowd. The people separated good-humoredly to let her through; two or
three people said, in voices just loud enough to be heard across the crowd,
"Here comes your Missus, Hutchinson," and "Bill, she made it after all."
Mrs. Hutchinson reached her husband, and Mr. Summers, who had been
waiting, said cheerfully, "Thought we were going to have to get on without
you, Tessie." Mrs. Hutchinson said, grinning, "Wouldn't have me leave
m'dishes in the sink, now, would you, Joe?," and soft laughter ran through
the crowd as the people stirred back into position after Mrs. Hutchinson's
arrival.

10   "Well, now," Mr. Summers said soberly, "guess we better get started,
get this over with, so's we can go back to work. Anybody ain't here?"

"Dunbar," several people said. "Dunbar, Dunbar."

Mr. Summers consulted his list. "Clyde Dunbar," he said. "That's
right. He's broke his leg, hasn't he? Who's drawing for him?"

"Me, I guess," a woman said, and Mr. Summers turned to look at her.
"Wife draws for her husband," Mr. Summers said. "Don't you have a
grown boy to do it for you, Janey?" Although Mr. Summers and everyone
else in the village knew the answer perfectly well, it was the business of
the official of the lottery to ask such questions formally. Mr. Summers
waited with an expression of polite interest while Mrs. Dunbar answered.

"Horace's not but sixteen yet," Mrs. Dunbar said regretfully. "Guess I
gotta fill in for the old man this year."

15   "Right," Mr. Summers said. He made a note on the list he was holding.
Then he asked, "Watson boy drawing this year?"

A tall boy in the crowd raised his hand. "Here," he said. "I'm drawing
for m'mother and me." He blinked his eyes nervously and ducked his head
as several voices in the crowd said things like "Good fellow, Jack," and
"Glad to see your mother's got a man to do it."

"Well," Mr. Summers said, "guess that's everyone. Old Man Warner
make it?"

"Here," a voice said, and Mr. Summers nodded.

A sudden hush fell on the crowd as Mr. Summers cleared his throat
and looked at the list. "All ready?" he called. "Now, I'll read the names—
heads of families first—and the men come up and take a paper out of the
box. Keep the paper folded in your hand without looking at it until everyone has had a turn. Everything clear?"

20   The people had done it so many times that they only half listened to
the directions; most of them were quiet, wetting their lips, not looking
around. Then Mr. Summers raised one hand high and said, "Adams." A

man disengaged himself from the crowd and came forward. "Hi, Steve," Mr. Summers said, and Mr. Adams said, "Hi, Joe." They grinned at one another humorlessly and nervously. Then Mr. Adams reached into the black box and took out a folded paper. He held it firmly by one corner as he turned and went hastily back to his place in the crowd, where he stood a little apart from his family, not looking down at his hand.

"Allen," Mr. Summers said. "Anderson. . . . Bentham."

"Seems like there's no time at all between lotteries any more," Mrs. Delacroix said to Mrs. Graves in the back row. "Seems like we got through with the last one only last week."

"Time sure goes fast," Mrs. Graves said.

"Clark. . . . Delacroix."

25   "There goes my old man," Mrs. Delacroix said. She held her breath while her husband went forward.

"Dunbar," Mr. Summers said, and Mrs. Dunbar went steadily to the box while one of the women said, "Go on, Janey," and another said, "There she goes."

"We're next," Mrs. Graves said. She watched while Mr. Graves came around from the side of the box, greeted Mr. Summers gravely, and selected a slip of paper from the box. By now, all through the crowd there were men holding the small folded papers in their large hands, turning them over and over nervously. Mrs. Dunbar and her two sons stood together, Mrs. Dunbar holding the slip of paper.

"Harburt. . . . Hutchinson."

"Get up there, Bill," Mrs. Hutchinson said, and the people near her laughed.

30   "Jones."

"They do say," Mr. Adams said to Old Man Warner, who stood next to him, "that over in the north village they're talking of giving up the lottery."

Old Man Warner snorted. "Pack of crazy fools," he said. "Listening to the young folks, nothing's good enough for *them*. Next thing you know, they'll be wanting to go back to living in caves, nobody work any more, live *that* way for a while. Used to be a saying about 'Lottery in June, corn be heavy soon.' First thing you know, we'd all be eating stewed chickweed and acorns. There's *always* been a lottery," he added petulantly. "Bad enough to see young Joe Summers up there joking with everybody."

"Some places have already quit lotteries," Mrs. Adams said.

"Nothing but trouble in *that*," Old Man Warner said stoutly. "Pack of young fools."

35   "Martin." And Bobby Martin watched his father go forward. "Overdyke. . . . Percy."

"I wish they'd hurry," Mrs. Dunbar said to her older son. "I wish they'd hurry."

"They're almost through," her son said.

"You get ready to run tell Dad," Mrs. Dunbar said.

Mr. Summers called his own name and then stepped forward precisely and selected a slip from the box. Then he called, "Warner."

40   "Seventy-seventh year I been in the lottery," Old Man Warner said as he went through the crowd. "Seventy-seventh time."

"Watson." The tall boy came awkwardly through the crowd. Someone said, "Don't be nervous, Jack," and Mr. Summers said, "Take your time, son."

"Zanini."

After that, there was a long pause, a breathless pause, until Mr. Summers, holding his slip of paper in the air, said, "All right, fellows." For a minute, no one moved, and then all the slips of paper were opened. Suddenly, all the women began to speak at once, saying, "Who is it?," "Who's got it?," "Is it the Dunbars?," "Is it the Watsons?" Then the voices began to say, "It's Hutchinson. It's Bill," "Bill Hutchinson's got it."

"Go tell your father," Mrs. Dunbar said to her older son.

45   People began to look around to see the Hutchinsons. Bill Hutchinson was standing quiet, staring down at the paper in his hand. Suddenly, Tessie Hutchinson shouted to Mr. Summers, "You didn't give him time enough to take any paper he wanted. I saw you. It wasn't fair!"

"Be a good sport, Tessie," Mrs. Delacroix called, and Mrs. Graves said, "All of us took the same chance."

"Shut up, Tessie," Bill Hutchinson said.

"Well, everyone," Mr. Summers said, "that was done pretty fast, and now we've got to be hurrying a little more to get done in time." He consulted his next list. "Bill," he said, "you draw for the Hutchinson family. You got any other households in the Hutchinsons?"

"There's Don and Eva," Mrs. Hutchinson yelled, "Make *them* take their chance!"

50   "Daughters draw with their husbands' families, Tessie," Mr. Summers said gently. "You know that as well as anyone else."

"It wasn't *fair*," Tessie said.

"I guess not, Joe," Bill Hutchinson said regretfully. "My daughter draws with her husband's family, that's only fair. And I've got no other family except the kids."

"Then, as far as drawing for families is concerned, it's you," Mr. Summers said in explanation, "and as far as drawing for households is concerned, that's you, too. Right?"

"Right," Bill Hutchinson said.

55   "How many kids, Bill?" Mr. Summers asked formally.

"Three," Bill Hutchinson said. "There's Bill, Jr., and Nancy, and little Dave. And Tessie and me."

"All right, then," Mr. Summers said. "Harry, you got their tickets back?"

Mr. Graves nodded and held up the slips of paper. "Put them in the box, then," Mr. Summers directed. "Take Bill's and put it in."

"I think we ought to start over," Mrs. Hutchinson said, as quietly as she could. "I tell you it wasn't *fair*. You didn't give him time enough to choose. *Every*body saw that."

60   Mr. Graves had selected the five slips and put them in the box, and he dropped all the papers but those onto the ground, where the breeze caught them and lifted them off.

"Listen, everybody," Mrs. Hutchinson was saying to the people around her.

"Ready, Bill?" Mr. Summers asked, and Bill Hutchinson, with one quick glance around at his wife and children, nodded.

"Remember," Mr. Summers said, "take the slips and keep them folded until each person has taken one. Harry, you help little Dave." Mr. Graves took the hand of the little boy, who came willingly with him up to the box. "Take a paper out of the box, Davy," Mr. Summers said. Davy put his hand into the box and laughed. "Take just *one* paper," Mr. Summers said. "Harry, you hold it for him." Mr. Graves took the child's hand and removed the folded paper from the tight fist and held it while little Dave stood next to him and looked at him wonderingly.

"Nancy next," Mr. Summers said. Nancy was twelve, and her school friends breathed heavily as she went forward, switching her skirt, and took a slip daintily from the box. "Bill, Jr.," Mr. Summers said, and Billy, his face red and his feet overlarge, nearly knocked the box over as he got a paper out. "Tessie," Mr. Summers said. She hesitated for a minute, looking around defiantly, and then set her lips and went up to the box. She snatched a paper out and held it behind her.

65   "Bill," Mr. Summers said, and Bill Hutchinson reached into the box and felt around, bringing his hand out at last with the slip of paper in it.

The crowd was quiet. A girl whispered, "I hope it's not Nancy," and the sound of the whisper reached the edges of the crowd.

"It's not the way it used to be," Old Man Warner said clearly. "People ain't the way they used to be."

"All right," Mr. Summers said. "Open the papers. Harry, you open little Dave's."

Mr. Graves opened the slip of paper and there was a general sigh through the crowd as he held it up and everyone could see that it was blank. Nancy and Bill, Jr., opened theirs at the same time, and both beamed and laughed, turning around to the crowd and holding their slips of paper above their heads.

70   "Tessie," Mr. Summers said. There was a pause, and then Mr. Summers looked at Bill Hutchinson, and Bill unfolded his paper and showed it. It was blank.

"It's Tessie," Mr. Summers said, and his voice was hushed. "Show us her paper, Bill."

Bill Hutchinson went over to his wife and forced the slip of paper out of her hand. It had a black spot on it, the black spot Mr. Summers had made the night before with the heavy pencil in the coal-company office. Bill Hutchinson held it up, and there was a stir in the crowd.

"All right, folks," Mr. Summers said. "Let's finish quickly."

Although the villagers had forgotten the ritual and lost the original black box, they still remembered to use stones. The pile of stones the boys had made earlier was ready; there were stones on the ground with the blowing scraps of paper that had come out of the box. Mrs. Delacroix selected a stone so large she had to pick it up with both hands and turned to Mrs. Dunbar. "Come on," she said. "Hurry up."

75   Mrs. Dunbar had small stones in both hands, and she said, gasping for breath, "I can't run at all. You'll have to go ahead and I'll catch up with you."

The children had stones already, and someone gave little Davy Hutchinson a few pebbles.

Tessie Hutchinson was in the center of a cleared space by now, and she held her hands out desperately as the villagers moved in on her. "It isn't fair," she said. A stone hit her on the side of the head.

Old Man Warner was saying, "Come on, come on, everyone." Steve Adams was in the front of the crowd of villagers, with Mrs. Graves beside him.

"It isn't fair, it isn't right," Mrs. Hutchinson screamed, and then they were upon her.

READING AND REACTING

1. What possible significance, beyond their literal meaning, might each of these items have: the village square, Mrs. Hutchinson's apron, Old Man Warner, the slips of paper, the black spot.

2. "The Lottery" takes place in June, and summer, a conventional symbol, has a positive connotation. What does this setting contribute to the story's plot? To its atmosphere?

3. What, if anything, might the names *Graves, Adams, Summers,* and *Delacroix* signify in the context of this story? Do you think these names are intended to have any special significance? Why or why not?

4. What role do the children play in the ritual? How can you explain their presence in the story? Do they have any symbolic role in the story?

5. What symbolic significance might be found in the way the characters are dressed? In their conversation?

6. In what sense is the story's title ironic?

7. Throughout the story there is a general atmosphere of excitement. What indication is there of nervousness or apprehension?

8. Early in the story, the boys stuff their pockets with stones, foreshadowing the attack in the story's conclusion. What other examples of foreshadowing can you identify?

9. **JOURNAL ENTRY**   How can a ritual like the lottery continue to be held year after year? Why does no one move to end it? Can you think of a modern-day parallel to this lottery—a situation in which people continue to act in ways they know to be wrong rather than challenge the status quo? How can you account for such behavior?

10. **CRITICAL PERSPECTIVE**   When "The Lottery" was published in the June 26, 1948, issue of *The New Yorker,* its effect was immediate. The story, as the critic Judy Oppenheimer notes in her book *Private Demons: The Life of Shirley Jackson,* "provoked an unprecedented outpouring of fury, horror, rage, disgust, and intense fascination." As a result, Jackson received hundreds of letters, which contained (among others) the following interpretations of the story:

   ◆ The story is an attack on small-town America.

   ◆ The story is a parable about the perversion of democracy.

   ◆ The story is a criticism of prejudice, particularly anti-Semitism.

   ◆ The story has no point at all.

   How plausible do you think each of these explanations is? Which comes closest to your interpretation of the story? Why?

ALICE WALKER (1944–   ) is an accomplished writer of poetry, fiction, and criticism. Her characters are mainly rural African-Americans, often living in her native Georgia, who struggle to survive in hostile environments. Her writing displays a particular sensitivity to the emotions of people who suffer physical or psychological harm in their efforts to assert their own identities.

Walker was the youngest of five boys and three girls born to Willie Lee and Minnie Tallulah Grant Walker, sharefarmers who raised cotton. She left the rural South to attend Atlanta's Spelman College (1961–1963) and Sarah Lawrence College in Bronxville, New York (1963–1965).

In 1967, Walker moved to Mississippi, where she was supported in the writing of her first novel, *The Third Life of Grange Copeland* (1970), by a National Endowment of the Arts grant. Her short story "Everyday Use" was included in *Best American Short Stories* in 1973. Other novels and short story collections followed, including *In Love and Trouble: Stories of Black Women* (1973), *Meridian* (1976), *You Can't Keep a Good Woman Down* (short stories, 1981), *The Temple of My Familiar* (1989), *Possessing the Secret of Joy* (1993), and *The Complete Stories* (short stories, 1994). Walker's third novel, *The Color Purple* (1982) won the American Book Award and a Pulitzer Prize.

In the third year of her marriage, Walker took back her maiden name because she wanted to honor her great-great-great-grandmother who walked, carrying her two children, from Virginia to Georgia. Walker's renaming is consistent with one of her goals in writing, which is to further the process of reconnecting people to their ancestors. She has said that "it is fatal to see yourself as separate," and that if people can reaffirm the past, they can "make a different future."

A L I C E   W A L K E R

Everyday Use
(1973)

for your grandma

I will wait for her in the yard that Maggie and I made so clean and wavy yesterday afternoon. A yard like this is more comfortable than most people know. It is not just a yard. It is like an extended living room. When the hard clay is swept clean as a floor and the fine sand around the edges lined with tiny, irregular grooves, anyone can come and sit and look up into the elm tree and wait for the breezes that never come inside the house.

Maggie will be nervous until after her sister goes: she will stand hopelessly in corners, homely and ashamed of the burn scars down her arms and legs, eying her sister with a mixture of envy and awe. She thinks her sister has held life always in the palm of one hand, that "no" is a word the world never learned to say to her.

You've no doubt seen those TV shows where the child who has "made it" is confronted, as a surprise, by her own mother and father, tottering in weakly from backstage. (A pleasant surprise, of course: What would they do if parent and child came on the show only to curse out and insult each other?) On TV mother and child embrace and smile into each other's faces. Sometimes the mother and father weep, the child wraps them in her arms and leans across the table to tell how she would not have made it without their help. I have seen these programs.

Sometimes I dream a dream in which Dee and I are suddenly brought together on a TV program of this sort. Out of a dark and soft-seated limousine I am ushered into a bright room filled with many people. There I meet a smiling, gray, sporty man like Johnny Carson who shakes my hand and tells me what a fine girl I have. Then we are on the stage and Dee is embracing me with tears in her eyes. She pins on my dress a large orchid, even though she has told me once that she thinks orchids are tacky flowers.

5   In real life I am a large, big-boned woman with rough, man-working hands. In the winter I wear flannel nightgowns to bed and overalls during the day. I can kill and clean a hog as mercilessly as a man. My fat keeps me hot in zero weather. I can work outside all day, breaking ice to get water for

washing; I can eat pork liver cooked over the open fire minutes after it comes steaming from the hog. One winter I knocked a bull calf straight in the brain between the eyes with a sledge hammer and had the meat hung up to chill before nightfall. But of course all this does not show on television. I am the way my daughter would want me to be: a hundred pounds lighter, my skin like an uncooked barley pancake. My hair glistens in the hot bright lights. Johnny Carson has much to do to keep up with my quick and witty tongue.

But that is a mistake. I know even before I wake up. Who ever knew a Johnson with a quick tongue? Who can even imagine me looking a strange white man in the eye? It seems to me I have talked to them always with one foot raised in flight, with my head turned in whichever way is farthest from them. Dee, though. She would always look anyone in the eye. Hesitation was no part of her nature.

"How do I look, Mama?" Maggie says, showing just enough of her thin body enveloped in pink skirt and red blouse for me to know she's there, almost hidden by the door.

"Come out into the yard," I say.

Have you ever seen a lame animal, perhaps a dog run over by some careless person rich enough to own a car, sidle up to someone who is ignorant enough to be kind to him? That is the way my Maggie walks. She has been like this, chin on chest, eyes on ground, feet in shuffle, ever since the fire that burned the other house to the ground.

10   Dee is lighter than Maggie, with nicer hair and a fuller figure. She's a woman now, though sometimes I forget. How long ago was it that the other house burned? Ten, twelve years? Sometimes I can still hear the flames and feel Maggie's arms sticking to me, her hair smoking and her dress falling off her in little black papery flakes. Her eyes seemed stretched open, blazed open by the flames reflected in them. And Dee. I see her standing off under the sweet gum tree she used to dig gum out of; a look of concentration on her face as she watched the last dingy gray board of the house fall in toward the red-hot brick chimney. Why don't you do a dance around the ashes? I'd wanted to ask her. She had hated the house that much.

I used to think she hated Maggie, too. But that was before we raised the money, the church and me, to send her to Augusta to school. She used to read us without pity; forcing words, lies, other folks' habits, whole lives upon us two, sitting trapped and ignorant underneath her voice. She washed us in a river of make-believe, burned us with a lot of knowledge we didn't necessarily need to know. Pressed us to her with the serious way she read, to shove us away at just the moment, like dimwits, we seemed about to understand.

Dee wanted nice things. A yellow organdy dress to wear to her graduation from high school; black pumps to match a green suit she'd made from an old suit somebody gave me. She was determined to stare down any disaster in her efforts. Her eyelids would not flicker for minutes at a time. Often I fought off the temptation to shake her. At sixteen she had a style of her own, and knew what style was.

I never had an education myself. After second grade the school was closed down. Don't ask me why: in 1927 colored asked fewer questions than they do now. Sometimes Maggie reads to me. She stumbles along good-naturedly but can't see well. She knows she is not bright. Like good looks and money, quickness passed her by. She will marry John Thomas (who has mossy teeth in an earnest face) and then I'll be free to sit here and I guess just sing church songs to myself. Although I never was a good singer. Never could carry a tune. I was always better at a man's job. I used to love to milk till I was hooked in the side in '49. Cows are soothing and slow and don't bother you, unless you try to milk them the wrong way.

I have deliberately turned my back on the house. It is three rooms, just like the one that burned, except the roof is tin; they don't make shingle roofs any more. There are no real windows, just some holes cut in the sides, like the portholes in a ship, but not round and not square, with rawhide holding the shutters up on the outside. This house is in a pasture, too, like the other one. No doubt when Dee sees it she will want to tear it down. She wrote me once that no matter where we "choose" to live, she will manage to come see us. But she will never bring her friends. Maggie and I thought about this and Maggie asked me, "Mama, when did Dee ever *have* any friends?"

15 She had a few. Furtive boys in pink shirts hanging about on washday after school. Nervous girls who never laughed. Impressed with her they worshiped the well-turned phrase, the cute shape, the scalding humor that erupted like bubbles in lye. She read to them.

When she was courting Jimmy T she didn't have much time to pay to us, but turned all her faultfinding power on him. He *flew* to marry a cheap city girl from a family of ignorant flashy people. She hardly had time to recompose herself.

When she comes I will meet—but there they are!

Maggie attempts to make a dash for the house, in her shuffling way, but I stay her with my hand. "Come back here," I say. And she stops and tries to dig a well in the sand with her toe.

It is hard to see them clearly through the strong sun. But even the first glimpse of leg out of the car tells me it is Dee. Her feet were always neat-looking, as if God himself had shaped them with a certain style. From the other side of the car comes a short, stocky man. Hair is all over his head a foot long and hanging from his chin like a kinky mule tail. I hear Maggie suck in her breath. "Uhnnnh," is what it sounds like. Like when you see the wriggling end of a snake just in front of your foot on the road. "Uhnnnh."

20 Dee next. A dress down to the ground, in this hot weather. A dress so loud it hurts my eyes. There are yellows and oranges enough to throw back

the light of the sun. I feel my whole face warming from the heat waves it throws out. Earrings gold, too, and hanging down to her shoulders. Bracelets dangling and making noises when she moves her arm up to shake the folds of the dress out of her armpits. The dress is loose and flows, and as she walks closer, I like it. I hear Maggie go "Uhnnnh" again. It is her sister's hair. It stands straight up like the wool on a sheep. It is black as night and around the edges are two long pigtails that rope about like small lizards disappearing behind her ears.

"Wa-su-zo-Tean-o!"[1] she says, coming on in that gliding way the dress makes her move. The short stocky fellow with the hair to his navel is all grinning and he follows up with "Asalamalakim,[2] my mother and sister!" He moves to hug Maggie but she falls back, right up against the back of my chair. I feel her trembling there and when I look up I see the perspiration falling off her chin.

"Don't get up," says Dee. Since I am stout it takes something of a push. You can see me trying to move a second or two before I make it. She turns, showing white heels through her sandals, and goes back to the car. Out she peeks next with a Polaroid. She stoops down quickly and lines up picture after picture of me sitting there in front of the house with Maggie cowering behind me. She never takes a shot without making sure the house is included. When a cow comes nibbling around the edge of the yard she snaps it and me and Maggie *and* the house. Then she puts the Polaroid in the back seat of the car, and comes up and kisses me on the forehead.

Meanwhile Asalamalakim is going through motions with Maggie's hand. Maggie's hand is as limp as a fish, and probably as cold, despite the sweat, and she keeps trying to pull it back. It looks like Asalamalakim wants to shake hands but wants to do it fancy. Or maybe he don't know how people shake hands. Anyhow, he soon gives up on Maggie.

"Well," I say. "Dee."

25   "No, Mama," she says. "Not 'Dee,' Wangero Leewanika Kemanjo!"

"What happened to 'Dee'?" I wanted to know.

"She's dead," Wangero said. "I couldn't bear it any longer, being named after the people who oppress me."

"You know as well as me you was named after your aunt Dicie," I said. Dicie is my sister. She named Dee. We called her "Big Dee" after Dee was born.

"But who was *she* named after?" asked Wangero.

30   "I guess after Grandma Dee," I said.

"And who was she named after?" asked Wangero.

"Her mother," I said, and saw Wangero was getting tired. "That's about as far back as I can trace it," I said. Though, in fact, I probably could have carried it back beyond the Civil War through the branches.

---

[1] Greeting in Swahili; Dee sounds it out one syllable at a time.

[2] Greeting in Arabic: "Peace be upon you."

"Well," said Asalamalakim, "there you are."

"Uhnnnh," I heard Maggie say.

35   "There I was not," I said, "before 'Dicie' cropped up in our family, so why should I try to trace it that far back?"

He just stood there grinning, looking down on me like somebody inspecting a Model A car. Every once in a while he and Wangero sent eye signals over my head.

"How do you pronounce this name?" I asked.

"You don't have to call me by it if you don't want to," said Wangero.

"Why shouldn't I?" I asked. "If that's what you want us to call you, we'll call you."

40   "I know it might sound awkward at first," said Wangero.

"I'll get used to it," I said. "Ream it out again."

Well, soon we got the name out of the way. Asalamalakim had a name twice as long and three times as hard. After I tripped over it two or three times he told me to just call him Hakim-a-barber. I wanted to ask him was he a barber, but I didn't really think he was, so I didn't ask.

"You must belong to those beef-cattle peoples down the road," I said. They said "Asalamalakim" when they met you, too, but they didn't shake hands. Always too busy: feeding the cattle, fixing the fences, putting up salt-lick shelters, throwing down hay. When the white folks poisoned some of the herd the men stayed up all night with rifles in their hands. I walked a mile and a half just to see the sight.

Hakim-a-barber said, "I accept some of their doctrines, but farming and raising cattle is not my style." (They didn't tell me, and I didn't ask, whether Wangero [Dee] had really gone and married him.)

45   We sat down to eat and right away he said he didn't eat collards and pork was unclean. Wangero, though, went on through the chitlins and corn bread, the greens and everything else. She talked a blue streak over the sweet potatoes. Everything delighted her. Even the fact that we still used the benches her daddy made for the table when we couldn't afford to buy chairs.

"Oh, Mama!" she cried. Then turned to Hakim-a-barber. "I never knew how lovely these benches are. You can feel the rump prints," she said, running her hands underneath her and along the bench. Then she gave a sigh and her hand closed over Grandma Dee's butter dish. "That's it!" she said. "I knew there was something I wanted to ask you if I could have." She jumped up from the table and went over in the corner where the churn stood, the milk in it clabber by now. She looked at the churn and looked at it.

"This churn top is what I need," she said. "Didn't Uncle Buddy whittle it out of a tree you all used to have?"

"Yes," I said.

"Uh huh," she said happily. "And I want the dasher, too."

50   "Uncle Buddy whittle that, too?" asked the barber.

Dee (Wangero) looked up at me.

"Aunt Dee's first husband whittled the dash," said Maggie so low you almost couldn't hear her. "His name was Henry, but they called him Stash."

"Maggie's brain is like an elephant's," Wangero said, laughing. "I can use the churn top as a centerpiece for the alcove table," she said, sliding a plate over the churn, "and I'll think of something artistic to do with the dasher."

When she finished wrapping the dasher the handle stuck out. I took it for a moment in my hands. You didn't even have to look close to see where hands pushing the dasher up and down to make butter had left a kind of sink in the wood. In fact, there were a lot of small sinks; you could see where thumb and fingers had sunk into the wood. It was beautiful light yellow wood, from a tree that grew in the yard where Big Dee and Stash had lived.

55   After dinner Dee (Wangero) went to the trunk at the foot of my bed and started rifling through it. Maggie hung back in the kitchen over the dishpan. Out came Wangero with two quilts. They had been pieced by Grandma Dee and then Big Dee and me had hung them on the quilt frames on the front porch and quilted them. One was in the Lone Star pattern. The other was Walk Around the Mountain. In both of them were scraps of dresses Grandma Dee had worn fifty and more years ago. Bits and pieces of Grandpa Jarrell's Paisley shirts. And one teeny faded blue piece, about the size of a penny matchbox, that was from Great Grandpa Ezra's uniform that he wore in the Civil War.

"Mama," Wangero said sweet as a bird. "Can I have these old quilts?"

I heard something fall in the kitchen, and a minute later the kitchen door slammed.

"Why don't you take one or two of the others?" I asked. "These old things was just done by me and Big Dee from some tops your grandma pieced before she died."

"No," said Wangero. "I don't want those. They are stitched around the borders by machine."

60   "That'll make them last better," I said.

"That's not the point," said Wangero. "These are all pieces of dresses Grandma used to wear. She did all this stitching by hand. Imagine!" She held the quilts securely in her arms, stroking them.

"Some of the pieces, like those lavender ones, come from old clothes her mother handed down to her," I said, moving up to touch the quilts. Dee (Wangero) moved back just enough so that I couldn't reach the quilts. They already belonged to her.

"Imagine!" she breathed again, clutching them closely to her bosom.

"The truth is," I said, "I promised to give them quilts to Maggie, for when she marries John Thomas."

65   She gasped like a bee had stung her.

"Maggie can't appreciate these quilts!" she said. "She'd probably be backward enough to put them to everyday use."

"I reckon she would," I said. "God knows I been saving 'em for long enough with nobody using 'em. I hope she will!" I didn't want to bring up how I had offered Dee (Wangero) a quilt when she went away to college. Then she had told me they were old-fashioned, out of style.

"But, they're *priceless!*" she was saying now, furiously; for she has a temper. "Maggie would put them on the bed and in five years they'd be in rags. Less than that!"

"She can always make some more," I said. "Maggie knows how to quilt."

Dee (Wangero) looked at me with hatred. "You just will not understand. The point is these quilts, *these* quilts!"

70   "Well," I said, stumped. "What would *you* do with them?"

"Hang them," she said. As if that was the only thing you *could* do with quilts.

Maggie by now was standing in the door. I could almost hear the sound her feet made as they scraped over each other.

"She can have them, Mama," she said, like somebody used to never winning anything, or having anything reserved for her. "I can 'member Grandma Dee without the quilts."

I looked at her hard. She had filled her bottom lip with checkerberry snuff and it gave her face a kind of dopey, hangdog look. It was Grandma Dee and Big Dee who taught her how to quilt herself. She stood there with her scarred hands hidden in the folds of her skirt. She looked at her sister with something like fear but she wasn't mad at her. This was Maggie's portion. This was the way she knew God to work.

75   When I looked at her like that something hit me in the top of my head and ran down to the soles of my feet. Just like when I'm in church and the spirit of God touches me and I get happy and shout. I did something I never had done before: hugged Maggie to me, then dragged her on into the room, snatched the quilts out of Miss Wangero's hands and dumped them into Maggie's lap. Maggie just sat there on my bed with her mouth open.

"Take one or two of the others," I said to Dee.

But she turned without a word and went out to Hakim-a-barber.

"You just don't understand," she said, as Maggie and I came out to the car.

"What don't I understand?" I wanted to know.

80   "Your heritage," she said. And then she turned to Maggie, kissed her, and said, "You ought to try to make something of yourself, too, Maggie. It's really a new day for us. But from the way you and Mama still live you'd never know it."

She put on some sunglasses that hid everything above the tip of her nose and her chin.

Maggie smiled; maybe at the sunglasses. But a real smile, not scared. After we watched the car dust settle I asked Maggie to bring me a dip of snuff. And then the two of us sat there just enjoying, until it was time to go in the house and go to bed.

READING AND REACTING

1. What is the conventional symbolic significance of a patchwork quilt in American culture?

2. What is the *literal* meaning of the two quilts to Maggie and her mother? To Dee? Beyond this literal meaning, what symbolic meaning, if any, do they have to Maggie and her mother? Do the quilts have any symbolic meaning to Dee?

3. How does the contrast between the two sisters' appearances, personalities, lifestyles, and feelings about the quilts help to convey the story's theme?

4. What does the name *Wangero* signify to Dee? To her mother and sister? Could the name be considered a symbol? Why or why not?

5. Why do you think Maggie relinquishes the quilts to her sister?

6. What is Dee's opinion of her mother and sister? Do you agree with her assessment?

7. What does the story's title suggest to you? Do you see it as ironic? What other titles would be effective?

8. What possible meanings, aside from their literal meanings, might each of the following suggest: the family's yard, Maggie's burn scars, the trunk in which the quilts are kept, Dee's Polaroid camera? What symbolic functions, if any, do these items serve in the story?

9. **JOURNAL ENTRY**   What other objects have the kind of symbolic value to you that the quilts have to Maggie? What gives these objects this value?

10. **CRITICAL PERSPECTIVE**   According to Barbara Christian in her article "The Black Woman Artist as Wayward," "Everyday Use" is a story in which Alice Walker examines the "creative legacy" of ordinary African-American women. According to Christian, the story "is about the use and misuse of the concept of heritage. The mother of two daughters, one selfish and stylish, the other scarred and caring, passes on to us its true definition." What definition of heritage does the mother attempt to pass on to her children? In what ways is this definition like or unlike Dee's definition?

JOHN STEINBECK (1902–1968), winner of the 1962 Nobel Prize in literature, is noted for his sympathetic portraits of hardscrabble working people, particularly farm laborers, and for his evocation of rural landscapes that reflect the geography of the Salinas Valley in California, where he grew up. After attending Stanford University, Steinbeck worked as a journalist before publishing his first novel, *Cup of Gold* (1929), an adventure story, followed by *Tortilla Flat* (1935), about a poor Mexican-

American community in Monterey, and *In Dubious Battle* (1936), about a farmworkers' strike. After the success of *Of Mice and Men* (1937), his tragic story set among migrant farmworkers, Steinbeck travelled with a group of farmers migrating to the "paradise" of California from the dustbowl of Oklahoma, an experience that provided the basis for his most enduring work, *The Grapes of Wrath* (1939), winner of a Pulitzer Prize. Other well-known Steinbeck novels include *Cannery Row* (1945), *East of Eden* (1952), and *The Winter of Our Discontent* (1961). A number of Steinbeck's works have been adapted for the stage and for film.

"The Chrysanthemums," from the collection *The Long Valley*, is not set in the social milieu generally associated with Steinbeck's work, but it has been hailed as containing one of his richest character studies.

JOHN STEINBECK

The Chrysanthemums

(1937)

The high grey-flannel fog of winter closed off the Salinas Valley from the sky and from all the rest of the world. On every side it sat like a lid on the mountains and made of the great valley a closed pot. On the broad, level land floor the gang plows bit deep and left the black earth shining like metal where the shares had cut. On the foothill ranches across the Salinas River, the yellow stubble fields seemed to be bathed in pale cold sunshine, but there was no sunshine in the valley now in December. The thick willow scrub along the river flamed with sharp and positive yellow leaves.

It was a game of quiet and of waiting. The air was cold and tender. A light wind blew up from the southwest so that the farmers were mildly hopeful of a good rain before long; but fog and rain do not go together.

Across the river, on Henry Allen's foothill ranch there was little work to be done, for the hay was cut and stored and the orchards were plowed up to receive the rain deeply when it should come. The cattle on the higher slopes were becoming shaggy and rough-coated.

Elisa Allen, working in her flower garden, looked down across the yard and saw Henry, her husband, talking to two men in business suits. The three of them stood by the tractor shed, each man with one foot on the side of the little Fordson. They smoked cigarettes and studied the machine as they talked.

5   Elisa watched them for a moment and then went back to her work. She was thirty-five. Her face was lean and strong and her eyes were as clear as water. Her figure looked blocked and heavy in her gardening costume, a man's black hat pulled low down over her eyes, clod-hopper shoes,[1] a

---

[1] Heavy shoes, such as the ones that might be worn by a plowman.

figured print dress almost completely covered by a big corduroy apron with four big pockets to hold the snips, the trowel and scratcher, the seeds and the knife she worked with. She wore heavy leather gloves to protect her hands while she worked.

She was cutting down the old year's chrysanthemum stalks with a pair of short and powerful scissors. She looked down toward the men by the tractor shed now and then. Her face was eager and mature and handsome; even her work with the scissors was over-eager, over-powerful. The chrysanthemum stems seemed too small and easy for her energy.

She brushed a cloud of hair out of her eyes with the back of her glove, and left a smudge of earth on her cheek in doing it. Behind her stood the neat white farm house with red geraniums close-banked around it as high as the windows. It was a hard-swept looking little house with hard-polished windows, and a clean mud-mat on the front steps.

Elisa cast another glance toward the tractor shed. The strangers were getting into their Ford coupe. She took off a glove and put her strong fingers down into the forest of new green chrysanthemum sprouts that were growing around the old roots. She spread the leaves and looked down among the close-growing stems. No aphids were there, no sowbugs or snails or cutworms. Her terrier fingers destroyed such pests before they could get started.

Elisa started at the sound of her husband's voice. He had come near quietly, and he leaned over the wire fence that protected her flower garden from cattle and dogs and chickens.

10   "At it again," he said. "You've got a strong new crop coming."

Elisa straightened her back and pulled on the gardening glove again. "Yes. They'll be strong this coming year." In her tone and on her face there was a little smugness.

"You've got a gift with things," Henry observed. "Some of those yellow chrysanthemums you had this year were ten inches across. I wish you'd work out in the orchard and raise some apples that big."

Her eyes sharpened. "Maybe I could do it, too. I've a gift with things, all right. My mother had it. She could stick anything in the ground and make it grow. She said it was having planters' hands that knew how to do it."

"Well, it sure works with flowers," he said.

15   "Henry, who were those men you were talking to?"

"Why, sure, that's what I came to tell you. They were from the Western Meat Company. I sold those thirty head of three-year-old steers. Got nearly my own price, too."

"Good," she said. "Good for you."

"And I thought," he continued, "I thought how it's Saturday afternoon, and we might go into Salinas for dinner at a restaurant, and then to a picture show—to celebrate, you see."

"Good," she repeated. "Oh, yes. That will be good."

20   Henry put on his joking tone. "There's fights tonight. How'd you like to go to the fights?"

"Oh, no," she said breathlessly. "No, I wouldn't like fights."

"Just fooling, Elisa. We'll go to a movie. Let's see. It's two now. I'm going to take Scotty and bring down those steers from the hill. It'll take us maybe two hours. We'll go in town about five and have dinner at the Cominos Hotel. Like that?"

"Of course I'll like it. It's good to eat away from home."

"All right, then. I'll go get up a couple of horses."

25   She said, "I'll have plenty of time to transplant some of these sets, I guess."

She heard her husband calling Scotty down by the barn. And a little later she saw the two men ride up the pale yellow hillside in search of the steers.

There was a little square sandy bed kept for rooting the chrysanthemums. With her trowel she turned the soil over and over, and smoothed it and patted it firm. Then she dug ten parallel trenches to receive the sets. Back at the chrysanthemum bed she pulled out the little crisp shoots, trimmed off the leaves of each one with her scissors and laid it on a small orderly pile.

A squeak of wheels and plod of hoofs came from the road. Elisa looked up. The country road ran along the dense bank of willows and cottonwoods that bordered the river, and up this road came a curious vehicle, curiously drawn. It was an old spring-wagon, with a round canvas top on it like the cover of a prairie schooner.[2] It was drawn by an old bay horse and a little grey-and-white burro. A big stubble-bearded man sat between the cover flaps and drove the crawling team. Underneath the wagon, between the hind wheels, a lean and rangy mongrel dog walked sedately. Words were printed on the canvas, in clumsy, crooked letters. "Pots, pans, knives, sisors, lawn mores, Fixed." Two rows of articles, and the triumphantly definitive "Fixed" below. The black paint had run down in little sharp points beneath each letter.

Elisa, squatting on the ground, watched to see the crazy, loose-jointed wagon pass by. But it didn't pass. It turned into the farm road in front of her house, crooked old wheels skirling and squeaking. The rangy dog darted from between the wheels and ran ahead. Instantly the two ranch shepherds flew out at him. Then all three stopped, and with stiff and quivering tails, with taut straight legs, with ambassadorial dignity, they slowly circled, sniffing daintily. The caravan pulled up to Elisa's wire fence and stopped. Now the newcomer dog, feeling outnumbered, lowered his tail and retired under the wagon with raised hackles and bared teeth.

30   The man on the wagon seat called out, "That's a bad dog in a fight when he gets started."

Elisa laughed. "I see he is. How soon does he generally get started?"

---

[2] Covered wagon used by American pioneers.

The man caught up her laughter and echoed it heartily. "Sometimes not for weeks and weeks," he said. He climbed stiffly down, over the wheel. The horse and the donkey drooped like unwatered flowers.

Elisa saw that he was a very big man. Although his hair and beard were greying, he did not look old. His worn black suit was wrinkled and spotted with grease. The laughter had disappeared from his face and eyes the moment his laughing voice ceased. His eyes were dark, and they were full of the brooding that gets in the eyes of teamsters and of sailors. The calloused hands he rested on the wire fence were cracked, and every crack was a black line. He took off his battered hat.

"I'm off my general road, ma'am," he said. "Does this dirt road cut over across the river to the Los Angeles highway?"

35   Elisa stood up and shoved the thick scissors in her apron pocket. "Well, yes, it does, but it winds around and then fords the river. I don't think your team could pull through the sand."

He replied with some asperity. "It might surprise you what them beasts can pull through."

"When they get started?" she asked.

He smiled for a second. "Yes. When they get started."

"Well," said Elisa, "I think you'll save time if you go back to the Salinas road and pick up the highway there."

40   He drew a big finger down the chicken wire and made it sing. "I ain't in any hurry, ma'am. I go from Seattle to San Diego and back every year. Takes all my time. About six months each way. I aim to follow nice weather."

Elisa took off her gloves and stuffed them in the apron pocket with the scissors. She touched the under edge of her man's hat, searching for fugitive hairs. "That sounds like a nice kind of a way to live," she said.

He leaned confidentially over the fence. "Maybe you noticed the writing on my wagon. I mend pots and sharpen knives and scissors. You got any of them things to do?"

"Oh, no," she said quickly. "Nothing like that." Her eyes hardened with resistance.

"Scissors is the worst thing," he explained. "Most people just ruin scissors trying to sharpen 'em, but I know how. I got a special tool. It's a little bobbit kind of thing, and patented. But it sure does the trick."

45   "No. My scissors are all sharp."

"All right, then. Take a pot," he continued earnestly, "a bent pot, or a pot with a hole. I can make it like new so you don't have to buy no new ones. That's a saving for you."

"No," she said shortly. "I tell you I have nothing like that for you to do."

His face fell to an exaggerated sadness. His voice took on a whining undertone. "I ain't had a thing to do today. Maybe I won't have no supper tonight. You see I'm off my regular road. I know folks on the highway clear from Seattle to San Diego. They save their things for me to sharpen up because they know I do it so good and save them money."

"I'm sorry," Elisa said irritably. "I haven't anything for you to do."

50   His eyes left her face and fell to searching the ground. They roamed about until they came to the chrysanthemum bed where she had been working. "What's them plants, ma'am?"

The irritation and resistance melted from Elisa's face. "Oh, those are chrysanthemums, giant whites and yellows. I raise them every year, bigger than anybody around here."

"Kind of a long-stemmed flower? Looks like a quick puff of colored smoke?" he asked.

"That's it. What a nice way to describe them."

"They smell kind of nasty till you get used to them," he said.

55   "It's a good bitter smell," she retorted, "not nasty at all."

He changed his tone quickly. "I like the smell myself."

"I had ten-inch blooms this year," she said.

The man leaned farther over the fence. "Look. I know a lady down the road a piece, has got the nicest garden you ever seen. Got nearly every kind of flower but no chrysanthemums. Last time I was mending a copper-bottom washtub for her (that's a hard job but I do it good), she said to me, 'If you ever run acrost some nice chrysanthemums I wish you'd try to get me a few seeds.' That's what she told me."

Elisa's eyes grew alert and eager. "She couldn't have known much about chrysanthemums. You *can* raise them from seed, but it's much easier to root the little sprouts you see there."

60   "Oh," he said. "I s'pose I can't take none to her, then."

"Why yes you can," Elisa cried. "I can put some in damp sand, and you can carry them right along with you. They'll take root in the pot if you keep them damp. And then she can transplant them."

"She'd sure like to have some, ma'am. You say they're nice ones?"

"Beautiful," she said. "Oh, beautiful." Her eyes shone. She tore off the battered hat and shook out her dark pretty hair. "I'll put them in a flower pot, and you can take them right with you. Come into the yard."

While the man came through the picket gate Elisa ran excitedly along the geranium-bordered path to the back of the house. And she returned carrying a big red flower pot. The gloves were forgotten now. She kneeled on the ground by the starting bed and dug up the sandy soil with her fingers and scooped it into the bright new flower pot. Then she picked up the little pile of shoots she had prepared. With her strong fingers she pressed them into the sand and tamped around them with her knuckles. The man stood over her. "I'll tell you what to do," she said. "You remember so you can tell the lady."

65   "Yes, I'll try to remember."

"Well, look. These will take root in about a month. Then she must set them out, about a foot apart in good rich earth like this, see?" She lifted a handful of dark soil for him to look at. "They'll grow fast and tall. Now remember this: In July tell her to cut them down, about eight inches from the ground."

"Before they bloom?" he asked.

"Yes, before they bloom." Her face was tight with eagerness. "They'll grow right up again. About the last of September the buds will start."

She stopped and seemed perplexed. "It's the budding that takes the most care," she said hesitantly. "I don't know how to tell you." She looked deep into his eyes, searchingly. Her mouth opened a little, and she seemed to be listening. "I'll try to tell you," she said. "Did you ever hear of planting hands?"

70   "Can't say I have, ma'am."

"Well, I can only tell you what it feels like. It's when you're picking off the buds you don't want. Everything goes right down into your fingertips. You watch your fingers work. They do it themselves. You can feel how it is. They pick and pick the buds. They never make a mistake. They're with the plant. Do you see? Your fingers and the plant. You can feel that, right up your arm. They know. They never make a mistake. You can feel it. When you're like that you can't do anything wrong. Do you see that? Can you understand that?"

She was kneeling on the ground looking up at him. Her breast swelled passionately.

The man's eyes narrowed. He looked away self-consciously. "Maybe I know," he said. "Sometimes in the night in the wagon there—"

Elisa's voice grew husky. She broke in on him, "I've never lived as you do, but I know what you mean. When the night is dark—why, the stars are sharp-pointed, and there's quiet. Why, you rise up and up! Every pointed star gets driven into your body. It's like that. Hot and sharp and—lovely."

75   Kneeling there, her hand went out toward his legs in the greasy black trousers. Her hesitant fingers almost touched the cloth. Then her hand dropped to the ground. She crouched low like a fawning dog.

He said, "It's nice, just like you say. Only when you don't have no dinner, it ain't."

She stood up then, very straight, and her face was ashamed. She held the flower pot out to him and placed it gently in his arms. "Here. Put it in your wagon, on the seat, where you can watch it. Maybe I can find something for you to do."

At the back of the house she dug in the can pile and found two old and battered aluminum saucepans. She carried them back and gave them to him. "Here, maybe you can fix these."

His manner changed. He became professional. "Good as new I can fix them." At the back of his wagon he sat a little anvil, and out of an oily tool box dug a small machine hammer. Elisa came through the gate to watch him while he pounded out the dents in the kettles. His mouth grew sure and knowing. At a difficult part of the work he sucked his under-lip.

80   "You sleep right in the wagon?" Elisa asked.

"Right in the wagon, ma'am. Rain or shine I'm dry as a cow in there."

"It must be nice," she said. "It must be very nice. I wish women could do such things."

"It ain't the right kind of a life for a woman."

Her upper lip raised a little, showing her teeth. "How do you know? How can you tell?" she said.

85   "I don't know, ma'am," he protested. "Of course I don't know. Now here's your kettles, done. You don't have to buy no new ones."

"How much?"

"Oh, fifty cents'll do. I keep my prices down and my work good. That's why I have all them satisfied customers up and down the highway."

Elisa brought him a fifty-cent piece from the house and dropped it in his hand. "You might be surprised to have a rival some time. I can sharpen scissors, too. And I can beat the dents out of little pots. I could show you what a woman might do."

He put his hammer back in the oily box and shoved the little anvil out of sight. "It would be a lonely life for a woman, ma'am, and a scarey life, too, with animals creeping under the wagon all night." He climbed over the singletree,[3] steadying himself with a hand on the burro's white rump. He settled himself in the seat, picked up the lines. "Thank you kindly, ma'am," he said. "I'll do like you told me; I'll go back and catch the Salinas road."

90   "Mind," she called, "if you're long in getting there, keep the sand damp."

"Sand, ma'am? . . . Sand? Oh, sure. You mean around the chrysanthemums. Sure I will." He clucked his tongue. The beasts leaned luxuriously into their collars. The mongrel dog took his place between the back wheels. The wagon turned and crawled out the entrance road and back the way it had come, along the river.

Elisa stood in front of her wire fence watching the slow progress of the caravan. Her shoulders were straight, her head thrown back, her eyes half-closed, so that the scene came vaguely into them. Her lips moved silently, forming the words "Good-bye—good-bye." Then she whispered, "That's a bright direction. There's a glowing there." The sound of her whisper startled her. She shook herself free and looked about to see whether anyone had been listening. Only the dogs had heard. They lifted their heads toward her from their sleeping in the dust, and then stretched out their chins and settled asleep again. Elisa turned and ran hurriedly into the house.

In the kitchen she reached behind the stove and felt the water tank. It was full of hot water from the noonday cooking. In the bathroom she tore off her soiled clothes and flung them into the corner. And then she scrubbed herself with a little block of pumice, legs and thighs, loins and chest and arms, until her skin was scratched and red. When she had dried herself she stood in front of a mirror in her bedroom and looked at her body. She tightened her stomach and threw out her chest. She turned and looked over her shoulder at her back.

---

[3] A wooden bar that connects a wagon to the horses' harnesses.

After a while she began to dress, slowly. She put on her newest under-clothing and her nicest stockings and the dress which was the symbol of her prettiness. She worked carefully on her hair, penciled her eyebrows and rouged her lips.

95   Before she was finished she heard the little thunder of hoofs and the shouts of Henry and his helper as they drove the red steers into the corral. She heard the gate bang shut and set herself for Henry's arrival.

His step sounded on the porch. He entered the house calling, "Elisa, where are you?"

"In my room, dressing. I'm not ready. There's hot water for your bath. Hurry up. It's getting late."

When she heard him splashing in the tub, Elisa laid his dark suit on the bed, and shirt and socks and tie beside it. She stood his polished shoes on the floor beside the bed. Then she went to the porch and sat primly and stiffly down. She looked toward the river road where the willow-line was still yellow with frosted leaves so that under the high grey fog they seemed a thin band of sunshine. This was the only color in the grey afternoon. She sat unmoving for a long time. Her eyes blinked rarely.

Henry came banging out of the door, shoving his tie inside his vest as he came. Elisa stiffened and her face grew tight. Henry stopped short and looked at her. "Why—why, Elisa. You look so nice!"

100   "Nice? You think I look nice? What do you mean by 'nice'?"

Henry blundered on. "I don't know. I mean you look different, strong and happy."

"I am strong? Yes, strong. What do you mean 'strong'?"

He looked bewildered. "You're playing some kind of a game," he said helplessly. "It's a kind of a play. You look strong enough to break a calf over your knee, happy enough to eat it like a watermelon."

For a second she lost her rigidity. "Henry! Don't talk like that. You didn't know what you said." She grew complete again. "I'm strong," she boasted. "I never knew before how strong."

105   Henry looked down toward the tractor shed, and when he brought his eyes back to her, they were his own again. "I'll get out the car. You can put on your coat while I'm starting."

Elisa went into the house. She heard him drive to the gate and idle down his motor, and then she took a long time to put on her hat. She pulled it here and pressed it there. When Henry turned the motor off she slipped into her coat and went out.

The little roadster[4] bounced along on the dirt road by the river, raising the birds and driving the rabbits into the brush. Two cranes flapped heavily over the willow-line and dropped into the river-bed.

Far ahead on the road Elisa saw a dark speck. She knew.

---

[4] An early roofless automobile, with a single seat for two or three passengers.

She tried not to look as they passed it, but her eyes would not obey. She whispered to herself sadly, "He might have thrown them off the road. That wouldn't have been much trouble, not very much. But he kept the pot," she explained. "He had to keep the pot. That's why he couldn't get them off the road."

110   The roadster turned a bend and she saw the caravan ahead. She swung full around toward her husband so she could not see the little covered wagon and the mismatched team as the car passed them.

In a moment it was over. The thing was done. She did not look back.

She said loudly, to be heard above the motor, "It will be good, tonight, a good dinner."

"Now you're changed again," Henry complained. He took one hand from the wheel and patted her knee. "I ought to take you in to dinner oftener. It would be good for both of us. We get so heavy out on the ranch."

"Henry," she asked, "could we have wine at dinner?"

115   "Sure we could. Say! That will be fine."

She was silent for a while; then she said, "Henry, at those prize fights, do the men hurt each other very much?"

"Sometimes a little, not often. Why?"

"Well, I've read how they break noses, and blood runs down their chests. I've read how the fighting gloves get heavy and soggy with blood."

He looked around at her. "What's the matter, Elisa? I didn't know you read things like that." He brought the car to a stop, then turned to the right over the Salinas River bridge.

120   "Do any women ever go to the fights?" she asked.

"Oh, sure, some. What's the matter, Elisa? Do you want to go? I don't think you'd like it, but I'll take you if you really want to go."

She relaxed limply in the seat. "Oh, no. No. I don't want to go. I'm sure I don't." Her face was turned away from him. "It will be enough if we can have wine. It will be plenty." She turned up her coat collar so he could not see that she was crying weakly—like an old woman.

READING AND REACTING

1. The first few paragraphs establish the setting of the story. What details does Steinbeck choose to emphasize? Why?

2. What symbolic significance does the image of the pot have at various points in the story? (Notice that in paragraph 1, the valley where Eliza and Henry Allen live is described as a "closed pot.")

3. Throughout the story Mrs. Allen says she has a gift. What is her gift? How is her gift important to the story?

4. What effect does the man in the wagon have on Mrs. Allen? What does he symbolize to her?

5. What do the chrysanthemums mean to Mrs. Allen? To the man in the wagon? Why do you think the man in the wagon takes such an interest in Mrs. Allen's chrysanthemums?

6. In paragraphs 64 through 71 Steinbeck describes Eliza's planting of the chrysanthemums, and in paragraphs 93 and 94 he describes her preparation for her night out with her husband. Why does he dwell on these details? What do they tell readers about Mrs. Allen?

7. Why do you think the man in the wagon throws away the chrysanthemum shoots? Why does Eliza react the way she does when she sees the chrysanthemums in the road? When she passes the wagon?

8. Why is Mrs. Allen so insistent on ordering wine with dinner? Why does she ask about the prize fights? What do you think she means in the last paragraph when she says, "It will be enough to have wine." Do you see these as symbolic gestures? Explain.

9. **JOURNAL ENTRY**   Do you think Mrs. Allen is as trapped as she thinks she is? What, if anything, could she have done to improve her situation?

10. **CRITICAL PERSPECTIVE**   In her article "Steinbeck's Strong Women in Short Stories," critic Marilyn L. Mitchell points out that Eliza feels frustrated by the fact that she and her work are not taken seriously by the men around her. According to Mitchell, Eliza is frustrated "in her role as a rancher's wife; and part of Eliza's sense of frustration stems from the fact that her work, even the dirty work of gardening, remains 'woman's work.' " Are there any hints in the story that the men, like Eliza, are also frustrated and victimized?

WRITING SUGGESTIONS: SYMBOL AND ALLEGORY

1. Select a story that you have read in this chapter, and discuss its use of symbols.

2. Strangers figure prominently in "Young Goodman Brown" and "The Chrysanthemums." Write an essay in which you discuss the possible symbolic significance of strangers in each story.

3. Write an essay in which you discuss the conflicts present in "Young Goodman Brown." In your essay show how the allegorical elements in the story reflect and reinforce these conflicts.

4. If Shirley Jackson had wished to write "The Lottery" as an allegory whose purpose was to expose the evils of Nazi Germany, what revisions would she have had to make to convey the dangers of blind obedience to authority? Consider the story's symbols, the characters (and their names), and the setting.

5. In a number of works in this anthology, prized possessions function as symbols—for example, the quilt in "Everyday Use," the grinding ball in "The Secret Lion," the clock and de Spain's rug in "Barn Burning," and the animals in *The Glass Menagerie*. Write an essay in which you discuss the symbolic significance of a prized possession in any two works in this text.

CHAPTER 10

Theme

I think a writer's job is to provoke questions. I like to think that if someone's read a book of mine, they've had—I don't know—the literary equivalent of a shower. Something that would start them thinking in a slightly different way perhaps. That's what I think writers are for.

DORIS LESSING, *WRITERS AT WORK*, 9TH ED.

Reduced to its simplest and most general terms, theme for Negro writers will rise from understanding the meaning of their being transplanted from a "savage" to a "civilized" culture in all of its social, political, economic, and emotional implications. It means that Negro writers must have in their consciousness the foreshortened picture of the whole, *nourishing culture from which they were torn in Africa, and of the long, complex (and for the most part, unconscious) struggle to regain in some form and under alien conditions of life a* whole *culture again.*

It is not only this picture they must have, but also a knowledge of the social and emotional milieu that gives it tone and solidity of detail. Theme for Negro writers will emerge when they have begun to feel the meaning of the history of their race as though they in one life time had lived it themselves throughout all the long centuries.

RICHARD WRIGHT, "BLUEPRINT FOR NEGRO WRITING"

A work of art encountered as a work of art is an experience, not a statement or an answer to a question. Art is not only about something; it is something. A work of art is a thing in the world, not just a text or commentary on the world.

SUSAN SONTAG, "ON STYLE" IN *AGAINST INTERPRETATION*

In testing and validating the idea of greatness in any short story, the reader can quickly come to one conclusion: there is no absolute set of criteria for a great short story; each has its own special imprint. But any great short story must have staying power, depth, range, or scope, where its form and content merge to produce a highly individualized, living, and vital portrait from life. It either entices or forces the reader to come back to it—as though it were a strong magnet—for further profit. In the end, it may still remain a mystery or open-ended, "offering everything and confirming nothing." Not singly but in combination—whether in subject, style, setting, mood, tone, plot, character, action, or theme—the great short story evolves, and as it strikes out in new directions, it makes a case (often unconsciously) for its own immortality.

THOMAS A. GULLASON, "WHAT MAKES A SHORT STORY GREAT?"

One of the most difficult things is the first paragraph. I have spent many months on a first paragraph, and once I get it, the rest just comes out very easily. In the first paragraph you solve most of the problems with your book. The theme is defined, the style, the tone. At least in my case, the first paragraph is a kind of sample of what the rest of the book is going to be. That's why writing a book of short stories is much more difficult than writing a novel. Every time you write a short story, you have to begin all over again.

GABRIEL GARCÍA MÁRQUEZ, *WRITERS AT WORK*, 6TH ED.

The **theme** of a work of literature is its central or dominant idea. *Theme* is not the same as *plot* or *subject,* two terms with which it is sometimes confused. A simple *plot summary* of Tadeusz Borowski's "Silence" (p. 356) could be "Prisoners are liberated from a concentration camp and, despite the admonitions of the American officer, they kill a captured German guard." The statement " 'Silence' is about freed prisoners and a guard" could define the *subject* of the story. A statement of the *theme* of "Silence," however, would have to do more than summarize its plot or identify its subject; it would have to convey the values and ideas expressed by the story. Many effective stories are complex, expressing more than one theme, and "Silence" is no exception. You could say, for example, that "Silence" suggests that human beings have a need for vengeance. You could also say the story demonstrates that silence is sometimes the only response possible when one is confronting unspeakable horrors. Although both these themes—and others—are present in the story, one theme seems to dominate—the idea that under extreme conditions the oppressed can become as morally bankrupt as their oppressors.

When writing about theme, be certain you are not merely telling what happens in the story. The theme you identify should be an idea that extends beyond the story, applying to you and to your world. Compare these two statements about Edgar Allan Poe's "The Cask of Amontillado" (p. 209):

> *Poe's "The Cask of Amontillado" is about a man who loses his humanity because of his obsessive desire to avenge himself on Fortunato.*

> *Poe's "The Cask of Amontillado" suggests that when the desire for revenge becomes obsessive, it can deprive individuals of all that makes them human.*

The first statement merely tells what the story is about; the second statement identifies the story's theme, making a general observation about humanity and thereby giving the theme meaning outside the story itself.

Granted, some short works (fairy tales, fables, and some popular fiction, for example) have themes that can be summed up as **clichés**—overused phrases or expressions—or as morals—lessons dramatized by the work. The fairy tale "Cinderella," for example, expresses the clichéd theme that a virtuous girl who endures misfortune will eventually achieve her just reward; the fable "The Tortoise and the Hare" illustrates the moral "Slow and steady wins the race." Like "The Cask of Amontillado," however, most of the stories in this anthology have themes that require more complex expression than clichés or morals allow.

Interpreting Themes

Contemporary critical theory holds that the theme of a work of fiction is as much the creation of the reader as of the writer. The readers' backgrounds, knowledge, values, and beliefs all determine the theme or themes they will perceive in a work. Most readers, for example, will realize that David Michael Kaplan's story "Doe Season" (p. 342)—in which the main character goes hunting, kills her first deer, and is forced to confront suffering and death—expresses a conventional **initiation theme,** revealing growing up to be a disillusioning and painful process. Still, different readers bring different perspectives to the story and, in some cases, see different themes.

During a classroom discussion of "Doe Season," a student familiar with hunting saw more than his classmates did in the story's conventional initiation theme. He knew that in many states there really is a doe season, which lasts approximately three days. Shorter than the ten-day buck season, its purpose is to enable hunters to control the size of the deer herd by killing females. This knowledge enabled the student to conclude that by the end of the story the female child's innocence must inevitably be destroyed, just as the doe must be.

Another student pointed out that Andy is a female who uses a male name. Andy's participation in hunting, a traditional male rite of passage, leads to her killing the deer and to her subsequent disillusionment. It also leads to her decision to abandon her nickname. By contrasting "Andrea" with "Andy," the story pits the child's female perspective, illustrated by her compassion, against the other characters' male perspective, associated with killing and death. This interpretation led the student to conclude that the theme of "Doe Season" was that males' and females' different outlooks on life ultimately cannot be reconciled.

Other students did not accept the condemnation of the father and the other male characters implied by the interpretation discussed above. They pointed out that the father is a sympathetic figure who is extremely supportive; he encourages and defends his daughter. He takes her hunting because he loves her, not because he wants to initiate her into life or to hurt her. One student mentioned that Andy's reaction when she sees the doe, common in children who kill their first deer, is called *buck fever*. In light of this information, several students thought that far from being about irreconcilable male and female perspectives, "Doe Season" makes a statement about a young girl who is hunting for her own identity and who in the process discovers her own mortality. Her father is therefore the agent who enables her to confront the inevitability of death, a fact she must accept if she is going to take her place in the adult world. In this sense the theme of the story is the idea that in order to mature, a child must reconcile life with the reality of death.

Different readers may see different themes in a story, but your interpretation of a theme must make sense in light of what is actually in the story. Evidence from the work, not just your own feelings or assumptions, must support your interpretation, and a single symbol or one statement by a character is not enough in itself to reveal a story's theme. Therefore, you must identify a cross section of examples from the text to support your interpretation of the story's theme. If you say that the theme of James Joyce's "Araby" (p. 249) is that an innocent idealist is inevitably doomed to disillusionment, you have to find examples from the text to support your statement. You could begin with the title, concluding that the word *Araby* suggests dreams of exotic beauty that the boy tries to find when he goes to the fair. You could reinforce your idea about the elusiveness of beauty by pointing out that Mangan's unattainable sister is a symbol of this beauty that the boy wants so desperately to find. Finally, you could show how idealism is ultimately crushed by society: At the end of the story the boy stands alone in the darkness and realizes that his dreams of beauty are childish fantasies. Although other readers may have different responses to "Araby," they should concede that your interpretation is reasonable if you support your interpretation with enough examples.

IDENTIFYING THEMES

Every element of a story can shed light on its themes. As you analyze a short story, look for features that reveal and reinforce what you perceive to be the story's most important ideas.

The *title* of a story can often provide insight into the theme or themes of a story. The title of an F. Scott Fitzgerald story, "Babylon Revisited," emphasizes a major idea in the story—that Paris of the 1920s is like Babylon, the ancient city the Bible singles out as the epitome of evil and corruption. The story's protagonist, Charlie Wales, comes to realize that no matter how much money he lost after the stock market crash, he lost more—his wife and his daughter—during the boom, when he was in Paris. Charlie's search through his past—his return to "Babylon"—provides new meaning to his life and offers at least a small bit of hope for the future.

Sometimes a *narrator's or character's statement* can lead you to a theme. For example, at the beginning of Alberto Alvaro Ríos's "The Secret Lion" (p. 43) the first-person narrator says, "I was twelve and in junior high school and something happened that we didn't have a name for, but it was there nonetheless like a lion, and roaring, roaring that way the biggest things do. Everything changed." Although the narrator does not directly announce the story's theme, he does suggest that the story will communicate the idea that the price children pay for growing up is realizing that everything changes, that nothing stays the way it is.

The *arrangement of events* in a story can suggest a story's theme, as it does in an Ernest Hemingway story, "The Short Happy Life of Francis Macomber." At the beginning of the story the title character is a coward who is stuck in an unhappy marriage. As the story progresses, he gradually learns the nature of courage and, finally, finds it in himself. At the moment of his triumph, however, Francis is killed; his "happy life" is short indeed. The way the events of the story are presented, through foreshadowing and flashbacks, provides insight into the connection between Macomber's marriage and his behavior as a hunter. This connection in turn helps to reveal a possible theme: Sometimes courage can be more important than life itself.

Conflict, a central plot element in short fiction, can offer clues to the themes expressed in a story. In "Araby" the young boy believes that his society neglects art and beauty and glorifies the mundane. This conflict between the boy's idealism and his world can help readers understand why the boy cloisters himself in his room reading books and why he retreats into dreams of idealized love. A major theme of the story—that growing up leads to the loss of youthful idealism—is revealed by this central conflict.

Similarly, the main character in "The Yellow Wall-Paper" (p. 160), a woman who has recently had a baby, is set in opposition to the larger nineteenth-century society in which she lives. She is suffering from "temporary nervous depression," what doctors today recognize as postpartum depression. Following the practice of the time, her physician has ordered complete bed rest and has instructed her husband to deprive her of all mental and physical stimulation. This harsh treatment leads the narrator to lose her grasp on reality; eventually she begins to hallucinate. The central conflict of the story is clearly between the woman and her society, controlled by men. This conflict communicates the story's theme: In nineteenth-century America, women are dominated not just by their husbands and the male medical establishment, but also by society as a whole.

The *point of view* of a story can help shed light on theme. For instance, a writer's use of an unreliable first-person narrator can help to communicate the theme of a story. Thus, Montresor's self-serving first-person account of his crime in "The Cask of Amontillado," and his convincing attempts to justify his actions, enable readers to understand the dangers of irrational anger and misplaced ideas about honor. The voice of a third-person narrator can also help to convey a story's theme. For example, the detachment of the narrator in Stephen Crane's Civil War novel *The Red Badge of Courage* reinforces the theme of the novel: Bravery, cowardice, battle, and even life itself are insignificant when set beside the indifference of the universe.

Quite often a story will give names, places, and objects symbolic significance. These *symbols* can not only enrich the story, but also help to convey a central theme. For example, the rocking horse in D. H. Lawrence's "The Rocking-Horse Winner" (p. 512) can be seen as a symbol of the boy's desperate desire to remain a child. Interpreted in this way, it reinforces the theme that innocence cannot survive when it confronts forces such as greed and selfishness. Similarly, Hawthorne's "Young Goodman Brown" (p. 298) uses symbols such as the walking stick, the woods, sunset and night, and the vague shadows to develop one of its central themes: If a person strays from the path of faith, evil is everywhere.

Finally, *changes in a character* can shed light on the theme or themes of the story. In the course of Raymond Carver's "Cathedral" (p. 405), for example, the main character alters his preconceptions about blind people. The shift in attitude that precipitates this change conveys the story's central theme: Sometimes people have to shut their eyes to see the beauty and mystery of the things around them that they take for granted. Similarly, the main character in Charles Baxter's "Gryphon" (p. 125) comes to realize that the "lies" Miss Ferenczi tells may be closer to the truth than the "facts" his teachers present. Thus, the narrator's changing attitude toward Miss Ferenczi helps to communicate the story's central theme about the nature of truth.

▼▼

CHECKLIST FOR WRITING ABOUT THEME

- ◆ What is the central theme of the story?
- ◆ What other themes can you identify?
- ◆ Does the title of the story suggest a theme?
- ◆ Does the narrator, or any character, make statements that express or imply a theme?
- ◆ In what way does the arrangement of events in the story suggest a theme?
- ◆ In what way does the central conflict of the story suggest a theme?
- ◆ How does the point of view shed light on the story's central theme?
- ◆ Do any symbols suggest a theme?
- ◆ Do any characters in the story change in any significant way? Do their changes convey a particular theme?

◆ Have you clearly identified the story's central theme, rather than just summarized the plot or stated the subject?

◆ Does your statement of the story's central theme make a general observation that has an application beyond the story itself?

▲▲

DAVID MICHAEL KAPLAN (1946–   ) is one of a group of American writers who, along with South American writers such as García Márquez of Colombia, are called "magic realists." Magic realists work outside of the "hobbits and wizards" borders of traditional fantasy writing, seamlessly interweaving magical elements and detailed, realistically drawn "everyday" settings. These elements, says a reviewer of Kaplan's work, are invoked "to illuminate and underscore heightened moments of reality." The story "Doe Season," which appears in Kaplan's debut short story collection, *Comfort* (1987), was selected as one of the Best American Short Stories of 1985. Kaplan's first novel, *Skating in the Dark,* was published in 1991.

Interestingly, the stories in *Comfort* break from classic "first-time author" tradition by sidestepping the autobiographical, young-man-comes-of-age theme. Instead, these stories are about young girls or young women—coming to grips with parents (present or absent) and with loss and searching for ways to resolve their ambivalence about becoming women. In "Doe Season" Andy's surreal encounter with the doe may be a dream, but the beauty and horror of their meeting will affect the rest of her life.

DAVID MICHAEL KAPLAN

Doe Season

(1985)

They were always the same woods, she thought sleepily as they drove through the early morning darkness—deep and immense, covered with yesterday's snowfall, which had frozen overnight. They were the same woods that lay behind her house, *and they stretch all the way to here,* she thought, *for miles and miles, longer than I could walk in a day, or a week even, but they are still the same woods.* The thought made her feel good: it was like thinking of God; it was like thinking of the space between here and the moon; it was like thinking of all the foreign countries from her geography book where even now, Andy knew, people were going to bed, while they—she and her father and Charlie Spoon and Mac, Charlie's eleven-year-old son— were driving deeper into the Pennsylvania countryside, to go hunting.

They had risen long before dawn. Her mother, yawning and not trying to hide her sleepiness, cooked them eggs and French toast. Her father smoked a cigarette and flicked ashes into his saucer while Andy listened, wondering *Why doesn't he come?* and *Won't he ever come?* until at last a car pulled into the graveled drive and honked. "That will be Charlie Spoon," her father said; he always said "Charlie Spoon," even though his real name was Spreun, because Charlie was, in a sense, shaped like a spoon, with a large head and a narrow waist and chest.

Andy's mother kissed her and her father and said, "Well, have a good time" and "Be careful." Soon they were outside in the bitter dark, loading gear by the back-porch light, their breath steaming. The woods behind the house were then only a black streak against the wash of night.

Andy dozed in the car and woke to find that it was half light. Mac— also sleeping—had slid against her. She pushed him away and looked out the window. Her breath clouded the glass, and she was cold; the car's heater didn't work right. They were riding over gentle hills, the woods on both sides now—the same woods, she knew, because she had been watching the whole way, even while she slept. They had been in her dreams, and she had never lost sight of them.

5   Charlie Spoon was driving. "I don't understand why she's coming," he said to her father. "How old is she anyway—eight?"

"Nine," her father replied. "She's small for her age."

"So—nine. What's the difference? She'll just add to the noise and get tired besides."

"No, she won't," her father said. "She can walk me to death. And she'll bring good luck, you'll see. Animals—I don't know how she does it, but they come right up to her. We go walking in the woods, and we'll spot more raccoons and possums and such than I ever see when I'm alone."

Charlie grunted.

10   "Besides, she's not a bad little shot, even if she doesn't hunt yet. She shoots the .22 real good."

"Popgun," Charlie said, and snorted. "And target shooting ain't deer hunting."

"Well, she's not gonna be shooting anyway, Charlie," her father said. "Don't worry. She'll be no bother."

"I still don't know why she's coming," Charlie said.

"Because she wants to, and I want her to. Just like you and Mac. No difference."

15   Charlie turned onto a side road and after a mile or so slowed down. "That's it!" he cried. He stopped, backed up, and entered a narrow dirt road almost hidden by trees. Five hundred yards down, the road ran parallel to a

fenced-in field. Charlie parked in a cleared area deeply rutted by frozen tractor tracks. The gate was locked. *In the spring,* Andy thought, *there will be cows here, and a dog that chases them,* but now the field was unmarked and bare.

"This is it," Charlie Spoon declared. "Me and Mac was up here just two weeks ago, scouting it out, and there's deer. Mac saw the tracks."

"That's right," Mac said.

"Well, we'll just see about that," her father said, putting on his gloves. He turned to Andy. "How you doing, honeybun?"

"Just fine," she said.

20   Andy shivered and stamped as they unloaded: first the rifles, which they unsheathed and checked, sliding the bolts, sighting through scopes, adjusting the slings; then the gear, their food and tents and sleeping bags and stove stored in four backpacks—three big ones for Charlie Spoon and her father and Mac, and a day pack for her.

"That's about your size," Mac said, to tease her.

She reddened and said, "Mac, I can carry a pack big as yours any day." He laughed and pressed his knee against the back of hers, so that her leg buckled. "Cut it out," she said. She wanted to make an iceball and throw it at him, but she knew that her father and Charlie were anxious to get going, and she didn't want to displease them.

Mac slid under the gate, and they handed the packs over to him. Then they slid under and began walking across the field toward the same woods that ran all the way back to her home, where even now her mother was probably rising again to wash their breakfast dishes and make herself a fresh pot of coffee. *She is there, and we are here:* the thought satisfied Andy. There was no place else she would rather be.

Mac came up beside her. "Over there's Canada," he said, nodding toward the woods.

25   "Huh!" she said. "Not likely."

"I don't mean *right* over there. I mean farther up north. You think I'm dumb?"

Dumb as your father, she thought.

"Look at that," Mac said, pointing to a piece of cow dung lying on a spot scraped bare of snow. "A frozen meadow muffin." He picked it up and sailed it at her. "Catch!"

"Mac!" she yelled. His laugh was as gawky as he was. She walked faster. He seemed different today somehow, bundled in his yellow-and-black-checkered coat, a rifle in hand, his silly floppy hat not quite covering his ears. They all seemed different as she watched them trudge through the snow—Mac and her father and Charlie Spoon—bigger, maybe, as if the cold landscape enlarged rather than diminished them, so that they, the only figures in that landscape, took on size and meaning just by being there. If they weren't there, everything would be quieter, and the woods would be the same as before. *But they are here,* Andy thought, looking behind her at the boot prints in the snow, *and I am too, and so it's all different.*

30   "We'll go down to the cut where we found those deer tracks," Charlie said as they entered the woods. "Maybe we'll get lucky and get a late one coming through."

The woods descended into a gully. The snow was softer and deeper here, so that often Andy sank to her knees. Charlie and Mac worked the top of the gully while she and her father walked along the base some thirty yards behind them. "If they miss the first shot, we'll get the second," her father said, and she nodded as if she had known this all the time. She listened to the crunch of their boots, their breathing, and the drumming of a distant woodpecker. And the crackling. In winter the woods crackled as if everything were straining, ready to snap like dried chicken bones.

We are hunting, Andy thought. The cold air burned her nostrils.

They stopped to make lunch by a rock outcropping that protected them from the wind. Her father heated the bean soup her mother had made for them, and they ate it with bread already stiff from the cold. He and Charlie took a few pulls from a flask of Jim Beam while she scoured the plates with snow and repacked them. Then they all had coffee with sugar and powdered milk, and her father poured her a cup too. "We won't tell your momma," he said, and Mac laughed. Andy held the cup the way her father did, not by the handle but around the rim. The coffee tasted smoky. She felt a little queasy, but she drank it all.

Charlie Spoon picked his teeth with a fingernail. "Now, you might've noticed one thing," he said.

35   "What's that?" her father asked.

"You might've noticed you don't hear no rifles. That's because there ain't no other hunters here. We've got the whole damn woods to ourselves. Now, I ask you—do I know how to find 'em?"

"We haven't seen deer yet, neither."

"Oh, we will," Charlie said, "but not for a while now." He leaned back against the rock. "Deer're sleeping, resting up for the evening feed."

"I seen a deer behind our house once, and it was afternoon," Andy said.

40   "Yeah, honey, but that was *before* deer season," Charlie said, grinning. "They know something now. They're smart that way."

"That's right," Mac said.

Andy looked at her father—had she said something stupid?

"Well, Charlie," he said, "if they know so much, how come so many get themselves shot?"

"Them's the ones that don't *believe* what they know," Charlie replied. The men laughed. Andy hesitated, and then laughed with them.

45   They moved on, as much to keep warm as to find a deer. The wind became even stronger. Blowing through the treetops, it sounded like the ocean, and once Andy thought she could smell salt air. But that was impossible; the ocean was *hundreds* of miles away, farther than Canada even. She and her parents had gone last summer to stay for a week at a motel on the New Jersey shore. That was the first time she'd seen the ocean, and it

frightened her. It was huge and empty, yet always moving. Everything lay hidden. If you walked in it, you couldn't see how deep it was or what might be below; if you swam, something could pull you under and you'd never be seen again. Its musky, rank smell made her think of things dying. Her mother had floated beyond the breakers, calling to her to come in, but Andy wouldn't go farther than a few feet into the surf. Her mother swam and splashed with animal-like delight while her father, smiling shyly, held his white arms above the waist-deep water as if afraid to get them wet. Once a comber rolled over and sent them both tossing, and when her mother tried to stand up, the surf receding behind, Andy saw that her mother's swimsuit top had come off, so that her breasts swayed free, her nipples like two dark eyes. Embarrassed, Andy looked around: except for two women under a yellow umbrella farther up, the beach was empty. Her mother stood up unsteadily, regained her footing. Taking what seemed the longest time, she calmly refixed her top. Andy lay on the beach towel and closed her eyes. The sound of the surf made her head ache.

And now it was winter; the sky was already dimming, not just with the absence of light but with a mist that clung to the hunters' faces like cobwebs. They made camp early. Andy was chilled. When she stood still, she kept wiggling her toes to make sure they were there. Her father rubbed her arms and held her to him briefly, and that felt better. She unpacked the food while the others put up the tents.

"How about rounding us up some firewood, Mac?" Charlie asked.

"I'll do it," Andy said. Charlie looked at her thoughtfully and then handed her the canvas carrier.

There wasn't much wood on the ground, so it took her a while to get a good load. She was about a hundred yards from camp, near a cluster of high, lichen-covered boulders, when she saw through a crack in the rock a buck and two does walking gingerly, almost daintily, through the alder trees. She tried to hush her breathing as they passed not more than twenty yards away. There was nothing she could do. If she yelled, they'd be gone; by the time she got back to camp, they'd be gone. The buck stopped, nostrils quivering, tail up and alert. He looked directly at her. Still she didn't move, not one muscle. He was a beautiful buck, the color of late-turned maple leaves. Unafraid, he lowered his tail, and he and his does silently merged into the trees. Andy walked back to camp and dropped the firewood.

50   "I saw three deer," she said. "A buck and two does."

"Where?" Charlie Spoon cried, looking behind her as if they might have followed her into camp.

"In the woods yonder. They're gone now."

"Well, hell!" Charlie banged his coffee cup against his knee.

"Didn't I say she could find animals?" her father said, grinning.

55   "Too late to go after them," Charlie muttered. "It'll be dark in a quarter hour. Damn!"

"Damn," Mac echoed.

"They just walk right up to her," her father said.

"Well, leastwise this proves there's deer here." Charlie began snapping long branches into shorter ones. "You know, I think I'll stick with you," he told Andy, "since you're so good at finding deer and all. How'd that be?"

"Okay, I guess," Andy murmured. She hoped he was kidding; no way did she want to hunt with Charlie Spoon. Still, she was pleased he had said it.

60   Her father and Charlie took one tent, she and Mac the other. When they were in their sleeping bags, Mac said in the darkness, "I bet you really didn't see no deer, did you?"

She sighed. "I did, Mac. Why would I lie?"

"How big was the buck?"

"Four point. I counted."

Mac snorted.

65   "You just believe what you want, Mac," she said testily.

"Too bad it ain't buck season," he said. "Well, I got to go pee."

"So pee."

She heard him turn in his bag. "You ever see it?" he asked.

"It? What's 'it'?"

70   "It. A pecker."

"Sure," she lied.

"Whose? Your father's?"

She was uncomfortable. "No," she said.

"Well, whose then?"

75   "Oh I don't know! Leave me be, why don't you?"

"Didn't see a deer, didn't see a pecker," Mac said teasingly.

She didn't answer right away. Then she said, "My cousin Lewis. I saw his."

"Well, how old's he?"

"One and a half."

80   "Ha! A baby! A baby's is like a little worm. It ain't a real one at all."

If he says he'll show me his, she thought, *I'll kick him. I'll just get out of my bag and kick him.*

"I went hunting with my daddy and Versh and Danny Simmons last year in buck season," Mac said, "and we got ourselves one. And we hog-dressed the thing. You know what that is, don't you?"

"No," she said. She was confused. What was he talking about now?

"That's when you cut him open and take out all his guts, so the meat don't spoil. Makes him lighter to pack out, too."

85   She tried to imagine what the deer's guts might look like, pulled from the gaping hole. "What do you do with them?" she said. "The guts?"

"Oh, just leave 'em for the bears."

She ran her finger like a knife blade along her belly.

"When we left them on the ground," Mac said, "they smoked. Like they were cooking."

"Huh," she said.

90   "They cut off the deer's pecker, too, you know."

Andy imagined Lewis's pecker and shuddered. "Mac, you're disgusting."

He laughed. "Well, I gotta go pee." She heard him rustle out of his bag. "Broo!" he cried, flapping his arms. "It's cold!"

He makes so much noise, she thought, *just noise and more noise.*

Her father woke them before first light. He warned them to talk softly and said that they were going to the place where Andy had seen the deer, to try to cut them off on their way back from their night feeding. Andy couldn't shake off her sleep. Stuffing her sleeping bag into its sack seemed to take an hour, and tying her boots was the strangest thing she'd ever done. Charlie Spoon made hot chocolate and oatmeal with raisins. Andy closed her eyes and, between beats of her heart, listened to the breathing of the forest. *When I open my eyes, it will be lighter,* she decided. But when she did, it was still just as dark, except for the swaths of their flashlights and the hissing blue flame of the stove. *There has to be just one moment when it all changes from dark to light,* Andy thought. She had missed it yesterday, in the car; today she would watch more closely.

95 But when she remembered again, it was already first light and they had moved to the rocks by the deer trail and had set up shooting positions—Mac and Charlie Spoon on the up-trail side, she and her father behind them, some six feet up on a ledge. The day became brighter, the sun piercing the tall pines, raking the hunters, yet providing little warmth. Andy now smelled alder and pine and the slightly rotten odor of rock lichen. She rubbed her hand over the stone and considered that it must be very old, had probably been here before the giant pines, *before anyone was in these woods at all.* A chipmunk sniffed on a nearby branch. She aimed an imaginary rifle and pressed the trigger. The chipmunk froze, then scurried away. Her legs were cramping on the narrow ledge. Her father seemed to doze, one hand in his parka, the other cupped lightly around the rifle. She could smell his scent of old wool and leather. His cheeks were speckled with gray-black whiskers, and he worked his jaws slightly, as if chewing a small piece of gum.

Please let us get a deer, she prayed.

A branch snapped on the other side of the rock face. Her father's hand stiffened on the rifle, startling her—*He hasn't been sleeping at all,* she marveled—and then his jaw relaxed, as did the lines around his eyes, and she heard Charlie Spoon call, "Yo, don't shoot, it's us." He and Mac appeared from around the rock. They stopped beneath the ledge. Charlie solemnly crossed his arms.

"I don't believe we're gonna get any deer here," he said drily.

Andy's father lowered his rifle to Charlie and jumped down from the ledge. Then he reached up for Andy. She dropped into his arms and he set her gently on the ground.

100 Mac sidled up to her. "I knew you didn't see no deer," he said.

"Just because they don't come when you want 'em to don't mean she didn't see them," her father said.

Still, she felt bad. Her telling about the deer had caused them to spend the morning there, cold and expectant, with nothing to show for it.

They tramped through the woods for another two hours, not caring much about noise. Mac found some deer tracks, and they argued about how old they were. They split up for a while and then rejoined at an old logging road that deer might use, and followed it. The road crossed a stream, which had mostly frozen over but in a few spots still caught leaves and twigs in an icy swirl. They forded it by jumping from rock to rock. The road narrowed after that, and the woods thickened.

They stopped for lunch, heating up Charlie's wife's corn chowder. Andy's father cut squares of applesauce cake with his hunting knife and handed them to her and Mac, who ate his almost daintily. Andy could faintly taste knife oil on the cake. She was tired. She stretched her leg; the muscle that had cramped on the rock still ached.

"Might as well relax," her father said, as if reading her thoughts. "We won't find deer till suppertime."

Charlie Spoon leaned back against his pack and folded his hands across his stomach. "Well, even if we don't get a deer," he said expansively, "it's still great to be out here, breathe some fresh air, clomp around a bit. Get away from the house and the old lady." He winked at Mac, who looked away.

"That's what the woods are all about, anyway," Charlie said. "It's where the women don't want to go." He bowed his head toward Andy. "With your exception, of course, little lady." He helped himself to another piece of applesauce cake.

"She ain't a woman," Mac said.

"Well, she damn well's gonna be," Charlie said. He grinned at her. "Or will you? You're half a boy anyway. You go by a boy's name. What's your real name? Andrea, ain't it?"

"That's right," she said. She hoped that if she didn't look at him, Charlie would stop.

"Well, which do you like? Andy or Andrea?"

"Don't matter," she mumbled. "Either."

"She's always been Andy to me," her father said.

Charlie Spoon was still grinning. "So what are you gonna be, Andrea? A boy or a girl?"

"I'm a girl," she said.

"But you want to go hunting and fishing and everything, huh?"

"She can do whatever she likes," her father said.

"Hell, you might as well have just had a boy and be done with it!" Charlie exclaimed.

"That's funny," her father said, and chuckled. "That's just what her momma tells me."

120   They were looking at her, and she wanted to get away from them all, even from her father, who chose to joke with them.

"I'm going to walk a bit," she said.

She heard them laughing as she walked down the logging trail. She flapped her arms; she whistled. *I don't care how much noise I make,* she thought. Two grouse flew from the underbrush, startling her. A little farther down, the trail ended in a clearing that enlarged into a frozen meadow; beyond it the woods began again. A few moldering posts were all that was left of a fence that had once enclosed the field. The low afternoon sunlight reflected brightly off the snow, so that Andy's eyes hurt. She squinted hard. A gust of wind blew across the field, stinging her face. And then, as if it had been waiting for her, the doe emerged from the trees opposite and stepped cautiously into the field. Andy watched: it stopped and stood quietly for what seemed a long time and then ambled across. It stopped again about seventy yards away and began to browse in a patch of sugar grass uncovered by the wind. Carefully, slowly, never taking her eyes from the doe, Andy walked backward, trying to step into the boot prints she'd already made. When she was far enough back into the woods, she turned and walked faster, her heart racing. *Please let it stay,* she prayed.

"There's doe in the field yonder," she told them.

They got their rifles and hurried down the trail.

125   "No use," her father said. "We're making too much noise any way you look at it."

"At least we got us the wind in our favor," Charlie Spoon said, breathing heavily.

But the doe was still there, grazing.

"Good Lord," Charlie whispered. He looked at her father. "Well, whose shot?"

"Andy spotted it," her father said in a low voice. "Let her shoot it."

130   "What!" Charlie's eyes widened.

Andy couldn't believe what her father had just said. She'd only shot tin cans and targets; she'd never even fired her father's .30-.30, and she'd never killed anything.

"I can't," she whispered.

"That's right, she can't," Charlie Spoon insisted. "She's not old enough and she don't have a license even if she was!"

"Well, who's to tell?" her father said in a low voice. "Nobody's going to know but us." He looked at her. "Do you want to shoot it, punkin?"

135   *Why doesn't it hear us?* she wondered. *Why doesn't it run away?* "I don't know," she said.

"Well, I'm sure as hell gonna shoot it," Charlie said. Her father grasped Charlie's rifle barrel and held it. His voice was steady.

"Andy's a good shot. It's her deer. She found it, not you. You'd still be sitting on your ass back in camp." He turned to her again. "Now—do you want to shoot it, Andy? Yes or no."

He was looking at her; they were all looking at her. Suddenly she was angry at the deer, who refused to hear them, who wouldn't run away even when it could. "I'll shoot it," she said. Charlie turned away in disgust.

She lay on the ground and pressed the rifle stock against her shoulder bone. The snow was cold through her parka; she smelled oil and wax and damp earth. She pulled off one glove with her teeth. "It sights just like the .22," her father said gently. "Cartridge's already chambered." As she had done so many times before, she sighted down the scope; now the doe was in the reticle. She moved the barrel until the cross hairs lined up. Her father was breathing beside her.

140   "Aim where the chest and legs meet, or a little above, punkin," he was saying calmly. "That's the killing shot."

But now, seeing it in the scope, Andy was hesitant. Her finger weakened on the trigger. Still, she nodded at what her father said and sighted again, the cross hairs lining up in exactly the same spot—the doe had hardly moved, its brownish-gray body outlined starkly against the blue-backed snow. *It doesn't know,* Andy thought. *It just doesn't know.* And as she looked, deer and snow and faraway trees flattened within the circular frame to become like a picture on a calendar, not real, and she felt calm, as if she had been dreaming everything—the day, the deer, the hunt itself. And she, finger on trigger, was only a part of that dream.

"Shoot!" Charlie hissed.

Through the scope she saw the deer look up, ears high and straining.

Charlie groaned, and just as he did, and just at the moment when Andy knew—*knew*—the doe would bound away, as if she could feel its haunches tensing and gathering power, she pulled the trigger. Later she would think, *I felt the recoil, I smelled the smoke, but I don't remember pulling the trigger.* Through the scope the deer seemed to shrink into itself, and then slowly knelt, hind legs first, head raised as if to cry out. It trembled, still straining to keep its head high, as if that alone would save it; failing, it collapsed, shuddered, and lay still.

145   "Whoee!" Mac cried.

"One shot! One shot!" her father yelled, clapping her on the back. Charlie Spoon was shaking his head and smiling dumbly.

"I told you she was a great little shot!" her father said. "I told you!" Mac danced and clapped his hands. She was dazed, not quite understanding what had happened. And then they were crossing the field toward the fallen doe, she walking dreamlike, the men laughing and joking, released now from the tension of silence and anticipation. Suddenly Mac pointed and cried out, "Look at that!"

The doe was rising, legs unsteady. They stared at it, unable to comprehend, and in that moment the doe regained its feet and looked at them, as if it too were trying to understand. Her father whistled softly. Charlie Spoon unslung his rifle and raised it to his shoulder, but the doe was already bounding away. His hurried shot missed, and the deer disappeared into the woods.

"Damn, damn, damn," he moaned.

150   "I don't believe it," her father said. "That deer was dead."

"Dead, hell!" Charlie yelled. "It was gutshot, that's all. Stunned and gutshot. Clean shot, my ass!"

What have I done? Andy thought.

Her father slung his rifle over his shoulder. "Well, let's go. It can't get too far."

"Hell, I've seen deer run ten miles gutshot," Charlie said. He waved his arms. "We may never find her!"

155   As they crossed the field, Mac came up to her and said in a low voice, "Gutshoot a deer, you'll go to hell."

"Shut up, Mac," she said, her voice cracking. It was a terrible thing she had done, she knew. She couldn't bear to think of the doe in pain and frightened. *Please let it die,* she prayed.

But though they searched all the last hour of daylight, so that they had to recross the field and go up the logging trail in a twilight made even deeper by thick, smoky clouds, they didn't find the doe. They lost its trail almost immediately in the dense stands of alderberry and larch.

"I am cold, and I am tired," Charlie Spoon declared. "And if you ask me, that deer's in another county already."

"No one's asking you, Charlie," her father said.

160   They had a supper of hard salami and ham, bread, and the rest of the applesauce cake. It seemed a bother to heat the coffee, so they had cold chocolate instead. Everyone turned in early.

"We'll find it in the morning, honeybun," her father said, as she went to her tent.

"I don't like to think of it suffering." She was almost in tears.

"It's dead already, punkin. Don't even think about it." He kissed her, his breath sour and his beard rough against her cheek.

Andy was sure she wouldn't get to sleep; the image of the doe falling, falling, then rising again, repeated itself whenever she closed her eyes. Then she heard an owl hoot and realized that it had awakened her, so she must have been asleep after all. She hoped the owl would hush, but instead it hooted louder. She wished her father or Charlie Spoon would wake up and do something about it, but no one moved in the other tent, and suddenly she was afraid that they had all decamped, wanting nothing more to do with her. She whispered, "Mac, Mac," to the sleeping bag where he should be, but no one answered. She tried to find the flashlight she always kept by her side, but couldn't, and she cried in panic, "Mac, are you there?" He mumbled something, and immediately she felt foolish and hoped he wouldn't reply.

165   When she awoke again, everything had changed. The owl was gone, the woods were still, and she sensed light, blue and pale, light where before there had been none. *The moon must have come out,* she thought. And it was warm, too, warmer than it should have been. She got out of her sleeping bag and took off her parka—it was that warm. Mac was asleep, wheezing like an old man. She unzipped the tent and stepped outside.

The woods were more beautiful than she had ever seen them. The moon made everything ice-rimmed glimmer with a crystallized, immanent light, while underneath that ice the branches of trees were as stark as skeletons. She heard a crunching in the snow, the one sound in all that silence, and there, walking down the logging trail into their camp, was the doe. Its body, like everything around her, was silvered with frost and moonlight. It walked past the tent where her father and Charlie Spoon were sleeping and stopped no more than six feet from her. Andy saw that she had shot it, yes, had shot it cleanly, just where she thought she had, the wound a jagged, bloody hole in the doe's chest.

A heart shot, she thought.

The doe stepped closer, so that Andy, if she wished, could have reached out and touched it. It looked at her as if expecting her to do this, and so she did, running her hand, slowly at first, along the rough, matted fur, then down to the edge of the wound, where she stopped. The doe stood still. Hesitantly, Andy felt the edge of the wound. The torn flesh was sticky and warm. The wound parted under her touch. And then, almost without her knowing it, her fingers were within, probing, yet still the doe didn't move. Andy pressed deeper, through flesh and muscle and sinew, until her whole hand and more was inside the wound and she had found the doe's heart, warm and beating. She cupped it gently in her hand. *Alive,* she marveled. *Alive.*

The heart quickened under her touch, becoming warmer and warmer until it was hot enough to burn. In pain, Andy tried to remove her hand, but the wound closed about it and held her fast. Her hand was burning. She cried out in agony, sure they would all hear and come help, but they didn't. And then her hand pulled free, followed by a steaming rush of blood, more blood than she ever could have imagined—it covered her hand and arm, and she saw to her horror that her hand was steaming. She moaned and fell to her knees and plunged her hand into the snow. The doe looked at her gently and then turned and walked back up the trail.

170   In the morning, when she woke, Andy could still smell the blood, but she felt no pain. She looked at her hand. Even though it appeared unscathed, it felt weak and withered. She couldn't move it freely and was afraid the others would notice. *I will hide it in my jacket pocket,* she decided, *so nobody can see.* She ate the oatmeal that her father cooked and stayed apart from them all. No one spoke to her, and that suited her. A light snow began to fall. It was the last day of their hunting trip. She wanted to be home.

Her father dumped the dregs of his coffee. "Well, let's go look for her," he said.

Again they crossed the field. Andy lagged behind. She averted her eyes from the spot where the doe had fallen, already filling up with snow. Mac and Charlie entered the woods first, followed by her father. Andy remained in the field and considered the smear of gray sky, the nearby flock of crows pecking at unyielding stubble. *I will stay here,* she thought, *and not move for a long while.* But now someone—Mac—was yelling. Her father appeared at the woods' edge and waved for her to come. She ran and pushed through a brake of alderberry and larch. The thick underbrush scratched her face. For a moment she felt lost and looked wildly about. Then, where the brush thinned, she saw them standing quietly in the falling snow. They were staring down at the dead doe. A film covered its upturned eye, and its body was lightly dusted with snow.

"I told you she wouldn't get too far," Andy's father said triumphantly. "We must've just missed her yesterday. Too blind to see."

"We're just damn lucky no animal got to her last night," Charlie muttered.

175   Her father lifted the doe's foreleg. The wound was blood-clotted, brown, and caked like frozen mud. "Clean shot," he said to Charlie. He grinned. "My little girl."

Then he pulled out his knife, the blade gray as the morning. Mac whispered to Andy, "Now watch this," while Charlie Spoon lifted the doe from behind by its forelegs so that its head rested between his knees, its underside exposed. Her father's knife sliced thickly from chest to belly to crotch, and Andy was running from them, back to the field and across, scattering the crows who cawed and circled angrily. And now they were all calling to her—Charlie Spoon and Mac and her father—crying *Andy, Andy* (but that wasn't her name, she would no longer be called that); yet louder than any of them was the wind blowing through the treetops, like the ocean where her mother floated in green water, also calling *Come in, come in,* while all around her roared the mocking of the terrible, now inevitable, sea.

READING AND REACTING

1. The initiation of a child into adulthood is a very common literary theme. In this story hunting is presented as an initiation rite. Why do you think hunting is an appropriate coming-of-age ritual?

2. Which characters are in conflict in this story? What ideas are in conflict? How do these conflicts help to communicate the story's initiation theme?

3. In the story's opening paragraph and elsewhere, Andy finds comfort and reassurance in the idea that the woods are "always the same"; later in the story, she remembers the ocean, "huge and empty, yet always moving. Everything lay hidden . . ." (45). How does the contrast between the woods and the ocean suggest the transition from childhood to adulthood?

4. How do references to blood suggest the story's initiation theme? Do they suggest another theme as well?

5. Throughout the story references are made to Andy's ability to inspire the trust of animals. As her father says, "I don't know how she does it, but they come right up to her" (8). How does his comment foreshadow later events?

6. Why do you think Andy prays that she and the others will get a deer? What makes her change her mind? How does the change in Andy's character help to convey the story's theme?

7. Andy's mother is not an active participant in the story's events. Still, her presence is important to the story. *Why* is it important? How does paragraph 45 reveal the importance of the mother's role?

8. What would you say Andy has learned as a result of her experience? What else do you think she has to learn?

9. **JOURNAL ENTRY**   How would the story be different if Andy were a boy? What would be the same?

10. **CRITICAL PERSPECTIVE**   In a review of *Comfort,* the book in which "Doe Season" appears, Susan Wood makes the following observation:

    The dozen or so stories in David Michael Kaplan's affecting first collection share a common focus on the extraordinary moments of recognition in ordinary lives. He is at his best suggesting how such moments may alter, for better or for worse, our relationships with those to whom we are most deeply bound—children, parents, lovers—in love and guilt.

    At what point does "the extraordinary moment of recognition" occur in "Doe Season"? How does this moment alter Andy's relationship with both her parents?

TADEUSZ BOROWSKI* (1922–1951),   Polish short story writer, poet, essayist, and journalist, was a survivor of the Nazi concentration camps at Auschwitz and Dachau. He is one of a group of European-born writers (including Elie Wiesel and Primo Levi) who drew on their personal experiences to create a unique body of writing sometimes called the "literature of atrocity." Borowski's stories are among the most brutal to come out of the camps, and critics in his lifetime denounced what they saw as his "cynical detachment" in the face of human suffering, notably in his short story collections *Pozegnanie z Maria* [*Farewell to Mary*] (1948) and *Kamienny swiat* (1948) [published in English as *This Way for the Gas, Ladies and Gentlemen, and Other Short Stories,* 1967].

More recent critics, including the well-known Czech writer Jan Kott, have agreed that Borowski's Auschwitz stories are minor masterpieces in which the writer works toward a redefinition of tragedy in light of the Holocaust. "The hero of Borowski's stories is a hero *deprived of all choice,*" writes critic Andrej Wirth. "He finds himself in a situation without choice because every choice is base [evil]." In Borowski's camps, neither victims nor executioners are portrayed as wholly good or evil. Borowski could not even absolve himself of guilt: His frequent use of a first-person narrator who collaborates in the crimes of the camps, writes Kott, "was the moral

---

* No photograph available for this author.

decision of a prisoner who had lived through Auschwitz [by working for the Nazis as a hospital orderly]—an acceptance of mutual responsibility, mutual participation, and mutual guilt. . . ." The final irony of Borowski's life is that having survived the gas chambers of Auschwitz, he chose to take his own life by asphyxiation when he was just twenty-nine years old.

TADEUSZ   BOROWSKI

Silence

(1959)

Translated by Barbara Vedder

At last they seized him inside the German barracks, just as he was about to climb over the window ledge. In absolute silence they pulled him down to the floor and panting with hate dragged him into a dark alley. Here, closely surrounded by a silent mob, they began tearing at him with greedy hands.

Suddenly from the camp gate a whispered warning was passed from one mouth to another. A company of soldiers, their bodies leaning forward, their rifles on the ready, came running down the camp's main road, weaving between the clusters of men in stripes standing in the way. The crowd scattered and vanished inside the blocks. In the packed, noisy barracks the prisoners were cooking food pilfered during the night from neighbouring farmers. In the bunks and in the passageways between them, they were grinding grain in small flour-mills, slicing meat on heavy slabs of wood, peeling potatoes and throwing the peels on to the floor. They were playing cards for stolen cigars, stirring batter for pancakes, gulping down hot soup, and lazily killing fleas. A stifling odour of sweat hung in the air, mingled with the smell of food, with smoke and with steam that liquified along the ceiling beams and fell on the men, the bunks and the food in large, heavy drops, like autumn rain.

There was a stir at the door. A young American officer with a tin helmet on his head entered the block and looked with curiosity at the bunks and the tables. He wore a freshly pressed uniform; his revolver was hanging down, strapped in an open holster that dangled against his thigh. He was assisted by the translator who wore a yellow band reading "interpreter" on the sleeve of his civilian coat, and by the chairman of the Prisoners' Committee, dressed in a white summer coat, a pair of tuxedo trousers and tennis shoes. The men in the barracks fell silent. Leaning out of their bunks and lifting their eyes from the kettles, bowls and cups, they gazed attentively into the officer's face.

"Gentlemen," said the officer with a friendly smile, taking off his helmet—and the interpreter proceeded at once to translate sentence after sentence—"I know, of course, that after what you have gone through and after what you have seen, you must feel a deep hate for your tormentors. But we, the soldiers of America, and you, the people of Europe, have fought so that law should prevail over lawlessness. We must show our respect for the law. I assure you that the guilty will be punished, in this camp as well as in all the others. You have already seen, for example, that the S.S.[1] men were made to bury the dead."

5   ". . . right, we could use the lot at the back of the hospital. A few of them are still around," whispered one of the men in a bottom bunk.

". . . or one of the pits," whispered another. He sat straddling the bunk, his fingers firmly clutching the blanket.

"Shut up! Can't you wait a little longer? Now listen to what the American has to say," a third man, stretched across the foot of the same bunk, spoke in an angry whisper. The American officer was now hidden from their view behind the thick crowd gathered at the other end of the block.

"Comrades, our new Kommandant gives you his word of honour that all the criminals of the S.S. as well as among the prisoners will be punished," said the translator. The men in the bunks broke into applause and shouts. In smiles and gestures they tried to convey their friendly approval of the young man from across the ocean.

"And so the Kommandant requests," went on the translator, his voice turning somewhat hoarse, "that you try to be patient and do not commit lawless deeds, which may only lead to trouble, and please pass the sons of bitches over to the camp guards. How about it, men?"

10   The block answered with a prolonged shout. The American thanked the translator and wished the prisoners a good rest and an early reunion with their dear ones. Accompanied by a friendly hum of voices, he left the block and proceeded to the next.

Not until after he had visited all the blocks and returned with the soldiers to his headquarters did we pull our man off the bunk—where covered with blankets and half-smothered with the weight of our bodies he lay gagged, his face buried in the straw mattress—and dragged him on to the cement floor under the stove, where the entire block, grunting and growling with hatred, trampled him to death.

READING AND REACTING

1. What is the narrative point of view of "Silence"? How does this point of view help to communicate the story's theme? How do you account for the shift in point of view in the last paragraph?

2. How does Borowski suggest his story's theme has a universal application, one that extends beyond the specific set of circumstances

---

[1] The Schutzstaffel (SS) or "Defense Squad" was the elite Nazi military corps. Created in 1925 as Hitler's bodyguards, the SS, or Black Shirts, controlled German security, including the Gestapo (secret state police) and concentration camp guards.

he describes? For example, what do you make of the fact that the characters have no names?

3. How does the behavior of the prisoners change when the American officer arrives? How do you account for this change?

4. How do the prisoners react to the American officer's speech? What is their opinion of him? What does he think of them? How do we know?

5. What judgments does the narrator make about the prisoners' treatment of the guard? How accurate do you believe these judgments are?

6. What comment does "Silence" make about the prisoners' need for vengeance? About the Americans' ability to understand the horrors of the concentration camps? Do you believe these comments are accurate?

7. Do you think this story is too short to convey its points effectively? What could be added? What would the advantages and disadvantages of such additions be?

8. In what way does its title express the story's central theme?

9. **JOURNAL ENTRY**   Do you think the prisoners' response is justified? Do you believe such violent actions can ever be justified? If so, under what circumstances?

10. **CRITICAL PERSPECTIVE**   In the introduction to *This Way to the Gas, Ladies and Gentlemen,* the book in which "Silence" first appeared, Czech critic Jan Kott points out that Borowski's Auschwitz stories reflected his understanding that all prisoners had to compromise their humanity in order to survive. "In Borowski's Auschwitz stories," says Kott, "the difference between executioner and victim is stripped of all greatness and pathos. . . . [E]veryone was assigned a double part: executioner and victim." In what sense are the prisoners in "Silence" playing a "double part"? Does Kott's observation in any way lessen the moral and ethical responsibility of those who built and ran the concentration camps?

HISAYE YAMAMOTO (1921–   ) was born in Redondo Beach, California, the daughter of immigrants from Kuamamota, Japan, and studied languages at Compton Junior College. She began writing as a teenager, contributing to columns in the English sections of Japanese-language newspapers. Forced by the United States government to relocate with her family to an internment camp in Poston, Arizona, during World War II, Yamamoto authored the camp newsletter, *The Poston Chronicle,* as well as a mystery serial, "Death Rides the Rails to Poston."

After her release Yamamoto worked from 1945 to 1948 as a columnist for the *Los Angeles Tribune,* a weekly newspaper directed toward the black community. At the same time, she was submitting short stories about Japanese-American life to literary magazines such as *Partisan Review,* which in 1949 published "Seventeen Syllables." Yamamoto's output has been very small but nonetheless influential. She was, according to one editor, "one of the first Japanese-American writers to gain national recognition after the war, at a time when anti-Japanese sentiment was still rampant," and her story "Yoneko's Earthquake" was included in *Best American Short Stories, 1952.*

Of the widely anthologized "Seventeen Syllables" Yamamoto has said that, although the incidents are invented, it is the story of her mother.

HISAYE YAMAMOTO

Seventeen Syllables

(1949)

The first Rosie knew that her mother had taken to writing poems was one evening when she finished one and read it aloud for her daughter's approval. It was about cats, and Rosie pretended to understand it thoroughly and appreciate it no end, partly because she hesitated to disillusion her mother about the quantity and quality of Japanese she had learned in all the years now that she had been going to Japanese school every Saturday (and Wednesday, too, in the summer). Even so, her mother must have been skeptical about the depth of Rosie's understanding, because she explained afterwards about the kind of poem she was trying to write.

See, Rosie, she said, it was a *haiku,*[1] a poem in which she must pack all her meaning into seventeen syllables only, which were divided into three lines of five, seven, and five syllables. In the one she had just read, she had tried to capture the charm of a kitten, as well as comment on the superstition that owning a cat of three colors meant good luck.

"Yes, yes, I understand. How utterly lovely," Rosie said, and her mother, either satisfied or seeing through the deception and resigned, went back to composing.

The truth was that Rosie was lazy; English lay ready on the tongue but Japanese had to be searched for and examined, and even then put forth tentatively (probably to meet with laughter). It was so much easier to say yes, yes, even when one meant no, no. Besides, this was what was in her mind to say: I was looking through one of your magazines from Japan last night, Mother, and toward the back I found some *haiku* in English that delighted me. There was one that made me giggle off and on until I fell asleep—

---

[1] A classical Japanese poetical form.

It is morning, and lo!
I lie awake, comme il faut,
sighing for some dough.

5   Now, how to reach her mother, how to communicate the melancholy song? Rosie knew formal Japanese by fits and starts, her mother had even less English, no French. It was much more possible to say yes, yes.

It developed that her mother was writing the *haiku* for a daily newspaper, the *Mainichi Shimbun,* that was published in San Francisco. Los Angeles, to be sure, was closer to the farming community in which the Hayashi family lived and several Japanese vernaculars[2] were printed there, but Rosie's parents said they preferred the tone of the northern paper. Once a week, the *Mainichi* would have a section devoted to *haiku,* and her mother became an extravagant contributor, taking for herself the blossoming pen name, Ume Hanazono.

So Rosie and her father lived for a while with two women, her mother and Ume Hanazono. Her mother (Tome Hayashi by name) kept house, cooked, washed, and, along with her husband and the Carrascos, the Mexican family hired for the harvest, did her ample share of picking tomatoes out in the sweltering fields and boxing them in tidy strata in the cool packing shed. Ume Hanazono, who came to life after the dinner dishes were done, was an earnest, muttering stranger who often neglected speaking when spoken to and stayed busy at the parlor table as late as midnight scribbling with pencil on scratch paper or carefully copying characters on good paper with her fat, pale-green Parker.

The new interest had some repercussions on the household routine. Before, Rosie had been accustomed to her parents and herself taking their hot baths early and going to bed almost immediately afterwards, unless her parents challenged each other to a game of flower cards or unless company dropped in. Now if her father wanted to play cards, he had to resort to solitaire (at which he always cheated fearlessly), and if a group of friends came over, it was bound to contain someone who was also writing *haiku,* and the small assemblage would be split in two, her father entertaining the non-literary members and her mother comparing ecstatic notes with the visiting poet.

If they went out, it was more of the same thing. But Ume Hanazono's life span, even for a poet's, was very brief—perhaps three months at most.

10   One night they went over to see the Hayano family in the neighboring town to the west, an adventure both painful and attractive to Rosie. It was attractive because there were four Hayano girls, all lovely and each one named after a season of the year (Haru, Natsu, Aki, Fuyu), painful because something had been wrong with Mrs. Hayano ever since the birth of her

---

[2] Dialects, usually associated with particular regions.

first child. Rosie would sometimes watch Mrs. Hayano, reputed to have been the belle of her native village, making her way about a room, stooped, slowly shuffling, violently trembling (*always* trembling), and she would be reminded that this woman, in this same condition, had carried and given issue to three babies. She would look wonderingly at Mr. Hayano, handsome, tall, and strong, and she would look at her four pretty friends. But it was not a matter she could come to any decision about.

On this visit, however, Mrs. Hayano sat all evening in the rocker, as motionless and unobtrusive as it was possible for her to be, and Rosie found the greater part of the evening practically anaesthetic. Too, Rosie spent most of it in the girls' room, because Haru, the garrulous one, said almost as soon as the bows and other greetings were over, "Oh, you must see my new coat!"

It was a pale plaid of grey, sand, and blue, with an enormous collar, and Rosie, seeing nothing special in it, said, "Gee, how nice."

"Nice?" said Haru, indignantly. "Is that all you can say about it? It's gorgeous! And so cheap, too. Only seventeen ninety-eight, because it was a sale. The saleslady said it was twenty-five dollars regular."

"Gee," said Rosie. Natsu, who never said much and when she said anything said it shyly, fingered the coat covetously and Haru pulled it away.

15 "Mine," she said, putting it on. She minced in the aisle between the two large beds and smiled happily. "Let's see how your mother likes it."

She broke into the front room and the adult conversation and went to stand in front of Rosie's mother, while the rest watched from the door. Rosie's mother was properly envious. "May I inherit it when you're through with it?"

Haru, pleased, giggled, and said yes, she could, but Natsu reminded gravely from the door, "You promised me, Haru."

Everyone laughed but Natsu, who shamefacedly retreated into the bedroom. Haru came in laughing, taking off the coat. "We were only kidding, Natsu," she said. "Here, you try it on now."

After Natsu buttoned herself into the coat, inspected herself solemnly in the bureau mirror, and reluctantly shed it, Rosie, Aki, and Fuyu got their turns, and Fuyu, who was eight, drowned in it while her sisters and Rosie doubled up in amusement. They all went into the front room later, because Haru's mother quaveringly called to her to fix the tea and rice cakes and open a can of sliced peaches for everybody. Rosie noticed that her mother and Mr. Hayano were talking together at the little table—they were discussing a *haiku* that Mr. Hayano was planning to send to the *Mainichi*, while her father was sitting at one end of the sofa looking through a copy of *Life*, the new picture magazine. Occasionally, her father would comment on a photograph, holding it toward Mrs. Hayano and speaking to her as he always did—loudly, as though he thought someone such as she must surely be at least a trifle deaf also.

20 The five girls had their refreshments at the kitchen table, and it was while Rosie was showing the sisters her trick of swallowing peach slices

without chewing (she chased each slippery crescent down with a swig of tea) that her father brought his empty teacup and untouched saucer to the sink and said, "Come on, Rosie, we're going home now."

"Already?" asked Rosie.

"Work tomorrow," he said.

He sounded irritated, and Rosie, puzzled, gulped one last yellow slice and stood up to go, while the sisters began protesting, as was their wont.

"We have to get up at five-thirty," he told them, going into the front room quickly, so that they did not have their usual chance to hang onto his hands and plead for an extension of time.

25   Rosie, following, saw that her mother and Mr. Hayano were sipping tea and still talking together, while Mrs. Hayano concentrated, quivering, on raising the handleless Japanese cup to her lips with both her hands and lowering it back to her lap. Her father, saying nothing, went out the door, onto the bright porch, and down the steps. Her mother looked up and asked, "Where is he going?"

"Where is he going?" Rosie said. "He said we were going home now."

"Going home?" Her mother looked with embarrassment at Mr. Hayano and his absorbed wife and then forced a smile. "He must be tired," she said.

Haru was not giving up yet. "May Rosie stay overnight?" she asked, and Natsu, Aki, and Fuyu came to reinforce their sister's plea by helping her make a circle around Rosie's mother. Rosie, for once having no desire to stay, was relieved when her mother, apologizing to the perturbed Mr. and Mrs. Hayano for her father's abruptness at the same time, managed to shake her head no at the quartet, kindly but adamant, so that they broke their circle and let her go.

Rosie's father looked ahead into the windshield as the two joined him. "I'm sorry," her mother said. "You must be tired." Her father, stepping on the starter, said nothing. "You know how I get when it's *haiku*," she continued, "I forget what time it is." He only grunted.

30   As they rode homeward silently, Rosie, sitting between, felt a rush of hate for both—for her mother for begging, for her father for denying her mother. I wish this old Ford would crash, right now, she thought, then immediately, no, no, I wish my father would laugh, but it was too late: already the vision had passed through her mind of the green pick-up crumpled in the dark against one of the mighty eucalyptus trees they were just riding past, of the three contorted, bleeding bodies, one of them hers.

Rosie ran between two patches of tomatoes, her heart working more rambunctiously than she had ever known it to. How lucky it was that Aunt Taka and Uncle Gimpachi had come tonight, though, how very lucky. Otherwise she might not have really kept her half-promise to meet Jesus Carrasco. Jesus was going to be a senior in September at the same school she went to, and his parents were the ones helping with the tomatoes this year. She and Jesus, who hardly remembered seeing each other at Cleveland

High where there were so many other people and two whole grades between them, had become great friends this summer—he always had a joke for her when he periodically drove the loaded pick-up up from the fields to the shed where she was usually sorting while her mother and father did the packing, and they laughed a great deal together over infinitesimal repartee[3] during the afternoon break for chilled watermelon or ice cream in the shade of the shed.

What she enjoyed most was racing him to see which could finish picking a double row first. He, who could work faster, would tease her by slowing down until she thought she would surely pass him this time, then speeding up furiously to leave her several sprawling vines behind. Once he had made her screech hideously by crossing over, while her back was turned, to place atop the tomatoes in her green-stained bucket a truly monstrous, pale green worm (it had looked more like an infant snake). And it was when they had finished a contest this morning, after she had pantingly pointed a green finger at the immature tomatoes evident in the lugs[4] at the end of his row and he had returned the accusation (with justice), that he had startlingly brought up the matter of their possibly meeting outside the range of both their parents' dubious eyes.

"What for?" she had asked.

"I've got a secret I want to tell you," he said.

35 "Tell me now," she demanded.

"It won't be ready till tonight," he said.

She laughed. "Tell me tomorrow then."

"It'll be gone tomorrow," he threatened.

"Well, for seven hakes, what is it?" she had asked, more than twice, and when he had suggested that the packing shed would be an appropriate place to find out, she had cautiously answered maybe. She had not been certain she was going to keep the appointment until the arrival of mother's sister and her husband. Their coming seemed a sort of signal of permission, of grace, and she had definitely made up her mind to lie and leave as she was bowing them welcome.

40 So as soon as everyone appeared settled back for the evening, she announced loudly that she was going to the privy outside, "I'm going to the *benjo!*"[5] and slipped out the door. And now that she was actually on her way, her heart pumped in such an undisciplined way that she could hear it with her ears. It's because I'm running, she told herself, slowing to a walk. The shed was up ahead, one more patch away, in the middle of the fields. Its bulk, looming in the dimness, took on a sinisterness that was funny

---

3 Witty conversation.

4 Shallow boxes in which produce is shipped to market.

5 A lavatory with a flush toilet (Japanese).

when Rosie reminded herself that it was only a wooden frame with a canvas roof and three canvas walls that made a slapping noise on breezy days.

Jesus was sitting on the narrow plank that was the sorting platform and she went around to the other side and jumped backwards to seat herself on the rim of a packing stand. "Well, tell me," she said without greeting, thinking her voice sounded reassuringly familiar.

"I saw you coming out the door," Jesus said. "I heard you running part of the way, too."

"Uh-huh," Rosie said. "Now tell me the secret."

"I was afraid you wouldn't come," he said.

45   Rosie delved around on the chicken-wire bottom of the stall for number two tomatoes, ripe, which she was sitting beside, and came up with a left-over that felt edible. She bit into it and began sucking out the pulp and seeds. "I'm here," she pointed out.

"Rosie, are you sorry you came?"

"Sorry? What for?" she said. "You said you were going to tell me something."

"I will, I will," Jesus said, but his voice contained disappointment, and Rosie fleetingly felt the older of the two, realizing a brand-new power which vanished without category under her recognition.

"I have to go back in a minute," she said. "My aunt and uncle are here from Wintersburg. I told them I was going to the privy."

50   Jesus laughed. "You funny thing," he said. "You slay[6] me!"

"Just because you have a bathroom *inside*," Rosie said. "Come on, tell me."

Chuckling, Jesus came around to lean on the stand facing her. They still could not see each other very clearly, but Rosie noticed that Jesus became very sober again as he took the hollow tomato from her hand and dropped it back into the stall. When he took hold of her empty hand, she could find no words to protest; her vocabulary had become distressingly constricted and she thought desperately that all that remained intact now was yes and no and oh, and even these few sounds would not easily out. Thus, kissed by Jesus, Rosie fell for the first time entirely victim to a helplessness delectable beyond speech. But the terrible, beautiful sensation lasted no more than a second, and the reality of Jesus' lips and tongue and teeth and hands made her pull away with such strength that she nearly tumbled.

Rosie stopped running as she approached the lights from the windows of home. How long since she had left? She could not guess, but gasping yet, she went to the privy in back and locked herself in. Her own breathing deafened her in the dark, close space, and she sat and waited until she could hear at last the nightly calling of the frogs and crickets. Even then,

---

[6] Amuse, delight (slang).

all she could think to say was oh, my, and the pressure of Jesus' face against her face would not leave.

No one had missed her in the parlor, however, and Rosie walked in and through quickly, announcing that she was next going to take a bath. "Your father's in the bathhouse," her mother said, and Rosie, in her room, re-called that she had not seen him when she entered. There had been only Aunt Taka and Uncle Gimpachi with her mother at the table, drinking tea. She got her robe and straw sandals and crossed the parlor again to go out-side. Her mother was telling them about the *haiku* competition in the *Mainichi* and the poem she had entered.

55   Rosie met her father coming out of the bathhouse. "Are you through, Father?" she asked. "I was going to ask you to scrub my back."

"Scrub your own back," he said shortly, going toward the main house.

"What have I done now?" she yelled after him. She suddenly felt like doing a lot of yelling. But he did not answer, and she went into the bath-house. Turning on the dangling light, she removed her denims and T-shirt and threw them in the big carton for dirty clothes standing next to the washing machine. Her other things she took with her into the bath com-partment to wash after her bath. After she had scooped a basin of hot water from the square wooden tub, she sat on the grey cement of the floor and soaped herself at exaggerated leisure, singing "Red Sails in the Sunset" at the top of her voice and using da-da-da where she suspected her words. Then, standing up, still singing, for she was possessed by the notion that any attempt now to analyze would result in spoilage and she believed that the larger her volume the less she would be able to hear herself think, she obtained more hot water and poured it on until she was free of lather. Only then did she allow herself to step into the steaming vat, one leg first, then the remainder of her body inch by inch until the water no longer stung and she could move around at will.

She took a long time soaking, afterwards remembering to go around outside to stoke the embers of the tin-lined fireplace beneath the tub and to throw on a few more sticks so that the water might keep its heat for her mother, and when she finally returned to the parlor, she found her mother still talking *haiku* with her aunt and uncle, the three of them on another round of tea. Her father was nowhere in sight.

At Japanese school the next day (Wednesday it was), Rosie was grave and giddy by turns. Preoccupied at her desk in the row for students on Book Eight, she made up for it at recess by performing wild mimicry for the benefit of her friend Chizuko. She held her nose and whined a witticism or two in what she considered was the manner of Fred Allen;[7] she as-sumed intoxication and a British accent to go over the climax of the

---

[7] American humorist (1894–1956) and radio personality.

Rudy Vallee[8] recording of the pub conversation about William Ewart Gladstone;[9] she was the child Shirley Temple[10] piping, "On the Good Ship Lollipop"; she was the gentleman soprano of the Four Inkspots trilling, "If I Didn't Care." And she felt reasonably satisfied when Chizuko wept and gasped, "Oh, Rosie, you ought to be in the movies!"

60   Her father came after her at noon, bringing her sandwiches of minced ham and two nectarines to eat while she rode, so that she could pitch right into the sorting when they got home. The lugs were piling up, he said, and the ripe tomatoes in them would probably have to be taken to the cannery tomorrow if they were not ready for the produce haulers tonight. "This heat's not doing them any good. And we've got no time for a break today."

It *was* hot, probably the hottest day of the year, and Rosie's blouse stuck damply to her back even under the protection of the canvas. But she worked as efficiently as a flawless machine and kept the stalls heaped, with one part of her mind listening in to the parental murmuring about the heat and the tomatoes and with another part planning the exact words she would say to Jesus when he drove up with the first load of the afternoon. But when at last she saw that the pick-up was coming, her hands went berserk and the tomatoes started falling in the wrong stalls, and her father said, "Hey, hey! Rosie, watch what you're doing!"

"Well, I have to go to the *benjo*," she said, hiding panic.

"Go in the weeds over there," he said, only half-joking.

"Oh, Father!" she protested.

65   "Oh, go on home," her mother said. "We'll make out for awhile."

In the privy[11] Rosie peered through a knothole toward the fields, watching as much as she could of Jesus. Happily she thought she saw him look in the direction of the house from time to time before he finished unloading and went back toward the patch where his mother and father worked. As she was heading for the shed, a very presentable black car purred up the dirt driveway to the house and its driver motioned to her. Was this the Hayashi home, he wanted to know. She nodded. Was she a Hayashi? Yes, she said, thinking that he was a good-looking man. He got out of the car with a huge, flat package and she saw that he warmly wore a business suit. "I have something here for your mother then," he said, in a more elegant Japanese than she was used to.

She told him where her mother was and he came along with her, patting his face with an immaculate white handkerchief and saying something about the coolness of San Francisco. To her surprised mother and father, he bowed and introduced himself as, among other things, the *haiku*

---

[8]   American singer (1901–   ), stage, radio, and movie personality.

[9]   English politician (1809–1902) and reformer.

[10]   Child actress (1928–   ) of the 1930s, known for her ringlets and dimples.

[11]   Outbuilding containing a toilet.

editor of the *Mainichi Shimbun,* saying that since he had been coming as far as Los Angeles anyway, he had decided to bring her the first prize she had won in the recent contest.

"First prize?" her mother echoed, believing and not believing, pleased and overwhelmed. Handed the package with a bow, she bobbed her head up and down numerous times to express her utter gratitude.

"It is nothing much," he added, "but I hope it will serve as a token of our great appreciation for your contributions and our great admiration of your considerable talent."

70   "I am not worthy," she said, falling easily into his style. "It is I who should make some sign of my humble thanks for being permitted to contribute."

"No, no, to the contrary," he said, bowing again.

But Rosie's mother insisted, and then saying that she knew she was being unorthodox, she asked if she might open the package because her curiosity was so great. Certainly she might. In fact, he would like her reaction to it, for personally, it was one of his favorite *Hiroshiges.*

Rosie thought it was a pleasant picture, which looked to have been sketched with delicate quickness. There were pink clouds, containing some graceful calligraphy,[12] and a sea that was a pale blue except at the edges, containing four sampans[13] with indications of people in them. Pines edged the water and on the far-off beach there was a cluster of thatched huts towered over by pine-dotted mountains of grey and blue. The frame was scalloped and gilt.

After Rosie's mother pronounced it without peer and somewhat prodded her father into nodding agreement, she said Mr. Kuroda must at least have a cup of tea after coming all this way, and although Mr. Kuroda did not want to impose, he soon agreed that a cup of tea would be refreshing and went along with her to the house, carrying the picture for her.

75   "Ha, your mother's crazy!" Rosie's father said, and Rosie laughed uneasily as she resumed judgment on the tomatoes. She had emptied six lugs when he broke into an imaginary conversation with Jesus to tell her to go and remind her mother of the tomatoes, and she went slowly.

Mr. Kuroda was in his shirtsleeves expounding some *haiku* theory as he munched a rice cake, and her mother was rapt. Abashed in the great man's presence, Rosie stood next to her mother's chair until her mother looked up inquiringly, and then she started to whisper the message, but her mother pushed her gently away and reproached, "You are not being very polite to our guest."

"Father says the tomatoes . . ." Rosie said aloud, smiling foolishly.

"Tell him I shall only be a minute," her mother said, speaking the language of Mr. Kuroda.

---

[12] Graceful or artistic handwriting.

[13] Flatbottomed Asian boats.

When Rosie carried the reply to her father, he did not seem to hear and she said again, "Mother says she'll be back in a minute."

80 "All right, all right," he nodded, and they worked again in silence. But suddenly, her father uttered an incredible noise, exactly like the cork of a bottle popping, and the next Rosie knew, he was stalking angrily toward the house, almost running in fact, and she chased after him crying, "Father! Father! What are you going to do?"

He stopped long enough to order her back to the shed. "Never mind!" he shouted. "Get on with the sorting!"

And from the place in the fields where she stood, frightened and vacillating, Rosie saw her father enter the house. Soon Mr. Kuroda came out alone, putting on his coat. Mr. Kuroda got into his car and backed out down the driveway onto the highway. Next her father emerged, also alone, something in his arms (it was the picture, she realized), and, going over to the bathhouse woodpile, he threw the picture on the ground and picked up the axe. Smashing the picture, glass and all (she heard the explosion faintly), he reached over for the kerosene that was used to encourage the bath fire and poured it over the wreckage. I am dreaming, Rosie said to herself, I am dreaming, but her father, having made sure that his act of cremation was irrevocable, was even then returning to the fields.

Rosie ran past him and toward the house. What had become of her mother? She burst into the parlor and found her mother at the back window watching the dying fire. They watched together until there remained only a feeble smoke under the blazing sun. Her mother was very calm.

"Do you know why I married your father?" she said without turning.

85 "No," said Rosie. It was the most frightening question she had ever been called upon to answer. Don't tell me now, she wanted to say, tell me tomorrow, tell me next week, don't tell me today. But she knew she would be told now, that the telling would combine with the other violence of the hot afternoon to level her life, her world to the very ground.

It was like a story out of the magazines illustrated in sepia,[14] which she had consumed so greedily for a period until the information had somehow reached her that those wretchedly unhappy autobiographies, offered to her as the testimonials of living men and women, were largely inventions: Her mother, at nineteen, had come to America and married her father as an alternative to suicide.

At eighteen she had been in love with the first son of one of the well-to-do families in her village. The two had met whenever and wherever they could, secretly, because it would not have done for his family to see him favor her—her father had no money; he was a drunkard and a gambler besides. She had learned she was with child; an excellent match had already been arranged for her lover. Despised by her family, she had given premature birth to a stillborn son, who would be seventeen now. Her

---

[14] Dark brown ink or pigment.

family did not turn her out, but she could no longer project herself in any direction without refreshing in them the memory of her indiscretion. She wrote to Aunt Taka, her favorite sister in America, threatening to kill herself if Aunt Taka would not send for her. Aunt Taka hastily arranged a marriage with a young man of whom she knew, but lately arrived from Japan, a young man of simple mind, it was said, but of kindly heart. The young man was never told why his unseen betrothed was so eager to hasten the day of meeting.

The story was told perfectly, with neither groping for words nor untoward passion. It was as though her mother had memorized it by heart, reciting it to herself so many times over that its nagging vileness had long since gone.

"I had a brother then?" Rosie asked, for this was what seemed to matter now; she would think about the other later, she assured herself, pushing back the illumination which threatened all that darkness that had hitherto been merely mysterious or even glamorous. "A half-brother?"

90   "Yes."

"I would have liked a brother," she said.

Suddenly, her mother knelt on the floor and took her by the wrists. "Rosie," she said urgently, "promise me you will never marry!" Shocked more by the request than the revelation, Rosie stared at her mother's face. Jesus, Jesus, she called silently, not certain whether she was invoking the help of the son of the Carrascos or of God, until there returned sweetly the memory of Jesus' hand, how it had touched her and where. Still her mother waited for an answer, holding her wrists so tightly that her hands were going numb. She tried to pull free. Promise, her mother whispered fiercely, promise. Yes, yes, I promise, Rosie said. But for an instant she turned away, and her mother, hearing the familiar glib agreement, released her. Oh, you, you, you, her eyes and twisted mouth said, you fool. Rosie, covering her face, began at last to cry, and the embrace and consoling hand came much later than she expected.

READING AND REACTING

1. Why do you think Rosie's mother begins writing *haiku?* Why does she stop?

2. What does the narrator mean when she says, "So Rosie and her father lived for a while with two women, her mother and Ume Hanazono" (7)? How are these two women different?

3. In what way does writing *haiku* reveal the differences between Rosie's mother and father? Why does Rosie's father destroy the prize his wife won? Do you think his actions are understandable? Do you think they are justified?

4. What role does Mrs. Hayano play in the story? How does she shed light on Rosie's mother's life, and on her motivation?

5. Explain how each of these conflicts contributes to your understanding of the story: the conflict between husband and wife, mother and daughter, Japanese and American cultures, Rosie's mother and Ume Hanazono, farm work and poetry.

6. Who is the story's main character?

7. What is the story really about? Creativity? Communication? Tradition? Work? Gender roles?

8. How would you sum up the story's major theme? In what why does the title express that theme?

9. **JOURNAL ENTRY**   In paragraphs 84 through 88, Rosie's mother tells her daughter the story of her life. What is the significance of this story? In what sense is this tale—"told perfectly"—the heart of the story?

10. **CRITICAL PERSPECTIVE**   In his article "The *Issei* Father in the Fiction of Hisaye Yamamoto," Charles Crow observes that Yamamoto's stories deal with the disruptions of Japanese-American life caused by the Second World War. Parents, who in many cases were born in Japan, came into conflict with children, who had assimilated into the American mainstream. "Like most Japanese-American authors," says Crow, "Yamamoto explores the frustrated relationship between these two generations—a relationship which changed abruptly and forever in the relocation centers during the war."

   In what sense is "Seventeen Syllables" about the struggle between two generations of Japanese-Americans? How do the different perspectives of the two generations frustrate their attempts to communicate with each other? Is this generational struggle the story's primary focus, or is it really about something else?

EUDORA WELTY (1909–   ) was born and raised in Jackson, Mississippi, where she still lives in her family's home. After attending the Mississippi College for Women, the University of Wisconsin, and Columbia University (where she studied advertising), she returned to Jackson to pursue her long career as a writer, beginning as a journalist. In 1936 she wrote the first of her many short stories, which are gathered in *Collected Stories* (1980). Welty has also authored several novels, including *Delta Wedding* (1946), *Losing Battles* (1970), and the Pulitzer Prize-winning *The Optimist's Daughter* (1972). Her volume of memoirs, *One Writer's Beginnings* (1984), was a bestseller.

One of the country's most accomplished writers, Welty has focused much of her fiction on life in southern towns and villages peopled with dreamers, eccentrics, and close-knit families. Her sharply observed characters are sometimes presented with great humor, sometimes with poignant lyricism, but always with clarity and sympathy. "Of course any writer is in part all of his characters," she has written. "How otherwise would they be known to him, occur to him, become what they are?" In "A Worn Path," Welty creates a particularly memorable character in the tenacious Phoenix Jackson and explores a theme that transcends race and region.

EUDORA WELTY

A Worn Path

(1940)

It was December—a bright frozen day in the early morning. Far out in the country there was an old Negro woman with her head tied in a red rag, coming along a path through the pinewoods. Her name was Phoenix Jackson. She was very old and small and she walked slowly in the dark pine shadows, moving a little from side to side in her steps, with the balanced heaviness and lightness of a pendulum in a grandfather clock. She carried a thin, small cane made from an umbrella, and with this she kept tapping the frozen earth in front of her. This made a grave and persistent noise in the still air, that seemed meditative like the chirping of a solitary little bird.

She wore a dark striped dress reaching down to her shoe tops, and an equally long apron of bleached sugar sacks, with a full pocket: all neat and tidy, but every time she took a step she might have fallen over her shoelaces, which dragged from her unlaced shoes. She looked straight ahead. Her eyes were blue with age. Her skin had a pattern all its own of numberless branching wrinkles and as though a whole little tree stood in the middle of her forehead, but a golden color ran underneath, and the two knobs of her cheeks were illumined by a yellow burning under the dark. Under the red rag her hair came down on her neck in the frailest of ringlets, still black, and with an odor like copper.

Now and then there was a quivering in the thicket. Old Phoenix said, "Out of my way, all you foxes, owls, beetles, jack rabbits, coons and wild animals! . . . Keep out from under these feet, little bob-whites. . . . Keep the big wild hogs out of my path. Don't let none of those come running my direction. I got a long way." Under her small black-freckled hand her cane, limber as a buggy whip, would switch at the brush as if to rouse up any hiding things.

On she went. The woods were deep and still. The sun made the pine needles almost too bright to look at, up where the wind rocked. The cones dropped as light as feathers. Down in the hollow was the mourning dove—it was not too late for him.

5   The path ran up a hill. "Seem like there is chains about my feet, time I get this far," she said, in the voice of argument old people keep to use with themselves. "Something always take a hold of me on this hill—pleads I should stay."

After she got to the top she turned and gave a full, severe look behind her where she had come. "Up through pines," she said at length. "Now down through oaks."

Her eyes opened their widest, and she started down gently. But before she got to the bottom of the hill a bush caught her dress.

Her fingers were busy and intent, but her skirts were full and long, so that before she could pull them free in one place they were caught in another. It was not possible to allow the dress to tear. "I in the thorny bush," she said. "Thorns, you doing your appointed work. Never want to let folks pass, no sir. Old eyes thought you was a pretty little *green* bush."

Finally, trembling all over, she stood free, and after a moment dared to stoop for her cane.

10   "Sun so high!" she cried, leaning back and looking, while the thick tears went over her eyes. "The time getting all gone here."

At the foot of this hill was a place where a log was laid across the creek.

"Now comes the trial," said Phoenix.

Putting her right foot out, she mounted the log and shut her eyes. Lifting her skirt, leveling her cane fiercely before her, like a festival figure in some parade, she began to march across. Then she opened her eyes and she was safe on the other side.

"I wasn't as old as I thought," she said.

15   But she sat down to rest. She spread her skirts on the bank around her and folded her hands over her knees. Up above her was a tree in a pearly cloud of mistletoe. She did not dare to close her eyes, and when a little boy brought her a plate with a slice of marble-cake on it she spoke to him. "That would be acceptable," she said. But when she went to take it there was just her own hand in the air.

So she left that tree, and had to go through a barbed-wire fence. There she had to creep and crawl, spreading her knees and stretching her fingers like a baby trying to climb the steps. But she talked loudly to herself: she could not let her dress be torn now, so late in the day, and she could not pay for having her arm or her leg sawed off if she got caught fast where she was.

At last she was safe through the fence and risen up out in the clearing. Big dead trees, like black men with one arm, were standing in the purple stalks of the withered cotton field. There sat a buzzard.

"Who you watching?"

In the furrow she made her way along.

20   "Glad this not the season for bulls," she said, looking sideways, "and the good Lord made his snakes to curl up and sleep in the winter. A pleasure I

don't see no two-headed snake coming around that tree, where it come once. It took a while to get by him, back in the summer."

She passed through the old cotton and went into a field of dead corn. It whispered and shook and was taller than her head. "Through the maze now," she said, for there was no path.

Then there was something tall, black, and skinny there, moving before her.

At first she took it for a man. It could have been a man dancing in the field. But she stood still and listened, and it did not make a sound. It was as silent as a ghost.

"Ghost," she said sharply, "who be you the ghost of? For I have heard of nary death close by."

25   But there was no answer—only the ragged dancing in the wind.

She shut her eyes, reached out her hand, and touched a sleeve. She found a coat and inside that an emptiness, cold as ice.

"You scarecrow," she said. Her face lighted. "I ought to be shut up for good," she said with laughter. "My senses is gone. I too old. I the oldest people I ever know. Dance, old scarecrow," she said, "while I dancing with you."

She kicked her foot over the furrow, and with mouth drawn down, shook her head once or twice in a little strutting way. Some husks blew down and whirled in streamers about her skirts.

Then she went on, parting her way from side to side with the cane, through the whispering field. At last she came to the end, to a wagon track where the silver grass blew between the red ruts. The quail were walking around like pullets, seeming all dainty and unseen.

30   "Walk pretty," she said. "This is the easy place. This the easy going."

She followed the track, swaying through the quiet bare fields, through the little strings of trees silver in their dead leaves, past cabins silver from weather, with the doors and windows boarded shut, all like old women under a spell sitting there. "I walking in their sleep," she said, nodding her head vigorously.

In a ravine she went where a spring was silently flowing through a hollow log. Old Phoenix bent and drank. "Sweet-gum makes the water sweet," she said, and drank more. "Nobody know who made this well, for it was here when I was born."

The track crossed a swampy part where the moss hung as white as lace from every limb. "Sleep on, alligators, and blow your bubbles." Then the track went into the road.

Deep, deep the road went down between the high green-colored banks. Overhead the live-oaks met, and it was as dark as a cave.

35   A black dog with a lolling tongue came up out of the weeds by the ditch. She was meditating, and not ready, and when he came at her she only hit him a little with her cane. Over she went in the ditch, like a little puff of milkweed.

Down there, her senses drifted away. A dream visited her, and she reached her hand up, but nothing reached down and gave her a pull. So she lay there and presently went to talking. "Old woman," she said to herself, "that black dog come up out of the weeds to stall you off, and now there he sitting on his fine tail, smiling at you."

A white man finally came along and found her—a hunter, a young man, with his dog on a chain.

"Well, Granny!" he laughed. "What are you doing there?"

"Lying on my back like a June-bug waiting to be turned over, mister," she said, reaching up her hand.

40   He lifted her up, gave her a swing in the air, and set her down. "Anything broken, Granny?"

"No sir, them old dead weeds is springy enough," said Phoenix, when she had got her breath. "I thank you for your trouble."

"Where do you live, Granny?" he asked, while the two dogs were growling at each other.

"Away back yonder, sir, behind the ridge. You can't even see it from here."

"On your way home?"

45   "No sir, I going to town."

"Why, that's too far! That's as far as I walk when I come out myself, and I get something for my trouble." He patted the stuffed bag he carried, and there hung down a little closed claw. It was one of the bob-whites, with its beak hooked bitterly to show it was dead. "Now you go on home, Granny!"

"I bound to go to town, mister," said Phoenix. "The time come around."

He gave another laugh, filling the whole landscape. "I know you old colored people! Wouldn't miss going to town to see Santa Claus!"

But something held old Phoenix very still. The deep lines in her face went into a fierce and different radiation. Without warning, she had seen with her own eyes a flashing nickel fall out of the man's pocket onto the ground.

50   "How old are you, Granny?" he was saying.

"There is no telling, mister," she said, "no telling."

Then she gave a little cry and clapped her hands and said, "Git on away from here, dog! Look! Look at that dog!" She laughed as if in admiration. "He ain't scared of nobody. He a big black dog." She whispered, "Sic him!"

"Watch me get rid of that cur," said the man. "Sic him, Pete! Sic him!"

Phoenix heard the dogs fighting, and heard the man running and throwing sticks. She even heard a gunshot. But she was slowly bending forward by that time, further and further forward, the lid stretched down over her eyes, as if she were doing this in her sleep. Her chin was lowered almost to her knees. The yellow palm of her hand came out from the fold of her apron. Her fingers slid down and along the ground under the piece of money with the grace and care they would have in lifting an egg from under a setting hen. Then she slowly straightened up, she stood erect, and the nickel was in her apron pocket. A bird flew by. Her lips moved. "God watching me the whole time. I come to stealing."

55   The man came back, and his own dog panted about them. "Well, I scared him off that time," he said, and then he laughed and lifted his gun and pointed it at Phoenix.

She stood straight and faced him.

"Doesn't the gun scare you?" he said, still pointing it.

"No, sir, I seen plenty go off closer by, in my day, and for less than what I done," she said, holding utterly still.

He smiled, and shouldered the gun. "Well, Granny," he said, "you must be a hundred years old, and scared of nothing. I'd give you a dime if I had any money with me. But you take my advice and stay home, and nothing will happen to you."

60   "I bound to go on my way, mister," said Phoenix. She inclined her head in the red rag. Then they went in different directions, but she could hear the gun shooting again and again over the hill.

She walked on. The shadows hung from the oak trees to the road like curtains. Then she smelled wood-smoke, and smelled the river, and she saw a steeple and the cabins on their steep steps. Dozens of little black children whirled around her. There ahead was Natchez shining. Bells were ringing. She walked on.

In the paved city it was Christmas time. There were red and green electric lights strung and crisscrossed everywhere, and all turned on in the daytime. Old Phoenix would have been lost if she had not distrusted her eyesight and depended on her feet to know where to take her.

She paused quietly on the sidewalk where people were passing by. A lady came along in the crowd, carrying an armful of red-, green- and silver-wrapped presents; she gave off perfume like the red roses in hot summer, and Phoenix stopped her.

"Please, missy, will you lace up my shoe?" She held up her foot.

65   "What do you want, Grandma?"

"See my shoe," said Phoenix. "Do all right for out in the country, but wouldn't look right to go in a big building."

"Stand still then, Grandma," said the lady. She put her packages down on the sidewalk beside her and laced and tied both shoes tightly.

"Can't lace 'em with a cane," said Phoenix. "Thank you, missy. I doesn't mind asking a nice lady to tie up my shoe, when I gets out on the street."

Moving slowly and from side to side, she went into the big building, and into a tower of steps, where she walked up and around and around until her feet knew to stop.

70   She entered a door, and there she saw nailed up on the wall the document that had been stamped with the gold seal and framed in the gold frame, which matched the dream that was hung up in her head.

"Here I be," she said. There was a fixed and ceremonial stiffness over her body.

"A charity case, I suppose," said an attendant who sat at the desk before her.

But Phoenix only looked above her head. There was sweat on her face, the wrinkles in her face shone like a bright net.

"Speak up, Grandma," the woman said. "What's your name? We must have your history, you know. Have you been here before? What seems to be the trouble with you?"

75   Old Phoenix only gave a twitch to her face as if a fly were bothering her.

"Are you deaf?" cried the attendant.

But then the nurse came in.

"Oh, that's just old Aunt Phoenix," she said. "She doesn't come for herself—she has a little grandson. She makes these trips just as regular as clockwork. She lives away back off the Old Natchez Trace." She bent down. "Well, Aunt Phoenix, why don't you just take a seat? We won't keep you standing after your long trip." She pointed.

The old woman sat down, bolt upright in the chair.

80   "Now, how is the boy?" asked the nurse.

Old Phoenix did not speak.

"I said, how is the boy?"

But Phoenix only waited and stared straight ahead, her face very solemn and withdrawn into rigidity.

"Is his throat any better?" asked the nurse. "Aunt Phoenix, don't you hear me? Is your grandson's throat any better since the last time you came for the medicine?"

85   With her hands on her knees, the old woman waited, silent, erect and motionless, just as if she were in armor.

"You mustn't take up our time this way, Aunt Phoenix," the nurse said. "Tell us quickly about your grandson, and get it over. He isn't dead, is he?"

At last there came a flicker and then a flame of comprehension across her face, and she spoke.

"My grandson. It was my memory had left me. There I sat and forgot why I made my long trip."

"Forgot?" The nurse frowned. "After you came so far?"

90   Then Phoenix was like an old woman begging a dignified forgiveness for waking up frightened in the night. "I never did go to school, I was too old at the Surrender,"[1] she said in a soft voice. "I'm an old woman without an education. It was my memory fail me. My little grandson, he is just the same, and I forgot it in the coming."

"Throat never heals, does it?" said the nurse, speaking in a loud, sure voice to old Phoenix. By now she had a card with something written on it,

---

[1] Of General Robert E. Lee to General Ulysses S. Grant at the end of the Civil War, April 9, 1865.

a little list. "Yes. Swallowed lye. When was it?—January—two–three years ago—"

Phoenix spoke unasked now. "No, missy, he not dead, he just the same. Every little while his throat begin to close up again, and he not able to swallow. He not get his breath. He not able to help himself. So the time come around, and I go on another trip for the soothing medicine."

"All right. The doctor said as long as you came to get it, you could have it," said the nurse. "But it's an obstinate case."

"My little grandson, he sit up there in the house all wrapped up, waiting by himself," Phoenix went on. "We is the only two left in the world. He suffer and it don't seem to put him back at all. He got a sweet look. He going to last. He wear a little patch quilt and peep out holding his mouth open like a little bird. I remembers so plain now. I not going to forget him again, no, the whole enduring time. I could tell him from all the others in creation."

95   "All right." The nurse was trying to hush her now. She brought her a bottle of medicine. "Charity," she said, making a check mark in a book.

Old Phoenix held the bottle close to her eyes, and then carefully put it into her pocket.

"I thank you," she said.

"It's Christmas time, Grandma," said the attendant. "Could I give you a few pennies out of my purse?"

"Five pennies is a nickel," said Phoenix stiffly.

100   "Here's a nickel," said the attendant.

Phoenix rose carefully and held out her hand. She received the nickel and then fished the other nickel out of her pocket and laid it beside the new one. She stared at her palm closely, with her head on one side.

Then she gave a tap with her cane on the floor.

"This is what come to me to do," she said. "I going to the store and buy my child a little windmill they sells, made out of paper. He going to find it hard to believe there such a thing in the world. I'll march myself back where he waiting, holding it straight up in this hand."

She lifted her free hand, gave a little nod, turned around, and walked out of the doctor's office. Then her slow step began on the stairs, going down.

READING AND REACTING

1. In what way does the first paragraph set the scene for the story? How does it foreshadow the events that will take place later on?

2. Traditionally, a quest is an expedition in which a knight overcomes a series of obstacles in order to perform a prescribed feat. In what way is Phoenix's journey like a quest? What obstacles does she face? What feat must she perform?

3. Because Phoenix is so old, she has trouble seeing. What things does she have difficulty seeing? In what ways do her mistakes shed light on her character? How do they contribute to the impact of the story?

4. What is the major theme of this story? What other themes are expressed in the story?

5. A phoenix is a mythical bird that would live for five hundred years, be consumed by fire, and then rise from its own ashes. In what way is this name appropriate for the main character of this story?

6. Throughout the story, Phoenix demonstrates nobility. She is not intimidated by the man with the gun and has no difficulty asking a white woman to tie her shoe. In spite of this nobility, however, Phoenix has no qualms about stealing a nickel or taking charity from the doctor. How do you account for this apparent contradiction?

7. How do the various people Phoenix encounters react to her? Do they treat her with respect? With disdain? Why do you think they react the way they do?

8. In paragraph 90 Phoenix says that she is an old woman without an education. Does she nevertheless seem to have any knowledge that the other characters lack?

9. **JOURNAL ENTRY**   Do you think Phoenix is a fully developed character?

10. **CRITICAL PERSPECTIVE**   Writing about "A Worn Path," Eudora Welty says that the question she is asked most frequently by both students and teachers is whether Phoenix Jackson's grandson is actually dead. Here she attempts to answer this question:

     I had not meant to mystify readers by withholding any fact; it is not a writer's business to tease. The story is told through Phoenix's mind and she undertakes her errand. As the author at one with the character as I tell it, I must assume that the boy is alive. As the reader, you are free to think as you like, of course; the story invites you to believe that no matter what happens, Phoenix for as long as she is able to walk and can hold to her purpose will make her journey.

     Do you think Phoenix's grandson is alive or dead? Why? How does your viewpoint affect your reading of the story?

WRITING SUGGESTIONS: THEME

1. The major characters in both "Doe Season" and "Seventeen Syllables" learn a hard lesson. Write an essay in which you compare the lessons that Andy and Rosie learn and discuss the effects their knowledge has on them.

2. All four of this chapter's stories deal with the importance of patience and persistence. Write an essay in which you examine the value of enduring despite difficulties, citing the main characters in "The Chrysanthemums" (p. 326), "Silence" (p. 356), "A Worn Path" (p. 371), and "Doe Season." Which character is the most successful? Which is the least? How do you explain their relative degrees of success?

3. Both "Seventeen Syllables" and "The Chrysanthemums" are about farm wives. In what ways are these wives similar? How are they different? What comment do these stories make on the condition of women in general and of rural women in particular? If you like, you may also discuss the narrator's mother in Alice Munro's "Boys and Girls" (p. 531).

4. Both "Doe Season" and "Silence" deal with violence. How do the two stories' treatments of this subject differ?

5. Like "Doe Season," the poem "Rainbow" by Robert Huff (printed below) also focuses on a child's experience with hunting. How is its central theme different from the central theme of "Doe Season"?

RAINBOW

After the shot the driven feathers rock
In the air and are by sunlight trapped.
Their moment of descent is eloquent.
It is the rainbow echo of a bird
5 *Whose thunder, stopped, puts in my daughter's eyes*
A question mark. She does not see the rainbow,
And the folding bird-fall was for her too quick.
It is about the stillness of the bird
Her eyes are asking. She is three years old;
10 *Has cut her fingers; found blood tastes of salt;*
But she has never witnessed quiet blood,
Nor ever seen before the peace of death.
I say: "The feathers—Look!" but she is torn
And wretched and draws back. And I am glad
15 *That I have wounded her, have winged her heart,*
And that she goes beyond my fathering.

Fiction

FOR FURTHER READING

JULIA ALVAREZ*

Daughter of Invention

(1991)

For a period after they arrived in this country, Laura García tried to invent something. Her ideas always came after the sightseeing visits she took with her daughters to department stores to see the wonders of this new country. On his free Sundays, Carlos carted the girls off to the Statue of Liberty or the Brooklyn Bridge or Rockefeller Center, but as far as Laura was concerned, these were men's wonders. Down in housewares were the true treasures women were after.

Laura and her daughters would take the escalator, marveling at the moving staircase, she teasing them that this might be the ladder Jacob saw with angels moving up and down to heaven.[1] The moment they lingered by a display, a perky saleslady approached, no doubt thinking a young mother with four girls in tow fit the perfect profile for the new refrigerator with automatic defrost or the heavy duty washing machine with the pre-wash soak cycle. Laura paid close attention during the demonstrations, asking intelligent questions, but at the last minute saying she would talk it over with her husband. On the drive home, try as they might, her daughters could not engage their mother in conversation, for inspired by what she had just seen, Laura had begun inventing.

She never put anything actual on paper until she had settled her house down at night. On his side of the bed her husband would be conked out[2] for an hour already, his Spanish newspapers draped over his chest, his glasses propped up on his bedside table, looking out eerily at the darkened room like a disembodied bodyguard. In her lighted corner, pillows

---

* Author birth date not available.

[1] Refers to Jacob's dream described in Genesis 28:12.

[2] Asleep (slang).

propped behind her, Laura sat up inventing. On her lap lay one of those innumerable pads of paper her husband brought home from his office, compliments of some pharmaceutical company, advertising tranquilizers or antibiotics or skin cream. She would be working on a sketch of something familiar but drawn at such close range so she could attach a special nozzle or handier handle, the thing looked peculiar. Her daughters would giggle over the odd doodles they found in kitchen drawers or on the back shelf of the downstairs toilet. Once Yoyo was sure her mother had drawn a picture of a man's you-know-what; she showed her sisters her find, and with coy, posed faces they inquired of their mother what she was up to. *Ay,*[3] that was one of her failures, she explained to them, a child's double-compartment drinking glass with an outsized, built-in straw.

Her daughters would seek her out at night when she seemed to have a moment to talk to them: they were having trouble at school or they wanted her to persuade their father to give them permission to go into the city or to a shopping mall or a movie—in broad daylight, Mami! Laura would wave them out of her room. "The problem with you girls . . ." The problem boiled down to the fact that they wanted to become Americans and their father—and their mother, too, at first—would have none of it.

5   "You girls are going to drive me crazy!" she threatened, if they kept nagging. "When I end up in Bellevue,[4] you'll be safely sorry!"

She spoke in English when she argued with them. And her English was a mishmash[5] of mixed-up idioms and sayings that showed she was "green behind the ears," as she called it.

If her husband insisted she speak in Spanish to the girls so they wouldn't forget their native tongue, she'd snap, "When in Rome, do unto the Romans."

Yoyo, the Big Mouth, had become the spokesman for her sisters, and she stood her ground in that bedroom. "We're not going to that school anymore, Mami!"

"You have to." Her eyes would widen with worry. "In this country, it is against the law not to go to school. You want us to get thrown out?"

10   "You want us to get killed? Those kids were throwing stones today!"

"Sticks and stones don't break bones," she chanted. Yoyo could tell, though, by the look on her face, it was as if one of those stones the kids had aimed at her daughters had hit her. But she always pretended they were at fault. "What did you do to provoke them? It takes two to tangle, you know."

"Thanks, thanks a lot, Mom!" Yoyo stormed out of that room and into her own. Her daughters never called her *Mom* except when they wanted her to feel how much she had failed them in this country. She was a good

---

[3] Alas (Spanish).

[4] A hospital for the mentally ill, located in New York City.

[5] Jumble.

enough Mami, fussing and scolding and giving advice, but a terrible girl-friend parent, a real failure of a Mom.

Back she went to her pencil and pad, scribbling and tsking[6] and tear-ing off sheets, finally giving up, and taking up her *New York Times*. Some nights, though, if she got a good idea, she rushed into Yoyo's room, a flushed look on her face, her tablet of paper in her hand, a cursory knock on the door she'd just thrown open. "Do I have something to show you, Cuquita!"

This was Yoyo's time to herself, after she finished her homework, while her sisters were still downstairs watching TV in the basement. Hunched over her small desk, the overhead light turned off, her desk lamp poignantly lighting only her paper, the rest of the room in warm, soft, un-created darkness, she wrote her secret poems in her new language.

15   "You're going to ruin your eyes!" Laura began, snapping on the overly bright overhead light, scaring off whatever shy passion Yoyo, with the blue thread of her writing, had just begun coaxing out of a labyrinth of feelings.

"Oh, Mami!" Yoyo cried out, her eyes blinking up at her mother, "I'm writing."

"*Ay* Cuquita." This was her communal pet name for whoever was in her favor. "Cuquita, when I make a million, I'll buy you your very own typewriter." (Yoyo had been nagging her mother for one just like the one her father had bought to do his order forms at home.) "Gravy on the turkey" was what she called it when someone was buttering her up. She buttered and poured. "I'll hire you your very own typist."

Down she plopped on the bed and held out her pad. "Take a guess, Cuquita!" Yoyo studied the rough sketch a moment. Soap sprayed from the nozzle head of a shower when you turned the knob a certain way? Instant coffee with creamer already mixed in? Time-released water capsules for your potted plants when you were away? A keychain with a timer that would go off when your parking meter was about to expire? (The ticking would help you find your keys easily if you mislaid them.) The famous one, famous only in hindsight, was the stick person dragging a square by a rope—a suitcase with wheels? "Oh, of course," Yoyo said, humoring her. "What every household needs: a shower like a car wash, keys ticking like a bomb, luggage on a leash!" By now, it had become something of a family joke, their Thomas Edison[7] Mami, their Benjamin Franklin[8] Mom.

Her face fell. "Come on now! Use your head." One more wrong guess, and she'd show Yoyo, pointing with her pencil to the different highlights of this incredible new wonder. "Remember that time we took the car to

---

6 Clicking sound that expresses disapproval.

7 American inventor (1847–1931) known for developing the electric light bulb and the phonograph.

8 American statesman (1706–1790) scientist, inventor, and writer.

Bear Mountain, and we re-ah-lized that we had forgotten to pack an opener with our pick-a-nick!" (Her daughters kept correcting her, but she insisted this was how it should be said.) "When we were ready to eat we didn't have any way to open the refreshments cans?" (This before fliptop lids, which she claimed had crossed her mind.) "You know what this is now?" Yoyo shook her head. "Is a car bumper, but see this part is a removable can opener. So simple and yet so necessary, eh?"

20   "Yeah, Mami. You should patent it." Yoyo shrugged as her mother tore off the scratch paper and folded it, carefully, corner to corner, as if she were going to save it. But then, she tossed it in the wastebasket on her way out of the room and gave a little laugh like a disclaimer. "It's half of one or two dozen of another."

None of her daughters was very encouraging. They resented her spending time on those dumb inventions. Here they were trying to fit in America among Americans; they needed help figuring out who they were, why the Irish kids whose grandparents had been micks[9] were calling them spics.[10] Why had they come to this country in the first place? Important, crucial, final things, and here was their own mother, who didn't have a second to help them puzzle any of this out, inventing gadgets to make life easier for the American Moms.

Sometimes Yoyo challenged her. "Why, Mami? Why do it? You're never going to make money. The Americans have already thought of everything, you know that."

"Maybe not. Maybe, just maybe, there's something they've missed that's important. With patience and calm, even a burro can climb a palm." This last was one of her many Dominican sayings she had imported into her scrambled English.

"But what's the point?" Yoyo persisted.

25   "Point, point, does everything need a point? Why do you write poems?"

Yoyo had to admit it was her mother who had the point there. Still, in the hierarchy of things, a poem seemed much more important than a potty that played music when a toilet-training toddler went in its bowl.

They talked about it among themselves, the four girls, as they often did now about the many puzzling things in this new country.

"Better she reinvents the wheel than be on our cases all the time," the oldest, Carla, observed. In the close quarters of an American nuclear family, their mother's prodigious energy was becoming a real drain on their self-determination. Let her have a project. What harm could she do, and besides, she needed that acknowledgement. It had come to her automatically in the old country from being a de la Torre. "García de la Torre," Laura would enunciate carefully, giving her maiden as well as married

---

[9]   Derogatory term for people of Irish descent.

[10] Derogatory term for people of Hispanic heritage.

name when they first arrived. But the blank smiles had never heard of her name. She would show them. She would prove to these Americans what a smart woman could do with a pencil and pad.

She had a near miss once. Every night, she liked to read *The New York Times* in bed before turning off her light, to see what the Americans were up to. One night, she let out a yelp to wake up her husband beside her. He sat bolt upright, reaching for his glasses which in his haste, he knocked across the room. *"¿Qué pasa? ¿Qué pasa?"*[11] What is wrong? There was terror in his voice, the same fear she'd heard in the Dominican Republic before they left. They had been watched there; he was followed. They could not talk, of course, though they had whispered to each other in fear at night in the dark bed. Now in America, he was safe, a success even; his Centro de Medicina[12] in the Bronx was thronged with the sick and the homesick yearning to go home again. But in dreams, he went back to those awful days and long nights, and his wife's screams confirmed his secret fear: they had not gotten away after all; the SIM had come for them at last.

30   *"Ay,* Cuco! Remember how I showed you that suitcase with little wheels so we should not have to carry those heavy bags when we traveled? Someone stole my idea and made a million!" She shook the paper in his face. "See, see! This man was no *bobo!*[13] He didn't put all his pokers on a back burner. I kept telling you, one of these days my ship would pass me by in the night!" She wagged her finger at her husband and daughters, laughing all the while, one of those eerie laughs crazy people in movies laugh. The four girls had congregated in her room. They eyed their mother and each other. Perhaps they were all thinking the same thing, wouldn't it be weird and sad if Mami did end up in Bellevue?

"¡Ya, ya!"[14] She waved them out of her room at last. "There is no use trying to drink spilt milk, that's for sure."

It was the suitcase rollers that stopped Laura's hand; she had weather-vaned[15] a minor brainstorm. And yet, this plagiarist had gotten all the credit, and the money. What use was it trying to compete with the Americans: they would always have the head start. It was their country, after all. Best stick close to home. She cast her sights about—her daughters ducked—and found her husband's office in need. Several days a week, dressed professionally in a white smock with a little name tag pinned on the lapel, a shopping bag full of cleaning materials and rags, she rode with her husband in his car to the Bronx. On the way, she organized the glove compartment or took off the address stickers from the magazines for the

---

[11] "What's happening?" (Spanish).

[12] Medical Center (Spanish).

[13] Fool (Spanish).

[14] "Now, now." (Spanish)

[15] Pointed towards.

waiting room because she had read somewhere how by means of these stickers drug addict patients found out where doctors lived and burglarized their homes looking for syringes. At night, she did the books, filling in columns with how much money they had made that day. Who had time to be inventing silly things!

She did take up her pencil and pad one last time. But it was to help one of her daughters out. In ninth grade, Yoyo was chosen by her English teacher, Sister Mary Joseph, to deliver the Teacher's Day address at the school assembly. Back in the Dominican Republic growing up, Yoyo had been a terrible student. No one could ever get her to sit down to a book. But in New York, she needed to settle somewhere, and since the natives were unfriendly, and the country inhospitable, she took root in the language. By high school, the nuns were reading her stories and compositions out loud in English class.

But the spectre of delivering a speech brown-nosing the teachers jammed her imagination. At first she didn't want to and then she couldn't seem to write that speech. She should have thought of it as "a great honor," as her father called it. But she was mortified. She still had a slight accent, and she did not like to speak in public, subjecting herself to her classmates' ridicule. It also took no great figuring to see that to deliver a eulogy for a convent full of crazy, old, overweight nuns was no way to endear herself to her peers.

35   But she didn't know how to get out of it. Night after night, she sat at her desk, hoping to polish off some quick, noncommittal little speech. But she couldn't get anything down.

The weekend before the assembly Monday morning Yoyo went into a panic. Her mother would just have to call in tomorrow and say Yoyo was in the hospital, in a coma.

Laura tried to calm her down. "Just remember how Mister Lincoln couldn't think of anything to say at the Gettysburg, but then, bang! *Four score and once upon a time ago,*" she began reciting. "Something is going to come if you just relax. You'll see, like the Americans say, *Necessity is the daughter of invention.* I'll help you."

That weekend, her mother turned all her energy towards helping Yoyo write her speech. "Please, Mami, just leave me alone, please," Yoyo pleaded with her. But Yoyo would get rid of the goose only to have to contend with the gander. Her father kept poking his head in the door just to see if Yoyo had "fulfilled your obligations," a phrase he had used when the girls were younger and he'd check to see whether they had gone to the bathroom before a car trip. Several times that weekend around the supper table, he recited his own high school valedictorian speech. He gave Yoyo pointers on delivery, notes on the great orators and their tricks. (Humbleness and praise and falling silent with great emotion were his favorites.)

Laura sat across the table, the only one who seemed to be listening to him. Yoyo and her sisters were forgetting a lot of their Spanish, and their father's formal, florid diction was hard to understand. But Laura smiled softly to herself, and turned the lazy Susan[16] at the center of the table around and around as if it were the prime mover, the first gear of her attention.

40   That Sunday evening, Yoyo was reading some poetry to get herself inspired: Whitman's poems in an old book with an engraved cover her father had picked up in a thrift shop next to his office. *I celebrate myself and sing myself. . . . He most honors my style who learns under it to destroy the teacher.* The poet's words shocked and thrilled her. She had gotten used to the nuns, a literature of appropriate sentiments, poems with a message, expurgated texts. But here was a flesh and blood man, belching and laughing and sweating in poems. *Who touches this book touches a man.*

That night, at last, she started to write, recklessly, three, five pages, looking up once only to see her father passing by the hall on tiptoe. When Yoyo was done, she red over her words, and her eyes filled. She finally sounded like herself in English!

As soon as she had finished that first draft, she called her mother to her room. Laura listened attentively while Yoyo read the speech out loud, and in the end, her eyes were glistening too. Her face was soft and warm and proud. "*Ay*, Yoyo, you are going to be the one to bring our name to the headlights in this country! That is a beautiful, beautiful speech I want for your father to hear it before he goes to sleep. Then I will type it for you, all right?"

Down the hall they went, mother and daughter, faces flushed with accomplishment, into the master bedroom where Carlos was propped up on his pillows, still awake, reading the Dominican papers, already days old. Now that the dictatorship had been toppled, he had become interested in his country's fate again. The interim government was going to hold the first free elections in thirty years. History was in the making, freedom and hope were in the air again! There was still some question in his mind whether or not he might move his family back. But Laura had gotten used to the life here. She did not want to go back to the old country where, de la Torre or not, she was only a wife and a mother (and a failed one at that, since she had never provided the required son). Better an independent nobody than a high-class houseslave. She did not come straight out and disagree with her husband's plans. Instead, she fussed with him about reading the papers in bed, soiling their sheets with those poorly printed, foreign tabloids. "*The Times* is not that bad!" she'd claim if her husband tried to humor her by saying they shared the same dirty habit.

The minute Carlos saw his wife and daughter filing in, he put his paper down, and his face brightened as if at long last his wife had delivered the son, and that was the news she was bringing him. His teeth were

---

[16] Revolving tray.

already grinning from the glass of water next to his bedside lamp, so he lisped when he said, "Eh-speech, eh-speech!"

45   "It is so beautiful, Cuco," Laura coached him, turning the sound on his TV off. She sat down at the foot of the bed. Yoyo stood before both of them, blocking their view of the soldiers in helicopters landing amid silenced gun reports and explosions. A few weeks ago it had been the shores of the Dominican Republic. Now it was the jungles of Southeast Asia they were saving. Her mother gave her the nod to begin reading.

Yoyo didn't need much encouragement. She put her nose to the fire, as her mother would have said, and read from start to finish without looking up. When she concluded, she was a little embarrassed at the pride she took in her own words. She pretended to quibble with a phrase or two, then looked questioningly to her mother. Laura's face was radiant. Yoyo turned to share her pride with her father.

The expression on his face shocked both mother and daughter. Carlos's toothless mouth had collapsed into a dark zero. His eyes bored into Yoyo, then shifted to Laura. In barely audible Spanish, as if secret microphones or informers were all about, he whispered to his wife, "You will permit her to read *that?*"

Laura's eyebrows shot up, her mouth fell open. In the old country, any whisper of a challenge to authority could bring the secret police in their black V.W.'s. But this was America. People could say what they thought. "What is wrong with her speech?" Laura questioned him.

"What ees wrrrong with her eh-speech?" Carlos wagged his head at her. His anger was always more frightening in his broken English. As if he had mutilated the language in his fury—and now there was nothing to stand between them and his raw, dumb anger. "What is wrong? I will tell you what is wrong. It show no gratitude. It is boastful. *I celebrate myself? The best student learns to destroy the teacher?*" He mocked Yoyo's plagiarized words. "That is insubordinate. It is improper. It is disrespecting of her teachers—" In his anger he had forgotten his fear of lurking spies: each wrong he voiced was a decibel higher than the last outrage. Finally, he shouted at Yoyo, "As your father, I forbid you to make that eh-speech!"

50   Laura leapt to her feet, a sign that *she* was about to deliver her own speech. She was a small woman, and she spoke all her pronouncements standing up, either for more projection or as a carry-over from her girlhood in convent schools where one asked for, and literally, took the floor in order to speak. She stood by Yoyo's side, shoulder to shoulder. They looked down at Carlos. "That is no tone of voice—" she began.

But now, Carlos was truly furious. It was bad enough that his daughter was rebelling, but here was his own wife joining forces with her. Soon he would be surrounded by a houseful of independent American women. He too leapt from the bed, throwing off his covers. The Spanish newspapers flew across the room. He snatched the speech out of Yoyo's hands, held it before the girl's wide eyes, a vengeful, mad look in his own, and then once, twice, three, four, countless times, he tore the speech into shreds.

"Are you crazy?" Laura lunged at him. "Have you gone mad? That is her speech for tomorrow you have torn up!"

"Have *you* gone mad?" He shook her away. "You were going to let her read that . . . that insult to her teachers?"

"Insult to her teachers!" Laura's face had crumpled up like a piece of paper. On it was written a love note to her husband, an unhappy, haunted man. "This is America, Papi, America! You are not in a savage country anymore!"

55   Meanwhile, Yoyo was on her knees, weeping wildly, collecting all the little pieces of her speech, hoping that she could put it back together before the assembly tomorrow morning. But not even a sibyl[17] could have made sense of those tiny scraps of paper. All hope was lost. "He broke it, he broke it," Yoyo moaned as she picked up a handful of pieces.

Probably, if she had thought a moment about it, she would not have done what she did next. She would have realized her father had lost brothers and friends to the dictator Trujillo. For the rest of his life, he would be haunted by blood in the streets and late night disappearances. Even after all these years, he cringed if a black Volkswagen passed him on the street. He feared anyone in uniform: the meter maid giving out parking tickets, a museum guard approaching to tell him not to get too close to his favorite Goya.[18]

On her knees, Yoyo thought of the worst thing she could say to her father. She gathered a handful of scraps, stood up, and hurled them in his face. In a low, ugly whisper, she pronounced Trujillo's hated nickname: "Chapita! You're just another Chapita!"

It took Yoyo's father only a moment to register the loathsome nickname before he came after her. Down the halls they raced, but Yoyo was quicker than he and made it into her room just in time to lock the door as her father threw his weight against it. He called down curses on her head, ordered her on his authority as her father to open that door! He throttled that doorknob, but all to no avail. Her mother's love of gadgets saved Yoyo's hide that night. Laura had hired a locksmith to install good locks on all the bedroom doors after the house had been broken into once while they were away. Now if burglars broke in again, and the family were at home, there would be a second round of locks for the thieves to contend with.

"Lolo," she said, trying to calm him down. "Don't you ruin my new locks."

60   Finally he did calm down, his anger spent. Yoyo heard their footsteps retreating down the hall. Their door clicked shut. Then, muffled voices, her mother's rising in anger, in persuasion, her father's deeper murmurs of

---

17 Female prophet or fortuneteller.

18 Spanish painter Francisco Goya (1746–1828).

explanation and self-defense. The house fell silent a moment, before Yoyo heard, far off, the gun blasts and explosions, the serious, self-important voices of newscasters reporting their TV war.

A little while later, there was a quiet knock at Yoyo's door, followed by a tentative attempt at the door knob. "Cuquita?" her mother whispered. "Open up, Cuquita."

"Go away," Yoyo wailed, but they both knew she was glad her mother was there, and needed only a moment's protest to save face.

Together they concocted a speech: two brief pages of stale compliments and the polite commonplaces on teachers, a speech wrought by necessity and without much invention by mother and daughter late into the night on one of the pads of paper Laura had once used for her own inventions. After it was drafted, Laura typed it up while Yoyo stood by, correcting her mother's misnomers and mis-sayings.

Yoyo came home the next day with the success story of the assembly. The nuns had been flattered, the audience had stood up and given "our devoted teachers a standing ovation," what Laura had suggested they do at the end of the speech.

65   She clapped her hands together as Yoyo recreated the moment. "I stole that from your father's speech, remember? Remember how he put that in at the end?" She quoted him in Spanish, then translated for Yoyo into English.

That night, Yoyo watched him from the upstairs hall window, where she'd retreated the minute she heard his car pull up in front of the house. Slowly, her father came up the driveway, a grim expression on his face as he grappled with a large, heavy cardboard box. At the front door, he set the package down carefully and patted all his pockets for his house keys. (If only he'd had Laura's ticking key chain!) Yoyo heard the snapping open of locks downstairs. She listened as he struggled to maneuver the box through the narrow doorway. He called her name several times, but she did not answer him.

"My daughter, your father, he love you very much," he explained from the bottom of the stairs. "He just want to protect you." Finally, her mother came up and pleaded with Yoyo to go down and reconcile with him. "Your father did not mean to harm. You must pardon him. Always it is better to let bygones by forgotten, no?"

Downstairs, Yoyo found her father setting up a brand new electric typewriter on the kitchen table. It was even better than her mother's. He had outdone himself with all the extra features: a plastic carrying case with Yoyo's initials decaled below the handle, a brace to lift the paper upright while she typed, an erase cartridge, an automatic margin tab, a plastic hood like a toaster cover to keep the dust away. Not even her mother could have invented such a machine!

But Laura's inventing days were over just as Yoyo's were starting up with her school-wide success. Rather than the rolling suitcase everyone else in the family remembers, Yoyo thinks of the speech her mother wrote as her last invention. It was as if, after that, her mother had passed on to Yoyo her pencil and pad and said, "Okay, Cuquita, here's the buck. You give it a shot."

M A R G A R E T   A T W O O D

(1939–   )

Rape Fantasies

(1977)

The way they're going on about it in the magazines you'd think it was just invented, and not only that but it's something terrific, like a vaccine for cancer. They put it in capital letters on the front cover, and inside they have these questionnaires like the ones they used to have about whether you were a good enough wife or an endomorph[1] or an ectomorph,[2] remember that? with the scoring upside down on page 73, and then these numbered do-it-yourself dealies, you know? RAPE, TEN THINGS TO DO ABOUT IT, like it was ten new hairdos or something. I mean, what's so new about it?

So at work they all have to talk about it because no matter what magazine you open, there it is, staring you right between the eyes, and they're beginning to have it on the television, too. Personally I'd prefer a June Allyson[3] movie anytime but they don't make them any more and they don't even have them that much on the Late Show. For instance, day before yesterday, that would be Wednesday, thank god it's Friday as they say, we were sitting around in the women's lunch room—the *lunch* room, I mean you'd think you could get some peace and quiet in there—and Chrissy closes up the magazine she's been reading and says, "How about it, girls, do you have rape fantasies?"

The four of us were having our game of bridge the way we always do, and I had a bare twelve points counting the singleton with not that much of a bid in anything. So I said one club, hoping Sondra would remember about the one club convention, because the time before when I used that she thought I really meant clubs and she bid us up to three, and all I had was four little ones with nothing higher than a six, and we went down two and on top of that we were vulnerable. She is not the world's best bridge player. I mean, neither am I but there's a limit.

---

[1] A person with a short, soft body.

[2] A person with a long, lean body.

[3] American actress (1917–   ) known for her portrayals of sweet, innocent girls in movies of the 1940s and 1950s.

Darlene passed but the damage was done, Sondra's head went round like it was on ball bearings and she said, "*What* fantasies?"

5   "Rape fantasies," Chrissy said. She's a receptionist and she looks like one; she's pretty but cool as a cucumber, like she's been painted all over with nail polish, if you know what I mean. Varnished. "It says here all women have rape fantasies."

"For Chrissake, I'm eating an egg sandwich," I said, "and I bid one club and Darlene passed."

"You mean, like some guy jumping you in an alley or something," Sondra said. She was eating her lunch, we all eat our lunches during the game, and she bit into a piece of that celery she always brings and started to chew away on it with this thoughtful expression in her eyes and I knew we might as well pack it in as far as the game was concerned.

"Yeah, sort of like that," Chrissy said. She was blushing a little, you could see it even under her makeup.

"I don't think you should go out alone at night," Darlene said, "you put yourself in a position," and I may have been mistaken but she was looking at me. She's the oldest, she's forty-one though you wouldn't know it and neither does she, but I looked it up in the employees' file. I like to guess a person's age and then look it up to see if I'm right. I let myself have an extra pack of cigarettes if I am, though I'm trying to cut down. I figure it's harmless as long as you don't tell. I mean, not everyone has access to that file, it's more or less confidential. But it's all right if I tell you, I don't expect you'll ever meet her, though you never know, it's a small world. Anyway.

10   "For *heaven's* sake, it's only *Toronto*," Greta said. She worked in Detroit for three years and she never lets you forget it, it's like she thinks she's a war hero or something, we should all admire her just for the fact that she's still walking this earth, though she was really living in Windsor[4] the whole time, she just worked in Detroit. Which for me doesn't really count. It's where you sleep, right?

"Well, do you?" Chrissy said. She was obviously trying to tell us about hers but she wasn't about to go first, she's cautious, that one.

"I certainly don't," Darlene said, and she wrinkled up her nose, like this, and I had to laugh. "I think its disgusting." She's divorced, I read that in the file too, she never talks about it. It must've been years ago anyway. She got up and went over to the coffee machine and turned her back on us as though she wasn't going to have anything more to do with it.

"Well," Greta said. I could see it was going to be between her and Chrissy. They're both blondes, I don't mean that in a bitchy way but they do try to outdress each other. Greta would like to get out of Filing, she'd like to be a receptionist too so she could meet more people. You don't meet

---

[4] The southernmost city in Canada, south of Detroit, Michigan.

much of anyone in Filing except other people in Filing. Me, I don't mind it so much, I have outside interests.

"Well," Greta said, "I sometimes think about, you know my apartment? It's got this little balcony, I like to sit out there in the summer and I have a few plants out there. I never bother that much about locking the door to the balcony, it's one of those sliding glass ones, I'm on the eighteenth floor for heaven's sake, I've got a good view of the lake and the CN Tower and all. But I'm sitting around one night in my housecoat, watching TV with my shoes off, you know how you do, and I see this guy's feet, coming down past the window, and the next thing you know he's standing on the balcony, he's let himself down by a rope with a hook on the end of it from the floor above, that's the nineteenth, and before I can even get up off the chesterfield he's inside the apartment. He's all dressed in black with black gloves on"—I knew right away what show she got the black gloves off because I saw the same one—"and then he, well, you know."

15   "You know what?" Chrissy said, but Greta said, "And afterwards he tells me that he goes all over the outside of the apartment building like that, from one floor to another, with his rope and his hook . . . and then he goes out to the balcony and tosses his rope, and he climbs up it and disappears."

"Just like Tarzan," I said, but nobody laughed.

"Is that all?" Chrissy said. "Don't you ever think about, well, I think about being in the bathtub, with no clothes on . . ."

"So who takes a bath in their clothes?" I said, you have to admit it's stupid when you come to think of it, but she just went on, ". . . with lots of bubbles, what I use is Vitabath, it's more expensive but it's so relaxing, and my hair pinned up, and the door opens and this fellow's standing there. . . ."

"How'd he get in?" Greta said.

20   "Oh, I don't know, through a window or something. Well, I can't very well get out of the bathtub, the bathroom's too small and besides he's blocking the doorway, so I just *lie* there, and he starts to very slowly take his own clothes off, and then he gets into the bathtub with me."

"Don't you scream or anything?" said Darlene. She'd come back with her cup of coffee, she was getting really interested. "I'd scream like bloody murder."

"Who'd hear me?" Chrissy said. "Besides, all the articles say it's better not to resist, that way you don't get hurt."

"Anyway you might get bubbles up your nose," I said, "from the deep breathing," and I swear all four of them looked at me like I was in bad taste, like I'd insulted the Virgin Mary or something. I mean, I don't see what's wrong with a little joke now and then. Life's too short, right?

"Listen," I said, "those aren't *rape* fantasies. I mean, you aren't getting *raped*, it's just some guy you haven't met formally who happens to be more attractive than Derek Cummins"—he's the Assistant Manager, he wears elevator shoes or at any rate they have these thick soles and he has this funny way of talking, we call him Derek Duck—"and you have a good time. Rape is when they've got a knife or something and you don't want to."

25   "So what about you, Estelle," Chrissy said, she was miffed because I laughed at her fantasy, she thought I was putting her down. Sondra was miffed too, by this time she'd finished her celery and she wanted to tell about hers, but she hadn't got in fast enough.

"All right, let me tell you one," I said. "I'm walking down this dark street at night and this fellow comes up and grabs my arm. Now it so happens that I have a plastic lemon in my purse, you know how it always says you should carry a plastic lemon in your purse? I don't really do it, I tried it once but the darn thing leaked all over my checkbook, but in this fantasy I have one, and I say to him, 'You're intending to rape me, right?' and he nods, so I open my purse to get the plastic lemon, and I can't find it! My purse is full of all this junk, Kleenex and cigarettes and my change purse and my lipstick and my driver's license, you know the kind of stuff, so I ask him to hold out his hands, like this, and I pile all this junk into them and down at the bottom there's the plastic lemon, and I can't get the top off. So I hand it to him and he's very obliging, he twists the top off and hands it back to me, and I squirt him in the eye."

I hope you don't think that's too vicious. Come to think of it, it is a bit mean, especially when he was so polite and all.

"*That's* your rape fantasy?" Chrissy says. "I don't believe it."

"She's a card," Darlene says, she and I are the ones that've been here the longest and she never will forget the time I got drunk at the office party and insisted I was going to dance under the table instead of on top of it, I did a sort of Cossack number[5] but then I hit my head on the bottom of the table—actually it was a desk—when I went to get up, and I knocked myself out cold. She's decided that's the mark of an original mind and she tells everyone new about it and I'm not sure that's fair. Though I did do it.

30   "I'm being totally honest," I say. I always am and they know it. There's no point in being anything else, is the way I look at it, and sooner or later the truth will get out so you might as well not waste the time, right? "You should hear the one about the Easy-Off Cleaner."

But that was the end of the lunch hour, with one bridge game shot to hell, and the next day we spent most of the time arguing over whether to start a new game or play out the hands we had left over from the day before, so Sondra never did get a chance to tell about her rape fantasy.

It started me thinking though, about my own rape fantasies. Maybe I'm abnormal or something, I mean I have fantasies about handsome strangers coming in through the window too, like Mr. Clean,[6] I wish one would, please god somebody without flat feet and big sweat marks on his shirt, and over five feet five, believe me being tall is a handicap though it's

---

[5] Ukrainian folk dance that involves squatting and kicking.

[6] Muscular, bald genie featured in ads for detergent.

getting better, tall guys are starting to like someone whose nose reaches higher than their belly button. But if you're being totally honest you can't count those as rape fantasies. In a real rape fantasy, what you should feel is this anxiety, like when you think about your apartment building catching on fire and whether you should use the elevator or the stairs or maybe just stick your head under a wet towel, and you try to remember everything you've read about what to do but you can't decide.

For instance, I'm walking along this dark street at night and this short, ugly fellow comes up and grabs my arm, and not only is he ugly, you know, with a sort of puffy nothing face, like those fellows you have to talk to in the bank when your account's overdrawn—of course I don't mean they're all like that—but he's absolutely covered in pimples. So he gets me pinned against the wall, he's short but he's heavy, and he starts to undo himself and the zipper gets stuck. I mean, one of the most significant moments in a girl's life, it's almost like getting married or having a baby or something, and he sticks the zipper.

So I say, kind of disgusted, "Oh for Chrissake," and he starts to cry. He tells me he's never been able to get anything right in his entire life, and this is the last straw, he's going to go jump off a bridge.

35   "Look," I say, I feel so sorry for him, in my rape fantasies I always end up feeling sorry for the guy, I mean there has to be something *wrong* with them, if it was Clint Eastwood[7] it'd be different but worse luck it never is. I was the kind of little girl who buried dead robins, know what I mean? It used to drive my mother nuts, she didn't like me touching them, because of the germs I guess. So I say, "Listen, I know how you feel. You really should do something about those pimples, if you got rid of them you'd be quite good looking, honest; then you wouldn't have to go around doing stuff like this. I had them myself once," I say, to comfort him, but in fact I did, and it ends up I give him the name of my old dermatologist, the one I had in high school, that was back in Leamington,[8] except I used to go to St. Catharine's for the dermatologist. I'm telling you, I was really lonely when I first came here; I thought it was going to be such a big adventure and all, but it's a lot harder to meet people in a city. But I guess it's different for a guy.

Or I'm lying in bed with this terrible cold, my face is all swollen up, my eyes are red and my nose is dripping like a leaky tap, and this fellow comes in through the window and *he* has a terrible cold too, it's a new kind of flu that's been going around. So he says, "I'b goig do rabe you"—I hope you don't mind me holding my nose like this but that's the way I imagine it—and he lets out this terrific sneeze, which slows him down a bit, also I'm no object of beauty myself, you'd have to be some kind of

---

[7] American actor (1930–   ) known primarily for his tough-guy roles in movie westerns and detective stories.

[8] Town southeast of Windsor, Ontario, on the north shore of Lake Erie.

pervert to want to rape someone with a cold like mine, it'd be like raping a bottle of LePage's mucilage the way my nose is running. He's looking wildly around the room, and I realize it's because he doesn't have a piece of Kleenex! "Id's ride here," I say, and I pass him the Kleenex, god knows why he even bothered to get out of bed, you'd think if you were going to go around climbing in windows you'd wait till you were healthier, right? I mean, that takes a certain amount of energy. So I ask him why doesn't he let me fix him a Neo-Citran[9] and scotch, that's what I always take, you still have the cold but you don't feel it, so I do and we end up watching the Late Show together. I mean, they aren't all sex maniacs, the rest of the time they must lead a normal life. I figure they enjoy watching the Late Show just like anybody else.

I do have a scarier one though . . . where the fellow says he's hearing angel voices that're telling him he's got to kill me, you know, you read about things like that all the time in the papers. In this one I'm not in the apartment where I live now, I'm back in my mother's house in Leamington and the fellow's been hiding in the cellar, he grabs my arm when I go downstairs to get a jar of jam and he's got hold of the axe too, out of the garage, that one is really scary. I mean, what do you say to a nut like that?

So I start to shake but after a minute I get control of myself and I say, is he sure the angel voices have got the right person, because I hear the same angel voices and they've been telling me for some time that I'm going to give birth to the reincarnation of St. Anne[10] who in turn has the Virgin Mary and right after that comes Jesus Christ and the end of the world, and he wouldn't want to interfere with that, would he? So he gets confused and listens some more, and then he asks for a sign and I show him my vaccination mark, you can see it's sort of an odd-shaped one, it got infected because I scratched the top off, and that does it, he apologizes and climbs out the coal chute[11] again, which is how he got in in the first place, and I say to myself there's some advantage in having been brought up a Catholic even though I haven't been to church since they changed the service into English,[12] it just isn't the same, you might as well be a Protestant. I must write to Mother and tell her to nail up that coal chute, it always has bothered me. Funny, I couldn't tell you at all what this man looks like but I know exactly what kind of shoes he's wearing, because that's the last I see of him, his shoes going up the coal chute, and they're the old-fashioned kind that lace up the ankles, even though he's a young fellow. That's strange, isn't it?

---

[9] Citrus-flavored cold medicine.

[10] Mother of the Virgin Mary.

[11] Trough through which coal is dropped from a delivery truck into a basement bin.

[12] The Roman Catholic mass was performed in Latin before the Second Vatican Council (1962–1965).

Let me tell you though I really sweat until I see him safely out of there and I go upstairs right away and make myself a cup of tea. I don't think about that one much. My mother always said you shouldn't dwell on unpleasant things and I generally agree with that, I mean, dwelling on them doesn't make them go away. Though not dwelling on them doesn't make them go away either, when you come to think of it.

40   Sometimes I have these short ones where the fellow grabs my arm but I'm really a Kung-Fu[13] expert, can you believe it, in real life I'm sure it would just be a conk on the head and that's that, like getting your tonsils out, you'd wake up and it would be all over except for the sore places, and you'd be lucky if your neck wasn't broken or something, I could never even hit the volleyball in gym and a volleyball is fairly large, you know?— and I just go *zap* with my fingers into his eyes and that's it, he falls over, or I flip him against a wall or something. But I could never really stick my fingers in anyone's eyes, could you? It would feel like hot jello and I don't even like cold jello, just thinking about it gives me the creeps. I feel a bit guilty about that one, I mean how would you like walking around knowing someone's been blinded for life because of you?

But maybe it's different for a guy.

The most touching one I have is when the fellow grabs my arm and I say sad and kind of dignified, "You'd be raping a corpse." That pulls him up short and I explain that I've just found out I have leukemia and the doctors have only given me a few months to live. That's why I'm out pacing the streets alone at night, I need to think, you know, come to terms with myself. I don't really have leukemia but in the fantasy I do, I guess I chose that particular disease because a girl in my grade four class died of it, the whole class sent her flowers when she was in the hospital. I didn't understand then that she was going to die and I wanted to have leukemia too so I could get flowers. Kids are funny, aren't they? Well, it turns out that he has leukemia himself, and *he* only has a few months to live, that's why he's going around raping people, he's very bitter because he's so young and his life is being taken from him before he's really lived it. So we walk along gently under the street lights, it's spring and sort of misty, and we end up going for coffee, we're happy we've found the only other person in the world who can understand what we're going through, it's almost like fate, and after a while we just sort of look at each other and our hands touch, and he comes back with me and moves into my apartment and we spend our last months together before we die, we just sort of don't wake up in the morning, though I've never decided which one of us gets to die first. If it's him I have to go on and fantasize about the funeral, if it's me I don't have to worry about that, so it just about depends on how tired I am at the time. You may not believe this but sometimes I even start crying. I cry at the end of movies, even the ones that aren't all that sad, so I guess it's the same thing. My mother's like that too.

---

[13] Chinese art of self-defense; resembles karate.

The funny thing about these fantasies is that the man is always some-one I don't know, and the statistics in the magazines, well, most of them anyway, they say it's often someone you do know, at least a little bit, like your boss or something—I mean, it wouldn't be *my* boss, he's over sixty and I'm sure he couldn't rape his way out of a paper bag, poor old thing, but it might be someone like Derek Duck, in his elevator shoes, perish the thought—or someone you just met, who invites you up for a drink, it's getting so you can hardly be sociable any more, and how are you supposed to meet people if you can't trust them even that basic amount? You can't spend your whole life in the Filing Department or cooped up in your own apartment with all the doors and windows locked and the shades down. I'm not what you would call a drinker but I like to go out now and then for a drink or two in a nice place, even if I am by myself, I'm with Women's Lib on that even though I can't agree with a lot of the other things they say. Like here for instance, the waiters all know me and if anyone, you know, bothers me. . . . I don't know why I'm telling you all this, except I think it helps you get to know a person, especially at first, hearing some of the things they think about. At work they call me the office worry wart, but it isn't so much like worrying, it's more like figuring out what you should do in an emergency, like I said before.

Anyway, another thing about it is that there's a lot of conversation, in fact I spend most of my time, in the fantasy that is, wondering what I'm going to say and what he's going to say, I think it would be better if you could get a conversation going. Like, how could a fellow do that to a per-son he's just had a long conversation with, once you let them know you're human, you have a life too, I don't see how they could go ahead with it, right? I mean, I know it happens but I just don't understand it, that's the part I really don't understand.

T. CORAGHESSAN BOYLE

(1948–   )

Greasy Lake

(1985)

It's about a mile down on the dark side of Route 88.

BRUCE SPRINGSTEEN

There was a time when courtesy and winning ways went out of style, when it was good to be bad, when you cultivated decadence like a taste. We were all dangerous characters then. We wore torn-up leather jackets, slouched around with toothpicks in our mouths, sniffed glue and ether and what somebody claimed was cocaine. When we wheeled our parents' whining station wagons out into the street we left a patch of rubber half a block long. We drank gin and grape juice, Tango, Thunderbird, and Bali Hai. We were nineteen. We were bad. We read André Gide[1] and struck elaborate poses to show that we didn't give a shit about anything. At night, we went up to Greasy Lake.

Through the center of town, up the strip, past the housing developments and shopping malls, street lights giving way to the thin streaming illumination of the headlights, trees crowding the asphalt in a black unbroken wall: that was the way out to Greasy Lake. The Indians had called it Wakan, a reference to the clarity of its waters. Now it was fetid and murky, the mud banks glittering with broken glass and strewn with beer cans and the charred remains of bonfires. There was a single ravaged island a hundred yards from shore, so stripped of vegetation it looked as if the air force had strafed it. We went up to the lake because everyone went there, because we wanted to snuff the rich scent of possibility on the breeze, watch a girl take off her clothes and plunge into the festering murk, drink beer, smoke pot, howl at the stars, savor the incongruous full-throated roar of rock and roll against the primeval susurrus of frogs and crickets. This was nature.

I was there one night, late, in the company of two dangerous characters. Digby wore a gold star in his right ear and allowed his father to pay his tuition at Cornell; Jeff was thinking of quitting school to become a painter/musician/head-shop proprietor. They were both expert in the social graces, quick with a sneer, able to manage a Ford with lousy shocks over a rutted and gutted blacktop road at eighty-five while rolling a joint as compact as a Tootsie Roll Pop stick. They could lounge against a bank of booming speakers and trade "man's with the best of them or roll out across the dance floor as if their joints worked on bearings. They were slick and quick and they wore their mirror shades at breakfast and dinner, in the shower, in closets and caves. In short, they were bad.

I drove. Digby pounded the dashboard and shouted along with Toots & the Maytals while Jeff hung his head out the window and streaked the side of my mother's Bel Air with vomit. It was early June, the air soft as a hand on your cheek, the third night of summer vacation. The first two nights we'd been out till dawn, looking for something we never found. On this, the third night, we'd cruised the strip sixty-seven times, been in and out of every bar and club we could think of in a twenty-mile radius, stopped twice for bucket chicken and forty-cent hamburgers, debated going to a party at the house of a girl Jeff's sister knew, and chucked two dozen raw eggs at mailboxes and hitchhikers. It was 2:00 A.M.; the bars were closing. There was nothing to do but take a bottle of lemon-flavored gin up to Greasy Lake.

---

[1] André Gide (1869–1951). French novelist and critic whose work—much of it semi-autobiographical—examines the conflict between desire and discipline and shows individuals battling conventional morality.

5   The taillights of a single car winked at us as we swung into the dirt lot
with its tufts of weed and washboard corrugations; '57 Chevy, mint,
metallic blue. On the far side of the lot, like the exoskeleton of some gaunt
chrome insect, a chopper leaned against its kickstand. And that was it for
excitement: some junkie half-wit biker and a car freak pumping his girlfriend. Whatever it was we were looking for, we weren't about to find it at
Greasy Lake. Not that night.

But then all of a sudden Digby was fighting for the wheel. "Hey, that's
Tony Lovett's car! Hey!" he shouted, while I stabbed at the brake pedal and
the Bel Air nosed up to the gleaming bumper of the parked Chevy. Digby
leaned on the horn, laughing, and instructed me to put my brights on. I
flicked on the brights. This was hilarious. A joke. Tony would experience
premature withdrawal and expect to be confronted by grim-looking state
troopers with flashlights. We hit the horn, strobed the lights, and then
jumped out of the car to press our witty faces to Tony's windows; for all we
knew we might even catch a glimpse of some little fox's tit, and then we
could slap backs with red-faced Tony, roughhouse a little, and go on to
new heights of adventure and daring.

The first mistake, the one that opened the whole floodgate, was losing
my grip on the keys. In the excitement, leaping from the car with the gin
in one hand and a roach clip in the other, I spilled them in the grass—in
the dark, rank, mysterious nighttime grass of Greasy Lake. This was a tactical error, as damaging and irreversible in its way as Westmoreland's decision to dig in at Khe Sanh.[2] I felt it like a jab of intuition, and I stopped
there by the open door, peering vaguely into the night that puddled up
round my feet.

The second mistake—and this was inextricably bound up with the
first—was identifying the car as Tony Lovett's. Even before the very bad
character in greasy jeans and engineer boots ripped out of the driver's
door, I began to realize that this chrome blue was much lighter than the
robin's-egg of Tony's car, and that Tony's car didn't have rear-mounted
speakers. Judging from their expressions, Digby and Jeff were privately
groping toward the same inevitable and unsettling conclusion as I was.

In any case, there was no reasoning with this bad greasy character—
clearly he was a man of action. The first lusty Rockette[3] kick of his steel-
toed boot caught me under the chin, chipped my favorite tooth, and left
me sprawled in the dirt. Like a fool, I'd gone down on one knee to comb
the stiff hacked grass for the keys, my mind making connections in the

---

[2] In late 1967 North Vietnamese and Viet Cong forces mounted a strong attack against
American troops at Khe Sanh, thereby causing General William C. Westmoreland,
commander of U.S. forces in Vietnam, to "dig in" to defend an area of relatively little
tactical importance.

[3] Famed dancing troupe at New York's Radio City Music Hall, noted for their precision
and can-can-like high kicks.

most dragged-out, testudineous way, knowing that things had gone wrong, that I was in a lot of trouble, and that the lost ignition key was my grail and my salvation. The three or four succeeding blows were mainly absorbed by my right buttock and the tough piece of bone at the base of my spine.

10   Meanwhile, Digby vaulted the kissing bumpers and delivered a savage kung-fu blow to the greasy character's collarbone. Digby had just finished a course in martial arts for phys-ed credit and had spent the better part of the past two nights telling us apocryphal tales of Bruce Lee types and of the raw power invested in lightning blows shot from coiled wrists, ankles, and elbows. The greasy character was unimpressed. He merely backed off a step, his face like a Toltec mask, and laid Digby out with a single whistling roundhouse blow . . . but by now Jeff had got into the act, and I was beginning to extricate myself from the dirt, a tinny compound of shock, rage, and impotence wadded in my throat.

Jeff was on the guy's back, biting at his ear. Digby was on the ground, cursing. I went for the tire iron I kept under the driver's seat. I kept it there because bad characters always keep tire irons under the driver's seat, for just such an occasion as this. Never mind that I hadn't been involved in a fight since sixth grade, when a kid with a sleepy eye and two streams of mucus depending from his nostrils hit me in the knee with a Louisville slugger,[4] never mind that I'd touched the tire iron exactly twice before, to change tires: it was there. And I went for it.

I was terrified. Blood was beating in my ears, my hands were shaking, my heart turning over like a dirtbike in the wrong gear. My antagonist was shirtless, and a single cord of muscle flashed across his chest as he bent forward to peel Jeff from his back like a wet overcoat. "Motherfucker," he spat, over and over, and I was aware in that instant that all four of us—Digby, Jeff, and myself included—were chanting "motherfucker, motherfucker," as if it were a battle cry. (What happened next? the detective asks the murderer from beneath the turned-down brim of his porkpie hat. I don't know, the murderer says, something came over me. Exactly.)

Digby poked the flat of his hand in the bad character's face and I came at him like a kamikaze, mindless, raging, stung with humiliation—the whole thing, from the initial boot in the chin to this murderous primal instant involving no more than sixty hyperventilating, gland-flooding seconds—I came at him and brought the tire iron down across his ear. The effect was instantaneous, astonishing. He was a stunt man and this was Hollywood, he was a big grimacing toothy balloon and I was a man with a straight pin. He collapsed. Wet his pants. Went loose in his boots.

A single second, big as a zeppelin, floated by. We were standing over him in a circle, gritting our teeth, jerking our necks, our limbs and hands and feet twitching with glandular discharges. No one said anything. We just stared down at the guy, the car freak, the lover, the bad greasy character laid

---

[4] A popular brand of baseball bat.

low. Digby looked at me; so did Jeff. I was still holding the tire iron, a tuft of hair clinging to the crook like dandelion fluff, like down. Rattled, I dropped it in the dirt, already envisioning the headlines, the pitted faces of the police inquisitors, the gleam of handcuffs, clank of bars, the big black shadows rising from the back of the cell . . . when suddenly a raw torn shriek cut through me like all the juice in all the electric chairs in the country.

15   It was the fox. She was short, barefoot, dressed in panties and a man's shirt. "Animals!" she screamed, running at us with her fists clenched and wisps of blow-dried hair in her face. There was a silver chain round her ankle, and her toenails flashed in the glare of the headlights. I think it was the toenails that did it. Sure, the gin and the cannabis and even the Kentucky Fried may have had a hand in it, but it was the sight of those flaming toes that set us off—the toad emerging from the loaf in *Virgin Spring*,[5] lipstick smeared on a child: she was already tainted. We were on her like Bergman's deranged brothers—see no evil, hear none, speak none—panting, wheezing, tearing at her clothes, grabbing for flesh. We were bad characters, and we were scared and hot and three steps over the line—anything could have happened.

It didn't.

Before we could pin her to the hood of the car, our eyes masked with lust and greed and the purest primal badness, a pair of headlights swung into the lot. There we were, dirty, bloody, guilty, dissociated from humanity and civilization, the first of the Ur-crimes behind us, the second in progress, shreds of nylon panty and spandex brassiere dangling from our fingers, our flies open, lips licked—there we were, caught in the spotlight. Nailed.

We bolted. First for the car, and then, realizing we had no way of starting it, for the woods. I thought nothing. I thought escape. The headlights came at me like accusing fingers. I was gone.

Ram-bam-bam, across the parking lot, past the chopper and into the feculent undergrowth at the lake's edge, insects flying up in my face, weeds whipping, frogs and snakes and red-eyed turtles splashing off into the night: I was already ankle-deep in muck and tepid water and still going strong. Behind me, the girl's screams rose in intensity, disconsolate, incriminating, the screams of the Sabine women,[6] the Christian martyrs, Anne Frank[7] dragged from the garret. I kept going, pursued by those cries,

---

[5]   Film by Swedish director Ingmar Bergman.

[6]   According to legend, members of an ancient Italian tribe abducted by Romans who took them for wives. The "Rape of the Sabine Women" has been depicted by various artists, most notably by seventeenth-century French painter Nicolas Poussin.

[7]   Anne Frank (1929–1945). German Jewish girl whose family was forced to hide in an attic in Amsterdam during the Nazi occupation of the Netherlands. Frank, who along with her family was discovered by storm troopers and sent to die at the concentration camp at Belsen, is famous for her diary, which recounts her days in hinding.

imagining cops and bloodhounds. The water was up to my knees when I realized what I was doing: I was going to swim for it. Swim the breadth of Greasy Lake and hide myself in the thick clot of woods on the far side. They'd never find me there.

20   I was breathing in sobs, in gasps. The water lapped at my waist as I looked out over the moon-burnished ripples, the mats of algae that clung to the surface like scabs. Digby and Jeff had vanished. I paused. Listened. The girl was quieter now, screams tapering to sobs, but there were male voices, angry, excited, and the high-pitched ticking of the second car's engine. I waded deeper, stealthy, hunted, the ooze sucking at my sneakers. As I was about to take the plunge—at the very instant I dropped my shoulder for the first slashing stroke—I blundered into something. Something unspeakable, obscene, something soft, wet, moss-grown. A patch of weed? A log? When I reached out to touch it, it gave like a rubber duck, it gave like flesh.

In one of those nasty little epiphanies for which we are prepared by films and TV and childhood visits to the funeral home to ponder the shrunken painted forms of dead grandparents, I understood what it was that bobbed there so inadmissibly in the dark. Understood, and stumbled back in horror and revulsion, my mind yanked in six different directions (I was nineteen, a mere child, an infant, and here in the space of five minutes I'd struck down one greasy character and blundered into the waterlogged carcass of a second), thinking, The keys, the keys, why did I have to go and lose the keys? I stumbled back, but the muck took hold of my feet—a sneaker snagged, balance lost—and suddenly I was pitching face forward into the buoyant black mass, throwing out my hands in desperation while simultaneously conjuring the image of reeking frogs and muskrats revolving in slicks of their own deliquescing juices. AAAAArrrgh! I shot from the water like a torpedo, the dead man rotating to expose a mossy beard and eyes cold as the moon. I must have shouted out, thrashing around in the weeds, because the voices behind me suddenly became animated.

"What was that?"

"It's them, it's them: they tried to, tried to . . . *rape* me!" Sobs.

A man's voice, flat Midwestern accent. "You sons a bitches, we'll kill you!"

25   Frogs, crickets.

Then another voice, harsh, *r*-less, Lower East Side: "Motherfucker!" I recognized the verbal virtuosity of the bad greasy character in the engineer boots. Tooth chipped, sneakers gone, coated in mud and slime and worse, crouching breathless in the weeds waiting to have my ass thoroughly and definitively kicked and fresh from the hideous stinking embrace of a three-days-dead-corpse, I suddenly felt a rush of joy and vindication: the son of a bitch was alive! Just as quickly, my bowels turned to ice. "Come on out of there, you pansy mothers!" the bad greasy character was screaming. He shouted curses till he was out of breath.

The crickets started up again, then the frogs. I held my breath. All at once there was a sound in the reeds, a swishing, a splash: thunk-a-thunk.

They were throwing rocks. The frogs fell silent. I cradled my head. Swish, swish, thunk-a-thunk. A wedge of feldspar the size of a cue ball glanced off my knee. I bit my finger.

It was then that they turned to the car. I heard a door slam, a curse, and then the sound of the headlights shattering—almost a good-natured sound, celebratory, like corks popping from the necks of bottles. This was succeeded by the dull booming of the fenders, metal on metal, and then the icy crash of the windshield. I inched forward, elbows and knees, my belly pressed to the muck, thinking of guerrillas and commandos and *The Naked and the Dead*.[8] I parted the weeds and squinted the length of the parking lot.

The second car—it was a Trans-Am—was still running, its high beams washing the scene in a lurid stagy light. Tire iron flailing, the greasy bad character was laying into the side of my mother's Bel Air like an avenging demon, his shadow riding up the trunks of the trees. Whomp. Whomp. Whomp-whomp. The other two guys—blond types, in fraternity jackets—were helping out with tree branches and skull-sized boulders. One of them was gathering up bottles, rocks, muck, candy wrappers, used condoms, pop-tops, and other refuse and pitching it through the window on the driver's side. I could see the fox, a white bulb behind the windshield of the '57 Chevy. "Bobbie," she whined over the thumping, "come *on*." The greasy character paused a moment, took one good swipe at the left taillight, and then heaved the tire iron halfway across the lake. Then he fired up the '57 and was gone.

30 Blond head nodded at blond head. One said something to the other, too low for me to catch. They were no doubt thinking that in helping to annihilate my mother's car they'd committed a fairly rash act, and thinking too that there were three bad characters connected with that very car watching them from the woods. Perhaps other possibilities occurred to them as well—police, jail cells, justices of the peace, reparations, lawyers, irate parents, fraternal censure. Whatever they were thinking, they suddenly dropped branches, bottles, and rocks and sprang for their car in unison, as if they'd choreographed it. Five seconds. That's all it took. The engine shrieked, the tires squealed, a cloud of dust rose from the rutted lot and then settled back on darkness.

I don't know how long I lay there, the bad breath of decay all around me, my jacket heavy as a bear, the primordial ooze subtly reconstituting itself to accommodate my upper thighs and testicles. My jaws ached, my knee throbbed, my coccyx was on fire. I contemplated suicide, wondered if I'd need bridgework, scraped the recesses of my brain for some sort of excuse to give my parents—a tree had fallen on the car, I was blindsided by a bread truck, hit and run, vandals had got to it while we were playing chess at Digby's. Then I thought of the dead man. He was probably the

---

8 A popular and critically successful 1948 novel by Norman Mailer, depicting U.S. Army life during World War II.

only person on the planet worse off than I was. I thought about him, fog on the lake, insects chirring eerily, and felt the tug of fear, felt the darkness opening up inside me like a set of jaws. Who was he, I wondered, this victim of time and circumstance bobbing sorrowfully in the lake at my back. The owner of the chopper, no doubt, a bad older character come to this. Shot during a murky drug deal, drowned while drunkenly frolicking in the lake. Another headline. My car was wrecked; he was dead.

When the eastern half of the sky went from black to cobalt and the trees began to separate themselves from the shadows, I pushed myself up from the mud and stepped out into the open. By now the birds had begun to take over for the crickets, and dew lay slick on the leaves. There was a smell in the air, raw and sweet at the same time, the smell of the sun firing buds and opening blossoms. I contemplated the car. It lay there like a wreck along the highway, like a steel sculpture left over from a vanished civilization. Everything was still. This was nature.

I was circling the car, as dazed and bedraggled as the sole survivor of an air blitz, when Digby and Jeff emerged from the trees behind me. Digby's face was crosshatched with smears of dirt; Jeff's jacket was gone and his shirt was torn across the shoulder. They slouched across the lot, looking sheepish, and silently came up beside me to gape at the ravaged automobile. No one said a word. After a while Jeff swung open the driver's door and began to scoop the broken glass and garbage off the seat. I looked at Digby. He shrugged. "At least they didn't slash the tires," he said.

It was true: the tires were intact. There was no windshield, the headlights were staved in, and the body looked as if it had been sledgehammered for a quarter a shot at the county fair, but the tires were inflated to regulation pressure. The car was drivable. In silence, all three of us bent to scrape the mud and shattered glass from the interior. I said nothing about the biker. When we were finished, I reached in my pocket for the keys, experienced a nasty stab of recollection, cursed myself, and turned to search the grass. I spotted them almost immediately, no more than five feet from the open door, glinting like jewels in the first tapering shaft of sunlight. There was no reason to get philosophical about it: I eased into the seat and turned the engine over.

35   It was at that precise moment that the silver Mustang with the flame decals rumbled into the lot. All three of us froze; then Digby and Jeff slid into the car and slammed the door. We watched as the Mustang rocked and bobbed across the ruts and finally jerked to a halt beside the forlorn chopper at the far end of the lot. "Let's go," Digby said. I hesitated, the Bel Air wheezing beneath me.

Two girls emerged from the Mustang. Tight jeans, stiletto heels, hair like frozen fur. They bent over the motorcycle, paced back and forth aimlessly, glanced once or twice at us, and then ambled over to where the reeds sprang up in a green fence round the perimeter of the lake. One of them cupped her hands to her mouth. "Al," she called, "Hey, Al!"

"Come on," Digby hissed. "Let's get out of here."

But it was too late. The second girl was picking her way across the lot, unsteady on her heels, looking up at us and then away. She was older— twenty-five or -six—and as she came closer we could see there was something wrong with her: she was stoned or drunk, lurching now and waving her arms for balance. I gripped the steering wheel as if it were the ejection lever of a flaming jet, and Digby spat out my name, twice, terse and impatient.

"Hi," the girl said.

40   We looked at her like zombies, like war veterans, like deaf-and-dumb pencil peddlers.

She smiled, her lips cracked and dry. "Listen," she said, bending from the waist to look in the window, "you guys seen Al?" Her pupils were pinpoints, her eyes glass. She jerked her neck. "That's his bike over there— Al's. You seen him?"

Al. I didn't know what to say. I wanted to get out of the car and retch, I wanted to go home to my parents' house and crawl into bed. Digby poked me in the ribs. "We haven't seen anybody," I said.

The girl seemed to consider this, reaching out a slim veiny arm to brace herself against the car. "No matter," she said, slurring the *t*'s, "he'll turn up." And then, as if she'd just taken stock of the whole scene—the ravaged car and our battered faces, the desolation of the place—she said: "Hey, you guys look like some pretty bad characters—been fightin', huh?" We stared straight ahead, rigid as catatonics. She was fumbling in her pocket and muttering something. Finally she held out a handful of tablets in glassine wrappers: "Hey, you want to party, you want to do some of these with me and Sarah?"

I just looked at her. I thought I was going to cry. Digby broke the silence. "No, thanks," he said, leaning over me. "Some other time."

45   I put the car in gear and it inched forward with a groan, shaking off pellets of glass like an old dog shedding water after a bath, heaving over the ruts on its worn springs, creeping toward the highway. There was a sheen of sun on the lake. I looked back. The girl was still standing there, watching us, her shoulders slumped, hand outstretched.

RAYMOND CARVER

(1938–1988)

Cathedral

(1983)

This blind man, an old friend of my wife's, he was on his way to spend the night. His wife had died. So he was visiting the dead wife's relatives in Connecticut. He called my wife from his in-laws'. Arrangements were made. He would come by train, a five-hour trip, and my wife would meet him at the station. She hadn't seen him since she worked for him one summer in Seattle ten years ago. But she and the blind man had kept in touch. They made tapes and mailed them back and forth. I wasn't enthusiastic about his visit. He was no one I knew. And his being blind bothered me. My idea of blindness came from the movies. In the movies, the blind moved slowly and never laughed. Sometimes they were led by seeing-eye dogs. A blind man in my house was not something I looked forward to.

That summer in Seattle she had needed a job. She didn't have any money. The man she was going to marry at the end of the summer was in officers' training school. He didn't have any money, either. But she was in love with the guy, and he was in love with her, etc. She'd seen something in the paper: HELP WANTED—*Reading to Blind Man,* and a telephone number. She phoned and went over, was hired on the spot. She'd worked with this blind man all summer. She read stuff to him, case studies, reports, that sort of thing. She helped him organize his little office in the county social-service department. They'd become good friends, my wife and the blind man. How do I know these things? She told me. And she told me something else. On her last day in the office, the blind man asked if he could touch her face. She agreed to this. She told me he touched his fingers to every part of her face, her nose—even her neck! She never forgot it. She even tried to write a poem about it. She was always trying to write a poem. She wrote a poem or two every year, usually after something really important had happened to her.

When we first started going out together, she showed me the poem. In the poem, she recalled his fingers and the way they had moved around over her face. In the poem, she talked about what she had felt at the time, about what went through her mind when the blind man touched her nose and lips. I can remember I didn't think much of the poem. Of course, I didn't tell her that. Maybe I just don't understand poetry. I admit it's not the first thing I reach for when I pick up something to read.

Anyway, this man who'd first enjoyed her favors, the officer-to-be, he'd been her childhood sweetheart. So okay. I'm saying that at the end of the summer she let the blind man run his hands over her face, said good-bye to him, married her childhood etc., who was now a commissioned officer, and she moved away from Seattle. But they'd kept in touch, she and the blind man. She made the first contact after a year or so. She called him up one night from an Air Force base in Alabama. She wanted to talk. They talked. He asked her to send a tape and tell him about her life. She did this. She sent the tape. On the tape, she told the blind man about her husband and about their life together in the military. She told the blind man she loved her husband but she didn't like it where they lived and she didn't like it that he was part of the military-industrial thing. She told the blind man she'd written a poem and he was in it. She told him that she was writing a poem about what it was like to be an Air Force officer's wife. The poem wasn't finished yet. She was still writing it. The blind man made a tape. He sent her the tape. She made a tape. This went on for years. My wife's office was posted to one base and then another. She sent tapes from Moody AFB, McGuire, McConnell, and finally Travis,[1] near Sacramento, where one night she got to feeling lonely and cut off from people she kept losing in that moving-around life. She got to feeling she couldn't go it another step. She went in and swallowed all the pills and capsules in the medicine chest and washed them down with a bottle of gin. Then she got into a hot bath and passed out.

5   But instead of dying, she got sick. She threw up. Her officer—why should he have a name? he was the childhood sweetheart, and what more does he want?—came home from somewhere, found her, and called the ambulance. In time, she put it all on a tape and sent the tape to the blind man. Over the years, she put all kinds of stuff on tapes and sent the tapes off lickety-split. Next to writing a poem every year, I think it was her chief means of recreation. On one tape, she told the blind man she'd decided to live away from her officer for a time. On another tape, she told him about her divorce. She and I began going out, and of course she told her blind man about it. She told him everything, or so it seemed to me. Once she asked me if I'd like to hear the latest tape from the blind man. This was a year ago. I was on the tape, she said. So I said okay, I'd listen to it. I got us drinks and we settled down in the living room. We made ready to listen. First she inserted the tape into the player and adjusted a couple of dials. Then she pushed a lever. The tape squeaked and someone began to talk in this loud voice. She lowered the volume. After a few minutes of harmless chitchat, I heard my own name in the mouth of this stranger, this blind man I didn't even know! And then this: "From all you've said about him, I can only conclude—" But we were interrupted, a knock at the door, something, and we didn't ever get back to the tape. Maybe it was just as well. I'd heard all I wanted to.

Now this same blind man was coming to sleep in my house.

"Maybe I could take him bowling," I said to my wife. She was at the draining board doing scalloped potatoes. She put down the knife she was using and turned around.

"If you love me," she said, "you can do this for me. If you don't love me, okay. But if you had a friend, any friend, and the friend came to visit, I'd make him feel comfortable." She wiped her hands with the dish towel.

"I don't have any blind friends," I said.

10   "You don't have *any* friends," she said. "Period. Besides," she said, "goddamn it, his wife's just died! Don't you understand that? The man's lost his wife!"

I didn't answer. She'd told me a little about the blind man's wife. Her name was Beulah. Beulah! That's a name for a colored woman.

"Was his wife a Negro?" I asked.

---

[1] Names of U.S. Air Force bases.

"Are you crazy?" my wife said. "Have you just flipped or something?" She picked up a potato. I saw it hit the floor, then roll under the stove. "What's wrong with you?" she said. "Are you drunk?"

"I'm just asking," I said.

15   Right then my wife filled me in with more detail than I cared to know. I made a drink and sat at the kitchen table to listen. Pieces of the story began to fall into place.

Beulah had gone to work for the blind man the summer after my wife had stopped working for him. Pretty soon Beulah and the blind man had themselves a church wedding. It was a little wedding—who'd want to go to such a wedding in the first place?—just the two of them, plus the minister and the minister's wife. But it was a church wedding just the same. It was what Beulah had wanted, he'd said. But even then Beulah must have been carrying the cancer in her glands. After they had been inseparable for eight years—my wife's word, *inseparable*—Beulah's health went into a rapid decline. She died in a Seattle hospital room, the blind man sitting beside the bed and holding on to her hand. They'd married, lived and worked together, slept together—had sex, sure—and then the blind man had to bury her. All this without his having ever seen what the god-damned woman looked like. It was beyond my understanding. Hearing this, I felt sorry for the blind man for a little bit. And then I found myself thinking what a pitiful life this woman must have led. Imagine a woman who could never see herself as she was seen in the eyes of her loved one. A woman who could go on day after day and never receive the smallest compliment from her beloved. A woman whose husband could never the expression on her face, be it misery or something better. Someone who could wear makeup or not—what difference to him? She could, if she wanted, wear green eye-shadow around one eye, a straight pin in her nostril, yellow slacks, and purple shoes, no matter. And then to slip off into death, the blind man's hand on her hand, his blind eyes streaming tears—I'm imagining now—her last thought maybe this: that he never even knew what she looked like, and she on an express to the grave. Robert was left with a small insurance policy and a half of a twenty-peso Mexican coin. The other half of the coin went into the box with her. Pathetic.

So when the time rolled around, my wife went to the depot to pick him up. With nothing to do but wait—sure, I blamed him for that—I was having a drink and watching the TV when I heard the car pull into the drive. I got up from the sofa with my drink and went to the window to have a look.

I saw my wife laughing as she parked the car. I saw her get out of the car and shut the door. She was still wearing a smile. Just amazing. She went around to the other side of the car to where the blind man was already starting to get out. This blind man, feature this, he was wearing a full beard! A beard on a blind man! Too much, I say. The blind man reached into the backseat and dragged out a suitcase. My wife took his arm, shut the car door, and, talking all the way, moved him down the drive and then up the steps to the front porch. I turned off the TV. I finished my drink, rinsed the glass, dried my hands. Then I went to the door.

My wife said, "I want you to meet Robert. Robert, this is my husband. I've told you all about him." She was beaming. She had this blind man by his coat sleeve.

20 The blind man let go of his suitcase and up came his hand.

I took it. He squeezed hard, held my hand, and then he let it go.

"I feel like we've already met," he boomed.

"Likewise," I said. I didn't know what else to say. Then I said, "Welcome. I've heard a lot about you." We began to move then, a little group, from the porch into the living room, my wife guiding him by the arm. The blind man was carrying his suitcase in his other hand. My wife said things like, "To your left here, Robert. That's right. Now watch it, there's a chair. That's it. Sit down right here. This is the sofa. We just bought this sofa two weeks ago."

I started to say something about the old sofa. I'd liked that old sofa. But I didn't say anything. Then I wanted to say something else, small-talk, about the scenic ride along the Hudson.[2] How going *to* New York, you should sit on the right-hand side of the train, and coming *from* New York, the left-hand side.

25 "Did you have a good train ride?" I said. "Which side of the train did you sit on, by the way?"

"What a question, which side!" my wife said. "What's it matter which side?" she said.

"I just asked," I said.

"Right side," the blind man said. "I hadn't been on a train in nearly forty years. Not since I was a kid. With my folks. That's been a long time. I'd nearly forgotten the sensation. I have winter in my beard now," he said. "So I've been told, anyway. Do I look distinguished, my dear?" the blind man said to my wife.

"You look distinguished, Robert," she said. "Robert," she said. "Robert, it's just so good to see you."

30 My wife finally took her eyes off the blind man and looked at me. I had the feeling she didn't like what she saw. I shrugged.

I've never met, or personally known, anyone who was blind. This blind man was late forties, a heavy-set, balding man with stooped shoulders, as if he carried a great weight there. He wore brown slacks, brown shoes, a light-brown shirt, a tie, a sports coat. Spiffy. He also had this full beard. But he didn't use a cane and he didn't wear dark glasses. I'd always thought dark glasses were a must for the blind. Fact was, I wished he had a pair. At first glance, his eyes looked like anyone else's eyes. But if you looked close, there was something different about them. Too much white

---

[2] River that flows from the Adirondack Mountains southward into the Upper New York Bay.

in the iris, for one thing, and the pupils seemed to move around in the sockets without his knowing it or being able to stop it. Creepy. As I stared at his face, I saw the left pupil turn in toward his nose while the other made an effort to keep in one place. But it was only an effort, for that eye was on the roam without his knowing it or wanting it to be.

I said, "Let me get you a drink. What's your pleasure? We have a little of everything. It's one of our pastimes."

"Bub, I'm a Scotch man myself," he said fast enough in this big voice.

"Right," I said. Bub! "Sure you are. I knew it."

35 He let his fingers touch his suitcase, which was sitting alongside the sofa. He was taking his bearings. I didn't blame him for that.

"I'll move that up to your room," my wife said.

"No, that's fine," the blind man said loudly. "It can go up when I go up."

"A little water with the Scotch?" I said.

"Very little," he said.

40 "I knew it," I said.

He said, "Just a tad. The Irish actor, Barry Fitzgerald? I'm like that fellow. When I drink water, Fitzgerald said, I drink water. When I drink whiskey, I drink whiskey." My wife laughed. The blind man brought his hand up under his beard. He lifted his beard slowly and let it drop.

I did the drinks, three big glasses of Scotch with a splash of water in each. Then we made ourselves comfortable and talked about Robert's travels. First the long flight from the West Coast to Connecticut, we covered that. Then from Connecticut up here by train. We had another drink concerning that leg of the trip.

I remembered having read somewhere that the blind didn't smoke because, as speculation had it, they couldn't see the smoke they exhaled. I thought I knew that much and that much only about blind people. But this blind man smoked his cigarette down to the nubbin and then lit another one. This blind man filled his ashtray and my wife emptied it.

When we sat down at the table for dinner, we had another drink. My wife heaped Robert's plate with cube steak, scalloped potatoes, green beans. I buttered him up two slices of bread. I said, "Here's bread and butter for you." I swallowed some of my drink. "Now let us pray," I said, and the blind man lowered his head. My wife looked at me, her mouth agape. "Pray the phone won't ring and the food doesn't get cold," I said.

45 We dug in. We ate everything there was to eat on the table. We ate like there was no tomorrow. We didn't talk. We ate. We scarfed. We grazed that table. We were into serious eating. The blind man had right away located his foods, he knew just where everything was on his plate. I watched with admiration as he used his knife and fork on the meat. He'd cut two pieces of meat, fork the meat into his mouth, and then go all out for the scalloped potatoes, the beans next, and then he'd tear off a hunk of buttered bread and eat that. He'd follow this up with a big drink of milk. It didn't seem to bother him to use his fingers once in a while, either.

We finished everything, including half a strawberry pie. For a few moments, we sat as if stunned. Sweat beaded on our faces. Finally, we got up from the table and left the dirty plates. We didn't look back. We took ourselves into the living room and sank into our places again. Robert and my wife sat on the sofa. I took the big chair. We had us two or three more drinks while they talked about the major things that had come to pass for them in the past ten years. For the most part, I just listened. Now and then I joined in. I didn't want him to think I'd left the room, and I didn't want her to think I was feeling left out. They talked of things that had happened to them—to them!—these past ten years. I waited in vain to hear my name on my wife's sweet lips: "And then my dear husband came into my life"—something like that. But I heard nothing of the sort. More talk of Robert. Robert had done a little of everything, it seemed, a regular blind jack-of-all-trades. But most recently he and his wife had had an Amway distributorship, from which, I gathered, they'd earned their living, such as it was. The blind man was also a ham radio operator.[3] He talked in his loud voice about conversations he'd had with fellow operators in Guam, in the Philippines, in Alaska, and even in Tahiti. He said he'd have a lot of friends there if he ever wanted to go visit those places. From time to time, he'd turn his blind face toward me, put his hand under his beard, ask me something. How long had I been in my present position? (Three years.) Did I like my work? (I didn't.) Was I going to stay with it? (What were the options?) Finally, when I thought he was beginning to run down, I got up and turned on the TV.

My wife looked at me with irritation. She was heading toward a boil. Then she looked at the blind man and said, "Robert, do you have a TV?"

The blind man said, "My dear, I have two TVs. I have a color set and a black-and-white thing, an old relic. It's funny, but if I turn the TV on, and I'm always turning it on, I turn on the color set. It's funny, don't you think?"

I didn't know what to say to that. I had absolutely nothing to say to that. No opinion. So I watched the news program and tried to listen to what the announcer was saying.

50   "This is a color TV," the blind man said. "Don't ask me how, but I can tell."

"We traded up a while ago," I said.

The blind man had another taste of his drink. He lifted his beard, sniffed it, and let it fall. He leaned forward on the sofa. He positioned his ashtray on the coffee table, then put the lighter to his cigarette. He leaned back on the sofa and crossed his legs at the ankles.

My wife covered her mouth, and then she yawned. She stretched. She said, "I think I'll go upstairs and put on my robe. I think I'll change into something else. Robert, you make yourself comfortable," she said.

---

[3] Amateur radio operator.

"I'm comfortable," the blind man said.

55 "I want you to feel comfortable in this house," she said.

"I am comfortable," the blind man said.

After she'd left the room, he and I listened to the weather report and then to the sports roundup. By that time, she'd been gone so long I didn't know if she was going to come back. I thought she might have gone to bed. I wished she'd come back downstairs. I didn't want to be left alone with a blind man. I asked him if he wanted another drink, and he said sure. Then I asked if he wanted to smoke some dope with me. I said I'd just rolled a number. I hadn't, but I planned to do so in about two shakes.

"I'll try some with you," he said.

"Damn right," I said. "That's the stuff."

60 I got our drinks and sat down on the sofa with him. Then I rolled us two fat numbers. I lit one and passed it. I brought it to his fingers. He took it and inhaled.

"Hold it as long as you can," I said. I could tell he didn't know the first thing.

My wife came back downstairs wearing her pink robe and her pink slippers.

"What do I smell?" she said.

"We thought we'd have us some cannabis," I said.

65 My wife gave me a savage look. Then she looked at the blind man and said, "Robert, I didn't know you smoked."

He said, "I do now, my dear. There's a first time for everything. But I don't feel anything yet."

"This stuff is pretty mellow," I said. "This stuff is mild. It's dope you can reason with," I said. "It doesn't mess you up."

"Not much it doesn't, bub," he said, and laughed.

My wife sat on the sofa between the blind man and me. I passed her the number. She took it and toked[4] and then passed it back to me. "Which way is this going?" she said. Then she said, "I shouldn't be smoking this. I can hardly keep my eyes open as it is. That dinner did me in. I shouldn't have eaten so much."

70 "It was the strawberry pie," the blind man said. "That's what did it," he said, and he laughed his big laugh. Then he shook his head.

"There's more strawberry pie," I said.

"Do you want some more, Robert?" my wife said.

"Maybe in a little while," he said.

We gave our attention to the TV. My wife yawned again. She said, "Your bed is made up when you feel like going to bed, Robert. I know you must have had a long day. When you're ready to go to bed, say so." She pulled his arm. "Robert?"

75 He came to and said, "I've had a real nice time. This beats tapes, doesn't it?"

---

4 Inhaled.

I said, "Coming at you," and I put the number between his fingers. He inhaled, held the smoke, and then let it go. It was like he'd been doing it since he was nine years old.

"Thanks, bub," he said. "But I think this is all for me. I think I'm beginning to feel it," he said. He held the burning roach out for my wife.

"Same here," she said. "Ditto.[5] Me, too." She took the roach[6] and passed it to me. "I may just sit here for a while between you two guys with my eyes closed. But don't let me bother you, okay? Either one of you. If it bothers you, say so. Otherwise, I may just sit here with my eyes closed until you're ready to go to bed," she said. "Your bed's made up, Robert, when you're ready. It's right next to our room at the top of the stairs. We'll show you up when you're ready. You wake me up now, you guys, if I fall asleep." She said that and then she closed her eyes and went to sleep.

The news program ended. I got up and changed the channel. I sat back down on the sofa. I wished my wife hadn't pooped out. Her head lay across the back of the sofa, her mouth open. She'd turned so that her robe slipped away from her legs, exposing a juicy thigh. I reached to draw her robe back over her, and it was then that I glanced at the blind man. What the hell! I flipped the robe open again.

80   "You say when you want some strawberry pie," I said.

"I will," he said.

I said, "Are you tired? Do you want me to take you up to your bed? Are you ready to hit the hay?"

"Not yet," he said. "No, I'll stay up with you, bub. If that's all right. I'll stay up until you're ready to turn in. We haven't had a chance to talk. Know what I mean? I feel like me and her monopolized the evening." He lifted his beard and he let it fall. He picked up his cigarettes and his lighter.

"That's all right," I said. Then I said, "I'm glad for the company."

85   And I guess I was. Every night I smoked dope and stayed up as long as I could before I fell asleep. My wife and I hardly ever went to bed at the same time. When I did go to sleep, I had these dreams. Sometimes I'd wake up from one of them, my heart going crazy.

Something about the church and the Middle Ages was on the TV. Not your run-of-the-mill TV fare. I wanted to watch something else. I turned to the other channels. But there was nothing on them, either. So I turned back to the first channel and apologized.

"Bub, it's all right," the blind man said. "It's fine with me. Whatever you want to watch is okay. I'm always learning something. Learning never ends. It won't hurt me to learn something tonight. I got ears," he said.

We didn't say anything for a time. He was leaning forward with his head turned at me, his right ear aimed in the direction of the set. Very

---

[5] As said before; likewise.

[6] Cigarette.

disconcerting. Now and then his eyelids drooped and then they snapped open again. Now and then he put his fingers into his beard and tugged, like he was thinking about something he was hearing on the television.

On the screen, a group of men wearing cowls was being set upon and tormented by men dressed in skeleton costumes and men dressed as devils. The men dressed as devils wore devil masks, horns, and long tails. This pageant was part of a procession. The Englishman who was narrating the thing said it took place in Spain once a year. I tried to explain to the blind man what was happening.

90   "Skeletons," he said. "I know about skeletons," he said, and nodded.

The TV showed this one cathedral. Then there was a long, slow look at another one. Finally, the picture switched to the famous one in Paris, with its flying buttresses and its spires reaching up to the clouds. The camera pulled away to show the whole of the cathedral rising above the skyline.

There were times when the Englishman who was telling the thing would shut up, would simply let the camera move around the cathedrals. Or else the camera would tour the countryside, men in fields walking behind oxen. I waited as long as I could. Then I felt I had to say something. I said, "They're showing the outside of this cathedral now. Gargoyles. Little statues carved to look like monsters. Now I guess they're in Italy. Yeah, they're in Italy. There's paintings on the walls of this one church."

"Are those fresco[7] paintings, bub?" he asked, and he sipped from his drink.

I reached for my glass. But it was empty. I tried to remember what I could remember. "You're asking me are those frescoes?" I said. "That's a good question. I don't know."

95   The camera moved to a cathedral outside Lisbon.[8] The differences in the Portuguese cathedral compared with the French and Italian were not that great. But they were there. Mostly the interior stuff. Then something occurred to me, and I said, "Something has occurred to me. Do you have any idea what a cathedral is? What they look like, that is? Do you follow me? If somebody says cathedral to you, do you have any notion what they're talking about? Do you know the difference between that and a Baptist church, say?"

He let the smoke dribble from his mouth. "I know they took hundreds of workers fifty or a hundred years to build," he said. "I just heard the man say that, of course. I know generations of the same families worked on a cathedral. I heard him say that, too. The men who began their life's work on them, they never lived to see the completion of their work. In that wise, bub, they're no different from the rest of us, right?" He laughed. Then his eyelids drooped again. His head nodded. He seemed to be snoozing. Maybe he was imagining himself in Portugal. The TV was showing

---

[7] Plaster painted with watercolors.

[8] The capital of Portugal.

another cathedral now. This one was in Germany. The Englishman's voice droned on. "Cathedrals," the blind man said. He sat up and rolled his head back and forth. "If you want the truth, bub, that's about all I know. What I just said. What I heard him say. But maybe you could describe one to me? I wish you'd do it. I'd like that. If you want to know, I really don't have a good idea."

I stared hard at the shot of the cathedral on the TV. How could I even begin to describe it? But say my life depended on it. Say my life was being threatened by an insane guy who said I had to do it or else.

I stared some more at the cathedral before the picture flipped off into the countryside. There was no use. I turned to the blind man and said, "To begin with, they're very tall." I was looking around the room for clues. "They reach way up. Up and up. Toward the sky. They're so big, some of them, they have to have these supports. To help hold them up, so to speak. These supports are called buttresses. They remind me of viaducts,[9] for some reason. But maybe you don't know viaducts, either? Sometimes the cathedrals have devils and such carved into the front. Sometimes lords and ladies. Don't ask me why this is," I said.

He was nodding. The whole upper part of his body seemed to be moving back and forth.

100   "I'm not doing so good, am I?" I said.

He stopped nodding and leaned forward on the edge of the sofa. As he listened to me, he was running his fingers through his beard. I wasn't getting through to him, I could see that. But he waited for me to go on just the same. He nodded, like he was trying to encourage me. I tried to think what else to say. "They're really big," I said. "They're massive. They're built of stone. Marble, too, sometimes. In those olden days, when they built cathedrals, men wanted to be close to God. In those olden days, God was an important part of everyone's life. You could tell this from their cathedral-building. I'm sorry," I said, "but it looks like that's the best I can do for you. I'm just no good at it."

"That's all right, bub," the blind man said. "Hey, listen. I hope you don't mind my asking you. Can I ask you something? Let me ask you a simple question, yes or no. I'm just curious and there's no offense. You're my host. But let me ask if you are in any way religious? You don't mind my asking?"

I shook my head. He couldn't see that, though. A wink is the same as a nod to a blind man. "I guess I don't believe in it. In anything. Sometimes it's hard. You know what I'm saying?"

"Sure, I do," he said.

100   "Right," I said.

The Englishman was still holding forth. My wife sighed in her sleep. She drew a long breath and went on with her sleeping.

---

[9] Bridges that cross over roads or railroads.

"You'll have to forgive me," I said. "But I can't tell you what a cathedral looks like. It just isn't in me to do it. I can't do any more than I've done."

The blind man sat very still, his head down, as he listened to me.

I said, "The truth is, cathedrals don't mean anything special to me. Nothing. Cathedrals. They're something to look at on late-night TV. That's all they are."

110   It was then that the blind man cleared his throat. He brought something up. He took a handkerchief from his back pocket. Then he said, "I get it, bub. It's okay. It happens. Don't worry about it," he said. "Hey, listen to me. Will you do me a favor? I got an idea. Why don't you find us some heavy paper? And a pen. We'll do something. We'll draw one together. Get us a pen and some heavy paper. Go on, bub, get the stuff," he said.

So I went upstairs. My legs felt like they didn't have any strength in them. They felt like they did after I'd done some running. In my wife's room, I looked around. I found some ballpoints in a little basket on her table. And then I tried to think where to look for the kind of paper he was talking about.

Downstairs, in the kitchen, I found a shopping bag with onion skins in the bottom of the bag. I emptied the bag and shook it. I brought it into the living room and sat down with it near his legs. I moved some things, smoothed the wrinkles from the bag, spread it out on the coffee table.

The blind man got down from the sofa and sat next to me on the carpet.

He ran his fingers over the paper. He went up and down the sides of the paper. The edges, even the edges. He fingered the corners.

115   "All right," he said. "All right, let's do her."

He found my hand, the hand with the pen. He closed his hand over my hand. "Go ahead, bub, draw," he said. "Draw. You'll see. I'll follow along with you. It'll be okay. Just begin now like I'm telling you. You'll see. Draw," the blind man said.

So I began. First I drew a box that looked like a house. It could have been the house I lived in. Then I put a roof on it. At either end of the roof, I drew spires. Crazy.

"Swell," he said. "Terrific. You're doing fine," he said. "Never thought anything like this could happen in your lifetime, did you, bub? Well, it's a strange life, we all know that. Go on now. Keep it up."

I put in windows with arches. I drew flying buttresses. I hung great doors. I couldn't stop. The TV station went off the air. I put down the pen and closed and opened my fingers. The blind man felt around over the paper. He moved the tips of his fingers over the paper, all over what I had drawn, and he nodded.

120   "Doing fine," the blind man said.

I took up the pen again, and he found my hand. I kept at it. I'm no artist. But I kept drawing just the same.

My wife opened up her eyes and gazed at us. She sat up on the sofa, her robe hanging open. She said, "What are you doing? Tell me, I want to know."

I didn't answer her.

The blind man said, "We're drawing a cathedral. Me and him are working on it. Press hard," he said to me. "That's right. That's good," he said. "Sure. You got it, bub, I can tell. You didn't think you could. But you can, can't you? You're cooking with gas now. You know what I'm saying? We're going to really have us something here in a minute. How's the old arm?" he said. "Put some people in there now. What's a cathedral without people?"

125   My wife said, "What's going on? Robert, what are you doing? What's going on?"

"It's all right," he said to her. "Close your eyes now," the blind man said to me.

I did it. I closed them just like he said.

"Are they closed?" he said. "Don't fudge."

"They're closed," I said.

130   "Keep them that way," he said. He said, "Don't stop now. Draw."

So we kept on with it. His fingers rode my fingers as my hand went over the paper. It was like nothing else in my life up to now.

Then he said, "I think that's it. I think you got it," he said. "Take a look. What do you think?"

But I had my eyes closed. I thought I'd keep them that was for a little longer. I thought it was something I ought to do.

"Well?" he said. "Are you looking?"

135   My eyes were still closed. I was in my house. I knew that. But I didn't feel like I was inside anything.

"It's really something," I said.

S A N D R A   C I S N E R O S

(1954–   )

Mericans

(1991)

We're waiting for the awful grandmother who is inside dropping pesos[1] into *la ofrenda*[2] box before the altar to La Divina Providencia. Lighting votive candles and genuflecting.[3] Blessing herself and kissing her thumb.

---

[1] Mexican currency.

[2] Offering (Spanish).

[3] Bending the knee in reverence or worship.

Running a crystal rosary between her fingers. Mumbling, mumbling, mumbling.

There are so many prayers and promises and thanks-be-to-God to be given in the name of the husband and the sons and the only daughter who never attend mass. It doesn't matter. Like La Virgen de Guadalupe,[4] the awful grandmother intercedes on their behalf. For the grandfather who hasn't believed in anything since the first PRI[5] elections. For my father, El Periquín, so skinny he needs his sleep. For Auntie Light-skin, who only a few hours before was breakfasting on brain and goat tacos after dancing all night in the pink zone.[6] For Uncle Fat-face, the blackest of the black sheep—*Always remember your Uncle Fat-face in your prayers.* And Uncle Baby—*You go for me, Mamá—God listens to you.*

The awful grandmother has been gone a long time. She disappeared behind the heavy leather outer curtain and the dusty velvet inner. We must stay near the church entrance. We must not wander over to the balloon and punch-ball vendors. We cannot spend our allowance on fried cookies or Familia Burrón comic books or those clear cone-shaped suckers that make everything look like a rainbow when you look through them. We cannot run off and have our picture taken on the wooden ponies. We must not climb the steps up the hill behind the church and chase each other through the cemetery. We have promised to stay right where the awful grandmother left us until she returns.

There are those walking to church on their knees. Some with fat rags tied around their legs and others with pillows, one to kneel on, and one to flop ahead. There are women with black shawls crossing and uncrossing themselves. There are armies of penitents carrying banners and flowered arches while musicians play tinny trumpets and tinny drums.

5   La Virgen de Guadalupe is waiting inside behind a plate of thick glass. There's also a gold crucifix bent crooked as a mesquite tree when someone once threw a bomb. La Virgen de Guadalupe on the main altar because she's a big miracle, the crooked crucifix on a side altar because that's a little miracle.

But we're outside in the sun. My big brother Junior hunkered against the wall with his eyes shut. My little brother Keeks running around in circles.

Maybe and most probably my little brother is imagining he's a flying feather dancer, like the ones we saw swinging high up from a pole on the Virgin's birthday. I want to be a flying feather dancer too, but when he circles past me he shouts, "I'm a B-Fifty-two bomber, you're a German," and

---

[4] The Virgin Mary as Mexican Catholics believed she appeared to a young boy in Mexico City in the sixteenth century.

[5] The Institutional Revolutionary Party, which dominated the 1985 political elections in Mexico.

[6] Mexican-American cultural district.

shoots me with an invisible machine gun. I'd rather play flying feather dancers, but if I tell my brother this, he might not play with me at all.

"*Girl*. We can't play with a *girl*." *Girl*. It's my brothers' favorite insult now instead of "sissy." "You *girl*," they yell at each other. "You throw that ball like a *girl*."

I've already made up my mind to be a German when Keeks swoops past again, this time yelling, "I'm Flash Gordon. You're Ming the Merciless and the Mud People."[7] I don't mind being Ming the Merciless, but I don't like being the Mud People. Something wants to come out of the corners of my eyes, but I don't let it. Crying is what *girls* do.

10   I leave Keeks running around in circles—"I'm the Lone Ranger, you're Tonto." I leave Junior squatting on his ankles and go look for the awful grandmother.

Why do churches smell like the inside of an ear? Like incense and the dark and candles in blue glass? And why does holy water smell of tears? The awful grandmother makes me kneel and fold my hands. The ceiling high and everyone's prayers bumping up there like balloons.

If I stare at the eyes of the saints long enough, they move and wink at me, which makes me a sort of saint too. When I get tired of winking saints, I count the awful grandmother's mustache hairs while she prays for Uncle Old, sick from the worm,[8] and Auntie Cuca, suffering from a life of troubles that left half her face crooked and the other half sad.

There must be a long, long list of relatives who haven't gone to church. The awful grandmother knits the names of the dead and the living into one long prayer fringed with the grandchildren born in that barbaric country with its barbarian ways.

I put my weight on one knee, then the other, and when they both grow fat as a mattress of pins, I slap them each awake. *Micaela, you may wait outside with Alfredito and Enrique.* The awful grandmother says it all in Spanish, which I understand when I'm paying attention. "What?" I say, though it's neither proper nor polite. "What?" which the awful grandmother hears as "*¿Güat?*" But she only gives me a look and shoves me toward the door.

15   After all that dust and dark, the light from the plaza makes me squinch my eyes like if I just came out of the movies. My brother Keeks is drawing squiggly lines on the concrete with a wedge of glass and the heel of his shoe. My brother Junior squatting against the entrance, talking to a lady and man.

They're not from here. Ladies don't come to church dressed in pants. And everybody knows men aren't supposed to wear shorts.

"*¿Quieres chicle?*"[9] the lady asks in a Spanish too big for her mouth.

---

[7] A comic-book superhero and his enemies.

[8] Hung over.

[9] "Would you like a chiclet?" (Spanish)

"*Gracias.*"[10] The lady gives him a whole handful of gum for free, little cellophane cubes of Chiclets, cinnamon and aqua and the white ones that don't taste like anything but are good for pretend buck teeth.

"*Por favor,*"[11] says the lady. "*¿Un foto?*"[12] pointing to her camera.

20 "*Sí.*"[13]

She's so busy taking Junior's picture, she doesn't notice me and Keeks.

"Hey, Michele, Keeks. You guys want gum?"

"But you speak English!"

"Yeah," my brother says, "we're Mericans."

25 We're Mericans, we're Mericans, and inside the awful grandmother prays.

STEPHEN CRANE

(1871–1900)

The Open Boat

1897

A Tale Intended to be after the Fact:
Being the Experience of Four Men from the Sunk Steamer Commodore

I

None of them knew the color of the sky. Their eyes glanced level, and were fastened upon the waves that swept toward them. These waves were of the hue of slate,[1] save for the tops, which were of foaming white, and all of the men knew the colors of the sea. The horizon narrowed and widened, and dipped and rose, and at all times its edge was jagged with waves that seemed thrust up in points like rocks.

Many a man ought to have a bathtub larger than the boat which here rode upon the sea. These waves were most wrongfully and barbarously abrupt and tall and each frothtop was a problem in small-boat navigation.

The cook squatted in the bottom, and looked with both eyes at the six inches of gunwale which separated him from the ocean. His sleeves were rolled over his fat forearms, and the two flaps of his unbuttoned vest dangled as he bent to bail out the boat. Often he said, "Gawd! that was a narrow clip." As he remarked it he invariably gazed eastward over the broken sea.

---

10 "Thank you." (Spanish)

11 "Please." (Spanish)

12 "A photo?" (Spanish)

13 "Yes." (Spanish)

1 Hard, bluish-grey rock.

The oiler, steering with one of the two oars in the boat, sometimes raised himself suddenly to keep clear of water that swirled in over the stern. It was a thin little oar, and it seemed often ready to snap.

5   The correspondent,[2] pulling at the other oar, watched the waves and wondered why he was there.

The injured captain, lying in the bow, was at this time buried in that profound dejection and indifference which comes, temporarily at least, to even the bravest and most enduring when, willy-nilly, the firm fails, the army loses, the ship goes down. The mind of the master of a vessel is rooted deep in the timbers of her, though he command for a day or a decade; and this captain had on him the stern impression of a scene in the grays of dawn of seven turned faces, and later a stump of a topmast with a white ball on it, that slashed to and fro at the waves, went low and lower, and down. Thereafter there was something strange in his voice. Although steady, it was deep with mourning, and of a quality beyond oration or tears.

"Keep 'er a little more south, Billie," said he.

"A little more south, sir," said the oiler in the stern.

A seat in this boat was not unlike a seat upon a bucking broncho, and by the same token a broncho is not much smaller. The craft pranced and reared and plunged like an animal. As each wave came, and she rose for it, she seemed like a horse making at a fence outrageously high. The manner of her scramble over these walls of water is a mystic thing, and, moreover, at the top of them were ordinarily these problems in white water, the foam racing down from the summit of each wave requiring a new leap, and a leap from the air. Then, after scornfully bumping a crest, she would slide and race and splash down a long incline, and arrive bobbing and nodding in front of the next menace.

10   A singular disadvantage of the sea lies in the fact that after successfully surmounting one wave you discover that there is another behind it just as important and just as nervously anxious to do something effective in the way of swamping boats. In a ten-foot dinghy[3] one can get an idea of the resources of the sea in the line of waves that is not possible to the average experience which is never at sea in a dinghy. As each slaty wall of water approached, it shut all else from the view of the men in the boat, and it was not difficult to imagine that this particular wave was the final outburst of the ocean, the last effort of the grim water. There was a terrible grace in the move of the waves, and they came in silence, save for the snarling of the crests.

In the wan light the faces of the men must have been gray. Their eyes must have glinted in strange ways as they gazed steadily astern. Viewed from a balcony, the whole thing would doubtless have been weirdly picturesque. But the men in the boat had no time to see it, and if they had

---

[2] Newspaper reporter.

[3] Small rowboat.

had leisure, there were other things to occupy their minds. The sun swung steadily up the sky, and they knew it was broad day because the color of the sea changed from slate to emerald green streaked with amber lights, and the foam was like tumbling snow. The process of the breaking day was unknown to them. They were aware only of this effect upon the color of the waves that rolled toward them.

In disjointed sentences the cook and the correspondent argued as to the difference between a life-saving station and a house of refuge. The cook had said: "There's a house of refuge just north of the Mosquito Inlet Light, and as soon as they see us they'll come off in their boat and pick us up."

"As soon as who see us?" said the correspondent.

"The crew," said the cook.

15   "Houses of refuge don't have crews," said the correspondent. "As I understand them, they are only places where clothes and grub are stored for the benefit of shipwrecked people. They don't carry crews."

"Oh, yes, they do," said the cook.

"No, they don't," said the correspondent.

"Well, we're not there yet, anyhow," said the oiler, in the stern.

"Well," said the cook, "perhaps it's not a house of refuge that I'm thinking of as being near Mosquito Inlet Light; perhaps it's a life-saving station."

20   "We're not there yet," said the oiler in the stern.

II

As the boat bounced from the top of each wave the wind tore through the hair of the hatless men, and as the craft plopped her stern down again the spray splashed past them. The crest of each of these waves was a hill, from the top of which the men surveyed for a moment a broad tumultuous expanse, shining and wind-riven. It was probably splendid, it was probably glorious, this play of the free sea, wild with lights of emerald and white and amber.

"Bully good thing it's an on-shore wind," said the cook. "If not, where would we be? Wouldn't have a show."

"That's right," said the correspondent.

The busy oiler nodded his assent.

25   Then the captain, in the bow, chuckled in a way that expressed humor, contempt, tragedy, all in one. "Do you think we've got much of a show now, boys?" said he.

Whereupon the three were silent, save for a trifle of hemming and hawing.[4] To express any particular optimism at this time they felt to be childish and stupid, but they all doubtless possessed this sense of the

---

[4] Sounds made while searching for the right words to speak.

situation in their minds. A young man thinks doggedly at such times. On the other hand, the ethics of their condition was decidedly against any open suggestion of hopelessness. So they were silent.

"Oh, well," said the captain, soothing his children, "we'll get ashore all right."

But there was that in his tone which made them think; so the oiler quoth,[5] "Yes! if this wind holds."

The cook was bailing. "Yes! if we don't catch hell in the surf."

30   Canton-flannel gulls flew near and far. Sometimes they sat down on the sea, near patches of brown seaweed that rolled over the waves with a movement like carpets on a line in a gale. The birds sat comfortably in groups, and they were envied by some in the dinghy, for the wrath of the sea was no more to them than it was to a covey of prairie chickens a thousand miles inland. Often they came very close and stared at the men with black bead-like eyes. At these times they were uncanny and sinister in their unblinking scrutiny, and the men hooted angrily at them, telling them to be gone. One came, and evidently decided to alight on the top of the captain's head. The bird flew parallel to the boat and did not circle, but made short sidelong jumps in the air in chicken-fashion. His black eyes were wistfully fixed upon the captain's head. "Ugly brute," said the oiler to the bird. "You look as if you were made with a jacknife." The cook and the correspondent swore darkly at the creature. The captain naturally wished to knock it away with the end of the heavy painter, but he did not dare do it, because anything resembling an emphatic gesture would have capsized this freighted boat; and so, with his open hand, the captain gently and carefully waved the gull away. After it had been discouraged from the pursuit the captain breathed easier on account of his hair, and others breathed easier because the bird struck their minds at this time as being somehow gruesome and ominous.

In the meantime the oiler and the correspondent rowed. And also they rowed. They sat together in the same seat, and each rowed an oar. Then the oiler took both oars; then the correspondent took both oars; then the oiler; then the correspondent. They rowed and they rowed. The very ticklish part of the business was when the time came for the reclining one in the stern to take his turn at the oars. By the very last star of truth, it is easier to steal eggs from under a hen than it was to change seats in the dinghy. First the man in the stern slid his hand along the thwart and moved with care, as if he were of Sèvres.[6] Then the man in the rowing-seat slid his hand along the other thwart. It was all done with the most extraordinary care. As the two sidled past each other, the whole party kept watchful eyes on the coming wave, and the captain cried: "Look out, now! Steady, there!"

---

[5] Said.

[6] French porcelain.

The brown mats of seaweed that appeared from time to time were like islands, bits of earth. They were travelling, apparently, neither one way nor the other. They were, to all intents, stationary. They informed the men in the boat that it was making progress slowly toward the land.

The captain, rearing cautiously in the bow after the dinghy soared on a great swell, said that he had seen the lighthouse at Mosquito Inlet. Presently the cook remarked that he had seen it. The correspondent was at the oars then, and for some reason he too wished to look at the lighthouse; but his back was toward the far shore, and the waves were important, and for some time he could not seize an opportunity to turn his head. But at last there came a wave more gentle than the others, and when at the crest of it he swiftly scoured the western horizon.

"See it?" said the captain.

35   "No," said the correspondent, slowly; "I didn't see anything."

"Look again," said the captain. He pointed. "It's exactly in that direction."

At the top of another wave the correspondent did as he was bid, and this time his eyes chanced on a small, still thing on the edge of the swaying horizon. It was precisely like the point of a pin. It took an anxious eye to find a lighthouse so tiny.

"Think we'll make it, Captain?"

"If this wind holds and the boat don't swamp,[7] we can't do much else," said the captain.

40   The little boat, lifted by each towering sea and splashed viciously by the crests, made progress that in the absence of seaweed was not apparent to those in her. She seemed just a wee thing wallowing, miraculously top up, at the mercy of five oceans. Occasionally a great spread of water, like white flames, swarmed into her.

"Bail her, cook," said the captain, serenely.

"All right, Captain," said the cheerful cook.

III

It would be difficult to describe the subtle brotherhood of men that was here established on the seas. No one said that it was so. No one mentioned it. But it dwelt in the boat, and each man felt it warm him. They were a captain, an oiler, a cook, and a correspondent, and they were friends—friends in a more curiously iron-bound degree than may be common. The hurt captain, lying against the water-jar in the bow, spoke always in a low voice and calmly; but he could never command a more ready and swiftly obedient crew than the motley three of the dinghy. It was more than a mere recognition of what was best for the common safety. There was surely in it a quality that was personal and heart-felt.

---

[7] Sink by filling with water.

And after this devotion to the commander of the boat, there was this comradeship, that the correspondent, for instance, who had been taught to be cynical of men, knew even at the time was the best experience of his life. But no one said that it was so. No one mentioned it.

"I wish we had a sail," remarked the captain. "We might try my overcoat on the end of an oar, and give you two boys a chance to rest." So the cook and the correspondent held the mast and spread wide the overcoat; the oiler steered; and the little boat made good way with her new rig. Sometimes the oiler had to scull sharply to keep a sea from breaking into the boat, but otherwise sailing was a success.

45   Meanwhile the lighthouse had been growing slowly larger. It had now almost assumed color, and appeared like a little gray shadow on the sky. The man at the oars could not be prevented from turning his head rather often to try for a glimpse of this little gray shadow.

At last, from the top of each wave, the men in the tossing boat could see land. Even as the lighthouse was an upright shadow on the sky, this land seemed but a long black shadow on the sea. It certainly was thinner than paper. "We must be about opposite New Smyrna," said the cook, who had coasted this shore often in schooners. "Captain, by the way, I believe they abandoned that life-saving station there about a year ago."

"Did they?" said the captain.

The wind slowly died away. The cook and the correspondent were not now obliged to slave in order to hold high the oar. But the waves continued their old impetuous swooping at the dinghy, and the little craft, no longer under way, struggled woundily over them. The oiler or the correspondent took the oars again.

Shipwrecks are apropos of[8] nothing. If men could only train for them and have them occur when the men had reached pink[9] condition, there would be less drowning at sea. Of the four in the dinghy none had slept any time worth mentioning for two days and two nights previous to embarking in the dinghy, and in the excitement of clambering about the deck of a foundering ship they had also forgotten to eat heartily.

50   For these reasons, and for others, neither the oiler nor the correspondent was fond of rowing at this time. The correspondent wondered ingenuously how in the name of all that was sane could there be people who thought it amusing to row a boat. It was not an amusement; it was a diabolical punishment, and even a genius of mental aberrations could never conclude that it was anything but a horror to the muscles and crime against the back. He mentioned to the boat in general how the amusement of rowing struck him, and the weary-faced oiler smiled in full sympathy. Previously to the foundering, by the way, the oiler had worked double watch in the engine-room of the ship.

---

[8] With regard to.

[9] Highest or finest.

"Take her easy now, boys," said the captain. "Don't spend yourselves. If we have to run a surf you'll need all your strength, because we'll sure have to swim for it. Take your time."

Slowly the land arose from the sea. From a black line it became a line of black and a line of white—trees and sand. Finally the captain said that he could make out a house on the shore. "That's the house of refuge, sure," said the cook. "They'll see us before long, and come out after us."

The distant lighthouse reared high. "The keeper ought to be able to make us out now, if he's looking through a glass," said the captain. "He'll notify the life-saving people."

"None of those other boats could have got ashore to give word of the wreck," said the oiler, in a low voice, "else the life-boat would be out hunting us."

55   Slowly and beautifully the land loomed out of the sea. The wind came again. It had veered from the north-east to the south-east. Finally a new sound struck the ears of the men in the boat. It was the low thunder of the surf on the shore. "We'll never be able to make the lighthouse now," said the captain. "Swing her head a little more north, Billie."

"A little more north, sir," said the oiler.

Whereupon the little boat turned her nose once more down the wind, and all but the oarsman watched the shore grow. Under the influence of this expansion doubt and direful apprehension were leaving the minds of the men. The management of the boat was still most absorbing, but it could not prevent a quiet cheerfulness. In an hour, perhaps, they would be ashore.

Their backbones had become thoroughly used to balancing in the boat, and they now rode this wild colt of a dinghy like circus men. The correspondent thought that he had been drenched to the skin, but happening to feel in the top pocket of his coat, he found therein eight cigars. Four of them were soaked with seawater; four were perfectly scatheless. After a search, somebody produced three dry matches; and thereupon the four waifs rode impudently in their little boat and, with an assurance of an impending rescue shining in their eyes, puffed at the big cigars, and judged well and ill of all men. Everybody took a drink of water.

IV

"Cook," remarked the captain, "there don't seem to be any signs of life about your house of refuge."

60   "No," replied the cook. "Funny they don't see us!"

A broad stretch of lowly coast lay before the eyes of the men. It was of low dunes topped with dark vegetation. The roar of the surf was plain, and sometimes they could see the white lip of a wave as it spun up the beach. A tiny house was blocked out black upon the sky. Southward, the slim lighthouse lifted its little gray length.

Tide, wind, and waves were swinging the dinghy northward. "Funny they don't see us," said the men.

The surf's roar was here dulled, but its tone was nevertheless thunderous and mighty. As the boat swam over the great rollers the men sat listening to this roar. "We'll swamp sure," said everybody.

It is fair to say here that there was not a life-saving station within twenty miles in either direction; but the men did not know this fact, and in consequence they made dark and opprobrious remarks concerning the eyesight of the nation's life-savers. Four scowling men sat in the dinghy and surpassed records in the invention of epithets.

65   "Funny they don't see us."

The light-heartedness of a former time had completely faded. To their sharpened minds it was easy to conjure pictures of all kinds of incompetency and blindness and, indeed, cowardice. There was the shore of the populous land, and it was bitter and bitter to them that from it came no sign.

"Well," said the captain, ultimately, "I suppose we'll have to make a try for ourselves. If we stay out here too long, we'll none of us have strength left to swim after the boat swamps."

And so the oiler, who was at the oars, turned the boat straight for the shore. There was a sudden tightening of muscles. There was some thinking.

"If we don't all get ashore," said the captain—"if we don't all get ashore, I suppose you fellows know where to send news of my finish?"

70   They then briefly exchanged some addresses and admonitions. As for the reflections of the men, there was a great deal of rage in them. Perchance they might be formulated thus: "If I am going to be drowned—if I am going to be drowned—if I am going to be drowned, why, in the name of the seven mad gods who rule the sea, was I allowed to come thus far and contemplate sand and trees? Was I brought here merely to have my nose dragged away as I was about to nibble the sacred cheese of life? It is preposterous. If this old ninny-woman, Fate, cannot do better than this, she should be deprived of the management of men's fortunes. She is an old hen who knows not her intention. If she has decided to drown me, why did she not do it in the beginning and save me all this trouble? The whole affair is absurd.—But no; she cannot mean to drown me. She dare not drown me. She cannot drown me. Not after all this work." Afterward the man might have had an impulse to shake his fist at the clouds. "Just you drown me, now, and then hear what I call you!"

The billows that came at this time were more formidable. They seemed always just about to break and roll over the little boat in a turmoil of foam. There was a preparatory and long growl in the speech of them. No mind unused to the sea would have concluded that the dinghy could ascend these sheer heights in time. The shore was still afar. The oiler was a wily surfman. "Boys," he said swiftly, "she won't live three minutes more, and we're too far out to swim. Shall I take her to sea again, Captain?"

"Yes; go ahead!" said the captain.

This oiler, by a series of quick miracles and fast and steady oarsmanship, turned the boat in the middle of the surf and took her safely to sea again.

There was a considerable silence as the boat bumped over the furrowed sea to deeper water. Then somebody in gloom spoke: "Well, anyhow, they must have seen us from the shore by now."

75   The gulls went in slanting flight up the wind toward the gray, desolate east. A squall, marked by dinghy clouds and clouds brick-red like smoke from a burning building, appeared from the south-east.

"What do you think of those life-saving people? Ain't they peaches?"

"Funny they haven't seen us."

"Maybe they think we're out here for sport! Maybe they think we're fishin'. Maybe they think we're damned fools."

It was a long afternoon. A changed tide tried to force them southward, but wind and wave said northward. Far ahead, where coast-line, sea, and sky formed their mighty angle, there were little dots which seemed to indicate a city on the shore.

80   "St. Augustine?"

The captain shook his head. "Too near Mosquito Inlet."

And the oiler rowed, and then the correspondent rowed; then the oiler rowed. It was a weary business. The human back can become the seat of more aches and pains than are registered in books for the composite anatomy of a regiment. It is a limited area, but it can become the theatre of innumerable muscular conflicts, tangles, wrenches, knots, and other comforts.

"Did you ever like to row, Billie?" asked the correspondent.

"No," said the oiler; "hang it!"

85   When one exchanged the rowing-seat for a place in the bottom of the boat, he suffered a bodily depression that caused him to be careless of everything save an obligation to wiggle one finger. There was cold sea-water swashing to and fro in the boat, and he lay in it. His head, pillowed on a thwart, was within an inch of the swirl of a wave-crest, and sometimes a particularly obstreperous sea came inboard and drenched him once more. But these matters did not annoy him. It is almost certain that if the boat had capsized he would have tumbled comfortably upon the ocean as if he felt sure that it was a great soft mattress.

"Look! There's a man on the shore!"

"Where?"

"There! See 'im?"

"Yes, sure! He's walking along."

90   "Now he's stopped. Look! He's facing us!"

"He's waving at us!"

"So he is! By thunder!"

"Ah, now we're all right! Now we're all right! There'll be a boat out here for us in half an hour."

"He's going on. He's running. He's going up to that house there."

95   The remote beach seemed lower than the sea, and it required a searching glance to discern the little black figure. The captain saw a floating stick, and they rowed to it. A bath towel was by some weird chance in the

boat, and, tying this on the stick, the captain waved it. The oarsman did not dare turn his head, so he was obliged to ask questions.

"What's he doing now?"

"He's standing still again. He's looking, I think.—There he goes again—toward the house.—Now he's stopped again."

"Is he waving at us?"

"No, not now; he was, though."

"Look! There comes another man!"

"He's running."

"Look at him go, would you!"

"Why, he's on a bicycle. Now he's met the other man. They're both waving at us. Look!"

"There comes something up the beach."

"What the devil is that thing?"

"Why, it looks like a boat."

"Why, certainly, it's a boat."

"No; it's on wheels."

"Yes, so it is. Well, that must be the life-boat. They drag them along shore on a wagon."

"That's the life-boat, sure."

"No, by God, it's—it's an omnibus."

"I tell you it's a life-boat."

"It is not! It's an omnibus. I can see it plain. See? One of the these big hotel omnibuses."

"By thunder, you're right. It's an omnibus, sure as fate. What do you suppose they are doing with an omnibus? Maybe they are going around collecting the life-crew, hey?"

"That's it, likely. Look! There's a fellow waving a little black flag. He's standing on the steps of the omnibus. There come those other two fellows. Now they're all talking together. Look at the fellow with the flag. Maybe he ain't waving it!"

"That ain't a flag, is it? That's his coat. Why, certainly, that's his coat."

"So it is; it's his coat. He's taken it off and is waving it around his head. But would you look at him swing it!"

"Oh, say, there isn't any life-saving station there. That's just a winter-resort hotel omnibus that has brought over some of the boarders to see us drown."

"What's that idiot with the coat mean? What's he signalling, anyhow?"

"It looks as if he were trying to tell us to go north. There must be a life-saving station up there."

"No; he thinks we're fishing. Just giving us a merry hand. See? Ah, there, Willie!"

"Well, I wish I could make something out of those signals. What do you suppose he means?"

"He don't mean anything; he's just playing."

"Well, if he'd just signal us to try the surf again, or to go to sea and wait, or go north, or go south, or go to hell, there would be some reason in it. But look at him! He just stands there and keeps his coat revolving like a wheel. The ass!"

125   "There come more people."

"Now there's quite a mob. Look! Isn't that a boat?"

"Where? Oh, I see where you mean. No, that's no boat."

"That fellow is still waving his coat."

"He must think we like to see him do that. Why don't he quit it? It don't mean anything."

130   "I don't know. I think he is trying to make us go north. It must be that there's a life-saving station there somewhere."

"Say, he ain't tired yet. Look at 'im wave!"

"Wonder how long he can keep that up. He's been revolving his coat ever since he caught sight of us. He's an idiot. Why aren't they getting men to bring a boat out? A fishing boat—one of those big yawls—could come out here all right. Why don't he do something?"

"Oh, it's all right now."

"They'll have a boat out here for us in less than no time, now that they've seen us."

135   A faint yellow tone came into the sky over the low land. The shadows on the sea slowly deepened. The wind bore coldness with it, and the men began to shiver.

"Holy smoke!" said one, allowing his voice to express his impious mood, "If we keep on monkeying out here! If we've got to flounder out here all night!"

"Oh, we'll never have to stay here all night! Don't you worry. They've seen us now, and it won't be long before they'll come chasing out after us."

The shore grew dusky. The man waving a coat blended gradually into this gloom, and it swallowed in the same manner the omnibus and the group of people. The spray, when it dashed uproariously over the side, made the voyagers shrink and swear like men who were being branded.

"I'd like to catch the chump who waved the coat. I feel like socking him one, just for luck."

140   "Why? What did he do?"

"Oh, nothing, but then he seemed so damned cheerful."

In the meantime the oiler rowed, and then the correspondent rowed, and then the oiler rowed. Gray-faced and bowed forward, they mechanically, turn by turn, plied the leaden oars. The form of the lighthouse had vanished from the southern horizon, but finally a pale star appeared, just lifting from the sea. The streaked saffron[10] in the west passed before the all-merging darkness, and the sea to the east was black. The land had vanished, and was expressed only by the low and drear thunder of the surf.

---

[10] Orange-yellow.

"If I am going to be drowned—if I am going to be drowned—if I am going to be drowned, why, in the name of the seven gods who rule the sea, was I allowed to come thus far and contemplate sand and trees? Was I brought here merely to have my nose dragged away as I was about to nibble the sacred cheese of life?"

The patient captain, drooped over the water-jar, was sometimes obliged to speak to the oarsman.

145   "Keep her head up! Keep her head up!"

"Keep her head up, sir." The voices were weary and low.

This was surely a quiet evening. All save the oarsman lay heavily and listlessly in the boat's bottom. As for him, his eyes were just capable of noting the tall black waves that swept forward in a most sinister silence, save for an occasional subdued growl of a crest.

The cook's head was on a thwart, and he looked without interest at the water under his nose. He was deep in other scenes. Finally he spoke. "Billie," he murmured, dreamfully, "what kind of pie do you like best?"

V

"Pie!" said the oiler and the correspondent, agitatedly. "Don't talk about those things, blast you!"

150   "Well," said the cook, "I was just thinking about ham sandwiches, and—"

A night on the sea in an open boat is a long night. As darkness settled finally, the shine of the light, lifting from the sea in the south, changed to full gold. On the northern horizon a new light appeared, a small bluish gleam on the edge of the waters. These two lights were the furniture of the world. Otherwise there was nothing but waves.

Two men huddled in the stern, and distances were so magnificent in the dinghy that the rower was enabled to keep his feet partly warm by thrusting them under his companions. Their legs indeed extended far under the rowingseat until they touched the feet of the captain forward. Sometimes, despite the efforts of the tired oarsman, a wave came piling into the boat, an icy wave of the night, and the chilling water soaked them anew. They would twist their bodies for a moment and groan, and sleep the dead sleep once more, while the water in the boat gurgled about them as the craft rocked.

The plan of the oiler and the correspondent was for one to row until he lost the ability, and then arouse the other from his sea-water couch in the bottom of the boat.

The oiler plied the oars until his head drooped forward and the overpowering sleep blinded him; and he rowed yet afterward. Then he touched a man in the bottom of the boat, and called his name. "Will you spell[11] me for a little while?" he said meekly.

---

[11] Relieve.

155   "Sure, Billie," said the correspondent, awaking and dragging himself to a sitting position. They exchanged places carefully, and the oiler, cuddling down in the sea-water at the cook's side, seemed to go to sleep instantly.

The particular violence of the sea had ceased. The waves came without snarling. The obligation of the man at the oars was to keep the boat headed so that the tilt of the roller would not capsize her, and to preserve her from filling when the crests rushed past. The black waves were silent and hard to be seen in the darkness. Often one was almost upon the boat before the oarsman was aware.

In a low voice the correspondent addressed the captain. He was not sure that the captain was awake, although this iron man seemed to be always awake. "Captain, shall I keep her making for that light north, sir?"

The same steady voice answered him. "Yes. Keep it about two points off the port bow."

The cook had tied a life-belt around himself in order to get even the warmth which this clumsy cork contrivance could donate, and he seemed almost stovelike when a rower, whose teeth invariably chattered wildly as soon as he ceased his labor, dropped down to sleep.

160   The correspondent, as he rowed, looked down at the two men sleeping underfoot. The cook's arm was around the oiler's shoulders, and, with their fragmentary clothing and haggard faces, they were the babes of the sea—a grotesque rendering of the old babes in the wood.

Later he must have grown stupid at his work, for suddenly there was a growling of water, and a crest came with a roar and a swash into the boat, and it was a wonder that it did not set the cook afloat in his life-belt. The cook continued to sleep, but the oiler sat up, blinking his eyes and shaking with the new cold.

"Oh, I'm awful sorry, Billie," said the correspondent, contritely.

"That's all right, old boy," said the oiler, and lay down again and was asleep.

Presently it seemed that even the captain dozed, and the correspondent thought that he was the one man afloat on all the oceans. The wind had a voice as it came over the waves, and it was sadder than the end.

165   There was a long, loud swishing astern of the boat, and a gleaming trail of phosphorescence, like blue flame, was furrowed on the black waters. It might have been made by a monstrous knife.

Then there came a stillness, while the correspondent breathed with open mouth and looked at the sea.

Suddenly there was another swish and another long flash of bluish light, and this time it was alongside the boat, and might almost have been reached with an oar. The correspondent saw an enormous fin speed like a shadow through the water, hurling the crystalline spray and leaving the long glowing trail.

The correspondent looked over his shoulder at the captain. His face was hidden, and he seemed to be asleep. He looked at the babes of the sea.

They certainly were asleep. So, being bereft of sympathy, he leaned a little way to one side and swore softly into the sea.

But the thing did not then leave the vicinity of the boat. Ahead or astern on one side or the other, at intervals long or short, fled the long sparkling streak and there was to be heard the *whirroo* of the dark fin. The speed and power of the thing was greatly to be admired. It cut the water like a gigantic and keen projectile.

170   The presence of this biding thing did not affect the man with the same horror that it would if he had been a picnicker. He simply looked at the sea dully and swore in an undertone.

Nevertheless, it is true that he did not wish to be alone with the thing. He wished one of his companions to awake by chance and keep him company with it. But the company hung motionless over the water-jar, and the oiler and the cook in the bottom of the boat were plunged in slumber.

VI

"If I am going to be drowned—if I am going to be drowned—if I am going to be drowned, why, in the name of the seven mad gods who rule the sea, was I allowed to come thus far and contemplate sand and trees?"

During this dismal night, it may be remarked that a man would conclude that it was really the intention of the seven mad gods to drown him, despite the abominable injustice of it. For it was certainly an abominable injustice to drown a man who had worked so hard, so hard. The man felt it would be a crime most unnatural. Other people had drowned at sea since galleys swarmed with painted sails, but still—

When it occurs to a man that nature does not regard him as important, and that she feels she would not maim the universe by disposing of him, he at first wishes to throw bricks at the temple, and he hates deeply the fact that there are no bricks and no temples. Any visible expression of nature would surely be pelleted with his jeers.

175   Then, if there be no tangible thing to hoot, he feels, perhaps, the desire to confront a personification and indulge in pleas, bowed to one knee, and with hands supplicant, saying, "Yes, but I love myself."

A high cold star on a winter's night is the word he feels that she says to him. Thereafter he knows the pathos[12] of his situation.

The men in the dinghy had not discussed these matters, but each had, no doubt, reflected upon them in silence and according to his mind. There was seldom any expression upon their faces save the general one of complete weariness. Speech was devoted to the business of the boat.

To chime the notes of his emotion, a verse mysteriously entered the correspondent's head. He had even forgotten that he had forgotten this verse, but it suddenly was in his mind.

---

[12] Pity, sorrow, compassion.

A soldier of the Legion lay dying in Algiers;
There was lack of woman's nursing, there was dearth of woman's tears;
But a comrade stood beside him, and he took that comrade's hand,
And he said, "I never more shall see my own, my native land."[13]

In his childhood the correspondent had been made acquainted with the fact that a soldier of the Legion lay dying in Algiers, but he had never regarded the fact as important. Myriads of his school-fellows had informed him of the soldier's plight, but the dinning had naturally ended by making him perfectly indifferent. He had never considered it his affair that a soldier of the Legion lay dying in Algiers, nor had it appeared to him as a matter for sorrow. It was less to him than the breaking of a pencil's point.

180   Now, however, it quaintly came to him as a human, living thing. It was no longer merely a picture of a few throes in the breast of a poet, meanwhile drinking tea and warming his feet at the grate; it was an actuality—stern, mournful, and fine.

The correspondent plainly saw the soldier. He lay on the sand with his feet out straight and still. While his pale left hand was upon his chest in an attempt to thwart the going of his life, the blood came between his fingers. In the far Algerian distance, a city of low square forms was set against a sky that was faint with the last sunset hues. The correspondent, plying the oars and dreaming of the slow and slower movements of the lips of the soldier, was moved by a profound and perfectly impersonal comprehension. He was sorry for the soldier of the Legion who lay dying in Algiers.

The thing which had followed the boat and waited had evidently grown bored at the delay. There was no longer to be heard the slash of the cutwater, and there was no longer the flame of the long trail. The light in the north still glimmered, but it was apparently no nearer to the boat. Sometimes the boom of the surf rang in the correspondent's ears, and he turned the craft seaward then and rowed harder. Southward, some one had evidently built a watch-fire on the beach. It was too low and too far to be seen, but it made a shimmering, roseate reflection upon the bluff in back of it, and this could be discerned from the boat. The wind came stronger, and sometimes a wave suddenly raged out like a mountain cat, and there was to be seen the sheen and sparkle of a broken crest.

The captain, in the bow, moved on his water-jar and sat erect. "Pretty long night," he observed to the correspondent. He looked at the shore. "Those life-saving people take their time."

"Did you see that shark playing around?"

185   "Yes, I saw him. He was a big fellow, all right."

"Wish I had known you were awake."

Later the correspondent spoke into the bottom of the boat.

"Billie!" There was a slow and gradual disentanglement.

"Billie, will you spell me?"

---

[13] Lines from "Bingen on the Rhine," a Victorian ballad about the death of a German soldier in the French Foreign Legion.

190 "Sure," said the oiler.

As soon as the correspondent touched the cold, comfortable sea-water in the bottom of the boat and had huddled close to the cook's life-belt he was deep in sleep, despite the fact that his teeth played all the popular airs. This sleep was so good to him that it was but a moment before he heard a voice call his name in a tone that demonstrated the last stages of exhaustion. "Will you spell me?"

"Sure, Billie."

The light in the north had mysteriously vanished, but the correspondent took his course from the wide-awake captain.

Later in the night they took the boat farther out to sea, and the captain directed the cook to take one oar at the stern and keep the boat facing the seas. He was to call out if he should hear the thunder of the surf. This plan enabled the oiler and the correspondent to get respite together. "We'll give those boys a chance to get into shape again," said the captain. They curled down and, after a few preliminary chatterings and trembles, slept once more the dead sleep. Neither knew they had bequeathed to the cook the company of another shark, or perhaps the same shark.

195 As the boat caroused on the waves, spray occasionally bumped over the side and gave them a fresh soaking, but this had no power to break their repose. The ominous slash of the wind and the water affected them as it would have affected mummies.

"Boys," said the cook, with the notes of every reluctance in his voice, "she drifted in pretty close. I guess one of you had better take her to sea again." The correspondent, aroused, heard the crash of the toppled crests.

As he was rowing, the captain gave him some whisky-and-water, and this steadied the chills out of him. "If I ever get ashore and anybody shows me even a photograph of an oar—"

At last there was a short conversation.

"Billie!—Billie, will you spell me?"

200 "Sure," said the oiler.

VII

When the correspondent again opened his eyes, the sea and sky were each the gray hue of the dawning. Later, carmine[14] and gold was painted upon the waters. The morning appeared finally, in its splendor, with a sky of pure blue, and the sunlight flamed on the tips of the waves.

On the distant dunes were set many little black cottages, and a tall white windmill reared above them. No man, nor dog, nor bicycle appeared on the beach. The cottages might have formed a deserted village.

The voyagers scanned the shore. A conference was held in the boat. "Well," said the captain, "if no help is coming, we might better try a run through the surf right away. If we stay out here much longer we will be too

---

[14] Purplish-red.

weak to do anything for ourselves at all." The others silently acquiesced in this reasoning. The boat was headed for the beach. The correspondent wondered if none ever ascended the tall wind-tower, and if they never looked seaward. This tower was a giant, standing with its back to the plight of the ants. It represented in a degree, to the correspondent, the serenity of nature amid the struggles of the individual—nature in the wind, and nature in the vision of men. She did not seem cruel to him then, nor beneficent, nor treacherous, nor wise. But she was indifferent, flatly indifferent. It is, perhaps, plausible that a man in this situation, impressed with the unconcern of the universe, should see the innumerable flaws of life, and have them taste wickedly in his mind, and wish for another chance. A distinction between right and wrong seems absurdly clear to him, then, in this new ignorance of the grave-edge, and he understands that if he were given another opportunity he would mend his conduct and his words, and be better and brighter during an introduction or at a tea.

"Now, boys," said the captain, "she is going to swamp sure. All we can do is to work her in as far as possible, and then when she swamps, pile out and scramble for the beach. Keep cool now, and don't jump until she swamps sure."

205   The oiler took the oars. Over his shoulders he scanned the surf. "Captain," he said, "I think I'd better bring her about and keep her head-on to the seas and back her in."

"All right, Billie," said the captain. "Back her in." The oiler swung the boat then, and, seated in the stern, the cook and the correspondent were obliged to look over their shoulders to contemplate the lonely and indifferent shore.

The monstrous inshore rollers heaved the boat high until the men were again enabled to see the white sheets of water scudding up the slanted beach. "We won't get in very close," said the captain. Each time a man could wrest his attention from the rollers, he turned his glance toward the shore, and in the expression of the eyes during this contemplation there was a singular quality. The correspondent, observing the others, knew that they were not afraid, but the full meaning of their glances was shrouded.

As for himself, he was too tired to grapple fundamentally with the fact. He tried to coerce his mind into thinking of it, but the mind was dominated at this time by the muscles, and the muscles said they did not care. It merely occurred to him that if he should drown it would be a shame.

There were no hurried words, no pallor, no plain agitation. The men simply looked at the shore. "Now, remember to get well clear of the boat when you jump," said the captain.

210   Seaward the crest of a roller suddenly fell with a thunderous crash, and the long white comber[15] came roaring down upon the boat.

---

[15] Large wave.

"Steady now," said the captain. The men were silent. They turned their eyes from the shore to the comber and waited. The boat slid up the incline, leaped at the furious top, bounced over it, and swung down the long back of the wave. Some water had been shipped, and the cook bailed it out.

But the next crest crashed also. The tumbling, boiling flood of white water caught the boat and whirled it almost perpendicular. Water swarmed in from all sides. The correspondent had his hands on the gunwale[16] at this time, and when the water entered at that place he swiftly withdrew his fingers, as if he objected to wetting them.

The little boat, drunken with this weight of water, reeled and snuggled deeper into the sea.

"Bail her out, cook! Bail her out!" said the captain.

215   "All right, Captain," said the cook.

"Now, boys, the next one will do for us sure," said the oiler, "Mind to jump clear of the boat."

The third wave moved forward, huge, furious, implacable. It fairly swallowed the dinghy, and almost simultaneously the men tumbled into the sea. A piece of life-belt had lain in the bottom of the boat, and as the correspondent went overboard he held this to his chest with his left hand.

The January water was icy, and he reflected immediately that it was colder than he had expected to find it off the coast of Florida. This appeared to his dazed mind as a fact important enough to be noted at the time. The coldness of the water was sad; it was tragic. This fact was somehow mixed and confused with his opinion of his own situation, so that it seemed almost a proper reason for tears. The water was cold.

When he came to the surface he was conscious of little but the noisy water. Afterward he saw his companions in the sea. The oiler was ahead in the race. He was swimming strongly and rapidly. Off to the correspondent's left, the cook's great white and corked back bulged out of the water; and in the rear the captain was hanging with his one good hand to the keel of the overturned dinghy.

220   There is a certain immovable quality to a shore, and the correspondent wondered at it amid the confusion of the sea.

It seemed also very attractive; but the correspondent knew that it was a long journey, and he paddled leisurely. The piece of life-preserver lay under him, and sometimes he whirled down the incline of a wave as if he were on a handsled.

But finally he arrived at a place in the sea where travel was beset with difficulty. He did not pause swimming to inquire what manner of current had caught him, but there his progress ceased. The shore was set before him like a bit of scenery on a stage, and he looked at it and understood with his eyes each detail of it.

---

[16] The upper edge of a boat's side.

As the cook passed, much farther to the left, the captain was calling to him. "Turn over on your back, cook! Turn over on your back and use the oar."

"All right, sir." The cook turned on his back, and, paddling with an oar went ahead as if he were a canoe.

225   Presently the boat also passed to the left of the correspondent, with the captain clinging with one hand to the keel. He would have appeared like a man raising himself to look over a board fence if it were not for the extraordinary gymnastics of the boat. The correspondent marvelled that the captain could still hold to it.

They passed on nearer to shore—the oiler, the cook, the captain—and following them went the water-jar, bouncing gaily over the seas.

The correspondent remained in the grip of this strange new enemy—a current. The shore, with its white slope of sand and its green bluff topped with little silent cottages, was spread like a picture before him. It was very near to him then, but he was impressed as one who, in a gallery, looks at a scene from Brittany or Algiers.

He thought: "I am going to drown? Can it be possible? Can it be possible? Can it be possible?" Perhaps an individual must consider his own death to be the final phenomenon of nature.

But later a wave perhaps whirled him out of this small deadly current, for he found suddenly that he could again make progress toward the shore. Later still he was aware that the captain, clinging with one hand to the keel of the dinghy, had his face turned away from the shore and toward him, and was calling his name. "Come to the boat! Come to the boat!"

230   In his struggle to reach the captain and the boat, he reflected that when one gets properly wearied drowning must really be a comfortable arrangement—a cessation of hostilities accompanied by a large degree of relief; and he was glad of it, for the main thing in his mind for some moments had been horror of the temporary agony. He did not wish to be hurt.

Presently he saw a man running along the shore. He was undressing with most remarkable speed. Coat, trousers, shirt, everything flew magically off him.

"Come to the boat!" called the captain.

"All right, Captain." As the correspondent paddled, he saw the captain let himself down to bottom and leave the boat. Then the correspondent performed his one little marvel of the voyage. A large wave caught him and flung him with ease and supreme speed completely over the boat and far beyond it. It struck him even then as an event in gymnastics and a true miracle of the sea. An overturned boat in the surf is not a plaything to a swimming man.

The correspondent arrived in water that reached only to his waist, but his condition did not enable him to stand for more than a moment. Each wave knocked him into a heap, and the undertow pulled at him.

235   Then he saw the man who had been running and undressing, and undressing and running, come bounding into the water. He dragged ashore

the cook, and then waded toward the captain; but the captain waved him away and sent him to the correspondent. He was naked—naked as a tree in winter; but a halo was about his head, and he shone like a saint. He gave a strong pull, and a long drag, and a bully heave at the correspondent's hand. The correspondent, schooled in the minor formulae, said, "Thanks, old man." But suddenly the man cried, "What's that?" He pointed a swift finger. The correspondent said, "Go."

In the shallows, face downward, lay the oiler. His forehead touched sand that was periodically, between each wave, clear of the sea.

The correspondent did not know all that transpired afterward. When he achieved safe ground he fell, striking the sand with each particular part of his body. It was as if he had dropped from a roof, but the thud was grateful to him.

It seems that instantly the beach was populated with men with blankets, clothes, and flasks, and women with coffee-pots and all the remedies sacred to their minds. The welcome of the land to the men from the sea was warm and generous; but a still and dripping shape was carried slowly up the beach, and the land's welcome for it could only be the different and sinister hospitality of the grave.

When it came night, the white waves paced to and fro in the moonlight, and the wind brought the sound of the great sea's voice to the men on the shore, and they felt that they could then be interpreters.

L O U I S E   E R D R I C H

(1954–   )

Fleur

(1986)

The first time she drowned in the cold and glassy waters of Lake Turcot, Fleur Pillager was only a girl. Two men saw the boat tip, saw her struggle in the waves. They rowed over to the place she went down, and jumped in. When they dragged her over the gunwales, she was cold to the touch and stiff, so they slapped her face, shook her by the heels, worked her arms back and forth, and pounded her back until she coughed up lake water. She shivered all over like a dog, then took a breath. But it wasn't long afterward that those two men disappeared. The first wandered off, and the other, Jean Hat, got himself run over by a cart.

It went to show, my grandma said. It figured to her, all right. By saving Fleur Pillager, those two men had lost themselves.

The next time she fell in the lake, Fleur Pillager was twenty years old and no one touched her. She washed onshore, her skin a dull dead gray, but when George Many Women bent to look closer, he saw her chest move. Then her eyes spun open, sharp black riprock, and she looked at him.

"You'll take my place," she hissed. Everybody scattered and left her there, so no one knows how she dragged herself home. Soon after that we noticed Many Women changed, grew afraid, wouldn't leave his house, and would not be forced to go near water. For his caution, he lived until the day that his sons brought him a new tin bathtub. Then the first time he used the tub he slipped, got knocked out, and breathed water while his wife stood in the other room frying breakfast.

Men stayed clear of Fleur Pillager after the second drowning. Even though she was good-looking, nobody dared to court her because it was clear that Misshepeshu, the waterman, the monster, wanted her for himself. He's a devil, that one, love-hungry with desire and maddened for the touch of young girls, the strong and daring especially, the ones like Fleur.

5   Our mothers warn us that we'll think he's handsome, for he appears with green eyes, copper skin, a mouth tender as a child's. But if you fall into his arms, he sprouts horns, fangs, claws, fins. His feet are joined as one and his skin, brass scales, rings to the touch. You're fascinated, cannot move. He casts a shell necklace at your feet, weeps gleaming chips that harden into mica on your breasts. He holds you under. Then he takes the body of a lion or a fat brown worm. He's made of gold. He's made of beach moss. He's a thing of dry foam, a thing of death by drowning, the death a Chippewa cannot survive.

Unless you are Fleur Pillager. We all knew she couldn't swim. After the first time, we thought she'd never go back to Lake Turcot. We thought she'd keep to herself, live quiet, stop killing men off by drowning in the lake. After the first time, we thought she'd keep the good ways. But then, after the second drowning, we knew that we were dealing with something much more serious. She was haywire, out of control. She messed with evil, laughed at the old women's advice, and dressed like a man. She got herself into some half-forgotten medicine, studied ways we shouldn't talk about. Some say she kept the finger of a child in her pocket and a powder of unborn rabbits in a leather thong around her neck. She laid the heart of an owl on her tongue so she could see at night, and went out, hunting, not even in her own body. We know for sure because the next morning, in the snow or dust, we followed the tracks of her bare feet and saw where they changed, where the claws sprang out, the pad broadened and pressed into the dirt. By night we heard her chuffing cough, the bear cough. By day her silence and the wide grin she threw to bring down our guard made us frightened. Some thought that Fleur Pillager should be driven off the reservation, but not a single person who spoke like this had the nerve. And finally, when people were just about to get together and throw her out, she left on her own and didn't come back all summer. That's what this story is about.

During that summer, when she lived a few miles south in Argus, things happened. She almost destroyed that town.

When she got down to Argus in the year of 1920, it was just a small grid of six streets on either side of the railroad depot. There were two elevators, one central, the other a few miles west. Two stores competed for the trade of the three hundred citizens, and three churches quarreled with one another for their souls. There was a frame building for Lutherans, a heavy brick one for Episcopalians, and a long narrow shingled Catholic church. This last had a tall slender steeple, twice as high as any building or tree.

No doubt, across the low, flat wheat, watching from the road as she came near Argus on foot, Fleur saw that steeple rise, a shadow thin as a needle. Maybe in that raw space it drew her the way a lone tree draws lightning. Maybe, in the end, the Catholics are to blame. For if she hadn't seen that sign of pride, that slim prayer, that marker, maybe she would have kept walking.

10   But Fleur Pillager turned, and the first place she went once she came into town was to the back door of the priest's residence attached to the landmark church. She didn't go there for a handout, although she got that, but to ask for work. She got that too, or the town got her. It's hard to tell which came out worse, her or the men or the town, although the upshot of it all was that Fleur lived.

The four men who worked at the butcher's had carved up about a thousand carcasses between them, maybe half of that steers and the other half pigs, sheep, and game animals like deer, elk, and bear. That's not even mentioning the chickens, which were beyond counting. Pete Kozka owned the place, and employed Lily Veddar, Tor Grunewald, and my stepfather, Dutch James, who had brought my mother down from the reservation the year before she disappointed him by dying. Dutch took me out of school to take her place. I kept house half the time and worked the other in the butcher shop, sweeping floors, putting sawdust down, running a hambone across the street to a customer's bean pot or a package of sausage to the corner. I was a good one to have around because until they needed me, I was invisible. I blended into the stained brown walls, a skinny, big-nosed girl with staring eyes. Because I could fade into a corner or squeeze beneath a shelf, I knew everything, what the men said when no one was around, and what they did to Fleur.

Kozka's Meats served farmers for a fifty-mile area, both to slaughter, for it had a stock pen and chute, and to cure the meat by smoking it or spicing it in sausage. The storage locker was a marvel, made of many thicknesses of brick, earth insulation, and Minnesota timber, lined inside with sawdust and vast blocks of ice cut from Lake Turcot, hauled down from home each winter by horse and sledge.

A ramshackle board building, part slaughterhouse, part store, was fixed to the low, thick square of the lockers. That's where Fleur worked. Kozka hired her for her strength. She could lift a haunch or carry a pole of sausages without stumbling, and she soon learned cutting from Pete's wife, a string-thin blonde who chain-smoked and handled the razor-sharp knives with nerveless precision, slicing close to her stained fingers. Fleur and Fritzie Kozka worked afternoons, wrapping their cuts in paper, and Fleur hauled the packages to the lockers. The meat was left outside the heavy oak doors that were only opened at 5:00 each afternoon, before the men ate supper.

Sometimes Dutch, Tor, and Lily ate at the lockers, and when they did I stayed too, cleaned floors, restoked the fires in the front smokehouses, while the men sat around the squat cast-iron stove spearing slats of herring onto hardtack bread. They played long games of poker or cribbage on a board made from the planed end of a salt crate. They talked and I listened, although there wasn't much to hear since almost nothing ever happened in Argus. Tor was married, Dutch had lost my mother, and Lily read circulars. They mainly discussed about the auctions to come, equipment, or women.

15   Every so often, Pete Kozka came out front to make a whist, leaving Fritzie to smoke cigarettes and fry raised doughnuts in the back room. He sat and played a few rounds but kept his thoughts to himself. Fritzie did not tolerate him talking behind her back, and the one book he read was the New Testament. If he said something, it concerned weather or a surplus of sheep stomachs, a ham that smoked green or the markets for corn and wheat. He had a good-luck talisman, the opal-white lens of a cow's eye. Playing cards, he rubbed it between his fingers. That soft sound and the slap of cards was about the only conversation.

Fleur finally gave them a subject.

Her cheeks were wide and flat, her hands large, chapped, muscular. Fleur's shoulders were broad as beams, her hips fishlike, slippery, narrow. An old green dress clung to her waist, worn thin where she sat. Her braids were thick like the tails of animals, and swung against her when she moved, deliberately, slowly in her work, held in and half-tamed, but only half. I could tell, but the others never saw. They never looked into her sly brown eyes or noticed her teeth, strong and curved and very white. Her legs were bare, and since she padded around in beadwork moccasins they never saw that her fifth toes were missing. They never knew she'd drowned. They were blinded, they were stupid, they only saw her in the flesh.

And yet it wasn't just that she was a Chippewa, or even that she was a woman, it wasn't that she was good-looking or even that she was alone that made their brains hum. It was how she played cards.

Women didn't usually play with men, so the evening that Fleur drew a chair up to the men's table without being so much as asked, there was a shock of surprise.

20   "What's this," said Lily. He was fat, with a snake's cold pale eyes and precious skin, smooth and lily-white, which is how he got his name. Lily had a dog, a stumpy mean little bull of a thing with a belly drum-tight from eating pork rinds. The dog liked to play cards just like Lily, and straddled his barrel thighs through games of stud, rum poker, vingt-un.[1]

---

[1] Vingt-un—twenty-one, a card game.

The dog snapped at Fleur's arm that first night, but cringed back, its snarl frozen, when she took her place.

"I thought," she said, her voice soft and stroking, "you might deal me in."

There was a space between the heavy bin of spiced flour and the wall where I just fit. I hunkered down there, kept my eyes open, saw her black hair swing over the chair, her feet solid on the wood floor. I couldn't see up on the table where the cards slapped down, so after they were deep in their game I raised myself up in the shadows, and crouched on a sill of wood.

I watched Fleur's hands stack and ruffle, divide the cards, spill them to each player in a blur, rake them up and shuffle again. Tor, short and scrappy, shut one eye and squinted the other at Fleur. Dutch screwed his lips around a wet cigar.

"Gotta see a man," he mumbled, getting up to go out back to the privy. The others broke, put their cards down, and Fleur sat alone in the lamplight that glowed in a sheen across the push of her breasts. I watched her closely, then she paid me a beam of notice for the first time. She turned, looked straight at me, and grinned the white wolf grin a Pillager turns on its victims, except that she wasn't after me.

25   "Pauline there," she said, "how much money you got?"

We'd all been paid for the week that day. Eight cents was in my pocket.

"Stake me," she said, holding out her long fingers. I put the coins in her palm and then I melted back to nothing, part of the walls and tables. It was a long time before I understood that the men would not have seen me no matter what I did, how I moved. I wasn't anything like Fleur. My dress hung loose and my back was already curved, an old woman's. Work had roughened me, reading made my eyes sore, caring for my mother before she died had hardened my face. I was not much to look at, so they never saw me.

When the men came back and sat around the table, they had drawn together. They shot each other small glances, stuck their tongues in their cheeks, burst out laughing at odd moments, to rattle Fleur. But she never minded. They played their vingt-un, staying even as Fleur slowly gained. Those pennies I had given her drew nickels and attracted dimes until there was a small pile in front of her.

Then she hooked them with five-card draw, nothing wild. She dealt, discarded, drew, and then she sighed and her cards gave a little shiver. Tor's eye gleamed, and Dutch straightened in his seat.

30   "I'll pay to see that hand," said Lily Veddar.

Fleur showed, and she had nothing there, nothing at all.

Tor's thin smile cracked open, and he threw his hand in too.

"Well, we know one thing," he said, leaning back in his chair, "the squaw can't bluff."

With that I lowered myself into a mound of swept sawdust and slept. I woke up during the night, but none of them had moved yet, so I couldn't either. Still later, the men must have gone out again, or Fritzie come out to break the game, because I was lifted, soothed, cradled in a woman's arms and rocked so quiet that I kept my eyes shut while Fleur rolled me into a closet of grimy ledgers, oiled paper, balls of string, and thick files that fit beneath me like a mattress.

35   The game went on after work the next evening. I got my eight cents back five times over, and Fleur kept the rest of the dollar she'd won for a stake. This time they didn't play so late, but they played regular, and then kept going at it night after night. They played poker now, or variations, for one week straight, and each time Fleur won exactly one dollar, no more and no less, too consistent for luck.

By this time, Lily and the other men were so lit with suspense that they got Pete to join the game with them. They concentrated, the fat dog sitting tense in Lily Veddar's lap, Tor suspicious, Dutch stroking his huge square brow, Pete steady. It wasn't that Fleur won that hooked them in so, because she lost hands too. It was rather that she never had a freak hand or even anything above a straight. She only took on her low cards, which didn't sit right. By chance, Fleur should have gotten a full or flush by now. The irritating thing was she beat with pairs and never bluffed, because she couldn't, and still she ended up each night with exactly one dollar. Lily couldn't believe, first of all, that a woman could be smart enough to play cards, but even if she was, that she would then be stupid enough to cheat for a dollar a night. By day I watched him turn the problem over, his hard white face dull, small fingers probing at his knuckles, until he finally thought he had Fleur figured out as a bit-time player, caution her game. Raising the stakes would throw her.

More than anything now, he wanted Fleur to come away with something but a dollar. Two bits less or ten more, the sum didn't matter, just so he broke her streak.

Night after night she played, won her dollar, and left to stay in a place that just Fritzie and I knew about. Fleur bathed in the slaughtering tub, then slept in the unused brick smokehouse behind the lockers, a windowless place tarred on the inside with scorched fats. When I brushed against her skin I noticed that she smelled of the walls, rich and woody, slightly burnt. Since that night she put me in the closet I was no longer afraid of her, but followed her close, stayed with her, became her moving shadow that the men never noticed, the shadow that could have saved her.

August, the month that bears fruit, closed around the shop, and Pete and Fritzie left for Minnesota to escape the heat. Night by night, running, Fleur had won thirty dollars, and only Pete's presence had kept Lily at bay. But Pete was gone now, and one payday, with the heat so bad no one could move but Fleur, the men sat and played and waited while she finished work. The cards sweat, limp in their fingers, the table was slick with grease, and even the walls were warm to the touch. The air was motionless. Fleur was in the next room boiling heads.

40   Her green dress, drenched, wrapped her like a transparent sheet. A skin of lakeweed. Black snarls of veining clung to her arms. Her braids were loose, half-unraveled, tied behind her neck in a thick loop. She stood in steam, turning skulls through a vat with a wooden paddle. When scraps boiled to the surface, she bent with a round tin sieve and scooped them out. She'd filled two dishpans.

"Ain't that enough now?" called Lily. "We're waiting." The stump of a dog trembled in his lap, alive with rage. It never smelled me or noticed me above Fleur's smoky skin. The air was heavy in my corner, and pressed me down. Fleur sat with them.

"Now what do you say?" Lily asked the dog. It barked. That was the signal for the real game to start.

"Let's up the ante," said Lily, who had been stalking this night all month. He had a roll of money in his pocket. Fleur had five bills in her dress. The men had each saved their full pay.

"Ante a dollar then," said Fleur, and pitched hers in. She lost, but they let her scrape along, cent by cent. And then she won some. She played unevenly, as if chance was all she had. She reeled them in. The game went on. The dog was stiff now, poised on Lily's knees, a ball of vicious muscle with its yellow eyes slit in concentration. It gave advice, seemed to sniff the lay of Fleur's cards, twitched and nudged. Fleur was up, then down, saved by a scratch. Tor dealt seven cards, three down. The pot grew, round by round, until it held all the money. Nobody folded. Then it all rode on one last card and they went silent. Fleur picked hers up and blew a long breath. The heat lowered like a bell. Her card shook, but she stayed in.

45   Lily smiled and took the dog's head tenderly between his palms.

"Say, Fatso," he said, crooning the words, "you reckon that girl's bluffing?"

The dog whined and Lily laughed. "Me too," he said, "let's show." He swept his bills and coins into the pot and then they turned their cards over.

Lily looked once, looked again, then he squeezed the dog up like a fist of dough and slammed it on the table.

Fleur threw her arms out and drew the money over, grinning that same wolf grin that she'd used on me, the grin that had them. She jammed the bills in her dress, scooped the coins up in waxed white paper that she tied with string.

50   "Let's go another round," said Lily, his voice choked with burrs. But Fleur opened her mouth and yawned, then walked out back to gather slops for the one big hog that was waiting in the stock pen to be killed.

The men sat still as rocks, their hands spread on the oiled wood table. Dutch had chewed his cigar to damp shreds, Tor's eye was dull. Lily's gaze was the only one to follow Fleur. I didn't move. I felt them gathering, saw my stepfather's veins, the ones in his forehead that stood out in anger. The dog had rolled off the table and curled in a knot below the counter, where none of the men could touch it.

Lily rose and stepped out back to the closet of ledgers where Pete kept his private stock. He brought back a bottle, uncorked and tipped it between his fingers. The lump in his throat moved, then he passed it on. They drank, quickly felt the whiskey's fire, and planned with their eyes things they couldn't say out loud.

When they left, I followed. I hid out back in the clutter of broken boards and chicken crates beside the stock pen, where they waited. Fleur could not be seen at first, and then the moon broke and showed her, slipping cautiously along the rough board chute with a bucket in her hand. Her hair fell, wild and coarse, to her waist, and her dress was a floating patch in the dark. She made a pig-calling sound, rang the tin pail lightly against the wood, froze suspiciously. But too late. In the sound of the ring Lily moved, fat and nimble, stepped right behind Fleur and put out his creamy hands. At his first touch, she whirled and doused him with the bucket of sour slops. He pushed her against the big fence and the package of coins split, went clinking and jumping, winked against the wood. Fleur rolled over once and vanished in the yard.

The moon fell behind a curtain of ragged clouds, and Lily followed into the dark muck. But he tripped, pitched over the huge flank of the pig, who lay mired to the snout, heavily snoring. I sprang out of the weeds and climbed the side of the pen, stuck like glue. I saw the sow rise to her neat, knobby knees, gain her balance, and sway, curious, as Lily stumbled forward. Fleur had backed into the angle of rough wood just beyond, and when Lily tried to jostle past, the sow tipped up on her hind legs and struck, quick and hard as a snake. She plunged her head into Lily's thick side and snatched a mouthful of his shirt. She lunged again, caught him lower, so that he grunted in pained surprise. He seemed to ponder, breathing deep. Then he launched his huge body in a swimmer's dive.

55   The sow screamed as his body smacked over hers. She rolled, striking out with her knife-sharp hooves, and Lily gathered himself upon her, took her foot-long face by the ears and scraped her snout and cheeks against the trestles of the pen. He hurled the sow's tight skull against an iron post, but instead of knocking her dead, he merely woke her from her dream.

She reared, shrieked, drew him with her so that they posed standing upright. They bowed jerkily to each other, as if to begin. Then his arms swung and flailed. She sank her black fangs into his shoulder, clasping him, dancing him forward and backward through the pen. Their steps picked up pace, went wild. The two dipped as one, box-stepped, tripped each other. She ran her split foot through his hair. He grabbed her kinked tail. They went down and came up, the same shape and then the same color, until the men couldn't tell one from the other in that light and Fleur was able to launch herself over the gates, swing down, hit gravel.

The men saw, yelled, and chased her at a dead run to the smokehouse. And Lily too, once the sow gave up in disgust and freed him. That is where I should have gone to Fleur, saved her, thrown myself on Dutch. But I went stiff with fear and couldn't unlatch myself from the trestles or move at all.

I closed my eyes and put my head in my arms, tried to hide, so there is nothing to describe but what I couldn't block out, Fleur's hoarse breath, so loud it filled me, her cry in the old language, and my name repeated over and over among the words.

The heat was still dense the next morning when I came back to work. Fleur was gone but the men were there, slack-faced, hung over. Lily was paler and softer than ever, as if his flesh had steamed on his bones. They smoked, took pulls off a bottle. It wasn't noon yet. I worked awhile, waiting shop and sharpening steel. But I was sick, I was smothered, I was sweating so hard that my hands slipped on the knives, and I wiped my fingers clean of the greasy touch of the customers' coins. Lily opened his mouth and roared once, not in anger. There was no meaning to the sound. His boxer dog, sprawled limp beside his foot, never lifted its head. Nor did the other men.

They didn't notice when I stepped outside, hoping for a clear breath. And then I forgot them because I knew that we were all balanced, ready to tip, to fly, to be crushed as soon as the weather broke. The sky was so low that I felt the weight of it like a yoke. Clouds hung down, witch teats, a tornado's green-brown cones, and as I watched one flicked out and became a delicate probing thumb. Even as I picked up my heels and ran back inside, the wind blew suddenly, cold, and then came rain.

60 Inside, the men had disappeared already and the whole place was trembling as if a huge hand was pinched at the rafters, shaking it. I ran straight through, screaming for Dutch or for any of them, and then I stopped at the heavy doors of the lockers, where they had surely taken shelter. I stood there a moment. Everything went still. Then I heard a cry building in the wind, faint at first, a whistle and then a shrill scream that tore through the walls and gathered around me, spoke plain so I understood that I should move, put my arms out, and slam down the great iron bar that fit across the hasp and lock.

Outside, the wind was stronger, like a hand held against me. I struggled forward. The bushes tossed, the awnings flapped off storefronts, the rails of porches rattled. The odd cloud became a fat snout that nosed along the earth and sniffled, jabbed, picked at things, sucked them up, blew them apart, rooted around as if it was following a certain scent, then stopped behind me at the butcher shop and bored down like a drill.

I went flying, landed somewhere in a ball. When I opened my eyes and looked, stranger things were happening.

A herd of cattle flew through the air like giant birds, dropping dung, their mouths opened in stunned bellows. A candle, still lighted, blew past, and tables, napkins, garden tools, a whole school of drifting eyeglasses, jackets on hangers, hams, a checkerboard, a lampshade, and at last the sow from behind the lockers, on the run, her hooves a blur, set free, swooping, diving, screaming as everything in Argus fell apart and got turned upside down, smashed, and thoroughly wrecked.

Days passed before the town went looking for the men. They were bachelors, after all, except for Tor, whose wife had suffered a blow to the head that made her forgetful. Everyone was occupied with digging out, in high relief because even though the Catholic steeple had been torn off like a peaked cap and sent across five fields, those huddled in the cellar were unhurt. Walls had fallen, windows were demolished, but the stores were intact and so were the bankers and shop owners who had taken refuge in their safes or beneath their cash registers. It was a fair-minded disaster, no one could be said to have suffered much more than the next, at least not until Fritzie and Pete came home.

65   Of all the businesses in Argus, Kozka's Meats had suffered worst. The boards of the front building had been split to kindling, piled in a huge pyramid, and the shop equipment was blasted far and wide. Pete paced off the distance the iron bathtub had been flung—a hundred feet. The glass candy case went fifty, and landed without so much as a cracked pane. There were other surprises as well, for the back rooms where Fritzie and Pete lived were undisturbed. Fritzie said the dust still coated her china figures, and upon her kitchen table, in the ashtray, perched the last cigarette she'd put out in haste. She lit it up and finished it, looking through the window. From there, she could see that the old smokehouse Fleur had slept in was crushed to a reddish sand and the stockpens were completely torn apart, the rails stacked helter-skelter. Fritzie asked for Fleur. People shrugged. Then she asked about the others and, suddenly, the town understood that three men were missing.

There was a rally of help, a gathering of shovels and volunteers. We passed boards from hand to hand, stacked them, uncovered what lay beneath the pile of jagged splinters. The lockers, full of the meat that was Pete and Fritzie's investment, slowly came into sight, still intact. When enough room was made for a man to stand on the roof, there were calls, a general urge to hack through and see what lay below. But Fritzie shouted that she wouldn't allow it because the meat would spoil. And so the work continued, board by board, until at last the heavy oak doors of the freezer were revealed and people pressed to the entry. Everyone wanted to be the first, but since it was my stepfather lost, I was let go in when Pete and Fritzie wedged through into the sudden icy air.

Pete scraped a match on his boot, lit the lamp Fritzie held, and then the three of us stood still in its circle. Light glared off the skinned and hanging carcasses, the crates of wrapped sausages, the bright and cloudy blocks of lake ice, pure as winter. The cold bit into us, pleasant at first, then numbing. We must have stood there a couple of minutes before we saw the men, or more rightly, the humps of fur, the iced and shaggy hides they wore, the bearskins they had taken down and wrapped around themselves. We stepped closer and tilted the lantern beneath the flaps of fur into their faces. The dog was there, perched among them, heavy as a doorstop. The three had hunched around a barrel where the game was still laid out, and a dead lantern and an empty bottle, too. But they had thrown down their last hands and hunkered tight, clutching one another, knuckles raw from beating at the door they had also attacked with hooks. Frost stars gleamed off their eyelashes and the stubble of their beards. Their faces were set in concentration, mouths open as if to speak some careful thought, some agreement they'd come to in each other's arms.

▲ ▲ ▲

Power travels in the bloodlines, handed out before birth. It comes down through the hands, which in the Pillagers were strong and knotted, big, spidery, and rough, with sensitive fingertips good at dealing cards. It comes through the eyes, too, belligerent, darkest brown, the eyes of those in the bear clan, impolite as they gaze directly at a person.

In my dreams, I look straight back at Fleur, at the men. I am no longer the watcher on the dark sill, the skinny girl.

70   The blood draws us back, as if it runs through a vein of earth. I've come home and, except for talking to my cousins, live a quiet life. Fleur lives quiet too, down on Lake Turcot with her boat. Some say she's married to the waterman, Misshepeshu, or that she's living in shame with white men or windigos, or that she's killed them all. I'm about the only one here who ever goes to visit her. Last winter, I went to help out in her cabin when she bore the child, whose green eyes and skin the color of an old penny made more talk, as no one could decide if the child was mixed blood or what, fathered in a smokehouse, or by a man with brass scales, or by the lake. The girl is bold, smiling in her sleep, as if she knows what people wonder, as if she hears the old men talk, turning the story over. It comes up different every time and has no ending, no beginning. They get the middle wrong too. They only know that they don't know anything.

GABRIEL GARCÍA MÁRQUEZ

(1928–   )

A Very Old Man with Enormous Wings: A Tale for Children

(1968)

translated from the Spanish by Gregory Rabassa

On the third day of rain they had killed so many crabs inside the house that Pelayo had to cross his drenched courtyard and throw them into the sea, because the newborn child had a temperature all night and they thought it was due to the stench. The world had been sad since Tuesday. Sea and sky were a single ash-gray thing and the sands of the beach, which on March nights glimmered like powdered light, had become a stew of mud and rotten shellfish. The light was so weak at noon that when Pelayo was coming back to the house after throwing away the crabs, it was hard for him to see what it was that was moving and groaning in the rear of the courtyard. He had to go very close to see that it was an old man, a very old man, lying face down in the mud, who, in spite of his tremendous efforts, couldn't get up, impeded by his enormous wings.

Frightened by that nightmare, Pelayo ran to get Elisenda, his wife, who was putting compresses on the sick child, and he took her to the rear of the courtyard. They both looked at the fallen body with mute stupor. He was dressed like a ragpicker.[1] There were only a few faded hairs left on his bald skull and very few teeth in his mouth, and his pitiful condition of a drenched great-grandfather had taken away any sense of grandeur he might have had. His huge buzzard wings, dirty and half-plucked, were forever entangled in the mud. They looked at him so long and so closely that Pelayo and Elisenda very soon overcame their surprise and in the end found him familiar. Then they dared speak to him, and he answered in an incomprehensible dialect with a strong sailor's voice. That was how they skipped over the inconvenience of the wings and quite intelligently concluded that he was a lonely castaway from some foreign ship wrecked by the storm. And yet, they called in a neighbor woman who knew everything about life and death to see him, and all she needed was one look to show them their mistake.

"He's an angel," she told them. "He must have been coming for the child, but the poor fellow is so old that the rain knocked him down."

On the following day everyone knew that a flesh-and-blood angel was held captive in Pelayo's house. Against the judgment of the wise neighbor woman, for whom angels in those times were the fugitive survivors of a celestial conspiracy, they did not have the heart to club him to death. Pelayo watched over him all afternoon from the kitchen, armed with his bailiff's club, and before going to bed he dragged him out of the mud and locked him up with the hens in the wire chicken coop. In the middle of the night, when the rain stopped, Pelayo and Elisenda were still killing crabs. A short time afterward the child woke up without a fever and with a desire to eat. Then they felt magnanimous and decided to put the angel on a raft with fresh water and provisions for three days and leave him to his fate on the high seas. But when they went out into the courtyard with the first light of dawn, they found the whole neighborhood in front of the chicken coop having fun with the angel, without the slightest reverence, tossing him things to eat through the openings in the wire as if he weren't a supernatural creature but a circus animal.

5   Father Gonzaga arrived before seven o'clock, alarmed by the strange news. By that time onlookers less frivolous than those at dawn had already arrived and they were making all kinds of conjectures concerning

----

[1] Someone who makes a living collecting rags and other refuse.

the captive's future. The simplest among them thought that he should be named mayor of the world. Others of sterner mind felt that he should be promoted to the rank of five-star general in order to win all wars. Some visionaries hoped that he could be put to stud in order to implant on earth a race of winged wise men who could take charge of the universe. But Father Gonzaga, before becoming a priest, had been a robust woodcutter. Standing by the wire, he reviewed his catechism[2] in an instant and asked them to open the door so that he could take a close look at that pitiful man who looked more like a huge decrepit hen among the fascinated chickens. He was lying in a corner drying his open wings in the sunlight among the fruit peels and breakfast leftovers that the early risers had thrown him. Alien to the impertinences of the world, he only lifted his antiquarian[3] eyes and murmured something in his dialect when Father Gonzaga went into the chicken coop and said good morning to him in Latin. The parish priest had his first suspicion of an imposter when he saw that he did not understand the language of God or know how to greet His ministers. Then he noticed that seen close up he was much too human; he had an unbearable smell of the outdoors, the back side of his wings was strewn with parasites and his main feathers had been mistreated by terrestrial winds, and nothing about him measured up to the proud dignity of angels. Then he came out of the chicken coop and in a brief sermon warned the curious against the risks of being ingenuous. He reminded them that the devil had the bad habit of making use of carnival tricks in order to confuse the unwary. He argued that if wings were not the essential element in determining the difference between a hawk and an airplane, they were even less so in the recognition of angels. Nevertheless, he promised to write a letter to his bishop so that the latter would write to his primate so that the latter would write to the Supreme Pontiff[4] in order to get the final verdict from the highest courts.

His prudence fell on sterile hearts. The news of the captive angel spread with such rapidity that after a few hours the courtyard had the bustle of a marketplace and they had to call in troops with fixed bayonets to disperse the mob that was about to knock the house down. Elisenda, her spine all twisted from sweeping up so much marketplace trash, then got the idea of fencing in the yard and charging five cents admission to see the angel.

The curious came from far away. A traveling carnival arrived with a flying acrobat who buzzed over the crowd several times, but no one paid any attention to him because his wings were not those of an angel but,

---

[2] A book that summarizes the doctrines of Roman Catholicism in question-and-answer form.

[3] Refers to someone who studies antiquities, particularly old books.

[4] The Pope.

rather, those of a sidereal[5] bat. The most unfortunate invalids on earth came in search of health: a poor woman who since childhood had been counting her heartbeats and had run out of numbers; a Portuguese man who couldn't sleep because the noise of the stars disturbed him; a sleep-walker who got up at night to undo the things he had done while awake; and many others with less serious ailments. In the midst of that shipwreck disorder that made the earth tremble, Pelayo and Elisenda were happy with fatigue, for in less than a week they had crammed their rooms with money and the line of pilgrims waiting their turn to enter still reached beyond the horizon.

The angel was the only one who took no part in his own act. He spent his time trying to get comfortable in his borrowed nest, befuddled by the hellish heat of the oil lamps and sacramental candles that had been placed alone the wire. At first they tried to make him eat some mothballs, which, according to the wisdom of the wise neighbor woman, were the food pre-scribed for angels. But he turned them down, just as he turned down the papal lunches that the penitents brought him, and they never found out whether it was because he was an angel or because he was an old man that in the end he ate nothing but eggplant mush. His only supernatural virtue seemed to be patience. Especially during the first days, when the hens pecked at him, searching for the stellar parasites that proliferated in his wings, and the cripples pulled out feathers to touch their defective parts with, and even the most merciful threw stones at him, trying to get him to rise so they could see him standing. The only time they succeeded in arousing him was when they burned his side with an iron for branding steers, for he had been motionless for so many hours that they thought he was dead. He awoke with a start, ranting in his hermetic[6] language and with tears in his eyes, and he flapped his wings a couple of times, which brought on a whirlwind of chicken dung and lunar dust and a gale of panic that did not seem to be of this world. Although many thought that his reaction had been one not of rage but of pain, from then on they were careful not to annoy him, because the majority understood that his pas-sivity was not that of a hero taking his ease but that of a cataclysm in repose.

Father Gonzaga held back the crowd's frivolity with formulas of maid-servant inspiration while awaiting the arrival of a final judgment on the nature of the captive. But the mail from Rome showed no sense of urgency. They spent their time finding out if the prisoner had a navel, if his dialect had any connection with Aramaic,[7] how many times he could fit on the head of a pin, or whether he wasn't just a Norwegian with wings. Those

---

[5] Relating to the stars.

[6] Occult, magical.

[7] An ancient Middle Eastern language, believed to have been the language spoken by Jesus.

meager letters might have come and gone until the end of time if a providential event had not put an end to the priest's tribulations.

10   It so happened that during those days, among so many other carnival attractions, there arrived in town the traveling show of the woman who had been changed into a spider for having disobeyed her parents. The admission to see her was not only less than the admission to see the angel, but people were permitted to ask her all manner of questions about her absurd state and to examine her up and down so that no one would ever doubt the truth of her horror. She was a frightful tarantula the size of a ram and with the head of a sad maiden. What was most heart-rending, however, was not her outlandish shape but the sincere affliction with which she recounted the details of her misfortune. While still practically a child she had sneaked out of her parents' house to go to a dance, and while she was coming back through the woods after having danced all night without permission, a fearful thunderclap rent the sky in two and through the crack came the lightening bolt of brimstone that changed her into a spider. Her only nourishment came from the meatballs that charitable souls chose to toss into her mouth. A spectacle like that, full of so much human truth and with such a fearful lesson, was bound to defeat without even trying that of a haughty angel who scarcely deigned to look at mortals. Besides, the few miracles attributed to the angel showed a certain mental disorder, like the blind man who didn't recover his sight but grew three new teeth, or the paralytic who didn't get to walk but almost won the lottery, and the leper whose sores sprouted sunflowers. Those consolation miracles, which were more like mocking fun, had already ruined the angel's reputation when the woman who had been changed into a spider finally crushed him completely. That was how Father Gonzaga was cured forever of his insomnia and Pelayo's courtyard went back to being as empty as during the time it had rained for three days and crabs walked through the bedrooms.

The owners of the house had no reason to lament. With the money they saved they built a two-story mansion with balconies and gardens and high netting so that crabs wouldn't get in during the winter, and with iron bars on the windows so that angels wouldn't get in. Pelayo also set up a rabbit warren close to town and gave up his job as bailiff for good, and Elisenda bought some satin pumps with high heels and many dresses of iridescent silk, the kind worn on Sunday by the most desirable women in those times. The chicken coop was the only thing that didn't receive any attention. If they washed it down with creolin[8] and burned tears of myrrh[9] inside it every so often, it was not in homage to the angel but to drive away the dungheap stench that still hung everywhere like a ghost and was turning the new house into an old one. At first, when the child learned to

---

[8]   A disinfectant.

[9]   A type of incense.

walk, they were careful that he not get too close to the chicken coop. But then they began to lose their fears and got used to the smell, and before the child got his second teeth he'd gone inside the chicken coop to play, where the wires were falling apart. The angel was no less standoffish with him than with other mortals, but he tolerated the most ingenious infamies with the patience of a dog who had no illusions. They both came down with chicken pox at the same time. The doctor who took care of the child couldn't resist the temptation to listen to the angel's heart, and he found so much whistling in the heart and so many sounds in his kidneys that it seemed impossible for him to be alive. What surprised him most, however, was the logic of his wings. They seemed so natural on that completely human organism that he couldn't understand why other men didn't have them too.

When the child began school it had been some time since the sun and rain had caused the collapse of the chicken coop. The angel went dragging himself about here and there like a stray dying man. They would drive him out of the bedroom with a broom and a moment later find him in the kitchen. He seemed to be in so many places at the same time that they grew to think that he'd been duplicated, that he was reproducing himself all through the house, and the exasperated and unhinged Elisenda shouted that it was awful living in that hell full of angels. He could scarcely eat and his antiquarian eyes had also become so foggy that he went about bumping into posts. All he had left were the bare cannulae[10] of his last feathers. Pelayo threw a blanket over him and extended him the charity of letting him sleep in the shed, and only then did they notice that he had a temperature at night, and was delirious with the tongue twisters of an old Norwegian. That was one of the few times they became alarmed, for they thought he was going to die and not even the wise neighbor woman had been able to tell them what to do with dead angels.

And yet he not only survived his worst winter, but seemed improved with the first sunny days. He remained motionless for several days in the farthest corner of the courtyard, where no one would see him, and at the beginning of December some large, stiff feathers began to grow on his wings, the feathers of a scarecrow, which looked more like another misfortune of decrepitude. But he must have known the reason for those changes, for he was quite careful that no one should notice them, that no one should hear the sea chanteys that he sometimes sang under the stars. One morning Elisenda was cutting some bunches of onions for lunch when a wind that seemed to come from the high seas blew into the kitchen. Then she went to the window and caught the angel in his first attempt at flight. They were so clumsy that his fingernails opened a furrow in the vegetable patch and he was on the point of knocking the shed down with the ungainly flapping that slipped on the light and couldn't get a

---

[10] Tubes at the base of feathers.

grip on the air. But he did manage to gain altitude. Elisenda let out a sigh of relief, for herself and for him, when she saw him pass over the last houses, holding himself up in some way with the risky flapping of a senile vulture. She kept watching him even when she was through cutting the onions and she kept on watching until it was no longer possible for her to see him, because then he was no longer an annoyance in her life but an imaginary dot on the horizon of the sea.

S U S A N   G L A S P E L L

(1882–1948)

A Jury of Her Peers

(1917)

When Martha Hale opened the storm-door and got a cut of the north wind, she ran back for her big woolen scarf. As she hurriedly wound that round her head her eye made a scandalized sweep of her kitchen. It was no ordinary thing that called her away—it was probably further from ordinary than anything that had ever happened in Dickson County. But what her eye took in was that her kitchen was in no shape for leaving: her bread all ready for mixing, half the flour sifted and half unsifted.

She hated to see things half done; but she had been at that when the team from town stopped to get Mr. Hale, and then the sheriff came running in to say his wife wished Mrs. Hale would come too—adding, with a grin, that he guessed she was getting scary and wanted another woman along. So she had dropped everything right where it was.

"Martha!" now came her husband's impatient voice. "Don't keep folks waiting out here in the cold."

She again opened the storm-door, and this time joined the three men and the one woman waiting for her in the big two-seated buggy.

5   After she had the robes tucked around her she took another look at the woman who sat beside her on the back seat. She had met Mrs. Peters the year before at the county fair, and the thing she remembered about her was that she didn't seem like a sheriff's wife. She was small and thin and didn't have a strong voice. Mrs. Gorman, sheriff's wife before Gorman went out and Peters came in, had a voice that somehow seemed to be backing up the law with every word. But if Mrs. Peters didn't look like a sheriff's wife, Peters made it up in looking like a sheriff. He was to a dot the kind of man who could get himself elected sheriff—a heavy man with a big voice, who was particularly genial with the law-abiding, as if to make it plain that he knew the difference between criminals and non-criminals. And right there it came into Mrs. Hale's mind, with a stab, that this man who was so pleasant and lively with all of them was going to the Wrights' now as a sheriff.

"The country's not very pleasant this time of year," Mrs. Peters at last ventured, as if she felt they ought to be talking as well as the men.

Mrs. Hale scarcely finished her reply, for they had gone up a little hill and could see the Wright place now, and seeing it did not make her feel like talking. It looked very lonesome this cold March morning. It had always been a lonesome-looking place. It was down in a hollow, and the poplar trees around it were lonesome-looking trees. The men were looking at it and talking about what had happened. The county attorney was bending to one side of the buggy, and kept looking steadily at the place as they drew up to it.

"I'm glad you came with me," Mrs. Peters said nervously, as the two women were about to follow the men in through the kitchen door.

Even after she had her foot on the door-step, her hand on the knob, Martha Hale had a moment of feeling she could not cross that threshold. And the reason it seemed she couldn't cross it now was simply because she hadn't crossed it before. Time and time again it had been in her mind, "I ought to go over and see Minnie Foster"—she still thought of her as Minnie Foster, though for twenty years she had been Mrs. Wright. And then there was always something to do and Minnie Foster would go from her mind. But *now* she could come.

10   The men went over to the stove. The women stood close together by the door. Young Henderson, the county attorney, turned around and said, "Come up to the fire, ladies."

Mrs. Peters took a step forward, then stopped. "I'm not—cold," she said.

And so the two women stood by the door, at first not even so much as looking around the kitchen.

The men talked for a minute about what a good thing it was the sheriff had sent his deputy out that morning to make a fire for them, and then Sheriff Peters stepped back from the stove, unbuttoned his outer coat, and leaned his hands on the kitchen table in a way that seemed to mark the beginning of official business. "Now, Mr. Hale," he said in a sort of semi-official voice, "before we move things about, you tell Mr. Henderson just what it was you saw when you came here yesterday morning."

The county attorney was looking around the kitchen.

15   "By the way," he said, "has anything been moved?" He turned to the sheriff. "Are things just as you left them yesterday?"

Peters looked from cupboard to sink; from that to a small worn rocker a little to one side of the kitchen table.

"It's just the same."

"Somebody should have been left here yesterday," said the county attorney.

"Oh—yesterday," returned the sheriff, with a little gesture as of yesterday having been more than he could bear to think of. "When I had to send Frank to Morris Center for that man who went crazy—let me tell you, I had my hands full *yesterday*. I knew you could get back from Omaha by today, George, and as long as I went over everything here myself—"

20   "Well, Mr. Hale," said the county attorney, in a way of letting what was past and gone go, "tell just what happened when you came here yesterday morning."

Mrs. Hale, still leaning against the door, had that sinking feeling of the mother whose child is about to speak a piece. Lewis often wandered along and got things mixed up in a story. She hoped he would tell this straight and plain, and not say unnecessary things that would just make things harder for Minnie Foster. He didn't begin at once, and she noticed that he looked queer—as if standing in that kitchen and having to tell what he had seen there yesterday morning made him almost sick.

"Yes, Mr. Hale?" the county attorney reminded.

"Harry and I had started to town with a load of potatoes," Mrs. Hale's husband began.

Harry was Mrs. Hale's oldest boy. He wasn't with them now, for the very good reason that those potatoes never got to town yesterday and he was taking them this morning, so he hadn't been home when the sheriff stopped to say he wanted Mr. Hale to come over to the Wright place and tell the county attorney his story there, where he could point it all out. With all Mrs. Hale's other emotions came the fear now that maybe Harry wasn't dressed warm enough—they hadn't any of them realized how that north wind did bite.

25   "We come along this road," Hale was going on, with a motion of his hand to the road over which they had just come, "and as we got in sight of the house I says to Harry, 'I'm goin' to see if I can't get John Wright to take a telephone.' You see," he explained to Henderson, "unless I can get somebody to go in with me they won't come out this branch road except for a price *I* can't pay. I'd spoke to Wright about it once before; but he put me off, saying folks talked too much anyway, and all he asked was peace and quiet—guess you know about how much he talked himself. But I thought maybe if I went to the house and talked about it before his wife, and said all the women-folks liked the telephones, and that in this lonesome stretch of road it would be a good thing—well, I said to Harry that that was what I was going to say—though I said at the same time that I didn't know as what his wife wanted made much difference to John—"

Now there he was!—saying things he didn't need to say. Mrs. Hale tried to catch her husband's eye, but fortunately the county attorney interrupted with:

"Let's talk about that a little later, Mr. Hale. I do want to talk about that, but I am anxious now to get along to just what happened when you got here."

When he began this time, it was very deliberately and carefully:

"I didn't see or hear anything. I knocked at the door. And still it was all quiet inside. I knew they must be up—it was past eight o'clock. So I knocked again, louder, and I thought I heard somebody say, 'Come in.' I wasn't sure—I'm not sure yet. But I opened the door—this door," jerking a hand toward the door by which the two women stood, "and there, in that rocker"—pointing to it—"sat Mrs. Wright."

30   Everyone in the kitchen looked at the rocker. It came into Mrs. Hale's mind that that rocker didn't look in the least like Minnie Foster—the Minnie Foster of twenty years before. It was a dingy red, with wooden rungs up the back, and the middle rung was gone, and the chair sagged to one side.

"How did she—look?" the county attorney was inquiring.

"Well," said Hale, "she looked—queer."

"How do you mean—queer?"

As he asked it he took out a note-book and pencil. Mrs. Hale did not like the sight of that pencil. She kept her eye fixed on her husband, as if to keep him from saying unnecessary things that would go into that note-book and make trouble.

35   Hale did speak guardedly, as if the pencil had affected him too.

"Well, as if she didn't know what she was going to do next. And kind of—done up."

"How did she seem to feel about your coming?"

"Why, I don't think she minded—one way or other. She didn't pay much attention. I said 'Ho' do, Mrs. Wright? It's cold, ain't it?' And she said, 'Is it?'—and went on pleatin' at her apron.

"Well, I was surprised. She didn't ask me to come up to the stove, or to sit down, but just set there, not even lookin' at me. And so I said: 'I want to see John.'

40   "And then she—laughed. I guess you would call it a laugh.

"I thought of Harry and the team outside, so I said, a little sharp, 'Can I see John?' 'No,' says she—kind of dull like. 'Ain't he home?' says I. Then she looked at me. 'Yes,' says she, 'he's home.' 'Then why can't I see him?' I asked her, out of patience with her now. ''Cause he's dead,' says she, just as quiet and dull—and fell to pleatin' her apron. 'Dead?' says I, like you do when you can't take in what you've heard.

"She just nodded her head, not getting a bit excited, but rockin' back and forth.

"'Why—where is he?' says I, not knowing *what* to say.

"She just pointed upstairs—like this"—pointing to the room above.

45   "I got up, with the idea of going up there myself. By this time I—didn't know what to do. I walked from there to here; then I says: 'Why, what did he die of?'

"'He died of a rope around his neck,' says she; and just went on pleatin' at her apron."

Hale stopped speaking, and stood staring at the rocker, as if he were still seeing the woman who had sat there the morning before. Nobody spoke; it was as if every one were seeing the woman who had sat there the morning before.

"And what did you do then?" the county attorney at last broke the silence.

"I went out and called Harry. I thought I might—need help. I got Harry in, and we went upstairs." His voice fell almost to a whisper. "There he was—lying over the—"

50   "I think I'd rather have you go into that upstairs," the county attorney interrupted, "where you can point it all out. Just go on now with the rest of the story."

"Well, my first thought was to get that rope off. It looked—"

He stopped, his face twitching.

"But Harry, he went up to him, and he said, 'No, he's dead all right, and we'd better not touch anything.' So we went downstairs.

"She was still sitting that same way. 'Has anybody been notified?' I asked. 'No,' says she, unconcerned."

55   "'Who did this, Mrs. Wright?' said Harry. He said it business-like, and she stopped pleatin' at her apron. 'I don't know,' she says. 'You don't *know?*' says Harry. 'Weren't you sleepin' in the bed with him?' 'Yes,' says she, 'but I was on the inside.' 'Somebody slipped a rope round his neck and strangled him, and you didn't wake up?' says Harry. 'I didn't wake up,' she said after him.

"We may have looked as if we didn't see how that could be, for after a minute she said, 'I sleep sound.'

"Harry was going to ask her more questions, but I said maybe that weren't our business; maybe we ought to let her tell her story first to the coroner or the sheriff. So Harry went fast as he could over to High Road— the Rivers's place, where there's a telephone."

"And what did she do when she knew you had gone for the coronor?" The attorney got his pencil in his hand all ready for writing.

"She moved from that chair to this one over here"—Hale pointed to a small chair in the corner—"and just sat there with her hands held together and looking down. I got a feeling that I ought to make some conversation, so I said I had come to see if John wanted to put in a telephone; and at that she started to laugh, and then she stopped and looked at me—scared."

60   At the sound of a moving pencil the man who was telling the story looked up.

"I dunno—maybe it wasn't scared," he hastened; "I wouldn't like to say it was. Soon Harry got back, and then Dr. Lloyd came, and you, Mr. Peters, and so I guess that's all I know that you don't."

He said that last with relief, and moved a little, as if relaxing. Every one moved a little. The county attorney walked toward the stair door.

"I guess we'll go upstairs first—then out to the barn and around there."

He paused and looked around the kitchen.

65   "You're convinced there was nothing important here?" he asked the sheriff. "Nothing that would—point to any motive?"

The sheriff too looked all around, as if to re-convince himself.

"Nothing here but kitchen things," he said, with a little laugh for the insignificance of kitchen things.

The county attorney was looking at the cupboard—a peculiar, ungainly structure, half closet and half cupboard, the upper part of it being built in the wall, and the lower part just the old-fashioned kitchen cupboard. As if its queerness attracted him, he got a chair and opened the upper part and looked in. After a moment he drew his hand away sticky.

"Here's a nice mess," he said resentfully.

70   The two women had drawn nearer, and now the sheriff's wife spoke.

"Oh—her fruit," she said, looking to Mrs. Hale for sympathetic understanding. She turned back to the county attorney and explained: "She worried about that when it turned so cold last night. She said the fire would go out and her jars might burst."

Mrs. Peters' husband broke into a laugh.

"Well, can you beat the woman! Held for murder, and worrying about her preserves!"

The young attorney set his lips.

75   "I guess before we're through with her she may have something more serious than preserves to worry about."

"Oh, well," said Mrs. Hale's husband, with good-natured superiority, "women are used to worrying over trifles."

The two women moved a little closer together. Neither of them spoke. The county attorney seemed suddenly to remember his manners—and think of his future.

"And yet," said he, with the gallantry of a young politician, "for all their worries, what would we do without the ladies?"

The women did not speak, did not unbend. He went to the sink and began washing his hands. He turned to wipe them on the roller wheel— whirled it for a cleaner place.

80   "Dirty towels! Not much of a housekeeper, would you say, ladies?"

He kicked his foot against some dirty pans under the sink.

"There's a great deal of work to be done on a farm," said Mrs. Hale stiffly.

"To be sure. And yet"—with a little bow to her—"I know there are some Dickson County farm-houses that do not have such roller towels." He gave it a pull to expose its full length again.

"Those towels get dirty awful quick. Men's hands aren't always as clean as they might be."

85   "Ah, loyal to your sex, I see," he laughed. He stopped and gave her a keen look. "But you and Mrs. Wright were neighbors. I suppose you were friends, too."

Martha Hale shook her head.

"I've seen little enough of her of late years. I've not been in this house—it's more than a year."

"And why was that? You didn't like her?"

"I liked her well enough," she replied with spirit. "Farmers' wives have their hands full, Mr. Henderson. And then—" She looked around the kitchen.

90   "Yes?" he encouraged.

"It never seemed a very cheerful place," said she, more to herself than to him.

"No," he agreed; "I don't think anyone would call it cheerful. I shouldn't say she had the home-making instinct."

"Well, I don't know as Wright had, either," she muttered.

"You mean they didn't get on very well?" he was quick to ask.

95   "No; I don't mean anything," she answered, with decision. As she turned a little away from him, she added: "But I don't think a place would be any the cheerfuler for John Wright's bein' in it."

"I'd like to talk to you about that a little later, Mrs. Hale," he said. "I'm anxious to get the lay of things upstairs now."

He moved toward the stair door, followed by the two men.

"I suppose anything Mrs. Peters does'll be all right?" the sheriff inquired. "She was to take in some clothes for her, you know—and a few little things. We left in such a hurry yesterday."

The county attorney looked at the two women whom they were leaving alone there among the kitchen things.

100   "Yes—Mrs. Peters," he said, his glance resting on the woman who was not Mrs. Peters, the big farmer woman who stood behind the sheriff's wife. "Of course Mrs. Peters is one of us," he said, in a manner of entrusting responsibility. "And keep your eye out, Mrs. Peters, for anything that might be of use. No telling; you women might come upon a clue to the motive—and that's the thing we need."

Mr. Hale rubbed his face after the fashion of a showman getting ready for a pleasantry.

"But would the women know a clue if they did come upon it?" he said; and, having delivered himself of this, he followed the others through the stair door.

The women stood motionless and silent, listening to the footsteps, first up the stairs, then in the room above them.

Then, as if releasing herself from something strange, Mrs. Hale began to arrange the dirty pans under the sink, which the county attorney's disdainful push of the foot had deranged.

105   "I'd hate to have men comin' into my kitchen," she said testily— "snoopin' round and criticizin'."

"Of course it's no more than their duty," said the sheriff's wife, in her manner of timid acquiescence.

"Duty's all right," replied Mrs. Hale bluffly; "but I guess that deputy sheriff that come out to make the fire might have got a little of this on." She gave the roller towel a pull. "Wish I'd thought of that sooner! Seems mean to talk about her for not having things slicked up, when she had to come away in such a hurry."

She looked around the kitchen. Certainly it was not "slicked up." Her eye was held by a bucket of sugar on a low shelf. The cover was off the wooden bucket, and beside it was a paper bag—half full.

Mrs. Hale moved toward it.

110   "She was putting this in here," she said to herself—slowly.

She thought of the flour in her kitchen at home—half sifted, half not sifted. She had been interrupted, and had left things half done. What had interrupted Minnie Foster? Why had that work been left half done? She made a move as if to finish it,—unfinished things always bothered her,— and then she glanced around and saw that Mrs. Peters was watching her— and she didn't want Mrs. Peters to get that feeling she had got of work begun and then—for some reason—not finished.

"It's a shame about her fruit," she said, and walked toward the cupboard that the county attorney had opened, and got on the chair, murmuring: "I wonder if it's all gone."

It was a sorry enough looking sight, but "Here's one that's all right," she said at last. She held it toward the light. "This is cherries, too." She looked again. "I declare I believe that's the only one."

With a sigh, she got down from the chair, went to the sink, and wiped off the bottle.

115   "She'll feel awful bad, after all her hard work in the hot weather. I remember the afternoon I put up my cherries last summer."

She set the bottle on the table, and, with another sigh, started to sit down in the rocker. But she did not sit down. Something kept her from sitting down in that chair. She straightened—stepped back, and, half turned away, stood looking at it, seeing the woman who had sat there "pleatin' at her apron."

The thin voice of the sheriff's wife broke in upon her: "I must be getting those things from the front room closet." She opened the door into the other room, started in, stepped back. "You coming with me, Mrs. Hale?" she asked nervously. "You—you could help me get them."

They were soon back—the stark coldness of that shut-up room was not a thing to linger in.

"My!" said Mrs. Peters, dropping the things on the table and hurrying to the stove.

120   Mrs. Hale stood examining the clothes the woman who was being detained in town had said she wanted.

"Wright was close![1]" she exclaimed, holding up a shabby black shirt that bore the marks of much making over. "I think maybe that's why she kept so much to herself. I s'pose she felt she couldn't do her part; and then, you don't enjoy things when you feel shabby. She used to

---

[1] Not generous in giving or spending.

wear pretty clothes and be lively—when she was Minnie Foster, one of the town girls, singing in the choir. But that—oh, that was twenty years ago."

With a carefulness in which there was something tender, she folded the shabby clothes and piled them at one corner of the table. She looked at Mrs. Peters, and there was something in the other woman's look that irritated her.

"She don't care," she said to herself. "Much difference it makes to her whether Minnie Foster had pretty clothes when she was a girl."

Then she looked again, and she wasn't so sure; in fact, she hadn't at any time been perfectly sure about Mrs. Peters. She had that shrinking manner, and yet her eyes looked as if they could see a long way into things.

125   "This all you was to take in?" asked Mrs. Hale.

"No," said the sheriff's wife; "she said she wanted an apron. Funny thing to want," she ventured in her nervous little way, "for there's not much to get you dirty in jail, goodness knows. But I suppose just to make her feel more natural. If you're used to wearing an apron—. She said they were in the bottom drawer of this cupboard. Yes—here they are. And then her little shawl that always hung on the stair door."

She took the small gray shawl from behind the door leading upstairs, and stood a minute looking at it.

Suddenly Mrs. Hale took a quick step toward the other woman.

"Mrs. Peters!"

130   "Yes, Mrs. Hale?"

"Do you think she—did it?"

A frightened look blurred the other thing in Mrs. Peters's eyes.

"Oh, I don't know," she said, in a voice that seemed to shrink away from the subject.

"Well, I don't think she did," affirmed Mrs. Hale stoutly. "Asking for an apron, and her little shawl. Worryin' about her fruit."

135   "Mr. Peters says—." Footsteps were heard in the room above; she stopped, looked up, then went on in a lowered voice: "Mr. Peters says—it looks bad for her. Mr. Henderson is awful sarcastic in a speech, and he's going to make fun of her saying she didn't—wake up."

For a moment Mrs. Hale had no answer. Then, "Well, I guess John Wright didn't wake up—when they was slippin' that rope under his neck," she muttered.

"No, it's *strange*," breathed Mrs. Peters. "They think it was such a—funny way to kill a man."

She began to laugh; at sound of the laugh, abruptly stopped.

"That's just what Mr. Hale said," said Mrs. Hale, in a resolutely natural voice. "There was a gun in the house. He says that's what he can't understand."

140   "Mr. Henderson said, coming out, that what was needed for the case was a motive. Something to show anger—or sudden feeling."

"Well, I don't see any signs of anger around here," said Mrs. Hale. "I don't—"

She stopped. It was as if her mind tripped on something. Her eye was caught by a dish-towel in the middle of the kitchen table. Slowly she moved toward the table. One half of it was wiped clean, the other half messy. Her eyes made a slow, almost unwilling turn to the bucket of sugar and the half empty bag beside it. Things begun—and not finished.

After a moment she stepped back, and said, in that manner of releasing herself:

"Wonder how they're finding things upstairs? I hope she had it a little more red up[2] up there. You know,"—she paused, and feeling gathered,—"it seems kind of *sneaking;* locking her up in town and coming out here to get her own house to turn against her!"

145   "But, Mrs. Hale," said the sheriff's wife, "the law is the law."

"I s'pose 'tis," answered Mrs. Hale shortly.

She turned to the stove, saying something about that fire not being much to brag of. She worked with it a minute, and when she straightened up she said aggressively:

"The law is the law—and a bad stove is a bad stove. How'd you like to cook on this?"—pointing with the poker to the broken lining. She opened the oven door and started to express her opinion of the oven; but she was swept into her own thoughts, thinking of what it would mean, year after year, to have that stove to wrestle with. The thought of Minnie Foster trying to bake in that oven—and the thought of her never going over to see Minnie Foster—.

She was startled by hearing Mrs. Peters say: "A person gets discouraged—and loses heart."

150   The sheriff's wife had looked from the stove to the sink—to the pail of water which had been carried in from outside. The two women stood there silent, above them the footsteps of the men who were looking for evidence against the woman who had worked in that kitchen. That look of seeing into things, of seeing through a thing to something else, was in the eyes of the sheriff's wife now. When Mrs. Hale next spoke to her, it was gently:

"Better loosen up your things, Mrs. Peters. We'll not feel them when we go out."

Mrs. Peters went to the back of the room to hang up the fur tippet she was wearing. A moment later she exclaimed, "Why, she was piecing a quilt," and held up a large sewing basket piled high with quilt pieces.

Mrs. Hale spread some of the blocks on the table.

"It's log-cabin pattern," she said, putting several of them together, "Pretty, isn't it?"

155   They were so engaged with the quilt that they did not hear the footsteps on the stairs. Just as the stair door opened Mrs. Hale was saying:

---

[2] Neat, tidy.

"Do you suppose she was going to quilt it or just knot it?"

The sheriff threw up his hands.

"They wonder whether she was going to quilt it or just knot it!"

There was a laugh for the ways of women, a warming of hands over the stove, and then the county attorney said briskly:

160 "Well, let's go right out to the barn and get that cleared up."

"I don't see as there's anything so strange," Mrs. Hale said resentfully, after the outside door had closed on the three men—"our taking up our time with little things while we're waiting for them to get the evidence. I don't see as it's anything to laugh about."

"Of course they've got awful important things on their minds," said the sheriff's wife apologetically.

They returned to an inspection of the blocks for the quilt. Mrs. Hale was looking at the fine, even sewing, and preoccupied with thoughts of the woman who had done that sewing, when she heard the sheriff's wife say, in a queer tone:

"Why, look at this one."

165 She turned to take the block held out to her.

"The sewing," said Mrs. Peters, in a troubled way, "All the rest of them have been so nice and even—but—this one. Why, it looks as if she didn't know what she was about!"

Their eyes met—something flashed to life, passed between them; then, as if with an effort they seemed to pull away from each other. A moment Mrs. Hale sat there, her hands folded over that sewing which was so unlike all the rest of the sewing. Then she had pulled a knot and drawn the threads.

"Oh, what are you doing, Mrs. Hale?" asked the sheriff's wife, startled.

"Just pulling out a stitch or two that's not sewed very good," said Mrs. Hale mildly.

170 "I don't think we ought to touch things," Mrs. Peters said, a little helplessly.

"I'll just finish up this end," answered Mrs. Hale, still in that mild, matter-of-fact fashion.

She threaded a needle and started to replace bad sewing with good. For a little while she sewed in silence. Then, in that thin, timid voice, she heard:

"Mrs. Hale!"

"Yes, Mrs. Peters?"

175 "What do you suppose she was so—nervous about?"

"Oh, *I* don't know," said Mrs. Hale, as if dismissing a thing not important enough to spend much time on. "I don't know as she was—nervous. I sew awful queer sometimes when I'm just tired."

She cut a thread, and out of the corner of her eye looked up at Mrs. Peters. The small, lean face of the sheriff's wife seemed to have tightened up. Her eyes had that look of peering into something. But the next moment she moved, and said in her thin, indecisive way:

"Well, I must get those clothes wrapped. They may be through sooner than we think. I wonder where I could find a piece of paper—and string."

"In that cupboard, maybe," suggested Mrs. Hale, after a glance around.

180   One piece of the crazy sewing remained unripped. Mrs. Peters's back turned; Martha Hale now scrutinized that piece, compared it with the dainty, accurate sewing of the other blocks. The difference was startling. Holding this block made her feel queer, as if the distracted thoughts of the woman who had perhaps turned to it to try and quiet herself were communicating themselves to her.

Mrs. Peters's voice roused her.

"Here's a bird-cage," she said. "Did she have a bird, Mrs. Hale?"

"Why, I don't know whether she did or not." She turned to look at the cage Mrs. Peters was holding up. "I've not been here in so long." She sighed. "There was a man round last year selling canaries cheap—but I don't know as she took one. Maybe she did. She used to sing real pretty herself."

Mrs. Peters looked around the kitchen.

185   "Seems kind of funny to think of a bird here." She half laughed—an attempt to put up a barrier. "But she must have had one—or why would she have a cage? I wonder what happened to it."

"I suppose maybe the cat got it," suggested Mrs. Hale, resuming her sewing.

"No, she didn't have a cat. She's got that feeling some people have about cats—being afraid of them. When they brought her to our house yesterday, my cat got in the room, and she was real upset and asked me to take it out."

"My sister Bessie was like that," laughed Mrs. Hale.

The sheriff's wife did not reply. The silence made Mrs. Hale turn round. Mrs. Peters was examining the bird-cage.

190   "Look at this door," she said slowly. "It's broke. One hinge has been pulled apart."

Mrs. Hale came nearer.

"Looks as if someone must have been—rough with it."

Again their eyes met—startled, questioning, apprehensive. For a moment neither spoke nor stirred. Then Mrs. Hale, turning away, said brusquely:

"If they're going to find any evidence, I wish they'd be about it. I don't like this place."

"But I'm awful glad you came with me, Mrs. Hale." Mrs. Peters put the bird-cage on the table and sat down. "It would be lonesome for me—sitting here alone."

195   "Yes, it would, wouldn't it?" agreed Mrs. Hale, a certain determined naturalness in her voice. She had picked up the sewing, but now it dropped in her lap, and she murmured in a different voice: "But I tell you what I *do* wish, Mrs. Peters. I wish I had come over sometimes when she was here. I wish—I had."

"But of course you were awful busy, Mrs. Hale. Your house—and your children."

"I could've come," retorted Mrs. Hale shortly. "I stayed away because it weren't cheerful—and that's why I ought to have come. I"—she looked around—"I've never liked this place. Maybe because it's down in a hollow and you don't see the road. I don't know what it is, but it's a lonesome place, and always was. I wish I had come over to see Minnie Foster sometimes. I can see now—" She did not put it into words.

"Well, you mustn't reproach yourself," counseled Mrs. Peters. "Somehow, we just don't see how it is with other folks till—something comes up."

200   "Not having children makes less work," mused Mrs. Hale, after a silence, "but it makes a quiet house—and Wright out to work all day—and no company when he did come in. Did you know John Wright, Mrs. Peters?"

"Not to know him. I've seen him in town. They say he was a good man."

"Yes—good," conceded John Wright's neighbor grimly. "He didn't drink, and kept his word as well as most, I guess, and paid his debts. But he was a hard man, Mrs. Peters. Just to pass the time of day with him—." She stopped, shivered a little. "Like a raw wind that gets to the bone." Her eye fell upon the cage on the table before her, and she added, almost bitterly: "I should think she would've wanted a bird!"

Suddenly she leaned forward, looking intently at the cage. "But what do you s'pose went wrong with it?"

"I don't know," returned Mrs. Peters; "unless it got sick and died."

205   But after she said it she reached over and swung the broken door. Both women watched it as if somehow held by it.

"You didn't know—her?" Mrs. Hale asked, a gentler note in her voice.

"Not till they brought her yesterday," said the sheriff's wife.

"She—come to think of it, she was kind of like a bird herself. Real sweet and pretty, but kind of timid and—fluttery. How—she—did—change."

That held her for a long time. Finally, as if struck with a happy thought and relieved to get back to everyday things, she exclaimed:

210   "Tell you what, Mrs. Peters, why don't you take the quilt in with you? It might take up her mind."

"Why, I think that's a real nice idea, Mrs. Hale," agreed the sheriff's wife, as if she were too glad to come into the atmosphere of a simple kindness. "There couldn't possibly be any objection to that, could there? Now, just what will I take? I wonder if her patches are in here—and her things?"

They turned to the sewing basket.

"Here's some red," said Mrs. Hale, bringing out a roll of cloth. Underneath that was a box. "Here, maybe her scissors are in here—and her things." She held it up. "What a pretty box! I'll warrant that was something she had a long time ago—when she was a girl."

She held it in her hand a moment; then, with a little sigh, opened it.

215   Instantly her hand went to her nose.

"Why—!"

Mrs. Peters drew nearer—then turned away.

"There's something wrapped up in this piece of silk," faltered Mrs. Hale.

"This isn't her scissors," said Mrs. Peters, in a shrinking voice.

220   Her hand not steady, Mrs. Hale raised the piece of silk. "Oh, Mrs. Peters!" she cried. "It's—"

Mrs. Peters bent closer.

"It's the bird," she whispered.

"But, Mrs. Peters!" cried Mrs. Hale. "*Look* at it! Its neck—look at its neck! It's all—other side *to*."

She held the box away from her.

225   The sheriff's wife again bent closer.

"Somebody wrung its neck," said she, in a voice that was slow and deep.

And then again the eyes of the two women met—this time clung together in a look of dawning comprehension, of growing horror. Mrs. Peters looked from the dead bird to the broken door of the cage. Again their eyes met. And just then there was a sound at the outside door.

Mrs. Hale slipped the box under the quilt pieces in the basket, and sank into the chair before it. Mrs. Peters stood holding to the table. The county attorney and the sheriff came in from outside.

"Well, ladies," said the county attorney, as one turning from serious things to little pleasantries, "have you decided whether she was going to quilt it or knot it?"

230   "We think," began the sheriff's wife in a flurried voice, "that she was going to—knot it."

He was too preoccupied to notice the change that came in her voice on this last.

"Well, that's very interesting, I'm sure," he said tolerantly. He caught sight of the bird-cage. "Has the bird flown?"

"We think the cat got it," said Mrs. Hale in a voice curiously even.

He was walking up and down, as if thinking something out.

235   "Is there a cat?" he asked absently.

Mrs. Hale shot a look up at the sheriff's wife.

"Well, not *now*," said Mrs. Peters. "They're superstitious, you know; they leave."

She sank into the chair.

The county attorney did not heed her. "No sign at all of anyone having come in from the outside," he said to Peters, in the manner of continuing an interrupted conversation. "Their own rope. Now let's go upstairs again and go over it, piece by piece. It would have to have been someone who knew just the—"

240   The stair door closed behind them and their voices were lost.

The two women sat motionless, not looking at each other, but as if peering into something and at the same time holding back. When they spoke now it was as if they were afraid of what they were saying, but as if they could not help saying it.

"She liked the bird," said Martha Hale, low and slowly. "She was going to bury it in that pretty box."

"When I was a girl," said Mrs. Peters, under her breath, "my kitten— there was a boy took a hatchet, and before my eyes—before I could get there—" She covered her face an instant. "If they hadn't held me back I would have"—she caught herself, looked upstairs where footsteps were heard, and finished weakly—"hurt him."

They they sat without speaking or moving.

245   "I wonder how it would seem," Mrs. Hale at last began, as if feeling her way over strange ground—"never to have had any children around?" Her eyes made a slow sweep of the kitchen, as if seeing what that kitchen had meant through all the years. "No, Wright wouldn't like the bird," she said after that—"a thing that sang. She used to sing. He killed that too." Her voice tightened.

Mrs. Peters moved uneasily.

"Of course we don't know who killed the bird."

"I knew John Wright," was Mrs. Hale's answer.

"It was an awful thing was done in this house that night, Mrs. Hale," said the sheriff's wife. "Killing a man while he slept—slipping a thing round his neck that choked the life out of him."

250   Mrs. Hale's hand went out to the bird-cage.

"His neck. Choked the life out of him."

"We don't *know* who killed him," whispered Mrs. Peters wildly. "We don't *know*."

Mrs. Hale had not moved. "If there had been years and years of—nothing, then a bird to sing to you, it would be awful—still—after the bird was still."

It was as if something within her not herself had spoken, and it found in Mrs. Peters something she did not know as herself.

255   "I know what stillness is," she said, in a queer, monotonous voice. "When we homesteaded in Dakota, and my first baby died—after he was two years old—and me with no other then—"

Mrs. Hale stirred.

"How soon do you suppose they'll be through looking for the evidence?"

"I know what stillness is," repeated Mrs. Peters, in just that same way. Then she too pulled back. "The law has got to punish crime, Mrs. Hale," she said in her tight little way.

"I wish you'd seen Minnie Foster," was the answer, "when she wore a white dress with blue ribbons, and stood up there in the choir and sang."

260   The picture of that girl, the fact that she had lived neighbor to that girl for twenty years, and had let her die for lack of life, was suddenly more than she could bear.

"Oh, I *wish* I'd come over here once in a while!" she cried. "That was a crime! That was a crime! Who's going to punish that?"

"We mustn't take on," said Mrs. Peters, with a frightened look toward the stairs.

"I might 'a' *known* she needed help! I tell you, it's *queer*, Mrs. Peters. We live close together, and we live far apart. We all go through the same things—it's all just a different kind of the same thing! If it weren't—why do you and I *understand*? Why do we *know*—what we know this minute?"

She dashed her hand across her eyes. Then, seeing the jar of fruit on the table, she reached for it and choked out:

265   "If I was you I wouldn't *tell* her her fruit was gone! Tell her it *ain't*. Tell her it's all right—all of it. Here—take this in to prove it to her! She—she may never know whether it was broke or not."

She turned away.

Mrs. Peters reached out for the bottle of fruit as if she were glad to take it—as if touching a familiar thing, having something to do, could keep her from something else. She got up, looking about for something to wrap the fruit in, took a petticoat from the pile of clothes she had brought from the front room, and nervously started winding that round the bottle.

"My!" she began, in a high, false voice, "it's a good thing the men couldn't hear us! Getting all stirred up over a little thing like a—dead canary." She hurried over that. "As if that could have anything to do with—with—My, wouldn't they *laugh*?"

Footsteps were heard on the stairs.

270   "Maybe they would," muttered Mrs. Hale—"maybe they wouldn't."

"No, Peters," said the county attorney incisively; "it's all perfectly clear, except the reason for doing it. But you know juries when it comes to women. If there was some definite thing—something to show. Something to make a story about. A thing that would connect up with this clumsy way of doing it."

In a covert way Mrs. Hale looked at Mrs. Peters. Mrs. Peters was looking at her. Quickly they looked away from each other. The outer door opened and Mr. Hale came in.

"I've got the team[3] round now," he said. "Pretty cold out there."

"I'm going to stay here awhile by myself," the county attorney suddenly announced. "You can send Frank out for me, can't you?" he asked the sheriff. "I want to go over everything. I'm not satisfied we can't do better."

275   Again, for one brief moment, the two women's eyes found one another. The sheriff came up to the table.

"Did you want to see what Mrs. Peters was going to take in?"

The county attorney picked up the apron. He laughed.

"Oh, I guess they're not very dangerous things the ladies have picked out."

280   Mrs. Hale's hand was on the sewing basket in which the box was concealed. She felt that she ought to take her hand off the basket. She did not

---

[3] Horses.

seem able to. He picked up one of the quilt blocks which she had piled on to cover the box. Her eyes felt like fire. She had a feeling that if he took up the basket she would snatch it from him.

But he did not take it up. With another little laugh, he turned away, saying:

"No; Mrs. Peters doesn't need supervising. For that matter, a sheriff's wife is married to the law. Ever think of it that way, Mrs. Peters?"

Mrs. Peters was standing beside the table. Mrs. Hale shot a look up at her; but she could not see her face. Mrs. Peters had turned away. When she spoke, her voice was muffled.

"Not—just that way," she said.

285   "Married to the law!" chuckled Mrs. Peters's husband. He moved toward the door into the front room, and said to the county attorney:

"I just want you to come in here a minute, George. We ought to take a look at these windows."

"Oh—windows," said the county attorney scoffingly.

"We'll be right out, Mr. Hale," said the sheriff to the farmer, who was still waiting by the door.

Hale went to look after the horses. The sheriff followed the county attorney into the other room. Again—for one moment—the two women were alone in that kitchen.

290   Martha Hale sprang up, her hands tight together, looking at that other woman, with whom it rested. At first she could not see her eyes, for the sheriff's wife had not turned back since she turned away at that suggestion of being married to the law. But now Mrs. Hale made her turn back. Her eyes made her turn back. Slowly, unwillingly, Mrs. Peters turned her head until her eyes met the eyes of the other woman. There was a moment when they held each other in a steady, burning look in which there was no evasion nor flinching. Then Martha Hale's eyes pointed the way to the basket in which was hidden the thing that would make certain the conviction of the other woman—that woman who was not there and yet who had been there with them all through that hour.

For a moment Mrs. Peters did not move. And then she did it. With a rush forward, she threw back the quilt pieces, got the box, tried to put it in her handbag. It was too big. Desperately she opened it, started to take the bird out. But there she broke—she could not touch the bird. She stood there helpless, foolish.

There was the sound of a knob turning in the inner door. Martha Hale snatched the box from the sheriff's wife, and got it in the pocket of her big coat just as the sheriff and the county attorney came back into the kitchen.

"Well, Henry," said the county attorney facetiously, "at least we found out that she was not going to quilt it. She was going to—what is it you call it, ladies?"

Mrs. Hale's hand was against the pocket of her coat.

295   "We call it—knot it, Mr. Henderson."

J A M E S   J O Y C E

(1884–1941)

Eveline

(1914)

She sat at the window watching the evening invade the avenue. Her head was leaned against the window curtains and in her nostrils was the odor of dusty cretonne.[1] She was tired.

Few people passed. The man out of the last house passed on his way home; she heard his footsteps clacking along the concrete pavement and afterwards crunching on the cinder path before the new red houses. One time there used to be a field there in which they used to play every evening with other people's children. Then a man from Belfast[2] bought the field and built houses in it—not like their little brown houses but bright brick houses with shining roofs. The children of the avenue used to play together in that field—the Devines, the Waters, the Dunns, little Keogh the cripple, she and her brothers and sisters. Ernest, however, never played: he was too grown up. Her father used often to hunt them in out of the field with his blackthorn stick; but usually little Keogh used to keep *nix*[3] and call out when he saw her father coming. Still they seemed to have been rather happy then. Her father was not so bad then; and besides, her mother was alive. That was a long time ago; she and her brothers and sisters were all grown up; her mother was dead. Tizzie Dunn was dead, too, and the Waters had gone back to England. Everything changes. Now she was going to go away like the others, to leave her home.

Home! She looked around the room, reviewing all its familiar objects which she had dusted once a week for so many years, wondering where on earth all the dust came from. Perhaps she would never see again those familiar objects from which she had never dreamed of being divided. And yet during all those years she had never found out the name of the priest whose yellowing photograph hung on the wall above the broken harmonium beside the colored print of the promises made to Blessed Margaret Mary Alacoque. He had been a school friend of her father. Whenever he showed the photograph to a visitor her father used to pass it with a casual word:

---

[1] Heavy cloth used for curtains and upholstery.

[2] Capital of present-day Northern Ireland. This story refers to a time before the Partition of Ireland.

[3] Keep watch (slang).

"He is in Melbourne now."

5   She had consented to go away, to leave her home. Was that wise? She tried to weigh each side of the question. In her home anyway she had shelter and food; she had those whom she had known all her life about her. Of course she had to work hard both in the house and at business. What would they say of her in the Stores when they found out that she had run away with a fellow? Say she was a fool, perhaps; and her place would be filled up by advertisement. Miss Gavan would be glad. She had always had an edge on her, especially whenever there were people listening.

"Miss Hill, don't you see these ladies are waiting?"

"Look lively, Miss Hill, please."

She would not cry many tears at leaving the Stores.

But in her new home, in a distant unknown country, it would not be like that. Then she would be married—she, Eveline. People would treat her with respect then. She would not be treated as her mother had been. Even now, though she was over nineteen, she sometimes felt herself in danger of her father's violence. She knew it was that that had given her the palpitations. When they were growing up he had never gone for her, like he used to go for Harry and Ernest, because she was a girl; but latterly he had begun to threaten her and say what he would do to her only for her dead mother's sake. And now she had nobody to protect her. Ernest was dead and Harry, who was in the church decorating business, was nearly always down somewhere in the country. Besides, the invariable squabble for money on Saturday nights had begun to weary her unspeakably. She always gave her entire wages—seven shillings—and Harry always sent up what he could but the trouble was to get any money from her father. He said she used to squander the money, that she had no head, that he wasn't going to give her his hard-earned money to throw about the streets, and much more, for he was usually fairly bad of a Saturday night. In the end he would give her the money and ask her had she any intention of buying Sunday dinner. Then she had to rush out as quickly as she could and do her marketing, holding her black leather purse tightly in her hand as she elbowed her way through the crowds and returning home late under her load of provisions. She had hard work to keep the house together and to see that the two young children, who had been left to her charge went to school regularly and got their meals regularly. It was hard work—a hard life—but now that she was about to leave it she did not find it a wholly undesirable life.

10   She was about to explore another life with Frank. Frank was very kind, manly, open-hearted. She was to go away with him by the night-boat to be his wife and to live with him in Buenos Aires where he had a home waiting for her. How well she remembered the first time she had seen him; he was lodging in a house on the main road where she used to visit. It seemed a few weeks ago. He was standing at the gate, his peaked cap pushed back on his head and his hair tumbled forward over a face of bronze. Then they had come to know each other. He used to meet her outside the Stores every

evening and see her home. He took her to see *The Bohemian Girl* and she felt elated as she sat in an unaccustomed part of the theater with him. He was awfully fond of music and sang a little. People knew that they were courting and, when he sang about the lass that loves a sailor, she always felt pleasantly confused. He used to call her Poppens out of fun. First of all it had been an excitement for her to have a fellow and then she had begun to like him. He had tales of distant countries. He had started as a deck boy at a pound a month on a ship of the Allan Line going out to Canada. He told her the names of the ships he had been on and the names of the different services. He had sailed through the Straits of Magellan[4] and he told her stories of the terrible Patagonians.[5] He had fallen on his feet in Buenos Aires, he said, and had come over to the old country just for a holiday. Of course, her father had found out the affair and had forbidden her to have anything to say to him.

"I know these sailor chaps," he said.

One day he had quarreled with Frank and after that she had to meet her lover secretly.

The evening deepened in the avenue. The white of two letters in her lap grew indistinct. One was to Harry; the other was to her father. Ernest had been her favorite but she liked Harry too. Her father was becoming old lately, she noticed; he would miss her. Sometimes he could be very nice. Not long before, when she had been laid up for a day, he had read her out a ghost story and made toast for her at the fire. Another day, when their mother was alive, they had all gone for a picnic to the Hill of Howth. She remembered her father putting on her mother's bonnet to make the children laugh.

Her time was running out but she continued to sit by the window, leaning her head against the window curtain, inhaling the odor of dusty cretonne. Down far in the avenue she could hear a street organ playing. She knew the air. Strange that it should come that very night to remind her of the promise to her mother, her promise to keep the home together as long as she could. She remembered the last night of her mother's illness; she was again in the close dark room at the other side of the hall and outside she heard a melancholy air of Italy. The organ player had been ordered to go away and given sixpence. She remembered her father strutting back into the sickroom saying:

15   "Damned Italians! coming over here!"

As she mused the pitiful vision of her mother's life laid its spell on the very quick of her being—that life of commonplace sacrifices closing in

---

4   Sea channel at the southern tip of South America.

5   People from Patagonia, a tableland region in southern Argentina and Chile.

final craziness. She trembled as she heard again her mother's voice saying constantly with foolish insistence:

"Derevaun Seraun! Derevaun Seraun!"[6]

She stood up in a sudden impulse of terror. Escape! She must escape! Frank would save her. He would give her life, perhaps love, too. But she wanted to live. Why should she be unhappy? She had a right to happiness. Frank would take her in his arms, fold her in his arms. He would save her.

She stood among the swaying crowd in the station at the North Wall. He held her hand and she knew that he was speaking to her, saying something about the passage over and over again. The station was full of soldiers with brown baggages. Through the wide doors of the sheds she caught a glimpse of the black mass of the boat, lying in beside the quay[7] wall, with illumined portholes. She answered nothing. She felt her cheek pale and cold and, out of a maze of distress, she prayed to God to direct her, to show her what was her duty. The boat blew a long mournful whistle into the mist. If she went, tomorrow she would be on the sea with Frank, steaming toward Buenos Aires. Their passage had been booked. Could she still draw back after all he had done for her? Her distress awoke a nausea in her body and she kept moving her lips in silent, fervent prayer.

20   A bell clanged upon her heart. She felt him seize her hand:

"Come!"

All the seas of the world tumbled about her heart. He was drawing her into them: he would drown her. She gripped with both hands at the iron railing.

"Come!"

No! No! No! It was impossible. Her hands clutched the iron in frenzy. Amid the seas she sent a cry of anguish!

25   "Eveline! Evvy!"

He rushed beyond the barrier and called to her to follow. He was shouted at to go on but he still called to her. She set her white face to him, passive, like a helpless animal. Her eyes gave him no sign of love or farewell or recognition.

---

6 "The end of pleasure is pain!" (Irish).

7 A paved stretch of shoreline facing navigable water, used for loading and unloading ships.

FRANZ KAFKA

(1883–1924)

The Metamorphosis

(1915)

I

As Gregor Samsa awoke one morning from uneasy dreams he found himself transformed in his bed into a gigantic insect. He was lying on his hard, as it were armor-plated, back and when he lifted his head a little he could see his dome-like brown belly divided into stiff arched segments on top of which the bed quilt could hardly keep in position and was about to slide off completely. His numerous legs, which were pitifully thin compared to the rest of his bulk, waved helplessly before his eyes.

What has happened to me? he thought. It was no dream. His room, a regular human bedroom, only rather too small, lay quiet between the four familiar walls. Above the table on which a collection of cloth samples was unpacked and spread out—Samsa was a commercial traveler—hung the picture which he had recently cut out of an illustrated magazine and put into a pretty gilt frame. It showed a lady, with a fur cap on and a fur stole, sitting upright and holding out to the spectator a huge fur muff into which the whole of her forearm had vanished!

Gregor's eyes turned next to the window, and the overcast sky—one could hear rain drops beating on the window gutter—made him quite melancholy. What about sleeping a little longer and forgetting all this nonsense, he thought, but it could not be done, for he was accustomed to sleep on his right side and in his present condition he could not turn himself over. However violently he forced himself towards his right side he always rolled on to his back again. He tried it at least a hundred times, shutting his eyes to keep from seeing his struggling legs, and only desisted when he began to feel in his side a faint dull ache he had never experienced before.

Oh God, he thought, what an exhausting job I've picked on! Traveling about day in, day out. It's much more irritating work than doing the actual business in the office, and on top of that there's the trouble of constant traveling, of worrying about train connections, the bed and irregular meals, casual acquaintances that are always new and never become intimate friends. The devil take it all! He felt a slight itching up on his belly; slowly pushed himself on his back nearer to the top of the bed so that he could lift his head more easily; identified the itching place which was surrounded by many small white spots the nature of which he could not understand and made to touch it with a leg, but drew the leg back immediately, for the contact made a cold shiver run through him.

5   He slid down again into his former position. This getting up early, he thought, makes one quite stupid. A man needs his sleep. Other commercials live like harem women. For instance, when I come back to the hotel of a morning to write up the orders I've got, these others are only sitting down to breakfast. Let me just try that with my chief; I'd be sacked on the spot. Anyhow, that might be quite a good thing for me, who can tell? If I didn't have to hold my hand because of my parents I'd have given notice long ago, I'd have gone to the chief and told him exactly what I think of him. That would knock him endways from his desk! It's a queer way of doing, too, this sitting on high at a desk and talking down to employees, especially when they have to come quite near because the chief is hard of hearing. Well, there's still hope; once I've saved enough money to pay back my parents' debts to him—that should take another five or six years—I'll do it without fail. I'll cut myself completely loose then. For the moment, though, I'd better get up, since my train goes at five.

He looked at the alarm clock ticking on the chest. Heavenly Father! he thought. It was half-past six o'clock and the hands were quietly moving on, it was even past the half-hour, it was getting on toward a quarter to seven. Had the alarm clock not gone off? From the bed one could see that it had been properly set for four o'clock; of course it must have gone off. Yes, but was it possible to sleep quietly through that ear-splitting noise? Well, he had not slept quietly, yet apparently all the more soundly for that. But what was he to do now? The next train went at seven o'clock; to catch that he would need to hurry like mad and his samples weren't even packed up, and he himself wasn't feeling particularly fresh and active. And even if he did catch the train he wouldn't avoid a row with the chief, since the firm's porter would have been waiting for the five o'clock train and would have long since reported his failure to turn up. The porter was a creature of the chief's, spineless and stupid. Well, supposing he were to say he was sick? But that would be most unpleasant and would look suspicious, since during his five years' employment he had not been ill once. The chief himself would be sure to come with the sick-insurance doctor, would reproach his parents with their son's laziness and would cut all excuses short by referring to the insurance doctor, who of course regarded all mankind as perfectly healthy malingerers. And would he be so far wrong on this occasion? Gregor really felt quite well, apart from a drowsiness that was utterly superfluous after such a long sleep, and he was even unusually hungry.

As all this was running through his mind at top speed without his being able to decide to leave his bed—the alarm clock had just struck a quarter to seven—there came a cautious tap at the door behind the head of his bed. "Gregor," said a voice—it was his mother's—"it's a quarter to seven. Hadn't you a train to catch?" That gentle voice! Gregor had a shock as he heard his own voice answering hers, unmistakably his own voice, it was true, but with a persistent horrible twittering squeak behind it like an undertone, that left the words in their clear shape only for the first moment and then rose up reverberating round them to destroy their sense, so that one could not be sure one had heard them rightly. Gregor wanted to answer at length and explain everything, but in the circumstances he confined himself to saying: "Yes, yes, thank you, Mother, I'm getting up now." The wooden door between them must have kept the change in his voice from being noticeable outside, for his mother contented herself with this statement and shuffled away. Yet this brief exchange of words had made the other members of the family aware that Gregor was still in the house, as they had not expected, and at one of the side doors his father was already knocking, gently, yet with his fist. "Gregor, Gregor," he called, "what's the matter with you?" And after a little while he called again in a deeper voice: "Gregor! Gregor!" At the other side door his sister was saying in a low, plaintive tone: "Gregor? Aren't you well? Are you needing anything?" He answered them both at once: "I'm just ready," and did his best to make his voice sound as normal as possible by enunciating the words very clearly and leaving long pauses between them. So his father went back to his breakfast, but his sister whispered: "Gregor, open the door, do." However, he was not thinking of opening the door, and felt thankful for the prudent habit he had acquired in traveling of locking all doors during the night, even at home.

His immediate intention was to get up quietly without being disturbed, to put on his clothes and above all eat his breakfast, and only then to consider what else was to be done, since in bed, he was well aware, his meditations would come to no sensible conclusion. He remembered that often enough in bed he had felt small aches and pains, probably caused by awkward postures, which had proved purely imaginary once he got up, and he looked forward eagerly to seeing this morning's delusions gradually fall away. That the change in his voice was nothing but the precursor of a severe chill, a standing ailment of commercial travelers, he had not the least possible doubt.

To get rid of the quilt was quite easy; he had only to inflate himself a little and it fell off by itself. But the next move was difficult, especially because he was so uncommonly broad. He would have needed arms and hands to hoist himself up; instead he had only the numerous little legs which never stopped waving in all directions and which he could not control in the least. When he tried to bend one of them it was the first to stretch itself straight; and did he succeed at last in making it do what he wanted, all the other legs meanwhile waved the more wildly in a high degree of unpleasant agitation. "But what's the use of lying idle in bed," said Gregor to himself.

10   He thought that he might get out of bed with the lower part of his body first, but this lower part, which he had not yet seen and of which he could form no clear conception, proved too difficult to move; it shifted so slowly; and when finally, almost wild with annoyance, he gathered his forces together and thrust out recklessly, he had miscalculated the direction and bumped heavily against the lower end of the bed,

and the stinging pain he felt informed him that precisely this lower part of his body was at the moment probably the most sensitive.

So he tried to get the top part of himself out first, and cautiously moved his head towards the edge of the bed. That proved easy enough, and despite its breadth and mass the bulk of his body at last slowly followed the movement of his head. Still, when he finally got his head free over the edge of the bed he felt too scared to go on advancing, for after all if he let himself fall in this way it would take a miracle to keep his head from being injured. And at all costs he must not lose consciousness now, precisely now; he would rather stay in bed.

But when after a repetition of the same efforts he lay in his former position again, sighing, and watched his little legs struggling against each other more wildly than ever, if that were possible, and saw no way of bringing any order into this arbitrary confusion, he told himself again that it was impossible to stay in bed and that the most sensible course was to risk everything for the smallest hope of getting away from it. At the same time he did not forget meanwhile to remind himself that cool reflection, the coolest possible, was much better than desperate resolves. In such moments he focused his eyes as sharply as possible on the window, but, unfortunately, the prospect of the morning fog, which muffled even the other side of the narrow street, brought him little encouragement and comfort. "Seven o'clock already," he said to himself when the alarm clock chimed again, "seven o'clock already and still such a thick fog." And for a little while he lay quiet, breathing lightly, as if perhaps expecting such complete repose to restore all things to their real and normal condition.

But then he said to himself: "Before it strikes a quarter past seven I must be quite out of this bed, without fail. Anyhow, by that time someone will have come from the office to ask for me, since it opens before seven." And he set himself to rocking his whole body at once in a regular rhythm, with the idea of swinging it out of the bed. If he tipped himself out in that way he could keep his head from injury by lifting it at an acute angle when he fell. His back seemed to be hard and was not likely to suffer from a fall on the carpet. His biggest worry was the loud crash he would not be able to help making, which would probably cause anxiety, if not terror, behind all the doors. Still, he must take the risk.

When he was already half out of the bed—the new method was more a game than an effort, for he needed only to hitch himself across by rocking to and fro—it struck him how simple it would be if he could get help. Two strong people—he thought of his father and the servant girl—would be amply sufficient; they would only have to thrust their arms under his convex back, lever him out of the bed, bend down with their burden and then be patient enough to let him turn himself right over on to the floor, where it was to be hoped his legs would then find their proper function. Well, ignoring the fact that the doors were all locked, ought he really to call for help? In spite of his misery he could not suppress a smile at the very idea of it.

15   He had got so far that he could barely keep his equilibrium when he rocked himself strongly, and he would have to nerve himself very soon for the final decision since in five minutes' time it would be a quarter past seven—when the front door bell rang. "That's someone from the office," he said to himself, and grew almost rigid, while his little legs only jigged about all the faster. For a moment everything stayed quiet. "They're not going to open the door," said Gregor to himself, catching at some kind of irrational hope. But then of course the servant girl went as usual to the door with her heavy tread and opened it. Gregor needed only to hear the first good morning of the visitor to know immediately who it was—the chief clerk himself. What a fate, to be condemned to work for a firm where the smallest omission at once gave rise to the gravest suspicion! Were all employees in a body nothing but scoundrels, was there not among them one single loyal devoted man who, had he wasted only an hour or so of the firm's time in a morning, was so tormented by conscience as to be driven out of his mind and actually incapable of leaving his bed? Wouldn't it really have been sufficient to send an apprentice to inquire—if any inquiry were necessary at all—did the chief clerk himself have to come and thus indicate to the entire family, an innocent family, that this suspicious circumstance could be investigated by no one less versed in affairs than himself? And more through the agitation caused by these reflections than through any act of will Gregor swung himself out of bed with all his strength. There was a loud thump, but it was not really a crash. His fall was broken to some extent by the carpet, his back, too, was less stiff than he thought, and so there was merely a dull thud, not so very startling. Only he had not lifted his head carefully enough and had hit it; he turned it and rubbed it on the carpet in pain and irritation.

"That was something falling down in there," said the chief clerk in the next room to the left. Gregor tried to suppose to himself that something like what had happened to him today might some day happen to the chief clerk; one really could not deny that it was possible. But as if in brusque reply to this supposition the chief clerk took a couple of firm steps in the next-door room and his patent leather boots creaked. From the right-hand room his sister was whispering to inform him of the situation: "Gregor, the chief clerk's here." "I know," muttered Gregor to himself; but he didn't dare to make his voice loud enough for his sister to hear it.

"Gregor," said his father now from the left-hand room, "the chief clerk has come and wants to know why you didn't catch the early train. We don't know what to say to him. Besides, he wants to talk to you in person. So open the door, please. He will be good enough to excuse the untidiness of your room." "Good morning, Mr. Samsa," the chief clerk was calling amiably meanwhile. "He's not well," said his mother to the visitor, while his father was still speaking through the door, "he's not well, sir, believe me. What else would make him miss a train! The boy thinks about nothing but his work. It makes me almost cross the way he never goes out in the evenings; he's been here the last eight days and has stayed at home every single evening. He just sits there quietly at the table reading a news-paper or looking through railway timetables. The only amusement he gets is doing fretwork. For instance, he spent two or three evenings cutting out a little picture frame; you would be surprised to see how pretty it is; it's hanging in his room; you'll see it in a minute when Gregor opens the door. I must say I'm glad you've come, sir; we should never have got him to unlock the door by ourselves; he's so obstinate; and I'm sure he's unwell, though he wouldn't have it to be so this morning." "I'm just coming," said Gregor slowly and carefully, not moving an inch for fear of losing one word of the conversation. "I can't think of any other explanation, madam," said the chief clerk, "I hope it's nothing serious. Although on the other hand I must say that we men of business—fortunately or unfor-tunately—very often simply have to ignore any slight indisposition, since business must be attended to." "Well, can the chief clerk come in now?" asked Gregor's father impatiently, again knocking on the door. "No," said Gregor. In the left-hand room a painful silence followed this refusal, in the right-hand room his sister began to sob.

Why didn't his sister join the others? She was probably newly out of bed and hadn't even begun to put on her clothes yet. Well, why was she crying? Because he wouldn't get up and let the chief clerk in, because he was in danger of losing his job, and because the chief would begin dun-ning his parents again for the old debts? Surely these were things one didn't need to worry about for the present. Gregor was still at home and not in the least thinking of deserting the family. At the moment, true, he was lying on the carpet and no one who knew the condition he was in could seriously expect him to admit the chief clerk. But for such a small discourtesy, which could plausibly be explained away somehow later on, Gregor could hardly be dismissed on the spot. And it seemed to Gregor that it would be much more sensible to leave him in peace for the present than to trouble him with tears and entreaties. Still, of course, their uncer-tainty bewildered them all and excused their behavior.

"Mr. Samsa," the chief clerk called now in a louder voice, "what's the matter with you? Here you are, barricading yourself in your room, giving only 'yes' and 'no' for answers, causing your parents a lot of unnecessary trouble and neglecting—I mention this only in passing—neglecting your business duties in an incredible fashion. I am speaking here in the name of your parents and of your chief, and I beg you quite seriously to give me an immediate and precise explanation. You amaze me, you amaze me. I thought you were a quiet, dependable person, and now all at once you seem bent on making a disgraceful exhibition of yourself. The chief did hint to me early this morning a possible explanation for your disappear-ance—with reference to the cash payments that were entrusted to you re-cently—but I almost pledged my solemn word of honor that this could not be so. But now that I see how incredibly obstinate you are, I no longer have the slightest desire to take your part at all. And your position in the firm is not so unassailable. I came with the intention of telling you all this in private, but since you are wasting my time so needlessly I don't see why your parents shouldn't hear it too. For some time past your work has been most unsatisfactory; this is not the season of the year for a business boom, of course, we admit that, but a season of the year for doing no business at all, that does not exist, Mr. Samsa, must not exist."

20   "But, sir," cried Gregor, beside himself and in his agitation forgetting everything else, "I'm just going to open the door this very minute. A slight illness, an attack of giddiness, has kept me from getting up. I'm still lying in bed. But I feel all right again. I'm getting out of bed now. Just give me a moment or two longer! I'm not quite so well as I thought. But I'm all right, really. How a thing like that can suddenly strike one down! Only last night I was quite well, my parents can tell you, or rather I did have a slight presentiment. I must have showed some sign of it. Why didn't I report it at the office! But one always thinks that an indisposition can be got over without staying in the house. Oh sir, do spare my parents! All that you're reproaching me with now has no foundation; no one has ever said a word to me about it. Perhaps you haven't looked at the last orders I sent in. Anyhow, I can still catch the eight o'clock train, I'm much the better for my few hours' rest. Don't let me detain you here, sir; I'll be attending to business very soon, and do be good enough to tell the chief so and to make my excuses to him!"

And while all this was tumbling out pell-mell and Gregor hardly knew what he was saying, he had reached the chest quite easily, perhaps because of the practice he had had in bed, and was now trying to lever himself upright by means of it. He meant actually to open the door, actually to show himself and speak to the chief clerk; he was eager to find out what the others, after all their insistence, would say at the sight of him. If they were horrified then the responsibility was no longer his and he could stay quiet. But if they took it calmly, then he had no reason either to be upset, and could really get to the station for the eight o'clock train if he hurried. At first he slipped down a few times from the polished surface of the chest, but at length with a last heave he stood upright; he paid no more attention to the pains in the lower part of his body, however they smarted. Then he let himself fall against the back of a near-by chair, and clung with his little legs to the edges of it. That brought him into control of himself again and he stopped speaking, for now he could listen to what the chief clerk was saying.

"Did you understand a word of it?" the chief clerk was asking; "surely he can't be trying to make fools of us?" "Oh dear," cried his mother, in tears, "perhaps he's terribly ill and we're tormenting him. Grete! Grete!" she called out then. "Yes Mother?" called his sister from the other side. They were calling to each other across Gregor's room. "You must go this minute for the doctor. Gregor is ill. Go for the doctor, quick. Did you hear how he was speaking?" "That was no human voice," said the chief clerk in a voice noticeably low beside the shrillness of the mother's. "Anna! Anna!" his father was calling through the hall to the kitchen, clapping his hands, "get a locksmith at once!" And the two girls were already running through the hall with a swish of skirts—how could his sister have got dressed so quickly?—and were tearing the front door open. There was no sound of its closing again; they had evidently left it open, as one does in houses where some great misfortune has happened.

But Gregor was now much calmer. The words he uttered were no longer understandable, apparently, although they seemed clear enough to him, even clearer than before, perhaps because his ear had grown accustomed to the sound of them. Yet at any rate people now believed that something was wrong with him, and were ready to help him. The positive certainty with which these first measures had been taken comforted him. He felt himself drawn once more into the human circle and hoped for great and remarkable results from both the doctor and the locksmith, without really distinguishing precisely between them. To make his voice as clear as possible for the decisive conversation that was now imminent he coughed a little, as quietly as he could, of course, since this noise too might not sound like a human cough for all he was able to judge. In the next room meanwhile there was complete silence. Perhaps his parents were sitting at the table with the chief clerk, whispering, perhaps they were all leaning against the door and listening.

Slowly Gregor pushed the chair towards the door, then let go of it, caught hold of the door for support—the soles at the end of his little legs were somewhat sticky—and rested against it for a moment after his efforts. Then he set himself to turning the key in the lock with his mouth. It seemed, unhappily, that he hadn't really any teeth—what could he grip the key with?—but on the other hand his jaws were certainly very strong; with their help he did manage to set the key in motion, heedless of the fact that he was undoubtedly damaging them somewhere, since a brown fluid issued from his mouth, flowed over the key and dripped on the floor. "Just listen to that," said the chief clerk next door; "he's turning the key." That was a great encouragement to Gregor; but they should all have shouted encouragement to him, his father and mother too: "Go on, Gregor," they should have called out, "keep going, hold on to that key!" And in the belief that they were all following his efforts intently, he clenched his jaws recklessly on the key with all the force at his command. As the turning of the key progressed he circled round the lock, holding on now only with his mouth, pushing on the key, as required, or pulling it down again with all the weight of his body. The louder click of the finally yielding lock literally quickened Gregor. With a deep breath of relief he said to himself: "So I didn't need the locksmith," and laid his head on the handle to open the door wide.

25   Since he had to pull the door towards him, he was still invisible when it was really wide open. He had to edge himself slowly round the near half of the double door, and to do it very carefully if he was not to fall plump upon his back just on the threshold. He was still carrying out this difficult manoeuvre, with no time to observe anything else, when he heard the

chief clerk utter a loud "Oh!"—it sounded like a gust of wind—and how he could see the man, standing as he was nearest to the door, clapping one hand before his open mouth and slowly backing away as if driven by some invisible steady pressure. His mother—in spite of the chief clerk's being there her hair was still undone and sticking up in all directions—first clasped her hands and looked at his father, then took two steps towards Gregor and fell on the floor among her outspread skirts, her face quite hidden on her breast. His father knotted his fist with a fierce expression on his face as if he meant to knock Gregor back into his room, then looked uncertainly round the living room, covered his eyes with his hands and wept till his great chest heaved.

Gregor did not go now into the living room, but leaned against the inside of the firmly shut wing of the door, so that only half his body was visible and his head above it bending sideways to look at the others. The light had meanwhile strengthened; on the other side of the street one could see clearly a section of the endlessly long, dark gray building opposite—it was a hospital—abruptly punctuated by its row of regular windows; the rain was still falling, but only in large singly discernible and literally singly splashing drops. The breakfast dishes were set out on the table lavishly, for breakfast was the most important meal of the day to Gregor's father, who lingered it out for hours over various newspapers. Right opposite Gregor on the wall hung a photograph of himself on military service, as a lieutenant, hand on sword, a carefree smile on his face, inviting one to respect his uniform and military bearing. The door leading to the hall was open, and one could see that the front door stood open too, showing the landing beyond and the beginning of the stairs going down.

"Well," said Gregor, knowing perfectly that he was the only one who had retained any composure, "I'll put my clothes on at once, pack up my samples and start off. Will you only let me go? You see, sir, I'm not obstinate, and I'm willing to work; traveling is a hard life, but I couldn't live without it. Where are you going, sir? To the office? Yes? Will you give a true account of all this? One can be temporarily incapacitated, but that's just the moment for remembering former services and bearing in mind that later on, when the incapacity has been got over, one will certainly work with all the more industry and concentration. I'm loyally bound to serve the chief, you know that very well. Besides, I have to provide for my parents and my sister. I'm in great difficulties, but I'll get out of them again. Don't make things any worse for me than they are. Stand up for me in the firm. Travelers are not popular there, I know. People think they earn sacks of money and just have a good time. A prejudice there's no particular reason for revising. But you, sir, have a more comprehensive view of affairs than the rest of the staff, yes, let me tell you in confidence, a more comprehensive view than the chief himself, who, being the owner, lets his judgment easily be swayed against one of his employees. And you know very well that the traveler, who is never seen in the office almost the whole year round, can so easily fall a victim to gossip and ill luck and unfounded complaints, which he mostly knows nothing about, except when he comes back exhausted from his rounds, and only then suffers in person from their evil consequences, which he can no longer trace back to the original causes. Sir, sir, don't go away without a word to me to show that you think me in the right at least to some extent!"

But at Gregor's very first words the chief clerk had already backed away and only stared at him with parted lips over one twitching shoulder. And while Gregor was speaking he did not stand still one moment but stole away towards the door, without taking his eyes off Gregor, yet only an inch at a time, as if obeying some secret injunction to leave the room. He was already at the hall, and the suddenness with which he took his last step out of the living room would have made one believe he had burned the sole of his foot. Once in the hall he stretched his right arm before him towards the staircase, as if some supernatural power were waiting there to deliver him.

Gregor perceived that the chief clerk must on no account be allowed to go away in this frame of mind if his position in the firm were not to be endangered to the utmost. His parents did not understand this so well; they had convinced themselves in the course of years that Gregor was settled for life in this firm, and besides they were so occupied with their immediate troubles that all foresight had forsaken them. Yet Gregor had this foresight. The chief clerk must be detained, soothed, persuaded and finally won over; the whole future of Gregor and his family depended on it! If only his sister had been there! She was intelligent; she had begun to cry while Gregor was still lying quietly on his back. And no doubt the chief clerk, so partial to ladies, would have been guided by her; she would have shut the door of the flat and in the hall talked him out of his horror. But she was not there, and Gregor would have to handle the situation himself. And without remembering that he was still unaware what powers of movement he possessed, without even remembering that his words in all possibility, indeed in all likelihood, would again be unintelligible, he let go the wing of the door, pushed himself through the opening, started to walk towards the chief clerk, who was already ridiculously clinging with both hands to the railing on the landing; but immediately, as he was feeling for a support, he fell down with a little cry upon all his numerous legs. Hardly was he down when he experienced for the first time this morning a sense of physical comfort; his legs had firm ground under them; they were completely obedient, as he noted with joy; they even strove to carry him forward in whatever direction he chose; and he was inclined to believe that a final relief from all his sufferings was at hand. But in the same moment as he found himself on the floor, rocking with suppressed eagerness to move, not far from his mother, indeed just in front of her, she, who had seemed so completely crushed, sprang all at once to her feet, her arms and fingers outspread, cried: "Help, for God's sake, help!" bent her head down as if to see Gregor better, yet on the contrary kept backing senselessly away; had quite forgotten that the laden table stood behind her; sat upon it hastily, as if in absence of mind, when she bumped into it; and seemed altogether unaware that the big coffee pot beside her was upset and pouring coffee in a flood over the carpet.

30   "Mother, Mother," said Gregor in a low voice, and looked up at her. The chief clerk, for the moment, had quite slipped from his mind; instead, he could not resist snapping his jaws together at the sight of the streaming coffee. That made his mother scream again, she fled from the table and fell into the arms of his father, who hastened to catch her. But Gregor had now no time to spare for his parents; the chief clerk was already on the stairs; with his chin on the banisters he was taking one last backward look. Gregor made a spring, to be as sure as possible of overtaking him; the chief clerk must have divined his intention, for he leaped down several steps and vanished; he was still yelling "Ugh!" and it echoed through the whole staircase.

Unfortunately, the flight of the chief clerk seemed completely to upset Gregor's father, who had remained relatively calm until now, for instead of running after the man himself, or at least not hindering Gregor in his pursuit, he seized in his right hand the walking stick which the chief clerk had left behind on a chair, together with a hat and greatcoat, snatched in his left hand a large newspaper from the table and began stamping his feet and flourishing the stick and the newspaper to drive Gregor back into his room. No entreaty of Gregor's availed, indeed no entreaty was even understood, however humbly he bent his head his father only stamped on the floor the more loudly. Behind his father his mother had torn open a window, despite the cold weather, and was leaning far out of it with her face in her hands. A strong draught set in from the street to the staircase, the window curtains blew in, the newspapers on the table fluttered, stray pages whisked over the floor. Pitilessly Gregor's father drove him back, hissing and crying "Shoo!" like a savage. But Gregor was quite unpracticed in walking backwards, it really was a slow business. If he only had a chance to turn around he could get back to his room at once, but he was afraid of exasperating his father by the slowness of such a rotation and at any moment the stick in his father's hand might hit him a fatal blow on the back or on the head. In the end, however, nothing else was left for him to do since to his horror he observed that in moving backwards he could not even control the direction he took; and so, keeping an anxious eye on his father all the time over his shoulder, he began to turn round as quickly as he could, which was in reality very slowly. Perhaps his father noted his good intentions, for he did not interfere except every now and then to help him in the manoeuvre from a distance with the point of the stick. If only he would have stopped making that unbearable hissing noise! It made Gregor quite lose his head. He had turned almost completely round when the hissing noise so distracted him that he even turned a little the wrong way again. But when at last his head was fortunately right in front of the doorway, it appeared that his body was too broad simply to get through the opening. His father, of course, in his present mood was far from thinking

of such a thing as opening the other half of the door, to let Gregor have
enough space. He had merely the fixed idea of driving Gregor back into
his room as quickly as possible. He would never have suffered Gregor to
make the circumstantial preparations for standing up on end and perhaps
slipping his way through the door. Maybe he was now making more noise
than ever to urge Gregor forward, as if no obstacle impeded him; to Gregor, anyhow, the noise in his rear sounded no longer like the voice of one
single father; this was really no joke, and Gregor thrust himself—come
what might—into the doorway. One side of his body rose up, he was tilted
at an angle in the doorway, his flank was quite bruised, horrid blotches
stained the white door, soon he was stuck fast and, left to himself, could
not have moved at all, his legs on one side fluttered trembling to the air,
those on the other were crushed painfully to the floor—when from behind
his father gave him a strong push which was literally a deliverance and he
flew far into the room, bleeding freely. The door was slammed behind him
with the stick, and then at last there was silence.

II

Not until it was twilight did Gregor awake out of a deep sleep, more like a
swoon than a sleep. He would certainly have waked up of his own accord
not much later, for he felt himself sufficiently rested and well-slept, but it
seemed to him as if a fleeting step and a cautious shutting of the door
leading into the hall had aroused him. The electric lights in the street cast
a pale sheen here and there on the ceiling and the upper surfaces of the
furniture, but down below, where he lay, it was dark. Slowly, awkwardly
trying out his feelers, which he now first learned to appreciate, he pushed
his way to the door to see what had been happening there. His left side felt
like one single long, unpleasantly tense scar, and he had actually to limp
on his two rows of legs. One little leg, moreover, had been severely damaged in the course of that morning's events—it was almost a miracle that
only one had been damaged—and trailed uselessly behind him.

   He had reached the door before he discovered what had really drawn
him to it: the smell of food. For there stood a basin filled with fresh
milk in which floated little sops of white bread. He could almost have
laughed with joy, since he was now still hungrier than in the morning,
and he dipped his head almost over the eyes straight into the milk. But
soon in disappointment he withdrew it again; not only did he find it
difficult to feed because of his tender left side—and he could only feed
with the palpitating collaboration of his whole body—he did not like
the milk either, although milk had been his favorite drink and that was
certainly why his sister had set it there for him, indeed it was almost
with repulsion that he turned away from the basin and crawled back to
the middle of the room.

   He could see through the crack of the door that the gas was turned on
in the living room, but while usually at this time his father made a habit

of reading the afternoon newspaper in a loud voice to his mother and occasionally to his sister as well, not a sound was now to be heard. Well, perhaps his father had recently given up this habit of reading aloud, which his sister had mentioned so often in conversation and in her letters. But there was the same silence all around, although the flat was certainly not empty of occupants. "What a quiet life our family has been leading," said Gregor to himself, and as he sat there motionless staring into the darkness he felt great pride in the fact that he had been able to provide such a life for his parents and sister in such a fine flat. But what if all the quiet, the comfort, the contentment were now to end in horror? To keep himself from being lost in such thoughts Gregor took refuge in movement and crawled up and down the room.

35   Once during the long evening one of the side doors was opened a little and quickly shut again, later the other side door too; someone had apparently wanted to come in and then thought better of it. Gregor now stationed himself immediately before the living room door, determined to persuade any hesitating visitor to come in or at least to discover who it might be; but the door was not opened again and he waited in vain. In the early morning, when the doors were locked, they had all wanted to come in, now that he had opened one door and the other had apparently been opened during the day, no one came in and even the keys were on the other side of the doors.

It was late at night before the gas went out in the living room, and Gregor could easily tell that his parents and his sister had all stayed awake until then, for he could clearly hear the three of them stealing away on tiptoe. No one was likely to visit him, not until the morning, that was certain; so he had plenty of time to meditate at his leisure on how he was to arrange his life afresh. But the lofty, empty room in which he had to lie flat on the floor filled him with an apprehension he could not account for, since it had been his very own room for the past five years—and with a half-unconscious action, not without a slight feeling of shame, he scuttled under the sofa, where he felt comfortable at once, although his back was a little cramped and he could not lift his head up, and his only regret was that his body was too broad to get the whole of it under the sofa.

He stayed there all night, spending the time partly in a light slumber, from which his hunger kept waking him up with a start, and partly in worrying and sketching vague hopes, which all led to the same conclusion, that he must lie low for the present and, by exercising patience and the utmost consideration, help the family to bear the inconvenience he was bound to cause them in his present condition.

Very early in the morning, it was still almost night, Gregor had the chance to test the strength of his new resolutions, for his sister, nearly fully dressed, opened the door from the hall and peered in. She did not see him at once, yet when she caught sight of him under the sofa—well, he had to be somewhere, he couldn't have flown away, could he?—she was so startled that without being able to help it she slammed the door shut again. But as if regretting her behavior she opened the door again immediately and came in on tiptoe, as if she were visiting an invalid or even a stranger. Gregor had pushed his head forward to the very edge of the sofa and watched her. Would she notice that he had left the milk standing, and not for lack of hunger, and would she bring in some other kind of food more to his taste? If she did not do it of her own accord, he would rather starve than draw her attention to the fact, although he felt a wild impulse to dart out from under the sofa, throw himself at her feet and beg her for something to eat. But his sister at once noticed, with surprise, that the basin was still full, except for a little milk that had been spilt all around it, she lifted it immediately, not with her bare hands, true, but with a cloth and carried it away. Gregor was wildly curious to know what she would bring instead, and made various speculations about it. Yet what she actually did next, in the goodness of her heart, he could never have guessed at. To find out what he liked she brought him a whole selection of food, all set out on an old newspaper. There were old, half-decayed vegetables, bones from last night's supper covered with a white sauce that had thickened; some raisins and almonds; a piece of cheese that Gregor would have called uneatable two days ago; a dry roll of bread, a buttered roll, and a roll both buttered and salted. Besides all that, she set down again the same basin, into which she had poured some water, and which was apparently to be reserved for his exclusive use. And with fine tact, knowing that Gregor would not eat in her presence, she withdrew quickly and even turned the key, to let him understand that he could take his ease as much as he liked. Gregor's legs all whizzed towards the food. His wounds must have healed completely, moreover, for he felt no disability, which amazed him and made him reflect how more than a month ago he had cut one finger a little with a knife and had still suffered pain from the wound only the day before yesterday. Am I less sensitive now? he thought, and sucked greedily at the cheese, which above all the other edibles attracted him at once and strongly. One after another and with tears of satisfaction in his eyes he quickly devoured the cheese, the vegetables and the sauce; the fresh food, on the other hand, had no charms for him, he could not even stand the smell of it and actually dragged away to some little distance the things he could eat. He had long finished his meal and was only lying lazily on the same spot when his sister turned the key slowly as a sign for him to retreat. That roused him at once, although he was nearly asleep, and he hurried under the sofa again. But it took considerable self-control for him to stay under the sofa, even for the short time his sister was in the room, since the large meal had swollen his body somewhat and he was so cramped he could hardly breathe. Slight attacks of breathlessness afflicted him and his eyes were starting a little out of his head as he watched his unsuspecting sister sweeping together with a broom not only the remains of what he had eaten but even the things he had not touched, as if these were now of no use to anyone, and hastily shoveling it all into a bucket, which she covered with a wooden lid and carried away. Hardly had she turned her back when Gregor came from under the sofa and stretched and puffed himself out.

In this manner Gregor was fed, once in the early morning while his parents and the servant girl were still asleep, and a second time after they had all had their midday dinner, for then his parents took a short nap and the servant girl could be sent out on some errand or other by his sister. Not that they would have wanted him to starve, of course, but perhaps they could not have borne to know more about his feeding than from hearsay, perhaps too his sister wanted to spare them such little anxieties wherever possible, since they had quite enough to bear as it was.

40   Under what pretext the doctor and the locksmith had been got rid of on that first morning Gregor could not discover, for since what he said was not understood by the others it never struck any of them, not even his sister, that he could understand what they said, and so whenever his sister came into his room he had to content himself with hearing her utter only a sigh now and then and an occasional appeal to the saints. Later on, when she had got a little used to the situation—of course she could never get completely used to it—she sometimes threw out a remark which was kindly meant or could be so interpreted. "Well, he liked his dinner today," she would say when Gregor had made a good clearance of his food; and when he had not eaten, which gradually happened more and more often, she would say almost sadly: "Everything's been left standing again."

But although Gregor could get no news directly, he overheard a lot from the neighboring rooms, and as soon as voices were audible, he would run to the door of the room concerned and press his whole body against it. In the first few days especially there was no conversation that did not refer to him somehow, even if only indirectly. For two whole days there were family consultations at every mealtime about what should be done; but also between meals the same subject was discussed, for there were always at least two members of the family at home, since no one wanted to be alone in the flat and to leave it quite empty was unthinkable. And on the very first of these days the household cook—it was not quite clear what and how much she knew of the situation—went down on her knees to his mother and begged leave to go, and when she departed, a quarter of an hour later, gave thanks for her dismissal with tears in her eyes as if for the greatest benefit that could have been conferred on her, and without any prompting swore a solemn oath that she would never say a single word to anyone about what had happened.

Now Gregor's sister had to cook too, helping her mother; true, the cooking did not amount to much, for they ate scarcely anything. Gregor was always hearing one of the family vainly urging another to eat and getting no answer but: "Thanks, I've had all I want," or something similar. Perhaps they drank nothing either. Time and again his sister kept asking his father if he wouldn't like some beer and offered kindly to go and fetch it herself, and when he made no answer suggested that she could ask the concierge to fetch it, so that he need feel no sense of obligation, but then a round "No" came from his father and no more was said about it.

In the course of that very first day Gregor's father explained the family's financial position and prospects to both his mother and his sister. Now and then he rose from the table to get some voucher or memorandum out of the small safe he had rescued from the collapse of his business five years earlier. One could hear him opening the complicated lock and rustling papers out and shutting it again. This statement made by his father was the first cheerful information Gregor had heard since his imprisonment. He had been of the opinion that nothing at all was left over from his father's business, at least his father had never said anything to the contrary, and of course he had not asked him directly. At that time Gregor's sole desire was to do his utmost to help the family to forget as soon as possible the catastrophe which had overwhelmed the business and thrown them all into a state of complete despair. And so he had set to work with unusual ardor and almost overnight had become a commercial traveler instead of a little clerk, with of course much greater chances of earning money, and his success was immediately translated into good round coin which he could lay on the table for his amazed and happy family. These had been fine times, and they had never recurred, at least not with the same sense of glory, although later on Gregor had earned so much money that he was able to meet the expenses of the whole household and did so. They had simply got used to it, both the family and Gregor; the money was gratefully accepted and gladly given, but there was no special uprush of warm feeling. With his sister alone had he remained intimate, and it was a secret plan of his that she, who loved music, unlike himself, and could play movingly on the violin, should be sent next year to study at the Conservatorium, despite the great expense that would entail, which must be made up in some other way. During his brief visits home the Conservatorium was often mentioned in the talks he had with his sister, but always merely as a beautiful dream which could never come true, and his parents discouraged even these innocent references to it; yet Gregor had made up his mind firmly about it and meant to announce the fact with due solemnity on Christmas Day.

Such were the thoughts, completely futile in his present condition, that went through his head as he stood clinging upright to the door and listening. Sometimes out of sheer weariness he had to give up listening and let his head fall negligently against the door, but he always had to pull himself together again at once, for even the slight sound his head made was audible next door and brought all conversation to a stop. "What can he be doing now?" his father would say after a while, obviously turning towards the door, and only then would the interrupted conversation gradually be set going again.

45   Gregor was now informed as amply as he could wish—for his father tended to repeat himself in his explanations, partly because it was a long time since he had handled such matters and partly because his mother could not always grasp things at once—that a certain amount of investments, a very small amount it was true, had survived the wreck of their fortunes and had even increased a little because the dividends had not

been touched meanwhile. And besides that, the money Gregor brought home every month—he had kept only a few dollars for himself—had never been quite used up and now amounted to a small capital sum. Behind the door Gregor nodded his head eagerly, rejoiced at this evidence of unexpected thrift and foresight. True, he could really have paid off some more of his father's debts to the chief with his extra money, and so brought much nearer the day on which he could quit his job, but doubtless it was better the way his father had arranged it.

Yet this capital was by no means sufficient to let the family live on the interest of it; for one year, perhaps, or at the most two, they could live on the principal, that was all. It was simply a sum that ought not to be touched and should be kept for a rainy day; money for living expenses would have to be earned. Now his father was still hale enough but an old man, and he had done no work for the past five years and could not be expected to do much; during these five years, the first years of leisure in his laborious though unsuccessful life, he had grown rather fat and become sluggish. And Gregor's old mother, how was she to earn a living with her asthma, which troubled her even when she walked through the flat and kept her lying on a sofa every other day panting for breath beside an open window? And was his sister to earn her bread, she who was still a child of seventeen and whose life hitherto had been so pleasant, consisting as it did in dressing herself nicely, sleeping long, helping in the housekeeping, going out to a few modest entertainments and above all playing the violin? At first whenever the need for earning money was mentioned Gregor let go his hold on the door and threw himself down on the cool leather sofa beside it, he felt so hot with shame and grief.

Often he just lay there the long nights through without sleeping at all, scrabbling for hours on the leather. Or he nerved himself to the great effort of pushing an armchair to the window, then crawled up over the window sill and, braced against the chair, leaned against the window panes, obviously in some recollection of the sense of freedom that looking out of a window always used to give him. For in reality day by day things that were even a little way off were growing dimmer to his sight; the hospital across the street, which he used to execrate for being all too often before his eyes, was now quite beyond his range of vision, and if he had not known that he lived in Charlotte Street, a quiet street but still a city street, he might have believed that his window gave on a desert waste where gray sky and gray land blended indistinguishably into each other. His quick-witted sister only needed to observe twice that the armchair stood by the window; after that whenever she had tidied the room she always pushed the chair back to the same place at the window and even left the inner casements open.

If he could have spoken to her and thanked her for all she had to do for him, he could have borne her ministrations better; as it was, they oppressed him. She certainly tried to make as light as possible of whatever was disagreeable in her task, and as time went on she succeeded, of course, more and more, but time brought more enlightenment to Gregor too. The very way she came in distressed him. Hardly was she in the room when she rushed to the window, without even taking time to shut the door, careful as she was usually to shield the sight of Gregor's room from the others, and as if she were almost suffocating tore the casements open with hasty fingers, standing then in the open draught for a while even in the bitterest cold and drawing deep breaths. This noisy scurry of hers upset Gregor twice a day; he would crouch trembling under the sofa all the time, knowing quite well that she would certainly have spared him such a disturbance had she found it at all possible to stay in his presence without opening a window.

On one occasion, about a month after Gregor's metamorphosis, when there was surely no reason for her to be still startled at his appearance, she came a little earlier than usual and found him gazing out of the window, quite motionless, and thus well placed to look like a bogey. Gregor would not have been surprised had she not come in at all, for she could not immediately open the window while he was there, but not only did she retreat, she jumped back as if in alarm and banged the door shut; a stranger might well have thought that he had been lying in wait for her there meaning to bite her. Of course he hid himself under the sofa at once, but he had to wait until midday before she came again, and she seemed more ill at ease than usual. This made him realize how repulsive the sight of him still was to her, and that it was bound to go on being repulsive, and what an effort it must cost her not to run away even from the sight of the small portion of his body that stuck out from under the sofa. In order to spare her that, therefore, one day he carried a sheet on his back to the sofa—it cost him four hours' labor—and arranged it there in such a way as to hide him completely, so that even if she were to bend down she could not see him. Had she considered the sheet unnecessary, she would certainly have stripped it off the sofa again, for it was clear enough that this curtaining and confining of himself was not likely to conduce Gregor's comfort, but she left it where it was, and Gregor even fancied that he caught a thankful glance from her eye when he lifted the sheet carefully a very little with his head to see how she was taking the new arrangement.

50   For the first fortnight his parents could not bring themselves to the point of entering his room, and he often heard them expressing their appreciation of his sister's activities, whereas formerly they had frequently scolded her for being as they thought a somewhat useless daughter. But now, both of them often waited outside the door, his father and his mother, while his sister tidied his room, and as soon as she came out she had to tell them exactly how things were in the room, what Gregor had eaten, how he had conducted himself this time and whether there was not perhaps some slight improvement in his condition. His mother, moreover, began relatively soon to want to visit him, but his father and sister dissuaded her at first with arguments which Gregor listened to very attentively and altogether approved. Later, however, she had to be held back by

main force, and when she cried out: "Do let me in to Gregor, he is my unfortunate son! Can't you understand that I must go to him?" Gregor thought it might be well to have her come in, not every day, of course, but perhaps once a week; she understood things, after all, much better than his sister, who was only a child despite the efforts she was making and had perhaps taken on so difficult a task merely out of childish thoughtlessness.

Gregor's desire to see his mother was soon fulfilled. During the daytime he did not want to show himself at the window, out of consideration for his parents, but he could not crawl very far around the few square yards of floor space he had, nor could he bear lying quietly at rest all during the night, while he was fast losing any interest he had ever taken in food, so that for mere recreation he had formed the habit of crawling crisscross over the walls and ceiling. He especially enjoyed hanging suspended from the ceiling; it was much better than lying on the floor; one could breathe more freely; one's body swung and rocked lightly; and in the almost blissful absorption induced by this suspension it could happen to his own surprise that he let go and fell plump on the floor. Yet he now had his body much better under control than formerly, and even such a big fall did him no harm. His sister at once remarked the new distraction Gregor had found for himself—he left traces behind him of the sticky stuff on his soles wherever he crawled—and she got the idea in her head of giving him as wide a field as possible to crawl in and of removing the pieces of furniture that hindered him, above all the chest of drawers and the writing desk. But that was more than she could manage all by herself; she did not dare ask her father to help her; and as for the servant girl, a young creature of sixteen who had had the courage to stay on after the cook's departure, she could not be asked to help, for she had begged as an especial favor that she might keep the kitchen door locked and open it only on a definite summons; so there was nothing left but to apply to her mother at an hour when her father was out. And the old lady did come, with exclamations of joyful eagerness, which, however, died away at the door of Gregor's room. Gregor's sister, of course, went in first, to see that everything was in order before letting his mother enter. In great haste Gregor pulled the sheet lower and rucked it more in folds so that it really looked as if it had been thrown accidentally over the sofa. And this time he did not peer out from under it; he renounced the pleasure of seeing his mother on this occasion and was only glad that she had come at all. "Come in, he's out of sight," said his sister, obviously leading her mother in by the hand. Gregor could now hear the two women struggling to shift the heavy old chest from its place, and his sister claiming the greater part of the labor for herself, without listening to the admonitions of her mother who feared she might overstrain herself. It took a long time. After at least a quarter of an hour's tugging his mother objected that the chest had better be left where it was, for in the first place it was too heavy and could never be got out before his father came home, and standing in the middle of the room like that it would only hamper Gregor's movements, while in the second place it was not at all certain that removing the furniture would be doing a service to

Gregor. She was inclined to think to the contrary; the sight of the naked walls made her own heart heavy, and why shouldn't Gregor have the same feeling, considering that he had been used to his furniture for so long and might feel forlorn without it. "And doesn't it look," she concluded in a low voice—in fact she had been almost whispering all the time as if to avoid letting Gregor, whose exact whereabouts she did not know, hear even the tones of her voice, for she was convinced that he could not understand her words—"doesn't it look as if we were showing him, by taking away his furniture, that we have given up hope of his ever getting better and are just leaving him coldly to himself? I think it would be best to keep his room exactly as it has always been, so that when he comes back to us he will find everything unchanged and be able all the more easily to forget what has happened in between."

On hearing these words from his mother Gregor realized that the lack of all direct human speech for the past two months together with the monotony of family life must have confused his mind, otherwise he could not account for the fact that he had quite earnestly looked forward to having his room emptied of furnishing. Did he really want his warm room, so comfortably fitted with old family furniture, to be turned into a naked den in which he would certainly be able to crawl unhampered in all directions but at the price of shedding simultaneously all recollection of his human background? He had indeed been so near the brink of forgetfulness that only the voice of his mother, which he had not heard for so long, had drawn him back from it. Nothing should be taken out of his room; everything must stay as it was; he could not dispense with the good influence of the furniture on his state of mind; and even if the furniture did hamper him in his senseless crawling round and round, that was no drawback but a great advantage.

Unfortunately his sister was of the contrary opinion; she had grown accustomed, and not without reason, to consider herself an expert in Gregor's affairs as against her parents, and so her mother's advice was now enough to make her determined on the removal not only of the chest and the writing desk, which had been her first intention, but of all the furniture except the indispensable sofa. This determination was not, of course, merely the outcome of childish recalcitrance and of the self-confidence she had recently developed so unexpectedly and at such cost; she had in fact perceived that Gregor needed a lot of space to crawl about in, while on the other hand he never used the furniture at all, so far as could be seen. Another factor might have been also the enthusiastic temperament of an adolescent girl, which seeks to indulge itself on every opportunity and which now tempted Grete to exaggerate the horror of her brother's circumstances in order that she might do all the more for him. In a room where Gregor lorded it all alone over empty walls no one save herself was likely ever to set foot.

And so she was not to be moved from her resolve by her mother who seemed moreover to be ill at ease in Gregor's room and therefore unsure of herself, was soon reduced to silence and helped her daughter as best she could to push the chest outside. Now, Gregor could do without the chest, if need be, but the writing desk he must retain. As soon as the two women had got the chest out of his room, groaning as they pushed it, Gregor stuck his head out from under the sofa to see how he might intervene as kindly and cautiously as possible. But as bad luck would have it, his mother was the first to return, leaving Grete clasping the chest in the room next door where she was trying to shift it all by herself, without of course moving it from the spot. His mother however was not accustomed to the sight of him, it might sicken her and so in alarm Gregor backed quickly to the other end of the sofa, yet could not prevent the sheet from swaying a little in front. That was enough to put her on the alert. She paused, stood still for a moment and then went back to Grete.

55   Although Gregor kept reassuring himself that nothing out of the way was happening, but only a few bits of furniture were being changed round, he soon had to admit that all this trotting to and fro of the two women, their little ejaculations and the scraping of furniture along the floor affected him like a vast disturbance coming from all sides at once, and however much he tucked in his head and legs and cowered to the very floor he was bound to confess that he would not be able to stand it for long. They were clearing his room out; taking away everything he loved; the chest in which he kept his fret saw and other tools was already dragged off; they were now loosening the writing desk which had almost sunk into the floor, the desk at which he had done all his homework when he was at the commercial academy, at the grammar school before that, and, yes, even at the primary school—he had no more time to waste in weighing the good intentions of the two women, whose existence he had by now almost forgotten, for they were so exhausted that they were laboring in silence and nothing could be heard but the heavy scuffling of their feet.

And so he rushed out—the women were just leaning against the writing desk in the next room to give themselves a breather—and four times changed his direction, since he really did not know what to rescue first, then on the wall opposite, which was already otherwise cleared, he was struck by the picture of the lady muffled in so much fur and quickly crawled up to it and pressed himself to the glass, which was a good surface to hold on to and comforted his hot belly. This picture at least, which was entirely hidden beneath him, was going to be removed by nobody. He turned his head towards the door of the living room so as to observe the women when they came back.

They had not allowed themselves much of a rest and were already coming; Grete had twined her arm round her mother and was almost supporting her. "Well, what shall we take now?" said Grete, looking round. Her eyes met Gregor's from the wall. She kept her composure, presumably because of her mother, bent her head down to her mother, to keep her from looking up, and said, although in a fluttering, unpremeditated voice: "Come, hadn't we better go back to the living room for a moment?" Her intentions were clear enough to Gregor, she wanted to bestow her mother in safety and then chase him down from the wall. Well, just let her try it! He clung to his picture and would not give it up. He would rather fly in Grete's face.

But Grete's words had succeeded in disquieting her mother, who took a step to one side, caught sight of the huge brown mass on the flowered wallpaper, and before she was really conscious that what she saw was Gregor screamed in a loud, hoarse voice: "Oh God, oh God!" fell with outspread arms over the sofa as if giving up and did not move. "Gregor!" cried his sister, shaking her fist and glaring at him. This was the first time she had directly addressed him since his metamorphosis. She ran into the next room for some aromatic essence with which to rouse her mother from her fainting fit. Gregor wanted to help too—there was still time to rescue the picture—but he was stuck fast to the glass and had to tear himself loose; he then ran after his sister into the next room as if he could advise her, as he used to do; but then had to stand helplessly behind her; she meanwhile searched among various small bottles and when she turned round started in alarm at the sight of him; one bottle fell on the floor and broke; a splinter of glass cut Gregor's face and some kind of corrosive medicine splashed him; without pausing a moment longer Grete gathered up all the bottles she could carry and ran to her mother with them; she banged the door shut with her foot. Gregor was now cut off from his mother, who was perhaps nearly dying because of him; he dared not open the door for fear of frightening away his sister, who had to stay with her mother; there was nothing he could do but wait; and harassed by self-reproach and worry he began now to crawl to and fro, over everything, walls, furniture and ceiling, and finally in his despair, when the whole room seemed to be reeling round him, fell down on to the middle of the big table.

A little while elapsed, Gregor was still lying there feebly and all around was quiet, perhaps that was a good omen. Then the doorbell rang. The servant girl was of course locked in her kitchen, and Grete would have to open the door. It was his father. "What's been happening?" were his first words; Grete's face must have told him everything. Grete answered in a muffled voice, apparently hiding her head on his breast: "Mother has been fainting, but she's better now. Gregor's broken loose." "Just what I expected," said his father, "just what I've been telling you, but you women would never listen." It was clear to Gregor that his father had taken the worst interpretation of Grete's all too brief statement and was assuming that Gregor had been guilty of some violent act. Therefore Gregor must now try to propitiate his father, since he had neither time nor means for an explanation. And so he fled to the door of his own room and crouched against it, to let his father see as soon as he came in from the hall that his son had the good intention of getting back into his room immediately and that it was not necessary to drive him there, but that if only the door were opened he would disappear at once.

60   Yet his father was not in the mood to perceive such fine distinctions. "Ah!" he cried as soon as he appeared, in a tone which sounded at once

angry and exultant. Gregor drew his head back from the door and lifted it to look at his father. Truly, this was not the father he had imagined to himself; admittedly he had been too absorbed of late in his new recreation of crawling over the ceiling to take the same interest as before in what was happening elsewhere in the flat, and he ought really to be prepared for some changes. And yet, and yet, could that be his father? The man who used to lie wearily sunk in bed whenever Gregor set out on a business journey; who welcomed him back of an evening lying in a long chair in a dressing gown; who could not really rise to his feet but only lifted his arms in greeting, and on the rare occasions when he did go out with his family, on one or two Sundays a year and on high holidays, walked between Gregor and his mother, who were slow walkers anyhow, even more slowly than they did, muffled in his old greatcoat, shuffling laboriously forward with the help of his crookhandled stick which he set down most cautiously at every step and, whenever he wanted to say anything, nearly always came to a full stop and gathered his escort around him? Now he was standing there in fine shape; dressed in a smart blue uniform with gold buttons, such as bank messengers wear; his strong double chin bulged over the stiff high collar of his jacket; from under his bushy eyebrows his black eyes darted fresh and penetrating glances; his onetime tangled white hair had been combed flat on either side of a shining and carefully exact parting. He pitched his cap, which bore a gold monogram, probably the badge of some bank, in a wide sweep across the whole room on to a sofa and with the tail-ends of his jacket thrown back, his hands in his trouser pockets, advanced with a grim visage towards Gregor. Likely enough he did not himself know what he meant to do; at any rate he lifted his feet uncommonly high, and Gregor was dumbfounded at the enormous size of his shoe soles. But Gregor could not risk standing up to him, aware as he had been from the very first day of his new life that his father believed only the severest measures suitable for dealing with him. And so he ran before his father, stopping when he stopped and scuttling forward again when his father made any kind of move. In this way they circled the room several times without anything decisive happening; indeed the whole operation did not even look like a pursuit because it was carried out so slowly. And so Gregor did not leave the floor, for he feared that his father might take as a piece of peculiar wickedness any excursion of his over the walls or the ceiling. All the same, he could not stay this course much longer, for while his father took one step he had to carry out a whole series of movements. He was already beginning to feel breathless, just as in his former life his lungs had not been very dependable. As he was staggering along, trying to concentrate his energy on running, hardly keeping his eyes open; in his dazed state never even thinking of any other escape than simply going forward; and having almost forgotten that the walls were free to him, which in this room were well provided with finely carved pieces of furniture full of knobs and crevices—suddenly something lightly flung landed close behind him and rolled before him. It was an apple; a second apple followed immediately; Gregor came to a stop in alarm; there was no point in running on, for his father was determined to bombard him. He had filled his pockets with fruit from the dish on the sideboard and was now shying apple after apple, without taking particularly good aim for the moment. The small red apples rolled about the floor as if magnetized and cannoned into each other. An apple thrown without much force grazed Gregor's back and glanced off harmlessly. But another following immediately landed right on his back and sank in; Gregor wanted to drag himself forward, as if this startling, incredible pain could be left behind him: but he felt as if nailed to the spot and flattened himself out in a complete derangement of all his senses. With his last conscious look he saw the door of his room being torn open and his mother rushing out ahead of his screaming sister, in her underbodice, for her daughter had loosened her clothing to let her breathe more freely and recover from her swoon, he saw his mother rushing towards his father, leaving one after another behind her on the floor her loosened petticoats, stumbling over her petticoats straight to his father and embracing him, in complete union with him—but here Gregor's sight began to fail—with her hands clasped round his father's neck as she begged for her son's life.

III

The serious injury done to Gregor, which disabled him for more than a month—the apple went on sticking in his body as a visible reminder, since no one ventured to remove it—seemed to have made even his father recollect that Gregor was a member of the family, despite his present unfortunate and repulsive shape, and ought not to be treated as an enemy, that, on the contrary, family duty required the suppression of disgust and the exercise of patience, nothing but patience.

And although his injury had impaired, probably for ever, his power of movement, and for the time being it took him long, long minutes to creep across his room like an old invalid—there was no question now of crawling up the wall—yet in his own opinion he was sufficiently compensated for this worsening of his condition by the fact that towards evening the living-room door, which he used to watch intently for an hour or two beforehand, was always thrown open, so that lying in the darkness of his room, invisible to the family, he could see them all at the lamp-lit table and listen to their talk, by general consent as it were, very different from his earlier eavesdropping.

True, their intercourse lacked the lively character of former times, which he had always called to mind with a certain wistfulness in the small hotel bedrooms where he had been wont to throw himself down, tired out, on damp bedding. They were now mostly very silent. Soon after supper his father would fall asleep in his armchair; his mother and sister would admonish each other to be silent; his mother, bending low over the lamp, stitched at fine sewing for an underwear firm; his sister, who had taken a job as a salesgirl, was learning shorthand and French in the evenings on the chance of bettering herself. Sometimes his father woke up, and as if quite unaware that he had been sleeping said to his mother: "What a lot of sewing you're doing today!" and at once fell asleep again, while the two women exchanged a tired smile.

With a kind of mulishness his father persisted in keeping his uniform on even in the house; his dressing gown hung uselessly on its peg and he slept fully dressed where he sat, as if he were ready for service at any moment and even here only at the beck and call of his superior. As a result, his uniform, which was not brand-new to start with, began to look dirty, despite all the loving care of the mother and sister to keep it clean, and Gregor often spent whole evenings gazing at the many greasy spots on the garment, gleaming with gold buttons always in a high state of polish, in which the old man sat sleeping in extreme discomfort and yet quite peacefully.

65   As soon as the clock struck ten his mother tried to rouse his father with gentle words and to persuade him after that to get into bed, for sitting there he could not have a proper sleep and that was what he needed most, since he had to go to duty at six. But with the mulishness that had obsessed him since he became a bank messenger he always insisted on staying longer at the table, although he regularly fell asleep again and in the end only with the greatest trouble could be got out of his armchair and into his bed. However insistently Gregor's mother and sister kept urging him with gentle reminders, he would go on slowly shaking his head for a quarter of an hour, keeping his eyes shut, and refuse to get to his feet. The mother plucked at his sleeve, whispering endearments in his ear, the sister left her lessons to come to her mother's help, but Gregor's father was not to be caught. He would only sink down deeper in his chair. Not until the two women hoisted him up by the armpits did he open his eyes and look at them both, one after the other, usually with the remark: "This is a life. This is the peace and quiet of my old age." And leaning on the two of them he would heave himself up, with difficulty, as if he were a great burden to himself, suffer them to lead him as far as the door and then wave them off and go on alone, while the mother abandoned her needlework and the sister her pen in order to run after him and help him farther.

Who could find time, in this overworked and tired-out family, to bother about Gregor more than was absolutely needful? The household was reduced more and more; the servant girl was turned off; a gigantic bony charwoman with white hair flying round her head came in morning and evening to do the rough work; everything else was done by Gregor's mother, as well as great piles of sewing. Even various family ornaments, which his mother and sister used to wear with pride at parties and celebrations, had to be sold, as Gregor discovered of an evening from hearing them all discuss the prices obtained. But what they lamented most was the fact that they could not leave the flat which was much too big for their present circumstances, because they could not think of any way to shift

Gregor. Yet Gregor saw well enough that consideration for him was not the main difficulty preventing the removal, for they could have easily shifted him in some suitable box with a few air holes in it; what really kept them from moving into another flat was rather their own complete hopelessness and the belief that they had been singled out for a misfortune such as had never happened to any of their relations or acquaintances. They fulfilled to the uttermost all that the world demands of poor people, the father fetched breakfast for the small clerks in the bank, the mother devoted her energy to making underwear for strangers, the sister trotted to and fro behind the counter at the behest of customers, but more than this they had not the strength to do. And the wound in Gregor's back began to nag at him afresh when his mother and sister, after getting his father into bed came back again, left their work lying, drew close to each other and sat cheek by cheek; when his mother, pointing towards his room, said: "Shut that door now, Grete," and he was left again in darkness, while next door the women mingled their tears or perhaps sat dry-eyed staring at the table.

Gregor hardly slept at all by night or by day. He was often haunted by the idea that next time the door opened he would take the family's affairs in hand again just as he used to do; once more, after this long interval, there appeared in his thoughts the figures of the chief and the chief clerk, the commercial travelers and the apprentices, the porter who was so dull-witted, two or three friends in other firms, a chambermaid in one of the rural hotels, a sweet and fleeting memory, a cashier in a milliner's shop, whom he had wooed earnestly but too slowly—they all appeared, together with strangers or people he had quite forgotten, but instead of helping him and his family they were one and all unapproachable and he was glad when they vanished. At other times he would not be in the mood to bother about his family, he was only filled with rage at the way they were neglecting him, and although he had no clear idea of what he might care to eat he would make plans for getting into the larder to take the food that was after all his due, even if he were not hungry. His sister no longer took thought to bring him what might especially please him, but in the morning and at noon before she went to business hurriedly pushed into his room with her foot any food that was available, and in the evening cleared it out again with one sweep of the broom, heedless of whether it had been merely tasted, or—as most frequently happened—left untouched. The cleaning of his room, which she now did always in the evenings, could not have been more hastily done. Streaks of dirt stretched along the walls, here and there lay balls of dust and filth. At first Gregor used to station himself in some particularly filthy corner when his sister arrived, in order to re-proach her with it, so to speak. But he could have sat there for weeks without getting her to make any improvements; she could see the dirt as well as he did, but she had simply made up her mind to leave it alone. And yet, with a touchiness that was new to her, which seemed anyhow to have in-fected the whole family, she jealously guarded her claim to be the sole care-taker of Gregor's room. His mother once subjected his room to a thorough

cleaning, which was achieved only by means of several buckets of water—
all this dampness of course upset Gregor too and he lay widespread, sulky
and motionless on the sofa—but she was well punished for it. Hardly had
his sister noticed the changed aspect of his room that evening than she
rushed in high dudgeon into the living room and, despite the imploringly
raised hands of her mother, burst into a storm of weeping, while her parents—her father had of course been startled out of his chair—looked on at
first in helpless amazement; then they too began to go into action; the father reproached the mother on his right for not having left the cleaning of
Gregor's room to his sister; shrieked at the sister on his left that never
again was she to be allowed to clean Gregor's room; while the mother tried
to pull the father into his bedroom, since he was beyond himself with agitation; the sister, shaken with sobs, then beat upon the table with her
small fists; and Gregor hissed loudly with rage because not one of them
thought of shutting the door to spare him such a spectacle and so much
noise.

Still, even if the sister, exhausted by her daily work, had grown tired
of looking after Gregor as she did formerly, there was no need for his
mother's intervention or for Gregor's being neglected at all. The charwoman was there. This old widow, whose strong bony frame had enabled
her to survive the worst a long life could offer, by no means recoiled from
Gregor. Without being in the least curious she had once by chance opened
the door of his room and at the sight of Gregor, who, taken by surprise,
began to rush to and fro although no one was chasing him, merely stood
there with her arms folded. From that time she never failed to open his
door a little for a moment, morning and evening, to have a look at him. At
first she even used to call him to her, with words which apparently she
took to be friendly, such as: "Come along, then, you old dung beetle!" or
"Look at the old dung beetle, then!" To such allocutions Gregor made no
answer, but stayed motionless where he was, as if the door had never been
opened. Instead of being allowed to disturb him so senselessly whenever
the whim took her, she should rather have been ordered to clean out his
room daily, that charwoman! Once, early in the morning—heavy rain was
lashing on the windowpanes, perhaps a sign that spring was on the way—
Gregor was so exasperated when she began addressing him again that he
ran at her, as if to attack her, although slowly and feebly enough. But the
charwoman instead of showing fright merely lifted high a chair that happened to be beside the door, and as she stood there with her mouth wide
open it was clear that she meant to shut it only when she brought the chair
down on Gregor's back. "So you're not coming any nearer?" she asked, as
Gregor turned away again, and quietly put the chair back into the corner.

Gregor was now eating hardly anything. Only when he happened to
pass the food laid out for him did he take a bit of something in his mouth
as a pastime, kept it there for an hour at a time and usually spat it out
again. At first he thought it was chagrin over the state of his room that
prevented him from eating, yet he soon got used to the various changes in

his room. It had become a habit in the family to push into his room things there was no room for elsewhere, and there were plenty of these now, since one of the rooms had been let to three lodgers. These serious gentlemen— all three of them with full beards, as Gregor once observed through a crack in the door—had a passion for order, not only in their own room but, since they were now members of the household, in all its arrangements, especially in the kitchen. Superfluous, not to say dirty, objects they could not bear. Besides, they had brought with them most of the furnishings they needed. For this reason many things could be dispensed with that it was no use trying to sell but that should not be thrown away either. All of them found their way into Gregor's room. The ash can likewise and the kitchen garbage can. Anything that was not needed for the moment was simply flung into Gregor's room by the charwoman, who did everything in a hurry; fortunately Gregor usually saw only the object, whatever it was, and the hand that held it. Perhaps she intended to take the things away again as time and opportunity offered, or to collect them until she could throw them all out in a heap, but in fact they just lay wherever she happened to throw them, except when Gregor pushed his way through the junk heap and shifted it somewhat, at first out of necessity, because he had not room enough to crawl, but later with increasing enjoyment, although after such excursions, being sad and weary to death, he would lie motionless for hours. And since the lodgers often ate their supper at home in the common living room, the living-room door stayed shut many an evening, yet Gregor reconciled himself quite easily to the shutting of the door, for often enough on evenings when it was opened he had disregarded it entirely and lain in the darkest corner of his room, quite unnoticed by the family. But on one occasion the charwoman left the door open a little and it stayed ajar even when the lodgers came in for supper and the lamp was lit. They set themselves at the top end of the table where formerly Gregor and his father and mother had eaten their meals, unfolded their napkins and took knife and fork in hand. At once his mother appeared in the other doorway with a dish of meat and close behind her his sister with a dish of potatoes piled high. The food steamed with a thick vapor. The lodgers bent over the food set before them as if to scrutinize it before eating, in fact the man in the middle, who seemed to pass for an authority with the other two, cut a piece of meat as it lay on the dish, obviously to discover if it were tender or should be sent back to the kitchen. He showed satisfaction, and Gregor's mother and sister, who had been watching anxiously, breathed freely and began to smile.

70   The family itself took its meals in the kitchen. Nonetheless, Gregor's father came into the living room before going into the kitchen and with one prolonged bow, cap in hand, made a round of the table. The lodgers all stood up and murmured something in their beards. When they were alone again they ate their food in almost complete silence. It seemed remarkable to Gregor that among the various noises coming from the table he could always distinguish the sound of their masticating teeth, as if this were a

sign to Gregor that one needed teeth in order to eat, and that with tooth-less jaws even of the finest make one could do nothing. "I'm hungry enough," said Gregor sadly to himself, "But not for that kind of food. How these lodgers are stuffing themselves, and here am I dying of starvation!"

On that very evening—during the whole of his time there Gregor could not remember ever having heard the violin—the sound of violin-playing came from the kitchen. The lodgers had already finished their sup-per, the one in the middle had brought out a newspaper and given the other two a page apiece, and now they were leaning back at ease reading and smoking. When the violin began to play they pricked up their ears, got to their feet, and went on tiptoe to the hall door where they stood hud-dled together. Their movements must have been heard in the kitchen, for Gregor's father called out: "Is the violin-playing disturbing you, gentle-men? It can be stopped at once." "On the contrary," said the middle lodger, "could not Fräulein Samsa come and play in this room, beside us, where it is much more convenient and comfortable?" "Oh certainly," cried Gregor's father, as if he were the violin-player. The lodgers came back into the living room and waited. Presently Gregor's father arrived with the music stand, his mother carrying the music and his sister with the violin. His sister quietly made everything ready to start playing; his parents, who had never let rooms before and so had an exaggerated idea of the courtesy due to lodgers, did not venture to sit down on their own chairs; his father leaned against the door, the right hand thrust between two buttons of his livery coat, which was formally buttoned up; but his mother was offered a chair by one of the lodgers and, since she left the chair just where he had happened to put it, sat down in a corner to one side.

Gregor's sister began to play; the father and mother, from either side, intently watched the movements of her hands. Gregor, attracted by the playing, ventured to move forward a little until his head was actually in-side the living room. He felt hardly any surprise at his growing lack of consideration for the others; there had been a time when he prided himself on being considerate. And yet just on this occasion he had more reason than ever to hide himself, since owing to the amount of dust which lay thick in his room and rose into the air at the slightest movement, he too was covered with dust; fluff and hair and remnants of food trailed with him, caught on his back and along his sides; his indifference to everything was much too great for him to turn on his back and scrape himself clean on the carpet, as once he had done several times a day. And in spite of his condition, no shame deterred him from advancing a little over the spotless floor of the living room.

To be sure, no one was aware of him. The family was entirely absorbed in the violin-playing; the lodgers, however, who first of all had stationed themselves, hands in pockets, much too close behind the music stand so that they could all have read the music, which must have bothered his sis-ter, had soon retreated to the window, half-whispering with downbent heads, and stayed there while his father turned an anxious eye on them.

Indeed, they were making it more than obvious that they had been disappointed in their expectation of hearing good or enjoyable violin-playing, that they had had more than enough of the performance and only out of courtesy suffered a continued disturbance of their peace. From the way they all kept blowing the smoke of their cigars high in the air through nose and mouth one could divine their irritation. And yet Gregor's sister was playing so beautifully. Her face leaned sideways, intently and sadly her eyes followed the notes of music. Gregor crawled a little farther forward and lowered his head to the ground so that it might be possible for his eyes to meet hers. Was he an animal, that music had such an effect upon him? He felt as if the way were opening before him to the unknown nourishment he craved. He was determined to push forward till he reached his sister, to pull at her skirt and so let her know that she was to come into his room with her violin, for no one here appreciated her playing as he would appreciate it. He would never let her out of his room, at least, not so long as he lived; his frightful appearance would become, for the first time, useful to him; he would watch all the doors of his room at once and spit at intruders; but his sister should need no constraint, she should stay with him of her own free will; she should sit beside him on the sofa, bend down her ear to him and hear him confide that he had had the firm intention of sending her to the Conservatorium, and that, but for his mishap, last Christmas—surely Christmas was long past?—he would have announced it to everybody without allowing a single objection. After this confession his sister would be so touched that she would burst into tears, and Gregor would then raise himself to her shoulder and kiss her on the neck, which, now that she went to business, she kept free of any ribbon or collar.

"Mr. Samsa!" cried the middle lodger, to Gregor's father, and pointed, without wasting any more words, at Gregor, now working himself slowly forwards. The violin fell silent, the middle lodger first smiled to his friends with a shake of the head and then looked at Gregor again. Instead of driving Gregor out, his father seemed to think it more needful to begin by soothing down the lodgers, although they were not at all agitated and apparently found Gregor more entertaining than the violin-playing. He hurried toward them and, spreading out his arms, tried to urge them back into their own room and at the same time to block their view of Gregor. They now began to be really a little angry, one could not tell whether because of the old man's behavior or because it had just dawned on them that all unwittingly they had such a neighbor as Gregor next door. They demanded explanations of his father, they waved their arms like him, tugged uneasily at their beards, and only with reluctance backed towards their room. Meanwhile Gregor's sister, who stood there as if lost when her playing was so abruptly broken off, came to life again, pulled herself together all at once after standing for a while holding violin and bow in nervelessly hanging hands and staring at her music, pushed her violin into the lap of her mother, who was still sitting in her chair fighting asthmatically for breath, and ran into the lodgers' room to which they were now being shepherded by her father rather more quickly than before. One could see the pillows and blankets on the beds flying under her accustomed fingers and being laid in order. Before the lodgers had actually reached their room she had finished making the beds and slipped out.

75   The old man seemed once more to be so possessed by his mulish self-assertiveness that he was forgetting all the respect he should show to his lodgers. He kept driving them on and driving them on until in the very door of the bedroom the middle lodger stamped his foot loudly on the floor and so brought him to a halt. "I beg to announce," said the lodger, lifting one hand and looking also at Gregor's mother and sister, "that because of the disgusting conditions prevailing in this household and family"—here he spat on the floor with emphatic brevity—"I give you notice on the spot. Naturally I won't pay you a penny for the days I have lived here, on the contrary I shall consider bringing an action for damages against you, based on claims—believe me—that will be easily susceptible of proof." He ceased and stared straight in front of him, as if he expected something. In fact his two friends at once rushed into the breach with these words: "And we too give notice on the spot." On that he seized the door-handle and shut the door with a slam.

Gregor's father, groping with his hands, staggered forward and fell into his chair; it looked as if he were stretching himself there for his ordinary evening nap, but the marked jerkings of his head, which was as if uncontrollable, showed that he was far from asleep. Gregor had simply stayed quietly all the time on the spot where the lodgers had espied him. Disappointment at the failure of his plan, perhaps also the weakness arising from extreme hunger, made it impossible for him to move. He feared, with a fair degree of certainty, that at any moment the general tension would discharge itself in a combined attack upon him, and he lay waiting. He did not react even to the noise made by the violin as it fell off his mother's lap from under her trembling fingers and gave out a resonant note.

"My dear parents," said his sister, slapping her hand on the table by way of introduction, "things can't go on like this. Perhaps you don't realize that, but I do. I won't utter my brother's name in the presence of this creature, and so all I say is: we must try to get rid of it. We've tried to look after it and to put up with it as far as is humanly possible, and I don't think anyone could reproach us in the slightest."

"She is more than right," said Gregor's father to himself. His mother, who was still choking for lack of breath, began to cough hollowly into her hand with a wild look in her eyes.

His sister rushed over to her and held her forehead. His father's thoughts seemed to have lost their vagueness at Grete's words, he sat more upright, fingering his service cap that lay among the plates still lying on the table from the lodgers' supper, and from time to time looked at the still form of Gregor.

80   "We must try to get rid of it," his sister now said explicitly to her father, since her mother was coughing too much to hear a word, "it will be

the death of both of you, I can see that coming. When one has to work as hard as we do, all of us, one can't stand this continual torment at home on top of it. At least I can't stand it any longer." And she burst into such a passion of sobbing that her tears dropped on her mother's face, where she wiped them off mechanically.

"My dear," said the old man sympathetically, and with evident under-standing, "but what can we do?"

Gregor's sister merely shrugged her shoulders to indicate the feeling of helplessness that had now overmastered her during her weeping fit, in contrast to her former confidence.

"If he could understand us," said her father, half questioningly; Grete, still sobbing, vehemently waved a hand to show how unthinkable that was.

"If he could understand us," repeated the old man, shutting his eyes to consider his daughter's conviction that understanding was impossible, "then perhaps we might come to some agreement with him. But as it is—"

85   "He must go," cried Gregor's sister, "That's the only solution, Father. You must try to get rid of the idea that this is Gregor. The fact that we've believed it for so long is the root of all our trouble. But how can it be Gre-gor? If this were Gregor, he would have realized long ago that human be-ings can't live with such a creature, and he'd have gone away on his own accord. Then we wouldn't have any brother, but we'd be able to go on liv-ing and keep his memory in honor. As it is, this creature persecutes us, drives away our lodgers, obviously wants the whole apartment to himself and would have us all sleep in the gutter. Just look, Father," she shrieked all at once, "he's at it again!" And in an access of panic that was quite in-comprehensible to Gregor she even quitted her mother, literally thrusting the chair from her as if she would rather sacrifice her mother than stay so near to Gregor, and rushed behind her father, who also rose up, being sim-ply upset by her agitation, and half-spread his arms out as if to protect her.

Yet Gregor had not the slightest intention of frightening anyone, far less his sister. He had only begun to turn round in order to crawl back to his room, but it was certainly a startling operation to watch, since because of his disabled condition he could not execute the difficult turning move-ments except by lifting his head and then bracing it against the floor over and over again. He paused and looked round. His good intentions seemed to have been recognized; the alarm had only been momentary. Now they were all watching him in melancholy silence. His mother lay in her chair, her legs stiffly outstretched and pressed together, her eyes almost closing for sheer weariness; his father and his sister were sitting beside each other, his sister's arm around the old man's neck.

Perhaps I can go on turning round now, thought Gregor, and began his labors again. He could not stop himself from panting with the effort, and had to pause now and then to take breath. Nor did anyone harass him, he was left entirely to himself. When he had completed the turn-round he began at once to crawl straight back. He was amazed at the distance sepa-rating him from his room and could not understand how in his weak state he had managed to accomplish the same journey so recently, almost without remarking it. Intent on crawling as fast as possible, he barely noticed that not a single word, not an ejaculation from his family, interfered with his progress. Only when he was already in the doorway did he turn his head round, not completely, for his neck muscles were getting stiff, but enough to see that nothing had changed behind him except that his sister had risen to her feet. His last glance fell on his mother, who was not quite overcome by sleep.

Hardly was he well inside his room when the door was hastily pushed shut, bolted and locked. The sudden noise in his rear startled him so much that his little legs gave beneath him. It was his sister who had shown such haste. She had been standing ready waiting and made a light spring forward, Gregor had not even heard her coming, and she cried "At last!" to her parents as she turned the key in the lock.

"And what now?" said Gregor to himself, looking round in the darkness. Soon he made the discovery that he was now unable to stir a limb. This did not surprise him, rather it seemed unnatural that he should ever actually have been able to move on these feeble little legs. Otherwise he felt relatively comfortable. True, his whole body was aching, but it seemed that the pain was gradually growing less and would finally pass away. The rotting apple in his back and the inflamed area around it, all covered with soft dust, already hardly troubled him. He thought of his family with tenderness and love. The decision that he must disappear was one that he held to even more strongly than his sister, if that were possible. In this state of vacant and peaceful meditation he remained until the tower clock struck three in the morning. The first broadening of light in the world outside the window entered his consciousness once more. Then his head sank to the floor of its own accord and from his nostrils came the last faint flicker of his breath.

90   When the charwoman arrived early in the morning—what between her strength and her impatience she slammed all the doors so loudly, never mind how often she had been begged not to do so, that no one in the whole apartment could enjoy any quiet sleep after her arrival—she noticed nothing unusual as she took her customary peep into Gregor's room. She thought he was lying motionless on purpose, pretending to be in the sulks; she credited him with every kind of intelligence. Since she happened to have the longhanded broom in her hand she tried to tickle him up with it from the doorway. When that too produced no reaction she felt provoked and poked at him a little harder, and only when she had pushed him along the floor without meeting any resistance was her attention aroused. It did not take her long to establish the truth of the matter, and her eyes widened, she let out a whistle, yet did not waste much time over it but tore open the door of the Samsas' bedroom and yelled into the darkness at the top of her voice: "Just look at this, it's dead; it's lying here dead and done for!"

Mr. and Mrs. Samsa started up in their double bed and before they realized the nature of the charwoman's announcement had some difficulty in overcoming the shock of it. But then they got out of bed quickly, one on either side, Mr. Samsa throwing a blanket over his shoulders, Mrs. Samsa in nothing but her nightgown; in this array they entered Gregor's room. Meanwhile the door of the living room opened, too, where Grete had been sleeping since the advent of the lodgers; she was completely dressed as if she had not been to bed, which seemed to be confirmed also by the paleness of her face. "Dead?" said Mrs. Samsa, looking questioningly at the charwoman, although she could have investigated for herself, and the fact was obvious enough without investigation. "I should say so," said the charwoman, proving her words by pushing Gregor's corpse a long way to one side with her broomstick. Mrs. Samsa made a movement as if to stop her, but checked it. "Well," said Mr. Samsa, "now thanks be to God." He crossed himself, and the three women followed his example. Grete, whose eyes never left the corpse, said: "Just see how thin he was. It's such a long time since he's eaten anything. The food came out again just as it went in." Indeed, Gregor's body was completely flat and dry, as could only now be seen when it was no longer supported by the legs and nothing prevented one from looking closely at it.

"Come in beside us, Grete, for a little while," said Mrs. Samsa with a tremulous smile, and Grete, not without looking back at the corpse, followed her parents into their bedroom. The charwoman shut the door and opened the window wide. Although it was so early in the morning a certain softness was perceptible in the fresh air. After all, it was already the end of March.

The three lodgers emerged from their room and were surprised to see no breakfast; they had been forgotten. "Where's our breakfast?" said the middle lodger peevishly to the charwoman. But she put her finger to her lips and hastily, without a word, indicated by gestures that they should go into Gregor's room. They did so and stood, their hands in the pockets of their somewhat shabby coats, around Gregor's corpse in the room where it was now fully light.

At that the door of the Samsas' bedroom opened and Mr. Samsa appeared in his uniform, his wife on one arm, his daughter on the other. They all looked a little as if they had been crying; from time to time Grete hid her face on her father's arm.

95   "Leave my house at once!" said Mr. Samsa, and pointed to the door without disengaging himself from the women. "What do you mean by that?" said the middle lodger, taken somewhat aback, with a feeble smile. The two others put their hands behind them and kept rubbing them together, as if in gleeful expectation of a fine set-to in which they were bound to come off the winners. "I mean just what I say," answered Mr. Samsa, and advanced in a straight line with his two companions towards the lodger. He stood his ground at first quietly, looking at the floor as if his thoughts were taking a new pattern in his head. "Then let us go, by all means," he said, and looked up at Mr. Samsa as if in a sudden access of humility he were expecting some renewed sanction for this decision. Mr. Samsa merely nodded briefly once or twice with meaning eyes. Upon that the lodger really did go

with long strides into the hall, his two friends had been listening and had quite stopped rubbing their hands for some moments and now went scuttling after him as if afraid that Mr. Samsa might get into the hall before them and cut them off from their leader. In the hall they all three took their hats from the rack, their sticks from the umbrella stand, bowed in silence and quitted the apartment. With a suspiciousness which proved quite unfounded Mr. Samsa and the two women followed them out to the landing; leaning over the banister they watched the three figures slowly but surely going down the long stairs, vanishing from sight at a certain turn of the staircase on every floor and coming into view again after a moment or so; the more they dwindled, the more the Samsa family's interest in them dwindled, and when a butcher's boy met them and passed them on the stairs coming up proudly with a tray on his head, Mr. Samsa and the two women soon left the landing and as if a burden had been lifted from them went back into their apartment.

They decided to spend this day in resting and going for a stroll; they had not only deserved such a respite from work, but absolutely needed it. And so they sat down at the table and wrote three notes of excuse, Mr. Samsa to his board of management, Mrs. Samsa to her employer and Grete to the head of her firm. While they were writing, the charwoman came in to say that she was going now, since her morning's work was finished. At first they only nodded without looking up, but as she kept hovering there they eyed her irritably. "Well?" said Mr. Samsa. The charwoman stood grinning in the doorway as if she had good news to impart to the family but meant not to say a word unless properly questioned. The small ostrich feather standing upright on her hat, which had annoyed Mr. Samsa ever since she was engaged, was waving gaily in all directions. "Well, what is it then?" asked Mrs. Samsa, who obtained more respect from the charwoman than the others. "Oh," said the charwoman, giggling so amiably that she could not at once continue, "just this, you don't need to bother about how to get rid of the thing next door. It's been seen to already." Mrs. Samsa and Grete bent over their letters again, as if preoccupied; Mr. Samsa, who perceived that she was eager to begin describing it all in detail, stopped her with a decisive hand. But since she was not allowed to tell her story, she remembered the great hurry she was in, being obviously deeply huffed: "Bye, everybody," she said, whirling off violently, and departed with a frightful slamming of doors.

"She'll be given notice tonight," said Mr. Samsa, but neither from his wife nor his daughter did he get any answer, for the charwoman seemed to have shattered again the composure they had barely achieved. They rose, went to the window and stayed there, clasping each other tight. Mr. Samsa turned to his chair to look at them and quietly observed them for a little. Then he called out: "Come along, now, do. Let bygones be bygones. And you might have some consideration for me." The two of them complied at once, hastened to him, caressed him and quickly finished their letters.

Then they all three left the apartment together, which was more than they had done for months, and went by tram into the open country outside the town. The tram, in which they were the only passengers, was filled with warm sunshine. Leaning comfortably back in their seats they canvassed their prospects for the future, and it appeared on closer inspection that these were not at all bad, for the jobs they had got, which so far they had never really discussed with each other, were all three admirable and likely to lead to better things later on. The greatest immediate improvement in their condition would of course arise from moving to another house; they wanted to take a smaller and cheaper but also better situated and more easily run apartment than the one they had, which Gregor had selected. While they were thus conversing, it struck both Mr. and Mrs. Samsa, almost at the same moment, as they became aware of their daughter's increasing vivacity, that in spite of all the sorrow of recent times, which had made her cheeks pale, she had bloomed into a pretty girl with a good figure. They grew quieter and half unconsciously exchanged glances of complete agreement, having come to the conclusion that it would soon be time to find a good husband for her. And it was like a confirmation of their new dreams and excellent intentions that at the end of their journey their daughter sprang to her feet first and stretched her young body.

JAMAICA KINCAID

(1949–   )

Girl

(1984)

Wash the white clothes on Monday and put them on the stone heap; wash the color clothes on Tuesday and put them on the clothesline to dry; don't walk barehead in the hot sun; cook pumpkin fritters in very hot sweet oil; soak your little clothes right after you take them off; when buying cotton to make yourself a nice blouse, be sure that it doesn't have gum on it, because that way it won't hold up well after a wash; soak salt fish overnight before you cook it; is it true that you sing benna[1] in Sunday School?; always eat your food in such a way that it won't turn someone else's stomach; on Sundays try to walk like a lady and not like the slut you are so bent on becoming; don't sing benna in Sunday School; you mustn't speak to wharf-rat boys, not even to give directions; don't eat fruits on the street— flies will follow you; *but I don't sing benna on Sundays at all and never in Sunday school;* this is how to sew on a button; this is how to make a buttonhole for the button you have just sewed on; this is how to hem a dress when you see the hem coming down and so to prevent yourself from looking like the slut I know you are so bent on becoming; this is how you iron your father's khaki shirt so that it doesn't have a crease; this is how you

---

[1] Calypso music.

iron your father's khaki pants so that they don't have a crease; this is how you grow okra—far from the house, because okra tree harbors red ants; when you are growing dasheen, make sure it gets plenty of water or else it makes your throat itch when you are eating it; this is how you sweep a corner; this is how you sweep a whole house; this is how you sweep a yard; this is how you smile to someone you don't like too much; this is how you smile to someone you don't like at all; this is how you smile to someone you like completely; this is how you set a table for tea; this is how you set a table for dinner; this is how you set a table for dinner with an important guest; this is how you set a table for lunch; this is how you set a table for breakfast; this is how to behave in the presence of men who don't know you very well, and this way they won't recognize immediately the slut I have warned you against becoming; be sure to wash every day, even if it is with your own spit; don't squat down to play marbles—you are not a boy, you know; don't pick people's flowers—you might catch something; don't throw stones at blackbirds, because it might not be a blackbird at all; this is how to make a bread pudding; this is how to make doukona;[2] this is how to make pepper pot; this is how to make a good medicine for a cold; this is how to make a good medicine to throw away a child before it even becomes a child; this is how to catch a fish; this is how to throw back a fish you don't like, and that way something bad won't fall on you; this is how to bully a man; this is how a man bullies you; this is how to love a man, and if this doesn't work there are other ways, and if they don't work don't feel too bad about giving up; this is how to spit up in the air if you feel like it, and this is how to move quick so that it doesn't fall on you; this is how to make ends meet; always squeeze bread to make sure it's fresh; *but what if the baker won't let me feel the bread?;* you mean to say that after all you are really going to be the kind of woman who the baker won't let near the bread?

D. H. L A W R E N C E

(1885–1930)

The Rocking-Horse Winner

(1920)

There was a woman who was beautiful, who started with all the advantages, yet she had no luck. She married for love, and the love turned to dust. She had bonny children, yet she felt they had been thrust upon her, and she could not love them. They looked at her coldly, as if they were finding fault with her. And hurriedly she felt she must cover up some fault in herself. Yet what it was that she must cover up she never knew. Nevertheless,

---

[2] Spicy plantain pudding.

when her children were present, she always felt the centre of her heart go hard. This troubled her, and in her manner she was all the more gentle and anxious for her children, as if she loved them very much. Only she herself knew that at the centre of her heart was a hard little place that could not feel love, no, not for anybody. Everybody else said of her: "She is such a good mother. She adores her children." Only she herself, and her children themselves, knew it was not so. They read it in each other's eyes.

There were a boy and two little girls. They lived in a pleasant house, with a garden, and they had discreet servants, and felt themselves superior to anyone in the neighbourhood.

Although they lived in style, they felt always an anxiety in the house. There was never enough money. The mother had a small income, and the father had a small income, but not nearly enough for the social position which they had to keep up. The father went into town to some office. But though he had good prospects, these prospects never materialised. There was always the grinding sense of the shortage of money, though the style was always kept up.

At last the mother said: "I will see if *I* can't make something." But she did not know where to begin. She racked her brains, and tried this thing and the other, but could not find anything successful. The failure made deep lines come into her face. Her children were growing up, they would have to go to school. There must be more money, there must be more money. The father, who was always very handsome and expensive in his tastes, seemed as if he never *would* be able to do anything worth doing. And the mother, who had a great belief in herself, did not succeed any better, and her tastes were just as expensive.

5   And so the house came to be haunted by the unspoken phrase: *There must be more money! There must be more money!* The children could hear it all the time, though nobody said it aloud. They heard it at Christmas, when the expensive and splendid toys filled the nursery. Behind the shining modern rocking-horse, behind the smart doll's house, a voice would start whispering: "There *must* be more money! There *must* be more money!" And the children would stop playing, to listen for a moment. They would look into each other's eyes, to see if they had all heard. And each one saw in the eyes of the other two that they too had heard. "There *must* be more money! There *must* be more money!"

It came whispering from the springs of the still-swaying rocking-horse, and even the horse, bending his wooden, champing head, heard it. The big doll, sitting so pink and smirking in her new pram, could hear it quite plainly, and seemed to be smirking all the more self-consciously because of it. The foolish puppy, too, that took the place of the teddybear, he was looking so extraordinarily foolish for no other reason but that he heard the secret whisper all over the house: "There *must* be more money!"

Yet nobody ever said it aloud. The whisper was everywhere, and therefore no one spoke it. Just as no one ever says: "We are breathing!" in spite of the fact that breath is coming and going all the time.

"Mother," said the boy Paul one day, "why don't we keep a car of our own? Why do we always use uncle's, or else a taxi?"

"Because we're the poor members of the family," said the mother.

10 "But why *are* we, mother?"

"Well—I suppose," she said slowly and bitterly, "it's because your father has no luck."

The boy was silent for some time.

"Is luck money, mother?" he asked, rather timidly.

"No, Paul. Not quite. It's what causes you to have money."

15 "Oh!" said Paul vaguely. "I thought when Uncle Oscar said *filthy lucker*, it meant money."

"*Filthy lucre* does mean money," said the mother. "But it's lucre, not luck."

"Oh!" said the boy. "Then what *is* luck, mother?"

"It's what causes you to have money. If you're lucky you have money. That's why it's better to be born lucky than rich. If you're rich, you may lose your money. But if you're lucky, you will always get more money."

"Oh! Will you? And is father not lucky?"

20 "Very unlucky, I should say," she said bitterly.

The boy watched her with unsure eyes.

"Why?" he asked.

"I don't know. Nobody ever knows why one person is lucky and another unlucky."

"Don't they? Nobody at all? Does *nobody* know?"

25 "Perhaps God. But He never tells."

"He ought to, then. And aren't you lucky either, mother?"

"I can't be, if I married an unlucky husband."

"But by yourself, aren't you?"

"I used to think I was, before I married. Now I think I am very unlucky indeed."

30 "Why?"

"Well—never mind! Perhaps I'm not really," she said.

The child looked at her to see if she meant it. But he saw, by the lines of her mouth, that she was only trying to hide something from him.

"Well, anyhow," he said stoutly, "I'm a lucky person."

"Why?" said his mother, with a sudden laugh.

35 He stared at her. He didn't even know why he had said it.

"God told me," he asserted, brazening it out.

"I hope He did, dear!" she said, again with a laugh, but rather bitter.

"He did, mother!"

"Excellent!" said the mother, using one of her husband's exclamations.

40 The boy saw she did not believe him; or rather, that she paid no attention to his assertion. This angered him somewhat, and made him want to compel her attention.

He went off by himself, vaguely, in a childish way, seeking for the clue to "luck." Absorbed, taking no heed of other people, he went about with a sort of stealth, seeking inwardly for luck. He wanted luck, he wanted it, he wanted it. When the two girls were playing dolls in the nursery, he would sit on his big rocking-horse, charging madly into space, with a frenzy that made the little girls peer at him uneasily. Wildly the horse careered, the waving dark hair of the boy tossed, his eyes had a strange glare in them. The little girls dared not speak to him.

When he had ridden to the end of his mad little journey, he climbed down and stood in front of his rocking-horse, staring fixedly into its lowered face. Its red mouth was slightly open, its big eye was wide and glassy-bright.

"Now!" he would silently command the snorting steed. "Now, take me to where there is luck! Now take me!"

And he would slash the horse on the neck with the little whip he had asked Uncle Oscar for. He *knew* the horse could take him to where there was luck, if only he forced it. So he would mount again and start on his furious ride, hoping at last to get there. He knew he could get there.

45 "You'll break your horse, Paul!" said the nurse.

"He's always riding like that! I wish he'd leave off!" said his elder sister Joan.

But he only glared down on them in silence. Nurse gave him up. She could make nothing of him. Anyhow, he was growing beyond her.

One day his mother and his Uncle Oscar came in when he was on one of his furious rides. He did not speak to them.

"Hallo, you young jockey! Riding a winner?" said his uncle.

50 "Aren't you growing too big for a rocking-horse? You're not a very little boy any longer, you know," said his mother.

But Paul only gave a blue glare from his big, rather close-set eyes. He would speak to nobody when he was in full tilt. His mother watched him with an anxious expression on her face.

At last he suddenly stopped forcing his horse into the mechanical gallop and slid down.

"Well, I got there!" he announced fiercely, his blue eyes still flaring, and his sturdy long legs straddling apart.

"Where did you get to?" asked his mother.

55 "Where I wanted to go," he flared back at her.

"That's right, son!" said Uncle Oscar. "Don't you stop till you get there. What's the horse's name?"

"He doesn't have a name," said the boy.

"Gets on without all right?" asked the uncle.

"Well, he has different names. He was called Sansovino last week."

60 "Sansovino, eh? Won the Ascot.[1] How did you know this name?"

"He always talks about horse-races with Bassett," said Joan.

The uncle was delighted to find that his small nephew was posted with all the racing news. Bassett, the young gardener, who had been wounded in the left foot in the war and had got his present job through Oscar Cresswell,

---

[1] The annual horse race at Ascot Heath in England.

whose batman he had been, was a perfect blade of the "turf." He lived in the racing events, and the small boy lived with him.

Oscar Cresswell got it all from Bassett.

"Master Paul comes and asks me, so I can't do more than tell him, sir," said Bassett, his face terribly serious, as if he were speaking of religious matters.

65   "And does he ever put anything on a horse he fancies?"

"Well—I don't want to give him away—he's a young sport, a fine sport, sir. Would you mind asking him himself? He sort of takes a pleasure in it, and perhaps he'd feel I was giving him away, sir, if you don't mind."

Bassett was serious as a church.

The uncle went back to his nephew and took him off for a ride in the car.

"Say, Paul, old man, do you ever put anything on a horse?" the uncle asked.

70   The boy watched the handsome man closely.

"Why, do you think I oughtn't to?" he parried.

"Not a bit of it! I thought perhaps you might give me a tip for the Lincoln."[2]

The car sped on into the country, going down to Uncle Oscar's place in Hampshire.

"Honour bright?" said the nephew.

75   "Honour bright, son!" said the uncle.

"Well, then, Daffodil."

"Daffodil! I doubt it, sonny. What about Mirza?"

"I only know the winner," said the boy. "That's Daffodil."

"Daffodil, eh?"

80   There was a pause. Daffodil was an obscure horse comparatively.

"Uncle!"

"Yes, son?"

"You won't let it go any further, will you? I promised Bassett."

"Bassett be damned, old man! What's he got to do with it?"

85   "We're partners. We've been partners from the first. Uncle, he lent me my first five shillings, which I lost. I promised him, honour bright, it was only between me and him; only you gave me that ten-shilling note I started winning with, so I thought you were lucky. You won't let it go any further, will you?"

The boy gazed at his uncle from those big, hot, blue eyes, set rather close together. The uncle stirred and laughed uneasily.

"Right you are, son! I'll keep your tip private. Daffodil, eh? How much are you putting on him?"

"All except twenty pounds," said the boy. "I keep that in reserve."

The uncle thought it a good joke.

---

[2] The Lincolnshire Handicap.

90 "You keep twenty pounds in reserve, do you, you young romancer? What are you betting, then?"

"I'm betting three hundred," said the boy gravely. "But it's between you and me, Uncle Oscar! Honour bright?"

The uncle burst into a roar of laughter.

"It's between you and me all right, you young Nat Gould,"[3] he said, laughing. "But where's your three hundred?"

"Bassett keeps it for me. We're partners."

95 "You are, are you! And what is Bassett putting on Daffodil?"

"He won't go quite as high as I do, I expect. Perhaps he'll go a hundred and fifty."

"What, pennies?" laughed the uncle.

"Pounds," said the child, with a surprised look at his uncle. "Bassett keeps a bigger reserve than I do."

Between wonder and amusement Uncle Oscar was silent. He pursued the matter no further, but he determined to take his nephew with him to the Lincoln races.

100 "Now, son," he said, "I'm putting twenty on Mirza, and I'll put five on for you on any horse you fancy. What's your pick?"

"Daffodil, uncle."

"No, not the fiver on Daffodil!"

"I should if it was my own fiver," said the child.

"Good! Good! Right you are! A fiver for me and a fiver for you on Daffodil."

105 The child had never been to a race-meeting before, and his eyes were blue fire. He pursed his mouth tight and watched. A Frenchman just in front had put his money on Lancelot. Wild with excitement, he flayed his arms up and down, yelling *"Lancelot! Lancelot!"* in his French accent.

Daffodil came in first, Lancelot second, Mirza third. The child, flushed and with eyes blazing, was curiously serene. His uncle brought him four five-pound notes, four to one.

"What am I to do with these?" he cried, waving them before the boy's eyes.

"I suppose we'll talk to Bassett," said the boy. "I expect I have fifteen hundred now; and twenty in reserve; and this twenty."

His uncle studied him for some moments.

110 "Look here, son!" he said. "You're not serious about Bassett and that fifteen hundred, are you?"

"Yes, I am. But it's between you and me, uncle. Honour bright?"

"Honour bright all right, son! But I must talk to Bassett."

"If you'd like to be a partner, uncle, with Bassett and me, we could all be partners. Only, you'd have to promise, honour bright, uncle, not to let

---

[3] Nathaniel Gould (1857–1919). British journalist and writer known for his stories about horse racing.

it go beyond us three. Bassett and I are lucky, and you must be lucky, because it was your ten shillings I started winning with. . . ."

Uncle Oscar took both Bassett and Paul into Richmond Park for an afternoon, and there they talked.

115   "It's like this, you see, sir," Bassett said. "Master Paul would get me talking about racing events, spinning yarns, you know, sir. And he was always keen on knowing if I'd made or if I'd lost. It's about a year since, now, that I put five shillings on Blush of Dawn for him: and we lost. Then the luck turned, with that ten shillings he had from you: that we put on Singhalese. And since that time, it's been pretty steady, all things considering. What do you say, Master Paul?"

"We're all right when we're sure," said Paul. "It's when we're not quite sure that we go down."

"Oh, but we're careful then," said Bassett.

"But when are you *sure?*" smiled Uncle Oscar.

"It's Master Paul, sir," said Bassett in a secret, religious voice. "It's as if he had it from heaven. Like Daffodil, now, for the Lincoln. That was as sure as eggs."

120   "Did you put anything on Daffodil?" asked Oscar Cresswell.

"Yes, sir. I made my bit."

"And my nephew?"

Bassett was obstinately silent, looking at Paul.

"I made twelve hundred, didn't I, Bassett? I told uncle I was putting three hundred on Daffodil."

125   "That's right," said Bassett, nodding.

"But where's the money?" asked the uncle.

"I keep it safe locked up, sir. Master Paul can have it any minute he likes to ask for it."

"What, fifteen hundred pounds?"

"And twenty! And *forty*, that is, with the twenty he made on the course."

130   "It's amazing!" said the uncle.

"If Master Paul offers you to be partners, sir, I would, if I were you: if you'll excuse me," said Bassett.

Oscar Cresswell thought about it.

"I'll see the money," he said.

They drove home again, and, sure enough, Bassett came round to the garden-house with fifteen hundred pounds in notes. The twenty pounds reserve was left with Joe Glee, in the Turf Commission deposit.

135   "You see, it's all right, uncle, when I'm *sure!* Then we go strong, for all we're worth. Don't we, Bassett?"

"We do that, Master Paul."

"And when are you sure?" said the uncle, laughing.

"Oh, well, sometimes I'm *absolutely* sure, like about Daffodil," said the boy; "and sometimes I have an idea; and sometimes I haven't even an idea, have I, Bassett? Then we're careful, because we mostly go down."

"You do, do you! And when you're sure, like about Daffodil, what makes you sure, sonny?"

140   "Oh, well, I don't know," said the boy uneasily. "I'm sure, you know, uncle; that's all."

"It's as if he had it from heaven, sir," Bassett reiterated.

"I should say so!" said the uncle.

But he became a partner. And when the Leger[4] was coming on Paul was "sure" about Lively Spark, which was a quite inconsiderable horse. The boy insisted on putting a thousand on the horse, Bassett went for five hundred, and Oscar Cresswell two hundred. Lively Spark came in first, and the betting had been ten to one against him. Paul had made ten thousand.

"You see," he said, "I was absolutely sure of him."

145   Even Oscar Cresswell had cleared two thousand.

"Look here, son," he said, "this sort of thing makes me nervous."

"It needn't, uncle! Perhaps I shan't be sure again for a long time."

"But what are you going to do with your money?" asked the uncle.

"Of course," said the boy, "I started it for mother. She said she had no luck, because father is unlucky, so I thought if *I* was lucky, it might stop whispering."

150   "What might stop whispering?"

"Our house. I *hate* our house for whispering."

"What does it whisper?"

"Why—why"—the boy fidgeted—"why, I don't know. But it's always short of money, you know, uncle."

"I know it, son, I know it."

155   "You know people send mother writs,[5] don't you, uncle?"

"I'm afraid I do," said the uncle.

"And then the house whispers, like people laughing at you behind your back. It's awful, that is! I thought if I was lucky ____ "

"You might stop it," added the uncle.

The boy watched him with big blue eyes, that had an uncanny cold fire in them, and he said never a word.

160   "Well, then!" said the uncle. "What are we doing?"

"I shouldn't like mother to know I was lucky," said the boy.

"Why not, son?"

"She'd stop me."

"I don't think she would."

165   "Oh!"—and the boy writhed in an odd way—"I *don't* want her to know, uncle."

"All right, son! We'll manage it without her knowing."

They managed it very easily. Paul, at the other's suggestion, handed over five thousand pounds to his uncle, who deposited it with the family

---

4 The St. Leger Stakes.

5 Letters from creditors requesting payment.

lawyer, who was then to inform Paul's mother that a relative had put five thousand pounds into his hands, which sum was to be paid out a thousand pounds at a time, on the mother's birthday, for the next five years.

"So she'll have a birthday present of a thousand pounds for five successive years," said Uncle Oscar. "I hope it won't make it all the harder for her later."

Paul's mother had her birthday in November. The house had been 'whispering' worse than ever lately, and, even in spite of his luck, Paul could not bear up against it. He was very anxious to see the effect of the birthday letter, telling his mother about the thousand pounds.

170   When there were no visitors, Paul now took his meals with his parents, as he was beyond the nursery control. His mother went into town nearly every day. She had discovered that she had an odd knack of sketching furs and dress materials, so she worked secretly in the studio of a friend who was the chief 'artist' for the leading drapers. She drew the figures of ladies in furs and ladies in silk and sequins for the newspaper advertisements. This young woman artist earned several thousand pounds a year, but Paul's mother only made several hundreds, and she was again dissatisfied. She so wanted to be first in something, and she did not succeed, even in making sketches for drapery advertisements.

She was down to breakfast on the morning of her birthday. Paul watched her face as she read her letters. He knew the lawyer's letter. As his mother read it, her face hardened and became more expressionless. Then a cold, determined look came on her mouth. She hid the letter under the pile of others, and said not a word about it.

"Didn't you have anything nice in the post for your birthday, mother?" said Paul.

"Quite moderately nice," she said, her voice cold and absent.

She went away to town without saying more.

175   But in the afternoon Uncle Oscar appeared. He said Paul's mother had had a long interview with the lawyer, asking if the whole five thousand could not be advanced at once, as she was in debt.

"What do you think, uncle?" asked the boy.

"I leave it to you, son."

"Oh, let her have it, then! We can get some more with the other," said the boy.

"A bird in the hand is worth two in the bush, laddie!" said Uncle Oscar.

180   "But I'm sure to *know* for the Grand National; or the Lincolnshire; or else the Derby.[6] I'm sure to know for *one* of them," said Paul.

So Uncle Oscar signed the agreement, and Paul's mother touched the whole five thousand. Then something very curious happened. The

---

[6] Famous British horse races. The Grand National is run at Aintree, the Derby at Epsom Downs.

voices in the house suddenly went mad, like a chorus of frogs on a spring evening. There was certain new furnishings, and Paul had a tutor. He was *really* going to Eton, his father's school, in the following autumn. There were flowers in the winter, and a blossoming of the luxury Paul's mother had been used to. And yet the voices in the house, behind the sprays of mimosa and almond-blossom, and from under the piles of iridescent cushions, simply trilled and screamed in a sort of ecstasy: "There *must* be more money! Oh-h-h; there *must* be more money. Oh, now, now-w! Now-w-w—there *must* be more money!—more than ever! More than ever!"

It frightened Paul terribly. He studied away at his Latin and Greek with his tutor. But his intense hours were spent with Bassett. The Grand National had gone by: he had not "known," and had lost a hundred pounds. Summer was at hand. He was in agony for the Lincoln. But even for the Lincoln he didn't "know," and he lost fifty pounds. He became wild-eyed and strange, as if something were going to explode in him.

"Let it alone, son! Don't you bother about it!" urged Uncle Oscar. But it was as if the boy couldn't really hear what his uncle was saying.

"I've got to know for the Derby! I've got to know for the Derby!" the child reiterated, his big blue eyes blazing with a sort of madness.

185   His mother noticed how overwrought he was.

"You'd better go to the seaside. Wouldn't you like to go now to the seaside, instead of waiting? I think you'd better," she said, looking down at him anxiously, her heart curiously heavy because of him.

But the child lifted his uncanny blue eyes.

"I couldn't possibly go before the Derby, mother!" he said. "I couldn't possibly!"

"Why not?" she said, her voice becoming heavy when she was opposed. "Why not? You can still go from the seaside to see the Derby with your Uncle Oscar, if that's what you wish. No need for you to wait here. Besides, I think you care too much about these races. It's a bad sign. My family has been a gambling family, and you won't know till you grow up how much damage it has done. But it has done damage. I shall have to send Bassett away, and ask Uncle Oscar not to talk racing to you, unless you promise to be reasonable about it: go away to the seaside and forget it. You're all nerves!"

190   "I'll do what you like, mother, so long as you don't send me away till after the Derby," the boy said.

"Send you away from where? Just from this house?"

"Yes," he said, gazing at her.

"Why, you curious child, what makes you care about this house so much, suddenly? I never knew you loved it."

He gazed at her without speaking. He had a secret within a secret, something he had not divulged, even to Bassett or to his Uncle Oscar.

195   But his mother, after standing undecided and a little bit sullen for some moments, said:

"Very well, then! Don't go to the seaside till after the Derby, if you don't wish it. But promise me you won't let your nerves go to pieces. Promise you won't think so much about horse-racing and *events,* as you call them!"

"Oh no," said the boy casually. "I won't think much about them, mother. You needn't worry. I wouldn't worry, mother, if I were you."

"If you were me and I were you," said his mother, "I wonder what we *should* do!"

"But you know you needn't worry, mother, don't you?" the boy repeated.

200   "I should be awfully glad to know it," she said wearily.

"Oh, well, you *can,* you know. I mean, you *ought* to know you needn't worry," he insisted.

"Ought I? Then I'll see about it," she said.

Paul's secret of secrets was his wooden horse, that which had no name. Since he was emancipated from a nurse and a nursery-governess, he had had his rocking-horse removed to his own bedroom at the top of the house.

"Surely you're too big for a rocking-horse!" his mother had remonstrated.

205   "Well, you see, mother, till I can have a *real* horse, I like to have *some* sort of animal about," had been his quaint answer.

"Do you feel he keeps you company?" she laughed.

"Oh yes! He's very good, he always keeps me company, when I'm there," said Paul.

So the horse, rather shabby, stood in an arrested prance in the boy's bedroom.

The Derby was drawing near, and the boy grew more and more tense. He hardly heard what was spoken to him, he was very frail, and his eyes were really uncanny. His mother had sudden strange seizures of uneasiness about him. Sometimes, for half an hour, she would feel a sudden anxiety about him that was almost anguish. She wanted to rush to him at once, and know he was safe.

210   Two nights before the Derby, she was at a big party in town, when one of her rushes of anxiety about her boy, her firstborn, gripped her heart till she could hardly speak. She fought with the feeling, might and main, for she believed in common sense. But it was too strong. She had to leave the dance and go downstairs to telephone to the country. The children's nursery-governess was terribly surprised and startled at being rung up in the night.

"Are the children all right, Miss Wilmot?"

"Oh yes, they are quite all right."

"Master Paul? Is he all right?"

"He went to bed as right as a trivet. Shall I run up and look at him?"

215   "No," said Paul's mother reluctantly. "No! Don't trouble. It's all right. Don't sit up. We shall be home fairly soon." She did not want her son's privacy intruded upon.

"Very good," said the governess.

It was about one o'clock when Paul's mother and father drove up to their house. All was still. Paul's mother went to her room and slipped off her white fur cloak. She had told her maid not to wait up for her. She heard her husband downstairs, mixing a whisky and soda.

And then, because of the strange anxiety at her heart, she stole upstairs to her son's room. Noiselessly she went along the upper corridor. Was there a faint noise? What was it?

She stood, with arrested muscles, outside his door, listening. There was a strange, heavy, and yet not loud noise. Her heart stood still. It was a soundless noise, yet rushing and powerful. Something huge, in violent, hushed motion. What was it? What in God's name was it? She ought to know. She felt that she knew the noise. She knew what it was.

220   Yet she could not place it. She couldn't say what it was. And on and on it went, like a madness.

Softly, frozen with anxiety and fear, she turned the door-handle.

The room was dark. Yet in the space near the window, she heard and saw something plunging to and fro. She gazed in fear and amazement.

Then suddenly she switched on the light, and saw her son, in his green pyjamas, madly surging on the rocking-horse. The blaze of light suddenly lit him up, as he urged the wooden horse, and lit her up, as she stood, blonde, in her dress of pale green and crystal, in the doorway.

"Paul!" she cried. "Whatever are you doing?"

225   "It's Malabar!" he screamed in a powerful, strange voice. "It's Malabar!"

His eyes blazed at her for one strange and senseless second, as he ceased urging his wooden horse. Then he fell with a crash to the ground, and she, all her tormented motherhood flooding upon her, rushed to gather him up.

But he was unconscious, and unconscious he remained, with some brain-fever. He talked and tossed, and his mother sat stonily by his side.

"Malabar! It's Malabar! Bassett, Bassett, I *know!* It's Malabar!"

So the child cried, trying to get up and urge the rocking-horse that gave him his inspiration.

230   "What does he mean by Malabar?" asked the heart-frozen mother.

"I don't know," said the father stonily.

"What does he mean by Malabar?" she asked her brother Oscar.

"It's one of the horses running for the Derby," was the answer.

And, in spite of himself, Oscar Cresswell spoke to Bassett, and himself put a thousand on Malabar: at fourteen to one.

235   The third day of the illness was critical: they were waiting for a change. The boy, with his rather long, curly hair, was tossing ceaselessly on the pillow. He neither slept nor regained consciousness, and his eyes were like blue stones. His mother sat, feeling her heart had gone, turned actually into a stone.

In the evening, Oscar Cresswell did not come, but Bassett sent a message, saying could he come up for one moment, just one moment? Paul's mother was very angry at the intrusion, but on second thoughts she agreed. The boy was the same. Perhaps Bassett might bring him to consciousness.

The gardener, a shortish fellow with a little brown moustache and sharp little brown eyes, tiptoed into the room, touched his imaginary cap to Paul's mother, and stole to the bedside, staring with glittering, smallish eyes at the tossing, dying child.

"Master Paul!" he whispered. "Master Paul! Malabar came in first all right, a clean win. I did as you told me. You've made over seventy thousand pounds, you have; you've got over eighty thousand. Malabar came in all right, Master Paul."

"Malabar! Malabar! Did I say Malabar, mother? Did I say Malabar? Do you think I'm lucky, mother? I knew Malabar, didn't I? Over eighty thousand pounds! I call that lucky, don't you, mother? Over eighty thousand pounds! I knew, didn't I know I knew? Malabar came in all right. If I ride my horse till I'm sure, then I tell you, Bassett, you can go as high as you like. Did you go for all you were worth, Bassett?"

240   "I went a thousand on it, Master Paul."

"I never told you, mother, that if I can ride my horse, and *get there*, then I'm absolutely sure—oh, absolutely! Mother, did I ever tell you? I *am* lucky!"

"No, you never did," said his mother.

But the boy died in the night.

And even as he lay dead, his mother heard her brother's voice saying to her: "My God, Hester, you're eighty-odd thousand to the good, and a poor devil of a son to the bad. But, poor devil, poor devil, he's best gone out of a life where he rides his rocking-horse to find a winner."

D O R I S   L E S S I N G

(1919–   )

A Woman on the Roof

(1963)

It was during the week of hot sun, that June.

Three men were at work on the roof, where the leads got so hot they had the idea of throwing water on to cool them. But the water steamed, then sizzled; and they made jokes about getting an egg from some woman in the flats under them, to poach it for their dinner. By two it was not possible to touch the guttering they were replacing, and they speculated about what workmen did in regularly hot countries. Perhaps they should borrow kitchen gloves with the egg? They were all a bit dizzy, not used to the heat; and they shed their coats and stood side by side squeezing themselves into a foot-wide patch of shade against a chimney, careful to keep their feet in the thick socks and boots out of the sun. There was a fine view across several acres of roofs. Not far off a man sat in a deck chair reading the newspapers. Then they saw her, between chimneys, about fifty yards away. She lay face down on a brown blanket. They could see the top part of her: black hair, a flushed solid back, arms spread out.

"She's stark naked," said Stanley, sounding annoyed.

Harry, the oldest, a man of about forty-five, said: "Looks like it."

5   Young Tom, seventeen, said nothing, but he was excited and grinning. Stanley said: "Someone'll report her if she doesn't watch out."

"She thinks no one can see," said Tom, craning his head all ways to see more.

At this point the woman, still lying prone, brought her two hands up behind her shoulders with the ends of a scarf in them, tied it behind her back, and sat up. She wore a red scarf tied around her breasts and brief red bikini pants. This being the first day of the sun she was white, flushing red. She sat smoking, and did not look up when Stanley let out a wolf whistle. Harry said: "Small things amuse small minds," leading the way back to their part of the roof, but it was scorching. Harry said: "Wait, I'm going to rig up some shade," and disappeared down the skylight into the building. Now that he'd gone, Stanley and Tom went to the farthest point they could to peer at the woman. She had moved, and all they could see were two pink legs stretched on the blanket. They whistled and shouted but the legs did not move. Harry came back with a blanket and shouted: "Come on, then." He sounded irritated with them. They clambered back to him and he said to Stanley: "What about your missus?" Stanley was newly married, about three months. Stanley said, jeering: "What about my missus?"—preserving his independence. Tom said nothing, but his mind was full of the nearly naked woman. Harry slung the blanket, which he had borrowed from a friendly woman downstairs, from the stem of a television aerial to a row of chimney-pots. This shade fell across the piece of gutter they had to replace. But the shade kept moving, they had to adjust the blanket, and not much progress was made. At last some of the heat left the roof, and they worked fast, making up for lost time. First Stanley, then Tom, made a trip to the end of the roof to see the woman. "She's on her back," Stanley said, adding a jest which made Tom snicker, and the older man smile tolerantly. Tom's report was that she hadn't moved, but it was a lie. He wanted to keep what he had seen to himself: he had caught her in the act of rolling down the little red pants over her hips, till they were no more than a small triangle. She was on her back, fully visible, glistening with oil.

Next morning, as soon as they came up, they went to look. She was already there, face down, arms spread out, naked except for the little red pants. She had turned brown in the night. Yesterday she was a scarlet-and-white woman, today she was a brown woman. Stanley let out a whistle. She lifted her head, startled, as if she'd been asleep, and looked straight over at them. The sun was in her eyes, she blinked and stared, then she dropped her head again. At this gesture of indifference, they all three,

Stanley, Tom and old Harry, let out whistles and yells. Harry was doing it in parody of the younger men, making fun of them, but he was also angry. They were all angry because of her utter indifference to the three men watching her.

10   "Bitch," said Stanley.

"She should ask us over," said Tom, snickering.

Harry recovered himself and reminded Stanley: "If she's married, her old man wouldn't like that."

"Christ," said Stanley virtuously, "if my wife lay about like that, for everyone to see, I'd soon stop her."

Harry said, smiling: "How do you know, perhaps she's sunning herself at this very moment?"

15   "Not a chance, not on our roof." The safety of his wife put Stanley into a good humor, and they went to work. But today it was hotter than yesterday; and several times one or the other suggested they should tell Matthew, the foreman, and ask to leave the roof until the heat wave was over. But they didn't. There was work to be done in the basement of the big block of flats, but up here they felt free, on a different level from ordinary humanity shut in the streets or the buildings. A lot more people came out on to the roofs that day, for an hour at midday. Some married couples sat side by side in deck chairs, the women's legs stockingless and scarlet, the men in vests with reddening shoulders.

The woman stayed on her blanket, turning herself over and over. She ignored them, no matter what they did. When Harry went off to fetch more screws, Stanley said: "Come on." Her roof belonged to a different system of roofs, separated from theirs at one point by about twenty feet. It meant a scrambling climb from one level to another, edging along parapets, clinging to chimneys, while their big boots slipped and slithered, but at last they stood on a small square projecting roof looking straight down at her, close. She sat smoking, reading a book. Tom thought she looked like a poster, or a magazine cover, with the blue sky behind her and her legs stretched out. Behind her a great crane at work on a new building in Oxford Street swung its black arm across roofs in a great arc. Tom imagined himself at work on the crane, adjusting the arm to swing over and pick her up and swing her back across the sky to drop her near him.

They whistled. She looked up at them, cool and remote, then went on reading. Again, they were furious. Or, rather, Stanley was. His sun-heated face was screwed into a rage as he whistled again and again, trying to make her look up. Young Tom stopped whistling. He stood beside Stanley, excited, grinning; but he felt as if he were saying to the woman: Don't associate me with *him*, for his grin was apologetic. Last night he had thought of the unknown woman before he slept, and she had been tender with him. This tenderness he was remembering as he shifted his feet by the jeering, whistling Stanley, and watched the indifferent, healthy brown woman a few feet off, with the gap that plunged to the street between them. Tom thought it was romantic, it was like being high on two hilltops.

But there was a shout from Harry, and they clambered back. Stanley's face was hard, really angry. The boy kept looking at him and wondered why he hated the woman so much, for by now he loved her.

They played their little games with the blanket, trying to trap shade to work under; but again it was not until nearly four that they could work seriously, and they were exhausted, all three of them. They were grumbling about the weather by now. Stanley was in a thoroughly bad humor. When they made their routine trip to see the woman before they packed up for the day, she was apparently asleep, face down, her back all naked save for the scarlet triangle on her buttocks. "I've got a good mind to report her to the police," said Stanley, and Harry said: "What's eating you? What harm's she doing?"

"I tell you, if she was my wife!"

20 "But she isn't, is she?" Tom knew that Harry, like himself, was uneasy at Stanley's reaction. He was normally a sharp young man, quick at his work, making a lot of jokes, good company.

"Perhaps it will be cooler tomorrow," said Harry.

But it wasn't; it was hotter, if anything, and the weather forecast said the good weather would last. As soon as they were on the roof, Harry went over to see if the woman was there, and Tom knew it was to prevent Stanley going, to put off his bad humor. Harry had grownup children, a boy the same age as Tom, and the youth trusted and looked up to him.

Harry came back and said: "She's not there."

"I bet her old man has put his foot down," said Stanley, and Harry and Tom caught each other's eyes and smiled behind the young married man's back.

25 Harry suggested they should get permission to work in the basement, and they did, that day. But before packing up Stanley said: "Let's have a breath of fresh air." Again Harry and Tom smiled at each other as they followed Stanley up to the roof. Tom in the devout conviction that he was there to protect the woman from Stanley. It was about five-thirty, and a calm, full sunlight lay over the roofs. The great crane still swung its black arm from Oxford Street to above their heads. She was not there. Then there was a flutter of white from behind a parapet, and she stood up, in a belted, white dressing-gown. She had been there all day, probably, but on a different patch of roof, to hide from them. Stanley did not whistle; he said nothing, but watched the woman bend to collect papers, books, cigarettes, then fold the blanket over her arm. Tom was thinking: If they weren't here, I'd go over and say . . . what? But he knew from his nightly dreams of her that she was kind and friendly. Perhaps she would ask him down to her flat? Perhaps . . . He stood watching her disappear down the skylight. As she went, Stanley let out a shrill derisive yell; she started, and it seemed as if she nearly fell. She clutched to save herself, they could hear things falling. She looked straight at them, angry. Harry said, facetiously: "Better be careful on those slippery ladders, love." Tom knew he said it to save her from Stanley, but she could not know it. She vanished, frowning.

Tom was full of a secret delight, because he knew her anger was for the others, not for him.

"Roll on some rain," said Stanley, bitter, looking at the blue evening sky.

Next day was cloudless, and they decided to finish the work in the basement. They felt excluded, shut in the grey cement basement fitting pipes, from the holiday atmosphere of London in a heat wave. At lunchtime they came up for some air, but while the married couples, and the men in shirtsleeves or vests, were there, she was not there, either on her usual patch of roof or where she had been yesterday. They all, even Harry, clambered about, between chimney-pots, over parapets, the hot leads stinging their fingers. There was not a sign of her. They took off their shirts and vests and exposed their chests, feeling their feet sweaty and hot. They did not mention the woman. But Tom felt alone again. Last night she had him into her flat: it was big and had fitted white carpets and a bed with a padded white leather headboard. She wore a black filmy negligée and her kindness to Tom thickened his throat as he remembered it. He felt she had betrayed him by not being there.

And again after work they climbed up, but still there was nothing to be seen of her. Stanley kept repeating that if it was as hot as this tomorrow he wasn't going to work and that's all there was to it. But they were all there next day. By ten the temperature was in the middle seventies, and it was eighty long before noon. Harry went to the foreman to say it was impossible to work on the leads in that heat; but the foreman said there was nothing else he could put them on, and they'd have to. At midday they stood, silent, watching the skylight on her roof open, and then she slowly emerged in her white gown, holding a bundle of blanket. She looked at them, gravely, then went to the part of the roof where she was hidden from them. Tom was pleased. He felt she was more his when the other men couldn't see her. They had taken off their shirts and vests, but now they put them back again, for they felt the sun bruising their flesh. "She must have the hide of a rhino," said Stanley, tugging at guttering and swearing. They stopped work, and sat in the shade, moving around behind chimney stacks. A woman came to water a yellow window box opposite them. She was middleaged, wearing a flowered summer dress. Stanley said to her: "We need a drink more than them." She smiled and said: "Better drop down to the pub quick, it'll be closing in a minute." They exchanged pleasantries, and she left them with a smile and a wave.

"Not like Lady Godiva,"[1] said Stanley. "She can give us a bit of a chat and a smile."

30   "You didn't whistle at *her*," said Tom, reproving.

"Listen to him," said Stanley, "you didn't whistle, then?"

---

[1] According to legend, Lady Godiva rode naked through the streets of Coventry in an effort to win relief for the townspeople from an exorbitant tax.

But the boy felt as if he hadn't whistled, as if only Harry and Stanley had. He was making plans, when it was time to knock off work, to get left behind and somehow make his way over to the woman. The weather report said the hot spell was due to break, so he had to move quickly. But there was no chance of being left. The other two decided to knock off work at four, because they were exhausted. As they went down, Tom quickly climbed a parapet and hoisted himself higher by pulling his weight up a chimney. He caught a glimpse of her lying on her back, her knees up, eyes closed, a brown woman lolling in the sun. He slipped and clattered down, as Stanley looked for information: "She's gone down," he said. He felt as if he had protected her from Stanley, and that she must be grateful to him. He could feel the bond between the woman and himself.

Next day, they stood around on the landing below the roof, reluctant to climb up into the heat. The woman who had lent Harry the blanket came out and offered them a cup of tea. They accepted gratefully, and sat around Mrs. Pritchett's kitchen an hour or so, chatting. She was married to an airline pilot. A smart blonde, of about thirty, she had an eye for the handsome sharp-faced Stanley; and the two teased each other while Harry sat in a corner, watching, indulgent, though his expression reminded Stanley that he was married. And young Tom felt envious of Stanley's ease in badinage;[2] felt, too, that Stanley's getting off with Mrs. Pritchett left his romance with the woman on the roof safe and intact.

"I thought they said the heat wave'd break," said Stanley, sullen, as the time approached when they really would have to climb up into the sunlight.

35 "You don't like it, then?" asked Mrs. Pritchett.

"All right for some," said Stanley. "Nothing to do but lie about as if it was a beach up there. Do you ever go up?"

"Went up once," said Mrs. Pritchett. "But it's a dirty place up there, and it's too hot."

"Quite right too," said Stanley.

Then they went up, leaving the cool neat little flat and the friendly Mrs. Pritchett.

40 As soon as they were up they saw her. The three men looked at her, resentful at her ease in this punishing sun. Then Harry said, because of the expression on Stanley's face: "Come on, we've got to pretend to work, at least."

They had to wrench another length of guttering that ran beside a parapet out of its bed, so that they could replace it. Stanley took it in his two hands, tugged, swore, stood up. "Fuck it," he said, and sat down under a chimney. He lit a cigarette. "Fuck them," he said. "What do they think we are, lizards? I've got blisters all over my hands." Then he jumped up and climbed over the roofs and stood with his back to them. He put his fingers either side of his mouth and let out a shrill whistle.

---

[2] Playful banter.

Tom and Harry squatted, not looking at each other, watching him. They could just see the woman's head, the beginnings of her brown shoulders. Stanley whistled again. Then he began stamping with his feet, and whistled and yelled and screamed at the woman, his face getting scarlet. He seemed quite mad, as he stamped and whistled, while the woman did not move, she did not move a muscle.

"Barmy," said Tom.

"Yes," said Harry, disapproving.

Suddenly the older man came to a decision. It was, Tom knew, to save some sort of scandal or real trouble over the woman. Harry stood up and began packing tools into a length of oily cloth. "Stanley," he said, commanding. At first Stanley took no notice, but Harry said: "Stanley, we're packing it in, I'll tell Matthew."

45   Stanley came back, cheeks mottled, eyes glaring.

"Can't go on like this," said Harry. "It'll break in a day or so. I'm going to tell Matthew we've got sunstroke, and if he doesn't like it, it's too bad." Even Harry sounded aggrieved, Tom noted. The small, competent man, the family man with his grey hair, who was never at a loss, sounded really off balance. "Come on," he said, angry. He fitted himself into the open square in the roof, and went down, watching his feet on the ladder. Then Stanley went, with not a glance at the woman. Then Tom, who, his throat beating with excitement, silently promised her on a backward glance: Wait for me, wait, I'm coming.

On the pavement Stanley said: "I'm going home." He looked white now, so perhaps he really did have sunstroke. Harry went off to find the foreman, who was at work on the plumbing of some flats down the street. Tom slipped back, not into the building they had been working on, but the building on whose roof the woman lay. He went straight up, no one stopping him. The skylight stood open, with an iron ladder leading up. He emerged on to the roof a couple of yards from her. She sat up, pushing back her black hair with both hands. The scarf across her breasts bound them tight, and brown flesh bulged around it. Her legs were brown and smooth. She stared at him in silence. The boy stood grinning, foolish, claiming the tenderness he expected from her.

"What do you want?" she asked.

"I . . . I came to . . . make your acquaintance," he stammered, grinning, pleading with her.

50   They looked at each other, the slight, scarlet-faced excited boy, and the serious, nearly naked woman. Then, without a word, she lay down on her brown blanket, ignoring him.

"You like the sun, do you?" he enquired of her glistening back.

Not a word. He felt panic, thinking of how she had held him in her arms, stroked his hair, brought him where he sat, lordly, in her bed, a glass of some exhilarating liquor he had never tasted in life. He felt that if he knelt down, stroked her shoulders, her hair, she would turn and clasp him in her arms.

He said: "The sun's all right for you, isn't it?"

She raised her head, set her chin on two small fists. "Go away," she said. He did not move. "Listen," she said, in a slow reasonable voice, where anger was kept in check, though with difficulty; looking at him, her face weary with anger, "if you get a kick out of seeing women in bikinis, why don't you take a sixpenny bus ride to the Lido?[3] You'd see dozens of them, without all this mountaineering."

55   She hadn't understood him. He felt her unfairness pale him. He stammered: "But I like you, I've been watching you and . . ."

"Thanks," she said, and dropped her face again, turned away from him.

She lay there. He stood there. She said nothing. She had simply shut him out. He stood, saying nothing at all, for some minutes. He thought: She'll have to say something if I stay. But the minutes went past, with no sign of them in her, except in the tension of her back, her thighs, her arms—the tension of waiting for him to go.

He looked up at the sky, where the sun seemed to spin in heat; and over the roofs where he and his mates had been earlier. He could see the heat quivering where they had worked. And they expect us to work in these conditions! he thought, filled with righteous indignation. The woman hadn't moved. A bit of hot wind blew her black hair softly; it shone, and was iridescent. He remembered how he had stroked it last night.

Resentment of her at last moved him off and away down the ladder, through the building, into the street. He got drunk then, in hatred of her.

60   Next day when he woke the sky was grey. He looked at the wet grey and thought, vicious: Well, that's fixed you, hasn't it now? That's fixed you good and proper.

The three men were at work early on the cool leads, surrounded by damp drizzling roofs where no one came to sun themselves, black roofs, slimy with rain. Because it was cool now, they would finish the job that day, if they hurried.

A L I C E   M U N R O

(1931–   )

Boys and Girls

(1968)

My father was a fox farmer. That is, he raised silver foxes, in pens; and in the fall and early winter, when their fur was prime, he killed them and skinned them and sold their pelts to the Hudson's Bay Company or the Montreal Fur Traders. These companies supplied us with heroic calendars to hang, one on each side of the kitchen door. Against a background of cold blue sky and black pine forests and treacherous northern rivers,

---

[3] A bathing area in London's Hyde Park.

plumed adventurers planted the flags of England or of France; magnificent savages bent their backs to the portage.[1]

For several weeks before Christmas, my father worked after supper in the cellar of our house. The cellar was whitewashed, and lit by a hundred-watt bulb over the worktable. My brother Laird and I sat on the top step and watched. My father removed the pelt inside-out from the body of the fox, which looked surprisingly small, mean and rat-like, deprived of its arrogant weight of fur. The naked, slippery bodies were collected in a sack and buried at the dump. One time the hired man, Henry Bailey, had taken a swipe at me with this sack, saying, "Christmas present!" My mother thought that was not funny. In fact she disliked the whole pelting operation—that was what the killing, skinning, and preparation of the furs was called—and wished it did not have to take place in the house. There was the smell. After the pelt had been stretched inside-out on a long board my father scraped away delicately, removing the little clotted webs of blood vessels, the bubbles of fat; the smell of blood and animal fat, with the strong primitive odour of the fox itself, penetrated all parts of the house. I found it reassuringly seasonal, like the smell of oranges and pine needles.

Henry Bailey suffered from bronchial troubles. He would cough and cough until his narrow face turned scarlet, and his light blue, derisive eyes filled up with tears; then he took the lid off the stove, and, standing well back, shot out a great clot of phlegm—hsss—straight into the heart of the flames. We admired him for his performance and for his ability to make his stomach growl at will, and for his laughter, which was full of high whistlings and gurglings and involved the whole faulty machinery of his chest. It was sometimes hard to tell what he was laughing at, and always possible that it might be us.

After we had been sent to bed we could still smell fox and still hear Henry's laugh, but these things, reminders of the warm, safe, brightly lit downstairs world, seemed lost and diminished, floating on the stale cold air upstairs. We were afraid at night in the winter. We were not afraid of *outside* though this was the time of year when snowdrifts curled around our house like sleeping whales and the wind harassed us all night, coming up from the buried fields, the frozen swamp, with its old bugbear chorus of threats and misery. We were afraid of *inside,* the room where we slept. At this time the upstairs of our house was not finished. A brick chimney went up one wall. In the middle of the floor was a square hole, with a wooden railing around it; that was where the stairs came up. On the other side of the stairwell were the things that nobody had any use for any more—a soldiery roll of linoleum, standing on end, a wicker baby carriage, a fern basket, china jugs and basins with cracks in them, a picture of the Battle of Balaclava, very sad to look at. I had told Laird, as soon as he was

---

[1] Carrying boats or goods overland from one body of water to another or around an obstacle such as rapids.

old enough to understand such things, that bats and skeletons lived over
there; whenever a man escaped from the county jail, twenty miles away, I
imagined that he had somehow let himself in the window and was hiding
behind the linoleum. But we had rules to keep us safe. When the light was
on, we were safe as long as we did not step off the square of worn carpet
which defined our bedroom-space; when the light was off no place was
safe but the beds themselves. I had to turn out the light kneeling on the
end of my bed, and stretching as far as I could to reach the cord.

5   In the dark we lay on our beds, our narrow life rafts, and fixed our
eyes on the faint light coming up the stairwell, and sang songs. Laird sang
"Jingle Bells," which he would sing any time, whether it was Christmas or
not, and I sang "Danny Boy." I love the sound of my own voice, frail and
supplicating, rising in the dark. We could make out the tall frosted shapes
of the windows now, gloomy and white. When I came to the part, *When I
am dead, as dead I well may be*—a fit of shivering caused not by the cold
sheets but by pleasurable emotion almost silenced me. *You'll kneel and say,
an Ave there above me*—What was an Ave? Every day I forgot to find out.

Laird went straight from singing to sleep. I could hear his long, satisfied, bubbly breaths. Now for the time that remained to me, the most perfectly private and perhaps the best time of the whole day, I arranged
myself tightly under the covers and went on with one of the stories I was
telling myself from night to night. These stories were about myself, when
I had grown a little older; they took place in a world that was recognizably
mine, yet one that presented opportunities for courage, boldness and self-
sacrifice, as mine never did. I rescued people from a bombed building (it
discouraged me that the real war had gone on so far away from Jubilee). I
shot two rabid wolves who were menacing the schoolyard (the teachers
cowered terrified at my back). I rode a fine horse spiritedly down the main
street of Jubilee, acknowledging the towns-people's gratitude for some yet-
to-be-worked-out piece of heroism (nobody ever rode a horse there, except
King Billy in the Orangemen's Day parade). There was always riding and
shooting in these stories, though I had only been on a horse twice—bare-
back because we did not own a saddle—and the second time I had slid
right around and dropped under the horse's feet; it had stepped placidly
over me. I really was learning to shoot, but I could not hit anything yet,
not even tin cans on fence posts.

Alive, the foxes inhabited a world my father made for them. It was surrounded by a high guard fence, like a medieval town, with a gate that was
padlocked at night. Along the streets of this town were ranged large,
sturdy pens. Each of them had a real door that a man could go through, a
wooden ramp along the wire, for the foxes to run up and down on, and a
kennel—something like a clothes chest with airholes—where they slept
and stayed in winter and had their young. There were feeding and watering dishes attached to the wire in such a way that they could be emptied
and cleaned from the outside. The dishes were made of old tin cans, and

the ramps and kennels of odds and ends of old lumber. Everything was tidy and ingenious; my father was tirelessly inventive and his favourite book in the world was Robinson Crusoe. He had fitted a tin drum on a wheelbarrow, for bringing water down to the pens. This was my job in summer, when the foxes had to have water twice a day. Between nine and ten o'clock in the morning, and again after supper, I filled the drum at the pump and trundled it down through the barnyard to the pens, where I parked it, and filled my watering can and went along the streets. Laird came too, with his little cream and green gardening can, filled too full and knocking against his legs and slopping water on his canvas shoes. I had the real watering can, my father's, though I could only carry it three-quarters full.

The foxes all had names, which were printed on a tin plate and hung beside their doors. They were not named when they were born, but when they survived the first year's pelting and were added to the breeding stock. Those my father had named were called names like Prince, Bob, Wally and Betty. Those I had named were called Star or Turk, or Maureen or Diana. Laird named one Maud after a hired girl we had when he was little, one Harold after a boy at school, and one Mexico, he did not say why.

Naming them did not make pets out of them, or anything like it. Nobody but my father ever went into the pens, and he had twice had blood-poisoning from bites. When I was bringing them their water they prowled up and down on the paths they had made inside their pens, barking seldom—they saved that for nighttime, when they might get up a chorus of community frenzy—but always watching me, their eyes burning, clear gold, in their pointed, malevolent faces. They were beautiful for their delicate legs and heavy, aristocratic tails and the bright fur sprinkled on dark down their backs—which gave them their name—but especially for their faces, drawn exquisitely sharp in pure hostility, and their golden eyes.

10   Besides carrying water I helped my father when he cut the long grass, and the lamb's quarter and flowering money-musk, that grew between the pens. He cut with the scythe and I raked into piles. Then he took a pitch-fork and threw fresh-cut grass all over the top of the pens, to keep the foxes cooler and shade their coats, which were browned by too much sun. My father did not talk to me unless it was about the job we were doing. In this he was quite different from my mother, who, if she was feeling cheerful, would tell me all sorts of things—the name of a dog she had had when she was a little girl, the names of boys she had gone out with later on when she was grown up, and what certain dresses of hers had looked like—she could not imagine now what had become of them. Whatever thoughts and stories my father had were private, and I was shy of him and would never ask him questions. Nevertheless I worked willingly under his eyes, and with a feeling of pride. One time a feed salesman came down into the pens to talk to him and my father said, "Like to have you meet my new hired man." I turned away and raked furiously, red in the face with pleasure.

"Could of fooled me," said the salesman. "I thought it was only a girl."

After the grass was cut, it seemed suddenly much later in the year. I walked on stubble in the earlier evening, aware of the reddening skies, the entering silences, of fall. When I wheeled the tank out of the gate and put the padlock on, it was almost dark. One night at this time I saw my mother and father standing talking on the little rise of ground we called the gangway, in front of the barn. My father had just come from the meathouse; he had his stiff bloody apron on, and a pail of cut-up meat in his hand.

It was an odd thing to see my mother down at the barn. She did not often come out of the house unless it was to do something—hang out the wash or dig potatoes in the garden. She looked out of place, with her bare lumpy legs, not touched by the sun, her apron still on and damp across the stomach from the supper dishes. Her hair was tied up in a kerchief, wisps of it falling out. She would tie her hair up like this in the morning, saying she did not have time to do it properly, and it would stay tied up all day. It was true, too; she really did not have time. These days our back porch was piled with baskets of peaches and grapes and pears, bought in town, and onions and tomatoes and cucumbers grown at home, all waiting to be made into jelly and jam and preserves, pickles and chili sauce. In the kitchen there was a fire in the stove all day, jars clinked in boiling water, sometimes a cheesecloth bag was strung on a pole between two chairs, straining blue-black grape pulp for jelly. I was given jobs to do and I would sit at the table peeling peaches that had been soaked in the hot water, or cutting up onions, my eyes smarting and streaming. As soon as I was done I ran out of the house, trying to get out of earshot before my mother thought of what she wanted me to do next. I hated the hot dark kitchen in summer, the green blinds and the flypapers, the same old oilcloth table and wavy mirror and bumpy linoleum. My mother was too tired and preoccupied to talk to me, she had no heart to tell about the Normal School Graduation Dance; sweat trickled over her face and she was always counting under her breath, pointing at jars, dumping cups of sugar. It seemed to me that work in the house was endless, dreary and peculiarly depressing; work done out of doors, and in my father's service, was ritualistically important.

I wheeled the tank up to the barn, where it was kept, and I heard my mother saying, "Wait till Laird gets a little bigger, then you'll have a real help."

15   What my father said I did not hear. I was pleased by the way he stood listening, politely as he would to a salesman or a stranger, but with an air of wanting to get on with his real work. I felt my mother had no business down here and I wanted him to feel the same way. What did she mean about Laird? He was no help to anybody. Where was he now? Swinging himself sick on the swing, going around in circles, or trying to catch caterpillars. He never once stayed with me till I was finished.

"And then I can use her more in the house," I heard my mother say. She had a dead-quiet, regretful way of talking about me that always made me uneasy. "I just get my back turned and she runs off. It's not like I had a girl in the family at all."

I went and sat on a feedbag in the corner of the barn, not wanting to appear when this conversation was going on. My mother, I felt, was not to be trusted. She was kinder than my father and more easily fooled, but you could not depend on her, and the real reasons for the things she said and did were not to be known. She loved me, and she sat up late at night making a dress of the difficult style I wanted, for me to wear when school started, but she was also my enemy. She was always plotting. She was plotting now to get me to stay in the house more, although she knew I hated it (*because* she knew I hated it) and keep me from working for my father. It seemed to me she would do this simply out of perversity, and to try her power. It did not occur to me that she could be lonely, or jealous. No grown-up could be; they were too fortunate. I sat and kicked my heels monotonously against a feedbag, raising dust, and did not come out till she was gone.

At any rate, I did not expect my father to pay any attention to what she said. Who could imagine Laird doing my work—Laird remembering the padlock and cleaning out the watering-dishes with a leaf on the end of a stick, or even wheeling the tank without it tumbling over? It showed how little my mother knew about the way things really were.

I have forgotten to say what the foxes were fed. My father's bloody apron reminded me. They were fed horsemeat. At this time most farmers still kept horses, and when a horse got too old to work, or broke a leg or got down and would not get up, as they sometimes did, the owner would call my father, and he and Henry went out to the farm in the truck. Usually they shot and butchered the horse there, paying the farmer from five to twelve dollars. If they had already too much meat on hand, they would bring the horse back alive, and keep it for a few days or weeks in our stable, until the meat was needed. After the war the farmers were buying tractors and gradually getting rid of horses altogether, so it sometimes happened that we got a good healthy horse, that there was just no use for any more. If this happened in the winter we might keep the horse in our stable till spring, for we had plenty of hay and if there was a lot of snow— and the plow did not always get our road cleared—it was convenient to be able to go to town with a horse and cutter.

20   The winter I was eleven years old we had two horses in the stable. We did not know what names they had had before, so we called them Mack and Flora. Mack was an old black workhorse, sooty and indifferent. Flora was a sorrel mare, a driver. We took them both out in the cutter. Mack was slow and easy to handle. Flora was given to fits of violent alarm, veering at cars and even at other horses, but we loved her speed and high-stepping, her general air of gallantry and abandon. On Saturdays we went down to the stable and as soon as we opened the door on its cosy, animal-smelling darkness Flora threw up her head, rolled her eyes, whinnied despairingly

and pulled herself through a crisis of nerves on the spot. It was not safe to go into her stall; she would kick.

This winter also I began to hear a great deal more on the theme my mother had sounded when she had been talking in front of the barn. I no longer felt safe. It seemed that in the minds of the people around me there was a steady undercurrent of thought, not to be deflected, on this one subject. The word *girl* had formerly seemed to me innocent and unburdened, like the word *child*; now it appeared that it was no such thing. A girl was not, as I had supposed, simply what I was; it was what I had to become. It was a definition, always touched with emphasis, with reproach and disappointment. Also it was a joke on me. Once Laird and I were fighting, and for the first time ever I had to use all my strength against him; even so, he caught and pinned my arm for a moment, really hurting me. Henry saw this, and laughed, saying, "Oh, that there Laird's gonna show you, one of these days!" Laird was getting a lot bigger. But I was getting bigger too.

My grandmother came to stay with us for a few weeks and I heard other things. "Girls don't slam doors like that." "Girls keep their knees together when they sit down." And worse still, when I asked some questions, "That's none of girls' business." I continued to slam the doors and sit as awkwardly as possible, thinking that by such measures I kept myself free.

When spring came, the horses were let out in the barnyard. Mack stood against the barn wall trying to scratch his neck and haunches, but Flora trotted up and down and reared at the fences, clattering her hooves against the rails. Snow drifts dwindled quickly, revealing the hard grey and brown earth, the familiar rise and fall of the ground, plain and bare after the fantastic landscape of winter. There was a great feeling of opening-out, of release. We just wore rubbers now, over our shoes; our feet felt ridiculously light. One Saturday we went out to the stable and found all the doors open, letting in the unaccustomed sunlight and fresh air. Henry was there, just idling around looking at his collection of calendars which were tacked up behind the stalls in a part of the stable my mother had probably never seen.

"Come to say goodbye to your old friend Mack?" Henry said. "Here, you give him a taste of oats." He poured some oats into Laird's cupped hands and Laird went to feed Mack. Mack's teeth were in bad shape. He ate very slowly, patiently shifting the oats around in his mouth, trying to find a stump of a molar to grind it on. "Poor old Mack," said Henry mournfully. "When a horse's teeth's gone, he's gone. That's about the way."

25   "Are you going to shoot him today?" I said. Mack and Flora had been in the stable so long I had almost forgotten they were going to be shot.

Henry didn't answer me. Instead he started to sing in a high, trembly, mocking-sorrowful voice, *Oh, there's no more work, for poor Uncle Ned, he's gone where the good darkies go.* Mack's thick, blackish tongue worked diligently at Laird's hand. I went out before the song was ended and sat down on the gangway.

I had never seen them shoot a horse, but I knew where it was done. Last summer Laird and I had come upon a horse's entrails before they were buried. We had thought it was a big black snake, coiled up in the sun. That was around in the field that ran up beside the barn. I thought that if we went inside the barn, and found a wide crack or a knothole to look through, we would be able to see them do it. It was not something I wanted to see; just the same, if a thing really happened, it was better to see it, and know.

My father came down from the house, carrying the gun.

"What are you doing here?" he said.

30   "Nothing."

"Go on up and play around the house."

He sent Laird out of the stable. I said to Laird, "Do you want to see them shoot Mack?" and without waiting for an answer led him around to the front door of the barn, opened it carefully, and went in. "Be quiet or they'll hear us," I said. We could hear Henry and my father talking in the stable, then the heavy, shuffling steps of Mack being backed out of his stall.

In the loft it was cold and dark. Thin, crisscrossed beams of sunlight fell through the cracks. The hay was low. It was a rolling country, hills and hollows, slipping under our feet. About four feet up was a beam going around the walls. We piled hay up in one corner and I boosted Laird up and hoisted myself. The beam was not very wide; we crept along it with our hands flat on the barn walls. There were plenty of knotholes, and I found one that gave me the view I wanted—a corner of the barnyard, the gate, part of the field. Laird did not have a knothole and began to complain.

I showed him a widened crack between two boards. "Be quiet and wait. If they hear you you'll get us in trouble."

35   My father came in sight carrying the gun. Henry was leading Mack by the halter. He dropped it and took out his cigarette papers and tobacco; he rolled cigarettes for my father and himself. While this was going on Mack nosed around in the old, dead grass along the fence. Then my father opened the gate and they took Mack through. Henry led Mack away from the path to a patch of ground and they talked together, not loud enough for us to hear. Mack again began searching for a mouthful of fresh grass, which was not to be found. My father walked away in a straight line, and stopped short at a distance which seemed to suit him. Henry was walking away from Mack too, but sideways, still negligently holding on to the halter. My father raised the gun and Mack looked up as if he had noticed something and my father shot him.

Mack did not collapse at once but swayed, lurched sideways and fell, first on his side; then he rolled over on his back and, amazingly, kicked his legs for a few seconds in the air. At this Henry laughed, as if Mack had done a trick for him. Laird, who had drawn a long, groaning breath of surprise when the shot was fired, said out loud, "He's not dead." And it seemed to me it might be true. But his legs stopped, he rolled on his side again, his muscles quivered and sank. The two men walked over and looked at him in a businesslike way; they bent down and examined his forehead where the bullet had gone in, and now I saw his blood on the brown grass.

"Now they just skin him and cut him up," I said. "Let's go." My legs were a little shaky and I jumped gratefully down into the hay. "Now you've seen how they shoot a horse," I said in a congratulatory way, as if I had seen it many times before. "Let's see if any barn cat's had kittens in the hay." Laird jumped. He seemed young and obedient again. Suddenly I remembered how, when he was little, I had brought him into the barn and told him to climb the ladder to the top beam. That was in the spring, too, when the hay was low. I had done it out of a need for excitement, a desire for something to happen so that I could tell about it. He was wearing a little bulky brown and white checked coat, made down from one of mine. He went all the way up, just as I told him, and sat down on the top beam with the hay far below him on one side, and the barn floor and some old machinery on the other. Then I ran screaming to my father, "Laird's up on the top beam!" My father came, my mother came, my father went up the ladder talking very quietly and brought Laird down under his arm, at which my mother leaned against the ladder and began to cry. They said to me, "Why weren't you watching him?" but nobody ever knew the truth. Laird did not know enough to tell. But whenever I saw the brown and white checked coat hanging in the closet, or at the bottom of the rag bag, which was where it ended up, I felt a weight in my stomach, the sadness of unexorcized guilt.

I looked at Laird who did not even remember this, and I did not like the look on his thin, winter-pale face. His expression was not frightened or upset, but remote, concentrating. "Listen," I said, in an unusually bright and friendly voice, "you aren't going to tell, are you?"

"No," he said absently.

40   "Promise."

"Promise," he said. I grabbed the hand behind his back to make sure he was not crossing his fingers. Even so, he might have a nightmare; it might come out that way. I decided I had better work hard to get all thoughts of what he had seen out of his mind—which, it seemed to me, could not hold very many things at a time. I got some money I had saved and that afternoon we went into Jubilee and saw a show, with Judy Canova, at which we both laughed a great deal. After that I thought it would be all right.

Two weeks later I knew they were going to shoot Flora. I knew from the night before, when I heard my mother ask if the hay was holding out all right, and my father said, "Well, after to-morrow there'll just be the cow, and we should be able to put her out to grass in another week." So I knew it was Flora's turn in the morning.

This time I didn't think of watching it. That was something to see just one time. I had not thought about it very often since, but sometimes when

I was busy, working at school, or standing in front of the mirror combing my hair and wondering if I would be pretty when I grew up, the whole scene would flash into my mind: I would see the easy, practised way my father raised the gun, and hear Henry laughing when Mack kicked his legs in the air. I did not have any great feeling of horror and opposition, such as a city child might have had; I was too used to seeing the death of animals as a necessity by which we lived. Yet I felt a little ashamed, and there was a new wariness, a sense of holding-off, in my attitude to my father and his work.

It was a fine day, and we were going around the yard picking up tree branches that had been torn off in winter storms. This was something we had been told to do, and also we wanted to use them to make a teepee. We heard Flora whinny, and then my father's voice and Henry's shouting, and we ran down to the barnyard to see what was going on.

45   The stable door was open. Henry had just brought Flora out, and she had broken away from him. She was running free in the barnyard, from one end to the other. We climbed up on the fence. It was exciting to see her running, whinnying, going up on her hind legs, prancing and threatening like a horse in a Western movie, an unbroken ranch horse, though she was just an old driver, an old sorrel mare. My father and Henry ran after her and tried to grab the dangling halter. They tried to work her into a corner, and they had almost succeeded when she made a run between them, wild-eyed, and disappeared around the corner of the barn. We heard the rails clatter down as she got over the fence, and Henry yelled, "She's into the field now!"

That meant she was in the long L-shaped field that ran up by the house. If she got around the center, heading towards the lane, the gate was open; the truck had been driven into the field this morning. My father shouted to me, because I was on the other side of the fence, nearest the lane, "Go shut the gate!"

I could run very fast. I ran across the garden, past the tree where our swing was hung, and jumped across a ditch into the lane. There was the open gate. She had not got out, I could not see her up on the road; she must have run to the other end of the field. The gate was heavy. I lifted it out of the gravel and carried it across the roadway. I had it half-way across when she came in sight, galloping straight towards me. There was just time to get the chain on. Laird came scrambling through the ditch to help me.

Instead of shutting the gate, I opened it as wide as I could. I did not make any decision to do this, it was just what I did. Flora never slowed down; she galloped straight past me, and Laird jumped up and down, yelling, "Shut it, shut it!" even after it was too late. My father and Henry appeared in the field a moment too late to see what I had done. They only saw Flora heading for the township road. They would think I had not got there in time.

They did not waste any time asking about it. They went back to the barn and got the gun and the knives they used, and put these in the truck;

then they turned the truck around and came bouncing up the field toward us. Laird called to them, "Let me go too, let me go too!" and Henry stopped the truck and they took him in. I shut the gate after they were all gone.

50   I supposed Laird would tell. I wondered what would happen to me. I had never disobeyed my father before, and I could not understand why I had done it. Flora would not really get away. They would catch up with her in the truck. Or if they did not catch her this morning somebody would see her and telephone us this afternoon or tomorrow. There was no wild country here for her to run to, only farms. What was more, my father had paid for her, we needed the meat to feed the foxes, we needed the foxes to make our living. All I had done was make more work for my father who worked hard enough already. And when my father found out about it he was not going to trust me any more; he would know that I was not entirely on his side. I was on Flora's side, and that made me no use to anybody, not even to her. Just the same, I did not regret it; when she came running at me and I held the gate open, that was the only thing I could do.

I went back to the house, and my mother said, "What's all the commotion?" I told her that Flora had kicked down the fence and got away. "Your poor father," she said, "now he'll have to go chasing over the countryside. Well, there isn't any use planning dinner before one." She put up the ironing board. I wanted to tell her, but thought better of it and went upstairs and sat on my bed.

Lately I had been trying to make my part of the room fancy, spreading the bed with old lace curtains, and fixing myself a dressing-table with some leftovers of cretonne for a skirt. I planned to put up some kind of barricade between my bed and Laird's, to keep my section separate from his. In the sunlight, the lace curtains were just dusty rags. We did not sing at night any more. One night when I was singing Laird said, "You sound silly," and I went right on but the next night I did not start. There was not so much need to anyway, we were no longer afraid. We knew it was just old furniture over there, old jumble and confusion. We did not keep to the rules. I still stayed awake after Laird was asleep and told myself stories, but even in these stories something different was happening, mysterious alterations took place. A story might start off in the old way, with a spectacular danger, a fire or wild animals, and for a while I might rescue people; then things would change around, and instead, somebody would be rescuing me. It might be a boy from our class at school, or even Mr. Campbell, our teacher, who tickled girls under the arms. And at this point the story concerned itself at great length with what I looked like—how long my hair was, and what kind of dress I had on; by the time I had these details worked out the real excitement of the story was lost.

It was later than one o'clock when the truck came back. The tarpaulin was over the back, which meant there was meat in it. My mother had to heat dinner up all over again. Henry and my father had changed from their bloody overalls into ordinary working overalls in the barn, and they washed their arms and necks and faces at the sink, and splashed water on their hair and combed it. Laird lifted his arm to show off a streak of blood. "We shot old Flora," he said, "and cut her up in fifty pieces."

"Well, I don't want to hear about it," my mother said. "And don't come to my table like that."

55   My family made him go and wash the blood off.

We sat down and my father said grace and Henry pasted his chewing-gum on the end of his fork, the way he always did; when he took it off he would have us admire the pattern. We began to pass the bowls of steaming, overcooked vegetables. Laird looked across the table at me and said proudly, distinctly, "Anyway it was her fault Flora got away."

"What?" my father said.

"She could of shut the gate and she didn't. She just open' it up and Flora run out."

"Is that right?" my father said.

60   Everybody at the table was looking at me. I nodded, swallowing food with great difficulty. To my shame, tears flooded my eyes.

My father made a curt sound of disgust. "What did you do that for?"

I did not answer. I put down my fork and waited to be sent from the table, still not looking up.

But this did not happen. For some time nobody said anything, then Laird said matter-of-factly, "She's crying."

"Never mind," my father said. He spoke with resignation, even good humour, the words which absolved and dismissed me for good. "She's only a girl," he said.

65   I didn't protest that, even in my heart. Maybe it was true.

EDGAR ALLAN POE

(1809–1849)

The Tell-Tale Heart

(1850)

True!—nervous—very, very dreadfully nervous I had been and am; but why *will* you say that I am mad? The disease had sharpened my senses—not destroyed—not dulled them. Above all was the sense of hearing acute. I heard all things in the heaven and in the earth. I heard many things in hell. How, then, am I mad? Hearken! and observe how healthily—how calmly I can tell you the whole story.

It is impossible to say how first the idea entered my brain; but once conceived, it haunted me day and night. Object there was none. Passion there was none. I loved the old man. He had never wronged me. He had never given me insult. For his gold I had no desire. I think it was his eye! yes, it was this! One of his eyes resembled that of a vulture—a pale blue eye, with a film over it. Whenever it fell upon me, my blood ran cold; and so by degrees—very gradually—I made up my mind to take the life of the old man, and thus rid myself of the eye for ever.

Now this is the point. You fancy me mad. Madmen know nothing. But you should have seen *me*. You should have seen how wisely I proceeded— with what caution—with what foresight—with what dissimulation I went to work! I was never kinder to the old man than during the whole week before I killed him. And every night, about midnight, I turned the latch of his door and opened it—oh, so gently! And then, when I had made an opening sufficient for my head, I put in a dark lantern, all closed, closed, so that no light shone out, and then I thrust in my head. Oh, you would have laughed to see how cunningly I thrust it in! I moved it slowly—very, very slowly, so that I might not disturb the old man's sleep. It took me an hour to place my whole head within the opening so far that I could see him as he lay upon his bed. Ha!—would a madman have been so wise as this? And then, when my head was well in the room, I undid the lantern cautiously—oh, so cautiously—cautiously (for the hinges creaked)—I undid it just so much that a single thin ray fell upon the vulture eye. And this I did for seven long nights—every night just at midnight—but I found the eye always closed; and so it was impossible to do the work; for it was not the old man who vexed me, but his Evil Eye. And every morning, when the day broke, I went boldly into the chamber, and spoke courageously to him, calling him by name in a hearty tone, and inquiring how he had passed the night. So you see he would have been a very profound old man, indeed, to suspect that every night, just at twelve, I looked in upon him while he slept.

Upon the eighth night I was more than usually cautious in opening the door. A watch's minute hand moves more quickly than did mine. Never before that night had I *felt* the extent of my own powers—of my sagacity. I could scarcely contain my feelings of triumph. To think that there I was, opening the door, little by little, and he not even to dream of my secret deeds or thoughts. I fairly chuckled at the idea; and perhaps he heard me; for he moved on the bed suddenly, as if startled. Now you may think that I drew back—but no. His room was as black as pitch with the thick darkness (for the shutters were close fastened, through fear of robbers), and so I knew that he could not see the opening of the door, and I kept pushing it on steadily, steadily.

5   I had my head in, and was about to open the lantern, when my thumb slipped upon the tin fastening, and the old man sprang up in the bed, crying out—"Who's there?"

I kept quite still and said nothing. For a whole hour I did not move a muscle, and in the meantime I did not hear him lie down. He was still sitting up in the bed listening;—just as I have done, night after night, hearkening to the death watches[1] in the wall.

---

[1] Beetles that infest timbers. Their clicking sound was thought to be an omen of death.

Presently I heard a slight groan, and I knew it was the groan of mortal terror. It was not a groan of pain or of grief—oh, no!—it was the low stifled sound that arises from the bottom of the soul when overcharged with awe. I knew the sound well. Many a night, just at midnight, when all the world slept, it has welled up from my own bosom, deepening, with its dreadful echo, the terrors that distracted me. I say I knew it well. I knew what the old man felt, and pitied him, although I chuckled at heart. I knew that he had been lying awake ever since the first slight noise, when he had turned in the bed. His fears had been ever since growing upon him. He had been trying to fancy them causeless, but could not. He had been saying to himself—"It is nothing but the wind in the chimney—it is only a mouse crossing the floor," or "it is merely a cricket which has made a single chirp." Yes, he had been trying to comfort himself with these suppositions; but he had found all in vain. *All in vain;* because Death, in approaching him, had stalked with his black shadow before him, and enveloped the victim. And it was the mournful influence of the unperceived shadow that caused him to feel—although he neither saw nor heard—to *feel* the presence of my head within the room.

When I had waited a long time, very patiently, without hearing him lie down, I resolved to open a little—a very, very little crevice in the lantern. So I opened it—you cannot imagine how stealthily, stealthily— until, at length, a single dim ray, like the thread of the spider, shot from out the crevice and full upon the vulture eye.

It was open—wide, wide open—and I grew furious as I gazed upon it. I saw it with perfect distinctness—all a dull blue, with a hideous veil over it that chilled the very marrow in my bones; but I could see nothing else of the old man's face or person: for I had directed the ray as if by instinct, precisely upon the damned spot.

10   And now have I not told you that what you mistake for madness is but over-acuteness of the senses?—now, I say, there came to my ears a low, dull, quick sound, such as a watch makes when enveloped in cotton. I knew *that* sound well too. It was the beating of the old man's heart. It increased my fury, as the beating of a drum stimulates the soldier into courage.

But even yet I refrained and kept still. I scarcely breathed. I held the lantern motionless. I tried how steadily I could maintain the ray upon the eye. Meantime the hellish tattoo of the heart increased. It grew quicker and quicker, and louder and louder every instant. The old man's terror *must* have been extreme! It grew louder, I say, louder every moment!—do you mark me well? I have told you that I am nervous: so I am. And now at the dead hour of the night, amid the dreadful silence of that old house, so strange a noise as this excited me to uncontrollable terror. Yet, for some minutes longer I refrained and stood still. But the beating grew louder, louder! I thought the heart must burst. And now a new anxiety seized me—the sound would be heard by a neighbor! The old man's hour had come! With a loud yell, I threw open the lantern and leaped into the room.

He shrieked once—once only. In an instant I dragged him to the floor, and pulled the heavy bed over him. I then smiled gaily, to find the deed so far done. But, for many minutes, the heart beat on with a muffled sound. This, however, did not vex me; it would not be heard through the wall. At length it ceased. The old man was dead. I removed the bed and examined the corpse. Yes, he was stone, stone dead. I placed my hand upon the heart and held it there many minutes. There was no pulsation. He was stone dead. His eye would trouble me no more.

If still you think me mad, you will think so no longer when I describe the wise precautions I took for the concealment of the body. The night waned, and I worked hastily, but in silence. First of all I dismembered the corpse. I cut off the head and the arms and the legs.

I then took up three planks from the flooring of the chamber, and deposited all between the scantlings. I then replaced the boards so cleverly, so cunningly, that no human eye—not even *his*—could have detected anything wrong. There was nothing to wash out—no stain of any kind—no blood-spot whatever. I had been too wary for that. A tub had caught all— ha! ha!

When I had made an end of these labors, it was four o'clock—still dark as midnight. As the bell sounded the hour, there came a knocking at the street door. I went down to open it with a light heart,—for what had I *now* to fear? There entered three men, who introduced themselves, with perfect suavity, as officers of the police. A shriek had been heard by a neighbor during the night; suspicion of foul play had been aroused; information had been lodged at the police office, and they (the officers) had been deputed to search the premises.

15 I smiled,—for *what* had I to fear? I bade the gentlemen welcome. The shriek, I said, was my own in a dream. The old man, I mentioned, was absent in the country. I took my visitors all over the house. I bade them search—search *well*. I led them, at length, to *his* chamber. I showed them his treasures, secure, undisturbed. In the enthusiasm of my confidence, I brought chairs into the room, and desired them *here* to rest from their fatigues, while I myself, in the wild audacity of my perfect triumph, placed my own seat upon the very spot beneath which reposed the corpse of the victim.

The officers were satisfied. My *manner* had convinced them. I was singularly at ease. They sat, and while I answered cheerily, they chatted familiar things. But, ere long, I felt myself getting pale and wished them gone. My head ached, and I fancied a ringing in my ears: but still they sat and still chatted. The ringing became more distinct:—it continued and became more distinct: I talked more freely to get rid of the feeling: but it continued and gained definitiveness—until, at length, I found that the noise was *not* within my ears.

No doubt I now grew *very* pale:—but I talked more fluently, and with a heightened voice. Yet the sound increased—and what could I do? It was *a low, dull, quick sound—much such a sound as a watch makes when enveloped in cotton.* I gasped for breath—and yet the officers heard it not. I talked more quickly—more vehemently; but the noise steadily increased. I arose and argued about trifles, in a high key and with violent gesticulations, but the noise steadily increased. Why *would* they not be gone? I paced the floor to and fro with heavy strides, as if excited to fury by the observation of the men—but the noise steadily increased. On God! what *could* I do? I foamed—I raved—I swore! I swung the chair upon which I had been sitting, and grated it upon the boards, but the noise arose over all and continually increased. It grew louder—louder—*louder!* And still the men chatted pleasantly, and smiled. Was it possible they heard not? Almighty God!—no, no! They heard!—they suspected!—they *knew!*—they were making a mockery of my horror!—this I thought, and this I think. But any thing was better than this agony! Any thing was more tolerable than this derision! I could bear those hypocritical smiles no longer! I felt that I must scream or die!—and now—again!—hark! louder! louder! louder! *louder!*—

"Villains!" I shrieked, "dissemble no more! I admit the deed!—tear up the planks!—here, here!—it is the beating of his hideous heart!"

KATHERINE ANNE PORTER

(1890–1980)

The Jilting of Granny Weatherall

(1930)

She flicked her wrist neatly out of Doctor Harry's pudgy careful fingers and pulled the sheet up to her chin. The brat ought to be in knee breeches. Doctoring around the country with spectacles on his nose! "Get along now, take your schoolbooks and go. There's nothing wrong with me."

Doctor Harry spread a warm paw like a cushion on her forehead where the forked green vein danced and made her eyelids twitch. "Now, now, be a good girl, and we'll have you up in no time."

"That's no way to speak to a woman nearly eighty years old just because she's down. I'd have you respect your elders, young man."

"Well, Missy, excuse me." Doctor Harry patted her cheek. "But I've got to warn you, haven't I? You're a marvel, but you must be careful or you're going to be good and sorry."

5   "Don't tell me what I'm going to be. I'm on my feet now, morally speaking. It's Cornelia. I had to go to bed to get rid of her."

Her bones felt loose, and floated around in her skin, and Doctor Harry floated like a balloon around the foot of the bed. He floated and pulled down his waistcoat and swung his glasses on a cord. "Well, stay where you are, it certainly can't hurt you."

"Get along and doctor your sick," said Granny Weatherall. "Leave a well woman alone. I'll call for you when I want you. . . . Where were you forty years ago when I pulled through milk-leg and double pneumonia? You weren't even born. Don't let Cornelia lead you on," she shouted, because Doctor Harry appeared to float up to the ceiling and out. "I pay my own bills, and I don't throw my money away on nonsense!"

She meant to wave good-by, but it was too much trouble. Her eyes closed of themselves, it was like a dark curtain drawn around the bed. The pillow rose and floated under her, pleasant as a hammock in a light wind. She listened to the leaves rustling outside the window. No, somebody was swishing newspapers: no, Cornelia and Doctor Harry were whispering together. She leaped broad awake, thinking they whispered in her ear.

"She was never like this, *never* like this!" "Well, what can we expect?" "Yes, eighty years old. . . ."

10 Well, and what if she was? She still had ears. It was like Cornelia to whisper around doors. She always kept things secret in such a public way. She was always being tactful and kind. Cornelia was dutiful; that was the trouble with her. Dutiful and good: "So good and dutiful," said Granny, "that I'd like to spank her." She saw herself spanking Cornelia and making a fine job of it.

"What'd you say, Mother?"

Granny felt her face tying up in hard knots.

"Can't a body think, I'd like to know?"

"I thought you might want something."

15 "I do. I want a lot of things. First off, go away and don't whisper."

She lay and drowsed, hoping in her sleep that the children would keep out and let her rest a minute. It had been a long day. Not that she was tired. It was always pleasant to snatch a minute now and then. There was always so much to be done, let me see: tomorrow.

Tomorrow was far away and there was nothing to trouble about. Things were finished somehow when the time came; thank God there was always a little margin over for peace: then a person could spread out the plan of life and tuck in the edges orderly. It was good to have everything clean and folded away, with the hair brushes and tonic bottles sitting straight on the white embroidered linen: the day started without fuss and the pantry shelves laid out with rows of jelly glasses and brown jugs and white stone-china jars with blue whirligigs and words painted on them: coffee, tea, sugar, ginger, cinnamon, allspice: and the bronze clock with the lion on top nicely dusted off. The dust that lion could collect in twenty-four hours! The box in the attic with all those letters tied up, well, she'd have to go through that tomorrow. All those letters—George's letters and John's letters and her letters to them both—lying around for the children to find afterwards made her uneasy. Yes, that would be tomorrow's business. No use to let them know how silly she had been once.

While she was rummaging around she found death in her mind and it felt clammy and unfamiliar. She had spent so much time preparing for death there was no need for bringing it up again. Let it take care of itself now. When she was sixty she had felt very old, finished, and went around making farewell trips to see her children and grandchildren, with a secret in her mind: This is the very last of your mother, children! Then she made her will and came down with a long fever. That was all just a notion like a lot of other things, but it was lucky too, for she had once and for all got over the idea of dying for a long time. Now she couldn't be worried. She hoped she had better sense now. Her father had lived to be one hundred and two years old and had drunk a noggin of strong hot toddy on his last birthday. He told the reporters it was his daily habit, and he owed his long life to that. He had made quite a scandal and was very pleased about it. She believed she'd just plague Cornelia a little.

"Cornelia! Cornelia!" No footsteps, but a sudden hand on her cheek. "Bless you, where have you been?"

20   "Here, Mother."

"Well, Cornelia, I want a noggin of hot toddy."

"Are you cold, darling?"

"I'm chilly, Cornelia. Lying in bed stops the circulation. I must have told you that a thousand times."

Well, she could just hear Cornelia telling her husband that Mother was getting a little childish and they'd have to humor her. The thing that most annoyed her was that Cornelia thought she was deaf, dumb, and blind. Little hasty glances and tiny gestures tossed around her and over her head saying, "Don't cross her, let her have her way, she's eighty years old," and she sitting there as if she lived in a thin glass cage. Sometimes Granny almost made up her mind to pack up and move back to her own house where nobody could remind her every minute that she was old. Wait, wait, Cornelia, till your own children whisper behind your back!

25   In her day she had kept a better house and had got more work done. She wasn't too old yet for Lydia to be driving eighty miles for advice when one of the children jumped the track, and Jimmy still dropped in and talked things over: "Now, Mammy, you've a good business head, I want to know what you think of this? . . ." Old. Cornelia couldn't change the furniture around without asking. Little things, little things! They had been so sweet when they were little. Granny wished the old days were back again with the children young and everything to be done over. It had been a hard pull, but not too much for her. When she thought of all the food she had cooked, and all the clothes she had cut and sewed, and all the gardens she had made—well, the children showed it. There they were, made out of her, and they couldn't get away from that. Sometimes she wanted to see John again and point to them and say, Well, I didn't do so badly, did I? But that would have to wait. That was for tomorrow. She used to think of him as a man, but now all the children were older than their father, and he would be a child beside her if she saw him now. It seemed strange and there was something wrong in the idea. Why, he couldn't possibly recognize her. She had fenced in a hundred acres once, digging the post holes herself and clamping the wires with just a negro boy to help. That changed a woman. John would be looking for a young woman with the peaked Spanish comb in her hair and the painted fan. Digging post holes

changed a woman. Riding country roads in the winter when women had their babies was another thing: sitting up nights with sick horses and sick negroes and sick children and hardly ever losing one. John, I hardly ever lost one of them! John would see that in a minute, that would be something he could understand, she wouldn't have to explain anything!

It made her feel like rolling up her sleeves and putting the whole place to rights again. No matter if Cornelia was determined to be everywhere at once, there were a great many things left undone on this place. She would start tomorrow and do them. It was good to be strong enough for everything, even if all you made melted and changed and slipped under your hands, so that by the time you finished you almost forgot what you were working for. What was it I set out to do? she asked herself intently, but she could not remember. A fog rose over the valley, she saw it marching across the creek swallowing the trees and moving up the hill like an army of ghosts. Soon it would be at the near edge of the orchard, and then it was time to go in and light the lamps. Come in, children, don't stay out in the night air.

Lighting the lamps had been beautiful. The children huddled up to her and breathed like little calves waiting at the bars in the twilight. Their eyes followed the match and watched the flame rise and settle in a blue curve, then they moved away from her. The lamp was lit, they didn't have to be scared and hang on to mother any more. Never, never, never more. God, for all my life I thank Thee. Without Thee, my God, I could never have done it. Hail, Mary, full of grace.

I want you to pick all the fruit this year and see that nothing is wasted. There's always someone who can use it. Don't let good things rot for want of using. You waste life when you waste good food. Don't let things get lost. It's bitter to lose things. Now, don't let me get to thinking, not when I am tired and taking a little nap before supper. . . .

The pillow rose about her shoulders and pressed against her heart and the memory was being squeezed out of it: oh, push down the pillow, somebody: it would smother her if she tried to hold it. Such a fresh breeze blowing and such a green day with no threats in it. But he had not come, just the same. What does a woman do when she has put on the white veil and set out the white cake for a man and he doesn't come? She tried to remember. No, I swear he never harmed me but in that. He never harmed me but in that . . . and what if he did? There was the day, the day, but a whirl of dark smoke rose and covered it, crept up and over into the bright field where everything was planted so carefully in orderly rows. That was hell, she knew hell when she saw it. For sixty years she had prayed against remembering him and against losing her soul in the deep pit of hell, and now the two things were mingled in one and the thought of him was a smoky cloud from hell that moved and crept in her head when she had just got rid of Doctor Harry and was trying to rest a minute. Wounded vanity, Ellen, said a sharp voice in the top of her mind. Don't let your wounded vanity get the upper hand of you. Plenty of girls get jilted. You were jilted, weren't you? Then stand up to it. Her eyelids wavered and let in streamers of blue-gray light like tissue paper over her eyes. She must get up and pull the shades down or she'd never sleep. She was in bed again and the shades were not down. How could that happen? Better turn over, hide from the light, sleeping in the light gave you nightmares. "Mother, how do you feel now?" and a stinging wetness on her forehead. But I don't like having my face washed in cold water!

30 Hapsy? George? Lydia? Jimmy? No, Cornelia, and her features were swollen and full of little puddles. "They're coming, darling, they'll all be here soon." Go wash your face, child, you look funny.

Instead of obeying, Cornelia knelt down and put her head on the pillow. She seemed to be talking but there was no sound. "Well, are you tongue-tied? Whose birthday is it? Are you going to give a party?"

Cornelia's mouth moved urgently in strange shapes. "Don't do that, you bother me, daughter."

"O, no, Mother. Oh, no. . . ."

Nonsense. It was strange about children. They disputed your every word. "No what, Cornelia?"

35 "Here's Doctor Harry."

"I won't see that boy again. He just left five minutes ago."

"That was this morning, Mother. It's night now. Here's the nurse."

"This is Doctor Harry, Mrs. Weatherall. I never saw you look so young and happy!"

"Ah, I'll never be young again—but I'd be happy if they'd let me lie in peace and get rested."

40 She thought she spoke up loudly, but no one answered. A warm weight on her forehead, a warm bracelet on her wrist, and a breeze went on whispering, trying to tell her something. A shuffle of leaves in the everlasting hand of God. He blew on them and they danced and rattled. "Mother, don't mind, we're going to give you a little hypodermic." "Look here, daughter, how do ants get in this bed? I saw sugar ants yesterday." Did you send for Hapsy too?

It was Hapsy she really wanted. She had to go a long way back through a great many rooms to find Hapsy standing with a baby on her arm. She seemed to herself to be Hapsy also, and the baby on Hapsy's arm was Hapsy and himself and herself, all at once, and there was no surprise in the meeting. Then Hapsy melted from within and turned flimsy as gray gauze and the baby was a gauzy shadow, and Hapsy came up close and said, "I thought you'd never come," and looked at her very searchingly and said, "You haven't changed a bit!" They leaned forward to kiss, when Cornelia began whispering from a long way off, "Oh, is there anything you want to tell me? Is there anything I can do for you?"

Yes, she had changed her mind after sixty years and she would like to see George. I want you to find George. Find him and be sure to tell him I forgot him. I want him to know I had my husband just the same and my children and my house like any other woman. A good house too and a good husband that I loved and fine children out of him. Better than I hoped for even. Tell him I was given back everything he took away and more. Oh, no, oh, God, no, there was something else besides the house and the man and the children. Oh, surely they were not all? What was it? Something not given back. . . . Her breath crowded down under her ribs and grew into a monstrous frightening shape with cutting edges; it bored up into her head, and the agony was unbelievable: Yes, John, get the Doctor now, no more talk, my time has come.

When this one was born it should be the last. The last. It should have been born first, for it was the one she had truly wanted. Everything came in good time. Nothing left out, left over. She was strong, in three days she would be as well as ever. Better. A woman needed milk in her to have her full health.

"Mother, do you hear me?"

45   "I've been telling you—"

"Mother, Father Connolly's here."

"I went to Holy Communion last week. Tell him I'm not so sinful as all that."

"Father just wants to speak to you."

He could speak as much as he pleased. It was like him to drop in and inquire about her soul as if it were a teething baby, and then stay on for a cup of tea and a round of cards and gossip. He always had a funny story of some sort, usually about an Irishman who made his little mistakes and confessed them, and the point lay in some absurd thing he would blurt out in the confessional showing his struggles between native piety and original sin. Granny felt easy about her soul. Cornelia, where are your manners? Give Father Connolly a chair. She had her secret comfortable understanding with a few favorite saints who cleared a straight road to God for her. All as surely signed and sealed as the papers for the new Forty Acres. Forever . . . heirs and assigns forever. Since the day the wedding cake was not cut, but thrown out and wasted. The whole bottom dropped out of the world, and there she was blind and sweating with nothing under her feet and the walls falling away. His hand had caught her under the breast, she had not fallen, there was the freshly polished floor with the green rug on it, just as before. He had cursed like a sailor's parrot and said, "I'll kill him for you." Don't lay a hand on him, for my sake leave something to God. "Now, Ellen, you must believe what I tell you. . . ."

50   So there was nothing, nothing to worry about any more, except sometimes in the night one of the children screamed in a nightmare, and they both hustled out shaking and hunting for the matches and calling, "There, wait a minute, here we are!" John, get the doctor now, Hapsy's time has come. But there was Hapsy standing by the bed in a white cap. "Cornelia, tell Hapsy to take off her cap. I can't see her plain."

Her eyes opened very wide and the room stood out like a picture she had seen somewhere. Dark colors with the shadows rising towards the ceiling in long angles. The tall black dresser gleamed with nothing on it but

John's picture, enlarged from a little one, with John's eyes very black when they should have been blue. You never saw him, so how do you know how he looked? But the man insisted the copy was perfect, it was very rich and handsome. For a picture, yes, but it's not my husband. The table by the bed had a linen cover and a candle and a crucifix. The light was blue from Cornelia's silk lampshades. No sort of light at all, just frippery. You had to live forty years with kerosene lamps to appreciate honest electricity. She felt very strong and she saw Doctor Harry with a rosy nimbus around him.

"You look like a saint, Doctor Harry, and I vow that's as near as you'll ever come to it."

"She's saying something."

"I heard you, Cornelia. What's all this carrying-on?"

55   "Father Connolly's saying—"

Cornelia's voice staggered and bumped like a cart in a bad road. It rounded corners and turned back again and arrived nowhere. Granny stepped up in the cart very lightly and reached for the reins, but a man sat beside her and she knew him by his hands, driving the cart. She did not look in his face, for she knew without seeing, but looked instead down the road where the trees leaned over and bowed to each other and a thousand birds were singing a Mass. She felt like singing too, but she put her hand in the bosom of her dress and pulled out a rosary, and Father Connolly murmured Latin in a very solemn voice and tickled her feet. My God, will you stop that nonsense? I'm a married woman. What if he did run away and leave me to face the priest by myself? I found another a whole world better. I wouldn't have exchanged my husband for anybody except St. Michael himself, and you may tell him that for me with a thank you in the bargain.

Light flashed on her closed eyelids, and a deep roaring shook her. Cornelia, is that lightning? I hear thunder. There's going to be a storm. Close all the windows. Call the children in. . . . "Mother, here we are, all of us." "Is that you, Hapsy?" "Oh, no, I'm Lydia. We drove as fast as we could." Their faces drifted above her, drifted away. The rosary fell out of her hands and Lydia put it back. Jimmy tried to help, their hands fumbled together, and Granny closed two fingers around Jimmy's thumb. Beads wouldn't do, it must be something alive. She was so amazed her thoughts ran round and round. So, my dear Lord, this is my death and I wasn't even thinking about it. My children have come to see me die. But I can't, it's not time. Oh, I always hated surprises. I wanted to give Cornelia the amethyst set— Cornelia, you're to have the amethyst set, but Hapsy's to wear it when she wants, and, Doctor Harry, do shut up. Nobody sent for you. Oh, my dear Lord, do wait a minute. I meant to do something about the Forty Acres, Jimmy doesn't need it and Lydia will later on, with that worthless husband of hers. I meant to finish the altar cloth and send six bottles of wine to Sister Borgia for her dyspepsia. I want to send six bottles of wine to Sister Borgia, Father Connolly, now don't let me forget.

Cornelia's voice made short turns and tilted over and crashed. "Oh, Mother, oh, Mother, oh, Mother. . . ."

"I'm not going, Cornelia. I'm taken by surprise. I can't go."

60   You'll see Hapsy again. What about her? "I thought you'd never come." Granny made a long journey outward, looking for Hapsy. What if I don't find her? What then? Her heart sank down and down, there was no bottom to death, she couldn't come to the end of it. The blue light from Cornelia's lampshade drew into a tiny point in the center of her brain, it flickered and winked like an eye, quietly it fluttered and dwindled. Granny lay curled down within herself, amazed and watchful, staring at the point of light that was herself; her body was now only a deeper mass of shadow in an endless darkness and this darkness would curl around the light and swallow it up. God, give a sign!

For the second time there was no sign. Again no bridegroom and the priest in the house. She could not remember any other sorrow because this grief wiped them all away. Oh, no, there's nothing more cruel than this— I'll never forgive it. She stretched herself with a deep breath and blew out the light.

A M Y   T A N

(1952–   )

Two Kinds

(1989)

My mother believed you could be anything you wanted to be in America. You could open a restaurant. You could work for the government and get good retirement. You could buy a house with almost no money down. You could become rich. You could become instantly famous.

"Of course you can be prodigy, too," my mother told me when I was nine. "You can be best anything. What does Auntie Lindo know? Her daughter, she is only best tricky."

America was where all my mother's hopes lay. She had come here in 1949 after losing everything in China: her mother and father, her family home, her first husband, and two daughters, twin baby girls. But she never looked back with regret. There were so many ways for things to get better.

We didn't immediately pick the right kind of prodigy. At first my mother thought I could be a Chinese Shirley Temple. We'd watch Shirley's old movies on TV as though they were training films. My mother would poke my arm and say, *"Ni kan"*—You watch. And I would see Shirley tapping her feet, or singing a sailor song, or pursing her lips into a very round O while saying, "Oh my goodness."

5　　　"*Ni kan,*" said my mother as Shirley's eyes flooded with tears. "You already know how. Don't need talent for crying!"

Soon after my mother got this idea about Shirley Temple, she took me to a beauty training school in the Mission district and put me in the hands of a student who could barely hold the scissors without shaking. Instead of getting big fat curls, I emerged with an uneven mass of crinkly black fuzz. My mother dragged me off to the bathroom and tried to wet down my hair.

"You look like Negro Chinese," she lamented, as if I had done this on purpose.

The instructor of the beauty training school had to lop off these soggy clumps to make my hair even again. "Peter Pan is very popular these days," the instructor assured my mother. I now had hair the length of a boy's, with straight-across bangs that hung at a slant two inches above my eyebrows. I liked the haircut and it made me actually look forward to my future fame.

In fact, in the beginning, I was just as excited as my mother, maybe even more so. I pictured this prodigy part of me as many different images, trying each one on for size. I was a dainty ballerina girl standing by the curtains, waiting to hear the right music that would send me floating on my tiptoes. I was like the Christ child lifted out of the straw manger, crying with holy indignity. I was Cinderella stepping from her pumpkin carriage with sparkly cartoon music filling the air.

10　　　In all of my imaginings, I was filled with a sense that I would soon become *perfect.* My mother and father would adore me. I would be beyond reproach. I would never feel the need to sulk for anything.

But sometimes the prodigy in me became impatient. "If you don't hurry up and get me out of here, I'm disappearing for good," it warned. "And then you'll always be nothing."

Every night after dinner, my mother and I would sit at the Formica kitchen table. She would present new tests, taking her examples from stories of amazing children she had read in *Ripley's Believe It or Not,* or *Good Housekeeping, Reader's Digest,* and a dozen other magazines she kept in a pile in our bathroom. My mother got these magazines from people whose houses she cleaned. And since she cleaned many houses each week, we had a great assortment. She would look through them all, searching for stories about remarkable children.

The first night she brought out a story about a three-year-old boy who knew the capitals of all the states and even most of the European countries. A teacher was quoted as saying the little boy could also pronounce the names of the foreign cities correctly.

"What's the capital of Finland?" my mother asked me, looking at the magazine story.

15　　　All I knew was the capital of California, because Sacramento was the name of the street we lived on in Chinatown. "Nairobi!" I guessed, saying the most foreign word I could think of. She checked to see if that was possibly one way to pronounce "Helsinki" before showing me the answer.

The tests got harder—multiplying numbers in my head, finding the queen of hearts in a deck of cards, trying to stand on my head without using my hands, predicting the daily temperatures in Los Angeles, New York, and London.

One night I had to look at a page from the Bible for three minutes and then report everything I could remember. "Now Jehoshaphat had riches and honor in abundance and . . . that's all I remember, Ma," I said.

And after seeing my mother's disappointed face once again, something inside of me began to die. I hated the tests, the raised hopes and failed expectations. Before going to bed that night, I looked in the mirror above the bathroom sink and when I saw only my face staring back—and that it would always be this ordinary face—I began to cry. Such a sad, ugly girl! I made high-pitched noises like a crazed animal, trying to scratch out the face in the mirror.

And then I saw what seemed to be the prodigy side of me—because I had never seen that face before. I looked at my reflection, blinking so I could see more clearly. The girl staring back at me was angry, powerful. This girl and I were the same. I had new thoughts, willful thoughts, or rather thoughts filled with lots of won'ts. I won't let her change me, I promised myself. I won't be what I'm not.

20   So now on nights when my mother presented her tests, I performed listlessly, my head propped on one arm. I pretended to be bored. And I was. I got so bored I started counting the bellows of the foghorns out on the bay while my mother drilled me in other areas. The sound was comforting and reminded me of the cow jumping over the moon. And the next day, I played a game with myself, seeing if my mother would give up on me before eight bellows. After a while I usually counted only one, maybe two bellows at most. At last she was beginning to give up hope.

Two or three months had gone by without any mention of my being a prodigy again. And then one day my mother was watching *The Ed Sullivan Show* on TV. The TV was old and the sound kept shorting out. Every time my mother got halfway up from the sofa to adjust the set, the sound would go back on and Ed would be talking. As soon as she sat down, Ed would go silent again. She got up, the TV broke into loud piano music. She sat down. Silence. Up and down, back and forth, quiet and loud. It was like a stiff embraceless dance between her and the TV set. Finally she stood by the set with her hand on the sound dial.

She seemed entranced by the music, a little frenzied piano piece with this mesmerizing quality, sort of quick passages and then teasing lilting ones before it returned to the quick playful parts.

"*Ni kan,*" my mother said, calling me over with hurried hand gestures, "Look here."

I could see why my mother was fascinated by the music. It was being pounded out by a little Chinese girl, about nine years old, with a Peter Pan haircut. The girl had the sauciness of a Shirley Temple. She was proudly modest like a proper Chinese child. And she also did this fancy sweep of a curtsy, so that the fluffy skirt of her white dress cascaded slowly to the floor like the petals of a large carnation.

25   In spite of these warning signs, I wasn't worried. Our family had no piano and we couldn't afford to buy one, let alone reams of sheet music and piano lessons. So I could be generous in my comments when my mother bad-mouthed the little girl on TV.

"Play note right, but doesn't sound good! No singing sound," complained my mother.

"What are you picking on her for?" I said carelessly. "She's pretty good. Maybe she's not the best, but she's trying hard." I knew almost immediately I would be sorry I said that.

"Just like you," she said. "Not the best. Because you not trying." She gave a little huff as she let go of the sound dial and sat down on the sofa.

The little Chinese girl sat down also to play an encore of "Anitra's Dance" by Grieg. I remember the song, because later on I had to learn how to play it.

30   Three days after watching *The Ed Sullivan Show,* my mother told me what my schedule would be for piano lessons and piano practice. She had talked to Mr. Chong, who lived on the first floor of our apartment building. Mr. Chong was a retired piano teacher and my mother had traded house-cleaning services for weekly lessons and a piano for me to practice on every day, two hours a day, from four until six.

When my mother told me this, I felt as though I had been sent to hell. I whined and then kicked my foot a little when I couldn't stand it anymore.

"Why don't you like me the way I am? I'm *not* a genius! I can't play the piano. And even if I could, I wouldn't go on TV if you paid me a million dollars!" I cried.

My mother slapped me. "Who ask you be genius?" she shouted. "Only ask you be your best. For you sake. You think I want you be genius? Hnnh! What for! Who ask you!"

"So ungrateful," I heard her mutter in Chinese. "If she had as much talent as she has temper, she would be famous now."

35   Mr. Chong, whom I secretly nicknamed Old Chong, was very strange, always tapping his fingers to the silent music of an invisible orchestra. He looked ancient in my eyes. He had lost most of the hair on top of his head and he wore thick glasses and had eyes that always looked tired and sleepy. But he must have been younger than I thought, since he lived with his mother and was not yet married.

I met Old Lady Chong once and that was enough. She had this peculiar smell like a baby that had done something in its pants. And her fingers felt like a dead person's, like an old peach I once found in the back of the refrigerator; the skin just slid off the meat when I picked it up.

I soon found out why Old Chong had retired from teaching piano. He was deaf. "Like Beethoven!" he shouted to me. "We're both listening only in our head!" And he would start to conduct his frantic silent sonatas.

Our lessons went like this. He would open the book and point to different things, explaining their purpose: "Key! Treble! Bass! No sharps or flats! So this is C major! Listen now and play after me!"

And then he would play the C scale a few times, a simple chord, and then, as if inspired by an old, unreachable itch, he gradually added more notes and running trills and a pounding bass until the music was really something quite grand.

40 I would play after him, the simple scale, the simple chord, and then I just played some nonsense that sounded like a cat running up and down on top of garbage cans. Old Chong smiled and applauded and then said, "Very good! But now you must learn to keep time!"

So that's how I discovered that Old Chong's eyes were too slow to keep up with the wrong notes I was playing. He went through the motions in half-time. To help me keep rhythm, he stood behind me, pushing down on my right shoulder for every beat. He balanced pennies on top of my wrists so I would keep them still as I slowly played scales and arpeggios. He had me curve my hand around an apple and keep that shape when playing chords. He marched stiffly to show me how to make each finger dance up and down, staccato like an obedient little soldier.

He taught me all these things, and that was how I also learned I could be lazy and get away with mistakes, lots of mistakes. If I hit the wrong notes because I hadn't practiced enough, I never corrected myself. I just kept playing in rhythm. And Old Chong kept conducting his own private reverie.

So maybe I never really gave myself a fair chance. I did pick up the basics pretty quickly, and I might have become a good pianist at that young age. But I was so determined not to try, not to be anybody different that I learned to play only the most ear-splitting preludes, the most discordant hymns.

Over the next year, I practiced like this, dutifully in my own way. And then one day I heard my mother and her friend Lindo Jong both talking in a loud bragging tone of voice so others could hear. It was after church, and I was leaning against the brick wall wearing a dress with stiff white petticoats. Auntie Lindo's daughter, Waverly, who was about my age, was standing farther down the wall about five feet away. We had grown up together and shared all the closeness of two sisters squabbling over crayons and dolls. In other words, for the most part, we hated each other. I thought she was snotty. Waverly Jong had gained a certain amount of fame as "Chinatown's Littlest Chinese Chess Champion."

45 "She bring home too many trophy," lamented Auntie Lindo that Sunday. "All day she play chess. All day I have no time do nothing but dust off

her winnings." She threw a scolding look at Waverly, who pretended not to see her.

"You lucky you don't have this problem," said Auntie Lindo with a sigh to my mother.

And my mother squared her shoulders and bragged: "Our problem worser than yours. If we ask Jing-mei wash dish, she hear nothing but music. It's like you can't stop this natural talent."

And right then, I was determined to put a stop to her foolish pride.

A few weeks later, Old Chong and my mother conspired to have me play in a talent show which would be held in the church hall. By then, my parents had saved up enough to buy me a secondhand piano, a black Wurlitzer spinet with a scarred bench. It was the showpiece of our living room.

50   For the talent show, I was to play a piece called "Pleading Child" from Schumann's *Scenes from Childhood*. It was a simple, moody piece that sounded more difficult than it was. I was supposed to memorize the whole thing, playing the repeat parts twice to make the piece sound longer. But I dawdled over it, playing a few bars and then cheating, looking up to see what notes followed. I never really listened to what I was playing. I daydreamed about being somewhere else, about being someone else.

The part I liked to practice best was the fancy curtsy: right foot out, touch the rose on the carpet with a pointed foot, sweep to the side, left leg bends, look up and smile.

My parents invited all the couples from the Joy Luck Club[1] to witness my debut. Auntie Lindo and Uncle Tin were there. Waverly and her two older brothers had also come. The first two rows were filled with children both younger and older than I was. The little ones got to go first. They recited simple nursery rhymes, squawked out tunes on miniature violins, twirled Hula Hoops, pranced in pink ballet tutus, and when they bowed or curtsied, the audience would sigh in unison, "Awww," and then clap enthusiastically.

When my turn came, I was very confident. I remember my childish excitement. It was as if I knew, without a doubt, that the prodigy side of me really did exist. I had no fear whatsoever, no nervousness. I remember thinking to myself, This is it! This is it! I looked out over the audience, at my mother's blank face, my father's yawn, Auntie Lindo's stiff-lipped smile, Waverly's sulky expression. I had on a white dress layered with sheets of lace, and a pink bow in my Peter Pan haircut. As I sat down I envisioned people jumping to their feet and Ed Sullivan rushing up to introduce me to everyone on TV.

And I started to play. It was so beautiful. I was so caught up in how lovely I looked that at first I didn't worry how I would sound. So it was a surprise to me when I hit the first wrong note and I realized something

---

[1] A name denoting the mother's circle of friends, all of whom were Chinese immigrants to the United States.

didn't sound quite right. And then I hit another and another followed that. A chill started at the top of my head and began to trickle down. Yet I couldn't stop playing, as though my hands were bewitched. I kept thinking my fingers would adjust themselves back, like a train switching to the right track. I played this strange jumble through two repeats, the sour notes staying with me all the way to the end.

55   When I stood up, I discovered my legs were shaking. Maybe I had just been nervous and the audience, like Old Chong, had seen me go through the right motions and had not heard anything wrong at all. I swept my right foot out; went down on my knee, looked up and smiled. The room was quiet, except for Old Chong, who was beaming and shouting, "Bravo! Bravo! Well done!" But then I saw my mother's face, her stricken face. The audience clapped weakly, and as I walked back to my chair, with my whole face quivering as I tried not to cry, I heard a little boy whisper loudly to his mother, "That was awful," and the mother whispered back, "Well, she certainly tried."

And now I realized how many people were in the audience, the whole world it seemed. I was aware of eyes burning into my back. I felt the shame of my mother and father as they sat stiffly throughout the rest of the show.

We could have escaped during intermission. Pride and some strange sense of honor must have anchored my parents to their chairs. And so we watched it all: the eighteen-year-old boy with a fake mustache who did a magic show and juggled flaming hoops while riding a unicycle. The breasted girl with white makeup who sang from *Madama Butterfly* and got honorable mention. And the eleven-year-old boy who won first prize playing a tricky violin song that sounded like a busy bee.

After the show, the Hsus, the Jongs, and the St. Clairs from the Joy Luck Club came up to my mother and father.

"Lots of talented kids," Auntie Lindo said vaguely, smiling broadly.

60   "That was somethin' else," said my father, and I wondered if he was referring to me in a humorous way, or whether he even remembered what I had done.

Waverly looked at me and shrugged her shoulders. "You aren't a genius like me," she said matter-of-factly. And if I hadn't felt so bad, I would have pulled her braids and punched her stomach.

But my mother's expression was what devastated me: a quiet, blank look that said she had lost everything. I felt the same way, and it seemed as if everybody were now coming up, like gawkers at the scene of an accident, to see what parts were actually missing. When we got on the bus to go home, my father was humming the busy-bee tune and my mother was silent. I kept thinking she wanted to wait until we got home before shouting at me. But when my father unlocked the door to our apartment, my mother walked in and then went to the back, into the bedroom. No accusations. No blame. And in a way, I felt disappointed. I had been waiting for her to start shouting, so I could shout back and cry and blame her for all my misery.

I assumed my talent-show fiasco meant I never had to play the piano again. But two days later, after school, my mother came out of the kitchen and saw me watching TV.

"Four clock," she reminded me as if it were any other day. I was stunned, as though she were asking me to go through the talent-show torture again. I wedged myself more tightly in front of the TV.

65   "Turn off TV," she called from the kitchen five minutes later.

I didn't budge. And then I decided. I didn't have to do what my mother said anymore. I wasn't her slave. This wasn't China. I had listened to her before and look what happened. She was the stupid one.

She came out from the kitchen and stood in the arched entryway of the living room. "Four clock," she said once again, louder.

"I'm not going to play anymore," I said nonchalantly. "Why should I? I'm not a genius."

She walked over and stood in front of the TV. I saw her chest was heaving up and down in an angry way.

70   "No!" I said, and I now felt stronger, as if my true self had finally emerged. So this was what had been inside me all along.

"No! I won't!" I screamed.

She yanked me by the arm, pulled me off the floor, snapped off the TV. She was frighteningly strong, half pulling, half carrying me toward the piano as I kicked the throw rugs under my feet. She lifted me up and onto the hard bench. I was sobbing by now, looking at her bitterly. Her chest was heaving even more and her mouth was open, smiling crazily as if she were pleased I was crying.

"You want me to be someone that I'm not!" I sobbed. "I'll never be the kind of daughter you want me to be!"

"Only two kinds of daughters," she shouted in Chinese. "Those who are obedient and those who follow their own mind! Only one kind of daughter can live in this house. Obedient daughter!"

75   "Then I wish I wasn't your daughter. I wish you weren't my mother," I shouted. As I said these things I got scared. It felt like worms and toads and slimy things crawling out of my chest, but it also felt good, as if this awful side of me had surfaced, at last.

"Too late change this," said my mother shrilly.

And I could sense her anger rising to its breaking point. I wanted to see it spill over. And that's when I remembered the babies she had lost in China, the ones we never talked about. "Then I wish I'd never been born!" I shouted. "I wish I were dead! Like them."

It was as if I had said the magic words. Alakazam!—and her face went blank, her mouth closed, her arms went slack, and she backed out of the room, stunned, as if she were blowing away like a small brown leaf, thin, brittle, lifeless.

It was not the only disappointment my mother felt in me. In the years that followed, I failed her so many times, each time asserting my own will, my right to fall short of expectations. I didn't get straight As. I didn't become class president. I didn't get into Stanford. I dropped out of college.

80   For unlike my mother, I did not believe I could be anything I wanted to be. I could only be me.

And for all those years, we never talked about the disaster at the recital or my terrible accusations afterward at the piano bench. All that remained unchecked, like a betrayal that was now unspeakable. So I never found a way to ask her why she had hoped for something so large that failure was inevitable.

And even worse, I never asked her what frightened me the most: Why had she given up hope?

For after our struggle at the piano, she never mentioned my playing again. The lessons stopped. The lid to the piano was closed, shutting out the dust, my misery, and her dreams.

So she surprised me. A few years ago, she offered to give me the piano, for my thirtieth birthday. I had not played in all those years. I saw the offer as a sign of forgiveness, a tremendous burden removed.

85   "Are you sure?" I asked shyly. "I mean, won't you and Dad miss it?"

"No, this your piano," she said firmly. "Always your piano. You only one can play."

"Well, I probably can't play anymore," I said. "It's been years."

"You pick up fast," said my mother, as if she knew this was certain. "You have natural talent. You could been genius if you want to."

"No I couldn't."

90   "You just not trying," said my mother. And she was neither angry nor sad. She said it as if to announce a fact that could never be disproved. "Take it," she said.

But I didn't at first. It was enough that she had offered it to me. And after that, every time I saw it in my parents' living room, standing in front of the bay windows, it made me feel proud, as if it were a shiny trophy I had won back.

Last week I sent a tuner over to my parents' apartment and had the piano reconditioned, for purely sentimental reasons. My mother had died a few months before and I had been getting things in order for my father, a little bit at a time. I put the jewelry in special silk pouches. The sweaters she had knitted in yellow, pink, bright orange—all the colors I hated—I put those in moth-proof boxes. I found some old Chinese silk dresses, the kind with little slits up the sides. I rubbed the old silk against my skin, then wrapped them in tissue and decided to take them home with me.

After I had the piano tuned, I opened the lid and touched the keys. It sounded even richer than I remembered. Really, it was a very good piano. Inside the bench were the same exercise notes with handwritten scales, the same secondhand music books with their covers held together with yellow tape.

I opened up the Schumann book to the dark little piece I had played at the recital. It was on the left-hand side of the page, "Pleading Child." It looked more difficult than I remembered. I played a few bars, surprised at how easily the notes came back to me.

95   And for the first time, or so it seemed, I noticed the piece on the right-hand side. It was called "Perfectly Contented." I tried to play this one as well. It had a lighter melody but the same flowing rhythm and turned out to be quite easy. "Pleading Child" was shorter but slower; "Perfectly Contented" was longer, but faster. And after I played them both a few times, I realized they were two halves of the same song.

J A M E S   T H U R B E R

(1894–1961)

The Catbird Seat

(1943)

Mr. Martin bought the pack of Camels on Monday night in the most crowded cigar store on Broadway. It was theater time and seven or eight men were buying cigarettes. The clerk didn't even glance at Mr. Martin, who put the pack in his overcoat pocket and went out. If any of the staff at F & S had seen him buy the cigarettes, they would have been astonished, for it was generally known that Mr. Martin did not smoke, and never had. No one saw him.

It was just a week to the day since Mr. Martin had decided to rub out Mrs. Ulgine Barrows. The term "rub out" pleased him because it suggested nothing more than the correction of an error—in this case an error of Mr. Fitweiler. Mr. Martin had spent each night of the past week working out his plan and examining it. As he walked home now he went over it again. For the hundredth time he resented the element of imprecision, the margin of guesswork that entered into the business. The project as he had worked it out was casual and bold, the risks were considerable. Something might go wrong anywhere along the line. And therein lay the cunning of his scheme. No one would ever see in it the cautious, painstaking hand of Erwin Martin, head of the filing department at F & S, of whom Mr. Fitweiler had once said, "Man is fallible but Martin isn't." No one would see his hand, that is, unless it were caught in the act.

Sitting in his apartment, drinking a glass of milk, Mr. Martin reviewed his case against Mrs. Ulgine Barrows, as he had every night for seven nights. He began at the beginning. Her quacking voice and braying laugh had first profaned the halls of F & S on March 7, 1941 (Mr. Martin had a head for dates). Old Roberts, the personnel chief, had introduced her as the newly appointed special adviser to the president of the firm, Mr.

Fitweiler. The woman had appalled Mr. Martin instantly, but he hadn't shown it. He had given her his dry hand, a look of studious concentration, and a faint smile. "Well," she had said, looking at the papers on his desk, "are you lifting the oxcart out of the ditch?" As Mr. Martin recalled that moment, over his milk, he squirmed slightly. He must keep his mind on her crimes as a special adviser, not on her peccadillos as a personality. This he found difficult to do, in spite of entering an objection and sustaining it. The faults of the woman as a woman kept chattering on in his mind like an unruly witness. She had, for almost two years now, baited him. In the halls, in the elevator, even in his own office, into which she romped now and then like a circus horse, she was constantly shouting these silly questions at him. "Are you lifting the oxcart out of the ditch? Are you tearing up the pea patch? Are you hollering down the rain barrel? Are you scraping around the bottom of the pickle barrel? Are you sitting in the catbird seat?"

It was Joey Hart, one of Mr. Martin's two assistants, who had explained what the gibberish meant. "She must be a Dodger fan," he had said. "Red Barber announces the Dodger games over the radio and he uses those expressions—picked 'em up down South." Joey had gone on to explain one or two. "Tearing up the pea patch" meant going on a rampage; "sitting in the catbird seat" meant sitting pretty, like a batter with three balls and no strikes on him. Mr. Martin dismissed all this with an effort. It had been annoying, it had driven him near to distraction, but he was too solid a man to be moved to murder by anything so childish. It was fortunate, he reflected as he passed on to the important charges against Mrs. Barrows, that he had stood up under it so well. He had maintained always an outward appearance of polite tolerance. "Why, I even believe you like the woman," Miss Paird, his other assistant, had once said to him. He had simply smiled.

5   A gavel rapped in Mr. Martin's mind and the case proper was resumed. Mrs. Ulgine Barrows stood charged with willful, blatant, and persistent attempts to destroy the efficiency and system of F & S. It was competent, material, and relevant to review her advent and rise to power. Mr. Martin had got the story from Miss Paird, who seemed always able to find things out. According to her, Mrs. Barrows had met Mr. Fitweiler at a party, where she had rescued him from the embraces of a powerfully built drunken man who had mistaken the president of F & S for a famous retired Middle Western football coach. She had led him to a sofa and somehow worked upon him a monstrous magic. The aging gentleman had jumped to the conclusion there and then that this was a woman of singular attainments, equipped to bring out the best in him and in the firm. A week later he had introduced her into F & S as his special adviser. On that day confusion got its foot in the door. After Miss Tyson, Mr. Brundage, and Mr. Bartlett had been fired and Mr. Munson had taken his hat and stalked out, mailing in his resignation later, old Roberts had been emboldened to speak to Mr. Fitweiler. He mentioned that Mr. Munson's department had been "a little

disrupted" and hadn't they perhaps better resume the old system there? Mr. Fitweiler had said certainly not. He had the greatest faith in Mrs. Barrow's ideas. "They require a little seasoning, a little seasoning, is all," he had added. Mr. Roberts had given it up. Mr. Martin reviewed in detail all the changes wrought by Mrs. Barrows. She had begun chipping at the cornices of the firm's edifice and now she was swinging at the foundation stones with a pickaxe.

Mr. Martin came now, in his summing up, to the afternoon of Monday, November 2, 1942—just one week ago. On that day, at 3 P.M., Mrs. Barrows had bounced into his office. "Boo!" she had yelled. "Are you scraping around the bottom of the pickle barrel?" Mr. Martin had looked at her from under his green eyeshade, saying nothing. She had begun to wander about the office, taking it in with her great, popping eyes. "Do you really need *all* these filing cabinets?" she had demanded suddenly. Mr. Martin's heart had jumped. "Each of these files," he had said, keeping his voice even, "plays an indispensable part in the system of F & S." She had brayed at him, "Well, don't tear up the pea patch!" and gone to the door. From there she had bawled, "But you sure have got a lot of fine scrap in here!" Mr. Martin could no longer doubt that the finger was on his beloved department. Her pickaxe was on the upswing, poised for the first blow. It had not come yet; he had received no blue memo from the enchanted Mr. Fitweiler bearing nonsensical instructions deriving from the obscene woman. But there was no doubt in Mr. Martin's mind that one would be forthcoming. He must act quickly. Already a precious week had gone by. Mr. Martin stood up in his living room, still holding his milk glass. "Gentlemen of the jury," he said to himself, "I demand the death penalty for this horrible person."

The next day Mr. Martin followed his routine, as usual. He polished his glasses more often and once sharpened an already sharp pencil, but not even Miss Paird noticed. Only once did he catch sight of his victim; she swept past him in the hall with a patronizing "Hi!" At five-thirty he walked home, as usual, and had a glass of milk, as usual. He had never drunk anything stronger in his life—unless you could count ginger ale. The late Sam Schlosser, the S of F & S, had praised Mr. Martin at a staff meeting several years before for his temperate habits. "Our most efficient worker neither drinks nor smokes," he had said. "The results speak for themselves." Mr. Fitweiler had sat by, nodding approval.

Mr. Martin was still thinking about that red-letter day as he walked over to the Schrafft's on Fifth Avenue near Forty-sixth Street. He got there, as he always did, at eight o'clock. He finished his dinner and the financial page of the *Sun* at a quarter to nine, as he always did. It was his custom after dinner to take a walk. This time he walked down Fifth Avenue at a casual pace. His gloved hands felt moist and warm, his forehead cold. He transferred the Camels from his overcoat to a jacket pocket. He wondered, as he did so, if they did not represent an unnecessary note of strain. Mrs. Barrows smoked only Luckies. It was his idea to puff a few puffs on a

Camel (after the rubbing-out), stub it out in the ashtray holding her lip-stick-stained Luckies, and thus drag a small red herring across the trail. Perhaps it was not a good idea. It would take time. He might even choke, too loudly.

Mr. Martin had never seen the house on West Twelfth Street where Mrs. Barrows lived, but he had a clear enough picture of it. Fortunately, she had bragged to everybody about her ducky first-floor apartment in the perfectly darling three-story red-brick. There would be no doorman or other attendants; just the tenants of the second and third floors. As he walked along, Mr. Martin realized that he would get there before nine-thirty. He had considered walking north on Fifth Avenue from Schrafft's to a point from which it would take him until ten o'clock to reach the house. At that hour people were less likely to be coming in or going out. But the procedure would have made an awkward loop in the straight thread of his casualness, and he had abandoned it. It was impossible to fig-ure when people would be entering or leaving the house, anyway. There was a great risk at any hour. If he ran into anybody, he would simply have to place the rubbing-out of Ulgine Barrows in the inactive file forever. The same thing would hold true if there were someone in her apartment. In that case he would just say that he had been passing by, recognized her charming house and thought to drop in.

10   It was eighteen minutes after nine when Mr. Martin turned into Twelfth Street. A man passed him, and a man and a woman talking. There was no one within fifty paces when he came to the house, halfway down the block. He was up the steps and in the small vestibule in no time, press-ing the bell under the card that said "Mrs. Ulgine Barrows." When the clicking in the lock started, he jumped forward against the door. He got inside fast, closing the door behind him. A bulb in a lantern hung from the hall ceiling on a chain seemed to give a monstrously bright light. There was nobody on the stair, which went up ahead of him along the left wall. A door opened down the hall in the wall on the right. He went to-ward it swiftly, on tiptoe.

"Well, for God's sake, look who's here!" bawled Mrs. Barrows, and her braying laugh rang out like the report of a shotgun. He rushed past her like a football tackle, bumping her. "Hey, quit shoving!" she said, closing the door behind them. They were in her living room, which seemed to Mr. Martin to be lighted by a hundred lamps. "What's after you?" she said. "You're as jumpy as a goat." He found he was unable to speak. His heart was wheezing in his throat. "I—yes," he finally brought out. She was jab-bering and laughing as she started to help him off with his coat. "No, no," he said. "I'll put it here." He took it off and put it on a chair near the door. "Your hat and gloves, too," she said. "You're in a lady's house." He put his hat on top of the coat. Mrs. Barrows seemed larger than he had thought. He kept his gloves on. "I was passing by," he said. "I recognized—is there anyone here?" She laughed louder than ever. "No," she said, "we're all alone. You're as white as a sheet, you funny man. Whatever *has* come over you? I'll mix you a toddy." She started toward a door across the room. "Scotch-and-soda be all right? But say, you don't drink, do you?" She turned and gave him her amused look. Mr. Martin pulled himself together. "Scotch-and-soda will be all right," he heard himself say. He could hear her laughing in the kitchen.

Mr. Martin looked quickly around the living room for the weapon. He had counted on finding one there. There were andirons and a poker and something in a corner that looked like an Indian club. None of them would do. It couldn't be that way. He began to pace around. He came to a desk. On it lay a metal paper knife with an ornate handle. Would it be sharp enough? He reached for it and knocked over a small brass jar. Stamps spilled out of it and it fell to the floor with a clatter. "Hey," Mrs. Barrows yelled from the kitchen, "are you tearing up the pea patch?" Mr. Martin gave a strange laugh. Picking up the knife, he tried its point against his left wrist. It was blunt. It wouldn't do.

When Mrs. Barrows reappeared, carrying two highballs, Mr. Martin, standing there with his gloves on, became acutely conscious of the fantasy he had wrought. Cigarettes in his pocket, a drink prepared for him—it was all too grossly improbable. It was more than that; it was impossible. Somewhere in the back of his mind a vague idea stirred, sprouted. "For heaven's sake, take off those gloves," said Mrs. Barrows. "I always wear them in the house," said Mr. Martin. The idea began to bloom, strange and wonderful. She put the glasses on a coffee table in front of a sofa and sat on the sofa. "Come over here, you odd little man," she said. Mr. Martin went over and sat beside her. It was difficult getting a cigarette out of the pack of Camels, but he managed it. She held a match for him, laughing. "Well," she said, handing him his drink, "this is perfectly marvelous. You with a drink and a cigarette."

Mr. Martin puffed, not too awkwardly, and took a gulp of the highball. "I drink and smoke all the time," he said. He clinked his glass against hers. "Here's nuts to that old windbag, Fitweiler," he said, and gulped again. The stuff tasted awful, but he made no grimace. "Really, Mr. Martin," she said, her voice and posture changing, "you are insulting our employer." Mrs. Barrows was now all special adviser to the president. "I am preparing a bomb," said Mr. Martin, "which will blow the old goat higher than hell." He had only had a little of the drink, which was not strong. It couldn't be that. "Do you take dope or something?" Mrs. Barrows asked coldly. "Heroin," said Mr. Martin. "I'll be coked to the gills when I bump that old buzzard off." "Mr. Martin!" she shouted, getting to her feet. "That will be all of that. You must go at once." Mr. Martin took another swallow of his drink. He tapped his cigarette out in the ashtray and put the pack of Camels on the coffee table. Then he got up. She stood glaring at him. He walked over and put on his hat and coat. "Not a word about this," he said, and laid an index finger against his lips. All Mrs.

Barrows could bring out was "Really!" Mr. Martin put his hand on the doorknob. "I'm sitting in the catbird seat," he said. He stuck his tongue out at her and left. Nobody saw him go.

15   Mr. Martin got to his apartment, walking, well before eleven. No one saw him go in. He had two glasses of milk after brushing his teeth, and he felt elated. It wasn't tipsiness, because he hadn't been tipsy. Anyway, the walk had worn off all effects of the whisky. He got in bed and read a magazine for a while. He was asleep before midnight.

Mr. Martin got to the office at eight-thirty the next morning, as usual. At a quarter to nine, Ulgine Barrows, who had never before arrived at work before ten, swept into his office. "I'm reporting to Mr. Fitweiler now!" she shouted. "If he turns you over to the police, it's no more than you deserve!" Mr. Martin gave her a look of shocked surprise. "I beg your pardon?" he said. Mrs. Barrows snorted and bounced out of the room, leaving Miss Paird and Joey Hart staring after her. "What's the matter with that old devil now?" asked Miss Paird. "I have no idea," said Mr. Martin, resuming his work. The other two looked at him and then at each other. Miss Paird got up and went out. She walked slowly past the closed door of Mr. Fitweiler's office. Mrs. Barrows was yelling inside, but she was not braying. Miss Paird could not hear what the woman was saying. She went back to her desk.

Forty-five minutes later, Mrs. Barrows left the president's office and went into her own, shutting the door. It wasn't until half an hour later that Mr. Fitweiler sent for Mr. Martin. The head of the filing department, neat, quiet, attentive, stood in front of the old man's desk. Mr. Fitweiler was pale and nervous. He took his glasses off and twiddled them. He made a small, bruffing sound in his throat. "Martin," he said, "you have been with us more than twenty years." "Twenty-two, sir," said Mr. Martin. "In that time," pursued the president, "your work and your—uh—manner have been exemplary." "I trust so, sir," said Mr. Martin. "I have understood, Martin," said Mr. Fitweiler, "that you have never taken a drink or smoked." "That is correct, sir," said Mr. Martin. "Ah, yes." Mr. Fitweiler polished his glasses. "You may describe what you did after leaving the office yesterday, Martin," he said. Mr. Martin allowed less than a second for his bewildered pause. "Certainly, sir," he said. "I walked home. Then I went to Schrafft's for dinner. Afterward I walked home again. I went to bed early, sir, and read a magazine for a while. I was asleep before eleven." "Ah, yes," said Mr. Fitweiler again. He was silent for a moment, searching for the proper words to say to the head of the filing department. "Mrs. Barrows," he said finally, "Mrs. Barrows has worked hard, Martin, very hard. It grieves me to report that she has suffered a severe breakdown. It has taken the form of a persecution complex accompanied by distressing hallucinations." "I am very sorry, sir," said Mr. Martin. "Mrs. Barrows is under the delusion," continued Mr. Fitweiler, "that you visited her last evening and behaved yourself in an—uh—unseemly manner." He raised his hand to silence Mr. Martin's little pained outcry. "It is the nature of these psychological diseases," Mr. Fitweiler said, "to fix upon the least likely and most innocent party as the—uh—source of persecution. These matters are not for the lay mind to grasp, Martin. I've just had my psychiatrist, Dr. Fitch, on the phone. He would not, of course, commit himself, but he made enough generalizations to substantiate my suspicions. I suggested to Mrs. Barrows when she had completed her—uh—story to me this morning, that she visit Dr. Fitch, for I suspected a condition at once. She flew, I regret to say, into a rage, and demanded—uh—requested that I call you on the carpet. You may not know, Martin, but Mrs. Barrows had planned a reorganization of your department—subject to my approval, of course, subject to my approval. This brought you, rather than anyone else, to her mind—but again that is a phenomenon for Dr. Fitch and not for us. So, Martin, I am afraid Mrs. Barrows' usefulness here is at an end." "I am dreadfully sorry, sir," said Mr. Martin.

It was at this point that the door to the office blew open with the suddenness of a gas-main explosion and Mrs. Barrows catapulted through it. "Is the little rat denying it?" she screamed. "He can't get away with that!" Mr. Martin got up and moved discreetly to a point beside Mr. Fitweiler's chair. "You drank and smoked at my apartment," she bawled at Mr. Martin, "and you know it! You called Mr. Fitweiler an old windbag and said you were going to blow him up when you got coked to the gills on your heroin!" She stopped yelling to catch her breath and a new glint came into her popping eyes. "If you weren't such a drab, ordinary little man," she said, "I'd think you'd planned it all. Sticking your tongue out at me, saying you were sitting in the catbird seat, because you thought no one would believe me when I told it! My God, it's really too perfect!" She brayed loudly and hysterically, and the fury was on her again. She glared at Mr. Fitweiler. "Can't you see how he has tricked us, you old fool? Can't you see his little game?" But Mr. Fitweiler had been surreptitiously pressing all the buttons under the top of his desk and employees of F & S began pouring into the room. "Stockton," said Mr. Fitweiler, "you and Fishbein will take Mrs. Barrows to her home. Mrs. Powell, you will go with them." Stockton, who had played a little football in high school, blocked Mrs. Barrows as she made for Mr. Martin. It took him and Fishbein together to force her out of the door into the hall, crowded with stenographers and office boys. She was still screaming imprecations at Mr. Martin, tangled and contradictory imprecations. The hubbub finally died out down the corridor.

"I regret that this has happened," said Mr. Fitweiler. "I shall ask you to dismiss it from your mind, Martin." "Yes, sir," said Mr. Martin, anticipating his chief's "That will be all" by moving to the door. "I will dismiss it." He went out and shut the door, and his step was light and quick in the hall. When he entered his department he had slowed down to his customary gait, and he walked quietly across the room to the W20 file, wearing a look of studious concentration.

A N N E   T Y L E R

(1941–   )

Teenage Wasteland

(1984)

He used to have very blond hair—almost white—cut shorter than other children's so that on his crown a little cowlick always stood up to catch the light. But this was when he was small. As he grew older, his hair grew darker, and he wore it longer—past his collar even. It hung in lank, taffy-colored ropes around his face, which was still an endearing face, fine-featured, the eyes an unusual aqua blue. But his cheeks, of course, were no longer round, and a sharp new Adam's apple jogged in his throat when he talked.

In October, they called from the private school he attended to request a conference with his parents. Daisy went alone; her husband was at work. Clutching her purse, she sat on the principal's couch and learned that Donny was noisy, lazy, and disruptive; always fooling around with his friends, and he wouldn't respond in class.

In the past, before her children were born, Daisy had been a fourth-grade teacher. It shamed her now to sit before this principal as a parent, a delinquent parent, a parent who struck Mr. Lanham, no doubt, as unseeing or uncaring. "It isn't that we're not concerned," she said. "Both of us are. And we've done what we could, whatever we could think of. We don't let him watch TV on school nights. We don't let him talk on the phone till he's finished his homework. But he tells us he doesn't *have* any homework or he did it all in study hall. How are we to know what to believe?"

From early October through November, at Mr. Lanham's suggestion, Daisy checked Donny's assignments every day. She sat next to him as he worked, trying to be encouraging, sagging inwardly as she saw the poor quality of everything he did—the sloppy mistakes in math, the illogical leaps in his English themes, the history questions left blank if they required any research.

5   Daisy was often late starting supper, and she couldn't give as much attention to Donny's younger sister. "You'll never guess what happened at . . ." Amanda would begin, and Daisy would have to tell her, "Not now, honey."

By the time her husband, Matt, came home, she'd be snappish. She would recite the day's hardships—the fuzzy instructions in English, the botched history map, the morass of unsolvable algebra equations. Matt would look surprised and confused, and Daisy would gradually wind down. There was no way, really, to convey how exhausting all this was.

In December, the school called again. This time, they wanted Matt to come as well. She and Matt had to sit on Mr. Lanham's couch like two bad children and listen to the news: Donny had improved only slightly, raising a D in history to a C, and a C in algebra to a B-minus. What was worse, he had developed new problems. He had cut classes on at least three occasions. Smoked in the furnace room. Helped Sonny Barnett break into a freshman's locker. And last week, during athletics, he and three friends had been seen off the school grounds; when they returned, the coach had smelled beer on their breath.

Daisy and Matt sat silent, shocked. Matt rubbed his forehead with his fingertips. Imagine, Daisy thought, how they must look to Mr. Lanham: an overweight housewife in a cotton dress and a too-tall, too-thin insurance agent in a baggy, frayed suit. Failures, both of them—the kind of people who are always hurrying to catch up, missing the point of things that everyone else grasps at once. She wished she'd worn nylons instead of knee socks.

It was arranged that Donny would visit a psychologist for testing. Mr. Lanham knew just the person. He would set this boy straight, he said.

10   When they stood to leave, Daisy held her stomach in and gave Mr. Lanham a firm, responsible handshake.

Donny said the psychologist was a jackass and the tests were really dumb; but he kept all three of his appointments, and when it was time for the follow-up conference with the psychologist and both parents, Donny combed his hair and seemed unusually sober and subdued. The psychologist said Donny had no serious emotional problems. He was merely going through a difficult period in his life. He required some academic help and a better sense of self-worth. For this reason, he was suggesting a man named Calvin Beadle, a tutor with considerable psychological training.

In the car going home, Donny said he'd be damned if he'd let them drag him to some stupid fairy tutor. His father told him to watch his language in front of his mother.

That night, Daisy lay awake pondering the term "self-worth." She had always been free with her praise. She had always told Donny he had talent, was smart, was good with his hands. She had made a big to-do over every little gift he gave her. In fact, maybe she had gone too far, although, Lord knows, she had meant every word. Was that his trouble?

She remembered when Amanda was born. Donny had acted lost and bewildered. Daisy had been alert to that, of course, but still, a new baby keeps you so busy. Had she really done all she could have? She longed—she ached—for a time machine. Given one more chance, she'd do it perfectly— hug him more, praise him more, or perhaps praise him less. Oh, who can say . . .

15   The tutor told Donny to call him Cal. All his kids did, he said. Daisy thought for a second that he meant his own children, then realized her mistake. He seemed too young, anyhow, to be a family man. He wore a heavy brown handlebar mustache. His hair was as long and stringy as Donny's, and his jeans as faded. Wire-rimmed spectacles slid down his nose. He lounged in a canvas director's chair with his fingers laced across

his chest, and he casually, amiably questioned Donny, who sat upright and glaring in an armchair.

"So they're getting on your back at school," said Cal. "Making a big deal about anything you do wrong."

"Right," said Donny.

"Any idea why that would be?"

"Oh, well, you know, stuff like homework and all," Donny said.

20   "You don't do your homework?"

"Oh, well, I might do it sometimes but not just exactly like they want it." Donny sat forward and said, "It's like a prison there, you know? You've got to go to every class, you can never step off the school grounds."

"You cut classes sometimes?"

"Sometimes," Donny said, with a glance at his parents.

Cal didn't seem perturbed. "Well," he said, "I'll tell you what. Let's you and me try working together three nights a week. Think you can handle that? We'll see if we can show that school of yours a thing or two. Give it a month; then if you don't like it, we'll stop. If *I* don't like it, we'll stop. I mean, sometimes people just don't get along, right? What do you say to that?"

25   "Okay," Donny said. He seemed pleased.

"Make it seven o'clock till eight, Monday, Wednesday, and Friday," Cal told Matt and Daisy. They nodded. Cal shambled to his feet, gave them a little salute, and showed them to the door.

This was where he lived as well as worked, evidently. The interview had taken place in the dining room, which had been transformed into a kind of office. Passing the living room, Daisy winced at the rock music she had been hearing, without registering it, ever since she had entered the house. She looked in and saw a boy about Donny's age lying on a sofa with a book. Another boy and a girl were playing Ping-Pong in front of the fireplace. "You have several here together?" Daisy asked Cal.

"Oh, sometimes they stay on after their sessions, just to rap. They're a pretty sociable group, all in all. Plenty of goof-offs like young Donny here."

He cuffed Donny's shoulder playfully. Donny flushed and grinned.

30   Climbing into the car, Daisy asked Donny, "Well? What do you think?"

But Donny had returned to his old evasive self. He jerked his chin toward the garage. "Look," he said. "He's got a basketball net."

Now on Mondays, Wednesdays, and Fridays, they had supper early— the instant Matt came home. Sometimes, they had to leave before they were really finished. Amanda would still be eating her dessert. "Bye, honey. Sorry," Daisy would tell her.

Cal's first bill sent a flutter of panic through Daisy's chest, but it was worth it, of course. Just look at Donny's face when they picked him up: alight and full of interest. The principal telephoned Daisy to tell her how Donny had improved. "Of course, it hasn't shown up in his grades yet, but several of the teachers have noticed how his attitude's changed. Yes, sir, I think we're onto something here."

At home, Donny didn't act much different. He still seemed to have a low opinion of his parents. But Daisy supposed that was unavoidable—part of being fifteen. He said his parents were too "controlling"—a word that made Daisy give him a sudden look. He said they acted like wardens. On weekends, they enforced a curfew. And any time he went to a party, they always telephoned first to see if adults would be supervising. "For God's sake!" he said. "Don't you trust me?"

35   "It isn't a matter of trust, honey . . ." But there was no explaining to him.

His tutor called one afternoon. "I get the sense," he said, "that this kid's feeling . . . underestimated, you know? Like you folks expect the worst of him. I'm thinking we ought to give him more rope."

"But see, he's still so suggestible," Daisy said. "When his friends suggest some mischief—smoking or drinking or such—why, he just finds it hard not to go along with them."

"Mrs. Coble," the tutor said, "I think this kid is hurting. You know? Here's a serious, sensitive kid, telling you he'd like to take on some grown-up challenges, and you're giving him the message that he can't be trusted. Don't you understand how that hurts?"

"Oh," said Daisy.

40   "It undermines his self-esteem—don't you realize that?"

"Well, I guess you're right," said Daisy. She saw Donny suddenly from a whole new angle: his pathetically poor posture, that slouch so forlorn that his shoulders seemed about to meet his chin . . . oh, wasn't it awful being young? She'd had a miserable adolescence herself and had always sworn no child of hers would ever be that unhappy.

They let Donny stay out later, they didn't call ahead to see if the parties were supervised, and they were careful not to grill him about his evening. The tutor had set down so many rules! They were not allowed any questions at all about any aspect of school, nor were they to speak with his teachers. If a teacher had some complaint, she should phone Cal. Only one teacher disobeyed—the history teacher, Miss Evans. She called one morning in February. "I'm a little concerned about Donny, Mrs. Coble."

"Oh, I'm sorry, Miss Evans, but Donny's tutor handles these things now . . ."

"I always deal directly with the parents. You are the parent," Miss Evans said, speaking very slowly and distinctly. "Now, here is the problem. Back when you were helping Donny with his homework, his grades rose from a D to a C, but now they've slipped back, and they're closer to an F."

45   "They are?"

"I think you should start overseeing his homework again."

"But Donny's tutor says . . ."

"It's nice that Donny has a tutor, but you should still be in charge of his homework. With you, he learned it. Then he passed his tests. With the tutor, well, it seems the tutor is more of a crutch. 'Donny,' I say, 'a quiz is coming up on Friday. Hadn't you better be listening instead of talking?'

'That's okay, Miss Evans,' he says. 'I have a tutor now.' Like a talisman! I really think you ought to take over, Mrs. Coble."

"I see," said Daisy. "Well, I'll think about that. Thank you for calling."

50　　Hanging up, she felt a rush of anger at Donny. A talisman! For a talisman, she'd given up all luxuries, all that time with her daughter, her evenings at home!

She dialed Cal's number. He sounded muzzy. "I'm sorry if I woke you," she told him, "but Donny's history teacher just called. She says he isn't doing well."

"She should have dealt with me."

"She wants me to start supervising his homework again. His grades are slipping."

"Yes," said the tutor, "but you and I both know there's more to it than mere grades, don't we? I care about the *whole* child—his happiness, his self-esteem. The grades will come. Just give them time."

55　　When she hung up, it was Miss Evans she was angry at. What a narrow woman!

It was Cal this, Cal that, Cal says this, Cal and I did that. Cal lent Donny an album by The Who. He took Donny and two other pupils to a rock concert. In March, when Donny began to talk endlessly on the phone with a girl named Miriam, Cal even let Miriam come to one of the tutoring sessions. Daisy was touched that Cal would grow so involved in Donny's life, but she was also a little hurt, because she had offered to have Miriam to dinner and Donny had refused. Now he asked them to drive her to Cal's house without a qualm.

This Miriam was an unappealing girl with blurry lipstick and masses of rough red hair. She wore a short, bulky jacket that would not have been out of place on a motorcycle. During the trip to Cal's she was silent, but coming back, she was more talkative. "What a neat guy, and what a house! All those kids hanging out, like a club. And the stereo playing rock . . . gosh, he's not like a grown-up at all! Married and divorced and everything, but you'd think he was our own age."

"Mr. Beadle was married?" Daisy asked.

"Yeah, to this really controlling lady. She didn't understand him a bit."

60　　"No, I guess not," Daisy said.

Spring came, and the students who hung around at Cal's drifted out to the basketball net above the garage. Sometimes, when Daisy and Matt arrived to pick up Donny, they'd find him there with the others—spiky and excited, jittering on his toes beneath the backboard. It was staying light much longer now, and the neighboring fence cast narrow bars across the bright grass. Loud music would be spilling from Cal's windows. Once it was The Who, which Daisy recognized from the time that Donny had borrowed the album. *"Teenage Wasteland,"*[1] she said aloud, identifying the

---

[1] The song is actually "Baba O'Riley," from the band's *Who's Next* album.

song, and Matt gave a short, dry laugh. "It certainly is," he said. He'd misunderstood; he thought she was commenting on the scene spread before them. In fact, she might have been. The players looked like hoodlums, even her son. Why, one of Cal's students had recently been knifed in a tavern. One had been shipped off to boarding school in midterm; two had been withdrawn by their parents. On the other hand, Donny had mentioned someone who'd been studying with Cal for five years. "Five years!" said Daisy. "Doesn't anyone ever stop needing him?"

Donny looked at her. Lately, whatever she said about Cal was read as criticism. "You're just feeling competitive," he said. "And controlling."

She bit her lip and said no more.

In April, the principal called to tell her that Donny had been expelled. There had been a locker check, and in Donny's locker they found five cans of beer and half a pack of cigarettes. With Donny's previous record, his offense meant expulsion.

65 Daisy gripped the receiver tightly and said, "Well, where is he now?"

"We've sent him home," said Mr. Lanham. "He's packed up all his belongings, and he's coming home on foot."

Daisy wondered what she would say to him. She felt him looming closer and closer, bringing this brand-new situation that no one had prepared her to handle. What other place would take him? Could they enter him in public school? What were the rules? She stood at the living room window, waiting for him to show up. Gradually, she realized that he was taking too long. She checked the clock. She stared up the street again.

When an hour had passed, she phoned the school. Mr. Lanham's secretary answered and told her in a grave, sympathetic voice that yes, Donny Coble had most definitely gone home. Daisy called her husband. He was out of the office. She went back to the window and thought awhile, and then she called Donny's tutor.

"Donny's been expelled from school," she said, "and now I don't know where he's gone. I wonder if you've heard from him?"

70 There was a long silence. "Donny's with me, Mrs. Coble," he finally said.

"With you? How'd he get there?"

"He hailed a cab, and I paid the driver."

"Could I speak to him, please?"

There was another silence. "Maybe it'd be better if we had a conference," Cal said.

75 "I don't *want* a conference. I've been standing at the window picturing him dead or kidnapped or something, and now you tell me you want a—"

"Donny is very, very upset. Understandably so," said Cal. "Believe me, Mrs. Coble, this is not what it seems. Have you asked Donny's side of the story?"

"Well, of course not, how could I? He went running off to you instead."

"Because he didn't feel he'd be listened to."

"But I haven't even—"

80 "Why don't you come out and talk? The three of us," said Cal, "will try to get this thing in perspective."

"Well, all right," Daisy said. But she wasn't as reluctant as she sounded. Already, she felt soothed by the calm way Cal was taking this.

Cal answered the doorbell at once. He said, "Hi, there," and led her into the dining room. Donny sat slumped in a chair, chewing the knuckle of one thumb. "Hello, Donny," Daisy said. He flicked his eyes in her direction.

"Sit here, Mrs. Coble," said Cal, placing her opposite Donny. He himself remained standing, restlessly pacing. "So," he said.

Daisy stole a look at Donny. His lips were swollen, as if he'd been crying.

85 "You know," Cal told Daisy, "I kind of expected something like this. That's a very punitive school you've got him in—you realize that. And any half-decent lawyer will tell you they've violated his civil rights. Locker checks! Where's their search warrant?"

"But if the rule is—" Daisy said.

"Well, anyhow, let him tell you his side."

She looked at Donny. He said, "It wasn't my fault. I promise."

"They said your locker was full of beer."

90 "It was a put-up job! See, there's this guy that doesn't like me. He put all these beers in my locker and started a rumor going, so Mr. Lanham ordered a locker check."

"What was the boy's name?" Daisy asked.

"Huh?"

"Mrs. Coble, take my word, the situation is not so unusual," Cal said. "You can't imagine how vindictive kids can be sometimes."

"What was the boy's *name*," said Daisy, "so that I can ask Mr. Lanham if that's who suggested he run a locker check."

95 "You don't believe me," Donny said.

"And how'd this boy get your combination in the first place?"

"Frankly," said Cal, "I wouldn't be surprised to learn the school was in on it. Any kid that marches to a different drummer, why, they'd just love an excuse to get rid of him. The school is where I lay the blame."

"Doesn't *Donny* ever get blamed?"

"Now, Mrs. Coble, you heard what he—"

100 "Forget it," Donny told Cal. "You can see she doesn't trust me."

Daisy drew in a breath to say that of course she trusted him—a reflex. But she knew that bold-faced, wide-eyed look of Donny's. He had worn that look when he was small, denying some petty misdeed with the evidence plain as day all around him. Still, it was hard for her to accuse him outright. She temporized and said, "The only thing I'm sure of is that they've kicked you out of school, and now I don't know what we're going to do."

"We'll fight it," said Cal.

"We can't. Even you must see we can't."

"I could apply to Brantly," Donny said.

105   Cal stopped his pacing to beam down at him. "Brantly! Yes. They're really onto where a kid is coming from, at Brantly. Why, *I* could get you into Brantly. I work with a lot of their students."

Daisy had never heard of Brantly, but already she didn't like it. And she didn't like Cal's smile, which struck her now as feverish and avid—a smile of hunger.

On the fifteenth of April, they entered Donny in a public school, and they stopped his tutoring sessions. Donny fought both decisions bitterly. Cal, surprisingly enough, did not object. He admitted he'd made no headway with Donny and said it was because Donny was emotionally disturbed.

Donny went to his new school every morning, plodding off alone with his head down. He did his assignments, and he earned average grades, but he gathered no friends, joined no clubs. There was something exhausted and defeated about him.

The first week in June, during final exams, Donny vanished. He simply didn't come home one afternoon, and no one at school remembered seeing him. The police were reassuring, and for the first few days, they worked hard. They combed Donny's sad, messy room for clues; they visited Miriam and Cal. But then they started talking about the number of kids who ran away every year. Hundreds, just in this city. "He'll show up, if he wants to," they said. "If he doesn't, he won't."

110   Evidently, Donny didn't want to.

It's been three months now and still no word. Matt and Daisy still look for him in every crowd of awkward, heartbreaking teenage boys. Every time the phone rings, they imagine it might be Donny. Both parents have aged. Donny's sister seems to be staying away from home as much as possible.

At night, Daisy lies awake and goes over Donny's life. She is trying to figure out what went wrong, where they made their first mistake. Often, she finds herself blaming Cal, although she knows he didn't begin it. Then at other times she excuses him, for without him, Donny might have left earlier. Who really knows? In the end, she can only sigh and search for a cooler spot on the pillow. As she falls asleep, she occasionally glimpses something in the corner of her vision. It's something fleet and round, a ball—a basketball. It flies up, it sinks through the hoop, descends, lands in a yard littered with last year's leaves and striped with bars of sunlight as white as bones, bleached and parched and cleanly picked.

Fiction Casebook

This section contains the 1966 short story "Where Are You Going, Where Have You Been?" by Joyce Carol Oates, a collection of source materials,* thirteen questions to stimulate discussion and writing, and a student paper.

Source Materials

- ◆ Oates, Joyce Carol. "When Characters from the Page Are Made Flesh on the Screen." *New York Times* 23 Mar. 1986, sec. 2:1+. An article by the author in which she discusses her feelings about the film *Smooth Talk,* based on her story. (p. 592)

- ◆ Schulz, Gretchen, and R. J. R. Rockwood. "In Fairyland, without a Map: Connie's Exploration Inward in Joyce Carol Oates' 'Where Are You Going, Where Have You Been?' " *Literature and Psychology* 30 (1980): 155–67. A psychological interpretation of the story from a scholarly journal. (p. 595)

- ◆ Tierce, Mike, and John Michael Crafton. "Connie's Tambourine Man: A New Reading of Arnold Friend." *Studies in Short Fiction* 22 (1985): 219–24. A critical interpretation of the character of Arnold Friend. (p. 607)

- ◆ Dylan, Bob. "It's All Over Now, Baby Blue." Los Angeles: Warner Bros., 1965. Lyrics from a popular folk song, which, according to Oates, inspired the story. (This and other Dylan songs are discussed in Tierce and Crafton's article.) (p. 613)

- ◆ Wegs, Joyce M. " 'Don't You Know Who I Am?' The Grotesque in Oates's 'Where Are You Going, Where Have You Been?' " *Journal of Narrative Technique* 5 (1975): 66–72. An examination of the cultural context of the story. (p. 614)

---

* Note that some of the critical articles in this casebook were written before the current MLA documentation style was adopted. See Appendix A for current MLA format. Page references to specific editions of the Oates story have been deleted to avoid confusion.

Each of these sources provides insights (sometimes contradictory ones) into the short story "Where Are You Going, Where Have You Been?" Other kinds of sources can also enrich your understanding of the work—for instance, other stories by Oates, biographical data about the author, or stories by other writers dealing with similar themes. In addition, nonprint sources—such as the film *Smooth Talk*—can provide suggestions about how to approach the story. Although no analytical or biographical source—not even the author's comments—can give you the magical key that will unlock a story's secrets, such sources can enhance your enjoyment and aid your understanding of a work; they can also suggest topics to explore in writing.

In preparation for writing an essay on a topic of your choice about the story "Where Are You Going, Where Have You Been?" read the story and the accompanying source materials carefully. Then, consider the questions at the end of this casebook (p. 619) in light of what you have read. These questions are *not* presented as writing assignments but rather as spring-boards to a topic you can develop in a three- to five-page essay. For guidelines on evaluating literary criticism, see p. 15; for guidelines on using source materials, see Appendix A. Be sure to document any words or ideas borrowed from the story or from another source, and remember to place any words that are not your own in quotation marks.

A complete student paper, "Mesmerizing Men and Vulnerable Teens: Power Relationships in 'Where Are You Going, Where Have You Been?' and 'Teenage Wasteland,' " based on the source materials in this casebook, begins on p. 621.

JOYCE CAROL OATES (1938–   ) is one of contemporary America's most prolific novelists and short story writers. Born and raised in rural Erie County, New York, Oates first gained prominence in the 1960s with publication of *A Garden of Earthly Delights* (1967), *Expensive People* (1968), and *them* (1969), which won the National Book Award. In these and other works, Oates began to explore the multilay-ered nature of American society—writing of urban slums, decaying rural communities, and exclusive suburbs in a dense and compellingly realistic prose style. In some of her more recent novels, including *Belle-fleur* (1980) and *Mysteries of Winterthurn* (1984), Oates reveals her deep

Photo of Joyce Carol Oates reprinted by permission of the author and Blanche C. Gregory, Inc.

fascination with the traditions of nineteenth-century gothic writers—Edgar Allan Poe, Fyodor Dostoevski, Mary Shelley, and others. Oates's recent works include *Lock My Door upon Myself* (1990), *The Rise of Life on Earth* (1991), *Black Water* (1992), and *Foxfire* (1993), *What I Lived For* (1994), *Haunted* (1994), *Zombie* (1995), and *First Love* (1996).

Oates, wrote *Washington Post* critic Susan Wood, "attempts more than most of our writers . . . to explore the profound issues of evil and innocence, betrayal and revenge and atonement, as they are manifest in contemporary American experience. . . ." Although Oates frequently centers her novels around larger issues and moral questions, she can also focus on the private worlds of her characters, as in *Black Water* (1992).

Critics responding to Oates's work have called it violent, lurid, even depraved. Yet, asks Laura Z. Hobson in a review of Oates's 1981 novel, *Angel of Light,* "Would there be such a hullabaloo about the violence in her books if they had been written by a man? From her earliest books onward, reviewers too often struck an insulting tone of surprise: *What's a nice girl like you doing in a place like this?* . . . [Oates] replies that in these violent times only tales of violence have reality. Well, maybe. But the critics' preoccupation with a single facet of her work ignores everything else: her inventiveness, her insider's knowledge of college life, her evocations of nature . . . her ability to tell a story, to write a spellbinder. . . ."

JOYCE CAROL OATES

Where Are You Going, Where Have You Been?

(1966)

For Bob Dylan

Her name was Connie. She was fifteen and she had a quick nervous giggling habit of craning her neck to glance into mirrors, or checking other people's faces to make sure her own was all right. Her mother, who noticed everything and knew everything and who hadn't much reason any longer to look at her own face, always scolded Connie about it. "Stop gawking at yourself, who are you? You think you're so pretty?" she would say. Connie would raise her eyebrows at these familiar complaints and look right through her mother, into a shadowy vision of herself as she was right at that moment: she knew she was pretty and that was everything. Her mother had been pretty once too, if you could believe those old snapshots in the album, but now her looks were gone and that was why she was always after Connie.

"Why don't you keep your room clean like your sister? How've you got your hair fixed—what the hell stinks? Hair spray? You don't see your sister using that junk."

Her sister June was twenty-four and still lived at home. She was a secretary in the high school Connie attended, and if that wasn't bad enough—with her in the same building—she was so plain and chunky and steady that Connie had to hear her praised all the time by her mother and her mother's sisters. June did this, June did that, she saved money and helped clean the house and cooked and Connie couldn't do a thing, her mind was all filled with trashy day-dreams. Their father was away at work most of the time and when he came home he wanted supper and he read the newspaper at supper and after supper he went to bed. He didn't bother talking much to them, but around his bent head Connie's mother kept picking at her until Connie wished her mother was dead and she herself was dead and it was all over. "She makes me want to throw up sometimes," she complained to her friends. She had a high, breath-less, amused voice which made everything she said sound a little forced, whether it was sincere or not.

There was one good thing: June went places with girl friends of hers, girls who were just as plain and steady as she, and so when Connie wanted to do that her mother had no objections. The father of Connie's best girl friend drove the girls the three miles to town and left them off at a shopping plaza, so that they could walk through the stores or go to a movie, and when he came to pick them up again at eleven he never bothered to ask what they had done.

5   They must have been familiar sights, walking around that shopping plaza in their shorts and flat ballerina slippers that always scuffed the sidewalk, with charm bracelets jingling on their thin wrists; they would lean together to whisper and laugh secretly if someone passed by who amused or interested them. Connie had long dark blond hair that drew anyone's eye to it, and she wore part of it pulled up on her head and puffed out and the rest of it she let fall down her back. She wore a pull-over jersey blouse that looked one way when she was at home and another way when she was away from home. Everything about her had two sides to it, one for home and one for anywhere that was not home: her walk that could be childlike and bobbing, or languid enough to make anyone think she was hearing music in her head, her mouth which was pale and smirking most of the time, but bright and pink on these evenings out, her laugh which was cynical and drawling at home—"Ha, ha, very funny"—but high-pitched and nervous anywhere else, like the jingling of the charms on her bracelet.

Sometimes they did go shopping or to a movie, but sometimes they went across the highway, ducking fast across the busy road, to a drive-in restaurant where older kids hung out. The restaurant was shaped like a big bottle, though squatter than a real bottle, and on its cap was a revolving figure of a grinning boy who held a hamburger aloft. One night in mid-summer they ran across, breathless with daring, and right away someone leaned out a car window and invited them over, but it was just a boy from high school they didn't like. It made them feel good to be able to ignore him. They went up through the maze of parked and cruising cars to the bright-lit, fly-infested restaurant, their faces pleased and expectant as if they were entering a sacred building that loomed out of the night to give them what haven and what blessing they yearned for. They sat at the counter and crossed their legs at the ankles, their thin shoulders rigid with excitement, and listened to the music that made everything so good: the music was always in the background like music at a church service, it was something to depend upon.

A boy named Eddie came in to talk with them. He sat backwards on his stool, turning himself jerkily around in semi-circles and then stopping and turning again, and after a while he asked Connie if she would like something to eat. She said she did and so she tapped her friend's arm on her way out—her friend pulled her face up into a brave droll look—and Connie said she would meet her at eleven, across the way. "I just hate to leave her like that," Connie said earnestly, but the boy said that she wouldn't be alone for long. So they went out to his car and on the way Connie couldn't help but let her eyes wander over the windshields and faces all around her, her face gleaming with a joy that had nothing to do with Eddie or even this place; it might have been the music. She drew her shoulders up and sucked in her breath with the pure pleasure of being alive, and just at that moment she happened to glance at a face just a few feet from hers. It was a boy with shaggy black hair, in a convertible jalopy painted gold. He stared at her and then his lips widened into a grin. Connie slit her eyes at him and turned away, but she couldn't help glancing back and there he was still watching her. He wagged a finger and laughed and said, "Gonna get you, baby," and Connie turned away again without Eddie noticing anything.

She spent three hours with him, at the restaurant where they ate hamburgers and drank Cokes in wax cups that were always sweating, and then down an alley a mile or so away, and when he left her off at five to eleven only the movie house was still open at the plaza. Her girl friend was there, talking with a boy. When Connie came up the two girls smiled at each other and Connie said, "How was the movie?" and the girl said, "*You* should know." They rode off with the girl's father, sleepy and pleased, and Connie couldn't help but look at the darkened shopping plaza with its big empty parking lot and its signs that were faded and ghostly now, and over at the drive-in restaurant where cars were still circling tirelessly. She couldn't hear the music at this distance.

Next morning June asked her how the movie was and Connie said, "So-so."

10   She and that girl and occasionally another girl went out several times a week that way, and the rest of the time Connie spent around the house—it was summer vacation—getting in her mother's way and thinking, dreaming, about the boys she met. But all the boys fell back and dissolved into a single face that was not even a face, but an idea, a feeling, mixed up with the urgent insistent pounding of the music and the humid night air of July. Connie's mother kept dragging her back to the daylight by finding things for her to do or saying, suddenly, "What's this about the Pettinger girl?"

And Connie would say nervously, "Oh, her. That dope." She always drew thick clear lines between herself and such girls, and her mother was simple and kindly enough to believe her. Her mother was so simple, Connie thought, that it was maybe cruel to fool her so much. Her mother went scuffling around the house in old bedroom slippers and complained over the telephone to one sister about the other, then the other called up and the two of them complained about the third one. If June's name was mentioned her mother's tone was approving, and if Connie's name was mentioned it was disapproving. This did not really mean she disliked Connie and actually Connie thought that her mother preferred her to June because she was prettier, but the two of them kept up a pretense of exasperation, a sense that they were tugging and struggling over something of little value to either of them. Sometimes, over coffee, they were almost friends, but something would come up—some vexation that was like a fly buzzing suddenly around their heads—and their faces went hard with contempt.

One Sunday Connie got up at eleven—none of them bothered with church—and washed her hair so that it could dry all day long, in the sun. Her parents and sister were going to a barbecue at an aunt's house and Connie said no, she wasn't interested, rolling her eyes to let her mother know just what she thought of it. "Stay home alone then," her mother said sharply. Connie sat out back in a lawn chair and watched them drive away, her father quiet and bald, hunched around so that he could back the car out, her mother with a look that was still angry and not at all softened through the windshield, and in the back seat poor old June all dressed up as if she didn't know what a barbecue was, with all the running yelling kids and the flies. Connie sat with her eyes closed in the sun, dreaming and dazed with the warmth about her as if this were a kind of love, the caresses of love, and her mind slipped over onto thoughts of the boy she had been with the night before and how nice he had been, how sweet it always was, not the way someone like June would suppose but sweet, gentle, the way it was in movies and promised in songs; and when she opened her eyes she hardly knew where she was, the back yard ran off into weeds and a fence-line of trees and behind it the sky was perfectly blue and still. The asbestos "ranch house" that was now three years old startled her—it looked small. She shook her head as if to get awake.

It was too hot. She went inside the house and turned on the radio to drown out the quiet. She sat on the edge of her bed, barefoot, and listened for an hour and a half to a program called XYZ Sunday Jamboree, record after record of hard, fast, shrieking songs she sang along with, interspersed by exclamations from "Bobby King": "An' look here you girls at Napoleon's—Son and Charley want you to pay real close attention to this song coming up!"

And Connie paid close attention herself, bathed in a glow of slow-pulsed joy that seemed to rise mysteriously out of the music itself and lay languidly about the airless little room, breathed in and breathed out with each gentle rise and fall of her chest.

15   After a while she heard a car coming up the drive. She sat up at once, startled, because it couldn't be her father so soon. The gravel kept crunching all the way in from the road—the driveway was long—and Connie ran to the window. It was a car she didn't know. It was an open jalopy, painted a bright gold that caught the sunlight opaquely. Her heart began to pound and her fingers snatched at her hair, checking it, and she whispered "Christ. Christ," wondering how bad she looked. The car came to a stop at the side door and the horn sounded four short taps as if this were a signal Connie knew.

She went into the kitchen and approached the door slowly, then hung out the screen door, her bare toes curling down off the step. There were two boys in the car and now she recognized the driver: he had shaggy, shabby black hair that looked crazy as a wig and he was grinning at her.

"I ain't late, am I?" he said.

"Who the hell do you think you are?" Connie said.

"Toldja I'd be out, didn't I?"

20 "I don't even know who you are."

She spoke sullenly, careful to show no interest or pleasure, and he spoke in a fast bright monotone. Connie looked past him to the other boy, taking her time. He had fair brown hair, with a lock that fell onto his forehead. His sideburns gave him a fierce, embarrassed look, but so far he hadn't even bothered to glance at her. Both boys wore sunglasses. The driver's glasses were metallic and mirrored everything in miniature.

"You wanta come for a ride?" he said.

Connie smirked and let her hair fall loose over one shoulder.

"Don'tcha like my car? New paint job," he said. "Hey."

25 "What?"

"You're cute."

She pretended to fidget, chasing flies away from the door.

"Don'tcha believe me, or what?" he said.

"Look, I don't even know who you are," Connie said in disgust.

30 "Hey, Ellie's got a radio, see. Mine's broke down." He lifted his friend's arm and showed her the little transistor the boy was holding, and now Connie began to hear the music. It was the same program that was playing inside the house.

"Bobby King?" she said.

"I listen to him all the time. I think he's great."

"He's kind of great," Connie said reluctantly.

"Listen, that guy's *great.* He knows where the action is."

35 Connie blushed a little, because the glasses made it impossible for her to see just what this boy was looking at. She couldn't decide if she liked him or if he was just a jerk, and so she dawdled in the doorway and wouldn't come down or go back inside. She said, "What's all that stuff painted on your car?"

"Can'tcha read it?" He opened the door very carefully, as if he was afraid it might fall off. He slid out just as carefully, planting his feet firmly on the ground, the tiny metallic world in his glasses slowing down like gelatine hardening and in the midst of it Connie's bright green blouse. "This here is my name, to begin with," he said. ARNOLD FRIEND was written in tarlike black letters on the side, with a drawing of a round grinning face that reminded Connie of a pumpkin, except it wore sunglasses. "I wanta introduce myself, I'm Arnold Friend and that's my real name and I'm gonna be your friend, honey, and inside the car's Ellie Oscar, he's kinda shy." Ellie brought his transistor radio up to his shoulder and balanced it there. "Now these numbers are a secret code, honey," Arnold Friend explained. He read off the numbers 33, 19, 17 and raised his eyebrows at her to see what she thought of that, but she didn't think much of it. The left rear fender had been smashed and around it was written, on the gleaming gold background: DONE BY CRAZY WOMAN DRIVER. Connie had to laugh at that. Arnold Friend was pleased at her laughter and looked up at her. "Around the other side's a lot more—you wanta come and see them?"

"No."

"Why not?"

"Why should I?"

40 "Don'tcha wanta see what's on the car? Don'tcha wanta go for a ride?"

"I don't know."

"Why not?"

"I got things to do."

"Like what?"

45 "Things."

He laughed as if she had said something funny. He slapped his thighs. He was standing in a strange way, leaning back against the car as if he were balancing himself. He wasn't tall, only an inch or so taller than she would be if she came down to him. Connie liked the way he was dressed, which was the way all of them dressed: tight faded jeans stuffed into black, scuffed boots, a belt that pulled his waist in and showed how lean he was, and a white pull-over shirt that was a little soiled and showed the hard small muscles of his arms and shoulders. He looked as if he probably did hard work, lifting and carrying things. Even his neck looked muscular. And his face was a familiar face, somehow: the jaw and chin and cheeks slightly darkened, because he hadn't shaved for a day or two, and the nose long and hawk-like, sniffing as if she were a treat he was going to gobble up and it was all a joke.

"Connie, you ain't telling the truth. This is your day set aside for a ride with me and you know it," he said, still laughing. The way he straightened and recovered from his fit of laughing showed that it had been all fake.

"How do you know what my name is?" she said suspiciously.

"It's Connie."

50 "Maybe and maybe not."

"I know my Connie," he said, wagging his finger. Now she remembered him even better, back at the restaurant, and her cheeks warmed at the thought of how she sucked in her breath just at the moment she passed him—how she must have looked to him. And he had remembered her. "Ellie and I come out here especially for you," he said. "Ellie can sit in back. How about it?"

"Where?"

"Where what?"

"Where're we going?"

55 He looked at her. He took off the sunglasses and she saw how pale the skin around his eyes was, like holes that were not in shadow but instead in light. His eyes were chips of broken glass that catch the light in an amiable way. He smiled. It was as if the idea of going for a ride somewhere, to some place, was a new idea to him.

"Just for a ride, Connie sweetheart."

"I never said my name was Connie," she said.

"But I know what it is. I know your name and all about you, lots of things," Arnold Friend said. He had not moved yet but stood still leaning back against the side of his jalopy. "I took a special interest in you, such a pretty girl, and found out all about you like I know your parents and sister are gone some- wheres and I know where and how long they're going to be gone, and I know who you were with last night, and your best girl friend's name is Betty. Right?"

He spoke in a simple lilting voice, exactly as if he were reciting the words to a song. His smile assured her that everything was fine. In the car Ellie turned up the volume on his radio and did not bother to look around at them.

60   "Ellie can sit in the back seat," Arnold Friend said. He indicated his friend with a casual jerk of his chin, as if Ellie did not count and she should not bother with him.

"How'd you find out all that stuff?" Connie said.

"Listen: Betty Schultz and Tony Fitch and Jimmy Pettinger and Nancy Pet- tinger," he said, in a chant. "Raymond Stanley and Bob Hutter—"

"Do you know all those kids?"

"I know everybody."

65   "Look, you're kidding. You're not from around here."

"Sure."

"But—how come we never saw you before?"

"Sure you saw me before," he said. He looked down at his boots, as if he were a little offended. "You just don't remember."

"I guess I'd remember you," Connie said.

70   "Yeah?" He looked up at this, beaming. He was pleased. He began to mark time with the music from Ellie's radio, tapping his fists lightly together. Connie looked away from his smile to the car, which was painted so bright it almost hurt her eyes to look at it. She looked at that name, ARNOLD FRIEND. And up at the front fender was an expression that was familiar—MAN THE FLYING SAUCERS. It was an expression kids had used the year before, but didn't use this year. She looked at it for a while as if the words meant something to her that she did not yet know.

"What're you thinking about? Huh?" Arnold Friend demanded. "Not wor- ried about your hair blowing around in the car, are you?"

"No."

"Think I maybe can't drive good?"

"How do I know?"

75   "You're a hard girl to handle. How come?" he said. "Don't you know I'm your friend? Didn't you see me put my sign in the air when you walked by?"

"What sign?"

"My sign." And he drew an X in the air, leaning out toward her. They were maybe ten feet apart. After his hand fell back to his side the X was still in the air, almost visible. Connie let the screen door close and stood perfectly still in- side it, listening to the music from her radio and the boy's blend together. She stared at Arnold Friend. He stood there so stiffly relaxed, pretending to be re- laxed, with one hand idly on the door handle as if he were keeping himself up that way and had no intention of ever moving again. She recognized most things about him, the tight jeans that showed his thighs and buttocks and the greasy leather boots and the tight shirt, and even that slippery friendly smile of his, that sleepy dreamy smile that all the boys used to get across ideas they didn't want to put into words. She recognized all this and also the singsong way he talked, slightly mocking, kidding, but serious and a little melancholy, and she recognized the way he tapped one fist against the other in homage to the perpetual music behind him. But all these things did not come together.

She said suddenly, "Hey, how old are you?"

His smile faded. She could see then that he wasn't a kid, he was much older—thirty, maybe more. At this knowledge her heart began to pound faster.

80   "That's a crazy thing to ask. Can'tcha see I'm your own age?"

"Like hell you are."

"Or maybe a coupla years older, I'm eighteen."

"Eighteen?" she said doubtfully.

He grinned to reassure her and lines appeared at the corners of his mouth. His teeth were big and white. He grinned so broadly his eyes became slits and she saw how thick the lashes were, thick and black as if painted with a black tarlike material. Then he seemed to become embarrassed, abruptly, and looked over his shoulder at Ellie. "*Him,* he's crazy," he said. "Ain't he a riot, he's a nut, a real character." Ellie was still listening to the music. His sunglasses told nothing about what he was thinking. He wore a bright orange shirt unbuttoned halfway to show his chest, which was a pale, bluish chest and not muscular like Arnold Friend's. His shirt collar was turned up all around and the very tips of the collar pointed out past his chin as if they were protecting him. He was pressing the transistor radio up against his ear and sat there in a kind of daze, right in the sun.

85   "He's kinda strange," Connie said.

"Hey, she says you're kinda strange! Kinda strange!" Arnold Friend cried. He pounded on the car to get Ellie's attention. Ellie turned for the first time and Connie saw with shock that he wasn't a kid either—he had a fair, hairless face, cheeks reddened slightly as if the veins grew too close to the surface of his skin, the face of a forty-year-old baby. Connie felt a wave of dizziness rise in her at this sight and she stared at him as if waiting for something to change the shock of the moment, make it all right again. Ellie's lips kept shaping words, mumbling along with the words blasting in his ear.

"Maybe you two better go away," Connie said faintly.

"What? How come?" Arnold Friend cried. "We come out here to take you for a ride. It's Sunday." He had the voice of the man on the radio now. It was the same voice, Connie thought. "Don'tcha know it's Sunday all day and honey, no matter who you were with last night today you're with Arnold Friend and don't you forget it!—Maybe you better step out here," he said, and this last was in a different voice. It was a little flatter, as if the heat was finally getting to him.

"No. I got things to do."

90   "Hey."

"You two better leave."

"We ain't leaving until you come with us."

"Like hell I am—"

"Connie, don't fool around with me. I mean, I mean, don't fool *around,*" he said, shaking his head. He laughed incredulously. He placed his sunglasses on top of his head, carefully, as if he were indeed wearing a wig, and brought the stems down behind his ears. Connie stared at him, another wave of dizziness and fear rising in her so that for a moment he wasn't even in focus but was just a blur, standing there against his gold car, and she had the idea that he had driven up the driveway all right but had come from nowhere before that and belonged nowhere and that everything about him and even about the music that was so familiar to her was only half real.

95   "If my father comes and sees you—"

"He ain't coming. He's at a barbecue."

"How do you know that?"

"Aunt Tillie's. Right now they're—uh—they're drinking. Sitting around," he said vaguely, squinting as if he were staring all the way to town and over to Aunt Tillie's backyard. Then the vision seemed to get clear and he nodded energetically. "Yeah. Sitting around. There's your sister in a blue dress, huh? And high heels, the poor sad bitch—nothing like you sweetheart! And your mother's helping some fat woman with the corn, they're cleaning the corn—husking the corn—"

"What fat woman?" Connie cried.

100   "How do I know what fat woman. I don't know every goddam fat woman in the world!" Arnold Friend laughed.

"Oh, that's Mrs. Hornby. . . . Who invited her?" Connie said. She felt a little light-headed. Her breath was coming quickly.

"She's too fat. I don't like them fat. I like them the way you are, honey," he said, smiling sleepily at her. They stared at each other for a while, through the screen door. He said softly, "Now what you're going to do is this: you're going to come out that door. You're going to sit up front with me and Ellie's going to sit in the back, the hell with Ellie, right? This isn't Ellie's date. You're my date. I'm your lover, honey."

"What? You're crazy—"

"Yes, I'm your lover. You don't know what that is but you will," he said. "I know that too. I know all about you. But look: it's real nice and you couldn't ask for nobody better than me, or more polite. I always keep my word. I'll tell you how it is, I'm always nice at first, the first time. I'll hold you so tight you won't think you have to try to get away or pretend anything because you'll know you can't. And I'll come inside you where it's all secret and you'll give in to me and you'll love me—"

105   "Shut up! You're crazy!" Connie said. She backed away from the door. She put her hands against her ears as if she'd heard something terrible, something not meant for her. "People don't talk like that, you're crazy," she muttered. Her heart was almost too big now for her chest and its pumping made sweat break out all over her. She looked out to see Arnold Friend pause and then take

a step toward the porch lurching. He almost fell. But, like a clever drunken man, he managed to catch his balance. He wobbled in his high boots and grabbed hold of one of the porch posts.

"Honey?" he said. "You still listening?"

"Get the hell out of here!"

"Be nice, honey. Listen."

"I'm going to call the police—"

110 He wobbled again and out of the side of his mouth came a fast spat curse, an aside not meant for her to hear. But even this "Christ!" sounded forced. Then he began to smile again. She watched this smile come, awkward as if he were smiling from inside a mask. His whole face was a mask, she thought wildly, tanned down onto his throat but then running out as if he had plastered make-up on his face but had forgotten about his throat.

"Honey—? Listen, here's how it is. I always tell the truth and I promise you this: I ain't coming in that house after you."

"You better not! I'm going to call the police if you—if you don't—"

"Honey," he said, talking right through her voice, "honey, I'm not coming in there but you are coming out here. You know why?"

She was panting. The kitchen looked like a place she had never seen before, some room she had run inside but which wasn't good enough, wasn't going to help her. The kitchen window had never had a curtain, after three years, and there were dishes in the sink for her to do—probably—and if you ran your hand across the table you'd probably feel something sticky there.

115 "You listening, honey? Hey?"

"—going to call the police—"

"Soon as you touch the phone I don't need to keep my promise and can come inside. You won't want that."

She rushed forward and tried to lock the door. Her fingers were shaking. "But why lock it," Arnold Friend said gently, talking right into her face. "It's just a screen door. It's just nothing." One of his boots was at a strange angle, as if his foot wasn't in it. It pointed out to the left, bent at the ankle. "I mean, anybody can break through a screen door and glass and wood and iron or anything else if he needs to, anybody at all and specially Arnold Friend. If the place got lit up with a fire honey you'd come running out into my arms, right into my arms and safe at home—like you knew I was your lover and'd stopped fooling around. I don't mind a nice shy girl but I don't like no fooling around." Part of those words were spoken with a slight rhythmic lilt, and Connie somehow recognized them—the echo of a song from last year, about a girl rushing into her boy friend's arms and coming home again—

Connie stood barefoot on the linoleum floor, staring at him. "What do you want?" she whispered.

120 "I want you," he said.

"What?"

"Seen you that night and thought, that's the one, yes sir. I never needed to look any more."

"But my father's coming back. He's coming to get me. I had to wash my hair first—" She spoke in a dry, rapid voice, hardly raising it for him to hear.

"No, your daddy is not coming and yes, you had to wash your hair and you washed it for me. It's nice and shining and all for me, I thank you, sweetheart," he said, with a mock bow, but again he almost lost his balance. He had to bend and adjust his boots. Evidently his feet did not go all the way down; the boots must have been stuffed with something so that he would seem taller. Connie stared out at him and behind him Ellie in the car, who seemed to be looking off toward Connie's right, into nothing. This Ellie said, pulling the words out of the air one after another as if he were just discovering them, "You want me to pull out the phone?"

125   "Shut your mouth and keep it shut," Arnold Friend said, his face red from bending over or maybe from embarrassment because Connie had seen his boots. "This ain't none of your business."

"What—what are you doing? What do you want?" Connie said. "If I call the police they'll get you, they'll arrest you—"

"Promise was not to come in unless you touch that phone, and I'll keep that promise," he said. He resumed his erect position and tried to force his shoulders back. He sounded like a hero in a movie, declaring something important. He spoke too loudly and it was as if he were speaking to someone behind Connie. "I ain't made plans for coming in that house where I don't belong but just for you to come out to me, the way you should. Don't you know who I am?"

"You're crazy," she whispered. She backed away from the door but did not want to go into another part of the house, as if this would give him permission to come through the door. "What do you. . . . You're crazy, you . . ."

"Huh? What're you saying, honey?"

130   Her eyes darted everywhere in the kitchen. She could not remember what it was, this room.

"This is how it is, honey: you come out and we'll drive away, have a nice ride. But if you don't come out we're gonna wait till your people come home and then they're all going to get it."

"You want that telephone pulled out?" Ellie said. He held the radio away from his ear and grimaced, as if without the radio the air was too much for him.

"I toldja shut up, Ellie," Arnold Friend said, "you're deaf, get a hearing aid, right? Fix yourself up. This little girl's no trouble and's gonna be nice to me, so Ellie keep to yourself, this ain't your date—right? Don't hem in on me. Don't hog. Don't crush. Don't bird dog. Don't trail me," he said in a rapid meaningless voice, as if he were running through all the expressions he'd learned but was no longer sure which one of them was in style, then rushing on to new ones, making them up with his eyes closed, "Don't crawl under my fence, don't squeeze in my chipmunk hole, don't sniff my glue, suck my popsicle, keep your own greasy fingers on yourself!" He shaded his eyes and peered in at Connie, who was backed against the kitchen table. "Don't mind him honey he's just a creep. He's a dope. Right? I'm the boy for you and like I said you come out here nice like a lady and give me your hand, and nobody else gets hurt, I mean, your nice old bald-headed daddy and your mummy and your sister in her high heels. Because listen: why bring them in this?"

"Leave me alone," Connie whispered.

135 "Hey, you know that old woman down the road, the one with the chickens and stuff—you know her?"

"She's dead!"

"Dead? What? You know her?" Arnold Friend said.

"She's dead—"

"Don't you like her?"

140 "She's dead—she's—she isn't here any more—"

"But don't you like her, I mean, you got something against her? Some grudge or something?" Then his voice dipped as if he were conscious of a rudeness. He touched the sunglasses perched on top of his head as if to make sure they were still there. "Now you be a good girl."

"What are you going to do?"

"Just two things, or maybe three," Arnold Friend said. "But I promise it won't last long and you'll like me that way you get to like people you're close to. You will. It's all over for you here, so come on out. You don't want your people in any trouble, do you?"

She turned and bumped against a chair or something, hurting her leg, but she ran into the back room and picked up the telephone. Something roared in her ear, a tiny roaring, and she was so sick with fear that she could do nothing but listen to it—the telephone was clammy and very heavy and her fingers groped down to the dial but were too weak to touch it. She began to scream into the phone, into the roaring. She cried out, she cried for her mother, she felt her breath start jerking back and forth in her lungs as if it were something Arnold Friend were stabbing her with again and again with no tenderness. A noisy sorrowful wailing rose all about her and she was locked inside it the way she was locked inside the house.

145 After a while she could hear again. She was sitting on the floor with her wet back against the wall.

Arnold Friend was saying from the door, "That's a good girl. Put the phone back."

She kicked the phone away from her.

"No, honey. Pick it up. Put it back right."

She picked it up and put it back. The dial tone stopped.

150 "That's a good girl. Now you come outside."

She was hollow with what had been fear, but what was now just an emptiness. All that screaming had blasted it out of her. She sat, one leg cramped under her, and deep inside her brain was something like a pinpoint of light that kept going and would not let her relax. She thought, I'm not going to see my mother again. She thought, I'm not going to sleep in my bed again. Her bright green blouse was all wet.

Arnold Friend said, in a gentle-loud voice that was like a stage voice, "The place where you came from ain't there any more, and where you had in mind to go is cancelled out. This place you are now—inside your daddy's house—is nothing but a cardboard box I can knock down any time. You know that and always did know it. You hear me?"

She thought, I have got to think. I have to know what to do.

"We'll go out to a nice field, out in the country here where it smells so nice and it's sunny," Arnold Friend said. "I'll have my arms around you so you won't need to try to get away and I'll show you what love is like, what it does. The hell with this house! It looks solid all right," he said. He ran a fingernail down the screen and the noise did not make Connie shiver, as it would have the day before. "Now put your hand on your heart, honey. Feel that? That feels solid too but we know better, be nice to me, be sweet like you can because what else is there for a girl like you but to be sweet and pretty and give in?—and get away before her people come back?"

155 She felt her pounding heart. Her hand seemed to enclose it. She thought for the first time in her life that it was nothing that was hers, that belonged to her, but just a pounding, living thing inside this body that wasn't really hers either.

"You don't want them to get hurt," Arnold Friend went on. "Now get up, honey. Get up all by yourself."

She stood.

"Now turn this way. That's right. Come over here to me—Ellie, put that away, didn't I tell you? You dope. You miserable creepy dope," Arnold Friend said. His words were not angry but only part of an incantation. The incantation was kindly. "Now come out through the kitchen to me honey and let's see a smile, try it, you're a brave sweet little girl and now they're eating corn and hotdogs cooked to bursting over an outdoor fire, and they don't know one thing about you and never did and honey you're better than them because not a one of them would have done this for you."

Connie felt the linoleum under her feet; it was cool. She brushed her hair back out of her eyes. Arnold Friend let go of the post tentatively and opened his arms for her, his elbows pointing in toward each other and his wrists limp, to show that this was an embarrassed embrace and a little mocking, he didn't want to make her self-conscious.

160 She put out her hand against the screen. She watched herself push the door slowly open as if she were safe back somewhere in the other doorway, watching this body and this head of long hair moving out into the sunlight where Arnold Friend waited.

"My sweet little blue-eyed girl," he said, in a half-sung sigh that had nothing to do with her brown eyes but was taken up just the same by the vast sunlit reaches of the land behind him and on all sides of him, so much land that Connie had never seen before and did not recognize except to know that she was going to it.

When Characters from the Page Are Made Flesh on the Screen

BY JOYCE CAROL OATES

Some years ago in the American Southwest there surfaced a tabloid psychopath known as "The Pied Piper of Tucson." I have forgotten his name but his specialty was the seduction and occasional murder of teen-age girls. He may or may not have had actual accomplices, but his bizarre activities were known among a circle of teen-agers in the Tucson area; for some reason they kept his secrets, deliberately did not inform parents or police. It was this fact, not the fact of the mass murderer himself, that struck me at the time. And this was a pre-Manson time, this was early or mid-1960's.

The "Pied Piper" mimicked teen-agers in their talk, dress and behavior, but he was not a teen-ager—he was a man in his early 30's. Rather short, he stuffed rags in his leather boots to give himself height. (And sometimes walked unsteadily as a consequence: did none among his admiring constituency notice?) He charmed his victims, to the bewilderment of others who fancy themselves free of all lunatic attractions. "The Pied Piper of Tucson": a trashy dream, a tabloid archetype, sheer artifice, comedy, cartoon—surrounded, however improbably, and finally tragically, by real people. You think that, if you look twice, he won't be there. But there he is.

I don't remember any longer where I first read about "The Pied Piper"—very likely in *Life* magazine. I do recall deliberately not reading the full article because I didn't want to be distracted by too much detail.

It was not after all the mass murderer himself who intrigued me, but the disturbing fact that a number of teen-agers—from "good" families—aided and abetted his crimes. This is the sort of thing authorities and responsible citizens invariably call "inexplicable" because they can't find explanations for it. *They* would not have fallen under this maniac's spell, after all.

An early draft of my short story "Where Are You Going, Where Have You Been?"—from which the current film "Smooth Talk" has been adapted by Joyce Chopra and Tom Cole—had the rather too explicit title "Death and the Maiden." It was cast in a mode of fiction to which I am still partial—indeed, every third or fourth story of mine is probably in this mode—"realistic allegory," it might be called. It is Hawthornian, romantic, shading into parable. Like the medieval German engraving from which my title was taken the story was minutely detailed yet clearly an allegory of the fatal attractions of death (or the devil). An innocent young girl is seduced by way of her own vanity; she mistakes death for erotic romance of a particularly American/trashy sort.

In subsequent drafts the story changed its tone, its focus, its language, its title. It became "Where Are You Going, Where Have You Been?" Written at a time when the author was intrigued by the music of Bob Dylan, particularly the hauntingly elegiac song "It's All Over Now, Baby Blue," it was dedicated to

Bob Dylan. The charismatic mass murderer drops into the background and his innocent victim, a 15-year-old, moves into the foreground. She becomes the true protagonist of the tale, courting and being courted by her fate, a self-styled 1950's pop figure, alternately absurd and winning.

There is no suggestion in the published story that "Arnold Friend" has seduced and murdered other young girls, or even that he necessarily intends to murder Connie. Is his interest "merely" sexual? (Nor is there anything about the complicity of other teen-agers. I saved that yet more provocative note for a current story, "Testimony.") Connie is shallow, vain, silly, hopeful, doomed—perhaps as I saw, and still see, myself?—but capable nonetheless of an unexpected gesture of heroism at the story's end.

Her smooth-talking seducer, who cannot lie, promises her that her family will be unharmed if she gives herself to him; and so she does. The story ends abruptly at the point of her "crossing over." We don't know the nature of her sacrifice, only that she is generous enough to make it.

In adapting a narrative so spare and thematically foreshortened as "Where Are You Going, Where Have You Been?" film director Joyce Chopra and screenwriter Tom Cole were required to do a good deal of filling in, expanding, inventing. Connie's story becomes lavishly, and lovingly, textured; she is not an allegorical figure so much as a "typical" teen-age girl (if Laura Dern, spectacularly good-looking, can be so defined).

Joyce Chopra, who has done documentary films on contemporary teen-age culture, and, yet more authoritatively, has an adolescent daughter of her own, creates in "Smooth Talk" a believable world for Connie to inhabit. Or worlds: as in the original story there is Connie-at-home, and there is Connie-with-her-friends. Two 15-year-old girls, two finely honed styles, two voices, sometimes but not often overlapping. It is one of the marvelous visual features of the film that we *see* Connie and her friends transform themselves, once they are safely free of parental observation. What freedom, what joy! The girls claim their true identities in the neighborhood shopping mall!

"Smooth Talk" is, in a way, as much Connie's mother's story as it is Connie's; its center of gravity, its emotional nexus, is frequently with the mother—played by Mary Kay Place. (Though the mother's sexual jealousy of her daughter is slighted in the film.) Connie's ambiguous relationship with her affable, somewhat mysterious father (played by Levon Helm) is an excellent touch: I had thought, subsequent to the story's publication, that I should have built up the father, suggesting, as subtly as I could, an attraction there paralleling the attraction Connie feels for her seducer Arnold Friend.

Treat Williams impersonates Arnold Friend as Arnold Friend impersonates—is it James Dean? James Dean regarding himself in mirrors, doing James Dean impersonations? Laura Dern is so right as "my" Connie that I may come to think I modeled the fictitious girl on her, in the way that writers frequently delude themselves about notions of causality.

My difficulties with "Smooth Talk" have primarily to do with my chronic hesitation—a justifiable shyness, I'm sure—about seeing/hearing work of mine abstracted from its contexture of language. All writers know that language is their subject; quirky word choices, patterns of rhythm, enigmatic pauses, punctuation marks. Where the quick-scanner sees "quick" writing, the writer conceals nine-tenths of his iceberg.

Of course we all have "real" subjects, and we will fight to the death to defend these subjects, but beneath the tale-telling it is the tale-telling that grips us so very fiercely: "the soul at the *white heat*" in Emily Dickinson's words. Because of this it is always an eerie experience for me, as a writer, to hear "my" dialogue floating back to me from the external world; particularly when it is surrounded, as of course it must be, by "other" dialogue I seem not to recall having written. Perhaps a panic reaction sets in—perhaps I worry that I might be responsible for knowing what "I" meant, in writing things "I" didn't write? Like a student who has handed in work not entirely his own, and dreads interrogation from his teacher?

It is startling too to *see* fictitious characters inhabiting, with such seeming aplomb, roles that until now seemed private, flat on the page. (I don't, like many of my writing colleagues, feel affronted, thinking, "*That* isn't how he/she looks!" I think instead, guiltily, "Is *that* how he/she really looks?")

I have also had a number of plays produced and so characteristically doubtful am I about intruding into my directors' territories that I nearly always abrogate my authority to them. The writer works in a single dimension, the director works in three. I assume that they are professionals to their fingertips; authorities in their medium as I am an authority (if I am) in mine. I would fiercely defend the placement of a semicolon in one of my novels, but I would probably have deferred fairly quickly to Joyce Chopra's decision to reverse the story's ending, turn it upside-down, in a sense, so that the film ends not with death, not with a sleepwalker's crossing-over to her fate, but upon a sense of reconciliation, rejuvenation. Laura Dern's Connie is no longer "my" Connie at the film's conclusion; she is very much alive, assertive, strong-willed—a girl, perhaps, of the mid-1980's, and not of the mid-1960's.

A girl's loss of virginity, bittersweet but not necessarily tragic. Not today. A girl's coming of age that involves her succumbing to, but then rejecting, the "trashy dreams" of her pop teen-age culture. "Where Are You Going, Where Have You Been?" deliberately betrays itself as allegorical in its conclusion: Death and Death's chariot (a funky souped-up convertible) have come for the Maiden. Awakening is, in the story's final lines, moving out into the sunlight where Arnold Friend waits:

"My sweet little blue-eyed girl," he said in a half-sung sigh that had nothing to do with (Connie's) brown eyes but was taken up just the same by the vast sunlit reaches of the land behind him and on all sides of him—so much land that Connie had never seen before and did not recognize except to know that she was going to it.

I quite understand that this is an unfilmable conclusion, and "Where Are You Going, Where Have You Been?" is in fact an unfilmable short story. But Joyce Chopra's "Smooth Talk" is an accomplished and sophisticated movie that attempts to do just that.

In Fairyland, without a Map: Connie's Exploration Inward in Joyce Carol Oates' "Where Are You Going, Where Have You Been?"

GRETCHEN SCHULZ
R. J. R. ROCKWOOD

Joyce Carol Oates has stated that her prize-winning story *Where Are You Going, Where Have You Been?* (Fall, 1966) came to her "more or less in a piece" after hearing Bob Dylan's song *It's All Over Now, Baby Blue,* and then reading about a "killer in some Southwestern state," and thinking about "the old legends and folk songs of Death and the Maiden."[1] The "killer" that Miss Oates had in mind, the one on whom her character Arnold Friend is modeled, was twenty-three-year-old Charles Schmid of Tucson, Arizona. Schmid had been charged with the murders of three teen-age girls, and was the subject of a lengthy article in the March 4, 1966, issue of *Life* magazine. It is not surprising that this account should have generated mythic musings in Miss Oates—musings that culminated in a short story which has depths as mythic as any of the "old legends and folk songs." The *Life* reporter, Don Moser, himself had found in this raw material such an abundance of the reality which is the stuff of myth, that he entitled his article "The Pied Piper of Tucson."

The article states that Schmid—or "Smitty," as he was called—had sought deliberately "to create an exalted, heroic image of himself." To the teen-agers in Smitty's crowd, who "had little to do but look each other over," their leader was a "folk hero . . . more dramatic, more theatrical, more *interesting* than anyone

else in their lives," and seemed to embody the very lyrics of a then popular song: "Hey, c'mon babe, follow me,/ I'm the Pied Piper, follow me,/ I'm the Pied Piper,/ And I'll show you where it's at." With a face which was "his own creation: the hair dyed raven black, the skin darkened to a deep tan with pancake make-up, the lips whitened, the whole effect heightened by a mole he had painted on one cheek," Smitty would cruise "in a golden car," haunting "all the teen-age hangouts," looking for pretty girls, especially ones with long blond hair. Because he was only five-foot-three, Smitty "habitually stuffed three or four inches of old rags and tin cans into the bottoms of his high-topped boots to make himself taller," even though the price he paid for that extra height was an awkward, stumbling walk that made people think he had "wooden feet."[2]

In his transformation into the Arnold Friend of *Where Are You Going, Where Have You Been?*, Smitty underwent the kind of apotheosis[3] which he had tried, by means of bizarre theatrics, to achieve in actuality, for Arnold is the exact transpersonal[4] counterpart of the real-life "Pied Piper of Tucson." Thus, although Arnold is a "realistic" figure, drawn from the life of a specific psychopathic killer, that superficial realism is only incidental to the more essential realism of the mythic characteristics—the archetypal qualities—he shares with the man who was his model. Asked to comment on Arnold, Miss Oates reveals that, to her, the character is *truly* mythological. No longer quite human, he functions as a personified subjective factor: "Arnold Friend," she says, "is a fantastic figure: he is Death, he is the 'elf-[king]' of the ballads, he is the Imagination, he is a Dream, he is a Lover, a Demon, *and all that.*"[5]

If *'Where Are You Going, Where Have You Been?'* is a "portrait of a psychopathic killer masquerading as a teenager,"[6] it is clear that this portrait is created in the mind of Connie, the teen-age protagonist of the story, and that it exists *there only*. It is thus Connie's inner world that determines how Arnold is, or has to be, at least in her eyes, for her personal problems are so compelling that they effectively rearrange and remodel the world of objective reality. Arnold Friend's own part in the creation of his image—whether he deliberately set about to become the "fantastic" figure he is, or seems to be, as his model, Smitty, did—Miss Oates ignores altogether. She is interested only in Connie, Arnold's young victim, and in how Connie's psychological state shapes her perceptions. We find—as we might expect with a writer who characterizes the mode in which she writes as "psychological realism"[7]—that the "fantastic" or mythological qualities of Arnold Friend (and of all those in the story) are presented as subjective rather than objective facts, aspects of the transpersonal psyche projected outward, products of the unconscious mental processes of a troubled adolescent girl.

Toward Arnold Friend, and what he represents, Connie is ambivalent:

she is both fascinated and frightened. She is, after all, at that confusing age when a girl feels, thinks, and acts both like a child, put off by a possible lover, and like a woman, attracted to him. Uncertain how to bridge the chasm between "home" and "anywhere that was not home," she stands—or wavers—at the boundary between childhood and adulthood, hesitant and yet anxious to enter the new world of experience which is opening before her:

> Everything about her had two sides to it, one for home and one for anywhere that was not home: her walk, which could be childlike and bobbing, or languid enough to make anyone think she was hearing music in her head; her mouth, which was pale and smirking most of the time, but bright and pink on these evenings out; her laugh, which was cynical and drawling at home—"Ha, ha, very funny,"—but high-pitched and nervous anywhere else, like the jingling of the charms on her bracelet.[8]

That her laugh is "high-pitched and nervous" when she is "any- where that was not home" betrays the fact that Connie, like all young people, needs help as she begins to move from the past to the future, as she begins the perilous inward journey towards maturity. This journey is an essential part of the adolescent's search for personal identity, and though it is a quest that he must undertake by himself, traditionally it has been the responsibility of culture to help by providing symbolic maps of the territory through which he will travel, territory that lies on the other side of consciousness.

Such models of behavior and maps of the unknown are generally provided by the products of fantasy—myth, legend, and folklore.

Folk fairy tales have been especially useful in this way. In his book, *The Uses of Enchantment: The Meaning and Importance of Fairy Tales* (1976), Bruno Bettelheim argues that children's fairy tales offer "symbolic images" that suggest "happy solutions"[9] to the problems of adolescence. Indeed, Joyce Carol Oates herself has Hugh Petrie, the caricaturist in her novel *The Assassins* (1975) observe that "fairy tales are analogous to life as it is lived in the family."[10] In her fiction both short and long Miss Oates makes frequent use of fairy tale material. Again and again she presents characters and situations which parallel corresponding motifs from the world of folk fantasy. And never is this more true than in the present story—never in all the eight novels and eleven collections of short stories which she has written at last count. Woven into the complex texture of *Where Are You Going, Where Have You Been?* are motifs from such tales as *The Spirit in the Bottle, Snow White, Cinderella, Sleeping Beauty, Rapunzel, Little Red Riding Hood,* and *The Three Little Pigs.*[11] *The Pied Piper of Hamelin,* which ends tragically and so according to Bettelheim does not qualify as a proper fairy tale,[12] serves as the "frame device" that contains all the other tales.

There is a terrible irony here, for although the story is full of fairy tales, Connie, its protagonist, is not. Connie represents an entire generation of young people who have grown up—or tried to—without the help of those bedtime stories which not only entertain the child, but also enable him vicariously to experience and work through problems which he will encounter in adolescence. The only "stories" Connie knows are those of the sexually provocative but superficial lyrics of the popular songs she loves or of the equally insubstantial movies she attends. Such songs and movies provide either no models of behavior for her to imitate, or dangerously inappropriate ones. Connie has thus been led to believe that life and, in particular, love will be "sweet, gentle, the way it was in the movies and promised in songs." She has no idea that life actually can be just as grim as in folk fairy tales. The society that is depicted in *Where Are You Going, Where Have You Been?* has failed to make available to children like Connie maps of the unconscious such as fairy tales provide, because it has failed to recognize that in the unconscious past and future coalesce,[13] and that, psychologically, where the child is going is where he has already been. Since Connie has been left—in the words of yet another of the popular songs—to "wander through that wonderland alone"—it is small wonder, considering her lack of spiritual preparation, that Connie's journey there soon becomes a terrifying schizophrenic separation from reality, with prognosis for recovery extremely poor.

The fact that the Oates story, like the magazine article which inspired it, is framed around the motif of the Pied Piper is significant, for this device serves to fix blame for the catastrophe which the story describes. The motif suggests that the adults of Connie's world have made the same mistake as the Burghers[14] of Hamelin seven centuries before: having failed to live up to their moral obligations by refusing to "pay the piper," they themselves—albeit unknowingly—have unleashed the very force which will prove destructive to their children. What kind of force this is, and its particular implications for Connie, we can understand more clearly by interpreting the symbolism underlying the fate of the legendary children of Hamelin: led outside the comfortable sanity of their walled city, the children disappear into that emblem of the devouring unconscious, the Koppenberg . . . victims, we would say, of an acute, collective psychosis. Assuming that the eternal patterns recur, each time as though for the first and last time, then this will be Connie's fate too, and her own psychosis will likewise have no remission. Certainly Arnold Friend is such that Connie cannot keep from following him, perhaps because in following him she is following the popular music she loves, music with which he is not only closely identified, but of which he is the personification. Thus, when Connie, "hearing music in her head," wanders into the bottle-shaped drive-in restaurant, charmed by "the music that made everything so good: the music . . . always in the background, like music at a church service," it is there that she first sees him. He later arrives at her house with a transistor radio which is playing "the same program that was playing inside the house," a program which leaves Connie feeling "bathed in a glow of slow-pulsed joy that seemed to rise mysteriously out of the music itself." Arnold even talks in a "simple lilting voice, exactly as if he were reciting the words to a song." There are many more passages of this kind, but let these suffice to show that Arnold is, indeed, depicted as a Pied Piper, incarnated by society's refusal to live up to its cultural obligation to provide what is needed to help the adolescent make it safely through to adulthood.

The help provided by fairy tales proper is such that a child can learn to compensate even when adult society makes errors of the gravest sort, capping with a happy ending a situation which might otherwise prove tragic for the child. Accordingly, the force which lures all save one of the unwitting children of Hamelin to their psychological death in the Koppenberg[15] is identical to that which the child is taught to tame in the fairy tale *Spirit in the Bottle*. For Connie, the "bottle" is the drive-in restaurant where the teen-agers hang out, a restaurant "shaped like a big bottle, though squatter than a real bottle . . . [and] on its cap a revolving figure of a grinning boy holding a hamburger aloft." The boy on the bottle-cap reminds us of "the boy named Eddie" inside the restaurant who, appropriately, sits *eddying* on his stool, "turning himself jerkily around in semi-circles and then stopping and turning back again," motion which suggests that bottled up sexual pressures are building, ever more insistent in their demand for release. Eddie takes Connie off for some petting, some rubbing that arouses her sexuality, too, until in her mind his face dissolves "into a single face that was not even a face but an idea, a feeling, mixed up with the urgent insistent pounding of the music and the humid night air of July." On this same visit to the restaurant Connie arouses Arnold Friend, who wags his finger at her, laughs, and says, " 'Gonna get you, baby'," and who at this moment reveals that he is not only the Pied Piper, but also that hostile spirit in the bottle which is described in the fairy tale.

When the woodcutter's son discovers *his* mysterious bottle and releases a spirit which likewise threatens to destroy *him,* he manages to entrap the spirit once again, agreeing to release it only when it agrees to share its special powers with him, powers which enable the boy to become the "greatest physician in the land." As in the fairy tale, Connie has uncorked the bottle, but because she is unacquainted with this part of the psyche, she is not equipped to recognize the grinning boy atop the bottle-cap or the laughing Arnold Friend as a potentially destructive force which must be controlled if it is to make a positive contribution to her personality. What complicates the attempt to control this force is that it disguises itself as mere sexuality, as is evident from the fairy tale in the fact that the bottle is clearly phallic and the boy's handling of it masturbatory: if we consider that what leads to the boy's taking flight and finding the bottle is his father's belittling him for incompetence at chopping wood, we can say that, psychologically, the boy is seeking compensation in an eroticised flood of negative content from the unconscious. Bettelheim points out that a fairy tale like *Spirit in the Bottle* deals with two problems that confront the child as he struggles to establish a sense of identity: parental belittlement, and integration of a divided personality.[16] In Connie's case, her mother's belittling remarks that "Connie couldn't do a thing, her mind was all filled with trashy daydreams," certainly have contributed to Connie's two-sidedness, with her one personality "for home" and another for "anywhere that was not home," a division also apparent in the relationship between Connie and the "girl friend" who accompanies her to the bottle-shaped restaurant— the two are so poorly differentiated

as to suggest a mere *doubling* of Connie, rather than two separate individuals. While such personality division may at first glance seem pathological, it is not, according to Bettelheim, necessarily abnormal, since "the manner in which the child can bring some order into his world view is by dividing everything into opposites," and that "in the later oedipal[17] and post oedipal ages, this splitting extends to the child himself."[18] In *Spirit in the Bottle,* the degraded hero, reacting to the anguish of being regarded by his parent as stupid and incompetent, withdraws into himself, undergoes a split into positive and negative aspects, de-energizes the negative (as represented by the spirit that comes out of the bottle), and then successfully reintegrates his personality, achieving a durable and socially productive synthesis. Had Connie been familiar with this fairy tale, she would have known that however deplorable her situation might seem at a given moment, the means toward an eventual happy solution is in learning to interact with the unconscious in such a way as to emulate the woodcutter's son, who, *by asserting rational control over the terms of the spirit's release into consciousness,* is able to demonstrate to himself and the world that he is not only wiser and better than his parent, but positively the "greatest physician in the land."

Knowledge of this tale alone, however, would not suffice, for it is merely a beginning: to be assured of safe passage through what Bettelheim terms "that thorniest of thickets, the oedipal period,"[19] a child like Connie would need to have absorbed the wisdom of the other fairy tales to which Miss Oates alludes, tales such as *Snow White, Cinderella,*

Rapunzel, and *Little Red Riding Hood.* By their applicability to Connie's situation, these tales reveal that at its deepest level Connie's most compelling psychological problem is *unresolved oedipal conflict, aggravated by sibling rivalry.*

Suggestive of *Snow White* is Connie's "habit of craning her neck to glance into mirrors, or checking other people's faces to make sure her own was all right" (as though other people's faces were mirrors, too); and we are told also that her mother, "who noticed everything and knew everything"—as though with the wicked queen's magic power— "hadn't much reason any longer to look at her own face," and so was jealous of her daughter's beauty and "always after Connie." Arnold Friend's sunglasses also mirror everything, which means that, in this instance, he personifies the Magic Mirror, and, of course, he finds Connie the fairest one of all. In his words, "Seen you that night and thought, that's the one, yes sir, I never needed to look anymore." Though he thus serves as Prince, there is a hint of the dwarf motif in Arnold's short stature and obvious phallicism; and most particularly is this true of his friend, Ellie Oscar, a case of arrested development, whose face is that of a "forty-year-old baby." Connie's "Someday My Prince Will Come" daydreams, plus the many references to how dazed and sleepy she always is, especially the day Arnold comes for her, when she "lay languidly about the airless little room" and "breathed in and breathed out with each gentle rise and fall of her chest"—these, too, suggest *Snow White* and, for that matter, *Sleeping Beauty,* whose heroine in the Brothers Grimm is, like Connie, fifteen.

The oedipal implications of *Snow White* are evident in the fact that, as Bettelheim points out, the queen's Magic Mirror speaks not with the mother's but the daughter's voice, revealing the jealous child's own sense of inferiority and frustration projected onto her mother. The father's romantic feelings for the daughter are never at issue in such a fairy tale, and he is generally depicted as weak, ineffectual, and oblivious to the struggle that ensues between mother and daughter[20]—exactly as in Miss Oates' story:

> Their father was away at work most of the time and when he came home he wanted supper and he read the newspaper at supper and after supper he went to bed. He didn't bother talking much to them, but around his bent head Connie's mother kept picking at her until Connie wished her mother was dead and she herself was dead and it was all over.

It would be difficult to find a more striking emblem of mother-daughter oedipal conflict than in this passage, where the second death wish serves as punishment for the first.

Bettelheim observes that whenever the child's feeling of "degradation" is the result of "oedipal entanglement of father and daughter," the "Cinderella" theme emerges.[21] Unlike *Snow White,* however, *Cinderella* centers on the "agonies and hopes which form the essential content of sibling rivalry . . . [since] 'having lived among the ashes' was a symbol of being debased in comparison to one's siblings."[22] In this case, the relationship between Connie and her sister June is a classical statement of the pattern:

> Her sister June was twenty-four and still lived at home. She was a

secretary in the high school Connie attended, and if that wasn't bad enough—with her in the same building—she was so plain and chunky and steady that Connie had to hear her praised all the time by her mother and her mother's sisters. June did this, June did that. . . .

Although grown up, June has not only not left home, but, in a sense, she is still in high school: this suggests that June is an even greater victim of oedipal entanglement than Connie—or, to put it another way, that June is Connie projected nine years into the future. What we have is thus a feminine version of the tale *Two Brothers* in which the personality is split between "striving for independence and self-assertion" (Connie) and "the opposite tendency to remain safely home, tied to the parents" (June).[23] Implied also is the dichotomy underlying *Sinbad the Seaman and Sinbad the Porter,* in which the former character represents the "pleasure-oriented id" (Connie) and the latter the "reality-oriented ego" (June).[24] In this instance the ego is oriented toward the reality of permanent oedipal fixation, and therefore constitutes a negative personality, conforming to the Jungian concept of the *shadow.*[25] Perhaps the saddest commentary on the situation in Miss Oates' story is the fact that the personality receiving positive reinforcement is Connie's shadow: "If June's name was mentioned her mother's tone was approving, and if Connie's name was mentioned it was disapproving."

The theme of debasement with respect to one's siblings is, of course, not the only link between this story and *Cinderella.* Connie, with her other personality for "anywhere that was not home," suggests *Cinderella,* too, especially in the magical transformation from child to woman which she undergoes on her nights out. The description of the drive-in restaurant, with its music, and the boys with whom the girls pair up, and their feeling that the event is a wonderful experience which must end too soon—all of this brings to mind Cinderella's ball, particularly since it is here that Connie meets Arnold Friend, her "Prince Charming." And it is this meeting which sends him seeking her out and finding her, barefoot, in the kitchen. Certainly the "convertible jalopy painted gold" suggests *Cinderella,* though in the fairy tale it is Cinderella herself who has the "convertible" vehicle. This gold-painted car reminds us of a royal chariot, too, especially with the horn sounding as though to announce the arrival of royalty when the car comes up Connie's drive. Still more obvious in its reference to the fairy tale is the drawing on the car of "a round, grinning face that reminded Connie of a pumpkin, except it wore sunglasses" and was signed "ARNOLD FRIEND." It is also pertinent that Arnold proclaims that he has come to take her away, and that, as he talks, Connie notices "He had the voice of the man on the radio now," a man who has been mentioned several times, whose name suggests royalty epitomized, a man called "Bobby King."

If Connie is Cinderella, she is also, by virtue of her "long dark blond hair that drew anyone's eye to it," Rapunzel. On the day of Arnold's arrival, Connie "washed her hair so that it could dry all day long in the sun." At the first sound of the car, "her fingers snatched at her hair, checking it, and she whispered, 'Christ. Christ,' wondering how she looked." While she talks with

Arnold, she makes the most of her hair: "Connie smirked and let her hair fall loose over one shoulder." Later, frightened by the desire she has aroused in him, she argues that her father is coming back to the house for her, that she has had to wash her hair in preparation for his return, but Arnold says, "No, your daddy is not coming and yes, you had to wash your hair and you washed it for me. It's nice and shining and all for me. I thank you sweetheart." Again, at the very end of the story, Connie watches "this body and this head of long hair moving out into the sunlight where Arnold Friend waited." It is obvious that Connie's *crowning glory* is, indeed, her hair, that she uses it to draw boys to her, among them Arnold Friend, and that Arnold, like the Prince in the fairy tale, takes her away from a place where she feels "locked inside." The fact that in the fairy tale the Prince is temporarily blinded by thorns when he falls from the tower where Rapunzel is locked is perhaps echoed in Arnold's peculiar eyes, "like holes . . . like chips of broken glass," which he covers with those dark glasses.

Why Arnold Friend is conjured up when it is, as she claims, her father that Connie is waiting for, becomes clear if we consider that Arnold, the Prince of *Snow White, Sleeping Beauty, Cinderella,* and *Rapunzel,* is also the Big Bad Wolf of *Little Red Riding Hood,* a tale which, according to Bettelheim, "deals with the daughter's unconscious wish to be seduced by her father (the wolf)."[26] If Arnold represents an erotic transformation of Connie's father, then this suggests that Connie's oedipal death-wish for her mother has undergone psychological realization. This in turn sheds light on that curious conversation between Arnold and Connie concerning "that old woman down the road" whom Connie insists is dead (" 'She's dead—she's—she isn't here any more—' "), but about whom Arnold says " 'But don't you like her, I mean, you got something against her? Some grudge or something?' " Connie's overreaction, so revealing in its guilt and terror, tells us that she has displaced onto the "old woman" the homicidal impulses unconsciously intended for her mother, an indiscretion for which she is already punishing herself through Arnold Friend. Bettelheim observes that when Little Red Riding Hood is swallowed up by the wolf, she is being "punished for arranging for the wolf to do away with a mother figure."[27]

Since one of Arnold's more lupine[28] characteristics is his *hairiness,* it is odd, though appropriate psychologically, considering that Arnold is experienced as a transformation of her "nice old bald-headed daddy," that Connie cannot keep from seeing "as a wig" Arnold's shaggy, shabby, black hair." But Arnold's hairiness is not the only sign that Connie's daddy-substitute is wolvish. He also has trouble standing and moving about, which suggests a four-footed animal masquerading as a man. When he first gets out of his car, he moves "carefully, planting his feet firmly on the ground." Later, he stands "in a strange way, leaning back against the car as if he were balancing himself." Later still, "He wobble[s] in his high boots and grab[s] hold of one of the porch posts." No wonder Connie has the uneasy feeling that "his feet do not go all the way down" into those boots as they should. Then, of course, there are Arnold's teeth, so "big and white," and his way of "sniffing" at Connie as though "she were a treat he was going to gobble up." What could be more reminiscent of the Wolf in *Little Red Riding Hood?* And we should add that Arnold's talk of tearing Connie's house down reminds us of the Wolf in *The Three Little Pigs,* also. When Connie tries to lock the screen, Arnold says:

> "But why lock it . . . It's just a screen door. It's just nothing . . . I mean, anybody can break through a screen door and glass and wood and iron or anything else if he needs to, anybody at all, and specially Arnold Friend. If the place got lit up with a fire, honey, you'd come runnin' out into my arms."

Later, in a statement that accurately epitomizes Connie's entire situation, he says: " 'This place you are now—inside your daddy's house—is nothing but a cardboard box I can knock down any time. You know that and always did know it'."

If the structure of Connie's life—and of her psyche—were not, indeed, as flimsy as cardboard, she might be able to deal with Arnold Friend even as Beauty deals with the Beast who is *her* daddy-substitute; she might learn to love him for himself and so transform him into a Prince again. But Connie lacks the familial and psychic strength which allows Beauty and her love to mature.[29] She is still just as "little" as Little Red Riding Hood. And, as we shall see, her confrontation with "the Beast"—with the wolvish Arnold Friend—makes her more childlike, not less; she regresses to what Bettelheim describes as a "more primitive, earlier form of existence,"[30] as Red Riding Hood does

under similar circumstances. Of course, "in typical fairy-story fashion" Red Riding Hood's regression is "impressively exaggerated." She goes all the way back to "the pre-birth existence in the womb" when she is swallowed by the Wolf (an act which has sexual significance, too). And she must then be cut from that "womb" by the Woodcutter, to emerge as a "born again" Red Riding Hood, a child who has learned that she is a child and still too young to deal with the Wolf.[31] Miss Oates is not free to exaggerate so fantastically, but she can and does suggest that Connie's psychological experience parallels Red Riding Hood's—in all respects save one. In Connie's case, Arnold Friend is the Woodcutter as well as the Wolf.

Connie begins to regress to a more childlike state as soon as she realizes that Arnold is more Wolf than Prince, more interested in animal sex than happy-ever-after romance. When he suddenly announces, " 'I'm your lover. You don't know what that is yet but you will'," she is frightened, and when he proceeds to explain "what that is" in some detail, she is more frightened still. Her flirtatious words and gestures give way to the frantic words and gestures of a child—and a very young child at that: " 'Shut up! You're crazy!' Connie said. . . . She put her hands up against her ears as if she'd heard something terrible, something not meant for her. 'People don't talk like that, you're crazy,' she muttered." Furthermore, while she is saying this, she "back[s] away from the door," and so backs away from that symbolic threshold between "home" and "not home," childhood and womanhood, where she has been hovering ever since Arnold arrived. She has not locked the door, though, and when she remembers that fact and tries to do so, with fingers clumsy as a child's, she fails. A "wave of dizziness and fear" has left her sweating, "panting," "shaking"—utterly unable to save herself from the Wolf. Of course, we must not forget that this Wolf actually embodies Connie's own sexual impulses, a fact which implies that her childlike inability to save herself from him is complicated by a womanly desire to give herself to him. And, indeed, the very portions of the text which suggest that Connie is feeling like a terrified child simultaneously suggest that she is feeling like a woman thoroughly aroused by Arnold Friend and the sex he offers. The "wave of dizziness," the sweating, "panting," and "shaking" all characterize a woman well on the way to orgasm.

Connie's progression towards orgasm and her regression towards the womb both reach their climax in that decidedly schizophrenic moment when she tries to call her mother on the telephone. Miss Oates describes it thus:

> . . . she ran into the back room and picked up the telephone. Something roared in her ear, a tiny roaring, and she was so sick with fear that she could do nothing but listen to it—the telephone was clammy and very heavy and her fingers groped down to the dial but were too weak to touch it. She began to scream into the phone, into the roaring. She cried out, she cried for her mother, she felt her breath start jerking back and forth in her lungs as if it were something Arnold Friend was stabbing her with again and again with no tenderness. A noisy sorrowful wailing rose all

about her and she was locked inside it the way she was locked inside this house.

> After a while she could hear again. She was sitting on the floor with her wet back against the wall.

If the spasms which set Connie's "breath . . . jerking back and forth" as if Arnold were "stabbing her . . . again and again" suggest that she is experiencing something like the moment of climax in the sexual act, they also indicate that she is succumbing to sexual appetite exactly as Red Riding Hood does when she climbs into bed with the Wolf. Of course, Red Riding Hood is seeking the safety of a mother-figure's arms, the safety of a womb, not sex. This is true of Connie, too. The little girl in her is acting littler all the time, and now, more like a baby than a child, she is crying for her mother, trying to reach her mother through the umbilical-like cord on a phone she has forgotten how to use. She cannot reach her mother, but she does manage to reach the momentary safety of a womb of sorts. The lines which suggest that she is experiencing something like orgasm also suggest that she is experiencing something like birth—but in reverse. The description of the "breath . . . jerking back and forth in her lungs" in spasms that set her "wailing" reminds us of the moment of birth; and it is followed by a description that makes Connie sound like an unborn baby (rather than a newborn one), for she collapses into an unconscious and embryonic heap on the floor of the house where she feels "locked inside," even as a baby is "locked inside" a womb.

Connie does not stay in that "womb," however. The child in Connie may want to stay there, but the woman in Connie wants to be born. And the same spasms that suggest a birth-in-reverse suggest a birth-in-progress, too, a birth in which the two Connies who have thus far existed together in the one Connie, with the woman "locked inside" the womb of the child, are finally torn apart. As the story moves towards its conclusion, we note that the child who has thus become mother of the woman feels "hollow." She feels as if her "heart" and "body" are not "really hers" any more. They belong to that womanly part of her which now seems to be someone else entirely—someone who pushes her way out of the womb-like house where she has spent her formative years even as she has pushed her way out of the womb of the child:

> She put out her hand against the screen. She watched herself push the door slowly open as if she were back safe somewhere inside the house . . . watching this body and this head of long hair moving out into the sunlight where Arnold Friend waited.

Arnold Friend has not had to pull Connie out of the womb with the physical force which the Woodcutter uses in the fairy tale. We should remember that he has threatened to use such physical force if necessary, but his psychological force (as an embodiment of Connie's own impulses) proves to be more than sufficient to ensure that the birth takes place, whether the embryonic woman is really ready to be born or not.

Of course she is not ready to be born—despite the fact that it is only as a newborn that brown-eyed Connie can be Arnold's "sweet little blue-eyed girl." Connie has not developed enough to survive in the world outside the womb—in the world outside the conscious personality—and it is not surprising that she gazes upon this world in utter bewilderment: "—so much land that Connie had never seen before and did not recognize except to know that she was going to it."[32] Had she been nurtured on fairy tales instead of popular songs and movies she would not feel at such a loss; she would have "been" to this world before, through the vicarious experience offered by fairy tales, and she would have some sense of how to survive there now. Connie lacks the benefit of such experience, however, and even Arnold Friend appears to realize how that lack has hampered her development. He certainly speaks to the supposed woman as though she were still a child: " 'Now, turn this way. That's right. Come over here to me. . . . and let's see a smile, try it, you're a brave, sweet little girl'." How fatherly he sounds. And how like the Woodcutter. But we know that he is still the Wolf, and that he still intends to "gobble up" this "little girl" as soon as he gets the chance. Connie is not going to live happily ever after. Indeed, it would seem that she is not going to live at all. She simply does not know how. She is stranded in Fairyland, without a map.[33]

Notes

[1] "Interview with Joyce Carol Oates about Where Are You Going, Where Have You Been?" in *Mirrors: An Introduction to Literature*, ed. John R. Knott, Jr., and Christopher R. Keaske, 2nd ed. (San Francisco: Canfield Press, 1975), pp. 18–19.

[2] Don Moser, "The Pied Piper of Tucson," *Life,* 60, no. 9 (March 4, 1966), 18–19, 22–24, 80c–d.

[3] The raising of a human to divine status—Ed.

[4] Going beyond the individual or personal—Ed.

[5] Interview in Mirrors, p. 19. For a perceptive analysis of Arnold Friend as a demonic figure, a subject which will not be developed here, see Joyce M. Wegs, "Don't You Know Who I Am?" The Grotesque in Oates's 'Where Are You Going, Where Have You Been?'," The Journal of Narrative Technique, 5 (January 1975), pp. 66–72.

[6] Wegs, p. 69.

[7] Joyce Carol Oates, "Preface," Where Are You Going, Where Have You Been?: Stories of Young America (Greenwich, CT: Fawcett Publications, 1974), p. 10.

[8] Joyce Carol Oates, "Where Are You Going, Where Have You Been?," Where Are You Going, Where Have You Been?: Stories of Young America (Greenwich, CT: Fawcett Publications, 1974), p. 13. All further references are to this edition of the story and will appear in the text of the essay. The story was originally published in Epoch, Fall 1966. It has since been included in Prize Stories: The O. Henry Awards 1968; in The Best American Short Stories of 1967; and in a collection of Oates' stories, The Wheel of Love (New York: Vanguard Press, 1970; Greenwich, CT: Fawcett Publications, 1972). The story is also being anthologized with increasing frequency in collections intended for use in the classroom, such as Donald McQuade and Robert Atwan, Popular Writing in America: The Interaction of Style and Audience (New York: Oxford University Press, 1974).

[9] Bruno Bettelheim, The Uses of Enchantment: The Meaning and Importance of Fairy Tales (New York: Alfred A. Knopf, 1976), p. 39.

[10] Joyce Carol Oates, The Assassins (New York: Vanguard Press, 1975), p. 378.

[11] At the MLA convention in New York, on December 26, 1976, I got a chance to ask Joyce Carol Oates if the many allusions to various fairy tales in "Where Are You Going, Where Have You Been?" were intentional. She replied that they were. (Gretchen Schulz)

[12] Bettelheim, n. 34, p. 316.

[13] Grow together; unite—Ed.

[14] Townspeople—Ed.

[15] According to the legend, one of the children of Hamelin does survive, though against his will. He is a lame boy who falls so far behind the other children that before he can reach the opening into the Koppenberg, it closes, swallowing all but himself. Psychologically, the boy's "lameness" can be interpreted as an unconscious protective mechanism which is capable of thwarting the boy's conscious will, thus saving him from destruction. This is protection exactly of the sort that properly internalized fairy tales provide, and its chief advantage is that it is not subject to the ego's often erring judgment, since it operates beyond the effective jurisdiction of consciousness.

[16] Bettelheim, pp. 66 ff.; n. 6, pp. 311–312; and passim.

[17] Refers to ages from about 3 to 6 when a child often has sexual feelings toward the parent of the opposite sex, while fearing the parent of the same sex as a rival—Ed.

[18] Bettelheim, p. 74.

[19] Bettelheim, p. 73.

20 Bettelheim, pp. 207, 114.

21 Bettelheim, p. 245.

22 Bettelheim, p. 236.

23 Bettelheim, p. 91.

24 Bettelheim, p. 85.

25 C. G. Jung, The Archetypes and the Collective Unconscious, 2nd ed., and Aion, 2nd ed., Collected Works of C. G. Jung, Vol. IX, pts. I & II (Princeton, NJ: Princeton University Press, 1968), passim.

26 Bettelheim, p. 175.

27 Bettelheim, p. 172.

28 Wolfish.

29 Bettelheim, pp. 303–309, passim.

30 Bettelheim, p. 180.

31 Bettelheim, p. 180.

32 There is a fascinating and, it seems, rather significant echo between this line and the passage in Hemingway's "The Snows of Kilimanjaro," where at the moment of his death from gangrene, Harry imagines that the overdue plane that was to take him to the hospital in Arusha arrives, and shortly after taking off with Harry aboard, turns to the left (away from Arusha), and heads instead for the summit of Mt. Kilimanjaro: "Then they began to climb and they were going to the East it seemed, and then it darkened and they were in a storm, the rain so thick it seemed like flying through a waterfall, and then they were out and Compie [the pilot] turned his head and grinned and pointed and there, ahead, all he could see, as wide as all the world, great, high, and unbelievably white in the sun, was the square top of Kilimanjaro. *And then he knew that there was where he was going* [italics mine]." Ernest Hemingway, "The Snows of Kilimanjaro," *The Fifth Column and the First Forty-nine Stories* (New York: Charles Scribner's Sons, 1938), p. 174.

33 Concerning the plight of the Connie's of the world, Bettelheim states thus: ". . . unfed by our common fantasy heritage, the folk fairy tale, the child cannot invent stories on his own which help him cope with life's problems. All the stories he can invent are just expressions of his own wishes and anxieties. Relying on his own resources, all the child can imagine are elaborations of where he presently is, since he cannot know where he needs to go, or how to go about getting there" (pp. 121–122).

Connie's Tambourine Man: A New Reading of Arnold Friend

MIKE TIERCE AND JOHN MICHAEL CRAFTON

The critical reception of Joyce Carol Oates' "Where Are You Going, Where Have You Been?" reveals a consistent pattern for reducing the text to a manageable, univocal[1] reading. Generally, this pattern involves two assumptions: Arnold *must* symbolize Satan and Connie *must* be raped and murdered. No critic has yet questioned Joyce Wegs' assertion that "Arnold is clearly a symbolic Satan."[2] Marie Urbanski argues that Arnold's "feet resemble the devil's cloven hoofs," Joan Winslow calls the story "an encounter with the devil," Tom Quirk maintains the story describes a "demoniac character," and Christina Marsden Gillis refers to "the satanic visitor's incantation."[3] Wegs' assertion that Arnold is "a criminal with plans to rape and probably murder Connie"[4] is also accepted at face value. Gillis assumes that Arnold "leads his victim . . . to a quick and violent sexual assault,"[5] and Quirk refers to "the rape and subsequent murder of Connie."[6] Even though Gretchen Schulz and R. J. R. Rockwood correctly claim that the portrait of Arnold "is created in the mind of Connie . . . and that it exists *there only*," they still persist in having Arnold as a demon and Connie as doomed: "But we know that he is still the Wolf, and that he still intends to 'gobble up' this 'little girl' as soon as he gets the chance. Connie is not going to live happily ever after. Indeed, it would seem that she is not going to live at all."[7]

While all of these critics insist on seeing satanic traces in Arnold, they refuse, on the other hand, to see that these traces are only part of a much more complex, more dynamic symbol. There are indeed diabolic shades to Arnold, but just as Blake and Shelley could see in Milton's Satan[8] a positive, attractive symbol of the poet, the rebellious embodiment of creative energy, so we should also be sensitive to Arnold's multifaceted and creative nature. Within the frame of the story, the fiction of Arnold burns in the day as the embodiment of poetic energy. The story is dedicated to Bob Dylan,

the troubadour, the artist. Friend is the artist, the actor, the rhetorician, the teacher, all symbolized by Connie's overheated imagination. We should not assume that Arnold is completely evil because she is afraid of him. Her limited perceptions remind us of Blake's questioner in "The Tyger" who begins to perceive the frightening element of the experiential world but also is rather duped into his fear by his own limitations. Like the figure in Blake, Connie is the framer, the story creator—and the diabolic traces in her fiction frighten her not because they are the manifestations of an outside evil but because they are the symbolic extrapolations of her own psyche.

If the adamant insistence that Arnold Friend is Satan is rejected, then who is this intriguing mysterious visitor? In *Enter Mysterious Stranger: American Cloistral Fiction*, Roy Male asserts that many mysterious intruders throughout American literature "are almost always potential saviors, destroyers, or ambiguous combinations of both, and their initial entrance, however much it may be displaced toward realism, amounts to the entrance of God or the devil on a machine."[9] And if Arnold Friend is *not* satanic, then his arrival could be that of a savior. This possibility moreover is suggested by Connie's whispering "Christ. Christ"[10] when Arnold first arrives in his golden "machine." Not only is "33" part of Arnold's "secret code" of numbers, but his sign, an "X" that seems to hover in the air, is also one of the symbols for Christ. Because music is closely associated with religion—"the music was always in the background, like music at a church service"—it also adds a religious element to Arnold's arrival. The key question then is who is this musical messiah, and the key to the answer is the dedication "For Bob Dylan"—the element of the story so unsatisfactorily accounted for by our predecessors. Not only does the description of Arnold Friend also fit Bob Dylan—a type of rock-and-roll messiah—but three of Dylan's songs (popular when the story was written) are very similar to the story itself.

In the mid-sixties Bob Dylan's followers perceived him to be a messiah. According to his biographer, Dylan was "a rock-and-roll king."[11] It is no wonder then that Arnold speaks with "the voice of the man on the radio," the disc jockey whose name, Bobby King, is a reference to "Bobby" Dylan, the "king" of rock-and-roll. Dylan was more than just a "friend" to his listeners; he was "Christ revisited," "the prophet leading [his followers] into [a new] Consciousness."[12] In fact, "people were making him an idol; . . . thousands of men and women, young and old, felt their lives entwined with his because they saw him as a mystic, a messiah who would lead them to salvation.[13]

That Oates consciously associates Arnold Friend with Bob Dylan is clearly suggested by the similarities of their physical descriptions. Arnold's "shaggy, shabby black hair that looked crazy as a wig," his "long and hawklike nose," his unshavened face, his "big and white" teeth, his lashes, "thick and black as if painted with a black tarlike material" and his size ("only an inch or so taller than Connie") are all characteristic of Bob Dylan. Even Arnold's "fast, bright monotone voice" is suggestive of Dylan, especially since he speaks "in a simple

lilting voice, exactly as if he were reciting the words to a song."

Dylan then provides a physical model for Arnold's appearance and a historical referent for Arnold's existence. Yet more profoundly, the myth of Dylan's being organized or somehow controlled by his music is reflected by Connie, Arnold, and Ellie being organized or perhaps even unified by the almost mystical music heard throughout the story. Connie, for example, notices the way Arnold "tapped one fist against another in homage to the perpetual music behind him." Since this "perpetual music" is the one thing that Connie can "depend upon," it even becomes her breath of life; she is "bathed in a glow of slow-pulsed joy that seemed to rise mysteriously out of the music itself, . . . breathed in and breathed out with each gentle rise of her chest." Paying "close attention" to the words and singing along with the songs played on the "*XYZ* Sunday Jamboree," Connie spends her Sunday afternoon worshiping "the music that made everything so good." And when her two visitors arrive, "the same program . . . playing inside the house" is also playing on Ellie Oscar's radio. In fact, "the music from [Connie's] radio and [Ellie's] blend together." Ellie is so closely associated with the radio that without it pressed up against his ear, he grimaces "as if . . . the air was too much for him." Both Ellie's and Arnold's existences seem to depend completely on the "perpetual music"; consequently, Oates appears to be suggesting that they are not literally present. They are instead part of Connie's musically induced fantasy—another of her so-called "trashy daydreams."

Oates points out that Connie spends her summer "thinking, dreaming of the boys she met." But because of Connie's gradually changing desires, "all the boys fell back and dissolved into a single face that was not even a face but an idea, a feeling, mixed up with the urgent insistent pounding of the music." This "urgent" feeling reflects Connie's desire for something more sexually stimulating than the kissing sessions she spends with "boys" like Eddie. As Freud points out, "the motive forces of phantasies are unsatisfied wishes, and every single phantasy is the fulfillment of a wish, a correlation of unsatisfying realty. . . . In young women the erotic wishes predominate almost exclusively."[14] Although we acknowledge the sexist nature of Freud's generalization, his point seems to apply to Connie. Furthermore, Roy Male suggests that even though "there is no logical reason for the entrance of a stranger, it is equally true that he comes as if in answer to some unuttered call." Arnold is described as "talking right through Connie's voice" because that is the only voice he has. His arrival is the answer to Connie's "unuttered" call and to her "erotic" desires. Arnold's "face" is therefore "familiar" because it is the "face" that replaces the "boys" in her fantasies. Not only is the emphasis placed on Arnold's face reinforced by "a drawing of a round grinning face" on his car, but when Connie first encounters Arnold at Napoleon's drive-in restaurant, he is described as "a face just a few feet from hers"—perhaps her own distorted reflection in a car windshield.

Connie not only turns away from Arnold's face "without Eddie noticing anything," but many other elements in the story suggest that Arnold is just another "shadowy vision of [Connie] herself." For example, Arnold is described as being "just a blur . . . that . . . had come from nowhere . . . and belonged nowhere and that everything about him . . . was only half real." His "fake" laughter suggests that his threatening presence is "all a joke." He opens the door to his car carefully because it might fall off, he cannot walk without stumbling, his feet seem not to be in his boots, and he wears a mask and make-up. He even touches his sunglasses "as if to make sure they were still there." He also magically knows Connie's name, her best friend's name, her other friends' names, and where her parents are and when they will return. Part of the action that takes place also suggests a dream-like experience. Arnold's asking Connie if she has something against a dead woman, Connie's inability to dial the telephone, and Arnold's promise not to come into the house are all tinged with a sense of unreality. Even the fact that the phrase "as if" is used over thirty times suggests that there is something dubious about Connie's experience.

In order to reinforce the idea that Arnold's visit is another fantasy, Oates parallels the actual description of one of Connie's other daydreams to the description of her finally joining Arnold Friend at the story's end:

> Connie sat with her eyes closed in the sun, dreaming and dazed with the warmth about her as if this were a kind of love, the caresses of love, and her mind slipped over onto thoughts of the boy she had been with the night before and how nice

he had been, how sweet it always was, not the way someone like June would suppose but sweet, gentle, the way it was in movies and promised in songs; and when she opened her eyes she hardly knew where she was, the back yard ran off into weeds and a fence-like line of trees and behind it the sky was perfectly blue and still. The asbestos "ranch house" that was now three years old startled her—it looked small. She shook her head as if to get awake. . . .

"My sweet little blue-eyed girl," he said in a half-sung sigh that had nothing to do with her brown eyes but was taken up just the same by the vast sunlit reaches of the land behind him and on all sides of him—so much land that Connie had never seen before and did not recognize except to know that she was going to it.

The fence-like line of trees is replaced by "the vast sunlit reaches of the land" surrounding Arnold Friend. Through her encounter with this mysterious stranger, Connie frees herself from the sense of confinement she feels in her father's house. As Roy Male so aptly explains it, the "mysterious strangers who are potential saviors" force the "insider" to undergo a transformation, which "may involve the effort of the insider to break out of his fixed orientation."[15] The Dylanesque music initiates such a breakthrough for Connie. She no longer has to "dawdle in the doorway." As Dylan suggests in "Mister Tambourine Man," once she answers the call by forcing open the screen door, "there are no fences facin' " her any longer. She broadens her horizons to include the "vast sunlit reaches of the land" all around her.

The reference to "Mister Tambourine Man" implies another connection between the story and Dylan. A few of his song lyrics are very similar to the story itself. Oates herself suggests that part of the story's inspiration was "hearing for some weeks Dylan's song 'It's All Over Now, Baby Blue.' "[16] Such lines as "you must leave now," "something calls for you," "the vagabond who's rapping at your door," and "go start anew" are suggestive of the impending change awaiting Connie. Two other Dylan songs are equally as applicable though. The following lines from "Like a Rolling Stone"— the second most popular song of 1965 (the story was first published in 1966)—are also very similar to Connie's situation at the end of the story:

> You used to be so amused
> At Napoleon in rags and the
>   language that he used
> Go to him now, he calls you, you
>   can't refuse
> When you got nothing, you got
>   nothing to lose
> You're invisible now, you got no
>   secrets to conceal.

But Dylan's "Mr. Tambourine Man" —the number ten song in 1965—is even more similar. The following stanza establishes the notion of using music to rouse one's imagination into a blissful fantasy world:

> Take me on a trip upon your magic
>   swirlin' ship,
> My senses have been stripped,
> My hands can't feel to grip,
> My toes too numb to step,
> Wait only for my boot heels to be
>   wanderin'.
> I'm ready to go anywhere,
> I'm ready for to fade
> Into my own parade.

Cast your dancin' spell my way,
I promise to go under it.
Hey, Mister Tambourine Man, play a
    song for me,
I'm not sleepy and there ain't no
    place I'm going to.
Hey, Mister Tambourine Man, play a
    song for me.
In the jingle, jangle morning I'll
    come followin' you.

Arnold Friend's car—complete with the phrase "MAN THE FLYING SAUCERS"—is just such "a magic swirlin' ship." Arnold is the personification of popular music, particularly Bob Dylan's music; and as such, Connie's interaction with him is a musically induced fantasy, a kind of "magic carpet ride" in "a convertible jalopy painted gold." Rising out of Connie's radio, Arnold Friend/Bob Dylan is a magical, musical messiah; he persuades Connie to abandon her father's house. As a manifestation of her own desires, he frees her from the limitations of a fifteen-year-old girl, assisting her maturation by stripping her of her childlike vision.

NOTES

1 Having only one meaning.

2 Joyce M. Wegs, " 'Don't You Know Who I Am?' The Grotesque in Oates's, 'Where Are You Going, Where Have You Been?' " in *Critical Essays on Joyce Carol Oates,* ed. Linda W. Wagner (Boston: G. K. Hall, 1979), p. 90. First printed in *Journal of Narrative Technique,* 5 (1975), pp. 66–72.

3 Marie Urbanski, "Existential Allegory: Joyce Carol Oates' 'Where Are You Going, Where Have You Been?' " *Studies in Short Fiction,* 15 (1978), p. 202; Joan Winslow, "The Stranger Within: Two Stories by Oates and Hawthorne," *Studies in Short Fiction,* 17 (1980), p. 264; Tom Quirk, "A Source for 'Where Are You Going, Where Have You Been?' " *Studies in Short Fiction,* 18 (1981), p. 416; Christina Marsden Gillis, " 'Where Are You Going, Where Have You Been?': Seduction, Space, and a Fictional Mode," *Studies in Short Fiction,* 18 (1981), p. 70.

4 Wegs, p. 89.

5 Gillis, p. 65.

6 Quirk, p. 416.

7 Gretchen Schulz and R. J. R. Rockwood, "In Fairyland, without a Map: Connie's Exploration Inward in Joyce Carol Oates' 'Where Are You Going, Where Have You Been?' " *Literature and Psychology,* 30 (1980), pp. 156, 165, & 166, respectively.

8 In *Paradise Lost,* Milton clearly intends Satan to be a symbol of archetypal evil. Blake and Shelley, as true Romantics, saw in their predecessor's portrait of Lucifer a duality that embodied positive as well as negative traits.

9 Roy Male, *Enter Mysterious Stranger: American Cloistral Fiction* (Norman: University of Oklahoma Press, 1979), p. 21.

10 Joyce Carol Oates, "Where Are You Going, Where Have You Been?" in *The Wheel of Love* (New York: Vanguard Press, 1970), p. 40. Hereafter cited parenthetically within the text.

[11] Anthony Scaduto, *Bob Dylan* (New York: Grosset and Dunlop, 1971), p. 222.

[12] Scaduto, p. 274.

[13] Scaduto, p. 229.

[14] Sigmund Freud, "Creative Writers and Day-Dreamers," in *Criticism: The Major Statements,* ed. Charles Kaplan (New York: St. Martin's Press, 1975), p. 468.

[15] Male, p. 10.

[16] "Interview with Joyce Carol Oates about 'Where Are You Going, Where Have You Been?' " in *Mirrors: An Introduction to Literature,* eds. John R. Knott, Jr., and Christopher R. Keaske, 2nd ed. (San Francisco: Canfield Press, 1975), pp. 18–19.

It's All Over Now, Baby Blue
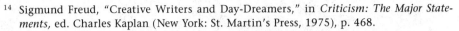

BOB DYLAN

You must leave now, take what you need you think will last
But whatever you wish to keep, you better grab it fast
Yonder stands your orphan with his gun
Crying like a fire in the sun.
Look out, the saints are comin' through
And it's all over now, baby blue.

The highway is for gamblers, better use your sins
Take what you have gathered from coincidence
The empty-handed painter from your streets
Is drawing crazy patterns on your sheets
This sky too is folding under you
And it's all over now, baby blue.

All your seasick sailors they are rowing home
Your empty-handed army men are going home
The lover who has just walked out your door
Has taken all his blankets from the floor
The carpet too is moving under you
And it's all over now, baby blue.

Leave your stepping stones behind, something calls for you
Forget the dead you've left, they will not follow you
The vagabond who's rapping at your door
Is standing in the clothes that you once wore
Strike another match, go start anew
And it's all over now, baby blue.

"Don't You Know Who I Am?" The Grotesque in Oates's "Where Are You Going, Where Have You Been?"

JOYCE M. WEGS

Joyce Carol Oates's ability to absorb and then to transmit in her fiction the terror which is often a part of living in America today has been frequently noted and admired. For instance, Walter Sullivan praises her skill by noting that "horror resides in the transformation of what we know best, the intimate and comfortable details of our lives made suddenly threatening."[1] Although he does not identify it as such, Sullivan's comment aptly describes a classic instance of a grotesque intrusion: a familiar world suddenly appears alien. Oates frequently evokes the grotesque in her fiction, drawing upon both its traditional or demonic and its contemporary or psychological manifestations.[2] In the prize-winning short story, "Where Are You Going, Where Have You Been?", Oates utilizes the grotesque in many of its forms to achieve a highly skillful integration of the multiple levels of the story and, in so doing, to suggest a transcendent reality which reaches beyond surface realism to evoke the simultaneous mystery and reality of the contradictions of the human heart. Full of puzzling and perverse longings, the heart persists in mixing lust and love, life and death, good and evil. Oates's teenage protagonist, Connie, discovers that her dream love-god also wears the face of lust, evil and death.

Centering the narrative on the world of popular teenage music and culture, Oates depicts the tawdry world of drive-in restaurants and shopping plazas blaring with music with a careful eye for authentic surface detail. However, her use of popular music as a thematic referent is typical also of her frequent illumination of the illusions and grotesquely false values which may arise from excessive devotion to such aspects of popular culture as rock music, movies, and romance magazines. In all of her fiction as in this story, she frequently employs a debased religious imagery to suggest the gods which modern society has substituted for conventional religion. Oates delineates the moral poverty of Connie, her fifteen-year-old protagonist, by imaging a typical evening Connie spends at a drive-in restaurant as a grotesquely parodied religious pilgrimage. Left by her friend's father to stroll at the shopping center or go to a movie, Connie and her girlfriend immediately cross the highway to the restaurant frequented by older teenagers. A grotesque parody of a church, the building is bottle-shaped and has a grinning boy holding a hamburger aloft on top of it. Unconscious of any ludicrousness, Connie and her friend enter it as if going into a "sacred building"[3] which will give them "what haven and blessing they yearned for." It is the music which is "always in the background, like music at a church service" that has invested this "bright-lit, fly-infested" place with such significance. Indeed, throughout the story the music is given an almost mystical character, for it evokes in Connie a mysterious pleasure, a "glow of slow-pulsed joy that seemed to rise mysteriously out of the music itself."

Although the story undoubtedly has a moral dimension,[4] Oates does not take a judgmental attitude toward Connie. In fact, much of the terror of the story comes from the recognition that there must be thousands of Connies. By carefully including telltale phrases, Oates demonstrates in an understated fashion why Connies exist. Connie's parents, who seem quite typical, have disqualified themselves as moral guides for her. At first reading, the reader may believe Connie's mother to be concerned about her daughter's habits, views, and friends; but basically their arguments are little more than a "pretense of exasperation, a sense that they . . . [are] tugging and struggling over something of little value to either of them." Connie herself is uncertain of her mother's motives for constantly picking at her; she alternates between a view that her mother's harping proceeds from jealousy of Connie's good looks now that her own have faded and a feeling that her mother really prefers her over her plain older sister June because she is prettier. In other words, to Connie and her mother, real value lies in beauty. Connie's father plays a small role in her life, but by paralleling repeated phrases, Oates suggests that this is precisely the problem. Because he does not "bother talking much" to his family, he can hardly ask the crucial parental questions, "Where are you going?" or "Where have you been?"

The moral indifference of the entire adult society is underscored by Oates's parallel description of the father of Connie's friend, who also "never . . . [bothers] to ask" what they did when he picks up the pair at the end of one of their evenings out. Similarly, on Sunday morning, "none of them bothered with church," not even that supposed paragon, June.

Since her elders do not bother about her, Connie is left defenseless against the temptations represented by Arnold Friend. A repeated key phrase emphasizes her helplessness. As she walks through the parking lot of the restaurant with Eddie, she can not "help but" look about happily, full of joy in a life characterized by casual pickups and constant music. When she sees Arnold in a nearby car, she looks away, but her instinctive flirtatiousness triumphs and she can not "help but" look back. Later, like Lot's wife leaving Sodom and Gomorrah,[5] she cannot "help but look back" at the plaza and drive-in as her friend's father drives them home. In Connie's case, the consequences of the actions she can not seem to help are less biblically swift to occur and can not be simply labeled divine retribution.

Since music is Connie's religion, its values are hers also. Oates does not include the lyrics to any popular songs here, for any observer of contemporary America could surely discern the obvious link between Connie's high esteem for romantic love and youthful beauty and the lyrics of scores of hit tunes. The superficiality of Connie's values becomes terrifyingly apparent when Arnold Friend, the external embodiment of the teenage ideal celebrated in popular songs, appears at Connie's home in the country one Sunday afternoon when she is home alone, listening to music and drying her hair. It is no accident that Arnold's clothes, car, speech, and taste in music reflect current teenage chic almost exactly, for they constitute part of a careful disguise intended to reflect Arnold's self-image as an accomplished youthful lover.

Suspense mounts in the story as the reader realizes along with Connie that Arnold is not a teenager and is really thirty or more. Each part of his disguise is gradually revealed to be grotesquely distorted in some way. His shaggy black hair, "crazy as a wig," is evidently really a wig. The mask-like appearance of his face has been created by applying a thick coat of makeup; however, he has carelessly omitted his throat. Even his eyelashes appear to be made-up, but with some tarlike material. In his clothing, his disguise appears more successful, for Connie approves of the way he dresses, as "all of them dressed," in tight jeans, boots, and pullover. When he walks, however, Connie realizes that the runty Arnold, conscious that the ideal teenage dream lover is tall, has stuffed his boots; the result is, however, that he can hardly walk and staggers ludicrously. Attempting to bow, he almost falls. Similarly, the gold jalopy covered with teenage slang phrases seems authentic until Connie notices that one of them is no longer in vogue. Even his speech is not his own, for it recalls lines borrowed from disc jockeys, teenage slang, and lines from popular songs. Arnold's strange companion, Ellie Oscar, is just as grotesque as Arnold. Almost totally absorbed in listening to music and interrupting this activity only to offer threatening

assistance to Arnold, Ellie is no youth either; he has the "face of a forty-year-old baby." Although Arnold has worked out his disguise with great care, he soon loses all subtlety in letting Connie know of his evil intentions; he is not simply crazy but a criminal with plans to rape and probably to murder Connie.

However, Arnold is far more than a grotesque portrait of a psychopathic killer masquerading as a teenager; he also has all the traditional sinister traits of that arch-deceiver and source of grotesque terror, the devil. As is usual with Satan, he is in disguise; the distortions in his appearance and behavior suggest not only that his identity is faked but also hint at his real self. Equating Arnold and Satan is not simply a gratuitous connection designed to exploit traditional demonic terror, for the early pages of the story explicitly prepare for this linking by portraying popular music and its values as Connie's perverted version of religion. When Arnold comes up the drive, her first glance makes Connie believe that a teenage boy with his jalopy, the central figure of her religion, has arrived; therefore, she murmurs "Christ. Christ" as she wonders about how her newly-washed hair looks. When the car—a parodied golden chariot?—stops, a horn sounds "as if this were a signal Connie knew." On one level, the horn honks to announce the "second coming" of Arnold, a demonic Day of Judgment.[6] Although Connie never specifically recognizes Arnold as Satan, her first comment to him both hints at his infernal origins and faithfully reproduces teenage idiom: "Who the *hell* do you think you are?" (emphasis mine). When he introduces himself, his name too hints at his identity, for "friend" is uncomfortably close to "fiend"; his initials could well stand for Arch Fiend. The frightened Connie sees Arnold as "only half real": he "had driven up her driveway all right but had come from nowhere before that and belonged nowhere." Especially supernatural is his mysterious knowledge about her, her family, and her friends. At one point, he even seems to be able to see all the way to the barbecue which Connie's family is attending and to get a clear vision of what all the guests are doing. Typical of his ambiguous roles is his hint that he had something to do with the death of the old woman who lived down the road. It is never clear whether Arnold has killed her, has simply heard of her death, or knows about it in his devil role of having come to take her away to hell. Although Arnold has come to take Connie away, in his traditional role as evil spirit, he may not cross a threshold uninvited; he repeatedly mentions that he is not going to come in after Connie, and he never does. Instead, he lures Connie out to him. Part of his success may be attributed to his black magic in having put his sign on her—X for victim. Because the devil is not a mortal being, existing as he does in all ages, it is not surprising that he slips in remembering what slang terms are in vogue. Similarly, his foolish attempt at a bow may result from a mixup in temporal concepts of the ideal lover. In addition, his clumsy bow may be due to the fact that it must be difficult to manipulate boots if one has cloven feet!

Although Oates attempts to explain the existence of Connie, she makes no similar effort to explain the existence of Arnold, for that would constitute an answer to the timeless and insoluble problem of evil in the world. As this story shows, Oates would agree with Pope Paul VI's recent commentary on the "terrible reality" of evil in the world, but she would not, I feel sure, endorse his view of this evil as being literally embodied in a specific being. Pope Paul describes evil as "not merely a lack of something, but an effective agent, a living spiritual being, perverted and perverting. A terrible reality. Mysterious and frightening."[7] Oates's description of her own views on religion is in terms strikingly similar to the language used by Pope Paul. To her, religion is a "kind of psychological manifestation of deep powers, deep imaginative, mysterious powers, which are always with us, and what has in the past been called supernatural. I would prefer simply to call natural. However, though these things are natural, they are still inaccessible and cannot be understood, cannot be controlled."[8] Thus, although Arnold is clearly a symbolic Satan, he also functions on a psychological level.

On this level, Arnold Friend is the incarnation of Connie's unconscious erotic desires and dreams, but in uncontrollable nightmare form. When she first sees Arnold in the drive-in, she instinctively senses his sinister attraction, for she cannot "help glancing back" at him. Her "trashy daydreams" are largely filled with blurred recollections of the caresses of the many boys she has dated. That her dreams are a kind of generalized sexual desire—although Connie does not consciously identify them as such—is made evident by Oates's description of Connie's summer dreams: "But all the boys fell back and dissolved into a single face that was not even a face but an idea, a feeling, mixed up with the urgent insistent pounding of the music and the humid night air of July." What is frightening about Arnold is that he voices and makes explicit her own sexual desires; teenage boys more usually project their similar message with "that sleepy dreamy smile that all the boys used to get across ideas they didn't want to put into words." Connie's reaction to his bluntness is one of horror: "People don't talk like that, you're crazy."

Connie's fear drives her into a grotesque separation of mind from body in which her unconscious self takes over and betrays her. Terror-stricken, she cannot even make her weak fingers dial the police; she can only scream into the phone. In the same way that she is Arnold's prisoner, locked inside the house he alternately threatens to knock down or burn down, she is also a prisoner of her own body: "A noisy sorrowful wailing rose all about her and she was locked inside it the way she was locked inside this house." Finally, her conscious mind rejects any connection with her body and its impulses; her heart seems "nothing that was hers" "but just a pounding, living thing inside this body that wasn't really hers either." In a sense, her body with its puzzling desires "decides" to go with Arnold although her rational self is terrified of him: "She watched herself push the door slowly open as if she were back safe somewhere in the other doorway, watching this body and this head of long hair moving out into the sunlight where Arnold Friend waited."

Oates encourages the reader to look for multiple levels in this story and to consider Arnold and Connie at more than face value by her repeated emphasis on the question of identity. The opening of the story introduces the concept to which both Connie and her mother seem to subscribe—being pretty means being someone. In fact, her mother's acid questions as she sees Connie at her favorite activity of mirror-gazing—"Who are you? You think you're so pretty?"—also introduce the converse of this idea, namely, that those who lack physical beauty have no identity. As does almost everything in the story, everything about Connie has "two sides to it." However, Connie's nature, one for at home and one for "anywhere that was not home," is simple in comparison to that of Arnold. Connie's puzzled questions at first query what role Arnold thinks he is playing: "Who the hell do you think you are?" Then she realizes that he sees himself all too literally as the man of her dreams, and she becomes more concerned about knowing his real identity. By the time that Arnold asks, "Don't you know who I am?" Connie realizes that it is no longer a simple question of whether he is a "jerk" or someone worth her attention but of just how crazy he is. By the end she knows him to be a murderer, for she realizes that she will never see her family again. However, only the reader sees Arnold's Satan identity. Connie's gradual realization of Arnold's identity brings with it a recognition of the actual significance of physical beauty: Arnold is indeed someone to be concerned about, even if he is no handsome youth. At the conclusion Connie has lost all identity except that of victim, for Arnold's half-sung sigh about her blue eyes ignores the reality of her brown ones. In Arnold's view, Connie's personal identity is totally unimportant.

Dedicated to contemporary balladeer Bob Dylan, this story in a sense represents Oates's updated prose version of a ballad in which a demon lover carries away his helpless victim. By adding modern psychological insights, she succeeds in revealing the complex nature of the victim of a grotesque intrusion by an alien force; on one level, the victim actually welcomes and invites this demonic visitation. Like Bob Dylan, she grafts onto the ballad tradition a moral commentary which explores but does not solve the problems of the evils of our contemporary society; an analogous Dylan ballad is his "It's a Hard Rain's a Gonna' Fall." Even the title records not only the ritual parental questions but also suggests that there is a moral connection between the two questions: where Connie goes is related to where she has been. Oates does not judge Connie in making this link, however; Connie is clearly not in complete control over where she has been. The forces of her society, her family, and her self combine to make her fate inescapable.

NOTES

1 Walter Sullivan, "The Artificial Demon: Joyce Carol Oates and the Dimensions of the Real," *The Hollins Critic*, 9, No. 4 (Dec., 1972), p. 2.

2 Joyce Markert Wegs, "The Grotesque in Some American Novels of the Nineteen-Sixties: Ken Kesey, Joyce Carol Oates, Sylvia Plath," Diss., University of Illinois, 1973.

3 Joyce Carol Oates, "Where Are You Going, Where Have You Been?" *The Wheel of Love* (1970; rpt. Greenwich, CT: Fawcett, 1972), p. 31. All subsequent references to the story appear within parentheses in the text.

4 See Walter Sullivan, "Where Have All the Flowers Gone?: The Short Story in Search of Itself," *Sewanee Review*, 78, No. 3 (Summer, 1970), p. 537.

5 Lot and his family were spared when God destroyed the wicked cities of Sodom and Gomorrah, but Lot's wife was turned into a pillar of salt when she disobeyed God's injunction not to look back at the cities. See Genesis 19:24–26.

6 The time of Christ's return; when all people on earth will be judged.

7 Andrew M. Greeley, "The Devil, You Say," *The New York Times Magazine*, 4 Feb., 1973, p. 26, quotes an address by Pope Paul on 15 Nov., 1972, as reported in the Vatican newspaper.

8 Linda Kuehl, "An Interview with Joyce Carol Oates," *Commonweal*, 91 (5 Dec., 1969), p. 308.

Questions

1. How is "Where Are You Going, Where Have You Been?" similar to and different from Anne Tyler's "Teenage Wasteland"?

2. Is Arnold Friend meant to be the devil? Is he an antisocial hoodlum? Is he a rapist and murderer (see the March 4, 1966, *Life* magazine article "The Pied Piper of Tucson" and "Killing for Kicks" in the March 14, 1966, issue of *Newsweek*)? Is he actually Bob Dylan (as Tierce and Crafton suggest in their article)? Or is he just a misunderstood social misfit who terrifies Connie more because of her innocence than because of his evil?

3. In a note accompanying the article she coauthored, Gretchen Schulz says that Oates told her the references to fairy tales in the story are intentional. Do you think Oates's comment is accurate? Does it matter whether or not the allusions are intentional?

4. Many critical articles see "Where Are You Going, Where Have You Been?" as heavily symbolic, even allegorical, with elements of myth, dream, and fairy tale woven throughout. Is this kind of analysis necessary, or could the story be seen in much simpler terms?

5. Who is the story's central character, Arnold Friend or Connie?

6. Dark undertones aside, in what sense is this simply an initiation story, the coming of age of a typical 1960s teenager?

7. What roles are played in the story by music, sex, the weather, contemporary slang, and physical appearance?

8. Why does Connie's family play such a minor role in the story? How would expanding their roles change the story?

9. Which aspects of teenage culture have changed in the more than thirty years since Oates wrote the story? Which have stayed the same? Given the scope of the changes, is the story dated?

10. Most critics (like Oates herself) see the end of the story as alarmingly negative, suggesting rape and even murder. Do you see it this way?

11. Feminist critics might see this story as a familiar tale of a young woman's seduction by a man who uses threats of physical violence to coerce her into giving in to his will. In what sense is this a story of male power and female powerlessness?

12. Do you agree with Oates that the dramatic differences in the endings of the film and the story are justified by the differences between the 1960s and the 1980s?

13. How is the so-called generation gap—the failure of one generation to understand another's culture, customs, and heroes—important to the story?

Michele Olivari
Professor Biemiller
English 102
8 March 1996

Mesmerizing Men and Vulnerable Teens: Power
Relationships in "Where Are You Going, Where Have
You Been?" and "Teenage Wasteland"

Both Joyce Carol Oates's "Where Are You Going,
Where Have You Been?" (1966) and Anne Tyler's "Teenage
Wasteland" (1984) feature adolescents engaged in constant
conflict with their parents. Both stories are set in "teenage
wastelands" in which the protagonists ignore limits established by authority figures and avoid making decisions or
finding a direction for their lives. The most striking similarity between the two stories, however, is the presence of a
hypnotic older man—one who exerts enormous influence
over the teenagers, pushing them out of their passive states
and causing them to take action. Ironically, the actions in
both cases, although decisive, have terrifying consequences.

Arnold Friend, the mysterious loner who pursues Connie in "Where Are You Going, Where Have You Been?" is
characterized by Gretchen Schulz and R. J. R. Rockwood as
the fairy tale wolf who "intends to 'gobble up' this 'little
girl' as soon as he gets the chance" (603). Many other critics, as Mike Tierce and John Michael Crafton point out, see
Arnold as the devil; Tierce and Crafton, however, prefer to
see him as a Bob Dylan figure "--a type of rock and roll mes-
siah--" (609). Oates herself, in stating that Arnold is based
on a "charismatic mass murderer" (593), acknowledges both

the threat he poses and his seductive powers. Regardless of whether Arnold is murderer, devil, wolf, or musical messiah, it is clear that he is a strong, controlling personality who has an unnaturally powerful hold over Connie. In a less dramatic way, Cal, the tutor in "Teenage Wasteland," has just such a hold over Donny. Both men, supported by background music, use their power to mesmerize young people, separating them from home and family and seducing them into following different--and dangerous--paths. In both stories, it is the adolescents' tendency to drift without an anchor that makes them vulnerable.

Both Connie and Donny are passive dreamers, stuck in numbing adolescence, waiting for something to happen. Meanwhile, both break the rules set by their parents. Connie is fifteen, and her mind is "all filled with trashy daydreams" (581). At night she sneaks out to forbidden hangouts, lying to her parents about where she is going. As she drifts through her unstructured summer days, she is "dazed with the warmth about her" (584) and caught up in the music she listens to and in her romantic fantasies. Donny is also stalled, caught in a cycle of failure and defeat, "noisy, lazy, and disruptive" (571) and unresponsive in school, cutting classes, smoking, and drinking beer.

Both Connie and Donny are emotionally separated from their parents. Connie's mother constantly nags her and compares her unfavorably to her sister June; her father does not even talk to them, choosing instead to read his newspaper and avoid conflict. In "Teenage Wasteland" Daisy's primary attitude toward her son Donny is disappointment.

Olivari 3

Ignoring his potential, she sees only "his pathetically poor posture, that slouch so forlorn that his shoulders [seem] about to meet his chin" (574). She feels sorry for him, but she is helpless to rescue him, let alone give him the emotional support he needs. Like Connie's mother, she clearly disapproves of her child's behavior. Despite her efforts to defend and encourage him, she is ashamed of his failures and upset at how they reflect upon her as a parent. Both Connie and Donny are drifting, unconnected to people or social institutions, and both are allowed to drift by weak, ineffective parents whom they neither respect nor admire. Both Connie and Donny, therefore, are vulnerable to the power of a hypnotic older man.

Arnold Friend, a strange-looking man who acts like a teenager, has great power over Connie. Initially, she is drawn to him by how he looks and dresses, and because of the music they share; later, his claims to know all about her, to know what she wants (which she herself does not know) draw her closer to him. Although she begins by flirting with him as she does with other boys, it does not take her long to realize he is different. At first "his face [is] a familiar face, somehow" (584), and "she recognize[s] most things about him" (586), but her confidence turns to fear when she realizes he is older than he appears (586). By now, though, she is under his spell. Little by little, things that have been comforting and familiar--the music, Arnold's clothing and mannerisms, even Connie's own kitchen--become "only half real" (589), as Arnold himself is. As Arnold becomes more and more threatening, Connie becomes more and more helpless; toward the end of the story, cut off from everything she has known, she is "hollow with what had been fear, but what [is] now an emptiness" (593). With Arnold's power the only thing she can recognize, she crosses the line into uncertainty--and, perhaps, death.

Cal Beadle, Donny's tutor, has none of the frightening mannerisms of Arnold Friend, and he has no sinister intentions. Nevertheless, he is also a controlling figure. Like Arnold, Cal is an older man who dresses and acts as adolescents do and listens to the music they like. He immediately sides with Donny, setting himself in opposition to authority figures and social institutions, such as school and the family. This attitude makes it possible--and even acceptable--for Donny to do the same thing. Never blaming or even criticizing Donny, Cal suggests that Donny's parents are too controlling and advises they "give him more rope" (574). But many of Cal's "kids," like Donny, are allowed to continue their anti-social and self-destructive patterns of behavior, remaining under Cal's loose supervision for years. Cal does not help Donny to function in his world; he shelters him from it. Still, Donny sides with Cal, adopting his attitudes and expressions: it becomes "Cal this, Cal that, Cal says this, Cal and I did that" (575). Eventually, Cal becomes the role model Donny's own parents have failed to provide. Donny comes to depend on Cal, even going straight to Cal's house when he is expelled from school, and Cal comes to enjoy that dependence. But Cal does not necessarily have Donny's best interests at heart. Daisy, who despite her

Olivari 5

own failures with Donny seems to know him (and Cal) well, sees Cal as predatory and controlling, characterizing his smile as "feverish and avid--a smile of hunger" (576). Although Cal does not cause Donny to leave home, he makes it impossible for him to stay. Once he has convinced Donny that it is acceptable to reject the values established by his parents and teachers, Donny's departure becomes inevitable. Having removed all Donny's anchors, Cal then removes himself from Donny's life, deciding the teenager is "emotionally disturbed" (576) and thus absolving himself of blame. At this point, Donny, "exhausted and defeated" (576), has no real choice but to disappear.

Both Arnold Friend and Cal Beadle--Arnold odd-looking and out of date, Cal estranged from his "controlling" wife and surrounded by teenagers--seem to exist outside the adult world and its rules and values. Perhaps as a result, each has a need for power, a desire to control. Each selects someone weaker, less confident, and more confused than himself, a teenager with strained family relationships and no focused goals. Clearly, critics' characterization of Arnold Friend, and the hypnotic power those characterizations suggest, apply not just to Arnold but also to Cal. Even though Cal is just a catalyst and means Donny no harm, his casual dismissal of him after he has separated the boy from all that is familiar to him pushes Donny from the known and safe to the unknown and dangerous. It is to this uncertain world that Connie too is driven: a place she "[does] not recognize except to know that she [is] going to it" (593).

Olivari 6

Works Cited

Kirszner, Laurie G., and Stephen R. Mandell, eds. <u>Litera-ture: Reading, Reacting, Writing</u>. 3rd ed. Fort Worth: Harcourt Brace, 1997.

Oates, Joyce Carol. "When Characters from the Page Are Made Flesh on the Screen." Ed. Kirszner and Mandell. 592–94.

---. "Where Are You Going, Where Have You Been?" Kirszner and Mandell. 579–91.

Schulz, Gretchen and R. J. R. Rockwood. "In Fairyland, without a Map: Connie's Exploration Inward in Joyce Carol Oates's 'Where Are You Going, Where Have You Been?' " Kirszner and Mandell. 595–607.

Tierce, Mike, and John Michael Crafton. "Connie's Tambourine Man: A New Reading of Arnold Friend." Kirszner and Mandell. 607–13.

Tyler, Anne. "Teenage Wasteland." Kirszner and Mandell. 569–76.

Poetry

CHAPTER 11

Understanding Poetry

NIKKI GIOVANNI

(1945–   )

Poetry

(1975)

poetry is motion graceful
as a fawn
gentle as a teardrop
strong like the eye
5 finding peace in a crowded room
we poets tend to think
our words are golden
though emotion speaks too
loudly to be defined
10 by silence

sometimes after midnight or just before
the dawn
we sit typewriter in hand
pulling loneliness around us
15 forgetting our lovers or children
who are sleeping
ignoring the weary wariness
of our own logic
to compose a poem

20   no one understands it
it never says "love me" for poets are
beyond love
it never says "accept me" for poems seek not
acceptance but controversy

25 it only says "i am" and therefore
   i concede that you are too
   a poem is pure energy
   horizontally contained
   between the mind
30 of the poet and the ear of the reader
   if it does not sing discard the ear
   for poetry is song
   if it does not delight discard
   the heart for poetry is joy
35 if it does not inform then close
   off the brain for it is dead
   if it cannot heed the insistent message
   that life is precious

   which is all we poets
40 wrapped in our loneliness
   are trying to say

ARCHIBALD MACLEISH

(1892–1982)

Ars Poetica[1]

(1926)

A poem should be palpable and mute
As a globed fruit,

Dumb
As old medallions to the thumb,

5 Silent as the sleeve-worn stone
Of casement ledges where the moss has grown—

A poem should be wordless
As the flight of birds.

A poem should be motionless in time
10 As the moon climbs,

---

[1] Art of Poetry.

Leaving, as the moon releases
Twig by twig the night-entangled trees,

Leaving, as the moon behind the winter leaves,
Memory by memory the mind—

15 A poem should be motionless in time
As the moon climbs.

A poem should be equal to:
Not true.

For all the history of grief
20 An empty doorway and a maple leaf.

For love
The leaning grasses and two lights above the sea—

A poem should not mean
But be.

MARIANNE MOORE

(1887–1972)

Poetry

(1921)

I, too, dislike it: there are things that are important beyond all this
    fiddle.
  Reading it, however, with a perfect contempt for it, one discovers
    in it
after all, a place for the genuine.

    Hands that can grasp, eyes
5   that can dilate, hair that can rise
      if it must, these things are important not because a

high-sounding interpretation can be put upon them but because they are
  useful. When they become so derivative as to become unintelligible,
  the same thing may be said for all of us, that we

10   do not admire what
            we cannot understand: the bat
                  holding on upside down or in quest of something to
 eat, elephants pushing, a wild horse taking a roll, a tireless wolf under
    a tree, the immovable critic twitching his skin like a horse that
        feels a
15   flea, the base-
    ball fan, the statistician—
        nor is it valid
            to discriminate against "business documents and

school-books";[1] all these phenomena are important. One must make a
20   distinction
        however: when dragged into prominence by half poets, the result is
          not poetry,
       nor till the poets among us can be
        "literalists of
25   the imagination"[2]—above
            insolence and triviality and can present

for inspection, "imaginary gardens with real toads in them," shall
    we have
    it. In the meantime, if you demand on the one hand,
    the raw material of poetry in
30   all its rawness and
        that which is on the other hand
            genuine, you are interested in poetry.

---

[1] Moore quotes the *Diaries of Tolstoy* (New York, 1917): "Where the boundary between prose and poetry lies, I shall never be able to understand. . . . Poetry is verse; prose is not verse. Or else poetry is everything with the exception of business documents and school books."

[2] A reference (given by Moore) to W. B. Yeats's "William Blake and His Illustrations" (in *Ideas of Good and Evil*, 1903): "The limitation of his view was from the very intensity of his vision; he was a too literal realist of the imagination as others are of nature; and because he believed that the figures seen by the mind's eye, when exhalted by inspiration, were 'external existences,' symbols of divine essences, he hated every grace of style that might obscure their linieaments."

Defining Poetry

Throughout history and across various national and cultural boundaries, poetry has held an important place. In ancient China and Japan, for example, poetry was prized above all else. One story tells of a samurai warrior who, when defeated, asked for a pen and paper. Thinking that he wanted to write a will before being executed, his captor granted his wish. Instead of writing a will, however, the warrior wrote a farewell poem which so moved his captor that he immediately released him.

To the ancient Greeks and Romans, poetry was the medium of spiritual and philosophical expression. Epics such as the *Iliad* and the *Aeneid* are written in verse, and so are dramas such as *Oedipus the King* (p. 1590) and *Antigone* (p. 1708). Passages of the Bible, the Koran, and the Hindu holy books are also written in poetry. Today, throughout the world, poetry continues to delight and to inspire. For many people, in many places, poetry is the language of the emotions, the medium of expression they use when they speak from the heart.

Despite the longstanding place of poetry in our lives, however, many people—including poets themselves—have difficulty deciding just what poetry is. Is a poem "pure energy / horizontally contained / between the mind / of the poet and the ear of the reader" as Nikki Giovanni describes it? Or is a poem, as Archibald MacLeish says, "Dumb," "Silent," "wordless," and "motionless in time"? Or is it simply what Marianne Moore calls "all this fiddle"?

One way of defining poetry is to say that it uses language to condense experience into an intensely concentrated package, with each sound, each word, each image, and each line carrying great weight. But beyond this, it is difficult to pin down what makes a particular arrangement of words or lines a poem. Part of the problem is that poetry has many guises: A poem may be short or long, accessible or obscure; it may express a mood or tell a story; it may conform to a familiar poetic form—a sonnet, a couplet, a haiku—or follow no conventional pattern; it may or may not have a regular, identifiable meter or a rhyme scheme; it may depend heavily on elaborate imagery, figures of speech, irony, complex allusions or symbols, or repeated sounds—or it may include none of these features conventionally associated with poetry.

To further complicate the issue, different readers, different poets, different generations of readers and poets, and different cultures may have different expectations about poetry. As a result, they have different assumptions about poetry, and these conflicting assumptions raise questions. Must poetry be written to delight or inspire, or can a poem have a political or social message? And must this message be conveyed subtly, embellished with imaginatively chosen sounds and words, or can it be explicit and straightforward? These questions, which have been debated by literary critics as well as by poets for many years, have no easy answers—

and perhaps no answers at all. A haiku—short, rich in imagery, adhering to a rigid formal structure—is certainly poetry, and so is a political poem like Wole Soyinka's "Telephone Conversation" (p. 7). To some Western readers, however, a haiku might seem too plain and understated to be poetic, and Soyinka's poem might seem to be a political tract masquerading as poetry. Still, most of these readers would agree that the following lines qualify as poetry.

WILLIAM SHAKESPEARE

(1564–1616)

That Time of Year Thou Mayst in Me Behold

(1609)

That time of year thou mayst in me behold
When yellow leaves, or none, or few, do hang
Upon those boughs which shake against the cold,
Bare ruined choirs, where late the sweet birds sang.
5 In me thou see'st the twilight of such day
As after sunset fadeth in the west,
Which by and by black night doth take away,
Death's second self that seals up all in rest.
In me thou see'st the glowing of such fire,
10 That on the ashes of his youth doth lie,
As the deathbed whereon it must expire,
Consumed with that which it was nourished by
This thou perceiv'st, which makes thy love more strong,
To love that well which thou must leave ere long.

This poem possesses many of the characteristics that Western readers have come to associate with poetry. For instance, its lines have a regular pattern of rhyme and meter that identifies it as a **sonnet.** The poem also includes a complex network of related imagery and figurative language that compares the lost youth of the aging speaker to the sunset and to autumn. Finally, the pair of rhyming lines at the end of the poem states a familiar poetic theme: The lovers' knowledge that they must die makes their love stronger.

Even though the next poem is quite different from the sonnet above, most readers would probably agree that it, too, is a poem.

L O U I S   Z U K O F S K Y

(1904–1978)

I Walk in the Old Street

(1944)

I walk in the old street
to hear the beloved songs
afresh
this spring night.
5 Like the leaves—my loves wake—

not to be the same
or look tireless to the stars
and a ripped doorbell.

Unlike Shakespeare's sonnet, Zukofsky's poem does not have a regular metrical pattern or rhyme scheme. Its diction is more conversational than poetic, and one of its images—a "ripped doorbell"—stands in stark contrast to the other, more conventionally "poetic" images. Nevertheless, the subject—love—is a traditional one; in fact, Zukofsky's poem echoes some of the sentiments of the Shakespeare sonnet. Finally, the poem's division into two four-line stanzas and its use of imaginative comparisons ("Like the leaves—my loves wake—") are unmistakably poetic.

Although the two preceding works can easily be classified as poems, readers might have trouble with the following lines.

E .   E .   C U M M I N G S

(1894–1962)

l(a

(1923)

l(a

le
af
fa

5 ll

s)
one
l

iness

Unlike the two poems above, "l(a" does not seem to have any of the characteristics normally associated with poetry. It has no meter, rhyme, or imagery. It has no repeated sounds, no figures of speech, no symbols. It cannot even be read aloud because its "lines" are fragments of words. In spite of its odd appearance, however, "l(a" does present an idea that is poetic. Reconstructed, the words Cummings broke apart—"l (a leaf falls) one l iness"—express a conventional poetic theme: the loneliness and isolation of the individual. At the same time, by breaking words into bits and pieces, Cummings suggests the flexibility of language and conveys the need to break out of customary ways of using words to define experience.

It is true that most poems, particularly those divided into stanzas, look like poems, and it is also true that poems tend to use compressed language. Beyond this, however, what makes a poem a poem is more a matter of degree than a question of whether or not it conforms to a strict set of rules. A poem is likely to use *more* imagery, figurative language, rhyme, and so on than a prose piece—but, then again, it may not.

A Note on Reading Poetry

Some readers say they do not like poetry because they find it obscure or intimidating. One reason some people have difficulty reading poetry is that it often presents information in subtle (and therefore potentially confusing) ways; it does not immediately "get to the point" as journalistic articles or business letters do. One could argue, however, that by concentrating experience, poetry actually "gets to the point" in ways—and to degrees—that other kinds of writing do not. Even so, some readers see poetry as an alien form. They have the misconception that poetry is always filled with obscure allusions, complex metrical schemes, and flowery diction. Others feel excluded from what they see as its secret language and mysterious structure, approaching poetry as something that must be deciphered. Certainly, reading poetry often requires hard work and concentration. Because it is compressed, poetry often omits exposition and explanation; consequently, readers must be willing to take the time to read closely—to interpret ideas and supply missing connections. Many readers are simply not motivated to dig deeply for what they perceive to be uncertain rewards. But not all poems are difficult, and even those that are, often are well worth the effort. (For specific suggestions about how to read poetry, see Chapter 12.)

Recognizing Kinds of Poetry

Most poems are either *narrative* poems, which recount a story, or *lyric* poems, which communicate a speaker's mood, feelings, or state of mind.

Narrative Poetry

Although any brief poem that tells a story, such as Edwin Arlington Robinson's "Richard Cory" (p. 992), or even a popular song like Bruce Springsteen's "My Hometown" (p. 1009) may be considered a narrative poem, the two most familiar forms of narrative poetry are the *epic* and the *ballad.*

Epic poems recount the accomplishments of heroic figures, typically including expansive settings, superhuman feats, and gods and supernatural beings. The language of epic poems tends to be formal, even elevated, and often quite elaborate. Epics span many cultures—from the *Odyssey* (Greek) to *Beowulf* (Anglo-Saxon) to *The Epic of Gilgamesh* (Babylonian). In ancient times, epics were handed down orally; more recently, poets have written literary epics, such as John Milton's 1667 *Paradise Lost* and Nobel Prize–winning poet Derek Walcott's 1990 *Omeros,* which follow many of the same conventions.

The **ballad** is another type of narrative poetry with roots in an oral tradition. Originally intended to be sung, a ballad uses repeated words and phrases, including a refrain, to advance its story. Some—but not all—ballads use the **ballad stanza** (p. 830). For examples of traditional ballads in this text, see "Bonny Barbara Allen" (p. 891), "Sir Patrick Spence" (p. 893), and "Western Wind" (p. 894). Dudley Randall's "Ballad of Birmingham" (p. 703) and Gwendolyn Brooks's "The Ballad of Chocolate Mabbie" (p. 1073) are examples of contemporary ballads.

Lyric Poetry

Like narrative poems, lyric poems take various forms.

An **elegy** is a poem in which a poet mourns the death of a specific person, as in Robert Hayden's "Homage to the Empress of the Blues" (p. 947), about the singer Bessie Smith. Other examples of this type of elegy include Edna St. Vincent Millay's "Elegy Before Death" (p. 738) and A. E. Housman's "To an Athlete Dying Young" (p. 952). Sometimes, however, an elegy's subject is more general. Thomas Gray's "Elegy Written in a Country Churchyard" (p. 938), for example, mourns the inevitable death of all people.

An **ode** is a long lyric poem, formal and serious in style, tone, and subject matter. An ode typically has a fairly complex stanzaic pattern, such as the **terza rima** used by Percy Bysshe Shelley in "Ode to the West Wind" (p. 997). Other odes in this text include John Keats's "Ode to a Nightingale" (p. 960) and "Ode on a Grecian Urn" (p. 958).

An **aubade** is a poem about morning, usually celebrating the coming of dawn. An example is Philip Larkin's "Aubade" (p. 964).

A **meditation** is a lyric poem that focuses on a physical object, using this object as a vehicle for considering larger issues. Edmund Waller's "Go, Lovely Rose" (p. 1019) is a meditation.

A **pastoral**—for example, Christopher Marlowe's "The Passionate Shepherd to His Love" (p. 971)—is a lyric poem that celebrates the simple, idyllic pleasures of country life.

Finally, a **dramatic monologue** is a poem whose speaker addresses one or more listeners, often revealing much more than he or she intends. Robert Browning's "My Last Duchess" (p. 676) and "Porphyria's Lover" (p. 693) and Alfred, Lord Tennyson's "Ulysses" (p. 1015) are three dramatic monologues that appear in this text.

Discovering Themes in Poetry

A poem can be about anything, from the mysteries of the universe to poetry itself. Although no subject is really inappropriate for poetic treatment, certain conventional subjects recur frequently. For example, poets often write about love, nature, death, family, the folly of human desires, and the inevitability of growing old.

A poem's **theme,** however, is more than its general subject matter. It includes the ideas the poet explores, the concerns the poem examines. More specifically, a poem's theme is its main point or idea. Poems "about nature," for instance, may praise the beauty of nature, assert the superiority of its simplest creatures over humans, consider its evanescence, or mourn its destruction. Similarly, poems "about death" may examine the difficulty of facing one's own mortality, eulogize a friend, assert the need for the acceptance of life's cycles, cry out against death's inevitability, or explore the **carpe diem** theme ("life is brief, so let us seize the day").

In order to discover the theme of a poem, readers look at its form, its voice, its language, its images, its allusions, its sound—all of its individual elements. Together, these elements convey the ideas that are important in the poem. Of course, a poem may not communicate the same meaning to every reader. Different readers bring different backgrounds, attitudes, and experiences to a poem, and therefore they see different things and give weight to different ideas.

The following poem is rich enough in language and content to suggest a variety of different interpretations.

A D R I E N N E   R I C H

(1929–   )

A Woman Mourned by Daughters

(1984)

Now, not a tear begun,
we sit here in your kitchen,
spent, you see, already.
You are swollen till you strain
5 this house and the whole sky.
You, whom we so often
succeeded in ignoring!
You are puffed up in death
like a corpse pulled from the sea;
10 we groan beneath your weight.
And yet you were a leaf,
a straw blown on the bed,
you had long since become
crisp as a dead insect.
15 What is it, if not you,
that settles on us now
like satins you pulled down
over our bridal heads?
What rises in our throats
20 like food you prodded in?
Nothing could be enough.
You breathe upon us now
through solid assertions
of yourself: teaspoons, goblets,
25 seas of carpet, a forest
of old plants to be watered,
an old man in an adjoining
room to be touched and fed.
And all this universe
30 dares us to lay a finger
anywhere, save exactly
as you would wish it done.

In general terms "A Woman Mourned by Daughters" is, of course, about the speaker's mother. More specifically, this poem explores a number of different ideas: the passing of time; the relationships between mother and daughters, father and daughters, husband and wife; the power of memory. Its central theme, however, may be expressed as a **paradox:** "After death, a person may be a stronger presence than she was when she was alive."

Many different elements in the poem suggest this interpretation. The poem's speaker directly addresses her mother. Her voice is searching, questioning, and the poem's unpoetic diction ("You, whom we so often / succeeded in ignoring") and metrical irregularities give it a halting, uncertain quality. The words, images, and figurative language work together to establish the central idea: Alive, the mother was light as a leaf or a straw or a dead insect; dead, she seems "swollen" and "puffed up," and the daughters feel crushed by her weight. The concrete details of her life—"teaspoons, goblets, / seas of carpet . . ."—weigh on her survivors and keep them under her spell. In her kitchen, her memory is alive; in death, she has tremendous power over her daughters.

Like most complex poems, this one supports several alternate readings. Some readers will focus on the negative language used to describe the mother; others might emphasize the images of domesticity; still others might concentrate on the role of the absent sisters and the almost-absent father. Any of these focuses can lead to a redefinition of the poem's theme.

The following poem is also about a parent who inspires ambivalent feelings in a child.

RAYMOND CARVER

(1938–1988)

Photograph of My Father in His Twenty-Second Year

(1983)

October. Here in this dank, unfamiliar kitchen
I study my father's embarrassed young man's face.
Sheepish grin, he holds in one hand a string
of spiny yellow perch, in the other
5 a bottle of Carlsbad beer.

In jeans and denim shirt, he leans
against the front fender of a 1934 Ford.
He would like to pose bluff and hearty for his posterity,
wear his old hat cocked over his ear.
10 All his life my father wanted to be bold.

But the eyes give him away, and the hands
that limply offer the string of dead perch
and the bottle of beer. Father, I love you,
yet how can I say thank you, I who can't hold my liquor either,
15 and don't even know the places to fish?

Like Rich's speaker, Carver's is also in a kitchen. Studying a picture, this speaker sees through his father's façade. Instead of seeing the "bold," "bluff and hearty" young man his father wanted to be, he sees him as he was: "embarrassed" and "sheepish," with limp hands. In the last three lines of the poem, the speaker addresses his father directly, drawing an analogy between his father's shortcomings and his own. This frank acknowledgment of his own vulnerability and the explicit comparison between father and son suggest that the poem has more to do with the speaker than with his father. Still, it is clear that the poem has something universal to say about the link between parents and children—specifically, about the ambivalent feelings that children have for parents who pass on to them their own faults and failings.

The poem below also looks back on a parent, but here the adult speaker assumes a child's point of view.

JUDITH ORTIZ COFER

(1952–   )

My Father in the Navy: A Childhood Memory

(1982)

Stiff and immaculate
in the white cloth of his uniform
and a round cap on his head like a halo,
he was an apparition on leave from a shadow-world
5 and only flesh and blood when he rose from below
the waterline where he kept watch over the engines
and dials making sure the ship parted the waters
on a straight course.
Mother, brother and I kept vigil
10 on the nights and dawns of his arrivals,
watching the corner beyond the neon sign of a quasar
for the flash of white our father like an angel
heralding a new day.
His homecomings were the verses

15 we composed over the years making up
the siren's song that kept him coming back
from the bellies of iron whales
and into our nights
like the evening prayer.

Even as an adult the speaker seems still not to know her father, whom she remembers as "stiff and immaculate," dressed in white, "an apparition on leave from a shadow-world." She remembers him as being "like an angel," wearing his cap "like a halo." In lines 14–16, the speaker gives the father a mythical quality by associating him with the long-missing, long-awaited wanderer—Odysseus, hero of Homer's *Odyssey*. The reference to the "siren's song" in line 16, also an allusion to the *Odyssey*, suggests the adult speaker's realization that the father is drawn back—perhaps against his will—to the family. Together, the poem's tone and imagery convey the child's view of the father as elusive and unreal—an impression the adult speaker neither confirms nor corrects. Perhaps, then, the poem suggests that the speaker is still struggling to understand her father's complex role in her life; perhaps, too, it suggests the universal difficulty of a child's trying to understand a parent.

EXERCISE: DISCOVERING THEMES IN POETRY

The seven poems that follow share a common subject—each is about a parent—yet each explores different ideas. Read each poem, keeping the following questions in mind.

1. What is the speaker's attitude toward his or her parent?

2. Which words and images suggest positive associations? Which help to create a negative impression?

3. How does the poem's title characterize the parent? How does it contribute to the poem's overall effect?

4. How would you characterize the poem's tone? For example, is the poem sentimental, humorous, angry, resentful, or regretful?

5. What ideas about parents and children are explored in the poem? What do you think is the poem's central theme?

6. What does the poem say about the parent? What does it reveal about the speaker?

THEODORE ROETHKE

(1908–1963)

My Papa's Waltz

(1948)

The whiskey on your breath
Could make a small boy dizzy;
But I hung on like death:
Such waltzing was not easy.

5 We romped until the pans
Slid from the kitchen shelf;
My mother's countenance
Could not unfrown itself.

The hand that held my wrist
10 Was battered on one knuckle;
At every step you missed
My right ear scraped a buckle.

You beat time on my head
With a palm caked hard by dirt,
15 Then waltzed me off to bed
Still clinging to your shirt.

DYLAN THOMAS

(1914–1953)

Do Not Go Gentle into That Good Night[1]

(1952)

Do not go gentle into that good night,
Old age should burn and rave at close of day;
Rage, rage against the dying of the light.

---

[1] This poem was written during the last illness of the poet's father, D. J. Thomas.

Though wise men at their end know dark is right,
5 Because their words had forked no lightning they
Do not go gentle into that good night.

Good men, the last wave by, crying how bright
Their frail deeds might have danced in a green bay,
Rage, rage against the dying of the light.

10 Wild men who caught and sang the sun in flight,
And learn, too late, they grieved it on its way,
Do not go gentle into that good night.

Grave men, near death, who see with blinding sight
Blind eyes could blaze like meteors and be gay,
15 Rage, rage against the dying of the light.

And you, my father, there on the sad height,
Curse, bless, me now with your fierce tears, I pray,
Do not go gentle into that good night.
Rage, rage against the dying of the light.

SIMON J. ORTIZ

(1941–   )

My Father's Song

(1976)

Wanting to say things,
I miss my father tonight.
His voice, the slight catch,
the depth from his thin chest,
5 the tremble of emotion
in something he has just said
to his son, his song:

We planted corn one Spring at Acu—
we planted several times
10 but this one particular time
I remember the soft damp sand
in my hand.

My father had stopped at one point
to show me an overturned furrow;
15 the plowshare had unearthed
the burrow nest of a mouse
in the soft moist sand.

Very gently, he scooped tiny pink animals
into the palm of his hand
20 and told me to touch them.
We took them to the edge
of the field and put them in the shade
of a sand moist clod.

I remember the very softness
25 of cool and warm sand and tiny alive mice
and my father saying things.

COLLEEN J. MCELROY

(1935–   )

My Father's Wars

(1984)

Once he followed simple rules
of casual strength,
summoned violence with the flick
of combat ribbon or hash mark;
5 now he forces a pulse into treasonous muscles
and commands soap opera villains.
He is camped in a world regimented
by glowing tubes,
his olive-black skin begging for the fire
10 of unlimited color.
In towns where he can follow
the orders of silence,
gunfights are replayed
in thirty-minute intervals
15 familiar as his stiff right arm
or the steel brace scaffolding his leg.

By midday the room is filled
with game shows and private eyes hurling
questions against all those who swear
20 their innocence;
his wife is in full retreat
and jumps when he answers in half-formed words
of single grunts deadly as shrapnel.
He need not remind her
25 he is always the hero;
the palms of his hands
are muddy with old battle lines.
He has fallen
heir to brutal days where he moves
30 battalions of enemies;
his mornings are shattered with harsh echoes
of their electronic voices.

Here he is on neutral ground
and need not struggle to capture words
35 he can no longer force his brain to master;
he plans his roster
and does not attend to his wife's
rapid-fire review of the neighbor's behavior.
He recalls too clearly the demarcation of blacks,
40 of Buffalo Soldier and 93rd Division.
By late afternoon he is seen rigidly
polishing his car in broad one-arm swipes,
its side windows and bumpers emblazoned
with stickers: US ARMY RETIRED REGULAR

LUCILLE CLIFTON

(1936–   )

My Mama Moved among the Days

(1969)

My Mama moved among the days
like a dreamwalker in a field;
seemed like what she touched was hers
seemed like what touched her couldn't hold,
5 she got us almost through the high grass

then seemed like she turned around and ran
right back in
right back on in

ROBERT HAYDEN

(1913–1980)

Those Winter Sundays

(1962)

Sundays too my father got up early
and put his clothes on in the blueblack cold,
then with cracked hands that ached
from labor in the weekday weather made
5 banked fires blaze. No one ever thanked him.

I'd wake and hear the cold splintering, breaking.
When the rooms were warm, he'd call,
and slowly I would rise and dress,
fearing the chronic angers of that house,

10 Speaking indifferently to him,
who had driven out the cold
and polished my good shoes as well.
What did I know, what did I know
of love's austere and lonely offices?

SEAMUS HEANEY[1]

(1939–   )

Digging

(1966)

Between my finger and my thumb
The squat pen rests; snug as a gun.

---

[1] Winner of the 1995 Nobel Prize in Literature.

Under my window, a clean rasping sound
When the spade sinks into gravelly ground:
5   My father, digging. I look down

Till his straining rump among the flowerbeds
Bends low, comes up twenty years away
Stooping in rhythm through potato drills
Where he was digging.

10   The coarse boot nestled on the lug, the shaft
Against the inside knee was levered firmly.
He rooted out tall tops, buried the bright edge deep
To scatter new potatoes that we picked
Loving their cool hardness in our hands.
15   By God, the old man could handle a spade.
Just like his old man.

My grandfather cut more turf in a day
Than any other man on Toner's bog.
Once I carried him milk in a bottle
20   Corked sloppily with paper. He straightened up
To drink it, then fell to right away

Nicking and slicing neatly, heaving sods
Over his shoulder, going down and down
For the good turf. Digging.

25   The cold smell of potato mould, the squelch and slap
Of soggy peat, the curt cuts of an edge
Through living roots awaken in my head.
But I've no spade to follow men like them.

Between my finger and my thumb
30   The squat pen rests.
I'll dig with it.

CHAPTER 12

Reading and Writing
about Poetry

Reading Poetry

Sometimes readers approach poetry purely for pleasure. At other times, however, reading a poem is the first step toward writing about it—and, through writing, toward learning more about it. The following guidelines, which focus on issues discussed elsewhere in this section, may help direct your approach and enrich your reading of a poem.

- Rephrase the poem in your own words. What does your paraphrase reveal about the poem's subject and central concerns? What is lost or gained in your paraphrase of the poem?

- Consider the poem's **voice.** Who is the poem's persona or speaker? How would you characterize the poem's tone? Is the poem ironic? (See Chapter 13.)

- Study the poem's **diction** and look up unfamiliar words in a dictionary. How does word choice affect your reaction to the poem? What do the connotations of words reveal about the poem? What level of diction is used? Is dialect used? Is word order unusual or unexpected? How does the arrangement of words contribute to your understanding of the poem? (See Chapter 14.)

- Examine the poem's **imagery.** What kind of imagery predominates? What specific images are used? Is a pattern of imagery present? How does use of imagery enrich the poem? (See Chapter 15.)

- Identify the poem's **figures of speech.** Does the poet use metaphor? Simile? Personification? Hyperbole? Understatement? Metonymy or synecdoche? Apostrophe? How do figures of speech affect your reading of the poem? (See Chapter 16.)

- Listen to the **sound** of the poem. Are rhythm and meter regular or irregular? How do rhythm and meter reinforce the poem's central concerns? Does the poem use alliteration? Assonance? Rhyme? How do these elements enhance the poem? (See Chapter 17.)

◆ Look at the poem's **form.** Is the poem written in closed or open form? Is the poem constructed as a sonnet? A sestina? A villanelle? An epigram? A haiku? Is the poem an example of concrete poetry? How does the poem's form reinforce its ideas? (See Chapter 18.)

◆ Consider the poem's use of **symbol, allegory, allusion,** or **myth.** Does the poem make use of symbols? Allusions? How do symbols or allusions support its theme? Is the poem an allegory? Does the poem retell or interpret a myth? (See Chapter 19.)

◆ Identify the poem's **theme.** What central theme or themes does the poem explore? How are the themes expressed? (See Chapter 11.)

ACTIVE READING

When you approach a poem that you plan to write about, you engage in the same active reading strategies you use when you read a short story or a play. When you finish recording your reactions to the poem, you focus on a topic, develop ideas about that topic, decide on a thesis, prepare an outline, and draft and revise your essay.

Catherine Wittaker, a student in an introduction to literature course, was asked to write a three- to five-page essay comparing any *two* of the seven poems about parents that appear in the exercise in Chapter 11 (pp. 641–647). Her instructor told the class that the essay should reflect students' own reactions to the poem, not the opinions of literary critics. As Catherine planned and wrote her paper, she was guided by the process described in Chapter 2, Reading and Writing about Literature.

Previewing

Catherine began her work by previewing each poem and then reading it more closely to see which two she wanted to write about. She knew she wanted to study poems with an affectionate, straightforward tone, so she began by eliminating those she considered obscure or difficult and those whose portrait of the speaker's parent did not seem sympathetic.

Previewing helped Catherine to narrow down her choices. As she looked through "Those Winter Sundays," she was drawn immediately to words in the opening lines ("Sundays too . . ."; "blueblack cold"). She had the same reaction to "The squat pen rests; snug as a gun" in line 2 of "Digging." In each case, the words made Catherine want to examine the poem further. She noticed too that both poems were divided into stanzas of varying lengths and that both focused on a father. Keeping these features in mind, Catherine began a close reading of each poem.

Highlighting and Annotating

As Catherine read and reread "Those Winter Sundays" and "Digging," she recorded her comments and questions. The highlighted and annotated poems follow.

ROBERT HAYDEN

(1913–1980)

Were there many Sundays like these?

Those Winter Sundays

(1962)

Like all other days of the week?

Sundays (too) my father got up early
and put his clothes on in the blueblack cold,
Why did he get up before dawn?
then with cracked hands that ached
from labor in the weekday weather made
What kind of job did the father have?
5   banked fires blaze. No one ever thanked him.
Was there a large family?

I'd wake and hear the cold splintering, breaking.
When the rooms were warm, he'd call,
and slowly I would rise and dress,
fearing the chronic angers of that house,
Were there problems in the family?

10 Speaking indifferently to him,
Why did he do this?
who had driven out the cold
and polished my good shoes as well.
What did I know, what did I know
Was there a mother around?
of love's austere and lonely offices?
offices = duties or functions assigned to someone

austere = without adornment or ornamentation, simple, bare — simple, without luxury, harsh

SEAMUS HEANEY

(1939–   )

Digging

(1966)

Between my finger and my thumb
The squat pen rests; snug as a gun.

→ Why use this expression?.
→ Why a "squat" pen?

Under my window, a clean rasping sound
When the spade sinks into gravelly ground:
5 My father, digging. I look down

Till his straining rump among the flowerbeds
Bends low, comes up twenty years away
Stooping in rhythm through potato drills
Where he was digging.

Is he thinking about the past?

10 The coarse boot nestled on the lug, the shaft
Against the inside knee was levered firmly.
He rooted out tall tops, buried the bright edge deep
To scatter new potatoes that we picked
Loving their cool hardness in our hands.

Is this like the poet's pen?

Was this a family task?

15 By God, the old man could handle a spade.
Just like his old man.

Two generations could "handle a spade." Can the poet dig?

My grandfather cut more turf in a day
Than any other man on Toner's bog.
Once I carried him milk in a bottle
20 Corked sloppily with paper. He straightened up
To drink it, then fell to right away

Was he a young child at the time?

The grandfather was a hard worker

Nicking and slicing neatly, heaving sods
Over his shoulder, going down and down
For the good turf. Digging.

Almost like an art of digging?

25 The cold smell of potato mould, the squelch and slap
Of soggy peat, the curt cuts of an edge
Through living roots awaken in my head.
But I've no spade to follow men like them.

What does it make him remember?

What are "men like them" like?

Same as first 2 lines {
Between my finger and my thumb
30 The squat pen rests. → Why is this repeated?
I'll dig with it. → Dig for what?
}

Catherine found the language of both poems appealing, and she believed her highlighting and annotating had given her some valuable insights. For example, she noticed some parallels between the two poems: Both focus on the past, both portray fathers as hard workers, and neither mentions a mother.

Writing about Poetry

Planning an Essay

Even though Catherine still had to find a specific topic for her paper, her preliminary work did suggest some interesting possibilities. She was especially intrigued by the way both poems depict fathers as actively engaged in physical tasks.

Choosing a Topic

One idea Catherine thought she might want to write about in her paper was the significance of the speakers' attitudes toward their fathers: Although both see their fathers as hard workers, the speaker in "Those Winter Sundays" has mixed feelings about his father's devotion to his family, while the speaker in "Digging" is more appreciative. Catherine explored this idea in the two journal entries below.

"Those Winter Sundays"
Why did the father get up early every morning? One could imagine that he had a large family and little money. There is no mention of a mother. Images are created of the utter coldness and "chronic angers" of the house. The father not only made fires to warm the house but also polished his child's (or children's) shoes—maybe for church. And yet, the child seems not to care or appreciate the father's efforts. Is he too young to say thank you, or are there other problems in the house for which the child blames the father?

"Digging"
In the poem, the poet seems to be contemplating the subject about which to write when the sounds of digging capture his attention. He remembers the steady, artful rhythm of his

father's digging of the potatoes and how they (probably the poet and his brothers and sisters) picked out the cool potatoes. His memories appear to be entirely appreciative of his father's and grandfather's hard work and skill. He does, however, feel regret that he is not like these dedicated men. Even though he cannot use a shovel, he hopes to use his pen in order to make his own contributions as a writer.

When Catherine reread her journal entries, she thought she had moved closer to a specific topic for her paper. The more she reviewed the two poems, the more confident she felt exploring their similar views of the fathers' roles and their contrasting attitudes toward these fathers. Before she could write a draft of her paper, however, Catherine needed to generate a list of specific similarities and differences between the two poems:

Finding Something to Say

Brainstorming   Catherine returned to the highlighted and annotated poems in order to compile the following brainstorming notes:

DIFFERENCES

"Those Winter Sundays"	"Digging"
— memories of family problems	— only happy memories are involved
— the child acts ambiguously toward his father	— the child admires his father
— atmosphere of tension	— atmosphere of happiness and togetherness

SIMILARITIES

— the fathers are hard workers
— the fathers appear to love their children
— similar time—impression that the events happened years ago
— children, now grown, appreciate their fathers' dedication
— children, now grown, are inspired by their fathers' determination

After finishing her brainstorming, Catherine reviewed her notes carefully. As connections between the two poems came into focus, she was able to decide on a possible thesis and on a tentative order in which to present her ideas.

Deciding on a Thesis

The more Catherine thought about the two poems, the more she focused on their similarities. She expressed a possible main idea for her paper in the following tentative thesis statement:

Although their family backgrounds are different, both now-grown poets realize the determination and dedication of their fathers and are consequently impassioned in their writings.

Preparing an Outline

Before preparing a scratch outline, Catherine reviewed her notes to identify the specific ideas she wanted to address in her first draft. Then she arranged those ideas in a logical order in a scratch outline.

"Those Winter Sundays"

Poet reflects back on childhood
— father's hard work
— his misunderstanding and lack of appreciation for everything his father did

Family setting in childhood
— tension in the house
— no mother mentioned in the poem

Poet's realization of father's love and dedication

"Digging"

Poet reminisces
— father's skill and hard work
— grandfather's steady heaving of sods
— children's participation and acceptance

Happiness of the family

The desire for the poet to continue the tradition

Drafting

With a thesis statement and scratch outline to guide her, Catherine wrote the following first draft of her essay. Her instructor's comments appear in the margins and at the end of the paper.

(first draft)

A Comparison of Two Poems about Fathers

Robert Hayden's "Those Winter Sundays" and "Digging" by Seamus Heaney are poems that were inspired by fathers and composed as tributes to fathers. Although their family backgrounds are different, both now-grown (poets) realize the determination and dedication of their fathers and are consequently impassioned in their writings.

Careful you're confusing poet and speaker

In "Those Winter Sundays," Hayden reflects back on his childhood. He remembers the many Sundays when his father got up early to start the fires to make the house warm for his children's awakening. The poet pictures his father's hands made rough by his weekday work. These same hands not only made the fires on Sunday but also polished his son's good shoes, in preparation, no doubt, for church.

Hayden also quite clearly remembers that his father was never thanked for his work. The reader imagines that the father had many children and may have been poor. There were inner tensions in the house and, quite noticeably, there is no mention of a mother.

Looking back, the poet now realizes the dedication and austere care with which his father took care of the family. As a child, he never thanked his father, but now, as an adult, the poet seems to appreciate the simple kindness of his father.

In a similar sense, Seamus Heaney writes "Digging" as a tribute to his father and grandfather. He also reminisces about his father and remembers with clarity the skill with which his father dug potatoes. The grandfather, too, is remembered, as is his technique for neatly heaving sods.

Here too quotations from the poem would strengthen your discussion

There is an atmosphere of happiness in this poem. With the children helping the father harvest the potatoes, a sense of family togetherness is created. The reader feels that this family is a hard-working, but nevertheless happy, one.

As the poet reminisces about his childhood, he realizes that, unlike his father and grandfather, he will never be a master of shovelling or a person using physical strength to earn a living. He wishes to be like his father before him, desiring to accomplish and contribute. However, for the poet, any "digging" to be done will be by his pen, in the form of literature.

To conclude, the fathers in these poets' pasts inspire them to write. An appreciation and admiration for their fathers' dedication is achieved only after the children mature into adults. It is then that the fathers' impact on their children's lives is realized for its true importance.

Good start! When you revise, focus on the following:

— Edit use of "poet" and "speaker" carefully. You cannot assume that these poems reflect the poets' own lives or attitudes toward their fathers.

— Add more specific references to the poems, particularly quotations.

— Consider adding brief references to other poems about parents.

— Consider rearranging your material into a point-by-point comparison, which will make the specific points of similarity and difference clearer.

Let's discuss this draft in a Conference.

First Draft: Commentary

After submitting her first draft, Catherine met with her instructor for a pre-revision conference. Together, they reviewed not only her first draft, but also her annotations, journal entries, brainstorming notes, and scratch outline. During the meeting, her instructor elaborated on his marginal comments and, building on ideas Catherine herself had discovered, helped her develop a plan for revision.

Catherine's instructor liked her approach to the poems, and he agreed that their similarities were worth exploring in detail. He thought, however, that her references to the poems' language and ideas needed to be much more specific, and that her current pattern of organization—discussing "Those Winter Sundays" first and then moving on to consider "Digging"—made the specific similarities between the two poems difficult to see.

Because the class had studied other poems in which speakers try to resolve their ambivalent feelings toward their parents, Catherine's instructor also suggested that she mention these poems to provide a wider context for her ideas. Finally, he explained the difference between the perspective of the poet and that of the **speaker,** a persona the poet creates, reminding her to edit carefully with this distinction in mind.

As she reexamined her ideas in light of her discussion with her instructor, Catherine looked again at both the annotated poems and her brainstorming notes. She then recorded her thoughts about her progress in an additional journal entry.

> After reviewing the poems again and talking to Professor Jackson, I discovered some additional points that I want to include in my final draft. The connection between the poet's pen and the shovel is evident in "Digging," as are the cold and the tensions in the house in "Those Winter Sundays." The tone of each poem should also be discussed. Specifically, I think that the poet's choice of "austere" in "Those Winter Sundays" has significance and should be included. In my next draft, I'll expand my first draft—hopefully, without reading into the poems too much. I also need to reorganize my ideas so parallels between the two poems will be clearer.

Because this journal entry suggested a new arrangement of ideas within her essay, Catherine prepared a new scratch outline to guide her revision.

Reflections on their fathers
    Both Poems
        — fathers' dedication and hard work

Family similarities and differences
"Digging"
— loving and caring
"Those Winter Sundays"
— family problems (tone of the poem)
Lessons learned from father
"Digging"
— inspiration (symbolism of pen and shovel)
— realization of father's inner strength
"Those Winter Sundays"
— realization of father's inner strength
— "austere" caring (images of cold)
Brief discussion of other poems about fathers

After once again reviewing all the material she had accumulated, Catherine prepared a second draft.

Second draft

A Comparison of Two Poems about Fathers

Robert Hayden's "Those Winter Sundays" and Seamus Heaney's "Digging" are two literary pieces that are tributes to their fathers. The inspiration and admiration wrought from the dedication of the fathers is an element evident in each poem. Although the nature of the two family relationships may differ, the common thread of the love of fathers for their children weaves through each poem.

Reflections on one's childhood can bring assorted memories to light. Presumably, Hayden and Heaney are now adults and reminisce on their childhood with a mature sense of enlightenment not found in childhood. Both poets describe their fathers' hard work and dedication to their families. Hayden remembers that even after working hard all week, his father would get up early on Sunday to warm the house in preparation for his children's rising. The poet vividly portrays his father's hands, describing "cracked hands that ached from labor in the weekday weather" (3–4). And yet, these same hands not only built the fires that drove out the cold but also polished his children's good shoes.

In a similar way, Heaney reminisces about his father's and grandfather's digging of soil and sod, elaborating on their skill and dedication to their task.

The fathers in these poems appear to be the hardest of workers, laborers who sought to support their families. Not only did they have a dedication to their work, but they also cared about and undoubtedly loved their children. Looking back, Hayden realizes that, although his childhood may not have been perfect nor his family life entirely without problems, his father loved him. Heaney's depiction of the potato picking makes us imagine a loving family led by a father and grandfather who worked together and included the children in both work and celebration. Heaney grows to become a man who has nothing but respect for his father and grandfather, wishing to emulate them and somehow follow their greatness.

Although similarities exist between the sons and fathers in the poems, the family life differs between the two. Perhaps it is the tone of the poems that best typifies the family atmosphere. The tone of "Digging" is wholesome, earthy, natural, and happy, emphasizing the healthy and caring nature of the poet's childhood. In reminiscing, Heaney seems to have no negative memories concerning his father or family. In contrast, the tone of Hayden's poem is very much like the coldness of the Sunday mornings. Even though the father warmed the house, the "chronic angers of that house" (9) did not leave with the cold. The poet, as a child, seems full of resentment toward the father, no doubt blaming him for the family problems. (Curiously, it is the father and not a mother who polishes the children's good shoes. Was there no mother?) The reader senses that the father-son communication evident in Heaney's family is missing in Hayden's.

There are many other poets who have written about their fathers. Simon J. Ortiz in "My Father's Song" writes a touching tribute to his father, who taught him to respect and care for the lives of animals and to appreciate earthly wonders. In other poems, such as Theodore Roethke's "My Papa's Waltz" and Colleen J. McElroy's "My Father's Wars," the fathers are depicted as imperfect, vulnerable people who try to cope with life as well as possible.

"Digging" and "Those Winter Sundays" are poems written from the inspirations of sons, admiring and appreciating their fathers. Childhood memories act not only as images of the past but also as aids for the poets' self-realization and enlightenment. Even after childhood, the fathers' influence over their sons is evident; only now do the poets appreciate its true importance.

Second Draft: Commentary

When she reread her second draft, Catherine thought she had accomplished some of what she had set out to do: She had, for example, tightened her thesis statement, rearranged her discussion, and added specific details. However, she still was not satisfied with her analysis of the poem's language and tone (she had not, for example, considered the importance of the word *austere* or examined the significance of Heaney's equation of spade and pen). In addition, she realized she was still confusing the poet with the speaker. She also thought that the material in paragraph 5 about other poems, although interesting, was distracting, so she decided to try to relocate it. Finally, she planned to edit and proofread carefully as she prepared her final draft.

Catherine Wittaker

Professor Jackson

English 102

5 March 1996

Digging for Memories

Robert Hayden's "Those Winter Sundays" and Seamus Heaney's "Digging" are two literary pieces that are tributes to the speakers' fathers. Although the depiction of the families and the tones of the two poems are different, the common thread of love between fathers and children is woven through the two poems, and each speaker is inspired by his father's example.

Many other poets have written about children and their fathers. Simon J. Ortiz in "My Father's Song" writes a touching tribute to a father who taught the speaker to respect and care for the lives of animals and to appreciate earthly wonders. In other poems, such as Theodore Roethke's "My Papa's Waltz" and Colleen J. McElroy's "My Father's Wars," the fathers are depicted as imperfect, vulnerable people who try to cope with life as well as possible.

As all these poems reveal, reflections on childhood can bring assorted memories to light, as they do for Hayden's and Heaney's speakers. Now adults, they reminisce about their childhoods with a mature sense of enlightenment not found in childhood. Both speakers describe their fathers' hard work and dedication to their families. Hayden's speaker remembers that even after working hard all week, his father would get up early on Sunday to warm the house in preparation for his children's rising. The speaker vividly

Thesis

¶ 5 from second draft has been relocated. References to poems in Chapter 11 of this text include complete authors' names and titles.

Speaker and author are clearly distinguished.

Wittaker 2

Parenthetical references cite line numbers.

portrays his father's hands, describing "cracked hands that ached from labor in the weekday weather" (3–4). And yet, these same hands not only built the fires that drove out the cold, but also polished his children's good shoes. In a similar way, Heaney's speaker reminisces about his father's and grandfather's digging of soil and sod, elaborating on their skill and their dedication to their tasks.

The fathers in these poems appear to be the hardest of workers, laborers who sought to support their families. Not only were they dedicated to their work, but they also seem to have cared about and to have loved their children. Looking back, Hayden's speaker realizes that, although his childhood may not have been perfect and his family life was not entirely without problems, his father loved him. Heaney's depiction of the potato picking makes us imagine a loving family led by a father and grandfather who worked together and included the children in both work and celebration. Heaney's speaker grows to become a man who has nothing but respect for his father and grandfather, wishing to emulate them and somehow fill their shoes.

Although similarities exist between the sons and fathers in the poems, the family life the two poems depict is very different. Perhaps it is the tone of the poems that best reveals the family atmosphere. The tone of "Digging" is wholesome, earthy, natural, and happy, emphasizing the healthy and caring nature of the speaker's childhood. In reminiscing, Heaney's speaker seems to have no negative memories concerning his father or family. In contrast, the tone of Hayden's poem is very much like the coldness of

Wittaker 3

the Sunday mornings. Even though the father warmed the house, the "chronic angers of that house" (9) did not leave with the cold. The speaker, as a child, seems to have been full of resentment toward the father, no doubt blaming him for the family problems. The reader senses that the father-son communication evident in Heaney's poem is missing in Hayden's.

Topic sentence stresses paper's emphasis on similarities.

In spite of these differences, the reader cannot go away from either poem without the impression that both speakers learned important lessons from their fathers. Both fathers had a great amount of inner strength and dedication to their families. As the years pass, Hayden's speaker now realizes the depth of his father's devotion to his family. He uses the description of the "blueblack cold" (2) that was splintered and broken by the fires lovingly prepared by his father to suggest the strength and compassion with which his father tried to keep his family free from harm and tension. The cold suggests the tensions of the family which the father is determined to force out of the house through his "austere and lonely offices" (14).

In Heaney's poem, the father and grandfather also had a profound impact on the young speaker. As the memories come pouring back, the speaker's admiration for the men who came before him forces him to reflect on his own life and work. He realizes that he will never have the proficiency to do the physical labor of his relatives: "I've no spade to follow men like them" (28). However, just as the shovel was the tool of his father and grandfather, the pen will be the tool with which the speaker will work. The

Wittaker 4

shovel suggests the hard work, effort, and determination of the men who came before him, while the pen is the literary equivalent of the shovel. Heaney's speaker has been inspired by his father and grandfather and hopes to accomplish with a pen in the world of literature what they accomplished with a shovel on the land.

Conclusion   "Digging" and "Those Winter Sundays" are poems written from the perspective of sons, admiring and appreciating their fathers. Childhood memories act not only as images of the past but also as aids for the speakers' self-realization and enlightenment. Even after childhood, the fathers' influence over their sons is evident; only now, however, do the speakers appreciate its true importance.

Final Draft: Commentary

As she wrote her final draft, Catherine expanded her analysis, looking more closely at the language and tone of the two poems. To support and clarify her points, she added more direct quotations, taking care to reproduce words and punctuation marks accurately and to cite line numbers in parentheses after each quotation. She also moved her discussion of other poems to paragraph 2, where it provides a smooth transition from her introduction to her discussion of Hayden and Heaney. Her final draft is more fully developed and more convincing than her earlier drafts were.

CHAPTER 13

Voice

What makes a poem significant? What makes it memorable? Passion and thought, emotionally charged language, fresh imagery, surprising use of metaphor . . . yes. But also, I think, the very sure sense that the moment we enter the world of the poem we are participating in another episode of the myth-journey of humankind; that a voice has taken up the tale once more. The individual experience as related or presented in the poem renews our deep, implicit faith in that greater experience. A poem remains with us to the extent that it allows us to feel that we are listening to a voice at once contemporary and ancient. This makes all the difference.

JOHN HAINES, "THE HOLE IN THE BUCKET"

I have been ruminating about "personal poems"—I am inclined to agree that one turns back to less personal poems yet you surely would not remove Shakespeare's sonnets, all of Donne, much of Yeats, all of Emily Dickinson, Sappho, Millay, Wylie (or most), Wyatt from the canon, would you? The trouble is that one does not choose what one is to write about: poetry is a seizure, and not done on will. The point is I think that a "personal" poem has to go deep enough to touch the universal: the "I" *is only a device like any other. This is not to argue—as I agree that it would be better if the muse provided more* less *personal poems.*

MAY SARTON, "AMONG THE VISUAL DAYS"

Of women's poetry [it] . . . may be said [that] insofar as it attempts timidly to adjust itself to literary standards which exclude the female, it dooms itself to insignificance. Where it speaks in its own array of voices, it enlarges literature. . . . I therefore make the assumption that "women's poetry" exists in much the same sense that "American poetry" exists. It has a history. It has a terrain. Many of its practitioners believe it has something like a language.

ALICIA SUSAN OSTRIKER, *STEALING THE LANGUAGE*

This dynamic interplay between musician and audience, or between speaker and audience is crucial to an understanding and appreciation of the Black poetry of the 1960s. Significantly, many of the poets, especially the poets of Black Consciousness, have emphasized the fact that they were writing primarily for a Black audience. They wished to speak to other Black people and they wished to do it on terms to

668

which the people were accustomed. They wanted to reach "the community," they said, the Black masses, and as they looked for models they patterned their work on their people's music. They wanted to scream like James Brown, to blow like Trane [jazz saxophonist and composer John Coltrane]. In the process, they found their roots. They discovered the African griot and rediscovered the Baptist preacher.

STEPHEN E. HENDERSON, "CLICHÉ, MONOTONY, AND TOUCHSTONE"

Someone writing a poem believes in a reader, in readers, of that poem. The "who" of that reader quivers like a jellyfish. Self-reference is always possible: that my "I" is a universal "we," that the reader is my clone. That sending letters to myself is enough for attention to be paid. That my chip of mirror contains the world.

But most often someone writing a poem believes in, depends on, a delicate, vibrating range of difference, that an "I" can become a "we" without extinguishing others, that a partly common language exists to which strangers can bring their own heartbeat, memories, images. A language that itself has learned from the heartbeat, memories, images of strangers.

ADRIENNE RICH, *WHAT IS FOUND THERE*

E M I L Y   D I C K I N S O N

(1830–1886)

I'm Nobody! Who Are You?

(1891)

I'm Nobody! Who are you?
Are you—Nobody—Too?
Then there's a pair of us?
Don't tell! they'd advertise—you know!

5 How dreary—to be—Somebody!
How public—like a Frog—
To tell one's name—the livelong June—
To an admiring Bog!

The Speaker in the Poem

In fiction, the author's careful choice and arrangement of words enable readers to form an impression of the narrator and to decide whether he or she is sophisticated or unsophisticated, trustworthy or untrustworthy, innocent or experienced. Like fiction, poetry depends on a **speaker** who describes events, feelings, and ideas to readers. Finding out as much as possible about this speaker can help readers to interpret the poem. For example, the speaker in Emily Dickinson's "I'm Nobody! Who are you?" seems at once shy and playful. The first stanza of the poem suggests that the speaker is a private person, perhaps with little self-esteem. As the poem continues, however, the voice becomes almost defiant. In a sense the speaker's two voices represent two ways of relating to the world. The first voice expresses the private self—internal, isolated, and revealed through poetry; the second expresses the public self—external, self-centered, and inevitably superficial. Far from being defeated by shyness, the speaker claims to have chosen her status as "nobody."

One question readers might ask about "I'm Nobody! Who are you?" is how close the speaker's voice is to the poet's. Readers who conclude that the poem is about the conflict between a poet's public and private responsibilities may be tempted to see the speaker and the poet as one. But this is not necessarily the case. Like the narrator of a short story, the speaker of a poem is a **persona,** or mask, that the poet assumes within the poem. Some readers mistakenly believe that the speaker is always the poet and that the ideas expressed by the speaker are the poet's. Granted, in some poems little distance exists between the poet and the speaker. Without hard evidence to support a link between speaker and poet, however, readers should not assume they are one and the same.

In most cases the speaker is quite different from the poet. And even when the speaker's voice conveys the attitude of the poet, it may do so only indirectly. In "The Chimney Sweeper" (p. 897), for example, William Blake assumes the voice of a child to criticize the system of child labor that existed in eighteenth-century England. Even though the child speaker does not understand the conditions that cause his misery, readers sense the poet's attitude as the trusting speaker describes the conditions under which he works. The poet's indignation is especially apparent in the biting irony of the last line, in which the victimized speaker innocently assures readers that if all people do their duty, "they need not fear harm."

Sometimes the poem's speaker is anonymous, using the third person and remaining outside the poem. In this case—as in William Carlos Williams's "Red Wheelbarrow" (p. 747), for instance—the first-person voice is absent. At other times, the speaker has a set identity—a king, a beggar, a highwayman, a sheriff, a husband, a wife, a rich man, a chimney sweep, a child, a mythical figure, an explorer, a teacher, a faithless lover, a saint, or even a flower, an animal, or a clod of earth. Whatever the case, the speaker is not necessarily the poet, but a creation that the poet uses to convey his or her ideas. (For this reason a group of poems by a single poet may have very different voices.) Notice in the following poem how the poet assumes the mask of a fictional character, Gretel from the fairy tale "Hansel and Gretel."

LOUISE GLÜCK

(1943–   )

Gretel in Darkness

(1971)

This is the world we wanted. All who would have seen us dead
Are dead. I hear the witch's cry
Break in the moonlight through a sheet of sugar: God rewards.
Her tongue shrivels into gas. . . .

5   Now, far from women's arms
And memory of women, in our father's hut
We sleep, are never hungry.
Why do I not forget?
My father bars the door, bars harm
10 From this house, and it is years.

No one remembers. Even you, my brother.
Summer afternoons you look at me as though you meant
To leave, as though it never happened. But I killed for you.
I see armed firs, the spires of that gleaming kiln come back, come back—

15 Nights I turn to you to hold me but you are not there.
Am I alone? Spies
Hiss in the stillness, Hansel we are there still, and it is real, real,
That black forest, and the fire in earnest.

The speaker in this poem comments on her life in the years after her encounter with the witch in the forest. Speaking to her brother, Gretel observes that they now live in the world they wanted: They live with their father in his hut, and the witch and the wicked stepmother are dead. Even so, the memory of the events in the forest haunt Gretel and make it impossible for her to live "happily ever after." The "armed firs," the "gleaming kiln," and "the black forest" break through the "sheet of sugar" that her life has become.

By assuming the persona of Gretel, Louise Glück is able to convey some interesting and complex ideas. On one level Gretel represents any person who has lived through a traumatic experience. Memories of the event keep breaking through into the present, frustrating her attempts to reestablish her belief in the goodness of the world. The voice we hear is sad, alone, and frightened: "Nights I turn to you to hold me," she says, "but you are not there." Although the murder Gretel committed for her brother was justified, it seems to haunt her. "No one remembers," laments Gretel, not even her brother. At some level she realizes that by killing the witch she has killed a part of herself, perhaps the part of women that men fear and so transform into witches and wicked step-mothers. The world that is left after the killing is the father's and the brother's, not hers, and she is now alone in a dark world haunted by the memories of the black forest. In this sense Gretel—"Now, far from women's arms / And memory of women"—may be the voice of all vic-timized women who, because of men, act against their own best inter-ests—and regret it.

Various elements in a poem can help readers to discover information about its speaker. For instance, the title can shed light on the speaker's identity, as Glück's title does. Word choice can also provide information about the speaker. Notice in the following poem, for example, how Span-ish words help to define the poem's frame of reference and to characterize the speaker.

LEONARD ADAMÉ

(1947–   )

My Grandmother Would Rock Quietly and Hum

(1973)

> in her house
> she would rock quietly and hum
> until her swelled hands
> calmed
>
> 5 in summer
> she wore thick stockings
> sweaters
> and grey braids

(when "el cheque"[1] came
10 we went to Payless
and I laughed greedily
when given a quarter)

mornings,
sunlight barely lit
15 the kitchen
and where
there were shadows
it was not cold

she quietly rolled
20 flour tortillas—
the "papas"[2]
cracking in hot lard
would wake me

she had lost her teeth
25 and when we ate
she had bread
soaked in "café"[3]

always her eyes
were clear
30 and she could see
as I cannot yet see—
through her eyes
she gave me herself

she would sit
35 and talk
of her girlhood—
of things strange to me:
    México
    epidemics
40   relatives shot
    her father's hopes
    of this country—
how they sank
with cement dust
45 to his insides

---

[1] The check.

[2] Potatoes.

[3] Coffee.

now
when I go
to the old house
the worn spots
50　by the stove
echo of her shuffling
and
México
still hangs in her
55　fading
calendar pictures

In this poem the speaker is an adult recalling childhood memories of his grandmother. Spanish words—*el cheque, tortillas, papas,* and *café*—identify the speaker as Latino. His easy use of English, his comment that talk of Mexico is strange to him, and his observation that he cannot yet see through his grandmother's eyes suggest, however, that he is not in touch with his ethnic identity. At one level, the grandmother evokes nostalgic memories of the speaker's youth. At another level, as a living symbol of his ties with Mexico, she connects him to the ethnic culture he is trying to recover. The poem ends on an ambivalent note: Even though the speaker is able to return to "the old house," the pictures of Mexico are fading, perhaps suggesting the speaker's assimilation into mainstream American culture.

Direct statements by the speaker can also help to establish his or her identity. Notice in the poem that follows how the first line of each stanza establishes the identity of the speaker—and defines his perspective.

LANGSTON HUGHES

(1902–1967)

Negro

(1926)

I am a Negro:
　　Black as the night is black,
　　Black like the depths of my Africa.

I've been a slave:
5　　Caesar told me to keep his door-steps clean.
　　I brushed the boots of Washington.

I've been a worker:
    Under my hand the pyramids arose.
    I made mortar for the Woolworth Building.

10 I've been a singer:
    All the way from Africa to Georgia
    I carried my sorrow songs.
    I made ragtime.

I've been a victim:
15   The Belgians cut off my hands in the Congo.
    They lynch me still in Mississippi.

I am a Negro:
    Black as the night is black,
    Black like the depths of my Africa.

Here the speaker, identifying himself as "a Negro," assumes each of the roles African-Americans have historically played in Western society— slave, worker, singer, and victim. By so doing, he gives voice to his ancestors who, by being forced to serve others, were deprived of their identities. By presenting not just their suffering, but also their accomplishments, the speaker asserts his pride in being black. The speaker also implies that the suffering of black people has been caused by economic exploitation: Romans, Egyptians, Belgians, and Americans all used black labor to help build their societies. In this context the speaker's implied warning is clear: Except for the United States, all the societies that have exploited blacks have declined, and long after these empires have fallen, black people still endure.

In each of the preceding poems, the speaker is alone. The following poem, a **dramatic monologue,** presents a more complex situation in which the poet creates a complete dramatic scene. The speaker is developed as a character whose distinctive temperament is revealed through his words as he addresses a silent listener.

ROBERT BROWNING

(1812–1889)

My Last Duchess

(1842)

Ferrara

That's my last Duchess painted on the wall,
Looking as if she were alive. I call
That piece a wonder, now: Frà Pandolf's[1] hands
Worked busily a day, and there she stands.
5 Will't please you sit and look at her? I said
"Frà Pandolf" by design, for never read
Strangers like you that pictured countenance,
The depth and passion of its earnest glance,
But to myself they turned (since none puts by
10 The curtain I have drawn for you, but I)
And seemed as they would ask me, if they durst,
How such a glance came there; so, not the first
Are you to turn and ask thus. Sir, 'twas not
Her husband's presence only, called that spot
15 Of joy into the Duchess' cheek: perhaps
Frà Pandolf chanced to say "Her mantle laps
Over my lady's wrist too much," or "Paint
Must never hope to reproduce the faint
Half-flush that dies along her throat": such stuff
20 Was courtesy, she thought, and cause enough
For calling up that spot of joy. She had
A heart—how shall I say?—too soon made glad,
Too easily impressed; she liked whate'er
She looked on, and her looks went everywhere.
25 Sir, 'twas all one! My favor at her breast,
The dropping of the daylight in the West,
The bough of cherries some officious fool
Broke in the orchard for her, the white mule
She rode with round the terrace—all and each
30 Would draw from her alike the approving speech,
Or blush, at least. She thanked men—good! but thanked
Somehow—I know not how—as if she ranked
My gift of a nine-hundred-years-old name
With anybody's gift. Who'd stoop to blame
35 This sort of trifling? Even had you skill

---

[1] "Brother" Pandolf, a fictive painter.

In speech—(which I have not)—to make your will
Quite clear to such an one, and say, "Just this
Or that in you disgusts me; here you miss,
Or there exceed the mark"—and if she let
40 Herself be lessoned so, nor plainly set
Her wits to yours, forsooth, and made excuse
—E'en then would be some stooping; and I choose
Never to stoop. Oh sir, she smiled, no doubt,
Whene'er I passed her; but who passed without
45 Much the same smile? This grew; I gave commands;
Then all smiles stopped together. There she stands
As if alive. Will't please you rise? We'll meet
The company below, then. I repeat,
The Count your master's known munificence
50 Is ample warrant that no just pretense
Of mine for dowry will be disallowed;
Though his fair daughter's self, as I avowed
At starting, is my object. Nay, we'll go
Together down, sir. Notice Neptune,[2] though,
55 Taming a sea horse, thought a rarity,
Which Claus of Innsbruck[3] cast in bronze for me!

The Duke referred to in the poem is most likely Alfonso II, Duke of Ferrara, Italy, whose young wife, Lucrezia, died in 1561 after only three years of marriage. Shortly after her death, the Duke began negotiations to marry again. The poem opens with the Duke showing a portrait of his late wife to an emissary of an unnamed Count who is there to arrange a marriage between the Duke and the Count's daughter. The Duke remarks that the artist, Frà Pandolf, has caught a certain look upon the Duchess's face. This look aroused the jealousy of the Duke, who thought that it should have been for him alone. According to the Duke, the Duchess's crime was to have a heart "too soon made glad," "Too easily impressed." Eventually the Duke could stand the situation no longer; he "gave commands," and the smiles "stopped together."

Much of what readers learn about the Duke's state of mind comes from what is implied by his words. As he discusses the painting, the Duke unintentionally reveals himself to be obsessively possessive and jealous, referring to "*my* last Duchess," "*my* favor at her breast," and "*my* gift of a nine-hundred-years-old name." He keeps the picture of his late wife well hidden behind a curtain that no one draws except him. His interest in the picture has little to do with the memory of his wife, however. In death the

---

[2] God of the sea.

[3] An imaginary—or unidentified—sculptor. The Count of Tyrol's capital was at Innsbrück, Austria.

Duchess has become just what the Duke always wanted her to be: a personal possession that reflects his good taste.

The listener plays a subtle but important role in the poem: His presence establishes the dramatic situation that allows the character of the Duke to be revealed. The purpose of the story is to communicate to the emissary exactly what the Duke expects from his prospective bride, and from her father. As he speaks, the Duke conveys only the information that he wants the emissary to take back to his master, the Count. Although he appears vain and superficial, the Duke is actually extraordinarily shrewd. Throughout the poem he turns the conversation to his own ends and gains the advantage through flattery and false modesty. Notice, for example, that he claims he has little skill in speaking when actually he is cleverly manipulating the conversation. The success of the poem lies in the poet's ability to develop the voice of this complex character, who embodies both superficial elegance and shocking cruelty.

Poems for Further Reading: The Speaker in the Poem

L E S L I E   M A R M O N   S I L K O

(1948–   )

Where Mountain Lion Lay Down with Deer

(1973)

I climb the black rock mountain
    stepping from day to day
            silently.
I smell the wind for my ancestors
5   pale blue leaves
    crushed wild mountain smell.
Returning
    up the gray stone cliff
    where I descended
10   a thousand years ago.
Returning to faded black stone.
    where mountain lion lay down with deer.
It is better to stay up here
          watching wind's reflection
          in tall yellow flowers.

The old ones who remember me are gone
     the old songs are all forgotten
and the story of my birth.
How I danced in snow-frost moonlight
20   distant stars to the end of the Earth,
How I swam away
           in freezing mountain water
           narrow mossy canyon tumbling down
               out of the mountain
25   out of the deep canyon stone
       down
          the memory
            spilling out
              into the world.

READING AND REACTING

1. Whom does the speaker's voice represent in line 4? In line 9? Can you explain this shift?

2. From where is the speaker returning? What is she trying to recover?

3. **JOURNAL ENTRY**   The poet is of Native American descent. How important is it for you to know this information about her? In what way does information about the poet's ancestry affect your interpretation of the poem?

4. **CRITICAL PERSPECTIVE**   In her 1983 essay "Answering the Deer," Native American poet and critic Paula Gunn Allen observes that the possibility of cultural extinction is a basic reality Native Americans must face. Native American women writers, says Allen, face this fact directly, but with a kind of hope:

   The sense of hope . . . comes about when one has faced ultimate disaster time and time again over the ages and has emerged . . . stronger and more certain of the endurance of the people, the spirits, and the land from which they both arise and which informs both with life. Transformation, or more directly, metamorphosis, is the oldest tribal ceremonial theme. . . . And it comes once again into use within American Indian poetry of extinction and regeneration that is ultimately the only poetry any contemporary Indian woman can write.

   Does Silko's poem address the issue of cultural extinction and the possibility of regeneration or metamorphosis? How?

JANICE MIRIKITANI

(1942–   )

Suicide Note

(1987)

*. . . An Asian-American college student was reported to
have jumped to her death from her dormitory window. Her
body was found two days later under a deep cover of snow.
Her suicide note contained an apology to her
parents for having received less than a perfect
four point grade average. . . .*

How many notes written . . .
ink smeared like birdprints in snow.

    not good enough   not pretty enough   not smart enough
dear mother and father.
5 I apologize
for disappointing you.
I've worked very hard,
        not good enough
harder, perhaps to please you.
10 If only I were a son, shoulders broad
as the sunset threading through pine,
I would see the light in my mother's
eyes, or the golden pride reflected
in my father's dream
15 of my wide, male hands worthy of work
and comfort.
I would swagger through life
muscled and bold and assured,
drawing praises to me
20 like currents in the bed of wind, virile
with confidence.
    not good enough   not strong enough   not good enough

I apologize.
Tasks do not come easily.
25 Each failure, a glacier.
Each disapproval, a bootprint.
Each disappointment,
ice above my river.
So I have worked hard.

30   not good enough
My sacrifice I will drop
bone by bone, perched
on the ledge of my womanhood,
fragile as wings.
35   not strong enough
It is snowing steadily
surely not good weather
for flying—this sparrow
sillied and dizzied by the wind
40 on the edge.
     not smart enough
I make this ledge my altar
to offer penance.
This air will not hold me,
45 the snow burdens my crippled wings,
my tears drop like bitter cloth
softly into the gutter below.
  not good enough   not strong enough   not smart enough
    Choices thin as shaved
50   ice. Notes shredded
    drift like snow
on my broken body,
covers me like whispers
of sorries
55 sorries.
Perhaps when they find me
they will bury
my bird bones beneath
a sturdy pine
60 and scatter my feathers like
unspoken song
over this white and cold and silent
breast of earth.

READING AND REACTING

1. This poem presents a suicide note that is also an apology. Why does the speaker feel she must apologize?

2. What attitude does the speaker convey toward her parents? What emotions do you think she feels toward them?

3. **JOURNAL ENTRY** Is the college student who speaks in this poem a stranger to you? Or is her voice in any way like that of students you know?

The Tone of the Poem

Not only does a poem have a speaker, but it also has a **tone** which conveys the speaker's attitude toward his or her subject or audience. In speech, stressing a word in a sentence can modify or color a statement, drastically affecting the meaning of a sentence. For example, the statement "Of course you would want to go to that restaurant" seems relatively straightforward, but changing the emphasis to "Of course *you* would want to go to *that* restaurant" suggests sarcasm or criticism. For poets, however, conveying a particular tone to readers represents a challenge because readers rarely hear their spoken voices. Instead, poets indicate tone by using techniques such as rhyme, meter, word choice, sentence structure, figures of speech, and imagery.

The range of possible tones is wide. For example, a poem's speaker may be joyful, sad, playful, serious, comic, intimate, formal, relaxed, condescending, or ironic. Consider how the tone of the following poem conveys the speaker's attitude.

ROBERT FROST

(1874–1963)

Fire and Ice

(1923)

> Some say the world will end in fire,
> Some say in ice.
> From what I've tasted of desire
> I hold with those who favor fire.
> 5 But if it had to perish twice,
> I think I know enough of hate
> To say that for destruction ice
> Is also great
> And would suffice.

Here the speaker uses word choice, rhyme, and understatement to comment on the human condition. The conciseness and the simple, regular meter and rhyme suggest an **epigram**—a short poem that makes a pointed comment in an unusually clear, and often witty, manner. This pointedness is consistent with the speaker's glib, unemotional tone, as is the last line's wry understatement that ice "would suffice." The contrast between the poem's serious message—that active hatred and indifference are equally destructive—and its informal style and offhand tone is consistent with the speaker's detached, almost smug, posture.

Sometimes shifts in tone reveal changes in the speaker's attitude. Consider how changes in tone in the following poem reveal a shift in the speaker's attitude toward war.

THOMAS HARDY

(1840–1928)

The Man He Killed

(1902)

"Had he and I but met
By some old ancient inn,
We should have sat us down to wet
Right many a nipperkin![1]

5   "But ranged as infantry,
And staring face to face,
I shot at him as he at me,
And killed him in his place.

"I shot him dead because—
10   Because he was my foe,
Just so: my foe of course he was;
That's clear enough; although

"He thought he'd 'list,[2] perhaps,
Off-hand-like—just as I—
15 Was out of work—had sold his traps—
No other reason why.

"Yes; quaint and curious war is!
You shoot a fellow down
You'd treat if met where any bar is,
20   Or help to half-a crown."

The speaker in this poem is a soldier who tells his story about war in the first person. Quotation marks indicate that the speaker is engaged in conversation—perhaps in a pub—and his dialect indicates that he is probably of the English working class. For him the object of war is simple: Kill or be killed. To Hardy, the speaker seems to represent all men who are thrust

---

[1] A small container of liquor.

[2] Enlist.

into a war without understanding its underlying economic or ideological causes. In this sense the speaker and his enemy are both victims of forces beyond their comprehension or control.

The tone of "The Man He Killed" is not consistent throughout; it changes as the speaker tells his story. As the poem unfolds, its sentence structure deteriorates, and this in turn helps to convey the attitude of the speaker toward his subject. In the first two stanzas of the poem, sentences are smooth and unbroken, establishing the speaker's matter-of-fact tone and reflecting his confidence that he has done what he had to do. In the third and fourth stanzas, however, broken syntax reflects the narrator's increasingly disturbed state of mind as he tells about the man he killed. The poem's singsong meter and regular rhyme scheme *(met/wet, inn/nipperkin)* suggest that the speaker is trying hard to maintain his composure; the smooth sentence structure of the last stanza, and the use of a cliché in an attempt to trivialize the incident ("Yes; quaint and curious war is!") show the speaker's efforts to regain his control.

Sometimes a shift in tone can set up an ironic contrast between the speaker and his or her subject. In the next poem, the speaker's abrupt change of tone at the end of the poem establishes just such a contrast.

A M Y   L O W E L L

(1874–1925)

Patterns

(1915)

I walk down the garden paths,
And all the daffodils
Are blowing, and the bright blue squills.
I walk down the patterned garden-paths
5 In my stiff, brocaded gown.
With my powdered hair and jewelled fan,
I too am a rare
Pattern. As I wander down
The garden paths.

10 My dress is richly figured,
And the train
Makes a pink and silver stain
On the gravel, and the thrift
Of the borders.
15 Just a plate of current fashion
Tripping by in high-heeled, ribboned shoes.

Not a softness anywhere about me,
Only whalebone[1] and brocade.
And I sink on a seat in the shade
20 Of a lime tree. For my passion
Wars against the stiff brocade.
The daffodils and squills
Flutter in the breeze
As they please.
25 And I weep;
For the lime-tree is in blossom
And one small flower has dropped upon my bosom.
And the plashing of waterdrops
In the marble fountain
30 Comes down the garden-paths.
The dripping never stops.
Underneath my stiffened gown
Is the softness of a woman bathing in a marble basin,
A basin in the midst of hedges grown
35 So thick, she cannot see her lover hiding,
But she guesses he is near,
And the sliding of the water
Seems the stroking of a dear
Hand upon her.
40 What is Summer in a fine brocaded gown!
I should like to see it lying in a heap upon the ground.
All the pink and silver crumpled up on the ground.

I would be the pink and silver as I ran along the paths,
And he would stumble after,
45 Bewildered by my laughter.
I should see the sun flashing from his sword-hilt and buckles
    on his shoes.
I would choose
To lead him in a maze along the patterned paths,
A bright and laughing maze for my heavy-booted lover.
50 Till he caught me in the shade,
And the buttons of his waistcoat bruised my body as he clasped me,
Aching, melting, unafraid.
With the shadows of the leaves and the sundrops,
And the plopping of the waterdrops,
55 All about us in the open afternoon—
I am very like to swoon

---

[1] Used in making corsets.

With the weight of this brocade,
For the sun sifts through the shade.

Underneath the fallen blossom
60 In my bosom,
Is a letter I have hid.
It was brought to me this morning by a rider from the Duke.
Madam, we regret to inform you that Lord Hartwell
Died in action Thursday se'nnight.[2]
65 As I read it in the white, morning sunlight,
The letters squirmed like snakes.
"Any answer, Madam," said my footman.
"No," I told him.
"See that the messenger takes some refreshment.
70 No, no answer."
And I walked into the garden,
Up and down the patterned paths,
In my stiff, correct brocade.
The blue and yellow flowers stood up proudly in the sun,
75 Each one.
I stood upright too,
Held rigid to the pattern
By the stiffness of my gown.
Up and down I walked.
80 Up and down.

In a month he would have been my husband.
In a month, here, underneath this lime,
We would have broken the pattern;
He for me, and I for him,
85 He as Colonel, I as Lady,
On this shady seat.
He had a whim
That sunlight carried blessing.
And I answered, "It shall be as you have said."
90 Now he is dead.

In Summer and in Winter I shall walk
Up and down
The patterned garden-paths
In my stiff, brocaded gown.

---

[2] "Seven night," or a week ago Thursday.

95 The squills and daffodils
Will give place to pillared roses, and to asters, and to snow.
I shall go
Up and down,
In my gown.
100 Gorgeously arrayed,
Boned and stayed.
And the softness of my body will be guarded from embrace
By each button, hook, and lace.
For the man who should loose me is dead,
105 Fighting with the Duke in Flanders,[3]
In a pattern called a war.
Christ! What are patterns for?

The speaker begins by describing herself walking down garden paths. She wears a stiff brocaded gown, has powdered hair, and carries a jewelled fan. By her own admission she is "a plate of current fashion." Although her tone is controlled, she is preoccupied by sensual thoughts. Beneath her "stiffened gown" is the "softness of a woman bathing in a marble basin," and the "sliding of the water" in a fountain reminds the speaker of the stroking of her lover's hand. She imagines herself shedding her brocaded gown and running with her lover along the maze of "patterned paths." The sensuality of the speaker's thoughts stands in ironic contrast to the images of stiffness and control that dominate the poem; her passion "wars against the stiff brocade." She is also full of repressed rage. After all, she knows that her lover has been killed, and she realizes the meaninglessness of the patterns of her life, patterns to which she has conformed, just as her lover has by going to war and doing what he was supposed to do. Throughout the poem, the speaker's tone reflects her barely contained anger and frustration. In the last line of the poem, when she finally lets out her rage, the irony of the situation becomes apparent.

---

[3] Region in northwestern Europe, including part of northern France and western Belgium. Flanders was the site of a historic World War I battle.

Poems for Further Reading: Tone

SIMON J. ORTIZ

(1941–   )

Speaking

(1977)

I take him outside
under the trees,
have him stand on the ground.
We listen to the crickets,
5 cicadas, million years old sound.
Ants come by us.
I tell them,
"This is he, my son.
This boy is looking at you.
10 I am speaking for him."

The crickets, cicadas,
the ants, the millions of years
are watching us,
hearing us.
15 My son murmurs infant words,
speaking, small laughter
bubbles from him.
Tree leaves tremble.
They listen to this boy
20 speaking for me.

READING AND REACTING

1. How would you characterize the speaker's tone? Is it consistent throughout? Should it be?

2. What do you think the speaker means when he says, "the millions of years / are watching us"? What does this comment suggest about the speaker's purpose?

3. The first stanza ends with the father speaking for his infant son, and the last stanza ends with the son speaking for the father. In what sense does each speak for the other?

4. **JOURNAL ENTRY** What do you think the poem's real subject is? Nature? Communication? Parenthood? Tradition? Something else?

WILLIAM WORDSWORTH

(1770–1850)

The World Is Too Much with Us

(1807)

The world is too much with us; late and soon,
Getting and spending, we lay waste our powers;
Little we see in Nature that is ours;
We have given our hearts away, a sordid boon!
5 This Sea that bares her bosom to the moon;
The winds that will be howling at all hours,
And are up-gathered now like sleeping flowers;
For this, for everything, we are out of tune;
It moves us not. Great God! I'd rather be
10 A Pagan suckled in a creed outworn;
So might I, standing on this pleasant lea,
Have glimpses that would make me less forlorn;
Have sight of Proteus[1] rising from the sea;
Or hear old Triton[2] blow his wreathèd horn.

READING AND REACTING

1. What is the speaker's attitude toward the contemporary world? How is this attitude revealed through the poem's tone?

2. This poem is a **sonnet,** a highly structured traditional form. How do the rhyme scheme and the regular meter help to establish the poem's tone?

3. **JOURNAL ENTRY**   Imagine you are a modern-day environmentalist, labor organizer, or corporate executive. Write a response to the sentiments expressed in this poem.

4. **CRITICAL PERSPECTIVE**   According to M. H. Abrams in his 1972 essay "Two Roads to Wordsworth," critics have tended to follow one of two different paths to the poet, and these approaches have yielded two different versions of the poet:

   One Wordsworth is simple, elemental, forthright, the other is complex, paradoxical, problematic; one is an affirmative poet of life, love, and joy, the other is an equivocal or self-divided poet whose affirmations are

---

[1]   Sometimes said to be Poseidon's son, this Greek sea god had the ability to change shapes at will and to tell the future.

[2]   The trumpeter of the sea, this sea god is usually pictured blowing on a conch shell. Triton was the son of Poseidon, ruler of the sea.

implicitly qualified . . . by a pervasive sense of morality and an ever-incipient despair of life; . . . one is the Wordsworth of light, the other the Wordsworth of [shadow], or even darkness.

Does your reading of "The World Is Too Much with Us" support one of these versions of Wordsworth over the other? Which one? Why?

SYLVIA PLATH

(1932–1963)

Morning Song

(1962)

Love set you going like a fat gold watch.
The midwife slapped your footsoles, and your bald cry
Took its place among the elements.

Our voices echo, magnifying your arrival. New statue.
5 In a drafty museum, your nakedness
Shadows our safety. We stand round blankly as walls.

I'm no more your mother
Than the cloud that distills a mirror to reflect its own slow
Effacement at the wind's hand.

10 All night your moth-breath
Flickers among the flat pink roses. I wake to listen:
A far sea moves in my ear.

One cry, and I stumble from bed, cow-heavy and floral
In my Victorian nightgown.
15 Your mouth opens clean as a cat's. The window square
Whitens and swallows its dull stars. And now you try
Your handful of notes;
The clear vowels rise like balloons.

READING AND REACTING

1. Who is the speaker? To whom is she speaking? What does the poem reveal about her?

2. What is the poem's subject? What attitudes about her subject do you suppose the poet expects her readers to have?

3. How is the tone of the first stanza different from that of the third? How does the tone reflect the content of each stanza?

4. **JOURNAL ENTRY**   In what sense does this poem reinforce traditional ideas about motherhood? How does it undercut them?

5. **CRITICAL PERSPECTIVE**   Sylvia Plath's life, which ended in suicide, was marked by emotional turbulence and instability. According to Anne Stevenson in *Bitter Fame*, her 1988 biography of Plath, in the weeks immediately preceding the composition of "Morning Song" a fit of rage over his supposed infidelity caused Plath to destroy many of her husband's books and poetic works in progress. Then, only a few days later, she suffered a miscarriage. According to Stevenson, "Morning Song" is about sleepless nights and surely reflects Plath's depression. However, in a 1991 biography, *Rough Magic,* Paul Alexander says, "Beautiful, simple, touching, 'Morning Song' was Plath's— then—definitive statement of motherhood."

How does this biographical information affect your response to "Morning Song"? Which biographer's assessment of the poem do you think makes more sense?

R O B E R T   H E R R I C K

(1591–1674)

To the Virgins, to Make Much of Time

(1646)

Gather ye rosebuds while ye may,
  Old Time is still a-flying;
And this same flower that smiles today,
  Tomorrow will be dying.

5 The glorious lamp of heaven, the sun,
  The higher he's a-getting,
The sooner will his race be run,
  And nearer he's to setting.

That age is best which is the first,
10 When youth and blood are warmer;
But being spent, the worse, and worst
  Times still succeed the former.

Then be not coy, but use your time,
  And while ye may, go marry;
15 For having lost but once your prime,
  You may forever tarry.

READING AND REACTING

1. How would you characterize the speaker? Do you think he expects his listeners to share his views? How might his expectations affect his tone?

2. This poem is developed almost like an argument. What is the speaker's main point? How does he support it?

3. What effect does the poem's use of rhyme have on its tone?

4. **JOURNAL ENTRY**   Whose side are you on—the speaker's or those he addresses?

A Special Case of Tone: Irony

Just as in fiction and drama, **irony** in poetry occurs when a discrepancy exists between two levels of meaning or experience. Consider the tone of the following lines by Stephen Crane:

> *Do not weep, maiden, for war is kind.*
> *Because your lover threw wild hands toward the sky*
> *And the afrightened steed ran on alone,*
> *Do not weep.*
> *War is kind.*

How can war be "kind"? Isn't war exactly the opposite of "kind"? Surely the speaker does not intend his words to be taken literally. By making this statement, the speaker actually conveys the opposite idea: War is a cruel, mindless exercise of violence.

Skillfully used, irony is a powerful way of making a pointed comment about a situation or of manipulating a reader's emotions. Implicit in irony is the writer's assumption that readers will not be misled by the literal meaning of a statement. In order for irony to work, readers must recognize the disparity between what is said and what is meant, or between what a character or speaker thinks is occurring and what readers know to be happening.

One kind of irony that appears in poetry is **dramatic irony**, which occurs when a speaker believes one thing and readers realize something else. In the following poem the poet uses a deranged speaker to tell a story that is filled with irony.

ROBERT BROWNING

(1812–1889)

Porphyria's Lover

(1836)

The rain set early in to-night,
    The sullen wind was soon awake,
It tore the elm-tops down for spite,
    And did its worst to vex the lake:
5   I listened with heart fit to break.
When glided in Porphyria; straight
    She shut the cold out and the storm,
And kneeled and made the cheerless grate
    Blaze up, and all the cottage warm;
10   Which done, she rose, and from her form
Withdrew the dripping cloak and shawl,
    And laid her soiled gloves by, untied
Her hat and let the damp hair fall,
    And, last, she sat down by my side
15   And called me. When no voice replied,
She put my arm about her waist,
    And made her smooth white shoulder bare,
And all her yellow hair displaced,
    And, stooping, made my cheek lie there,
20   And spread, o'er all, her yellow hair,
Murmuring how she loved me—she
    Too weak, for all her heart's endeavour,
To set its struggling passion free
    From pride, and vainer ties dissever,
25   And give herself to me for ever.
But passion sometimes would prevail,
    Nor could to-night's gay feast restrain
A sudden thought of one so pale
    For love of her, and all in vain:
30 So, she was come through wind and rain.
Be sure I looked up at her eyes
    Happy and proud; at last I knew
Porphyria worshipped me; surprise
    Made my heart swell, and still it grew
35   While I debated what to do.
That moment she was mine, mine, fair,
    Perfectly pure and good: I found

A thing to do, and all her hair
    In one long yellow string I wound
40   Three times her little throat around,
And strangled her. No pain felt she;
    I am quite sure she felt no pain.
As a shut bud that holds a bee,
    I warily oped her lids: again
45   Laughed the blue eyes without a stain.
And I untightened next the tress
    About her neck; her cheek once more
Blushed bright beneath my burning kiss:
    I propped her head up as before,
50   Only, this time my shoulder bore
Her head, which droops upon it still:
    The smiling rosy little head,
So glad it has its utmost will,
    That all it scorned at once is fled,
55   And I, its love, am gained instead!
Porphyria's love: she guessed not how
    Her darling one wish would be heard.
And thus we sit together now,
    And all night long we have not stirred,
60   And yet God has not said a word!

Like Browning's "My Last Duchess" (p. 676) this poem is a **dramatic monologue.** The speaker recounts his story in a straightforward manner, seemingly unaware of the horror of his tale. In fact, much of the effect of this poem comes from the speaker's telling his tale of murder in a flat, unemotional tone—and from readers' gradual realization that the speaker is mad.

The irony of the poem and of its title becomes apparent as the monologue progresses. At first the speaker fears that Porphyria is too weak to free herself from pride and vanity to love him. As he looks in her eyes, however, he comes to believe that she worships him. To preserve the perfection of Porphyria's love, the speaker strangles her with her own hair. He assures his silent listener, "I am quite sure she felt no pain." Like many of Browning's narrators, the speaker in this poem exhibits a selfish and perverse need to possess another person totally. The moment the speaker realizes that Porphyria loves him, he feels compelled to kill her and keep her his forever. According to him, she is at this point "mine, mine, fair, / Perfectly pure and good," and he believes that by murdering her he actually fulfills "Her darling one wish"—to preserve the purity of her love forever. As he attempts to justify his actions, the speaker reveals himself to be a deluded psychopathic killer.

Another kind of irony is **situational irony,** which occurs when the situation itself contradicts readers' expectations. For example, in "Porphyria's Lover" the meeting of two lovers results not in joy and passion but in murder. Notice in the next poem too how the situation creates irony.

PERCY BYSSHE SHELLEY

(1792–1822)

Ozymandias

(1818)

I met a traveler from an antique land
Who said: Two vast and trunkless legs of stone
Stand in the desert. Near them, on the sand,
Half sunk, a shattered visage lies, whose frown,
5 And wrinkled lip, and sneer of cold command,
Tell that its sculptor well those passions read
Which yet survive, stamped on these lifeless things,
The hand that mocked them, and the heart that fed;
And on the pedestal these words appear:
10 "My name is Ozymandias,[1] king of kings:
Look on my works, ye Mighty, and despair!"
Nothing beside remains. Round the decay
Of that colossal wreck, boundless and bare
The lone and level sands stretch far away.

The speaker tells a tale about a colossal statue that lies shattered in the desert. Its head lies separated from the trunk, and the face has a wrinkled lip and a "sneer of cold command." On the pedestal of the monument are words exhorting all those who pass: "Look on my works, ye Mighty, and despair!" The situational irony of the poem has its source in the contrast between the "colossal wreck" and the boastful inscription on its base. To the speaker, Ozymandias stands for the vanity of those who mistakenly think they can withstand the ravages of time.

Perhaps the most common kind of irony found in poetry is **verbal irony,** which is created when words say one thing but mean another, often exactly the opposite. When verbal irony is particularly biting, it is called **sarcasm**—for example, Stephen Crane's use of the word *kind* in his antiwar poem "War Is Kind." In speech verbal irony is easy to detect

---

[1] The Greek name for Ramses II, ruler of Egypt in the thirteenth century B.C.

through the speaker's change in tone or emphasis. In writing, when these signals are absent, verbal irony becomes more difficult to convey. Poets must depend on the context of a remark or on the contrast between a word and other images in the poem to create irony.

Consider how verbal irony is established in the following poem.

ARIEL DORFMAN

(1942–   )

Hope

(1988)

Translated by Edith Grossman with the author

My son has been
missing
since May 8
of last year.

5   They took him
just for a few hours
they said
just for some routine
questioning.

10 After the car left,
the car with no license plate,
we couldn't

find out

anything else
15 about him.
But now things have changed.
We heard from a compañero
who just got out
that five months later
20 they were torturing him
in Villa Grimaldi,
at the end of September
they were questioning him
in the red house
25 that belonged to the Grimaldis.

They say they recognized
his voice his screams
they say.

Somebody tell me frankly
30 what times are these
what kind of world
what country?
What I'm asking is
how can it be
35 that a father's
joy
a mother's
joy
is knowing
40 that they
that they are still
torturing
their son?
Which means
45 that he was alive
five months later
and our greatest
hope
will be to find out
50 next year
that they're still torturing him
eight months later

and he may   might   could
still be alive.

Although it is not necessary to know the background of the poet to appreciate this poem, it does help to know that Ariel Dorfman is a native of
Chile. After the assassination of Salvador Allende, Chile's elected socialist
president, in September 1973, the civilian government was replaced by a
military dictatorship. Civil rights were suspended, and activists, students,
and members of opposition parties were arrested and frequently detained
indefinitely; sometimes they simply disappeared. The irony of this poem
originates in the discrepancy between the way the word *hope* is used in the
poem and the way it is usually used. For most people, hope has positive associations, but in the poem it takes on a different meaning. This irony is
not lost on the speaker.

Poems for Further Reading: Irony

W. H. AUDEN

(1907–1973)

The Unknown Citizen

(1939)

(To JS/07/M/378
This Marble Monument Is Erected by the State)

He was found by the Bureau of Statistics to be
One against whom there was no official complaint,
And all the reports on his conduct agree
That, in the modern sense of an old-fashioned word, he was a saint,
5 For in everything he did he served the Greater Community.
Except for the War till the day he retired
He worked in a factory and never got fired,
But satisfied his employers, Fudge Motors Inc.
Yet he wasn't a scab or odd in his views,
10 For his Union reports that he paid his dues,
(Our report on his Union shows it was sound)
And our Social Psychology workers found
That he was popular with his mates and liked a drink.
The Press are convinced that he bought a paper every day
15 And that his reactions to advertisements were normal in every way.
Policies taken out in his name prove that he was fully insured,
And his Health-card shows he was once in hospital but left it cured.
Both Producers Research and High-Grade Living declare
He was fully sensible to the advantages of the Installment Plan
20 And had everything necessary to the Modern Man,
A phonograph, a radio, a car and a frigidaire.
Our researchers into Public Opinion are content
That he held the proper opinions for the time of year;
When there was peace, he was for peace; when there was war, he went.
25 He was married and added five children to the population,
Which our Eugenist[1] says was the right number for a parent of his
    generation,
And our teachers report that he never interfered with their education.
Was he free? Was he happy? The question is absurd:
Had anything been wrong, we should certainly have heard.

---

[1] One who studies the science of human improvement, especially through genetic control.

READING AND REACTING

1. The "unknown citizen" represents modern citizens, who, according to the poem, are programmed like machines. How does the title help to establish the tone of the poem? How does the inscription on the monument help to establish the tone?

2. Who is the speaker? What is his attitude toward the unknown citizen? How can you tell?

3. What kinds of irony are present in the poem? Identify several examples.

4. **JOURNAL ENTRY** This poem was written in 1939. Does its criticism apply to contemporary society, or does it seem dated?

5. **CRITICAL PERSPECTIVE** In 1939, the same year this poem was published, Auden argued in his essay "The Public vs. The Late Mr. William Butler Yeats" that poetry can never really change anything. He reiterated this point as late as 1971 in his biographical *A Certain World:*

   By all means let a poet, if he wants to, write poems . . . [that protest] against this or that political evil or social injustice. But let him remember this. The only person who will benefit from them is himself; they will enhance his literary reputation among those who feel as he does. The evil or injustice, however, will remain exactly what it would have been if he had kept his mouth shut.

   Do you believe that poetry—or any kind of literature—has the power to combat "evil or injustice" in the world? Do you consider "The Unknown Citizen" a political poem? How might this poem effect social or political change?

ANNE SEXTON

(1928–1974)

Cinderella

(1970)

You always read about it:
the plumber with twelve children
who wins the Irish Sweepstakes.
From toilets to riches.
5 That story.

Or the nursemaid,
some luscious sweet from Denmark
who captures the oldest son's heart.

From diapers to Dior.[1]
10 That story.

Or a milkman who serves the wealthy,
eggs, cream, butter, yogurt, milk,
the white truck like an ambulance
who goes into real estate
15 and makes a pile.
From homogenized to martinis at lunch.

Or the charwoman
who is on the bus when it cracks up
and collects enough from the insurance.
20 From mops to Bonwit Teller.[2]
That story.

Once
the wife of a rich man was on her deathbed
and she said to her daughter Cinderella:
25 Be devout. Be good. Then I will smile
down from heaven in the seam of a cloud.
The man took another wife who had
two daughters, pretty enough
but with hearts like blackjacks.
30 Cinderella was their maid.
She slept on the sooty hearth each night
and walked around looking like Al Jolson.[3]
Her father brought presents home from town,
jewels and gowns for the other women
35 but the twig of a tree for Cinderella.
She planted that twig on her mother's grave
and it grew to a tree where a white dove sat.
Whenever she wished for anything the dove
would drop it like an egg upon the ground.
40 The bird is important, my dears, so heed him.

Next came the ball, as you all know.
It was a marriage market.
The prince was looking for a wife.
All but Cinderella were preparing
45 and gussying up for the big event.

---

[1] Fashion designer Christian Dior.

[2] Exclusive department store.

[3] Al Jolson (Asa Yoelson; 1886–1950)—American singer and songwriter, famous for his "black-face" minstrel performances.

Cinderella begged to go too.
Her stepmother threw a dish of lentils
into the cinders and said: Pick them
up in an hour and you shall go.
50 The white dove brought all his friends;
all the warm wings of the fatherland came,
and picked up the lentils in a jiffy.
No, Cinderella, said the stepmother,
you have no clothes and cannot dance.
55 That's the way with stepmothers.

Cinderella went to the tree at the grave
and cried forth like a gospel singer:
Mama! Mama! My turtledove,
send me to the prince's ball!
60 The bird dropped down a golden dress
and delicate little gold slippers.
Rather a large package for a simple bird.
So she went. Which is no surprise.
Her stepmother and sisters didn't
65 recognize her without her cinder face
and the prince took her hand on the spot
and danced with no other the whole day.

As nightfall came she thought she'd better
get home. The prince walked her home
70 and she disappeared into the pigeon house
and although the prince took an axe and broke
it open she was gone. Back to her cinders.
These events repeated themselves for three days.
However on the third day the prince
75 covered the palace steps with cobbler's wax
and Cinderella's gold shoe stuck upon it.
Now he would find whom the shoe fit
and find his strange dancing girl for keeps.
He went to their house and the two sisters
80 were delighted because they had lovely feet.
The eldest went into a room to try the slipper on
but her big toe got in the way so she simply
sliced it off and put on the slipper.
The prince rode away with her until the white dove
85 told him to look at the blood pouring forth.
That is the way with amputations.
They don't just heal up like a wish.
The other sister cut off her heel
but the blood told as blood will.
90 The prince was getting tired.

He began to feel like a shoe salesman.
But he gave it one last try.
This time Cinderella fit into the shoe
like a love letter into its envelope.
95 At the wedding ceremony
the two sisters came to curry favor
and the white dove pecked their eyes out.
Two hollow spots were left
like soup spoons.

100 Cinderella and the prince
lived, they say, happily ever after,
like two dolls in a museum case
never bothered by diapers or dust,
never arguing over the timing of an egg,
105 never telling the same story twice,
never getting a middle-aged spread,
their darling smiles pasted on for eternity
Regular Bobbsey Twins.[4]
That story.

READING AND REACTING

1. The first twenty-one lines of the poem act as a prelude. How does this prelude help to establish the speaker's ironic tone?

2. At times the speaker talks directly to readers. What effect do these statements have on you? Would the poem be more effective without them?

3. Throughout the poem, the speaker mixes contemporary colloquial expressions with the conventional diction of a fairy tale. How does the juxtaposition of these different levels of diction create irony?

4. **JOURNAL ENTRY** What details of the fairy tale does Sexton change in her poem? Why do you think she makes these changes?

5. **CRITICAL PERSPECTIVE** In his 1973 book *Confessional Poets*, Robert Phillips comments on Anne Sexton's use of the Grimm Brothers' fairy tales in her book *Transformations*. According to Phillips, by transforming the Grimms' stories into symbols of our own time, Sexton "has managed to offer us understandable images of the world around us."

   ["Cinderella"] she takes to be a prototype of the old rags to riches theme ("From diapers to Dior. / That story."). Cinderella is said to have slept on the sooty hearth each night and "walked around looking like Al Jolson"—a

---

[4] The two sets of twins—Nan and Bert, Flossie and Freddie—in a popular series of early twentieth-century children's books. They led an idealized, problem-free life.

*comparison indicative of the level of invention and humor in the book. At
the end, when Cinderella marries the handsome prince to live happily every
after, Mrs. Sexton pulls a double whammy and reveals that the ending, in
itself, is another fairy tale within a fairy tale, totally unreal and unlikely.*

Is "Cinderella," written in 1970, a "symbol of our own time"? In
what way does it offer us "understandable images of the world
around us"?

DUDLEY RANDALL

(1914–   )

Ballad of Birmingham

(1969)

(On the bombing of a church in Birmingham, Alabama, 1963)

"Mother dear, may I go downtown
Instead of out to play,
And march the streets of Birmingham
In a Freedom March today?"

5 "No, baby, no, you may not go,
For the dogs are fierce and wild,
And clubs and hoses, guns and jails
Aren't good for a little child."

"But, mother, I won't be alone.
10 Other children will go with me,
And march the streets of Birmingham
To make our country free."

"No, baby, no, you may not go,
For I fear those guns will fire.
15 But you may go to church instead
And sing in the children's choir."

She has combed and brushed her night-dark hair,
And bathed rose petal sweet,
And drawn white gloves on her small brown hands,
20 And white shoes on her feet.

The mother smiled to know her child
Was in the sacred place,

But that smile was the last smile
To come upon her face.

25 For when she heard the explosion,
Her eyes grew wet and wild.
She raced through the streets of Birmingham
Calling for her child.

She clawed through bits of glass and brick,
30 Then lifted out a shoe.
"O, here's the shoe my baby wore,
But, baby, where are you?"

READING AND REACTING

1. Who are the two speakers in the poem? How do their attitudes differ? How does the tone of the poem convey their attitudes?

2. What kinds of irony are present in the poem? Give examples of each kind you identify.

3. This poem is a **ballad**, a form of poetry traditionally written to be sung or recited. Ballads typically repeat words and phrases and have regular meter and rhyme. How do the regular rhyme, repeated words, and singsong meter affect the poem's tone?

4. **JOURNAL ENTRY**   This poem was written in response to the 1963 bombing of the 16th Street Baptist Church in Birmingham, Alabama, a bombing that killed four African-American children. How does this historical background help you to understand the irony of the poem?

▼▼▼

CHECKLIST FOR WRITING ABOUT VOICE

THE SPEAKER IN THE POEM

♦ Who is the speaker? What do we know about him or her?

♦ Is the speaker anonymous, or does he or she have a particular identity?

♦ How does assuming a particular persona help the poet to convey his or her ideas?

♦ Does the title give information about the speaker's identity?

♦ In what way does word choice provide information about the speaker?

♦ Does the speaker make any direct statements that help you to establish his or her identity or character?

♦ Does the speaker address anyone? How can you tell? Does the presence of a listener seem to affect the speaker?

TONE

♦ What is the speaker's attitude toward his or her subject?

♦ How do word choice, rhyme, meter, sentence structure, figures of speech, and imagery help to convey the attitude of the speaker?

♦ Is the tone of the poem consistent? How do shifts in tone reflect the changing moods or attitudes of the speaker?

♦ Does any dramatic irony exist in the poem? Are there any examples of situational irony?

♦ Does verbal irony appear in the poem?

▲▲▲

WRITING SUGGESTIONS: VOICE

1. Write an essay in which you discuss your attitude toward your cultural identity in light of that of the speaker in "My Grandmother Would Rock Quietly and Hum" (p. 672) or "Where Mountain Lion Lay Down with Deer" (p. 678).

2. Compare the women's voices in "Cinderella" (p. 699) and "Gretel in Darkness" (p. 671). In what way are their attitudes toward men similar? In what way are they different?

3. The theme of Herrick's poem "To the Virgins, to Make Much of Time" (p. 691) is known as **carpe diem** or "seize the day." Read Andrew Marvell's "To His Coy Mistress" (p. 785), which has the same theme, and compare its tone with that of "To the Virgins, to Make Much of Time."

4. Read the following poem by Emily Dickinson, and compare her speaker's use of the word *hope* with Ariel Dorfman's (p. 696).

"Hope" is the thing with feathers—
That perches in the soul—
And sings the tune without the words—
And never stops—at all—

And sweetest—in the Gale—is heard—
And sore must be the storm—
That could abash the little Bird—
That kept so many warm—

I've heard it in the chillest land—
And on the strangest Sea—
Yet, never, in Extremity,
It asked a crumb—of Me.

5. Because the speaker and the poet are not necessarily the same, poems by the same author can have different voices. Compare the voices of "Morning Song" (p. 690), "Metaphors" (p. 984), and "Daddy" (p. 779), all by Sylvia Plath.

CHAPTER 14

Word Choice, Word Order

If the language of commerce is a parade, then the language of the poem is that of a hive where one may be stung into recognition by words that have the power to create images strong enough to change our own lives as we imagine and live them.

TESS GALLAGHER, "THE POEM AS TIME MACHINE"

The poet's love of language must, if language is to reward him with unlooked-for miracles, that is, with poetry, amount to a passion. The passion for the things of the world and the passion for naming them must be in him indistinguishable. I think that Wordsworth's intensity of feeling lay as much in his naming of the waterfall as in his physical apprehension of it, when he wrote:

. . . The sounding cataract
Haunted me like a passion. . . .

DENISE LEVERTOV, "ORIGINS OF A POEM"

What is known in a poem is its language, that is, the words it uses. Yet those words seem different in a poem. Even the most familiar will seem strange. In a poem, each word, being equally important, exists in absolute focus, having a weight it rarely achieves in fiction. . . . Words in a novel are subordinate to broad slices of action or characterization that push the plot forward. In a poem, they are the action. That is why poems establish themselves right away—in a line or two—and why experienced readers of poetry can tell immediately if the poem they are reading possesses any authority. On the other hand, it would be hard to know much about a novel on the basis of its first sentence. We usually give it a dozen or so pages to earn its right to our attention. And, paradoxically, it has our attention when its language has all but disappeared into the events it generated.

MARK STRAND, INTRODUCTION TO *BEST AMERICAN POEMS OF 1991*

I like mountain and prairie and sky. When I write poetry, I use such words and I also use abstract words. But it is difficult to give you a list of favorite words because words become vital—they come alive—within a certain context. A given word is extremely important and vital in one context and not very interesting in another. It

706

depends upon what's around the word. The environment. Although some words are naturally interesting, in my opinion. Like some creatures. The fox, I think, is a creature of almost immediate interest to most people. Other words are not as immediately interesting, or are even negatively received. Like some other creatures. The lizard, for example, is a creature most people wouldn't ordinarily care about. But in its natural habitat and in its dimension of wilderness, the lizard can be seen as a beautiful thing. Its movements are very wonderful to watch. Similarly, you can take almost any word and make it interesting by the way in which you use it.

N. SCOTT MOMADAY, IN *ANCESTRAL VOICES*

I will say this, you can't write poetry unless you're willing to immerse yourself in language—not just in words, but in words of a certain potency. It's like learning a foreign language.

There was a time when I couldn't understand any poetry beyond simple narrative verse. I remember reading modern poems and being completely baffled by them, not knowing what they meant or how they worked. You try and try and all of a sudden you know how they work.

MARGARET ATWOOD, IN "A QUESTION OF METAMORPHOSIS"

Q: In your poetry some words seem to have a different meaning than in most poetry in English. Take the word "sugar," for example. The costs of sugar, the human costs are alive in the poetry, which makes the word new, in a sense, or reveals what the word really means.

A: Well, the word "wheat" for me will always be a literary word. It's a word out of poetry; it's not a word out of agriculture for me. It's not a word that I know—it's not a world or word that I know. When you plant wheat, that's work, but wheat in tapestries, wheat in literature becomes a pastoral word that has no work in it, in a sense. I think that may be the difference, because sugar is not a pastoral, though it may appear to be a pastoral thing. The fields of sugar in the Caribbean are divinely beautiful, are supremely calm and so on, but there's a lot of blood and sweat in the earth for it. I think the same is true of wheat, and when a northern writer writes about wheat, he's writing close to the idea of bread, of survival. The wheat in the Bible is hard-work wheat; it's not a literary word. The same thing would be true, I imagine, of olive oil in Greece or, if you change places, of the coconut. For one person it's picturesque and archaic and literary. For another person it's something that smells and grows.

DEREK WALCOTT, INTERVIEWED IN *PARTISAN REVIEW*

SIPHO SEPAMLA

(1932–   )

Words, Words, Words[1]

We don't speak of tribal wars anymore
we say simple faction fights
there are no tribes around here
only nations
5 it makes sense you see
'cause from there
one moves to multinational
it makes sense you get me
'cause from there
10 one gets one's homeland
which is a reasonable idea
'cause from there
one can dabble with independence
which deserves warm applause
15 —the bloodless revolution

we are talking of words
words tossed around as if
denied location by the wind
we mean those words some spit
20 others grab
dress them up for the occasion
fling them on the lap of an audience
we are talking of those words
that stalk our lives like policemen
25 words no dictionary can embrace
words that change sooner than seasons
we mean words
that spell out our lives
words, words, words
30 for there's a kind of poetic licence
doing the rounds in these parts

Words identify and name, characterize and distinguish, compare and contrast. Words describe, limit, and embellish; words locate and measure. Without words, there cannot be a poem. Even though words may be elusive and uncertain and changeable, "tossed around as if / denied location

---

[1] Publication date is not available. This title is possibly an allusion to *Hamlet* 2. 2. 189.

by the wind" and "can change sooner than seasons," they still can "stalk our lives like policemen." In poetry, as in love and politics, words matter.

Beyond the quantitative—how many words, how many letters and syllables—is the much more important quality of words: Which are chosen, and why? Why are certain words placed next to others? What does a word suggest in a particular context? How are the words arranged? What exactly constitutes the right word?

Word Choice

In poetry, even more than in fiction or drama, words tend to become the focus—sometimes even the true subject—of a work. For this reason, the choice of one word over another can be crucial. Because poems are brief, they must compress many ideas into a few lines; poets know how much weight each individual word carries, and so they choose with great care, trying to select words that imply more than they state.

A poet may choose a word because of its sound. For instance, a word may echo another word's sound, and such repetition may place emphasis on both words; it may rhyme with another word and therefore be needed to preserve the poem's rhyme scheme; or, it may have a certain combination of stressed and unstressed syllables needed to maintain the poem's metrical pattern. Occasionally, a poet may even choose a word because of how it looks on the page. Most often, poets select words because they help to communicate the poem's ideas.

At the same time, poets may choose words for their degree of concreteness or abstraction, specificity or generality. A *concrete* word denotes an item that is a perceivable, tangible entity—for example, a kiss or a flag. An *abstract* word refers to an intangible idea, condition, or quality, something that cannot be perceived by the senses—love, patriotism, and so on. *Specific* words denote particular items; *general* words refer to entire classes or groups of items. As the following example illustrates, whether a word is specific or general is relative; its degree of specificity or generality depends on its relationship to other words.

> Poem → closed form poem → sonnet → seventeenth-century sonnet →
> Elizabethan sonnet → sonnet by Shakespeare → "My Mistress' Eyes Are
> Nothing Like the Sun"

Sometimes a poet wants a precise word, one that is specific and concrete. At other times, however, a poet might prefer general or abstract language, which may allow for more subtlety—or even for intentional ambiguity.

Finally, a word may be chosen for its **connotation**—what it suggests. Every word has one or more **denotations**—what it signifies without emotional associations, judgments, or opinions. The word *family*, for example, denotes "a group of related things or people." Connotation is a more complex matter, however, for a single word may have many different associations. In general terms, a word may have a connotation that is positive, neutral, or negative. Thus, *family* may have a positive connotation when it describes a group of loving relatives, a neutral connotation when it describes a biological category, and an ironically negative connotation when it describes an organized crime family. Beyond this distinction, *family,* like any other word, may have a variety of emotional and social associations, suggesting loyalty, warmth, home, security, or duty. In fact, many words have somewhat different meanings in different contexts. To help guide their word choice, poets consider what a particular word may suggest to readers as well as what it denotes.

In the poem that follows, the poet chooses words for their sounds, their relationships to other words, and their connotations.

WALT WHITMAN

(1819–1892)

When I Heard the Learn'd Astronomer

(1865)

When I heard the learn'd astronomer,
When the proofs, the figures, were ranged in columns before me,
When I was shown the charts and diagrams, to add, divide, and
    measure them,
5 When I sitting heard the astronomer where he lectured with much
    applause in the lecture-room,
How soon unaccountable I became tired and sick,
Till rising and gliding out I wander'd off by myself,
In the mystical moist night-air, and from time to time,
10 Look'd up in perfect silence at the stars.

This poem might be paraphrased as follows: "When I grew restless listening to an astronomy lecture, I went outside, where I found I learned more just by looking at the stars than I had learned inside." But the paraphrase is neither as rich nor as complex as the poem. Through careful use of diction, Whitman establishes a dichotomy that supports the poem's central theme about the relative merits of two ways of learning.

The poem can be divided into two groups of four lines. The first four lines, unified by the repetition of "When," introduce the astronomer and his tools: "proofs," "figures," and "charts and diagrams" to be added, divided, and measured. In this section of the poem, the speaker is passive: He sits and listens ("I heard"; "I was shown"; "I sitting heard"). The repetition of "When" reinforces the dry monotony of the lecture. In the next four lines, the choice of words signals the change in the speaker's actions and reactions. The confined lecture hall is replaced by "the mystical moist night-air," and the dry lecture and automatic applause give way to "perfect silence"; instead of sitting passively, the speaker becomes active (he rises, glides, wanders); instead of listening, he looks. The mood of the first half of the poem is restrained: The language is concrete and physical, and the speaker is studying, receiving information from a "learn'd" authority. The rest of the poem, celebrating intuitive knowledge and feelings, is more abstract, freer. Throughout the poem, the lecture hall contrasts sharply with the natural world outside its walls.

After considering the poem as a whole, readers should not find it hard to understand why the poet selected certain words. Whitman's use of "lectured" in line 4 rather than a more neutral word like "spoke" is appropriate both because it suggests formality and distance and because it echoes "lecture-room" in the same line. The word "sick" in line 5 is striking because it connotes physical as well as emotional distress, more effectively conveying the extent of the speaker's discomfort than "bored" or "restless" would. "Rising" and "gliding" (6) are used rather than "standing" and "walking out" both because of the way their stressed vowel sounds echo each other (and echo "time to time" in the next line) and because of their connotation of dreaminess, which is consistent with "wander'd" (6) and "mystical" (7). The word "moist" (7) is chosen not only because its consonant sounds echo the m and st sounds in "mystical," but also to establish a contrast with the dry, airless lecture hall. Finally, line 8's "perfect silence" is a better choice than a reasonable substitute like "complete silence" or "total silence," which would suggest the degree of the silence but not its quality.

In the next poem the poet also pays careful attention to word choice.

WILLIAM STAFFORD

(1914–1993)

For the Grave of Daniel Boone

(1957)

The farther he went the farther home grew.
Kentucky became another room;
the mansion arched over the Mississippi;
flowers were spread all over the floor.
5 He traced ahead a deepening home,
and better, with goldenrod:

Leaving the snakeskin of place after place,
going on—after the trees
the grass, a bird flying after a song.
10 Rifle so level, sighting so well
his picture freezes down to now,
a story-picture for children.

They go over the velvet falls
into the tapestry of his time,
15 heirs to the landscape, feeling no jar:
it is like evening; they are the quail
surrounding his fire, coming in for the kill;
their little feet move sacred sand.

Children, we live in a barbwire time
20 but like to follow the old hands back—
the ring in the light, the knuckle, the palm,
all the way to Daniel Boone,
hunting our own kind of deepening home.
From the land that was his I heft this rock.

25 Here on his grave I put it down.

A number of words in "For the Grave of Daniel Boone" are noteworthy for their multiple denotations and connotations. In the first stanza, for example, "home" does not mean Boone's residence; it connotes an abstract state, a dynamic concept that grows and deepens, encompassing states and rivers while becoming paradoxically more and more elusive. In literal terms, Boone's "home" at the poem's end is a narrow, confined space: his grave. In a wider sense, his home is the United States, particularly the natural landscape he explored. Thus, the word "home" comes to have a variety of associations to readers beyond its denotative meaning: It suggests both the infinite possibilities beyond the frontier and the realities of civilization's walls and fences.

The word "snakeskin" denotes "the skin of a snake"; its most immediate connotations are smoothness and slipperiness. In this poem, however, the snakeskin signifies more, for it is Daniel Boone who is "leaving the snakeskin of place after place." Like a snake, Boone belongs to the natural world—and, like a snake, wanders from place to place, shedding his skin as he goes. Thus, the word "snakeskin," with its connotation of rebirth and its links to nature, passing time, and the inevitability of change, is consistent with the image of Boone as both a man of nature and a restless wanderer, "a bird flying after a song."

In the poem's third stanza, the phrases "velvet falls" and "tapestry of time" seem at first to have been selected solely for their pleasing repetition of sounds ("v<u>e</u>lvet fa<u>ll</u>s"; "<u>t</u>apestry of <u>t</u>ime"). But both of these phrases also support the poem's theme: Alive, Boone was in constant movement; he was also larger than life. Now he has been reduced; "his picture freezes down to . . . / a story-picture for children" (11–12), and he is as static and inorganic as velvet or tapestry—no longer dynamic, like "falls" and "time."

The word "barbwire" (in line 19's phrase "barbwire time") is another word whose multiple meanings enrich the poem's theme. In the simplest terms "barbwire" denotes a metal fencing material. In light of the poem's concern with space and distance, however, "barbwire" (with its connotations of sharpness, danger, and confinement) is also the antithesis of Boone's free or peaceful wilderness, evoking images of prisons and concentration camps and reinforcing the poem's central dichotomy between past freedom and present restriction.

The phrase "old hands" (20) also has multiple meanings in the context of the poem. On one level, the hands could belong to an elderly person holding a storybook; on another level, "old hands" could refer to those with considerable life experience—like Boone, who was an "old hand" at scouting. On still another level, given the poem's concern with time, "old hands" could suggest the hands of a clock.

Through what it says literally and through what its words suggest, "For the Grave of Daniel Boone" communicates a good deal about the speaker's identification with Daniel Boone and with the nation he called home. Boone's horizons, his concept of "home," expanded as he wandered. Now, when he is frozen in time and space, a character in a child's picture book, a body in a grave, we are still "hunting our own kind of deepening home," but our horizons, like Boone's, have narrowed in this "barbwire time."

Poems for Further Reading: Word Choice

RUSSELL ENDO

(1956–   )

Susumu, My Name

(1988)

You are entitled to overhear
Susumu, my name, means
    "progress" in Japanese,
The progress of prosperity
5   and of good fortune.

The dust that seeped through
makeshift barracks in Arizona[1]
Whet my parents' taste for the
American Dream.
10 But my luck shall have to be
different
I want my wheels to skim like
the blades of the wind
Across all ruts.
15 I want my wheels to spin so fast
That we stand still.
Are you with me?
Then may we whisper in the
summer breeze
20 Susumu.

READING AND REACTING

1. Why does Endo use "overhear" in line 1? What connotations does this word have? What other words might he have substituted?

2. Do any words seem to have been chosen for their sounds? What else do these words contribute to the poem?

3. **JOURNAL ENTRY**   Write a paragraph in which you explore the denotations and connotations of a word that has special meaning to members of your family or ethnic group. (If you like, you may turn your paragraph into a poem.)

JAMES WRIGHT   -

(1927–1980)

Autumn Begins in Martins Ferry, Ohio

1963

In the Shreve High football stadium,
I think of Polacks nursing long beers in Tiltonsville,
And gray faces of Negroes in the blast furnace at Benwood,
And the ruptured night watchman of Wheeling Steel,
5 Dreaming of heroes.

---

[1] Camps where Japanese-Americans were confined during World War II.

All the proud fathers are ashamed to go home.
Their women cluck like starved pullets,
Dying for love.
Therefore,
10   Their sons grow suicidally beautiful
At the beginning of October,
And gallop terribly against each other's bodies.

READING AND REACTING

1. Evaluate Wright's decision to use each of the following words:
   "Polacks" (2), "ruptured" (4), "pullets" (7), "suicidally" (10), "gallop"
   (12). Do any of these words strike you as unexpected, even unsettling,
   in the context in which he uses them? Can you explain why each is
   used instead of a more conventional word?

2. What thematic relationship, if any, do you see between line 5
   ("Dreaming of heroes") and line 8 ("Dying for love")? What do these
   lines reveal about the people who live in Martins Ferry?

3. **JOURNAL ENTRY**   What comment does this poem seem to be making
   about small towns? About high school football?

4. **CRITICAL PERSPECTIVE**   In her 1980 essay "James Wright:
   Returning to the Heartland," Bonnie Costello discusses the poet's
   complex relationship to place and its effect on "Autumn Begins in
   Martins Ferry, Ohio," characterizing Wright as a kind of "fugitive" or
   "exile" from the past his poems reveal:

   *James Wright was an elegaic poet of place. Place names echo through his
   lines as through deserted villages and wintry valleys, for Martins Ferry,
   Ohio; Fargo, North Dakota; Wheeling, West Virginia, are all dying. While
   he admired D. H. Lawrence's essay "The Spirit of Place" and tried to follow
   its guidelines, his own subject raised a special problem since it was the
   departure of spirit that he best portrayed. Wright tried repeatedly to call his
   spirit back, but his finest poems are those which catch it crossing the last
   hill crest or disappearing into the mist. One might argue that there is,
   indeed, a spirit in this place, one hopeless, ignorant, and long suffering,
   nonetheless beautiful and mysterious.*

   How does "Autumn Begins in Martins Ferry, Ohio" convey the
   elegaic sense of place Costello describes?

ADRIENNE RICH

(1929–)

Living in Sin

(1955)

She had thought the studio would keep itself,
no dust upon the furniture of love.
Half heresy, to wish the taps less vocal,
the panes relieved of grime. A plate of pears,
5 a piano with a Persian shawl, a cat
stalking the picturesque amusing mouse
had risen at his urging.
Not that at five each separate stair would writhe
under the milkman's tramp; that morning light
10 so coldly would delineate the scraps
of last night's cheese and three sepulchral bottles;
that on the kitchen shelf among the saucers
a pair of beetle-eyes would fix her own—
envoy from some black village in the mouldings . . .
15 Meanwhile, he, with a yawn,
sounded a dozen notes upon the keyboard,
declared it out of tune, shrugged at the mirror,
rubbed at his beard, went out for cigarettes;
while she, jeered by the minor demons,
20 pulled back the sheets and made the bed and found
a towel to dust the table-top,
and let the coffee-pot boil over on the stove.
By evening she was back in love again,
though not so wholly but throughout the night
25 she woke sometimes to feel the daylight coming
like a relentless milkman up the stairs.

READING AND REACTING

1. How might the poem's impact change if each of these words were deleted: "Persian" (5), "picturesque" (6), "sepulchral" (11), "minor" (19), "sometimes" (25)?

2. What words in the poem have strongly negative connotations? What do these words suggest about the relationship the poem describes?

3. This poem, about a woman in love, uses very few words conventionally associated with love poems. Instead, many of its words denote the everyday routine of housekeeping. Give examples of such words. Why do you think they are used?

4. **JOURNAL ENTRY**   What connotations does the title have? What other phrases have similar denotative meanings? How do their connotations differ? Why do you think Rich chose the title she did?

5. **CRITICAL PERSPECTIVE**   In "Her Cargo: Adrienne Rich and the Common Language," a 1979 essay examining the poet's work over almost thirty years, Alicia Ostriker notes that early poems by Rich, including "Living in Sin," reflect popular male poets' "resigned sense of life as a diminished thing" and only "tremble on the brink of indignation":

   They seem about to state explicitly . . . a connection between feminine subordination in male-dominated middle-class relationships, and emotionally lethal inarticulateness for both sexes. But the poetry . . . is minor because it is polite. It illustrates symptoms but does not probe sources. There is no disputing the ideas of the predecessors, and Adrienne Rich at this point is a cautious good poet in the sense of being a good girl, a quality noted with approval by her reviewers.

   Does your reading of "Living in Sin" support Ostriker's characterization of it as "resigned," "polite," and "cautious"? Do you think Rich is "being a good girl"?

KARL SHAPIRO

(1913–   )

Auto Wreck

(1941)

Its quick soft silver bell beating, beating,
And down the dark one ruby flare
Pulsing out red light like an artery,
The ambulance at top speed floating down
5 Past beacons and illuminated clocks
Wings in a heavy curve, dips down,
And brakes speed, entering the crowd.
The doors leap open, emptying light;
Stretchers are laid out, the mangled lifted
10 And stowed into the little hospital.
Then the bell, breaking the hush, tolls once,
And the ambulance with its terrible cargo
Rocking, slightly rocking, moves away,
As the doors, an afterthought, are closed.

15 We are deranged, walking among the cops
Who sweep glass and are large and composed.
One is still making notes under the light.
One with a bucket douches ponds of blood
Into the street and gutter.
20 One hangs lanterns on the wrecks that cling,
Empty husks of locusts, to iron poles.

Our throats were tight as tourniquets,
Our feet were bound with splints, but now,
Like convalescents intimate and gauche,
25 We speak through sickly smiles and warn
With the stubborn saw of common sense,
The grim joke and the banal resolution.
The traffic moves around with care,
But we remain, touching a wound
30 That opens to our richest horror.
Already old, the question Who shall die?
Becomes unspoken Who is innocent?
For death in war is done by hands;
Suicide has cause and stillbirth, logic;
35 And cancer, simple as a flower, blooms.
But this invites the occult mind,
Cancels our physics with a sneer,
And spatters all we knew of denouement
Across the expedient and wicked stones.

READING AND REACTING

1. Comment on the verbs used in this poem. In what sense are they appropriate for a poem about an automobile accident?

2. Why is each of these words particularly startling or vivid in the context of the poem: "little" (10), "terrible" (12), "ponds" (18), "occult" (36), "wicked" (39)?

3. Comment on the logic of the pairing of these words: "large and composed" (16), "intimate and gauche" (24). What effect do you think the poet is trying to create?

4. **JOURNAL ENTRY** How accurately do you think this poem's language conveys the experience of viewing an auto accident? Explain.

E. E. CUMMINGS

(1894–1962)

in Just-[1]

(1923)

in Just-
spring   when the world is mud-
luscious the little
lame balloonman

5 whistles   far   and wee

and eddieandbill come
running from marbles and
piracies and it's
spring

10 when the world is puddle-wonderful
the queer
old balloonman whistles
far   and   wee
and bettyandisbel come dancing

15 from hop-scotch and jump-rope and

it's
spring
and
    the

20   goat-footed

balloonMan   whistles
far
and
wee

READING AND REACTING

1. In this poem Cummings coins a number of words that he uses to modify other words. Identify these coinages. What other, more conventional, words could be used in their place? What does Cummings accomplish by using the coined words instead?

---

[1] Also known as "Chansons Innocentes I."

2. What do you think Cummings means by "far and wee" in lines 5, 13, and 22–24? Why do you think he arranges the three words in a different way each time he uses them?

3. **CRITICAL PERSPECTIVE**   In "Latter-Day Notes on E. E. Cummings' Language" (1955), Robert E. Maurer suggests that Cummings often coined new words in the same way that children do: for example, "by adding the normal -er or -est *(beautifuler, chiefest),* or stepping up the power of a word such as *last,* which is already superlative, and saying *lastest,"* creating words such as *givingest* and *whirlingest.* In addition to "combining two or more words to form a single new one . . . to give an effect of wholeness, of one quality" (for example, *yellowgreen),* "in the simplest of his word coinages, he merely creates a new word by analogy as a child would without adding any shade of meaning other than that inherent in the prefix or suffix he utilizes, as in the words *unstrength* and *untimid. . . ."* Many early reviewers, Maurer notes, criticized such coinages because they "convey a thrill but not a precise impression," a criticism also leveled at Cummings's poetry more broadly.

Consider the coinages in "in Just-." Do you agree that many do not add "shades of meaning" or provide a "precise impression"? Or, do you find that the coinages contribute to the whole in a meaningful way?

THEODORE ROETHKE

(1908–1963)

I Knew a Woman

(1958)

I knew a woman, lovely in her bones,
When small birds sighed, she would sigh back at them;
Ah, when she moved, she moved more ways than one:
The shapes a bright container can contain!
5 Of her choice virtues only gods should speak,
Or English poets who grew up on Greek
(I'd have them sing in chorus, cheek to cheek).

How well her wishes went! She stroked my chin,
She taught me Turn, and Counter-turn, and Stand;
10 She taught me Touch, that undulant white skin;
I nibbled meekly from her proffered hand;
She was the sickle; I, poor I, the rake,
Coming behind her for her pretty sake
(But what prodigious mowing we did make).

15 Love likes a gander, and adores a goose:
   Her full lips pursed, the errant note to seize;
   She played it quick, she played it light and loose;
   My eyes, they dazzled at her flowing knees;
   Her several parts could keep a pure repose,
20 Or one hip quiver with a mobile nose
   (She moved in circles, and those circles moved).

   Let seed be grass, and grass turn into hay:
   I'm martyr to a motion not my own;
   What's freedom for? To know eternity.
25 I swear she cast a shadow white as stone.
   But who would count eternity in days?
   These old bones live to learn her wanton ways:
   (I measure time by how a body sways).

READING AND REACTING

1. Many of the words in Roethke's poem have double meanings—for example, "gander" and "goose" in line 15. Identify other words that have more than one meaning, and consider the function these multiple meanings serve.

2. The poem's language contains many surprises; often the word we expect is not the one we get. For example, "container" in line 4 is not a conventional means of describing a women. What other words are used in unusual ways? What does Roethke achieve by choosing such words?

3. Is there a difference between the denotation or connotation of the word "bones" in the phrases "lovely in her bones" (1) and "These old bones" (27)? Explain.

4. **JOURNAL ENTRY**   How does this poem differ from your idea of what a love poem should be?

EXERCISE: REVISIONS AND WORD CHOICE

Writing a poem can be hard work, typically requiring many revisions. In writing drafts of a poem, a poet moves closer and closer to what he or she considers to be "the right words." The questions that follow ask you to focus on one poet's decisions.

Read Robert Frost's "In White" and a later version of the poem, called "Design," and then answer the questions that follow.

ROBERT FROST

(1874–1963)

In White

(1912)

A dented spider like a snowdrop white
On a white Heal-all, holding up a moth
Like a white piece of lifeless satin cloth—
Saw ever curious eye so strange a sight?

5 Portent in little, assorted death and blight
Like the ingredients of a witches' broth?
The beady spider, the flower like a froth,
And the moth carried like a paper kite.

What had that flower to do with being white,
10 The blue Brunella every child's delight?
What brought the kindred spider to that height?
(Make we no thesis of the miller's plight.)
What but design of darkness and of night?
Design, design! Do I use the word aright?

Design

(1936)

I found a dimpled spider, fat and white,
On a white heal-all, holding up a moth
Like a white piece of rigid satin cloth—
Assorted characters of death and blight
5 Mixed ready to begin the morning right,
Like the ingredients of a witches' broth—
A snow-drop spider, a flower like a froth,
And dead wings carried like a paper kite.

What had that flower to do with being white,
10 The wayside blue and innocent heal-all?
What brought the kindred spider to that height,
Then steered the white moth thither in the night?
What but design of darkness to appall?—
If design govern in a thing so small.

1. What is suggested by the title "Design" that is not suggested by the title "In White"? Does each title suit the poem it introduces? Explain.

2. The word "white" is used several times in each poem; each poem also includes words that rhyme with "white" and other words that indicate color or relative shades of light and darkness. Do Frost's revisions change the significance of the color white? Explain.

3. What does the word "design" denote? What connotations does it have? Does it suggest the same thing in both versions of the poem?

4. Study the poem's last two lines. How can you explain the changes the poet made, particularly in the use of the word "design"?

5. What other changes in word choice did Frost make as he revised? What reasons might he have had for each change?

6. Do you think any words or phrases in "Design" should be restored to their original equivalents? Should any words be changed? Explain.

Levels of Diction

Like other writers, poets use various levels of diction to convey their ideas. The diction of a poem may be formal or informal or fall anywhere in between, depending on the identity of the speaker and on the speaker's attitude toward the reader and toward his or her subject. At one extreme, highly informal poems can be full of jargon, regionalisms, and slang. At the other extreme, very formal poems can be far removed in style and vocabulary from everyday speech. Many poems, of course, use language that falls somewhere between formal and informal diction. Still, to understand the range of poets' options, it is helpful to identify and contrast the two extremes of formal and informal diction.

FORMAL DICTION

Formal diction typically uses a learned vocabulary and grammatically correct forms. In general, formal diction does not include colloquialisms, such as contractions and shortened word forms (*phone* for *telephone*). As the following poem illustrates, a speaker who uses formal diction can sound aloof and impersonal.

MARGARET ATWOOD

(1939–   )

The City Planners

(1966)

Cruising these residential Sunday
streets in dry August sunlight:
what offends us is
the sanities:
5 the houses in pedantic rows, the planted
sanitary trees, assert
levelness of surface like a rebuke
to the dent in our car door.
No shouting here, or
10 shatter of glass; nothing more abrupt
than the rational whine of a power mower
cutting a straight swath in the discouraged grass.

But though the driveways neatly
sidestep hysteria
15 by being even, the roofs all display
the same slant of avoidance to the hot sky,
certain things:
the smell of spilled oil a faint

sickness lingering in the garages,
20 a splash of paint on brick surprising as a bruise,
a plastic hose poised in a vicious
coil; even the too-fixed stare of the wide windows

give momentary access to
the landscape behind or under
25 the future cracks in the plaster

when the houses, capsized, will slide
obliquely into the clay seas, gradual as glaciers
that right now nobody notices.

That is where the City Planners
30 with the insane faces of political conspirators
are scattered over unsurveyed
territories, concealed from each other,
each in his own private blizzard;

guessing directions, they sketch
35 transitory lines rigid as wooden borders
on a wall in the white vanishing air

tracing the panic of suburb
order in a bland madness of snows.

Atwood's speaker is clearly concerned about the poem's central issue, but rather than use *I*, she uses the first-person plural (*us*) to maintain distance and to give the impression of avoiding emotional involvement. Although phrases such as "sickness lingering in the garages" and "insane faces of political conspirators" do convey the speaker's disapproval, the use of formal words—"pedantic," "rebuke," "display," "poised," "obliquely," "conspirators," "transitory"—helps her to maintain her distance. Both the speaker herself and her attack on the misguided city planners gain credibility through her balanced tone and through the use of language that is as "professional" as theirs, with no slang, nonstandard diction, or colloquialisms.

INFORMAL DICTION

Informal diction is the language closest to everyday conversation. It includes colloquialisms—contractions, shortened word forms, and the like— and may also include slang, regional expressions, and even nonstandard words.

In the poem that follows, the speaker uses informal diction to highlight the contrast between James Baca, a law student speaking to the graduating class of his old high school, and the graduating seniors.

JIM SAGEL

(1947–   )

Baca Grande[1]

(1982)

Una vaca se topó con un ratón y le dice:
"Tú—¿tan chiquito y con bigote?" Y le responde el ratón:
"Y tú tan grandota—¿y sin brassiere?"[2]

---

[1] *Baca* is both a phonetic spelling of the Spanish word "vaca" (cow) and the last name of one of the poem's characters. *Grande* means "large."

[2] A cow ran into a rat and said: "You—so small and with a moustache?" The rat responded: "And you—so big and without a bra?"

It was nearly a miracle
James Baca remembered anyone at all
from the old hometown gang
having been two years at Yale
5 no less
and halfway through law school
at the University of California at Irvine

They hardly recognized him either
in his three-piece grey business suit
10 and surfer-swirl haircut
with just the menacing hint
of a tightly trimmed Zapata moustache
 for cultural balance
and relevance

15 He had come to deliver the keynote address
to the graduating class of 80
at his old alma mater
and show off his well-trained lips
which laboriously parted
20 each Kennedyish "R"
and drilled the first person pronoun
through the microphone
like an oil bit
with the slick, elegantly honed phrases
25 that slid so smoothly
off his meticulously bleached
 tongue
He talked Big Bucks
with astronautish fervor and if he
30 the former bootstrapless James A. Baca
could dazzle the ass
off the universe
then even you
 yes you

35 Joey Martinez toying with your yellow
 tassle
and staring dumbly into space
could emulate Mr. Baca someday
 possibly
40 well
there was of course
such a thing
as being an outrageously successful

gas station attendant too
45   let us never forget
it doesn't really matter what you do
so long as you excel
    James said
never believing a word
50 of it
for he had already risen
    as high as they go

Wasn't nobody else
from this deprived environment
55 who'd ever jumped
    straight out of college
into the Governor's office
and maybe one day
he'd sit in that big chair
60   himself
and when he did
he'd forget this damned town
and all the petty little people
in it
65 once and for all

That much he promised himself

"Baca Grande" uses numerous colloquialisms, including contractions; conversational placeholders, such as "no less" and "well"; shortened word forms, such as "gas station"; slang terms, such as "Big Bucks"; whimsical coinages ("Kennedyish," "astronautish," "bootstrapless"); nonstandard grammatical constructions, such as "Wasn't nobody else"; and even profanity. The level of language is perfectly appropriate for the students Baca addresses—suspicious, streetwise, and unimpressed by Baca's "three-piece grey business suit" and "surfer-swirl haircut." In fact, the informal diction is a key element in the poem, expressing the gap between the slick James Baca, with "his well-trained lips / which laboriously parted / each Kennedyish 'R'" and his audience, with their unpretentious, forthright speech. In this sense "Baca Grande" is as much a linguistic commentary as a social one.

Poems for Further Reading:
Levels of Diction

BARBARA L. GREENBERG
(1932-   )

The Faithful Wife
(1978)

But if I *were* to have a lover, it would be someone
who could take nothing from you. I would, in conscience,
not dishonor you. He and I would eat at Howard Johnson's

which you and I do not enjoy. With him I would go
5 fishing because it is not your sport. He would wear blue
which is your worst color; he would have none of your virtues.

Not strong, not proud, not just, not provident, my lover
would blame me for his heart's distress, which you would never
think to do. He and I would drink too much and weep together

10 and I would bruise his face as I would not bruise your face
even in my dreams. Yes I would dance with him, but to a music
you and I would never choose to hear, and in a place

where you and I would never wish to be. He and I would speak
Spanish, which is not your tongue, and we would take
15 long walks in fields of burdock, to which you are allergic.

We would make love only in the morning. It would be
altogether different. I would know him with my other body,
the one that you have never asked to see.

READING AND REACTING

1. In what respect does this poem sound like everyday speech? What
   colloquial elements usually present in conversation are absent here?

2. The speaker seems to be addressing her husband. What words or
   phrases in the poem sound out of place given the identities of the
   participants in the conversation?

3. **JOURNAL ENTRY**   How do you interpret the poem's title? In what
   sense is it ironic? In what sense is it not?

RICHARD WILBUR

(1921–   )

For the Student Strikers

(1970)

Go talk with those who are rumored to be unlike you,
And whom, it is said, you are so unlike.
Stand on the stoops of their houses and tell them why
You are out on strike.

5 It is not yet time for the rock, the bullet, the blunt
Slogan that fuddles the mind toward force.
Let the new sound in our streets be the patient sound
Of your discourse.

Doors will be shut in your faces, I do not doubt.
10 Yet here or there, it may be, there will start,
Much as the lights blink on in a block at evening,
Changes of heart.

They are your houses; the people are not unlike you;
Talk with them, then, and let it be done
15 Even for the grey wife of your nightmare sheriff
And the guardsman's son.

READING AND REACTING

1. Is this poem's diction primarily formal or informal? List the words
   that support your conclusion.

2. What elements in the poem besides its vocabulary might lead you to
   characterize it as formal or informal?

3. **JOURNAL ENTRY**   This poem is an *exhortation,* a form of discourse
   intended to incite or encourage listeners to take action. Given the
   speaker's audience and subject matter, is its level of diction
   appropriate? Explain.

CHARLES BUKOWSKI

(1920–1994)

Dog Fight

(1984)

he draws up against my rear bumper in the fast lane,
I can see his head in the rear view mirror, his eyes
are blue and he sucks upon a dead cigar.
I pull over. he passes, then slows. I don't like
5 this.
I pull back into the fast lane, engage myself upon
his rear bumper. we are as a team passing through
Compton.
I turn the radio on and light a cigarette.
10 he ups it 5 mph, I do likewise. we are as a team
entering Inglewood.
he pulls out of the fast lane and I drive past.
then I slow. when I check the rear view he is
upon my bumper again.
15 he has almost made me miss my turnoff at Century.
I hit the blinker and fire across 3 lanes of
traffic, just make the off-ramp . . .
blazing past the front of an inflammable tanker.
blue eyes comes down from behind the tanker and
20 we veer down the ramp in separate lanes to the signal
and we sit there side by side, not looking at each
other.
I am caught behind an empty school bus as he idles
behind a Mercedes.
25 the signal switches and he is gone. I cut to the
inner lane behind him, then I see that the parking
lane is open and I flash by inside of him and the
Mercedes, turn up the radio, make the green as the
Mercedes and blue eyes run the yellow into the red.
30 they make it as I power it and switch back ahead of
them in their lane in order to miss a parked vegetable
truck.
now we are running 1-2-3, not a cop in sight, we are
moving through a 1980 California July
35 we are driving with skillful nonchalance
we are moving in perfect anger
we are as a team

approaching LAX:[1]
1-2-3
40   2-3-1
3-2-1.

READING AND REACTING

1. "Dog Fight" describes a car race from the emotionally charged perspective of a driver. Given this persona, comment on the appropriateness of the level of diction of the following words: "likewise" (10), "upon" (14), "nonchalance" (35), "perfect" (36).

2. Many of the words in the poem are **jargon**—specialized language associated with a particular trade or profession. In this case, Bukowski uses automotive terms and the action words and phrases that typically describe driving maneuvers. Would you characterize these words as formal, informal, or neither? Explain.

3. What colloquialisms are present in the poem? Could noncolloquial expressions be substituted for any of them? How would such substitutions change the poem?

4. **CRITICAL PERSPECTIVE**   In a 1978 review in the *Village Voice*, critic Michael Lally defended Bukowski's poetry:

   Despite what some criticize as prose in Bukowski's poetry, there is in much of his work a poetic sensibility that, though arrogantly smart-ass and self-protective as well as self-promotional (he's the granddaddy of "punk" sensibility for sure), is also sometimes poignant, emotionally revealing, uniquely "American". . . .

   Do you see "Dog Fight" as prose, or do you see in it a "poetic sensibility"? In what sense, if any, do you find it "uniquely 'American'"? Give examples from the poem to support your conclusions.

DIALECT

Dialect denotes a regional variety of language, which may differ from the most widely used standard spoken or written language in its pronunciation, grammar, or vocabulary. (Dialect also differs from *slang*, which tends to be associated with groups determined by age or special interest rather than by region. In addition, slang is calculated to call attention to itself and its user, whereas dialect is not.) Dialect is generally used in poetry to suggest an authentic, unedited voice. Because it is associated with a particular region, dialect can also create a sense of place.

The poem that follows is told in the voice of a rural mountain woman.

---

[1] Los Angeles International Airport.

FAYE KICKNOSWAY

(1939–   )

Gracie

(1986)

I mean, I'm a no shoes hillbilly an' home
is deeper in the map than Kentucky or Tennessee an'
all I been raised to do is walk the chicken
yard, spillin' grain from ma's
5 apron, maybe once a week wear a bonnet
into town. I have red hair an' white skin;

men lean on their elbows lookin' at me. Ma's
voice tells me, "Don't breathe so deep," an'
the preacher says how happy I'll be when I'm dead. Skin
10 touchin' skin is evil. I'm to keep inside the chicken
yard, no eye's to see beneath my bonnet.
Farm boys suck their cheeks an' call, "Come home

with me, I'll give you your own chicken
yard an' take you proudly once a week to town." Home
15 ain't enough. As I spill grain from ma's
apron, I see city streets hung with lights an'
a dark room with a window lookin' on the bonnet
of the sky. Voices stroke at my skin

through its walls. When the grain's gone from ma's
20 apron, I hang it on its hook by her bonnet.
I figure to be my own fare North an' leave home.
My legs are crossed under a counter. I smell chicken
fry. A man leans on his elbows; his eyes drink my skin.
In a dark room, my dress undoes my body an'

25 I lie with him. His hot mouth comes home
on mine. I expect to hear the preacher's or ma's
voice yellin' at me, but the only voices in the wall's
 skin
are strange an' soft. I have beer an' chicken
30 for breakfast. All day I wear his body like a bonnet.
My stockins are run. The streets are hung with lights an'
he sleeps. I stand by the window an'
look into the night's skin, fancy home an' the chicken
yard, ma's apron an' my head cool in its bonnet.

"Gracie" juxtaposes nonstandard grammatical forms such as "I been," "ain't," and "My stockins are run" with rich, understated figurative language such as "the bonnet / of the sky" and "Voices stroke at my skin." The speaker uses contractions; shortened word forms ("ma"); colloquialisms, such as "I mean," "a no shoes hillbilly," "deep" (for "deeply"), and "I figure"; and regionalisms, such as "chicken fry" and "I . . . fancy." Apostrophes indicate conversational pronunciation in words such as "an'," "touchin'," and "lookin'." The natural, colorful diction reveals the speaker's personality, and the apparent guilelessness of the dialect imparts a sense of authenticity and directness to her voice.

Poems for Further Reading: Dialect

ROBERT BURNS

(1759–1796)

John Anderson My Jo, John

(1790)

John Anderson my jo,[1] John,
  When we were first acquent,[2]
Your locks were like the raven,
  Your bonny brow was brent;[3]
5 But now your brow is beld,[4] John,
  Your locks are like the snaw;
But blessings on your frosty pow,[5]
  John Anderson my jo.

John Anderson my jo, John,
10   We clamb the hill thegither;
And mony a canty[6] day, John,
  We've had wi' ane anither:

---

[1] Dear.

[2] Acquainted.

[3] Unwrinkled.

[4] Bald.

[5] Head.

[6] Happy.

   Now we maun[7] totter down, John,
      And hand in hand we'll go,
15 And sleep thegither at the foot,
      John Anderson my jo.

READING AND REACTING

1. Reread the definition of dialect on page 731. In what respects do the words in Burns's poem conform to this definition?

2. **JOURNAL ENTRY** "Translate" the poem into modern colloquial English.

GWENDOLYN BROOKS

(1917–   )

We Real Cool

(1960)

The Pool Players.
Seven at the Golden Shovel.

   We real cool. We
   Left School. We

   Lurk late. We
   Strike straight. We
5 Sing sin. We
   Thin gin. We

   Jazz June. We
   Die soon.

READING AND REACTING

1. This poem is written in an urban dialect. What elements identify its diction as dialect rather than simply informal?

2. How does the poem's use of dialect affect your attitude toward the speaker?

3. **CRITICAL PERSPECTIVE** In *Gwendolyn Brooks: Poetry and the Heroic Voice*, critic D. H. Malhem writes of "We Real Cool," "Despite presentation in the voice of the gang, this is a maternal poem, gently scolding yet deeply sorrowing for the hopelessness of the boys." Do you agree?

---

[7] Must.

Word Order

The order in which words are arranged in a poem can be just as important as the choice of words. Because English sentences nearly always have a subject-verb-object sequence, with adjectives preceding the nouns they modify, any departures from this order call attention to themselves. Thus, poets can use readers' expectations about word order to their advantage. Syntax can be natural, or it can be manipulated, with words intentionally placed out of conventional order. A poet may place emphasis on a word by locating it first or last in a line, or by placing it in a stressed position in the line. If its placement departs from conventional sequence, the word will have even greater emphasis. Choosing a particular word order can cause two related—or startlingly unrelated—words to fall in adjacent or parallel positions, calling attention to the similarity—or the difference—between them. Unconventional syntax can also serve a poem's rhyme or meter or highlight sound correspondences that might otherwise not be noticeable. Finally, irregular syntax throughout a poem can reveal a speaker's mood—for example, giving a playful quality to a poem or suggesting a speaker's disoriented state.

In the poem that follows, the placement of many words departs from conventional English syntax.

EDMUND SPENSER

(1552–1599)

One Day I Wrote Her Name
upon the Strand

(1595)

One day I wrote her name upon the strand,[1]
But came the waves and washed it away:
Again I wrote it with a second hand,
But came the tide and made my pains his prey.
5 "Vain man," said she, "that doest in vain assay,
A mortal thing so to immortalize,
For I myself shall like to this decay,
And eek[2] my name be wiped out likewise."

---

[1] Beach.

[2] Also, indeed.

"Not so," quod[3] I, "let baser things devise,
10 To die in dust, but you shall live by fame:
My verse your virtues rare shall eternize,
And in the heavens write your glorious name.
Where whenas death shall all the world subdue,
Our love shall live, and later life renew."

"One Day I Wrote Her Name upon the Strand," a sonnet, has a fixed metrical pattern and rhyme scheme. To accommodate the sonnet's rhyme and meter, Spenser makes a number of adjustments in syntax. For example, to make sure certain rhyming words fall at the ends of lines, the poet sometimes moves words out of their conventional order, as the following three comparisons illustrate.

CONVENTIONAL WORD ORDER	INVERTED SEQUENCE
"'Vain man,' she said, that doest *assay in vain*."	"'Vain man,' said she, that doest *in vain assay*." ("Assay" appears at end of line 5, to rhyme with line 7's "decay.")
"My verse shall *eternize your rare virtues*."	"My verse *your virtues rare shall eternize*." ("Eternize" appears at end of line 11 to rhyme with line 9's "devise.")
"Where whenas death shall *subdue all the world*, / Our love shall live, and *later renew life*."	"Where whenas death shall *all the world subdue*, / Our love shall live, and *later life renew*." (Rhyming words "subdue" and "renew" are placed at ends of lines.)

To make sure the metrical pattern stresses certain words, the poet occasionally moves a word out of order so it will fall on a stressed syllable. The following comparison illustrates this technique.

CONVENTIONAL WORD ORDER	INVERTED SEQUENCE
"But *the waves came* and washed it away."	"But *came the waves* and washed it away." (stress in line 2 falls on "waves" rather than on "the.")

As the comparisons show, Spenser's adjustments in syntax are motivated in part by a desire to preserve the sonnet's rhyme and meter.

The following poem does more than simply invert words: It presents an intentionally disordered syntax.

---

[3] Said.

E. E. CUMMINGS

(1894–1962)

anyone lived in a pretty how town

(1940)

anyone lived in a pretty how town
(with up so floating many bells down)
spring summer autumn winter
he sang his didn't he danced his did.

5 Women and men (both little and small)
cared for anyone not at all
they sowed their isn't they reaped their same
sun moon stars rain

children guessed (but only a few
10 and down they forgot as up they grew
autumn winter spring summer)
that noone loved him more by more

when by now and tree by leaf
she laughed his joy she cried his grief
15 bird by snow and stir by still
anyone's any was all to her

someones married their everyones
laughed their cryings and did their dance
(sleep wake hope and then) they
20 said their nevers they slept their dream

stars rain sun moon
(and only the snow can begin to explain
how children are apt to forget to remember
with up so floating many bells down)

25 one day anyone died i guess
(and noone stooped to kiss his face)
busy folk buried them side by side
little by little and was by was

all by all and deep by deep
30 and more by more they dream their sleep
noone and anyone earth by april
wish by spirit and if by yes.

Women and men (both dong and ding)
summer autumn winter spring
35 reaped their sowing and went their came
sun moon stars rain

At times Cummings, like Spenser, manipulates syntax in response to the demands of rhyme and meter—for example, in line 10. But Cummings goes much further: He uses unconventional syntax as part of a scheme that encompasses other unusual elements of the poem, such as its unexpected departures from the musical metrical pattern (for example, in line 3 and line 8) and from the rhyme scheme (for example, in lines 3 and 4), and its use of parts of speech in unfamiliar contexts. Together, these techniques create a playful quality. The refreshing disorder of the syntax (for instance, in lines 1–2, line 10, and line 24) adds to the poem's whimsical effect.

Poems for Further Reading: Word Order

EDNA ST. VINCENT MILLAY

(1892–1950)

Elegy before Death

(1921)

There will be rose and rhododendron
    When you are dead and under ground;
Still will be heard from white syringas
    Heavy with bees, a sunny sound;

5 Still will the tamaracks be raining
    After the rain has ceased, and still
Will there be robins in the stubble,
    Grey sheep upon the warm green hill.

Spring will not ail nor autumn falter;
10   Nothing will know that you are gone,—
Saving alone some sullen plough-land
    None but yourself sets foot upon;

Saving the may-weed and the pig-weed
    Nothing will know that you are dead,—
15 These, and perhaps a useless wagon
    Standing beside some tumbled shed.

Oh, there will pass with your great passing
    Little of beauty not your own,—
Only the light from common water,
20   Only the grace from simple stone!

READING AND REACTING

1. Reword the poem using conventional syntax. What words and phrases in the poem are presented out of expected order?

2. Where do the poem's meter and rhyme scheme require the poet to depart from conventional syntax?

EMILY DICKINSON

(1830–1886)

My Life Had Stood— A Loaded Gun

(c. 1863)

My Life had stood—a Loaded Gun—
In Corners—till a Day
The Owner passed—identified—
And carried Me away—

5 And now We roam in Sovereign Woods—
And now We hunt the Doe—
And every time I speak for Him—
The Mountains straight reply—

And do I smile, such cordial light
10 Upon the Valley glow—
It is as a Vesuvian[1] face
Had let its pleasure through—

---

[1] Refers to Mount Vesuvius, a volcano that erupted in 79 A.D., destroying the city of Pompeii.

And when at Night—Our good Day done—
I guard My Master's Head—
15   'Tis better than the Eider-Duck's[2]
Deep Pillow—to have shared—

To foe of His—I'm deadly foe—
None stir the second time—
On whom I lay a Yellow Eye—
20   Or an emphatic Thumb—

Though I than He—may longer live
He longer must—than I—
For I have but the power to kill,
Without—the power to die—

READING AND REACTING

1. Identify lines in which word order departs from conventional English syntax. Can you explain in each case why the word order has been manipulated?

2. Do any words gain added emphasis by virtue of their unexpected position? Which ones? How are these words important to the poem's meaning?

3. **JOURNAL ENTRY**   Why do you think the speaker might be comparing her life to a loaded gun?

4. **CRITICAL PERSPECTIVE**   In "Vesuvius at Home: The Power of Emily Dickinson," feminist poet and critic Adrienne Rich sees "My Life Had Stood—A Loaded Gun" as "a central poem in understanding Emily Dickinson, and ourselves, and the condition of the woman artist, particularly in the 19th century." She offers a feminist interpretation of the poem:

I think it is a poem about possession by the daemon, about the dangers and risks of such possession if you are a woman, about the knowledge that power in a woman can seem destructive, and that you cannot live without the daemon once it has possessed you. The archetype of the daemon as masculine is beginning to change, but it has been real for women up until now. But this woman poet also perceives herself as a lethal weapon. . . . The poet experiences herself as loaded gun, imperious energy; yet without the Owner, the possessor, she is merely lethal.

Do you think this is a plausible reading of the poem, or do you feel more comfortable with conventional readings, which would interpret the "He" of this poem simply as Dickinson's unique version of God? Can you develop a reading that incorporates both interpretations?

[2]   Refers to the duck that produces eiderdown, used for stuffing pillows.

▼▼▼

CHECKLIST FOR WRITING ABOUT WORD
CHOICE AND WORD ORDER

WORD CHOICE

◆ What words are of central importance in the poem?

◆ What is the denotative meaning of each of these key words?

◆ Why is each word chosen instead of a synonym? (For example, is
the word chosen for its sound? Its connotation? Its relationship to
other words in the poem? Its contribution to the poem's metrical
pattern?)

◆ What other words could be effectively used in place of words now
in the poem?

◆ How would substitutions change the poem's meaning?

◆ Which key words have neutral connotations? Which have negative
connotations? Which have positive connotations? Beyond its
literal meaning, what does each word suggest?

◆ Are any words repeated? Why?

◆ How would you characterize the poem's level of diction? Why is
this level of diction used? Is it effective?

◆ Does the poem mix different levels of diction? To what end?

◆ Does the poem use dialect? For what purpose?

WORD ORDER

◆ Is the poem's syntax conventional, or are words arranged in
unexpected order?

◆ What phrases represent departures from conventional syntax?

◆ What is the purpose of the unusual syntax? (For example, is it
necessary to preserve the poem's meter or rhyme scheme? To
highlight particular sound correspondences? To place emphasis on
a particular word or phrase? To reflect the speaker's mood?)

◆ How would the poem's impact change if conventional syntax
were used?

▲▲▲

WRITING SUGGESTIONS: WORD CHOICE, WORD ORDER

1. Reread the two poems in this chapter by E. E. Cummings: "in Just-"
(p. 719) and "anyone lived in a pretty how town" (p. 737). If you like,
you may also read one or two additional poems in this text by
Cummings. Do you believe Cummings chose words primarily for their
sound? For their appearance on the page? What other factors might
have influenced his choices?

2. The tone of "We Real Cool" (p. 734) is flat and unemotional; the problem on which it focuses, however, is a serious one. Expand this concise poem into an essay or story that uses more detailed, more emotional language to communicate the speaker's hopeless situation.

3. Reread "Gracie" (p. 732) and choose another poem in the text whose speaker is a woman. Compare the two speakers' levels of diction and choice of words. What does their speech reveal about their lives?

4. Reread "For the Grave of Daniel Boone" (p. 711) alongside either Andrew Suknaski's "The Bitter Word" (p. 1014) or Delmore Schwartz's "The True-Blue American" (p. 880). What does each poem's choice of words reveal about the speaker's attitude toward his subject?

5. Analyze the choice of words and the level of diction in Margaret Atwood's "The City Planners" (p. 724), William Blake's "London" (p. 899), and Denise Levertov's "What Were They Like?" (p. 966). Pay particular attention to each poem's use of language to express social or political criticism.

CHAPTER 15

Imagery

Images are probably the most important part of the poem. First of all, you want to tell a story, but images are what are going to shore it up and get to the heart of the matter. . . . If they're not coming, I'm not even writing a poem, it's pointless.

ANNE SEXTON, *WRITERS AT WORK* 4TH EDITION

The difference between a literature that includes the image, and a literature that excludes the image (such as the newspaper or the scientific Newtonian essay) is that the first helps us to bridge the gap between ourselves and nature, and the second encourages us to remain isolated, living despairingly in the gap. Many philosophers and critics urge us to remain in the gap, and let the world of nature and the world of men fall further and further apart. We can do that; or a human being can reach out with his right hand to the natural world, and with his left hand to the world of human intelligence, and touch both at the same moment. Apparently no one but human beings can do this. What is the power that enables us to do that reaching? Barfield says it is imagination.

ROBERT BLY, "WHAT THE IMAGE CAN DO"

The poet sits before a blank piece of paper with a need to say many things in the small space of the poem. The world is huge, the poet is alone, and the poem is just a bit of language, a few scratchings of a pen surrounded by the silence of the night.

It could be that the poet wishes to tell you about his or her life. A few images of some fleeting moment when one was happy or exceptionally lucid. The secret wish of poetry is to stop time. The poet wants to retrieve a face, a mood, a cloud in the sky, a tree in the wind, and take a kind of mental photograph of that moment in which you as a reader recognize yourself. Poems are other people's snapshots in which we recognize ourselves.

CHARLES SIMIC, INTRODUCTION TO *BEST AMERICAN POETRY OF 1992*

The poet, contemplating the experience of love, creates an expression of the irrefutable unity of opposites; that is, the poet seeks to discover the third thing, the bond that binds, the "sacramental relationship" that can, through the poem, be rediscovered again and again. When Buson writes his poem,

> *By white chrysanthemums*
> *scissors hesitate*
> *only an instant*

his poem is not "about" scissors and chrysanthemums. It is an essay on birth and life and death and the rhythm of days and seasons, and it suggests profound unity. He balances action against perfect stillness, life against death, beauty against emptiness. But he excludes none of them. Against the death of chrysanthemums, he places the human hand with all its implications of beauty and life in flowers which the human mind holds dear. Against the cutting, he places the moment's hesitation, a perfect stillness. And in that perfect stillness, we glimpse the great void of which we are a part. Through the poem, we are invited into the reality of the "other" life.

SAM HAMILL, *A POET'S WORK*

J A N E   F L A N D E R S

(1940–   )

Cloud Painter

(1984)

Suggested by the life and art of John Constable[1]

At first, as you know, the sky is incidental—
a drape, a backdrop for trees and steeples.
Here an oak clutches a rock (already he works outdoors),
a wall buckles but does not break,
5 water pearls through a lock, a haywain[2] trembles.

The pleasures of landscape are endless. What we see
around us should be enough.
Horizons are typically high and far away.

Still, clouds let us drift and remember. He is, after all,
10 a miller's son, used to trying
to read the future in the sky, seeing instead

---

[1] John Constable (1776–1837)—British painter noted for his landscapes.

[2] An open horse-drawn wagon for carrying hay.

ships, horses, instruments of flight.
Is that his mother's wash flapping on the line?
His schoolbook, smudged, illegible?

15 In this period the sky becomes significant.
Cloud forms are technically correct—mares' tails,
sheep-in-the-meadow, thunderheads.
You can almost tell which scenes have been interrupted
by summer showers.

20 Now his young wife dies.
His landscapes achieve belated success.
He is invited to join the Academy. I forget
whether he accepts or not.

In any case, the literal forms give way
25 to something spectral, nameless. His palette shrinks
to gray, blue, white—the colors of charity.
Horizons sink and fade,
trees draw back till they are little more than frames,
then they too disappear.

30 Finally the canvas itself begins to vibrate
with waning light,
as if the wind could paint.
And we too, at last, stare into a space
which tell us nothing,
35 except that the world can vanish along with our need for it.

Because the purpose of poetry—and, for that matter, of all literature—is to expand the perception of readers, poets try to appeal to the senses. In "Cloud Painter," for example, Flanders uses details, such as the mother's wash on the line and the smudged schoolbook, to enable readers to visualize a particular scene in John Constable's early work. Clouds are described so readers can easily picture them—"mares' tails, / sheep-in-the-meadow, thunderheads." Thus, "Cloud Painter" is not just about the work of John Constable; it is also about the ability of the artist—poet or painter—to call up images in the minds of an audience. To achieve this end, a poet uses **imagery,** language that evokes a physical sensation produced by one of the five senses—sight, hearing, taste, touch, or smell.

Although the effect can be quite complex, the way images work is simple: When you read the word *red,* your memory of the various red things that you have seen determines how you picture the image. In addition, the word *red* may have emotional associations, or **connotations,** that define your response. A red sunset, for example, can have a positive connotation or a negative one depending on whether it is associated with the end of a

John Constable. *Landscape, Noon, The Haywain*. 1821. Oil on canvas, 130.5 ×
185.5 cm. London, National Gallery.

perfect day or with air pollution. By choosing an image carefully, then,
poets not only create pictures in a reader's mind, but also suggest a great
number of imaginative associations. These associations help poets to establish the **atmosphere** or **mood** of the poem. (The falling snow in
"Stopping by Woods on a Snowy Evening" [p. 936], for example, creates a
quiet, almost mystical mood.)

Readers come to a poem with their own individual sets of experiences,
so an image in a poem does not always suggest the same thing to all readers. In "Cloud Painter," for example, the poet presents the image of an oak
tree clutching a rock. Although most readers will probably see a picture
that is consistent with the one the poet sees, no two images will be identical. Every reader will have his or her own distinct mental image of a tree
clinging to a rock; some will be remembered experiences, while others
will be imaginative creations. Some readers may even be familiar enough
with the work of the painter John Constable to visualize a particular tree
clinging to a particular rock in one of his paintings.

By conveying what the poet sees and experiences, images enable readers to participate in the poet's mental processes. Through this interaction,
readers' minds are opened and enriched by perceptions and associations
different from—and possibly more original and complex than—their own.

One advantage of imagery is its extreme economy. Just a few words enable poets to evoke specific emotions and reactions. Consider in the following poem how just a few visual images create a picture.

WILLIAM CARLOS WILLIAMS

(1883–1963)

Red Wheelbarrow

(1923)

so much depends
upon

a red wheel
barrow

5 glazed with rain
water

beside the white
chickens

This poem asks readers to pause for a moment to consider the uniqueness and mystery of everyday objects. What is immediately apparent is the poem's verbal economy. The poet does not tell readers what the barnyard smells like or what sounds the animals make. In fact, he does not even paint a detailed picture of the scene. How large is the wheelbarrow? What is it made of? How many chickens are in the barnyard? Without answering these questions, the poet is able to use imagery to create a scene upon which, he says, "so much depends."

The red wheelbarrow establishes a momentary connection between the poet and his world. Like a still-life painting, the wheelbarrow beside the white chickens gives order to a world that is full of seemingly unrelated objects. By asserting the importance of the objects in the poem, the poet suggests that our ability to perceive the objects of this world gives our lives meaning and that our ability to convey our perceptions to others is central to our lives as well as to art.

Another advantage of images is that they enable poets to present ideas that would be difficult to convey in any other way. Just one look at a dictionary will illustrate that concepts such as *beauty* and *mystery* are so abstract that they are difficult to define, let alone to discuss in specific terms. By choosing an image or series of images that embodies these ideas, however, poets can effectively and persuasively make their feelings known. Consider, for example, the following brief poem.

E Z R A   P O U N D

(1885–1972)

In a Station of the Metro

(1916)

The apparition of these faces in the crowd;
Petals on a wet, black bough.

This poem is almost impossible to paraphrase because the facts it communicates are less important than the feelings associated with these facts. The poem's title indicates that the first line is meant to suggest a group of people gathered in a station of the Paris subway. The scene, however, is presented not as a clear picture but as an apparition, suggesting that it is somehow unexpected or even dreamlike. In contrast with the image of the subway platform is the image of the people's faces as flower petals on the dark branch of a tree. Thus, the subway platform—dark, cold, wet, subterranean (associated with baseness, death, and hell)—is juxtaposed with white flowers—delicate, pale, radiant, lovely (associated with the ideal, life, and heaven). These contrasting images, presented without comment, bear the entire weight of the poem.

Although images can be strikingly visual, they can also appeal to the senses of hearing, smell, taste, and touch. The following poem uses images of sound and taste as well as visual images.

G A R Y   S N Y D E R

(1930–   )

Some Good Things to Be Said
for the Iron Age

(1970)

A ringing tire iron
 dropped on the pavement
Whang of a saw
brusht on limbs
5 the taste
of rust

This poem presents two commonplace aural images: the ringing of a tire iron and the sound of a saw. These somewhat ordinary images gain power, however, through their visual isolation in the poem. Together they produce a harsh and jarring chord that in turn creates a sense of uneasiness in the reader. This poem does more than present sensory images, though. It also conveys the speaker's interpretations of these images. The last two lines of the poem imply not only that the time in which we live (the Iron Age) is base and mundane, but also that it is declining into an age of rust. This idea is reinforced by the repeated consonant sounds in *taste* and *rust*, which encourage readers to hold the final image of the poem on their tongues. The title of the poem makes an ironic comment, suggesting that compared to the time that is approaching, the age of iron may be "good." Thus, in the mind of the poet, ordinary events gain added significance, and images that spring from everyday experience become sources of enlightenment and insight.

In shorter poems, such as most of those discussed above, one or two images may serve as focal points. Longer poems may introduce groups of related images, creating a more complex tapestry of sensory impressions. Notice in the following poem how several images are woven together.

S U Z A N N E   E .   B E R G E R

(1944–   )

The Meal

(1984)

They have washed their faces until they are pale,
their homework is beautifully complete.
They wait for the adults to lean towards each other.
The hands of the children are oval
5 and smooth as pine-nuts.

The girls have braided and rebraided their hair,
and tied ribbons without a single mistake.
The boy has put away his coin collection.
They are waiting for the mother to straighten her lipstick,
10 and for the father to speak.

They gather around the table, carefully
as constellations waiting to be named.
Their minds shift and ready, like dunes.
It is so quiet, all waiting stars and dunes.

15   Their forks move across their plates without scraping,
      they wait for the milk and the gravy
      at the table with its forgotten spices.
      They are waiting for a happiness to lift their eyes,
      like sudden light flaring in the trees outside.

20   The white miles of the meal continue,
      the figures still travel across a screen:
      the father carving the Sunday roast,
      her mouth uneven as a torn hibiscus,
      their braids still gleaming in the silence.

This poem groups related images that evoke silence, order, and emptiness. It begins with the image of faces washed "until they are pale" and goes on to describe the children's oval hands as "smooth as pine-nuts." Forks move across plates "without scraping," and the table hints at the memory of "forgotten spices." Despite the poem's title, these children are emotionally starved. The attentive, well-scrubbed children sit at a table where, neither eating nor speaking, they wait for "the milk and the gravy" and for happiness that never comes. The "white miles of the meal" seem to go on forever, reinforcing the sterility and emptiness of the Sunday ritual. Suggesting an absence of sensation or feeling, a kind of paralysis, the poem's images challenge conventional assumptions about the family and its rituals.

Much visual imagery is **static,** freezing the moment and thereby giving it the timeless quality of painting or sculpture. ("The Meal" presents just such a tableau, and so do "Red Wheelbarrow" and "In a Station of the Metro.") Some imagery, however, is **kinetic,** conveying a sense of motion or change.

WILLIAM CARLOS WILLIAMS
(1883–1963)

The Great Figure
(1938)

      Among the rain
      and lights
      I saw the figure 5
      in gold
5   on a red
      firetruck
      moving

                    tense
                    unheeded
            10 to gong clangs
                    siren howls
                    and wheels rumbling
                    through the dark city.

Commenting on this poem in his autobiography, Williams explains that while walking in New York, he heard the sound of a fire engine. As he turned the corner, he saw a golden figure 5 on a red background speed by. The impression was so forceful that he immediately jotted down a poem about it. In the poem Williams attempts to recreate the sensation the figure 5 made as it moved into his consciousness. Notice that he presents the

Charles Demuth (1883–1935) *I Saw the Figure 5 in Gold*. Oil on composition board, h. 36, w. 29¾ in. The Metropolitan Museum of Art, The Alfred Steiglitz Collection, 1949. (49.59.1) All rights reserved, The Metropolitan Museum of Art.

image as if it were a picture taken by a camera with a high-speed shutter. Readers are asked to see the speeding engine with the number 5 caught in tense focus by the camera. Notice too that the poet presents images in the order in which he perceived them: first the 5 and then the image of the red fire truck howling and clanging into the darkness. Thus, "The Great Figure" uses images of sight, sound, and movement to recreate for readers the poet's experience. The American painter Charles Demuth was fascinated by the kinetic quality of the poem. Working closely with his friend Williams, he attempted to capture the stop-action feature of the poem in the painting reproduced on page 751.

A special use of imagery, called **synesthesia,** occurs when one sense is described in a way that is appropriate for another—for instance, when a sound is described with color. When people say they are feeling *blue* or describe music as *hot,* they are using synesthesia. The poet John Keats uses this technique in the following lines from "Ode to a Nightingale" (p. 960):

> *O, for a draught of vintage! that hath been*
> > *Cool'd a long age in the deep-delvéd earth,*
> *Tasting of Flora and the country green,*
> > *Dance and Provençal song, and sunburnt mirth!*

In this passage the speaker describes the taste of wine in terms of images that appeal to a variety of senses: flowers, a grassy field, dance, song, and sun.

Poems for Further Reading: Imagery

MICHELLE CLIFF

(1946–   )

A Visit to the Secret Annex[1]

(1979)

> *What kinds of times are these, when*
> *A talk about trees is almost a crime*
> *Because it implies a silence about so many*
> > *horrors?*

BERTOLT BRECHT, "FOR THOSE BORN LATER"

---

[1] An apartment in Amsterdam where Anne Frank and her family hid to avoid being sent to a concentration camp during World War II.

I was born later
not into this world.
The trees were not the same
The horrors not exact—but similar

5   I walk along the *Prinsengracht*[2]—a late-spring afternoon
a visitor—cooled by the air from the canals.

I sight my destination—pass it by
Return on the heels of a group of schoolchildren.

The stairs stretch up
10 into perpendicular flights
I begin my climb.

I had not expected my feelings to be so. . . . What?
(Then why did I turn around?)

Cold sweat pours out of my head and through the cloth of my
15 burgundy shirt. The back of my shirt sticks flat. I can feel it
darkening.

(By now I have learned to fight
pretending I am not touched.)

Here in these narrow, empty rooms
20 (Why do I say "empty"? The place is filled with other people—
silent people reading the legends and walking back and forth—
past the ornamental toilet—baroque, green scrolls curl around
two birds with tails entwined on the bowl. Delft? I wonder.)

Here in these rooms alone I am terrified of tears (and what
25 follows? shame? embarrassment?) and feel an onslaught
coming if I give in.

I lock my eyes. Sweat pours out instead   tidal   salt.
Redirected by my bitten lips and tongue from the pinpoints at
the corners of my eyes to the entire surface of my body. My
30 skin.

Yes, my girl. I say this to myself. (Because part of me is a girl
and part of me is a woman speaking to her.) Here is the heroine
you once had and wondered about.

---

2   The street where the secret annex was located.

The girl you loved.
35 I meet her suspended in this place. At thirteen, fourteen, fifteen.
At four or so a Montessori student. A baby held by an elegant
mother.

Would I have changed places
were that the only choice?

40 I glance at the two walls where she fixed her pinups.
Norma Shearer, Deanna Durbin, Ginger Rogers—lips reddened
wildly from the rotogravure.[3]
There are pictures of the "little princesses"[4]—Elizabeth and
Margaret Rose.
45 Another picture showing roses. In the foreground of a country
house. Her dream house? Didn't we all have dream houses?

The *Westerkerk* [5] next-door strikes four. A window is open wide
onto a huge flowering chestnut in the garden of the church.

I turn to the tree. Breathe in its blossoms. Watch its fat leaves
50 move against a bright-blue sky.

I do not know how to calculate the ages of trees. (I have
studied closely how to calculate the ages of churches.)

I remember the childhood advice about the rings in a tree's
insides. But I can't slice the tree open. Just to tell if it's forty or
55 so.

I hold a conversation with myself about trees.
To see if she might have had a living tree as a companion—
even a tree in a churchyard—instead of one cut from colored
paper.

60 Still, she would have only sensed the tree, had the tree been
there.

Still, she might have listened for the hard drop of the fruit in fall,
while her father tracked the advance of the allies on his little
map. Imagined gathering the chestnuts and roasting them at
65 the side of a canal busy with barges and small family boats.

---

[3] A section of the newspaper produced by a special printing process.

[4] Princess Elizabeth, now Queen Elizabeth II, and her sister, Princess Margaret.

[5] A church with a clock tower that could be seen from the attic window.

But she would never have seen her tree—the windows of the
hiding place were always shaded, covered with paper or
painted blue.
To keep their existences secret   safe.

70 Had she cracked the pane to peek as her tree flowered, or shed
its fruit or leaves, she would have been killed.
Sooner.

Ah . . . the congregations of the *Westerkerk,* not knowing a group
of Jews hovered above them, above their chestnut tree.
75 Thinking they were *Judenrein.*[6]

READING AND REACTING

1. What do the recurring images of trees contribute to the poem?

2. Give examples of nonvisual images that occur in the poem—for
   example, the sound of the clock striking. How are these nonvisual
   images related to one another? To other images in the poem?

3. **JOURNAL ENTRY**   The speaker reacts to the scene she describes with
   anger and sadness. Describe a contemporary scene that would elicit a
   similar response from you, selecting images that communicate your
   response.

4. **CRITICAL PERSPECTIVE**   In May of 1944, after her family had been
   in hiding for almost two years and only a few months before they
   were captured by the Gestapo, Anne Frank wrote in her diary:

   *Again and again I ask myself, would it not have been better for us all if we
   had not gone into hiding, and we were dead now and not going through all
   this misery. . . . But we all recoil from these thoughts too, for we still love
   life. . . . I hope something will happen soon now, shooting if need be—
   nothing can crush us more than this restlessness. Let the end come, even if
   it's hard; then at least we shall know whether we are finally going to win
   through or go under.*

   How well do you think "A Visit to the Secret Annex" conveys the
   difficulty of the Franks' situation?

---

[6] German for free or "clean" of Jews.

MATSUO BASHO

(1644?–1694)

Four Haiku[1]

translated by Geoffrey Bownas and Anthony Thwaite

Spring:
A hill without a name
Veiled in morning mist.

The beginning of autumn:
5   Sea and emerald paddy
Both the same green.

The winds of autumn
Blow: yet still green
The chestnut husks.

10   A flash of lightning:
Into the gloom
Goes the heron's cry.

READING AND REACTING

1. A **haiku** is a three-line poem, a Japanese form that traditionally has seventeen syllables. Haiku are admired for their extreme economy and their striking images. What are the central images in each of Basho's haiku? To what senses do these images appeal?

2. In another poem Basho says that art begins with "The depths of the country / and a rice-planting song." What do you think he means? In what way do the poems above exemplify this idea?

3. Do you think the brevity of these poems increases or decreases the impact of their images?

4. **JOURNAL ENTRY**   "In a Station of the Metro" (p. 748) is Ezra Pound's version of a haiku. How successful do you think Pound was? Do you think a longer poem would have been more or less effective?

---

[1] Publication date is not available.

CAROLYN KIZER

(1925–   )

After Basho

(1984)

Tentatively, you
slip onstage this evening,
pallid, famous moon.

READING AND REACTING

1. What possible meanings does the word "After" have in the title? What does the title tell readers about the writer's purpose?
2. What visual picture does the poem suggest? What mood does the poem's central image create?
3. What is the impact of "tentatively" in the first line and "famous" in the last line? How do the connotations of these words affect the image of the moon?

RICHARD WILBUR

(1921–   )

Sleepless at Crown Point

(1973)

All night, this headland
Lunges into the rumpling
Capework of the wind.

READING AND REACTING

1. What scene is the speaker describing?
2. What is the significance of the title?
3. How do the words "lunges" and "capework" help to establish the poem's central image?

H . D . [H I L D A   D O O L I T T L E]

(1886–1961)

Heat

(1916)

O wind, rend open the heat,
cut apart the heat,
rend it to tatters.

Fruit cannot drop
5 through this thick air—
fruit cannot fall into heat
that presses up and blunts
the points of pears
and rounds the grapes.

10 Cut the heat—
plough through it,
turning it on either side
of your path.

READING AND REACTING

1. Why is heat a difficult concept to describe? What specific difficulties face a poet trying to describe heat?

2. What images does H. D. use to convey her ideas? Are all these images visual?

3. In this poem, the speaker addresses the wind. Could the poem be entitled "Wind"?

4. **JOURNAL ENTRY**   What other qualities of heat could H. D. have evoked? What images could she have used to convey these qualities?

5. **CRITICAL PERSPECTIVE**   H. D. was one of a school of poets, influenced by Japanese haiku, who called themselves "Imagists." Like haiku, their poems tried to present a highly concentrated image of an object or scene. In her 1982 study *H.D.: The Life and Work of An American Poet* Janice S. Robinson notes that "the Imagists believed in presentation rather than representation. One thing does not "stand for" another thing in H.D.'s early poems. Rather, all things are emanations, as it were, of life itself. . . ."

   In your opinion, how accurately does this description of H.D.'s imagism apply to "Heat"?

ROBERT FROST

(1874–1963)

Nothing Gold Can Stay

(1923)

Nature's first green is gold,
Her hardest hue to hold.
Her early leaf's a flower;
But only so an hour.
5 Then leaf subsides to leaf.
So Eden sank to grief.
So dawn goes down to day.
Nothing gold can stay.

READING AND REACTING

1. What central idea does this poem express?

2. What do you think the first line of the poem means? In what sense is this line ironic?

3. What is the significance of the colors green and gold in this poem? What do these colors have to do with "Eden" and "dawn"?

4. **JOURNAL ENTRY**   In what way do the various images in the poem prepare readers for the last line?

5. **CRITICAL PERSPECTIVE**   In "The Figure a Poem Means," the introduction to the first edition of his *Collected Poems* (1930), Frost laid out a theory of poetry:

   It begins in delight, it inclines to the impulse, it assumes direction with the first line laid down, it runs a course of lucky events, and ends in a clarification of life—not necessarily a great clarification . . . but a momentary stay against confusion. . . . Like a piece of ice on a hot stove the poem must ride on its own melting. . . . Read it a hundred times: it will forever keep its freshness as a metal keeps its fragrance. It can never lose its sense of a meaning that once unfolded by surprise as it went.

   Do you find Frost's remarks true of "Nothing Gold Can Stay"?

JEAN TOOMER

(1894–1967)

Reapers

(1923)

Black reapers with the sound of steel on stones
Are sharpening scythes. I see them place the hones[1]
In their hip-pockets as a thing that's done,
And start their silent swinging, one by one.
5 Black horses drive a mower through the weeds,
And there, a field rat, startled, squealing bleeds,
His belly close to ground. I see the blade,
Blood-stained, continue cutting weeds and shade.

READING AND REACTING

1. What determines the order in which the speaker arranges the images in this poem? At what point does he comment on these images?

2. The first four lines of the poem seem to suggest that the workers are content. What image contradicts this impression? How does it do so?

3. What ideas are traditionally associated with the image of the reaper? The scythe? The harvest? (You may want to consult a reference work, such as *A Dictionary of Symbols* by J. E. Cirlot, in your college library.) In what way does the speaker rely on these conventional associations to help him convey his ideas? Can you appreciate the poem without understanding the associations?

4. **CRITICAL PERSPECTIVE**   According to Brian Joseph Benson and Mabel Mayle Dillard, in their 1980 study *Jean Toomer,* the poet disagreed with some other artists of the Harlem Renaissance, choosing not to focus on "Negro" themes for a primarily black audience, but rather to try to make his work universal in scope. Do you think he has achieved this goal in "Reapers"?

---

[1] Stones used to sharpen cutting instruments.

WILFRED OWEN

(1893–1918)

Dulce et Decorum Est[1]

(1920)

Bent double, like old beggars under sacks,
Knock-kneed, coughing like hags, we cursed through sludge,
Till on the haunting flares we turned our backs
And towards our distant rest began to trudge.
5 Men marched asleep. Many had lost their boots
But limped on, blood-shod. All went lame; all blind;
Drunk with fatigue; deaf even to the hoots
Of tired, outstripped Five-Nines[2] that dropped behind.

Gas! Gas! Quick, boys!—An ecstasy of fumbling,
10 Fitting the clumsy helmets just in time;
But someone still was yelling out and stumbling
And flound'ring like a man in fire or lime . . .
Dim, through the misty panes and thick green light,
As under a green sea, I saw him drowning.
15 In all my dreams, before my helpless sight,
He plunges at me, guttering, choking, drowning.

If in some smothering dreams you too could pace
Behind the wagon that we flung him in,
And watch the white eyes writhing in his face,
20 His hanging face, like a devil's sick of sin;
If you could hear, at every jolt, the blood
Come gargling from the froth-corrupted lungs,
Obscene as cancer, bitter as the cud
Of vile, incurable sores on innocent tongues,—
25 My friend, you would not tell with such high zest
To children ardent for some desperate glory,
The old Lie: Dulce et decorum est
Pro patria mori.

---

[1] The title and last lines are from Horace, Odes 3.2: "Sweet and fitting it is to die for one's country."

[2] Shells that explode on impact and release poison gas.

READING AND REACTING

1. Who is the speaker in this poem? What is his attitude toward his subject?

2. What images are traditionally associated with soldiers? How do the images in this poem depart from convention? Why do you think Owen selected such images?

3. What senses does the poem appeal to other than sight? Is any of the imagery kinetic?

4. **JOURNAL ENTRY** Does the knowledge that Owen died in World War I change your reaction to the poem, or are the poem's images compelling enough to eliminate the need for biographical background?

5. **CRITICAL PERSPECTIVE** Like many other British poets who experienced fighting in the European trenches during World War I, Owen struggled to find a new poetic idiom to describe the horrors of this new kind of war. In his 1986 biography *Owen the Poet,* Dominic Hibberd praises the "controlled and powerful anger in 'Dulce et Decorum Est' which for some readers will be the poem's most valuable quality" and goes on to note that the "organization and clarity of the first half is replaced [beginning at line 15] by confused, choking syntax and a vocabulary of sickness and disgust, matching the nightmare which is in progress." How does this movement from control to confusion serve the meaning of the poem?

▼▼▼

CHECKLIST FOR WRITING ABOUT IMAGERY

◆ Do the images in the poem appeal to the sense of sight, touch, hearing, smell, or taste?

◆ Does the poem depend on a single image or a variety of different images?

◆ Does the poem depend on a pattern of related imagery?

◆ What details make the images memorable?

◆ What mood do the images create?

◆ Do the images define or exemplify abstract concepts?

◆ Are the images static or kinetic? Are there any examples of synesthesia?

◆ How do the poem's images help to convey its theme?

◆ How effective are the images? In what way do the images enhance your enjoyment of the poem?

▲▲▲

WRITING SUGGESTIONS: IMAGERY

1. How are short poems such as "Some Good Things to Be Said for the Iron Age" (p. 748) and "In a Station of the Metro" (p. 748) like and unlike haiku?

2. Reread "Cloud Painter" (p. 744) and "The Great Figure" (p. 750), and read "Musée des Beaux Arts" (p. 888). Study the paintings accompanying the poems in the text. Then, write a paper in which you draw some conclusions about the differences between artistic and poetic images.

3. Analyze the role of imagery in the depiction of the parent/child relationships in "The Meal" (p. 749), "My Papa's Waltz" (p. 642), and "Daddy" (p. 779). How does each poem's imagery convey the nature of the relationship it describes?

4. Write an essay in which you discuss the color imagery in "Nothing Gold Can Stay" (p. 759), "Reapers" (p. 760), and "In a Station of the Metro" (p. 748). In what way does color reinforce the themes of the poems?

5. Sometimes, as in "A Visit to the Secret Annex," imagery can be used to make a comment about the society in which a scene takes place. Choose two poems in which imagery functions in this way—"For the Union Dead" (p. 967), "The Colonel" (p. 856), "The *Chicago Defender* Sends a Man to Little Rock" (p. 1077), or "Composed upon Westminster Bridge, September 3, 1802" (p. 1026), for example—and discuss how images contribute to the social statement each poem makes.

CHAPTER 16

Figures of Speech

When I was a young man I was always hunting for new metaphors. Then I found out that really good metaphors are always the same. I mean you compare time to a road, death to sleeping, life to dreaming, and those are the great metaphors in literature because they correspond to something essential. If you invent metaphors, they are apt to be surprising during the fraction of a second, but they strike no deep emotion whatever. If you think of life as a dream, that is a thought, a thought that is real, or at least that most men are bound to have, no? "What oft was thought but ne'er so well expressed." I think that's better than the idea of shocking people, than finding connections between things that have never been connected before, because there is no real connection, so the whole thing is a kind of juggling.

JORGE LUIS BORGES, *WRITERS AT WORK,* 4TH EDITION

Poetry begins in trivial metaphors, pretty metaphors, "grace" metaphors, and goes on to the profoundest thinking that we have. Poetry provides the one permissible way of saying one thing and meaning another. People say, "Why don't you say what you mean?" We never do that, do we, being all of us too much poets. We like to talk in parables and in hints and in indirections—whether from diffidence or some other instinct.

I have wanted in late years to go further and further in making metaphor the whole of thinking.

ROBERT FROST, "A MEDITATIVE MONOLOGUE"

Poetry is made of comparisons, simple or complex, open or concealed. The richness of poetry is obtained by mixing or interweaving or juxtaposing these comparisons. The mixture is either a mechanical mixture or a chemical mixture: when the mechanical becomes chemical the explosion takes place. That is the difference between prose and poetry. In prose all comparisons are simple and uncompounded. In poetry all metaphors are mixed metaphors.

J. ISAACS, *THE BACKGROUND OF MODERN POETRY*

I suppose we shall never be able to distinguish absolutely and with a hard edge the image from the metaphor, any more than anyone has so distinguished prose from poetry or perception from thought (these are instances, not necessarily parallels). We shall very often be able to tell, just as we can very often tell the difference between snow and rain; but there are some weathers which are either-neither, and so here there is an area where our differences will mingle. If the poet says, simply, "The red bird," we shall probably take that as an image. But as soon as we read the rest of the line—"The red bird flies across the golden floor"—there arise obscure thoughts of relationships that lead in the direction of parable: the line alone is not, strictly, a metaphor, but its resonances take it prospectively beyond a pure perception, if perception could ever be quite that. Metaphor stands somewhat as a mediating term squarely between a thing and a thought, which may be why it is so likely to compose itself about a word of sense and a word of thought, as in this example of a common Shakespearean formula: "Even to the teeth and forehead of my fault."

HOWARD NEMEROV, "ON METAPHOR"

Metaphor is not to be considered, . . . as the alternative of the poet, which he may elect to use or not, since he may state the matter directly and straightforwardly if he chooses. It is frequently the only means available if he is to write at all. . . .

CLEANTH BROOKS, "METAPHOR AND THE TRADITION"

WILLIAM SHAKESPEARE

(1564–1616)

Shall I Compare Thee to a Summer's Day?

(1609)

Shall I compare thee to a summer's day?
Thou art more lovely and more temperate.
Rough winds do shake the darling buds of May,
And summer's lease hath all too short a date.
5 Sometime too hot the eye of heaven shines,
And often is his gold complexion dimmed;
And every fair from fair sometimes declines,
By chance, or nature's changing course, untrimmed.
But thy eternal summer shall not fade,
10 Nor lose possession of that fair thou ow'st;[1]

---

[1] Beauty you possess.

Nor shall death brag thou wand'rest in his shade,
When in eternal lines to time thou grow'st.
So long as men can breathe or eyes can see,
So long lives this, and this gives life to thee.

Although figurative language is used in all kinds of writing, poets in particular recognize the power of a figure of speech to take readers beyond the literal meaning of a word. For this reason, **figures of speech**—expressions that describe one thing in terms of something else—are more prominent in poetry than in other kinds of writing. For example, the sonnet by Shakespeare that is printed above compares a loved one to a summer's day in order to make the point that, unlike the fleeting summer, the loved one will—within the poem—remain forever young. But this sonnet goes beyond the obvious equation (loved one = summer's day); the speaker's assertion that his loved one will live forever in his poem actually says more about his confidence in his own talent and reputation (and about the power of figurative language) than about the loved one's beauty.

Simile, Metaphor, and Personification

When William Wordsworth opens a poem with "I wandered lonely as a cloud" (p. 1026), he conveys a good deal more than he would if he simply said "I wandered, lonely." By comparing himself in his loneliness to a cloud, he suggests that like the cloud he is a part of nature, and that he too is drifting, passive, blown by winds, and lacking will or substance. With such figures of speech, poets can suggest a wide variety of feelings and associations in very few words. The phrase "I wandered lonely as a cloud" is a **simile,** a comparison between two unlike items that includes *like* or *as*. When an imaginative comparison between two unlike things does not include *like* or *as*—that is, when it says "a is b" rather than "a is like b"—it is a **metaphor.**

Accordingly, when the speaker in Adrienne Rich's "Living in Sin" (p. 716) speaks of "daylight coming / like a relentless milkman up the stairs," she is using a strikingly original simile to suggest that daylight brings not the conventional associations of promise and awakening, but rather a stale, neverending routine that is greeted without enthusiasm. This idea is consistent with the rest of the poem, which is a grim account of an unhappy relationship. However, when the speaker in Audre Lorde's poem says "Rooming houses are old women" (p. 769), she uses a metaphor, equating two elements to stress their common associations with emptiness, transience, and hopelessness. In addition, by identifying rooming houses as old women, Lorde is using a special kind of comparison called **personification**—endowing inanimate objects or abstract ideas with life or with human characteristics.

Sometimes, as in Wordsworth's "I wandered lonely as a cloud," a single brief simile or metaphor can be appreciated for what it communicates on its own. At other times, however, a simile or metaphor may be one of several related figurative comparisons that work together to communicate a poem's meaning. The following poem presents just such a series of related figurative comparisons. Together, they suggest the depth of the problem the poem explores in a manner that each individual comparison could not do alone.

LANGSTON HUGHES

(1902–1967)

Dream Deferred

(1951)

What happens to a dream deferred?

  Does it dry up
  like a raisin in the sun?
  Or fester like a sore—
5 And then run?
  Does it stink like rotten meat?
  Or crust and sugar over—
  like a syrupy sweet?

  Maybe it just sags
10 like a heavy load.

  Or does it explode?

The dream to which Hughes alludes in his 1951 poem is the dream of racial equality. By extension, it is also the American Dream—or any important unrealized dream. His speaker offers six tentative answers to the question asked in the poem's first line, and five of the six are presented as similes. As the poem unfolds, the speaker considers different alternatives: The dream can shrivel up and die, fester, decay, crust over—or just sag under the weight of the burden those who hold the dream must carry. In each case, the speaker transforms an abstract entity—a dream—into a concrete item—a raisin in the sun, a sore, rotten meat, syrupy candy, a heavy load. The final line of the poem, italicized for emphasis, gains power less from what it says than for what it leaves unsaid. Unlike the other alternatives explored in the poem, *"Or does it explode?"* is not presented as a simile. Nevertheless, because of the pattern of figurative language the poem has established, readers supply the other, unspoken half of the comparison: ". . . like a bomb."

Sometimes a singe *extended simile* or *extended metaphor* is developed throughout a poem. The poem that follows, for example, develops an extended simile, comparing a poet to an acrobat.

L A W R E N C E   F E R L I N G H E T T I

(1919–   )

Constantly Risking Absurdity

(1958)

<pre>
Constantly risking absurdity
                    and death
        whenever he performs
                    above the heads
5   of his audience
        the poet like an acrobat
                    climbs on rime
                    to a high wire of his own making
        and balancing on eyebeams
10   above a sea of faces
                paces his way
                    to the other side of day
            performing entrechats
                    and sleight-of-foot tricks
15 and other high theatrics
                    and all without mistaking
                any thing
                    for what it may not be

                For he's the super realist
20   who must perforce perceive
                taut truth
                    before the taking of each stance or step
        in his supposed advance
                    toward that still higher perch
25 where Beauty stands and waits
                    with gravity
                                to start her death-defying leap
</pre>

And he
        a little charleychaplin man
30   who may or may not catch
    her fair eternal form
            spreadeagled in the empty air
  of existence

In his extended comparison between a poet and an acrobat, Ferlinghetti characterizes the poet as a kind of all-purpose circus performer, at once swinging recklessly on a trapeze and balancing carefully on a tightrope. The simile is introduced in line 6 ("The poet like an acrobat"), and the poem follows the poet/acrobat through fanciful gymnastics, always in some sense referring to both poet and acrobat.

What the poem suggests is that the poet, like an acrobat, works hard at his craft but manages to make it all look easy. Something of an exhibition-ist, the poet is innovative and creative, taking impossible chances yet also building on traditional skills in his quest for truth and beauty. Moreover, like an acrobat, the poet is balanced "on eyebeams / above a sea of faces," for he too depends on audience reaction to help him keep his performance focused. The poet may be "the super realist," but he also has plenty of play-ful tricks up his sleeve: *entrechats / and sleight-of-foot tricks / and other high theatrics*," including puns ("above the heads / of his audience"), un-expected rhyme ("climbs on rime"), alliteration ("taut truth"), coinages ("a little charleychaplin man"), and all the other linguistic acrobatics available to creators of poems. (Even the arrangement of the poem's words on the page suggests the acrobatics it describes.) Like these tricks, the poem's cen-tral simile is a whimsical one, perhaps suggesting that Ferlinghetti is pok-ing fun at poets who take their craft too seriously. In any case, the simile helps him to illustrate the acrobatic possibilities of language in a fresh and original manner.

The following poem develops an extended metaphor that equates inanimate objects with human beings.

AUDRE LORDE

(1934–1992)

Rooming Houses Are Old Women

(1968)

Rooming houses are old women
rocking dark windows into their whens
waiting incomplete circles
rocking

5 rent office to stoop to
community bathrooms to gas rings and
under-bed boxes of once useful garbage
city issued with a twice monthly check
and the young men next door
10 with their loud midnight parties
and fishy rings left in the bathtub
no longer arouse them
from midnight to mealtime no stops inbetween
light breaking to pass through jumbled up windows
15 and who was it who married the widow that Buzzie's son messed with?

To Welfare and insult form the slow shuffle
from dayswork to shopping bags
heavy with leftovers
Rooming houses
20 are old women waiting
searching
through darkening windows
the end or beginning of agony
old women seen through half-ajar doors
25 hoping
they are not waiting
but being
the entrance to somewhere
unknown and desired
30 but not new.

So closely does Lorde equate rooming houses and women in this poem that at times it is difficult to tell which of the two is actually the poem's subject. Despite the poem's assertion, rooming houses are *not* old women; however, they are *comparable to* the old women who live there, for their walls enclose a lifetime of disappointments as well as the physical detritus of life. Like old women, rooming houses are in decline, rocking away their remaining years. Like the houses they inhabit, these women's boundaries are fixed—"rent office to stoop to / community bathrooms to gas rings"— and their hopes and expectations are few. They are surrounded by other people's loud parties, but their own lives have been reduced to a "slow shuffle" to nowhere, a hopeless, frightened—and perhaps pointless— "waiting / searching." Over time, the women and the places in which they live have become one. By using an unexpected comparison between two seemingly unrelated entities, the poem illuminates both the essence of the rooming houses and the essence of their elderly occupants.

Poems for Further Reading: Simile, Metaphor, and Personification

ROBERT BURNS

(1759–1796)

Oh, My Love Is Like a Red, Red Rose

(1796)

Oh, my love is like a red, red rose
    That's newly sprung in June;
My love is like the melody
    That's sweetly played in tune.

5 So fair art thou, my bonny lass,
    So deep in love am I;
And I will love thee still, my dear,
    Till a' the seas gang[1] dry.

Till a' the seas gang dry, my dear,
10   And the rocks melt wi' the sun;
And I will love thee still, my dear,
    While the sands o' life shall run.

And fare thee weel, my only love!
    And fare thee weel awhile!
15 And I will come again, my love
    Though it were ten thousand mile.

READING AND REACTING

1. Why does the speaker compare his love to a rose? What other simile is used in the poem? For what purpose is it used?

2. Why do you suppose Burns begins with similes? Would moving them to the end change the poem's impact?

3. Where does the speaker seem to exaggerate the extent of his love? Why does he exaggerate? Do you think this exaggeration weakens the effectiveness of the poem? Explain.

---

[1] Go.

J O H N   U P D I K E

(1932–   )

Ex-Basketball Player

(1958)

Pearl Avenue runs past the high-school lot,
Bends with the trolley tracks, and stops, cut off
Before it has a chance to go two blocks,
At Colonel McComsky Plaza. Berth's Garage
5 Is on the corner facing west, and there,
Most days, you'll find Flick Webb, who helps Berth out.

Flick stands tall among the idiot pumps—
Five on a side, the old bubble-head style,
Their rubber elbows hanging loose and low.
10 One's nostrils are two S's, and his eyes
An E and O. And one is squat, without
A head at all—more of a football type.

Once Flick played for the high-school team, the Wizards.
He was good: in fact, the best. In '46
15 He bucketed three hundred ninety points,
A county record still. The ball loved Flick.
I saw him rack up thirty-eight or forty
In one home game. His hands were like wild birds.

He never learned a trade, he just sells gas,
20 Checks oil, and changes flats. Once in a while,
As a gag, he dribbles an inner tube,
But most of us remember anyway.
His hands are fine and nervous on the lug wrench.
It makes no difference to the lug wrench, though.

25 Off work, he hangs around Mae's luncheonette.
Grease-gray and kind of coiled, he plays pinball,
Smokes those thin cigars, nurses lemon phosphates.
Flick seldom says a word to Mae, just nods
Beyond her face toward bright applauding tiers
30 Of Necco Wafers, Nibs, and Juju Beads.

READING AND REACTING

1. Explain the use of personification in the second stanza and in the poem's last two lines. What two elements make up each figurative comparison? How are the two elements in each pair alike?

2. What kind of figure of speech is each of the following: "His hands were like wild birds" (18); "Grease-gray and kind of coiled" (26)? What other figures of speech can you identify in the poem?

3. **JOURNAL ENTRY**   Who do you think this poem's speaker might be? What is his attitude toward Flick Webb? Do you think Flick himself shares this assessment? Explain.

ADRIENNE RICH

(1929–   )

The Roofwalker

(1961)

for Denise

Over the half-finished houses
night comes. The builders
stand on the roof. It is
quiet after the hammers,
5 the pulleys hang slack.
Giants, the roofwalkers,
on a listing deck, the wave
of darkness about to break
on their heads. The sky
10 is a torn sail where figures
pass magnified, shadows
on a burning deck.

I feel like them up there:
exposed, larger than life,
15 and due to break my neck.
Was it worth while to lay—
with infinite exertion—
a roof I can't live under?
—All those blueprints,
20 closings of gaps,
measurings, calculations?
A life I didn't choose

chose me: even
my tools are the wrong ones
25 for what I have to do.
I'm naked, ignorant,
a naked man fleeing
across the roofs
who could with a shade of difference
30 be sitting in the lamplight
against the cream wallpaper
reading—not with indifference—
about a naked man
fleeing across the roofs.

READING AND REACTING

1. Is the speaker's comparison of herself with a roofwalker a metaphor or a simile? Explain. Do you find this comparison plausible, or do you see it as forced? What characteristics does the speaker share with the roofwalkers?

2. What other comparisons are made in the poem? Are these comparisons metaphors or similes? Explain.

3. **JOURNAL ENTRY** Do you think the speaker is examining her personal life or her professional life? Why?

4. **CRITICAL PERSPECTIVE** In a 1971 speech for a forum on women writers in the twentieth century, later published as "When We Dead Awaken: Writing As Re-Vision," Rich made the following comments:

   A radical critique of literature, feminist in its impulse, would take the work first of all as a clue to . . . how we have been led to imagine ourselves, how our language has trapped as well as liberated us. . . . [A]t this moment for women writers in particular, there is the challenge and promise of a whole new psychic geography to be explored. But there is also a difficult and dangerous walking on the ice, as we try to find language and images for the consciousness we are just coming into, and with little in the past to support us.

   How does "The Roofwalker," written prior to the emergence of the feminist movement, reflect Rich's struggle with this changing "consciousness"?

RANDALL JARRELL

(1914–1965)

The Death of the Ball Turret Gunner

(1945)

From my mother's sleep I fell into the State
And I hunched in its belly till my wet fur froze.
Six miles from earth, loosed from its dream of life,
I woke to black flak and the nightmare fighters.
5 When I died they washed me out of the turret with a hose.

READING AND REACTING

1. Who is the speaker? To what does he compare himself in the poem's first two lines? What words establish this comparison?

2. Contrast the speaker's actual identity with the one he creates for himself in lines 1–2. What elements of his actual situation do you think lead him to characterize himself as he does in lines 1–2?

3. **JOURNAL ENTRY**   Both this poem and "Dulce et Decorum Est" (p. 000) use figurative language to describe the horrors of war. Which poem has a greater impact on you? How does the poem's figurative language contribute to this impact?

4. **CRITICAL PERSPECTIVE**   In a 1974 article, Frances Ferguson criticizes "The Death of the Ball Turret Gunner," arguing that the poem "thoroughly manifests the lack of a middle between the gunner's birth and his death. . . . Because the poem presents a man who seems to have lived in order to die, we forget the fiction that he must have lived." However, in a 1978 explication, Patrick J. Horner writes that the "manipulation of time reveals the stunning brevity of the gunner's waking life and the State's total disregard for that phenomenon. . . . Because of the telescoping of time, . . . [the poem] resonates with powerful feeling."

  With which critic do you agree? That is, do you see the "lack of a middle" as a positive or negative quality of this poem?

MARGE PIERCY

(1934–   )

The Secretary Chant

(1973)

My hips are a desk.
From my ears hang
chains of paper clips.
Rubber bands form my hair.
5 My breasts are wells of mimeograph ink.
My feet bear casters.
Buzz. Click.
My head is a badly organized file.
My head is a switchboard
10 where crossed lines crackle.
Press my fingers
and in my eyes appear
credit and debit.
Zing. Tinkle.
15 My navel is a reject button.
From my mouth issue canceled reams.
Swollen, heavy, rectangular
I am about to be delivered
of a baby
20 Xerox machine.
File me under W
because I wonce
was
a woman.

READING AND REACTING

1. Examine each of the poem's figures of speech. Do they all make
   reasonable comparisons, or are some far-fetched or hard to visualize?
   Explain the relationship between the secretary and each item with
   which she is compared.

2. **JOURNAL ENTRY**   The speaker's frequent use of metaphor rather
   than simile (as in line 1's "My hips are a desk") creates a distorted
   physical image of the secretary. Does this image undermine, or even
   trivialize, the poem's point, or does it strengthen the poem? Would
   similes be more effective? Explain.

3. **CRITICAL PERSPECTIVE**   In a review of a recent collection of
   Piercy's poetry, Sandra Gilbert notes instances of "a kind of bombast"

(pompous language) and remarks, "As most poets realize, political verse is almost the hardest kind to write." In what sense can "The Secretary Chant" be seen as "political verse"? Do you think Piercy successfully achieves her political purpose, or does she undercut it with "bombast"?

JOHN DONNE

(1572–1631)

A Valediction: Forbidding Mourning

(1611)

As virtuous men pass mildly away,
　　And whisper to their souls to go,
Whilst some of their sad friends do say
　　The breath goes now, and some say no:

5　So let us melt, and make no noise,
　　No tear-floods, nor sigh-tempests move;
'Twere profanation of our joys
　　To tell the laity[1] our love.

Moving of th' earth brings harms and fears;
10　　Men reckon what it did and meant;
But trepidation of the spheres,
　　Though greater far, is innocent.

Dull sublunary lovers' love
　　(Whose soul is sense) cannot admit
15　Absence, because it doth remove
　　Those things which elemented it.

But we, by a love so much refined
　　That ourselves know not what it is,
Inter-assurèd of the mind,
20　　Care less, eyes, lips, and hands to miss.

Our two souls, therefore, which are one,
　　Though I must go, endure not yet
A breach, but an expansion,
　　Like gold to airy thinness beat.

---

[1] Here, "common people."

25 If they be two, they are two so
        As stiff twin compasses are two:
    Thy soul, the fixed foot, makes no show
        To move, but doth, if th' other do.

    And though it in the center sit,
30   Yet when the other far doth roam,
    It leans and harkens after it,
        And grows erect as that comes home.

    Such wilt thou be to me, who must,
        Like th' other foot, obliquely run;
35 Thy firmness makes my circle just,[2]
        And makes me end where I begun.

READING AND REACTING

1. Beginning with line 25 the poem develops an extended metaphor, called a **conceit,** which compares the speaker and his loved one to "twin compasses" (26), attached and yet separate. Why is the compass an especially apt metaphor? What qualities of the compass does the poet emphasize?

2. The poem uses other figures of speech to characterize both the lovers' union and their separation. To what other events does the speaker compare his separation from his loved one? To what other elements does he compare their attachment? Do you think these comparisons are effective?

3. **JOURNAL ENTRY**   Does the poem's use of figurative language strike you as appropriate or excessive? Explain.

4. **CRITICAL PERSPECTIVE**   In *John Donne and the Metaphysical Poets* (1970), Judah Stampfer writes of this poem's "thin, dry texture, its stanzas of pinched music," noting that its form "has too clipped a brevity to qualify as a song" and that its "music wobbles on a dry, measured beat." Yet, he argues, "the poem comes choked with emotional power" because "the speaker reads as a naturally reticent man, leaving his beloved in uncertainty and deep trouble." Stampfer concludes, "Easy self-expression here would be self-indulgent, if not reprehensible. . . . For all his careful dignity, we feel a heart is breaking here."

    Do you find such emotional power in this highly intellectual poem?

_____

[2] Perfect.

Hyperbole and Understatement

Two additional kinds of figurative language, *hyperbole* and *understatement,* also give poets opportunities to suggest meaning beyond the literal level of language.

Hyperbole is intentional exaggeration—saying more than is actually meant. In the poem "Oh, My Love Is Like a Red, Red Rose" (p. 771), when the speaker says that he will love his lady until all the seas go dry, he is using hyperbole. **Understatement** is just the opposite—saying less than is meant. When the speaker in the poem "Fire and Ice" (p. 682), weighing two equally grim alternatives for the end of the world, says that "for destruction ice / Is also great / And would suffice," he is using understatement. In both cases, poets rely on their readers to understand that their words are not to be taken literally.

By using hyperbole, poets attract readers' attention—for example, with exaggerated anger or graphic images of horror. But poets use hyperbole to ridicule and satirize as well as to inflame and shock. With understatement, poets can convey powerful emotions subtly, without unnecessary artifice or embellishment, allowing the ideas to speak for themselves.

The emotionally charged poem that follows uses hyperbole to attract attention, conveying anger and bitterness that seem almost beyond the power of words.

SYLVIA PLATH

(1932–1963)

Daddy

(1965)

You do not do, you do not do
Any more, black shoe
In which I have lived like a foot
For thirty years, poor and white,
5 Barely daring to breathe or Achoo.

Daddy, I have had to kill you.
You died before I had time—
Marble-heavy, a bag full of God,
Ghastly statue with one grey toe
10 Big as a Frisco seal

And a head in the freakish Atlantic
Where it pours bean green over blue
In the waters off beautiful Nauset.
I used to pray to recover you.
15 Ach, du.[1]

In the German tongue, in the Polish town[2]
Scraped flat by the roller
Of wars, wars, wars.
But the name of the town is common.
20 My Polack friend

Says there are a dozen or two.
So I never could tell where you
Put your foot, your root,
I never could talk to you.
25 The tongue stuck in my jaw.

It stuck in a barb wire snare.
Ich, ich, ich, ich,[3]
I could hardly speak.
I thought every German was you.
30 And the language obscene

An engine, an engine
Chuffing me off like a Jew.
A Jew to Dachau, Auschwitz, Belsen.[4]
I began to talk like a Jew.
35 I think I may well be a Jew.

The snows of the Tyrol, the clear beer of Vienna
Are not very pure or true.
With my gypsy ancestress and my weird luck
And my Taroc pack and my Taroc pack
40 I may be a bit of a Jew.

I have always been scared of *you*,
With your Luftwaffe,[5] your gobbledygoo.

---

[1] Ah, you. (German)

[2] Grabôw, where Plath's father was born.

[3] I. (German)

[4] Nazi concentration camps.

[5] The German air force.

And your neat moustache
And your Aryan eye, bright blue.
45 Panzer[6]-man, panzer-man, O You—

Not God but a swastika
So black no sky could squeak through.
Every woman adores a Fascist,
The boot in the face, the brute
50 Brute heart of a brute like you.

You stand at the blackboard, daddy,
In the picture I have of you,
A cleft in your chin instead of your foot
But no less a devil for that, no not
55 Any less the black man who

Bit my pretty red heart in two.
I was ten when they buried you.
At twenty I tried to die
And get back, back, back to you.
60 I thought even the bones would do.

But they pulled me out of the sack,
And they stuck me together with glue.
And then I knew what to do.
I made a model of you,
65 A man in black with a Meinkampf[7] look

And a love of the rack and the screw.
And I said I do, I do.
So daddy, I'm finally through.
The black telephone's off at the root,
70 The voices just can't worm through.

If I've killed one man, I've killed two—
The vampire who said he was you
And drank my blood for a year,
Seven years, if you want to know.
75 Daddy, you can lie back now.

---

6 Protected by armor. The Panzer division was the German armored division.

7 *Mein Kampf* (My Struggle) is Adolf Hitler's autobiography.

> There's a stake in your fat black heart
> And the villagers never liked you.
> They are dancing and stamping on you.
> They always *knew* it was you.
> 80 Daddy, daddy, you bastard, I'm through.

In her anger and frustration, the speaker sees herself as a helpless victim—a foot entrapped in a shoe, a Jew in a concentration camp—of her father's (and, later, her husband's) absolute tyranny. Thus, her hated father is characterized as a "black shoe," "a bag full of God," a "ghastly statue," and, eventually, a Nazi, a torturer, the devil, a vampire. The poem "Daddy" is widely accepted by scholars as autobiographical, and the fact that Plath's own father was actually neither a Nazi nor a sadist (nor, obviously, the devil or a vampire) makes it clear that the figurative comparisons in the poem are wildly exaggerated. Even so, they may convey the poet's true feelings toward her father—and, perhaps, toward the patriarchal society in which she lived.

Plath uses hyperbole as the medium through which to communicate these emotions to readers who she knows cannot possibly feel the way she does. Her purpose, therefore, is not just to shock but also to enlighten, to persuade, and perhaps even to empower her readers. Throughout the poem, the inflammatory language is set in ironic opposition to the childish, affectionate term "Daddy"—most strikingly in the last line's choked out "Daddy, daddy, you bastard, I'm through." The result of the exaggerated rhetoric is a poem that is vivid and shocking. And, although some might believe that Plath's almost wild exaggeration undermines the poem's impact, others would argue that the powerful figurative language is necessary to convey the extent of the speaker's rage.

Like "Daddy," the next poem presents a situation whose emotional impact is devastating. In this case, however, the poet does not use emotional language; instead, he uses understatement, presenting the events without embellishment.

D A V I D   H U D D L E

(1942–   )

Holes Commence Falling

(1979)

> The lead & zinc company
> owned the mineral rights
> to the whole town anyway,

and after drilling holes
5 for 3 or 4 years,
they finally found the right
place and sunk a mine shaft.
We were proud
of all that digging,
10 even though nobody from
town got hired. They
were going to dig right
under New River and hook up
with the mine at Austinville.
15 Then people's wells
started drying up just like
somebody'd shut off a faucet,
and holes commenced falling,
big chunks of people's yards
20 would drop 5 or 6 feet,
houses would shift and crack.
Now and then the company'd
pay out a little money
in damages; they got a truck
25 to haul water and sell it
to the people whose wells
had dried up, but most
everybody agreed the
situation wasn't
30 serious.

Although "Holes Commence Falling" relates a tragic sequence of events, the tone of the poem is matter-of-fact and the language is understated. Certainly the speaker could have overdramatized the events, using inflated rhetoric to denounce big business and to predict disastrous events for the future. At the very least, he could have colored the events with realistic emotions, assigning blame to the lead and zinc company with justifiable anger. Instead, the speaker is so restrained, so nonchalant, so passive that readers must supply the missing emotions themselves—realizing, for example, that when the speaker concludes "everybody agreed the / situation wasn't / serious," he means just the opposite.

Throughout the poem, unpleasant events are presented without comment and without emotion. As it proceeds, the poem traces the high and low points in the town's fortunes, but for every hope ("We were proud / of all that digging") there is a disappointment ("even though nobody from / town got hired"). The lead and zinc company offers some compensation for the damage it does, but it is never enough. The present tense verb of the poem's title indicates that the problems the town

faces—wells drying up, yards dropping, houses shifting and cracking—
are regular occurrences. Eventually, readers come to see that what is not
expressed, what lurks just below the surface—anger, powerlessness, resentment, hopelessness—is the poem's real subject. The speaker's laconic
speech and flat tone seem to suggest an attitude of resignation, but the
obvious contrast between the understated tone and the seriousness of the
problem creates a sense of irony that makes the speaker's real attitude toward the lead and zinc company clear.

Poems for Further Reading: Hyperbole and Understatement

ANNE BRADSTREET

(1612?–1672)

To My Dear and Loving Husband

(1678)

If ever two were one, then surely we.
If ever man were lov'd by wife, then thee;
If ever wife was happy in a man,
Compare with me ye women if you can.
5 I prize thy love more than whole Mines of gold,
Or all the riches that the East doth hold.
My love is such that Rivers cannot quench,
Nor ought but love from thee, give recompence.
Thy love is such I can no way repay,
10 The heavens reward thee manifold I pray.
Then while we live, in love lets so persever,
That when we live no more, we may live ever.

READING AND REACTING

1. Review the claims the poem's speaker makes about her husband in
   lines 5–8. Are such exaggerated declarations of love necessary, or
   would the rest of the poem be sufficient to convey the extent of her
   devotion to her husband?

2. **JOURNAL ENTRY**   Compare this poem's declarations of love to those
   of John Donne's speaker in "A Valediction: Forbidding Mourning"
   (p. 777). Which speaker do you believe is more convincing? Why?

A N D R E W   M A R V E L L

(1621–1678)

To His Coy Mistress

(1681)

Had we but world enough and time,
This coyness, lady, were no crime.
We would sit down and think which way
To walk, and pass our long love's day.
5 Thou by the Indian Ganges' side
Should'st rubies find; I by the tide
Of Humber[1] would complain. I would
Love you ten years before the Flood,
And you should, if you please, refuse
10 Till the conversion of the Jews.
My vegetable love should grow
Vaster than empires, and more slow.
An hundred years should go to praise
Thine eyes, and on thy forehead gaze,
15 Two hundred to adore each breast,
But thirty thousand to the rest.
An age at least to every part,
And the last age should show your heart.
For, lady, you deserve this state,
20 Nor would I love at lower rate.
　　　But at my back I always hear
Time's wingèd chariot hurrying near,
And yonder all before us lie
Deserts of vast eternity.
25 Thy beauty shall no more be found,
Nor in thy marble vault shall sound
My echoing song; then worms shall try
That long preserved virginity,
And your quaint honor turn to dust,
30 And into ashes all my lust.
The grave's a fine and private place,
But none, I think, do there embrace.
　　　Now therefore, while the youthful hue
Sits on thy skin like morning glew[2]

---

[1] An estuary in the east coast of England.

[2] Dew.

35 And while thy willing soul transpires
At every pore with instant fires,
Now let us sport us while we may;
And now, like amorous birds of prey,
Rather at once our time devour
40 Than languish in his slow-chapped[3] power.
Let us roll all our strength and all
Our sweetness up into one ball
And tear our pleasures with rough strife
Thorough the iron gates of life.
45 Thus, though we cannot make our sun
Stand still, yet we will make him run.

READING AND REACTING

1. In this poem Marvell's speaker sets out to convince a reluctant woman to become his lover. In order to make his case more convincing, he uses hyperbole, exaggerating time periods, sizes, spaces, and the possible fate of the woman, should she refuse him. Identify as many examples of hyperbole as you can.

2. The tone of "To His Coy Mistress" is more whimsical than serious. Given this tone, what do you see as the purpose of Marvell's use of hyperbole?

ROBERT FROST

(1874–1963)

"Out, Out—"

(1916)

The buzz saw snarled and rattled in the yard
And made dust and dropped stove-length sticks of wood,
Sweet-scented stuff when the breeze drew across it.
And from there those that lifted eyes could count
5 Five mountain ranges one behind the other
Under the sunset far into Vermont.
And the saw snarled and rattled, snarled and rattled,
As it ran light, or had to bear a load.
And nothing happened: day was all but done.
10 Call it a day, I wish they might have said
To please the boy by giving him the half hour

---

[3] Slowly crushing.

That a boy counts so much when saved from work.
His sister stood beside them in her apron
To tell them 'Supper.' At the word, the saw,
15 As if to prove saws knew what supper meant,
Leaped out at the boy's hand, or seemed to leap—
He must have given the hand. However it was,
Neither refused the meeting. But the hand!
The boy's first outcry was a rueful laugh,
20 As he swung toward them holding up the hand
Half in appeal, but half as if to keep
The life from spilling. Then the boy saw all—
Since he was old enough to know, big boy
Doing a man's work, though a child at heart—
25 He saw all spoiled. 'Don't let him cut my hand off—
The doctor, when he comes. Don't let him, sister!'
So. But the hand was gone already.
The doctor put him in the dark of ether.
He lay and puffed his lips out with his breath.
30 And then—the watcher at his pulse took fright.
No one believed. They listened at his heart.
Little—less—nothing!—and that ended it.
No more to build on there. And they, since they
Were not the one dead, turned to their affairs.

READING AND REACTING

1. The poem's title is an **allusion** to a passage in Shakespeare's *Macbeth* (5.5.23–28) which attacks the brevity and meaninglessness of life in very emotional terms:

> "Out, out brief candle!
> *Life's but a walking shadow, a poor player,*
> *That struts and frets his hour upon the stage*
> *And then is heard no more. It is a tale*
> *Told by an idiot, full of sound and fury,*
> *Signifying nothing."*

What idea do you think Frost wants to convey through the title *"Out, Out—"*?

2. Explain why each of the following qualifies as understatement:

"Neither refused the meeting." (18)

"He saw all spoiled." (25)

". . . that ended it." (32)

"No more to build on there." (33)

Can you identify any other examples of understatement in the poem?

3. **JOURNAL ENTRY**   Do you think the poem's impact is strengthened or weakened by its understated tone? Explain your conclusion.

4. **CRITICAL PERSPECTIVE**   In an essay on Frost in his 1985 book *Affirming Limits*, Robert Pack focuses on the single word "So" in line 27 of "Out, Out—":

> *For a moment, his narration is reduced to the impotent word "So," and in that minimal word all his restrained grief is held. . . . That "So" is the narrator's cry of bearing witness to a story that must be what it is in a scene he cannot enter. He cannot rescue or protect the boy. . . . In the poem's sense of human helplessness in an indifferent universe, we are all "watchers," and what we see is death without redemption, "signifying nothing." So. So? So! How shall we read that enigmatic word?*

How do you read this "enigmatic word" in the poem?

DONALD HALL

(1928–   )

My Son, My Executioner

(1955)

My son, my executioner,
    I take you in my arms,
Quiet and small and just astir,
    And whom my body warms.

5 Sweet death, small son, our instrument
    Of immortality,
Your cries and hungers document
    Our bodily decay.

We twenty-five and twenty-two,
10   Who seemed to live forever,
Observe enduring life in you
    And start to die together.

READING AND REACTING

1. Because the speaker is a young man holding his newborn son in his arms, the equation in line 1 comes as a shock. What is Hall's purpose in opening with such a startling statement?

2. In what sense is the comparison between baby and executioner a valid one? Could you argue that, given the underlying similarities between the two, Hall is *not* using hyperbole? Explain.

MARGARET ATWOOD

(1939–   )

You Fit into Me

(1971)

you fit into me
like a hook into an eye

a fish hook
an open eye

READING AND REACTING

1. What connotations does Atwood expect readers to associate with the phrase "you fit into me"? What does the speaker seem at first to mean by "like a hook into an eye" in line 2?

2. The speaker's shift to the brutal suggestions of lines 3 and 4 is calculated to shock readers. Does the use of hyperbole here have another purpose in the context of the poem? Explain.

Metonymy and Synecdoche

Metonymy and synecdoche are two related figures of speech. **Metonymy** is the substitution of the name of one thing for the name of another thing that most readers associate with the first—for example, using *hired gun* to mean "paid assassin" or using *suits* for "business executives." A specific kind of metonymy, called **synecdoche,** involves the substitution of a part for the whole (for example, using *bread*—as in "Give us this day our daily bread"—to mean "food") or the whole for a part (for example, saying "You can take the boy out of Brooklyn, but you can't take Brooklyn [meaning its distinctive traits] out of the boy"). Instead of describing something by saying it is like something else (as in simile) or by equating it with something else (as in metaphor), writers can characterize an object or concept by using a term that evokes it. The following poem illustrates the use of synecdoche.

RICHARD LOVELACE

(1618–1658)

To Lucasta Going to the Wars

(1649)

Tell me not, Sweet, I am unkind
   That from the nunnery
Of thy chaste breast and quiet mind,
   To war and arms I fly.

5 True, a new mistress now I chase,
   The first foe in the field;
And with a stronger faith embrace
   A sword, a horse, a shield.

Yet this inconstancy is such
10   As you too shall adore;
I could not love thee, Dear, so much,
   Loved I not Honor more.

In this poem the use of synecdoche allows the poet to condense a number of complex ideas into a very few words. In line 3, when he says that he is flying from his loved one's "chaste breast and quiet mind," the speaker is using "breast" and "mind" to stand for all his loved one's physical and intellectual attributes. In line 8, when he says that he is embracing "A sword, a horse, a shield," he is using these three items to represent all the trappings of war—and, thus, to represent war itself.

Poem for Further Reading:
Metonymy and Synecdoche

DYLAN THOMAS

(1914–1953)

The Hand That Signed the Paper

(1936)

The hand that signed the paper felled a city;
Five sovereign fingers taxed the breath,
Doubled the globe of dead and halved a country;
These five kings did a king to death.

5 The mighty hand leads to a sloping shoulder,
The finger joints are cramped with chalk;
A goose's quill has put an end to murder
That put an end to talk.

The hand that signed the treaty bred a fever,
10 And famine grew, and locusts came;
Great is the hand that holds dominion over
Man by a scribbled name.

The five kings count the dead but do not soften
The crusted wound nor stroke the brow;
15 A hand rules pity as a hand rules heaven;
Hands have no tears to flow.

READING AND REACTING

1. When the speaker uses the word "hand" in the expression "the hand that signed the paper," to what larger entity is he really referring? Why does he use "hand" instead of what it stands for?

2. Does "hand" stand for the same thing throughout the poem, or does its meaning change? Explain.

Apostrophe

With **apostrophe**, a poem's speaker addresses an absent person or thing— for example, a historical or literary figure or even an inanimate object or an abstract concept.

In the following poem, for example, the speaker uses apostrophe when she addresses Vincent Van Gogh.

SONIA SANCHEZ

(1934–   )

On Passing thru Morgantown, Pa.

(1984)

i saw you
vincent van
gogh perched
on those pennsylvania

5 cornfields communing
amid secret black
bird societies. yes.
i'm sure that was
you exploding your
10 fantastic delirium
while in the
distance
red indian
hills beckoned.

Expecting her readers to be aware that Van Gogh is a Dutch postimpressionist painter known for his mental instability as well as for his art, Sanchez is able to give added meaning to a phrase such as "fantastic delirium" as well as to the poem's visual images. The speaker sees Van Gogh perched like a black bird on a fence, and at the same time she also sees what he sees. Like Van Gogh, then, the speaker sees the Pennsylvania cornfields as both a natural landscape and an "exploding" work of art.

Poems for Further Reading: Apostrophe

ALLEN GINSBERG

(1926–   )

A Supermarket in California

(1956)

What thoughts I have of you tonight, Walt Whitman,[1] for I walked down the sidestreets under the trees with a headache self-conscious looking at the full moon.

In my hungry fatigue, and shopping for images, I went into the neon
5 fruit supermarket, dreaming of your enumerations!

What peaches and what penumbras! Whole families shopping at night! Aisles full of husbands! Wives in the avocados, babies in the tomatoes!—and you, Garcia Lorca,[2] what were you doing down by the watermelons?

---

[1] Walt Whitman (1819–1892)—American poet. Whitman's poems frequently praise the commonplace and often contain lengthy "enumerations."

[2] Federico García Lorca (1899–1936)—Spanish poet and dramatist.

10   I saw you, Walt Whitman, childless, lonely old grubber, poking among the meats in the refrigerator and eyeing the grocery boys.[3]

I heard you asking questions of each: Who killed the pork chops? What price bananas? Are you my Angel?

I wandered in and out of the brilliant stacks of cans following you, and
15 followed in my imagination by the store detective.

We strode down the open corridors together in our solitary fancy tasting artichokes, possessing every frozen delicacy, and never passing the cashier.

Where are we going, Walt Whitman? The doors close in an hour.
20 Which way does your beard point tonight?

(I touch your book[4] and dream of our odyssey in the supermarket and feel absurd.)

Will we walk all night through solitary streets? The trees add shade to shade, lights out in the houses, we'll both be lonely.

25   Will we stroll dreaming of the lost America of love past blue automobiles in driveways, home to our silent cottage?

Ah, dear father, graybeard, lonely old courage-teacher, what America did you have when Charon[5] quit poling his ferry and you got out on a smoking bank and stood watching the boat disappear on the black waters
30 of Lethe?[6]

READING AND REACTING

1. In this poem Ginsberg's speaker addresses Walt Whitman, a nineteenth-century American poet. What attitude does the speaker seem to have toward Whitman?

2. Is this poem serious, or is it supposed to be read as a playful experiment? How can you tell?

3. **JOURNAL ENTRY**   Read the excerpt from Walt Whitman's "Song of Myself" on page 1022. In what way does your reading of this excerpt help you to understand Ginsberg's purpose in having his speaker address Whitman?

---

[3] Whitman's sexual orientation is the subject of much debate. Ginsberg is suggesting here that Whitman was homosexual.

[4] *Leaves of Grass.*

[5] In Greek mythology, the ferryman who transported the souls of the dead across the Styx and Acheron rivers to the underworld.

[6] The mythological underworld river whose waters caused the dead to forget their former lives.

WALT WHITMAN

(1819–1892)

A Noiseless Patient Spider

(1881)

A noiseless patient spider,
I mark'd where on a little promontory it stood isolated,
Mark'd how to explore the vacant vast surrounding,
It launch'd forth filament, filament, filament, out of itself,
5 Ever unreeling them, ever tirelessly speeding them.

And you O my soul where you stand,
Surrounded, detached, in measureless oceans of space,
Ceaselessly musing, venturing, throwing, seeking the spheres to
    connect them,
Till the bridge you will need be form'd, till the ductile anchor
    hold,
10 Till the gossamer thread you fling catch somewhere, O my soul.

READING AND REACTING

1. This poem has at its center a figurative comparison between the soul
   and a spider. In what respects are the two comparable?

2. Where in the poem does the poet use apostrophe? What does its
   presence contribute to the poem? Would the poem be as effective
   without this use of apostrophe? Explain.

▼▼▼▼▼▼▼▼▼▼▼▼▼▼▼▼▼▼▼▼▼▼▼▼▼▼▼▼▼▼▼▼▼▼▼▼▼▼▼

CHECKLIST FOR WRITING ABOUT FIGURES OF SPEECH

◆ Are any figures of speech present in the poem? Identify each
   example of simile, metaphor, personification, hyperbole,
   understatement, metonymy, synecdoche, and apostrophe.

◆ What two elements are being compared in each use of simile,
   metaphor, and personification? Is the comparison logical? What
   characteristics do the two items being compared share?

◆ How do figurative comparisons contribute to the impact of the
   poem as a whole?

◆ Does the poet use hyperbole? Why? For example, is it used to
   move or to shock readers, or is its use intended to produce a
   humorous or satirical effect?

♦ Does the poet use understatement? For what purpose? Would more straightforward language be more effective?

♦ In metonymy and synecdoche, what item is being substituted for another? What purpose does the substitution serve?

♦ If the poem includes apostrophe, whom or what does the speaker address? What is accomplished through the use of apostrophe?

▲▲

WRITING SUGGESTIONS: FIGURES OF SPEECH

1. Various figures of speech are often used to portray characters in a poem. Choose two or three poems that focus on a single character—for example, "Ex-Basketball Player" (p. 772), "Richard Cory" (p. 992), or "Gracie" (p. 732)—and explain how figures of speech are used to characterize the poem's central figure.

2. Write an essay in which you discuss the different ways poets use figures of speech to examine the nature of poetry itself. What kinds of figures of speech do poets use to describe their craft? (You might begin by reading the three poems about poetry that open Chapter 11.)

3. Write an essay in which you compare Adrienne Rich's "The Roofwalker" (p. 773) with Lawrence Ferlinghetti's "Constantly Risking Absurdity" (p. 768). Pay particular attention to the similarities between Ferlinghetti's identification of the poet with an acrobat and Rich's identification of her speaker with a roofwalker.

4. Write a letter replying to Marvell's, Bradstreet's, Donne's, or Burns's speaker. Use figurative language to express the depth of your love and the extent of your devotion.

5. Choose two or three poems that share a common subject—for example, love, nature, war, or mortality—and write a paper in which you draw some general conclusions about the relative effectiveness of the poems' use of figurative language to examine that subject.

CHAPTER 17

Sound

A primary pleasure in poetry is . . . the pleasure of saying something over for its own sweet sake and because it sounds just right. For myself, certainly, and for you if you will remember how it truly was, the thing said over will not necessarily be A Great Thought, though great thoughts are not necessarily excluded either; it may be as near as not to meaningless, especially if one says it without much attention to its context. For instance, a riddling song has the refrain: Sing ninety-nine and ninety. I can remember being charmed enough with that to say it over and over to myself for days, without ever having a single thought about its meaning except for a certain bemused wonder about how different it was from singing a hundred and eighty-nine.

HOWARD NEMEROV, "POETRY AND MEANING"

I don't think of poetry as a "rational" activity but as an aural one. My poems usually begin with words or phrases which appeal more because of their sound than their meaning, and the movement and phrasing of a poem are very important to me. But like many modern poets I tend to conceal rhymes by placing them in the middle of lines, and to avoid immediate alliteration and assonance in favor of echoes placed later in the poems. For me, every poem has a texture of sound which is at least as important to me as the "argument." This is not to minimize "statement." But it does annoy me when students, prompted by the approach of their teacher, ask, "What is the poet trying to say?" It implies that the poet is some kind of verbal cripple who can't quite "say" what he "means" and has to resort to a lot of round-the-mulberry-bush, thereby putting the student to a great deal of trouble extracting his "meaning," like a prize out of a box of Cracker Jack.

MARGARET ATWOOD, "MY MOTHER WOULD RATHER
SKATE THAN SCRUB FLOORS"

Let us concede that the effects of the meters are mysterious, from moment to moment imprecise, often enough uncertain or ambiguous. Meters do accompany the sense, like a kind of percussion only, mostly noise. Over and above syntax, they bind the individual words together, and the larger structural parts as well, over and above whatever appearance of logic survives in the argument; as a result, the words and parts seem to cohere, more perhaps than in plain fact may be the case. How they assist the recollection is by fixing it in permanent, or would-be permanent, form.

This, for the poet, may be the large and rather sentimental purpose which gives force to all their various combining and intersecting functions.

DONALD JUSTICE, "METERS AND MEMORY"

I've never taught a poetry writing class that has not suffered my reiteration of Duke Ellington's line: "It don't mean a thing if it ain't got that swing." How can you describe the feeling of reading a Roethke poem, . . . when the rhythm is so palpable it is as if the poem could be cupped in your hands? Those poems move great distances in meaning between sentences and yet they hold together, largely because of the sound. The same thing is operating in a song that makes you want to get up and dance. From the poet's point of view, the rhythm helps the poem to get written; the poet feels the right word, its sound tugging against its meaning, and doesn't think of it, at least in the ways we usually think of thinking. Rhythm and sound and arrangement—the formal properties of words—allow the poet to get beyond thought, or beneath it.

MICHAEL RYAN, "ON THE NATURE OF POETRY"

The most obvious function of the line-break is rhythmic: it can record the slight (but meaningful) hesitations between word and word that are characteristic of the mind's dance among perceptions but which are not noted by grammatical punctuation. Regular punctuation is a part of regular sentence structure, that is, of the expression of completed thoughts; and this expression is typical of prose, even though prose is not at all times bound by its logic. But in poems one has the opportunity not only, as in expressive prose, to depart from the syntactic norm, but . . . to present the dynamics of perception along with its arrival at full expression. The line-break is a form of punctuation additional to the punctuation that forms part of the logic of completed thoughts. Line-breaks—together with intelligent use of indentation and other devices of scoring—represent a peculiarly poetic, a-logical, parallel (not competitive) punctuation.

DENISE LEVERTOV, "ON THE FUNCTION OF LINE"

W A L T   W H I T M A N

(1819–1892)

Had I the Choice[1]

Had I the choice to tally greatest bards,
To limn[2] their portraits, stately, beautiful, and emulate at will,
Homer with all his wars and warriors—Hector, Achilles, Ajax,
Or Shakespeare's woe-entangled Hamlet, Lear, Othello—Tennyson's
    fair ladies,
5 Meter or wit the best, or choice conceit to wield in perfect rhyme,
    delight of singers;
These, these, O sea, all these I'd gladly barter,
Would you the undulation of one wave, its trick to me transfer,
Or breathe one breath of yours upon my verse,
And leave its odor there.

Rhythm

Rhythm—the regular recurrence of sounds—is at the heart of all natural phenomena: the beating of a heart, the lapping of waves against the shore, the croaking of frogs on a summer's night, the whisper of wheat swaying in the wind. In fact, even mechanical phenomena, such as the movement of rush-hour traffic through a city's streets, have a kind of rhythm. Poetry, which explores these phenomena, often tries to reflect the same rhythms. Walt Whitman makes this point in "Had I the Choice" when he says that he would gladly trade the "perfect rhyme" of Shakespeare for the ability to reproduce "the undulation of one wave" in his verse.

Effective public speakers frequently repeat key words and phrases to create a rhythm. In his speech "I Have a Dream," for example, Martin Luther King, Jr., repeats the phrase "I have a dream" to create a cadence that ties the central section of the speech together:

> *I say to you today, my friends, even though we face the difficulties of today
> and tomorrow, I still have a dream. It is a dream deeply rooted in the
> American dream. I have a dream that one day this nation will rise up and live
> out the true meaning of its creed: "We hold these truths to be self-evident,
> that all men are created equal." I have a dream that one day, on the red hills
> of Georgia, sons of former slaves and the sons of former slave owners will be
> able to sit down together at the table of brotherhood. I have a dream that one*

---

[1] Publication date is not available.

[2] To describe, depict.

day even the state of Mississippi, a state sweltering with the heat of injustice,
sweltering with the heat of oppression, will be transformed into an oasis of
freedom and justice. I have a dream that my four little children will one day
live in a nation where they will not be judged by the color of their skin, but by
the content of their character.

Poets, too, create rhythm by using repeated words and phrases. Consider
the use of repetition in the following poem.

GWENDOLYN BROOKS

(1917–   )

Sadie and Maud

(1945)

Maud went to college.
Sadie stayed at home.
Sadie scraped life
With a fine-tooth comb.

5 She didn't leave a tangle in.
Her comb found every strand.
Sadie was one of the livingest chits
In all the land.

Sadie bore two babies
10 Under her maiden name.
Maud and Ma and Papa
Nearly died of shame.

When Sadie said her last so-long
Her girls struck out from home.
15 (Sadie had left as heritage
Her fine-tooth comb.)

Maud, who went to college,
Is a thin brown mouse.
She is living all alone
20 In this old house.

Much of the force of this poem comes from its balanced structure and regular rhyme and meter, underscored by the repeated words "Sadie" and
"Maud," which shift the focus from one subject to the other and back
again ("Maud went to college / Sadie stayed home"). The poem's singsong

rhythm recalls the rhymes children recite when jumping rope. This evocation of carefree childhood ironically contrasts with the adult realities that both Sadie and Maud face as they grow up: Sadie stays at home and has two children out of wedlock; Maud goes to college and ends up "a thin brown mouse." The speaker implies that the alternatives Sadie and Maud represent are both undesirable. Although Sadie "scraped life / with a fine-tooth comb," she dies young and leaves nothing to her girls but her desire to experience life. Maud, who graduated from college, shuts out life and cuts herself off from her roots.

Just as repetition of words and phrases can create rhythm, so can the distribution of words among the lines of a poem—and even the appearance of words on a printed page. How a poem looks is especially important in **open form** poetry (Chapter 18), which dispenses with traditional patterns of versification. In the following excerpt from a poem by E. E. Cummings, for example, an unusual arrangement of words forces readers first to slow down and then to speed up, creating a rhythm that emphasizes a key phrase—"The / lily":

> *the moon is hiding*
> *in her hair.*
> *The*
> *lily*
> *of heaven*
> *full of all dreams,*
> *draws down.*

Poetic rhythm—the repetition of stresses and pauses—is an essential element in poetry. Rhythm helps to establish a poem's mood and, in combination with other poetic elements, it conveys the poet's emphasis and communicates the poem's meaning. Although rhythm can be affected by the regular repetition of words and phrases or by the arrangement of words into lines, poetic rhythm is largely created by **meter,** the pattern of stressed and unstressed syllables that governs a poem's lines.

Meter

A **stress** (or accent) occurs when one syllable is emphasized more than another, unstressed, syllable: *fór • ceps, bá • sic, il • lú • sion, ma • lár • i • a.* In a poem, even one-syllable words can be stressed to create a particular effect. For example, in Elizabeth Barrett Browning's line "How do I love thee? Let me count the ways," the metrical pattern that places stress on "love" creates one meaning; stressing "I" would create another.

Scansion is the process of analyzing patterns of stressed and unstressed syllables within a line. The most common method of poetic notation involves indicating stressed syllables with a ' and unstressed syllables with a ⌣. Although scansion gives readers the "beat" of the poem, it only approximates the sound of spoken language, which contains an infinite variety of stresses. By providing a graphic representation of the stressed and unstressed syllables of a poem, scansion aids understanding, but it is no substitute for reading the poem aloud and experimenting with varying degrees of emphasis.

The basic unit of meter is a **foot**—a group of syllables with a fixed pattern of stressed and unstressed syllables. The following chart illustrates the most common types of feet in English and American verse.

FOOT	STRESS PATTERN	EXAMPLE
Iamb	⌣ ´	They pace │ in sleek │ chi val│ric cer│tain ty (Adrienne Rich)
Trochee	´ ⌣	Thou, when │ thou re│turn'st, wilt │ tell me. (John Donne)
Anapest	⌣ ⌣ ´	With a hey, │ and a ho, │ and a hey │ nonino (William Shakespeare)
Dactyl	´ ⌣ ⌣	Constantly │ risking ab│surdity (Lawrence Ferlinghetti)

Iambic and *anapestic* meters are called *rising meters* because they progress from unstressed to stressed syllables. *Trochaic* and *dactylic* meters are known as *falling meters* because they move from stressed to unstressed syllables.

The following types of metrical feet, less common than those above, are used for emphasis or to provide variety rather than to create the dominant meter of a poem.

	STRESS PATTERN	EXAMPLE
Spondee	´ ´	Pomp, pride │ and circumstance of glorious war! (William Shakespeare)
Pyrrhic	⌣ ⌣	A horse! a horse! My king│dom for │ a horse! (William Shakespeare)

A line of poetry has **meter** when the feet form a definite, rhythmic pattern. Each line is measured by the number of feet it contains.

monometer one foot	**pentameter** five feet
dimeter two feet	**hexameter** six feet
trimeter three feet	**heptameter** seven feet
tetrameter four feet	**octameter** eight feet

The name for a metrical pattern of a line of verse identifies the name of the foot used and the number of feet the line contains. For example, the most common foot in English poetry is the **iamb,** most often occurring in lines of three or five feet.

˘ ′ ˘ ′ ˘ ′
Eight hun|dred of | the brave   Iambic trimeter

(William Cowper)

˘ ′ ˘ ′ ˘
O, how | much more | doth   Iambic pentameter
′ ˘ ′ ˘ ′
beau|ty beau|teous seem

(William Shakespeare)

Because **iambic pentameter** is so well suited to the rhythms of English speech, writers frequently use it in plays and poems. Shakespeare's plays, for example, are written in unrhymed lines of iambic pentameter called **blank verse.**

Many other metrical combinations are also possible; a few are illustrated below.

′ ˘ ′ ˘ ′ ˘
Like a | high-born | maiden   Trochaic trimeter

(Percy Bysshe Shelley)

˘ ˘ ′ ˘ ˘ ′
The As sy|rian came down | Anapestic tetrameter
˘ ˘ ′ ˘ ˘ ′
like the wolf | on the fold

(Lord Byron)

′ ˘ ˘ ′ ˘ ˘
Maid en most | beau ti ful | Dactylic hexameter
′ ˘ ˘ ′ ˘ ˘ ′
mother most | boun ti ful, | la
˘ ˘ ′
dy of | lands, (A. C.

Swinburne)

˘ ′ ˘ ′ ˘ ′ ˘
The yel|low fog | that rubs | its   Iambic heptameter
′ ˘ ′ ˘ ′
back | upon | the win |
˘ ′
dow-panes (T. S. Eliot)

Scansion can be an extremely technical process, and when readers become bogged down with anapests and dactyls, they can easily forget that poetic meter is not an end in itself. Meter should be appropriate for the ideas expressed by the poem, and it should help to create a suitable tone. A light skipping rhythm, for example, would be inappropriate for an **elegy,** and a slow, heavy rhythm would surely be out of place in an **epigram** or a limerick. The following poem illustrates the different types of metrical feet.

SAMUEL TAYLOR COLERIDGE

(1772–1834)

Metrical Feet

(1806)

Lesson for a Boy

Trochee trips from long to short;
From long to long in solemn sort
Slow Spondee stalks; strong foot! yet ill able
Ever to come up with Dactyl trisyllable.
5 Iambics march from short to long—
With a leap and a bound the swift Anapests throng;
One syllable long, with one short at each side,
Amphibrachys hastes with a stately stride—
First and last being long, middle short, Amphimacer
10 Strikes his thundering hoofs like a proud high-bred Racer.
If Derwent[1] be innocent, steady, and wise,
And delight in the things of earth, water, and skies;
Tender warmth at his heart, with these meters to show it,
With sound sense in his brains, may make Derwent a poet—
15 May crown him with fame, and must win him the love
Of his father on earth and his Father above.
        My dear, dear child!
Could you stand upon Skiddaw,[2] you would not from its whole ridge
See a man who so loves you as your fond s. t. COLERIDGE.

---

[1] Coleridge's son.
[2] A mountain in the Lake District of England.

Each line of Coleridge's poem illustrates the characteristics of the particular metrical foot he describes. Thus, Coleridge makes the point that different meters enable poets to achieve different effects.

Even poems with regular meter may contain individual lines of varying lengths because poets may vary the line length to relieve monotony or to accommodate the demands of meaning or emphasis. Consider in the following poem how the poet uses iambic lines of different lengths.

E M I L Y   D I C K I N S O N

(1830–1886)

I Like to See It Lap the Miles

(1891)

I like to see it lap the Miles—
And lick the Valleys up—
And stop to feed itself at Tanks—
And then—prodigious step

5 Around a Pile of Mountains—
And supercilious peer
In Shanties—by the sides of Roads—
And then a Quarry pare

To fit its Ribs
10 And crawl between
Complaining all the while
In horrid—hooting stanza—
Then chase itself down Hill—

And neigh like Boanerges[1]—
15 Then—punctual as a Star
Stop—docile and omnipotent
At its own stable door—

This poem is a single sentence that, except for some short pauses, stretches unbroken from beginning to end. Iambic lines of varying lengths actually suggest the movements of the train that the poet describes. Iambic tetrameter lines, such as the first, give readers a sense of the train's steady, rhythmic movement across a flat landscape, and shorter lines ("To fit its Ribs /

---

[1] A vociferous preacher and orator. Also, the name, meaning "son of thunder," Jesus gave to apostles John and James because of their fiery zeal.

And crawl between") suggest its slowing motion. Beginning with two iambic dimeter lines and progressing to iambic trimeter lines, the third stanza increases in speed just like the train that is racing downhill "In horrid—hooting stanza—."

A poet can also use more than one type of metrical foot. Any variation in a metrical pattern—the substitution of a trochee for an iamb, for instance—immediately calls attention to itself. Poets are aware of this fact and use it to their advantage. For example, in line 16 of "I Like to See It Lap the Miles," the poet departs from iambic meter by placing unexpected stress on the first word, *stop*. By emphasizing this word, the poet brings the flow of the poem to an abrupt halt, suggesting the jolt riders experience when a train comes to a stop. In the following segment from "The Rime of the Ancient Mariner," Samuel Taylor Coleridge also departs from his poem's dominant meter.

> The ship | was cheered, | the har|bor cleared,
> Merri|ly did | we drop
> Below | the kirk, | below | the hill,
> Below | the light|house top.

Although these lines are arranged in iambic tetrameter, the poet uses a trochee in the second line, breaking the meter in order to accommodate the natural pronunciation of "merrily" as well as to place stress on the word.

Another way of varying the meter is to introduce a pause in the rhythm known as a **caesura**—a Latin word meaning "a cutting"—within a line. When scanning a poem, you indicate a caesura with two parallel lines: ‖. Unless a line of poetry is extremely short, it probably will contain a caesura.

A caesura occurs after a punctuation mark or at a natural break in phrasing:

> How do I love thee? ‖ Let me count the ways.
>
> Elizabeth Barrett Browning

> Two loves I have ‖ of comfort and despair.
>
> William Shakespeare

> High on a throne of royal state, ‖ which far
> Outshone the wealth of Ormus ‖ and of Ind
>
> John Milton

Sometimes, more than one caesura occurs in a single line:

> 'Tis good. ‖ Go to the gate. ‖ Somebody knocks.
>
> William Shakespeare

Although the end of a line may mark the end of a metrical unit, it does not always coincide with the end of a sentence. Poets may choose to indicate a pause at this point, or they may continue, without a break, to the next line. Lines that have distinct pauses at the end—usually signaled by punctuation—are called **end-stopped lines.** Lines that do not end with strong pauses are called **run-on lines.** (Sometimes the term **enjambment** is used to describe this type of line.) End-stopped lines can seem formal, or even forced, because their length is rigidly dictated by the poem's meter, rhythm, and rhyme scheme. In the following excerpt from John Keats's "La Belle Dame Sans Merci" (p. 955), for example, rhythm, meter, and rhyme dictate the pauses that occur at the ends of the lines:

> *O, what can ail thee, knight-at-arms,*
>   *Alone and palely loitering?*
> *The sedge has withered from the lake,*
>   *And no birds sing.*

In contrast to end-stopped lines, run-on lines seem more natural. Because their ending points are determined by the rhythms of speech and by the meaning and emphasis the poet wishes to convey rather than by meter and rhyme, run-on lines are suited to the open form of much modern poetry. In the following lines from the 1967 poem "We Have Come Home," by the Gambian poet Lenrie Peters, run-on lines give the poem a conversational tone:

> *We have come home*
> *From the bloodless war*
> *With sunken hearts*
> *Our boots full of pride—*
> *From the true massacre of the soul*
> *When we have asked*
> *'What does it cost*
> *To be loved and left alone?'*

Rather than relying exclusively on end-stopped or run-on lines, poets often use a combination of the two to produce the effects they want. In the following lines from "Pot Roast" by Mark Strand, for example, the juxtaposition of end-stopped and run-on lines controls the rhythm:

> *I gaze upon the roast,*
> *that is sliced and laid out*
> *on my plate*
> *and over it*
> *I spoon the juices*
> *of carrot and onion.*
> *And for once I do not regret*
> *the passage of time.*

Poems for Further Reading: Rhythm and Meter

ADRIENNE RICH

(1929–   )

Aunt Jennifer's Tigers

(1951)

Aunt Jennifer's tigers prance across a screen,
Bright topaz denizens of a world of green.
They do not fear the men beneath the tree;
They pace in sleek chivalric certainty.

5 Aunt Jennifer's fingers fluttering through her wool
Find even the ivory needle hard to pull.
The massive weight of Uncle's wedding band
Sits heavily upon Aunt Jennifer's hand.

When Aunt is dead, her terrified hands will lie
10 Still ringed with ordeals she was mastered by.
The tigers in the panel that she made
Will go on prancing, proud and unafraid.

READING AND REACTING

1. What is the dominant metrical pattern of the poem? In what way does the meter enhance the ironic contrast the poem develops?

2. The lines in the first stanza are end-stopped, and those in the second and third stanzas combine end-stopped and run-on lines. What does the poet achieve by varying the rhythm?

3. What ideas do the caesuras in the first and fourth lines of the last stanza emphasize?

4. **JOURNAL ENTRY** What is the speaker's opinion of Aunt Jennifer's marriage? Do you think she is commenting on this particular marriage or on marriage in general?

5. **CRITICAL PERSPECTIVE** In her 1986 study of Rich's work, *The Aesthetics of Power*, Claire Keyes writes of this poem that although it is formally beautiful, almost perfect, its voice creates problems:

   [T]he tone seldom approaches intimacy, the speaker seeming fairly detached from the fate of Aunt Jennifer. . . . The dominant voice of the poem asserts the traditional theme that art outlives the person who produces it. . . . The

speaker is almost callous in her disregard for Aunt's death. . . . Who cares that Aunt Jennifer dies? The speaker does not seem to; she gets caught up in those gorgeous tigers. . . . Here lies the dominant voice: Aunt is not compelling; her creation is.

Do you agree with Keyes's reading of the poem?

ETHERIDGE KNIGHT

(1931–1991)

For Malcolm,[1] A Year After

(1986)

> Compose for Red[2] a proper verse;
> Adhere to foot and strict iamb;
> Control the burst of angry words
> Or they might boil and break the dam.
> 5 Or they might boil and overflow
> And drench me, drown me, drive me mad.
> So swear no oath, so shed no tear,
> And sing no song blue Baptist sad.
> Evoke no image, stir no flame,
> 10 And spin no yarn across the air.
> Make empty anglo tea lace words—
> Make them dead white and dry bone bare.
>
> Compose a verse for Malcolm man,
> And make it rime and make it prim.
> 15 The verse will die—as all men do—
> But not the memory of him!
> Death might come singing sweet like C,
> Or knocking like the old folk say,
> The moon and stars may pass away,
> 20 But not the anger of that day.

READING AND REACTING

1. Why do you think Knight chooses to write a "proper verse" in "strict iamb"? Do you think this meter is an appropriate choice for his subject?

---

[1] Malcolm X.

[2] Malcolm X's nickname when he was a young man.

2. What sounds and words are repeated in this poem? How does this repetition enhance the poem's rhythm?

3. Where in the poem does Knight use caesuras? Why does he use this device in each instance?

4. **JOURNAL ENTRY**   How would you describe the mood of the speaker? Is the poem's meter consistent with his mood or in conflict with it? Explain.

Alliteration and Assonance

Just as poetry depends on rhythm, it also depends on the sounds of individual words. An effect pleasing to the ear, such as "Did he who made the Lamb make thee?" from William Blake's "The Tyger" (p. 899), is called **euphony.** A jarring or discordant effect, such as "The vorpal blade went snicker-snack!" from Lewis Carroll's "Jabberwocky" (p. 822), is called **cacophony.**

One of the earliest, and perhaps the most primitive, methods of enhancing sound is **onomatopoeia,** which occurs when the sound of a word echoes its meaning, as it does in common words such as *bang, crash,* and *hiss.* Poets make broad application of this technique by using combinations of words that suggest a correspondence between sound and meaning. Notice how Edgar Allan Poe uses this device in the following segment from his poem "The Bells":

> Yet the ear, it fully knows,
>   By the twanging
>   And the clanging,
> How the danger ebbs and flows;
> Yet the ear distinctly tells,
>   In the jangling
>   And the wrangling
> How the danger sinks and swells
> By the sinking or the swelling in the anger of the bells—
>   Of the bells,—
> Of the bells, bells, bells, bells. . . .

Poe's primary objective in this poem is to recreate the sound of ringing bells. Although he succeeds, the poem (113 lines long in its entirety) is extremely tedious. A more subtle use of onomatopoetic words appears in the following passage from *An Essay on Criticism* by Alexander Pope:

> Soft is the strain when Zephyr gently blows,
> And the smooth stream in smoother numbers flows;
> But when the loud surges lash the sounding shore,
> The hoarse, rough verse should like the torrent roar:

When Ajax strives some rock's vast weight to throw,
The line too Labors, and the words move slow.

After earlier admonishing readers that sound must echo sense, Pope uses onomatopoetic words such as *lash* and *roar* to convey the fury of the sea, and he uses repeated consonants to echo the sounds these words suggest. Notice, for example, how the *s* and *m* sounds suggest the gently blowing Zephyr and the flowing of the smooth stream and how the series of *r* sounds echoes the torrent's roar.

Alliteration—the repetition of consonant sounds in consecutive or neighboring words, usually at the beginning of words—is another device used to enhance sound in a poem. Both Poe ("sinks and swells") and Pope ("smooth stream") make use of alliteration in the preceding excerpts, and so does Alfred, Lord Tennyson in the following poem.

ALFRED, LORD TENNYSON

(1809–1892)

The Eagle

(1851)

He clasps the crag with crooked hands;
Close to the sun in lonely lands,
Ringed with the azure world, he stands.

The wrinkled sea beneath him crawls:
5 He watches from his mountain walls,
And like a thunderbolt he falls.

Repeated hard *c* sounds in the first two lines of the poem give the lines a harsh, flinty quality that echoes the sharp sound of the eagle's claws holding fast to his rocky perch. The *l* sounds in line 2 ("lonely lands") slow down the rhythm of the line and thus reflect the expansiveness and isolation of the world in which the eagle lives.

The following poem also uses alliteration to create special aural effects.

N. SCOTT MOMADAY

(1934–   )

Comparatives

(1976)

Sunlit sea,
the drift of fronds,
and banners
of bobbing boats—
5 the seaside
upon the planks,
the coil and
crescent of flesh
extending
10 just into death.

Even so,
in the distant,
inland sea,
a shadow runs,
15 radiant,
rude in the rock:
fossil fish,
fissure of bone
forever.
20 It is perhaps
the same thing,
an agony
twice perceived.

It is most like
25 wind on waves—
mere commotion,
mute and mean,
perceptible—
that is all.

Throughout the poem, Momaday uses alliteration to create a subtle effect.
Repeated *s* sounds in line 1 echo the fluid motion of the sea, and in lines 3
and 4 *b* sounds suggest the bobbing of boats. In the second stanza, *r* sounds
evoke the smooth movement of a shadow across a rock. And finally, in the
third stanza, repeated *w* and *m* sounds suggest the wind blowing across the
waves.

Assonance—the repetition of the same or similar vowel sounds, especially in stressed syllables—can also enrich a poem. When used solely to produce aural effects, assonance can be distracting. Consider, for example, the monotony and clumsiness of the repeated vowel sounds in Tennyson's "Many a morning on the moorland did we hear the copses ring. . . ." When used more subtly, however, assonance can enhance the effectiveness of a poem, as it does in John Keats's "Bright Star" (p. 957).

> The moving waters at their priest-like task
>   Of pure ablution round earth's human shores

Notice how the repeated long vowel sounds suggest the liquid flow of the "moving waters." Certainly Keats could have used other words to describe the sea, but had he done so, he might have lost the aural reinforcement (and the beauty) that assonance provides.

Assonance can also unify an entire poem. In the following poem, assonance emphasizes the thematic connections among words and thus unifies the poem's ideas.

ROBERT HERRICK

(1591–1674)

Delight in Disorder

(1648)

A sweet disorder in the dress
Kindles in clothes a wantonness.
A lawn[1] about the shoulders thrown
Into a fine distractión;
5 An erring lace, which here and there
Enthralls the crimson stomacher;[2]
A cuff neglectful, and thereby
Ribbons to flow confusedly;
A winning wave, deserving note,
10 In the tempestuous petticoat;
A careless shoestring, in whose tie
I see a wild civility;
Do more bewitch me than when art
Is too precise in every part.

---

[1] A shawl made of fine fabric.

[2] A heavily embroidered garment worn by females over the chest and stomach.

Repeated vowel sounds extend throughout this poem—for instance, "sh<u>ou</u>lders" and "thr<u>ow</u>n" in line 3; and "t<u>ie</u>," "w<u>i</u>ld," and "prec<u>i</u>se" in lines 11, 12, and 14. Using alliteration as well as assonance, Herrick subtly links certain words—"<u>t</u>em<u>p</u>e<u>s</u>tuous <u>p</u>e<u>tt</u>icoat," for example. By connecting these words, he calls attention to the pattern of imagery that helps to convey the poem's theme.

Rhyme

In addition to alliteration and assonance, poets create sound patterns with **rhyme**—the use of matching sounds in two or more words: "tight" and "might"; "born" and "horn"; "sleep" and "deep." For a rhyme to be **perfect**, final vowel and consonant sounds must be the same, as they are in each of the preceding examples. **Imperfect rhyme** (sometimes called *near rhyme, slant rhyme, approximate rhyme,* or *consonance*) occurs when the final consonant sounds in two words are the same but vowel sounds are different—"learn/barn," or "pads/lids," for example. William Stafford uses imperfect rhyme in "Traveling through the Dark" (p. 1010) when he rhymes "road" with "dead." Finally, **eye rhyme** occurs when two words look alike but are pronounced differently—for example, "watch" and "catch."

Rhyme can also be classified according to the position of the rhyming syllables in a line of verse. The most common type of rhyme is **end rhyme,** which occurs at the end of a line.

> *Tyger! Tyger! burning <u>bright</u>*
> *In the forests of the <u>night</u>*
> > William Blake, "The Tyger"

Internal rhyme occurs within a line.

> *The Sun came up upon the left,*
> *Out of the <u>sea</u> came <u>he</u>!*
> *And he shone <u>bright</u> and on the <u>right</u>*
> *Went down into the sea.*
> > Samuel Taylor Coleridge, "The Rime
> > of the Ancient Mariner"

Beginning rhyme occurs at the beginning of a line.

> *Red River, red river,*
> *<u>Slow</u> flow heat is silence*
> *<u>No</u> will is still as a river*
> *Still. Will heat move*
> > T. S. Eliot, "Virginia"

Rhyme can also be classified according to the number of syllables that correspond. **Masculine rhyme** (also called **rising rhyme**) occurs when single syllables correspond ("can"/"ran"; "descend"/"contend"). **Feminine rhyme** (also called **double rhyme** or **falling rhyme**) occurs when two syllables, a stressed one followed by an unstressed one, correspond ("ocean"/"motion"; "leaping"/"sleeping"). Finally, **triple rhyme** occurs when three syllables correspond. Less common than the other two, triple rhyme is frequently used for humorous or satiric purposes, as in the following lines from the long poem *Don Juan* by Lord Byron:

> *Sagest of women, even of widows, she*
> > *Resolved that Juan should be quite a <u>paragon</u>,*
> *And worthy of the noblest pedigree:*
> > *(His sire of Castile, his dam from <u>Aragon</u>).*

In some cases—for example, when it is overused or used in unexpected places—rhyme can create unusual and even comic effects. In the following poem, humor is created by the incongruous connections established by rhymes such as "priest"/"beast" and "pajama"/"lllama."

OGDEN NASH

(1902–1971)

The Lama

(1931)

> The one-l lama
> He's a priest.
> The two-l llama,
> He's a beast.
> 5 And I will bet
> A silk pajama
> There isn't any
> Three-l lllama.

The conventional way to describe a poem's rhyme scheme is to chart rhyming sounds that appear at the ends of lines. The sound that ends the first line is designated *a*, and all subsequent lines that end in that sound are also labeled *a*. The next sound to appear at the end of a line, and all other lines whose last sounds rhyme with it, are designated *b*, and so on. The lines of the poem that follows have been labeled in this manner.

RICHARD WILBUR

(1921–   )

A Sketch

(1975)

Into the lower right   *a*
Square of the window frame   *b*
There came   *b*
            with scalloped flight   *a*

5   A goldfinch, lit upon   *c*
The dead branch of a pine,   *d*
Shining,   *d*
            and then was gone,   *c*

Tossed in a double arc   *e*
10 Upward into the thatched   *f*
And cross-hatched   *f*
            pine-needle dark.   *e*

Briefly, as fresh drafts stirred   *g*
The tree, he dulled and gleamed   *h*
15 And seemed   *h*
            more coal than bird,   *g*

Then, dodging down, returned   *i*
In a new light, his perch   *j*
A birch—   *j*
20   twig, where he burned   *i*

In the sun's broadside ray,   *k*
Some seed pinched in his bill.   *l*
Yet still   *l*
            he did not stay,   *k*

25 But into a leaf-choken pane,   *m*
Changeful as even in heaven,   *n*
Even   *n*
            in Saturn's reign,   *m*

Tunneled away and hid.   *o*
30 And then? But I cannot well   *p*
Tell   *p*
            you all that he did.   *o*

It was like glancing at rough   *q*
Sketches tacked on a wall,   *r*
35 And all   *r*
         so less than enough   *q*

Of gold on beaten wing,   *s*
I could not choose that one   *t*
Be done   *t*
40   as the finished thing.   *s*

Although the rhyme scheme of this poem (*abba, cddc,* etc.) is regular, it is hardly noticeable until it is charted. This does not mean, however, that the rhyme is unimportant. On the contrary, the rhyme scheme reinforces the poem's meaning and binds lines into structural units, connecting the first and fourth as well as the second and third lines of each stanza. In stanza 1 "right" and "flight" draw lines 1 and 4 of the stanza together, enclosing "fame" and "came" in lines 2 and 3. The pattern begins again with the next stanza and continues through the rest of the poem. Like the elusive goldfinch the poet describes, the rhymes are difficult to follow with the eye. In this sense the rhyme reflects the central theme of the poem: the difficulty of capturing in words a reality which, like the goldfinch, is forever shifting.

Naturally, rhyme does not have to be subtle to enrich a poem. An obvious rhyme scheme can communicate meaning by forcing attention on a relationship between ideas that are not normally linked. Notice how Alexander Pope uses this technique in the following excerpt from *An Essay on Man:*

> *Honour and shame from no condition rise;*
> *Act well your part, there all the honour lies.*
> *Fortune in men has some small diff'rence made,*
> *One flaunts in rags, one flutters in brocade;*
> *The cobbler aproned, and the parson gowned,*
> *The friar hooded, and the monarch crowned.*
> *"What differ more (you cry) than crown and cowl?"*
> *I'll tell you, friend; a wise man and a fool.*
>
> *You'll find, if once the monarch acts the monk,*
> *Or, cobbler-like, the parson will be drunk,*
> *Worth makes the man, and want of it, the fellow;*
> *The rest is all but leather or prunella.*[1]
> *   Stuck o'er with titles and hung round with strings,*
> *That thou mayest be by kings, or whores of kings.*
> *Boast the pure blood of an illustrious race,*

---

[1] Heavy cloth the color of prunes.

In quiet flow from Lucrece[2] to Lucrece;
But by your fathers' worth if yours you rate,
Count me those only who were good and great.

The lines of this poem are written in **heroic couplets,** with a rhyme scheme of *aa, bb, cc, dd,* and so on. In heroic couplets, greater stress falls on the second line of each pair, usually on the last word of the line. Coming at the end of the line, this word receives double emphasis: It is strengthened both because of its position in the line and because it is rhymed with the last word of the couplet's first line. In some cases rhyme joins opposing ideas, thereby reinforcing a theme that runs through the passage: the contrast between the high and the low, the virtuous and the immoral. For example, "gowned" and "crowned" in lines 5 and 6 convey the opposite conditions of the parson and the monarch and exemplify the idea expressed in lines 3 and 4 that fortune, not virtue, determines one's station. Throughout this passage, then, rhyme emphasizes key ideas and helps to convey the meaning of the poem.

Poems for Further Reading: Alliteration, Assonance, and Rhyme

ALICE WALKER

(1944–   )

Revolutionary Petunias

(1972)

Sammy Lou of Rue
sent to his reward
the exact creature who
murdered her husband,
5 using a cultivator's hoe
with verve and skill;
and laughed fit to kill
in disbelief
at the angry, militant
10 pictures of herself
the Sonneteers quickly drew:
not any of them people that
she knew.

---

[2] In Roman legend, she stabbed herself after being defiled by Sextus Tarquinius.

> A backwoods woman
> 15 her house was papered with
> funeral home calendars and
> faces appropriate for a Mississippi
> Sunday School. She raised a George,
> a Martha, a Jackie and a Kennedy. Also
> 20 a John Wesley Junior.[1]
> "Always respect the word of God,"
> she said on her way to she didn't
> know where, except it would be by
> electric chair, and she continued
> 25 "Don't yall forget to *water*
> my purple petunias."

READING AND REACTING

1. Although this poem has no definite rhyme scheme, it does contain some words that rhyme. Why do you think Walker uses rhyme in each case? What, if anything, do these rhymes add to the poem?

2. The first line contains an example of internal rhyme. Are there other examples? What does the internal rhyme in this poem accomplish?

3. **JOURNAL ENTRY** What is the significance of Sammy Lou's last words? How do they help you interpret the poem's title?

GERARD MANLEY HOPKINS

(1844–1889)

Pied Beauty

(1918)

> Glory be to God for dappled things—
> For skies of couple-color as a brinded[1] cow;
>   For rose-moles all in stipple upon trout that swim;
> Fresh-firecoal chestnut-falls; finches' wings;
> 5   Landscape plotted and pieced—fold, fallow, and plow;
>   And áll trádes, their gear and tackle and trim.[2]

---

[1] John Wesley (1730–1791), a British religious leader and the founder of Methodism.

[1] Brindled (streaked).

[2] Equipment.

All things counter, original, spare, strange;
  Whatever is fickle, freckled (who knows how?)
   With swift, slow; sweet, sour; adazzle, dim;
10 He fathers-forth whose beauty is past change:
    Praise him.

READING AND REACTING

1. Identify examples of onomatopoeia, alliteration, assonance, imperfect rhyme, and perfect rhyme. Do you think all these techniques are essential to the poem? Are any of them annoying or distracting?

2. What is the central theme of this poem? In what way do the sounds of the poem help to communicate this idea?

3. Identify examples of masculine and feminine rhyme.

4. **JOURNAL ENTRY** Hopkins uses both pleasing and discordant sounds in his poem. Identify uses of euphony and cacophony, and explain how these techniques affect your reactions to the poem.

W. H. AUDEN

(1907–1973)

As I Walked Out One Evening
(1940)

As I walked out one evening,
  Walking down Bristol Street,
The crowds upon the pavement
  Were fields of harvest wheat.

5 And down by the brimming river
  I heard a lover sing
Under an arch of the railway:
  "Love has no ending.

  "I'll love you, dear, I'll love you
10 Till China and Africa meet,
And the river jumps over the mountain
  And the salmon sing in the street,

  "I'll love you till the ocean
  Is folded and hung up to dry,
15 And the seven stars go squawking
  Like geese about the sky.

"The years shall run like rabbits,
    For in my arms I hold
The Flower of the Ages,
20   And the first love of the world."

But all the clocks in the city
    Began to whirr and chime:
"O let not Time deceive you,
    You cannot conquer Time.

25 "In the burrows of the Nightmare
    Where Justice naked is,
Time watches from the shadow
    And coughs when you would kiss.

"In headaches and in worry
30   Vaguely life leaks away,
And Time will have his fancy
    Tomorrow or today.

"Into many a green valley
    Drifts the appalling snow;
35 Time breaks the threaded dances
    And the diver's brilliant bow.

"O plunge your hands in water,
    Plunge them in up to the wrist;
Stare, stare in the basin
40   And wonder what you've missed.

"The glacier knocks in the cupboard,
    The desert sighs in the bed,
And the crack in the teacup opens
    A lane to the land of the dead.

45 "Where the beggars raffle the banknotes
    And the Giant is enchanting to Jack,
And the Lily-white Boy is a Roarer,
    And Jill goes down on her back.

"O look, look in the mirror,
50   O look in your distress;
Life remains a blessing
    Although you cannot bless.

"O stand, stand at the window
          As the tears scald and start;
55 You shall love your crooked neighbor
          With your crooked heart."

          It was late, late in the evening,
          The lovers they were gone;
          The clocks had ceased their chiming,
60   And the deep river ran on.

READING AND REACTING

1. In lines 2 and 4 of almost every stanza Auden uses perfect end rhyme. In stanzas 5 and 7, however, he uses imperfect rhyme. Should he have been more consistent in his use of rhyme? Would the poetic effect have been better had he consistently used perfect rhyme?

2. What is the poem's rhyme scheme? Where does Auden use alliteration and assonance? Does he use internal rhyme? In what other ways does he use sound?

3. Does Auden's use of sound reinforce the poem's content or undercut it?

4. **JOURNAL ENTRY**   Could this poem be considered a love poem? How are its sentiments about love different from those conventionally expressed in poems about love?

5. **CRITICAL PERSPECTIVE**   In a 1940 British review of Auden's work, T. C. Worlsey made the following comments about this poem:

   There is no technical reason why such a poem as [this] should not be popular; the metre and the rhythm are easy and helpful, and the symbols have reference to a world of experience common to every inhabitant of these islands. Here . . . the poet has gone as far as he can along the road to creating a popular poetry.

   Does Auden's poem strike you as a model for "popular" poetry—that is, poetry for people who don't usually read poetry?

LEWIS CARROLL

(1832–1898)

Jabberwocky

(1871)

'Twas brillig, and the slithy toves
    Did gyre and gimble in the wabe:
All mimsy were the borogoves,
    And the mome raths outgrabe.

5 "Beware the Jabberwock, my son!
    The jaws that bite, the claws that catch!
Beware the Jubjub bird, and shun
    The frumious Bandersnatch!"

He took his vorpal sword in hand;
10   Long time the manxome foe he sought—
So rested he by the Tumtum tree
    And stood awhile in thought.

And, as in uffish thought he stood,
    The Jabberwock, with eyes of flame,
15 Came whiffling through the tulgey wood,
    And burbled as it came!

One, two! One, two! And through and through
    The vorpal blade went snicker-snack!
He left it dead, and with its head
20   He went galumphing back.

"And hast thou slain the Jabberwock?
    Come to my arms, my beamish boy!
O frabjous day! Callooh, Callay!"
    He chortled in his joy.

25 'Twas brillig, and the slithy toves
    Did gyre and gimble in the wabe:
All mimsy were the borogoves,
    And the mome raths outgrabe.

READING AND REACTING

1. Many words in this poem may be unfamiliar to you. Are they actual
words? Use a dictionary to check before you dismiss any. Do some

words seem to have meaning in the context of the poem regardless of whether or not they appear in the dictionary? Explain.

2. This poem contains many examples of onomatopoeia. What ideas do the various words' sounds suggest?

3. **JOURNAL ENTRY** Summarize the story the poem tells. In what sense is this poem a story of a young man's initiation into adulthood?

4. **CRITICAL PERSPECTIVE** According to Humpty Dumpty in Carroll's *Alice in Wonderland,* the nonsense words in the poem are *portmanteau words* (that is, words whose form and meaning are derived from two other distinct words—as *smog* is a portmanteau of *smoke* and *fog*). Critic Elizabeth Sewell, however, rejects this explanation: "*[F]rumious,* for instance, is not a word, and does not have two meanings packed up in it; it is a group of letters without any meaning at all. . . . [I]t looks like other words, and almost certainly more than two."

Which nonsense words in the poem seem to you to be portmanteau words, and which do not? Can you suggest possible sources for those words that are not portmanteau words?

▼▼▼

CHECKLIST FOR WRITING ABOUT SOUND

RHYTHM AND METER

◆ Does the poem contain repeated words and phrases? If so, how do they help to create rhythm?

◆ Does the poem have regular meter, or does the meter vary from line to line?

◆ How does the meter contribute to the overall effect of the poem?

◆ Which lines of the poem contain caesuras? What effect do they have?

◆ Are the lines of the poem end-stopped, run-on, or a combination of the two? What effects are produced by the presence or absence of pauses at the ends of lines?

ALLITERATION, ASSONANCE, AND RHYME

◆ Does the poem contain any examples of onomatopoeia?

◆ Are there any examples of alliteration or assonance?

◆ Does the poem have a regular rhyme scheme?

◆ Does the poem use internal rhyme? Beginning rhyme?

◆ Does the poem include examples of masculine, feminine, or triple rhyme?

◆ In what ways does rhyme create unity?

◆ How does the rhyme reinforce the ideas in the poem?

▲▲▲

WRITING SUGGESTIONS: SOUND

1. William Blake's "The Tyger" appeared in a collection entitled *Songs of Experience*. Compare this poem (p. 899) to "The Lamb" (p. 898), which appeared in a collection called *Songs of Innocence*. In what way are the speakers in these two poems relatively "innocent" or "experienced"? How does sound help to convey the voice of the speakers in these two poems?

2. Write an essay in which you compare the themes of "Aunt Jennifer's Tigers" (p. 807) and "Revolutionary Petunias" (p. 817). In what ways does sound reinforce each poem's themes?

3. "Sadie and Maud" (p. 799), like "The Faithful Wife" (p. 728), "My Papa's Waltz" (p. 642), and "Daddy" (p. 779), communicates attitudes toward home and family. How does the presence or absence of rhyme in these poems help to convey their respective ideas about this subject?

4. Robert Frost once said that writing poems that have no meter is like playing tennis without a net. What do you think he meant? Do you agree? After reading "Out, Out—" (p. 786), "Stopping By Woods on a Snowy Evening" (p. 936), and "The Road Not Taken" (p. 934), write an essay in which you assess Frost's use of meter.

5. Select two or three contemporary poems that have no end rhyme. Write an essay in which you discuss what these poets gain and lose by not using rhyme.

CHAPTER 18

Form

Dryden chose the couplet because he thought it the plainest mode available, the verse "nearest prose," and he chose it in conscious reaction against the artificial stanzaic modes that had dominated English poetry during most of the sixteenth and seventeenth centuries. In short, he and his followers thought they were liberating poetry, just as Coleridge and Wordsworth liberated it a hundred years later, or Pound and Williams a hundred years after that. The history of poetry is a continual fixing and freeing of conventions.

HAYDEN CARRUTH, "THE QUESTION OF POETIC FORM"

Yeats said that the finished poem made a sound like the click of the lid on a perfectly made box. One-hundred-and-forty syllables, organized into a sonnet, do not necessarily make a click; the same number of syllables, dispersed in asymmetric lines of free verse, will click like a lid if the poem is good. In the sonnet and in the free verse poem, the poet improvises toward that click, and achieves his resolution in unpredictable ways. The rhymes and line lengths of the sonnet are too gross to contribute greatly to that sense of resolution. The click is our sense of lyric form.

DONALD HALL, "GOATFOOT, MILKTONGUE, TWINBIRD"

No verse can be free, it must be governed by some measure, but not by the old measure.

WILLIAM CARLOS WILLIAMS, "ON MEASURE"

As for poetic form, Black writers have experimented with all forms and with no traditional form. Afro-American literature in its most indigenous expression is not written in any Anglo-Saxon form, but takes the form of all Oriental literature (this is particularly true of the poetry), that literature from which all Western writers have copied or modified forms, the free alliterative verse that includes the use of any or all devices used to get music into free verse along with the key to wisdom literature—that key of parallelism of structure and thought.

The folk ballad is not as Oriental as that free line of alliterative verse, but it is still the oldest form of poetry. The Arabs were masters of the nomadic song, the love lyric, and the song of praise (more than 3,000 years of songs of praise exist); all Asia and Africa sang before the Saxons recorded their epics and romances. The Black writer in the United States does have a heritage, a literary heritage as ancient as the first record of life; and in a new land, in a strange land, even as slaves, Black people sang songs in a new language and made a new art to express their pain.

MARGARET WALKER, *THE HUMANISTIC TRADITION
OF AFRO-AMERICAN LITERATURE*

Poetic forms—meters, rhyming patterns, the shaping of poems into symmetrical blocks of lines called couplets or stanzas—have existed since poetry was an oral activity. Such forms can easily become format, of course, where the dynamics of experience and desire are forced to fit a pattern to which they have no organic relationship. People are often taught in school to confuse closed poetic forms (or formulas) with poetry itself, the lifeblood of the poem. Or, that a poem consists merely in a series of sentences broken (formatted) into short lines called "free verse." But a closed form like the sestina, the sonnet, the villanelle remains inert formula or format unless the "triggering subject," as Richard Hugo called it, acts on the imagination to make the form evolve, become responsive, or works almost in resistance to the form. It's a struggle not to let the form take over, lapse into format, assimilate the poetry; and that very struggle can produce a movement, a music, of its own.

ADRIENNE RICH, "WHAT IS FOUND THERE"

JOHN KEATS
(1795–1821)

On the Sonnet

(1819)

> If by dull rhymes our English must be chained,
> And like Andromeda,[1] the sonnet sweet
> Fettered, in spite of painéd loveliness,
> Let us find, if we must be constrained,
> 5 Sandals more interwoven and complete
> To fit the naked foot of Poesy:
> Let us inspect the lyre, and weigh the stress
> Of every chord, and see what may be gained
> By ear industrious, and attention meet;

---

[1] In Greek mythology, Andromeda was chained to a rock to appease a sea monster.

10 Misers of sound and syllable, no less
   Than Midas[2] of his coinage, let us be
   Jealous of dead leaves in the bay-wreath crown;
   So, if we may not let the Muse be free,
   She will be bound with garlands of her own.

The **form** of a literary work is its structure or shape, the way its parts fit together to form a whole; **poetic form** is the design of a poem described in terms of rhyme, meter, and stanzaic pattern.

Until the twentieth century, most poetry was written in **closed form** (sometimes called **fixed form**), characterized by regular patterns of meter, rhyme, line length, and stanzaic divisions. Early poems that were passed down through the oral tradition—epics and ballads, for example—relied on regular form to facilitate memorization. Even after poems were written down, poets tended to favor regular patterns. In fact, until relatively recently, regular form was what distinguished poetry from prose. Of course, strict adherence to regular patterns sometimes produced poems that were, in John Keats's words, "chained" by "dull rhymes" and "fettered" by the rules governing a particular form. But rather than feeling "constrained" by form, many poets experimented with imagery, figures of speech, allusion, and other techniques—stretching closed form to its limits.

As they sought new means of expression, poets turned to forms used by poets in other cultures, adapting them to the demands of their own languages. English and American poets, for example, adopted (and still use) early French forms, such as the villanelle and the sestina, and early Italian forms, such as the Petrarchan sonnet and terza rima. More recently, the nineteenth-century American poet Henry Wadsworth Longfellow studied Icelandic epics; the twentieth-century poet Ezra Pound studied the works of French troubadours; and Pound and other twentieth-century American poets, such as Richard Wright and Carolyn Kizer, were inspired by Japanese haiku. Other American poets, such as Vachel Lindsay, Langston Hughes, and Maya Angelou, looked closer to home—to the rhythms of blues, jazz, and spirituals—for inspiration.

As time went on, more and more poets moved away from closed form to experiment with **open form** poetry (sometimes called **free verse** or *vers libre*), varying line length within a poem, dispensing with stanzaic divisions, breaking lines in unexpected places, and even abandoning any semblance of formal structure. In English, nineteenth-century poets—such as William Blake and Matthew Arnold—experimented with lines of irregular meter and length, and Walt Whitman wrote **prose poems,** open form poems whose long lines made them look like prose. (Well before this time,

---

[2] King Midas was granted his wish that all he touched would turn to gold.

Asian poetry and some biblical passages had used a type of free verse.) In nineteenth-century France, Symbolist poets such as Baudelaire, Rimbaud, Verlaine, and Mallarmé also used free verse. Later, in the early twentieth century, a group of American poets including Ezra Pound, William Carlos Williams, and Amy Lowell, who were associated with a movement known as **imagism,** wrote poetry that dispensed with traditional principles of English versification, creating new rhythms and meters.

Although much contemporary English and American poetry is composed in open form, many poets also write in closed form—even in very traditional, highly structured patterns. Still, new forms, and new variations of old forms, are being created all the time. And, because contemporary poets do not feel bound by rules or restrictions about what constitutes "acceptable" poetic form, they are free to discover the form that best suits the poem's purpose, subject, language, and theme.

Closed Form

A **closed form** (or *fixed form*) poem looks symmetrical; it has an identifiable, repeated pattern, with lines of similar length arranged in groups of two, three, four, or more. Such poems also tend to rely on regular metrical patterns and rhyme schemes.

Despite what its name suggests, closed form poetry does not have to be confining or conservative. Sometimes contemporary poets experiment by using characteristics of open form poetry (such as lines of varying length) within a closed form, or by moving back and forth within a single poem from open to closed to open form. Sometimes they (like their eighteenth-century counterparts) experiment with closed form by combining different stanzaic forms (stanzas of two and three lines, for example) within a single poem.

Even when poets work within a traditional closed form, such as a **sonnet,** they can still break new ground. For example, they can create a sonnet with an unexpected meter or rhyme scheme, add an extra line or even extra stanzas to a traditional sonnet form, combine two different traditional sonnet forms in a single poem, or write an abbreviated version of a lengthy form, such as a **sestina** or a **villanelle.** (See the section on Traditional Closed Forms in this chapter for examples of such experiments.) In other words, poets can use traditional forms as building blocks, combining them in innovative ways to create new patterns and new forms.

Sometimes a pattern simply determines the meter of a poem's individual lines. At other times the pattern extends to the stanza level, with lines arranged into groups. At still other times, as in the case of traditional closed forms, a poetic pattern gives shape to an entire poem.

Blank Verse

Blank verse is unrhymed poetry with each line written in a set pattern of five stressed and five unstressed syllables called **iambic pentameter** (see p. 802). Many passages from Shakespeare's plays, such as the following lines from *Hamlet*, are written in blank verse:

> *To sleep, perchance to dream, ay there's the rub,*
> *For in that sleep of death what dreams may come*
> *When we have shuffled off this mortal coil*
> *Must give us pause—there's the respect*
> *That makes calamity of so long life:*

For a contemporary use of blank verse, see John Updike's "Ex-Basketball Player" (p. 772).

Stanza

A **stanza** is a group of two or more lines with the same metrical pattern—and often with a regular rhyme scheme as well—separated by blank space from other such groups of lines. The stanza in poetry is like the paragraph in prose: It groups related thoughts into units.

A two-line stanza with rhyming lines of similar length and meter is called a **couplet**. The **heroic couplet**, first used by Chaucer and especially popular throughout the eighteenth century, consists of two rhymed lines of iambic pentameter, with a weak pause after the first line and a strong pause after the second. The following example, from Alexander Pope's *An Essay on Criticism*, is a heroic couplet:

> *True ease in writing comes from art, not chance,*
> *As those move easiest who have learned to dance.*

Contemporary poems composed of couplets include Maxine Kumin's "Morning Swim" (p. 963) and Barry Spacks's "Finding a Yiddish Paper on the Riverside Line" (p. 1009).

A three-line stanza with lines of similar length and a set rhyme scheme is called a **tercet**. Percy Bysshe Shelley's "Ode to the West Wind" (p. 997) is built largely of tercets:

> *O wild West Wind, thou breath of Autumn's being,*
> *Thou, from whose unseen presence the leaves dead*
> *Are driven, like ghosts from an enchanter fleeing,*
>
> *Yellow, and black, and pale, and hectic red,*
> *Pestilence-stricken multitudes: O Thou,*
> *Who chariotest to their dark wintry bed*

Although in many tercets all three lines rhyme, "Ode to the West Wind" uses a special rhyme scheme, also used by Dante, called **terza rima.** This rhyme scheme (*aba, bcb, cdc, ded,* and so on) creates an interlocking series of stanzas: Line 2's *dead* looks ahead to the rhyming words *red* and *bed,* which close lines 4 and 6, and the pattern continues throughout the poem.

A four-line stanza with lines of similar length and a set rhyme scheme is called a **quatrain.** The quatrain, the most widely used and versatile unit in English and American poetry, is used by William Wordsworth in the following excerpt from "She Dwelt among the Untrodden Ways" (p. 1027):

> *A violet by a mossy stone*
> > *Half hidden from the eye!*
> *Fair as a star, when only one*
> > *Is shining in the sky.*

Quatrains are frequently used by contemporary poets as well—for instance, in Theodore Roethke's "My Papa's Waltz" (p. 642), Adrienne Rich's "Aunt Jennifer's Tigers" (p. 807), and William Stafford's "Traveling through the Dark" (p. 1010).

One special kind of quatrain, called the **ballad stanza,** alternates lines of eight and six syllables; typically, only the second and fourth lines rhyme. The following lines from "Sir Patrick Spence" (p. 893) illustrate the ballad stanza:

> *The king sits in Dumferling toune,*
> > *Drinking the blude-reid wine:*
> *'O whar will I get guid sailor*
> > *To sail this schip of mine?'*

Common measure, a four-line stanzaic pattern closely related to the ballad stanza, is used in hymns as well as in poetry. It differs from the ballad stanza in that its rhyme scheme is *abab* rather than *abcb.* In contemporary poetry this pattern appears in Donald Hall's "My Son, My Executioner" (p. 788).

Other stanzaic forms include **rhyme royal,** a seven-line stanza *(ababbcc)* set in iambic pentameter, used in Sir Thomas Wyatt's sixteenth-century poem "They Flee from Me That Sometimes Did Me Seke" as well as in Theodore Roethke's twentieth-century "I Knew a Woman" (p. 720); **ottava rima,** an eight-line stanza *(abababcc)* set in iambic pentameter; and the Spenserian stanza, a nine-line form *(ababbcbcc)* whose first eight lines are set in iambic pentameter and whose last line is in iambic hexameter. The Romantic poets John Keats and Percy Bysshe Shelley were among those who used this form. (See Chapter 17 for definitions and examples of various metrical patterns.)

Traditional Closed Forms

The Sonnet

Perhaps the most familiar kind of traditional closed form poem written in English is the **sonnet,** a fourteen-line poem with a distinctive rhyme scheme and metrical pattern. The English or **Shakespearean sonnet,** which consists of fourteen lines divided into three quatrains and a concluding couplet, is written in iambic pentameter and follows the rhyme scheme *abab cdcd efef gg.* The **Petrarchan sonnet,** popularized in the fourteenth century by the Italian Francesco Petrarch, also consists of fourteen lines of iambic pentameter, but these lines are divided into an eight-line unit called an **octave** and a six-line unit (composed of two tercets) called a **sestet.** The rhyme scheme of the octave is *abba abba;* the rhyme scheme of the sestet is *cde cde.*

The conventional structures of these sonnet forms reflect the arrangement of ideas within a poem: In the Shakespearean sonnet the poet typically presents three "paragraphs" of related thoughts, introducing an idea in the first quatrain, developing it in the two remaining quatrains, and summing up in a succinct closing couplet. In the Petrarchan sonnet the octave introduces a problem that is resolved in the sestet. (Many Shakespearean sonnets also have a problem-solution structure.) Some poets vary the traditional patterns somewhat to suit the poem's language or ideas. For example, they may depart from the pattern to sidestep a forced rhyme or unnatural stress on a syllable, or they may not place the problem-solution break between octave and sestet.

The following poem follows the form of a traditional English sonnet.

WILLIAM SHAKESPEARE

(1564–1616)

When, in Disgrace with Fortune and Men's Eyes

(1609)

When, in disgrace with Fortune and men's eyes,
I all alone beweep my outcast state,
And trouble deaf heaven with my bootless[1] cries,
And look upon myself and curse my fate,
5 Wishing me like to one more rich in hope,
Featured like him, like him with friends possessed,
Desiring this man's art, and that man's scope,
With what I most enjoy contented least,
Yet in these thoughts myself almost despising,
10 Haply[2] I think on thee, and then my state,

---

[1] Futile.

[2] Luckily.

> Like to the lark at break of day arising
> From sullen earth, sings hymns at heaven's gate;
>   For thy sweet love rememb'red such wealth brings
>   That then I scorn to change my state with kings.

This sonnet is written in iambic pentameter and has a conventional rhyme scheme: *abab* (eyes-state-cries-fate), *cdcd* (hope-possessed-scope-least), *efef* (despising-state-arising-gate), *gg* (brings-kings). In this poem, in which the speaker explains how thoughts of his loved one can rescue him from despair, each quatrain is unified by rhyme as well as by subject. In the first quatrain the speaker presents his problem: He is down on his luck and out of favor with his peers, isolated in self-pity and cursing his fate. In the second quatrain he develops this idea further: He is envious of others and dissatisfied with things that usually please him. In the third quatrain the focus shifts: Although the first two quatrains develop a dependent clause ("When. . . .") that introduces a problem, line 9 begins to present the resolution. In the third quatrain the speaker explains how, in the midst of his despair and self-hatred, he thinks of his loved one, and his spirits soar. The closing couplet sums up the mood transformation the poem describes and explains its significance: When the speaker realizes the emotional riches his loved one gives him, he is no longer envious of others.

Poems for Further Reading: The Sonnet

CLAUDE MCKAY

(1890–1948)

The White City

(1922)

> I will not toy with it nor bend an inch.
> Deep in the secret chambers of my heart
> I muse my life-long hate, and without flinch
> I bear it nobly as I live my part.
> 5 My being would be a skeleton, a shell,
> If this dark Passion that fills my every mood,
> And makes my heaven in the white world's hell,
> Did not forever feed me vital blood.
> I see the mighty city through a mist—

10 The strident trains that speed the goaded mass,
The poles and spires and towers vapor-kissed,
The fortressed port through which the great ships pass,
The tides, the wharves, the dens I contemplate,
Are sweet like wanton loves because I hate.

READING AND REACTING

1. In what sense is the speaker's mood similar to that of the speaker in "When, in Disgrace with Fortune and Men's Eyes" (p. 831)? How is it different?

2. How is the speaker's description of the city in the third quatrain consistent with the emotions he expresses in lines 1–8?

3. The closing couplet of a Shakespearean sonnet traditionally sums up the sonnet's concerns. Is this true here? Explain.

4. **JOURNAL ENTRY**   Given the speaker's passionate anger at "the white world's hell" in which he lives, what, if anything, do you think McKay would have gained by writing his poem in open form—for example, in a **prose poem**—instead of in a sonnet?

5. **CRITICAL PERSPECTIVE**   According to Tyrone Tillery's 1992 biography of McKay, the poet chose the sonnet form because "he found [it] admirable for a moment's thought. He understood that he had a tendency to be diffuse and repetitive, and he felt that tight rhythmic and metric forms helped him check these faults." Critic Onwuchekwa Jemie, in a 1973 survey of Harlem Renaissance poets, saw a paradox in McKay's use of the "old-fashioned" sonnet form to contain "venom and rage." Noting that "[e]ach of his protest sonnets just about explodes from the page," Jemie observes that "McKay's attacks on the white world are carried out in one of that culture's most entrenched and conservative poetic forms. McKay's words deny the white world, but his form, style, language, and poetic attitude tend to affirm it." Jemie concludes, "It is the mark of his achievement that he is able to work that fragile sonnet frame into a vehicle of dynamite."

   How do these observations help you to understand why McKay chose to express his ideas in a sonnet? Do you think he made the right choice?

JOHN KEATS

(1795–1821)

On First Looking into
Chapman's Homer[1]

(1816)

Much have I traveled in the realms of gold,
    And many goodly states and kingdoms seen;
    Round many western islands have I been
Which bards in fealty to Apollo[2] hold.
5 Oft of one wide expanse had I been told
    That deep-browed Homer ruled as his demesne,[3]
    Yet did I never breathe its pure serene[4]
Till I heard Chapman speak out loud and bold.
Then felt I like some watcher of the skies
10   When a new planet swims into his ken;
Or like stout Cortez[5] when with eagle eyes
    He stared at the Pacific—and all his men
Looked at each other with a wild surmise—
    Silent, upon a peak in Darien.[6]

READING AND REACTING

1. Is this a Petrarchan or a Shakespearean sonnet? Explain your conclusion.

2. **JOURNAL ENTRY** The sestet's change of focus is introduced with the word "Then" in line 9. How does the mood of the sestet differ from the mood of the octave? How does the language differ?

3. **CRITICAL PERSPECTIVE** Biographer Aileen Ward offers an interesting explanation to suggest the reason for the excitement Keats felt "On First Looking into Chapman's Homer." Homer's epic tales of gods and heroes were known to most readers of Keats's day only in a

---

[1] The translation of Homer by Elizabethan poet George Chapman.

[2] Greek god of light, truth, reason, male beauty; associated with music and poetry.

[3] Realm, domain.

[4] Air, atmosphere.

[5] It was Vasco de Balboa (not Hernando Cortez as Keats suggests) who first saw the Pacific Ocean, from "a peak in Darien."

[6] Former name of the Isthmus of Panama.

very formal eighteenth-century translation by Alexander Pope. For instance, this is Pope's description of Ulysses escaping from a shipwreck:

> *his knees no more*
> *Perform'd their office, or his weight upheld:*
> *His swoln heart heav'd, his bloated body swell'd:*
> *From mouth to nose the briny torrent ran,*
> *And lost in lassitude lay all the man,*
> *Deprived of voice, of motion, and of breath,*
> *The soul scarce waking in the arms of death . . .*

In a rare 1616 edition of Chapman's translation, Keats discovered a very different poem:

> *both knees falt'ring, both*
> *His strong hands hanging down, and all with froth*
> *His cheeks and nostrils flowing, voice and breath*
> *Spent to all use, and down he sank to death.*
> *The sea had soak'd his heart through. . . .*

This, as Ward notes, was "poetry of a kind that had not been written in England for two hundred years."

Do you think Keats's own poem seems closer in its form and language to Pope or to Chapman?

GWENDOLYN BROOKS

(1917–   )

First Fight. Then Fiddle

(1949)

First fight. Then fiddle. Ply the slipping string
With feathery sorcery; muzzle the note
With hurting love; the music that they wrote
Bewitch, bewilder. Qualify to sing
5 Threadwise. Devise no salt, no hempen thing
For the dear instrument to bear. Devote
The bow to silks and honey. Be remote
A while from malice and from murdering.
But first to arms, to armor. Carry hate
10 In front of you and harmony behind.
Be deaf to music and to beauty blind.
Win war. Rise bloody, maybe not too late
For having first to civilize a space
Wherein to play your violin with grace.

Reading and Reacting

1. What is the subject of Brooks's poem? What do you think she means by "fight" and "fiddle"?

2. What is the poem's rhyme scheme? Is it an essential element of the poem? Would the poem be equally effective if it did not include end rhyme? Explain your position.

3. Study the poem's use of capitalization and punctuation carefully. Why do you think Brooks chooses to end many of her sentences in mid-line? How do her choices determine how you read the poem?

The Sestina

The **sestina,** introduced in thirteenth-century France, is composed of six six-line stanzas and a three-line conclusion called an **envoi.** Although the sestina does not require end rhyme, it does require that each line end with one of six key words, which are repeated throughout the poem in a fixed order. The alternation of these six words in different positions—but always at the ends of lines—in each of the poem's six stanzas creates a rhythmic verbal pattern that unifies the poem.

ALBERTO ALVARO RÍOS

(1952–   )

Nani

(1982)

Sitting at her table, she serves
the sopa de arroz[1] to me
instinctively, and I watch her,
the absolute mamá, and eat words
5   I might have had to say more
out of embarrassment. To speak,
now-foreign words I used to speak,
too, dribble down her mouth as she serves
me albóndigas.[2] No more
10   than a third are easy to me.
By the stove she does something with words
and looks at me only with her
back. I am full. I tell her

_____

[1] Rice soup.

[2] Meatballs.

I taste the mint, and watch her speak
15 smiles at the stove. All my words
make her smile. Nani never serves
herself, she only watches me
with her skin, her hair. I ask for more.

I watch the mamá warming more
20 tortillas for me. I watch her
fingers in the flame for me.
Near her mouth, I see a wrinkle speak
of a man whose body serves
the ants like she serves me, then more words
25 from more wrinkles about children, words
about this and that, flowing more
easily from these other mouths. Each serves
as a tremendous string around her,
holding her together. They speak
30 nani was this and that to me
and I wonder just how much of me
will die with her, what were the words
I could have been, was. Her insides speak
through a hundred wrinkles, now, more
35 than she can bear, steel around her,
shouting, then, What is this thing she serves?

She asks me if I want more.
I own no words to stop her.
Even before I speak, she serves.

In many respects Rios's poem closely follows the form of the traditional sestina. For instance, it interweaves six key words—"serves," "me," "her," "words," "more," and "speak"—through six groups of six lines each, rearranging the order in which the words appear so that the first line of each group of six lines ends with the key word that closed the preceding group of lines. The poem repeats the key words in exactly the order prescribed: *abcdef, faebdc, cfdabe,* and so on. In addition, the sestina closes with a three-line envoi that includes all six of the poem's key words, three at the ends of lines and three within the lines. However, Rios departs from the sestina form by grouping his six sets of six lines not into six separate stanzas but rather into two eighteen-line stanzas.

The sestina form suits Rios's subject matter well. The focus of the poem, on the verbal and nonverbal interaction between the poem's "me" and "her," is reinforced by each of the related words. "Nani" is a poem about communication, and the key words return to probe this theme again and again. Throughout the poem these repeated words help to create a fluid, melodic, and tightly woven work.

Poem for Further Reading: The Sestina

ELIZABETH BISHOP

(1911–1979)

Sestina

(1965)

September rain falls on the house.
In the failing light, the old grandmother
sits in the kitchen with the child
beside the Little Marvel Stove,
5 reading the jokes from the almanac,
laughing and talking to hide her tears.

She thinks that her equinoctial tears
and the rain that beats on the roof of the house
were both foretold by the almanac,
10 but only known to a grandmother.
The iron kettle sings on the stove.
She cuts some bread and says to the child,

It's time for tea now; but the child
is watching the teakettle's small hard tears
15 dance like mad on the hot black stove,
the way the rain must dance on the house.
Tidying up, the old grandmother
hangs up the clever almanac

on its string. Birdlike, the almanac
20 hovers half open above the child,
hovers above the old grandmother
and her teacup full of dark brown tears.
She shivers and says she thinks the house
feels chilly, and puts more wood in the stove.

25 *It was to be,* says the Marvel Stove.
I know what I know, says the almanac.
With crayons the child draws a rigid house
and a winding pathway. Then the child
puts in a man with buttons like tears
30 and shows it proudly to the grandmother.

But secretly, while the grandmother
busies herself about the stove,
the little moons fall down like tears
from between the pages of the almanac
35 into the flower bed the child
has carefully placed in the front of the house.

Time to plant tears, says the almanac.
The grandmother sings to the marvellous stove
and the child draws another inscrutable house.

READING AND REACTING

1. Does the poet's adherence to the traditional form create any problems? For example, do you think the syntax is strained at any point? Explain.

2. How does this sestina use sound—meter, rhyme, alliteration, assonance, and so on? Could sound have been used more effectively? How?

3. **JOURNAL ENTRY** How are the six key words related to the poem's theme?

4. **CRITICAL PERSPECTIVE** In a 1992 biography, Lorrie Goldensohn says this of Bishop's poetry:

   In all of her published work, the more volcanic emotions required containment within the vessel of form; overtly autobiographical feeling is poured into sestinas or villanelles, cooled into rhyme. . . . Her poems, wary of post-romantic subjectivity, insist on the distance and relative impersonality of the tie between reader and writer, between poem and audience, and between poem and experience all the while that the poetry itself speaks in one of the most idiosyncratic of voices yet to be invented in American poetry.

   Do you believe the sestina form creates a "distance" between you and the poet, or are you able to sense the intensity of the poet's feelings?

The Villanelle

The **villanelle**, first introduced in France in the Middle Ages, is a nineteen-line poem composed of five tercets and a concluding quatrain; its rhyme scheme is *aba aba aba aba aba abaa.* Two different lines are systematically repeated in the poem: Line 1 appears again in lines 6, 12, and 18, and line 3 reappears as lines 9, 15, and 19. Thus, each tercet concludes with an exact (or close) duplication of either line 1 or line 3, and the final quatrain concludes by repeating both line 1 and line 3.

THEODORE ROETHKE

(1908–1963)

The Waking

(1953)

I wake to sleep, and take my waking slow.
I feel my fate in what I cannot fear.
I learn by going where I have to go.

We think by feeling. What is there to know?
5 I hear my being dance from ear to ear.
I wake to sleep, and take my waking slow.

Of those so close beside me, which are you?
God bless the Ground! I shall walk softly there,
And learn by going where I have to go.

10 Light takes the Tree; but who can tell us how?
The lowly worm climbs up a winding stair;
I wake to sleep, and take my waking slow.

Great Nature has another thing to do
To you and me; so take the lively air,
15 And, lovely, learn by going where to go.

This shaking keeps me steady. I should know.
What falls away is always. And is near.
I wake to sleep, and take my waking slow.
I learn by going where I have to go.

"The Waking," like all villanelles, closely intertwines threads of sounds and words. The repeated lines and the very regular rhyme and meter give the poem a monotonous, almost hypnotic, rhythm. Not only does this poem use end rhyme and repetition of lines, but it also makes extensive use of alliteration (I feel my fate in what I cannot fear") and internal rhyme ("I hear my being dance from ear to ear"; "I wake to sleep and take my waking slow"). The result is a tightly constructed poem of overlapping sounds and images. (For another well-known example of a villanelle, see Dylan Thomas's "Do Not Go Gentle into That Good Night," p. 642.)

Poem for Further Reading: The Villanelle

WILLIAM MEREDITH

(1919–   )

In Memory of Donald A. Stauffer

(1987)

Armed with an indiscriminate delight
His ghost left Oxford five summers ago,
Still on the sweet, obvious side of right.

How many friends and students talked all night
5 With this remarkable teacher? How many go
Still armed with his indiscriminate delight?

He liked, but often could not reach, the bright:
Young people sometimes prefer not to know
About the sweet or obvious sides of right.

10 But how all arrogance involves a slight
To knowledge, his humility would show
Them, and his indiscriminate delight

In what was true. This was why he could write
Commonplace books: his patience lingered so
15 Fondly on the sweet, obvious side of right.

What rare anthology of ghosts sits till first light
In the understanding air where he talks now,
Armed with his indiscriminate delight
There on the sweet and obvious side of right?

READING AND REACTING

1. Review the definition of *villanelle* and explain how Meredith's poem expands the possibilities of the traditional villanelle.

2. Try to make the changes you believe are necessary to make Meredith's poem absolutely consistent with the prescribed form of the villanelle. How does your editing change the poem?

3. **JOURNAL ENTRY**   What kinds of subjects do you think would be most appropriate for villanelles? Why? What subjects, if any, do you think would not be suitable? Explain.

The Epigram

Originally, an epigram was an inscription carved in stone on a monument or statue. As a literary form, an **epigram** is a very brief poem that makes a pointed, often sarcastic, comment in a surprising twist at the end. In a sense, it is a poem with a punch line. Although some epigrams rhyme, others do not. Many are only two lines long, but others are somewhat longer. What they have in common is their economy of language and their tone. One of the briefest of epigrams, written by Ogden Nash, appeared in *The New Yorker* magazine in 1931:

> The Bronx?
> No thonx.

In just four words, Nash manages to convey the unexpected, using rhyme and creative spelling to characterize a borough of New York City. The poem's two lines are perfectly balanced, making the contrast between the noncommittal tone of the first and the negative tone of the second quite striking.

Poems for Further Reading: The Epigram

Read the two epigrams that follow and explain the point each one makes. Then evaluate each poem. What qualities do you conclude make an epigram effective?

SAMUEL TAYLOR COLERIDGE

(1772–1834)

What Is an Epigram?

(1802)

What is an epigram? a dwarfish whole,
Its body brevity, and wit its soul.

WILLIAM BLAKE

(1757–1827)

Her Whole Life Is an Epigram

(c. 1793–1811)

Her whole life is an epigram: smack, smooth & neatly penned,
Platted[1] quite neat to catch applause, with a sliding noose at the end.

Haiku

Like an epigram, a haiku compresses words into a very small package. Unlike an epigram, however, a haiku focuses not on the idea but on the image. A traditional Japanese form, the **haiku** is a brief unrhymed poem that presents the essence of some aspect of nature, concentrating a vivid image in just three lines. Although in the strictest sense the haiku consists of seventeen syllables divided into lines of five, seven, and five syllables, respectively, not all poets conform to this rigid form.

The poem below is a translation of a classic Japanese haiku by Matsuo Basho:

Silent and still: then
Even sinking into the rocks,
The cicada's screech.

Notice that this poem conforms to the haiku's three-line structure and traditional subject matter, vividly depicting a natural scene without comment or analysis.

As the next poem illustrates, haiku in English is not always consistent with the traditional haiku in form or subject matter.

RICHARD BRAUTIGAN

(1935–1984)

Widow's Lament*

It's not quite cold enough
to go borrow some firewood
from the neighbors.

---

[1] Braided.

* Publication date is not available.

Brautigan's haiku adheres to the traditional pattern's number of lines and syllables, and its central idea is expressed in very concentrated terms. The poem's focus, however, is not the natural world but human psychology. Moreover, without the title, the poem would be so ambiguous as to be meaningless. In this sense, the poet "cheats" the form, depending on the title's four syllables as well as on the seventeen of the poem itself to convey his ideas.

Poem for Further Reading: Haiku

RICHARD WRIGHT
(1908–1960)

Hokku Poems
(1960)

I am nobody
A red sinking autumn sun
Took my name away

    *

Make up your mind snail!
You are half inside your house
And halfway out!

    *

In the falling snow
A laughing boy holds out his palms
Until they are white

    *

Keep straight down this block
Then turn right where you will find
A peach tree blooming

    *

With a twitching nose
A dog reads a telegram
On a wet tree trunk

    *

The spring lingers on
In the scent of a damp log
Rotting in the sun

*

Whose town did you leave
O wild and drowning spring rain
And where do you go?

*

The crow flew so fast
That he left his lonely caw
Behind in the fields

READING AND REACTING

1. The poems in this group of modern English haiku differ in several respects from the traditional Japanese form. Consider the form and subject matter of each haiku carefully, and explain how each is like and unlike a classic haiku.

2. **JOURNAL ENTRY**   Referring to the additional haiku poems in Chapter 15 as well as to those in this chapter, write a broad definition of haiku that applies to all of them.

Open Form

An **open form** poem (sometimes called **free verse** or *vers libre*) makes occasional use of rhyme and meter, but it has no familiar, easily identifiable pattern or design—that is, it has no conventional stanzaic divisions, no consistent metrical pattern, and no repeated rhyme scheme. Still, although open form poetry does lack a distinguishable pattern of meter, rhyme, or line length, it is not necessarily shapeless, untidy, or randomly ordered. All poems have form, and the form of a poem may be determined by factors such as the appearance of words on the printed page or pauses in natural speech as well as by conventional metrical patterns or rhyme schemes.

Open form poetry invites readers to participate in the creative process, to discover the relationship between form and meaning. Some modern poets believe that only open form offers them freedom to express their ideas or that the subject matter or mood of their poetry demands a relaxed, experimental approach to form. For example, when Lawrence Ferlinghetti portrays the poet as an acrobat who "climbs on rime" (p. 768), he constructs his poem in a way that is consistent with the poet/acrobat's willingness to take risks. Thus, the poem's idiosyncratic form supports its ideas about the possibilities of poetry and the poet as experimenter.

Without a predetermined pattern, however, poets must create forms that suit their needs, and they must continue to shape and reshape the look of the poem on the page as they revise its words. Sometimes this absence of prescribed form presents a problem. More often, though, open form represents a challenge, a way to experiment with fresh arrangements of words and new juxtapositions of ideas.

For some poets, such as Carl Sandburg, open form provided an opportunity to create **prose poems.**

CARL SANDBURG

(1878–1967)

Chicago

(1914)

Hog Butcher for the World,
Tool Maker, Stacker of Wheat,
Player with Railroads and the Nation's Freight Handler;
Stormy, husky, brawling,
5   City of the Big Shoulders:
They tell me you are wicked and I believe them, for I have seen
    your painted women under the gas lamps luring the farm boys.
And they tell me you are crooked and I answer: Yes, it is true I
    have seen the gunman kill and go free to kill again.
10 And they tell me you are brutal and my reply is: On the faces of
    women and children I have seen the marks of wanton hunger.
And having answered so I turn once more to those who sneer at this
    my city, and I give them back the sneer and say to them:
Come and show me another city with lifted head singing so proud
15   to be alive and coarse and strong and cunning.
Flinging magnetic curses amid the toil of piling job on job, here is a tall
    bold slugger set vivid against the little soft cities;
Fierce as a dog with tongue lapping for action, cunning as a savage
    pitted against the wilderness,
20   Bareheaded,
    Shoveling,
    Wrecking,
    Planning,
    Building, breaking, rebuilding,
25 Under the smoke, dust all over his mouth, laughing with white teeth,
Under the terrible burden of destiny laughing as a young man laughs,
Laughing even as an ignorant fighter laughs who has never lost a battle,

Bragging and laughing that under his wrist is the pulse, and under his
ribs
the heart of the people,
30   Laughing!
Laughing the stormy, husky, brawling laughter of Youth, half-naked,
sweating, proud to be Hog Butcher, Tool Maker, Stacker of
Wheat, Player with railroads and Freight Handler to the Nation.

Although "Chicago" does not wander aimlessly all over the page, it
does represent a departure from traditional closed form. It uses capitalization and punctuation conventionally, and it generally (but not always) divides words into lines consistent with the natural divisions of phrases and
sentences. However, the poem is not divided into stanzas, and its lines
vary widely in length—from a single word isolated on a line to a line
crowded with words—and follow no particular metrical pattern. Instead,
its form is created through its pattern of alternating sections of long and
short lines; through its repeated words and phrases ("They tell me" in lines
6–10, "under" in lines 25–26, and "laughing" in lines 25–31, for example); through alliteration (for instance, "slugger set vivid against the little
soft cities" in line 17); and, most of all, through the piling up of words
into catalogs in lines 1–5, 20–24, and 32–33.

In order to understand Sandburg's reasons for choosing such a form, we
must consider the poem's subject matter and theme. "Chicago" celebrates
the scope and power of a "stormy, husky, brawling" city, one that is exuberant and outgoing, not sedate and civilized. Chicago the city does not
conform to anyone else's rules; it is, after all, "Bareheaded, / Shoveling, /
Wrecking, / Planning, / Building, breaking," constantly active, in flux, on
the move, "proud to be alive." "Fierce as a dog . . . cunning as a savage," the
city is characterized as, among other things, a worker, a fighter, and a har-
borer of "painted women" and killers and hungry women and children.
Such characterizations clearly demand a departure from the orderly confines of stanzaic form and measured rhyme and meter, a kind of form better suited to "the little soft cities" than to the "tall / bold slugger" that is
Chicago.

Of course, open form poetry does not have to look like Sandburg's
prose poem. The next poem experiments with a different kind of open
form.

L O U I S E   G L Ü C K

(1943–   )

Life Is a Nice Place

(1966)

Life is a nice place (They change
the decorations
every season; and the music,
my dear, is just too
5   marvellous, they play you
anything from birds to Bach. And
every day the Host
arranges for some clever sort
of contest and they give
10   the most
fantastic prizes; I go absolutely
green. Of course, celebrities abound;
I've even seen Love waltzing around
in amusing disguises.) to
15   visit. But
I wouldn't want to live there.

Glück's poem includes several end rhymes ("too"/"you"; "Host"/"most"; "abound"/"around"). It also has a visible pattern on the page, broadening and narrowing with some regularity. Moreover, it has a clear syntactical structure, with one main sentence interrupted by parenthetical comments, and it uses capitalization and punctuation conventionally. The poem clearly has a form, but it is fresh and idiosyncratic, with neither stanzaic divisions nor repeated patterns of rhyme or meter to anchor it to tradition.

The poem's unusual form suits both its subject and its sarcastic tone. It is divided into five sentences, but only the final sentence ends at the end of a line. Moreover, the first sentence ("Life is a nice place . . . to visit") begins in line 1 but does not conclude until the end of the poem. The long parenthetical intrusion, unusual in itself, keeps readers from seeing at first that the poem is a grim new twist on an old cliché: "Life is a nice place . . . / to visit. But / I wouldn't want to live there."

The poem's first line is ironic, for the life the speaker presents is shallow, false, and ultimately meaningless. It is a cross between a stage set and a cocktail party, where love is elusive ("waltzing around / in amusing disguises") and nature is artificially recreated by piped-in music and painted backdrops. Although a traditional structure and regular rhyme and meter could, through their contrast with the subject matter, create ironic tension,

Glück chooses an unconventional form that visually reinforces the empty cycles of the life the poem describes. Breaks in lines are not determined by conventional phrasing or punctuation but largely by the demands of form, which create unusual word groups such as "every season; and the music, is just too" and "fantastic prizes; I go absolutely." These odd juxtapositions suggest the random quality of the speaker's encounters and, perhaps, the unpredictability of her life.

The poem that follows, an extreme example of open form, looks almost as if it has spilled out of a box of words.

E. E. CUMMINGS

(1894–1962)

the sky was can dy

(1925)

        the
            sky
                was
        can   dy   lu
     5 minous
                edible
        spry
            pinks shy
        lemons
    10 greens   coo   l choc
        olate
        s.

            un   der,
            a   lo
    15 co
        mo
                tive   s pout
                        ing
                        vi
    20   o
                        lets

Like many of Cummings's poems, this one seems ready to skip off the page. Its irregular line length and unconventional capitalization, punctuation, and word divisions immediately draw readers' attention to its form. Despite these oddities, and despite the absence of orderly rhyme and

meter, the poem does have its conventional elements. A closer examination reveals that the poem's theme—the beauty of the sky—is quite conventional; that the poem is divided, although somewhat crudely, into two
sections; and that the poet does use some rhyme—"spry" and "shy," for
example. However, Cummings's sky is described not in traditional terms,
but rather as something "edible," not only in terms of color but of flavor
as well. The breaks within words ("can dy lu / minous"; "coo l choc / olate
/ s" seem to expand each word's possibilities, visually stretching them to
the limit, extending their taste and visual image over several lines and, in
the case of the last two words, visually reinforcing the picture the words
describe. In addition, the isolation of syllables exposes hidden rhyme, as
in "lo / co / mo" and "lu" / "coo." By using open form, Cummings makes
a clear statement about the capacity of a poem to move beyond the traditional boundaries set by words and lines.

Poems for Further Reading: Open Form

WALT WHITMAN

(1819–1892)

from Out of the Cradle Endlessly Rocking

(1881)

Out of the cradle endlessly rocking,
Out of the mocking-bird's throat, the musical shuttle,
Out of the Ninth-month[1] midnight,
Over the sterile sands and the fields beyond, where the child leaving his
  bed wander'd alone, bareheaded, barefoot,
5 Down from the shower'd halo,
Up from the mystic play of shadows twining and twisting as if they were
  alive,
Out from the patches of briers and blackberries,
From the memories of the bird that chanted to me,
From your memories sad brother, from the fitful risings and fallings I
  heard,
10 From under that yellow half-moon late-risen and swollen as if with tears,

---

[1] The Quaker designation for September. In context, an allusion to the human birth
cycle.

From those beginning notes of yearning and love there in the mist,
From the thousand responses of my heart never to cease,
From the myriad thence-arous'd words,
From the word stronger and more delicious than any,
15 From such as now they start the scene revisiting,
As a flock, twittering, rising, or overhead passing,
Borne hither, ere all eludes me, hurriedly,
A man, yet by these tears a little boy again,
Throwing myself on the sand, confronting the waves,
20 I, chanter of pains and joys, uniter of here and hereafter,
Taking all hints to use them, but swiftly leaping beyond them,
A reminiscence sing.

READING AND REACTING

1. This excerpt, the first twenty-two lines of a poem nearly two hundred lines long, has no regular metrical pattern or rhyme scheme. What gives it form?

2. How might you explain why the poem's lines vary in length?

3. **JOURNAL ENTRY** Compare this excerpt with the excerpt from Whitman's "Song of Myself" (p. 1022). In what respects are the forms of the two poems similar?

4. **CRITICAL PERSPECTIVE** Reviewing a recent biography of Whitman, Geoffrey O'Brien writes of a paradox in Whitman's poetry:

   [N]either fiction nor verse as they then existed could provide Whitman with what he needed, so he invented out of necessity his own form, a reversion to what he conceived of as the most archaic bardic impulses, representing itself as the poetry of the future.

   Can you see the form of "Out of the Cradle" as both "archaic" and "of the future"?

DIANE WAKOSKI

(1937–)

Sleep

(1966)

The mole
lifting snouts—
full of strained black dirt
—his perfect tunnel
5   sculptured
to fit

the fat
body. Sleep
fits tight
10   —must keep bringing out.
the fine grit
to keep size
for even one day.

READING AND REACTING

1. This poem's form seems to be in direct conflict with the logical divisions its syntax and punctuation suggest. For instance, the words in lines 4–9 are set between dashes, indicating a parenthetical comment, yet only lines 4–8 are visually aligned. Also, line 10 ends with a period, but lines 11–13 are clearly part of the same sentence as line 10. How can you account for such discrepancies?

2. How might the poem's discussion of the mole's constant search for the perfect size tunnel have suggested the form of the poem?

3. **JOURNAL ENTRY**   Why do you believe the poet placed the words "Sleep / fits tight" (8–9) where she did? Could—or should—these words be relocated? If so, where could they be placed, and what changes in form or punctuation would the poet have to make?

ROBERT HAYDEN

(1913–   )

Monet's "Waterlilies"[1]

(1966)

(for Bill and Sonja)

Today as the news from Selma[2] and Saigon[3]
poisons the air like fallout,

---

[1] Claude Monet (1840–1926), French impressionist painter. The poet's description of the painter's use of light in this particular painting is equally applicable to most of Monet's work.

[2] Selma, a city in central Alabama. In 1965 a peaceful demonstration in support of voting rights for blacks was brutally broken up by the Selma police. Two civil rights supporters were killed: one, minister James Reeb, was beaten to death on a town street; the other, homemaker Viola Liuzzo, was shot by Ku Klux Klansmen as she was driving along a highway.

[3] Saigon, the capital of the former South Vietnam, now known as Ho Chi Minh City. All news of the Vietnam War was cleared through Saigon by U.S. authorities.

I come again to see
the serene great picture that I love.
5 Here space and time exist in light
the eye like the eye of faith believes.
    The seen, the known
dissolve in irridescence, become
illusive flesh of light
10   that was not, was, forever is.

O light beheld as through refracting tears.
Here is the aura of that world
    each of us has lost.
Here is the shadow of its joy.

READING AND REACTING

1. The speaker stands before Monet's "Waterlilies," where he takes temporary refuge from the turbulent world. Why do you suppose Hayden chose not to use the soothing rhythms and comforting shape of closed form to convey the serenity of the moment? Do you think he made the right choice?

2. Hayden indents lines 3, 7, 10, and 13. What purpose, if any, do these indentations serve?

3. Why do you think the last four lines are separated from the rest of the poem?

WILLIAM CARLOS WILLIAMS

(1883–1963)

Spring and All

(1923)

By the road to the contagious hospital
under the surge of the blue
mottled clouds driven from the
northeast—a cold wind. Beyond, the
5 waste of broad, muddy fields
brown with dried weeds, standing and fallen

patches of standing water
the scattering of tall trees

All along the road the reddish
10 purplish, forked, upstanding, twiggy
stuff of bushes and small trees
with dead, brown leaves under them
leafless vines—

Lifeless in appearance, sluggish
15 dazed spring approaches—

They enter the new world naked,
cold, uncertain of all
save that they enter. All about them
the cold, familiar wind—

20 Now the grass, tomorrow
the stiff curl of wildcarrot leaf
One by one objects are defined—
It quickens: clarity, outline of leaf

But now the stark dignity of
25 entrance—Still, the profound change
has come upon them: rooted, they
grip down and begin to awaken

READING AND REACTING

1. What elements of traditional closed form poems are present in "Spring and All"? What elements are absent?

2. Why is the poem divided into sections? What does Williams accomplish by isolating two sets of two lines each (7–8; 14–15)?

3. "Spring and All" uses assonance, alliteration, and repetition. Give several examples of each technique, and explain what each adds to the poem.

4. **JOURNAL ENTRY**   "Spring and All" includes only two periods. Elsewhere, where readers might expect to find end punctuation, the poet uses colons, dashes, or no punctuation at all. Why do you think the poet made these decisions about the use of punctuation?

5. **CRITICAL PERSPECTIVE**   In the book *Spring and All,* in which this poem appeared, Williams claimed to be staking out a "new world" of poetry addressed "to the imagination." However, in *Lives of the Modern Poets* (1980), William H. Pritchard challenges this claim:

   [T]o believe that Williams's talk about the Imagination, the "new world," points to some radical way in which this poem is in advance of more traditional versifiers seems to me mistaken. Consider the last five lines of a *poem [Robert] Frost had written, in conventional meters, a few years before:*

    How Love burns through the Putting in the Seed
    On through the watching for that early birth
    When, just as the soil tarnishes with weed,
    The sturdy seedling with arched body comes
    Shouldering its way and shedding the earth crumbs.

This birth is every bit as imaginative, every bit as much of a new world, as anything in ["Spring and All"].

What do you think of Pritchard's evaluation?

LAWRENCE FERLINGHETTI

(1919–   )

Don't Let That Horse
Eat That Violin

(1958)

Don't let that horse
                 eat that violin
    cried Chagall's[1] mother
                    But he
5   kept right on
                    painting

And became famous

And kept on painting
               The Horse With Violin In Mouth

10 And when he finally finished it
he jumped up upon the horse
                 and rode away
     waving the violin

And then with a low bow gave it
15 to the first naked nude he ran across

And there were no strings
                  attached

---

[1] Marc Chagall (1887–1985), Russian-born painter and printmaker.

READING AND REACTING

1. In what respects is the poem's form appropriate for its language, tone, and subject matter?

2. What factors determine the arrangement of words in lines? Are the breaks between lines purely arbitrary, or is there some logic to the poet's word groupings?

3. **JOURNAL ENTRY**   Marc Chagall is an artist known for whimsical paintings in which people, animals, and even buildings float in space. How does the form of Ferlinghetti's poem reflect the form of Chagall's work? (If possible, try to examine a reproduction of one of Chagall's paintings.)

CAROLYN   FORCHÉ

(1950–   )

The Colonel

(1978)

What you have heard is true. I was in his house. His wife carried
a tray of coffee and sugar. His daughter filed her nails, his son went
out for the night. There were daily papers, pet dogs, a pistol on the
cushion beside him. The moon swung bare on its black cord over
5 the house. On the television was a cop show. It was in English.
Broken bottles were embedded in the walls around the house to
scoop the kneecaps from a man's legs or cut his hands to lace. On
the windows there were gratings like those in liquor stores. We had
dinner, rack of lamb, good wine, a gold bell was on the table for
10 calling the maid. The maid brought green mangoes, salt, a type of
bread. I was asked how I enjoyed the country. There was a brief
commercial in Spanish. His wife took everything away. There was
some talk then of how difficult it had become to govern. The parrot
said hello on the terrace. The colonel told it to shut up, and pushed
15 himself from the table. My friend said to me with his eyes: say
nothing. The colonel returned with a sack used to bring groceries
home. He spilled many human ears on the table. They were like
dried peach halves. There is no other way to say this. He took one
of them in his hands, shook it in our faces, dropped it into a water

20 glass. It came alive there. I am tired of fooling around he said. As
for the rights of anyone, tell your people they can go fuck themselves. He swept the ears to the floor with his arm and held the last
of his wine in the air. Something for your poetry, no? he said. Some
of the ears on the floor caught this scrap of his voice. Some of the
25 ears on the floor were pressed to the ground.

READING AND REACTING

1. Treating Forché's prose poem as prose rather than poetry, try dividing
   it into paragraphs. What determines where you make your divisions?

2. If you were to reshape "The Colonel" into a more conventional looking
   poem, what options might you have? Rewrite the poem so it "looks
   like poetry," and compare your revision to the original. Which
   version do you find more effective? Why?

3. What is the main point of "The Colonel"? How does the form help
   Forché to communicate this point?

4. **JOURNAL ENTRY**   Do you think "The Colonel" should be considered
   poetry or prose? Consider its subject matter and language as well as its
   form.

Concrete Poetry

With roots in the ancient Greek *pattern poems* and the sixteenth- and
seventeenth-century *emblem poems*, contemporary **concrete poetry** uses
words—and, sometimes, different fonts and type sizes—to shape a picture
on the page. The form of a concrete poem is not something that emerges
from the poem's words and images, but something predetermined by the
visual image the poet has decided to create. Although some concrete
poems are little more than novelties, others—like the poem that follows—
can be original and enlightening.

MAY SWENSON

(1913–1989)

Women

(1970)

Women	Or they
should be	should be
pedestals	little horses
moving	those wooden
5 pedestals	sweet
moving	oldfashioned
to the	painted
motions	rocking
of men	horses

10   the gladdest things in the toyroom

The	feelingly
pegs	and then
of their	unfeelingly
ears	To be
15 so familiar	joyfully
and dear	ridden
to the trusting	rockingly
fists	ridden until
To be chafed	the restored

20 egos dismount and the legs stride away

Immobile	willing
sweetlipped	to be set
sturdy	into motion
and smiling	Women
25 women	should be
should always	pedestals
be waiting	to men

The curved shape of the poem immediately reinforces its title, and the arrangement of words on the page suggests a variety of visual directions readers might follow. The two columns seem at first to suggest two alternatives: "Women should be. . . ." / "Or they should be. . . ." A closer look, however, reveals that the poem's central figures of speech, such as woman as rocking horse and woman as pedestal, move back and forth between the two columns of images. This exchange of positions might suggest that the two possibilities are really just two ways of looking at one limited role. Thus, the experimental form of the poem visually challenges the apparent complacency of its words, suggesting that women, like words, need not fall into traditional roles or satisfy conventional expectations.

Poems for Further Reading: Concrete Poetry

GEORGE HERBERT

(1593–1633)

Easter Wings

(1633)

Lord, who createdst man in wealth and store,
Though foolishly he lost the same,
Decaying more and more
Till he became
Most poor;
With thee
Oh, let me rise
As larks, harmoniously,
And sing this day thy victories;
Then shall the fall further the flight in me.

My tender age in sorrow did begin;
And still with sicknesses and shame
Thou didst so punish sin,
That I became
Most thin.
With thee
Let me combine,
And feel this day thy victory;
For if I imp my wing on thine,
Affliction shall advance the flight in me.

READING AND REACTING

1. In this example of an emblem poem, lines are arranged so that shape and language reinforce each other. Explain how this is accomplished. (For example, how does line length support the poem's images and ideas?)

2. This poem has a definite rhyme scheme. How would you describe it? What relationship do you see between the rhyme scheme and the poem's visual divisions?

(1933-   )

You Too? Me Too—
Why Not? Soda Pop

(1968)

I am
look
ing at
the Co
5   caCola
bottle
which is
green wi
th ridges
10   just like

c   c   c
o   o   o
l   l   l
u   u   u
15   m   m   m
n   n   n
s   s   s
and on itself it says

COCA-COLA
20   reg.u.s.pat.off.

exactly like an art pop
statue of that kind of
bottle but not so green
that the juice inside
25   gives other than the co
lor it has when I pour
it out in a clear glass
glass on this table top
(It's making me thirsty
30   all this winking and
beading of Hippocrene
please let me pause
drinking the fluid in)
ah! it is enticing how
35   each color is the same
brown in green bottle
brown in uplifted glass
making each utensil on
the table laid a brown
40   fork in a brown shade
making me long to watch
them harvesting the crop
which makes the deep-aged
rich brown wine of America
45 that is to say which makes
soda   pop

READING AND REACTING

1. **JOURNAL ENTRY** Is this a poem, or is it just a clever novelty? Explain your position, and give examples to support it.

▼▼▼

CHECKLIST FOR WRITING ABOUT FORM

◆ Is the poem written in open or closed form? On what characteristics do you base your conclusion?

◆ Why did the poet choose open or closed form? For example, is the poem's form consistent with its subject matter, tone, or theme? Is it determined by the conventions of the era in which it was written?

◆ If the poem is arranged in closed form, does the pattern apply to single lines, groups of lines, or the entire poem? What factors determine the breaks between groups of lines?

◆ Is the poem a sonnet? A sestina? A villanelle? An epigram? A haiku? How do the traditional form's conventions suit the poet's language and theme? Is the poem consistent with the requirements of the form at all times, or does it break any new ground?

◆ If the poem is arranged in open form, what determines the breaks at the ends of lines?

◆ Are certain words or phrases isolated on lines? Why?

◆ How do elements such as assonance, alliteration, rhyme, and repetition of words give the poem form?

◆ What use does the poet make of punctuation and capitalization? Of white space on the page?

◆ Is the poem a prose poem? How does this form support the poem's subject matter?

◆ Is the poem a concrete poem? How does the poet use the visual shape of the poem to convey meaning?

▲▲▲

WRITING SUGGESTIONS: FORM

1. Reread the definitions of closed and open form in this chapter. Do you consider concrete poetry to be open or closed? Explain your position in a short essay, supporting your conclusion with specific references to the three concrete poems in this chapter.

2. Some poets—for example, Emily Dickinson and Robert Frost—write both open and closed form poems. Choose one open and one closed form poem by a single poet, and explain the poet's possible reasons for choosing each type of form. In your analysis of the two poems, defend the poet's choices if you can.

3. Do you see complex forms, such as the villanelle and the sestina, as just exercises, or even merely opportunities for poets to show off their skills, or do you believe the special demands of the forms add something valuable to the poem? To help you answer this question, read "Do Not Go Gentle into That Good Night" (p. 642), and analyze Dylan Thomas's use of the villanelle's structure to enhance his poem's theme. Or, study Elizabeth Bishop's "Sestina" (p. 838), and consider how her use of the sestina's form helps her to convey her ideas.

4. The following open form poem is an alternate version of May Swenson's "Women" (p. 858). Read the two versions carefully, and write an essay in which you compare them. What differences do you notice? Which do you think was written first? Why? Do the two poems make the same point? Which makes the point with less ambiguity? Which is more effective? Why?

Women Should Be Pedestals

Women should be pedestals
moving pedestals
moving to the motions of men
Or they should be little horses
5 those wooden sweet oldfashioned painted rocking horses
the gladdest things in the toyroom
The pegs of their ears so familiar and dear
to the trusting fists
To be chafed feelingly
10 and then unfeelingly
To be joyfully ridden
until the restored egos dismount and the legs stride away
Immobile sweetlipped sturdy and smiling
women should always be waiting
15 willing to be set into motion
Women should be pedestals to men

5. Look through the Poems for Further Reading section that follows Chapter 19 of this text, and identify a few prose poems. Write an essay in which you consider why the form seems suitable for each poem. Is there a particular kind of subject matter that seems especially appropriate for a prose poem?

Symbol, Allegory, Allusion, Myth

What the reader gets from a symbol depends not only upon what the author has put into it but upon the reader's sensitivity and his consequent apprehension of what is there. The feeling of profundity that accompanies it comes from a gradual but never final penetration of the form.

WILLIAM YORK TINDALL, "EXCELLENT DUMB DISCOURSE"

"Symbols plunge us into the shadowy experience of power. Metaphors are just the linguistic surface of symbols, and they owe their power to relate the semantic surface to the presemantic surface in the depths of human experience to the two-dimensional structure of the symbol."

PAUL RICOEUR, *INTERPRETATION THEORY*

Chicano literature has gone beyond its beginnings. It no longer simply asserts and defines an identity. It now paints its context and carries out its visions. . . .

The symbols and images have already become familiar—we speak a common mythological language. Critics have begun to explain and nourish motifs, visions, and symbols [in Chicano literature] such as the mirror (symbol of self-knowledge), the creative serpent (cyclical nature of energy and transformation, rather than a linear definition of progress), in lak ech (Mayan principle of behavior) and, of course, the parent earth, la tierra, *as birther, burier, and healer.*

CARMEN TAFOLLA, *CHICANO LITERATURE*

Myth is an expression of "primitive" people. People in the process of making what we call civilization, and its purpose is to explain and support them against darkness. . . . Myth is also a counter against morality in a world in which life is "solitary, nasty, poor, brutish, and short." . . . Myths are also composed—if they are "composed" and not built by accretion, like deltas—by anonymous authors. It would never occur to us to wonder, for example, who wrote about Demeter and Persephone. Nobody wrote it. Everybody did. It doesn't matter.

ADRIÀN OKTENBERG, *FROM THE BOTTOM UP*

A myth is not "a large controlling image." The future of mythical poetry does not depend upon reconciling poetry with an image. It depends rather upon making of poetry something it is always striving against human bias and superficiality to become. The poetical imagination when it attains any consistent fire and efficacy is always displacing the texture of the mind into the external world so that it becomes a theater of preternatural forces. A certain control and direction given the poetical emotions, and poetry, as it always has, becomes mythical.

RICHARD CHASE, "NOTES ON THE STUDY OF MYTH"

W I L L I A M   B L A K E

(1757–1827)

The Sick Rose

(1794)

O Rose thou art sick.
The invisible worm
That flies in the night,
In the howling storm:

5 Has found out thy bed
Of crimson joy:
And his dark secret love
Does thy life destroy.

Symbol

As in fiction and drama, symbols in poetry function as a kind of short-hand, as a subtle way of introducing a significant idea or attitude. A **symbol** is an idea or image that suggests something else—but not in the simple way that a dollar sign stands for money or a flag represents a country. A symbol is an image that transcends its literal, or denotative, meaning in a complex way. For instance, if someone gives a rose to a loved one, it could simply be a sign of love. But in the William Blake poem "The Sick Rose," the rose has a range of contradictory and complementary meanings. For what does the rose stand? Beauty? Perfection? Passion? Something else? As this poem illustrates, the distinguishing characteristic of a symbol is that its meaning cannot easily be pinned down or defined.

Such ambiguity can be frustrating, but it is precisely this characteristic of a symbol that enables it to enrich a work and to give it additional layers of meaning. As Robert Frost has said, a symbol is a little thing that touches a larger thing. Notice in the following poem how the central symbol does just this.

ROBERT FROST

(1874–1963)

For Once, Then, Something

(1923)

> Others taunt me with having knelt at well-curbs
> Always wrong to the light, so never seeing
> Deeper down in the well than where the water
> Gives me back in a shining surface picture
> 5 Me myself in the summer heaven, godlike,
> Looking out of a wreath of fern and cloud puffs.
> *Once,* when trying with chin against a well-curb,
> I discerned, as I thought, beyond the picture,
> Through the picture, a something white, uncertain,
> 10 Something more of the depths—and then I lost it.
> Water came to rebuke the too clear water.
> One drop fell from a fern, and lo, a ripple
> Shook whatever it was lay there at bottom,
> Blurred it, blotted it out. What was that whiteness?
> 15 Truth? A pebble of quartz? For once, then, something.

The central symbol in this poem is the "something" that the speaker thinks he discerns at the bottom of a well. Traditionally, the act of looking down a well suggests a search for truth. In this poem the speaker remarks that he always seems to look down the well at the wrong angle, so that all he can see is his own reflection—the surface, not the depths. Once, the speaker tells us, he thought he saw something "beyond the picture," something "white, uncertain," but the image remained indistinct, disappearing when a drop of water from a fern caused the water to ripple. The poem ends with the speaker questioning the significance of what he saw. Like a reader encountering a symbol, the speaker is left trying to come to terms with images that cannot be clearly perceived and suggestions that cannot be readily understood. In light of the elusive nature of truth, all the speaker can do is ask questions that have no definite answers.

Symbols that appear in works of fiction, poetry, or drama can be *conventional, universal,* or *private.* **Conventional symbols** are those recognized by people who share certain cultural and social assumptions. National flags, for example, evoke a general and agreed-upon response in most people of a particular country and, for better or for worse, American children perceive the golden arches of McDonald's as a symbol of food, fun, and happiness. **Universal symbols** are those likely to be recognized by people regardless of their culture. In 1890, the noted Scottish anthropologist Sir James George Frazer wrote the first version of his work *The Golden Bough,* in which he showed parallels between the rites and beliefs of early cultures and those of Christianity. Fascinated by Frazer's work, the psychologist Carl Jung sought to explain these similarities by formulating a theory of **archetypes,** which held that certain images or ideas reside in the subconscious of all people. According to Jung, archetypal, or universal, symbols include water, symbolizing rebirth; spring, symbolizing growth; and winter, symbolizing death.

Sometimes symbols can be obscure or highly idiosyncratic **private symbols.** The works of William Blake and W. B. Yeats, for example, combine symbols from different cultural, theological, and philosophical sources to form complex networks of symbolic associations. To Blake, for example, the scientist Isaac Newton represents the tendency of scientists to quantify experience while ignoring the beauty and mystery of nature. Readers cannot begin to understand Blake's use of Newton as a symbol until they have read a number of his more challenging poems.

Most often, however, symbols in poems are not this challenging. In the following poem, for instance, the poet introduces a cross—a symbol that has specific associations to those familiar with Christianity—and makes his own use of it.

JIM SIMMERMAN [1]

Child's Grave, Hale County, Alabama

(1983)

Someone drove a two-by-four
through the heart of this hard land
that even in a good year
will notch a plow blade worthless,
5 snap the head off a shovel,
or bow a stubborn back.

---

[1] Birth date is not available.

He'd have had to steal
the wood from a local mill
or steal, by starlight, across
10 his landlord's farm, to worry
a fencepost out of its well
and lug it the three miles home.
He'd have had to leave his wife
asleep on a corn shuck mat,
15 leave his broken brogans[2]
by the stove, to slip outside,
quiet as sin, with the child
bundled in a burlap sack.
What a thing to have to do
20 on a cold night in December,
1936, alone
but for a raspy wind
and the red, rock-ridden dirt
things come down to in the end.
25 Whoever it was pounded
this shabby half-cross
into the ground must have toiled
all night to root it so:
five feet buried with the child
30 for the foot of it that shows.
And as there are no words
carved here, it's likely that
the man was illiterate,
or addled with fatigue,
35 or wrenched simple-minded
by the one simple fact.
Or else the unscored lumber
driven deep into the land
and the hump of busted rock
40 spoke too plainly of his grief:
forty years layed by and still
there are no words for this.

Even in non-Christian cultures, the cross on a grave is a readily identifiable symbol of death and rebirth. In this poem, however, the cross is not simply presented as a conventional Christian symbol; it is also associated with the tenant farmer's hard work and difficult life. In this sense the cross also suggests the poverty that helped bring about the death of the child and the social conditions that existed during the Depression. These

---

[2] Sturdy, heavy work shoes, frequently ankle high.

associations take readers through many layers of meaning, so that the cross may ultimately stand for the tenant farmer's whole life (the cross *he* has to bear), not just for the death of the child. This interpretation by no means exhausts the possible symbolic significance of the cross in the poem. For example, the crude cross might also suggest the rage and grief of the individual who made it, or it might call to mind the poor who live and die in anonymity. Certainly the poet could have assigned a fixed meaning to the cross that marks the child's grave, but he chose instead, by suggesting various ideas through a single powerful symbol, to let readers arrive at their own conclusions.

How do you know when an idea or image is a symbol? At what point do you decide that a particular object or idea goes beyond the literal level and takes on symbolic significance? When, that is, is a rose more than a rose or a cross more than a cross? Frequently you can recognize a symbol by its prominence or repetition. In "Child's Grave, Hale County, Alabama," for example, the cross is introduced in the first line of the poem, and it is the focal point of the poem; in "The Sick Rose" the importance of the rose is emphasized by the title.

It is not enough, however, to identify an image or idea that seems to suggest something else. Your decision that a particular item has some symbolic significance must be supported by the details of the poem and make sense within the context of the ideas developed in the poem. Moreover, the symbol must support the poem's theme. Notice in the following poem how the image of the volcano helps readers to understand the poem's central theme.

E M I L Y   D I C K I N S O N

(1830–1886)

Volcanoes Be in Sicily

(1914)

Volcanoes be in Sicily
And South America
I judge from my Geography—
Volcanoes nearer here
5 A Lava step at any time
Am I inclined to climb—
A Crater I may contemplate
Vesuvius at Home.

This poem opens with a statement of fact: Volcanoes are located in Sicily and South America. In lines 3 and 4, however, the speaker makes the improbable observation that volcanoes are located near where she is at the moment. Readers familiar with Dickinson know that her poems are highly autobiographical and that she lived in Amherst, Massachusetts, a town with no volcanoes. This information leads readers to suspect they should not take the speaker's observation literally and that in the context of the poem volcanoes may have symbolic significance. But what do volcanoes suggest here? On the one hand, volcanoes represent the awesome creative power of nature; on the other hand, they suggest its destructiveness. The speaker's contemplation of the crater of Vesuvius—the volcano that buried the ancient Roman city of Pompeii in A.D. 79—is therefore filled with contradictory associations. Since Dickinson was a recluse, volcanoes—active, destructive, unpredictable, and dangerous—may be seen as symbolic of everything she fears in the outside world and, perhaps, within herself. She has a voyeur's attraction to danger and power, but she is also afraid of them. For this reason she (and her speaker) may feel safer contemplating Vesuvius at home—not experiencing exotic lands, but simply reading a geography book.

Poems for Further Reading: Symbol

LANGSTON HUGHES

(1902–1967)

Island

(1951)

Wave of sorrow,
Do not drown me now:

I see the island
Still ahead somehow.

5 I see the island
And its sands are fair:

Wave of sorrow,
Take me there.

READING AND REACTING

1. What makes you suspect that the island has symbolic significance in this poem? Is it a universal, conventional, or private symbol? Explain your answer.

2. Is the "wave of sorrow" also a symbol?

3. **JOURNAL ENTRY**   Beyond its literal meaning, what might the island in this poem suggest? Consider several possibilities.

4. **CRITICAL PERSPECTIVE**   In *Langston Hughes,* a 1973 study of the poet's work, Onwuchekwa Jemie writes that "the black writer's problem is . . . how to actualize the oral tradition in written form":

The black writer . . . has no long written tradition of his own to emulate; and for him to abandon the effort to translate into written form that oral medium which is the full reservoir of his culture would be to annihilate his identity and become a zombie, a programmed vehicle for "the message of another people."

Do you think "Island" successfully "actualizes the oral tradition in written form"? What elements help it to qualify as "oral" poetry?

THEODORE ROETHKE

(1908–1963)

Night Crow

(1944)

When I saw that clumsy crow
Flap from a wasted tree,
Over the gulfs of dream
Flew a tremendous bird
5 Further and further away
Into a moonless black,
Deep in the brain, far back.

READING AND REACTING

1. What is the significance of the title? In what way does it help you to interpret the symbolic significance of the crow?

2. How is the "clumsy crow" different from the crow "Deep in the brain"? What visual image does each suggest?

3. **JOURNAL ENTRY**   It has been suggested that "Night Crow" is a commentary on the difference between reality and imagination. Does the poem's use of symbol support such an interpretation? Explain.

LOUISE BOGAN

The Dragonfly

(1961)

You are made of almost nothing
But of enough
To be great eyes
And diaphanous double vans[1];
5 To be ceaseless movement,
Unending hunger
Grappling love.

Link between water and air,
Earth repels you.
10 Light touches you only to shift into iridescence
Upon your body and wings.
Twice-born, predator,
You split into the heat.
Swift beyond calculation or capture
15 You dart into the shadow
Which consumes you.

You rocket into the day.
But at last, when the wind flattens the grasses,
For you, the design and purpose stop.

20 And you fall
With the other husks of summer.

READING AND REACTING

1. What details of the poem suggest that the dragonfly has symbolic significance?

2. List three possible interpretations of the symbol of the dragonfly. How does the poem support each interpretation?

3. Do you think the seasons alluded to in the poem have symbolic significance? Why or why not?

4. **JOURNAL ENTRY**   What qualities does Bogan give the dragonfly? Are these the same qualities you associate with a dragonfly? How do you account for any differences?

---

[1] Wings.

5. **CRITICAL PERSPECTIVE**   In her book *A Separate Vision* (1984), Deborah Pope makes the following observation about Bogan's poetry:

> *[F]requently, Louise Bogan creates barren, ominous landscapes that evoke a state of isolation in space and time. Her artistic fidelity is not so much to actual nature as it is to the inner world of the psyche, colored by emotional and psychological response. . . . [S]he negates nature and exerts her control over it by transforming it in her work. Ironically, the result is . . . an even greater powerlessness.*

In what sense is "The Dragonfly" less a depiction of "actual nature" than of "the inner world of the psyche"? Does the poem suggest a sense of powerlessness?

Allegory

Allegory is a form of narrative that equates abstract ideas with people, places, and things, turning them into a story. Allegorical elements, each with a strict equivalent on a literal level, form a network that offers a political or moral lesson. Like symbolism, allegory uses things to suggest other things. But unlike symbols, which have a range of possible meanings, allegorical elements can always be assigned specific meanings. (Because writers use allegory to instruct, they gain nothing by hiding its significance.) In this sense, symbols open us possibilities for interpretation while allegories tend to restrict possibilities.

Quite often an allegory involves a journey or an adventure, as in the case of Dante's *Divine Comedy,* which traces a journey through Hell, Purgatory, and Heaven. Within an allegory everything can have meaning: the road upon which the characters walk, the people they encounter, or a phrase that one of them repeats throughout the journey. Once you understand the **allegorical framework**—the allegory's system of correspondences—your main task is to see how the various elements fit within this system. Some poems can be relatively straightforward, but others can be so complicated that it takes a great deal of time and effort to unlock their meaning. In the following poem, a journey is central to the allegory.

CHRISTINA ROSSETTI

(1830–1894)

Uphill

(1861)

Does the road wind uphill all the way?
    Yes, to the very end.
Will the day's journey take the whole long day?
    From morn to night, my friend.

5 But is there for the night a resting-place?
    A roof for when the slow dark hours begin.
May not the darkness hide it from my face?
    You cannot miss that inn.

Shall I meet other wayfarers at night?
10   Those who have gone before.
Then must I knock, or call when just in sight?
    They will not keep you standing at that door.

Shall I find comfort, travel-sore and weak?
    Of labor you shall find the sum.
15 Will there be beds for me and all who seek?
    Yea, beds for all who come.

"Uphill" uses a question-and-answer structure to describe a journey along
an uphill road. Like the journey described in John Bunyan's seventeenth-
century allegory *The Pilgrim's Progress*, this is a spiritual one that suggests
a person's uphill journey through life. The day and night duration of the
journey stands for life and death, and the inn at the end of the road stands
for the grave, the final resting place.

Poem for Further Reading: Allegory

ADRIENNE RICH

(1929–   )

Diving into the Wreck

(1973)

First having read the book of myths,
and loaded the camera,
and checked the edge of the knife-blade,
I put on
5   the body-armor of black rubber
the absurd flippers
the grave and awkward mask.
I am having to do this
not like Cousteau with his
10   assiduous team
aboard the sun-flooded schooner
but here alone.

There is a ladder.
The ladder is always there
15   hanging innocently
close to the side of the schooner.
We know what it is for,
we who have used it.
Otherwise
20   it's a piece of maritime floss
some sundry equipment.

I go down.
Rung after rung and still
the oxygen immerses me
25   the blue light
the clear atoms
of our human air.
I go down.
My flippers cripple me,
30   I crawl like an insect down the ladder
and there is no one
to tell me when the ocean
will begin.

First the air is blue and then
35 it is bluer and then green and then
black I am blacking out and yet
my mask is powerful
it pumps my blood with power
the sea is another story
40 the sea is not a question of power
I have to learn alone
to turn my body without force
in the deep element.

And now: it is easy to forget
45 what I came for
among so many who have always
lived here
swaying their crenellated fans
between the reefs
50 and besides
you breathe differently down here.

I came to explore the wreck.
The words are purposes.
The words are maps.
55 I came to see the damage that was done
and the treasures that prevail.
I stroke the beam of my lamp
slowly along the flank
of something more permanent
60 than fish or weed

the thing I came for:
the wreck and not the story of the wreck
the thing itself and not the myth
the drowned face always staring
65 toward the sun
the evidence of damage
worn by salt and sway into this threadbare beauty
the ribs of the disaster
curving their assertion
70 among the tentative haunters.

This is the place.
And I am here, the mermaid whose dark hair
streams black, the merman in his armored body
We circle silently
75 about the wreck

we dive into the hold.
I am she: I am he
whose drowned face sleeps with open eyes
whose breasts still bear the stress
80 whose silver, copper, vermeil cargo lies
obscurely inside barrels
half-wedged and left to rot
we are the half-destroyed instruments
that once held to a course
85 the water-eaten log
the fouled compass

We are, I am, you are
by cowardice or courage
the one who finds our way
90 back to this scene
carrying a knife, a camera
a book of myths
in which
our names do not appear.

READING AND REACTING

1. On one level this poem is about a deep-sea diver's exploration of a wrecked ship. What details suggest that the poet wants you to see something more?

2. Explain the allegorical elements presented in the poem. What, for example, might the diver and the wreck represent?

3. Does the poem contain any symbols? How can you tell they are symbols and not allegorical elements?

4. **JOURNAL ENTRY** In lines 62–63, the speaker says that she came for "the wreck and not the story of the wreck / the thing itself and not the myth." What do you think the speaker is really looking for?

5. **CRITICAL PERSPECTIVE** A number of critics have noted that "Diving into the Wreck" represents an attempt by Rich to reimagine or reinvent the myths of the dominant culture. Rachel Blau DuPlessis makes this observation:

In this poem of journey and transformation Rich is tapping the energies and plots of myth, while re-envisioning the content. While there is a hero, a quest, and a buried treasure, the hero is a woman; the quest is a critique of old myths; the treasure is knowledge. . . .

Why do you suppose Rich decided to "reinvent" myth?

Allusion

An **allusion** is a brief reference to a person, place, or event, historical or actual, that readers are expected to recognize. Like symbols and allegories, allusions enrich a work by introducing associations and attitudes from another context.

When poets use allusions, they assume that they and their readers share a common body of knowledge. If, when reading a poem, you come across a reference with which you are not familiar, take the time to look it up in a dictionary or an encyclopedia. As you have probably realized by now, a large part of the meaning of a poem may depend on an unfamiliar reference.

Although poets usually expect readers to recognize their references, some use allusions to exclude readers from their work. In his 1922 poem "The Waste Land," for example, T. S. Eliot makes allusions to historical events, ancient languages, and obscure literary works. He even includes a set of notes to accompany his poem, but they do little more than complicate an already complicated text. (As you might expect, critical response to this poem was mixed, with some critics saying that it was a work of genius and others saying that it was pretentious.)

Allusions can come from any source: history, the arts, other works of literature, the Bible, current events, or even the personal life of the poet. In the following poem, the Nigerian poet and playwright Wole Soyinka alludes to contemporary political figures.

WOLE SOYINKA

(1934–   )

Future Plans

(1972)

The meeting is called
To odium: Forgers, framers
Fabricators Inter-
national. Chairman,
5 A dark horse, a circus nag turned blinkered sprinter

Mach Three
We rate him—one for the Knife
Two for 'iavelli, Three—
Breaking speed
10 Of the truth barrier by a swooping detention decree

Projects in view:
Mao Tse Tung in league
With Chiang Kai. Nkrumah
Makes a secret
15 Pact with Verwood, sworn by Hastings Banda.
Proven: Arafat
In flagrante cum
Golda Meir. Castro drunk
With Richard Nixon
20 Contraceptives stacked beneath the papal bunk . . .
                                    . . . and more to come

This poem is structured like an agenda for a meeting. From the moment it announces that a meeting has been called "To odium" (a pun on "to order"), it is clear that the poem will be a bitter political satire. Those in attendance are "Forgers, framers / Fabricators." The second stanza contains three allusions that shed light on the character of the chairman. The first is to Mack the Knife, a petty criminal in Bertolt Brecht and Kurt Weill's 1933 Threepenny Opera. The second is to Niccolò Machiavelli, whose 1532 book The Prince advocates the use of unscrupulous means to strengthen the State. The last is to the term mach, which denotes the speed of an airplane in relation to the speed of sound—mach one, two, three, and so on. Through these allusions the poem implies that the meeting's chairman has been chosen for his ability to engage in violence, to be ruthless, and to break the "truth barrier"—that is, to lie.

The rest of the poem alludes to individuals involved in global politics—specifically, the politics of developing nations. According to the speaker, instead of fighting for the rights of the oppressed, these people consolidate their own political power by collaborating with those who oppose their positions. Thus, Mao Tse-tung, the former communist leader of China, is in league with Chiang Kai-shek, his old Nationalist Chinese enemy; Yassir Arafat, the leader of the Palestine Liberation Organization, is linked with Golda Meir, the former prime minister of Israel; Kwame Nkrumah, the first president of Ghana, conspires with Hendrick Verwoerd, the former prime minister of South Africa, assassinated in 1966; and former President Richard Nixon gets drunk with Cuba's communist leader, Fidel Castro. These allusions suggest the self-serving nature of political alliances and the extreme disorder of world politics. The ideological juxtapositions show the underlying sameness and interchangeability of various political philosophies, none of which has the answer to the world's problems. Whether the poem is satirizing the United Nations and its idealistic agenda, criticizing the tendency of politics to make strange bedfellows, or showing how corrupt all politicians are, its allusions enable the poet to broaden his frame of reference and thus make the poem more meaningful to readers.

The following poem uses allusions to writers, as well as to a myth, to develop its theme.

W I L L I A M   M E R E D I T H

(1919–   )

Dreams of Suicide

(1980)

(in sorrowful memory of Ernest Hemingway, Sylvia Plath, and John Berryman)

i

I reach for the awkward shotgun not to disarm
you, but to feel the metal horn,
furred with the downy membrane of dream.
More surely than the unicorn,
5 you are the mythical beast.

ii

Or I am sniffing an oven. On all fours
I am imitating a totemic animal
but she is not my totem or the totem
of my people, this is not my magic oven.

iii

10 If I hold you tight by the ankles,
still you fly upward from the iron railing.
Your father made these wings,
after he made his own, and now from beyond
he tells you *fly down,* in the voice
15 my own father might say *walk, boy.*

This poem is dedicated to the memory of three writers who committed suicide. In each stanza the speaker envisions in a dream the death of one of the writers. In the first stanza he dreams of Ernest Hemingway, who killed himself with a shotgun. The speaker grasps the metal horn of Hemingway's shotgun and transforms him into a mythical beast who, like a unicorn, represents the rare, unique talent of the artist. In the second stanza the speaker dreams of Sylvia Plath, who asphyxiated herself in a gas oven. He sees himself, like Plath, on his knees imitating an animal sniffing an oven. Finally, in the third stanza, the speaker dreams of John Berryman, who leaped to his death. Berryman is characterized as Icarus, a mythological figure who, along with his father Daedalus, fled Crete by building wings made of feathers and wax. Together they flew away, but, ignoring his father's warning, Icarus flew too close to the sun and, when the wax melted, fell to his death in the sea. Like Icarus, Berryman ignores the warning of his father and, like Daedalus, the speaker tries to stop Berryman. In this poem, then, the speaker uses allusions to make a point about the difficult lives of writers—and, perhaps, to convey his own empathy for those who could not survive the struggle to reconcile art and life.

Poem for Further Reading: Allusion

DELMORE SCHWARTZ

(1913–1966)

The True-Blue American

(1959)

Jeremiah Dickson was a true-blue American,
For he was a little boy who understood America, for he felt that he must
Think about *everything;* because that's *all* there is to think about,
Knowing immediately the intimacy of truth and comedy,
5 Knowing intuitively how a sense of humor was a necessity
For one and for all who live in America. Thus, natively, and
Naturally when on an April Sunday in an ice cream parlor Jeremiah
Was requested to choose between a chocolate sundae and a banana split
He answered unhesitatingly, having no need to think of it
10 Being a true-blue American, determined to continue as he began:
Rejecting the either-or of Kierkegaard,[1] and many another European;
Refusing to accept alternatives, refusing to believe the choice of
        between;
Rejecting selection; denying dilemma; electing absolute affirmation:
        knowing
15   in his breast
                The infinite and the gold
                Of the endless frontier, the deathless West.
"Both: I will have them both!" declared this true-blue American
In Cambridge, Massachusetts, on an April Sunday, instructed

---

[1] Søren Kierkegaard (1813–1855)—Danish philosopher who greatly influenced twentieth-century existentialism. *Either-Or* (1841) is one of his best-known works.

20   By the great department stores, by the Five-and-Ten,
Taught by Christmas, by the circus, by the vulgarity and grandeur of
        Niagara Falls and the Grand Canyon,
Tutored by the grandeur, vulgarity, and infinite appetite gratified and
        Shining in the darkness, of the light
25 On Saturdays at the double bills of the moon pictures,
The consummation of the advertisements of the imagination of the light
Which is as it was—the infinite belief in infinite hope—of Columbus,
        Barnum, Edison, and Jeremiah Dickson.

READING AND REACTING

1. To what does the poem's title refer? Do you think this title has
   meaning beyond its identification of Jeremiah Dickson?

2. Read an encyclopedia article about Kierkegaard. Why do you suppose
   Schwartz alludes to him in line 11?

3. Is the name Jeremiah Dickson an allusion? What do you think the
   significance of this name might be? What would be the effect of
   using a more obviously ethnic name? A more common name?

4. What is the significance of the allusions to places in lines 19–22 and
   to individuals in lines 27 and 28?

5. **JOURNAL ENTRY** How do you define a "true-blue" American? How
   do you think the poem's speaker would define this term?

6. **CRITICAL PERSPECTIVE** In his 1977 biography of Schwartz, James
   Atlas remarks on the poet's affinity with mass culture:

   *Delmore's interest in the products of the popular mind, while in part
   motivated by a desire to ally himself with a wider public than was
   ordinarily available to poets, had none of the moralizing condescension [of
   other 1950s intellectuals]; it was a natural expression of his own affinities
   with all that was American, affinities derived from his early infatuation
   with baseball, tabloids, the movies, and whatever else he thought animated
   the drama of history. . . . He was genuinely democratic. . . .*

   Do you see "The True-Blue American" as a celebration of mass
   culture? If not, what do you think Schwartz's purpose might have
   been?

Myth

A **myth** is a narrative that embodies—and in some cases helps to explain—
the religious, philosophical, moral, and political values of a culture. Using
gods and supernatural beings, myths try to make sense of occurrences in
the natural world. More generally, the term *myth* can also refer to a private

belief system invented by an individual poet as well as to any fully realized fictitious setting in which a literary work takes place, such as the myths of William Faulkner's Yoknapatawpha County or Lawrence Durrell's Alexandria. Contrary to popular usage, however, *myth* is not the same as *falsehood*. In the broadest sense, myths are stories—usually whole groups of stories— that can be true or partly true as well as false; regardless of their degree of accuracy, however, myths express the deepest beliefs of a culture. According to this definition, then, the *Iliad* and the *Odyssey,* the Koran, and the Old and New Testaments can all be regarded as myths.

According to the mythologist Joseph Campbell, the appeal of myths is that they contain truths that link people together, whether they live today or lived 2,500 years ago. Myths do, after all, attempt to explain phenomena that human beings care about regardless of when and where they live. It is not surprising, then, that myths frequently contain archetypal images that cut across cultural and racial boundaries and touch us on a very deep and basic level. Many Greek myths illustrate this power. For example, when Orpheus descends into Hades to rescue his wife, Eurydice, he acts out the human desire to transcend death; and when Telemachus sets out in search of his father, Odysseus, he reminds readers that we all are lost children searching for parents. When Icarus ignores his father and flies too near the sun and when Pandora cannot resist looking into a box that she has been told not to open, we are reminded of the fundamental weaknesses we all share.

When poets use myths, they are actually making allusions. They expect readers to bring to the poem the cultural, emotional, and ethical context of the myths to which the poem alludes. At one time, when educated individuals studied the Greek and Latin classics as well as the Bible, poets could be reasonably sure that readers would recognize the mythological allusions they made. Because this is no longer the case, readers usually have to consult dictionaries, encyclopedias, or collections of myths, such as the *New Larousse Encyclopedia of Mythology* or *Bullfinch's Mythology,* to identify a mythological allusion. Without this background information, many readers are unable to understand the full significance of an allusion or its application within the poem. Although many of the poems in this anthology are accompanied by notes, these notes may not provide all the information you will need to understand each mythological allusion and determine its significance within a poem. Occasionally you may have to look for answers beyond this text.

Sometimes a poet will allude to a myth in a title; sometimes references to various myths will appear throughout a poem; at other times, an entire poem will focus on a single myth. In each case, as in the following poem, the use of myth can help to communicate the poem's theme.

C O U N T E E   C U L L E N

(1903–1946)

Yet Do I Marvel

(1925)

I doubt not God is good, well-meaning, kind,
And did He stoop to quibble could tell why
The little buried mole continues blind,
Why flesh that mirrors Him must some day die,
5   Make plain the reason tortured Tantalus
Is baited by the fickle fruit, declare
If merely brute caprice dooms Sisyphus
To struggle up a never-ending stair.
Inscrutable His ways are, and immune
10   To catechism by a mind too strewn
With petty cares to slightly understand
What awful brain compels His awful hand.
Yet do I marvel at this curious thing:
To make a poet black, and bid him sing!

The speaker in this poem begins by affirming his belief in the benevolence of God, but he then goes on to question why God engages in what appear to be capricious acts. As part of his catalog of questions, the speaker mentions Tantalus and Sisyphus, two figures from Greek mythology. Tantalus was a king who was admitted to the society of the gods. Because he behaved so badly, he was condemned to stand up to his chin in a pool of water over which hung a branch laden with fruit. When he got thirsty and tried to drink, the level of the water would drop, and when he got hungry and reached for fruit, it would move just out of his grasp. Thus, Tantalus was doomed to be near what he most desired, but forever unable to obtain it. Like Tantalus, Sisyphus was also condemned to Hades. For his disrespect to Zeus he was sentenced to endless toil. Every day, Sisyphus would push a gigantic boulder up a steep hill. As he neared the top, the boulder would slip down the hill, and he would have to begin again. Like Tantalus, the speaker cannot have what he wants; like Sisyphus, he is forced to toil in vain. He wonders why a well-meaning God would "make a poet black and bid him sing" in a racist society that does not listen to his voice. Thus, the poet's two allusions to Greek mythology enrich the poem by connecting the suffering of the speaker to a universal drama that has been acted out again and again.

Poems for Further Reading: Myth

L O U I S E   E R D R I C H

(1954–   )

Windigo

(1984)

For Angela
The Windigo is a flesh-eating, wintry demon with a man buried deep
inside of it. In some Chippewa stories, a young girl vanquishes
this monster by forcing boiling lard down its throat, thereby
releasing the human at the core of ice.

You knew I was coming for you, little one,
when the kettle jumped into the fire.
Towels flapped on the hooks,
and the dog crept off, groaning,
5   to the deepest part of the woods.

In the hackles of dry brush a thin laughter started up.
Mother scolded the food warm and smooth in the pot
and called you to eat.
But I spoke in the cold trees:
10   *New one, I have come for you, child hide and lie still.*

The sumac pushed sour red cones through the air.
Copper burned in the raw wood.
You saw me drag toward you.
Oh touch me, I murmured, and licked the soles of your feet.
15   You dug your hands into my pale, melting fur.

I stole you off, a huge thing in my bristling armor.
Steam rolled from my wintry arms, each leaf shivered
from the bushes we passed
until they stood, naked, spread like the cleaned spines of fish.

20   Then your warm hands hummed over and shoveled themselves full
of the ice and the snow. I would darken and spill
all night running, until at last morning broke the cold earth
and I carried you home,
a river shaking in the sun.

READING AND REACTING

1. Because Erdrich writes for a diverse audience, she cannot reasonably expect all her readers to be familiar with the Native American myth in the poem. Does her introduction provide enough information for those who are not?

2. Who is the speaker in the poem? How would you characterize the speaker? What advantage does Erdrich gain by assuming this persona?

3. What is the major theme of this poem? How does the myth of the Windigo express this theme?

4. **JOURNAL ENTRY**   How is the Windigo described in the introduction like and unlike the one portrayed in the poem?

5. **CRITICAL PERSPECTIVE**   In her 1987 examination of various emerging American literatures, "The Bones of This Body Say, Dance," Lynda Koolish discusses Native American poetry:

   Earlier historical periods of Native American culture provide images of vision and power for many American Indian writers. Poetry, like prayers, chants, the telling of dreams, folktales, tribal lore, or oral history, is an essential part of the spiritual and aesthetic survival of American Indian people. . . . Like myth or folklore, legend or dream, poetry makes the unknowable intelligible. In Native American poetry, as in all these language art forms, access is provided to the mysterious and creative powers of the universe and thus to one's own inner power.

   Does "Windigo" offer this kind of access to you? Why or why not?

W I L L I A M   B U T L E R   Y E A T S

(1865–1939)

Leda and the Swan

(1924)

A sudden blow: the great wings beating still
Above the staggering girl, her thighs caressed
By the dark webs, her nape caught in his bill,
He holds her helpless breast upon his breast.

5 How can those terrified vague fingers push
The feathered glory from her loosening thighs?
And how can body, laid in that white rush,
But feel the strange heart beating where it lies?

A shudder in the loins engenders there
10 The broken wall, the burning roof and tower
And Agamemnon dead.
                              Being so caught up,
So mastered by the brute blood of the air,
Did she put on his knowledge with his power
Before the indifferent beak could let her drop?

READING AND REACTING

1. Look up the myth of Leda in an encyclopedia. What event is described in this poem? What is the mythological significance of the event?

2. How is Leda portrayed? Why is the swan described as a "feathered glory" (6)? Why in the poem's last line is Leda dropped by his "indifferent beak"?

3. The third stanza refers to the Trojan War, which was indirectly caused by the event described in the poem. How does the allusion to the Trojan War develop the theme of the poem?

4. **JOURNAL ENTRY**   Does the poem answer the questions asked in its last two lines? Explain.

5. **CRITICAL PERSPECTIVE**   According to Richard Ellmann this poem deals with "transcendence of opposites." The bird's rape of the human, the coupling of god and woman, the moment at which one epoch ended and another began . . . : "in the act which included all these Yeats had the violent symbol for the transcendence of opposites which he needed."

   What opposite or contrary forces exist in the myth of Leda and the swan? Do you think the poem implies that these forces can be reconciled?

DEREK WALCOTT [1]

(1930–   )

Sea Grapes [2]

(1971)

That sail which leans on light,
tired of islands,
a schooner beating up the Caribbean

---

[1] Winner of the 1992 Nobel Prize in literature.

[2] Small trees found on tropical sandy beaches.

for home, could be Odysseus,
5 home-bound on the Aegean;
that father and husband's

longing, under gnarled sour grapes, is
like the adulterer hearing Nausicaa's[3] name
in every gull's outcry.

10 This brings nobody peace. The ancient war
between obsession and responsibility
will never finish and has been the same

for the sea-wanderer or the one on shore
now wriggling on his sandals to walk home,
15 since Troy sighed its last flame,

and the blind giant's boulder heaved the trough
from whose ground-swell the great hexameters come
to the conclusions of exhausted surf.

The classics can console. But not enough.

READING AND REACTING

1. Locate a plot summary of the *Odyssey* in an encyclopedia. In the context of the myth of Odysseus, what is the "ancient war / between obsession and responsibility" (10–11) to which the speaker refers? Does this conflict have a wider application in the context of the poem? Explain.

2. Consider the following lines from the poem: "and the blind giant's boulder heaved the trough / from whose ground-swell the great hexameters come / to the conclusions of exhausted surf" (16–18). In what sense does the blind giant's boulder create the "great hexameters"? In what way does the trough end up as "exhausted surf"?

3. **JOURNAL ENTRY** This poem includes many references to Homer's *Odyssey*. Do you think a reader can appreciate the poem without having read Homer?

4. **CRITICAL PERSPECTIVE** Asked in an interview about the final line of "Sea Grapes," Derek Walcott made the following comments:

   All of us have been to the point where, in extreme agony and distress, you turn to a book, and look for parallels, and you look for a greater grief than maybe your own. . . . But the truth of human agony is that a book does not assuage a toothache. It isn't that things don't pass and heal. Perhaps the

---

[3] A young woman who befriended Odysseus.

only privilege that a poet has is that, in that agony, whatever chafes and
hurts, if the person survives, [he] produces something that is hopefully
lasting and moral from the experience.

How do Walcott's remarks help to explain the poem's last line?

W . H . A U D E N

(1907–1973)

Musée des Beaux Arts

(1940)

About suffering they were never wrong,
The Old Masters: how well they understood
Its human position; how it takes place
While someone else is eating or opening a window or just walking
    dully along
5 How, when the aged are reverently, passionately waiting
For the miraculous birth, there always must be
Children who did not specially want it to happen, skating
On a pond at the edge of the wood:
They never forgot
10 That even the dreadful martyrdom must run its course
Anyhow in a corner, some untidy spot
Where the dogs go on with their doggy life and the torturer's horse
Scratches its innocent behind on a tree.
In Brueghel's *Icarus,* for instance: how everything turns away
15 Quite leisurely from the disaster; the ploughman may
Have heard the splash, the forsaken cry,
But for him it was not an important failure; the sun shone
As it had to on the white legs disappearing into the green
Water; and the expensive delicate ship that must have seen
20 Something amazing, a boy falling out of the sky,
Had somewhere to get to and sailed calmly on.

READING AND REACTING

1. Reread the summary of the myth of Icarus on p. 880. Is Auden's
   allusion to the myth essential to the poem?

2. What point does the poet make by reffering to the "Old Masters" (2)?

3. **JOURNAL ENTRY**   Look at the painting on page 889. How does
   looking at Brueghel's *Fall of Icarus* help you to understand the poem?
   To what specific details in the painting does the poet refer?

The Fall of Icarus, by Brueghel. Photograph by Giraudon. Art Resource, N.Y.

▼▼▼▼▼▼▼▼▼▼▼▼▼▼▼▼▼▼▼▼▼▼▼▼▼▼▼▼▼▼▼▼▼▼▼▼

CHECKLIST FOR WRITING ABOUT SYMBOL, ALLEGORY, ALLUSION, MYTH

SYMBOL

◆ Are there any symbols in the poem? What leads you to believe they are symbols?

◆ Are these symbols conventional?

◆ Are they universal or archetypal?

◆ Does the work contain any private symbols?

◆ What is the literal meaning of the symbol in the context of the poem?

◆ Beyond its literal meaning, what else could the symbol suggest?

◆ How does your interpretation of the symbol enhance your understanding of the poem?

ALLEGORY

◆ Are there any allegorical elements within the poem? How can you tell?

◆ What do the allegorical elements signify on a literal level?

◆ What lesson does the allegory illustrate?

ALLUSION

◆ Are there any allusions in the poem?

◆ Do you recognize the names, places, historical events, or literary works to which the poet alludes?

◆ What does each allusion add to the poem? In what way does each deepen the poem's meaning? Does any allusion interfere with your understanding or enjoyment of the poem?

◆ Would the poem be more effective without a particular allusion?

MYTH

◆ What myths or mythological figures are alluded to?

◆ How does the poem use myth to convey its meaning?

◆ How faithful is the poem to the myth? Does the poet add material to the myth? Are any details from the original myth omitted? Is any information distorted? Why?

▲▲

WRITING SUGGESTIONS: SYMBOL, ALLEGORY, ALLUSION, MYTH

1. Read "Aunt Jennifer's Tigers" (p. 807) and "Diving into the Wreck" (p. 874) by Adrienne Rich. Then, write an essay in which you discuss similarities and the differences in Rich's use of symbols in the two works.

2. Many popular songs make use of allusion. Choose one or two popular songs that you know well, and analyze their use of allusion, paying particular attention to whether the allusions expand the impact and meaning of the song or create barriers to your understanding.

3. Read the Emily Dickinson poem "Because I Could Not Stop for Death" (p. 913), and then write an interpretation of the poem, supplying allegorical equivalents for the concrete objects in the poem.

4. What applications do the lessons of myth have for twentieth-century life? Choose two or three poems from the section on myth, and consider how you can use myth to make generalizations about your own life.

5. Both Judith Ortiz Cofer's "My Father in the Navy: A Childhood Memory" (p. 640) and Derek Walcott's "Sea Grapes" (p. 886) allude to Homer's *Odyssey*. Read a summary of this story in an encyclopedia or other reference book, and then write an essay in which you discuss the poets' treatments of Homer's tale. What specific use does each poet make of the story?

Poetry

ANNA AKHMATOVA

(1889–1966)

He Loved Three Things Alone

(1911)

He loved three things alone:
White peacocks, evensong,
Old maps of America.
He hated children crying,
5 And raspberry jam with his tea,
And womanish hysteria.
. . . And he had married me.

ANONYMOUS

Bonny Barbara Allan

(traditional Scottish ballad)

It was in and about the Martinmas[1] time,
  even the green leaves were afalling,
That Sir John Graeme, in the West Country,
  Fell in love with Barbara Allan.

---

[1] Saint Martin's Day, November 11.

5 He sent his men down through the town,
       To the place where she was dwelling;
   "O haste and come to my master dear,
       Gin² ye be Barbara Allan."

O hooly,³ hooly rose she up,
10   To the place where he was lying,
   And when she drew the curtain by:
       "Young man, I think you're dying."

"O it's I'm sick, and very, very sick,
       And 'tis a' for Barbara Allan."—
15 "O the better for me ye's never be,
       Tho your heart's blood were aspilling.

"O dinna ye mind,⁴ young man," said she,
       "When ye was in the tavern adrinking,
   That ye made the health gae round and round,
20   And slighted Barbara Allan?"

He turned his face unto the wall,
       And death was with him dealing:
   "Adieu, adieu, my dear friends all,
       And be kind to Barbara Allan."

25 And slowly, slowly raise she up,
       And slowly, slowly left him,
   And sighing said she could not stay,
       Since death of life had reft him.

She had not gane a mile but twa,⁵
30   When she heard the dead-bell ringing,
   And every jow⁶ that the dead-bell geid,
       It cried, "Woe to Barbara Allan!"

"O mother, mother, make my bed!
       O make it saft and narrow!
35 Since my love died for me today,
       I'll die for him tomorrow."

---

² If.

³ Slowly.

⁴ Don't you remember.

⁵ Two.

⁶ Stroke.

Sir Patrick Spence

(traditional Scottish ballad)

The king sits in Dumferling toune,
    Drinking the blude-reid wine:
"O whar will I get guid sailor
    To sail this schip of mine?"

5 Up and spak an eldern knicht,
    Sat at the kings richt kne:
"Sir Patrick Spence is the best sailor
    That sails upon the se."

The king has written a braid letter,
10   And signed it wi' his hand,
And sent it to Sir Patrick Spence,
    Was walking on the sand.

The first line that Sir Patrick red,
    A loud lauch lauchèd he;
15 The next line that Sir Patrick red,
    The teir blinded his ee.

"O wha[1] is this has don this deid,
    This ill deid don to me,
To send me out this time o' the yeir,
20   To sail upon the se!

"Mak haste, mak haste, my mirry men all,
    Our guid schip sails the morne."
"O say na sae[2] my master deir,
    For I feir a deadlie storme.

25 "Late late yestreen I saw the new moone,
    Wi' the auld moone in hir arme,
And I feir, I feir, my deir master,
    That we will cum to harme."

---

[1] Who.

[2] Not so.

O our Scots nobles wer richt laith[3]
30   To weet[4] their cork-heild schoone;[5]
Bot lang owre[6] a' the play wer playd,
     Their hats they swam aboone.[7]

O lang, lang may their ladies sit,
     Wi' their fans into their hand,
35 Or ere they se Sir Patrick Spence
     Cum sailing to the land.

O lang, lang may the ladies stand,
     Wi' their gold kems[8] in their hair,
Waiting for their ain[9] deir lords,
40   For they'll se thame na mair.

Haf owre,[10] haf owre to Aberdour,
     It's fiftie fadom deip,
And thair lies guid Sir Patrick Spence,
     Wi' the Scots lords at his feit.

Western Wind

(English lyric)

Western wind, when wilt thou blow,
The[1] small rain down can rain?
Christ, if my love were in my arms,
And I in my bed again!

---

[3] Loath.

[4] Wet.

[5] Shoes.

[6] Before.

[7] Above.

[8] Combs.

[9] Own.

[10] Halfway over.

[1] [So that] the.

M A T T H E W   A R N O L D

(1822–1888)

Dover Beach

(1867)

The sea is calm tonight.
The tide is full, the moon lies fair
Upon the straits;—on the French coast the light
Gleams and is gone; the cliffs of England stand,
5 Glimmering and vast, out in the tranquil bay.
Come to the window, sweet is the night-air!
Only, from the long line of spray
Where the sea meets the moon-blanched[1] land,
Listen! you hear the grating roar
10 Of pebbles which the waves draw back, and fling,
At their return, up the high strand,[2]
Begin, and cease, and then again begin,
With tremulous cadence slow, and bring
The eternal note of sadness in.

15 Sophocles[3] long ago
Heard it on the Aegean,[4] and it brought
Into his mind the turbid ebb and flow
Of human misery; we
Find also in the sound a thought,
20 Hearing it by this distant northern sea.

The Sea of Faith
Was once, too, at the full, and round earth's shore
Lay like the folds of a bright girdle furled.
But now I only hear
25 Its melancholy, long, withdrawing roar,
Retreating, to the breath
Of the night-wind, down the vast edges drear
And naked shingles[5] of the world.

---

[1] Whitened by the moon.

[2] Beach.

[3] Greek playwright (496–406 B.C.), author of tragedies including *Oedipus Rex* and *Antigone*.

[4] Sea between Greece and Turkey.

[5] Gravel beaches.

Ah, love, let us be true
30 To one another! for the world, which seems
To lie before us like a land of dreams,
So various, so beautiful, so new,
Hath really neither joy, nor love, nor light,
Nor certitude, nor peace, nor help for pain;
35 And we are here as on a darkling[6] plain
Swept with confused alarms of struggle and flight,
Where ignorant armies clash by night.

J O H N   B E R R Y M A N

(1914–1972)

Dream Song #14

(1964)

Life, friends, is boring. We must not say so.
After all, the sky flashes, the great sea yearns,
we ourselves flash and yearn,
and moreover my mother told me as a boy
5 (repeatedly) "Ever to confess you're bored
means you have no

Inner Resources." I conclude now I have no
inner resources, because I am heavy bored.
Peoples bore me,
10 literature bores me, especially great literature,
Henry bores me, with his plights & gripes
as bad as achilles,[1]

who loves people and valiant art, which bores me.
And the tranquil hills, & gin, look like a drag
15 and somehow a dog
has taken itself & its tail considerably away
into mountains or sea or sky, leaving
behind: me, wag.

---

[6] Darkening.

[1] Temperamental Greek hero of the Trojan War who was vulnerable only at the heel.

WILLIAM BLAKE

(1757–1827)

The Chimney Sweeper

(1789)

When my mother died I was very young,
And my father sold me while yet my tongue
Could scarcely cry "'weep! 'weep! 'weep! 'weep!"
So your chimneys I sweep, and in soot I sleep.

5 There's little Tom Dacre, who cried when his head,
That curled like a lamb's back, was shaved: so I said
"Hush, Tom! never mind it, for when your head's bare
You know that the soot cannot spoil your white hair."

And so he was quiet, and that very night,
10 As Tom was a-sleeping, he had such a sight!
That thousands of sweepers, Dick, Joe, Ned, and Jack,
Were all of them locked up in coffins of black.

And by came an Angel who had a bright key,
And he opened the coffins and set them all free;
15 Then down a green plain leaping, laughing, they run,
And wash in a river, and shine in the sun.

Then naked and white, all their bags left behind,
They rise upon clouds and sport in the wind;
And the Angel told Tom, if he'd be a good boy,
20 He'd have God for his father, and never want joy.

And so Tom awoke; and we rose in the dark,
And got with our bags and our brushes to work.
Though the morning was cold, Tom was happy and warm;
So if all do their duty they need not fear harm.

The Garden of Love

(1794)

I went to the Garden of Love,
And saw what I never had seen:
A Chapel was built in the midst,
Where I used to play on the green.

5 And the gates of this Chapel were shut,
And "Thou shalt not" writ over the door;
So I turned to the Garden of Love
That so many sweet flowers bore;

And I saw it was filled with graves,
10 And tomb-stones where flowers should be;
And Priests in black gowns were walking their rounds,
And binding with briars my joys and desires.

The Lamb

(1789)

Little Lamb, who made thee?
Dost thou know who made thee?
Gave thee life & bid thee feed,
By the stream & o'er the mead;
5 Gave thee clothing of delight,
Softest clothing wooly bright;
Gave thee such a tender voice,
Making all the vales rejoice!
Little Lamb who made thee?
10   Dost thou know who made thee?

Little Lamb I'll tell thee,
Little Lamb I'll tell thee!
He is callèd by thy name,
For he calls himself a Lamb:
15 He is meek & he is mild,
He became a little child:
I a child & thou a lamb,
We are callèd by his name.
Little Lamb God bless thee.
20   Little Lamb God bless thee.

London

(1794)

I wander through each chartered street,
Near where the chartered Thames does flow,
And mark in every face I meet
Marks of weakness, marks of woe.

5 In every cry of every man,
In every infant's cry of fear,
In every voice, in every ban,
The mind-forged manacles I hear.

How the chimney-sweeper's cry
10 Every black'ning church appalls;
And the hapless soldier's sigh
Runs in blood down palace walls.

But most through midnight streets I hear
How the youthful harlot's curse
15 Blasts the new born infant's tear,
And blights with plagues the marriage hearse.

The Tyger

(1794)

Tyger! Tyger! burning bright
In the forests of the night,
What immortal hand or eye
Could frame thy fearful symmetry?

5 In what distant deeps or skies
Burnt the fire of thine eyes?
On what wings dare he aspire?
What the hand dare seize the fire?

And what shoulder, and what art,
10 Could twist the sinews of thy heart?
And when thy heart began to beat,
What dread hand? and what dread feet?

What the hammer? what the chain?
In what furnace was thy brain?
15 What the anvil? what dread grasp
Dare its deadly terrors clasp?

When the stars threw down their spears,
And watered heaven with their tears,
Did he smile his work to see?
20 Did he who made the Lamb make thee?

Tyger! Tyger! burning bright
In the forests of the night,
What immortal hand or eye
Dare frame thy fearful symmetry?

ROBERT BLY

(1926–   )

Snowfall in the Afternoon

(1962)

1

The grass is half-covered with snow.
It was the sort of snowfall that starts in late afternoon.
And now the little houses of the grass are growing dark.

2

If I reached my hands down, near the earth,
5 I could take handfuls of darkness!
A darkness was always there, which we never noticed.

3

As the snow grows heavier, the cornstalks fade further away,
And the barn moves nearer to the house.
The barn moves all alone in the growing storm.

4

10 The barn is full of corn, and moving toward us now,
Like a hulk blown toward us in a storm at sea;
All the sailors on deck have been blind for many years.

L O U I S E   B O G A N

(1879–1970)

Women

(1923)

Women have no wilderness in them,
They are provident instead,
Content in the tight hot cell of their hearts
To eat dusty bread.

5 They do not see cattle cropping red winter grass,
They do not hear
Snow water going down under culverts
Shallow and clear.

They wait, when they should turn to journeys,
10 They stiffen, when they should bend.
They use against themselves that benevolence
To which no man is friend.

They cannot think of so many crops to a field
Or of clean wood cleft by an axe.
15 Their love is an eager meaninglessness
Too tense, or too lax.

They hear in every whisper that speaks to them
A shout and a cry.
As like as not, when they take life over their door-sills
20 They should let it go by.

ANNE BRADSTREET

(1612?–1672)

The Author to Her Book[1]

(1678)

Thou ill-formed offspring of my feeble brain,
Who after birth did'st by my side remain,
Till snatched from thence by friends, less wise than true,
Who thee abroad exposed to public view;
5 Made thee in rags, halting, to the press to trudge,
Where errors were not lessened, all may judge.
At thy return my blushing was not small,
My rambling brat (in print) should mother call;
I cast thee by as one unfit for light,
10 Thy visage was so irksome in my sight;
Yet being mine own, at length affection would
Thy blemishes amend, if so I could:
I washed thy face, but more defects I saw,
And rubbing off a spot, still made a flaw.
15 I stretched thy joints to make thee even feet,[2]
Yet still thou run'st more hobbling than is meet;[3]
In better dress to trim thee was my mind,
But nought save homespun cloth in the house I find.
In this array, 'mongst vulgars[4] may'st thou roam;
20 In critics' hands beware thou dost not come;
And take thy way where yet thou are not known.
If for thy Father asked, say thou had'st none;
And for thy Mother, she alas is poor,
Which caused her thus to send thee out of door.

---

[1] Bradstreet addresses *The Tenth Muse,* a collection of her poetry, which was published without her consent in 1650.

[2] Metrical feet.

[3] Appropriate or decorous.

[4] Common people.

ELIZABETH BARRETT BROWNING

(1806–1861)

How Do I Love Thee?

(1850)

How do I love thee? Let me count the ways.
I love thee to the depth and breadth and height
My soul can reach, when feeling out of sight
For the ends of being and ideal grace.
5 I love thee to the level of every day's
Most quiet need, by sun and candle-light.
I love thee freely, as men strive for right.
I love thee purely, as they turn from praise.
I love thee with the passion put to use
10 In my old griefs, and with my childhood's faith.
I love thee with a love I seemed to lose
With my lost saints. I love thee with the breath,
Smiles, tears, of all my life; and, if God choose,
I shall but love thee better after death.

ROBERT BROWNING

(1812–1889)

Meeting at Night

(1845)

The gray sea and the long black land;
And the yellow half-moon large and low;
And the startled little waves that leap
In fiery ringlets from their sleep,
5 As I gain the cove with pushing prow,
And quench its speed i' the slushy sand.

Then a mile of warm sea-scented beach;
Three fields to cross till a farm appears;
A tap at the pane, the quick sharp scratch
10 And blue spurt of a lighted match,
And a voice less loud, through its joys and fears,
Than the two hearts beating each to each!

Parting at Morning

(1845)

Round the cape of a sudden came the sea,
And the sun looked over the mountain's rim:
And straight was a path of gold for him,
And the need of a world of men for me.

GEORGE GORDON, LORD BYRON

(1788–1824)

She Walks in Beauty

(1815)

1

She walks in beauty, like the night
    Of cloudless climes and starry skies;
And all that's best of dark and bright
    Meet in her aspect and her eyes:
5 Thus mellowed to that tender light
    Which heaven to gaudy day denies.

2

One shade the more, one ray the less,
    Had half impaired the nameless grace
Which waves in every raven tress,
10   Or softly lightens o'er her face;
Where thoughts serenely sweet express
    How pure, how dear their dwelling place.

3

And on that cheek, and o'er that brow,
    So soft, so calm, yet eloquent,
15 The smiles that win, the tints that glow,
    But tell of days in goodness spent,
A mind at peace with all below,
    A heart whose love is innocent!

THOMAS CAMPION

(1567–1620)

There Is a Garden in Her Face

(1617)

There is a garden in her face
Where roses and white lilies grow;
   A heav'nly paradise is that place
Wherein all pleasant fruits do flow.
5   There cherries grow which none may buy
   Till "Cherry-ripe" themselves do cry.

Those cherries fairly do enclose
Of orient pearl a double row,
   Which when her lovely laughter shows,
10 They look like rose-buds filled with snow;
     Yet them nor peer nor prince can buy,
   Till "Cherry-ripe" themselves do cry.

Her eyes like angels watch them still;
Her brows like bended bows do stand,
15   Threat'ning with piercing frowns to kill
All that attempt, with eye or hand
     Those sacred cherries to come nigh
   Till "Cherry-ripe" themselves do cry.

GEOFFREY CHAUCER

(1343–1400)

from The Canterbury Tales

(1386–1387)

(General Prologue)

Whan that Aprill with his shoures soote[1]
The droghte of March[2] hath perced to the roote,
And bathed every veyne[3] in swich licour[4]
Of which vertu[5] engendred is the flour;
5   Whan Zephirus[6] eek with his sweete breeth
Inspired hath in every holt and heeth[7]
The tendre croppes,[8] and the yonge sonne[9]
Hath in the Ram his halfe cours yronne,[10]
And smale foweles maken melodye,
10 That slepen al the nyght with open ye
(So priketh hem nature in hir corages);
Thanne longen folk to goon on pilgrimages,
And palmeres[11] for to seken straunge strondes[12]
To ferne halwes, kowthe[13] in sondry londes;
15 And specially from every shires ende

---

[1] Gentle showers.

[2] Dryness of March.

[3] Veins in the plants.

[4] Such liquid.

[5] Potency.

[6] The west wind; in classical mythology, husband of Flora, goddess of flowers, and father of Carpus, god of fruit.

[7] Woodland and plain.

[8] New foliage.

[9] Just beginning its annual journey after the vernal equinox. In Chaucer's time the English legal year began on March 25.

[10] The zodiacal house of Aries (the Ram) in Chaucer's time extended from March 12 to April 11.

[11] Professional pilgrims whose emblem was a palm frond.

[12] Lands.

[13] Faraway saints (or shrines), known.

Of Engelond to Caunterbury they wende
The hooly blisful martir[14] for to seke
That hem hath holpen whan that they were seeke.[15]
    Bifil that in that seson on a day
20 In Southwerk[16] at the Tabard[17] as I lay
Redy to wenden on my pilgrymage
To Caunterbury with ful devout corage,
At nyght was come into that hostelrye
Wel nyne and twenty in a compaignye
25 Of sondry folk, by aventure[18] yfalle
In felaweshipe, and pilgrimes were they alle,
That toward Caunterbury wolden ryde.
The chambres and the stables weren wyde,
And wel we weren esed atte beste.[19]
30 And shortly,[20] whan the sonne was to reste,
So hadde I spoken with hem everichon
That I was of hir felaweship anon,[21]
And made forward[22] erly for to ryse,
To take oure wey ther as I yow devyse.[23]
35   But nathelees, whil I have tyme and space,
Er that I ferther in this tale pace,
Me thynketh it acordaunt to resoun
To telle yow al the condicioun[24]
Of ech of hem, so as it semed me,
40 And whiche they weren, and of what degree,[25]
And eek in what array that they were inne,
And at a knyght than wol I first bigynne.

---

[14] Blessed St. Thomas à Becket, martyred in Canterbury Cathedral in 1170.

[15] Helped, sick.

[16] The borough south of London bridge.

[17] Inn identified by a sign shaped like a smock.

[18] Chance.

[19] Accommodated in the best manner.

[20] To be brief about it.

[21] Immediately.

[22] (We) made an agreement.

[23] (Will) relate.

[24] Circumstances.

[25] Status (rank).

LUCILLE CLIFTON

(1936–   )

come home from the movies

(1974)

come home from the movies,
black girls and boys,
the picture be over and the screen
be cold as our neighborhood.
5 come home from the show,
don't be the show.
take off some flowers and plant them,
pick us some papers and read them,
stop making some babies and raise them.
10 come home from the movies
black girls and boys,
show our fathers how to walk like men,
they already know how to dance.

SAMUEL TAYLOR COLERIDGE

(1772–1834)

Kubla Khan[1]

(1797–1798)

Or, a Vision in a Dream. A Fragment.

In Xanadu did Kubla Khan
A stately pleasure-dome decree:
Where Alph,[2] the sacred river, ran
Through caverns measureless to man
5 Down to a sunless sea.

---

[1] Coleridge mythologizes the actual Kublai Khan, a thirteenth-century Mongol emperor, as well as the Chinese city of Xanadu.

[2] Probably derived from the Greek river Alpheus, whose waters, according to legend, rose from the Ionian Sea in Sicily as the fountain of Arethusa.

So twice five miles of fertile ground
With walls and towers were girdled round;
And there were gardens bright with sinuous rills,
Where blossomed many an incense-bearing tree;
10 And here were forests ancient as the hills,
Enfolding sunny spots of greenery.

But oh! that deep romantic chasm which slanted
Down the green hill athwart a cedarn cover!
A savage place! as holy and enchanted
15 As e'er beneath a waning moon was haunted
By woman wailing for her demon-lover!
And from this chasm, with ceaseless turmoil seething,
As if this earth in fast thick pants were breathing,
A mighty fountain momently was forced:
20 Amid whose swift half-intermitted burst
Huge fragments vaulted like rebounding hail,
Or chaffy grain beneath the thresher's flail:
And 'mid these dancing rocks at once and ever
It flung up momently the sacred river.
25 Five miles meandering with a mazy motion
Through wood and dale the sacred river ran,
Then reached the caverns measureless to man,
And sank in tumult to a lifeless ocean:
And 'mid this tumult Kubla heard from far
30 Ancestral voices prophesying war!
    The shadow of the dome of pleasure
    Floated midway on the waves;
    Where was heard the mingled measure
    From the fountain and the caves.
35 It was a miracle of rare device,
A sunny pleasure-dome with caves of ice!

    A damsel with a dulcimer
    In a vision once I saw:
    It was an Abyssinian maid,
40   And on her dulcimer she played,
    Singing of Mount Abora.[3]
    Could I revive within me
    Her symphony and song,
    To such a deep delight 'twould win me,

---

[3] Some scholars see a reminiscence here of John Milton's *Paradise Lost IV*, 280–82: "where Abassin kings their issue guard / Mount Amara, though this by some supposed / True Paradise under the Ethiop Line."

45 That with music loud and long,
I would build that dome in air,
That sunny dome! those caves of ice!
And all who heard should see them there,
And all should cry, Beware! Beware!
50 His flashing eyes, his floating hair!
Weave a circle round him thrice,[4]
And close your eyes with holy dread,
For he on honey-dew hath fed,
And drunk the milk of Paradise.

V I C T O R   H E R N Á N D E Z   C R U Z
(1949–   )

Anonymous
(1982)

And if I lived in those olden times
With a funny name like Choicer or
Henry Howard, Earl of Surrey, what chimes!
I would spend my time in search of rhymes
5 Make sure the measurement termination surprise
In the court of kings snapping till woo sunrise
Plus always be using the words *alas* and *hath*
And not even knowing that that was my path
Just think on the Lower East Side of Manhattan
10 It would have been like living in satin
Alas! The projects hath not covered the river
Thou see-est vision to make thee quiver
Hath I been delivered to that "wildernesse"
So past
15 I would have been the last one in the
Dance to go
Taking note the minuet so slow
All admire my taste
Within thou *mambo* of much more haste.

---

[4] A magic ritual, to keep away intruding spirits.

COUNTEE CULLEN

(1903–1946)

For a Lady I Know

(1925)

She even thinks that up in heaven
Her class lies late and snores,
While poor black cherubs rise at seven
To do celestial chores.

E. E. CUMMINGS

(1894–1962)

Buffalo Bill's

(1923)

Buffalo Bill's
defunct
            who used to
            ride a watersmooth-silver
5   stallion
and break onetwothreefourfive pigeonsjustlikethat
                                                Jesus
he was a handsome man
                    and what i want to know is
10 how do you like your blueeyed boy
Mister Death

---

next to of course god america i

(1926)

"next to of course god america i
love you land of the pilgrims' and so forth oh

say can you see by the dawn's early my
country 'tis of centuries come and go
5 and are no more what of it we should worry
in every language even deafanddumb
thy sons acclaim your glorious name by gorry
by jingo by gee by gosh by gum
why talk of beauty what could be more beaut-
10 iful than these heroic happy dead
who rushed like lions to the roaring slaughter
they did not stop to think they died instead
then shall the voice of liberty be mute?"

He spoke. And drank rapidly a glass of water

EMILY DICKINSON

(1830–1886)

After Great Pain, a Formal Feeling Comes—

(c. 1862)

After great pain, a formal feeling comes—
The Nerves sit ceremonious, like Tombs—
The stiff Heart questions was it He, that bore,
And Yesterday, or Centuries before?

5 The Feet, mechanical, go round—
Of Ground, or Air, or Ought—
A Wooden way
Regardless grown,
A Quartz contentment, like a stone—

10 This is the Hour of Lead—
Remembered, if outlived,
As Freezing persons, recollect the Snow—
First—Chill—then Stupor—then the letting go—

Because I Could Not Stop for Death

(1863)

Because I could not stop for Death—
He kindly stopped for me—
The Carriage held but just Ourselves—
And Immortality.

5 We slowly drove—He knew no haste
And I had put away
My labor and my leisure too,
For His Civility—

We passed the School, where Children strove
10 At Recess—in the Ring—
We passed the Fields of Gazing Grain—
We passed the Setting Sun—
Or rather—He passed Us—
The Dews drew quivering and chill—

15 For only Gossamer, my Gown—
My Tippet[1]—only Tulle—

We paused before a House that seemed
A Swelling of the Ground—
The Roof was scarcely visible—
20 The Cornice—in the Ground—

Since then—'tis Centuries—and yet
Feels shorter than the Day
I first surmised the Horses' Heads
Were toward Eternity—

---

[1] Cape.

I Heard a Fly Buzz—When I Died

(c. 1862)

I heard a Fly buzz—when I died—
The Stillness in the Room
Was like the Stillness in the Air—
Between the Heaves of Storm—

5 The Eyes around—had wrung them dry—
And Breaths were gathering firm
For that last Onset—when the King
Be witnessed—in the Room—

I willed my Keepsakes—Signed away
10 What portion of me be
Assignable—and then it was
There interposed a Fly—

With Blue—uncertain stumbling Buzz—
Between the light—and me—
15 And then the Windows failed—and then
I could not see to see—

I Never Saw a Moor—

(c. 1865)

I never saw a Moor—
I never saw the Sea—
Yet know I how the Heather looks
And what a Billow be.

5 I never spoke with God
Nor visited in Heaven—
Yet certain am I of the spot
As if the Checks were given—

I Taste a Liquor Never Brewed

(1861)

I taste a liquor never brewed—
From Tankards scooped in Pearl—
Not all the Frankfort Berries[1]
Yield such an Alcohol!

5 Inebriate of Air—am I—
And Debauchee of Dew—
Reeling—thro endless summer days—
From inns of Molten Blue—

When "Landlords" turn the drunken Bee
10 Out of the Foxglove's door—
When Butterflies—renounce their "drams"—
I shall but drink the more!

Till Seraphs swing their snowy Hats—
And Saints—to windows run—
15 To see the little Tippler
From Manzanilla[2] come!

Much Madness is Divinest Sense—

(c. 1862)

Much Madness is divinest Sense—
To a discerning Eye—
Much Sense—the starkest Madness—
'Tis the Majority
5 In this, as All, prevail—
Assent—and you are sane—
Demur—you're straightway dangerous—
And handled with a Chain—

---

[1] This line is a variant reading for the usually accepted "Not all the Vats upon the Rhine." In both cases, the poet refers to German wine.

[2] A pale Spanish sherry.

The Soul Selects Her Own Society

(1862)

The Soul selects her own Society—
Then—shuts the Door—
To her divine Majority—
Present no more—

5 Unmoved—she notes the Chariots—pausing—
At her low Gate—
Unmoved—an Emperor be kneeling
Upon her Mat—

I've known her—from an ample nation—
10 Choose One—
Then—close the Valves of her attention—
Like Stone—

There's a Certain Slant of Light

(c. 1861)

There's a certain Slant of light,
Winter Afternoons—
That oppresses, like the Heft
Of Cathedral Tunes—

5 Heavenly Hurt, it gives us—
We can find no scar,
But internal difference,
Where the Meanings, are—

None may teach it—Any—
10 'Tis the Seal Despair—
An imperial affliction
Sent us of the Air—

When it comes, the Landscape listens—
Shadows—hold their breath—
15 When it goes, 'tis like the Distance
On the look of Death—

Wild Nights—Wild Nights!

(1890, c. 1861)

Wild Nights—Wild Nights!
Were I with thee
Wild Nights should be
Our luxury!

5 Futile—the Winds—
To a Heart in port—
Done with the Compass—
Done with the Chart!

Rowing in Eden—
10 Ah, the Sea!
Might I but moor—Tonight—
In Thee!

JOHN DONNE

(1572–1631)

Batter My Heart, Three-Personed God

(c. 1610)

Batter my heart, three-personed God, for You
As yet but knock, breathe, shine, and seek to mend.
That I may rise and stand, o'erthrow me, and bend
Your force to break, blow, burn, and make me new.
5 I, like an usurped town to another due,
Labor to admit You, but Oh! to no end.
Reason, Your viceroy in me, me should defend,
But is captived, and proves weak or untrue.
Yet dearly I love You, and would be lovèd fain,
10 But am betrothed unto Your enemy;
Divorce me, untie or break that knot again;
Take me to You, imprison me, for I,
Except You enthrall me, never shall be free,
Nor ever chaste, except You ravish me.

Death Be Not Proud

(c. 1610)

Death be not proud, though some have callèd thee
Mighty and dreadful, for thou art not so;
For those whom thou think'st thou dost overthrow
Die not, poor death, nor yet canst thou kill me.
5 From rest and sleep, which but thy pictures be,
Much pleasure, then from thee much more must flow,
And soonest our best men with thee do go,
Rest of their bones, and soul's delivery.
Thou art slave to fate, chance, kings, and desperate men,
10 And dost with poison, war, and sickness dwell,
And poppy, or charms can make us sleep as well,
And better than thy stroke; why swell'st thou then?
One short sleep past, we wake eternally,
And death shall be no more; death, thou shalt die.

Hymn to God, My God, in My Sickness

(1633)

Since I am coming to that Holy Room,[1]
    Where, with Thy choir of saints for evermore,
I shall be made thy music; as I come
    I tune the instrument here at the door,
5   And what I must do then, think here before.

Whilst my physicians by their love are grown
    Cosmographers, and I their map, who lie
Flat on this bed, that by them may be shown
    That this is my southwest discovery
10   *Per fretum febris,*[2] by these straits[3] to die,

---

[1] See John 14:2–7.

[2] Of or by a fever (Latin).

[3] Difficulties.

I joy, that in these straits,[4] I see my West;[5]
    For, though their currents yield return to none,
What shall my West hurt me? As West and East[6]
    In all flat maps (and I am one) are one,
15   So death doth touch the Resurrection.

Is the Pacific Sea my home? Or are
    The Eastern riches? Is Jerusalem?
Anyan,[7] and Magellan,[8] and Gibraltar,[9]
    All straits, and none but straits, are ways to them,
20   Whether where Japhet dwelt, or Cham, or Sem.[10]

We think that Paradise and Calvary
    Christ's cross, and Adam's tree, stood in one place;
Look, Lord, and find both Adams met in me;
    As the first Adam's[11] sweat surrounds my face,
25   May the last Adam's[12] blood my soul embrace.

So, in his purple wrapped,[13] receive me, Lord,
    By these his thorns give me his other crown;
And as to others' souls I preached thy word,
    Be this my text, my sermon to mine own,
30   Therefore that He may raise, the Lord throws down.

---

[4] Narrow channels that connect larger bodies of water.

[5] Refers to the setting sun; suggests death.

[6] Refers to the rising sun; suggests resurrection.

[7] Anyang, a Chinese center of trade in Donne's time.

[8] The Strait of Magellan, which connects the Atlantic and Pacific Oceans at the southernmost tip of South America; part of the sea route commonly used in trade between Europe and Asia in Donne's time.

[9] The Strait of Gibraltar, which connects the Atlantic Ocean and the Mediterranean Sea.

[10] The three sons of Noah, whose descendants, according to the Bible, established tribes throughout the ancient Middle East.

[11] Refers to the first man, according to the biblical book of Genesis.

[12] Refers to Christ. See I Corinthians 15:45.

[13] Alludes to the blood-drenched linen found in the tomb of the risen Christ; also a royal color.

Song

(1633)

Go and catch a falling star,
    Get with child a mandrake root,[1]
Tell me where all past years are,
    Or who cleft the Devil's foot,
5 Teach me to hear mermaids singing,
    Or to keep off envy's stinging,
        And find
        What wind
Serves to advance an honest mind.

10 If thou be'st borne to strange sights,
    Things invisible to see,
Ride ten thousand days and nights,
    Till age snow white hairs on thee,
Thou, when thou return'st, wilt tell me
15   All strange wonders that befell thee,
        And swear
        Nowhere
Lives a woman true, and fair.

If thou findst one, let me know,
20   Such a pilgrimage were sweet—
Yet do not, I would not go,
    Though at next door we might meet;
Though she were true, when you met her,
    And last, till you write your letter,
25   Yet she
       Will be
False, ere I come, to two, or three.

---

[1] The mandrake root (or mandragora), which is forked and resembles the lower part of the human body, was thought to be an aphrodisiac.

R I T A   D O V E

(1952–   )

The Satisfaction Coal Company

(1986)

1

What to do with a day.
Leaf through *Jet*. Watch T.V.
Freezing on the porch
but he goes anyhow, snow too high
5 for a walk, the ice treacherous.
Inside, the gas heater takes care of itself;
he doesn't even notice being warm.

Everyone says he looks great.
Across the street a drunk stands smiling
10 at something carved in a tree.
The new neighbor with the floating hips
scoots out to get the mail
and waves once, brightly,
storm door clipping her heel on the way in.

2

15 Twice a week he had taken the bus down Glendale hill
to the corner of Market. Slipped through
the alley by the canal and let himself in.
Started to sweep
with terrible care, like a woman
20 brushing shine into her hair,
same motion, same lullaby.
No curtains—the cop on the beat
stopped outside once in the hour
to swing his billy club and glare.

25 It was better on Saturdays
when the children came along:
he mopped while they emptied
ashtrays, clang of glass on metal
then a dry scutter. Next they counted
30 nailheads studding the leather cushions.
Thirty-four! they shouted,
that was the year and
they found it mighty amusing.

But during the week he noticed more—
35 lights when they gushed or dimmed
at the Portage Hotel, the 10:32
picking up speed past the B & O switchyard,
floorboards trembling and the explosive
kachook kachook kachook kachook
40 and the oiled rails ticking underneath.

3

They were poor then but everyone had been poor.
He hadn't minded the sweeping,
just the thought of it—like now
when people ask him what he's thinking
45 and he says *I'm listening.*

Those nights walking home alone,
the bucket of coal scraps banging his knee,
he'd hear a roaring furnace
with its dry, familiar heat. Now the nights
50 take care of themselves—as for the days,
there is the canary's sweet curdled song,
the wino smiling through his dribble.
Past the hill, past the gorge
choked with wild sumac in summer,
55 the corner has been upgraded.
Still, he'd like to go down there someday
to stand for a while, and get warm.

M I C H A E L   D R A Y T O N

(1563–1631)

Since There's No Help

(1619)

Since there's no help, come let us kiss and part;
Nay, I have done, you get no more of me,
And I am glad, yea, glad with all my heart
That thus so cleanly I myself can free;
5 Shake hands for ever, cancel all our vows,

And when we meet at any time again,
Be it not seen in either of our brows
That we one jot of former love retain.
Now at the last gasp of Love's latest breath,
10 When, his pulse failing, Passion speechless lies,
When Faith is kneeling by his bed of death,
And Innocence is closing up his eyes,
    Now if thou wouldst, when all have given him over,
    From death to life thou mightst him yet recover.

PAUL LAURENCE DUNBAR

(1872–1906)

We Wear the Mask

(1913)

We wear the mask that grins and lies,
It hides our cheeks and shades our eyes—
This debt we pay to human guile;
With torn and bleeding hearts we smile,
5 And mouth with myriad subtleties.

Why should the world be over-wise,
In counting all our tears and sighs?
Nay, let them only see us, while
  We wear the mask.

10 We smile, but, O great Christ, our cries
To thee from tortured souls arise.
We sing, but oh the clay is vile
Beneath our feet, and long the mile;
But let the world dream otherwise,
15 We wear the mask!

T. S. ELIOT

(1888–1965)

Journey of the Magi[1]

(1927)

"A cold coming we had of it,
Just the worst time of the year
For a journey, and such a long journey:
The ways deep and the weather sharp,
5 The very dead of winter."[2]
And the camels galled, sore-footed, refractory,
Lying down in the melting snow.
There were times we regretted
The summer palaces on slopes, the terraces,
10 And the silken girls bringing sherbet.
Then the camel men cursing and grumbling
And running away, and wanting their liquor and women,
And the night-fires going out, and the lack of shelters,
And the cities hostile and the towns unfriendly
15 And the villages dirty and charging high prices:
A hard time we had of it.
At the end we preferred to travel all night,
Sleeping in snatches,
With the voices singing in our ears, saying
20 That this was all folly.

Then at dawn we came down to a temperate valley,
Wet, below the snow line, smelling of vegetation;
With a running stream and a water-mill beating the darkness,
And three trees[3] on the low sky,
25 And an old white horse[4] galloped away in the meadow.
Then we came to a tavern with vine-leaves over the lintel,
Six hands at an open door dicing for pieces of silver,[5]

---

[1] In the poem, one of the three wise men who ventured east to pay tribute to the infant Jesus (see Matthew 12:1–12) recalls the experience.

[2] The five quoted lines are adapted from a passage in a 1622 Christmas Day sermon by Bishop Lancelot Andrewes.

[3] Refers to the three crosses at Calvary (see Luke 23:32–33).

[4] Refers to the white horse of the conquering Christ in Revelation 19:11–16.

[5] Echoes the soldiers dicing for Christ's garments, as well as his betrayal by Judas.

And feet kicking the empty wine-skins.
But there was no information, and so we continued
30 And arrived at evening, not a moment too soon
Finding the place; it was (you may say) satisfactory.
All this was a long time ago, I remember,
And I would do it again, but set down
This set down
35 This: were we led all that way for
Birth or Death? There was a Birth, certainly,
We had evidence and no doubt. I had seen birth and death,
But had thought they were different; this Birth was
Hard and bitter agony for us, like Death, our death.
40 We returned to our places, these Kingdoms,
But no longer at ease here, in the old dispensation,
With an alien people clutching their gods.
I should be glad of another death.

The Love Song of
J. Alfred Prufrock

(1917)

S'io credessi che mia risposta fosse
A persona che mai tornasse al mondo,
Questa fiamma staria senza piu scosse.
Ma perciocche giammai di questo fondo
Non torno vivo alcun, s'i'odo il vero,
Senza tema d'infamia ti rispondo.[1]

Let us go then, you and I,
When the evening is spread out against the sky
Like a patient etherized upon a table;
Let us go, through certain half-deserted streets,
5 The muttering retreats
Of restless nights in one-night cheap hotels

---

[1] The epigraph is from Dante's *Inferno*, Canto XXVII. In response to the poet's question about his identity, Guido da Montefelto, who for his sin of fraud must spend eternity wrapped in flames, replies: "If I thought that I was speaking to someone who could go back to the world, this flame would shake me no more. But since from this place nobody ever returns alive, if what I hear is true, I answer you without fear of infamy."

And sawdust restaurants with oyster-shells:
Streets that follow like a tedious argument
Of insidious intent
10   To lead you to an overwhelming question . . .
Oh, do not ask, "What is it?"
Let us go and make our visit.

In the room the women come and go
Talking of Michelangelo.

15   The yellow fog that rubs its back upon the window-panes,
The yellow smoke that rubs its muzzle on the window-panes
Licked its tongue into the corners of the evening,
Lingered upon the pools that stand in drains,
Let fall upon its back the soot that falls from chimneys,
20   Slipped by the terrace, made a sudden leap,
And seeing that it was a soft October night,
Curled once about the house, and fell asleep.

And indeed there will be time
For the yellow smoke that slides along the street,
25   Rubbing its back upon the window-panes;
There will be time, there will be time
To prepare a face to meet the faces that you meet;
There will be time to murder and create,
And time for all the works and days[2] of hands
30   That lift and drop a question on your plate;
Time for you and time for me,
And time yet for a hundred indecisions,
And for a hundred visions and revisions,
Before the taking of a toast and tea.

35   In the room the women come and go
Talking of Michelangelo.

And indeed there will be time
To wonder, "Do I dare?" and, "Do I dare?"
Time to turn back and descend the stair,
40   With a bald spot in the middle of my hair—
(They will say: "How his hair is growing thin!")
My morning coat, my collar mounting firmly to the chin,
My necktie rich and modest, but asserted by a simple pin—
(They will say: "But how his arms and legs are thin!")

---

2   "Works and Days" is the title of a work by the eighth-century B.C. Greek Hesiod,
whose poem celebrates farmwork.

45   Do I dare
    Disturb the universe?
    In a minute there is time
    For decisions and revisions which a minute will reverse.

    For I have known them all already, known them all—
50   Have known the evenings, mornings, afternoons,
    I have measured out my life with coffee spoons;
    I know the voices dying with a dying fall[3]
    Beneath the music from a farther room.
        So how should I presume?

55   And I have known the eyes already, known them all—
    The eyes that fix you in a formulated phrase,
    And when I am formulated, sprawling on a pin,
    When I am pinned and wriggling on the wall,
    Then how should I begin
60   To spit out all the butt-ends of my days and ways?
        And how should I presume?

    And I have known the arms already, known them all—
    Arms that are braceleted and white and bare
    (But in the lamplight, downed with light brown hair!)
65   Is it perfume from a dress
    That makes me so digress?
    Arms that lie along a table, or wrap about a shawl.
        And should I then presume?
        And how should I begin?

        *   *   *   *   *

70   Shall I say, I have gone at dusk through narrow streets
    And watched the smoke that rises from the pipes
    Of lonely men in shirt-sleeves, leaning out of windows? . . .

    I should have been a pair of ragged claws
    Scuttling across the floors of silent seas.

        *   *   *   *   *

75   And the afternoon, the evening, sleeps so peacefully!
    Smoothed by long fingers,
    Asleep . . . tired . . . or it malingers,
    Stretched on the floor, here beside you and me.
    Should I, after tea and cakes and ices,
80   Have the strength to force the moment to its crisis?

---

[3] Allusion to Orsino's speech in *Twelfth Night* (I, i), "That strain again! It had a dying fall."

But though I have wept and fasted, wept and prayed,
Though I have seen my head (grown slightly bald) brought in upon
    a platter,[4]
I am no prophet—and here's no great matter;
I have seen the moment of my greatness flicker,
85 And I have seen the eternal Footman[5] hold my coat, and snicker,
And in short, I was afraid.
And would it have been worth it, after all,
After the cups, the marmalade, the tea,
Among the porcelain, among some talk of you and me,
90 Would it have been worth while,
To have bitten off the matter with a smile,
To have squeezed the universe into a ball
To roll it toward some overwhelming question,
To say: "I am Lazarus,[6] come from the dead,
95 Come back to tell you all, I shall tell you all"—
If one, settling a pillow by her head,
    Should say: "That is not what I meant at all.
    That is not it, at all."

And would it have been worth it, after all,
100 Would it have been worth while,
After the sunsets and the dooryards and the sprinkled streets,
After the novels, after the teacups, after the skirts that trail along the
    floor—
And this, and so much more?—
It is impossible to say just what I mean!
105 But as if a magic lantern threw the nerves in patterns on a screen:
Would it have been worth while
If one, settling a pillow or throwing off a shawl,
And turning toward the window, should say:
    "That is not it at all,
110   That is not what I meant, at all."

*　*　*　*　*

No! I am not Prince Hamlet, nor was meant to be;
Am an attendant lord, one that will do
To swell a progress,[7] start a scene or two,
Advise the prince; no doubt, an easy tool,
115 Deferential, glad to be of use,

---

[4] Like John the Baptist, who was beheaded by King Herod (see Matthew 14:3–11).

[5] Perhaps death, or fate.

[6] Lazarus was raised from the dead by Christ (see John 11:1–44).

[7] Here, in the Elizabethan sense of a royal journey.

Politic, cautious, and meticulous;
Full of high sentence,[8] but a bit obtuse;
At times, indeed, almost ridiculous—
Almost, at times, the Fool.

120 I grow old . . . I grow old . . .
I shall wear the bottoms of my trousers rolled.

Shall I part my hair behind? Do I dare to eat a peach?
I shall wear white flannel trousers, and walk upon the beach.
I have heard the mermaids singing, each to each.

125 I do not think that they will sing to me.

I have seen them riding seaward on the waves
Combing the white hair of the waves blown back
When the wind blows the water white and black.

We have lingered in the chambers of the sea
130 By sea-girls wreathed with seaweed red and brown
Till human voices wake us, and we drown.

JAMES A. EMANUEL

(1921–   )

Emmett Till[1]

(1968)

I hear a whistling
Through the water.
Little Emmett
Won't be still.
5 He keeps floating
Round the darkness,
Edging through

---

[8] Opinions.

[1] Emmett Till, a fourteen-year-old black youth from Chicago, was visiting relatives in Mississippi in 1955 when he made what he thought was an innocent remark to a white woman. Several days later his body was found in the river with a heavy cotton gin fan tied around his neck with barbed wire.

> The silent chill.
> Tell me, please,
> 10 That bedtime story
> Of the fairy
> River Boy
> Who swims forever,
> Deep in treasures,
> 15 Necklaced in
> A coral toy.

ROBERT FRANCIS
(1901–   )

Pitcher
(1953)

His art is eccentricity, his aim
How not to hit the mark he seems to aim at,

His passion how to avoid the obvious,
His technique how to vary the avoidance.

5 The others throw to be comprehended. He
Throws to be a moment misunderstood.

Yet not too much. Not errant, arrant, wild,
But every seeming aberration willed.

Not to, yet still, still to communicate
10 Making the batter understand too late.

R O B E R T   F R O S T

(1874–1963)

Acquainted with the Night

(1928)

I have been one acquainted with the night.
I have walked out in rain—and back in rain.
I have outwalked the furthest city light.

I have looked down the saddest city lane.
5 I have passed by the watchman on his beat
And dropped my eyes, unwilling to explain.

I have stood still and stopped the sound of feet
When far away an interrupted cry
Came over houses from another street,

10 But not to call me back or say good-by;
And further still at an unearthly height,
One luminary clock against the sky

Proclaimed the time was neither wrong nor right.
I have been one acquainted with the night.

Birches

(1915)

When I see birches bend to left and right
Across the lines of straighter darker trees,
I like to think some boy's been swinging them.
But swinging doesn't bend them down to stay
5 As ice-storms do. Often you must have seen them
Loaded with ice a sunny winter morning
After a rain. They click upon themselves
As the breeze rises, and turn many-colored
As the stir cracks and crazes their enamel.
10 Soon the sun's warmth makes them shed crystal shells
Shattering and avalanching on the snow-crust—
Such heaps of broken glass to sweep away
You'd think the inner dome of heaven had fallen.

They are dragged to the withered bracken by the load,
15 And they seem not to break; though once they are bowed
So low for long, they never right themselves:
You may see their trunks arching in the woods
Years afterwards, trailing their leaves on the ground
Like girls on hands and knees that throw their hair
20 Before them over their heads to dry in the sun.
But I was going to say when Truth broke in
With all her matter-of-fact about the ice-storm
I should prefer to have some boy bend them
As he went out and in to fetch the cows—
25 Some boy too far from town to learn baseball,
Whose only play was what he found himself,
Summer or winter, and could play alone.
One by one he subdued his father's trees
By riding them down over and over again
30 Until he took the stiffness out of them,
And not one but hung limp, not one was left
For him to conquer. He learned all there was
To learn about not launching out too soon
And so not carrying the tree away
35 Clear to the ground. He always kept his poise
To the top branches, climbing carefully
With the same pains you use to fill a cup
Up to the brim, and even above the brim.
Then he flung outward, feet first, with a swish,
40 Kicking his way down through the air to the ground.
So was I once myself a swinger of birches.
And so I dream of going back to be.
It's when I'm weary of considerations,
And life is too much like a pathless wood
45 Where your face burns and tickles with the cobwebs
Broken across it, and one eye is weeping
From a twig's having lashed across it open.
I'd like to get away from earth awhile
And then come back to it and begin over.
50 May no fate willfully misunderstand me
And half grant what I wish and snatch me away
Not to return. Earth's the right place for love:
I don't know where it's likely to go better.
I'd like to go by climbing a birch tree,
55 And climb black branches up a snow-white trunk
Toward Heaven, till the tree could bear no more,
But dipped its top and set me down again.
That would be good both going and coming back.
One could do worse than be a swinger of birches.

Desert Places

(1936)

Snow falling and night falling fast, oh, fast
In a field I looked into going past,
And the ground almost covered smooth in snow,
But a few weeds and stubble showing last.

5 The woods around it have it—it is theirs.
All animals are smothered in their lairs,
I am too absent-spirited to count;
The loneliness includes me unawares.

And lonely as it is, that loneliness
10 Will be more lonely ere it will be less—
A blanker whiteness of benighted snow
With no expression, nothing to express.

They cannot scare me with their empty spaces
Between stars—on stars where no human race is.
15 I have it in me so much nearer home
To scare myself with my own desert places.

Mending Wall

(1914)

Something there is that doesn't love a wall,
That sends the frozen-ground-swell under it,
And spills the upper boulders in the sun;
And makes gaps even two can pass abreast.
5 The work of hunters is another thing:
I have come after them and made repair
Where they have left not one stone on a stone,
But they would have the rabbit out of hiding,
To please the yelping dogs. The gaps I mean,
10 No one has seen them made or heard them made,
But at spring mending-time we find them there.
I let my neighbor know beyond the hill;
And on a day we meet to walk the line
And set the wall between us once again.

15 We keep the wall between us as we go.
   To each the boulders that have fallen to each.
   And some are loaves and some so nearly balls
   We have to use a spell to make them balance:
   "Stay where you are until our backs are turned!"
20 We wear our fingers rough with handling them.
   Oh, just another kind of outdoor game,
   One on a side. It comes to little more:
   There where it is we do not need the wall:
   He is all pine and I am apple orchard.
25 My apple trees will never get across
   And eat the cones under his pines, I tell him.
   He only says, "Good fences make good neighbors."
   Spring is the mischief in me, and I wonder
   If I could put a notion in his head:
30 "*Why* do they make good neighbors? Isn't it
   Where there are cows? But here there are no cows.
   Before I built a wall I'd ask to know
   What I was walling in or walling out,
   And to whom I was like to give offense.
35 Something there is that doesn't love a wall,
   That wants it down." I could say "Elves" to him,
   But it's not elves exactly, and I'd rather
   He said it for himself. I see him there
   Bringing a stone grasped firmly by the top
40 In each hand, like an old-stone savage armed.
   He moves in darkness as it seems to me,
   Not of woods only and the shade of trees.
   He will not go behind his father's saying,
   And he likes having thought of it so well
45 He says again, "Good fences make good neighbors."

The Road Not Taken

(1915)

Two roads diverged in a yellow wood,
And sorry I could not travel both
And be one traveler, long I stood
And looked down one as far as I could
5 To where it bent in the undergrowth;

Then took the other, as just as fair,
And having perhaps the better claim,
Because it was grassy and wanted wear;
Though as for that the passing there
10 Had worn them really about the same,

And both that morning equally lay
In leaves no step had trodden black.
Oh, I kept the first for another day!
Yet knowing how way leads on to way,
15 I doubted if I should ever come back.

I shall be telling this with a sigh
Somewhere ages and ages hence:
Two roads diverged in a wood, and I—
I took the one less traveled by,
20 And that has made all the difference.

The Silken Tent

(1942)

She is as in a field a silken tent
At midday when a sunny summer breeze
Has dried the dew and all its ropes relent,
So that in guys it gently sways at ease,
5 And its supporting central cedar pole,
That is its pinnacle to heavenward
And signifies the sureness of the soul,
Seems to owe naught to any single cord,
But strictly held by none, is loosely bound
10 By countless silken ties of love and thought
To everything on earth the compass round,
And only by one's going slightly taut
In the capriciousness of summer air
Is of the slightest bondage made aware.

Stopping by Woods on a Snowy Evening

(1923)

Whose woods these are I think I know.
His house is in the village though;
He will not see me stopping here
To watch his woods fill up with snow.

5　My little horse must think it queer
To stop without a farmhouse near
Between the woods and frozen lake
The darkest evening of the year.

He gives his harness bells a shake
10　To ask if there is some mistake.
The only other sound's the sweep
Of easy wind and downy flake.

The woods are lovely, dark and deep,
But I have promises to keep,
15　And miles to go before I sleep,
And miles to go before I sleep.

JERRY GARCIA AND ROBERT HUNTER

Ripple

If my words did glow with the gold of sunshine
And my tunes were played on the harp unstrung
Would you hear my voice come through the music
Would you hold it near as it were your own?

5　It's a hand-me-down, the thoughts are broken
Perhaps they're better left unsung
I don't know, don't really care
Let there be songs to fill the air

(Chorus)

Ripple in still water
10 Where there is no pebble tossed
Nor wind to blow

Reach out your hand if your cup be empty
If your cup is full may it be again
Let it be known there is a fountain
15 That was not made by the hands of men

There is a road, no simple highway
Between the dawn and the dark of night
And if you go no one may follow
That path is for your steps alone

(Chorus)

20 You who choose to lead must follow
But if you fall you fall alone
If you should stand then who's to guide you?
If I knew the way I would take you home

NIKKI GIOVANNI

(1943–   )

Nikki-Rosa

(1968)

childhood remembrances are always a drag
if you're Black
you always remember things like living in Woodlawn[1]
with no inside toilet
5 and if you become famous or something
they never talk about how happy you were to have your mother
all to yourself and
how good the water felt when you got your bath from one of those
big tubs that folk in chicago barbecue in
10 and somehow when you talk about home
it never gets across how much you
understood their feelings

---

[1] A predominantly black suburb of Cincinnati, Ohio.

as the whole family attended meetings about Hollydale
and even though you remember
15 your biographers never understand
your father's pain as he sells his stock
and another dream goes
and though you're poor it isn't poverty that
concerns you
20 and though they fought a lot
it isn't your father's drinking that makes any difference
but only that everybody is together and you
and your sister have happy birthdays and very good christmasses
and I really hope no white person ever has cause to write about me
25 because they never understand Black love is Black wealth and they'll
probably talk about my hard childhood and never understand that
all the while I was quite happy

THOMAS GRAY

(1716–1771)

Elegy Written in a Country Churchyard

(1753)

The curfew tolls the knell of parting day,
　　The lowing herd wind slowly o'er the lea,
The plowman homeward plods his weary way,
　　And leaves the world to darkness and to me.

5 Now fades the glimmering landscape on the sight,
　　And all the air a solemn stillness holds,
Save where the beetle wheels his droning flight,
　　And drowsy tinklings lull the distant folds;

Save that from yonder ivy-mantled tower
10　　The moping owl does to the moon complain
Of such, as wand'ring near her secret bower,
　　Molest her ancient solitary reign.

Beneath those rugged elms, that yew tree's shade,
　　Where heaves the turf in many a mold'ring heap,

15 Each in his narrow cell forever laid,
    The rude[1] forefathers of the hamlet sleep.

The breezy call of incense-breathing morn,
    The swallow twitt'ring from the straw-built shed,
The cock's shrill clarion, or the echoing horn[2]
20   No more shall rouse them from their lowly bed.

For them no more the blazing hearth shall burn,
    Or busy housewife ply her evening care;
No children run to lisp their sire's return,
    Or climb his knees the envied kiss to share.

25 Oft did the harvest to their sickle yield,
    Their furrow oft the stubborn glebe[3] has broke;
How jocund did they drive their team afield!
    How bowed the woods beneath their sturdy stroke!

Let not Ambition mock their useful toil,
30   Their homely joys, and destiny obscure;
Nor Grandeur hear with a disdainful smile
    The short and simple annals of the poor.

The boast of heraldry[4] the pomp of pow'r,
    And all that beauty, all that wealth e'er gave,
35 Awaits alike th' inevitable hour.
    The paths of glory lead but to the grave.

Nor you, ye proud, impute to these the fault,
    If Mem'ry o'er their tomb no trophies raise,
Where through the long-drawn aisle and fretted[5] vault
40   The pealing anthem swells the note of praise.

Can storied urn or animated bust
    Back to its mansion call the fleeting breath?
Can Honor's voice provoke the silent dust,
    Or Flatt'ry soothe the dull cold ear of Death?

---

[1] Simple.

[2] Of the fox-hunters.

[3] Sod.

[4] Nobility.

[5] Inlaid with designs.

45 Perhaps in this neglected spot is laid
    Some heart once pregnant with celestial fire;
Hands that the rod of empire might have swayed,
    Or waked to ecstasy the living lyre.

But knowledge to their eyes her ample page
50   Rich with the spoils of time did ne'er unroll;
Chill Penury[6] repressed their noble rage,
    And froze the genial current of the soul.

Full many a gem of purest ray serene,
    The dark unfathomed caves of ocean bear:
55 Full many a flower is born to blush unseen,
    And waste its sweetness on the desert air.

Some village Hampden,[7] that with dauntless breast
    The little tyrant of his field withstood;
Some mute inglorious Milton[8] here may rest,
60   Some Cromwell,[9] guiltless of his country's blood.

Th' applause of list'ning senates to command,
    The threats of pain and ruin to despise,
To scatter plenty o'er a smiling land,
    And read their hist'ry in a nation's eyes,

65 Their lot forbade; nor circumscribed alone
    Their growing virtues, but their crimes confined;
Forbade to wade through slaughter to a throne,
    And shut the gates of mercy on mankind,

---

[6] Poverty.

[7] John Hampden (1594–1643), English statesman, cousin of Oliver Cromwell and popular hero of the parliamentarians after his arrest by Charles I in 1642, helped begin the civil war.

[8] John Milton (1608–1674), British poet.

[9] Oliver Cromwell (1599–1658), English statesman, Lord Protector of England (1653–1658). Cromwell first attempted to reconcile differences among Charles I, Parliament, and the army; following the king's defeat in 1648, Cromwell subjugated the Irish and invaded Scotland to defeat Charles II. He established the Protectorate (1653) but ultimately failed to find constitutional grounds for his rule. Despite his genius and forceful character, Cromwell was forced by the necessities of governing to commit many acts that can only be described as cruel and intolerant.

The struggling pangs of conscious truth to hide,
70   To quench the blushes of ingenuous[10] shame,
Or heap the shrine of Luxury and Pride
      With incense kindled at the Muse's[11] flame.

Far from the madding[12] crowd's ignoble strife,
      Their sober wishes never learned to stray;
75 Along the cool sequestered vale of life
      They kept the noiseless tenor of their way.

Yet ev'n these bones from insult to protect
      Some frail memorial still erected nigh,
With uncouth rhymes and shapeless sculpture decked,
80   Implores the passing tribute of a sigh.

Their name, their years, spelt by th' unlettered Muse,
      The place of fame and elegy supply:
And many a holy text around she strews,
      That teach the rustic moralist to die.

85 For who to dumb Forgetfulness a prey,
      This pleasing anxious being e'er resigned,
Left the warm precincts of the cheerful day,
      Nor cast one longing ling'ring look behind?

On some fond breast the parting soul relies,
90   Some pious drops the closing eye requires;
Ev'n from the tomb the voice of Nature cries,
      Ev'n in our ashes live their wonted fires.

For thee, who mindful of th' unhonored dead
      Dost in these lines their artless tale relate;
95 If chance[13] by lonely contemplation led,
      Some kindred spirit shall inquire thy fate,

---

10 Innocent.

11 In Greek mythology, any of the nine daughters of Mnemosyne and Zeus, each of
whom presided over a different art or science.

12 Frenzied.

13 If by chance.

Haply[14] some hoary-headed swain[15] may say,
   "Oft have we seen him at the peep of dawn
Brushing with hasty steps the dews away
100   To meet the sun upon the upland lawn.

"There at the foot of yonder nodding beech
   That wreathes its old fantastic roots so high,
His listless length at noontide would he stretch,
   And pore upon the brook that babbles by.

105 "Hard by yon wood, now smiling as in scorn,
   Mutt'ring his wayward fancies he would rove,
Now drooping, woeful wan, like one forlorn,
   Or crazed with care, or crossed in hopeless love.

"One morn I missed him, on the customed hill,
110   Along the heath and near his fav'rite tree;
Another came; not yet beside the rill,[16]
   Nor up the lawn, nor at the wood was he;

"The next with dirges due in sad array
   Slow through the churchway path we saw him borne.
115 Approach and read (for thou canst read) the lay,[17]
   Graved on the stone beneath yon aged thorn."

The Epitaph

Here rests his head upon the lap of Earth
   A youth to Fortune and to Fame unknown.
Fair Science[18] frowned not on his humble birth,
120   *And Melancholy marked him for her own.*

Large was his bounty, and his soul sincere,
   Heav'n did a recompense as largely send:
He gave to Mis'ry all he had, a tear,
   He gained from Heav'n ('twas all he wished) a friend.

---

[14] Perhaps.

[15] Gray-haired shepherd.

[16] Brook.

[17] Song, poem.

[18] Knowledge.

125 *No farther seek his merits to disclose,*
    Or draw his frailties from their dread abode,
    (There they alike in trembling hope repose),
    The bosom of His Father and his God.

T H O M A S   H A R D Y

(1840–1928)

Channel Firing

(1914)

That night your great guns, unawares,
Shook all our coffins[1] as we lay,
And broke the chancel window-squares,
We thought it was the Judgment Day

5 And sat upright. While drearisome
Arose the howl of wakened hounds:
The mouse let fall the altar-crumb,
The worms drew back into the mounds,

The glebe[2] cow drooled. Till God called, "No;
10 It's gunnery practice out at sea
Just as before you went below;
The world is as it used to be:

"All nations striving strong to make
Red war yet redder. Mad as hatters
15 They do no more for Christés sake
Than you who are helpless in such matters.

"That this is not the judgment hour
For some of them's a blessed thing,
For if it were they'd have to scour
20 Hell's floor for so much threatening. . . .

---

[1] For centuries, it has been the practice in England to bury people under the flooring or in the basements of churches.

[2] A small field.

"Ha, ha. It will be warmer when
I blow the trumpet (if indeed
I ever do; for you are men,
And rest eternal sorely need)."

25 So down we lay again. "I wonder,
Will the world ever saner be,"
Said one, "than when He sent us under
In our indifferent century!"

And many a skeleton shook his head.
30 "Instead of preaching forty year,"
My neighbor Parson Thirdly said,
"I wish I had stuck to pipes and beer."

Again the guns disturbed the hour,
Roaring their readiness to avenge,
35 As far inland as Stourton Tower.[3]
And Camelot,[4] and starlit Stonehenge.[5]

The Convergence of the Twain

(Lines on the loss of the 'Titanic')

I

In a solitude of the sea
Deep from human vanity,
And the Pride of Life that planned her, stilly couches she.

---

[3] Erected in the eighteenth century in Wiltshire, England, to commemorate King Alfred the Great's defeat of the Danes in 878.

[4] Legendary site of King Arthur's court.

[5] A group of stones on Salisbury Plain, believed by many, including Hardy, to be the site of ancient druidic rituals.

II

Steel chambers, late the pyres[1]
Of her salamandrine fires,[2]
Cold currents thrid,[3] and turn to rhythmic tidal lyres.

III

Over the mirrors meant
To glass the opulent
The sea-worm crawls—grotesque, slimed, dumb, indifferent.

IV

Jewels in joy designed
To ravish the sensuous mind
Lie lightless, all their sparkles bleared and black and blind.

V

Dim moon-eyed fishes near
Gaze at the gilded gear
And query: 'What does this vaingloriousness down here?' . . .

VI

Well: while was fashioning
This creature of cleaving wing,
The Immanent[4] Will that stirs and urges everything

VII

Prepared a sinister mate
For her—so gaily great—
A Shape of Ice, for the time far and dissociate.

---

[1] Funeral pyres; piles of wood on which corpses were burned in ancient rites.

[2] Refers to the old belief that salamanders could live in fire.

[3] Thread (archaic verb form).

[4] Inherent, dwelling within.

VIII

And as the smart ship grew
In stature, grace, and hue,
In shadowy silent distance grew the Iceberg too.

IX

25   Alien they seemed to be:
No mortal eye could see
The intimate welding of their later history,

X

Or sign that they were bent
By paths coincident
30 On being anon[5] twin halves of one august[6] event,

XI

Till the Spinner of the Years
Said 'Now!' And each one hears,
And consummation comes, and jars two hemispheres.

Hap

(1866)

If but some vengeful god would call to me
From up the sky, and laugh: 'Thou suffering thing,
Know that thy sorrow is my ecstasy,
That thy love's loss is my hate's profiting!'

5 Then would I bear it, clench myself, and die,
Steeled by the sense of ire unmerited;
Half-eased in that a Powerfuller than I
Had willed and meted me the tears I shed.

---

5 Soon.

6 Awe-inspiring, majestic.

But not so. How arrives it joy lies slain,
10 And why unblooms the best hope ever sown?
—Crass Casualty obstructs the sun and rain,
And dicing Time for gladness casts a moan. . . .
These purblind Doomsters had as readily strown
Blisses about my pilgrimage as pain.

ROBERT HAYDEN

(1913–   )

Homage to the Empress
of the Blues[1]

(1966)

Because there was a man somewhere in a candystripe silk shirt,
gracile and dangerous as a jaguar and because a woman moaned
for him in sixty-watt gloom and mourned him Faithless Love
Twotiming Love Oh Love Oh Careless Aggravating Love,

5   She came out on the stage in yards of pearls, emerging like
a favorite scenic view, flashed her golden smile and sang.

Because grey laths began somewhere to show from underneath
torn hurdygurdy lithographs of dollfaced heaven;
and because there were those who feared alarming fists of snow
10 on the door and those who feared the riot-squad of statistics,

She came out on the stage in ostrich feathers, beaded satin,
and shone that smile on us and sang.

---

[1] An epitaph for Bessie Smith, American jazz singer, 1894–1937.

SEAMUS HEANEY

(1939–   )

Lightenings viii

(1995)

The annals[1] say: when the monks of Clonmacnoise[2]
Were all at prayers inside the oratory
A ship appeared above them in the air.

The anchor dragged along behind so deep
5 It hooked itself into the altar rails
And then, as the big hull[3] rocked to a standstill,

A crewman shinned and grappled down a rope
And struggled to release it. But in vain.
'This man can't bear our life here and will drown,'

10 The abbot[4] said, 'Unless we help him.' So
They did, the freed ship sailed and the man climbed back
Out of the marvelous as he had known it.

GERARD MANLEY HOPKINS

(1844–1889)

God's Grandeur

(1877)

The world is charged with the grandeur of God.
    It will flame out, like shining from shook foil;
    It gathers to a greatness, like the ooze of oil
Crushed. Why do men then now not reck his rod?

---

[1] Journals containing yearly records.

[2] An Irish abbey founded in 541, destroyed by the English in 1552.

[3] The frame or body of a ship.

[4] The monk in authority over a community of monks.

5 Generations have trod, have trod, have trod;
     And all is seared with trade; bleared, smeared with toil;
     And wears man's smudge and shares man's smell: the soil
Is bare now, nor can foot feel, being shod.
And for all this, nature is never spent;
10   There lives the dearest freshness deep down things;
And though the last lights off the black West went
     Oh, morning, at the brown brink eastward, springs—
Because the Holy Ghost over the bent
     World broods with warm breast and with ah! bright wings.

The Windhover[1]

(1877)

To Christ Our Lord

I caught this morning morning's minion,[2] kingdom of daylight's
     dauphin, dapple-dawn-drawn Falcon, in his riding
     Of the rolling level underneath him steady air, and striding
High there, how he rung upon the rein[3] of a wimpling[4] wing
5 In his ecstasy! then off, off forth on swing,
     As a skate's heel sweeps smooth on a bow-bend: the hurl and gliding
     Rebuffed the big wind. My heart in hiding
Stirred for a bird,—the achieve of, the mastery of the thing!
Brute beauty and valor and act, oh, air, pride, plume, here
10   Buckle! and the fire that breaks from thee then, a billion
Times told lovelier, more dangerous, O my chevalier!
     No wonder of it: shéer plód, makes plow down sillion[5]
Shine, and blue-bleak embers, ah my dear,
     Fall, gall themselves, and gash gold-vermilion.

[1] The kestrel, a European falcon, so called for its ability to hover in the air with its head to the wind.

[2] Favorite.

[3] A horse is "rung upon the rein" when it circles at the end of a long rein held by the trainer.

[4] Rippling.

[5] The ridge between two furrows.

A. E. HOUSMAN

(1859–1936)

Terence, This Is Stupid Stuff

(1896)

"Terence,[1] this is stupid stuff:
You eat your victuals fast enough;
There can't be much amiss, 'tis clear,
To see the rate you drink your beer.
5 But oh, good Lord, the verse you make,
It gives a chap the belly-ache.
The cow, the old cow, she is dead;
It sleeps well, the horned head:
We poor lads, 'tis our turn now
10 To hear such tunes as killed the cow.
Pretty friendship 'tis to rhyme
Your friends to death before their time
Moping melancholy mad:
Come, pipe a tune to dance to, lad."

15　　Why, if 'tis dancing you would be,
There's brisker pipes than poetry.
Say, for what were hop-yards meant,
Or why was Burton built on Trent?
Oh many a peer of England brews
20 Livelier liquor than the Muse,[2]
And malt does more than Milton can
To justify God's ways to man.[3]
Ale, man, ale's the stuff to drink
For fellows whom it hurts to think:
25 Look into the pewter pot
To see the world as the world's not.
And faith, 'tis pleasant till 'tis past:

---

[1] The original title of Housman's *A Shropshire Lad* was *The Poems of Terence Hearsay*. Terence was a Roman poet, author of satiric comedies; here, Terence is used as the poet's name for himself.

[2] The lines here compare the Muses, mythological figures who inspire artists, with the products of the breweries of Burton-on-Trent. (Many of the brewery owners were named "peers of England"—that is, dukes, earls, viscounts, barons, or marquis.)

[3] Alludes to Milton's promise in *Paradise Lost* (I:17–26) to "justify the ways of God to men."

The mischief is that 'twill not last.
Oh I have been to Ludlow[4] fair
30 And left my necktie God knows where,
And carried half-way home, or near,
Pints and quarts of Ludlow beer:
Then the world seemed none so bad,
And I myself a sterling lad;
35 And down in lovely muck I've lain,
Happy till I woke again.
Then I saw the morning sky:
Heigho, the tale was all a lie;
The world, it was the old world yet,
40 I was I, my things were wet,
And nothing now remained to do
But begin the game anew.

Therefore, since the world has still
Much good, but much less good than ill,
45 And while the sun and moon endure
Luck's a chance, but trouble's sure,
I'd face it as a wise man would,
And train for ill and not for good.
'Tis true, the stuff I bring for sale
50 Is not so brisk a brew as ale:
Out of a stem that scored the hand
I wrung it in a weary land.
But take it: if the smack is sour,
The better for the embittered hour;
55 It should do good to heart and head
When your soul is in my soul's stead;
And I will friend you, if I may,
In the dark and cloudy day.

There was a king reigned in the East:
60 There, when kings will sit to feast,
They get their fill before they think
With poisoned meat and poisoned drink.
He gathered all that springs to birth
From the many-venomed earth;
65 First a little, thence to more,
He sampled all her killing store;
And easy, smiling, seasoned sound,
Sate the king when healths went round.

---

4 A Shropshire town.

They put arsenic in his meat
70 And stared aghast to watch him eat;
They poured strychnine in his cup
And shook to see him drink it up:
They shook, they stared as white's their shirt:
Them it was their poison hurt.
75 —I tell the tale that I heard told.
Mithridates, he died old.[5]

To an Athlete Dying Young

(1896)

The time you won your town the race
We chaired you through the market-place;
Man and boy stood cheering by,
And home we brought you shoulder-high.

5 Today, the road all runners come,
Shoulder-high we bring you home,
And set you at your threshold down,
Townsman of a stiller town.

Smart lad, to slip betimes away
10 From fields where glory does not stay,
And early though the laurel grows
It withers quicker than the rose.

Eyes the shady night has shut
Cannot see the record cut,
15 And silence sounds no worse than cheers
After earth has stopped the ears.

Now you will not swell the rout
Of lads that wore their honors out,
Runners whom renown outran
20 And the name died before the man.

---

[5] Mithridates VI, a pre-Christian king of Pontus, supposedly took small doses of poison daily to make him immune.

So set, before its echoes fade,
The fleet foot on the sill of shade,
And hold to the low lintel up
The still-defended challenge-cup.

25 And round that early-laureled head
Will flock to gaze the strengthless dead,
And find unwithered on its curls
The garland briefer than a girl's.

BEN JONSON

(1573?–1637)

On My First Son

(1603)

Farewell, thou child of my right hand,[1] and joy.
My sin was too much hope of thee, loved boy;
Seven years thou wert lent to me, and I thee pay,
Exacted by thy fate, on the just day.[2]
5 Oh, could I lose all father now. For why
Will man lament the state he should envỳ?—
To have so soon 'scaped world's and flesh's rage,
And, if no other misery, yet age.
Rest in soft peace, and asked, say, "Here doth lie
10 Ben Jonson his best piece of poetry,"
For whose sake henceforth all his vows be such
As what he loves may never like[3] too much.

---

[1] Translation of the Hebrew name of Benjamin, Jonson's son.

[2] The very day.

[3] Thrive.

To Celia
(1616)

Drink to me only with thine eyes,
    And I will pledge with mine;
Or leave a kiss but in the cup,
    And I'll not ask for wine.
5 The thirst that from the soul doth rise
    Doth ask a drink divine;
But might I of Jove's nectar sup,
    I would not change for thine.

I sent thee late a rosy wreath,
10   Not so much honoring thee
As giving it a hope that there
    It could not withered be.
But thou thereon didst only breathe,
    And sent'st it back to me;
15 Since when it grows, and smells, I swear,
    Not of itself but thee.

DONALD JUSTICE

(1925–   )

On the Death of
Friends in Childhood
(1960)

We shall not ever meet them bearded in heaven,
Nor sunning themselves among the bald of hell;
If anywhere, in the deserted schoolyard at twilight,
Forming a ring, perhaps, or joining hands
5 In games whose very names we have forgotten.
Come, memory, let us seek them there in the shadows.

JOHN KEATS

(1795–1821)

La Belle Dame Sans Merci:[1] A Ballad

(1819, 1820)

1

O what can ail thee, knight at arms,
    Alone and palely loitering?
The sedge has wither'd from the lake,
    And no birds sing.

2

5 O what can ail thee, knight at arms,
    So haggard and so woe-begone?
The squirrel's granary is full,
    And the harvest's done.

3

I see a lily on thy brow
10   With anguish moist and fever dew,
And on thy cheeks a fading rose
    Fast withereth too.

4

I met a lady in the meads,
    Full beautiful, a fairy's child;
15 Her hair was long, her foot was light,
    And her eyes were wild.

5

I made a garland for her head,
    And bracelets too, and fragrant zone;[2]
She look'd at me as she did love,
20   And made sweet moan.

---

[1] The title, which means "The Lovely Lady Without Pity," was taken from a medieval poem by Alain Chartier.

[2] Belt.

6

I set her on my pacing steed,
And nothing else saw all day long,
For sidelong would she bend, and sing
A fairy's song.

7

25 She found me roots of relish sweet,
And honey wild, and manna dew,
And sure in language strange she said—
I love thee true.

8

She took me to her elfin grot,[3]
30 And there she wept, and sigh'd full sore,
And there I shut her wild wild eyes
With kisses four.

9

And there she lullèd me asleep,
And there I dream'd—Ah! woe betide!
35 The latest[4] dream I ever dream'd
On the cold hill's side.

10

I saw pale kings, and princes too,
Pale warriors, death pale were they all;
They cried—"La belle dame sans merci
40 Hath thee in thrall!"

11

I saw their starv'd lips in the gloam[5]
With horrid warning gapèd wide,
And I awoke and found me here
On the cold hill's side.

---

[3] Grotto.

[4] Last.

[5] Twilight.

12

45 And this is why I sojourn here,
　　Alone and palely loitering,
Though the sedge is wither'd from the lake,
　　And no birds sing.

Bright Star! Would I Were Steadfast as Thou Art

(1819)

Bright star! would I were steadfast as thou art—
　　Not in lone splendor hung aloft the night,
And watching, with eternal lids apart,
　　Like nature's patient, sleepless Eremite[1]
5 The moving waters at their priest-like task
　　Of pure ablution[2] round earth's human shores,
Or gazing on the new soft-fallen mask
　　Of snow upon the mountains and the moors—
No—yet still steadfast, still unchangeable,
10　　Pillowed upon my fair love's ripening breast,
　　To feel for ever its soft fall and swell,
　　Awake for ever in a sweet unrest,
Still, still to hear her tender-taken breath,
And so live ever—or else swoon to death.

---

[1] Hermit, religious recluse.

[2] Washing, cleansing.

Ode on a Grecian Urn[1]

(1819, 1820)

1

Thou still unravish'd bride of quietness,
   Thou foster-child of silence and slow time,
Sylvan[2] historian, who canst thus express
A flowery tale more sweetly than our rhyme:
5 What leaf-fring'd legend haunts about thy shape
   Of deities or mortals, or of both,
      In Tempe[3] or the dales of Arcady?[4]
   What men or gods are these? What maidens loth?
What mad pursuit? What struggle to escape?
10   What pipes and timbrels? What wild ecstasy?

2

Heard melodies are sweet, but those unheard
   Are sweeter; therefore, ye soft pipes, play on;
Not to the sensual ear, but, more endear'd,
   Pipe to the spirit ditties of no tone:
15 Fair youth, beneath the trees, thou canst not leave
   Thy song, nor ever can those trees be bare;
      Bold lover, never, never canst thou kiss,
Though winning near the goal—yet, do not grieve;
      She cannot fade, though thou hast not thy bliss,
20   For ever wilt thou love, and she be fair!

3

Ah, happy, happy boughs! that cannot shed
   Your leaves, nor ever bid the spring adieu;
And, happy melodist, unwearied,
   For ever piping songs for ever new;
25 More happy love! more happy, happy love!

---

[1] Though many urns similar to the one Keats describes actually exist, the subject of the poem is purely imaginary.

[2] Pertaining to woods or forests.

[3] A beautiful valley in Greece.

[4] The valleys of Arcadia, a mountainous region on the Greek peninsula. Like Tempe, they represent a rustic pastoral ideal.

For ever warm and still to be enjoy'd,
    For ever panting, and for ever young;
All breathing human passion far above,
    That leaves a heart high-sorrowful and cloy'd,
30   A burning forehead, and a parching tongue.

4

Who are these coming to the sacrifice?
    To what green altar, O mysterious priest,
Lead'st thou that heifer lowing at the skies,
    And all her silken flanks with garlands drest?
35 What little town by river or sea shore,
    Or mountain-built with peaceful citadel,
        Is emptied of this folk, this pious morn?
And, little town, thy streets for evermore
    Will silent be; and not a soul to tell
40   Why thou art desolate, can e'er return.

5

O Attic⁵ shape! Fair attitude! with brede⁶
    Of marble men and maidens overwrought,⁷
With forest branches and the trodden weed;
    Thou, silent form, dost tease us out of thought
45 As doth eternity: Cold Pastoral!
    When old age shall this generation waste,
        Thou shalt remain, in midst of other woe
Than ours, a friend to man, to whom thou say'st,
    "Beauty is truth, truth beauty,"—that is all
50   Ye know on earth, and all ye need to know.

---

⁵ Characteristic of Athens or Athenians.

⁶ Braid.

⁷ Elaborately ornamented.

Ode to a Nightingale

(1819)

1

My heart aches, and a drowsy numbness pains
   My sense, as though of hemlock I had drunk,
Or emptied some dull opiate to the drains
   One minute past, and Lethe-wards[1] had sunk:
5 Tis not through envy of thy happy lot,
   But being too happy in thine happiness,—
      That thou, light-winged Dryad[2] of the trees,
      In some melodious plot
   Of beechen green, and shadows numberless,
10   Singest of summer in full-throated ease.

2

O, for a draught of vintage! that hath been
   Cool'd a long age in the deep-delved earth,
Tasting of Flora[3] and the country green,
   Dance, and Provençal song,[4] and sunburnt mirth!
15 O for a beaker full of the warm South,
   Full of the true, the blushful Hippocrene,[5]
      With beaded bubbles winking at the brim,
      And purple-stained mouth;
That I might drink, and leave the world unseen,
20   And with thee fade away into the forest dim:

3

Fade far away, dissolve, and quite forget
   What thou among the leaves hast never known,
The weariness, the fever, and the fret
   Here, where men sit and hear each other groan;
25 Where palsy shakes a few, sad, last gray hairs,

---

[1] Toward Lethe, the river in Hades whose waters cause forgetfulness.

[2] In Greek mythology, a tree spirit, a wood nymph.

[3] Roman goddess of flowers; also, the flowers themselves.

[4] Provence, in southern France, was famous in medieval times for its troubadours, who wrote and performed love songs.

[5] Fountain of the Muses on Mt. Helicon; a source of poetic inspiration.

Where youth grows pale, and spectre-thin, and dies;
    Where but to think is to be full of sorrow
      And leaden-eyed despairs,
    Where Beauty cannot keep her lustrous eyes,
30   Or new Love pine at them beyond to-morrow.

4

Away! away! for I will fly to thee,
    Not charioted by Bacchus[6] and his pards,
But on the viewless wings of Poesy,
    Though the dull brain perplexes and regards:
35 Already with thee! tender is the night,
    And haply the Queen-Moon is on her throne,
      Cluster'd around by all her starry Fays;[7]
        But here there is no light,
    Save what from heaven is with the breezes blown
40   Through verdurous glooms and winding mossy ways.

5

I cannot see what flowers are at my feet,
    Nor what soft incense hangs upon the boughs,
But, in embalmed[8] darkness, guess each sweet
    Wherewith the seasonable month endows
45 The grass, the thicket, and the fruit-tree wild;
    White hawthorn, and the pastoral eglantine;[9]
      Fast fading violets cover'd up in leaves;
        And mid-May's eldest child,
    The coming musk-rose, full of dewy wine,
50   The murmurous haunt of flies on summer eves.

6

Darkling[10] I listen; and, for many a time
    I have been half in love with easeful Death,

---

[6] Greek god of wine.

[7] Fairies.

[8] Perfumed.

[9] Sweetbrier, or honeysuckle.

[10] In the dark.

Call'd him soft names in many a mused[11] rhyme,
    To take into the air my quiet breath;
55 Now more than ever seems it rich to die,
    To cease upon the midnight with no pain,
      While thou art pouring forth thy soul abroad
        In such an ecstasy!
    Still wouldst thou sing, and I have ears in vain—
60   To thy high requiem become a sod.

7

Thou wast not born for death, immortal Bird!
    No hungry generations tread thee down;
The voice I hear this passing night was heard
    In ancient days by emperor and clown:
65 Perhaps the self-same song that found a path
    Through the sad heart of Ruth,[12] when, sick for home,
      She stood in tears amid the alien corn;[13]
        The same that oft-times hath
Charm'd magic casements, opening on the foam
70   Of perilous seas, in faery lands forlorn.

8

Forlorn! the very word is like a bell
    To toll me back from thee to my sole self!
Adieu! the fancy[14] cannot cheat so well
    As she is fam'd to do, deceiving elf.
75 Adieu! adieu! thy plaintive anthem[15] fades
    Past the near meadows, over the still stream,
      Up the hill-side; and now 'tis buried deep
        In the next valley-glades:
Was it a vision, or a waking dream?
80   Fled is that music:—Do I wake or sleep?

---

[11] Meditated.

[12] The widow of Mahlon in the biblical Book of Ruth. She is sad and homesick because she left her home with her mother-in-law to go to Bethlehem. While there she married Boaz, a rich landowner. She was the great-grandmother of King David.

[13] Wheat.

[14] Imagination. Compare "the viewless wings of Poesy," line 33.

[15] Hymn.

When I Have Fears
(1818)

When I have fears that I may cease to be
    Before my pen has gleaned my teeming brain,
Before high-piléd books, in charact'ry,[1]
    Hold like rich garners the full-ripened grain;
5 When I behold, upon the night's starred face,
    Huge cloudy symbols of a high romance,
And think that I may never live to trace
    Their shadows, with the magic hand of chance;
And when I feel, fair creature of an hour,
10   That I shall never look upon thee more,
Never have relish in the faery power
    Of unreflecting love!—then on the shore
Of the wide world I stand alone, and think
Till Love and Fame to nothingness do sink.

MAXINE KUMIN

(1925–   )

Morning Swim
(1965)

Into my empty head there come
a cotton beach, a dock wherefrom

I set out, oily and nude
through mist, in chilly solitude.

5 There was no line, no roof or floor
to tell the water from the air.

Night fog thick as terry cloth
closed me in its fuzzy growth.

---

[1] Print.

I hung my bathrobe on two pegs.
10 I took the lake between my legs.

Invaded and invader, I
went overhand on that flat sky.

Fish twitched beneath me, quick and tame.
In their green zone they sang my name

15 and in the rhythm of the swim
I hummed a two-four-time slow hymn.

I hummed *Abide with Me*. The beat
rose in the fine thrash of my feet,

rose in the bubbles I put out
20 slantwise, trailing through my mouth.

My bones drank water; water fell
through all my doors. I was the well

that fed the lake that met my sea
in which I sang *Abide with Me*.

PHILIP LARKIN

(1922–1985)

Aubade

(1977)

I work all day, and get half-drunk at night.
Waking at four to soundless dark, I stare.
In time the curtain-edges will grow light.
Till then I see what's really always there:
5 Unresting death, a whole day nearer now,
Making all thought impossible but how
And where and when I shall myself die.
Arid interrogation: yet the dread
Of dying, and being dead,
10 Flashes afresh to hold and horrify.

The mind blanks at the glare. Not in remorse
—The good not done, the love not given, time
Torn off unused—nor wretchedly because
An only life can take so long to climb
15 Clear of its wrong beginnings, and may never;
But at the total emptiness for ever,
The sure extinction that we travel to
And shall be lost in always. Not to be here,
Not to be anywhere,
20 And soon; nothing more terrible, nothing more true.

This is a special way of being afraid
No trick dispels. Religion used to try,
That vast moth-eaten musical brocade
Created to pretend we never die,
25 And specious stuff that says *No rational being
Can fear a thing it will not feel,* not seeing
That this is what we fear—no sight, no sound,
No touch or taste or smell, nothing to think with,
Nothing to love or link with,
30 The anaesthetic from which none come round.

And so it stays just on the edge of vision,
A small unfocused blur, a standing chill
That slows each impulse down to indecision.
Most things may never happen: this one will,
35 And realization of it rages out
In furnace-fear when we are caught without
People or drink. Courage is no good:
It means not scaring others. Being brave
Lets no one off the grave.
40 Death is no different whined at than withstood.

Slowly light strengthens, and the room takes shape.
It stands plain as a wardrobe, what we know,
Have always known, know that we can't escape,
Yet can't accept. One side will have to go.
45 Meanwhile telephones crouch, getting ready to ring
In locked-up offices, and all the uncaring
Intricate rented world begins to rouse.
The sky is white as clay, with no sun.
Work has to be done.
50 Postmen like doctors go from house to house.

D. H. LAWRENCE

(1885–1930)

Piano

(1918)

Softly, in the dusk, a woman is singing to me;
Taking me back down the vista of years, till I see
A child sitting under the piano, in the boom of the tingling strings
And pressing the small, poised feet of a mother who smiles as she sings.

5 In spite of myself, the insidious mastery of song
Betrays me back, till the heart of me weeps to belong
To the old Sunday evenings at home, with winter outside
And hymns in the cozy parlor, the tinkling piano our guide.

So now it is vain for the singer to burst into clamor
10 With the great black piano appassionato.[1] The glamor
Of childish days is upon me, my manhood is cast
Down in the flood of remembrance, I weep like a child for the past.

DENISE LEVERTOV

(1923–   )

What Were They Like?

(1966)

    1) Did the people of Viet Nam
        use lanterns of stone?
    2) Did they hold ceremonies
        to reverence the opening of buds?
5 3) Were they inclined to rippling laughter?
    4) Did they use bone and ivory,
        jade and silver, for ornament?
    5) Had they an epic poem?
    6) Did they distinguish between speech and singing?

---

[1] Impassioned (Italian).

10 1) Sir, their light hearts turned to stone.
       It is not remembered whether in gardens
       stone lanterns illumined pleasant ways.

   2) Perhaps they gathered once to delight in blossom,
       but after the children were killed
15   there were no more buds.

   3) Sir, laughter is bitter to the burned mouth.

   4) A dream ago, perhaps. Ornament is for joy.
       All the bones were charred.

   5) It is not remembered. Remember,
20   most were peasants; their life
       was in rice and bamboo.
       When peaceful clouds were reflected in the paddies
       and the water buffalo stepped surely along terraces,
       maybe fathers told their sons old tales.
25   When bombs smashed the mirrors
       there was time only to scream.

   6) There is an echo yet, it is said,
       of their speech which was like a song.
       It is reported their singing resembled
30   the flight of moths in moonlight.
       Who can say? It is silent now.

ROBERT   LOWELL

(1917–1977)

For the Union Dead

(1959)

*"Relinquunt omnia
servare rem publicam."*[1]

The old South Boston Aquarium stands
in a Sahara of snow now. Its broken windows are boarded.
The bronze weathervane cod has lost half its scales.
The airy tanks are dry.

---

[1] "They gave up everything to preserve the Republic." A monument in Boston Common bears a similar form of this quotation. Designed by Augustus Saint-Gaudens, the monument is dedicated to Colonel Robert Gould Shaw and the African-American troops he commanded during a Civil War battle at Fort Wagner, South Carolina, on July 18, 1863.

5 Once my nose crawled like a snail on the glass;
my hand tingled
to burst the bubbles
drifting from the noses of the cowed, compliant fish.

My hand draws back. I often sigh still
10 for the dark downward and vegetating kingdom
of the fish and reptile. One morning last March,
I pressed against the new barbed and galvanized

fence on the Boston Common. Behind their cage,
yellow dinosaur steamshovels were grunting
15 as they cropped up tons of mush and grass
to gouge their underworld garage.

Parking spaces luxuriate like civic
sandpiles in the heart of Boston.
A girdle of orange, Puritan-pumpkin colored girders
20 braces the tingling Statehouse,

shaking over the excavations, as it faces Colonel Shaw
and his bell-cheeked Negro infantry
on St. Gauden's shaking Civil War relief,
propped by a plank splint against the garage's earthquake.

25 Two months after marching through Boston,
half the regiment was dead;
at the dedication,
William James[2] could almost hear the bronze Negroes breathe.

Their monument sticks like a fishbone
30 in the city's throat.
Its Colonel is as lean
as a compass-needle.

He has an angry wrenlike vigilance,
a greyhound's gentle tautness;
35 he seems to wince at pleasure,
and suffocate for privacy.

He is out of bounds now. He rejoices in man's lovely,
peculiar power to choose life and death—
when he leads his black soldiers to death,
40 he cannot bend his back.

---

[2] Harvard psychologist and philosopher (1842–1910).

On a thousand small town New England greens,
the old white churches hold their air
of sparse, sincere rebellion; frayed flags
quilt the graveyards of the Grand Army of the Republic.

45 The stone statues of the abstract Union Soldier
grow slimmer and younger each year—
wasp-waisted, they doze over muskets
and muse through their sideburns . . .

Shaw's father wanted no monument
50 except the ditch,
where his son's body was thrown
and lost with his "niggers."

The ditch is nearer.
There are no statues for the last war here;
55 on Boylston Street, a commercial photograph
shows Hiroshima boiling

ever a Mosler Safe,[3] the "Rock of Ages"
that survived the blast. Space is nearer.
When I crouch to my television set,
60 the drained faces of Negro school-children rise like balloons.

Colonel Shaw
is riding on his bubble,
he waits
for the blessed break.

65 The Aquarium is gone. Everywhere,
giant finned cars nose forward like fish;
a savage servility
slides by on grease.

---

[3] A brand of safe known for being especially strong.

BOB MARLEY

Get Up, Stand Up

Get up, stand up, stand up for your rights
Get up, stand up, stand up for your rights
Get up, stand up, stand up for your rights
Get up, stand up, don't give up the fight

5 Preacher man don't tell me
Heaven is under the earth
I know you don't know
What life is really worth
It's not all that glitters is gold
10 Half the story has never been told
So now you see the light
Stand up for your rights

Get up, stand up, stand up for your rights
Get up, stand up, stand up for your rights
15 Get up, stand up, stand up for your rights
Get up, stand up, don't give up the fight

Most people think
Great good will come from the skies
Take away everything
20 And make everybody feel high
But if you know what life is worth
You would look for yours on earth
And now you've seen the light
You stand up for your rights

25 Get up, stand up (yeah yeah)
Stand up for your rights (oh)
Get up, stand up (get up, stand up)
Don't give up the fight (life is your right)
Get up, stand up (so we can't give up the fight)
30 Stand up for your right (lord lord)
Get up, stand up (people struggling on)
Don't give up the fight (yeah)

We're sick and tired of your easing kissing game
To die and go to heaven in jesus' name
35 We know and we understand
Almighty god is a living man

You can fool some people sometimes
But you can't fool all the people all the time

And now we've seen the light (what you gonna do)
40 We gonna stand up for our rights

Get up, stand up, stand up for your rights
Get up, stand up, stand up for your rights
Get up, stand up, stand up for your rights
Get up, stand up, don't give up the fight

CHRISTOPHER MARLOWE

(1564–1593)

The Passionate Shepherd to His Love

(1600)

Come live with me and be my love,
And we will all the pleasures prove
That valleys, groves, hills, and fields,
Woods, or steepy mountain yields.

5 And we will sit upon the rocks,
Seeing the shepherds feed their flocks
By shallow rivers, to whose falls
Melodious birds sing madrigals.

And I will make thee beds of roses
10 And a thousand fragrant posies,
A cap of flowers and a kirtle[1]
Embroidered all with leaves of myrtle;

A gown made of the finest wool
Which from our pretty lambs we pull;
15 Fair-linèd slippers for the cold,
With buckles of the purest gold;

---

[1] Skirt.

A belt of straw and ivy buds,
With coral clasps and amber studs.
And if these pleasures may thee move,
20 Come live with me and be my love.

The shepherds' swains shall dance and sing
For thy delight each May morning.
If these delights thy mind may move,
Then live with me and be my love.

CLAUDE MCKAY

(1890–1948)

If We Must Die

(1922)

If we must die, let it not be like hogs
Hunted and penned in an inglorious spot,
While round us bark the mad and hungry dogs,
Making their mock at our accursed lot.
5 If we must die, O let us nobly die,
So that our precious blood may not be shed
In vain; then even the monsters we defy
Shall be constrained to honor us though dead!
O kinsmen! we must meet the common foe!
10 Though far outnumbered let us show us brave,
And for their thousand blows deal one deathblow!
What though before us lies the open grave?
Like men we'll face the murderous, cowardly pack,
Pressed to the wall, dying, but fighting back!

E D N A   S T .   V I N C E N T   M I L L A Y

(1892–1950)

What Lips My Lips
Have Kissed

(1923)

What lips my lips have kissed, and where, and why,
I have forgotten, and what arms have lain
Under my head till morning; but the rain
Is full of ghosts tonight, that tap and sigh
5 Upon the glass and listen for reply,
And in my heart there stirs a quiet pain
For unremembered lads that not again
Will turn to me at midnight with a cry.
Thus in the winter stands the lonely tree,
10 Nor knows what birds have vanished one by one,
Yet knows its boughs more silent than before:
I cannot say what loves have come and gone,
I only know that summer sang in me
A little while, that in me sings no more.

J O H N   M I L T O N

(1608–1674)

When I Consider How
My Light Is Spent[1]

(1655?)

When I consider how my light is spent,
     Ere half my days in this dark world and wide,
     And that one talent[2] which is death to hide
Lodged with me useless, though my soul more bent

---

1 A meditation on his blindness.

2 See Jesus' parable of the talents in Matthew 25:14–30.

5 To serve therewith my Maker, and present
    My true account, lest He returning chide;
    "Doth God exact day-labor, light denied?"
I fondly[3] ask. But Patience, to prevent
That murmur, soon replies, "God doth not need
10   Either man's work or His own gifts. Who best
    Bear His mild yoke, they serve Him best. His state
Is kingly: thousands at His bidding speed,
    And post o'er land and ocean without rest;
    They also serve who only stand and wait."

JANICE MIRIKITANI

(1942–)

Breaking Silence

(1981)

*After forty years of silence about the experience of Japanese
Americans in World War II concentration camps, my mother
testified before the Commission on Wartime Relocation and
Internment of Japanese American Civilians in 1981.
(Quoted excerpts from my mother's testimony,
modified with her permission)*

FOR MY MOTHER

There are miracles that happen
she said.
From the silences
in the glass caves of our ears,
5 from the crippled tongue,
from the mute, wet eyelash,
testimonies waiting like winter.
    We were told
that silence was better
10 golden like our skin,
    useful like
go quietly,
    easier like

---

[3] Foolishly.

don't make waves,
15   expedient like
horsestalls and deserts.

          "Mr. Commissioner. . .
          . . . the U.S. Army Signal Corps confiscated
          our property. . . it was subjected to
20   vandalism and ravage. All improvements
          we had made before our incarceration
          was stolen or destroyed. . .
          I was coerced into signing documents
          giving you authority to take. . . "
25   to take
          to take.

My mother,
soft as tallow,
words peeling from her
30 like slivers of yellow flame.
Her testimony,
a vat of boiling water
surging through the coldest
bluest vein.
35   She had come to her land
as shovel, hoe and sickle searing
reed and rock and dead brush
labored to sinew the ground
to soften gardens pregnant with seed
40 awaiting each silent morning
birthing
fields of flowers,
mustard greens and tomatoes
throbbing like the sea.
45   And then
All was hushed for announcements:
    "Take only what you can carry. . . "
We were made to believe our faces
betrayed us.
50 Our bodies were loud
with yellow screaming flesh
needing to be silenced
behind barbed wire.

          "Mr. Commissioner. . .
55   . . . it seems we were singled out
          from others who were under suspicion.

Our neighbors were of German and
Italian descent, some of whom were
not citizens. . . It seems we were
60   singled out. . . "

She had worn her work
like lemon leaves,
shining in her sweat,
driven by her dreams that honed
65 the blade of her plow.
The land she built
like hope
grew quietly
irises, roses, sweet peas
70 opening, opening.
        And then
all was hushed for announcements:
    ". . . to be incarcerated for your own good"
The sounds of her work
75 bolted in barracks. . .
silenced.

Mr. Commissioner. . .
So when you tell me I must limit
testimony,
80   when you tell me my time is up,
I tell you this:
Pride has kept my lips
pinned by nails
my rage coffined.
85   But I exhume my past
to claim this time.
My youth is buried in Rohwer,[1]
Obachan's ghost visits Amache Gate.[1]
My niece haunts Tule Lake.[1]
90   Words are better than tears,
so I spill them.
I kill this,
the silence. . .

There are miracles that happen
95 she said,
and everything is made visible.

---

[1] During World War II, Japanese-Americans were interned in camps in these places.

We see the cracks and fissures in our soil:
We speak of suicides and intimacies,
of longings lush like wet furrows,
100 of oceans bearing us toward imagined riches,
of burning humiliations and
crimes by the government.
Of self hate and of love that breaks
through silences.
105   We are lightning and justice.
Our souls become transparent like glass
revealing tears for war-dead sons
red ashes of Hiroshima
jagged wounds from barbed wire.
110   We must recognize ourselves at last.
We are a rainforest of color
and noise.
We hear everything.
We are unafraid.

115   Our language is beautiful.

N . S C O T T M O M A D A Y

The Bear

What ruse of vision,
escarping the wall of leaves,
rending incision
into countless surfaces,

5   would cull and color
his somnolence, whose old age
has outworn valor,
all but the fact of courage?

Seen, he does not come,
10 move, but seems forever there,
dimensionless, dumb,
in the windless noon's hot glare.

More scarred than others
these years since the trap maimed him,
15   pain slants his withers,
drawing up the crooked limb.

Then he is gone, whole,
without urgency, from sight,
      as buzzards control,
20 imperceptibly, their flight.

HOWARD NEMEROV

(1920–1991)

Life Cycle of Common Man

(1960)

Roughly figured, this man of moderate habits,
This average consumer of the middle class,
Consumed in the course of his average life span
Just under half a million cigarettes,
5 Four thousand fifths of gin and about
A quarter as much vermouth; he drank
Maybe a hundred thousand cups of coffee,
And counting his parents' share it cost
Something like half a million dollars
10 To put him through life. How many beasts
Died to provide him with meat, belt and shoes
Cannot be certainly said.

                    But anyhow,
It is in this way that a man travels through time,
Leaving behind him a lengthening trail
15 Of empty bottles and bones, of broken shoes,
Frayed collars and worn out or outgrown
Diapers and dinnerjackets, silk ties and slickers.
Given the energy and security thus achieved,
He did . . . ? What? The usual things, of course,
20 The eating, dreaming, drinking and begetting,
And he worked for the money which was to pay
For the eating, et cetera, which were necessary

If he were to go on working for the money, et cetera,
But chiefly he talked. As the bottles and bones
25 Accumulated behind him, the words proceeded
Steadily from the front of his face as he
Advanced into the silence and made it verbal.
Who can tally the tale of his words? A lifetime
Would barely suffice for their repetition;
30 If you merely printed all his commas the result
Would be a very large volume, and the number of times
He said "thank you" or "very little sugar, please,"
Would stagger the imagination. There were also
Witticisms, platitudes, and statements beginning
35 "It seems to me" or "As I always say."
Consider the courage in all that, and behold the man
Walking into deep silence, with the ectoplastic
Cartoon's balloon of speech proceeding
Steadily out of the front of his face, the words
40 Borne along on the breath which is his spirit
Telling the numberless tale of his untold Word
Which makes the world his apple, and forces him to eat.

PABLO NERUDA

(1904–1973)

The United Fruit Co.[1]

(1950)

translated by Robert Bly

When the trumpet sounded, it was
all prepared on the earth,
and Jehovah parceled out the earth
to Coca-Cola, Inc., Anaconda,
5 Ford Motors, and other entities:
The Fruit Company, Inc.
reserved for itself the most succulent,
the central coast of my own land,

---

[1] Incorporated in New Jersey in 1899 by Andrew Preston and Minor C. Keith, United Fruit became the major force in growing, transporting, and merchandising Latin American produce, especially bananas. The company is also notorious for its involvement in politics and is a symbol for many people of "Yankee" imperialism and oppression.

the delicate waist of America.
10 It rechristened its territories
as the "Banana Republics"
and over the sleeping dead,
over the restless heroes
who brought about the greatness,
15 the liberty and the flags,
it established the comic opera:
abolished the independencies,
presented crowns of Caesar,
unsheathed envy, attracted
20 the dictatorship of the flies,
Trujillo flies, Tacho flies,
Carias flies, Martinez flies,
Ubico flies,[2] damp flies
of modest blood and marmalade,
25 drunken flies who zoom
over the ordinary graves,
circus flies, wise flies
well trained in tyranny.

Among the bloodthirsty flies
30 the Fruit Company lands its ships,
taking off the coffee and the fruit;
the treasure of our submerged
territories flows as though
on plates into the ships.

35 Meanwhile Indians are falling
into the sugared chasms
of the harbors, wrapped
for burial in the mist of the dawn:
a body rolls, a thing
40 that has no name, a fallen cipher,
a cluster of dead fruit
thrown down on the dump.

---

[2] Trujillo, Tacho, Carias, Martinez, and Ubico are all political dictators.

WILFRED OWEN

(1893–1918)

Anthem for Doomed Youth

(1917?)

What passing-bells for these who die as cattle?
    Only the monstrous anger of the guns.
Only the stuttering rifles' rapid rattle
Can patter out their hasty orisons.
5 No mockeries now for them; no prayers nor bells,
    Nor any voice of mourning save the choirs,—
The shrill, demented choirs of wailing shells;
    And bugles calling for them from sad shires.

What candles may be held to speed them all?
10   Not in the hands of boys, but in their eyes
    Shall shine the holy glimmers of good-byes.
The pallor of girls' brows shall be their pall;
Their flowers the tenderness of patient minds,
And each slow dusk a drawing-down of blinds.

SHARON OLDS

(1942–   )

Rites of Passage

(1983)

As the guests arrive at my son's party
they gather in the living room—
short men, men in first grade
with smooth jaws and chins.
5 Hands in pockets, they stand around
jostling, jockeying for place, small fights
breaking out and calming. One says to another
How old are you? Six. I'm seven. So?
They eye each other, seeing themselves
10 tiny in the other's pupils. They clear their
throats a lot, a room of small bankers,

they fold their arms and frown. *I could beat you
up,* a seven says to a six,
the dark cake, round and heavy as a
15 turrent, behind them on the table. My son,
freckles like specks of nutmeg on his cheeks,
chest narrow as the balsa[1] keel[2] of a
model boat, long hands
cool and thin as the day they guided him
20 out of me, speaks up as a host
for the sake of the group.
We could easily kill a two-year-old,
he says in his clear voice. The other
men agree, they clear their throats
25 like Generals, they relax and get down to
playing war, celebrating my son's life.

L I N D A   P A S T A N

(1932–   )

Ethics

(1980)

In ethics class so many years ago
our teacher asked this question every fall:
if there were a fire in a museum
which would you save, a Rembrandt painting
5 or an old woman who hadn't many
years left anyhow? Restless on hard chairs
caring little for pictures or old age
we'd opt one year for life, the next for art
and always half-heartedly. Sometimes
10 the woman borrowed my grandmother's face
leaving her usual kitchen to wander
some drafty, half imagined museum.
One year, feeling clever, I replied
why not let the woman decide herself?
15 Linda, the teacher would report, eschews

---

[1] A lightweight wood.

[2] The piece of wood that runs lengthwise along the center of a ship's bottom.

the burdens of responsibility.
This fall in a real museum I stand
before a real Rembrandt, old woman,
or nearly so, myself. The colors
20 within this frame are darker than autumn,
darker even than winter—the browns of earth,
though earth's most radiant elements burn
through the canvas. I know now that woman
and painting and season are almost one
25 and all beyond saving by children.

MARGE PIERCY

(1934–   )

A Work of Artifice

(1973)

The bonsai tree
in the attractive pot
could have grown eighty feet tall
on the side of a mountain
5   till split by lightning.
But a gardener
carefully pruned it.
It is nine inches high.
Every day as he
10 whittles back the branches
the gardener croons,
It is your nature
to be small and cozy
domestic and weak;
15 how lucky, little tree,
to have a pot to grow in.
With living creatures
one must begin very early
to dwarf their growth:
20 the bound feet,
the crippled brain,
the hair in curlers,
the hands you
love to touch.

SYLVIA PLATH

(1932–1963)

Metaphors

(1960)

I'm a riddle in nine syllables,
An elephant, a ponderous house,
A melon strolling on two tendrils.
O red fruit, ivory, fine timbers!
5 This loaf's big with its yeasty rising.
Money's new-minted in this fat purse.
I'm a means, a stage, a cow in calf.
I've eaten a bag of green apples,
Boarded the train there's no getting off.

Mirror

(1963)

I am silver and exact. I have no preconceptions.
Whatever I see I swallow immediately
Just as it is, unmisted by love or dislike.
I am not cruel, only truthful—
5 The eye of a little god, four-cornered.
Most of the time I meditate on the opposite wall.
It is pink, with speckles. I have looked at it so long
I think it is a part of my heart. But it flickers.
Faces and darkness separate us over and over.

10 Now I am a lake. A woman bends over me,
Searching my reaches for what she really is.
Then she turns to those liars, the candles or the moon.
I see her back, and reflect it faithfully.
She rewards me with tears and an agitation of hands.
15 I am important to her. She comes and goes.
Each morning it is her face that replaces the darkness.
In me she has drowned a young girl, and in me an old woman
Rises toward her day after day, like a terrible fish.

EZRA POUND

(1885–1972)

The River-Merchant's Wife: A Letter[1]

(1515)

While my hair was still cut straight across my forehead
I played about the front gate, pulling flowers.
You came by on bamboo stilts, playing horse,
You walked about my seat, playing with blue plums.
5 And we went on living in the village of Chokan:[2]
Two small people, without dislike or suspicion.
At fourteen I married My Lord you.
I never laughed, being bashful.
Lowering my head, I looked at the wall.
10 Called to, a thousand times, I never looked back.

At fifteen I stopped scowling,
I desired my dust to be mingled with yours
Forever and forever and forever.
Why should I climb the lookout?
15 At sixteen you departed,
You went into far Ku-to-yen,[3] by the river of swirling eddies,
And you have been gone five months.
The monkeys make sorrowful noise overhead.

You dragged your feet when you went out.
20 By the gate now, the moss is grown, the different mosses,
Too deep to clear them away!
The leaves fall early this autumn, in wind.
The paired butterflies are already yellow with August
Over the grass in the West garden;
25 They hurt me. I grow older.

---

[1] This is one of the many translations Pound made of Chinese poems. The poem is a free translation of Li Po's (701–762) "Two Letters from Chang-Kan."

[2] Chang-Kan.

[3] An island in the river Ch'ū-t'ang.

If you are coming down through the narrows of the river Kiang,[4]
Please let me know beforehand,
And I will come out to meet you
    As far as Cho-fu-sa.[5]

SIR WALTER RALEIGH
(1552?–1618)

The Nymph's Reply
to the Shepherd

(1589?)

If all the world and love were young,
And truth in every shepherd's tongue,
These pretty pleasures might me move
To live with thee and be thy love.

5 Time drives the flocks from field to fold,
When rivers rage and rocks grow cold;
And Philomel[1] becometh dumb;
The rest complains of cares to come.

The flowers do fade, and wanton fields
10 To wayward winter reckoning yields:
A honey tongue, a heart of gall,
Is fancy's spring, but sorrow's fall.

Thy gowns, thy shoes, thy beds of roses,
Thy cap, thy kirtle, and thy posies
15 Soon break, soon wither, soon forgotten,
In folly ripe, in reason rotten.

---

[4] The Japanese name for the river Ch'ū-t'ang (see note 3). Pound's translations are based on commentaries derived from Japanese scholars; therefore, he usually uses Japanese instead of Chinese names.

[5] A beach several hundred miles upstream of Nanking.

[1] The nightingale.

Thy belt of straw and ivy buds,
Thy coral clasps and amber studs,
All these in me no means can move
20 To come to thee and be thy love.

But could youth last, and love still breed,
Had joys no date, nor age no need,
Then these delights my mind might move
To live with thee and be thy love.

JOHN CROWE RANSOM

(1888–1974)

Bells for John Whiteside's Daughter

(1924)

There was such speed in her little body,
And such lightness in her footfall,
It is no wonder her brown study
Astonishes us all.

5 Her wars were bruited in our high window.
We looked among orchard trees and beyond,
Where she took arms against her shadow,
Or harried unto the pond

The lazy geese, like a snow cloud
10 Dripping their snow on the green grass,
Tricking and stopping, sleepy and proud,
Who cried in goose, Alas,

For the tireless heart within the little
Lady with rod that made them rise
15 From their noon apple-dreams, and scuttle
Goose-fashion under the skies!

But now go the bells, and we are ready;
In one house we are sternly stopped
To say we are vexed at her brown study,
20 Lying so primly propped.

HENRY   REED

(1914–   )

Naming of Parts

(1946)

Today we have naming of parts. Yesterday,
We had daily cleaning. And tomorrow morning,
We shall have what to do after firing. But today,
Today we have naming of parts. Japonica[1]
5 Glistens like coral in all of the neighboring gardens,
    And today we have naming of parts.

This is the lower sling swivel. And this
Is the upper sling swivel, whose use you will see,
When you are given your slings. And this is the piling swivel,
10 Which in your case you have not got. The branches
Hold in the gardens their silent, eloquent gestures,
    Which in our case we have not got.

This is the safety-catch, which is always released
With an easy flick of the thumb. And please do not let me
15 See anyone using his finger. You can do it quite easy
If you have any strength in your thumb. The blossoms
Are fragile and motionless, never letting anyone see
    Any of them using their finger.

And this you can see is the bolt. The purpose of this
20 Is to open the breech, as you see. We can slide it
Rapidly backwards and forwards: we call this
Easing the spring. And rapidly backwards and forwards
The early bees are assaulting and fumbling the flowers:
    They call it easing the Spring.

25 They call it easing the Spring: it is perfectly easy
If you have any strength in your thumb: like the bolt,
And the breech, and the cocking-piece, and the point of balance,
Which in our case we have not got; and the almond-blossom
Silent in all of the gardens and the bees going backwards and forwards,
30   For today we have the naming of parts.

------

[1] A shrub having waxy flowers in a variety of colors.

EDWIN ARLINGTON ROBINSON

(1869–1935)

Miniver Cheevy

(1910)

Miniver Cheevy, child of scorn,
    Grew lean while he assailed the seasons;
He wept that he was ever born,
    And he had reasons.

5 Miniver loved the days of old
    When swords were bright and steeds were prancing;
The vision of a warrior bold
    Would set him dancing.

Miniver sighed for what was not,
10   And dreamed, and rested from his labors;
He dreamed of Thebes[1] and Camelot,[2]
    And Priam's[3] neighbors.

Miniver mourned the ripe renown
    That made so many a name so fragrant;
15 He mourned Romance, now on the town,
    And Art, a vagrant.

Miniver loved the Medici,[4]
    Albeit he had never seen one;
He would have sinned incessantly
20   Could he have been one.

Miniver cursed the commonplace
    And eyed a khaki suit with loathing;
He missed the medieval grace
    Of iron clothing.

---

[1] The setting of many Greek legends, including that of Oedipus.

[2] The legendary site of King Arthur's court.

[3] Priam was the last King of Troy; his "neighbors" included Helen, Aeneas, and Hector.

[4] Rulers of Florence, Italy, from the fifteenth through the eighteenth centuries. During the Renaissance, Lorenzo de Medici was a renowned patron of the arts.

25 Miniver scorned the gold he sought,
        But sore annoyed was he without it;
    Miniver thought, and thought, and thought,
        And thought about it.

    Miniver Cheevy, born too late,
30   Scratched his head and kept on thinking;
    Miniver coughed, and called it fate,
        And kept on drinking.

Mr. Flood's Party

(1921)

    Old Eben Flood, climbing alone one night
    Over the hill between the town below
    And the forsaken upland hermitage
    That held as much as he should ever know
5   On earth again of home, paused warily.
    The road was his with not a native near;
    And Eben, having leisure, said aloud,
    For no man else in Tilbury Town to hear:

    "Well, Mr. Flood, we have the harvest moon
10 Again, and we may not have many more;
    The bird is on the wing, the poet[1] says,
    And you and I have said it here before.
    Drink to the bird." He raised up to the light
    The jug that he had gone so far to fill,
15 And answered huskily: "Well, Mr. Flood,
    Since you propose it, I believe I will."

    Alone, as if enduring to the end
    A valiant armor of scarred hopes outworn,
    He stood there in the middle of the road
20 Like Roland's ghost winding a silent horn.[2]
    Below him, in the town among the trees,

---

[1] Edward FitzGerald, trans., *The Rubáiyát of Omar Khayyám.*

[2] In the *Chanson de Roland,* a medieval French romance, Roland and his soldiers are trapped and killed at a mountain pass; Roland waits until the last minute before his death to sound his horn to signal for help from his emperor, Charlemagne.

Where friends of other days had honored him,
A phantom salutation of the dead
Rang thinly till old Eben's eyes were dim.

25 Then, as a mother lays her sleeping child
Down tenderly, fearing it may awake,
He set the jug down slowly at his feet
With trembling care, knowing that most things break;
And only when assured that on firm earth
30 It stood, as the uncertain lives of men
Assuredly did not, he paced away,
And with his hand extended paused again:

"Well, Mr. Flood, we have not met like this
In a long time; and many a change has come
35 To both of us, I fear, since last it was
We had a drop together. Welcome home!"
Convivially returning with himself,
Again he raised the jug up to the light;
And with an acquiescent quaver said:
40 "Well, Mr. Flood, if you insist, I might.

"Only a very little, Mr. Flood—
For auld lang syne. No more, sir; that will do."
So, for the time, apparently it did,
And Eben evidently thought so too;
45 For soon amid the silver loneliness
Of night he lifted up his voice and sang,
Secure, with only two moons listening,
Until the whole harmonious landscape rang—

"For auld lang syne." The weary throat gave out,
50 The last word wavered; and the song being done,
He raised again the jug regretfully
And shook his head, and was again alone.
There was not much that was ahead of him,
And there was nothing in the town below—
55 Where strangers would have shut the many doors
That many friends had opened long ago.

Richard Cory

(1897)

Whenever Richard Cory went down town,
We people on the pavement looked at him:
He was a gentleman from sole to crown,
Clean favored, and imperially slim.

5 And he was always quietly arrayed,
And he was always human when he talked;
But still he fluttered pulses when he said,
"Good-morning," and he glittered when he walked.

And he was rich—yes, richer than a king—
10 And admirably schooled in every grace:
In fine, we thought that he was everything
To make us wish that we were in his place.

So on we worked, and waited for the light,
And went without the meat, and cursed the bread;
15 And Richard Cory, one calm summer night,
Went home and put a bullet through his head.

SONIA SANCHEZ

(1934–   )

right on: white america

(1970)

this country might have
been a pio
        neer land
once.
5   but.   there ain't
no mo
        indians   blowing
custer's[1] mind

---

[1] General George Armstrong Custer (1839–1876) was killed by Sioux in his "last stand" at the Little Bighorn in Montana.

<pre>
               with a different
10 image of america.
                      this country
          might have
                      needed shoot/
          outs/ daily/
15   once.
                            but. there ain't
          no mo real/ white/   allamerican
                                  bad/guys.
          just.
20   u & me.
                      blk/ and un/armed.
          this country might have
          been a pion
                      eer land.   once.
25   and it still is.
          check out
                      the falling
          gun/shells   on our blk/tomorrows.
</pre>

CARL SANDBURG

(1878–1967)

Fog

(1916)

<pre>
          The fog comes
          on little cat feet.
          It sits looking
          over harbor and city
5 on silent haunches
          and then moves on.
</pre>

MONGONE WALLY SEROTE

(1944–   )

For Don M.—Banned

(1982)

it is a dry white season
dark leaves don't last, their brief lives dry out
and with a broken heart they dive down gently headed for earth,
not even bleeding.
5 it is a dry white season brother,
only the trees know the pain as they still stand erect
dry like steel, their branches dry like wire,
indeed, it is a dry white season
but seasons come to pass.

ANNE SEXTON

(1928–1974)

Her Kind

(1960)

I have gone out, a possessed witch,
haunting the black air, braver at night;
dreaming evil, I have done my hitch[1]
over the plain houses, light by light:
5 lonely thing, twelve-fingered, out of mind.
A woman like that is not a woman, quite.
I have been her kind.

I have found the warm caves in the woods,
filled them with skillets, carvings, shelves,
10 closets, silks, innumerable goods;
fixed the suppers for the worms and the elves:
whining, rearranging the disaligned.
A woman like that is misunderstood.
I have been her kind.

---

[1] Period of service (military slang).

15 I have ridden in your cart, driver,
  waved my nude arms at villages going by,
  learning the last bright routes, survivor
  where your flames still bite my thigh
  and my ribs crack where your wheels wind.
20 A woman like that is not ashamed to die.
  I have been her kind.

WILLIAM SHAKESPEARE

(1564–1616)

Let Me Not to the Marriage of True Minds

(1609)

Let me not to the marriage of true minds
Admit impediments.[1] Love is not love
Which alters when it alteration finds,
Or bends with the remover to remove:
5 Oh, no! it is an ever-fixéd mark,
That looks on tempests and is never shaken;
It is the star to every wandering bark,
Whose worth's unknown, although his height[2] be taken.
Love's not Time's fool,[3] though rosy lips and cheeks
10 Within his bending sickle's compass come;
Love alters not with his brief hours and weeks,
But bears it out even to the edge of doom.[4]
If this be error and upon me proved,
I never writ, nor no man ever loved.

---

[1] A reference to "The Order of Solemnization of Matrimony" in the Anglican *Book of Common Prayer:* "I require that if either of you know any impediments why ye may not be lawfully joined together in Matrimony, ye do now confess it."

[2] Although the altitude of a star may be measured, its worth is unknowable.

[3] That is, mocked by Time.

[4] Doomsday.

My Mistress' Eyes Are Nothing Like the Sun

(1609)

My mistress' eyes are nothing like the sun;
Coral is far more red than her lips' red;
If snow be white, why then her breasts are dun;
If hairs be wires, black wires grow on her head.
5　I have seen roses damasked red and white,
But no such roses see I in her cheeks;
And in some perfumes is there more delight
Than in the breath that from my mistress reeks.
I love to hear her speak, yet well I know
10　That music hath a far more pleasing sound;
I grant I never saw a goddess go:
My mistress, when she walks, treads on the ground.
　　And yet, by heaven, I think my love as rare
　　As any she, belied with false compare.

Not Marble, Nor the Gilded Monuments

(1609)

Not marble, nor the gilded monuments
Of princes, shall outlive this powerful rhyme;
But you shall shine more bright in these contents
Than unswept stone, besmeared with sluttish time.
5　When wasteful war shall statues overturn,
And broils root out the work of masonry,
Nor Mars[1] his sword nor war's quick fire shall burn
The living record of your memory.
'Gainst death and all-oblivious enmity
10　Shall you pace forth; your praise shall still find room
Even in the eyes of all posterity
That wear this world out to the ending doom.
So, till the judgment that yourself arise,
You live in this, and dwell in lovers' eyes.

---

[1] God of War.

Shall I Compare Thee to a Summer's Day?

(1609)

Shall I compare thee to a summer's day?
Thou art more lovely and more temperate:
Rough winds do shake the darling buds of May,
And summer's lease hath all too short a date.
5 Sometime too hot the eye of heaven shines,
And often in his gold complexion dimmed;
And every fair from fair sometimes declines,
By chance, or nature's changing course, untrimmed.
But thy eternal summer shall not fade,
10 Nor lose possession of that fair thou ow'st
Nor shall death brag thou wand'rest in his shade,
When in eternal lines to time thou grow'st.
      So long as men can breathe or eyes can see,
      So long lives this, and this gives life to thee.

PERCY BYSSHE SHELLEY

(1792–1822)

Ode to the West Wind

(1820)

I

O wild West Wind, thou breath of Autumn's being,
Thou, from whose unseen presence the leaves dead
Are driven, like ghosts from an enchanter fleeing,

Yellow, and black, and pale, and hectic[1] red,
5 Pestilence-stricken multitudes: O Thou,
Who chariotest to their dark wintry bed

The winged seeds, where they lie cold and low,
Each like a corpse within its grave, until
Thine azure sister of the Spring[2] shall blow

---

[1] Reference to a tubercular fever that produces flushed cheeks.

[2] The west wind of the spring.

10 Her clarion o'er the dreaming earth, and fill
(Driving sweet buds like flocks to feed in air)
With living hues and odours plain and hill:

Wild Spirit, which art moving everywhere;
Destroyer and Preserver; hear, O hear!

II

15 Thou on whose stream, mid the steep sky's commotion,
Loose clouds like Earth's decaying leaves are shed,
Shook from the tangled boughs of Heaven and Ocean,

Angels of rain and lightning: there are spread
On the blue surface of thine aery surge,
20 Like the bright hair uplifted from the head

Of some fierce Maenad,[3] even from the dim verge
Of the horizon to the zenith's height,
The locks of the approaching storm. Thou Dirge

Of the dying year, to which this closing night
25 Will be the dome of a vast sepulchre,
Vaulted with all thy congregated might

Of vapours, from whose solid atmosphere
Black rain and fire and hail will burst: O hear!

III

Thou who didst waken from his summer dreams
30 The blue Mediterranean, where he lay,
Lulled by the coil of his crystalline streams,

Beside a pumice isle in Baiae's bay,[4]
And saw in sleep old palaces and towers
Quivering within the wave's intenser day,

---

[3] A female votary who danced wildly in ceremonies for Dionysus (or Bacchus), Greek god of wine and vegetation, who according to legend died in the fall and was reborn in the spring.

[4] A bay in the Mediterranean Sea, west of Naples. It was known for the opulent villas built by Roman emperors along its shores.

35 All overgrown with azure moss and flowers
So sweet, the sense faints picturing them! Thou
For whose path the Atlantic's level powers

Cleave themselves into chasms, while far below
The sea-blooms and the oozy woods which wear
40 The sapless foliage of the ocean, know

Thy voice, and suddenly grow grey with fear,
And tremble and despoil themselves: O hear!

IV

If I were a dead leaf thou mightest bear;
If I were a swift cloud to fly with thee;
45 A wave to pant beneath thy power, and share

The impulse of thy strength, only less free
Than thou, O Uncontrollable! If even
I were as in my boyhood, and could be

The comrade of thy wanderings over Heaven,
50 As then, when to outstrip thy skiey speed
Scarce seemed a vision; I would ne'er have striven

As thus with thee in prayer in my sore need,
Oh! lift me as a wave, a leaf, a cloud!
I fall upon the thorns of life! I bleed!

55 A heavy weight of hours has chained and bowed
One too like thee: tameless, and swift, and proud.

V

Make me thy lyre,[5] even as the forest is:
What if my leaves are falling like its own!
The tumult of thy mighty harmonies

60 Will take from both a deep, autumnal tone,
Sweet though in sadness. Be thou, Spirit fierce,
My spirit! Be thou me, impetuous one!

---

[5] An Aeolian harp, a stringed instrument that produces musical sounds when exposed to the wind.

Drive my dead thoughts over the universe
Like withered leaves to quicken a new birth!
65 And, by the incantation of this verse,

Scatter, as from an unextinguished hearth
Ashes and sparks, my words among mankind!
Be through my lips to unawakened Earth

The trumpet of a prophecy! O Wind,
70 If Winter comes, can Spring be far behind?

SIR PHILIP SIDNEY

(1554–1586)

Astrophel and Stella

(1591)

Who will in fairest book of Nature know,
How Virtue may best lodged in beauty be,
Let him but learn of Love to read in thee,
Stella, those fair lines, which true goodness show.
5 There shall he find all vices' overthrow,
Not by rude force, but sweetest sovereignty
Of reason, from whose light those night birds fly;
That inward sun in thine eyes shineth so.
And not content to be Perfection's heir
10 Thyself, dost strive all minds that way to move,
Who mark in thee what is in thee most fair.
So while thy beauty draws the heart to love,
As fast thy Virtue bends that love to good:
"But ah," desire still cries, "give me some food."

CHARLES SIMIC

(1938–   )

Birthday Star Atlas

(1986)

Wildest dream, Miss Emily,
Then the coldly dawning suspicion—
Always at the loss—come day
Large black birds overtaking men who sleep in ditches.

5 A whiff of winter in the air. Sovereign blue,
Blue that stands for intellectual clarity
Over a street deserted except for a far off dog,
A police car, a light at the vanishing point

For the children to solve on the blackboard today—
10 Blind children at the school you and I know about.
Their gray nightgowns creased by the north wind;
Their fingernails bitten from time immemorial.

We're in a long line outside a dead letter office.
We're dustmice under a conjugal bed carved with exotic fishes and
monkeys.
15 We're in a slow drifting coalbarge huddled around the television set
Which has a wire coat-hanger for an antenna.

A quick view (by satellite) of the polar regions
Maternally tucked in for the long night.
Then some sort of interference—parallel lines
20 Like the ivory-boned needles of your grandmother knitting our fates
together.

All things ambiguous and lovely in their ambiguity,
Like the nebulae in my new star atlas—
Pale ovals where the ancestral portraits have been taken down.
The gods with their goatees and their faint smiles

25 In company of their bombshell spouses,
Naked and statuesque as if entering a death camp.
They smile, too, stroke the Triton wrapped around the mantle clock
When they are not showing the whites of their eyes in theatrical ecstasy.

Nostalgias for the theological vaudeville.
30 A false springtime cleverly painted on cardboard
For the couple in the last row to sigh over
While holding hands which unknown to them

Flutter like bird-shaped scissors . . .
Emily, the birthday atlas!
35 I kept turning its pages awed
And delighted by the size of the unimaginable;

The great nowhere, the everlasting nothing—
Pure and serene doggedness
For the hell of it—and love,
40 Our nightly stroll the color of silence and time.

B O R I S   S L U T S K Y [1]

How Did They Kill
My Grandmother?

translated by Elaine Feinstein

How did they kill my grandmother?
I'll tell you how they killed her.
One morning a tank rolled up to
a building where
5 the hundred and fifty Jews of our town who,
weightless
        from a year's starvation,
and white
        with the knowledge of death,
10 were gathered holding their bundles.
And the German polizei[2] were
herding the old people briskly;
and their tin mugs clanked as
the young men led them away
15   far away.

---

[1] Birth date of author and publication date of poem are not available.

[2] Police.

But my small grandmother
my seventy-year-old grandmother
began to curse and
scream at the Germans;
20 shouting that I was a soldier.
She yelled at them: My grandson
is off at the front fighting!
Don't you dare
touch me!
25 Listen, you
              can hear our guns!

Even as she went off, my grandmother
cried abuse,
              starting all over again
30 with her curses.
From every window then
Ivanovnas and Andreyevnas
Sidorovnas and Petrovnas
sobbed: You tell them, Polina
35 Matveyevna, keep it up!
They all yelled together:
              "What can we do against
this enemy, the Hun?"
Which was why the Germans chose
40 to kill her inside the town.

A bullet struck her hair
and kicked her grey plait down.
My grandmother fell to the ground.
That is how she died there.

STEVIE SMITH

(1902–1971)

Not Waving But Drowning

(1957)

Nobody heard him, the dead man,
But still he lay moaning:
I was much further out than you thought
And not waving but drowning.

5 Poor chap, he always loved larking
And now he's dead
It must have been too cold for him his heart gave way,
They said.

Oh, no no no, it was too cold always
10 (Still the dead one lay moaning)
I was much too far out all my life
And not waving but drowning.

CATHY SONG

(1955–   )

Lost Sister

(1983)

1

In China,
even the peasants
named their first daughters
Jade—
5 the stone that in the far fields
could moisten the dry season,
could make men move mountains
for the healing green of the inner hills
glistening like slices of winter melon.

10 And the daughters were grateful:
they never left home.
To move freely was a luxury
stolen from them at birth.
Instead, they gathered patience,
15 learning to walk in shoes
the size of teacups,[1]
without breaking—
the arc of their movements
as dormant as the rooted willow,

---

[1] A reference to the practice of binding young girls' feet so that they remain small. This practice, which crippled women, was common in China until the communist revolution.

20 as redundant as the farmyard hens.
But they traveled far
in surviving,
learning to stretch the family rice,
to quiet the demons,
25 the noisy stomachs.

2

There is a sister
across the ocean,
who relinquished her name,
diluting jade green
30 with the blue of the Pacific.
Rising with a tide of locusts,
she swarmed with others
to inundate another shore.
In America,
35 there are many roads
and women can stride along with men.

But in another wilderness,
the possibilities,
the loneliness,
40 can strangulate like jungle vines.
The meager provisions and sentiments
of once belonging—
fermented roots, Mah-Jongg[2] tiles and firecrackers—
set but a flimsy household
45 in a forest of nightless cities.
A giant snake rattles above,
spewing black clouds into your kitchen.
Dough-faced landlords
slip in and out of your keyholes,
50 making claims you don't understand,
tapping into your communication systems
of laundry lines and restaurant chains.

You find you need China:
your one fragile identification,
55 a jade link
handcuffed to your wrist.
You remember your mother

---

[2] Or mahjong, an ancient Chinese game played with dice and tiles.

who walked for centuries,
footless—
60 and like her,
you have left no footprints,
but only because
there is an ocean in between,
the unremitting space of your rebellion.

G A R Y   S O T O

(1952–   )

Black Hair

(1985)

At eight I was brilliant with my body.
In July, that ring of heat
We all jumped through, I sat in the bleachers
Of Romain Playground, in the lengthening
5 Shade that rose from our dirty feet.
The game before us was more than baseball.
It was a figure—Hector Moreno
Quick and hard with turned muscles,
His crouch the one I assumed before an altar
10 Of worn baseball cards, in my room.
I came here because I was Mexican, a stick
Of brown light in love with those
Who could do it—the triple and hard slide,
The gloves eating balls into double plays.
15 What could I do with 50 pounds, my shyness,
My black torch of hair, about to go out?
Father was dead, his face no longer
Hanging over the table or our sleep,
And mother was the terror of mouths
20 Twisting hurt by butter knives.

In the bleachers I was brilliant with my body,
Waving players in and stomping my feet,
Growing sweaty in the presence of white shirts.
I chewed sunflower seeds. I drank water
25 And bit my arm through the late innings.
When Hector lined balls into deep

Center, in my mind I rounded the bases
With him, my face flared, my hair lifting
Beautifully, because we were coming home
30 To the arms of brown people.

History

(1977)

Grandma lit the stove.
Morning sunlight
Lengthened in spears
Across the linoleum floor.
5 Wrapped in a shawl,
Her eyes small
With sleep.
She sliced papas,[1]
Pounded chiles
10 With a stone
Brought from Guadalajara.[2]

                              After
Grandpa left for work,
She hosed down
15 The walk her sons paved
And in the shade
Of a chinaberry,
Unearthed her
Secret cigar box
20 Of bright coins
And bills, counted them
In English,
Then in Spanish,
And buried them elsewhere.
25 Later, back
From the market,
Where no one saw her,
She pulled out
Pepper and beet, spines

---

[1] Potatoes.

[2] A city in Mexico.

30 Of asparagus
From her blouse,
Tiny chocolates
From under a paisley bandana,
And smiled.

35 That was the '50s,
And Grandma in her '50s,
A face streaked
From cutting grapes
And boxing plums.
40 I remember her insides
Were washed of tapeworm,
Her arms swelled into knobs
Of small growths—
Her second son
45 Dropped from a ladder
And was dust.
And yet I do not know
The sorrows
That sent her praying
50 In the dark of a closet,
The tear that fell
At night
When she touched
Loose skin
55 Of belly and breasts.
I do not know why
Her face shines
Or what goes beyond this shine,
Only the stories
60 That pulled her
From Taxco[3] to San Joaquin,
Delano to Westside,[4]
The places
In which we all begin.

---

[3] A city in Mexico.

[4] Places in California.

BARRY SPACKS

(1931–   )

Finding a Yiddish[1] Paper on the Riverside Line

(1978)

Again I hold these holy letters,
Never learned. Dark candelabras.

Once they glowed in the yellow light
Through the chicken smell of Friday night,[2]

5   My father in his peach-stained shirt
Scrubbing off twelve hours' dirt

While I drew my name on misted glass.
Now trim suburban houses pass

And on my lap the headlines loom
10   Like strangers in the living room.

BRUCE SPRINGSTEEN

(1949–   )

My Hometown

(1984)

I was eight years old and running with a dime in my hand
Into the bus stop to pick up a paper for my old man
I'd sit on his lap in that big old Buick and steer as we drove through town
He'd tousle my hair and say son take a good look around
5   This is your hometown

---

[1] Yiddish, a language derived from High German and spoken by Eastern European Jews, is written in Hebrew characters.

[2] The Jewish Sabbath begins at sundown on Friday. Chicken is traditionally served at the Sabbath meal.

This is your hometown
This is your hometown
This is your hometown

In '65 tension was running high at my high school
10 There was a lot of fights between the black and white
There was nothing you could do
Two cars at a light on a Saturday night in the back seat there was a gun
Words were passed in a shotgun blast
Troubled times had come to my hometown
15 My hometown
My hometown
My hometown

Now Main Street's whitewashed windows and vacant stores
Seems like there ain't nobody wants to come down here no more
20 They're closing down the textile mill across the railroad tracks
Foreman says these jobs are going boys and they ain't coming back to
    your hometown
Your hometown
Your hometown
Your hometown

25 Last night me and Kate we laid in bed talking about getting out
Packing up our bags maybe heading south
I'm thirty-five we got a boy of our own now
Last night I sat him up behind the wheel and said son take a good look
    around this is your hometown

WILLIAM STAFFORD

(1914–1993)

Traveling through the Dark

(1962)

Traveling through the dark I found a deer
dead on the edge of the Wilson River road.
It is usually best to roll them into the canyon:
that road is narrow; to swerve might make more dead.

5 By glow of the tail-light I stumbled back of the car
and stood by the heap, a doe, a recent killing;
she had stiffened already, almost cold.
I dragged her off; she was large in the belly.

My fingers touching her side brought me the reason—
10 her side was warm; her fawn lay there waiting,
alive, still, never to be born.
Beside that mountain road I hesitated.

The car aimed ahead its lowered parking lights;
under the hood purred the steady engine.
15 I stood in the glare of the warm exhaust turning red;
around our group I could hear the wilderness listen.

I thought hard for us all—my only swerving—
then pushed her over the edge into the river.

DONA STEIN

(1935–   )

Putting Mother By

(1977)

We are in her kitchen;
we have one enormous
pot and all the spices
are together.

5 We are too tiny and take
so long to sterilize
the jar; finally, more
water is boiling, waiting.
We don't have to call,
10 she hears and comes
into her kitchen.

We lift her over the pot;
she slips into the water
without a murmur.
15 She does not try to get out.

Later, we stand on tiptoes
and watch her inside
the Mason jar floating
in liquid by bay leaves
20 and flakes of pepper.
Dill weed floats like
a pine tree around her hair.

We look at each other, we
press our noses against
25 the jar and see she is more
surprised than anything else.

Carefully we carry her down
into the cellar; we store
her next to the peaches and plums;
30 we have her now.

WALLACE STEVENS

(1879–1955)

Anecdote of the Jar

(1923)

I placed a jar in Tennessee,
And round it was, upon a hill.
It made the slovenly wilderness
Surround that hill.

5 The wilderness rose up to it,
And sprawled around, no longer wild.
The jar was round upon the ground
And tall and of a port in air.

It took dominion everywhere.
10 The jar was gray and bare.
It did not give of bird or bush,
Like nothing else in Tennessee.

Disillusionment of Ten o'clock

(1923)

The houses are haunted
By white night-gowns.
None are green,
Or purple with green rings,
5 Or green with yellow rings,
Or yellow with blue rings.
None of them are strange,
With socks of lace
And beaded ceintures.[1]
10 People are not going
To dream of baboons and periwinkles.
Only, here and there, an old sailor,
Drunk and asleep in his boots,
Catches tigers
15 In red weather.

The Emperor of Ice-Cream

(1923)

Call the roller of big cigars,
The muscular one, and bid him whip
In kitchen cups concupiscent curds.
Let the wenches dawdle in such dress
5 As they are used to wear, and let the boys
Bring flowers in last month's newspapers.
Let be be finale of seem.
The only emperor is the emperor of ice-cream.

Take from the dresser of deal,[1]
10 Lacking the three glass knobs, that sheet
On which she embroidered fantails[2] once
And spread it so as to cover her face.

---

[1] Girdles, or belts, around the waist.

[1] Fir or pine wood.

[2] According to Stevens, "the word fantails does not mean fans, but fantail pigeons."

If her horny feet protrude, they come
To show how cold she is, and dumb.
15 Let the lamp affix its beam.
The only emperor is the emperor of ice-cream.

ANDREW SUKNASKI

(1942–   )

The Bitter Word

(1976)

from fort walsh
colonel irvine brings the bitter word
to sitting bull at wood mountain
makes clear the government welcomes the teton—
5 yet they must not expect provisions
or food from canada

sitting bull proudly replies:
when did i ever ask you for provisions?
before i beg
10 *i will cut willows for my young men to use*
while killing mice to survive

in the spring of 1881
sitting bull gathers his remaining 1200 sioux
and treks to fort qu'appelle to make
15 the final request for a reservation—
inspector sam steele tells them
the great white mother wishes them to return
to their own country
(a rather curious view of a people
20 whose meaning of country changes with
the migrations of tatanka)[1]
steele politely refuses the request
and supplies enough provisions for the return
to wood mountain

---

[1] A Lakota-Nakota (Sioux) word meaning "god-animal" and referring to the buffalo.

₂₅ death by summer is certain
while irvine makes sure
provisions and seed never arrive
seeing the migrating game
sitting bull knew the tatanka
₃₀ would never return
though his people dreamed of white tatanka rising
from the subterranean meadows others fled to
(hideous shrieks of red river carts grating in
their ears)
₃₅ he must have sensed the hunger to follow
which was exactly what the authorities hoped for
on both sides of the border

ALFRED, LORD TENNYSON

(1809–1892)

Ulysses[1]

(1833)

It little profits that an idle king,
By this still hearth, among these barren crags,
Matched with an agèd wife, I mete and dole
Unequal laws unto a savage race
₅ That hoard, and sleep, and feed, and know not me.
I cannot rest from travel; I will drink
Life to the lees. All times I have enjoyed
Greatly, have suffered greatly, both with those
That loved me, and alone; on shore, and when
₁₀ Through scudding drifts the rainy Hyades[2]
Vexed the dim sea. I am become a name;
For always roaming with a hungry heart
Much have I seen and known—cities of men
And manners, climates, councils, governments,

---

[1] A legendary Greek king of Ithaca and hero of Homer's *Odyssey*, Ulysses (or Odysseus) is noted for his daring and cunning. After his many adventures—including encounters with the Cyclops, the cannibalistic Laestrygones, and the enchantress Circe—Ulysses returned home to his faithful wife, Penelope. Tennyson portrays an older Ulysses pondering his situation.

[2] A group of stars whose rising was supposedly followed by rain, and hence stormy seas.

15 Myself not least, but honored of them all—
And drunk delight of battle with my peers,
Far on the ringing plains of windy Troy.[3]
I am a part of all that I have met;
Yet all experience is an arch wherethrough
20 Gleams that untraveled world whose margin fades
Forever and forever when I move.
How dull it is to pause, to make an end,
To rust unburnished, not to shine in use!
As though to breathe were life! Life piled on life
25 Were all too little, and of one to me
Little remains; but every hour is saved
From that eternal silence, something more,
A bringer of new things; and vile it were
For some three suns to store and hoard myself,
30 And this grey spirit yearning in desire
To follow knowledge like a sinking star,
Beyond the utmost bound of human thought.
    This is my son, mine own Telemachus,
To whom I leave the scepter and the isle—
35 Well-loved of me, discerning to fulfill
This labor, by slow prudence to make mild
A rugged people, and through soft degrees
Subdue them to the useful and the good.
Most blameless is he, centered in the sphere
40 Of common duties, decent not to fail
In offices of tenderness, and pay
Meet adoration to my household gods,
When I am gone. He works his work, I mine.
    There lies the port; the vessel puffs her sail;
45 There gloom the dark, broad seas. My mariners,
Souls that have toiled, and wrought, and thought with me—
That ever with a frolic welcome took
The thunder and the sunshine, and opposed
Free hearts, free foreheads—you and I are old;
50 Old age hath yet his honor and his toil.
Death closes all; but something ere the end,
Some work of noble note, may yet be done,
Not unbecoming men that strove with Gods.
The lights begin to twinkle from the rocks;
55 The long day wanes; the low moon climbs; the deep
Moans round with many voices. Come, my friends,

---

[3] An ancient city in Asia Minor. According to legend, Paris, King of Troy, abducted Helen, initiating the famed Trojan war, in which numerous Greek heroes, including Ulysses, fought.

'Tis not too late to seek a newer world.
Push off, and sitting well in order smite
The sounding furrows; for my purpose holds
60 To sail beyond the sunset, and the baths
Of all the western stars, until I die.
It may be that the gulfs will wash us down;
It may be we shall touch the Happy Isles,[4]
And see the great Achilles,[5] whom we knew.
65 Though much is taken, much abides; and though
We are not now that strength which in old days
Moved earth and heaven, that which we are, we are—
One equal temper of heroic hearts,
Made weak by time and fate, but strong in will
70 To strive, to seek, to find, and not to yield.

DYLAN THOMAS

(1914–1953)

Fern Hill

(1946)

Now as I was young and easy under the apple boughs
About the lilting house and happy as the grass was green,
   The night above the dingle[1] starry,
    Time let me hail and climb
5   Golden in the heydays of his eyes,
And honored among wagons I was prince of the apple towns
And once below a time I lordly had the trees and leaves
   Trail with daisies and barley
   Down the rivers of the windfall light.

10 And as I was green and carefree, famous among the barns
About the happy yard and singing as the farm was home,
   In the sun that is young once only,
    Time let me play and be
   Golden in the mercy of his means,

---

4 Elysium, or Paradise, believed to be in the far western ocean.

5 Famed Greek hero of the Trojan War.

1 Wooded valley.

15 And green and golden I was huntsman and herdsman, the calves
Sang to my horn, the foxes on the hills barked clear and cold,
　　And the sabbath rang slowly
　　In the pebbles of the holy streams.

All the sun long it was running, it was lovely, the hay
20 Fields high as the house, the tunes from the chimneys, it was air
　　And playing, lovely and watery
　　　And fire green as grass.
　　And nightly under the simple stars
As I rode to sleep the owls were bearing the farm away,
25 All the moon long I heard, blessed among stables, the nightjars
　　Flying with the ricks, and the horses
　　　Flashing into the dark.

And then to awake, and the farm, like a wanderer white
With the dew, come back, the cock on his shoulder: it was all
30 　Shining, it was Adam and maiden,
　　　The sky gathered again
　　And the sun grew round that very day.
So it must have been after the birth of the simple light
In the first, spinning place, the spellbound horses walking warm
35 　Out of the whinnying green stable
　　　On to the fields of praise.

And honored among foxes and pheasants by the gay house
Under the new made clouds and happy as the heart was long,
　　In the sun born over and over,
40 　　I ran my heedless ways,
　　My wishes raced through the house high hay
And nothing I cared, at my sky blue trades, that time allows
In all his tuneful turning so few and such morning songs
　　Before the children green and golden
45 　　Follow him out of grace,

Nothing I cared, in the lamb white days, that time would take me
Up to the swallow thronged loft by the shadow of my hand,
　　In the moon that is always rising,
　　　Nor that riding to sleep
50 　I should hear him fly with the high fields
And wake to the farm forever fled from the childless land.
Oh as I was young and easy in the mercy of his means,
　　Time held me green and dying
　　Though I sang in my chains like the sea.

MARGARET WALKER

(1915–   )

Lineage

(1942)

My grandmothers were strong.
They followed plows and bent to toil.
They moved through fields sowing seed.
They touched earth and grain grew.
5 They were full of sturdiness and singing.
My grandmothers were strong.

My grandmothers are full of memories
Smelling of soap and onions and wet clay
With veins rolling roughly over quick hands
10 They have many clean words to say.
My grandmothers were strong.
Why am I not as they?

EDMUND WALLER

(1606–1687)

Go, Lovely Rose

(1645)

Go, lovely rose,
Tell her that wastes her time and me
That now she knows,
When I resemble her to thee,
5 How sweet and fair she seems to be.

Tell her that's young
And shuns to have her graces spied,
That hadst thou sprung
In deserts where no men abide,
10 Thou must have uncommended died.

Small is the worth
Of beauty from the light retired:
Bid her come forth,
Suffer herself to be desired,
15 And not blush so to be admired.

Then die, that she
The common fate of all things rare
May read in thee,
How small a part of time they share
20 That are so wondrous sweet and fair.

JAMES WELCH

(1940–   )

Going to Remake This World

(1976)

Morning and the snow might fall forever.
I keep busy. I watch the yellow dogs
chase creeping cars filled with Indians
on their way to the tribal office.
5 Grateful trees tickle the busy underside
of our snow-fat sky. My mind is right,
I think, and you will come today
for sure, this day when the snow falls.

From my window, I see bundled Doris Horseman,
10 black in the blowing snow, her raving son,
Horace, too busy counting flakes to hide his face.
He doesn't know. He kicks my dog
and glares at me, too dumb to thank the men
who keep him on relief and his mama drunk.

15 My radio reminds me that Hawaii calls
every afternoon at two. Moose Jaw is overcast,
twelve below and blowing. Some people . . .
Listen: if you do not come this day, today
of all days, there is another time
20 when breeze is tropic and riffs the green sap

forever up these crooked cottonwoods.
    Sometimes,
you know, the snow never falls forever.

The Man from Washington

(1976)

The end came easy for most of us.
Packed away in our crude beginnings
in some far corner of a flat world,
we didn't expect much more
5 than firewood and buffalo robes
to keep us warm. The man came down,
a slouching dwarf with rainwater eyes,
and spoke to us. He promised
that life would go on as usual,
10 that treaties would be signed, and everyone—
man, woman and child—would be inoculated
against a world in which we had no part,
a world of money, promise and disease.

PHYLLIS WHEATLEY

(1754–1784)

On Being Brought from Africa to America

(1773)

'Twas mercy brought me from my *Pagan* land,
Taught my benighted soul to understand
That there's a God, that there's a *Saviour* too:
Once I redemption neither sought nor knew.
5 Some view our sable race with scornful eye,
"Their colour is a diabolic die."
Remember, *Christians*, *Negroes*, black as *Cain*,
May be refin'd, and join th' angelic train.

WALT WHITMAN

(1819–1892)

Cavalry Crossing a Ford

(1865)

A line in long array where they wind betwixt green islands,
They take a serpentine course, their arms flash in the sun—hark to the
    musical clank,
Behold the silvery river, in it the splashing horses loitering stop to drink,
Behold the brown-faced men, each group, each person a picture, the
negligent rest on the saddles,
5 Some emerge on the opposite bank, others are just entering the ford—
    while,
Scarlet and blue and snowy white,
The guidon flags flutter gayly in the wind.

from Song of Myself

(1855)

1

I celebrate myself, and sing myself,
And what I assume you shall assume,
For every atom belonging to me as good belongs to you.

I loafe and invite my soul,
5 I lean and loafe at my ease observing a spear of summer grass.

My tongue, every atom of my blood, form'd from this soil, this air,
Born here of parents born here from parents the same, and their parents
    the same,
I, now thirty-seven years old in perfect health begin,
Hoping to cease not till death.

10 Creeds and schools in abeyance,
Retiring back a while suffied at what they are, but never forgotten,
I harbor for good or bad, I permit to speak at every hazard,
Nature without check with original energy.

2

Houses and rooms are full of perfumes, the shelves are crowded with
    perfumes,
15 I breathe the fragrance myself and know it and like it,
The distillation would intoxicate me also, but I shall not let it.

The atmosphere is not a perfume, it has no taste of the distillation, it is
    odorless,
It is for my mouth forever, I am in love with it,
I will go to the bank by the wood and become undisguised and naked,
20 I am mad for it to be in contact with me.

The smoke of my own breath,
Echoes, ripples, buzz'd whispers, love-root, silk-thread, crotch and vine,
My respiration and inspiration, the beating of my heart, the passing of
    blood and air through my lungs,
The sniff of green leaves and dry leaves, and of the shore and dark-color'd
    sea-rocks, and of hay in the barn,
25 The sound of the belch'd words of my voice loos'd to the eddies of the
    wind,
A few light kisses, a few embraces, a reaching around of arms,
The play of shine and shade on the trees as the supple boughs wag,
The delight alone or in the rush of the streets, or along the fields and
    hill-sides,
The feeling of health, the full-noon trill, the song of me rising from bed
    and meeting the sun.

30 Have you reckon'd a thousand acres much? have you reckon'd the earth
    much?
Have you practis'd so long to learn to read?
Have you felt so proud to get at the meaning of poems?

Stop this day and night with me and you shall possess the origin of all
    poems,
You shall possess the good of the earth and sun, (there are millions of
    suns left,)
35 You shall no longer take things at second or third hand, nor look through
    the eyes of the dead, nor feed on the spectres in books,
You shall not look through my eyes either, nor take things from me,
You shall listen to all sides and filter them from your self.

RICHARD WILBUR

(1921–   )

Museum Piece

(1950)

The good gray guardians of art
Patrol the halls on spongy shoes,
Impartially protective, though
Perhaps suspicious of Toulouse.[1]

5 Here dozes one against the wall,
Disposed upon a funeral chair.
A Degas[2] dancer pirouettes
Upon the parting of his hair.

See how she spins! The grace is there,
10 But strain as well is plain to see.
Degas loved the two together:
Beauty joined to energy.

Edgar Degas purchased once
A fine El Greco,[3] which he kept
15 Against the wall beside his bed
To hang his pants on while he slept.

---

[1] Henri de Toulouse-Lautrec (1864–1901)—French artist, famous for his paintings of Parisian café life, prostitutes, and popular entertainers.

[2] Edgar Degas (1834–1871)—French painter and sculptor, noted for his many studies of ballet dancers.

[3] El Greco (Domenikos Theotokopoulos; 1541–1614)—Greek-born painter who worked mainly in Spain.

WILLIAM CARLOS WILLIAMS

(1883–1963)

The Dance

(1944)

In Breughel's[1] great picture, The Kermess,[2]
the dancers go round, they go round and
around, the squeal and the blare and the
tweedle of bagpipes, a bugle and fiddles
5 tipping their bellies (round as the thick-
sided glasses whose wash they impound)
their hips and their bellies off balance
to turn them. Kicking and rolling about
the Fair Grounds, swinging their butts, those
10 shanks must be sound to bear up under such
rollicking measures, prance as the dance
in Breughel's great picture, The Kermess.

This Is Just to Say

(1938)

I have eaten
the plums
that were in
the icebox
5 and which
you were probably
saving
for breakfast

Forgive me
10 they were delicious
so sweet
and so cold

---

[1] Refers to the Flemish painter Peter Breughel (1525–1569).

[2] The Church Mass; Breughel's painting (1567) of peasants dancing at a church festival.

WILLIAM WORDSWORTH

(1770–1850)

Composed upon Westminster Bridge, September 3, 1802

(1807)

Earth has not anything to show more fair:
Dull would he be of soul who could pass by
A sight so touching in its majesty:
This City now doth, like a garment, wear
5 The beauty of the morning; silent, bare,
Ships, towers, domes, theatres, and temples lie
Open unto the fields, and to the sky;
All bright and glittering in the smokeless air.
Never did sun more beautifully steep
10 In his first splendor, valley, rock, or hill;
Ne'er saw I, never felt, a calm so deep!
The river glideth at his own sweet will:
Dear God! the very houses seem asleep;
And all that mighty heart is lying still!

I Wandered Lonely as a Cloud

(1807)

I wandered lonely as a cloud
    That floats on high o'er vales and hills,
When all at once I saw a crowd,
    A host, of golden daffodils,
5 Beside the lake, beneath the trees,
Fluttering and dancing in the breeze.

Continuous as the stars that shine
    And twinkle on the milky way,
They stretched in never-ending line
10   Along the margin of a bay:
Ten thousand saw I at a glance,
Tossing their heads in sprightly dance.

The waves beside them danced; but they
    Out-did the sparkling waves in glee;
15 A poet could not but be gay,
    In such a jocund company;
I gazed—and gazed—but little thought
What wealth the show to me had brought:

For oft, when on my couch I lie
20   In vacant or in pensive mood,
They flash upon that inward eye
    Which is the bliss of solitude;
And then my heart with pleasure fills,
And dances with the daffodils.

She Dwelt among the Untrodden Ways

(1800)

She dwelt among the untrodden ways
    Beside the springs of Dove,[1]
A Maid whom there were none to praise
    And very few to love:
5 A violet by a mossy stone
    Half hidden from the eye!
—Fair as a star, when only one
    Is shining in the sky.

The Solitary Reaper[1]

(1807)

Behold her, single in the field,
Yon solitary Highland lass!
Reaping and singing by herself;

---

[1] River in the Lake District of England.

[1] A person who harvests grain.

Stop here, or gently pass!
5 Alone she cuts and binds the grain,
And sings a melancholy strain;
O listen! for the vale profound
Is overflowing with the sound.

No nightingale did ever chaunt
10 More welcome notes to weary bands
Of travelers in some shady haunt
Among Arabian sands.
A voice so thrilling ne'er was heard
In springtime from the cuckoo-bird,
15 Breaking the silence of the seas
Among the farthest Herbrides.[2]

Will no one tell me what she sings?—
Perhaps the plaintive numbers flow
For old, unhappy, far-off things,
20 And battles long ago.
Or is it some more humble lay,
Familiar matter of today?
Some natural sorrow, loss, or pain,
That has been, and may be again?

25 Whate'er the theme, the maiden sang
As if her song could have no ending;
I saw her singing at her work,
And o'er the sickle[3] bending—
I listened, motionless and still;
30 And, as I mounted up the hill,
The music in my heart I bore
Long after it was heard no more.

---

[2] A group of islands off the west coast of Scotland.

[3] A curved blade used for harvesting grain or cutting grass.

JAMES WRIGHT

(1927–1980)

A Blessing

(1961)

Just off the highway to Rochester, Minnesota,
Twilight bounds softly forth on the grass.
And the eyes of those two Indian ponies
Darken with kindness.
5 They have come gladly out of the willows
To welcome my friend and me.
We step over the barbed wire into the pasture
Where they have been grazing all day, alone.
They ripple tensely, they can hardly contain their happiness
10 That we have come.
They bow shyly as wet swans. They love each other.
There is no loneliness like theirs.
At home once more,
They begin munching the young tufts of spring in the darkness.
15 I would like to hold the slenderer one in my arms,
For she has walked over to me
And nuzzled my left hand.
She is black and white,
Her mane falls wild on her forehead,
20 And the light breeze moves me to caress her long ear
That is delicate as the skin over a girl's wrist.
Suddenly I realize
That if I stepped out of my body I would break
Into blossom.

WILLIAM BUTLER YEATS

(1865–1939)

Crazy Jane Talks with the Bishop

(1933)

I met the Bishop on the road
And much said he and I.

"Those breasts are flat and fallen now,
Those veins must soon be dry;
5   Live in a heavenly mansion,
Not in some foul sty."

"Fair and foul are near of kin,
And fair needs foul," I cried.
"My friends are gone, but that's a truth
10 Nor grave nor bed denied,
Learned in bodily lowliness
And in the heart's pride.

"A woman can be proud and stiff
When on love intent;
15 But Love has pitched his mansion in
The place of excrement;
For nothing can be sole or whole
That has not been rent."

An Irish Airman
Foresees His Death

(1919)

I know that I shall meet my fate
Somewhere among the clouds above;
Those that I fight I do not hate,
Those that I guard I do not love;
5   My country is Kiltartan Cross
My countrymen Kiltartan's poor,
No likely end could bring them loss
Or leave them happier than before.
Nor law, nor duty bade me fight,
10 Nor public men, nor cheering crowds,
A lonely impulse of delight
Drove to this tumult in the clouds;
I balanced all, brought all to mind,
The years to come seemed waste of breath,
15 A waste of breath the years behind
In balance with this life, this death.

The Lake Isle of Innisfree

(1892)

I will arise and go now, and go to Innisfree,[1]
And a small cabin build there, of clay and wattles[2] made:
Nine bean-rows will I have there, a hive for the honey-bee,
And live alone in the bee-loud glade.

5 And I shall have some peace there, for peace comes dropping slow,
Dropping from the veils of the morning to where the cricket sings;
There midnight's all a glimmer, and noon a purple glow,
And evening full of the linnet's wings.

I will arise and go now, for always night and day
10 I hear lake water lapping with low sounds by the shore;
While I stand on the roadway, or on the pavements grey,
I hear it in the deep heart's core.

The Rose of Peace

If Michael,[1] leader of God's host,
When Heaven and Hell are met,
Looked down on you from Heaven's door-post
He would his deeds forget.

5 Brooding no more upon God's wars
In his divine homestead,
He would go weave out of the stars
A chaplet[2] for your head.

And all folk seeing him bow down,
10 And white stars tell your praise,
Would come at last to God's great town,
Led on by gentle ways;

---

[1] An island in Lough (Lake) Gill, County Sligo, in Ireland.

[2] Stakes interwoven with twigs or branches, used for walls and roofing.

[1] The Archangel Michael, who is traditionally represented as the leader of God's army in the battle against Satan.

[2] Wreath or garland.

And God would bid His warfare cease,
Saying all things were well;
15 And softly make a rosy peace,
A peace of Heaven with Hell.

Sailing to Byzantium

(1927)

That is no country for old men. The young
In one another's arms, birds in the trees
—Those dying generations—at their song,
The salmon-falls, the mackerel-crowded seas,
5 Fish, flesh, or fowl, commend all summer long
Whatever is begotten, born, and dies.
Caught in that sensual music all neglect
Monuments of unaging intellect.

An aged man is but a paltry thing,
10 A tattered coat upon a stick, unless
Soul clap its hands and sing, and louder sing
For every tatter in its mortal dress,
Nor is there singing school but studying
Monuments of its own magnificence;
15 And therefore I have sailed the seas and come
To the holy city of Byzantium.

O sages standing in God's holy fire
As in the gold mosaic of a wall,
Come from the holy fire, perne in a gyre,
20 And be the singing-masters of my soul.
Consume my heart away; sick with desire
And fastened to a dying animal
It knows not what it is; and gather me
Into the artifice of eternity.

25 Once out of nature I shall never take
My bodily form from any natural thing,
But such a form as Grecian goldsmiths make
Of hammered gold and gold enameling

To keep a drowsy Emperor awake;
30 Or set upon a golden bough to sing
To lords and ladies of Byzantium
Of what is past, or passing, or to come.

The Second Coming[1]

(1921)

Turning and turning in the widening gyre[2]
The falcon cannot hear the falconer;
Things fall apart; the center cannot hold;
Mere anarchy is loosed upon the world,
5 The blood-dimmed tide is loosed, and everywhere
The ceremony of innocence is drowned;
The best lack all conviction, while the worst
Are full of passionate intensity.[3]

Surely some revelation is at hand;
10 Surely the Second Coming is at hand;
The Second Coming! Hardly are those words out
When a vast image out of *Spiritus Mundi* [4]
Troubles my sight: somewhere in sands of the desert
A shape with lion body and the head of a man,
15 A gaze blank and pitiless as the sun,
Is moving its slow thighs, while all about it
Reel shadows of the indignant desert birds.
The darkness drops again; but now I know
That twenty centuries[5] of stony sleep
20 Were vexed to nightmare by a rocking cradle,
And what rough beast, its hour come round at last,
Slouches towards Bethlehem to be born?

---

[1] The Second Coming usually refers to the return of Christ. Yeats theorized cycles of history, much like the turning of a wheel. Here he offers a poetic comment on his view of the dissolution of civilization at the end of one such cycle.

[2] Spiral.

[3] Lines 4–8 refer to the Russian Revolution (1917).

[4] The Spirit of the World. Yeats believed all souls to be connected by a "Great Memory."

[5] The centuries since the birth of Christ.

Poets' Corner

MAYA ANGELOU (1928–   ), born Marguerita Johnson in St. Louis, grew up with her grandmother in Stamps, Arkansas, where she graduated from Lafayette County Training School. She has worked as a cook, streetcar conductor, dancer, screenwriter, singer, and actress. She has written numerous volumes of poetry as well as the much-acclaimed autobiographical series that begins with *I Know Why the Caged Bird Sings* (1970). Her works have been nominated for the National Book Award and the Pulitzer Prize. A notable distinction came to Angelou when she read her poem "On the Pulse of Morning" at the inauguration of President Bill Clinton. Critic Carol E. Neubauer notes that "through all of her verse, Angelou reaches out to touch the lives of others and to offer them hope and confidence in place of humiliation and despair." Angelou herself summarizes her work best: "I speak to the black experience, but I am always talking about the human condition—about what we can endure, dream, fail at, and still survive."

MARGARET ATWOOD (1939–   ) was born in Ottawa, Canada, and grew up in Toronto, where she attended the University of Toronto. Although her poetry won the Governor General's Award, Canada's highest literary honor, for *The Circle Game* in 1966, Atwood has become better known for her critical essays and novels, such as *The Handmaid's Tale* (1986). Critic Carolyn Allen compares Atwood to such feminist writers as Marge Piercy, Alice Munro, and Adrienne Rich, noting that "Atwood's increasingly unmistakable voice comes in part from her willingness to create women who attempt transformations and almost—but not quite—

become trees, roots, foxes. By failing to change themselves into what they cannot be, they become instead what they most truly are." In an interview with Linda Sandler, Atwood explains, "You can't write poetry unless you're willing to immerse yourself in language—not just in words, but in words of a certain potency. It's like learning a foreign language."

W(YSTAN) H(UGH) AUDEN (1907–1973), son of an English physician, earned a scholarship to Oxford University, where he became interested in the modernist poetry of T. S. Eliot; his circle of friends (dubbed the "Auden Generation") included writers Stephen Spender, Cecil Day-Lewis, Christopher Isherwood, and Louis MacNeice. Prior to leaving England and becoming a U.S. citizen, Auden published several volumes of poetry. In the United States he published *The Age of Anxiety*, which won the Pulitzer Prize (1945), and *The Shield of Achilles*, which won the National Book Award (1956). Noted critic and Nobel Prize-winning poet Seamus Heaney describes Auden as "an epoch-making poet on public themes, the register of a new sensibility, a great sonneteer, a writer of perfect light verse, a prospector of literature at its most illiterate roots and a dandy of lexicography at its most extravagant reaches." In an interview with Daniel Halpern in 1971, Auden said, "Truth in poetry is very important to me. I think you must feel, when you read a poem, that it says something about life which you recognize to be true."

WILLIAM BLAKE (1757–1827) displayed artistic abilities as a very young boy in London. His parents allowed him to leave school at age ten to study at Henry Pars's Drawing School for several years before he was apprenticed at age fourteen to the engraver James Basire. He also studied briefly at the Royal Academy of Arts. Blake made his living as an illustrator of Milton, Dante, and other writers. In addition, he wrote, illustrated, and printed his own lyrical and visionary poetical works and eventually developed his own mythology. Blake was little known during his lifetime, but he is now regarded as one of the earliest and most important figures of British Romanticism. His major works include *Songs of Innocence* (1789), *The Marriage of Heaven and Hell* (1793), *Songs of Experience* (1794), *Milton* (ca. 1804–1810), and *Jerusalem* (ca. 1815–1820). Attempting to explain Blake's obscurity among his contemporaries, who admired him more for his engravings than for his poetry, noted poet William Butler Yeats described Blake as one of those "men who loved the future like a mistress, and . . . if he spoke confusedly and obscurely it was because he spoke things for whose speaking he could find no models in the world about him." In defense of his work, Blake once remarked, "What is Grand is necessarily obscure to Weak men. That which can be made Explicit to the Idiot is not worth my care."

LOUISE BOGAN (1897–1970), who was born in Livermore Falls, Maine, had an extremely traumatic and unstable life, including depression so severe that for a short time she was voluntarily hospitalized. Bogan worked as poetry editor for the *New Yorker* from 1931 to 1970 and was elected to the American Academy of Arts and Letters. Her works include *Dark Summer* (1929), *Poems and New Poems* (1941), and *Collected Poems* (1954). In a memorial tribute to Bogan and her work, well-known poet and critic W. H. Auden noted: "What, aside from their technical excellence, is most impressive about her poems is the unflinching courage with which she faced her problems, her determination never to surrender to self-pity, but to wrest beauty and joy out of dark places." In her journal Bogan revealed how she used her experiences in her writing by repressing "the outright narrative" of her life and absorbing it "along with life itself": "The repressed becomes the poem. Actually, I have written down my experience in the closest detail. But the rough and vulgar facts of it are not there."

ANNE BRADSTREET (1612[?]–1672), America's first published poet, was born in England but moved with her husband and parents in 1630 to Puritan New England. Her first volume of poetry, *The Tenth Muse, Lately Sprung Up in America,* was published without her consent in 1650 by her brother-in-law. Dissatisfied with these poems, Bradstreet began to rework them, and after her death these revisions were published along with new poems as *Several Poems Compiled with Great Variety of Wit and Learning, Full of Delight* (1678). Acclaimed poet and critic Adrienne Rich calls Bradstreet "the first nondidactic American poet, the first to give an embodiment to American nature, the first in whom personal intention appears to precede Puritan dogma as an impulse to verse." Bradstreet herself declared, "I have not studied in this you read to show my skill, but to declare the truth, not to set forth myself, but the glory of God."

GWENDOLYN BROOKS (1917–   ) (See p. 1073 for biographical information.) In a review of her poetry collection *Annie Allen*, Langston Hughes, prominent poet of the Harlem Renaissance, noted that "the people and the poems in Gwendolyn Brooks's book are alive, reaching and very much of today." Brooks's desire to reach all African-American people is revealed in a 1974 interview in which she explained that she wanted "to develop a style that will appeal to black people in taverns, black people in gutters, schools, offices, factories, prisons, the consulate; I wish to reach black people in pulpits, black people in mines, on farms, on thrones."

ELIZABETH BARRETT BROWNING (1806–1861) was born into a large, wealthy, and very protective English family. Following a childhood riding accident, she suffered ill health for the remainder of her life. As a young woman, she achieved a considerable literary reputation and corresponded with many of the best-known writers of the time. In the 1840's she began to correspond with another young poet, Robert Browning. In 1846 the couple eloped to Italy, where they lived happily until her death. By 1850, the publication year of her best-known collection, *Sonnets from the Portuguese*, Browning's poetry was so highly regarded that she was seriously considered to replace William Wordsworth as Poet Laureate of England. American critic and poet Edgar Allan Poe observed: "That Miss Barrett has done more, in poetry, than any woman living or dead will scarcely be questioned. That she has surpassed all her poetical contemporaries of either sex (with a single exception) is our deliberate opinion—not idly entertained, we think, nor founded on any visionary basis." In light of negative critical comments made concerning her work, Browning explained, "My poems, while full of faults, . . . have my soul and life in them."

ROBERT BROWNING (1812–1889) grew up in London. His father was a clerk for the Bank of England; his mother was a strict Congregationalist, so he was unable to attend the major Anglican universities. Browning entered London University, where he stayed for a short time before leaving to devote himself to his poetry. Browning's reputation as a poet was established by *The Ring and the Book* (1868–1869). During the 1860's he and Alfred, Lord

Tennyson were considered England's greatest living poets. Late in life Browning received a degree from Oxford and an audience with Queen Victoria. He also saw the establishment of the Browning Society, a group that read and studied his work. Perhaps his greatest honor came after his death, when he was buried in Poets' Corner in Westminster Abbey. G. K. Chesterton, one of England's most prominent writers, praised Browning's "boldly designed poems, every one of which taken separately might have founded an artistic school." In a letter to Joseph Milsand, Browning expressed his desire to be read and understood: "I am writing lyrics . . . with more music and painting in them than before so as to get people to hear and see."

ROBERT BURNS (1759–1796), son of a poor tenant farmer in Alloway, Scotland, learned first-hand about the social injustices imposed upon common people, and this experience, along with his disagreement with such Calvinist tenets as predestination and humankind's innate sinfulness, furnished material for his poetry. In 1786 Burns published *Poems, Chiefly in the Scottish Dialect,* but after his marriage to Jean Armour, who had previously borne his illegitimate twins, Burns produced no poetry except for "Tam o' Shanter." Burns collected and revised Scottish folk songs and rediscovered such tunes as "Auld Lange Syne." Iain Crichton Smith, one of Scotland's best-known contemporary poets, has observed that "the lyrics of Burns are perfect of their kind, and their perfection, poised precariously between sentiment and universal truth, tells us that nothing more can be added." In a letter to Dr. John Moore, Burns noted: "To know myself had been all along my constant study."

RAYMOND CARVER (1938–1988), born in Clatskanie, Oregon, and raised in Yakima, Washington, became interested in writing as he listened to his father's stories. Carver took John Gardner's creative writing course at Chico State College, published stories and poems in literary magazines while a student at Humboldt State College in California, and attended the University of Iowa Writers' Workshop. Carver's short story "Will You Please Be Quiet, Please?" was selected as one of *The Best American Short Stories of 1967,* and in 1984, his 1983 collection *Cathedral: Stories* was nominated for both the National Book Critics Circle Award for fiction and the Pulitzer Prize. Carver is known as one of the most important practitioners and innovators of minimalist fiction. Critic Ted Solotaroff explains that Carver has "the kind of gift that travels: the common touch raised to the next power, the power, of art, that can be conveyed intact to his readers and brings out . . . the giftedness in them, the possibility of getting down to the charged and freighted roots of our lives." In an interview with the *Paris Review,* Carver explained how a writer extracts subject matter from personal sources: "You have to be immensely daring, very skilled and imaginative and willing to tell everything on yourself. . . . What do you know better than your own secrets?"

MICHELLE CLIFF (1946–   ) was born in Kingston, Jamaica, and educated at Wagner College and the Warburg Institute in London. In the early 1980s she moved to Montague, Massachusetts, and with poet Adrienne Rich co-edited *Sinister Wisdom,* a journal devoted to feminist issues. Cliff has received such fellowships as the MacDowell, the National Endowment for the Arts, and the Eli Kantor at Yaddo. Her publications include poetry collections, such as *Claiming an Identity They Taught Me to Despise* and *The Land of Look Behind,* as well as a novel, *Abeng.* Critic Françoise Lionnet comments on the fluidity of language in *Abeng:* "[Cliff's] move from Standard English to creole speech is meant to underscore class and racial differences among protagonists, but it also makes manifest the double consciousness of the postcolonial, bilingual, and bicultural writer who lives and writes across margins of different traditions and cultural universes." Cliff has said, "In my writing I am concerned most of all with social issues and political realities and how they affect the lives of people."

LUCILLE CLIFTON (1936–   ), born in Depew, New York, attended Howard University and graduated from Fredonia State Teachers College. She recalls with fondness her childhood, especially the poems her mother wrote to read to her and the stories her father told about his ancestors. In addition to being named Poet Laureate of Maryland, Clifton has been nominated for the Pulitzer Prize and has won two grants from the National Endowment for the Arts (1969, 1973). Her book *Good Times* was recognized by the New York *Times* as one of the best books of 1969. Critic Haki Madhubti describes Clifton as "a poet of *mean* talent who has not let her gifts separate her from the work at hand. She is a teacher and an example. To read her is to give birth to bright seasons." Clifton has described her style as follows: "I use a simple language. I have never believed that for anything to be valid or true or intellectual or 'deep' it had to first be complex. . . . I am not interested if anyone knows whether or not I am familiar with big words; I am interested in trying to render big ideas in a simple way. I am interested in being understood, not admired. I wish to celebrate and not to be celebrated."

SAMUEL TAYLOR COLERIDGE (1772–1834) was born in Devon in southern England, the thirteenth child in his family. After the death of his clergyman father, Coleridge was sent to London to attend Christ's Hospital, a boarding school. He received a scholarship to Jesus College, Cambridge, but he left without taking a degree. In 1796 he met William Wordsworth, and the two collaborated on *Lyrical Ballads,* the 1798 edition of which contains in its Preface one of the best-known definitions of literary Romanticism. Coleridge's greatest piece of literary criticism, *Biographia Literaria,* appeared in 1817. Noted critic Harold Bloom has remarked that though Coleridge's poetry "is a testament of defeat, a yielding to the anxiety of influence and to the fear of self-glorification, it is one of the most enduringly poignant of such testaments that literature affords us." In *Biographica Literaria* Coleridge distinguishes poetry from scientific writing, saying that "a poem . . . [has] for its immediate object pleasure, not truth."

COUNTEE CULLEN (1903–1946) was born Countee LeRoy Porter in New York City. (Some sources say Louisville, Kentucky, or Baltimore, Maryland.) When his paternal grandmother died in 1918, he was taken into the home of the Reverend Frederic A. Cullen, pastor of Harlem's largest Methodist-Episcopal congregation and later president of the NAACP. Cullen came of age at the center of African-American politics and culture. He received a bachelor's degree from New York University and a master's degree from Harvard. He earned a Guggenheim Fellowship and lived in France for a time, during which he was married briefly to Yolande DuBois, daughter of W. E. B. DuBois. Cullen, one of the leading voices of the Harlem Renaissance, was a novelist and a writer of children's books as well as a poet. In a review of *Color,* Cullen's best known volume of poetry, noted critic Babette Deutsch observes: "Mr. Cullen's poems are intensely race-conscious. He writes out of the pain of inflamed memories and with a wistful harking back to the primitive heritage of his own folk." Cullen acknowledged that his subject was always "the heights and depths of emotions which I feel as a Negro."

E(DWARD) E(STLIN) CUMMINGS (1894–1962) was born in Cambridge, Massachusetts, and completed undergraduate and graduate degrees at Harvard in 1915 and 1916. Although best known as a poet, Cummings was also a prose writer, translator, playwright, creator of a ballet, and visual artist. Among his honors and awards are two Guggenheim fellowships (1933 and 1951), a special citation from the National Book Awards in 1955, and the Bollingen Prize in Poetry (1957). According to Malcolm Cowley, Cummings "suffers from comparison with those who built on a larger scale . . . but still he is unsurpassed in his field." Randall Darrell said of Cummings, "No one else . . . has ever made avant-garde, experimental poems so attractive to the general and special reader."

EMILY DICKINSON (1830–1886) was born into a prominent family in Amherst, Massachusetts, where she attended Amherst Academy and Mount Holyoke Female Seminary. Except for brief trips to Boston, Philadelphia, and Washington, Dickinson rarely left her hometown, and after 1862 she rarely left her home. Only a handful of Dickinson's poems were published during her lifetime, and most of these had undergone editorial changes to make them more "conventional." The Dickinson canon was not completely established until 1955, when editor Thomas H. Johnson produced the definitive edition of Dickinson's *Collected Poems*. The texts and chronological numbering system of the 1,775 poems are still accepted today. Although obscure during the nineteenth century, Dickinson is now considered among the greatest of American poets. Joyce Carol Oates calls Dickinson "the most paradoxical of poets" because, despite "the extraordinary intimacy of her poetry," and even her letters, her voice has "a tone of the purest anonymity"; thus, if "anonymity is the soul's essential voice—its seductive, mesmerizing, fatal voice—then Emily Dickinson is our poet of the soul: our most endlessly fascinating American poet." Johnson describes her genius as follows: "A prosodist experimenting in meters, rhyme, capitals, grammar, and punctuation. [She] exhibited a boldness which doomed her to obscurity in her lifetime. Yet the stature she continues to take . . . is notable in the history of literary reputations." Dickinson saw poetry as a moment of great intensity. She told her literary adviser Thomas Wentworth Higginson, "If I read a book and it makes my whole body so cold no fire can warm me, I know *that* is poetry. If I feel physically as if the top of my head were taken off, I know *that* is poetry."

JOHN DONNE (1572–1631) was born into a Roman Catholic family in London. As a precocious twelve-year-old, Donne entered Oxford, but he was forced to leave in 1587 because of his Catholicism; he completed his degree in 1596. After he married sixteen-year-old Ann More, Donne was imprisoned (1601–1602) and then had difficulty supporting his wife and twelve children. Having converted to the Anglican religion in 1592 and having become an Anglican priest in 1615, he had many political opportunities, leading to his appointment in 1621 as Dean of St. Paul's Cathedral in London. Donne's later poems are more deeply religious than his earlier love poems. In 1633, two years after Donne's death, his collection, entitled *Poems,* was published, prefaced with elegies by Izaak Walton, Thomas Carew, and other admiring friends who honored him as a master poet; however, Ben Jonson's criticism of Donne's innovative meter, use of profanity, and obsequious verse continued to influence later critics. For instance, Samuel Johnson faulted Donne and other metaphysical writers for "a voluntary deviation from nature in pursuit of something new and strange." Therefore, Johnson claimed, they "fail to give delight by their desire of exciting admiration." Donne's famous epigram might well comment on this negative assessment: "John Donne / Ann Donne / Undonne."

RITA DOVE (1952–   ) was born in Akron, Ohio, earned her bachelor's degree at Miami University of Ohio in 1973, studied at Tubingen University in Germany on a Fulbright scholarship in 1974, and did graduate work at the University of Iowa Writers' Workshop. Dove was the nation's youngest (and first African American) Poet Laureate and was also Consultant in Poetry at the Library of Congress. She began her professional literary career by publishing several poetry chapbooks. Her first full-length volume of poetry, *The Yellow House on the Corner,* appeared in 1980; another collection, *Thomas and Beulah,* was awarded the 1987 Pulitzer Prize in poetry. Noted critic and Langston Hughes biographer Arnold Rampersad observes that Dove's "brilliant mind" is reinforced by "very wide reading," yet when she writes of "black experience," it is "in the course of 'ordinary' things" and situations "almost always very close to the poet's private experience, part of her personal and family history. . . ." Dove has explained that her themes transcend racial boundaries: "Obviously, as a black woman, I am concerned with race. . . . But certainly not every poem of mine mentions the fact of being black. They are poems about humanity, and sometimes humanity happens to be black."

T(HOMAS) S(TEARNS) ELIOT (1888–1965), born in St. Louis, Missouri, received undergraduate, master's, and doctoral degrees from Harvard before emigrating to London, where he worked as a bank clerk and then an influential book editor. In 1927 he became a British citizen. Among his many honors are prestigious professorships at Cambridge and Harvard, the Nobel Prize in Literature and the British Order of Merit (1948), the Emerson-Thoreau Medal from the American Academy of Arts and Sciences (1959), and the U.S. Medal of Freedom (1964). Among his best-known works are "The Love Song of J. Alfred Prufrock" (1917), *The Waste Land* (1922), and *The Four Quartets* (1943). For nearly three decades Eliot held a position of eminence among modern writers. In recent years he has received attention because of *Cats,* the long-running musical based on his 1939 *Old Possum's Book of Practical Cats,* a collection of verse. Ezra Pound, upon reading the manuscript of *The Waste Land,* suggested revisions to his friend but immediately recognized it as a work of genius, saying Eliot's poem was enough "to make the rest of us shut up shop." Eliot's assessment was more modest; he responded to critics who called *The Waste Land* social criticism by saying it was merely "the relief of a personal and wholly insignificant grouse against life . . . just a piece of rhythmical grumbling."

LOUISE ERDRICH (1954–   ) was born in Little Falls, Minnesota, the daughter of a German-American father and a Chippewa mother. She is a member of the Turtle Mountain Band of the Chippewa people. She attended Dartmouth College (B.A., 1976) and Johns Hopkins University (M.A., 1977). Her first novel, *Love Medicine* (1984), composed of fourteen interlocking stories, is the first in a four-volume saga that also includes *The Beet Queen,* (1986), *Tracks* (1988), and *The Bingo Palace* (1994). *Love Medicine* received the 1984 National Book Critics Circle Award, the Virginia McCormick Scully Prize, the Los Angeles *Times* Award, and the American Academy and Institute of Arts and Letters Award. Erdrich credits her family for teaching her how to tell stories about strong female characters: "Everybody in my family is a storyteller . . . whether a liar or a storyteller—whatever." Critic Carolyne Wright praises Erdrich's first volume of poetry, *Jacklight,* for its use of family and tribal history and for attaining "the enduring and universal via the minute particulars of individual and community experience [, which] has been a stated aim of poetry written in English since Wordsworth's Preface to the *Lyrical Ballads.*" Erdrich recalls her father's giving her a nickel for each story she wrote and her mother's stapling them into book covers: "At an early age I felt myself to be a published author earning substantial royalties."

LAWRENCE FERLINGHETTI (1919–   ) was born in Yonkers, New York, and brought up in France. Following a tumultuous childhood, this most scholarly writer of the Beat movement attended the University of North Carolina at Chapel Hill, Columbia University, and the Sorbonne. He settled in San Francisco and began his literary career writing book reviews for the San Francisco *Chronicle* and articles for Peter Martin's *City Lights*. In 1953 he joined with Martin to open City Lights Books, which became associated with the Beat Generation of writers. In 1955 Ferlinghetti's first book of poetry, *Pictures of the Gone World,* was published under the City Lights imprint. The following year he was charged with obscenity and arrested for publishing Allen Ginsberg's *Howl*. This publicity helped make a bestseller of Ferlinghetti's poetry collection *A Coney Island of the Mind* (1958). Years later Ginsberg noted that Ferlinghetti "ought to receive some sort of Pulitzer Prize" for publishing so many important anti-establishment writers. Ferlinghetti has expressed his belief in an ideal community transcending nationalism and forming only one continent on earth: "Under it all, after all, all colors of skin at length blended into one skin with one tongue."

CAROLYN FORCHÉ (1950–   ) was born in Detroit, Michigan. She studied at Michigan State University (B.A., 1972) and at Bowling Green State University (M.F.A., 1975). She has taught at several prestigious universities, including the University of Virginia, New York University, Vassar College, and Columbia University. Her first collection of poetry, *Gathering the Tribes* (1976), was published in the Yale Series of Younger Poets. Her poems have appeared in major magazines and journals, and she has received several grants and awards, including a Tennessee Williams Fellowship to the Bread Loaf Writers' Conference (1976), a National Endowment for the Arts grant (1977), and a Guggenheim Fellowship (1978). Critic Mark Harris has noted that although Forché "seeks her subjects in the common sources of human life and experience," her poems "have the effect of making the commonplace seem disturbingly unfamiliar." According to Harris, one of Forché's major themes is "the communication that takes place in silence, beyond the terse language of her poems."

Forché affirms this idea in these lines from "Taking Off My Clothes" (in *Gathering the Tribes*): "I have hundreds / of names for the snow, for this, all of them quiet."

ROBERT FROST (1874–1963) was born in San Francisco but moved in his youth to New England, where he briefly attended Dartmouth College, and later Harvard, without taking a degree. In 1900 he settled his family on a dairy farm near Derry, New Hampshire, where a large number of his poems originated. Twenty years later he helped establish the Bread Loaf School of English at Middlebury College, Vermont, which was near his home at Ripton.

As an established poet, Frost enjoyed enormous popularity, receiving honorary degrees from Oxford and Cambridge. He won Pulitzer Prizes for *New Hampshire, Collected Poems, A Further Range,* and *A Witness Tree* (in 1924, 1931, 1937, and 1943) and the Bollingen Prize in 1963. In 1950 he was nominated for, but did not win, the Nobel Prize in Literature. Named Consultant in Poetry for the Library of Congress, Frost became the unofficial poet laureate of America. He is perhaps best remembered for reciting his poem "The Gift Outright" from memory at the inauguration of President John F. Kennedy in 1961. (At age eighty-seven his poor eyesight prevented his reading the poem.) Critic Donald J. Greiner observes that "Stopping by Woods on a Snowy Evening," one of American literature's most explicated poems, "has immortality written all over it" and "deserves its place alongside the many novels and stories that ponder the fate of those who dare to plunge beyond the safety of the clearing to the darkness of the woods." Frost himself wrote poet and critic Louis Untermeyer in 1923 that this poem was his "best bid for remembrance."

NIKKI (YOLANDE CORNELIA) GIOVANNI (1943–) was born in Knoxville, Tennessee, and grew up in Wyoming and Lincoln Heights, near Cincinnati. She studied at Fisk University (B.A., 1967), the Columbia School of Arts, and the University of Pennsylvania School of Social Work. Grants from the Ford Foundation and other organizations supported her writing; she published *Black Feeling, Black Talk* in 1968 and *Black Judgment* in 1969. Giovanni has written a syndicated column for the New York *Times,* published essays in several magazines and journals, and edited *Night Comes Softly: An Anthology of Black Voices* (1970). Giovanni has had an enormous impact on African-American literature. Critic Alex Bateman observes that her poetry has shifted away from an earlier focus on militancy and revolution towards reflection on personal relationships and concern for her craft; "it is on finding the right words to correspond to the poetry, internal perceptions, that Giovanni expends her energy." Giovanni has this to say about her writing: "poetry is a trestle / spanning the distance between / what i tell / and what i say."

LOUISE GLÜCK (1943–), born in New York City, attended Sarah Lawrence College and Columbia University and then taught at the University of North Carolina at Greensboro, the University of Virginia, the University of Iowa, and the University of Cincinnati. Among her many awards and honors are Columbia University's Academy of American Poets Prize (1967), a Rockefeller Foundation grant (1968), a National Endowment for the Arts grant (1969–1970), and a Guggenheim Fellowship (1975–1976). Glück's first collection of poetry, *First Born*, appeared in 1968, followed in 1975 by *The House on Marshland*, which brought her national recognition. She won the American Academy Award in 1981 and the National Book Critics Circle Award in 1985 for *The Triumph of Achilles*. Her most recent collection is *Meadowlands* (1996). Critic Deno Trakis suggests that although the world of Glück's poems is "bleak"—portraying people "isolated from family, or bitter from rejected love, or disappointed with what life has to offer"—it is "depicted with a lyrical grace, and her poems are attractive if disturbing." Perhaps Glück's outlook on her career is expressed by her persona in "To Autumn": "I am no longer young. What / of it? Summer approaches and the long / decaying days of autumn when I shall begin / the great poems of my middle period."

H(ILDA) D(OOLITTLE) (1886–1961), born in Bethlehem, Pennsylvania, attended Bryn Mawr College briefly. Her first love was Ezra Pound, who considered her an "imagist" poet, a label from which she never freed herself. During her literary career, which encompassed five decades, H. D. wrote prodigiously but published modestly. Her work was diverse: numerous translations, a screenplay, a verse drama, short prose works, several autobiographical novels, and a children's novel. In 1916 H. D. published her first book of poems, *Sea Garden*, followed by *Hymen* (1921), *Heliodora and Other Poems* (1924), and *Collected Poems of H. D.* (1924); she received the Award of Merit Medal for Poetry from the American Academy of Arts and Letters in 1960. Not until after her death did H. D.'s long poems surface and provide insights from yet another point of view. Susan

Stanford Friedman considers H. D. "a major poet belonging both to the modernist mainstream and the tradition of women's writing"—indeed, a "poet's poet." Recounting her steady, disciplined routine of writing, H. D. told a friend in the 1920s, "I sit at my typewriter until I drop. I have, in some way, to justify my existence."

THOMAS HARDY (1840–1928), born in Dorsetshire, England, practiced architecture in London until he decided to write full-time. A versatile writer, Hardy published fourteen novels, eight volumes of poetry, four collections of short stories, two plays, and a variety of essays, prefaces, and non-fiction prose. His best known novels are *Far from the Madding Crowd* (1874), *The Return of the Native* (1878), *The Mayor of Casterbridge* (1886), *Tess of the D'Urbervilles* (1891), and *Jude the Obscure* (1896). In 1909 he became president of the prestigious Society of Authors, and the next year King George V conferred upon him the Order of Merit; in 1912 W. B. Yeats presented him with the Royal Society of Literature's gold medal. In his later years he was considered the last great writer of the Victorian era. Poet John Crowe Ransom connected Hardy to the succeeding generation "by reason of his naturalism and rebellion against the dogma," and poets Ezra Pound, W. H. Auden, and D. H. Lawrence acknowledged Hardy's influence on them. Hardy is often called a pessimist, but he regarded himself as a "meliorist," a person who believes the world can be improved by human effort. In his preface to *Late Lyrics and Earlier* (1922) Hardy wrote that "pain . . . shall be kept down to a minimum by loving kindness, operating through scientific knowledge, and actuated by the modicum of free will . . . possessed by organic life when the mighty or necessitating forces . . . happen to be in equilibrium, which may or may not be often."

ROBERT HAYDEN (1913–1980), born Asa Bundy Sheffey in Detroit, was renamed by his adoptive parents. Following his studies at Detroit City College (now Wayne State University) and the University of Michigan, Hayden taught at Fisk University for twenty-two years and then taught at the University of Michigan until his death. He published four significant volumes of poetry and in 1966 won the Grand Prize for Poetry in English at the First World Festival of Negro Arts in Dakar, Senegal, for *A Ballad of Remembrance*, thus gaining international recognition. He was elected in 1975 to the Academy of American Poets and in 1976 became the first African-American to be appointed Poetry Consultant at the

Library of Congress. Critic Wilburn Williams notes that "Hayden's characteristically soft-spoken and fluid voice derives much of its power from the evident contrast between the maelstrom of anguish [from] which it originates and the quiet reflecting pool of talk into which it is inevitably channeled." In explaining his inspiration to write poetry, Hayden commented that he sought to "experiment with forms and techniques I have not used before to arrive at something really my own, something patterned, wild, and free."

SEAMUS HEANEY (1939–   ) was born into a Roman Catholic family in the predominantly Protestant town of Mossbawn, County Derry, Northern Ireland. He was educated at Queen's University, Belfast, and St. Joseph's College of Education. In 1972 Heaney left Northern Ireland and eventually settled in Dublin in the Irish Republic. One of the most influential contemporary Irish poets, Heaney has received most of the literary prizes to be won in Ireland and England as well as the 1995 Nobel Prize in Literature—the third Irish writer to win this award (after W. B. Yeats in 1923 and Samuel Beckett in 1969). Heaney's poetry, according to critic William Grimes, "is rooted in the Irish soil . . . as though Ireland's wet peat were a storehouse of images and memories. At the same time [he] moves easily from the homely images of farm and village to larger issues of history, language, and national identity." Poet Derek Walcott, who won the Nobel Prize in 1992, calls Heaney "the guardian spirit of Irish poetry." Heaney metaphorically depicts the hard, patient work of poetry in "Digging," the first poem in his first book, *Death of a Naturalist* (1966): "Between my fingers and my thumb / The squat pen rests. / I'll dig with it."

ROBERT HERRICK (1591–1674), the son of a London goldsmith, studied at Cambridge University and then associated for nearly a decade with poets such as his mentor Ben Jonson. In 1629 Herrick took Anglican orders and became a parish priest in rural Devonshire. During the English Civil War in the 1640s, Puritans in power removed him from this office because he remained loyal to King Charles I, but he was restored to his post after the Restoration of Charles II in 1660. In 1648 Herrick published over 1,200 poems in one volume with two titles: *Hesperides* for the secular subjects and *Noble Numbers* for the sacred ones. However, as critic Robert M. Adams has observed, the "harsh weather of Puritanism" was not right for Herrick's "tiny, playful lyrics," so "nobody noticed

Hesperides, either to applaud or deplore." Herrick's best poems praise beautiful girls and the powers of wine and fellowship; many of them, like those of Jonson, follow Greek and Latin pastoral models. His best known lines are from the *carpe diem* poem "To the Virgins, to Make Much of Time": "Gather ye rosebuds while ye may / Old Time is still a flying: / And this same flower that smiles to day, / To morrow will be dying."

GERARD MANLEY HOPKINS (1844–1889) was a member of a cultivated London family who sent him to the Highgate School and to Oxford, where he was influenced by both Walter Pater, the aesthetic critic, and the Anglican High Church movement led by Cardinal John Henry Newman. Hopkins converted to Roman Catholicism at twenty-two and became a Jesuit priest. His long poem, *The Wreck of the Deutschland,* appeared in 1875; his shorter, more accessible nature poems were published in 1918 by his friend Robert Bridges. His most famous sonnet is "The Windhover," which explores ways to praise, revere, and serve God. Hopkins is best known for his unusual metrical system, which he named "sprung rhythm." His poems boldly experiment with imagery, syntax, and rhythm that join nature and Christianity together with passionate, sometimes anguished, intensity. Critic Jerome Bump suggests that such "idiosyncratic creativity" made his style "so radically different from that of his contemporaries" that his best work was not published in his lifetime and his achievements were "not fully recognized until after World War I." In the following comment, Hopkins revealed his belief that nature, like the Bible, offers moral instruction: "This world is word, expression, news of God" and "it is a book he has written . . . a poem of beauty. . . ."

A(LFRED) E(DWARD) HOUSMAN (1859–1936) was born in Shropshire, England. He studied classics at Oxford but failed his exams. After establishing himself as an independent Latin scholar, in 1911 he won an appointment as Professor of Latin at Cambridge, where he spent the rest of his life. He disdained numerous honors and awards, including the Royal Order of Merit, because, according to critic William G. Holzberger, "he would be condescended to by no one, not even by the King." Besides two brief books of poetry—*A Shropshire Lad* (1896) and *Last Poems* (1922)—he wrote a volume of criticism, *The Name and Nature of Poetry* (1933). Influenced by classical Greek and Latin lyrics as well as English ballads, his best works express melancholy over the brevity of youth, beauty, and love.

Holzberger calls Housman's treatment of nature "basically romantic," yet not quite "romantic worship of nature," and he finds Housman to be classical "in terms of conciseness and economy of language, precision of form, and in the Epicurean stoicism. . . ." Housman described the process of creating his poetry as one of intuition from inexplicable sources, as when he called the creative spell of 1895 a period of "continuous excitement."

LANGSTON HUGHES (1902–1967), from Joplin, Missouri, studied at Columbia University for a year but left school and worked his way to Europe as a cook on a steamship. In 1929 he completed his B.A. at Lincoln University in Pennsylvania. Widely regarded as the most important writer of the Harlem Renaissance, Hughes wrote novels, short stories, an autobiography, plays, translations, newspaper columns, and fourteen volumes of poetry. He was influenced by the rhythms and devices, as well as the subject matter, of blues, jazz, and gospel music. Critic Jessie Fauset said that "no other poet . . . would ever write as tenderly, understandingly, and humorously about life in Harlem" as Hughes has done. According to Hughes, "The only way to get a thing done is to start to do it, then keep doing it, and finally you'll finish it, even if in the beginning you think you can't do it at all."

BEN JONSON (1572–1637) was born in London, where he attended the Westminster School and learned the classics from the great classical scholar William Camden. After working as a bricklayer, he took up acting and writing plays. In 1598 he killed a fellow actor in a duel and escaped hanging only because an ancient law, commonly referred to as the Neck Verse, prevented the execution of anyone who could read and write Latin. Jonson became well known for his wit, his erudition, and his friendships with Shakespeare and John Donne. He was admired by a group of younger poets, including Thomas Carew and Robert Herrick, who called themselves the Sons of Ben. Jonson's lyrics are both learned and simple, both witty and tender. His dramas, particularly the comedies, such as *Volpone,* are greatly admired today. In 1619 Jonson was named the first Poet Laureate of England. Alexander Pope, comparing Jonson to Shakespeare, correctly predicted that the world would "exalt the one at the expense of the other." Jonson, who was also an actor, a playwright, a scholar, a critic, and a translator, took his calling as a poet very seriously; he spoke of his Epigrammes (1616) as "the ripest of my verses."

JOHN KEATS (1795–1821) grew up in a large working-class family in London. He began writing poems at eighteen, while apprenticed to an apothecary and surgeon. His collection *Poems* (1817) was soon followed by *Endymion* (1818). In 1819, a "year of miracles," Keats wrote his great odes along with narrative poems, such as the unfinished *Hyperion*, that have secured his place among the major English Romantic poets. Keats believed fervently in a life of sensations, and his poems and letters show unparalleled richness of diction and imagery. In 1820 Keats traveled to Italy, hoping to regain his health, but he died there of tuberculosis the next year, at age twenty-five. The epigraph that opens *Adonais*, Shelley's elegy on the death of Keats, begins, "Thou went the morning star among the living, / ere thy fair light had fled." On his tomb in Rome is engraved the epitaph Keats wrote for himself: "Here lies one whose name was writ in water."

AUDRE LORDE (1934–1992) was born in New York of West Indian parents. She earned a B.A. from Hunter College and a Master's degree in Library Science from Columbia University. Her "biomythography," *Zami: A New Spelling of My Name* (1982), frankly discusses her life as a lesbian. Lorde's poetry expresses her rage at injustices against blacks, women, and homosexuals. Her more than ten books of poetry include *The First Cities* (1968), *Between Our Selves* (1976), and *Our Dead Behind Us* (1986). Lorde's best poems achieve a balance between passionate primitive and personal mythologies. As Joan Martin has observed, Lorde "is a rare creature . . . the Black Unicorn, magical and mysterious bearer of fantasy draped in beauty and truth." Lorde expresses the danger of turning her powerful style into political statement alone in her poem "Power": "unless I learn to use / the difference between poetry and rhetoric / my power too will run corrupt as poisonous mold."

ROBERT LOWELL (1917–1977) came from a famous Boston family that included distinguished poets James Russell Lowell and Amy Lowell. He studied briefly at Harvard and then at Kenyon College, where he came under the influence of John Crowe Ransom and Allen Tate, both well-known poet-critics. Besides serving as Consultant in Poetry to the Library of Congress, Lowell won many awards, including a Guggenheim Fellowship (1947), a Pulitzer Prize (1947) for *Lord Weary's Castle,* the National Book Award (1960) for *Life Studies,* and the Bollingen Poetry Translation Prize (1962) for Racine's *Phaedra.* Critic Ashley Brown notes that in the volume *For the Union Dead* (1964), personal emotion merges magnificently with public themes. In 1965 Lowell made a public statement of protest against America's involvement in Vietnam by rejecting President Johnson's invitation to the White House Festival of the Arts. Lowell told novelist V. S. Naipaul in 1969 that America is "beyond any country, it's an empire. I feel very bitter about it, but pious, and baffled by it." The subject matter of Lowell's poetry covers a wide range of topics in history and personal experience, including his own recurring mental illness. In the "Afterthought" to *Notebook 1967–68,* Lowell wrote: ". . . in truth I seem to have felt mostly the joys of living; in remembering, in recording, thanks to the gift of the Muse, it is the pain."

CLAUDE MCKAY (1890–1948) was born in Jamaica, where he received part of his education from a well-read older brother. After winning an award and stipend from the Jamaican Institute of Arts and Sciences for two early volumes of poetry, he studied at the Tuskeegee Institute and at Kansas State College. In 1914 he left school and traveled to New York City. His early poems make him an important member of the Harlem Renaissance of the 1920s. His poetry is collected in *The Passion of Claude McKay: Selected Poetry and Prose, 1912–1948.* McKay wrote in traditional meter and rhyme. His poetry expresses powerful, compressed passion, both personal and social; his anger is disguised by his elegant control, as in his descriptions of the New York he both loved and hated. According to Arthur D. Prayton, "McKay does not seek to hide his bitterness, but having preserved his vision as a poet and his status as a human being, he can transcend bitterness." Something of this transcendence is apparent in the words of McKay's poem "If We Must Die": "Like men will face the murderous, cowardly push. / Press to the wall, dying, but fighting back."

WILLIAM MEREDITH (1919–   ),   born in New York City, received his B.A. from Princeton and served as a pilot in World War II; his war experiences color much of his work. His many awards include several prizes from *Poetry* magazine, a Rockefeller grant for poetry, and Guggenheim and Ford fellowships; he also served as a Consultant in Poetry to the Library of Congress. Meredith's most important books are *Love Letter from an Impossible Land* (1944), winner of the Yale Series of Younger Poets competition—*The Wreck of the Thresher and Other Poems* (1964); *Earth Walk: New and Selected Poems* (1970); and *The Cheer* (1980). His poems are serene and confident accounts of the relationships between people and their surroundings, with a calm and sometimes fervent tone of joy. Poet Archibald MacLeish launched Meredith's literary career by publishing his first book; he praised the way Meredith creates "the live idiom of a poet's speech reaching for poetry." When Meredith reviewed poetry recordings in 1961, he commented on the "unique authority" of a poet's performance that projects "the liveliest sense of character." For Meredith, "This rapport between person and poem is the mark of the truest poetry."

EDNA ST. VINCENT MILLAY (1892–1950),   born in Rockland, Maine, studied at Barnard and then Vassar. She spent much of her life in Greenwich Village, where she was admired for her bohemian ways as well for the poems she wrote during the period of her greatest popularity, the 1920s and 1930s. In addition to poems, she wrote nine plays, most of which were performed by the Provincetown Players. Millay's poems are consistent, eloquent, and romantic; they contain few topical references. Her typical themes are universal ones—love and death. American poet and critic Allen Tate, noting Millay's use of nineteenth-century vocabulary to express twentieth-century emotions, wrote: "She has been from the beginning the one poet of our time who has successfully stood athwart two ages." The watchword of the "flaming youth" of the 1920s was a line from Millay: "My candle burns at both ends."

Janice Mirikitani (1942–   ) was born in Stockton, California. A third-generation Japanese-American, she was incarcerated from 1942 to 1945 with her family in an internment camp. Mirikitani attended the University of California at both Los Angeles and Berkeley. Inspired by a student strike for Asian-American and Ethnic Studies, she became an activist and editor, founding in 1970 the first Asian-American literary journal, *Aion,* and editing anthologies of Japanese-American writers—*Ayumi: A Japanese-American Anthology* (1980) and *Making Waves: An Anthology of Writings by and about Asian-American Women* (1989). The internment experience is central to her own poetry and prose in *Awake in the River* (1978) and *Shedding Silence* (1987). Russell C. Leong credits her for enlightening readers to "Third World communities, cultures, and conflicts as transformed through the visions and writing of women." Mirikitani writes that when her mother broke forty years of silence by testifying during the 1981–82 congressional hearings about her experiences in the internment camp, she "called us to history, memory and an inner anger that gave us new voice to unearth injustices."

N(avarre) Scott Momaday (1934–   ) was born in Lawton, Oklahoma, and studied at the University of New Mexico and at Stanford University (Ph.D., 1963). In 1969 Momaday became the first Native American writer to be awarded a Pulitzer Prize, for his first novel, *House Made of Dawn* (1968). *The Names: A Memoir* (1976) recounts his growing up in New Mexico. His other works include two volumes of poetry, *Angle of Geese and Other Poems* (1974) and *Gourd Dancer* (1976); *The Way to Rainy Mountain* (1969), a unique collection of personal and historical narratives interwoven with tales from Kiowa mythology and illustrated by Momaday's father; *The Ancient Child* (1989), a novel; and *In the Presence of the Sun* (1992), a collection of poems and narratives illustrated by Momaday. Critic Roger Dickinson-Brown has referred to Momaday's work as "a fusion of alien cultures and . . . extraordinary experiments in different literary forms." In spite of his great versatility, Momaday considers himself primarily a poet, and he returns again and again to Kiowa culture for inspiration because he says it has "a certain strength and beauty I find missing in the modern world."

MARIANNE MOORE (1887–1972) was born in St. Louis and educated at Bryn Mawr. After teaching stenography and working as a librarian, she became an editor of the *Dial,* an outstanding literary magazine of the 1920s. Her *Collected Poems* (1951) won the Pulitzer Prize. In all, she published more than a dozen volumes of poetry, which can be found in her *Complete Poems* (1981). Famed for her originality of style and format—her poems are usually elaborately composed, with complex line lengths—Moore considers hundreds of apparent "curiosities" as subjects, her most typical being strange animals. Poet James Dickey has praised the way she remakes "our world from particulars that we have never adequately understood on our own." Poet John Ashberry believes that despite the "obvious grandeur" of Moore's chief contemporary competitors, William Carlos Williams and Wallace Stevens, she is "our greatest modern poet." Although her poetry deceptively resembles prose, its apparent oddity and prosaic quality set off the metaphorical daring of her work. A line from her work "Poetry" epitomizes what she says all poetry should be: "imaginary gardens with real toads in them."

SHARON OLDS (1942–) was born in San Francisco, attended Stanford and Columbia (Ph.D., 1972), and has taught at many schools in New York City. Her best-known poetry collection is *The Dead and the Living* (1984), which won both the Lamont Poetry Award and the National Book Critics Circle Award. She has won major grants from New York State, the National Endowment for the Arts, and the Guggenheim Foundation. *The Father* (1992) is a more recent volume of poetry. Because she graphically details personal traumas, some critics place her in the literary tradition of Sylvia Plath, though Olds has a less tormented tone and her poems are more accessible. Her poetry celebrates and explores family life, erotic experience, and feminist topics through frequently grotesque humor combined with straightforward reporting, in a manner that *Poetry* magazine critic Lisel Mueller has called "a proud, urgent human voice." A good example of this can be found in Olds's poem "35/10," published just a few years after Olds turned 35: "Brushing out my daughter's dark / silken hair before the mirror / I see the grey gleaming on my head, / . . . it's an old / story—the oldest we have on our planet— / the story of replacement."

SIMON J. ORTIZ (1941–   ) was born in Albuquerque, the son of a Native American potter from the Acoma Pueblo. Ortiz attended Ft. Lewis College, the University of New Mexico, and the University of Iowa in the 1960s; he served in the U.S. Army from 1963 to 1966. His poetry collections include *Naked in the Wind* (1971), *Going for the Rain* (1976), *From Sand Creek: Rising in This Heart Which Is Our America* (1981), *After and Before the Lightning* (1991), and *Woven Stone* (1992). Among the critics who have applauded his optimism for the survival of mankind and nature is Harold Jaffe, who finds his work "not of gloom and despair, but of a renewed faith in the prospect of relationship with the land and solidarity among the dispossessed." Reflecting on how his community and his homeland inform his writing, Ortiz has said, "I've tried to consider most importantly my life as a Native American who is absolutely related to the land and all that that means culturally, politically, personally."

WILFRED OWEN (1893–1918) was born in Plas Wilmot, near Oswestry in Shropshire, England, where his father worked on the railway. He was educated at the Birkenhead Institute and the Shrewsbury Technical School. Unable to afford the University of London, he joined the army in 1915, was injured, and was sent to recuperate at a hospital near Edinburgh, where he wrote most of his poems. Owen returned to battle in France and won the Military Cross for bravery; he died one week before the Armistice, having published only five poems in periodicals. His friend and fellow World War I "trench poet" Sigfried Sassoon published Owen's *Poems* in 1920, and another collection (with Edmund Blunden's memoir) appeared in 1931. *Collected Poems*, edited by Cecil Day-Lewis, was published in 1963. According to S. R. Welland, Owen's work was a major influence on 1930s poets, because it is "powerfully realistic poetry of social protest charged with pity for human suffering." Owen portrayed himself as "a conscientious objector with a very seared conscience," a label that reflects his intense hatred for the evils of war and his sympathy for its victims.

LINDA PASTAN (1932–) grew up in a middle-class family in the Bronx, New York. She received her B.A. from Radcliffe College, her M.L.S. from Simmons College, and an M.A. from Brandeis University. Her publications include *A Perfect Circle of Sun* (1971); *On the Way to the Zoo* (1975); *Aspects of Eve* (1977); *The Five Stages of Grief* (1978), winner of the Poetry Society of America award; *PM/AM: Newly Selected Poems* (1983), American Book Award nominee; *The Imperfect Paradise* (1988); *Heroes in Disguise* (1991); and *An Early Afterlife* (1995). She has received fellowships from the Bread Loaf Writers' Conference, the state of Maryland, and the National Endowment for the Arts. According to prominent feminist critic Sandra M. Gilbert, Pastan "broods on the rewards as well as the risks of domesticity" because she is "quite self-consciously a *woman* poet" who "austerely ordains the necessity of acquiescence in the ordinary." Pastan explains how she writes poetry: "By allowing myself to follow a poem wherever it wants to take me, I find that I often stumble upon truths about myself, my world, that I scarcely suspected I knew"; Pastan then compares the writing process to "following the thread through the labyrinth, trying at all costs to avoid the minotaur."

MARGE PIERCY (1936–) grew up poor and white, in a predominantly black neighborhood in Detroit. She received a bachelor's degree from the University of Michigan in 1957 and a master's degree from Northwestern University in 1958. Her publications include novels, nonfiction, and poetry collections, such as *Hard Loving* (1969), *Living in the Open* (1976), *Woman on the Edge of Time* (1976), *The Moon Is Always Female* (1980), *Parti-Colored Blocks for a Quilt: Poets on Poetry* (1982), *Circles on the Water* (1982), *Braided Lives* (1982), *My Mother's Body* (1985), and *The Longings of Women* (1994). She has received the Shaeffer-Eaton-PEN New England award (1989) and the Shalom Center award (1992). Author Erica Jong has remarked that the often-controversial Piercy is "an immensely gifted poet and novelist whose range and versatility have made it hard for her talents to be adequately appreciated critically." Piercy affirms her purpose in writing is to be "useful" so "readers will find poems that speak to and for them, will take those poems into their lives and say them to each other and put them up on the bathroom wall and remember bits and pieces of them in stressful or quiet moments."

SYLVIA PLATH (1932–1963)   was born in Boston to Polish-German immigrant parents who were both teachers. Plath won a scholarship to Smith College and then a Fulbright to Cambridge University, where she met and married poet Ted Hughes. Following her anonymously published first work, *A Winter Ship,* came *The Colossus and Other Poems* (1962), *Ariel* (1965), *The Bell Jar* [U.K. (1963), U.S. (1971)], and *Crossing the Water* (1971). Plath's mother published *Letters Home by Sylvia Plath: Correspondence 1950–1963* in 1975; then Hughes edited *Johnny Panic and the Bible of Dreams and Other Prose Writings* and *Sylvia Plath: The Collected Poems,* the 1982 Pulitzer Prize winner. Plath won a *Mademoiselle* magazine prize while a guest editor in 1953, the Bess Hokin Award from *Poetry* in 1957, a Yaddo fellowship in 1959, and the Eugene F. Saxon Fellowship in 1961. Poet Robert Lowell, who contributed the introduction to *Ariel,* praised her as "one of those super-real, hypnotic, great classical heroines." In a 1958 journal entry, Plath prophesied: "coming again to make and make in the face of the flux; making of the moment something of permanence. That is the lifework. . . . My life, I feel, will not be lived until there are books and stories which relive it perpetually in time." Plath committed suicide at the age of thirty-one.

EZRA POUND (1885–1972)   was born in Hailey, Idaho, and grew up near Philadelphia. He graduated from Hamilton College (Ph.B., 1905) and the University of Pennsylvania (M.A., 1906). After his first publication, *A Lume Spento* (1908), came *Personae and Exultations of Ezra Pound* (1913), *Homage to Sextus Propertius* (1919), and *Hugh Selwyn Mauberley* (1920). In 1917 he began his best-known work: a series of cantos that eventually included *The Pisan Cantos* (1948) and *Thrones: Cantos 96-109* (1959). During World War II Pound became a fervent supporter of Mussolini and broadcast fascist propaganda over Italian radio. After the war, he was arrested for treason and incarcerated in a mental hospital from 1946 to 1958. A fair assessment must include both critics who praise Pound and those who damn him. T. S. Eliot called Pound a motivating force behind modern poetry; however, when Eliot, W. H. Auden, Allen Tate, Robert Penn Warren, and Katherine Anne Porter awarded Pound the Bollingen-Library of Congress Award for the best poetry by an American for 1948, Robert Hillyer protested bitterly that Pound's poems "are the vehicle of contempt for America, [of] Fascism, anti-Semitism and, in the prize-winning *Pisan Cantos* themselves, ruthless mockery of our . . . war dead." Leader of a small group of poets who called themselves Imagists, Pound experimented with poetic images (such as Chinese ideograms) to express "an intellectual and emotional complex in an instant of time"; he once told an interviewer, "You cannot have literature without curiosity, and when a writer's curiosity dries out he is finished."

ADRIENNE RICH (1929–   ) was born and raised in Baltimore. Her first book, *A Change of World,* was published by W. H. Auden in the Yale Series of Younger Poets during her senior year at Radcliffe. She graduated in 1951 and continued her studies at Oxford. Among her awards are two Guggenheim fellowships, the Poetry Society of America award, a National Institute of Arts and Letters award, a Bollingen Foundation grant, and a National Endowment for the Arts grant. Rich writes about gender, power, and women's conflicting roles in works such as *Twenty-one Love Poems* (1976), *The Dream of a Common Language, Poems 1974–1977* (1978), *A Wild Patience Has Taken Me This Far* (1981), *The Fact of a Doorframe: Poems Selected and New 1950–1984* (1985), and *Time's Power: Poems 1985–88* (1989). *The Diamond Cutters and Other Poems* (1955) won the Poetry Society of America award, and *Diving into the Wreck: Poems 1971–1972* (1973) won the 1974 National Book Award. William Heyen has noted that Rich's work describes years of conflict in her life as a woman, wife, mother, and poet. As Rich once commented about her writing, "Instead of poems *about* experiences I am getting poems that *are* experiences, that contribute to my knowledge and my emotional life even while they reflect and assimilate it."

EDWIN ARLINGTON ROBINSON (1869–1935)   was born in Head Tide, Maine, a descendant of the poet Anne Bradstreet. He grew up in Gardiner, Maine (the inspiration for his Tilbury Town) and then studied for two years at Harvard before his family's financial difficulties halted his education. He published *The Torrent and the Night Before* (1896), *The Children of the Night* (1897), and *Captain Craig* (1902) before *The Man Against the Sky* (1916) confirmed his reputation as a major poet. Pulitzer Prizes were awarded to his *Collected Poems* (1922), *The Man Who Died Twice* (1924), and *Tristram* (1928). Robert Frost, in his introduction to Robinson's posthumous *King Jasper* (1935), characterized Robinson as a poet who "stayed content with the old-fashioned way to be new," unlike contemporary experimentalists who used poetry for their grievances against "un-Utopian" society; Frost then praised Robinson's skillful blending of playful humor and profound melancholy. Robinson commented in a 1916 interview with poet Joyce Kilmer that poetry is both "undefinable" and "unmistakable: a language which tell us, through a more or less emotional experience, something that cannot be said."

THEODORE ROETHKE (1908–1963) was born in Saginaw, Michigan, where his father owned a twenty-five-acre greenhouse complex that inspired much of his symbolism. After his education at Michigan University and Harvard, he taught English at Lafayette College; he became poet-in-residence at the University of Washington a year before he died. He won the Pulitzer Prize in 1954 for *The Waking* (1953) and two National Book Awards (1959 and 1965) for *Words for the Wind* and *The Far Field*, respectively. Stanley Kunitz has praised Roethke's rare gifts as a writer: "The ferocity of Roethke's imagination makes most contemporary poetry seem pale and tepid in contrast. Even his wit is murderous. . . . What Roethke brings us is news of the root, of the minimal, of the primordial. The subhuman is given tongue; and the tongue proclaims the agony of coming alive, the painful miracle of growth." Roethke once explained that he writes about "trivial and vulgar" details and has put down in poems "as barely and honestly as possible, symbolically, what few nuggets of observation and, let us hope, spiritual wisdom I have managed to seize upon in the course of a conventional albeit sometimes disordered existence."

SONIA SANCHEZ (1934–   ) was born in Birmingham, Alabama, grew up in Harlem, and studied political science and poetry at Hunter College (B.A., 1955) and New York University. Her publications include *Homecoming* (1969), *It's a New Day: Poems for Young Brothas and Sistuhs* (1971), *Love Poems* (1973), *A Blues Book for Blue Black Magical Women* (1973), *I'm Black When I'm Singing, I'm Blue When I Ain't* (1982), and *homegirls & handgrenades* (1984). She has been honored with the PEN writing award, National Institute of Arts and Letters and National Endowment for the Arts grants, and the American Book Award. C.W.E. Bigsby believes that her work is distinguished by "language which catches the nuance of the spoken word, the rhythms of the street, and of a music which is partly jazz and partly a lyricism which underlies ordinary conversation." Sanchez—one of the strongest black feminist voices advocating change not through rage, violence, or substance abuse, but through political astuteness, moral power, and strong family relationships—has declared, "I recognize that my writing must serve a dual purpose. It must be a clarion call to the values of change while it also speaks to the beauty of a non-exploitative age."

CARL SANDBURG (1878–1967) was born in Galesburg, Illinois, to Swedish parents. He studied at Lombard College and later wrote for *Poetry* magazine. His volumes of verse, often about industrialized America, include *Chicago Poems* (1915), *Corn Huskers* (1918), *Smoke and Steel* (1920), and *Good Morning, America* (1928); in 1951 he won the Pulitzer Prize for his *Complete Poems*. He also wrote prose works such as *Abraham Lincoln: The Prairie Years* (1926) and *Abraham Lincoln: The War Years* (1940). On his seventy-fifth birthday in 1953 Governor Adlai Stevenson proclaimed "Carl Sandburg Day" in Illinois, and a representative of King Gustav VI of Sweden decorated Sandburg with the Commander Order of the Northern Star. He was named Poet Laureate of Illinois in 1962 and received the Presidential Medal of Freedom in 1964. According to Henry Steele Commager, Sandburg "celebrates what is best in us, and recalls us to our heritage and our humanity." In his notes to his *Complete Poems,* Sandburg has affirmed his purpose as a poet "of streets and struggles, of dust and combat, of violence wanton or justified, of plain folk living close to a hard earth." On his eighty-fifth birthday in 1963, upon the publication of his final book, *Honey and Salt,* Sandburg said, "Being a poet is a damn dangerous business."

WILLIAM SHAKESPEARE (1564–1616) was born in Stratford-upon-Avon, England. He grew up in a middle class family, his father being a glover and wool dealer and later an alderman and bailiff (mayor). The Bard probably attended Stratford Grammar School, where he learned the classics, but no documented record of his youth exists. By 1592 he had been recognized as a successful actor and playwright in London. Best known for his plays, he proved his genius also in his nondramatic poetry: *Venus and Adonis* (1593), *The Rape of Lucrece* (1594), and *The Phoenix and the Turtle* (1601). Equally renowned are the lyric poems (songs) in his plays and the 154 sonnets probably written in the late 1590s but not published until 1609. Commenting on these sonnets, William Wordsworth stated that "with this key Shakespeare unlocked his heart"; however, according to Terence Spencer, Shakespeare the man remains "elusive" in the sonnets despite their great "poetic power," their "exploration of intimate relationships," and their "sensitivity to the tragedy of human aspirations and the triumph of time." Because Shakespeare's letters have not survived, he speaks through his art.

PERCY BYSSHE SHELLEY (1792–1822) was the son of a conservative, aristocratic Member of Parliament from Sussex, England. Shelley was expelled from Oxford in 1811 after six months when he refused to repudiate writing the anti-religious pamphlet *The Necessity of Atheism*. In 1819, near despair from bad health, rejection from the public and his family, and the tragic loss of two children from his marriage to Mary Wollstonecraft Godwin (the daughter of two well-known English writers), he produced his dramatic masterpiece *Prometheus Unbound* and the great lyric poem "Ode to the West Wind"; he also wrote the tragedy *The Cenci* and *The Mask of Anarchy,* which calls for a proletarian revolution. Then he published *Epipsychidion* ("soul out of my soul"), *Adonais* (an elegy for John Keats), and the prose treatise *A Defence of Poetry.* William Wordsworth praised Shelley as "one of the best *artists* of us all: I mean in workmanship of style," yet Shelley satirized Wordsworth in *Peter Bell the Third* and the sonnet "To Wordsworth," which laments the senior poet's compromising his youthful idealism. Shelley's *A Defence of Poetry* proclaims that a poem "is the very image of life expressed in its eternal truth" and that poets "are the unacknowledged legislators of the World."

LESLIE MARMON SILKO (1948–   ) describes her ancestry as Native American, Mexican, and Anglo. She was born in Albuquerque and grew up on the Laguna Pueblo Reservation, where she attended the Bureau of Indian Affairs school. She graduated from the University of New Mexico, attended law school and completed graduate work in English, and taught writing at Navajo Community College and the University of Arizona. In 1981 Silko received a MacArthur Foundation fellowship that granted her five years of financial support. Her writings include *Laguna Woman* (1974), *Ceremony* (1977), *Storyteller* (1981), and *Almanac of the Dead* (1991). As Edith Blicksilver observes, Silko explores "the imaginative richness and beauty of tribal folk tales. The relationships between people and natural forces, the animal and vegetable kingdoms, are the subject of a series of poems describing different types of love relationships." Having listened as a child to her family's retelling of folklore, such as trickster

Coyote's misadventures and accounts of Apache and Navajo raids on Pueblo people, Silko affirms that stories define her cultural traditions and ceremonies: "There have to be stories. It's stories that make this a community."

GARY SOTO (1952–   ) was born in Fresno, California. He worked in the fields, as did his Mexican-American parents and grandparents. He attended Fresno City College and California State University and earned an M.F.A. degree in creative writing from the University of California at Irvine. He recreates the Fresno barrios in works such as *The Elements of San Joaquin* (1977), *The Tale of Sunlight* (1978), *Where Sparrows Work Hard* (1981), *Home Course in Religion: New Poems* (1991), *Neighborhood Odes* (1992), and *New and Selected Poems* (1995). Soto has received the Academy of American Poets prize (1975), *The Nation* prize (1975), the International Poetry Forum award (1976), the American Book Award (1985), a Best Book for Young Adults citation from the American Library Association (1990), and Guggenheim and National Endowment for the Arts fellowships. Maeve Visser Knoth has commented that his "simple poems of childhood, adolescence, and adulthood . . . [are] about ordinary events and emotions made remarkable by Soto's skilled use of words and images." Soto explains, "I like the youth in my poetry, sort of a craziness. For me that's really important. I don't want to take a dreary look at the world."

(AKINWANDE OLUWOLE) WOLE SOYINKA (1934–   ) was born in Abeokuta in western Nigeria. His father was a primary school principal; his mother was a primary school teacher. Soyinka attended the University College of Ibadan and the University of Leeds. His *Collected Plays,* along with major works such as *Death and the King's Horseman* (1976), *The Bacchae,* and *The Interpreters,* led to his winning the Nobel Prize in Literature in 1986. The Swedish Academy described him as "a writer who in a wide cultural perspective and with poetic overtures fashions the drama of existence." A deeply committed political writer and activist who has since 1965 been repeatedly imprisoned in his homeland, Soyinka has said, "I would be frankly ill at ease with myself if I failed to call attention to the public for . . . its . . . abdication of basic rights to official crooks, thugs, touts and other . . . scum of society."

WILLIAM STAFFORD (1914–1993) was born in Hutchinson, Kansas, and grew up in a number of small Kansas towns. He received his bachelor's and master's degrees from the University of Kansas and his Ph.D. from the University of Iowa. *Traveling through the Dark* won the National Book Award in 1963. His other awards include the Shelley Memorial Award, a Yaddo Foundation fellowship, a Danforth Foundation grant, and the American Academy and Institute of Arts Award in Literature. Critic Paul Zweig has called Stafford "one of the finest poets of the conversational style. His poems are limpid and controlled, with a sort of narrative plainness that recalls Robert Frost." Stafford observes in *Writing the Australian Crawl: Views on the Writer's Vocation* that poetry "is the kind of thing you have to see from the corner of your eye. You can be too well prepared for poetry. . . . It's like a very faint star. If you look straight at it you can't see it, but if you look a little to one side it is there."

WALLACE STEVENS (1879–1955) was born in Reading, Pennsylvania, the son of a prominent attorney and a schoolteacher. He attended Harvard, where he began writing poetry, and the New York Law School. In 1916 he took a job with the Hartford Accident and Indemnity Company that afforded him and his family a prosperous life. Stevens won the Bollingen Prize in 1949 for his life's work. In 1955 he won both the Pulitzer Prize and the National Book Award for his *Collected Poems*. Fusing elements of the ancient, the Romantic, and the American poet, as Richard Gray has noted, "Stevens returned the poet to his ancient role of bard or myth-maker, offering purpose and a sense of meaning to his tribe. And to this he added another more peculiarly Romantic and American dimension, which was that of hero." In a letter to his wife Elsie, Stevens wrote, "The priest in me worshipped one God at one shrine; the poet another God at another shrine. The priest worshipped Mercy and Love; the poet Beauty and Might." In his poem "Of Modern Poetry" he defines "the poem of the act of the mind."

ALFRED, LORD TENNYSON (1809–1892) was born in Tennyshire, England. He attended Louth Grammar School between 1815 and 1820 and afterwards was educated at home by his father. Tennyson entered Trinity College, Cambridge, in 1827, but left in 1831 without a degree. While at Cambridge Tennyson received the Chancellor's Gold Medal for "Timbuctoo" (1829). In 1850, following the success of *In Memoriam,* he was chosen as Poet Laureate of England, succeeding William Wordsworth, and in 1883 he became a baron. Tennyson's poetry dominated Victorian England, catching the spirit of the age with its focus on social, moral, and democratic progress; as Brian Southam has suggested, "There is a sufficient body of his finest work to place him among the great poets of English literature." Tennyson's reliance on the idea of progress in an inventive and energetic age is nowhere more evident than in "Locksley Hall" (1842), in which the speaker exclaims: "Not in vain the distance beacons. Forward, forward let us range, / Let the great world spin forever down the ringing grooves of change." Tennyson said he wrote his 1859 masterpiece *Idylls of the King* (an Arthurian saga) "to teach men the need of an ideal."

DYLAN THOMAS (1914–1953) was born in the seaside town of Swansea, Wales, to an indulgent mother and a bitter, atheistic father who was a schoolmaster in English at the Swansea Grammar School. Thomas benefited from his father's dramatic readings of Shakespeare, an extensive library of modern and nineteenth-century poets, and the relaxed atmosphere of the Swansea Grammar School, which he attended from 1925 to 1931, when he left to become a copyreader and then reporter for the South Wales *Evening Post.* Awards and honors bestowed on Thomas include the Blumenthal Poetry Prize (1938), the Levinson Poetry Prize (1945), and the Foyle's Poetry Prize (1952). In assessing Thomas's career, poet Karl Shapiro has observed, "Thomas was the first modern romantic you could put your finger on, the first whose journeys and itineraries became part of his own mythology, the first who offered himself up as a public, not a private sacrifice." Reflecting on the nature of his own poetry, Thomas asserted, "My poetry is, or should be, useful to me for one reason: it is the record of my individual struggle from darkness towards some measure of light."

ALICE WALKER (1944–   )   (See p. 317 for biographical information.) Walker's legacy as a black woman author has led Henry Louis Gates, Jr., to describe her connection with African-American writer and folklorist Zora Neale Hurston as a "literary bonding quite unlike anything that has ever happened within the Afro-American tradition." Because Walker was so inspired by Hurston's work (long since forgotten by the 1970s), she edited a Hurston anthology—*I Love Myself When I Am Laughing . . . And Then Again When I Am Looking Mean and Impressive* (1979)—bringing both Walker and Hurston into national prominence and leading to the reissuing of Hurston's works, such as her novel *Their Eyes Were Watching God* (1937). Walker has described her own writing as an effort to capture "a sense of community," one of "solidarity and sharing."

MARGARET WALKER (1915–   ),   born in Birmingham, Alabama, attended Northwestern University (B.A., 1935), the University of Iowa (M.A., 1940; Ph.D., 1965) and Yale University. In 1942 her first and most influential collection of poetry, *For My People,* won the prestigious Yale Series of Younger Poets Award; it was followed by *Prophets for a New Day* (1970) and *October Journey* (1973), which include ballads and sonnets about the struggle for civil rights. Her 1966 historical novel *Jubilee* (winner of the Houghton Mifflin Literary Fellowship), uses slave narrative to celebrate a heroic woman's journey to freedom. Theodore Hudson has described Walker's poetry as "insightful, compassionate, and sincere." Walker has sought to capture in her work the strength of African-American women, to live out the rhetorical maxim expressed in her 1942 poem "Lineage": "My mothers were strong. / Why am I not as they?" Her dedication to *For My People* makes clear her indebtedness to and responsibility for "my people everywhere singing their slave songs repeatedly: their dirges and their ditties and their blues and jubilees."

JAMES WELCH (1940–   ) was born in Browning, Montana, and educated at the University of
Montana. He is one of the best known Native American writers in the United States. Welch's works
usually involve contemporary Native American experience with its emphasis on consciousness of
nature and the earth. His publications include the
poetry collection *Riding the Earthboy 40* (1971) and
four novels—*Winter in the Blood* (1974), *The Death
of Jim Loney* (1979), *Fools Crow* (1986), and *The In-
dian Lawyer* (1990). In 1994 he published *Killing Custer,* a work of nonfiction. Joseph Bruchac has written that Welch's poems are "always
memorable and, in some cases, close to great. It seems he will continue to
be a vital force in American writing." The closing lines of "Never Give a
Bum an Even Break" (the last poem in *Riding the Earthboy 40*) suggest the
purpose of Welch's writing: "Any day we will crawl out to settle / old
scores or create new roles / our mask glittering in a comic rain."

WALT WHITMAN (1819–1892)   was born in West
Hills, Long Island, New York. His formal education
ended after six years; he then became an office boy
and a printer's apprentice at two newspapers, an experience that gave him access to a circulating library and prepared him to be a newspaper reporter
and editor. He worked as a part-time carpenter
while writing his major work, *Leaves of Grass*
(1855), which he continued to revise and expand
until his death. In 1862 when his brother was
wounded in the Civil War, Whitman went to the war front and remained
in Washington as a volunteer nurse, visiting hospitals daily. This experience led to *Drum-Taps* (1865); the second issue of this book included
"When Lilacs Last in the Door-Yard Bloom'd." Critic Harold Bloom has
concluded that "Whitman has been an inescapable influence not only
for most significant American poets after him . . . but also for the most
gifted writers of narrative fiction." Commenting on the validity of nontraditional forms of poetry, of which he was a very important innovator,
Whitman asserted: "The rhyme and conformity of perfect poems show the
free growth of metrical laws and bud from them as unerringly and loosely
as lilacs or roses on a bush, and take shapes as compact as the shapes of
chestnuts and oranges and melons and peas, and shed the perfume impal-
pable to form."

RICHARD WILBUR (1921–   ), born in New York City, grew up on a farm in North Caldwell, New Jersey, and was educated at Amherst and Harvard. He began writing poetry while serving in the army during World War II and has published translations, nonfiction prose, and several volumes of poetry, including *Things of This World* (1956), for which he won the Pulitzer Prize, the Edna St. Vincent Millay Memorial Award, and the National Book Award in 1957; *The Beautiful Changes and Other Poems* (1947); *Ceremony and Other Poems* (1950); and *The Poems of Richard Wilbur* (1963). He also wrote the lyrics to Leonard Bernstein's comic operetta *Candide*. Wilbur was named Poet Laureate of the United Sates in 1987. Poet and critic Donald Hall has praised Wilbur's "capacity for drawing sympathetically on the world of the past without getting out of touch with the present." A professor of English, Wilbur seeks activities that he calls "non-verbal" because, he says, "It is good for a writer to move into words out of silence as much as he can."

WILLIAM CARLOS WILLIAMS (1883–1963) was born in Rutherford, New Jersey, to a stern British father and a French-Dutch-Spanish-Jewish mother. He read the classics at home; traveled to Europe, where he attended private schools in Geneva and Paris; and then returned to New York City and attended the prestigious Horace Mann High School before entering the University of Pennsylvania to study medicine (M.D., 1906). As poet, playwright, novelist, autobiographer, and essayist, Williams published widely. His awards include the National Book Award (1950), the Bollingen Prize in Poetry (1952), the Levinson Prize (1954), the Blumenthal Prize (1955), and a posthumous Pulitzer Prize (1963) for *Pictures from Brueghel and Other Poems*. According to poet Randall Jarrell, "Williams' poetry is more remarkable for its empathy, sympathy, its muscular and emotional identification with its subjects, than any other modern poetry except Rilke's." Reflecting on the origins of his own work, Williams revealed, "I think it was the French painters rather than the writers who influenced us, and their influence was very great; they created an atmosphere of release, color-release, from stereotypical forms, trite subjects."

WILLIAM WORDSWORTH (1770–1850) grew up in a middle-class English family and was educated at St. John's College, Cambridge. His life in the beautiful Lake District of northern England inspired him to write poems celebrating the individual in nature and the democratic spirit. A prolific poet whose definitive edition runs five full volumes, Wordsworth is best known for *Lyrical Ballads with a Few Other Poems* (1798), which he wrote in collaboration with Samuel Taylor Coleridge. One of the poets credited with the Romantic revolution in poetry, Wordsworth was honored for his achievements by the British government in 1843, when was named Poet Laureate of England. Critic F. W. Bateson has identified two voices that come together in the greatest of Wordsworth's poetry: "(i) an essentially objective poetry, evincing a strong sense of social responsibility, but crude, naive and often bathetic (the Augustan manner), [and] (ii) an essentially subjective poetry, egocentric, sentimental, and escapist, but often charming because of its spontaneity (the Romantic manner)." Wordsworth's famous Preface to *Lyrical Ballads* supports both subjective and objective voices: "all good poetry is the spontaneous overflow of powerful feelings: but though this be true, poems to which any value can be attached, were never produced on any variety of subjects but by a man who, being possessed of more than usual organic sensibility, had also thought long and deeply."

JAMES WRIGHT (1927–1980) was born in Martins Ferry, Ohio. After serving in the U.S. Army in Japan during World War II, he graduated from Kenyon College, where he won the Robert Frost Poetry Prize, and received his M.A. and Ph.D. from the University of Washington at Seattle. His numerous volumes of poetry include *Saint Judas* (1959), *Shall We Gather at the River* (1968), and the Pulitzer Prize-winning *Collected Poems* (1971). Among his other awards are two Borestone Mountain Poetry Awards, the Eunice Tietjens Memorial Award from *Poetry* magazine, a Guggenheim Fellowship, the *Kenyon Review* poetry fellowship, and a Longview Foundation Award. Critic Keith Walters observes that "Wright was always haunted by human suffering, not only his own, but also the suffering of the social outcast—the murderer, the rapist, the untrue lover, the Judas." In a 1975 *Paris Review* interview he commented, "I do not have a talent for happiness. . . . I tried to come to terms with that in the clearest and most ferociously perfect form that I could find and in all the traditional ways."

RICHARD WRIGHT (1908–1960)   (See p. 196 for biographical information.) According to James Baldwin, "Wright's unrelenting bleak landscape was not merely that of the Deep South, or of Chicago, but that of the world of the human heart." Wright himself regarded what he wrote as essentially American, declaring that "The Negro is America's metaphor." *American Hunger* (1977), the second part of his autobiography, focuses on themes of manhood, freedom, and oppression, based on his experiences in Chicago and connections with the Communist Party. As Wright once explained, "I wanted to be a Communist but my kind of Communist. I wanted to share people's feelings"; consequently, he requested that his name be removed from Party rolls but continued to work for organizations affiliated with the Communist Party.

WILLIAM BUTLER YEATS (1865–1939)   was born in Dublin, Ireland, into an upper-middle-class Anglo-Irish family. He was educated in London and in Dublin, where he attended the Metropolitan School of Art (1884–86). *The Tower* (1928) and *The Winding Stair and Other Poems* (1929) are two of the most highly praised of his many volumes of poetry. In addition to poetry, Yeats also wrote essays and plays. Many prestigious colleges and universities in England and Ireland bestowed honors on Yeats, and in 1923 he won the Nobel Prize for Literature in recognition not only of his accomplishment as a poet but also of his tireless efforts to promote Irish literature. T. S. Eliot has said of Yeats: "He was one of the few [poets] whose history was the history of our own time, who are part of the consciousness of our age, which cannot be understood without them." Yeats's *Autobiographies* contains this comment on the link between art and artist: "When great artists were at their most creative the result was not simply a work of art, but rather the 're-creation of the man through that art.'"

Poetry Casebook

This casebook contains ten poems by Gwendolyn Brooks, a collection of source materials,* twelve questions to stimulate discussion and writing, and a student paper offering insights into various aspects of Brooks's work.

Poems

(Other poems by Brooks included elsewhere in this text are "Sadie and Maud," from *A Street in Bronzeville* (p. 799); "First Fight. Then Fiddle," from *Annie Allen* (p. 835); and "We Real Cool," from *The Bean Eaters* (p. 734).)

---

* Note that the articles in this casebook do not use current MLA documentation style. See Appendix A for new MLA format.

Source Materials

◆ Brooks, Gwendolyn. "An Interview with Myself." *Triquarterly* 60 (1984): 405–10. An interview with Gwendolyn Brooks, conducted by the poet herself, in which she discusses her background and her ideas about poetry in general and the role of African-American poets in particular. (p. 1084)

◆ Brooks, Gwendolyn. From *Report from Part One*. Detroit: Broadside Press, 1972. An excerpt from a book in which Brooks discusses her African-American identity. (p. 1088)

◆ Baker, Houston, A., Jr. "The Achievement of Gwendolyn Brooks." *A Life Distilled: Gwendolyn Brooks, Her Poetry and Fiction*. Ed. Maria K. Mootry and Gary Smith. Urbana: U of Illinois P, 1987. 21–29. A discussion of Brooks's use of traditional forms to explore the African-American experience. (p. 1090)

◆ Stavros, George. "An Interview with Gwendolyn Brooks." *Contemporary Literature* 11.1 (Winter 1970): 1–20. Excerpts from an interview with the poet conducted in 1969. (p. 1097)

◆ Smith, Gary. "Gwendolyn Brooks's 'Children of the Poor,' Metaphysical Poetry and the Inconditions of Love." *A Life Distilled: Gwendolyn Brooks, Her Poetry and Fiction*. Ed. Maria K. Mootry and Gary Smith. Urbana: U of Illinois P, 1987. 165–76. A critical article that examines Gwendolyn Brooks's use of the sonnet form. (p. 1099)

◆ Mootry, Maria K. "'Chocolate Mabbie' and 'Pearl May Lee': Gwendolyn Brooks and the Ballad Tradition." *CLA Journal* 30.3 (March 1987): 278–93. An excerpt from a critical article about Gwendolyn Brooks's use of ballad themes and techniques as well as new variations on the ballad tradition. (p. 1108)

◆ Smith, Gary. "Gwendolyn Brooks's *A Street in Bronzeville*, the Harlem Renaissance and the Mythologies of Black Women." *American Women Poets*. Ed. Harold Bloom. New York: Chelsea, 1986. 86–89. Excerpts from a critical article about the relationship between Brooks's poetry and the poetry of the Harlem Renaissance. (p. 1114)

After reading the poems and the source materials that follow them, carefully consider the questions at the end of the casebook (p. 1119). Then, decide on a topic for a three- to five-page essay on the work of Gwendolyn Brooks. For guidelines on evaluating literary criticism, see p. 14; for guidelines on using source materials, see p. 34. Make sure your paper follows the conventions for documenting sources outlined in Appendix A.

A complete student paper, "Racial Consciousness in 'The Ballad of Rudolph Reed,'" which uses some of the sources included in this casebook, begins on p. 1121.

GWENDOLYN BROOKS (1917–) was, in 1950, the first African-American to win a Pulitzer Prize (for her second book of poems, *Annie Allen*). Born in Topeka, Kansas, Brooks was raised in a section of Chicago called "Bronzeville," which provided the setting for her first published poetry collection, *A Street in Bronzeville* (1945). She remembers "a sparkly childhood with two fine parents" who encouraged their daughter to love music and poetry. When Brooks was barely twenty years old, her mother showed her poems to Langston Hughes and James Weldon Johnson, two of the most distinguished writers of the Harlem Renaissance, who became Brooks's literary and personal mentors. Brooks, who ran poetry workshops for radical black activists during the late 1960s, continues to be deeply involved in the intellectual and artistic development of the young people around her. She is also the poet laureate of Illinois. Beyond the collections cited in the casebook, Brooks is known for her volumes *Riot* (1969), *Family Pictures* (1970), *Aloneness* (1971), *Aurora* (1972), *Beckonings* (1975), *Primer for Blacks* (1980), *Black Love* (1982), *Mayor Harold Washington* and *Chicago, The I Will City* (1983), and *The Near Johannesburg Boy, and Other Poems* (1987). Collected works include *Selected Poems* (1963), *The World of Gwendolyn Brooks* (1971), and *Blacks* (1987). She also published a novel, *Maud Martha* (1953), and *Report from Part One: An Autobiography* (1972).

From her earliest work, Brooks showed a remarkable ability to blend elements of traditional and modernist poetry with the language and rhythms of African-American life. Yet whether the voice is cool and restrained (as in "People Who Have No Children Can Be Hard") or ironically colloquial (as in "We Real Cool"), Brooks's poems are dense, complex, and often surprising explorations that offer the deepest rewards to her readers.

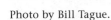

Photo by Bill Tague.

The Ballad of Chocolate Mabbie

(1945)

It was Mabbie without the grammar school gates.
And Mabbie was all of seven.
And Mabbie was cut from a chocolate bar.
And Mabbie thought life was heaven.

5 The grammar school gates were the pearly gates,
For Willie Boone went to school.
When she sat by him in history class
Was only her eyes were cool.

It was Mabbie without the grammar school gates
10 Waiting for Willie Boone.
Half hour after the closing bell!
He would surely be coming soon.

Oh, warm is the waiting for joys, my dears!
And it cannot be too long.
15 Oh, pity the little poor chocolate lips
That carry the bubble of song!

Out came the saucily bold Willie Boone.
It was woe for our Mabbie now.
He wore like a jewel a lemon-hued lynx
20 With sand-waves loving her brow.

It was Mabbie alone by the grammar school gates.
Yet chocolate companions had she:
Mabbie on Mabbie with hush in the heart.
Mabbie on Mabbie to be.

A Song in the Front Yard

(1945)

I've stayed in the front yard all my life.
I want a peek at the back
Where it's rough and untended and hungry weed grows.
A girl gets sick of a rose.

5 I want to go in the back yard now
And maybe down the alley,
To where the charity children play.
I want a good time today.

They do some wonderful things.
10 They have some wonderful fun.
My mother sneers, but I say it's fine
How they don't have to go in at quarter to nine.

My mother, she tells me that Johnnie Mae
Will grow up to be a bad woman.
15 That George'll be taken to Jail soon or late
(On account of last winter he sold our back gate).

But I say it's fine. Honest, I do.
And I'd like to be a bad woman, too,
And wear the brave stockings of night-black lace
20 And strut down the streets with paint on my face.

People Who Have No Children Can Be Hard

(1949)

People who have no children can be hard:
Attain a mail of ice and insolence:
Need not pause in the fire, and in no sense
Hesitate in the hurricane to guard.
5 And when wide world is bitten and bewarred
They perish purely, waving their spirits hence
Without a trace of grace or of offense
To laugh or fail, diffident, wonder-starred.
While through a throttling dark we others hear
10 The little lifting helplessness, the queer
Whimper-whine; whose unridiculous
Lost softness softly makes a trap for us.
And makes a curse. And makes a sugar of
The malocclusions, the inconditions of love.

What Shall I Give My Children?

(1949)

What shall I give my children? who are poor,
Who are adjudged the leastwise of the land,
Who are my sweetest lepers, who demand
No velvet and no velvety velour;
5 But who have begged me for a brisk contour,
Crying that they are quasi, contraband
Because unfinished, graven by a hand
Less than angelic, admirable or sure.
My hand is stuffed with mode, design, device.
10 But I lack access to my proper stone.
And plenitude of plan shall not suffice
Nor grief nor love shall be enough alone
To ratify my little halves who bear
Across an autumn freezing everywhere.

The Bean Eaters

(1960)

They eat beans mostly, this old yellow pair.
Dinner is a casual affair.
Plain chipware on a plain and creaking wood,
Tin flatware.
5 Two who are Mostly Good.
Two who have lived their day,
But keep on putting on their clothes
And putting things away.

And remembering . . .
10 Remembering, with twinklings and twinges,
As they lean over the beans in their rented back room that
is full of beads and receipts and dolls and cloths,
tobacco crumbs, vases and fringes.

The Chicago Defender[1] Sends a Man to Little Rock

(1960)

Fall, 1957[2]

In Little Rock the people bear
Babes, and comb and part their hair
And watch the want ads, put repair
To roof and latch. While wheat toast burns
5 A woman waters multiferns.

Time upholds or overturns
The many, tight, and small concerns.

In Little Rock the people sing
Sunday hymns like anything,
10 Through Sunday pomp and polishing.

And after testament and tunes,
Some soften Sunday afternoons
With lemon tea and Lorna Doones.

I forecast
15 And I believe
Come Christmas Little Rock will cleave
To Christmas tree and trifle, weave,
From laugh and tinsel, texture fast.

In Little Rock is baseball; Barcarolle.[3]
20 That hotness in July . . . the uniformed figures raw and implacable
And not intellectual,
Batting the hotness or clawing the suffering dust.
The Open Air Concert, on the special twilight green. . . .
When Beethoven is brutal or whispers to lady-like air.
25 Blanket-sitters are solemn, as Johann troubles to lean

To tell them what to mean. . . .

---

[1] A weekly newspaper for African-American readers.

[2] When black students first entered the high school in Little Rock, Arkansas, in 1957, the city erupted in race riots protesting desegregation.

[3] A Venetian gondolier's song, or one suggesting the rhythm of rowing.

There is love, too, in Little Rock. Soft women softly
Opening themselves in kindness,
Or, pitying one's blindness,
30 Awaiting one's pleasure
In azure
Glory with anguished rose at the root. . . .
To wash away old semi-discomfitures.
They re-teach purple and unsullen blue.
35 The wispy soils go. And uncertain
Half-havings have they clarified to sures.

In Little Rock they know
Not answering the telephone is a way of rejecting life,
That it is our business to be bothered, is our business
40 To cherish bores or boredom, be polite
To lies and love and many-faceted fuzziness.
I scratch my head, massage the hate-I-had.
I blink across my prim and pencilled pad.
The saga I was sent for is not down.
45 Because there is a puzzle in this town.
The biggest News I do not dare
Telegraph to the Editor's chair:
"They are like people everywhere."

The angry Editor would reply
50 In hundred harryings of Why.

And true, they are hurling spittle, rock,
Garbage and fruit in Little Rock.
And I saw coiling storm a-writhe
On bright madonnas. And a scythe
55 Of men harassing brownish girls.
(The bows and barrettes in the curls
And braids declined away from joy.)

I saw a bleeding brownish boy. . . .

The lariat lynch-wish I deplored.

60 The loveliest lynchee was our Lord.

The Blackstone Rangers[1]

(1968)

I

As Seen by Disciplines

There they are.
Thirty at the corner.
Black, raw, ready.
Sores in the city
5 that do not want to heal.

II

The Leaders

Jeff. Gene. Geronimo. And Bop.
They cancel, cure and curry.
Hardly the dupes of the downtown thing
the cold bonbon,
10 the rhinestone thing. And hardly
in a hurry.
Hardly Belafonte, King,
Black Jesus, Stokely, Malcolm X or Rap.
Bungled trophies.
15 Their country is a Nation on no map.

Jeff, Gene, Geronimo and Bop
in the passionate noon,
in bewitching night
are the detailed men, the copious men.
20 They curry, cure,
they cancel, cancelled images whose Concerts
are not divine, vivacious; the different tins
are intense last entries; pagan argument;
translations of the night.

25 The Blackstone bitter bureaus
(bureaucracy is footloose) edit, fuse
unfashionable damnations and descent;
and exulting, monstrous hand on monstrous hand,
construct, strangely, a monstrous pearl or grace.

---

[1] A Chicago street gang.

III

GANG GIRLS

A Rangerette

30 Gang Girls are sweet exotics.
Mary Ann
uses the nutrients of her orient,
but sometimes sighs for Cities of blue and jewel
beyond her Ranger rim of Cottage Grove.
35 (Bowery Boys, Disciples, Whip-Birds will
dissolve no margins, stop no savory sanctities.)

Mary is
a rose in a whiskey glass.

Mary's
40 Februaries shudder and are gone. Aprils
fret frankly, lilac hurries on.
Summer is a hard irregular ridge.
October looks away.
And that's the Year!
45   Save for her bugle-love.
Save for the bleat of not-obese devotion.
Save for Somebody Terribly Dying, under
the philanthropy of robins. Save for her Ranger
bringing
50 an amount of rainbow in a string-drawn bag.
"Where did you get the diamond?" Do not ask:
but swallow, straight, the spirals of his flask
and assist him at your zipper; pet his lips
and help him clutch you.

55 Love's another departure.
Will there be any arrivals, confirmations?
Will there be gleaming?

Mary, the Shakedancer's child
from the rooming-flat, pants carefully, peers at
60 her laboring lover. . . .
    Mary! Mary Ann!
Settle for sandwiches! settle for stocking caps!
for sudden blood, aborted carnival,
the props and niceties of non-loneliness—
65 the rhymes of Leaning.

The Ballad of Rudolph Reed

(1960)

Rudolph Reed was oaken.
His wife was oaken too.
And his two girls and his good little man
Oakened as they grew.

5 "I am not hungry for berries.
I am not hungry for bread.
But hungry hungry for a house
Where at night a man in bed

"May never hear the plaster
10 Stir as if in pain.
May never hear the roaches
Falling like fat rain.

"Where never wife and children need
Go blinking through the gloom.
15 Where every room of many rooms
Will be full of room.

"Oh my home may have its east or west
Or north or south behind it.
All I know is I shall know it,
20 And fight for it when I find it."

It was in a street of bitter white
That he made his application.
For Rudolph Reed was oakener
Than others in the nation.

25 The agent's steep and steady stare
Corroded to a grin.
Why, you black old, tough old hell of a man,
Move your family in!

Nary a grin grinned Rudolph Reed,
30 Nary a curse cursed he,
But moved in his House. With his dark little wife,
And his dark little children three.

A neighbor would *look*, with a yawning eye
That squeezed into a slit.

35 But the Rudolph Reeds and the children three
   Were too joyous to notice it.

For were they not firm in a home of their own
   With windows everywhere
   And a beautiful banistered stair
40 And a front yard for flowers and a back yard for grass?

The first night, a rock, big as two fists.
   The second, a rock big as three.
   But nary a curse cursed Rudolph Reed.
   (Though oaken as man could be.)

45 The third night, a silvery ring of glass.
   Patience ached to endure.
   But he looked, and lo! small Mabel's blood
   Was staining her gaze so pure.

Then up did rise our Rudolph Reed
50 And pressed the hand of his wife,
   And went to the door with a thirty-four
   And a beastly butcher knife.

He ran like a mad thing into the night.
   And the words in his mouth were stinking.
55 By the time he had hurt his first white man
   He was no longer thinking.

By the time he had hurt his fourth white man
   Rudolph Reed was dead.
   His neighbors gathered and kicked his corpse.
60 "Nigger—" his neighbors said.

Small Mabel whimpered all night long,
   For calling herself the cause.
   Her oak-eyed mother did no thing
   But change the bloody gauze.

Medgar Evers[1]

(1964)

For Charles Evers[2]

The man whose height his fear improved he
arranged to fear no further. The raw
intoxicated time was time for better birth or a final death.
Old styles, old tempos, all the engagement of
5 the day—the sedate, the regulated fray—
the antique light, the Moral rose, old gusts,
tight whistlings from the past, the mothballs
in the Love at last our man forswore.

Medgar Evers annoyed confetti and assorted
10 brands of businessmen's eyes.

The shows came down: to maxims and surprise.
And palsy.

Roaring no rapt arise-ye to the dead, he
leaned across tomorrow. People said that
15 he was holding clean globes in his hands.

The Boy Died in My Alley

(1981)

Without my having known.
Policeman said, next morning,
"Apparently died Alone."
"You heard a shot?" Policeman said.
5 Shots I hear and Shots I hear.
I never see the dead.

The Shot that killed him yes I heard
as I heard the Thousand shots before;
careening tinnily down the nights
10 across my years and arteries.

---

[1] African-American civil rights leader who was killed by a sniper in 1963.

[2] Medgar Evers's brother.

Policeman pounded on my door.
"Who is it?" "POLICE!" Policeman yelled.
"A Boy was dying in your alley.
A Boy is dead, and in your alley.
15 And have you known this Boy before?"

I have known this Boy before.
I have known this Boy before, who
ornaments my alley.
I never saw his face at all.
20 I never saw his futurefall.
But I have known this Boy.

I have always heard him deal with death.
I have always heard the shout, the volley.
I have closed my heart-ears late and early.
25 And I have killed him ever.

I joined the Wild and killed him
with knowledgeable unknowing.
I saw where he was going.
I saw him Crossed. And seeing,
30 I did not take him down.

He cried not only "Father!"
but "Mother!
Sister!
Brother."
35 The cry climbed up the alley.
It went up to the wind.
It hung upon the heaven
for a long
stretch-strain of Moment.

40 The red floor of my alley
is a special speech to me.

An Interview with Myself

GWENDOLYN BROOKS

QUESTION: Why are you inter-
viewing yourself?

GB: Because I know the facts and
nuances.

Q: Describe your "background."

GB: Nothing Strange. No child
abuse, no prostitution, no Mafia
membership. A sparkly childhood,

with two fine parents and one brother, in a plain but warmly enclosing two-storey gray house (we always rented the top floor). Our house, regularly painted by my father (sometimes with the help of his friend Berry Thompson), had a back yard and a front yard, both pleasant with hedges and shrubs and trees and flowers. My father recited fascinating poetry, and sang to us jolly or haunting songs. My favorite was "Asleep in the Deep": "Many brave hearts are asleep in the deep, so beware—be-e-e-e WARE"; his voice went down sincerely, down and down and down; suddenly the living room was a theater. My mother sang, too, and played the piano almost every day. She loved music. Classical, popular, spiritual, *all* music. She wrote music; she had gone to a class to study harmony. My parents and my brother and I observed all the holidays. We made much of the Table. It entertained, variously, turkey and pumpkin pie, fruitcake and mince pie, "Easter ham," birthday-cake creations. My brother and my mother and I (not my father) enjoyed family and church picnics, went to Riverview, Sunday School, the Regal Theatre and the Metropolitan and Harmony theaters, neighborhood parties, the Field Museum. . . . Our life was family-oriented, so we did a lot of family visiting. Aunt Ella and Uncle Ernest, Aunt Gertie and Uncle Paul lived in Chicago (all near each other now, out in Lincoln Cemetery), so we saw them frequently; but there were also aunts, uncles and cousins in Milwaukee, Topeka, and Kalamazoo, so in the summer, sometimes, we

would get on a train and go visit those folks. We children enjoyed those visits so—enjoyed watching, deciphering! We enjoyed our schooltimes, too. As soon as we were old enough, my mother got us library cards; and there were many books in the house, including the Harvard Classics. Our parents were intelligent and courageous; they subscribed to duty, decency, dignity, industry—*kindness.*

Q: Why is your name, almost always, followed by the phrase "Pulitzer Prize"?

GB: Because I was the first black to be given a Pulitzer of any kind. That was in 1950, for my second book of poetry, *Annie Allen.* Thirty-three years later, another black woman has received a Pulitzer, this time for a novel, *The Color Purple* (multitalented Alice Walker). Several estimable black males won the prize in those intervening years—starting with the remarkable *Ebony* photographer, Moneta Sleet Jr. (In 1971 *Ebony* sent the two of us to Montgomery, Alabama, to work up a feature on "After-the-Storm" Montgomery. We would dash into the street; I would seize and question anyone who looked storyful, while amiable Moneta photographed away. One of the most enjoyable adventures of my life; I've always thanked Senior Editor Herb Nipson for choosing me to share that trip with Moneta.)

Q: You promised a nice little Pulitzer story.

GB: Here is a nice little Pulitzer story, one of many Pulitzer stories

I'll tell you later. On Pulitzer announcement day, this past spring, I heard Alice's award mentioned on radio, minutes before I was to address an audience at the University of Missouri in Kansas City. I announced this Happening—mentioning the strange thirty-three-year gap—and asked the audience to celebrate with applause. The audience applauded. And some of the audience tsk-tsked appropriately: because, you see, in those thirty-three years black women writers had not been idle. We had Paule Marshall. We had Mari Evans. We had Margaret Walker, Toni Cade Bambara, Audre Lorde, Lucille Clifton, Toni Morrison, Ai, Dolores Kendrick, Sonia Sanchez. Many others. Talented women. Writers of poetry *and* prose, strikingly effective *and* interesting *and* English-nourishing *and* blackness-preserving. When you really think of thirty-three years stretching between myself in 1950 and Alice in 1983, you have to gasp.

Q: Talk about the late sixties.

GB: Speaking of nourishment— my nourishment of nourishments was in the years 1967 to 1972. As I've said of those years, the "new" black ideal italicized black identity, solidarity, self-possession, self-address. Furthermore, the *essential* black ideal vitally acknowledged African roots. Came Oscar Brown Jr.'s variety show, "Opportunity, Please Knock." I met many of the Blackstone Rangers comprising, chiefly, that cast. They liked me and respected me. I started a poetry workshop for interested Rangers, college students, teen organizers. Later I paid Walter Bradford, a young organizer-friend of Oscar's, to run a one-year workshop for Rangers only. It was highly successful. My original group stayed with me several years. Eventually, many of them got teaching jobs here and there, across the country.

Among them, I had two good *Sons of the Revolution.* That's irony. We had no Revolution. We had a healthy rebellion. These "Sons," Walter Bradford and Don L. (Haki) Lee, taught me a little of what I needed to know about The Great World around me. I found myself reading, with profit, the books Haki recommended: such books as Fanon's *The Wretched of the Earth,* Lundberg's *The Rich and the Super-Rich,* DuBois' *The Souls of Black Folk,* Zora Neale Hurston's novels. We talked, we walked, we read our work in taverns and churches and jail. I invited writers like James Baldwin and John O. Killens to my house to meet them, to exchange views with them. At such parties, and at our own regular meetings, and at our street festivals, the air was hot, heavy with logic, illogic, zeal, construction. What years those were—years of hot-breathing hope, clean planning, and sizable black cross-reference and reliance. OF COURSE I know those years couldn't and shouldn't "return"! The flaws have been witnessed and cataloged, with great energy (and inventiveness). I needn't repeat. Much is gone and forgotten, the good and the not-good. But there's something under-river; pride surviving, pride and self-respect surviving, however wobbly or wondering.

Well, those young people adopted and instructed me. They put me on The Wall of Respect! (Forty-third and Langley.)

The theme poem of that Black-time's essence was Haki's "New Integrationist":

I
seek
integration
of
negroes
with
Black
people

Q: Talk about the Poet Laureate Awards.

GB: When I was made Poet Laureate of Illinois, following Carl Sandburg's death, I wanted to substantiate the honor with assistance to the young. I spend about $2,000 each spring on a competition that involves at least twenty high-school and elementary-school awards, and a ceremony—for many years now—at the University of Chicago, with presentations, recitations. The Chicago newspapers have been cooperative, giving my young poets a forum every year.

Q: Do you feel you've had your share of honors?

GB: Indeed! There's even the Gwendolyn Brooks Junior High School at 147th and Wallace (Harvey), and the Gwendolyn Brooks Cultural Center at Western Illinois University.

Q: Have you written fiction?

GB: Short stories and novellas I am not proud of. And a novel, *Maud Martha,* published by Harper & Row. *Maud Martha* is a lovely little novel about a lovely little person, wrestling with the threads of her milieu. Of course this "lovely little person" was the essence of myself, or aspects of myself tied with as neat a ribbon as my innocence could manage. The novel is very funny, very often!—and not at all disappointing, even *though* my heroine was never raped, did not become a lady of the evening, did not enter the world of welfare mothers (I admire Diahann Carroll's under-rated movie "Claudine"), did not murder the woman who stepped on her toe in the bus. I said in my autobiographical novel "an auto-biographical novel is a better testament, a better thermometer, than a memoir can be. For who, in presenting a 'factual' account, is going to tell the absolute, the horrifying or exquisite, the incredible Truth?" An autobiographical novel is allowing. There's fact-meat in the soup, among the chunks of fancy: but, generally, definite identification will be difficult. . . . Much that happened to Maudie has not happened to me; and she is a nicer and a better-co-ordinated creature than I am. I can say that lots in the "story" was taken out of my own life and twisted, highlighted or dimmed, dressed up or down.

Q: What is a poet? What is poetry?

GB: There are hundreds of definitions. A poet is one who distils experience—strains experience. A poet looks—sees. Poets oblige themselves to see. Poetry is siren, prose is survey. I keep telling children: "Poetry comes out of life. What happened to you yesterday and last week and six years ago and ten minutes ago and what you *surmise* may happen tomorrow is poetry-in-the-rough. Strain it—distil—work the magic of carefully-chosen *words* upon it—and there's poetry."

Q: What is the meaning of T.H.E.M.?

GB: "Trying Hard to Express Myself." I organized the eighteen teenagers on my block into a forum. T.H.E.M. was their choice of a name. They met at my house, flopped on the floor when chairage was exhausted, discussed numbers of things: school, sex, drugs, politics—Africa. One of them tired of discussions on Africa this, Africa that. She judged, "We're never going there. We're going *no*where. We're folks who have nothing at all to do with Africa." So I sent her to Ghana, with another girl from our "club," and my daughter as chaperone. Couldn't have had a better chaperone! My daughter Nora Blakely writes prose and poetry, has taught in elementary school and at Roosevelt University, dances and teaches dancing, choreographs. On the way, my voyagers had a few days in London and in Paris. I wanted to help extend the horizons of these young people, and they met with me for about four years. During that time I gave them scholarships, took them to black plays and movies, bought books and educational magazines for them, brought "career people" to speak to them—writers, a senator, a photographer, an editor, an actress. They were not shy in the presence of these "career people": they challenged, corrected, extended. (These youngsters were also "watch-workers," who kept a collective eye on the block and reported disturbances to the police.) Our best-enjoyed nourishment, however, was the unrestricted exhilaration of "mere" communication.

from Report from Part One

GWENDOLYN BROOKS

Until 1967 my own blackness did not confront me with a shrill spelling of itself. I knew that I was what most people were calling "a Negro"; I called myself that, although always the word fell awkwardly on a poet's ear; I had never liked the sound of it (Caucasian has an ugly sound, too, while the name Indian is beautiful to look at and to hear.) *And* I knew that people of my coloration and distinctive history had been bolted to trees and sliced or burned or shredded; knocked to the back of the line; provided with separate toilets, schools, neighborhoods:

denied, when possible, voting rights: hounded, hooted at, or shunned, or patronizingly patted (often the patting-hand was, I knew, surreptitiously wiped after the Kindness, so that unspeakable contamination might be avoided). America's social climate, it seemed, was trying to tell me something. It was trying to tell me something Websterian. Yet, although almost secretly, I had always felt that to be black was good. Sometimes, there would be an approximate whisper around me: *others* felt, it seemed, that to be black was good. The translation would have been something like "Hey—being black is *fun.*" Or something like "Hey—our folks have got stuff to be proud of!" Or something like "Hey—since we are so good why aren't we treated like the other 'Americans?' "

Suddenly there was New Black to meet. In the spring of 1967 I met some of it at the Fisk University Writers' Conference in Nashville. Coming from white white white South Dakota State College I arrived in Nashville, Tennessee, to give one more "reading." But blood-boiling surprise was in store for me. First, I was aware of a general energy, an electricity, in look, walk, speech, *gesture* of the young blackness I saw all about me. I had been "loved" at South Dakota State College. Here, I was coldly Respected. Here, the heroes included the novelist-director, John Killens, editors David Llorens, and Hoyt Fuller, playwright Ron Milner, historians John Henrik Clarke and Lerone Bennett (and even poor Lerone was taken to task, by irate members of a no-nonsense young audience, for affiliating himself with *Ebony Magazine,* considered at that time a traitor for allowing

skin-bleach advertisements in its pages, and for over-featuring light-skinned women). Imamu Amiri Baraka, then "LeRoi Jones," was expected. He arrived in the middle of my own offering, and when I called attention to his presence there was jubilee in Jubilee Hall.

All that day and night, Margaret Danner Cunningham—another Old Girl, another coldly Respected old Has-been—and an almost hysterical Gwendolyn B. walked about in amazement, listening, looking, learning. *What was going on!*

In my cartoon basket I keep a cartoon of a stout, dowager-hatted, dowager-furred Helen Hokinson woman. She is on parade in the world. She is a sign-carrier in the wild world. Her sign says "Will someone please tell me what is going on?" Well, although I cannot give a full-blooded answer to that potent question, I have been supplied—the sources are plural—with helpful materials: hints, friendly *and* inimical clues, approximations, statistics, "proofs" of one kind and another; from these I am trying to weave the coat that I shall wear. In 1967's Nashville, however, the somewhat dotty expression in the eyes of the cartoon-woman, the *agapeness,* were certainly mine. I was in some inscrutable and uncomfortable wonderland. I didn't know what to make of what surrounded me, of what with hot sureness began almost immediately to invade me. *I* had never been, before, in the general presence of such insouciance, such live firmness, such confident vigor, such determination to mold or carve something DEFINITE.

Up against the wall, white man! was the substance of the Baraka shout, at the evening reading he shared with fierce Ron Milner among intoxicating drumbeats, heady incense and organic underhumming. Up against the wall! And a pensive (until that moment) white man of thirty or thirty-three abruptly shot himself into the heavy air, screaming "Yeah! *Yeah!* Up against the wall, Brother! KILL 'EM ALL! KILL 'EM *ALL!*"

I thought that was interesting.

There is indeed a new black today. He is different from any the world has known. He's a tall-walker. Almost firm. By many of his own *brothers* he is not understood. And he is understood by *no* white. Not the wise white; not the Schooled white; not the Kind white. Your *least* prerequisite toward an understanding of the new black is an exceptional

Doctorate which can be conferred only upon those with the proper properties of bitter birth and intrinsic sorrow. I know this is infuriating, especially to those professional Negro-understanders, some of them so *very* kind, with special portfolio, special savvy. But I cannot say anything other, because nothing other is the truth.

I—who have "gone the gamut" from an almost angry rejection of my dark skin by some of my brainwashed brothers and sisters to a surprised queenhood in the new black sun—am qualified to enter at least the kindergarten of new consciousness now. New consciousness and trudge-toward-progress.

I have hopes for myself.

The Achievement of Gwendolyn Brooks

HOUSTON A. BAKER, JR.

A writer writes out of his own family background, out of his own immediate community, during his formative period. And he writes out of his own talent and his own individual vision. Now if he doesn't, if he tries to get away from that by bending it to some ideological line, then he is depriving the group of its uniqueness. What we need is individuals. If the white society has tried to do anything to us, it has tried to keep us from being individuals.[1]

—RALPH ELLISON

Gwendolyn Brooks, like W. E. B. Du Bois, seems caught between two worlds. And both she and Du Bois

manifest the duality of their lives in their literary works; Du Bois wrote in a beautiful, impressionistic style set off by quotations from the world's literary masters. Brooks writes tense, complex, rhythmic verse that contains the metaphysical complexities of John Donne and the word magic of Apollinaire, Eliot, and Pound. The high style of both authors, however, is often used to explicate the condition of black Americans trapped behind a veil that separates them from the white world. What one seems to have is white style and black content—two warring ideals in one dark body.

This apparent dichotomy has produced a confusing situation for

Gwendolyn Brooks. The world of white arts and letters has pointed to her with pride; it has bestowed kudos and a Pulitzer Prize. The world of black arts and letters has looked on with mixed emotion, and pride has been only one part of the mixture. There have also been troubling questions about the poet's essential "blackness," her dedication to the melioration of the black Americans' social conditions. The real duality appears when we realize that Gwendolyn Brooks—although praised and awarded—does not appear on the syllabi of most American literature courses, and her name seldom appears in the annual scholarly bibliographies of the academic world. It would seem she is a black writer after all, *not* an American writer. Yet when one listens to the voice of today's black-revolutionary consciousness, one often hears that Brooks's early poetry fits the white, middle-class patterns that Imamu Baraka has seen as characteristic of "Negro literature."[2]

When one turns to her canon, one finds that she has abided the questions of both camps. Etheridge Knight has perfectly captured her enduring quality in the following lines:

O courier on pegasus, O Daughter
   of Parnassus
O Splendid woman of the purple
   stitch.
When beaten and blue,
   despairingly we sink
Within obfuscating mire,
O, cradle in your bosom us, hum
   your lullabies
And soothe our souls with kisses
   of verse
That stir us on to search for light.
O Mother of the world. Effulgent
   lover of the Sun!
For ever speak the truth.[3]

She has the Parnassian inspiration and the earth-mother characteristics noted by the poet; her strength has come from a dedication to truth. The truth that concerns her does not amount to a facile realism or a heavy naturalism, although "realism" is the word that comes to mind when one reads a number of poems in *A Street in Bronzeville* (1945).

Poems, or segments, such as "kitchenette building," "a song in the front yard," and "the vacant lot," all support the view that the writer was intent on a realistic, even a naturalistic, portrayal of the life of lower-echelon urban dwellers:

We are things of dry hours and
   the involuntary plan,
Grayed in, and gray. "Dream"
   makes a giddy sound, not
   strong
Like "rent," "feeding a wife,"
   "satisfying a man."[4]

My mother, she tells me that
   Johnnie Mae
Will grow up to be a bad woman.
That George'll be taken to Jail
   soon or late
(On account of last winter he sold
   our back gate.)
                         (*WGB*, p. 12)

And with seeing the squat fat
   daughter
Letting in the men
When majesty has gone for the
   day—
And letting them out again.
                         (*WGB*, p. 25)

These passages reinforce the designation of Brooks as a realist, and poems such as "The Sundays of Satin-Legs Smith," "We Real Cool," "A Lovely Love," and the volume *Annie Allen* can be added to the list. If she had insisted on a strict realism and nothing more, she could perhaps be written off as a limited poet. But she is no mere chronicler of the condition of the black American poor. Even her most vividly descriptive verses contain an element that removes them from the realm of a cramped realism. All of her characters have both ratiocinative and imaginative capabilities; they have the ability to reason, dream, muse, and remember. This ability distinguishes them from the naturalistic literary victim caught in an environmental maze. From the realm of "raw and unadorned life," Satin-Legs Smith creates his own world of bright colors, splendid attire, and soft loves in the midst of a cheap hotel's odor and decay. The heroine of "The Anniad" conjures up a dream world, covers it in silver plate, populates it with an imaginary prince, and shores up magnificent fragments against the ruins of war. And Jessie Mitchell's mother seeks refuge from envy and death in a golden past:

> She revived for the moment
>   settled and dried-up
>   triumphs,
> Forced perfume into old petals,
>   pulled up the droop,
> Refueled
> Triumphant long-exhaled breaths.
> Her exquisite yellow youth. . . .
>
> (*WGB*, p. 329)

Gwendolyn Brooks's characters, in short, are infinitely human because at the core of their existence is the imaginative intellect.

Given the vision of such characters, it is impossible to agree with David Littlejohn, who wishes to view them as simplistic mouthpieces for the poet's sensibility;[5] moreover, it is not surprising that the characters'

concerns transcend the ghetto life of many black Americans. They reflect the joy of childhood, the burdens and contentment of motherhood, the distortions of the war-torn psyche, the horror of blood-guiltiness, and the pains of the anti-hero confronted with a heroic ideal. Brooks's protagonists, personae, and speakers, in short, capture all of life's complexities, particularly the complexity of an industrialized age characterized by swift change, depersonalization, and war.

In "Gay Chaps at the Bar," the poet shows her concern for a theme that has had a great influence on twentieth-century British and American art. In one section, "my dreams, my works, must wait till after hell," she employs the food metaphors characteristic of her writing to express the incompleteness that accompanies war:

> I hold my honey and I store my
>   bread
> In little jars and cabinets of my
>   will.
> I label clearly, and each latch and
>   lid
> I bid, Be firm till I return from
>   hell.
> I am very hungry. I am
>   incomplete.
>
> (*WGB*, p. 50)

In another section, "piano after war," she captures the mental anguish occasioned by war. The rejuvenation the speaker has felt in the "golden rose" music feeding his "old hungers" suddenly ends:

> But suddenly, across my climbing
>   fever
> Of proud delight—a multiplying
>   cry.
> A cry of bitter dead men who will
>   never

Attend a gentle maker of musical
   joy.
Then my thawed eye will go again
   to ice.
And stone will shove the softness
   from my face.

(WGB, p. 52)

In "The Anniad" and the "Appendix to the Anniad," the poet deals once again with the chaos of arms: War destroys marriage, stifles fertility, and turns men to creatures of "untranslatable ice." Her work, therefore, joins the mainstream of twentieth-century poetry in its treatment of the terrors of war, and her message comes to us through, as I have mentioned, the imaginative intellect of characters who evoke sympathy and identification.

War, however, is not the only theme that allies Gwendolyn Brooks with the mainstream. One finds telling and ironical speculation in "the preacher: ruminates behind the sermon":

Perhaps—who knows?—He tires
   of looking down.
Those eyes are never lifted. Never
   straight.
Perhaps sometimes He tires of
   being great
In solitude. Without a hand to
   hold.

(WGB, p. 15)

In "Strong Men, Riding Horses," we have a Prufrockian portrait of the anti-hero. After his confrontation with the ideals of a Western film, the persona comments:

I am not like that. I pay rent, am
   addled
By illegible landlords, run, if
   robbers call.

What mannerisms I present,
   employ,

Are camouflage, and what my
   mouths remark
To word-wall off that broadness of
   the dark
Is pitiful.
I am not brave at all.

(WGB, p. 313)

In "Mrs. Small," one has a picture of the "Mr. Zeros" (or Willie Lomans) of a complex century, and in "A Bronzeville Mother Loiters in Mississippi. Meanwhile a Mississippi Mother Burns Bacon," we have an evocation of the blood-guiltiness of the white psyche in an age of dying colonialism. Brooks presents these themes with skill because she has the ability to endow each figure with a unique, individualizing vision of the world.

If they were considered in isolation, however, the characters and concerns of the verse would not mark the poet as an outstanding writer. Great poetry demands word magic, a sense of the infinite possibilities of language. In this technical realm Brooks is superb. Her ability to dislocate and mold language into complex patterns of meaning can be observed in her earliest poems and in her latest volumes—In The Mecca (1968), Riot (1969), and Family Pictures (1970). The first lines of "The Sundays of Satin-Legs Smith" are illustrative:

INAMORATAS, with an approbation,
Bestowed his title. Blessed his
   inclination.

He wakes, unwinds, elaborately:
   a cat
Tawny, reluctant, royal. He is fat
And fine this morning. Definite.
   Reimbursed.

(WGB, p. 26)

The handling of polysyllabics is not in the least strained, and the movement is so graceful that one scarcely notices the rhymed couplets. Time and again this word magic is at work, and the poet's varying rhyme schemes lend a subtle resonance that is not found in the same abundance in the works of other acknowledged American writers. It is important to qualify this judgment, however, for while Brooks employs polysyllabics and forces words into striking combinations, she preserves colloquial rhythms. Repeatedly one is confronted by a realistic voice—not unlike that in Robert Frost's poetry—that carries one along the dim corridors of the human psyche or down the rancid halls of a decaying tenement. Brooks's colloquial narrative voice, however, is more prone to complex juxtapositions than Frost's, as a stanza from "The Anniad" illustrates:

> Doomer, though, crescendo-comes
> Prophesying hecatombs.
> Surrealist and cynical.
> Garrulous and guttural.
> Spits upon the silver leaves.
> Denigrates the dainty eves
> Dear dexterity achieves.
>
> (*WGB*, pp. 85–86)

This surely differs from Frost's stanzas, and the difference resides in the poet's obvious joy in words. She fuses the most elaborate words into contexts that allow them to speak naturally or to sing beautifully her meaning.

Brooks is not indebted to Frost alone for technical influences; she also acknowledges her admiration for Langston Hughes. Although a number of her themes and techniques set her work in the twentieth-

century mainstream, there are those that place it firmly in the black American literary tradition. One of her most effective techniques is a sharp, black, comic irony that is closely akin to the scorn Hughes directed at the ways of white folks throughout his life. When added to her other skills, this irony proves formidable. "The Lovers of the Poor" is unsparing in its portrayal of ineffectual, middle-age, elitist philanthropy:

> Their guild is giving money to
> the poor.
> The worthy poor. The very very
> worthy
> And beautiful poor. Perhaps just
> not too swarthy?
> Perhaps just not too dirty nor too
> dim
> Nor—passionate. In truth, what
> they could wish
> Is—something less than derelict
> or dull.
> Not staunch enough to stab,
> though, gaze for gaze!
> God shield them sharply from the
> beggar-bold!
>
> (*WGB*, p. 334)

Hughes could not have hoped for better. And the same vitriol is directed at whites who seek the bizarre and exotic by "slumming" among blacks in "I love those little booths at Benvenuti's":

> But how shall they tell people
> they have been
> Out Bronzeville way? For all the
> nickels in
> Have not bought savagery or
> defined a "folk."
> The colored people will not
> "clown."
> The colored people arrive, sit
> firmly down,

Eat their Express Spaghetti, their
    T-bone steak,
Handling their steel and crockery
    with no clatter,
Laugh punily, rise, go firmly out
    of the door.

                (*WGB*, p. 111)

The poet's chiding, however, is not always in the derisive mode. She often turns an irony of loving kindness on black Americans. "We Real Cool" would fit easily into the canon of Hughes or Sterling Brown:

We real cool. We
Left School. We

Lurk late. We
Strike straight. We

Sing sin. We
Thin gin. We

Jazz June. We
Die soon.

                (*WGB*, p. 315)

The irony is patent, but the poet's sympathy and admiration for the folk are no less obvious (the bold relief of "We," for example). A sympathetic irony in dealing with the folk has characterized some of the most outstanding works in the black American literary tradition, from Paul Laurence Dunbar's "Jimsella" and the novels of Claude McKay to Ralph Ellison's *Invisible Man* and the work of recent writers such as George Cain and Louise Meriwether. All manifest a concern with the black man living in the "promised land" of the American city, and Brooks's *A Street in Bronzeville, Annie Allen,* "The Bean Eaters," and "Bronzeville Woman in a Red Hat" likewise reveal the employment of kindly laughter to veil the tears of a desperate situation. In her autobiography, *Report from Part One,* she attests to having been in the situation and to having felt its deeper pulsations: "I lived on 63rd Street [in Chicago] . . . and there was a good deal of life in the raw all about me. You might feel that this would be disturbing, but it was not. It contributed to my writing progress. I wrote about what I saw and heard in the street."[6]

Finally, there are the poems of protest. A segregated military establishment comes under attack in both "The Negro Hero" and "the white troops had their orders but the Negroes looked like men." The ignominies of lynching are exposed in "A Bronzeville Mother Loiters in Mississippi. Meanwhile, a Mississippi Mother Burns Bacon." And in poems like "Riders to the Blood-red Wrath" and "The Second Sermon on the Warpland," Brooks expresses the philosophy of militant resistance that has characterized the black American literary tradition from the day a black slave first sang of Pharaoh's army. The poet, in short, has spoken forcefully against the indignities suffered by black Americans in a racialistic society. Having undertaken a somewhat thorough revaluation of her role as a black poet in an era of transition, she has stated and proved her loyalty to the task of creating a new consciousness in her culture. Her shift from a major white publishing firm to an independent black one (Broadside Press) for her autobiography is an indication of her commitment to the cause of black institution-building that has been championed by a number of today's black artists. One might, however, take issue with her recent statement that she was "ignorant" until enlightened by the black activities and concerns of the 1960s. Although she is currently serving as one of the most engaged artistic guides for a culture, she is more justly described as a herald than as an uninformed convert. She has mediated the dichotomy that left Paul Laurence Dunbar (whose *Complete Poems* she read at an early age) a torn and agonized man. Of course, she had the example of Dunbar, the Harlem Renaissance writers, and others to build upon, but at times even superior talents have been incapable of employing the accomplishments of the past for their own ends. Unlike the turn-of-the-century poet and a number of Renaissance writers, Brooks has often excelled the surrounding white framework, and she has been able to see clearly beyond it to the strengths and beauties of her own unique cultural tradition.

Gwendolyn Brooks represents a singular achievement. Beset by a double consciousness, she has kept herself from being torn asunder by crafting poems that equal the best in the black and white American literary traditions. Her characters are believable, her themes manifold, and her technique superb. The critic (whether black or white) who comes to her work seeking only support for his ideology will be disappointed for, as Etheridge Knight pointed out, she has ever spoken the truth. And truth, one likes to feel, always lies beyond the boundaries of any one ideology. Perhaps Brooks's most significant achievement is her endorsement of this point of view. From her hand and fertile imagination have come volumes that transcend the dogma on either side of the American veil. In their transcendence, they are fitting representatives of an "Effulgent lover of the Sun!"

Notes

1 Ralph Ellison and James Alan McPherson, "Indivisible Man," *The Atlantic* 226 (Dec. 1970): p. 60.

2 Imamu Amiri Baraka (LeRoi Jones), "The Myth of a 'Negro Literature,'" *Home: Social Essays* (New York: William Morrow, 1966), pp. 105–15.

3 Etheridge Knight, "To Gwendolyn Brooks," *Poems from Prison* (Detroit: Broadside Press, 1968), p. 30.

4 Gwendolyn Brooks, "kitchenette building," *The World of Gwendolyn Brooks* (New York: Harper & Row, 1971), p. 4.

5 David Littlejohn, *Black on White: A Critical Survey of Writings by American Negroes* (New York: Viking Press, 1969), pp. 89–94.

6 Gwendolyn Brooks, *Report from Part One* (Detroit: Broadside Press, 1972), p. 133.

An Interview with Gwendolyn Brooks

GEORGE STAVROS

Q. There is a quality of pathos about all of your characters and compassion in your treatment of them. Many of them make a pitiful attempt to be what they cannot be.

A. Some of them. Not all of them; some of them are very much interested in just the general events of their own lives.

Q. Let me suggest one of the frequently anthologized poems, "A Song in the Front Yard," about a girl who "gets sick of a rose" and decides she'd like to leave the comfort and pleasure of the front yard to see what life would be like in the back.

A. Or out in the alley, where the charity children play, based on my own resentment when I was a little girl, having to come inside the front gate after nine—oh, earlier than that in my case.

Q. Isn't there a yearning to get away in many such portraits?

A. I wouldn't attach any heavy significance to that particular poem, because that was the lightest kind of a little poem.

Q. How about a poem like "Sadie and Maud," a little lyric, I think in quatrains, contrasting Maud, who turns out to be a lonely brown "mouse," and Sadie, who "scraped life/With a fine tooth comb"?

A. Those are imaginary characters, purely imaginary.

. . .

Q. How about the seven pool players in the poem "We Real Cool"?

A. They have no pretensions to any glamour. They are supposedly dropouts, or at least they're in the poolroom when they should possibly be in school, since they're probably young enough, or at least those I saw were when I looked in a poolroom, and they. . . . First of all, let me tell you how that's supposed to be said, because there's a reason why I set it out as I did. These are people who are essentially saying, "Kilroy is here. We are." But they're a little uncertain of the strength of their identity. [Reads:]

We real cool. We
Left school. We

Lurk late. We
Strike straight. We

Sing sin. We
Thin gin. We

Jazz June. We
Die soon.

The "We"—you're supposed to stop after the "We" and think about their validity, and of course there's no way for you to tell whether it should be said softly or not, I suppose, but I say it rather softly because I want to represent their basic uncertainty, which they don't bother to question every day, of course.

Q. Are you saying that the form of this poem, then, was determined by the colloquial rhythm you were trying to catch?

A. No, determined by my feeling about these boys, these young men.

Q. These short lines, then, are your own invention at this point? You don't have any literary model in mind; you're not thinking of Eliot or Pound or anybody in particular. . . ?

A. My gosh, no! I don't even admire Pound, but I do like, for instance, Eliot's "Prufrock" and *The Waste Land,* "Portrait of a Lady," and some others of those earlier poems. But nothing of the sort ever entered my mind. When I start writing a poem, I don't think about models or about what anybody else in the world has done.

. . .

Q. How do you feel about that climate in regard to what the black writer is doing now? Do you think his task is becoming easier, more difficult, more important?

A. I think it is the task or job or responsibility or pleasure or pride of any writer to respond to his climate. You write about what is in the world. I think I would be silly, and so would LeRoi Jones, to sit down now under the trees and write about the Victorian age,

unless there's some special reference we could make to what's going on now.

Q. Then your poems about Malcolm X and Medgar Evers, for example, are part of a continuing interest in poetry that involved you with matters of the day. Is that correct?

A. No, I didn't involve myself with Medgar Evers' assassination—I merely reacted to it, and I described what he had done, the effects he had had on the assaulting elements of his society, and I ended, most beautifully, I thought: "People said that / he was holding clean globes in his hands."

Q. What did you mean when you said he had departed from "Old styles, old tempos, all the engagement of / the day—the sedate, the regulated fray . . . "?

A. [Reads:] ". . . the antique light, the Moral rose, old gusts, / tight whistlings from the past, the mothballs / in the Love at last our man forswore." He just up and decided he wasn't going to have anything else to do with the stale traditions of the past and the hindrances and restrictions that American response to horrors had been concerned with.

Q. In other words, an impatience with injustice and continuing oppression.

A. Yes, he decided he would just "have none" of it anymore and would do something about righting things for his people.

Gwendolyn Brooks's "Children of the Poor," Metaphysical Poetry and the Inconditions of Love

GARY SMITH

> It is not a permanent necessity that poets should be interested in philosophy, or in any other subject. We can only say that it appears likely that poets in our civilization, as it exists at present, must be *difficult*. Our civilization comprehends great variety and complexity, and this variety and complexity, playing upon a refined sensibility, must produce various and complex results. The poet must become more and more comprehensive, more allusive, more indirect, in order to force, to dislocate if necessary, language into his meaning.
>
> —T. S. ELIOT, THE METAPHYSICAL POETS[1]

Despite Gwendolyn Brooks's recent protest that the sonnet is irrelevant to her artistic goal of blackening English,[2] she is arguably one of America's finest sonneteers. Throughout the early phases of her writing career, before her association with the Black Arts Movement of the 1960s, she repeatedly turned to the sonnet to express her dual commitment to socially relevant and well-crafted poetry. Moreover, she was able to sustain these two often contradictory purposes without creating polemical verse or writing in an art for art's sake mode. Her success in achieving both commitment and craftsmanship is underscored by the many awards she has received for her poetry—especially her sonnets. Her initial public recognition as a sonneteer came in the form of the Eunice Tietjens Award (1944) for "Gay Chaps at the Bar"; this poem along with nine others form the antiwar sonnet cycle that concludes her first published volume, *A Street in Bronzeville* (1945). Her second volume, *Annie Allen* (1949), for which she won a Pulitzer Prize (1950), contains no less than eight sonnets. And in her third volume, *The Bean Eaters* (1960), Brooks includes two of her most critically acclaimed sonnets, "A Lovely Love" and "The Egg Boiler."

In part, Brooks's attraction to the sonnet might be traced to the influence of the New Negro poets, her immediate literary predecessors during the Harlem Renaissance, had upon her work. From these poets, Brooks learned that the four-hundred-year-old and largely genteel sonnet form could be used as a devastating instrument of social protest and that the inherent tensions in the sonnet's syllogistic structure could be used to argue against racism and social injustice. She also knew that the sonnet form had been mastered by most of the major poets writing in the English language.

For example, Claude McKay and Countee Cullen, two of the leading sonneteers among the New Negro poets, primarily used the English romantic poets as models for their sonnets. In two of their most famous sonnets, "If We Must Die" and "From the Dark Tower," the poets freely adapted the Romantic themes and literary styles of Keats, Wordsworth, and Shelley.[3] Their poems, written in iambic pentameter with exact rhymes, are models of traditional Shakespearean and Petrarchan sonnets. However, both poets were obviously immune to the modernist rebellion against romantic lyricism, pastoral imagery, and traditional versification that was underway when their poems were written. Nonetheless, their sonnets indirectly address the paradoxical questions of racism and socioeconomic injustice in America. The metaphorical language of McKay's sonnets—"hogs," "dogs," "monsters," and "kinsmen,"—has inspired any number of outcries against oppression and injustice; whereas the "Dark Tower" of Cullen's sonnet describes any place of forced labor and captivity. The two sonnets are not only timeless in their social protest but also noticeably colorless.

While the New Negro poets demonstrated to Brooks that race was incidental to the tradition of well-crafted and universal poetry, two other individuals had decisive influences upon her distinctly modern poetic voice. The first was the distinguished poet and statesman, James Weldon Johnson; the second was Inez Stark, the Chicago socialite and reader for *Poetry* magazine. In his brief but incisive commentary on several poems Brooks sent him, Johnson wrote: "You have an unquestionable talent and feeling for poetry. Continue to write—at the same time, study carefully the work of the best modern poets—not to imitate them, but to help cultivate the highest possible standard of self-criticism."[4] The immediate effect of Johnson's advice was to provide a "standard" for Brooks's poetry other than the one she found in the New Negro poetry. To her substantial reading list that already included Milton, Spenser, Donne, and Shakespeare, Brooks added Frost, Eliot, Cummings, and Pound.[5]

Stark complemented Johnson's theoretical advice with practical criticism of Brooks's poetry. In the poetry workshop she organized for a group of aspiring poets on Chicago's Southside, Stark gave Brooks lessons in traditional versification as well as modernist poetics. Her classroom texts included Robert Hillyer's *First Principles of Verse* as well as *Poetry*, the magazine that featured many of the modernist poets. As the following quotation indicates, Stark translated into plain, outspoken English the very essence of modernist poetics:

All you need in this poem are the last four lines. . . . You must be careful not to list the obvious things. They, in these days (wartime) are more than ever a weakening influence on the strengths we need. Use them only to illustrate boredom and inanity.

I don't understand too well what it's all about but it has three FINE lines.

Dig at this until you have us see all the skeleton and no fat.

(Report, pp. 66–67, emphasis in the original)

The criticism Stark offered Brooks emphasizes imagistic compression, ironic understatement, and temporal and spatial dislocations. These characteristics, of course, were radical departures from the romantic and generally discursive styles of McKay and Cullen.

Johnson and Stark's stylistic advice provides a partial explanation for Brooks's difficulty as a modern poet. Her best work comprehends not only the protest tradition of the New Negro poetry, but also the traditional and contemporary styles of European and American poetry. To be sure, it is the precise juggling of these various and complex traditions that contributes to the metaphysical quality of her verse. Like John Donne, the seventeenth-century metaphysical poet, Brooks creates a depth and range of feeling in her poetry that often overshadows her commonplace subject matter; she also displays a metaphysical wit that features startling and incongruent figures of speech; and she uses poetic diction that is a mixture of formal and colloquial speech.[6]

Donne's *Holy Sonnet XIV*[7] offers a striking example of the difficulties associated with metaphysical poetry. Its octave summarizes the persona's paradoxical religious feelings:

> Batter my heart, three-personed
>   God; for you
> As yet but knock, breathe, shine,
>   and seek to mend;
> That I may rise and stand,
>   o'erthrow me, and bend
> Your force, to break, blow, burn,
>   and make me new.
> I, like an usurped town, to
>   another due,
> Labor to admit You, but Oh, to no
>   end!
> Reason, Your viceroy in me, me
>   should defend,
> But is captivated, and proves weak
>   or untrue.

The speaker literally implores God to save him from the inner forces that threaten to destroy his religious faith. His heart-felt desperation is dramatized by the plosives that accompany his penitential outburst: "break," "blow," and "burn." However, the ninth line, with its volta, begins the turn toward a partial resolution of the persona's ordeal:

> Yet dearly I love You and would be
>   loved fain,
> But am betrothed unto Your
>   enemy:
> Divorce me, untie or break that
>   knot again
> Take me to You, imprison me, for
>   I,
> Except You enthrall me, never
>   shall be free,
> Nor ever chaste, except You ravish
>   me.

In a voice less strident than the one that controls the poem, the persona finally resolves his predicament with a simple declaration of love: "Yet dearly I love You."

The initial difficulty one experiences while reading the sonnet is structural. Donne has altered the conventional Petrarchan rhyme pattern by adding a Shakespearean couplet to the final quatrain. Within the sonnet, this structural change creates two voltas: at the end of the second and third quatrains; whereas, in the conventional Petrarchan sonnet, the volta usually occurs at the first point, and in the Shakespearean sonnet, it is withheld until the penultimate line. On one level, one doubling of the volta thwarts the reader's expectation for an early resolution of the persona's paradoxical dilemma; on another level, it lessens the dramatic distance between the opening conceit, "Batter my heart, three-personed God," and the final one, "Except you enthrall me, never shall be free."

This structural complexity is compounded by the sonnet's metaphorical language. In the initial quatrain, God is prefigured as an artisan capable of transforming the persona, who imagines himself a misshapen vessel. But rather than draw this metaphorical analogy to a point of conclusion, the second quatrain introduces another conceit: The speaker is a beleaguered town and God a liberating force. And in the final quatrain, the speaker equates God to a lover. Of course, this triunal metaphor, vessel-town-woman, lends itself to a multitude of interpretations, none of which totally answers the sonnet's paradoxical question: How can the persona's fractured religious faith be restored by a three-personed God? One possible answer—that the speaker's love negotiates the logical gaps between the three different conceits—is plausible on an emotional or metaphysical level but not a rational one.

The final complexity within the sonnet is Donne's poetic diction. In the opening lines, he takes his words from the metal arts: "batter," "knock," "shine," and "mend"; whereas in the second quatrain, he turns to the military: "usurped town," "viceroy," "defend," and "captived." Finally, he utilizes the diction of love and courtship: "betrothed," "enthrall," "chaste," and "ravish." These disparate choices are intended, in part, to startle the reader into an awareness of the subliminal relationships between words and ideas. They reinforce the complex and paradoxical nature of Donne's religious faith. But more important, the words, like the sonnet's structure and metaphorical conceits, characterize Donne's metaphysical sensibility.

Brooks's sonnet sequence, *The Children of the Poor,*[8] contains many of the same stylistic difficulties one finds in Donne's *Holy Sonnets,* but it also presents a distinct departure from many of his themes. While Brooks consistently experiments with the sonnet's syllogistic structure, she does not always adhere to the theme of resolution. Her sonnets do not attempt to resolve their paradoxical dilemmas as much as they graphically display a mind that alternately associates and disassociates itself from the dilemmas. Like Donne, Brooks also entertains questions of religious faith in her sonnets, yet she rejects religion as a viable means of resolving complex social problems. Finally, as in Donne's *Holy Sonnets,* love plays a decisive role in Brooks's sonnets, but she is most adept at describing its absence. Indeed, her overriding theme, "the inconditions of love," examines the sociopsychological forces in modern society that deny love.

The Children of the Poor consists of five sonnets. As protest sonnets, they address the question of socioeconomic injustice. Brooks's thematic focus is upon the most vulnerable members of society—black children. Throughout *The Children of the Poor,* Brooks manipulates form to underscore her theme. In each sonnet, she uses a mixture of both Petrarchan and Shakespearean forms. While the octave conforms to the Petrarchan rhyme pattern, *abba* and *abba,* the sestet offers a series of complex variations on the Shakespearean rhyme pattern: *efef* and *gg.* This diversity reinforces the complexity of the emotional responses to the paradoxical questions within each sonnet. Furthermore, the multiple couplets that Brooks employs in the sestet—especially in the first three sonnets—thwart the expected resolution of the sonnets' dilemmas; instead they heighten the sense of the mother's frustration and her inability to provide meaningful answers to her children.

In the first sonnet, for example, the Petrarchan rhyme pattern of the octave underscores the ordered yet constrained lives of childless people:

> People who have no children can
> be hard:
> Attain a mail of ice and insolence:
> Need not pause in the fire, and in
> no sense
> Hesitate in the hurricane to
> guard.
> And when wide world is bitten
> and bewarred
> They perish purely, waving their
> spirits hence
> Without a trace of grace or of
> offense
> To laugh or fail, diffident,
> wonder-starred.

Here, the world of childless people is characterized as essentially callous and ingrown. Without children, they are indifferent to human and natural disasters, "pause in the fire," and "hesitate in the hurricane," as well as to their own lives, "they perish purely." The world of people with children, however, is marked ironically by self-containing contradictions:

> While through a throttling dark
> we others hear
> The little lifting helplessness, the
> queer
> Whimper-whine; whose
> unridiculous
> Lost softness softly makes a trap
> for us.
> And makes a curse. And makes a
> sugar of
> The malocclusions, the
> inconditions of love.
>
> (*WGB*, p. 99)

In this sestet, Brooks uses multiple couplets to reinforce the mother's feeling of enclosure. As opposed to a "mail of ice," parents are entrapped by the emotional needs of their children. The multiple couplets also thwart an expected resolution to the sonnet's implied, paradoxical question: Is human life more fulfilling with or without children? Rather than offering a possible answer, the couplets present a series of oxymorons: soft trap, soft curse, and sugary malocclusions. These oxymorons become the metaphorical equivalents for the inconditions of love.

In the second sonnet, ingenious and incongruent figures of speech also reinforce the anti-love theme. The mother begins by comparing her children with lepers; this conceit is raised to a level of abstraction when she further compares them with "contraband"; and, finally, in the last quatrain, the speaker employs the mythological conceit of the alchemist's stone:[9]

> What shall I give my children?
> who are poor,
> Who are adjudged the leastwise
> of the land,
> Who are my sweetest lepers, who
> demand
> No velvet and no velvety velour;
> But who have begged me for a
> brisk contour,
> Crying that they are quasi,
> contraband
> Because unfinished, graven by a
> hand
> Less than angelic, admirable or
> sure,
> My hand is stuffed with mode,
> design, device.
> But I lack access to my proper
> stone.
> And plenitude of plan shall not
> suffice
> Nor grief nor love shall be enough
> alone

To ratify my little halves who
    bear
Across an autumn freezing
    everywhere.

(*WGB*, p. 100)

At first reading, these heterogeneous metaphors startle the reader into a more acute awareness of the complex social problems of poverty; the disjunction, however, creates certain historical parallels that add to the richness of the mother's emotional stress in response to her paradoxical question: "What shall I give my children? who are poor?" Indeed, the movement of metaphors is from simple abstractions, "leastwise" and "poor," to Biblical and historical referents, "lepers" and "contraband,"[10] and finally to mythology, "proper stone." These figures of speech obviously avoid a concrete description of poverty and help distance the persona from her painful dilemma. Psychologically, her children are not simply shoeless and malnourished; they are freely associated with other outcasts in the Bible and in Afro-American history. The mother's awareness is further underscored by the descriptive terms she uses for her children, "sweetest lepers" and "little halves." These euphemisms connote a tacit acceptance of the judgment of her children as social undesirables. More important, they suggest the mother's "sweet" refusal to counter the social images of her children or, perhaps, to accept them as mirror images of herself. Thus, the sonnet's paradoxical question precipitates not an unequivocal defense of human love apart from poverty, but rather a dramatization of the mother's inner conflicts: how poverty has weakened the emotional underpinnings of her love.

Brooks's use of both colloquial and literary poetic diction plays a part in dramatizing the psychological problems of love and poverty. The octave of the third sonnet is particularly suggestive of this mixture of two poetic dictions:

And shall I prime my children,
    pray, to pray?
Mites, come invade most frugal
    vestibules
Spectered with crusts of penitents'
    renewals
And all hysterics arrogant for a
    day.
Instruct yourselves here is no devil
    to pay.
Children, confine your lights in
    jellied rules;
Resemble graves; be metaphysical
    mules;
Learn Lord will not distort nor leave
    the fray.

(*WGB*, p. 101)

In the first line, the sonnet's paradoxical question contains an implied answer. The word "prime" is an elliptical expression that implies teaching at a primary level; when combined with the other two accented words in the line, "pray, to pray," it becomes an alliterative but sarcastic answer to the question. In the second line, "mites" is both a reference to insect pests and a diminutive qualifier for "children" as well as an ingenious reference to the small boxes used for special, Sunday school offerings. These connotations coalesce in the phrase, "invade most frugal vestibules," the nearly empty anteroom of the church where the children have come to pray.

In the third line, "spectered" connotes the mysterious, ghostly nature of Christian mythology, while "crusts of penitents' renewals" suggests bits of the sacramental wafer as well as the more domestic image of a nearly empty food closet. Moreover, in keeping with the mother's pessimism about religious belief, "all hysterics" infers an emotional catharsis that, "for a day," accompanies the children's intense religious worship.

While the word choices in the initial quatrain are allusively literary, those in the second are colloquial. The mother sarcastically admonishes her children, "instruct yourselves here is no devil to pay" and "confine your lights in jellied rules." The word "lights" signifies both religious enlightenment and self-knowledge, but ironically the mother instructs her children to confine their self-knowledge in the "jellied rules" of their religious training. This spiritual food, like the earlier "crust," does not, however, respond to the basic need of the poor children for nourishment. Without food, the children will "resemble graves." Finally, in a striking example of Brooks's use of colloquial and literary diction, the mother commands her children, "be metaphysical mules." She encourages her children to accept religion's meager offerings, and as the final two lines of the sonnet suggest, the mother will apply a "bandage" on their eyes to conceal their spiritual impoverishment.

While the first three sonnets dramatize the emotional paralysis and pessimism of a mother whose love has been undermined by poverty, the fourth sonnet presents a radical shift in tone and viewpoint. The poetic diction is more forceful and less encumbered by allusive figures of speech. Its perspective omits the dichotomies that characterize the mother's ambivalence in the earlier sonnets; its point of view is the collective, second person plural, "you." Its deliberate, self-assertive tone suggests someone who is actively engaged in the life struggles of her children:

> First fight. Then fiddle. Ply the
> slipping string
> With feathery sorcery; muzzle the
> note
> With hurting love; the music that
> they wrote
> Bewitch, bewilder. Qualify to sing
> Threadwise. Devise no salt, no
> hempen thing
> For the dear instrument to bear.
> Devote
> The bow to silks and honey. Be
> remote
> A while from malice and from
> murdering.
> But first to arms, to armor. Carry
> hate
> In front of you and harmony
> behind.
> Be deaf to music and to beauty
> blind.
> Win war. Rise bloody, maybe not
> too late
> For having first to civilize a space
> Wherein to play your violin with
> grace.
>
> (*WGB*, p. 102)

The spondee, "First fight. Then fiddle," interrupts the regular iambic pentameter of the initial line. As plosives and imperatives, they underscore an emotional commitment to militant action as a response to the sonnet's implied, paradoxical question: How can the ideals of art—beauty and truth—be reconciled with the demands for socioeconomic justice?

This commitment is also conveyed in the sonnet's form and imagery. The octave, for example, argues that music-making and the discipline it involves have certain sociopsychological virtues: "Ply the slipping string," "muzzle the note," "Qualify to sing," and "Devote the bow to silks and honey." However, the sestet, with its volta in the ninth line, defiantly argues that militant action is necessary "to civilize a space / Wherein to play your violin with grace." Unlike the incongruent and heterogeneous figures of speech in the earlier sonnets, the images are neatly divided between militancy and music: "Carry hate in front of you and harmony behind."

The introspective and elegaic tone of the initial three sonnets returns in the final poem. As a protest sonnet, its paradoxical question, how can the poor—who have lived marginal lives—accept death, is perhaps a response to the previous sonnet's exhortation to militant social action.[11] The mother's commitment to socioeconomic justice for her children is still firm:

> When my dears die, the
>   festival-colored brightness
> That is their motion and mild
>   repartee
> Enchanted, a macabre mockery
> Charming the rainbow radiance
>   into tightness
> And into a remarkable politeness
> That is not kind and does not
>   want to be,
> May not they in the crisp
>   encounter see
> Something to recognize and read
>   as rightness?
> I say they may, so granitely
>   discreet,
> The little crooked questionings
>   inbound,
> Concede themselves on most
>   familiar ground,
> Cold an old predicament of the
>   breath:
> Adriot, the shapely prefaces
>   complete,
> Accept the university of death.
>   (*WGB*, p. 103)

In the octave, the euphemism, "dears die," replaces the earlier oxymoron, "sweetest lepers," as a descriptive term for the mother's children. The alliterative and playful word choices, "motion and mild" and "rainbow radiance," also help create an optimistic and enchanting tone in the poem. Furthermore, death becomes another euphemism, "crisp encounter."

The sestet, then, with its volta, "I say they may," answers the paradoxical question in the affirmative. The poverty and "crooked questionings" that characterize the children's lives have prepared them to accept death as a natural consequence of living. But by placing a couplet after the volta, Brooks thwarts our expectation for a stoic resolution of the sonnet. The last three lines further imply that death will actually begin life, because its "university" will provide answers that have eluded the mother. Death is a universal that ignores matters of race and class.

In retrospect, *The Children of the Poor* demonstrates Brooks's success in writing poetry that is both socially conscious and intricately crafted. Her sonnets belong to the modernist tradition in that they contain the variety, complexity, indirection, and dislocation T. S. Eliot suggests are the hallmarks of poets in our civilization. Nonetheless, she subscribes to the New Negro's faith in art as an instrument for social change. Like Cullen and McKay, her protest sonnets avoid specific mention of race as a social issue inextricably tied to poverty; moreover, as illustrated by the abrupt tonal shifts between the third and fourth sonnets, she often vacillates between overt militancy and painful introspection. Finally, if Brooks has abandoned the sonnet form as a means of addressing the socioeconomic concerns of blacks in her latest poetry, she remains committed to art as a means of negotiating racial differences. And in this sense, her commitment to art remains, by implication, a commitment to human life.

NOTES

1 T. S. Eliot, "The Metaphysical Poets," in *Selected Essays* (New York: Harcourt, Brace, 1950), p. 248.

2 See Martha H. Brown, "Interview with Gwendolyn Brooks," *The Great Lakes Review 6* (Summer 1979): 55.

3 See Blyden Jackson and Louis D. Rubin, Jr., *Black Poetry in America: Two Essays in Historical Interpretation* (Baton Rouge: Louisiana State University Press, 1974), pp. 46–47.

4 Gwendolyn Brooks, *Report from Part One* (Detroit: Broadside Press, 1972), p. 202. Hereinafter cited in the text as *Report.*

5 See George Stavros, "An Interview with Gwendolyn Brooks," *Contemporary Literature* II (Winter 1970): 10.

6 See Herbert J. C. Grierson, *Metaphysical Lyrics and Poems of the Seventeenth Century* (New York: Oxford University Press, 1959), pp. xiii–xxviii.

7 For an interesting discussion of John Donne's *Holy Sonnets,* especially "Sonnet XIV," see *John Donne's Poetry,* ed. A. L. Clements (New York: W. W. Norton, 1966), pp. 246–59.

8 Gwendolyn Brooks, *The World of Gwendolyn Brooks* (New York: Harper & Row, 1971), pp. 99–103. Hereinafter cited in the text as *WGB.*

9 See R. Baxter Miller, " 'Does Man Love Art?': The Humanistic Aesthetic of Gwendolyn Brooks," in *Black American Literature and Humanism,* ed. R. Baxter Miller (Lexington: University Press of Kentucky, 1981), pp. 104–6.

10 Besides the usual meaning of goods forbidden by law, "contraband" was also used during the Civil War to identify slaves who fled to, or were smuggled behind, the Union lines or remained in territory captured by the Union Army.

11 See Harry B. Shaw, *Gwendolyn Brooks* (Boston: Twayne Publishers, 1980), pp. 114–15.

"Chocolate Mabbie" and "Pearl May Lee": Gwendolyn Brooks and the Ballad Tradition

MARIA K. MOOTRY

Among the five major volumes of Gwendolyn Brooks' poetry, one of the notably recurring poetic forms is the ballad. From "The Ballad of Chocolate Mabbie," in her first volume, to "The Ballad of Edie Barrow" in her last major book,[1] Brooks shows a continued interest in this popular or folk art form. Brooks' attraction to ballads is not unique. In their revolt against the artifice, formalism, and abstraction of eighteenth-century classicist poetry, romantic poets like Coleridge and Wordsworth often turned to folk ballads for subjects and techniques. They liked the fact that the ballad, as a folk form, focused on the outcasts of society, including abandoned mothers, prisoners, and beggars. At the same time, they valued the ballad's language and structure because it seemed to avoid the pretensions of eighteenth-century classicist poetry. In his famous preface to the second edition of *Lyrical Ballads,* Wordsworth maintains that the language of all poetry, like the language of the ballad, should be neutral, simple, and essentially the same as everyday speech. Coleridge and Wordsworth, however, aimed merely to *imitate* the ballad form in order to demonstrate the value of their new theory of poetics. Brooks' use of the ballad reflects a similar desire to recover a simpler, more direct, poetic form; it

also reflects her belief that the poet should "vivify the commonplace."[2]

However, Brooks goes beyond the mere imitation of ballad themes and techniques to create more varied and complex structures. The result is that while on one level her ballads are simple and direct, on another level they are deeply ironic and complex, both in theme and technique. Thus through her use of ballads, Brooks meets the demands of two ostensibly disparate audiences: the "art for art's sake" audience with its emphasis on the poem as its own excuse for being and the "common" audience who looks for familiar structures and social or moral messages.[3] In the process, Brooks recovers the ballad tradition by using its themes and techniques; she reinvigorates that tradition by infusing it with new themes and variations; and finally, she critiques the tradition by using parodic techniques. The overall effect, however, is the revelation of contemporary, often unpleasant, truths about Afro-American and American society.

In this essay, observations of Brooks' use of the Western folk ballad tradition in her poetry will be based on the analysis of the [poem] "The Ballad of Chocolate Mabbie" (*WGB*, p. 14), which appeared in her first volume, *A Street in Bronzeville* (1945). [This poem was] selected not only because [it is a literary ballad] but because, as [its title suggests, it] is Brooksian in its emphasis on a "woman-identified" vision.[4] Gordon Hall Gerould, in his study of the European folk ballad, notes that "the sorrows peculiar to women serve the ballad poets . . . for some of their most poignant moments."[5] Brooks continues this thematic aspect of the European folk ballad tradition, often infusing into her own literary ballads the complex use of additional folk elements from the Afro-American spirituals and blues (sacred and secular) traditions. Before analyzing the poems, however, it may be useful to review briefly the major folk ballad conventions.

I. THE BALLAD TRADITION

The original popular (or folk) ballad is anonymous, transmitted by oral tradition, and tells a story, often about events well known to its audience. Whatever affects the thoughts and emotions of a community may become the subject of a ballad, but the most frequent themes are unfaithful lovers, shocking murders, mysterious happenings, and political oppression. For example, the latter theme is expressed in the English ballads of Robin Hood, who defended the rights of the common people against the predatory rich. Perhaps because the story is usually well known to the audience, the ballad poet tends to present his narrative in a series of dramatically striking episodes. The audience is left to fill out the complete narrative since characterization is brief, transitions are abrupt, and action is often developed through dialogue.

The language of folk ballads is usually simple in diction and meter. However, because many ballads have been handed down from generation to generation, the diction often ranges from the Scottish or Anglo-Saxon vernacular to archaisms reflecting past poetic oral conventions or everyday usage. Inversions of syntactical structures are also common, perhaps to maintain earlier narrative conventions. Regarding stanzaic form, the typical folk ballad uses the ballad stanza, an *abcb* four-line stanza with alternating four-stress and three-stress lines. However, even where the ballad stanza is not employed, there tends to be the use of refrains and repetition of phrases or parallel phrasing. Often a refrain is repeated with only a slight change, creating what is called an incremental refrain.

Although many ballads begin *in medias res,* just as frequently the ballad employs stock opening phrases to establish its narrative structure. In any event, because of its elliptical episodic structure, colors, actions, and even dialogue are often metonymic and multifunctional. Finally, ballads often also close with some kind of summary stanza. This final stanza often continues the incremental nature of ballad repetition, as well as the simplicity with which tragic situations are presented.

These are some of the major features of the Western European folk ballad. Of course, there are many variations and exceptions to these rules, but for the purpose of this essay, these core conventions may serve as a guide in assessing how Brooks uses the folk ballad tradition and how she departs from it in two of her most powerful literary ballads.

II. "THE BALLAD OF CHOCOLATE MABBIE" AND THE AFRO-AMERICAN SACRED TRADITION

In "The Ballad of Chocolate Mabbie," Brooks deals with the pathos of intraracial discrimination, one of her recurring themes. Seven-year-old Mabbie falls in love with her classmate, Willie Boone, moons over him in history class, and waits for him outside the grammar school gates. In an epiphanic scene, Mabbie's erstwhile "lover" appears insouciantly in the company of a light-skinned, long-haired beauty. At the poem's conclusion, Mabbie is left to "chocolate companions" and to her own resources.

In "The Ballad of Chocolate Mabbie," Brooks uses many of the European ballad conventions mentioned above. For instance, the poem begins with an opening phrase which establishes its narrative character: "*It was* Mabbie without the grammar school gates. . . . " The use of the connective "and" reinforces both the poem's plot structure and its apparent simplicity. An almost childlike progression of sentences makes up this first stanza:

> *It was Mabbie* without the
> grammar school gates.
> *And* Mabbie was all of seven.
> *And* Mabbie was cut from a
> chocolate bar.
> *And* Mabbie thought life was
> heaven. (*WGB*, p. 14; emphasis
> mine)

Repetition appears in the phrasing "It was Mabbie . . . / And Mabbie was . . . / And Mabbie thought . . . . " This parallel repetition recurs in the third stanza, which repeats the opening line: "It was Mabbie without the grammar school gates." The repetition becomes incremental with the closing stanza, where the opening line is again repeated with the meaningful change of one word, "without," to the word "alone," i.e., "It was Mabbie *without* the grammar school gates" (first stanza) becomes "It was Mabbie *alone* by the grammar school gates" (sixth and last stanza—emphasis mine).

Archaic or somewhat outdated usages appear unobstrusively in "Chocolate Mabbie." The word "without" in the poem's first line is clearly archaic; and certain words have an archaic aura, e.g., "saucily," "woe," and "lemon-*hued*" in the fifth stanza. To this suggestion of the old ballad tradition, Brooks juxtaposes modern vernacular language, particularly in the key phrase, "cut from a chocolate bar." Also noteworthy is Brook's use of predominantly Anglo-Saxon words. Often monosyllabic, often with hard consonants, and often used alliteratively, these words with Anglo-Saxon roots create a harsh if vigorous tone and reinforce Brooks' debt to the European (English) folk tradition. Examples of these key words occurring in "Chocolate Mabbie" include "without," "gates," "seven," "cut," "thought," "heaven," "school," "cool," "soon," "brow," and "alone." Also, the preponderance of "to be" verbs and pronouns reflects an Anglo-Saxon linguistic base. One of the few interpolations of an Afro-American vernacular phrasing in the poem occurs in the fourth line of the second stanza where Brooks describes Mabbie's ardor for Willie: "Was only her eyes were cool" is at once a balladic inversion and a Black English construction. The very absence of sustained Black English in the poem accentuates this line, which interestingly anticipates the masterful title of one of Brooks' most famous poems, "We Real Cool."

Turning to its stanzaic form, "Chocolate Mabbie," like the traditional ballad, uses the *abcb* rhyme scheme with rhythmic alternating four-stress and three-stress lines. For instance, the first stanza of the poem scans as follows:

It was, Mabbie without the
   grammar school gates.
And Mabbie was all of seven.
And Mabbie was cut from a
   chocolate bar.
And Mabbie thought life was
   heaven.

Further balladic elements include the repetition of phrases and the use of parallelisms mentioned above, particularly the incrementally juxtaposed line which opens the first and last stanzas:

It was Mabbie *without* the
   grammar school gates.

. . . .

It was Mabbie *alone* by the
   grammar school gates.

Balladic epithets also appear in such phrases as "the pearly gates," "bold Willie Boone," "lemon-hued lynx" and "sand-waves." Yet while these epithets merely *adorn* the traditional ballad, in "Chocolate Mabbie" they become hyperbolic, a mockery within a mock-tragedy. "Bold Willie Boone" and his "lemon-hued lynx" are inflated references to school children which infuse "Chocolate Mabbie" with a satiric tone. The foreshadowing voice of the narrator deepens the sense of satire when describing Mabbie's school gate vigil in the fourth stanza:

Oh, warm is the waiting for joys,
   my dears,
And it cannot be too long.
Oh, pity the little poor chocolate
   lips
That carry the bubble of song!

If exaggerated language in "Chocolate Mabbie" mocks the ballad tradition when it is applied to these prepubescent ordinary characters, the poem's understated plot similarly burlesques another major ballad feature, the episodic, sensationalist plot. While the plot of "Chocolate Mabbie" is "cinematic" in that it offers a montage-like series of images, in actuality the story is minimal. The reader observes a love-sick Mabbie outside the gates, observes Mabbie in the history class, and observes Mabbie desolately watching Willie leave with his "lemon-hued lynx." These everyday "events" in "Chocolate Mabbie" pale before the far more shocking events of such traditional ballads as "Sir Patrick Spence," in which a heroic sailor is involuntarily sent to his death, or "Child-Waters," where a young woman's consuming love ends in an illegitimate baby and public humiliation.

In spite of her occasional parodic stance, Brooks adds to the traditional ballad conventions a theme that is at once universal and particularized. "Chocolate Mabbie," at its core, is a poem about unrequited love. To the theme of unrequited love is added the theme of intraracial discrimination within the black community. As Arthur P. Davis has noted, this is a recurring issue in Brooks' poetry.[6] When this theme is linked to the theme of a female child's developing identity within the black community, it may not be sensationalist, but it does take on the power of a harsh revelation. The result, ultimately, is that "Chocolate Mabbie" is not only about the loss of love, but even more so, it is about the loss of innocence.

It is in addressing the theme of "innocence versus experience" that Brooks further modifies her use of the European ballad tradition by drawing on subjects and themes common to the Afro-American sacred folk tradition. The opening lines of "Chocolate Mabbie" express Mabbie's delusions of love in quasi-religious terms. To Mabbie, who "thought life was heaven," the grammar school gates have become "the pearly gates." References to "pearly gates" recur frequently in Afro-American spirituals, usually when linked to the theme of the Second Coming. This messianic theme and its attendant imagery are parodically and mockingly reconstructed in the third stanza, where Mabbie's hopes for Willie's attention are expressed in the final line: "He would surely be coming soon." Thus, in another hyperbolic strategy, Mabbie is shown as having made a religion of love. Yet, from another perspective, the folk spirituals or sacred tradition is not so much mocked as used as an analogue of secular dilemma. In a further analogy to the biblical tradition, Mabbie, like Adam and Eve, is banished from her prelapsarian state. Thus if the imagery suggests apocalyptic visions, it also looks backward to the Fall. Mabbie's "guilt" is a moot point because she, like all humans, is original sin personified, being "graven by a hand less than angelic."[7] However, the implications are twofold. Brooks is not only speaking of original sin in a Calvinistic sense, but primarily of the social "sin" of being born black

and female. In addressing this theme of loss of innocence, Brooks resorts neither to a sense of predestined fate nor to the romantic transcendence of ideal black womanhood so common to her predecessors during the Harlem Renaissance. Rather, the bitterness of Mabbie's rejection by Willie and the collapse of Mabbie's naive worldview is balanced by the implied possibility of the reconstruction of self in society. Mabbie must learn to use her personal resources, to cherish her "chocolate companions" and not to waste her personal resources, to cherish her "chocolate companions" and not to waste her time brooding over male "betrayal." As Brooks advised in her autobiography,

> [b]lack women must remember . . . [t]hat her [sic] personhood precedes her femalehood, that, sweet as sex may be, she cannot endlessly brood on Black man's blondes, blues and blunders. She is a person in the world—with wrongs to right, stupidities to outwit, *with* her man when possible, on her own when not. . . . Therefore she must, in the midst of tragedy and hatred and neglect . . . mightily enjoy the readily available: sunshine and pets and children and conversation and games and travel (tiny or large) and books and walks and chocolate cake. . . .

By infusing satire and parody into "Chocolate Mabbie" Brooks establishes the poem's distance from the simple folk ballad tradition. Despite the ballad conventions and sacred imagery, the poem has a mocking quality, which gives it a complex cutting edge and reinforces its ideas. The childlike syntax of the opening stanza goes beyond balladic simplicity to a primerlike quality. It is as if an elementary school child is adding sentence to sentence with no sense of subordination. This simplicity underscores the fact that on one level Brooks is writing about "puppy-love" and humorously focusing on a transitory childish crush and its inevitable demise. Yet, in the final stanza the narrator loses her sardonic tone. Thus the reader is reminded that if this is, from one perspective, childish subject matter, ultimately it is a serious poetic statement about the dilemma of growing up black and female in America.[8]

. . .

In conclusion, Brooks' use of folk traditions varies considerably. At times, it is straightforward, at other times parodic; and often it is a complex mixture of both. Further analysis of her use of the traditions of ballads, blues, and spirituals needs to be made before any full understanding of her art can be achieved. The relationship between the blues tradition and the ballad tradition, for instance, needs further exploration. At this point, based on [a powerful example], it can be argued that Brooks turned to folk forms— ballad, blues, and spirituals—not out of any sentimental attachment to a given tradition but to deepen her poetic structure. While, on the surface, these folk elements make her poetry more accessible to the reader, a closer examination reveals insinuations and refinements of technique that augment the complexity so characteristic of her work. In so doing, Brooks has met her own criteria expressed in this early statement for an effective black poet:

> The Negro poet's most urgent duty, at present, is to polish his technique, his way of presenting his truths and his beauties, that these may be more insinuating, and therefore, more overwhelming.[9]

NOTES

[1] Unless noted differently, all citations of primary texts refer to Gwendolyn Brooks, *The World of Gwendolyn Brooks* (New York: Harper, 1971), hereafter cited with pagination in the text as *WGB*. This omnibus includes *A Street in Bronzeville* (1945), *Annie Allen* (1949), *Maud Martha* (1953), *The Bean Eaters* (1960), and *In the Mecca* (1968).

[2] Remarks made during a reading in Carbondale, Illinois, at the Newman Center in October 1980.

[3] For Brooks' conscious attempt to weld craft to "humanity," see Frank Harriot, "The Life of a Pulitzer Poet," *Negro Digest,* August 1950, pp. 14–16.

[4] See Bethel's essay, " 'This Infinity of Conscious Pain': Zora N. Hurston and the Black Female Literary Tradition," from *All the Women Are White; All the Blacks Are Men, but Some of Us Are Brave: Black Women's Studies,* ed. Gloria T. Hull, Patricia Bill Scott, and Barbara Smith (Old Westbury, NY: The Feminist Press, 1982), pp. 176–88. Bethel, p. 180.

[5] Gordon Hall Gerould, *The Ballad of Tradition* (Oxford: Clarendon, 1932), p. 48; hereafter cited in the text as Gerould. I am heavily indebted to Gerould for my discussion of the European ballad tradition.

[6] Arthur P. Davis, "The Black-and-Tan Motif in the Poetry of Gwendolyn Brooks," *CLA Journal,* 6, No. 2 (December 1962), pp. 90–97.

[7] See Brooks' Sonnet #2 from "The Children of the Poor" sequence in which the mother complains that her children are "sweetest lepers" because "graven by a hand less than angelic, admirable or sure" (*WGB*, p. 100).

8 Gwendolyn Brooks, *Report from Part One: An Autobiography* (Detroit: Broadside Press, 1972), p. 204.

9 Gwendolyn Brooks, "Poets Who Are Negroes," *Phylon,* 2 (December 1950), p. 312.

Gwendolyn Brooks's A Street in Bronzeville, the Harlem Renaissance and the Mythologies of Black Women

GARY SMITH

When Gwendolyn Brooks published her first collection of poetry *A Street in Bronzeville* (1945) with Harper and Brothers, she already enjoyed a substantial reputation in the literary circles of Chicago. Nearly a decade earlier, her mother, Keziah Brooks, had arranged meetings between her daughter and James Weldon Johnson and Langston Hughes, two of the most distinguished Black writers of America's Harlem Renaissance. Determined to mold Gwendolyn into a *lady Paul Laurence Dunbar,* Mrs. Brooks proffered poems for the famous writers to read. While Johnson's advice to the young poet was abrupt, eventually he exerted an incisive influence on her later work. In a letter and a marginal note included on the returned poems, addressed to her on 30 August 1937, Johnson praised Brooks's obvious talent and pointed her in the direction of Modernist poetry:

> My dear Miss Brooks: I have read the poems you sent me last. Of them I especially liked *Reunion* and *Myself. Reunion* is very good, and *Myself* is good. You should, by all means, continue you[r] study and work. I shall always be glad to give

you any assistance that I can. Sincerely yours. James Weldon Johnson.

> Dear Miss Brooks—You have an unquestionable talent and feeling for poetry. Continue to write—at the same time, study carefully the work of the best modern poets—not to imitate them, but to help cultivate the highest possible standards of self-criticism. Sincerely, James Weldon Johnson.

Of course, the irony in Johnson's advice, addressed as it is to the future *lady* Dunbar, is that he actually began his own career by conspicuously imitating Dunbar's dialect poems, *Lyrics of a Lowly Life;* yet he encourages Brooks to study the work of the "best Modern poets." He was, perhaps, reacting to the latent elements of modernism already found in her poetry; but the effect was to turn Brooks momentarily away from the Black aesthetic of Hughes's *Weary Blues* (1926) and Countee Cullen's *Color* (1925) toward the Modernist aesthetics of T. S. Eliot, Ezra Pound, and e. e. cummings. It is interesting to note, however, that, even though Johnson's second letter admonishes Brooks to study the Modernist poets, he cautions her "not to imitate them," but to read them with the intent of cultivating the "highest possible standards of self-criticism." Flattered by the older poet's attention and advice, Brooks embarked upon a serious attempt to absorb as much Modernist poetry as she could carry from the public library.

If Johnson played the part of literary mentor, Brooks's relationship with Hughes was more personal, warmer, and longer lasting. She was already on familiar terms with *Weary Blues,* so their first meeting was particularly inspirational. Brooks showed Hughes a packet of her poems, and he praised her talent and encouraged her to continue to write. Years later, after Brooks's reputation was firmly established by a Pulitzer Prize for *Annie Allen* (1949), her relationship with Hughes blossomed into mutual admiration. Hughes dedicated his collection of short stories, *Something in Common* (1963), to her. While Hughes's poetic style had an immeasurable influence on Brooks's poetry, she also respected his personal values and lifestyle. As she noted in her autobiography *[Report],* Hughes was her idol:

> Langston Hughes! The words and deeds of Langston Hughes were rooted in kindness, and in pride. His point of departure was always a clear pride in his race. Race pride may be craft, art, or a music that combines the best of jazz and hymn. Langston frolicked and chanted to the measure of his own race-reverence.

> He was an easy man. You could rest in his company. No one possessed a more serious understanding

of life's immensities. No one was firmer in recognition of the horrors man imposes upon man, in hardy insistence on reckonings. But when those who knew him remember him the memory inevitably will include laughter of an unusually warm and tender kind. The wise man, he knew, will take some juice out of this one life that is his gift.

> Mightily did he use the street. He found its multiple heart, its tastes, smells, alarms, formulas, flowers, garbage and convulsions. He brought them all to his tabletop. He crushed them to a writing paste. He himself became the pen.

In other words, while Johnson encouraged Brooks to find "standards for self-criticism" in Modernism, Hughes underscored the value of cultivating the ground upon which she stood. In Hughes, in both the poet and man, Brooks found standards for living: he was a model of witty candor and friendly unpretentiousness and, most importantly, a literary success. Hughes convinced Brooks that a Black poet need not travel outside the realm of his own experiences to create a poetic vision and write successful poetry. Unlike the Modernist Eliot who gathered much of his poetic material from the drawingrooms and salons of London, Hughes found his material in the coldwater flats and backstreets of Harlem. And Brooks, as is self-evident in nearly all her poetry, learned Hughes's example by heart.

II

The critical reception of *A Street in Bronzeville* contained, in embryo, many of the central issues in the scholarly debate that continues to engage Brooks's poetry. As in the following quotation from *The New York Times Book Review,* most reviewers were able to recognize Brooks's versatility and craft as a poet:

> If the idiom is colloquial, the language is universal. Brooks commands both the colloquial and more austere rhythms. She can vary manner and tone. In form, she demonstrates a wide range: quatrains, free verse, ballads, and sonnets—all appropriately controlled. The longer line suits her better than the short, but she is not verbose. In some of the sonnets, she uses an abruptness of address that is highly individual.

Yet, while noting her stylistic successes, not many critics fully understood her achievement in her first book. This difficulty was not only characteristic of critics who examined the formal aspects of prosody in her work, but also of critics who addressed themselves to the social realism in her poetry. Moreover, what Brooks gained at the hands of critics who focused on her technique, she lost to critics who chose to emphasize the exotic, Negro features of the book, as the following quote illustrates:

> *A Street in Bronzeville* ranges from blues ballads and funeral chants to verse in high humor. With both clarity and insight, it mirrors the impressions of life in an urban Negro community. The best poem is "The Sundays of Satin-Legs Smith," a poignant and hour-by-hour page out of a zoot-suiter's life. A subtle change of pace proves Brooks' facility in a variety of poetic forms.

The poems in *A Street in Bronzeville* actually served notice that Brooks had learned her craft well enough to combine successfully themes and styles from both the Harlem Renaissance and Modernist poetry. She even achieves some of her more interesting effects in the book by parodying the two traditions. She juggles the pessimism of Modernist poetry with the general optimism of the Harlem Renaissance. Three of her more notable achievements, "kitchenette building," "the mother," and "Sundays of Satin-Legs Smith," are parodic challenges to T. S. Eliot's dispirited anti-hero J. Alfred Prufrock. "[K]itchenette building" begins with Eliot-like emphasis on the dry infertility of modern life: "We are things of dry hours and the involuntary plan." The poem concludes with the humored optimism that "Since Number 5 is out of the bathroom / we think of lukewarm water, we hope to get in it." Another example is the alienated, seemingly disaffected narrator of "the mother" who laments the loss of her children but with the resurgent, hopeful voice that closes the poem: "Believe me, I loved you all." Finally a comparison could be made between the elaborate, self-assertive manner with which Satin-legs Smith dresses himself for his largely purposeless Sunday outing and the tentative efforts of his counterpart, J. Alfred Prufrock.

Because of the affinities *A Street in Bronzeville* shares with Modernist poetry and the Harlem Renaissance, Brooks was initiated not only into the vanguard of American literature, but also into what had been the inner circle of Harlem writers. Two of the Renaissance's leading poets, Claude McKay and Countee Cullen, addressed letters to her to mark the publication of *A Street in Bronzeville.* McKay welcomed her into a dubious but potentially rewarding career:

> I want to congratulate you again on the publication of 'A Street in Bronzeville' [sic] and welcome you among the band of hard working poets who do have something to say. It is a pretty rough road we have to travel, but I suppose much compensation is derived from the joy of being able to sing. Yours sincerely, Claude McKay. (October 10, 1945)

Cullen pinpointed her dual place in American literature:

> I have just finished reading, 'A Street in Bronzeville' [sic] and want you to know that I enjoyed it thoroughly. There can be no doubt that you are a poet, a good one, with every indication of becoming a better. I am glad to be able to say 'welcome' to you to that too small group of Negro poets, and to the larger group of American ones. No one can deny you your place there. (August 24, 1945)

The immediate interest in these letters is how both poets touch upon the nerve ends of the critical debate that surrounded *A Street in Bronzeville.* For McKay, while Brooks has "something to say," she can also "sing"; and for Cullen, she belongs not only to the minority of Negro poets, but also to the majority of American ones. Nonetheless, the critical question for both poets might well have been Brooks's relationship to the Harlem Renaissance. What had she absorbed of the important tenets of the Black aesthetic as expressed during the New Negro Movement? And how had she addressed herself, as a poet, to the literary movement's assertion of the folk and African culture, and its promotion of the arts as the agent to define racial integrity and to fuse racial harmony?

Aside from its historical importance, the Harlem Renaissance—as a literary movement—is rather difficult to define. There is, for example, no fixed or generally agreed upon date or event that serves as a point of origin for the movement. One might easily assign this date to the publication of McKay's poems *Harlem Shadows* (1922), Alaine Locke's anthology *The New Negro* (1925), or Cullen's anthology *Caroling Dusk* (1927). Likewise, the general description of the movement as a Harlem Renaissance is often questioned, since most of the major writers, with the notable exceptions of Hughes and Cullen, actually did not live and work in Harlem. Finally, many of the themes and literary conventions defy definition in terms of what was and what was not a New Negro poet. Nonetheless, there was a common ground of purpose and meaning in the works of the individual writers that permits a broad definition of the spirit and intent of the Harlem Renaissance. Indeed, the New Negro poets expressed a deep pride in being Black; they found reasons for this pride in ethnic identity and heritage; and they shared a common faith in the fine arts as a means of defining and reinforcing racial pride. But in the literal expression of these artistic impulses, the poets were either romantics or realists and, quite often within a single poem, both. The realistic impulse, as defined best in the poems of McKay's *Harlem Shadows*, was a sober reflection upon Blacks as second class citizens, segregated from the mainstream of American socioeconomic life, and largely unable to realize the wealth and opportunity that America promised. The romantic impulse, on the other hand, as defined in the poems of Sterling Brown's *Southern Road* (1932), often found these unrealized dreams in the collective strength and will of the folk masses. In comparing the poems in *A Street in Bronzeville* with various poems from the Renaissance, it becomes apparent that Brooks agrees, for the most part, with their prescriptions for the New Negro. Yet the unique contributions she brings to bear upon this tradition are extensive: 1) the biting ironies of intraracial discrimination, 2) the devaluation of love in heterosexual relationships between Blacks, and 3) the primacy of suffering in the lives of poor Black women.

III

The first clue that *A Street in Bronzeville* was, at the time of its publication, unlike any other book of poems by a Black American is its insistent emphasis on demystifying romantic love between Black men and women.

. . .

In *A Street in Bronzeville*, this romantic impulse for idealizing the Black woman runs headlong into the biting ironies of intraracial discrimination. In poem after poem in *A Street in Bronzeville*, within the well-observed caste lines of skin color, the consequences of dark pigmentation are revealed in drastic terms. One of the more popular of these poems, "The Ballad of Chocolate Mabbie," explores the tragic ordeal of Mabbie, the Black female heroine, who is victimized by her dark skin

and her "saucily bold" lover, Willie Boone:

> It was Mabbie without the
>   grammar school gates.
> And Mabbie was all of seven.
> And Mabbie was cut from a
>   chocolate bar.
> And Mabbie thought life was
>   heaven.

Mabbie's life, of course, is one of unrelieved monotony; her social contacts are limited to those who, like her, are dark skinned, rather than "lemon-hued" or light skinned. But as Brooks makes clear, the larger tragedy of Mabbie's life is the human potential that is squandered:

> Oh, warm is the waiting for joys,
>   my dears!
> And it cannot be too long.
> Oh, pity the little poor chocolate
>   lips
> That carry the bubble of song!

. . .

For Brooks, unlike the Renaissance poets, the victimization of poor Black women becomes not simply a minor chord but a predominant theme of *A Street in Bronzeville*. Few, if any, of her female characters are able to free themselves from the web of poverty and racism that threatens to strangle their lives. The Black heroine in "obituary for a living lady" was "decently wild / As a child," but as a victim of society's hypocritical, puritan standards, she

> fell in love with a man who didn't
>   know
> That even if she wouldn't let him
>   touch her breasts she
> was still worth his hours.

In another example of the complex life-choices confronting Brooks's women, the two sisters of "Sadie and

Maud" must choose between death-in-life and life-in-death. Maud, who went to college, becomes a "thin brown mouse," presumably resigned to spinsterhood, "living all alone / In this old house," while Sadie who "scraped life / With a fine-tooth comb" bears two illegitimate children and dies, leaving as a heritage for her children her "fine-tooth comb." What is noticeable in the lives of these Black women is a mutual identity that is inextricably linked with race and poverty.

. . .

Brooks's relationship with the Harlem Renaissance poets, as *A Street in Bronzeville* ably demonstrates, was hardly imitative. As one of the important links with the Black poetic tradition of the 1920s and 1930s, she enlarged the element of realism that was an important part of the Renaissance worldview. Although her poetry is often conditioned by the optimism that was also a legacy of the period, Brooks rejects outright their romantic prescriptions for the lives of Black women. And in this regard, she serves as a vital link with the Black Arts Movement of the 1960s that, while it witnessed the flowering of Black women as poets and social activists as well as the rise of Black feminist aesthetics in the 1970s, brought about a curious revival of romanticism in the Renaissance mode.

However, since the publication of *A Street in Bronzeville,* Brooks has not eschewed the traditional roles and values of Black women in American society; on the contrary, in her subsequent works, *Annie Allen* (1949), *The Bean Eaters* (1960), and *In the Mecca* (1968), she has been remarkably consistent in identifying the root cause of intraracial problems with the Black community as white racism and its pervasive socioeconomic effects. Furthermore, as one of the chief voices of the Black Arts Movement, she has developed a social vision, in such works as *Riot* (1969), *Family Pictures* (1970), and *Beckonings* (1975), that describes Black women and men as equally integral parts of the struggle for social and economic justice.

Questions

1. Consider the voice in Brooks's poetry. Is a consistent, recognizable voice present throughout, or does the voice of the speaker vary from poem to poem?

2. Study Brooks's comments about her own work. Do you believe her assessments and explanations are always accurate, or do you question her conclusions at times?

3. Do Brooks's poems apply only to the lives of African-Americans, or do they also have relevance to the lives of other Americans—or to the lives of people in other countries? That is, to what degree are her themes universal, and to what degree are they race- or culture-specific?

4. Gwendolyn Brooks does not focus on conventional poetic subjects such as love, nature, or death. Could you argue that these subjects are nevertheless present in many of her poems?

5. Brooks is essentially a formalist poet, relying on traditional closed forms that have regular rhyme, meter, and stanzaic divisions—for example, the ballad and the sonnet. Are such traditional forms appropriate for her subject matter?

6. What patterns of imagery and figurative language recur in Brooks's poems?

7. Consider the effects of Brooks's use of **caesura** in her sonnets. What do these stops in mid-line contribute to the poems?

8. What is the significance of the religious references in Brooks's poetry—for example, the one at the end of "The *Chicago Defender* Sends a Man to Little Rock" (p. 1077)?

9. What is Brooks's motive in using regular—at times singsong—meter and rhyme in poems with serious subjects, such as "The Ballad of Rudolph Reed" (p. 1081) and "Sadie and Maud" (p. 799)? Does the poem's sound undercut or enhance its meaning in such cases?

10. What other poets might you compare with Brooks? Why are they comparable?

11. To what degree are Brooks's poems concerned with "women's issues"—or even with feminism? Are such themes central to her poetry, merely incidental, or nonexistent?

12. Many of Brooks's most recent poems focus explicitly on social issues. For example, "Jane Addams," an unpublished 1989 poem, is about the woman who founded the first settlement house in the United States, and a 1987 poem, "Thinking of Elizabeth Steinberg," focuses on a six-year-old victim of child abuse. How do the poems in this casebook address issues of social justice?

Adam Goren
Professor West
Literature 201
8 April 1996

Racial Consciousness in
"The Ballad of Rudolph Reed"

According to Gwendolyn Brooks, she did not come to terms with the implications of being a black writer in America until 1967. At that time she was forced to confront the fact that although she was accepted by the white world of letters, she was regarded as irrelevant by militant blacks (Brooks, <u>Report</u> 1088). Certainly much in Brooks's poetry shows she is a poet who values the themes and forms of the traditional Western literary canon. She writes poetry that reflects universal human concerns; she writes in traditional poetic forms, such as the sonnet and the ballad; and she uses white writers as models (Baker 1090). Even so, the body of Brooks's work--including many poems written before 1967--illustrates that race has always been a major concern (Baker 1090). Her 1960 poem "The Ballad of Rudolph Reed," typical of her early poetry, illustrates how Brooks uses a conventional poetic form--the ballad--to treat an unconventional poetic subject: racial intolerance.

In "The Ballad of Rudolph Reed," Gwendolyn Brooks tells of an African-American family's encounter with racial violence when they move into a white neighborhood. The strength of Rudolph Reed, the protagonist of the poem, and his family is clearly evoked with the use of the word <u>oaken</u> in the first stanza of the poem:

> Rudolph Reed was oaken.
> His wife was oaken too.
> And his two good girls and his good little man
> Oakened as they grew. (1–4)

Reed and his family move to the white neighborhood to escape the deplorable conditions of their former home. According to Reed, he is hungry for the peace and security that most white people take for granted. All he wants is a house in which he "May never hear the roaches / Falling like fat rain" and "Where never wife and children need / Go blinking through the gloom" (11–14). In other words, Reed, like other Americans, is taking the United States government at its word and trying to claim a piece of the American dream for himself and his family.

The traditional meter and the simple, direct language of the ballad are well suited to communicating Reed's hope and determination. Brooks's use of traditional ballad rhyme scheme and meter suggests a link between Reed's quest and the subjects of other romantic ballads. For example, like Robin Hood, a subject of many English ballads, Reed confronts political oppression and fights for the rights of the common person (Mootry 1109). This evocation of an idealized romantic past stands in direct contrast, however, to the contemporary racial brutality that exists outside Reed's new house. "[T]oo joyous to notice it" (36), the family is oblivious to the racism that will destroy their short-lived happiness.

Soon after the family moves into its new house, neighbors begin throwing rocks through their windows. Reed withstands these assaults for three nights until his child is injured by a piece of broken glass. Grabbing a gun and a butcher knife, he runs out to defend his house:

> He ran like a mad thing into the night.
> And the words in his mouth were stinking.
> By the time he had hurt his first white man
> He was no longer thinking.
> By the time he had hurt his fourth white man
> Rudolph Reed was dead. (53–58)

One of the ironies of the poem emerges from the fact that Reed, who is repeatedly described as <u>oaken</u>, is unable to endure the rocks and insults of his white neighbors. Throughout the poem the word <u>oaken</u> is repeated like a ballad refrain. Reed and his wife are <u>oaken</u>; his children <u>oaken</u> as they grow; and Reed is <u>oakener</u> than others. Traditionally, the oak tree is known for its strength. The oak, however, is unable to bend and, as a result, it can be uprooted in a storm. The duality of this image embodies the dilemma facing African-Americans in 1960. On the one hand, they had to be strong to survive the kind of racial brutality described in the poem. On the other hand, being too strong made it likely that they, like Reed, would confront the white power structure and be broken by it. "The Ballad of Rudolph Reed" offers no way out of this dilemma; indeed, it suggests that as long as the racial situation in the United States remains polarized, men and women, like Reed and his wife, will be oppressed and even killed.

The ballad structure that so easily communicates the hopeful mood of the first part of the poem is also able to convey the brutality of the final part of the poem. The quaintness of the ballad's old-fashioned language--"nary a curse"(30)--and inverted sentence structure--"Then up did rise our Rudolph Reed"(49)--by evoking an earlier, more innocent time, emphasizes the fundamental irony of Reed's predicament: He is attacked simply for wanting to improve his life. Obviously, the American Dream, as well as all it implies, was not meant to include African-Americans. Running like "a mad thing into the night" (53), Reed seems like a character in a B movie or a nightmare. In this case, however, the situation as well as the brutality is all too real: "His neighbors gathered and kicked his corpse. / 'Nigger--' his neighbors said" (59–60).

By the last stanza, violence, grief, and resignation have replaced the hope and determination expressed at the beginning of the poem. All that remains of Reed and his dream is the image of a mother comforting her wounded child:

> Small Mabel whimpered all night long
> For calling herself the cause.
> Her oak-eyed mother did no thing
> But change her bloody gauze. (61–64)

Despite its bitterness, however, the poem does offer some comfort. Reed's wife remains "oak-eyed" (63)--that is, strong--and both she and her daughter survive the attack. The implication is that they will continue the struggle and possibly triumph over those who killed Reed.

"The Ballad of Rudolph Reed" was written in 1960, well before Brooks says she understood the implications of being a black writer in America. Despite Brooks's assertions to the contrary, the themes she explores in this poem are similar to those she explores in many poems written after 1967 (Smith 1099). Brooks's impatience with the white power structure and her anger about the oppression of African-Americans--ideas apparent in "Medgar Evers" and "A Boy Died in My Alley"--clearly dominate "The Ballad of Rudolph Reed." Using the ballad to express her ideas, Brooks combines her mastery of traditional forms with her need to create a poetry that is relevant to African-Americans. Houston A. Baker, Jr., sums up her achievement when he says that throughout her career Brooks has created works "that equal the best in the black and white American literary traditions" (Baker 1096).

Goren 6

Works Cited

Baker, Houston A., Jr. "The Achievement of Gwendolyn Brooks." Ed. Kirszner and Mandell. 1090–96.

Brooks, Gwendolyn. From <u>Report from Part One.</u> Ed. Kirszner and Mandell. 1088–90.

---. "The Ballad of Rudolph Reed." Ed. Kirszner and Mandell. 1081–82.

Kirszner, Laurie G., and Stephen R. Mandell, eds. <u>Literature: Reading, Reacting, Writing.</u> 3rd. ed. Fort Worth: Harcourt, 1997.

Mootry, Maria K. " 'Chocolate Mabbie' and 'Pearl May Lee': Gwendolyn Brooks and the Ballad Tradition." Ed. Kirszner and Mandell. 1108–14.

Smith, Gary. "Gwendolyn Brooks's 'Children of the Poor,' Metaphysical Poetry and the Inconditions of Love." Ed. Kirszner and Mandell. 1099–1107.

Drama

CHAPTER 20

Understanding Drama

Dramatic Literature

The distinctive appearance of a script, with its stage directions, character parts, and divisions into acts and scenes, identifies **drama** as a unique form of literature. A play is written to be performed in front of an audience by actors who take on the roles of the characters and who present the story through dialogue and action. (An exception is **closet drama,** which is meant to be read, not performed.) Indeed, the term *theater* comes from the Greek word *theasthai,* which means "to view" or "to see." Thus, drama is different from novels and short stories, which are meant to be read.

Dramatic works differ from other prose works in a number of significant ways. Unlike novels and short stories, plays do not usually have narrators to tell the audience what a character is thinking or what happened in the past; the audience knows only what the characters reveal. Drama develops primarily by means of **dialogue,** the lines spoken by the characters. The plot and the action of drama unfold on the stage as the characters interact. In addition, playwrights employ various techniques to compensate for the absence of a narrator. For example, playwrights use **monologues**—extended speeches by one character. (A monologue in which a character expresses private thoughts while alone on the stage is called a **soliloquy.**) Playwrights can also use **asides**—brief comments by an actor who addresses the audience but is assumed not to be heard by the other characters on the stage—to reveal the thoughts of the speaker. Like the observations of a narrator, these dramatic techniques give the audience insight into a character's motives and attitudes. In addition, makeup, costumes, scenery, and lighting enhance a dramatic performance, as do actors' and directors' interpretations of dialogue and stage directions.

The Origins of the Modern Theater

THE ANCIENT GREEK THEATER

The dramatic presentations of ancient Greece developed out of religious rites performed to honor gods or to mark the coming of spring. Playwrights such as Aeschylus (525–456 B.C.), Sophocles (496–406 B.C.), and Euripides (480?–406 B.C.) composed plays to be performed and judged at competitions held during the yearly Dionysian festivals. Works to be produced were chosen by a selection board and evaluated by a panel of judges. To compete in the contest, authors had to submit three tragedies, which could either be unrelated thematically or based on a common theme, and one comedy. Unfortunately, relatively few of these ancient Greek plays survive today.

The open-air semicircular ancient Greek theater, built into the side of a hill, looked much like a primitive version of a modern sports stadium. Some Greek theaters, such as the Athenian theater, could seat almost seventeen thousand spectators. Sitting in tiered seats, the audience would look down on the *orchestra,* or "dancing place," occupied by the **chorus**— originally a group of men (led by an individual called the *choragos*) who danced and chanted and later a group of onlookers who commented on

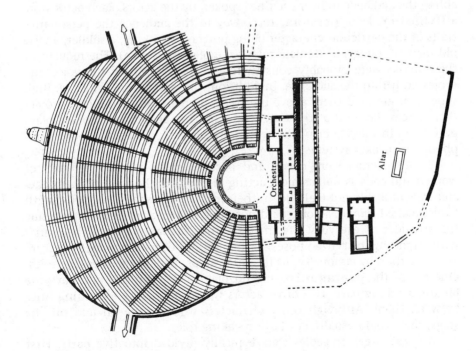

The Theater of Dionysus at Athens. Redrawn from a drawing by R. C. Flickinger, *The Greek Theater and Its Drama* (1918).

the drama. Raised a few steps above the orchestra was a platform on which the actors performed, behind which was a *skene,* or building, that originally served as a resting place or dressing room. (The modern term *scene* is derived from the Greek skene.) Behind the skene was a line of pillars called a *colonnade,* which was covered by a roof. Actors used the skene for entrances and exits; beginning with the plays of Sophocles, painted backdrops were hung there. These backdrops, however, were most likely more decorative than realistic. Historians believe that realistic props and scenery were probably absent from the ancient Greek theater. Instead, the setting was suggested by the play's dialogue, so the audience had to imagine the specific physical details of a scene.

Two mechanical devices were used: One, a rolling cart or platform, was sometimes employed to introduce action that had occurred offstage. For example, actors frozen in position could be rolled onto the roof of the skene to illustrate an event such as the killing of Oedipus's father, which occurred before the play began. Another mechanical device, a small crane, was used to show gods ascending to or descending from heaven. Such devices enabled playwrights to dramatize many of the myths that were celebrated at the Dionysian festivals.

The ancient Greek theater was designed to enhance acoustics. The flat stone wall of the skene reflected the sound from the orchestra and the stage, and the curved shape of the amphitheater captured the sound, enabling the audience to hear the lines spoken by the actors. Each actor wore a stylized mask, or **persona,** to convey to the audience the personality traits of the particular character being portrayed—a king, a soldier, a wise old man, a young girl (female roles were played by men). The mouths of these masks were probably constructed so they amplified the voice and projected it into the audience. In addition, the actors wore *kothernoi,* high shoes that elevated them above the stage, perhaps also helping to project their voices. Because of the excellent acoustics, audiences who see plays performed in these ancient theaters today can hear clearly without microphones or speaker systems.

Because actors wore masks and because males played the parts of women and gods as well as men, acting methods in the ancient Greek theater were probably not realistic. In their masks, high shoes, and full-length tunics (called *chiton*), actors could not hope to appear natural or to mimic the attitudes of everyday life. Instead, they probably recited their lines while standing in stylized poses, with emotions conveyed more by gesture and tone than by action. Typically, three actors had all the speaking roles. One actor—the **protagonist**—would play the central role and have the largest speaking part. Two other actors would divide the remaining lines between them. Although other characters would come on and off the stage, they would usually not have speaking roles.

Ancient Greek tragedies were typically divided into five parts. First came the *prologos,* in which an actor gave the background or explanations that the audience needed to follow the rest of the drama. Then came the *párodos,* in which the chorus entered and commented on the events presented in the prologue. Following this were several *episodia,* or episodes, in which characters spoke to one another on the stage and developed the central conflict of the play. Alternating with episodes were *stasimon* (choral odes), in which the chorus commented on the exchanges that had taken place during the preceding episode. Frequently the choral odes were divided into *strophes,* or stanzas, that were recited or sung as the chorus moved across the orchestra in one direction and *antistrophes* that were recited as it moved in the opposite direction. (Interestingly, the chorus stood between the audience and the actors, often functioning as an additional audience, expressing the political, social, and moral views of the community.) Finally came the *exodos,* the last scene of the play, during which the conflict was resolved and the actors left the stage.

Using music, dance, and verse—as well as a variety of architectural and technical innovations—the ancient Greek theater was able to convey traditional themes of tragedy. Thus, the theater powerfully expressed ideas that were central to the religious festivals in which they first appeared: the reverence for the cycles of life and death, the unavoidable dictates of the gods, and the inscrutable workings of fate.

THE ELIZABETHAN THEATER

The Elizabethan theater, influenced by the classical traditions of Roman and Greek dramatists, traces its roots back to local religious pageants performed at medieval festivals during the twelfth and thirteenth centuries. The town guilds, organizations of craftsmen who worked in the same profession, reenacted Old and New Testament stories: the fall of man, Noah and the flood, David and Goliath, and the crucifixion of Christ, for example. Church fathers encouraged these plays because they brought the Bible to a largely illiterate audience. Sometimes these spectacles, called **mystery plays,** were presented in the market square or on the church steps, and at other times actors appeared on movable stages or wagons called *pageants,* which could be wheeled to a given location. (Some of these wagons were quite elaborate, with trapdoors and pulleys, and an upper tier that simulated heaven.) As mystery plays became more popular, they were performed in series over several days, presenting an entire cycle of a holiday—the death and resurrection of Christ during Easter, for example.

Related to mystery plays are **morality plays,** which developed in the fourteenth and fifteenth centuries. Unlike mystery plays, which depict scenes from the Bible, morality plays allegorize the Christian way of life. Typically, characters representing various virtues and vices struggle or debate over the soul of man. *Everyman* (1500), the best known of these plays, dramatizes the good and bad qualities of Everyman and shows his struggle to determine what is of value to him as he journeys toward death.

By the middle of the sixteenth century, mystery and morality plays had lost ground to a new secular drama. One reason for this decline was that mystery and morality plays were associated with Catholicism and consequently discouraged by the Protestant clergy. In addition, newly discovered plays of ancient Greece and Rome introduced a dramatic tradition that supplanted the traditions of religious drama. English plays that followed the classic model were sensational and bombastic, often dealing with murder, revenge, and blood retribution. Appealing to privileged classes and commoners alike, these plays were extremely popular. (One source estimates that between 20,000 and 25,000 people attended the London theaters each week.) Companies of professional actors performed works such as Christopher Marlowe's *Tamburlaine* and Thomas Kyd's *The Spanish Tragedy* in tavern courtyards and then eventually in theaters. According to scholars, the structure of the Elizabethan theater evolved from these courtyards.

The Globe Theater (a corner of which was unearthed in 1989), where Shakespeare's plays were performed, consisted of a large main stage that extended out into the open-air *yard* where the *groundlings*, or common people, stood. Spectators who paid more sat on small stools in two or three levels of galleries that extended in front of and around the stage. (The theater could probably seat almost two thousand people at a performance.) Most of the play's action occurred on the stage, which had no curtain and could be seen from three sides. Beneath the stage was a space called the *hell*, which could be reached when the floorboards were removed. This space enabled actors to "disappear" or descend into a hole or grave when the play called for such action. Above the stage was a roof called the *heavens*, which protected the actors from the weather and contained ropes and pulleys used to lower props or to create special effects.

At the rear of the stage was a narrow alcove covered by a curtain that could be open or closed. This curtain, often painted, functioned as a decorative rather than a realistic backdrop. The main function of this alcove was to enable actors to hide when the script called for them to do so. Some Elizabethan theaters contained a rear stage instead of an alcove. Because the rear stage was concealed by a curtain, props could be arranged on it ahead of time. When the action on the rear stage was finished, the curtain would be drawn and the action would continue on the front stage.

On either side of the rear stage was a door through which the actors could enter and exit the front stage. Above the rear stage was an upper, curtained stage called the *chamber,* which functioned as a balcony or as any other setting located above the action taking place on the stage below. On either side of the chamber were casement windows, which actors could use when a play called for a conversation with someone leaning out a window or standing on a balcony. Above the chamber was the *music gallery,* a balcony that housed the musicians who provided musical interludes throughout the play (and doubled as a stage if the play required it). The *huts,* windows located above the music gallery, could be used by characters playing lookouts or sentries. Because of the many acting sites, more than one action could take place simultaneously. For example, lookouts could stand in the towers of Hamlet's castle while Hamlet and Horatio walked the walls below.

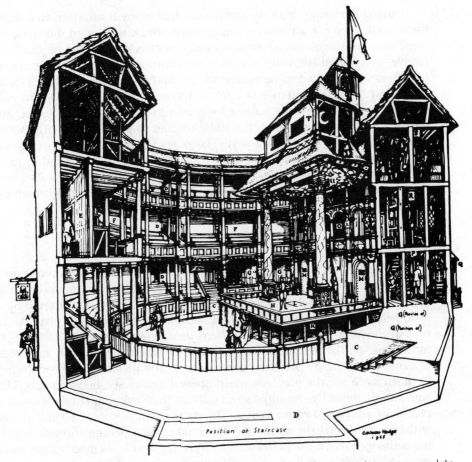

The Globe Playhouse,

1599-1613

A CONJECTURAL

RECONSTRUCTION

KEY

AA Main entrance
B   The Yard
CC Entrances to lowest gallery
D   Entrances to staircase and upper
    galleries
E   Corridor serving the different sections
    of the middle gallery
F   Middle gallery ('Twopenny Rooms')
G   'Gentlemen's Rooms' or 'Lords' Rooms'
H   The stage

J   The hanging being put up round the
    stage
K   The 'Hell' under the stage
L   The stage trap, leading down to the
    Hell
MM Stage doors
N   Curtained 'place behind the stage'
O   Gallery above the stage, used as re-
    quired sometimes by musicians, some-
    times by spectators, and often as part
    of the play
P   Back-stage area (the tiring-house)
Q   Tiring-house door
R   Dressing-rooms
S   Wardrobe and storage
T   The hut housing the machine for
    lowering enthroned gods, etc., to the
    stage
U   The 'Heavens'
W   Hoisting the playhouse flag

The Globe Playhouse, 1599–1613; A Conjectural Reconstruction. From
C. Walter Hodges, *The Global Restored.*

During Shakespeare's time the theater had many limitations that must have challenged the audience's imagination. Because women did not perform on the stage, young boys—usually between the ages of ten and twelve—played all the women's parts. In addition, there was no artificial lighting, so plays had to be performed in daylight. Rain, wind, or clouds could disrupt a performance or ruin an image—such as "the morn in russet mantle clad"—that the audience was asked to imagine. Finally, because few sets and props were used, the audience had to visualize the high walls of a castle or the trees of a forest. The plays themselves were performed without intermission, except for musical interludes that occurred at various points. Thus, the experience of seeing one of Shakespeare's plays staged in the Elizabethan theater was different from seeing it presented today in a modern theater.

THE MODERN THEATER

Unlike the theaters of ancient Greece and Elizabethan England, seventeenth- and eighteenth-century theaters—such as the Palais Royal, where the great French playwright Molière presented many of his plays—were covered by a roof, beautifully decorated, and illuminated by candles so that plays could be performed at night. The theater remained brightly lit even during performances, partly because there was no easy way to extinguish hundreds of candles and partly because people went to the theater to see each other as much as to see the play. A curtain opened and closed between acts. The audience of about five hundred spectators sat in a long room and viewed the play on a **picture-frame stage.** This type of stage contained the action within a **proscenium arch** that surrounded the opening through which the audience viewed the performance. Thus, the action seemed to take place in an adjoining room with one of its walls cut away. Painted scenery and elaborate costumes were commonplace, and for the first time women performed female roles. Because the theaters were small, audiences were relatively close to the stage, so actors could use subtle movements and facial expressions to enhance their performances.

Many of the first innovations in the theater were quite basic. For example, the first stage lighting was produced by candles lining the front of the stage. This method of lighting was not only ineffective—actors were lit from below and had to step forward to be fully illuminated—but also dangerous. Costumes and even entire theaters could and did accidentally catch fire. Later, covered lanterns with reflectors provided more light. In the nineteenth century a device that used an oxyhydrogen flame directed on a cylinder of lime created extremely bright illumination that could, with the aid of a lens, be concentrated into a spotlight. (It is from this method of stage lighting that we get the expression *to be in the limelight.*) Eventually, in the twentieth century, electric lights provided a dependable and safe way of lighting the stage. Electric spotlights, footlights, and ceiling light bars made the actors clearly visible and enabled playwrights to create special effects. In Arthur Miller's *Death of a Salesman* (p. 1458), for example, lighting focuses attention on action in certain areas of the stage while leaving other areas in complete darkness.

Along with electric lighting came other innovations, such as electronic amplification. Microphones made it possible for actors to speak conversationally and to avoid using unnaturally loud "stage diction" to project their voices to the rear of the theater. Microphones placed at various points around the stage enabled actors and actresses to interact naturally and to deliver their lines audibly even without facing the audience. More recently, small wireless microphones eliminated the unwieldy wires and the "dead spaces" left between upright or hanging microphones, allowing characters to move freely around the stage.

The true revolutions in staging came with the advent of **realism** in the middle of the nineteenth century. Until this time scenery was painted on canvas backdrops that trembled visibly, especially when they were intersected by doors through which actors and actresses entered. With realism came settings that were accurate down to the smallest detail. (Improved lighting, which revealed the inadequacies of painted backdrops, also contributed to the introduction of realistic stage settings.) Backdrops were replaced by the **box set,** three flat panels arranged to form connected walls, with the fourth wall removed so the audience had the illusion of looking into a room. The room itself was decorated with real furniture, plants, and pictures on the walls; the door of one room might connect to another completely furnished room, or a window might open to a garden filled with realistic foliage. In addition, new methods of changing scenery were employed. Elevator stages, hydraulic lifts, and moving platforms enabled directors to make complicated changes in scenery out of the audience's view.

During the late nineteenth and early twentieth centuries, however, some playwrights reacted against what they saw as the excesses of realism. They introduced **surrealistic** stage settings, in which color and scenery were designed to mirror the uncontrolled images of dreams, and **expressionistic** stage settings, in which costumes and scenery were exaggerated and distorted to reflect the workings of a troubled, even unbalanced mind. In addition, playwrights used lighting to create areas of light, shadow, and color that reinforced the themes of the play or reflected the emotions of the protagonist. In *The Emperor Jones,* for example, Eugene O'Neill used a series of expressionistic scenes to show the mental state of the terrified protagonist.

Sets in contemporary plays run the gamut from realistic to fantastic, from a detailed recreation of a room in a production of Tennessee Williams's *The Glass Menagerie* (p. 1898) to a stark, dreamlike set for Edward Albee's *The Sandbox* (p. 1695). Motorized devices, such as revolving turntables, and *wagons*—scenery mounted on wheels—make possible rapid changes of scenery. The Broadway musical *Les Miserables*, for example, requires scores of elaborate sets—Parisian slums, barricades, walled gardens— to be shifted as the audience watches. A gigantic barricade constructed on stage at one point in the play is later rotated to show the carnage that has taken place on both sides of a battle. Light, sound, and smoke are used to heighten the impact of the scene.

Today, as dramatists attempt to break down the barriers that separate audiences from the action they are viewing, plays are not limited to the picture-frame stage; in fact, they are performed on many different kinds of stages. Some plays, for example, take place on a **thrust stage,** which has an area that projects out into the audience. Others are performed on an **arena stage,** with the audience surrounding the actors. This kind of performance is often called **theater in the round.** In addition, experiments have been done with *environmental staging,* in which the stage surrounds the audience or several stages are situated at various locations throughout the audience. Plays may also be performed outdoors in settings ranging from parks to city streets. Some playwrights even try to blur the line that divides the audience from the stage by having actors move through or sit in the audience—or even by eliminating the stage entirely. For example, *Tony 'n Tina's Wedding,* a 1988 "participatory drama" created by the theater group Artificial Intelligence, takes place not in a theater but at a church where a wedding is performed and then at a catering hall where the wedding reception is held. Throughout the play the members of the audience function as guests, joining in the wedding celebration and mingling with the actors, who improvise freely. More recent examples of such "interactive" drama include *Grandma Sylvia's Funeral* and *Off the Wall,* in which audiences "attend" an art auction. Today, no single architectural

Thrust-Stage Theater. With seats on three sides of the stage area, the thrust stage and its background can assume many forms other than the conventional living-room interior in the illustration. Entrances can be made from the aisles, from the sides, through the stage floor, and from the back.

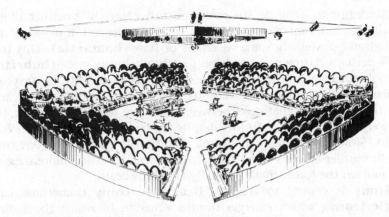

Arena Theater. The audience surrounds the stage area, which may or may not be raised. Use of scenery is limited—perhaps to a single piece of scenery standing alone in the middle of the stage.

form defines the theater. Perhaps the most that can be said is that the modern stage is a flexible space suited to the many varieties of contemporary theatrical production.

Kinds of Drama

TRAGEDY

In his *Poetics,* Aristotle (384–322 B.C.) sums up ancient Greek thinking about drama when he writes that a **tragedy** is a drama treating a serious subject and involving persons of significance. According to Aristotle, when the members of an audience see a tragedy, they should feel both pity (and thus closeness to the protagonist) and fear (and thus revulsion) because they recognize in themselves the potential for similar reactions. The purging of these emotions that the audience experiences as they see the dramatic action unfold before them is called **catharsis.** For this catharsis to occur, the protagonist of a tragedy must be worthy of the audience's attention and sympathy. Because of his or her exalted position, the fall of a tragic protagonist is greater than that of an average person; therefore, it arouses more pity and fear in the audience. Often the entire society suffers as a result of the actions of the protagonist. Before the action of Sophocles' *Oedipus the King* (p. 1590), for example, Oedipus has freed Thebes from the deadly grasp of the Sphinx by answering her riddle and, as a result, he has been welcomed as king. But because of his sins, Oedipus is an affront to the gods and brings famine and pestilence to the city. When it finally comes, his fall is sudden and absolute.

According to Aristotle, the protagonist of a tragedy is neither all good nor all evil, but a mixture of the two. He is like the rest of us—only more exalted and possessing some weakness or flaw **(hamartia).** This tragic flaw—perhaps narrowness of vision or overwhelming pride **(hubris)**—is typically the element that creates the conditions for tragedy. Shakespeare's Romeo and Juliet, for example, are so much in love they think they can ignore the blood feud that rages between their two families. However, their naive efforts to sustain their love despite the feud lead them to their tragic deaths. Similarly, Richard III's blind ambition to gain the throne causes him to murder all those who stand in his way. His unscrupulousness sets into motion the forces that eventually cause his death.

Irony is central to tragedy. **Dramatic irony** (sometimes called **tragic irony**), which emerges from a situation in which the audience knows more about the dramatic situation than a character does. As a result, the character's words and actions may be consistent with what he or she expects but at odds with what the audience knows will happen. Thus, a character may say or do something that causes the audience to infer a meaning beyond what the character intends or realizes. The dramatic irony is clear, for example, when Oedipus announces that whoever has disobeyed the dictates of the gods will be exiled. The audience knows, although Oedipus does not, that he has just condemned himself. **Cosmic irony,** sometimes called **irony of fate,** occurs when God, fate, or some larger, uncontrollable force seems to be intentionally deceiving characters into believing they can escape their fate. Too late, they realize that trying to avoid their destiny is futile. Years before Oedipus was born, for example, the oracle of Apollo foretold that Oedipus would kill his father and become his mother's husband. Naturally, his parents attempted to thwart the prophesy, but ironically, their actions ensured that the prophesy would be fulfilled.

At some point in a tragedy—usually after the climax—the protagonist recognizes the reasons for his or her downfall. It is this recognition (and the accompanying acceptance) that elevates tragic protagonists to grandeur and gives their suffering meaning. Without this recognition there would be no tragedy, just **pathos**—suffering that exists simply to satisfy the sentimental or morbid sensibilities of the audience. In spite of the death of the protagonist, then, tragedy enables the audience to see the nobility of the character and thus to experience a sense of elation. In Shakespeare's King Lear, for example, a king at the height of his powers decides to divide his kingdom among his daughters. Too late he realizes that without his power, he is just a bothersome old man to his ambitious children. Only after going mad does he understand the vanity of his former existence; he dies a humbled but enlightened man.

According to Aristotle, a tragedy achieves the illusion of reality only when it has *unity of action*—that is, when the play contains only those actions that lead to its tragic outcome. Later critics concluded that a subplot destroys this unity and that tragic and comic elements should not be mixed. To the concept of unity of action, these later critics added two other requirements: *unity of place*—that the play have a single setting—and *unity of time*—that the events depicted by the play take no longer than the actual duration of the play (or, at most, a single day).

The three unities have had a long and rather uneven history. In some of his plays—*The Tempest* and *The Comedy of Errors*, for example—Shakespeare observed the unities. Shakespeare, however, had no compunctions about writing plays with subplots and frequent changes of location. He also wrote **tragicomedies,** such as *The Merchant of Venice*, that have a serious theme appropriate for tragedy but end happily, usually because of a sudden turn of events. During the eighteenth century, with its emphasis on classic form, the unities were adhered to quite strictly, but with the onset of romanticism and its emphasis on the natural in the late eighteenth and early nineteenth centuries, interest in the unities of place and time waned. Even though some modern dramatists occasionally observe the unities—*The Sandbox*, for instance, has a single setting and takes place during a period of time that corresponds to the length of the play—few adhere to them strictly.

Ideas about appropriate subjects for tragedy have also changed. For Aristotle, the protagonist of a tragedy had to be exceptional—a king, for example. The protagonists of Greek tragedies were usually historical or mythical figures. Shakespeare often used kings and princes as protagonists—Richard II and Hamlet, for example—but he also used people of lesser rank, as in *Romeo and Juliet*. In our times interest in the lives of monarchs has been overshadowed by involvement in the lives of ordinary people. Modern tragedies—*Death of a Salesman*, for example—are more likely to focus on a traveling salesman than on a king.

With the rise of the middle class in the nineteenth century, ideas about the nature of tragedy changed. Responding to the age's desire for sentimentality, playwrights produced **melodramas,** sensational plays that appealed mainly to the emotions. Melodramas contain many of the elements of tragedy but end happily and often rely on conventional plots and stock characters. Because the protagonists in melodramas—often totally virtuous heroines suffering at the hands of impossibly wicked villains—helplessly endure their tribulations without ever gaining insight or enlightenment, they never achieve tragic status. As a result, they remain cardboard cutouts who exist only to exploit the emotions of the audience. Melodrama survives today in many films and in television soap operas.

Realism, which arose in the late nineteenth century as a response to the artificiality of melodrama, developed serious (and sometimes tragic) themes and believable characters in the context of everyday contemporary life. Writers of realistic drama used their plays to educate their audiences about the problems of the society in which they lived. For this reason, realistic drama focuses on the commonplace and eliminates the unlikely coincidences and excessive sentimentality of melodrama. Dramatists like Henrik Ibsen scrutinize the lives of ordinary people, not larger-than-life characters. After great suffering, these characters rise above the limitations of their mediocre lives and exhibit courage or emotional strength. The insight they gain often focuses attention on a social problem—the restrictive social conventions that define the behavior of women in nineteenth-century marriages, for example. Realistic drama also features settings and props similar to those used in people's daily lives and includes dialogue that reflects the way people actually speak.

Developing alongside realism was another literary movement called **naturalism.** Like realism, naturalism rejected the unrealistic plots and sentimentality of melodrama, but unlike realism, naturalism sought to explore the depths of the human condition. Influenced by Charles Darwin's ideas about evolution and natural selection and Karl Marx's ideas about economic forces that shape people's lives, naturalism is a pessimistic philosophy that presents a world which at worst is hostile and at best is indifferent to human concerns. It pictures human beings as higher-order animals who are driven by basic instincts—especially hunger, fear, and sexuality—and are subject to economic, social, and biological forces beyond their understanding or control. It is, therefore, well suited to tragic themes.

The nineteenth-century French writer Émile Zola did much to develop the theory of naturalism, and later so did the American writers Stephen Crane, Frank Norris, and Theodore Dreiser. Naturalism also finds its way into the work of contemporary dramatists, such as Arthur Miller. Unlike other tragic protagonists, the protagonists of naturalist works are crushed not by the gods or by fate, but by poverty, animal drives, or social class. Willy Loman in *Death of a Salesman,* for example, is subject to the economic forces of a society that does not value its workers and discards those it no longer finds useful.

COMEDY

A **comedy** is a dramatic work that treats themes and characters with humor and typically has a happy ending. Whereas tragedy focuses on the hidden dimensions of the tragic hero's character, comedy concentrates on the public persona, the protagonist as a social being. Tragic figures are typically seen in isolation, questioning the meaning of their lives and trying to comprehend their suffering. Hamlet—draped in sable, longing for death, and self-consciously contemplating his duty—illustrates the isolation of the tragic hero.

Unlike tragic heroes, comic figures are seen in the public arena, where people intentionally assume the masks of pretension and self-importance. The purpose of comedy is to strip away these masks and expose human beings for what they are. Whereas tragedy reveals the nobility of the human condition, comedy demonstrates its inherent folly, portraying human beings as selfish, hypocritical, vain, weak, irrational, and capable of self-delusion. Thus, the basic function of comedy is critical—to tell people that things are not what they seem and that appearances are not necessarily reality. In the comic world nothing is solid or predictable, and accidents and coincidences are more important to the plot than reason. Many of Shakespeare's comedies, for example, depend on exchanged or confused identities. The wordplay and verbal nonsense of comedy adds to this general confusion.

Comedies typically rely on certain familiar plot devices. Many comedies begin with a startling or unusual situation that attracts the audience's attention. In Shakespeare's *A Midsummer Night's Dream,* for example, Theseus, the Duke of Athens, rules that Hermia will either marry the man her father has chosen for her or be put to death. Such an event could lead to tragedy if comedy did not intervene to save the day.

Comedy often depends on obstacles and hindrances to further its plot: The more difficult the problems the lovers face, the more satisfying their eventual triumph will be. For this reason, the plot of a comedy is usually more complex than the plot of a tragedy. Compare the rather straightforward plot of *Hamlet* (p. 1355)—a prince ordered to avenge his murdered father's death is driven mad with indecision and, after finally acting decisively, is killed himself—with the mix-ups, mistaken identities, and general confusion of *Much Ado about Nothing* (p. 1633).

Finally, comedies have happy endings. Whereas tragedy ends with death, comedy ends by affirming life. Eventually the confusion and misunderstandings reach a point where some resolution must be achieved: The difficulties of the lovers are overcome, the villains are banished, and the lovers marry—or at least express their intention to do so. In this way the lovers establish their connection with the rest of society, and its values are affirmed.

The first comedies, written in Greece in the fifth century B.C., heavily satirized the religious and social issues of the day. In the fourth and third centuries B.C., this **Old Comedy** gave way to **New Comedy,** a comedy of romance with stock characters—lovers and untrustworthy servants, for example—and conventional settings. Lacking the bitter satire and bawdiness of Old Comedy, New Comedy depends on outrageous plots, mistaken identities, young lovers, interfering parents, and conniving servants. Ultimately the young lovers outwit all those who stand between them and in so doing affirm the primacy of youth and love over old age and death.

Old and New Comedy represent two distinct lines of humor that extend to modern times. Old Comedy depends on **satire**—bitter humor that diminishes a person, idea, or institution by ridiculing it or holding it up to scorn. Unlike comedy, which exists simply to make people laugh, satire is social criticism, deriding hypocrisy, pretension, and vanity or condemning vice. At its best, satire appeals to the intellect, has a serious purpose, and arouses thoughtful laughter. New Comedy may also be satiric, but it frequently contains elements of **farce,** comedy in which stereotypical characters engage in boisterous horseplay and slapstick humor, all the while making jokes and sexual innuendoes—as they do in Anton Chekhov's *The Brute* (p. 1342).

English comedy got its start in the sixth century A.D. in the form of farcical episodes that appeared in morality plays. During the Renaissance comedy developed rapidly, beginning in 1533 with Nicholas Udall's *Ralph Roister Doister* and eventually evolving into Shakespeare's **romantic**

comedy—such as *Much Ado about Nothing,* in which love is the main subject and idealized heroines and lovers endure great difficulties until the inevitable happy ending is reached.

Also during the Renaissance, particularly in the latter part of the sixteenth century, writers like Ben Jonson experimented with a different type of comedy—the **comedy of humours,** which focuses on characters whose behavior is controlled by a characteristic trait, or *humour.* During the Renaissance a person's temperament was thought to be determined by the mix of fluids, or humours, in the body. When one humour dominated, a certain type of disposition resulted. Playwrights capitalized on this belief, writing comedies in which characters are motivated by stereotypical behaviors that result from the imbalance of the humours. In comedies such as Jonson's *Volpone* and *The Alchemist,* characters such as the suspicious husband and the miser can be manipulated by others because of their predictable dispositions.

Closely related to the comedy of humours is the satiric **comedy of manners,** which developed during the sixteenth century and achieved great popularity in the nineteenth century. This form focuses on the manners and customs of society and directs its satire against characters who violate social conventions and rules of behavior. These plays tend to be memorable more for their witty and sparkling dialogue than for their development of characters or setting. Oliver Goldsmith's *She Stoops to Conquer* and George Bernard Shaw's *Pygmalion* are examples of this type of comedy.

In the eighteenth century a reaction against the perceived immorality of the comedy of manners led to **sentimental comedy,** which eventually achieved great popularity. This kind of comedy relies on sentimental emotion rather than on wit or humor to move an audience. It also dwells on the virtues rather than on the vices of life. The heroes of sentimental comedy are unimpeachably noble, moral, and honorable; the pure, virtuous, middle-class heroines suffer trials and tribulations calculated to move the audience to tears rather than laughter. Eventually the distress of the hero and heroine is resolved in a sometimes contrived but always happy ending.

In his 1877 essay *The Idea of Comedy,* novelist and critic George Meredith suggests that comedy that appeals to the intellect should be called **high comedy.** Shakespeare's *As You Like It* and Shaw's *Pygmalion* can be characterized in this way. When comedy has little or no intellectual appeal, according to Meredith, it is **low comedy.** Low comedy appears in parts of Shakespeare's *The Taming of the Shrew* and as comic relief in *Macbeth.*

The twentieth century has developed its own characteristic comic forms. Most reflect the uncertainty and pessimism of a century that has seen two world wars, the Holocaust, and nuclear destruction, as well as threats posed by environmental pollution and ethnic and racial conflict. Combining laughter and hints of tragedy, these modern tragicomedies feature **antiheroes,** characters who possess the opposite attributes of a hero and whose plight frequently elicits laughter, not pity and fear, from the audience. **Black comedies,** for example, rely for their comedy on the morbid and the absurd. These works are usually so satiric and bitter that they threaten to slip over the edge into tragedy. The screenplay of Joseph Heller's novel *Catch 22*, which ends with a character dropping bombs on his own men, is a classic example of black comedy. **Theater of the absurd,** which includes comedies such as *The Sandbox*, begins with the assumption that the human condition is irrational. Typically, this type of drama does not have a discernible plot; instead, it presents a series of apparently unrelated images and illogical exchanges of dialogue meant to reinforce the idea that human beings live in a remote, confusing, and often incomprehensible universe. Absurdist dramas seem to go in circles, never progressing to a climax or achieving a resolution, reinforcing the theme of the endless and meaningless repetition that characterizes modern life.

A Note on Translations

Many dramatic works that we read or see are translations. For example, Ibsen wrote in Norwegian, Sophocles in Greek, Molière in French, and Chekhov in Russian. Before English-speaking viewers or readers can evaluate the language of a translated play, they must understand that the language they hear or read is the translator's interpretation of what the playwright intended to communicate. Translation is interpretation, not just a search for literal equivalents; as a result, a translation is always different from the original. Moreover, different translations are different from one another. During the course of Henrik Ibsen's 1879 play *A Doll House* (p. 1185), for instance, Nora, the main character, refers several times to a symbolic gesture of support she expects from her husband Torvald. In the translation in this text, that gesture is translated as "the miracle"; in another translation, it is translated as "the wonderful." Not only is *miracle* more consistent with idiomatic English usage, but it is also a more absolute, and therefore more forceful, term.

The choices translators make can be very different. Compare these two versions of an exchange of dialogue from two different translations of the same Chekhov play, called *The Brute* in the translation which begins on p. 1342 and *The Bear* in the alternate version.

—*From* The Brute:

SMIRNOV: You'd like me to come simpering to you in French, I suppose. *'Enchanté, madame! Merci beaucoup* for not paying zee money, *madame! Pardonnez-moi* if I 'ave disturbed you, *madame!* How *charmante* you look in mourning, *madame!'*

Mrs. Popov: Now you're being silly, Mr. Smirnov.

Smirnov: *(mimicking)* 'Now you're being silly, Mr. Smirnov.' 'You don't know how to talk to a lady, Mr. Smirnov.' Look here, Mrs. Popov. I've known more women than you've known pussy cats. I've fought three duels on their account. I've jilted twelve, and been jilted by nine others. Oh, yes, Mrs. Popov, I've played the fool in my time, whispered sweet nothings, bowed and scraped and endeavoured to please. Don't tell me I don't know what it is to love, to pine away with longing, to have the blues, to melt like butter, to be weak as water. I was full of tender emotion. I was carried away with passion. I squandered half my fortune on the sex. I chattered about women's emancipation. But there's an end to everything, dear madam.

—*From* The Bear:

Smirnov: Ach, it's astonishing! How would you like me to talk to you? In French, perhaps? *(Lisps in anger.) Madame, je vous prie. . . . how happy I am that you're not paying me the money. . . . Ah, pardon, I've made you uneasy! Such lovely weather we're having today! And you look so becoming in your mourning dress. (Bows and scrapes.)*

Mrs. Popov: That's rude and not very clever!

Smirnov: *(teasing)* Rude and not very clever! I don't know how to behave in the company of ladies. Madam, in my time I've seen far more women than you've seen sparrows. Three times I've fought duels over women; I've jilted twelve women, nine have jilted me! Yes! There was a time when I played the fool; I became sentimental over women, used honeyed words, fawned on them, bowed and scraped. . . . I loved, suffered, sighed at the moon; I became limp, melted, shivered . . . I loved passionately, madly, every which way, devil take me, I chattered away like a magpie about the emancipation of women, ran through half my fortune as a result of my tender feelings; but now, if you will excuse me, I'm on to your ways! I've had enough!

Although both translations convey Smirnov's anger and frustration, they use different words (with different connotations), different phrasing—and even different stage directions. In *The Bear,* for instance, only one French phrase is used, while *The Brute* uses several and specifies a French accent as well; other differences between the two translations include *The Bear*'s use of "teasing," "sparrows," and "I've had enough!" where *The Brute* uses "mimicking," "pussy cats," and "But there's an end to everything, dear madam." (Elsewhere in the play *The Bear* uses profanity while *The Brute* uses more polite language.) Many words and idiomatic expressions used in daily speech cannot be translated exactly from one language to another, and here the two translators make different choices.

CHAPTER 21

Reading and Writing
about Drama

Reading Drama

When you read a play, you will notice features it shares with works of fiction—for instance, its use of language and symbols, the interaction among its characters, and its development of a theme or themes. In addition, you will encounter features that distinguish it from fiction—for example, the presence of stage directions and the division into acts and scenes.

The following guidelines, designed to help you explore works of dramatic literature, focus on issues that will be examined in depth in chapters to come.

- ◆ Trace the play's **plot.** What conflicts are present? Where does the rising action reach a climax? Where does the falling action begin? What techniques move the action along? (See Chapter 22.)

- ◆ Analyze the play's **characters.** Who are the central characters? What are their most distinctive traits? How do you learn about their personalities, backgrounds, appearances, and strengths and weaknesses? (See Chapter 23.)

- ◆ Examine the play's **language.** How does dialogue reveal characters' emotions, conflicts, opinions, and motivation? (See Chapter 23.)

- ◆ Does the play include soliloquies or asides? What do they contribute to your knowledge of the play's characters and events? (See Chapter 23.)

- ◆ How do the characters interact with one another? Do the characters change and grow in response to the play's events, or do they remain essentially unchanged? (See Chapter 23.)

- ◆ Read the play's **stage directions.** What do you learn from the descriptions of the characters, including their dress, gestures, and facial expressions? (See Chapter 23.) What information do you gain from studying the playwright's descriptions of the play's setting? Do the stage directions include information about lighting, props, music, or sound effects? (See Chapter 24.)

◆ Consider the play's **staging.** Where and when does the action take place? What techniques are used to convey a sense of time and place to the audience? (See Chapter 24.)

◆ Identify any **symbolic elements** in the play. How do such symbols enhance the play's central ideas? (See Chapter 25.)

◆ Try to interpret the play's **themes.** What is the main idea the play communicates? What additional themes are explored? (See Chapter 25.)

ACTIVE READING

As you read a play about which you plan to write, you follow the same process that guides you when you read any work of literature: You read actively, marking the text as you proceed. Then, you go on to select a topic and generate ideas about it, decide on a thesis, prepare an outline, and write and revise several drafts.

Kimberly Allison, a student in an introduction to literature course, was given the following assignment:

> Write a three- to five-page essay about any play read for this course. In choosing your topic, you may focus on action, character, staging, or theme, or you may consider more than one of these elements.

The instructor specifically asked students not to consult outside sources.

Previewing

Kim decided to write her paper on Susan Glaspell's play *Trifles,* which begins on page 1172. She began by previewing *Trifles,* taking note of its brief length; its one-act structure; its cast of characters; and its setting in the home of Mrs. Wright, who has been arrested for the murder of her husband. In addition, Kim noticed a few unusual features—in particular, the fact that Mr. and Mrs. Wright do not appear in the play.

Highlighting and Annotating

As Kim read *Trifles,* she highlighted the lines of dialogue and stage directions she thought she might want to examine more closely, identified possible links among ideas and patterns of action and language, and jotted down questions and observations. She found herself especially interested in the different ways in which the female and male characters react to the objects discovered in the house and in how the women and men interact.

The following highlighted and annotated passage shows some of her responses to the play.

The men laugh; the women looked abashed. [handwritten: Why do the men and Women react so differently?]

County Attorney: *(rubbing his hands over the stove)* Frank's fire didn't do much up there, did it? Well, let's go out to the barn and get that cleared up.

The men go outside.

[handwritten left margin: Why do the men and the women stay?]

Mrs. Hale: *(resentfully)* I don't know as there's anything so strange, our taken' up our time with little things while we're waiting for them to get the evidence. *(She sits down at the big table smoothing out a block with decision.)* I don't see as it's anything to laugh about.

Mrs. Peters: *(apologetically)* Of course they've got awful important things on their minds. [handwritten: Like what? Why does she make excuses for the men?]

Pulls up a chair and joins Mrs. Hale at the table.

Mrs. Hale: *(examining another block)* Mrs. Peters, look at this one. Here, this is the one she was working on, and look at the sewing! All the rest of it has been so nice and even. And look at this! It's all over the place! Why, it looks as if she didn't know what she was about!

[handwritten: What do the women guess about Mrs. Wright by looking at her sewing?]

Kim's highlighting and annotating of the entire play raised a number of questions. For instance, she wondered why the quilt seems so important to the women, and why the men leave the kitchen but the women do not. Most of Kim's notes focused on the play's characters, suggesting some interesting possibilities for her essay.

Writing about Drama

Planning an Essay

Even after Kim decided to write about the play's characters, she knew she had to narrow her focus. The highlighting and annotating she had done suggested that gender roles in general, and the women's role in particular, would make an interesting topic, so she decided to explore this idea further.

Choosing a Topic

To help her decide on a direction for her paper, Kim wrote the following journal entry.

What is the role of the women in this play? Although the women have accompanied their husbands to retrieve items for Mrs. Wright, they seem to be primarily interested in why Mrs. Wright would leave her house in such disarray. They find several objects that suggest that Mrs. Wright was lonely and that she was at the mercy of her husband's wishes. But these women are left on their own and seem to band together. Their guilt about not visiting Mrs. Wright also seems to ally them with the murder suspect. Mrs. Hale even begins to empathize with Mrs. Wright's loss of her bird. The women seem to find the details, or "trifles," of Mrs. Wright's life interesting and learn from them the facts surrounding the murder while the men wander aimlessly around the house and yard. The real clue to the murder appears to be Mrs. Wright's untended house, but the men do not notice the implications of the disorder. The women appear to have an understanding that comes from their own experiences as women, which the men are unable to tap into.

At this point, Kim concluded that the idea of the women's role in *Trifles* would be the best focus for her paper. As she went on to gather ideas to write about, she planned to examine the women characters in terms of their interaction with the men as well as with each other.

Finding Something to Say

Brainstorming   Kim's next step was to generate the specific ideas she would discuss in her paper. She reread the text of the play and her annotations, brainstorming about her topic and jotting down ideas as she proceeded. Some of her brainstorming notes appear below.

> Sheriff Peters says there is nothing in the kitchen but kitchen stuff; he thinks Mrs. Wright is a typical woman, worried about her preserves while imprisoned for murder.
> Mr. Henderson eventually sides with the other two men, claiming that women's worries are trifles.
> Mr. Hale mentions Mr. Wright's cheapness; he seems to know Mr. Wright best.
> Men think women are shallow and worry only about trifles.
>
> Women empathize with Mrs. Wright because they understand her treatment.
> Mrs. Hale feels animosity toward the men for laughing about the women's interest in the quilt; she regrets not visiting Mrs. Wright; feels sorry for Mrs. Wright because she had no children; she realizes that Sheriff dirtied the towels.
> Mrs. Peters = wife of Sheriff; empathizes with Mrs. Wright's loss of bird; notes that keeping house was Mrs. Wright's duty.
> Mrs. Wright restricted by husband; never leaves the house; loses control after her bird is killed.

John Wright strips wife of her identity; controls her every
mood; stops her from singing, which she enjoys; kills canary.

The first thing Kim noticed when she reread her notes was that the
women and men have two entirely different attitudes about women's lives
and concerns: The men think their work is much more important than
that of the women, whom they see as simply concerned with trivialities;
the women realize they are not much different from Mrs. Wright. Now
Kim saw that in order to discuss the women's role in the play, she must
first define that role in relation to the role of the men. To do so, she needed
to find a logical arrangement for the ideas she had collected—an arrangement that would enable her to clarify the differences between men's and
women's roles.

Listing   At this point, Kim decided that listing ideas could make the contrast between men's and women's roles clear.

MEN'S ROLE	WOMEN'S ROLE
working outside the home	making preserves
making decisions about financial expenditures	cleaning house
	making quilts
think women are to do only housework	raising children
	going to ladies clubs for socializing
create and enforce law	
dictate wives' actions	must follow laws that men create and enforce
have separate identities and power	subordinate to their husbands
actions are accepted by society	must act defiantly to break boundaries of social role

After listing, Kim was able to confirm her idea that men's and
women's roles are portrayed very differently in *Trifles.* Both men and
women seem to agree that they have different responsibilities, and both
seem to understand and accept the fact that power and freedom are unevenly distributed between the two genders.

Deciding on a Thesis

Kim's listing helped her to understand the nature of women's limited role
in the society portrayed in *Trifles.* This in turn enabled her to develop the
following tentative thesis statement, which she could use to help guide her
essay's first draft.

The central focus of <u>Trifles</u> is not on finding out who killed
Mr. Wright, but on the limited, even subservient, role of women
like Mrs. Wright.

Preparing an Outline

Guided by her thesis statement and the information she had collected in her notes, Kim made the following scratch outline, arranging her supporting details in a logical order under appropriate headings.

<u>Mrs. Hale and Mrs. Peters had limited roles</u>
-- Subservient to husbands
-- Do domestic chores
-- Confined to kitchen
-- Identify with Minnie Wright's loneliness

<u>Minnie Wright had limited role</u>
-- Does what husband tells her to do
-- Had no link with outside world
-- Couldn't sing
-- Had no friends
-- Had no identity

Drafting

Using her tentative thesis statement and her scratch outline as guides, Kimberly Allison wrote the following first draft of her essay. Before she began, she reviewed her highlighting to search for details that would illustrate and support her generalizations about the play.

Women's Role in <u>Trifles</u>

Susan Glaspell's <u>Trifles</u> seems to focus on the murder of John Wright. Mr. Wright had little concern for his wife's opinions. Mr. Hale suggested that Minnie Wright was powerless against her husband, and Sheriff Henry Peters questioned whether Minnie was allowed to quilt her log cabin pattern. Perhaps, since Mr. Wright did not spend his money freely, he would have made Minnie knot the quilt because it cost less. Minnie was controlled by her husband. He forced her to perform repetitive domestic chores. The central focus of <u>Trifles</u> is not on who killed Mr. Wright, but on the limited, even subservient role of women like Mrs. Wright.

Mrs. Peters and Mrs. Hale were similar to Minnie. Mrs. Peters and Mrs. Hale also performed domestic chores and had to do what their husbands wanted them to do, and they too were confined to Mrs. Wright's kitchen. The kitchen was the focal point of the play. Ironically, the women found that the kitchen held the clues to Mrs. Wright's loneliness and to the details of the murder. Mrs. Peters and Mrs. Hale remained confined to the kitchen while their husbands exercised their freedom to enter and exit the house at will. This mirrored Minnie's life since she stayed home while her husband went to work and into town. The two women discussed Minnie's isolation. Beginning to identify with Minnie's loneliness, Mrs. Peters and Mrs. Hale recognized that while they were busy in their own homes, they had, in fact, participated in isolating and confining Minnie.

The two women discovered that Minnie's only connection to the outside world was her bird. Minnie too was a caged bird because she was kept from singing and communicating with others by her husband. And piecing together the evidence, the women came to believe that John Wright had broken the bird's neck.

At the same time, Mrs. Peters and Mrs. Hale discovered the connection between the dead canary and Minnie's situation, and they began to recognize that they had to band together in order to exert their strength against the men. They realized that Minnie's independence and identity were crushed by her husband, and that their own husbands believed women's lives were trivial and unimportant. The revelation that Mrs. Peters and Mrs. Hale experienced urged them to commit an act as rebellious as the one that got Minnie in trouble: They concealed their discovery from their husbands and from the law.

Because Mrs. Hale and Mrs. Peters empathized with Minnie's condition, they suppressed the evidence they found and endured their husbands' insults rather than confronting their husbands. And through this, the women attempted to break through the boundaries of their social roles, just as Minnie had done before them.

First Draft: Commentary

When Kim distributed copies of her draft to other students in a formal peer review session, they suggested that her paper be developed further, pointing to paragraph 3 in particular. They also agreed that her paper's sentences seemed choppy; many needed to be linked with transitional words and phrases.

When Kim read over her first draft, one thing was obvious to her: She had gone beyond the scope of her tentative thesis statement and scratch outline by considering not just the women's roles but also the actions they take to break free of this role. She decided to revise her thesis statement to reflect this new emphasis—and, then, to expand her paper to develop this aspect of her thesis more fully.

When she met with her instructor to discuss her new ideas, he encouraged her to expand her paper's focus and to use direct quotations and specific examples to support her ideas. He also reminded her that present tense is used for discussions of literary works—not "Mrs. Peters and Mrs. Hale *were* similar to Minnie" but "Mrs. Peters and Mrs. Hale *are* similar to Minnie." (Only events that occurred *before* the time in which the play takes place—for example, the murder or Minnie's girlhood experiences—should be described in past tense.)

After her meeting with her instructor, Kim made a new scratch outline to guide her as she continued to revise:

Subservient role of women
- -- Minnie's husband didn't respect her opinion
- -- Didn't let her sing
- -- Could only perform domestic chores

Confinement of women in home
- -- Mrs. Hale and Mrs. Peters are confined to kitchen
- -- Minnie is concerned about her preserves
- -- Minnie didn't belong to Ladies Aid
- -- Minnie lonely at home because she had no children
- -- Minnie was a caged bird

Women's defiance
- -- Mrs. Hale and Mrs. Peters solve "mystery"
- -- Realize they must band together
- -- Take action
- -- Defy men's law

Revising and Editing

Before she wrote her next draft, Kim reviewed the suggestions she had recorded in meetings with classmates and with her instructor. Then she incorporated this material, along with her own new ideas, into her second draft, which appears on pages 1154–1157.

(Second draft)

Confinement and Rebellion in <u>Trifles</u>

Susan Glaspell's play <u>Trifles</u> involves the solving of a murder. Two women, Mrs. Peters and Mrs. Hale, discover that Mrs. Wright, who remains in jail throughout the play, has indeed murdered her husband. Interestingly, the women make this discovery through the examination of evidence in Mrs. Wright's kitchen, which their husbands, Sheriff Henry Peters and farmer Lewis Hale, along with the county attorney, Mr. Henderson, dismiss as women's "trifles." The focus of <u>Trifles</u>, however, is not on the murder of John Wright but on the subservient role of women, the confinement of the wife in the home, and the desperate acts necessary for achieving autonomy.

The role of Minnie Foster (Mrs. Wright) becomes evident in the first few minutes of the play, when Mr. Hale declares, "I didn't know as what his wife wanted made much difference to John--" (1173). Minnie's powerlessness is revealed further when the women discuss how Mr. Wright forced Minnie to give up the thing she loved--singing. Both of these observations suggest that Minnie's every action was controlled and stifled by her husband. She was not allowed to make decisions or be an individual; instead, she was only to perform domestic chores.

Doing domestic chores was the only part of life that Minnie was allowed to exert some power over, a condition that is shared by Mrs. Peters and Mrs. Hale, especially since these two women can be assumed to work only in the home and since their behavior as wives is also determined by their husbands.

The men are free to walk throughout the house and

outside of it while the women are, not surprisingly, confined to the kitchen, just as Minnie had been confined to the
house. Early in the play, Mrs. Hale refers to Minnie's isolation: "[S]he kept so much to herself. She didn't even belong
to the Ladies Aid" (1176–77). Mrs. Hale goes on to mention
Minnie's lack of nice clothing, which further suggests her
confinement in the home: If she never left her home, she
wouldn't need to look nice, and why would she want to leave
home if she had no nice clothes? Minnie's isolation is further revealed when Mrs. Hale contemplates Minnie's lack of
children: "Not having children makes less work--but it
makes a quiet house, and Wright out to work all day, and no
company when he did come in" (1179). As a result, Minnie's
only connection to the outside world was her bird, which becomes the symbol of Minnie's confinement, for Minnie herself was a caged bird. In a sense, Mr. Wright strangled her,
as he did the bird, by preventing her from talking to other
people in the community. Unlike the men, Mrs. Peters and
Mrs. Hale realize the connection between the dead canary
and Minnie's situation as "Their eyes meet" and they share
"A look of growing comprehension, of horror" (1180).

The comprehension that Mrs. Peters and Mrs. Hale experience is one that urges them to rebel by concealing their
discovery from their husbands and from the law. Mrs. Peters does concede that "the law is the law," but she also understands that because Mr. Wright treated his wife badly,
treating her as a domestic slave and isolating her from the
world, Minnie is justified in killing him. And even if Minnie
had been able to communicate the abuse she suffered, the
law would not take the abuse into account because the men

on the jury would not be sympathetic to a woman who complained about how her husband treated her.

The dialogue in <u>Trifles</u> reveals a huge difference in how women and men view their experiences. From the opening of the play, the gulf between the men and women emerges, and as the play progresses, the polarization of the male and female characters becomes clearer. Once the men leave the kitchen to find what they consider to be significant criminal evidence, the men and women are divided physically as well as emotionally. The men create their own community, as do the women, leading them to separate according to gender. With the women alone in the kitchen, the focus of the dialogue is on the female experience. The women discuss the quilt and the disarray in the kitchen, emphasizing that Mrs. Wright would not leave her home in disorder unless she was distracted by some more pressing situation.

The men further trivialize Mrs. Wright's and other women's significance when Mrs. Peters brings to bear another force that keeps women subservient: women's attempt to fill the role of homemaker. Women accept servitude voluntarily, making the work in the home their main interest. But the county attorney condemns Minnie, sarcastically observing, "I shouldn't say she had the homemaking instinct" (1175). Minnie has attempted to keep her home clean and do her chores, but the lack of heat has exploded her preserves, and her husband has dirtied the towels. What has caused Minnie to neglect her chores is something of great importance: her desire for independence and freedom from the servitude she once accepted voluntarily.

What makes this play most interesting is that the

women come to realize that they too have volunteered to be subservient to their husbands. They even accept the fact that their husbands will trivialize their discovery about the murder, as the men earlier trivialized their discussions of Minnie's daily tasks. Therefore, the women band together and conceal the information, breaking through their subservient roles as wives. And in the end, they find their own independence and significance in society.

Second Draft: Commentary

When she read her second draft, Kim had mixed feelings. She thought it was an improvement over her first draft, primarily because she had expanded the focus of her thesis and added specific details and quotations to support her points. She also believed her essay was now clearer, with smoother transitions.

Even though she knew what she wanted to say, however, Kim thought her paper's logic was somewhat difficult to follow, and she thought clearer topic sentences might correct his problem by guiding readers more smoothly through her essay. She also thought that her organization, which did not follow her revised scratch outline, was somewhat confusing. (For example, she had discussed the women's subservient role in two different parts of her essay—paragraphs 2 and 7.) In addition, Kim thought her third paragraph needed further development, and she still believed her essay could use additional supporting details and quotations throughout. After rereading her notes, she wrote her final draft, which appears on the following pages.

Allison 1

Kimberly Allison

English 1013

Professor Johnson

March 1, 1995

Breaking through the Boundaries:

Acts of Defiance in <u>Trifles</u>

Double-
space

Opening 1
sentence
identifies
author
and work.

Intro-
duction
places
play in
historical 2
context.

Thesis
statement.

Susan Glaspell wrote her best-known play, <u>Trifles</u>, in 1916, at a time when women were beginning to challenge their socially defined roles, realizing that their identities as wives and domestics kept them in a subordinate position in society. Because women were demanding more autonomy, traditional institutions such as marriage, which confined women to the home and made them mere extensions of their husbands, were beginning to be reexamined.

As a married woman, Glaspell was evidently touched by these concerns, perhaps because when she wrote <u>Trifles</u> she was at the mercy of her husband's wishes and encountered barriers in pursuing her career as a writer because she was a woman. But for whatever reason, Glaspell chose as the play's protagonist a married woman, Minnie Foster (Mrs. Wright), who has challenged society's expectations in a very extreme way: by murdering her husband. Minnie's defiant act has occurred before the action begins, and as the play unfolds two women, Mrs. Peters and Mrs. Hale, who accompany their husbands on an investigation of the murder scene, piece together the details of the situation surrounding the murder. As the events unfold, however, it becomes clear that the focus of <u>Trifles</u> is not on who killed John Wright, but on the themes of the subordinate role of

Allison 2

women, the confinement of the wife in the home, and the desperate acts necessary for achieving autonomy.

Topic sentence identifies first point paper will discuss: women's subordinate role.

3   The subordinate role of women, particularly Minnie's role in her marriage, becomes evident in the first few minutes of the play when Mr. Hale observes that the victim, John Wright, had little concern for his wife's opinions: "I didn't know as what his wife wanted made much difference to John" (1173). Here Mr. Hale suggests that Minnie was powerless against the wishes of her husband. Indeed, as these characters imply, Minnie's every act and thought were controlled by her husband, who strove to break her spirit by forcing her to perform repetitive domestic chores alone in the home. Minnie's only power in the household remained her kitchen work, a situation which Mrs. Peters and Mrs. Hale share since each of these women's behavior is determined by her husband. Therefore, when Sheriff Peters condemns Minnie's concern about her preserves, saying, "Well, can you beat the women! Held for murder and worrying about her preserves" (1175), he is, in a sense, condemning all three of the women for worrying over domestic matters rather than the murder that has been committed. Indeed, the sheriff's comment suggests that he assumes women's lives are trivial, an assumption which pervades the thoughts and dialogue of all three men.

Topic sentence introduces second point paper will discuss: women's confinement.

4   Mrs. Peters and Mrs. Hale are similar to Minnie in another way as well: Throughout the play, they are confined to the kitchen of the Wrights' house. Therefore, the kitchen becomes the focal point of the play. The women find that the kitchen holds the clues to Mrs. Wright's loneliness and

Allison 3

to the details of the murder. Mrs. Peters and Mrs. Hale remain confined to the kitchen while their husbands enter and exit the house at will. This scenario mirrors Minnie's daily life, as she remained in the home while her husband went to work and into town. The two women discuss Minnie's isolation in being housebound: "Not having children makes less work--but it makes a quiet house, and Wright out to work all day, and no company when he did come in" (1179). Beginning to identify with Minnie's loneliness, Mrs. Peters and Mrs. Hale recognize that, busy in their own homes, they have, in fact, participated in isolating and confining Minnie. Mrs. Hale declares, "I wish I had come over once in a while! That was a crime! That was a crime! Who's going to punish that? . . . I might have known she needed help" (1182)!

Transitional paragraph discusses women's observations and conclusions.

5   Soon the two women discover that Minnie's only connection to the outside world was her bird, the symbol of her confinement; Minnie was a caged bird who was kept from singing and communicating with others because of her restrictive husband. And piecing together the evidence--the disorderly kitchen, the mis-stitched quilt pieces, and the dead canary--the women come to believe that John Wright broke the bird's neck just as he had broken Minnie's spirit. Likewise, Mrs. Peters and Mrs. Hale discern the connection between the dead canary and Minnie's situation. The stage directions describe the moment when the women become aware of the truth behind the murder: "<u>Their eyes meet</u>," and the women share "<u>A look of growing comprehension, of horror</u>" (1180).

Allison 4

Topic
sentence
intro-
duces
third
point
paper
will
discuss:
common-
ality of
women's
exper-
iences.

6   Through their observations and discussions in Mrs. Wright's kitchen, Mrs. Hale and Mrs. Peters come to understand the commonality of women's experiences. Mrs. Hale speaks for both of them when she says, "I know how things can be--for women. . . . We all go through the same things-- it's all just a different kind of the same thing" (1182). And, once the two women realize the experiences they share, they begin to recognize that they must band together in order to challenge a male-oriented society; while their experiences may seem trivial to the men, the "trifles" of their lives are significant to them. They realize that Minnie's independence and identity were crushed by her husband, and that their own husbands have asserted that women's lives are trivial and unimportant as well. Thus, the revelation that Mrs. Peters and Mrs. Hale experience is one that urges them to commit an act as defiant as the one that has gotten Minnie into trouble: They conceal their discovery from their husbands and from the law.

7   Significantly, Mrs. Peters does acknowledge that "the law is the law," but she also understands that because Mr. Wright treated his wife badly, Minnie is justified in killing him. They also realize, however, that for men the law is black and white, and that an all-male jury will not take into account the extenuating circumstances that prompted Minnie to kill her husband. And even if Minnie were allowed to communicate to the male-dominated court the abuses she has suffered, the law would undoubtedly view her experience as trivial because a woman who complained about how her husband treated her would be considered ungrateful.

8   Nevertheless, because Mrs. Hale and Mrs. Peters empathize with Minnie's condition, they suppress the evidence
they find, enduring their husbands' condescension rather
than standing up to them. And, through this action, the
women attempt to break through the boundaries of their social role, just as Minnie has done. While Minnie is imprisoned for her crime, she has freed herself; and, while
Mrs. Peters and Mrs. Hale appear to conceal their knowledge, fearing the men will laugh at them, these women are
really challenging society and freeing themselves as well.

Conclu- 9   Susan Glaspell addressed many of the issues impor-
sion   tant to early twentieth-century women in <u>Trifles</u>, including
places   women's subordinate status, the wife's confinement in the
play in home, and the desperate acts necessary for women to break
historical out of restrictive social roles. In order to emphasize the
context.   pervasiveness of these issues, Glaspell does more than
focus on the plight of the woman who has ended her isolation and loneliness by committing a heinous crime against
society. By presenting three male and two female characters who demonstrate the vast differences between male
and female experience, she illustrates how men define the
roles of women and how women can challenge these roles in
search of their own significance in society and their eventual independence.

Final Draft: Commentary

Kim made many changes in her final draft. Although her thesis statement is much the same as it was in her previous draft, she has expanded her paper considerably. For example, she added a discussion of the commonality of women's experience in paragraph 5 and elsewhere, and this material helps to explain what motivates Mrs. Hale and Mrs. Peters to conceal evidence from their husbands. As she expanded her essay, Kim added illustrative explanations, details, and quotations. She also worked hard to make her topic sentences clearer, and she used information from her class notes to help her write a new introduction and conclusion that discussed the situation of women at the time in which *Trifles* was written. Finally, she added a new title to emphasize the expanded focus of her essay on the "desperate acts" all three women are driven to in response to their subjugation and confinement.

CHAPTER 22

Plot

We assume that, for the finest form of tragedy, the plot must be not simple but complex; and further, that it must imitate actions arousing fear and pity, since that is the distinctive function of this kind of imitation. It follows, therefore, that there are three forms of plot to be avoided. (1) A good man must not be seen passing from happiness to misery, or (2) a bad man from misery to happiness. The first situation is not fear-inspiring or piteous, but simply odious to us. The second is the most untragic that can be; it has not one of the requisites of tragedy; it does not appeal either to the human feeling in us, or to our pity, or to our fears. Nor, on the other hand, should (3) an extremely bad man be seen falling from happiness into misery. Such a story may arouse the human feeling in us, but it will not move us to either pity or fear; pity is occasioned by undeserved misfortune, and fear by that of one like ourselves; so that there will be nothing either piteous or fear-inspiring in the situation. . . .

The tragic fear and pity may be aroused by the spectacle; but they may also be aroused by the very structure and incidents of the play—which is the better way and shows the better poet. The plot in fact should be so framed that, even without seeing the things take place, he who simply hears the account of them shall be filled with horror and pity at the incidents.

ARISTOTLE, *POETICS*, TRANS. INGRAM BYWATER

Great character creation is a fine thing in a drama, but the sum of all its characters is the story that they enact. Aristotle puts the plot at the head of the dramatic elements; of all these he thinks plot the most difficult and the most expressive. And he is right. Not that every plot stands first, or any and every plot is more important than the characters in the play; any plot counts only in so far as it is expressive. But the fact remains, nevertheless, that the plot is the most important of all the elements in drama because of them all it can be most completely expressive of the characteristic idea behind the play.

STARK YOUNG, *THE THEATRE*

What is the common aim of all dramatists? . . . First, as promptly as possible to win the attention of the audience; secondly, to hold that interest steady or, better, to increase it till the final curtain falls. It is the time limit to which all dramatists are subject which makes the immediate winning of attention necessary. The dramatist

*has no time to waste. How is he to win this attention? By what is done in the play;
by characterization; by the language the people of his play speak; or by a combination of two or more of these. Today we hear much discussion whether it is what is
done, i.e. action, or characterization, or dialogue which most interests a public.
Which is the chief essential in good drama? History shows indisputably that the
drama in its beginnings, no matter where we look, depended most on action.*

GEORGE PIERCE BAKER, *DRAMATIC TECHNIQUE*

*Put in its simplest and most mundane terms, the basic task of anyone concerned
with presenting any kind of drama to any audience consists in capturing their attention and holding it as long as required. Only when that fundamental objective
has been achieved can the more lofty and ambitious intentions be fulfilled: the im-
parting of wisdom and insight, poetry and beauty, amusement and relaxation, illumination and purging of emotion. If you lose their attention, if you fail to make
them concentrate on what is happening, on what is being said, all is lost.*

*The creation of interest and suspense (in their very widest sense) thus underlies
all dramatic construction. Expectations must be aroused, but never, until the last
curtain, wholly fulfilled; the action must seem to be getting nearer to the objective
yet never reach it entirely before the end; and, above all, there must be constant
variation of pace and rhythm, monotony of any kind being certain to lull the attention and induce boredom and somnolence.*

MARTIN ESSLIN, *AN ANATOMY OF DRAMA*

*One major shift from earlier drama is seen in dramatic structure. In recent years, it
has become increasingly difficult to find new plays that tell a clearly articulated
story by first setting forth necessary information about characters and situation
and then going on to develop a series of complications leading to a climax and resolution. This traditional method of ordering events has for the most part been abandoned in favor of thematic unity achieved by introducing an idea or motif and then
developing variations upon it in order to increase perceptions about it. Unfortunately
this kind of structure often remains obscure to the uninitiated and so to them the
plays may seem merely confused; consequently, they are apt to feel more annoyed or
outraged than enlightened.*

OSCAR BROCKETT, *PERSPECTIVES ON CONTEMPORARY THEATRE*

Plot denotes the way events are arranged in a work of literature. Although
the accepted conventions of drama require that the plot of a play be presented somewhat differently from the plot of a short story, the same components of plot are present in both. Plot in a dramatic work, like plot in a
short story, presents conflicts that are revealed, intensified, and resolved

during the course of the play through the characters' actions. (See Chapter 4 for a discussion of conflict.)

PLOT STRUCTURE

In 1863 the German critic Gustav Freytag devised a pyramid to represent a prototype for the plot of a dramatic work. According to Freytag, a play typically begins with **exposition,** which presents characters and setting and introduces the basic situation in which the characters are involved. Then, during the **rising action,** complications develop, conflicts emerge, suspense builds, and crises occur. The rising action culminates in a **climax,** at which point the plot's tension peaks. Finally, during the **falling action,** the intensity subsides, eventually winding down to a **resolution,** or **denouement,** in which all loose ends are tied up.

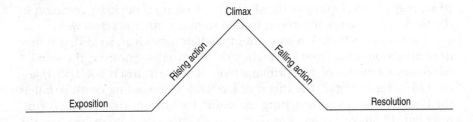

The plot of Susan Glaspell's one-act play *Trifles* (p. 1172), which resembles that of a detective story, is consistent with Freytag's model. As in the familiar detective story plot, the exposition section includes the introduction of the detective and the explanation of the crime. The rising action develops as the investigation of the crime proceeds, with suspense increasing as the solution approaches. The high point of the action, the climax, comes with the revelation of the crime's solution, and the falling action presents the explanation of the solution. The story concludes with a resolution typically characterized by the apprehension of the criminal and the restoration of order.

According to Freytag's model, the action of *Trifles* can be diagrammed as follows:

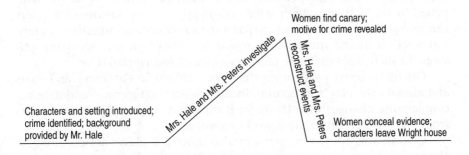

Of course the actual structure of a play is rarely if ever as neat as the first of the two diagrams on page 1167 suggests. In fact, a diagram of a play's action is more likely to look like the lopsided pyramid that represents *Trifles*—or even like a choppy line graph, with little or no exposition and truncated falling action. Because long stretches of exposition can be dull, a playwright may arouse audience interest by moving directly into conflict. *Oedipus the King* (p. 1590), for example, begins with the conflict, and so does *The Cuban Swimmer* (p. 1576). Similarly, because audiences tend to lose interest after the play's climax is reached, a playwright may choose to dispense with extended falling action. Thus, after Hamlet's death, the play ends abruptly.

Plot and Subplot

While the main plot is developing, another, parallel plot, called a **subplot,** may be developing alongside it. This structural device is common in the works of Shakespeare, and it is used in many other plays as well.

The subplot's function may not immediately be clear, so at first it may draw attention away from the main plot. Eventually, however, the subplot reinforces elements of the primary plot. In Henrik Ibsen's *A Doll House* (p. 1185), for example, the threat of Dr. Rank's impending death parallels the threat of Nora's approaching exposure; for both of them, time is running out. In Shakespeare's *King Lear* a more elaborate subplot involves the Earl of Gloucester who, like Lear, misjudges his children, favoring a deceitful son who does not deserve his support and overlooking a more deserving one. Both families suffer greatly as a result of the fathers' misplaced loyalties. Thus, the parallel plot places additional emphasis on Lear's poor judgment and magnifies the consequences of his misguided acts: Both fathers, and all but one of the five children, are dead by the play's end.

PLOT DEVELOPMENT

In a dramatic work plot unfolds through **action,** what characters say and do. Generally, a play does not include a narrator whose commentary ensures that events will move smoothly along. Instead, exchanges of dialogue reveal what is happening—and, sometimes, indicate what has happened in the past or suggest what will happen in the future. Characters can recount past events to other characters, announce an intention to take some action in the future, or summarize events that are occurring offstage. In such cases dialogue takes the place of formal narrative.

On the printed page, stage directions chronicle entrances and exits and identify the play's structural divisions—acts and scenes—and their accompanying changes of setting. Such directions efficiently move readers from one location and time period to another.

Certain staging techniques can also move the play's action along. A change in lighting, for instance, can efficiently shift viewer focus to another part of the stage—and thus to another place and time. Similarly, an adjustment of **scenery** or **props**—for instance, a breakfast table, complete with morning paper, replacing a bedtime setting—can indicate that the action has moved forward in time, as can a change of costumes. In Tennessee Williams's *The Glass Menagerie* (p. 1198) various devices—such as words projected on a screen that preview words to be spoken by a character, and visual images on screen that predict scenes to follow—help to keep the action moving. For example, a screen image of blue roses leads into a scene in which Laura tells her mother how Jim gave her the nickname "Blue Roses." Music can also advance a play's action. It may be used to introduce excitement or doom or a romantic interlude, and a repeated musical theme can predict a particular character's entrance. In Scene 5 of *The Glass Menagerie,* for example, stage directions announce "The Dance-Hall Music Changes To A Tango That Has A Minor And Somewhat Ominous Tone"; a "music legend" repeated throughout the play serves as a signature in scenes focusing on Laura.

Less traditional elements can also advance the action. In Thornton Wilder's 1938 play *Our Town*, for example, a character known as the Stage Manager functions as a narrator, not only describing the play's setting and introducing the audience to the characters, but also soliciting questions from characters scattered around the audience, prompting characters, and interrupting dialogue. In *The Glass Menagerie* the protagonist, Tom Wingfield, also serves as a narrator, summarizing what has happened and moving readers on to the next scene: "After the fiasco at Rubicam's Business College, the idea of getting a gentleman caller for Laura began to play a more important part in Mother's calculations" (Scene 3).

Flashbacks

Unlike incidents related in short stories or novels, incidents presented in plays are generally presented in the order in which they occur. However, many plays—such as *The Glass Menagerie* and Arthur Miller's *Death of a Salesman* (p. 1458)—include **flashbacks,** which depict events that occur before the play's main action. In addition, dialogue can overcome the limitations set by the chronological action on stage by recounting events that occurred earlier. Thus, Mr. Hale in *Trifles* tells the other characters how he discovered John Wright's murder, and Nora in *A Doll House* confides her secret to her friend Kristine. As characters on stage are brought up to date, the audience is also given necessary information—facts that are essential to an understanding of the characters' motivations. Naturally, characters must have plausible reasons for explaining past events: In *Trifles* Mr. Hale is the only character who has witnessed the events he describes, and in *A Doll House* Kristine, formerly Nora's friend and confidante, has not seen her in years. A character's need for information provides playwrights with a convenient excuse for supplying readers with necessary background. In less realistic dramas, however, no such excuse is necessary: Characters can interrupt the action to deliver long monologues or soliloquies that fill in background details—or even address the audience directly, as Tom does in *The Glass Menagerie.*

Foreshadowing

In addition to revealing past events, dialogue can **foreshadow,** or look ahead to, future action. In many cases, seemingly unimportant comments have thematic significance that becomes clear as the play develops. For example, in Act III of *A Doll House* Torvald Helmer says to Kristine, "An exit should always be effective, Mrs. Linde, but that's what I can't get Nora to grasp." At the end of the play, Nora's exit is not only effective, but also memorable.

Elements of staging can also suggest events to come. In *The Glass Menagerie,* for instance, the ever-present photograph of the absent father— who, Tom tells the audience, may be seen as a symbol of "the long delayed but always expected something that we live for"—foreshadows Tom's escape. Various bits of **stage business**—gestures or movements designed to attract the audience's attention—may also foreshadow future events. In *A Doll House,* for instance, Nora's sneaking forbidden macaroons seems at first to suggest her fear of her husband, but her actions actually foreshadow her eventual defiance of his authority.

A FINAL NOTE

Because of a play's limited performance time, and because of space limitations, not every action can be represented on stage. Frequently, incidents that would involve many actors or require elaborate scenery are only suggested—for example, a violent political riot by a single scuffle, a full-scale wedding by the kiss between bride and groom, a gala evening at the opera by a well-dressed group in box seats, a trip to an exotic locale by a departure scene—or are said to occur offstage, with the roar of a crowd suggesting an athletic event, for instance.

▼▼

CHECKLIST FOR WRITING ABOUT PLOT

- ◆ Summarize the play's events.
- ◆ What is the play's central conflict? How is it resolved? What other conflicts are present?
- ◆ What section of the play constitutes its rising action?
- ◆ Where does the play's climax occur?
- ◆ What crises can you identify?
- ◆ How is suspense created?
- ◆ What section of the play constitutes its falling action?

- ◆ Does the play contain a subplot? What is its purpose? How is it related to the main plot?

- ◆ Does the play include flashbacks? Does the play's dialogue contain summaries of past events or references to events in the future? How does the use of flashbacks or foreshadowing advance the play's plot?

- ◆ Does the play include a narrator? Does it provide a substitute for formal narrative through any other device?

- ◆ How does the dialogue advance the play's plot?

- ◆ How do characters' actions advance the play's plot?

- ◆ How do stage directions advance the play's plot?

- ◆ How does staging advance the play's plot?

- ◆ Does the play use any unconventional devices to advance the plot?

- ◆ What events occur offstage? Why?

▲▲▲

SUSAN GLASPELL (1882–1948) was born in Davenport, Iowa, and graduated from Drake University in 1899. First a reporter and then a freelance writer, she lived in Chicago (where she was part of the Chicago Renaissance that included poet Carl Sandburg and novelist Theodore Dreiser) and later in Greenwich Village. Her works include two plays in addition to *Trifles, The Verge* (1921) and *Alison's House* (1930), and several novels, including *Fidelity* (1915) and *The Morning Is Near Us* (1939). With her husband, George Cram Cook, she founded the Provincetown Players, which became the staging ground for innovative plays by Eugene O'Neill, among others.

Glaspell herself wrote plays for the Provincetown Players, beginning with *Trifles*, which she created for the 1916 season although she had previously never written a drama. The play opened on August 8, 1916, with Glaspell and her husband in the cast. Glaspell said she wrote *Trifles* in one afternoon, sitting in the empty theater and looking at the bare stage: "After a time, the stage became a kitchen—a kitchen there all by itself." She remembered a murder trial she had covered in Iowa in her days as a reporter, and the story began to play itself out on the stage as she gazed. Throughout her revisions, she said, she returned to look at the stage to see whether the events she was recording came to life on it. Although Glaspell later rewrote *Trifles* in short story form ("A Jury of Her Peers," p. 455), the play version remains her most successful and memorable work.

SUSAN GLASPELL

Trifles

(1916)

CHARACTERS

GEORGE HENDERSON, *county attorney*   **MRS. PETERS**
HENRY PETERS, *sheriff*   **MRS. HALE**
LEWIS HALE, *a neighboring farmer*

SCENE

The kitchen in the now abandoned farmhouse of John Wright, a gloomy kitchen, and left without having been put in order—unwashed pans under the sink, a loaf of bread outside the breadbox, a dish towel on the table—other signs of incompleted work. At the rear the outer door opens and the Sheriff comes in followed by the County Attorney and Hale. The Sheriff and Hale are men in middle life, the County Attorney is a young man; all are much bundled up and go at once to the stove. They are followed by two women—the Sheriff's wife first; she is a slight wiry woman, a thin nervous face. Mrs. Hale is larger and would ordinarily be called more comfortable looking, but she is disturbed now and looks fearfully about as she enters. The women have come in slowly, and stand close together near the door.

COUNTY ATTORNEY: *(rubbing his hands)* This feels good. Come up to the fire, ladies.

MRS. PETERS: *(after taking a step forward)* I'm not—cold.

SHERIFF: *(unbuttoning his overcoat and stepping away from the stove as if to mark the beginning of official business)* Now, Mr. Hale, before we move things about, you explain to Mr. Henderson just what you saw when you came here yesterday morning.

COUNTY ATTORNEY: By the way, has anything been moved? Are things just as you left them yesterday?

5 **SHERIFF:**   *(looking about)* It's just the same. When it dropped below zero last night I thought I'd better send Frank out this morning to make a fire for us—no use getting pneumonia with a big case on, but I told him not to touch anything except the stove—and you know Frank.

COUNTY ATTORNEY: Somebody should have been left here yesterday.

SHERIFF: Oh—yesterday. When I had to send Frank to Morris Center for that man who went crazy—I want you to know I had my hands full yesterday. I knew you could get back from Omaha by today and as long as I went over everything here myself—

COUNTY ATTORNEY: Well, Mr. Hale, tell just what happened when you came here yesterday morning.

HALE: Harry and I had started to town with a load of potatoes. We came along the road from my place and as I got here I said, "I'm going to see if I can't get John Wright to go in with me on a party telephone." I spoke to Wright about it once before and he put me off, saying folks talked too much anyway, and all he asked was peace and quiet—I guess you know about how much he talked himself; but I thought maybe if I went to the house and talked about it before his wife, though I said to Harry that I didn't know as what his wife wanted made much difference to John—

10 **COUNTY ATTORNEY:** Let's talk about that later, Mr. Hale. I do want to talk about that, but tell now just what happened when you got to the house.

HALE: I didn't hear or see anything; I knocked at the door, and still it was all quiet inside. I knew they must be up, it was past eight o'clock. So I knocked again, and I thought I heard somebody say, "Come in." I wasn't sure, I'm not sure yet, but I opened the door—this door *(Indicating the door by which the two women are still standing.)* and there in that rocker—*(Pointing to it.)* sat Mrs. Wright.

They all look at the rocker.

COUNTY ATTORNEY: What—was she doing?

HALE: She was rockin' back and forth. She had her apron in her hand and was kind of—pleating it.

COUNTY ATTORNEY: And how did she—look?

15 **HALE:** Well, she looked queer.

COUNTY ATTORNEY: How do you mean—queer?

HALE: Well, as if she didn't know what she was going to do next. And kind of done up.

COUNTY ATTORNEY: How did she seem to feel about your coming?

HALE: Why, I don't think she minded—one way or other. She didn't pay much attention. I said, "How do, Mrs. Wright, it's cold, ain't it?" And she said, "Is it?"—and went on kind of pleating at her apron. Well, I was surprised; she didn't ask me to come up to the stove, or to set down, but just sat there, not even looking at me, so I said, "I want to see John." And then she—laughed. I guess you would call it a laugh. I thought of Harry and the team outside, so I said a little sharp: "Can't I see John?" "No," she says, kind o' dull like. "Ain't he home?" says I. "Yes," says she, "he's home." "Then why can't I see him?" I asked her, out of patience. " 'Cause he's dead," says she. *"Dead?"* says I. She just nodded her head, not getting a bit excited, but rockin' back and forth. "Why—where is he?" says I, not knowing what to say. She just pointed upstairs—like that *(Himself pointing to the room above.)*. I got up, with the idea of going up there. I walked from there to here—then I says, "Why, what did he die of?" "He died of a rope round his neck," says she, and just went on pleatin' at her apron. Well, I went out and called Harry. I thought I might—need help. We went upstairs and there he was lyin'—

20 **COUNTY ATTORNEY:**   I think I'd rather have you go into that upstairs, where you can point it all out. Just go on now with the rest of the story.

HALE: Well, my first thought was to get that rope off. It looked . . . *(Stops, his face twitches.)* . . . but Harry, he went up to him, and he said, "No, he's dead all right, and we'd better not touch anything." So we went back down stairs. She was still sitting that same way. "Has anybody been notified?" I asked. "No," says she, unconcerned. "Who did this, Mrs. Wright?" said Harry. He said it businesslike—and she stopped pleatin' of her apron. "I don't know," she says. "You don't *know?*" says Harry. "No," says she. "Weren't you sleepin' in the bed with him?" says Harry. "Yes," says she, "but I was on the inside." "Somebody slipped a rope round his neck and strangled him and you didn't wake up?" says Harry. "I didn't wake up," she said after him. We must 'a looked as if we didn't see how that could be, for after a minute she said, "I sleep sound." Harry was going to ask her more questions but I said maybe we ought to let her tell her story first to the coroner, or the sheriff, so Harry went fast as he could to Rivers' place, where there's a telephone.

COUNTY ATTORNEY: And what did Mrs. Wright do when she knew that you had gone for the coroner?

HALE: She moved from that chair to this one over here *(Pointing to a small chair in the corner.)* and just sat there with her hands held together and looking down. I got a feeling that I ought to make some conversation, so I said I had come in to see if John wanted to put in a telephone, and at that she started to laugh, and then she stopped and looked at me—scared. *(The County Attorney, who has had his notebook out, makes a note.)* I dunno, maybe it wasn't scared. I wouldn't like to say it was. Soon Harry got back, and then Dr. Lloyd came, and you, Mr. Peters, and so I guess that's all I know that you don't.

COUNTY ATTORNEY: *(looking around)* I guess we'll go upstairs first—and then out to the barn and around there. *(To the Sheriff.)* You're convinced that there was nothing important here—nothing that would point to any motive.

25 **SHERIFF:**   Nothing here but kitchen things.

The County Attorney, after again looking around the kitchen, opens the door of a cupboard closet. He gets up on a chair and looks on a shelf. Pulls his hand away, sticky.

COUNTY ATTORNEY: Here's a nice mess.

The women draw nearer.

MRS. PETERS: *(to the other woman)* Oh, her fruit; it did freeze. *(To the County Attorney.)* She worried about that when it turned so cold. She said the fire'd go out and her jars would break.

SHERIFF: Well, can you beat the women! Held for murder and worryin' about her preserves.

COUNTY ATTORNEY: I guess before we're through she may have something more serious than preserves to worry about.

30 **HALE:** Well, women are used to worrying over trifles.

The two women move a little closer together.

COUNTY ATTORNEY: *(with the gallantry of a young politician)* And yet, for all their worries, what would we do without the ladies? *(The women do not unbend. He goes to the sink, takes a dipperful of water from the pail and pouring it into a basin, washes his hands. Starts to wipe them on the roller towel, turns it for a cleaner place.)* Dirty towels! *(Kicks his foot against the pans under the sink.)* Not much of a housekeeper, would you say, ladies?

MRS. HALE: *(stiffly)* There's a great deal of work to be done on a farm.

COUNTY ATTORNEY: To be sure. And yet *(With a little bow to her)* I know there are some Dickson county farmhouses which do not have such roller towels.

He gives it a pull to expose its full length again.

MRS. HALE: Those towels get dirty awful quick. Men's hands aren't always as clean as they might be.

35 **COUNTY ATTORNEY:** Ah, loyal to your sex, I see. But you and Mrs. Wright were neighbors. I suppose you were friends, too.

MRS. HALE: *(shaking her head)* I've not seen much of her of late years. I've not been in this house—it's more than a year.

COUNTY ATTORNEY: And why was that? You didn't like her?

MRS. HALE: I liked her all well enough. Farmers' wives have their hands full, Mr. Henderson. And then—

COUNTY ATTORNEY: Yes—?

40 **MRS. HALE:** *(looking about)* It never seemed a very cheerful place.

COUNTY ATTORNEY: No—it's not cheerful. I shouldn't say she had the homemaking instinct.

MRS. HALE: Well, I don't know as Wright had, either.

COUNTY ATTORNEY: You mean that they didn't get on very well?

MRS. HALE: No, I don't mean anything. But I don't think a place'd be any cheerfuller for John Wright's being in it.

45 **COUNTY ATTORNEY:** I'd like to talk more of that a little later. I want to get the lay of things upstairs now.

He goes to the left, where three steps lead to a stair door.

SHERIFF: I suppose anything Mrs. Peters does'll be all right. She was to take in some clothes for her, you know, and a few little things. We left in such a hurry yesterday.

COUNTY ATTORNEY: Yes, but I would like to see what you take, Mrs. Peters, and keep an eye out for anything that might be of use to us.

MRS. PETERS: Yes, Mr. Henderson.

The women listen to the men's steps on the stairs, then look about the kitchen.

MRS. HALE: I'd hate to have men coming into my kitchen, snooping around and criticizing.

She arranges the pans under sink which the County Attorney had shoved out of place.

50 **MRS. PETERS:** Of course it's no more than their duty.

MRS. HALE: Duty's all right, but I guess that deputy sheriff that came out to make the fire might have got a little of this on. *(Gives the roller towel a pull.)* Wish I'd thought of that sooner. Seems mean to talk about her for not having things slicked up when she had to come away in such a hurry.

MRS. PETERS: *(who has gone to a small table in the left rear corner of the room, and lifted one end of a towel that covers a pan)* She had bread set.

Stands still.

MRS. HALE: *(eyes fixed on a loaf of bread beside the breadbox, which is on a low shelf at the other side of the room. Moves slowly toward it.)* She was going to put this in there. *(Picks up loaf, then abruptly drops it. In a manner of returning to familiar things.)* It's a shame about her fruit. I wonder if it's all gone. *(Gets up on the chair and looks.)* I think there's some here that's all right, Mrs. Peters. Yes—here; *(Holding it toward the window)* this is cherries, too. *(Looking again.)* I declare I believe that's the only one. *(Gets down, bottle in her hand. Goes to the sink and wipes it off on the outside.)* She'll feel awful bad after all her hard work in the hot weather. I remember the afternoon I put up my cherries last summer.

She puts the bottle on the big kitchen table, center of the room. With a sigh, is about to sit down in the rocking-chair. Before she is seated realizes what chair it is; with a slow look at it, steps back. The chair which she has touched rocks back and forth.

MRS. PETERS: Well, I must get those things from the front room closet. *(She goes to the door at the right, but after looking into the other room, steps back.)* You coming with me, Mrs. Hale? You could help me carry them.

They go in the other room; reappear, Mrs. Peters carrying a dress and skirt, Mrs. Hale following with a pair of shoes.

55 **MRS. PETERS:** My, it's cold in there.

She puts the clothes on the big table, and hurries to the stove.

MRS. HALE: *(examining her skirt)* Wright was close. I think maybe that's why she kept so much to herself. She didn't even belong to the Ladies

Aid. I suppose she felt she couldn't do her part, and then you don't enjoy things when you feel shabby. She used to wear pretty clothes and be lively, when she was Minnie Foster, one of the town girls singing in the choir. But that—oh, that was thirty years ago. This all you was to take in?

MRS. PETERS: She said she wanted an apron. Funny thing to want, for there isn't much to get you dirty in jail, goodness knows. But I suppose just to make her feel more natural. She said they was in the top drawer in this cupboard. Yes, here. And then her little shawl that always hung behind the door. *(Opens stair door and looks.)* Yes, here it is.

Quickly shuts door leading upstairs.

MRS. HALE: *(abruptly moving toward her)* Mrs. Peters?

MRS. PETERS: Yes, Mrs. Hale?

60 **MRS. HALE:** Do you think she did it?

MRS. PETERS: *(in a frightened voice)* Oh, I don't know.

MRS. HALE: Well, I don't think she did. Asking for an apron and her little shawl. Worrying about her fruit.

MRS. PETERS: *(starts to speak, glances up, where footsteps are heard in the room above. In a low voice.)* Mr. Peters says it looks bad for her. Mr. Henderson is awful sarcastic in a speech and he'll make fun of her sayin' she didn't wake up.

MRS. HALE: Well, I guess John Wright didn't wake when they was slipping that rope under his neck.

65 **MRS. PETERS:** No, it's strange. It must have been done awful crafty and still. They say it was such a—funny way to kill a man, rigging it all up like that.

MRS. HALE: That's just what Mr. Hale said. There was a gun in the house. He says that's what he can't understand.

MRS. PETERS: Mr. Henderson said coming out that what was needed for the case was a motive; something to show anger, or—sudden feeling.

MRS. HALE: *(who is standing by the table)* Well, I don't see any signs of anger around here. *(She puts her hand on the dish towel which lies on the table, stands looking down at table, one half of which is clean, the other half messy.)* It's wiped to here. *(Makes a move as if to finish work, then turns and looks at loaf of bread outside the breadbox. Drops towel. In that voice of coming back to familiar things.)* Wonder how they are finding things upstairs. I hope she had it a little more red-up[1] up there. You know, it seems kind of *sneaking.* Locking her up in town and then coming out here and trying to get her own house to turn against her!

MRS. PETERS: But Mrs. Hale, the law is the law.

70 **MRS. HALE:** I s'pose 'tis. *(Unbuttoning her coat.)* Better loosen up your things, Mrs. Peters. You won't feel them when you go out.

---

[1] (slang) spruced up.

Mrs. Peters takes off her fur tippet, goes to hang it on hook at back of room, stands looking at the under part of the small corner table.

MRS. PETERS: She was piecing a quilt.

She brings the large sewing basket and they look at the bright pieces.

MRS. HALE: It's log cabin pattern. Pretty, isn't it? I wonder if she was goin' to quilt it or just knot it?

Footsteps have been heard coming down the stairs. The Sheriff enters followed by Hale and the County Attorney.

SHERIFF: They wonder if she was going to quilt it or just knot it!

The men laugh; the women look abashed.

COUNTY ATTORNEY: *(rubbing his hands over the stove)* Frank's fire didn't do much up there, did it? Well, let's go out to the barn and get that cleared up.

The men go outside.

75 **MRS. HALE:** *(resentfully)* I don't know as there's anything so strange, our takin' up our time with little things while we're waiting for them to get the evidence. *(She sits down at the big table smoothing out a block with decision.)* I don't see as it's anything to laugh about.

MRS. PETERS: *(apologetically)* Of course they've got awful important things on their minds.

Pulls up a chair and joins Mrs. Hale at the table.

MRS. HALE: *(examining another block)* Mrs. Peters, look at this one. Here, this is the one she was working on, and look at the sewing! All the rest of it has been so nice and even. And look at this! It's all over the place! Why, it looks as if she didn't know what she was about!

After she has said this they look at each other, then start to glance back at the door. After an instant Mrs. Hale has pulled at a knot and ripped the sewing.

MRS. PETERS: Oh, what are you doing, Mrs. Hale?

MRS. HALE: *(mildly)* Just pulling out a stitch or two that's not sewed very good. *(Threading a needle.)* Bad sewing always made me fidgety.

80 **MRS. PETERS:** *(nervously)* I don't think we ought to touch things.

MRS. HALE: I'll just finish up this end. *(Suddenly stopping and leaning forward.)* Mrs. Peters?

MRS. PETERS: Yes, Mrs. Hale?

MRS. HALE: What do you suppose she was so nervous about?

MRS. PETERS: Oh—I don't know. I don't know as she was nervous. I sometimes sew awful queer when I'm just tired. *(Mrs. Hale starts to say something, looks at Mrs. Peters, then goes on sewing.)* Well, I must get these things wrapped up. They may be through sooner than we think.

(Putting apron and other things together.) I wonder where I can find a piece of paper, and string.

85 **Mrs. Hale:** In that cupboard, maybe.

Mrs. Peters: *(looking in cupboard)* Why, here's a birdcage. *(Holds it up.)* Did she have a bird, Mrs. Hale?

Mrs. Hale: Why, I don't know whether she did or not—I've not been here for so long. There was a man around last year selling canaries cheap, but I don't know as she took one; maybe she did. She used to sing real pretty herself.

Mrs. Peters: *(glancing around)* Seems funny to think of a bird here. But she must have had one, or why would she have a cage? I wonder what happened to it.

Mrs. Hale: I s'pose maybe the cat got it.

90 **Mrs. Peters:** No, she didn't have a cat. She's got that feeling some people have about cats—being afraid of them. My cat got in her room and she was real upset and asked me to take it out.

Mrs. Hale: My sister Bessie was like that. Queer, ain't it?

Mrs. Peters: *(examining the cage)* Why, look at this door. It's broke. One hinge is pulled apart.

Mrs. Hale: *(looking too)* Looks as if someone must have been rough with it.

Mrs. Peters: Why, yes.

She brings the cage forward and puts it on the table.

95 **Mrs. Hale:** I wish if they're going to find any evidence they'd be about it. I don't like this place.

Mrs. Peters: But I'm awful glad you came with me, Mrs. Hale. It would be lonesome for me sitting here alone.

Mrs. Hale: It would, wouldn't it? *(Dropping her sewing.)* But I tell you what I do wish, Mrs. Peters. I wish I had come over sometimes when *she* was here. I—*(Looking around the room)*—wish I had.

Mrs. Peters: But of course you were awful busy, Mrs. Hale—your house and your children.

Mrs. Hale: I could've come. I stayed away because it weren't cheerful—and that's why I ought to have come. I—I've never liked this place. Maybe because it's down in a hollow and you don't see the road. I dunno what it is but it's a lonesome place and always was. I wish I had come over to see Minnie Foster sometimes. I can see now—

Shakes her head.

100 **Mrs. Peters:** Well, you mustn't reproach yourself, Mrs. Hale. Somehow we just don't see how it is with other folks until—something comes up.

Mrs. Hale: Not having children makes less work—but it makes a quiet house, and Wright out to work all day, and no company when he did come in. Did you know John Wright, Mrs. Peters?

MRS. PETERS: Not to know him; I've seen him in town. They say he was a good man.

MRS. HALE: Yes—good; he didn't drink, and kept his word as well as most, I guess, and paid his debts. But he was a hard man, Mrs. Peters. Just to pass the time of day with him—(*Shivers.*) Like a raw wind that gets to the bone. (*Pauses, her eye falling on the cage.*) I should think she would 'a wanted a bird. But what do you suppose went with it?

MRS. PETERS: I don't know, unless it got sick and died.

She reaches over and swings the broken door, swings it again. Both women watch it.

105 MRS. HALE: You weren't raised round here, were you? (*Mrs. Peters shakes her head.*) You didn't know—her?

MRS. PETERS: Not till they brought her yesterday.

MRS. HALE: She—come to think of it, she was kind of like a bird herself—real sweet and pretty, but kind of timid and—fluttery. How—she—did—change. (*Silence; then as if struck by a happy thought and relieved to get back to everyday things.*) Tell you what, Mrs. Peters, why don't you take the quilt in with you? It might take up her mind.

MRS. PETERS: Why, I think that's a real nice idea, Mrs. Hale. There couldn't possibly be any objection to it, could there? Now, just what would I take? I wonder if her patches are in here—and her things.

They look in the sewing basket.

MRS. HALE: Here's some red. I expect this has got sewing things in it. (*Brings out a fancy box.*) What a pretty box. Looks like something somebody would give you. Maybe her scissors are in here. (*Opens box. Suddenly puts her hand to her nose.*) Why—(*Mrs. Peters bends nearer, then turns her face away.*) There's something wrapped up in this piece of silk.

110 MRS. PETERS: Why, this isn't her scissors.

MRS. HALE: (*lifting the silk*) Oh, Mrs. Peters—it's—

Mrs. Peters bends closer.

MRS. PETERS: It's the bird.

MRS. HALE: (*jumping up*) But, Mrs. Peters—look at it! Its neck! Look at its neck! It's all—other side *to*.

MRS. PETERS: Somebody—wrung—its—neck.

Their eyes meet. A look of growing comprehension, of horror. Steps are heard outside. Mrs. Hale slips box under quilt pieces, and sinks into her chair. Enter Sheriff and County Attorney. Mrs. Peters rises.

115 COUNTY ATTORNEY: (*as one turning from serious things to little pleasantries*) Well, ladies, have you decided whether she was going to quilt it or knot it?

MRS. PETERS: We think she was going to—knot it.

County Attorney: Well, that's interesting, I'm sure. *(Seeing the birdcage.)* Has the bird flown?

Mrs. Hale: *(putting more quilt pieces over the box)* We think the—cat got it.

County Attorney: *(preoccupied)* Is there a cat?

Mrs. Hale glances in a quick covert way at Mrs. Peters.

120 **Mrs. Peters:** Well, not *now*. They're superstitious, you know. They leave.

County Attorney: *(to Sheriff Peters, continuing an interrupted conversation)* No sign at all of anyone having come from the outside. Their own rope. Now let's go up again and go over it piece by piece. *(They start upstairs.)* It would have to have been someone who knew just the—

Mrs. Peters sits down. The two women sit there not looking at one another, but as if peering into something and at the same time holding back. When they talk now it is in the manner of feeling their way over strange ground, as if afraid of what they are saying, but as if they can not help saying it.

Mrs. Hale: She liked the bird. She was going to bury it in that pretty box.

Mrs. Peters: *(in a whisper)* When I was a girl—my kitten—there was a boy took a hatchet, and before my eyes—and before I could get there—*(Covers her face an instant)* If they hadn't held me back I would have—*(Catches herself, looks upstairs where steps are heard, falters weakly)*—hurt him.

Mrs. Hale: *(with a slow look around her)* I wonder how it would seem never to have had any children around. *(Pause.)* No, Wright wouldn't like the bird—a thing that sang. She used to sing. He killed that, too.

125 **Mrs. Peters:** *(moving uneasily)* We don't know who killed the bird.

Mrs. Hale: I knew John Wright.

Mrs. Peters: It was an awful thing was done in this house that night, Mrs. Hale. Killing a man while he slept, slipping a rope around his neck that choked the life out of him.

Mrs. Hale: His neck. Choked the life out of him.

Her hand goes out and rests on the birdcage.

Mrs. Peters: *(with rising voice)* We don't know who killed him. We don't know.

130 **Mrs. Hale:** *(her own feeling not interrupted)* If there'd been years and years of nothing, then a bird to sing to you, it would be awful—still, after the bird was still.

Mrs. Peters: *(something within her speaking)* I know what stillness is. When we homesteaded in Dakota, and my first baby died—after he was two years old, and me with no other then—

Mrs. Hale: *(moving)* How soon do you suppose they'll be through, looking for the evidence?

Mrs. Peters: I know what stillness is. *(Pulling herself back.)* The law has got to punish crime, Mrs. Hale.

Mrs. Hale: *(not as if answering that)* I wish you'd seen Minnie Foster when she wore a white dress with blue ribbons and stood up there in the choir and sang. *(A look around the room.)* Oh, I *wish* I'd come over here once in a while! That was a crime! That was a crime! Who's going to punish that?

135 **Mrs. Peters:** *(looking upstairs)* We mustn't—take on.

Mrs. Hale: I might have known she needed help! I know how things can be—for women. I tell you, it's queer, Mrs. Peters. We live close together and we live far apart. We all go through the same things— it's all just a different kind of the same thing. *(Brushes her eyes; noticing the bottle of fruit, reaches out for it.)* If I was you I wouldn't tell her her fruit was gone. Tell her it *ain't*. Tell her it's all right. Take this in to prove it to her. She—she may never know whether it was broke or not.

Mrs. Peters: *(takes the bottle, looks about for something to wrap it in; takes petticoat from the clothes brought from the other room, very nervously begins winding this around the bottle. In a false voice)* My, it's a good thing the men couldn't hear us. Wouldn't they just laugh! Getting all stirred up over a little thing like a—dead canary. As if that could have anything to do with—with—wouldn't they *laugh*!

The men are heard coming down stairs.

Mrs. Hale: *(under her breath)* Maybe they would—maybe they wouldn't.

County Attorney: No, Peters, it's all perfectly clear except a reason for doing it. But you know juries when it comes to women. If there was some definite thing. Something to show—something to make a story about—a thing that would connect up with this strange way of doing it—

The women's eyes meet for an instant. Enter Hale from outer door.

140 **Hale:** Well, I've got the team around. Pretty cold out there.

County Attorney: I'm going to stay here a while by myself. *(To the Sheriff.)* You can send Frank out for me, can't you? I want to go over everything. I'm not satisfied that we can't do better.

Sheriff: Do you want to see what Mrs. Peters is going to take in?

The County Attorney goes to the table, picks up the apron, laughs.

County Attorney: Oh, I guess they're not very dangerous things the ladies have picked out. *(Moves a few things about, disturbing the quilt pieces which cover the box. Steps back.)* No, Mrs. Peters doesn't need supervising. For that matter, a sheriff's wife is married to the law. Ever think of it that way, Mrs. Peters?

MRS. PETERS: Not—just that way.

145 **SHERIFF:** *(chuckling)* Married to the law. *(Moves toward the other room.)* I just want you to come in here a minute, George. We ought to take a look at these windows.

COUNTY ATTORNEY: *(scoffingly)* Oh, windows!

SHERIFF: We'll be right out, Mr. Hale.

Hale goes outside. The Sheriff follows the County Attorney into the other room. Then Mrs. Hale rises, hands tight together, looking intensely at Mrs. Peters, whose eyes make a slow turn, finally meeting Mrs. Hale's. A moment Mrs. Hale holds her, then her own eyes point the way to where the box is concealed. Suddenly Mrs. Peters throws back quilt pieces and tries to put the box in the bag she is wearing. It is too big. She opens box, starts to take bird out, cannot touch it, goes to pieces, stands there helpless. Sound of a knob turning in the other room. Mrs. Hale snatches the box and puts it in the pocket of her big coat. Enter County Attorney and Sheriff.

COUNTY ATTORNEY: *(facetiously)* Well, Henry, at least we found out that she was not going to quilt it. She was going to—what is it you call it, ladies?

MRS. HALE: *(her hand against her pocket)* We call it—knot it, Mr. Henderson.

READING AND REACTING

1. What key events occur before the play begins? Why do you suppose these events are not presented in the play itself?

2. What are the "trifles" to which the title refers? How do these "trifles" advance the play's plot?

3. Glaspell's short story version of *Trifles* is called "A Jury of Her Peers" (p. 455). Who are Mrs. Wright's peers? What do you suppose the verdict would be if she were tried for her crime in 1916, when only men were permitted to serve on juries? If the trial were held today, do you think the jury might reach a different decision?

4. *Trifles* is a one-act play, and all its action occurs in the Wrights' kitchen. Does this static setting in any way slow down the flow of the plot? Are there any advantages to this setting? Explain.

5. All background information about Mrs. Wright is provided by Mrs. Hale. Do you consider her to be a reliable source of information? Why or why not?

6. Mr. Hale's summary of his conversation with Mrs. Wright is the reader's only encounter with her. How would Mrs. Wright's presence change the play?

7. *Trifles* is a relatively slow moving, "talky" play, with very little physical action. Is this a weakness of the play, or is the slow development consistent with the effect Glaspell is trying to achieve? Explain.

8. How does each of the following events advance the play's action: the men's departure from the kitchen, the discovery of the quilt pieces, the discovery of the dead bird?

9. How do the County Attorney's sarcastic comments and his patronizing attitude toward Mrs. Hale and Mrs. Peters advance the play's action?

10. How do Mrs. Peters's memories of her own life advance the action?

11. What assumptions about women do the male characters make? In what ways do the female characters conform to or depart from these assumptions?

12. In what sense is the process of making a quilt an appropriate metaphor for the plot of *Trifles?*

13. **JOURNAL ENTRY**   Do you think Mrs. Hale and Mrs. Peters do the right thing by concealing evidence?

14. **CRITICAL PERSPECTIVE**   Gary A. Richardson writes in *American Drama from the Colonial Period through World War I* that in *Trifles,* Glaspell "developed a new structure for her action . . . ."

While action in the traditional sense is minimal, Glaspell is nevertheless able to rivet attention on the two women, wed the audience to their perspective, and make a compelling case for the fairness of their actions. Existing on the margins of their society, Mrs. Peters and Mrs. Hale become emotional surrogates for the jailed Minnie Wright, effectively exonerating her action as "justifiable homicide."

Trifles is carefully crafted to match Glaspell's subject matter—the action meanders, without a clearly delineated beginning, middle, or end. . . .

Exactly how does Glaspell "rivet attention on" Mrs. Hale and Mrs. Peters? Do you agree that the play is "without a clearly delineated beginning, middle, and end"? If so, do you too see this "meandering" as appropriate for Glaspell's subject matter?

HENRIK IBSEN (1828–1906) is Norway's foremost dramatist. He was born in Skien, Norway, into a prosperous family, but his father lost his fortune when Ibsen was six; when he was fifteen, he was apprenticed to an apothecary away from home and was permanently estranged from his family. He studied to enter the university and wrote plays during his apprenticeship; though he did not pass the university entrance exam, his second play, *The Warrior's Barrow,* was produced by the Christiania Theatre in 1850. He began a life in the theater, writing plays and serving as artistic director of a theatrical company. Disillusioned by the public's lack of interest in theater, he moved to Italy and Germany with his wife and son between 1864 and 1891. By the time he returned to Norway, he was famous and revered. Ibsen's most notable plays include *Brand* (1865), *Peer Gynt* (1867), *A Doll House* (1879), *Ghosts* (1881), *An Enemy of the People* (1882), *The Wild Duck* (1884), *Hedda Gabler* (1890), and *When We Dead Awaken* (1899).

A Doll House marks the beginning of Ibsen's successful realist period, during which he explored the ordinary lives of small-town people, in this case what he called "a modern tragedy." The issue, he said, is that there are "two kinds of moral law, . . . one in man and a completely different one in woman. They do not understand each other. . . ." Nora and Helmer destroy their marriage because they cannot comprehend or accept their differences. Though the play begins conventionally, it does not fulfill its audience's expectations for a tidy resolution; as a result, the play was not very successful when first performed. Nevertheless, the publication of *A Doll House* made Ibsen internationally famous.

H E N R I K   I B S E N

A Doll House

(1879)

translated by Rolf Fjelde

CHARACTERS

TORVALD HELMER, *a lawyer*
NORA, *his wife*
DR. RANK
MRS. LINDE
A DELIVERY BOY

NILS KROGSTAD, *a bank clerk*
THE HELMERS' THREE SMALL CHILDREN
ANNE-MARIE, *their nurse*
HELENE, *a maid*

The action takes place in Helmer's residence.

ACT I

A comfortable room, tastefully but not expensively furnished. A door to the right in the back wall leads to the entryway; another to the left leads to Helmer's study. Between these doors, a piano. Midway in the left-hand wall a door, and further back a window. Near the window a round table with an armchair and a small sofa. In the right-hand wall, toward the rear, a door, and nearer the foreground a porcelain stove with two armchairs and a rocking chair beside it. Between the stove and the side door, a small table. Engravings on the walls. An étagère with china figures and other small art objects; a small bookcase with richly bound books; the floor carpeted; a fire burning in the stove. It is a winter day.

A bell rings in the entryway; shortly after we hear the door being unlocked. Nora comes into the room, humming happily to herself; she is wearing street clothes and carries an armload of packages, which she puts down on the table to the right. She has left the hall door open; and through it a Delivery Boy is seen, holding a Christmas tree and a basket, which he gives to the Maid who let them in.

NORA: Hide the tree well, Helene. The children mustn't get a glimpse of it till this evening, after it's trimmed. *(To the Delivery Boy, taking out her purse.)* How much?

DELIVERY BOY: Fifty, ma'am.

NORA: There's a crown. No, keep the change. *(The Boy thanks her and leaves. Nora shuts the door. She laughs softly to herself while taking off her street things. Drawing a bag of macaroons from her pocket, she eats a couple, then steals over and listens at her husband's study door.)* Yes, he's home. *(Hums again as she moves to the table right.)*

HELMER: *(from the study)* Is that my little lark twittering out there?

5 **NORA:** *(busy opening some packages)* Yes, it is.

HELMER: Is that my squirrel rummaging around?

NORA: Yes!

HELMER: When did my squirrel get in?

NORA: Just now. *(Putting the macaroon bag in her pocket and wiping her mouth.)* Do come in, Torvald, and see what I've bought.

10 **HELMER:** Can't be disturbed. *(After a moment he opens the door and peers in, pen in hand.)* Bought, you say? All that there? Has the little spendthrift been out throwing money around again?

NORA: Oh, but Torvald, this year we really should let ourselves go a bit. It's the first Christmas we haven't had to economize.

HELMER: But you know we can't go squandering.

NORA: Oh yes, Torvald, we can squander a little now. Can't we? Just a tiny, wee bit. Now that you've got a big salary and are going to make piles and piles of money.

HELMER: Yes—starting New Year's. But then it's a full three months till the raise comes through.

15 **NORA:** Pooh! We can borrow that long.

HELMER: Nora! *(Goes over and playfully takes her by the ear.)* Are your scatterbrains off again? What if today I borrowed a thousand crowns, and you squandered them over Christmas week, and then on New Year's Eve a roof tile fell on my head, and I lay there—

NORA: *(putting her hand on his mouth)* Oh! Don't say such things!

HELMER: Yes, but what if it happened—then what?

NORA: If anything so awful happened, then it just wouldn't matter if I had debts or not.

20 **HELMER:** Well, but the people I'd borrowed from?

NORA: Them? Who cares about them! They're strangers.

HELMER: Nora, Nora, how like a woman! No, but seriously, Nora, you know what I think about that. No debts! Never borrow! Something of

freedom's lost—and something of beauty, too—from a home that's
founded on borrowing and debt. We've made a brave stand up to
now, the two of us; and we'll go right on like that the little while we
have to.

NORA: *(going toward the stove)* Yes, whatever you say, Torvald.

HELMER: *(following her)* Now, now, the little lark's wings mustn't droop.
Come on, don't be a sulky squirrel. *(Taking out his wallet.)* Nora, guess
what I have here.

25 **NORA:** *(turning quickly)* Money!

HELMER: There, see. *(Hands her some notes.)* Good grief, I know how
costs go up in a house at Christmastime.

NORA: Ten—twenty—thirty—forty. Oh, thank you, Torvald; I can
manage no end on this.

HELMER: You really will have to.

NORA: Oh yes, I promise I will! But come here so I can show you
everything I bought. And so cheap! Look, new clothes for Ivar here—
and a sword. Here a horse and a trumpet for Bob. And a doll and a
doll's bed here for Emmy; they're nothing much, but she'll tear them
to bits in no time anyway. And here I have dress material and
handkerchiefs for the maids. Old Anne-Marie really deserves
something more.

30 **HELMER:** And what's in that package there?

NORA: *(with a cry)* Torvald, no! You can't see that till tonight!

HELMER: I see. But tell me now, you little prodigal, what have you
thought of for yourself?

NORA: For myself? Oh, I don't want anything at all.

HELMER: Of course you do. Tell me just what—within reason—you'd
most like to have.

35 **NORA:** I honestly don't know. Oh, listen, Torvald—

HELMER: Well?

NORA: *(fumbling at his coat buttons, without looking at him)* If you want
to give me something, then maybe you could—you could—

HELMER: Come on, out with it.

NORA: *(hurriedly)* You could give me money, Torvald. No more than you
think you can spare; then one of these days I'll buy something with it.

40 **HELMER:** But Nora—

NORA: Oh, please, Torvald darling, do that! I beg you, please. Then I
could hang the bills in pretty gilt paper on the Christmas tree.
Wouldn't that be fun?

HELMER: What are those little birds called that always fly through their
fortunes?

NORA: Oh yes, spendthrifts; I know all that. But let's do as I say,
Torvald; then I'll have time to decide what I really need most. That's
very sensible, isn't it?

HELMER: *(smiling)* Yes, very—that is, if you actually hung onto the
money I give you, and you actually used it to buy yourself something.

But it goes for the house and for all sorts of foolish things, and then I only have to lay out some more.

45 **NORA:** Oh, but Torvald—

HELMER: Don't deny it, my dear little Nora. *(Putting his arm around her waist.)* Spendthrifts are sweet, but they use up a frightful amount of money. It's incredible what it costs a man to feed such birds.

NORA: Oh, how can you say that! Really, I save everything I can.

HELMER: *(laughing)* Yes, that's the truth. Everything you can. But that's nothing at all.

NORA: *(humming, with a smile of quiet satisfaction)* Hm, if you only knew what expenses we larks and squirrels have, Torvald.

50 **HELMER:** You're an odd little one. Exactly the way your father was. You're never at a loss for scaring up money; but the moment you have it, it runs right out through your fingers; you never know what you've done with it. Well, one takes you as you are. It's deep in your blood. Yes, these things are hereditary, Nora.

NORA: Ah, I could wish I'd inherited many of Papa's qualities.

HELMER: And I couldn't wish you anything but just what you are, my sweet little lark. But wait; it seems to me you have a very—what should I call it?—a very suspicious look today—

NORA: I do?

HELMER: You certainly do. Look me straight in the eye.

55 **NORA:** *(looking at him)* Well?

HELMER: *(shaking an admonitory finger)* Surely my sweet tooth hasn't been running riot in town today, has she?

NORA: No. Why do you imagine that?

HELMER: My sweet tooth really didn't make a little detour through the confectioner's?

NORA: No, I assure you, Torvald—

60 **HELMER:** Hasn't nibbled some pastry?

NORA: No, not at all.

HELMER: Nor even munched a macaroon or two?

NORA: No, Torvald, I assure you, really—

HELMER: There, there now. Of course I'm only joking.

65 **NORA:** *(going to the table, right)* You know I could never think of going against you.

HELMER: No, I understand that; and you *have* given me your word. *(Going over to her.)* Well, you keep your little Christmas secrets to yourself, Nora darling. I expect they'll come to light this evening, when the tree is lit.

NORA: Did you remember to ask Dr. Rank?

HELMER: No. But there's no need for that; it's assumed he'll be dining with us. All the same, I'll ask him when he stops by here this morning. I've ordered some fine wine. Nora, you can't imagine how I'm looking forward to this evening.

NORA: So am I. And what fun for the children, Torvald!

70 **HELMER:** Ah, it's so gratifying to know that one's gotten a safe, secure job, and with a comfortable salary. It's a great satisfaction, isn't it?

NORA: Oh, it's wonderful!

HELMER: Remember last Christmas? Three whole weeks before, you shut yourself in every evening till long after midnight, making flowers for the Christmas tree, and all the other decorations to surprise us. Ugh, that was the dullest time I've ever lived through.

NORA: It wasn't at all dull for me.

HELMER: *(smiling)* But the outcome *was* pretty sorry, Nora.

75 **NORA:** Oh, don't tease me with that again. How could I help it that the cat came in and tore everything to shreds.

HELMER: No, poor thing, you certainly couldn't. You wanted so much to please us all, and that's what counts. But it's just as well that the hard times are past.

NORA: Yes, it's really wonderful.

HELMER: Now I don't have to sit here alone, boring myself, and you don't have to tire your precious eyes and your fair little delicate hands—

NORA: *(clapping her hands)* No, is it really true, Torvald, I don't have to? Oh, how wonderfully lovely to hear! *(Taking his arm.)* Now I'll tell you just how I've thought we should plan things. Right after Christmas— *(The doorbell rings.)* Oh, the bell. *(Straightening the room up a bit.)* Somebody would have to come. What a bore!

80 **HELMER:** I'm not at home to visitors, don't forget.

MAID: *(from the hall doorway)* Ma'am, a lady to see you—

NORA: All right, let her come in.

MAID: *(to Helmer)* And the doctor's just come too.

HELMER: Did he go right to my study?

85 **MAID:** Yes, he did.

Helmer goes into his room. The Maid shows in Mrs. Linde, dressed in traveling clothes, and shuts the door after her.

MRS. LINDE: *(in a dispirited and somewhat hesitant voice)* Hello, Nora.

NORA: *(uncertain)* Hello—

MRS. LINDE: You don't recognize me.

NORA: No, I don't know—but wait, I think—*(Exclaiming.)* What! Kristine! Is it really you?

90 **MRS. LINDE:** Yes, it's me.

NORA: *Kristine!* To think I didn't recognize you. But then, how could I? *(More quietly.)* How you've changed, Kristine!

MRS. LINDE: Yes, no doubt I have. In nine—ten long years.

NORA: Is it so long since we met! Yes, it's all of that. Oh, these last eight years have been a happy time, believe me. And so now you've come in to town, too. Made the long trip in the winter. That took courage.

MRS. LINDE: I just got here by ship this morning.

95 **NORA:**   To enjoy yourself over Christmas, of course. Oh, how lovely! Yes, enjoy ourselves, we'll do that. But take your coat off. You're not still cold? *(Helping her.)* There now, let's get cozy here by the stove. No, the easy chair there! I'll take the rocker here. *(Seizing her hands.)* Yes, now you have your old look again; it was only in that first moment. You're a bit more pale, Kristine—and maybe a bit thinner.

MRS. LINDE: And much, much older, Nora.

NORA: Yes, perhaps a bit older; a tiny, tiny bit; not much at all. *(Stopping short; suddenly serious.)* Oh, but thoughtless me, to sit here, chattering away. Sweet, good Kristine, can you forgive me?

MRS. LINDE: What do you mean, Nora?

NORA: *(softly)* Poor Kristine, you've become a widow.

100 **MRS. LINDE:**   Yes, three years ago.

NORA: Oh, I knew it, of course: I read it in the papers. Oh, Kristine, you must believe me; I often thought of writing you then, but I kept postponing it, and something always interfered.

MRS. LINDE: Nora dear, I understand completely.

NORA: No, it was awful of me, Kristine. You poor thing, how much you must have gone through. And he left you nothing?

MRS. LINDE: No.

105 **NORA:**   And no children?

MRS. LINDE: No.

NORA: Nothing at all, then?

MRS. LINDE: Not even a sense of loss to feed on.

NORA: *(looking incredulously at her)* But Kristine, how could that be?

110 **MRS. LINDE:**   *(smiling wearily and smoothing her hair)* Oh, sometimes it happens, Nora.

NORA: So completely alone. How terribly hard that must be for you. I have three lovely children. You can't see them now; they're out with the maid. But now you must tell me everything—

MRS. LINDE: No, no, no, tell me about yourself.

NORA: No, you begin. Today I don't want to be selfish. I want to think only of you today. But there *is* something I must tell you. Did you hear of the wonderful luck we had recently?

MRS. LINDE: No, what's that?

115 **NORA:**   My husband's been made manager in the bank, just think!

MRS. LINDE: Your husband? How marvelous!

NORA: Isn't it? Being a lawyer is such an uncertain living, you know, especially if one won't touch any cases that aren't clean and decent. And of course Torvald would never do that, and I'm with him completely there. Oh, we're simply delighted, believe me! He'll join the bank right after New Year's and start getting a huge salary and lots of commissions. From now on we can live quite differently—just as we want. Oh, Kristine, I feel so light and happy! Won't it be lovely to have stacks of money and not a care in the world?

Mrs. Linde: Well, anyway, it would be lovely to have enough for necessities.

Nora: No, not just for necessities, but stacks and stacks of money!

120 **Mrs. Linde:**   *(smiling)* Nora, Nora, aren't you sensible yet? Back in school you were such a free spender.

Nora: *(with a quiet laugh)* Yes, that's what Torvald still says. *(Shaking her finger.)* But "Nora, Nora" isn't as silly as you all think. Really, we've been in no position for me to go squandering. We've had to work, both of us.

Mrs. Linde: You too?

Nora: Yes, at odd jobs—needlework, crocheting, embroidery, and such—*(casually)* and other things too. You remember that Torvald left the department when we were married? There was no chance of promotion in his office, and of course he needed to earn more money. But that first year he drove himself terribly. He took on all kinds of extra work that kept him going morning and night. It wore him down, and then he fell deathly ill. The doctors said it was essential for him to travel south.

Mrs. Linde: Yes, didn't you spend a whole year in Italy?

125 **Nora:**   That's right. It wasn't easy to get away, you know. Ivar had just been born. But of course we had to go. Oh, that was a beautiful trip, and it saved Torvald's life. But it cost a frightful sum, Kristine.

Mrs. Linde: I can well imagine.

Nora: Four thousand, eight hundred crowns it cost. That's really a lot of money.

Mrs. Linde: But it's lucky you had it when you needed it.

Nora: Well, as it was, we got it from Papa.

130 **Mrs. Linde:**   I see. It was just about the time your father died.

Nora: Yes, just about then. And, you know, I couldn't make that trip out to nurse him. I had to stay here, expecting Ivar any moment, and with my poor sick Torvald to care for. Dearest Papa, I never saw him again, Kristine. Oh, that was the worst time I've known in all my marriage.

Mrs. Linde: I know how you loved him. And then you went off to Italy?

Nora: Yes. We had the means now, and the doctors urged us. So we left a month after.

Mrs. Linde: And your husband came back completely cured?

135 **Nora:**   Sound as a drum!

Mrs. Linde: But—the doctor?

Nora: Who?

Mrs. Linde: I thought the maid said he was a doctor, the man who came in with me.

Nora: Yes, that was Dr. Rank—but he's not making a sick call. He's our closest friend, and he stops by at least once a day. No, Torvald hasn't had a sick moment since, and the children are fit and strong, and I am, too. *(Jumping up and clapping her hands.)* Oh, dear God, Kristine, what a lovely thing to live and be happy! But how disgusting of me— I'm talking of nothing but my own affairs. *(Sits on a stool close by Kristine, arms resting across her knees.)* Oh, don't be angry with me! Tell me, is it really true that you weren't in love with your husband? Why did you marry him, then?

140 **MRS. LINDE:** My mother was still alive, but bedridden and helpless— and I had my two younger brothers to look after. In all conscience, I didn't think I could turn him down.

NORA: No, you were right there. But was he rich at the time?

MRS. LINDE: He was very well off, I'd say. But the business was shaky, Nora. When he died, it all fell apart, and nothing was left.

NORA: And then—?

MRS. LINDE: Yes, so I had to scrape up a living with a little shop and a little teaching and whatever else I could find. The last three years have been like one endless workday without a rest for me. Now it's over, Nora. My poor mother doesn't need me, for she's passed on. Nor the boys, either; they're working now and can take care of themselves.

145 **NORA:** How free you must feel—

MRS. LINDE: No—only unspeakably empty. Nothing to live for now. *(Standing up anxiously.)* That's why I couldn't take it any longer out in that desolate hole. Maybe here it'll be easier to find something to do and keep my mind occupied. If I could only be lucky enough to get a steady job, some office work—

NORA: Oh, but Kristine, that's so dreadfully tiring, and you already look so tired. It would be much better for you if you could go off to a bathing resort.

MRS. LINDE: *(going toward the window)* I have no father to give me travel money, Nora.

NORA: *(rising)* Oh, don't be angry with me.

150 **MRS. LINDE:** *(going to her)* Nora dear, don't you be angry with me. The worst of my kind of situation is all the bitterness that's stored away. No one to work for, and yet you're always having to snap up your opportunities. You have to live; and so you grow selfish. When you told me the happy change in your lot, do you know I was delighted less for your sakes than for mine?

NORA: How so? Oh, I see. You think Torvald could do something for you.

MRS. LINDE: Yes, that's what I thought.

NORA: And he will, Kristine! Just leave it to me; I'll bring it up so delicately—find something attractive to humor him with. Oh, I'm so eager to help you.

MRS. LINDE: How very kind of you, Nora, to be so concerned over me— doubly kind, considering you really know so little of life's burdens yourself.

155 **NORA:** I—? I know so little—?

MRS. LINDE: *(smiling)* Well my heavens—a little needlework and such—
   Nora, you're just a child.

NORA: *(tossing her head and pacing the floor)* You don't have to act so
   superior.

MRS. LINDE: Oh?

NORA: You're just like the others. You all think I'm incapable of
   anything serious—

160 **MRS. LINDE:** Come now—

NORA: That I've never had to face the raw world.

MRS. LINDE: Nora dear, you've just been telling me all your troubles.

NORA: Hm! Trivial! *(Quietly.)* I haven't told you the big thing.

MRS. LINDE: Big thing? What do you mean?

165 **NORA:** You look down on me so, Kristine, but you shouldn't. You're
   proud that you worked so long and hard for your mother.

MRS. LINDE: I don't look down on a soul. But it *is* true: I'm proud—and
   happy, too—to think it was given to me to make my mother's last
   days almost free of care.

NORA: And you're also proud thinking of what you've done for your
   brothers.

MRS. LINDE: I feel I've a right to be.

NORA: I agree. But listen to this, Kristine—I've also got something to be
   proud and happy for.

170 **MRS. LINDE:** I don't doubt it. But whatever do you mean?

NORA: Not so loud. What if Torvald heard! He mustn't, not for anything
   in the world. Nobody must know, Kristine. No one but you.

MRS. LINDE: But what is it, then?

NORA: Come here. *(Drawing her down beside her on the sofa.)* It's true—
   I've also got something to be proud and happy for. I'm the one who
   saved Torvald's life.

MRS. LINDE: Saved—? Saved how?

175 **NORA:** I told you about the trip to Italy. Torvald never would have lived
   if he hadn't gone south—

MRS. LINDE: Of course; your father gave you the means—

NORA: *(smiling)* That's what Torvald and all the rest think, but—

MRS. LINDE: But—?

NORA: Papa didn't give us a pin. I was the one who raised the money.

180 **MRS. LINDE:** You? That whole amount?

NORA: Four thousand, eight hundred crowns. What do you say to that?

MRS. LINDE: But Nora, how was it possible? Did you win the lottery?

NORA: *(disdainfully)* The lottery? Pooh! No art to that.

MRS. LINDE: But where did you get it from then?

185 **NORA:** *(humming, with a mysterious smile)* Hmm, tra-la-la-la.

MRS. LINDE: Because you couldn't have borrowed it.

NORA: No? Why not?

Mrs. Linde: A wife can't borrow without her husband's consent.

Nora: *(tossing her head)* Oh, but a wife with a little business sense, a wife who knows how to manage—

190 **Mrs. Linde:** Nora, I simply don't understand—

Nora: You don't have to. Whoever said I *borrowed* the money? I could have gotten it other ways. *(Throwing herself back on the sofa.)* I could have gotten it from some admirer or other. After all, a girl with my ravishing appeal—

Mrs. Linde: You lunatic.

Nora: I'll bet you're eaten up with curiosity, Kristine.

Mrs. Linde: Now listen here, Nora—you haven't done something indiscreet?

195 **Nora:** *(sitting up again)* Is it indiscreet to save your husband's life?

Mrs. Linde: I think it's indiscreet that without his knowledge you—

Nora: But that's the point: he mustn't know! My Lord, can't you understand? He mustn't ever know the close call he had. It was to *me* the doctors came to say his life was in danger—that nothing could save him but a stay in the south. Didn't I try strategy then! I began talking about how lovely it would be for me to travel abroad like other young wives; I begged and I cried; I told him please to remember my condition, to be kind and indulge me; and then I dropped a hint that he could easily take out a loan. But at that, Kristine, he nearly exploded. He said I was frivolous, and it was his duty as man of the house not to indulge me in whims and fancies—as I think he called them. Aha, I thought, now you'll just have to be saved—and that's when I saw my chance.

Mrs. Linde: And your father never told Torvald the money wasn't from him?

Nora: No, never. Papa died right about then. I'd considered bringing him into my secret and begging him never to tell. But he was too sick at the time—and then, sadly, it didn't matter.

200 **Mrs. Linde:** And you've never confided in your husband since?

Nora: For heaven's sake, no! Are you serious? He's so strict on that subject. Besides—Torvald, with all his masculine pride—how painfully humiliating for him if he ever found out he was in debt to me. That would just ruin our relationship. Our beautiful, happy home would never be the same.

Mrs. Linde: Won't you ever tell him?

Nora: *(thoughtfully, half smiling)* Yes—maybe sometime, years from now, when I'm no longer so attractive. Don't laugh! I only mean when Torvald loves me less than now, when he stops enjoying my dancing and dressing up and reciting for him. Then it might be wise to have something in reserve—*(Breaking off.)* How ridiculous! That'll never happen—Well, Kristine, what do you think of my big secret? I'm capable of something too, hm? You can imagine, of course, how this thing hangs over me. It really hasn't been easy meeting the payments on time. In the business world there's what they call quarterly interest and what they call amortization, and these are always so terribly hard to manage. I've had to skimp a little here and there, wherever I could, you know. I could hardly spare anything from my house allowance, because Torvald has to live well. I couldn't let the children go poorly dressed; whatever I got for them, I felt I had to use up completely—the darlings!

MRS. LINDE: Poor Nora, so it had to come out of your own budget, then?

205 **NORA:**   Yes, of course. But I was the one most responsible, too. Every time Torvald gave me money for new clothes and such, I never used more than half; always bought the simplest, cheapest outfits. It was a godsend that everything looks so well on me that Torvald never noticed. But it did weigh me down at times, Kristine. It *is* such a joy to wear fine things. You understand.

MRS. LINDE: Oh, of course.

NORA: And then I found other ways of making money. Last winter I was lucky enough to get a lot of copying to do. I locked myself in and sat writing every evening till late in the night. Ah, I was tired so often, dead tired. But still it was wonderful fun, sitting and working like that, earning money. It was almost like being a man.

MRS. LINDE: But how much have you paid off this way so far?

NORA: That's hard to say, exactly. These accounts, you know, aren't easy to figure. I only know that I've paid out all I could scrape together. Time and again I haven't known where to turn. *(Smiling.)* Then I'd sit here dreaming of a rich old gentleman who had fallen in love with me—

210 **MRS. LINDE:**   What! Who is he?

NORA: Oh, really! And that he'd died, and when his will was opened, there in big letters it said, "All my fortune shall be paid over in cash, immediately, to that enchanting Mrs. Nora Helmer."

MRS. LINDE: But Nora dear—who *was* this gentleman?

NORA: Good grief, can't you understand? The old man never existed; that was only something I'd dream up time and again whenever I was at my wits' end for money. But it makes no difference now; the old fossil can go where he pleases for all I care; I don't need him or his will—because now I'm free. *(Jumping up.)* Oh, how lovely to think of that, Kristine! Carefree! To know you're carefree, utterly carefree; to be able to romp and play with the children, and to keep up a beautiful, charming home—everything just the way Torvald likes it! And think, spring is coming, with big blue skies. Maybe we can travel a little then. Maybe I'll see the ocean again. Oh yes, it *is* so marvelous to live and be happy!

(The front doorbell rings.)

MRS. LINDE: *(rising)* There's the bell. It's probably best that I go.

215 **NORA:**   No, stay. No one's expected. It must be for Torvald.

MAID: *(from the hall doorway)* Excuse me, ma'am—there's a gentleman here to see Mr. Helmer, but I didn't know—since the doctor's with him—

NORA: Who is the gentleman?

KROGSTAD: *(from the doorway)* It's me, Mrs. Helmer.

Mrs. Linde starts and turns away toward the window.

NORA: *(stepping toward him, tense, her voice a whisper)* You? What is it? Why do you want to speak to my husband?

220 **KROGSTAD:** Bank business—after a fashion. I have a small job in the investment bank, and I hear now your husband is going to be our chief—

NORA: In other words, it's—

KROGSTAD: Just dry business, Mrs. Helmer. Nothing but that.

NORA: Yes, then please be good enough to step into the study. *(She nods indifferently as she sees him out by the hall door, then returns and begins stirring up the stove.)*

MRS. LINDE: Nora—who was that man?

225 **NORA:** That was a Mr. Krogstad—a lawyer.

MRS. LINDE: Then it really was him.

NORA: Do you know that person?

MRS. LINDE: I did once—many years ago. For a time he was a law clerk in our town.

NORA: Yes, he's been that.

230 **MRS. LINDE:** How he's changed.

NORA: I understand he had a very unhappy marriage.

MRS. LINDE: He's a widower now.

NORA: With a number of children. There now, it's burning. *(She closes the stove door and moves the rocker a bit to one side.)*

MRS. LINDE: They say he has a hand in all kinds of business.

235 **NORA:** Oh? That may be true: I wouldn't know. But let's not think about business. It's so dull.

Dr. Rank enters from Helmer's study.

RANK: *(still in the doorway)* No, no, really—I don't want to intrude, I'd just as soon talk a little while with your wife. *(Shuts the door, then notices Mrs. Linde.)* Oh, beg pardon. I'm intruding here too.

NORA: No, not at all. *(Introducing him.)* Dr. Rank, Mrs. Linde.

RANK: Well now, that's a name much heard in this house. I believe I passed the lady on the stairs as I came.

MRS. LINDE: Yes, I take the stairs very slowly. They're rather hard on me.

240 **RANK:** Uh-hm, some touch of internal weakness?

MRS. LINDE: More overexertion, I'd say.

RANK: Nothing else? Then you're probably here in town to rest up in a round of parties?

MRS. LINDE: I'm here to look for work.

RANK: Is that the best cure for overexertion?

245 **MRS. LINDE:**   One has to live, Doctor.

RANK: Yes, there's a common prejudice to that effect.

NORA: Oh, come on, Dr. Rank—you really do want to live yourself.

RANK: Yes, I really do. Wretched as I am, I'll gladly prolong my torment indefinitely. All my patients feel like that. And it's quite the same, too, with the morally sick. Right at this moment there's one of those moral invalids in there with Helmer—

MRS. LINDE: *(softly)* Ah!

250 **NORA:**   Who do you mean?

RANK: Oh, it's a lawyer, Krogstad, a type you wouldn't know. His character is rotten to the root—but even he began chattering all-importantly about how he had to *live*.

NORA: Oh? What did he want to talk to Torvald about?

RANK: I really don't know. I only heard something about the bank.

NORA: I didn't know that Krog—that this man Krogstad had anything to do with the bank.

255 **RANK:**   Yes, he's gotten some kind of berth down there. *(To Mrs. Linde.)* I don't know if you also have, in your neck of the woods, a type of person who scuttles about breathlessly, sniffing out hints of moral corruption, and then maneuvers his victim into some sort of key position where he can keep an eye on him. It's the healthy these days that are out in the cold.

MRS. LINDE: All the same, it's the sick who most need to be taken in.

RANK: *(with a shrug)* Yes, there we have it. That's the concept that's turning society into a sanatorium.

Nora, lost in her thoughts, breaks out into quiet laughter and claps her hands.

RANK: Why do you laugh at that? Do you have any real idea of what society is?

NORA: What do I care about dreary old society? I was laughing at something quite different—something terribly funny. Tell me, Doctor—is everyone who works in the bank dependent now on Torvald?

260 **RANK:**   Is that what you find so terribly funny?

NORA: *(smiling and humming)* Never mind, never mind! *(Pacing the floor.)* Yes, that's really immensely amusing: that we—that Torvald has so much power now over all those people. *(Taking the bag out of her pocket.)* Dr. Rank, a little macaroon on that?

RANK: See here, macaroons! I thought they were contraband here.

NORA: Yes, but these are some that Kristine gave me.

MRS. LINDE: What? I—?

265 **NORA:**   Now, now, don't be afraid. You couldn't possibly know that Torvald had forbidden them. You see, he's worried they'll ruin my teeth. But hmp! Just this once! Isn't that so, Dr. Rank? Help yourself! *(Puts a macaroon in his mouth.)* And you too, Kristine. And I'll also have one, only a little one—or two, at the most. *(Walking about*

again.) Now I'm really tremendously happy. Now there's just one last thing in the world that I have an enormous desire to do.

RANK: Well! And what's that?

NORA: It's something I have such a consuming desire to say so Torvald could hear.

RANK: And why can't you say it?

NORA: I don't dare. It's quite shocking.

270 **MRS. LINDE:** Shocking?

RANK: Well, then it isn't advisable. But in front of us you certainly can. What do you have such a desire to say so Torvald could hear?

NORA: I have such a huge desire to say—to hell and be damned!

RANK: Are you crazy?

MRS. LINDE: My goodness, Nora!

275 **RANK:** Go on, say it. Here he is.

NORA: (*hiding the macaroon bag*) Shh, shh, shh!

Helmer comes in from his study, hat in hand, overcoat over his arm.

NORA: (*going toward him*) Well, Torvald dear, are you through with him?

HELMER: Yes, he just left.

NORA: Let me introduce you—this is Kristine, who's arrived here in town.

280 **HELMER:** Kristine—? I'm sorry, but I don't know—

NORA: Mrs. Linde, Torvald dear. Mrs. Kristine Linde.

HELMER: Of course. A childhood friend of my wife's, no doubt?

MRS. LINDE: Yes, we knew each other in those days.

NORA: And just think, she made the long trip down here in order to talk with you.

285 **HELMER:** What's this?

MRS. LINDE: Well, not exactly—

NORA: You see, Kristine is remarkably clever in office work, and so she's terribly eager to come under a capable man's supervision and add more to what she already knows—

HELMER: Very wise, Mrs. Linde.

NORA: And then when she heard that you'd become a bank manager—the story was wired out to the papers—then she came in as fast as she could and—Really, Torvald, for my sake you can do a little something for Kristine, can't you?

290 **HELMER:** Yes, it's not at all impossible. Mrs. Linde, I suppose you're a widow?

MRS. LINDE: Yes.

HELMER: Any experience in office work?

MRS. LINDE: Yes, a good deal.

HELMER: Well, it's quite likely that I can make an opening for you—

295 **NORA:** (*clapping her hands*) You see, you see!

HELMER: You've come at a lucky moment, Mrs. Linde.

MRS. LINDE: Oh, how can I thank you?

HELMER: Not necessary. (*Putting his overcoat on.*) But today you'll have
to excuse me—

RANK: Wait, I'll go with you. (*He fetches his coat from the hall and warms
it at the stove.*)

300 **NORA:**   Don't stay out long, dear.

HELMER: An hour; no more.

NORA: Are you going too, Kristine?

MRS. LINDE: (*putting on her winter garments*) Yes, I have to see about a
room now.

HELMER: Then perhaps we can all walk together.

305 **NORA:**   (*helping her*) What a shame we're so cramped here, but it's quite
impossible for us to—

MRS. LINDE: Oh, don't even think of it! Good-bye, Nora dear, and
thanks for everything.

NORA: Good-bye for now. Of course you'll be back this evening. And
you too, Dr. Rank. What? If you're well enough? Oh, you've got to
be! Wrap up tight now.

*In a ripple of small talk the company moves out into the hall; children's voices
are heard outside on the steps.*

NORA: There they are! There they are! (*She runs to open the door. The
children come in with their nurse, Anne-Marie.*) Come in, come in!
(*Bends down and kisses them.*) Oh, you darlings—! Look at them,
Kristine. Aren't they lovely!

RANK: No loitering in the draft here.

310 **HELMER:**   Come, Mrs. Linde—this place is unbearable now for anyone
but mothers.

*Dr. Rank, Helmer, and Mrs. Linde go down the stairs. Anne-Marie goes into the
living room with the children. Nora follows, after closing the hall door.*

NORA: How fresh and strong you look. Oh, such red cheeks you have!
Like apples and roses. (*The children interrupt her throughout the
following.*) And it was so much fun? That's wonderful. Really? You
pulled both Emmy and Bob on the sled? Imagine, all together! Yes,
you're a clever boy, Ivar. Oh, let me hold her a bit, Anne-Marie. My
sweet little doll baby! (*Takes the smallest from the nurse and dances with
her.*) Yes, yes, Mama will dance with Bob as well. What? Did you
throw snowballs? Oh, if I'd only been there! No, don't bother, Anne-
Marie—I'll undress them myself. Oh yes, let me. It's such fun. Go in
and rest; you look half frozen. There's hot coffee waiting for you on
the stove. (*The nurse goes into the room to the left. Nora takes the
children's winter things off, throwing them about, while the children talk
to her all at once.*) Is that so? A big dog chased you? But it didn't bite?
No, dogs never bite little, lovely doll babies. Don't peek in the
packages, Ivar! What is it? Yes, wouldn't you like to know. No, no,
it's an ugly something. Well? Shall we play? What shall we play?

Hide-and-seek? Yes, let's play hide-and-seek. Bob must hide first. I must? Yes, let me hide first. *(Laughing and shouting, she and the children play in and out of the living room and the adjoining room to the right. At last Nora hides under the table. The children come storming in, search, but cannot find her, then hear her muffled laughter, dash over to the table, lift the cloth up and find her. Wild shouting. She creeps forward as if to scare them. More shouts. Meanwhile, a knock at the hall door; no one has noticed it. Now the door half opens, and Krogstad appears. He waits a moment; the game goes on.)*

KROGSTAD: Beg pardon, Mrs. Helmer—

NORA: *(with a strangled cry, turning and scrambling to her knees)* Oh! What do you want?

KROGSTAD: Excuse me. The outer door was ajar; it must be someone forgot to shut it—

315 **NORA:** *(rising)* My husband isn't home, Mr. Krogstad.

KROGSTAD: I know that.

NORA: Yes—then what do you want here?

KROGSTAD: A word with you.

NORA: With—? *(To the children, quietly.)* Go in to Anne-Marie. What? No, the strange man won't hurt Mama. When he's gone, we'll play some more. *(She leads the children into the room to the left and shuts the door after them. Then, tense and nervous)* You want to speak to me?

320 **KROGSTAD:** Yes, I want to.

NORA: Today? But it's not yet the first of the month—

KROGSTAD: No, it's Christmas Eve. It's going to be up to you how merry a Christmas you have.

NORA: What is it you want? Today I absolutely can't—

KROGSTAD: We won't talk about that till later. This is something else. You do have a moment to spare, I suppose?

325 **NORA:** Oh yes, of course—I do, except—

KROGSTAD: Good. I was sitting over at Olsen's Restaurant when I saw your husband go down the street—

NORA: Yes?

KROGSTAD: With a lady.

NORA: Yes. So?

330 **KROGSTAD:** If you'll pardon my asking: wasn't that lady a Mrs. Linde?

NORA: Yes.

KROGSTAD: Just now come into town?

NORA: Yes, today.

KROGSTAD: She's a good friend of yours?

335 **NORA:** Yes, she is. But I don't see—

KROGSTAD: I also knew her once.

NORA: I'm aware of that.

KROGSTAD: Oh? You know all about it. I thought so. Well, then let me ask you short and sweet: is Mrs. Linde getting a job in the bank?

NORA: What makes you think you can cross-examine me, Mr. Krogstad—you, one of my husband's employees? But since you ask, you might as well know—yes, Mrs. Linde's going to be taken on at the bank. And I'm the one who spoke for her, Mr. Krogstad. Now you know.

340 **KROGSTAD:**   So I guessed right.

NORA: *(pacing up and down)* Oh, one does have a tiny bit of influence, I should hope. Just because I am a woman, don't think it means that— When one has a subordinate position, Mr. Krogstad, one really ought to be careful about pushing somebody who—hm—

KROGSTAD: Who has influence?

NORA: That's right.

KROGSTAD: *(in a different tone)* Mrs. Helmer, would you be good enough to use your influence on my behalf?

345 **NORA:**   What? What do you mean?

KROGSTAD: Would you please make sure that I keep my subordinate position in the bank?

NORA: What does that mean? Who's thinking of taking away your position?

KROGSTAD: Oh, don't play the innocent with me. I'm quite aware that your friend would hardly relish the chance of running into me again; and I'm also aware now whom I can thank for being turned out.

NORA: But I promise you—

350 **KROGSTAD:**   Yes, yes, yes, to the point: there's still time, and I'm advising you to use your influence to prevent it.

NORA: But Mr. Krogstad, I have absolutely no influence.

KROGSTAD: You haven't? I thought you were just saying—

NORA: You shouldn't take me so literally. I! How can you believe that I have any such influence over my husband?

KROGSTAD: Oh, I've known your husband from our student days. I don't think the great bank manager's more steadfast than any other married man.

355 **NORA:**   You speak insolently about my husband, and I'll show you the door.

KROGSTAD: The lady has spirit.

NORA: I'm not afraid of you any longer. After New Year's, I'll soon be done with the whole business.

KROGSTAD: *(restraining himself)* Now listen to me, Mrs. Helmer. If necessary, I'll fight for my little job in the bank as if it were life itself.

NORA: Yes, so it seems.

360 **KROGSTAD:**   It's not just a matter of income; that's the least of it. It's something else—All right, out with it! Look, this is the thing. You know, just like all the others, of course, that once, a good many years ago, I did something rather rash.

NORA: I've heard rumors to that effect.

KROGSTAD: The case never got into court; but all the same, every door was closed in my face from then on. So I took up those various activities you know about. I had to grab hold somewhere; and I dare say I haven't been among the worst. But now I want to drop all that. My boys are growing up. For their sakes, I'll have to win back as much respect as possible here in town. That job in the bank was like the first rung in my ladder. And now your husband wants to kick me right back down in the mud again.

NORA: But for heaven's sake, Mr. Krogstad, it's simply not in my power to help you.

KROGSTAD: That's because you haven't the will to—but I have the means to make you.

365 **NORA:** You certainly won't tell my husband that I owe you money?

KROGSTAD: Hm—what if I told him that?

NORA: That would be shameful of you. *(Nearly in tears.)* This secret—my joy and my pride—that he should learn it in such a crude and disgusting way—learn it from you. You'd expose me to the most horrible unpleasantness—

KROGSTAD: Only unpleasantness?

NORA: *(vehemently)* But go on and try. It'll turn out the worse for you, because then my husband will really see what a crook you are, and then you'll *never* be able to hold your job.

370 **KROGSTAD:** I asked if it was just domestic unpleasantness you were afraid of.

NORA: If my husband finds out, then of course he'll pay what I owe at once, and then we'd be through with you for good.

KROGSTAD: *(a step closer)* Listen, Mrs. Helmer—you've either got a very bad memory, or else no head at all for business. I'd better put you a little more in touch with the facts.

NORA: What do you mean?

KROGSTAD: When your husband was sick, you came to me for a loan of four thousand, eight hundred crowns.

375 **NORA:** Where else could I go?

KROGSTAD: I promised to get you that sum—

NORA: And you got it.

KROGSTAD: I promised to get you that sum, on certain conditions. You were so involved in your husband's illness, and so eager to finance your trip, that I guess you didn't think out all the details. It might just be a good idea to remind you. I promised you the money on the strength of a note I drew up.

NORA: Yes, and that I signed.

380 **KROGSTAD:** Right. But at the bottom I added some lines for your father to guarantee the loan. He was supposed to sign down there.

NORA: Supposed to? He did sign.

KROGSTAD: I left the date blank. In other words, your father would have dated his signature himself. Do you remember that?

NORA: Yes, I think—

KROGSTAD: Then I gave you the note for you to mail to your father. Isn't that so?

385 **NORA:** Yes.

KROGSTAD: And naturally you sent it at once—because only some five,
six days later you brought me the note, properly signed. And with
that, the money was yours.

NORA: Well, then; I've made my payments regularly, haven't I?

KROGSTAD: More or less. But—getting back to the point—those were
hard times for you then, Mrs. Helmer.

NORA: Yes, they were.

390 **KROGSTAD:**   Your father was very ill, I believe.

NORA: He was near the end.

KROGSTAD: He died soon after?

NORA: Yes.

KROGSTAD: Tell me, Mrs. Helmer, do you happen to recall the date of
your father's death? The day of the month, I mean.

395 **NORA:**   Papa died the twenty-ninth of September.

KROGSTAD: That's quite correct; I've already looked into that. And now
we come to a curious thing—*(taking out a paper)* which I simply
cannot comprehend.

NORA: Curious thing? I don't know—

KROGSTAD: This is the curious thing: that your father co-signed the
note for your loan three days after his death.

NORA: How—? I don't understand.

400 **KROGSTAD:**   Your father died the twenty-ninth of September. But look.
Here your father dated his signature October second. Isn't that
curious, Mrs. Helmer? *(Nora is silent.)* Can you explain it to me? *(Nora
remains silent.)* It's also remarkable that the words "October second"
and the year aren't written in your father's hand, but rather in one
that I think I know. Well, it's easy to understand. Your father forgot
perhaps to date his signature, and then someone or other added it, a
bit sloppily, before anyone knew of his death. There's nothing wrong
in that. It all comes down to the signature. And there's no question
about *that,* Mrs. Helmer. It really *was* your father who signed his own
name here, wasn't it?

NORA: *(after a short silence, throwing her head back and looking squarely at
him)* No, it wasn't. *I* signed Papa's name.

KROGSTAD: Wait, now—are you fully aware that this is a dangerous
confession?

NORA: Why? You'll soon get your money.

KROGSTAD: Let me ask you a question—why didn't you send the paper
to your father?

405 **NORA:**   That was impossible. Papa was so sick. If I'd asked him for his
signature, I also would have had to tell him what the money was for.
But I couldn't tell him, sick as he was, that my husband's life was in
danger. That was just impossible.

KROGSTAD: Then it would have been better if you'd given up the trip
abroad.

NORA: I couldn't possibly. The trip was to save my husband's life. I
couldn't give that up.

KROGSTAD: But didn't you ever consider that this was a fraud against me?

NORA: I couldn't let myself be bothered by that. You weren't any concern of mine. I couldn't stand you, with all those cold complications you made, even though you knew how badly off my husband was.

410 **KROGSTAD:** Mrs. Helmer, obviously you haven't the vaguest idea of what you've involved yourself in. But I can tell you this: it was nothing more and nothing worse than I once did—and it wrecked my whole reputation.

NORA: You? Do you expect me to believe that you ever acted bravely to save your wife's life?

KROGSTAD: Laws don't inquire into motives.

NORA: Then they must be very poor laws.

KROGSTAD: Poor or not—if I introduce this paper in court, you'll be judged according to law.

415 **NORA:** This I refuse to believe. A daughter hasn't a right to protect her dying father from anxiety and care? A wife hasn't a right to save her husband's life? I don't know much about laws, but I'm sure that somewhere in the books these things are allowed. And you don't know anything about it—you who practice the law? You must be an awful lawyer, Mr. Krogstad.

KROGSTAD: Could be. But business—the kind of business we two mixed up in—don't you think I know about that? All right. Do what you want now. But I'm telling you *this*: if I get shoved down a second time, you're going to keep me company. *(He bows and goes out through the hall.)*

NORA: *(pensive for a moment, then tossing her head)* Oh, really! Trying to frighten me! I'm not so silly as all that. *(Begins gathering up the children's clothes, but soon stops.)* But—? No, but that's impossible! I did it out of love.

THE CHILDREN: *(in the doorway, left)* Mama, that strange man's gone out the door.

NORA: Yes, yes, I know it. But don't tell anyone about the strange man. Do you hear? Not even Papa!

420 **THE CHILDREN:** No, Mama. But now will you play again?

NORA: No, not now.

THE CHILDREN: Oh, but Mama, you promised.

NORA: Yes, but I can't now. Go inside; I have too much to do. Go in, go in, my sweet darlings. *(She herds them gently back in the room and shuts the door after them. Settling on the sofa, she takes up a piece of embroidery and makes some stitches, but soon stops abruptly.)* No! *(Throws the work aside, rises, goes to the hall door and calls out.)* Helene! Let me have the tree in here. *(Goes to the table, left, opens the table drawer, and stops again.)* No, but that's utterly impossible!

MAID: *(with the Christmas tree)* Where should I put it, ma'am?

425 **NORA:** There. The middle of the floor.

Maid: Should I bring anything else?

Nora: No, thanks. I have what I need.

The Maid, who has set the tree down, goes out.

Nora: *(absorbed in trimming the tree)* Candles here—and flowers here. That terrible creature! Talk, talk, talk! There's nothing to it at all. The tree's going to be lovely. I'll do anything to please you, Torvald. I'll sing for you, dance for you—

Helmer comes in from the hall, with a sheaf of papers under his arm.

Nora: Oh! You're back so soon?

430 **Helmer:**   Yes. Has anyone been here?

Nora: Here? No.

Helmer: That's odd. I saw Krogstad leaving the front door.

Nora: So? Oh yes, that's true. Krogstad was here a moment.

Helmer: Nora, I can see by your face that he's been here, begging you to put in a good word for him.

435 **Nora:**   Yes.

Helmer: And it was supposed to seem like your own idea? You were to hide it from me that he'd been here. He asked you that, too, didn't he?

Nora: Yes, Torvald, but—

Helmer: Nora, Nora, and you could fall for that? Talk with that sort of person and promise him anything? And then in the bargain, tell me an untruth.

Nora: An untruth—?

440 **Helmer:**   Didn't you say that no one had been here? *(Wagging his finger.)* My little songbird must never do that again. A songbird needs a clean beak to warble with. No false notes. *(Putting his arm about her waist.)* That's the way it should be, isn't it? Yes, I'm sure of it. *(Releasing her.)* And so, enough of that. *(Sitting by the stove.)* Ah, how snug and cozy it is here. *(Leafing among his papers.)*

Nora: *(busy with the tree, after a short pause)* Torvald!

Helmer: Yes.

Nora: I'm so much looking forward to the Stenborgs' costume party, day after tomorrow.

Helmer: And I can't wait to see what you'll surprise me with.

445 **Nora:**   Oh, that stupid business!

Helmer: What?

Nora: I can't find anything that's right. Everything seems so ridiculous, so inane.

Helmer: So my little Nora's come to *that* recognition?

Nora: *(going behind his chair, her arms resting on its back)* Are you very busy, Torvald?

450 **Helmer:**   Oh—

Nora: What papers are those?

Helmer: Bank matters.

NORA: Already?

HELMER: I've gotten full authority from the retiring management to make all necessary changes in personnel and procedure. I'll need Christmas week for that. I want to have everything in order by New Year's.

455   NORA: So that was the reason this poor Krogstad—

HELMER: Hm.

NORA: (still leaning on the chair and slowly stroking the nape of his neck) If you weren't so very busy, I would have asked you an enormous favor, Torvald.

HELMER: Let's hear. What is it?

NORA: You know, there isn't anyone who has your good taste—and I want so much to look well at the costume party. Torvald, couldn't you take over and decide what I should be and plan my costume?

460   HELMER: Ah, is my stubborn little creature calling for a lifeguard?

NORA: Yes, Torvald, I can't get anywhere without your help.

HELMER: All right—I'll think it over. We'll hit on something.

NORA: Oh, how sweet of you. (Goes to the tree again. Pause.) Aren't the red flowers pretty—? But tell me, was it really such a crime that this Krogstad committed?

HELMER: Forgery. Do you have any idea what that means?

465   NORA: Couldn't he have done it out of need?

HELMER: Yes, or thoughtlessness, like so many others. I'm not so heartless that I'd condemn a man categorically for just one mistake.

NORA: No, of course not, Torvald!

HELMER: Plenty of men have redeemed themselves by openly confessing their crimes and taking their punishment.

NORA: Punishment—?

470   HELMER: But now Krogstad didn't go that way. He got himself out by sharp practices, and that's the real cause of his moral breakdown.

NORA: Do you really think that would—?

HELMER: Just imagine how a man with that sort of guilt in him has to lie and cheat and deceive on all sides, has to wear a mask even with the nearest and dearest he has, even with his own wife and children. And with the children, Nora—that's where it's most horrible.

NORA: Why?

HELMER: Because that kind of atmosphere of lies infects the whole life of a home. Every breath the children take in is filled with the germs of something degenerate.

475   NORA: (coming closer behind him) Are you sure of that?

HELMER: Oh, I've seen it often enough as a lawyer. Almost everyone who goes bad early in life has a mother who's a chronic liar.

NORA: Why just—the mother?

HELMER: It's usually the mother's influence that's dominant, but the father's works in the same way, of course. Every lawyer is quite familiar with it. And still this Krogstad's been going home year in, year out, poisoning his own children with lies and pretense; that's why I call him morally lost. *(Reaching his hands out toward her.)* So my sweet little Nora must promise me never to plead his cause. Your hand on it. Come, come, what's this? Give me your hand. There, now. All settled. I can tell you it'd be impossible for me to work alongside of him. I literally feel physically revolted when I'm anywhere near such a person.

NORA: *(withdraws her hand and goes to the other side of the Christmas tree)* How hot it is here! And I've got so much to do.

480 **HELMER:**   *(getting up and gathering his papers)* Yes, and I have to think about getting some of these read through before dinner. I'll think about your costume, too. And something to hang on the tree in gilt paper, I may even see about that. *(Putting his hand on her head.)* Oh you, my darling little songbird. *(He goes into his study and closes the door after him.)*

NORA: *(softly, after a silence)* Oh, really! It isn't so. It's impossible. It must be impossible.

ANNE-MARIE: *(in the doorway, left)* The children are begging so hard to come in to Mama.

NORA: No, no, no, don't let them in to me! You stay with them, Anne-Marie.

ANNE-MARIE: Of course, ma'am. *(Closes the door.)*

485 **NORA:**   *(pale with terror)* Hurt my children—! Poison my home? *(A moment's pause; then she tosses her head.)* That's not true. Never. Never in all the world.

ACT II

Same room. Beside the piano the Christmas tree now stands stripped of ornaments, burned-down candle stubs on its ragged branches. Nora's street clothes lie on the sofa. Nora, alone in the room, moves restlessly about; at last she stops at the sofa and picks up her coat.

NORA: *(dropping the coat again)* Someone's coming! *(Goes toward the door, listens.)* No—there's no one. Of course—nobody's coming today, Christmas Day—or tomorrow, either. But maybe—(*Opens the door and looks out.)* No, nothing in the mailbox. Quite empty. *(Coming forward.)* What nonsense! He won't do anything serious. Nothing terrible could happen. It's impossible. Why, I have three small children.

Anne-Marie, with a large carton, comes in from the room to the left.

ANNE-MARIE: Well, at last I found the box with the masquerade clothes.

NORA: Thanks. Put it on the table.

ANNE-MARIE: *(does so)* But they're all pretty much of a mess.

5 **NORA:** Ahh! I'd love to rip them in a million pieces!

ANNE-MARIE: Oh, mercy, they can be fixed right up. Just a little patience.

NORA: Yes, I'll go get Mrs. Linde to help me.

ANNE-MARIE: Out again now? In this nasty weather? Miss Nora will catch cold—get sick.

NORA: Oh, worse things could happen—How are the children?

10 **ANNE-MARIE:** The poor mites are playing with their Christmas presents, but—

NORA: Do they ask for me much?

ANNE-MARIE: They're so used to having Mama around, you know.

NORA: Yes. But Anne-Marie, I *can't* be together with them as much as I was.

ANNE-MARIE: Well, small children get used to anything.

15 **NORA:** You think so? Do you think they'd forget their mother if she was gone for good?

ANNE-MARIE: Oh, mercy—gone for good!

NORA: Wait, tell me, Anne-Marie—I've wondered so often—how could you ever have the heart to give your child over to strangers?

ANNE-MARIE: But I had to, you know, to become little Nora's nurse.

NORA: Yes, but how could you *do* it?

20 **ANNE-MARIE:** When I could get such a good place? A girl who's poor and who's gotten in trouble is glad enough for that. Because that slippery fish, he didn't do a thing for me, you know.

NORA: But your daughter's surely forgotten you.

ANNE-MARIE: Oh, she certainly has not. She's written to me, both when she was confirmed and when she was married.

NORA: *(clasping her about the neck)* You old Anne-Marie, you were a good mother for me when I was little.

ANNE-MARIE: Poor little Nora, with no other mother but me.

25 **NORA:** And if the babies didn't have one, then I know that you'd—What silly talk! *(Opening the carton.)* Go in to them. Now I'll have to— Tomorrow you can see how lovely I'll look.

ANNE-MARIE: Oh, there won't be anyone at the party as lovely as Miss Nora. *(She goes off into the room, left.)*

NORA: *(begins unpacking the box, but soon throws it aside)* Oh, if I dared to go out. If only nobody would come. If only nothing would happen here while I'm out. What craziness—nobody's coming. Just don't think. This muff—needs a brushing. Beautiful gloves, beautiful gloves. Let it go. Let it go! One, two, three, four, five, six—*(With a cry.)* Oh, there they are! *(Poises to move toward the door, but remains irresolutely standing. Mrs. Linde enters from the hall, where she has removed her street clothes.)*

NORA: Oh, it's you, Kristine. There's no one else out there? How good that you've come.

Mrs. Linde: I hear you were up asking for me.

30 **Nora:**   Yes, I just stopped by. There's something you really can help me with. Let's get settled on the sofa. Look, there's going to be a costume party tomorrow evening at the Stenborgs' right above us, and now Torvald wants me to go as a Neapolitan peasant girl and dance the tarantella that I learned in Capri.

Mrs. Linde: Really, are you giving a whole performance?

Nora: Torvald says yes, I should. See, here's the dress. Torvald had it made for me down there; but now it's all so tattered that I just don't know—

Mrs. Linde: Oh, we'll fix that up in no time. It's nothing more than the trimmings—they're a bit loose here and there. Needle and thread? Good, now we have what we need.

Nora: Oh, how sweet of you!

35 **Mrs. Linde:**   (sewing) So you'll be in disguise tomorrow, Nora. You know what? I'll stop by then for a moment and have a look at you all dressed up. But listen, I've absolutely forgotten to thank you for that pleasant evening yesterday.

Nora: (getting up and walking about) I don't think it was as pleasant as usual yesterday. You should have come to town a bit sooner, Kristine—Yes, Torvald really knows how to give a home elegance and charm.

Mrs. Linde: And you do, too, if you ask me. You're not your father's daughter for nothing. But tell me, is Dr. Rank always so down in the mouth as yesterday?

Nora: No, that was quite an exception. But he goes around critically ill all the time—tuberculosis of the spine, poor man. You know, his father was a disgusting thing who kept mistresses and so on—and that's why the son's been sickly from birth.

Mrs. Linde: (lets her sewing fall to her lap) But my dearest Nora, how do you know about such things?

40 **Nora:**   (walking more jauntily) Hmp! When you've had three children, then you've had a few visits from—from women who know something of medicine, and they tell you this and that.

Mrs. Linde: (resumes sewing; a short pause) Does Dr. Rank come here every day?

Nora: Every blessed day. He's Torvald's best friend from childhood, and *my* good friend, too. Dr. Rank almost belongs to this house.

Mrs. Linde: But tell me—is he quite sincere? I mean, doesn't he rather enjoy flattering people?

Nora: Just the opposite. Why do you think that?

45 **Mrs. Linde:**   When you introduced us yesterday, he was proclaiming that he'd often heard my name in this house; but later I noticed that your husband hadn't the slightest idea who I really was. So how could Dr. Rank—?

NORA: But it's all true, Kristine. You see, Torvald loves me beyond words, and, as he puts it, he'd like to keep me all to himself. For a long time he'd almost be jealous if I even mentioned any of my old friends back home. So of course I dropped that. But with Dr. Rank I talk a lot about such things, because he likes hearing about them.

MRS. LINDE: Now listen, Nora; in many ways you're still like a child. I'm a good deal older than you, with a little more experience. I'll tell you something: you ought to put an end to all this with Dr. Rank.

NORA: What should I put an end to?

MRS. LINDE: Both parts of it, I think. Yesterday you said something about a rich admirer who'd provide you with money—

50 **NORA:** Yes, one who doesn't exist—worse luck. So?

MRS. LINDE: Is Dr. Rank well off?

NORA: Yes, he is.

MRS. LINDE: With no dependents?

NORA: No, no one. But—

55 **MRS. LINDE:** And he's over here every day?

NORA: Yes, I told you that.

MRS. LINDE: How can a man of such refinement be so grasping?

NORA: I don't follow you at all.

MRS. LINDE: Now don't try to hide it, Nora. You think I can't guess who loaned you the forty-eight hundred crowns?

60 **NORA:** Are you out of your mind? How could you think such a thing! A friend of ours, who comes here every single day. What an intolerable situation that would have been!

MRS. LINDE: Then it really wasn't him.

NORA: No, absolutely not. It never even crossed my mind for a moment—And he had nothing to lend in those days; his inheritance came later.

MRS. LINDE: Well, I think that was a stroke of luck for you, Nora dear.

NORA: No, it never would have occurred to me to ask Dr. Rank—Still, I'm quite sure that if I had asked him—

65 **MRS. LINDE:** Which you won't, of course.

NORA: No, of course not. I can't see that I'd ever need to. But I'm quite positive that if I talked to Dr. Rank—

MRS. LINDE: Behind your husband's back?

NORA: I've got to clear up this other thing; *that's* also behind his back. I've *got* to clear it all up.

MRS. LINDE: Yes, I was saying that yesterday, but—

70 **NORA:** *(pacing up and down)* A man handles these problems so much better than a woman—

MRS. LINDE: One's husband does, yes.

NORA: Nonsense. *(Stopping.)* When you pay everything you owe, then you get your note back, right?

MRS. LINDE: Yes, naturally.

NORA: And can rip it into a million pieces and burn it up—that filthy scrap of paper!

75 **MRS. LINDE:**   *(looking hard at her, laying her sewing aside, and rising slowly)* Nora, you're hiding something from me.

NORA: You can see it in my face?

MRS. LINDE: Something's happened to you since yesterday morning. Nora, what is it?

NORA: *(hurrying toward her)* Kristine! *(Listening.)* Shh! Torvald's home. Look, go in with the children a while. Torvald can't bear all this snipping and stitching. Let Anne-Marie help you.

MRS. LINDE: *(gathering up some of the things)* All right, but I'm not leaving here until we've talked this out. *(She disappears into the room, left, as Torvald enters from the hall.)*

80 **NORA:**   Oh, how I've been waiting for you, Torvald dear.

HELMER: Was that the dressmaker?

NORA: No, that was Kristine. She's helping me fix up my costume. You know, it's going to be quite attractive.

HELMER: Yes, wasn't that a bright idea I had?

NORA: Brilliant! But then wasn't I good as well to give in to you?

85 **HELMER:**   Good—because you give in to your husband's judgment? All right, you little goose, I know you didn't mean it like that. But I won't disturb you. You'll want to have a fitting, I suppose.

NORA: And you'll be working?

HELMER: Yes. *(Indicating a bundle of papers.)* See. I've been down to the bank. *(Starts toward his study.)*

NORA: Torvald.

HELMER: *(stops)* Yes.

90 **NORA:**   If your little squirrel begged you, with all her heart and soul, for something—?

HELMER: What's that?

NORA: Then would you do it?

HELMER: First, naturally, I'd have to know what it was.

NORA: Your squirrel would scamper about and do tricks, if you'd only be sweet and give in.

95 **HELMER:**   Out with it.

NORA: Your lark would be singing high and low in every room—

HELMER: Come on, she does that anyway.

NORA: I'd be a wood nymph and dance for you in the moonlight.

HELMER: Nora—don't tell me it's that same business from this morning?

100 **NORA:**   *(coming closer)* Yes, Torvald, I beg you, please!

HELMER: And you actually have the nerve to drag that up again?

NORA: Yes, yes, you've got to give in to me; you *have* to let Krogstad keep his job in the bank.

HELMER: My dear Nora, I've slated his job for Mrs. Linde.

Nora: That's awfully kind of you. But you could just fire another clerk instead of Krogstad.

105 **Helmer:**   This is the most incredible stubbornness! Because you go and give an impulsive promise to speak up for him, I'm expected to—

Nora: That's not the reason, Torvald. It's for your own sake. That man does writing for the worst papers; you said it yourself. He could do you any amount of harm. I'm scared to death of him—

Helmer: Ah, I understand. It's the old memories haunting you.

Nora: What do you mean by that?

Helmer: Of course, you're thinking about your father.

110 **Nora:**   Yes, all right. Just remember how those nasty gossips wrote in the papers about Papa and slandered him so cruelly. I think they'd have had him dismissed if the department hadn't sent you up to investigate, and if you hadn't been so kind and open-minded toward him.

Helmer: My dear Nora, there's a notable difference between your father and me. Your father's official career was hardly above reproach. But mine is; and I hope it'll stay that way as long as I hold my position.

Nora: Oh, who can ever tell what vicious minds can invent? We could be so snug and happy now in our quiet, carefree home—you and I and the children, Torvald! That's why I'm pleading with you so—

Helmer: And just by pleading for him you make it impossible for me to keep him on. It's already known at the bank that I'm firing Krogstad. What if it's rumored around now that the new bank manager was vetoed by his wife—

Nora: Yes, what then—?

115 **Helmer:**   Oh yes—as long as our little bundle of stubbornness gets her way—! I should go and make myself ridiculous in front of the whole office—give people the idea I can be swayed by all kinds of outside pressure. Oh, you can bet I'd feel the effects of that soon enough! Besides—there's something that rules Krogstad right out at the bank as long as I'm the manager.

Nora: What's that?

Helmer: His moral failings I could maybe overlook if I had to—

Nora: Yes, Torvald, why not?

Helmer: And I hear he's quite efficient on the job. But he was a crony of mine back in my teens—one of those rash friendships that crop up again and again to embarrass you later in life. Well, I might as well say it straight out: we're on a first-name basis. And that tactless fool makes no effort at all to hide it in front of others. Quite the contrary—he thinks that entitles him to take a familiar air around me, and so every other second he comes booming out with his "Yes, Torvald!" and "Sure thing, Torvald!" I tell you, it's been excruciating for me. He's out to make my place in the bank unbearable.

120 **Nora:**   Torvald, you can't be serious about all this.

Helmer: Oh no? Why not?

NORA: Because these are such petty considerations.

HELMER: What are you saying? Petty? You think I'm petty!

NORA: No, just the opposite, Torvald dear. That's exactly why—

125 **HELMER:**   Never mind. You call my motives petty; then I might as well be just that. Petty! All right! We'll put a stop to this for good. *(Goes to the hall door and calls.)* Helene!

NORA: What do you want?

HELMER: *(searching among his papers)* A decision. *(The Maid comes in.)* Look here; take this letter; go out with it at once. Get hold of a messenger and have him deliver it. Quick now. It's already addressed. Wait, here's some money.

MAID: Yes, sir. *(She leaves with the letter.)*

HELMER: *(straightening his papers)* There, now, little Miss Willful.

130 **NORA:**   *(breathlessly)* Torvald, what was that letter?

HELMER: Krogstad's notice.

NORA: Call it back, Torvald! There's still time. Oh, Torvald, call it back! Do it for my sake—for your sake, for the children's sake! Do you hear, Torvald; do it! You don't know how this can harm us.

HELMER: Too late.

NORA: Yes, too late.

135 **HELMER:**   Nora dear, I can forgive you this panic, even though basically you're insulting me. Yes, you are! Or isn't it an insult to think that *I* should be afraid of a courtroom hack's revenge? But I forgive you anyway, because this shows so beautifully how much you love me. *(Takes her in his arms.)* This is the way it should be, my darling Nora. Whatever comes, you'll see: when it really counts, I have strength and courage enough as a man to take on the whole weight myself.

NORA: *(terrified)* What do you mean by that?

HELMER: The whole weight, I said.

NORA: *(resolutely)* No, never in all the world.

HELMER: Good. So we'll share it, Nora, as man and wife. That's as it should be. *(Fondling her.)* Are you happy now? There, there, there— not these frightened dove's eyes. It's nothing at all but empty fantasies—Now you should run through your tarantella and practice your tambourine. I'll go to the inner office and shut both doors, so I won't hear a thing; you can make all the noise you like. *(Turning in the doorway.)* And when Rank comes, just tell him where he can find me. *(He nods to her and goes with his papers into the study, closing the door.)*

140 **NORA:**   *(standing as though rooted, dazed with fright, in a whisper)* He really could do it. He will do it. He'll do it in spite of everything. No, not that, never, never! Anything but that! Escape! A way out—*(The doorbell rings.)* Dr. Rank! Anything but that! *Anything,* whatever it is! *(Her hands pass over her face, smoothing it; she pulls herself together, goes over and opens the hall door. Dr. Rank stands outside, hanging his fur coat up. During the following scene, it begins getting dark.)*

NORA: Hello, Dr. Rank. I recognized your ring. But you mustn't go in to
Torvald yet; I believe he's working.

RANK: And you?

NORA: For you, I always have an hour to spare—you know that. *(He has
entered, and she shuts the door after him.)*

RANK: Many thanks. I'll make use of these hours while I can.

145 **NORA:** What do you mean by that? While you can?

RANK: Does that disturb you?

NORA: Well, it's such an odd phrase. Is anything going to happen?

RANK: What's going to happen is what I've been expecting so long—
but I honestly didn't think it would come so soon.

NORA: *(gripping his arm)* What is it you've found out? Dr. Rank, you
have to tell me!

150 **RANK:** *(sitting by the stove)* It's all over with me. There's nothing to be
done about it.

NORA: *(breathing easier)* Is it you—then—?

RANK: Who else? There's no point in lying to one's self. I'm the most
miserable of all my patients, Mrs. Helmer. These past few days I've
been auditing my internal accounts. Bankrupt! Within a month I'll
probably be laid out and rotting in the churchyard.

NORA: Oh, what a horrible thing to say.

RANK: The thing itself is horrible. But the worst of it is all the other
horror before it's over. There's only one final examination left; when
I'm finished with that, I'll know about when my disintegration will
begin. There's something I want to say. Helmer with his sensitivity
has such a sharp distaste for anything ugly. I don't want him near my
sickroom.

155 **NORA:** Oh, but Dr. Rank—

RANK: I won't have him in there. Under no condition. I'll lock my door
to him—As soon as I'm completely sure of the worst, I'll send you my
calling card marked with a black cross, and you'll know then the
wreck has started to come apart.

NORA: No, today you're completely unreasonable. And I wanted you so
much to be in a really good humor.

RANK: With death up my sleeve? And then to suffer this way for
somebody else's sins. Is there any justice in that? And in every single
family, in some way or another, this inevitable retribution of nature
goes on—

NORA: *(her hands pressed over her ears)* Oh, stuff! Cheer up! Please—be
gay!

160 **RANK:** Yes, I'd just as soon laugh at it all. My poor, innocent spine,
serving time for my father's gay army days.

NORA: *(by the table, left)* He was so infatuated with asparagus tips and
pâté de foie gras, wasn't that it?

RANK: Yes—and with truffles.

Nora: Truffles, yes. And then with oysters, I suppose?

Rank: Yes, tons of oysters, naturally.

165 **Nora:** And then the port and champagne to go with it. It's so sad that all these delectable things have to strike at our bones.

Rank: Especially when they strike at the unhappy bones that never shared in the fun.

Nora: Ah, that's the saddest of all.

Rank: *(looks searchingly at her)* Hm.

Nora: *(after a moment)* Why did you smile?

170 **Rank:** No, it was you who laughed.

Nora: No, it was you who smiled, Dr. Rank!

Rank: *(getting up)* You're even a bigger tease than I'd thought.

Nora: I'm full of wild ideas today.

Rank: That's obvious.

175 **Nora:** *(putting both hands on his shoulders)* Dear, dear Dr. Rank, you'll never die for Torvald and me.

Rank: Oh, that loss you'll easily get over. Those who go away are soon forgotten.

Nora: *(looks fearfully at him)* You believe that?

Rank: One makes new connections, and then—

Nora: Who makes new connections?

180 **Rank:** Both you and Torvald will when I'm gone. I'd say you're well under way already. What was that Mrs. Linde doing here last evening?

Nora: Oh, come—you can't be jealous of poor Kristine?

Rank: Oh yes, I am. She'll be my successor here in the house. When I'm down under, that woman will probably—

Nora: Shh! Not so loud. She's right in there.

Rank: Today as well. So you see.

185 **Nora:** Only to sew on my dress. Good gracious, how unreasonable you are. *(Sitting on the sofa.)* Be nice now, Dr. Rank. Tomorrow you'll see how beautifully I'll dance; and you can imagine then that I'm dancing only for you—yes, and of course for Torvald, too—that's understood. *(Takes various items out of the carton.)* Dr. Rank, sit over here and I'll show you something.

Rank: *(sitting)* What's that?

Nora: Look here. Look.

Rank: Silk stockings.

Nora: Flesh-colored. Aren't they lovely? Now it's so dark here, but tomorrow—No, no, no, just look at the feet. Oh well, you might as well look at the rest.

190 **Rank:** Hm—

Nora: Why do you look so critical? Don't you believe they'll fit?

Rank: I've never had any chance to form an opinion on that.

Nora: *(glancing at him a moment)* Shame on you. *(Hits him lightly on the ear with the stockings.)* That's for you. *(Puts them away again.)*

RANK: And what other splendors am I going to see now?

195 **NORA:** Not the least bit more, because you've been naughty. *(She hums a little and rummages among her things.)*

RANK: *(after a short silence)* When I sit here together with you like this, completely easy and open, then I don't know—I simply can't imagine—whatever would have become of me if I'd never come into this house.

NORA: *(smiling)* Yes, I really think you feel completely at ease with us.

RANK: *(more quietly, staring straight ahead)* And then to have to go away from it all—

NORA: Nonsense, you're not going away.

200 **RANK:** *(his voice unchanged)*—and not even be able to leave some poor show of gratitude behind, scarcely a fleeting regret—no more than a vacant place that anyone can fill.

NORA: And if I asked you now for—? No—

RANK: For what?

NORA: For a great proof of your friendship—

RANK: Yes, yes?

205 **NORA:** No, I mean—for an exceptionally big favor—

RANK: Would you really, for once, make me so happy?

NORA: Oh, you haven't the vaguest idea what it is.

RANK: All right, then tell me.

NORA: No, but I can't, Dr. Rank—it's all out of reason. It's advice and help, too—and a favor—

210 **RANK:** So much the better. I can't fathom what you're hinting at. Just speak out. Don't you trust me?

NORA: Of course. More than anyone else. You're my best and truest friend, I'm sure. That's why I want to talk to you. All right, then, Dr. Rank: there's something you can help me prevent. You know how deeply, how inexpressibly dearly Torvald loves me; he'd never hesitate a second to give up his life for me.

RANK: *(leaning close to her)* Nora—do you think he's the only one—

NORA: *(with a slight start)* Who—?

RANK: Who'd gladly give up his life for you.

215 **NORA:** *(heavily)* I see.

RANK: I swore to myself you should know this before I'm gone. I'll never find a better chance. Yes, Nora, now you know. And also you know now that you can trust me beyond anyone else.

NORA: *(rising, natural and calm)* Let me by.

RANK: *(making room for her, but still sitting)* Nora—

NORA: *(in the hall doorway)* Helene, bring the lamp in. *(Goes over to the stove.)* Ah, dear Dr. Rank, that was really mean of you.

220 **RANK:** *(getting up)* That I've loved you just as deeply as somebody else? Was *that* mean?

NORA: No, but that you came out and told me. That was quite unnecessary—

RANK: What do you mean? Have you known—?

The Maid comes in with the lamp, sets it on the table, and goes out again.

RANK: Nora—Mrs. Helmer—I'm asking you: have you known about it?

NORA: Oh, how can I tell what I know or don't know? Really, I don't know what to say—Why did you have to be so clumsy, Dr. Rank! Everything was so good.

225 **RANK:** Well, in any case, you now have the knowledge that my body and soul are at your command. So won't you speak out?

NORA: *(looking at him)* After that?

RANK: Please, just let me know what it is.

NORA: You can't know anything now.

RANK: I have to. You mustn't punish me like this. Give me the chance to do whatever is humanly possible for you.

230 **NORA:** Now there's nothing you can do for me. Besides, actually, I don't need any help. You'll see—it's only my fantasies. That's what it is. Of course! *(Sits in the rocker, looks at him, and smiles.)* What a nice one you are, Dr. Rank. Aren't you a little bit ashamed, now that the lamp is here?

RANK: No, not exactly. But perhaps I'd better go—for good?

NORA: No, you certainly can't do that. You must come here just as you always have. You know Torvald can't do without you.

RANK: Yes, but *you?*

NORA: You know how much I enjoy it when you're here.

235 **RANK:** That's precisely what threw me off. You're a mystery to me. So many times I've felt you'd almost rather be with me than with Helmer.

NORA: Yes—you see, there are some people that one loves most and other people that one would almost prefer being with.

RANK: Yes, there's something to that.

NORA: When I was back home, of course I loved Papa most. But I always thought it was so much fun when I could sneak down to the maids' quarters, because they never tried to improve me, and it was always so amusing, the way they talked to each other.

RANK: Aha, so it's *their* place that I've filled.

240 **NORA:** *(jumping up and going to him)* Oh, dear, sweet Dr. Rank, that's not what I mean at all. But you can understand that with Torvald it's just the same as with Papa—

The Maid enters from the hall.

MAID: Ma'am—please! *(She whispers to Nora and hands her a calling card.)*

NORA: *(glancing at the card)* Ah! *(Slips it into her pocket.)*

RANK: Anything wrong?

NORA: No, no, not at all. It's only some—it's my new dress—

245 **RANK:** Really? But—there's your dress.

NORA: Oh, that. But this is another one—I ordered it—Torvald mustn't know—

RANK: Ah, now we have the big secret.

NORA: That's right. Just go in with him—he's back in the inner study. Keep him there as long as—

RANK: Don't worry. He won't get away. *(Goes into the study.)*

250 **NORA:** *(to the Maid)* And he's standing waiting in the kitchen?

MAID: Yes, he came up by the back stairs.

NORA: But didn't you tell him somebody was here?

MAID: Yes, but that didn't do any good.

NORA: He won't leave?

255 **MAID:** No, he won't go till he's talked with you, ma'am.

NORA: Let him come in, then—but quietly. Helene, don't breathe a word about this. It's a surprise for my husband.

MAID: Yes, yes, I understand—*(Goes out.)*

NORA: This horror—it's going to happen. No, no, no, it can't happen, it mustn't. *(She goes and bolts Helmer's door. The Maid opens the hall door for Krogstad and shuts it behind him. He is dressed for travel in a fur coat, boots, and a fur cap.)*

NORA: *(going toward him)* Talk softly. My husband's home.

260 **KROGSTAD:** Well, good for him.

NORA: What do you want?

KROGSTAD: Some information.

NORA: Hurry up, then. What is it?

KROGSTAD: You know, of course, that I got my notice.

265 **NORA:** I couldn't prevent it, Mr. Krogstad. I fought for you to the bitter end, but nothing worked.

KROGSTAD: Does your husband's love for you run so thin? He knows everything I can expose you to, and all the same he dares to—

NORA: How can you imagine he knows anything about this?

KROGSTAD: Ah, no—I can't imagine it either, now. It's not at all like my fine Torvald Helmer to have so much guts—

NORA: Mr. Krogstad, I demand respect for my husband!

270 **KROGSTAD:** Why, of course—all due respect. But since the lady's keeping it so carefully hidden, may I presume to ask if you're also a bit better informed than yesterday about what you've actually done?

NORA: More than you ever could teach me.

KROGSTAD: Yes, I *am* such an awful lawyer.

NORA: What is it you want from me?

KROGSTAD: Just a glimpse of how you are, Mrs. Helmer. I've been thinking about you all day long. A cashier, a night-court scribbler, a—well, a type like me also has a little of what they call a heart, you know.

275 **NORA:** Then show it. Think of my children.

KROGSTAD: Did you or your husband ever think of mine? But never mind. I simply wanted to tell you that you don't need to take this

thing too seriously. For the present, I'm not proceeding with any
action.

Nora: Oh no, really! Well—I knew that.

Krogstad: Everything can be settled in a friendly spirit. It doesn't
have to get around town at all; it can stay just among us three.

Nora: My husband must never know anything of this.

280 **Krogstad:** How can you manage that? Perhaps you can pay me the
balance?

Nora: No, not right now.

Krogstad: Or you know some way of raising the money in a day or two?

Nora: No way that I'm willing to use.

Krogstad: Well, it wouldn't have done you any good, anyway. If you
stood in front of me with a fistful of bills, you still couldn't buy your
signature back.

285 **Nora:** Then tell me what you're going to do with it.

Krogstad: I'll just hold onto it—keep it on file. There's no outsider
who'll even get wind of it. So if you've been thinking of taking some
desperate step—

Nora: I have.

Krogstad: Been thinking of running away from home—

Nora: I have!

290 **Krogstad:** Or even of something worse—

Nora: How could you guess that?

Krogstad: You can drop those thoughts.

Nora: How could you guess I was thinking of *that?*

Krogstad: Most of us think about *that* at first. I thought about it too,
but I discovered I hadn't the courage—

295 **Nora:** *(lifelessly)* I don't either.

Krogstad: *(relieved)* That's true, you haven't the courage? You too?

Nora: I don't have it—I don't have it.

Krogstad: It would be terribly stupid, anyway. After that first storm at
home blows out, why, then—I have here in my pocket a letter for
your husband—

Nora: Telling everything?

300 **Krogstad:** As charitably as possible.

Nora: *(quickly)* He mustn't ever get that letter. Tear it up. I'll find some
way to get money.

Krogstad: Beg pardon, Mrs. Helmer, but I think I just told you—

Nora: Oh, I don't mean the money I owe you. Let me know how much
you want from my husband, and I'll manage it.

Krogstad: I don't want any money from your husband.

305 **Nora:** What do you want, then?

Krogstad: I'll tell you what. I want to recoup, Mrs. Helmer; I want to
get on in the world—and there's where your husband can help me.
For a year and a half I've kept myself clean of anything disreputable—
all that time struggling with the worst conditions; but I was satisfied,

working my way up step by step. Now I've been written right off, and I'm just not in the mood to come crawling back. I tell you, I want to move on. I want to get back in the bank—in a better position. Your husband can set up a job for me—

NORA: He'll never do that!

KROGSTAD: He'll do it. I know him. He won't dare breathe a word of protest. And once I'm in there together with him, you just wait and see! Inside of a year, I'll be the manager's right-hand man. It'll be Nils Krogstad, not Torvald Helmer, who runs the bank.

NORA: You'll never see the day!

310 **KROGSTAD:** Maybe you think you can—

NORA: I have the courage now—for *that.*

KROGSTAD: Oh, you don't scare me. A smart, spoiled lady like you—

NORA: You'll see; you'll see!

KROGSTAD: Under the ice, maybe? Down in the freezing, coal-black water? There, till you float up in the spring, ugly, unrecognizable, with your hair falling out—

315 **NORA:** You don't frighten me.

KROGSTAD: Nor do you frighten me. One doesn't do these things, Mrs. Helmer. Besides, what good would it be? I'd still have him safe in my pocket.

NORA: Afterwards? When I'm no longer—?

KROGSTAD: Are you forgetting that *I'll* be in control then over your final reputation? *(Nora stands speechless, staring at him.)* Good; now I've warned you. Don't do anything stupid. When Helmer's read my letter, I'll be waiting for his reply. And bear in mind that it's your husband himself who's forced me back to my old ways. I'll never forgive him for that. Good-bye, Mrs. Helmer. *(He goes out through the hall.)*

NORA: *(goes to the hall door, opens it a crack, and listens)* He's gone. Didn't leave the letter. Oh no, no, that's impossible too! *(Opening the door more and more.)* What's that? He's standing outside—not going downstairs. He's thinking it over? Maybe he'll—? *(A letter falls in the mailbox; then Krogstad's footsteps are heard, dying away down a flight of stairs. Nora gives a muffled cry and runs over toward the sofa table. A short pause.)* In the mailbox. *(Slips warily over to the hall door.)* It's lying there. Torvald, Torvald—now we're lost!

320 **MRS. LINDE:** *(entering with the costume from the room, left)* There now, I can't see anything else to mend. Perhaps you'd like to try—

NORA: *(in a hoarse whisper)* Kristine, come here.

MRS. LINDE: *(tossing the dress on the sofa)* What's wrong? You look upset.

NORA: Come here. See that letter? *There!* Look—through the glass in the mailbox.

MRS. LINDE: Yes, yes, I see it.

325 **NORA:** That letter's from Krogstad—

MRS. LINDE: Nora—it's Krogstad who loaned you the money!

Nora: Yes, and now Torvald will find out everything.

Mrs. Linde: Believe me, Nora, it's best for both of you.

Nora: There's more you don't know. I forged a name.

330 **Mrs. Linde:**   But for heaven's sake—?

Nora: I only want to tell you that, Kristine, so that you can be my witness.

Mrs. Linde: Witness? Why should I—?

Nora: If I should go out of my mind—it could easily happen—

Mrs. Linde: Nora!

335 **Nora:**   Or anything else occurred—so I couldn't be present here—

Mrs. Linde: Nora, Nora, you aren't yourself at all!

Nora: And someone should try to take on the whole weight, all of the guilt, you follow me—

Mrs. Linde: Yes, of course, but why do you think—?

Nora: Then you're the witness that it isn't true, Kristine. I'm very much myself; my mind right now is perfectly clear; and I'm telling you: nobody else has known about this; I alone did everything. Remember that.

340 **Mrs. Linde:**   I will. But I don't understand all this.

Nora: Oh, how could you ever understand it? It's the miracle now that's going to take place.

Mrs. Linde: The miracle?

Nora: Yes, the miracle. But it's so awful, Kristine. It mustn't take place, not for anything in the world.

Mrs. Linde: I'm going right over and talk with Krogstad.

345 **Nora:**   Don't go near him; he'll do you some terrible harm!

Mrs. Linde: There was a time once when he'd gladly have done anything for me.

Nora: He?

Mrs. Linde: Where does he live?

Nora: Oh, how do I know? Yes. *(Searches in her pocket.)* Here's his card. But the letter, the letter—!

350 **Helmer:**   *(from the study, knocking on the door)* Nora!

Nora: *(with a cry of fear)* Oh! What is it? What do you want?

Helmer: Now, now, don't be so frightened. We're not coming in. You locked the door—are you trying on the dress?

Nora: Yes, I'm trying it. I'll look just beautiful, Torvald.

Mrs. Linde: *(who has read the card)* He's living right around the corner.

355 **Nora:**   Yes, but what's the use? We're lost. The letter's in the box.

Mrs. Linde: And your husband has the key?

Nora: Yes, always.

Mrs. Linde: Krogstad can ask for his letter back unread; he can find some excuse—

Nora: But it's just this time that Torvald usually—

360 **Mrs. Linde:**   Stall him. Keep him in there. I'll be back as quick as I can. *(She hurries out through the hall entrance.)*

NORA: *(goes to Helmer's door, opens it, and peers in)* Torvald!

HELMER: *(from the inner study)* Well—does one dare set foot in one's own living room at last? Come on, Rank, now we'll get a look—*(In the doorway.)* But what's this?

NORA: What, Torvald dear?

HELMER: Rank had me expecting some grand masquerade.

365 **RANK:**   *(in the doorway)* That was my impression, but I must have been wrong.

NORA: No one can admire me in my splendor—not till tomorrow.

HELMER: But Nora dear, you look so exhausted. Have you practiced too hard?

NORA: No, I haven't practiced at all yet.

HELMER: You know, it's necessary—

370 **NORA:**   Oh, it's absolutely necessary, Torvald. But I can't get anywhere without your help. I've forgotten the whole thing completely.

HELMER: Ah, we'll soon take care of that.

NORA: Yes, take care of me, Torvald, please! Promise me that? Oh, I'm so nervous. That big party—You must give up everything this evening for me. No business—don't even touch your pen. Yes? Dear Torvald, promise?

HELMER: It's a promise. Tonight I'm totally at your service—you little helpless thing. Hm—but first there's one thing I want to—*(Goes toward the hall door.)*

NORA: What are you looking for?

375 **HELMER:**   Just to see if there's any mail.

NORA: No, no, don't do that, Torvald!

HELMER: Now what?

NORA: Torvald, please. There isn't any.

HELMER: Let me look, though. *(Starts out. Nora, at the piano, strikes the first notes of the tarantella. Helmer, at the door, stops.)* Aha!

380 **NORA:**   I can't dance tomorrow if I don't practice with you.

HELMER: *(going over to her)* Nora dear, are you really so frightened?

NORA: Yes, so terribly frightened. Let me practice right now; there's still time before dinner. Oh, sit down and play for me, Torvald. Direct me. Teach me, the way you always have.

HELMER: Gladly, if it's what you want. *(Sits at the piano.)*

NORA: *(snatches the tambourine up from the box, then a long, varicolored shawl, which she throws around herself, whereupon she springs forward and cries out)* Play for me now! Now I'll dance!

Helmer plays and Nora dances. Rank stands behind Helmer at the piano and looks on.

385 **HELMER:**   *(as he plays)* Slower. Slow down.

NORA: Can't change it.

HELMER: Not so violent, Nora!

NORA: Has to be just like this.

HELMER: *(stopping)* No, no, that won't do at all.
390 **NORA:** *(laughing and swinging her tambourine)* Isn't that what I told you?
RANK: Let me play for her.
HELMER: *(getting up)* Yes, go on. I can teach her more easily then.

Rank sits at the piano and plays; Nora dances more and more wildly. Helmer has stationed himself by the stove and repeatedly gives her directions; she seems not to hear them; her hair loosens and falls over her shoulders; she does not notice, but goes on dancing. Mrs. Linde enters.

MRS. LINDE: *(standing dumbfounded at the door)* Ah—!
NORA: *(still dancing)* See what fun, Kristine!
395 **HELMER:** But Nora darling, you dance as if your life were at stake.
NORA: And it is.
HELMER: Rank, stop! This is pure madness. Stop it, I say!

Rank breaks off playing, and Nora halts abruptly.

HELMER: *(going over to her)* I never would have believed it. You've
forgotten everything I taught you.
NORA: *(throwing away the tambourine)* You see for yourself.
400 **HELMER:** Well, there's certainly room for instruction here.
NORA: Yes, you see how important it is. You've got to teach me to the
very last minute. Promise me that, Torvald?
HELMER: You can bet on it.
NORA: You mustn't, either today or tomorrow, think about anything
else but me; you mustn't open any letters—or the mailbox—
HELMER: Ah, it's still the fear of that man—
405 **NORA:** Oh yes, yes, that too.
HELMER: Nora, it's written all over you—there's already a letter from
him out there.
NORA: I don't know. I guess so. But you mustn't read such things now;
there mustn't be anything ugly between us before it's all over.
RANK: *(quietly to Helmer)* You shouldn't deny her.
HELMER: *(putting his arm around her)* The child can have her way. But
tomorrow night, after you've danced—
410 **NORA:** Then you'll be free.
MAID: *(in the doorway, right)* Ma'am, dinner is served.
NORA: We'll be wanting champagne, Helene.
MAID: Very good, ma'am. *(Goes out.)*
HELMER: So—a regular banquet, hm?
415 **NORA:** Yes, a banquet—champagne till daybreak! *(Calling out.)* And
some macaroons, Helene. Heaps of them—just this once.
HELMER: *(taking her hands)* Now, now, now—no hysterics. Be my own
little lark again.
NORA: Oh, I will soon enough. But go on in—and you, Dr. Rank.
Kristine, help me put up my hair.

RANK: *(whispering, as they go)* There's nothing wrong—really wrong, is there?

HELMER: Oh, of course not. It's nothing more than this childish anxiety I was telling you about. *(They go out, right.)*

420 NORA: Well?

MRS. LINDE: Left town.

NORA: I could see by your face.

MRS. LINDE: He'll be home tomorrow evening. I wrote him a note.

NORA: You shouldn't have. Don't try to stop anything now. After all, it's a wonderful joy, this waiting here for the miracle.

425 MRS. LINDE: What is it you're waiting for?

NORA: Oh, you can't understand that. Go in to them: I'll be along in a moment.

Mrs. Linde goes into the dining room. Nora stands a short while as if composing herself; then she looks at her watch.

NORA: Five. Seven hours to midnight. Twenty-four hours to the midnight after, and then the tarantella's done. Seven and twenty-four? Thirty-one hours to live.

HELMER: *(in the doorway, right)* What's become of the little lark?

NORA: *(going toward him with open arms)* Here's your lark!

ACT III

Same scene. The table, with chairs around it, has been moved to the center of the room. A lamp on the table is lit. The hall door stands open. Dance music drifts down from the floor above. Mrs. Linde sits at the table, absently paging through a book, trying to read, but apparently unable to focus her thoughts. Once or twice she pauses, tensely listening for a sound at the outer entrance.

MRS. LINDE: *(glancing at her watch)* Not yet—and there's hardly any time left. If only he's not—*(Listening again.)* Ah, there he is. *(She goes out in the hall and cautiously opens the outer door. Quiet footsteps are heard on the stairs. She whispers:)* Come in. Nobody's here.

KROGSTAD: *(in the doorway)* I found a note from you at home. What's back of all this?

MRS. LINDE: I just *had* to talk to you.

KROGSTAD: Oh? And it just *had* to be here in this house?

5 MRS. LINDE: At my place it was impossible; my room hasn't a private entrance. Come in; we're all alone. The maid's asleep, and the Helmers are at the dance upstairs.

KROGSTAD: *(entering the room)* Well, well, the Helmers are dancing tonight? Really?

MRS. LINDE: Yes, why not?

KROGSTAD: How true—why not?

Mrs. Linde: All right, Krogstad, let's talk.

10 **Krogstad:**   Do we two have anything more to talk about?

Mrs. Linde: We have a great deal to talk about.

Krogstad: I wouldn't have thought so.

Mrs. Linde: No, because you've never understood me, really.

Krogstad: Was there anything more to understand—except what's all too common in life? A calculating woman throws over a man the moment a better catch comes by.

15 **Mrs. Linde:**   You think I'm so thoroughly calculating? You think I broke it off lightly?

Krogstad: Didn't you?

Mrs. Linde: Nils—is that what you really thought?

Krogstad: If you cared, then why did you write me the way you did?

Mrs. Linde: What else could I do? If I had to break off with you, then it was my job as well to root out everything you felt for me.

20 **Krogstad:**   *(wringing his hands)* So that was it. And this—all this, simply for money!

Mrs. Linde: Don't forget I had a helpless mother and two small brothers. We couldn't wait for you, Nils; you had such a long road ahead of you then.

Krogstad: That may be; but you still hadn't the right to abandon me for somebody else's sake.

Mrs. Linde: Yes—I don't know. So many, many times I've asked myself if I did have that right.

Krogstad: *(more softly)* When I lost you, it was as if all the solid ground dissolved from under my feet. Look at me; I'm a half-drowned man now, hanging onto a wreck.

25 **Mrs. Linde:**   Help may be near.

Krogstad: It was near—but then you came and blocked it off.

Mrs. Linde: Without my knowing it, Nils. Today for the first time I learned that it's you I'm replacing at the bank.

Krogstad: All right—I believe you. But now that you know, will you step aside?

Mrs. Linde: No, because that wouldn't benefit you in the slightest.

30 **Krogstad:**   Not "benefit" me, hm! I'd step aside anyway.

Mrs. Linde: I've learned to be realistic. Life and hard, bitter necessity have taught me that.

Krogstad: And life's taught me never to trust fine phrases.

Mrs. Linde: Then life's taught you a very sound thing. But you do have to trust in actions, don't you?

Krogstad: What does that mean?

35 **Mrs. Linde:**   You said you were hanging on like a half-drowned man to a wreck.

Krogstad: I've good reason to say that.

Mrs. Linde: I'm also like a half-drowned woman on a wreck. No one to suffer with; no one to care for.

KROGSTAD: You made your choice.

MRS. LINDE: There wasn't any choice then.

40 **KROGSTAD:**   So—what of it?

MRS. LINDE: Nils, if only we two shipwrecked people could reach across to each other.

KROGSTAD: What are you saying?

MRS. LINDE: Two on one wreck are at least better off than each on his own.

KROGSTAD: Kristine!

45 **MRS. LINDE:**   Why do you think I came into town?

KROGSTAD: Did you really have some thought of me?

MRS. LINDE: I have to work to go on living. All my born days, as long as I can remember, I've worked, and it's been my best and my only joy. But now I'm completely alone in the world; it frightens me to be so empty and lost. To work for yourself—there's no joy in that. Nils, give me something—someone to work for.

KROGSTAD: I don't believe all this. It's just some hysterical feminine urge to go out and make a noble sacrifice.

MRS. LINDE: Have you ever found me to be hysterical?

50 **KROGSTAD:**   Can you honestly mean this? Tell me—do you know everything about my past?

MRS. LINDE: Yes.

KROGSTAD: And you know what they think I'm worth around here.

MRS. LINDE: From what you were saying before, it would seem that with me you could have been another person.

KROGSTAD: I'm positive of that.

55 **MRS. LINDE:**   Couldn't it happen still?

KROGSTAD: Kristine—you're saying this in all seriousness? Yes, you are! I can see it in you. And do you really have the courage, then—?

MRS. LINDE: I need to have someone to care for; and your children need a mother. We both need each other. Nils, I have faith that you're good at heart—I'll risk everything together with you.

KROGSTAD: *(gripping her hands)* Kristine, thank you, thank you—Now I know I can win back a place in their eyes. Yes—but I forgot—

MRS. LINDE: *(listening)* Shh! The tarantella. Go now! Go on!

60 **KROGSTAD:**   Why? What is it?

MRS. LINDE: Hear the dance up there? When that's over, they'll be coming down.

KROGSTAD: Oh, then I'll go. But—it's all pointless. Of course, you don't know the move I made against the Helmers.

MRS. LINDE: Yes, Nils, I know.

KROGSTAD: And all the same, you have the courage to—?

65 **MRS. LINDE:**   I know how far despair can drive a man like you.

KROGSTAD: Oh, if I only could take it all back.

MRS. LINDE: You easily could—your letter's still lying in the mailbox.

KROGSTAD: Are you sure of that?

MRS. LINDE: Positive. But—

70 **KROGSTAD:**   *(looks at her searchingly)* Is that the meaning of it, then? You'll save your friend at any price. Tell me straight out. Is that it?

MRS. LINDE: Nils—anyone who's sold herself for somebody else once isn't going to do it again.

KROGSTAD: I'll demand my letter back.

MRS. LINDE: No, no.

KROGSTAD: Yes, of course. I'll stay here till Helmer comes down; I'll tell him to give me my letter again—that it only involves my dismissal—that he shouldn't read it—

75 **MRS. LINDE:**   No, Nils, don't call the letter back.

KROGSTAD: But wasn't that exactly why you wrote me to come here?

MRS. LINDE: Yes, in that first panic. But it's been a whole day and night since then, and in that time I've seen such incredible things in this house. Helmer's got to learn everything; this dreadful secret has to be aired; those two have to come to a full understanding; all these lies and evasions can't go on.

KROGSTAD: Well, then, if you want to chance it. But at least there's one thing I can do, and do right away—

MRS. LINDE: *(listening)* Go now, go, quick! The dance is over. We're not safe another second.

80 **KROGSTAD:**   I'll wait for you downstairs.

MRS. LINDE: Yes, please do; take me home.

KROGSTAD: I can't believe it; I've never been so happy. *(He leaves by way of the outer door; the door between the room and the hall stays open.)*

MRS. LINDE: *(straightening up a bit and getting together her street clothes)* How different now! How different! Someone to work for, to live for— a home to build. Well, it is worth the try! Oh, if they'd only come! *(Listening.)* Ah, there they are. Bundle up. *(She picks up her hat and coat. Nora's and Helmer's voices can be heard outside; a key turns in the lock, and Helmer brings Nora into the hall almost by force. She is wearing the Italian costume with a large black shawl about her; he has on evening dress, with a black domino open over it.)*

NORA: *(struggling in the doorway)* No, no, no, not inside! I'm going up again. I don't want to leave so soon.

85 **HELMER:**   But Nora dear—

NORA: Oh, I beg you, please, Torvald. From the bottom of my heart, *please*—only an hour more!

HELMER: Not a single minute, Nora darling. You know our agreement. Come on, in we go; you'll catch cold out here. *(In spite of her resistance, he gently draws her into the room.)*

MRS. LINDE: Good evening.

NORA: Kristine!

90 **HELMER:**   Why, Mrs. Linde—are you here so late?

MRS. LINDE: Yes, I'm sorry, but I did want to see Nora in costume.

NORA: Have you been sitting here, waiting for me?

MRS. LINDE: Yes. I didn't come early enough; you were all upstairs; and then I thought I really couldn't leave without seeing you.

HELMER: *(removing Nora's shawl)* Yes, take a good look. She's worth looking at, I can tell you that, Mrs. Linde. Isn't she lovely?

95 **MRS. LINDE:**   Yes, I should say—

HELMER: A dream of loveliness, isn't she? That's what everyone thought at the party, too. But she's horribly stubborn—this sweet little thing. What's to be done with her? Can you imagine, I almost had to use force to pry her away.

NORA: Oh, Torvald, you're going to regret you didn't indulge me, even for just a half hour more.

HELMER: There, you see. She danced her tarantella and got a tumultuous hand—which was well earned, although the performance may have been a bit too naturalistic—I mean it rather overstepped the proprieties of art. But never mind—what's important is, she made a success, an overwhelming success. You think I could let her stay on after that and spoil the effect? Oh no; I took my lovely little Capri girl—my capricious little Capri girl, I should say—took her under my arm; one quick tour of the ballroom, a curtsy to every side, and then—as they say in novels—the beautiful vision disappeared. An exit should always be effective, Mrs. Linde, but that's what I can't get Nora to grasp. Phew, it's hot in here. *(Flings the domino on a chair and opens the door to his room.)* Why's it dark in here? Oh yes, of course. Excuse me. *(He goes in and lights a couple of candles.)*

NORA: *(in a sharp, breathless whisper)* So?

100 **MRS. LINDE:**   *(quietly)* I talked with him.

NORA: And—?

MRS. LINDE: Nora—you must tell your husband everything.

NORA: *(dully)* I knew it.

MRS. LINDE: You've got nothing to fear from Krogstad, but you have to speak out.

105 **NORA:**   I won't tell.

MRS. LINDE: Then the letter will.

NORA: Thanks, Kristine. I know now what's to be done. Shh!

HELMER: *(reentering)* Well, then, Mrs. Linde—have you admired her?

MRS. LINDE: Yes, and now I'll say good night.

110 **HELMER:**   Oh, come, so soon? Is this yours, this knitting?

MRS. LINDE: Yes, thanks. I nearly forgot it.

HELMER: Do you knit, then?

MRS. LINDE: Oh yes.

HELMER: You know what? You should embroider instead.

115 **MRS. LINDE:**   Really? Why?

HELMER: Yes, because it's a lot prettier. See here, one holds the embroidery so, in the left hand, and then one guides the needle with the right—so—in an easy, sweeping curve—right?

Mrs. Linde: Yes, I guess that's—

Helmer: But, on the other hand, knitting—it can never be anything
   but ugly. Look, see here, the arms tucked in, the knitting needles
   going up and down—there's something Chinese about it. Ah, that was
   really a glorious champagne they served.

Mrs. Linde: Yes, good night, Nora, and don't be stubborn any more.

120 **Helmer:**   Well put, Mrs. Linde!

Mrs. Linde: Good night, Mr. Helmer.

Helmer: *(accompanying her to the door)* Good night, good night. I hope
   you get home all right. I'd be very happy to—but you don't have far
   to go. Good night, good night. *(She leaves. He shuts the door after her
   and returns.)* There, now, at last we got her out the door. She's a
   deadly bore, that creature.

Nora: Aren't you pretty tired, Torvald?

Helmer: No, not a bit.

125 **Nora:**   You're not sleepy?

Helmer: Not at all. On the contrary, I'm feeling quite exhilarated. But
   you? Yes, you really look tired and sleepy.

Nora: Yes, I'm very tired. Soon now I'll sleep.

Helmer: See! You see! I was right all along that we shouldn't stay
   longer.

Nora: Whatever you do is always right.

130 **Helmer:**   *(kissing her brow)* Now my little lark talks sense. Say, did you
   notice what a time Rank was having tonight?

Nora: Oh, was he? I didn't get to speak with him.

Helmer: I scarcely did either, but it's a long time since I've seen him in
   such high spirits. *(Gazes at her a moment, then comes nearer her.)* Hm—
   it's marvelous, though, to be back home again—to be completely
   alone with you. Oh, you bewitchingly lovely young woman!

Nora: Torvald, don't look at me like that!

Helmer: Can't I look at my richest treasure? At all that beauty that's
   mine, mine alone—completely and utterly.

135 **Nora:**   *(moving around to the other side of the table)* You mustn't talk to
   me that way tonight.

Helmer: *(following her)* The tarantella is still in your blood, I can see—
   and it makes you even more enticing. Listen. The guests are
   beginning to go. *(Dropping his voice.)* Nora—it'll soon be quiet
   through this whole house.

Nora: Yes, I hope so.

Helmer: You do, don't you, my love? Do you realize—when I'm out at a
   party like this with you—do you know why I talk to you so little, and
   keep such a distance away; just send you a stolen look now and
   then—you know why I do it? It's because I'm imagining then that
   you're my secret darling, my secret young bride-to-be, and that no
   one suspects there's anything between us.

NORA: Yes, yes; oh, yes, I know you're always thinking of me.

140 **HELMER:**   And then when we leave and I place the shawl over those fine young rounded shoulders—over that wonderful curving neck—then I pretend that you're my young bride, that we're just coming from the wedding, that for the first time I'm bringing you into my house—that for the first time I'm alone with you—completely alone with you, your trembling young beauty! All this evening I've longed for nothing but you. When I saw you turn and sway in the tarantella— my blood was pounding till I couldn't stand it—that's why I brought you down here so early—

NORA: Go away, Torvald! Leave me alone. I don't want all this.

HELMER: What do you mean? Nora, you're teasing me. You will, won't you? Aren't I your husband—?

A knock at the outside door.

NORA: *(startled)* What's that?

HELMER: *(going toward the hall)* Who is it?

145 **RANK:**   *(outside)* It's me. May I come in a moment?

HELMER: *(with quiet irritation)* Oh, what does he want now? *(Aloud.)* Hold on. *(Goes and opens the door.)* Oh, how nice that you didn't just pass us by!

RANK: I thought I heard your voice, and then I wanted so badly to have a look in. *(Lightly glancing about.)* Ah, me, these old familiar haunts. You have it snug and cozy in here, you two.

HELMER: You seemed to be having it pretty cozy upstairs, too.

RANK: Absolutely. Why shouldn't I? Why not take in everything in life? As much as you can, anyway, and as long as you can. The wine was superb—

150 **HELMER:**   The champagne especially.

RANK: You noticed that too? It's amazing how much I could guzzle down.

NORA: Torvald also drank a lot of champagne this evening.

RANK: Oh?

NORA: Yes, and that always makes him so entertaining.

155 **RANK:**   Well, why shouldn't one have a pleasant evening after a well spent day?

HELMER: Well spent? I'm afraid I can't claim that.

RANK: *(slapping him on the back)* But I can, you see!

NORA: Dr. Rank, you must have done some scientific research today.

RANK: Quite so.

160 **HELMER:**   Come now—little Nora talking about scientific research!

NORA: And can I congratulate you on the results?

RANK: Indeed you may.

NORA: Then they were good?

RANK: The best possible for both doctor and patient—certainty.

165 **NORA:** *(quickly and searchingly)* Certainty?

RANK: Complete certainty. So don't I owe myself a gay evening afterwards?

NORA: Yes, you're right, Dr. Rank.

HELMER: I'm with you—just so long as you don't have to suffer for it in the morning.

RANK: Well, one never gets something for nothing in life.

170 **NORA:** Dr. Rank—are you very fond of masquerade parties?

RANK: Yes, if there's a good array of odd disguises—

NORA: Tell me, what should we two go as at the next masquerade?

HELMER: You little featherhead—already thinking of the next!

RANK: We two? I'll tell you what: you must go as Charmed Life—

175 **HELMER:** Yes, but find a costume for *that!*

RANK: Your wife can appear just as she looks every day.

HELMER: That was nicely put. But don't you know what you're going to be?

RANK: Yes, Helmer, I've made up my mind.

HELMER: Well?

180 **RANK:** At the next masquerade I'm going to be invisible.

HELMER: That's a funny idea.

RANK: They say there's a hat—black, huge—have you never heard of the hat that makes you invisible? You put it on, and then no one on earth can see you.

HELMER: *(suppressing a smile)* Ah, of course.

RANK: But I'm quite forgetting what I came for. Helmer, give me a cigar, one of the dark Havanas.

185 **HELMER:** With the greatest of pleasure. *(Holds out his case.)*

RANK: Thanks. *(Takes one and cuts off the tip.)*

NORA: *(striking a match)* Let me give you a light.

RANK: Thank you. *(She holds the match for him; he lights the cigar.)* And now good-bye.

HELMER: Good-bye, good-bye, old friend.

190 **NORA:** Sleep well, Doctor.

RANK: Thanks for that wish.

NORA: Wish me the same.

RANK: You? All right, if you like—Sleep well. And thanks for the light. *(He nods to them both and leaves.)*

HELMER: *(his voice subdued)* He's been drinking heavily.

195 **NORA:** *(absently)* Could be. *(Helmer takes his keys from his pocket and goes out in the hall.)* Torvald—what are you after?

HELMER: Got to empty the mailbox; it's nearly full. There won't be room for the morning papers.

NORA: Are you working tonight?

HELMER: You know I'm not. Why—what's this? Someone's been at the lock.

NORA: At the lock—?

200 **HELMER:** Yes, I'm positive. What do you suppose—? I can't imagine one of the maids—? Here's a broken hairpin. Nora, it's yours—

NORA: *(quickly)* Then it must be the children—

HELMER: You'd better break them of that. Hm, hm—well, opened it after all. *(Takes the contents out and calls into the kitchen.)* Helene! Helene, would you put out the lamp in the hall. *(He returns to the room, shutting the hall door, then displays the handful of mail.)* Look how it's piled up. *(Sorting through them.)* Now what's this?

NORA: *(at the window)* The letter! Oh, Torvald, no!

HELMER: Two calling cards—from Rank.

205 **NORA:** From Dr. Rank?

HELMER: *(examining them)* "Dr. Rank, Consulting Physician." They were on top. He must have dropped them in as he left.

NORA: Is there anything on them?

HELMER: There's a black cross over the name. See? That's a gruesome notion. He could almost be announcing his own death.

NORA: That's just what he's doing.

210 **HELMER:** What! You've heard something? Something he's told you?

NORA: Yes. That when those cards came, he'd be taking his leave of us. He'll shut himself in now and die.

HELMER: Ah, my poor friend! Of course I knew he wouldn't be here much longer. But so soon—And then to hide himself away like a wounded animal.

NORA: If it has to happen, then it's best it happens in silence—don't you think so, Torvald?

HELMER: *(pacing up and down)* He'd grown right into our lives. I simply can't imagine him gone. He with his suffering and loneliness—like a dark cloud setting off our sunlit happiness. Well, maybe it's best this way. For him, at least. *(Standing still.)* And maybe for us too, Nora. Now we're thrown back on each other, completely. *(Embracing her.)* Oh you, my darling wife, how can I hold you close enough? You know what, Nora—time and again I've wished you were in some terrible danger, just so I could stake my life and soul and everything, for your sake.

215 **NORA:** *(tearing herself away, her voice firm and decisive)* Now you must read your mail, Torvald.

HELMER: No, no, not tonight. I want to stay with you, dearest.

NORA: With a dying friend on your mind?

HELMER: You're right. We've both had a shock. There's ugliness between us—these thoughts of death and corruption. We'll have to get free of them first. Until then—we'll stay apart.

NORA: *(clinging about his neck)* Torvald—good night! Good night!

220 **HELMER:** *(kissing her on the cheek)* Good night, little songbird. Sleep well, Nora. I'll be reading my mail now. *(He takes the letters into his room and shuts the door after him.)*

NORA: *(with bewildered glances, groping about, seizing Helmer's domino, throwing it around her, and speaking in short, hoarse, broken whispers)* Never see him again. Never, never. *(Putting her shawl over her head.)* Never see the children either—them, too. Never, never. Oh, the freezing black water! The depths—down—Oh, I wish it were over—He has it now; he's reading it—now. Oh no, no, not yet. Torvald, goodbye, you and the children—*(She starts for the hall; as she does, Helmer throws open his door and stands with an open letter in his hand.)*

HELMER: Nora!

NORA: *(screams)* Oh—!

HELMER: What is this? You know what's in this letter?

225 NORA: Yes, I know. Let me go! Let me out!

HELMER: *(holding her back)* Where are you going?

NORA: *(struggling to break loose)* You can't save me, Torvald!

HELMER: *(slumping back)* True! Then it's true what he writes? How horrible! No, no, it's impossible—it can't be true.

NORA: It *is* true. I've loved you more than all this world.

230 HELMER: Ah, none of your slippery tricks.

NORA: *(taking one step toward him)* Torvald—!

HELMER: What *is* this you've blundered into!

NORA: Just let me loose. You're not going to suffer for my sake. You're not going to take on my guilt.

HELMER: No more playacting. *(Locks the hall door.)* You stay right here and give me a reckoning. You understand what you've done? Answer! You understand?

235 NORA: *(looking squarely at him, her face hardening)* Yes. I'm beginning to understand everything now.

HELMER: *(striding about)* Oh, what an awful awakening! In all these eight years—she who was my pride and joy—a hypocrite, a liar—worse, worse—a criminal! How infinitely disgusting it all is! The shame! *(Nora says nothing and goes on looking straight at him. He stops in front of her.)* I should have suspected something of the kind. I should have known. All your father's flimsy values—Be still! All your father's flimsy values have come out in you. No religion, no morals, no sense of duty—Oh, how I'm punished for letting him off! I did it for your sake, and you repay me like this.

NORA: Yes, like this.

HELMER: Now you've wrecked all my happiness—ruined my whole future. Oh, it's awful to think of. I'm in a cheap little grafter's hands; he can do anything he wants with me, ask for anything, play with me like a puppet—and I can't breathe a word. I'll be swept down miserably into the depths on account of a featherbrained woman.

NORA: When I'm gone from this world, you'll be free.

240 HELMER: Oh, quit posing. Your father had a mess of those speeches too. What good would that ever do me if you were gone from this world, as you say? Not the slightest. He can still make the whole thing

known; and if he does, I could be falsely suspected as your accomplice. They might even think that I was behind it—that I put you up to it. And all that I can thank you for—you that I've coddled the whole of our marriage. Can you see now what you've done to me?

Nora: *(icily calm)* Yes.

Helmer: It's so incredible, I just can't grasp it. But we'll have to patch up whatever we can. Take off the shawl. I said, take if off! I've got to appease him somehow or other. The thing has to be hushed up at any cost. And as for you and me, it's got to seem like everything between us is just as it was—to the outside world, that is. You'll go right on living in this house, of course. But you can't be allowed to bring up the children; I don't dare trust you with them—Oh, to have to say this to someone I've loved so much! Well, that's done with. From now on happiness doesn't matter; all that matters is saving the bits and pieces, the appearance—*(The doorbell rings. Helmer starts.)* What's that? And so late. Maybe the worst—? You think he'd—? Hide, Nora! Say you're sick. *(Nora remains standing motionless. Helmer goes and opens the door.)*

Maid: *(half dressed, in the hall)* A letter for Mrs. Helmer.

Helmer: I'll take it. *(Snatches the letter and shuts the door.)* Yes, it's from him. You don't get it; I'm reading it myself.

245 **Nora:** Then read it.

Helmer: *(by the lamp)* I hardly dare. We may be ruined, you and I. But—I've got to know. *(Rips open the letter, skims through a few lines, glances at an enclosure, then cries out joyfully.)* Nora! *(Nora looks inquiringly at him.)* Nora! Wait—better check it again—Yes, yes, it's true. I'm saved. Nora, I'm saved!

Nora: And I?

Helmer: You too, of course. We're both saved, both of us. Look. He's sent back your note. He says he's sorry and ashamed—that a happy development in his life—oh, who cares what he says! Nora, we're saved! No one can hurt you. Oh, Nora, Nora—but first, this ugliness all has to go. Let me see—*(Takes a look at the note.)* No, I don't want to see it; I want the whole thing to fade like a dream. *(Tears the note and both letters to pieces, throws them into the stove and watches them burn.)* There—now there's nothing left—He wrote that since Christmas Eve you—Oh, they must have been three terrible days for you, Nora.

Nora: I fought a hard fight.

250 **Helmer:** And suffered pain and saw no escape but—No, we're not going to dwell on anything unpleasant. We'll just be grateful and keep on repeating: it's over now, it's over! You hear me, Nora? You don't seem to realize—it's over. What's it mean—that frozen look? Oh, poor little Nora, I understand. You can't believe I've forgiven you. But I have, Nora; I swear I have. I know that what you did, you did out of love for me.

NORA: That's true.

HELMER: You loved me the way a wife ought to love her husband. It's simply the means that you couldn't judge. But you think I love you any the less for not knowing how to handle your affairs? No, no—just lean on me; I'll guide you and teach you. I wouldn't be a man if this feminine helplessness didn't make you twice as attractive to me. You mustn't mind those sharp words I said—that was all in the first confusion of thinking my world had collapsed. I've forgiven you, Nora; I swear I've forgiven you.

NORA: My thanks for your forgiveness. *(She goes out through the door, right.)*

HELMER: No, wait—*(Peers in.)* What are you doing in there?

255 **NORA:** *(inside)* Getting out of my costume.

HELMER: *(by the open door)* Yes, do that. Try to calm yourself and collect your thoughts again, my frightened little songbird. You can rest easy now; I've got wide wings to shelter you with. *(Walking about close by the door.)* How snug and nice our home is, Nora. You're safe here; I'll keep you like a hunted dove I've rescued out of a hawk's claws. I'll bring peace to your poor, shuddering heart. Gradually it'll happen, Nora; you'll see. Tomorrow all this will look different to you; then everything will be as it was. I won't have to go on repeating I forgive you; you'll feel it for yourself. How can you imagine I'd ever conceivably want to disown you—or even blame you in any way? Ah, you don't know a man's heart, Nora. For a man there's something indescribably sweet and satisfying in knowing he's forgiven his wife—and forgiven her out of a full and open heart. It's as if she belongs to him in two ways now: in a sense he's given her fresh into the world again, and she's become his wife and his child as well. From now on that's what you'll be to me—you little, bewildered, helpless thing. Don't be afraid of anything, Nora; just open your heart to me, and I'll be conscience and will to you both—*(Nora enters in her regular clothes.)* What's this? Not in bed? You've changed your dress?

NORA: Yes, Torvald, I've changed my dress.

HELMER: But why now, so late?

NORA: Tonight I'm not sleeping.

260 **HELMER:** But Nora dear—

NORA: *(looking at her watch)* It's still not so very late. Sit down, Torvald; we have a lot to talk over. *(She sits at one side of the table.)*

HELMER: Nora—what is this? That hard expression—

NORA: Sit down. This'll take some time. I have a lot to say.

HELMER: *(sitting at the table directly opposite her)* You worry me, Nora. And I don't understand you.

265 **NORA:** No, that's exactly it. You don't understand me. And I've never understood you either—until tonight. No, don't interrupt. You can just listen to what I say. We're closing out accounts, Torvald.

HELMER: How do you mean that?

NORA: *(after a short pause)* Doesn't anything strike you about our sitting here like this?

HELMER: What's that?

NORA: We've been married now eight years. Doesn't it occur to you that this is the first time we two, you and I, man and wife, have ever talked seriously together?

270 **HELMER:**   What do you mean—seriously?

NORA: In eight whole years—longer even—right from our first acquaintance, we've never exchanged a serious word on any serious thing.

HELMER: You mean I should constantly go and involve you in problems you couldn't possibly help me with?

NORA: I'm not talking of problems. I'm saying that we've never sat down seriously together and tried to get to the bottom of anything.

HELMER: But dearest, what good would that ever do you?

275 **NORA:**   That's the point right there: you've never understood me. I've been wronged greatly, Torvald—first by Papa, and then by you.

HELMER: What! By us—the two people who've loved you more than anyone else?

NORA: *(shaking her head)* You never loved me. You've thought it fun to be in love with me, that's all.

HELMER: Nora, what a thing to say!

NORA: Yes, it's true now, Torvald. When I lived at home with Papa, he told me all his opinions, so I had the same ones too; or if they were different I hid them, since he wouldn't have cared for that. He used to call me his doll-child, and he played with me the way I played with my dolls. Then I came into your house—

280 **HELMER:**   How can you speak of our marriage like that?

NORA: *(unperturbed)* I mean, then I went from Papa's hands into yours. You arranged everything to your own taste, and so I got the same taste as you—or I pretended to; I can't remember. I guess a little of both, first one, then the other. Now when I look back, it seems as if I'd lived here like a beggar—just from hand to mouth. I've lived by doing tricks for you, Torvald. But that's the way you wanted it. It's a great sin what you and Papa did to me. You're to blame that nothing's become of me.

HELMER: Nora, how unfair and ungrateful you are! Haven't you been happy here?

NORA: No, never. I thought so—but I never have.

HELMER: Not—not happy!

285 **NORA:**   No, only lighthearted. And you've always been so kind to me. But our home's been nothing but a playpen. I've been your doll-wife here, just as at home I was Papa's doll-child. And in turn the children have been my dolls. I thought it was fun when you played with me,

just as they thought it fun when I played with them. That's been our marriage, Torvald.

HELMER: There's some truth in what you're saying—under all the raving exaggeration. But it'll all be different after this. Playtime's over; now for the schooling.

NORA: Whose schooling—mine or the children's?

HELMER: Both yours and the children's, dearest.

NORA: Oh, Torvald, you're not the man to teach me to be a good wife to you.

290 HELMER: And you can say that?

NORA: And I—how am I equipped to bring up children?

HELMER: Nora!

NORA: Didn't you say a moment ago that that was no job to trust me with?

HELMER: In a flare of temper! Why fasten on that?

295 NORA: Yes, but you were so very right. I'm not up to the job. There's another job I have to do first. I have to try to educate myself. You can't help me with that. I've got to do it alone. And that's why I'm leaving you now.

HELMER: *(jumping up)* What's that?

NORA: I have to stand completely alone, if I'm ever going to discover myself and the world out there. So I can't go on living with you.

HELMER: Nora, Nora!

NORA: I want to leave right away. Kristine should put me up for the night—

300 HELMER: You're insane! You've no right! I forbid you!

NORA: From here on, there's no use forbidding me anything. I'll take with me whatever is mine. I don't want a thing from you, either now or later.

HELMER: What kind of madness is this!

NORA: Tomorrow I'm going home—I mean, home where I came from. It'll be easier up there to find something to do.

HELMER: Oh, you blind, incompetent child!

305 NORA: I must learn to be competent, Torvald.

HELMER: Abandon your home, your husband, your children! And you're not even thinking what people will say.

NORA: I can't be concerned about that. I only know how essential this is.

HELMER: Oh, it's outrageous. So you'll run out like this on your most sacred vows.

NORA: What do you think are my most sacred vows?

310 HELMER: And I have to tell you that! Aren't they your duties to your husband and children?

NORA: I have other duties equally sacred.

HELMER: That isn't true. What duties are they?

NORA: Duties to myself.

HELMER: Before all else, you're a wife and a mother.

315 **NORA:** I don't believe in that any more. I believe that, before all else, I'm a human being, no less than you—or anyway, I ought to try to become one. I know the majority thinks you're right, Torvald, and plenty of books agree with you, too. But I can't go on believing what the majority says, or what's written in books. I have to think over these things myself and try to understand them.

HELMER: Why can't you understand your place in your own home? On a point like that, isn't there one everlasting guide you can turn to? Where's your religion?

NORA: Oh, Torvald, I'm really not sure what religion is.

HELMER: What—?

NORA: I only know what the minister said when I was confirmed. He told me religion was this thing and that. When I get clear and away by myself, I'll go into that problem too. I'll see if what the minister said was right, or, in any case, if it's right for me.

320 **HELMER:** A young woman your age shouldn't talk like that. If religion can't move you, I can try to rouse your conscience. You do have some moral feeling? Or, tell me—has that gone too?

NORA: It's not easy to answer that, Torvald. I simply don't know. I'm all confused about these things. I just know I see them so differently from you. I find out, for one thing, that the law's not at all what I'd thought—but I can't get it through my head that the law is fair. A woman hasn't a right to protect her dying father or save her husband's life! I can't believe that.

HELMER: You talk like a child. You don't know anything of the world you live in.

NORA: No, I don't. But now I'll begin to learn for myself. I'll try to discover who's right, the world or I.

HELMER: Nora, you're sick; you've got a fever. I almost think you're out of your head.

325 **NORA:** I've never felt more clearheaded and sure in my life.

HELMER: And—clearheaded and sure—you're leaving your husband and children?

NORA: Yes.

HELMER: Then there's only one possible reason.

NORA: What?

330 **HELMER:** You no longer love me.

NORA: No. That's exactly it.

HELMER: Nora! You can't be serious!

NORA: Oh, this is so hard, Torvald—you've been so kind to me always. But I can't help it. I don't love you any more.

HELMER: *(struggling for composure)* Are you also clearheaded and sure about that?

335 **NORA:** Yes, completely. That's why I can't go on staying here.

HELMER: Can you tell me what I did to lose your love?

NORA: Yes, I can tell you. It was this evening when the miraculous thing didn't come—then I knew you weren't the man I'd imagined.

HELMER: Be more explicit; I don't follow you.

NORA: I've waited now so patiently eight long years—for, my Lord, I know miracles don't come every day. Then this crisis broke over me, and such a certainty filled me: *now* the miraculous event would occur. While Krogstad's letter was lying out there, I never for an instant dreamed that you could give in to his terms. I was so utterly sure you'd say to him: go on, tell your tale to the whole wide world. And when he'd done that—

340 **HELMER:**   Yes, what then? When I'd delivered my own wife into shame and disgrace—!

NORA: When he'd done that, I was so utterly sure that you'd step forward, take the blame on yourself and say: I am the guilty one.

HELMER: Nora—!

NORA: You're thinking I'd never accept such a sacrifice from you? No, of course not. But what good would my protests be against you? That was the miracle I was waiting for, in terror and hope. And to stave that off, I would have taken my life.

HELMER: I'd gladly work for you day and night, Nora—and take on pain and deprivation. But there's no one who gives up honor for love.

345 **NORA:**   Millions of women have done just that.

HELMER: Oh, you think and talk like a silly child.

NORA: Perhaps. But you neither think nor talk like the man I could join myself to. When your big fright was over—and it wasn't from any threat against me, only for what might damage you—when all the danger was past, for you it was just as if nothing had happened. I was exactly the same, your little lark, your doll, that you'd have to handle with double care now that I'd turned out so brittle and frail. *(Gets up.)* Torvald—in that instant it dawned on me that for eight years I've been living here with a stranger, and that I'd even conceived three children—oh, I can't stand the thought of it! I could tear myself to bits.

HELMER: *(heavily)* I see. There's a gulf that's opened between us—that's clear. Oh, but Nora, can't we bridge it somehow?

NORA: The way I am now, I'm no wife for you.

350 **HELMER:**   I have the strength to make myself over.

NORA: Maybe—if your doll gets taken away.

HELMER: But to part! To part from you! No, Nora, no—I can't imagine it.

NORA: *(going out, right)* All the more reason why it has to be. *(She reenters with her coat and a small overnight bag, which she puts on a chair by the table.)*

HELMER: Nora, Nora, not now! Wait till tomorrow.

355 **NORA:**   I can't spend the night in a strange man's room.

HELMER: But couldn't we live here like brother and sister—

NORA: You know very well how long that would last. *(Throws her shawl about her.)* Good-bye, Torvald. I won't look in on the children. I know they're in better hands than mine. The way I am now, I'm no use to them.

HELMER: But someday, Nora—someday—?

NORA: How can I tell? I haven't the least idea what'll become of me.

360 **HELMER:** But you're my wife, now and wherever you go.

NORA: Listen, Torvald—I've heard that when a wife deserts her husband's house just as I'm doing, then the law frees him from all responsibility. In any case, I'm freeing you from being responsible. Don't feel yourself bound, any more than I will. There has to be absolute freedom for us both. Here, take your ring back. Give me mine.

HELMER: That too?

NORA: That too.

HELMER: There it is.

365 **NORA:** Good. Well, now it's all over. I'm putting the keys here. The maids know all about keeping up the house—better than I do. Tomorrow, after I've left town, Kristine will stop by to pack up everything that's mine from home. I'd like those things shipped up to me.

HELMER: Over! All over! Nora, won't you ever think about me?

NORA: I'm sure I'll think of you often, and about the children and the house here.

HELMER: May i write you?

NORA: No—never. You're not to do that.

370 **HELMER:** Oh, but let me send you—

NORA: Nothing. Nothing.

HELMER: Or help you if you need it.

NORA: No. I accept nothing from strangers.

HELMER: Nora—can I never be more than a stranger to you?

375 **NORA:** *(picking up the overnight bag)* Ah, Torvald—it would take the greatest miracle of all—

HELMER: Tell me the greatest miracle!

NORA: You and I both would have to transform ourselves to the point that—Oh, Torvald, I've stopped believing in miracles.

HELMER: But I'll believe. Tell me! Transform ourselves to the point that—?

NORA: That our living together could be a true marriage. *(She goes out down the hall.)*

380 **HELMER:** *(sinks down on a chair by the door, face buried in his hands)* Nora! Nora! *(Looking about and rising.)* Empty. She's gone. *(A sudden hope leaps in him.)* The greatest miracle—?

(From below, the sound of a door slamming shut.)

READING AND REACTING

1. What is your attitude toward Nora at the beginning of the play? How does your attitude toward her change as the play progresses? What events and/or lines of dialogue change your assessment of her?

2. List the key events that occur before the play begins. How do we learn of each event?

3. In Act 1, how do the various references to macaroons in the stage directions reinforce plot developments?

4. Evaluate the role of the following in advancing the play's action: the Christmas tree, the locked mailbox, the telegram Dr. Rank receives, Dr. Rank's calling cards.

5. In Act 2 Torvald says, "Whatever comes, you'll see: when it really counts, I have strength and courage enough as a man to take on the whole weight myself." How does this statement influence Nora's subsequent actions?

6. How do the upcoming costume party and Nora's dance function in the play's plot? Where does the play's climax occur?

7. Explain how the following foreshadow events that will occur later in the play: Torvald's comments about Krogstad's children (Act 1); Torvald's attitude toward Nora's father (Act 2); Krogstad's suggestions about suicide (Act 2).

8. In addition to the play's central plot—which concerns the blackmail of Nora by Krogstad and her attempts to keep her crime secret from Torvald—the play contains several subplots, some of which have developed before the play begins and some of which unfold alongside the central plot. Identify these subplots. How do they advance the themes of survival, debt, sacrifice, and duty that run through the play?

9. Is Kristine Linde essential to the play? How might the play be different without her?

10. Is Mrs. Linde as much of a "modern woman" as Nora? Is she actually *more* of a modern woman?

11. Do you think *A Doll House* is primarily about the struggle between the needs of the individual and the needs of society or about the conflict between women's roles in the family and in the larger society? Explain.

12. **JOURNAL ENTRY** Nora makes a drastic decision at the end of the play. Do you think she overreacts? What other options does she have? What additional options might she have today?

13. **CRITICAL PERSPECTIVE** Since its earliest performances, there has been much comment on the conclusion of *A Doll House*. In fact, Ibsen based the play on a true story, which closely paralleled the main events of the play: A wife borrows money to finance a trip for an

ailing husband, repayment is demanded, she forges a check and is discovered. (In the real-life story, however, the husband demanded a divorce, and the wife had a nervous breakdown and was committed to a mental institution.)

Many viewers found the play's ending unrealistically harsh. In fact, a famous German actress refused to play the scene as written because she insisted she would never leave her children. (Ibsen reluctantly rewrote the ending for her; in this version, Helmer forces Nora to the doorway of the children's bedroom, and she sinks to the floor as the curtain falls.) Moreover, many critics have found it hard to accept Nora's transformation from, in Elizabeth Hardwick's words, "the girlish, charming wife to the radical, courageous heroine setting out alone" ("Ibsen's Women" in *Seduction and Betrayal*).

What is your response to the play's ending? Do you think it makes sense in light of what we have learned about Nora and her marriage? Or do you, for example, agree with Hardwick that Nora's abandonment of her children is not only implausible but a "rather casual" gesture that "drops a stain on our admiration of Nora"?

SAM SHEPARD (1943–   ) was born Samuel Shepard Rogers, Jr., in Fort Sheridan, Illinois. He lived in the San Bernadino Valley in Southern California until, at nineteen, he moved to New York to pursue a career in acting. In 1972, following a successful run of plays but disillusioned with theater politics, Shepard moved to London. After his return to the United States, Shepard accompanied Bob Dylan on his 1976 Rolling Thunder Tour. Living in San Francisco, Shepard began acting in films and in 1983 portrayed of the test pilot Chuck Yeager in *The Right Stuff*. Shepard now lives in Virginia.

Shepard has won many awards for his dramas and screenplays. Since the performance of his first one-act drama, *Cowboys* (1964), he has won eleven Obie awards for his plays, including *Chicago* (1965); *Curse of the Starving Class* (1976); *Buried Child* (1978), which won a Pulitzer Prize for 1979; and *Fool for Love* (1983). Shepard's *A Lie of the Mind* (1985) was named the outstanding new play of the 1985–86 season by the Drama Desk. His more recent plays include *States of Shock* (1991) and *Simpatico* (1994). Shepard's screenplays include *Zabrinski Point* (1969) and *Paris, Texas* (1984), which won the Palme d'Or at the Cannes Film Festival.

Shepard's plays focus on American culture and myth, particularly in the contexts of country music, rock and roll music, Hollywood films, the American West, and the suburban middle-class family. Many of his plays reflect dysfunctional American families—marked by conflict between siblings, passion and violence of lovers, and the cycle of generational problems. In *True West*, Shepard explores sibling rivalry, the mythology of the American West, and the destructive potential of inherited family patterns.

SAM SHEPARD

True West

(1981)

CHARACTERS

Austin, *early thirties, light blue sports shirt, light tan cardigan sweater, clean blue jeans, white tennis shoes*

Lee, *his older brother, early forties, filthy white t-shirt, tattered brown overcoat covered with dust, dark blue baggy suit pants from the Salvation Army, pink suede belt, pointed black forties dress shoes scuffed up, holes in the soles, no socks, no hat, long pronounced sideburns, "Gene Vincent" hairdo, two days' growth of beard, bad teeth*

Saul Kimmer, *late forties, Hollywood producer, pink and white flower print sports shirt, white sports coat with matching polyester slacks, black and white loafers*

Mom, *early sixties, mother of the brothers, small woman, conservative white skirt and matching jacket, red shoulder bag, two pieces of matching red luggage*

True West was first performed at the Magic Theatre in San Francisco on July 10, 1980. The director was Robert Woodruff, and the cast was as follows:

Austin	*Peter Coyote*
Lee	*Jim Haynie*
Saul Kimmer	*Tom Dahlgren*
Mom	*Carol McElheney*

SCENE
All nine scenes take place on the same set; a kitchen and adjoining alcove of an older home in a Southern California suburb, about 40 miles east of Los Angeles. The kitchen takes up most of the playing area to stage left. The kitchen consists of a sink, upstage center, surrounded by counter space, a wall telephone, cupboards, and a small window just above it bordered by neat yellow curtains. Stage left of sink is a stove. Stage right, a refrigerator. The alcove adjoins the kitchen to stage right. There is no wall division or door to the alcove. It is open and easily accessible from the kitchen and defined only by the objects in it: a small round glass breakfast table mounted on white iron legs, two matching white iron chairs set across from each other. The two exterior walls of the alcove which prescribe a corner in the upstage right are composed of many small windows, beginning from a solid wall about three feet high and extending to the ceiling. The

windows look out to bushes and citrus trees. The alcove is filled with all sorts of house plants in various pots, mostly Boston ferns hanging in planters at different levels. The floor of the alcove is composed of green synthetic grass.

All entrances and exits are made stage left from the kitchen. There is no door. The actors simply go off and come onto the playing area.

NOTE ON SET AND COSTUME

The set should be constructed realistically with no attempt to distort its dimensions, shapes, objects, or colors. No objects should be introduced which might draw special attention to themselves other than the props demanded by the script. If a stylistic "concept" is grafted onto the set design it will only serve to confuse the evolution of the characters' situation, which is the most important focus of the play.

Likewise, the costumes should be exactly representative of who the characters are and not added onto for the sake of making a point to the audience.

NOTE ON SOUND

The Coyote of Southern California has a distinct yapping, dog-like bark, similar to a Hyena. This yapping grows more intense and maniacal as the pack grows in numbers, which is usually the case when they lure and kill pets from suburban yards. The sense of growing frenzy in the pack should be felt in the background, particularly in Scenes 7 and 8. In any case, these Coyotes never make the long, mournful, solitary howl of the Hollywood stereotype.

The sound of Crickets can speak for itself.

These sounds should also be treated realistically even though they sometimes grow in volume and numbers.

A C T   O N E

S C E N E   1

Night. Sound of crickets in dark. Candlelight appears in alcove, illuminating Austin, seated at glass table hunched over a writing notebook, pen in hand, cigarette burning in ashtray, cup of coffee, typewriter on table, stacks of paper, candle burning on table.

Soft moonlight fills kitchen illuminating Lee, beer in hand, six-pack on counter behind him. He's leaning against the sink, mildly drunk; takes a slug of beer.

Lee: So, Mom took off for Alaska, huh?

Austin: Yeah.

Lee: Sorta' left you in charge.

Austin: Well, she knew I was coming down here so she offered me the place.

5 **Lee:** You keepin' the plants watered?

AUSTIN: Yeah.

LEE: Keepin' the sink clean? She don't like even a single tea leaf in the sink ya' know.

AUSTIN: *(trying to concentrate on writing)* Yeah, I know.

(pause)

LEE: She gonna' be up there a long time?

10 **AUSTIN:**   I don't know.

LEE: Kinda' nice for you, huh? Whole place to yourself.

AUSTIN: Yeah, it's great.

LEE: Ya' got crickets anyway. Tons a' crickets out there. *(looks around kitchen)* Ya' got groceries? Coffee?

AUSTIN: *(looking up from writing)* What?

15 **LEE:**   You got coffee?

AUSTIN: Yeah.

LEE: At's good. *(short pause)* Real coffee? From the bean?

AUSTIN: Yeah. You want some?

LEE: Naw. I brought some uh—*(motions to beer)*

20 **AUSTIN:**   Help yourself to whatever's—*(motions to refrigerator)*

LEE: I will. Don't worry about me. I'm not the one to worry about. I mean I can uh—*(pause)* You always work by candlelight?

AUSTIN: No—uh—Not always.

LEE: Just sometimes?

AUSTIN: *(puts pen down, rubs his eyes)* Yeah. Sometimes it's soothing.

25 **LEE:**   Isn't that what the old guys did?

AUSTIN: What old guys?

LEE: The Forefathers. You know.

AUSTIN: Forefathers?

LEE: Isn't that what they did? Candlelight burning into the night? Cabins in the wilderness.

30 **AUSTIN:**   *(rubs hand through his hair)* I suppose.

LEE: I'm not botherin' you am I? I mean I don't wanna break into yer uh—concentration or nothin'.

AUSTIN: No, it's all right.

LEE: That's good. I mean I realize that yer line a' work demands a lota' concentration.

AUSTIN: It's okay.

35 **LEE:**   You probably think that I'm not fully able to comprehend somethin' like that, huh?

AUSTIN: Like what?

LEE: That stuff yer doin'. That art. You know. Whatever you call it.

AUSTIN: It's just a little research.

LEE: You may not know it but I did a little art myself once.

40 **AUSTIN:**   You did?

LEE: Yeah! I did some a' that. I fooled around with it. No future in it.

AUSTIN: What'd you do?

LEE: Never mind what I did! Just never mind about that. *(pause)* It was
   ahead of its time.

(pause)

AUSTIN: So, you went out to see the old man, huh?

45   LEE: Yeah, I seen him.

AUSTIN: How's he doing?

LEE: Same. He's doin' just about the same.

AUSTIN: I was down there too, you know.

LEE: What d'ya' want, an award? You want some kinda' medal? You
   were down there. He told me all about you.

50   AUSTIN: What'd he say?

LEE: He told me. Don't worry.

(pause)

AUSTIN: Well—

LEE: You don't have to say nothin'.

AUSTIN: I wasn't.

55   LEE: Yeah, you were gonna' make somethin' up. Somethin' brilliant.

(pause)

AUSTIN: You going to be down here very long, Lee?

LEE: Might be. Depends on a few things.

AUSTIN: You got some friends down here?

LEE: *(laughs)* I know a few people. Yeah.

60   AUSTIN: Well, you can stay here as long as I'm here.

LEE: I don't need your permission do I?

AUSTIN: No.

LEE: I mean she's my mother too, right?

AUSTIN: Right.

65   LEE: She might've just as easily asked me to take care of her place as you.

AUSTIN: That's right.

LEE: I mean I know how to water plants.

(long pause)

AUSTIN: So you don't know how long you'll be staying then?

LEE: Depends mostly on houses, ya' know.

70   AUSTIN: Houses?

LEE: Yeah. Houses. Electric devices. Stuff like that. I gotta' make a little
   tour first.

(short pause)

AUSTIN: Lee, why don't you just try another neighborhood, all right?

LEE: *(laughs)* What'sa' matter with this neighborhood? This is a great
   neighborhood. Lush. Good class a' people. Not many dogs.

AUSTIN: Well, our uh—Our mother just happens to live here. That's all.

75 **LEE:**   Nobody's gonna' know. All they know is somethin's missing.
That's all. She'll never even hear about it. Nobody's gonna' know.

AUSTIN: You're going to get picked up if you start walking around here
at night.

LEE: Me? I'm gonna' git picked up? What about you? You stick out like
a sore thumb. Look at you. You think yer regular lookin'?

AUSTIN: I've got too much to deal with here to be worrying about—

LEE: Yer not gonna' have to worry about me! I've been doin' all right
without you. I haven't been anywhere near you for five years! Now
isn't that true?

80 **AUSTIN:**   Yeah.

LEE: So you don't have to worry about me. I'm a free agent.

AUSTIN: All right.

LEE: Now all I wanna' do is borrow yer car.

AUSTIN: No!

85 **LEE:**   Just fer a day. One day.

AUSTIN: No!

LEE: I won't take it outside a twenty mile radius. I promise ya'. You can
check the speedometer.

AUSTIN: You're not borrowing my car! That's all there is to it.

(pause)

LEE: Then I'll just take the damn thing.

90 **AUSTIN:**   Lee, look—I don't want any trouble, all right?

LEE: That's a dumb line. That is a dumb fuckin' line. You git paid fer
dreamin' up a line like that?

AUSTIN: Look, I can give you some money if you need money.

*(Lee suddenly lunges at Austin, grabs him violently by the shirt and shakes him
with tremendous power)*

LEE: Don't you say that to me! Don't you ever say that to me! *(just as
suddenly he turns him loose, pushes him away and backs off)* You may be
able to git away with that with the Old Man. Git him tanked up for a
week! Buy him off with yer Hollywood blood money, but not me! I
can git my own money my own way. Big money!

AUSTIN: I was just making an offer.

95 **LEE:**   Yeah, well keep it to yourself!

(long pause)

Those are the most monotonous fuckin' crickets I ever heard in my life.

AUSTIN: I kinda' like the sound.

LEE: Yeah. Supposed to be able to tell the temperature by the number
a' pulses. You believe that?

AUSTIN: The temperature?

LEE: Yeah. The air. How hot it is.

100 **AUSTIN:**   How do you do that?

LEE: I don't know. Some woman told me that. She was a Botanist. So I believed her.

AUSTIN: Where'd you meet her?

LEE: What?

AUSTIN: The woman Botanist?

105 **LEE:** I met her on the desert. I been spendin' a lota' time on the desert.

AUSTIN: What were you doing out there?

LEE: *(pause, stares in space)* I forgit. Had me a Pit Bull there for a while but I lost him?

AUSTIN: Pit Bull?

LEE: Fightin' dog. Damn I made some good money off that little dog. Real good money.

(pause)

110 **AUSTIN:** You could come up north with me, you know.

LEE: What's up there?

AUSTIN: My family.

LEE: Oh, that's right, you got the wife and kiddies now don't ya! The house, the car, the whole slam. That's right.

AUSTIN: You could spend a couple days. See how you like it. I've got an extra room.

115 **LEE:** Too cold up there.

(pause)

AUSTIN: You want to sleep for a while?

LEE: *(pause, stares at Austin)* I don't sleep.

(lights to black)

SCENE 2

Morning. Austin is watering plants with a vaporizer, Lee sits at glass table in alcove drinking beer.

LEE: I never realized the old lady was so security-minded.

AUSTIN: How do you mean?

120 **LEE:** Made a little tour this morning. She's got locks on everything. Locks and double-locks and chain locks and—What's she got that's so valuable?

AUSTIN: Antiques I guess. I don't know.

LEE: Antiques? Brought everything with her from the old place, huh. Just the same crap we always had around. Plates and spoons.

AUSTIN: I guess they have personal value to her.

LEE: Personal value. Yeah. Just a lota' junk. Most of it's phony anyway. Idaho decals. Now who in the hell wants to eat offa' plate with the

State of Idaho starin' ya' in the face. Every time ya' take a bite ya' get to see a little bit more.

125 **AUSTIN:**   Well it must mean something to her or she wouldn't save it.

LEE: Yeah, well personally I don't wann' be invaded by Idaho when I'm eatin'. When I'm eatin' I'm home. Ya' know what I'm sayin'? I'm not driftin', I'm home. I don't need my thoughts swept off to Idaho. I don't need that!

(pause)

AUSTIN: Did you go out last night?

LEE: Why?

AUSTIN: I thought I heard you go out.

130 **LEE:**   Yeah, I went out. What about it?

AUSTIN: Just wondered.

LEE: Damn coyotes kept me awake.

AUSTIN: Oh yeah, I heard them. They must've killed somebody's dog or something.

LEE: Yappin' their fool heads off. They don't yap like that on the desert. They howl. These are city coyotes here.

135 **AUSTIN:**   Well, you don't sleep anyway do you?

(pause, Lee stares at him)

LEE: You're pretty smart aren't ya?

AUSTIN: How do you mean?

LEE: I mean you never had any more on the ball than I did. But here you are gettin' invited into prominent people's houses. Sittin' around talkin' like you know somethin'.

AUSTIN: They're not so prominent.

140 **LEE:**   They're a helluva' lot more prominent than the houses I get invited into.

AUSTIN: Well you invite yourself.

LEE: That's right. I do. In fact I probably got a wider range a' choices than you do, come to think of it.

AUSTIN: I wouldn't doubt it.

LEE: In fact I been inside some pretty classy places in my time. And I never even went to an Ivy League school either.

145 **AUSTIN:**   You want some breakfast or something?

LEE: Breakfast?

AUSTIN: Yeah. Don't you eat breakfast?

LEE: Look, don't worry about me pal. I can take care a' myself. You just go ahead as though I wasn't even here, all right?

(Austin goes into kitchen, makes coffee)

AUSTIN: Where'd you walk to last night?

(pause)

150 **LEE:**   I went up in the foothills there. Up in the San Gabriels. Heat was
        drivin' me crazy.
    AUSTIN: Well, wasn't it hot out on the desert?
    LEE: Different kinda' heat. Out there it's clean. Cools off at night.
        There's a nice little breeze.
    AUSTIN: Where were you, the Mojave?[1]
    LEE: Yeah. The Mojave. That's right.
155 **AUSTIN:**   I haven't been out there in years.
    LEE: Out past Needles there.
    AUSTIN: Oh yeah.
    LEE: Up here it's different. This country's real different.
    AUSTIN: Well, it's been built up.
160 **LEE:**   Built up? Wiped out is more like it. I don't even hardly recognize it.
    AUSTIN: Yeah. Foothills are the same though, aren't they?
    LEE: Pretty much. It's funny goin' up in there. The smells and
        everything. Used to catch snakes up there, remember?
    AUSTIN: You caught snakes.
    LEE: Yeah. And you'd pretend you were Geronimo[2] or some damn thing.
        You used to go right out to lunch.
165 **AUSTIN:**   I enjoyed my imagination.
    LEE: That what you call it? Looks like yer still enjoyin' it.
    AUSTIN: So you just wandered around up there, huh?
    LEE: Yeah. With a purpose.
    AUSTIN: See any houses?

(pause)

170 **LEE:**   Couple. Couple a' real nice ones. One of 'em didn't even have a
        dog. Walked right up and stuck my head in the window. Not a peep.
        Just a sweet kinda' suburban silence.
    AUSTIN: What kind of a place was it?
    LEE: Like a paradise. Kinda' place that sorta' kills ya' inside. Warm
        yellow lights. Mexican tile all around. Copper pots hangin' over the
        stove. Ya' know like they got in the magazines. Blonde people movin'
        in and outa' the rooms, talkin' to each other. *(pause)* Kinda' place you
        wish you sorta' grew up in, ya' know.
    AUSTIN: That's the kind of place you wish you'd grown up in?
    LEE: Yeah, why not?
175 **AUSTIN:**   I thought you hated that kind of stuff.
    LEE: Yeah, well you never knew too much about me did ya'?

(pause)

---

[1] Desert in southeastern California, east of Los Angeles and south of Death Valley.

[2] Chiricahua Apache (1829–1909) known for resisting Mexican and U.S. efforts to control the American Southwest.

AUSTIN: Why'd you go out to the desert in the first place?

LEE: I was on my way to see the old man.

AUSTIN: You mean you just passed through there?

180 **LEE:** Yeah. That's right. Three months of passin' through.

AUSTIN: Three months?

LEE: Somethin' like that. Maybe more. Why?

AUSTIN: You lived on the Mojave for three months?

LEE: Yeah. What'sa' matter with that?

185 **AUSTIN:** By yourself?

LEE: Mostly. Had a couple a' visitors. Had that dog for a while.

AUSTIN: Didn't you miss people?

LEE: *(laughs)* People?

AUSTIN: Yeah. I mean I go crazy if I have to spend three nights in a motel by myself.

190 **LEE:** Yer not in a motel now.

AUSTIN: No, I know. But sometimes I have to stay in motels.

LEE: Well, they got people in motels don't they?

AUSTIN: Strangers.

LEE: Yer friendly aren't ya'? Aren't you the friendly type?

(pause)

195 **AUSTIN:** I'm going to have somebody coming by here later, Lee.

LEE: Ah! Lady friend?

AUSTIN: No, a producer.

LEE: Aha! What's he produce?

AUSTIN: Film. Movies. You know.

200 **LEE:** Oh, movies. Motion Pictures! A Big Wig huh?

AUSTIN: Yeah.

LEE: What's he comin' by here for?

AUSTIN: We have to talk about a project.

LEE: Whadya' mean, "a project"? What's "a project"?

205 **AUSTIN:** A script.

LEE: Oh. That's what yer doin' with all these papers?

AUSTIN: Yeah.

LEE: Well, what's the project about?

AUSTIN: We're uh—it's a period piece.

210 **LEE:** What's "a period piece"?

AUSTIN: Look, it doesn't matter. The main thing is we need to discuss this alone. I mean—

LEE: Oh, I get it. You want me outa' the picture.

AUSTIN: Not exactly. I just need to be alone with him for a couple of hours. So we can talk.

LEE: Yer afraid I'll embarrass ya' huh?

215 **AUSTIN:** I'm not afraid you'll embarrass me!

LEE: Well, I tell ya' what—Why don't you just gimme the keys to yer car and I'll be back here around six o'clock or so. That give ya' enough time?

AUSTIN: I'm not loaning you my car, Lee.

LEE: You want me to just git lost huh? Take a hike? Is that it? Pound the pavement for a few hours while you bullshit yer way into a million bucks.

AUSTIN: Look, it's going to be hard enough for me to face this character on my own without—

220   **LEE:**   You don't know this guy?

AUSTIN: No I don't know—He's a producer. I mean I've been meeting with him for months but you never get to know a producer.

LEE: Yer tryin' to hustle him? Is that it?

AUSTIN: I'm not trying to hustle him! I'm trying to work out a deal! It's not easy.

LEE: What kinda' deal?

225   **AUSTIN:**   Convince him it's a worthwhile story.

LEE: He's not convinced? How come he's comin' over here if he's not convinced? I'll convince him for ya'.

AUSTIN: You don't understand the way things work down here.

LEE: How do things work down here?

(pause)

AUSTIN: Look, if I loan you my car will you have it back here by six?

230   **LEE:**   On the button. With a full tank a' gas.

AUSTIN: *(digging in his pocket for keys)* Forget about the gas.

LEE: Hey, these days gas is gold, old buddy.

(Austin hands the keys to Lee)

You remember that car I used to loan you?

AUSTIN: Yeah.

LEE: Forty Ford. Flathead.

235   **AUSTIN:**   Yeah.

LEE: Sucker hauled ass didn't it?

AUSTIN: Lee, it's not that I don't want to loan you my car—

LEE: You are loanin' me yer car.

(Lee gives Austin a pat on the shoulder, pause)

AUSTIN: I know. I just wish—

240   **LEE:**   What? You wish what?

AUSTIN: I don't know. I wish I wasn't—I wish I didn't have to be doing business down here. I'd like to just spend some time with you.

LEE: I thought it was "Art" you were doin'.

(Lee moves across kitchen toward exit, tosses keys in his hand)

AUSTIN: Try to get it back here by six, okay?

LEE: No sweat. Hey, ya' know, if that uh—story of yours doesn't go over with the guy—tell him I got a couple a' "projects" he might be interested in. Real commercial. Full a' suspense. True-to-life stuff.

(Lee exits, Austin stares after Lee then turns, goes to papers at table, leafs through pages, lights fade to black)

SCENE 3

Afternoon. Alcove, Saul Kimmer and Austin seated across from each other at table.

245 **SAUL:** Well, to tell you the truth Austin, I have never felt so confident about a project in quite a long time.

AUSTIN: Well, that's good to hear, Saul.

SAUL: I am absolutely convinced we can get this thing off the ground. I mean we'll have to make a sale to television and that means getting a major star. Somebody bankable. But I think we can do it. I really do.

AUSTIN: Don't you think we need a first draft before we approach a star?

SAUL: No, no, not at all. I don't think it's necessary. Maybe a brief synopsis. I don't want you to touch the typewriter until we have some seed money.

250 **AUSTIN:** That's fine with me.

SAUL: I mean it's a great story. Just the story alone. You've really managed to capture something this time.

AUSTIN: I'm glad you like it, Saul.

(Lee enters abruptly into kitchen carrying a stolen television set, short pause)

LEE: Aw shit, I'm sorry about that. I am really sorry Austin.

AUSTIN: *(standing)* That's all right.

255 **LEE:** *(moving toward them)* I mean I thought it was way past six already. You said to have it back here by six.

AUSTIN: We were just finishing up. *(to Saul)* This is my, uh—brother, Lee.

SAUL: *(standing)* Oh, I'm very happy to meet you.

(Lee sets T.V. on sink counter, shakes hands with Saul)

LEE: I can't tell ya' how happy I am to meet you sir.

SAUL: Saul Kimmer.

260 **LEE:** Mr. Kipper.

SAUL: Kimmer.

AUSTIN: Lee's been living out on the desert and he just uh—

SAUL: Oh, that's terrific! *(to Lee)* Palm Springs?

LEE: Yeah. Yeah, right. Right around in that area. Near uh—Bob Hope Drive there.

265 **SAUL:** Oh I love it out there. I just love it. The air is wonderful.

LEE: Yeah. Sure is. Healthy.

SAUL: And the golf. I don't know if you play golf, but the golf is just about the best.

Lee: I play a lota' golf.

Saul: Is that right?

270 **Lee:**   Yeah. In fact I was hoping I'd run into somebody out here who played a little golf. I've been lookin' for a partner.

Saul: Well, I uh—

Austin: Lee's just down for a visit while our mother's in Alaska.

Saul: Oh, your mother's in Alaska?

Austin: Yes. She went up there on a little vacation. This is her place.

275 **Saul:**   I see. Well isn't that something. Alaska.

Lee: What kinda' handicap do ya' have, Mr. Kimmer?

Saul: Oh I'm just a Sunday duffer really. You know.

Lee: That's good 'cause I haven't swung a club in months.

Saul: Well we ought to get together sometime and have a little game. Austin, do you play?

(Saul mimes a Johnny Carson golf swing for Austin)

280 **Austin:**   No, I don't uh—I've watched it on T.V.

Lee: *(to Saul)* How 'bout tomorrow morning? Bright and early. We could get out there and put in eighteen holes before breakfast.

Saul: Well, I've got uh—I have several appointments—

Lee: No, I mean real early. Crack a'dawn. While the dew's still thick on the fairway.

Saul: Sounds really great.

285 **Lee:**   Austin could be our caddie.

Saul: Now that's an idea. *(laughs)*

Austin: I don't know the first thing about golf.

Lee: There's nothin' to it. Isn't that right, Saul? He'd pick it up in fifteen minutes.

Saul: Sure. Doesn't take long. 'Course you have to play for years to find your true form. *(chuckles)*

290 **Lee:**   *(to Austin)* We'll give ya' a quick run-down on the club faces. The irons, the woods. Show ya' a couple pointers on the basic swing. Might even let ya' hit the ball a couple times. Whadya' think, Saul?

Saul: Why not. I think it'd be great. I haven't had any exercise in weeks.

Lee: 'At's the spirit! We'll have a little orange juice right afterwards.

(pause)

Saul: Orange juice?

Lee: Yeah! Vitamin C! Nothin' like a shot a' orange juice after a round a' golf. Hot shower. Snappin' towels at each others' privates. Real sense a' fraternity.

295 **Saul:**   *(smiles at Austin)* Well, you make it sound very inviting. I must say. It really does sound great.

Lee: Then it's a date.

Saul: Well, I'll call the country club and see if I can arrange something.

LEE: Great! Boy, I sure am sorry that I busted in on ya' all in the middle of yer meeting.

SAUL: Oh that's quite all right. We were just about finished anyway.

300 **LEE:**   I can wait out in the other room if you want.

SAUL: No really—

LEE: Just got Austin's color T.V. back from the shop. I can watch a little amateur boxing now.

(Lee and Austin exchange looks)

SAUL: Oh—Yes.

LEE: You don't fool around in Television, do you Saul?

305 **SAUL:**   Uh—I have in the past. Produced some T.V. Specials. Network stuff. But it's mainly features now.

LEE: That's where the big money is, huh?

SAUL: Yes. That's right.

AUSTIN: Why don't I call you tomorrow, Saul and we'll get together. We can have lunch or something.

SAUL: That'd be terrific.

310 **LEE:**   Right after the golf.

(pause)

SAUL: What?

LEE: You can have lunch right after the golf.

SAUL: Oh, right.

LEE: Austin was tellin' me that yer interested in stories.

315 **SAUL:**   Well, we develop certain projects that we feel have commercial potential.

LEE: What kinda' stuff do ya' go in for?

SAUL: Oh, the usual. You know. Good love interest. Lots of action.
    (chuckles at Austin)

LEE: Westerns?

SAUL: Sometimes.

320 **AUSTIN:**   I'll give you a ring, Saul.

(Austin tries to move Saul across the kitchen but Lee blocks their way)

LEE: I got a Western that'd knock yer lights out.

SAUL: Oh really?

LEE: Yeah. Contemporary Western. Based on a true story. 'Course I'm not a writer like my brother here. I'm not a man of the pen.

SAUL: Well—

325 **LEE:**   I mean I can tell ya' a story off the tongue but I can't put it down on paper. That don't make any difference though does it?

SAUL: No, not really.

LEE: I mean plenty a' guys have stories don't they? True-life stories. Musta' been a lota' movies made from real life.

SAUL: Yes. I suppose so.

LEE: I haven't seen a good Western since "Lonely Are the Brave." You remember that movie?

330 **SAUL:** No, I'm afraid I—

LEE: Kirk Douglas.[3] Helluva' movie. You remember that movie, Austin?

AUSTIN: Yes.

LEE: *(to Saul)* The man dies for the love of a horse.

SAUL: Is that right.

335 **LEE:** Yeah. Ya' hear the horse screamin' at the end of it. Rain's comin' down. Horse is screamin'. Then there's a shot. BLAM! Just a single shot like that. Then nothin' but the sound of rain. And Kirk Douglas is ridin' in the ambulance. Ridin' away from the scene of the accident. And when he hears that shot he knows that his horse has died. He knows. And you see his eyes. And his eyes die. Right inside his face. And then his eyes close. And you know that he's died too. You know that Kirk Douglas has died from the death of his horse.

SAUL: *(eyes Austin nervously)* Well, it sounds like a great movie. I'm sorry I missed it.

LEE: Yeah, you shouldn't a' missed that one.

SAUL: I'll have to try to catch it some time. Arrange a screening or something. Well, Austin, I'll have to hit the freeway before rush hour.

AUSTIN: *(ushers him toward exit)* It's good seeing you, Saul.

(Austin and Saul shake hands)

340 **LEE:** So ya' think there's room for a real Western these days? A true-to-life Western?

SAUL: Well, I don't see why not. Why don't you uh—tell the story to Austin and have him write a little outline.

LEE: You'd take a look at it then?

SAUL: Yes. Sure. I'll give it a read-through. Always eager for new material. *(smiles at Austin)*

LEE: That's great! You'd really read it then huh?

345 **SAUL:** It would just be my opinion of course.

LEE: That's all I want. Just an opinion. I happen to think it has a lota' possibilities.

SAUL: Well, it was great meeting you and I'll—

(Saul and Lee shake)

LEE: I'll call you tomorrow about the golf.

SAUL: Oh. Yes, right.

350 **LEE:** Austin's got your number, right?

SAUL: Yes.

LEE: So long Saul. *(gives Saul a pat on the back)*

(Saul exits, Austin turns to Lee, looks at T.V. then back to Lee)

---

[3] Actor (1916–) known for his tough-guy appearances in movie westerns.

AUSTIN: Give me the keys.

(Austin extends his hand toward Lee, Lee doesn't move, just stares at Austin, smiles, lights to black)

SCENE 4

Night. Coyotes in distance, fade, sound of typewriter in dark, crickets, candle-light in alcove, dim light in kitchen, lights reveal Austin at glass table typing, Lee sits across from him, foot on table, drinking beer and whiskey, the T.V. is still on sink counter, Austin types for a while, then stops.

LEE: All right, now read it back to me.

355 **AUSTIN:**   I'm not reading it back to you, Lee. You can read it when we're finished. I can't spend all night on this.

LEE: You got better things to do?

AUSTIN: Let's just go ahead. Now what happens when he leaves Texas?

LEE: Is he ready to leave Texas yet? I didn't know we were that far along. He's not ready to leave Texas.

AUSTIN: He's right at the border.

360 **LEE:**   *(sitting up)* No, see this is one a' the crucial parts. Right here. *(taps paper with beer can)* We can't rush through this. He's not right at the border. He's a good fifty miles from the border. A lot can happen in fifty miles.

AUSTIN: It's only an outline. We're not writing an entire script now.

LEE: Well ya' can't leave things out even if it is an outline. It's one a' the most important parts. Ya' can't go leavin' it out.

AUSTIN: Okay, okay. Let's just—get it done.

LEE: All right. Now. He's in the truck and he's got his horse trailer and his horse.

365 **AUSTIN:**   We've already established that.

LEE: And he sees this other guy comin' up behind him in another truck. And that truck is pullin' a gooseneck.

AUSTIN: What's a gooseneck?

LEE: Cattle trailer. You know the kind with a gooseneck, goes right down in the bed a' the pick-up.

AUSTIN: Oh. All right. *(types)*

370 **LEE:**   It's important.

AUSTIN: Okay. I got it.

LEE: All these details are important.

(Austin types as they talk)

AUSTIN: I've got it.

LEE: And this other guy's got his horse all saddled up in the back a' the gooseneck.

375 **AUSTIN:**   Right.

LEE: So both these guys have got their horses right along with 'em, see.

AUSTIN: I understand.

LEE: Then this first guy suddenly realizes two things.

AUSTIN: The guy in front?

380 **LEE:**   Right. The guy in front realizes two things almost at the same time. Simultaneous.

AUSTIN: What were the two things?

LEE: Number one, he realizes that the guy behind him is the husband of the woman he's been—

(Lee makes gesture of screwing by pumping his arm)

AUSTIN: *(sees Lee gesture)* Oh. Yeah.

LEE: And number two, he realizes he's in the middle of Tornado Country.

385 **AUSTIN:**   What's "Tornado Country"?

LEE: Panhandle.

AUSTIN: Panhandle?

LEE: Sweetwater. Around in that area. Nothin'. Nowhere. And number three—

AUSTIN: I thought there was only two.

390 **LEE:**   There's three. There's a third unforeseen realization.

AUSTIN: And what's that?

LEE: That he's runnin' outa' gas.

AUSTIN: *(stops typing)* Come on, Lee.

(Austin gets up, moves to kitchen, gets a glass of water)

LEE: Whadya' mean, "come on"? That's what it is. Write it down! He's runnin' outa' gas.

395 **AUSTIN:**   It's too—

LEE: What? It's too what? It's too real! That's what ya' mean isn't it? It's too much like real life!

AUSTIN: It's not like real life! It's not enough like real life. Things don't happen like that.

LEE: What! Men don't fuck other men's women?

AUSTIN: Yes. But they don't end up chasing each other across the Panhandle. Through "Tornado Country."

400 **LEE:**   They do in this movie!

AUSTIN: And they don't have horses conveniently along with them when they run out of gas! And they don't run out of gas either!

LEE: These guys run outa' gas! This is my story and one a' these guys runs outa' gas!

AUSTIN: It's just a dumb excuse to get them into a chase scene. It's contrived.

LEE: It is a chase scene! It's already a chase scene. They been chasin' each other fer days.

405 **AUSTIN:**   So now they're supposed to abandon their trucks, climb on
their horses and chase each other into the mountains?

LEE: *(standing suddenly)* There aren't any mountains in the Panhandle!
It's flat!

(Lee turns violently toward windows in alcove and throws beer can at them)

LEE: Goddamn these crickets! *(yells at crickets)* Shut up out there! *(pause,
turns back toward table)* This place is like a fuckin' rest home here.
How're you supposed to think!

AUSTIN: You wanna' take a break?

LEE: No, I don't wanna' take a break! I wanna' get this done! This is my
last chance to get this done.

410 **AUSTIN:**   *(moves back into alcove)* All right. Take it easy.

LEE: I'm gonna' be leavin' this area. I don't have time to mess around
here.

AUSTIN: Where are you going?

LEE: Never mind where I'm goin'! That's not nothin' to do with you. I
just gotta' get this done. I'm not like you. Hangin' around bein' a
parasite offa' other fools. I gotta' do this thing and get out.

(pause)

AUSTIN: A parasite? Me?

415 **LEE:**   Yeah, you!

AUSTIN: After you break into people's houses and take their televisions?

LEE: They don't need their televisions! I'm doin' them a service.

AUSTIN: Give me back my keys, Lee.

LEE: Not until you write this thing! You're gonna' write this outline
thing for me or that car's gonna' wind up in Arizona with a different
paint job.

420 **AUSTIN:**   You think you can force me to write this? I was doing you a
favor.

LEE: Get off yer high horse will ya'! Favor! Big favor. Handin' down
favors from the mountain top.

AUSTIN: Let's just write it, okay? Let's sit down and not get upset and
see if we can just get through this.

(Austin sits at typewriter)

(long pause)

LEE: Yer not gonna' even show it to him, are ya'?

AUSTIN: What?

425 **LEE:**   This outline. You got no intention of showin' it to him. Yer just
doin' this 'cause yer afraid a' me.

AUSTIN: You can show it to him yourself.

LEE: I will, boy! I'm gonna' read it to him on the golf course.

AUSTIN: And I'm not afraid of you either.

LEE: Then how come yer doin' it?

430 **AUSTIN:**   *(pause)* So I can get my keys back.

(pause as Lee takes keys out of his pocket slowly and throws them on table, long pause, Austin stares at keys)

LEE: There. Now you got yer keys back.

(Austin looks up at Lee but doesn't take keys)

LEE: Go ahead. There's yer keys.

(Austin slowly takes keys off table and puts them back in his own pocket)

Now what're you gonna' do? Kick me out?

AUSTIN: I'm not going to kick you out, Lee.

LEE: You couldn't kick me out, boy.

435 **AUSTIN:**   I know.

LEE: So you can't even consider that one. *(pause)* You could call the police. That'd be the obvious thing.

AUSTIN: You're my brother.

LEE: That don't mean a thing. You go down to the L.A. Police Department there and ask them what kinda' people kill each other the most. What do you think they'd say?

AUSTIN: Who said anything about killing?

440 **LEE:**   Family people. Brothers. Brothers-in-law. Cousins. Real American-type people. They kill each other in the heat mostly. In the Smog-Alerts. In the Brush Fire Season. Right about this time a' year.

AUSTIN: This isn't the same.

LEE: Oh no? What makes it different?

AUSTIN: We're not insane. We're not driven to acts of violence like that. Not over a dumb movie script. Now sit down.

(long pause, Lee considers which way to go with it)

LEE: Maybe not. *(he sits back down at table across from Austin)* Maybe you're right. Maybe we're too intelligent, huh? *(pause)* We got our heads on our shoulders. One of us has even got a Ivy League diploma. Now that means somethin' don't it? Doesn't that mean somethin'?

445 **AUSTIN:**   Look, I'll write this thing for you, Lee. I don't mind writing it. I just don't want to get all worked up about it. It's not worth it. Now, come on. Let's just get through it, okay?

LEE: Nah. I think there's easier money. Lotsa' places I could pick up thousands. Maybe millions. I don't need this shit. I could go up to Sacramento Valley[4] and steal me a diesel. Ten thousand a week dismantling one a' those suckers. Ten thousand a week!

---

4 Valley in north-central California.

(Lee opens another beer, puts his foot back up on table)

AUSTIN: No, really, look, I'll write it out for you. I think it's a great idea.

LEE: Nah, you got yer own work to do. I don't wanna interfere with yer life.

AUSTIN: I mean it'd be really fantastic if you could sell this. Turn it into a movie. I mean it.

(pause)

450 **LEE:**   Ya' think so huh?

AUSTIN: Absolutely. You could really turn your life around, you know. Change things.

LEE: I could get me a house maybe.

AUSTIN: Sure you could get a house. You could get a whole ranch if you wanted to.

LEE: *(laughs)* A ranch? I could get a ranch?

AUSTIN: 'Course you could. You know what a screenplay sells for these days?

455 **LEE:**   No. What's it sell for?

AUSTIN: A lot. A whole lot of money.

LEE: Thousands?

AUSTIN: Yeah. Thousands.

LEE: Millions?

460 **AUSTIN:**   Well—

LEE: We could get the old man outa' hock then.

AUSTIN: Maybe.

LEE: Maybe? Whadya' mean, maybe?

AUSTIN: I mean it might take more than money.

465 **LEE:**   You were just tellin' me it'd change my whole life around. Why wouldn't it change his?

AUSTIN: He's different.

LEE: Oh, he's of a different ilk[5] huh?

AUSTIN: He's not gonna' change. Let's leave the old man out of it.

LEE: That's right. He's not gonna' change but I will. I'll just turn myself right inside out. I could be just like you then, huh? Sittin' around dreamin' stuff up. Gettin' paid to dream. Ridin' back and forth on the freeway just dreamin' my fool head off.

470 **AUSTIN:**   It's not all that easy.

LEE: It's not, huh?

AUSTIN: No. There's a lot of work involved.

LEE: What's the toughest part? Deciding whether to jog or play tennis?

(long pause)

---

5 Sort, kind.

AUSTIN: Well, look. You can stay here—do whatever you want to. Borrow the car. Come in and out. Doesn't matter to me. It's not my house. I'll help you write this thing or—not. Just let me know what you want. You tell me.

475 **LEE:** Oh. So now suddenly you're at my service. Is that it?

AUSTIN: What do you want to do Lee?

(long pause, Lee stares at him then turns and dreams at windows)

LEE: I tell ya' what I'd do if I still had that dog. Ya' wanna' know what I'd do?

AUSTIN: What?

LEE: Head out to Ventura. Cook up a little match. God that little dog could bear down. Lota' money in dog fightin'. Big money.

(pause)

AUSTIN: Why don't we try to see this through, Lee. Just for the hell of it. Maybe you've really got something here. What do you think?

(pause, Lee considers)

480 **LEE:** Maybe so. No harm in tryin' I guess. You think it's such a hot idea. Besides, I always wondered what'd be like to be you.

AUSTIN: You did?

LEE: Yeah, sure. I used to picture you walkin' around some campus with yer arms fulla' books. Blondes chasin' after ya'.

AUSTIN: Blondes? That's funny.

LEE: What's funny about it?

485 **AUSTIN:** Because I always used to picture you somewhere.

LEE: Where'd you picture me?

AUSTIN: Oh, I don't know. Different places. Adventures. You were always on some adventure.

LEE: Yeah.

AUSTIN: And I used to say to myself, "Lee's got the right idea. He's out there in the world and here I am. What am I doing?"

490 **LEE:** Well you were settin' yourself up for somethin'.

AUSTIN: I guess.

LEE: We better get started on this thing then.

AUSTIN: Okay.

(Austin sits up at typewriter, puts new paper in)

LEE: Oh. Can I get the keys back before I forget?

(Austin hesitates)

You said I could borrow the car if I wanted, right? Isn't that what you said?

495 **AUSTIN:** Yeah. Right.

(Austin takes keys out of his pocket, sets them on table, Lee takes keys slowly, plays with them in his hand)

Lee: I could get a ranch, huh?

Austin: Yeah. We have to write it first though.

Lee: Okay. Let's write it.

(lights start dimming slowly to end of scene as Austin types, Lee speaks)

So they take off after each other straight into an endless black prairie. The sun is just comin' down and they can feel the night on their backs. What they don't know is that each one of 'em is afraid, see. Each one separately thinks that he's the only one that's afraid. And they keep ridin' like that straight into the night. Not knowing. And the one who's chasin' doesn't know where the other one is taking him. And the one who's being chased doesn't know where he's going.

(lights to black, typing stops in the dark, crickets fade)

A C T   T W O

S C E N E   5

Morning. Lee at the table in alcove with a set of golf clubs in a fancy leather bag, Austin at sink washing a few dishes.

Austin: He really liked it, huh?

Lee: He wouldn't a' gave me these clubs if he didn't like it.

Austin: He gave you the clubs?

Lee: Yeah. I told ya' he gave me the clubs. The bag too.

5 **Austin:** I thought he just loaned them to you.

Lee: He said it was part a' the advance. A little gift like. Gesture of his good faith.

Austin: He's giving you an advance?

Lee: Now what's so amazing about that? I told ya' it was a good story. You even said it was a good story.

Austin: Well that is really incredible Lee. You know how many guys spend their whole lives down here trying to break into this business? Just trying to get in the door?

10 **Lee:** *(pulling clubs out of bag, testing them)* I got no idea. How many?

(pause)

Austin: How much of an advance is he giving you?

Lee: Plenty. We were talkin' big money out there. Ninth hole is where I sealed the deal.

Austin: He made a firm commitment?

LEE: Absolutely.

15 **AUSTIN:**   Well, I know Saul and he doesn't fool around when he says he likes something.

LEE: I thought you said you didn't know him.

AUSTIN: Well, I'm familiar with his tastes.

LEE: I let him get two up on me goin' into the back nine. He was sure he had me cold. You shoulda' seen his face when I pulled out the old pitching wedge and plopped it pin-high, two feet from the cup. He 'bout shit his pants. "Where'd a guy like you ever learn how to play golf like that?" he says.

(Lee laughs, Austin stares at him)

AUSTIN: 'Course there's no contract yet. Nothing's final until it's on paper.

20 **LEE:**   It's final, all right. There's no way he's gonna back out of it now. We gambled for it.

AUSTIN: Saul, gambled?

LEE: Yeah, sure. I mean he liked the outline already so he wasn't risking that much. I just guaranteed it with my short game.

(pause)

AUSTIN: Well, we should celebrate or something. I think Mom left a bottle of champagne in the refrigerator. We should have a little toast.

(Austin gets glasses from cupboard, goes to refrigerator, pulls out bottle of champagne)

LEE: You shouldn't oughta' take her champagne, Austin. She's gonna' miss that.

25 **AUSTIN:**   Oh, she's not going to mind. She'd be glad we put it to good use. I'll get her another bottle. Besides, it's perfect for the occasion.

(pause)

LEE: Yer gonna' get a nice fee fer writin' the script a' course. Straight fee.

(Austin stops, stares at Lee, puts glasses and bottle on table, pause)

AUSTIN: I'm writing the script?

LEE: That's what he said. Said we couldn't hire a better screenwriter in the whole town.

AUSTIN: But I'm already working on a script. I've got my own project. I don't have time to write two scripts.

30 **LEE:**   No, he said he was gonna' drop that other one.

(pause)

AUSTIN: What? You mean mine? He's going to drop mine and do yours instead?

LEE: *(smiles)* Now look, Austin, it's jest beginner's luck ya' know. I mean I sank a fifty foot putt for this deal. No hard feelings.

(Austin goes to phone on wall, grabs it, starts dialing)

He's not gonna' be in, Austin. Told me he wouldn't be in 'till late this afternoon.

AUSTIN: *(stays on phone, dialing, listens)* I can't believe this. I just can't believe it. Are you sure he said that? Why would he drop mine?

LEE: That's what he told me.

35 **AUSTIN:** He can't do that without telling me first. Without talking to me at least. He wouldn't just make a decision like that without talking to me!

LEE: Well I was kinda' surprised myself. But he was real enthusiastic about my story.

(Austin hangs up phone violently, paces)

AUSTIN: What'd he say! Tell me everything he said!

LEE: I been tellin' ya! He said he liked the story a whole lot. It was the first authentic Western to come along in a decade.

AUSTIN: He liked that story! Your story?

40 **LEE:** Yeah! What's so surprisin' about that?

AUSTIN: It's stupid! It's the dumbest story I ever heard in my life.

LEE: Hey, hold on! That's my story yer talkin' about!

AUSTIN: It's a bullshit story! It's idiotic. Two lamebrains chasing each other across Texas! Are you kidding? Who do you think's going to go see a film like that?

LEE: It's not a film! It's a movie. There's a big difference. That's somethin' Saul told me.

45 **AUSTIN:** Oh he did, huh?

LEE: Yeah, he said, "In this business we make movies, American movies. Leave the films to the French."

AUSTIN: So you got real intimate with old Saul huh? He started pouring forth his vast knowledge of Cinema.

LEE: I think he liked me a lot, to tell ya' the truth. I think he felt I was somebody he could confide in.

AUSTIN: What'd you do, beat him up or something?

50 **LEE:** *(stands fast)* Hey, I've about had it with the insults buddy! You think yer the only one in the brain department here? Yer the only one that can sit around and cook things up? There's other people got ideas too, ya' know!

AUSTIN: You must've done something. Threatened him or something. Now what'd you do Lee?

LEE: I convinced him!

(Lee makes sudden menacing lunge toward Austin, wielding golf club above his head, stops himself, frozen moment, long pause, Lee lowers club)

AUSTIN: Oh, Jesus. You didn't hurt him did you?

(long silence, Lee sits back down at table)

Lee! Did you hurt him?

LEE: I didn't do nothin' to him! He liked my story. Pure and simple. He said it was the best story he's come across in a long, long time.

55 **AUSTIN:**   That's what he told me about my story! That's the same thing he said to me.

LEE: Well, he musta' been lyin'. He musta' been lyin' to one of us anyway.

AUSTIN: You can't come into this town and start pushing people around. They're gonna' put you away!

LEE: I never pushed anybody around! I beat him fair and square. *(pause)* They can't touch me anyway. They can't put a finger on me. I'm gone. I can come in through the window and go out through the door. They never knew what hit 'em. You, yer stuck. Yer the one that's stuck. Not me. So don't be warnin' me what to do in this town.

(pause, Austin crosses to table, sits at typewriter, rests)

AUSTIN: Lee, come on, level with me will you? It doesn't make any sense that suddenly he'd throw my idea out the window. I've been talking to him for months. I've got too much at stake. Everything's riding on this project.

60 **LEE:**   What's yer idea?

AUSTIN: It's just a simple love story.

LEE: What kinda' love story?

AUSTIN: *(stands, crosses into kitchen)* I'm not telling you!

LEE: Ha! 'Fraid I'll steal it huh? Competition's gettin' kinda' close to home isn't it?

65 **AUSTIN:**   Where did Saul say he was going?

LEE: He was gonna' take my story to a couple studios.

AUSTIN: That's *my* outline you know! I wrote that outline! You've got no right to be peddling it around.

LEE: You weren't ready to take credit for it last night.

AUSTIN: Give me my keys!

70 **LEE:**   What?

AUSTIN: The keys! I want my keys back!

LEE: Where you goin'?

AUSTIN: Just give me my keys! I gotta' take a drive. I gotta' get out of here for a while.

LEE: Where you gonna' go, Austin?

75 **AUSTIN:**   *(pause)* I might just drive out to the desert for a while. I gotta' think.

LEE: You can think here just as good. This is the perfect setup for thinkin'. We got some writin' to do here, boy. Now let's just have us a little toast. Relax. We're partners now.

(Lee pops the cork of the champagne bottle, pours two drinks as the lights fade to black)

SCENE 6

Afternoon. Lee and Saul in kitchen, Austin in alcove

LEE: Now you tell him. You tell him, Mr. Kipper.

SAUL: Kimmer.

LEE: Kimmer. You tell him what you told me. He don't believe me.

80 **AUSTIN:** I don't want to hear it.

SAUL: It's really not a big issue, Austin. I was simply amazed by your brother's story and—

AUSTIN: Amazed? You lost a bet! You gambled with my material!

SAUL: That's really beside the point, Austin. I'm ready to go all the way with your brother's story. I think it has a great deal of merit.

AUSTIN: I don't want to hear about it, okay? Go tell it to the executives! Tell it to somebody who's going to turn it into a package deal or something. A T.V. series. Don't tell it to me.

85 **SAUL:** But I want to continue with your project too, Austin. It's not as though we can't do both. We're big enough for that aren't we?

AUSTIN: "We"? *I* can't do both! I don't know about "we."

LEE: *(to Saul)* See, what'd I tell ya'. He's totally unsympathetic.

SAUL: Austin, there's no point in our going to another screenwriter for this. It just doesn't make sense. You're brothers. You know each other. There's a familiarity with the material that just wouldn't be possible otherwise.

AUSTIN: There's no familiarity with the material! None! I don't know what "Tornado Country" is. I don't know what a "gooseneck" is. And I don't want to know! *(pointing to Lee)* He's a hustler! He's a bigger hustler than you are! If you can't see that, then—

90 **LEE:** *(to Austin)* Hey, now hold on. I didn't have to bring this bone back to you, boy. I persuaded Saul here that you were the right man for the job. You don't have to go throwin' up favors in my face.

AUSTIN: Favors! I'm the one who wrote the fuckin' outline! You can't even spell.

SAUL: *(to Austin)* Your brother told me about the situation with your father.

(pause)

AUSTIN: What? *(looks at Lee)*

SAUL: That's right. Now we have a clear-cut deal here, Austin. We have big studio money standing behind this thing. Just on the basis of your outline.

95 **AUSTIN:** *(to Saul)* What'd he tell you about my father?

SAUL: Well—that he's destitute. He needs money.

LEE: That's right. He does.

(Austin shakes his head, stares at them both)

AUSTIN: *(to Lee)* And this little assignment is supposed to go toward the old man? A charity project? Is that what this is? Did you cook this up on the ninth green too?

SAUL: It's a big slice, Austin.

100   **AUSTIN:**   *(to Lee)* I gave him money! I already gave him money. You know that. He drank it all up!

LEE: This is a different deal here.

SAUL: We can set up a trust for your father. A large sum of money. It can be doled out to him in parcels so he can't misuse it.

AUSTIN: Yeah, and who's doing the doling?

SAUL: Your brother volunteered.

(Austin laughs)

105   **LEE:**   That's right. I'll make sure he uses it for groceries.

AUSTIN: *(to Saul)* I'm not doing this script! I'm not writing this crap for you or anybody else. You can't blackmail me into it. You can't threaten me into it. There's no way I'm doing it. So just give it up. Both of you.

(long pause)

SAUL: Well, that's it then. I mean this is an easy three hundred grand. Just for a first draft. It's incredible, Austin. We've got three different studios all trying to cut each other's throats to get this material. In one morning. That's how hot it is.

AUSTIN: Yeah, well you can afford to give me a percentage on the outline then. And you better get the genius here an agent before he gets burned.

LEE: Saul's gonna' be my agent. Isn't that right, Saul?

110   **SAUL:**   That's right. *(to Austin)* Your brother has really got something, Austin. I've been around too long not to recognize it. Raw talent.

AUSTIN: He's got a lota' balls is what he's got. He's taking you right down the river.

SAUL: Three hundred thousand, Austin. Just for a first draft. Now you've never been offered that kind of money before.

AUSTIN: I'm not writing it.

(pause)

SAUL: I see. Well—

115   **LEE:**   We'll just go to another writer then. Right, Saul? Just hire us somebody with some enthusiasm. Somebody who can recognize the value of a good story.

SAUL: I'm sorry about this, Austin.

AUSTIN: Yeah.

SAUL: I mean I was hoping we could continue both things but now I don't see how it's possible.

AUSTIN: So you're dropping my idea altogether. Is that it? Just trade horses in midstream? After all these months of meetings.

120 **SAUL:**   I wish there was another way.

AUSTIN: I've got everything riding on this, Saul. You know that. It's my only shot. If this falls through—

SAUL: I have to go with what my instincts tell me—

AUSTIN: Your instincts!

SAUL: My gut reaction.

125 **AUSTIN:**   You lost! That's your gut reaction. You lost a gamble. Now you're trying to tell me you like his story? How could you possibly fall for that story? It's as phony as Hoppalong Cassidy. What do you see in it? I'm curious.

SAUL: It has the ring of truth, Austin.

AUSTIN: *(laughs)* Truth?

LEE: It is true.

SAUL: Something about the real West.

130 **AUSTIN:**   Why? Because it's got horses? Because it's got grown men acting like little boys?

SAUL: Something about the land. Your brother is speaking from experience.

AUSTIN: So am I!

SAUL: But nobody's interested in love these days, Austin. Let's face it.

LEE: That's right.

135 **AUSTIN:**   *(to Saul)* He's been camped out on the desert for three months. Talking to cactus. What's he know about what people wanna' see on the screen! I drive on the freeway every day. I swallow the smog. I watch the news in color. I shop in the Safeway. I'm the one who's in touch! Not him!

SAUL: I have to go now, Austin.

(Saul starts to leave)

AUSTIN: There's no such thing as the West anymore! It's a dead issue! It's dried up, Saul, and so are you.

(Saul stops and turns to Austin)

SAUL: Maybe you're right. But I have to take the gamble, don't I?

AUSTIN: You're a fool to do this, Saul.

140 **SAUL:**   I've always gone on my hunches. Always. And I've never been wrong. *(to Lee)* I'll talk to you tomorrow, Lee.

LEE: All right, Mr. Kimmer.

SAUL: Maybe we could have some lunch.

LEE: Fine with me. *(smiles at Austin)*

SAUL: I'll give you a ring.

(Saul exits, lights to black as brothers look at each other from a distance)

SCENE 7

Night. Coyotes, crickets, sound of typewriter in dark, candlelight up on Lee at typewriter struggling to type with one finger system, Austin sits sprawled out on kitchen floor with whiskey bottle, drunk.

145 **AUSTIN:**   *(singing, from floor)*
"Red sails in the sunset
Way out on the blue
Please carry my loved one
Home safely to me
Red sails in the sunset—"
LEE: *(slams fist on table)* Hey! Knock it off will ya'! I'm tryin' to concentrate here.
AUSTIN: *(laughs)* You're tryin' to concentrate?
LEE: Yeah. That's right.
AUSTIN: Now you're tryin' to concentrate.
150 **LEE:**   Between you, the coyotes and the crickets a thought don't have much of a chance.
AUSTIN: "Between me, the coyotes and the crickets." What a great title.
LEE: I don't need a title! I need a thought.
AUSTIN: *(laughs)* A thought! Here's a thought for ya'—
LEE: I'm not askin' fer yer thoughts! I got my own. I can do this thing on my own.
155 **AUSTIN:**   You're going to write an entire script on your own?
LEE: That's right.

(pause)

AUSTIN: Here's a thought. Saul Kimmer—
LEE: Shut up will ya'!
AUSTIN: He thinks we're the same person.
160 **LEE:**   Don't get cute.
AUSTIN: He does! He's lost his mind. Poor old Saul. *(giggles)* Thinks we're one and the same.
LEE: Why don't you ease up on that champagne.
AUSTIN: *(holding up bottle)* This isn't champagne anymore. We went through the champagne a long time ago. This is serious stuff. The days of champagne are long gone.
LEE: Well, go outside and drink it.
165 **AUSTIN:**   I'm enjoying your company, Lee. For the first time since your arrival I am finally enjoying your company. And now you want me to go outside and drink alone?
LEE: That's right.

(Lee reads through paper in typewriter, makes an erasure)

AUSTIN: You think you'll make more progress if you're alone? You might drive yourself crazy.

LEE: I could have this thing done in a night if I had a little silence.

AUSTIN: Well you'd still have the crickets to contend with. The coyotes. The sounds of the Police Helicopters prowling above the neighborhood. Slashing their searchlights down through the streets. Hunting for the likes of you.

170 **LEE:**   I'm a screenwriter now! I'm legitimate.

AUSTIN: *(laughing)* A screenwriter!

LEE: That's right. I'm on salary. That's more'n I can say for you. I got an advance coming.

AUSTIN: This is true. This is very true. An advance. *(pause)* Well, maybe I oughta' go out and try my hand at your trade. Since you're doing so good at mine.

LEE: Ha!

(Lee attempts to type some more but gets the ribbon tangled up, starts trying to re-thread it as they continue talking)

175 **AUSTIN:**   Well why not? You don't think I've got what it takes to sneak into people's houses and steal their T.V.s?

LEE: You couldn't steal a toaster without losin' yer lunch.

(Austin stands with a struggle, supports himself by the sink)

AUSTIN: You don't think I could sneak into somebody's house and steal a toaster?

LEE: Go take a shower or somethin' will ya!

(Lee gets more tangled up with the typewriter ribbon, pulling it out of the machine as though it was fishing line)

AUSTIN: You really don't think I could steal a crumby toaster? How much you wanna' bet I can't steal a toaster! How much? Go ahead! You're a gambler aren't you? Tell me how much yer willing to put on the line. Some part of your big advance? Oh, you haven't got that yet have you. I forgot.

180 **LEE:**   All right. I'll bet you your car that you can't steal a toaster without gettin' busted.

AUSTIN: You already got my car!

LEE: Okay, your house then.

AUSTIN: What're you gonna' give me! I'm not talkin' about my house and my car, I'm talkin' about what are you gonna' give me. You don't have nothin' to give me.

LEE: I'll give you—shared screen credit. How 'bout that? I'll have it put in the contract that this was written by the both of us.

185 **AUSTIN:**   I don't want my name on that piece of shit! I want something of value. You got anything of value? You got any tidbits from the desert? Any Rattlesnake bones? I'm not a greedy man. Any little personal treasure will suffice.

LEE: I'm gonna' just kick yer ass out in a minute.

AUSTIN: Oh, so now you're gonna' kick me out! Now I'm the intruder. I'm the one who's invading your precious privacy.

LEE: I'm trying to do some screenwriting here!!

(Lee stands, picks up typewriter, slams it down hard on table, pause, silence except for crickets)

AUSTIN: Well, you got everything you need. You got plenty a' coffee? Groceries. You got a car. A contract. *(pause)* Might need a new typewriter ribbon but other than that you're pretty well fixed. I'll just leave ya' alone for a while.

(Austin tries to steady himself to leave, Lee makes a move toward him)

190 **LEE:**   Where you goin'?

AUSTIN: Don't worry about me. I'm not the one to worry about.

(Austin weaves toward exit, stops)

LEE: What're you gonna' do? Just go wander out into the night?

AUSTIN: I'm gonna' make a little tour.

LEE: Why don't ya' just go to bed for Christ's sake. Yer makin' me sick.

195 **AUSTIN:**   I can take care a' myself. Don't worry about me.

(Austin weaves badly in another attempt to exit, he crashes to the floor, Lee goes to him but remains standing)

LEE: You want me to call your wife for ya' or something?

AUSTIN: *(from floor)* My wife?

LEE: Yeah. I mean maybe she can help ya' out. Talk to ya' or somethin'.

AUSTIN: *(struggles to stand again)* She's five hundred miles away. North. North of here. Up in the North country where things are calm. I don't need any help. I'm gonna' go outside and I'm gonna' steal a toaster. I'm gonna' steal some other stuff too. I might even commit bigger crimes. Bigger than you ever dreamed of. Crimes beyond the imagination!

(Austin manages to get himself vertical, tries to head for exit again)

200 **LEE:**   Just hang on a minute, Austin.

AUSTIN: Why? What for? You don't need my help, right? You got a handle on the project. Besides, I'm lookin' forward to the smell of the night. The bushes. Orange blossoms. Dust in the driveways. Rain bird sprinklers. Lights in people's houses. You're right about the lights, Lee. Everybody else is livin' the life. Indoors. Safe. This is a Paradise down here. You know that? We're livin' in a Paradise. We've forgotten about that.

LEE: You sound just like the old man now.

AUSTIN: Yeah, well we all sound alike when we're sloshed. We just sorta' echo each other.

LEE: Maybe if we could work on this together we could bring him back out here. Get him settled down some place.

(Austin turns violently toward Lee, takes a swing at him, misses and crashes to the floor again, Lee stays standing)

AUSTIN: I don't want him out here! I've had it with him! I went all the way out there! I went out of my way. I gave him money and all he did was play Al Jolson[6] records and spit at me! I gave him money!

(pause)

205 **LEE:** Just help me a little with the characters, all right? You know how to do it, Austin.

AUSTIN: *(on floor, laughs)* The characters!

LEE: Yeah. You know. The way they talk and stuff. I can hear it in my head but I can't get it down on paper.

AUSTIN: What characters?

LEE: The guys. The guys in the story.

210 **AUSTIN:** Those aren't characters.

LEE: Whatever you call 'em then. I need to write somethin' out.

AUSTIN: Those are illusions of characters.

LEE: I don't give a damn what ya' call 'em! You know what I'm talkin' about!

AUSTIN: Those are fantasies of a long lost boyhood.

215 **LEE:** I gotta' write somethin' out on paper!!

(pause)

AUSTIN: What for? Saul's gonna' get you a fancy screenwriter isn't he?

LEE: I wanna' do it myself!

AUSTIN: Then do it! Yer on your own now, old buddy. You bulldogged yer way into contention. Now you gotta' carry it through.

LEE: I will but I need some advice. Just a couple a' things. Come on, Austin. Just help me get 'em talkin' right. It won't take much.

220 **AUSTIN:** Oh, now you're having a little doubt huh? What happened? The pressure's on, boy. This is it. You gotta' come up with it now. You don't come up with a winner on your first time out they just cut your head off. They don't give you a second chance ya' know.

LEE: I got a good story! I know it's a good story. I just need a little help is all.

AUSTIN: Not from me. Not from yer little old brother. I'm retired.

LEE: You could save this thing for me, Austin. I'd give ya' half the money. I would. I only need half anyway. With this kinda' money I could be a long time down the road. I'd never bother ya' again. I promise. You'd never even see me again.

---

6 Lithuanian-born singer and actor (1886–1950); appeared in the first sound film, *The Jazz Singer* (1927).

AUSTIN: *(still on floor)* You'd disappear?

225 **LEE:** I would for sure.

AUSTIN: Where would you disappear to?

LEE: That don't matter. I got plenty a' places.

AUSTIN: Nobody can disappear. The old man tried that. Look where it got him. He lost his teeth.

LEE: He never had any money.

230 **AUSTIN:** I don't mean that. I mean his teeth! His real teeth. First he lost his real teeth, then he lost his false teeth. You never knew that did ya'? He never confided in you.

LEE: Nah, I never knew that.

AUSTIN: You wanna' drink?

(Austin offers bottle to Lee, Lee takes it, sits down on kitchen floor with Austin, they share the bottle)

Yeah, he lost his real teeth one at a time. Woke up every morning with another tooth lying on the mattress. Finally, he decides he's gotta' get 'em all pulled out but he doesn't have any money. Middle of Arizona with no money and no insurance and every morning another tooth is lying on the mattress. *(takes a drink)* So what does he do?

LEE: I dunno'. I never knew about that.

AUSTIN: He begs the government. G.I. Bill or some damn thing. Some pension plan he remembers in the back of his head. And they send him out the money.

235 **LEE:** They did?

(they keep trading the bottle between them, taking drinks)

AUSTIN: Yeah. They send him the money but it's not enough money. Costs a lot to have all yer teeth yanked. They charge by the individual tooth, ya' know. I mean one tooth isn't equal to another tooth. Some are more expensive. Like the big ones in the back—

LEE: So what happened?

AUSTIN: So he locates a Mexican dentist in Juarez who'll do the whole thing for a song. And he takes off hitchhiking to the border.

LEE: Hitchhiking?

240 **AUSTIN:** Yeah. So how long you think it takes him to get to the border? A man his age.

LEE: I dunno.

AUSTIN: Eight days it takes him. Eight days in the rain and the sun and every day he's droppin' teeth on the blacktop and nobody'll pick him up 'cause his mouth's full a' blood.

(pause, they drink)

So finally he stumbles into the dentist. Dentist takes all his money and all his teeth. And there he is, in Mexico, with his gums sewed up and his pockets empty.

(long silence, Austin drinks)

LEE: That's it?

AUSTIN: Then I go out to see him, see. I go out there and I take him out
for a nice Chinese dinner. But he doesn't eat. All he wants to do is
drink Martinis outa' plastic cups. And he takes his teeth out and lays
'em on the table 'cause he can't stand he feel of 'em. And we ask the
waitress for one a' those doggie bags to take the Chop Suey home in.
So he drops his teeth in the doggie bag along with the Chop Suey.
And then we go out to hit all the bars up and down the highway. Says
he wants to introduce me to all his buddies. And in one a' those bars,
in one a' those bars up and down the highway, he left that doggie bag
with his teeth laying in the Chop Suey.

245 **LEE:** You never found it?

AUSTIN: We went back but we never did find it. *(pause)* Now that's a
true story. True to life.

(they drink as lights fade to black)

SCENE 8

*Very early morning, between night and day. No crickets, coyotes yapping fever-
ishly in distance before light comes up, a small fire blazes up in the dark from
alcove area, sound of Lee smashing typewriter with a golf club, lights coming up,
Lee seen smashing typewriter methodically then dropping pages of his script into
a burning bowl set on the floor of alcove, flames leap up, Austin has a whole
bunch of stolen toasters lined up on the sink counter along with Lee's stolen T.V.,
the toasters are of a wide variety of models, mostly chrome, Austin goes up and
down the line of toasters, breathing on them and polishing them with a dish
towel, both men are drunk, empty whiskey bottles and beer cans litter floor of
kitchen, they share a half empty bottle on one of the chairs in the alcove, Lee
keeps periodically taking deliberate ax-chops at the typewriter using a nine-iron
as Austin speaks, all of their mother's house plants are dead and drooping.*

AUSTIN: *(polishing toasters)* There's gonna be a general lack of toast in
the neighborhood this morning. Many, many unhappy, bewildered
breakfast faces. I guess it's best not to even think of the victims. Not
to even entertain it. Is that the right psychology?

LEE: *(pauses)* What?

AUSTIN: Is that the correct criminal psychology? Not to think of the
victims?

250 **LEE:** What victims?

(Lee takes another swipe at typewriter with nine-iron, adds pages to the fire)

AUSTIN: The victims of crime. Of breaking and entering. I mean is it a
prerequisite for a criminal not to have a conscience?

LEE: Ask a criminal.

(pause, Lee stares at Austin)

What're you gonna' do with all those toasters? That's the dumbest thing I ever saw in my life.

Austin: I've got hundreds of dollars worth of household appliances here. You may not realize that.

Lee: Yeah, and how many hundreds of dollars did you walk right past?

255 **Austin:**   It was toasters you challenged me to. Only toasters. I ignored every other temptation.

Lee: I never challenged you! That's no challenge. Anybody can steal a toaster.

(Lee smashes typewriter again)

Austin: You don't have to take it out on my typewriter ya' know. It's not the machine's fault that you can't write. It's a sin to do that to a good machine.

Lee: A sin?

Austin: When you consider all the writers who never even had a machine. Who would have given an eyeball for a good typewriter. Any typewriter.

(Lee smashes typewriter again)

260 **Austin:**   *(polishing toasters)* All the ones who wrote on matchbook covers. Paper bags. Toilet paper. Who had their writing destroyed by their jailers. Who persisted beyond all odds. Those writers would find it hard to understand your actions.

(Lee comes down on typewriter with one final crushing blow of the nine-iron then collapses in one of the chairs, takes a drink from bottle, pause)

Austin: *(after pause)* Not to mention demolishing a perfectly good golf club. What about all the struggling golfers? What about Lee Trevino?[7] What do you think he would've said when he was batting balls around with broomsticks at the age of nine. Impoverished.

(pause)

Lee: What time is it anyway?

Austin: No idea. Time stands still when you're havin' fun.

Lee: Is it too late to call a woman? You know any women?

265 **Austin:**   I'm a married man.

Lee: I mean a local woman.

(Austin looks out at light through window above sink)

---

7 U.S. professional golfer (1939–   ); first golfer to win the Hickock award for outstanding athlete, in 1971.

AUSTIN: It's either too late or too early. You're the nature enthusiast. Can't you tell the time by the light in the sky? Orient yourself around the North Star or something?

LEE: I can't tell anything.

AUSTIN: Maybe you need a little breakfast. Some toast! How 'bout some toast?

(Austin goes to cupboard, pulls out loaf of bread and starts dropping slices into every toaster, Lee stays sitting, drinks, watches Austin)

270 **LEE:** I don't need toast. I need a woman.

AUSTIN: A woman isn't the answer. Never was.

LEE: I'm not talkin' about permanent. I'm talkin' about temporary.

AUSTIN: *(putting toast in toasters)* We'll just test the merits of these little demons. See which brands have a tendency to burn. See which one can produce a perfectly golden piece of fluffy toast.

LEE: How much gas you got in yer car?

275 **AUSTIN:** I haven't driven my car for days now. So I haven't had an opportunity to look at the gas gauge.

LEE: Take a guess. You think there's enough to get me to Bakersfield?

AUSTIN: Bakersfield? What's in Bakersfield?

LEE: Just never mind what's in Bakersfield! You think there's enough goddamn gas in the car!

AUSTIN: Sure.

280 **LEE:** Sure. You could care less, right. Let me run outa' gas on the Grapevine. You could give a shit.

AUSTIN: I'd say there was enough gas to get you just about anywhere, Lee. With your determination and guts.

LEE: What the hell time is it anyway?

(Lee pulls out his wallet, starts going through dozens of small pieces of paper with phone numbers written on them, drops some on the floor, drops others in the fire)

AUSTIN: Very early. This is the time of morning when the coyotes kill people's cocker spaniels. Did you hear them? That's what they were doing out there. Luring innocent pets away from their homes.

LEE: *(searching through his papers)* What's the area code for Bakersfield? You know?

285 **AUSTIN:** You could always call the operator.

LEE: I can't stand that voice they give ya'.

AUSTIN: What voice?

LEE: That voice that warns you that if you'd only tried harder to find the number in the phone book you wouldn't have to be calling the operator to begin with.

(Lee gets up, holding a slip of paper from his wallet, stumbles toward phone on wall, yanks receiver, starts dialing)

AUSTIN: Well I don't understand why you'd want to talk to anybody else anyway. I mean you can talk to me. I'm your brother.

290 **LEE:**   *(dialing)* I wanna' talk to a woman. I haven't heard a woman's voice in a long time.

AUSTIN: Not since the Botanist?

LEE: What?

AUSTIN: Nothing. *(starts singing as he tends toast)*

"Red sails in the sunset

Way out on the blue

Please carry my loved one

Home safely to me"

LEE: Hey, knock it off will ya'! This is long distance here.

295 **AUSTIN:**   Bakersfield?

LEE: Yeah, Bakersfield. It's Kern County.

AUSTIN: Well, what County are *we* in?

LEE: You better get yourself a 7-Up, boy.

AUSTIN: One County's as good as another.

(Austin hums "Red Sails" softly as Lee talks on phone)

300 **LEE:**   *(to phone)* Yeah, operator look—first off I wanna' know the area code for Bakersfield. Right. Bakersfield! Okay. Good. Now I wanna' know if you can help me track somebody down. *(pause)* No, no I mean a phone number. Just a phone number. Okay. *(holds a piece of paper up and reads it)* Okay, the name is Melly Ferguson. Melly. *(pause)* I dunno'. Melly. Maybe. Yeah. Maybe Melanie. Yeah. Melanie Ferguson. Okay. *(pause)* What? I can't hear ya' so good. Sounds like yer under the ocean. *(pause)* You got ten Melanie Fergusons? How could that be? Ten Melanie Fergusons in Bakersfield? Well gimme all of 'em then. *(pause)* What d'ya' mean? Gimme all ten Melanie Fergusons! That's right. Just a second. *(to Austin)* Gimme a pen.

AUSTIN: I don't have a pen.

LEE: Gimme a pencil then!

AUSTIN: I don't have a pencil.

LEE: *(to phone)* Just a second, operator. *(to Austin)* Yer a writer and ya' don't have a pen or a pencil!

305 **AUSTIN:**   I'm not a writer. You're a writer.

LEE: I'm on the phone here! Get me a pen or a pencil.

AUSTIN: I gotta' watch the toast.

LEE: *(to phone)* Hang on a second, operator.

(Lee lets the phone drop then starts pulling all the drawers in the kitchen out on the floor and dumping the contents, searching for a pencil, Austin watches him casually)

LEE: *(crashing through drawers, throwing contents around kitchen)* This is the last time I try to live with people, boy! I can't believe it. Here I am! Here I am again in a desperate situation! This would never happen out on the desert. I would never be in this kinda' situation

out on the desert. Isn't there a pen or a pencil in this house! Who
lives in this house anyway!

310 **AUSTIN:**   Our mother.

LEE: How come she don't have a pen or a pencil. She's a social person
isn't she? Doesn't she have to make shopping lists? She's gotta' have a
pencil. *(finds a pencil)* Aaha! *(he rushes back to phone, picks up receiver)*
All right operator. Operator? Hey! Operator! Goddamnit!

*(Lee rips the phone off the wall and throws it down, goes back to chair and falls
into it, drinks, long pause)*

AUSTIN: She hung up?

LEE: Yeah, she hung up. I knew she was gonna' hang up. I could hear it
in her voice.

(Lee starts going through his slips of paper again)

AUSTIN: Well, you're probably better off staying here with me anyway.
I'll take care of you.

315 **LEE:**   I don't need takin' care of! Not by you anyway.

AUSTIN: Toast is almost ready.

(Austin starts buttering all the toast as it pops up)

LEE: I don't want any toast!

(long pause)

AUSTIN: You gotta' eat something. Can't just drink. How long have we
been drinking, anyway?

LEE: *(looking through slips of paper)* Maybe it was Fresno. What's the area
code for Fresno? How could I have lost that number! She was beautiful.

(pause)

320 **AUSTIN:**   Why don't you just forget about that, Lee. Forget about the
woman.

LEE: She had green eyes. You know what green eyes do to me?

AUSTIN: I know but you're not gonna' get it on with her now anyway.
It's dawn already. She's in Bakersfield for Christ's sake.

(long pause, Lee considers the situation)

LEE: Yeah. *(looks at windows)* It's dawn?

AUSTIN: Let's just have some toast and—

325 **LEE:**   What is this bullshit with the toast anyway! You make it sound like
salvation or something. I don't want any goddamn toast! How many
times I gotta' tell ya'! *(Lee gets up, crosses upstage to windows in alcove,
looks out, Austin butters toast)*

AUSTIN: Well it is like salvation sort of. I mean the smell. I love the
smell of toast. And the sun's coming up. It makes me feel like
anything's possible. Ya' know?

Lee: *(back to Austin, facing windows upstage)* So go to church why don't ya'.

Austin: Like a beginning. I love beginnings.

Lee: Oh yeah. I've always been kinda' partial to endings myself.

330 **Austin:** What if I come with you, Lee?

Lee: *(pause as Lee turns toward Austin)* What?

Austin: What if I come with you out to the desert?

Lee: Are you kiddin'?

Austin: No. I'd just like to see what it's like.

335 **Lee:** You wouldn't last a day out there pal.

Austin: That's what you said about the toasters. You said I couldn't steal a toaster either.

Lee: A toaster's got nothin' to do with the desert.

Austin: I could make it, Lee. I'm not that helpless. I can cook.

Lee: Cook?

340 **Austin:** I can.

Lee: So what! You can cook. Toast.

Austin: I can make fires. I know how to get fresh water from condensation.

(Austin stacks buttered toast up in a tall stack on plate)

(Lee slams table)

Lee: It's not somethin' you learn out of a Boy Scout handbook!

Austin: Well how do you learn it then! How're you supposed to learn it!

(pause)

345 **Lee:** Ya' just learn it, that's all. Ya' learn it 'cause ya' have to learn it. You don't *have* to learn it.

Austin: You could teach me.

Lee: *(stands)* What're you, crazy or somethin'? You went to college. Here, you are down here, rollin' in bucks. Floatin' up and down in elevators. And you wanna' learn how to live on the desert!

Austin: I do, Lee. I really do. There's nothin' down here for me. There never was. When we were kids here it was different. There was a life here then. But now—I keep comin' down here thinkin' it's the fifties or somethin'. I keep finding myself getting off the freeway at familiar landmarks that turn out to be unfamiliar. On the way to appointments. Wandering down streets I thought I recognized that turn out to be replicas of streets I remember. Streets I misremember. Streets I can't tell if I lived on or saw in a postcard. Fields that don't even exist anymore.

Lee: There's no point cryin' about that now.

350 **Austin:** There's nothin' real down here, Lee! Least of all me!

Lee: Well I can't save you from that!

Austin: You can let me come with you.

LEE: No dice, pal.

AUSTIN: You could let me come with you, Lee!

355 **LEE:** Hey, do you actually think I chose to live out in the middle a'
nowhere? Do ya'? Ya' think it's some kinda' philosophical decision I
took or somethin'? I'm livin' out there 'cause I can't make it here!
And yer bitchin' to me about all yer success!

AUSTIN: I'd cash it all in in a second. That's the truth.

LEE: *(pause, shakes his head)* I can't believe this.

AUSTIN: Let me go with you.

LEE: Stop sayin' that will ya'! Yer worse than a dog.

(Austin offers out the plate of neatly stacked toast to Lee)

360 **AUSTIN:** You want some toast?

(Lee suddenly explodes and knocks the plate out of Austin's hand, toast goes fly-ing, long frozen moment where it appears Lee might go all the way this time when Austin breaks it by slowly lowering himself to his knees and begins gathering the scattered toast from the floor and stacking it back on the plate, Lee begins to cir-cle Austin in a slow, predatory way, crushing pieces of toast in his wake, no words for a while, Austin keeps gathering toast, even the crushed pieces)

LEE: Tell ya' what I'll do, little brother. I might just consider makin'
you a deal. Little trade. *(Austin continues gathering toast as Lee circles
him through this)* You write me up this screenplay thing just like I tell
ya'. I mean you can use all yer usual tricks and stuff. Yer fancy
language. Yer artistic hocus pocus. But ya' gotta' write everything
like I say. Every move. Every time they run outa' gas, they run outa'
gas. Every time they wanna' jump on a horse, they do just that. If
they wanna' stay in Texas, by God they'll stay in Texas! *(Keeps
circling)* And you finish the whole thing up for me. Top to bottom.
And you put my name on it. And I own all the rights. And every dime
goes in my pocket. You do that and I'll sure enough take ya' with me
to the desert. *(Lee stops, pause, looks down at Austin)* How's that sound?

*(pause as Austin stands slowly holding plate of demolished toast, their faces are
very close, pause)*

AUSTIN: It's a deal.

*(Lee stares straight into Austin's eyes, then he slowly takes a piece of toast off
the plate, raises it to his mouth and takes a huge crushing bite never taking his
eyes off Austin, as Lee crunches into the toast the lights black out)*

S C E N E   9

*Mid-day. No sound, blazing heat, the stage is ravaged; bottles, toasters, smashed
typewriter, ripped out telephone, etc. All the debris from previous scene is now*

starkly visible in intense yellow light, the effect should be like a desert junkyard at high noon, the coolness of the preceding scenes is totally obliterated. Austin is seated at table in alcove, shirt open, pouring with sweat, hunched over a writing notebook, scribbling notes desperately with a ballpoint pen. Lee with no shirt, beer in hand, sweat pouring down his chest, is walking a slow circle around the table, picking his way through the objects, sometimes kicking them aside.

LEE: *(as he walks)* All right, read it back to me. Read it back to me!

AUSTIN: *(scribbling at top speed)* Just a second.

365 **LEE:** Come on, come on! Just read what ya' got.

AUSTIN: I can't keep up! It's not the same as if I had a typewriter.

LEE: Just read what we got so far. Forget about the rest.

AUSTIN: All right. Let's see—okay—*(wipes sweat from his face, reads as Lee circles)* Luke says uh—

LEE: Luke?

370 **AUSTIN:** Yeah.

LEE: His name's Luke? All right, all right—we can change the names later. What's he say? Come on, come on.

AUSTIN: He says uh—*(reading)* "I told ya' you were a fool to follow me in here. I know this prairie like the back a' my hand."

LEE: No, no, no! That's not what I said. I never said that.

AUSTIN: That's what I wrote.

375 **LEE:** It's not what I said. I never said "like the back a' my hand." That's stupid. That's one a' those—whadya' call it? Whadya' call that?

AUSTIN: What?

LEE: Whadya' call it when somethin's been said a thousand times before. Whadya' call that?

AUSTIN: Um—a cliché?

LEE: Yeah. That's right. Cliché. That's what that is. A cliché. "The back a' my hand." That's stupid.

380 **AUSTIN:** That's what you said.

LEE: I never said that! And even if I did, that's where yer supposed to come in. That's where yer supposed to change it to somethin' better.

AUSTIN: Well how am I supposed to do that and write down what you say at the same time?

LEE: Ya' just do, that's all! You hear a stupid line you change it. That's yer job.

AUSTIN: All right. *(makes more notes)*

385 **LEE:** What're you changin' it to?

AUSTIN: I'm not changing it. I'm just trying to catch up.

LEE: Well change it! We gotta' change that, we can't leave that in there like that. ". . . the back a' my hand." That's dumb.

AUSTIN: *(stops writing, sits back)* All right.

LEE: *(pacing)* So what'll we change it to?

390 **AUSTIN:** Um—How 'bout—"I'm on intimate terms with this prairie."

LEE: *(to himself considering line as he walks)* "I'm on intimate terms with this prairie." Intimate terms, intimate terms. Intimate—that means like uh—sexual right?

AUSTIN: Well—yeah—or—

LEE: He's on sexual terms with the prairie? How dya' figure that?

AUSTIN: Well it doesn't necessarily have to mean sexual.

395 **LEE:** What's it mean then?

AUSTIN: It means uh—close—personal—

LEE: All right. How's it sound? Put it into the uh—the line there. Read it back. Let's see how it sounds. *(to himself)* "Intimate terms."

AUSTIN: *(scribbles in notebook)* Okay. It'd go something like this: *(reads)* "I told ya' you were a fool to follow me in here. I'm on intimate terms with this prairie."

LEE: That's good. I like that. That's real good.

400 **AUSTIN:** You do?

LEE: Yeah. Don't you?

AUSTIN: Sure.

LEE: Sounds original now. "Intimate terms." That's good. Okay. Now we're cookin! That has a real ring to it.

(Austin makes more notes, Lee walks around, pours beer on his arms and rubs it over his chest feeling good about the new progress, as he does this Mom enters unobtrusively down left with her luggage, she stops and stares at the scene still holding luggage as the two men continue, unaware of her presence, Austin absorbed in his writing, Lee cooling himself off with beer)

LEE: *(continues)* "He's on intimate terms with this prairie." Sounds real mysterious and kinda' threatening at the same time.

405 **AUSTIN:** *(writing rapidly)* Good.

LEE: Now—*(Lee turns and suddenly sees Mom, he stares at her for a while, she stares back, Austin keeps writing feverishly, not noticing, Lee walks slowly over to Mom and takes a closer look, long pause)*

LEE: Mom?

(Austin looks up suddenly from his writing, sees Mom, stands quickly, long pause, Mom surveys the damage)

AUSTIN: Mom. What're you doing back?

MOM: I'm back.

410 **LEE:** Here, lemme take those for ya.

(Lee sets beer on counter then takes both her bags but doesn't know where to set them down in the sea of junk so he just keeps holding them)

AUSTIN: I wasn't expecting you back so soon. I thought uh—How was Alaska?

MOM: Fine.

LEE: See any igloos?

Mom: No. Just glaciers.

415   **Austin:**   Cold huh?

Mom: What?

Austin: It must've been cold up there?

Mom: Not really.

Lee: Musta' been colder than this here. I mean we're havin' a real
scorcher here.

420   **Mom:**   Oh? *(she looks at damage)*

Lee: Yeah. Must be in the hundreds.

Austin: You wanna' take your coat off, Mom?

Mom: No. *(pause, she surveys space)* What happened in here?

Austin: Oh um—Me and Lee were just sort of celebrating and uh—

425   **Mom:**   Celebrating?

Austin: Yeah. Uh—Lee sold a screenplay. A story, I mean.

Mom: Lee did?

Austin: Yeah.

Mom: Not you?

430   **Austin:**   No. Him.

Mom: *(to Lee)* You sold a screenplay?

Lee: Yeah. That's right. We're just sorta' finishing it up right now.
That's what we're doing here.

Austin: Me and Lee are going out to the desert to live.

Mom: You and Lee?

435   **Austin:**   Yeah. I'm taking off with Lee.

Mom: *(she looks back and forth at each of them, pause)* You gonna go live
with your father?

Austin: No. We're going to a different desert Mom.

Mom: I see. Well, you'll probably wind up on the same desert sooner or
later. What're all these toasters doing here?

Austin: Well—we had kind of a contest.

440   **Mom:**   Contest?

Lee: Yeah.

Austin: Lee won.

Mom: Did you win a lot of money, Lee?

Lee: Well not yet. It's comin' in any day now.

445   **Mom:**   *(to Lee)* What happened to your shirt?

Lee: Oh. I was sweatin' like a pig and I took it off.

(Austin grabs Lee's shirt off the table and tosses it to him, Lee sets down suit-
cases and puts his shirt on)

Mom: Well it's one hell of a mess in here isn't it?

Austin: Yeah, I'll clean it up for you, Mom. I just didn't know you were
coming back so soon.

Mom: I didn't either.

450   **Austin:**   What happened?

Mom: Nothing. I just started missing all my plants.

(she notices dead plants)

Austin: Oh.

Mom: Oh, they're all dead aren't they. *(she crosses toward them, examines them closely)* You didn't get a chance to water I guess.

Austin: I was doing it and then Lee came and—

455 **Lee:**   Yeah I just distracted him a whole lot here, Mom. It's not his fault.

(pause, as Mom stares at plants)

Mom: Oh well, one less thing to take care of I guess. *(turns toward brothers)* Oh, that reminds me—You boys will probably never guess who's in town. Try and guess.

(long pause, brothers stare at her)

Austin: Whadya' mean, Mom?

Mom: Take a guess. Somebody very important has come to town. I read it, coming down on the Greyhound.

Lee: Somebody very important?

460 **Mom:**   See if you can guess. You'll never guess.

Austin: Mom—we're trying to uh—*(points to writing pad)*

Mom: Picasso.[8] *(pause)* Picasso's in town. Isn't that incredible? Right now.

(pause)

Austin: Picasso's dead, Mom.

Mom: No, he's not dead. He's visiting the museum. I read it on the bus. We have to go down there and see him.

465 **Austin:**   Mom—

Mom: This is the chance of a lifetime. Can you imagine? We could all go down and meet him. All three of us.

Lee: Uh—I don't think I'm really up fer meetin' anybody right now. I'm uh—What's his name?

Mom: Picasso! Picasso! You've never heard of Picasso? Austin, you've heard of Picasso.

Austin: Mom, we're not going to have time.

470 **Mom:**   It won't take long. We'll just hop in the car and go down there. An opportunity like this doesn't come along every day.

Austin: We're gonna' be leavin' here, Mom!

(pause)

Mom: Oh.

Lee: Yeah.

(pause)

Mom: You're both leaving?

---

8   Spanish-born painter (1881–1973) known for his abstract, geometric style (cubism).

475 **LEE:** *(looks at Austin)* Well we were thinkin' about that before but now I—

AUSTIN: No, we are! We're both leaving. We've got it all planned.

MOM: *(to Austin)* Well you can't leave. You have a family.

AUSTIN: I'm leaving. I'm getting out of here.

LEE: *(to Mom)* I don't really think Austin's cut out for the desert do you?

480 **MOM:** No. He's not.

AUSTIN: I'm going with you, Lee!

MOM: He's too thin.

LEE: Yeah, he'd just burn up out there.

AUSTIN: *(to Lee)* We just gotta' finish this screenplay and then we're gonna' take off. That's the plan. That's what you said. Come on, let's get back to work, Lee.

485 **LEE:** I can't work under these conditions here. It's too hot.

AUSTIN: Then we'll do it on the desert.

LEE: Don't be tellin' me what we're gonna do!

MOM: Don't shout in the house.

LEE: We're just gonna' have to postpone the whole deal.

490 **AUSTIN:** I can't postpone it! It's gone past postponing! I'm doing everything you said. I'm writing down exactly what you tell me.

LEE: Yeah, but you were right all along see. It is a dumb story. "Two lamebrains chasin' each other across Texas." That's what you said, right?

AUSTIN: I never said that.

(Lee sneers in Austin's face then turns to Mom)

LEE: I'm gonna' just borrow some a' your antiques, Mom. You don't mind do ya'? Just a few plates and things. Silverware.

(Lee starts going through all the cupboards in kitchen pulling out plates and stacking them on counter as Mom and Austin watch)

MOM: You don't have any utensils on the desert?

495 **LEE:** Nah, I'm fresh out.

AUSTIN: *(to Lee)* What're you doing?

MOM: Well some of those are very old. Bone China.[9]

LEE: I'm tired of eatin' outa' my bare hands, ya' know. It's not civilized.

AUSTIN: *(to Lee)* What're you doing? We made a deal!

500 **MOM:** Couldn't you borrow the plastic ones instead? I have plenty of plastic ones.

LEE: *(as he stacks plates)* It's not the same. Plastic's not the same at all. What I need is somethin' authentic. Somethin' to keep me in touch.

---

[9] Porcelain made of clay mixed with bone ash.

It's easy to get outa' touch out there. Don't worry I'll get em' back to ya'.

(Austin rushes up to Lee, grabs him by shoulders)

AUSTIN: You can't just drop the whole thing, Lee!

(Lee turns, pushes Austin in the chest knocking him backwards into the alcove, Mom watches numbly, Lee returns to collecting the plates, silverware, etc.)

MOM: You boys shouldn't fight in the house. Go outside and fight.
LEE: I'm not fightin'. I'm leavin'.
505 **MOM:**   There's been enough damage done already.
LEE: *(his back to Austin and Mom, stacking dishes on counter)* I'm clearin' outa' here once and for all. All this town does is drive a man insane. Look what it's done to Austin there. I'm not lettin' that happen to me. Sell myself down the river. No sir. I'd rather be a hundred miles from nowhere than let that happen to me.

(during this Austin has picked up the ripped-out phone from the floor and wrapped the cord tightly around both his hands, he lunges at Lee whose back is still to him, wraps the cord around Lee's neck, plants a foot in Lee's back and pulls back on the cord, tightening it, Lee chokes desperately, can't speak and can't reach Austin with his arms, Austin keeps applying pressure on Lee's back with his foot, bending him into the sink, Mom watches)

AUSTIN: *(tightening cord)* You're not goin' anywhere! You're not takin' anything with you. You're not takin' my car! You're not takin' the dishes! You're not takin' anything! You're stayin' right here!
MOM: You'll have to stop fighting in the house. There's plenty of room outside to fight. You've got the whole outdoors to fight in.

(Lee tries to tear himself away, he crashes across the stage like an enraged bull dragging Austin with him, he snorts and bellows but Austin hangs on and manages to keep clear of Lee's attempts to grab him, they crash into the table, to the floor, Lee is face down thrashing wildly and choking, Austin pulls cord tighter, stands with one foot planted on Lee's back and the cord stretched taut)

AUSTIN: *(holding cord)* Gimme back my keys, Lee! Take the keys out! Take 'em out!

(Lee desperately tries to dig in his pockets, searching for the car keys, Mom moves closer)

510 **MOM:**   *(calmly to Austin)* You're not killing him are you?
AUSTIN: I don't know. I don't know if I'm killing him. I'm stopping him. That's all. I'm just stopping him.

(Lee thrashes but Austin is relentless)

MOM: You oughta' let him breathe a little bit.
AUSTIN: Throw the keys out, Lee!

(Lee finally gets keys out and throws them on floor but out of Austin's reach, Austin keeps pressure on cord, pulling Lee's neck back, Lee gets one hand to the cord but can't relieve the pressure)

Reach me those keys would ya', Mom.

MOM: *(not moving)* Why are you doing this to him?

515 **AUSTIN:** Reach me the keys!

MOM: Not until you stop choking him.

AUSTIN: I can't stop choking him! He'll kill me if I stop choking him!

MOM: He won't kill you. He's your brother.

AUSTIN: Just get me the keys would ya'!

(pause, Mom picks keys up off floor, hands them to Austin)

520 **AUSTIN:** *(to Mom)* Thanks.

MOM: Will you let him go now?

AUSTIN: I don't know. He's not gonna' let me get outa' here.

MOM: Well you can't kill him.

AUSTIN: I can kill him! I can easily kill him. Right now. Right here. All I gotta' do is just tighten up. See? *(he tightens cord, Lee thrashes wildly, Austin releases pressure a little, maintaining control)* Ya' see that?

525 **MOM:** That's a savage thing to do.

AUSTIN: Yeah well don't tell me I can't kill him because I can. I can just twist. I can just keep twisting. *(Austin twists the cord tighter, Lee weakens, his breathing changes to a short rasp)*

MOM: Austin!

(Austin relieves pressure, Lee breathes easier but Austin keeps him under control)

AUSTIN: *(eyes on Lee, holding cord)* I'm goin' to the desert. There's nothing stopping me. I'm going by myself to the desert.

(Mom moving toward her luggage)

MOM: Well, I'm going to go check into a motel. I can't stand this anymore.

530 **AUSTIN:** Don't go yet!

(Mom pauses)

MOM: I can't stay here. This is worse than being homeless.

AUSTIN: I'll get everything fixed up for you, Mom. I promise. Just stay for a while.

MOM: *(picking up luggage)* You're going to the desert.

AUSTIN: Just wait!

(Lee thrashes, Austin subdues him, Mom watches holding luggage, pause)

535 **MOM:** It was the worst feeling being up there. In Alaska. Staring out a window. I never felt so desperate before. That's why when I saw that article on Picasso I thought—

AUSTIN: Stay here, Mom. This is where you live.

(she looks around the stage)

MOM: I don't recognize it at all.

(she exits with luggage, Austin makes a move toward her but Lee starts to struggle and Austin subdues him again with cord, pause)

AUSTIN: (holding cord) Lee? I'll make ya' a deal. You let me get outa' here. Just let me get to my car. All right, Lee? Gimme a little headstart and I'll turn you loose. Just gimme a little headstart. All right?

(Lee makes no response, Austin slowly releases tension cord, still nothing from Lee)

AUSTIN: Lee?

Lee is motionless, Austin very slowly begins to stand, still keeping a tenuous hold on the cord and his eyes riveted to Lee for any sign of movement, Austin slowly drops the cord and stands, he stares down at Lee who appears to be dead)

540 **AUSTIN:** (whispers) Lee?

(pause, Austin considers, looks toward exit, back to Lee, then makes a small movement as if to leave. Instantly Lee is on his feet and moves toward exit, blocking Austin's escape. They square off to each other, keeping a distance between them. Pause, a single coyote heard in distance, lights fade softly into moonlight, the figures of the brothers now appear to be caught in a vast desert-like landscape, they are very still but watchful for the next move, lights go slowly to black as the after-image of the brothers pulses in the dark, coyote fades)

READING AND REACTING

1. What exactly happens in *True West?* Summarize the play's plot, including all significant events. What do you see as the play's most important event? Why?

2. What possible meanings does the play's title suggest?

3. What is the nature of the conflict between Lee and Austin? On what specific issues do they disagree? How do their values differ? How does the conflict between them advance the plot?

4. Why does Lee decide to write a screenplay? Why does Austin agree to help him? Consider all their possible motives.

5. How does Lee's golf game with Saul Kimmer, a scene that occurs offstage between Acts I and II, advance the play's action? Why do you suppose this scene does not appear in the play?

6. Summarize the plot of the "Contemporary Western" Lee describes in Scene 4. How "true"—that is, how believable—do you think it is? How does it parallel the plot of *True West?*

7. Explain how each of the following props helps to develop the play's plot: Lee's stolen T.V.s, Austin's typewriter, Austin's car keys, the golf clubs Saul Kimmer gives to Lee, the toasters.

8. In Scene 6 Austin says to Saul, "He's been camped out on the desert for three months. Talking to cactus. What's he know about what people wanna see on the screen! I drive on the freeway every day. I swallow the smog. I watch the news in color. I shop in the Safeway. I'm the one who's in touch! Not him!" Is Austin right?

9. In Scene 7 Austin tells Lee a story about his father's teeth. What is the significance of this story? In what sense is it a comment on Lee's screenplay (summarized in Scene 4)?

10. The mother of the two men does not appear until the last scene of the play. Should she have appeared earlier? Should she not have appeared at all?

11. Austin and Lee's mother has been to Alaska on vacation; their father and Lee himself have been living on the desert; Austin lives in Los Angeles. What, if anything, do these settings reveal about each character? Do you think these settings have symbolic significance, or are they just places?

12. **JOURNAL ENTRY** What motivates Austin to steal the toasters? Do you see this as a "true to life" plot development?

13. **CRITICAL PERSPECTIVE** In an introduction to a collection of Shepard's plays, Richard Gilman characterizes them as fragmentary and elusive:

Most of his plays seem like fragments, chunks of various sizes thrown out from some mother lode of urgent and heterogeneous imagination in which he has scrabbled with pick, shovel, gunbutt and hands. The reason so many of them seem incomplete is that they lack the clear boundaries as artifact, the internal order, the progress toward a denouement (of some kind: a crystallization, a summarizing image, a poise in the mind) and the consistency of tone and procedure that ordinarily characterize good drama, even most avant-garde drama of the postwar time.

Many of his plays seem partial, capricious, arbitrarily brought to an end and highly unstable. They spill over, they leak. They change, chameleon-like, in self-protection as we look at them. This is a source of the difficulty one has in writing about them, as it's also a source of their originality. Another difficulty is that we tend to look at all plays for their single "meanings" or ruling ideas but find this elusive in Shepard. . . .

Do you find this to be an accurate description of *True West?* If so, do you think the qualities Gilman identifies make the play stronger or weaker?

ATHOL FUGARD (1932–   ) grew up in Port Elizabeth, South Africa, a product of two national strains in South Africa. His mother is an Afrikaaner, and his father is of English descent. His work has always been critical of apartheid's effects on those it touches, but it is not usually overtly political: Fugard simply demonstrates how apartheid limited the lives and spirits of individuals. Fugard's other plays include *The Blood Knot* (1964), *Boesman and Lena* (1969), *A Lesson from Aloes* (1981), *The Road to Mecca*, *My Children! My Africa!* (1985), and *Playland* (1993). The South African actor Zakes Mokae is featured in the original productions of nearly every Fugard play.

"Master Harold" . . . and the Boys (1983) is based on an autobiographical incident recounted in *Notebooks 1960–1977*, a collection of diaries Fugard published in 1977. The play received its first production at the Yale Repertory Theatre, with Zakes Mokae in the role of Sam.

ATHOL FUGARD

"Master Harold" . . . and the Boys

(1983)

The St. George's Park Tea Room on a wet and windy Port Elizabeth[1] afternoon.

Tables and chairs have been cleared and are stacked on one side except for one which stands apart with a single chair. On this table a knife, fork, spoon and side plate in anticipation of a simple meal, together with a pile of comic books.

Other elements: a serving counter with a few stale cakes under glass and a not very impressive display of sweets, cigarettes and cool drinks, etc.; a few cardboard advertising handouts—Cadbury's Chocolate, Coca-Cola—and a blackboard on which an untrained hand has chalked up the prices of Tea, Coffee, Scones, Milkshakes—all flavors—and Cool Drinks; a few sad ferns in pots; a telephone; an old-style jukebox.

There is an entrance on one side and an exit into a kitchen on the other.

Leaning on the solitary table, his head cupped in one hand as he pages through one of the comic books, is Sam. A black man in his mid-forties. He

---

[1] City on the southeast coast of South Africa.

wears the white coat of a waiter. Behind him on his knees, mopping down the floor with a bucket of water and a rag, is Willie. Also black and about the same age as Sam. He has his sleeves and trousers rolled up.

The year: 1950

WILLIE: (Singing as he works.)
"She was scandalizin' my name,
She took my money
She called me honey
But she was scandalizin' my name.
Called it love but was playin' a game . . ."

He gets up and moves the bucket. Stands thinking for a moment, then, raising his arms to hold an imaginary partner, he launches into an intricate ballroom dance step. Although a mildly comic figure, he reveals a reasonable degree of accomplishment.

Hey, Sam.

Sam, absorbed in the comic book, does not respond.

Hey, Boet Sam!

Sam looks up.

I'm getting it. The quickstep. Look now and tell me. (*He repeats the step.*) Well?

SAM: (*Encouragingly.*) Show me again.

WILLIE: Okay, count for me.

SAM: Ready?

5 **WILLIE:** Ready.

SAM: Five, six, seven, eight . . . (*Willie starts to dance.*) A-n-d one two three four . . . and one two three four . . . (*Ad libbing as Willie dances.*) Your shoulders, Willie . . . your shoulders! Don't look down! Look happy, Willie! Relax, Willie!

WILLIE: (*Desperate but still dancing.*) I am relax.

SAM: No, you're not.

WILLIE: (*He falters.*) Ag no man, Sam! Mustn't talk. You make me make mistakes.

10 **SAM:** But you're too stiff.

WILLIE: Yesterday I'm not straight . . . today I'm too stiff!

SAM: Well, you are. You asked me and I'm telling you.

WILLIE: Where?

SAM: Everywhere. Try to glide through it.

15 **WILLIE:** Glide?

SAM: Ja, make it smooth. And give it more style. It must look like you're enjoying yourself.

WILLIE: (*Emphatically.*) I wasn't.

SAM: Exactly.

WILLIE: How can I enjoy myself? Not straight, too stiff and now it's
also glide, give it more style, make it smooth. . . . Haai! Is hard to
remember all those things, Boet Sam.

20 **SAM:**   That's your trouble. You're trying too hard.

WILLIE: I try hard because it *is* hard.

SAM: But don't let me see it. The secret is to make it look easy. Ballroom
must look happy, Willie, not like hard work. It must . . . Ja! . . . it
must look like romance.

WILLIE: Now another one! What's romance?

SAM: Love story with happy ending. A handsome man in tails, and in
his arms, smiling at him, a beautiful lady in evening dress!

25 **WILLIE:**   Fred Astaire, Ginger Rogers.

SAM: You got it. Tapdance or ballroom, it's the same. Romance. In two
weeks' time when the judges look at you and Hilda, they must see a
man and a woman who are dancing their way to a happy ending.
What I saw was you holding her like you were frightened she was
going to run away.

WILLIE: Ja! Because that is what she wants to do! I got no romance left
for Hilda anymore, Boet Sam.

SAM: Then pretend. When you put your arms around Hilda, imagine she
is Ginger Rogers.

WILLIE: With no teeth? You try.

30 **SAM:**   Well, just remember, there's only two weeks left.

WILLIE: I know, I know! *(To the jukebox.)* I do it better with music. You
got sixpence for Sarah Vaughan?[2]

SAM: That's a slow foxtrot. You're practicing the quickstep.

WILLIE: I'll practice slow foxtrot.

SAM: *(Shaking his head.)* It's your turn to put money in the jukebox.

35 **WILLIE:**   I only got bus fare to go home. *(He returns disconsolately to his
work.)* Love story and happy ending! She's doing it all right, Boet
Sam, but is not me she's giving happy endings. Fuckin' whore! Three
nights now she doesn't come practice. I wind up gramophone, I get
record ready and I sit and wait. What happens? Nothing. Ten o'clock
I start dancing with my pillow. You try and practice romance by
yourself, Boet Sam. Struesgod, she doesn't come tonight I take back
my dress and ballroom shoes and I find me new partner. Size twenty-
six. Shoes size seven. And now she's also making trouble for me with
the baby again. Reports me to Child Wellfed, that I'm not giving her
money. She lies! Every week I am giving her money for milk. And
how do I know is my baby? Only his hair looks like me. She's fucking
around all the time I turn my back. Hilda Samuels is a bitch! *(Pause.)*
Hey, Sam!

SAM: Ja.

---

[2] Sarah Vaughan (b. 1924)—U.S. jazz and blues singer.

WILLIE: You listening?

SAM: Ja.

WILLIE: So what you say?

40 **SAM:**   About Hilda?

WILLIE: Ja.

SAM: When did you last give her a hiding?

WILLIE: *(Reluctantly.)* Sunday night.

SAM: And today is Thursday.

45 **WILLIE:**   *(He knows what's coming.)* Okay.

SAM: Hiding on Sunday night, then Monday, Tuesday and Wednesday she doesn't come to practice . . . and you are asking me why?

WILLIE: I said okay, Boet Sam!

SAM: You hit her too much. One day she's going to leave you for good.

WILLIE: So? She makes me the hell-in too much.

50 **SAM:**   *(Emphasizing his point.)* *Too* much and *too* hard. You had the same trouble with Eunice.

WILLIE: Because she also make the hell-in, Boet Sam. She never got the steps right. Even the waltz.

SAM: Beating her up every time she makes a mistake in the waltz? *(Shaking his head.)* No, Willie! That takes the pleasure out of ballroom dancing.

WILLIE: Hilda is not too bad with the waltz, Boet Sam. Is the quickstep where the trouble starts.

SAM: *(Teasing him gently.)* How's your pillow with the quickstep?

55 **WILLIE:**   *(Ignoring the tease.)* Good! And why? Because it got no legs. That's her trouble. She can't move them quick enough, Boet Sam. I start the record and before halfway Count Basie[3] is already winning. Only time we catch up with him is when gramophone runs down.

Sam laughs.

Haaikona, Boet Sam, is not funny.

SAM: *(Snapping his fingers.)* I got it! Give her a handicap.

WILLIE: What's that?

SAM: Give her a ten-second start and then let Count Basie go. Then I put my money on her. Hot favorite in the Ballroom Stakes: Hilda Samuels ridden by Willie Malopo.

WILLIE: *(Turning away.)* I'm not talking to you no more.

60 **SAM:**   *(Relenting.)* Sorry, Willie . . .

WILLIE: It's finish between us.

SAM: Okay, okay . . . I'll stop.

WILLIE: You can also fuck off.

SAM: Willie, listen! I want to help you!

65 **WILLIE:**   No more jokes?

---

[3] William "Count" Basie (b. 1904)—U.S. jazz pianist, composer, and bandleader.

SAM: I promise.

WILLIE: Okay. Help me.

SAM: *(His turn to hold an imaginary partner.)* Look and learn. Feet together. Back straight. Body relaxed. Right hand placed gently in the small of her back and wait for the music. Don't start worrying about making mistakes or the judges or the other competitors. It's just you, Hilda and the music, and you're going to have a good time. What Count Basie do you play?

WILLIE: "You the cream in my coffee, you the salt in my stew."

70 **SAM:** Right. Give it to me in strict tempo.

WILLIE: Ready?

SAM: Ready.

WILLIE: A-n-d . . . *(Singing.)*
"You the cream in my coffee.
You the salt in my stew.
You will always be my
necessity.
I'd be lost without
you. . . ." (etc.)

Sam launches into the quickstep. He is obviously a much more accomplished dancer than Willie. Hally enters. A seventeen-year-old white boy. Wet raincoat and school case. He stops and watches Sam. The demonstration comes to an end with a flourish. Applause from Hally and Willie.

HALLY: Bravo! No question about it. First place goes to Mr. Sam Semela.

75 **WILLIE:** *(In total agreement.)* You was gliding with style, Boet Sam.

HALLY: *(Cheerfully.)* How's it, chaps?

SAM: Okay, Hally.

WILLIE: *(Springing to attention like a soldier and saluting.)* At your service, Master Harold!

HALLY: Not long to the big event, hey!

80 **SAM:** Two weeks.

HALLY: You nervous?

SAM: No.

HALLY: Think you stand a chance?

SAM: Let's just say I'm ready to go out there and dance.

85 **HALLY:** It looked like it. What about you, Willie?

Willie groans.

What's the matter?

SAM: He's got leg trouble.

HALLY: *(Innocently.)* Oh, sorry to hear that, Willie.

WILLIE: Boet Sam! You promised. *(Willie returns to his work.)*

Hally deposits his school case and takes off his raincoat. His clothes are a little neglected and untidy: black blazer with school badge, gray flannel trousers in need of an ironing, khaki shirt and tie, black shoes. Sam has fetched a towel for Hally to dry his hair.

HALLY: God, what a lousy bloody day. It's coming down cats and dogs out there. Bad for business, chaps . . . *(Conspiratorial whisper.)* . . . but it also means we're in for a nice quiet afternoon.

90 **SAM:**   You can speak loud. Your Mom's not here.

HALLY: Out shopping?

SAM: No. The hospital.

HALLY: But it's Thursday. There's no visiting on Thursday afternoons. Is my Dad okay?

SAM: Sounds like it. In fact, I think he's going home.

95 **HALLY:**   *(Stopped short by Sam's remark.)* What do you mean?

SAM: The hospital phoned.

HALLY: To say what?

SAM: I don't know. I just heard your Mom talking.

HALLY: So what makes you say he's going home?

100 **SAM:**   It sounded as if they were telling her to come and fetch him.

Hally thinks about what Sam has said for a few seconds.

HALLY: When did she leave?

SAM: About an hour ago. She said she would phone you. Want to eat?

Hally doesn't respond.

Hally, want your lunch?

HALLY: I suppose so. *(His mood has changed.)* What's on the menu? . . . as if I don't know.

SAM: Soup, followed by meat pie and gravy.

105 **HALLY:**   Today's?

SAM: No.

HALLY: And the soup?

SAM: Nourishing pea soup.

HALLY: Just the soup. *(The pile of comic books on the table.)* And these?

110 **SAM:**   For your Dad. Mr. Kempston brought them.

HALLY: You haven't been reading them, have you?

SAM: Just looking.

HALLY: *(Examining the comics.)* Jungle Jim . . . Batman and Robin . . . Tarzan . . . God, what rubbish! Mental pollution. Take them away.

Sam exits waltzing into the kitchen. Hally turns to Willie.

HALLY: Did you hear my Mom talking on the telephone, Willie?

115 **WILLIE:**   No, Master Hally. I was at the back.

HALLY: And she didn't say anything to you before she left?

WILLIE: She said I must clean the floors.

HALLY: I mean about my Dad.

WILLIE: She didn't say nothing to me about him, Master Hally.

120 **HALLY:** *(With conviction.)* No! It can't be. They said he needed at least
        another three weeks of treatment. Sam's definitely made a mistake.
        *(Rummages through his school case, finds a book and settles down at the
        table to read.)* So, Willie!
WILLIE: Yes, Master Hally! Schooling okay today?
HALLY: Yes, okay. . . . *(He thinks about it.)* . . . No, not really. Ag, what's
        the difference? I don't care. And Sam says you've got problems.
WILLIE: Big problems.
HALLY: Which leg is sore?

Willie groans.

        Both legs.
125 **WILLIE:** There is nothing wrong with my legs. Sam is just making jokes.
HALLY: So then you *will* be in the competition.
WILLIE: Only if I can find me a partner.
HALLY: But what about Hilda?
SAM: *(Returning with a bowl of soup.)* She's the one who's got trouble
        with her legs.
130 **HALLY:** What sort of trouble, Willie?
SAM: From the way he describes it, I think the lady has gone a bit lame.
HALLY: Good God! Have you taken her to see a doctor?
SAM: I think a vet would be better.
HALLY: What do you mean?
135 **SAM:** What do you call it again when a racehorse goes very fast?
HALLY: Gallop?
SAM: That's it!
WILLIE: Boet Sam!
HALLY: "A gallop down the homestretch to the winning post." But
        what's that got to do with Hilda?
140 **SAM:** Count Basie always gets there first.

Willie lets fly with his slop rag. It misses Sam and hits Hally.

HALLY: *(Furious.)* For Christ's sake, Willie! What the hell do you think
        you're doing!
WILLIE: Sorry, Master Hally, but it's him. . . .
HALLY: Act your bloody age! *(Hurls the rag back at Willie.)* Cut out the
        nonsense now and get on with your work. And you too, Sam. Stop
        fooling around.

Sam moves away.

        No. Hang on. I haven't finished! Tell me exactly what my Mom said.
SAM: I have. "When Hally comes, tell him I've gone to the hospital and
        I'll phone him."
145 **HALLY:** She didn't say anything about taking my Dad home?
SAM: No. It's just that when she was talking on the phone . . .
HALLY: *(Interrupting him.)* No, Sam. They can't be discharging him.
        She would have said so if they were. In any case, we saw him last

night and he wasn't in good shape at all. Staff nurse even said there was talk about taking more X-rays. And now suddenly today he's better? If anything, it sounds more like a bad turn to me . . . which I sincerely hope it isn't. Hang on . . . how long ago did you say she left?

SAM: Just before two . . . *(His wrist watch.)* . . . hour and a half.

HALLY: I know how to settle it. *(Behind the counter to the telephone. Talking as he dials.)* Let's give her ten minutes to get to the hospital, ten minutes to load him up, another ten, at the most, to get home and another ten to get him inside. Forty minutes. They should have been home for at least half an hour already. *(Pause—he waits with the receiver to his ear.)* No reply, chaps. And you know why? Because she's at his bedside in hospital helping him pull through a bad turn. You definitely heard wrong.

150 **SAM:**   Okay.

As far as Hally is concerned, the matter is settled. He returns to his table, sits down and divides his attention between the book and his soup. Sam is at his school case and picks up a textbook Modern Graded Mathematics for Standards Nine and Ten. Opens it at random and laughs at something he sees.

Who is this supposed to be?

HALLY: Old fart-face Prentice.

SAM: Teacher?

HALLY: Thinks he is. And believe me, that is not a bad likeness.

SAM: Has he seen it?

155 **HALLY:**   Yes.

SAM: What did he say?

HALLY: Tried to be clever, as usual. Said I was no Leonardo da Vinci and that bad art had to be punished. So, six of the best, and his are bloody good.

SAM: On your bum?

HALLY: Where else? The days when I got them on my hands are gone forever, Sam.

160 **SAM:**   With your trousers down!

HALLY: No. He's not quite that barbaric.

SAM: That's the way they do it in jail.

HALLY: *(Flicker of morbid interest.)* Really?

SAM: Ja. When the magistrate sentences you to "strokes with a light cane."

165 **HALLY:**   Go on.

SAM: They make you lie down on a bench. One policeman pulls down your trousers and holds your ankles, another one pulls your shirt over your head and holds your arms . . .

HALLY: Thank you! That's enough.

SAM: . . . and the one that gives you the strokes talks to you gently and for a long time between each one. *(He laughs.)*

HALLY: I've heard enough, Sam! Jesus! It's a bloody awful world when you come to think of it. People can be real bastards.

170 **SAM:**   That's the way it is, Hally.

HALLY: It doesn't *have* to be that way. There is something called progress, you know. We don't exactly burn people at the stake anymore.

SAM: Like Joan of Arc.

HALLY: Correct. If she was captured today, she'd be given a fair trial.

SAM: And then the death sentence.

175 **HALLY:**   *(A world-weary sigh.)* I know, I know! I oscillate between hope and despair for this world as well, Sam. But things will change, you wait and see. One day somebody is going to get up and give history a kick up the backside and get it going again.

SAM: Like who?

HALLY: *(After thought.)* They're called social reformers. Every age, Sam, has got its social reformer. My history book is full of them.

SAM: So where's ours?

HALLY: Good question. And I hate to say it, but the answer is: I don't know. Maybe he hasn't even been born yet. Or is still only a babe in arms at his mother's breast. God, what a thought.

180 **SAM:**   So we just go on waiting.

HALLY: Ja, looks like it. *(Back to his soup and the book.)*

SAM: *(Reading from the textbook.)* "Introduction: In some mathematical problems only the magnitude . . ." *(He mispronounces the word "magnitude.")*

HALLY: *(Correcting him without looking up.)* Magnitude.

SAM: What's it mean?

185 **HALLY:**   How big it is. The size of the thing.

SAM: *(Reading.)* ". . . a magnitude of the quantities is of importance. In other problems we need to know whether these quantities are negative or positive. For example, whether there is a debit or credit bank balance . . ."

HALLY: Whether you're broke or not.

SAM: ". . . whether the temperature is above or below Zero . . ."

HALLY: Naught degrees. Cheerful state of affairs! No cash and you're freezing to death. Mathematics won't get you out of that one.

190 **SAM:**   "All these quantities are called . . ." *(Spelling the word.)* . . . s-c-a-l . . .

HALLY: Scalars.

SAM: Scalars! *(Shaking his head with a laugh.)* You understand all that?

HALLY: *(Turning a page.)* No. And I don't intend to try.

SAM: So what happens when the exams come?

195 **HALLY:**   Failing a maths exam isn't the end of the world, Sam. How many times have I told you that examination results don't measure intelligence?

SAM: I would say about as many times as you've failed one of them.

HALLY: *(Mirthlessly.)* Ha, ha, ha.

SAM: *(Simultaneously.)* Ha, ha, ha.

HALLY: Just remember Winston Churchill didn't do particularly well at school.

200 **SAM:** You've also told me that one many times.

HALLY: Well, it just so happens to be the truth.

SAM: *(Enjoying the word.)* Magnitude! Magnitude! Show me how to use it.

HALLY: *(After thought.)* An intrepid social reformer will not be daunted by the magnitude of the task he has undertaken.

SAM: *(Impressed.)* Couple of jaw-breakers in there!

205 **HALLY:** I gave you three for the price of one. Intrepid, daunted and magnitude. I did that once in an exam. Put five of the words I had to explain in one sentence. It was half a page long.

SAM: Well, I'll put my money on you in the English exam.

HALLY: Piece of cake. Eighty percent without even trying.

SAM: *(Another textbook from Hally's case.)* And history?

HALLY: So-so. I'll scrape through. In the fifties if I'm lucky.

210 **SAM:** You didn't do too badly last year.

HALLY: Because we had World War One. That at least had some action. You try to find that in the South African Parliamentary system.

SAM: *(Reading from the history textbook.)* "Napoleon and the principle of equality." Hey! This sounds interesting. "After concluding peace with Britain in 1802, Napoleon used a brief period of calm to in-sti-tute . . ."

HALLY: Introduce.

SAM: ". . . many reforms. Napoleon regarded all people as equal before the law and wanted them to have equal opportunities for advancement. All ves-ti-ges of the feu-dal system with its oppression of the poor were abolished." Vestiges, feudal system and abolished. I'm all right on oppression.

215 **HALLY:** I'm thinking. He swept away . . . abolished . . . the last remains . . . vestiges . . . of the bad old days . . . feudal system.

SAM: Ha! There's the social reformer we're waiting for. He sounds like a man of some magnitude.

HALLY: I'm not so sure about that. It's a damn good title for a book, though. A man of magnitude!

SAM: He sounds pretty big to me, Hally.

HALLY: Don't confuse historical significance with greatness. But maybe I'm being a bit prejudiced. Have a look in there and you'll see he's two chapters long. And hell! . . . has he only got dates, Sam, all of which you've got to remember! This campaign and that campaign, and then, because of all the fighting, the next thing is we get Peace Treaties all over the place. And what's the end of the story? Battle of Waterloo, which he loses. Wasn't worth it. No, I don't know about him as a man of magnitude.

220 **SAM:** Then who would you say was?

HALLY: To answer that, we need a definition of greatness, and I suppose
that would be somebody who . . . somebody who benefited all
mankind.

SAM: Right. But like who?

HALLY: *(He speaks with total conviction.)* Charles Darwin. Remember
him? That big book from the library. *The Origin of the Species.*

SAM: Him?

225 **HALLY:** Yes. For his Theory of Evolution.

SAM: You didn't finish it.

HALLY: I ran out of time. I didn't finish it because my two weeks was
up. But I'm going to take it out again after I've digested what I read.
It's safe. I've hidden it away in the Theology section. Nobody ever
goes in there. And anyway who are you to talk? You hardly even
looked at it.

SAM: I tried. I looked at the chapters in the beginning and I saw one
called "The Struggle for an Existence." Ah ha, I thought. At last! But
what did I get? Something called the mistletoe which needs the apple
tree and there's too many seeds and all are going to die except one
. . . ! No, Hally.

HALLY: *(Intellectually outraged.)* What do you mean, No! The poor man
had to start somewhere. For God's sake, Sam, he revolutionized
science. Now we know.

230 **SAM:** What?

HALLY: Where we come from and what it all means.

SAM: And that's a benefit to mankind? Anyway, I still don't believe it.

HALLY: God, you're impossible. I showed it to you in black and white.

SAM: Doesn't mean I got to believe it.

235 **HALLY:** It's the likes of you that kept the Inquisition in business. It's
called bigotry. Anyway, that's my man of magnitude. Charles
Darwin! Who's yours?

SAM: *(Without hesitation.)* Abraham Lincoln.

HALLY: I might have guessed as much. Don't get sentimental, Sam.
You've never been a slave, you know. And anyway we freed your
ancestors here in South Africa long before the Americans. But if you
want to thank somebody on their behalf, do it to Mr. William
Wilberforce.[4] Come on. Try again. I want a real genius. *(Now enjoying
himself, and so is Sam. Hally goes behind the counter and helps himself to
a chocolate.)*

SAM: William Shakespeare.

HALLY: *(No enthusiasm.)* Oh. So you're also one of them, are you? You're
basing that opinion on only one play, you know. You've only read my
Julius Caesar and even I don't understand half of what they're talking

---

4 William Wilberforce (1759–1833)—English abolitionist.

about. They should do what they did with the old Bible: bring the language up to date.

240 **SAM:** That's all you've got. It's also the only one *you've* read.

HALLY: I know. I admit it. That's why I suggest we reserve our judgment until we've checked up on a few others. I've got a feeling, though, that by the end of this year one is going to be enough for me, and I can give you the names of twenty-nine other chaps in the Standard Nine class of the Port Elizabeth Technical College who feel the same. But if you want him, you can have him. My turn now. *(Pacing.)* This is a damned good exercise, you know! It started off looking like a simple question and here it's got us really probing into the intellectual heritage of our civilization.

SAM: So who is it going to be?

HALLY: My next man . . . and he gets the title on two scores: social reform and literary genius . . . is Leo Nikolaevich Tolstoy.

SAM: That Russian.

245 **HALLY:** Correct. Remember the picture of him I showed you?

SAM: With the long beard.

HALLY: *(Trying to look like Tolstoy.)* And those burning, visionary eyes. My God, the face of a social prophet if ever I saw one! And remember my words when I showed it to you? Here's a *man*, Sam!

SAM: Those were words, Hally.

HALLY: Not many intellectuals are prepared to shovel manure with the peasants and then go home and write a "little book" called *War and Peace*. Incidentally, Sam, he was somebody else who, to quote, ". . . did not distinguish himself scholastically."

250 **SAM:** Meaning?

HALLY: He was also no good at school.

SAM: Like you and Winston Churchill.

HALLY: *(Mirthlessly.)* Ha, ha, ha.

SAM: *(Simultaneously.)* Ha, ha, ha.

255 **HALLY:** Don't get clever, Sam. That man freed his serfs of his own free will.

SAM: No argument. He was a somebody, all right. I accept him.

HALLY: I'm sure Count Tolstoy will be very pleased to hear that. Your turn. Shoot. *(Another chocolate from behind the counter.)* I'm waiting, Sam.

SAM: I've got him.

HALLY: Good. Submit your candidate for examination.

260 **SAM:** Jesus.

HALLY: *(Stopped dead in his tracks.)* Who?

SAM: Jesus Christ.

HALLY: Oh, come on, Sam!

SAM: The Messiah.

265 **HALLY:** Ja, but still . . . No, Sam. Don't let's get started on religion. We'll just spend the whole afternoon arguing again. Suppose I turn around and say Mohammed?

SAM: All right.

HALLY: You can't have them both on the same list!

SAM: Why not? You like Mohammed, I like Jesus.

HALLY: I *don't* like Mohammed. I never have. I was merely being hypothetical. As far as I'm concerned, the Koran is as bad as the Bible. No. Religion is out! I'm not going to waste my time again arguing with you about the existence of God. You know perfectly well I'm an atheist . . . and I've got homework to do.

270 **SAM:** Okay, I take him back.

HALLY: You've got time for one more name.

SAM: *(After thought.)* I've got one I know we'll agree on. A simple straightforward great Man of Magnitude . . . and no arguments. And *he* really *did* benefit all mankind.

HALLY: I wonder. After your last contribution I'm beginning to doubt whether anything in the way of an intellectual agreement is possible between the two of us. Who is he?

SAM: Guess.

275 **HALLY:** Socrates? Alexandre Dumas? Karl Marx? Dostoevsky? Nietzsche?

Sam shakes his head after each name.

Give me a clue.

SAM: The letter P is important . . .

HALLY: Plato!

SAM: . . . and his name begins with an F.

HALLY: I've got it. Freud and Psychology.

280 **SAM:** No. I didn't understand him.

HALLY: That makes two of us.

SAM: Think of mouldy apricot jam.

HALLY: *(After a delighted laugh.)* Penicillin and Sir Alexander Fleming! And the title of the book: *The Microbe Hunters. (Delighted.)* Splendid, Sam! Splendid. For once we are in total agreement. The major breakthrough in medical science in the Twentieth Century. If it wasn't for him, we might have lost the Second World War. It's deeply gratifying, Sam, to know that I haven't been wasting my time in talking to you. *(Strutting around proudly.)* Tolstoy may have educated his peasants, but I've educated you.

SAM: Standard Four to Standard Nine.

285 **HALLY:** Have we been at it as long as that?

SAM: Yep. And my first lesson was geography.

HALLY: *(Intrigued.)* Really? I don't remember.

SAM: My room there at the back of the old Jubilee Boarding House. I had just started working for your Mom. Little boy in short trousers walks in one afternoon and asks me seriously: "Sam, do you want to see South Africa?" Hey man! Sure I wanted to see South Africa!

HALLY: Was that me?

290 **SAM:** . . . So the next thing I'm looking at a map you had just done for homework. It was your first one and you were very proud of yourself.

HALLY: Go on.

SAM: Then came my first lesson. "Repeat after me, Sam: Gold in the Transvaal, mealies in the Free State, sugar in Natal and grapes in the Cape." I still know it!

HALLY: Well, I'll be buggered. So that's how it all started.

SAM: And your next map was one with all the rivers and the mountains they came from. The Orange, the Vaal, the Limpopo, the Zambezi . . .

295 **HALLY:** You've got a phenomenal memory!

SAM: You should be grateful. That is why you started passing your exams. You tried to be better than me.

They laugh together. Willie is attracted by the laughter and joins them.

HALLY: The old Jubilee Boarding House. Sixteen rooms with board and lodging, rent in advance and one week's notice. I haven't thought about it for donkey's years . . . and I don't think that's an accident. God, was I glad when we sold it and moved out. Those years are not remembered as the happiest ones of an unhappy childhood.

WILLIE: *(Knocking on the table and trying to imitate a woman's voice.)* "Hally, are you there?"

HALLY: Who's that supposed to be?

300 **WILLIE:** "What you doing in there, Hally? Come out at once!"

HALLY: *(To Sam.)* What's he talking about?

SAM: Don't you remember?

WILLIE: "Sam, Willie . . . is he in there with you boys?"

SAM: Hiding away in our room when your mother was looking for you.

305 **HALLY:** *(Another good laugh.)* Of course! I used to crawl and hide under your bed! But finish the story, Willie. Then what used to happen? You chaps would give the game away by telling her I was in there with you. So much for friendship.

SAM: We couldn't lie to her. She knew.

HALLY: Which meant I got another rowing for hanging around the "servants' quarters." I think I spent more time in there with you chaps than anywhere else in that dump. And do you blame me? Nothing but bloody misery wherever you went. Somebody was always complaining about the food, or my mother was having a fight with Micky Nash because she'd caught her with a petty officer in her room. Maud Meiring was another one. Remember those two? They were prostitutes, you know. Soldiers and sailors from the troopships. Bottom fell out of the business when the war ended. God, the flotsam and jetsam that life washed up on our shores! No joking, if it wasn't for your room, I would have been the first certified ten-year-old in medical history. Ja, the memories are coming back now. Walking home from school and thinking: "What can I do this afternoon?" Try out a few ideas, but sooner or later I'd end up in there with you fellows. I bet you I could still find my way to your room with my eyes closed. *(He does exactly that.)* Down the corridor . . . telephone on the

right, which my Mom keeps locked because somebody is using it on
the sly and not paying . . . past the kitchen and unappetizing cooking
smells . . . around the corner into the backyard, hold my breath again
because there are more smells coming when I pass your lavatory, then
into that little passageway, first door on the right and into your
room. How's that?

SAM: Good. But, as usual, you forgot to knock.

HALLY: Like that time I barged in and caught you and Cynthia . . . at it.
Remember? God, was I embarrassed! I didn't know what was going on
at first.

310 **SAM:**   Ja, that taught you a lesson.

HALLY: And about a lot more than knocking on doors, I'll have you
know, and I don't mean geography either. Hell, Sam, couldn't you
have waited until it was dark?

SAM: No.

HALLY: Was it that urgent?

SAM: Yes, and if you don't believe me, wait until your time comes.

315 **HALLY:**   No, thank you. I am not interested in girls. *(Back to his memories
. . . Using a few chairs he recreates the room as he lists the items.)* A gray
little room with a cold cement floor. Your bed against that wall . . .
and I now know why the mattress sags so much! . . . Willie's bed . . .
it's propped up on bricks because one leg is broken . . . that wobbly
little table with the washbasin and jug of water . . . Yes! . . . stuck
to the wall above it are some pin-up pictures from magazines. Joe
Louis . . .

WILLIE: Brown Bomber. World Title. *(Boxing pose.)* Three rounds and
knockout.[5]

HALLY: Against who?

SAM: Max Schmeling.

HALLY: Correct. I can also remember Fred Astaire and Ginger Rogers,
and Rita Hayworth in a bathing costume which always made me hot
and bothered when I looked at it. Under Willie's bed is an old
suitcase with all his clothes in a mess, which is why I never hide
there. Your things are neat and tidy in a trunk next to your bed, and
on it there is a picture of you and Cynthia in your ballroom clothes,
your first silver cup for third place in a competition and an old radio
which doesn't work anymore. Have I left out anything?

320 **SAM:**   No.

HALLY: Right, so much for the stage directions. Now the characters.
(Sam and Willie move to their appropriate positions in the bedroom.)

---

[5] In 1938, U.S. boxer Joe Louis (Joseph Louis Barrows; 1914–1981), the "Brown
Bomber," reclaimed the heavyweight title from German Max Schmeling (1905–   )
by a decisive knockout. Schmeling had won the title from Louis in 1936. Because of
the rise of Nazism and Hitler's well-known disdain for so-called impure races, Louis's
victory was highly symbolic.

Willie is in bed, under his blankets with his clothes on, complaining nonstop about something, but we can't make out a word of what he's saying because he's got his head under the blankets as well. You're on your bed trimming your toenails with a knife—not a very edifying sight—and as for me . . . What am I doing?

SAM: You're sitting on the floor giving Willie a lecture about being a good loser while you get the checker board and pieces ready for a game. Then you go to Willie's bed, pull off the blankets and make him play with you first because you know you're going to win, and that gives you the second game with me.

HALLY: And you certainly were a bad loser, Willie!

WILLIE: Haai!

325 **HALLY:**   Wasn't he, Sam? And so slow! A game with you almost took the whole afternoon. Thank God I gave up trying to teach you how to play chess.

WILLIE: You and Sam cheated.

HALLY: I never saw Sam cheat, and mine were mostly the mistakes of youth.

WILLIE: Then how is it you two was always winning?

HALLY: Have you ever considered the possibility, Willie, that it was because we were better than you?

330 **WILLIE:**   Every time better?

HALLY: Not every time. There were occasions when we deliberately let you win a game so that you would stop sulking and go on playing with us. Sam used to wink at me when you weren't looking to show me it was time to let you win.

WILLIE: So then you two didn't play fair.

HALLY: It was for your benefit, Mr. Malopo, which is more than being fair. It was an act of self-sacrifice. *(To Sam.)* But you know what my best memory is, don't you?

SAM: No.

335 **HALLY:**   Come on, guess. If your memory is so good, you must remember it as well.

SAM: We got up to a lot of tricks in there, Hally.

HALLY: This one was special, Sam.

SAM: I'm listening.

HALLY: It started off looking like another of those useless nothing-to-do afternoons. I'd already been down to Main Street looking for adventure, but nothing had happened. I didn't feel like climbing trees in the Donkin Park or pretending I was a private eye and following a stranger . . . so as usual: See what's cooking in Sam's room. This time it was you on the floor. You had two thin pieces of wood and you were smoothing them down with a knife. It didn't look particularly interesting, but when I asked you what you were doing, you just said, "Wait and see, Hally. Wait . . . and see" . . . in that secret sort of way of yours, so I knew there was a surprise coming. You teased me, you bugger, by being deliberately slow and not answering my questions!

Sam laughs.

And whistling while you worked away! God, it was infuriating! I could have brained you! It was only when you tied them together in a cross and put that down on the brown paper that I realized what you were doing. "Sam is making a kite?" And when I asked you and you said "Yes" . . . ! (*Shaking his head with disbelief.*) The sheer audacity of it took my breath away. I mean, seriously, what the hell does a black man know about flying a kite? I'll be honest with you, Sam, I had no hopes for it. If you think I was excited and happy, you got another guess coming. In fact, I was shit-scared that we were going to make fools of ourselves. When we left the boarding house to go up onto the hill, I was praying quietly that there wouldn't be any other kids around to laugh at us.

340 **SAM:**   (*Enjoying the memory as much as Hally.*) Ja, I could see that.

HALLY: I made it obvious, did I?

SAM: Ja. You refused to carry it.

HALLY: Do you blame me? Can you remember what the poor thing looked like? Tomato-box wood and brown paper! Flour and water for glue! Two of my mother's old stockings for a tail, and then all those bits and pieces of string you made me tie together so that we could fly it! Hell, no, that was now only asking for a miracle to happen.

SAM: Then the big argument when I told you to hold the string and run with it when I let go.

345 **HALLY:**   I was prepared to run, all right, but straight back to the boarding house.

SAM: (*Knowing what's coming.*) So what happened?

HALLY: Come on, Sam, you remember as well as I do.

SAM: I want to hear it from you.

Hally pauses. He wants to be as accurate as possible.

HALLY: You went a little distance from me down the hill, you held it up ready to let it go. . . . "This is it," I thought. "Like everything else in my life, here comes another fiasco." Then you shouted, "Go, Hally!" and I started to run. (*Another pause.*) I don't know how to describe it, Sam. Ja! The miracle happened! I was running, waiting for it to crash to the ground, but instead suddenly there was something alive behind me at the end of the string, tugging at it as if it wanted to be free. I looked back . . . (*Shakes his head.*) . . . I still can't believe my eyes. It was flying! Looping around and trying to climb even higher into the sky. You shouted to me to let it have more string. I did, until there was none left and I was just holding that piece of wood we had tied it to. You came up and joined me. You were laughing.

350 **SAM:**   So were you. And shouting, "It works, Sam! We've done it!"

HALLY: And we had! I was so proud of us! It was the most splendid thing I had ever seen. I wished there were hundreds of kids around to watch us. The part that scared me, though, was when you showed me how to make it dive down to the ground and then just when it was on the point of crashing, swoop up again!

SAM: You didn't want to try yourself.

HALLY: Of course not! I would have been suicidal if anything had happened to it. Watching you do it made me nervous enough. I was quite happy just to see it up there with its tail fluttering behind it. You left me after that, didn't you? You explained how to get it down, we tied it to the bench so that I could sit and watch it, and you went away. I wanted you to stay, you know. I was a little scared of having to look after it by myself.

SAM: *(Quietly.)* I had work to do, Hally.

355 **HALLY:** It was sort of sad bringing it down, Sam. And it looked sad again when it was lying there on the ground. Like something that had lost its soul. Just tomato-box wood, brown paper and two of my mother's old stockings! But, hell, I'll never forget that first moment when I saw it up there. I had a stiff neck the next day from looking up so much.

Sam laughs. Hally turns to him with a question he never thought of asking before.

Why did you make that kite, Sam?

SAM: *(Evenly.)* I can't remember.

HALLY: Truly?

SAM: Too long ago, Hally.

HALLY: Ja, I suppose it was. It's time for another one, you know.

360 **SAM:** Why do you say that?

HALLY: Because it feels like that. Wouldn't be a good day to fly it, though.

SAM: No. You can't fly kites on rainy days.

HALLY: *(He studies Sam. Their memories have made him conscious of the man's presence in his life.)* How old are you, Sam?

SAM: Two score and five.

365 **HALLY:** Strange, isn't it?

SAM: What?

HALLY: Me and you.

SAM: What's strange about it?

HALLY: Little white boy in short trousers and a black man old enough to be his father flying a kite. It's not every day you see that.

370 **SAM:** But why strange? Because the one is white and the other black?

HALLY: I don't know. Would have been just as strange, I suppose, if it had been me and my Dad . . . cripple man and a little boy! Nope! There's no chance of me flying a kite without it being strange. *(Simple* *statement of fact—no self-pity.)* There's a nice little short story there. "The Kite-Flyers." But we'd have to find a twist in the ending.

SAM: Twist?

HALLY: Yes. Something unexpected. The way it ended with us was too straightforward . . . me on the bench and you going back to work. There's no drama in that.

WILLIE: And me?

375 **HALLY:** You?

WILLIE: Yes me.

HALLY: You want to get into the story as well, do you? I got it! Change the title: "Afternoons in Sam's Room" . . . expand it and tell all the stories. It's on its way to being a novel. Our days in the old Jubilee. Sad in a way that they're over. I almost wish we were still in that little room.

SAM: We're still together.

HALLY: That's true. It's just that life felt the right size in there . . . not too big and not too small. Wasn't so hard to work up a bit of courage. It's got so bloody complicated since then.

The telephone rings. Sam answers it.

380 **SAM:** St. George's Park Tea Room . . . Hello, Madam . . . Yes, Madam, he's here . . . Hally, it's your mother.

HALLY: Where is she phoning from?

SAM: Sounds like the hospital. It's a public telephone.

HALLY: *(Relieved.)* You see! I told you. *(The telephone.)* Hello, Mom . . . Yes . . . Yes no fine. Everything's under control here. How's things with poor old Dad? . . . Has he had a bad turn? . . . What? . . . Oh, God! . . . Yes, Sam told me, but I was sure he'd made a mistake. But what's this all about, Mom? He didn't look at all good last night. How can he get better so quickly? . . . Then very obviously you must say no. Be firm with him. You're the boss. . . . You know what it's going to be like if he comes home. . . . Well, then, don't blame me when I fail my exams at the end of the year. . . . Yes! How am I expected to be fresh for school when I spend half the night massaging his gammy leg? . . . So am I! . . . So tell him a white lie. Say Dr. Colley wants more X-rays of his stump. Or bribe him. We'll sneak in double tots of brandy in future. . . . What? . . . Order him to get back into bed at once! If he's going to behave like a child, treat him like one. . . . All right, Mom! I was just trying to . . . I'm sorry. . . . I said I'm sorry. . . . Quick, give me your number. I'll phone you back. *(He hangs up and waits a few seconds.)* Here we go again! *(He dials.)* I'm sorry, Mom. . . . Okay . . . But now listen to me carefully. All it needs is for you to put your foot down. Don't take no for an answer. . . . Did you hear me? And whatever you do, don't discuss it with him. . . . Because I'm frightened you'll give in to him. . . . Yes,

Sam gave me lunch. . . . I ate all of it! . . . No, Mom not a soul. It's still raining here. . . . Right, I'll tell them. I'll just do some homework and then lock up. . . . But remember now, Mom. Don't listen to anything he says. And phone me back and let me know what happens. . . . . Okay. Bye, Mom. *(He hangs up. The men are staring at him.)* My Mom says that when you're finished with the floors you must do the windows. *(Pause.)* Don't misunderstand me, chaps. All I want is for him to get better. And if he was, I'd be the first person to say: "Bring him home." But he's not, and we can't give him the medical care and attention he needs at home. That's what hospitals are there for. *(Brusquely.)* So don't just stand there! Get on with it!

Sam clears Hally's table.

You heard right. My Dad wants to go home.

SAM: Is he better?

385 **HALLY:**   *(Sharply.)* No! How the hell can he be better when last night he was groaning with pain? This is not an age of miracles!

SAM: Then he should stay in hospital.

HALLY: *(Seething with irritation and frustration.)* Tell me something I don't know, Sam. What the hell do you think I was saying to my Mom? All I can say is fuck-it-all.

SAM: I'm sure he'll listen to your Mom.

HALLY: You don't know what she's up against. He's already packed his shaving kit and pajamas and is sitting on his bed with his crutches, dressed and ready to go. I know him when he gets in that mood. If she tries to reason with him, we've had it. She's no match for him when it comes to a battle of words. He'll tie her up in knots. *(Trying to hide his true feelings.)*

390 **SAM:**   I suppose it gets lonely for him in there.

HALLY: With all the patients and nurses around? Regular visits from the Salvation Army? Balls! It's ten times worse for him at home. I'm at school and my mother is here in the business all day.

SAM: He's at least got you at night.

HALLY: *(Before he can stop himself.)* And we've got him! Please! I don't want to talk about it anymore. *(Unpacks his school case, slamming down books on the table.)* Life is just a plain bloody mess, that's all. And people are fools.

SAM: Come on, Hally.

395 **HALLY:**   Yes, they are! They bloody well deserve what they get.

SAM: Then don't complain.

HALLY: Don't try to be clever, Sam. It doesn't suit you. Anybody who thinks there's nothing wrong with this world needs to have his head examined. Just when things are going along all right, without fail someone or something will come along and spoil everything. Somebody should write that down as a fundamental law of the

Universe. The principle of perpetual disappointment. If there is a
God who created this world, he should scrap it and try again.

Sam: All right, Hally, all right. What you got for homework?

Hally: Bullshit, as usual. (*Opens an exercise book and reads.*) "Write five
hundred words describing an annual event of cultural or historical
significance."

400 **Sam:**   That should be easy enough for you.

Hally: And also plain bloody boring. You know what he wants, don't
you? One of their useless old ceremonies. The commemoration of the
landing of the 1820 Settlers,[6] or if it's going to be culture, Carols by
Candlelight every Christmas.

Sam: It's an impressive sight. Make a good description, Hally. All those
candles glowing in the dark and the people singing hymns.

Hally: And it's called religious hysteria. (*Intense irritation.*) Please, Sam!
Just leave me alone and let me get on with it. I'm not in the mood for
games this afternoon. And remember my Mom's orders . . . you're to
help Willie with the windows. Come on now, I don't want any more
nonsense in here.

Sam: Okay, Hally, okay.

*Hally settles down to his homework; determined preparations . . . pen, ruler, ex-
ercise book, dictionary, another cake . . . all of which will lead to nothing.*

(*Sam waltzes over to Willie and starts to replace tables and chairs. He
practices a ballroom step while doing so. Willie watches. When Sam is
finished, Willie tries.*) Good! But just a little bit quicker on the turn
and only move in to her after she's crossed over. What about this
one?

Another step. When Sam is finished, Willie again has a go.

Much better. See what happens when you just relax and enjoy
yourself? Remember that in two weeks' time and you'll be all right.

405 **Willie:**   But I haven't got partner, Boet Sam.

Sam: Maybe Hilda will turn up tonight.

Willie: No, Boet Sam. (*Reluctantly.*) I gave her a good hiding.

Sam: You mean a bad one.

Willie: Good bad one.

410 **Sam:**   Then you mustn't complain either. Now you pay the price for
losing your temper.

Willie: I also pay two pounds ten shilling entrance fee.

Sam: They'll refund you if you withdraw now.

Willie: (*Appalled.*) You mean, don't dance?

---

6 In 1820 the British government paid for 4,000 Britons to travel to the Cape and allot-
ted each family 100 acres.

SAM: Yes.

415 **WILLIE:**   No! I wait too long and I practice too hard. If I find me new partner, you think I can be ready in two weeks? I ask Madam for my leave now and we practice every day.

SAM: Quickstep non-stop for two weeks. World record, Willie, but you'll be mad at the end.

WILLIE: No jokes, Boet Sam.

SAM: I'm not joking.

WILLIE: So then what?

420 **SAM:**   Find Hilda. Say you're sorry and promise you won't beat her again.

WILLIE: No.

SAM: Then withdraw. Try again next year.

WILLIE: No.

SAM: Then I give up.

425 **WILLIE:**   Haaikona, Boet Sam, you can't.

SAM: What do you mean, I can't? I'm telling you: I give up.

WILLIE: *(Adamant.)* No! *(Accusingly.)* It was you who start me ballroom dancing.

SAM: So?

WILLIE: Before that I use to be happy. And is you and Miriam who bring me to Hilda and say here's partner for you.

430 **SAM:**   What are you saying, Willie?

WILLIE: You!

SAM: But me what? To blame?

WILLIE: Yes.

SAM: Willie . . . ? *(Bursts into laughter.)*

435 **WILLIE:**   And now all you do is make jokes at me. You wait. When Miriam leaves you is my turn to laugh. Ha! Ha! Ha!

SAM: *(He can't take Willie seriously any longer.)* She can leave me tonight! I know what to do. *(Bowing before an imaginary partner.)* May I have the pleasure? *(He dances and sings.)*
"Just a fellow with his pillow . . .
Dancin' like a willow . . .
In an autumn breeze . . ."

WILLIE: There you go again!

Sam goes on dancing and singing.

Boet Sam!

SAM: There's the answer to your problem! Judges' announcement in two weeks' time: "Ladies and gentlemen, the winner in the open section . . . Mr. Willie Malopo and his pillow!"

This is too much for a now really angry Willie. He goes for Sam, but the latter is too quick for him and puts Hally's table between the two of them.

HALLY: *(Exploding.)* For Christ's sake, you two!

440 **WILLIE:**   *(Still trying to get at Sam.)* I donner you, Sam! Struesgod!

SAM: *(Still laughing.)* Sorry, Willie . . . Sorry . . .

HALLY: Sam! Willie! *(Grabs his ruler and gives Willie a vicious whack on the bum.)* How the hell am I supposed to concentrate with the two of you behaving like bloody children!

WILLIE: Hit him too!

HALLY: Shut up, Willie.

445 **WILLIE:** He started jokes again.

HALLY: Get back to your work. You too, Sam. *(His ruler.)* Do you want another one, Willie?

Sam and Willie return to their work. Hally uses the opportunity to escape from his unsuccessful attempt at homework. He struts around like a little despot, ruler in hand, giving vent to his anger and frustration.

Suppose a customer had walked in then? Or the Park Superintendent. And seen the two of you behaving like a pair of hooligans. That would have been the end of my mother's license, you know. And your jobs! Well, this is the end of it. From now on there will be no more of your ballroom nonsense in here. This is a business establishment, not a bloody New Brighton dancing school. I've been far too lenient with the two of you. *(Behind the counter for a green cool drink and a dollop of ice cream. He keeps up his tirade as he prepares it.)* But what really makes me bitter is that I allow you chaps a little freedom in here when business is bad and what do you do with it? The foxtrot! Specially you, Sam. There's more to life than trotting around a dance floor and I thought at least you knew it.

SAM: It's a harmless pleasure, Hally. It doesn't hurt anybody.

HALLY: It's also a rather simple one, you know.

SAM: You reckon so? Have you ever tried?

450 **HALLY:** Of course not.

SAM: Why don't you? Now.

HALLY: What do you mean? Me dance?

SAM: Yes. I'll show you a simple step—the waltz—then you try it.

HALLY: What will that prove?

455 **SAM:** That it might not be as easy as you think.

HALLY: I didn't say it was easy. I said it was simple—like in simple-minded, meaning mentally retarded. You can't exactly say it challenges the intellect.

SAM: It does other things.

HALLY: Such as?

SAM: Make people happy.

460 **HALLY:** *(The glass in his hand.)* So do American cream sodas with ice cream. For God's sake, Sam, you're not asking me to take ballroom dancing serious, are you?

SAM: Yes.

HALLY: *(Sigh of defeat.)* Oh, well, so much for trying to give you a decent education. I've obviously achieved nothing.

SAM: You still haven't told me what's wrong with admiring something that's beautiful and then trying to do it yourself.

HALLY: Nothing. But we happen to be talking about a foxtrot, not a thing of beauty.

465 **SAM:** But that is just what I'm saying. If you were to see two champions doing, two masters of the art . . . !

HALLY: Oh, God, I give up. So now it's also art!

SAM: Ja.

HALLY: There's a limit, Sam. Don't confuse art and entertainment.

SAM: So then what is art?

470 **HALLY:** You want a definition?

SAM: Ja.

HALLY: *(He realizes he has got to be careful. He gives the matter a lot of thought before answering.)* Philosophers have been trying to do that for centuries. What is Art? What is Life? But basically I suppose it's . . . the giving of meaning to matter.

SAM: Nothing to do with beautiful?

HALLY: It goes beyond that. It's the giving of form to the formless.

475 **SAM:** Ja, well, maybe it's not art, then. But I still say it's beautiful.

HALLY: I'm sure the word you mean to use is entertaining.

SAM: *(Adamant.)* No. Beautiful. And if you want proof, come along to the Centenary Hall in New Brighton in two weeks' time.

The mention of the Centenary Hall draws Willie over to them.

HALLY: What for? I've seen the two of you prancing around in here often enough.

SAM: *(He laughs.)* This isn't the real thing, Hally. We're just playing around in here.

480 **HALLY:** So? I can use my imagination.

SAM: And what do you get?

HALLY: A lot of people dancing around and having a so-called good time.

SAM: That all?

HALLY: Well, basically it is that, surely.

485 **SAM:** No, it isn't. Your imagination hasn't helped you at all. There's a lot more to it than that. We're getting ready for the championships, Hally, not just another dance. There's going to be a lot of people, all right, and they're going to have a good time, but they'll only be spectators, sitting around and watching. It's just the competitors out there on the dance floor. Party decorations and fancy lights all around the walls! The ladies in beautiful evening dresses!

HALLY: My mother's got one of those, Sam, and quite frankly, it's an embarrassment every time she wears it.

SAM: *(Undeterred.)* Your imagination left out the excitement.

Hally scoffs.

Oh, yes. The finalists are not going to be out there just to have a good time. One of those couples will be the 1950 Eastern Province Champions. And your imagination left out the music.

WILLIE: Mr. Elijah Gladman Guzana and his Orchestral Jazzonions.

SAM: The sound of the big band, Hally. Trombone, trumpet, tenor and alto sax. And then, finally, your imagination also left out the climax of the evening when the dancing is finished, the judges have stopped whispering among themselves and the Master of Ceremonies collects their scorecards and goes up onto the stage to announce the winners.

490 **HALLY:**   All right. So you make it sound like a bit of a do. It's an occasion. Satisfied?

SAM: *(Victory.)* So you admit that!

HALLY: Emotionally yes, intellectually no.

SAM: Well, I don't know what you mean by that, all I'm telling you is that it is going to be *the* event of the year in New Brighton. It's been sold out for two weeks already. There's only standing room left. We've got competitors coming from Kingwilliamstown, East London, Port Alfred.

Hally starts pacing thoughtfully.

HALLY: Tell me a bit more.

495 **SAM:**   I thought you weren't interested . . . intellectually.

HALLY: *(Mysteriously.)* I've got my reasons.

SAM: What do you want to know?

HALLY: It takes place every year?

SAM: Yes. But only every third year in New Brighton. It's East London's turn to have the championships next year.

500 **HALLY:**   Which, I suppose, makes it an even more significant event.

SAM: Ah ha! We're getting somewhere. Our "occasion" is now a "significant event."

HALLY: I wonder.

SAM: What?

HALLY: I wonder if I would get away with it.

505 **SAM:**   But what?

HALLY: *(To the table and his exercise book.)* "Write five hundred words describing an annual event of cultural or historical significance." Would I be stretching poetic license a little too far if I called your ballroom championships a cultural event?

SAM: You mean . . . ?

HALLY: You think we could get five hundred words out of it, Sam?

SAM: Victor Sylvester has written a whole book on ballroom dancing.

510 **WILLIE:**   You going to write about it, Master Hally?

HALLY: Yes, gentlemen, that is precisely what I am considering doing. Old Doc Bromely—he's my English teacher—is going to argue with me, of course. He doesn't like natives. But I'll point out to him that in strict anthropological terms the culture of a primitive black society includes its dancing and singing. To put my thesis in a nutshell: The war-dance has been replaced by the waltz. But it still amounts to the same thing: the release of primitive emotions through movement. Shall we give it a go?

SAM: I'm ready.

WILLIE: Me also.

HALLY: Ha! This will teach the old bugger a lesson. (*Decision taken.*) Right. Let's get ourselves organized. (*This means another cake on the table. He sits.*) I think you've given me enough general atmosphere, Sam, but to build the tension and suspense I need facts. (*Pencil poised.*)

515 **WILLIE:**   Give him facts, Boet Sam.

HALLY: What you called the climax . . . how many finalists?

SAM: Six couples.

HALLY: (*Making notes.*) Go on. Give me the picture.

SAM: Spectators seated right around the hall. (*Willie becomes a spectator.*)

520 **HALLY:**   . . . and it's a full house.

SAM: At one end, on the stage, Gladman and his Orchestral Jazzonions. At the other end is a long table with the three judges. The six finalists go onto the dance floor and take up their positions. When they are ready and the spectators have settled down, the Master of Ceremonies goes to the microphone. To start with, he makes some jokes to get the people laughing . . .

HALLY: Good touch! (*As he writes.*) ". . . creating a relaxed atmosphere which will change to one of tension and drama as the climax is approached."

SAM: (*Onto a chair to act out the M.C.*) "Ladies and gentlemen, we come now to the great moment you have all been waiting for this evening. . . . The finals of the 1950 Eastern Province Open Ballroom Dancing Championships. But first let me introduce the finalists! Mr. and Mrs. Welcome Tchabalala from Kingwilliamstown . . ."

WILLIE: (*He applauds after every name.*) Is when the people clap their hands and whistle and make a lot of noise, Master Hally.

525 **SAM:**   "Mr. Mulligan Njikelane and Miss Nomhle Nkonyeni of Grahamstown; Mr. and Mrs. Norman Nchinga from Port Alfred; Mr. Fats Bokolane and Miss Dina Plaatjies from East London; Mr. Sipho Dugu and Mrs. Mable Magada from Peddie; and from New Brighton our very own Mr. Willie Malopo and Miss Hilda Samuels."

Willie can't believe his ears. He abandons his role as spectator and scrambles into position as a finalist.

WILLIE: Relaxed and ready to romance!

SAM: The applause dies down. When everybody is silent, Gladman lifts up his sax, nods at the Orchestral Jazzonions . . .

WILLIE: Play the jukebox please, Boet Sam!

SAM: I also only got bus fare, Willie.

530 **HALLY:**   Hold it, everybody. (*Heads for the cash register behind the counter.*) How much is in the till, Sam?

SAM: Three shillings. Hally . . . your Mom counted it before she left.

Hally hesitates.

HALLY: Sorry, Willie. You know how she carried on the last time I did it. We'll just have to pool our combined imaginations and hope for the best. (*Returns to the table.*) Back to work. How are the points scored, Sam?

SAM: Maximum of ten points each for individual style, deportment, rhythm and general appearance.

WILLIE: Must I start?

535 **HALLY:**   Hold it for a second, Willie. And penalties?

SAM: For what?

HALLY: For doing something wrong. Say you stumble or bump into somebody . . . do they take off any points?

SAM: (*Aghast.*) Hally . . . !

HALLY: When you're dancing. If you and your partner collide into another couple.

Hally can get no further. Sam has collapsed with laughter. He explains to Willie.

540 **SAM:**   If me and Miriam bump into you and Hilda . . .

Willie joins him in another good laugh.

Hally, Hally . . . !

HALLY: (*Perplexed.*) Why? What did I say?

SAM: There's no collisions out there, Hally. Nobody trips or stumbles or bumps into anybody else. That's what that moment is all about. To be one of those finalists on that dance floor is like . . . like being in a dream about a world in which accidents don't happen.

HALLY: (*Genuinely moved by Sam's image.*) Jesus, Sam! That's beautiful!

WILLIE: (*Can endure waiting no longer.*) I'm starting! (*Willie dances while Sam talks.*)

545 **SAM:**   Of course it is. That's what I've been trying to say to you all afternoon. And it's beautiful because that is what we want life to be like. But instead, like you said, Hally, we're bumping into each other all the time. Look at the three of us this afternoon: I've bumped into Willie, the two of us have bumped into you, you've bumped into your mother, she bumping into your Dad. . . . None of us knows the steps and there's no music playing. And it doesn't stop with us. The whole world is doing it all the time. Open a newspaper and what do you read? America has bumped into Russia, England is bumping into India, rich man bumps into poor man. Those are big collisions, Hally. They make for a lot of bruises. People get hurt in all that bumping, and we're sick and tired of it now. It's been going on for too long. Are

we never going to get it right? . . . . Learn to dance life like champions
instead of always being just a bunch of beginners at it?

HALLY: *(Deep and sincere admiration of the man.)* You've got a vision,
Sam!

SAM: Not just me. What I'm saying to you is that everybody's got it.
That's why there's only standing room left for the Centenary Hall in
two weeks' time. For as long as the music lasts, we are going to see six
couples get it right, the way we want life to be.

HALLY: But is that the best we can do, Sam . . . watch six finalists
dreaming about the way it should be?

SAM: I don't know. But it starts with that. Without the dream we won't
know what we're going for. And anyway I reckon there are a few
people who have got past just dreaming about it and are trying for
something real. Remember that thing we read once in the paper about
the Mahatma Gandhi? Going without food to stop those riots in
India?

550 **HALLY:**   You're right. He certainly was trying to teach people to get the
steps right.

SAM: And the Pope.

HALLY: Yes, he's another one. Our old General Smuts as well, you know.
He's also out there dancing. You know, Sam, when you come to think
of it, that's what the United Nations boils down to . . . a dancing
school for politicians!

SAM: And let's hope they learn.

HALLY: *(A little surge of hope.)* You're right. We mustn't despair. Maybe
there's some hope for mankind after all. Keep it up, Willie. *(Back to
his table with determination.)* This is a lot bigger than I thought. So
what have we got? Yes, our title: "A World Without Collisions."

555 **SAM:**   That sounds good! "A World Without Collisions."

HALLY: Subtitle: "Global Politics on the Dance Floor." No. A bit too
heavy, hey? What about "Ballroom Dancing as a Political Vision"?

The telephone rings. Sam answers it.

SAM: St. George's Park Tea Room . . . Yes, Madam . . . Hally, it's your
Mom.

HALLY: *(Back to reality.)* Oh, God, yes! I'd forgotten all about that. Shit!
Remember my words, Sam? Just when you're enjoying yourself,
someone or something will come along and wreck everything.

SAM: You haven't heard what she's got to say yet.

560 **HALLY:**   Public telephone?

SAM: No.

HALLY: Does she sound happy or unhappy?

SAM: I couldn't tell. *(Pause.)* She's waiting, Hally.

HALLY: *(To the telephone.)* Hello, Mom . . . No, everything is okay here.
Just doing my homework. . . . What's your news? . . . You've what?
. . . *(Pause. He takes the receiver away from his ear for a few seconds. In*

the course of Hally's telephone conversation, Sam and Willie discreetly position the stacked tables and chairs. Hally places the receiver back to his ear.) Yes, I'm still here. Oh, well, I give up now. Why did you do it, Mom? . . . Well, I just hope you know what you've let us in for. . . . *(Loudly.)* I said I hope you know what you've let us in for! It's the end of the peace and quiet we've been having. *(Softly.)* Where is he? *(Normal voice.)* He can't hear us from in there. But for God's sake, Mom, what happened? I told you to be firm with him. . . . Then you and the nurses should have held him down, taken his crutches away. . . . I know only too well he's my father! . . . I'm not being disrespectful, but I'm sick and tired of emptying stinking chamberpots full of phlegm and piss. . . . Yes, I do! When you're not there, he asks *me* to do it. . . . If you really want to know the truth, that's why I've got no appetite for my food. . . . Yes! There's a lot of things you don't know about. For your information, I still haven't got that science textbook I need. And you know why? He borrowed the money you gave me for it. . . . Because I didn't want to start another fight between you two. . . . He says that every time. . . . All right, Mom! *(Viciously.)* Then just remember to start hiding your bag away again, because he'll be at your purse before long for money for booze. And when he's well enough to come down here, you better keep an eye on the till as well, because that is also going to develop a leak. . . . Then don't complain to me when he starts his old tricks. . . . Yes, you do. I get it from you on one side and from him on the other, and it makes life hell for me. I'm not going to be the peacemaker anymore. I'm warning you now: when the two of you start fighting again, I'm leaving home. . . . Mom, if you start crying, I'm going to put down the receiver. . . . Okay . . . *(Lowering his voice to a vicious whisper.)* Okay, Mom. I heard you. *(Desperate.)* No. . . . Because I don't want to. I'll see him when I get home! Mom! . . . *(Pause. When he speaks again, his tone changes completely. It is not simply pretense. We sense a genuine emotional conflict.)* Welcome home, chum! . . . What's that? . . . Don't be silly, Dad. You being home is just about the best news in the world. . . . I bet you are. Bloody depressing there with everybody going on about their ailments, hey! . . . How you feeling? . . . Good . . . Here as well, pal. Coming down cats and dogs. . . . That's right. Just the day for a kip and a toss in your old Uncle Ned. . . . Everything's just hunky-dory on my side, Dad. . . . Well, to start with, there's a nice pile of comics for you on the counter. . . . Yes, old Kemple brought them in. *Batman and Robin, Submariner* . . . just your cup of tea . . . I will. . . . Yes, we'll spin a few yarns tonight. . . . Okay, chum, see you in a little while. . . . No, I promise. I'll come straight home. . . . *(Pause—his mother comes back on the phone.)* Mom? Okay. I'll lock up now. . . . What? . . . Oh, the brandy . . . Yes, I'll remember! . . . I'll put it in my suitcase now, for God's sake. I know well enough what will happen if he doesn't get it. . . . *(Places a bottle of brandy on the counter.)* I was kind to him, Mom. I didn't say anything nasty! . . . All right. Bye. *(End of telephone conversation. A desolate Hally doesn't move. A strained silence.)*

565 **SAM:**   *(Quietly.)* That sounded like a bad bump, Hally.

HALLY: *(Having a hard time controlling his emotions. He speaks carefully.)* Mind your own business, Sam.

SAM: Sorry. I wasn't trying to interfere. Shall we carry on? Hally? *(He indicates the exercise book. No response from Hally.)*

WILLIE: *(Also trying.)* Tell him about when they give out the cups, Boet Sam.

SAM: Ja! That's another big moment. The presentation of the cups after the winners have been announced. You've got to put that in.

Still no response from Hally.

570 **WILLIE:**   A big silver one, Master Hally, called floating trophy for the champions.

SAM: We always invite some big-shot personality to hand them over. Guest of honor this year is going to be His Holiness Bishop Jabulani of the All African Free Zionist Church.

Hally gets up abruptly, goes to his table and tears up the page he was writing on.

HALLY: So much for a bloody world without collisions.

SAM: Too bad. It was on its way to being a good composition.

HALLY: Let's stop bullshitting ourselves, Sam.

575 **SAM:**   Have we been doing that?

HALLY: Yes! That's what all our talk about a decent world has been . . . just so much bullshit.

SAM: We did say it was still only a dream.

HALLY: And a bloody useless one at that. Life's a fuck-up and it's never going to change.

SAM: Ja, maybe that's true.

580 **HALLY:**   There's no maybe about it. It's a blunt and brutal fact. All we've done this afternoon is waste our time.

SAM: Not if we'd got your homework done.

HALLY: I don't give a shit about my homework, so, for Christ's sake, just shut up about it. *(Slamming books viciously into his school case.)* Hurry up now and finish your work. I want to lock up and get out of here. *(Pause.)* And then go where? Home-sweet-fucking-home. Jesus, I hate that word.

Hally goes to the counter to put the brandy bottle and comics in his school case. After a moment's hesitation, he smashes the bottle of brandy. He abandons all further attempts to hide his feelings. Sam and Willie work away as unobtrusively as possible.

Do you want to know what is really wrong with your lovely little dream, Sam? It's not just that we are all bad dancers. That does happen to be perfectly true, but there's more to it than just that. You left out the cripples.

SAM: Hally!

HALLY: *(Now totally reckless.)* Ja! Can't leave them out, Sam. That's why we always end up on our backsides on the dance floor. They're also out there dancing . . . like a bunch of broken spiders trying to do the quickstep! *(An ugly attempt at laughter.)* When you come to think of it, it's a bloody comical sight. I mean, it's bad enough on two legs . . . but one and a pair of crutches! Hell, no, Sam. That's guaranteed to turn that dance floor into a shambles. Why you shaking your head? Picture it, man. For once this afternoon let's use our imaginations sensibly.

585 **SAM:**   Be careful, Hally.

HALLY: Of what? The truth? I seem to be the only one around here who is prepared to face it. We've had the pretty dream, it's time now to wake up and have a good long look at the way things really are. Nobody knows the steps, there's no music, the cripples are also out there tripping up everybody and trying to get into the act, and it's all called the All-Comers-How-to-Make-a-Fuckup-of-Life Championships. *(Another ugly laugh.)* Hang on, Sam! The best bit is still coming. Do you know what the winner's trophy is? A beautiful big chamber-pot with roses on the side, and it's full to the brim with piss. And guess who I think is going to be this year's winner.

SAM: *(Almost shouting.)* Stop now!

HALLY: *(Suddenly appalled by how far he has gone.)* Why?

SAM: Hally? It's your father you're talking about.

590 **HALLY:**   So?

SAM: Do you know what you've been saying?

Hally can't answer. He is rigid with shame. Sam speaks to him sternly.

No, Hally, you mustn't do it. Take back those words and ask for forgiveness! It's a terrible sin for a son to mock his father with jokes like that. You'll be punished if you carry on. Your father is your father, even if he is a . . . cripple man.

WILLIE: Yes, Master Hally. Is true what Sam say.

SAM: I understand how you are feeling, Hally, but even so . . .

HALLY: No, you don't!

595 **SAM:**   I think I do.

HALLY: And I'm telling you you don't. Nobody does. *(Speaking carefully as his shame turns to rage at Sam.)* It's your turn to be careful, Sam. Very careful! You're treading on dangerous ground. Leave me and my father alone.

SAM: I'm not the one who's been saying things about him.

HALLY: What goes on between me and my Dad is none of your business!

SAM: Then don't tell me about it. If that's all you've got to say about him, I don't want to hear.

For a moment Hally is at loss for a response.

600 **HALLY:** Just get on with your bloody work and shut up.
SAM: Swearing at me won't help you.
HALLY: Yes, it does! Mind your own fucking business and shut up!
SAM: Okay. If that's the way you want it, I'll stop trying.

He turns away. This infuriates Hally even more.

HALLY: Good. Because what you've been trying to do is meddle in something you know nothing about. All that concerns you in here, Sam, is to try and do what you get paid for—keep the place clean and serve the customers. In plain words, just get on with your job. My mother is right. She's always warning me about allowing you to get too familiar. Well, this time you've gone too far. It's going to stop right now.

No response from Sam.

You're only a servant in here, and don't forget it.

Still no response. Hally is trying hard to get one.

And as far as my father is concerned, all you need to remember is that he is your boss.
605 **SAM:** *(Needled at last.)* No, he isn't. I get paid by your mother.
HALLY: Don't argue with me, Sam!
SAM: Then don't say he's my boss.
HALLY: He's a white man and that's good enough for you.
SAM: I'll try to forget you said that.
610 **HALLY:** Don't! Because you won't be doing me a favor if you do. I'm telling you to remember it.

A pause. Sam pulls himself together and makes one last effort.

SAM: Hally, Hally . . . ! Come on now. Let's stop before it's too late. You're right. We *are* on dangerous ground. If we're not careful, somebody is going to get hurt.
HALLY: It won't be me.
SAM: Don't be so sure.
HALLY: I don't know what you're talking about, Sam.
615 **SAM:** Yes, you do.
HALLY: *(Furious.)* Jesus, I wish you would stop trying to tell me what I do and what I don't know.

Sam gives up. He turns to Willie.

SAM: Let's finish up.
HALLY: Don't turn your back on me! I haven't finished talking.

He grabs Sam by the arm and tries to make him turn around. Sam reacts with a flash of anger.

SAM: Don't do that, Hally! *(Facing the boy.)* All right, I'm listening. Well? What do you want to say to me?

620 **HALLY:**   *(Pause as Hally looks for something to say.)* To begin with, why don't you also start calling me Master Harold, like Willie.

SAM: Do you mean that?

HALLY: Why the hell do you think I said it?

SAM: And if I don't.

HALLY: You might just lose your job.

625 **SAM:**   *(Quietly and very carefully.)* If you make me say it once, I'll never call you anything else again.

HALLY: So? *(The boy confronts the man.)* Is that meant to be a threat?

SAM: Just telling you what will happen if you make me do that. You must decide what it means to you.

HALLY: Well, I have. It's good news. Because that is exactly what Master Harold wants from now on. Think of it as a little lesson in respect, Sam, that's long overdue, and I hope you remember it as well as you do your geography. I can tell you now that somebody who will be glad to hear I've finally given it to you will be my Dad. Yes! He agrees with my Mom. He's always going on about it as well. "You must teach the boys to show you more respect, my son."

SAM: So now you can stop complaining about going home. Everybody is going to be happy tonight.

630 **HALLY:**   That's perfectly correct. You see, you mustn't get the wrong idea about me and my Dad, Sam. We also have our good times together. Some bloody good laughs. He's got a marvelous sense of humor. Want to know what our favorite joke is? He gives out a big groan, you see, and says: "It's not fair, is it, Hally?" Then I have to ask: "What, chum?" And then he says: "A nigger's arse" . . . and we both have a good laugh.

The men stare at him with disbelief.

What's the matter, Willie? Don't you catch the joke? You always were a bit slow on the uptake. It's what is called a pun. You see, fair means both light in color and to be just and decent. *(He turns to Sam.)* I thought *you* would catch it, Sam.

SAM: Oh ja, I catch it all right.

HALLY: But it doesn't appeal to your sense of humor.

SAM: Do you really laugh?

HALLY: Of course.

635 **SAM:**   To please him? Make him feel good?

HALLY: No, for heaven's sake! I laugh because I think it's a bloody good joke.

SAM: You're really trying hard to be ugly, aren't you? And why drag poor old Willie into it? He's done nothing to you except show you the respect you want so badly. That's also not being fair, you know . . . and *I* mean just or decent.

WILLIE: It's all right, Sam. Leave it now.

SAM: It's me you're after. You should just have said "Sam's arse" . . . because that's the one you're trying to kick. Anyway, how do you know it's not fair? You've never seen it. Do you want to? (*He drops his trousers and underpants and presents his backside for Hally's inspection.*) Have a good look. A real Basuto[7] arse . . . which is about as nigger as they can come. Satisfied? (*Trousers up.*) Now you can make your Dad even happier when you go home tonight. Tell him I showed you my arse and he is quite right. It's not fair. And if it will give him an even better laugh next time, I'll also let *him* have a look. Come, Willie, let's finish up and go.

Sam and Willie start to tidy up the tea room. Hally doesn't move. He waits for a moment when Sam passes him.

640 **HALLY:** (*Quietly.*) Sam . . .

Sam stops and looks expectantly at the boy. Hally spits in his face. A long and heartfelt groan from Willie. For a few seconds Sam doesn't move.

SAM: (*Taking out a handkerchief and wiping his face.*) It's all right, Willie.

To Hally.

Ja, well, you've done it . . . Master Harold. Yes, I'll start calling you that from now on. It won't be difficult anymore. You've hurt yourself, Master Harold. I saw it coming. I warned you, but you wouldn't listen. You've just hurt yourself *bad.* And you're a coward, Master Harold. The face you should be spitting in is your father's . . . but you used mine, because you think you're safe inside your fair skin . . . and this time I don't mean just or decent. (*Pause, then moving violently towards Hally.*) Should I hit him, Willie?

WILLIE: (*Stopping Sam.*) No, Boet Sam.

SAM: (*Violently.*) Why not?

WILLIE: It won't help, Boet Sam.

645 **SAM:** I don't want to help! I want to hurt him.

WILLIE: You also hurt yourself.

SAM: And if he had done it to you, Willie?

WILLIE: Me? Spit at me like I was a dog? (*A thought that had not occurred to him before. He looks at Hally.*) Ja. Then I want to hit him. I want to hit him hard!

A dangerous few seconds as the men stand staring at the boy. Willie turns away, shaking his head.

But maybe all I do is go cry at the back. He's little boy, Boet Sam. Little *white* boy. Long trousers now, but he's still little boy.

---

[7] Any of a Bantu people living in Basutoland, or Lesotho, in Southeast Africa.

SAM: *(His violence ebbing away into defeat as quickly as it flooded.)* You're right. So go on, then: groan again, Willie. You do it better than me. *(To Hally.)* You don't know all of what you've just done . . . Master Harold. It's not just that you've made me feel dirtier than I've ever been in my life . . . I mean, how do I wash off yours and your father's filth? . . . I've also failed. A long time ago I promised myself I was going to try and do something, but you've just shown me . . . Master Harold . . . that I've failed. *(Pause.)* I've also got a memory of a little white boy when he was still wearing short trousers and a black man, but they're not flying a kite. It was the old Jubilee days, after dinner one night. I was in my room. You came in and just stood against the wall, looking down at the ground, and only after I'd asked you what you wanted, what was wrong, I don't know how many times, did you speak and even then so softly I almost didn't hear you. "Sam, please help me to go and fetch my Dad." Remember? He was dead drunk on the floor of the Central Hotel Bar. They'd phoned for your Mom, but you were the only one at home. And do you remember how we did it? You went in first by yourself to ask permission for me to go into the bar. Then I loaded him onto my back like a baby and carried him back to the boarding house with you following behind carrying his crutches. *(Shaking his head as he remembers.)* A crowded Main Street with all the people watching a little white boy following his drunk father on a nigger's back! I felt for that little boy . . . Master Harold. I felt for him. After that we still had to clean him up, remember? He'd messed in his trousers, so we had to clean him up and get him into bed.

650 **HALLY:** *(Great pain.)* I love him, Sam.

SAM: I know you do. That's why I tried to stop you from saying these things about him. It would have been so simple if you could have just despised him for being a weak man. But he's your father. You love him and you're ashamed of him. You're ashamed of so much! . . . And now that's going to include yourself. That was the promise I made to myself: to try and stop that happening. *(Pause.)* After we got him to bed you came back with me to my room and sat in a corner and carried on just looking down at the ground. And for days after that! You hadn't done anything wrong, but you went around as if you owed the world an apology for being alive. I didn't like seeing that! That's not the way a boy grows up to be a man! . . . But the one person who should have been teaching you what that means was the cause of your shame. If you really want to know, that's why I made you that kite. I wanted you to look up, be proud of something, of yourself . . . *(Bitter smile at the memory.)* . . . and you certainly were that when I left you with it up there on the hill. Oh, ja . . . something else! . . . If you ever do write it as a short story, there was a twist in our ending. I couldn't sit down there and stay with you. It was a "Whites Only" bench. You were too young, too excited to notice then. But not anymore. If you're not careful . . . Master Harold . . . you're going to be sitting up there by yourself for a long time to come, and there won't be a kite in the sky. *(Sam has got nothing more to say. He exits into the kitchen, taking off his waiter's jacket.)*

WILLIE: Is bad. Is all all bad in here now.

HALLY: *(Books into his school case, raincoat on.)* Willie . . . *(It is difficult to speak.)* Will you lock up for me and look after the keys?

WILLIE: Okay.

Sam returns. Hally goes behind the counter and collects the few coins in the cash register. As he starts to leave . . .

655 **SAM:** Don't forget the comic books.

Hally returns to the counter and puts them in his case. He starts to leave again.

SAM: *(To the retreating back of the boy.)* Stop . . . Hally . . .

Hally stops, but doesn't turn to face him.

Hally . . . I've got no right to tell you what being a man means if I don't behave like one myself, and I'm not doing so well at that this afternoon. Should we try again, Hally?

HALLY: Try what?

SAM: Fly another kite, I suppose. It worked once, and this time I need it as much as you do.

HALLY: It's still raining, Sam. You can't fly kites on rainy days, remember.

660 **SAM:** So what do we do? Hope for better weather tomorrow?

HALLY: *(Helpless gesture.)* I don't know. I don't know anything anymore.

SAM: You sure of that, Hally? Because it would be pretty hopeless if that was true. It would mean nothing has been learnt in here this afternoon, and there was a hell of a lot of teaching going on . . . one way or the other. But anyway, I don't believe you. I reckon there's one thing you know. You don't *have* to sit up there by yourself. You know what that bench means now, and you can leave it any time you choose. All you've got to do is stand up and walk away from it.

Hally leaves. Willie goes up quietly to Sam.

WILLIE: Is okay, Boet Sam. You see. Is . . . *(He can't find any better words.)* . . . is going to be okay tomorrow. *(Changing his tone.)* Hey, Boet Sam! *(He is trying hard.)* You right. I think about it and you right. Tonight I find Hilda and say sorry. And make promise I won't beat her no more. You hear me, Boet Sam?

SAM: I hear you, Willie.

665 **WILLIE:** And when we practice I relax and romance with her from beginning to end. Non-stop! You watch! Two weeks' time: "First prize for promising newcomers: Mr. Willie Malopo and Miss Hilda Samuels." *(Sudden impulse.)* To hell with it! I walk home. *(He goes to the jukebox, puts in a coin and selects a record. The machine comes to life*

in the gray twilight, blushing its way through a spectrum of soft, romantic colors.) How did you say it, Boet Sam? Let's dream. *(Willie sways with the music and gestures for Sam to dance.)*

Sarah Vaughan sings.

"Little man you're crying,
I know why you're blue,
Someone took your kiddy car away;
Better go to sleep now,
Little man you've had a busy day." *(etc. etc.)*
     You lead. I follow.

The men dance together.

"Johnny won your marbles,
Tell you what we'll do;
Dad will get you new ones
     right away;
Better go to sleep now,
Little man you've had a
     busy day."

READING AND REACTING

1. How has Hally's character been shaped by his father's inadequacies? In what sense is he his father's son? In what sense has he tried to compensate for his father's shortcomings?

2. In what respects is the relationship between Hally and Sam like and unlike a father-son relationship?

3. The play uses a personal relationship to make a statement about a social and political situation. In what way can it be seen as also using political tensions to make a point about personal relationships?

4. Is the background of apartheid and South African social and cultural mores essential to the play, or could you imagine other settings and contexts in which Sam might be vulnerable to Hally's mistreatment? Do you think the play is dated now that apartheid has been abolished in South Africa?

5. At what point does the play's climax occur? How would you expect a live audience to react to this climax? How did you react?

6. Is Sam's failure to resort to violence believable? Do you think he is motivated by anything other than fear or self-preservation?

7. What is Willie's function in the play? Does his presence affect the dynamics between Hally and Sam? Does it give the audience any essential information about the other two characters? How would the play be different without him?

8. What are the advantages and disadvantages of the play's focusing on only three characters and using a single setting? What could Fugard

have gained by showing Hally, Sam, and Willie in other contexts? By having them interact with other characters? What additional characters and settings could be added?

9. Is the play's ending hopeful? Pessimistic? Cynical?

10. Hally seems obsessed with past events. What comment do you think Fugard is making through Hally about the past and its impact on the present? In what way do the past events Hally recalls prepare us for the play's climactic scene? Why do you think Hally tends to recall past events as scenes from a play or short story?

11. **JOURNAL ENTRY** What has Sam learned from Hally? What has Hally learned from Sam? What else does each learn during the course of the play?

12. **CRITICAL PERSPECTIVE** In an interview with Fugard, Heinrich von Staden suggests to the playwright that his portrait of Hally is likely to be disturbing to the audience:

> [Y]ou leave your audience feeling quite ambivalent about your protagonist. . . . Here is a fundamentally good kid who went much further than a lot of white people in South Africa would: in being open to blacks, being willing to teach them, to communicate with them. Essentially, Hally was not a racist until he becomes unveiled as Master Harold. And at that point the ratio of good to evil becomes very unclear, becomes very fuzzy.

Do you have ambivalent feelings about Hally/Master Harold? Do you think he is a racist?

WRITING SUGGESTIONS: PLOT

1. Central to the plots of both *Trifles* and *A Doll House* is a woman who commits a crime. Compare and contrast the reactions of the two plays' other characters, particularly each woman's friends, to her crime.

2. Write an essay in which you consider the influence of the main characters' fathers on the plots of *True West, A Doll House,* or *"Master Harold" . . . and the Boys.*

3. All four of the plays in this chapter portray dysfunctional families. Analyze the family relationships in one or more of these plays, and consider what steps might be taken (and by whom) to solve the family's problems.

4. Since *"Master Harold" . . . and the Boys* was written, apartheid has been abolished in South Africa. Does this fact make the play dated, or does the play deal with issues that reach beyond a specific time and place?

5. In both *Trifles* and *A Doll House,* the plot depends to some extent on the fact that male characters misjudge—and perhaps underestimate—women. Write an essay in which you compare and contrast the attitudes the men in these plays hold toward women, the ways in which they reveal these attitudes, and the ways in which the women react.

CHAPTER 23

Character

What playwrights do perhaps is to file away in their semi-conscious minds any un-
usual, exciting, provocative people they encounter in their day-to-day existence.
Later, much later, they find occasion to remember this one's face, that one's way of
walking, somebody's gravelly voice, an old woman lighting up a cigarette, a rotund
man with a ruddy face looking as if it had just been rubbed down with baby oil, who
sprawled across two seats of a subway train and read the Bible. Indeed one of the
great pleasures that plays and movies have to offer is the instinctive response we all
have to the role-playing of others. Since role-casting seems to be a deeply rooted
mechanism, we are entertained in theaters by the mere awareness that a figure up
there on the stage or on the screen has a certain definite identity. The more "strik-
ing" the identity, the more we should be entertained; and "striking" in this instance
does not mean the run-of-the-mill roles with which we cast the drama of everyday
living.

THELMA ALTSHULER AND RICHARD PAUL JANERO, *RESPONSES TO DRAMA*

A character living onstage is a union of the creative talents of the actor and the
dramatist. Any argument over which of the two is more important is futile because
they are completely interdependent. The actor requires the character created by the
dramatist to provide the initial and vital stimulus. The dramatist requires the em-
bodiment of the character by the actor to bring his creation to fulfillment. The result
of this collaboration is the finished performance to which both the actor and the
dramatist have made a unique contribution. The result can be neither Shakespeare's
Macbeth nor the actor's Macbeth. It must be the actor as Shakespeare's Macbeth. An
audience can never see a character as the dramatist conceived him. They always see
whatever significance a particular actor has been able to find. . . .

In beginning his study, the actor should keep in mind two basic questions for
which he must find answers:

1) What primarily does the character want?
2) What is he willing to do to get it? . . .

In the answer to what a person wants *and* what he is willing to do to get it
lies the key to his character. Here is to be found the *motivating force* behind what
a character does and says. And that is what the actor is most eager to discover as he
studies the play!

Failure to understand the desire that motivates the behavior of the character means failure to understand the dramatist's intention. This, in turn, means failure to interpret the play truthfully.

CHARLES MCGRAW, *ACTING IS BELIEVING* 2ND ED.

Shakespeare is above all writers, at least above all modern writers, the poet of nature: the poet that holds up to his readers a faithful mirror of manners and life. His characters are not modified by the customs of particular places, unpracticed by the rest of the world; by the peculiarities of studies or professions, which can operate but upon small numbers; or by the accidents of transient fashions or temporary opinions: they are the genuine progeny of common humanity, such as the world will always supply, and observation will always find. His persons act and speak by the influence of those general passions and principles by which all minds are agitated, and the whole system of life is continued in motion. In the writings of other poets a character is too often an individual; in those of Shakespeare it is commonly a species.

FROM THE PREFACE TO SAMUEL JOHNSON'S EDITION OF SHAKESPEARE

Last week Equity torpedoed a musical called "Miss Saigon," which includes parts for dozens of Asian actors. The celebrated actor Jonathan Pryce plays the Engineer in the London production, and was to do so on Broadway. Equity said it could not approve of Mr. Pryce playing the role, which he apparently does brilliantly, because the Engineer is Eurasian and Mr. Pryce is Caucasian. . . .

Let's be clear: this wish for politically correct casting goes only one way, the way designed to redress the injuries of centuries. When Pat Carroll, who is a woman, plays Falstaff, who is not, the casting is considered a stroke of brilliance. When Josette Simon, who is black, plays Maggie in "After the Fall" a part Arthur Miller patterned after Marilyn Monroe and which has traditionally been played, not by white women, but by blonde white women, it is hailed as a breakthrough.

But when the pendulum moves the other way, the actors' union balks. It is noted, quite correctly, that it is insufferable that roadshow companies of "The King and I" habitually use Caucasian men wearing eyeliner to play the King, rather than searching for suitable Asian actors. But the conclusion drawn from this is that a white man should never be permitted inside the skin of an Asian one, although all of acting is about getting inside someone else's skin, someone different, someone somehow foreign.

ANNA QUINDLEN, "ERROR, STAGE LEFT," *NEW YORK TIMES*

In Tennessee Williams's 1945 play *The Glass Menagerie* (p. 1898) the protagonist, Tom Wingfield, functions as the play's narrator. Stepping out of his role as character and speaking directly to the audience, he directs the play's action, music, lighting, and other elements. In addition, he summarizes characters' actions, explains their motivation, and discusses the significance of their behavior in the context of the play—commenting on his own character's actions as well. In his role as narrator, Tom also presents useful background information about the characters. For instance, when he introduces his co-worker, Jim, he prepares readers for Jim's entrance and helps them to understand his subsequent actions:

> *In high school Jim was a hero. He had tremendous Irish good nature and vitality with the scrubbed and polished look of white chinaware. He seemed to move in a continual spotlight. . . . But Jim apparently ran into more interference after his graduation. . . . His speed had definitely slowed. Six years after he left high school he was holding a job that wasn't much better than mine.*

Most plays, however, do not include narrators who present background. Instead, readers learn about characters from their own words and from comments by others about them, from the characters' actions, and from the playwright's stage directions. At a performance, the audience has the added advantage of learning from the actors' interpretations of the characters.

Characters in plays, like characters in novels and short stories, may be **round** or **flat, static** or **dynamic.** Generally speaking, major characters are likely to be round, while minor characters are apt to be flat. Through the language and the actions of the characters, readers learn whether the characters are multidimensional, skimpily developed, or perhaps merely **foils,** players whose main purpose is to shed light on more important characters. Readers also learn about the emotions, attitudes, and values that help to shape the characters—their hopes and fears, their strengths and weaknesses. In addition, readers learn from the play whether or not characters grow and change emotionally, and they are able to trace a character's development by comparing his or her early words and actions with later ones. In short, observant readers can learn a good deal about a play's characters—and thus about the play itself—from those characters' words and actions.

CHARACTERS' WORDS

Characters' words reveal the most about their attitudes, feelings, beliefs, and values. For example, a **monologue**—an extended speech by one character—can reveal the character's feelings, communicating information to other characters and to the audience. A **soliloquy**—a monologue revealing a character's thoughts and feelings, directed at the audience and presumed not to be heard by other characters—can also convey information about a character. Hamlet's well-known soliloquy that begins "To be or not to be" eloquently communicates his distraught mental state—his resentment toward his mother and uncle, his confusion about what course of action to take, his suicidal thoughts. Finally, **dialogue**—an exchange of words between two characters—can reveal misunderstanding or conflict between them, or it can show their agreement, mutual support, or similar beliefs. Thus, characters' statements can convey information important to the play's action and to the development of its theme.

In Henrik Ibsen's *A Doll House* (p. 1185) the characters' words reveal a good deal about them. Nora Helmer, the spoiled young wife, has broken the law and kept her crime secret from her husband. Through her words we learn about her motivation, her emotions, and her reactions to other characters and to her potentially dangerous situation. We learn, for instance, that she is flirtatious ("If your little squirrel begged you, with all her heart and soul. . . ." [Act 2]) and that she is childishly unrealistic about the consequences of her actions. When her husband, Torvald, asks what she would do if he was seriously injured, leaving her in debt, she says, "If anything so awful happened, then it just wouldn't matter if I had debts or not" (Act 1). When Torvald presses, "Well, but the people I'd borrowed from?" she dismisses them: "Them? Who cares about them! They're strangers." As the play progresses, Nora's lack of understanding of the power of the law becomes more and more significant as she struggles with her moral and ethical dilemma.

The inability of both Nora and Torvald to confront ugly truths is also revealed through their words. When, in Act 1, Nora tells Krogstad, her blackmailer, that his revealing her secret could expose her to "the most horrible unpleasantness," he responds, "Only unpleasantness?" Yet later on, in Act 3, Torvald uses the same word, fastidiously dismissing the horror with, "No, we're not going to dwell on anything unpleasant."

The ease with which Torvald is able to dismiss his dying friend Dr. Rank in Act 3 ("He with his suffering and loneliness—like a dark cloud setting off our sunlit happiness. Well, maybe it's best this way.") exposes his egocentrism and foreshadows the lack of support he will give Nora immediately thereafter. Especially revealing is his use of *I* and *my* and *me,* which convey his self-centeredness:

> Now you've wrecked all my happiness—ruined my whole future. Oh, it's awful to think of. I'm in a cheap little grafter's hands; he can do anything he wants with me, ask for anything, play with me like a puppet—and I can't breathe a word. I'll be swept down miserably into the depths on account of a featherbrained woman.

Just as Torvald's words reveal that he has not been changed by the play's events, Nora's words show that she has changed significantly. Her dialogue near the end of Act III shows that she has become a responsible, determined woman—one who more fully understands her situation and her options and is no longer blithely oblivious to her duties. When she says, "I've never felt more clearheaded and sure in my life," she is calm and decisive; when she says, "Our home's been nothing but a playpen. I've been your doll-wife here, just as at home I was Papa's doll-child," she reveals her newly found self-awareness. When she confronts her husband, she displays complete honesty—perhaps for the first time in her relationship with Torvald.

Sometimes what other characters say to or about a character can reveal more to an audience than the character's own words. (Keep in mind, however, that you should measure the accuracy of characters' comments against what you already know about them.) For instance, in Act 2 of *A Doll House,* when the dying Dr. Rank says, apparently without malice, "[Torvald] Helmer with his sensitivity has such a sharp distaste for anything ugly," readers not only think ill of the man who is too "sensitive" to visit his sick friend but also question his ability to withstand situations that may be emotionally or morally "ugly" as well.

Susan Glaspell's *Trifles* (p. 1172) focuses on an absent character, describing her solely through other characters' remarks. The evidence suggests that Mrs. Wright has killed her husband, and only Mrs. Hale's and Mrs. Peters's comments about Mrs. Wright's dreary life can delineate her character and suggest a likely motive for the murder. Although we never meet Mrs. Wright, we learn essential information from the other women: that as a young girl she liked to sing, and that more recently she was so distraught about the lack of beauty in her life that even her sewing revealed her distress.

Similarly, the father in *The Glass Menagerie* never appears (and therefore never speaks), but the play's other characters describe him as "A telephone man who—fell in love with long-distance" (Scene 6)—the absent husband and father who symbolizes abandonment and instability to Laura and Amanda and the possibility of freedom and escape to Tom.

Whether or not language is central to a play's theme, words are always revealing: Explicitly or implicitly, they convey a character's nature, attitudes, and relationships with other characters. A character may, for instance, use learned words, foreign words, elaborate figurative language, irony or sarcasm, regionalisms, slang, jargon, clichés, or profanity. Words can also be used to indicate tone—for example, to express irony. Any of these uses of language may communicate vital information to the audience about a character's background, attitudes, and motivation. And, of course, a character's language may change as a play progresses, and this change, too, may be revealing.

Formal and Informal Language

One character in a dramatic work may be very formal and aloof, using absolutely correct grammar, a learned vocabulary, and long, complex sentences; another may be informal, using conversational speech, colloquialisms, and slang. At times, two characters with different levels of language may be set in opposition for dramatic effect, as they are in Irish playwright George Bernard Shaw's 1912 play *Pygmalion,* which updates the ancient Greek myth of a sculptor who creates (and falls in love with) a statue of a woman. In Shaw's version a linguistics professor sets out to teach "proper" speech and manners to a lowly flower seller. Throughout the play the contrasting language of Henry Higgins, the professor, and Eliza Doolittle, the flower seller, indicates their differing social standing:

> **LIZA:**   I ain't got no mother. Her that turned me out was my sixth
> stepmother. But I done without them. And I'm a good girl, I am.
>
> **HIGGINS:**   Very well, then, what on earth is all this fuss about?

A character's accent or dialect may also be significant. In comedies of
manners, for instance, rustic or provincial characters, identified by their
speech, were often objects of humor. In *Pygmalion* Eliza Doolittle uses
cockney dialect, the dialect spoken in the East End of London. Her colorful, distinctive language (complete with expressions like *Nah-ow, garn,* and
ah-ah-ah-ow-ow-ow-oo) and her nonstandard grammatical constructions at
first make her an object of ridicule; later, the transformation of her speech
parallels the dramatic changes in her character.

Plain and Elaborate Style

Dialogue can be plain and unadorned, or it can be quite elaborate, with
figurative language such as similes and other imaginative comparisons
embellishing a character's words. Depending on the context of a speech
and on the other characters' language, the complexity or lack of complexity can have different effects. A character whose language is simple and
unsophisticated may seem to be unintelligent, unenlightened, gullible, or
naive—especially if the character also uses slang, dialect, or colloquial
expressions. Conversely, a character's plain, down-to-earth language can
convey common sense or intelligence. Plain language can also be quite
emotionally powerful. Thus, Willy Loman's speech in Act 2 of *Death of a
Salesman* (p. 1458), about an eighty-four-year-old salesman named Dave
Singleman, moves the audience with its sincerity and directness:

> Do you know? When he died—and by the way he died the death of a
> salesman, in his green velvet slippers in the smoker of the New York,
> New Haven and Hartford, going into Boston—when he died, hundreds
> of salesmen and buyers were at his funeral. Things were sad on a lotta
> trains for months after that.

Like plain speech, elaborate language may have different effects in different contexts. Figurative language can add to a character's nobility,
making him or her seem to have depth and insight and analytical skills
absent in other characters. In the following excerpt from a soliloquy from
Shakespeare's *Hamlet* (p. 1355), notice how complex language reveals
Hamlet's tendency to engage in self-analysis:

> **HAMLET:**   O, that this too too solid flesh would melt,
> Thaw, and resolve itself into a dew!
> Or that the Everlasting had not fix'd
> His canon 'gainst self-slaughter! O God! O God!
> How weary, stale, flat, and unprofitable
> Seem to me all the uses of this world!

Fie on't, O fie, 'tis an unweeded garden,
That grows to seed. . . . (1.2.129–36)

In the preceding lines, Hamlet compares the world to a garden gone to seed. His use of imagery and figurative language vividly communicates his feelings about the world and his internal struggle against the temptation to commit suicide.

Sometimes, elaborate figurative language may make a character seem pompous or untrustworthy. In the following passages from Shakespeare's *King Lear*, for example, Goneril and Regan, the deceitful daughters, use elaborate language to conceal their true feelings from their father, King Lear. However, Cordelia—the loyal, loving daughter—uses simple, straightforward prose that suggests her sincerity and lack of artifice. Compare the three speeches:

GONERIL: Sir, I love you more than words can wield the matter;
Dearer than eyesight, space, and liberty;
Beyond what can be valued, rich or rare;
No less than life, with grace, health, beauty, honour;
As much as child e'er lov'd, or father found;
A love that makes breath poor, and speech unable.
Beyond all manner of so much I love you. (1.1.56–62)

REGAN: Sir, I am made
Of the selfsame metal that my sister is,
And prize me at her worth. In my true heart
I find she names my very deed of love;
Only she comes too short, that I profess
Myself an enemy to all other joys
Which the most precious square of sense possesses,
And find I am alone felicitate
In your dear Highness' love. (1.1.70–78)

CORDELIA: Unhappy that I am, I cannot heave
My heart into my mouth. I love your Majesty
According to my bond; no more no less. (1.1.93–95)

Cordelia's unwillingness, even when she is prodded by Lear, to exaggerate her feelings or misrepresent her love through inflated language shows the audience her honesty and nobility. The contrast between her language and that of her sisters makes their motivation clear.

Tone

Tone reveals a character's mood or attitude. Tone can be flat or hysterical, bitter or accepting, affectionate or aloof, anxious or calm. Contrasts in tone can indicate differences in outlook or emotional state between two characters; changes in tone from one point in the play to another can suggest corresponding changes within a character. At the end of *A Doll House*, for instance, Nora is resigned to what she must do, and her language is appropriately controlled. Her husband, however, is desperate to change her mind, and his language reflects this desperation. The following exchanges from Act 3 of the play illustrate their contrasting emotional states:

> **HELMER:**   But to part! To part from you! No, Nora, no—I can't imagine it.
> **NORA:**   *(going out, right)* All the more reason why it has to be.

> **HELMER:**   Over! All over! Nora, won't you ever think about me?
> **NORA:**   I'm sure I'll think of you often, and about the children and the house here.

In earlier scenes between the two characters, Nora is emotional—at times, hysterical—and her husband is considerably more controlled. As the dialogue above indicates, both Nora and Torvald Helmer change dramatically during the course of the play.

Irony

Irony, a contradiction or discrepancy between two different levels of meaning, can reveal a great deal about character. **Verbal irony**—a contradiction between what a character says and what he or she means—is very important in drama, where the verbal interplay between characters carries the weight of the play. For example, when Nora and Dr. Rank discuss the latest news about his health in *A Doll House,* there is deep irony in his use of the phrase "complete certainty." Although the phrase usually suggests reassuring news, here it is meant to suggest death, and both Nora and Dr. Rank understand this.

   Dramatic irony depends on the audience's knowing something that a character has not yet realized, or on one character's knowing something other characters do not know. In some cases dramatic irony is created by an audience's awareness of historical background or events of which characters are unaware. (Familiar with the story of Oedipus, for instance, the audience knows that the man who has caused all the problems in Thebes— the man Oedipus vows to find and take revenge on—is Oedipus himself.) In other cases dramatic irony emerges when the audience learns something from a play's unfolding action. The central irony in *A Doll House,* for example, is that the family's "happy home" rests on a foundation of secrets, lies, and deception. Torvald does not know about the secrets, and Nora does not understand how they have poisoned her marriage. The audience, however, quickly becomes aware of the atmosphere of deceit—and aware of how it threatens the family's happiness.

   Dramatic irony may also be conveyed through words—in dialogue or asides, for example. Typically, dramatic irony is revealed when a character, in conversation, delivers lines that give the audience information that other characters, offstage at the time, do not know. In *A Doll House* the audience knows—because she has explained her situation to Kristine—that Nora has spent the previous Christmas season hard at work, earning money to pay her secret debt. Torvald, however, remains unaware of her activities and believes her story that she was using the time to make holiday decorations, which the cat destroyed. This belief is consistent with his impression of her as an irresponsible child, yet the audience has quite a different impression of Nora. This discrepancy, one of many contradictions between the audience's view of Nora and Torvald's impression of her, helps to create dramatic tension in the play.

Asides create dramatic irony by undercutting dialogue, providing ironic contrast between what the characters on stage know and what the audience knows. In Anton Chekhov's *The Brute* (p. 1342), for example, the audience knows that Mr. Smirnov is succumbing to Mrs. Popov's charms because he says, in an aside, "My god, what eyes she has! They're setting me on fire." Mrs. Popov, however, is not yet aware of his infatuation. The discrepancy between the audience's awareness and the character's adds to the play's humor.

CHARACTERS' ACTIONS

How characters act—and how they react to other characters or to particular events—conveys their values and attitudes. Actions may also reveal a character's personality. When Laura Wingfield, a character in *The Glass Menagerie*, hides rather than face the "gentleman caller" her brother Tom has brought home, readers see just how shy she is; when Nora in *A Doll House* plays hide-and-seek with her children, eats forbidden macaroons, and takes childish joy in Christmas, her immaturity is apparent.

Readers also learn about characters from what they do *not* do. Thus, Nora's failure to remain in touch with her friend Kristine, who has had such a hard life, reveals her selfishness, and the failure of Mrs. Peters and Mrs. Hale in *Trifles* to communicate their evidence to the sheriff indicates their support for Mrs. Wright and their understanding of what motivated her to take such drastic action.

Naturally, actions do not exist in isolation; they affect other characters. In William Shakespeare's *Othello* Iago is the embodiment of evil, and we discover his true nature through his interactions with other characters: He reveals the secret marriage of Othello and Desdemona to her father; he schemes to arouse Othello's jealousy, making him believe Desdemona has been unfaithful with his lieutenant, Cassio; he persuades Cassio to ask Desdemona to plead his case with Othello, knowing this act will further arouse Othello's suspicions; he encourages Othello to be suspicious of Desdemona's defense of Cassio; he plants Desdemona's handkerchief in Cassio's room; and, finally, he persuades Othello to kill Desdemona and then kills his own wife, Emilia, to prevent her from exposing his role in the intrigue. As the play progresses, then, Iago's dealings with others consistently reveal him to be evil and corrupt.

STAGE DIRECTIONS

When we read a play, we also read the playwright's italicized **stage directions,** the notes that concern **staging**—the scenery, props, lighting, music, sound effects, costumes, and other elements that contribute to the way the play looks and sounds to an audience (Chapter 24). In addition to commenting on staging, stage directions may supply physical details about the characters, suggesting their age, appearance, movements, gestures, relative positions, and facial expressions. These details may in turn convey additional information about characters: Appearance may reveal social position or economic status, expressions may reveal attitudes, and so on. Stage directions may also indicate the manner in which a line of dialogue is to be delivered—haltingly, confidently, hesitantly, or loudly, for instance. The way a line is spoken may reveal a character to be excited, upset, angry, shy, or disappointed. Finally, stage directions may indicate *changes* in characters—for instance, a character whose speech is described as timid in early scenes may deliver lines emphatically and forcefully later on in the play.

Some plays' stage directions provide a good deal of detail about character; others do little more than list characters' names. Arthur Miller often chooses to provide detailed information about character through stage directions. In *Death of a Salesman,* for instance, Miller's stage directions characterize Willy Loman immediately and specifically:

He is past sixty years of age, dressed quietly. Even as he crosses the stage to the doorway of the house, his exhaustion is apparent. He unlocks the door, comes into the kitchen, and thankfully lets his burden down, feeling the soreness of his palms. A word-sigh escapes his lips—

Subsequent stage directions provide information about how lines are to be spoken. For example, in the play's opening lines Willy's wife Linda calls out to him *"with some trepidation";* Linda speaks *"very carefully, delicately,"* and Willy speaks *"with casual irritation."* These instructions to readers (and actors) are meant to suggest the strained relationship between the two characters.

George Bernard Shaw is notorious for the particularly full character description in his stage directions. In these notes—seen by readers of the play but not heard by audiences—he communicates complex information about characters' attitudes and values, strengths and weaknesses, motivation and reactions, and relationships with other characters. In doing so Shaw functions as a narrator, explicitly communicating his own attitudes toward various characters. (Unlike the voice of Tom Wingfield in *The Glass Menagerie,* however, the voice in Shaw's stage directions is not also the voice of a character in the play; it is the voice of the playwright.) Shaw's stage directions for *Pygmalion* initially describe Eliza Doolittle as follows:

She is not at all an attractive person. She is perhaps eighteen, perhaps twenty, hardly older. She wears a little sailor hat of black straw that has long been exposed to the dust and soot of London and has seldom if ever been brushed. Her hair needs washing rather badly; its mousy color can hardly be natural. She wears a shoddy black coat that reaches nearly to her knees and is shaped to her waist. She has a brown skirt with a coarse apron. Her boots are much the worse for wear. She is no doubt as clean as she can afford to be; but compared to the ladies she is very dirty. Her features are no worse than theirs; but their condition leaves something to be desired; and she needs the services of a dentist.

Rather than providing an unobtrusive, objective summary of the character's most notable physical attributes, Shaw injects subjective comments (*"seldom if ever brushed"*; *"color can hardly be natural"*; *"no doubt as clean as she can afford to be"*) that reveal his attitude toward Eliza. This initially supercilious attitude, which he shares with Professor Higgins, is tempered considerably by the end of the play, helping to make Eliza's transformation more obvious than it would be if measured by her words and actions alone. In Act V the tone of the stage directions characterizing Eliza has changed to something approaching admiration: *"Eliza enters, sunny, self-possessed, and giving a staggeringly convincing exhibition of ease of manner."*

Stage directions in *Hamlet* are not nearly as comprehensive. Characters are introduced with only the barest identifying tags: "Claudius, *King of Denmark*"; "Hamlet, *Son to the former, and nephew to the present King*"; "Gertrude, *Queen of Denmark, mother to Hamlet.*" Most stage directions do little more than chronicle the various characters' entrances and exits or specify particular physical actions: *"Enter Ghost"*; *"Spreads his arms"*; *"Ghost beckons Hamlet"*; *"He kneels"*; *"Sheathes his sword"*; *"Leaps in the grave."* Occasionally, stage directions specify a prop (*"Puts down the skull"*); a sound effect (*"A noise within"*); or a costume (*"Enter the ghost in his night-gown"*). Such brevity is typical of Shakespeare's plays, in which characters are delineated almost solely by their words—and, not incidentally, by the way actors have interpreted the characters over the years. In fact, because these stage directions only suggest characters' gestures, physical reactions, movements, and facial expressions, actors have been left quite free to experiment, reading various interpretations into Shakespeare's characters.

ACTORS' INTERPRETATIONS

When we watch a play, we gain insight into a character not merely through what the character says and does or how other characters react, but also through the way an actor interprets the role. If a playwright does not specify a character's mannerisms, gestures, or movements, or does not indicate how a line is to be delivered (or sometimes even if he or she does), an actor is free to interpret the role as he or she believes it should be played. Even when a playwright *does* specify such actions, the actor has a good deal of freedom to decide which gestures or expressions will convey a certain emotion.

In "Some Thoughts on Playwrighting," American playwright Thornton Wilder argues that "the theatre is an art which reposes upon the work of many collaborators" rather than on "one governing selecting will." Citing examples from Shakespeare and Ibsen, Wilder illustrates the great degree of "intervention" that may occur in dramatic productions. For instance, Wilder observes, Shakespeare's Shylock has been portrayed by two different actors as "noble, wronged and indignant" and as "a vengeful and hysterical buffoon"—and both performances were positive contributions to the theater. As noted earlier, the absence of detailed stage directions in Shakespeare's plays makes possible (and perhaps even encourages) such widely diverging interpretations. However, as Wilder notes, even when playing roles created by a playwright such as Ibsen, whose stage directions are typically quite specific, actors and directors may choose to depart from, or even to disregard, instructions about actors' appearances or mannerisms and still stage fine performances. Wilder sees this disregard for playwrights' wishes as the result of a completely healthy collaboration between playwright and actor. In fact, Wilder believes, "Characterization in a play is like a blank check which the dramatist accords to the actor for him to fill in—not entirely blank, for a number of indications of individuality are already there, but to a far less definite and absolute degree than in the novel." In many ways, then, the playwright's words on the page are just the beginning of the characters' lives.

Irish playwright Samuel Beckett devotes a good deal of attention to indicating actors' movements and gestures and their physical reactions to one another. In his 1952 play *Waiting for Godot,* for example, Beckett seems to choreograph every gesture, every emotion, every intention, with stage directions such as the following:

♦ *(he looks at them ostentatiously in turn to make it clear they are both meant)*

♦ *Vladimir seizes Lucky's hat. Silence of Lucky. He falls. Silence. Panting of the victors.*

♦ *Estragon hands him the boot. Vladimir inspects it, throws it down angrily.*

♦ *Estragon pulls, stumbles, falls. Long silence.*

♦ *He goes feverishly to and fro, halts finally at extreme left, broods.*

Clearly, Beckett provides full and obviously carefully thought-out stage directions and, in so doing, attempts to retain a good deal of control over his characters. Still, in a 1988 production of *Godot,* director Mike Nichols and comic actors Robin Williams and Steve Martin felt free to improvise, adding gestures and movements not specified or even hinted at—and most critics believed that this production managed to remain true to the tragicomic spirit of Beckett's existentialist play.

▼▼▼▼▼▼▼▼▼▼▼▼▼▼▼▼▼▼▼▼▼▼▼▼▼▼▼▼▼▼▼▼▼▼▼▼▼

CHECKLIST FOR WRITING ABOUT CHARACTER

◆ Does any character serve as a narrator? If so, what information does this narrator supply about the other characters? How reliable is the narrator?

◆ Are the major characters fully developed?

◆ Do the major characters change and grow during the course of the play, or do they remain essentially unchanged?

◆ What function does each of the minor characters serve in the play?

◆ What elements reveal changes in the characters?

◆ What is revealed about the characters through their words?

◆ Do characters use foreign words, regionalisms, slang, jargon, clichés, or profanity? What does such use of language reveal about characters? About theme?

◆ Is the language formal or informal?

◆ Do characters speak in dialect? With accents?

◆ Is the language elaborate or plain?

◆ Do different characters exhibit contrasting styles or levels of language? What is the significance of these differences?

◆ In what way does language reveal characters' emotional states?

◆ Does the tone or style of any character's language change significantly as the play progresses? What does this change reveal?

◆ Does the play include verbal irony? Dramatic irony? How is irony conveyed? What purpose does irony achieve?

◆ What is revealed about the characters through what others say about them?

◆ Do other characters like or dislike the character?

◆ Is the audience encouraged to react sympathetically to the character?

◆ What is revealed about the characters through their actions?

◆ What is revealed about the characters through the playwright's stage directions?

◆ How might different actors' interpretations change an audience's understanding of the characters?

▲▲▲▲▲▲▲▲▲▲▲▲▲▲▲▲▲▲▲▲▲▲▲▲▲▲▲▲▲▲▲▲▲▲▲▲▲

ANTON CHEKHOV (1860–1904) is the major nineteenth-century Russian playwright and short story writer. He became a doctor and, as a young adult, supported the rest of his family following his father's bankruptcy. After his early adult years in Moscow, Chekhov spent the rest of his life in the country, moving to Yalta, a resort town in Crimea, for his health (he suffered from tuberculosis). He continued to write plays, mostly for the Moscow Art Theatre, although he could not supervise their production as he would have wished. His important plays include *The Seagull* (1896), *Uncle Vanya* (1898), *The Three Sisters* (1901), and *The Cherry Orchard* (1904).

The Brute, or *The Bear* (1888), is one of a number of one-act farces Chekhov wrote just before his major plays. It is based on a French farce (*Les Jurons de Cadillac* by Pierre Breton) about a man who cannot refrain from swearing. The woman he loves offers to marry him if he can avoid swearing for one hour; though he can't do it, he fails so charmingly that she agrees to marry him anyway.

ANTON CHEKHOV
....

The Brute

(1888)

A Joke in One Act

English Version by Eric Bentley

CHARACTERS
....

MRS. POPOV, *widow and landowner, small, with dimpled cheeks*
MR. GRIGORY S. SMIRNOV, *gentleman farmer, middle-aged*
LUKA, *Mrs. Popov's footman, an old man*
GARDENER
COACHMAN
HIRED MEN

SCENE
....

The drawing room of a country house. Mrs. Popov, in deep mourning, is staring hard at a photograph. Luka is with her.

Luka: It's not right, ma'am, you're killing yourself. The cook has gone off with the maid to pick berries. The cat's having a high old time in the yard catching birds. Every living thing is happy. But you stay moping here in the house like it was a convent, taking no pleasure in nothing. I mean it, ma'am! It must be a full year since you set foot out of doors.

Mrs. Popov: I must never set foot out of doors again, Luka. Never! I have nothing to set foot out of doors *for.* My life is done. *He* is in his grave. I have buried myself alive in this house. We are *both* in our graves.

Luka: You're off again, ma'am. I just won't listen to you no more. Mr. Popov is dead, but what can we do about that? It's God's doing. God's will be done. You've cried over him, you've done your share of mourning, haven't you? There's a limit to everything. You can't go on weeping and wailing forever. My old lady died, for that matter, and I wept and wailed over her a whole month long. Well, that was it. I couldn't weep and wail all my life. She just wasn't worth it. *(He sighs.)* As for the neighbors, you've forgotten all about them, ma'am. You don't visit them and you don't let them visit you. You and I are like a pair of spiders—excuse the expression, ma'am—here we are in this house like a pair of spiders, we never see the light of day. And it isn't like there was no nice people around either. The whole county's swarming with 'em. There's a regiment quartered at Riblov, and the officers are so good-looking! The girls can't take their eyes off them— There's a ball at the camp every Friday—The military band plays most every day of the week—What do you say, ma'am? You're young, you're pretty, you could enjoy yourself! Ten years from now you may want to strut and show your feathers to the officers, and it'll be too late.

Mrs. Popov: *(firmly)* You must never bring this subject up again, Luka. Since Popov died, life has been an empty dream to me, you know that. *You* may think I am alive. Poor ignorant Luka! You are wrong. I am dead. I'm in my grave. Never more shall I see the light of day, never strip from my body this . . . raiment of death! Are you listening, Luka? Let his ghost learn how I love him! Yes, *I* know, and *you* know, he was often unfair to me, he was cruel to me, and he was unfaithful to me. What of it? *I* shall be faithful to *him,* that's all. I will show him how *I* can love. Hereafter, in a better world than this, he will welcome me back, the same loyal girl I always was—

5 **Luka:** Instead of carrying on this way, ma'am, you should go out in the garden and take a bit of a walk, ma'am. Or why not harness Toby and take a drive? Call on a couple of the neighbours, ma'am?

Mrs. Popov: *(breaking down)* Oh, Luka!

Luka: Yes, ma'am? What have I said, ma'am? Oh, dear!

Mrs. Popov: Toby! You said Toby! He adored that horse. When he drove me out to the Korchagins and the Vlasovs, it was always with Toby!

He was a wonderful driver, do you remember, Luka? So graceful! So strong! I can see him now, pulling at those reins with all his might and main! Toby! Luka, tell them to give Toby an extra portion of oats today.

LUKA: Yes, ma'am.

A bell rings.

10 **MRS. POPOV:** Who is that? Tell them I'm not at home.

LUKA: Very good, ma'am. *(Exit.)*

MRS. POPOV: *(gazing again at the photograph)* You shall see, my Popov, how a wife can love and forgive. Till death do us part. Longer than that. Till death re-unite us forever! *(Suddenly a titter breaks through her tears.)* Aren't you ashamed of yourself, Popov? Here's your little wife, being good, being faithful, so faithful she's locked up here waiting for her own funeral, while you—doesn't it make you ashamed, you naughty boy? You were terrible, you know. You were unfaithful, and you made those awful scenes about it, you stormed out and left me alone for weeks—

Enter Luka.

LUKA: *(upset)* There's someone asking for you, ma'am. Says he must—

MRS. POPOV: I suppose you told him that since my husband's death I see no one?

15 **LUKA:** Yes, ma'am. I did, ma'am. But he wouldn't listen, ma'am. He says it's urgent.

MRS. POPOV: *(shrilly)* I see no one!!

LUKA: He won't take no for an answer, ma'am. He just curses and swears and comes in anyway. He's a perfect monster, ma'am. He's in the dining room right now.

MRS. POPOV: In the dining room, is he? I'll give him his come-uppance. Bring him in here this minute.

Exit Luka.

(Suddenly sad again.) Why do they do this to me? Why? Insulting my grief, intruding on my solitude? *(She sighs.)* I'm afraid I'll have to enter a convent. I will, I *must* enter a convent!

Enter Mr. Smirnov and Luka.

SMIRNOV: *(to Luka)* Dolt! Idiot! You talk too much! *(Seeing Mrs. Popov. With dignity.)* May I have the honor of introducing myself, madam? Grigory S. Smirnov, landowner and lieutenant of artillery, retired. Forgive me, madam, if I disturb your peace and quiet, but my business is both urgent and weighty.

20 **MRS. POPOV:** *(declining to offer him her hand)* What is it you wish, sir?

SMIRNOV: At the time of his death, your late husband—with whom I had the honor to be acquainted, ma'am—was in my debt to the tune of twelve hundred rubles. I have two notes to prove it. Tomorrow, ma'am, I must pay the interest on a bank loan. I have therefore no alternative, ma'am, but to ask you to pay me the money today.

MRS. POPOV: Twelve hundred rubles? But what did my husband owe it to you for?

SMIRNOV: He used to buy his oats from me, madam.

MRS. POPOV: *(to Luka, with a sigh)* Remember what I said, Luka: tell them to give Toby an extra portion of oats today!

Exit Luka.

My dear Mr.—what was the name again?

25 **SMIRNOV:** Smirnov, ma'am.

MRS. POPOV: My dear Mr. Smirnov, if Mr. Popov owed you money, you shall be paid—to the last ruble, to the last kopeck. But today—you must excuse me, Mr.—what was it?

SMIRNOV: Smirnov, ma'am.

MRS. POPOV: Today, Mr. Smirnov, I have no ready cash in the house. *(Smirnov starts to speak.)* Tomorrow, Mr. Smirnov, no, the day after tomorrow, all will be well. My steward will be back from town. I shall see that he pays what is owing. Today, no. In any case, today is exactly seven months from Mr. Popov's death. On such a day you will understand that I am in no mood to think of money.

SMIRNOV: Madam, if you don't pay up now, you can carry me out feet foremost. They'll seize my estate.

30 **MRS. POPOV:** You can have your money. *(He starts to thank her.)* Tomorrow. *(He again starts to speak.)* That is: the day after tomorrow.

SMIRNOV: I don't need the money the day after tomorrow. I need it today.

MRS. POPOV: I'm sorry, Mr.—

SMIRNOV: *(shouting)* Smirnov!

MRS. POPOV: *(sweetly)* Yes, of course. But you can't have it today.

35 **SMIRNOV:** But I can't wait for it any longer!

MRS. POPOV: Be sensible, Mr. Smirnov. How can I pay you if I don't have it?

SMIRNOV: You don't have it?

MRS. POPOV: I don't have it.

SMIRNOV: Sure?

40 **MRS. POPOV:** Positive.

SMIRNOV: Very well. I'll make a note to that effect. *(Shrugging.)* And then they want me to keep cool. I meet the tax commissioner on the street, and he says, "Why are you always in such a bad humor, Smirnov?" Bad humor! How can I help it, in God's name? I need money, I need it desperately. Take yesterday: I leave home at the crack of dawn, I call on all my debtors. Not a one of them pays up. Footsore and weary. I creep at midnight into some little dive, and try to snatch a few winks of sleep on the floor by the vodka barrel. Then today, I come here, fifty miles from home, saying to myself, "At last, at last, I can be sure of something," and you're not in the mood! You give me a mood! Christ, how can I help getting all worked up?

Mrs. Popov: I thought I'd made it clear, Mr. Smirnov, that you'll get your money the minute my steward is back from town.

Smirnov: What the hell do I care about your steward? Pardon the expression, ma'am. But it was you I came to see.

Mrs. Popov: What language! What a tone to take to a lady! I refuse to hear another word. *(Quickly, exit.)*

45 **Smirnov:** Not in the mood, huh? "Exactly seven months since Popov's death," huh? How about me? *(Shouting after her.)* Is there this interest to pay, or isn't there? I'm asking you a question: is there this interest to pay, or isn't there? So your husband died, and you're not in the mood, and your steward's gone off some place, and so forth and so on, but what can *I* do about all that, huh? What do *you* think I should do? Take a running jump and shove my head through the wall? Take off in a balloon? You don't know my *other* debtors. I call on Gruzdeff. Not at home. I look for Yaroshevitch. He's hiding out. I find Kooritsin. He kicks up a row, and I have to throw him through the window. I work my way right down the list. Not a kopeck. Then I come to you, and God damn it to hell, if you'll pardon the expression, you're not in the mood! *(Quietly, as he realizes he's talking to air.)* I've spoiled them all, that's what, I've let them play me for a sucker. Well, I'll show them. I'll show this one. I'll stay right here till she pays up. Ugh! *(He shudders with rage.)* I'm in a rage! I'm in a positively towering rage! Every nerve in my body is trembling at forty to the dozen! I can't breathe, I feel ill, I think I'm going to faint, hey, you there!

Enter Luka.

Luka: Yes, sir? Is there anything you wish, sir?

Smirnov: Water! Water! No, make it vodka.

Exit Luka.

Consider the logic of it. A fellow creature is desperately in need of cash, so desperately in need that he has to seriously contemplate hanging himself, and this woman, this mere chit of a girl, won't pay up, and why not? Because, forsooth, she isn't in the mood! Oh, the logic of women! Come to that, I never have liked them, I could do without the whole sex. Talk to a woman? I'd rather sit on a barrel of dynamite, the very thought gives me gooseflesh. Women! Creatures of poetry and romance! Just to see one in the distance gets me mad. My legs start twitching with rage. I feel like yelling for help.

Enter Luka, handing Smirnov a glass of water.

Luka: Mrs. Popov is indisposed, sir. She is seeing no one.

Smirnov: Get out.

Exit Luka.

Indisposed, is she? Seeing no one, huh? Well, she can see me or not, but I'll be here, I'll be right here till she pays up. If you're sick for a week, I'll be here for a week. If you're sick for a year, I'll be here for a year. You won't get around *me* with your widow's weeds and your schoolgirl dimples. I know all about dimples. *(Shouting through the window.)* Semyon, let the horses out of those shafts, we're not leaving, we're staying, and tell them to give the horses some oats, yes, oats, you fool, what do you think? *(Walking away from the window.)* What a mess, what an unholy mess! I didn't sleep last night, the heat is terrific today, not a damn one of 'em has paid up, and here's this— this skirt in mourning that's not in the mood! My head aches, where's that—*(He drinks from the glass.)* Water, ugh! You there!

Enter Luka.

50 **Luka:** Yes, sir. You wish for something, sir?
Smirnov: Where's that confounded vodka I asked for?

Exit Luka.

(Smirnov sits and looks himself over.) Oof! A fine figure of a man *I* am! Unwashed, uncombed, unshaven, straw on my vest, dust all over me. The little woman must've taken me for a highwayman. *(Yawns.)* I suppose it wouldn't be considered polite to barge into a drawing room in this state, but who cares? I'm not a visitor, I'm a creditor— most unwelcome of guests, second only to Death.

Enter Luka.

Luka: *(handing him the vodka)* If I may say so, sir, you take too many liberties, sir.
Smirnov: What?!
Luka: Oh, nothing, sir, nothing.
55 **Smirnov:** Who in hell do you think you're talking to? Shut your mouth!
Luka: *(aside)* There's an evil spirit abroad. The Devil must have sent him. Oh! *(Exit Luka.)*
Smirnov: What a rage I'm in! I'll grind the whole world to powder. Oh, I feel ill again. You there!

Enter Mrs. Popov.

Mrs. Popov: *(looking at the floor)* In the solitude of my rural retreat, Mr. Smirnov, I've long since grown unaccustomed to the sound of the human voice. Above all, I cannot bear shouting. I must beg you not to break the silence.
Smirnov: Very well. Pay me my money and I'll go.

60 **MRS. POPOV:**　I told you before, and I tell you again, Mr. Smirnov. I have no cash, you'll have to wait till the day after tomorrow. Can I express myself more plainly?

SMIRNOV:　And *I* told *you* before, and *I* tell *you* again, that I need the money today, that the day after tomorrow is too late, and that if you don't pay, and pay now, I'll have to hang myself in the morning!

MRS. POPOV:　But I have no cash. This is quite a puzzle.

SMIRNOV:　You won't pay, huh?

MRS. POPOV:　I *can't* pay, Mr. Smirnov.

65 **SMIRNOV:**　In that case, I'm going to sit here and wait. *(Sits down.)* You'll pay up the day after tomorrow? Very good. Till the day after tomorrow, here I sit. *(Pause. He jumps up.)* Now look, do I have to pay that interest tomorrow, or don't I? Or do you think I'm joking?

MRS. POPOV:　I must ask you not to raise your voice, Mr. Smirnov. This is not a stable.

SMIRNOV:　Who said it was? Do I have to pay the interest tomorrow or not?

MRS. POPOV:　Mr. Smirnov, do you know how to behave in the presence of a lady?

SMIRNOV:　No, madam, I do not know how to behave in the presence of a lady.

70 **MRS. POPOV:**　Just what I thought. I look at you, and I say: ugh! I hear you talk, and I say to myself: "That man doesn't know how to talk to a lady."

SMIRNOV:　You'd like me to come simpering to you in French, I suppose. "*Enchanté, madame! Merci beaucoup* for not paying zee money, *madame! Pardonnez-moi* if I 'ave disturbed you, *madame!* How *charmante* you look in mourning, *madame!*"

MRS. POPOV:　Now you're being silly, Mr. Smirnov.

SMIRNOV:　*(mimicking)* "Now you're being silly, Mr. Smirnov." "You don't know how to talk to a lady, Mr. Smirnov." Look here, Mrs. Popov, I've known more women than you've known pussy cats. I've fought three duels on their account. I've jilted twelve, and been jilted by nine others. Oh, yes, Mrs. Popov, I've played the fool in my time, whispered sweet nothings, bowed and scraped and endeavored to please. Don't tell me I don't know what it is to love, to pine away with longing, to have the blues, to melt like butter, to be weak as water. I was full of tender emotion. I was carried away with passion. I squandered half my fortune on the sex. I chattered about women's emancipation. But there's an end to everything, dear madam. Burning eyes, dark eyelashes, ripe, red lips, dimpled cheeks, heaving bosoms, soft whisperings, the moon above; the lake below—I don't give a rap for that sort of nonsense any more, Mrs. Popov. I've found out about women. Present company excepted, they're liars. Their behavior is mere play acting; their conversation is sheer gossip. Yes, dear lady, women, young or old, are false, petty, vain, cruel, malicious, unreasonable. As for intelligence, any sparrow could give them points. Appearances, I admit, can be deceptive. In appearance, a woman may be all poetry and romance, goddess and angel, muslin and fluff. To look at her exterior is to be transported to heaven. But I have looked at her interior, Mrs. Popov, and what did I find there—in her very soul? A crocodile. *(He has gripped the back of the chair so firmly that it snaps.)* And, what is more revolting, a crocodile with an illusion, a crocodile that imagines tender sentiments are its own special province, a crocodile that thinks itself queen of the realm of love! Whereas, in sober fact, dear madam, if a woman can love anything except a lapdog you can hang me by the feet on that nail. For a man, love is suffering, love is sacrifice. A woman just swishes her train around and tightens her grip on your nose. Now, you're a woman, aren't you, Mrs. Popov? You must be an expert on some of this. Tell me, quite frankly, did you ever know a woman to be—faithful, for instance? Or even sincere? Only old hags, huh? Though some women are old hags from birth. But as for the others? You're right: a faithful woman is a freak of nature—like a cat with horns.

MRS. POPOV: Who *is* faithful, then? Who *have* you cast for the faithful lover? Not man?

75 **SMIRNOV:** Right first time, Mrs. Popov: man.

MRS. POPOV: *(going off into a peal of bitter laughter)* Man! Man is faithful! that's a new one! *(Fiercely.)* What right do you have to say this, Mr. Smirnov? Men faithful? Let me tell you something. Of all the men I have ever known my late husband Popov was the best. I loved him, and there are women who know how to love, Mr. Smirnov. I gave him my youth, my happiness, my life, my fortune. I worshipped the ground he trod on—and what happened? The best of men was unfaithful to me, Mr. Smirnov. Not once in a while. All the time. After he died, I found his desk drawer full of love letters. While he was alive, he was always going away for the week-end. He squandered my money. He made love to other women before my very eyes. But, in spite of all, Mr. Smirnov, *I* was faithful. Unto death. And beyond. I am *still* faithful, Mr. Smirnov! Buried alive in this house, I shall wear mourning till the day I, too, am called to my eternal rest.

SMIRNOV: *(laughing scornfully)* Expect me to believe that? As if I couldn't see through all this hocus-pocus. Buried alive! Till you're called to your eternal rest! Till when? Till some little poet—or some little subaltern with his first moustache—comes riding by and asks: "Can that be the house of the mysterious Tamara who for love of her late husband has buried herself alive, vowing to see no man?" Ha!

MRS. POPOV: *(flaring up)* How dare you? How dare you insinuate—?

SMIRNOV: You may have buried yourself alive, Mrs. Popov, but you haven't forgotten to powder your nose.

80　**MRS. POPOV:**　*(incoherent)* How dare you? How—?

SMIRNOV:　Who's raising his voice now? Just because I call a spade a spade. Because I shoot straight from the shoulder. Well, don't shout at me, I'm not your steward.

MRS. POPOV:　I'm not shouting, you're shouting! Oh, leave me alone!

SMIRNOV:　Pay me the money, and I will.

MRS. POPOV:　You'll get no money out of me!

85　**SMIRNOV:**　Oh, so that's it!

MRS. POPOV:　Not a ruble, not a kopeck. Get out! Leave me alone!

SMIRNOV:　Not being your husband, I must ask you not to make scenes with me. *(He sits.)* I don't like scenes.

MRS. POPOV:　*(choking with rage)* You're sitting down?

SMIRNOV:　Correct, I'm sitting down.

90　**MRS. POPOV:**　I asked you to leave!

SMIRNOV:　Then give me the money. *(Aside.)* Oh, what a rage I'm in, what a rage!

MRS. POPOV:　The impudence of the man! I won't talk to you a moment longer. Get out. *(Pause.)* Are you going?

SMIRNOV:　No.

MRS. POPOV:　No?!

95　**SMIRNOV:**　No.

MRS. POPOV:　On your head be it. Luka!

Enter Luka.

Show the gentleman out, Luka.

LUKA:　*(approaching)* I'm afraid, sir, I'll have to ask you, um, to leave, sir, now, um—

SMIRNOV:　*(jumping up)* Shut your mouth, you old idiot! Who do you think you're talking to? I'll make mincemeat of you.

LUKA:　*(clutching his heart)* Mercy on us! Holy saints above! *(He falls into an armchair.)* I'm taken sick! I can't breathe!!

100　**MRS. POPOV:**　Then where's Dasha? Dasha! Dasha! Come here at once! *(She rings.)*

LUKA:　They gone picking berries, ma'am, I'm alone here—Water, water, I'm taken sick!

MRS. POPOV:　*(to Smirnov)* Get out, you!

SMIRNOV:　Can't you even be polite with me, Mrs. Popov?

MRS. POPOV:　*(clenching her fists and stamping her feet)* With you? You're a wild animal, you were never house-broken!

105　**SMIRNOV:**　What? What did you say?

MRS. POPOV:　I said you were a wild animal, you were never house-broken.

SMIRNOV:　*(advancing upon her)* And what right do you have to talk to me like that?

MRS. POPOV:　Like what?

SMIRNOV:　You have insulted me, madam.

110 **Mrs. Popov:** What of it? Do you think I'm scared of you?

Smirnov: So you think you can get away with it because you're a woman. A creature of poetry and romance, huh? Well, it doesn't go down with me. I hereby challenge you to a duel.

Luka: Mercy on us! Holy saints alive! Water!

Smirnov: I propose we shoot it out.

Mrs. Popov: Trying to scare me again? Just because you have big fists and a voice like a bull? You're a brute.

115 **Smirnov:** No one insults Grigory S. Smirnov with impunity! And I don't care if you *are* a female.

Mrs. Popov: *(trying to outshout him)* Brute, brute, brute!

Smirnov: The sexes are equal, are they? Fine: then it's just prejudice to expect men alone to pay for insults. I hereby challenge—

Mrs. Popov: *(screaming)* All right! You want to shoot it out? All right! Let's shoot it out!

Smirnov: And let it be here and now!

120 **Mrs. Popov:** Here and now! All right! I'll have Popov's pistols here in one minute! *(Walks away, then turns.)* Putting one of Popov's bullets through your silly head will be a pleasure! Au revoir. *(Exit.)*

Smirnov: I'll bring her down like a duck, a sitting duck. I'm not one of your little poets, I'm no little subaltern with his first moustache. No, sir, there's no weaker sex where I'm concerned!

Luka: Sir! Master! *(He goes down on his knees.)* Take pity on a poor old man, and do me a favor: go away. It was bad enough before, you nearly scared me to death. But a duel—!

Smirnov: *(ignoring him)* A duel! That's equality of the sexes for you! That's women's emancipation! Just as a matter of principle I'll bring her down like a duck. But what a woman! "Putting one of Popov's bullets through your silly head . . ." Her cheeks were flushed, her eyes were gleaming! And, by God, she's accepted the challenge! I never knew a woman like this before!

Luka: Sir! Master! Please go away! I'll always pray for you!

125 **Smirnov:** *(again ignoring him)* What a woman! Phew!! *She's* no sour puss, *she's* no cry baby. She's fire and brimstone. She's a human cannon ball. What a shame I have to kill her!

Luka: *(weeping)* Please, kind sir, please, go away!

Smirnov: *(as before)* I like her, isn't that funny? With those dimples and all? I like her. I'm even prepared to consider letting her off that debt. And where's my rage? It's gone. I never knew a woman like this before.

Enter Mrs. Popov with pistols.

Mrs. Popov: *(boldly)* Pistols, Mr. Smirnov! *(Matter of fact.)* But before we start, you'd better show me how it's done. I'm not too familiar with these things. In fact I never gave a pistol a second look.

Luka: Lord, have mercy on us, I must go hunt up the gardener and the coachman. Why has this catastrophe fallen upon us, O Lord? *(Exit.)*

130 **SMIRNOV:** *(examining the pistols)* Well, it's like this. There are several makes: one is the Mortimer, with capsules, especially constructed for dueling. What you have here are Smith and Wesson triple-action revolvers, with extractor, first-rate job, worth ninety rubles at the very least. You hold it this way. *(Aside.)* My God, what eyes she has! They're setting me on fire.

 MRS. POPOV: This way?

 SMIRNOV: Yes, that's right. You cock the trigger, take aim like this, head up, arm out like this. Then you just press with this finger here, and it's all over. The main thing is, keep cool, take slow aim, and don't let your arm jump.

 MRS. POPOV: I see. And if it's inconvenient to do the job here, we can go out in the garden.

 SMIRNOV: Very good. Of course, I should warn you: I'll be firing in the air.

135 **MRS. POPOV:** What? This is the end. Why?

 SMIRNOV: Oh, well—because—for private reasons.

 MRS. POPOV: Scared, huh? *(She laughs heartily.)* Now don't you try to get out of it, Mr. Smirnov. My blood is up. I won't be happy till I've drilled a hole through that skull of yours. Follow me. What's the matter? Scared?

 SMIRNOV: That's right. I'm scared.

 MRS. POPOV: Oh, come on, what's the matter with you?

140 **SMIRNOV:** Well, um, Mrs. Popov, I, um, I like you.

 MRS. POPOV: *(laughing bitterly)* Good God! He likes me, does he? The gall of the man. *(Showing him the door.)* You may leave, Mr. Smirnov.

 SMIRNOV: *(Quietly puts the gun down, takes his hat, and walks to the door. Then he stops and the pair look at each other without a word. Then, approaching gingerly.)* Listen, Mrs. Popov. Are you still mad at me? I'm in the devil of a temper myself, of course. But then, you see—what I mean is—it's this way—the fact is—(Roaring.)* Well, is it my fault, damn it, if I like you? *(Clutches the back of a chair. It breaks.)* Christ, what fragile furniture you have here. I like you. Know what I mean? I could fall in love with you.

 MRS. POPOV: I hate you. Get out!

 SMIRNOV: What a woman! I never saw anything like it. Oh, I'm lost, I'm done for, I'm a mouse in a trap.

145 **MRS. POPOV:** Leave this house, or I shoot!

 SMIRNOV: Shoot away! What bliss to die of a shot that was fired by that little velvet hand! To die gazing into those enchanting eyes. I'm out of my mind. I know: you must decide at once. Think for one second, then decide. Because if I leave now, I'll never be back. Decide! I'm a pretty decent chap. Landed gentleman, I should say. Ten thousand a year. Good stable. Throw a kopeck up in the air, and I'll put a bullet through it. Will you marry me?

 MRS. POPOV: *(indignant, brandishing the gun).* We'll shoot it out! Get going! Take your pistol!

SMIRNOV: I'm out of my mind. I don't understand anything any more. *(Shouting.)* You there! That vodka!

MRS. POPOV: No excuses! No delays! We'll shoot it out!

150 **SMIRNOV:** I'm out of my mind. I'm falling in love. I *have* fallen in love. *(He takes her hand vigorously; she squeals.)* I love you. *(He goes down on his knees.)* I love you as I've never loved before. I jilted twelve, and was jilted by nine others. But I didn't love a one of them as I love you. I'm full of tender emotion. I'm melting like butter. I'm weak as water. I'm on my knees like a fool, and I offer you my hand. It's a shame, it's a disgrace. I haven't been in love in five years. I took a vow against it. And now, all of a sudden, to be swept off my feet, it's a scandal. I offer you my hand, dear lady. Will you or won't you? You won't? Then don't! *(He rises and walks toward the door.)*

MRS. POPOV: I didn't say anything.

SMIRNOV: *(stopping)* What?

MRS. POPOV: Oh, nothing, you can go. Well, no, just a minute. No, you can go. Go! I detest you! But, just a moment. Oh, if you knew how furious I feel! *(Throws the gun on the table.)* My fingers have gone to sleep holding that horrid thing. *(She is tearing her handkerchief to shreds.)* And what are you standing around for? Get out of here!

SMIRNOV: Goodbye.

155 **MRS. POPOV:** Go, go, go! *(Shouting.)* Where are you going? Wait a minute! No, no, it's all right, just go. I'm fighting mad. Don't come near me, don't come near me!

SMIRNOV: *(who is coming near her)* I'm pretty disgusted with myself— falling in love like a kid, going down on my knees like some moongazing whippersnapper, the very thought gives me gooseflesh. *(Rudely.)* I love you. But it doesn't make sense. Tomorrow, I have to pay that interest, and we've already started mowing. *(He puts his arm about her waist.)* I shall never forgive myself for this.

MRS. POPOV: Take your hands off me, I hate you! Let's shoot it out!

A long kiss. Enter Luka with an axe, the Gardener with a rake, the coachman with a pitchfork, hired men with sticks.

LUKA: *(seeing the kiss)* Mercy on us! Holy saints above!

MRS. POPOV: *(dropping her eyes)* Luka, tell them in the stable that Toby is *not* to have any oats today.

READING AND REACTING

1. Are Mr. Smirnov and Mrs. Popov round or flat characters? Are they static or dynamic?

2. Which of the two would you characterize as the stronger? That is, who (if anyone) has the upper hand in their relationship?

3. Although Mrs. Popov's husband is dead, he is, in a sense, an important character in *The Brute*. How does he influence the play's two main characters?

4. Why are Mrs. Popov and Mr. Smirnov distrustful of members of the opposite sex? How is this distrust revealed to the audience?

5. Do you think this play reinforces gender stereotypes or questions their validity? Explain.

6. Because *The Brute* is a farce, Chekhov's characters frequently exaggerate for comic effect. For instance, Smirnov tells Mrs. Popov, "I've known more women than you've known pussy cats. I've fought three duels on their account. I've jilted twelve, and been jilted by nine others." Give some additional examples of such broadly exaggerated language, and explain its function.

7. Give some examples of physical actions used to reinforce emotions or attitudes in *The Brute*.

8. Explain and illustrate how the characters' words reveal each of the following moods: Mrs. Popov's anger at Mr. Smirnov, Mrs. Popov's ambivalence toward her late husband, Mr. Smirnov's impatience with Mrs. Popov, Mr. Smirnov's stubbornness.

9. As the play progresses, Mrs. Popov's changing language communicates her changing feelings toward her husband. Give examples to illustrate these changes.

10. What can you infer about Mrs. Popov's relationship with Luka from the language she uses when she addresses him? From the language he uses with her? What function does Luka serve in the play?

11. At what point in the play does Mr. Smirnov's speech become more elaborate? What does his use of figurative language suggest?

12. Where in the play does dramatic irony occur? Is verbal irony present?

13. Where in the play do asides occur? What is their function?

14. **JOURNAL ENTRY**   If you had to take a side in the dispute between Mrs. Popov and Mr. Smirnov, whose side would you be on? Why?

15. **CRITICAL PERSPECTIVE**   Critic Harvey Pilcher characterizes *The Brute*, like Chekhov's other one-act "farce-vaudevilles," as a "comedy of situation":

> *Although they contain an assortment of comic ingredients—parody, slapstick, misunderstandings, the absurd, the grotesque, irony, and social satire—the vaudevilles still belong to the genre of "comedy of situation." This is because . . . the emphasis for an audience is 'not on mystery and surprise, but on the working-out of a known situation . . . not so much on what will happen next as to how it will happen.' In the best of the comedy of situation stories, the situation itself opens the door to comedy of characterization. There is a comic psychological inevitability about the way Smirnov . . . fails to live up to his misogynistic principles and [Mrs. Popov] abandons the role of the faithful widow. . . .*

   In what way is the "comedy of situation" Pilcher describes similar to today's television "situation comedies"?

WILLIAM SHAKESPEARE (1564–1616) was born in Stratford-on-Avon, England, and raised his family there, although he spent most of his adult life in London. Though relatively little is known of his daily life, he was deeply involved in all aspects of the theater: He was an actor who joined the Lord Chamberlain's Men (an acting company) in 1594, a shareholder in that company, a part owner of the Globe Theater from 1599, and, most significantly, the author of at least thirty-six plays. Most of his plays were not published during his lifetime; his friends issued the first legitimate version of his collected plays, the First Folio edition, in 1623.

It is difficult to date many of Shakespeare's plays exactly since they must be dated by records of their first performance (often hard to come by) and topical references in the text. We do know from an entry in the *Stationers' Register* that a play called the *Revenge of Hamlett Prince Denmarke* was presented around July 26, 1602, though Shakespeare's company probably first staged the play at the Globe Theater in 1600 or 1601. Some scholars believe the play was composed as early as 1598, though no earlier, since it was not among Shakespeare's plays listed in Francis Meres's *Palladis Tamis,* published in 1598.

WILLIAM SHAKESPEARE

Hamlet
Prince of Denmark*

(c. 1600)

CHARACTERS

CLAUDIUS, *King of Denmark*
HAMLET, *son to the former and*
  nephew to the present King
POLONIUS, *Lord Chamberlain*
HORATIO, *friend to Hamlet*
LAERTES, *son to Polonius*
VOLTIMAND
CORNELIUS
ROSENCRANTZ } *courtiers*
GUILDENSTERN
OSRIC

REYNALDO, *servant to Polonius*
PLAYERS
TWO CLOWNS, *grave-diggers*
FORTINBRAS, *Prince of Norway*
A CAPTAIN
ENGLISH AMBASSADORS
GHOST OF HAMLET'S FATHER
GERTRUDE, *Queen of Denmark and*
  mother of Hamlet
OPHELIA, *daughter to Polonius*
LORDS, LADIES, OFFICERS,

---

* Note that individual lines are numbered in the following play. When a line is shared by one or more characters, it is counted as one line.

A GENTLEMAN   SOLDIERS, SAILORS,
A PRIEST   MESSENGERS, AND OTHER
FRANCISCO, *a soldier*   ATTENDANTS
MARCELLUS ⎫
BERNARDO ⎭ *officers*

ACT I SCENE I

Elsinore. A platform before the castle.

(Francisco at his post. Enter to him Bernardo.)

BERNARDO: Who's there?
FRANCISCO: Nay, answer me: stand, and unfold yourself.
BERNARDO: Long live the king!
FRANCISCO: Bernardo?
BERNARDO: He.
FRANCISCO: You come most carefully upon your hour.
5 **BERNARDO:** 'Tis now struck twelve; get thee to bed, Francisco.
FRANCISCO: For this relief much thanks: 'tis bitter cold,
    And I am sick at heart.
BERNARDO: Have you had quiet guard?
FRANCISCO: Not a mouse stirring.
BERNARDO: Well, good-night.
10   If you do meet Horatio and Marcellus,
    The rivals of my watch, bid them make haste.
FRANCISCO: I think I hear them.—Stand, ho! Who is there?

(Enter Horatio and Marcellus.)

HORATIO: Friends to this ground.
MARCELLUS: And liegemen to the Dane.
15 **FRANCISCO:** Give you good-night.
MARCELLUS: O, farewell, honest soldier:
    Who hath reliev'd you?
FRANCISCO: Bernardo has my place.
    Give you good-night.

(Exit.)

MARCELLUS: Holla! Bernardo!
BERNARDO: Say.
    What, is Horatio there?
HORATIO: A piece of him.
BERNARDO: Welcome, Horatio:—welcome, good Marcellus.
20 **MARCELLUS:** What, has this thing appear'd again to-night?
BERNARDO: I have seen nothing.

Marcellus: Horatio says 'tis but our fantasy,
And will not let belief take hold of him
Touching this dreaded sight, twice seen of us:
25 Therefore I have entreated him along
With us to watch the minutes of this night;
That, if again this apparition come
He may approve our eyes and speak to it.
Horatio: Tush, tush, 'twill not appear.
Bernardo: Sit down awhile,
30 And let us once again assail your ears,
That are so fortified against our story,
What we two nights have seen.
Horatio: Well, sit we down,
And let us hear Bernardo speak of this.
Bernardo: Last night of all,
35 When yon same star that's westward from the pole
Had made his course to illume that part of heaven
Where now it burns, Marcellus and myself,
The bell then beating one,—
Marcellus: Peace, break thee off; look where it comes again!

(Enter Ghost, armed.)

40 **Bernardo:** In the same figure, like the king that's dead.
Marcellus: Thou art a scholar; speak to it, Horatio.
Bernardo: Looks it not like the king? mark it, Horatio.
Horatio: Most like:—it harrows me with fear and wonder.
Bernardo: It would be spoke to.
Marcellus: Question it, Horatio.
45 **Horatio:** What art thou, that usurp'st this time of night,
Together with that fair and warlike form
In which the majesty of buried Denmark
Did sometimes march? by heaven I charge thee, speak!
Marcellus: It is offended.
Bernardo: See, it stalks away!
50 **Horatio:** Stay! speak, speak! I charge thee, speak!

(Exit Ghost.)

Marcellus: 'Tis gone, and will not answer.
Bernardo: How now, Horatio! you tremble and look pale:
Is not this something more than fantasy?
What think you on't?
55 **Horatio:** Before my God, I might not this believe
Without the sensible and true avouch
Of mine own eyes.
Marcellus: Is it not like the king?

HORATIO: As thou art to thyself:
  Such was the very armor he had on
60 When he the ambitious Norway combated;
  So frown'd he once when, in an angry parle,[1]
  He smote the sledded Polacks on the ice.
  'Tis strange.
MARCELLUS: Thus twice before, and just at this dead hour,
65 With martial stalk hath he gone by our watch.
HORATIO: In what particular thought to work I know not;
  But, in the gross and scope of my opinion,
  This bodes some strange eruption to our state.
MARCELLUS: Good now, sit down, and tell me, he that knows,
70 Why this same strict and most observant watch
  So nightly toils the subject of the land;
  And why such daily cast of brazen cannon,
  And foreign mart for implements of war;
  Why such impress of shipwrights, whose sore task
75 Does not divide the Sunday from the week;
  What might be toward, that this sweaty haste
  Doth make the night joint-laborer with the day:
  Who is't that can inform me?
HORATIO: That can I;
  At least, the whisper goes so. Our last king,
80 Whose image even but now appear'd to us,
  Was, as you know, by Fortinbras of Norway,
  Thereto prick'd on by a most emulate pride,
  Dar'd to the combat; in which our valiant Hamlet,—
  For so this side of our known world esteem'd him,—
85 Did slay this Fortinbras; who, by a seal'd compact,
  Well ratified by law and heraldry,
  Did forfeit, with his life, all those his lands.
  Which he stood seiz'd of,[2] to the conqueror:
  Against the which, a moiety competent[3]
90 Was gagéd[4] by our king; which had return'd
  To the inheritance of Fortinbras,
  Had he been vanquisher; as by the same cov'nant,
  And carriage of the article design'd,
  His fell to Hamlet. Now, sir, young Fortinbras,
95 Of unimproved mettle hot and full,
  Hath in the skirts of Norway, here and there,
  Shark'd up a list of landless resolutes,
  For food and diet, to some enterprise

---

[1] Parley, or conference.   [2] Possessed.   [3] A sufficient portion of his lands.
[4] Engaged or pledged.

That hath a stomach in't: which is no other,—
100 As it doth well appear unto our state,—
But to recover of us by strong hand,
And terms compulsatory, those foresaid lands
So by his father lost: and this, I take it,
Is the main motive of our preparations,
105 The source of this our watch, and the chief head
Of this post-haste and romage[5] in the land.
BERNARDO: I think it be no other, but e'en so:
Well may it sort that this portentous figure
Comes armed through our watch; so like the king
110 That was and is the question of these wars.
HORATIO: A mote it is to trouble the mind's eye.
In the most high and palmy state of Rome,
A little ere the mightiest Julius fell,
The graves stood tenantless, and the sheeted dead
115 Did squeak and gibber in the Roman streets:
As, stars with trains of fire and dews of blood,
Disasters in the sun; and the moist star,
Upon whose influence Neptune's empire stands,
Was sick almost to doomsday with eclipse:
120 And even the like precurse of fierce events,—
As harbingers preceding still the fates,
And prologue to the omen coming on,—
Have heaven and earth together demonstrated
Unto our climature and countrymen.—
125 But, soft, behold! lo, where it comes again!

(Re-enter Ghost.)

I'll cross it, though it blast me.—Stay, illusion!
If thou hast any sound or use of voice,
Speak to me:
If there be any good thing to be done,
130 That may to thee do ease, and grace to me,
Speak to me:
If thou art privy to thy country's fate,
Which, happily,[6] foreknowing may avoid,
O, speak!
135 Or if thou has uphoarded in thy life
Extorted treasure in the womb of earth,
For which, they say, you spirits oft walk in death,

(Cock crows.)

---

[5] General activity.   [6] Haply, or perhaps.

Speak of it:—stay, and speak!—Stop it, Marcellus.

MARCELLUS: Shall I strike at it with my partisan?[7]

140 **HORATIO:** Do, if it will not stand.

BERNARDO: 'Tis here!

HORATIO: 'Tis here!

MARCELLUS: 'Tis gone!

(Exit Ghost.)

We do it wrong, being so majestical,
To offer it the show of violence;
For it is, as the air, invulnerable,
145 And our vain blows malicious mockery.

BERNARDO: It was about to speak when the cock crew.

HORATIO: And then it started like a guilty thing
Upon a fearful summons. I have heard,
The cock, that is the trumpet to the morn,
150 Doth with his lofty and shrill-sounding throat
Awake the god of day; and at his warning,
Whether in sea or fire, in earth or air,
The extravagant and erring spirit hies
To his confine: and of the truth herein
155 This present object made probation.[8]

MARCELLUS: It faded on the crowing of the cock.
Some say that ever 'gainst that season comes
Wherein our Saviour's birth is celebrated,
The bird of dawning singeth all night long:
160 And then, they say, no spirit can walk abroad;
The nights are wholesome; then no planets strike,
No fairy takes, nor witch hath power to charm;
So hallow'd and so gracious is the time.

HORATIO: So have I heard, and do in part believe.
165 But, look, the morn, in russet mantle clad,
Walks o'er the dew of yon high eastern hill:
Break we our watch up: and, by my advice,
Let us impart what we have seen to-night
Unto young Hamlet; for, upon my life,
170 This spirit, dumb to us, will speak to him:
Do you consent we shall acquaint him with it,
As needful in our loves, fitting our duty?

MARCELLUS: Let's do't, I pray; and I this morning know
Where we shall find him most conveniently.

(Exeunt.)

---

[7] Pike.   [8] Proof.

SCENE II

Elsinore. A room of state in the castle.

(Enter the King, Queen, Hamlet, Polonius, Laertes, Voltimand, Cornelius, Lords, and Attendants.)

KING: Though yet of Hamlet our dear brother's death
The memory be green; and that it us befitted
To bear our hearts in grief, and our whole kingdom
To be contracted in one brow of woe;
5   Yet so far hath discretion fought with nature
That we with wisest sorrow think on him,
Together with remembrance of ourselves.
Therefore our sometime sister, now our queen,
The imperial jointress of this warlike state,
10   Have we, as 'twere with defeated joy,—
With one auspicious and one dropping eye,
With mirth and funeral, and with dirge in marriage,
In equal scale weighing delight and dole,—
Taken to wife: nor have we herein barr'd
15   Your better wisdoms, which have freely gone
With this affair along:—for all, our thanks.
Now follows that you know, young Fortinbras,
Holding a weak supposal of our worth,
Or thinking by our late dear brother's death
20   Our state to be disjoint and out of frame,
Colleagued with the dream of his advantage,
He hath not fail'd to pester us with message,
Importing the surrender of those lands
Lost by his father, with all bonds of law,
25   To our most valiant brother. So much for him.—
Now for ourself, and for this time of meeting:
Thus much the business is:—we have here writ
To Norway, uncle of young Fortinbras,—
Who, impotent and bed-rid, scarcely hears
30   Of this his nephew's purpose,—to suppress
His further gait herein; in that the levies,
The lists, and full proportions, are all made
Out of his subject:—and we here despatch
You, good Cornelius, and you, Voltimand,
35   For bearers of this greeting to old Norway;
Giving to you no further personal power
To business with the king more than the scope
Of these dilated articles allow.
Farewell; and let your haste commend your duty.

40 **CORNELIUS** and **VOLTIMAND:**   In that and all things will we show our
duty.

KING: We doubt it nothing: heartily farewell.

(Exeunt Voltimand and Cornelius.)

And now, Laertes, what's the news with you?
You told us of some suit; what is't, Laertes?
You cannot speak of reason to the Dane,
45 And lose your voice: what wouldst thou beg, Laertes,
That shall not be my offer, nor thy asking?
The head is not more native to the heart,
The hand more instrumental to the mouth,
Than is the throne of Denmark to thy father.
50 What wouldst thou have, Laertes?

LAERTES: Dread my lord,
Your leave and favor to return to France;
From whence though willingly I came to Denmark,
To show my duty in your coronation;
Yet now, I must confess, that duty done,
55 My thoughts and wishes bend again toward France.
And bow them to your gracious leave and pardon.

KING: Have you your father's leave? What says Polonius?

POLONIUS: He hath, my lord, wrung from me my slow leave
By laborsome petition; and at last
60 Upon his will I seal'd my hard consent:
I do beseech you, give him leave to go.

KING: Take thy fair hour, Laertes; time be thine,
And thy best graces spend it at thy will!—
But now, my cousin Hamlet, and my son,—

65 **HAMLET:**   *(Aside)* A little more than kin, and less than kind.

KING: How is it that the clouds still hang on you?

HAMLET: Not so, my lord; I am too much i' the sun.

QUEEN: Good Hamlet, cast thy nighted color off,
And let thine eye look like a friend on Denmark.
70 Do not for ever with thy vailed[1] lids
Seek for thy noble father in the dust:
Thou know'st 'tis common,—all that live must die,
Passing through nature to eternity.

HAMLET: Ay, madam, it is common.

QUEEN: If it be,
75 Why seems it so particular with thee?

HAMLET: Seems, madam! nay, it is; I know not seems.
'Tis not alone my inky cloak, good mother,

---

[1] Downcast.

Nor customary suits of solemn black,
Nor windy suspiration of forc'd breath,
80   No, nor the fruitful river in the eye,
Nor the dejected 'havior of the visage,
Together with all forms, moods, shows of grief,
That can denote me truly: these, indeed, seem;
For they are actions that a man might play:
85   But I have that within which passeth show;
These but the trappings and the suits of woe.

KING: 'Tis sweet and cómmendable in your nature, Hamlet,
To give these mourning duties to your father:
But, you must know, your father lost a father;
90   That father lost, lost his; and the survivor bound,
In filial obligation, for some term
To do obsequious sorrow: but to persever
In obstinate condolement is a course
Of impious stubbornness; 'tis unmanly grief:
95   It shows a will most incorrect to heaven;
A heart unfortified, a mind impatient;
An understanding simple and unschool'd:
For what we know must be, and is as common
As any the most vulgar thing to sense,[2]
100   Why should we, in our peevish opposition,
Take it to heart? Fie! 'tis a fault to heaven,
A fault against the dead, a fault to nature,
To reason most absurd; whose common theme
Is death of fathers, and who still[3] hath cried,
105   From the first corse till he that died to-day,
This must be so. We pray you, throw to earth
This unprevailing woe; and think of us
As of a father: for let the world take note
You are the most immediate to our throne;
110   And with no less nobility of love
Than that which dearest father bears his son
Do I impart toward you. For your intent
In going back to school in Wittenberg,
It is most retrograde to our desire:
115   And we beseech you bend you to remain
Here, in the cheer and comfort of our eye,
Our chiefest courtier, cousin, and our son.

QUEEN: Let not thy mother lose her prayers, Hamlet:
I pray thee, stay with us; go not to Wittenberg.
120 **HAMLET:**   I shall in all my best obey you, madam.

---

[2] Anything that is very commonly seen or heard.   [3] Ever, or always.

KING: Why, 'tis a loving and a fair reply:
Be as ourself in Denmark.—Madam, come;
This gentle and unforc'd accord of Hamlet
Sits smiling to my heart: in grace whereof,
125   No jocund health that Denmark drinks to-day
But the great cannon to the clouds shall tell;
And the king's rouse[4] the heavens shall bruit[5] again,
Re-speaking earthly thunder. Come away.

(Exeunt all but Hamlet.)

HAMLET: O, that this too too solid flesh would melt,
130   Thaw, and resolve itself into a dew!
Or that the Everlasting had not fix'd
His canon 'gainst self-slaughter! O God! O God!
How weary, stale, flat, and unprofitable
Seem to me all the uses of this world!
135   Fie on't! O fie! 'tis an unweeded garden,
That grows to seed; things rank and gross in nature
Possess it merely. That it should come to this!
But two months dead!—nay, not so much, not two:
So excellent a king; that was, to this,
140   Hyperion[6] to a satyr: so loving to my mother,
That he might not beteem the winds of heaven
Visit her face too roughly. Heaven and earth!
Must I remember? why, she would hang on him
As if increase of appetite had grown
145   By what it fed on: and yet, within a month,—
Let me not think on't,—Frailty, thy name is woman!—
A little month; or ere those shoes were old
With which she follow'd my poor father's body
Like Niobe, all tears;—why she, even she,—
150   O God! a beast, that wants discourse of reason,
Would have mourn'd longer,—married with mine uncle,
My father's brother; but no more like my father
Than I to Hercules: within a month;
Ere yet the salt of most unrighteous tears
155   Had left the flushing in her galled eyes,
She married:—O, most wicked speed, to post
With such dexterity to incestuous sheets!
It is not, nor it cannot come to good;
But break, my heart,—for I must hold my tongue!

(Enter Horatio, Marcellus, and Bernardo.)

---

[4] Drink.   [5] Echo.   [6] The Greek sun god, the brightest and most beautiful of the gods.

160 **HORATIO:**   Hail to your lordship!
HAMLET: I am glad to see you well:
    Horatio,—or I do forget myself.
HORATIO: The same, my lord, and your poor servant ever.
HAMLET: Sir, my good friend; I'll change that name with you:
    And what make you from Wittenberg, Horatio?—Marcellus?
165 **MARCELLUS:**   My good lord,—
HAMLET: I am very glad to see you.—Good even, sir.—
    But what, in faith, make you from Wittenberg?
HORATIO: A truant disposition, good my lord.
HAMLET: I would not hear your enemy say so;
170   Nor shall you do mine ear that violence,
    To make it truster of your own report
    Against yourself: I know you are no truant.
    But what is your affair in Elsinore?
    We'll teach you to drink deep ere you depart.
175 **HORATIO:**   My lord, I came to see your father's funeral.
HAMLET: I pray thee, do not mock me, fellow-student;
    I think it was to see my mother's wedding.
HORATIO: Indeed, my lord, it follow'd hard upon.
HAMLET: Thrift, thrift, Horatio! the funeral-bak'd meats
180   Did coldly furnish forth the marriage tables.
    Would I had met my dearest foe[7] in heaven
    Ere I had ever seen that day, Horatio!—
    My father,—methinks I see my father.
HORATIO: Where, my lord?
HAMLET: In my mind's eye, Horatio.
185 **HORATIO:**   I saw him once; he was a goodly[8] king.
HAMLET: He was a man, take him for all in all,
    I shall not look upon his like again.
HORATIO: My lord, I think I saw him yester-night.
HAMLET: Saw who?
190 **HORATIO:**   My lord, the king your father.
HAMLET: The king my father!
HORATIO: Season your admiration[9] for awhile
    With an attent ear, till I may deliver,
    Upon the witness of these gentlemen,
    This marvel to you.
HAMLET: For God's love, let me hear.
195 **HORATIO:**   Two nights together had these gentlemen,
    Marcellus and Bernardo, in their watch,
    In the dead vast and middle of the night,
    Been thus encounter'd. A figure like your father,

---

[7] Worst enemy.   [8] Handsome.   [9] Astonishment.

Arm'd at all points exactly, cap-a-pe,[10]
200 Appears before them, and with solemn march
Goes slow and stately by them: thrice he walk'd
By their oppress'd[11] and fear-surprised eyes,
Within his truncheon's length; whilst they, distill'd
Almost to jelly with the act of fear,
205 Stand dumb, and speak not to him. This to me
In dreadful secrecy impart they did;
And I with them the third night kept the watch:
Where, as they had deliver'd, both in time,
Form of the thing, each word made true and good,
210 The apparition comes: I knew your father;
These hands are not more like.

HAMLET: But where was this?
MARCELLUS: My lord, upon the platform where we watch'd.
HAMLET: Did you not speak to it?
HORATIO: My lord, I did;
But answer made it none: yet once methought
215 It lifted up its head, and did address
Itself to motion, like as it would speak:
But even then the morning cock crew loud,
And at the sound it shrunk in haste away,
And vanish'd from our sight.
HAMLET: 'Tis very strange.
220 **HORATIO:** As I do live, my honor'd lord, 'tis true;
And we did think it writ down in our duty
To let you know of it.
HAMLET: Indeed, indeed, sirs, but this troubles me.
Hold you the watch to-night?
225 **MARCELLUS** and **BERNARDO:** We do, my lord.
HAMLET: Arm'd, say you?
MARCELLUS and **BERNARDO:** Arm'd, my lord.
HAMLET: From top to toe?
MARCELLUS and **BERNARDO:** My lord, from head to foot.
230 **HAMLET:** Then saw you not his face?
HORATIO: O yes, my lord; he wore his beaver up.
HAMLET: What, look'd he frowningly?
HORATIO: A countenance more in sorrow than in anger.
HAMLET: Pale or red?
235 **HORATIO:** Nay, very pale.
HAMLET: And fix'd his eyes upon you?
HORATIO: Most constantly.
HAMLET: I would I had been there.

---

[10] *Cap-a-pie,* from head to toe.   [11] Overwhelmed.

HORATIO: It would have much amaz'd you.

HAMLET: Very like, very like. Stay'd it long?

HORATIO: While one with moderate haste might tell[12] a hundred.

240 **MARCELLUS** and **BERNARDO:**   Longer, longer.

HORATIO: Not when I saw't.

HAMLET: His beard was grizzled,—no?

HORATIO: It was, as I have seen it in his life,
A sable silver'd.

HAMLET: I will watch to-night;
Perchance 'twill walk again.

HORATIO: I warrant it will.

245 **HAMLET:**   If it assume my noble father's person
I'll speak to it, though hell itself should gape
And bid me hold my peace. I pray you all,
If you have hitherto conceal'd this sight,
Let it be tenable in your silence still;

250 And whatsoever else shall hap to-night,
Give it an understanding, but no tongue:
I will requite your loves. So, fare ye well:
Upon the platform, 'twixt eleven and twelve,
I'll visit you.

ALL: Our duty to your honor.

255 **HAMLET:**   Your loves, as mine to you: farewell.

(Exeunt Horatio, Marcellus, and Bernardo.)

My father's spirit in arms; all is not well;
I doubt some foul play: would the night were come!
Till then sit still, my soul: foul deeds will rise,
Though all the earth o'erwhelm them, to men's eyes.

(Exit.)

SCENE III

A room in Polonius' house.

(Enter Laertes and Ophelia.)

LAERTES: My necessaries are embark'd: farewell:
And, sister, as the winds give benefit,
And convoy[1] is assistant, do not sleep,
But let me hear from you.

OPHELIA: Do you doubt that?

---

[12] Count.   [1] Means of conveyance.

5 **LAERTES:**   For Hamlet, and the trifling of his favor,
Hold it a fashion and a toy in blood:
A violet in the youth of primy nature,
Forward, not permanent, sweet, not lasting,
The perfume and suppliance of a minute;
10   No more.
OPHELIA: No more but so?
LAERTES: Think it no more:
For nature, crescent,[2] does not grow alone
In thews and bulk; but as this temple[3] waxes,
The inward service of the mind and soul
Grows wide withal. Perhaps he loves you now;
15   And now no soil nor cautel[4] doth besmirch
The virtue of his will: but you must fear,
His greatness weigh'd, his will is not his own;
For he himself is subject to his birth:
He may not, as unvalu'd persons do,
20   Carve for himself; for on his choice depends
The safety and the health of the whole state;
And therefore must his choice be circumscrib'd
Unto the voice and yielding of that body
Whereof he is the head. Then if he says he loves you,
25   It fits your wisdom so far to believe it
As he in his particular act and place
May give his saying deed; which is no further
Than the main[5] voice of Denmark goes withal.
Then weigh what loss your honor may sustain
30   If with too credent ear you list his songs,
Or lose your heart, or your chaste treasure open
To his unmaster'd importunity.
Fear it, Ophelia, fear it, my dear sister;
And keep within the rear of your affection,
35   Out of the shot and danger of desire.
The chariest maid is prodigal enough
If she unmask her beauty to the moon:
Virtue itself scrapes not calumnious strokes:
The canker galls the infants of the spring
40   Too oft before their buttons be disclos'd;
And in the morn and liquid dew of youth
Contagious blastments are most imminent.
Be wary, then; best safety lies in fear:
Youth to itself rebels, though none else near.
45 **OPHELIA:**   I shall the effect of this good lesson keep
As watchman to my heart. But, good my brother,

---

[2] Growing.   [3] Body.   [4] Deceit.   [5] Strong, or mighty.

Do not, as some ungracious pastors do,
Show me the steep and thorny way to heaven;
Whilst like a puff'd and reckless libertine,
50 Himself the primrose path of dalliance treads,
And recks not his own rede.[6]
LAERTES: O, fear me not.
I stay too long:—but here my father comes.

(Enter Polonius.)

A double blessing is a double grace;
Occasion smiles upon a second leave.
55 **POLONIUS:**   Yet here, Laertes! aboard, aboard, for shame!
The wind sits in the shoulder of your sail,
And you are stay'd for. There,—my blessing with you!

(Laying his hand on Laertes' head.)

And these few precepts in thy memory
See thou character.[7] Give thy thoughts no tongue,
60 Nor any unproportion'd thought his act.
Be thou familiar, but by no means vulgar.
The friends thou hast, and their adoption tried,
Grapple them to thy soul with hoops of steel;
But do not dull thy palm with entertainment
65 Of each new-hatch'd, unfledg'd comrade. Beware
Of entrance to a quarrel; but, being in,
Bear't that the opposèd may beware of thee.
Give every man thine ear, but few thy voice:
Take each man's censure,[8] but reserve thy judgment.
70 Costly thy habit as thy purse can buy,
But not express'd in fancy; rich, not gaudy:
For the apparel oft proclaims the man;
And they in France of the best rank and station
Are most select and generous chief in that.
75 Neither a borrower nor a lender be:
For a loan oft loses both itself and friend;
And borrowing dulls the edge of husbandry.
This above all,—to thine own self be true;
And it must follow, as the night the day,
80 Thou canst not then be false to any man.
Farewell: my blessing season this in thee!
LAERTES: Most humbly do I take my leave, my lord.
POLONIUS: The time invites you; go, your servants tend.[9]
LAERTES: Farewell, Ophelia; and remember well
85   What I have said to you.

---

[6] Counsel.   [7] Engrave in your mind.   [8] Opinion.   [9] Wait.

OPHELIA: 'Tis in my memory lock'd,
And you yourself shall keep the key of it.
LAERTES: Farewell. *(Exit.)*
POLONIUS: What is't, Ophelia, he hath said to you?
OPHELIA: So please you, something touching the Lord Hamlet.
90 **POLONIUS:** Marry, well bethought:
'Tis told me he hath very oft of late
Given private time to you; and you yourself
Have of your audience been most free and bounteous:
If it be so,—as so 'tis put on me,
95 And that in way of caution,—I must tell you,
You do not understand yourself so clearly
As it behoves my daughter and your honor.
What is between you? give me up the truth.
OPHELIA: He hath, my lord, of late made many tenders
100 Of his affection to me.
POLONIUS: Affection! pooh! you speak like a green girl,
Unsifted in such perilous circumstance.
Do you believe his tenders,[10] as you call them?
OPHELIA: I do not know, my lord, what I should think.
105 **POLONIUS:** Marry, I'll teach you: think yourself a baby;
That you have ta'en these tenders for true pay,
Which are not sterling. Tender yourself more dearly;
Or,—not to crack the wind of the poor phrase,
Wronging it thus,—you'll tender me a fool.
110 **OPHELIA:** My lord, he hath impórtun'd me with love
In honorable fashion.
POLONIUS: Ay, fashion you may call it; go to, go to.
OPHELIA: And hath given countenance to his speech, my lord,
With almost all the holy vows of heaven.
115 **POLONIUS:** Ay, springes to catch woodcocks. I do know,
When the blood burns, how prodigal the soul
Lends the tongue vows: these blazes, daughter,
Giving more light than heat,—extinct in both,
Even in their promise, as it is a-making,—
120 You must not take for fire. From this time
Be somewhat scanter of your maiden presence;
Set your entreatments at a higher rate
Than a command to parley. For Lord Hamlet,
Believe so much in him, that he is young;
125 And with a larger tether may he walk
Than may be given you: in few, Ophelia,
Do not believe his vows; for they are brokers,[11]—

---

[10] Offers. [11] Procurers.

Not of that die which their investments show,
But mere implorators of unholy suits,
130 Breathing like sanctified and pious bawds,
The better to beguile. This is for all,—
I would not, in plain terms, from this time forth,
Have you so slander any moment leisure
As to give words or talk with the Lord Hamlet.
135 Look to't, I charge you; come your ways.
OPHELIA: I shall obey, my lord.

(Exeunt.)

SCENE IV

The platform.

(Enter Hamlet, Horatio, and Marcellus.)

HAMLET: The air bites shrewdly; it is very cold.
HORATIO: It is a nipping and an eager air.
HAMLET: What hour now?
HORATIO: I think it lacks of twelve.
MARCELLUS: No, it is struck.
5 **HORATIO:** Indeed? I heard it not: then it draws near the season
Wherein the spirit held his wont to walk.

(A flourish of trumpets, and ordnance shot off within.)

What does this mean, my lord?
HAMLET: The king doth wake to-night, and takes his rouse,
Keeps wassail, and the swaggering upspring[1] reels;
10 And, as he drains his draughts of Rhenish down,
The kettle-drum and trumpet thus bray out
The triumph of his pledge.[2]
HORATIO: Is it a custom?
HAMLET: Ay, marry, is't:
But to my mind,—though I am native here,
15 And to the manner born,—it is a custom
More honor'd in the breach than the observance.
This heavy-headed revel east and west
Makes us traduc'd and tax'd of other nations:
They clepe us drunkards, and with swinish phrase
20 Soil our addition;[3] and, indeed, it takes
From our achievements, though perform'd at height,
The pith and marrow of our attribute.

---

[1] A dance.   [2] The glory of his toasts.   [3] Reputation.

So oft it chances in particular men
That, for some vicious mole of nature in them,
25   As in their birth,—wherein they are not guilty,
Since nature cannot choose his origin,—
By the o'ergrowth of some complexion,
Oft breaking down the pales and forts of reason;
Or by some habit, that too much o'erleavens
30   The form of plausive[4] manners;—that these men,—
Carrying, I say, the stamp of one defect,
Being nature's livery or fortune's star,—
Their virtues else,—be they as pure as grace,
As infinite as man may undergo,—
35   Shall in the general censure take corruption
From that particular fault: the dram of evil
Doth all the noble substance of a doubt
To his own scandal.

HORATIO: Look, my lord, it comes!

(Enter Ghost.)

HAMLET: Angels and ministers of grace defend us!—
40   Be thou a spirit of health or goblin damn'd,
Bring with thee airs from heaven or blasts from hell,
Be thy intents wicked or charitable,
Thou com'st in such a questionable shape
That I will speak to thee: I'll call thee Hamlet,
45   King, father, royal Dane: O, answer me!
Let me not burst in ignorance; but tell
Why thy canóniz'd bones, hearsèd in death,
Have burst their cerements; why the sepulchre,
Wherein we saw thee quietly in-urn'd,
50   Hath op'd his ponderous and marble jaws
To cast thee up again! What may this mean,
That thou, dead corse, again in còmplete steel,
Revisit'st thus the glimpses of the moon,
Making night hideous and we[5] fools of nature
55   So horridly to shake our disposition
With thoughts beyond the reaches of our souls?
Say, why is this? wherefore? what should we do?

(Ghost beckons Hamlet.)

HORATIO: It beckons you to go away with it,
As if it some impartment did desire
60   To you alone.

---

[4] Pleasing.   [5] Us.

MARCELLUS: Look, with what courteous action
It waves you to a more removed ground:
But do not go with it.
HORATIO: No, by no means.
HAMLET: It will not speak; then will I follow it.
HORATIO: Do not, my lord.
HAMLET: Why, what should be the fear?
65 I do not set my life at a pin's fee;
And for my soul, what can it do to that,
Being a thing immortal as itself?
It waves me forth again;—I'll follow it.
HORATIO: What if it tempt you toward the flood, my lord.
70 Or to the dreadful summit of the cliff
That beetles o'er his base into the sea,
And there assume some other horrible form,
Which might deprive your sovereignty of reason,
And draw you into madness? think of it:
75 The very place puts toys of desperation,
Without more motive, into every brain
That looks so many fathoms to the sea
And hears it roar beneath.
HAMLET: It waves me still.—
Go on; I'll follow thee.
80 **MARCELLUS:** You shall not go, my lord.
HAMLET: Hold off your hands.
HORATIO: Be rul'd; you shall not go.
HAMLET: My fate cries out,
And makes each petty artery in this body
As hardy as the Némean lion's[6] nerve.—

(Ghost beckons.)

Still am I call'd;—unhand me, gentlemen;—*(Breaking from them)*
85 By heaven, I'll make a ghost of him that lets[7] me.
I say, away!—Go on; I'll follow thee.

(Exeunt Ghost and Hamlet.)

HORATIO: He waxes desperate with imagination.
MARCELLUS: Let's follow; 'tis not fit thus to obey him.
HORATIO: Have after.—To what issue will this come?
90 **MARCELLUS:** Something is rotten in the state of Denmark.
HORATIO: Heaven will direct it.
MARCELLUS: Nay, let's follow him.

(Exeunt.)

---

[6] The fierce lion that Hercules was called upon to slay as one of his "twelve labors."
[7] Hinders.

SCENE V

A more remote part of the platform.

(Enter Ghost and Hamlet.)

HAMLET: Where wilt thou lead me? speak, I'll go no further.
GHOST: Mark me.
HAMLET: I will.
GHOST: My hour is almost come,
    When I to sulphurous and tormenting flames
    Must render up myself.
HAMLET: Alas, poor ghost!
5 **GHOST:**   Pity me not, but lend thy serious hearing
    To what I shall unfold.
HAMLET: Speak; I am bound to hear.
GHOST: So art thou to revenge, when thou shalt hear.
HAMLET: What?
GHOST: I am thy father's spirit;
10   Doom'd for a certain term to walk the night,
    And, for the day, confin'd to waste in fires
    Till the foul crimes[1] done in my days of nature
    Are burnt and purg'd away. But that I am forbid
    To tell the secrets of my prison-house,
15   I could a tale unfold whose lightest word
    Would harrow up thy soul; freeze thy young blood;
    Make thy two eyes, like stars, start from their spheres;
    Thy knotted and combined locks to part,
    And each particular hair to stand on end,
20   Like quills upon the fretful porcupine:
    But this eternal blazon[2] must not be
    To ears of flesh and blood.—List, list, O, list!—
    If thou didst ever thy dear father love,—
HAMLET: O God!
25 **GHOST:**   Revenge his foul and most unnatural murder.
HAMLET: Murder!
GHOST: Murder—most foul, as in the best it is;
    But this most foul, strange, and unnatural.
HAMLET: Haste me to know't, that I, with wings as swift
30   As meditation or the thoughts of love,
    May sweep to my revenge.
GHOST: I find thee apt;
    And duller shouldst thou be than the fat weed

---

[1] Rather, sins or faults.   [2] Disclosure of information concerning the other world.

That rots itself in ease on Lethe[3] wharf,
Wouldst thou not stir in this. Now, Hamlet,
35   'Tis given out that, sleeping in mine orchard,
A serpent stung me; so the whole ear of Denmark
Is by a forged process of my death
Rankly abus'd: but know, thou noble youth,
The serpent that did sting thy father's life
40   Now wears his crown.
HAMLET: O my prophetic soul! mine uncle!
GHOST: Ay, that incestuous, that adulterate beast,
With witchcraft of his wit, with traitorous gifts,—
O wicked wit and gifts that have the power
So to seduce!—won to his shameful lust
45   The will of my most seeming virtuous queen:
O Hamlet, what a falling-off was there!
From me, whose love was of that dignity
That it went hand in hand even with the vow
I made to her in marriage: and to decline
50   Upon a wretch whose natural gifts were poor
To those of mine!
But virtue, as it never will be mov'd,
Though lewdness court it in a shape of heaven;
So lust, though to a radiant angel link'd,
55   Will sate itself in a celestial bed
And prey on garbage.
But, soft! methinks I scent the morning air;
Brief let me be.—Sleeping within mine orchard,
My custom always in the afternoon,
60   Upon my sécure hour thy uncle stole,
With juice of cursed hebenon[4] in a vial,
And in the porches of mine ears did pour
The leperous distilment; whose effect
Holds such an enmity with blood of man
65   That, swift as quicksilver, it courses through
The natural gates and alleys of the body;
And with a sudden vigor it doth posset[5]
And curd, like eager[6] droppings into milk,
The thin and wholesome blood: so did it mine;
70   And a most instant tetter bark'd about,
Most lazar-like,[7] with vile and loathsome crust,
All my smooth body.
Thus was I, sleeping, by a brother's hand,
Of life, of crown, of queen, at once despatch'd:

---

[3] The river of forgetfulness of the past, out of which the dead drink.   [4] Ebony.
[5] Coagulate.   [6] Acid.   [7] Like a leper, whose skin is rough.

75   Cut off even in the blossoms of my sin,
        Unhousel'd, unanointed, unanel'd;
        No reckoning made, but sent to my account
        With all my imperfections on my head:
        O, horrible! O, horrible! most horrible!
80   If thou hast nature in thee, bear it not;
        Let not the royal bed of Denmark be
        A couch for luxury[8] and damned incest.
        But, howsoever thou pursu'st this act,
        Taint not thy mind, nor let thy soul contrive
85   Against thy mother aught: leave her to heaven,
        And to those thorns that in her bosom lodge,
        To prick and sting her. Fare thee well at once!
        The glowworm shows the matin to be near,
        And 'gins to pale his uneffectual fire:
90   Adieu, adieu! Hamlet, remember me. *(Exit.)*
   HAMLET: O all you host of heaven! O earth! what else?
        And shall I couple hell?—O, fie!—Hold, my heart;
        And you, my sinews, grow not instant old,
        But bear me stiffly up.—Remember thee!
95   Ay, thou poor ghost, while memory holds a seat
        In this distracted globe. Remember thee!
        Yea, from the table of my memory
        I'll wipe away all trivial fond[9] recórds,
        All saws of books, all forms, all pressures past,
100   That youth and observation copied there;
        And thy commandment all alone shall live
        Within the book and volume of my brain,
        Unmix'd with baser matter: yes, by heaven.—
        O most pernicious woman!
105   O villain, villain, smiling, damned villain!
        My tables,—meet it is I set it down,
        That one may smile, and smile, and be a villain;
        At least, I am sure, it may be so in Denmark:

  (Writing)

        So, uncle, there you are. Now to my word;
110   It is, *Adieu, adieu! remember me:*
        I have sworn't.
   HORATIO: *(Within)* My lord, my lord,—
   MARCELLUS: *(Within)*   Lord Hamlet,—
   HORATIO: *(Within)*   Heaven secure
        him!

---

[8] Lechery.   [9] Foolish.

Marcellus: *(Within)* So be it!

Horatio: *(Within)* Illo, ho, ho, my lord!

115 **Hamlet:** Hillo, ho, ho, boy! come, bird, come.[10]

(Enter Horatio and Marcellus.)

Marcellus: How is't, my noble lord?

Horatio: What news, my lord?

Hamlet: O, wonderful!

Horatio: Good my lord, tell it.

Hamlet: No; you'll reveal it.

Horatio: Not I, my lord, by heaven.

Marcellus: Nor I, my lord.

120 **Hamlet:** How say you, then; would heart of man once think it?—
But you'll be secret?

Horatio and **Marcellus:** Ay, by heaven, my lord.

Hamlet: There's ne'er a villain dwelling in all Denmark
But he's an arrant knave.

125 **Horatio:** There needs no ghost, my lord, come from the grave
To tell us this.

Hamlet: Why, right; you are i' the right;
And so, without more circumstance at all,
I hold it fit that we shake hands and part:

130 You, as your business and desire shall point you,—
For every man has business and desire,
Such as it is;—and for mine own poor part,
Look you, I'll go pray.

Horatio: These are but wild and whirling words, my lord.

135 **Hamlet:** I'm sorry they offend you, heartily;
Yes, faith, heartily.

Horatio: There's no offence, my lord.

Hamlet: Yes, by Saint Patrick, but there is, Horatio,
And much offence too. Touching this vision here,—
It is an honest ghost, that let me tell you:

140 For you desire to know what is between us,
O'ermaster't as you may. And now, good friends,
As you are friends, scholars, and soldiers,
Give me one poor request.

Horatio: What is't, my lord? we will.

145 **Hamlet:** Never make known what you have seen to-night.

Horatio and **Marcellus:** My lord, we will not.

Hamlet: Nay, but swear't.

Horatio: In faith,
My lord, not I.

---

10 Hamlet used the word "bird" because this is a falconer's call.

MARCELLUS: Nor I, my lord, in faith.

HAMLET: Upon my sword.

MARCELLUS: We have sworn, my lord, already.

HAMLET: Indeed, upon my sword, indeed.

150 **GHOST:** *(Beneath)* Swear.

HAMLET: Ha, ha, boy! say'st thou so? art thou there, truepenny?—
Come on,—you hear this fellow in the cellarage,—
Consent to swear.

HORATIO: Propose the oath, my lord.

HAMLET: Never to speak of this that you have seen,
155 Swear by my sword.

GHOST: *(Beneath)* Swear.

HAMLET: *Hic et ubique?*[11] then we'll shift our ground.—
Come hither, gentlemen,
And lay your hands again upon my sword:
160 Never to speak of this that you have heard,
Swear by my sword.

GHOST: *(Beneath)* Swear.

HAMLET: Well said! old mole! canst work i' the earth so fast?
A worthy pioneer![12]—Once more remove, good friends.

165 **HORATIO:** O day and night, but this is wondrous strange!

HAMLET: And therefore as a stranger give it welcome.
There are more things in heaven and earth, Horatio,
Than are dreamt of in your philosophy.
But come;—
170 Here, as before, never, so help you mercy,
How strange or odd soe'er I bear myself,—
As I, perchance, hereafter shall think meet
To put an antic disposition on,—
That you, at such times seeing me, never shall,
175 With arms encumber'd[13] thus, or this headshake,
Or by pronouncing of some doubtful phrase,
As, *Well, well, we know;*—or, *We could, an if we would;*—
Or, *If we list to speak;*—or, *There be, an if they might;*—
Or such ambiguous giving out, to note
180 That you know aught of me:—this not to do,
So grace and mercy at your most need help you,
Swear.

GHOST: *(Beneath)* Swear.

HAMLET: Rest, rest, perturbed spirit!—So, gentlemen,
185 With all my love I do commend to you:
And what so poor a man as Hamlet is
May do, to express his love and friending to you,

---

[11] Here and everywhere?   [12] A soldier who digs trenches and undermines fortresses.
[13] Folded.

God willing, shall not lack. Let us go in together;
And still your fingers on your lips, I pray.
190   The time is out of joint:—O cursed spite,
That ever I was born to set it right!—
Nay, come, let's go together.

(Exeunt.)

ACT II   SCENE I

A room in Polonius' house.

(Enter Polonius and Reynaldo.)

POLONIUS: Give him this money and these notes, Reynaldo.
REYNALDO: I will, my lord.
POLONIUS: You shall do marvelous wisely, good Reynaldo,
Before you visit him, to make inquiry
5   On his behavior.
REYNALDO: My lord, I did intend it.
POLONIUS: Marry, well said; very well said. Look you, sir,
Inquire me first what Danskers[1] are in Paris;
And how, and who, what means, and where they keep,
What company, at what expense; and finding,
10   By this encompassment and drift of question,
That they do know my son, come you more nearer
Than your particular demands will touch it:
Take you, as 'twere, some distant knowledge of him;
As thus, *I know his father and his friends,*
15   *And in part him;*—do you mark this, Reynaldo?
REYNALDO: Ay, very well, my lord.
POLONIUS: *And in part him;—but,* you may say, *not well:*
But if't be he I mean, he's very wild;
Addicted so and so; and there put on him
20   What forgeries you please; marry, none so rank
As may dishonor him; take heed of that;
But, sir, such wanton, wild, and usual slips
As are companions noted and most known
To youth and liberty.
REYNALDO: As gaming, my lord.
25 **POLONIUS:**   Ay, or drinking, fencing, swearing, quarreling,
Drabbing:[2]—you may go so far.
REYNALDO: My lord, that would dishonor him.
POLONIUS: Faith, no; as you may season it in the charge.
You must not put another scandal on him,

---

[1] Danes.   [2] Going about with loose women.

30   That he is open to incontinency;
   That's not my meaning: but breathe his faults so quaintly
   That they may seem the taints of liberty;
   The flash and outbreak of a fiery mind;
   A savageness in unreclaimed blood,
35   Of general assault.
REYNALDO: But, my good lord,—
POLONIUS: Wherefore should you do this?
REYNALDO: Ay, my lord,
   I would know that.
POLONIUS: Marry, sir, here's my drift;
   And I believe it is a fetch of warrant:[3]
   You laying these slight sullies on my son.
40   As 'twere a thing a little soil'd i' the working,
   Mark you,
   Your party in converse, him you would sound,
   Having ever seen in the prenominate crimes
   The youth you breathe of guilty, be assur'd
45   He closes with you in this consequence;
   Good sir, or so; or *friend,* or *gentleman,*—
   According to the phrase or the addition[4]
   Of man and country.
REYNALDO: Very good, my lord.
POLONIUS: And then, sir, does he this,—he does,—
50   What was I about to say?—By the mass, I was
   About to say something:—where did I leave?
REYNALDO: At *closes in the consequence,*
   At *friend or so,* and *gentleman.*
POLONIUS: At—closes in the consequence,—ay, marry;
55   He closes with you thus:—*I know the gentleman;*
   I saw him yesterday, or t'other day,
   Or then, or then; with such, or such; and, as you say,
   There was he gaming; there o'ertook in's rouse;
   There falling out at tennis: or perchance,
60   *I saw him enter such a house of sale,*—
   Videlicet, a brothel,—or so forth.—
   See you now;
   Your bait of falsehood takes this carp of truth:
   And thus do we of wisdom and of reach,
65   With windlasses, and with assays of bias,
   By indirections find directions out:
   So, by my former lecture and advice,
   Shall you my son. You have me, have you not?

---

[3] A good device.   [4] Form of address.

REYNALDO: My lord, I have.

POLONIUS: God b' wi' you; fare you well.

70 REYNALDO: Good my lord!

POLONIUS: Observe his inclination in yourself.

REYNALDO: I shall, my lord.

POLONIUS: And let him ply his music.

REYNALDO: Well, my lord.

POLONIUS: Farewell!

(Exit Reynaldo.)

(Enter Ophelia.)

75   How now, Ophelia! what's the matter?

OPHELIA: Alas, my lord, I have been so affrighted.

POLONIUS: With what, i' the name of God?

OPHELIA: My lord, as I was sewing in my chamber,
Lord Hamlet,—with his doublet all unbrac'd;

80 No hat upon his head; his stockings foul'd,
Ungarter'd, and down-gyved[5] to his ankle;
Pale as his shirt; his knees knocking each other;
And with a look so piteous in purport
As if he had been loosed out of hell

85 To speak of horrors,—he comes before me.

POLONIUS: Mad for thy love?

OPHELIA: My lord, I do not know;
But truly I do fear it.

POLONIUS: What said he?

OPHELIA: He took me by the wrist, and held me hard;
Then goes he to the length of all his arm;

90 And with his other hand thus o'er his brow,
He falls to such perusal of my face
As he would draw it. Long stay'd he so;
At last,—a little shaking of mine arm,
And thrice his head thus waving up and down,—

95 He rais'd a sigh so piteous and profound
That it did seem to shatter all his bulk
And end his being; that done, he lets me go:
And, with his head over his shoulder turn'd,
He seem'd to find his way without his eyes;

100 For out o' doors he went without their help,
And to the last bended their light on me.

POLONIUS: Come, go with me: I will go seek the king.
This is the very ecstasy[6] of love;
Whose violent property fordoes itself,[7]

---

[5] Dangling like chains.   [6] Madness.   [7] Destroys itself.

105   And leads the will to desperate undertakings,
         As oft as any passion under heaven
         That does afflict our nature. I am sorry,—
         What, have you given him any hard words of late?
     OPHELIA: No, my good lord; but, as you did command,
110   I did repel his letters, and denied
         His access to me.
     POLONIUS: That hath made him mad.
         I am sorry that with better heed and judgment
         I had not quoted him: I fear'd he did but trifle,
         And meant to wreck thee; but, beshrew my jealousy!
115   It seems it is as proper to our age
         To cast beyond ourselves in our opinions
         As it is common for the younger sort
         To lack discretion. Come, go we to the king:
         This must be known; which, being kept close, might move
120   More grief to hide than hate to utter love.

     (Exeunt.)

                         SCENE II

A room in the castle.

(Enter King, Queen, Rosencrantz, Guildenstern, and Attendants.)

     KING: Welcome, dear Rosencrantz and Guildenstern!
         Moreover that we much did long to see you,
         The need we have to use you did provoke
         Our hasty sending. Something have you heard
5   Of Hamlet's transformation; so I call it,
         Since nor the exterior nor the inward man
         Resembles that it was. What it should be,
         More than his father's death, that thus hath put him
         So much from the understanding of himself,
10   I cannot dream of: I entreat you both,
         That being of so young days brought up with him,
         And since so neighbor'd to his youth and humor,
         That you vouchsafe your rest here in our court
         Some little time: so by your companies
15   To draw him on to pleasures, and to gather,
         So much as from occasion you may glean,
         Whether aught, to us unknown, afflicts him thus,
         That, open'd, lies within our remedy.
     QUEEN: Good gentlemen, he hath much talk'd of you;
20   And sure I am two men there are not living

To whom he more adheres. If it will please you
To show us so much gentry and good-will
As to expend your time with us awhile,
For the supply and profit of our hope,
25   Your visitation shall receive such thanks
As fits a king's remembrance.
ROSENCRANTZ: Both your majesties
Might, by the sovereign power you have of us,
Put your dread pleasures more into command
Than to entreaty.
GUILDENSTERN: We both obey,
30   And here give up ourselves, in the full bent,
To lay our service freely at your feet,
To be commanded.
KING: Thanks, Rosencrantz and gentle Guildenstern.
QUEEN: Thanks, Guildenstern and gentle Rosencrantz:
35   And I beseech you instantly to visit
My too-much-changed son.—Go, some of you,
And bring these gentlemen where Hamlet is.
GUILDENSTERN: Heavens make our presence and our practices
Pleasant and helpful to him!
QUEEN: Ay, amen!

(Exeunt Rosencrantz, Guildenstern, and some Attendants.)

(Enter Polonius.)

40 **POLONIUS:**   The ambassadors from Norway, my good lord,
Are joyfully return'd.
KING: Thou still has been the father of good news.
POLONIUS: Have I, my lord? Assure you, my good liege,
I hold my duty, as I hold my soul,
45   Both to my God and to my gracious king:
And I do think,—or else this brain of mine
Hunts not the trail of policy[1] so sure
As it hath us'd to do,—that I have found
The very cause of Hamlet's lunacy.
50 **KING:**   O, speak of that; that do I long to hear.
POLONIUS: Give first admittance to the ambassadors;
My news shall be the fruit to that great feast.
KING: Thyself do grace to them, and bring them in.

(Exit Polonius.)

He tells me, my sweet queen, that he hath found
55   The head and source of all your son's distemper.

---

[1] Statecraft.

QUEEN: I doubt it is no other but the main,—
　　His father's death and our o'erhasty marriage.
KING: Well, we shall sift him.

(Re-enter Polonius, with Voltimand and Cornelius.)

　　　　　　　　　　　　　　　Welcome, my good friends!
　　Say, Voltimand, what from our brother Norway?
60 **VOLTIMAND:**   Most fair return of greetings and desires.
　　Upon our first, he sent out to suppress
　　His nephew's levies; which to him appear'd
　　To be a preparation 'gainst the Polack;
　　But, better look'd into, he truly found
65　　It was against your highness: whereat griev'd,—
　　That so his sickness, age, and impotence
　　Was falsely borne in hand,—sends out arrests
　　On Fortinbras; which he, in brief, obeys;
　　Receives rebuke from Norway; and, in fine,
70　　Makes vows before his uncle never more
　　To give the assay of arms against your majesty.
　　Whereon old Norway, overcome with joy,
　　Gives him three thousand crowns in annual fee;
　　And his commission to employ those soldiers,
75　　So levied as before, against the Polack:
　　With an entreaty, herein further shown, *(gives a paper)*
　　That it might please you to give quiet pass
　　Through your dominions for this enterprise,
　　On such regards of safety and allowance
80　　As therein are set down.
KING:　　　　　　　　　It likes us well;
　　And at our more consider'd time we'll read,
　　Answer, and think upon this business.
　　Meantime we thank you for your well-took labor:
　　Go to your rest; at night we'll feast together:
85　　Most welcome home!

(Exeunt Voltimand and Cornelius.)

POLONIUS:　　　　　　　This business is well ended.—
　　My liege, and madam,—to expostulate
　　What majesty should be, what duty is,
　　Why day is day, night night, and time is time,
　　Were nothing but to waste night, day, and time.
90　　Therefore, since brevity is the soul of wit,
　　And tediousness the limbs and outward flourishes,
　　I will be brief:—your noble son is mad:
　　Mad call I it; for to define true madness,
　　What is't but to be nothing else but mad?
95　　But let that go.

QUEEN: More matter with less art.
POLONIUS: Madam, I swear I use no art at all.
  That he is mad, 'tis true 'tis pity;
  And pity 'tis 'tis true: a foolish figure;
  But farewell it, for I will use no art.
100   Mad let us grant him, then: and now remains
  That we find out the cause of this effect;
  Or rather say, the cause of this defect,
  For this effect defective comes by cause:
  Thus it remains, and the remainder thus.
105   Perpend.
  I have a daughter,—have whilst she is mine,—
  Who, in her duty and obedience, mark,
  Hath given me this: now gather, and surmise

(Reads)

To the celestial, and my soul's idol, the most beautified Ophelia,—
110   That's an ill phrase, a vile phrase,—*beautified* is a vile phrase: but
    you shall hear. Thus:

(Reads)

  In her excellent white bosom, these, &c.
QUEEN: Came this from Hamlet to her?
POLONIUS: Good madam, stay a while; I will be faithful.

(Reads)

115   *Doubt thou the stars are fire;*
    Doubt that the sun doth move;
  Doubt truth to be a liar;
    But never doubt I love.
    O dear Ophelia, I am ill at these numbers,
120   *I have not art to reckon my groans: but that I love thee best, O most*
    best, believe it. Adieu.
    Thine evermore, most dear lady, whilst this machine is to him, Hamlet

  This, in obedience, hath my daughter show'd me:
  And more above, hath his solicitings,
125   As they fell out by time, by means, and place,
  All given to mine ear.
KING: But how hath she
  Receiv'd his love?
POLONIUS: What do you think of me?
KING: As of a man faithful and honorable.
POLONIUS: I would fain prove so. But what might you think,
130   When I had seen this hot love on the wing,—
  As I perceiv'd it, I must tell you that,
  Before my daughter told me,—what might you,

Or my dear majesty your queen here, think,
If I had play'd the desk or table-book;[2]
135   Or given my heart a winking, mute and dumb;
Or look'd upon this love with idle sight;—
What might you think? No, I went round to work,
And my young mistress thus I did bespeak:
Lord Hamlet is a prince out of thy sphere;
140   *This must not be:* and then I precepts gave her,
That she should lock herself from his resort,
Admit no messengers, receive no tokens.
Which done, she took the fruits of my advice;
And he, repulsed,—a short tale to make,—
145   Fell into a sadness; then into a fast;
Thence to a watch; thence into a weakness;
Thence to a lightness; and, by this declension,
Into the madness wherein now he raves
And all we wail for.
KING: Do you think 'tis this?
150 **QUEEN:**   It may be, very likely.
POLONIUS: Hath there been such a time,—I'd fain know that,—
That I have positively said, *'Tis so,*
When it prov'd otherwise?
KING: Not that I know.
POLONIUS: Take this from this, if this be otherwise: *(Pointing to his head*
and shoulder)
155   If circumstances lead me, I will find
Where truth is hid, though it were hid indeed
Within the center.
KING: How may we try it further?
POLONIUS: You know, sometimes he walks for hours together
Here in the lobby.
QUEEN: So he does, indeed.
160 **POLONIUS:**   At such a time I'll loose my daughter to him:
Be you and I behind an arras[3] then;
Mark the encounter: if he love her not,
And be not from his reason fall'n thereon,
Let me be no assistant for a state,
165   But keep a farm and carters.
KING: We will try it.
QUEEN: But look, where sadly the poor wretch comes reading.
POLONIUS: Away, I do beseech you, both away:
I'll board[4] him presently:—O, give me leave.

---

[2] Memorandum pad.   [3] Tapestry, hung some distance away from a wall.   [4] Address.

(Exeunt King, Queen, and Attendants.)

(Enter Hamlet, reading.)

How does my good Lord Hamlet?

170 **HAMLET:** Well, God-a-mercy.

POLONIUS: Do you know me, my lord?

HAMLET: Excellent, excellent well; you're a fishmonger.

POLONIUS: Not I, my lord.

HAMLET: Then I would you were so honest a man.

175 **POLONIUS:** Honest, my lord!

HAMLET: Ay, sir; to be honest, as this world goes, is to be one man picked out of ten thousand.

POLONIUS: That's very true, my lord.

HAMLET: For if the sun breed maggots in a dead dog, being a god

180 kissing carrion,—Have you a daughter?

POLONIUS: I have, my lord.

HAMLET: Let her not walk i' the sun: conception is a blessing; but not as your daughter may conceive:—friend, look to't.

POLONIUS: How say you by that?—*(Aside)* Still harping on my

185 daughter:—yet he knew me not at first; he said I was a fishmonger: he is far gone, far gone: and truly in my youth I suffered much extremity for love; very near this. I'll speak to him again.—What do you read, my lord?

HAMLET: Words, words, words.

190 **POLONIUS:** What is the matter, my lord?

HAMLET: Between who?

POLONIUS: I mean, the matter that you read, my lord.

HAMLET: Slanders, sir: for the satirical slave says here that old men have gray beards; that their faces are wrinkled; their eyes purging

195 thick amber and plum-tree gum; and that they have a plentiful lack of wit, together with most weak hams: all which, sir, though I most powerfully and potently believe, yet I hold it not honesty to have it thus set down; for you yourself, sir, should be old as I am, if, like a crab, you could go backward.

200 **POLONIUS:** *(Aside)* Though this be madness, yet there is method in't.— ill you walk out of the air, my lord?

HAMLET: Into my grave?

POLONIUS: Indeed, that is out o' the air.—*(Aside)* How pregnant[5] sometimes his replies are! a happiness that often madness hits on,

205 which reason and sanity could not so prosperously be delivered of. I will leave him, and suddenly contrive the means of meeting between him and my daughter.—More honorable lord, I will most humbly take my leave of you.

---

[5] Ready, and clever.

HAMLET: You cannot, sir, take from me anything that I will more
210   willingly part withal,—except my life, except my life, except my life.
POLONIUS: Fare you well, my lord.
HAMLET: These tedious old fools!

(Enter Rosencrantz and Guildenstern.)

POLONIUS: You go to seek the Lord Hamlet; there he is.
ROSENCRANTZ: *(To Polonius)* God save you, sir!

(Exit Polonius.)

215 **GUILDENSTERN:** Mine honored lord!
ROSENCRANTZ: My most dear lord!
HAMLET: My excellent good friends! How dost thou, Guildenstern?
     Ah, Rosencrantz? Good lads, how do ye both?
ROSENCRANTZ: As the indifferent children of the earth.
220 **GUILDENSTERN:** Happy in that we are not overhappy; on fortune's cap
     we are not the very button.
HAMLET: Nor the soles of her shoe?
ROSENCRANTZ: Neither, my lord.
HAMLET: Then you live about her waist, or in the middle of her favors?
225 **GUILDENSTERN:** Faith, her privates we.
HAMLET: In the secret parts of fortune? O, most true; she is a strumpet.
     What's the news?
ROSENCRANTZ: None, my lord, but that the world's grown honest.
HAMLET: Then is doomsday near: but your news is not true. Let me
230 question more in particular: what have you, my good friends,
     deserved at the hands of fortune, that she sends you to prison
     hither?
GUILDENSTERN: Prison, my lord!
HAMLET: Denmark's a prison.
235 **ROSENCRANTZ:** Then is the world one.
HAMLET: A goodly one; in which there are many confines, wards, and
     dungeons, Denmark being one o' the worst.
ROSENCRANTZ: We think not so, my lord.
HAMLET: Why, then, 'tis none to you; for there is nothing either good
240 or bad, but thinking makes it so: to me it is a prison.
ROSENCRANTZ: Why, then, your ambition makes it one; 'tis too
     narrow for your mind.
HAMLET: O God, I could be bounded in a nutshell, and count myself
     a king of infinite space, were it not that I have bad dreams.
245 **GUILDENSTERN:** Which dreams, indeed, are ambition; for the very
     substance of the ambitious is merely the shadow of a dream.
HAMLET: A dream itself is but a shadow.
ROSENCRANTZ: Truly, and I hold ambition of so airy and light a quality
     that it is but a shadow's shadow.

250 **HAMLET:**   Then are our beggars bodies, and our monarchs and
         outstretched heroes the beggars' shadows. Shall we to the court? for,
         by my fay, I cannot reason.
      ROSENCRANTZ and **GUILDENSTERN:**   We'll wait upon you.
      HAMLET: No such matter: I will not sort you with the rest of my
255   servants, for, to speak to you like an honest man, I am most
         dreadfully attended. But, in the beaten way of friendship, what make
         you at Elsinore?
      ROSENCRANTZ: To visit you, my lord; no other occasion.
      HAMLET: Beggar that I am, I am even poor in thanks; but I thank you:
260   and sure, dear friends, my thanks are too dear a halfpenny. Were
         you not sent for? Is it your own inclining? Is it a free visitation?
         Come, deal justly with me: come, come; nay, speak.
      GUILDENSTERN: What should we say, my lord?
      HAMLET: Why, anything—but to the purpose. You were sent for; and
265   there is a kind of confession in your looks, which your modesties
         have not craft enough to color: I know the good king and queen
         have sent for you.
      ROSENCRANTZ: To what end, my lord?
      HAMLET: That you must teach me. But let me conjure you, by the rights
270   of our fellowship, by the consonancy of our youth, by the obligation
         of our ever-preserved love, and by what more dear a better proposer
         could charge you withal, be even and direct with me, whether you
         were sent for or no?
      ROSENCRANTZ: What say you? *(To Guildenstern)*
275 **HAMLET:**   *(Aside)* Nay, then, I have an eye of you.—If you love me,
         hold not off.
      GUILDENSTERN: My lord, we were sent for.
      HAMLET: I will tell you why; so shall my anticipation prevent your
         discovery, and your secrecy to the king and queen moult no
280   feather. I have of late,—but wherefore I know not,—lost all my
         mirth, forgone all custom of exercises; and, indeed, it goes so
         heavily with my disposition that this goodly frame, the earth,
         seems to me a sterile promontory; this most excellent canopy, the
         air, look you, this brave o'erhanging firmament, this majestical
285   roof fretted[6] with golden fire,—why, it appears no other thing to
         me than a foul and pestilent congregation of vapors. What a piece
         of work is man! How noble in reason! how infinite in faculties! in
         form and moving, how express and admirable! in action, how like
         an angel! in apprehension, how like a god! the beauty of the world!
290   the paragon of animals! And yet, to me, what is this quintessence
         of dust? man delights not me; no, nor woman neither, though by
         your smiling you seem to say so.

---

[6] A roof with fretwork.

ROSENCRANTZ: My lord, there was no such stuff in my thoughts.

HAMLET: Why did you laugh, then, when I said, *Man delights not me?*

295 **ROSENCRANTZ:**   To think, my lord, if you delight not in man, what lenten entertainment[7] the players shall receive from you: we coted[8] them on the way; and hither are they coming, to offer you service.

HAMLET: He that plays the king shall be welcome,—his majesty shall have tribute of me; the adventurous knight shall use his foil and

300 target; the lover shall not sigh gratis; the humorous[9] man shall end his part in peace; the clown shall make those laugh whose lungs are tickled o' the sere;[10] and the lady shall say her mind freely, or the blank verse shall halt[11] for't.—What players are they?

ROSENCRANTZ: Even those you were wont to take delight in,—the

305 tragedians of the city.

HAMLET: How chances it they travel? their residence, both in reputation and profit, was better both ways.

ROSENCRANTZ: I think their inhibition[12] comes by the means of the late innovation.

310 **HAMLET:**   Do they hold the same estimation they did when I was in the city? Are they so followed?

ROSENCRANTZ: No, indeed, they are not.

HAMLET: How comes it? do they grow rusty?

ROSENCRANTZ: Nay, their endeavor keeps in the wonted pace; but there

315 is, sir, an aery[13] of children, little eyases,[14] that cry out on the top of question, and are most tyrannically clapped for't: these are now the fashion; and so berattle the common stages,—so they call them,— that many wearing rapiers are afraid of goose-quills, and dare scarce come thither.

320 **HAMLET:**   What, are they children? who maintains 'em? how are they escoted?[15] Will they pursue the quality[16] no longer than they can sing? will they not say afterwards, if they should grow themselves to common players,—as it is most like, if their means are no better, —their writers do them wrong, to make them exclaim against

325 their own succession?

ROSENCRANTZ: Faith, there has been much to do on both sides; and the nation holds it no sin to tarre[17] them to controversy: there was for awhile no money bid for argument, unless the poet and the player went to cuffs in the question.

330 **HAMLET:**   Is't possible?

GUILDENSTERN: O, there has been much throwing about of brains.

HAMLET: Do the boys carry it away?

---

[7] Poor reception.   [8] Passed.   [9] Eccentric.   [10] Whose lungs, for laughter, are easily tickled.   [11] Limp.   [12] Difficulty, preventing them from remaining in the capital.   [13] Aerie: brood of birds of prey.   [14] Young hawks; a reference to the boys' companies that became popular rivals of Shakespeare's company of players.   [15] Financially supported.   [16] Profession.   [17] Egg them on.

ROSENCRANTZ: Ay, that they do, my lord; Hercules and his load[18] too.

HAMLET: It is not strange; for mine uncle is king of Denmark, and those
335   that would make mouths at him while my father lived, give twenty,
forty, fifty, an hundred ducats a-piece for his picture in little.
'Sblood, there is something in this more than natural, if philosophy
could find it out.

(Flourish of trumpets within.)

GUILDENSTERN: There are the players.

340 **HAMLET:** Gentlemen, you are welcome to Elsinore. Your hands, come:
the appurtenance of welcome is fashion and ceremony: let me comply
with you in this garb; lest my extent[19] to the players, which, I
tell you, must show fairly outward, should more appear like
entertainment[20] than yours. You are welcome: but my uncle-father
345   and aunt-mother are deceived.

GUILDENSTERN: In what, my dear lord?

HAMLET: I am but mad north-north-west: when the wind is southerly
I know a hawk from a handsaw.

(Enter Polonius.)

POLONIUS: Well be with you, gentlemen!

350 **HAMLET:** Hark you, Guildenstern;—and you too;—at each ear a hearer:
that great baby you see there is not yet out of his swathing-clouts.

ROSENCRANTZ: Happily he's the second time come to them; for they
say an old man is twice a child.

HAMLET: I will prophesy he comes to tell me of the players; mark it.
355   You say right, sir: o' Monday morning; 'twas so indeed.

POLONIUS: My lord, I have news to tell you.

HAMLET: My lord, I have news to tell you. When Roscius was an actor
in Rome,—

POLONIUS: The actors are come hither, my lord.

360 **HAMLET:** Buzz, buzz!

POLONIUS: Upon mine honor,—

HAMLET: Then came each actor on his ass,—

POLONIUS: The best actors in the world, either for tragedy, comedy,
history, pastoral, pastoral-comical, historical-pastoral, tragical-
365   historical, tragical-comical-historical-pastoral, scene individable,[21]
or poem unlimited:[22] Seneca cannot be too heavy nor Plautus too
light. For the law of writ and the liberty,[23] these are the only men.

---

[18] The globe, or the world.   [19] Show of friendliness.   [20] Welcome.   [21] A play
that observes the unities of time and place.   [22] A typical multiscened Elizabethan
type of drama, not restricted by the unities. Examples are *Hamlet, Macbeth, King Lear*,
and virtually any other play by Shakespeare.   [23] For the laws of the unities and for
playwriting that is not so restricted.

HAMLET: O Jephthah, judge of Israel, what a treasure hadst thou!

POLONIUS: What a treasure had he, my lord?

370 **HAMLET:** Why—

>One fair daughter, and no more,
>The which he loved passing well.

POLONIUS: *(Aside)* Still on my daughter.

HAMLET: Am I not i' the right, old Jephthah?

375 **POLONIUS:** If you call me Jephthah, my lord, I have a daughter that I
love passing well.

HAMLET: Nay, that follows not.

POLONIUS: What follows, then, my lord?

HAMLET: Why—

380
>As by lot, God wot,

and then, you know,

>It came to pass, as most like it was,

the first row of the pious chanson will show you more; for look
where my abridgement comes.

(Enter four or five Players.)

385   You are welcome, masters; welcome, all:—I am glad to see thee
well:—welcome, good friends.—O, my old friend! Thy face is
valanced since I saw thee last; comest thou to beard me in
Denmark?—What, my young lady and mistress! By'r lady, your
ladyship is nearer heaven than when I saw you last, by the altitude
390   of a chopine.[24] Pray God, your voice, like a piece of uncurrent gold,
be not cracked within the ring.—Masters, you are all welcome.
We'll e'en to't like French falconers, fly at anything we see: we'll
have a speech straight: come, give us a taste of your quality; come,
a passionate speech.

395 **1ST PLAYER:** What speech, my lord?

HAMLET: I heard thee speak me a speech once,—but it was never
acted; or, if it was, not above once; for the play, I remember,
pleased not the million; 'twas caviare to the general: but it was,—
as I received it, and others whose judgments in such matters cried
400   in the top of mine,—an excellent play, well digested in the scenes,
set down with as much modesty as cunning. I remember, one said
there were no sallets in the lines to make the matter savory, nor no
matter in the phrase that might indite the author of affectation;
but called it an honest method, as wholesome as sweet, and by
405   very much more handsome than fine. One speech in it I chiefly
loved: 'twas Aeneas' tale to Dido; and thereabout of it especially
where he speaks of Priam's slaughter: if it live in your memory,
begin at this line;—let me see, let me see:—

---

[24] A wooden stilt more than a foot high used under a woman's shoe; a Venetian fashion introduced into England.

The rugged Pyrrhus, like the Hyrcanian beast,[25]

410 —it is not so:—it begins with Pyrrhus:—

The rugged Pyrrhus,—he whose sable arms,
Black as his purpose, did the night resemble
When he lay couched in the ominous horse,—
Hath now this dread and black complexion smear'd
415 With heraldry more dismal; head to foot
Now is he total gules; horridly trick'd
With blood of fathers, mothers, daughters, sons,
Bak'd and impasted with the parching streets,
That lend a tyrannous and damned light
420 To their vile murders: roasted in wrath and fire,
And thus o'er-sized with coagulate gore,
With eyes like carbuncles, the hellish Pyrrhus
Old grandsire Priam seeks.—

So proceed you.
425 **POLONIUS:** 'Fore God, my lord, well spoken, with good accent and
good discretion.
1ST PLAYER: Anon he finds him
Striking too short at Greeks; his antique sword,
Rebellious to his arm, lies where it falls,
430 Repugnant to command: unequal match'd,
Pyrrhus at Priam drives; in rage strikes wide;
But with the whiff and wind of his fell sword
The unnerved father falls. Then senseless Ilium,
Seeming to feel this blow, with flaming top
435 Stoops to his base; and with a hideous crash
Takes prisoner Pyrrhus' ear: for, lo! his sword,
Which was declining on the milky head
Of reverend Priam, seem'd i' the air to stick:
So, as a painted tyrant, Pyrrhus stood;
440 And, like a neutral to his will and matter,
Did nothing.
But as we often see, against some storm,
A silence in the heavens, the rack stand still,
The blood winds speechless, and the orb below
445 As hush as death, anon the dreadful thunder
Doth rend the region; so, after Pyrrhus' pause,
A roused vengeance sets him new a-work;
And never did the Cyclops' hammers fall
On Mars his armor, forg'd for proof eterne,

---

[25] This speech is an example of the declamatory style of drama, which Shakespeare
surely must have considered outmoded.

450   With less remorse than Pyrrhus' bleeding sword
        Now falls on Priam.—
        Out, out, thou strumpet, Fortune! All you gods,
        In general synod, take away her power;
        Break all the spokes and fellies from her wheel,
455   And bowl the round knave down the hill of heaven,
        As low as to the fiends!
    POLONIUS: This is too long.
    HAMLET: It shall to the barber's, with your beard.—Pr'ythee, say
        on.—He's for a jig, or a tale of bawdry, or he sleeps:—say on; come
460   to Hecuba.
    1ST PLAYER: But who, O, who had seen the mobled queen,—
    HAMLET: *The mobled queen?*
    POLONIUS: That's good; *mobled queen* is good.
    1ST PLAYER: Run barefoot up and down, threatening the flames
465   With bissom rheum; a clout upon that head
        Where late the diadem stood; and, for a robe,
        About her lank and all o'er-teemed loins,
        A blanket, in the alarm of fear caught up;—
        Who this had seen, with tongue in venom steep'd,
470   'Gainst Fortune's state would treason have pronounc'd:
        But if the gods themselves did see her then,
        When she saw Pyrrhus make malicious sport
        In mincing with his sword her husband's limbs,
        The instant burst of clamor that she made,—
475   Unless things mortal move them not at all,—
        Would have made milch the burning eyes of heaven,
        And passion in the gods.
    POLONIUS: Look, whether he has not turn'd his color, and has tears
        in's eyes.—Pray you, no more.
480 HAMLET: 'Tis well; I'll have thee speak out the rest soon.—Good my
        lord, will you see the players well bestowed? Do you hear, let them
        be well used; for they are the abstracts and brief chronicles of the
        time; after your death you were better have a bad epitaph than
        their ill report while you live.
485 POLONIUS: My lord, I will use them according to their desert.
    HAMLET: Odd's bodikin, man, better: use every man after his desert,
        and who should scape whipping? Use them after your own honor
        and dignity: the less they deserve the more merit is in your
        bounty. Take them in.
490 POLONIUS: Come, sirs.
    HAMLET: Follow him, friends: we'll hear a play to-morrow.

    (Exit Polonius with all the Players but the First.)

        Dost thou hear me, old friend; can you play the Murder of Gonzago?
    1ST PLAYER: Ay, my lord.

HAMLET: We'll ha't to-morrow night. You could, for a need, study a
495   speech of some dozen or sixteen lines which I would set down and
insert in't? could you not?

1ST PLAYER: Ay, my lord.

HAMLET: Very well.—Follow that lord; and look you mock him not.

(Exit First Player.)

    —My good friends, *(to Rosencrantz and Guildenstern)* I'll leave you
500   till night: you are welcome to Elsinore.

ROSENCRANTZ: Good my lord!

(Exeunt Rosencrantz and Guildenstern.)

HAMLET: Ay, so God b' wi' ye!—Now I am alone.
    O, what a rogue[26] and peasant slave am I!
    Is it not monstrous that this player here,
505   But in a fiction, in a dream of passion,
    Could force his soul so to his own conceit[27]
    That from her working all his visage wan'd;
    Tears in his eyes, distraction in's aspéct,
    A broken voice, and his whole function suiting
510   With forms to his conceit? And all for nothing!
    For Hecuba!
    What's Hecuba to him or he to Hecuba,
    That he should weep for her? What would he do,
    Had he the motive and the cue for passion
515   That I have? He would drown the stage with tears,
    And cleave the general ear with horrid speech;
    Make mad the guilty, and appal the free;
    Confound the ignorant, and amaze, indeed,
    The very faculties of eyes and ears.
520   Yet I,
    A dull and muddy-mettled rascal, peak,
    Like John-a-dreams, unpregnant of my cause,
    And can say nothing; no, not for a king
    Upon whose property and most dear life
525   A damn'd defeat was made. Am I a coward?
    Who calls me villain? breaks my pate across?
    Plucks off my beard and blows it in my face?
    Tweaks me by the nose? gives me the lie i' the throat,
    As deep as to the lungs? who does me this, ha?
530   'Swounds, I should take it: for it cannot be
    But I am pigeon-liver'd, and lack gall
    To make oppression bitter; or ere this

---

[26] Wretched creature.   [27] Conception.

I should have fatted all the region kites
With this slave's offal:—bloody, bawdy villain!
535 Remorseless, treacherous, lecherous, kindless villain!
O, vengeance!
Why, what an ass am I! This is most brave,
That I, the son of a dear father murder'd,
Prompted to my revenge by heaven and hell,
540 Must, like a whore, unpack my heart with words,
And fall a-cursing like a very drab,
A scullion!
Fie upon't! foh!—About, my brain! I have heard
That guilty creatures, sitting at a play,
545 Have by the very cunning of the scene
Been struck so to the soul that presently
They have proclaim'd their malefactions;
For murder, though it have no tongue, will speak
With most miraculous organ. I'll have these players
550 Play something like the murder of my father
Before mine uncle: I'll observe his looks;
I'll tent[28] him to the quick: if he but blench,
I know my course. The spirit that I have seen
May be the devil: and the devil hath power
555 To assume a pleasing shape; yea, and perhaps
Out of my weakness and my melancholy,—
As he is very potent with such spirits,—
Abuses me to damn me: I'll have grounds
More relative than this:—the play's the thing
560 Wherein I'll catch the conscience of the king. *(Exit.)*

ACT III SCENE I

A room in the castle.

(Enter King, Queen, Polonius, Ophelia, Rosencrantz, and Guildenstern.)

KING: And can you, by no drift of circumstance,
Get from him why he puts on this confusion,
Grating so harshly all his days of quiet
With turbulent and dangerous lunacy?
5 **ROSENCRANTZ:** He does confess he feels himself distracted;
But from what cause he will by no means speak.
GUILDENSTERN: Nor do we find him forward to be sounded;
But, with a crafty madness, keeps aloof

---

[28] Probe.

When we would bring him on to some confession
10   Of his true state.
QUEEN: Did he receive you well?
ROSENCRANTZ: Most like a gentleman.
GUILDENSTERN: But with much forcing of his disposition.
ROSENCRANTZ: Niggard of question; but, of our demands,
        Most free in his reply.
QUEEN: Did you assay him
15   To any pastime?
ROSENCRANTZ: Madam, it so fell out that certain players
        We o'er-raught on the way: of these we told him;
        And there did seem in him a kind of joy
        To hear of it: they are about the court;
20   And, as I think, they have already order
        This night to play before him.
POLONIUS: 'Tis most true:
        And he beseech'd me to entreat your majesties
        To hear and see the matter.
KING: With all my heart; and it doth much content me
25   To hear him so inclin'd.
        Good gentlemen, give him a further edge,
        And drive his purpose on to these delights.
ROSENCRANTZ: We shall, my lord.

(Exeunt Rosencrantz and Guildenstern.)

KING: Sweet Gertrude, leave us too;
        For we have closely sent for Hamlet hither
30   That he, as 'twere by accident, may here
        Affront Ophelia:
        Her father and myself,—lawful espials,[1]—
        Will so bestow ourselves that, seeing, unseen,
        We may of their encounter frankly judge;
35   And gather by him, as he is behav'd,
        If't be the affliction of his love or no
        That thus he suffers for.
QUEEN: I shall obey you:—
        And for your part, Ophelia, I do wish
        That your good beauties be the happy cause
40   Of Hamlet's wildness: so shall I hope your virtues
        Will bring him to his wonted way again,
        To both your honors.
OPHELIA: Madam, I wish it may.

(Exit Queen.)

---

[1] Spies.

POLONIUS: Ophelia, walk you here.—Gracious, so please you,
We will bestow ourselves.—*(To Ophelia)* Read on this book;
45   That show of such an exercise may color
Your loneliness.—We are oft to blame in this,—
'Tis too much prov'd,—that with devotion's visage
And pious action we do sugar o'er
The devil himself.
KING: *(Aside)*   O, 'tis too true!
50   How smart a lash that speech doth give my conscience!
The harlot's cheek, beautied with plastering art,
Is not more ugly to the thing that helps it
Than is my deed to my most painted word:
O heavy burden!
55 **POLONIUS:**   I hear him coming: let's withdraw, my lord.

(Exeunt King and Polonius.)

(Enter Hamlet.)

HAMLET: To be, or not to be,—that is the question:
Whether 'tis nobler in the mind to suffer
The slings and arrows of outrageous fortune,
Or to take arms against a sea of troubles,
60   And by opposing end them?—To die,—to sleep,—
No more; and by a sleep to say we end
The heart-ache and the thousand natural shocks
That flesh is heir to,—'tis a consummation
Devoutly to be wish'd. To die,—to sleep;—
65   To sleep! perchance to dream:—ay, there's the rub;
For in that sleep of death what dreams may come,
When we have shuffled off this mortal coil,
Must give us pause: there's the respect
That makes a calamity of so long life;
70   For who would bear the whips and scorns of time,
The oppressor's wrong, the proud man's contumely,
The pangs of déspis'd love, the law's delay,
The insolence of office, and the spurns
That patient merit of the unworthy takes,
75   When he himself might his quietus make
With a bare bodkin?[2] who would fardels[3] bear,
To grunt[4] and sweat under a weary life,
But that the dread of something after death,—
The undiscover'd country, from whose bourn[5]
80   No traveler returns,—puzzles the will,
And makes us rather bear those ills we have

---

[2] Stiletto.   [3] Burdens.   [4] Groan.   [5] Boundary.

Than to fly to others that we know not of?
Thus conscience does make cowards of us all;
And thus the native hue of resolution
85   Is sicklied o'er with the pale cast of thought;
And enterprises of great pith and moment,
With this regard, their currents turn awry,
And lose the name of action.—Soft you now!
The fair Ophelia.—Nymph, in thy orisons[6]
90   Be all my sins remember'd.

OPHELIA: Good my lord,
How does your honor for this many a day?

HAMLET: I humbly thank you; well, well, well.

OPHELIA: My lord, I have remembrances of yours,
That I have longed long to re-deliver;
95   I pray you, now receive them.

HAMLET: No, not I;
I never gave you aught.

OPHELIA: My honor'd lord, you know right well you did;
And with them, words of so sweet breath compos'd
As made the things more rich: their perfume lost,
100   Take these again; for to the noble mind
Rich gifts wax poor when givers prove unkind.
There, my lord.

HAMLET: Ha, ha! are you honest?

OPHELIA: My lord?

105 **HAMLET:** Are you fair?

OPHELIA: What means your lordship?

HAMLET: That if you be honest and fair, your honesty should admit
no discourse to your beauty.

OPHELIA: Could beauty, my lord, have better commerce than with
110 honesty?

HAMLET: Ay, truly; for the power of beauty will sooner transform
honesty from what it is to a bawd than the force of honesty can
translate beauty into his likeness: this was sometime a paradox,
but now the time gives it proof. I did love you once.

115 **OPHELIA:** Indeed, my lord, you made me believe so.

HAMLET: You should not have believed me; for virtue cannot so
inoculate our old stock but we shall relish of it: I loved you not.

OPHELIA: I was the more deceived.

HAMLET: Get thee to a nunnery: why wouldst thou be a breeder of
120 sinners? I am myself indifferent[7] honest; but yet I could accuse me
of such things that it were better my mother had not borne me: I
am very proud, revengeful, ambitious; with more offences at my

---

6 Prayers.   7 Tolerably.

beck than I have thoughts to put them in, imagination to give
them shape, or time to act them in. What should such fellows as I
125   do crawling between heaven and earth? We are arrant knaves, all;
believe none of us. Go thy ways to a nunnery. Where's your father?

OPHELIA: At home, my lord.

HAMLET: Let the doors be shut upon him, that he may play the fool
nowhere but in's own house. Farewell.

130 **OPHELIA:**   O, help him, you sweet heavens!

HAMLET: If thou dost marry, I'll give thee this plague for thy
dowry,—be thou as chaste as ice, as pure as snow, thou shalt not
escape calumny. Get thee to a nunnery, go: farewell. Or, if thou
wilt needs marry, marry a fool; for wise men know well enough
135   what monsters you make of them. To a nunnery, go; and quickly
too. Farewell.

OPHELIA: O heavenly powers, restore him!

HAMLET: I have heard of your paintings too, well enough; God has
given you one face and you make yourselves another: you jig, you
140   amble, and you lisp, and nickname God's creatures, and make your
wantonness your ignorance. Go to, I'll no more on't; it hath made
me mad. I say, we will have no more marriages: those that are
married already, all but one, shall live; the rest shall keep as they are.
To a nunnery, go. *(Exit.)*

145 **OPHELIA:**   O, what a noble mind is here o'erthrown!
The courtier's, soldier's, scholar's eye, tongue, sword:
The expectancy and rose of the fair state,
The glass of fashion and the mould of form,
The observ'd of all observers,—quite, quite down!
150   And I, of ladies most deject and wretched
That suck'd the honey of his music vows,
Now see that noble and most sovereign reason,
Like sweet bells jangled, out of tune and harsh;
That unmatch'd form and feature of blown[8] youth
155   Blasted with ecstasy: O, woe is me,
To have seen what I have seen, see what I see!

(Re-enter King and Polonius.)

KING: Love! his affections do not that way tend;
Nor what he spake, though it lack'd form a little,
Was not like madness. There's something in his soul
160   O'er which his melancholy sits on brood;
And I do doubt[9] the hatch and the disclose
Will be some danger: which for to prevent,
I have in quick determination
Thus set it down:—he shall with speed to England

---

[8] Full-blown.   [9] Fear.

165 For the demand of our neglected tribute:
Haply, the seas and countries different,
With variable objects, shall expel
This something-settled matter in his heart;
Whereon his brains still beating puts him thus
170 From fashion of himself. What think you on't?
POLONIUS: It shall do well: but yet do I believe
The origin and commencement of his grief
Sprung from neglected love.—How now, Ophelia!
You need not tell us what Lord Hamlet said;
175 We heard it all.—My lord, do as you please;
But if you hold it fit, after the play,
Let his queen mother all alone entreat him
To show his grief: let her be round with him;
And I'll be plac'd, so please you, in the ear
180 Of all their conference. If she finds him not,[10]
To England send him; or confine him where
Your wisdom best shall think.
KING: It shall be so:
Madness in great ones must not unwatch'd go.

(Exeunt.)

SCENE II

A hall in the castle.

(Enter Hamlet and certain Players.)

HAMLET: Speak the speech, I pray you, as I pronounced it to you,
trippingly on the tongue: but if you mouth it, as many of your
players do, I had as lief the town-crier spoke my lines. Nor do not
saw the air too much with your hand, thus; but use all gently: for
5 in the very torrent, tempest, and, as I may say, the whirlwind of
passion, you must acquire and beget a temperance that may give it
smoothness. O, it offends me to the soul, to hear a robustious
periwigpated fellow tear a passion to tatters, to very rags, to split
the ears of the groundlings, who, for the most part, are capable of
10 nothing but inexplicable dumb shows and noise: I could have such
a fellow whipped for o'erdoing Termagant;[1] it out-herods Herod:[2]
pray you, avoid it.
1ST PLAYER: I warrant your honor.
HAMLET: Be not too tame neither, but let your own discretion be
15 your tutor; suit the action to the word, the word to the action;

---

[10] Does not find him out.   [1] A violent pagan deity, supposedly Mohammedan.
[2] Outrants the ranting Herod, who figures in medieval drama.

with this special observance, that you o'erstep not the modesty of
nature: for anything so overdone is from the purpose of playing,
whose end, both at the first and now, was and is, to hold, as
'twere, the mirror up to nature; to show virtue her own feature,
20   scorn her own image, and the very age and body of the time his
form and pressure. Now, this overdone or come tardy off, though it
make the unskilful laugh, cannot but make the judicious grieve;
the censure of the which one must, in your allowance, o'erweigh
a whole theater of others. O, there be players that I have seen
25   play,—and heard others praise, and that highly,—not to speak it
profanely, that, neither having the accent of Christians, nor the
gait of Christian, pagan, nor man, have so strutted and bellowed
that I have thought some of nature's journeymen had made men,
and not made them well, they imitated humanity so abominably.
30 **1ST PLAYER:**   I hope we have reformed that indifferently with us, sir.
HAMLET: O, reform it altogether. And let those that play your clowns
speak no more than is set down for them: for there be of them that
will themselves laugh, to set on some quantity of barren spectators
to laugh too; though, in the meantime, some necessary question of
35   the play be then to be considered: that's villainous, and shows a
most pitiful ambition in the fool that uses it. Go, make you ready.

(Exeunt Players.)

(Enter Polonius, Rosencrantz, and Guildenstern.)

How now, my lord! will the king hear this piece of work?
POLONIUS: And the queen, too, and that presently.
HAMLET: Bid the players make haste.

(Exit Polonius.)

40   Will you two help to hasten them?
ROSENCRANTZ and **GUILDENSTERN:**   We will, my lord. *(Exeunt.)*
HAMLET: What, ho, Horatio!

(Enter Horatio.)

HORATIO: Here, sweet lord, at your service.
HAMLET: Horatio, thou art e'en as just a man
45   As e'er my conversation cop'd withal.
HORATIO: O, my dear lord,—
HAMLET: Nay, do not think I flatter;
For what advancement may I hope from thee,
That no revénue hast, but thy good spirits,
To feed and clothe thee? Why should the poor be flatter'd?
50   No, let the candied tongue lick ábsurd pomp;
And crook the pregnant hinges of the knee
Where thrift may follow fawning. Dost thou hear?

Since my dear soul was mistress of her choice,
And could of men distinguish, her election
55   Hath seal'd thee for herself: for thou hast been
As one, in suffering all, that suffers nothing;
A man that Fortune's buffets and rewards
Hast ta'en with equal thanks: and bless'd are those
Whose blood and judgment are so well commingled
60   That they are not a pipe for Fortune's finger
To sound what stop she please. Give me that man
That is not passion's slave, and I will wear him
In my heart's core, ay, in my heart of heart,
As I do thee.—Something too much of this.—
65   There is a play to-night before the king;
One scene of it comes near the circumstance
Which I have told thee of my father's death:
I pr'ythee, when thou see'st that act a-foot,
Even with the very comment of thy soul
70   Observe mine uncle: if this his occulted guilt
Do not itself unkennel in one speech,
It is a damned ghost that we have seen;
And my imaginations are as foul
As Vulcan's stithy.[3] Give him heedful note:
75   For I mine eyes will rivet to his face;
And, after, we will both our judgments join
In censure of his seeming.

HORATIO: Well, my lord:
If he steal aught the whilst this play is playing,
And scape detecting, I will pay the theft.

80 **HAMLET:**   They are coming to the play; I must be idle:[4]
Get you a place.

*(Danish march. A flourish. Enter King, Queen, Polonius, Ophelia, Rosencrantz,
Guildenstern, and others.)*

KING: How fares our cousin Hamlet?
HAMLET: Excellent, i'faith; of the chameleon's dish:[5] I eat the air,
promise-crammed: you cannot feed capons so.
85 **KING:**   I have nothing with this answer, Hamlet; these words are not
mine.
HAMLET: No, nor mine now. *(To Polonius)* My lord, you played once
i'the university, you say?
POLONIUS: That did I, my lord, and was accounted a good actor.
90 **HAMLET:**   And what did you enact?
POLONIUS: I did enact Julius Caesar: I was killed i' the Capitol; Brutus
killed me.

---

[3] Smithy.   [4] Foolish.   [5] Chameleons were supposed to live on air.

HAMLET: It was a brute part of him to kill so capital a calf there.—Be the players ready.

95 **ROSENCRANTZ:** Ay, my lord; they stay upon your patience.

QUEEN: Come hither, my good Hamlet, sit by me.

HAMLET: No, good mother, here's metal more attractive.

POLONIUS: O, ho! do you mark that? *(To the King)*

HAMLET: Lady, shall I lie in your lap? *(Lying down at Ophelia's feet)*

100 **OPHELIA:** No, my lord.

HAMLET: I mean, my head upon your lap?

OPHELIA: Ay, my lord.

HAMLET: Do you think I meant country matters?

OPHELIA: I think nothing, my lord.

105 **HAMLET:** That's a fair thought to lie between maids' legs.

OPHELIA: What is, my lord?

HAMLET: Nothing.

OPHELIA: You are merry, my lord.

HAMLET: Who, I?

110 **OPHELIA:** Ay, my lord.

HAMLET: O, your only jig-maker. What should a man do but be merry? for, look you, how cheerfully my mother looks, and my father died within's two hours.

OPHELIA: Nay, 'tis twice two months, my lord.

115 **HAMLET:** So long? Nay, then, let the devil wear black, for I'll have a suit of sables. O heavens! die two months ago, and not forgotten yet? Then there's hope a great man's memory may outlive his life half a year: but, by'r lady, he must build churches, then; or else shall he suffer not thinking on, with the hobby-horse, whose epitaph is,

120 *For, O, for, O, the hobby-horse is forgot.*

(Trumpets sound. The dumb show enters.)

(Enter a King and a Queen, very lovingly; the Queen embracing him and he her. She kneels, and makes show of protestation unto him. He takes her up, and declines his head upon her neck: lays him down upon a bank of flowers: she, seeing him asleep, leaves him. Anon comes in a fellow, takes off his crown, kisses it, and pours poison in the King's ears, and exit. The Queen returns; finds the King dead, and makes passionate action. The Poisoner, with some two or three Mutes, comes in again, seeming to lament with her. The dead body is carried away. The Poisoner woos the Queen with gifts: she seems loth and unwilling awhile, but in the end accepts his love.)

(Exeunt.)

OPHELIA: What means this, my lord?

HAMLET: Marry, this is miching mallecho;[6] it means mischief.

OPHELIA: Belike this show imports the argument of the play.

---

[6] A sneaking misdeed.

(Enter Prologue.)

HAMLET: We shall know by this fellow: the players cannot keep counsel;
125   they'll tell all.
OPHELIA: Will he tell us what this show meant?
HAMLET: Ay, or any show that you'll show him: be not you ashamed
     to show, he'll not shame to tell you what it means.
OPHELIA: You are naught, you are naught: I'll mark the play.
130 **PROLOGUE:**   *For us, and for our tragedy,*
               Here stooping to your clemency,
               We beg your hearing patiently.
HAMLET: Is this a prologue, or the posy[7] of a ring?
OPHELIA: 'Tis brief, my lord.
135 **HAMLET:** As woman's love.

(Enter a King and a Queen.)

PROLOGUE KING: Full thirty times hath Phoebus' cart gone round
     Neptune's salt wash and Tellus' orbed ground,[8]
     And thirty dozen moons with borrow'd sheen
     About the world have times twelve thirties been,
140   Since love our hearts, and Hymen did our hands
     Unite commutual in most sacred bands.
PROLOGUE QUEEN: So many journeys may the sun and moon
     Make us again count o'er ere love be done!
     But, woe is me, you are so sick of late,
145   So far from cheer and from your former state
     That I distrust you.[9] Yet, though I distrust,
     Discomfort you, my lord, it nothing must:
     For women's fear and love holds quantity,[10]
     In neither aught, or in extremity.
150   Now, what my love is, proof hath made you know;
     And as my love is siz'd, my fear is so:
     Where love is great, the littlest doubts are fear;
     Where little fears grow great, great love grows there.
PROLOGUE KING: Faith, I must leave thee, love, and shortly too;
155   My operant powers their functions leave[11] to do:
     And thou shalt live in this fair world behind,
     Honor'd, belov'd; and haply one as kind
     For husband shalt thou,—
PROLOGUE QUEEN: O, confound the rest!
     Such love must needs be treason in my breast:
160   In second husband let me be accurst!
     None wed the second but who kill'd the first.

---

[7] Motto or inscription.   [8] The globe.   [9] Worry about you.   [10] Correspond in degree.   [11] Cease.

HAMLET: *(Aside)* Wormwood, wormwood.

PROLOGUE QUEEN: The instances that second marriage move
Are base respects of thrift, but none of love:
165   A second time I kill my husband, dead,
When second husband kisses me in bed.

PROLOGUE KING: I do believe you think what now you speak;
But what we do determine oft we break.
Purpose is but the slave to memory;
170   Of violent birth, but poor validity:
Which now, like fruit unripe, sticks on the tree;
But fall unshaken when they mellow be.
Most necessary 'tis that we forget
To pay ourselves what to ourselves is debt:
175   What to ourselves in passion we propose,
The passion ending, doth the purpose lose.
The violence of either grief or joy
Their own enactures with themselves destroy:
Where joy most revels grief doth most lament;
180   Grief joys, joy grieves, on slender accident.
This world is not for aye; nor 'tis not strange
That even our loves should with our fortunes change;
For 'tis a question left us yet to prove
Whether love lead fortune or else fortune love.
185   The great man down, you mark his favorite flies;
The poor advanc'd makes friends of enemies.
And hitherto doth love on fortune tend:
For who not needs shall never lack a friend;
And who in want a hollow friend doth try,
190   Directly seasons him his enemy.
But, orderly to end where I begun,—
Our wills and fates do so contrary run
That our devices still are overthrown;
Our thoughts are ours, their ends none of our own:
195   So think thou wilt no second husband wed;
But die thy thoughts when thy first lord is dead.

PROLOGUE QUEEN: Nor earth to me give food, nor heaven light!
Sport and repose lock from me day and night!
To desperation turn my trust and hope!
200   An anchor's[12] cheer in prison be my scope!
Each opposite, that blanks the face of joy,
Meet what I would have well, and it destroy!
Both here and hence, pursue me lasting strife,
If, once a widow, ever I be wife!

---

[12] Anchorite's, or hermit's.

205 **HAMLET:**   If she should break it now! *(To Ophelia)*
   PROLOGUE KING: 'Tis deeply sworn. Sweet, leave me here awhile;
       My spirits grow dull, and fain I would beguile
       The tedious day with sleep. *(Sleeps)*
   PROLOGUE QUEEN: Sleep rock thy brain,
       And never come mischance between us twain! *(Exit.)*
210 **HAMLET:**   Madam, how like you this play?
   QUEEN: The lady doth protest too much, methinks.
   HAMLET: O, but she'll keep her word.
   KING: Have you heard the argument? Is there no offence in't?
   HAMLET: No, no, they do but jest, poison in jest; no offence i' the
215   world.
   KING: What do you call the play?
   HAMLET: The Mouse-trap. Marry, how? Tropically.[13] This play is the
       image of a murder done in Vienna: Gonzago is the duke's name:
       his wife, Baptista: you shall see anon; 'tis a knavish piece of work:
220   but what o' that? your majesty, and we that have free souls, it
       touches us not: let the galled jade wince, our withers are unwrung.

   (Enter Lucianus.)

       This is one Lucianus, nephew to the king.
   OPHELIA: You are a good chorus, my lord.
   HAMLET: I could interpret between you and your love, if I could see
225   the puppets dallying.
   OPHELIA: You are keen, my lord, you are keen.
   HAMLET: It would cost you a groaning to take off my edge.
   OPHELIA: Still better, and worse.
   HAMLET: So you must take your husbands.—Begin, murderer; pox,
230   leave thy damnable faces and begin. Come:—*The croaking raven
       doth bellow for revenge.*
   LUCIANUS: Thoughts black, hands apt, drugs fit, and time agreeing;
       Confederate season, else no creature seeing;
       Thou mixture rank, of midnight weeds collected,
235   With Hecate's ban[14] thrice blasted, thrice infected,
       Thy natural magic and dire property
       On wholesome life usurp immediately.

   (Pours the poison into the sleeper's ears.)

   HAMLET: He poisons him i' the garden for's estate. His name's Gonzago:
       the story is extant, and writ in choice Italian: you shall see anon how
240   the murderer gets the love of Gonzago's wife.
   OPHELIA: The king rises.

---

[13] Figuratively, or metaphorically; by means of a "trope."   [14] The spell of the goddess of witchcraft.

HAMLET: What, frighted with false fire!

QUEEN: How fares my lord?

POLONIUS: Give o'er the play.

245 **KING:**   Give me some light:—away!

ALL: Lights, lights, lights!

(Exeunt all but Hamlet and Horatio.)

HAMLET: Why, let the stricken deer go weep,
    The hart ungalled play;
    For some must watch, while some must sleep:
250   So runs the world away.—
    Would not this, sir, and a forest of feathers,
    If the rest of my fortunes turn Turk with me,
    With two Provencial roses on my razed shoes,
    Get me a fellowship in a cry[15] of players, sir?

255 **HORATIO:**   Half a share.

HAMLET: A whole one, I.
                    For thou dost know, O Damon dear,
                        This realm dismantled was
                        Of Jove himself; and now reigns here
260   A very, very—pajock.[16]

HORATIO: You might have rhymed.

HAMLET: O good Horatio, I'll take the ghost's word for a thousand
    pound. Didst perceive?

HORATIO: Very well, my lord.

265 **HAMLET:**   Upon the talk of the poisoning,—

HORATIO: I did very well note him.

HAMLET: Ah, ha!—Come, some music! come, the recorders!—
    For if the king like not the comedy,
    Why, then, belike,—he likes it not, perdy. Come, some music!

(Re-enter Rosencrantz and Guildenstern.)

270 **GUILDENSTERN:**   Good my lord, vouchsafe me a word with you.

HAMLET: Sir, a whole history.

GUILDENSTERN: The king, sir,—

HAMLET: Ay, sir, what of him?

GUILDENSTERN: Is, in his retirement, marvelous distempered.

275 **HAMLET:**   With drink, sir?

GUILDENSTERN: No, my lord, rather with choler.

HAMLET: Your wisdom should show itself more richer to signify this
    to his doctor; for, for me to put him to his purgation would perhaps
    plunge him into far more choler.

280 **GUILDENSTERN:**   Good my lord, put your discourse into some frame,
    and start not so wildly from my affair.

---

[15] Company.   [16] Peacock.

HAMLET: I am tame, sir:—pronounce.

GUILDENSTERN: The queen, your mother, in most great affliction of spirit, hath sent me to you.

285 **HAMLET:** You are welcome.

GUILDENSTERN: Nay, good my lord, this courtesy is not of the right breed. If it shall please you to make me a wholesome answer, I will do you mother's commandment: if not, your pardon and my return shall be the end of my business.

290 **HAMLET:** Sir, I cannot.

GUILDENSTERN: What, my lord?

HAMLET: Make you a wholesome answer; my wit's diseas'd: but, sir, such answer as I can make, you shall command; or, rather, as you say, my mother: therefore no more, but to the matter: my mother,

295 you say,—

ROSENCRANTZ: Then thus she says: your behavior hath struck her into amazement and admiration.

HAMLET: O wonderful son, that can so astonish a mother!—But is there no sequel at the heels of this mother's admiration?

300 **ROSENCRANTZ:** She desires to speak with you in her closet[17] ere you go to bed.

HAMLET: We shall obey, were she ten times our mother. Have you any further trade with us?

ROSENCRANTZ: My lord, you once did love me.

305 **HAMLET:** So I do still, by these pickers and stealers.[18]

ROSENCRANTZ: Good, my lord, what is your cause of distemper? you do, surely, bar the door upon your own liberty if you deny your griefs to your friend.

HAMLET: Sir, I lack advancement.

310 **ROSENCRANTZ:** How can that be, when you have the voice of the king himself for your succession in Denmark?

HAMLET: Ay, but *While the grass grows,*—the proverb is something musty.

(Re-enter the Players, with recorders.)

O, the recorders:—let me see one.—To withdraw with you:—why

315 do you go about to recover the wind of me, as if you would drive me into a toil?

GUILDENSTERN: O, my lord, if my duty be too bold, my love is too unmannerly.

HAMLET: I do not well understand that. Will you play upon this pipe?

320 **GUILDENSTERN:** My lord, I cannot.

HAMLET: I pray you.

GUILDENSTERN: Believe me, I cannot.

---

17 Boudoir.   18 Fingers.

HAMLET: I do beseech you.

GUILDENSTERN: I know no touch of it, my lord.

325 **HAMLET:**   'Tis as easy as lying: govern these ventages[19] with your finger and thumb, give it breath with your mouth, and it will discourse most eloquent music. Look you, these are the stops.

GUILDENSTERN: But these cannot I command to any utterance of harmony; I have not the skill.

330 **HAMLET:**   Why, look you now, how unworthy a thing you make of me! You would play upon me; you would seem to know my stops; you would pluck out the heart of my mystery; you would sound me from my lowest note to the top of my compass: and there is much music, excellent voice, in this little organ; yet cannot you make it

335 speak. 'Sblood, do you think that I am easier to be played on than a pipe? Call me what instrument you will, though you can fret me you cannot play upon me.

(Enter Polonius.)

God bless you, sir!

POLONIUS: My lord, the queen would speak with you, and

340 presently.

HAMLET: Do you see yonder cloud that's almost in shape of a camel?

POLONIUS: By the mass, and 'tis like a camel indeed.

HAMLET: Methinks it is like a weasel.

POLONIUS: It is backed like a weasel.

345 **HAMLET:**   Or like a whale?

POLONIUS: Very like a whale.

HAMLET: Then will I come to my mother by and by.—They fool me to the top of my bent.—I will come by and by.

POLONIUS: I will say so.

350 **HAMLET:**   By and by is easily said.

(Exit Polonius.)

Leave me, friends.

(Exeunt Rosencrantz, Guildenstern, Horatio, and Players.)

'Tis now the very witching time of night,
When churchyards yawn, and hell itself breathes out
Contagion to this world: now could I drink hot blood,

355 And do such bitter business as the day
Would quake to look on. Soft! now to my mother.—
O heart, lose not thy nature; let not ever
The soul of Nero[20] enter this firm bosom:

---

[19] Holes.   [20] Nero killed his mother, a crime of which Hamlet does not want to be guilty.

360
Let me be cruel, not unnatural:
I will speak daggers to her, but use none;
My tongue and soul in this be hypocrites,—
How in my words soever she be shent,
To give them seals never, my soul, consent! *(Exit.)*

SCENE III

A room in the castle.

(Enter King, Rosencrantz, and Guildenstern.)

KING: I like him not; nor stands it safe with us
To let his madness range. Therefore prepare you;
I your commission with forthwith despatch,
And he to England shall along with you:
5
The terms of our estate may not endure
Hazard so dangerous as doth hourly grow
Out of his lunacies.
GUILDENSTERN: We will ourselves provide:
Most holy and religious fear it is
To keep those many many bodies safe
10
That live and feed upon your majesty.
ROSENCRANTZ: The single and peculiar life is bound,
With all the strength and armor of the mind,
To keep itself from 'noyance; but much more
That spirit upon whose weal depend and rest
15
The lives of many. The cease of majesty
Dies not alone; but like a gulf doth draw
What's near it with it: it is a massy wheel,
Fix'd on the summit of the highest mount,
To whose huge spokes ten thousand lesser things
20
Are mortis'd and adjoin'd; which, when it falls,
Each small annexment, petty consequence,
Attends the boisterous ruin. Never alone
Did the king sigh, but with a general groan.
KING: Arm you, I pray you, to this speedy voyage;
25
For we will fetters put upon this fear,
Which now goes too free-footed.
ROSENCRANTZ and **GUILDENSTERN:**   We will haste us.

(Exeunt Rosencrantz and Guildenstern.)

(Enter Polonius.)

POLONIUS: My lord, he's going to his mother's closet:
Behind the arras I'll convey myself

To hear the process; I'll warrant she'll tax him home:[1]
30   And, as you said, and wisely was it said,
'Tis meet that some more audience than a mother,
Since nature makes them partial, should o'erhear
The speech, of vantage. Fare you well, my liege:
I'll call upon you ere you go to bed,
35   And tell you what I know.

KING: Thanks, dear my lord.

(Exit Polonius.)

O, my offence is rank, it smells to heaven;
It hath the primal eldest curse upon't,—
A brother's murder!—Pray can I not,
Though inclination be as sharp as will:
40   My stronger guilt defeats my strong intent;
And, like a man to double business bound,
I stand in pause where I shall first begin,
And both neglect. What if this cursed hand
Were thicker than itself with brother's blood,—
45   Is there not rain enough in the sweet heavens
To wash it white as snow? Whereto serves mercy
But to confront the visage of offence?
And what's in prayer but this twofold force,—
To be forestalled ere we come to fall,
50   Or pardon'd being down? Then I'll look up;
My fault is past. But, O, what form of prayer
Can serve my turn? Forgive me my foul murder?—
That cannot be; since I am still possess'd
Of those effects for which I did the murder,—
55   My crown, mine own ambition, and my queen.
May one be pardon'd and retain the offence?[2]
In the corrupted currents of this world
Offence's gilded hand may shove by justice;
And oft 'tis seen the wicked prize itself
60   Buys out the law: but 'tis not so above;
There is no shuffling,—there the action lies
In his true nature; and we ourselves compell'd,
Even to the teeth and forehead of our faults,
To give in evidence. What then? what rests?[3]
65   Try what repentance can: what can it not?
Yet what can it when one can not repent?
O wretched state! O bosom black as death!
O limed[4] soul, that, struggling to be free,

---

[1] Reprove him properly.   [2] That is, the gains won by the offense.   [3] Remains.
[4] Snared.

Art more engag'd! Help, angels! make assay:
70 Bow, stubborn knees; and, heart, with strings of steel,
Be soft as sinews of the new-born babe!
All may be well. *(Retires and kneels)*

(Enter Hamlet.)

HAMLET: Now might I do it pat, now he is praying;
And now I'll do't—and so he goes to heaven;
75 And so am I reveng'd:—that would be scann'd:
A villain kills my father; and for that,
I, his sole son, do this same villain send
To heaven.
O, this is hire and salary, not revenge.
80 He took my father grossly, full of bread;
With all his crimes broad blown, as flush as May;
And how his audit stands who knows save heaven?
But in our circumstance and course of thought
'Tis heavy with him: and am I, then, reveng'd,
85 To take him in the purging of his soul,
When he is fit and season'd for his passage?
No.
Up, sword; and know thou a more horrid hent:[5]
When he is drunk, asleep, or in his rage;
90 Or in the incestuous pleasure of his bed;
At gaming, swearing; or about some act
That has no relish of salvation in't;—
Then trip him, that his heels may kick at heaven;
And that his soul may be as damn'd and black
95 As hell, whereto it goes. My mother stays:
This physic but prolongs thy sickly days. *(Exit.)*

(The King rises and advances.)

KING: My words fly up, my thoughts remain below:
Words without thoughts never to heaven go. *(Exit.)*

SCENE IV
....

Another room in the castle.

(Enter Queen and Polonius.)

POLONIUS: He will come straight. Look you lay home to him:
Tell him his pranks have been too broad to bear with,
And that your grace hath screen'd and stood between

---

[5] Opportunity.

Much heat and him. I'll silence me e'en here.
5   Pray you, be round with him.
HAMLET: *(Within)* Mother, mother, mother!
QUEEN: I'll warrant you:
Fear me not:—withdraw, I hear him coming.

(Polonius goes behind the arras.)

(Enter Hamlet.)

HAMLET: Now, mother, what's the matter?
QUEEN: Hamlet, thou hast thy father much offended.
10 **HAMLET:**   Mother, you have my father much offended.
QUEEN: Come, come, you answer with an idle tongue.
HAMLET: Go, go, you question with a wicked tongue.
QUEEN: Why, how now, Hamlet!
HAMLET: What's the matter now?
QUEEN: Have you forgot me?
HAMLET: No, by the rood, not so:
15   You are the queen, your husband's brother's wife;
And,—would it were not so!—you are my mother.
QUEEN: Nay, then, I'll set those to you that can speak.
HAMLET: Come, come, and sit you down; you shall not budge;
You go not till I set you up a glass
20   Where you may see the inmost part of you.
QUEEN: What wilt thou do? thou wilt not murder me?—
Help, help, ho!
POLONIUS: *(Behind)* What, ho! help, help, help!
HAMLET: How now! a rat?
(Draws.)
Dead, for a ducat, dead! *(Makes a pass through the arras)*
25 **POLONIUS:**   *(Behind)* O, I am slain! *(Falls and dies.)*
QUEEN: O me, what hast thou done?
HAMLET: Nay, I know not:
Is it the king? *(Draws forth Polonius)*
QUEEN: O, what a rash and bloody deed is this!
HAMLET: A bloody deed!—almost as bad, good mother,
30   As kill a king and marry with his brother.
QUEEN: As kill a king!
HAMLET: Ay, lady, 'twas my word.—
Thou wretched, rash, intruding fool, farewell! *(To Polonius)*
I took thee for thy better: take thy fortune;
Thou find'st to be too busy is some danger.—
35   Leave wringing of your hands: peace; sit you down,
And let me wring your heart: for so I shall,
If it be made of penetrable stuff;
If damned custom have not braz'd it so
That it is proof and bulwark against sense.

40 **QUEEN:**   What have I done, that thou dar'st wag thy tongue
         In noise so rude against me?
      HAMLET: Such an act
         That blurs the grace and blush of modesty;
         Calls virtue hypocrite; takes off the rose
         From the fair forehead of an innocent love,
45   And sets a blister there; makes marriage-vows
         As false as dicers' oaths: O, such a deed
         As from the body of contraction plucks
         The very soul, and sweet religion makes
         A rhapsody of words: heaven's face doth glow;
50   Yea, this solidity and compound mass,
         With tristful[1] visage, as against the doom,
         Is thought-sick at the act.
      QUEEN: Ah me, what act,
         That roars so loud, and thunders in the index?
      HAMLET: Look here upon this picture and on this,—
55   The counterfeit presentment of two brothers.
         See what grace was seated on this brow;
         Hyperion's curls; the front of Jove himself;
         An eye like Mars, to threaten and command;
         A station like the herald Mercury
60   New-lighted on a heaven-kissing hill;
         A combination and a form, indeed,
         Where every god did seem to set his seal,
         To give the world assurance of a man:
         This was your husband.—Look you now, what follows:
65   Here is your husband, like a mildew'd ear
         Blasting his wholesome brother. Have you eyes?
         Could you on this fair mountain leave to feed,
         And batten on this moor? Ha! have you eyes?
         You cannot call it love; for at your age
70   The hey-day in the blood is tame, it's humble,
         And waits upon the judgment: and what judgment
         Would step from this to this? Sense, sure, you have,
         Else could you not have motion: but sure that sense
         Is apoplex'd: for madness would not err;
75   Nor sense to ecstasy was ne'er so thrill'd
         But it reserv'd some quantity of choice
         To serve in such a difference. What devil was't
         That thus hath cozen'd you at hoodman-blind?[2]
         Eyes without feeling, feeling without sight,
80   Ears without hand or eyes, smelling sans all,
         Or but a sickly part of one true sense

---

[1] Gloomy.   [2] Tricked you at blindman's buff.

Could not so mope.
O shame! where is thy blush! Rebellious hell,
If thou canst mutine in a matron's bones,
85 To flaming youth let virtue be as wax,
And melt in her own fire: proclaim no shame
When the compulsive ardor gives the charge,
Since frost itself as actively doth burn,
And reason panders[3] will.

QUEEN: O Hamlet, speak no more:
90 Thou turn'st mine eyes into my very soul;
And there I see such black and grained spots
As will not leave their tinct.[4]

HAMLET: Nay, but to live
In the rank sweat of an enseamed bed,
Stew'd in corruption, honeying and making love
95 Over the nasty sty,—

QUEEN: O, speak to me no more;
These words like daggers enter in mine ears;
No more, sweet Hamlet.

HAMLET: A murderer and a villain;
A slave that is not twentieth part the tithe
Of your precedent lord; a vice of kings;[5]
100 A cutpurse of the empire and the rule,
That from a shelf the precious diadem stole,
And put it in his pocket!

QUEEN: No more.

HAMLET: A king of shreds and patches,—

(Enter Ghost.)

Save me, and hover o'er me with your wings,
105 You heavenly guards!—What would your gracious figure?

QUEEN: Alas, he's mad!

HAMLET: Do you not come your tardy son to chide,
That, laps'd in time and passion, lets go by
The important acting of your dread command?
110 O, say!

GHOST: Do not forget: this visitation
Is but to whet thy almost blunted purpose.
But, look, amazement on thy mother sits:
O, step between her and her fighting soul,—
115 Conceit in weakest bodies strongest works,—
Speak to her, Hamlet.

---

[3] Becomes subservient to.   [4] As will not yield up their color.   [5] A buffoon among kings. The "Vice" in morality plays.

HAMLET: How is it with you, lady?
QUEEN: Alas, how is't with you,
That you do bend your eye on vacancy,
And with the incorporal air do hold discourse?
120 Forth at your eyes your spirits wildly peep;
And, as the sleeping soldiers in the alarm,
Your bedded hair, like life in excrements,[6]
Starts up and stands on end. O gentle son,
Upon the heat and flame of thy distemper
125 Sprinkle cool patience. Whereon do you look?
HAMLET: On him, on him! Look you, how pale he glares!
His form and cause conjoin'd, preaching to stones,
Would make them capable.—Do not look upon me;
Lest with this piteous action you convert
130 My stern effects: then what I have to do
Will want true color; tears perchance for blood.
QUEEN: To whom do you speak this?
HAMLET: Do you see nothing there?
QUEEN: Nothing at all; yet all that is I see.
HAMLET: Nor did you nothing hear?
135 QUEEN: No, nothing but ourselves.
HAMLET: Why, look you there! look, how it steals away!
My father, in his habit as he liv'd!
Look, where he goes, even now, out at the portal!

(Exit Ghost.)

QUEEN: This is the very coinage of your brain:
140 This bodiless creation ecstasy
Is very cunning in.
HAMLET: Ecstasy!
My pulse, as yours, doth temperately keep time.
And makes as healthful music: it is not madness
That I have utter'd: bring me to the test,
145 And I the matter will re-word; which madness
Would gambol from. Mother, for love of grace,
Lay not that flattering unction to your soul,
That not your trespass, but my madness speaks:
It will but skin and film the ulcerous place,
150 Whilst rank corruption, mining all within,
Infects unseen. Confess yourself to Heaven;
Repent what's past; avoid what is to come;
And do not spread the compost on the weeds,
To make them ranker. Forgive me this my virtue;

---

[6] In outgrowths or extremities.

155 For in the fatness[7] of these pursy times
Virtue itself of vice must pardon beg,
Yea, curb and woo for leave to do him good.
   QUEEN: O Hamlet, thou hast cleft my heart in twain.
   HAMLET: O, throw away the worser part of it,
160 And live the purer with the other half.
Good-night: but go not to mine uncle's bed;
Assume a virtue, if you have it not.
That monster custom, who all sense doth eat,
Of habits devil, is angel yet in this,—
165 That to the use of actions fair and good
He likewise gives a frock or livery
That aptly is put on. Refrain to-night;
And that shall lend a kind of easiness
To the next abstinence: the next more easy;
170 For use almost can change the stamp of nature,
And either curb the devil, or throw him out
With wondrous potency. Once more, good-night:
And when you are desirous to be bless'd,
I'll blessing beg of you.—For this same lord *(pointing to Polonius)*
175 I do repent: but Heaven hath pleas'd it so,
To punish me with this, and this with me,
That I must be their[8] scourge and minister.
I will bestow him, and will answer well
The death I gave him. So, again, good-night.—
180 I must be cruel only to be kind:
Thus bad begins and worse remains behind.—
One word more, good lady.
   QUEEN: What shall I do?
   HAMLET: Not this, by no means, that I bid you do:
Let the bloat king tempt you again to bed;
185 Pinch wanton on your cheek; call you his mouse;
And let him, for a pair of reechy kisses,
Or paddling in your neck with his damn'd fingers,
Make you to ravel all this matter out,
That I essentially am not in madness,
190 But mad in craft. 'Twere good you let him know;
For who that's but a queen, fair, sober, wise,
Would from a paddock,[9] from a bat, a gib,
Such dear concernings hide? who would do so?
No, in despite of sense and secrecy,
195 Unpeg the basket on the house's top,
Let the birds fly, and, like the famous ape,

---

[7] Corruption.   [8] Heaven's, or the heavens'.   [9] Paddock: toad; gib: tomcat.

To try conclusions, in the basket creep,
And break your own neck down.

QUEEN: Be thou assur'd, if words be made of breath
200 And breath of life, I have not life to breathe
What thou hast said to me.

HAMLET: I must to England; you know that?

QUEEN: Alack,
I had forgot: 'tis so concluded on.

HAMLET: There's letters seal'd: and my two school-fellows,—
205 Whom I will trust as I will adders fang'd,
They bear the mandate; they must sweep my way,
And marshal me to knavery. Let it work;
For 'tis the sport to have the éngineer
Hoist with his own petard: and't shall go hard
210 But I will delve one yard below their mines,
And blow them at the moon: O, 'tis most sweet,
When in one line two crafts directly meet.—
This man shall set me packing:
I'll lug the guts into the neighbor room.—
215 Mother, good-night.—Indeed, this counsellor
Is now most still, most secret, and most grave,
Who was in life a foolish prating knave.
Come, sir, to draw toward an end with you:—
Good-night, mother.

(Exeunt severally; Hamlet dragging out Polonius.)

ACT IV SCENE I

A room in the castle.

(Enter King, Queen, Rosencrantz, and Guildenstern.)

KING: There's matter in these sighs, these prófound heaves:
You must translate: 'tis fit we understand them.
Where is your son?

QUEEN: Bestow this place on us a little while. *(To Rosencrantz and*
5 *Guildenstern, who go out)* Ah, my good lord, what have I seen to-night!

KING: What, Gertrude? How does Hamlet?

QUEEN: Mad as the sea and wind, when both contend
Which is the mightier: in his lawless fit,
Behind the arras hearing something stir,
10 He whips his rapier out, and cries, *A rat, a rat!*
And, in this brainish apprehension,[1] kills
The unseen good old man.

---

[1] Mad notion.

KING: O heavy deed!
It had been so with us had we been there:
His liberty is full of threats to all;
15   To you yourself, to us, to every one.
Alas, how shall this bloody deed be answer'd?
It will be laid to us, whose providence
Should have kept short, restrain'd, and out of haunt
This mad young man: but so much was our love,
20   We would not understand what was most fit;
But, like the owner of a foul disease,
To keep it from divulging, let it feed
Even on the pith of life. Where is he gone?
QUEEN: To draw apart the body he hath kill'd:
25   O'er whom his very madness, like some ore
Among a mineral of metals base,
Shows itself pure; he weeps for what is done.
KING: O Gertrude, come away!
The sun no sooner shall the mountains touch
30   But we will ship him hence: and this vile deed
We must, with all our majesty and skill,
Both countenance and excuse.—Ho, Guildenstern!

(Enter Rosencrantz and Guildenstern.)

Friends both, go join you with some further aid:
Hamlet in madness hath Polonius slain,
35   And from his mother's closet hath he dragg'd him:
Go seek him out; speak fair, and bring the body
Into the chapel. I pray you, haste in this.

(Exeunt Rosencrantz and Guildenstern.)

Come, Gertrude, we'll call up our wisest friends;
And let them know both what we mean to do
40   And what's untimely done: so haply slander,—
Whose whisper o'er the world's diameter,
As level as the cannon to his blank,
Transports his poison'd shot,—may amiss our name,
And hit the woundless air.—O, come away!
45   My soul is full of discord and dismay.

(Exeunt.)

SCENE II

Another room in the castle.

(Enter Hamlet.)

HAMLET: Safely stowed.

ROSENCRANTZ and **GUILDENSTERN:**   *(Within)* Hamlet! Lord Hamlet!

HAMLET: What noise? who calls on Hamlet?
O, here they come.

(Enter Rosencrantz and Guildenstern.)

5   **ROSENCRANTZ:**   What have you done, my lord, with the dead body?

HAMLET: Compounded it with dust, whereto 'tis kin.

ROSENCRANTZ: Tell us where 'tis, that we may take it thence,
And bear it to the chapel.

HAMLET: Do not believe it.

10   **ROSENCRANTZ:**   Believe what?

HAMLET: That I can keep your counsel, and not mine own. Besides, to
be demanded of a sponge!—what replication should be made by the
son of a king?

ROSENCRANTZ: Take you me for a sponge, my lord?

15   **HAMLET:**   Ay, sir; that soaks up the king's countenance, his rewards,
his authorities. But such officers do the king best service in the
end: he keeps them, like an ape, in the corner of his jaw; first
mouthed, to be last swallowed: when he needs what you have
gleaned, it is but squeezing you, and, sponge, you shall be dry
20   again.

ROSENCRANTZ: I understand you not, my lord.

HAMLET: I am glad of it: a knavish speech sleeps in a foolish ear.

ROSENCRANTZ: My lord, you must tell us where the body is, and go
with us to the king.

25   **HAMLET:**   The body is with the king, but the king is not with the
body. The king is a thing,—

GUILDENSTERN: A thing, my lord!

HAMLET: Of nothing: bring me to him.
Hide fox, and all after.

(Exeunt.)

SCENE III

Another room in the castle.

(Enter King, attended.)

KING: I have sent to seek him, and to find the body.
How dangerous is it that this man goes loose!
Yet must not we put the strong law on him:
He's lov'd of the distracted multitude,
5   Who like not in their judgment, but their eyes;
And where 'tis so, the offender's scourge is weigh'd,

But never the offence. To bear all smooth and even,
This sudden sending him away must seem
Deliberate pause: diseases desperate grown
10   By desperate appliance are reliev'd,
Or not at all.

(Enter Rosencrantz.)

How now! what hath befallen!

ROSENCRANTZ: Where the dead body is bestow'd, my lord,
We cannot get from him.

KING: But where is he?

15 **ROSENCRANTZ:**   Without, my lord; guarded, to know your pleasure.

KING: Bring him before us.

ROSENCRANTZ: Ho, Guildenstern! bring in my lord.

(Enter Hamlet and Guildenstern.)

KING: Now, Hamlet, where's Polonius?

HAMLET: At supper.

20 **KING:**   At supper! where?

HAMLET: Not where he eats, but where he is eaten: a certain
convocation of politic worms are e'en at him. Your worm is your
only emperor for diet: we fat all creatures else to fat us, and we fat
ourselves for maggots: your fat king and your lean beggar is but
25   variable service,—two dishes, but to one table: that's the end.

KING: Alas, alas!

HAMLET: A man may fish with the worm that hath eat of a king, and
eat of the fish that hath fed of that worm.

KING: What does thou mean by this?

30 **HAMLET:**   Nothing but to show you how a king may go a progress
through the guts of a beggar.

KING: Where is Polonius?

HAMLET: In heaven; send thither to see: if your messenger find him
not there, seek him i' the other place yourself. But, indeed, if you
35   find him not within this month, you shall nose him as you go up
the stairs into the lobby.

KING: Go seek him there. *(To some Attendants)*

HAMLET: He will stay till ye come.

(Exeunt Attendants.)

KING: Hamlet, this deed, for thine especial safety,—
40   Which we do tender, as we dearly grieve
For that which thou hast done,—must send thee hence
With fiery quickness: therefore prepare thyself;
The bark is ready, and the wind at help,
The associates tend, and everything is bent
45   For England.

HAMLET: For England!

KING: Ay, Hamlet.

HAMLET: Good.

KING: So is it, if thou knew'st our purposes.

HAMLET: I see a cherub that sees them.—But, come; for England!—
Farewell, dear mother.

KING: Thy loving father, Hamlet.

50 **HAMLET:**   My mother: father and mother is man and wife; man and
wife is one flesh; and so, my mother.—Come, for England! *(Exit.)*

KING: Follow him at foot; tempt him with speed aboard;
Delay it not; I'll have him hence to-night:
Away! for everything is seal'd and done

55   That else leans on the affair, pray you, make haste.

(Exeunt Rosencrantz and Guildenstern.)

And, England, if my love thou hold'st at aught,—
As my great power thereof may give thee sense,
Since yet thy cicatrice looks raw and red
After the Danish sword, and thy free awe

60   Pays homage to us,—thou mayst not coldly set
Our sovereign process; which imports at full,
By letters conjuring to that effect,
The present death of Hamlet. Do it, England;
For like the hectic in my blood he rages,

65   And thou must cure me: till I know 'tis done,
Howe'er my haps, my joys will ne'er begin. *(Exit)*

SCENE IV

A plain in Denmark.

(Enter Fortinbras, and Forces marching.)

FORTINBRAS: Go, from me greet the Danish king:
Tell him that, by his license, Fortinbras
Craves the conveyance of a promis'd march
Over his kingdom. You know the rendezvous,

5   If that his majesty would aught with us,
We shall express our duty in his eye,
And let him know so.

CAPTAIN: I will do't, my lord.

FORTINBRAS: Go softly on.

(Exeunt Fortinbras and Forces.)

(Enter Hamlet, Rosencrantz, Guildenstern, &c.)

HAMLET: Good sir, whose powers are these?
10 **CAPTAIN:** They are of Norway, sir.
HAMLET: How purpos'd, sir, I pray you?
CAPTAIN: Against some part of Poland.
HAMLET: Who commands them, sir?
CAPTAIN: The nephew to old Norway, Fortinbras.
15 **HAMLET:** Goes it against the main of Poland, sir,
        Or for some frontier?
CAPTAIN: Truly to speak, and with no addition,
        We go to gain a little patch of ground
        That hath in it no profit but the name.
20   To pay five ducats, five, I would not farm it;
        Nor will it yield to Norway or the Pole
        A ranker[1] rate should it be sold in fee.
HAMLET: Why, then the Polack never will defend it.
CAPTAIN: Yes, it is already garrison'd.
25 **HAMLET:** Two thousand souls and twenty thousand ducats
        Will not debate the question of this straw:
        This is the imposthume[2] of much wealth and peace,
        That inward breaks, and shows no cause without
        Why the man dies.—I humbly thank you, sir.
30 **CAPTAIN:** God b' wi' you, sir. *(Exit.)*
ROSENCRANTZ: Will't please you go, my lord?
HAMLET: I'll be with you straight. Go a little before.

(Exeunt all but Hamlet.)

        How all occasions do inform against me,
        And spur my dull revenge! What is a man,
35   If his chief good and market of his time
        Be but to sleep and feed? a beast, no more.
        Sure he that made us with such large discourse,[3]
        Looking before and after, gave us not
        That capability and godlike reason
40   To fust[4] in us unus'd. Now, whether it be
        Bestial oblivion or some craven scruple
        Of thinking too precisely on the event,—
        A thought which, quarter'd, hath but one part wisdom
        And ever three parts coward,—I do not know
45   Why yet I live to say, *This thing's to do;*
        Sith[5] I have cause, and will, and strength, and means
        To do't. Examples, gross as earth, exhort me:
        Witness this army, of such mass and charge,
        Led by a delicate and tender prince;

---

[1] Dearer.   [2] Ulcer.   [3] Reasoning faculty.   [4] Grow musty.   [5] Since.

50   Whose spirit, with divine ambition puff'd,
        Makes mouths at the invisible event;
        Exposing what is mortal and unsure
        To all that fortune, death, and danger dare,
        Even for an egg-shell. Rightly to be great
55   Is not to stir without great argument,
        But greatly to find quarrel in a straw
        When honor's at the stake. How stand I, then,
        That have a father kill'd, a mother stain'd,
        Excitements of my reason and my blood,
60   And let all sleep? while, to my shame, I see
        The imminent death of twenty thousand men,
        That, for a fantasy and trick of fame,
        Go to their graves like beds; fight for a plot
        Whereon the numbers cannot try the cause,
65   Which is not tomb enough and continent[6]
        To hide the slain?—O, from this time forth,
        My thoughts be bloody, or be nothing worth! *(Exit.)*

SCENE V

Elsinore. A room in the castle.

(Enter Queen and Horatio.)

QUEEN: I will not speak with her.
HORATIO: She is importunate; indeed, distract:
    Her mood will needs be pitied.
QUEEN: What would she have?
HORATIO: She speaks much of her father; says she hears
5   There's tricks i' the world; and hems, and beats her heart;
    Spurns enviously at straws; speaks things in doubt,
    That carry but half sense: her speech is nothing,
    Yet the unshapéd use of it doth move
    The hearers to collection; they aim at it,
10   And botch the words up fit to their own thoughts;
    Which, as her winks, and nods, and gestures yield them,
    Indeed would make one think there might be thought,
    Though nothing sure, yet much unhappily.
    'Twere good she were spoken with; for she may strew
15   Dangerous conjectures in ill-breeding minds.
QUEEN: Let her come in.

(Exit Horatio.)

---

[6] Container.

To my sick soul, as sin's true nature is,
Each toy seems prologue to some great amiss:
So full of artless jealousy is guilt,
20   It spills itself in fearing to be spilt.

(Re-enter Horatio and Ophelia.)

OPHELIA: Where is the beauteous majesty of Denmark?
QUEEN: How now, Ophelia!
OPHELIA: *(Sings)*

> How should I your true love know
> From another one?
> 25   By his cockle hat and staff,
> And his sandal shoon.

QUEEN: Alas, sweet lady, what imports this song?
OPHELIA: Say you? nay, pray you, mark.

(Sings)

> He is dead and gone, lady,
> 30   He is dead and gone;
> At his head a grass green turf,
> At his heels a stone.

QUEEN: Nay, but, Ophelia,—
OPHELIA: Pray you, mark.

(Sings)

> White his shroud as the mountain snow,

(Enter King.)

35   **QUEEN:**   Alas, look here, my lord.
OPHELIA: *(Sings)*

> Larded with sweet flowers;
> Which bewept to the grave did go
> With true-love showers.

KING: How do you, pretty lady?
40   **OPHELIA:**   Well, God 'ild[1] you! They say the owl was a baker's daughter.
Lord, we know what we are, but know not what we may be.
God be at your table!
KING: Conceit upon her father.
OPHELIA: Pray you, let's have no words of this; but when they ask
45   you what it means, say you this:

(Sings.)

---

[1] Yield you—that is, reward you.

> To-morrow is Saint Valentine's day
>   All in the morning betime,
> And I a maid at your window,
>   To be your Valentine.

50   Then up he rose, and donn'd his clothes,
>   And dupp'd the chamber-door;
> Let in the maid, that out a maid
>   Never departed more.

KING: Pretty Ophelia!

55 **OPHELIA:** Indeed, la, without an oath, I'll make an end on't;

(Sings)

> By Gis[2] and by Saint Charity,
>   Alack, and fie for shame!
> Young men will do't, if they come to't;
>   By cock, they are to blame.

60   Quoth she, before you tumbled me,
>   You promis'd me to wed.
> So would I ha' done, by yonder sun,
>   An thou hadst not come to my bed.

KING: How long hath she been thus?

65 **OPHELIA:** I hope all will be well. We must be patient: but I cannot
choose but weep, to think they should lay him i' the cold ground.
My brother shall know of it: and so I thank you; for your good
counsel.—Come, my coach!—Good-night, ladies; good-night,
sweet ladies; good-night, good-night. *(Exit.)*

70 **KING:** Follow her close; give her good watch, I pray you.

(Exit Horatio.)

> O, this is the poison of deep grief; it springs
> All from her father's death. O Gertrude, Gertrude,
> When sorrows come, they come not single spies,
> But in battalions! First, her father slain:
75   Next, your son gone; and he most violent author
> Of his own just remove: the people muddied,
> Thick and unwholesome in their thoughts and whispers
> For good Polonius' death; and we have done but greenly
> In hugger-mugger[3] to inter him: poor Ophelia
80   Divided from herself and her fair judgment,
> Without the which we are pictures, or mere beasts:
> Last, and as much containing as all these,

---

[2] A contraction for "by Jesus."   [3] In great secrecy and haste.

Her brother is in secret come from France;
Feeds on his wonder, keeps himself in clouds,
85   And wants not buzzers to infect his ear
With pestilent speeches of his father's death;
Wherein necessity, of matter beggar'd,
Will nothing stick our person to arraign
In ear and ear. O my dear Gertrude, this,
90   Like to a murdering piece,[4] in many places
Gives me superfluous death.

(A noise within.)

QUEEN: Alack, what noise is this?
KING: Where are my Switzers?[5] let them guard the door.

(Enter a Gentleman.)

What is the matter?
GENTLEMAN: Save yourself, my lord:
The ocean, overpeering of his list,
95   Eats not the flats with more impetuous haste
Than young Laertes, in a riotous head,
O'erbears your officers. The rabble call him lord;
And, as the world were now but to begin,
Antiquity forgot, custom not known,
100   The ratifiers and props of every word,
They cry, *Choose we, Laertes shall be king!*
Caps, hands, and tongues applaud it to the clouds,
Laertes shall be king, Laertes king!
QUEEN: How cheerfully on the false trail they cry!
105   O, this is counter, you false Danish dogs!
KING: The doors are broke.

(Noise within)

(Enter Laertes armed; Danes following.)

LAERTES: Where is this king?—Sirs, stand you all without.
DANES: No, let's come in.
LAERTES: I pray you, give me leave.
DANES: We will, we will. *(They retire without the door.)*
110 **LAERTES:**   I thank you:—keep the door.—O thou vile king,
Give me my father!
QUEEN: Calmly, good Laertes.
LAERTES: That drop of blood that's calm proclaims me bastard;
Cries cuckold to my father; brands the harlot

---

[4] A cannon.   [5] Bodyguard of Swiss mercenaries.

Even here, between the chaste unsmirched brow
115 Of my true mother.
KING: What is the cause, Laertes,
That thy rebellion looks so giant-like?—
Let him go, Gertrude; do not fear our person:
There's such divinity doth hedge a king,
That treason can but peep to what it would,
120 Acts little of his will.—Tell me, Laertes,
Why thou art thus incens'd.—Let him go, Gertrude:—
Speak, man.
LAERTES: Where is my father?
KING: Dead.
QUEEN: But not by him.
KING: Let him demand his fill.
125 LAERTES: How came he dead? I'll not be juggled with:
To hell, allegiance! vows, to the blackest devil!
Conscience and grace, to the profoundest pit!
I dare damnation:—to this point I stand,—
That both the worlds I give to negligence,
130 Let come what comes; only I'll be reveng'd
Most thoroughly for my father.
KING: Who shall stay you?
LAERTES: My will, not all the world:
And for my means, I'll husband them so well,
They shall go far with little.
KING: Good Laertes,
135 If you desire to know the certainty
Of your dear father's death, is't writ in your revenge
That, sweepstake, you will draw both friend and foe,
Winner or loser?
LAERTES: None but his enemies.
KING: Will you know them, then?
140 LAERTES: To his good friends thus wide I'll ope my arms;
And, like the kind life-rendering pelican,[6]
Repast them with my blood.
KING: Why, now you speak
Like a good child and a true gentleman.
That I am guiltless of your father's death,
145 And am most sensible in grief for it,
It shall as level to your judgment pierce
As day does to your eye.
DANES: *(Within)*   Let her come in.
LAERTES: How now! what noise is that?

---

[6] The pelican mother was believed to draw blood from itself to feed its young.

(Re-enter Ophelia, fantastically dressed with straws and flowers.)

O heat, dry up my brains! tears seven times salt
150   Burn out the sense and virtue of mine eyes!—
By heaven, thy madness shall be paid by weight
Till our scale turn the beam. O rose of May!
Dear maid, kind sister, sweet Ophelia!—
O heavens! is't possible a young maid's wits
155   Should be as mortal as an old man's life!
Nature is fine in love; and where 'tis fine
It sends some precious instance of itself
After the thing it loves.

OPHELIA: *(Sings)*

They bore him barefac'd on the bier;
160   Hey no nonny, nonny, hey nonny;
And on his grave rain'd many a tear,—
Fare you well, my dove!

LAERTES: Hadst thou thy wits, and didst persuade revenge,
It could not move thus.

165 **OPHELIA:**   You must sing, *Down-a-down, an you call him a-down-a.* O,
how the wheel becomes it! It is the false steward, that stole his
master's daughter.

LAERTES: This nothing's more than matter.

OPHELIA: There's rosemary, that's for remembrance; pray, love,
170   remember: and there is pansies that's for thoughts.

LAERTES: A document in madness,—thoughts and remembrance fitted.

OPHELIA: There's fennel for you, and columbines:—there's rue for
you; and here's some for me:—we may call it herb-grace o' Sundays:—
O, you must wear your rue with a difference.—There's a
175   daisy:—I would give you some violets, but they withered all when
my father died:—they say, he made a good end,—

(Sings)

For bonny sweet Robin is all my joy,—

LAERTES: Thoughts and affliction, passion, hell itself,
She turns to favor and to prettiness.

OPHELIA: *(Sings)*

180   And will he not come again?
And will he not come again?
No, no, he is dead,
Go to thy death-bed,
He never will come again.

185   His beard was as white as snow
All flaxen was his poll:
He is gone, he is gone,

And we cast away moan:
God ha' mercy on his soul!

190 And of all Christian souls, I pray God.—God b' wi' ye. *(Exit.)*
LAERTES: Do you see this, O God?
KING: Laertes, I must commune with your grief,
Or you deny me right. Go but apart,
Make choice of whom your wisest friends you will,
195 And they shall hear and judge 'twixt you and me:
If by direct or by collateral hand
They find us touch'd, we will our kingdom give,
Our crown, our life, and all that we call ours,
To you in satisfaction; but if not,
200 Be you content to lend your patience to us,
And we shall jointly labor with your soul
To give it due content.
LAERTES: Let this be so;
His means of death, his obscure burial,—
No trophy, sword, nor hatchment[7] o'er his bones
205 No noble rite nor formal ostentation,—
Cry to be heard, as 'twere from heaven to earth,
That I must call't in question.
KING: So you shall;
And where the offence is, let the great axe fall.
I pray you, go with me.

(Exeunt.)

SCENE VI

Another room in the castle.

(Enter Horatio and a Servant.)

HORATIO: What are they that would speak with me?
SERVANT: Sailors, sir: they say they have letters for you.
HORATIO: Let them come in.—

(Exit Servant.)

I do not know from what part of the world
5 I should be greeted, if not from Lord Hamlet.

(Enter Sailors.)

1ST SAILOR: God bless you, sir.
HORATIO: Let him bless thee too.

---

[7] A tablet with coat of arms.

1ST SAILOR: He shall, sir, an't please him. There's a letter for you, sir; it comes from the ambassador that was bound for England; if your
10   name be Horatio, as I am let to know it is.

HORATIO: *(Reads) Horatio, when thou shalt have overlooked this, give these fellows some means to the king: they have letters for him. Ere we were two days old at sea, a pirate of very warlike appointment gave us chase. Finding ourselves too slow of sail, we put on a compelled valor; and in*
15   *the grapple I boarded them; on the instant they got clear of our ship; so I alone became their prisoner. They have dealt with me like thieves of mercy: but they knew what they did; I am to do a good turn for them. Let the king have the letters I have sent; and repair thou to me with as much haste as thou wouldst fly death. I have words to speak in thine ear*
20   *will make thee dumb; yet are they much too light for the bore of the matter. These good fellows will bring thee where I am. Rosencrantz and Guildenstern hold their course for England: of them I have much to tell thee. Farewell. He that thou knowest thine.*   Hamlet
Come, I will give you way for these your letters;
25   And do't the speedier, that you may direct me
To him from whom you brought them.

(Exeunt.)

SCENE VII

Another room in the castle.

(Enter King and Laertes.)

KING: Now must your conscience my acquittance seal,
And you must put me in your heart for friend,
Sith you have heard, and with a knowing ear,
That he which hath your noble father slain
5   Pursu'd my life.
LAERTES: It well appears:—but tell me
Why you proceeded not against these feats,
So crimeful and so capital in nature.
As by your safety, wisdom, all things else,
You mainly were stirr'd up.
KING: O, for two special reasons;
10   Which may to you, perhaps, seem much unsinew'd,
But yet to me they are strong. The queen his mother
Lives almost by his looks; and for myself,—
My virtue or my plague, be it either which,—
She's so conjunctive to my life and soul,
15   That, as the star moves not but in his sphere,
I could not but by her. The other motive,

Why to a public count I might not go,
Is the great love the general gender bear him;
Who, dipping all his faults in their affection,
20 Would, like the spring that turneth wood to stone,
Convert his gyves to graces; so that my arrows,
Too slightly timber'd for so loud a wind,
Would have reverted to my bow again,
And not where I had aim'd them.
25 **LAERTES:** And so have I a noble father lost;
A sister driven into desperate terms,—
Whose worth, if praises may go back again,
Stood challenger on mount of all the age
For her perfections:—but my revenge will come.
30 **KING:** Break not your sleeps for that: you must not think
That we are made of stuff so flat and dull
That we can let our beard be shook with danger,
And think it pastime. You shortly shall hear more:
I lov'd your father, and we love ourself;
35 And that, I hope, will teach you to imagine,—

(Enter a Messenger.)

How now! what news?
MESSENGER: Letters, my lord, from Hamlet:
This to your majesty; this to the queen.
KING: From Hamlet! Who brought them?
MESSENGER: Sailors, my lord, they say; I saw them not:
40 They were given me by Claudio,—he receiv'd them
Of him that brought them.
KING: Laertes, you shall hear them.—Leave us.

(Exit Messenger.)

(Reads) High and mighty,—You shall know I am set naked on your
kingdom. To-morrow shall I beg leave to see your kingly eyes: when I shall,
45 *first asking your pardon thereunto, recount the occasions of my sudden*
and more strange return.   Hamlet
What should this mean? Are all the rest come back?
Or is it some abuse,[1] and no such thing?
LAERTES: Know you the hand?
50 **KING:** 'Tis Hamlet's character:[2]—*Naked,*—
And in a postscript here, he says, *alone.*
Can you advise me?
LAERTES: I am lost in it, my lord. But let him come;
It warms the very sickness in my heart,

---

[1] Ruse.   [2] Handwriting.

55   That I shall live, and tell him to his teeth,
        Thus diddest thou.

KING: If it be so, Laertes,—
        As how should it be so? how otherwise?—
        Will you be rul'd by me?

LAERTES: Ay, my lord:
        So you will not o'errule me to a peace.

60 KING: To thine own peace. If he be now return'd,—
        As checking at his voyage, and that he means
        No more to undertake it,—I will work him
        To an exploit, now ripe in my device,
        Under the which he shall not choose but fall:

65   And for his death no wind of blame shall breathe;
        But even his mother shall uncharge the practice
        And call it accident.

LAERTES: My lord, I will be rul'd;
        The rather if you could devise it so
        That I might be the organ.

KING: It falls right.

70   You have been talk'd of since your travel much,
        And that in Hamlet's hearing, for a quality
        Wherein they say you shine: your sum of parts
        Did not together pluck such envy from him
        As did that one; and that, in my regard,

75   Of the unworthiest siege.

LAERTES: What part is that, my lord?

KING: A very riband in the cap of youth,
        Yet needful too; for youth no less becomes
        The light and careless livery that it wears
        Than settled age his sables and his weeds,

80   Importing health and graveness.—Two months since,
        Here was a gentleman of Normandy,—
        I've seen myself, and serv'd against, the French,
        And they can well on horseback: but this gallant
        Had witchcraft in't; he grew unto his seat;

85   And to such wondrous doing brought his horse,
        As he had been incorps'd and demi-natur'd[3]
        With the brave beast: so far he topp'd my thought,
        That I, in forgery of shapes and tricks,[4]
        Come short of what he did.

LAERTES: A Norman was't?

90 KING: A Norman.

---

[3] Made as one body and formed into half man, half horse—or centaur.   [4] In imagining tricks of horsemanship.

LAERTES: Upon my life, Lamond.
KING: The very same.
LAERTES: I know him well: he is the brooch, indeed,
    And gem of all the nation.
KING: He made confession of you;
95   And gave you such a masterly report
    For art and exercise in your defence,
    And for your rapier most especially,
    That he cried out, 'twould be a sight indeed
    If one could match you: the scrimers[5] of their nation,
100   He swore, had neither motion, guard, nor eye,
    If you oppos'd them. Sir, this report of his
    Did Hamlet so envenom with his envy,
    That he could nothing do but wish and beg
    Your sudden coming o'er, to play with him.
105   Now, out of this,—
LAERTES: What out of this, my lord?
KING: Laertes, was your father dear to you?
    Or are you like the painting of a sorrow,
    A face without a heart?
LAERTES: Why ask you this?
KING: Not that I think you did not love your father;
110   But that I know love is begun by time;
    And that I see, in passages of proof,[6]
    Time qualifies the spark and fire of it.
    There lives within the very flame of love
    A kind of wick or snuff that will abate it;
115   And nothing is at a like goodness still;
    For goodness, growing to a pleurisy,[7]
    Dies in his own too much: that we would do
    We should do when we would; for this *would* changes,
    And hath abatements and delays as many
120   As there are tongues, or hands, or accidents;
    And then this *should* is like a spendthrift sigh
    That hurts by easing. But to the quick o' the ulcer:
    Hamlet comes back: what would you undertake
    To show yourself your father's son in deed
125   More than in words?
LAERTES: To cut his throat i' the church.
KING: No place, indeed, should murder sanctuarize;
    Revenge should have no bounds. But, good Laertes,
    Will you do this, keep close within your chamber.
    Hamlet return'd shall know you are come home:

---

[5] Fencers.   [6] The evidence of experience.   [7] Plethora, an excess of blood.

130 We'll put on those shall praise your excellence,
And set a double varnish on the fame
The Frenchman gave you; bring you, in fine, together,
And wager on yours heads: he, being remiss,[8]
Most generous, and free from all contriving,
135 Will not peruse the foils; so that, with ease,
Or with a little shuffling, you may choose
A sword unbated, and, in a pass of practice,
Requite him for your father.

LAERTES: I will do't it:
And, for that purpose, I'll anoint my sword.
140 I bought an unction of a mountebank,
So mortal that but dip a knife in it,
Where it draws blood no cataplasm so rare,[9]
Collected from all simples that have virtue
Under the moon, can save the thing from death
145 That is but scratch'd withal: I'll touch my point
With this contagion, that, if I gall him slightly,
It may be death.

KING: Let's further think of this;
Weigh what convenience both of time and means
May fit us to our shape: if this should fail,
150 And that our drift look through our bad performance,
'Twere better not assay'd: therefore this project
Should have a back or second, that might hold
If this should blast in proof. Soft! let me see:—
We'll make a solemn wager on your cunnings,—
155 I ha't:
When in your motion you are hot and dry,—
As make your bouts more violent to that end,—
And that he calls for drink, I'll have prepar'd him
A chalice for the nonce;[10] whereon but sipping,
160 If he by chance escape your venom'd stuck
Our purpose may hold there.

(Enter Queen.)

How now, sweet queen!

QUEEN: One woe doth tread upon another's heel,
So fast they follow:—your sister's drown'd, Laertes.

LAERTES: Drown'd! O, where?

165 QUEEN: There is a willow grows aslant a brook,
That shows his hoar leaves in the glassy stream;

---

[8] Unguarded and free from suspicion.   [9] No poultice, however remarkably effica-
cious.   [10] Purpose.

There with fantastic garlands did she come
Of crowflowers, nettles, daisies, and long purples,
That liberal shepherds give a grosser name,
170 But our cold maids do dead men's fingers call them.
There, on the pendant boughs her coronet weeds
Clambering to hang, an envious[11] sliver broke;
When down her weedy trophies and herself
Fell in the weeping brook. Her clothes spread wide;
175 And, mermaid-like, awhile they bore her up:
Which time she chanted snatches of old tunes;
As one incapable of her own distress,
Or like a creature native and indu'd
Unto that element: but long it could not be
180 Till that her garments, heavy with their drink,
Pull'd the poor wretch from her melodious lay
To muddy death.

LAERTES: Alas, then, she is drown'd?

QUEEN: Drown'd, drown'd.

LAERTES: Too much of water hast thou, poor Ophelia,
185 And therefore I forbid my tears: but yet
It is our trick; nature her custom holds,
Let shame say what it will: when these are gone,
The woman will be out.[12]—Adieu, my lord:
I have a speech of fire, that fain would blaze,
190 But that this folly douts it.[13] *(Exit.)*

KING: Let's follow, Gertrude;
How much I had to do to calm his rage!
Now fear I this will give it start again;
Therefore let's follow.

(Exeunt.)

ACT V SCENE I

A churchyard.

(Enter two Clowns[1] with spades, &c.)

1ST CLOWN: Is she to be buried in Christian burial that wilfully seeks
her own salvation?

2ND CLOWN: I tell thee she is; and therefore make her grave straight:
the crowner[2] hath sat on her, and finds it Christian burial.

5 **1ST CLOWN:**   How can that be, unless she drowned herself in her own
defence?

---

[11] Malicious.   [12] That is, "I shall be ruthless."   [13] Drowns it.   [1] Rustic fellows.   [2] Coroner.

2ND CLOWN: Why, 'tis found so.

1ST CLOWN: It must be *se offendendo,*[3] it cannot be else. For here lies
the point: if I drown myself wittingly, it argues an act: and an act
hath three branches; it is to act, to do, and to perform: argal,[4] she
drowned herself wittingly.

2ND CLOWN: Nay, but hear you, goodman delver,—

1ST CLOWN: Give me leave. Here lies the water; good: here stands the
man; good: if the man go to this water and drown himself, it is,
will he, nill he, he goes,—mark you that: but if the water come to
him and drown him, he drowns not himself: argal, he that is not
guilty of his own death shortens not his own life.

2ND CLOWN: But is this law?

1ST CLOWN: Ay, marry, is't; crowner's quest law.

2ND CLOWN: Will you ha' the truth on't? If this had not been a
gentlewoman she should have been buried out of Christian burial.

1ST CLOWN: Why, there thou say'st: and the more pity that great folks
should have countenance in this world to drown or hang themselves
more than their even-Christian.[5]—Come, my spade. There is
no ancient gentlemen but gardeners, ditchers, and grave-makers;
they hold up Adam's profession.

2ND CLOWN: Was he a gentleman?

1ST CLOWN: He was the first that ever bore arms.

2ND CLOWN: Why, he had none.

1ST CLOWN: What, art a heathen? How dost thou understand the
Scripture? The Scripture says, Adam digged: could he dig without
arms? I'll put another question to thee: if thou answerest me not
to the purpose, confess thyself,[6]—

2ND CLOWN: Go to.

1ST CLOWN: What is he that builds stronger than either the mason,
the shipwright, or the carpenter?

2ND CLOWN: The gallows-maker; for that frame outlives a thousand
tenants.

1ST CLOWN: I like thy wit well, in good faith: the gallows does well;
but how does it well? it does well to those that do ill: now thou
dost ill to say the gallows is built stronger than the church: argal,
the gallows may do well to thee. To't again, come.

2ND CLOWN: Who builds stronger than a mason, a shipwright, or a
carpenter?

1ST CLOWN: Ay, tell me that, and unyoke.

2ND CLOWN: Marry, now I can tell.

1ST CLOWN: To't.

2ND CLOWN: Mass, I cannot tell.

------

[3] In self-offense; he means *se defendendo,* in self-defense.   [4] He means *ergo,* therefore.   [5] Fellow Christian.   [6] Confess thyself an ass," perhaps.

(Enter Hamlet and Horatio, at a distance.)

1st Clown: Cudgel thy brains no more about it, for your dull ass will
50   not mend his pace with beating; and when you are asked this
question next, say a grave-maker; the houses that he makes last till
doomsday. Go, get thee to Yaughan: fetch me a stoup of liquor.

(Exit Second Clown.)

(Digs and sings)

> In youth, when I did love, did love,
>   Methought it was very sweet,
55   To contract, O, the time, for, ah, my behove,[7]
>   O, methought there was nothing meet.

Hamlet: Has this fellow no feeling of his business, that he sings at
grave-making?
Horatio: Custom hath made it in him a property of easiness.
60 **Hamlet:**   'Tis e'en so: the hand of little employment hath the daintier
sense.
1st Clown: *(Sings)*

> But age, with his stealing steps,
>   Hath claw'd me in his clutch,
> And hath shipp'd me intil the land,
65   As if I had never been such.

(Throws up a skull)

Hamlet: That skull had a tongue in it, and could sing once: how the
knave joels[8] it to the ground, as if it were Cain's jawbone, that did
the first murder! This might be the pate of a politician, which this
ass now o'erreaches; one that would circumvent God, might it not?
70 **Horatio:**   It might, my lord.
Hamlet: Or of a courtier; which could say, *Good-morrow, sweet lord!*
How dost thou, good lord? This might be my lord such-a-one, that
praised my lord such-a-one's horse, when he meant to beg it,—
might it not?
75 **Horatio:**   Ay, my lord.
Hamlet: Why, e'en so: and now my Lady Worm's; chapless,[9] and
knocked about the mazard[10] with a sexton's spade: here's fine
revolution, an we had the trick to see't. Did these bones cost no
more the breeding but to play at loggats[11] with 'em? Mine ache
80   to think on't.

---

[7] Behoof, or advantage.   [8] Throws.   [9] Without a lower jaw.   [10] Head.   [11] A
game in which small pieces of wood are hurled at a stake.

1st Clown: *(Sings)*
> A pick-axe and a spade, a spade,
> For and a shrouding sheet:
> O, a pit of clay for to be made
> For such a guest is meet.

(Throws up another)

85 **Hamlet:**   There's another: why may not that be the skull of a lawyer? Where be his quiddits[12] now, his quillets,[13] his cases, his tenures, and his tricks? why does he suffer this rude knave now to knock him about the sconce with a dirty shovel, and will not tell him of his action of battery? Hum! This fellow might be in's time a great
90 buyer of land, with his statutes, his recognizances, his fines, his double vouchers, his recoveries: is this the fine of his fines, and the recovery of his recoveries, to have his fine pate full of fine dirt? will his vouchers vouch him no more of his purchases, and double ones too, than the length and breadth of a pair of indentures? The
95 very conveyances of his lands will hardly lie in this box; and must the inheritor himself have no more, ha?

Horatio: Not a jot more, my lord.

Hamlet: Is not parchment made of sheep-skins?

Horatio: Ay, my lord, and of calf-skins too.

100 **Hamlet:**   They are sheep and calves which seek out assurance in that. I will speak to this fellow.—Whose grave's this, sir?

1st Clown: Mine, sir.—*(Sings)*
> O, a pit of clay for to be made
> For such a guest is meet.

105 **Hamlet:**   I think it be thine indeed; for thou liest in't.

1st Clown: You lie out on't, sir, and therefore it is not yours: for my part, I do not lie in't, and yet it is mine.

Hamlet: Thou dost lie in't, to be in't, and say it is thine: 'tis for the dead, not for the quick; therefore thou liest.

110 **1st Clown:**   'Tis a quick lie, sir: 'twill away again from me to you.

Hamlet: What man dost thou dig it for?

1st Clown: For no man, sir.

Hamlet: What woman, then?

1st Clown: For none, neither.

115 **Hamlet:**   Who is to be buried in't?

1st Clown: One that was a woman, sir; but, rest her soul, she's dead.

Hamlet: How absolute the knave is! we must speak by the card, or equivocation will undo us. By the Lord, Horatio, these three years I

---

12 "Whatnesses"—that is, hair-splittings.   13 Quibbling distinctions.

have taken note of it; the age is grown so picked[14] that the toe of
120   the peasant comes so near the heel of the courtier, he galls his
kibe.[15]—How long hast thou been a grave-maker?

1st Clown: Of all the days i' the year, I came to't that day that our
last King Hamlet o'ercame Fortinbras.

Hamlet: How long is that since?

125 **1st Clown:**   Cannot you tell that? every fool can tell that: it was the
very day that young Hamlet was born,—he that is mad, and sent
into England.

Hamlet: Ay, marry, why was he sent into England?

1st Clown: Why, because he was mad: he shall recover his wits there;
130   or, if he do not, it's no great matter there.

Hamlet: Why?

1st Clown: 'Twill not be seen in him there; there the men are as mad
as he.

Hamlet: How came he mad?

135 **1st Clown:**   Very strangely, they say.

Hamlet: How strangely?

1st Clown: Faith, e'en with losing his wits.

Hamlet: Upon what ground?

1st Clown: Why, here in Denmark: I have been sexton here, man
140   and boy, thirty years.

Hamlet: How long will a man lie i' the earth ere he rot?

1st Clown: Faith, if he be not rotten before he die,—as we have many
pocky corses now-a-days, that will scarce hold the laying in,—he
will last you some eight year or nine year: a tanner will last you nine
145   year.

Hamlet: Why he more than another?

1st Clown: Why, sir, his hide is so tanned with his trade that he will
keep out water a great while; and your water is a sore decayer of
your whoreson dead body. Here's a skull now; this skull has lain in
150   the earth three-and-twenty years.

Hamlet: Whose was it?

1st Clown: A whoreson mad fellow's it was: whose do you think
it was?

Hamlet: Nay, I know not.

155 **1st Clown:**   A pestilence on him for a mad rogue! 'a poured a flagon
of Rhenish on my head once. This same skull, sir, was Yorick's
skull, the king's jester.

Hamlet: This?

1st Clown: E'en that.

---

[14] Refined or educated.   [15] Rubs and irritates the chilblain sore on the courtier's
heel.

160 **HAMLET:** Let me see. *(Takes the skull)*—Alas, poor Yorick!—I knew
him, Horatio; a fellow of infinite jest, of most excellent fancy: he
hath borne me on his back a thousand times; and now, how abhorred
in my imagination it is! my gorge rises at it. Here hung
those lips that I have kissed I know not how oft. Where be your
165 gibes now? your gambols? your songs? your flashes of merriment,
that were wont to set the table on a roar? Not one now, to mock
your own grinning? quite chap-fallen? Now get you to my lady's
chamber, and tell her, let her paint an inch thick, to this favor[16]
she must come; make her laugh at that.—Pr'ythee, Horatio, tell me
170 one thing.

   HORATIO: What's that, my lord?

   HAMLET: Dost thou think Alexander looked o' this fashion i' the earth?

   HORATIO: E'en so.

   HAMLET: And smelt so? pah! *(Throws down the skull)*

175 **HORATIO:** E'en so, my lord.

   HAMLET: To what base uses we may return, Horatio! Why may not
imagination trace the noble dust of Alexander till he find it stopping
a bung-hole?

   HORATIO: 'Twere to consider too curiously to consider so.

180 **HAMLET:** No, faith, not a jot; but to follow him thither with modesty
enough, and likelihood to lead it: as thus; Alexander died, Alexander
was buried, Alexander returneth into dust; the dust is earth; of earth
we make loam; and why of that loam whereto he was converted
might they not stop a beer-barrel?

185   Imperious Caesar, dead and turn'd to clay,
       Might stop a hole to keep the wind away:
       O, that that earth which kept the world in awe
        Should patch a wall to expel the winter's flaw!—

But soft! but soft! aside.—Here comes the king.

*(Enter Priests, &c., in procession; the corpse of Ophelia, Laertes and Mourners
following; King, Queen, their Trains, &c.)*

190   The queen, the courtiers: who is that they follow?
   And with such maimed rites? This doth betoken
   The corse they follow did with desperate hand
   Fordo its own life: 'twas of some estate.
   Couch we awhile and mark. *(Retiring with Horatio)*

195 **LAERTES:** What ceremony else?

   HAMLET: That is Laertes,
   A very noble youth: mark.

   LAERTES: What ceremony else?

---

[16] Face.

1ST PRIEST: Her obsequies have been as far enlarg'd
       As we have warrantise: her death was doubtful,
200   And, but that great command o'ersways the order,
       She should in ground unsanctified have lodg'd
       Till the last trumpet; for charitable prayers,
       Shards, flints, and pebbles, should be thrown on her,
       Yet here she is allowed her virgin rites,
205   Her maiden strewments, and the bringing home
       Of bell and burial.
LAERTES: Must there no more be done?
1ST PRIEST: No more be done:
       We should profane the service of the dead
       To sing a *requiem,* and such rest to her
210   As to peace-parted souls.
LAERTES: Lay her i' the earth;—
       And from her fair and unpolluted flesh
       May violets spring!—I tell thee, churlish priest,
       A ministering angel shall my sister be
       When thou liest howling.
HAMLET: What, the fair Ophelia!
215 **QUEEN:** Sweets to the sweet: farewell! *(Scattering flowers)*
       I hop'd thou shouldst have been my Hamlet's wife;
       I thought thy bride-bed to have deck'd, sweet maid,
       And not have strew'd thy grave.
LAERTES: O, treble woe
       Fall ten times treble on that cursed head
220   Whose wicked deed thy most ingenious sense
       Depriv'd thee of!—Hold off the earth awhile,
       Till I have caught her once more in mine arms:

(Leaps into the grave)

       Now pile your dust upon the quick and dead,
       Till of this flat a mountain you have made,
225   To o'er-top old Pelion[17] or the skyish head
       Of blue Olympus.
HAMLET: *(Advancing)* What is he whose grief
       Bears such an emphasis? whose phrase of sorrow
       Conjures the wandering stars, and makes them stand
230   Like wonder-wounded hearers? this is I, Hamlet the
       Dane. *(Leaps into the grave)*
LAERTES: The devil take thy soul! *(Grappling with him)*
HAMLET: Thou pray'st not well.
       I pr'ythee, take thy fingers from my throat;

---

17 A mountain in Greece.

235   For, though I am not splenetive and rash,
      Yet have I in me something dangerous,
      Which let thy wiseness fear: away thy hand.
KING: Pluck them asunder.
QUEEN: Hamlet! Hamlet!
ALL: Gentlemen,—
HORATIO: Good my lord, be quiet.

(The Attendants part them, and they come out of the grave.)

240 **HAMLET:** Why, I will fight with him upon this theme
      Until my eyelids will no longer wag.
QUEEN: O my son, what theme?
HAMLET: I lov'd Ophelia; forty thousand brothers
      Could not, with all their quantity of love,
245   Make up my sum.—What wilt thou do for her?
KING: O, he is mad, Laertes.
QUEEN: For love of God, forbear him.
HAMLET: 'Swounds, show me what thou'lt do:
      Woul't weep? woul't fight? woul't fast? woul't tear thyself?
250   Woul't drink up eisel?[18] eat a crocodile?
      I'll do't.—Dost thou come here to whine?
      To outface me with leaping in her grave?
      Be buried quick[19] with her, and so will I:
      And, if thou prate of mountains, let them throw
255   Millions of acres on us, till our ground,
      Singeing his pate against the burning zone,[20]
      Make Ossa[21] like a wart! Nay, an thou'lt mouth,
      I'll rant as well as thou.
QUEEN: This is mere madness:
      And thus awhile the fit will work on him;
260   Anon, as patient as the female dove,
      When that her golden couplets are disclos'd,[22]
      His silence will sit drooping.
HAMLET: Hear you, sir;
      What is the reason that you use me thus?
      I lov'd you ever: but it is no matter;
265   Let Hercules himself do what he may,
      The cat will mew, and dog will have his day. *(Exit.)*
KING: I pray thee, good Horatio, wait upon him.—

(Exit Horatio.)

    (To Laertes) Strengthen your patience in our last night's speech;
    We'll put the matter to the present push.—

---

[18] Vinegar.   [19] Alive.   [20] The fiery zone of the celestial sphere.   [21] A high mountain in Greece.   [22] When the golden twins are hatched.

270　Good Gertrude, set some watch over your son.—
　　This grave shall have a living monument:
　　An hour of quiet shortly shall we see;
　　Till then, in patience our proceeding be.

(Exeunt.)

S C E N E　I I

A hall in the castle.

(Enter Hamlet and Horatio.)

HAMLET:　So much for this, sir: now let me see the other;
　　You do remember all the circumstance?
HORATIO:　Remember it, my lord!
HAMLET:　Sir, in my heart there was a kind of fighting
5　　That would not let me sleep: methought I lay
　　Worse than the mutines in the bilboes.[1] Rashly,
　　And prais'd be rashness for it,—let us know,
　　Our indiscretion sometimes serves us well,
　　When our deep plots do fail: and that should teach us
10　　There's a divinity that shapes our ends,
　　Rough-hew them how we will.
HORATIO:　　　　　　　　　　　　This is most certain.
HAMLET:　Up from my cabin,
　　My sea-gown scarf'd about me, in the dark
　　Grop'd I to find out them: had my desire;
15　　Finger'd their packet; and, in fine, withdrew
　　To mine own room again: making so bold,
　　My fears forgetting manners, to unseal
　　Their grand commission; where I found, Horatio,
　　O royal knavery! an exact command,—
20　　Larded with many several sorts of reasons,
　　Importing Denmark's health and England's too,
　　With, ho! such bugs[2] and goblins in my life,—
　　That, on the supervise, no leisure bated,
　　No, not to stay the grinding of the axe,
25　　My head should be struck off.
HORATIO:　　　　　　　　　　　Is't possible?
HAMLET:　Here's the commission: read it at more leisure.
　　But wilt thou hear me how I did proceed?
HORATIO:　I beseech you.

---

[1] Mutineers in the iron stocks on board ship.　　[2] Bugbears.

HAMLET: Being thus benetted round with villainies,—
30   Ere I could make a prologue to my brains,
    They had begun the play,—I sat me down;
    Devis'd a new commission; wrote it fair:
    I once did hold it, as our statists do,
    A baseness to write fair, and labor'd much
35   How to forget that learning; but, sir, now
    It did me yeoman's service. Wilt thou know
    The effect of what I wrote?
HORATIO: Ay, good my lord.
HAMLET: An earnest conjuration from the king,—
    As England was his faithful tributary;
40   As love between them like the palm might flourish;
    As peace should still her wheaten garland wear
    And stand a comma[3] 'tween their amities;
    And many such like as's of great charge,—
    That, on the view and know of these contents,
45   Without debatement further, more or less,
    He should the bearers put to sudden death,
    Not shriving-time allow'd.
HORATIO: How was this seal'd?
HAMLET: Why, even in that was heaven ordinant.
    I had my father's signet in my purse,
50   Which was the model of that Danish seal:
    Folded the writ up in form of the other;
    Subscrib'd it; gav't the impression; plac'd it safely,
    The changeling never known. Now, the next day
    Was our sea-fight; and what to this was sequent
55   Thou know'st already.
HORATIO: So Guildenstern and Rosencrantz go to't.
HAMLET: Why, man, they did make love to this employment;
    They are not near my conscience; their defeat
    Does by their own insinuation[4] grow:
60   'Tis dangerous when the baser nature[5] comes
    Between the pass and fell[6] incensed points
    Of mighty opposites.
HORATIO: Why, what a king is this!
HAMLET: Does it not, think'st thee, stand me now upon,[7]
    He that hath kill'd my king and whor'd my mother;
65   Popp'd in between the election and my hopes;
    Thrown out his angle for my proper life,
    And with such cozenage,[8]—is't not perfect conscience

---

[3] Link.   [4] By their own "sticking their noses" into the business.   [5] Men of lower
rank.   [6] Fierce.   [7] That is, "Don't you think it is my duty?"   [8] Deceit.

To quit him with this arm? and is't not to be damn'd,
To let this canker of our nature come
70   In further evil?
HORATIO: It must be shortly known to him from England
What is the issue of the business there.
HAMLET: It will be short: the interim is mine;
And a man's life's no more than to say One.
75   But I am very sorry, good Horatio,
That to Laertes I forgot myself;
For by the image of my cause I see
The portraiture of his: I'll court his favors:
But, sure, the bravery[9] of his grief did put me
Into a towering passion.
80 **HORATIO:**   Peace; who comes here?

(Enter Osric.)

OSRIC: Your lordship is right welcome back to Denmark.
HAMLET: I humbly thank you, sir.—Dost know this water-fly?
HORATIO: No, my good lord.
HAMLET: Thy state is the more gracious; for 'tis a vice to know him.
85   He hath much land, and fertile: let a beast be lord of beasts, and
his crib shall stand at the king's mess: 'tis a chough;[10] but, as I say,
spacious in the possession of dirt.
OSRIC: Sweet lord, if your lordship were at leisure, I should impart a
thing to you from his majesty.
90 **HAMLET:**   I will receive it with all diligence of spirit. Put your bonnet
to his right use; 'tis for the head.
OSRIC: I thank your lordship, 'tis very hot.
HAMLET: No, believe me, 'tis very cold; the wind is northerly.
OSRIC: It is indifferent cold, my lord, indeed.
95 **HAMLET:**   Methinks it is very sultry and hot for my complexion.
OSRIC: Exceedingly, my lord; it is very sultry,—as't were,—I cannot
tell how.—But, my lord, his majesty bade me signify to you that he
has laid a great wager on your head. Sir, this is the matter,—
HAMLET: I beseech you, remember,—

(Hamlet moves him to put on his hat.)

100 **OSRIC:**   Nay, in good faith; for mine ease, in good faith. Sir, here is
newly come to court Laertes; believe me, an absolute gentleman, full
of most excellent differences, of very soft society and great showing:
indeed, to speak feelingly of him, he is the card or calendar of gentry,

---

[9] Ostentation.   [10] He shall have his trough at the king's table: he is a chattering fool.

for you shall find in him the continent of what part a gentleman
would see.

HAMLET: Sir, his definement suffers no perdition in you;—though, I
know, to divide him inventorially would dizzy the arithmetic of
memory, and yet but yaw neither, in respect of his quick sail. But,
in the verity of extolment, I take him to be a soul of great article;
and his infusion of such dearth[11] and rareness as, to make true
diction of him, his semblable is his mirror; and who else would
trace him, his umbrage,[12] nothing more.

OSRIC: Your lordship speaks most infallibly of him.

HAMLET: The concernancy, sir? why do we wrap the gentleman in our
more rawer breath?

OSRIC: Sir?

HORATIO: Is't not possible to understand in another tongue? You will
do't sir, really.

HAMLET: What imports the nomination[13] of this gentleman?

OSRIC: Of Laertes?

HORATIO: His purse is empty already; all's golden words are spent.

HAMLET: Of him, sir.

OSRIC: I know, you are not ignorant,—

HAMLET: I would you did, sir; yet, in faith, if you did, it would not
much approve me.[14]—Well, sir.

OSRIC: You are not ignorant of what excellence Laertes is,—

HAMLET: I dare not confess that, lest I should compare with him in
excellence; but to know a man well were to know himself.

OSRIC: I mean, sir, for his weapon; but in the imputation laid on him
by them, in his meed he's unfellowed.[15]

HAMLET: What's his weapon?

OSRIC: Rapier and dagger.

HAMLET: That's two of his weapons: but, well.

OSRIC: The king, sir, hath wagered with him six Barbary horses:
against the which he has imponed,[16] as I take it, six French rapiers
and poniards, with their assigns, as girdle, hangers, and so: three
of the carriages, in faith, are very dear to fancy, very responsive to
the hilts, most delicate carriages, and of very liberal conceit.

HAMLET: What call you the carriages?

HORATIO: I knew you must be edified by the margent ere you had
done.[17]

OSRIC: The carriages, sir, are the hangers.

HAMLET: The phrase would be more german to the matter if we could
carry cannon by our sides: I would it might be hangers till then.

---

[11] Rareness, or excellence.   [12] Shadow.   [13] Naming.   [14] If you, who are a fool,
thought me not ignorant, that would not be particularly to my credit.   [15] In his
worth he has no equal.   [16] Staked.   [17] Informed by a note in the margin of your
instructions.

145   But, on: six Barbary horses against six French swords, their assigns, and three liberal conceited carriages; that's the French bet against the Danish: why is this imponed, as you call it?

Osric: The king, sir, hath laid, that in a dozen passes between you and him he shall not exceed you three hits: he hath laid on twelve

150   for nine; and it would come to immediate trial if your lordship would vouchsafe the answer.

Hamlet: How if I answer no?

Osric: I mean, my lord, the opposition of your person in trial.[18]

Hamlet: Sir, I will walk here in the hall: if it please his majesty, it is

155   the breathing time of day with me: let the foils be brought, the gentleman willing, and the king hold his purpose, I will win for him if I can; if not, I will gain nothing but my shame and the odd hits.

Osric: Shall I re-deliver you[19] e'en so?

Hamlet: To this effect, sir; after what flourish your nature will.

160 **Osric:**   I commend my duty to your lordship.

Hamlet: Yours, yours.

(Exit Osric.)

He does well to commend it himself; there are no tongues else for's turn.

Horatio: This lapwing runs away with the shell on his head.[20]

165 **Hamlet:**   He did comply with his dug before he sucked it.[21] Thus has he,—and many more of the same bevy, that I know the drossy age dotes on,—only got the tune of the time, and outward habit of encounter; a kind of yesty collection,[22] which carries them through and through the most fanned and winnowed opinions; and do but

170   blow them to their trial, the bubbles are out.

(Enter a Lord.)

Lord: My lord, his majesty commended him to you by young Osric, who brings back to him that you attend him in the hall: he sends to know if your pleasure hold to play with Laertes, or that you will take longer time.

175 **Hamlet:**   I am constant to my purposes; they follow the king's pleasure: if his fitness speaks, mine is ready; now or whensoever, provided I be so able as now.

Lord: The king and queen and all are coming down.

Hamlet: In happy time.

180 **Lord:**   The queen desires you to use some gentle entertainment to Laertes before you fall to play.

---

[18] That is, the presence of your person as Laertes' opponent in the fencing contest.
[19] Carry back your answer.   [20] This precocious fellow is like a lapwing that starts running when it is barely out of the shell.   [21] He paid compliments to his mother's breast before he sucked it.   [22] Yeasty or frothy affair.

HAMLET: She well instructs me.

(Exit Lord.)

HORATIO: You will lose this wager, my lord.

HAMLET: I do not think so; since he went into France I have been in
185   continual practice: I shall win at the odds. But thou wouldst not
    think how ill all's here about my heart: but it is no matter.

HORATIO: Nay, good my lord,—

HAMLET: It is but foolery; but it is such a kind of gain-giving[23] as
    would perhaps trouble a woman.

190 **HORATIO:** If your mind dislike anything, obey it: I will forestall their
    repair hither, and say you are not fit.

HAMLET: Not a whit, we defy augury: there's a special providence in
    the fall of a sparrow. If it be now, 'tis not to come; if it be not to
    come, it will be now; if it be not now, yet it will come: the readiness
195   is all. Since no man has aught of what he leaves, what is't to leave
    betimes?[24]

(Enter King, Queen, Laertes, Lords, Osric, and Attendants with foils, &c.)

KING: Come, Hamlet, come, and take this hand from me.

(The King puts Laertes' hand into Hamlet's.)

HAMLET: Give me your pardon, sir: I have done you wrong:
    But pardon't, as you are a gentleman.
200   This presence knows, and you must needs have heard,
    How I am punish'd with sore distraction.
    What I have done,
    That might your nature, honor, and exception
    Roughly awake, I here proclaim was madness.
205   Was't Hamlet wrong'd Laertes? Never Hamlet:
    If Hamlet from himself be ta'en away,
    And when he's not himself does wrong Laertes,
    Then Hamlet does it not, Hamlet denies it.
    Who does it, then? His madness: if't be so,
210   Hamlet is of the faction that is wrong'd;
    His madness is poor Hamlet's enemy.
    Sir, in this audience,
    Let my disclaiming from a purpos'd evil
    Free me so far in your most generous thoughts
215   That I have shot mine arrow o'er the house
    And hurt my brother.

LAERTES: I am satisfied in nature,
    Whose motive, in this case, should stir me most

---

[23] Misgiving.   [24] What does an early death matter?

To my revenge: but in my terms of honor
I stand aloof; and will no reconcilement
220   Till by some elder masters of known honor
I have a voice and precedent of peace
To keep my name ungor'd. But till that time
I do receive your offer'd love like love,
And will not wrong it.
HAMLET: I embrace it freely;
225   And will this brother's wager frankly play.[25]—
Give us the foils; come on.
LAERTES: Come, one for me.
HAMLET: I'll be your foil, Laertes; in mine ignorance
Your skill shall, like a star in the darkest night,
Stick fiery off indeed.
LAERTES: You mock me, sir.
230 **HAMLET:** No, by this hand.
KING: Give them the foils, young Osric.
Cousin Hamlet,
You know the wager?
HAMLET: Very well, my lord;
Your grace hath laid the odds o' the weaker side.
235 **KING:** I do not fear it; I have seen you both;
But since he's better'd, we have therefore odds.
LAERTES: This is too heavy, let me see another.
HAMLET: This likes we well. These foils have all a length?

(They prepare to play.)

OSRIC: Ay, my good lord.
240 **KING:** Set me the stoups of wine upon that table,—
If Hamlet give the first or second hit,
Or quit in answer of the third exchange,
Let all the battlements their ordnance fire;
The king shall drink to Hamlet's better breath;
245   And in the cup an union[26] shall he throw,
Richer than that which four successive kings
In Denmark's crown have worn. Give me the cups;
And let the kettle[27] to the trumpet speak,
The trumpet to the cannoneer without,
250   The cannons to the heavens, the heavens to earth,
Now the king drinks to Hamlet.—Come, begin;—
And you, the judges, bear a wary eye.
HAMLET: Come on, sir.
LAERTES: Come, my lord.

---

[25] Fence with a heart free from resentment.   [26] A pearl.   [27] Kettledrum.

(They play.)

HAMLET:	One.
LAERTES:	No.
HAMLET:	Judgment.

OSRIC: A hit, a very palpable hit.

LAERTES: Well;—again.

255   **KING:**   Stay, give me a drink.—Hamlet, this pearl is thine;
Here's to thy health.—

(Trumpets sound, and cannon shot off within.)

Give him the cup.

HAMLET: I'll play this bout first; set it by awhile.—
Come.—Another hit; what say you?

(They play.)

260   **LAERTES:**   A touch, a touch, I do confess.

KING: Our son shall win.

QUEEN: He's fat, and scant of breath.—
Here, Hamlet, take my napkin, rub thy brows:
The queen carouses to thy fortune, Hamlet.

HAMLET: Good madam!

KING: Gertrude, do not drink.

265   **QUEEN:**   I will, my lord; I pray you, pardon me.

KING: *(Aside)* It is the poison'd cup; it is too late.

HAMLET: I dare not drink yet, madam; by and by.

QUEEN: Come, let me wipe thy face.

LAERTES: My lord, I'll hit him now.

KING: I do not think't.

270   **LAERTES:**   *(Aside)* And yet 'tis almost 'gainst my conscience.

HAMLET: Come, for the third, Laertes: you but dally;
I pray you, pass with your best violence:
I am afeard you make a wanton of me.

LAERTES: Say you so? come on.

(They play.)

275   **OSRIC:**   Nothing, neither way.

LAERTES: Have at you now!

(Laertes wounds Hamlet; then, in scuffling, they change rapiers, and Hamlet wounds Laertes.)

KING: Part them; they are incens'd.

HAMLET: Nay, come, again.

(The Queen falls.)

OSRIC: Look to the queen there, ho!

HORATIO: They bleed on both sides.—How is it, my lord?

OSRIC: How is't, Laertes?

280 **LAERTES:**   Why, as a woodcock to my own springe, Osric;
     I am justly kill'd with mine own treachery.

HAMLET: How does the queen?

KING: She swoons to see them bleed.

QUEEN: No, no, the drink, the drink,—O my dear Hamlet,—
     The drink, the drink!—I am poison'd. *(Dies.)*

285 **HAMLET:**   O villainy!—Ho! let the door be lock'd:
     Treachery! seek it out.

(Laertes falls.)

LAERTES: It is here, Hamlet: Hamlet, thou art slain;
     No medicine in the world can do thee good;
     In thee there is not half an hour of life;
290 The treacherous instrument is in thy hand,
     Unbated and envenom'd: the foul practice
     Hath turn'd itself on me; lo, here I lie,
     Never to rise again: thy mother's poison'd:
     I can no more:—the king, the king's to blame.

295 **HAMLET:**   The point envenom'd too!—
     Then venom to thy work. *(Stabs the King.)*

OSRIC and **LORDS:**   Treason! treason!

KING: O, yet defend me, friends; I am but hurt.

HAMLET: Here, thou incestuous, murderous, damned Dane,
300 Drink off this potion.—Is thy union here?
     Follow my mother.

(King dies.)

LAERTES: He is justly serv'd;
     It is a poison temper'd by himself.—
     Exchange forgiveness with me, noble Hamlet:
305 Mine and my father's death come not upon thee,
     Nor thine on me! *(Dies.)*

HAMLET: Heaven make thee free of it! I follow thee.—
     I am dead, Horatio.—Wretched queen, adieu!—
     You that look pale and tremble at this chance,
310 That art but mutes or audience to this act,
     Had I but time,—as this fell sergeant, death,
     Is strict in his arrest,—O, I could tell you,—
     But let it be.—Horatio, I am dead;
     Thou liv'st; report me and my cause aright
315 To the unsatisfied.[28]

---

[28] The uninformed.

HORATIO: Never believe it:
I am more an antique Roman than a Dane,—
Here's yet some liquor left.

HAMLET: As thou'rt a man,
Give me the cup; let go; by heaven, I'll have't.—
O good Horatio, what a wounded name,
320   Things standing thus unknown, shall live behind me!
If thou didst ever hold me in thy heart,
Absent thee from felicity awhile,
And in this harsh world draw thy breath in pain,
To tell my story.—

(March afar off, and shot within.)

What warlike noise is this?

325 **OSRIC:** Young Fortinbras, with conquest come from Poland,
To the ambassadors of England gives
This warlike volley.

HAMLET: O, I die, Horatio;
The potent poison quite o'er-crows my spirit:
I cannot live to hear the news from England;
330   But I do prophesy the election lights
On Fortinbras: he has my dying voice;
So tell him, with the occurrents, more and less,
Which have solicited.[29]—The rest is silence. *(Dies.)*

HORATIO: Now cracks a noble heart.—Good-night, sweet prince,
335   And flights of angels sing thee to thy rest!
Why does the drum come hither?

(March within. Enter Fortinbras, the English Ambassadors, and others.)

FORTINBRAS: Where is this sight?

HORATIO: What is it you would see?
If aught of woe or wonder, cease your search.

FORTINBRAS: This quarry cries on havoc.[30]—O proud death,
340   What feast is toward in thine eternal cell,
That thou so many princes at a shot
So bloodily hast struck?

1ST AMBASSADOR: The sight is dismal;
And our affairs from England come too late:
The ears are senseless that should give us hearing,
345   To tell him his commandment is fulfill'd,
That Rosencrantz and Guildenstern are dead:
Where should we have our thanks?

---

[29] So tell him, together with the events, more or less, that have brought on this tragic affair.   [30] This collection of dead bodies cries out havoc.

HORATIO: Not from his mouth,
    Had it the ability of life to thank you:
    He never gave commandment for their death.
350   But since, so jump[31] upon this bloody question,
    You from the Polack wars, and you from England,
    Are here arriv'd, give order that these bodies
    High on a stage be placed to the view;
    And let me speak to the yet unknowing world
355   How these things came about: so shall you hear
    Of carnal, bloody, and unnatural acts;
    Of accidental judgments, casual slaughters;
    Of deaths put on by cunning and forc'd cause;
    And, in this upshot, purposes mistook
360   Fall'n on the inventors' heads: all this can I
    Truly deliver.
FORTINBRAS: Let us haste to hear it,
    And call the noblest to the audience.
    For me, with sorrow I embrace my fortune:
    I have some rights of memory in this kingdom,[32]
365   Which now to claim my vantage doth invite me.
HORATIO: Of that I shall have also cause to speak,
    And from his mouth whose voice will draw on more:
    But let this same be presently perform'd,
    Even while men's minds are wild: lest more mischance
370   On plots and errors happen.
FORTINBRAS: Let four captains
    Bear Hamlet like a soldier to the stage;
    For he was likely, had he been put on,[33]
    To have prov'd most royally: and, for his passage,
    The soldier's music and the rites of war
375   Speak loudly for him.—
    Take up the bodies.—Such a sight as this
    Becomes the field, but here shows much amiss.
    Go, bid the soldiers shoot.

(A dead march)

(Exeunt, bearing off the dead bodies: after which a peal of ordnance is shot off.)

READING AND REACTING

    1. What are Hamlet's most notable character traits?

    2. Review each of Hamlet's soliloquies. Judging from his own words, do
       you believe his assessments of his own problems are accurate? Are his

---

[31] Opportunely.   [32] I have some unforgotten rights to this kingdom.   [33] Tested
by succession to the throne.

assessments of other characters' behavior accurate? Point to examples from the soliloquies that reveal Hamlet's insight (or lack of insight).

3. Is Hamlet a sympathetic character? Where (if anywhere) do you find yourself growing impatient with him or disagreeing with him?

4. What is the emotional effect on the audience of having Hamlet behave so cruelly toward Ophelia after his "To be or not to be" soliloquy?

5. What do other characters' comments reveal about Hamlet's character *before* the key events in the play begin to unfold? For example, in what way has he changed since he returned to the castle and found out about his father's death?

6. Claudius is presented as the play's villain. Is he all bad, or does he have any redeeming qualities?

7. List those in the play whom you believe to be flat characters. Why do you characterize each individual in this way? What does each of these flat characters contribute to the play?

8. Is Fortinbras simply Hamlet's foil, or does he have another essential role? Explain.

9. Each of the play's major characters has one or more character flaws that influence plot development. What specific weaknesses do you see in Claudius, Gertrude, Polonius, Laertes, Ophelia, and Hamlet himself? Through what words or actions is each weakness revealed? How does each weakness contribute to the play's action?

10. Why doesn't Hamlet kill Claudius when he has the chance in Act 3? What words or actions reveal his motivation for hesitating? What are the implications of his failure to act?

11. Why does Hamlet pretend to be insane? Why does he arrange for the "play within a play" to be performed? Why does he agree to the duel with Laertes? In each case, what words or actions reveal his motivation to the audience?

12. Is the ghost an essential character, or could the information he reveals and the reactions he arouses come from another source? Explain. (Keep in mind that the ghost is a stock character in Elizabethan drama.)

13. Describe Hamlet's relationship with his mother. Do you consider this a typical mother/son relationship? Why or why not?

14. In the graveyard scene, the gravedigger makes many ironic comments. In what way do these statements shed light on the events taking place in the play?

15. **JOURNAL ENTRY**   Both Gertrude and Ophelia are portrayed as weak women, firmly under the influence of the men in their lives. Are these characterizations of them as passive and dependent absolutely essential to the play's plot? Explain.

16. **CRITICAL PERSPECTIVE**   In a 1951 book, *The Meaning of Shakespeare*, Harold Goddard reads *Hamlet* as, in part, a play about war, with a grimly ironic conclusion in that "all the Elder Hamlet's conquests have been for nothing—for less than nothing. Fortinbras, his former enemy, is to inherit the kingdom! Such is the end to which the Ghost's thirst for vengeance has led." He goes on to describe the play's ending:

> *The dead Hamlet is borne out "like a soldier" and the last rites over his body are to be the rites of war. The final word of the text is "shoot." The last sounds we hear are a dead march and the reverberations of ordnance being shot off. The end crowns the whole. The sarcasm of fate could go no further. Hamlet, who aspired to nobler things, is treated at death as if he were the mere image of his father: a warrior. Shakespeare knew what he was about in making the conclusion of his play martial. Its theme has been war as well as revenge. It is the story of the Minotaur over again, of that monster who from the beginning of human strife has exacted his annual tribute of youth. No sacrifice ever offered to it was more precious than Hamlet. But he was not the last.*
>
> *If ever a play seems expressly written for the twentieth century, it is Hamlet. It should be unnecessary to underscore its pertinence to an age in which, twice within three decades, the older generation has called on the younger generation to settle a quarrel with the making of which it had nothing to do. So taken, Hamlet is an allegory of our time. Imagination or violence, Shakespeare seems to say, there is no other alternative.*

Can you find other evidence in the play to support the idea that one of its major themes is war?

 **ARTHUR MILLER** (1915–   ) was born in New York City and graduated in 1938 from the University of Michigan, where he began to write plays. His first big success, which won the New York Drama Critics Circle award, was *All My Sons* (1947), about a man who has knowingly manufactured faulty airplane parts. Other significant plays are *The Crucible* (1953), based on the Salem witch trials of 1692, which Miller saw as parallel to contemporary investigations by the House Un-American Activities Committee; *A View from the Bridge* (1955); and *After the Fall* (1955). He was married for a time to actress Marilyn Monroe and wrote the screenplay for her movie *The Misfits* (1961). His play *The Last Yankee* opened off-Broadway in 1993, and *Broken Glass* was both published and performed in 1994.

Death of a Salesman is his most significant work, a play that quickly became an American classic. Miller has said he is very much influenced by the structure of Greek tragedy, and in his play he shows that a tragedy can also be the story of an ordinary person told in realistic terms. The play is frequently produced, and Miller continues to be involved in new productions because, as he says, with each production he learns to see the play differently. When he directed *Death of a Salesman* in China in 1983, audiences perceived it as primarily the story of the mother, and in the 1983 Broadway production Miller himself realized "at a certain point that it was far more the story of Biff, the son, than it was of Willy Loman, the salesman of the title."

ARTHUR MILLER

Death of a Salesman

Certain Private Conversations in Two Acts and a Requiem

(1949)

CHARACTERS

WILLY LOMAN	**THE WOMAN**
LINDA, *his wife*	**HOWARD WAGNER**
BIFF ⎱ *his sons*	**JENNY**
HAPPY ⎰	**STANLEY**
UNCLE BEN	**MISS FORSYTHE**
CHARLEY	**LETTA**
BERNARD	

The action takes place in Willy Loman's house and yard and in various places he visits in the New York and Boston of today.

Throughout the play, in the stage directions, left and right mean stage left and stage right.

ACT I

A melody is heard, played upon a flute. It is small and fine, telling of grass and trees and the horizon. The curtain rises.

Before us is the Salesman's house. We are aware of towering, angular shapes behind it, surrounding it on all sides. Only the blue light of the sky falls upon the house and forestage; the surrounding area shows an angry glow of orange. As more light appears, we see a solid vault of apartment houses around the small, fragile-seeming home. An air of the dream clings to the place, a dream rising out of reality. The kitchen at center seems actual enough, for there is a kitchen table with three chairs, and a refrigerator. But no other fixtures are seen. At the back of the kitchen there is a draped entrance, which leads to the livingroom. To the right of the kitchen, on a level raised two feet, is a bedroom furnished only with a brass bedstead and a straight chair. On a shelf over the bed a silver athletic trophy stands. A window opens onto the apartment house at the side.

Behind the kitchen, on a level raised six and a half feet, is the boys' bedroom, at present barely visible. Two beds are dimly seen, and at the back of the room a dormer window. (This bedroom is above the unseen livingroom.) At the left a stairway curves up to it from the kitchen.

The entire setting is wholly or, in some places, partially transparent. The roofline of the house is one-dimensional; under and over it we see the apartment buildings. Before the house lies an apron, curving beyond the forestage into the orchestra. This forward area serves as the back yard as well as the locale of all Willy's imaginings and of his city scenes. Whenever the action is in the present the actors observe the imaginary wall-lines, entering the house only through the door at the left. But in the scenes of the past these boundaries are broken, and characters enter or leave a room by stepping "through" a wall onto the forestage.

From the right, Willy Loman, the Salesman, enters, carrying two large sample cases. The flute plays on. He hears but is not aware of it. He is past sixty years of age, dressed quietly. Even as he crosses the stage to the doorway of the house, his exhaustion is apparent. He unlocks the door, comes into the kitchen, and thankfully lets his burden down, feeling the soreness of his palms. A word-sigh escapes his lips—it might be "Oh, boy, oh, boy." He closes the door, then carries his cases out into the livingroom, through the draped kitchen doorway.

Linda, his wife, has stirred in her bed at the right. She gets out and puts on a robe, listening. Most often jovial, she has developed an iron repression of her exceptions to Willy's behavior—she more than loves him, she admires him, as though his mercurial nature, his temper, his massive dreams and little cruelties, served her only as sharp reminders of the turbulent longings within him, longings which she shares but lacks the temperament to utter and follow to their end.

LINDA: *(hearing Willy outside the bedroom, calls with some trepidation)* Willy!

WILLY: It's all right. I came back.

LINDA: Why? What happened? *(Sight pause.)* Did something happen, Willy?

WILLY: No, nothing happened.

5 **LINDA:** You didn't smash the car, did you?

WILLY: *(with casual irritation)* I said nothing happened. Didn't you hear me?

LINDA: Don't you feel well?

WILLY: I am tired to the death. *(The flute has faded away. He sits on the bed beside her, a little numb.)* I couldn't make it. I just couldn't make it, Linda.

LINDA: *(very carefully, delicately)* Where were you all day? You look terrible.

10 **WILLY:** I got as far as a little above Yonkers. I stopped for a cup of coffee. Maybe it was the coffee.

LINDA: What?

WILLY: *(after a pause)* I suddenly couldn't drive any more. The car kept going onto the shoulder, y'know?

LINDA: *(helpfully)* Oh. Maybe it was the steering again. I don't think Angelo knows the Studebaker.

WILLY: No, it's me, it's me. Suddenly I realize I'm goin' sixty miles an hour and I don't remember the last five minutes. I'm—I can't seem to—keep my mind to it.

15 LINDA: Maybe it's your glasses. You never went for your new glasses.

WILLY: No, I see everything. I came back ten miles an hour. It took me nearly four hours from Yonkers.

LINDA: *(resigned)* Well, you'll just have to take a rest, Willy, you can't continue this way.

WILLY: I just got back from Florida.

LINDA: But you didn't rest your mind. Your mind is overactive, and the mind is what counts, dear.

20 WILLY: I'll start out in the morning. Maybe I'll feel better in the morning. *(She is taking off his shoes.)* These goddam arch supports are killing me.

LINDA: Take an aspirin. Should I get you an aspirin? It'll soothe you.

WILLY: *(with wonder)* I was driving along, you understand? And I was fine. I was even observing the scenery. You can imagine, me looking at scenery, on the road every week of my life. But it's so beautiful up there, Linda, the trees are so thick, and the sun is warm. I opened the windshield and just let the warm air bathe over me. And then all of a sudden I'm goin' off the road! I'm tellin' ya, I absolutely forgot I was driving. If I'd've gone the other way over the white line I might've killed somebody. So I went on again—and five minutes later I'm dreamin' again, and I nearly—*(He presses two fingers against his eyes.)* I have such thoughts, I have such strange thoughts.

LINDA: Willy, dear. Talk to them again. There's no reason why you can't work in New York.

WILLY: They don't need me in New York. I'm the New England man. I'm vital in New England.

25 LINDA: But you're sixty years old. They can't expect you to keep traveling every week.

WILLY: I'll have to send a wire to Portland. I'm supposed to see Brown and Morrison tomorrow morning at ten o'clock to show the line. Goddammit, I could sell them! *(He starts putting on his jacket.)*

LINDA: *(taking the jacket from him)* Why don't you go down to the place tomorrow and tell Howard you've simply got to work in New York? You're too accommodating, dear.

WILLY: If old man Wagner was alive I'd a been in charge of New York now! That man was a prince, he was a masterful man. But that boy of his, that Howard, he don't appreciate. When I went north the first time, the Wagner Company didn't know where New England was!

LINDA: Why don't you tell those things to Howard, dear?

30 **WILLY:**   *(encouraged)* I will, I definitely will. Is there any cheese?

LINDA: I'll make you a sandwich.

WILLY: No, go to sleep. I'll take some milk. I'll be up right away. The boys in?

LINDA: They're sleeping. Happy took Biff on a date tonight.

WILLY: *(interested)* That so?

35 **LINDA:**   It was so nice to see them shaving together, one behind the other, in the bathroom. And going out together. You notice? The whole house smells of shaving lotion.

WILLY: Figure it out. Work a lifetime to pay off a house. You finally own it, and there's nobody to live in it.

LINDA: Well, dear, life is a casting off. It's always that way.

WILLY: No, no, some people—some people accomplish something. Did Biff say anything after I went this morning?

LINDA: You shouldn't have criticized him, Willy, especially after he just got off the train. You mustn't lose your temper with him.

40 **WILLY:**   When the hell did I lose my temper? I simply asked him if he was making any money. Is that a criticism?

LINDA: But, dear, how could he make any money?

WILLY: *(worried and angered)* There's such an undercurrent in him. He became a moody man. Did he apologize when I left this morning?

LINDA: He was crestfallen, Willy. You know how he admires you. I think if he finds himself, then you'll both be happier and not fight any more.

WILLY: How can he find himself on a farm? Is that a life? A farmhand? In the beginning, when he was young, I thought, well, a young man, it's good for him to tramp around, take a lot of different jobs. But it's more than ten years now and he has yet to make thirty-five dollars a week!

45 **LINDA:**   He's finding himself, Willy.

WILLY: Not finding yourself at the age of thirty-four is a disgrace!

LINDA: Shh!

WILLY: The trouble is he's lazy, goddammit!

LINDA: Willy, please!

50 **WILLY:**   Biff is a lazy bum!

LINDA: They're sleeping. Get something to eat. Go on down.

WILLY: Why did he come home? I would like to know what brought him home.

LINDA: I don't know. I think he's still lost, Willy. I think he's very lost.

WILLY: Biff Loman is lost. In the greatest country in the world a young man with such—personal attractiveness, gets lost. And such a hard worker. There's one thing about Biff—he's not lazy.

55 **LINDA:**   Never.

WILLY: *(with pity and resolve)* I'll see him in the morning; I'll have a nice talk with him. I'll get him a job selling. He could be big in no time.

My God! Remember how they used to follow him around in high school? When he smiled at one of them their faces lit up. When he walked down the street . . . *(He loses himself in reminiscences.)*

LINDA: *(trying to bring him out of it)* Willy, dear, I got a new kind of American-type cheese today. It's whipped.

WILLY: Why do you get American when I like Swiss?

LINDA: I just thought you'd like a change—

60 **WILLY:** I don't want a change! I want Swiss cheese. Why am I always being contradicted?

LINDA: *(with a covering laugh)* I thought it would be a surprise.

WILLY: Why don't you open a window in here, for God's sake?

LINDA: *(with infinite patience)* They're all open, dear.

WILLY: The way they boxed us in here. Bricks and windows, windows and bricks.

65 **LINDA:** We should've bought the land next door.

WILLY: The street is lined with cars. There's not a breath of fresh air in the neighborhood. The grass don't grow any more, you can't raise a carrot in the back yard. They should've had a law against apartment houses. Remember those two beautiful elm trees out there? When I and Biff hung the swing between them?

LINDA: Yeah, like being a million miles from the city.

WILLY: They should've arrested the builder for cutting those down. They massacred the neighborhood. *(Lost.)* More and more I think of those days, Linda. This time of year it was lilac and wisteria. And then the peonies would come out, and the daffodils. What fragrance in this room!

LINDA: Well, after all, people had to move somewhere.

70 **WILLY:** No, there's more people now.

LINDA: I don't think there's more people. I think—

WILLY: There's more people! That's what's ruining this country! Population is getting out of control. The competition is maddening! Smell the stink from that apartment house! And another on the other side . . . How can they whip cheese?

On Willy's last line, Biff and Happy raise themselves up in their beds, listening.

LINDA: Go down, try it. And be quiet.

WILLY: *(turning to Linda, guiltily)* You're not worried about me, are you, sweetheart?

75 **BIFF:** What's the matter?

HAPPY: Listen!

LINDA: You've got too much on the ball to worry about.

WILLY: You're my foundation and my support, Linda.

LINDA: Just try to relax, dear. You make mountains out of molehills.

80 **WILLY:** I won't fight with him any more. If he wants to go back to Texas, let him go.

LINDA: He'll find his way.

WILLY: Sure. Certain men just don't get started till later in life. Like Thomas Edison, I think. Or B. F. Goodrich. One of them was deaf. *(He starts for the bedroom doorway.)* I'll put my money on Biff.

LINDA: And Willy—if it's warm Sunday we'll drive in the country. And we'll open the windshield, and take lunch.

WILLY: No, the windshields don't open on the new cars.

85 **LINDA:** But you opened it today.

WILLY: Me? I didn't. *(He stops.)* Now isn't that peculiar! Isn't that remarkable—*(He breaks off in amazement and fright as the flute is heard distantly.)*

LINDA: What, darling?

WILLY: That is the most remarkable thing.

LINDA: What, dear?

90 **WILLY:** I was thinking of the Chevvy. *(Slight pause.)* Nineteen twenty-eight . . . when I had that red Chevvy—*(Breaks off.)* That funny? I coulda sworn I was driving that Chevvy today.

LINDA: Well, that's nothing. Something must've reminded you.

WILLY: Remarkable. Ts. Remember those days? The way Biff used to simonize that car? The dealer refused to believe there was eighty thousand miles on it. *(He shakes his head.)* Heh! *(To Linda.)* Close your eyes, I'll be right up. *(He walks out of the bedroom.)*

HAPPY: *(to Biff)* Jesus, maybe he smashed up the car again!

LINDA: *(calling after Willy)* Be careful on the stairs, dear! The cheese is on the middle shelf! *(She turns, goes over to the bed, takes his jacket, and goes out of the bedroom.)*

Light has risen on the boys' room. Unseen, Willy is heard talking to himself, "Eighty thousand miles," and a little laugh. Biff gets out of bed, comes downstage a bit, and stands attentively. Biff is two years older than his brother Happy, well built, but in these days bears a worn air and seems less self-assured. He has succeeded less, and his dreams are stronger and less acceptable than Happy's. Happy is tall, powerfully made. Sexuality is like a visible color on him, or a scent that many women have discovered. He, like his brother, is lost, but in a different way, for he has never allowed himself to turn his face toward defeat and is thus more confused and hard-skinned, although seemingly more content.

95 **HAPPY:** *(getting out of bed)* He's going to get his license taken away if he keeps that up. I'm getting nervous about him, y'know, Biff?

BIFF: His eyes are going.

HAPPY: No, I've driven with him. He sees all right. He just doesn't keep his mind on it. I drove into the city with him last week. He stops at a green light and then it turns red and he goes. *(He laughs.)*

BIFF: Maybe he's color-blind.

HAPPY: Pop? Why he's got the finest eye for color in the business. You know that.

100 **BIFF:** *(sitting down on his bed)* I'm going to sleep.

HAPPY: You're not still sour on Dad, are you, Biff?

BIFF: He's all right, I guess.

WILLY: *(underneath them, in the livingroom)* Yes, sir, eighty thousand miles—eighty-two thousand!

BIFF: You smoking?

105 **HAPPY:** *(holding out a pack of cigarettes)* Want one?

BIFF: *(taking a cigarette)* I can never sleep when I smell it.

WILLY: What a simonizing job, heh!

HAPPY: *(with deep sentiment)* Funny, Biff, y'know? Us sleeping in here again? The old beds. *(He pats his bed affectionately.)* All the talk that went across those two beds, huh? Our whole lives.

BIFF: Yeah. Lotta dreams and plans.

110 **HAPPY:** *(with a deep and masculine laugh)* About five hundred women would like to know what was said in this room.

They share a soft laugh.

BIFF: Remember that big Betsy something—what the hell was her name—over on Bushwick Avenue?

HAPPY: *(combing his hair)* With the collie dog!

BIFF: That's the one. I got you in there, remember?

HAPPY: Yeah, that was my first time—I think. Boy, there was a pig! *(They laugh, almost crudely.)* You taught me everything I know about women. Don't forget that.

115 **BIFF:** I bet you forgot how bashful you used to be. Especially with girls.

HAPPY: Oh, I still am, Biff.

BIFF: Oh, go on.

HAPPY: I just control it, that's all. I think I got less bashful and you got more so. What happened, Biff? Where's the old humor, the old confidence? *(He shakes Biff's knee. Biff gets up and moves restlessly about the room.)* What's the matter?

BIFF: Why does Dad mock me all the time?

120 **HAPPY:** He's not mocking you, he—

BIFF: Everything I say there's a twist of mockery on his face. I can't get near him.

HAPPY: He just wants you to make good, that's all. I wanted to talk to you about Dad for a long time, Biff. Something's—happening to him. He—talks to himself.

BIFF: I noticed that this morning. But he always mumbled.

HAPPY: But not so noticeable. It got so embarrassing I sent him to Florida. And you know something? Most of the time he's talking to you.

125 **BIFF:** What's he say about me?

HAPPY: I can't make it out.

BIFF: What's he say about me?

HAPPY: I think the fact that you're not settled, that you're still kind of up in the air . . .

BIFF: There's one or two other things depressing him, Happy.

130 **HAPPY:**   What do you mean?

BIFF: Never mind. Just don't lay it all to me.

HAPPY: But I think if you just got started—I mean—is there any future for you out there?

BIFF: I tell ya, Hap, I don't know what the future is. I don't know—what I'm supposed to want.

HAPPY: What do you mean?

135 **BIFF:**   Well, I spent six or seven years after high school trying to work myself up. Shipping clerk, salesman, business of one kind or another. And it's a measly manner of existence. To get on that subway on the hot mornings in summer. To devote your whole life to keeping stock, or making phone calls, or selling or buying. To suffer fifty weeks of the year for the sake of a two-week vacation, when all you really desire is to be outdoors, with your shirt off. And always to have to get ahead of the next fella. And still—that's how you build a future.

HAPPY: Well, you really enjoy it on a farm? Are you content out there?

BIFF: *(with rising agitation)* Hap, I've had twenty or thirty different kinds of jobs since I left home before the war, and it always turns out the same. I just realized it lately. In Nebraska when I herded cattle, and the Dakotas, and Arizona, and now in Texas. It's why I came home now, I guess, because I realized it. This farm I work on, it's spring there now, see? And they've got about fifteen new colts. There's nothing more inspiring or—beautiful than the sight of a mare and a new colt. And it's cool there now, see? Texas is cool now, and it's spring. And whenever spring comes to where I am, I suddenly get the feeling, my God, I'm not gettin' anywhere! What the hell am I doing, playing around with horses, twenty-eight dollars a week! I'm thirty-four years old, I oughta be makin' my future. That's when I come running home. And now, I get here, and I don't know what to do with myself. *(After a pause.)* I've always made a point of not wasting my life, and every time I come back here I know that all I've done is to waste my life.

HAPPY: You're a poet, you know that, Biff? You're a—you're an idealist!

BIFF: No, I'm mixed up very bad. Maybe I oughta get married. Maybe I oughta get stuck into something. Maybe that's my trouble. I'm like a boy. I'm not married, I'm not in business, I just—I'm like a boy. Are you content, Hap? You're a success, aren't you? Are you content?

140 **HAPPY:**   Hell, no!

BIFF: Why? You're making money, aren't you?

HAPPY: *(moving about with energy, expressiveness)* All I can do now is wait for the merchandise manager to die. And suppose I get to be merchandise manager? He's a good friend of mine, and he just built a terrific estate on Long Island. And he lived there about two months and sold it, and now he's building another one. He can't enjoy it once it's finished. And I know that's just what I would do. I don't know what the hell I'm workin' for. Sometimes I sit in my apartment—all alone. And I think of the rent I'm paying. And it's crazy. But then, it's what I always wanted. My own apartment, a car, and plenty of women. And still, goddammit, I'm lonely.

BIFF: *(with enthusiasm)* Listen, why don't you come out West with me?

HAPPY: You and I, heh?

145   **BIFF:**   Sure, maybe we could buy a ranch. Raise cattle, use our muscles. Men built like we are should be working out in the open.

HAPPY: *(avidly)* The Loman Brothers, heh?

BIFF: *(with vast affection)* Sure, we'd be known all over the counties!

HAPPY: *(enthralled)* That's what I dream about, Biff. Sometimes I want to just rip my clothes off in the middle of the store and outbox that goddam merchandise manager. I mean I can outbox, outrun, and outlift anybody in that store, and I have to take orders from those common, petty sons-of-bitches till I can't stand it any more.

BIFF: I'm telln' you, kid, if you were with me I'd be happy out there.

150   **HAPPY:**   *(enthused)* See, Biff, everybody around me is so false that I'm constantly lowering my ideals . . .

BIFF: Baby, together we'd stand up for one another, we'd have someone to trust.

HAPPY: If I were around you—

BIFF: Hap, the trouble is we weren't brought up to grub for money. I don't know how to do it.

HAPPY: Neither can I!

155   **BIFF:**   Then let's go!

HAPPY: The only thing is—what can you make out there?

BIFF: But look at your friend. Builds an estate and then hasn't the peace of mind to live in it.

HAPPY: Yeah, but when he walks into the store the waves part in front of him. That's fifty-two thousand dollars a year coming through the revolving door, and I got more in my pinky finger than he's got in his head.

BIFF: Yeah, but you just said—

160   **HAPPY:**   I gotta show some of those pompous, self-important executives over there that Hap Loman can make the grade. I want to walk into the store the way he walks in. Then I'll go with you, Biff. We'll be together yet, I swear. But take those two we had tonight. Now weren't they gorgeous creatures?

BIFF: Yeah, yeah, most gorgeous I've had in years.

HAPPY: I get that any time I want, Biff. Whenever I feel disgusted. The only trouble is, it gets like bowling or something. I just keep knockin' them over and it doesn't mean anything. You still run around a lot?

BIFF: Naa. I'd like to find a girl—steady, somebody with substance.

HAPPY: That's what I long for.

165   **BIFF:**   Go on! You'd never come home.

HAPPY: I would! Somebody with character, with resistance! Like Mom, y'know? You're gonna call me a bastard when I tell you this. That girl

Charlotte I was with tonight is engaged to be married in five weeks.
(He tries on his new hat.)

BIFF: No kiddin'!

HAPPY: Sure, the guy's in line for the vice-presidency of the store. I
don't know what gets into me, maybe I just have an overdeveloped
sense of competition or something, but I went and ruined her, and
furthermore I can't get rid of her. And he's the third executive I've
done that to. Isn't that a crummy characteristic? And to top it all, I
go to their weddings! *(Indignantly, but laughing.)* Like I'm not
supposed to take bribes. Manufacturers offer me a hundred-dollar bill
now and then to throw an order their way. You know how honest I
am, but it's like this girl, see. I hate myself for it. Because I don't
want the girl, and, still, I take it and—I love it!

BIFF: Let's go to sleep.

170 **HAPPY:** I guess we didn't settle anything, heh?

BIFF: I just got one idea that I think I'm going to try.

HAPPY: What's that?

BIFF: Remember Bill Oliver?

HAPPY: Sure, Oliver is very big now. You want to work for him again?

175 **BIFF:** No, but when I quit he said something to me. He put his arm on
my shoulder, and he said, "Biff, if you ever need anything, come to
me."

HAPPY: I remember that. That sounds good.

BIFF: I think I'll go to see him. If I could get ten thousand or even seven
or eight thousand dollars I could buy a beautiful ranch.

HAPPY: I bet he'd back you. 'Cause he thought highly of you, Biff, I
mean, they all do. You're well liked, Biff. That's why I say to come
back here, and we both have the apartment. And I'm telln' you, Biff,
any babe you want . . .

BIFF: No, with a ranch I could do the work I like and still be something.
I just wonder though. I wonder if Oliver still thinks I stole that carton
of basketballs.

180 **HAPPY:** Oh, he probably forgot that long ago. It's almost ten years.
You're too sensitive. Anyway, he didn't really fire you.

BIFF: Well, I think he was going to. I think that's why I quit. I was
never sure whether he knew or not. I know he thought the world of
me, though. I was the only one he'd let lock up the place.

WILLY: *(below)* You gonna wash the engine, Biff?

HAPPY: Shh!

*Biff looks at Happy, who is gazing down, listening. Willy is mumbling in the
parlor.*

HAPPY: You hear that?

They listen. Willy laughs warmly.

185 **BIFF:** *(growing angry)* Doesn't he know Mom can hear that?

WILLY: Don't get your sweater dirty, Biff!

A look of pain crosses Biff's face.

HAPPY: Isn't that terrible? Don't leave again, will you? You'll find a job here. You gotta stick around. I don't know what to do about him, it's getting embarrassing.

WILLY: What a simonizing job!

BIFF: Mom's hearing that!

190 **WILLY:** No kiddin', Biff, you got a date? Wonderful!

HAPPY: Go on to sleep. But talk to him in the morning, will you?

BIFF: *(reluctantly getting into bed)* With her in the house. Brother!

HAPPY: *(getting into bed)* I wish you'd have a good talk with him.

The light on their room begins to fade.

BIFF: *(to himself in bed)* That selfish, stupid . . .

195 **HAPPY:** Sh . . . Sleep, Biff.

Their light is out. Well before they have finished speaking, Willy's form is dimly seen below in the darkened kitchen. He opens the refrigerator, searches in there, and takes out a bottle of milk. The apartment houses are fading out, and the entire house and surroundings become covered with leaves. Music insinuates itself as the leaves appear.

WILLY: Just wanna be careful with those girls, Biff, that's all. Don't make any promises. No promises of any kind. Because a girl, y'know, they always believe what you tell'em, and you're very young, Biff, you're too young to be talking seriously to girls.

Light rises on the kitchen. Willy, talking, shuts the refrigerator door and comes downstage to the kitchen table. He pours milk into a glass. He is totally immersed in himself, smiling faintly.

WILLY: Too young entirely, Biff. You want to watch your schooling first. Then when you're all set, there'll be plenty of girls for a boy like you. *(He smiles broadly at a kitchen chair.)* That so? The girls pay for you? *(He laughs.)* Boy, you must really be makin' a hit.

Willy is gradually addressing—physically—a point offstage, speaking through the wall of the kitchen, and his voice has been rising in volume to that of a normal conversation.

WILLY: I been wondering why you polish the car so careful. Ha! Don't leave the hubcaps, boys. Get the chamois to the hubcaps. Happy, use newspaper on the windows, it's the easiest thing. Show him how to do it, Biff! You see, Happy? Pad it up, use it like a pad. That's it, that's it, good work. You're doin' all right, Hap. *(He pauses, then nods in approbation for a few seconds, then looks upward.)* Biff, first thing we gotta do when we get time is clip that big branch over the house. Afraid it's gonna fall in a storm and hit the roof. Tell you what. We get a rope and sling her around, and then we climb up there with a couple of saws and take her down. Soon as you finish the car, boys, I wanna see ya. I got a surprise for you, boys.

BIFF: *(offstage)* Whatta ya got, Dad?

200 **WILLY:**   No, you finish first. Never leave a job till you're finished— remember that. *(Looking toward the "big trees.")* Biff, up in Albany I saw a beautiful hammock. I think I'll buy it next trip, and we'll hang it right between those two elms. Wouldn't that be something? Just swingin' there under those branches. Boy, that would be . . .

Young Biff and Young Happy appear from the direction Willy was addressing. Happy carries rags and a pail of water. Biff, wearing a sweater with a block "S," carries a football.

BIFF: *(pointing in the direction of the car offstage)* How's that, Pop, professional?

WILLY: Terrific. Terrific job, boys. Good work, Biff.

HAPPY: Where's the surprise, Pop?

WILLY: In the back seat of the car.

205 **HAPPY:**   Boy! *(He runs off.)*

BIFF: What is it, Dad? Tell me, what'd you buy?

WILLY: *(laughing, cuffs him)* Never mind, something I want you to have.

BIFF: *(turns and starts off)* What is it, Hap?

HAPPY: *(offstage)* It's a punching bag!

210 **BIFF:**   Oh, Pop!

WILLY: It's got Gene Tunney's[1] signature on it!

Happy runs onstage with a punching bag.

BIFF: Gee, how'd you know we wanted a punching bag?

WILLY: Well, it's the finest thing for the timing.

HAPPY: *(lies down on his back and pedals with his feet)* I'm losing weight, you notice, Pop?

215 **WILLY:**   *(to Happy)* Jumping rope is good too.

BIFF: Did you see the new football I got?

WILLY: *(examining the ball)* Where'd you get a new ball?

BIFF: The coach told me to practice my passing.

WILLY: That so? And he gave you the ball, heh?

220 **BIFF:**   Well, I borrowed it from the locker room. *(He laughs confidentially.)*

WILLY: *(laughing with him at the theft)* I want you to return that.

HAPPY: I told you he wouldn't like it!

BIFF: *(angrily)* Well, I'm bringing it back!

WILLY: *(stopping the incipient argument, to Happy)* Sure, he's gotta practice with a regulation ball, doesn't he? *(To Biff.)* Coach'll probably congratulate you on your initiative!

225 **BIFF:**   Oh, he keeps congratulating my initiative all the time, Pop.

---

[1] Gene (James Joseph) Tunney (1897–1978)—U.S. boxer, heavyweight champion from his defeat of Jack Dempsey in 1926 until his retirement in 1928.

WILLY: That's because he likes you. If somebody else took that ball there'd be an uproar. So what's the report, boys, what's the report?

BIFF: Where'd you go this time, Dad? Gee we were lonesome for you.

WILLY: *(pleased, puts an arm around each boy and they come down to the apron)* Lonesome, heh?

BIFF: Missed you every minute.

230 **WILLY:** Don't say? Tell you a secret, boys. Don't breathe it to a soul. Someday I'll have my own business, and I'll never have to leave home any more.

HAPPY: Like Uncle Charley, heh?

WILLY: Bigger than Uncle Charley! Because Charley is not—liked. He's liked, but he's not—well liked.

BIFF: Where'd you go this time, Dad?

WILLY: Well, I got on the road, and I went north to Providence. Met the Mayor.

235 **BIFF:** The Mayor of Providence!

WILLY: He was sitting in the hotel lobby.

BIFF: What'd he say?

WILLY: He said, "Morning!" And I said, "You've got a fine city here, Mayor." And then he had coffee with me. And then I went to Waterbury. Waterbury is a fine city. Big clock city, the famous Waterbury clock. Sold a nice bill there. And then Boston—Boston is the cradle of the Revolution. A fine city. And a couple of other towns in Mass., and on to Portland and Bangor and straight home!

BIFF: Gee, I'd love to go with you sometime, Dad.

240 **WILLY:** Soon as summer comes.

HAPPY: Promise?

WILLY: You and Hap and I, and I'll show you all the towns. America is full of beautiful towns and fine, upstanding people. And they know me, boys, they know me up and down New England. The finest people. And when I bring you fellas up, there'll be open sesame for all of us, 'cause one thing, boys: I have friends. I can park my car in any street in New England, and the cops protect it like their own. This summer, heh?

BIFF and **HAPPY:** *(together)* Yeah! You bet!

WILLY: We'll take our bathing suits.

245 **HAPPY:** We'll carry your bags, Pop!

WILLY: Oh, won't that be something! Me comin' into the Boston store with you boys carryin' my bags. What a sensation!

Biff is prancing around, practicing passing the ball.

WILLY: You nervous, Biff, about the game?

BIFF: Not if you're gonna be there.

WILLY: What do they say about you in school, now that they made you captain?

250 **HAPPY:** There's a crowd of girls behind him everytime the classes change.

BIFF: *(taking Willy's hand)* This Saturday, Pop, this Saturday—just for you, I'm going to break through for a touchdown.

HAPPY: You're supposed to pass.

BIFF: I'm takin' one play for Pop. You watch me, Pop, and when I take off my helmet, that means I'm breakin' out. Then you watch me crash through that line!

WILLY: *(kisses Biff)* Oh, wait'll I tell this in Boston!

Bernard enters in knickers. He is younger than Biff, earnest and loyal, a worried boy.

255 **BERNARD:** Biff, where are you? You're supposed to study with me today.

WILLY: Hey, looka Bernard. What're you lookin' so anemic about, Bernard?

BERNARD: He's gotta study, Uncle Willy. He's got Regents next week.

HAPPY: *(tauntingly, spinning Bernard around)* Let's box, Bernard!

BERNARD: Biff! *(He gets away from Happy.)* Listen, Biff, I heard Mr. Birnbaum say that if you don't start studyin' math he's gonna flunk you, and you won't graduate. I heard him!

260 **WILLY:** You better study with him, Biff. Go ahead now.

BERNARD: I heard him!

BIFF: Oh, Pop, you didn't see my sneakers! *(He holds up a foot for Willy to look at.)*

WILLY: Hey, that's a beautiful job of printing!

BERNARD: *(wiping his glasses)* Just because he printed University of Virginia on his sneakers doesn't mean they've got to graduate him, Uncle Willy!

265 **WILLY:** *(angrily)* What're you talking about? With scholarships to three universities they're gonna flunk him?

BERNARD: But I heard Mr. Birnbaum say—

WILLY: Don't be a pest, Bernard! *(To his boys.)* What an anemic!

BERNARD: Okay, I'm waiting for you in my house, Biff.

Bernard goes off. The Lomans laugh.

WILLY: Bernard is not well liked, is he?

270 **BIFF:** He's liked, but he's not well liked.

HAPPY: That's right, Pop.

WILLY: That's just what I mean. Bernard can get the best marks in school, y'understand, but when he gets out in the business world, y'understand, you are going to be five times ahead of him. That's why I thank Almighty God you're both built like Adonises. Because the man who makes an appearance in the business world, the man who creates personal interest, is the man who gets ahead. Be liked and you will never want. You take me, for instance. I never have to wait in line to see a buyer. "Willy Loman is here!" That's all they have to know, and I go right through.

BIFF: Did you knock them dead, Pop?

WILLY: Knocked 'em cold in Providence, slaughtered 'em in Boston.

275 **HAPPY:** *(on his back, pedaling again)* I'm losing weight, you notice, Pop?

Linda enters, as of old, a ribbon in her hair, carrying a basket of washing.

LINDA: *(with youthful energy)* Hello, dear!

WILLY: Sweetheart!

LINDA: How'd the Chevvy run?

WILLY: Chevrolet, Linda, is the greatest car ever built. *(To the boys.)* Since when do you let your mother carry wash up the stairs?

280 **BIFF:** Grab hold there, boy!

HAPPY: Where to, Mom?

LINDA: Hang them up on the line. And you better go down to your friends, Biff. The cellar is full of boys. They don't know what to do with themselves.

BIFF: Ah, when Pop comes home they can wait!

WILLY: *(laughs appreciatively)* You better go down and tell them what to do, Biff.

285 **BIFF:** I think I'll have them sweep out the furnace room.

WILLY: Good work, Biff.

BIFF: *(goes through wall-line of kitchen to doorway at back and calls down)* Fellas! Everybody sweep out the furnace room! I'll be right down!

VOICES: All right! Okay, Biff.

BIFF: George and Sam and Frank, come out back! We're hangin' up the wash! Come on, Hap, on the double! *(He and Happy carry out the basket.)*

290 **LINDA:** The way they obey him!

WILLY: Well, that's training, the training. I'm tellin' you, I was sellin' thousands and thousands, but I had to come home.

LINDA: Oh, the whole block'll be at that game. Did you sell anything?

WILLY: I did five hundred gross in Providence and seven hundred gross in Boston.

LINDA: No! Wait a minute, I've got a pencil. *(She pulls pencil and paper out of her apron pocket.)* That makes your commission . . . Two hundred—my God! Two hundred and twelve dollars!

295 **WILLY:** Well, I didn't figure it yet, but . . .

LINDA: How much did you do?

WILLY: Well, I—I did—about a hundred and eighty gross in Providence. Well, no—it came to—roughly two hundred gross on the whole trip.

LINDA: *(without hesitation)* Two hundred gross. That's . . . *(She figures.)*

WILLY: The trouble was that three of the stores were half closed for inventory in Boston. Otherwise I woulda broke records.

300 **LINDA:** Well, it makes seventy dollars and some pennies. That's very good.

WILLY: What do we owe?

LINDA: Well, on the first there's sixteen dollars on the refrigerator—

WILLY: Why sixteen?

LINDA: Well, the fan belt broke, so it was a dollar eighty.

305 **WILLY:** But it's brand new.

LINDA: Well, the man said that's the way it is. Till they work themselves in, y'know.

They move through the wall-line into the kitchen.

WILLY: I hope we didn't get stuck on that machine.

LINDA: They got the biggest ads of any of them!

WILLY: I know, it's a fine machine. What else?

310 **LINDA:** Well, there's nine-sixty for the washing machine. And for the vacuum cleaner there's three and a half due on the fifteenth. Then the roof, you got twenty-one dollars remaining.

WILLY: It don't leak, does it?

LINDA: No, they did a wonderful job. Then you owe Frank for the carburetor.

WILLY: I'm not going to pay that man! That goddam Chevrolet, they ought to prohibit the manufacture of that car!

LINDA: Well, you owe him three and a half. And odds and ends, comes to around a hundred and twenty dollars by the fifteenth.

315 **WILLY:** A hundred and twenty dollars! My God, if business don't pick up I don't know what I'm gonna do!

LINDA: Well, next week you'll do better.

WILLY: Oh, I'll knock them dead next week. I'll go to Hartford. I'm very well liked in Hartford. You know, the trouble is, Linda, people don't seem to take to me.

They move onto the forestage.

LINDA: Oh, don't be foolish.

WILLY: I know it when I walk in. They seem to laugh at me.

320 **LINDA:** Why? Why would they laugh at you? Don't talk that way, Willy.

Willy moves to the edge of the stage. Linda goes into the kitchen and starts to darn stockings.

WILLY: I don't know the reason for it, but they just pass me by. I'm not noticed.

LINDA: But you're doing wonderful, dear. You're making seventy to a hundred dollars a week.

WILLY: But I gotta be at it ten, twelve hours a day. Other men—I don't know—they do it easier. I don't know why—I can't stop myself—I talk too much. A man oughta come in with a few words. One thing about Charley. He's a man of few words, and they respect him.

LINDA: You don't talk too much, you're just lively.

325 **WILLY:** *(smiling)* Well, I figure, what the hell, life is short, a couple of jokes. *(To himself.)* I joke too much! *(The smile goes.)*

LINDA: Why? You're—

WILLY: I'm fat. I'm very—foolish to look at, Linda. I didn't tell you, but Christmas time I happened to be calling on F. H. Stewarts, and a salesman I know, as I was going in to see the buyer I heard him say something about—walrus. And I—I cracked him right across the face. I won't take that. I simply will not take that. But they do laugh at me. I know that.

LINDA: Darling . . .

WILLY: I gotta overcome it. I know I gotta overcome it. I'm not dressing to advantage, maybe.

330 **LINDA:** Willy, darling, you're the handsomest man in the world—

WILLY: Oh, no, Linda.

LINDA: To me you are. *(Slight pause.)* The handsomest.

From the darkness is heard the laughter of a woman. Willy doesn't turn to it, but it continues through Linda's lines.

LINDA: And the boys, Willy. Few men are idolized by their children the way you are.

Music is heard as behind a scrim, to the left of the house, The Woman, dimly seen, is dressing.

WILLY: *(with great feeling)* You're the best there is, Linda, you're a pal, you know that? On the road—on the road I want to grab you sometimes and just kiss the life outa you.

The laughter is loud now, and he moves into a brightening area at the left, where The Woman has come from behind the scrim and is standing, putting on her hat, looking into a "mirror" and laughing.

335 **WILLY:** 'Cause I get so lonely—especially when business is bad and there's nobody to talk to. I get the feeling that I'll never sell anything again, that I won't make a living for you, or a business, a business for the boys. *(He talks through The Woman's subsiding laughter; The Woman primps at the "mirror.")* There's so much I want to make for—

THE WOMAN: Me? You didn't make me, Willy. I picked you.

WILLY: *(pleased)* You picked me?

THE WOMAN: *(who is quite proper-looking, Willy's age)* I did. I've been sitting at that desk watching all the salesmen go by, day in, day out. But you've got such a sense of humor, and we do have such a good time together, don't we?

WILLY: Sure, sure. *(He takes her in his arms.)* Why do you have to go now?

340 **THE WOMAN:** It's two o'clock . . .

WILLY: No, come on in! *(He pulls her.)*

THE WOMAN: . . . my sisters'll be scandalized. When'll you be back?

WILLY: Oh, two weeks about. Will you come up again?

THE WOMAN: Sure thing. You do make me laugh. It's good for me. *(She squeezes his arm, kisses him.)* And I think you're a wonderful man.

345 **WILLY:** You picked me, heh?

THE WOMAN: Sure. Because you're so sweet. And such a kidder.

WILLY: Well, I'll see you next time I'm in Boston.

THE WOMAN: I'll put you right through to the buyers.

WILLY: *(slapping her bottom)* Right. Well, bottoms up!

350 **THE WOMAN:** *(slaps him gently and laughs)* You just kill me, Willy. *(He suddenly grabs her and kisses her roughly.)* You kill me. And thanks for the stockings. I love a lot of stockings. Well, good night.

WILLY: Good night. And keep your pores open!

THE WOMAN: Oh, Willy!

The Woman bursts out laughing, and Linda's laughter blends in. The Woman disappears into the dark. Now the area at the kitchen table brightens. Linda is sitting where she was at the kitchen table, but now is mending a pair of silk stockings.

LINDA: You are, Willy. The handsomest man. You've got no reason to feel that—

WILLY: *(coming out of The Woman's dimming area and going over to Linda)* I'll make it all up to you, Linda, I'll—

355 **LINDA:** There's nothing to make up, dear. You're doing fine, better than—

WILLY: *(noticing her mending)* What's that?

LINDA: Just mending my stockings. They're so expensive—

WILLY: *(angrily, taking them from her)* I won't have you mending stockings in this house! Now throw them out!

Linda puts the stockings in her pocket.

BERNARD: *(entering on the run)* Where is he? If he doesn't study!

360 **WILLY:** *(moving to the forestage, with great agitation)* You'll give him the answers!

BERNARD: I do, but I can't on a Regents! That's a state exam! They're liable to arrest me!

WILLY: Where is he? I'll whip him, I'll whip him!

LINDA: And he'd better give back that football, Willy, it's not nice.

WILLY: Biff! Where is he? Why is he taking everything?

365 **LINDA:** He's too tough with the girls, Willy. All the mothers are afraid of him!

WILLY: I'll whip him!

BERNARD: He's driving the car without a license!

The Woman's laugh is heard.

WILLY: Shut up!

LINDA: All the mothers—

370 **WILLY:** Shut up!

BERNARD: *(backing quietly away and out)* Mr. Birnbaum says he's stuck up.

WILLY: Get outa here!

BERNARD: If he doesn't buckle down he'll flunk math! *(He goes off.)*

LINDA: He's right, Willy, you've gotta—
375 **WILLY:** *(exploding at her)* There's nothing the matter with him! You want him to be a worm like Bernard? He's got spirit, personality . . .

As he speaks, Linda, almost in tears, exits into the livingroom. Willy is alone in the kitchen, wilting and staring. The leaves are gone. It is night again, and the apartment houses look down from behind.

WILLY: Loaded with it. Loaded! What is he stealing? He's giving it back, isn't he? Why is he stealing? What did I tell him? I never in my life told him anything but decent things.

Happy in pajamas has come down the stairs; Willy suddenly becomes aware of Happy's presence.

HAPPY: Let's go now, come on.
WILLY: *(sitting down at the kitchen table)* Huh! Why did she have to wax the floors herself? Everytime she waxes the floors she keels over. She knows that!
HAPPY: Shh! Take it easy. What brought you back tonight?
380 **WILLY:** I got an awful scare. Nearly hit a kid in Yonkers. God! Why didn't I go to Alaska with my brother Ben that time! Ben! That man was a genius, that man was success incarnate! What a mistake! He begged me to go.
HAPPY: Well, there's no use in—
WILLY: You guys! There was a man started with the clothes on his back and ended up with diamond mines!
HAPPY: Boy, someday I'd like to know how he did it.
WILLY: What's the mystery? The man knew what he wanted and went out and got it! Walked into a jungle, and comes out, the age of twenty-one, and he's rich! The world is an oyster, but you don't crack it open on a mattress!
385 **HAPPY:** Pop, I told you I'm gonna retire you for life.
WILLY: You'll retire me for life on seventy goddam dollars a week? And your women and your car and your apartment, and you'll retire me for life! Christ's sake, I couldn't get past Yonkers today! Where are you guys, where are you? The woods are burning! I can't drive a car!

Charley has appeared in the doorway. He is a large man, slow of speech, laconic, immovable. In all he says, despite what he says, there is pity, and now, trepidation. He has a robe over his pajamas, slippers on his feet. He enters the kitchen.

CHARLEY: Everything all right?
HAPPY: Yeah, Charley, everything's . . .
WILLY: What's the matter?
390 **CHARLEY:** I heard some noise. I thought something happened. Can't we do something about the walls? You sneeze in here, and in my house hats blow off.
HAPPY: Let's go to bed, Dad. Come on.

Charley signals to Happy to go.

WILLY: You go ahead, I'm not tired at the moment.

HAPPY: *(to Willy)* Take it easy, huh? *(He exits.)*

WILLY: What're you doin' up?

395 **CHARLEY:** *(sitting down at the kitchen table opposite Willy)* Couldn't sleep good. I had a heartburn.

WILLY: Well, you don't know how to eat.

CHARLEY: I eat with my mouth.

WILLY: No, you're ignorant. You gotta know about vitamins and things like that.

CHARLEY: Come on, let's shoot. Tire you out a little.

400 **WILLY:** *(hesitantly)* All right. You got cards?

CHARLEY: *(taking a deck from his pocket)* Yeah, I got them. Someplace. What is it with those vitamins?

WILLY: *(dealing)* They build up your bones. Chemistry.

CHARLEY: Yeah, but there's no bones in a heartburn.

WILLY: What are you talkin' about? Do you know the first thing about it?

405 **CHARLEY:** Don't get insulted.

WILLY: Don't talk about something you don't know anything about.

They are playing. Pause.

CHARLEY: What're you doin' home?

WILLY: A little trouble with the car.

CHARLEY: Oh. *(Pause.)* I'd like to take a trip to California.

410 **WILLY:** Don't say.

CHARLEY: You want a job?

WILLY: I got a job, I told you that. *(After a slight pause.)* What the hell are you offering me a job for?

CHARLEY: Don't get insulted.

WILLY: Don't insult me.

415 **CHARLEY:** I don't see no sense in it. You don't have to go on this way.

WILLY: I got a good job. *(Slight pause.)* What do you keep comin' in here for?

CHARLEY: You want me to go?

WILLY: *(after a pause, withering)* I can't understand it. He's going back to Texas again. What the hell is that?

CHARLEY: Let him go.

420 **WILLY:** I got nothin' to give him, Charley, I'm clean, I'm clean.

CHARLEY: He won't starve. None a them starve. Forget about him.

WILLY: Then what have I got to remember?

CHARLEY: You take it too hard. To hell with it. When a deposit bottle is broken you don't get your nickel back.

WILLY: That's easy enough for you to say.

425 **CHARLEY:** That ain't easy for me to say.

WILLY: Did you see the ceiling I put up in the livingroom?

CHARLEY: Yeah, that's a piece of work. To put up a ceiling is a mystery to me. How do you do it?

WILLY: What's the difference?

CHARLEY: Well, talk about it.

430 **WILLY:** You gonna put up a ceiling?

CHARLEY: How could I put up a ceiling?

WILLY: Then what the hell are you bothering me for?

CHARLEY: You're insulted again.

WILLY: A man who can't handle tools is not a man. You're disgusting.

435 **CHARLEY:** Don't call me disgusting, Willy.

Uncle Ben, carrying a valise and an umbrella, enters the forestage from around the right corner of the house. He is a stolid man, in his sixties, with a mustache and an authoritative air. He is utterly certain of his destiny, and there is an aura of far places about him. He enters exactly as Willy speaks.

WILLY: I'm getting awfully tired, Ben.

Ben's music is heard. Ben looks around at everything.

CHARLEY: Good, keep playing; you'll sleep better. Did you call me Ben?

Ben looks at his watch.

WILLY: That's funny. For a second there you reminded me of my brother Ben.

BEN: I have only a few minutes. *(He strolls, inspecting the place. Willy and Charley continue playing.)*

440 **CHARLEY:** You never heard from him again, heh? Since that time?

WILLY: Didn't Linda tell you? Couple of weeks ago we got a letter from his wife in Africa. He died.

CHARLEY: That so.

BEN: *(chuckling)* So this is Brooklyn, eh?

CHARLEY: Maybe you're in for some of his money.

445 **WILLY:** Naa, he had seven sons. There's just one opportunity I had with that man . . .

BEN: I must make a train, William. There are several properties I'm looking at in Alaska.

WILLY: Sure, sure! If I'd gone with him to Alaska that time, everything would've been totally different.

CHARLEY: Go on, you'd froze to death up there.

WILLY: What're you talking about?

450 **BEN:** Opportunity is tremendous in Alaska, William. Surprised you're not up there.

WILLY: Sure, tremendous.

CHARLEY: Heh?

WILLY: There was the only man I ever met who knew the answers.

CHARLEY: Who?

455 **BEN:** How are you all?

WILLY: *(taking a pot, smiling)* Fine, fine.

CHARLEY: Pretty sharp tonight.

BEN: Is Mother living with you?

WILLY: No, she died a long time ago.

460 **CHARLEY:** Who?

BEN: That's too bad. Fine specimen of a lady, Mother.

WILLY: *(to Charley)* Heh?

BEN: I'd hoped to see the old girl.

CHARLEY: Who died?

465 **BEN:** Heard anything from Father, have you?

WILLY: *(unnerved)* What do you mean, who died?

CHARLEY: *(taking a pot)* What're you talkin' about?

BEN: *(looking at his watch)* William, it's half-past eight!

WILLY: *(as though to dispel his confusion he angrily stops Charley's hand)* That's my build!

470 **CHARLEY:** I put the ace—

WILLY: If you don't know how to play the game I'm not gonna throw my money away on you!

CHARLEY: *(rising)* It was my ace, for God's sake!

WILLY: I'm through, I'm through!

BEN: When did Mother die?

475 **WILLY:** Long ago. Since the beginning you never knew how to play cards.

CHARLEY: *(picks up the cards and goes to the door)* All right! Next time I'll bring a deck with five aces.

WILLY: I don't play that kind of game!

CHARLEY: *(turning to him)* You should be ashamed of yourself!

WILLY: Yeah?

480 **CHARLEY:** Yeah! *(He goes out.)*

WILLY: *(slamming the door after him)* Ignoramus!

BEN: *(as Willy comes toward him through the wall-line of the kitchen)* So you're William.

WILLY: *(shaking Ben's hand)* Ben! I've been waiting for you so long! What's the answer? How did you do it?

BEN: Oh, there's a story in that.

Linda enters the forestage, as of old, carrying the wash basket.

485 **LINDA:** Is this Ben?

BEN: *(gallantly)* How do you do, my dear.

LINDA: Where've you been all these years? Willy's always wondered why you—

WILLY: *(pulling Ben away from her impatiently)* Where is Dad? Didn't you follow him? How did you get started?

BEN: Well, I don't know how much you remember.

490 **WILLY:** Well, I was just a baby, of course, only three or four years old—

BEN: Three years and eleven months.

WILLY: What a memory, Ben!

BEN: I have many enterprises, William, and I have never kept books.

WILLY: I remember I was sitting under the wagon in—was it Nebraska?

495 **BEN:** It was South Dakota, and I gave you a bunch of wild flowers.

WILLY: I remember you walking away down some open road.

BEN: *(laughing)* I was going to find Father in Alaska.

WILLY: Where is he?

BEN: At that age I had a very faulty view of geography, William. I discovered after a few days that I was heading due south, so instead of Alaska, I ended up in Africa.

500 **LINDA:** Africa!

WILLY: The Gold Coast!

BEN: Principally, diamond mines.

LINDA: Diamond mines!

BEN: Yes, my dear. But I've only a few minutes—

505 **WILLY:** No! Boys! Boys! *(Young Biff and Happy appear.)* Listen to this. This is your Uncle Ben, a great man! Tell my boys, Ben!

BEN: Why, boys, when I was seventeen I walked into the jungle, and when I was twenty-one I walked out. *(He laughs.)* And by God I was rich.

WILLY: *(to the boys)* You see what I been talking about? The greatest things can happen!

BEN: *(glancing at his watch)* I have an appointment in Ketchikan Tuesday week.

WILLY: No, Ben! Please tell about Dad. I want my boys to hear. I want them to know the kind of stock they spring from. All I remember is a man with a big beard, and I was in Mamma's lap, sitting around a fire, and some kind of high music.

510 **BEN:** His flute. He played the flute.

WILLY: Sure, the flute, that's right!

New music is heard, a high, rollicking tune.

BEN: Father was a very great and a very wild-hearted man. We would start in Boston, and he'd toss the whole family into the wagon, and then he'd drive the team right across the country; through Ohio, and Indiana, Michigan, Illinois, and all the Western states. And we'd stop in the towns and sell the flutes that he'd made on the way. Great inventor, Father. With one gadget he made more in a week than a man like you could make in a lifetime.

WILLY: That's just the way I'm bringing them up, Ben—rugged, well liked, all-around.

BEN: Yeah? *(To Biff.)* Hit that, boy—hard as you can. *(He pounds his stomach.)*

515 **BIFF:** Oh, no, sir!

BEN: *(taking boxing stance)* Come on, get to me! *(He laughs.)*

WILLY: Go to it, Biff! Go ahead, show him!

BIFF: Okay! *(He cocks his fist and starts in.)*

LINDA: *(to Willy)* Why must he fight, dear?

520 **BEN:**   *(sparring with Biff)* Good boy! Good boy!

WILLY: How's that, Ben, heh?

HAPPY: Give him the left, Biff!

LINDA: Why are you fighting?

BEN: Good boy! *(Suddenly comes in, trips Biff, and stands over him, the point of his umbrella poised over Biff's eye.)*

525 **LINDA:**   Look out, Biff!

BIFF: Gee!

BEN: *(patting Biff's knee)* Never fight fair with a stranger, boy. You'll never get out of the jungle that way. *(Taking Linda's hand and bowing.)* It was an honor and a pleasure to meet you, Linda.

LINDA: *(withdrawing her hand coldly, frightened)* Have a nice—trip.

BEN: *(to Willy)* And good luck with your—what do you do?

530 **WILLY:**   Selling.

BEN: Yes. Well . . . *(He raises his hand in farewell to all.)*

WILLY: No, Ben, I don't want you to think . . . *(He takes Ben's arm to show him.)* It's Brooklyn, I know, but we hunt too.

BEN: Really, now.

WILLY: Oh, sure, there's snakes and rabbits and—that's why I moved out here. Why, Biff can fell any one of these trees in no time! Boys! Go right over to where they're building the apartment house and get some sand. We're gonna rebuild the entire front stoop right now! Watch this, Ben!

535 **BIFF:**   Yes, sir! On the double, Hap!

HAPPY: *(as he and Biff run off)* I lost weight, Pop, you notice?

Charley enters in knickers, even before the boys are gone.

CHARLEY: Listen, if they steal any more from that building the watchman'll put the cops on them!

LINDA: *(to Willy)* Don't let Biff . . .

Ben laughs lustily.

WILLY: You shoulda seen the lumber they brought home last week. At least a dozen six-by-tens worth all kinds of money.

540 **CHARLEY:**   Listen, if that watchman—

WILLY: I gave them hell, understand. But I got a couple of fearless characters there.

CHARLEY: Willy, the jails are full of fearless characters.

BEN: *(clapping Willy on the back, with a laugh at Charley)* And the stock exchange, friend!

WILLY: *(joining in Ben's laughter)* Where are the rest of your pants?

545 **CHARLEY:**   My wife bought them.

WILLY: Now all you need is a golf club and you can go upstairs and go to sleep. *(To Ben.)* Great athlete! Between him and his son Bernard they can't hammer a nail!

BERNARD: *(rushing in)* The watchman's chasing Biff!

WILLY: *(angrily)* Shut up! He's not stealing anything!

LINDA: *(alarmed, hurrying off left)* Where is he? Biff, dear! *(She exits.)*

550 **WILLY:** *(moving toward the left, away from Ben)* There's nothing wrong. What's the matter with you?

BEN: Nervy boy. Good!

WILLY: *(laughing)* Oh, nerves of iron, that Biff!

CHARLEY: Don't know what it is. My New England man comes back and he's bleedin', they murdered him up there.

WILLY: It's contacts, Charley, I got important contacts!

555 **CHARLEY:** *(sarcastically)* Glad to hear it, Willy. Come in later, we'll shoot a little casino. I'll take some of your Portland money. *(He laughs at Willy and exits.)*

WILLY: *(turning to Ben)* Business is bad, it's murderous. But not for me, of course.

BEN: I'll stop by on my way back to Africa.

WILLY: *(longingly)* Can't you stay a few days? You're just what I need, Ben, because I—I have a fine position here, but I—well, Dad left when I was such a baby and I never had a chance to talk to him and I still feel—kind of temporary about myself.

BEN: I'll be late for my train.

They are at opposite ends of the stage.

560 **WILLY:** Ben, my boys—can't we talk? They'd go into the jaws of hell for me, see, but I—

BEN: William, you're being first-rate with your boys. Outstanding, manly chaps!

WILLY: *(hanging on to his words)* Oh, Ben, that's good to hear! Because sometimes I'm afraid that I'm not teaching them the right kind of— Ben, how should I teach them?

BEN: *(giving great weight to each word, and with a certain vicious audacity)* William, when I walked into the jungle, I was seventeen. When I walked out I was twenty-one. And, by God, I was rich! *(He goes off into darkness around the right corner of the house.)*

WILLY: . . . was rich! That's just the spirit I want to imbue them with! To walk into a jungle! I was right! I was right! I was right!

Ben is gone, but Willy is still speaking to him as Linda, in nightgown and robe, enters the kitchen, glances around for Willy, then goes to the door of the house, looks out and sees him. Comes down to his left. He looks at her.

565 **LINDA:** Willy, dear? Willy?

WILLY: I was right!

LINDA: Did you have some cheese? *(He can't answer.)* It's very late, darling. Come to bed, heh?

WILLY: *(looking straight up)* Gotta break your neck to see a star in this yard.

LINDA: You coming in?

570 **WILLY:** What ever happened to that diamond watch fob? Remember? When Ben came from Africa that time? Didn't he give me a watch fob with a diamond in it?

LINDA: You pawned it, dear. Twelve, thirteen years ago. For Biff's radio correspondence course.

WILLY: Gee, that was a beautiful thing. I'll take a walk.

LINDA: But you're in your slippers.

WILLY: *(starting to go around the house at the left)* I was right! I was! *(Half to Linda, as he goes, shaking his head.)* What a man! There was a man worth talking to. I was right!

575 **LINDA:** *(calling after Willy)* But in your slippers, Willy!

Willy is almost gone when Biff, in his pajamas, comes down the stairs and enters the kitchen.

BIFF: What is he doing out there?

LINDA: Sh!

BIFF: God Almighty, Mom, how long has he been doing this?

LINDA: Don't, he'll hear you.

580 **BIFF:** What the hell is the matter with him?

LINDA: It'll pass by morning.

BIFF: Shouldn't we do anything?

LINDA: Oh, my dear, you should do a lot of things, but there's nothing to do, so go to sleep.

Happy comes down the stairs and sits on the steps.

HAPPY: I never heard him so loud, Mom.

585 **LINDA:** Well, come around more often; you'll hear him. *(She sits down at the table and mends the lining of Willy's jacket.)*

BIFF: Why didn't you ever write me about this, Mom?

LINDA: How would I write to you? For over three months you had no address.

BIFF: I was on the move. But you know I thought of you all the time. You know that, don't you, pal?

LINDA: I know, dear, I know. But he likes to have a letter. Just to know that there's still a possibility for better things.

590 **BIFF:** He's not like this all the time, is he?

LINDA: It's when you come home he's always the worst.

BIFF: When I come home?

LINDA: When you write you're coming, he's all smiles, and talks about the future, and—he's just wonderful. And then the closer you seem to

come, the more shaky he gets, and then, by the time you get here,
he's arguing, and he seems angry at you. I think it's just that maybe
he can't bring himself to—to open up to you. Why are you so hateful
to each other? Why is that?

Biff: *(evasively)* I'm not hateful, Mom.

595 **Linda:** But you no sooner come in the door than you're fighting!

Biff: I don't know why. I mean to change. I'm tryin', Mom, you
understand?

Linda: Are you home to stay now?

Biff: I don't know. I want to look around, see what's doin'.

Linda: Biff, you can't look around all your life, can you?

600 **Biff:** I just can't take hold, Mom. I can't take hold of some kind of a
life.

Linda: Biff, a man is not a bird, to come and go with the springtime.

Biff: Your hair . . . *(He touches her hair.)* Your hair got so gray.

Linda: Oh, it's been gray since you were in high school. I just stopped
dyeing it, that's all.

Biff: Dye it again, will ya? I don't want my pal looking old. *(He smiles.)*

605 **Linda:** You're such a boy! You think you can go away for a year and . . .
You've got to get it into your head now that one day you'll knock on
this door and there'll be strange people here—

Biff: What are you talking about? You're not even sixty, Mom.

Linda: But what about your father?

Biff: *(lamely)* Well, I meant him too.

Happy: He admires Pop.

610 **Linda:** Biff, dear, if you don't have any feeling for him, then you can't
have any feeling for me.

Biff: Sure I can, Mom.

Linda: No. You can't just come to see me, because I love him. *(With a
threat, but only a threat, of tears.)* He's the dearest man in the world to
me, and I won't have anyone making him feel unwanted and low and
blue. You've got to make up your mind now, darling, there's no
leeway any more. Either he's your father and you pay him that
respect, or else you're not to come here. I know he's not easy to get
along with—nobody knows that better than me—but . . .

Willy: *(from the left, with a laugh)* Hey, hey, Biffo!

Biff: *(starting to go out after Willy)* What the hell is the matter with
him? *(Happy stops him.)*

615 **Linda:** Don't—don't go near him!

Biff: Stop making excuses for him! He always, always wiped the floor
with you. Never had an ounce of respect for you.

Happy: He's always had respect for—

Biff: What the hell do you know about it?

Happy: *(surlily)* Just don't call him crazy!

620 **Biff:** He's got no character—Charley wouldn't do this. Not in his own
house—spewing out that vomit from his mind.

HAPPY: Charley never had to cope with what he's got to.

BIFF: People are worse off than Willy Loman. Believe me, I've seen them!

LINDA: Then make Charley your father, Biff. You can't do that, can you? I don't say he's a great man. Willy Loman never made a lot of money. His name was never in the paper. He's not the finest character that ever lived. But he's a human being, and a terrible thing is happening to him. So attention must be paid. He's not to be allowed to fall into his grave like an old dog. Attention, attention must be finally paid to such a person. You called him crazy—

BIFF: I didn't mean—

625 **LINDA:** No, a lot of people think he's lost his—balance. But you don't have to be very smart to know what his trouble is. The man is exhausted.

HAPPY: Sure!

LINDA: A small man can be just as exhausted as a great man. He works for a company thirty-six years this March, opens up unheard-of-territories to their trademark, and now in his old age they take his salary away.

HAPPY: (*indignantly*) I didn't know that, Mom.

LINDA: You never asked, my dear! Now that you get your spending money someplace else you don't trouble your mind with him.

630 **HAPPY:** But I gave you money last—

LINDA: Christmas time, fifty dollars! To fix the hot water it cost ninety-seven fifty! For five weeks he's been on straight commission, like a beginner, an unknown!

BIFF: Those ungrateful bastards!

LINDA: Are they any worse than his sons? When he brought them business, when he was young, they were glad to see him. But now his old friends, the old buyers that loved him so and always found some order to hand him in a pinch—they're all dead, retired. He used to be able to make six, seven calls a day in Boston. Now he takes his valises out of the car and puts them back and takes them out again and he's exhausted. Instead of walking he talks now. He drives seven hundred miles, and when he gets there no one knows him any more, no one welcomes him. And what goes through a man's mind, driving seven hundred miles home without having earned a cent? Why shouldn't he talk to himself? Why? When he has to go to Charley and borrow fifty dollars a week and pretend to me that it's his pay? How long can that go on? How long? You see what I'm sitting here and waiting for? And you tell me he has no character? The man who never worked a day but for your benefit? When does he get the medal for that? Is this his reward—to turn around at the age of sixty-three and find his sons, who he loved better than his life, one a philandering bum—

HAPPY: Mom!

635 **LINDA:**   That's all you are, my baby! *(To Biff.)* And you! What happened
to the love you had for him? You were such pals! How you used to
talk to him on the phone every night! How lonely he was till he could
come home to you!

BIFF: All right, Mom. I'll live here in my room, and I'll get a job. I'll
keep away from him, that's all.

LINDA: No, Biff. You can't stay here and fight all the time.

BIFF: He threw me out of this house, remember that.

LINDA: Why did he do that? I never knew why.

640 **BIFF:**   Because I know he's a fake and he doesn't like anybody around
who knows!

LINDA: Why a fake? In what way? What do you mean?

BIFF: Just don't lay it all at my feet. It's between me and him—that's all
I have to say. I'll chip in from now on. He'll settle for half my pay
check. He'll be all right. I'm going to bed. *(He starts for the stairs.)*

LINDA: He won't be all right.

BIFF: *(turning on the stairs, furiously)* I hate this city and I'll stay here.
Now what do you want?

645 **LINDA:**   He's dying, Biff.

Happy turns quickly to her, shocked.

BIFF: *(after a pause)* Why is he dying?

LINDA: He's been trying to kill himself.

BIFF: *(with great horror)* How?

LINDA: I live from day to day.

650 **BIFF:**   What're you talking about?

LINDA: Remember I wrote you that he smashed up the car again? In
February?

BIFF: Well?

LINDA: The insurance inspector came. He said that they have evidence.
That all these accidents in the last year—weren't—weren't—accidents.

HAPPY: How can they tell that? That's a lie.

655 **LINDA:**   It seems there's a woman . . . *(She takes a breath as—)*

BIFF: *(sharply but contained)*   What woman?

LINDA: *(simultaneously)*   . . . and this woman . . .

LINDA: What?

BIFF: Nothing. Go ahead.

660 **LINDA:**   What did you say?

BIFF: Nothing. I just said what woman?

HAPPY: What about her?

LINDA: Well, it seems she was walking down the road and saw his car.
She says that he wasn't driving fast at all, and that he didn't skid. She
says he came to that little bridge, and then deliberately smashed into
the railing, and it was only the shallowness of the water that saved
him.

BIFF: Oh, no, he probably just fell asleep again.

665   **LINDA:**   I don't think he fell asleep.

      BIFF: Why not?

      LINDA: Last month . . . *(With great difficulty.)* Oh, boys, it's so hard to say a thing like this! He's just a big stupid man to you, but I tell you there's more good in him than in many other people. *(She chokes, wipes her eyes.)* I was looking for a fuse. The lights blew out, and I went down the cellar. And behind the fuse box—it happened to fall out—was a length of rubber pipe—just short.

      HAPPY: No kidding?

      LINDA: There's a little attachment on the end of it. I knew right away. And sure enough, on the bottom of the water heater there's a new little nipple on the gas pipe.

670   **HAPPY:**   *(angrily)* That—jerk.

      BIFF: Did you have it taken off?

      LINDA: I'm—I'm ashamed to. How can I mention it to him? Every day I go down and take away that little rubber pipe. But, when he comes home, I put it back where it was. How can I insult him that way? I don't know what to do. I live from day to day, boys. I tell you, I know every thought in his mind. It sounds so old-fashioned and silly, but I tell you he put his whole life into you and you've turned your backs on him. *(She is bent over in the chair, weeping, her face in her hands.)* Biff, I swear to God! Biff, his life is in your hands!

      HAPPY: *(to Biff)* How do you like that damned fool!

      BIFF: *(kissing her)* All right, pal, all right. It's all settled now. I've been remiss. I know that, Mom, but now I'll stay, and I swear to you, I'll apply myself. *(Kneeling in front of her, in a fever of self-reproach.)* It's just—you see, Mom, I don't fit in business. Not that I won't try. I'll try, and I'll make good.

675   **HAPPY:**   Sure you will. The trouble with you in business was you never tried to please people.

      BIFF: I know, I—

      HAPPY: Like when you worked for Harrison's. Bob Harrison said you were tops, and then you go and do some damn fool thing like whistling whole songs in the elevator like a comedian.

      BIFF: *(against Happy)* So what? I like to whistle sometimes.

      HAPPY: You don't raise a guy to a responsible job who whistles in the elevator!

680   **LINDA:**   Well, don't argue about it now.

      HAPPY: Like when you'd go off and swim in the middle of the day instead of taking the line around.

      BIFF: *(his resentment rising)* Well, don't you run off? You take off sometimes, don't you? On a nice summer day?

      HAPPY: Yeah, but I cover myself!

      LINDA: Boys!

685   **HAPPY:**   If I'm going to take a fade the boss can call any number where I'm supposed to be and they'll swear to him that I just left. I'll tell

you something that I hate to say, Biff, but in the business world some of them think you're crazy.

BIFF: *(angered)* Screw the business world!

HAPPY: All right, screw it! Great, but cover yourself!

LINDA: Hap, Hap!

BIFF: I don't care what they think! They've laughed at Dad for years, and you know why? Because we don't belong in this nut-house of a city! We should be mixing cement on some open plain, or—or carpenters. A carpenter is allowed to whistle!

Willy walks in from the entrance of the house, at left.

690 **WILLY:** Even your grandfather was better than a carpenter. *(Pause. They watch him.)* You never grew up. Bernard does not whistle in the elevator, I assure you.

BIFF: *(as though to laugh Willy out of it)* Yeah, but you do, Pop.

WILLY: I never in my life whistled in an elevator! And who in the business world thinks I'm crazy?

BIFF: I didn't mean it like that, Pop. Now don't make a whole thing out of it, will ya?

WILLY: Go back to the West! Be a carpenter, a cowboy, enjoy yourself!

695 **LINDA:** Willy, he was just saying—

WILLY: I heard what he said!

HAPPY: *(trying to quiet Willy)* Hey, Pop, come on now . . .

WILLY: *(continuing over Happy's line)* They laugh at me, heh? Go to Filene's, go to the Hub, go to Slattery's, Boston. Call out the name Willy Loman and see what happens! Big shot!

BIFF: All right, Pop.

700 **WILLY:** Big!

BIFF: All right!

WILLY: Why do you always insult me?

BIFF: I didn't say a word. *(To Linda.)* Did I say a word?

LINDA: He didn't say anything, Willy.

705 **WILLY:** *(going to the doorway of the livingroom)* All right, good night, good night.

LINDA: Willy, dear, he just decided . . .

WILLY: *(to Biff)* If you get tired hanging around tomorrow, paint the ceiling I put up in the livingroom.

BIFF: I'm leaving early tomorrow.

HAPPY: He's going to see Bill Oliver, Pop.

710 **WILLY:** *(interestedly)* Oliver? For what?

BIFF: *(with reserve, but trying, trying)* He always said he'd stake me. I'd like to go into business, so maybe I can take him up on it.

LINDA: Isn't that wonderful?

WILLY: Don't interrupt. What's wonderful about it? There's fifty men in the City of New York who'd stake him. *(To Biff.)* Sporting goods?

BIFF: I guess so. I know something about it and—

715 **WILLY:** He knows something about it! You know sporting goods better than Spalding, for God's sake! How much is he giving you?

BIFF: I don't know, I didn't even see him yet, but—

WILLY: Then what're you talkin' about?

BIFF: (getting angry) Well, all I said was I'm gonna see him, that's all!

WILLY: (turning away) Ah, you're counting your chickens again.

720 **BIFF:** (starting left for the stairs) Oh, Jesus, I'm going to sleep!

WILLY: (calling after him) Don't curse in this house!

BIFF: (turning) Since when did you get so clean!

HAPPY: (trying to stop them) Wait a . . .

WILLY: Don't use that language to me! I won't have it!

725 **HAPPY:** (grabbing Biff, shouts) Wait a minute! I got an idea. I got a feasible idea. Come here, Biff, let's talk this over now, let's talk some sense here. When I was down in Florida last time, I thought of a great idea to sell sporting goods. It just came back to me. You and I, Biff— we have a line, the Loman Line. We train a couple of weeks, and put on a couple of exhibitions, see?

WILLY: That's an idea!

HAPPY: Wait! We form two basketball teams, see? Two water-polo teams. We play each other. It's a million dollars' worth of publicity. Two brothers, see? The Loman Brothers. Displays in the Royal Palms—all the hotels. And banners over the ring and the basketball court: "Loman Brothers." Baby, we could sell sporting goods!

WILLY: That is a one-million-dollar idea.

LINDA: Marvelous!

730 **BIFF:** I'm in great shape as far as that's concerned.

HAPPY: And the beauty of it is, Biff, it wouldn't be like a business. We'd be out playin' ball again . . .

BIFF: (enthused) Yeah, that's . . .

WILLY: Million-dollar . . .

HAPPY: And you wouldn't get fed up with it, Biff. It'd be the family again. There'd be the old honor, and comradeship, and if you wanted to go off for a swim or somethin'—well, you'd do it! Without some smart cooky gettin' up ahead of you!

735 **WILLY:** Lick the world! You guys together could absolutely lick the civilized world.

BIFF: I'll see Oliver tomorrow. Hap, if we could work that out . . .

LINDA: Maybe things are beginning to—

WILLY: (wildly enthused, to Linda) Stop interrupting! (To Biff.) But don't wear sport jacket and slacks when you see Oliver.

BIFF: No, I'll—

740 **WILLY:** A business suit, and talk as little as possible, and don't crack any jokes.

BIFF: He did like me. Always liked me.

LINDA: He loved you!

WILLY: *(to Linda)* Will you stop! *(To Biff.)* Walk in very serious. You are not applying for a boy's job. Money is to pass. Be quiet, fine, and serious. Everybody likes a kidder, but nobody lends him money.

HAPPY: I'll try to get some myself, Biff. I'm sure I can.

745 **WILLY:** I can see great things for you, kids, I think your troubles are over. But remember, start big and you'll end big. Ask for fifteen. How much you gonna ask for?

BIFF: Gee, I don't know—

WILLY: And don't say "Gee." "Gee" is a boy's word. A man walking in for fifteen thousand dollars does not say "Gee!"

BIFF: Ten, I think, would be top though.

WILLY: Don't be so modest. You always started too low. Walk in with a big laugh. Don't look worried. Start off with a couple of your good stories to lighten things up. It's not what you say, it's how you say it—because personality always wins the day.

750 **LINDA:** Oliver always thought the highest of him—

WILLY: Will you let me talk?

BIFF: Don't yell at her, Pop, will ya?

WILLY: *(angrily)* I was talking, wasn't I!

BIFF: I don't like you yelling at her all the time, and I'm tellin' you, that's all.

755 **WILLY:** What're you, takin' over this house?

LINDA: Willy—

WILLY: *(turning on her)* Don't take his side all the time, goddammit!

BIFF: *(furiously)* Stop yelling at her!

WILLY: *(suddenly pulling on his cheek, beaten down, guilt ridden)* Give my best to Bill Oliver—he may remember me. *(He exits through the livingroom doorway.)*

760 **LINDA:** *(her voice subdued)* What'd you have to start that for? *(Biff turns away.)* You see how sweet he was as soon as you talked hopefully? *(She goes over to Biff.)* Come up and say good night to him. Don't let him go to bed that way.

HAPPY: Come on, Biff, let's buck him up.

LINDA: Please, dear. Just say good night. It takes so little to make him happy. Come. *(She goes through the livingroom doorway, calling upstairs from within the livingroom.)* Your pajamas are hanging in the bathroom. Willy!

HAPPY: *(looking toward where Linda went out)* What a woman! They broke the mold when they made her. You know that, Biff?

BIFF: He's off salary. My God, working on commission!

765 **HAPPY:** Well, let's face it: he's no hot-shot selling man. Except that sometimes, you have to admit, he's a sweet personality.

BIFF: *(deciding)* Lend me ten bucks, will ya? I want to buy some new ties.

HAPPY: I'll take you to a place I know. Beautiful stuff. Wear one of my striped shirts tomorrow.

Biff: She got gray. Mom got awful old. Gee, I'm gonna go in to Oliver tomorrow and knock him for a—

Happy: Come on up. Tell that to Dad. Let's give him a whirl. Come on.

770 **Biff:** *(steamed up)* You know, with ten thousand bucks, boy!

Happy: *(as they go into the livingroom)* That's the talk, Biff, that's the first time I've heard the old confidence out of you! *(From within the livingroom, fading off.)* You're gonna live with me, kid, and any babe you want you just say the word . . . *(The last lines are hardly heard. They are mounting the stairs to their parents' bedroom.)*

Linda: *(entering her bedroom and addressing Willy, who is in the bathroom. She is straightening the bed for him)* Can you do anything about the shower? It drips.

Willy: *(from the bathroom)* All of a sudden everything falls to pieces! Goddam plumbing, oughta be sued, those people. I hardly finished putting it in and the thing . . . *(His words rumble off.)*

Linda: I'm just wondering if Oliver will remember him. You think he might?

775 **Willy:** *(coming out of the bathroom in his pajamas)* Remember him? What's the matter with you, you crazy? If he'd've stayed with Oliver he'd be on top by now! Wait'll Oliver gets a look at him. You don't know the average caliber any more. The average young man today— *(he is getting into bed)*—is got a caliber of zero. Greatest thing in the world for him was to bum around.

Biff and Happy enter the bedroom. Slight pause.

Willy: *(stops short, looking at Biff)* Glad to hear it, boy.

Happy: He wanted to say good night to you, sport.

Willy: *(to Biff)* Yeah. Knock him dead, boy. What'd you want to tell me?

Biff: Just take it easy, Pop. Good night. *(He turns to go.)*

780 **Willy:** *(unable to resist)* And if anything falls off the desk while you're talking to him—like a package or something—don't you pick it up. They have office boys for that.

Linda: I'll make a big breakfast—

Willy: Will you let me finish? *(To Biff.)* Tell him you were in the business in the West. Not farm work.

Biff: All right, Dad.

Linda: I think everything—

785 **Willy:** *(going right through her speech)* And don't undersell yourself. No less than fifteen thousand dollars.

Biff: *(unable to bear him)* Okay. Good night, Mom. *(He starts moving.)*

Willy: Because you got a greatness in you, Biff, remember that. You got all kinds a greatness . . . *(He lies back, exhausted. Biff walks out.)*

Linda: *(calling after Biff)* Sleep well, darling!

Happy: I'm gonna get married, Mom. I wanted to tell you.

790 **Linda:** Go to sleep, dear.

HAPPY: *(going)* I just wanted to tell you.

WILLY: Keep up the good work. *(Happy exits.)* God . . . remember that Ebbets Field game? The championship of the city?

LINDA: Just rest. Should I sing to you?

WILLY: Yeah. Sing to me. *(Linda hums a soft lullaby.)* When that team came out—he was the tallest, remember?

795 **LINDA:** Oh, yes. And in gold.

Biff enters the darkened kitchen, takes a cigarette, and leaves the house. He comes downstage into a golden pool of light. He smokes, staring at the night.

WILLY: Like a young god. Hercules—something like that. And the sun, the sun all around him. Remember how he waved to me? Right up from the field, with the representatives of three colleges standing by? And the buyers I brought, and the cheers when he came out—Loman, Loman, Loman! God Almighty, he'll be great yet. A star like that, magnificent, can never really fade away!

The light on Willy is fading. The gas heater begins to glow through the kitchen wall, near the stairs, a blue flame beneath red coils.

LINDA: *(timidly)* Willy, dear, what has he got against you?

WILLY: I'm so tired. Don't talk any more.

Biff slowly returns to the kitchen. He stops, stares toward the heater.

LINDA: Will you ask Howard to let you work in New York?

800 **WILLY:** First thing in the morning. Everything'll be all right.

Biff reaches behind the heater and draws out a length of rubber tubing. He is horrified and turns his head toward Willy's room, still dimly lit, from which the strains of Linda's desperate but monotonous humming rise.

WILLY: *(staring through the window into the moonlight)* Gee, look at the moon moving between the buildings!

Biff wraps the tubing around his hand and quickly goes up the stairs. Curtain.

A C T   I I

Music is heard, gay and bright. The curtain rises as the music fades away. Willy, in shirt sleeves, is sitting at the kitchen table, sipping coffee, his hat in his lap. Linda is filling his cup when she can.

WILLY: Wonderful coffee. Meal in itself.

LINDA: Can I make you some eggs?

WILLY: No. Take a breath.

LINDA: You look so rested, dear.

5 **WILLY:** I slept like a dead one. First time in months. Imagine, sleeping till ten on a Tuesday morning. Boys left nice and early, heh?

LINDA: They were out of here by eight o'clock.

WILLY: Good work!

LINDA: It was so thrilling to see them leaving together. I can't get over the shaving lotion in this house.

WILLY: *(smiling)* Mmm—

10 **LINDA:** Biff was very changed this morning. His whole attitude seemed to be hopeful. He couldn't wait to get downtown to see Oliver.

WILLY: He's heading for a change. There's no question, there simply are certain men that take longer to get—solidified. How did he dress?

LINDA: His blue suit. He's so handsome in that suit. He could be a— anything in that suit!

Willy gets up from the table. Linda holds his jacket for him.

WILLY: There's no question, no question at all. Gee, on the way home tonight I'd like to buy some seeds.

LINDA: *(laughing)* That'd be wonderful. But not enough sun gets back there. Nothing'll grow any more.

15 **WILLY:** You wait, kid, before it's all over we're gonna get a little place out in the country, and I'll raise some vegetables, a couple of chickens . . .

LINDA: You'll do it yet, dear.

Willy walks out of his jacket. Linda follows him.

WILLY: And they'll get married, and come for a weekend. I'd build a little guest house. 'Cause I got so many fine tools, all I'd need would be a little lumber and some peace of mind.

LINDA: *(joyfully)* I sewed the lining . . .

WILLY: I could build two guest houses, so they'd both come. Did he decide how much he's going to ask Oliver for?

20 **LINDA:** *(getting him into the jacket)* He didn't mention it, but I imagine ten or fifteen thousand. You going to talk to Howard today?

WILLY: Yeah. I'll put it to him straight and simple. He'll just have to take me off the road.

LINDA: And Willy, don't forget to ask for a little advance, because we've got the insurance premium. It's the grace period now.

WILLY: That's a hundred . . . ?

LINDA: A hundred and eight, sixty-eight. Because we're a little short again.

25 **WILLY:** Why are we short?

LINDA: Well, you had the motor job on the car . . .

WILLY: That goddam Studebaker!

LINDA: And you got one more payment on the refrigerator . . .

WILLY: But it just broke again!

30 **LINDA:** Well, it's old, dear.

WILLY: I told you we should've bought a well-advertised machine. Charley bought a General Electric and it's twenty years old and it's still good, that son-of-a-bitch.

LINDA: But, Willy—

WILLY: Whoever heard of a Hastings refrigerator? Once in my life I would like to own something outright before it's broken! I'm always in a race with the junkyard! I just finished paying for the car and it's on its last legs. The refrigerator consumes belts like a goddam maniac. They time those things. They time them so when you finally paid for them, they're used up.

LINDA: *(buttoning up his jacket as he unbuttons it)* All told, about two hundred dollars would carry us, dear. But that includes the last payment on the mortgage. After this payment, Willy, the house belongs to us.

35   **WILLY:**   It's twenty-five years!

LINDA: Biff was nine years old when we bought it.

WILLY: Well, that's a great thing. To weather a twenty-five year mortgage is—

LINDA: It's an accomplishment.

WILLY: All the cement, the lumber, the reconstruction I put in this house! There ain't a crack to be found in it any more.

40   **LINDA:**   Well, it served its purpose.

WILLY: What purpose? Some stranger'll come along, move in, and that's that. If only Biff would take this house, and raise a family . . . *(He starts to go.)* Good-by, I'm late.

LINDA: *(suddenly remembering)* Oh, I forgot! You're supposed to meet them for dinner.

WILLY: Me?

LINDA: At Frank's Chop House on Forty-eighth near Sixth Avenue.

45   **WILLY:**   Is that so! How about you?

LINDA: No, just the three of you. They're gonna blow you to a big meal!

WILLY: Don't say! Who thought of that?

LINDA: Biff came to me this morning, Willy, and he said, "Tell Dad, we want to blow him to a big meal." Be there six o'clock. You and your two boys are going to have dinner.

WILLY: Gee whiz! That's really somethin'. I'm gonna knock Howard for a loop, kid. I'll get an advance, and I'll come home with a New York job. Goddammit, now I'm gonna do it!

50   **LINDA:**   Oh, that's the spirit, Willy!

WILLY: I will never get behind a wheel the rest of my life!

LINDA: It's changing, Willy, I can feel it changing!

WILLY: Beyond a question. G'by, I'm late. *(He starts to go again.)*

LINDA: *(calling after him as she runs to the kitchen table for a handkerchief)* You got your glasses?

55   **WILLY:**   *(feels for them, then comes back in)* Yeah, yeah, got my glasses.

LINDA: *(giving him the handkerchief)* And a handkerchief.

WILLY: Yeah, handkerchief.

LINDA: And your saccharine?

WILLY: Yeah, my saccharine.

60   **LINDA:**   Be careful on the subway stairs.

She kisses him, and a silk stocking is seen hanging from her hand. Willy notices it.

WILLY: Will you stop mending stockings? At least while I'm in the house. It gets me nervous. I can't tell you. Please.

Linda hides the stocking in her hand as she follows Willy across the forestage in front of the house.

LINDA: Remember, Frank's Chop House.
WILLY: *(passing the apron)* Maybe beets would grow out there.
LINDA: *(laughing)* But you tried so many times.
65 **WILLY:** Yeah. Well, don't work hard today. *(He disappears around the right corner of the house.)*
LINDA: Be careful!

As Willy vanishes, Linda waves to him. Suddenly the phone rings. She runs across the stage and into the kitchen and lifts it.

LINDA: Hello? Oh, Biff! I'm so glad you called, I just . . . Yes, sure, I just told him. Yes, he'll be there for dinner at six o'clock, I didn't forget. Listen, I was just dying to tell you. You know that little rubber pipe I told you about? That he connected to the gas heater? I finally decided to go down the cellar this morning and take it away and destroy it. But it's gone! Imagine? He took it away himself, it isn't there! *(She listens.)* When? Oh, then you took it. Oh—nothing, it's just that I'd hoped he'd taken it away himself. Oh, I'm not worried, darling, because this morning he left in such high spirits, it was like the old days! I'm not afraid any more. Did Mr. Oliver see you? . . . Well, you wait there then. And make a nice impression on him, darling. Just don't perspire too much before you see him. And have a nice time with Dad. He may have big news too! . . . That's right, a New York job. And be sweet to him tonight, dear. Be loving to him. Because he's only a little boat looking for a harbor. *(She is trembling with sorrow and joy.)* Oh, that's wonderful, Biff, you'll save his life. Thanks, darling. Just put your arm around him when he comes into the restaurant. Give him a smile. That's the boy . . . Good-by, dear. . . . You got your comb? . . . That's fine. Good-by, Biff dear.

In the middle of her speech, Howard Wagner, thirty-six, wheels in a small typewriter table on which is a wire-recording machine and proceeds to plug it in. This is on the left forestage. Light slowly fades on Linda as it rises on Howard. Howard is intent on threading the machine and only glances over his shoulder as Willy appears.

WILLY: Pst! Pst!
HOWARD: Hello, Willy, come in.
70 **WILLY:** Like to have a little talk with you, Howard.
HOWARD: Sorry to keep you waiting. I'll be with you in a minute.
WILLY: What's that, Howard?

HOWARD: Didn't you ever see one of these? Wire recorder.

WILLY: Oh. Can we talk a minute?

75 **HOWARD:**   Records things. Just got delivery yesterday. Been driving me crazy, the most terrific machine I ever saw in my life. I was up all night with it.

WILLY: What do you do with it?

HOWARD: I bought it for dictation, but you can do anything with it. Listen to this. I had it home last night. Listen to what I picked up. The first one is my daughter. Get this. *(He flicks the switch and "Roll out the Barrel" is heard being whistled.)* Listen to that kid whistle.

WILLY: That is lifelike, isn't it?

HOWARD: Seven years old. Get that tone.

80 **WILLY:**   Ts, ts. Like to ask a little favor if you . . .

The whistling breaks off, and the voice of Howard's Daughter is heard.

HIS DAUGHTER: "Now you, Daddy."

HOWARD: She's crazy for me! *(Again the same song is whistled.)* That's me! Ha! *(He winks.)*

WILLY: You're very good!

The whistling breaks off again. The machine runs silent for a moment.

HOWARD: Sh! Get this now, this is my son.

85 **HIS SON:**   "The capital of Alabama is Montgomery; the capital of Arizona is Phoenix; the capital of Arkansas is Little Rock; the capital of California is Sacramento . . ." *(And on, and on.)*

HOWARD: *(holding up five fingers)* Five years old, Willy!

WILLY: He'll make an announcer some day!

HIS SON: *(continuing)* "The capital . . ."

HOWARD: Get that—alphabetical order! *(The machine breaks off suddenly.)* Wait a minute. The maid kicked the plug out.

90 **WILLY:**   It certainly is a—

HOWARD: Sh, for God's sake!

HIS SON: "It's nine o'clock, Bulova watch time. So I have to go to sleep."

WILLY: That really is—

HOWARD: Wait a minute! The next is my wife.

They wait.

95 **HOWARD'S VOICE:**   "Go on, say something." *(Pause.)* "Well, you gonna talk?"

HIS WIFE: "I can't think of anything."

HOWARD'S VOICE: "Well, talk—it's turning."

HIS WIFE: *(shyly, beaten)* "Hello." *(Silence.)* "Oh, Howard, I can't talk into this . . ."

HOWARD: *(snapping the machine off)* That was my wife.

100 **WILLY:**   That is a wonderful machine. Can we—

HOWARD: I tell you, Willy, I'm gonna take my camera, and my bandsaw, and all my hobbies, and out they go. This is the most fascinating relaxation I ever found.

WILLY: I think I'll get one myself.

HOWARD: Sure, they're only a hundred and a half. You can't do without it. Supposing you wanna hear Jack Benny, see? But you can't be at home at that hour. So you tell the maid to turn the radio on when Jack Benny comes on, and this automatically goes on with the radio . . .

WILLY: And when you come home you . . .

105 **HOWARD:**   You can come home twelve o'clock, one o'clock, any time you like, and you get yourself a Coke and sit yourself down, throw the switch, and there's Jack Benny's program in the middle of the night!

WILLY: I'm definitely going to get one. Because lots of time I'm on the road, and I think to myself, what I must be missing on the radio!

HOWARD: Don't you have a radio in the car?

WILLY: Well, yeah, but who ever thinks of turning it on?

HOWARD: Say, aren't you supposed to be in Boston?

110 **WILLY:**   That's what I want to talk to you about, Howard. You got a minute?

(He draws a chair in from the wing.)

HOWARD: What happened? What're you doing here?

WILLY: Well . . .

HOWARD: You didn't crack up again, did you?

WILLY: Oh, no. No . . .

115 **HOWARD:**   Geez, you had me worried there for a minute. What's the trouble?

WILLY: Well, to tell you the truth, Howard, I've come to the decision that I'd rather not travel any more.

HOWARD: Not travel! Well, what'll you do?

WILLY: Remember, Christmas time, when you had the party here? You said you'd try to think of some spot for me here in town.

HOWARD: With us?

120 **WILLY:**   Well, sure.

HOWARD: Oh, yeah, yeah. I remember. Well, I couldn't think of anything for you, Willy.

WILLY: I tell ya, Howard. The kids are all grown up, y'know. I don't need much any more. If I could take home—well, sixty-five dollars a week, I could swing it.

HOWARD: Yeah, but Willy, see I—

WILLY: I tell ya why, Howard. Speaking frankly and between the two of us, y'know—I'm just a little tired.

125 **HOWARD:**   Oh, I could understand that, Willy. But you're a road man, Willy, and we do a road business. We've only got a half-dozen salesmen on the floor here.

WILLY: God knows, Howard, I never asked a favor of any man. But I was with the firm when your father used to carry you in here in his arms.

HOWARD: I know that, Willy, but—

WILLY: Your father came to me the day you were born and asked me what I thought of the name of Howard, may he rest in peace.

HOWARD: I appreciate that, Willy, but there just is no spot here for you. If I had a spot I'd slam you right in, but I just don't have a single, solitary spot.

He looks for his lighter. Willy has picked it up and gives it to him. Pause.

130   **WILLY:**   *(with increasing anger)* Howard, all I need to set my table is fifty dollars a week.

HOWARD: But where am I going to put you, kid?

WILLY: Look, it isn't a question of whether I can sell merchandise, is it?

HOWARD: No, but it's a business, kid, and everybody's gotta pull his own weight.

WILLY: *(desperately)* Just let me tell you a story, Howard—

135   **HOWARD:**   'Cause you gotta admit, business is business.

WILLY: *(angrily)* Business is definitely business, but just listen for a minute. You don't understand this. When I was a boy—eighteen, nineteen—I was already on the road. And there was a question in my mind as to whether selling had a future for me. Because in those days I had a yearning to go to Alaska. See, there were three gold strikes in one month in Alaska, and I felt like going out. Just for the ride, you might say.

HOWARD: *(barely interested)* Don't say.

WILLY: Oh, yeah, my father lived many years in Alaska. He was an adventurous man. We've got quite a little streak of self-reliance in our family. I thought I'd go out with my older brother and try to locate him, and maybe settle in the North with the old man. And I was almost decided to go, when I met a salesman in the Parker House. His name was Dave Singleman. And he was eighty-four years old, and he'd drummed merchandise in thirty-one states. And old Dave, he'd go up to his room, y'understand, put on his green velvet slippers—I'll never forget—and pick up his phone and call the buyers, and without ever leaving his room, at the age of eighty-four, he made his living. And when I saw that, I realized that selling was the greatest career a man could want. 'Cause what could be more satisfying than to be able to go, at the age of eighty-four, into twenty or thirty different cities, and pick up a phone, and be remembered and loved and helped by so many different people? Do you know? when he died—and by the way he died the death of a salesman, in his green velvet slippers in the smoker of the New York, New Haven and Hartford, going into Boston—when he died, hundreds of salesmen and buyers were at his funeral. Things were sad on a lotta trains for months after that. *(He stands up. Howard has not looked at him.)* In those days there was personality in it, Howard. There was respect, and comradeship, and gratitude in it. Today, it's all cut and dried, and there's no chance for bringing friendship to bear—or personality. You see what I mean? They don't know me any more.

HOWARD: *(moving away, to the right)* That's just the thing, Willy.

140 **WILLY:**   If I had forty dollars a week—that's all I'd need. Forty dollars, Howard.

HOWARD: Kid, I can't take blood from a stone, I—

WILLY: *(desperation is on him now)* Howard, the year Al Smith was nominated, your father came to me and—

HOWARD: *(starting to go off)* I've got to see some people, kid.

WILLY: *(stopping him)* I'm talking about your father! There were promises made across this desk! You mustn't tell me you've got people to see—I put thirty-four years into this firm, Howard, and now I can't pay my insurance! You can't eat the orange and throw the peel away—a man is not a piece of fruit! *(After a pause.)* Now pay attention. Your father—in 1928 I had a big year. I averaged a hundred and seventy dollars a week in commissions.

145 **HOWARD:**   *(impatiently)* Now, Willy, you never averaged—

WILLY: *(banging his hand on the desk)* I averaged a hundred and seventy dollars a week in the year of 1928! And your father came to me—or rather, I was in the office here—it was right over this desk—and he put his hand on my shoulder—

HOWARD: *(getting up)* You'll have to excuse me, Willy, I gotta see some people. Pull yourself together. *(Going out.)* I'll be back in a little while.

On Howard's exit, the light on his chair grows very bright and strange.

WILLY: Pull myself together! What the hell did I say to him? My God, I was yelling at him! How could I! *(Willy breaks off, staring at the light, which occupies the chair, animating it. He approaches this chair, standing across the desk from it.)* Frank, Frank, don't you remember what you told me that time? How you put your hand on my shoulder, and Frank . . . *(He leans on the desk and as he speaks the dead man's name he accidentally switches on the recorder, and instantly—)*

HOWARD'S SON: ". . . of New York is Albany. The capital of Ohio is Cincinnati, the capital of Rhode Island is . . ." *(The recitation continues.)*

150 **WILLY:**   *(leaping away with fright, shouting)* Ha! Howard! Howard! Howard!

HOWARD: *(rushing in)* What happened?

WILLY: *(pointing at the machine, which continues nasally, childishly, with the capital cities)* Shut it off! Shut it off!

HOWARD: *(pulling the plug out)* Look, Willy . . .

WILLY: *(pressing his hands to his eyes)* I gotta get myself some coffee. I'll get some coffee . . .

Willy starts to walk out. Howard stops him.

155 **HOWARD:** *(rolling up the cord)* Willy, look . . .
    WILLY: I'll go to Boston.
    HOWARD: Willy, you can't go to Boston for us.
    WILLY: Why can't I go?
    HOWARD: I don't want you to represent us. I've been meaning to tell
      you for a long time now.
160 **WILLY:** Howard, are you firing me?
    HOWARD: I think you need a good long rest, Willy.
    WILLY: Howard—
    HOWARD: And when you feel better, come back, and we'll see if we can
      work something out.
    WILLY: But I gotta earn money, Howard. I'm in no position—
165 **HOWARD:** Where are your sons? Why don't your sons give you a hand?
    WILLY: They're working on a very big deal.
    HOWARD: This is no time for false pride, Willy. You go to your sons and
      tell them that you're tired. You've got two great boys, haven't you?
    WILLY: Oh, no question, no question, but in the meantime . . .
    HOWARD: Then that's that, heh?
170 **WILLY:** All right, I'll go to Boston tomorrow.
    HOWARD: No, no.
    WILLY: I can't throw myself on my sons. I'm not a cripple!
    HOWARD: Look, kid, I'm busy this morning.
    WILLY: *(grasping Howard's arm)* Howard, you've got to let me go to
      Boston!
175 **HOWARD:** *(hard, keeping himself under control)* I've got a line of people
      to see this morning. Sit down, take five minutes, and pull yourself
      together, and then go home, will ya? I need the office, Willy. *(He
      starts to go, turns, remembering the recorder, starts to push off the table
      holding the recorder.)* Oh, yeah. Whenever you can this week, stop by
      and drop off the samples. You'll feel better, Willy, and then come
      back and we'll talk. Pull yourself together, kid, there's people
      outside.

*Howard exits, pushing the table off left. Willy stares into space, exhausted. Now
the music is heard—Ben's music—first distantly, then closer, closer. As Willy
speaks, Ben enters from the right. He carries valise and umbrella.*

    WILLY: Oh, Ben, how did you do it? What is the answer? Did you wind
      up the Alaska deal already?
    BEN: Doesn't take much time if you know what you're doing. Just a
      short business trip. Boarding ship in an hour. Wanted to say good-by.
    WILLY: Ben, I've got to talk to you.
    BEN: *(glancing at his watch)* Haven't the time, William.
180 **WILLY:** *(crossing the apron to Ben)* Ben, nothing's working out. I don't
      know what to do.

Ben: Now, look here, William. I've bought timberland in Alaska and I
need a man to look after things for me.

Willy: God, timberland! Me and my boys in those grand outdoors!

Ben: You've a new continent at your doorstep, William. Get out of
these cities, they're full of talk and time payments and courts of law.
Screw on your fists and you can fight for a fortune up there.

Willy: Yes, yes! Linda! Linda!

Linda enters as of old, with the wash.

185 **Linda:**   Oh, you're back?

Ben: I haven't much time.

Willy: No, wait! Linda, he's got a proposition for me in Alaska.

Linda: But you've got—*(To Ben.)* He's got a beautiful job here.

Willy: But in Alaska, kid, I could—

190 **Linda:**   You're doing well enough, Willy!

Ben: *(to Linda)* Enough for what, my dear?

Linda: *(frightened of Ben and angry at him)* Don't say those things to
him! Enough to be happy right here, right now. *(To Willy, while Ben
laughs.)* Why must everybody conquer the world? You're well liked,
and the boys love you, and someday—*(to Ben)*—why, old man Wagner
told him just the other day that if he keeps it up he'll be a member of
the firm, didn't he, Willy?

Willy: Sure, sure. I am building something with this firm, Ben, and if a
man is building something he must be on the right track, mustn't he?

Ben: What are you building? Lay your hand on it. Where is it?

195 **Willy:**   *(hesitantly)* That's true, Linda, there's nothing.

Linda: Why? *(To Ben.)* There's a man eighty-four years old—

Willy: That's right, Ben, that's right. When I look at that man I say,
what is there to worry about?

Ben: Bah!

Willy: It's true, Ben. All he has to do is go into any city, pick up the
phone, and he's making his living and you know why?

200 **Ben:**   *(picking up his valise)* I've got to go.

Willy: *(holding Ben back)* Look at this boy!

*Biff, in his high school sweater, enters carrying suitcase. Happy carries Biff's
shoulder guards, gold helmet, and football pants.*

Willy: Without a penny to his name, three great universities are
begging for him, and from there the sky's the limit, because it's not
what you do, Ben. It's who you know and the smile on your face! It's
contacts, Ben, contacts! The whole wealth of Alaska passes over the
lunch table at the Commodore Hotel, and that's the wonder, the
wonder of this country, that a man can end with diamonds here on
the basis of being liked! *(He turns to Biff.)* And that's why when you
get out on that field today it's important. Because thousands of
people will be rooting for you and loving you. *(To Ben, who has again*

begun to leave.) And Ben! when he walks into a business office his name will sound out like a bell and all the doors will open to him! I've seen it, Ben, I've seen it a thousand times! You can't feel it with your hand like timber, but it's there!

BEN: Good-by, William.

WILLY: Ben, am I right? Don't you think I'm right? I value your advice.

205 **BEN:**   There's a new continent at your doorstep, William. You could walk out rich. Rich. *(He is gone.)*

WILLY: We'll do it here, Ben! You hear me? We're gonna do it here!

Young Bernard rushes in. The gay music of the boys is heard.

BERNARD: Oh, gee, I was afraid you left already!

WILLY: Why? What time is it?

BERNARD: It's half-past one!

210 **WILLY:**   Well, come on, everybody! Ebbets Field[2] next stop! Where's the pennants? *(He rushes through the wall-line of the kitchen and out into the livingroom.)*

LINDA: *(to Biff)* Did you pack fresh underwear?

BIFF: *(who has been limbering up)* I want to go!

BERNARD: Biff, I'm carrying your helmet, ain't I?

HAPPY: No, I'm carrying the helmet.

215 **BERNARD:**   Oh, Biff, you promised me.

HAPPY: I'm carrying the helmet.

BERNARD: How am I going to get in the locker room?

LINDA: Let him carry the shoulder guards. *(She puts her coat and hat on in the kitchen.)*

BERNARD: Can I, Biff? 'Cause I told everybody I'm going to be in the locker room.

220 **HAPPY:**   In Ebbets Field it's the clubhouse.

BERNARD: I meant the clubhouse. Biff!

HAPPY: Biff!

BIFF: *(grandly, after a slight pause)* Let him carry the shoulder guards.

HAPPY: *(as he gives Bernard the shoulder guards)* Stay close to us now.

Willy rushes in with the pennants.

225 **WILLY:**   *(handing them out)* Everybody wave when Biff comes out on the field. *(Happy and Bernard run off.)* You set now, boy?

The music has died away.

BIFF: Ready to go, Pop. Every muscle is ready.

WILLY: *(at the edge of the apron)* You realize what this means?

BIFF: That's right, Pop.

---

[2] The home park of the Brooklyn dodgers.

WILLY: *(feeling Biff's muscles)* You're comin' home this afternoon
captain of the All-Scholastic Championship Team of the City of New
York.

230 **BIFF:** I got it, Pop. And remember, pal, when I take off my helmet, that
touchdown is for you.

WILLY: Let's go! *(He is starting out, with his arm around Biff, when
Charley enters, as of old, in knickers.)* I got no room for you, Charley.

CHARLEY: Room? For what?

WILLY: In the car.

CHARLEY: You goin' for a ride? I wanted to shoot some casino.

235 **WILLY:** *(furiously)* Casino! *(Incredulously.)* Don't you realize what
today is?

LINDA: Oh, he knows, Willy. He's just kidding you.

WILLY: That's nothing to kid about!

CHARLEY: No, Linda, what's goin' on?

LINDA: He's playing in Ebbets Field.

240 **CHARLEY:** Baseball in this weather?

WILLY: Don't talk to him. Come on, come on! *(He is pushing them out.)*

CHARLEY: Wait a minute, didn't you hear the news?

WILLY: What?

CHARLEY: Don't you listen to the radio? Ebbets Field just blew up.

245 **WILLY:** You go to hell! *(Charley laughs. Pushing them out.)* Come on,
come on! We're late.

CHARLEY: *(as they go)* Knock a homer, Biff, knock a homer!

WILLY: *(the last to leave, turning to Charley)* I don't think that was funny,
Charley. This is the greatest day of his life.

CHARLEY: Willy, when are you going to grow up?

WILLY: Yeah, heh? When this game is over, Charley, you'll be laughing
out of the other side of your face. They'll be calling him another Red
Grange.[3] Twenty-five thousand a year.

250 **CHARLEY:** *(kidding)* Is that so?

WILLY: Yeah, that's so.

CHARLEY: Well, then, I'm sorry, Willy. But tell me something.

WILLY: What?

CHARLEY: Who is Red Grange?

255 **WILLY:** Put up your hands. Goddam you, put up your hands!

*Charley, chuckling, shakes his head and walks away, around the left corner of
the stage. Willy follows him. The music rises to a mocking frenzy.*

WILLY: Who the hell do you think you are, better than everybody else?
You don't know everything, you big, ignorant, stupid . . . Put up your
hands!

---

[3] Red (Harold Edward) Grange (b. 1903)—U.S. football player. A running back for the
New York Yankees football team and the Chicago Bears, Grange was elected to the
Football Hall of Fame in 1963.

Light rises, on the right side of the forestage, on a small table in the reception room of Charley's office. Traffic sounds are heard. Bernard, now mature, sits whistling to himself. A pair of tennis rackets and an overnight bag are on the floor beside him.

WILLY: *(offstage)* What are you walking away for? Don't walk away! If you're going to say something say it to my face! I know you laugh at me behind my back. You'll laugh out of the other side of your goddam face after this game. Touchdown! Touchdown! Eighty thousand people! Touchdown! Right between the goal posts.

Bernard is a quiet, earnest, but self-assured young man. Willy's voice is coming from right upstage now. Bernard lowers his feet off the table and listens. Jenny, his father's secretary, enters.

JENNY: *(distressed)* Say, Bernard, will you go out in the hall?
BERNARD: What is that noise? Who is it?
260 **JENNY:** Mr. Loman. He just got off the elevator.
BERNARD: *(getting up)* Who's he arguing with?
JENNY: Nobody. There's nobody with him. I can't deal with him any more, and your father gets all upset everytime he comes. I've got a lot of typing to do, and your father's waiting to sign it. Will you see him?
WILLY: *(entering)* Touchdown! Touch—*(He sees Jenny.)* Jenny, Jenny, good to see you. How're ya? Workin'? Or still honest?
JENNY: Fine. How've you been feeling?
265 **WILLY:** Not much any more, Jenny. Ha, ha! *(He is surprised to see the rackets.)*
BERNARD: Hello, Uncle Willy.
WILLY: *(almost shocked)* Bernard! Well, look who's here! *(He comes quickly, guiltily, to Bernard and warmly shakes his hand.)*
BERNARD: How are you? Good to see you.
WILLY: What are you doing here?
270 **BERNARD:** Oh, just stopped by to see Pop. Get off my feet till my train leaves. I'm going to Washington in a few minutes.
WILLY: Is he in?
BERNARD: Yes, he's in his office with the accountant. Sit down.
WILLY: *(sitting down)* What're you going to do in Washington?
BERNARD: Oh, just a case I've got there, Willy.
275 **WILLY:** That so? *(indicating the rackets)* You going to play tennis there?
BERNARD: I'm staying with a friend who's got a court.
WILLY: Don't say. His own tennis court. Must be fine people, I bet.
BERNARD: They are, very nice. Dad tells me Biff's in town.
WILLY: *(with a big smile)* Yeah, Biff's in. Working on a very big deal, Bernard.
280 **BERNARD:** What's Biff doing?

WILLY: Well, he's been doing very big things in the West. But he
decided to establish himself here. Very big. We're having dinner. Did
I hear your wife had a boy?

BERNARD: That's right. Our second.

WILLY: Two boys! What do you know!

BERNARD: What kind of a deal has Biff got?

285 **WILLY:**   Well, Bill Oliver—very big sporting-goods man—he wants Biff
very badly. Called him in from the West. Long distance, carte
blanche, special deliveries. Your friends have their own private tennis
court?

BERNARD: You still with the old firm, Willy?

WILLY: *(after a pause)* I'm—I'm overjoyed to see how you made the
grade, Bernard, overjoyed. It's an encouraging thing to see a young
man really—really—Looks very good for Biff—very—*(He breaks off,
then.)* Bernard—*(He is so full of emotion, he breaks off again.)*

BERNARD: What is it, Willy?

WILLY: *(small and alone)* What—what's the secret?

290 **BERNARD:**   What secret?

WILLY: How—how did you? Why didn't he ever catch on?

BERNARD: I wouldn't know that, Willy.

WILLY: *(confidentially, desperately)* You were his friend, his boyhood
friend. There's something I don't understand about it. His life ended
after that Ebbets Field game. From the age of seventeen nothing good
ever happened to him.

BERNARD: He never trained himself for anything.

295 **WILLY:**   But he did, he did. After high school he took so many
correspondence courses. Radio mechanics; television; God knows
what, and never made the slightest mark.

BERNARD: *(taking off his glasses)* Willy, do you want to talk candidly?

WILLY: *(rising, faces Bernard)* I regard you as a very brilliant man,
Bernard. I value your advice.

BERNARD: Oh, the hell with the advice, Willy. I couldn't advise you.
There's just one thing I've always wanted to ask you. When he was
supposed to graduate, and the math teacher flunked him—

WILLY: Oh, that son-of-a-bitch ruined his life.

300 **BERNARD:**   Yeah, but, Willy, all he had to do was go to summer school
and make up that subject.

WILLY: That's right, that's right.

BERNARD: Did you tell him not to go to summer school?

WILLY: Me? I begged him to go. I ordered him to go!

BERNARD: Then why wouldn't he go?

305 **WILLY:**   Why? Why! Bernard, that question has been trailing me like a
ghost for the last fifteen years. He flunked the subject, and laid down
and died like a hammer hit him!

BERNARD: Take it easy, kid.

WILLY: Let me talk to you—I got nobody to talk to. Bernard, Bernard, was it my fault? Y'see? It keeps going around in my mind, maybe I did something to him. I got nothing to give him.

BERNARD: Don't take it so hard.

WILLY: Why did he lay down? What is the story there? You were his friend!

310 **BERNARD:** Willy, I remember, it was June, and our grades came out. And he'd flunked math.

WILLY: That son-of-a-bitch!

BERNARD: No, it wasn't right then. Biff just got very angry, I remember, and he was ready to enroll in summer school.

WILLY: *(surprised)* He was?

BERNARD: He wasn't beaten by it at all. But then, Willy, he disappeared from the block for almost a month. And I got the idea that he'd gone up to New England to see you. Did he have a talk with you then?

Willy stares in silence.

315 **BERNARD:** Willy?

WILLY: *(with a strong edge of resentment in his voice)* Yeah, he came to Boston. What about it?

BERNARD: Well, just that when he came back—I'll never forget this, it always mystifies me. Because I'd thought so well of Biff, even though he'd always taken advantage of me. I loved him, Willy, y'know? And he came back after that month and took his sneakers—remember those sneakers with "University of Virginia" printed on them? He was so proud of those, wore them every day. And he took them down in the cellar, and burned them up in the furnace. We had a fist fight. It lasted at least half an hour. Just the two of us, punching each other down the cellar, and crying right through it. I've often thought of how strange it was that I knew he'd given up his life. What happened in Boston, Willy?

Willy looks at him as at an intruder.

BERNARD: I just bring it up because you asked me.

WILLY: *(angrily)* Nothing. What do you mean, "What happened?" What's that got to do with anything?

320 **BERNARD:** Well, don't get sore.

WILLY: What are you trying to do, blame it on me? If a boy lays down is that my fault?

BERNARD: Now, Willy, don't get—

WILLY: Well, don't—don't talk to me that way! What does that mean, "What happened?"

Charley enters. He is in his vest, and he carries a bottle of bourbon.

CHARLEY: Hey, you're going to miss that train. *(He waves the bottle.)*

325 **BERNARD:** Yeah, I'm going. *(He takes the bottle.)* Thanks, Pop. *(He picks up his rackets and bag.)* Good-by, Willy, and don't worry about it. You know, "If at first you don't succeed . . ."

WILLY: Yes, I believe in that.

BERNARD: But sometimes, Willy, it's better for a man just to walk away.

WILLY: Walk away?

BERNARD: That's right.

330 **WILLY:** But if you can't walk away?

BERNARD: *(after a slight pause)* I guess that's when it's tough. *(Extending his hand.)* Good-by, Willy.

WILLY: *(shaking Bernard's hand)* Good-by, boy.

CHARLEY: *(an arm on Bernard's shoulder)* How do you like this kid? Gonna argue a case in front of the Supreme Court.

BERNARD: *(protesting)* Pop!

335 **WILLY:** *(genuinely shocked, pained, and happy)* No! The Supreme Court!

BERNARD: I gotta run, 'By, Dad!

CHARLEY: Knock 'em dead, Bernard!

Bernard goes off.

WILLY: *(as Charley takes out his wallet)* The Supreme Court! And he didn't even mention it!

CHARLEY: *(counting out money on the desk)* He don't have to—he's gonna do it.

340 **WILLY:** And you never told him what to do, did you? You never took any interest in him.

CHARLEY: My salvation is that I never took any interest in anything. There's some money—fifty dollars. I got an accountant inside.

WILLY: Charley, look . . . *(With difficulty.)* I got my insurance to pay. If you can manage it—I need a hundred and ten dollars.

Charley doesn't reply for a moment; merely stops moving.

WILLY: I'd draw it from my bank but Linda would know, and I . . .

CHARLEY: Sit down, Willy.

345 **WILLY:** *(moving toward the chair)* I'm keeping an account of everything, remember. I'll pay every penny back. *(He sits.)*

CHARLEY: Now listen to me, Willy.

WILLY: I want you to know I appreciate . . .

CHARLEY: *(sitting down on the table)* Willy, what're you doin'? What the hell is goin' on in your head?

WILLY: Why? I'm simply . . .

350 **CHARLEY:** I offered you a job. You can make fifty dollars a week. And I won't send you on the road.

WILLY: I've got a job.

CHARLEY: Without pay? What kind of a job is a job without pay? *(He rises.)* Now, look, kid, enough is enough. I'm no genius but I know when I'm being insulted.

WILLY: Insulted!

CHARLEY: Why don't you want to work for me?

355 **WILLY:** What's the matter with you? I've got a job.

CHARLEY: Then what're you walkin' in here every week for?

WILLY: *(getting up)* Well, if you don't want me to walk in here—

CHARLEY: I am offering you a job.

WILLY: I don't want your goddam job!

360 **CHARLEY:** When the hell are you going to grow up?

WILLY: *(furiously)* You big ignoramus, if you say that to me again I'll rap you one! I don't care how big you are! *(He's ready to fight.)*

Pause.

CHARLEY: *(kindly, going to him)* How much do you need, Willy?

WILLY: Charley, I'm strapped. I'm strapped. I don't know what to do. I was just fired.

CHARLEY: Howard fired you?

365 **WILLY:** That snotnose. Imagine that? I named him. I named him Howard.

CHARLEY: Willy, when're you gonna realize that them things don't mean anything? You named him Howard, but you can't sell that. The only thing you got in this world is what you can sell. And the funny thing is that you're a salesman, and you don't know that.

WILLY: I've always tried to think otherwise, I guess. I always felt that if a man was impressive, and well liked, that nothing—

CHARLEY: Why must everybody like you? Who liked J. P. Morgan?[4] Was he impressive? In a Turkish bath he'd look like a butcher. But with his pockets on he was very well liked. Now listen, Willy, I know you don't like me, and nobody can say I'm in love with you, but I'll give you a job because—just for the hell of it, put it that way. Now what do you say?

WILLY: I—I just can't work for you, Charley.

370 **CHARLEY:** What're you, jealous of me?

WILLY: I can't work for you, that's all, don't ask me why.

CHARLEY: *(angered, takes out more bills)* You been jealous of me all your life, you damned fool! Here, pay your insurance. *(He puts the money in Willy's hand.)*

WILLY: I'm keeping strict accounts.

CHARLEY: I've got some work to do. Take care of yourself. And pay your insurance.

375 **WILLY:** *(moving to the right)* Funny, y'know? After all the highways, and the trains, and the appointments, and the years, you end up worth more dead than alive.

---

[4] John Pierpont Morgan (1837–1913)—U.S. financier.

CHARLEY: Willy, nobody's worth nothin' dead. *(After a slight pause.)* Did you hear what I said?

Willy stands still, dreaming.

CHARLEY: Willy!

WILLY: Apologize to Bernard for me when you see him. I didn't mean to argue with him. He's a fine boy. They're all fine boys, and they'll end up big—all of them. Someday they'll all play tennis together. Wish me luck, Charley. He saw Bill Oliver today.

CHARLEY: Good luck.

380 **WILLY:** *(on the verge of tears)* Charley, you're the only friend I got. Isn't that a remarkable thing? *(He goes out.)*

CHARLEY: Jesus!

Charley stares after him a moment and follows. All light blacks out. Suddenly raucous music is heard, and a red glow rises behind the screen at right. Stanley, a young waiter, appears, carrying a table, followed by Happy, who is carrying two chairs.

STANLEY: *(putting the table down)* That's all right, Mr. Loman, I can handle it myself. *(He turns and takes the chairs from Happy and places them at the table.)*

HAPPY: *(glancing around)* Oh, this is better.

STANLEY: Sure, in the front there you're in the middle of all kinds a noise. Whenever you got a party, Mr. Loman, you just tell me and I'll put you back here. Y'know, there's a lotta people they don't like it private, because when they go out they like to see a lotta action around them because they're sick and tired to stay in the house by theirself. But I know you, you ain't from Hackensack. You know what I mean?

385 **HAPPY:** *(sitting down)* So, how's it coming, Stanley?

STANLEY: Ah, it's a dog's life. I only wish during the war they'd a took me in the Army. I coulda been dead by now.

HAPPY: My brother's back, Stanley.

STANLEY: Oh, he come back, heh? From the Far West.

HAPPY: Yeah, big cattle man, my brother, so treat him right. And my father's coming too.

390 **STANLEY:** Oh, your father too!

HAPPY: You got a couple of nice lobsters?

STANLEY: Hundred per cent, big.

HAPPY: I want them with the claws.

STANLEY: Don't worry, I don't give you no mice. *(Happy laughs.)* How about some wine? It'll put a head on the meal.

395 **HAPPY:** No. You remember, Stanley, that recipe I brought you from overseas? With the champagne in it?

STANLEY: Oh, yeah, sure. I still got it tacked up yet in the kitchen. But that'll have to cost a buck apiece anyways.

HAPPY: That's all right.

STANLEY: What'd you, hit a number or somethin'?

HAPPY: No, it's a little celebration. My brother is—I think he pulled off a big deal today. I think we're going into business together.

400 **STANLEY:** Great! That's the best for you. Because a family business, you know what I mean?—that's the best.

HAPPY: That's what I think.

STANLEY: 'Cause what's the difference? Somebody steals? It's in the family. Know what I mean? *(Sotto voce.)* Like this bartender here. The boss is goin' crazy what kinda leak he's got in the cash register. You put it in but it don't come out.

HAPPY: *(raising his head)* Sh!

STANLEY: What?

405 **HAPPY:** You notice I wasn't lookin' right or left, was I?

STANLEY: No.

HAPPY: And my eyes are closed.

STANLEY: So what's the—

HAPPY: Strudel's comin'.

410 **STANLEY:** *(catching on, looks around)* Ah, no, there's no—

He breaks off as a furred, lavishly dressed Girl enters and sits at the next table. Both follow her with their eyes.

STANLEY: Geez, how'd ya know?

HAPPY: I got radar or something. *(Staring directly at her profile.)* Oooooooo . . . Stanley.

STANLEY: I think that's for you, Mr. Loman.

HAPPY: Look at that mouth. Oh, God. And the binoculars.

415 **STANLEY:** Geez, you got a life, Mr. Loman.

HAPPY: Wait on her.

STANLEY: *(going to The Girl's table)* Would you like a menu, ma'am?

GIRL: I'm expecting someone, but I'd like a—

HAPPY: Why don't you bring her—excuse me, miss, do you mind? I sell champagne, and I'd like you to try my brand. Bring her a champagne, Stanley.

420 **GIRL:** That's awfully nice of you.

HAPPY: Don't mention it. It's all company money. *(He laughs.)*

GIRL: That's a charming product to be selling, isn't it?

HAPPY: Oh, gets to be like everything else. Selling is selling, y'know.

GIRL: I suppose.

425 **HAPPY:** You don't happen to sell, do you?

GIRL: No, I don't sell.

HAPPY: Would you object to a compliment from a stranger? You ought to be on a magazine cover.

GIRL: *(looking at him a little archly)* I have been.

Stanley comes in with a glass of champagne.

HAPPY: What'd I say before, Stanley? You see? She's a cover girl.
430 **STANLEY:**   Oh, I could see, I could see.
HAPPY: *(to The Girl)* What magazine?
GIRL: Oh, a lot of them. *(She takes the drink.)* Thank you.
HAPPY: You know what they say in France, don't you? "Champagne is
    the drink of the complexion"—Hya, Biff!

Biff has entered and sits with Happy.

BIFF: Hello, kid. Sorry I'm late.
435 **HAPPY:**   I just got here. Uh, Miss—?
GIRL: Forsythe.
HAPPY: Miss Forsythe, this is my brother.
BIFF: Is Dad here?
HAPPY: His name is Biff. You might've heard of him. Great football
    player.
440 **GIRL:**   Really? What team?
HAPPY: Are you familiar with football?
GIRL: No, I'm afraid I'm not.
HAPPY: Biff is quarterback with the New York Giants.
GIRL: Well, that is nice, isn't it? *(She drinks.)*
445 **HAPPY:**   Good health.
GIRL: I'm happy to meet you.
HAPPY: That's my name. Hap. It's really Harold, but at West Point they
    called me Happy.
GIRL: *(now really impressed)* Oh, I see. How do you do? *(She turns her
    profile.)*
BIFF: Isn't Dad coming?
450 **HAPPY:**   You want her?
BIFF: Oh, I could never make that.
HAPPY: I remember the time that idea would never come into your
    head. Where's the old confidence, Biff?
BIFF: I just saw Oliver—
HAPPY: Wait a minute. I've got to see that old confidence again. Do you
    want her? She's on call.
455 **BIFF:**   Oh, no. *(He turns to look at The Girl.)*
HAPPY: I'm telling you. Watch this. *(Turning to The Girl.)* Honey? *(She
    turns to him.)* Are you busy?
GIRL: Well, I am . . . but I could make a phone call.
HAPPY: Do that, will you, honey? And see if you can get a friend. We'll
    be here for a while. Biff is one of the greatest football players in the
    country.
GIRL: *(standing up)* Well, I'm certainly happy to meet you.
460 **HAPPY:**   Come back soon.
GIRL: I'll try.

HAPPY: Don't try, honey, try hard.

The Girl exits. Stanley follows, shaking his head in bewildered admiration.

HAPPY: Isn't that a shame now? A beautiful girl like that? That's why I
can't get married. There's not a good woman in a thousand. New York
is loaded with them, kid!

BIFF: Hap, look—

465 **HAPPY:** I told you she was on call!

BIFF: *(strangely unnerved)* Cut it out, will ya? I want to say something to
you.

HAPPY: Did you see Oliver?

BIFF: I saw him all right. Now look, I want to tell Dad a couple of things
and I want you to help me.

HAPPY: What? Is he going to back you?

470 **BIFF:** Are you crazy? You're out of your goddam head, you know that?

HAPPY: Why? What happened?

BIFF: *(breathlessly)* I did a terrible thing today, Hap. It's been the
strangest day I ever went through. I'm all numb, I swear.

HAPPY: You mean he wouldn't see you?

BIFF: Well, I waited six hours for him, see? All day. Kept sending my
name in. Even tried to date his secretary so she'd get me to him, but
no soap.

475 **HAPPY:** Because you're not showin' the old confidence, Biff. He
remembered you, didn't he?

BIFF: *(stopping Happy with a gesture)* Finally, about five o'clock, he comes
out. Didn't remember who I was or anything. I felt like such an idiot,
Hap.

HAPPY: Did you tell him my Florida idea?

BIFF: He walked away. I saw him for one minute. I got so mad I could've
torn the walls down! How the hell did I ever get the idea I was a
salesman there? I even believed myself that I'd been a salesman for
him! And then he gave me one look and—I realized what a ridiculous
lie my whole life has been! We've been talking in a dream for fifteen
years. I was a shipping clerk.

HAPPY: What'd you do?

480 **BIFF:** *(with great tension and wonder)* Well, he left, see. And the
secretary went out. I was all alone in the waiting-room. I don't
know what came over me, Hap. The next thing I know I'm in his
office—paneled walls, everything. I can't explain it. I—Hap, I took
his fountain pen.

HAPPY: Geez, did he catch you?

BIFF: I ran out. I ran down all eleven flights. I ran and ran and ran.

HAPPY: That was an awful dumb—what'd you do that for?

BIFF: *(agonized)* I don't know, I just—wanted to take something, I don't
know. You gotta help me, Hap. I'm gonna tell Pop.

485 **HAPPY:** You crazy? What for?

BIFF: Hap, he's got to understand that I'm not the man somebody lends that kind of money to. He thinks I've been spiting him all these years and it's eating him up.

HAPPY: That's just it. You tell him something nice.

BIFF: I can't.

HAPPY: Say you got a lunch date with Oliver tomorrow.

490 **BIFF:**   So what do I do tomorrow?

HAPPY: You leave the house tomorrow and come back at night and say Oliver is thinking it over. And he thinks it over for a couple of weeks, and gradually it fades away and nobody's the worse.

BIFF: But it'll go on forever!

HAPPY: Dad is never so happy as when he's looking forward to something!

Willy enters.

HAPPY: Hello, scout!

495 **WILLY:**   Gee, I haven't been here in years!

Stanley has followed Willy in and sets a chair for him. Stanley starts off but Happy stops him.

HAPPY: Stanley!

Stanley stands by, waiting for an order.

BIFF: *(going to Willy with guilt, as to an invalid)* Sit down, Pop. You want a drink?

WILLY: Sure, I don't mind.

BIFF: Let's get a load on.

500 **WILLY:**   You look worried.

BIFF: N-no. *(To Stanley.)* Scotch all around. Make it doubles.

STANLEY: Doubles, right. *(He goes.)*

WILLY: You had a couple already, didn't you?

BIFF: Just a couple, yeah.

505 **WILLY:**   Well, what happened, boy? *(Nodding affirmatively, with a smile.)* Everything go all right?

BIFF: *(takes a breath, then reaches out and grasps Willy's hand)* Pal . . . *(He is smiling bravely, and Willy is smiling too.)* I had an experience today.

HAPPY: Terrific, Pop.

WILLY: That so? What happened?

BIFF: *(high, slightly alcoholic, above the earth)* I'm going to tell you everything from first to last. It's been a strange day. *(Silence. He looks around, composes himself as best he can, but his breath keeps breaking the rhythm of his voice.)* I had to wait quite a while for him, and—

510 **WILLY:**   Oliver?

BIFF: Yeah, Oliver. All day, as a matter of cold fact. And a lot of— instances—facts, Pop, facts about my life came back to me. Who was it, Pop? Who ever said I was a salesman with Oliver?

WILLY: Well, you were.

BIFF: No, Dad, I was a shipping clerk.

WILLY: But you were practically—

515 **BIFF:** *(with determination)* Dad, I don't know who said it first, but I was never a salesman for Bill Oliver.

WILLY: What're you talking about?

BIFF: Let's hold on to the facts tonight, Pop. We're not going to get anywhere bullin' around. I was a shipping clerk.

WILLY: *(angrily)* All right, now listen to me—

BIFF: Why don't you let me finish?

520 **WILLY:** I'm not interested in stories about the past or any crap of that kind because the woods are burning, boys, you understand? There's a big blaze going on all around. I was fired today.

BIFF: *(shocked)* How could you be?

WILLY: I was fired, and I'm looking for a little good news to tell your mother, because the woman has waited and the woman has suffered. The gist of it is that I haven't got a story left in my head, Biff. So don't give me a lecture about facts and aspects. I am not interested. Now what've you got to say to me?

Stanley enters with three drinks. They wait until he leaves.

WILLY: Did you see Oliver?

BIFF: Jesus, Dad!

525 **WILLY:** You mean you didn't go up there?

HAPPY: Sure he went up there.

BIFF: I did. I—saw him. How could they fire you?

WILLY: *(on the edge of his chair)* What kind of a welcome did he give you?

BIFF: He won't even let you work on commission?

530 **WILLY:** I'm out! *(Driving.)* So tell me, he gave you a warm welcome?

HAPPY: Sure, Pop, sure!

BIFF: *(driven)* Well, it was kind of—

WILLY: I was wondering if he'd remember you. *(To Happy.)* Imagine, man doesn't see him for ten, twelve years and gives him that kind of a welcome!

HAPPY: Damn right!

535 **BIFF:** *(trying to return to the offensive)* Pop, look—

WILLY: You know why he remembered you, don't you? Because you impressed him in those days.

BIFF: Let's talk quietly and get this down to the facts, huh?

WILLY: *(as though Biff had been interrupting)* Well, what happened? It's great news, Biff. Did he take you into his office or'd you talk in the waiting-room?

BIFF: Well, he came in, see, and—

540 **WILLY:** *(with a big smile)* What'd he say? Betcha he threw his arm around you.

BIFF: Well, he kinda—

WILLY: He's a fine man. *(To Happy.)* Very hard man to see, y'know.

HAPPY: *(agreeing)* Oh, I know.

WILLY: *(to Biff)* Is that where you had the drinks?

545 **BIFF:**   Yeah, he gave me a couple of—no, no!

HAPPY: *(cutting in)* He told him my Florida idea.

WILLY: Don't interrupt. *(To Biff.)* How'd he react to the Florida idea?

BIFF: Dad, will you give me a minute to explain?

WILLY: I've been waiting for you to explain since I sat down here! What happened? He took you into his office and what?

550 **BIFF:**   Well—I talked. And—and he listened, see.

WILLY: Famous for the way he listens, y'know. What was his answer?

BIFF: His answer was—*(He breaks off, suddenly angry.)* Dad, you're not letting me tell you what I want to tell you!

WILLY: *(accusing, angered)* You didn't see him, did you?

BIFF: I did see him!

555 **WILLY:**   What'd you insult him or something? You insulted him, didn't you?

BIFF: Listen, will you let me out of it, will you just let me out of it!

HAPPY: What the hell!

WILLY: Tell me what happened!

BIFF: *(to Happy)* I can't talk to him!

A single trumpet note jars the ear. The light of green leaves stains the house, which holds the air of night and a dream. Young Bernard enters and knocks on the door of the house.

560 **YOUNG BERNARD:**   *(frantically)* Mrs. Loman, Mrs. Loman!

HAPPY: Tell him what happened!

BIFF: *(to Happy)* Shut up and leave me alone!

WILLY: No, no! You had to go and flunk math!

BIFF: What math? What're you talking about?

565 **YOUNG BERNARD:**   Mrs. Loman, Mrs. Loman!

Linda appears in the house, as of old.

WILLY: *(wildly)* Math, math, math!

BIFF: Take it easy, Pop!

YOUNG BERNARD: Mrs. Loman!

WILLY: *(furiously)* If you hadn't flunked you'd've been set by now!

570 **BIFF:**   Now, look, I'm gonna tell you what happened, and you're going to listen to me.

YOUNG BERNARD: Mrs. Loman!

BIFF: I waited six hours—

HAPPY: What the hell are you saying?

BIFF: I kept sending in my name but he wouldn't see me. So finally he . . . *(He continues unheard as light fades low on the restaurant.)*

575 **YOUNG BERNARD:**   Biff flunked math!

LINDA: No!

YOUNG BERNARD: Birnbaum flunked him! They won't graduate him!

LINDA: But they have to. He's gotta go to the university. Where is he? Biff! Biff!

YOUNG BERNARD: No, he left. He went to Grand Central.

580 **LINDA:**   Grand—You mean he went to Boston!

YOUNG BERNARD: Is Uncle Willy in Boston?

LINDA: Oh, maybe Willy can talk to the teacher. Oh, the poor, poor boy!

Light on house area snaps out.

BIFF: *(at the table, now audible, holding up a gold fountain pen)* . . . so I'm washed up with Oliver, you understand? Are you listening to me?

WILLY: *(at a loss)* Yeah, sure. If you hadn't flunked—

585 **BIFF:**   Flunked what? What're you talking about?

WILLY: Don't blame everything on me! I didn't flunk math—you did! What pen?

HAPPY: That was awful dumb, Biff, a pen like that is worth—

WILLY: *(seeing the pen for the first time)* You took Oliver's pen?

BIFF: *(weakening)* Dad, I just explained it to you.

590 **WILLY:**   You stole Bill Oliver's fountain pen!

BIFF: I didn't exactly steal it! That's just what I've been explaining to you!

HAPPY: He had it in his hand and just then Oliver walked in, so he got nervous and stuck it in his pocket!

WILLY: My God, Biff!

BIFF: I never intended to do it, Dad!

595 **OPERATOR'S VOICE:**   Standish Arms, good evening!

WILLY: *(shouting)* I'm not in my room!

BIFF: *(frightened)* Dad, what's the matter? *(He and Happy stand up.)*

OPERATOR: Ringing Mr. Loman for you!

WILLY: I'm not there, stop it!

600 **BIFF:**   *(horrified, gets down on one knee before Willy)* Dad, I'll make good, I'll make good. *(Willy tries to get to his feet. Biff holds him down.)* Sit down now.

WILLY: No, you're no good, you're no good for anything.

BIFF: I am, Dad, I'll find something else, you understand? Now don't worry about anything. *(He holds up Willy's face.)* Talk to me, Dad.

OPERATOR: Mr. Loman does not answer. Shall I page him?

WILLY: *(attempting to stand, as though to rush and silence the Operator)* No, no, no!

605 **HAPPY:**   He'll strike something, Pop.

WILLY: No, no . . .

BIFF: *(desperately, standing over Willy)* Pop, listen! Listen to me! I'm telling you something good. Oliver talked to his partner about the Florida idea. You listening? He—he talked to his partner, and he came to me . . . I'm going to be all right, you hear? Dad, listen to me, he said it was just a question of the amount!

WILLY: Then you . . . got it?

HAPPY: He's gonna be terrific, Pop!

610 **WILLY:** *(trying to stand)* Then you got it, haven't you? You got it! You got it!

BIFF: *(agonized, holds Willy down)* No, no. Look, Pop. I'm supposed to have lunch with them tomorrow. I'm just telling you this so you'll know that I can still make an impression, Pop. And I'll make good somewhere, but I can't go tomorrow, see?

WILLY: Why not? You simply—

BIFF: But the pen, Pop!

WILLY: You give it to him and tell him it was an oversight!

615 **HAPPY:** Sure, have lunch tomorrow!

BIFF: I can't say that—

WILLY: You were doing a crossword puzzle and accidentally used his pen!

BIFF: Listen, kid, I took those balls years ago, now I walk in with his fountain pen? That clinches it, don't you see? I can't face him like that! I'll try elsewhere.

PAGE'S VOICE: Paging Mr. Loman!

620 **WILLY:** Don't you want to be anything?

BIFF: Pop, how can I go back?

WILLY: You don't want to be anything, is that what's behind it?

BIFF: *(now angry at Willy for not crediting his sympathy)* Don't take it that way! You think it was easy walking into that office after what I'd done to him? A team of horses couldn't have dragged me back to Bill Oliver!

WILLY: Then why'd you go?

625 **BIFF:** Why did I go? Why did I go? Look at you! Look at what's become of you!

Off left, The Woman laughs.

WILLY: Biff, you're going to go to that lunch tomorrow, or—

BIFF: I can't go. I've got no appointment!

HAPPY: Biff, for . . . !

WILLY: Are you spiting me?

630 **BIFF:** Don't take it that way! Goddammit!

WILLY: *(strikes Biff and falters away from the table)* You rotten little louse! Are you spiting me?

THE WOMAN: Someone's at the door, Willy!

BIFF: I'm no good, can't you see what I am?

HAPPY: *(separating them)* Hey, you're in a restaurant! Now cut it out, both of you! *(The Girls enter.)* Hello, girls, sit down.

The Woman laughs, off left.

635   **MISS FORSYTHE:**   I guess we might as well. This is Letta.

    THE WOMAN: Willy, are you going to wake up?

    BIFF: *(ignoring Willy)* How're ya, miss, sit down. What do you drink?

    MISS FORSYTHE: Letta might not be able to stay long.

    LETTA: I gotta get up very early tomorrow. I got jury duty. I'm so excited! Were you fellows ever on a jury?

640   **BIFF:**   No, but I been in front of them! *(The Girls laugh.)* This is my father.

    LETTA: Isn't he cute? Sit down with us, Pop.

    HAPPY: Sit him down, Biff!

    BIFF: *(going to him)* Come on, slugger, drink us under the table. To hell with it! Come on, sit down, pal.

On Biff's last insistence, Willy is about to sit.

    THE WOMAN: *(now urgently)* Willy, are you going to answer the door!

The Woman's call pulls Willy back. He starts right, befuddled.

645   **BIFF:**   Hey, where are you going?

    WILLY: Open the door.

    BIFF: The door?

    WILLY: The washroom . . . the door . . . where's the door?

    BIFF: *(leading Willy to the left)* Just go straight down.

Willy moves left.

650   **THE WOMAN:**   Willy, Willy, are you going to get up, get up, get up, get up?

Willy exits left.

    LETTA: I think it's sweet you bring your daddy along.

    MISS FORSYTHE: Oh, he isn't really your father!

    BIFF: *(at left, turning to her resentfully)* Miss Forsythe, you've just seen a prince walk by. A fine, troubled prince. A hard-working, unappreciated prince. A pal, you understand? A good companion. Always for his boys.

    LETTA: That's so sweet.

655   **HAPPY:**   Well, girls, what's the program? We're wasting time. Come on, Biff. Gather round. Where would you like to go?

    BIFF: Why don't you do something for him?

    HAPPY: Me!

    BIFF: Don't you give a damn for him, Hap?

    HAPPY: What're you talking about? I'm the one who—

660   **BIFF:**   I sense it, you don't give a good goddam about him. *(He takes the rolled-up hose from his pocket and puts it on the table in front of Happy.)* Look what I found in the cellar, for Christ's sake. How can you bear to let it go on?

    HAPPY: Me? Who goes away? Who runs off and—

BIFF: Yeah, but he doesn't mean anything to you. You could help him—
I can't! Don't you understand what I'm talking about? He's going to
kill himself, don't you know that?

HAPPY: Don't I know it! Me!

BIFF: Hap, help him! Jesus . . . help him . . . Help me, help me, I can't
bear to look at his face! *(Ready to weep, he hurries out, up right.)*

665   **HAPPY:**   *(starting after him)* Where are you going?

MISS FORSYTHE: What's he so mad about?

HAPPY: Come on, girls, we'll catch up with him.

MISS FORSYTHE: *(as Happy pushes her out)* Say, I don't like that temper
of his!

HAPPY: He's just a little overstrung, he'll be all right!

670   **WILLY:**   *(off left, as The Woman laughs)* Don't answer! Don't answer!

LETTA: Don't you want to tell your father—

HAPPY: No, that's not my father. He's just a guy. Come on, we'll catch
Biff, and, honey, we're going to paint this town! Stanley, where's the
check! Hey, Stanley!

They exit. Stanley looks toward left.

STANLEY: *(calling to Happy indignantly)* Mr. Loman! Mr. Loman!

*Stanley picks up a chair and follows them off. Knocking is heard off left. The
Woman enters, laughing. Willy follows her. She is in a black slip; he is buttoning his shirt. Raw, sensuous music accompanies their speech.*

WILLY: Will you stop laughing? Will you stop?

675   **THE WOMAN:**   Aren't you going to answer the door? He'll wake the
whole hotel.

WILLY: I'm not expecting anybody.

THE WOMAN: Whyn't you have another drink, honey, and stop being
so damn self-centered?

WILLY: I'm so lonely.

THE WOMAN: You know you ruined me, Willy? From now on, whenever
you come to the office, I'll see that you go right through to the
buyers. No waiting at my desk any more, Willy. You ruined me.

680   **WILLY:**   That's nice of you to say that.

THE WOMAN: Gee, you are self-centered! Why so sad? You are the
saddest self-centeredest soul I ever did see-saw. *(She laughs. He kisses
her.)* Come on inside, drummer boy. It's silly to be dressing in the
middle of the night. *(As knocking is heard.)* Aren't you going to answer
the door?

WILLY: They're knocking on the wrong door.

THE WOMAN: But I felt the knocking. And he heard us talking in here.
Maybe the hotel's on fire!

WILLY: *(his terror rising)* It's a mistake.

685   **THE WOMAN:**   Then tell him to go away!

WILLY: There's nobody there.

THE WOMAN: It's getting on my nerves, Willy. There's somebody standing out there and it's getting on my nerves!

WILLY: *(pushing her away from him)* All right, stay in the bathroom here, and don't come out. I think there's a law in Massachusetts about it, so don't come out. It may be that new room clerk. He looked very mean. So don't come out. It's a mistake, there's no fire.

The knocking is heard again. He takes a few steps away from her, and she vanishes into the wing. The light follows him, and now he is facing Young Biff, who carries a suitcase. Biff steps toward him. The music is gone.

BIFF: Why didn't you answer?

690   **WILLY:**   Biff! What are you doing in Boston?

BIFF: Why didn't you answer? I've been knocking for five minutes, I called you on the phone—

WILLY: I just heard you. I was in the bathroom and had the door shut. Did anything happen home?

BIFF: Dad—I let you down.

WILLY: What do you mean?

695   **BIFF:**   Dad . . .

WILLY: Biffo, what's this about? *(Putting his arm around Biff.)* Come on, let's go downstairs and get you a malted.

BIFF: Dad, I flunked math.

WILLY: Not for the term?

BIFF: The term. I haven't got enough credits to graduate.

700   **WILLY:**   You mean to say Bernard wouldn't give you the answers?

BIFF: He did, he tried, but I only got a sixty-one.

WILLY: And they wouldn't give you four points?

BIFF: Birnbaum refused absolutely. I begged him, Pop, but he won't give me those points. You gotta talk to him before they close the school. Because if he saw the kind of man you are, and you just talked to him in your way, I'm sure he'd come through for me. The class came right before practice, see, and I didn't go enough. Would you talk to him? He'd like you, Pop. You know the way you could talk.

WILLY: You're on. We'll drive right back.

705   **BIFF:**   Oh, Dad, good work! I'm sure he'll change it for you!

WILLY: Go downstairs and tell the clerk I'm checkin' out. Go right down.

BIFF: Yes, Sir! See, the reason he hates me, Pop—one day he was late for class so I got up at the blackboard and imitated him. I crossed my eyes and talked with a lithp.

WILLY: *(laughing)* You did? The kids like it?

BIFF: They nearly died laughing!

710   **WILLY:**   Yeah? What'd you do?

BIFF: The thquare root of thixthy twee is . . . *(Willy bursts out laughing; Biff joins him.)* And in the middle of it he walked in!

Willy laughs and The Woman joins in offstage.

WILLY: *(without hesitating)* Hurry downstairs and—
BIFF: Somebody in there?
WILLY: No, that was next door.

The Woman laughs offstage.

715   **BIFF:**   Somebody got in your bathroom!
WILLY: No, it's the next room, there's a party—
THE WOMAN: *(enters, laughing. She lisps this)* Can I come in? There's something in the bathtub, Willy, and it's moving!

Willy looks at Biff, who is staring open-mouthed and horrified at The Woman.

WILLY: Ah—you better go back to your room. They must be finished painting by now. They're painting her room so I let her take a shower here. Go back, go back . . . *(He pushes her.)*
THE WOMAN: *(resisting)* But I've got to get dressed, Willy, I can't—
720   **WILLY:**   Get out of here! Go back, go back . . . *(Suddenly striving for the ordinary.)* This is Miss Francis, Biff, she's a buyer. They're painting her room. Go back, Miss Francis, go back . . .
THE WOMAN: But my clothes, I can't go out naked in the hall!
WILLY: *(pushing her offstage)* Get outa here! Go back, go back!

Biff slowly sits down on his suitcase as the argument continues offstage.

THE WOMAN: Where's my stockings? You promised me stockings, Willy!
WILLY: I have no stockings here!
725   **THE WOMAN:**   You had two boxes of size nine sheers for me, and I want them!
WILLY: Here, for God's sake, will you get outa here!
THE WOMAN: *(enters holding a box of stockings)* I just hope there's nobody in the hall. That's all I hope. *(To Biff.)* Are you football or baseball?
BIFF: Football.
THE WOMAN: *(angry, humiliated)* That's me too. G'night. *(She snatches her clothes from Willy, and walks out.)*
730   **WILLY:**   *(after a pause)* Well, better get going. I want to get to the school first thing in the morning. Get my suits out of the closet. I'll get my valise. *(Biff doesn't move.)* What's the matter? *(Biff remains motionless, tears falling.)* She's a buyer. Buys for J. H. Simmons. She lives down the hall—they're painting. You don't imagine—*(He breaks off. After a pause.)* Now listen, pal, she's just a buyer. She sees merchandise in her room and they have to keep it looking just so . . . *(Pause. Assuming command.)* All right, get my suits. *(Biff doesn't move.)* Now stop crying and do as I say. I gave you an order. Biff, I gave you an order! Is that what you do when I give you an order? How dare you cry! *(Putting his

arm around Biff.) Now look, Biff, when you grow up you'll understand about these things. You mustn't—you mustn't overemphasize a thing like this. I'll see Birnbaum first thing in the morning.

BIFF: Never mind.

WILLY: *(getting down beside Biff)* Never mind! He's going to give you those points. I'll see to it.

BIFF: He wouldn't listen to you.

WILLY: He certainly will listen to me. You need those points for the U. of Virginia.

735 **BIFF:** I'm not going there.

WILLY: Heh? If I can't get him to change that mark you'll make it up in summer school. You've got all summer to—

BIFF: *(his weeping breaking from him)* Dad . . .

WILLY: *(infected by it)* Oh, my boy . . .

BIFF: Dad . . .

740 **WILLY:** She's nothing to me, Biff. I was lonely, I was terribly lonely.

BIFF: You—you gave her Mama's stockings! *(His tears break through and he rises to go.)*

WILLY: *(grabbing for Biff)* I gave you an order!

BIFF: Don't touch me, you—liar!

WILLY: Apologize for that!

745 **BIFF:** You fake! You phony little fake! You fake! *(Overcome, he turns quickly and weeping fully goes out with his suitcase. Willy is left on the floor on his knees.)*

WILLY: I gave you an order! Biff, come back here or I'll beat you! Come back here! I'll whip you!

Stanley comes quickly in from the right and stands in front of Willy.

WILLY: *(shouts at Stanley)* I gave you an order . . .

STANLEY: Hey, let's pick it up, pick it up, Mr. Loman. *(He helps Willy to his feet.)* Your boys left with the chippies. They said they'll see you home.

A second waiter watches some distance away.

WILLY: But we were supposed to have dinner together.

Music is heard, Willy's theme.

750 **STANLEY:** Can you make it?

WILLY: I'll—sure, I can make it. *(Suddenly concerned about his clothes.)* Do I—I look all right?

STANLEY: Sure, you look all right. *(He flicks a speck off Willy's lapel.)*

WILLY: Here—here's a dollar.

STANLEY: Oh, your son paid me. It's all right.

755 **WILLY:** *(putting it in Stanley's hand)* No, take it. You're a good boy.

STANLEY: Oh, no, you don't have to . . .

WILLY: Here—here's some more, I don't need it any more. *(After a slight pause.)* Tell me—is there a seed store in the neighborhood?

STANLEY: Seeds? You mean like to plant?

As Willy turns, Stanley slips the money back into his jacket pocket.

WILLY: Yes. Carrots, peas . . .

760   **STANLEY:**   Well, there's hardware stores on Sixth Avenue, but it may be too late now.

WILLY: *(anxiously)* Oh, I'd better hurry. I've got to get some seeds. *(He starts off to the right.)* I've got to get some seeds, right away.
Nothing's planted. I don't have a thing in the ground.

Willy hurries out as the light goes down. Stanley moves over to the right after him, watches him off. The other waiter has been staring at Willy.

STANLEY: *(to the waiter)* Well, whatta you looking at?

The waiter picks up the chairs and moves off right. Stanley takes the table and follows him. The light fades on this area. There is a long pause, the sound of the flute coming over. The light gradually rises on the kitchen, which is empty. Happy appears at the door of the house, followed by Biff. Happy is carrying a large bunch of long-stemmed roses. He enters the kitchen, looks around for Linda. Not seeing her, he turns to Biff, who is just outside the house door, and makes a gesture with his hands, indicating "Not here, I guess." He looks into the livingroom and freezes. Inside, Linda, unseen, is seated, Willy's coat on her lap. She rises ominously and quietly and moves toward Happy, who backs up into the kitchen, afraid.

HAPPY: Hey, what're you doing up? *(Linda says nothing but moves toward him implacably.)* Where's Pop? *(He keeps backing to the right, and now Linda is in full view in the doorway to the livingroom.)* Is he sleeping?

LINDA: Where were you?

765   **HAPPY:**   *(trying to laugh it off)* We met two girls, Mom, very fine types. Here, we brought you some flowers. *(Offering them to her.)* Put them in your room, Ma.

She knocks them to the floor at Biff's feet. He has now come inside and closed the door behind him. She stares at Biff, silent.

HAPPY: Now what'd you do that for? Mom, I want you to have some flowers—

LINDA: *(cutting Happy off, violently to Biff)* Don't you care whether he lives or dies?

HAPPY: *(going to the stairs)* Come upstairs, Biff.

BIFF: *(with a flare of disgust, to Happy)* Go away from me! *(To Linda.)* What do you mean, lives or dies? Nobody's dying around here, pal.

770   **LINDA:**   Get out of my sight! Get out of here!

BIFF: I wanna see the boss.

LINDA: You're not going near him!

BIFF: Where is he? *(He moves into the livingroom and Linda follows.)*

LINDA: *(shouting after Biff)* You invite him for dinner. He looks forward to it all day—*(Biff appears in his parents' bedroom, looks around, and exits)*—and then you desert him there. There's no stranger you'd do that to!

775 **HAPPY:** Why? He had a swell time with us. Listen, when I—*(Linda comes back into the kitchen)*—desert him I hope I don't outlive the day!

LINDA: Get out of here!

HAPPY: Now look, Mom . . .

LINDA: Did you have to go to women tonight? You and your lousy rotten whores!

Biff re-enters the kitchen.

HAPPY: Mom, all we did was follow Biff around trying to cheer him up! *(To Biff.)* Boy, what a night you gave me!

780 **LINDA:** Get out of here, both of you, and don't come back! I don't want you tormenting him any more. Go on now, get your things together! *(To Biff.)* You can sleep in his apartment. *(She starts to pick up the flowers and stops herself.)* Pick up this stuff, I'm not your maid any more. Pick it up, you bum, you!

Happy turns his back to her in refusal. Biff slowly moves over and gets down on his knees, picking up the flowers.

LINDA: You're a pair of animals! Not one, not another living soul would have had the cruelty to walk out on that man in a restaurant!

BIFF: *(not looking at her)* Is that what he said?

LINDA: He didn't have to say anything. He was so humiliated he nearly limped when he came in.

HAPPY: But, Mom he had a great time with us—

785 **BIFF:** *(cutting him off violently)* Shut up!

Without another word, Happy goes upstairs.

LINDA: You! You didn't even go in to see if he was all right!

BIFF: *(still on the floor in front of Linda, the flowers in his hand; with self-loathing)* No. Didn't. Didn't do a damned thing. How do you like that, heh? Left him babbling in a toilet.

LINDA: You louse. You . . .

BIFF: Now you hit it on the nose! *(He gets up, throws the flowers in the wastebasket.)* The scum of the earth, and you're looking at him!

790 **LINDA:** Get out of here!

BIFF: I gotta talk to the boss, Mom. Where is he?

LINDA: You're not going near him. Get out of this house!

BIFF: *(with absolute assurance, determination)* No. We're gonna have an abrupt conversation, him and me.

LINDA: You're not talking to him!

Hammering is heard from outside the house, off right. Biff turns toward the noise.

795 **LINDA:**   *(suddenly pleading)* Will you please leave him alone?
BIFF: What's he doing out there?
LINDA: He's planting the garden!
BIFF: *(quietly)* Now? Oh, my God!

Biff moves outside, Linda following. The light dies down on them and comes up on the center of the apron as Willy walks into it. He is carrying a flashlight, a hoe and a handful of seed packets. He raps the top of the hoe sharply to fix it firmly, and then moves to the left, measuring off the distance with his foot. He holds the flashlight to look at the seed packets, reading off the instructions. He is in the blue of night.

WILLY: Carrots . . . quarter-inch apart. Rows . . . one-foot rows. *(He measures it off.)* One foot. *(He puts down a package and measures off.)* Beets. *(He puts down another package and measures again.)* Lettuce. *(He reads the package, puts it down.)* One foot—*(He breaks off as Ben appears at the right and moves slowly down to him.)* What a proposition, ts, ts. Terrific, terrific. 'Cause she's suffered, Ben, the woman has suffered. You understand me? A man can't go out the way he came in, Ben, a man has got to add up to something. You can't, you can't—*(Ben moves toward him as though to interrupt.)* You gotta consider, now. Don't answer so quick. Remember, it's a guaranteed twenty-thousand-dollar proposition. Now look, Ben, I want you to go through the ins and outs of this thing with me. I've got nobody to talk to, Ben, and the woman has suffered, you hear me?
800 **BEN:**   *(standing still, considering)* What's the proposition?
WILLY: It's twenty thousand dollars on the barrelhead. Guaranteed, gilt-edged, you understand?
BEN: You don't want to make a fool of yourself. They might not honor the policy.
WILLY: How can they dare refuse? Didn't I work like a coolie to meet every premium on the nose? And now they don't pay off? Impossible!
BEN: It's called a cowardly thing, William.
805 **WILLY:**   Why? Does it take more guts to stand here the rest of my life ringing up a zero?
BEN: *(yielding)* That's a point, William. *(He moves, thinking, turns.)* And twenty thousand—that *is* something one can feel with the hand, it is there.
WILLY: *(now assured, with rising power)* Oh, Ben, that's the whole beauty of it! I see it like a diamond, shining in the dark, hard and rough, that I can pick up and touch in my hand. Not like—like an appointment! This would not be another damned-fool appointment, Ben, and it changes all the aspects. Because he thinks I'm nothing, see, and so he spites me. But the funeral—*(Straightening up.)* Ben, that

funeral will be massive! They'll come from Maine, Massachusetts, Vermont, New Hampshire! All the old-timers with the strange license plates—that boy will be thunder-struck, Ben, because he never realized—I am known! Rhode Island, New York, New Jersey—I am known, Ben, and he'll see it with his eyes once and for all. He'll see what I am, Ben! He's in for a shock, that boy!

BEN: *(coming down to the edge of the garden)* He'll call you a coward.

WILLY: *(suddenly fearful)* No, that would be terrible.

810 **BEN:** Yes. And a damned fool.

WILLY: No, no, he mustn't, I won't have that! *(He is broken and desperate.)*

BEN: He'll hate you, William.

The gay music of the boys is heard.

WILLY: Oh, Ben, how do we get back to all the great times? Used to be so full of light, and comradeship, the sleigh-riding in winter, and the ruddiness on his cheeks. And always some kind of good news coming up, always something nice coming up ahead. And never even let me carry the valises in the house, and simonizing, simonizing that little red car! Why, why can't I give him something and not have him hate me?

BEN: Let me think about it. *(He glances at his watch.)* I still have a little time. Remarkable proposition, but you've got to be sure you're not making a fool of yourself.

Ben drifts off upstage and goes out of sight. Biff comes down from the left.

815 **WILLY:** *(suddenly conscious of Biff, turns and looks up at him, then begins picking up the packages of seeds in confusion)* Where the hell is that seed? *(Indignantly.)* You can't see nothing out here! They boxed in the whole goddam neighborhood!

BIFF: There are people all around here. Don't you realize that?

WILLY: I'm busy. Don't bother me.

BIFF: *(taking the hoe from Willy)* I'm saying good-by to you, Pop. *(Willy looks at him, silent, unable to move.)* I'm not coming back any more.

WILLY: You're not going to see Oliver tomorrow?

820 **BIFF:** I've got no appointment, Dad.

WILLY: He put his arm around you, and you've got no appointment?

BIFF: Pop, get this now, will you? Everytime I've left it's been a fight that sent me out of here. Today I realized something about myself and I tried to explain it to you and I—I think I'm just not smart enough to make any sense out of it for you. To hell with whose fault it is or anything like that. *(He takes Willy's arm.)* Let's just wrap it up, heh? Come on in, we'll tell Mom. *(He gently tries to pull Willy to the left.)*

WILLY: *(frozen, immobile, with guilt in his voice)* No, I don't want to see her.

BIFF: Come on! *(He pulls again, and Willy tries to pull away.)*

825 **WILLY:** *(highly nervous)* No, no, I don't want to see her.

BIFF: *(tries to look into Willy's face, as if to find the answer there)* Why don't you want to see her?

WILLY: *(more harshly now)* Don't bother me, will you?

BIFF: What do you mean, you don't want to see her? You don't want them calling you yellow, do you? This isn't your fault; it's me, I'm a bum. Now come inside! *(Willy strains to get away.)* Did you hear what I said to you?

Willy pulls away and quickly goes by himself into the house. Biff follows.

LINDA: *(to Willy)* Did you plant, dear?

830 **BIFF:** *(at the door, to Linda)* All right, we had it out. I'm going and I'm not writing any more.

LINDA: *(going to Willy in the kitchen)* I think that's the best way, dear. 'Cause there's no use drawing it out, you'll just never get along.

Willy doesn't respond.

BIFF: People ask where I am and what I'm doing, you don't know, and you don't care. That way it'll be off your mind and you can start brightening up again. All right? That clears it, doesn't it? *(Willy is silent, and Biff goes to him.)* You gonna wish me luck, scout? *(He extends his hand.)* What do you say?

LINDA: Shake his hand, Willy.

WILLY: *(turning to her, seething with hurt)* There's no necessity to mention the pen at all, y'know.

835 **BIFF:** *(gently)* I've got no appointment, Dad.

WILLY: *(erupting fiercely)* He put his arm around . . . ?

BIFF: Dad, you're never going to see what I am, so what's the use of arguing? If I strike oil I'll send you a check. Meantime forget I'm alive.

WILLY: *(to Linda)* Spite, see?

BIFF: Shake hands, Dad.

840 **WILLY:** Not my hand.

BIFF: I was hoping not to go this way.

WILLY: Well, this is the way you're going. Good-by.

Biff looks at him a moment, then turns sharply and goes to the stairs.

WILLY: *(stops him with)* May you rot in hell if you leave this house!

BIFF: *(turning)* Exactly what is it that you want from me?

845 **WILLY:** I want you to know, on the train, in the mountains, in the valleys, wherever you go, that you cut down your life for spite!

BIFF: No, no.

WILLY: Spite, spite, is the word of your undoing! And when you're down and out, remember what did it. When you're rotting somewhere beside the railroad tracks, remember, and don't you dare blame it on me!

BIFF: I'm not blaming it on you!
WILLY: I won't take the rap for this, you hear?

Happy comes down the stairs and stands on the bottom step, watching.

850 **BIFF:**   That's just what I'm telling you!
WILLY: *(sinking into a chair at the table, with full accusation)* You're trying
to put a knife in me—don't think I don't know what you're doing!
BIFF: All right, phony! Then let's lay it on the line. *(He whips the rubber
tube out of his pocket and puts it on the table.)*
HAPPY: You crazy—
LINDA: Biff! *(She moves to grab the hose, but Biff holds it down with his
hand.)*
855 **BIFF:**   Leave it there! Don't move it!
WILLY: *(not looking at it)* What is that?
BIFF: You know goddam well what that is.
WILLY: *(caged, wanting to escape)* I never saw that.
BIFF: You saw it. The mice didn't bring it into the cellar! What is this
supposed to do, make a hero out of you? This supposed to make me
sorry for you?
860 **WILLY:**   Never heard of it.
BIFF: There'll be no pity for you, you hear it? No pity!
WILLY: *(to Linda)* You hear the spite!
BIFF: No, you're going to hear the truth—what you are and what I am!
LINDA: Stop it!
865 **WILLY:**   Spite!
HAPPY: *(coming down toward Biff)* You cut it now!
BIFF: *(to Happy)* The man don't know who we are! The man is gonna
know! *(To Willy.)* We never told the truth for ten minutes in this
house!
HAPPY: We always told the truth!
BIFF: *(turning on him)* You big blow, are you the assistant buyer? You're
one of the two assistants to the assistant, aren't you?
870 **HAPPY:**   Well, I'm practically—
BIFF: You're practically full of it! We all are! And I'm through with it.
(To Willy.) Now hear this, Willy, this is me.
WILLY: I know you!
BIFF: You know why I had no address for three months? I stole a suit in
Kansas City and I was in jail. *(To Linda, who is sobbing.)* Stop crying.
I'm through with it.

Linda turns away from them, her hands covering her face.

WILLY: I suppose that's my fault!
875 **BIFF:**   I stole myself out of every good job since high school!
WILLY: And whose fault is that?
BIFF: And I never got anywhere because you blew me so full of hot air I
could never stand taking orders from anybody! That's whose fault it is!

WILLY: I hear that!

LINDA: Don't, Biff!

880 **BIFF:** It's goddam time you heard that! I had to be boss big shot in two weeks, and I'm through with it!

WILLY: Then hang yourself! For spite, hang yourself!

BIFF: No! Nobody's hanging himself, Willy! I ran down eleven flights with a pen in my hand today. And suddenly I stopped, you hear me? And in the middle of that office building, do you hear this? I stopped in the middle of that building and I saw—the sky. I saw the things that I love in this world. The work and the food and time to sit and smoke. And I looked at the pen and said to myself, what the hell am I grabbing this for? Why am I trying to become what I don't want to be? What am I doing in an office, making a contemptuous, begging fool of myself, when all I want is out there, waiting for me the minute I say I know who I am! Why can't I say that, Willy? *(He tries to make Willy face him, but Willy pulls away and moves to the left.)*

WILLY: *(with hatred, threateningly)* The door of your life is wide open!

BIFF: Pop! I'm a dime a dozen, and so are you!

885 **WILLY:** *(turning on him now in an uncontrolled outburst)* I am not a dime a dozen! I am Willy Loman, and you are Biff Loman!

Biff starts for Willy, but is blocked by Happy. In his fury, Biff seems on the verge of attacking his father.

BIFF: I am not a leader of men, Willy, and neither are you. You were never anything but a hard-working drummer who landed in the ash can like all the rest of them! I'm one dollar an hour, Willy! I tried seven states and couldn't raise it. A buck an hour! Do you gather my meaning? I'm not bringing home any prizes any more, and you're going to stop waiting for me to bring them home!

WILLY: *(directly to Biff)* You vengeful, spiteful mutt!

Biff breaks from Happy. Willy, in fright, starts up the stairs. Biff grabs him.

BIFF: *(at the peak of his fury)* Pop, I'm nothing! I'm nothing, Pop. Can't you understand that? There's no spite in it any more. I'm just what I am, that's all.

Biff's fury has spent itself, and he breaks down, sobbing, holding on to Willy, who dumbly fumbles for Biff's face.

WILLY: *(astonished)* What're you doing? What're you doing? *(To Linda.)* Why is he crying?

890 **BIFF:** *(crying, broken)* Will you let me go, for Christ's sake? Will you take that phony dream and burn it before something happens? *(Struggling to contain himself, he pulls away and moves to the stairs.)* I'll go in the morning. Put him—put him to bed. *(Exhausted, Biff moves up the stairs to his room.)*

WILLY: *(after a long pause, astonished, elevated)* Isn't that remarkable? Biff—he likes me!

LINDA: He loves you, Willy!

HAPPY: *(deeply moved)* Always did, Pop.

WILLY: Oh, Biff! *(Staring wildly.)* He cried! Cried to me! *(He is choking with his love, and now cries out his promise.)* That boy—that boy is going to be magnificent!

Ben appears in the light just outside the kitchen.

895   **BEN:**   Yes, outstanding, with twenty thousand behind him.

LINDA: *(sensing the racing of his mind, fearfully, carefully)* Now come to bed, Willy. It's all settled now.

WILLY: *(finding it difficult not to rush out of the house)* Yes, we'll sleep. Come on. Go to sleep, Hap.

BEN: And it does take a great kind of man to crack the jungle.

In accents of dread, Ben's idyllic music starts up.

HAPPY: *(his arm around Linda)* I'm getting married, Pop, don't forget it. I'm changing everything. I'm gonna run that department before the year is up. You'll see, Mom. *(He kisses her.)*

900   **BEN:**   The jungle is dark but full of diamonds, Willy.

Willy turns, moves, listening to Ben.

LINDA: Be good. You're both good boys, just act that way, that's all.

HAPPY: 'Night, Pop. *(He goes upstairs.)*

LINDA: *(to Willy)* Come, dear.

BEN: *(with greater force)* One must go in to fetch a diamond out.

905   **WILLY:**   *(to Linda, as he moves slowly along the edge of the kitchen, toward the door)* I just want to get settled down, Linda. Let me sit alone for a little.

LINDA: *(almost uttering her fear)* I want you upstairs.

WILLY: *(taking her in his arms)* In a few minutes, Linda. I couldn't sleep right now. Go on, you look awful tired. *(He kisses her.)*

BEN: Not like an appointment at all. A diamond is rough and hard to the touch.

WILLY: Go on now. I'll be right up.

910   **LINDA:**   I think this is the only way, Willy.

WILLY: Sure, it's the best thing.

BEN: Best thing!

WILLY: The only way. Everything is gonna be—go on, kid, get to bed. You look so tired.

LINDA: Come right up.

915   **WILLY:**   Two minutes.

Linda goes into the livingroom, then reappears in her bedroom. Willy moves just outside the kitchen door.

WILLY: Loves me. *(Wonderingly.)* Always loved me. Isn't that a remarkable thing? Ben, he'll worship me for it!

BEN: *(with promise)* It's dark there, but full of diamonds.

WILLY: Can you imagine that magnificence with twenty thousand dollars in his pocket?

LINDA: *(calling from her room)* Willy! Come up!

920 **WILLY:** *(calling from the kitchen)* Yes! Yes! Coming! It's very smart, you realize that, don't you, sweetheart? Even Ben sees it. I gotta go, baby. 'By! By! *(Going over to Ben, almost dancing.)* Imagine? When the mail comes he'll be ahead of Bernard again!

BEN: A perfect proposition all around.

WILLY: Did you see how he cried to me? Oh, if I could kiss him, Ben!

BEN: Time, William, time!

WILLY: Oh, Ben, I always knew one way or another we were gonna make it, Biff and I!

925 **BEN:** *(looking at his watch)* The boat. We'll be late. *(He moves slowly off into the darkness.)*

WILLY: *(elegiacally, turning to the house)* Now when you kick off, boy, I want a seventy-yard boot, and get right down the field under the ball, and when you hit, hit low and hit hard, because it's important, boy. *(He swings around and faces the audience.)* There's all kinds of important people in the stands, and the first thing you know . . . *(Suddenly realizing he is alone.)* Ben! Ben, where do I . . . ? *(He makes a sudden movement of search.)* Ben, how do I . . . ?

LINDA: *(calling)* Willy, you coming up?

WILLY: *(uttering a gasp of fear, whirling about as if to quiet her)* Sh! *(He turns around as if to find his way; sounds, faces, voices, seem to be swarming in upon him and he flicks at them, crying.)* Sh! Sh! *(Suddenly music, faint and high, stops him. It rises in intensity, almost to an unbearable scream. He goes up and down on his toes, and rushes off around the house.)* Shhh!

LINDA: Willy?

There is no answer. Linda waits. Biff gets up off his bed. He is still in his clothes. Happy sits up. Biff stands listening.

930 **LINDA:** *(with real fear)* Willy, answer me! Willy!

There is the sound of a car starting and moving away at full speed.

LINDA: No!

BIFF: *(rushing down the stairs)* Pop!

As the car speeds off, the music crashes down in a frenzy of sound, which becomes the soft pulsation of a single cello string. Biff slowly returns to his bedroom. He and Happy gravely don their jackets. Linda slowly walks out of her room. The music has developed into a dead march. The leaves of day are appearing over everything. Charley and Bernard, somberly dressed, appear and knock on the kitchen door. Biff and Happy slowly descend the stairs to the kitchen as Charley and Bernard enter. All stop a moment when Linda, in clothes of mourning, bearing a little bunch of roses, comes through the draped doorway into the kitchen. She goes to Charley and takes his arm. Now all move toward the audience, through the wall-line of the kitchen. At the limit of the apron, Linda lays down the flowers, kneels, and sits back on her heels. All stare down at the grave.

REQUIEM

CHARLEY: It's getting dark, Linda.

Linda doesn't react. She stares at the grave.

BIFF: How about it, Mom? Better get some rest, heh? They'll be closing the gate soon.

Linda makes no move. Pause.

HAPPY: *(deeply angered)* He had no right to do that! There was no necessity for it. We would've helped him.
CHARLEY: *(grunting)* Hmmm.
5 **BIFF:** Come along, Mom.
LINDA: Why didn't anybody come?
CHARLEY: It was a very nice funeral.
LINDA: But where are all the people he knew? Maybe they blame him.
CHARLEY: Naa. It's a rough world, Linda. They wouldn't blame him.
10 **LINDA:** I can't understand it. At this time especially. First time in thirty-five years we were just about free and clear. He only needed a little salary. He was even finished with the dentist.
CHARLEY: No man only needs a little salary.
LINDA: I can't understand it.
BIFF: There were a lot of nice days. When he'd come home from a trip; or on Sundays, making the stoop; finishing the cellar; putting on the new porch; when he built the extra bathroom; and put up the garage. You know something, Charley, there's more of him in that front stoop than in all the sales he ever made.
CHARLEY: Yeah. He was a happy man with a batch of cement.
15 **LINDA:** He was so wonderful with his hands.
BIFF: He had the wrong dreams. All, all, wrong.
HAPPY: *(almost ready to fight Biff)* Don't say that!
BIFF: He never knew who he was.
CHARLEY: *(stopping Happy's movement and reply. To Biff.)* Nobody dast blame this man. You don't understand: Willy was a salesman. And for a salesman, there is no rock bottom to the life. He don't put a bolt to a nut, he don't tell you the law or give you medicine. He's a man out there in the blue, riding on a smile and a shoeshine. And when they start not smiling back—that's an earthquake. And then you get

yourself a couple of spots on your hat, and you're finished. Nobody dast blame this man. A salesman is got to dream, boy. It comes with the territory.

20 **BIFF:** Charley, the man didn't know who he was.

HAPPY: *(infuriated)* Don't say that!

BIFF: Why don't you come with me, Happy?

HAPPY: I'm not licked that easily. I'm staying right in this city, and I'm gonna beat this racket! *(He looks at Biff, his chin set.)* The Loman Brothers!

BIFF: I know who I am, kid.

25 **HAPPY:** All right, boy. I'm gonna show you and everybody else that Willy Loman did not die in vain. He had a good dream. It's the only dream you can have—to come out number-one man. He fought it out here, and this is where I'm gonna win it for him.

BIFF: *(with a hopeless glance at Happy, bends toward his mother)* Let's go, Mom.

LINDA: I'll be with you in a minute. Go on, Charley. *(He hesitates.)* I want to, just for a minute. I never had a chance to say good-by.

Charley moves away, followed by Happy. Biff remains a slight distance up and left of Linda. She sits there, summoning herself. The flute begins, not far away, playing behind her speech.

LINDA: Forgive me, dear. I can't cry. I don't know what it is, but I can't cry. I don't understand it. Why did you ever do that? Help me, Willy, I can't cry. It seems to me that you're just on another trip. I keep expecting you. Willy, dear, I can't cry. Why did you do it? I search and search and I search, and I can't understand it, Willy. I made the last payment on the house today. Today, dear. And there'll be nobody home. *(A sob rises in her throat.)* We're free and clear. *(Sobbing more fully, released.)* We're free. *(Biff comes slowly toward her.)* We're free . . . We're free . . .

Biff lifts her to her feet and moves out up right with her in his arms. Linda sobs quietly. Bernard and Charley come together and follow them, followed by Happy. Only the music of the flute is left on the darkening stage as over the house the hard towers of the apartment buildings rise into sharp focus, and—

THE CURTAIN FALLS

READING AND REACTING

1. With which character in the play do you most identify? Why?

2. Is Willy a likeable character? What words and actions—both Willy's and those of other characters—help you form your conclusion?

3. How does the existence of The Woman affect our overall impression of Willy? What does she reveal about his character?

4. What does Willy's attitude toward his sons indicate about his character? How is this attitude revealed?

5. Does this play have a hero? A villain? Explain.

6. In the absence of a narrator, what devices does Miller use to provide exposition—basic information about character and setting?

7. The conversation between Biff and Happy in Act 1 reveals many of their differences. List some of the differences between these two characters.

8. In numerous remarks, Willy expresses his philosophy of business. Summarize some of his key ideas about the business world. How realistic do you think these ideas are? How do these attitudes help to delineate his character?

9. In Act 1 Linda tells Willy, "Few men are idolized by their children the way you are." Is she sincere, is she being ironic, or is she just trying to make Willy feel better?

10. How do the frequent flashbacks help to explain what motivates Willy? How else could this background information have been provided in the play? Are there advantages to using flashbacks instead of the alternative you suggest?

11. Is Linda simply a stereotype of the long-suffering wife, or is she an individualized, multidimensional character? Explain.

12. Willy Loman lives in Brooklyn, New York; his "territory" is New England. What is the significance to him of the "faraway places"—Africa, Alaska, California, Texas, and the like—mentioned in the play?

13. Explain the function of Bernard in the play.

14. The play concludes with a requiem. What is a requiem? What information about each of the major characters is supplied in this brief section? Is this information essential to your understanding or appreciation of the play, or would the play have been equally effective without the requiem? Explain.

15. **JOURNAL ENTRY** Do you think Willy Lomam is an innocent victim of the society in which he lives, or do you believe there are flaws in his character that make him at least partially responsible for his own misfortune? Explain.

16. **CRITICAL PERSPECTIVE** In his 1949 essay "Tragedy and the Common Man," Arthur Miller attempts to define modern tragedy:

There is a misconception of tragedy with which I have been struck in review after review, and in many conversations with writers and readers alike. It is the idea that tragedy is of necessity allied to pessimism. Even the dictionary says nothing more about the word than that it means a story with a sad or unhappy ending. This impression is so firmly fixed that I almost hesitate to claim that in truth tragedy implies more optimism in its author than does comedy, and that its final result ought to be the reinforcement of the onlooker's brightest opinions of the human animal.

For, if it is true to say that in essence the tragic hero is intent upon claiming his whole due as a personality, and if this struggle must be total and without reservation, then it automatically demonstrates the indestructible will of man to achieve his humanity.

The possibility of victory must be there in tragedy. Where pathos rules, where pathos is finally derived, a character has fought a battle he could not possibly have won. The pathetic is achieved when the protagonist is, by virtue of his witlessness, his insensitivity or the very air he gives off, incapable of grappling with a much superior force.

Pathos truly is the mode for the pessimist. But tragedy requires a nicer balance between what is possible and what is impossible. And it is curious, although edifying, that the plays we revere, century after century, are the tragedies. In them, and in them alone, lies the belief—optimistic, if you will, in the perfectibility of man.

In terms of this definition, do you see *Death of a Salesman* and its hero as truly tragic or simply pathetic? Do you find the play at all optimistic?

 **DAVID HENRY HWANG** (1957–   ) was born in Los Angeles and graduated from Stanford University in 1979, later attending the Yale School of Drama. *FOB* was written and first produced as part of a student festival in 1979 while he was an undergraduate. Later produced off-Broadway, it won an Obie for best play of the 1980–81 season. Hwang's most famous play is *M. Butterfly* (1988), which won the Tony Award for best play of the year. *M. Butterfly* deals with the true story of a French diplomat and his lover, a Chinese opera star, who years later was revealed to be a man; in this play, Hwang explores the cultural stereotype of the submissive Chinese woman and uses excerpts from Puccini's opera *Madame Butterfly*. His other works include *The Dance and the Railroad* (1981), *Family Devotions* (1981), and more recently *Face Value* (1993) and the one-act play *Bondage* (1991).

The son of Chinese immigrants, Hwang became fascinated as a college student by how a Chinese past and an American future can be reconciled. Most of his dramatic work has centered on this conflict. *FOB* (1978), for example, is the story of a "fresh-off-the-boat" Chinese immigrant and his more assimilated friends. Hwang mixes realism and symbolism in this play, evoking the powerful presence of Chinese mythic figures. In his 1982 introduction to a volume of four plays, including *FOB*, he wrote, "to Asian-American theater people across the nation . . . I dedicate this volume. I present these plays as an offering, with respect for the past and excitement for our future lives together."

DAVID HENRY HWANG

FOB

(1978)

For the warriors of my family

Playwright's Note: The roots of *FOB* are thoroughly American. The play began when a sketch I was writing about a limousine trip through Westwood, California, was invaded by two figures from American literature: Fa Mu Lan, the girl who takes her father's place in battle, from Maxine Hong Kingston's *The Woman Warrior,* and Gwan Gung, the god of fighters and writers, from Frank Chin's *Gee, Pop!*

This fact testifies to the existence of an Asian-American literary tradition. Japanese Americans, for instance, wrote plays in American concentration camps during World War II. Earlier, with the emergence of the railroads, came regular performances of Cantonese operas, featuring Gwan Gung, the adopted god of Chinese America.

CHARACTERS

(ALL IN EARLY TWENTIES)

DALE, *an American of Chinese descent, second generation*
GRACE, *his cousin, a first-generation Chinese American*
STEVE, *her friend, a Chinese newcomer*

SCENE
The back room of a small Chinese restaurant in Torrance, California.

TIME
The year 1980. Act I, Scene 1, takes place in the late afternoon. Act I, Scene 2, is a few minutes later. Act II is after dinner.

DEFINITIONS
Chong you bing *is a type of Chinese pancake, a Northern Chinese appetizer often made with dough and scallions, with a consistency similar to that of pita bread.*

Gung Gung *means "grandfather."*

Mei Guo *means "beautiful country," a Chinese term for America.*

Da dao *and* mao *are two swords, the traditional weapons of Gwan Gung and Fa Mu Lan, respectively.*

PROLOGUE

Lights Up on a blackboard. Enter Dale dressed preppie. The blackboard is the type which can flip around so both sides can be used. He lectures like a university professor, using the board to illustrate his points.

DALE: F-O-B. Fresh Off the Boat. FOB. What words can you think of that characterize the FOB? Clumsy, ugly, greasy FOB. Loud, stupid, four-eyed FOB. Big feet. Horny. Like Lenny in *Of Mice and Men.*[1] Very good. A literary reference. High-water pants. Floods, to be exact. Someone you wouldn't want your sister to marry. If you are a sister, someone you wouldn't want to marry. That assumes we're talking about boy FOBs, of course. But girl FOBs aren't really as . . . FOBish. Boy FOBs are the worst, the . . . pits. They are the sworn enemies of all ABC—oh, that's "American Born Chinese"—of all ABC girls. Before an ABC girl will be seen on Friday night with a boy FOB in Westwood, she would rather burn off her face.

He flips around the board. On the other side is written: "1. Where to find FOBs. 2. How to spot a FOB."

FOBs can be found in great numbers almost anyplace you happen to be, but there are some locations where they cluster in particularly large swarms. Community colleges, Chinese-club discos, Asian sororities, Asian fraternities, Oriental churches, shopping malls, and, of course, Bee Gee concerts. How can you spot a FOB? Look out! If you can't answer that, you might be one. *(He flips back the board, reviews.)* F-O-B. Fresh Off the Boat. FOB. Clumsy, ugly, greasy FOB. Loud, stupid, four-eyed FOB. Big feet. Horny. Like Lenny in *Of Mice and Men.* Floods. Like Lenny in *Of Mice and Men.* F-O-B. Fresh Off the Boat. FOB.

Lights fade to black. We hear American pop music, preferably in the funk— R&B—disco area.

ACT I

SCENE 1

The back room of a small Chinese restaurant in Torrance, California. Single table, with tablecloth; various chairs, supplies. One door leads outside, a back exit, another leads to the kitchen. Lights up on Grace, at the table. The music is coming from a small radio. On the table is a small, partially wrapped box, and

---

[1] A 1937 novel by American writer John Steinbeck (1902–1968), later dramatized for the stage. Lenny is a slow-witted but good-natured soul whose childlike simplicity allows him to be taken advantage of, and whose lack of awareness gets him in trouble.

a huge blob of discarded Scotch tape. As Grace tries to wrap the box, we see what has been happening: The tape she's using is stuck; so, in order to pull it out, she must tug so hard that an unusable quantity of tape is dispensed. Enter Steve, from the back door, unnoticed by Grace. He stands, waiting to catch her eye, tries to speak, but his voice is drowned out by the music. He is dressed in a stylish summer outfit.

GRACE: Aaaai-ya!
STEVE: Hey!

No response; he turns off the music.

GRACE: Huh? Look. Out of tape.
STEVE: *(in Chinese)* Yeah.
5 **GRACE:**   One whole roll. You know how much of it got on here? Look. That much. That's all.
STEVE: *(in Chinese)* Yeah. Do you serve *chong you bing* today?
GRACE: *(picking up box)* Could've skipped the wrapping paper, just covered it with tape.
STEVE: *(in Chinese)* Excuse me!
GRACE: Yeah? *(Pause.)* You wouldn't have any on you, would ya?
10 **STEVE:**   *(English from now onward)* Sorry? No. I don't have *bing*. I want to buy *bing*.
GRACE: Not *bing!* Tape. Have you got any tape?
STEVE: Tape? Of course I don't have tape.
GRACE: Just checking.
STEVE: Do you have any *bing?*

Pause.

15 **GRACE:**   Look, we're closed till five . . .
STEVE: Idiot girl.
GRACE: Why don't you take a menu?
STEVE: I want you to tell me!

Pause.

GRACE: *(ignoring Steve)* Working in a Chinese restaurant, you learn to deal with obnoxious customers.
20 **STEVE:**   Hey! You!
GRACE: If the customer's Chinese, you insult them by giving forks.
STEVE: I said I want you to tell me!
GRACE: If the customer's Anglo, you starve them by not giving forks.
STEVE: You serve *bing* or not?
25 **GRACE:**   But it's always easy just to dump whatever happens to be in your hands at the moment.

She sticks the tape blob on Steve's face.

STEVE: I suggest you answer my question at once!

GRACE: And I suggest you grab a menu and start doing things for yourself. Look, I'll get you one, even. How's that?

STEVE: I want it from your mouth!

GRACE: Sorry. We don't keep 'em there.

30 **STEVE:**   If I say they are there, they are there. *(He grabs her box.)*

GRACE: What—What're you doing? Give that back to me!

They parry around the table.

STEVE: Aaaah! Now it's different, isn't it? Now you're listening to me.

GRACE: 'Scuse me, but you really are an asshole, you know that? Who do you think you are?

STEVE: What are you asking me? Who I am?

35 **GRACE:**   Yes. You take it easy with that, hear?

STEVE: You ask who *I* am?

GRACE: One more second and I'm gonna call the cops.

STEVE: Very well, I will tell you.

She picks up the phone. He slams it down.

STEVE: I said, I'll tell you.

40 **GRACE:**   If this is how you go around meeting people, I think it's pretty screwed.

STEVE: Silence! I am Gwan Gung! God of warriors, writers, and prostitutes!

Pause.

GRACE: Bullshit!

STEVE: What?

GRACE: Bullshit! Bull-shit! You are not Gwan Gung. And gimme back my box.

45 **STEVE:**   I am Gwan Gung. Perhaps we should see what you have in here.

GRACE: Don't open that! *(Beat.)* You don't look like Gwan Gung. Gwan Gung is a warrior.

STEVE: I am a warrior!

GRACE: Yeah? Why are you so scrawny, then? You wouldn't last a day in battle.

STEVE: My credit! Many a larger man has been humiliated by the strength in one of my size.

50 **GRACE:**   Tell me, then. Tell me, if you are Gwan Gung. Tell me of your battles. Of one battle. Of Gwan Gung's favorite battle.

STEVE: Very well. Here is a living memory: One day, Gwan Gung woke up and saw the ring of fire around the sun and decided, "This is a good day to slay villagers." So he got up, washed himself, and looked over a map of the Three Kingdoms to decide where first to go. For those were days of rebellion and falling empires, so opportunity to slay was abundant. But planned slaughter required an order and restraint which soon became tedious. So Gwan Gung decided a change was in order. He called for his tailor, who he asked to make a beautiful blindfold of layered silk, fine enough to be weightless, yet thick enough to blind the wearer completely. The tailor complied, and soon produced a perfect piece of red silk, exactly suited to Gwan Gung's demands. In gratitude, Gwan Gung stayed the tailor's execution sentence. He then put on his blindfold, pulled out his sword, and began passing over the land, swiping at whatever got in his path. You see, Gwan Gung figured there was so much revenge and so much evil in those days that he could slay at random and still stand a good chance of fulfilling justice. This worked very well, until his sword, in its blind fury, hit upon an old and irritable atom bomb.

Grace catches Steve, takes back the box.

GRACE: Ha! Some Gwan Gung you are! Some warrior you are! You can't even protect a tiny box from the grasp of a woman! How could you have shielded your big head in battle?

STEVE: Shield! Shield! I still go to battle!

GRACE: Only your head goes to battle, 'cause only your head is Gwan Gung.

Pause.

55 **STEVE:** You made me think of you as a quiet listener. A good trick. What is your name?

GRACE: You can call me "The Woman Who Has Defeated Gwan Gung," if that's really who you are.

STEVE: Very well. But that name will change before long.

GRACE: That story you told—that wasn't a Gwan Gung story.

STEVE: What—you think you know all of my adventures through stories? All the books in the world couldn't record the life of one man, let alone a god. Now—do you serve *bing?*

60 **GRACE:** I won the battle; you go look yourself. There.

STEVE: You working here?

GRACE: Part time. It's my father's place. I'm also in school.

STEVE: School? University?

GRACE: Yeah. UCLA.

65 **STEVE:** Excellent. I have also come to America for school.

GRACE: Well, what use would Gwan Gung have for school?

STEVE: Wisdom. Wisdom makes a warrior stronger.

GRACE: Pretty good. If you are Gwan Gung, you're not the dumb jock I was expecting. Got a lot to learn about school, though.

STEVE: Expecting? You were expecting me?

70 **GRACE:** *(Quickly)* No, no. I meant, what I expected from the stories.

STEVE: Tell me, how do people think of Gwan Gung in America? Do they shout my name while rushing into battle, or is it too sacred to be used in such ostentatious display?

GRACE: Uh—no.

STEVE: No—what? I didn't ask a "no" question.

GRACE: What I mean is, neither. They don't do either of those.

75 **STEVE:** Not good. The name of Gwan Gung has been restricted for the use of leaders only?

GRACE: Uh—no. I think you better sit down.

STEVE: This is very scandalous. How are the people to take my strength? Gwan Gung might as well not exist, for all they know.

GRACE: You got it.

STEVE: I got what? You seem to be having trouble making your answers fit my questions.

80 **GRACE:** No, I think you're having trouble making your questions fit my answers.

STEVE: What is this nonsense? Speak clearly, or don't speak at all.

GRACE: Speak clearly?

STEVE: Yes. Like a warrior.

GRACE: Well, you see, Gwan Gung, god of warriors, writers, and prostitutes, no one gives a wipe about you 'round here. You're dead.

Pause.

85 **STEVE:** You . . . you make me laugh.

GRACE: You died way back . . . hell, no one even noticed when you died—that's how bad off your PR was. You died and no one even missed a burp.

STEVE: You lie! The name of Gwan Gung must be feared around the world—you jeopardize your health with such remarks. *(Pause)* You— you have heard of me, I see. How can you say—?

GRACE: Oh, I just study it a lot—Chinese American history, I mean.

STEVE: Ah. In the schools, in the universities, where new leaders are born, they study my ways.

90 **GRACE:** Well, fifteen of us do.

STEVE: Fifteen. Fifteen of the brightest, of the most promising?

GRACE: One wants to be a dental technician.

STEVE: A man studies Gwan Gung in order to clean teeth?

GRACE: There's also a middle-aged woman that's kinda bored with her kids.

95 **STEVE:** I refuse—I don't believe you—your stories. You're just angry at me for treating you like a servant. You're trying to sap my faith. The people—the people outside—they know me—they know the deeds of Gwan Gung.

GRACE: Check it out yourself.

STEVE: Very well. You will learn—learn not to test the spirit of Gwan Gung.

Steve exits. Grace picks up the box. She studies it.

GRACE: Fa Mu Lan sits and waits. She learns to be still while the emperors, the dynasties, the foreign lands flow past, unaware of her slender form, thinking it a tree in the woods, a statue to a goddess long abandoned by her people. But Fa Mu Lan, the Woman Warrior, is not ashamed. She knows that the one who can exist without movement while the ages pass is the one to whom no victory can be denied. It is training, to wait. And Fa Mu Lan, the Woman Warrior, must train, for she is no goddess, but girl—girl who takes her father's place in battle. No goddess, but woman—warrior-woman *(She breaks through the wrapping, reaches in, and pulls out another box, beautifully wrapped and ribboned.)*—and ghost. *(She puts the new box on the shelf, goes to the phone, dials.)* Hi, Dale? Hi, this is Grace . . . Pretty good. How 'bout you? . . . Good, good. Hey, listen, I'm sorry to ask you at the last minute and everything, but are you doing anything tonight? . . . Are you sure? . . . Oh, good. Would you like to go out with me and some of my friends? . . . Just out to dinner, then maybe we were thinking of going to a movie or something . . . Oh, good . . . Are you sure? . . . Yeah, okay. Um, we're all going to meet at the restaurant . . . No, *our* restaurant . . . right—as soon as possible. Okay, good . . . I'm really glad that you're coming. Sorry it's such short notice. Okay. Bye, now . . . Huh? Frank? Oh, okay. *(Pause)* Hi, Frank . . . Pretty good . . . Yeah? . . . No, I don't think so . . . Yeah . . . No, I'm sorry, I'd still rather not . . . I don't want to, okay? Do I have to be any clearer than that? . . . You are not! . . . You don't even know when they come—you'd have to lie on those tracks for hours . . . Forget it, okay? . . . Look, I'll get you a schedule so you can time it properly . . . It's not a favor, damn it. Now goodbye! *(She hangs up.)* Jesus!

Steve enters.

STEVE: Buncha weak boys, what do they know? One man—ChinaMan—wearing a leisure suit—green! I ask him, "You know Gwan Gung?" He says, "Hong Kong?" I say, "No, no. Gwan Gung." He says, "Yeah. They got sixty thousand people living on four acres. Went there last year." I say, "No, no. Gwan Gung." He says, "Ooooh! Gwan Gung?" I say, "Yes, yes, Gwan Gung." He says, "I never been there before."

100 **GRACE:** See? Even if you didn't die—who cares?

STEVE: Another kid—blue jeans and a T-shirt—I ask him, does he know Gwan Gung? He says, he doesn't need it, he knows Jesus Christ. What city is this now?

GRACE: Los Angeles.

STEVE: This isn't the only place where a new ChinaMan can land, is it?

GRACE: I guess a lot go to San Francisco.

105 **STEVE:** Good. This place got a bunch of weirdos around here.

GRACE: Yeah.

STEVE: They could never be followers of Gwan Gung. All who follow me must be loyal and righteous.

GRACE: Maybe you should try some other state.

STEVE: Huh? What you say?

110 GRACE: Never mind. You'll get used to it—like the rest of us.

Pause. Steve begins laughing.

STEVE: You are a very clever woman.

GRACE: Just average.

STEVE: No. You do a good job to make it seem like Gwan Gung has no followers here. At the university, what do you study?

GRACE: Journalism.

115 STEVE: Journalism—you are a writer, then?

GRACE: Of a sort.

STEVE: Very good. You are close to Gwan Gung's heart.

GRACE: As close as I'm gonna get.

STEVE: I would like to go out tonight with you.

120 GRACE: I knew it. Look, I've heard a lot of lines before, and yours is very creative, but . . .

STEVE: I will take you out.

GRACE: You will, huh?

STEVE: I do so because I find you worthy to be favored.

GRACE: You're starting to sound like any other guy now.

125 STEVE: I'm sorry?

GRACE: Look—if you're going to have any kinds of relationships with women in this country, you better learn to give us some respect.

STEVE: Respect? I give respect.

GRACE: The pushy, aggressive type is out, understand?

STEVE: Taking you out is among my highest tokens of respect.

130 GRACE: Oh, c'mon—they don't even say that in Hong Kong.

STEVE: You are being asked out by Gwan Gung!

GRACE: I told you, you're too wimpy to be Gwan Gung. And even if you were, you'd have to wait your turn in line.

STEVE: What?

GRACE: I already have something for tonight. My cousin and I are having dinner.

135 STEVE: You would turn down Gwan Gung for your cousin?

GRACE: Well, he has a X-1/9.

Pause.

STEVE: What has happened?

GRACE: Look—I tell you what. If you take both of us out, then it'll be okay, all right?

STEVE: I don't want to go out with your cousin!

140 GRACE: Well, sorry. It's part of the deal.

STEVE: Deal? What deals? Why am I made part of these deals?

GRACE: 'Cause you're in the U.S. in 1980, just like the rest of us. Now quit complaining. Will you take it or not?

Pause.

STEVE: Gwan Gung . . . bows to no one's terms but his own.

GRACE: Fine. Why don't you go down the street to Imperial Dragon Restaurant and see if they have *bing?*

145 **STEVE:** Do you have *bing?*

GRACE: See for yourself.

She hands him a menu. He exits. Grace moves with the box.

GRACE: Fa Mu Lan stood in the center of the village and turned round and round as the bits of fingers, the tips of tongues, the arms, the legs, the peeled skulls, the torn maidenheads, all whirled by. She pulled the loose gown closer to her body, stepped over the torsos, in search of the one of her family who might still be alive. Reaching the house that was once her home, crushing bones in her haste, only to find the doorway covered with the stretched and dried skin of that which was once her father. Climbing through an open window, noticing the shiny black thousand-day-old egg still floating in the shiny black sauce. Finding her sister tied spread-eagle on the mat, finding her mother in the basket in pieces, finding her brother nowhere. The Woman Warrior went to the mirror, which had stayed unbroken, and let her gown come loose and drop to the ground. She turned and studied the ideographs that had long ago been carved into the flesh of her young back . . . Carved by her mother, who lay carved in the basket.

Dale enters, approaches Grace.

She ran her fingers over the skin and felt the ridges where there had been pain.

Dale is behind Grace.

GRACE: But now they were firm and hard.

Dale touches Grace, who reacts by swinging around and knocking him to the ground. Only after he is down does she see his face.

GRACE: Dale! Shit! I'm sorry. I didn't . . . !

150 **DALE:** *(Groggy)* Am I late?

GRACE: I didn't know it was you, Dale.

DALE: Yeah. Well, I didn't announce myself.

GRACE: You shouldn't just come in here like that.

DALE: You're right. Never again.

155 **GRACE:** I mean, you should've yelled from the dining room.

DALE: Dangerous neighborhood, huh?

GRACE: I'm so sorry. Really.

DALE: Yeah. Uh—where're your other friends? They on the floor around here too?

GRACE: No. Uh—this is really bad, Dale. I'm really sorry.

160 **DALE:** What?—you can't make it after all?

GRACE: No, I can make it. It's just that . . .

DALE: They can't make it? Okay, so it'll just be us. That's cool.

GRACE: Well, not quite us.

DALE: Oh.

165 **GRACE:** See, what happened is—You know my friend Judy?

DALE: Uh—no.

GRACE: Well, she was gonna come with us—with me and this guy I know—his name is . . . Steve.

DALE: Oh, he's with you, right?

GRACE: Well, sort of. So since she was gonna come, I thought you should come too.

170 **DALE:** To even out the couples?

GRACE: But now my friend Judy, she decided she had too much work to do, so . . . oh, it's all messed up.

DALE: Well, that's okay. I can go home—or I can go with you, if this guy Steve doesn't mind. Where is he, anyway?

GRACE: I guess he's late. You know, he just came to this country.

DALE: Oh yeah? How'd you meet him?

175 **GRACE:** At a Chinese dance at U.C.L.A.

DALE: Hmmmm. Some of those FOBs get moving pretty fast.

Grace glares.

DALE: Oh. Is he . . . nice?

GRACE: He's okay. I don't know him that well. You know, I'm really sorry.

DALE: Hey, I said it's okay. Jesus, it's not like you hurt me or anything.

180 **GRACE:** For that, too.

DALE: Look—*(He hits himself.)* No pain!

GRACE: What I meant was, I'm sorry tonight's got so messed up.

DALE: Oh, it's okay. I wasn't doing anything anyway.

GRACE: I know, but still . . .

Silence.

185 **DALE:** Hey, that Frank is a joke, huh?

GRACE: Yeah. He's kind of a pain.

DALE: Yeah. What an asshole to call my friend.

GRACE: Did you hear him on the phone?

DALE: Yeah, all that railroad stuff?

190 **GRACE:** It was real dumb.

DALE: Dumb? He's dumb. He's doing it right now.

GRACE: Huh? Are you serious?

DALE: Yeah. I'm tempted to tie him down so, for once in his life, he won't screw something up.

GRACE: You're kidding!

195 **DALE:** Huh? Yeah, sure I'm kidding. Who would I go bowling with?

GRACE: No, I mean about him actually going out there—is that true?

DALE: Yeah—he's lying there. You know, right on Torrance Boulevard?

GRACE: No!

DALE: Yeah!

200 **GRACE:** But what if a train really comes?

DALE: I dunno. I guess he'll get up.

GRACE: I don't believe it!

DALE: Unless he's fallen asleep by that time or something.

GRACE: He's crazy.

205 **DALE:** Which is a real possibility for Frank, he's such a bore anyway.

GRACE: He's weird.

DALE: No, he just thinks he's in love with you.

GRACE: Is he?

DALE: I dunno. We'll see when the train comes.

210 **GRACE:** Do you think we should do something?

DALE: What?—You're not gonna fall for the twerp, are you?

GRACE: Well, no, but . . .

DALE: He's stupid—and ugly, to boot.

GRACE: . . . but staying on the tracks is kinda dangerous.

215 **DALE:** Let him. Teach him a lesson.

GRACE: You serious?

DALE: *(Moving closer to Grace)* Not to fool with my cousin.

He strokes her hair. They freeze in place, but his arm continues to stroke. Steve enters, oblivious of Dale and Grace, who do not respond to him. He speaks to the audience as if it were a panel of judges.

STEVE: No! Please! Listen to me! This is fifth time I come here. I tell you both my parents, I tell you their parents, I tell you their parents' parents and who was adopted great-granduncle. I tell you how many beggars in home town and name of their blind dogs. I tell you number of steps from my front door to temple, to well, to governor house, to fields, to whorehouse, to fifth cousin inn, to eighth neighbor toilet—you ask only: What for am I in whorehouse? I tell north, south, northeast, southwest, west, east, north-northeast, south-southwest, east-eastsouth—Why will you not let me enter in America? I come here five times—I raise lifetime fortune five times. Five times, I first come here, you say to me I am illegal, you return me on boat to fathers and uncles with no gold, no treasure, no fortune, no rice. I only want to come to America—come to "Mountain of Gold." And I hate Mountain and I hate America and I hate you! *(Pause)* But this year you call 1914—very bad for China.

Pause; light shift. Grace and Dale become mobile and aware of Steve's presence.

GRACE: Oh! Steve, this is Dale, my cousin. Dale, Steve.

220 **DALE:** Hey, nice to meet . . .

STEVE: *(Now speaking with Chinese accent)* Hello. Thank you. I am fine.

Pause.

DALE: Uh, yeah. Me too. So, you just got here, huh? What'cha think?

Steve smiles and nods, Dale smiles and nods; Steve laughs, Dale laughs; Steve hits Dale on the shoulder. They laugh some more. They stop laughing.

DALE: Oh. Uh—good. *(Pause)* Well, it looks like it's just gonna be the three of us, right? *(To Grace)* Where you wanna go?

GRACE: I think Steve's already taken care of that. Right, Steve?

225 **STEVE:** Excuse?

GRACE: You made reservations at a restaurant?

STEVE: Oh, reservations. Yes, yes.

DALE: Oh, okay. That limits the possibilities. Guess we're going to Chinatown or something, right?

GRACE: *(To Steve)* Where is the restaurant?

230 **STEVE:** Oh. The restaurant is a French restaurant. Los Angeles downtown.

DALE: Oh, we're going to a Western place? *(To Grace)* Are you sure he made reservations?

GRACE: We'll see.

DALE: Well, I'll get my car.

GRACE: Okay.

235 **STEVE:** No!

DALE: Huh?

STEVE: Please—allow me to provide car.

DALE: Oh. You wanna drive.

STEVE: Yes. I have car.

240 **DALE:** Look—why don't you let me drive? You've got enough to do without worrying about—you know—how to get around L.A., read the stop signs, all that.

STEVE: Please—allow me to provide car. No problem.

DALE: Well, let's ask Grace, okay? *(To Grace)* Grace, who do you think should drive?

GRACE: I don't really care. Why don't you two figure it out? But let's hurry, okay? We open pretty soon.

DALE: *(To Steve)* Look—you had to pick the restaurant we're going to, so the least I can do is drive.

245 **STEVE:** Uh, your car—how many people sit in it?

DALE: Well, it depends. Right now, none.

GRACE: *(To Dale)* He's got a point. Your car only seats two.

DALE: He can sit in the back. There's space there. I've fit luggage in it before.

GRACE: *(To Steve)* You want to sit in back?

250 **STEVE:** I sit—where?

DALE: Really big suitcases.

GRACE: Back of his car.

STEVE: X-1/9? Aaaai-ya!

DALE: X-1/9?

255 **STEVE:** No deal!

DALE: How'd he know that? How'd he know what I drive?

STEVE: Please. Use my car. Is . . . big.

DALE: Yeah? Well, how much room you got? *(Pause; slower)* How-big-your-car-is?

STEVE: Huh?

260 **DALE:** Your car—how is big?

GRACE: How big is your car?

STEVE: Oh! You go see.

DALE: 'Cause if it's, like, a Pinto or something, it's not that much of a difference.

STEVE: Big and black. Outside.

265 **GRACE:** Let's hurry.

DALE: Sure, sure. *(Exits.)*

GRACE: What you up to, anyway?

STEVE: *(Dropping accent)* Gwan Gung will not go into battle without equipment worthy of his position.

GRACE: Position? You came back, didn't you? What does that make you?

270 **DALE:** *(Entering)* Okay. There's only one black car out there—

STEVE: Black car is mine.

DALE: —and that's a Fleetwood limo. Now, you're not gonna tell me that's his.

STEVE: Cadillac. Cadillac is mine.

DALE: Limousine . . . Limousine is yours?

275 **STEVE:** Yes, yes. Limousine.

Pause.

DALE: *(To Grace)* You wanna ride in that black thing? People will think we're dead.

GRACE: It does have more room.

DALE: Well, it has to. It's built for passengers who can't bend.

GRACE: And the driver *is* expensive.

280 **DALE:** He could go home—save all that money.

GRACE: Well, I don't know. You decide.

DALE: *(To Steve)* Look, we take my car, savvy?

STEVE: Please—drive my car.

DALE: I'm not trying to be unreasonable or anything.

285 **STEVE:** My car—just outside.

DALE: I know where it is, I just don't know why it is.

GRACE: Steve's father manufactures souvenirs in Hong Kong.

DALE: *(To Steve)* Oh, and that's how you manage that out there, huh?—from thousands of aluminum Buddhas and striptease pens.

GRACE: Well, he can't drive and he has the money—

290 **DALE:** *(To Grace)* I mean, wouldn't you just feel filthy?

GRACE: —so it's easier for him.

DALE: Getting out of a limo in the middle of Westwood? People staring, thinking we're from 'SC? Wouldn't you feel like dirt?

GRACE: It doesn't matter either way to me.

Pause.

Dale: Where's your social conscience?

295 **Grace:**   Look—I have an idea. Why don't we just stay here.

Steve: We stay here to eat?

Grace: No one from the restaurant will bother us, and we can bring stuff in from the kitchen.

Steve: I ask you to go out.

Dale: Look, Grace, I can't put ya out like that.

300 **Grace:**   *(To Dale)* It's no problem, really. It should be fun. *(To Steve)* Since there are three of us—

Dale: Fun?

Grace: *(To Steve)*—it is easier to eat here.

Dale: How can it be fun? It's cheaper.

Steve: Does not seem right.

305 **Grace:**   I mean, unless our restaurant isn't nice enough.

Dale: No, no—that's not it.

Steve: *(Watching Dale)* No—this place, very nice.

Grace: Are you sure?

Dale: Yeah. Sure.

310 **Steve:**   *(Ditto)* Yeah. Sure.

Dale: Do you have . . . uh—those *burrito* things?

Grace: *Moo-Shoo?*

Dale: Yeah, that.

Grace: Yeah.

315 **Dale:**   And black mushrooms.

Grace: Sure.

Dale: And sea cucumber?

Steve: Do you have *bing?*

Pause.

Grace: Look, Dad and Russ and some of the others are gonna be setting up pretty soon, so let's get our place ready, okay?

320 **Dale:**   Okay. Need any help?

Grace: Well, yeah. That's what I just said.

Dale: Oh, right. I thought maybe you were just being polite.

Grace: Yeah. Meet me in the kitchen.

Dale: Are you sure your dad won't mind?

325 **Grace:**   What?

Dale: Cooking for us.

Grace: Oh, it's okay. He'll cook for anybody.

Exits. Silence.

Dale: So, how do you like America?

Steve: Very nice.

330 **DALE:** "Very nice." Good, colorful Hong Kong English. English—how much of it you got down, anyway?

STEVE: Please repeat?

DALE: English—you speak how much?

STEVE: Oh—very little.

DALE: *(Pause)* You feel like you're an American? Don't tell me. Lemme guess. Your father. *(He switches into a mock Hong Kong accent.)* Your fad-dah tink he sending you here so you get yo' M.B.A., den go back and covuh da world wit' trinkets and beads. Diversify. Franchise. Sell—ah—Hong Kong X-Ray glasses at tourist shop at Buckingham Palace. You know—ah—"See da Queen"? *(Switches back)* He's hoping your American education's gonna create an empire of defective goods and breakable merchandise. Like those little cameras with the slides inside? I bought one at Disneyland once and it ended up having pictures of Hong Kong in it. You know how shitty it is to expect the Magic Kingdom and wind up with the skyline of Kowloon? Part of your dad's plan, I'm sure. But you're gonna double-cross him. Coming to America, you're gonna jump the boat. You're gonna decide you like us. Yeah—you're gonna like having fifteen theaters in three blocks, you're gonna like West Hollywood and Newport Beach. You're gonna decide to become an American. Yeah, don't deny it—it happens to the best of us. You can't hold out—you're no different. You won't even know it's coming before it has you. Before you're trying real hard to be just like the rest of us—go dinner, go movie, go motel, bang-bang. And when your father writes you that do-it-yourself acupuncture sales are down, you'll throw that letter in the basket and burn it in your brain. And you'll write that you're gonna live in Monterey Park a few years before going back home—and you'll get your green card— and you'll build up a nice little stockbroker's business and have a few American kids before your dad realizes what's happened and dies, his hopes reduced to a few chattering teeth and a pack of pornographic playing cards. Yeah—great things come to the U.S. out of Hong Kong.

335 **STEVE:** *(Lights a cigarette, blows smoke, stands.)* Such as your parents?

Steve turns on the music, exits. Blackout.

SCENE 2

Lights Up on Dale and Steve eating. It is a few minutes later and food is on the table. Dale eats Chinese style, vigorously shoveling food into his mouth. Steve picks. Grace enters carrying a jar of hot sauce. Steve sees her.

STEVE: *(To Grace)* After eating, you like to go dance?

DALE: *(Face in bowl)* No, thanks. I think we'd be conspicuous.

STEVE: *(To Grace)* Like to go dance?

GRACE: Perhaps. We will see.

5 **DALE:** *(To Steve)* Wait a minute. Hold on. How can you just . . . ? I'm here, too, you know. Don't forget I exist just 'cuz you can't understand me.

STEVE: Please repeat?

DALE: I get better communication from my fish. Look, we go see movie. Three here. See? One, two, three. Three can see movie. Only two can dance.

STEVE: *(To Grace)* I ask you to go dance.

GRACE: True, but . . .

10 **DALE:** *(To Grace)* That would really be a screw, you know? You invite me down here, you don't have anyone for me to go out with, but you decide to go dancing.

GRACE: Dale, I understand.

DALE: Understand? That would really be a screw. *(To Steve)* Look, if you wanna dance, go find yourself some nice FOB partner.

STEVE: "FOB"? Has what meaning?

GRACE: Dale . . .

15 **DALE:** F-O-B. Fresh Off the Boat. FOB.

GRACE: Dale, I agree.

DALE: See, we both agree. *(To Grace)* He's a pretty prime example, isn't he? All those foreign students—

GRACE: I mean, I agree about going dancing.

DALE: —go swimming in their underwear and everything—What?

20 **GRACE:** *(To Steve)* Please understand. This is not the right time for dancing.

STEVE: Okay.

DALE: "Okay." It's okay when *she* says it's okay.

STEVE: *(To Dale)* "Fresh Off Boat" has what meaning?

Pause.

DALE: *(To Grace)* Did you ever hear about Dad his first year in the U.S.?

25 **GRACE:** Dale, he wants to know . . .

DALE: Well, Gung Gung was pretty rich back then, so Dad must've been a pretty disgusting . . . one, too. You know, his first year here, he spent, like, thirteen thousand dollars. And that was back 'round 1950.

GRACE: Well, Mom never got anything.

STEVE: FOB means what?

DALE: That's probably 'cause women didn't get anything back then. Anyway, he bought himself a new car—all kinds of stuff, I guess. But then Gung Gung went bankrupt, so Dad had to work.

30 **GRACE:** And Mom starved.

DALE: Couldn't hold down a job. Wasn't used to taking orders from anyone.

GRACE: Mom was used to taking orders from everyone.

STEVE: Please explain this meaning.

DALE: Got fired from job after job. Something like fifteen in a year. He'd just walk in the front door and out the back, practically.

35 **GRACE:**   Well, at least he had a choice of doors. At least he was educated.

STEVE: *(To Dale)* Excuse!

DALE: Huh?

GRACE: He was educated. Here. In America. When Mom came over, she couldn't quit just 'cause she was mad at her employer. It was work or starve.

DALE: Well, Dad had some pretty lousy jobs, too.

40 **STEVE:**   *(To Dale)* Explain, please!

GRACE: Do you know what it's like to work eighty hours a week just to feed yourself?

DALE: Do you?

STEVE: Dale!

DALE: *(To Steve)* It means you. You know how, if you go to a fish store or something, they have the stuff that just came in that day? Well, so have you.

45 **STEVE:**   I do not understand.

DALE: Forget it. That's part of what makes you one.

Pause.

STEVE: *(Picking up hot sauce, to Dale)* Hot. You want some?

Pause.

DALE: Well, yeah. Okay. Sure.

Steve puts hot sauce on Dale's food.

DALE: Hey, isn't that kinda a lot?

50 **GRACE:**   See, Steve's family comes from Shanghai.

DALE: Hmmmm. Well, I'll try it.

He takes a gulp, puts down his food.

GRACE: I think perhaps that was too much for him.

DALE: No.

GRACE: Want some water?

55 **DALE:**   Yes.

Grace exits.

DALE: You like hot sauce? You like your food hot? All right—here. *(He dumps the contents of the jar on Steve's plate, stirs.)* Fucking savage. Don't you ever worry about your intestines falling out?

Grace enters, gives water to Dale. Steve sits shocked.

DALE: Thanks. FOBs can eat anything, huh? They're specially trained. Helps maintain the characteristic greasy look.

Steve, cautiously, begins to eat his food.

DALE: What—? Look, Grace, he's eating that! He's amazing! A freak! What a cannibal!

GRACE: *(Taking Dale's plate)* Want me to throw yours out?

60 **DALE:** *(Snatching it back)* Huh? No. No, I can eat it.

Dale and Steve stare at each other across the table. In unison, they pick up as large a glob of food as possible, stuff it into their mouths. They cough and choke. They rest, repeat the face-off a second time. They continue in silent pain. Grace, who has been watching this, speaks to us.

GRACE: Yeah. It's tough trying to live in Chinatown. But it's tough trying to live in Torrance, too. It's true. I don't like being alone. You know, when Mom could finally bring me to the U.S., I was already ten. But I never studied my English very hard in Taiwan, so I got moved back to the second grade. There were a few Chinese girls in the fourth grade, but they were American-born, so they wouldn't even talk to me. They'd just stay with themselves and compare how much clothes they all had, and make fun of the way we all talked. I figured I had a better chance of getting in with the white kids than with them, so in junior high I started bleaching my hair and hanging out at the beach—you know, Chinese hair looks pretty lousy when you bleach it. After a while, I knew what beach was gonna be good on any given day, and I could tell who was coming just by his van. But the American-born Chinese, it didn't matter to them. They just giggled and went to their own dances. Until my senior year in high school—that's how long it took for me to get over this whole thing. One night I took Dad's car and drove on Hollywood Boulevard, all the way from downtown to Beverly Hills, then back on Sunset. I was looking and listening—all the time with the window down, just so I'd feel like I was part of the city. And that Friday, it was—I guess—I said, "I'm lonely. And I don't like it. I don't like being alone." And that was all. As soon as I said it, I felt all of the breeze—it was really cool on my face—and I heard all of the radio—and the music sounded really good, you know? So I drove home.

Pause. Dale bursts out coughing.

GRACE: Oh, I'm sorry. Want some more water, Dale?

DALE: It's okay. I'll get it myself. *(He exits.)*

STEVE: *(Looks at Grace)* Good, huh?

Steve and Grace stare at each other, as Lights Fade to Black.

ACT II

In blackout.

DALE: I am much better now. *(Single spot on Dale)* I go out now. Lots. I can, anyway. Sometimes I don't ask anyone, so I don't go out. But I could. *(Pause)* I am much better now. I have friends now. Lots. They drive Porsche Carreras. Well, one does. He has a house up in the Hollywood Hills where I can stand and look down on the lights of L.A. I guess I haven't really been there yet. But I could easily go. I'd just have to ask. *(Pause)* My parents—they don't know nothing about the world, about watching Benson at the Roxy, about ordering *hors d'oeuvres* at Scandia's, downshifting onto the Ventura Freeway at midnight. They're yellow ghosts and they've tried to cage me up with Chinese-ness when all the time we were in America. *(Pause)* So, I've had to work real hard—real hard—to be myself. To not be a Chinese, a yellow, a slant, a gook. To be just a human being, like everyone else, *(Pause)* I've paid my dues. And that's why I am much better now. I'm making it, you know? I'm making it in America.

A napkin is thrown in front of Dale's face from right. As it passes, the lights go up. The napkin falls on what we recognize as the dinner table from the last scene. We are in the back room. Dinner is over. Steve has thrown the napkin from where he is sitting in his chair. Dale is standing upstage of the table and had been talking to Steve.

DALE: So, look, will you just not be so . . . Couldn't you just be a little more . . . ? I mean, we don't have to do all this . . . You know what's gonna happen to us tomorrow morning? *(He burps.)* What kinda diarrhea . . . ? Look, maybe if you could just be a little more . . . *(He gropes.)* normal. Here—stand up.

Steve does.

DALE: Don't smile like that. Okay. You ever see *Saturday Night Fever?*
STEVE: Oh. *Saturday* . . .
5 **DALE:** Yeah.
STEVE: Oh. *Saturday Night Fever.* Disco.
DALE: That's it. Okay. You know . . .
STEVE: John Travolta.
DALE: Right. John Travolta. Now, maybe if you could be a little more like him.
10 **STEVE:** Uh—Bee Gees?
DALE: Yeah, right. Bee Gees. But what I mean is . . .
STEVE: You like Bee Gees?
DALE: I dunno. They're okay. Just stand a little more like him, you know, his walk? *(Dale tries to demonstrate.)*
STEVE: I believe Bee Gees very good.
15 **DALE:** Yeah. Listen.
STEVE: You see movie name of . . .
DALE: Will you listen for a sec?
STEVE: . . . *Grease?*
DALE: Hold on!
20 **STEVE:** Also Bee Gees.

DALE: I'm trying to help you!
STEVE: Also John Travolta?
DALE: I'm trying to get you normal!
STEVE: And—Oliver John-Newton.
25 **DALE:** WILL YOU SHUT UP? I'M TRYING TO HELP YOU! I'M
TRYING . . .
STEVE: Very good!
DALE: . . . TO MAKE YOU LIKE JOHN TRAVOLTA!

Dale grabs Steve by the arm. Pause. Steve coldly knocks Dale's hands away. Dale picks up the last of the dirty dishes on the table and backs into the kitchen. Grace enters from the kitchen with the box wrapped in Act I. She sits in a chair and goes over the wrapping, her back to Steve. He gets up and begins to go for the box, almost reaching her. She turns around suddenly, though, at which point he drops to the floor and pretends to be looking for something. She then turns back front, and he resumes his attempt. Just as he reaches the kitchen door, Dale enters with a wet sponge.

DALE: *(To Steve)* Oh, you finally willing to help? I already brought in all
the dishes, you know. Here—wipe the table.

Dale gives sponge to Steve, returns to kitchen. Steve throws the sponge on the floor, sits back at table. Grace turns around, sees sponge on the floor, picks it up, and goes to wipe the table. She brings the box with her and holds it in one hand.

GRACE: Look—you've been wanting this for some time now. Okay.
Here. I'll give it to you. *(She puts it on the table.)* A welcome to this
country. You don't have to fight for it—I'll give it to you instead.

Pause; Steve pushes the box off the table.

30 **GRACE:** Okay. Your choice.

Grace wipes the table.

DALE: *(Entering from kitchen; sees Grace)* What—you doing this?
GRACE: Don't worry, Dale.
DALE: I asked him to do it.
GRACE: I'll do it.
35 **DALE:** I asked him to do it. He's useless! *(Dale takes the sponge.)* Look, I
don't know how much English you know, but look-ee! *(He uses a mock
Chinese accent.)*
GRACE: Dale, don't do that.
DALE: *(Using sponge)* Look—makes table all clean, see?
GRACE: You have to understand . . .
DALE: Ooooh! Nice and clean!
40 **GRACE:** . . . he's not used to this.
DALE: "Look! I can see myself!"
GRACE: Look, I can do this. Really.

DALE: Here—now you do. (*Dale forces Steve's hand onto the sponge.*) Good. Very good. Now, move it around. (*Dale leads Steve's hand.*) Oh, you learn so fast. Get green card, no time flat, buddy.

Dale removes his hand; Steve stops.

DALE: Uh-uh-uh. You must do it yourself. Come. There—now doesn't that make you feel proud?

He takes his hand off; Steve stops. Dale gives up, crosses downstage. Steve remains at the table, still.

45 DALE: Jesus! I'd trade him in for a vacuum cleaner any day.
GRACE: You shouldn't humiliate him like that.
DALE: What humiliate? I asked him to wipe the table, that's all.
GRACE: See, he's different. He probably has a lot of servants at home.
DALE: Big deal. He's in America, now. He'd better learn to work.
50 GRACE: He's rich, you know.
DALE: So what? They all are. Rich FOBs.
GRACE: Does that include me?
DALE: Huh?
GRACE: Does that include me? Am I one of your "rich FOBs"?
55 DALE: What? Grace, c'mon, that's ridiculous. You're not rich. I mean, you're not poor, but you're not rich either. I mean, you're not a FOB. FOBs are different. You've been over here most of your life. You've had time to thaw out. You've thawed out really well, and, besides— you're my cousin.

Dale strokes Grace's hair, and they freeze as before. Steve, meanwhile, has almost imperceptibly begun to clean with his sponge. He speaks to the audience as if speaking with his family.

STEVE: Yes. I will go to America. "Mei Guo." (*Pause. He begins working.*) The white ghosts came into the harbor today. They promised that they would bring us to America, and that in America we would never want for anything. One white ghost told how the streets are paved with diamonds, how the land is so rich that pieces of gold lie on the road, and the worker-devils consider them too insignificant even to bend down for. They told of a land where there are no storms, no snow, but sunshine and warmth all year round, where a man could live out in the open and feel not even discomfort from the nature around him—a worker's paradise. A land of gold, a mountain of wealth, a land in which a man can make his fortune and grow without wrinkles into an old age. And the white ghosts are providing free passage both ways. (*Pause*) All we need to do is sign a worker's contract. (*Pause*) Yes, I am going to America.

At this point, Grace and Dale become mobile, but still fail to hear Steve. Grace picks up the box.

DALE: What's that?

STEVE: *(His wiping becomes increasingly frenzied.)* I am going to America because of its promises. I am going to follow the white ghosts because of their promises.

DALE: Is this for me?

60 **STEVE:** Because they promised! They promised! AND LOOK! YOU PROMISED! THIS IS SHIT! IT'S NOT TRUE.

DALE: *(Taking the box)* Let's see what's inside, is that okay?

STEVE: *(Shoves Dale to the ground and takes the box.)* IT IS NOT! *(With accent)* THIS IS MINE!

DALE: Well, what kind of shit is that?

STEVE: She gave this to me.

65 **DALE:** What kind of . . . we're not at your place. We're not in Hong Kong, you know. Look—look all around you—you see shit on the sidewalks?

STEVE: This is mine!

DALE: You see armies of rice-bowl haircuts?

STEVE: She gave this to me!

DALE: People here have their flies zipped up—see?

70 **STEVE:** You should not look in it.

DALE: So we're not in Hong Kong. And I'm not one of your servant boys that you can knock around—that you got by trading in a pack of pornographic playing cards—that you probably deal out to your friends. You're in America, understand?

STEVE: Quiet! Do you know who I am?

DALE: Yeah—you're a FOB. You're a rich FOB in the U.S. But you better watch yourself. 'Cause you can be sent back.

STEVE: Shut up! Do you know who I am?

75 **DALE:** You can be sent back, you know—just like that. 'Cause you're a guest here, understand?

STEVE: *(To Grace)* Tell him who I am.

DALE: I know who he is—heir to a fortune in junk merchandise. Big deal. Like being heir to Captain Crunch.

STEVE: Tell him!

Silence.

GRACE: You know it's not like that.

80 **STEVE:** Tell him!

DALE: Huh?

GRACE: All the stuff about rice bowls and—zippers—have you ever been there, Dale?

DALE: Well, yeah. Once. When I was ten.

GRACE: Well, it's changed a lot.

85 **DALE:** Remember getting heat rashes.

GRACE: People are dressing really well now—and the whole place has become really stylish—well, certainly not everybody, but the people

who are well-off enough to send their kids to American colleges—
they're really kinda classy.

DALE: Yeah.

GRACE: Sort of.

DALE: You mean, like him. So what? It's easy to be classy when you're
rich.

90 **GRACE:**   All I'm saying is . . . .

DALE: Hell, I could do that.

GRACE: Huh?

DALE: I could be classy, too, if I was rich.

GRACE: You *are* rich.

95 **DALE:**   No. Just upper-middle. Maybe.

GRACE: Compared to us, you're rich.

DALE: No, not really. And especially not compared to him. Besides,
when I was born we were still poor.

GRACE: Well, you're rich now.

DALE: Used to get one Life Saver a day.

100 **GRACE:**   That's all? One Life Saver?

DALE: Well, I mean, that's not all I lived on. We got normal food, too.

GRACE: I know, but . . .

DALE: Not like we were living in cardboard boxes or anything.

GRACE: All I'm saying is that the people who are coming in now—a lot
of them are different—they're already real Westernized. They don't
act like they're fresh off the boat.

105 **DALE:**   Maybe. But they're still FOBs.

STEVE: Tell him who I am!

DALE: Anyway, real nice dinner, Grace. I really enjoyed it.

GRACE: Thank you.

STEVE: Okay! I will tell myself.

110 **DALE:**   Go tell yourself—just don't bother us.

GRACE: (*Standing, to Steve*) What would you like to do now?

STEVE: Huh?

GRACE: You wanted to go out after dinner?

STEVE: Yes, yes. We go out.

115 **DALE:**   I'll drive. You sent the hearse home.

STEVE: I tell driver—return car after dinner.

DALE: How could you . . . ? What time did you . . . ? When did you tell
him to return? What time?

STEVE: (*Looks at his watch*) Seven-five.

DALE: No—not what time is it. What time you tell him to return?

120 **STEVE:**   Seven-five. Go see.

Dale exits through kitchen.

STEVE: (*No accent*) Why wouldn't you tell him who I am?

GRACE: Can Gwan Gung die?

Pause.

STEVE: No warrior can defeat Gwan Gung.

GRACE: Does Gwan Gung fear ghosts?

125   **STEVE:**   Gwan Gung fears no ghosts.

GRACE: Ghosts of warriors?

STEVE: No warrior ghosts.

GRACE: Ghosts that avenge?

STEVE: No avenging ghosts.

130   **GRACE:**   Ghosts forced into exile?

STEVE: No exiled ghosts.

GRACE: Ghosts that wait?

Pause.

STEVE: *(Quietly)* May I . . . take you out tonight? Maybe not tonight, but some other time? Another time? *(He strokes her hair.)* What has happened?

DALE: *(Entering)* I cannot believe it . . . *(He sees them.)* What do you think you're doing? *(He grabs Steve's hand. To Steve)* What . . . I step out for one second and you just go and—hell, you FOBs are sneaky. No wonder they check you so close at Immigration.

135   **GRACE:**   Dale, I can really take care of myself.

DALE: Yeah? What was his hand doing, then?

GRACE: Stroking my hair.

DALE: Well, yeah. I could see that. I mean, what was it doing stroking your hair? *(Pause)* Uh, never mind. All I'm saying is . . . *(He gropes.)* Jesus! If you want to be alone, why don't you just say so, huh? If that's what you really want, just say it, okay?

Pause.

DALE: Okay. Time's up.

140   **GRACE:**   Was the car out there?

DALE: Huh? Yeah. Yeah, it was. I could not believe it. I go outside and— thank God—there's no limousine. Just as I'm about to come back, I hear this sound like the roar of death and this big black shadow scrapes up beside me. I could not believe it!

STEVE: Car return—seven-five.

DALE: And when I asked him—I asked the driver, what time he'd been told to return. And he just looks at me and says, "Now."

STEVE: We go out?

145   **DALE:**   What's going on here? What is this?

STEVE: Time to go.

DALE: No! Not till you explain what's going on.

STEVE: *(To Grace)* You now want to dance?

DALE: *(To Grace)* Do you understand this? Was this coincidence?

150   **STEVE:**   *(Ditto)* I am told good things of American discos.

DALE: *(Ditto)* You and him just wanna go off by yourselves?

STEVE: I hear of Dillon's.

DALE: Is that it?

STEVE: You hear of Dillon's?
155 **DALE:** It's okay, you know.
STEVE: In Westwood.
DALE: I don't mind.
STEVE: Three—four stories.
DALE: Really.
160 **STEVE:** Live band.
DALE: Cousin.
STEVE: We go.

He takes Grace's hand.

DALE: He's just out to snake you, you know.

He takes the other hand. From this point on, almost unnoticeably, the lights begin to dim.

GRACE: Okay! That's enough! *(She pulls away.)* That's enough! I have to make all the decisions around here, don't I? When I leave it up to you two, the only place we go is in circles.
165 **DALE:** Well . . .
STEVE: No, I am suggesting place to go.
GRACE: Look, Dale, when I asked you here, what did I say we were going to do?
DALE: Uh—dinner and a movie—or something. But it was a different "we," then.
GRACE: It doesn't matter. That's what we're going to do.
170 **DALE:** I'll drive.
STEVE: My car can take us to movie.
GRACE: I think we better not drive at all. We'll stay right here. *(She removes Steve's tie.)* Do you remember this?
DALE: What—you think I borrow clothes or something? Hell, I don't even wear ties.

Grace takes the tie, wraps it around Dale's face like a blindfold.

DALE: Grace, what are you . . . ?
175 **GRACE:** *(To Steve)* Do you remember this?
DALE: I already told you. I don't need a closer look or nothing.
STEVE: Yes.
GRACE: *(Ties the blindfold, releases it)* Let's sit down.
DALE: Wait.
180 **STEVE:** You want me to sit here?
DALE: Grace, is he understanding you?
GRACE: Have you ever played Group Story?
STEVE: Yes, I have played that.
DALE: There—there he goes again! Grace, I'm gonna take . . .

He starts to remove the blindfold.

185 **GRACE:** *(Stopping him)* Dale, listen or you won't understand.

DALE: But how come *he's* understanding?

GRACE: Because he's listening.

DALE: But . . .

GRACE: Now, let's play Group Story.

190 **DALE:**   Not again. Grace, that's only good when you're stoned.

GRACE: Who wants to start? Steve, you know the rules?

STEVE: Yes—I understand.

DALE: See, we're talking normal speed—and he still understood.

GRACE: Dale, would you like to start?

Pause.

195 **DALE:**   All right.

By this time, the lights have dimmed, throwing shadows on the stage. Grace will strike two pots together to indicate each speaker change and the ritual will gradually take on elements of Chinese opera.

Uh, once upon a time . . . there were . . . three bears—Grace, this is ridiculous!

GRACE: Tell a story.

DALE: . . . three bears and they each had . . . cancer of the lymph nodes. Uh—and they were very sad. So the baby bear said, "I'll go to the new Cedar Sinai Hospital where they may have a cure for this fatal illness."

GRACE: But the new Cedar Sinai Hospital happened to be two thousand miles away—across the ocean.

STEVE: *(Gradually losing his accent)* That is very far.

200 **DALE:**   How did—? So, the bear tried to swim over, but his leg got chewed off by alligators—are there alligators in the Pacific Ocean?— Oh, well. So he ended up having to go for a leg *and* a cure for malignant cancer of the lymph nodes.

GRACE: When he arrived there, he came face to face with—

STEVE: With Gwan Gung, god of warriors, writers, and prostitutes.

DALE: And Gwan Gung looked at the bear and said . . .

GRACE: . . . strongly and with spirit . . .

205 **STEVE:**   "One-legged bear, what are you doing on my land? You are from America, are you not?"

DALE: And the bear said, "Yes. Yes."

GRACE: And Gwan Gung replied . . .

STEVE: *(Getting up)* By stepping forward, sword drawn, ready to wound, not kill, not end it so soon. To draw it out, play it, taunt it, make it feel like a dog.

DALE: Which is probably rather closely related to the bear.

210 **GRACE:**   Gwan Gung said—

STEVE: "When I came to America, did you lick my wounds? When I came to America, did you cure my sickness?"

DALE: And just as Gwan Gung was about to strike—

GRACE: There arrived Fa Mu Lan, the Woman Warrior. *(She stands, faces Steve. From here on in, striking pots together is not needed.)* "Gwan Gung."

STEVE: "What do you want? Don't interfere! Don't forget, I have gone before you into battle many times."

215 **DALE:**   But Fa Mu Lan seemed not to hear Gwan Gung's warning. She stood between him and the bear, drawing out her own sword.

GRACE: "You will learn I cannot forget. I don't forget, Gwan Gung. Spare the bear and I will present gifts."

STEVE: "Very well. He is hardly worth killing."

DALE: And the bear hopped off. Fa Mu Lan pulled a parcel from beneath her gown. *(She removes Dale's blindfold.)*

DALE: She pulled out two items.

220 **GRACE:**   "This is for you." *(She hands blindfold to Steve.)*

STEVE: "What is that?"

DALE: She showed him a beautiful piece of red silk, thick enough to be opaque, yet so light, he barely felt it in his hands.

GRACE: "Do you remember this?"

STEVE: "Why, yes. I used this silk for sport one day. How did you get hold of it?"

225 **DALE:**   Then she presented him with a second item. It was a fabric— thick and dried and brittle.

GRACE: "Do you remember this?"

STEVE: *(Turning away)* "No, no. I've never seen this before in my life. This has nothing to do with me. What is it—a dragon skin?"

DALE: Fa Mu Lan handed it to Gwan Gung.

GRACE: "Never mind. Use it—as a tablecloth. As a favor to me."

230 **STEVE:**   "It's much too hard and brittle. But, to show you my graciousness in receiving—I will use it tonight!"

DALE: That night, Gwan Gung had a large banquet, at which there was plenty, even for the slaves. But Fa Mu Lan ate nothing. She waited until midnight, till Gwan Gung and the gods were full of wine and empty of sense. Sneaking behind him, she pulled out the tablecloth, waving it above her head.

GRACE: *(Ripping the tablecloth from the table)* "Gwan Gung, you foolish boy. This thing you have used tonight as a tablecloth—it is the stretched and dried skins of my fathers. My fathers, whom you slew— for sport! And you have been eating their sins—you ate them!"

STEVE: "No. I was blindfolded. I did not know."

DALE: Fa Mu Lan waved the skin before Gwan Gung's face. It smelled suddenly of death.

235 **GRACE:**   "Remember the day you played? Remember? Well, eat that day, Gwan Gung."

STEVE: "I am not responsible. No. No."

Grace throws one end of the tablecloth to Dale, who catches it. Together, they become like Steve's parents. They chase him about the stage, waving the tablecloth like a net.

DALE: Yes!

GRACE: Yes!
STEVE: No!
240 DALE: You must!
GRACE: Go!
STEVE: Where?
DALE: To America!
GRACE: To work!
245 STEVE: Why?
DALE: Because!
GRACE: We need!
STEVE: No!
DALE: Why?
250 GRACE: Go.
STEVE: Hard!
DALE: So?
GRACE: Need.
STEVE: Far!
255 DALE: So?
GRACE: Need!
STEVE: Safe!
DALE: Here?
GRACE: No!
260 STEVE: Why?
DALE: Them.

Points.

GRACE: Them.

Points.

STEVE: Won't!
DALE: Must!
265 GRACE: Must!
STEVE: Won't!
DALE: Go!
GRACE: Go!
STEVE: Won't!
270 DALE: Bye!
GRACE: Bye!
STEVE: Won't!
DALE: Fare!
GRACE: Well!

Dale and Grace drop the tablecloth over Steve, who sinks to the floor. Grace then moves offstage, into the bathroom–storage room, while Dale goes upstage and stands with his back to the audience. Silence.

275 **STEVE:**   *(Begins pounding the ground)* Noooo! *(He throws off the tablecloth, standing up full. Lights up full, blindingly.)* I am GWAN GUNG!

DALE: *(Turning downstage suddenly)* What . . . ?

STEVE: I HAVE COME TO THIS LAND TO STUDY!

DALE: Grace . . .

STEVE: TO STUDY THE ARTS OF WAR, OF LITERATURE, OF RIGHTEOUSNESS!

280 **DALE:**   A movie's fine.

STEVE: I FOUGHT THE WARS OF THE THREE KINGDOMS!

DALE: An ordinary movie, let's go.

STEVE: I FOUGHT WITH THE FIRST PIONEERS, THE FIRST WARRIORS THAT CHOSE TO FOLLOW THE WHITE GHOSTS TO THIS LAND!

DALE: You can pick okay?

285 **STEVE:**   I WAS THEIR HERO, THEIR LEADER, THEIR FIRE!

DALE: I'll even let him drive, how's that?

STEVE: AND THIS LAND IS MINE! IT HAS NO RIGHT TO TREAT ME THIS WAY!

GRACE: No. Gwan Gung, *you* have no rights.

STEVE: Who's speaking?

290 **GRACE:**   *(Enters with a* da dao *and* mao, *two swords)* It is Fa Mu Lan. You are in a new land, Gwan Gung.

STEVE: Not new—I have been here before, many times. This time, I said I will have it easy. I will come as no ChinaMan before—on a plane, with money and rank.

GRACE: And?

STEVE: And—there is no change. I am still treated like this! This land . . . has no right. I AM GWAN GUNG!

GRACE: And I am Fa Mu Lan.

295 **DALE:**   I'll be Chiang Kai-shek, how's that?

STEVE: *(To Dale)* You! How can you—? I came over with your parents.

GRACE: *(Turning to Steve)* We are in America. And we have a battle to fight.

She tosses the da dao *to Steve. They square off.*

STEVE: I don't want to fight you.

GRACE: You killed my family.

300 **STEVE:**   You were revenged—I ate your father's sins.

GRACE: That's not revenge!

Swords strike.

GRACE: That was only the tease.

Strike.

GRACE: What's the point in dying if you don't know the cause of your death?

Series of strikes. Steve falls.

DALE: Okay! That's it!

Grace stands over Steve, her sword pointed at his heart. Dale snatches the sword from her hands. She does not move.

305 **DALE:**   Jesus! Enough is enough!

Dale takes Steve's sword; he also does not react.

DALE: What the hell kind of movie was that?

Dale turns his back on the couple, heads for the bathroom–storage room. Grace uses her now-invisible sword to thrust in and out of Steve's heart once.

DALE: That's it. Game's over. Now just sit down here. Breathe. One. Two. One. Two. Air. Good stuff. Glad they made it. Right, cousin?

Dale strokes Grace's hair. They freeze. Steve rises slowly to his knees and delivers a monologue to the audience.

STEVE: Ssssh! Please, miss! Please—quiet! I will not hurt you, I promise. All I want is . . . food . . . anything. You look full of plenty. I have not eaten almost one week now, but four days past when I found one egg and I ate every piece of it—including shell. Every piece, I ate. Please. Don't you have anything extra? *(Pause)* I want to. Now. This land does not want us any more than China. But I cannot. All work was done, then the bosses said they could not send us back. And I am running, running from Eureka, running from San Francisco, running from Los Angeles. And I been eating very little. One egg, only. *(Pause)* All America wants ChinaMen go home, but no one want it bad enough to pay our way. Now, please, can't you give even little? *(Pause)* I ask you, what you hate most? What work most awful for white woman? *(Pause)* Good. I will do that thing for you—you can give me food. *(Pause)* Think—you relax, you are given those things, clean, dry, press. No scrub, no dry. It is wonderful thing I offer you. *(Pause)* Good. Give me those and please bring food, or I be done before these things.

Grace steps away from Dale with box.

GRACE: Here—I've brought you something. *(She hands him the box.)* Open it.

He hesitates, then does, and takes out a small chong you bing.

310 **GRACE:**   Eat it.

He does, slowly at first, then ravenously.

GRACE: Good. Eat it all down. It's just food. Really. Feel better now? Good. Eat the *bing*. Hold it in your hands. Your hands . . . are beautiful. Lift it to your mouth. Your mouth . . . is beautiful. Bite it with your teeth. Your teeth . . . are beautiful. Crush it with your tongue. Your tongue . . . is beautiful. Slide it down your throat. Your throat . . . is beautiful.

STEVE: Our hands are beautiful.

She holds hers next to his.

GRACE: What do you see?

STEVE: I see . . . I see the hands of warriors.

315 **GRACE:**   Warriors? What of gods then?

STEVE: There are no gods that travel. Only warriors travel. *(Silence)* Would you like go dance?

GRACE: Yeah. Okay. Sure.

They start to leave. Dale speaks softly.

DALE: Well, if you want to be alone . . .

GRACE: I think we would, Dale. Is that okay? *(Pause)* Thanks for coming over. I'm sorry things got so screwed up.

320 **DALE:**   Oh—uh—that's okay. The evening was real . . . different, anyway.

GRACE: Yeah. Maybe you can take Frank off the tracks now?

DALE: *(laughing softly)* Yeah. Maybe I will.

STEVE: *(To Dale)* Very nice meeting you. *(Extends his hand)*

DALE: *(Does not take it)* Yeah. Same here.

Steve and Grace start to leave.

325 **DALE:**   You know . . . I think you picked up English faster than anyone I've ever met.

Pause.

STEVE: Thank you.

GRACE: See you.

STEVE: Good-bye.

DALE: Bye.

Grace and Steve exit.

CODA

Dale alone in the back room. He examines the swords, the tablecloth, the box. He sits down.

DALE: F-O-B. Fresh Off the Boat. FOB. Clumsy, ugly, greasy FOB. Loud, stupid, four-eyed FOB. Big feet. Horny. Like Lenny in *Of Mice and Men*. F-O-B. Fresh Off the Boat. FOB.

Slow fade to black

READING AND REACTING

1. Whom do you see as the central character in *FOB?* Why?

2. Are the characters in *FOB* developed as individuals, or are they presented simply as three different cultural points of view? Explain.

3. Why do you think the play has only three characters? What minor characters might Hwang have introduced? How might these characters have changed the play?

4. How do props and setting shed light on the play's characters?

5. At various points in the play, Steve switches from Chinese to English or from English to Chinese. How do these sudden changes in language help you to understand his character?

6. How does Grace change when she assumes the role of Fa Mu Lan? How does her language reveal this change? Consider in particular the tone, the level of formality, and the use of figurative language.

7. Dale is very impatient with Steve. Why? Cite examples of words and actions that illustrate this impatience.

8. When Steve speaks as Gwan Gung, he is quite emotional. Why is he so emotional? Identify lines of dialogue that convey his emotion.

9. What Chinese words and phrases do characters use in *FOB?* Why do you think each expression is used instead of its English equivalent?

10. Identify some examples of verbal irony. Why is irony used in each instance?

11. Choose one speech delivered by Grace, Dale, or Steve in the presence of another character. Make sure the speech is one you believe conceals the character's true feelings. Then suggest several asides—comments directed to the audience—that might reveal what you believe the character is thinking.

12. At the end of the play, do you think any character has changed? How can you tell? Is the change believable? Explain.

13. **JOURNAL ENTRY** *FOB* deals implicitly with the question of what it means to be an American. Does the play ever resolve this issue?

14. **CRITICAL PERSPECTIVE** A 1988 profile of Hwang in the *New York Times* noted that although *FOB* won several prestigious theatre awards, "not everyone was comfortable with his unboosterish portrayal of assimilation":

    My work has always been controversial within certain segments of the Asian-American community," says Hwang. "This is a community that is generally not represented well at all on the stage, in the media, etc. So on those few occasions when something comes along, everybody feels obligated to make sure that it represents his own point of view. And of course no artist can do that. . . . I find that sort of political criticism much more difficult and substantial than the esthetic criticism that I received . . .

that's nothing compared with being told that you've set the Asian-American back 10 years.

Do you see the play's portrayal of Asian-Americans as sympathetic? Can you see any reasons why the Asian-American community might have objected to Hwang's portrayals?

WRITING SUGGESTIONS: CHARACTER

1. In both *FOB* and *Death of a Salesman*, characters pursue their versions of the American Dream. Choose one character from each play, define his or her idea of the American Dream, and explain how each tries to make the dream a reality. In each case, consider the obstacles the character encounters and try to account for his or her success or lack of success.

2. The female characters in this chapter's plays—Mrs. Popov, Gertrude, Ophelia, Linda, and Grace—are all in one way or another in conflict with men. Focusing on the women in two different plays, define each conflict and consider whether or not it is resolved in the play. To what extent do you think the time in which each play was written determines how successful each woman is in resolving her basic conflict with a man? (If you like, you may discuss a female character in one of the plays in another chapter.)

3. Minor characters are often flat characters, or types; in many cases their sole function is to advance the plot or to highlight a particular trait in a major character. Sometimes, however, minor characters may be of more than minor importance. Choose one minor character from *Hamlet* or *Death of a Salesman*, (or from a play in another chapter), and write a paper in which you discuss how the play would be different without this character.

4. Locate several newspaper or magazine reviews analyzing different actors' interpretations of the same role (for example, Lee J. Cobb and Dustin Hoffman as Willy Loman). Based on your understanding of the play, which actor's interpretation seems most accurate? Explain your conclusion in an essay.

5. Review the explanation of tragedy in Chapter 20, "Understanding Drama." Using the discussion of the tragic hero as your guide, write an essay in which you discuss either Willy Loman or Hamlet as a tragic hero. (If you like, you may also consider the definition of tragedy offered by Professor Henry Harper in his final speech in *Another Antigone*, p. 1741.)

CHAPTER 24

Staging

In reading a play rather than witnessing it on stage, we . . . have to imagine what it might look like in performance, projecting in our mind's eye an image of the setting and the props, as well as the movements, gestures, facial expressions, and vocal intonations of the characters. . . . And we—like the director, designers, and actors— must develop our understanding of the play and our idea of the play in performance primarily from a careful reading of the dialogue, as well as from whatever stage directions and other information the dramatist might provide about the characters and the setting.

CARL H. KLAUS, MIRIAM GILBERT, AND BRAFORD S. FIELD, JR.,
STAGES OF DRAMA

The playwright as playwright is in part a director. If he is truly a man of the theatre (some playwrights only suffer the theatre but do not feel they belong to it) the playwright "sees" the play on the stage as he writes. His dialogue as well as his notations of stage behavior suggest movement and part of the total physical life that the script is to acquire when it is produced.

HAROLD CLURMON, ON *DIRECTING*

Whether the director sees . . . a play as tragedy, comedy or even farce will have an immediate and very practical effect on his handling of the production: it will influence his casting, the design of the set and costumes, the tone, rhythm and pacing of the performance. And, above all, the style in which it is to be acted.

MARTIN ESSLIN, *AN ANATOMY OF DRAMA*

The argument is sometimes advanced that the complete verisimilitude of the movies is more enjoyable than the necessarily limited illusionism of the live theater. Hollywood producers evidently believe the public in general holds such an opinion. Yet accepting conventions can be a source of pleasure for its own sake, just as children have always had fun putting on shows in the cellar by ignoring the steampipe or else turning it into the Brooklyn Bridge.

THELMA ALTSHULER AND RICHARD PAUL JENARO,
RESPONSES TO DRAMA

[W]hen first written and produced, A Doll's House was radical not only in its subject, which was certainly shocking at the time, but also in style. The premiere at the Royal Theatre in Copenhagen in December of 1879 was marked by the kind of realistic detail that still seemed revolutionary decades later at Stanislavski's Moscow Arts Theatre. On stage, fresh flowers, a fully stocked sewing basket, and a real woodpile gave life to Nora and Torvald's "cozy nest." What's more, even the offstage hallway and study were rendered in precise detail to further heighten the sense of reality on stage.

This astonishing realism made audiences of 1879 sit up and take notice. It forced them to face domestic issues as they never had before. Ever since, actors and directors have found new ways of achieving that freshness and connection.

VICTORIA ABRASH, *PLAYBILL: NORA*

Staging refers to the elements of a play's production that determine how the play looks and sounds to an audience. It encompasses the **stage settings** or **sets**—scenery and props—as well as the costumes, lighting, sound effects, and music that bring the play to life on the stage. In short, staging is everything that goes into making a written script a play.

Most contemporary staging in the West has concentrated on recreating the outside world. This concept of staging, which has dominated Western theatrical productions for centuries, would seem alien in many non-Western theaters. Japanese kabuki dramas (p. 2) and No plays, for example, depend on staging conventions that make no attempt to mirror reality or everyday speech. Scenery and costumes are largely symbolic, and often actors wear highly stylized makeup or masks. Although some European and American playwrights have been strongly influenced by non-Western staging, the majority of plays being produced in the West still try to create the illusion of reality.

STAGE DIRECTIONS

Usually a playwright presents instructions for the staging of a play in **stage directions**—remarks that comment on the scenery, the movements of the performers, the lighting, and the placement of props. (In the absence of detailed stage directions, dialogue can provide information about staging.) Sometimes these stage directions are quite simple, leaving much to the imagination of the director. Consider how little specific information about the staging of the play is provided in these stage directions from Samuel Beckett's 1952 absurdist play *Waiting for Godot*.

ACT I

A country road. A tree. Evening.

Of course you could say the stage directions provide all the information that is needed to stage *Waiting for Godot*. Often, however, playwrights furnish more information about staging. Consider these lines, which appear before Act I of Anton Chekhov's *The Cherry Orchard*.

ACT I

A room, which has always been called the nursery. One of the doors leads into Anya's room. Dawn, sun rises during the scene. May, the cherry trees in flower, but it is cold in the garden with the frost of the early morning. Windows closed.
   Enter Dunyasha with a candle and Lopahin with a book in his hand.

These comments indicate that the first act takes place in a room with more than one door and that several windows reveal cherry trees in bloom. They also specify that the lighting should simulate dawn and that certain characters should enter carrying particular props. Still, Chekhov leaves it up to those staging the play to decide on the costumes for the characters and on the furniture that will be placed around the room.

Some stage directions are even more specific. George Bernard Shaw's long, complex stage directions are legendary in the theater. Consider the detail he provides in this segment of the stage directions from his comedy *The Doctor's Dilemma*.

The consulting-room has two windows looking on Queen Anne Street. Between the two is a marble-topped console, with haunched gilt legs ending in sphinx claws. The huge pier-glass [a long narrow mirror that fits between two windows] which surmounts it is mostly disabled from reflection by elaborate painting on its surface of palms, ferns, lilies, tulips, and sunflowers. The adjoining wall contains the fireplace, with two arm-chairs before it. As we happen to face the corner we see nothing of the other two walls. On the right of the fireplace, or rather on the right of any person facing the fireplace, is the door. On the left is the writing-table at which Redpenny [a medical student] sits. It is an untidy table with a microscope, several test tubes, and a spirit lamp [an alcohol burner] standing up through its litter of papers. There is a couch in the middle of the room, at right angles to the console, and parallel to the fireplace. A chair stands between the couch and the window. Another in the corner. Another at the other end of the windowed wall. . . . The wallpaper and carpets are mostly green. . . . The house, in fact, was so well furnished in the middle of the XIXth century that it stands unaltered to this day and is still quite presentable.

Not only does Shaw describe the furniture to be placed in the room, but he also includes a good deal of detail—specifying, for example, "gilt legs ending in sphinx claws" and "test tubes and a spirit lamp" that clutter the writing table. In addition, maintaining a great degree of control over the stage setting of his play, he defines furniture placement and specifies color.

Regardless of how detailed the stage directions are, they do not eliminate the need for creative interpretations on the part of the producer, director, set designers, and actors (See "Actors' Interpretations," p. 1339). Stage directions—and, for that matter, the entire script—are the foundation on which to construct the play that the audience finally sees. Many directors, in fact, see stage directions as suggestions, not requirements, and some even consider them more confusing than helpful. Therefore, directors may choose to interpret a play's stage directions quite loosely—or even to ignore them.

THE USES OF STAGING

When audiences watch a play, it is easy for them to take staging for granted. But staging is a key element of drama, and details that are seen and heard—such as costumes, props, scenery, lighting, and music and sound effects—often reinforce the theme of the play or communicate important information about characters and their motivation.

Costumes   Costumes not only establish the historical period in which a play is set, but they also can provide insight into the character who wears them. When he first appears, Hamlet is profoundly disillusioned and quite melancholy. This fact was immediately apparent to Shakespeare's audience because Hamlet is dressed in sable, which to the Elizabethans signified a melancholy nature. In Tennessee Williams's *The Glass Menagerie* (p. 1898) Laura's dress of soft violet material and her hair ribbon reflect her delicate, childlike innocence. In contrast, her mother's "imitation velvety-looking cloth coat with imitation fur collar" and her "enormous black patent-leather pocketbook" reveal her somewhat pathetic attempt to achieve respectability. Later in the play, awaiting the "gentleman caller," Laura's mother wears a dress that is both outdated and inappropriately youthful, suggesting both her desire to relive her own past and her increasing desperation to marry off her daughter.

Props   **Props** (short for *properties*)—pictures, furnishings, objects and the like—can also be significant, helping audiences to interpret characters and themes. For example, the handkerchief in Shakespeare's *Othello* gains significance as the play progresses. It begins as an innocent object and ends as the piece of evidence that convinces Othello his wife is committing adultery. Sometimes props can have symbolic significance. During the Renaissance, for example, flowers had symbolic meaning. In Act 4 of *Hamlet* Ophelia, who is mad, gives flowers to various characters. In a note to the play the critic Thomas Parrott points out the symbolic significance of her gifts. To Claudius, the murderer of Hamlet's father, she gives fennel and columbines, which signify flattery and ingratitude; to the Queen she gives rue and daisies, which symbolize sadness and unfaithfulness. Although the full implications of the flowers are not apparent to modern audiences, many people in Shakespeare's audience would have been aware of their meaning.

The furnishings in a room can also reveal a lot about a play's characters and themes. Willy Loman's house in Arthur Miller's *Death of a Salesman* (p. 1458) is sparsely furnished, revealing the declining financial status of the family. The kitchen contains a table and three chairs, and the bedroom is furnished with only a brass bed and a straight chair. Over the bed on a shelf is Biff's silver athletic trophy, which is a constant reminder of his loss of status. Like Willy Loman's house, the Wingfield apartment in *The Glass Menagerie* reflects its inhabitants' modest economic circumstances. For example, the living room, which contains a sofa that unfolds into a bed, also serves as a bedroom for Laura. In addition, one piece of furniture highlights a central theme of the play: An old-fashioned cabinet in the living room displays a collection of transparent glass animals which, like Laura, are too fragile to be removed from their surroundings.

Scenery and Lighting   Playwrights often use scenery and lighting to create imaginative stage settings. In *Death of a Salesman* the house is surrounded by "towering angular shapes" of apartment houses that emphasize the "small, fragile-seeming home." Arthur Miller calls for a set that is "wholly, or in some places, transparent." Whenever the action is in the present, the actors observe the imaginary boundaries that separate rooms or mark the exterior walls of the house. But in scenes where the characters reenact events of the past, they walk over the boundaries and come to the front of the stage. By lighting up and darkening different parts of the stage, Miller is able to shift from the present to the past and back again.

The set of *The Glass Menagerie* is also innovative, combining imaginative backdrops with subtle lighting. As the curtain rises, the audience sees the dark rear wall of the Wingfield tenement, which is flanked on both sides by alleys lined with clotheslines, garbage cans, and fire escapes. After Tom delivers his opening narrative, the tenement wall becomes transparent, revealing the interior of the Wingfield apartment. To create this effect, Williams uses a **scrim,** a curtain that when illuminated from the front appears solid but when lit from the back becomes transparent. For Williams such "atmospheric touches" represented a new direction in theater that contrasted with the theater of "realistic conventions."

Contemporary playwrights often rely on sets that combine realistic and nonrealistic elements. In his 1988 Tony Award–winning play *M. Butterfly*, for example, David Henry Hwang uses not only scrims, but also a large red lacquered ramp that runs from the bottom to the top of the stage. The action takes place beneath, on, and above the ramp, creating an effect not unlike that created by Shakespeare's multiple stages. At several points in the play a character who acts as the narrator sits beneath the ramp, addressing the audience, while at the same time a character on top of the ramp acts out the narrator's words.

Music and Sound Effects   Staging involves more than visual elements such as costumes and scenery; it also includes music and sound effects. The stage directions for *Death of a Salesman,* for example, begin, *"A melody is heard, played upon a flute."* Although not specifically identified, the music is described as *"small and fine, telling of grass and trees and the horizon."* Interestingly, this music stands in stark contrast to the claustrophobic urban setting of the play. Music also has a major role in *The Glass Menagerie,* where a single recurring tune, like circus music, weaves in and out of the play. This musical motif not only gives emotional impact to certain lines, but also suggests the fantasy world into which Laura has retreated.

Sound effects play an important part in Henrik Ibsen's *A Doll House* (p. 1185). At the end of the play, after his wife has left him, Torvald Helmer sits alone on the stage. Notice in the following stage directions how the final sound effect cuts short Helmer's attempt at self-deluding optimism:

> **HELMER:**   *(Sinks down on a chair by the door, face buried in his hands.)* Nora! Nora! *(Looking about and rising.)* Empty. She's gone. *(A sudden hope leaps in him.)* The greatest miracle—?
>
> *From below, the sound of a door slamming shut.*

When you read a play, it may be difficult to appreciate the effect that staging can have on a performance. As you read, then, pay particular attention to the stage directions, and use your imagination to visualize the scenes the playwright describes. In addition, try to imagine the play's sights and sounds, and consider the options for staging that are suggested as characters speak to one another. Although even such careful reading cannot substitute for the actual experience of seeing a play performed, it will help you to go beyond the words on the page and to imagine the play the way it might appear on the stage.

▼▼

CHECKLIST FOR WRITING ABOUT STAGING

- ◆ What information about staging is contained in the stage directions of the play?
- ◆ What information about staging is suggested by the play's dialogue?
- ◆ What information about staging is left to the imagination?

◆ How might different decisions about staging affect the play?

◆ Do the stage directions provide information about how characters are supposed to look or behave?

◆ What costumes are specified? In what ways do costumes give insight into the characters who wear them?

◆ What props play an important part in the play? Do these props have symbolic meaning?

◆ Is the scenery used in the play special or unusual in any way?

◆ What lighting does the stage directions specify? In what way does this lighting affect your reaction to the play?

◆ In what ways are music and sound effects used in the play? Are musical themes associated with any characters? Do music and sound effects heighten the emotional impact of certain lines?

◆ How does staging help to communicate the play's themes?

▲▲

MILCHA SANCHEZ-SCOTT* (1949 or 1950–   )   is a Los Angeles–based writer of plays including *Dog Lady* and *The Cuban Swimmer,* both one act plays (1984); *Roosters,* published in *On New Ground: Contemporary Hispanic American Plays* (1987); and *Stone Wedding,* produced at the Los Angeles Theater Center (1988). Also produced by the Los Angeles Theater Center, her play *Carmen* was adapted from Georges Bizet's opera of the same title.

Sanchez-Scott, born in Bali, is the daughter of an Indonesian mother and a Colombian-Mexican father. Her early childhood was spent in Mexico, South America, and Britain, before her family moved to San Diego when she was fourteen. Since then, she has worked as an actress, as a maid, and at an employment agency.

According to William A. Henry in *Time,* visionary or hallucinatory elements in Sanchez-Scott's plays derive from the Latin American "magic realism" tradition of Jorge Luis Borges and Gabriel García Márquez. In *Roosters,* for example, what seems "a straightforward depiction of the life of farmlands gives way to mysterious visitations, symbolic cockfights enacted by dancers, virginal girls wearing wings, archetypal confrontations between father and son."

In 1984 the New York production of *The Cuban Swimmer* was noteworthy for an ingeniously designed set that realistically recreated on stage Pacific Ocean waves, a helicopter, and a tramp boat. According to the *New York Times,* "The audience can almost feel the resisting tides and the California oil slick that are represented by a watery-blue floor and curtain."

---

* No photograph available for this author.

Jeannette Mirabel, as the Cuban swimmer, made an "auspicious" debut in the play, according to the *Times;* "In a tour de force of balletic movements, she [kept] her arms fluttering in the imaginary waters throughout the play."

MILCHA SANCHEZ-SCOTT

The Cuban Swimmer

(1984)

CHARACTERS

MARGARITA SUÁREZ, *the swimmer*
EDUARDO SUÁREZ, *her father,*
   the coach
SIMÓN SUÁREZ, *her brother*
AÍDA SUÁREZ, *her mother*

ABUELA, *her grandmother*
VOICE OF MEL MUNSON
VOICE OF MARY BETH WHITE
VOICE OF RADIO OPERATOR

SETTING

The Pacific Ocean between San Pedro and Catalina Island.

TIME

Summer.

Live conga drums can be used to punctuate the action of the play.

SCENE 1

Pacific Ocean. Midday. On the horizon, in perspective, a small boat enters up-stage left, crosses to upstage right, and exits. Pause. Lower on the horizon, the same boat, in larger perspective, enters upstage right, crosses and exits upstage left. Blackout.

SCENE 2

Pacific Ocean. Midday. The swimmer, Margarita Suárez, is swimming. On the boat following behind her are her father, Eduardo Suárez, holding a megaphone, and Simón, her brother, sitting on top of the cabin with his shirt off, punk sunglasses on, binoculars hanging on his chest.

EDUARDO: *(Leaning forward, shouting in time to Margarita's swimming.)* Uno, dos, uno, dos. Y uno, dos . . . keep your shoulders parallel to the water.

SIMÓN: I'm gonna take these glasses off and look straight into the sun.

EDUARDO: *(Through megaphone.) Muy bien, muy bien* . . . but punch those arms in, baby.

SIMÓN: *(Looking directly at the sun through binoculars.)* Come on, come on, zap me. Show me something. *(He looks behind at the shoreline and ahead at the sea.)* Stop! Stop, *Papi!* Stop!

(Aída Suárez and Abuela, the swimmer's mother and grandmother, enter running from the back of the boat.)

5 **AÍDA AND ABUELA:** Qué? Qué es?

AÍDA: *Es un* shark?

EDUARDO: Eh?

ABUELA: Que es un shark dicen?

(Eduardo blows whistle. Margarita looks up at the boat.)

SIMÓN: No, *Papi,* no shark, no shark. We've reached the halfway mark.

10 **ABUELA:** *(Looking into the water.) A dónde está?*

AÍDA: It's not in the water.

ABUELA: Oh, no? Oh, no?

AÍDA: No! *A poco* do you think they're gonna have signs in the water to say you are halfway to Santa Catalina? No. It's done very scientific. *A ver, hijo,* explain it to your grandma.

SIMÓN: Well, you see, Abuela—*(He points behind.)* There's San Pedro. *(He points ahead.)* And there's Santa Catalina. Looks halfway to me.

(Abuela shakes her head and is looking back and forth, trying to make the decision, when suddenly the sound of a helicopter is heard.)

15 **ABUELA:** *(Looking up.)* Virgencita de la Caridad del Cobre. *Qué es eso?*

(Sound of helicopter gets closer. Margarita looks up.)

MARGARITA: Papi, Papi!

(A small commotion on the boat, with Everybody pointing at the helicopter above. Shadows of the helicopter fall on the boat. Simón looks up at it through binoculars.)

Papi—*qué es?* What is it?

EDUARDO: *(Through megaphone.)* Uh . . . uh . . . uh, *un momentico . . . mi hija.* . . . Your *papi's* got everything under control, understand? Uh . . . you just keep stroking. And stay . . . uh . . . close to the boat.

SIMÓN: Wow, *Papi!* We're on TV, man! Holy Christ, we're all over the fucking U.S.A.! It's Mel Munson and Mary Beth White!

Aída: *Por Dios!* Simón, don't swear. And put on your shirt.

(Aída fluffs her hair, puts on her sunglasses and waves to the helicopter. Simón leans over the side of the boat and yells to Margarita.)

20 **Simón:** Yo, Margo! You're on TV, man.

Eduardo: Leave your sister alone. Turn on the radio.

Margarita: *Papi! Qué está pasando?*

Abuela: *Que es la televisión dicen? (She shakes her head.) Porque como yo no puedo ver nada sin mis espejuelos.*

(Abuela rummages through the boat, looking for her glasses. Voices of Mel Munson and Mary Beth White are heard over the boat's radio.)

Mel's Voice: As we take a closer look at the gallant crew of *La Havana* . . . and there . . . yes, there she is . . . the little Cuban swimmer from Long Beach, California, nineteen-year-old Margarita Suárez. The unknown swimmer is our Cinderella entry . . . a bundle of tenacity, battling her way through the choppy, murky waters of the cold Pacific to reach the Island of Romance . . . Santa Catalina . . . where should she be the first to arrive, two thousand dollars and a gold cup will be waiting for her.

25 **Aída:** Doesn't even cover our expenses.

Abuela: *Qué dice?*

Eduardo: Shhhh!

Mary Beth's Voice: This is really a family effort, Mel, and—

Mel's Voice: Indeed it is. Her trainer, her coach, her mentor, is her father, Eduardo Suárez. Not a swimmer himself, it says here, Mr. Suárez is head usher of the Holy Name Society and the owner-operator of Suárez Treasures of the Sea and Salvage Yard. I guess it's one of those places—

30 **Mary Beth's Voice:** If I might interject a fact here, Mel, assisting in this swim is Mrs. Suárez, who is a former Miss Cuba.

Mel's Voice: And a beautiful woman in her own right. Let's try and get a closer look.

(Helicopter sound gets louder. Margarita, frightened, looks up again.)

Margarita: *Papi!*

Eduardo: *(Through megaphone.) Mi hija,* don't get nervous . . . it's the press. I'm handling it.

Aída: I see how you're handling it.

35 **Eduardo:** *(Through megaphone.)* Do you hear? Everything is under control. Get back into your rhythm. Keep your elbows high and kick and kick and kick and kick . . .

Abuela: *(Finds her glasses and puts them on.) Ay sí, es la televisión . . . (She points to helicopter.) Qué lindo mira . . . (She fluffs her hair, gives a big wave.) Aló América! Viva mi Margarita, viva todo los Cubanos en los Estados Unidos!*

Aída: *Ay por Dios,* Cecilia, the man didn't come all this way in his helicopter to look at you jumping up and down, making a fool of yourself.

Abuela: I don't care. I'm proud.

Aída: He can't understand you anyway.

40 **Abuela:**   *Viva . . . (She stops.) Simón, comó se dice viva?*

Simón: Hurray.

Abuela: Hurray for *mi Margarita y* for all the Cubans living *en* the United States, *y un abrazo . . . Simón, abrazo . . .*

Simón: A big hug.

Abuela: *Sí,* a big hug to all my friends in Miami, Long Beach, Union City, except for my son Carlos, who lives in New York in sin! He lives . . . *(She crosses herself.)* in Brooklyn with a Puerto Rican woman in sin! *No decente . . .*

45 **Simón:**   Decent.

Abuela: Carlos, *no decente.* This family, *decente.*

Aída: Cecilia, *por Dios.*

Mel's Voice: Look at that enthusiasm. The whole family has turned out to cheer little Margarita on to victory! I hope they won't be too disappointed.

Mary Beth's Voice: She seems to be making good time, Mel.

50 **Mel's Voice:**   Yes, it takes all kinds to make a race. And it's a testimonial to the all-encompassing fairness . . . the greatness of this, the Wrigley Invitational Women's Swim to Catalina, where among all the professionals there is still room for the amateurs . . . like these, the simple people we see below us on the ragtag *La Havana,* taking their long-shot chance to victory. *Vaya con Dios!*

(Helicopter sound fading as family, including Margarita, watch silently. Static as Simón turns radio off. Eduardo walks to bow of boat, looks out on the horizon.)

Eduardo: *(To himself.)* Amateurs.

Aída: Eduardo, that person insulted us. Did you hear, Eduardo? That he called us a simple people in a ragtag boat? Did you hear . . . ?

Abuela: *(Clenching her fist at departing helicopter.) Mal-Rayo los parta!*

Simón: *(Same gesture.)* Asshole!

(Aída follows Eduardo as he goes to side of boat and stares at Margarita.)

55 **Aída:**   This person comes in his helicopter to insult your wife, your family, your daughter . . .

Margarita: *(Pops her head out of the water.) Papi?*

Aída: Do you hear me, Eduardo? I am not simple.

Abuela: *Sí.*

Aída: I am complicated.

60 **Abuela:**   *Sí, demasiada complicada.*

Aída: Me and my family are not so simple.

Simón: Mom, the guy's an asshole.

ABUELA: *(Shaking her fist at helicopter.)* Asshole!

AÍDA: If my daughter was simple, she would not be in that water swimming.

65 **MARGARITA:**   Simple? *Papi . . . ?*

AÍDA: *Ahora,* Eduardo, this is what I want you to do. When we get to Santa Catalina, I want you to call the TV station and demand an apology.

EDUARDO: *Cállete mujer! Aquí mando yo.* I will decide what is to be done.

MARGARITA: *Papi,* tell me what's going on.

EDUARDO: Do you understand what I am saying to you, Aída?

70 **SIMÓN:**   *(Leaning over side of boat, to Margarita.)* Yo Margo! You know that Mel Munson guy on TV? He called you a simple amateur and said you didn't have a chance.

ABUELA: *(Leaning directly behind Simón.) Mi hija, insultó a la familia. Desgraciado!*

AÍDA: *(Leaning in behind Abuela.)* He called us peasants! And your father is not doing anything about it. He just knows how to yell at me.

EDUARDO: *(Through megaphone.)* Shut up! All of you! Do you want to break her concentration? Is that what you are after? Eh?

(Abuela, Aída, and Simón shrink back. Eduardo paces before them.)

Swimming is rhythm and concentration. You win a race *aquí.* *(Pointing to his head.)* Now . . . *(To Simón.)* you, take care of the boat, Aída *y Mama* . . . do something. Anything. Something practical.

(Abuela and Aída get on knees and pray in Spanish.)

Hija, give it everything, eh? . . . *por la familia. Uno . . . dos. . . . * You must win.

(Simón goes into cabin. The prayers continue as lights change to indicate bright sunlight, later in the afternoon.)

SCENE 3

Tableau for a couple of beats. Eduardo on bow with timer in one hand as he counts strokes per minute. Simón is in the cabin steering, wearing his sunglasses, baseball cap on backward. Abuela and Aída are at the side of the boat, heads down, hands folded, still muttering prayers in Spanish.

AÍDA and **ABUELA:**   *(Crossing themselves.) En el nombre del Padre, del Hijo y del Espíritu Santo amén.*

75 **EDUARDO:**   *(Through megaphone.)* You're stroking seventy-two!

SIMÓN: *(Singing.)* Mama's stroking, Mama's stroking seventy-two. . . .

EDUARDO: *(Through megaphone.)* You comfortable with it?

SIMÓN: *(Singing.)* Seventy-two, seventy-two, seventy-two for you.

AÍDA: *(Looking at the heavens.) Ay,* Eduardo, *ven acá,* we should be grateful that *Nuestro Señor* gave us such a beautiful day.

80 **ABUELA:**   *(Crosses herself.) Si, gracias a Dios.*

EDUARDO: She's stroking seventy-two, with no problem *(He throws a kiss to the sky.)* It's a beautiful day to win.

AÍDA: *Qué hermoso!* So clear and bright. Not a cloud in the sky. *Mira! Mira!* Even rainbows on the water . . . a sign from God.

SIMÓN: *(Singing.)* Rainbows on the water . . . you in my arms . . .

ABUELA and EDUARDO: *(Looking the wrong way.) Dónde?*

85 **AÍDA:**   *(Pointing toward Margarita.)* There, dancing in front of Margarita, leading her on . . .

EDUARDO: Rainbows on . . . *Ay coño!* It's an oil slick! You . . . you . . . *(To Simón.)* Stop the boat. *(Runs to bow, yelling.)* Margarita! Margarita!

(On the next stroke, Margarita comes up all covered in black oil.)

MARGARITA: *Papi! Papi . . . !*

(Everybody goes to the side and stares at Margarita, who stares back. Eduardo freezes.)

AÍDA: *Apúrate,* Eduardo, move . . . what's wrong with you . . . *no me oíste,* get my daughter out of the water.

EDUARDO: *(Softly.)* We can't touch her. If we touch her, she's disqualified.

90 **AÍDA:**   But I'm her mother.

EDUARDO: Not even by her own mother. Especially by her own mother. . . . You always want the rules to be different for you, you always want to be the exception. *(To Simón.)* And you . . . you didn't see it, eh? You were playing again?

SIMÓN: *Papi,* I was watching . . .

AÍDA: *(Interrupting.) Pues,* do something Eduardo. You are the big coach, the monitor.

SIMÓN: Mentor! Mentor!

95 **EDUARDO:**   How can a person think around you? *(He walks off to bow, puts head in hands.)*

ABUELA: *(Looking over side.) Mira como todos los* little birds are dead. *(She crosses herself.)*

AÍDA: Their little wings are glued to their sides.

SIMÓN: Christ, this is like the La Brea tar pits.

AÍDA: They can't move their little wings.

100 **ABUELA:**   *Esa niña tiene que moverse.*

SIMÓN: Yeah, Margo, you gotta move, man.

(Abuela and Simón gesture for Margarita to move. Aída gestures for her to swim.)

ABUELA: *Anda niña, muévete.*

AÍDA: Swim, *hija,* swim or the *aceite* will stick to your wings.

MARGARITA: *Papi?*

105 **ABUELA:**   *(Taking megaphone.)* Your *papi* say "move it!"

(Margarita with difficulty starts moving.)

ABUELA, AÍDA and **SIMÓN:** *(Laboriously counting.) Uno, dos . . . uno, dos . . . anda . . . uno, dos.*

EDUARDO: *(Running to take megaphone from Abuela.) Uno, dos . . .*

(Simón races into cabin and starts the engine. Abuela, Aída and Eduardo count together.)

SIMÓN: *(Looking ahead.) Papi,* it's over there!

EDUARDO: Eh?

110 **SIMÓN:** *(Pointing ahead and to the right.)* It's getting clearer over there.

EDUARDO: *(Through megaphone.)* Now pay attention to me. Go to the right.

(Simón, Abuela, Aída and Eduardo all lean over side. They point ahead and to the right, except Abuela, who points to the left.)

FAMILY: *(Shouting together.) Para yá! Para yá!*

(Lights go down on boat. A special light on Margarita, swimming through the oil, and on Abuela, watching her.)

ABUELA: *Sangre de mi sangre,* you will be another to save us. En Bolondron, where your great-grandmother Luz Suárez was born, they say one day it rained blood. All the people, they run into their houses. They cry, they pray, *pero* your great-grandmother Luz she had *cojones* like a man. She run outside. She look straight at the sky. She shake her fist. And she say to the evil one, "Mira . . . *(Beating her chest.) coño, Diablo, aquí estoy si me quieres."* And she open her mouth, and she drunk the blood.

Blackout.

<hr>

SCENE 4

Lights up on boat. Aída and Eduardo are on deck watching Margarita swim. We hear the gentle, rhythmic lap, lap, lap of the water, then the sound of inhaling and exhaling as Margarita's breathing becomes louder. Then Margarita's heartbeat is heard, with the lapping of the water and the breathing under it. These sounds continue beneath the dialogue to the end of the scene.

AÍDA: *Dios mío.* Look how she moves through the water. . . .

115 **EDUARDO:** You see, it's very simple. It is a matter of concentration.

AÍDA: The first time I put her in water she came to life, she grew before my eyes. She moved, she smiled, she loved it more than me. She didn't want my breast any longer. She wanted the water.

EDUARDO: And of course, the rhythm. The rhythm takes away the pain and helps the concentration.

(Pause. Aída and Eduardo watch Margarita.)

Aída: Is that my child or a seal. . . .

Eduardo: Ah, a seal, the reason for that is that she's keeping her arms
very close to her body. She cups her hands, and then she reaches and
digs, reaches and digs.

120 **Aída:**   To think that a daughter of mine . . .

Eduardo: It's the training, the hours in the water. I used to tie weights
around her little wrists and ankles.

Aída: A spirit, an ocean spirit, must have entered my body when I was
carrying her.

Eduardo: *(To Margarita.)* Your stroke is slowing down.

(Pause. We hear Margarita's heartbeat with the breathing under, faster now.)

Aída: Eduardo, that night, the night on the boat . . .

125 **Eduardo:**   Ah, the night on the boat again . . . the moon was . . .

Aída: The moon was full. We were coming to America. . . . *Qué
romantico.*

(Heartbeat and breathing continue.)

Eduardo: We were cold, afraid, with no money, and on top of
everything, you were hysterical, yelling at me, tearing at me with
your nails. *(Opens his shirt, points to the base of his neck.)* Look, I still
bear the scars . . . telling me that I didn't know what I was doing . . .
saying that we were going to die. . . .

Aída: You took me, you stole me from my home . . . you didn't give me
a chance to prepare. You just said we have to go now, now! Now, you
said. You didn't let me take anything. I left everything behind. . . . I
left everything behind.

Eduardo: Saying that I wasn't good enough, that your father didn't
raise you so that I could drown you in the sea.

130 **Aída:**   You didn't let me say even a good-bye. You took me, you stole
me, you tore me from my home.

Eduardo: I took you so we could be married.

Aída: That was in Miami. But that night on the boat, Eduardo. . . . We
were not married, that night on the boat.

Eduardo: *No pasó nada!* Once and for all get it out of your head, it was
cold, you hated me, and we were afraid. . . .

Aída: *Mentiroso!*

135 **Eduardo:**   A man can't do it when he is afraid.

Aída: Liar! You did it very well.

Eduardo: I did?

Aída: *Sí.* Gentle. You were so gentle and then strong . . . my passion for
you so deep. Standing next to you . . . I would ache . . . looking at
your hands I would forget to breathe, you were irresistible.

Eduardo: I was?

140 **Aída:**   You took me into your arms, you touched my face with your
fingertips . . . you kissed my eyes . . . *la esquina de la boca y . . .*

EDUARDO: *Sí, sí,* and then . . .

AÍDA: I look at your face on top of mine, and I see the lights of Havana in your eyes. That's when you seduced me.

EDUARDO: Shhh, they're gonna hear you.

(Lights go down. Special on Aída.)

AÍDA: That was the night. A woman doesn't forget those things . . . and later that night was the dream . . . the dream of a big country with fields of fertile land and big, giant things growing. And there by a green, slimy pond I found a giant pea pod and when I opened it, it was full of little, tiny baby frogs.

(Aída crosses herself as she watches Margarita. We hear louder breathing and heartbeat.)

145   **MARGARITA:**   Santa Teresa. Little Flower of God, pray for me. San Martín de Porres, pray for me. Santa Rosa de Lima, *Virgencita de la Caridad del Cobre,* pray for me. . . . Mother pray for me.

SCENE 5

Loud howling of wind is heard, as lights change to indicate unstable weather, fog and mist. Family on deck, braced and huddled against the wind. Simón is at the helm.

AÍDA: *Ay Dios mío, qué viento.*

EDUARDO: *(Through megaphone.)* Don't drift out . . . that wind is pushing you out. *(To Simón.)* You! Slow down. Can't you see your sister is drifting out?

SIMÓN: It's the wind, *Papi.*

AÍDA: Baby, don't go so far. . . .

150   **ABUELA:**   *(To heaven.) Ay Gran Poder de Dios, quita este maldito viento.*

SIMÓN: Margo! Margo! Stay close to the boat.

EDUARDO: Dig in. Dig in hard. . . . Reach down from your guts and dig in.

ABUELA: *(To heaven.) Ay Virgen de la Caridad del Cobre, por lo más tú quieres a pararla.*

AÍDA: *(Putting her hand out, reaching for Margarita.)* Baby, don't go far.

(Abuela crosses herself. Action freezes. Lights get dimmer, special on Margarita. She keeps swimming, stops, starts again, stops, then, finally exhausted, stops altogether. The boat stops moving.)

155   **EDUARDO:**   What's going on here? Why are we stopping?

SIMÓN: *Papi,* she's not moving! Yo Margo!

(The family all run to the side.)

EDUARDO: *Hija!* . . . *Hijita!* You're tired, eh?

Aída: *Por supuesto* she's tired. I like to see you get in the water, waving your arms and legs from San Pedro to Santa Catalina. A person isn't a machine, a person has to rest.

Simón: Yo, Mama! Cool out, it ain't fucking brain surgery.

160 **Eduardo:** *(To Simón.)* Shut up, you. *(Louder to Margarita.)* I guess your mother's right for once, huh? . . . I guess you had to stop, eh? . . . Give your brother, the idiot . . . a chance to catch up with you.

Simón: *(Clowning like Mortimer Snerd.)* Dum dee dum dee dum ooops, ah shucks . . .

Eduardo: I don't think he's Cuban.

Simón: *(Like Ricky Ricardo.)* Oye, Lucy! I'm home! Ba ba lu!

Eduardo: *(Joins in clowning, grabbing* Simón *in a headlock.)* What am I gonna do with this idiot, eh? I don't understand this idiot. He's not like us, Margarita. *(Laughing.)* You think if we put him into your bathing suit with a cap on his head . . . *(He laughs hysterically.)* You think anyone would know . . . huh? Do you think anyone would know? *(Laughs.)*

165 **Simón:** *(Vamping.)* Ay, mi amor. Anybody looking for tits would know.

(Eduardo slaps Simón across the face, knocking him down. Aída runs to Simón's aid. Abuela holds Eduardo back.)

Margarita: *Mía culpa! Mía culpa!*

Abuela: *Qué dices hija?*

Margarita: *Papi,* it's my fault, it's all my fault. . . . I'm so cold, I can't move. . . . I put my face in the water . . . and I hear them whispering . . . laughing at me. . . .

Aída: Who is laughing at you?

170 **Margarita:** The fish are all biting me . . . they hate me . . . they whisper about me. She can't swim, they say. She can't glide. She has no grace. . . . Yellowtails, bonita, tuna, man-o'-war, snub-nose sharks, *los baracudas* . . . they all hate me . . . only the dolphins care . . . and sometimes I hear the whales crying . . . she is lost, she is dead. I'm so numb, I can't feel. *Papi! Papi!* Am I dead?

Eduardo: *Vamos,* baby, punch those arms in. Come on . . . do you hear me?

Margarita: *Papi . . . Papi . . .* forgive me. . . .

(All is silent on the boat. Eduardo drops his megaphone, his head bent down in dejection. Abuela, Aída, Simón, all leaning over the side of the boat. Simón slowly walks away.)

Aída: *Mi hija, qué tienes?*

Simón: Oh, Christ, don't make her say it. Please don't make her say it.

175 **Abuela:** Say what? *Qué cosa?*

Simón: She wants to quit, can't you see she's had enough?

Abuela: *Mira, para eso. Esta niña* is turning blue.

Aída: *Oyeme, mi hija.* Do you want to come out of the water?

Margarita: *Papi?*

180 **SIMÓN:** *(To Eduardo.)* She won't come out until *you* tell her.

AÍDA: Eduardo . . . answer your daughter.

EDUARDO: *Le dije* to concentrate . . . concentrate on your rhythm. Then the rhythm would carry her . . . ay, it's a beautiful thing, Aída. It's like yoga, like meditation, the mind over matter . . . the mind controlling the body . . . that's how the great things in the world have been done. I wish you . . . I wish my wife could understand.

MARGARITA: *Papi?*

SIMÓN: *(To Margarita.)* Forget him.

185 **AÍDA:** *(Imploring.)* Eduardo, *por favor.*

EDUARDO: *(Walking in circles.)* Why didn't you let her concentrate? Don't you understand, the concentration, the rhythm is everything. But no, you wouldn't listen. *(Screaming to the ocean.)* Goddamn Cubans, why, God, why do you make us go everywhere with our families? *(He goes to back of boat.)*

AÍDA: *(Opening her arms.)* Mi hija, ven, come to *Mami. (Rocking.)* Your *mami* knows.

(Abuela has taken the training bottle, puts it in a net. She and Simón lower it to Margarita.)

SIMÓN: Take this. Drink it. *(As Margarita drinks, Abuela crosses herself.)*

ABUELA: *Sangre de mi sangre.*

(Music comes up softly. Margarita drinks, gives the bottle back, stretches out her arms, as if on a cross. Floats on her back. She begins a graceful backstroke. Lights fade on boat as special lights come up on Margarita. She stops. Slowly turns over and starts to swim, gradually picking up speed. Suddenly as if in pain she stops, tries again, then stops in pain again. She becomes disoriented and falls to the bottom of the sea. Special on Margarita at the bottom of the sea.)

190 **MARGARITA:** *Ya no puedo* . . . I can't. . . . A person isn't a machine . . . *es mi culpa* . . . Father forgive me . . . *Papi! Papi!* One, two. *Uno, dos. (Pause.) Papi! A dónde estás? (Pause.)* One, two, one, two. *Papi! Ay, Papi!* Where are you . . . ? Don't leave me. . . . Why don't you answer me? *(Pause. She starts to swim, slowly.) Uno, dos, uno, dos.* Dig in, dig in. *(Stops swimming.) Por favor, Papi! (Starts to swim again.)* One, two, one, two. Kick from your hip, kick from your hip. *(Stops swimming. Starts to cry.)* Oh God, please. . . . *(Pause.)* Hail Mary, full of grace . . . dig in, dig in . . . the Lord is with thee. . . . *(She swims to the rhythm of her Hail Mary.)* Hail Mary, full of grace . . . dig in, dig in . . . the Lord is with thee . . . dig in, dig in. . . . Blessed art thou among women. . . . *Mami,* it hurts. You let go of my hand. I'm lost. . . . And blessed is the fruit of thy womb, now and at the hour of our death. Amen. I don't want to die, I don't want to die.

(Margarita is still swimming. Blackout. She is gone.)

SCENE 6

Lights up on boat, we hear radio static. There is a heavy mist. On deck we see only black outline of Abuela with shawl over her head. We hear the voices of Eduardo, Aída, and Radio Operator.

EDUARDO'S VOICE: La Havana! Coming from San Pedro. Over.

RADIO OPERATOR'S VOICE: Right, DT6-6, you say you've lost a swimmer.

AÍDA'S VOICE: Our child, our only daughter . . . listen to me. Her name is Margarita Inez Suárez, she is wearing a black one-piece bathing suit cut high in the legs with a white racing stripe down the sides, a white bathing cap with goggles and her whole body covered with a . . . with a . . .

EDUARDO'S VOICE: With lanolin and paraffin.

195 **AÍDA'S VOICE:**   *Sí . . . con lanolin and paraffin.*

(More radio static. Special on Simón, on the edge of the boat.)

SIMÓN: Margo! Yo Margo! *(Pause.)* Man don't do this. *(Pause.)* Come on. . . . Come on. . . . *(Pause.)* God, why does everything have to be so hard? *(Pause.)* Stupid. You know you're not supposed to die for this. Stupid. It's his dream and he can't even swim. *(Pause.)* Punch those arms in. Come home. Come home. I'm your little brother. Don't forget what Mama said. You're not supposed to leave me behind. *Vamos,* Margarita, take your little brother, hold his hand tight when you cross the street. He's so little. *(Pause.)* Oh, Christ, give us a sign. . . . I know! I know! Margo, I'll send you a message . . . like mental telepathy. I'll hold my breath, close my eyes, and I'll bring you home. *(He takes a deep breath; a few beats.)* This time I'll beep . . . I'll send out sonar signals like a dolphin. *(He imitates dolphin sounds.)*

(The sound of real dolphins takes over from Simón, then fades into sound of Abuela saying the Hail Mary in Spanish, as full lights come up slowly.)

SCENE 7

Eduardo coming out of cabin, sobbing, Aída holding him. Simón anxiously scanning the horizon. Abuela looking calmly ahead.

EDUARDO: *Es mi culpa, sí, es mi culpa. (He hits his chest.)*

AÍDA: *Ya, ya viejo . . .* it was my sin . . . I left my home.

EDUARDO: Forgive me, forgive me. I've lost our daughter, our sister, our granddaughter, *mi carne, mi sangre, mis ilusiones. (To heaven.) Dios mío,* take me . . . take me, I say . . . Goddammit, take me!

200 **SIMÓN:**   I'm going in.

AÍDA and **EDUARDO:**   No!

EDUARDO: *(Grabbing and holding Simón, speaking to heaven.)* God, take me, not my children. They are my dreams, my illusions . . . and not this one, this one is my mystery . . . he has my secret dreams. In him are the parts of me I cannot see.

(Eduardo embraces Simón. Radio static becomes louder.)

AÍDA: I . . . I think I see her.
SIMÓN: No, it's just a seal.
205 **ABUELA:** *(Looking out with binoculars.) Mi nietacita, dónde estás? (She feels her heart.)* I don't feel the knife in my heart . . . my little fish is not lost.

(Radio crackles with static. As lights dim on boat, Voices of Mel and Mary Beth are heard over the radio.)

MEL'S VOICE: Tragedy has marred the face of the Wrigley Invitational Women's Race to Catalina. The Cuban swimmer, little Margarita Suárez, has reportedly been lost at sea. Coast Guard and divers are looking for her as we speak. Yet in spite of this tragedy the race must go on because . . .
MARY BETH'S VOICE: *(Interrupting loudly.)* Mel!
MEL'S VOICE: *(Startled.)* What!
MARY BETH'S VOICE: Ah . . . excuse me, Mel . . . we have a winner. We've just received word from Catalina that one of the swimmers is just fifty yards from the breakers . . . it's, oh, it's . . . Margarita Suárez!

(Special on family in cabin listening to radio.)

210 **MEL'S VOICE:** What? I thought she died!

(Special on Margarita, taking off bathing cap, trophy in hand, walking on the water.)

MARY BETH'S VOICE: Ahh . . . unless . . . unless this is a tragic . . . No . . . there she is, Mel. Margarita Suárez! The only one in the race wearing a black bathing suit cut high in the legs with a racing stripe down the side.

(Family cheering, embracing.)

SIMÓN: *(Screaming.)* Way to go, Margo!
MEL'S VOICE: This is indeed a miracle! It's a resurrection! Margarita Suárez, with a flotilla of boats to meet her, is now walking on the waters, through the breakers . . . onto the beach, with crowds of people cheering her on. What a jubilation! This is a miracle!

(Sound of crowds cheering. Lights and cheering sounds fade.)

Blackout.

READING AND REACTING

1. *The Cuban Swimmer* is a short play with a single setting. In what additional locations could Sanchez-Scott have set the play's action? What might she have gained or lost from these additional settings?

2. What lighting and sound effects does the play call for? In what way do these effects advance the action of the play? In what way—if any— do they help to communicate the play's theme?

3. Although most of the play is in English, the characters frequently speak Spanish. What are the advantages of this use of Spanish? Are there any drawbacks?

4. What function do the voices of Mel and Mary Beth serve in the play?

5. What conflicts develop among the family members as the play proceeds? In what way might these conflicts represent the problems of other immigrants to the United States?

6. In what sense is Mel's final comment "This is a miracle!" ironic?

7. Do you think this play comments on the position of women in American culture? In Cuban-American culture?

8. Could this play be seen as an **allegory?** What is the value of seeing it in this way?

9. Throughout much of the play Margarita is swimming in full view of the audience. Devise three ways in which a director could achieve this effect on stage. Which one would you choose if you were directing the play?

10. The 1984 New York production of *The Cuban Swimmer* had an extremely realistic set. Could the play be staged unrealistically, with the characters on a raised platform in make-believe water? How do you think this kind of set would affect the audience?

11. **JOURNAL ENTRY**   Are you able to empathize with Margarita's struggle? What elements of the play make it easy or difficult for you to do so?

12. **CRITICAL PERSPECTIVE**   In a review of the original New York production of *The Cuban Swimmer*—along with *Dog Lady,* another of the playwright's one-act plays—Herbert Mitgang devotes four paragraphs to the set ("The sets designed by Ming Cho Lee are the hit of the evening. . . ."), but of the plays he says only this:

    Hispanic-Americans use athletic skills to propel themselves into the mainstream of middle-class life in this country. It's a traditional theme. The basic plot was advanced a long time ago . . . and since then, in scores of films, books, and movies, members of ethnic groups have moved out of the slums.

    Do you think *The Cuban Swimmer* simply reworks this "traditional theme"? Or do you think it has a vision of its own?

SOPHOCLES (496–406 B.C.),   along with Aeschylus and Euripides, is one of the three great Greek tragic dramatists. He lived during virtually all of the great flowering and subsequent decline of fifth-century Athens—the high point of Greek civilization. Born as Greece struggled against the Persian empire and moved to adopt democracy, he lived as an adult under Pericles in the Golden Age of Athens and died as it became clear that Athens would lose the Peloponnesian War. Sophocles was an active participant in the public life of Athens, serving as a collector of tribute from Athenian subjects and later as a general. Though he wrote at least one hundred and twenty plays, only seven have survived, including three plays about Oedipus: *Oedipus the King* (c. 430 B.C.), *Oedipus at Colonus* (411? B.C.), and *Antigone* (441 B.C.).

Oedipus the King or Oedipus Rex, (sometimes called *Oedipus the Tyrant*), was performed shortly after a great plague in Athens (probably in 429 or 425 B.C.) and as Athens was falling into decline; the play opens with the account of a plague in Thebes, Oedipus's kingdom. Over the years, *Oedipus the King* has attracted impressive critical attention, from Aristotle's use of it as a model for his definition of tragedy to Freud's use of its power as evidence of the validity of the so-called Oedipus complex.

SOPHOCLES

Oedipus the King*

(c. 430 B.C.)

translated by Thomas Gould

CHARACTERS

OEDIPUS,[1] *The King of Thebes*
PRIEST OF ZEUS, *Leader of the Suppliants*
CREON, *Oedipus's Brother-in-law*
CHORUS, *a Group of Theban Elders*
CHORAGOS, *Spokesman of the Chorus*
TIRESIAS, *a blind Seer or Prophet*

---

* Note that individual lines are numbered in the following play. When a line is shared by two or more characters, it is counted as one line.

[1] *Oedipus:* The name means "swollen foot." It refers to the mutilation of Oedipus's feet done by his father, Laius, before the infant was sent to Mount Cithaeron to be put to death by exposure.

JOCASTA, *The Queen of Thebes*
MESSENGER, *from Corinth, once a Shepherd*
HERDSMAN, *once a Servant of Laius*
SECOND MESSENGER, *a Servant of Oedipus*

M U T E S

SUPPLIANTS, *Thebans seeking Oedipus's help*
ATTENDANTS, *for the Royal Family*
SERVANTS, *to lead Tiresias and Oedipus*
ANTIGONE, *Daughter of Oedipus and Jocasta*
ISMENE, *Daughter of Oedipus and Jocasta*

The action takes place during the day in front of the royal palace in Thebes. There are two altars (left and right) on the proscenium and several steps leading down to the orchestra. As the play opens, Thebans of various ages who have come to beg Oedipus for help are sitting on these steps and in part of the orchestra. These suppliants are holding branches of laurel or olive which have strips of wool[2] wrapped around them. Oedipus enters from the palace (the central door of the skene).

P R O L O G U E

OEDIPUS: My children, ancient Cadmus'[3] newest care,
why have you hurried to those seats, your boughs
wound with the emblems of the suppliant?
The city is weighed down with fragrant smoke,
5   with hymns to the Healer[4] and the cries of mourners.
I thought it wrong, my sons, to hear your words
through emissaries, and have come out myself,
I, Oedipus, a name that all men know.

(Oedipus addresses the Priest.)

Old man—for it is fitting that you speak
10   for all—what is your mood as you entreat me,
fear or trust? You may be confident
that I'll do anything. How hard of heart
if an appeal like this did not rouse my pity!
PRIEST: You, Oedipus, who hold the power here,
15   you see our several ages, we who sit

---

[2] *wool:* Branches wrapped with wool are traditional symbols of prayer or supplication.
[3] *Cadmus:* Oedipus's great great grandfather (although he does not know this) and the founder of Thebes.   [4] *Healer:* Apollo, god of prophecy, light, healing, justice, purification, and destruction.

before your altars—some not strong enough
to take long flight, some heavy in old age,
the priests, as I of Zeus,[5] and from our youths
a chosen band. The rest sit with their windings
20 in the markets, at the twin shrines of Pallas,[6]
and the prophetic embers of Ismēnos.[7]
Our city, as you see yourself, is tossed
too much, and can no longer lift its head
above the troughs of billows red with death.
25 It dies in the fruitful flowers of the soil,
it dies in its pastured herds, and in its women's
barren pangs. And the fire-bearing god[8]
has swooped upon the city, hateful plague,
and he has left the house of Cadmus empty.
30 Black Hades[9] is made rich with moans and weeping.
Not judging you an equal of the gods,
do I and the children sit here at your hearth,
but as the first of men, in troubled times
and in encounters with divinities.
35 You came to Cadmus' city and unbound
the tax we had to pay to the harsh singer,[10]
did it without a helpful word from us,
with no instruction; with a god's assistance
you raised up our life, so we believe.
40 Again now Oedipus, our greatest power,
we plead with you, as suppliants, all of us,
to find us strength, whether from a god's response,
or learned in some way from another man.
I know that the experienced among men
45 give counsels that will prosper best of all.
Noblest of men, lift up our land again!

---

[5] *Zeus:* father and king of the gods.   [6] *Pallas:* Athena, goddess of wisdom, arts, crafts, and war.   [7] *Ismenos:* a reference to the temple of Apollo near the river Ismēnos in Thebes. Prophecies were made here by "reading" the ashes of the altar fires. [8] *fire-bearing god:* contagious fever viewed as a god.   [9] *Black Hades:* refers to both the underworld where the spirits of the dead go and the god of the underworld. [10] *harsh singer:* the Sphinx, a monster with a woman's head, a lion's body, and wings. The "tax" that Oedipus freed Thebes from was the destruction of all the young men who failed to solve the Sphinx's riddle and were subsequently devoured. The Sphinx always asked the same riddle: "What goes on four legs in the morning, two legs at noon, and three legs in the evening, and yet is weakest when supported by the largest number of feet?" Oedipus discovered the correct answer—man, who crawls in infancy, walks in his prime, and uses a stick in old age—and thus ended the Sphinx's reign of terror. The Sphinx destroyed herself when Oedipus answered the riddle. Oedipus's reward for freeing Thebes of the Sphinx was the throne and the hand of the recently widowed Jocasta.

Think also of yourself; since now the land
calls you its Savior for your zeal of old,
oh let us never look back at your rule
50   as men helped up only to fall again!
Do not stumble! Put our land on firm feet!
The bird of omen was auspicious then,
when you brought that luck; be that same man again!
The power is yours; if you will rule our country,
55   rule over men, not in an empty land.
A towered city or a ship is nothing
if desolate and no man lives within.
OEDIPUS: Pitiable children, oh I know, I know
the yearnings that have brought you. Yes, I know
60   that you are sick. And yet, though you are sick,
there is not one of you so sick as I.
For your affliction comes to each alone,
for him and no one else, but my soul mourns
for me and for you, too, and for the city.
65   You do not waken me as from a sleep,
for I have wept, bitterly and long,
tried many paths in the wanderings of thought,
and the single cure I found by careful search
I've acted on: I sent Menoeceus' son,
70   Creon, brother of my wife, to the Pythian
halls of Phoebus,[11] so that I might learn
what I must do or say to save this city.
Already, when I think what day this is,
I wonder anxiously what he is doing.
75   Too long, more than is right, he's been away.
But when he comes, then I shall be a traitor
if I do not do all that the god reveals.
PRIEST: Welcome words! But look, those men have signaled
that it is Creon who is now approaching!
80 **OEDIPUS:**   Lord Apollo! May he bring Savior Luck,
a Luck as brilliant as his eyes are now!
PRIEST: His news is happy, it appears. He comes,
forehead crowned with thickly berried laurel.[12]
OEDIPUS: We'll know, for he is near enough to hear us.

(Enter Creon along one of the parados.)

85   Lord, brother in marriage, son of Menoeceus!
What is the god's pronouncement that you bring?

---

[11] *Pythian . . . Phoebus:* the temple of Phoebus Apollo's oracle or prophet at Delphi.
[12] *laurel:* Creon is wearing a garland of laurel leaves, sacred to Apollo.

CREON: It's good. For even troubles, if they chance
         to turn out well, I always count as lucky.
OEDIPUS: But what was the response? You seem to say
90   I'm not to fear—but not to take heart either.
CREON: If you will hear me with these men present,
         I'm ready to report—or go inside.

(Creon moves up the steps toward the palace.)

OEDIPUS: Speak out to all! The grief that burdens me
         concerns these men more than it does my life.
95 CREON: Then I shall tell you what I heard from the god.
         The task Lord Phoebus sets for us is clear:
         drive out pollution sheltered in our land,
         and do not shelter what is incurable.
OEDIPUS: What is our trouble? How shall we cleanse ourselves?
100 CREON: We must banish or murder to free ourselves
         from a murder that blows storms through the city.
OEDIPUS: What man's bad luck does he accuse in this?
CREON: My Lord, a king named Laius ruled our land
         before you came to steer the city straight.
105 OEDIPUS: I know. So I was told—I never saw him.
CREON: Since he was murdered, you must raise your hand
         against the men who killed him with their hands.
OEDIPUS: Where are they now? And how can we ever find
         the track of ancient guilt now hard to read?
110 CREON: In our own land, he said. What we pursue,
         that can be caught; but not what we neglect.
OEDIPUS: Was Laius home, or in the countryside—
         or was he murdered in some foreign land?
CREON: He left to see a sacred rite, he said;
115   He left, but never came home from his journey.
OEDIPUS: Did none of his party see it and report—
         someone we might profitably question?
CREON: They were all killed but one, who fled in fear,
         and he could tell us only one clear fact.
120 OEDIPUS: What fact? One thing could lead us on to more
         if we could get a small start on our hope.
CREON: He said that bandits chanced on them and killed him—
         with the force of many hands, not one alone.
OEDIPUS: How could a bandit dare so great an act—
125   unless this was a plot paid off from here!
CREON: We thought of that, but when Laius was killed,
         we had no one to help us in our troubles.
OEDIPUS: It was your very kingship that was killed!
         What kind of trouble blocked you from a search?
130 CREON: The subtle-singing Sphinx asked us to turn
         from the obscure to what lay at our feet.

OEDIPUS: Then I shall begin again and make it plain.
It was quite worthy of Phoebus, and worthy of you,
to turn our thoughts back to the murdered man,
135   and right that you should see me join the battle
for justice to our land and to the god.
Not on behalf of any distant kinships,
it's for myself I will dispel this stain.
Whoever murdered him may also wish
140   to punish me—and with the selfsame hand.
In helping him I also serve myself.
Now quickly, children: up from the altar steps,
and raise the branches of the suppliant!
Let someone go and summon Cadmus' people:
145   say I'll do anything.

(Exit an Attendant along one of the parados.)

Our luck will prosper
if the god is with us, or we have already fallen.
PRIEST: Rise, my children; that for which we came,
he has himself proclaimed he will accomplish.
May Phoebus, who announced this, also come
150   as Savior and reliever from the plague.

*(Exit Oedipus and Creon into the palace. The Priest and the Suppliants exit left
and right along the parados. After a brief pause, the Chorus (including the Choragos) enters the orchestra from the parados.)*

PARADOS

STROPHE 1[13]

CHORUS: Voice from Zeus,[14] sweetly spoken, what are you
that have arrived from golden
Pytho[15] to our shining
Thebes? I am on the rack, terror
155   shakes my soul.
Delian Healer,[16] summoned by "iē!"
I await in holy dread what obligation, something new
or something back once more with the revolving years,
        you'll bring about for me.
160   Oh tell me, child of golden Hope,
        deathless Response!

---

[13] *Strophe, Antistrophe:* probably refer to the direction in which the Chorus danced
while reciting specific stanzas. Strophe may have indicated dance steps to stage left,
antistrophe to stage right.   [14] *Voice from Zeus:* a reference to Apollo's prophecy.
Zeus taught Apollo how to prophesy.   [15] *Pytho:* Delphi.   [16] *Delian Healer:* Apollo.

ANTISTROPHE 1

I appeal to you first, daughter of Zeus,
  deathless Athena,
  and to your sister who protects this land,
165   Artemis,[17] whose famous throne is the whole circle
    of the marketplace,
  and Phoebus, who shoots from afar: iō!
  Three-fold defenders against death, appear!
  If ever in the past, to stop blind ruin
170   sent against the city,
    you banished utterly the fires of suffering,
      come now again!

STROPHE 2

Ah! Ah! Unnumbered are the miseries
I bear. The plague claims all
175   our comrades. Nor has thought found yet a spear
  by which a man shall be protected. What our glorious
  earth gives birth to does not grow. Without a birth
  from cries of labor
    do the women rise.
180   One person after another
      you may see, like flying birds,
  faster than indomitable fire, sped
  to the shore of the god that is the sunset.[18]

ANTISTROPHE 2

And with their deaths unnumbered dies the city.
185   Her children lie unpitied on the ground,
  spreading death, unmourned.
  Meanwhile young wives, and gray-haired mothers with them,
  on the shores of the altars, from this side and that,
  suppliants from mournful trouble,
190   cry out their grief.
  A hymn to the Healer shines,
    the flute a mourner's voice.
  Against which, golden goddess, daughter of Zeus,
    send lovely Strength.

---

[17] *Artemis:* goddess of virginity, childbirth, and hunting.   [18] *god . . . sunset:* Hades, god of the underworld.

STROPHE 3

195 Causing raging Ares[19]—who,
     armed now with no shield of bronze,
   burns me, coming on amid loud cries—
   to turn his back and run from my land,
   with a fair wind behind, to the great
200   hall of Amphitritē,[20]
   or to the anchorage that welcomes no one,
   Thrace's troubled sea!
   If night lets something get away at last,
      it comes by day.
205 Fire-bearing god . . .
      you who dispense the might of lightning,
   Zeus! Father! Destroy him with your thunderbolt!

(Enter Oedipus from the palace.)

ANTISTROPHE 3

   Lycēan Lord![21] From your looped
      bowstring, twisted gold,
210 I wish indomitable missiles might be scattered
   and stand forward, our protectors; also fire-bearing
   radiance of Artemis, with which
      she darts across the Lycian mountains.
   I call the god whose head is bound in gold,
215 with whom this country shares its name,
   Bacchus,[22] wine-flushed, summoned by "euoi!,"
      Maenads' comrade,
   to approach ablaze
      with gleaming . . .
220 pine, opposed to that god-hated god.

EPISODE 1

OEDIPUS: I hear your prayer. Submit to what I say
   and to the labors that the plague demands
   and you'll get help and a relief from evils.
   I'll make the proclamation, though a stranger
225 to the report and to the deed. Alone,
   had I no key, I would soon lose the track.
   Since it was only later that I joined you,

---

[19] *Ares:* god of war and destruction.   [20] *Amphitritē:* the Atlantic Ocean.
[21] *Lycēan Lord:* Apollo.   [22] *Bacchus:* Dionysus, god of fertility and wine.

to all the sons of Cadmus I say this:
whoever has clear knowledge of the man
230   who murdered Laius, son of Labdacus,
I command him to reveal it all to me—
nor fear if, to remove the charge, he must
accuse himself: his fate will not be cruel—
he will depart unstumbling into exile.
235   But if you know another, or a stranger,
to be the one whose hand is guilty, speak:
I shall reward you and remember you.
But if you keep your peace because of fear,
and shield yourself or kin from my command,
240   hear you what I shall do in that event:
I charge all in this land where I have throne
and power, shut out that man—no matter who—
both from your shelter and all spoken words,
nor in your prayers or sacrifices make
245   him partner, nor allot him lustral[23] water.
All men shall drive him from their homes: for he
is the pollution that the god-sent Pythian
response has only now revealed to me.
In this way I ally myself in war
250   with the divinity and the deceased.[24]
And this curse, too, against the one who did it,
whether alone in secrecy, or with others:
may he wear out his life unblest and evil!
I pray this, too: if he is at my hearth
255   and in my home, and I have knowledge of him,
may the curse pronounced on others come to me.
All this I lay to you to execute,
for my sake, for the god's, and for this land
nor ruined, barren, abandoned by the gods.
260   Even if no god had driven you to it,
you ought not to have left this stain uncleansed,
the murdered man a nobleman, a king!
You should have looked! But now, since, as it happens,
It's I who have the power that he had once,
265   and have his bed, and a wife who shares our seed,
and common bond had we had common children
(had not his hope of offspring had bad luck—
but as it happened, luck lunged at his head);
because of this, as if for my own father,
270   I'll fight for him, I'll leave no means untried,

---

[23] *lustral:* purifying.   [24] *the deceased:* Laius.

to catch the one who did it with his hand,
for the son of Labdacus, of Polydōrus,
of Cadmus before him, and of Agēnor.[25]
This prayer against all those who disobey:
275   the gods send out no harvest from their soil,
nor children from their wives. Oh, let them die
victims of this plague, or of something worse.
Yet for the rest of us, people of Cadmus,
we the obedient, may Justice, our ally,
280   and all the gods, be always on our side!

CHORAGOS: I speak because I feel the grip of your curse:
the killer is not I. Nor can I point
to him. The one who set us to this search,
Phoebus, should also name the guilty man.

285 **OEDIPUS:**   Quite right, but to compel unwilling gods—
no man has ever had that kind of power.

CHORAGOS: May I suggest to you a second way?

OEDIPUS: A second or a third—pass over nothing!

CHORAGOS: I know of no one who sees more of what
290   Lord Phoebus sees than Lord Tiresias.
My Lord, one might learn brilliantly from him.

OEDIPUS: Nor is this something I have been slow to do.
At Creon's word I sent an escort—twice now!
I am astonished that he has not come.

295 **CHORAGOS:**   The old account is useless. It told us nothing.

OEDIPUS: But tell it to me. I'll scrutinize all stories.

CHORAGOS: He is said to have been killed by travelers.

OEDIPUS: I have heard, but the one who did it no one sees.

CHORAGOS: If there is any fear in him at all,
300   he won't stay here once he has heard that curse.

OEDIPUS: He won't fear words: he had no fear when he did it.

(Enter Tiresias from the right, led by a Servant and two of Oedipus's Attendants.)

CHORAGOS: Look there! There is the man who will convict him!
It's the god's prophet they are leading here,
one gifted with the truth as no one else.

305 **OEDIPUS:**   Tiresias, master of all omens—
public and secret, in the sky and on the earth—
your mind, if not your eyes, sees how the city
lives with a plague, against which Thebes can find
no Saviour or protector, Lord, but you.
310   For Phoebus, as the attendants surely told you,
returned this answer to us: liberation

---

[25] *Son . . . Agēnor:* refers to Laius by citing his genealogy.

from the disease would never come unless
we learned without a doubt who murdered Laius—
put them to death, or sent them into exile.

315   Do not begrudge us what you may learn from birds
or any other prophet's path you know!
Care for yourself, the city, care for me,
care for the whole pollution of the dead!
We're in your hands. To do all that he can

320   to help another is man's noblest labor.

TIRESIAS: How terrible to understand and get
no profit from the knowledge! I knew this,
but I forgot, or I had never come.

OEDIPUS: What's this? You've come with very little zeal.

325 **TIRESIAS:** Let me go home! If you will listen to me,
You will endure your troubles better—and I mine.

OEDIPUS: A strange request, not very kind to the land
that cared for you—to hold back this oracle!

TIRESIAS: I see your understanding comes to you

330   inopportunely. So that won't happen to me . . .

OEDIPUS: Oh, by the gods, if you understand about this,
don't turn away! We're on our knees to you.

TIRESIAS: None of you understands! I'll never bring
my grief to light—I will not speak of yours.

335 **OEDIPUS:** You know and won't declare it! Is your purpose
to betray us and to destroy this land!

TIRESIAS: I will grieve neither of us. Stop this futile
cross-examination. I'll tell you nothing!

OEDIPUS: Nothing? You vile traitor! You could provoke

340   a stone to anger! You still refuse to tell?
Can nothing soften you, nothing convince you?

TIRESIAS: You blamed anger in me—you haven't seen.
The kind that lives with you, so you blame me.

OEDIPUS: Who wouldn't fill with anger, listening

345   to words like yours which now disgrace this city?

TIRESIAS: It will come, even if my silence hides it.

OEDIPUS: If it will come, then why won't you declare it?

TIRESIAS: I'd rather say no more. Now if you wish,
respond to that with all your fiercest anger!

350 **OEDIPUS:** Now I am angry enough to come right out
with this conjecture: you, I think, helped plot
the deed; you did it—even if your hand,
cannot have struck the blow. If you could see,
I should have said the deed was yours alone.

355 **TIRESIAS:** Is that right! Then I charge you to abide
by the decree you have announced: from this day
say no word to either these or me,
for you are the vile polluter of this land!

OEDIPUS: Aren't you appalled to let a charge like that
360   come bounding forth? How will you get away?
TIRESIAS: You cannot catch me. I have the strength of truth.
OEDIPUS: Who taught you this? Not your prophetic craft!
TIRESIAS: You did. You made me say it. I didn't want to.
OEDIPUS: Say what? Repeat it so I'll understand.
365 **TIRESIAS:** I made no sense? Or are you trying me?
OEDIPUS: No sense I understood. Say it again!
TIRESIAS: I say you are the murderer you seek.
OEDIPUS: Again that horror! You'll wish you hadn't said that.
TIRESIAS: Shall I say more, and raise your anger higher?
370 **OEDIPUS:** Anything you like! Your words are powerless.
TIRESIAS: You live, unknowing, with those nearest to you
    in the greatest shame. You do not see the evil.
OEDIPUS: You won't go on like that and never pay!
TIRESIAS: I can if there is any strength in truth.
375 **OEDIPUS:** In truth, but not in you! You have no strength,
    blind in your ears, your reason, and your eyes.
TIRESIAS: Unhappy man! Those jeers you hurl at me
    before long all these men will hurl at you.
OEDIPUS: You are the child of endless night; it's not
380   for me or anyone who sees to hurt you.
TIRESIAS: It's not my fate to be struck down by you.
    Apollo is enough. That's his concern.
OEDIPUS: Are these inventions Creon's or your own?
TIRESIAS: No, your affliction is yourself, not Creon.
385 **OEDIPUS:** Oh success!—in wealth, kingship, artistry,
    in any life that wins much admiration—
    the envious ill will stored up for you!
    to get at my command, a gift I did not
    seek, which the city put into my hands,
390   my loyal Creon, colleague from the start,
    longs to sneak up in secret and dethrone me.
    So he's suborned this fortuneteller—schemer!
    deceitful beggar-priest!—who has good eyes
    for gains alone, though in his craft he's blind.
395   Where were your prophet's powers ever proved?
    Why, when the dog who chanted verse[26] was here,
    did you not speak and liberate this city?
    Her riddle wasn't for a man chancing by
    to interpret; prophetic art was needed,
400   but you had none, it seems—learned from birds
    or from a god. I came along, yes I,
    Oedipus the ignorant, and stopped her—

---

[26] *dog . . . verse:* the Sphinx.

by using thought, not augury from birds.
And it is I whom you now wish to banish,
405   so you'll be close to the Creontian throne.
You—and the plot's concocter—will drive out
pollution to your grief: you look quite old
or you would be the victim of that plot!

CHORAGOS: It seems to us that this man's words were said
410   in anger, Oedipus, and yours as well.
Insight, not angry words, is what we need,
the best solution to the god's response.

TIRESIAS: You are the king, and yet I am your equal
in my right to speak. In that I too am Lord.
415   for I belong to Loxias,[27] not you.
I am not Creon's man. He's nothing to me.
Hear this, since you have thrown my blindness at me:
Your eyes can't see the evil to which you've come,
nor where you live, nor who is in your house.
420   Do you know your parents? Not knowing, you are
their enemy, in the underworld and here.
A mother's and a father's double-lashing
terrible-footed curse will soon drive you out.
Now you can see, then you will stare into darkness.
425   What place will not be harbor to your cry,
or what Cithaeron[28] not reverberate
when you have heard the bride-song in your palace
to which you sailed? Fair wind to evil harbor!
Nor do you see how many other woes
430   will level you to yourself and to your children.
So, at my message, and at Creon, too,
splatter muck! There will never be a man
ground into wretchedness as you will be.

OEDIPUS: Am I to listen to such things from him!
435   May you be damned! Get out of here at once!
Go! Leave my palace! Turn around and go!

(Tiresias begins to move away from Oedipus.)

TIRESIAS: I wouldn't have come had you not sent for me.
OEDIPUS: I did not know you'd talk stupidity,
or I wouldn't have rushed to bring you to my house.
440   **TIRESIAS:**   Stupid I seem to you, yet to your parents
who gave you natural birth I seemed quite shrewd.
OEDIPUS: Who? Wait! Who is the one who gave me birth?
TIRESIAS: This day will give you birth,[29] and ruin too.

---

[27] *Loxias:* Apollo.   [28] *Cithaeron:* reference to the mountain on which Oedipus was
to be exposed as an infant.   [29] *give you birth:* that is, identify your parents.

OEDIPUS:	What murky, riddling things you always say!
445 **TIRESIAS:**	Don't you surpass us all at finding out?
OEDIPUS:	You sneer at what you'll find has brought me greatness.
TIRESIAS:	And that's the very luck that ruined you.
OEDIPUS:	I wouldn't care, just so I saved the city.
TIRESIAS:	In that case I shall go. Boy, lead the way!
450 **OEDIPUS:**	Yes, let him lead you off. Here, underfoot,
	you irk me. Gone, you'll cause no further pain.

TIRESIAS: I'll go when I have said what I was sent for.
Your face won't scare me. You can't ruin me.
I say to you, the man whom you have looked for
455   as you pronounced your curses, your decrees
on the bloody death of Laius—he is here!
A seeming stranger, he shall be shown to be
a Theban born, though he'll take no delight
in that solution. Blind, who once could see,
460   a beggar who was rich, through foreign lands
he'll go and point before him with a stick.
To his beloved children, he'll be shown
a father who is also brother; to the one
who bore him, son and husband; to his father,
465   his seed-fellow and killer. Go in
and think this out; and if you find I've lied,
say then I have no prophet's understanding!

(Exit Tiresias, led by a Servant. Oedipus exits into the palace with his Attendants.)

STASIMON 1

STROPHE 1

CHORUS: Who is the man of whom the inspired
rock of Delphi[30] said
470   he has committed the unspeakable
with blood-stained hands?
Time for him to ply a foot
mightier than those of the horses
of the storm in his escape;
475   upon him mounts and plunges the weaponed
son of Zeus,[31] with fire and thunderbolts,
and in his train the dreaded goddesses
of Death, who never miss.

---

[30] *rock of Delphi:* Apollo's oracle at Delphi.   [31] *son of Zeus:* Apollo.

ANTISTROPHE 1

The message has just blazed,
480   gleaming from the snows
of Mount Parnassus: we must track
    everywhere the unseen man.
He wanders, hidden by wild
forests, up through caves
485   and rocks, like a bull,
anxious, with an anxious foot, forlorn.
He puts away from him the mantic[32] words come from earth's
navel,[33] at its center, yet these live
forever and still hover round him.

STROPHE 2

490 Terribly he troubles me,
    the skilled interpreter of birds![34]
I can't assent, nor speak against him.
    Both paths are closed to me.
I hover on the wings of doubt,
495   not seeing what is here nor what's to come.
What quarrel started in the house of Labdacus[35]
or in the house of Polybus,[36]
    either ever in the past
    or now, I never
500 heard, so that . . . with this fact for my touchstone
I could attack the public
    fame of Oedipus, by the side of the Labdaceans
an ally, against the dark assassination.

ANTISTROPHE 2

No, Zeus and Apollo
505   understand and know things
mortal; but that another man
    can do more as a prophet than I can—
for that there is no certain test,
    though, skill to skill,
510 one man might overtake another.
No, never, not until
    I see the charges proved,
when someone blames him shall I nod assent.

---

[32] *mantic:* prophetic.   [33] *earth's navel:* Delphi.   [34] *interpreter of birds:* Tiresias.
The Chorus is troubled by his accusations.   [35] *house of Labdacus:* the line of Laius.
[36] *Polybus:* Oedipus's foster father.

For once, as we all saw, the winged maiden[37] came
515   against him: he was seen then to be skilled,
        proved, by that touchstone, dear to the people. So,
        never will my mind convict him of the evil.

                    EPISODE 2

(Enter Creon from the right door of the skene and speaks to the Chorus.)

CREON: Citizens, I hear that a fearful charge
        is made against me by King Oedipus!
520   I had to come. If, in this crisis,
        he thinks that he has suffered injury
        from anything that I have said or done,
        I have no appetite for a long life—
        bearing a blame like that! It's no slight blow
525   the punishment I'd take from what he said:
        it's the ultimate hurt to be called traitor
        by the city, by you, by my own people!
CHORAGOS: The thing that forced that accusation out
        could have been anger, not the power of thought.
530 **CREON:**   But who persuaded him that thoughts of mine
        had led the prophet into telling lies?
CHORAGOS: I do not know the thought behind his words.
CREON: But did he look straight at you? Was his mind right
        when he said that I was guilty of this charge?
535 **CHORAGOS:**   I have no eyes to see what rulers do.
        But here he comes himself out of the house.

(Enter Oedipus from the palace.)

OEDIPUS: What? You here? And can you really have
        the face and daring to approach my house
        when you're exposed as its master's murderer
540   and caught, too, as the robber of my kingship?
        Did you see cowardice in me, by the gods,
        or foolishness, when you began this plot?
        Did you suppose that I would not detect
        your stealthy moves, or that I'd not fight back?
545   It's your attempt that's folly, isn't it—
        tracking without followers or connections,
        kingship which is caught with wealth and numbers?
CREON: Now wait! Give me as long to answer back!
        Judge me for yourself when you have heard me!

---

[37] *winged maiden:* the Sphinx.

550 **OEDIPUS:**   You're eloquent, but I'd be slow to learn
          from you, now that I've seen your malice toward me.
   CREON: That I deny. Hear what I have to say.
   OEDIPUS: Don't you deny it! You are the traitor here!
   CREON: If you consider mindless willfulness
555   a prized possession, you are not thinking sense.
   OEDIPUS: If you think you can wrong a relative
          and get off free, you are not thinking sense.
   CREON: Perfectly just, I won't say no. And yet
          what is this injury you say I did you?
560 **OEDIPUS:**   Did you persuade me, yes or no, to send
          someone to bring that solemn prophet here?
   CREON: And I still hold to the advice I gave.
   OEDIPUS: How many years ago did your King Laius . . .
   CREON: Laius! Do what? Now I don't understand.
565 **OEDIPUS:**   Vanish—victim of a murderous violence?
   CREON: That is a long count back into the past.
   OEDIPUS: Well, was this seer then practicing his art?
   CREON: Yes, skilled and honored just as he is today.
   OEDIPUS: Did he, back then, ever refer to me?
570 **CREON:**   He did not do so in my presence ever.
   OEDIPUS: You did inquire into the murder then.
   CREON: We had to, surely, though we discovered nothing.
   OEDIPUS: But the "skilled" one did not say this then? Why not?
   CREON: I never talk when I am ignorant.
575 **OEDIPUS:**   But you're not ignorant of your own part.
   CREON: What do you mean? I'll tell you if I know.
   OEDIPUS: Just this: if he had not conferred with you
          he'd not have told about my murdering Laius.
   CREON: If he said that, you are the one who knows.
580   But now it's fair that you should answer me.
   OEDIPUS: Ask on! You won't convict me as the killer.
   CREON: Well then, answer. My sister is your wife?
   OEDIPUS: Now there's a statement that I can't deny.
   CREON: You two have equal power in this country?
585 **OEDIPUS:**   She gets from me whatever she desires.
   CREON: And I'm a third? The three of us are equals?
   OEDIPUS: That's where you're treacherous to your kinship!
   CREON: But think about this rationally, as I do.
          First look at this: do you think anyone
590   prefers the anxieties of being king
          to untroubled sleep—if he has equal power?
          I'm not the kind of man who falls in love
          with kingship. I am content with a king's power.
          And so would any man who's wise and prudent.
595   I get all things from you, with no distress;

as king I would have onerous duties, too.
How could the kingship bring me more delight
than this untroubled power and influence?
I'm not misguided yet to such a point
600 that profitable honors aren't enough.
As it is, all wish me well and all salute;
those begging you for something have me summoned,
for their success depends on that alone.
Why should I lose all this to become king?
605 A prudent mind is never traitorous.
Treason's a thought I'm not enamored of;
nor could I join a man who acted so.
In proof of this, first go yourself to Pytho[38]
and ask if I brought back the true response.
610 Then, if you find I plotted with that portent
reader,[39] don't have me put to death by your vote
only—I'll vote myself for my conviction.
Don't let an unsupported thought convict me!
It's not right mindlessly to take the bad
615 for good or to suppose the good are traitors.
Rejecting a relation who is loyal
is like rejecting life, our greatest love.
In time you'll know securely without stumbling,
for time alone can prove a just man just,
620 though you can know a bad man in a day.
CHORAGOS: Well said, to one who's anxious not to fall.
Swift thinkers, Lord, are never safe from stumbling.
OEDIPUS: But when a swift and secret plotter moves
against me, I must make swift counterplot.
625 If I lie quiet and await his move,
he'll have achieved his aims and I'll have missed.
CREON: You surely cannot mean you want me exiled!
OEDIPUS: Not exiled, no. Your death is what I want!
CREON: If you would first define what envy is . . .
630 **OEDIPUS:** Are you still stubborn? Still disobedient?
CREON: I see you cannot think!
OEDIPUS: For me I can.
CREON: You should for me as well!
OEDIPUS: But you're a traitor!
CREON: What if you're wrong?
OEDIPUS: Authority must be maintained.
CREON: Not if the ruler's evil.
OEDIPUS: Hear that, Thebes!

---

[38] *Pytho:* Delphi.   [39] *portent reader:* Apollo's oracle or prophet.

635 **CREON:** It is my city too, not yours alone!

CHORAGOS: Please don't, my Lords! Ah, just in time, I see
Jocasta there, coming from the palace.
With her help you must settle your quarrel.

(Enter Jocasta from the palace.)

JOCASTA: Wretched men! What has provoked this ill-
640 advised dispute? Have you no sense of shame,
with Thebes so sick, to stir up private troubles?
Now go inside! And Creon, you go home!
Don't make a general anguish out of nothing!

CREON: My sister, Oedipus your husband here
645 sees fit to do one of two hideous things:
to have me banished from the land—or killed!

OEDIPUS: That's right: I caught him, Lady, plotting harm
against my person—with a malignant science.

CREON: May my life fail, may I die cursed, if I
650 did any of the things you said I did!

JOCASTA: Believe his words, for the god's sake, Oedipus,
in deference above all to his oath
to the gods. Also for me, and for these men!

K O M M O S [40]
....

STROPHE 1

CHORUS: Consent, with will and mind,
655 my king, I beg of you!

OEDIPUS: What do you wish me to surrender?

CHORUS: Show deference to him who was not feeble in time past
and is now great in the power of his oath!

OEDIPUS: Do you know what you're asking?

CHORUS: Yes.

OEDIPUS: Tell me then.

660 **CHORUS:** Never to cast into dishonored guilt, with an unproved
assumption, a kinsman who has bound himself by curse.

OEDIPUS: Now you must understand, when you ask this,
you ask my death or banishment from the land.

STROPHE 2

CHORUS: No, by the god who is the foremost of all gods,
665 the Sun! No! Godless,

---

[40] *Kommos:* a dirge or lament sung by the Chorus and one or more of the chief
characters.

friendless, whatever death is worst of all,
let that be my destruction, if this
   thought ever moved me!
But my ill-fated soul
670   this dying land
wears out—the more if to these older troubles
she adds new troubles from the two of you!

OEDIPUS: Then let him go, though it must mean my death,
or else disgrace and exile from the land.
675 My pity is moved by your words, not by his—
he'll only have my hate, wherever he goes.

CREON: You're sullen as you yield; you'll be depressed
when you've passed through this anger. Natures like yours
are hardest on themselves. That's as it should be.

680 **OEDIPUS:** Then won't you go and let me be?

CREON: I'll go.
Though you're unreasonable, they know I'm righteous.

(Exit Creon.)

ANTISTROPHE 1

CHORUS: Why are you waiting, Lady?
Conduct him back into the palace!

JOCASTA: I will, when I have heard what chanced.

685 **CHORUS:** Conjectures—words alone, and nothing based on thought.
But even an injustice can devour a man.

JOCASTA: Did the words come from both sides?

CHORUS: Yes.

JOCASTA: What was said?

CHORUS: To me it seems enough! enough! the land already troubled,
that this should rest where it has stopped.

690 **OEDIPUS:** See what you've come to in your honest thought,
in seeking to relax and blunt my heart?

ANTISTROPHE 2

CHORUS: I have not said this only once, my Lord.
That I had lost my sanity,
   without a path in thinking—
695 be sure this would be clear
   if I put you away
who, when my cherished land
   wandered crazed
with suffering, brought her back on course.
700 Now, too, be a lucky helmsman!

JOCASTA: Please, for the god's sake, Lord, explain to me
the reason why you have conceived this wrath?

OEDIPUS: I honor you, not them,[41] and I'll explain
    to you how Creon has conspired against me.

705 **JOCASTA:** All right, if that will explain how the quarrel started.

OEDIPUS: He says I am the murderer of Laius!

JOCASTA: Did he claim knowledge or that someone told him?

OEDIPUS: Here's what he did: he sent that vicious seer
    so he could keep his own mouth innocent.

710 **JOCASTA:** Ah then, absolve yourself of what he charges!
    Listen to this and you'll agree, no mortal
    is ever given skill in prophecy.
    I'll prove this quickly with one incident.
    It was foretold to Laius—I shall not say

715   by Phoebus himself, but by his ministers—
    that when his fate arrived he would be killed
    by a son who would be born to him and me.
    And yet, so it is told, foreign robbers
    murdered him, at a place where three roads meet.

720   As for the child I bore him, not three days passed
    before he yoked the ball-joints of its feet,[42]
    then cast it, by others' hands, on a trackless mountain.
    That time Apollo did not make our child
    a patricide, or bring about what Laius

725   feared, that he be killed by his own son.
    That's how prophetic words determined things!
    Forget them. The things a god must track
    he will himself painlessly reveal.

OEDIPUS: Just now, as I was listening to you, Lady,

730   what a profound distraction seized my mind!

JOCASTA: What made you turn around so anxiously?

OEDIPUS: I thought you said that Laius was attacked
    and butchered at a place where three roads meet.

JOCASTA: That is the story, and it is told so still.

735 **OEDIPUS:** Where is the place where this was done to him?

JOCASTA: The land's called Phocis, where a two-forked road
    comes in from Delphi and from Daulia.

OEDIPUS: And how much time has passed since these events?

JOCASTA: Just prior to your presentation here

740   as king this news was published to the city.

OEDIPUS: Oh, Zeus, what have you willed to do to me?

JOCASTA: Oedipus, what makes your heart so heavy?

OEDIPUS: No, tell me first of Laius' appearance,
    what peak of youthful vigor he had reached.

---

[41] *them:* the Chorus.   [42] *ball-joints of its feet:* the ankles.

745 **JOCASTA:**   A tall man, showing his first growth of white.
　　　　　He had a figure not unlike your own.
　　　OEDIPUS: Alas! It seems that in my ignorance
　　　　　I laid those fearful curses on myself.
　　　JOCASTA: What is it, Lord? I flinch to see your face.
750 **OEDIPUS:**   I'm dreadfully afraid the prophet sees.
　　　　　But I'll know better with one more detail.
　　　JOCASTA: I'm frightened too. But ask: I'll answer you.
　　　OEDIPUS: Was his retinue small, or did he travel
　　　　　with a great troop, as would befit a prince?
755 **JOCASTA:**   There were just five in all, one a herald.
　　　　　There was a carriage, too, bearing Laius.
　　　OEDIPUS: Alas! Now I see it! But who was it,
　　　　　Lady, who told you what you know about this?
　　　JOCASTA: A servant who alone was saved unharmed.
760 **OEDIPUS:**   By chance, could he be now in the palace?
　　　JOCASTA: No, he is not. When he returned and saw
　　　　　you had the power of the murdered Laius,
　　　　　he touched my hand and begged me formally
　　　　　to send him to the fields and to the pastures,
765 　　　so he'd be out of sight, far from the city.
　　　　　I did. Although a slave, he well deserved
　　　　　to win this favor, and indeed far more.
　　　OEDIPUS: Let's have him called back in immediately.
　　　JOCASTA: That can be done, but why do you desire it?
770 **OEDIPUS:**   I fear, Lady, I have already said
　　　　　too much. That's why I wish to see him now.
　　　JOCASTA: Then he shall come; but it is right somehow
　　　　　that I, too, Lord, should know what troubles you.
　　　OEDIPUS: I've gone so deep into the things I feared
775 　　　I'll tell you everything. Who has a right
　　　　　greater than yours, while I cross through this chance?
　　　　　Polybus of Corinth was my father,
　　　　　my mother was the Dorian Meropē.
　　　　　I was first citizen, until this chance
780 　　　attacked me—striking enough, to be sure,
　　　　　but not worth all the gravity I gave it.
　　　　　This: at a feast a man who'd drunk too much
　　　　　denied, at the wine, I was my father's son.
　　　　　I was depressed and all that day I barely
785 　　　held it in. Next day I put the question
　　　　　to my mother and father. They were enraged
　　　　　at the man who'd let this fiction fly at me.
　　　　　I was much cheered by them. And yet it kept
　　　　　grinding into me. His words kept coming back.
790 　　　Without my mother's or my father's knowledge

I went to Pytho. But Phoebus sent me away
dishonoring my demand. Instead, other
wretched horrors he flashed forth in speech.
He said that I would be my mother's lover,
795   show offspring to mankind they could not look at,
and be his murderer whose seed I am.[43]
When I heard this, and ever since, I gauged
the way to Corinth by the stars alone,
running to a place where I would never see
800   the disgrace in the oracle's words come true.
But I soon came to the exact location
where, as you tell of it, the king was killed.
Lady, here is the truth. As I went on,
when I was just approaching those three roads,
805   a herald and a man like him you spoke of
came on, riding a carriage drawn by colts.
Both the man out front and the old man himself[44]
tried violently to force me off the road.
The driver, when he tried to push me off,
810   I struck in anger. The old man saw this, watched
me approach, then leaned out and lunged down
with twin prongs[45] at the middle of my head!
He got more than he gave. Abruptly—struck
once by the staff in this my hand—he tumbled
815   out, head first, from the middle of the carriage.
And then I killed them all. But if there is
a kinship between Laius and this stranger,
who is more wretched than the man you see?
Who was there born more hated by the gods?
820   For neither citizen nor foreigner
may take me in his home or speak to me.
No, they must drive me off. And it is I
who have pronounced these curses on myself!
I stain the dead man's bed with these my hands,
825   by which he died. Is not my nature vile?
Unclean?—if I am banished and even
in exile I may not see my own parents,
or set foot in my homeland, or else be yoked
in marriage to my mother, and kill my father,
830   Polybus, who raised me and gave me birth?
If someone judged a cruel divinity
did this to me, would he not speak the truth?
You pure and awful gods, may I not ever

---

[43] *be . . . am:* that is, murder my father.   [44] *old man himself:* Laius.   [45] *lunged . . .*
prongs: Laius strikes Oedipus with a two-pronged horse goad, or whip.

see that day, may I be swept away
835 from men before I see so great and so
calamitous a stain fixed on my person!
CHORAGOS: These things seem fearful to us, Lord, and yet,
until you hear it from the witness, keep hope!
OEDIPUS: That is the single hope that's left to me,
840 to wait for him, that herdsman—until he comes.
JOCASTA: When he appears, what are you eager for?
OEDIPUS: Just this: if his account agrees with yours
then I shall have escaped this misery.
JOCASTA: But what was it that struck you in my story?
845 **OEDIPUS:**   You said he spoke of robbers as the ones
who killed him. Now: if he continues still
to speak of many, then I could not have killed him.
One man and many men just do not jibe.
But if he says one belted man, the doubt
850 is gone. The balance tips toward me. I did it.
JOCASTA: No! He told it as I told you. Be certain.
He can't reject that and reverse himself.
The city heard these things, not I alone.
But even if he swerves from what he said,
855 he'll never show that Laius' murder, Lord,
occurred just as predicted. For Loxias
expressly said my son was doomed to kill him.
The boy—poor boy—he never had a chance
to cut him down, for he was cut down first.
860 Never again, just for some oracle
will I shoot frightened glances right and left.
OEDIPUS: That's full of sense. Nonetheless, send a man
to bring that farm hand here. Will you do it?
JOCASTA: I'll send one right away. But let's go in.
865 Would I do anything against your wishes?

(Exit Oedipus and Jocasta through the central door into the palace.)

STASIMON   2
....

STROPHE 1

CHORUS: May there accompany me
the fate to keep a reverential purity in what I say,
in all I do, for which the laws have been set forth
and walk on high, born to traverse the brightest,
870 highest upper air; Olympus[46] only

---

[46] *Olympus:* Mount Olympus, home of the gods, treated as a god.

is their father, nor was it
mortal nature
that fathered them, and never will
oblivion lull them into sleep;
875   the god in them is great and never ages.

ANTISTROPHE 1

The will to violate, seed of the tyrant,
if it has drunk mindlessly of wealth and power,
without a sense of time or true advantage,
mounts to a peak, then
880   plunges to an abrupt . . . destiny,
where the useful foot
is of no use. But the kind
of struggling that is good for the city
I ask the god never to abolish.
885   The god is my protector: never will I give that up.

STROPHE 2

But if a man proceeds disdainfully
in deeds of hand or word
and has no fear of Justice
or reverence for shrines of the divinities
890   (may a bad fate catch him
for his luckless wantonness!),
if he'll not gain what he gains with justice
and deny himself what is unholy,
or if he clings, in foolishness, to the untouchable
895   (what man, finally, in such an action, will have strength
enough to fend off passion's arrows from his soul?),
if, I say, this kind of
deed is held in honor—
why should I join the sacred dance?

ANTISTROPHE 2

900   No longer shall I visit and revere
Earth's navel,[47] the untouchable,
nor visit Abae's[48] temple,
or Olympia,[49]
if the prophecies are not matched by events
905   for all the world to point to.

---

[47] *Earth's navel:* Delphi.   [48] *Abae:* a town in Phocis where there was another oracle of Apollo.   [49] *Olympia:* site of the oracle of Zeus.

No, you who hold the power, if you are rightly called
Zeus the king of all, let this matter not escape you
and your ever-deathless rule,
for the prophecies to Laius fade . . .
910   and men already disregard them;
nor is Apollo anywhere
      glorified with honors.
Religion slips away.

EPISODE 3

(Enter Jocasta from the palace carrying a branch wound with wool and a jar of incense. She is attended by two women.)

JOCASTA: Lords of the realm, the thought has come to me
915   to visit shrines of the divinities
with suppliant's branch in hand and fragrant smoke.
For Oedipus excites his soul too much
with alarms of all kinds. He will not judge
the present by the past, like a man of sense.
920   He's at the mercy of all terror-mongers.

(Jocasta approaches the altar on the right and kneels.)

Since I can do no good by counseling,
Apollo the Lycēan!—you are the closest—
I come a suppliant, with these my vows,
for a cleansing that will not pollute him.
925   For when we see him shaken we are all
afraid, like people looking at their helmsman.

(Enter a Messenger along one of the parados. He sees Jocasta at the altar and then addresses the Chorus.)

MESSENGER: I would be pleased if you would help me, stranger.
Where is the palace of King Oedipus?
Or tell me where he is himself, if you know.
930 **CHORUS:** This is his house, stranger. He is within.
This is his wife and mother of his children.
MESSENGER: May she and her family find prosperity,
if, as you say, her marriage is fulfilled.
JOCASTA: You also, stranger, for you deserve as much
935   for your gracious words. But tell me why you've come.
What do you wish? Or what have you to tell us?
MESSENGER: Good news, my Lady, both for your house and
    husband.
JOCASTA: What is your news? And who has sent you to us?

MESSENGER: I come from Corinth. When you have heard my
  news
940 you will rejoice, I'm sure—and grieve perhaps.
JOCASTA: What is it? How can it have this double power?
MESSENGER: They will establish him their king, so say
  the people of the land of Isthmia.[50]
JOCASTA: But is old Polybus not still in power?
945 **MESSENGER:** He's not, for death has clasped him in the tomb.
JOCASTA: What's this? Has Oedipus' father died?
MESSENGER: If I have lied then I deserve to die.
JOCASTA: Attendant! Go quickly to your master,
  and tell him this.

(Exit an Attendant into the palace.)

  Oracles of the gods!
950 Where are you now? The man whom Oedipus
  fled long ago, for fear that he should kill him—
  he's been destroyed by chance and not by him!

(Enter Oedipus from the palace.)

OEDIPUS: Darling Jocasta, my beloved wife,
  Why have you called me from the palace?
955 **JOCASTA:** First hear what this man has to say. Then see
  what the god's grave oracle has come to now!
OEDIPUS: Where is he from? What is this news he brings me?
JOCASTA: From Corinth. He brings news about your father:
  that Polybus is no more! that he is dead!
960 **OEDIPUS:** What's this, old man? I want to hear you say it.
MESSENGER: If this is what must first be clarified,
  please be assured that he is dead and gone.
OEDIPUS: By treachery or by the touch of sickness?
MESSENGER: Light pressures tip agéd frames into their sleep.
965 **OEDIPUS:** You mean the poor man died of some disease.
MESSENGER: And of the length of years that he had tallied.
OEDIPUS: Aha! Then why should we look to Pytho's vapors,[51]
  or to the birds that scream above our heads?[52]
  If we could really take those things for guides,
970 I would have killed my father. But he's dead!
  He is beneath the earth, and here am I,
  who never touched a spear. Unless he died
  of longing for me and I "killed" him that way!

---

[50] *land of Isthmia:* Corinth, which was on an isthmus.   [51] *Pytho's vapors:* the
prophecies of the oracle at Delphi.   [52] *birds . . . heads:* the prophecies derived from
interpreting the flights of birds.

No, in this case, Polybus, by dying, took
975 the worthless oracle to Hades with him.
JOCASTA: And wasn't I telling you that just now?
OEDIPUS: You were indeed. I was misled by fear.
JOCASTA: You should not care about this anymore.
OEDIPUS: I must care. I must stay clear of my mother's bed.
980 **JOCASTA:** What's there for man to fear? The realm of chance
prevails. True foresight isn't possible.
His life is best who lives without a plan.
This marriage with your mother—don't fear it.
How many times have men in dreams, too, slept
985 with their own mothers! Those who believe such things
mean nothing endure their lives most easily.
OEDIPUS: A fine, bold speech, and you are right, perhaps,
except that my mother is still living,
so I must fear her, however well you argue.
990 **JOCASTA:** And yet your father's tomb is a great eye.
OEDIPUS: Illuminating, yes. But I still fear the living.
MESSENGER: Who is the woman who inspires this fear?
OEDIPUS: Meropē, Polybus' wife, old man.
MESSENGER: And what is there about her that alarms you?
995 **OEDIPUS:** An oracle, god-sent and fearful, stranger.
MESSENGER: Is it permitted that another know?
OEDIPUS: It is. Loxias once said to me
I must have intercourse with my own mother
and take my father's blood with these my hands.
1000 So I have long lived far away from Corinth.
This has indeed brought much good luck, and yet,
to see one's parents' eyes is happiest.
MESSENGER: Was it for this that you have lived in exile?
OEDIPUS: So I'd not be my father's killer, sir.
1005 **MESSENGER:** Had I not better free you from this fear,
my Lord? That's why I came—to do you service.
OEDIPUS: Indeed, what a reward you'd get for that!
MESSENGER: Indeed, this is the main point of my trip,
to be rewarded when you get back home.
1010 **OEDIPUS:** I'll never rejoin the givers of my seed![53]
MESSENGER: My son, clearly you don't know what you're doing.
OEDIPUS: But how is that, old man? For the gods' sake, tell me!
MESSENGER: If it's because of them you won't go home.
OEDIPUS: I fear that Phoebus will have told the truth.
1015 **MESSENGER:** Pollution from the ones who gave you seed?

---

[53] *givers of my seed:* that is, my parents. Oedipus still thinks Meropē and Polybus are
his parents.

OEDIPUS: That is the thing, old man, I always fear.

MESSENGER: Your fear is groundless. Understand that.

OEDIPUS: Groundless? Not if I was born their son.

MESSENGER: But Polybus is not related to you.

1020 **OEDIPUS:** Do you mean Polybus was not my father?

MESSENGER: No more than I. We're both the same to you.

OEDIPUS: Same? One who begot me and one who didn't?

MESSENGER: He didn't beget you any more than I did.

OEDIPUS: But then, why did he say I was his son?

1025 **MESSENGER:** He got you as a gift from my own hands.

OEDIPUS: He loved me so, though from another's hands?

MESSENGER: His former childlessness persuaded him.

OEDIPUS: But had you bought me, or begotten me?

MESSENGER: Found you. In the forest hallows of Cithaeron.

1030 **OEDIPUS:** What were you doing traveling in that region?

MESSENGER: I was in charge of flocks which grazed those mountains.

OEDIPUS: A wanderer who worked the flocks for hire?

MESSENGER: Ah, but that day I was your savior, son.

OEDIPUS: From what? What was my trouble when you took me?

1035 **MESSENGER:** The ball-joints of your feet might testify.

OEDIPUS: What's that? What makes you name that ancient trouble?

MESSENGER: Your feet were pierced and I am your rescuer.

OEDIPUS: A fearful rebuke those tokens left for me!

MESSENGER: That was the chance that names you who you are.

1040 **OEDIPUS:** By the gods, did my mother or my father do this?

MESSENGER: That I don't know. He might who gave you to me.

OEDIPUS: From someone else? You didn't chance on me?

MESSENGER: Another shepherd handed you to me.

OEDIPUS: Who was he? Do you know? Will you explain!

1045 **MESSENGER:** They called him one of the men of—was it Laius?

OEDIPUS: The one who once was king here long ago?

MESSENGER: That is the one! The man was shepherd to him.

OEDIPUS: And is he still alive so I can see him?

MESSENGER: But you who live here ought to know that best.

1050 **OEDIPUS:** Does any one of you now present know
about the shepherd whom this man has named?
Have you seen him in town or in the fields? Speak out!
The time has come for the discovery!

CHORAGOS: The man he speaks of, I believe, is the same
1055 as the field hand you have already asked to see.
But it's Jocasta who would know this best.

OEDIPUS: Lady, do you remember the man we just
now sent for—is that the man he speaks of?

JOCASTA: What? The man he spoke of? Pay no attention!
1060 His words are not worth thinking about. It's nothing.

OEDIPUS: With clues like this within my grasp, give up?
Fail to solve the mystery of my birth?

JOCASTA: For the love of the gods, and if you love your life,
give up this search! My sickness is enough.
1065 **OEDIPUS:**   Come! Though my mothers for three generations
were in slavery, you'd not be lowborn!
JOCASTA: No, listen to me! Please! Don't do this thing!
OEDIPUS: I will not listen; I will search out the truth.
JOCASTA: My thinking is for you—it would be best.
1070 **OEDIPUS:**   This "best" of yours is starting to annoy me.
JOCASTA: Doomed man! Never find out who you are!
OEDIPUS: Will someone go and bring that shepherd here?
Leave her to glory in her wealthy birth!
JOCASTA: Man of misery! No other name
1075 shall I address you by, ever again.

(Exit Jocasta into the palace after a long pause.)

CHORAGOS: Why has your lady left, Oedipus,
hurled by a savage grief? I am afraid
disaster will come bursting from this silence.
OEDIPUS: Let it burst forth! However low this seed
1080 of mine may be, yet I desire to see it.
She, perhaps—she has a woman's pride—
is mortified by my base origins.
But I who count myself the child of Chance,
the giver of good, shall never know dishonor.
1085 She is my mother,[54] and the months my brothers
who first marked out my lowness, then my greatness.
I shall not prove untrue to such a nature
by giving up the search for my own birth.

STASIMON 3

STROPHE

CHORUS: If I have mantic power
1090 and excellence in thought,
by Olympus,
you shall not, Cithaeron, at tomorrow's
full moon,
fail to hear us celebrate you as the countryman
1095 of Oedipus, his nurse and mother,
or fail to be the subject of our dance,
since you have given pleasure
to our king.

---

[54] *She . . . mother:* Chance is my mother.

Phoebus, whom we summon by "iē!,"
1100   may this be pleasing to you!

ANTISTROPHE

Who was your mother, son?
which of the long-lived nymphs
after lying with Pan,[55]
        the mountain roaming . . . Or was it a bride
1105   of Loxias?[56]
For dear to him are all the upland pastures.
Or was it Mount Cyllēnē's lord,[57]
or the Bacchic god,[58]
        dweller of the mountain peaks,
1110   who received you as a joyous find
from one of the nymphs of Helicon,
the favorite sharers of his sport?

EPISODE 4

OEDIPUS: If someone like myself, who never met him,
    may calculate—elders, I think I see
1115   the very herdsman we've been waiting for.
    His many years would fit that man's age,
    and those who bring him on, if I am right,
    are my own men. And yet, in real knowledge,
    you can outstrip me, surely: you've seen him.

(Enter the old Herdsman escorted by two of Oedipus's Attendants. At first, the Herdsman will not look at Oedipus.)

1120 **CHORAGOS:**   I know him, yes, a man of the house of Laius,
    a trusty herdsman if he ever had one.
OEDIPUS: I ask you first, the stranger come from Corinth:
    is this the man you spoke of?
MESSENGER: That's he you see.
OEDIPUS: Then you, old man. First look at me! Now answer:
1125   did you belong to Laius' household once?
HERDSMAN: I did. Not a purchased slave but raised in the palace.
OEDIPUS: How have you spent your life? What is your work?
HERDSMAN: Most of my life now I have tended sheep.
OEDIPUS: Where is the usual place you stay with them?
1130 **HERDSMAN:**   On Mount Cithaeron. Or in that district.

---

[55] *Pan:* god of shepherds and woodlands, half man and half goat.   [56] *Loxias:* Apollo.
[57] *Mount Cyllēnē's lord:* Hermes, messenger of the gods.   [58] *Bacchic god:* Dionysus.

OEDIPUS: Do you recall observing this man there?

HERDSMAN: Doing what? Which is the man you mean?

OEDIPUS: This man right here. Have you had dealings with him?

HERDSMAN: I can't say right away. I don't remember.

1135 **MESSENGER:**   No wonder, master. I'll bring clear memory
to his ignorance. I'm absolutely sure
he can recall it, the district was Cithaeron,
he with a double flock, and I, with one,
lived close to him, for three entire seasons,
1140 six months along, from spring right to Arcturus.[59]
Then for the winter I'd drive mine to my fold,
and he'd drive his to Laius' pen again.
Did any of the things I say take place?

HERDSMAN: You speak the truth, though it's from long ago.

1145 **MESSENGER:**   Do you remember giving me, back then,
a boy I was to care for as my own?

HERDSMAN: What are you saying? Why do you ask me that?

MESSENGER: There, sir, is the man who was that boy!

HERDSMAN: Damn you! Shut your mouth! Keep your silence!

1150 **OEDIPUS:**   Stop! Don't you rebuke his words.
Your words ask for rebuke far more than his.

HERDSMAN: But what have I done wrong, most royal master?

OEDIPUS: Not telling of the boy of whom he asked.

HERDSMAN: He's ignorant and blundering toward ruin.

1155 **OEDIPUS:**   Tell it willingly—or under torture.

HERDSMAN: Oh god! Don't—I am old—don't torture me!

OEDIPUS: Here! Someone put his hands behind his back!

HERDSMAN: But why? What else would you find out, poor man?

OEDIPUS: Did you give him the child he asks about?

1160 **HERDSMAN:**   I did. I wish that I had died that day!

OEDIPUS: You'll come to that if you don't speak the truth.

HERDSMAN: It's if I speak that I shall be destroyed.

OEDIPUS: I think this fellow struggles for delay.

HERDSMAN: No, no! I said already that I gave him.

1165 **OEDIPUS:**   From your own home, or got from someone else?

HERDSMAN: Not from my own. I got him from another.

OEDIPUS: Which of these citizens? What sort of house?

HERDSMAN: Don't—by the gods!—don't, master, ask me more!

OEDIPUS: It means your death if I must ask again.

1170 **HERDSMAN:**   One of the children of the house of Laius.

OEDIPUS: A slave—or born into the family?

HERDSMAN: I have come to the dreaded thing, and I shall say it.

OEDIPUS: And I to hearing it, but hear I must.

---

[59] *Arcturus:* a star that is first seen in September in the Grecian sky.

HERDSMAN: He was reported to have been—his son.
1175   Your lady in the house could tell you best.
OEDIPUS: Because she gave him to you?
HERDSMAN: Yes, my lord.
OEDIPUS: What was her purpose?
HERDSMAN: I was to kill the boy.
OEDIPUS: The child she bore?
HERDSMAN: She dreaded prophecies.
OEDIPUS: What were they?
HERDSMAN: The word was that he'd kill his parents.
1180 **OEDIPUS:**   Then why did you give him up to this old man?
HERDSMAN: In pity, master—so he would take him home,
       to another land. But what he did was save him
       for this supreme disaster. If you are the one
       he speaks of—know your evil birth and fate!
1185 **OEDIPUS:**   Ah! All of it was destined to be true!
       Oh light, now may I look my last upon you,
       shown monstrous in my birth, in marriage monstrous,
       a murderer monstrous in those I killed.

(Exit Oedipus, running into the palace.)

STASIMON   4

STROPHE 1

CHORUS: Oh generations of mortal men,
1190   while you are living, I will
               appraise your lives at zero!
       What man
       comes closer to seizing lasting blessedness
       than merely to seize its semblance,
1195   and after living in this semblance, to plunge?
       With your example before us,
       with your destiny, yours,
               suffering Oedipus, no mortal
       can I judge fortunate.

ANTISTROPHE 1

1200   For he,[60] outranging everybody,
       shot his arrow[61] and became the lord
               of wide prosperity and blessedness,

---

[60] *he:* Oedipus.   [61] *shot his arrow:* took his chances; made a guess at the Sphinx's riddle.

oh Zeus, after destroying
the virgin with the crooked talons,[62]
1205   singer of oracles; and against death,
in my land, he arose a tower of defense.
From which time you were called my king
and granted privileges supreme—in mighty
Thebes the ruling lord.

STROPHE 2

1210   But now—whose story is more sorrowful than yours?
Who is more intimate with fierce calamities,
with labors, now that your life is altered?
Alas, my Oedipus, whom all men know:
one great harbor[63]—
1215   one alone sufficed for you,
as son and father,
when you tumbled,[64] plowman[65] of the woman's chamber.
How, how could your paternal
    furrows, wretched man,
1220   endure you silently so long.

ANTISTROPHE 2

Time, all-seeing, surprised you living an unwilled life
and sits from of old in judgment on the marriage, not a marriage,
where the begetter is the begot as well.
Ah, son of Laius . . . ,
1225   would that—oh, would that
I had never seen you!
I wail, my scream climbing beyond itself
from my whole power of voice. To say it straight:
    from you I got new breath—
1230   but I also lulled my eye to sleep.[66]

EXODOS

(Enter the Second Messenger from the palace.)

SECOND MESSENGER: You who are first among the citizens,
what deeds you are about to hear and see!
What grief you'll carry, if, true to your birth,

---

[62] *virgin . . . talons:* the Sphinx.   [63] *one great harbor:* metaphorical allusion to Jocasta's body.   [64] *tumbled:* were born and had sex.   [65] *plowman:* plowing is used
here as a sexual metaphor.   [66] *I . . . sleep:* I failed to see the corruption you brought.

you still respect the house of Labdacus!

1235   Neither the Ister nor the Phasis river
could purify this house, such suffering
does it conceal, or soon must bring to light—
willed this time, not unwilled. Griefs hurt worst
which we perceive to be self-chosen ones.

1240 **CHORAGOS:**   They were sufficient, the things we knew before,
to make us grieve. What can you add to those?

SECOND MESSENGER: The thing that's quickest said and quickest heard:
our own, our royal one, Jocasta's dead.

CHORAGOS: Unhappy queen! What was responsible?

1245 **SECOND MESSENGER:**   Herself. The bitterest of these events
is not for you, you were not there to see,
but yet, exactly as I can recall it,
you'll hear what happened to that wretched lady.
She came in anger through the outer hall,

1250   and then she ran straight to her marriage bed,
tearing her hair with the fingers of both hands.
Then, slamming shut the doors when she was in,
she called to Laius, dead so many years,
remembering the ancient seed which caused

1255   his death, leaving the mother to the son
to breed again an ill-born progeny.
She mourned the bed where she, alas, bred double—
husband by husband, children by her child.
From this point on I don't know how she died,

1260   for Oedipus then burst in with a cry,
and did not let us watch her final evil.
Our eyes were fixed on him. Wildly he ran
to each of us, asking for his spear
and for his wife—no wife: where he might find

1265   the double mother-field, his and his children's.
He raved, and some divinity then showed him—
for none of us did so who stood close by.
With a dreadful shout—as if some guide were leading—
he lunged through the double doors; he bent the hollow

1270   bolts from the sockets, burst into the room,
and there we saw her, hanging from above,
entangled in some twisted hanging strands.
He saw, was stricken, and with a wild roar
ripped down the dangling noose. When she, poor woman,

1275   lay on the ground, there came a fearful sight:
he snatched the pins of worked gold from her dress,
with which her clothes were fastened: these he raised

and struck into the ball-joints of his eyes.[67]
He shouted that they would no longer see
1280   the evils he had suffered or had done,
see in the dark those he should not have seen,
and know no more those he once sought to know.
While chanting this, not once but many times
he raised his hand and struck into his eyes.
1285   Blood from his wounded eyes poured down his chin,
not freed in moistening drops, but all at once
a stormy rain of black blood burst like hail.
These evils, coupling them, making them one,
have broken loose upon both man and wife.
1290   The old prosperity that they had once
was true prosperity, and yet today,
mourning, ruin, death, disgrace, and every
evil you could name—not one is absent.
CHORAGOS: Has he allowed himself some peace from all this grief?
1295 **SECOND MESSENGER:**   He shouts that someone slide the bolts and show
to all the Cadmeians the patricide,
his mother's—I can't say it, it's unholy—
so he can cast himself out of the land,
not stay and curse his house by his own curse.
1300   He lacks the strength, though, and he needs a guide,
for his is a sickness that's too great to bear.
Now you yourself will see: the bolts of the doors
are opening. You are about to see
a vision even one who hates must pity.

(Enter the blinded Oedipus from the palace, led in by a household Servant.)

1305 **CHORAGOS:**   Terrifying suffering for men to see,
more terrifying than any I've ever
come upon. Oh man of pain
what madness reached you? Which god from far off,
surpassing in range his longest spring,
1310   struck hard against your god-abandoned fate?
Oh man of pain,
I cannot look upon you—though there's so much
I would ask you, so much to hear,
so much that holds my eyes—
1315   such is the shudder you produce in me.

---

[67] *ball-joints of his eyes:* his eyeballs. Oedipus blinds himself in both eyes at the same time.

OEDIPUS: Ah! Ah! I am a man of misery.
Where am I carried? Pity me! Where
is my voice scattered abroad on wings?
Divinity, where has your lunge transported me?

1320 **CHORAGOS:** To something horrible, not to be heard or seen.

KOMMOS

STROPHE 1

OEDIPUS: Oh, my cloud
of darkness, abominable, unspeakable as it attacks me,
not to be turned away, brought by an evil wind!
Alas!
1325 Again alas! Both enter me at once:
the sting of the prongs,[68] the memory of evils!

CHORUS: I do not marvel that in these afflictions
you carry double griefs and double evils.

ANTISTROPHE 1

OEDIPUS: Ah, friend,
1330 so you at least are there, resolute servant!
Still with a heart to care for me, the blind man.
Oh! Oh!
I know that you are there. I recognize
even inside my darkness, that voice of yours.

1335 **CHORUS:** Doer of horror, how did you bear to quench
your vision? What divinity raised your hand?

STROPHE 2

OEDIPUS: It was Apollo there, Apollo, friends,
who brought my sorrows, vile sorrows to their perfection,
these evils that were done to me.
1340 But the one who struck them with his hand,
that one was none but I, in wretchedness.
For why was I to see
when nothing I could see would bring me joy?

CHORUS: Yes, that is how it was.

1345 **OEDIPUS:** What could I see, indeed,
or what enjoy—what greeting
is there I could hear with pleasure, friends?

---

[68] *prongs:* refers to both the whip that Laius used and the two gold pins Oedipus used
to blind himself.

Conduct me out of the land
    as quickly as you can!
1350   Conduct me out, my friends,
        the man utterly ruined,
    supremely cursed,
        the man who is by gods
    the most detested of all men!

1355 **CHORUS:**   Wretched in disaster and in knowledge:
    oh, I could wish you'd never come to know!

ANTISTROPHE 2

OEDIPUS: May he be destroyed, whoever freed the savage shackles
    from my feet when I'd been sent to the wild pasture,
        whoever rescued me from murder
1360   and became my savior—
        a bitter gift:
    if I had died then,
    I'd not have been such grief to self and kin.

CHORUS: I also would have had it so.

1365 **OEDIPUS:**   I'd not have returned to be my father's
    murderer; I'd not be called by men
    my mother's bridegroom.
    Now I'm without a god,
        child of a polluted parent,
1370   fellow progenitor with him
        who gave me birth in misery.
    If there's an evil that
        surpasses evils, that
    has fallen to the lot of Oedipus.

1375 **CHORAGOS:**   How can I say that you have counseled well?
    Better not to be than live a blind man.

OEDIPUS: That this was not the best thing I could do—
    don't tell me that, or advise me any more!
    Should I descend to Hades and endure
1380   to see my father with these eyes? Or see
    my poor unhappy mother? For I have done,
    to both of these, things too great for hanging.
    Or is the sight of children to be yearned for,
    to see new shoots that sprouted as these did?
1385   Never, never with these eyes of mine!
    Nor city, nor tower, nor holy images
    of the divinities! For I, all-wretched,
    most nobly raised—as no one else in Thebes—
    deprived myself of these when I ordained
1390   that all expel the impious one—god-shown

to be polluted, and the dead king's son![69]
Once I exposed this great stain upon me,
could I have looked on these with steady eyes?
No! No! And if there were a way to block
1395   the source of hearing in my ears, I'd gladly
have locked up my pitiable body,
so I'd be blind and deaf. Evils shut out—
that way my mind could live in sweetness.
Alas, Cithaeron,[70] why did you receive me?
1400   Or when you had me, not killed me instantly?
I'd not have had to show my birth to mankind.
Polybus, Corinth, halls—ancestral,
they told me—how beautiful was your ward,
a scar that held back festering disease!
1405   Evil my nature, evil my origin.
You, three roads, and you, secret ravine,
you oak grove, narrow place of those three paths
that drank my blood[71] from these hands, from him
who fathered me, do you remember still
1410   the things I did to you? When I'd come here,
what I then did once more? Oh marriages! Marriages!
You gave us life and when you'd planted us
you sent the same seed up, and then revealed
fathers, brothers, sons, and kinsman's blood,
1415   and brides, and wives, and mothers, all the most
atrocious things that happen to mankind!
One should not name what never should have been.
Somewhere out there, then, quickly, by the gods,
cover me up, or murder me, or throw me
1420   to the ocean where you will never see me more!

(Oedipus moves toward the Chorus and they back away from him.)

Come! Don't shrink to touch this wretched man!
Believe me, do not be frightened! I alone
of all mankind can carry these afflictions.

(Enter Creon from the palace with Attendants.)

CHORAGOS: Tell Creon what you wish for. Just when we need him
1425   he's here. He can act, he can advise you.
He's now the land's sole guardian in your place.

---

[69] *I . . . son:* Oedipus refers to his own curse against the murderer as well as his sins of patricide and incest.   [70] *Cithaeron:* the mountain on which the infant Oedipus was supposed to be exposed.   [71] *my blood:* that is, the blood of my father, Laius.

OEDIPUS: Ah! Are there words that I can speak to him?
What ground for trust can I present? It's proved
that I was false to him in everything.

1430 **CREON:** I have not come to mock you, Oedipus,
nor to reproach you for your former falseness.
You men, if you have no respect for sons
of mortals, let your awe for the all-feeding
flames of lordy Hēlius[72] prevent

1435 your showing unconcealed so great a stain,
abhorred by earth and sacred rain and light.
Escort him quickly back into the house!
If blood kin only see and hear their own
afflictions, we'll have no impious defilement.

1440 **OEDIPUS:** By the gods, you've freed me from one terrible fear,
so nobly meeting my unworthiness:
grant me something—not for me; for you!

CREON: What do you want that you should beg me so?

OEDIPUS: To drive me from the land at once, to a place

1445 where there will be no man to speak to me!

CREON: I would have done just that—had I not wished
to ask first of the god what I should do.

OEDIPUS: His answer was revealed in full—that I,
the patricide, unholy, be destroyed.

1450 **CREON:** He said that, but our need is so extreme,
it's best to have sure knowledge what must be done.

OEDIPUS: You'll ask about a wretched man like me?

CREON: Is it not time you put your trust in the god?

OEDIPUS: But I bid you as well, and shall entreat you.

1455 Give her who is within what burial
you will—you'll give your own her proper rites;
but me—do not condemn my fathers' land
to have me dwelling here while I'm alive,
but let me live on mountains—on Cithaeron

1460 famed as mine, for my mother and my father,
while they yet lived, made it my destined tomb,
and I'll be killed by those who wished my ruin!
And yet I know: no sickness will destroy me,
nothing will: I'd never have been saved

1465 when left to die unless for some dread evil.
Then let my fate continue where it will!
As for my children, Creon, take no pains
for my sons—they're men and they will never lack
the means to live, wherever they may be—

---

[72] *Hēlius:* the sun.

1470 but my two wretched, pitiable girls,
who never ate but at my table, never
were without me—everything that I
would touch, they'd always have a share of it—
please care for them! Above all, let me touch

1475 them with my hands and weep aloud my woes!
Please, my Lord!
Please, noble heart! Touching with my hands,
I'd think I held them as when I could see.

(Enter Antigone and Ismene from the palace with Attendants.)

What's this?

1480 Oh gods! Do I hear, somewhere, my two dear ones
sobbing? Has Creon really pitied me
and sent to me my dearest ones, my children?
Is that it?

CREON: Yes, I prepared this for you, for I knew

1485 you'd feel this joy, as you have always done.

OEDIPUS: Good fortune, then, and, for your care, be guarded
far better by divinity than I was!
Where are you, children? Come to me! Come here
to these my hands, hands of your brother, hands

1490 of him who gave you seed, hands that made
these once bright eyes to see now in this fashion.

(Oedipus embraces his daughters.)

He, children, seeing nothing, knowing nothing,
he fathered you where his own seed was plowed.
I weep for you as well, though I can't see you,

1495 imagining your bitter life to come,
the life you will be forced by men to live.
What gatherings of townsmen will you join,
what festivals, without returning home
in tears instead of watching holy rites?

1500 And when you've reached the time for marrying,
where, children, is the man who'll run the risk
of taking on himself the infamy
that will wound you as it did my parents?
What evil is not here? Your father killed

1505 his father, plowed the one who gave him birth,
and from the place where he was sown, from there
he got you, from the place he too was born.
These are the wounds: then who will marry you?
No man, my children. No, it's clear that you

1510 must wither in dry barrenness, unmarried.

(Oedipus addresses Creon.)

Son of Menoeceus! You are the only father
left to them—we two who gave them seed
are both destroyed: watch that they don't become
poor, wanderers, unmarried—they are your kin.
1515   Let not my ruin be their ruin, too!
No, pity them! You see how young they are,
bereft of everyone, except for you.
Consent, kind heart, and touch me with your hand!

(Creon grasps Oedipus's right hand.)

You, children, if you had reached an age of sense,
1520   I would have counseled much. Now, pray you may live
always where it's allowed, finding a life
better than his was, who gave you seed.
CREON: Stop this now. Quiet your weeping. Move away, into the
house.
OEDIPUS: Bitter words, but I obey them.
CREON: There's an end to all things.
1525 **OEDIPUS:**   I have first this request.
CREON: Tell me. I shall judge when
I will hear it.
OEDIPUS: Banish me from my homeland.
CREON: You must ask that of the god.
OEDIPUS: But I am the gods' most hated man!
CREON: Then you will soon get
what you want.
OEDIPUS: Do you consent?
CREON: I never promise when, as now, I'm ignorant.
1530 **OEDIPUS:**   Then lead me in.
CREON: Come. But let your hold fall from your
children.
OEDIPUS: Do not take them from me, ever!
CREON: Do not wish to keep all of
the power.
You had power, but that power did not follow you through life.

*(Oedipus's daughters are taken from him and led into the palace by Attendants.
Oedipus is led into the palace by a Servant. Creon and the other Attendants follow. Only the Chorus remains.)*

CHORUS: People of Thebes, my country, see: here is that Oedipus—
he who "knew" the famous riddle, and attained the highest power,
1535   whom all citizens admired, even envying his luck!
See the billows of wild troubles which he has entered now!

Here is the truth of each man's life: we must wait, and see his end,
scrutinize his dying day, and refuse to call him happy
till he has crossed the border of his life without pain.

(Exit the Chorus along each of the parados.)

READING AND REACTING

1. The ancient Greeks used no scenery in their theatrical productions. In the absence of scenery, how is the setting established at the beginning of *Oedipus the King?*

2. In order not to detract from the language of *Oedipus the King,* some contemporary productions use very simple costumes. Do you agree with this decision? If so, why? If not, what kind of costumes would you use?

3. In some recent productions of *Oedipus the King,* actors wear copies of ancient Greek masks. What are the advantages and disadvantages of using such masks in a contemporary production of the play?

4. In the ancient Greek theater the *strophe* and *antistrophe* were sung or chanted by the chorus as it danced back and forth across the stage. If you were staging the play today, would you place the chorus between the audience and the actors as the ancient Greeks did? How do you think modern audiences would react to the presence of the chorus?

5. Why does Sophocles have Oedipus blind himself offstage? What would be the effect of having Oedipus perform this act in full view of the audience?

6. In what ways does Sophocles observe the unities of time, place, and action described on pages 1138–39? How does Sophocles manage to present information about what happened years before the action of the play while still maintaining the three unities?

7. The ancient Greek audience that viewed *Oedipus the King* was familiar with the plot of the play. Given this situation, how does Sophocles create suspense? What are the advantages and disadvantages of using a story that the audience already knows?

8. At the end of the play, what has Oedipus learned about himself? About the gods? About the quest for truth? Is he a tragic or a pathetic figure? (See page 1138 for a discussion of these terms.)

9. Today, some directors employ *color-blind casting*—that is, they cast an actor in a role without regard to his or her race. Do you think this practice could be used in casting *Oedipus the King?* How, for example, would you react to an African-American cast as Oedipus or an Asian-American cast as Creon?

10. **JOURNAL ENTRY** Do you think Oedipus deserves his fate? Why or why not?

11. **CRITICAL PERSPECTIVE**   In "On Misunderstanding the *Oedipus Rex,*" F. R. Dodds argues that Sophocles did not intend that Oedipus's tragedy be seen as rising from a "grave moral flaw." Neither, says Dodds, was Oedipus a "mere puppet" of the gods. Rather, "what fascinates us is the spectacle of a man freely choosing, from the highest motives, a series of actions which lead to his own ruin":

> *Oedipus is great, not in virtue of a great worldly position—for his worldly position is an illusion which will vanish like a dream—but in virtue of his inner strength: strength to pursue the truth at whatever personal cost, and strength to accept and endure it when found. . . . Oedipus is great because he accepts the responsibility for all his acts, including those which are objectively most horrible, though subjectively innocent.*

Do you find Dodd's arguments persuasive? Or do you see Oedipus more as morally flawed or a victim of the gods?

WILLIAM SHAKESPEARE   (1564–1616) (picture and biography on p. 1355)

Much Ado about Nothing, which was probably written in 1598, begins with the return of Don Pedro, Prince of Aragon, to Messina after "the wars." The complex plot consists of three parallel stories: the romance of Don Pedro's daughter Hero and the young lord Claudio, which ends in apparent disaster; the trap set to make the young lord Benedick and Don Pedro's niece Beatrice fall in love; and Don John's scheme to keep Hero and Claudio apart, which is foiled by Dogberry and his Watch. Much of the success of this play on the stage depends on the actor in the role of Don John. The role contains relatively few words, but when well-acted, Don John is a conspicuous and sinister presence. However, clever word-play and surprising plot twists prevent the play from being taken too seriously. As its title indicates, *Much Ado about Nothing* is intended as varied and agreeable comic entertainment.

WILLIAM SHAKESPEARE

Much Ado about Nothing

DRAMATIS PERSONAE

DON PEDRO, *Prince of Aragon*
DON JOHN, *his bastard brother*
CLAUDIO, *a young lord of Florence*
BENEDICK, *a young lord of Padua*
LEONATO, *Governor of Messina*
ANTONIO, *his brother*
BALTHASAR, *attendant on Don Pedro*

CONRADE ⎱ *followers of Don John*
BORACHIO ⎰
FRIAR FRANCIS
DOGBERRY, *a constable*
VERGES, *a headborough*
A SEXTON
A BOY

HERO, *daughter to Leonato*
BEATRICE, *niece to Leonato*
MARGARET ⎤ *gentlewomen attending*
URSULA   ⎦ *on Hero*

MESSENGERS, WATCH,
ATTENDANTS, ETC.

SCENE—*Messina.*

ACT I

SCENE I. BEFORE LEONATO'S HOUSE.

(Enter Leonato, Hero, and Beatrice, with a Messenger.)

LEONATO: I learn in this letter that Don Pedro of Aragon comes this
night to Messina.

MESSENGER: He is very near by this. He was not three leagues off when
I left him.

5 **LEONATO:** How many gentlemen have you lost in this action?

MESSENGER: But few of any sort, and none of name.

LEONATO: A victory is twice itself when the achiever brings home full
numbers. I find here that Don Pedro hath bestowed much honor on a
young Florentine called Claudio.

10 **MESSENGER:** Much deserved on his part, and equally remembered by
Don Pedro. He hath borne himself beyond the promise of his age,
doing in the figure of a lamb the feats of a lion. He hath indeed better
bettered expectation than you must expect of me to tell you how.

LEONATO: He hath an uncle here in Messina will be very much glad of it.

15 **MESSENGER:** I have already delivered him letters, and there appears
much joy in him, even so much that joy could not show itself modest
enough without a badge of bitterness.

LEONATO: Did he break out into tears?

MESSENGER: In great measure.

20 **LEONATO:** A kind[1] overflow of kindness.[2] There are no faces truer than
those that are so washed. How much better is it to weep at joy than to
joy at weeping!

BEATRICE: I pray you, is Signior Mountanto returned from the wars,
or no?

25 **MESSENGER:** I know none of that name, lady. There was none such in
the army of any sort.

LEONATO: What is he that you ask for, Niece?

HERO: My cousin means Signior Benedick of Padua.

MESSENGER: Oh, he's returned, and as pleasant as ever he was.

30 **BEATRICE:** He set up his bills here in Messina and challenged Cupid at
the flight; and my uncle's fool, reading the challenge, subscribed for

---

[1] Natural.   [2] Affection.

Cupid and challenged him at the bird bolt. I pray you, how many
hath he killed and eaten in these wars? But how many hath he killed?
For indeed I promised to eat all of his killing.

35 **LEONATO:**   Faith, Niece, you tax[3] Signior Benedick too much. But he'll be
meet with you, I doubt it not.

MESSENGER: He hath done good service, lady, in these wars.

BEATRICE: You had musty victual, and he hath holp to eat it. He is a
very valiant trencherman,[4] he hath an excellent stomach.

40 **MESSENGER:**   And a good soldier too, lady.

BEATRICE: And a good soldier to a lady, but what is he to a lord?

MESSENGER: A lord to a lord, a man to a man, stuffed with all
honorable virtues.

BEATRICE: It is so indeed, he is no less than a stuffed man. But for the
45 stuffing—well, we are all mortal.

LEONATO: You must not, sir, mistake my niece. There is a kind of merry
war betwixt Signior Benedick and her. They never meet but there's a
skirmish of wit between them.

BEATRICE: Alas! he gets nothing by that. In our last conflict four of his
50 five wits[5] went halting off, and now is the whole man governed with
one. So that if he have wit enough to keep himself warm, let him
bear it for a difference between himself and his horse; for it is all the
wealth that he hath left, to be known a reasonable creature. Who is
his companion now? He hath every month a new sworn brother.

55 **MESSENGER:**   Is 't possible?

BEATRICE: Very easily possible. He wears his faith but as the fashion of
his hat, it ever changes with the next block.[6]

MESSENGER: I see, lady, the gentleman is not in your books.

BEATRICE: No, an he were, I would burn my study. But I pray you who
60 is his companion? Is there no young squarer now that will make a
voyage with him to the Devil?

MESSENGER: He is most in the company of the right noble Claudio.

BEATRICE: Oh Lord, he will hang upon him like a disease. He is sooner
caught than the pestilence, and the taker runs presently mad. God
65 help the noble Claudio! If he have caught the Benedick, it will cost
him a thousand pound ere a' be cured.

MESSENGER: I will hold friends with you, lady.

BEATRICE: Do, good friend.

LEONATO: You will never run mad, Niece.

70 **BEATRICE:**   No, not till a hot January.

MESSENGER: Don Pedro is approached.

(Enter Don Pedro, Don John, Claudio, Benedick, and Balthasar.)

---

[3] Satire.   [4] Eater.   [5] Common wit, fantasy, imagination, estimation, memory.
[6] Wooden mold for shaping felt hats.

DON PEDRO: Good Signior Leonato, you are come to meet your trouble. The fashion of the world is to avoid cost, and you encounter it.

LEONATO: Never came trouble to my house in the likeness of your
75 Grace; for trouble being gone, comfort should remain, but when you depart from me, sorrow abides and happiness takes his leave.

DON PEDRO: You embrace your charge too willingly. I think this is your daughter.

LEONATO: Her mother hath many times told me so.

80 **BENEDICK:** Were you in doubt, sir, that you asked her?

LEONATO: Signior Benedick, no, for then were you a child.

DON PEDRO: You have it full, Benedick. We may guess by this what you are, being a man. Truly, the lady fathers herself.[7] Be happy, lady, for you are like an honorable father.

85 **BENEDICK:** If Signior Leonato be her father, she would not have his head on her shoulders for all Messina, as like him as she is.

BEATRICE: I wonder that you will still be talking, Signior Benedick. Nobody marks you.

BENEDICK: What, my dear Lady Disdain! Are you yet living?

90 **BEATRICE:** Is it possible Disdain should die while she hath such meet food to feed it as Signior Benedick? Courtesy itself must convert to disdain if you come in her presence.

BENEDICK: Then is courtesy a turncoat. But it is certain I am loved of all ladies, only you excepted. And I would I could find in my heart that I
95 had not a hard heart, for truly I love none.

BEATRICE: A dear happiness to women. They would else have been troubled with a pernicious suitor. I thank God and my cold blood I am of your humor for that. I had rather hear my dog bark at a crow than a man swear he loves me.

100 **BENEDICK:** God keep your ladyship still in that mind! So some gentleman or other shall 'scape a predestinate scratched face.

BEATRICE: Scratching could not make it worse an 'twere such a face as yours were.

BENEDICK: Well, you are a rare parrot-teacher.

105 **BEATRICE:** A bird of my tongue is better than a beast of yours.

BENEDICK: I would my horse had the speed of your tongue, and so good a continuer. But keep your way, i' God's name. I have done.

BEATRICE: You always end with a jade's trick. I know you of old.

DON PEDRO: That is the sum of all, Leonato. Signior Claudio and
110 Signior Benedick, my dear friend Leonato hath invited you all. I tell him we shall stay here at the least a month, and he heartily prays some occasion may detain us longer. I dare swear he is no hypocrite, but prays from his heart.

---

[7] Resembles her father.

LEONATO: If you swear, my lord, you shall not be forsworn. *(To Don*
115   *John)* Let me bid you welcome, my lord. Being reconciled the Prince
your brother, I owe you all duty.
DON JOHN: I thank you. I am not of many words, but I thank you.
LEONATO: Please it your Grace lead on?
DON PEDRO: Your hand, Leonato. We will go together. *(Exeunt all except*
120   *Benedick and Claudio.)*
CLAUDIO: Benedick, didst thou note the daughter of Signior Leonato?
BENEDICK: I noted her not, but I looked on her.
CLAUDIO: Is she not a modest young lady?
BENEDICK: Do you question me, as an honest man should do, for my
125   simple true judgment? Or would you have me speak after my custom,
as being a professed tyrant to their sex?
CLAUDIO: No, I pray thee speak in sober judgment.
BENEDICK: Why, i' faith, methinks she's too low for a high praise, too
brown for a fair praise, and too little for a great praise. Only this
130   commendation I can afford her, that were she other than she is, she
were unhandsome; and being no other but as she is, I do not like her.
CLAUDIO: Thou thinkest I am in sport. I pray thee tell me truly how
thou likest her.
BENEDICK: Would you buy her, that you inquire after her?
135 **CLAUDIO:**   Can the world buy such a jewel?
BENEDICK: Yea, and a case to put it into. But speak you this with a sad
brow? Or do you play the flouting Jack,[8] to tell us Cupid is a good
hare-finder and Vulcan[9] a rare carpenter? Come, in what key shall a
man take you, to go in the song?
140 **CLAUDIO:**   In mine eye she is the sweetest lady that ever I looked on.
BENEDICK: I can see yet without spectacles, and I see no such matter.
There's her cousin, an she were not possessed with a fury, exceeds her
as much in beauty as the first of May doth the last of December. But I
hope you have no intent to turn husband, have you?
145 **CLAUDIO:**   I would scarce trust myself, though I had sworn the contrary,
if Hero would be my wife.
BENEDICK: Is 't come to this? In faith, hath not the world one man
but he will wear his cap with suspicion? Shall I never see a bachelor
of threescore again? Go to, i' faith. An thou wilt needs thrust thy
150   neck into a yoke, wear the print of it, and sigh away Sundays. Look,
Don Pedro is returned to seek you.

(Re-enter Don Pedro.)

DON PEDRO: What secret hath held you here, that you followed not to
Leonato's?

---

[8] Roman god of fire and metal work.   [9] Reckless, nieve trickster of a servant.

BENEDICK: I would your Grace would constrain me to tell.

155 **DON PEDRO:** I charge thee on thy allegiance.

BENEDICK: You hear, Count Claudio. I can be secret as a dumb man, I would have you think so, but, on my allegiance, mark you this, on my allegiance. He is in love. With who? Now that is your Grace's part. Mark how short his answer is—with Hero, Leonato's short daughter.

160 **CLAUDIO:** If this were so, so were it uttered.

BENEDICK: Like the old tale, my lord: "It is not so, nor 'twas not so, but, indeed, God forbid it should be so."

CLAUDIO: If my passion change not shortly, God forbid it should be otherwise.

165 **DON PEDRO:** Amen, if you love her, for the lady is very well worthy.

CLAUDIO: You speak this to fetch me in, my lord.

DON PEDRO: By my troth, I speak my thought.

CLAUDIO: And in faith, my lord, I spoke mine.

BENEDICK: And by my two faiths and troths, my lord, I spoke mine.

170 **CLAUDIO:** That I love her, I feel.

DON PEDRO: That she is worthy, I know.

BENEDICK: That I neither feel how she should be loved, nor know how she should be worthy, is the opinion that fire cannot melt out of me. I will die in it at the stake.

175 **DON PEDRO:** Thou wast ever an obstinate heretic in the despite of beauty.

CLAUDIO: And never could maintain his part but in the force of his will.

BENEDICK: That a woman conceived me, I thank her; that she brought me up, I likewise give her most humble thanks. But that I will have a recheat winded[10] in my forehead, or hang my bugle in an invisible baldric,[11] all women shall pardon me. Because I will not do them the wrong to mistrust any, I will do myself the right to trust none, and the fine is, for the which I may go the finer, I will live a bachelor.

DON PEDRO: I shall see thee, ere I die, look pale with love.

185 **BENEDICK:** With anger, with sickness, or with hunger, my lord, not with love. Prove that ever I lose more blood with love than I will get again with drinking, pick out mine eyes with a ballad-maker's pen, and hang me up at the door of a brothel house for the sign of blind Cupid.

190 **DON PEDRO:** Well, if ever thou dost fall from this faith, thou wilt prove a notable argument.

BENEDICK: If I do, hang me in a bottle like a cat and shoot at me, and he that hits me, let him be clapped on the shoulder and called Adam.

DON PEDRO: Well, as time shall try.

195 "In time the savage bull doth bear the yoke."

---

[10] Sounding of a hunter's horn.   [11] Sash or belt, worn across the chest, to hold a hunter's horn.

BENEDICK: The savage bull may, but if ever the sensible Benedick bear
it, pluck off the bull's horns and set them in my forehead. And let me
be vilely painted, and in such great letters as they write "Here is good
horse to hire" let them signify under my sign "Here you may see
200   Benedick the married man."

CLAUDIO: If this should ever happen, thou wouldst be horn-mad.

DON PEDRO: Nay, if Cupid have not spent all his quiver in Venice, thou
wilt quake for this shortly.

BENEDICK: I look for an earthquake too, then.

205 **DON PEDRO:**   Well, you will temporize with the hours. In the meantime,
good Signior Benedick, repair to Leonato's. Commend me to him, and
tell him I will not fail him at supper, for indeed he hath made great
preparation.

BENEDICK: I have almost matter enough in me for such an embassage,
210   and so I commit you—

CLAUDIO: To the tuition of God. From my house, if I had it—

DON PEDRO: The sixth of July. Your loving friend, Benedick.

BENEDICK: Nay, mock not, mock not. The body of your discourse is
sometime guarded with fragments, and the guards are but slightly
215   basted on neither. Ere you flout old ends any further, examine your
conscience. And so I leave you.

(Exit.)

CLAUDIO: My liege, your Highness now may do me good.

DON PEDRO: My love is thine to teach. Teach it but how
And thou shalt see how apt it is to learn
220   Any hard lesson that may do thee good.

CLAUDIO: Hath Leonato any son, my lord?

DON PEDRO: No child but Hero, she's his only heir. Dost thou affect
her, Claudio?

CLAUDIO: Oh, my lord,
When you went onward on this ended action,
225   I looked upon her with a soldier's eye,
That liked but had a rougher task in hand
Than to drive liking to the name of love.
But now I am returned and that war thoughts
Have left their places vacant, in their rooms
230   Come thronging soft and delicate desires,
All prompting me how fair young Hero is,
Saying I liked her ere I went to wars.

DON PEDRO: Thou wilt be like a lover presently,
And tire the hearer with a book of words.
235   If thou dost love fair Hero, cherish it,
And I will break with her and with her father,
And thou shalt have her. Was 't not to this end
That thou began'st to twist so fine a story?

CLAUDIO: How sweetly you do minister to love,
240   That know love's grief by his complexion!
     But lest my liking might too sudden seem,
     I would have salved it with a longer treatise.
DON PEDRO: What need the bridge much broader than the flood?
     The fairest grant is the necessity.
245   Look, what will serve is fit. 'Tis once thou lovest,
     And I will fit thee with the remedy.
     I know we shall have reveling tonight.
     I will assume thy part in some disguise,
     And tell fair Hero I am Claudio;
250   And in her bosom I'll unclasp my heart,
     And take her hearing prisoner with the force
     And strong encounter of my amorous tale.
     Then after to her father will I break,
     And the conclusion is, she shall be thine.
255   In practice let us put it presently. *(Exeunt.)*

SCENE II. A ROOM IN LEONATO'S HOUSE.

(Enter Leonato and Antonio, meeting.)

LEONATO: How now, Brother! Where is my cousin, your son? Hath he provided this music?
ANTONIO: He is very busy about it. But, Brother, I can tell you strange news, that you yet dreamed not of.
5 **LEONATO:** Are they good?
ANTONIO: As the event stamps them. But they have a good cover, they show well outward. The Prince and Count Claudio, walking in a thick-pleached alley in mine orchard, were thus much overheard by a man of mine. The Prince discovered to Claudio that he loved my
10 niece your daughter, and meant to acknowledge it this night in a dance; and if he found her accordant, he meant to take the present time by the top, and instantly break with you of it.
LEONATO: Hath the fellow any wit that told you this?
ANTONIO: A good sharp fellow. I will send for him, and question him
15 yourself.
LEONATO: No, no, we will hold it as a dream till it appear itself. But I will acquaint my daughter withal, that she may be the better prepared for an answer if peradventure this be true. Go you and tell her of it. *(Enter Attendants.)* Cousins, you know what you have to do.
20 Oh, I cry you mercy, friend—go you with me, and I will use your skill. Good Cousin, have a care this busy time.

(Exeunt.)

SCENE III. THE SAME.
....

(Enter Don John and Conrade.)

CONRADE: What the goodyear, my lord! Why are you thus out of
measure sad?

DON JOHN: There is no measure in the occasion that breeds, therefore
the sadness is without limit.

5 **CONRADE:**   You should hear reason.

DON JOHN: And when I have heard it, what blessing brings it?

CONRADE: If not a present remedy, at least a patient sufferance.

DON JOHN: I wonder that thou, being (as thou sayest thou art) born
under Saturn,[12] goest about to apply a moral medicine to a mortifying
10 mischief. I cannot hide what I am. I must be sad when I have cause,
and smile at no man's jests; eat when I have stomach, and wait for no
man's leisure; sleep when I am drowsy, and tend on no man's
business; laugh when I am merry, and claw[13] no man in his humor.

CONRADE: Yea, but you must not make the full show of this till you may
15 do it without controlment. You have of late stood out against your
brother, and he hath ta'en you newly into his grace, where it is
impossible you should take true root but by the fair weather that you
make yourself. It is needful that you frame the season for your own
harvest.

20 **DON JOHN:**   I had rather be a canker[14] in a hedge than a rose in his grace,
and it better fits my blood to be disdained of all than to fashion a
carriage to rob love from any. In this, though I cannot be said to be a
flattering honest man, it must not be denied but I am a plain-dealing
villain. I am trusted with a muzzle, and enfranchised with a clog;
25 therefore I have decreed not to sing in my cage. If I had my mouth, I
would bite; if I had my liberty, I would do my liking. In the meantime
let me be that I am, and seek not to alter me.

CONRADE: Can you make no use of your discontent?

DON JOHN: I make all use of it, for I use it only. Who comes here? *(Enter*
30 *Borachio.)* What news, Borachio?

BORACHIO: I came yonder from a great supper. The Prince your brother
is royally entertained by Leonato, and I can give you intelligence of
an intended marriage.

DON JOHN: Will it serve for any model to build mischief on? What is he
35 for a fool that betroths himself to unquietness?

BORACHIO: Marry, it is your brother's right hand.

DON JOHN: Who? The most exquisite Claudio?

BORACHIO: Even he.

DON JOHN: A proper squire! And who, and who? Which way looks he?

---

[12] Believed to indicate a grim temperment.   [13] Flatter.   [14] Wild rose.

40 **BORACHIO:**   Marry, on Hero, the daughter and heir of Leonato.

DON JOHN: A very forward March chick! How came you to this?

BORACHIO: Being entertained for a perfumer, as I was smoking a musty
room comes me the Prince and Claudio, hand in hand, in sad
conference. I whipped me behind the arras,[15] and there heard it
45   agreed upon that the Prince should woo Hero for himself, and having
obtained her, give her to Count Claudio.

DON JOHN: Come, come, let us thither. This may prove food to my
displeasure. That young start-up hath all the glory of my overthrow.
If I can cross him any way, I bless myself every way. You are both
50   sure, and will assist me?

CONRADE: To the death, my lord.

DON JOHN: Let us to the great supper. Their cheer is the greater that I
am subdued. Would the cook were of my mind! Shall we go prove
what's to be done?

55 **BORACHIO:**   We'll wait upon your lordship.

(Exeunt.)

ACT II

SCENE I. A HALL IN LEONATO'S HOUSE.

(Enter Leonato, Antonio, Hero, Beatrice, and others.)

LEONATO: Was not Count John here at supper?

ANTONIO: I saw him not.

BEATRICE: How tartly that gentleman looks! I never can see him but I
am heartburned an hour after.

5 **HERO:**   He is of a very melancholy disposition.

BEATRICE: He were an excellent man that were made just in the midway
between him and Benedick. The one is too like an image and says
nothing, and the other too like my lady's eldest son, evermore tattling.

LEONATO: Then half Signior Benedick's tongue in Count John's mouth,
10   and half Count John's melancholy in Signior Benedick's face—

BEATRICE: With a good leg and a good foot, Uncle, and money enough
in his purse, such a man would win any woman in the world, if a'
could get her goodwill.

LEONATO: By my troth, Niece, thou wilt never get thee a husband if
15   thou be so shrewd of thy tongue.

ANTONIO: In faith, she's too cursed.[16]

---

[15] Tapestries.   [16] Bitter.

BEATRICE: Too cursed is more than cursed. I shall lessen God's sending that way, for it is said "God sends a cursed cow short horns," but to a cow too cursed he sends none.

20 **LEONATO:**   So, by being too cursed, God will send you no horns.

BEATRICE: Just, if he send me no husband, for the which blessing I am at him upon my knees every morning and evening. Lord, I could not endure a husband with a beard on his face. I had rather lie in the woolen.[17]

25 **LEONATO:**   You may light on a husband that hath no beard.

BEATRICE: What should I do with him? Dress him in my apparel and make him my waiting gentlewoman? He that hath a beard is more than a youth, and he that hath no beard is less than a man. And he that is more than a youth is not for me, and he that is less than a

30 man, I am not for him. Therefore I will even take sixpence in earnest of the bearward, and lead his apes into Hell.

LEONATO: Well, then, go you into Hell?

BEATRICE: No, but to the gate, and there will the Devil meet me, like an old cuckold, with horns on his head, and say "Get you to Heaven,

35 Beatrice, get you to Heaven. Here's no place for you maids." So deliver I up my apes, and away to Saint Peter for the Heavens. He shows me where the bachelors sit, and there live we as merry as the day is long.

ANTONIO: *(To Hero)* Well, Niece, I trust you will be ruled by your father.

BEATRICE: Yes, faith, it is my cousin's duty to make curtsy and say,

40 "Father, as it please you." But yet for all that, Cousin, let him be a handsome fellow, or else make another curtsy and say, "Father, as it please me."

LEONATO: Well, Niece, I hope to see you one day fitted with a husband.

BEATRICE: Not till God make men of some other metal than earth.

45 Would it not grieve a woman to be overmastered with a piece of valiant dust? To make an account of her life to a clod of wayward marl? No, Uncle, I'll none. Adam's sons are my brethren, and truly, I hold it a sin to match in my kindred.

LEONATO: Daughter, remember what I told you. If the Prince do solicit

50 you in that kind, you know your answer.

BEATRICE: The fault will be in the music, Cousin, if you be not wooed in good time. If the Prince be too important, tell him there is measure in everything, and so dance out the answer. For, hear me, Hero. Wooing, wedding, and repenting is as a Scotch jig,[18] a

55 measure,[19] and a cinquepace.[20] The first suit is hot and hasty, like a Scotch jig, and full as fantastical; the wedding, mannerly modest, as a measure full of state and ancientry; and then comes repentance, and,

---

[17] Course blankets.   [18] Lively folk dance.   [19] Formal courtly dance.   [20] Steps of the galliard, an elaborate dance.

with his bad legs, falls into the cinquepace faster and faster till he
sink into his grave.

60 **LEONATO:**   Cousin, you apprehend passing shrewdly.

BEATRICE: I have a good eye, Uncle, I can see a church by daylight.

LEONATO: The revelers are entering, Brother. Make good room. *(All put
on their masks.)*

*(Enter Don Pedro, Claudio, Benedick, Balthasar, Don John, Borachio, Mar-
garet, Ursula, and others, masked.)*

DON PEDRO: Lady, will you walk about with your friend?

65 **HERO:**   So you walk softly, and look sweetly, and say nothing, I am
yours for the walk—and especially when I walk away.

DON PEDRO: With me in your company?

HERO: I may say so, when I please.

DON PEDRO: And when please you to say so?

70 **HERO:**   When I like your favor, for God defend the lute should be like
the case!

DON PEDRO: My visor is Philemon's roof.[21] Within the house is Jove.

HERO: Why, then, your visor should be thatched.

DON PEDRO: *(Drawing her aside)* Speak low, if you speak love.

75 **BALTHASAR:**   Well, I would you did like me.

MARGARET: So would not I, for your own sake, for I have many ill
qualities.

BALTHASAR: Which is one?

MARGARET: I say my prayers aloud.

80 **BALTHASAR:**   I love you the better. The hearers may cry "Amen."

MARGARET: God match me with a good dancer!

BALTHASAR: Amen.

MARGARET: And God keep him out of my sight when the dance is done!
Answer, clerk.

85 **BALTHASAR:**   No more words. The clerk is answered.

URSULA: I know you well enough. You are Signior Antonio.

ANTONIO: At a word, I am not.

URSULA: I know you by the waggling of your head.

ANTONIO: To tell you true, I counterfeit him.

90 **URSULA:**   You could never do him so ill-well unless you were the very
man. Here's his dry hand up and down. You are he, you are he.

ANTONIO: At a word, I am not.

URSULA: Come, come, do you think I do not know you by your
excellent wit? Can virtue hide itself? Go to, mum, you are he. Graces
95   will appear, and there's an end.

BEATRICE: Will you not tell me who told you so?

BENEDICK: No, you shall pardon me.

---

[21] Unknowingly housed the gods Jupiter and Mercury in his cottage.

BEATRICE: Nor will you not tell me who you are?

BENEDICK: Not now.

100 **BEATRICE:**   That I was disdainful, and that I had my good wit out of the
Hundred Merry Tales[22]—well, this was Signior Benedick that said so.

BENEDICK: What's he?

BEATRICE: I am sure you know him well enough.

BENEDICK: Not I, believe me.

105 **BEATRICE:**   Did he never make you laugh?

BENEDICK: I pray you, what is he?

BEATRICE: Why, he is the Prince's jester—a very dull fool, only his gift
is in devising impossible slanders. None but libertines delight in him,
and the commendation is not in his wit, but in his villainy; for he
110 both pleases men and angers them, and then they laugh at him and
beat him. I am sure he is in the fleet. I would he had boarded me.

BENEDICK: When I know the gentleman, I'll tell him what you say.

BEATRICE: Do, do. He'll but break a comparison or two on me, which,
peradventure not marked or not laughed at, strikes him into
115 melancholy—and then there's a partridge wing saved, for the fool
will eat no supper that night. *(Music)* We must follow the leaders.

BENEDICK: In every good thing.

BEATRICE: Nay, if they lead to any ill, I will leave them at the next
turning. *(Dance. Then exeunt all except Don John, Borachio, and Claudio.)*

120 **DON JOHN:**   Sure my brother is amorous on Hero, and hath withdrawn
her father to break with him about it. The ladies follow her, and but
one visor remains.

BORACHIO: And this is Claudio. I know him by his bearing.

DON JOHN: Are not you Signior Benedick?

125 **CLAUDIO:**   You know me well. I am he.

DON JOHN: Signior, you are very near my brother in his love. He is
enamored on Hero. I pray you, dissuade him from her. She is no equal
for his birth. You may do the part of an honest man in it.

CLAUDIO: How know you he loves her?

130 **DON JOHN:**   I heard him swear his affection.

BORACHIO: So did I too, and he swore he would marry her tonight.

DON JOHN: Come, let us to the banquet.

(Exeunt Don John and Borachio.)

CLAUDIO: Thus answer I in name of Benedick,
But hear these ill news with the ears of Claudio.
135 'Tis certain so. The Prince woos for himself.
Friendship is constant in all other things
Save in the office and affairs of love;
Therefore all hearts in love use their own tongues,

---

[22] Book of jokes (1526).

> Let every eye negotiate for itself,
> 140 And trust no agent, for beauty is a witch
> Against whose charms faith melteth into blood.[23]
> This is an accident of hourly proof,
> Which I mistrusted not. Farewell, therefore, Hero!

(Re-enter Benedick.)

BENEDICK: Count Claudio?

145 **CLAUDIO:** Yea, the same.

BENEDICK: Come, will you go with me?

CLAUDIO: Whither?

BENEDICK: Even to the next willow, about your own business, County. What fashion will you wear the garland of? About your neck, like a 150 usurer's chain? Or under your arm, like a lieutenant's scarf? You must wear it one way, for the Prince hath got your Hero.

CLAUDIO: I wish him joy of her.

BENEDICK: Why, that's spoken like an honest drovier.[24] So they sell bullocks. But did you think the Prince would have served you thus?

155 **CLAUDIO:** I pray you, leave me.

BENEDICK: Ho! Now you strike like the blind man. 'Twas the boy that stole your meat, and you'll beat the post.

CLAUDIO: If it will not be, I'll leave you.

(Exit.)

BENEDICK: Alas, poor hurt fowl! Now will he creep into sedges. But that 160 my Lady Beatrice should know me and not know me! The Prince's fool! Ha? It may be I go under that title because I am merry. Yea, but so I am apt to do myself wrong, I am not so reputed. It is the base, though bitter, disposition of Beatrice that puts the world into her person, and so gives me out. Well, I'll be revenged as I may.

(Re-enter Don Pedro.)

165 **DON PEDRO:** Now, signior, where's the Count? Did you see him?

BENEDICK: Troth, my lord, I have played the part of Lady Fame. I found him here as melancholy as a lodge in a warren.[25] I told him, and I think I told him true, that your Grace had got the goodwill of this young lady. And I offered him my company to a willow tree, either to 170 make him a garland, as being forsaken, or to bind him up a rod, as being worthy to be whipped.

DON PEDRO: To be whipped! What's his fault?

BENEDICK: The flat transgression of a schoolboy who, being overjoyed with finding a bird's nest, shows it his companion, and he steals it.

---

[23] Passion.　　[24] Cattle-driver.　　[25] Gamekeeper's hut.

175 **DON PEDRO:**   Wilt thou make a trust a transgression? The transgression
is in the stealer.

BENEDICK: Yet it had not been amiss the rod had been made, and the
garland too; for the garland he might have worn himself, and the rod
he might have bestowed on you, who, as I take it, have stolen his
180 birds' nest.

DON PEDRO: I will but teach them to sing and restore them to the owner.

BENEDICK: If their singing answer your saying, by my faith, you say
honestly.

DON PEDRO: The Lady Beatrice hath a quarrel to you. The gentleman
185 that danced with her told her she is much wronged by you.

BENEDICK: Oh, she misused me past the endurance of a block! An oak
but with one green leaf on it would have answered her. My very visor
began to assume life and scold with her. She told me, not thinking I
had been myself, that I was the Prince's jester, that I was duller than a
190 great thaw, huddling jest upon jest with such impossible conveyance
upon me that I stood like a man at a mark, with a whole army
shooting at me. She speaks poniards,[26] and every word stabs. If her
breath were as terrible as her terminations, there were no living
near her. She would infect to the North Star. I would not marry her
195 though she were endowed with all that Adam had left him before he
transgressed. She would have made Hercules have turned spit, yea, and
have cleft his club to make the fire, too. Come, talk not of her. You
shall find her the infernal Ate[27] in good apparel. I would to God some
scholar would conjure her; for certainly while she is here a man may
200 live as quiet in Hell as in a sanctuary, and people sin upon purpose
because they would go thither. So, indeed, all disquiet, horror, and
perturbation follows her.

DON PEDRO: Look, here she comes.

(Re-enter Claudio, Beatrice, Hero, and Leonato.)

BENEDICK: Will your Grace command me any service to the world's
205 end? I will go on the slightest errand now to the Antipodes[28] that you
can devise to send me on. I will fetch you a toothpicker now from the
furthest inch of Asia, bring you the length of Prester John's[29] foot,
fetch you a hair off the great Cham's[30] beard, do you any embassage
to the Pigmies, rather than hold three words' conference with this
210 harpy. You have no employment for me?

DON PEDRO: None but to desire your good company.

BENEDICK: Oh, God, sir, here's a dish I love not. I cannot endure my
Lady Tongue.

(Exit.)

---

[26] Daggers.   [27] Goddess of strife.   [28] The other side of the earth.   [29] Fabled
King of Abssinia.   [30] The Mongol Emperor.

Don Pedro: Come, lady, come, you have lost the heart of Signior
215   Benedick.
Beatrice: Indeed, my lord, he lent it me awhile, and I gave him use for
it, a double heart for his single one. Marry, once before he won it of
me with false dice, therefore your Grace may well say I have lost it.
Don Pedro: You have put him down, lady, you have put him down.
220 **Beatrice:**   So I would not he should do me, my lord, lest I should prove
the mother of fools. I have brought Count Claudio, whom you sent
me to seek.
Don Pedro: Why, how now, Count! Wherefore are you sad?
Claudio: Not sad, my lord.
225 **Don Pedro:**   How then? Sick?
Claudio: Neither, my lord.
Beatrice: The Count is neither sad, nor sick, nor merry, nor well, but
civil Count, civil as an orange,[31] and something of that jealous
complexion.
230 **Don Pedro:**   I' faith, lady, I think your blazon to be true, though I'll be
sworn, if he be so, his conceit[32] is false. Here, Claudio, I have wooed
in thy name, and fair Hero is won. I have broke with her father, and his
goodwill obtained. Name the day of marriage, and God give thee joy!
Leonato: Count, take of me my daughter, and with her my fortunes.
235   His Grace hath made the match, and all grace say "Amen" to it.
Beatrice: Speak, Count, 'tis your cue.
Claudio: Silence is the perfectest herald of joy. I were but little happy
if I could say how much. Lady, as you are mine, I am yours. I give
away myself for you, and dote upon the exchange.
240 **Beatrice:**   Speak, Cousin, or if you cannot, stop his mouth with a kiss,
and let not him speak neither.
Don Pedro: In faith, lady, you have a merry heart.
Beatrice: Yea, my lord, I thank it, poor fool—it keeps on the windy
side of care. My cousin tells him in his ear that he is in her heart.
245 **Claudio:**   And so she doth, Cousin.
Beatrice: Good Lord, for alliance! Thus goes everyone to the world but
I, and I am sunburned, I may sit in a corner and cry heigh-ho for a
husband!
Don Pedro: Lady Beatrice, I will get you one.
250 **Beatrice:**   I would rather have one of your father's getting. Hath your
Grace ne'er a brother like you? Your father got excellent husbands, if
a maid could come by them.
Don Pedro: Will you have me, lady?
Beatrice: No, my lord, unless I might have another for working days.
255   Your Grace is too costly to wear every day. But I beseech your Grace
pardon me. I was born to speak all mirth and no matter.

---

[31] Yellow color of Seville oranges.   [32] Imagination.

DON PEDRO: Your silence most offends me, and to be merry best
becomes you, for, out of question, you were born in a merry hour.

BEATRICE: No, sure, my lord, my mother cried; but then there was a star
260   danced, and under that was I born. Cousins, God give you joy!

LEONATO: Niece, will you look to those things I told you of?

BEATRICE: I cry you mercy, Uncle. By your Grace's pardon.

(Exit.)

DON PEDRO: By my troth, a pleasant-spirited lady.

LEONATO: There's little of the melancholy element in her, my lord. She
265   is never sad but when she sleeps, and not ever sad then, for I have
heard my daughter say she hath often dreamed of unhappiness and
waked herself with laughing.

DON PEDRO: She cannot endure to hear tell of a husband.

LEONATO: Oh, by no means. She mocks all her wooers out of suit.

270 **DON PEDRO:**   She were an excellent wife for Benedick.

LEONATO: Oh Lord, my lord, if they were but a week married they
would talk themselves mad.

DON PEDRO: County Claudio, when mean you to go to church?

CLAUDIO: Tomorrow, my lord. Time goes on crutches till love have all
275   his rites.

LEONATO: Not till Monday, my dear son, which is hence a just
sevennight,[33] and a time too brief, too, to have all things answer my
mind.

DON PEDRO: Come, you shake the head at so long a breathing. But I
280   warrant thee, Claudio, the time shall not go dully by us. I will, in the
interim, undertake one of Hercules' labors, which is to bring Signior
Benedick and the Lady Beatrice into a mountain of affection the one
with the other. I would fain have it a match, and I doubt not but to
fashion it if you three will but minister such assistance as I shall give
285   you direction.

LEONATO: My lord, I am for you, though it cost me ten nights'
watchings.

CLAUDIO: And I, my lord.

DON PEDRO: And you too, gentle Hero?

290 **HERO:**   I will do any modest office, my lord, to help my cousin to a good
husband.

DON PEDRO: And Benedick is not the unhopefulest husband that I
know. Thus far can I praise him. He is of a noble strain, of approved
valor and confirmed honesty. I will teach you how to humor your
295   cousin that she shall fall in love with Benedick. And I, with your two
helps, will so practice on Benedick that, in despite of his quick wit
and his queasy stomach, he shall fall in love with Beatrice. If we can

---

[33] A week.

do this, Cupid is no longer an archer. His glory shall be ours, for we are the only love gods. Go in with me, and I will tell you my drift. *(Exeunt.)*

SCENE II. THE SAME.

(Enter Don John and Borachio.)

DON JOHN: It is so. The Count Claudio shall marry the daughter of Leonato.

BORACHIO: Yea, my lord, but I can cross it.

DON JOHN: Any bar, any cross, any impediment will be medicinable to
5   me. I am sick in displeasure to him, and whatsoever comes athwart his affection ranges evenly with mine. How canst thou cross this marriage?

BORACHIO: Not honestly, my lord, but so covertly that no dishonesty shall appear in me.

10 **DON JOHN:** Show me briefly how.

BORACHIO: I think I told your lordship, a year since, how much I am in the favor of Margaret, the waiting gentlewoman to Hero.

DON JOHN: I remember.

BORACHIO: I can, at any unseasonable instant of the night, appoint her
15   to look out at her lady's chamber window.

DON JOHN: What life is in that, to be the death of this marriage?

BORACHIO: The poison of that lies in you to temper. Go you to the Prince your brother. Spare not to tell him that he hath wronged his honor in marrying the renowned Claudio—whose estimation do you
20   mightily hold up—to a contaminated stale,[34] such a one as Hero.

DON JOHN: What proof shall I make of that?

BORACHIO: Proof enough to misuse the Prince, to vex Claudio, to undo Hero, and kill Leonato. Look you for any other issue?

DON JOHN: Only to despite them I will endeavor anything.

25 **BORACHIO:** Go, then. Find me a meet hour to draw Don Pedro and the Count Claudio alone. Tell them that you know that Hero loves me, intend a kind of zeal both to the Prince and Claudio, as—in love of your brother's honor, who hath made this match, and his friend's reputation, who is thus like to be cozened[35] with the semblance of a
30   maid—that you have discovered thus. They will scarcely believe this without trial. Offer them instances, which shall bear no less likelihood than to see me at her chamber window, hear me call Margaret Hero, hear Margaret term me Claudio, and bring them to see this the very night before the intended wedding—for in the

---

[34] Whore.   [35] Cheated.

35 meantime I will so fashion the matter that Hero shall be absent. And
there shall appear such seeming truth of Hero's disloyalty that
jealousy shall be called assurance and all the preparation overthrown.

DON JOHN: Grow this to what adverse issue it can, I will put it in
practice. Be cunning in the working this and thy fee is a thousand
40 ducats.[36]

BORACHIO: Be you constant in the accusation and my cunning shall not
shame me.

DON JOHN: I will presently go learn their day of marriage. *(Exeunt.)*

SCENE III. LEONATO'S ORCHARD.

(Enter Benedick.)

BENEDICK: Boy!

(Enter Boy.)

BOY: Signior?

BENEDICK: In my chamber window lies a book. Bring it hither to me in
the orchard.

5 **BOY:** I am here already, sir.

BENEDICK: I know that, but I would have thee hence, and here again.
(Exit Boy.) I do much wonder that one man, seeing how much another
man is a fool when he dedicates his behaviors to love, will, after he
hath laughed at such shallow follies in others, become the argument
10 of his own scorn by falling in love—and such a man is Claudio. I have
known when there was no music with him but the drum and the fife,
and now had he rather hear the tabor and the pipe. I have known
when he would have walked ten mile afoot to see a good armor, and
now will he lie ten nights awake carving the fashion of a new
15 doublet.[37] He was wont to speak plain and to the purpose, like an
honest man and a soldier, and now is he turned orthography, his
words are a very fantastical banquet—just so many strange dishes.
May I be so converted, and see with these eyes? I cannot tell, I think
not. I will not be sworn but love may transform me to an oyster, but
20 I'll take my oath on it till he have made an oyster of me he shall
never make me such a fool. One woman is fair, yet I am well; another
is wise, yet I am well; another virtuous, yet I am well. But till all
graces be in one woman, one woman shall not come in my grace.
Rich she shall be, that's certain; wise, or I'll none; virtuous, or I'll
25 never cheapen her; fair, or I'll never look on her; mild, or come not
near me; noble, or not I for an angel; of good discourse, an excellent

---

36 Italian coins worth about $2.25 each.   37 Elaborately cut and embroidered jacket.

musician; and her hair shall be of what color it please God. Ha! The Prince and Monsieur Love! I will hide me in the arbor. *(Withdraws.)*

(Enter Don Pedro, Claudio, Leonato, and Balthasar.)

DON PEDRO: Come, shall we hear this music?
30 **CLAUDIO:** Yea, my good lord. How still the evening is,
    As hushed on purpose to grace harmony!
DON PEDRO: See you where Benedick hath hid himself?
CLAUDIO: Oh, very well, my lord, The music ended,
    We'll fit the kid fox with a pennyworth.
35 **DON PEDRO:** Come, Balthasar, we'll hear that song again.
BALTHASAR: Oh, good my lord, tax not so bad a voice
    To slander music any more than once.
DON PEDRO: It is the witness still of excellency
    To put a strange face on his own perfection.
40   I pray thee, sing, and let me woo no more.
BALTHASAR: Because you talk of wooing, I will sing.
    Since many a wooer doth commence his suit
    To her he thinks not worthy, yet he woos,
    Yet will he swear he loves.
DON PEDRO: Nay, pray thee, come.
    Or if thou wilt hold longer argument,
    Do it in notes.
BALTHASAR: Note this before my notes,
    There's not a note of mine that's worth the noting.
50 **DON PEDRO:** Why, these are very crotchets that he speaks—
    Note, notes, forsooth, and nothing.

(Plays the tune.)

BENEDICK: Now, divine air! Now is his soul ravished! Is it not strange that sheep's guts[38] should hale souls out of men's bodies? Well, a horn for my money, when all's done.
55 **BALTHASAR:** *(Sings.)*
        Sigh no more, ladies, sigh no more,
           Men were deceivers ever,
        One foot in sea and one on shore,
           To one thing constant never.
60   Then sigh not so, but let them go,
           And be you blithe and bonny,
        Converting all your sounds of woe
           Into Hey nonny, nonny.
        Sing no more ditties, sing no moe
65   Of dumps so dull and heavy.

---

[38] Material for musical strings.

    The fraud of men was ever so,
      Since summer first was leavy.
    Then sigh not so, but let them go,
      And be you blithe and bonny,
70   Converting all your sounds of woe
      Into Hey nonny, nonny.

DON PEDRO: By my troth, a good song.

BALTHASAR: And an ill singer, my lord.

DON PEDRO: Ha, no, no, faith, thou singest well enough for a shift.

75 **BENEDICK:** An he had been a dog that should have howled thus, they
would have hanged him. And I pray God his bad voice bode no
mischief. I had as lief have heard the night raven,[39] come what plague
could have come after it.

DON PEDRO: Yea, marry, dost thou hear, Balthasar? I pray thee get us
80 some excellent music, for tomorrow night we would have it at the
Lady Hero's chamber window.

BALTHASAR: The best I can, my lord.

DON PEDRO: Do so. Farewell. (*Exit Balthasar.*)
Come hither, Leonato. What was it you told me of today—that your
85 niece Beatrice was in love with Signior Benedick?

CLAUDIO: Oh, aye. Stalk on, stalk on, the fowl sits. I did never think
that lady would have loved any man.

LEONATO: No, nor I neither. But most wonderful that she should so dote
on Signior Benedick, whom she hath in all outward behaviors seemed
90 ever to abhor.

BENEDICK: Is 't possible? Sits the wind in that corner?

LEONATO: By my troth, my lord, I cannot tell what to think of it but
that she loves him with an enraged affection. It is past the infinite of
thought.

95 **DON PEDRO:** Maybe she doth but counterfeit.

CLAUDIO: Faith, like enough.

LEONATO: Oh, God, counterfeit! There was never counterfeit of passion
came so near the life of passion as she discovers it.

DON PEDRO: Why, what effects of passion shows she?

100 **CLAUDIO:** Bait the hook well—this fish will bite.

LEONATO: What effects, my lord? She will sit you, you heard my daughter
tell you how.

CLAUDIO: She did, indeed.

DON PEDRO: How, how, I pray you? You amaze me. I would have
105 thought her spirit had been invincible against all assaults of affection.

LEONATO: I would have sworn it had, my lord, especially against
Benedick.

---

[39] Melancholy.

BENEDICK: I should think this a gull[40] but that the white-bearded fellow speaks it. Knavery cannot, sure, hide himself in such reverence.

110 **CLAUDIO:** He hath ta'en the infection. Hold it up.

DON PEDRO: Hath she made her affection known to Benedick?

LEONATO: No, and swears she never will. That's her torment.

CLAUDIO: 'Tis true indeed, so your daughter says. "Shall I," says she, "that have so oft encountered him with scorn, write to him that I
115 love him?"

LEONATO: This says she now when she is beginning to write to him; for she'll be up twenty times a night, and there will she sit in her smock till she have writ a sheet of paper. My daughter tells us all.

CLAUDIO: Now you talk of a sheet of paper, I remember a pretty jest
120 your daughter told us of.

LEONATO: Oh, when she had writ it, and was reading it over, she found Benedick and Beatrice between the sheet?

CLAUDIO: That.

LEONATO: Oh, she tore the letter into a thousand half-pence, railed at
125 herself that she should be so immodest to write to one that she knew would flout her. "I measure him," says she, "by my own spirit, for I should flout him if he writ to me—yea, though I love him, I should."

CLAUDIO: Then down upon her knees she falls, weeps, sobs, beats her heart, tears her hair, prays, curses. "O sweet Benedick! God give me
130 patience!"

LEONATO: She doth indeed, my daughter says so. And the ecstasy hath so much overborne her that my daughter is sometime afeard she will do a desperate outrage to herself. It is very true.

DON PEDRO: It were good that Benedick knew of it by some other, if she
135 will not discover it.

CLAUDIO: To what end? He would make but a sport of it, and torment the poor lady worse.

DON PEDRO: An he should, it were an alms[41] to hang him. She's an excellent sweet lady, and out of all suspicion she is virtuous.

140 **CLAUDIO:** And she is exceeding wise.

DON PEDRO: In everything but in loving Benedick.

LEONATO: Oh, my lord, wisdom and blood combating in so tender a body, we have ten proofs to one that blood hath the victory. I am sorry for her, as I have just cause, being her uncle and her guardian.

145 **DON PEDRO:** I would she had bestowed this dotage on me. I would have daffed all other respects and made her half myself. I pray you tell Benedick of it, and hear what a' will say.

LEONATO: Were it good, think you?

CLAUDIO: Hero thinks surely she will die; for she says she will die if he
150 love her not, and she will die ere she make her love known, and she

---

[40] Trick.   [41] Good deed.

will die if he woo her rather than she will bate one breath of her accustomed crossness.

DON PEDRO: She doth well. If she should make tender of her love, 'tis very possible he'll scorn it, for the man, as you know all, hath a
155   contemptible spirit.

CLAUDIO: He is a very proper[42] man.

DON PEDRO: He hath indeed a good outward happiness.

CLAUDIO: Before God! And in my mind, very wise.

DON PEDRO: He doth indeed show some sparks that are like wit.

160   **CLAUDIO:**   And I take him to be valiant.

DON PEDRO: As Hector, I assure you. And in the managing of quarrels you may say he is wise, for either he avoids them with great discretion or undertakes them with a most Christianlike fear.

LEONATO: If he do fear God, a' must necessarily keep peace. If he break
165   the peace, he ought to enter into a quarrel with fear and trembling.

DON PEDRO: And so will he do, for the man doth fear God, howsoever it seems not in him by some large jests he will make. Well, I am sorry for your niece. Shall we go seek Benedick, and tell him of her love?

CLAUDIO: Never tell him, my lord. Let her wear it out with good
170   counsel.

LEONATO: Nay, that's impossible. She may wear her heart out first.

DON PEDRO: Well, we will hear further of it by your daughter. Let it cool the while. I love Benedick well, and I could wish he would modestly examine himself to see how much he is unworthy so good a
175   lady.

LEONATO: My lord, will you walk? Dinner is ready.

CLAUDIO: If he do not dote on her upon this, I will never trust my expectation.

DON PEDRO: Let there be the same net spread for her, and that must
180   your daughter and her gentlewomen carry. The sport will be when they hold one an opinion of another's dotage, and no such matter. That's the scene that I would see, which will be merely a dumb show. Let us send her to call him in to dinner.

(Exeunt Don Pedro, Claudio, and Leonato.)

BENEDICK: *(Coming forward)* This can be no trick. The conference was
185   sadly borne.[43] They have the truth of this from Hero. They seem to pity the lady. It seems her affections have their full bent. Love me! Why, it must be requited. I hear how I am censured. They say I will bear myself proudly if I perceive the love come from her. They say too that she will rather die than give any sign of affection. I did never
190   think to marry. I must not seem proud. Happy are they that hear their detractions and can put them to mending. They say the lady is fair—

---

[42] Handsome.   [43] Seriously maintained.

'tis a truth, I can bear them witness; and virtuous—'tis so, I cannot
reprove it; and wise, but for loving me—by my troth, it is no addition
to her wit, nor no great argument of her folly, for I will be horribly in
love with her. I may chance have some odd quirks and remnants of
195 wit broken on me because I have railed so long against marriage. But
doth not the appetite alter? A man loves the meat in his youth that
he cannot endure in his age. Shall quips[44] and sentences[45] and these
paper bullets of the brain awe a man from the career of his humor?
200 No, the world must be peopled. When I said I would die a bachelor, I
did not think I should live till I were married. Here comes Beatrice.
By this day, she's a fair lady! I do spy some marks of love in her.

(Enter Beatrice.)

BEATRICE: Against my will I am sent to bid you come in to dinner.
BENEDICK: Fair Beatrice, I thank you for your pains.
205 **BEATRICE:** I took no more pains for those thanks than you take pains to
thank me. If it had been painful, I would not have come.
BENEDICK: You take pleasure, then, in the message?
BEATRICE: Yea, just so much as you may take upon a knife's point and
choke a daw[46] withal. You have no stomach, signior. Fare you well.

(Exit.)

210 **BENEDICK:** Ha! "Against my will I am sent to bid you come in to
dinner." There's a double meaning in that. "I took no more pains for
those thanks than you took pains to thank me." That's as much as to
say, "Any pains that I take for you is as easy as thanks." If I do not
take pity of her, I am a villain; if I do not love her, I am a Jew.[47] I will
215 go get her picture.

(Exit.)

ACT III

SCENE I. LEONATO'S ORCHARD.

(Enter Hero, Margaret, and Ursula.)

HERO: Good Margaret, run thee to the parlor.
There shalt thou find my cousin Beatrice
Proposing with the Prince and Claudio.
Whisper her ear and tell her I and Ursula
5 Walk in the orchard, and our whole discourse

---

[44] Jokes.   [45] Proverbs.   [46] A jackdaw, a foolish bird.   [47] An unbeliever.

Is all of her—say that thou overheard'st us.
And bid her steal into the pleachèd[48] bower
Where honeysuckles, ripened by the sun,
Forbid the sun to enter, like favorites
10   Made proud by princes, that advance their pride
Against that power that bred it. There will she hide her,
To listen our propose. This is thy office.
Bear thee well in it, and leave us alone.

MARGARET: I'll make her come, I warrant you, presently.   *(Exit.)*

15 **HERO:**   Now, Ursula, when Beatrice doth come,
As we do trace this alley up and down
Our talk must only be of Benedick.
When I do name him, let it be thy part
To praise him more than ever man did merit.
20   My talk to thee must be how Benedick
Is sick in love with Beatrice. Of this matter
Is little Cupid's crafty arrow made,
That only wounds by hearsay.
(Enter Beatrice, behind.)   Now begin,
For look where Beatrice, like a lapwing,[49] runs
25   Close by the ground to hear our conference.

URSULA: The pleasant'st angling is to see the fish
Cut with her golden oars the silver stream,
And greedily devour the treacherous bait.
So angle we for Beatrice, who even now
30   Is couchèd in the woodbine coverture.[50]
Fear you not my part of the dialogue.

HERO: Then go we near her, that her ear lose nothing
Of the false sweet bait that we lay for it.

(Approaching the bower)

No, truly, Ursula, she is too disdainful.
35   I know her spirits are as coy and wild
As haggards[51] of the rock.

URSULA: But are you sure
That Benedick loves Beatrice so entirely?

HERO: So says the Prince and my new-trothèd lord.

URSULA: And did they bid you tell her of it, madam?

40 **HERO:**   They did entreat me to acquaint her of it.
But I persuaded them, if they loved Benedick,
To wish him wrestle with affection
And never to let Beatrice know of it.

---

[48] Covered with bleaches.   [49] Swift bird that runs close to the ground.   [50] Hiding place.   [51] Adult hawk caught wild.

URSULA: Why did you so? Doth not the gentleman
45   Deserve as full as fortunate a bed
        As ever Beatrice shall couch upon?
HERO: Oh god of love! I know he doth deserve
        As much as may be yielded to a man.
        But Nature never framed a woman's heart
50   Of prouder stuff than that of Beatrice.
        Disdain and scorn ride sparkling in her eyes,
        Misprizing what they look on, and her wit
        Values itself so highly that to her
        All matter else seems weak. She cannot love,
55   Nor take no shape nor project of affection,
        She is so self-endeared.
URSULA: Sure, I think so,
        And therefore certainly it were not good
        She knew his love, lest she make sport at it.
HERO: Why, you speak truth. I never yet saw man,
60   How wise, how noble, young, how rarely featured,
        But she would spell him backward. If fair-faced,
        She would swear the gentleman should be her sister;
        If black, why, Nature, drawing of an antique,[52]
        Made a foul blot; if tall, a lance ill-headed,
65   If low, an agate very vilely cut;
        If speaking, why, a vane blown with all winds,
        If silent, why, a block movèd with none.
        So turns she every man the wrong side out,
        And never gives to truth and virtue that
70   Which simpleness and merit purchaseth.
URSULA: Sure, sure, such carping is not commendable.
HERO: No, not to be so odd and from all fashions
        As Beatrice is cannot be commendable.
        But who dare tell her so? If I should speak,
75   She would mock me into air. Oh, she would laugh me
        Out of myself, press me to death with wit!
        Therefore let Benedick, like covered fire,
        Consume away in sighs, waste inwardly.
        It were a better death than die with mocks,
80   Which is as bad as die with tickling.
URSULA: Yet tell her of it. Hear what she will say.
HERO: No, rather I will go to Benedick
        And counsel him to fight against his passion.
        And truly I'll devise some honest slanders
85   To stain my cousin with. One doth not know
        How much an ill word may empoison liking.

---

[52] Grotesque.

URSULA:　Oh, do not do your cousin such a wrong!
　　She cannot be so much without true judgment—
　　Having so swift and excellent a wit
90　As she is prized to have—as to refuse
　　So rare a gentleman as Signior Benedick.
HERO:　He is the only man of Italy,
　　Always excepted my dear Claudio.
URSULA:　I pray you be not angry with me, madam,
95　Speaking my fancy. Signior Benedick,
　　For shape, for bearing, argument, and valor,
　　Goes foremost in report through Italy.
HERO:　Indeed he hath an excellent good name.
URSULA:　His excellence did earn it ere he had it.
100　When are you married, madam?
HERO:　Why, every day, tomorrow. Come, go in.
　　I'll show thee some attires, and have thy counsel
　　Which is the best to furnish[53] me tomorrow.
URSULA:　She's limed, I warrant you. We have caught her, madam.
105 **HERO:**　If it prove so, then loving goes by haps.
　　Some Cupid kills with arrows, some with traps.

　　(Exeunt Hero and Ursula.)

BEATRICE:　*(Coming forward)* What fire is in mine ears? Can this be true?
　　Stand I condemned for pride and scorn so much?
　　Contempt, farewell, and maiden pride, adieu!
110　No glory lives behind the back of such.
　　And, Benedick, love on, I will requite thee,
　　Taming my wild heart to thy loving hand.
　　If thou dost love, my kindness shall incite thee
　　To bind our loves up in a holy band,
115　For others say thou dost deserve and I
　　Believe it better than reportingly. *(Exit.)*

SCENE II. A ROOM IN LEONATO'S HOUSE.

(Enter Don Pedro, Claudio, Benedick, and Leonato.)

DON PEDRO:　I do but stay till your marriage be consummate, and then
　　go I toward Aragon.
CLAUDIO:　I'll bring you thither, my lord, if you'll vouchsafe me.
DON PEDRO:　Nay, that would be as great a soil in the new gloss of your
5　marriage as to show a child his new coat and forbid him to wear it. I
　　will only be bold with Benedick for his company, for from the crown

---

[53] Dress.

of his head to the sole of his foot he is all mirth. He hath twice or thrice cut Cupid's bowstring, and the little hangman dare not shoot at him. He hath a heart as sound as a bell, and his tongue is the clapper, for what his heart thinks his tongue speaks.

10

BENEDICK: Gallants, I am not as I have been.

LEONATO: So say I. Methinks you are sadder.

CLAUDIO: I hope he be in love.

DON PEDRO: Hang him, truant! There's no true drop of blood in him to be truly touched with love. If he be sad, he wants money.

15

BENEDICK: I have the toothache.

DON PEDRO: Draw it.

BENEDICK: Hang it!

CLAUDIO: You must hang it first and draw it afterward.

20

DON PEDRO: What! Sigh for the toothache?

LEONATO: Where is but a humor or a worm.

BENEDICK: Well, everyone can master a grief but he that has it.

CLAUDIO: Yet say I he is in love.

DON PEDRO: There is no appearance of fancy in him, unless it be a fancy that he hath to strange disguises—as to be a Dutchman today, a Frenchman tomorrow; or in the shape of two countries at once—as a German from the waist downward, all slops, and a Spaniard from the hip upward, no doublet. Unless he have a fancy to this foolery, as it appears he hath, he is no fool for fancy, as you would have it appear he is.

25

30

CLAUDIO: If he be not in love with some woman, there is no believing old signs. A' brushes his hat o' mornings. What should that bode?

DON PEDRO: Hath any man seen him at the barber's?

CLAUDIO: No, but the barber's man hath been seen with him, and the old ornament of his cheek hath already stuffed tennis balls.

35

LEONATO: Indeed, he looks younger than he did by the loss of a beard.

DON PEDRO: Nay, a' rubs himself with civet.[54] Can you smell him out by that?

CLAUDIO: That's as much as to say the sweet youth's in love.

40

DON PEDRO: The greatest note of it is his melancholy.

CLAUDIO: And when was he wont to wash his face?

DON PEDRO: Yea, or to paint himself? For the which, I hear what they say of him.

CLAUDIO: Nay, but his jesting spirit, which is now crept into a lute string and now governed by stops.

45

DON PEDRO: Indeed that tells a heavy tale for him. Conclude, conclude he is in love.

CLAUDIO: Nay, but I know who loves him.

DON PEDRO: That would I know too. I warrant one that knows him not.

---

[54] Cologne made of the secretions of the civet cat's glands.

50 **CLAUDIO:** Yes, and his ill conditions,[55] and, in despite of all, dies for him.

DON PEDRO: She shall be buried with her face upward.

BENEDICK: Yet is this no charm for the toothache. Old signior, walk aside with me. I have studied eight or nine wise words to speak to you, which these hobbyhorses must not hear.

(Exeunt Benedick and Leonato.)

55 **DON PEDRO:** For my life, to break with him about Beatrice.

CLAUDIO: 'Tis even so. Hero and Margaret have by this played their parts with Beatrice, and then the two bears will not bite one another when they meet.

(Enter Don John.)

DON JOHN: My lord and brother, God save you!

60 **DON PEDRO:** Good-den, Brother.

DON JOHN: If your leisure served, I would speak with you.

DON PEDRO: In private?

DON JOHN: If it please you. Yet Count Claudio may hear, for what I would speak of concerns him.

65 **DON PEDRO:** What's the matter?

DON JOHN: *(To Claudio)* Means your lordship to be married tomorrow?

DON PEDRO: You know he does.

DON JOHN: I know not that, when he knows what I know.

CLAUDIO: If there be any impediment, I pray you discover it.

70 **DON JOHN:** You may think I love you not. Let that appear hereafter, and aim better at me by that I now will manifest. For my brother, I think he holds you well, and in dearness of heart hath help to effect your ensuing marriage—surely suit ill spent and labor ill bestowed.

DON PEDRO: Why, what's the matter?

75 **DON JOHN:** I came hither to tell you, and, circumstances shortened, for she has been too long a-talking of, the lady is disloyal.

CLAUDIO: Who, Hero?

DON JOHN: Even she, Leonato's Hero, your Hero, every man's Hero.

CLAUDIO: Disloyal?

80 **DON JOHN:** The word is too good to paint out her wickedness, I could say she were worse. Think you of a worse title and I will fit her to it. Wonder not till further warrant. Go but with me tonight, you shall see her chamber window entered, even the night before her wedding day. If you love her then, tomorrow wed her, but it would better fit

85 your honor to change your mind.

CLAUDIO: May this be so?

DON PEDRO: I will not think it.

---

[55] Qualities.

DON JOHN: If you dare not trust that you see, confess not that you
know. If you will follow me, I will show you enough, and when you
90   have seen more, and heard more, proceed accordingly.
CLAUDIO: If I see anything tonight why I should not marry her
tomorrow, in the congregation where I should wed there will I shame
her.
DON PEDRO: And as I wooed for thee to obtain her, I will join with thee
95   to disgrace her.
DON JOHN: I will disparage her no farther till you are my witnesses.
Bear it coldly[56] but till midnight, and let the issue show itself.
DON PEDRO: Oh, day untowardly turned!
CLAUDIO: Oh, mischief strangely thwarting!
100 **DON JOHN:**   Oh, plague right well prevented! So will you say when you
have seen the sequel. *(Exeunt.)*

SCENE III.   A   STREET.

(Enter Dogberry and Verges with the Watch.)

DOGBERRY: Are you good men and true?
VERGES: Yea, or else it were pity but they should suffer salvation, body
and soul.
DOGBERRY: Nay, there were a punishment too good for them, if they
5   should have any allegiance in them, being chosen for the Prince's
watch.
VERGES: Well, give them their charge, Neighbor Dogberry.
DOGBERRY: First, who think you the most desartless[57] man to be
constable?
10 **FIRST WATCH:**   Hugh Otecake, sir, or George Seacole, for they can write
and read.
DOGBERRY: Come hither, Neighbor Seacole. God hath blessed you with
a good name. To be a well-favored[58] man is the gift of fortune, but to
write and read comes by nature.
15 **SECOND WATCH:**   Both which, Master Constable—
DOGBERRY: You have. I knew it would be your answer. Well, for your
favor, sir, why, give God thanks and make no boast of it. And for
your writing and reading, let that appear when there is no need of
such vanity. You are thought here to be the most senseless[59] and fit
20   man for the constable of the watch, therefore bear you the lantern.
This is your charge. You shall comprehend[60] all vagrom men. You are
to bid any man stand, in the Prince's name.
SECOND WATCH: How if a' will not stand?

---

[56] Patiently.   [57] Deserving, worthy.   [58] Attractive.   [59] Sensible.   [60] Capture.

DOGBERRY: Why, then take no note of him, but let him go, and
25   presently call the rest of the watch together and thank God you are
rid of a knave.

VERGES: If he will not stand when he is bidden, he is none of the
Prince's subjects.

DOGBERRY: True, and they are to meddle with none but the Prince's
30   subjects. You shall also make no noise in the streets, for for the watch
to babble and to talk is most tolerable[61] and not to be endured.

WATCH: We will rather sleep than talk. We know what belongs to a
watch.

DOGBERRY: Why, you speak like an ancient and most quiet watchman,
35   for I cannot see how sleeping should offend. Only have a care that
your bills be not stolen. Well, you are to call at all the alehouses and
bid those that are drunk get them to bed.

WATCH: How if they will not?

DOGBERRY: Why, then let them alone till they are sober. If they make
40   you not then the better answer, you may say they are not the men
you took them for.

WATCH: Well, sir.

DOGBERRY: If you meet a thief, you may suspect him, by virtue of your
office, to be no true man. And for such kind of men, the less you
45   meddle or make with them, why, the more is for your honesty.

WATCH: If we know him to be a thief, shall we not lay hands on him?

DOGBERRY: Truly, by your office you may, but I think they that touch
pitch will be defiled. The most peaceable way for you, if you do take a
thief, is to let him show himself what he is and steal out of your
50   company.

VERGES: You have been always called a merciful man, partner.

DOGBERRY: Truly, I would not hang a dog by my will, much more a
man who hath any honesty in him.

VERGES: If you hear a child cry in the night, you must call to the nurse
55   and bid her still it.

WATCH: How if the nurse be asleep and will not hear us?

DOGBERRY: Why, then depart in peace and let the child wake her with
crying; for the ewe that will not hear her lamb when it baas will
never answer a calf when he bleats.

60 **VERGES:**   'Tis very true.

DOGBERRY: This is the end of the charge: You, Constable, are to present
the Prince's own person. If you meet the Prince in the night, you may
stay him.

VERGES: Nay, by 'r Lady, that I think a' cannot.

65 **DOGBERRY:**   Five shillings to one on 't, with any man that knows the
statues, he may stay him. Marry, not without the Prince be willing,

---

[61] Intolerable.

for indeed the watch ought to offend no man, and it is an offense to stay a man against his will.

VERGES: By 'r Lady, I think it be so.

70 **DOGBERRY:** Ha, ah, ha! Well, masters, good night. An there be any matter of weight chances, call up me. Keep your fellows' counsels and your own, and good night. Come, neighbor.

WATCH: Well, masters, we hear our charge. Let us go sit here upon the church bench till two, and then all to bed.

75 **DOGBERRY:** One word more, honest neighbors. I pray you watch about Signior Leonato's door, for the wedding being there tomorrow, there is a great coil tonight. Adieu. Be vigilant, I beseech you. *(Exeunt Dogberry and Verges.)*

(Enter Borachio and Conrade.)

BORACHIO: What, Conrade!

80 **WATCH:** *(Aside)* Peace! Stir not.

BORACHIO: Conrade, I say!

CONRADE: Here, man, I am at thy elbow.

BORACHIO: Mass,[62] and my elbow itched. I thought there would a scab follow.

85 **CONRADE:** I will owe thee an answer for that. And now forward with thy tale.

BORACHIO: Stand thee close, then, under this penthouse,[63] for it drizzles rain, and I will, like a true drunkard, utter all to thee.

WATCH: *(Aside)* Some treason, masters. Yet stand close.

90 **BORACHIO:** Therefore know I have earned of Don John a thousand ducats.

CONRADE: Is it possible that any villainy should be so dear?

BORACHIO: Thou shouldst rather ask if it were possible any villainy should be so rich, for when rich villains have need of poor ones, poor ones may make what price they will.

95 **CONRADE:** I wonder at it.

BORACHIO: That shows thou art unconfirmed. Thou knowest that the fashion of a doublet, or a hat, or a cloak, is nothing to a man.

CONRADE: Yes, it is apparel.

BORACHIO: I mean, the fashion.

100 **CONRADE:** Yes, the fashion is the fashion.

BORACHIO: Tush! I may as well say the fool's the fool. But seest thou not what a deformed thief this fashion is?

WATCH: *(Aside)* I know that Deformed, a' has been a vile thief this seven year, a' goes up and down like a gentleman. I remember his

105 name.

BORACHIO: Didst thou not hear somebody?

CONRADE: No, 'twas the vane on the house.

---

[62] By the mass.   [63] Porch.

BORACHIO: Seest thou not, I say, what a deformed thief this fashion is? How giddily a' turns about all the hot bloods between fourteen and five and thirty? Sometimes fashioning them like Pharaoh's soldiers in the reechy[64] painting, sometime like god Bel's[65] priests in the old church window, sometime like the shaven Hercules in the smirched worm-eaten tapestry, where his codpiece seems as massy as his club?

CONRADE: All this I see, and I see that the fashion wears out more apparel than the man. But art not thou thyself giddy with the fashion too, that thou hast shifted out of thy tale into telling me of the fashion?

BORACHIO: Not so, neither. But know that I have tonight wooed Margaret, the Lady Hero's gentlewoman, by the name of Hero. She leans me out at her mistress' chamber window, bids me a thousand times good night.—I tell this tale vilely. I should first tell thee how the Prince, Claudio and my master, planted and placed and possessed by my master Don John, saw afar off in the orchard this amiable encounter.

CONRADE: And thought they Margaret was Hero?

BORACHIO: Two of them did, the Prince and Claudio, but the Devil my master knew she was Margaret. And partly by his oaths, which first possessed them, partly by the dark night, which did deceive them, but chiefly by my villainy, which did confirm any slander that Don John had made, away went Claudio enraged, swore he would meet her, as he was appointed, next morning at the temple and there before the whole congregation shame her with what he saw o'ernight, and send her home again without a husband.

FIRST WATCH: We charge you, in the Prince's name, stand!

SECOND WATCH: Call up the right master constable. We have here recovered[66] the most dangerous piece of lechery that was known in the commonwealth.

FIRST WATCH: And one Deformed is one of them. I know him, a' wears a lock.[67]

CONRADE: Masters, masters—

SECOND WATCH: You'll be made bring Deformed forth, I warrant you.

CONRADE: Masters—

FIRST WATCH: Never speak. We charge you let us obey you to go with us.

BORACHIO: We are like to prove a goodly commodity, being taken up of these men's bills.

CONRADE: A commodity in question, I warrant you. Come, we'll obey you. (*Exeunt.*)

---

[64] Covered with smoke residue.   [65] Character in Apocrypha.   [66] Discovered, found.   [67] Curled lock of hair by the ear.

SCENE IV. HERO'S APARTMENT.

(Enter Hero, Margaret, and Ursula.)

HERO: Good Ursula, wake my cousin Beatrice and desire her to rise.
URSULA: I will, lady.
HERO: And bid her come hither.
URSULA: Well.

(Exit.)

5 **MARGARET:** Troth, I think your other rebato were better.
HERO: No, pray thee, good Meg, I'll wear this.
MARGARET: By my troth's not so good, and I warrant your cousin will say so.
HERO: My cousin's a fool, and thou art another. I'll wear none but this.
10 **MARGARET:** I like the new tire[68] within excellently, if the hair were a thought browner, and your gown's a most rare fashion, i' faith. I saw the Duchess of Milan's gown that they praise so.
HERO: Oh, that exceeds, they say.
MARGARET: By my troth 's but a nightgown in respect of yours,—cloth
15 o' gold, and cuts, and laced with silver, set with pearls, down sleeves,[69] side sleeves,[70] and skirts round underborne with a bluish tinsel. But for a fine, quaint, graceful, and excellent fashion, yours is worth ten on't.
HERO: God give me joy to wear it! For my heart is exceeding heavy.
MARGARET: 'Twill be heavier soon by the weight of a man.
20 **HERO:** Fie upon thee! Are not ashamed?
MARGARET: Of what, lady? Of speaking honorably? Is not marriage honorable in a beggar? Is not your lord honorable without marriage? I think you would have me say, "saving your reverence, a husband." An bad thinking do not wrest true speaking, I'll offend nobody. Is there
25 any harm in "the heavier for a husband"? None, I think, an it be the right husband and the right wife; otherwise 'tis light, and not heavy. Ask my Lady Beatrice else—here she comes.

(Enter Beatrice.)

HERO: Good morrow, Coz.
BEATRICE: Good morrow, sweet Hero.
30 **HERO:** Why, how now? Do you speak in the sick tune?
BEATRICE: I am out of all other tune, methinks.
MARGARET: Clap 's into "Light-o'-love." That goes without a burden. Do you sing it, and I'll dance it.
BEATRICE: Ye light-o'-love, with your heels! Then, if your husband have
35 stables enough, you'll see he shall lack no barns.

---

[68] Headddress.   [69] Long sleeves.   [70] Sleeves hanging from the shoulder.

MARGARET: Oh, illegitimate construction! I scorn that with my heels.

BEATRICE: 'Tis almost five o'clock, Cousin, 'tis time you were ready. By my troth, I am exceeding ill. Heigh-ho!

MARGARET: For a hawk, a horse, or a husband?

40 **BEATRICE:** For the letter that begins them all, H.[71]

MARGARET: Well, an you be not turned Turk,[72] there's no more sailing by the star.

BEATRICE: What means the fool, trow?[73]

MARGARET: Nothing I, but God send everyone their heart's desire!

45 **HERO:** These gloves the Count sent me. They are an excellent perfume.

BEATRICE: I am stuffed, Cousin, I cannot smell.

MARGARET: A maid, and stuffed! There's goodly catching of cold.

BEATRICE: Oh, God help me! God help me! How long have you professed apprehension?[74]

50 **MARGARET:** Ever since you left it. Doth not my wit become me rarely?

BEATRICE: It is not seen enough, you should wear it in your cap. By my troth, I am sick.

MARGARET: Get you some of this distilled Carduus Benedictus,[75] and lay it to your heart. It is the only thing for a qualm.

55 **HERO:** There thou prickest her with a thistle.

BEATRICE: Benedictus! Why Benedictus? You have some moral in this Benedictus.

MARGARET: Moral! No, by my troth, I have no moral meaning, I meant plain holy thistle. You may think perchance that I think you are in
60 love. Nay, by 'r Lady, I am not such a fool to think what I list; nor I list not to think what I can; nor, indeed, I cannot think, if I would think my heart out of thinking, that you are in love, or that you will be in love, or that you can be in love. Yet Benedick was such another, and now is he become a man. He swore he would never marry, and
65 yet now, in despite of his heart, he eats his meat without grudging. And how you may be converted, I know not, but methinks you look with your eyes as other women do.

BEATRICE: What pace is this that thy tongue keeps?

MARGARET: Not a false gallop.

(Re-enter Ursula.)

75 **URSULA:** Madam, withdraw. The Prince, the Count, Signior Benedick, Don John, and all the gallants of the town, are come to fetch you to church.

HERO: Help to dress me, good Coz, good Meg, good Ursula. *(Exeunt.)*

---

[71] Pronounced as "ache."   [72] Heather.   [73] I wonder.   [74] Wit, intelligence.
[75] Thistle used as a cold remedy.

SCENE V. ANOTHER ROOM
IN LEONATO'S HOUSE.

(Enter Leonato, with Dogberry and Verges.)

LEONATO: What would you with me, honest neighbor?

DOGBERRY: Marry, sir, I would have some confidence with you that decerns you nearly.

LEONATO: Brief, I pray you, for you see it is a busy time with me.

5   **DOGBERRY:**   Marry, this it is, sir.

VERGES: Yes, in truth it is, sir.

LEONATO: What is it, my good friends?

DOGBERRY: Goodman Verges, sir, speaks a little off the matter—an old man, sir, and his wits are not so blunt as, God help, I would desire

10   they were, but, in faith, honest as the skin between his brows.

VERGES: Yes, I thank God I am as honest as any man living that is an old man and no honester than I.

DOGBERRY: Comparisons are odorous—*palabras*,[76] neighbor Verges.

LEONATO: Neighbors, you are tedious.

15   **DOGBERRY:**   It pleases your Worship to say so, but we are the poor Duke's officers. But truly, for mine own part, if I were as tedious as a king, I could find in my heart to bestow it all of your Worship.

LEONATO: All thy tediousness on me, ah?

DOGBERRY: Yea, an 'twere a thousand pound more than 'tis, for I hear

20   as good exclamation on your Worship as of any man in the city, and though I be but a poor man, I am glad to hear it.

VERGES: And so am I.

LEONATO: I would fain know what you have to say.

VERGES: Marry, sir, our watch tonight, excepting your Worship's

25   presence, ha' ta'en a couple of as arrant knaves as any in Messina.

DOGBERRY: A good old man, sir—he will be talking. As they say, "When the age is in, the wit is out." God help us! It is a world to see. Well said, i' faith, neighbor Verges. Well, God's a good man. An two men ride of a horse, one must ride behind. An honest soul, i' faith,

30   sir, by my troth he is, as ever broke bread. But God is to be worshiped, all men are not alike, alas, good neighbor!

LEONATO: Indeed, neighbor, he comes too short of you.

DOGBERRY: Gifts that God gives.

LEONATO: I must leave you.

35   **DOGBERRY:**   One word, sir. Our watch, sir, have indeed comprehended two aspicious persons, and we would have them this morning examined before your Worship.

LEONATO: Take their examination yourself, and bring it me. I am now in great haste, as it may appear unto you.

---

[76] Spanish for "words."

40 **DOGBERRY:** It shall be suffigance.[77]
LEONATO: Drink some wine ere you go. Fare you well.

(Enter a Messenger.)

MESSENGER: My lord, they stay for you to give your daughter to her husband.
LEONATO: I'll wait upon them. I am ready.

(Exeunt Leonato and Messenger.)

45 **DOGBERRY:** Go, good partner, go, get you to Francis Seacole. Bid him bring his pen and inkhorn to the jail. We are now to examination these men.
VERGES: And we must do it wisely.
DOGBERRY: We will spare for no wit, I warrant you, here's that shall
50 drive some of them to a noncome.[78] Only get the learned writer to set down our excommunication,[79] and meet me at the jail. *(Exeunt.)*

ACT IV

SCENE I. A CHURCH.

(Enter Don Pedro, Don John, Leonato, Friar Francis, Claudio, Benedick, Hero, Beatrice, and attendants.)

LEONATO: Come, Friar Francis, be brief—only to the plain form of marriage, and you shall recount their particular duties afterward.
FRIAR FRANCIS: You come hither, my lord, to marry this lady.
CLAUDIO: No.
5 **LEONATO:** To be married to her. Friar, you come to marry her.
FRIAR FRANCIS: Lady, you come hither to be married to this Count.
HERO: I do.
FRIAR FRANCIS: If either of you know any inward impediment why you should not be conjoined, I charge you, on your souls, to utter it.
10 **CLAUDIO:** Know you any, Hero?
HERO: None, my lord.
FRIAR FRANCIS: Know you any, Count?
LEONATO: I dare make his answer, none.
CLAUDIO: Oh, what men dare do! What men may do! What men daily
15 do, not knowing what they do!
BENEDICK: How now! Interjections? Why, then, some be of laughing, as ah, ha, he!

---

[77] Sufficient.   [78] Confused state.   [79] Examination.

CLAUDIO: Stand thee by, Friar. Father, by your leave,
Will you with free and unconstrainèd soul

20   Give me this maid, your daughter?

LEONATO: As freely, son, as God did give her me.

CLAUDIO: And what have I to give you back whose worth
May counterpoise this rich and precious gift?

DON PEDRO: Nothing, unless you render her again.

25   **CLAUDIO:**   Sweet Prince, you learn me noble thankfulness.
There, Leonato, take her back again.
Give not this rotten orange to your friend,
She's but the sign and semblance of her honor.
Behold how like a maid she blushes here!

30   Oh, what authority and show of truth
Can cunning sin cover itself withal!
Comes not that blood as modest evidence
To witness simple virtue? Would you not swear,
All you that see her, that she were a maid,

35   By these exterior shows? But she is none.
She knows the heat of a luxurious[80] bed.
Her blush is guiltiness, not modesty.

LEONATO: What do you mean, my lord?

CLAUDIO: Not to be married,
Not to knit my soul to an approved wanton.

40   **LEONATO:**   Dear my lord, if you, in your own proof,
Have vanquished the resistance of her youth,
And made defeat of her virginity—

CLAUDIO: I know what you would say. If I have known her,
You will say she did embrace me as a husband,

45   And so extenuate the 'forehand sin.
No, Leonato,
I never tempted her with word too large,
But, as a brother to his sister, showed
Bashful sincerity and comely love.

50   **HERO:**   And seemed I ever otherwise to you?

CLAUDIO: Out on thee! Seeming! I will write against it.
You seem to me as Dian[81] in her orb,
As chaste as is the bud ere it be blown,
But you are more intemperate in your blood

55   Than Venus, or those pampered animals
That rage in savage sensuality.

HERO: Is my lord well, that he doth speak so wide?

LEONATO: Sweet Prince, why speak not you?

---

[80] Lustful.   [81] Goddess of chastity.

DON PEDRO: What should I speak?
   I stand dishonored, that have gone about
60   To link my dear friend to a common stale.
LEONATO: Are these things spoken, or do I but dream?
DON JOHN: Sir, they are spoken, and these things are true.
BENEDICK: This looks not like a nuptial.
HERO: True! O God!
CLAUDIO: Leonato, stand I here?
65   Is this the Prince? Is this the Prince's brother?
   Is this face Hero's? Are our eyes our own?
LEONATO: All this is so, but what of this, my lord?
CLAUDIO: Let me but move one question to your daughter,
   And by that fatherly and kindly power
70   That you have in her, bid her answer truly.
LEONATO: I charge thee do so, as thou art my child.
HERO: Oh, God defend me! How am I beset! What kind of catechizing
   call you this?
CLAUDIO: To make you answer truly to your name.
75 **HERO:**   Is it not Hero? Who can blot that name
   With any just reproach?
CLAUDIO: Marry, that can Hero.
   Hero itself can blot out Hero's virtue.
   What man was he talked with you yesternight
   Out at your window betwixt twelve and one?
80   Now, if you are a maid, answer to this.
HERO: I talked with no man at that hour, my lord.
DON PEDRO: Why, then are you no maiden. Leonato, I am sorry you
   must hear. Upon mine honor,
   Myself, my brother, and this grievèd Count
85   Did see her, hear her, at that hour last night
   Talk with a ruffian at her chamber window,
   Who hath indeed, most like a liberal[82] villain,
   Confessed the vile encounters they have had
   A thousand times in secret.
90 **DON JOHN:**   Fie, fie! They are not to be named, my lord,
   Not to be spoke of,
   There is not chastity enough in language
   Without offense to utter them. Thus, pretty lady,
   I am sorry for thy much misgovernment.[83]
95 **CLAUDIO:**   O Hero, what a Hero hadst thou been
   If half thy outward graces had been placed
   About thy thoughts and counsels of thy heart!
   But fare thee well, most foul, most fair! Farewell,

---

[82] Gross.   [83] Evil acts.

Thou pure impiety and impious purity!
100　For thee I'll lock up all the gates of love,
And on my eyelids shall conjecture hang
To turn all beauty into thoughts of harm,
And never shall it more be gracious.

LEONATO: Hath no man's dagger here a point for me?

(Hero swoons.)

105　**BEATRICE:** Why, how now, Cousin! Wherefore sink you down?

DON JOHN: Come, let us go. These things, come thus to light,
Smother her spirits up.

(Exeunt Don Pedro, Don John, and Claudio.)

BENEDICK: How doth the lady?

BEATRICE:　　　　　　　　　　Dead, I think. Help, Uncle! Hero! Why,
Hero! Uncle! Signior Benedick! Friar!

110　**LEONATO:** O Fate! Take not away thy heavy hand.
Death is the fairest cover for her shame
That may be wished for.

BEATRICE:　　　　　　　　　　How now, Cousin Hero!

FRIAR FRANCIS: Have comfort, lady.

LEONATO: Dost thou look up?

115　**FRIAR FRANCIS:** Yea, wherefore should she not?

LEONATO: Wherefore! Why, doth not every earthly thing
Cry shame upon her? Could she here deny
The story that is printed in her blood?[84]
Do not live, Hero, do not ope thine eyes.
120　For did I think thou wouldst not quickly die,
Thought I thy spirits were stronger than thy shames,
Myself would, on the rearward of reproaches,
Strike at thy life. Grieved I, I had but one?
Chid I for that at frugal Nature's frame?
125　Oh, one too much by thee! Why had I one?
Why ever wast thou lovely in my eyes?
Why had I not with charitable hand
Took up a beggar's issue at my gates,
Who, smirchèd thus and mired with infamy,
130　I might have said, "No part of it is mine,
This shame derives itself from unknown loins"?
But mine, and mine I loved, and mine I praised,
And mine that I was proud on, mine so much
That I myself was to myself not mine,
135　Valuing of her—why, she, oh, she is fallen

---

[84] Blushing.

Into a pit of ink, that the wide sea
Hath drops too few to wash her clean again,
And salt too little which may season give
To her foul-tainted flesh!
BENEDICK: Sir, sir, be patient.
140 For my part, I am so attired in wonder
I know not what to say.
BEATRICE: Oh, on my soul, my cousin is belied!
BENEDICK: Lady, were you her bedfellow last night?
BEATRICE: No, truly not, although until last night I have this
145 twelvemonth been her bedfellow.
LEONATO: Confirmed, confirmed! Oh, that is stronger made
Which was before barred up with ribs of iron!
Would the two Princes lie, and Claudio lie,
Who loved her so, that, speaking of her foulness,
150 Washed it with tears? Hence from her! Let her die.
FRIAR FRANCIS: Hear me a little,
For I have only been silent so long
And given way unto this course of fortune
By noting of the lady. I have marked
155 A thousand blushing apparitions
To start into her face, a thousand innocent shames
In angel whiteness beat away those blushes.
And in her eye there hath appeared a fire
To burn the errors that these Princes hold
160 Against her maiden truth. Call me a fool,
Trust not my reading nor my observations,
Which with experimental seal doth warrant
The tenor of my book—trust not my age,
My reverence, calling, nor divinity—
165 If this sweet lady lie not guiltless here
Under some biting error.
LEONATO: Friar, it cannot be.
Thou seest that all the grace that she hath left
Is that she will not add to her damnation
A sin of perjury. She not denies it.
170 Why seek'st thou, then, to cover with excuse
That which appears in proper nakedness?
FRIAR FRANCIS: Lady, what man is he you are accused of?
HERO: They know that do accuse me, I know none.
If I know more of any man alive
175 Than that which maiden modesty doth warrant,
Let all my sins lack mercy! O my father,
Prove you that any man with me conversed
At hours unmeet, or that I yesternight
Maintained the change of words with any creature,
180 Refuse me, hate me, torture me to death!

FRIAR FRANCIS: There is some strange misprision[85] in the Princes.

BENEDICK: Two of them have the very bent of honor,
    And if their wisdoms be misled in this,
    The practice[86] of it lives in John the bastard,
185   Whose spirits toil in frame of villainies.

LEONATO: I know not. If they speak but truth of her,
    These hands shall tear her. If they wrong her honor,
    The proudest of them shall well hear of it.
    Time hath not yet so dried this blood of mine,
190   Nor age so eat up my invention,[87]
    Nor fortune made such havoc of my means,
    Nor my bad life reft me so much of friends,
    But they shall find, awaked in such a kind,
    Both strength of limb and policy of mind,
195   Ability in means and choice of friends,
    To quit me of them throughly.

FRIAR FRANCIS: Pause awhile,
    And let my counsel sway you in this case.
    Your daughter here the Princes left for dead.
    Let her awhile be secretly kept in,
200   And publish it that she is dead indeed.
    Maintain a mourning ostentation,
    And on your family's old monument
    Hang mournful epitaphs, and do all rites
    That appertain unto a burial.

205 **LEONATO:**   What shall become of this? What will this do?

FRIAR FRANCIS: Marry, this, well carried, shall on her behalf
    Change slander to remorse—that is some good.
    But not for that dream I on this strange course,
    But on this travail look for greater birth.
210   She dying, as it must be so maintained,
    Upon the instant that she was accused,
    Shall be lamented, pitied, and excused
    Of every hearer. For it so falls out,
    That what we have we prize not to the worth
215   Whiles we enjoy it; but being lacked and lost,
    Why, then we rack the value, then we find
    The virtue that possession would not show us
    Whiles it was ours. So will it fare with Claudio.
    When he shall hear she died upon his words,
220   The idea of her life shall sweetly creep
    Into his study of imagination;
    And every lovely organ of her life

---

[85] Misunderstanding.   [86] Planning, devising.   [87] Intellect.

Shall come apareled in more precious habit,
More moving-delicate and full of life,
225 Into the eye and prospect of his soul
Than when she lived indeed. Then shall he mourn,
If ever love had interest in his liver,[88]
And wish he had not so accused her,
No, though he thought his accusation true.
230 Let this be so, and doubt not but success
Will fashion the event in better shape
Than I can lay it down in likelihood.
But if all aim but this be leveled false,
The supposition of the lady's death
235 Will quench the wonder of her infamy.
And if it sort not well, you may conceal her,
As best befits her wounded reputation,
In some reclusive and religious life,
Out of all eyes, tongues, minds, and injuries.
240 **BENEDICK:** Signior Leonato, let the Friar advise you.
And though you know my inwardness and love
Is very much unto the Prince and Claudio,
Yet, by mine honor, I will deal in this
As secretly and justly as your soul
245 Should with your body.
LEONATO: Being that I flow in grief,
The smallest twine may lead me.
FRIAR FRANCIS: 'Tis well consented. Presently away,
For to strange sores strangely they strain the cure.
Come, lady, die to live. This wedding day
250 Perhaps is but prolonged. Have patience and endure. *(Exeunt all but
Benedick and Beatrice.)*
BENEDICK: Lady Beatrice, have you wept all this while?
BEATRICE: Yea, and I will weep awhile longer.
BENEDICK: I will not desire that.
255 **BEATRICE:** You have no reason, I do it freely.
BENEDICK: Surely I do believe your fair cousin is wronged.
BEATRICE: Ah, how much might the man deserve of me that would
right her!
BENEDICK: Is there any way to show such friendship?
260 **BEATRICE:** A very even way, but no such friend.
BENEDICK: May a man do it?
BEATRICE: It is a man's office, but not yours.
BENEDICK: I do love nothing in the world so well as you. Is not that
strange?

---

[88] Believed the origin of emotions.

265 **BEATRICE:**   As strange as the thing I know not. It were as possible for me
to say I loved nothing so well as you. But believe me not, and yet I lie
not, I confess nothing, nor I deny nothing. I am sorry for my cousin.

BENEDICK: By my sword, Beatrice, thou lovest me.

BEATRICE: Do not swear, and eat it.

270 **BENEDICK:**   I will swear by it that you love me, and I will make him eat
it that says I love not you.

BEATRICE: Will you not eat your word?

BENEDICK: With no sauce that can be devised to it. I protest I love thee.

BEATRICE: Why, then, God forgive me!

275 **BENEDICK:**   What offense, sweet Beatrice?

BEATRICE: You have stayed me in a happy hour. I was about to protest I
loved you.

BENEDICK: And do it with all thy heart.

BEATRICE: I love you with so much of my heart that none is left to
280   protest.

BENEDICK: Come, bid me do anything for thee.

BEATRICE: Kill Claudio.

BENEDICK: Ha! Not for the wide world.

BEATRICE: You kill me to deny it. Farewell.

285 **BENEDICK:**   Tarry, sweet Beatrice.

BEATRICE: I am gone, though I am here. There is no love in you. Nay, I
pray you let me go.

BENEDICK: Beatrice—

BEATRICE: In faith, I will go.

290 **BENEDICK:**   We'll be friends first.

BEATRICE: You dare easier be friends with me than fight with mine
enemy.

BENEDICK: Is Claudio thine enemy?

BEATRICE: Is he not approved in the height a villain that hath
295   slandered, scorned, dishonored my kinswoman? Oh, that I were a
man! What, bear her in hand until they come to take hands, and
then, with public accusation, uncovered slander, unmitigated
rancor—Oh, God, that I were a man! I would eat his heart in the
market place.

300 **BENEDICK:**   Hear me, Beatrice—

BEATRICE: Talk with a man out at a window! A proper saying!

BENEDICK: Nay, but, Beatrice—

BEATRICE: Sweet Hero! She is wronged, she is slandered, she is undone.

BENEDICK: Beat—

305 **BEATRICE:**   Princes and Counties! Surely, a princely testimony, a goodly
Count, Count Comfect,[89] a sweet gallant, surely! Oh, that I were a
man for his sake! Or that I had any friend would be a man for my

---

[89] Count candy.

sake! But manhood is melted into courtesies, valor into compliment, and men are only turned into tongue, and trim ones too. He is now
310 as valiant as Hercules that only tells a lie, and swears it. I cannot be a man with wishing, therefore I will die a woman with grieving.

BENEDICK: Tarry, good Beatrice. By this hand, I love thee.

BEATRICE: Use it for my love some other way than swearing by it.

BENEDICK: Think you in your soul the Count Claudio hath wronged
315 Hero?

BEATRICE: Yea, as sure as I have a thought or a soul.

BENEDICK: Enough, I am engaged, I will challenge him. I will kiss your hand, and so I leave you. By this hand, Claudio shall render me a dear account. As you hear of me, so think of me. Go, comfort your cousin.
320 I must say she is dead. And so farewell. *(Exeunt.)*

SCENE II.   A   PRISON.

(Enter Dogberry, Verges, and Sexton, in gowns; and the Watch, with Conrade and Borachio.)

DOGBERRY: Is our whole dissembly appeared?

VERGES: Oh, a stool and a cushion for the sexton.

SEXTON: Which be the malefactors?

DOGBERRY: Marry, that am I and my partner.

5 **VERGES:**   Nay, that's certain, we have the exhibition to examine.

SEXTON: But which are the offenders that are to be examined? Let them come before Master Constable.

DOGBERRY: Yea, marry, let them come before me. What is your name, friend?

10 **BORACHIO:**   Borachio.

DOGBERRY: Pray write down Borachio. Yours, sirrah?

CONRADE: I am a gentleman, sir, and my name is Conrade.

DOGBERRY: Write down master gentleman Conrade. Masters, do you serve God?

15 **CONRADE** and **BORACHIO:**   Yea, sir, we hope.

DOGBERRY: Write down that they hope they serve God. And write God first, for God defend[90] but God should go before such villains! Masters, it is proved already that you are little better than false knaves, and it will go near to be thought so shortly. How answer you for yourselves?

20 **CONRADE:**   Marry, sir, we say we are none.

DOGBERRY: A marvelous witty fellow, I assure you, but I will go about with him. Come you hither, sirrah, a word in your ear. Sir, I say to you, it is thought you are false knaves.

---

90 Forbid.

BORACHIO: Sir, I say to you we are none.

25 **DOGBERRY:** Well, stand aside. 'Fore God, they are both in a tale. Have you writ down that they are none?

SEXTON: Master Constable, you go not the way to examine. You must call forth the watch that are their accusers.

DOGBERRY: Yea, marry, that's the eftest[91] way. Let the watch come forth.

30 Masters, I charge you, in the Prince's name, accuse these men.

FIRST WATCH: This man said, sir, that Don John, the Prince's brother, was a villain.

DOGBERRY: Write down Prince John a villain. Why, this is flat perjury, to call a Prince's brother villain.

35 **BORACHIO:** Master Constable—

DOGBERRY: Pray thee, fellow, peace. I do not like thy look, I promise thee.

SEXTON: What heard you him say else?

SECOND WATCH: Marry, that he had received a thousand ducats of Don

40 John for accusing the Lady Hero wrongfully.

DOGBERRY: Flat burglary as ever was committed.

VERGES: Yea, by mass, that it is.

SEXTON: What else, fellow?

FIRST WATCH: And that Count Claudio did mean, upon his words, to

45 disgrace Hero before the whole assembly and not marry her.

DOGBERRY: O villain! Thou wilt be condemned into everlasting redemption for this.

SEXTON: What else?

WATCH: This is all.

50 **SEXTON:** And this is more, masters, than you can deny. Prince John is this morning secretly stolen away. Hero was in this manner accused, in this very manner refused, and upon the grief of this suddenly died. Master Constable, let these men be bound and brought to Leonato's. I will go before and show him their examination.

(Exit.)

55 **DOGBERRY:** Come, let them be opinioned.

VERGES: Let them be in the hands—

CONRADE: Off, coxcomb![92]

DOGBERRY: God's my life, where's the sexton? Let him write down the Prince's officer, coxcomb. Come, bind them. Thou naughty varlet!

60 **CONRADE:** Away! You are an ass, you are an ass.

DOGBERRY: Dost thou not suspect my place? Dost thou not suspect my years? Oh, that he were here to write me down an ass! But, masters, remember that I am an ass, though it be not written down, yet forget not that I am an ass. No, thou villain, thou art full of piety, as shall

---

[91] Neatest.   [92] Fool.

65 be proved upon thee by good witness. I am a wise fellow, and, which
is more, an officer; and, which is more, a householder; and, which is
more, as pretty a piece of flesh as any is in Messina; and one that
knows the law, go to; and a rich fellow enough, go to; and a fellow
that hath had losses; and one that hath two gowns, and everything
70 handsome about him. Bring him away. Oh, that I had been writ
down an ass!

(Exeunt.)

A C T   V

SCENE I. BEFORE LEONATO'S HOUSE.

(Enter Leonato and Antonio.)

ANTONIO: If you go on thus, you will kill yourself,
And 'tis not wisdom thus to second grief
Against yourself.
LEONATO: I pray thee, cease thy counsel,
Which falls into mine ears as profitless
5   As water in a sieve. Give not me counsel,
Nor let no comforter delight mine ear
But such a one whose wrongs do suit with mine.
Bring me a father that so loved his child,
Whose joy of her is overwhelmed like mine,
10   And bid him speak of patience.
Measure his woe the length and breadth of mine,
And let it answer every strain for strain,
As thus for thus, and such a grief for such,
In every lineament, branch, shape, and form.
15   If such a one will smile and stroke his beard,
Bid sorrow wag, cry "hem!" when he should groan,
Patch grief with proverbs, make misfortune drunk
With candlewasters,[93] bring him yet to me,
And I of him will gather patience.
20   But there is no such man. For, Brother, men
Can counsel and speak comfort to that grief
Which they themselves not feel; but, tasting it,
Their counsel turns to passion, which before
Would give preceptial medicine to rage,
25   Fetter strong madness in a silken thread,
Charm ache with air, and agony with words.
No, no, 'tis all men's office to speak patience

---

[93] People who stay up late.

To those that wring under the load of sorrow,
But no man's virtue nor sufficiency
30 To be so moral when he shall endure
The like himself. Therefore give me no counsel.
My griefs cry louder than advértisement.
ANTONIO: Therein do men from children nothing differ.
LEONATO: I pray thee, peace. I will be flesh and blood.
35 For there was never yet philosopher
That could endure the toothache patiently,
However they have writ the style of gods
And made a push at chance and sufferance.
ANTONIO: Yet bend not all the harm upon yourself.
40 Make those that do offend you suffer too.
LEONATO: There thou speak'st reason. Nay, I will do so.
My soul doth tell me Hero is belied,
And that shall Claudio know, so shall the Prince,
And all of them that thus dishonor her.
45 **ANTONIO:** Here comes the Prince and Claudio hastily.

(Enter Don Pedro and Claudio.)

DON PEDRO: Good-den, good-den.
CLAUDIO: Good day to both of you.
LEONATO: Hear you, my lords—
DON PEDRO: We have some haste, Leonato.
LEONATO: Some haste, my lord! Well, fare you well, my lord.
50 Are you so hasty now? Well, all is one.
DON PEDRO: Nay, do not quarrel with us, good old man.
ANTONIO: If he could right himself with quarreling,
Some of us would lie low.
CLAUDIO: Who wrongs him?
LEONATO: Marry, thou dost wrong me, thou dissembler, thou.—
55 Nay, never lay thy hand upon thy sword.
I fear thee not.
CLAUDIO: Marry,[94] beshrew[95] my hand
If it should give your age such cause of fear.
In faith, my hand meant nothing to my sword.
LEONATO: Tush, tush, man, never fleer[96] and jest at me.
60 I speak not like a dotard nor a fool,
As, under privilege of age, to brag
What I have done being young, or what would do
Were I not old. Know, Claudio, to thy head,
Thou hast so wronged mine innocent child and me

---

[94] Virgin Mary.   [95] Curse.   [96] Sneer.

65   That I am forced to lay my reverence by,
       And, with gray hairs and bruise of many days,
       Do challenge thee to trial of a man.
       I say thou hast belied mine innocent child.
       Thy slander hath gone through and through her heart,
70   And she lies buried with her ancestors,
       Oh, in a tomb where never scandal slept
       Save this of hers, framed by thy villainy!
CLAUDIO: My villainy?
LEONATO: Thine, Claudio, thine, I say.
DON PEDRO: You say not right, old man.
LEONATO: My lord, my lord,
75   I'll prove it on his body, if he dare,
       Despite his nice fence and his active practice,
       His May of youth and bloom of lustihood.[97]
CLAUDIO: Away! I will not have to do with you.
LEONATO: Canst thou so daff me? Thou hast killed my child.
80   If thou kill'st me, boy, thou shalt kill a man.
ANTONIO: He shall kill two of us, and men indeed.
       But that's no matter, let him kill one first,
       Win me and wear me. Let him answer me.
       Come, follow me, boy, come, sir boy, come, follow me.
85   Sir boy, I'll whip you from your foining[98] fence,
       Nay, as I am a gentleman, I will.
LEONATO: Brother—
ANTONIO: Content yourself. God knows I loved my niece,
       And she is dead, slandered to death by villains
90   That dare as well answer a man indeed
       As I dare take a serpent by the tongue.
       Boys, apes, braggarts, Jacks, milksops!
LEONATO: Brother Antony—
ANTONIO: Hold you content. What, man! I know them, yea,
95   And what they weigh, even to the utmost scruple
       Scambling, outfacing, fashion-monging boys
       That lie, and cog,[99] and flout, deprave and slander,
       Go antiquely[100] and show outward hideousness,
       And speak off half a dozen dangerous words,
100   How they might hurt their enemies if they durst—
       And this is all.
LEONATO: But, Brother Antony—
ANTONIO: Come, 'tis no matter.
       Do not you meddle, let me deal in this.

---

[97] Manhood.   [98] Thrusting.   [99] Cheat.   [100] As buffoons.

DON PEDRO: Gentlemen both, we will not wake your patience.
105   My heart is sorry for your daughter's death.
     But, on my honor, she was charged with nothing
     But what was true, and very full of proof.
LEONATO: My lord, my lord—
DON PEDRO: I will not hear you.
110 **LEONATO:** No? Come, Brother, away! I will be heard.
ANTONIO: And shall, or some of us will smart for it.

(Exeunt Leonato and Antonio.)

DON PEDRO: See, see, here comes the man we went to seek.

(Enter Benedick.)

CLAUDIO: Now, signior, what news?
BENEDICK: Good day, my lord.
115 **DON PEDRO:** Welcome, signior. You are almost come to part almost a
     fray.
CLAUDIO: We had like to have had our two noses snapped off with two
     old men without teeth.
DON PEDRO: Leonato and his brother. What thinkest thou? Had we
120   fought, I doubt we should have been too young for them.
BENEDICK: In a false quarrel there is no true valor. I came to seek you
     both.
CLAUDIO: We have been up and down to seek thee, for we are high-
     proof melancholy and would fain have it beaten away. Wilt thou use
125   thy wit?
BENEDICK: It is in my scabbard. Shall I draw it?
DON PEDRO: Dost thou wear thy wit by thy side?
CLAUDIO: Never any did so, though very many have been beside their
     wit. I will bid thee draw as we do the minstrels, draw to pleasure us.
130 **DON PEDRO:** As I am an honest man, he looks pale. Art thou sick, or
     angry?
CLAUDIO: What, courage, man! What though care killed a cat, thou hast
     mettle enough in thee to kill care.
BENEDICK: Sir, I shall meet your wit in the career, an you charge it
135   against me. I pray you choose another subject.
CLAUDIO: Nay, then, give him another staff. This last was broke cross.
DON PEDRO: By this light, he changes more and more. I think he be
     angry indeed.
CLAUDIO: If he be, he knows how to turn his girdle.
140 **BENEDICK:** Shall I speak a word in your ear?
CLAUDIO: God bless me from a challenge!
BENEDICK: *(Aside to Claudio)* You are a villain. I jest not. I will make it
     good how you dare, with what you dare, and when you dare. Do me
     right, or I will protest your cowardice. You have killed a sweet lady,
145   and her death shall fall heavy on you. Let me hear from you.

CLAUDIO: Well, I will meet you, so I may have good cheer.[101]

DON PEDRO: What, a feast, a feast?

CLAUDIO: I' faith, I thank him. He hath bid me to a calf's head and a capon, the which if I do not carve most curiously, say my knife's
150   naught. Shall I not find a woodcock[102] too?

BENEDICK: Sir, your wit ambles well, it goes easily.

DON PEDRO: I'll tell thee how Beatrice praised thy wit the other day. I said thou hadst a fine wit. "True," said she, "a fine little one." "No," said I, "a great wit." "Right," says she, "a great gross one." "Nay," said
155   I, "a good wit." "Just," said she, "it hurts nobody." "Nay," said I, "the gentleman is wise." "Certain," said she, "a wise gentleman." "Nay," said I, "he hath the tongues." "That I believe," said she, "for he swore a thing to me on Monday night which he forswore on Tuesday morning. There's a double tongue, there's two tongues." Thus did she,
160   an hour together, transshape thy particular virtues. Yet at last she concluded, with a sigh, thou wast the properest man in Italy.

CLAUDIO: For the which she wept heartily, and said she cared not.

DON PEDRO: Yea, that she did, but yet, for all that, an if she did not hate him deadly, she would love him dearly. The old man's daughter
165   told us all.

CLAUDIO: All, all, and, moreover, God saw him when he was hid in the garden.

DON PEDRO: But when shall we set the savage bull's horns on the sensible Benedick's head?

170   **CLAUDIO:**   Yea, and text underneath, "Here dwells Benedick the married man"?

BENEDICK: Fare you well, boy. You know my mind. I will leave you now to your gossiplike humor. You break jests as braggarts do their blades, which, God be thanked, hurt not. My lord, for your many courtesies I
175   thank you. I must discontinue your company. Your brother the bastard is fled from Messina. You have among you killed a sweet and innocent lady. For my Lord Lackbeard there, he and I shall meet, and till then peace be with him.

(Exit.)

DON PEDRO: He is in earnest.

180   **CLAUDIO:**   In most profound earnest, and I'll warrant you for the love of Beatrice.

DON PEDRO: And hath challenged thee.

CLAUDIO: Most sincerely.

DON PEDRO: What a pretty thing man is when he goes in his doublet
185   and hose and leaves off his wit!

---

[101] Entertainment.   [102] A foolish bird.

CLAUDIO: He is then a giant to an ape, but then is an ape a doctor to such a man.

DON PEDRO: But, soft you, let me be. Pluck up, my heart, and be sad.[103] Did he not say my brother was fled?

(Enter Dogberry, Verges, and the Watch, with Conrade and Borachio.)

190 **DOGBERRY:** Come, you, sir. If justice cannot tame you, she shall ne'er weigh more reasons in her balance. Nay, an you be a cursing hypocrite once, you must be looked to.

DON PEDRO: How now? Two of my brother's men bound! Borachio one!

CLAUDIO: Hearken after their offense, my lord.

195 **DON PEDRO:** Officers, what offense have these men done?

DOGBERRY: Marry, sir, they have committed false report; moreover, they have spoken untruths; secondarily, they are slanders; sixth and lastly, they have belied a lady; thirdly, they have verified unjust things; and, to conclude, they are lying knaves.

200 **DON PEDRO:** First, I ask thee what they have done; thirdly, I ask thee what's their offense; sixth and lastly, why they are committed; and, to conclude, what you lay to their charge.

CLAUDIO: Rightly reasoned, and in his own division, and, by my troth, there's one meaning well suited.

205 **DON PEDRO:** Who have you offended, masters, that you are thus bound to your answer? This learned constable is too cunning to be understood. What's your offense?

BORACHIO: Sweet Prince, let me go no farther to mine answer. Do you hear me, and let this Count kill me. I have deceived even your very
210 eyes. What your wisdoms could not discover, these shallow fools have brought to light, who in the night overheard me confessing to this man how Don John your brother incensed me to slander the Lady Hero; how you were brought into the orchard and saw me court Margaret in Hero's garments; how you disgraced her, when you
215 should marry her. My villainy they have upon record, which I had rather seal with my death than repeat over to my shame. The lady is dead upon mine and my master's false accusation, and, briefly, I desire nothing but the reward of a villain.

DON PEDRO: Runs not this speech like iron through your blood?

220 **CLAUDIO:** I have drunk poison whiles he uttered it.

DON PEDRO: But did my brother set thee onto this?

BORACHIO: Yea, and paid me richly for the practice of it.

DON PEDRO: He is composed and framed of treachery,
And fled he is upon this villainy.

225 **CLAUDIO:** Sweet Hero! Now thy image doth appear
In the rare semblance that I loved it first.

---

[103] Serious.

DOGBERRY: Come, bring away the plaintiffs.[104] By this time our sexton
hath reformed[105] Signior Leonato of the matter. And, masters, do not
forget to specify, when time and place shall serve, that I am an ass.

230 **VERGES:**   Here, here comes Master Signior Leonato, and the sexton too.

(Re-enter Leonato and Antonio, with the Sexton.)

LEONATO: Which is the villain? Let me see his eyes,
That when I note another man like him,
I may avoid him. Which of these is he?

BORACHIO: If you would know your wronger, look on me.

235 **LEONATO:**   Art thou the slave that with thy breath hast killed
Mine innocent child?

BORACHIO: Yea, even I alone.

LEONATO: No, not so, villain, thou beliest thyself.
Here stand a pair of honorable men,
A third is fled that had a hand in it.

240 I thank you, Princes, for my daughter's death.
Record it with your high and worthy deeds.
'Twas bravely done, if you bethink you of it.

CLAUDIO: I know not how to pray your patience,
Yet I must speak. Choose your revenge yourself,

245 Impose me to what penance your invention
Can lay upon my sin. Yet sinned I not
But in mistaking.

DON PEDRO: By my soul, nor I.
And yet to satisfy this good old man
I would bend under any heavy weight

250 That he'll enjoin me to.

LEONATO: I cannot bid you bid my daughter live,
That were impossible. But I pray you both
Possess the people in Messina here
How innocent she died, and if your love

255 Can labor aught in sad invention,
Hang her an epitaph upon her tomb,
And sing it to her bones, sing it tonight.
Tomorrow morning come you to my house,
And since you could not be my son-in-law,

260 Be yet my nephew. My brother hath a daughter,
Almost the copy of my child that's dead,
And she alone is heir to both of us.
Give her the right you should have given her cousin,
And so dies my revenge.

---

[104] Defendants, the accused.   [105] Informed.

Claudio: O noble sir,

265   Your overkindness doth wring tears from me!
       I do embrace your offer, and dispose
       For henceforth of poor Claudio.

Leonato: Tomorrow, then, I will expect your coming,
       Tonight I take my leave. This naughty man

270   Shall face to face be brought to Margaret,
       Who I believe was packed[106] in all this wrong,
       Hired to it by your brother.

Borachio: No, by my soul, she was not,
       Nor knew not what she did when she spoke to me,
       But always hath been just and virtuous

275   In anything that I do know by her.

Dogberry: Moreover, sir, which indeed is not under white and black,
       this plaintiff here, the offender, did call me ass. I beseech you, let it
       be remembered in his punishment. And also, the watch heard them
       talk of one Deformed. They say he wears a key in his ear, and a lock

280   hanging by it, and borrows money in God's name, the which he hath
       used so long and never paid that now men grow hardhearted and will
       lend nothing for God's sake. Pray you examine him upon that point.

Leonato: I thank thee for thy care and honest pains.

Dogberry: Your Worship speaks like a most thankful and reverend

285   youth, and I praise God for you.

Leonato: There's for thy pains.

Dogberry: God save the foundation![107]

Leonato: Go. I discharge thee of thy prisoner, and I thank thee.

Dogberry: I leave an arrant knave with your Worship, which I beseech

290   your Worship to correct yourself, for the example of others. God keep
       your Worship! I wish your Worship well. God restore you to health! I
       humbly give you leave to depart, and if a merry meeting may be
       wished, God prohibit it! Come, neighbor.

(Exeunt Dogberry and Verges.)

Leonato: Until tomorrow morning, lords, farewell.

295 **Antonio:**   Farewell, my lords. We look for you tomorrow.

Don Pedro: We will not fail.

Claudio: Tonight I'll mourn with Hero.

Leonato: *(To the Watch)* Bring you these fellows on. We'll talk with
       Margaret,
       How her acquaintance grew with this lewd fellow.

(Exeunt, severally.)

---

[106] Accomplice.   [107] This noble house.

SCENE II. LEONATO'S GARDEN.

(Enter Benedick and Margaret, meeting.)

BENEDICK: Pray thee, sweet Mistress Margaret, deserve well at my hand
  by helping me to the speech of Beatrice.
MARGARET: Will you, then, write me a sonnet in praise of my beauty?
BENEDICK: In so high a style, Margaret, that no man living shall come
5   over it, for, in most comely truth, thou deservest it.
MARGARET: To have no man come over me! Why, shall I always keep
  belowstairs?[108]
BENEDICK: Thy wit is as quick as the greyhound's mouth. It catches.
MARGARET: And yours as blunt as the fencer's foils, which hit but hurt
10   not.
BENEDICK: A most manly wit, Margaret. It will not hurt a woman. And
  so, I pray thee call Beatrice. I give thee the bucklers.
MARGARET: Give us the swords, we have bucklers of our own.
BENEDICK: If you use them, Margaret, you must put in the pikes[109] with
15   a vice, and they are dangerous weapons for maids.
MARGARET: Well, I will call Beatrice to you, who I think hath legs.
BENEDICK: And therefore will come.

(Exit Margaret.)

(Sings.)   "The god of love,
                                         That sits above,
20   And knows me, and knows me,
                                     How pitiful I deserve—"

I mean in singing, but in loving, Leander the good swimmer,
Troilus[110] the first employer of panders, and a whole bookful of these
quondam[111] carpetmongers[112] whose names yet run smoothly in the
25   even road of a blank verse, why, they were never so truly turned over
and over as my poor self in love. Marry, I cannot show it in rhyme. I
have tried. I can find out no rhyme to "lady" but "baby," an
innocent rhyme; for "scorn," "horn," a hard rhyme; for "school,"
"fool," a babbling rhyme—very ominous endings. No, I was not born
30   under a rhyming planet, nor I cannot woo in festival terms. *(Enter
Beatrice.)* Sweet Beatrice, wouldst thou come when I called thee?
BEATRICE: Yea, signior, and depart when you bid me.
BENEDICK: Oh, stay but till then!

---

[108] As the servants.   [109] Spikes.   [110] Character in *Troilus and Cryseida*.   [111] Former.   [112] Self-proclaimed generals who have distinguished themselves on the carpet and not on the field of battle.

BEATRICE: "Then" is spoken, fare you well now. And yet ere I go let me
35   go with that I came, which is, with knowing what hath passed
        between you and Claudio.

BENEDICK: Only foul words, and thereupon I will kiss thee.

BEATRICE: Foul words is but foul wind, and foul wind is but foul breath,
        and foul breath is noisome. Therefore I will depart unkissed.

40 **BENEDICK:** Thou hast frighted the word out of his right sense, so
        forcible is thy wit. But I must tell thee plainly, Claudio undergoes my
        challenge, and either I must shortly hear from him or I will subscribe
        him a coward. And I pray thee now, tell me for which of my bad parts
        didst thou first fall in love with me?

45 **BEATRICE:** For them all together, which maintained so politic a state of
        evil that they will not admit any good part to intermingle with them.
        But for which of my good parts did you first suffer love for me?

BENEDICK: Suffer love—a good epithet! I do suffer love indeed, for I love
        thee against my will.

50 **BEATRICE:** In spite of your heart, I think—alas, poor heart! If you spite
        it for my sake, I will spite it for yours, for I will never love that which
        my friend hates.

BENEDICK: Thou and I are too wise to woo peaceably.

BEATRICE: It appears not in this confession. There's not one wise man
55   among twenty that will praise himself.

BENEDICK: An old, an old instance, Beatrice, that lived in the time of
        good neighbors. If a man do not erect in this age his own tomb ere he
        dies, he shall live no longer in monument than the bell rings and the
        widow weeps.

60 **BEATRICE:** And how long is that, think you?

BENEDICK: Question. Why, an hour in clamor and a quarter in
        rheum.[113] Therefore is it most expedient for the wise, if Don Worm,
        his conscience, find no impediment to the contrary, to be the
        trumpet of his own virtues, as I am to myself. So much for praising
65   myself, who, I myself will bear witness, is praiseworthy. And now tell
        me, how doth your cousin?

BEATRICE: Very ill.

BENEDICK: And how do you?

BEATRICE: Very ill too.

70 **BENEDICK:** Serve God, love me, and mend. There will I leave you too,
        for here comes one in haste.

(Enter Ursula.)

URSULA: Madam, you must come to your uncle. Yonder's old coil at
        home. It is proved my Lady Hero hath been falsely accused, the

---

[113] Moisture.

Prince and Claudio mightily abused. And Don John is the author of
75   all, who is fled and gone. Will you come presently?
BEATRICE: Will you go hear this news, signior?
BENEDICK: I will live in thy heart, die in thy lap, and be buried in thy
eyes, and moreover I will go with thee to thy uncle's.

(Exeunt.)

SCENE III.   A CHURCH.

(Enter Don Pedro, Claudio, and three or four with tapers.)

CLAUDIO: Is this the monument of Leonato?
A LORD: It is, my lord.
CLAUDIO: *(Reading out of a scroll.)*
"Done to death by slanderous tongues
5   Was the Hero that here lies.
Death, in guerdon[114] of her wrongs,
    Gives her fame which never dies.
So the life that died with shame
Lives in death with glorious fame."
10   Hang thou there upon the tomb,
Praising her when I am dumb.
Now, music, sound, and sing your solemn hymn.

SONG

Pardon, goddess of the night,
15   Those that slew thy virgin knight,
For the which, with songs of woe,
Round about her tomb they go.
    Midnight, assist our moan,
    Help us to sigh and groan,
20   Heavily, heavily.
Graves, yawn, and yield your dead,
    Till death be utterèd,
        Heavily, heavily.

CLAUDIO: Now, unto thy bones good night!
25   Yearly will I do this rite.
DON PEDRO: Good morrow, masters. Put your torches out.
The wolves have preyed, and look, the gentle day,
Before the wheels of Phoebus,[115] round about

---

[114] Reward.   [115] The sungod's chariot wheels.

Dapples the drowsy east with spots of gray.
30   Thanks to you all, and leave us. Fare you well.
CLAUDIO: Good morrow, masters. Each his several way.
DON PEDRO: Come, let us hence and put on other weeds,
And then to Leonato's we will go.
CLAUDIO: And Hymen[116] now with luckier issue speed's
35   Than this for whom we rendered up this woe.

(Exeunt.)

SCENE IV. A ROOM IN
LEONATO'S HOUSE.

(Enter Leonato, Antonio, Benedick, Beatrice, Margaret, Ursula, Friar Frances, and Hero.)

FRIAR FRANCIS: Did I not tell you she was innocent?
LEONATO: So are the Prince and Claudio, who accused her
Upon the error that you heard debated.
But Margaret was in some fault for this,
5   Although against her will, as it appears
In the true course of all the question.
ANTONIO: Well, I am glad that all things sort so well.
BENEDICK: And so am I, being else by faith enforced
To call young Claudio to a reckoning for it.
10 **LEONATO:** Well, Daughter, and you gentlewomen all,
Withdraw into a chamber by yourselves,
And when I send for you, come hither masked.

(Exeunt Ladies.)

The Prince and Claudio promised by this hour
To visit me. You know your office, Brother.
15   You must be father to your brother's daughter,
And give her to young Claudio.
ANTONIO: Which I will do with confirmed countenance.
BENEDICK: Friar, I must entreat your pains, I think.
FRIAR FRANCIS: To do what, signior?
20 **BENEDICK:** To bind me, or undo me, one of them.
Signior Leonato, truth it is, good signior,
Your niece regards me with an eye of favor.
LEONATO: That eye my daughter lent her—'tis most true.
BENEDICK: And I do with an eye of love requite her.

---

[116] God of marriage.

25 **LEONATO:**   The sight whereof I think you had from me,
From Claudio, and the Prince. But what's your will?
BENEDICK: Your answer, sir, is enigmatical.
But, for my will, my will is, your goodwill
May stand with ours, this day to be conjoined
30 In the state of honorable marriage.
In which, good Friar, I shall desire your help.
LEONATO: My heart is with your liking.
FRIAR FRANCIS: And my help.
Here comes the Prince and Claudio.

(Enter Don Pedro and Claudio, and two or three others.)

DON PEDRO: Good morrow to this fair assembly.
35 **LEONATO:**   Good morrow, Prince. Good morrow, Claudio.
We here attend you. Are you yet determined
Today to marry with my brother's daughter?
CLAUDIO: I'll hold my mind, were she an Ethiope.
LEONATO: Call her forth, Brother, here's the Friar ready. *(Exit Antonio.)*
40 **DON PEDRO:**   Good morrow, Benedick. Why, what's the matter
That you have such a February face,
So full of frost, of storm, and cloudiness?
CLAUDIO: I think he thinks upon the savage bull.
Tush, fear not, man, we'll tip thy horns with gold,
45 And all Europa[117] shall rejoice at thee
As once Europa[118] did at lusty Jove
When he would play the noble beast in love.
BENEDICK: Bull Jove, sir, had an amiable low,
And some such strange bull leaped your father's cow
50 And got a calf in that same noble feat
Much like to you, for you have just his bleat.
CLAUDIO: For this I owe you. Here comes other reckonings.
(Re-enter Antonio, with the Ladies masked.) Which is the lady I must
seize upon?
55 **ANTONIO:**   This same is she, and I do give you her.
CLAUDIO: Why, then she's mine. Sweet, let me see your face.
LEONATO: No, that you shall not till you take her hand
Before this Friar and swear to marry her.
CLAUDIO: Give me your hand. Before this holy Friar,
60 I am your husband, if you like of me.
HERO: And when I lived, I was your other wife, *(Unmasking)*
And when you loved, you were my other husband.
CLAUDIO: Another Hero!

---

[117] Europe.   [118] The maiden whose love Jupiter won while disguised as a bull.

HERO: Nothing certainer.
One Hero died defiled, but I do live,
65   And surely as I live, I am a maid.
DON PEDRO: The former Hero! Hero that is dead!
LEONATO: She died, my lord, but whiles her slander lived.
FRIAR FRANCIS: All this amazement can I qualify.
When after that the holy rites are ended,
70   I'll tell you largely of fair Hero's death.
Meantime let wonder seem familiar,
And to the chapel let us presently.
BENEDICK: Soft and fair, Friar. Which is Beatrice?
BEATRICE: *(Unmasking)* I answer to that name. What is your will?
75 **BENEDICK:**   Do not you love me?
BEATRICE: Why, no, no more than reason.
BENEDICK: Why, then your uncle, and the Prince, and Claudio
Have been deceived. They swore you did.
BEATRICE: Do not you love me?
BENEDICK: Troth, no, no more than reason.
BEATRICE: Why, then my cousin, Margaret, and Ursula
80   Are much deceived, for they did swear you did.
BENEDICK: They swore that you were almost sick for me.
BEATRICE: They swore that you were well-nigh dead for me.
BENEDICK: 'Tis no such matter. Then you do not love me?
BEATRICE: No, truly, but in friendly recompense.
85 **LEONATO:**   Come, Cousin, I am sure you love the gentleman.
CLAUDIO: And I'll be sworn upon 't that he loves her,
For here's a paper, written in his hand,
A halting sonnet of his own pure brain,
Fashioned to Beatrice.
HERO.   And here's another,
90   Writ in my cousin's hand, stolen from her pocket,
Containing her affection unto Benedick.
BENEDICK: A miracle! Here's our own hands against our hearts. Come, I
will have thee, but, by this light, I take thee for pity.
BEATRICE: I would not deny you, but, by this good day, I yield upon
95   great persuasion, and partly to save your life, for I was told you were
in a consumption.
BENEDICK: Peace! I will stop your mouth. *(Kissing her)*
DON PEDRO: How dost thou, Benedick the married man?
BENEDICK: I'll tell thee what, Prince, a college of witcrackers cannot
100   flout me out of my humor. Dost thou think I care for a satire or an
epigram? No. If a man will be beaten with brains, a' shall wear
nothing handsome about him. In brief, since I do purpose to marry, I
will think nothing to any purpose that the world can say against it;
and therefore never flout at me for what I have said against it, for
105   man is a giddy thing, and this is my conclusion. For thy part,

Claudio, I did think to have beaten thee, but in that thou art like to be my kinsman, live unbruised, and love my cousin.

CLAUDIO: I had well hoped thou wouldst have denied Beatrice, that I might have cudgeled thee out of thy single life, to make thee a
110   double-dealer, which, out of question, thou wilt be if my cousin do not look exceeding narrowly to thee.

BENEDICK: Come, come, we are friends. Let's have a dance ere we are married, that we may lighten our own hearts and our wives' heels.

LEONATO: We'll have dancing afterward.

115 **BENEDICK:**   First, of my word, therefore play, music. Prince, thou art sad. Get thee a wife, get thee a wife. There is no staff[119] more reverend than one tipped with horn.

(Enter a Messenger.)

MESSENGER: My lord, your brother John is ta'en in flight,
And brought with armed men back to Messina.

120 **BENEDICK:**   Think not on him till tomorrow. I'll devise thee brave punishments for him. Strike up, pipers! *(Dance. Exeunt.)*

READING AND REACTING

1. *Much Ado about Nothing* contains very few stage directions. How does Shakespeare establish the settings of the play? How does he indicate the actions and appearances of the various characters?

2. What scenery would you use in the play? Would you use realistic scenery, or would you use unrealistic sets that just suggest objects and locations?

3. In the 1995 movie version of this play, Don Pedro was played by Denzel Washington, an African-American. What do you think of this choice? What contemporary actors would you cast as Beatrice, Benedick, Claudio, Hero, Don John, and Dogberry?

4. In Act 2, Scene 1, the characters attend a *masque,* a masquerade in which members of the court put on masks and costumes. How would you stage this event? For example, how would you use lighting and music?

5. What hints are there that Beatrice and Benedick care more for each other than they admit?

6. How is Beatrice and Benedick's relationship different from that of Hero and Claudio? Which couple would you say has more traditional ideas about love and marriage? Which couple's marriage do you think will be more successful?

7. The conversations between Claudio and Hero are written almost entirely in verse, whereas Beatrice and Benedick argue almost entirely

---

[119] Walking stick.

in prose. How might you account for this? What do you make of the fact that an exception occurs when Beatrice hears that Benedick loves her (3.1.107–116)?

8. *Much Ado about Nothing* was long known by the title *Beatrice and Benedick.* Which title do you think better represents the focus of the play? Why?

9. Is Don John a complex character or just a plot device? What function does he serve in the play?

10. **JOURNAL ENTRY** Do you think Hero should still marry Claudio, even after he humiliates her at their wedding? Why do you think she marries him?

11. **CRITICAL PERSPECTIVE** In *Shakespeare's Plays in Performance,* John Russell Brown discusses possible stage interpretations of Act 4, Scene 1, line 282 of *Much Ado about Nothing,* beginning when Beatrice implores Benedick to "Kill Claudio." Benedick refuses, saying, "Ha! Not for the wide world," and Beatrice replies, "You kill me to deny it. Farewell."

Dramatic interest is here dependent entirely on what has gone before, sustaining the words but not fully expressed by them. Some Beatrices break away to leave Benedick and the place where they have met, so that he has to cry out 'Tarry, sweet Beatrice,' and hurry to hold her back. But there are many ways of playing this moment. Beatrice may have been overcome by thoughts of love as soon as she spoke of them, and all that followed was a struggle to return to other concerns; so she might now find it impossible to leave Benedick and as she says 'Farewell' she does not move. Or she may have seized the opportunity to persuade Benedick to kill Claudio as a way of testing his worth, so that she spoke with conviction and energy and now adds to the pressure by leaving without sign of reluctance or indecision. Or the two may have been drawn together from the very start of this dialogue, while Beatrice was still weeping, and now hold each other in their arms; the whole exchange would then be very quiet, and Beatrice may now be telling herself to leave, but without any effect until she begins to regain her wits with: 'I am gone though I am here; there is no love in you; nay, I pray you, let me go.'

Reread the scene, and describe how you envision it.

EDWARD ALBEE (1928–) was abandoned by his parents as an infant and adopted by a wealthy couple, Reed and Frances Albee. He was always a writer, producing two unpublished novels in his teens, but did not turn to playwriting until his thirtieth birthday. A rebellious teenager, he was expelled from several schools and then lasted only a year at Trinity College. Now one of America's foremost and most controversial playwrights in the theater of the absurd, his most famous plays are *The Zoo Story* (1958), *The American Dream* (1961), *Who's Afraid of Virginia Woolf?* (1962), *The Marriage Play* (1992), and *Three Tall Women* (1994), which won Albee his third Pulitzer Prize. *The Sandbox* (1960), a one-act play, is closely related to *The American Dream.* Not only are the plays related thematically, but they also share the same characters. In 1985 Albee was playwright-in-residence at the University of Houston, where he wrote *Sand,* a collection of thematically related plays including *The Sandbox,* only fifteen minutes long. "With the possible exception of the little play *The Sandbox* . . . I don't think anything I've done has worked out to perfection," he said in an interview in 1966. In 1975, when an interviewer asked him which was his favorite play, he replied, "I'm terribly fond of *The Sandbox.* I think it's an absolutely beautiful, lovely little play."

EDWARD ALBEE

The Sandbox

(1960)

A Brief Play, in Memory of My Grandmother (1876–1959)

CHARACTERS

THE YOUNG MAN 25, *a good-looking, well-built boy in a bathing suit*
MOMMY 55, *a well-dressed, imposing woman*
DADDY 60, *a small man; gray, thin*
GRANDMA 86, *a tiny, wizened woman with bright eyes*
THE MUSICIAN *no particular age, but young would be nice*

NOTE. *When, in the course of the play, Mommy and Daddy call each other by these names, there should be no suggestion of regionalism. These names are of empty affection and point up the pre-senility and vacuity of their characters.*

THE SCENE. *A bare stage, with only the following: Near the footlights, far stage-right, two simple chairs set side by side, facing the audience; near the footlights, far stage-left, a chair facing stage-right with a music stand before it; farther back, and stage-center, slightly elevated and raked, a large child's sandbox with a toy pail and shovel; the background is the sky, which alters from brightest day to deepest night.*

At the beginning, it is brightest day; the Young Man is alone on stage to the rear of the sandbox, and to one side. He is doing calisthenics; he does calisthenics until quite at the very end of the play. These calisthenics, employing the arms only, should suggest the beating and fluttering of wings. The Young Man is, after all, the Angel of Death.

Mommy and Daddy enter from stage-left, Mommy first.

MOMMY: *(motioning to Daddy)* Well, here we are; this is the beach.

DADDY: *(whining)* I'm cold.

MOMMY: *(dismissing him with a little laugh)* Don't be silly; it's as warm as toast. Look at that nice young man over there: *he* doesn't think it's cold. *(Waves to the Young Man)* Hello.

YOUNG MAN: *(with an endearing smile)* Hi!

5   **MOMMY:**   *(looking about)* This will do perfectly . . . don't you think so, Daddy? There's sand there . . . and the water beyond. What do you think, Daddy?

DADDY: *(vaguely)* Whatever you say, Mommy.

MOMMY: *(with the same little laugh)* Well, of course . . . whatever I say. Then, it's settled, is it?

DADDY: *(shrugs)* She's *your* mother, not mine.

MOMMY: I know she's my mother. What do you take me for? *(A pause)* All right, now; let's get on with it. *(She shouts into the wings, stage-left)* You! Out there! You can come in now. *(The Musician enters, seats himself in the chair, stage-left, places music on the music stand, is ready to play. Mommy nods approvingly.)* Very nice; very nice. Are you ready, Daddy? Let's go get Grandma.

10   **DADDY:**   Whatever you say, Mommy.

MOMMY: *(leading the way out, stage-left)* Of course, whatever I say. *(To the Musician)* You can begin now. *(The Musician begins playing; Mommy and Daddy exit; the Musician, all the while playing, nods to the Young Man.)*

YOUNG MAN: *(with the same endearing smile)* Hi! *(After a moment, Mommy and Daddy re-enter, carrying Grandma. She is borne in by their hands under her armpits; she is quite rigid; her legs are drawn up; her feet do not touch the ground; the expression on her ancient face is that of puzzlement and fear.)*

DADDY: Where do we put her?

MOMMY: *(the same little laugh)* Wherever I say, of course. Let me see . . . well . . . all right, over there . . . in the sandbox. *(Pause)* Well, what are you waiting for, Daddy? . . . The sandbox! *(Together they carry Grandma over to the sandbox and more or less dump her in.)*

15   **GRANDMA:**   *(righting herself to a sitting position; her voice a cross between a baby's laugh and cry)* Ahhhhhh! Graaaaa!

DADDY: *(dusting himself)* What do we do now?

MOMMY: *(to the Musician)* You can stop now. *(The Musician stops.)* *(Back to Daddy)* What do you mean, what do we do now? We go over there and sit down, of course. *(To the Young Man)* Hello there.

YOUNG MAN: *(again smiling)* Hi! *(Mommy and Daddy move to the chairs, stage-right, and sit down. A pause.)*

GRANDMA: *(same as before)* Ahhhhhh! Ah-haaaaaa! Graaaaaa!

20   **DADDY:**   Do you think . . . do you think she's . . . comfortable?

MOMMY: *(impatiently)* How would I know?

DADDY: *(pause)* What do we do now?

MOMMY: *(as if remembering)* We . . . wait. We . . . sit here . . . and we wait . . . that's what we do.

DADDY: *(after a pause)* Shall we talk to each other?

25 **MOMMY:** *(with that little laugh; picking something off her dress)* Well, *you* can talk, if you want to . . . if you can think of anything to say . . . if you can think of anything *new*.

DADDY: *(thinks)* No . . . I suppose not.

MOMMY: *(with a triumphant laugh)* Of course not!

GRANDMA: *(banging the toy shovel against the pail)* Haaaaaa! Ah-ha-aaaaa!

MOMMY: *(out over the audience)* Be quiet, Grandma . . . just be quiet, and wait. *(Grandma throws a shovelful of sand at Mommy. Still out over the audience)* She's throwing sand at me! You stop that, Grandma; you stop throwing sand at Mommy! *(To Daddy)* She's throwing sand at me. *(Daddy looks around at Grandma, who screams at him.)*

30 **GRANDMA:** GRAAAAA!

MOMMY: Don't look at her. Just . . . sit here . . . be very still . . . and wait. *(To the Musician)* You . . . uh . . . you go ahead and do whatever it is you do. *(The Musician plays. Mommy and Daddy are fixed, staring out beyond the audience. Grandma looks at them, looks at the Musician, looks at the sandbox, throws down the shovel.)*

GRANDMA: Ah-haaaaaa! Graaaaaa! *(Looks for reaction; gets none. Now . . . directly to the audience)* Honestly! What a way to treat an old woman! Drag her out of the house . . . stick her in a car . . . bring her out here from the city . . . dump her in a pile of sand . . . and leave her here to set. I'm eighty-six years old! I was married when I was seventeen. To a farmer. He died when I was thirty. *(To the Musician)* Will you stop that, please? *(The Musician stops playing.)* I'm a feeble old woman . . . how do you expect anybody to hear me over that peep! peep! peep! *(To herself)* There's no respect around here. *(To the Young Man)* There's no respect around here!

YOUNG MAN: *(same smile)* Hi!

GRANDMA: *(after a pause, a mild double-take, continues, to the audience)* My husband died when I was thirty *(indicates Mommy)*, and I had to raise that big cow over there all by my lonesome. You can imagine what *that was* like. Lordy! *(To the Young Man)* Where'd they get *you*?

35 **YOUNG MAN:** Oh . . . I've been around for a while.

GRANDMA: I'll bet you have! Heh, heh, heh. Will you look at you!

YOUNG MAN: *(flexing his muscles)* Isn't that something? *(Continues his calisthenics.)*

GRANDMA: Boy, oh boy; I'll say. Pretty good.

YOUNG MAN: *(sweetly)* I'll say.

40 **GRANDMA:** Where ya from?

YOUNG MAN: Southern California.

GRANDMA: *(nodding)* Figgers; figgers. What's your name, honey?

YOUNG MAN: I don't know . . .

GRANDMA: *(to the audience)* Bright, too!

45 **YOUNG MAN:** I mean . . . I mean, they haven't given me one yet . . . the studio . . .

GRANDMA: *(giving him the once-over)* You don't say . . . you don't say. Well . . . uh, I've got to talk some more . . . don't you go 'way.

YOUNG MAN: Oh, no.

GRANDMA: *(turning her attention back to the audience)* Fine; fine. *(Then, once more, back to the Young Man)* You're . . . you're an actor, hunh?

YOUNG MAN: *(beaming)* Yes. I am.

50 **GRANDMA:** *(to the audience again, shrugs)* I'm smart that way. *Anyhow*, I had to raise . . . *that* over there all by my lonesome; and what's next to her there . . . that's what she married. Rich? I tell you . . . money, money, money. They took me off the *farm* . . . which was real decent of them . . . and they moved me into the big town house with *them* . . . fixed a nice place for me under the stove . . . gave me an army blanket . . . and my own dish . . . my very own dish! So, what have I got to complain about? Nothing, of course. I'm not complaining. *(She looks up at the sky, shouts to someone off stage)* Shouldn't it be getting dark now, dear? *(The lights dim, night comes on. The Musician begins to play; it becomes deepest night. There are spots on all the players, including the Young Man, who is, of course, continuing his calisthenics.)*

DADDY: *(stirring)* It's nighttime.

MOMMY: Shhhh. Be still . . . wait.

DADDY: *(whining)* It's so hot.

MOMMY: Shhhhhh. Be still . . . wait.

55 **GRANDMA:** *(to herself)* That's better. Night. *(To the Musician)* Honey, do you play all through this part? *(The Musician nods.)* Well, keep it nice and soft; that's a good boy. *(The Musician nods again; plays softly.)* That's nice. *(There is an off-stage rumble.)*

DADDY: *(starting)* What was that?

MOMMY: *(beginning to weep)* It was nothing.

DADDY: It was . . . it was . . . thunder . . . or a wave breaking . . . or something.

MOMMY: *(whispering, through her tears)* It was an off-stage rumble . . . and you know what *that* means . . .

60 **DADDY:** I forget . . .

MOMMY: *(barely able to talk)* It means the time has come for poor Grandma . . . and I can't bear it!

DADDY: *(vacantly)* I . . . I suppose you've got to be brave.

GRANDMA: *(mocking)* That's right, kid; be brave. You'll bear up; you'll get over it. *(Another off-stage rumble . . . louder.)*

MOMMY: Ohhhhhhhhhh . . . poor Grandma . . . poor Grandma . . .

65 **GRANDMA:** *(to Mommy)* I'm fine! I'm all right! It hasn't happened yet! *(A violent off-stage rumble. All the lights go out, save the spot on the Young Man; the Musician stops playing.)*

MOMMY: Ohhhhhhhhhh . . . Ohhhhhhhhhh . . . *(Silence.)*

GRANDMA: Don't put the lights up yet . . . I'm not ready; I'm not quite ready. *(Silence)* All right, dear . . . I'm about done. *(The lights come up again, to brightest day; the Musician begins to play. Grandma is discovered, still in the sandbox, lying on her side, propped up on an elbow, half covered, busily shoveling sand over herself.)*

GRANDMA: *(muttering)* I don't know how I'm supposed to do anything with this goddam toy shovel . . .

DADDY: Mommy! It's daylight!

70 **MOMMY:** *(brightly)* So it is! Well! Our long night is over. We must put away our tears, take off our mourning . . . and face the future. It's our duty.

GRANDMA: *(still shoveling; mimicking)* . . . take off our mourning . . . face the future . . . Lordy! *(Mommy and Daddy rise, stretch. Mommy waves to the Young Man.)*

YOUNG MAN: *(with that smile)* Hi! *(Grandma plays dead. [!] Mommy and Daddy go over to look at her; she is a little more than half buried in the sand; the toy shovel is in her hands, which are crossed on her breast.)*

MOMMY: *(before the sandbox; shaking her head)* Lovely! It's . . . it's hard to be sad . . . she looks . . . so happy. *(With pride and conviction)* It pays to do things well. *(To the Musician)* All right, you can stop now, if you want to. I mean, stay around for a swim, or something; it's all right with us. *(She sighs heavily.)* Well, Daddy . . . off we go.

DADDY: Brave Mommy!

75 **MOMMY:** Brave Daddy! *(They exit, stage left.)*

GRANDMA: *(after they leave; lying quite still)* It pays to do things well . . . Boy, oh boy! *(She tries to sit up)* . . . well, kids . . . *(but she finds she can't)* . . . I . . . I can't get up. I . . . I can't move . . . *(The Young Man stops his calisthenics, nods to the Musician, walks over to Grandma, kneels down by the sandbox.)*

GRANDMA: I . . . can't move . . .

YOUNG MAN: Shhhhh . . . be very still . . .

GRANDMA: I . . . I can't move . . .

80 **YOUNG MAN:** Uh . . . ma'am; I . . . I have a line here.

GRANDMA: Oh, I'm sorry, sweetie; you go right ahead.

YOUNG MAN: I am . . . uh . . .

GRANDMA: Take your time, dear.

YOUNG MAN: *(prepares; delivers the line like a real amateur)* I am the Angel of Death. I am . . . uh . . . I am come for you.

85 **GRANDMA:** What . . . wha . . . *(then, with resignation)* . . . ohhhh . . . ohhhh, I see. *(The Young Man bends over, kisses Grandma gently on the forehead.)*

GRANDMA: *(her eyes closed, her hands folded on her breast again, the shovel between her hands, a sweet smile on her face)* Well . . . that was very nice, dear . . .

YOUNG MAN: *(still kneeling)* Shhhhh . . . be still . . .

GRANDMA: What I meant was . . . you did that very well, dear . . .

YOUNG MAN: *(blushing)* . . . oh . . .

90 **GRANDMA:** No; I mean it. You've got that . . . you've got a quality.

YOUNG MAN: *(with his endearing smile)* Oh . . . thank you; thank you very much . . . ma'am.

GRANDMA: *(slowly; softly—as the Young Man puts his hands on top of Grandma's)* You're . . . you're welcome . . . dear.

(Tableau. The Musician continues to play as the curtain slowly comes down.)

READING AND REACTING

1. Albee's characters are two-dimensional. What does he gain by creating such flat characters? What does he lose?

2. Albee says that there should be "no suggestion of regionalism" in the speech of Mommy and Daddy. What do you believe he is trying to achieve with this stage direction?

3. Why do you think Albee recommends a bare stage with just a few props?

4. What purpose is served by each of the following props: the music stand, the sandbox, the toy pail and shovel? Do you think any of these props has symbolic significance?

5. In what way do changes in lighting affect the mood of the play?

6. What do costumes reveal about each character in the play? Why, for example, is The Young Man dressed in a bathing suit?

7. What function is served by the musician playing? By the offstage rumble?

8. Why does Grandma bury herself with sand? How would you stage this event?

9. At various points Grandma directly addresses the audience, gives lighting directions, and signals the musician. At one point, The Young Man interrupts her, saying, "I have a line here." How do you react to these characters' calling attention to the fact that they are actors in a play?

10. **JOURNAL ENTRY** What does *The Sandbox* seem to be saying about the American family? Do you think the play's assessment of the family is accurate?

11. **CRITICAL PERSPECTIVE** Critic Mickey Pearlman has argued that Albee's women "epitomize the worst stereotypes of American females—Mommy is the evil, all-powerful emasculator . . . and Grandma is the pathetic, ill-used, and nameless saint figure. Do you agree? Or do you believe Pearlman is overstating his case?

WRITING SUGGESTIONS: STAGING

1. Choose either *Oedipus the King* or *Much Ado about Nothing* and discuss the problems its original staging poses for contemporary audiences.

2. Write an essay in which you discuss what staging elements of *The Sandbox* strike you as "absurd" (see p. 1143 for a definition of **theater of the absurd**). How do these absurd elements help to communicate the play's ideas?

3. In all of the plays in this chapter, place is important. Write an essay in which you discuss how the settings in two of these plays help the playwrights to express their respective themes.

4. Write a detailed set of stage directions for either *The Cuban Swimmer* or the first act of *Much Ado about Nothing*.

5. Suppose you were asked to update the staging of either *Oedipus the King* or *Much Ado about Nothing* for a contemporary production. What scenery, props, and costumes would you use to transform the setting to the 1990s?

CHAPTER 25

Theme

Plays are like doors to me. They can be as massive and ornate as cathedrals or as small and intimate as keyholes. They can be as real as the kitchen sink or as ephemeral as dreams. When we read them in the quiet or sit in a darkened theatre space and listen we step over the threshold of the door that the playwright has opened for us. We walk into their secret garden or jungle and hopefully we are taken on an adventurous odyssey.

MARSHA MASON, *WOMEN PLAYWRIGHTS*

[D]rama is one of the things that makes possible a solution to the problem of social-izing people. In other words, we are born private, and we die private, but we live of necessity in direct relation to other people, even if we live alone. And dramatic con-flict of significance always verges on and deals with the way men live together. And this is incomprehensible to Man as a private person. He is always trying to find out where he stands in his society, whether he uses those terms or not. He always wants to know whether his life has a meaning, and that meaning is always in relation to others. It is always in relation to his society, it's always in relation to his choices, to the absence of his choices, which are dominated by other people. I think that when we speak of dramatic significance we're really talking about, either openly or unknow-ingly, about the dilemma of living together, of living a social existence, and the con-flict is endless between Man and his fellows and between his own instincts and the social necessity.

ARTHUR MILLER, *THE PLAYWRIGHTS SPEAK*

You can say what you like in the theater within any reasonable bounds. You have a liberty of speech and editorial expression you can't find in any other dramatic medium. And you can present an idea for the consideration of intelligent audiences, which, of course, is completely outside the gaudiest opium dreams of possibility in Hollywood. They wouldn't know an idea if they saw it on the Coast, and if by any chance they should recognize it the film people would be frightened right out of their suede shoes. I'm not patronizing in my attitude toward the films, just realistic. And I say again that the presentation of something besides mere entertainment and spec-tacle is the great function of the legitimate theater of the world today.

LILLIAN HELLMAN, *CONVERSATIONS WITH LILLIAN HELLMAN*

At the end of Fences *every person, with the exception of Raynell, is institutional-
ized. Rose is in a church. Lyons is in a penitentiary. Gabriel's in a mental hospital,
and Cory's in the marines. The only free person is the girl, Troy's daughter, the hope
for the future. That was conscious on my part because in '57 that's what I saw.
Blacks have relied on institutions which are really foreign—except for the black
church, which has been our saving grace. I have some problems with it but I recognize it as a central social organization and sometimes an economic organization for
the black community. I would like to see blacks develop their own institutions that
respond to their needs.*

AUGUST WILSON, *IN THEIR OWN VOICES*

*I'd rather talk about the "reading" of my plays than the "meaning." Every time I
talk about meaning to people it sounds like they're trying to substitute something
else for what I've written. I've had so many interviews where someone would say,
"so what does it mean? . . ." That's basically saying, "you're being obscure and why
don't you tell us what you want, what you really mean," thinking the writer has
some sort of agenda that hides somewhere behind or underneath the text or behind
the production somewhere. . . .*

SUZAN-LORI PARKS, *DRAMA REVIEW*

Like a short story or a novel, a play is open to interpretation. Readers' reactions are influenced by the language of the text, and audiences' reactions
are affected by the performance on stage. Just as in fiction, every element
of a play—its title, its conflicts, its dialogue, its characters, and its staging,
for instance—can shed light on its themes.

TITLES

The title of a play can provide insight into the themes of a play. The ironic
title of Susan Glaspell's *Trifles* (p. 1172), for example, suggests that
women's concern with "trifles" may get to the heart of the matter more
efficiently than the preoccupations of self-important men do. Edward
Albee's *The Sandbox* (p. 1695) is another title that offers clues to a theme
of the play, suggesting that individuals in modern society are like children
in a sandbox, concerned only with satisfying their physical and material
needs. Finally, Anton Chekhov's *The Brute* (p. 1342) effectively calls attention to that play's ideas about male-female relationships. The title
may refer to Smirnov, who says that he has never liked women—whom he
characterizes as "creatures of poetry and romance." Or it may refer to

Mrs. Popov's late husband, to whose memory she has dedicated her life despite the fact that he was repeatedly unfaithful. Either alternative reinforces the play's tongue-in-cheek characterization of men as "brutes."

CONFLICTS

The unfolding plot of a play—especially the conflicts that develop—can also reveal the play's themes. In Henrik Ibsen's *A Doll House* (p. 1185), for example, at least three major conflicts are present: one between Nora and her husband Torvald, one between Nora and Krogstad (an old acquaintance), and one between Nora and society. Each of these conflicts sheds light on the themes of the play.

Through Nora's conflict with Torvald, Ibsen examines the constraints placed on women and men by marriage in the nineteenth century. Both Nora and Torvald are imprisoned within their respective roles: Nora must be passive and childlike, and Torvald must be proper and always in control. Nora, therefore, expects her husband to be noble and generous and, in a crisis, to sacrifice himself for her. When he fails to live up to her expectations, she is profoundly disillusioned.

Nora's conflict with Krogstad underscores Ibsen's criticisms of the class system in nineteenth-century Norway. At the beginning of the play, Nora finds it "immensely amusing: that we—that Torvald has so much power over . . . people." Krogstad, a bank clerk who is in the employ of Torvald, visits Nora in Act 1 to enlist her aid in saving his job. It is clear that she sees him as her social inferior. When Krogstad questions her about a woman with whom he has seen her, she replies, "What makes you think you can cross-examine me, Mr. Krogstad—you, one of my husband's employees?" Nora does not realize that she and Krogstad are, ironically, very much alike: Both occupy subordinate positions and therefore have no power to determine their own destinies.

Finally, through Nora's conflict with society Ibsen examines the forces that subjugate women. Nineteenth-century society was male-dominated. Married women could not borrow money without their husband's signatures, own real estate in their own names, or enter into contracts. In addition, all their assets—including inheritances and trust funds—automatically became the property of their husbands at the time of marriage. As a result of her sheltered life, Nora is completely innocent of the consequences of her actions at the beginning of the play. More than one character shares Dr. Rank's confusion when he asks Nora, "Why do you laugh at that? Do you have any idea of what society is?" It is Nora's disillusionment at finding out that Torvald and the rest of society are not what she has been led to believe they are that ultimately causes her to rebel. By walking out the door at the end of the play, Nora not only rejects her husband and her children (to whom, incidentally, she has no legal right once she leaves), but also society and its laws.

These conflicts, then, underscore many of the themes that dominate *A Doll House*. First, the conflicts show that marriage in the nineteenth century imprisons both men and women in narrow, constricting roles. Next, the conflicts reveal that middle-class Norwegian society is narrow, smug, and judgmental. (Krogstad, for example, is looked down upon for a crime years after he committed it, and Nora is looked down upon because she borrows money to save her husband's life.) Finally, the conflicts show that society does not offer individuals—especially women—the freedom to lead happy and fulfilling lives. Only when the social and economic conditions that govern society change, Ibsen suggests, can women and men live together in mutual esteem.

DIALOGUE

The dialogue of a play can also give insight into its themes. Sometimes a character will suggest—or even explicitly state—a theme. In Act 3 of *A Doll House,* for example, Nora's friend, Mrs. Linde, comes as close as any character to expressing a central concern of the play when she says, "Helmer's got to learn everything; this dreadful secret has to be aired; those two have to come to a full understanding; all these lies can't go on." As the play goes on to demonstrate, the lies that exist both in marriage and in society are obstacles to love and happiness.

One of the main themes of Arthur Miller's *Death of a Salesman* (p. 1458)—the questionable validity of the American dream, given the social, political, and economic realities of contemporary America—is suggested by the play's dialogue. As his son Biff points out, Willy Loman's stubborn belief in upward mobility and material success is based more on fantasy than on fact:

WILLY: *(with hatred, threatening)* The door of your life is wide open!

BIFF: Pop! I am a dime a dozen, and so are you!

WILLY: *(turning on him now in an uncontrolled outburst)* I am not a dime a dozen! I am Willy Loman, and you are Biff Loman!

Biff starts for Willy, but is blocked by Happy. In his fury, Biff seems on the verge of attacking his father.

BIFF: I am not a leader of men, Willy, and neither are you. You were never anything but a hard-working drummer who landed in the ash can like all the rest of them! I'm one dollar an hour, Willy! I tried seven states and couldn't raise it. A buck an hour! Do you gather my meaning? I'm not bringing home any prizes any more, and you're going to stop waiting for me to bring them home!

Although not explicitly stating the theme of the play, this exchange strongly suggests that Biff rejects the flawed materialistic values to which Willy clings.

CHARACTERS

Because a dramatic work focuses on a central character, or protagonist, the development of this character can shed light on a play's themes. Willy Loman in *Death of a Salesman,* for example, is developed in great detail. At the beginning of the play he feels trapped, exhausted, and estranged from his surroundings. As Willy gradually sinks from depression into despair, the action of the play shifts from the present to the past, showing the events that shaped Willy's life. His attitudes, beliefs, dreams, and dashed hopes reveal him to be an embodiment of the major theme of the play— that an unquestioning belief in the American dream of success and upward mobility is unrealistic and possibly destructive.

Nora, the main character in *A Doll House,* changes a great deal during the course of the play. At the beginning of the play Nora is more her husband's possession than an adult capable of determining her own destiny. Nora's status becomes apparent in the first act when Torvald gently scolds his "little spendthrift" and refers to her as his "little lark" and his "squirrel." She is reduced to childish deceptions, such as hiding her macaroons from her husband when he enters the room. After Krogstad accuses her of committing forgery and threatens to expose her, she expects her husband to rise nobly to the occasion and take the blame for her. When Torvald instead accuses her of being a hypocrite, a liar, and a criminal, Nora's neat little world comes tumbling down. As a result of this experience, Nora changes; no longer is she the submissive and obedient wife. Instead, she becomes confident and assertive, ultimately telling Torvald that their marriage is a sham and that she can no longer stay with him. This abrupt shift in Nora's personality gives the audience a clear understanding of the major themes that are developed in the play.

Unlike Willy and Nora, Laura in Tennessee Williams's *The Glass Menagerie* (p. 1898) is a character who changes very little during the course of the play. Laura suffers from such pathological shyness that she is unable to attend typing class, let alone talk to a potential suitor. Although the "gentleman caller" does draw Laura out of her shell for a short time, she soon withdraws again. Laura's inability to change reinforces the play's theme that contemporary society, with its emphasis on progress, has no place for people like Laura who live in private worlds "of glass animals and old, worn-out phonograph records."

STAGING

Scenery and props may also convey the themes of a play. As the stage directions of *The Sandbox* indicate, the stage is relatively bare. Containing only two chairs and a sandbox, this bare stage suggests the play's frightening emptiness, a quality Albee believes characterizes the lives of all human beings. In *Death of a Salesman,* Biff's trophy, which is constantly in the audience's view, ironically underscores the futility of Willy's efforts to achieve success. Similarly, the miniature animals in *The Glass Menagerie* reflect the brittleness of Laura's character and the futility of her efforts to fit into the modern world.

Special lighting effects and music can also suggest a play's themes. Throughout *The Glass Menagerie*, for example, words and pictures are projected onto a section of the set between the front room and dining room walls. In Scene 1 of the play, as Tom's mother, Amanda, tells him about her experiences with her "gentlemen callers," an image of her as a girl greeting callers appears on the screen. As Amanda continues, the words *"Où sont Les Neiges"*—"Where are the snows [of yesteryear]?"—appear on the screen. Later in the play, when Laura and her mother discuss a boy Laura knew, his picture is projected on the screen, showing him as a high school hero carrying a silver cup. In addition to the slides, Williams uses music—a recurring tune, dance music, and "Ave Maria"—to increase the emotional impact of certain scenes. Williams also uses shafts of light focused on selected areas or characters to create a dreamlike atmosphere for the play. Collectively, the slides, the music, and the lighting reinforce the theme that those who retreat obsessively into the past eventually become estranged from the present.

A FINAL NOTE

As you read, your values and beliefs will influence your interpretation of a play's themes. For instance, your interest in feminism could lead you to focus your attention on the submissive, almost passive, role of Willy's wife Linda in *Death of a Salesman*. As a result, you could conclude that the play shows how in the post–World War II United States, women like Linda often sacrificed their own happiness for their husbands. Remember, however, that the details of a play, not just your own feelings or assumptions, must support your interpretation.

▼▼▼▼▼▼▼▼▼▼▼▼▼▼▼▼▼▼▼▼▼▼▼▼▼▼▼▼▼▼▼▼▼▼▼▼▼▼

CHECKLIST FOR WRITING ABOUT THEME

- What is the central theme of the play?
- What other themes can you identify?
- Does the title of the play suggest a theme?
- What conflicts exist in the play? In what way do they shed light on the themes of the play?
- Do any characters' statements express or imply a theme of the play?
- Do any characters change during the play? How do these changes suggest the play's themes?
- Do certain characters resist change? How do their actions suggest a theme of the play?

◆ Do scenery and props help to communicate the play's themes?

◆ Does music reinforce certain ideas in the play?

◆ Does lighting underscore the themes of the play?

▲▲

SOPHOCLES (496–406 B.C.)   (picture and biography on p. 1590)

Even though it was written long before *Oedipus the King*, *Antigone* traces the events that befall Oedipus's younger daughter after his banishment from Thebes. Antigone, caught between the laws of the gods and the edict of her uncle the king, follows her conscience despite the fatal consequences to herself. In the 1960s, the story of Antigone was especially meaningful to Americans who practiced civil disobedience in struggles for civil rights and against the war in Vietnam.

S O P H O C L E S *

Antigone

(441 B.C.)

An English Version by Dudley Fitts and Robert Fitzgerald

C H A R A C T E R S

ANTIGONE	**TEIRESIAS**
ISMENE	**A SENTRY**
EURYDICE	**A MESSENGER**
CREON	**CHORUS**
HAIMON	

SCENE
Before the palace of Creon, King of Thebes. A central double door, and two lateral doors. A platform extends the length of the façade, and from this platform three steps lead down into the "orchestra," or chorus-ground.

TIME
Dawn of the day after the repulse of the Argive army from the assault on Thebes.

---

* Note that individual lines are numbered in the following play. When a line is shared by two or more characters, it is counted as one line.

PROLOGUE[1]

Antigone and Ismene enter from the central door of the palace.

ANTIGONE: Ismene, dear sister,
You would think that we had already suffered enough
For the curse on Oedipus.[2]
I cannot imagine any grief
5   That you and I have not gone through. And now—
Have they told you of the new decree of our King Creon?

ISMENE: I have heard nothing: I know
That two sisters lost two brothers, a double death
In a single hour; and I know that the Argive army
10   Fled in the night; but beyond this, nothing.

ANTIGONE: I thought so. And that is why I wanted you
To come out here with me. There is something we must do.

ISMENE: Why do you speak so strangely?

ANTIGONE: Listen, Ismene:
15   Creon buried our brother Eteocles
With military honors, gave him a soldier's funeral,
And it was right that he should; but Polyneices,
Who fought as bravely and died as miserably,—
They say that Creon has sworn
20   No one shall bury him, no one mourn for him,
But his body must lie in the fields, a sweet treasure
For carrion birds to find as they search for food.
That is what they say, and our good Creon is coming here
To announce it publicly; and the penalty—
25   Stoning to death in the public square!
                                        There it is,
And now you can prove what you are:
A true sister, or a traitor to your family.

ISMENE: Antigone, you are mad! What could I possibly do?

---

[1] *Prologue:* Portion of the play containing the exposition, or explanation, of what has gone before and what is now happening.   [2] *the curse on Oedipus:* As Sophocles tells in *Oedipus the King,* the King of Thebes discovered that he had lived his life under a curse. Unknowingly, he had slain his father and married his mother. On realizing this terrible truth, Oedipus put out his own eyes and departed into exile. Now, years later, as *Antigone* opens, Antigone and Ismene, daughters of Oedipus, are recalling how their two brothers died. After the abdication of their father, the brothers had ruled Thebes together. But they fell to quarreling. When Eteocles expelled Polyneices, the latter returned with an army and attacked the city. The two brothers killed each other in combat, leaving the throne to Creon. The new king of Thebes has buried Eteocles with full honors, but, calling Polyneices a traitor, has decreed that his body shall be left to the crows—an especially terrible decree, for a rotting corpse might offend Zeus, bring down plague, blight, and barrenness upon Thebes, and prevent the soul of a dead hero from entering the Elysian Fields, abode of those favored by the gods.

ANTIGONE: You must decide whether you will help me or not.

30 **ISMENE:**   I do not understand you. Help you in what?

ANTIGONE: Ismene, I am going to bury him. Will you come?

ISMENE: Bury him! You have just said the new law forbids it.

ANTIGONE: He is my brother. And he is your brother, too.

ISMENE: But think of the danger! Think what Creon will do!

35 **ANTIGONE:**   Creon is not strong enough to stand in my way.

ISMENE: Ah sister!
     Oedipus died, everyone hating him
     For what his own search brought to light, his eyes
     Ripped out by his own hand; and Jocasta died,
40   His mother and wife at once: she twisted the cords
     That strangled her life; and our two brothers died,
     Each killed by the other's sword. And we are left:
     But oh, Antigone,
     Think how much more terrible than these
45   Our own death would be if we should go against Creon
     And do what he has forbidden! We are only women,
     We cannot fight with men, Antigone!
     The law is strong, we must give in to the law
     In this thing, and in worse. I beg the Dead
50   To forgive me, but I am helpless: I must yield
     To those in authority. And I think it is dangerous business
     To be always meddling.

ANTIGONE: If that is what you think,
     I should not want you, even if you asked to come.
     You have made your choice, you can be what you want to be.
55   But I will bury him; and if I must die,
     I say that this crime is holy: I shall lie down
     With him in death, and I shall be as dear
     To him as he to me.
                         It is the dead,
     Not the living, who make the longest demands:
60   We die for ever . . .
                         You may do as you like,
     Since apparently the laws of the gods mean nothing to you.

ISMENE: They mean a great deal to me; but I have no strength
     To break laws that were made for the public good.

ANTIGONE: That must be your excuse, I suppose. But as for me,
65   I will bury the brother I love.

ISMENE: Antigone,
     I am so afraid for you!

ANTIGONE: You need not be:
     You have yourself to consider, after all.

ISMENE: But no one must hear of this, you must tell no one!
     I will keep it a secret, I promise!

ANTIGONE: O tell it! Tell everyone!

70   Think how they'll hate you when it all comes out
        If they learn that you knew about it all the time!

ISMENE: So fiery! You should be cold with fear.

ANTIGONE: Perhaps. But I am doing only what I must.

ISMENE: But can you do it? I say that you cannot.

75 **ANTIGONE:**   Very well: when my strength gives out,
        I shall do no more.

ISMENE: Impossible things should not be tried at all.

ANTIGONE: Go away, Ismene:
        I shall be hating you soon, and the dead will too,

80   For your words are hateful. Leave me my foolish plan:
        I am not afraid of the danger; if it means death,
        It will not be the worst of deaths—death without honor.

ISMENE: Go then, if you feel that you must.
        You are unwise,

85   But a loyal friend indeed to those who love you.

Exit into the palace. Antigone goes off, left. Enter the Chorus.

PARADOS[3]

STROPHE 1

CHORUS: Now the long blade of the sun, lying
        Level east to west, touches with glory
        Thebes of the Seven Gates. Open, unlidded
        Eye of golden day! O marching light

90   Across the eddy and rush of Dirce's stream,[4]
        Striking the white shields of the enemy
        Thrown headlong backward from the blaze of morning!

CHORAGOS:[5]   Polyneices their commander
        Roused them with windy phrases,

95   He the wild eagle screaming
        Insults above our land,
        His wings their shields of snow,
        His crest their marshalled helms.

---

[3] *Parados:* a song sung by the chorus on the first entering. Its *strophe* (according to scholarly theory) was sung while the chorus danced from stage right to stage left; its *antistrophe,* while they danced back again. Another parados follows the prologue of *Oedipus the King.*   [4] *Dirce's stream:* river near Thebes.   [5] *Choragos:* leader of the Chorus and principal commentator on the play's action.

ANTISTROPHE 1

CHORUS: Against our seven gates in a yawning ring
100   The famished spears came onward in the night;
    But before his jaws were sated with our blood,
    Or pinefire took the garland of our towers,
    He was thrown back; and as he turned, great Thebes—
    No tender victim for his noisy power—
105   Rose like a dragon behind him, shouting war.
CHORAGOS: For God hates utterly
    The bray of bragging tongues;
    And when he beheld their smiling,
    Their swagger of golden helms,
110   The frown of his thunder blasted
    Their first man from our walls.

STROPHE 2

CHORUS: We heard his shout of triumph high in the air
    Turn to a scream; far out in a flaming arc
    He fell with his windy torch, and the earth struck him.
115   And others storming in fury no less than his
    Found shock of death in the dusty joy of battle.
CHORAGOS: Seven captains at seven gates
    Yielded their clanging arms to the god
    That bends the battle-line and breaks it.
120   These two only, brothers in blood,
    Face to face in matchless rage,
    Mirroring each the other's death,
    Clashed in long combat.

ANTISTROPHE 2

CHORUS: But now in the beautiful morning of victory
125   Let Thebes of the many chariots sing for joy!
    With hearts for dancing we'll take leave of war:
    Our temples shall be sweet with hymns of praise,
    And the long nights shall echo with our chorus.

SCENE I

CHORAGOS: But now at last our new King is coming:
130   Creon of Thebes, Menoeceus' son.
    In this auspicious dawn of his reign
    What are the new complexities
    That shifting Fate has woven for him?

135 What is his counsel? Why has he summoned
The old men to hear him?

Enter Creon from the palace, center. He addresses the Chorus from the top step.

CREON: Gentlemen: I have the honor to inform you that our Ship of
State, which recent storms have threatened to destroy, has come
safely to harbor at last, guided by the merciful wisdom of Heaven.
I have summoned you here this morning because I know that I can
140 depend upon you: your devotion to King Laius was absolute; you
never hesitated in your duty to our late ruler Oedipus; and when
Oedipus died, your loyalty was transferred to his children.
Unfortunately, as you know, his two sons, the princes Eteocles and
Polyneices, have killed each other in battle; and I, as the next in
145 blood, have succeeded to the full power of the throne.
  I am aware, of course, that no Ruler can expect complete loyalty
from his subjects until he has been tested in office. Nevertheless, I
say to you at the very outset that I have nothing but contempt for the
kind of Governor who is afraid, for whatever reason, to follow the
150 course that he knows is best for the State; and as for the man who
sets private friendship above the public welfare,—I have no use for
him, either. I call God to witness that I saw my country headed for
ruin, I should not be afraid to speak out plainly; and I need hardly
remind you that I would never have any dealings with an enemy of
155 the people. No one values friendship more highly than I; but we must
remember that friends made at the risk of wrecking our Ship are not
real friends at all.
  These are my principles, at any rate, and that is why I have made
the following decision concerning the sons of Oedipus: Eteocles, who
160 died as a man should die, fighting for his country, is to be buried
with full military honors, with all the ceremony that is usual when
the greatest heroes die; but his brother Polyneices, who broke his
exile to come back with fire and sword against his native city and the
shrines of his fathers' gods, whose one idea was to spill the blood of
165 his blood and sell his own people into slavery—Polyneices, I say, is to
have no burial: no man is to touch him or say the least prayer for
him; he shall lie on the plain, unburied; and the birds and the
scavenging dogs can do with him whatever they like.
  This is my command, and you can see the wisdom behind it.
170 As long as I am King, no traitor is going to be honored with the
loyal man. But whoever shows by word and deed that he is on the
side of the State,—he shall have my respect while he is living and
my reverence when he is dead.
CHORAGOS: If that is your will, Creon son of Menoeceus,
175 You have the right to enforce it: we are yours.
CREON: That is my will. Take care that you do your part.
CHORAGOS: We are old men: let the younger ones carry it out.

CREON: I do not mean that: the sentries have been appointed.
CHORAGOS: Then what is it that you would have us do?
180 **CREON:** You will give no support to whoever breaks this law.
CHORAGOS: Only a crazy man is in love with death!
CREON: And death it is; yet money talks, and the wisest
 Have sometimes been known to count a few coins too many.

Enter Sentry from left.

SENTRY: I'll not say that I'm out of breath from running, King, because
185 every time I stopped to think about what I have to tell you, I felt like
 going back. And all the time a voice kept saying, "You fool, don't you
 know you're walking straight into trouble?"; and then another voice:
 "Yes, but if you let somebody else get the news to Creon first, it will
 be even worse than that for you!" But good sense won out, at least I
190 hope it was good sense, and here I am with a story that makes no
 sense at all; but I'll tell it anyhow, because, as they say, what's going
 to happen's going to happen and—
CREON: Come to the point. What have you to say?
SENTRY: I did not do it. I did not see who did it. You must not punish
195 me for what someone else has done.
CREON: A comprehensive defense! More effective, perhaps,
 If I knew its purpose. Come: what is it?
SENTRY: A dreadful thing . . . I don't know how to put it—
CREON: Out with it!
SENTRY: Well, then;
200 The dead man—
        Polyneices—

Pause. The Sentry is overcome, fumbles for words. Creon waits impassively.

         out there—
            someone,—
 New dust on the slimy flesh!

Pause. No sign from Creon.

 Someone has given it burial that way, and
 Gone . . .

Long pause. Creon finally speaks with deadly control.

CREON: And the man who dared do this?
205 **SENTRY:**   I swear I
 Do not know! You must believe me!
       Listen:
 The ground was dry, not a sign of digging, no,
 Not a wheeltrack in the dust, no trace of anyone.
 It was when they relieved us this morning: and one of them,
210 The corporal, pointed to it.

There it was,

The strangest—

Look:

The body, just mounded over with light dust: you see?
Not buried really, but as if they'd covered it
Just enough for the ghost's peace. And no sign
215 Of dogs or any wild animal that had been there.
And then what a scene there was! Every man of us
Accusing the other: we all proved the other man did it,
We all had proof that we could not have done it.
We were ready to take hot iron in our hands,
220 Walk through fire, swear by all the gods,
It was not I!
I do not know who it was, but it was not I!

*Creon's rage has been mounting steadily, but the Sentry is too intent upon his
story to notice it.*

And then, when this came to nothing, someone said
A thing that silenced us and made us stare
225 Down at the ground: you had to be told the news,
And one of us had to do it! We threw the dice,
And the bad luck fell to me. So here I am,
No happier to be here than you are to have me:
Nobody likes the man who brings bad news.
230 **CHORAGOS:**   I have been wondering, King: can it be that the gods have
done this?

CREON: *(furiously)* Stop!
Must you doddering wrecks
Go out of your heads entirely? "The gods"!
Intolerable!
235 The gods favor this corpse? Why? How had he served them?
Tried to loot their temples, burn their images,
Yes, and the whole State, and its laws with it!
Is it your senile opinion that the gods love to honor bad men?
A pious thought!—

No, from the very beginning
240 There have been those who have whispered together,
Stiff-necked anarchists, putting their heads together,
Scheming against me in alleys. These are the men,
And they have bribed my own guard to do this thing.
(Sententiously.) Money!
245 There's nothing in the world so demoralizing as money.
Down go your cities,
Homes gone, men gone, honest hearts corrupted,
Crookedness of all kinds, and all for money!
(To Sentry.)   But you—

I swear by God and by the throne of God,
250   The man who has done this thing shall pay for it!
Find that man, bring him here to me, or your death
Will be the least of your problems: I'll string you up
Alive, and there will be certain ways to make you
Discover your employer before you die;
255   And the process may teach you a lesson you seem to have missed:
The dearest profit is sometimes all too dear:
That depends on the source. Do you understand me?
A fortune won is often misfortune.

SENTRY: King, may I speak?
CREON: Your very voice distresses me.
260   **SENTRY:**   Are you sure that it is my voice, and not your conscience?
CREON: By God, he wants to analyze me now!
SENTRY: It is not what I say, but what has been done, that hurts you.
CREON: You talk too much.
SENTRY: Maybe; but I've done nothing.
CREON: Sold your soul for some silver: that's all you've done.
265   **SENTRY:**   How dreadful it is when the right judge judges wrong!
CREON: Your figures of speech
May entertain you now; but unless you bring me the man,
You will get little profit from them in the end.

Exit Creon into the palace.

SENTRY: "Bring me the man"—!
270   I'd like nothing better than bringing him the man!
But bring him or not, you have seen the last of me here.
At any rate, I am safe! *(Exit Sentry.)*

ODE I [6]
....

STROPHE 1

CHORUS: Numberless are the world's wonders, but none
More wonderful than man; the stormgray sea
275   Yields to his prows, the huge crests bear him high;
Earth, holy and inexhaustible, is graven
With shining furrows where his plows have gone
Year after year, the timeless labor of stallions.

---

[6] *Ode I:* first song sung by the Chorus, who at the same time danced. Here again, as in the parados, *strophe* and *antistrophe* probably divide the song into two movements of the dance: right-to-left, then left-to-right.

Antistrophe 1

The lightboned birds and beasts that cling to cover,
The lithe fish lighting their reaches of dim water,
All are taken, tamed in the net of his mind;
The lion on the hill, the wild horse windy-maned,
Resign to him; and his blunt yoke has broken
The sultry shoulders of the mountain bull.

Strophe 2

Words also, and thought as rapid as air,
He fashions to his good use; statecraft is his,
And his the skill that deflects the arrows of snow,
The spears of winter rain: from every wind
He has made himself secure—from all but one:
In the late wind of death he cannot stand.

Antistrophe 2

O clear intelligence, force beyond all measure!
O fate of man, working both good and evil!
When the laws are kept, how proudly his city stands!
When the laws are broken, what of his city then?
Never may the anárchic man find rest at my hearth,
Never be it said that my thoughts are his thoughts.

SCENE II

Reenter Sentry leading Antigone.

CHORAGOS: What does this mean? Surely this captive woman
Is the Princess, Antigone. Why should she be taken?
SENTRY: Here is the one who did it! We caught her
In the very act of burying him.—Where is Creon?
CHORAGOS: Just coming from the house.

Enter Creon, center.

CREON: What has happened?
Why have you come back so soon?
SENTRY: *(expansively)*   O King,
A man should never be too sure of anything:
I would have sworn
That you'd not see me here again: your anger
Frightened me so, and the things you threatened me with;
But how could I tell then

That I'd be able to solve the case so soon?
310 No dice-throwing this time: I was only too glad to come!
Here is this woman. She is the guilty one:
We found her trying to bury him.
Take her, then; question her; judge her as you will.
I am through with the whole thing now, and glad of it.
315 **CREON:** But this is Antigone! Why have you brought her here?
SENTRY: She was burying him, I tell you!
CREON: *(severely)* Is this the truth?
SENTRY: I saw her with my own eyes. Can I say more?
CREON: The details: come, tell me quickly!
SENTRY: It was like this:
After those terrible threats of yours, King,
320 We went back and brushed the dust away from the body.
The flesh was soft by now, and stinking,
So we sat on a hill to windward and kept guard.
No napping this time! We kept each other awake.
But nothing happened until the white round sun
325 Whirled in the center of the round sky over us:
Then, suddenly,
A storm of dust roared up from the earth, and the sky
Went out, the plain vanished with all its tress
In the stinging dark. We closed our eyes and endured it.
330 The whirlwind lasted a long time, but it passed;
And then we looked, and there was Antigone!
I have seen
A mother bird come back to a stripped nest, heard
Her crying bitterly a broken note or two
335 For the young ones stolen. Just so, when this girl
Found the bare corpse, and all her love's work wasted,
She wept, and cried on heaven to damn the hands
That had done this thing.
And then she brought more dust
And sprinkled wine three times for her brother's ghost.
340 We ran and took her at once. She was not afraid,
Not even when we charged her with what she had done.
She denied nothing.
And this was a comfort to me,
And some uneasiness: for it is a good thing
To escape from death, but it is no great pleasure
345 To bring death to a friend.
Yet I always say
There is nothing so comfortable as your own safe skin!
CREON: *(slowly, dangerously)* And you, Antigone,
You with your head hanging,—do you confess this thing?
ANTIGONE: I do. I deny nothing.

CREON: *(to Sentry)*   You may go. *(Exit Sentry.)*
350   *(To Antigone.)* Tell me, tell me briefly:
       Had you heard my proclamation touching this matter?
ANTIGONE: It was public. Could I help hearing it?
CREON: And yet you dared defy the law.
ANTIGONE: I dared.
       It was not God's proclamation. That final Justice
355   That rules the world below makes no such laws.
       Your edict, King, was strong,
       But all your strength is weakness itself against
       The immortal unrecorded laws of God.
       They are not merely now: they were, and shall be,
360   Operative for ever, beyond man utterly.
       I knew I must die, even without your decree:
       I am only mortal. And if I must die
       Now, before it is my time to die,
       Surely this is no hardship: can anyone
365   Living, as I live, with evil all about me,
       Think Death less than a friend? This death of mine
       Is of no importance; but if I had left my brother
       Lying in death unburied, I should have suffered.
       Now I do not.
                     You smile at me. Ah Creon,
370   Think me a fool, if you like; but it may well be
       That a fool convicts me of folly.
CHORAGOS: Like father, like daughter: both headstrong, deaf to reason!
       She has never learned to yield:
CREON: She has much to learn.
       The inflexible heart breaks first, the toughest iron
375   Cracks first, and the wildest horses bend their necks
       At the pull of the smallest curb.
                                        Pride? In a slave?
       This girl is guilty of a double insolence,
       Breaking the given laws and boasting of it.
       Who is the man here,
380   She or I, if this crime goes unpunished?
       Sister's child, or more than sister's child,
       Or closer yet in blood—she and her sister
       Win bitter death for this!
       (To Servants.)   Go, some of you,
       Arrest Ismene. I accuse her equally.
385   Bring her: you will find her sniffling in the house there.
       Her mind's a traitor: crimes kept in the dark
       Cry for light, and the guardian brain shudders;
       But how much worse than this
       Is brazen boasting of barefaced anarchy!

390 **ANTIGONE:**   Creon, what more do you want than my death?

CREON: Nothing.

That gives me everything.

ANTIGONE: Then I beg you: kill me.

This talking is a great weariness: your words

Are distasteful to me, and I am sure that mine

Seem so to you. And yet they should not seem so:

395 I should have praise and honor for what I have done.

All these men here would praise me

Were their lips not frozen shut with fear of you.

(Bitterly.) Ah the good fortune of kings,

Licensed to say and do whatever they please!

400 **CREON:**   You are alone here in that opinion.

ANTIGONE: No, they are with me. But they keep their tongues in leash.

CREON: Maybe. But you are guilty, and they are not.

ANTIGONE: There is no guilt in reverence for the dead.

CREON: But Eteocles—was he not your brother too?

405 **ANTIGONE:**   My brother too.

CREON: And you insult his memory?

ANTIGONE: *(softly)* The dead man would not say that I insult it.

CREON: He would: for you honor a traitor as much as him.

ANTIGONE: His own brother, traitor or not, and equal in blood.

CREON: He made war on his country. Eteocles defended it.

410 **ANTIGONE:**   Nevertheless, there are honors due all the dead.

CREON: But not the same for the wicked as for the just.

ANTIGONE: Ah Creon, Creon

Which of us can say what the gods hold wicked?

CREON: An enemy is an enemy, even dead.

415 **ANTIGONE:**   It is my nature to join in love, not hate.

CREON: *(finally losing patience)* Go join them then; if you must have your love,

Find it in hell!

CHORAGOS: But see, Ismene comes:

Enter Ismene, guarded.

Those tears are sisterly, the cloud

That shadows her eyes rains down gentle sorrow.

420 **CREON:**   You too, Ismene,

Snake in my ordered house, sucking my blood

Stealthily—and all the time I never knew

That these two sisters were aiming at my throne!

                                                                                Ismene,

Do you confess your share in this crime, or deny it?

425 Answer me.

ISMENE: Yes, if she will let me say so. I am guilty.

ANTIGONE: *(coldly)* No, Ismene. You have no right to say so.

You would not help me, and I will not have you help me.

ISMENE: But now I know what you meant; and I am here
430   To join you, to take my share of punishment.
ANTIGONE: The dead man and the gods who rule the dead
         Know whose act this was. Words are not friends.
ISMENE: Do you refuse me, Antigone? I want to die with you:
         I too have a duty that I must discharge to the dead.
435 **ANTIGONE:**   You shall not lessen my death by sharing it.
ISMENE: What do I care for life when you are dead?
ANTIGONE: Ask Creon. You're always hanging on his opinions.
ISMENE: You are laughing at me. Why, Antigone?
ANTIGONE: It's a joyless laughter, Ismene.
ISMENE: But can I do nothing?
440 **ANTIGONE:**   Yes. Save yourself. I shall not envy you.
         There are those who will praise you; I shall have honor, too.
ISMENE: But we are equally guilty!
ANTIGONE: No more, Ismene.
         You are alive, but I belong to Death.
CREON: *(to the Chorus)* Gentlemen, I beg you to observe these girls:
445   One has just now lost her mind; the other
         It seems, has never had a mind at all.
ISMENE: Grief teaches the steadiest minds to waver, King.
CREON: Yours certainly did, when you assumed guilt with the guilty!
ISMENE: But how could I go on living without her?
CREON: You are.
450   She is already dead.
ISMENE: But your own son's bride!
CREON: There are places enough for him to push his plow.
         I want no wicked women for my sons!
ISMENE: O dearest Haimon, how your father wrongs you!
CREON: I've had enough of your childish talk of marriage!
455 **CHORAGOS:**   Do you really intend to steal this girl from your son?
CREON: No; Death will do that for me.
CHORAGOS: Then she must die?
CREON: *(ironically)* You dazzle me.
                                —But enough of this talk!
         (To Guards.) You, there, take them away and guard them well:
         For they are but women, and even brave men run
460   When they see Death coming. *Exeunt Ismene, Antigone, and Guards.*

                              ODE II
                        _____

STROPHE 1

CHORUS: Fortunate is the man who has never tasted God's vengeance!
         Where once the anger of heaven has struck, that house is shaken
         For ever: damnation rises behind each child

Like a wave cresting out of the black northeast,
465   When the long darkness under sea roars up
And bursts drumming death upon the windwhipped sand.

ANTISTROPHE 1

I have seen this gathering sorrow from time long past
Loom upon Oedipus' children: generation from generation
Takes the compulsive rage of the enemy god.
470   So lately this last flower of Oedipus' line
Drank the sunlight! but now a passionate word
And a handful of dust have closed up all its beauty.

STROPHE 2

What mortal arrogance
Transcends the wrath of Zeus?
475   Sleep cannot lull him nor the effortless long months
Of the timeless gods: but he is young for ever,
And his house is the shining day of high Olympos.
All that is and shall be,
And all the past, is his.
480   No pride on earth is free of the curse of heaven.

ANTISTROPHE 2

The straying dreams of men
May bring them ghosts of joy:
But as they drowse, the waking embers burn them;
Or they walk with fixed eyes, as blind men walk.
485   But the ancient wisdom speaks for our own time:
Fate works most for woe
With Folly's fairest show.
Man's little pleasure is the spring of sorrow.

SCENE III

CHORAGOS: But here is Haimon, King, the last of all your sons.
490   Is it grief for Antigone that brings him here,
And bitterness at being robbed of his bride?

Enter Haimon.

CREON: We shall soon see, and no need of diviners.

—Son,
You have heard my final judgment on that girl:
Have you come here hating me, or have you come
495   With deference and with love, whatever I do?

HAIMON: I am your son, father. You are my guide.
You make things clear for me, and I obey you.
No marriage means more to me than your continuing wisdom.
CREON: Good. That is the way to behave: subordinate
500 Everything else, my son, to your father's will.
This is what a man prays for, that he may get
Sons attentive and dutiful in his house,
Each one hating his father's enemies,
Honoring his father's friends. But if his sons
505 Fail him, if they turn out unprofitably,
What has he fathered but trouble for himself
And amusement for the malicious?
                                    So you are right
Not to lose your head over this woman.
Your pleasure with her would soon grow cold, Haimon,
510 And then you'd have a hellcat in bed and elsewhere.
Let her find her husband in Hell!
Of all the people in this city, only she
Has had contempt for my law and broken it.
Do you want me to show myself weak before the people?
515 Or to break my sworn word? No, and I will not.
The woman dies.
I suppose she'll plead "family ties." Well, let her.
If I permit my own family to rebel,
How shall I earn the world's obedience?
520 Show me the man who keeps his house in hand,
He's fit for public authority.
                                    I'll have no dealings
With lawbreakers, critics of the government:
Whoever is chosen to govern should be obeyed—
Must be obeyed, in all things, great and small,
525 Just and unjust! O Haimon,
The man who knows how to obey, and that man only,
Knows how to give commands when the time comes.
You can depend on him, no matter how fast
The spears come: he's a good soldier, he'll stick it out.

530 Anarchy, anarchy! Show me a greater evil!
This is why cities tumble and the great houses rain down,
This is what scatters armies!
No, no: good lives are made so by discipline.
We keep the laws then, and the lawmakers,
535 And no woman shall seduce us. If we must lose,
Let's lose to a man, at least! Is a woman stronger than we?
CHORAGOS: Unless time has rusted my wits,
What you say, King, is said with point and dignity.

HAIMON: *(boyishly earnest)* Father:

540   Reason is God's crowning gift to man, and you are right
       To warn me against losing mine. I cannot say—
       I hope that I shall never want to say!—that you
       Have reasoned badly. Yet there are other men
       Who can reason, too; and their opinions might be helpful.
545   You are not in a position to know everything
       That people say or do, or what they feel:
       Your temper terrifies—everyone
       Will tell you only what you like to hear.
       But I, at any rate, can listen; and I have heard them
550   Muttering and whispering in the dark about this girl.
       They say no woman has ever, so unreasonably,
       Died so shameful a death for a generous act:
       "She covered her brother's body. Is this indecent?
       She kept him from dogs and vultures. Is this a crime?
555   Death?—She should have all the honor that we can give her!"

       This is the way they talk out there in the city.

       You must believe me:
       Nothing is closer to me than your happiness.
       What could be closer? Must not any son
560   Value his father's fortune as his father does his?
       I beg you, do not be unchangeable:
       Do not believe that you alone can be right.
       The man who thinks that,
       The man who maintains that only he has the power
565   To reason correctly, the gift to speak, the soul—
       A man like that, when you know him, turns out empty.
       It is not reason never to yield to reason!

       In flood time you can see how some trees bend,
       And because they bend, even their twigs are safe,
570   While stubborn trees are torn up, roots and all.
       And the same thing happens in sailing:
       Make your sheet fast, never slacken,—and over you go,
       Head over heels and under: and there's your voyage.
       Forget you are angry! Let yourself be moved!
575   I know I am young; but please let me say this:
       The ideal condition
       Would be, I admit, that men should be right by instinct;
       But since we are all too likely to go astray,
       The reasonable thing is to learn from those who can teach.
580 **CHORAGOS:** You will do well to listen to him, King,
       If what he says is sensible. And you, Haimon,
       Must listen to your father.—Both speak well.

CREON: You consider it right for a man of my years and experience
To go to school to a boy?
HAIMON: It is not right
585 If I am wrong. But if I am young, and right,
What does my age matter?
CREON: You think it right to stand up for an anarchist?
HAIMON: Not at all. I pay no respect to criminals.
CREON: Then she is not a criminal?
590 **HAIMON:**   The City would deny it, to a man.
CREON: And the City proposes to teach me how to rule?
HAIMON: Ah. Who is it that's talking like a boy now?
CREON: My voice is the one voice giving orders in this City!
HAIMON: It is no City if it takes orders from one voice.
595 **CREON:**   The State is the King!
HAIMON: Yes, if the State is a desert.

Pause.

CREON: This boy, it seems, has sold out to a woman.
HAIMON: If you are a woman: my concern is only for you.
CREON: So? Your "concern"! In a public brawl with your father!
HAIMON: How about you, in a public brawl with justice?
600 **CREON:**   With justice, when all that I do is within my rights?
HAIMON: You have no right to trample on God's right.
CREON: *(completely out of control)* Fool, adolescent fool! Taken in by a
woman!
HAIMON: You'll never see me taken in by anything vile.
CREON: Every word you say is for her!
HAIMON: *(quietly, darkly)*   And for you.
605 And for me. And for the gods under the earth.
CREON: You'll never marry her while she lives.
HAIMON: Then she must die.—But her death will cause another.
CREON: Another?
Have you lost your senses? Is this an open threat?
610 **HAIMON:**   There is no threat in speaking to emptiness.
CREON: I swear you'll regret this superior tone of yours!
You are the empty one!
HAIMON: If you were not my father,
I'd say you were perverse.
CREON: You girl-struck fool, don't play at words with me!
615 **HAIMON:**   I am sorry. You prefer silence.
CREON: Now, by God—
I swear, by all the gods in heaven above us,
You'll watch it, I swear you shall!
(To the Servants.)   Bring her out!
Bring the woman out! Let her die before his eyes!
Here, this instant, with her bridegroom beside her!

620 **HAIMON:** Not here, no; she will not die here, King.
And you will never see my face again.
Go on raving as long as you've a friend to endure you.

(Exit Haimon.)

CHORAGOS: Gone, gone.
Creon, a young man in a rage is dangerous!
625 **CREON:** Let him do, or dream to do, more than a man can.
He shall not save these girls from death.
CHORAGOS: These girls?
You have sentenced them both?
CREON: No, you are right.
I will not kill the one whose hands are clean.
CHORAGOS: But Antigone?
CREON: *(somberly)* I will carry her far away
630 Out there in the wilderness, and lock her
Living in a vault of stone. She shall have food,
As the custom is, to absolve the State of her death.
And there let her pray to the gods of hell:
They are her only gods:
635 Perhaps they will show her an escape from death,
Or she may learn,
though late,
That piety shown the dead is pity in vain. *(Exit Creon.)*

ODE III

STROPHE

CHORUS: Love, unconquerable
Waster of rich men, keeper
640 Of warm lights and all-night vigil
In the soft face of a girl:
Sea-wanderer, forest-visitor!
Even the pure Immortals cannot escape you,
And mortal man, in his one day's dusk,
645 Trembles before your glory.

ANTISTROPHE

Surely you swerve upon ruin
The just man's consenting heart,
As here you have made bright anger
Strike between father and son—
650 And none has conquered but Love!
A girl's glánce wórking the will of heaven:

Pleasure to her alone who mocks us,
Merciless Aphrodite.[7]

SCENE IV

CHORAGOS: *(as Antigone enters guarded)* But I can no longer stand in
    awe of this,
655   Nor, seeing what I see, keep back my tears.
    Here is Antigone, passing to that chamber
    Where all find sleep at last.

STROPHE 1

ANTIGONE: Look upon me, friends, and pity me
    Turning back at the night's edge to say
660   Good-by to the sun that shines for me no longer;
    Now sleepy Death
    Summons me down to Acheron,[8] that cold shore:
    There is no bridesong there, nor any music.
CHORUS: Yet not unpraised, not without a kind of honor,
665   You walk at last into the underworld;
    Untouched by sickness, broken by no sword.
    What woman has ever found your way to death?

ANTISTROPHE 1

ANTIGONE: How often I have heard the story of Niobe,[9]
    Tantalos' wretched daughter, how the stone
670   Clung fast about her, ivy-close: and they say
    The rain falls endlessly
    And sifting soft snow; her tears are never done.
    I feel the loneliness of her death in mine.
CHORUS: But she was born of heaven, and you
675   Are woman, woman-born. If her death is yours,
    A mortal woman's, is this not for you
    Glory in our world and in the world beyond?

STROPHE 2

ANTIGONE: You laugh at me. Ah, friends, friends,
    Can you not wait until I am dead? O Thebes,

---

[7] *Aphrodite:* goddess of love and beauty.   [8] *Acheron:* river in Hades, domain of the
dead.   [9] *story of Niobe:* in which this mother, when her fourteen children were
slain, wept so copiously that she was transformed to a stone on Mount Sipylus. Her
tears became the mountain's streams.

680   O men many-charioted, in love with Fortune,
       Dear springs of Dirce, sacred Theban grove,
       Be witnesses for me, denied all pity,
       Unjustly judged! and think a word of love
       For her whose path turns
685   Under dark earth, where there are no more tears.
    CHORUS: You have passed beyond human daring and come at last
       Into a place of stone where Justice sits.
       I cannot tell
       What shape of your father's guilt appears in this.

ANTISTROPHE 2

690 **ANTIGONE:**   You have touched it at last: that bridal bed
       Unspeakable, horror of son and mother mingling:
       Their crime, infection of all our family!
       O Oedipus, father and brother!
       Your marriage strikes from the grave to murder mine.
695   I have been a stranger here in my own land:
       All my life
       The blasphemy of my birth has followed me.
    CHORUS: Reverence is a virtue, but strength
       Lives in established law: that must prevail.
700   You have made your choice,
       Your death is the doing of your conscious hand.

EPODE

    ANTIGONE: Then let me go, since all your words are bitter,
       And the very light of the sun is cold to me.
       Lead me to my vigil, where I must have
705   Neither love nor lamentation; no song, but silence.

Creon interrupts impatiently.

    CREON: If dirges and planned lamentations could put off death,
       Men would be singing for ever.
       (To the Servants.)   Take her, go!
       You know your orders: take her to the vault
       And leave her alone there. And if she lives or dies,
710   That's her affair, not ours: our hands are clean.
    ANTIGONE: O tomb, vaulted bride-bed in eternal rock,
       Soon I shall be with my own again
       Where Persephone[10] welcomes the thin ghosts underground:
       And I shall see my father again, and you, mother,

---

[10] *Persephone:* whom Pluto, god of the underworld, abducted to be his queen.

715 And dearest Polyneices—
dearest indeed
To me, since it was my hand
That washed him clean and poured the ritual wine:
And my reward is death before my time!

And yet, as men's hearts know, I have done no wrong,
720 I have not sinned before God. Or if I have,
I shall know the truth in death. But if the guilt
Lies upon Creon who judged me, then, I pray,
May his punishment equal my own.
CHORAGOS: O passionate heart,
Unyielding, tormented still by the same winds!
725 **CREON:**   Her guards shall have good cause to regret their delaying.
ANTIGONE: Ah! That voice is like the voice of death!
CREON: I can give you no reason to think you are mistaken.
ANTIGONE: Thebes, and you my fathers' gods,
And rulers of Thebes, you see me now, the last
730 Unhappy daughter of a line of kings,
Your kings, led away to death. You will remember
What things I suffer, and at what men's hands,
Because I would not transgress the laws of heaven.
(To the Guards, simply.) Come: let us wait no longer.

(Exit Antigone, left, guarded.)

O D E   I V

STROPHE 1

735 **CHORUS:**   All Danae's beauty was locked away
In a brazen cell where the sunlight could not come:
A small room still as any grave, enclosed her.
Yet she was a princess too,
And Zeus in a rain of gold poured love upon her.[11]
740 O child, child,
No power in wealth or war
Or tough sea-blackened ships
Can prevail against untiring Destiny!

---

[11] *All Danae's beauty . . . poured love upon her:* In legend, when an oracle told Acrisius, king of Argos, that his daughter Danae would bear a son who would grow up to slay him, he locked the princess into a chamber made of bronze, lest any man impregnate her. But Zeus, father of the gods, entered Danae's prison in a shower of gold. The resultant child, the hero Perseus, was accidentally to fulfill the prophecy by killing Acrisius with an ill-aimed discus throw.

ANTISTROPHE 1

745

And Dryas' son[12] also, that furious king,
Bore the god's prisoning anger for his pride:
Sealed up by Dionysos in deaf stone,
His madness died among echoes.
So at the last he learned what dreadful power
His tongue had mocked:

750

For he had profaned the revels,
And fired the wrath of the nine
Implacable Sisters[13] that love the sound of the flute.

STROPHE 2

And old men tell a half-remembered tale
Of horror[14] where a dark ledge splits the sea

755

And a double surf beats on the gráy shóres:
How a king's new woman, sick
With hatred for the queen he had imprisoned,
Ripped out his two sons' eyes with her bloody hands
While grinning Ares watched the shuttle plunge

760

Four times: four blind wounds crying for revenge,

ANTISTROPHE 2

Crying, tears and blood mingled.—Piteously born,
Those sons whose mother was of heavenly birth!
Her father was the god of the North Wind
And she was cradled by gales,

765

She raced with young colts on the glittering hills
And walked untrammeled in the open light:
But in her marriage deathless Fate found means
To build a tomb like yours for all her joy.

SCENE V

Enter blind Teiresias, led by a boy. The opening speeches of Teiresias should be in singsong contrast to the realistic lines of Creon.

---

[12] *Dryas' son:* King Lycurgus of Thrace, whom Dionysos, god of wine, caused to be stricken with madness.   [13] *Sisters:* the Muses, nine sister goddesses who presided over poetry and music, arts and sciences.   [14] *a half-remembered tale of horror:* As the Chorus recalls in the rest of this song, the point of this tale is that being nobly born will not save one from disaster. King Phineas cast off his first wife Cleopatra (not the later Egyptian queen, but the daughter of Boreas, god of the north wind) and imprisoned her in a cave. Out of hatred for Cleopatra, the cruel Eidothea, second wife of the king, blinded her stepsons. Ares, god of war, was said to gloat over bloodshed.

TEIRESIAS: This is the way the blind man comes, Princes, Princes,
770   Lockstep, two heads lit by the eyes of one.
CREON: What new thing have you to tell us, old Teiresias?
TEIRESIAS: I have much to tell you: listen to the prophet, Creon.
CREON: I am not aware that I have ever failed to listen.
TEIRESIAS: Then you have done wisely, King, and ruled well.
775 **CREON:**   I admit my debt to you. But what have you to say?
TEIRESIAS: This, Creon: you stand once more on the edge of fate.
CREON: What do you mean? Your words are a kind of dread.
TEIRESIAS: Listen, Creon:
         I was sitting in my chair of augury, at the place
780   Where the birds gather about me. They were all a-chatter,
         As is their habit, when suddenly I heard
         A strange note in their jangling, a scream, a
         Whirring fury; I knew that they were fighting,
         Tearing each other, dying
785   In a whirlwind of wings clashing. And I was afraid.
         I began the rites of burnt-offering at the altar,
         But Hephaistos[15] failed me: instead of bright flame,
         There was only the sputtering slime of the fat thigh-flesh
         Melting: the entrails dissolved in gray smoke,
790   The bare bone burst from the welter. And no blaze!

         This was a sign from heaven. My boy described it,
         Seeing for me as I see for others.

         I tell you, Creon, you yourself have brought
         This new calamity upon us. Our hearths and altars
795   Are stained with the corruption of dogs and carrion birds
         That glut themselves on the corpse of Oedipus' son.
         The gods are deaf when we pray to them, their fire
         Recoils from our offering, their birds of omen
         Have no cry of comfort, for they are gorged
800   With the thick blood of the dead.
                                        O my son,
         These are no trifles! Think: all men make mistakes,
         But a good man yields when he knows his course is wrong,
         And repairs the evil. The only crime is pride.
         Give in to the dead man, then: do not fight with a corpse—
805   What glory is it to kill a man who is dead?
         Think, I beg you:
         It is for your own good that I speak as I do.
         You should be able to yield for your own good.

---

[15] *Hephaistos:* god of fire.

CREON: It seems that prophets have made me their especial province.

810   All my life long
I have been a kind of butt for the dull arrows
Of doddering fortune-tellers!
                              No, Teiresias:
If your birds—if the great eagles of God himself
Should carry him stinking bit by bit to heaven,

815   I would not yield. I am not afraid of pollution:
No man can defile the gods.
                              Do what you will,
Go into business, make money, speculate
An India gold or that synthetic gold from Sardis,
Get rich otherwise than by my consent to bury him.

820   Teiresias, it is a sorry thing when a wise man
Sells his wisdom, lets out his words for hire!

TEIRESIAS: Ah Creon! Is there no man left in the world—

CREON: To do what?—Come, let's have the aphorism!

TEIRESIAS: No man who knows that wisdom outweighs any wealth?

825 **CREON:**   As surely as bribes are baser than any baseness.

TEIRESIAS: You are sick, Creon! You are deathly sick!

CREON: As you say: it is not my place to challenge a prophet.

TEIRESIAS: Yet you have said my prophecy is for sale.

CREON: The generation of prophets has always loved gold.

830 **TEIRESIAS:**   The generation of kings has always loved brass.

CREON: You forget yourself! You are speaking to your King.

TEIRESIAS: I know it. You are a king because of me.

CREON: You have a certain skill; but you have sold out.

TEIRESIAS: King, you will drive me to words that—

CREON: Say them, say them!

835   Only remember: I will not pay you for them.

TEIRESIAS: No, you will find them too costly.

CREON: No doubt. Speak:
Whatever you say, you will not change my will.

TEIRESIAS: Then take this, and take it to heart!
The time is not far off when you shall pay back

840   Corpse for corpse, flesh of your own flesh.
You have thrust the child of this world into living night,
You have kept from the gods below the child that is theirs:
The one in a grave before her death, the other,
Dead, denied the grave. This is your crime:

845   And the Furies and the dark gods of Hell
Are swift with terrible punishment for you.

Do you want to buy me now, Creon?
                              Not many days,
And your house will be full of men and women weeping,
And curses will be hurled at you from far

850   Cities grieving for sons unburied, left to rot
        Before the walls of Thebes.
        There are my arrows, Creon: they are all for you.

        (To Boy.) But come, child: lead me home.
        Let him waste his fine anger upon younger men.
855   Maybe he will learn at last
        To control a wiser tongue in a better head. *(Exit Teiresias.)*
     CHORAGOS: The old man has gone, King, but his words
        Remain to plague us. I am old, too,
        But I cannot remember that he was ever false.
860 **CREON:**   That is true. . . . It troubles me.
        Oh it is hard to give in! but it is worse
        To risk everything for stubborn pride.
     CHORAGOS: Creon: take my advice.
     CREON: What shall I do?
     CHORAGOS: Go quickly: free Antigone from her vault
865   And build a tomb for the body of Polyneices.
     CREON: You would have me do this!
     CHORAGOS: Creon, yes!
        And it must be done at once: God moves
        Swiftly to cancel the folly of stubborn men.
     CREON: It is hard to deny the heart! But I
870   Will do it: I will not fight with destiny.
     CHORAGOS: You must go yourself, you cannot leave it to others.
     CREON: I will go.
               —Bring axes, servants:
        Come with me to the tomb. I buried her, I
        Will set her free.
               Oh quickly!
875   My mind misgives—
        The laws of the gods are mighty, and a man must serve them
        To the last day of his life! *(Exit Creon.)*

PAEAN [16]

STROPHE 1

CHORAGOS: God of many names
CHORUS: O Iacchos
                               son
    of Kadmeian Sémele
                  O born of the Thunder!

---

[16] *Paean:* a song of praise or prayer, here to Dionysos, god of wine.

880   Guardian of the West
               Regent
      Of Eleusis' plain
               O Prince of maenad Thebes
      and the Dragon Field by rippling Ismenós:[17]

ANTISTROPHE 1

CHORAGOS: God of many names
CHORUS: the flame of torches
      flares on our hills
               the nymphs of Iacchos
885   dance at the spring of Castalia:[18]
      from the vine-close mountain
                  come ah come in ivy:
      Evohé evohé! [19] sings through the streets of Thebes

STROPHE 2

CHORAGOS: God of many names
CHORUS: Iacchos of Thebes
      heavenly Child
               of Sémele bride of the Thunderer!
890   The shadow of plague is upon us:
                    come
      with clement feet
               oh come from Parnasos
      down the long slopes
               across the lamenting water

---

[17] *God of many names . . . Dragon Field by rippling Ismenós:* Dionysos was also called Iacchos (or, by the Romans, Bacchus). He was the son of Zeus ("the Thunderer") and of Sémele, daughter of Kadmos (or Cadmus), legendary founder of Thebes. "Regent of Eleusis' plain" is another name for Dionysos, honored in secret rites at Eleusis, a town northwest of Athens. "Prince of maenad Thebes" is yet another: The Maenads were women of Thebes said to worship Dionysos with wild orgiastic rites. Kadmos, so the story goes, sowed dragon's teeth in a field beside the river Ismenós. Up sprang a crop of fierce warriors who fought among themselves until only five remained. These victors became the first Thebans.   [18] *Castalia:* a spring on Mount Parnassus, named for a maiden who drowned herself in it to avoid rape by the god Apollo. She became a nymph, or nature spirit, dwelling in its waters. In the temple of Delphi, at the mountain's foot, priestesses of Dionysos (the "nymphs of Iacchos") used the spring's waters in rites of purification.   [19] *Evohé evohé!:* cry of the Maenads in supplicating Dionysos: "Come forth, come forth!"

ANTISTROPHE 2

CHORAGOS: Io[20] Fire! Chorister of the throbbing stars!
     O purest among the voices of the night!
895   Thou son of God, blaze for us!
CHORUS: Come with choric rapture of circling Maenads
     Who cry *Iô Iacche!*
                    God of many names!

EXODUS [21]
....

Enter Messenger from left.

MESSENGER: Men of the line of Kadmos, you who live
     Near Amphion's citadel,[22]
                              I cannot say
900   Of any condition of human life "This is fixed,
     This is clearly good, or bad." Fate raises up,
     And Fate casts down the happy and unhappy alike:
     No man can foretell his Fate.
                         Take the case of Creon:
     Creon was happy once, as I count happiness:
905   Victorious in battle, sole governor of the land,
     Fortunate father of children nobly born.
     And now it has all gone from him! Who can say
     That a man is still alive when his life's joy fails?
     He is a walking dead man. Grant him rich,
910   Let him live like a king in his great house:
     If his pleasure is gone, I would not give
     So much as the shadow of smoke for all he owns.
CHORAGOS: Your words hint at sorrow: what is your news for us?
MESSENGER: They are dead. The living are guilty of their death.
915 CHORAGOS: Who is guilty? Who is dead? Speak!
MESSENGER: Haimon.
     Haimon is dead; and the hand that killed him
     Is his own hand.
CHORAGOS: His father's? or his own?
MESSENGER: His own, driven mad by the murder his father had done.
920 CHORAGOS: Teiresias, Teiresias, how clearly you saw it all!
MESSENGER: This is my news: you must draw what conclusions you can
     from it.

---

[20] *Io:* "Hail" or "Praise be to. . . ."   [21] *Exodus:* the final scene, containing the play's
resolution.   [22] *Amphion's citadel:* a name for Thebes. Amphion, son of Zeus, had
built a wall around the city by playing so beautifully on his lyre that the charmed
stones leaped into their slots.

CHORAGOS: But look: Eurydice, our Queen:
Has she overheard us?

Enter Eurydice from the palace, center.

EURYDICE: I have heard something, friends:
925   As I was unlocking the gate of Pallas'[23] shrine,
For I needed her help today, I heard a voice
Telling of some new sorrow. And I fainted
There at the temple with all my maidens about me.
But speak again: whatever it is, I can bear it:
930   Grief and I are no strangers.

MESSENGER: Dearest Lady,
I will tell you plainly all that I have seen.
I shall not try to comfort you: what is the use,
Since comfort could lie only in what is not true?
The truth is always best.

                          I went with Creon
935   To the outer plain where Polyneices was lying,
No friend to pity him, his body shredded by dogs.
We made our prayers in that place to Hecate
And Pluto,[24] that they would be merciful. And we bathed
The corpse with holy water, and we brought
940   Fresh-broken branches to burn what was left of it,
And upon the urn we heaped up a towering barrow
Of the earth of his own land.

                          When we were done, we ran
To the vault where Antigone lay on her couch of stone.
One of the servants had gone ahead,
945   And while he was yet far off he heard a voice
Grieving within the chamber, and he came back
And told Creon. And as the King went closer,
The air was full of wailing, the words lost,
And he begged us to make all haste. "Am I a prophet?"
950   He said, weeping, "And must I walk this road,
The saddest of all that I have gone before?
My son's voice calls me on. Oh quickly, quickly!
Look through the crevice there, and tell me
If it is Haimon, or some deception of the gods!"

955   We obeyed; and in the cavern's farthest corner
We saw her lying:
She had made a noose of her fine linen veil

---

[23] *Pallas:* Pallas Athene, goddess of wisdom, and hence an excellent source of advice.
[24] *Hecate and Pluto:* two fearful divinities—the goddess of witchcraft and sorcery and the king of Hades, underworld of the dead.

And hanged herself. Haimon lay beside her,
His arms about her waist, lamenting her,
960   His love lost under ground, crying out
That his father had stolen her away from him.

When Creon saw him the tears rushed to his eyes
And he called to him: "What have you done, child? Speak to me.
What are you thinking that makes your eyes so strange?
965   O my son, my son, I come to you on my knees!"
But Haimon spat in his face. He said not a word,
Staring—
             And suddenly drew his sword
And lunged. Creon shrank back, the blade missed; and the boy,
Desperate against himself, drove it half its length
970   Into his own side, and fell. And as he died
He gathered Antigone close in his arms again,
Choking, his blood bright red on her white cheek.
And now he lies dead with the dead, and she is his
At last, his bride in the house of the dead.

Exit Eurydice into the palace.

975 **CHORAGOS:**   She has left us without a word. What can this mean?
MESSENGER: It troubles me, too; yet she knows what is best,
Her grief is too great for public lamentation,
And doubtless she has gone to her chamber to weep
For her dead son, leading her maidens in his dirge.

Pause.

980 **CHORAGOS:**   It may be so: but I fear this deep silence.
MESSENGER: I will see what she is doing. I will go in.

Exit Messenger into the palace.

Enter Creon with attendants, bearing Haimon's body.

CHORAGOS: But here is the king himself: oh look at him,
Bearing his own damnation in his arms.
CREON: Nothing you say can touch me any more.
985   My own blind heart has brought me
From darkness to final darkness. Here you see
The father murdering, the murdered son—
And all my civic wisdom!

Haimon my son, so young, so young to die,
990   I was the fool, not you; and you died for me.
CHORAGOS: That is the truth; but you were late in learning it.
CREON: This truth is hard to bear. Surely a god
Has crushed me beneath the hugest weight of heaven,

And driven me headlong a barbaric way

995 To trample out the thing I held most dear.

The pains that men will take to come to pain!

Enter Messenger from the palace.

MESSENGER: The burden you carry in your hands is heavy,
But it is not all: you will find more in your house.

CREON: What burden worse than this shall I find there?

1000 **MESSENGER:** The Queen is dead.

CREON: O port of death, deaf world,
Is there no pity for me? And you, Angel of evil,
I was dead, and your words are death again.
Is it true, boy? Can it be true?

1005 Is my wife dead? Has death bred death?

MESSENGER: You can see for yourself.

The doors are opened and the body of Eurydice is disclosed within.

CREON: Oh pity!
All true, all true, and more than I can bear!
O my wife, my son!

1010 **MESSENGER:** She stood before the altar, and her heart
Welcomed the knife her own hand guided,
And a great cry burst from her lips for Megareus[25] dead,
And for Haimon dead, her sons; and her last breath
Was a curse for their father, the murderer of her sons.

1015 And she fell, and the dark flowed in through her closing eyes.

CREON: O God, I am sick with fear.
Are there no swords here? Has no one a blow for me?

MESSENGER: Her curse is upon you for the deaths of both.

CREON: It is right that it should be. I alone am guilty.

1020 I know it, and I say it. Lead me in,
Quickly, friends.
I have neither life nor substance. Lead me in.

CHORAGOS: You are right, if there can be right in so much wrong.
The briefest way is best in a world of sorrow.

1025 **CREON:** Let it come,
Let death come quickly, and be kind to me.
I would not ever see the sun again.

CHORAGOS: All that will come when it will; but we, meanwhile,

1030 Have much to do. Leave the future to itself.

CREON: All my heart was in that prayer!

---

[25] *Megareus:* Son of Creon and brother of Haimon, Megareus was slain in the unsuccessful attack on Thebes.

CHORAGOS: Then do not pray any more: the sky is deaf.
CREON: Lead me away. I have been rash and foolish.
    I have killed my son and my wife.
    I look for comfort; my comfort lies here dead.
1035   Whatever my hands have touched has come to nothing.
    Fate has brought all my pride to a thought of dust.

*As Creon is being led into the house, the Choragos advances and speaks directly
to the audience.*

CHORAGOS: There is no happiness where there is no wisdom;
    No wisdom but in submission to the gods.
    Big words are always punished,
1040   And proud men in old age learn to be wise.

READING AND REACTING

1. What ideas does *Antigone* express about duty? About obedience? In what ways do these ideas conform (or fail to conform) to your own concepts of duty and obedience?

2. The chorus expresses the values of the community. According to the chorus, is Antigone a danger to the community's values? How far do you believe a community should go to protect its values?

3. Both Creon and Antigone defend rights that they believe are sacred. What rights are in conflict? Is there any room for compromise?

4. Do you sympathize with Antigone or with Creon? What characteristics of each do you find noble? Do you ever lose patience with either of them? Explain.

5. Aristotle believed that tragic heroes must be neither all good nor all evil; to be effective, they must have elements of both good and evil. To what extent does Antigone conform to Aristotle's requirements?

6. What is Antigone's fatal flaw? How does this flaw lead to the tragic resolution of the play?

7. As the play progresses, do Creon and Antigone change, or do they remain essentially unchanged by events?

8. What lines of dialogue do you believe best express the play's central theme?

9. At the end of *Antigone* the chorus says, "Big words are always punished, / And proud men in old age learn to be wise." Do you think Creon has gained wisdom from his experiences? Why or why not?

10. In what way does Antigone's gender affect her actions? In what way does it determine how she is treated? Are the play's attitudes toward women consistent with those of contemporary American society? Explain.

11. **JOURNAL ENTRY** If you were Antigone, would you have stuck to your principles, or would you have given in? Explain your reasoning.

12. **CRITICAL PERSPECTIVE** In *Sophocles the Playwright*, S. M. Adams argues that, to the ancient Greek audience, Antigone and Creon were both tragic heroes. Do you agree that the two characters are *both* tragic heroes? If so, do you see the fact that the play has two tragic heroes as a problem?

A. R. (ARTHUR RAMSDELL) "PETE" GURNEY (1930–) stakes out dramatic territory occupied in fiction by writers such as John Updike and John Cheever, examining what the *Village Voice* once called "the dying lifestyle of wealthy WASPdom." Born to an affluent Buffalo family who "had sat in the same pew for a hundred years," Gurney was educated at St. Paul's prep school, Williams College, and Yale, where he wrote the first musical produced there. Gurney made a minor splash on Broadway with musical adaptations of *Tom Sawyer* (1958) and *Around the World in Eighty Days* (1962), taught American literature at M.I.T. (a post he kept until the mid-1980s), and had a number of short plays produced off-Broadway and for television.

Gurney's breakthrough came in 1971 with a Lincoln Center production of his play *Scenes from American Life*—a success followed by a string of others, including *Children* (1974), *Who Killed Richard Cory?* (1976), *Entertaining Strangers* (1977) and three plays produced during the 1982–1983 season: *The Middle Ages, What I Did Last Summer,* and *The Dining Room. Sweet Sue* was published in 1987; *The Cocktail Hour, Perfect Party,* and *Another Antigone* in 1989; and *Love Letters* and *The Golden Age* in 1990. Gurney writes, says one reviewer, "with an interweaving detachment and no small sense of nostalgia intricately crafted scenes of a Protestant culture challenged by Jews, blacks, women, and others seeking a share of the American pie." His more recent plays include *Later Life* (1993), *A Cheever Evening* (1994), *Sylvia* (1995), and *Overtime* (1996), a sequel to Shakespeare's *The Merchant of Venice*.

Gurney's *Another Antigone* (1988), notes *New York Times* critic Jeremy Gerard, is a significant departure for a playwright noted for his light, satiric touch. Like Sophocles' *Antigone*, the play deals with the cost of adhering to values.

A . R . G U R N E Y , J R .

Another Antigone

(1989)

To John Tillinger

C H A R A C T E R S

HENRY HARPER, *Professor of Classics*
JUDY MILLER, *a student*
DIANA EBERHART, *Dean of Humane Studies*
DAVID APPLETON, *a student*

The play takes place in a university in Boston during the latter half of the spring term.

It is designed, as Sophocles' Antigone *was, to be performed without an intermission. If one is deemed essential, however, it should occur after Dave's last line on page 1766.*

The general effect of the set should evoke the Greek Revival architecture of a typical New England college. There should be columns and steps and benches. Somewhere in the center there should be a slightly abstracted desk and two chairs, indicating both Henry's and Diana's office. Near it is a bookcase, a filing cabinet, on which is an old hotplate, a possibly tin coffee pot, and a couple of cracked mugs. The general effect should be multi-scenic, fluid and shifting, indoors and out, and vaguely Greek.

AT RISE: Henry sits at his desk, perusing a typewritten paper. Judy sits in the other chair. She watches intently. He is middle aged and conservatively dressed. She, in her early twenties, is casually dressed in whatever students are currently wearing.

HENRY: *(Finally, putting the document down neatly on the desk between them).* Another Antigone.
JUDY: Did someone else write one?
HENRY: Sophocles[1] wrote one.
JUDY: No, I mean someone in *class.*

---

[1] Sophocles (c. 496–406 B.C.)—Greek dramatist. Sophocles, Aeschylus, and Euripides are considered the greatest Athenian tragic dramatists.

5 **HENRY:** Aeschylus[2] wrote one, which is lost. Euripides[3] we *think* wrote one. Seneca[4] tried to write one. Voltaire[5] tried not to. Jean Anouilh[6] wrote a rather peculiar one in 1944, during the Nazi occupation of Paris.

JUDY: But I'm the only one in *class* who wrote one.

HENRY: *(Weak smile).* That's right. *(Pause.)* This year.

JUDY: You mean, other students wrote them in other years?

HENRY: Oh yes.

10 **JUDY:** Really?

HENRY: Of course. *(Henry goes to the filing cabinet. He pulls out a drawer.)* Let's see . . . Antigone . . . Antigone . . . *(He thumbs through a file of old folders and records.)* Here we are. Antigone. *(He takes out a particular folder.)* Now. I have a record of one in 1955, written during the McCarthy hearings. And another, by a student who I recall was black, about the Civil Rights movement in 1963. And of course there were two, no, three, which cropped up during the Vietnam war.

JUDY: Did anyone ever deal with the Nuclear Arms Race before?

HENRY: No. As far as I know, you are the first to apply the Antigone myth to that particular topic.

JUDY: The story really turned me on.

15 **HENRY:** I'm glad it did. It is one of the great works of Western literature. Antigone herself is the classic rebel, the ancestor to such figures as Saint Joan or Martin Luther.

JUDY: Oh yes. I see that.

HENRY: And Creon[7] is the ultimate image of uncompromising political authority.

JUDY: I got that, too.

HENRY: Their clash is inevitable and tragic.

20 **JUDY:** I understand. *(Indicating her manuscript.)* I tried to make them like Jane Fonda and Ronald Reagan.

HENRY: I know what you tried to do, Miss . . . uh . . . Miss . . . *(He glances at her title page.)* Miller. I read all . . . *(He glances at the last page.)* twelve pages of it, in preparation for this conference. *(He slides the script across the desk to her. She takes it, looks at the title page, flips through it, looks at the last page, then looks at him.)*

---

[2] Aeschylus (c. 525–456 B.C.)—Greek dramatist.

[3] Euripides (c. 480–406 B.C.)—Greek dramatist.

[4] Seneca (Lucius Annacus Seneca; c. 3 B.C.–A.D. 65)—Roman philosopher, statesman, and dramatist.

[5] François Marie Arouet de Voltaire (1674–1778)—French philosopher and writer.

[6] Jean Anouilh (1910–1987)—French dramatist. His version is also entitled *Antigone*.

[7] The antagonist in *Antigone*. Antigone opposes Creon's law.

JUDY: You didn't mark it.

HENRY: I most certainly did. I underlined several run-on sentences, and I circled a rather startling number of misspelled words.

JUDY: No, I mean you didn't *grade* it.

25 **HENRY:** No I didn't.

JUDY: Why not?

HENRY: Because this course is about Greek tragedy, and your paper isn't.

JUDY: Did you grade those other *Antigone's?*

HENRY: I most certainly did not. I simply keep a record of them on file, the way the Pope keeps a file on various heresies.

30 **JUDY:** Well mine isn't a heresy!

HENRY: It is, to me.

JUDY: Don't you believe in nuclear disarmament?

HENRY: Of course I do. I think the arms race is madness.

JUDY: Then don't you think these things should be said?

35 **HENRY:** Absolutely. And I believe I said them, back in February, when I was discussing the political background of Greek drama. Then, if you'll remember, I compared Athens and Sparta, and pointed out rather frightening analogies to the United States and the Soviet Union.

JUDY: I had mono in February.

HENRY: Mono?

JUDY: Nucleosis. I kept falling asleep at the Film Festival, even during *Psycho.*

HENRY: I'm sorry to hear that. You must get the notes, then, from a fellow student. You might need them when you write your term paper.

40 **JUDY:** But this *is* my term paper.

HENRY: It's not on an assigned topic.

JUDY: It's on *Antigone.*

HENRY: But it's not on Sophocles.

JUDY: But I spent two weeks working on it.

45 **HENRY:** Sophocles spent two years.

JUDY: But I'm taking other courses!

HENRY: And Sophocles didn't—I grant you.

JUDY: Yes, but . . .

HENRY: Miss Miller: At the beginning of the semester, I handed out a list of assigned topics. I stated specifically that any departures from these topics should be cleared through me. Now suddenly, long before the term is over, I discover this odd effort, stuffed under my door, with no previous permission whatsoever.

50 **JUDY:** I had to try it first. To see if it worked.

HENRY: Well, you did. And it didn't.

JUDY: So what do I do?

HENRY: You read the texts carefully. You attend class religiously. And in the middle of May, you hand in a fifteen-page, coherently organized, typewritten paper, with adequate margins and appropriate footnotes, on the main issues of this course.

JUDY: Couldn't you give me partial credit? For the idea?

55 **HENRY:**   Miss Miller, how can I? It's misguided. It's wrong. You have taken one of the world's great plays, and reduced it to a juvenile polemic on current events.

JUDY: Juvenile?

HENRY: I'm sorry.

JUDY: Of course that's your opinion.

HENRY: I'm afraid my opinion is the one that counts.

60 **JUDY:**   But what if I put it on?

HENRY: On?

JUDY: In front of the class—just reading it out loud.

HENRY: Miss Miller: we have only so much time before the end of the term. We have yet to absorb the very difficult concept of Greek tragedy. I doubt if there's time in class to play show-and-tell.

JUDY: Then I'll do it somewhere else.

65 **HENRY:**   I'd spend my time on a paper.

JUDY: I'll do my play instead. You could come and see.

HENRY: I'm afraid I'd see a great gap in your education, Miss Miller. As well as in my list of grades.

JUDY: You mean I'd fail?

HENRY: You'd receive an incomplete.

70 **JUDY:**   Which means, since I'm a senior, that I'd fail. I wouldn't graduate, Professor Harper.

HENRY: Which means you'd better not spend these last valuable days of your academic life on amateur theatrics. *(He gets up, begins organizing his books and notes.)* And now I have to teach a class. And I strongly suspect you have to go to one. *(Judy gets up, too.)*

JUDY: Professor Harper, I don't want to sound conceited or anything, but you should know that after I graduate, I've been accepted for a special training program in investment banking at Morgan Guaranty Trust in New York City.

HENRY: My congratulations.

JUDY: Well, in my interview, they were particularly impressed by my leadership qualities, my creativity, and my personal sense of commitment. They wrote me that in a letter, Professor Harper.

75 **HENRY:**   Congratulations again.

JUDY: I also heard, from someone who works there, that I'm only the second Jewish woman to be brought into that program at that level since its inception.

HENRY: I am virtually overwhelmed.

JUDY: Yes, well, I believe in my abilities, Professor Harper. I plan to apply them. I'm going to put this play *on*. I wrote it, and I like it, and I'm committed to what it says. And if it's no good now, I'll work to make it better. And I'll bet, by the end of the term, you'll be able to give me a straight A.

HENRY: *(Turning, as if at the door.)* Miss Miller: After such a magnificent display of American optimism and industry, I'm tempted to give you a straight A right now.

80 **JUDY:**   Thank you.

HENRY: And I believe I would if this were a course on comedy. But alas, it is not. It's a course on tragedy. And you have just demonstrated that you have no conception of tragedy at all! *(He goes off, with his books and notes. Judy looks at him, and looks at her paper. She goes off, reading it aloud.)*

JUDY:

People of this land, we suffer under a yoke.
(She begins to realize a new pertinence.)
A tyrant rules our city, and unjust laws
Now squelch all forms of perfectly plausible protest . . .

(She goes off. As she goes off, Diana comes on to address the audience. She is a harassed, nervous, middle-aged woman, dressed efficiently. She speaks to the audience as if it were a group of concerned students. She might speak from note cards.)

DIANA: Good morning . . . I spoke to you as freshmen. I speak to you now as seniors and what we hope will be very generous alumni . . . The topic of today's meeting is "Preparing for the Future." I'll be brief, since I know all of you are waiting to hear from the Placement people about the world beyond these walls. I do want to make a quick comment on our curriculum, however. A number of you have recently complained about the traditional courses which are still required. Why, you ask, with tuitions so high and the search for jobs so increasingly competitive, are you forced to take such impractical courses? You may be sure, by the way, that the recruiting offices at I.B.M. and General Electric are asking the same question: Why must you take these things? After all, they are concerned only with some book, some poem, some old play. "Only some work," as my special favorite Jane Austen[8] once said, "in which the best powers of the mind are displayed, in the best chosen language." Well, there you are. They're the best. And we need no reason beyond that to justify, for example, Professor Harper's course on Greek tragedy. It deals with the best. It exists. It is there. And will remain there, among several other valuable requirements, for what we hope is a very long time. *(She glances offstage.)* And now, Alice Zimmerman, from Placement, will talk to you about . . . *(She glances at her note card.)* "The Job Market Jungle versus the Graduate School Grind." Those of you who are tardy now be seated. *(The late members of the audience may be*

---

[8] Jane Austen (1775–1817)—English novelist.

seated here.) Have a good morning. *(She goes off as Dave comes on from another direction. He reads aloud from a typewritten script.)*

DAVE:

"No, Antigone, no. Please reconsider.
Do not take on this dangerous enterprise.
The risks are too great, the payoff insignificant."
(Judy comes on, as if down the steps of the library, carrying a stack of books.)

85 **JUDY:** *(Breathlessly.)* Look what I got. *(Reads off the titles.)* The Nuclear Insanity . . . A World Beyond War . . . Our Debt to the Future . . . I'm going to put all this in.

DAVE: You're racking up a lot of time on this thing.

JUDY: Well I want to make it good. Did you read the first scene?

DAVE: *(Reciting by heart.)*

"No, Antigone, no. Please reconsider."

JUDY: What do you think? *(Pause.)*

90 **DAVE:** You're in blank verse.

JUDY: I know that.

DAVE:

Every line.
(Accentuates it.)
"Do *not* take *on* this *dang'*rous *enter*prise."

JUDY: I know.

DAVE: How come?

95 **JUDY:** *(Accenting it.)* I *just* got *into* it and *couldn't stop.*

DAVE: *(Dramatically, as if it were Shakespeare.)*

"The risks are too great, the payoff insignificant."

JUDY: Want to do this?

DAVE: Me?

JUDY: Want to?

100 **DAVE:** *(Looking at script.)* This is a woman's part. This is her sister talking here.

JUDY: I've changed it. I've made it her lover.

DAVE: Get someone from Drama.

JUDY: I already did. Drama people are doing all the other roles. Please, Dave. Do it.

DAVE: *(Melodramatically.)*

"No, Antigone, no. Please reconsider."
(Pause.) I better not, Judy.

105 **JUDY:** I need company.

DAVE: No thanks.

JUDY: I thought you liked Greek stuff.

DAVE: I do.

JUDY: You even talked me into taking the course.

110 **DAVE:** I know, I know.

JUDY: You're always borrowing the books . . .

DAVE: Yeah, but I don't have time for anything anymore. I've got a
double lab in my major this term. And a brutal schedule in track
every weekend. And, as you know, I'm not doing too well in either.

JUDY: You're doing fine. You're just a slow starter. *(Slyly.)* Which is part
of your charm.

DAVE: All I know is, you get straight A's, you've got a great job waiting
for you on the outside, you can afford to fool around with drama.
Me? I've only had one interview so far, and I blew it.

115 **JUDY:** You didn't *blow* it, Dave. You just overslept.

DAVE: Yeah well, how can we live together next year if I can't nail down
a job in New York? I've got to get my grades up, Jude.

JUDY: All right, Dave. That's cool. I'll look for someone else. *(She takes
her own copy of her script out of her backpack, looks at it, looks at him.)*
Would you at least read it with me?

DAVE: Sure.

JUDY: From the top?

120 **DAVE:** Sure. Why not? *(Reading.)*
"Hello, Antigone. And what brings you here,
Worried and out of sorts on this spring morning?
You look like you've got something on—
(Pause.)
—your mind."

JUDY: *(Reading.)*
"My friend Lysander—"

DAVE: *(Looking at his script.)* Lysander? I have "Beloved sister."

JUDY: That's what I changed. I changed it to Lysander.

DAVE: Lysander? That's Shakespeare. It's from *Midsummer Night's Dream.*

125 **JUDY:** It's also Greek. I looked it up.

DAVE: But it primarily—

JUDY: *(Reads, with feeling.)*
"My friend Lysander, will you join with me
In picketing and protesting the bomb
At several local military bases
Where nuclear arms are stored? And would you be willing,
O my loyal Lysander—"

DAVE: Lysander. Sounds like a disinfectant.

JUDY: *(Insistently.)*
"Would you be willing, O my loyal Lysander
Even to chain yourself to a chain-link fence
Or lie down in the road in front of a gate
And so prevent all types of vehicular access?"

130 **DAVE:** I do.

JUDY:
"And if the state police or National Guard,
Accompanied by snarling German shepherds,
Attempted to dislodge us from our task,

Would you be willing, my lover and my friend . . .
To go to jail with me, and there remain
At least till our parents post appropriate bail.
(Pause.)

DAVE: Who'll you get for Lysander if I don't do it?

JUDY: Oh probably that blond fraternity type who lifts weights and played the lead in *Fool for Love.*[9]

DAVE: Mark Shapiro? *(Judy nods.)* I'll do Lysander.

135 **JUDY:** Now don't if you don't want to.

DAVE: So I get another C in another course.

JUDY: Now think positively, Dave.

DAVE: So I mess up another interview.

JUDY: *(Handing him her script.)* I'll buy you a new alarm clock. Read from here.

140 **DAVE:** *(Looking at it.)* This is all new.

JUDY: I rewrote it last night. With you in mind.

DAVE: You knew I'd do it.

JUDY: I hoped you would. *(Henry reenters his office, settles into a chair to read a book.)*

DAVE: *(Kissing her.)*
"Antigone . . .
(Then reading.)
Much as I've loved you, even since freshman year,
And lived with you since the second semester of sophomore,
Built you a loft for our bed in off-campus housing,
Prepared your pasta, shared your stereo,
Still I have fears about what you've just proposed.
The risks are too great, the payoff insignificant."

145 **JUDY:** What do you think?

DAVE: I love it.

JUDY: You do?

DAVE: I love you.

JUDY: *(Taking the script back.)* I don't like it.

150 **DAVE:** What's the matter?

JUDY: It sounds wrong. I'm going to rewrite it.

DAVE: Again?

JUDY: *(Gathering up her books and bag.)* I'll make it better.

DAVE: What if you cut Lysander?

155 **JUDY:** Why? You're good. I'm going to build up his part.

DAVE: *(Following her.)*
"No, Antigone, no. Please reconsider."
(They go off as Diana appears in the doorway to Henry's office.)

DIANA: Henry?

---

[9] A 1983 play by American playwright/actor Sam Shepard.

HENRY: Yes? Come in. *(He sees her and jumps to his feet.)* Ah. Our Dean. Empress of all Humanities, including Remedial Reading. *(He gives her an elaborately courtly salute and bow.)*

DIANA: Knock if off, Henry.

160 **HENRY:** You look particularly lovely today, Diana. What is it? New hairdo? New blouse? New something.

DIANA: It's the same old me, Henry.

HENRY: No, no. There's something different. Maybe it's your eyes. They blaze like beacons 'cross The Hellespont.[10]

DIANA: And it's the same old you, Henry. You've been saying things like that for twenty years.

HENRY: And meaning them, Diana.

165 **DIANA:** I used to think you meant them. Now I know different.

HENRY: Dear lady . . .

DIANA: Now I know that you just say these things by rote, Henry. You say them to the librarian in the reserve book room, and you say them to the Xerox woman, and you say them to the cashier in the cafeteria. You say them to keep us all at a distance, so you won't have to say anything else. If any of us *did* have a new blouse, you wouldn't notice it at all.

HENRY: Now, Diana . . .

DIANA: Let's change the channel, shall we, Henry? Something's come up.

170 **HENRY:** What dark words seek to escape through the gate of thy teeth?

DIANA: Judy Miller.

HENRY: Judy . . . ?

DIANA: Miller. *(Pause.)*

HENRY: Ah. Miss Miller. *(French accent.)* L'affaire Antigone.

175 **DIANA:** You know that's why I'm here, Henry.

HENRY: I swear I didn't. I have a number of students, a number of courses.

DIANA: You teach two courses, Henry. And you have relatively few students in each. Now let's focus, please, on the issue.

HENRY: Administration has made you cruel as Clytemnestra.[11]

DIANA: Henry, *please. (Pause.)*

180 **HENRY:** All right. Judy Miller.

DIANA: I understand—

HENRY: Would you like some coffee? *(He crosses to pour her some.)*

---

10 Ancient name for the Dardanelles, a strait dividing European and Asian Turkey, and connecting the Sea of Marmara with the Aegean Sea. British poet George Gordon, Lord Byron, swam the Hellespont (May 3, 1810) and later wrote a poem about it, "Written after Swimming from Sestos to Abydos." It is interesting—perhaps ironic—that Henry, a classicist, makes such a decidedly Romantic allusion.

11 In Greek legend, the daughter of the King of Sparta and wife to Agamemnon. She murders her husband and is in turn killed by her son, Orestes.

DIANA: Yes, please—I understand she brought in a rewritten version.

HENRY: She brought in *two* rewritten versions.

185 DIANA: Well she brought one to me, as well.

HENRY: The first? Or the second?

DIANA: A third.

HENRY: I said I wouldn't read that one.

DIANA: It's not bad, Henry. It's longer, it's getting better. It's now at least a play.

190 HENRY: It's hopeless.

DIANA: Give her a B for effort.

HENRY: A *B?* I won't give her any grade at all.

DIANA: A student takes our course, becomes inspired by an old play, writes a modern version . . .

HENRY: And demonstrates thereby that she knows nothing about Sophocles, nothing about the Greeks, nothing about tragedy.

195 DIANA: Henry, she tried.

HENRY: And failed. A B? A B means good. A B means very good. I am not so far lost in the current inflation of grades as to litter the campus with disposable Bs.

DIANA: Oh, Henry . . .

HENRY: I'm sorry. If I gave her a grade for that nonsense, Diana, it would make the whole course meaningless. *(Pause.)* It would make *me* meaningless. *(Pause. Diana lights a cigarette.)* Still smoking, I see.

DIANA: Sometimes.

200 HENRY: Don't.

DIANA: I smoke, Henry, when I find myself caught in the middle of something. Which seems to be the case a good deal lately with this job.

HENRY: Ah hah. Second thoughts from our Dean. You asked for that job, Diana. You agitated for it. All the chatter about the need for more women at the administrative level. Well, now you've sunk to that level and it's leveling you. Come back to the classroom where you belong.

DIANA: Sometimes I wish I could.

HENRY: *(Taking an ashtray out of a desk drawer, holding it out to her.)* At least put out that cigarette. Life is tragic enough without your contributing to it.

205 DIANA: Let me enjoy it, Henry.

HENRY: Your lungs or mine, Diana. *(He holds out the ashtray.)* Put it out.

DIANA: You win. *(She puts it out; he cleans out the ashtray, puts it away.)* Now let me win one.

HENRY: No.

DIANA: How about partial credit?

210 HENRY: No.

DIANA: She's a senior. She needs to graduate.

HENRY: I'm sorry. *(Pause.)*

DIANA: She's putting it on, you know.
HENRY: The play?
215 **DIANA:**   She's putting it on.
HENRY: Reading it? In some dining hall?
DIANA: Staging it. She asked my permission to use Spingler Auditorium.
HENRY: You said No.
DIANA: I said Yes.
220 **HENRY:**   You gave her permission?
DIANA: Of course I gave it to her. I had to give it to her. *(Pause.)* I wanted
     to give it to her.
HENRY: Traitor. Or is it, Traitress?
DIANA: Well, I'm sorry, Henry. But there seems to be a lot of interest
     cropping up for this thing. Several of the student antinuclear groups
     want to sponsor it. Bill Silverstein is writing some incidental music
     on the Moog Synthesizer. And someone over in Art has agreed to do
     simple neoclassic scenery. They plan to present it on the Friday night
     before graduation. For parents. And alumni. And friends.
HENRY: Poor Sophocles . . .
225 **DIANA:**   Oh now.
HENRY: Set to the tune of a Moog Synthesizer.
DIANA: Yes well, it should create quite a stir.
HENRY: Quite a stir! That's it, exactly, Diana! Quite a stir! It will stir up
     a lot of cheap liberal guilt and a lot of fake liberal piety and a lot of
     easy liberal anger at the poor Creons of this world who are really
     working on this nuclear thing, and frantically trying to keep the
     world from blowing itself up!
DIANA: Oh, Henry . . .
230 **HENRY:**   Do you know what tragedy is, Diana?
DIANA: I think I do, yes.
HENRY: I don't think you do, Diana. I don't think anyone in this happy-
     ending country really does. Tragedy means the universe is unjust and
     unfair, Diana. It means we are hedged about by darkness, doom, and
     death. It means the good, the just, and well-intentioned don't always
     win, Diana. That's what tragedy means. And if we can learn that, if I
     can teach that, if I can give these bright, beady-eyed students at least
     a glimmer of that, then perhaps someday we will be able to join
     hands with our enemies across the water, or our neighbors down
     below, or the outcasts in our own back*yard,* and create a common
     community against this darkness. That's what I believe, Diana. And
     that's what Sophocles believed in 443 B.C. when he wrote *Antigone.*
     That's what Shakespeare believed when he wrote *King Lear.* Tragedy
     keeps us honest, keeps us real, keeps us human. All great nations
     should have a tragic vision, Diana, and we have none. And that is
     why I cannot endorse what this woman, no, this *girl,* is doing when
     she puts on her strident little travesty for the passing parade in
     Spingler Auditorium on graduation weekend. That is not tragedy,

Diana. That is just trouble-making. And I cannot give her credit for it. *(Pause.)*

DIANA: May I have the ashtray back, please?

HENRY: No.

235 **DIANA:** I want it *back*, Henry. I don't want to tap ashes all over your floor.

HENRY: *(Handing it to her.)* Here. *(Gets up.)* I'll open the door.

DIANA: I'd leave the door closed, Henry. Open the window if you want. This is private. *(She smokes.)*

HENRY: *(Not opening anything.)* Private?

DIANA: Have you given any thoughts to your low enrollments, Henry?

240 **HENRY:** Thought? Of course I've given thought. In a world of television and Punk Rock, it's a little difficult to maintain—

DIANA: The Provost thinks there might be another reason, Henry.

HENRY: The Provost?

DIANA: He brought it up last fall, when he saw the registration figures.

HENRY: And what does the Provost think?

245 **DIANA:** Apparently . . . over the years . . . there've been complaints about you, Henry.

HENRY: Oh I'm sure. That I take attendance. That I take off for misspellings. That I actually *call* on people in class.

DIANA: No, it's something else, Henry. Some students . . . over the years . . . have complained that you're . . . biased.

HENRY: Biased?

DIANA: Prejudiced.

250 **HENRY:** *Prej*udiced?

DIANA: Anti-Semitic, Henry. *(Pause.)*

HENRY: Say that again.

DIANA: There's been a pattern of complaints.

HENRY: But on what *grounds?*

255 **DIANA:** Apparently the administration thinks you make certain remarks in the classroom. Which students pass on. And cause others to stay away. *(Pause.)*

HENRY: This is ridiculous.

DIANA: I agree.

HENRY: And outrageous.

DIANA: I think so, too.

260 **HENRY:** It's slander! I'm going to see the Provost right now!

DIANA: Hold on, Henry!

HENRY: I mean this is unconscionable. It's like the time five years ago when poor Bob Klein was accused of some late night unpleasantness in the lab by that little temptress in a T-shirt. He had to resign.

DIANA: He resigned because he was *guilty*, Henry.

HENRY: Well I'm not guilty of anti-Semitism. Or do you think I am?

265 **DIANA:** I think you . . . make remarks, Henry.

HENRY: Remarks?

DIANA: For example, in the curriculum meeting last fall . . .

HENRY: What did I say?

DIANA: You told that joke.

270 **HENRY:** It was a good joke. I got that joke from Jack Nathanson.

DIANA: Well no one laughed when *you* told it, Henry. And no one laughed when you delivered that diatribe against Israel last week at lunch.

HENRY: That wasn't supposed to be funny.

DIANA: Well it certainly wasn't.

HENRY: I mean, when you think how we let one small country so totally dominate our foreign policy . . .

275 **DIANA:** Henry!

HENRY: Well I mean it's insane! It's suicidal! Pericles[12] warned us about it in 426 B.C.: "Beware of entanglements in Asia Minor," he said.

DIANA: Henry, Dick Livingston was sitting right across the *table* when you said those things!

HENRY: Is Dick Jewish?

DIANA: *I'm* Jewish, Henry.

280 **HENRY:** *You're* Jewish?

DIANA: Half Jewish. My mother was an Austrian Jew.

HENRY: I didn't know that.

DIANA: Well I am. And Judy Miller is Jewish. *(Pause.)*

HENRY: Has she complained that I'm prejudiced?

285 **DIANA:** No. *She* hasn't . . .

HENRY: But you still think I'm some raving neo-Nazi who is pumping anti-Semitic propaganda into his courses three times a week?

DIANA: *(Quietly.)* No. I think you're a passionate teacher and scholar, whose lectures are loaded with extravagant analogies which are occasionally misinterpreted by sensitive Jewish students.

HENRY: And the Provost?

DIANA: The Provost thinks it's an issue which should never even arise. Seeing as how we're in the middle of a major fund drive. And more and more, it seems to be Jewish generosity that's keeping us all afloat.

290 **HENRY:** *(Thinking.)* I do the Auerbach[13] thing at the beginning of the term.

DIANA: The Auerbach thing?

HENRY: A great scholar. Jewish, Diana. And superb! He sees two fundamental themes in Western culture. The Greek and the Hebraic. Odysseus versus Abraham. Public honor versus private conscience.

DIANA: Well maybe that starts you off on the wrong foot.

---

[12] Pericles (c. 495–429 B.C.)—Greek statesman. He dominated Athens for over thirty years, and was noted for his skill at oratory, his leadership, and his honesty.

[13] Erich Auerbach, noted literary scholar, whose work includes *Mimesis*. Before his death in 1957, Auerbach was a professor at Yale University.

HENRY: No, no. It works marvelously. I carry it further. I build to the basic contrast between Athens and Jerusalem.

295 **DIANA:** Well maybe those generalizations could be taken the wrong way.

HENRY: Do you think so?

DIANA: Henry: This is a free country. And academic life is even more so. You may write four-letter words all over the blackboard. You may denounce the government, blaspheme God, take off your clothes . . .

HENRY: Good Heavens, Diana . . .

DIANA: You may do all of these things in here, and most of them out there. But there is one thing, here and there, you may not do. You may *not* be insensitive about the Jews. That is taboo. The twentieth century is still with us, Henry. We live in the shadow of the Holocaust. Remember that, please. And be warned. *(Pause.)*

300 **HENRY:** I hear you, Diana.

DIANA: Thank you.

HENRY: I'll stay simply with the Greeks. I'll lash myself to the mast, and avoid the Bible. I'll even avoid the Book of Job.[14]

DIANA: Thank you, Henry.

HENRY: I must say, Diana, I've never really understood the Old Testament anyway. All that brooding, internal self-laceration. And the sense of a special contract with God. The sense of being chosen. The sense of sure salvation somewhere on down the line. Have you ever felt that? I haven't. But the Jews must feel it. Even after Auschwitz,[15] they feel it. Perhaps because of Auschwitz, they feel it all the more. I suppose that's why they put so much stock in their children. They spoil them, you know. The children are generally spoiled. They bring them to dinner parties. They teach them to feel—what is that word?—"entitled." Perhaps that's why this girl, excuse me, this woman, this Miss Miller, feels so strongly she deserves special treatment.

305 **DIANA:** Henry.

HENRY: My children don't feel that way. I taught my children to toe the mark. To take their turn. To submit to authority. Of course, that hasn't worked out so well either. I mean, I don't hear from my children much anymore. The Jews hear from their children. Their children telephone them all the time. *(Turns to her.)* I'm painting myself into a corner, aren't I?

DIANA: Yes you are, Henry.

---

[14] The Book of Job recounts the sufferings of Job, who despite the trials and hardships God bestows on him, persists in his faith.

[15] Notorious World War II Nazi concentration camp, where many of the Holocaust victims died.

HENRY: Yes. Well. You're right. All this could be . . . misinterpreted. I'll try to be more careful.

DIANA: Yes, I would, Henry. Because the Provost is talking about cutting back.

310 **HENRY:** Cutting back?

DIANA: On courses that are—undersubscribed.

HENRY: My course on tragedy is required!

DIANA: Your course is on a *list* of *several* required courses. And the Provost can take it off that list any time.

HENRY: What? Tear from the Tree of Knowledge one of the last golden apples that still remain? A course that survived the ghastly chaos of the sixties? A course that—

315 **DIANA:** Henry, he can do it.

HENRY: I'll be more careful . . . "Whom the Gods would destroy,[16] they first drive mad."

DIANA: Yes, well, and it might be a good idea, Henry—just to avoid any misunderstanding—to give Judy Miller a grade for what she's done. *(Pause.)*

HENRY: You *think* so?

DIANA: Yes I do. Otherwise you might come out of this whole thing looking very much like Creon in that damn play.

320 **HENRY:** This is not a tragedy by Sophocles, Diana. It is a comedy by Aristophanes,[17] at best. I am not Creon, and that little Jewish princess is not Antigone, Princess of Thebes.

DIANA: Cool it, Henry!

HENRY: *(With great reluctance.)* I'll give her a D. For Determination.

DIANA: Henry . . .

HENRY: *(Angrily.)* All right. A C, then. For Commitment.

325 **DIANA:** I don't think she'll accept a C.

HENRY: Won't *accept?*

DIANA: She feels she deserves a good grade.

HENRY: She'll get a good grade when she shows me some small awareness of what tragedy is. Lord knows she's shown me what it isn't. *(Judy comes out now. She sits on some steps or a bench D., takes a spiral notebook out of her backpack, and writes in it, concentratedly. Diana sighs and gets up.)*

---

[16] Publius Syrus, in his Maxim 911, says "Fortune" rather than "the Gods." The line as recalled by Henry is a paraphrased version from British poet John Dryden (1631–1700).

[17] Aristophanes (c. 450–385 B.C.)—Greek comic dramatist. Note that when Henry says "that little Jewish princess," he is using a pejorative term. This usage is in ironic contrast to "Antigone, Princess of Thebes."

DIANA: If I were you, Henry, I'd head for the hills of New Hampshire after your last class. I wouldn't want to be around when the grades go in and that play goes on and that girl doesn't graduate. Go up to your cottage, chop wood, disconnect the telephone.

330 **HENRY:** I don't like to go up there alone.

DIANA: Oh dear. Trouble again?

HENRY: Elsa's moved out. Again.

DIANA: She'll be back.

HENRY: I don't think so. She says now the children have gone, I'm impossible to live with.

335 **DIANA:** Now where did she get an idea like that? *(She goes out. Henry exits, after a moment, another way. The lights come up more fully on Judy, hard at her writing on the steps in the sun. Dave comes on carrying a paperback book.)*

DAVE: Hi.

JUDY: *(Looking up from her work.)* Hey, aren't you supposed to be in Chemistry?

DAVE: Missed it. Lost track of the time.

JUDY: But you flunked the last quiz.

340 **DAVE:** I got hung up reading one of your books.

JUDY: Which one?

DAVE: *(Showing her.)* Sophocles . . . *Antigone.*

JUDY: Oh. *(Pause.)*

DAVE: It's good.

345 **JUDY:** It's fair.

DAVE: It's awesome.

JUDY: It's good.

DAVE: Maybe we should do that version.

JUDY: What about mine?

350 **DAVE:** Maybe you'd get your A if you did Sophocles.

JUDY: I've thought about that, Dave: In Sophocles, all she wants to do is bury one dead brother.

DAVE: True.

JUDY: In mine, she sees everyone in the *world* as her brother, and she's fighting to keep them all *alive.*

DAVE: O.K., Jude. *(He sits down beside her, takes out a banana.)* Want some?

355 **JUDY:** No thanks.

DAVE: *(As he eats.)* While I was reading, your dad called.

JUDY: Again?

DAVE: From the hospital. Between patients.

JUDY: What did he want?

360 **DAVE:** He wants you to graduate.

JUDY: I'll graduate.

DAVE: He wants to be sure.

JUDY: Did you tell him I'm appealing to the Grievance Committee? Did you say that the Dean herself is presenting my case?

DAVE: He said committees make him nervous.

365 **JUDY:**   Well, parents make *me* nervous.

DAVE: He said he hasn't spent thirty years in the lower intestine just so his daughter could flunk college.

JUDY: Sounds familiar.

DAVE: He said write the paper. Get the degree. Argue with the professor after.

JUDY: That's my father.

370 **DAVE:**   That's everyone's father.

JUDY: Actually, I got a letter from my mother today.

DAVE: Coordinated attack, huh.

JUDY: She wrote from her office. On her "Department of Mental Health" stationery. Saying I was just acting out my guilt for being so lucky in life.

DAVE: You are lucky.

375 **JUDY:**   I know and I know they've worked hard to keep it that way. Moving to Westport, so I could grow up in a "healthy suburban environment." Sending me to Andover, so I could frolic in preppy heaven. Europe last summer, so I could learn how to use a credit card. Hell, four years *here,* for God's sake. And now they're offering to pay a psychiatrist two hundred dollars a week so I can blame it all on them.

DAVE: You're kidding!

JUDY: My mother even enclosed a note from my grandmother saying that Jewish people should bend over backwards not to make waves.

DAVE: Got you surrounded, huh?

JUDY: Sure have.

380 **DAVE:**   They all just want you to do well.

JUDY: I know that. I appreciate that.

DAVE: Look. Why not hedge your bets? Do the play *and* write the paper.

JUDY: I *can't,* Dave. I've tried and I can't. It all comes out fake and phony and not me.

DAVE: Then take the C. The Dean says Harper will give you that. Take it, and run.

385 **JUDY:**   I can't do that either.

DAVE: Why *not?*

JUDY: I don't know, Dave. Here I am working with a bunch of really dedicated people . . . trying to reach out to the local community . . . on a subject which deals with the survival of the entire planet . . . don't you think that's worth a tad more than a C, Dave?

DAVE: Sure it is.

JUDY: Then let me go for it.

390 **DAVE:**   O.K. Let's rehearse. (*He tosses the banana peel into a trash can with a basketball leap.*)

JUDY: Thanks, Dave. (*She hugs him.*) Listen to this new stuff. (*She reads what she has just written.*)

"Lately I'm feeling very much alone.
Even you, Lysander, seem to be backing off,
Advising caution, counseling compromise."

DAVE: *(Reading over her shoulder.)*
"I just don't want to see you get in trouble.
Just think what they could do to you, Antigone:
They could throw you in jail, there to be beaten up
By roving gangs of angry lesbians.
Or worse:
They could banish you, and send you off
With no degree to grace your resume
To fritter away essential earning years
In waitressing or joining a typing pool."

JUDY: *(Reading.)*
"Still, my conscience tells me I am right.
And if I am to suffer—"
(She stops; looks at him.)

DAVE: What's the matter?

395 **JUDY:**   Maybe I *am* just being a brat.

DAVE: No, no . . .

JUDY: A spoiled little JAP, playing sixties-type games as a last gasp
before facing up to the real world . . .

DAVE: Naaa . . .

JUDY: Maybe I should just take a massive all-nighter in the library, and
grunt out one of those boring, studenty papers with a title like
"Tragic Irony in Sophocles" or some such thing.

400 **DAVE:**   Sounds good to me. Want me to help?

JUDY: You don't have time. *(Looking at her notebook; reading.)*
"And yet this stupid arms race still goes on.
Oh it appalls me! God, it makes me mad!
(She begins to gather steam.)
It's as if the United States and Soviet Russia
Were two small boys comparing penises
With the fate of the world dependent on the outcome!"

DAVE: *(Covering his crotch.)* Right on, Antigone!

JUDY: *(Cranking up.)*
"Oh men, men, men!
Why are you all—with only a few exceptions—
(A glance at Dave.)
So miserably hung up on competition?
The Air Force General, the Corporation Executive,
The College Professor tyrannizing his students . . ."

DAVE: *(Looking over her shoulder.)* Hey! Where's that line? I don't see that.

405 **JUDY:**   I'm improvising! I'm winging it!
"The College Professor tyrannizing his students,
It seems the entire world is under the thumb

Of self-important men. I fear, Lysander,
That one of these days, one of these little men
Will reach across his desk and push the button
Which will destroy us all!"

DAVE: Now that's pretty good.

JUDY: *(Gathering up her stuff.)* No it isn't. And you know it isn't. But I'll make it better. *(She starts off.)*

DAVE: *(Starting after her.)* I'll give you a hand.

JUDY: You better make up that chemistry. There's no reason for you to flunk out, even if I do. *(She goes.)*

410 **DAVE:**   *(Calling after her.)* But I really want to—*(He looks at the Sophocles still in his hand, gets an idea, concludes quietly.)* Help. *(He goes off the opposite way as Henry enters to teach his class. He carries an old, worn leather book, stuffed with scraps of paper. He might use half-lens reading glasses, so that he can peer out at the audience as necessary.)*

HENRY: It might be particularly appropriate at this point in the course to let Sophocles speak for himself. I will try to translate for you— directly from the Greek—portions of the great choral ode from the *Antigone.* I will attempt to make it speak as immediately as I can. And I hope, as you hear it, you will compare it to other local efforts on this subject that may have come to your attention in recent weeks. *(Opening his book, finding his place, translating with great feeling.)*

"There are many wondrous things in the world,
But nothing is more wondrous than Man."

(Looks up.) Deinos . . . "wondrous" . . . the other day I heard one of you use the word "awesome." All right. Let's try *awesome. (Returns to text.)*

"Nothing is more awesome than Man."

(Looks up; sighs.) Or yes. All right. Today: woman. The point is nothing is more awesome than the human being. Here I used to contrast this awesome view with the rather abject and quarrelsome vision of man emerging in the Old Testament. But I won't do that now. Rather, returning to the text . . . *(He does.)* I will simply call your attention to the series of magnificent images on the taming of nature: ships, plows, fishnets, ox-yokes . . . *(Looks up.)* Today planes, rockets, computers, laser beams . . . *(Returns to text.)*

"which man has created through his uncanny technology."

(Looks up.) And then come our social inventions, those things we have invented to tame ourselves . . . *(Translates.)* "language which leads to thought" . . . "laws" . . . "medicine" . . . "religion" . . . "cities" . . . *(Looks up.)* There it is. The city. The *polis.* The human community. The result of all this creative activity. We'll come back to that. *(Translates.)*

"Man—or woman—is resourceful in everything, and proudly prepares for the future. *But* . . ."

(Looks up.) There is a big But here . . . But . . . *(Translates.)*

"There is one thing he can't tame, can't control: and that is Death."
(Looks up.) All right now, death was terrifying—the Greeks loved life—but
  Sophocles goes on to mention something *worse* than death. *(Looks at
  text.)* And here comes the crack of the whip: *(Translates grimly.)*
"Yet if, for the sake of pride, he . . .
(Looks up; is glad to use the feminine this time.) Or *she* . . . *(Returns to text.)*
"Goes too far, then he becomes an exile . . ."
(Looks up.) Which to the Greek was far, far worse than death. *(Translates.)*
"An exile without a country,
Lost and alone,
Homeless and outlawed forever."
You see? Sophocles joyfully celebrates the lawful human community, the
  Greek *polis,* but then threatens those who defy it with a death beyond
  death—exile, banishment, ostracism. *(Returns to the text.)*
"Lost and alone.
Homeless and outlawed forever."
(Looks up.) Last year, I compared these grim lines to the Hebrews'
  lamentations in the Psalms. This year, I will try to conjure up other
  images of profound alienation: *(He thinks.)* The haunted Orestes . . .
  Napoleon dying his slow death on the desolate island of Saint
  Helena . . . some lost astronaut severed forever from the good, green
  earth . . . *(Returns to the text.)*
"Homeless and outlawed forever."
(Pause.) Those words were written over two thousand years ago. I have
  read and taught them countless times. I get shivers up and down my
  spine every time I do. *(The bell rings. He closes his book.)* I think even
  Sophocles would commend my theatrical timing. For the next
  session, read *The Trojan Women* by Euripides. Feminists will appreciate
  his sympathetic portrayal of women. Pacifists will admire his bitter
  attack on war. Classicists, however, prefer to reach beyond such
  limited responses. Thank you, and good afternoon. *(He gathers his
  books as Dave approaches him.)*
DAVE: Professor Harper?
HENRY: *(Turning.)* Yes?
DAVE: I'm a friend of Judy's.
415 **HENRY:**   Judy?
DAVE: Miss Miller.
HENRY: Ah.
DAVE: *(Holding out envelope.)* She asked me to give you this.
HENRY: "Has she sent poison or some other implement of dark death?"
420 **DAVE:**   Excuse me?
HENRY: A line from *Medea*.[18]
DAVE: It's just her term paper.
HENRY: She should be in class. She should hand it in herself.

---

[18] By Euripides (431).

DAVE: I think she's—a little mad at you, sir.
425 **HENRY:**   Mad? At me? Because I want her to learn? Oh dear. Would you
    tell her, please, that the quest for truth and beauty is a slow and
    painful climb, and she shouldn't bite the hand that leads her. *(His
    little pun.)*
DAVE: I'll—tell her something.
HENRY: Good. Meanwhile, I'll take that paper, in hopes she soon will
    return to the fold.
DAVE: Thank you, sir.
HENRY: *(Opening the envelope, sliding the paper out far enough to read the
    title.)* "Tragic Irony in Sophocles' *Antigone*." A good, no-nonsense title.
430 **DAVE:** I'll tell her, sir. *(He starts off.)*
HENRY: *(Pulling the paper out of the envelope.)* Lovely looking paper . . .
    Well typed.
DAVE: Mmm.
HENRY: Is this an electric typewriter?
DAVE: No actually, it's a word processor.
435 **HENRY:**   She can't come to class, but she seems to have found time to
    form a relationship with a computer.
DAVE: Actually, I did the typing, sir.
HENRY: Well let's hope the contents are as attractive as the form. *(He
    starts to thumb through the papers.)*
DAVE: I'll be going, then. *(He starts off.)*
HENRY: *(As he reads; calling out.)* Oh, ah, Mr.—
440 **DAVE:** *(Stopping, turning.)* Dave.
HENRY: Do you have a moment?
DAVE: Well I—
HENRY: Would you be so kind as to accompany me to my office?
DAVE: Me?
445 **HENRY:**   If you would.
DAVE: Now?
HENRY: If you'd be so kind. *(He turns and crosses slowly toward his office,
    still reading the paper. Dave hesitates a moment, and then follows. Henry
    enters his office, and sits at his desk, still reading. Dave stands in the
    doorway. As he reads, gesturing vaguely.)* Please sit down, Mr. . . . ah . . .
DAVE: Dave.
HENRY: Sit down, please.
450 **DAVE:** Thank you. *(He sits on the edge of the chair. Henry continues to read.
    Dave watches him.)*
HENRY: *(As he reads.)* This . . . appears to be . . . an excellent paper.
DAVE: Is it?
HENRY: *(Thumbing through to the end.)* Even a cursory glance tells me
    it's first-rate.
DAVE: I'll tell her, sir.
455 **HENRY:**   I've been around a long time. I've taught this course a good
    many years. I know a good paper when I see one, and I see one here.
DAVE: *(Almost at the door.)* That's great, sir.

HENRY: *(Quietly.)* Who wrote this?

DAVE: Huh?

HENRY: Who wrote this paper?

460 **DAVE:** Judy wrote it.

HENRY: No she didn't. I've also been around long enough to know that. She wrote a promising little essay for me at the start of the semester. She wrote a rather breathless hour exam. But she did not write this. She is not yet capable of the care and commitment I see emerging here.

DAVE: Maybe she's changed, sir.

HENRY: Ah. Then I would like to discuss this paper with her. Would you get her, please?

DAVE: I think she's rehearsing, sir.

465 **HENRY:** Then I must ask you to seek her out. Tell her I am passionate to engage in an intensive discussion with a kindred classicist.

DAVE: Sir . . .

HENRY: You might also tell her, *en passant,*[19] that I think this is plagiarism, pure and simple. She has tried to pass off as her own the work of somebody else. This is an offense punishable, according to the rules, by . . . *(He has found the college rule book and is already thumbing through it. He finds his place.)* "Automatic failure of the course involved."

DAVE: Sir . . .

HENRY: *(Reading.)* "And, after due deliberation by the Discipline Committee, possible expulsion from the University." *(Pause. He looks at Dave.)*

470 **DAVE:** *(Quietly.)* Oh boy.

HENRY: You might also be interested in the fact that . . . *(He reads again from the book.)* "persons aiding or contributing to a plagiaristic act will similarly be charged and punished." *(Looks up.)* You personally might be interested in that, Mr.—?

DAVE: Appleton.

HENRY: Well I'm not going to press charges against you, Mr. Appleton.

DAVE: Sir—

475 **HENRY:** Nor am I going to press charges against Miss Miller. Believe it or not, I would hate to prevent her from graduating. I would simply ask you to tell her to make an appointment at her earliest convenience, so that I may explain to her why, in the world of scholarship and learning, plagiarism is a dark and bloody crime. *(Dave stands at the door.)* That's all I have to say. You may go.

DAVE: She didn't write it.

HENRY: *(Infinitely patient.)* Yes I know. That's what I've been saying.

DAVE: No, I mean she doesn't even know about it.

---

[19] In passing.

HENRY: Doesn't know?

480 **DAVE:**   She still wants her play to be her paper. *(Pause.)*

HENRY: Then who wrote this?

DAVE: I did.

HENRY: Unbeknownst to her?

DAVE: Yes, sir.

485 **HENRY:**   Hoping I'd give it a good grade, and she'd go along with it, and the problem would be solved?

DAVE: I don't know what I hoped. *(Pause.)*

HENRY: *(Looking at paper again.)* And where did you get this paper? From some other student at some other college? From one of those companies who accept money and do your research?

DAVE: No! I wrote it myself.

HENRY: I don't believe that.

490 **DAVE:**   Well I did.

HENRY: How could you? You're not in my course.

DAVE: I still wrote it. *(Pause. Henry looks at the paper, looks at Dave.)*

HENRY: Sit down, please. *(Dave does. Henry is now all business.)* Name three plays by Sophocles beside the *Antigone.*

DAVE: *Oedipus Rex, Oedipus at Colonnus . . . Ajax.*

495 **HENRY:**   Describe Antigone's genealogy.

DAVE: Her father was Oedipus. Her mother, Jocasta. Her sister was Ismene. She had two brothers, Eteocles and Polyneices. *(Pause.)* Who killed each other. *(Pause.)* Fighting. *(Pause.)* For the throne. *(Pause.)* Of Thebes. *(Pause.)*

HENRY: And what, briefly, do you think *is* the "Tragic Irony in Sophocles' *Antigone"?*

DAVE: I don't think it's Antigone's tragedy at all. I think it's Creon's.

HENRY: And why do you think that?

500 **DAVE:**   Because she at least wins her point in the end.

HENRY: She dies.

DAVE: But she wins. He loses. Everything. The Gods are much more unfair to him. *(Pause.)*

HENRY: You're very good.

DAVE: Thank you.

505 **HENRY:**   Where did you learn all this?

DAVE: I read the play.

HENRY: *(Indicating paper.)* No. There's more here than just that.

DAVE: My grandfather liked the Greeks.

HENRY: Was he an academic?

510 **DAVE:**   No. He just liked the classics. He spent most of his spare time in the library, reading the Greeks.

HENRY: And he taught you?

DAVE: Right. And I kept it up when I had time.

HENRY: I could never get my own son to read anything but science fiction.

DAVE: That's what my dad reads. *(They laugh together.)*
515 **HENRY:** Why have you never taken a course from me?
DAVE: I couldn't fit it into my schedule.
HENRY: What's your major?
DAVE: Chemistry.
HENRY: Better worlds through chemistry, eh.
520 **DAVE:** Actually, my grades aren't too good.
HENRY: They'd be good in the classics.
DAVE: Not many jobs out there in that.
HENRY: Still, you should take my course.
DAVE: I wish I could.
525 **HENRY:** We could do a special seminar together. Study one play in depth. I'm fascinated with the *Antigone.* We could really dig in, you and I, next fall.
DAVE: I'm supposed to graduate this spring, sir.
HENRY: Oh dear . . . Then perhaps we might meet in the afternoon, from here on in. A small tutorial.
DAVE: I can't, sir. I'm on the track team.
HENRY: The track team? Splendid! The Greeks invented competitive sport!
530 **DAVE:** I know.
HENRY: *Hygies psyche meta somatos hygious.*
DAVE: Excuse me?
HENRY: We'll shift to Latin: *Mens sana in corpore sano.*
DAVE: *(Trying to translate.)* Sane mind . . .
535 **HENRY:** Sound mind in a sound body. The Tenth Satire by Juvenal.[20]
DAVE: Juvenal . . . Tenth . . .
HENRY: You don't by any chance throw the discus, do you? No, that would be too much.
DAVE: I just run the Four Hundred.
HENRY: Ah. Fleet of foot. A true Greek. "Skilled in all ways of contending."
540 **DAVE:** Thank you, sir.
HENRY: Well, then, I wonder if I might keep this fine paper long enough for Mrs. Murphy to make a Xerox copy.
DAVE: Sure. *(He gets up to leave.)*
HENRY: Just to remind me occasionally of what a good student can do.
DAVE: Sure. *(He starts for the door. At this point, Judy enters at another part of the stage. She sits on a bench, and waits impatiently, as if in a waiting room.)*
545 **HENRY:** You must be very fond of Miss Miller.
DAVE: I am.
HENRY: To have written this for her.

---

[20] Juvenal (Decimus Junius Juvenalis; c. A.D. 60–130)—Roman satirist.

DAVE: I liked writing it.

HENRY: Will you be seeing her soon?

550 **DAVE:** I think so.

HENRY: Would you remind her that she and I have yet to resolve our difficulties?

DAVE: She's stubborn, sir.

HENRY: I give you permission to help her. Be her tutor. See that she gets some small awareness of Greek tragedy.

DAVE: She thinks she already has, sir.

555 **HENRY:** But she *hasn't!* She sees answers, solutions, revisions. Tell her there are things beyond the world of management which are profoundly unmanageable!

DAVE: She wouldn't listen, sir.

HENRY: Then she and I are on a collision course.

DAVE: I'm afraid so, sir. *(Dave starts for the door again.)*

HENRY: One more minute, please *(Dave stops.)* Appleton, you said your name was?

560 **DAVE:** That's right.

HENRY: English, I suppose.

DAVE: Originally.

HENRY: The English love the classics.

DAVE: Yes.

565 **HENRY:** And Miss Miller's Jewish.

DAVE: That's right.

HENRY: May I speak classicist to classicist?

DAVE: Yeah. Sure.

HENRY: What you are witnessing here, Mr. Appleton, is once again the age-old clash between Athens and Jerusalem.

570 **DAVE:** I don't get you, sir.

HENRY: Read Tertullian.[21] Third century, A.D. "What is Athens to Jerusalem, or Jerusalem to Athens?" There it all is. The private conscience versus the communal obligation. Jew versus Greek. Miss Miller versus me.

DAVE: You think so?

HENRY: I do, but they tell me I shouldn't.

DAVE: It seems a little . . . exaggerated, sir.

575 **HENRY:** You're probably right. *(Henry gets up; takes his arm.)* Come, I'll walk with you down the hall. Plato and Aristotle, strolling through the colonnades of academe. We'll discuss simply Sophocles.

DAVE: O.K.

HENRY: *(As they go.)* And I hope Miss Miller appreciates this grand gesture you made on her behalf.

---

[21] Tertullian (Quintus Septimius Florens Tertullianus; c. A.D. 160–225)—African Father of the Church, born in Carthage.

DAVE: God, I hope she never finds out about it. *(They go out as Diana comes on, carrying a folder. Judy gets up expectantly.)*

JUDY: Well?

580 **DIANA:** The meeting's over.

JUDY: And?

DIANA: *(Deep breath.)* The Grievance Committee voted against you, Judy.

JUDY: Against?

DIANA: I'm sorry. *(They move into her office.)*

585 **JUDY:** Did the students on the committee vote against me?

DIANA: I can't reveal the specific vote.

JUDY: How about you? How did you vote?

DIANA: I abstained, of course. Since I was presenting your case.

JUDY: How would you have voted? If you could have? *(Pause.)*

590 **DIANA:** Against.

JUDY: What?!

DIANA: I put your case as fairly as I could, Judy. Really. But your argument simply didn't hold. The committee felt you were asking them to violate the integrity of the classroom. You want them to intrude on a principle that goes back to the Middle Ages.

JUDY: But other people do it all the time! There's a guy in Geology who got partial credit for skiing down Mount Washington!

DIANA: I know . . .

595 **JUDY:** And there's a girl who passed her Chemistry lab by cooking a crabmeat casserole.

DIANA: I know that, and I think it's disgraceful. But those are other instructors. We cannot dictate standards to *any* professor. You signed up for Greek tragedy. You bought the books. You read the syllabus. You agreed in effect to submit to the rules. There it is.

JUDY: There it is. Everyone seems to be backing off these days. You, my family, now the committee.

DIANA: Oh, Judy . . .

JUDY: *(Almost in tears.)* I guess I'm doomed to be alone.

600 **DIANA:** What about all those people working on your play?

JUDY: It's just extra curricular to them. I'm the one who's really on the line.

DIANA: Well what about that boy you go with?

JUDY: Oh, he just loves me, that's all.

DIANA: *(Lighting a cigarette.)* Well I'm sorry, Judy. I did what I could.

605 **JUDY:** Please don't smoke!

DIANA: I'm sorry.

JUDY: I think I'm allergic to it.

DIANA: All right, Judy.

JUDY: And it violates my air space.

610 **DIANA:** *(Putting cigarettes away.)* All right, all right. *(Pause.)*

JUDY: So what do I do?

DIANA: I told you: he's offered a C.

JUDY: I'm beyond a C.

DIANA: Beyond?

615 **JUDY:** I can't settle for a C.

DIANA: Then you won't graduate.

JUDY: Not in June. No.

DIANA: That's ridiculous!

JUDY: I'll make it up in summer school with that course on comedy where all they do is study *Annie Hall*. You can mail me my degree in September.

620 **DIANA:** That makes me a little angry, Judy. You told me you wanted to stand up with your class.

JUDY: I'm standing up, all right.

DIANA: But you'll lose your job! It depends on your graduating.

JUDY: I'll find another.

DIANA: That's not so easy these days.

625 **JUDY:** What's a job anyway? Is it the most important thing in the world? I suppose this is a hopelessly middle-class thing to say, but am I supposed to live and die over a job? Do you? You've been here a long time, worked your way up, now you're Dean of the whole department. Is that *it?* Are you in heaven now? Aren't there other things in your life beside your job?

DIANA: *(Taken aback.)* Of course there are, Judy . . .

JUDY: I mean, that's all I cared about, once upon a time. A *job*. I couldn't wait until I was scampering up and down Wall Street in my gray and white Adidas and a new suit from Saks, with my little leather briefcase swinging by my side. Meeting men for lunch and women for dinner, and both in the Health Club afterwards. A co-op on the East Side with a VCR and an answering machine with a funny message. Weekends at Sugarbush and Vineyard. Vacations in the Bahamas and France. Nailing down forty or fifty thou per annum within three years. Moving onward and upward through the corridors of power until I get an office with a corner view where I can look down on millions of women scampering up and down Wall Street in their gray and white Adidas.

DIANA: That's not the worst thing in the world!

JUDY: Isn't it? I'm not so sure. I'm beginning to think it's a con deal. All us women now killing ourselves to do those things that a lot of men decided not to do twenty years ago. I mean, here we are, the organization women, punching the clock, flashing the credit card, smoking our lungs out, while the really smart men are off making furniture or playing the clarinet or something. Look at you. Do you really want to be Dean, or are you just making some sort of feminist statement?

630 **DIANA:** Let's leave me out of this, please.

JUDY: Well all I know is I'm not so hung up on "The Job" anymore. It just seems like more of the same. More of what I did at Andover and

at Westport Junior High before that. More of what I've done every
summer, with my creative camps and Internships and my Special
Summer Projects. Touching all the bases, following all the rules, ever
since I can remember. And now here I am, about to graduate, or
rather *not* graduate, because I've come up with the first vaguely
unselfish idea I've ever had in my life, and this place, this
institution—in which my family has invested at least seventy
thousand dollars—won't give me credit for it.

DIANA: A C is a decent grade, Judy. We used to call it a gentleman's C.

JUDY: Well I'm no gentleman. *(She starts out.)*

DIANA: Judy . . . One more thing. *(Judy stops, turns.)*

635 **JUDY:** What?

DIANA: The Provost sat in on the Grievance Committee meeting.

JUDY: And?

DIANA: After it was over, he took me aside. He asked me to ask you a
question.

JUDY: Go ahead.

640 **DIANA:**   . . . the Provost wondered if your difficulty with Professor
Harper has anything to do with . . . ethnic issues.

JUDY: Say again?

DIANA: A student has recently complained that Professor Harper is
anti-Semitic?

JUDY: Anti-Se*mitic?*

DIANA: That's the complaint.

645 **JUDY:** Anti-Semitic? It's probably that Talmudic type who sits in the
front row and argues about everything. I bet he wears his yarmulke
even in the shower.

DIANA: Ah, but you don't feel that way?

JUDY: No way.

DIANA: Oh, Judy, I'm so glad to hear it.

JUDY: I never even thought of it.

650 **DIANA:** Good. Then I'll tell the Provost.

JUDY: I mean should I worry about that? My grandmother says you have
to watch out for that sort of thing at all times.

DIANA: Yes, well, times change.

JUDY: Unless it's there, and I didn't see it.

DIANA: No, no . . .

655 **JUDY:** I mean, maybe I'm so assimilated into white-bread middle-class
America that it passed me right by. Maybe I should reexamine this
whole issue with that in mind. Thanks a lot, Dean! *(She goes out.)*

DIANA: *(Calling after her.)* Judy! Judy! . . . Oh God! *(She makes up her
mind, opens a desk drawer, takes out a small tape recorder which she slams
onto the desk. She pushes the buttons determinedly and then begins to
dictate, pacing around her office as she smokes. Dictating.)* Monica,
please type a letter to the Provost . . . Dear Walter . . . I herewith
submit my resignation as Dean, to be effective at the end of this

school year. I find I long to return to the clear lines and concrete issues of the classroom. I especially yearn to resume my studies of Jane Austen, and the subordinate role of women in the 18th century. I will miss, of course, the sense of bustle and activity I've found here in Administration. There's something to be said, after all, for the friendships which come from working closely with other people during regular hours—among which I count my friendship with the other Deans, and you, Walter, and Monica, my fine assistant . . . Indeed, in some ways, I dread retreating to the hermetic world of bickering colleagues, sullen students, hopeless meetings, long hours of preparation . . . *(She slows down.)* . . . the loneliness of the library . . . the meals alone . . . the sense that something more important is going on everywhere else in the world . . . *(Long pause.)* Just type a rough draft of this, Monica. I'll look at it tomorrow. *(She clicks off the tape recorder, puts it back in her desk. Dave enters in a track suit, starts doing stretch exercises. Diana crosses to doorway, calls off.)* Monica, see if you can locate Professor Harper . . . *(Then she takes some computer printout sheets out of her briefcase and begins to go over them at her desk as the lights dim on her. The lights come up more fully on Dave, doing stretch exercises. We hear the distant sounds of students cheering. Judy comes on. It is by now late enough in the spring so she doesn't wear a jacket.)*

JUDY: Dave . . . *(She hugs him from behind.)*
DAVE: *(Through his stretches; pantingly.)* Hi . . .
JUDY: Am I bothering you?
660 **DAVE:** *(Grunting; stretching.)* Yes . . . But that's O.K.
JUDY: I just want to tell you something, David.
DAVE: *(Still exercising.)* Uh oh. When it's David, it's serious.
JUDY: I just want to tell you not to memorize any more of those speeches.
DAVE: Thank God.
665 **JUDY:** I'm changing everything.
DAVE: Again?
JUDY: I'm starting all over. From scratch.
DAVE: Why?
JUDY: I didn't like what we had. I can do better.
670 **DAVE:** Yeah?
JUDY: Now I'm on a totally different track. I mean, it's still *Antigone*. But I'm adding a whole new dimension.
DAVE: Are you throwing in acid rain?
JUDY: *(Laughing.)* No. I'm onto something much deeper. *(A whistle is heard offstage. Dave starts off.)*
DAVE: There's the Four Hundred. I've got to go.
675 **JUDY:** So throw away the old stuff.
DAVE: Is there a lot new to learn?
JUDY: Mostly for me.
DAVE: Can you tell me where you're taking it?

JUDY: Well I'm striving for a more natural style.

680 **DAVE:**   Way to go.

JUDY: And I'm connecting my attack on nuclear armaments with the issue of meaningful work.

DAVE: Excellent.

JUDY: And I'm making Antigone Jewish. *(She goes off. Another whistle from offstage. He looks after her, then runs off the opposite way as . . . the lights come up on Diana, who is still at her desk, working on printout sheets. After a moment, Henry appears in the doorway. He watches her affectionately for a moment.)*

HENRY: *(Finally.)* Woman at her work. I am reminded of Penelope at her loom.

685 **DIANA:**   *(Looking up; quickly putting away the sheets.)* Come in, Henry.

HENRY: *(Coming in.)* What a magnificent office, Diana! What corporate dimensions! *(As Diana puts her cigarette out.)* Thank you . . . A view of the Charles! The spires of Harvard dimly seen up the river! How different it is from the monkish cells assigned to those of us who teach.

DIANA: You've been here before, Henry.

HENRY: Never. I've scrupulously avoided all official contact with the bureaucracy, except on my own turf. I wouldn't be here now, dear Diana, but for a series of rather frantic telephone messages left under my door. *(He takes a stack of pink slips out of his pocket, reads.)* Call the Dean . . . See the Dean . . . Please call or see the Dean.

DIANA: Sit down, Henry.

690 **HENRY:**   *(Sitting.)* I will, but I must warn you I have very little time. We are now deep in the last plays of Euripides, particularly the *Bacchae*, which I continually find to be one of the more profoundly disturbing works of man. He has an even darker vision than Sophocles.

DIANA: Well maybe I've got some news that will cheer you up, Henry.

HENRY: Beware of Deans bearing gifts.

DIANA: Remember that grant you applied for two years ago?

HENRY: Ah yes. To go to Greece. To see the restorations at Epidaurus.[22] *(Pause.)* And to restore a ruin or two in my own life.

695 **DIANA:**   Well you've got that grant now, Henry.

HENRY: Now?

DIANA: I've been talking to the Provost. He's giving you next year off. All year. At full pay.

HENRY: Are you serious?

DIANA: I'm always serious, Henry. That's my problem, in case you ever notice. *(Pause.)*

700 **HENRY:**   Why suddenly now?

---

[22] Or Epidauros, an ancient city-state in Greece. The fourth-century B.C. theater there is preserved and still used for plays.

DIANA: Ours not to reason why, Henry.

HENRY: I begged for that leave two years ago. I practically fell to my knees and supplicated the Provost like old Priam before Achilles.[23] I thought if Elsa and I could just get away . . .

DIANA: Call her. Tell her you've lucked out, at long last.

HENRY: It's too late. She's . . . found someone. Apparently they sit and hold hands and watch television. Anyway, she wants a divorce.

705 **DIANA:** I am sorry.

HENRY: No, no, it's good. It's very good. The other shoe has dropped. Finally.

DIANA: Take one of your children then. Give them a trip.

HENRY: They wouldn't come. *(Pause.)* They have their own lives. *(Pause.)* Such as they are. *(Quietly.)* I'll go alone. *(Pause; he looks at her.)* Unless you'd come with me.

DIANA: Henry!

710 **HENRY:** Why not? Take a sabbatical. You're overdue.

DIANA: You mean, just—blip out into the blue Aegean?

HENRY: Exactly! Spend a naughty year abroad with an old satyr. Tell you what, I'd even let you smoke.

DIANA: I think I'd give it up if I went abroad.

HENRY: Then there we are!

715 **DIANA:** Oh gosh! To get away! To see something else besides these— walls! Just think, Henry . . . *(She stops.)* Just think. *(Pause. Sadly.)* It wouldn't work, Henry.

HENRY: It might.

DIANA: It already didn't, Henry. On that strange weekend in that gloomy hotel during the M.L.A. conference.

HENRY: That was a lovely weekend.

DIANA: It was not.

720 **HENRY:** Dido and Aeneas in their enchanted cave . . .

DIANA: Oh Henry, *please!*

HENRY: What's the matter?

DIANA: Dido, Penelope,[24] Clytemnestra! I am not a *myth,* Henry! I am not a *meta*phor!

HENRY: My dear lady . . .

725 **DIANA:** No, no, I'm *me,* Henry! I live and breathe in my own right! Do you know anything about my *life?* Do you know where I live? Do you know I have a daughter in Junior High?

---

23 In Greek legend, Priam, the last King of Troy, lost most of his sons in the Trojan War and was forced to beg Achilles for the body of Hector.

24 In Greek legend, Dido fled to Africa after her husband was murdered and founded Carthage. In one version of the myth she throws herself on a funeral pyre to avoid marriage to Iarras of Numidia; in Virgil's *Aeneid,* she kills herself after being abandoned by Aeneas, her lover. Penelope is the faithful wife of Odysseus (Ulysses), who rejected suitors and patiently awaited his return from his years of adventuring.

HENRY: Of course I know you have . . .

DIANA: What's her name, Henry? What's my daughter's *name?* It's not Electra and it's not Athena and it's not . . .

HENRY: Let me think . . .

DIANA: You don't *know,* Henry. And you don't know that my mother died last semester, and you don't know that I used to play the French horn. You don't *see* me, Henry. You don't see anyone. In your mind, everything is an example of something else! I suppose it's called stereotyping, but whatever it is, I don't like it, Henry! It makes me feel insignificant and unreal.

730 HENRY: Diana, dear friend . . . *(He moves toward her.)*

DIANA: No, now stay away from me, Henry. Don't touch me. Go to *Greece,* for God's sake! Find some young woman—excuse me, some sea nymph—who will throw herself into your arms on the topless shores of Mykonos. Really. Just go. *(Pause.)*

HENRY: Tell the Provost I'll take a raincheck.

DIANA: A raincheck?

HENRY: Maybe in a year or two. When my life is more in order.

735 DIANA: It doesn't work that way, Henry. It's now or not at all.

HENRY: Then I'll have to forgo it.

DIANA: Oh Henry . . .

HENRY: At this point in my life, I need my classes. Strange as that may seem. *(He starts out.)* And now, if you'll excuse me, the *Bacchae* call me to the dance.

DIANA: Henry! *(He stops.)* Other things go on in this university at the end of the school year besides discussions of the *Bacchae.*

740 HENRY: *(Stopping, turning.)* Such as?

DIANA: *(Taking the computer printouts from her desk.)* Well, for example, Henry, there's something called preregistration, when students give an indication of what courses they'd like to take next fall.

HENRY: The annual body count.

DIANA: *(Indicating sheets.)* Exactly, Henry. And we in the Humanities are down.

HENRY: We are always down. We are doomed to be down. We live in an age where a book—a good book—is as obsolete as an Aeolian harp.[25] All the more reason to keep standards *up.*

745 DIANA: You, particularly, are down, Henry. *(Pause.)*

HENRY: How many did I get?

DIANA: Two.

HENRY: Two? Two next fall? Two students to take through the entire rise and fall of the Roman Empire.

DIANA: Two, Henry.

750 HENRY: How many for my elective on Plato?

---

[25] Ancient instrument.

DIANA: Four.

HENRY: Four. Two for Rome, four for Plato. Six students, next fall, out of over four thousand, have shown some interest in the classical tradition. This, in a country founded by Washington and Jefferson and Madison precisely to reestablish that tradition.

DIANA: Shakespeare, on the other hand, is up.

HENRY: I must say, Diana, I fail to understand why students choose what they do. They land on courses like starlings on a telephone wire. It seems totally random.

755 **DIANA:** The Provost is cancelling all undergraduate courses with an enrollment of less than five, Henry.

HENRY: What?

DIANA: The Provost is cancelling your courses.

HENRY: He has no right!

DIANA: He has every right. It's a budgetary thing. There are clear rules about it. Jack Edwards's seminar on Racine goes. Sally Weiskopf's section on Keats.[26] The history department lost the entire seventeenth century.

760 **HENRY:** I'll talk to him. These things can change. Students can sign up in the fall.

DIANA: He's laid down the law, Henry. Jack Edwards has already gone up and been refused. *(Pause.)*

HENRY: Then I'll teach something else.

DIANA: Such as what, Henry?

HENRY: Dante. I'll teach Dante. I'm beginning to get a new understanding of Hell.

765 **DIANA:** Bill Brindisi's got Dante.

HENRY: Shakespeare, then. I'll do a section of Shakespeare.

DIANA: You don't like Shakespeare.

HENRY: Of course I like Shakespeare. He's just a bit . . . messy, that's all. And a bit over-picked. I refuse to spend an entire class focusing on the button image in *King Lear*. I'll do the Roman plays: *Julius Caesar, Coriolanus* . . .

DIANA: Jane Tillotson's got Shakespeare, Henry. All of him.

770 **HENRY:** All right then, what? Tolstoy? Joyce? I'm an educated man. I can do anything. Give me the freshman course—Introduction to Literature. I'll take it over. I'll muster that motley crew of junior instructors who teach it. We'll begin with the *Iliad*, and stride down the centuries, concluding with Conrad.

DIANA: I think they *start* with Conrad in that course, Henry.

HENRY: Oh really? Well, we'll change that. We'll—

DIANA: Henry. *(Pause.)* The Provost doesn't want you to teach. At all.

HENRY: Why not?

---

[26] Jean Racine (1639–1699)—French dramatist; John Keats (1795–1821)—British poet.

775 **DIANA:** He thinks your courses are becoming . . . problematic, Henry.

HENRY: The *Antigone* thing?

DIANA: And the anti-Semitic thing.

HENRY: I have scrupulously avoided anything controversial in my class.

DIANA: Apparently she hasn't, in her play. I hear it's more and more about being Jewish, and more and more about you.

780 **HENRY:** *(Quietly, with increasing anger.)* There is a law as old as Solon which allows a man to confront his accusers. I want to meet her, right now, in front of the Provost, and you, and Ariel Sharon, if he wants to be there!

DIANA: The Provost already met with her, Henry.

HENRY: And what did she say?

DIANA: Nothing! Everything! I don't know! He said it was all very general . . . He said you both deserve each other. He said if he didn't have the alumni breathing down his neck, he'd turn you both loose in the ring, and the hell with it. But right now, all he wants to do is get her graduated and you out of the country, so that things can simmer *down*. Now go to *Greece*, Henry, and enjoy it!

HENRY: And when I come back, he'll suggest early retirement.

785 **DIANA:** He might.

HENRY: He'll sweeten the pot. Buy me off with a few impressive benefits.

DIANA: You've been here a long time, Henry. I think they'd be very generous.

HENRY: I want to teach, Diana.

DIANA: I know.

790 **HENRY:** I need to teach.

DIANA: I know, I know . . .

HENRY: It's what I do.

DIANA: Henry, my old colleague . . .

HENRY: I am a classical scholar. I trained at Harvard. I have written three good books. I know a great deal, and I have to teach what I know, and I'm only good when I'm teaching it! My wife has left me, my children have scattered, I have nothing else but this! I have to teach, Diana. Have to. Or I'm dead.

795 **DIANA:** You need students, Henry.

HENRY: Then I'll have to get them, won't I? *(He goes off. Diana sits there for a moment, then opens her purse, takes out a pack of cigarettes. She shakes it, but it's empty. She gets up, and begins to walk toward the wings, calling out sweetly as she goes.)*

DIANA: Monica? . . . Did you bring any cigarettes in today? . . . Because if you did, even though you're down to your last one, I intend to get it, Monica. I intend to wrestle you to the ground! *(She goes off, as Judy comes on. She leans against a pillar in a rather theatrical pose and recites her lines, referring only occasionally to a script she carries, in her hand.)*

JUDY: "So Creon has determined I go to jail. I wonder if this is happening because I'm Jewish. I don't mean simply that Creon's prejudiced—though he probably is. I mean more because of me. Maybe it's built into my Jewish blood to rise up against the Creons of this world. All I know is for the first time in my life I've felt in tune with something larger than myself. I've been to the library lately. I've studied my roots. And I've learned how often we Jews have stood our ground against injustice. Pharaoh and Philistine, Hittite and Herod have fallen before us. Roman generals and Spanish Inquisitors, Venetian businessmen and Russian Cossacks, Nazis, Arabs, McCarthyites—all the arrogant authorities of this world have tried to subdue us. And when we protest, they throw us into jail. Well, what's jail these days? Maybe this is a jail right here. This so-called ivory tower. This labyrinth of curricular obligations. This festering nest of overpaid administrators. This rotten pit of dry and exhausted pedants. This winter camp which capitalism creates to keep its children off the job market. What job market? Where are the jobs? Where is there decent work in an economy so devoted to nonessential goods and destructive weapons?" *(Dave comes on.)*

DAVE: Judy—

800 **JUDY:** Wait. I'm almost done. *(She continues to recite.)* "Or maybe this whole damn country is a jail. Maybe we're all prisoners. Prisoners of these oppressive corporations, who capture us with their advertising, chain us to their products, and work us forever in meaningless jobs to pay for things we shouldn't even want."

DAVE: Judy. It's important.

JUDY: Hold it. *(She takes a deep breath.)* "And to protect this prison, this fortress America, this so-called way of life, we arm ourselves with weapons which, if they're used, could ten times over destroy the world, blot out the past, and turn the future into a desolate blank. Are we so sure we're right? Is life in these United States so great? Would the homeless hordes on the streets of New York agree? Would the hungry blacks in the South? Would the migrant workers breaking their backs to feed us go along with it? Oh God, Lysander, this might be a terrible thing to say, but I don't think our country is worth dying for any more. The world at large is worth dying for, not just us."

DAVE: Wow! That's tremendous.

JUDY: Thank you. *(Pause.)*

805 **DAVE:** *(Quietly.)* He wants to see you.

JUDY: The Provost? I know. I have a meeting with him in half an hour.

DAVE: No, *Harper! Harper* wants to see you.

JUDY: Harper?

DAVE: He called me at the lab.

810 **JUDY:** How come he called *you?*

DAVE: I don't know . . . I guess he knew I knew you. Anyway, he said he watched the rehearsal last night.

JUDY: *What?*

DAVE: He was there. And he wants to talk to you about it.

JUDY: Oh God. What did he think?

815 **DAVE:** Didn't say. *(The lights begin to come up on Henry's office, as Henry comes in, settles his desk.)*

JUDY: Oh Lord, he must have hated it. All that Creon stuff I put in. Well, maybe it'll do him good.

DAVE: He said he'd be in his office all afternoon. You better see him.

JUDY: *(Putting on lip gloss.)* I might. Then again I might not. First, of course, I have a major meeting with the Provost. *(She starts out.)*

DAVE: *(Calling after Judy.)* Hey, you're quite the Queen Bee around here these days.

820 **JUDY:** I'm another Antigone.

DAVE: Antigone dies in the end, remember.

JUDY: That's the old version. Mine ends happily ever after. *(She goes off.)*

DAVE: *(Calling after her.)* Ever hear of *hubris*, Judy? Know what that word means . . . *(He sees she's gone, speaks to himself.)* Pride. Overweening pride. For example, take a man whose father gives him a chemistry set when he's eight years old. This man takes Chemistry in high school, and majors in it in college. What makes this man think he can graduate if he doesn't study? What makes this man think he can find a job if he doesn't graduate? What makes this man stand around, talking to himself, when his final exam in Chemistry starts in five minutes, and he doesn't know the stuff at *all*? Pride, that's what. *Hubris.* Which leads to tragedy every time. *(He goes off grimly as the lights come up on Henry in his office. After a moment, Judy comes in.)*

JUDY: You wanted to see me, Professor Harper?

825 **HENRY:** *(Jumping up.)* Ah. Miss Miller. Yes. *(Indicates a chair.)* Please. *(Judy comes in.)* How well you look.

JUDY: Thank you.

HENRY: I am reminded of a line from the *Andromache:* "I now wear different robes."

JUDY: I don't know that one.

HENRY: No matter. You look lovely. Life on the wicked stage becomes you.

830 **JUDY:** Thanks. *(She sits.)*

HENRY: Yes, well, now I have recently had the opportunity to watch you practice your play.

JUDY: You mean, re*hearse.*

HENRY: Yes. Rehearse. Last night, in fact. I happen to know old Bill, who's the custodian of the Spingler Auditorium, and he took me up to the back of the balcony and let me sit there unobtrusively and watch you rehearse your play.

JUDY: I heard.

835 **HENRY:** Oh yes? Well that's where I was. All evening. *(Pause.)* I found it . . . *(This is tough for him.)* Interesting. *(Pause.)* Quite interesting. *(Pause.)* The crude poetry, the naive theatricality . . .

JUDY: Thank you.

HENRY: Your work also demonstrated an earnestness and commitment which I found . . . refreshing, in a world which seems too often concerned only with the meaning of meaning.

JUDY: You mean, you *liked* it? *(Pause.)*

HENRY: I . . . admired it.

840 **JUDY:**   Well thank you very much! I appreciate that.

HENRY: I have decided it may substitute after all for your term paper.

JUDY: That's great!

HENRY: Miss Miller, you might be interested to know that Sophocles himself was a practical man of the theatre. Not only did he write his plays, but he directed most of them, and sometimes acted in them as well, just as you are doing.

JUDY: Really?

845 **HENRY:**   Absolutely. And according to Aristotle—this might amuse you— he actually danced in a lost play of his called *Nausicaa.* He danced. He danced the part of a young woman playing ball.

JUDY: No kidding! That makes me feel very proud!

HENRY: Then I wonder if you would play ball with *me,* Miss Miller.

JUDY: What do you mean?

HENRY: Well now, last night, I noticed a number of people scurrying about, assisting with your production.

850 **JUDY:**   Yes . . .

HENRY: Good, practical souls, hard at work. I mean, not only did I notice your personal and particular friend . . .

JUDY: Dave . . .

HENRY: Yes, Dave. A fine, stalwart young man. I noticed him. But I also noticed other actors, and that odd cluster of people pretending to be the chorus.

JUDY: Right . . .

855 **HENRY:**   And then I hear there's to be an orchestra . . .

JUDY: A group. A combo, really . . .

HENRY: Well how many do you think are involved, in toto?

JUDY: In toto?

HENRY: Altogether.

860 **JUDY:**   Oh . . . maybe . . . thirty-five.

HENRY: And of course not all of them will graduate this year, will they?

JUDY: No. Some. Not all.

HENRY: Miss Miller, I wonder if you would announce to everyone in your production that I'm planning to give a special seminar next fall.

JUDY: Special seminar?

865 **HENRY:**   On the Greeks. And since these students have all been working on your *Antigone,* I'll give them the inside track. They *must,* however—you must tell them this—they *must* let the Dean's office know they're interested, so we'll have some indication of preenrollment.

JUDY: Professor Harper, I'm not sure they'd want to—

HENRY: Oh yes they would. Tell them this course will be—how shall I put it?—"project-oriented." They can put on plays. They can make models of the Parthenon. They can draw maps of the Peloponnesian Peninsula, I don't care!

JUDY: That doesn't sound like you, Professor Harper.

HENRY: Oh yes, yes. And tell them I'll grade it Pass/Fail, if they want. And I'll have very few papers. No papers at all, really, if that's what they want. Because the important thing is not papers, is it, it's the Greeks! We'll be studying the Greeks next year, that's the thing! We'll still be reading and discussing those fine old plays. We'll still be holding onto the heart of Western Civilization. That's what we'll be doing, Miss Miller, and you will have helped us do it! *(Pause.)*

870   **JUDY:**   You mean you want students next year.

HENRY: Yes, frankly, I do. *(Pause.)*

JUDY: Wow!

HENRY: There it is.

JUDY: I always thought we had to go through you. I never thought you had to go through *us.*

875   **HENRY:**   Well we do.

JUDY: You really *need* us, don't you? You have to have us.

HENRY: Without you, we'd die.

JUDY: I never knew that before.

HENRY: Now you do. *(Pause.)* So will you tell them about the course?

880   **JUDY:**   Yes I will.

HENRY: And you'll encourage them to come?

JUDY: I'll tell them, Professor Harper. I'll let them choose.

HENRY: But you won't . . . undercut me?

JUDY: No, I won't do that.

885   **HENRY:**   And you'll remind them to sign up immediately. So the administration will know.

JUDY: I'll do all that, sir. I mean, you have a right to live, too, after all.

HENRY: You're magnanimous in victory, Miss Miller.

JUDY: Thank you, sir.

HENRY: Now, before we turn to the crass topic of grades, suppose we celebrate the conclusion of these negotiations. *(Opens his drawer again, takes out a sherry bottle and two murky glasses.)* I keep this sherry around for those rare occasions when a fellow scholar stops by.

890   **JUDY:**   Oh I don't—

HENRY: *(Pouring.)* Please. It's important. Old Odysseus and the nymph Calypso, in Book Five of the *Odyssey,*[27] sharing a glass before they say

---

[27] In Homer's *Odyssey,* the nymph Calypso holds Odysseus captive for seven years; she treats him well, but he longs for his homeland and family. Finally, Zeus, prompted by Athena's intervention, orders Odysseus released. Calypso obeys, outfitting him with food and drink.

goodbye. *(He hands her her glass, raises his in a toast.)* To peace and reconciliation. *(They click glasses and drink.)* Doesn't that hit the spot?

JUDY: Actually, it does.

HENRY: Have some more.

JUDY: Oh, well. No. I mean, all right. *(He pours her more, and a touch more for himself. Judy gets up.)* You know, I was just thinking, Professor Harper . . .

895 **HENRY:**   *(His little joke.)* That's always a good sign.

JUDY: No, seriously, I was thinking that you and I are basically very much alike.

HENRY: Ah? And how so?

JUDY: I mean we both see too big a picture.

HENRY: Elucidate, please.

900 **JUDY:**   Sure. I mean, there you are, always talking about the Greeks versus the Jews, and here I am, talking about the Jews versus all authority.

HENRY: I see.

JUDY: Maybe we should both scale things down.

HENRY: Maybe we should. *(Settling back in his chair.)* In any case, I think you can count on receiving a B in my course, Miss Miller.

JUDY: A B.

905 **HENRY:**   A strong B. A solid B. A B which leans longingly toward a B plus.

JUDY: I was kind of hoping I'd get an A.

HENRY: I don't think your work quite warrants an A, Miss Miller.

JUDY: You don't think so?

HENRY: Let's reserve the A's for Sophocles, shall we? It gives us something to go for. *(Pause.)*

910 **JUDY:**   That's cool.

HENRY: I take it you agree.

JUDY: I guess a B from you is like an A from anyone else.

HENRY: Well, thank you, Miss Miller.

JUDY: *(Getting up.)* Besides, I don't really believe in grades anymore.

915 **HENRY:**   Good for you.

JUDY: I think I've grown beyond them.

HENRY: Unfortunately we live in a world which seems to require them. We have to toss them, like bones, to a ravenous administration.

JUDY: Oh God, I know. *They* even wanted me to take an A.

HENRY: And where did they propose you find that A?

920 **JUDY:**   A professor in Drama saw a rehearsal, and offered to give me a straight A.

HENRY: Ah, but of course that wouldn't count.

JUDY: Oh sure. He said I could register it under Special Topics.

HENRY: Well then, I'm afraid I'd have to go to the Provost. To protest this blatant interference in my course.

JUDY: I just came from the Provost. It was his idea, actually. *(Pause.)*

925 **HENRY:**   You mean you don't need a grade in my course to graduate.

JUDY: Not any more.

HENRY: You don't really need me at all.

JUDY: Technically, no.

HENRY: Why did you bother to come?

930 **JUDY:** I wanted your opinion of my *play!* I wanted to hear what you thought.

HENRY: And I told you: B.

JUDY: Right. Fine. And I'm accepting your B. I'll tell the Registrar. *(She starts out.)*

HENRY: Miss Miller. *(She stops.)* This professor who offered to intrude. Who was he?

JUDY: Who?

935 **HENRY:** Do I know him?

JUDY: He's new this year.

HENRY: What's his name?

JUDY: Bob Birnbaum.

HENRY: Bob—?

940 **JUDY:** Birnbaum. *(Pause.)*

HENRY: Of course.

JUDY: What do you mean?

HENRY: Once again Athens is forced to bow to Jerusalem.

JUDY: Explain that, please.

945 **HENRY:** I mean the Chosen People always choose to intrude.

JUDY: That's what I thought you meant. *(She strides for the door, then wheels on him.)* All bets are off, Professor Harper. I wouldn't recommend this course to a Nazi! And I'll take a good, solid, Jewish A from Birnbaum! *(She storms out.)*

HENRY: *(Quietly; to himself as he sits.)* Good God. What have I done? *(The lights dim on him as he sits at his desk. Diana crosses the stage hurriedly, carrying a stack of folders. Dave is following her.)*

DAVE: Dean . . . ? *(She turns.)* Could I speak to you for a minute, please?

DIANA: I'm sorry, but I'm late for an important meeting.

950 **DAVE:** The Committee on Academic Performance, right?

DIANA: That's the one.

DAVE: That's what I've got to speak to you about. *(She stops, looks at him.)*

DIANA: Aren't you that friend of Judy Miller's?

DAVE: David Appleton. My name's coming up before the committee today. I flunked the Chemistry final. I'm not graduating.

955 **DIANA:** Chemistry will take care of you. There's infinite salvation: makeup exams, summer school, degrees given out in the fall . . .

DAVE: I don't want any of that. I want to switch to your department and be here all next year.

DIANA: Studying what?

DAVE: The Greeks.

DIANA: But we don't have a Classics Department anymore.

960 **DAVE:** You have Professor Harper.

DIANA: He may be on sabbatical next year.

DAVE: Oh. Then I'll make up my general requirements till he returns and take Ancient Greek on my own.

DIANA: *(Starting out.)* If you'd make an appointment with Monica, my assistant, we'll discuss all this.

DAVE: No, I've thought it through. I just need your approval.

965 **DIANA:**   You're talking about another year's tuition.

DAVE: I know. And my dad's cutting me off. But I've gotten a double shift in the cafeteria. I'll get my degree next June, and apply for postgraduate studies with Professor Harper. *(Pause.)*

DIANA: I'll tell the committee you're staying on.

DAVE: Thank you.

DIANA: I envy you.

970 **DAVE:**   For studying with Harper?

DIANA: For being so sure. *(Judy enters.)*

JUDY: What's going on, Dave?

DAVE: I'm changing my life.

DIANA: Make an appointment if you want to change it back! *(She goes out.)*

975 **JUDY:**   We have a rehearsal, remember? I'm putting in the final rewrites.

DAVE: Can't make it. Got a class.

JUDY: At this hour? What class?

DAVE: Harper's actually.

JUDY: *Harper's? My* Harper?

980 **DAVE:**   I've been auditing it for the past three weeks.

JUDY: Why?

DAVE: I like him. I like the subject. I like myself when I'm working on it.

JUDY: You never told me that.

DAVE: I knew it would freak you out.

985 **JUDY:**   Damn right! He's a bigot, Dave.

DAVE: I don't think so.

JUDY: He's an anti-Semite.

DAVE: I don't think so, Judy.

JUDY: I *know* so! *Personally!* He made an anti-Semitic *slur!*

990 **DAVE:**   He just generalizes, Judy. It's his tragic flaw.

JUDY: I don't buy that, Dave.

DAVE: All right, so he made a crack? So what? People make ethnic digs all the time in this country. We all get it in the neck—the Poles, the Italians, now the Wasps.

JUDY: The Jews are different! All through history—

DAVE: So I keep hearing. Still, seems to me you're people, like everyone else. I think this Jewish thing is getting out of hand. Suddenly nothing counts except you're Jewish!

995 **JUDY:**   Dave . . .

DAVE: No, let me finish, for once in my life! I didn't fall in love with a Jewish Revolutionary, I fell in love with *you!* I fell in love with a particular person who liked Springsteen and Moo Sho Pork and staying in bed all day on Sunday. What happened to all that? What happens to us next *year?* These are the important things—not that you're Jewish, for God's sake!

JUDY: I think we're in a little hot water here.

DAVE: I guess we are. *(A bell rings.)* Saved by the bell. *(He starts off.)*

JUDY: Dave. *(He stops.)* We have a rehearsal now.

1000 **DAVE:** Work around me.

JUDY: It's too late for that.

DAVE: Look, it's his last class. The whole school knows about this. Everyone wants to see what he's going to say.

JUDY: Not if they're with *Antigone.*

DAVE: Give me an hour.

1005 **JUDY:** No! It's him or me, Dave. You choose.

DAVE: Be serious.

JUDY: I am. I'll put in Mark Shapiro. I'll replace you. Totally. *(Pause.)*

DAVE: Fair enough. *(He starts off again.)*

JUDY: *(Calling after him.)* Then it's true, what my grandmother said! You people always turn your backs when the chips are down! *(He turns, glares at her, then exits. She speaks softly, to herself.)* Oh Lord. I'm as bad as Harper. *(She goes off slowly the opposite way. The lights come up on Henry as he comes D., addressing the audience once again as if it were his class. Dave enters, to sit on the side and listen, as if he were in class.)*

1010 **HENRY:** *(To audience.)* This has been a course on tragedy. That is what this course is supposed to be about. *(Pause.)* First, let me remind you what tragedy is *not*. Tragedy has nothing to do with choice. If you can choose, it is not tragic. There are some people who think that our arms race with the Russians is tragic. It is not. It is not, because we have the choice, they have the choice, to say No, to stop, to disarm, to embrace each other in the name of peace at any time. So it is not tragic. It is stupid, yes. It is insane, it is suicidal, it is pathetic, but it is not—repeat Not—tragic, in the true Greek sense of the word. *(Pause.)* Tragedy occurs when you cannot choose, when you have no choice at all. This is hard for Americans to understand. Because most of us are free, or think we are. Nowhere else in the world, and never before in history, have so many people been so free to choose so many destinies. Perhaps, because of this freedom, it is impossible for us to sense what the Greeks called tragedy. We have no oracles, no gods, no real sense of ultimate authority to insist that if we do one thing, another will inevitably follow. We are free. *(Pause.)* On the other hand, there might come a time to some of us, to one or two, *(He glances at Dave.)* when we get an inkling, a glimmer, a faint shadow of a shadow of what it might have been like for the Greeks when they sat in a theatre and saw the universe close in on a man, or woman, because of some flaw, some excess, some overshooting of the mark . . . *(Pause.)* Then the net tightens, and as he struggles, tightens further, until he is crushed by forces total and absurd. *(Pause.)* Then we might be touching the outer borders of tragedy, as the Greeks once knew it. *(Pause. He takes up his book of Antigone.)* But I've just discovered something else about tragedy, or at least about Sophoclean tragedy. Something I thought I knew, but didn't understand till now. And that is what the tragic heroes do after the net has closed around them. What they do, even in the teeth of disaster, is accept responsibility, assert their own destiny, and mete out proudly their own punishments. This is what Oedipus does when he puts out his eyes. This is what Antigone does, when she hangs herself. And this is what Creon does, at the end of the same play. He has lost his wife, his children, all he holds dear. And he realizes why: that in his commitment to abstract and dehumanizing laws, he has neglected the very heart of life. And so he banishes himself from his own city. His Polis. He goes. He disappears. He leaves the stage, forever doomed now to wander far from the only community he knows, self-exiled and alone. *(Pause.)* I'll expect all papers under my door by five o'clock this evening. You may retrieve them, graded and with appropriate comments, from the Departmental office next Monday. Enjoy your summer. Read good books. Go to good plays. Think of the Greeks. Thank you and goodbye. *(He sees Dave go, then crosses to his desk, where he leaves his book of* Antigone. *Then he exits, as graduation music comes up loudly: an optimistic piece, played by a brass ensemble. Diana comes out in gown and colorful academic hood. She reads from a formal-looking document.)*

DIANA: Our final award is the Peabody Prize . . . *(Reads from card.)* "Offered annually to that student who best combines academic excellence with extracurricular commitment . . ." *(To audience.)* It is awarded this year to Judith Rachel Miller, of the graduating class, for her exceptional academic record as well as for her fascinating contemporary version of Sophocles' *Antigone. (Applause and cheers. Judy comes on, in academic robes. She accepts an envelope from Diana, who gives her a kiss.)* Congratulations, Judy . . . And now refreshments will be—

JUDY: May I say something, please?

DIANA: *(Very reluctantly.)* All right.

JUDY: *(To audience.)* First, I want to thank everyone involved for making our play possible. *(Looks at envelope.)* And I want to thank the Peabody Foundation for making this prize possible. *(Looks out.)* And I want to thank my parents for making *me* possible. *(Diana tries to step in.)* I'm not finished. *(Diana steps back. To audience.)* Lately I've been doing some thinking, and as someone once told me, that's always a good sign. I've been thinking about this prize, for example. I guess it stands for everything I used to believe in: personal ambition . . . success . . . *(She peeks into the envelope.)* And sure, why not? money . . . I mean, these are the things they tell us make our country great . . . *(Diana looks worried.)* Trouble is, I'm beginning to think these things aren't so important. Maybe my play hasn't influenced anyone else, but it sure has influenced me. I don't feel good about my life anymore. I don't feel good about my country. I can't accept all this *stuff* that's going on these days. I can't accept it. No, I'm sorry, but I just can't accept it. *(She hands the envelope back to Diana and hurries off.)*

1015 **DIANA:** Judy! *(She hurries off after Judy, as the lights come up on Henry's office. Dave enters, carrying a note. He finds Henry's book on the desk. He picks it up, looks at it, and starts deciphering the title.)*

DAVE: Alpha . . . Nu . . . Tau . . . Iota . . . Gamma . . . Omicron . . . Nu . . . Eta . . . *Antigone. (Diana enters, no longer in her robes, but still carrying the prize envelope.)*

DIANA: Mr. Appleton? Monica told me you got a note from Professor Harper.

DAVE: *(Indicating the book.)* He said he was leaving me his book.

DIANA: But did he say where he'd *be?* We can't locate him anywhere.

1020 **DAVE:** He just mentions the book.

DIANA: Oh dear.

DAVE: I'll find him. I'll track him down. Like Telemachus.[28] In the *Odyssey.*

DIANA: You're beginning to sound a little like him.

DAVE: Maybe. In some ways.

1025 **DIANA:** I suppose you heard about Judy.

DAVE: Saw it. From the sidelines.

DIANA: That girl seems to be interested in systematically hanging herself.

DAVE: She likes to go for broke.

DIANA: This prize is a sizable check. Do you know any cause she'd want to donate it to?

1030 **DAVE:** Tell you what: I'll ask her. It'll give me an excuse to open diplomatic relations.

DIANA: I have a feeling we may have lost them both forever.

DAVE: Oh God, I hope not.

DIANA: So do I . . . Meanwhile, I have no idea how to summarize all this for the Departmental report. What does Sophocles say at the end of that damn play?

DAVE: Well, he says that wisdom and reverence lead to happiness . . .

1035 **DIANA:** Oh good. I'll go along with that! Thank you. *(Dave starts out, then stops, turns back.)*

DAVE: But then he goes on to say that we only learn this when we're too old for it to make much difference.

DIANA: Then heaven help us all. *(They look at each other. Blackout.)*

THE END

---

[28] Odysseus's son, who searches for his father.

Reading and Reacting

1. The play introduces a number of opposing forces:
   - anarchy versus tyranny
   - individual versus community rights
   - Greek versus Hebraic sensibility

   Identify as many additional opposing forces as you can, and consider how each pair expresses the themes of the play.

2. What various meanings does the title of the play suggest? Is it necessary to be familiar with Sophocles' *Antigone* before reading *Another Antigone?* Explain.

3. In what way is Professor Harper like Creon? How is Judy like Antigone? In what ways are they different from their counterparts?

4. Is Professor Harper an effective teacher? What do his students and his colleagues think of him? What do you think of him?

5. In an interview A. R. Gurney said that the tendency to abstract or generalize dehumanizes the people who are placed in categories. What do you suppose Gurney meant by this statement? Can you think of any contemporary examples of this form of dehumanization? In what sense do Judy and Professor Harper dehumanize each other?

6. What power does professor Harper have? What power does Judy have? At what point does the balance of power shift?

7. Why does Diana, Professor Harper's dean, warn him that he must not be insensitive about the Jews? What does she mean when she says, "The 20th century is still with us, Henry. We live in the shadow of the Holocaust. Remember that, please, and be warned"? Do you think Professor Harper is anti-Semitic? Do you think Judy herself is?

8. Why is Professor Harper unable to keep his opinions to himself? Should he be censured for his remarks, or should he be able to express any opinion he wants to?

9. What is Dave's function in the play? Why does Dave choose Professor Harper over Judy? What does he realize about Harper that Judy fails to understand? Do you agree with his assessment of Professor Harper?

10. After accusing Dave of deserting her, Judy says to herself, "Oh Lord. I'm as bad as Harper." Do you think she is correct? What does this remark show about her?

11. At the end of the play Professor Harper points out that the essence of tragedy lies in the fact that tragic figures have no choice. "If you can choose," he says, "it is not tragic." According to Harper's definition, which of the characters in *Another Antigone* (if any) are tragic? Explain.

12. Is it significant that Judy is female and Professor Harper is male? Would the conflict have occurred if their roles had been reversed or if both Judy and Professor Harper were of the same gender?

13. **Journal Entry** Given all the problems confronting higher education today, do you think Judy's battle is really worth fighting?

14. **CRITICAL PERSPECTIVE**   In a review of the New York production of *Another Antigone*, Robert Feldberg observes that although neither Judy nor Professor Harper is a sympathetic character, Gurney favors Harper:

> *In most ways Harper is a fool. But there is a sense that Gurney, who shares a similar social background and is himself a teacher, has a feeling for the man. . . . Gurney may be trying to be evenhanded, but in his battle of the bores, the professor—and his values—easily win the sympathy vote.*

Do you think Gurney's depiction of the two central characters is "evenhanded," or do you agree that he seems to favor Harper?

BETH HENLEY (1952–   ) is a native of Mississippi. She studied at Southern Methodist University and the University of Illinois before beginning her career in theater as a teacher of drama. Henley is known for her realistic portrayals of Southern culture and ordinary people. The innocence of her characters causes them to respond to adversity in unexpected ways that create humorous situations.

Henley's plays include *Crimes of the Heart* (1979), *True Stories* (1986), *The Lucky Spot* (1987), *The Miss Firecracker Contest* (1989), and *Abundance* (1990). Many of her plays have been made into films. Her most popular play, *Crimes of the Heart,* was co-winner of the Great American Play Contest of the Actor's Theater of Louisville. The play also won a New York Drama Critics Circle Award and a Pulitzer Prize for 1980. In 1987 *Crimes of the Heart* was made into a movie starring, among others, dramatist and actor Sam Shepard.

In 1994 Henley interviewed another Mississippi writer whom she greatly admires—Eudora Welty—on the subject of Welty's short story "A Worn Path" (p. 577). The interview was produced by and is available from Harcourt Brace.

B E T H   H E N L E Y
....

Crimes of the Heart

(1979)

For Len, C.C., and Kayo.

T H E   C A S T
....

LENNY MAGRATH, *30, the oldest sister*
CHICK BOYLE, *29, the sisters' first cousin*
DOC PORTER, *30, Meg's old boyfriend*

MEG MAGRATH, *27, the middle sister*
BABE BOTRELLE, *24, the youngest sister*
BARNETTE LLOYD, *26, Babe's lawyer*

THE SETTING

The setting of the entire play is the kitchen in the MaGrath sisters' house in Hazlehurst, Mississippi, a small southern town. The old-fashioned kitchen is un-usually spacious, but there is a lived-in, cluttered look about it. There are four different entrances and exits to the kitchen: the back door; the door leading to the dining room and the front of the house; a door leading to the downstairs bed-room; and a staircase leading to the upstairs room. There is a table near the cen-ter of the room, and a cot has been set up in one of the corners.

THE TIME

In the fall; five years after Hurricane Camille

ACT I

The lights go up on the empty kitchen. It is late afternoon. Lenny MaGrath, a thirty-year-old woman with a round figure and face, enters from the back door carrying a white suitcase, a saxophone case, and a brown paper sack. She sets the suitcase and the sax case down and takes the brown sack to the kitchen table. After glancing quickly at the door, she gets the cookie jar from the kitchen counter, a box of matches from the stove and then brings both objects back down to the kitchen table. Excitedly, she reaches into the brown sack and pulls out a package of birthday candles. She quickly opens the package and removes a can-dle. She tries to stick the candle into a cookie—it falls off. She sticks the candle in again but the cookie is too hard and it crumbles. Frantically, she gets a second cookie from the jar. She strikes a match, lights the candle and beings dripping wax onto the cookie. Just as she is beginning to smile we hear Chick's voice from offstage.

CHICK'S VOICE: Lenny! Oh, Lenny! *(Lenny quickly blows out the candle and stuffs the cookie and candle into her dress pocket. Chick, 29, enters from the back door. She is a brightly dressed matron with yellow hair and shiny, red lips.)*
CHICK: Hi! I saw your car pull up.
LENNY: Hi.
CHICK: Well, did you see today's paper? *(Lenny nods.)* It's just too awful! It's just way too awful! How I'm gonna continue holding my head up high in this community, I do not know. Did you remember to pick up those pantyhose for me?
5 **LENNY:**   They're in the sack.
CHICK: Well, thank goodness, at least I'm not gonna have to go into town wearing holes in my stockings. *(Chick gets the package, tears it*

open and proceeds to take off one pair of stockings and put on another,
throughout the following scene. There should be something slightly
grotesque about this woman changing her stockings in the kitchen.)

LENNY: Did Uncle Watson call?

CHICK: Yes, Daddy has called me twice already. He said Babe's ready to
come home. We've got to get right over and pick her up before they
change their simple minds.

LENNY: *(hesitantly)* Oh, I know, of course, it's just—

10 **CHICK:**   What?

LENNY: Well, I was hoping Meg would call.

CHICK: Meg?

LENNY: Yes, I sent her a telegram: about Babe, and—

CHICK: A telegram?! Couldn't you just phone her up?

15 **LENNY:**   Well, no, 'cause her phone's . . . out of order.

CHICK: Out of order?

LENNY: Disconnected. I don't know what.

CHICK: Well, that sounds like Meg. My, these are snug. Are you sure you
bought my right size?

LENNY: *(looking at the box)* Size extra petite.

20 **CHICK:**   Well, they're skimping on the nylon material. *(Struggling to pull*
up the stockings.) That's all there is to it. Skimping on the nylon. *(She*
finishes on one leg and starts on the other.) Now, just what all did you
say in this "telegram" to Meg?

LENNY: I don't recall exactly. I, well, I just told her to come on home.

CHICK: To come on home! Why, Lenora Josephine, have you lost your
only brain, or what?

LENNY: *(nervously, as she begins to pick up the mess of dirty stockings and*
plastic wrappings) But Babe wants Meg home. She asked me to call her.

CHICK: I'm not talking about what Babe wants.

25 **LENNY:**   Well, what then?

CHICK: Listen, Lenora, I think it's pretty accurate to assume that after
this morning's paper, Babe's gonna be incurring some mighty
negative publicity around this town. And Meg's appearance isn't
gonna help out a bit.

LENNY: What's wrong with Meg?

CHICK: She had a loose reputation in high school.

LENNY: *(weakly)* She was popular.

30 **CHICK:**   She was known all over Copiah County as cheap Christmas
trash, and that was the least of it. There was that whole sordid affair
with Doc Porter, leaving him a cripple.

LENNY: A cripple—he's got a limp. Just, kind of, barely a limp.

CHICK: Well, his mother was going to keep *me* out of the Ladies' Social
League because of it.

LENNY: What?

CHICK: That's right. I never told you, but I had to go plead with that
mean old woman and convinced her that I was just as appalled and
upset with what Meg had done as she was, and that I was only a first

cousin anyway and I could hardly be blamed for all the skeletons in the Magraths' closet. It was humiliating. I tell you, she even brought up your mother's death. And that poor cat.

35 **LENNY:** Oh! Oh! Oh, please, Chick! I'm sorry. But you're in the Ladies' League now.

CHICK: Yes. That's true, I am. But frankly, if Mrs. Porter hadn't developed that tumor in her bladder, I wouldn't be in the club today, much less a committee head. (*As she brushes her hair.*) Anyway, you be a sweet potato and wait right here for Meg to call, so's you can convince her not to come back home. It would make things a whole lot easier on everybody. Don't you think it really would?

LENNY: Probably.

CHICK: Good, then suit yourself. How's my hair?

LENNY: Fine.

40 **CHICK:** Not pooching out in the back, is it?

LENNY: No.

CHICK: (*cleaning the hair from her brush*) All right then, I'm on my way. I've got Annie May over there keeping an eye on Peekay and Buck Jr., but I don't trust her with them for long periods of time. (*Dropping the ball of hair onto the floor.*) Her mind is like a loose sieve. Honestly it is. (*She puts the brush back into her purse.*) Oh! Oh! Oh! I almost forgot. Here's a present for you. Happy Birthday to Lenny, from the Buck Boyles! (*Chick takes a wrapped package from her bag and hands it to Lenny.*)

LENNY: Why, thank you, Chick. It's so nice to have you remember my birthday every year like you do.

CHICK: (*modestly*) Oh well, now, that's just the way I am, I suppose. That's just the way I was brought up to be. Well, why don't you go on and open up the present?

45 **LENNY:** All right. (*She starts to unwrap the gift.*)

CHICK: It's a box of candy—assorted crèmes.

LENNY: Candy—that's always a nice gift.

CHICK: And you have a sweet tooth, don't you?

LENNY: I guess.

50 **CHICK:** Well, I'm glad you like it.

LENNY: I do.

CHICK: Oh, speaking of which, remember that little polka-dot dress you got Peekay for her fifth birthday last month?

LENNY: The red-and-white one?

CHICK: Yes; well, the first time I put it in the washing machine, I mean the very first time, it fell all to pieces. Those little polka dots just dropped right off in the water.

55 **LENNY:** (*crushed*) Oh, no. Well, I'll get something else for her then—a little toy.

CHICK: Oh, no, no, no, no, no! We wouldn't hear of it! I just wanted to let you know so you wouldn't go and waste any more of your hard-earned money on that make of dress. Those inexpensive brands just don't hold up. I'm sorry, but not in these modern washing machines.

Doc Porter's voice: Hello! Hello, Lenny!

Chick: *(taking over)* Oh, look, it's Doc Porter! Come on in, Doc! Please come right on in! *(Doc Porter enters through the back door. He is carrying a large sack of pecans. Doc is an attractively worn man with a slight limp that adds rather than detracts from his quiet seductive quality. He is 30 years old, but appears slightly older.)* Well, how are you doing? How in the world are you doing?

Doc: Just fine, Chick.

60 **Chick:** And how are you liking it now that you're back in Hazlehurst?

Doc: Oh, I'm finding it somewhat enjoyable.

Chick: Somewhat! Only somewhat! Will you listen to him! What a silly, silly, silly man! Well, I'm on my way. I've got some people waiting on me. *(Whispering to Doc.)* It's Babe. I'm on my way to pick her up.

Doc: Oh.

Chick: Well, goodbye! Farewell and goodbye!

65 **Lenny:** 'Bye. *(Chick exits.)*

Doc: Hello.

Lenny: Hi. I guess you heard about the thing with Babe.

Doc: Yeah.

Lenny: It was in the newspaper.

70 **Doc:** Uh huh.

Lenny: What a mess.

Doc: Yeah.

Lenny: Well, come on and sit down. I'll heat us up some coffee.

Doc: That's okay. I can only stay a minute. I have to pick up Scott; he's at the dentist.

75 **Lenny:** Oh; well, I'll heat some up for myself. I'm kinda thirsty for a cup of hot coffee. *(Lenny puts the coffeepot on the burner.)*

Doc: Lenny—

Lenny: What?

Doc: *(not able to go on)* Ah . . .

Lenny: Yes?

80 **Doc:** Here, some pecans for you. *(He hands her the sack.)*

Lenny: Why, thank you, Doc. I love pecans.

Doc: My wife and Scott picked them up around the yard.

Lenny: Well, I can use them to make a pie. A pecan pie.

Doc: Yeah. Look, Lenny, I've got some bad news for you.

85 **Lenny:** What?

Doc: Well, you know, you've been keeping Billy Boy out on our farm; he's been grazing out there.

Lenny: Yes—

Doc: Well, last night, Billy Boy died.

Lenny: He died?

90 **Doc:** Yeah. I'm sorry to tell you when you've got all this on you, but I thought you'd want to know.

Lenny: Well, yeah. I do. He died?

Doc: Uh huh. He was struck by lightning.

Lenny: Struck by lightning? In that storm yesterday?

Doc: That's what we think.

95 **Lenny:** Gosh, struck by lightning. I've had Billy Boy so long. You know. Ever since I was ten years old.

Doc: Yeah. He was a mighty old horse.

Lenny: *(stung)* Mighty old.

Doc: Almost twenty years old.

Lenny: That's right, twenty years. 'Cause; ah, I'm thirty years old today. Did you know that?

100 **Doc:** No, Lenny, I didn't know. Happy Birthday.

Lenny: Thanks. *(She beings to cry.)*

Doc: Oh, come on now, Lenny. Come on. Hey, hey, now. You know I can't stand it when you Magrath women start to cry. You know it just gets me.

Lenny: Oh ho! Sure! You mean when Meg cries! Meg's the one you could never stand to watch cry! Not me! I could fill up a pig's trough!

Doc: Now, Lenny . . . stop it. Come on. Jesus!

105 **Lenny:** Okay! Okay! I don't know what's wrong with me. I don't mean to make a scene. I've been on this crying jag. *(She blows her nose.)* All this stuff with Babe, and old Granddaddy's gotten worse in the hospital and I can't get in touch with Meg.

Doc: You tried calling Meggy?

Lenny: Yes.

Doc: Is she coming home?

Lenny: Who knows. She hasn't called me. That's what I'm waiting here for—hoping she'll call.

110 **Doc:** She still living in California?

Lenny: Yes; in Hollywood.

Doc: Well, give me a call if she gets in. I'd like to see her.

Lenny: Oh, you would, huh?

Doc: Yeah, Lenny, sad to say, but I would.

115 **Lenny:** It is sad. It's very sad indeed. *(They stare at each other, then look away. There is a moment of tense silence.)*

Doc: Hey, Jell-O Face, your coffee's boiling.

Lenny: *(going to check)* Oh, it is? Thanks. *(After she checks the pot.)* Look, you'd better go on and pick Scott up. You don't want him to have to wait for you.

Doc: Yeah, you're right. Poor kid. It's his first time at the dentist.

Lenny: Poor thing.

120 **Doc:** Well, 'bye. I'm sorry to have to tell you about your horse.

Lenny: Oh, I know. Tell Joan thanks for picking up the pecans.

Doc: I will. *(He starts to leave.)*

LENNY: Oh, how's the baby?

DOC: She's fine. Real pretty. She, ah, holds your finger in her hand; like this.

125   **LENNY:**   Oh, that's cute.

DOC: Yeah. 'Bye, Lenny.

LENNY: 'Bye. *(Doc exits. Lenny stares after him for a moment, then goes and sits back down at the kitchen table. She reaches into her pocket and pulls out a somewhat crumbled cookie and a wax candle. She lights the candle again, lets the wax drip onto the cookie, then sticks the candle on top of the cookie. She begins to sing the "Happy Birthday" song to herself. At the end of the song she pauses, silently makes a wish, and blows out the candle. She waits a moment, then relights the candle, and repeats her actions, only this time making a different wish at the end of the song. She starts to repeat the procedure for the third time, as the phone begins to ring. She goes to answer it.)* Hello . . . oh, hello, Lucille, how's Zackery? . . . Oh, no! . . . Oh, I'm so sorry. Of course, it must be grueling for you . . . Yes, I understand. Your only brother . . . No, she's not here yet. Chick just went to pick her up . . . Oh, now, Lucille, she's still his wife, I'm sure she'll be interested . . . Well, you can just tell me the information and I'll relate it all to her . . . Uh hum, his liver's saved. Oh, that's good news! . . . Well, of course, when you look at it like that . . . Breathing stabilized . . . Damage to the spinal column, not yet determined . . . Okay . . . Yes, Lucille, I've got it all down . . . Uh huh, I'll give her that message. 'Bye, 'bye. *(Lenny drops the pencil and paper down. She sighs deeply, wipes her cheeks with the back of her hand, and goes to the stove to pour herself a cup of coffee. After a few moments, the front door is heard slamming. Lenny starts. A whistle is heard, then Meg's voice.)*

MEG'S VOICE: I'm home! *(She whistles the family whistle.)* Anybody home?

LENNY: Meg? Meg! *(Meg, 27, enters from the dining room. She has sad, magic eyes and wears a hat. She carries a worn-out suitcase.)*

130   **MEG:**   *(dropping her suitcase, running to hug Lenny)* Lenny—

LENNY: Well, Meg! Why, Meg! Oh, Meggy! Why didn't you call? Did you fly in? You didn't take a cab, did you? Why didn't you give us a call?

MEG: *(overlapping)* Oh, Lenny! Why, Lenny! Dear Lenny! *(Then she looks at Lenny's face.)* My God, we're getting so old! Oh, I called for heaven's sake. Of course, I called!

LENNY: Well, I never talked to you—

MEG: Well, I know! I let the phone ring right off the hook!

135   **LENNY:**   Well, as a matter of fact, I was out most of the morning seeing to Babe—

MEG: Now, just what's all this business about Babe? How could you send me such a telegram about Babe? And Zackery! You say somebody's shot Zackery?

LENNY: Yes, they have.

MEG: Well, good Lord! Is he dead?

LENNY: No. But he's in the hospital. He was shot in his stomach.

140 **MEG:**   In his stomach! How awful! Do they know who shot him? *(Lenny nods.)* Well, who? Who was it? Who? Who?

LENNY: Babe! They're all saying Babe shot him! They took her to jail! And they're saying she shot him! They're all saying it! It's horrible! It's awful!

MEG: *(overlapping)* Jail! Good Lord, jail! Well, who? Who's saying it? Who?

LENNY: Everyone! The policemen, the sheriff, Zackery, even Babe's saying it! Even Babe herself!

MEG: Well, for God's sake. For God's sake.

145 **LENNY:**   *(overlapping as she falls apart)* It's horrible! It's horrible! It's just horrible!

MEG: Now calm down, Lenny. Just calm down. Would you like a Coke? Here, I'll get you some Coke. *(Meg gets a Coke from the refrigerator. She opens it and downs a large swig.)* Why? Why would she shoot him? Why? *(Meg hands the Coke bottle to Lenny.)*

LENNY: I talked to her this morning and I asked her that very question. I said, "Babe, why would you shoot Zackery? He was your own husband. Why would you shoot him?" And do you know what she said? *(Meg shakes her head.)* She said, "'Cause I didn't like his looks. I just didn't like his looks."

MEG: *(after a pause)* Well, I don't like his looks.

LENNY: But you didn't shoot him! You wouldn't shoot a person 'cause you didn't like their looks! You wouldn't do that! Oh, I hate to say this—I do hate to say this—but I believe Babe is ill. I mean in-her-head ill.

150 **MEG:**   Oh, now, Lenny, don't you say that! There's plenty of good sane reasons to shoot another person and I'm sure that Babe had one. Now what we've got to do is get her the best lawyer in town. Do you have any ideas on who's the best lawyer in town?

LENNY: Well, Zackery is, of course; but he's been shot!

MEG: Well, count him out! Just count him and his whole firm out!

LENNY: Anyway, you don't have to worry, she's already got her lawyer.

MEG: She does? Who?

155 **LENNY:**   Barnette Lloyd. Annie Lloyd's boy. He just opened his office here in town. And Uncle Watson said we'd be doing Annie a favor by hiring him up.

MEG: Doing Annie a favor? Doing Annie a favor? Well, what about Babe? Have you thought about Babe? Do we want to do her a favor of thirty or forty years in jail? Have you thought about that?

LENNY: Now, don't snap at me! Just don't snap at me! I try to do what's right! All this responsibility keeps falling on my shoulders, and I try to do what's right!

Meg: Well, boo hoo, hoo, hoo! And how in the hell could you send me such a telegram about Babe!

Lenny: Well, if you had a phone, or if you didn't live way out there in Hollywood and not even come home for Christmas, maybe I wouldn't have to pay all that money to send you a telegram!

160 **Meg:**   *(overlapping)* "Babe's in terrible trouble—Stop! Zackery's been shot—Stop! Come home immediately—Stop! Stop! Stop!"

Lenny: And what was that you said about how old we're getting? When you looked at my face, you said, "My God, we're getting so old!" But you didn't mean we—you meant me! Didn't you? I'm thirty years old today and my face is getting all pinched up and my hair is falling out in the comb.

Meg: Why, Lenny! It's your birthday, October 23. How could I forget. Happy Birthday!

Lenny: Well, it's not. I'm thirty years old and Billy Boy died last night. He was struck by lightning. He was struck dead.

Meg: *(reaching for a cigarette)* Struck dead. Oh, what a mess. What a mess. Are you really thirty? Then I must be twenty-seven and Babe is twenty-four. My God, we're getting so old. *(They are silent for several moments as Meg drags off her cigarette and Lenny drinks her Coke.)* What's the cot doing in the kitchen?

165 **Lenny:**   Well, I rolled it out when Old Granddaddy got sick. So I could be close and hear him at night if he needed something.

Meg: *(glancing toward the door leading to the downstairs bedroom)* Is Old Granddaddy here?

Lenny: Why, no. Old Granddaddy's at the hospital.

Meg: Again?

Lenny: Meg!

170 **Meg:**   What?

Lenny: I wrote you all about it. He's been in the hospital over three months straight.

Meg: He has?

Lenny: Don't you remember? I wrote you about all those blood vessels popping in his brain?

Meg: Popping—

175 **Lenny:**   And how he was so anxious to hear from you and to find out about your singing career. I wrote it all to you. How they have to feed him through those tubes now. Didn't you get my letters?

Meg: Oh, I don't know, Lenny. I guess I did. To tell you the truth, sometimes I kinda don't read your letters.

Lenny: What?

Meg: I'm sorry. I used to read them. It's just, since Christmas reading them gives me these slicing pains right here in my chest.

Lenny: I see. I see. Is that why you didn't use that money Old Granddaddy sent you to come home Christmas; because you hate us so much? We never did all that much to make you hate us. We didn't!

180 **MEG:**   Oh, Lenny! Do you think I'd be getting slicing pains in my chest if I didn't care about you? If I hated you? Honestly, now, do you think I would?

LENNY: No.

MEG: Okay, then. Let's drop it. I'm sorry I didn't read your letters. Okay?

LENNY: Okay.

MEG: Anyway, we've got this whole thing with Babe to deal with. The first thing is to get her a good lawyer and get her out of jail.

185 **LENNY:**   Well, she's out of jail.

MEG: She is?

LENNY: That young lawyer, he's gotten her out.

MEG: Oh, he has?

LENNY: Yes, on bail. Uncle Watson's put it up. Chick's bringing her back right now—she's driving her home.

190 **MEG:**   Oh; well, that's a relief.

LENNY: Yes, and they're due home any minute now; so we can just wait right here for 'em.

MEG: Well, good. That's good. *(As she leans against the counter.)* So, Babe shot Zackery Botrelle, the richest and most powerful man in all of Hazlehurst, slap in the gut. It's hard to believe.

LENNY: It certainly is. Little Babe—shooting off a gun.

MEG: Little Babe.

195 **LENNY:**   She was always the prettiest and most perfect of the three of us. Old Granddaddy used to call her his Dancing Sugar Plum. Why, remember how proud and happy he was the day she married Zackery.

MEG: Yes, I remember. It was his finest hour.

LENNY: He remarked how Babe was gonna skyrocket right to the heights of Hazlehurst society. And how Zackery was just the right man for her whether she knew it now or not.

MEG: Oh, Lordy, Lordy. And what does Old Granddaddy say now?

LENNY: Well, I haven't had the courage to tell him all about this as yet. I thought maybe tonight we could go to visit him at the hospital, and you could talk to him and . . .

200 **MEG:**   Yeah; well, we'll see. We'll see. Do we have anything to drink around here—to the tune of straight bourbon?

LENNY: No. There's no liquor.

MEG: Hell. *(Meg gets a Coke from the refrigerator and opens it.)*

LENNY: Then you *will* go with me to see Old Granddaddy at the hospital tonight?

MEG: Of course. *(Meg goes to her purse and gets out a bottle of Empirin Compound. She takes out a tablet and puts it on her tongue.)* Brother, I know he's gonna go on about my singing career. Just like he always does.

205 **LENNY:**   Well, how is your career going?

MEG: It's not.

LENNY: Why, aren't you still singing at the club down on Malibu beach?

MEG: No. Not since Christmas.

LENNY: Well, then, are you singing someplace new?

210 MEG: No, I'm not singing. I'm not singing at all.

LENNY: Oh. Well, what do you do then?

MEG: What I do is I pay cold storage bills for a dog-food company.
That's what I do.

LENNY: *(trying to be helpful)* Gosh, don't you think it'd be a good idea to
stay in the show business field?

MEG: Oh, maybe.

215 LENNY: Like Old Granddaddy says, "With your talent, all you need is
exposure. Then you can make your own breaks!" Did you hear his
suggestion about getting your foot put in one of those blocks of
cement they've got out here? He thinks that's real important.

MEG: Yeh. I think I've heard that. And I'll probably hear it again when I
go to visit him at the hospital tonight; so let's just drop it. Okay?
(She notices the sack of pecans.) What's this? Pecans? Great, I love
pecans! *(Meg takes out two pecans and tries to open them by cracking
them together.)* Come on . . . Crack, you demons! Crack!

LENNY: We have a nutcracker!

MEG: *(trying with her teeth)* Ah, where's the sport in a nutcracker?
Where's the challenge?

LENNY: *(getting up to get the nutcracker)* It's over here in the utensil
drawer. *(As Lenny gets the nutcracker, Meg opens the pecan by stepping on
it with her shoe.)*

220 MEG: There! Open! *(Meg picks up the crumbled pecan and eats it.)* Mmmm,
delicious. Delicious. Where'd you get the fresh pecans?

LENNY: Oh . . . I don't know.

MEG: They sure are tasty.

LENNY: Doc Porter brought them over.

MEG: Doc. What's Doc doing here in town?

225 LENNY: Well, his father died a couple of months ago. Now he's back
home seeing to his property.

MEG: Gosh, the last I heard of Doc, he was up in the East painting the
walls of houses to earn a living. *(Amused.)* Heard he was living with
some Yankee woman who made clay pots.

LENNY: Joan.

MEG: What?

LENNY: Her name's Joan. She came down here with him. That's one of
her pots. Doc's married to her.

230 MEG: Married—

LENNY: Uh huh.

MEG: Doc married a Yankee?

LENNY: That's right; and they've got two kids.

MEG: Kids—

235 LENNY: A boy and a girl.

MEG: God. Then his kids must be half Yankee.

Lenny: I suppose.

Meg: God. That really gets me. I don't know why, but somehow that really gets me.

Lenny: I don't know why it should.

240 **Meg:**   And what a stupid-looking pot! Who'd buy it anyway?

Lenny: Wait—I think that's them. Yeah, that's Chick's car! Oh, there's Babe! Hello, Babe! They're home, Meg! They're home. *(Meg hides.)*

Babe's voice: Lenny! I'm home! I'm free! *(Babe, 24, enters exuberantly. She has an angelic face and fierce, volatile eyes. She carries a pink pocketbook.)* I'm home! *(Meg jumps out of hiding.)* Oh, Meg—Look, it's Meg! *(Running to hug her.)* Meg! When did you get home?

Meg: Just now!

Babe: Well, it's so good to see you! I'm so glad you're home! I'm so relieved. *(Chick enters.)*

245 **Meg:**   Why, Chick; hello.

Chick: Hello, Cousin Margaret. What brings you back to Hazlehurst?

Meg: Oh, I came on home . . . *(turning to Babe)* I came on home to see about Babe.

Babe: *(running to hug Meg)* Oh, Meg—

Meg: How are things with you, Babe?

250 **Chick:**   Well, they are dismal, if you want my opinion. She is refusing to cooperate with her lawyer, that nice-looking young Lloyd boy. She won't tell any of us why she committed this heinous crime, except to say that she didn't like Zackery's looks—

Babe: Oh, look, Lenny brought my suitcase from home! And my saxophone! Thank you! *(Babe runs over to the cot and gets out her saxophone.)*

Chick: Now, that young lawyer is coming over here this afternoon, and when he gets here he expects to get some concrete answers! That's what he expects! No more of this nonsense and stubbornness from you, Rebecca MaGrath, or they'll put you in jail and throw away the key!

Babe: *(overlapping to Meg)* Meg, come look at my new saxophone. I went to Jackson and bought it used. Feel it. It's so heavy.

Meg: *(overlapping to Chick)* It's beautiful. *(The room goes silent.)*

255 **Chick:**   Isn't that right, won't they throw away the key?

Lenny: Well, honestly, I don't know about that—

Chick: They will! And leave you there to rot. So, Rebecca, what are you going to tell Mr. Lloyd about shooting Zackery when he gets here? What are your reasons going to be?

Babe: *(glaring)* That I didn't like his looks! I just didn't like his stinking looks! And I don't like yours much either, Chick-the-Stick! So just leave me alone! I mean it! Leave me alone! Oooh! *(Babe exits up the stairs. There is a long moment of silence.)*

Chick: Well, I was only trying to warn her that she's going to have to help herself. It's just that she doesn't understand how serious the situation is. Does she? She doesn't have the vaguest idea. Does she now?

260 **LENNY:** Well, it's true, she does seem a little confused.

CHICK: And that's putting it mildly, Lenny honey. That's putting it mighty mild. So, Margaret, how's your singing career going? We keep looking for your picture in the movie magazines. *(Meg moves to light a cigarette.)* You know, you shouldn't smoke. It causes cancer. Cancer of the lungs. They say each cigarette is just a little stick of cancer. A little death stick.

MEG: That's what I like about it, Chick—taking a drag off of death. *(Meg takes a long, deep drag.)* Mmm! Gives me a sense of controlling my own destiny. What power! What exhilaration! Want a drag?

LENNY: *(trying to break the tension)* Ah, Zackery's liver's been saved! His sister called up and said his liver was saved. Isn't that good news?

MEG: Well, yes, that's fine news. Mighty fine news. Why, I've been told that the liver's a powerful important bodily organ. I believe it's used to absorb all our excess bile.

265 **LENNY:** Yes—well—it's been saved. *(The phone rings. Lenny gets it.)*

MEG: So! Did you hear all that good news about the liver, Little Chicken?

CHICK: I heard it. And don't you call me Chicken! *(Meg clucks like a chicken.)* I've told you a hundred times if I've told you once not to call me Chicken. You cannot call me Chicken.

LENNY: . . . Oh, no! . . . Of course, we'll be right over! 'Bye! *(She hangs up the phone.)* That was Annie May—Peekay and Buck Jr. have eaten paint!

CHICK: Oh, no! Are they all right? They're not sick? They're not sick, are they?

270 **LENNY:** I don't know. I don't know. Come on. We've got to run on next door.

CHICK: *(overlapping)* Oh, God! Oh, please! Please let them be all right! Don't let them die! Please, don't let them die!!

Chick runs off howling with Lenny following after. Meg sits alone, finishing her cigarette. After a moment, Babe's voice is heard.

BABE'S VOICE: Pst—Psst!

Meg looks around. Babe comes tiptoeing down the stairs.

BABE: Has she gone?

MEG: She's gone. Peekay and Buck Jr. just ate their paints.

275 **BABE:** What idiots.

MEG: Yeah.

BABE: You know, Chick's hated us ever since we had to move here from Vicksburg to live with Old Grandmama and Old Granddaddy.

MEG: She's an idiot.

BABE: Yeah. Do you know what she told me this morning while I was still behind bars and couldn't get away?

280 **MEG:** What?

BABE: She told me how embarrassing it was for her all those years ago, you know, when Mama—

MEG: Yeah, down in the cellar.

BABE: She said our mama had shamed the entire family, and we were known notoriously all through Hazlehurst. *(About to cry.)* Then she went on to say how I would now be getting just as much bad publicity, and humiliating her and the family all over again.

MEG: Ah, forget it, Babe. Just forget it.

285 **BABE:** I told her, "Mama got national coverage! National!" And if Zackery wasn't a senator from Copiah County, I probably wouldn't even be getting statewide.

MEG: Of course you wouldn't.

BABE: *(after a pause)* Gosh, sometimes I wonder . . .

MEG: What?

BABE: Why she did it. Why Mama hung herself.

290 **MEG:** I don't know. She had a bad day. A real bad day. You know how it feels on a real bad day.

BABE: And that old yellow cat. It was sad about that old cat.

MEG: Yeah.

BABE: I bet if Daddy hadn't of left us, they'd still be alive.

MEG: Oh, I don't know.

295 **BABE:** 'Cause it was after he left that she started spending whole days just sitting there and smoking on the back porch steps. She'd sling her ashes down onto the different bugs and ants that'd be passing by.

MEG: Yeah. Well, I'm glad he left.

BABE: That old yellow cat'd stay back there with her. I thought if she felt something for anyone it woulda been that old cat. Guess I musta been mistaken.

MEG: God, he was a bastard. Really, with his white teeth, Daddy was such a bastard.

BABE: Was he? I don't remember. *(Meg blows out a mouthful of smoke. After a moment, uneasily.)* I think I'm gonna make some lemonade. You want some?

300 **MEG:** Sure. *(Babe cuts lemons, dumps sugar, stirs ice cubes, etc. throughout the following exchange.)* Babe. Why won't you talk? Why won't you tell anyone about shooting Zackery?

BABE: Oooh—

MEG: Why not? You must have had a good reason. Didn't you?

BABE: I guess I did.

MEG: Well, what was it?

305 **BABE:** I . . . I can't say.

MEG: Why not? *(Pause)* Babe, why not? You can tell me.

BABE: 'Cause . . . I'm sort of . . . protecting someone.

MEG: Protecting someone? Oh, Babe, then you really didn't shoot him? I knew you couldn't have done it! I knew it!

BABE: No, I shot him. I shot him all right. I meant to kill him. I was aiming for his heart, but I guess my hands were shaking and I—just got him in the stomach.

310 **MEG:** *(collapsing)* I see.

BABE: *(stirring the lemonade)* So I'm guilty. And I'm just gonna have to take my punishment and go on to jail.

MEG: Oh, Babe—

BABE: Don't worry, Meg, jail's gonna be a relief to me. I can learn to play my new saxophone. I won't have to live with Zackery anymore. And I won't have his snoopy old sister, Lucille, coming over and pushing me around. Jail will be a relief. Here's your lemonade.

MEG: Thanks.

315 **BABE:** It taste okay?

MEG: Perfect.

BABE: I like a lot of sugar in mine. I'm gonna add some more sugar.
(Babe goes to add more sugar to her lemonade, as Lenny bursts through the back door in a state of excitement and confusion.)

LENNY: Well, it looks like the paint is primarily on their arms and faces, but Chick wants me to drive them all over to Doctor Winn's just to make sure. *(Lenny grabs her car keys off of the counter and as she does so, she notices the mess of lemons and sugar.)* Oh, now, Babe, try not to make a mess here; and be careful with this sharp knife. Honestly, all that sugar's gonna get you sick. Well, 'bye, 'bye. I'll be back as soon as I can.

MEG: 'Bye, Lenny.

320 **BABE:** 'Bye. *(Lenny exits.)* Boy, I don't know what's happening to Lenny.

MEG: What do you mean?

BABE: "Don't make a mess; don't make yourself sick; don't cut yourself with that sharp knife." She's turning into Old Grandmama.

MEG: You think so?

BABE: More and more. Do you know she's taken to wearing Old Grandmama's torn sunhat and her green garden gloves?

325 **MEG:** Those old lime-green ones?

BABE: Yeah; she works out in the garden wearing the lime-green gloves of a dead woman. Imagine wearing those gloves on your hands.

MEG: Poor Lenny. She needs some love in her life. All she does is work out at that brick yard and take care of Old Granddaddy.

BABE: Yeah. But she's so shy with men.

MEG: *(biting into an apple)* Probably because of that *shrunken* ovary she has.

330 **BABE:** *(slinging ice cubes)* Yeah, that *deformed* ovary.

MEG: Old Granddaddy's the one who's made her feel self-conscious about it. It's his fault. The old fool.

BABE: It's so sad.

MEG: God—you know what?

BABE: What?

335 **MEG:** I bet Lenny's never even slept with a man. Just think, thirty years old and never even had it once.

BABE: *(slyly)* Oh I don't know. Maybe she's . . . had it once.

MEG: She has?

BABE: Maybe. I think so.

MEG: When? When?

340 **BABE:** Well . . . maybe I shouldn't say—

MEG: Babe!

BABE: *(rapidly telling the story)* All right, then. It was after Old Granddaddy went back to the hospital this second time. Lenny was really in a state of deep depression, I could tell that she was. Then one day she calls me up and asks me to come over and to bring along my Polaroid camera. Well, when I arrive she's waiting for me out there in the sun parlor wearing her powder-blue Sunday dress and this old curled-up wig. She confided that she was gonna try sending in her picture to one of those lonely-hearts clubs.

MEG: Oh, my God.

BABE: Lonely Hearts of the South. She'd seen their ad in a magazine.

345 **MEG:** Jesus.

BABE: Anyway, I take some snapshots and she sends them on in to the club, and about two weeks later she receives in the mail this whole load of pictures of available men, most of 'em fairly odd-looking. But of course she doesn't call any of 'em up 'cause she's really shy. But one of 'em, this Charlie Hill from Memphis, Tennessee, he calls her.

MEG: He does?

BABE: Yeah. And time goes on and she says he's real funny on the phone, so they decide to get together to meet.

MEG: Yeah?

350 **BABE:** Well, he drives down here to Hazlehurst 'bout three or four different times and has supper with her; then one weekend she goes up to Memphis to visit him, and I think that is where it happened.

MEG: What makes you think so?

BABE: Well, when I went to pick her up from the bus depot, she ran off the bus and threw her arms around me and started crying and sobbing as though she'd like to never stop. I asked her, I said, "Lenny, what's the matter?" And she said, "I've done it, Babe! Honey, I've done it!"

MEG: *(whispering)* And you think she meant that she'd done *it*?

BABE: *(whispering back, slyly)* I think so.

355 **MEG:** Well, goddamn! *(They laugh with glee.)*

BABE: But she didn't say anything else about it. She just went on to tell me about the boot factory where Charlie worked and what a nice city Memphis was.

MEG: So, what happened to this Charlie?

BABE: Well, he came to Hazlehurst just one more time. Lenny took him over to meet Old Granddaddy at the hospital, and after that they broke it off.

MEG: 'Cause of Old Granddaddy?

360 **BABE:**   Well, she said it was on account of her missing ovary. That Charlie didn't want to marry her on account of it.

MEG: Ah, how mean. How hateful.

BABE: Oh, it was. He seemed like such a nice man, too—kinda chubby with red hair and freckles, always telling these funny jokes.

MEG: Hmmm, that just doesn't seem right. Something about that doesn't seem exactly right. *(Meg paces about the kitchen and comes across the box of candy Lenny got for her birthday.)* Oh, God. "Happy Birthday to Lenny, from the Buck Boyles."

BABE: Oh, no! Today's Lenny's birthday!

365 **MEG:**   That's right.

BABE: I forgot all about it!

MEG: I know. I did too.

BABE: Gosh, we'll have to order up a big cake for her. She always loves to make those wishes on her birthday cake.

MEG: Yeah, let's get her a big cake! A huge one! *(Suddenly noticing the plastic wrapper on the candy box.)* Oh, God, that Chick's so cheap!

370 **BABE:**   What do you mean?

MEG: This plastic has poinsettias on it!

BABE: *(running to see)* Oh, let me see—*(She looks at the package with disgust.)* Boy, oh, boy! I'm calling that bakery and ordering the very largest size cake they have! That Jumbo Deluxe!

MEG: Good!

BABE: Why, I imagine they can make one up to be about—*this* big. *(She demonstrates.)*

375 **MEG:**   Oh, at least; at least that big. Why, maybe, it'll even be *this* big. *(She makes a very, very, very large size cake.)*

BABE: You think it could be *that* big?

MEG: Sure!

BABE: *(after a moment, getting the idea)* Or, or what if it were *this* big? *(She maps out a cake that covers the room.)* What if we get the cake and it's *this* big? *(She gulps down a fistful of cake.)* Gulp! Gulp! Gulp! Tasty treat!

MEG: Hmmm—I'll have me some more! Give me some more of that birthday cake!

Suddenly there is a loud knock at the door.

380 **BARNETTE'S VOICE:**   Hello . . . hello! May I come in?

BABE: *(to Meg, in a whisper, as she takes cover)* Who's that?

MEG: I don't know.

BARNETTE'S VOICE: *(still knocking)* Hello! Hello, Mrs. Botrelle!

BABE: Oh, shoot! It's that lawyer. I don't want to see him.

385 **MEG:** Oh, Babe, come on. You've got to see him sometime.

BABE: No, I don't! *(She starts up the stairs.)* Just tell him I died. I'm going upstairs.

MEG: Oh, Babe! Will you come back here!

BABE: *(as she exits)* You talk to him, please, Meg. Please! I just don't want to see him—

MEG: Babe—Babe! Oh, shit . . . Ah, come on in! Door's open!

Barnette Lloyd, 26, enters carrying a briefcase. He is a slender, intelligent young man with an almost fanatical intensity that he subdues by sheer will.

390 **BARNETTE:** How do you do? I'm Barnette Lloyd.

MEG: Pleased to meet you. I've Meg MaGrath, Babe's older sister.

BARNETTE: Yes, I know. You're the singer.

MEG: Well, yes . . .

BARNETTE: I came to hear you five different times when you were singing at the club in Biloxi. Greeny's I believe was the name of it.

395 **MEG:** Yes, Greeny's.

BARNETTE: You were very good. There was something sad and moving about how you sang those songs. It was like you had some sort of vision. Some special sort of vision.

MEG: Well, thank you. You're very kind. Now . . . about Babe's case—

BARNETTE: Yes?

MEG: We've just got to win it.

400 **BARNETTE:** I intend to.

MEG: Of course. But, ah . . . *(She looks at him.)* Ah, you know, you're very young.

BARNETTE: Yes. I am. I'm young.

MEG: It's just, I'm concerned, Mr. Lloyd—

BARNETTE: Barnette. Please.

405 **MEG:** Barnette; that, ah, just maybe we need someone with, well, with more experience. Someone totally familiar with all the ins and outs and the this and thats of the legal dealings and such. As that.

BARNETTE: Ah, you have reservations.

MEG: *(relieved)* Reservations. Yes, I have . . . reservations.

BARNETTE: Well, possibly it would help you to know that I graduated first in my class from Ole Miss Law School. I also spent three different summers taking advanced courses in criminal law at Harvard Law School. I made A's in all the given courses. I was fascinated!

MEG: I'm sure.

410 **BARNETTE:** And even now, I've just completed one year working with Jackson's top criminal law firm, Manchester and Wayne. I was invaluable to them. Indispensable. They offered to double my percentage if I'd stay on; but I refused. I wanted to return to Hazelhurst and open my own office. The reason being, and this is a key point, that I have a personal vendetta to settle with one Zackery F. Botrelle.

MEG: A personal vendetta?

BARNETTE: Yes, ma'am. You are correct. Indeed, I do.

MEG: Hmmm. A personal vendetta . . . I think I like that. So you have some sort of a personal vendetta to settle with Zackery?

BARNETTE: Precisely. Just between the two of us, I not only intend to keep that sorry s.o.b. from ever being re-elected to the state senate by exposing his shady, criminal dealings; but I also intend to decimate his personal credibility by exposing him as a bully, a brute, and a red-neck thug!

415 **MEG:** Well; I can see that you're—fanatical about this.

BARNETTE: Yes, I am. I'm sorry, if I seem outspoken. But for some reason, I feel I can talk to you . . . those songs you sang. Excuse me; I feel like a jack-ass.

MEG: It's all right. Relax. Relax, Barnette. Let me think this out a minute. *(She takes out a cigarette. He lights it for her.)* Now just exactly how do you intend to get Babe off? You know, keep her out of jail.

BARNETTE: It seems to me that we can get her off with a plea of self-defense, or possibly we could go with innocent by reason of temporary insanity. But basically, I intend to prove that Zackery Botrelle brutalized and tormented this poor woman to such an extent that she had no recourse but to defend herself in the only way she knew how!

MEG: I like that!

420 **BARNETTE:** Then, of course, I'm hoping this will break the ice and we'll be able to go on to prove that the man's a total criminal, as well as an abusive bully and contemptible slob!

MEG: That sounds good! To me that sounds very good!

BARNETTE: It's just our basic game plan.

MEG: But now, how are you going to prove all this about Babe being brutalized? We don't want anyone perjured. I mean to commit perjury.

BARNETTE: Perjury? According to my sources, there'll be no need for perjury.

425 **MEG:** You mean it's the truth?

BARNETTE: This is a small town, Miss MaGrath. The word gets out.

MEG: It's really the truth?

BARNETTE: *(opening his briefcase)* Just look at this. It's a photostatic copy of Mrs. Botrelle's medical chart over the past four years. Take a good look at it, if you want your blood to boil!

MEG: *(looking over the chart)* What! What! This is maddening. This is madness! Did he do this to her? I'll kill him; I will—I'll fry his blood!! Did he do this?

430 **BARNETTE:** *(alarmed)* To tell you the truth, I can't say for certain what was accidental and what was not. That's why I need to talk with Mrs. Botrelle. That's why it's very important that I see her!

MEG: *(her eyes are wild, as she shoves him toward the door)* Well, look, I've got to see her first. I've got to talk to her first. What I'll do is I'll give you a call. Maybe you can come back over later on—

BARNETTE: Well, then, here's my card—

MEG: Okay. Goodbye.

BARNETTE: 'Bye!

435 **MEG:**   Oh, wait! Wait! There's one problem with you.

BARNETTE: What?

MEG: What if you get so fanatically obsessed with this vendetta thing that you forget about Babe? You forget about her and sell her down the river just to get at Zackery. What about that?

BARNETTE: I—wouldn't do that.

MEG: You wouldn't?

440 **BARNETTE:**   No.

MEG: Why not?

BARNETTE: Because, I'm—I'm fond of her.

MEG: What do you mean you're fond of her?

BARNETTE: Well, she . . . she sold me a pound cake at a bazaar once. And I'm fond of her.

445 **MEG:**   All right; I believe you. Goodbye.

BARNETTE: Goodbye. *(Barnette exits.)*

MEG: Babe! Babe, come down here! Babe!

Babe comes hurrying down the stairs.

BABE: What? What is it? I called about the cake—

MEG: What did Zackery do to you?

450 **BABE:**   They can't have it for today.

MEG: Did he hurt you? Did he? Did he do that?

BABE: Oh, Meg, please—

MEG: Did he? Goddamnit, Babe—

BABE: Yes, he did.

455 **MEG:**   Why? Why?

BABE: I don't know. He started hating me, 'cause I couldn't laugh at his jokes. I just started finding it impossible to laugh at his jokes the way I used to. And then the sound of his voice got to where it tired me out awful bad to hear it. I'd fall asleep just listening to him at the dinner table. He'd say, "Hand me some of that gravy!" Or, "This roast beef is too damn bloody." And suddenly I'd be out cold like a light.

MEG: Oh, Babe. Babe, this is very important. I want you to sit down here and tell me what all happened right before you shot Zackery. That's right, just sit down and tell me.

BABE: *(after a pause)* I told you, I can't tell you on account of I'm protecting someone.

MEG: But, Babe, you've just got to talk to someone about all this. You just do.

460 **BABE:**   Why?

MEG: Because it's a human need. To talk about our lives. It's an important human need.

BABE: Oh. Well, I do feel like I want to talk to someone. I do.

MEG: Then talk to me; please.

BABE: *(making a decision)* All right. *(After thinking a minute.)* I don't know where to start.

465 **MEG:**   Just start at the beginning. Just there at the beginning.

BABE: *(after a moment)* Well, do you remember Willie Jay? *(Meg shakes her head.)* Cora's youngest boy?

MEG: Oh, yeah, that little kid we used to pay a nickel to, to run down to the drugstore and bring us back a cherry Coke.

BABE: Right. Well, Cora irons at my place on Wednesdays now, and she just happened to mention that Willie Jay'd picked up this old stray dog and that he'd gotten real fond of him. But now they couldn't afford to feed him anymore, so she was gonna have to tell Willie Jay to set him loose in the woods.

MEG: *(trying to be patient)* Uh huh.

470 **BABE:**   Well, I said I liked dogs, and if he wanted to bring the dog over here, I'd take care of him. You see, I was alone by myself most of the time 'cause the senate was in session and Zackery was up in Jackson.

MEG: Uh huh. *(Meg reaches for Lenny's box of birthday candy. She takes little nibbles out of each piece throughout the rest of the scene.)*

BABE: So the next day, Willie Jay brings over this skinny, old dog with these little crossed eyes. Well, I asked Willie Jay what his name was, and he said they called him Dog. Well, I liked the name; so I thought I'd keep it.

MEG: *(getting up)* Uh huh. I'm listening. I'm just gonna get me a glass of cold water. Do you want one?

BABE: Okay.

475 **MEG:**   So you kept the name—Dog.

BABE: Yeah. Anyway, when Willie Jay was leaving he gave Dog a hug and said, "Goodbye, Dog. You're a fine ole dog." Well, I felt something for him, so I told Willie Jay he could come back and visit with Dog any time he wanted, and his face just kinda lit right up.

MEG: *(offering the candy)* Candy—

BABE: No thanks. Anyhow, time goes on and Willie Jay keeps coming over and over. And we talk about Dog and how fat he's getting, and then, well, you know, things start up.

MEG: No, I don't know. What things start up?

480 **BABE:**   Well, things start up. Like sex. Like that.

MEG: Babe, wait a minute—Willie Jay's a boy. A small boy, about this tall. He's about this tall!

BABE: No! Oh, no! He's taller now! He's fifteen now. When you knew him he was only about seven or eight.

MEG: But even so—fifteen. And he's a black boy; a colored boy; a Negro.

BABE: *(flustered)* Well, I realize that, Meg. Why do you think I'm so worried about his getting public exposure? I don't want to ruin his reputation!

485 **MEG:**   I'm amazed, Babe. I'm really, completely amazed. I didn't even know you were a liberal.

BABE: Well, I'm not! I'm not a liberal! I'm a democratic! I was just lonely! I was so lonely. And he was good. Oh, he was so, so good. I'd never had it that good. We'd always go out into the garage and—

MEG: It's okay. I've got the picture; I've got the picture! Now, let's just get back to the story. To yesterday, when you shot Zackery.

BABE: All right, then. Let's see . . . Willie Jay was over. And it was after we'd—

MEG: Yeah! Yeah.

490 **BABE:**   And we were just standing around on the back porch playing with Dog. Well, suddenly Zackery comes from around the side of the house. And he startled me 'cause he's supposed to be away at the office, and there he is coming from 'round the side of the house. Anyway, he says to Willie Jay, "Hey, boy, what are you doing back here?" And I said, "He's not doing anything. You just go on home. Willie Jay! You just run right on home." Well, before he can move, Zackery comes up and knocks him once right across the face and then shoves him down the porch steps, causing him to skin up his elbow real bad on that hard concrete. Then he says, "Don't you ever come around here again, or I'll have them cut out your gizzard!" Well, Willie Jay starts crying—these tears come streaming down his face— then he gets up real quick and runs away, with Dog following off after him. After that, I don't remember much too clearly; let's see . . . I went on into the living room, and I went right up to the davenport and opened the drawer where we keep the burglar gun . . . I took it out. Then I—I brought it up to my ear. That's right. I put it right inside my ear. Why, I was gonna shoot off my own head! That's what I was gonna do. Then I heard the back door slamming and suddenly, for some reason, I thought about Mama . . . how she'd hung herself. And here I was about ready to shoot myself. Then I realized—that's right, I realized how I didn't want to kill myself! And she—she probably didn't want to kill herself. She wanted to kill him, and I wanted to kill him, too. I wanted to kill Zackery, not myself. 'Cause I—I wanted to live! So I waited for him to come on into the living room. Then I held out the gun, and I pulled the trigger, aiming for his heart, but getting him in the stomach. *(After a pause.)* It's funny that I really did that.

MEG: It's a good thing that you did. It's a damn good thing that you did.

BABE: It was.

MEG: Please, Babe, talk to Barnette Lloyd. Just talk to him and see if he can help.

BABE: But how about Willie Jay?

495 **MEG:** *(starting towards the phone)* Oh, he'll be all right. You just talk to that lawyer like you did to me. *(Looking at the number on the card, she beings dialing.)* See, 'cause he's gonna be on your side.

BABE: No! Stop, Meg, stop! Don't call him up! Please don't call him up! You can't! It's too awful. *(She runs over and jerks the bottom half of the phone away from Meg. Meg stands, holding the receiver.)*

MEG: Babe! *(Babe slams her half of the phone into the refrigerator.)*

BABE: I just can't tell some stranger all about my personal life. I just can't.

MEG: Well, hell, Babe; you're the one who said you wanted to live.

500 **BABE:** That's right. I did. *(She takes the phone out of the refrigerator and hands it to Meg.)* Here's the other part of the phone. *(Babe moves to sit at the kitchen table. Meg takes the phone back to the counter. Babe fishes a lemon out of her glass and begins sucking on it.)* Meg.

MEG: What?

BABE: I called the bakery. They're gonna have Lenny's cake ready first thing tomorrow morning. That's the earliest they can get it.

MEG: All right.

BABE: I told them to write on it, "Happy Birthday Lenny—A Day Late." That sound okay?

505 **MEG:** *(at the phone)* It sounds nice.

BABE: I ordered up the very largest size cake they have. I told them chocolate cake with white icing and red trim. Think she'll like that?

MEG: *(dialing on the phone)* Yeah, I'm sure she will. She'll like it.

BABE: I'm hoping.

Curtain

ACT II

The lights go up on the kitchen. It is later that evening on the same day. Meg's suitcase has been moved upstairs. Babe's saxophone has been taken out of the case and put together. Babe and Barnette are sitting at the kitchen table. Barnette is writing and rechecking notes with explosive intensity. Babe, who has changed into a casual shift, sits eating a bowl of oatmeal, slowly.

BARNETTE: *(to himself)* Mmm huh! Yes! I see, I see! Well, we can work on that! And of course, this is mere conjecture! Difficult, if not impossible, to prove. Ha! Yes. Yes, indeed. Indeed—

BABE: Sure you don't want any oatmeal?

BARNETTE: What? Oh, no. No, thank you. Let's see; ah, where were we?

BABE: I just shot Zackery.

5 **BARNETTE:** *(looking at his notes)* Right. Correct. You've just pulled the trigger.

BABE: Tell me, do you think Willie Jay can stay out of all this?

BARNETTE: Believe me, it is in our interest to keep him as far out of this as possible.

BABE: Good.

BARNETTE: *(throughout the following, Barnette stays glued to Babe's every word)* All right, you've just shot one Zackery Botrelle, as a result of his continual physical and mental abuse—what happens now?

10 **BABE:**   Well, after I shot him, I put the gun down on the piano bench, and then I went out into the kitchen and made up a pitcher of lemonade.

BARNETTE: Lemonade?

BABE: Yes, I was dying of thirst. My mouth was just as dry as a bone.

BARNETTE: So in order to quench this raging thirst that was choking you dry and preventing any possibility of you uttering intelligible sounds or phrases, you went out to the kitchen and made up a pitcher of lemonade?

BABE: Right. I made it just the way I like it, with lots of sugar and lots of lemon—about ten lemons in all. Then I added two trays of ice and stirred it up with my wooden stirring spoon.

15 **BARNETTE:**   Then what?

BABE: Then I drank three glasses, one right after the other. They were large glasses—about this tall. Then suddenly my stomach kind of swole all up. I guess what caused it was all that sour lemon.

BARNETTE: Could be.

BABE: Then what I did was . . . I wiped my mouth off with the back of my hand, like this . . . *(She demonstrates.)*

BARNETTE: Hmmm.

20 **BABE:**   I did it to clear off those little beads of water that had settled there.

BARNETTE: I see.

BABE: Then I called out to Zackery. I said, "Zackery, I've made some lemonade. Can you use a glass?"

BARNETTE: Did he answer? Did you hear an answer?

BABE: No. He didn't answer.

25 **BARNETTE:**   So what'd you do?

BABE: I poured him a glass anyway and took it out to him.

BARNETTE: You took it out to the living room?

BABE: I did. And there he was, lying on the rug. He was looking up at me trying to speak words. I said, "What? . . . Lemonade? . . . You don't want it? Would you like a Coke instead?" Then I got the idea— he was telling me to call on the phone for medical help. So I got on the phone and called up the hospital. I gave my name and address and I told them my husband was shot and he was lying on the rug and there was plenty of blood. *(Babe pauses a minute, as Barnette works frantically on his notes.)* I guess that's gonna look kinda bad.

BARNETTE: What?

30 **BABE:**   Me fixing that lemonade before I called the hospital.

BARNETTE: Well, not . . . necessarily.

BABE: I tell you, I think the reason I made up the lemonade, I mean besides the fact that my mouth was bone dry, was that I was afraid to call the authorities. I was afraid. I—I really think I was afraid they would see that I had tried to shoot Zackery, in fact, that I *had* shot him, and they would accuse me of possible murder and send me away to jail.

BARNETTE: Well, that's understandable.

BABE: I think so. I mean, in fact, that's what did happen. That's what is happening—'cause here I am just about ready to go right off to the Parchment Prison Farm. Yes, here I am just practically on the brink of utter doom. Why, I feel so all alone.

35 **BARNETTE:** Now, now, look—Why, there's no reason for you to get yourself so all upset and worried. Please don't. Please. *(They look at each other for a moment.)* You just keep filling in as much detailed information as you can about those incidents on the medical reports. That's all you need to think about. Don't you worry, Mrs. Botrelle, we're going to have a solid defense.

BABE: Please, don't call me Mrs. Botrelle.

BARNETTE: All right.

BABE: My name's Becky. People in the family call be Babe; but my real name's Becky.

BARNETTE: All right, Becky. *(Barnette and Babe stare at each other for a long moment.)*

40 **BABE:** Are you sure you didn't go to Hazlehurst High?

BARNETTE: No, I went away to a boarding school.

BABE: Gosh, you sure do look familiar. You sure do.

BARNETTE: Well, I—I doubt you'll remember, but I did meet you once.

BABE: You did? When?

45 **BARNETTE:** At the Christmas bazaar, year before last. You were selling cakes and cookies and . . . candy.

BABE: Oh, yes! You bought the orange pound cake!

BARNETTE: Right.

BABE: Of course, and then we talked for a while. We talked about the Christmas angel.

BARNETTE: You do remember.

50 **BABE:** I remember it very well. You were even thinner than you are now.

BARNETTE: Well, I'm surprised. I'm certainly . . . surprised. *(The phone begins to ring.)*

BABE: *(as she goes to answer the phone)* This is quite a coincidence! Don't you think it is? Why, it's almost a fluke. *(She answers the phone.)* Hello . . . Oh, hello, Lucille . . . Oh, he is? . . . Oh, he does? . . . Okay. Oh, Lucille, wait! Has Dog come back to the house? . . . Oh, I see . . . Okay. Okay. *(After a brief pause.)* Hello, Zackery? How are you doing? . . . Uh huh . . . uh huh . . . Oh, I'm sorry . . . Please, don't scream . . . Uh huh . . . uh huh . . . You want what? . . . No, I can't come up there now . . . Well, for one thing, I don't even have the car. Lenny and Meg are up at the hospital right now, visiting with Old Granddaddy . . . What? . . . Oh, really? . . . Oh, really? . . . Well, I've got me a lawyer that's over here right now, and he's building me up a solid defense! . . . Wait just a minute. I'll see. *(To Barnette.)* He wants to talk to you. He says he's got some blackening evidence that's gonna convict me of attempting to murder him in the first degree!

BARNETTE: *(disgustedly)* Oh, bluff! He's bluffing! Here, hand me the phone. *(He takes the phone and becomes suddenly cool and suave.)* Hello, this is Mr. Barnette Lloyd speaking. I'm Mrs. . . . ah, Becky's attorney . . . Why, certainly, Mr. Botrelle, I'd be more than glad to check out any pertinent information that you may have . . . Fine, then I'll be right over. Goodbye. *(He hangs up the phone.)*

BABE: What did he say?

55 **BARNETTE:** He wants me to come to see him at the hospital this evening. Says he's got some sort of evidence. Sounds highly suspect to me.

BABE: Oooh! Didn't you just hate his voice? Doesn't he have the most awful voice! I just hate it! I can't bear to hear it!

BARNETTE: Well, now—now, wait. Wait just a minute.

BABE: What?

BARNETTE: I have a solution. From now on, I'll handle all communications between you two. You can simply refuse to speak with him.

60 **BABE:** All right—I will. I'll do that.

BARNETTE: *(starting to pack his briefcase)* Well, I'd better get over there and see just what he's got up his sleeve.

BABE: *(after a pause)* Barnette.

BARNETTE: Yes?

BABE: What's the personal vendetta about? You know, the one you have to settle with Zackery.

65 **BARNETTE:** Oh, it's—it's complicated. It's a very complicated matter.

BABE: I see.

BARNETTE: The major thing he did was to ruin my father's life. He took away his job, his home, his health, his respectability. I don't like to talk about it.

BABE: I'm sorry. I just wanted to say—I hope you win it. I hope you win your vendetta.

BARNETTE: Thank you.

70 **BABE:** I think it's an important thing that a person could win a lifelong vendetta.

BARNETTE: Yes. Well, I'd better be going.

BABE: All right. Let me know what happens.

BARNETTE: I will. I'll get back to you right away.

BABE: Thanks.

75 **BARNETTE:** Goodbye, Becky.

BABE: Goodbye, Barnette. *(Barnette exits. Babe looks around the room for a moment, then goes over to her white suitcase and open it up. She takes out her pink hair curlers and a brush. She begins brushing her hair.)* Goodbye, Becky. Goodbye, Barnette. Goodbye Becky. Oooh. *(Lenny enters. She is fuming. Babe is rolling her hair throughout most of the following scene.)* Lenny, hi!

LENNY: Hi.

BABE: Where's Meg?

LENNY: Oh, she had to go by the store and pick some things up. I don't know what.

80 **BABE:**   Well, how's Old Granddaddy?

LENNY: *(as she picks up Babe's bowl of oatmeal)* He's fine. Wonderful! Never been better!

BABE: Lenny, what's wrong? What's the matter?

LENNY: It's Meg! I could just wring her neck! I could just wring it!

BABE: Why? Wha'd she do?

85 **LENNY:**   She lied! She sat in that hospital room and shamelessly lied to Old Granddaddy. She went on and on telling such untrue stories and lies.

BABE: Well, what? What did she say?

LENNY: Well, for one thing she said she was gonna have a RCA record coming out with her picture on the cover, eating pineapples under a palm tree.

BABE: Well, gosh, Lenny, maybe she is! Don't you think she really is?

LENNY: Babe, she sat here this very afternoon and told me how all that she's done this whole year is work as a clerk for a dog-food company.

90 **BABE:**   Oh, shoot. I'm disappointed.

LENNY: And then she goes on to say that she'll be appearing on the Johnny Carson Show in two weeks' time. Two weeks' time! Why, Old Granddaddy's got a TV set right in his room. Imagine what a letdown it's gonna be.

BABE: Why, mercy me.

LENNY: *(slamming the coffeepot on)* Oh, and she told him the reason she didn't use the money he sent her to come home Christmas was that she was right in the middle of making a huge multimillion-dollar motion picture and was just under too much pressure.

BABE: My word!

95 **LENNY:**   The movie's coming out this spring. It's called, *Singing in a Shoe Factory*. But she only has a small leading role—not a large leading role.

BABE: *(laughing)* For heaven's sake—

LENNY: I'm sizzling. Oh, I just can't help it! I'm sizzling!

BABE: Sometimes Meg does such strange things.

LENNY: *(slowly, as she picks up the opened box of birthday candy)* Who ate this candy?

100 **BABE:**   *(hesitantly)* Meg.

LENNY: My one birthday present, and look what she does! Why, she's taken one little bite out of each piece and then just put it back in! Ooh! That's just like her! That is just like her!

BABE: Lenny, please—

LENNY: I can't help it! It gets me mad! It gets me upset! Why, Meg's always run wild—she started smoking and drinking when she was fourteen years old; she never made good grades—never made her own bed! But somehow she always seemed to get what she wanted. She's the one who got singing and dancing lessons, and a store-bought dress to wear to her senior prom. Why, do you remember how Meg always got to wear twelve jingle bells on her petticoats, while we were only allowed to wear three apiece? Why?! Why should Old Grandmama let her sew twelve golden jingle bells on her petticoats and us only three!

BABE: *(who has heard all this before)* I don't know! Maybe she didn't jingle them as much!

105 **LENNY:**   I can't help it! It gets me mad! I resent it. I do.

BABE: Oh, don't resent Meg. Things have been hard for Meg. After all, she was the one who found Mama.

LENNY: Oh, I know; she's the one who found Mama. But that's always been the excuse.

BABE: But, I tell you, Lenny, after it happened, Meg started doing all sorts of these strange things.

LENNY: She did? Like what?

110 **BABE:**   Like things I never wanted to tell you about.

LENNY: What sort of things?

BABE: Well, for instance, back when we used to go over to the library, Meg would spend all her time reading and looking through this old, black book called *Diseases of the Skin*. It was full of the most sickening pictures you'd ever seen. Things like rotting-away noses and eyeballs drooping off down the sides of people's faces and scabs and sores and eaten-away places all over *all* parts of people's bodies.

LENNY: *(trying to pour her coffee)* Babe, please! That's enough.

BABE: Anyway, she'd spend hours and hours just forcing herself to look through this book. Why, it was the same way she'd force herself to look at the poster of crippled children stuck up in the window at Dixieland Drugs. You know, that one where they want you to give a dime. Meg would stand there and stare at their eyes and look at the braces on their little crippled-up legs—then she'd purposely go and spend her dime on a double scoop ice cream cone and eat it all down. She's say to me, "See, I can stand it. I can stand it. Just look how I'm gonna be able to stand it."

115 **LENNY:**   That's awful.

BABE: She said she was afraid of being a weak person. I guess 'cause she cried in bed every night for such a long time.

LENNY: Goodness mercy. *(After a pause.)* Well, I suppose you'd have to be a pretty hard person to be able to do what she did to Doc Porter.

BABE: *(exasperated)* Oh, shoot! It wasn't Meg's fault that hurricane wiped Biloxi away. I never understood why people were blaming all that on Meg—just because that roof fell in and crunched Doc's leg. It wasn't her fault.

LENNY: Well, it was Meg who refused to evacuate. Jim Craig and some of Doc's other friends were all down there and they kept trying to get everyone to evacuate. But Meg refused. She wanted to stay on because she thought a hurricane would be—oh, I don't know—a lot of fun. Then everyone says she baited Doc into staying with her. She said she'd marry him if he'd stay.

120 **BABE:** *(taken aback by this new information)* Well, he has a mind of his own. He could have gone.

LENNY: But he didn't. 'Cause . . . 'cause he loved her. And then after the roof caved in and they got Doc to the high school gym, Meg just left. She just left him there to leave for California—'cause of her career, she says. I think it was a shameful thing to do. It took almost a year for his leg to heal and after that he gave up his medical career altogether. He said he was tired of hospitals. It's such a sad thing. Everyone always knew he was gonna be a doctor. We've called him Doc for years.

BABE: I don't know. I guess I don't have any room to talk; 'cause I just don't know. *(Pause.)* Gosh, you look so tired.

LENNY: I feel tired.

BABE: They say women need a lot of iron . . . so they won't feel tired.

125 **LENNY:** What's got iron in it? Liver?

BABE: Yeah, liver's got it. And vitamin pills.

After a moment, Meg enters. She carries a bottle of bourbon that is already minus a few slugs, and a newspaper. She is wearing black boots, a dark dress, and a hat. The room goes silent.

MEG: Hello.

BABE: *(fooling with her hair)* Hi, Meg. *(Lenny quietly sips her coffee.)*

MEG: *(handing the newspaper to Babe)* Here's your paper.

130 **BABE:** Thanks. *(She opens it.)* Oh, here it is, right on the front page. *(Meg lights a cigarette.)* Where's the scissors, Lenny?

LENNY: Look in there in the ribbon drawer.

BABE: Okay. *(Babe gets the scissors and glue out of the drawer and slowly begins cutting out the newspaper article.)*

MEG: *(after a few moments, filled only with the snipping of scissors)* All right—I lied! I lied! I couldn't help it . . . these stories just came pouring out of my mouth! When I saw how tired and sick Old Granddaddy'd gotten—they just flew out! All I wanted was to see him smiling and happy. I just wasn't going to sit there and look at him all miserable and sick and sad! I just wasn't!

BABE: Oh, Meg, he is sick, isn't he—

135 **MEG:** Why, he's gotten all white and milky—he's almost evaporated!

LENNY: *(gasping and turning to Meg)* But still you shouldn't have lied! It just was wrong for you to tell such lies—

MEG: Well, I know that! Don't you think I know that? I hate myself when I lie for that old man. I do. I feel so weak. And then I have to go and do at least three or four things that I know he'd despise just to get even with that miserable, old, bossy man!

LENNY: Oh, Meg, please, don't talk so about Old Granddaddy! It sounds so ungrateful. Why, he went out of his way to make a home for us, to treat us like we were his very own children. All he ever wanted was the best for us. That's all he ever wanted.

MEG: Well, I guess it was; but sometimes I wonder what we wanted.

140 **BABE:** *(taking the newspaper article and glue over to her suitcase)* Well, one thing I wanted was a team of white horses to ride Mama's coffin to her grave. That's one thing I wanted. *(Lenny and Meg exchange looks.)* Lenny, did you remember to pack my photo album?

LENNY: It's down there at the bottom, under all that night stuff.

BABE: Oh, I found it.

LENNY: Really, Babe, I don't understand why you have to put in the articles that are about the unhappy things in your life. Why would you want to remember them?

BABE: *(pasting the article in)* I don't know. I just like to keep an accurate record, I suppose. There. *(She begins flipping through the book.)* Look, here's a picture of me when I got married.

145 **MEG:** Let's see.

Babe brings the photo album over to the table. They all look at it.

LENNY: My word, you look about twelve years old.

BABE: I was just eighteen.

MEG: You're smiling, Babe. Were you happy then?

BABE: *(laughing)* Well, I was drunk on champagne punch. I remember that! *(They turn the page.)*

150 **LENNY:** Oh, there's Meg singing at Greeny's!

BABE: Oooh, I wish you were still singing at Greeny's! I wish you were!

LENNY: You're so beautiful!

BABE: Yes, you are. You're beautiful.

MEG: Oh, stop! I'm not—

155 **LENNY:** Look, Meg's starting to cry.

BABE: Oh, Meg—

MEG: I'm not—

BABE: Quick, better turn the page; we don't want Meg crying—*(She flips the pages.)*

LENNY: Why, it's Daddy.

160 **MEG:** Where'd you get that picture, Babe? I thought she burned them all.

BABE: Ah, I just found it around.

LENNY: What does it say here? What's that inscription?

BABE: It says "Jimmy—clowning at the beach—1952."

LENNY: Well, will you look at that smile.

165   **MEG:**   Jesus, those white teeth—turn the page, will you; we can't do any worse than this! *(They turn the page. The room goes silent.)*

BABE: It's Mama and the cat.

LENNY: Oh, turn the page—

BABE: That old yellow cat. You know, I bet if she hadn't of hung that old cat along with her, she wouldn't have gotten all that national coverage.

MEG: *(after a moment, hopelessly)* Why are we talking about this?

170   **LENNY:**   Meg's right. It was so sad. It was awfully sad. I remember how we all three just sat up on that bed the day of the service all dressed up in our black velveteen suits crying the whole morning long.

BABE: We used up one whole big box of Kleenexes.

MEG: And then Old Granddaddy came in and said he was gonna take us out to breakfast. Remember, he told us not to cry anymore 'cause he was gonna take us out to get banana splits for breakfast.

BABE: That's right—banana splits for breakfast!

MEG: Why, Lenny was fourteen years old, and he thought that would make it all better—

175   **BABE:**   Oh, I remember he said for us to eat all we wanted. I think I ate about five! He kept shoving them down us!

MEG: God, we were so sick!

LENNY: Oh, we were!

MEG: *(laughing)* Lenny's face turned green—

LENNY: I was just as sick as a dog!

180   **BABE:**   Old Grandmama was furious!

LENNY: Oh, she was!

MEG: The thing about Old Granddaddy is, he keeps trying to make us happy, and we end up getting stomachaches and turning green and throwing up in the flower arrangements.

BABE: Oh, that was me! I threw up in the flowers! Oh, no! How embarrassing!

LENNY: *(laughing)* Oh, Babe—

185   **BABE:**   *(hugging her sisters)* Oh, Lenny! Oh, Meg!

MEG: Oh, Babe! Oh, Lenny! It's so good to be home!

LENNY: Hey, I have an idea—

BABE: What?

LENNY: Let's play cards!!

190   **BABE:**   Oh, let's do!

MEG: All right!

LENNY: Oh, good! It'll be just like when we used to sit around the table playing hearts all night long.

BABE: I know! *(getting up)* I'll fix us up some popcorn and hot chocolate—

MEG: *(getting up)* Here, let me get out that old black popcorn pot.
195 **LENNY:**   *(getting up)* Oh, yes! Now, let's see, I think I have a deck of cards around here somewhere.
BABE: Gosh, I hope I remember all the rules—Are hearts good or bad?
MEG: Bad, I think. Aren't they, Lenny?
LENNY: That's right. Hearts are bad, but the Black Sister is the worst of all—
MEG: Oh, that's right! And the Black Sister is the Queen of Spades.
200 **BABE:**   *(figuring it out)* And spades are the black cards that aren't the puppy dog feet?
MEG: *(thinking for a moment)* Right. And she counts a lot of points.
BABE: And points are bad?
MEG: Right. Here, I'll get some paper so we can keep score.

The phone begins to ring.

LENNY: Oh, here they are!
205 **MEG:**   I'll get it—
LENNY: Why, look at these cards! They're years old!
BABE: Oh, let me see!
MEG: Hello . . . No, this is Meg MaGrath . . . Doc. How are you? . . . Well, good . . . You're where? . . . Well, sure. Come on over . . . Sure I'm sure. Yeah, come right on over . . . All right. 'Bye. *(She hangs up.)* That was Doc Porter. He's down the street at Al's Grill. He's gonna come on over.
LENNY: He is?
210 **MEG:**   He said he wanted to come see me.
LENNY: Oh. *(after a pause)* Well, do you still want to play?
MEG: No, I don't think so.
LENNY: All right. *(Lenny starts to shuffle the cards, as Meg brushes her hair.)* You know, it's really not much fun playing hearts with only two people.
MEG: I'm sorry; maybe after Doc leaves, I'll join you.
215 **LENNY:**   I know; maybe Doc'll want to play, then we can have a game of bridge.
MEG: I don't think so. Doc never liked cards. Maybe we'll just go out somewhere.
LENNY: *(putting down the cards; Babe picks them up)* Meg—
MEG: What?
LENNY: Well, Doc's married now.
220 **MEG:**   I know. You told me.
LENNY: Oh. Well, as long as you know that. *(Pause)* As long as you know that.
MEG: *(still primping)* Yes, I know. She made the pot.
BABE: How many cards do I deal out?
LENNY: *(leaving the table)* Excuse me.
225 **BABE:**   All of 'em, or what?

LENNY: Ah, Meg? Could I—could I ask you something? *(Babe proceeds to deal out all the cards.)*

MEG: What?

LENNY: I just wanted to ask you—

MEG: What?

Unable to go on with what she really wants to say, Lenny runs up and picks up the box of candy.

230   **LENNY:**   Well, just why did you take one little bite out of each piece of candy in this box and then just put it back in?

MEG: Oh. Well, I was looking for the ones with nuts.

LENNY: The ones with nuts.

MEG: Yeah.

LENNY: But there are none with nuts. It's a box of assorted crèmes—all it has in it are crèmes!

235   **MEG:**   Oh.

LENNY: Why couldn't you just read the box? It says right here, "Assorted Crèmes," not nuts! Besides, this was a birthday present to me! My one and only birthday present; my only one!

MEG: I'm sorry. I'll get you another box.

LENNY: I don't want another box. That's not the point!

MEG: What is the point?

240   **LENNY:**   I don't know; it's—it's—You have no respect for other people's property! You just take whatever you want. You just take it! Why, remember how you had layers and layers of jingle bells sewed onto your petticoats while Babe and I only had three apiece?!

MEG: Oh, God! She's starting up about those stupid jingle bells!

LENNY: Well, it's an example! A specific example of how you always got what you wanted!

MEG: Oh, come on, Lenny, you're just upset because Doc called.

LENNY: Who said anything about Doc? Do you think I'm upset about Doc? Why, I've long since given up worrying about you and all your men.

245   **MEG:**   *(turning in anger)* Look, I know I've had too many men. Believe me, I've had way too many men. But it's not my fault you haven't had any—or maybe just that one from Memphis.

LENNY: *(stopping)* What one from Memphis?

MEG: *(slowly)* The one Babe told me about. From the—club.

LENNY: Babe!

BABE: Meg!

250   **LENNY:**   How could you? I asked you not to tell anyone! I'm so ashamed! How could you? Who else have you told? Did you tell anyone else?

BABE: *(overlapping, to Meg)* Why'd you have to open your big mouth?

MEG: *(overlapping)* How am I supposed to know? You never said not to tell!

BABE: Can't you use your head just for once? (*Then to Lenny.*) No, I never told anyone else. Somehow it just slipped out to Meg. Really, it just flew out of my mouth—

LENNY: What do you two have—wings on your tongues?

255 **BABE:** I'm sorry, Lenny. Really sorry.

LENNY: I'll just never, never, never be able to trust you again—

MEG: (*furiously, coming to Babe's defense*) Oh, for heaven's sake, Lenny, we were just worried about you! We wanted to find a way to make you happy!

LENNY: Happy! Happy! I'll never be happy!

MEG: Well, not if you keep living your life as Old Granddaddy's nursemaid—

260 **BABE:** Meg, shut up!

MEG: I can't help it! I just know that the reason you stopped seeing this man from Memphis was because of Old Granddaddy.

LENNY: What—Babe didn't tell you the rest of the story—

MEG: Oh, she said it was something about your shrunken ovary.

BABE: Meg!

265 **LENNY:** Babe!

BABE: I just mentioned it!

MEG: But I don't believe a word of that story!

LENNY: Oh, I don't care what you believe! It's so easy for you—you always have men falling in love with you! But I have this underdeveloped ovary and I can't have children and my hair is falling out in the comb—so what man can love me? What man's gonna love me?

MEG: A lot of men!

270 **BABE:** Yeah, a lot! A whole lot!

MEG: Old Granddaddy's the only one who seems to think otherwise.

LENNY: 'Cause he doesn't want to see me hurt! He doesn't want to see me rejected and humiliated.

MEG: Oh, come on now, Lenny, don't be so pathetic! God, you make me angry when you just stand there looking so pathetic! Just tell me, did you really ask the man from Memphis? Did you actually ask that man from Memphis all about it?

LENNY: (*breaking apart*) No; I didn't. I didn't. Because I just didn't want him not to want me—

275 **MEG:** Lenny—

LENNY: (*furious*) Don't talk to me anymore! Don't talk to me! I think I'm gonna vomit—I just hope all this doesn't cause me to vomit! (*Lenny exits up the stairs sobbing.*)

MEG: See! See! She didn't even ask him about her stupid ovary! She just broke it all off 'cause of Old Granddaddy! What a jackass fool!

BABE: Oh, Meg, shut up! Why do you have to make Lenny cry? I just hate it when you make Lenny cry! (*Babe runs up the stairs.*) Lenny!

Oh, Lenny—*(Meg gives a long sigh and goes to get a cigarette and a drink.)*

MEG: I feel like hell. *(Meg sits in despair—smoking and drinking bourbon. There is a knock at the back door. Meg starts. She brushes her hair out of her face and goes to answer the door. It is Doc.)*

280 **Doc:** Hello, Meggy.

MEG: Well, Doc. Well, it's Doc.

Doc: *(after a pause)* You're home, Meggy.

MEG: Yeah, I've come home. I've come on home to see about Babe.

Doc: And how's Babe?

285 **MEG:** Oh, fine. Well, fair. She's fair. *(Doc nods.)* Hey, do you want a drink?

Doc: Whatcha got?

MEG: Bourbon.

Doc: Oh, don't tell me Lenny's stocking bourbon.

MEG: Well, no. I've been to the store. *(Meg gets him a glass and pours them each a drink. They click glasses.)* So, how's your wife?

290 **Doc:** She's fine.

MEG: I hear ya got two kids.

Doc: Yeah. Yeah, I got two kids.

MEG: A boy and a girl.

Doc: That's right, Meggy, a boy and a girl.

295 **MEG:** That's what you always said you wanted, wasn't it? A boy and a girl.

Doc: Is that what I said?

MEG: I don't know. I thought it's what you said. *(They finish their drinks in silence.)*

Doc: Whose cot?

MEG: Lenny's. She's taken to sleeping in the kitchen.

300 **Doc:** Ah. Where is Lenny?

MEG: She's in the upstairs room. I made her cry. Babe's up there seeing to her.

Doc: How'd you make her cry?

MEG: I don't know. Eating her birthday candy; talking on about her boyfriend from Memphis. I don't know. I'm upset about it. She's got a lot on her. Why can't I keep my mouth shut?

Doc: I don't know, Meggy. Maybe it's because you don't want to.

305 **MEG:** Maybe. *(They smile at each other. Meg pours each of them another drink.)*

Doc: Well, it's been a long time.

MEG: It has been a long time.

Doc: Let's see—when was the last time we saw each other?

MEG: I can't quite recall.

310 **Doc:** Wasn't it in Biloxi?

MEG: Ah, Biloxi. I believe so.

Doc: And wasn't there a—a hurricane going on at the time?

MEG: Was there?

DOC: Yes, there was, one hell of a hurricane. Camille, I believe they called it. Hurricane Camille.

315 **MEG:** Yes, now I remember. It was a beautiful hurricane.

DOC: We had a time down there. We had quite a time. Drinking vodka, eating oysters on the half shell, dancing all night long. And the wind was blowing.

MEG: Oh, God, was it blowing.

DOC: Goddamn, was it blowing.

MEG: There never has been such a wind blowing.

320 **DOC:** Oh, God, Meggy. Oh, God.

MEG: I know, Doc. It was my fault to leave you. I was crazy. I thought I was choking. I felt choked!

DOC: I felt like a fool.

MEG: No.

DOC: I just kept on wondering why.

325 **MEG:** I don't know why . . . 'Cause I didn't want to care. I don't know. I did care though. I did.

DOC: *(after a pause)* Ah, hell—*(He pours them both another drink.)* Are you still singing those sad songs?

MEG: No.

DOC: Why not?

MEG: I don't know, Doc. Things got worse for me. After a while, I just couldn't sing anymore. I tell you, I had one hell of a time over Christmas.

330 **DOC:** What do you mean?

MEG: I went nuts. I went insane. Ended up in L.A. County Hospital. Psychiatric ward.

DOC: Hell. Ah, hell, Meggy. What happened?

MEG: I don't really know. I couldn't sing anymore; so I lost my job. And I had a bad toothache. I had this incredibly painful toothache. For days I had it, but I wouldn't do anything about it. I just stayed inside my apartment. All I could do was sit around in chairs, chewing on my fingers. Then one afternoon I ran screaming out of the apartment with all my money and jewelry and valuables and tried to stuff it all into one of those March of Dimes collection boxes. That was when they nabbed me. Sad story. Meg goes mad. *(Doc stares at her for a long moment. He pours them both another drink.)*

DOC: *(after quite a pause)* There's a moon out.

335 **MEG:** Is there?

DOC: Wanna go take a ride in my truck and look out at the moon?

MEG: I don't know, Doc. I don't wanna start up. It'll be too hard, it we start up.

DOC: Who says we're gonna start up? We're just gonna look at the moon. For one night just you and me are gonna go for a ride in the country and look out at the moon.

MEG: One night?

340 **DOC:** Right.

MEG: Look out at the moon?

DOC: You got it.

MEG: Well . . . all right. *(She gets up.)*

DOC: Better take your coat. *(He helps her into her coat.)* And the bottle—
(He takes the bottle. Meg picks up the glasses.) Forget the glasses—

345 **MEG:** *(laughing)* Yeah—forget the glasses. Forget the goddamn glasses.

Meg shuts off the kitchen lights, leaving the kitchen lit by only a dim light over the kitchen sink. Meg and Doc leave. After a moment, Babe comes down the stairs in her slip.

BABE: Meg—Meg?

She stands for a moment in the moonlight wearing only a slip. She sees her saxophone then moves to pick it up. She plays a few shrieking notes. There is a loud knock on the back door.

BARNETTE'S VOICE: Becky! Becky, is that you? *(Babe puts down the saxophone.)*

BABE: Just a minute. I'm coming. *(She puts a raincoat on over her slip and goes to answer the door. It is Barnette.)* Hello, Barnette. Come on in. *(Barnette comes in. He is troubled but is making a great effort to hide the fact.)*

BARNETTE: Thank you.

350 **BABE:** What is it?

BARNETTE: I've, ah, I've just come from seeing Zackery at the hospital.

BABE: Oh?

BARNETTE: It seems . . . Well, it seems his sister, Lucille, was somewhat suspicious.

BABE: Suspicious?

355 **BARNETTE:** About you?

BABE: Me?

BARNETTE: She hired a private detective: he took these pictures. *(He hands Babe a small envelope containing several photographs. Babe opens the envelope and begins looking at the pictures in stunned silence.)* They were taken about two weeks ago. It seems she wasn't going to show them to Botrelle straight away. She, ah, wanted to wait till the time was right. *(The phone rings one and a half times. Barnette glances uneasily towards the phone.)* Becky? *(The phone stops ringing.)*

BABE: *(looking up at Barnette, slowly)* These are pictures of Willie Jay and me . . . out in the garage.

BARNETTE: *(looking away)* I know.

360 **BABE:** You looked at these pictures?

BARNETTE: Yes—I—well . . . professionally, I looked at them.

BABE: Oh, mercy. Oh, mercy! We can burn them, can't we? Quick, we can burn them—

BARNETTE: It won't do any good. They have the negatives.

BABE: *(holding the pictures, as she bangs herself hopelessly into the stove, table, cabinets, etc.)* Oh, no; oh, no; oh, no! Oh, no—

365 **BARNETTE:**   There—there, now—there—

LENNY'S VOICE: Babe? Are you all right? Babe—

BABE: *(hiding the pictures)* What? I'm all right. Go on back to bed. *(Lenny comes down the stairs. She is wearing a coat and wiping white night cream off of her face with a wash rag.)*

LENNY: What's the matter? What's going on down here?

BABE: Nothin! *(Then as she begins dancing ballet style around the room.)* We're—we're just dancing. We were just dancing around down here. *(Signaling to Barnette to dance.)*

370 **LENNY:**   Well, you'd better get your shoes on, 'cause we've got—

BABE: All right, I will! That's a good idea! *(As she goes to get her shoes, she hides the pictures.)* Now, you go on back to bed. It's pretty late and—

LENNY: Babe, will you listen a minute—

BABE: *(holding up her shoes)* I'm putting 'em on—

LENNY: That was the hospital that just called. We've got to get over there. Old Granddaddy's had himself another stroke.

375 **BABE:**   Oh. All right. My shoes are on. *(She stands. They all look at each other as the lights black out.)*

Curtain

A C T   I I I

The lights go up on the empty kitchen. It is the following morning. After a few moments, Babe enters from the back door. She is carrying her hair curlers in her hands. She goes and lies down on the cot. A few moments later, Lenny enters. She is tired and weary. Chick's voice is heard.

CHICK'S VOICE: Lenny! Oh, Lenny! *(Lenny turns to the door. Chick enters energetically.)* Well . . . how is he?

LENNY: He's stabilized; they say for now his functions are all stabilized.

CHICK: Well, is he still in the coma?

LENNY: Uh huh.

5 **CHICK:**   Hmmm. So do they think he's gonna be . . . passing on?

LENNY: He may be. He doesn't look so good. They said they'd phone us if there were any sudden changes.

CHICK: Well, it seems to me we'd better get busy phoning on the phone ourselves. *(Removing a list from her pocket.)* Now I've made out this list of all the people we need to notify about Old Granddaddy's predicament. I'll phone half if you'll phone half.

LENNY: But—what would we say?

CHICK: Just tell them the facts: that Old Granddaddy's got himself in a coma, and it could be he doesn't have long for this world.

10 **LENNY:**   I—I don't know. I don't feel like phoning.

CHICK: Why, Lenora, I'm surprised; how can you be this way? I went to all the trouble of making up the list. And I offered to phone half of the people on it, even though I'm only one-fourth of the granddaughters. I mean, I just get tired of doing more than my fair share, when people like Meg can suddenly just disappear to where they can't even be reached in case of emergency!

LENNY: All right; give me the list. I'll phone half.

CHICK: Well, don't do it just to suit me.

LENNY: *(she wearily tears the list into two halves)* I'll phone these here.

15 **CHICK:**   *(taking her half of the list)* Fine then. Suit yourself. Oh, wait—let me call Sally Bell. I need to talk to her anyway.

LENNY: All right.

CHICK: So you add Great-uncle Spark Dude to your list.

LENNY: Okay.

CHICK: Fine. Well, I've got to get on back home and see to the kids. It is gonna be an uphill struggle till I can find someone to replace that good-for-nothing Annie May Jenkins. Well, you let me know if you hear anymore.

20 **LENNY:**   All right.

CHICK: Goodbye, Rebecca. I said goodbye. *(Babe blows her sax. Chick starts to exit in a flurry, then pauses to add:)* And you really ought to try to get that phoning done before twelve noon. *(Chick exits.)*

LENNY: *(after a long pause)* Babe, I feel bad. I feel real bad.

BABE: Why, Lenny?

LENNY: Because yesterday I—I wished it.

25 **BABE:**   You wished what?

LENNY: I wished that Old Granddaddy would be put out of his pain. I wished it on one of my birthday candles. I did. And now he's in this coma, and they say he's feeling no pain.

BABE: Well, when did you have a cake yesterday? I don't remember you having any cake.

LENNY: Well, I didn't . . . have a cake. But I just blew out the candles, anyway.

BABE: Oh. Well, those birthday wishes don't count, unless you have a cake.

30 **LENNY:**   They don't?

BABE: No. A lot of times they don't even count when you do have a cake. It just depends.

LENNY: Depends on what?

BABE: On how deep your wish is, I suppose.

LENNY: Still, I just wish I hadn't of wished it. Gosh, I wonder when Meg's coming home.

35 **BABE:**   Should be soon.

LENNY: I just wish we wouldn't fight all the time. I don't like it when we do.

BABE: Me, neither.

LENNY: I guess it hurts my feelings, a little, the way Old Granddaddy's always put so much stock in Meg and all her singing talent. I think I've been, well, envious of her 'cause I can't seem to do too much.

BABE: Why, sure you can.

40 **LENNY:**   I can?

BABE: Sure. You just have to put your mind to it that's all. It's like how I went out and bought that saxophone, just hoping I'd be able to attend music school and start up my own career. I just went out and did it. Just on hope. Of course, now it looks like . . . Well, it just doesn't look like things are gonna work out for me. But I know they would for you.

LENNY: Well, they'll work out for you, too.

BABE: I doubt it.

LENNY: Listen, I heard up at the hospital that Zackery's already in fair condition. They say soon he'll probably be able to walk and everything.

45 **BABE:**   Yeah. And life sure can be miserable.

LENNY: Well, I know, 'cause—day before yesterday, Billy Boy was struck down by lightning.

BABE: He was?

LENNY: *(nearing sobs)* Yeah. He was struck dead.

BABE: *(crushed)* Life sure can be miserable.

(They sit together for several moments in morbid silence. Meg is heard singing a loud happy song. She suddenly enters through the dining room door. She is exuberant! Her hair is a mess and the heel of one shoe has broken off. She is laughing radiantly and limping as she sings into the broken heel.)

50 **MEG:**   *(spotting her sisters)* Good morning! Good morning! Oh, its a wonderful morning! I tell you, I am surprised I feel this good. I should feel like hell. By all accounts, I should feel like utter hell! *(She is looking for the glue.)* Where's that glue? This damn heel has broken off my shoe. La, la, la, la, la! Ah, here it is! Now let me just get these shoes off. Zip, zip, zip, zip, zip! Well, what's wrong with you two? My God, you look like doom! *(Babe and Lenny stare helplessly at Meg.)* Oh, I know, you're mad at me 'cause I stayed out all night long. Well, I did.

LENNY: No, we're—we're not mad at you. We're just . . . depressed. *(She starts to sob.)*

MEG: Oh, Lenny, listen to me, now; everything's all right with Doc. I mean, nothing happened. Well, actually a lot did happen, but it didn't come to anything. Not because of me, I'm afraid. *(Smearing glue on her heel.)* I mean, I was out there thinking, "What will I say when he begs me to run away with him? Will I have pity on his wife and those two half-Yankee children? I mean, can I sacrifice their happiness for mine? Yes! Oh, yes! Yes, I can!" But . . . he didn't ask me. He didn't even want to ask me. I could tell by this certain look in his eyes that he didn't even want to ask me. Why aren't I miserable! Why aren't I morbid! I should be humiliated! Devastated! Maybe these feelings are coming—I don't know. But for now it was . . . just such fun. I'm happy. I realized I could care about someone. I could want someone. And I sang! I sang all night long! I sang right up into the trees! But not for Old Granddaddy. None of it was to please Old Granddaddy! *(Lenny and Babe look at each other.)*

BABE: Ah, Meg—

MEG: What—

55 **BABE:** Well, it's just—It's . . .

LENNY: It's about Old Granddaddy—

MEG: Oh, I know; I know. I told him all those stupid lies. Well, I'm gonna go right over there this morning and tell him the truth. I mean every horrible thing. I don't care if he wants to hear it or not. He's just gonna have to take me like I am. And if he can't take it, if it sends him into a coma, that's just too damn bad!

Babe and Lenny look at each other; Babe cracks a smile. Lenny cracks a smile.

BABE: You're too late—Ha, ha, ha! *(They both break up laughing.)*

LENNY: Oh, stop! Please! Ha, ha, ha!

60 **MEG:** What is it? What's so funny?

BABE: *(still laughing)* It's not—It's not funny!

LENNY: *(still laughing)* No, it's not! It's not a bit funny!

MEG: Well, what is it, then? What?

BABE: *(trying to calm down)* Well, it's just—it's just—

65 **MEG:** What?

BABE: Well, Old Granddaddy—he—he's in a coma! *(Babe and Lenny break up laughing.)*

MEG: He's what?

BABE: *(shrieking)* In a coma!

MEG: My God! That's not funny!

70 **BABE:** *(calming down)* I know. For some reason, it just struck us as funny.

LENNY: I'm sorry. It's—it's not funny. It's sad. It's very sad. We've been up all night long.

BABE: We're really tired.

MEG: Well, my God. How is he? Is he gonna live?

(Babe and Lenny look at each other.)

BABE: They don't think so! *(They both break up again.)*

75 **LENNY:** Oh, I don't know why we're laughing like this. We're just sick! We're just awful!

BABE: We are—we're awful!

LENNY: *(as she collects herself)* Oh, good; now I feel bad. Now, I feel like
crying. I do; I feel like crying.

BABE: Me, too. Me, too.

MEG: Well, you've gotten me depressed!

80 **LENNY:** I'm sorry. I'm sorry. It, ah happened last night. He had another
stroke. *(They laugh again.)*

MEG: I see.

LENNY: But he's stabilized now. *(She chokes up once more.)*

MEG: That's good. You two okay? *(Babe and Lenny nod.)* You look like
you need some rest. *(Babe and Lenny nod again. Meg goes on, about her
heel.)* I hope that'll stay. *(Meg puts the top on the glue. A realization—)*
Oh, of course, now I won't be able to tell him the truth about all
those lies I told. I mean, finally I get my wits about me, and he conks
out. It's just like him. Babe, can I wear your slippers till this glue
dries?

BABE: Sure.

85 **LENNY:** *(after a pause)* Things sure are gonna be different around here . . .
when Old Granddaddy dies. Well, not for you two really, but for me.

BABE: *(depressed)* Yeah. It'll work out.

LENNY: I hope so. I'm afraid of being here all by myself. All alone.

MEG: Well, you don't have to be alone. Maybe Babe'll move back in here.

(Lenny looks at Babe hopefully.)

BABE: No, I don't think I'll be living here.

90 **MEG:** *(realizing her mistake)* Well, anyway, you're your own woman.
Invite some people over. Have some parties. Go out with strange men.

LENNY: I don't know any strange men.

MEG: Well . . . you know that Charlie.

LENNY: *(shaking her head)* Not anymore.

MEG: Why not?

95 **LENNY:** *(breaking down)* I told him we should never see each other again.

MEG: Well, if you told him, you can just untell him.

LENNY: Oh, no I couldn't. I'd feel like a fool.

MEG: Oh, that's not a good enough reason! All people in love feel like
fools. Don't they, Babe?

BABE: Sure.

100 **MEG:** Look, why don't you give him a call right now? See how things
stand.

LENNY: Oh, no! I'd be too scared—

MEG: But what harm could it possibly do? I mean, it's not gonna make
things any worse than this never seeing him again, at all, forever.

LENNY: I suppose that's true—

MEG: Of course it is; so call him up! Take a chance, will you? Just take
some sort of chance!

105 **LENNY:** You think I should?

MEG: Of course! You've got to try—You do! *(Lenny looks over at Babe.)*

BABE: You do, Lenny—I think you do.

LENNY: Really? Really, really?

MEG: Yes! Yes!

110 **BABE:**   You should!

LENNY: All right. I will! I will!

MEG: Oh, good!

BABE: Good!

LENNY: I'll call him right now, while I've got my confidence up!

115 **MEG:**   Have you got the number?

LENNY: Uh huh. But, ah, I think I wanna call him upstairs. It'll be more private.

MEG: Ah, good idea.

LENNY: I'm just gonna go on and call him up and see what happens— *(She has started up the stairs.)* Wish me good luck!

MEG: Good luck!

120 **BABE:**   Good luck, Lenny!

LENNY: Thanks.

(Lenny gets almost out of sight, when the phone begins to ring. She stops, Meg picks up the phone.)

MEG: Hello? *(Then in a whisper.)* Oh, thank you very much . . . Yes, I will. 'Bye, 'bye.

LENNY: Who was it?

MEG: Wrong number. They wanted Weed's Body Shop.

125 **LENNY:**   Oh. Well, I'll be right back down in a minute. *(Lenny exits.)*

MEG: *(after a moment, whispering to Babe)* That was the bakery; Lenny's cake is ready!

BABE: *(who has become increasingly depressed)* Oh.

MEG: I think I'll sneak on down to the corner and pick it up. *(She starts to leave.)*

BABE: Meg—

130 **MEG:**   What?

BABE: Nothing.

MEG: You okay? *(Babe shakes her head.)* What is it?

BABE: It's just—

MEG: What?

(Babe gets up and goes to her suitcase. She opens it and removes the envelope containing the photographs.)

135 **BABE:**   Here. Take a look.

MEG: *(taking the envelope)* What is it?

BABE: It's some evidence Zackery's collected against me. Looks like my goose is cooked. *(Meg opens the envelope and looks at the photographs.)*

MEG: My God, it's—it's you and . . . is *that* Willie Jay?

BABE: Yeh.

140 **MEG:**   Well, he certainly *has* grown. You were right about that. My, oh, my.

BABE: Please don't tell Lenny. She'd hate me.

MEG: I won't. I won't tell Lenny. *(Putting the pictures back into the envelope.)* What are you gonna do?

BABE: What can I do? *(There is a knock on the door. Babe grabs the envelope and hides it.)*

MEG: Who is it?

145 **BARNETTE'S VOICE:**   It's Barnette Lloyd.

MEG: Oh. Come on in, Barnette.

(Barnette enters. His eyes are ablaze with excitement.)

BARNETTE: *(as he paces around the room)* Well, good morning! *(Shaking Meg's hand.)* Good morning, Miss MaGrath. *(Touching Babe on the shoulder.)* Becky. *(Moving away.)* What I meant to say is . . . how are you doing this morning?

MEG: Ah—fine. Fine.

BARNETTE: Good. Good. I—I just had time to drop by for a minute.

150 **MEG:**   Oh.

BARNETTE: So, ah, how's your Granddad doing?

MEG: Well, not very, ah—ah, he's in this coma. *(She breaks up laughing.)*

BARNETTE: I see . . . I see. *(To Babe.)* Actually, the primary reason I came by was to pick up that—envelope. I left it here last night in all the confusion. *(Pause.)* You, ah, still do have it? *(Babe hands him the envelope.)* Yes. *(Taking the envelope.)* That's the one. I'm sure it'll be much better off in my office safe. *(He puts the envelope into his coat pocket.)*

MEG: I'm sure it will.

155 **BARNETTE:**   Beg your pardon?

BABE: It's all right. I showed her the pictures.

BARNETTE: Ah; I see.

MEG: So what's going to happen now, Barnette? What are those pictures gonna mean?

BARNETTE: *(after pacing a moment)* Hmmm. May I speak frankly and openly?

160 **BABE:**   Uh huh.

MEG: Please do—

BARNETTE: Well, I tell you now, at first glance, I admit those pictures had me considerably perturbed and upset. Perturbed to the point that I spent most of last night going over certain suspect papers and reports that had fallen into my hands—rather recklessly.

BABE: What papers do you mean?

BARNETTE: Papers that, pending word from three varied and unbiased experts, could prove graft, fraud, forgery, as well as a history of unethical behavior.

165 **MEG:** You mean about Zackery?

BARNETTE: Exactly. You see, I now intend to make this matter just as sticky and gritty for one Z. Botrelle as it is for us. Why, with the amount of scandal I'll dig up, Botrelle will be forced to settle this affair on our own terms!

MEG: Oh, Babe! Did you hear that?

BABE: Yes! Oh, yes! So you've won it! You've won your lifelong vendetta!

BARNETTE: Well . . . well, now of course it's problematic in that, well, in that we won't be able to expose him openly in the courts. That was the original game plan.

170 **BABE:** But why not? Why?

BARNETTE: Well, it's only that if, well, if a jury were to—to get, say, a glance at those, ah, photographs, well . . . well possibly . . .

BABE: We could be sunk.

BARNETTE: In a sense. But! On the other hand, if a newspaper were to get a hold of our little item, Mr. Zackery Botrelle could find himself boiling in some awfully hot water. So what I'm looking for very simply, is—a deal.

BABE: A deal?

175 **MEG:** Thank you, Barnette. It's a sunny day, Babe. *(Realizing she is in the way.)* Ooh, where's that broken shoe? *(She grabs her boots and runs upstairs.)*

BABE: So, you're having to give up your vendetta?

BARNETTE: Well, in a way. For the time. It, ah, seems to me you shouldn't always let your life be ruled by such things as, ah, personal vendettas. *(Looking at Babe with meaning.)* Other things can be important.

BABE: I don't know, I don't exactly know. How 'bout Willie Jay? Will he be all right?

BARNETTE: Yes, it's all been taken care of. He'll be leaving incognito on the midnight bus—heading north.

180 **BABE:** North.

BARNETTE: I'm sorry, it seemed the only . . . way. *(Barnette moves to her—She moves away.)*

BABE: Look, you'd better be getting on back to your work.

BARNETTE: *(awkwardly)* Right—'cause I—I've got those important calls out. *(Full of hope for her.)* They'll be pouring in directly. *(He starts to leave, then says to her with love.)* We'll talk.

MEG: *(reappearing in her boots)* Oh, Barnette—

185 **BARNETTE:** Yes?

MEG: Could you give me a ride just down to the corner? I need to stop at Helen's Bakery.

BARNETTE: Be glad to.

MEG: Thanks. Listen, Babe, I'll be right back with the cake. We're gonna have the best celebration! Now, ah, if Lenny asks where I've gone, just

say I'm . . . just say, I've gone out back to, ah, pick up some pawpaws!
Okay?

BABE: Okay.

190 **MEG:**   Fine; I'll be back in a bit. Goodbye.

BABE: 'Bye.

BARNETTE: Goodbye, Becky.

BABE: Goodbye, Barnette. Take care. *(Meg and Barnette exit. Babe sits
staring ahead, in a state of deep despair.)* Goodbye, Becky. Goodbye,
Barnette. Goodbye, Becky. *(She stops when Lenny comes down the stairs
in a fluster.)*

LENNY: Oh! Oh! Oh! I'm so ashamed! I'm such a coward! I'm such a
yellow-bellied chicken! I'm so ashamed! Where's Meg?

195 **BABE:**   *(suddenly bright)* She's, ah—gone out back—to pick up some
pawpaws.

LENNY: Oh. Well, at least I don't have to face her! I just couldn't do it!
I couldn't make the call! My heart was pounding like a hammer.
Pound! Pound! Pound! Why, I looked down and I could actually see
my blouse moving back and forth! Oh, Babe, you look so
disappointed. Are you?

BABE: *(despondently)* Uh huh.

LENNY: Oh, no! I've disappointed Babe! I can't stand it! I've gone and
disappointed my little sister, Babe! Oh, no! I feel like howling like
a dog!

CHICK'S VOICE: Oooh, Lenny! *(Chick enters dramatically; dripping with
sympathy.)* Well, I just don't know what to say! I'm so sorry! I am so
sorry for you! And for Little Babe, here, too. I mean to have such a
sister as that!

200 **LENNY:**   What do you mean?

CHICK: Oh, you don't need to pretend with me. I saw it all from over
there in my own backyard; I saw Meg stumbling out of Doc Porter's
pickup truck, not 15 minutes ago. And her looking such a disgusting
mess. You must be so ashamed! You must just want to die! Why, I
always said that girl was nothing but cheap Christmas trash!

LENNY: Don't talk that way about Meg.

CHICK: Oh, come on now, Lenny, honey, I know exactly how you feel
about Meg. Why, Meg's a low-class tramp and you need not have one
more blessed thing to do with her and her disgusting behavior.

LENNY: I said, don't you ever talk that way about my sister Meg again.

205 **CHICK:**   Well, my goodness gracious, Lenora, don't be such a noodle—
it's the truth!

LENNY: I don't care if it's the Ten Commandments. I don't want to hear
it in my home. Not ever again.

CHICK: In your home! Why, I never in all my life—This is my
Grandfather's home! And you're just living here on his charity; so
don't you get high-falutin' with me, Miss Lenora Josephine MaGrath!

LENNY: Get out of here—

CHICK: Don't you tell me to get out! What makes you think you can
order me around? Why, I've had just about my fill of you trashy
MaGraths and your trashy ways: hanging yourselves in cellars;
carrying on with married men; shooting your own husbands!

210 LENNY: Get out!

CHICK: *(to Babe)* And don't think she's not gonna end up at the state
prison farm or in some—mental institution. Why, it's a clear-cut case
of manslaughter with intent to kill!

LENNY: Out! Get out!

CHICK: *(running on)* That's what everyone's saying, deliberate intent to
kill! And you'll pay for that! Do you hear me? You'll pay!

LENNY: *(she picks up a broom and threatens Chick with it)* And I'm telling
you to get out!

215 CHICK: You—you put that down this minute—Are you a raving lunatic?

LENNY: *(beating Chick with the broom)* I said for you to get out! That
means out! And never, never, never come back!

CHICK: *(overlapping, as she runs around the room)* Oh! Oh! Oh! You're
crazy! You're crazy!

LENNY: *(chasing Chick out the door)* Do you hear me, Chick the Stick! This
is my home! This is my house! Get out! Out!

CHICK: *(overlapping)* Oh! Oh! Police! Police! You're crazy! Help! Help!
*(Lenny chases Chick out of the house. They are both screaming. The phone
rings. Babe goes and picks it up.)*

220 BABE: Hello? . . . Oh, hello, Zackery! . . . Yes, he showed them to
me! . . . You're what! . . . What do you mean? . . . What! . . . You can't
put me out to Whitfield . . . 'Cause I'm not crazy . . . I'm not! I'm
not! . . . She wasn't crazy, either . . . Don't you call my mother
crazy! . . . No, you're not! You're not gonna. You're not! *(She slams the
phone down and stares wildly ahead.)* He's not. He's not. *(As she walks
over to the ribbon drawer.)* I'll do it. I will. And he won't . . . *(She opens
the drawer; pulls out the rope; becomes terrified, throws the rope back in
the drawer and slams it shut. Lenny enters from the back door swinging
the broom and laughing.)*

LENNY: Oh, my! Oh, my! You should have seen us! Why, I chased Chick
the Stick right up the mimosa tree. I did! I left her right up there
screaming in the tree!

BABE: *(laughing; she is insanely delighted)* Oh, you did!

LENNY: Yes, I did! And I feel so good! I do! I feel good! I feel good!

BABE: *(overlapping)* Good! Good, Lenny! Good for you! *(They dance
around the kitchen.)*

225 LENNY: *(stopping)* You know what—

BABE: What?

LENNY: I'm gonna call Charlie! I'm gonna call him up right now!

BABE: You are?

LENNY: Yeah, I fell like I can really do it!

230 BABE: You do?

LENNY: My courage is up; my heart's in it; the time is right! No more beating around the bush! Let's strike while the iron is hot!

BABE: Right! Right! No more beating around the bush! Strike while the iron is hot! *(Lenny goes to the phone. Babe rushes over to the ribbon drawer. She begins tearing through it.)*

LENNY: *(with the receiver in her hand)* I'm calling him up, Babe—I'm really gonna do it!

BABE: *(still tearing through the drawer)* Good! Do it! Good!

235 **LENNY:** *(as she dials)* Look. My hands aren't even shaking.

BABE: *(pulling out a red cord of rope)* Don't we have any stronger rope than this?

LENNY: I guess not. All the rope we've got's in that drawer. *(About her hands.)* Now they're shaking a little. *(Babe takes the rope and goes up the stairs. Lenny finishes dialing the number. She waits for an answer.)* Hello? . . . Hello, Charlie. This is Lenny MaGrath . . . Well, I'm fine. I'm just fine. *(An awkward pause.)* I was, ah, just calling to see—how you're getting on . . . Well, good. Good . . . Yes, I know I said that. Now I wish I didn't say it . . . Well, the reason I said that before, about not seeing each other again, was 'cause of me, not you . . . Well, it's just I—I can't have any children. I—have this ovary problem . . . Why, Charlie, what a thing to say! . . . Well, they're not all little snot-nosed pigs! . . . You think they are! . . . Oh, Charlie, stop, stop! You're making me laugh . . . Yes, I guess I was. I can see now that I was . . . You are? . . . Well, I'm dying to see you, too . . . Well, I don't know when, Charlie . . . soon. How about, well, how about tonight? . . . You will? . . . Oh, you will! . . . All right, I'll be here. I'll be right here . . . Goodbye, then, Charlie. Goodbye for now. *(She hangs up the phone in a daze.)* Babe. Oh, Babe! He's coming. He's coming! Babe! Oh, Babe, where are you? Meg! Oh . . . out back—picking up pawpaws. *(As she exits through the back door.)* And those pawpaws are just ripe for picking up!

(There is a moment of silence, then a loud, horrible thud is heard coming from upstairs. The telephone begins ringing immediately. It rings five times before Babe comes hurrying down the stairs with a broken piece of rope hanging around her neck. The phone continues to ring.)

BABE: *(to the phone)* Will you shut up! *(She is jerking the rope from around her neck. She grabs a knife to cut it off.)* Cheap! Miserable! I hate you! I hate you! *(She throws the rope violently around the room. The phone stops ringing.)* Thank God. *(She looks at the stove, goes over to it, and turns the gas on. The sound of gas escaping is heard. Babe sniffs at it.)* Come on. Come on . . . Hurry up . . . I beg of you—hurry up! *(Finally, Babe feels the oven is ready; she takes a deep breath and opens the oven door to stick her head into it. She spots the rack and furiously jerks it out. Taking another breath, she sticks her head into the oven. She stands for several moments tapping her fingers furiously on top of the stove. She speaks from* *inside the oven . . .)* Oh, please. Please. *(After a few moments, she reaches for the box of matches with her head still in the oven. She tries to strike a match. It doesn't catch.)* Oh, Mama, please! *(She throws the match away and is getting a second one.)* Mama . . . Mama . . . So that's why you done it!

(In her excitement she starts to get up, bangs her head and falls back in the stove. Meg enters from the back door, carrying a birthday cake in a pink box.)

MEG: Babe! *(Meg throws the box down and runs to pull Babe's head out of the oven.)* Oh, my God! What are you doing? What the hell are you doing?

240 **BABE:**   *(dizzily)* Nothing. I don't know. Nothing. *(Meg turns off the gas and moves Babe to a chair near the open door.)*

MEG: Sit down. Sit down! Will you sit down!

BABE: I'm okay. I'm okay.

MEG: Put your head between your knees and breathe deep!

BABE: Meg—

245 **MEG:**   Just do it! I'll get you some water. *(Meg gets some water for Babe.)* Here.

BABE: Thanks.

MEG: Are you okay?

BABE: Uh huh.

MEG: Are you sure?

250 **BABE:**   Yeah, I'm sure. I'm okay.

MEG: *(getting a damp rag and putting it over her own face)* Well good. That's good.

BABE: Meg—

MEG: Yes?

BABE: I know why she did it.

255 **MEG:**   What? Why who did what?

BABE: *(with joy)* Mama. I know why she hung that cat along with her.

MEG: You do?

BABE: *(with enlightenment)* It's 'cause she was afraid of dying all alone.

MEG: Was she?

260 **BABE:**   She felt so unsure, you know, as to what was coming. It seems the best thing coming up would be a lot of angels and all of them singing. But I imagine they have high, scary voices and little gold pointed fingers that are as sharp as blades and you don't want to meet 'em all alone. You'd be afraid to meet 'em all alone. So it wasn't like what people were saying about her hating that cat. Fact is, she loved that cat. She needed him with her 'cause she felt so all alone.

MEG: Oh, Babe . . . Babe. Why, Babe? Why?

BABE: Why what?

MEG: Why did you stick your head into the oven?!

BABE: I don't know, Meg. I'm having a bad day. It's been a real bad day; those pictures, and Barnette giving up his vendetta; then Willie

Jay heading north; and—Zackery called me up. *(Trembling with terror.)* He says he's gonna have me classified insane and send me on out to the Whitfield asylum.

265 **MEG:**   What! Why, he could never do that!

BABE: Why not?

MEG: 'Cause you're not insane.

BABE: I'm not?

MEG: No! He's trying to bluff you. Don't you see it? Barnette's got him running scared.

270 **BABE:**   Really?

MEG: Sure. He's scared to death—calling you insane. Ha! Why, you're just as perfectly sane as anyone walking the streets of Hazlehurst, Mississippi.

BABE: I am?

MEG: More so! A lot more so!

BABE: Good!

275 **MEG:**   But, Babe, we've just got to learn how to get through these real bad days here. I mean, it's getting to be a thing in our family. *(Slight pause as she looks at Babe.)* Come on now. Look, we've got Lenny's cake right here. I mean don't you wanna be around to give her her cake, watch her blow out the candles?

BABE: *(realizing how much she wants to be here)* Yeah, I do, I do. 'Cause she always loves to make her birthday wishes on those candles.

MEG: Well, then we'll give her her cake and maybe you won't be so miserable.

BABE: Okay.

MEG: Good. Go on and take it out of the box.

280 **BABE:**   Okay. *(She takes the cake out of the box. It is a magical moment.)* Gosh, it's a pretty cake.

MEG: *(handing her some matches)* Here now. You can go on and light up the candles.

BABE: All right. *(She starts to light the candles.)* I love to light up candles. And there are so many here. Thirty pink ones in all plus one green one to grow on.

MEG: *(watching her light the candles)* They're pretty.

BABE: They are. *(She stops lighting the candles.)* And I'm not like Mama. I'm not so all alone.

285 **MEG:**   You're not.

BABE: *(as she goes back to lighting candles)* Well, you'd better keep an eye out for Lenny. She's supposed to be surprised.

MEG: All right. Do you know where she's gone?

BABE: Well, she's not here inside—so she must have gone on outside.

MEG: Oh, well, then I'd better run and find her.

290 **BABE:**   Okay; 'cause these candles are gonna melt down. *(Meg starts out the door.)*

MEG: Wait—there she is coming. Lenny! Oh, Lenny! Come on! Hurry up!

BABE: *(overlapping and improvising as she finishes lighting candles)* Oh, no! No! Well, yes—Yes! No, wait! Wait! Okay! Hurry up! *(Lenny enters. Meg covers Lenny's eyes with her hands.)*

LENNY: *(terrified)* What? What is it? What?

MEG & BABE: Surprise! Happy Birthday! Happy Birthday to Lenny!!

295 **LENNY:** Oh, no! Oh me! What a surprise! I could just cry! Oh, look: "Happy Birthday to Lenny—A Day Late!" How cute! My! Will you look at all those candles—it's absolutely frightening.

BABE: *(spontaneous thought)* Oh, no, Lenny, it's good! 'Cause—'cause the more candles you have on your cake, the stronger your wish is.

LENNY: Really?

BABE: Sure!

LENNY: Mercy. *(They start the song. Lenny, interrupting the song.)* Oh, but wait! I—can't think of my wish! My body's gone all nervous inside.

300 **MEG:** For God's sake, Lenny—Come on!

BABE: The wax is all melting!

LENNY: My mind is just a blank, a total blank!

MEG: Will you please just—

BABE: *(overlapping)* Lenny, hurry! Come on!

305 **LENNY:** Okay! Okay! Just go!! *(Meg and Babe burst into the "Happy Birthday" song. As it ends, Lenny blows out all of the candles on the cake. Meg and Babe applaud loudly.)*

MEG: Oh, you made it!

BABE: Hurray!

LENNY: Oh, me! Oh, me! I hope that wish comes true! I hope it does!

BABE: Why? What did you wish for?

310 **LENNY:** *(as she removes the candles from the cake)* Why, I can't tell you that.

BABE: Oh, sure you can—

LENNY: Oh, no! Then it won't come true.

BABE: Why, that's just superstition! Of course it will, if you made it deep enough.

MEG: Really? I didn't know that.

315 **LENNY:** Well, Babe's the regular expert on birthday wishes.

BABE: It's just I get these feelings. Now come on and tell us. What was it you wished for?

MEG: Yes, tell us. What was it?

LENNY: Well, I guess, it wasn't really a specific wish. This—this vision just sort of came into my mind.

BABE: A vision? What was it of?

320 **LENNY:** I don't know exactly. It was something about the three of us smiling and laughing together.

BABE: Well, when was it? Was it far away or near?

LENNY: I'm not sure, but it wasn't forever; it wasn't for every minute. Just this one moment and we were all laughing.

BABE: Then, what were we laughing about?

LENNY: I don't know. Just nothing, I guess.

325 **MEG:** Well, that's a nice wish to make. *(Lenny and Meg look at each other a moment.)* Here, now, I'll get a knife so we can go ahead and cut the cake in celebration of Lenny being born!

BABE: Oh, yes! And give each one of us a rose. A whole rose apiece!

LENNY: *(cutting the cake nervously)* Well, I'll try—I'll try!

MEG: *(licking the icing off a candle)* Mmmm—this icing is delicious! Here, try some!

BABE: Mmmm! It's wonderful! Here, Lenny!

330 **LENNY:** *(laughing joyously as she licks icing from her fingers and cuts huge pieces of cake that her sisters bite into ravenously)* Oh, how I do love having birthday cake for breakfast! How I do! *(The sisters freeze for a moment laughing and eating cake; the lights change and frame them in a magical, golden, sparkling glimmer; saxophone music is heard. The lights dim to blackout, and the saxophone continues to play.)*

CURTAIN

READING AND REACTING

1. *Crimes of the Heart* takes place entirely in the kitchen of the Magrath sisters' house. In what alternate settings could various scenes be staged? How might these settings improve the play?

2. Are the characters and situations in this play realistic or exaggerated? For example, what do you make of the fact that Barnette Lloyd fell in love with Babe years ago when she sold him a piece of cake at a bazaar or that Lenny's pet horse was killed by lightning?

3. *Crimes of the Heart* is set in Mississippi. How important is this setting? Could the play have been set in another part of the country? For example, how would the play be different if it were set in New England?

4. How much insight do the various characters have into their own situations? For example, does Babe ever come to terms with the fact that she shot her husband or that she could spend the rest of her life in jail?

5. What are the chief character flaws of Babe, Meg, Lenny, and Barnette?

6. What comment about life and relationships does the play seem to be making? Do you agree with these sentiments?

7. What are the "crimes" to which the play's title refers?

8. Do any of the characters change during the course of the play? How do these changes help to convey the main theme of the play?

9. The play begins with Lenny bringing a birthday cake into the kitchen and ends with all the sisters celebrating her birthday. Why do you think Henley chose to begin and end with these scenes? What idea is she trying to convey?

10. What function does music have in the play? (Remember that the play begins with the image of Lenny carrying a saxophone case and ends with saxophone music.)

11. **JOURNAL ENTRY** What do you think happens to the characters after the play is over? Which problems, if any, have they resolved, and which will they continue to face?

12. **CRITICAL PERSPECTIVE** In "Beth Henley: Female Quest and the Family Play Tradition," Jonnie Guerra notes that mothers "are literally absent from the action on stage" in Henley's plays. She observes, however, that "through the stories of other characters, usually their daughters, they become a strong presence. . . . Since the daughters dwell primarily on the very negative memories of their mothers, the images of these women that emerge from the shadows are consistently atrocious. . . ."

Do you think this observation applies to *Crimes of the Heart?*

AUGUST WILSON (1945–   ) was born in Pittsburgh, Pennsylvania, and lived in the African-American neighborhood known as the Hill. After leaving school at fifteen, he participated in the Black Arts movement in Pittsburgh, submitting poems to local African-American publications. In 1969, Wilson and his friend Rob Penny founded the Black Horizons Theatre Company, for which Wilson produced and directed plays. Although Wilson wrote plays while living in Pittsburgh, they began to gain recognition only after 1978, when he moved to St. Paul, Minnesota. There, in 1982, Lloyd Richards, dean of the Yale School of Drama and artistic director of the Yale Repertory Company, staged a performance of Wilson's *Ma Rainey's Black Bottom.* In 1990, Wilson moved to Seattle, Washington, where he continues to live.

Wilson's plays give powerful voice to the African-American experience by exploring the historical and metaphysical roots of African-American culture and by reflecting the rhythmic patterns of African-American storytelling. Wilson's plays include *Ma Rainey's Black Bottom* (1985), a Tony Award winner; *Fences* (1985), which won a Pulitzer Prize in 1987; *Joe Turner's Come and Gone* (1986); *Two Trains Running* (1989), which won Wilson his fifth New York Drama Critics Circle Award; *The Piano Lesson* (1987), which won a second Pulitzer Prize for Wilson in 1990; and *Seven Guitars* (1996).

Fences explores how the long-upheld color barrier in professional baseball affects the main character, Troy, who struggles with the pain of never realizing his dream of becoming a big-league player. Throughout the play Troy retreats behind literal and figurative barriers that impair his relations with his family but cannot shield him from his overwhelming disappointment.

A U G U S T   W I L S O N

Fences

(1985)

C H A R A C T E R S

TROY MAXSON
JIM BONO, *Troy's friend*
ROSE, *Troy's wife*
LYONS, *Troy's oldest son by previous marriage*
GABRIEL, *Troy's brother*
CORY, *Troy and Rose's son*
RAYNELL, *Troy's daughter*

SETTING

The setting is the yard which fronts the only entrance to the Maxson household, an ancient two-story brick house set back off a small alley in a big-city neighborhood. The entrance to the house is gained by two or three steps leading to a wooden porch badly in need of paint.

A relatively recent addition to the house and running its full width, the porch lacks congruence. It is a sturdy porch with a flat roof. One or two chairs of dubious value sit at one end where the kitchen window opens onto the porch. An old-fashioned icebox stands silent guard at the opposite end.

The yard is a small dirt yard, partially fenced, except for the last scene, with a wooden sawhorse, a pile of lumber, and other fence-building equipment set off to the side. Opposite is a tree from which hangs a ball made of rags. A baseball bat leans against the tree. Two oil drums serve as garbage receptacles and sit near the house at right to complete the setting.

THE PLAY

Near the turn of the century, the destitute of Europe sprang on the city with tenacious claws and an honest and solid dream. The city devoured them. They swelled its belly until it burst into a thousand furnaces and sewing machines, a thousand butcher shops and bakers' ovens, a thousand churches and hospitals and funeral parlors and money-lenders. The city grew. It nourished itself and offered each man a partnership limited only by his talent, his guile, and his willingness and capacity for hard work. For the immigrants of Europe, a dream dared and won true.

The descendants of African slaves were offered no such welcome or participation. They came from places called the Carolinas and the Virginias, Georgia, Alabama, Mississippi, and Tennessee. They came strong, eager, searching. The city rejected them and they fled and settled along the riverbanks and under bridges in shallow, ramshackle houses made of sticks and tarpaper. They collected rags and wood. They sold the use of their muscles and their bodies. They cleaned houses and washed clothes, they shined shoes, and in quiet desperation and vengeful pride, they stole, and lived in pursuit of their own dream. That they could breathe free, finally, and stand to meet life with the force of dignity and whatever eloquence the heart could call upon.

By 1957, the hard-won victories of the European immigrants had solidified the industrial might of America. War had been confronted and won with new energies that used loyalty and patriotism as its fuel. Life was rich, full, and flourishing. The Milwaukee Braves won the World Series, and the hot winds of change that would make the sixties a turbulent, racing, dangerous, and provocative decade had not yet begun to blow full.

ACT   I

SCENE   I

It is 1957. Troy and Bono enter the yard, engaged in conversation. Troy is fifty-three years old, a large man with thick, heavy hands; it is this largeness that he strives to fill out and make an accommodation with. Together with his blackness, his largeness informs his sensibilities and the choices he has made in his life.

Of the two men, Bono is obviously the follower. His commitment to their friendship of thirty-odd years is rooted in his admiration of Troy's honesty, capacity for hard work, and his strength, which Bono seeks to emulate.

It is Friday night, payday, and the one night of the week the two men engage in a ritual of talk and drink. Troy is usually the most talkative and at times he can be crude and almost vulgar, though he is capable of rising to profound heights of expression. The men carry lunch buckets and wear or carry burlap aprons and are dressed in clothes suitable to their jobs as garbage collectors.

Bono: Troy, you ought to stop that lying!

Troy: I ain't lying! The nigger had a watermelon this big. *(He indicates with his hands.)* Talking about . . . "What watermelon, Mr. Rand?" I liked to fell out! "What watermelon, Mr. Rand?" . . . And it sitting there big as life.

Bono: What did Mr. Rand say?

Troy: Ain't said nothing. Figure if the nigger too dumb to know he carrying a watermelon, he wasn't gonna get much sense out of him. Trying to hide that great big old watermelon under his coat. Afraid to let the white man see him carry it home.

5 **Bono:**   I'm like you . . . I ain't got no time for them kind of people.

Troy: Now what he look like getting mad cause he see the man from the union talking to Mr. Rand?

Bono: He come to me talking about . . . "Maxson gonna get us fired." I told him to get away from me with that. He walked away from me calling you a troublemaker. What Mr. Rand say?

TROY: Ain't said nothing. He told me to go down the Commissioner's office next Friday. They called me down there to see them.

BONO: Well, as long as you got your complaint filed, they can't fire you. That's what one of them white fellows tell me.

10 **TROY:** I ain't worried about them firing me. They gonna fire me cause I asked a question? That's all I did. I went to Mr. Rand and asked him, "Why? Why you got the white mens driving and the colored lifting?" Told him, "what's the matter, don't I count? You think only white fellows got sense enough to drive a truck. That ain't no paper job! Hell, anybody can drive a truck. How come you got all whites driving and the colored lifting?" He told me "take it to the union." Well, hell, that's what I done! Now they wanna come up with this pack of lies.

BONO: I told Brownie if the man come and ask him any questions . . . just tell the truth! It ain't nothing but something they done trumped up on you cause you filed a complaint on them.

TROY: Brownie don't understand nothing. All I want them to do is change the job description. Give everybody a chance to drive the truck. Brownie can't see that. He ain't got that much sense.

BONO: How you figure he be making out with that gal be up at Taylors' all the time . . . that Alberta gal?

TROY: Same as you and me. Getting just as much as we is. Which is to say nothing.

15 **BONO:** It is, huh? I figure you doing a little better than me . . . and I ain't saying what I'm doing.

TROY: Aw, nigger, look here . . . I know you. If you had got anywhere near that gal, twenty minutes later you be looking to tell somebody. And the first one you gonna tell . . . that you gonna want to brag to . . . is me.

BONO: I ain't saying that. I see where you be eyeing her.

TROY: I eye all the women. I don't miss nothing. Don't never let nobody tell you Troy Maxson don't eye the women.

BONO: You been doing more than eyeing her. You done bought her a drink or two.

20 **TROY:** Hell yeah, I bought her a drink! What that mean? I bought you one, too. What that mean cause I buy her a drink? I'm just being polite.

BONO: It's all right to buy her one drink. That's what you call being polite. But when you wanna be buying two or three . . . that's what you call eyeing her.

TROY: Look here, as long as you known me . . . you ever known me to chase after women?

BONO: Hell yeah! Long as I done known you. You forgetting I knew you when.

TROY: Naw, I'm talking about since I been married to Rose?

25 **BONO:** Oh, not since you been married to Rose. Now, that's the truth, there. I can say that.

TROY: All right then! Case closed.

BONO: I see you be walking up around Alberta's house. You supposed to be at Taylors' and you be walking up around there.

TROY: What you watching where I'm walking for? I ain't watching after you.

BONO: I seen you walking around there more than once.

30 **TROY:** Hell, you liable to see me walking anywhere! That don't mean nothing cause you see me walking around there.

BONO: Where she come from anyway? She just kinda showed up one day.

TROY: Tallahassee. You can look at her and tell she one of them Florida gals. They got some big healthy women down there. Grow them right up out the ground. Got a little bit of Indian in her. Most of them niggers down in Florida got some Indian in them.

BONO: I don't know about that Indian part. But she damn sure big and healthy. Woman wear some big stockings. Got them great big old legs and hips as wide as the Mississippi River.

TROY: Legs don't mean nothing. You don't do nothing but push them out of the way. But them hips cushion the ride!

35 **BONO:** Troy, you ain't got no sense.

TROY: It's the truth! Like you riding on Goodyears!

Rose enters from the house. She is ten years younger than Troy, her devotion to him stems from her recognition of the possibilities of her life without him: a succession of abusive men and their babies, a life of partying and running the streets, the Church, or aloneness with its attendant pain and frustration. She recognizes Troy's spirit as a fine and illuminating one and she either ignores or forgives his faults, only some of which she recognizes. Though she doesn't drink, her presence is an integral part of the Friday night rituals. She alternates between the porch and the kitchen, where supper preparations are under way.

ROSE: What you all out here getting into?

TROY: What you worried about what we getting into for? This is men talk, woman.

ROSE: What I care what you all talking about? Bono, you gonna stay for supper?

40 **BONO:** No, I thank you, Rose. But Lucille say she cooking up a pot of pigfeet.

TROY: Pigfeet! Hell, I'm going home with you! Might even stay the night if you got some pigfeet. You got something in there to top them pigfeet, Rose?

ROSE: I'm cooking up some chicken. I got some chicken and collard greens.[1]

TROY: Well, go on back in the house and let me and Bono finish what we was talking about. This is men talk. I got some talk for you later. You know what kind of talk I mean. You go on and powder it up.

---

[1] A leafy green vegetable.

ROSE: Troy Maxson, don't you start that now!

45 **TROY:** *(puts his arm around her)* Aw, woman . . . come here. Look here,
Bono . . . when I met this woman . . . I got out that place, say, "Hitch
up my pony, saddle up my mare . . . there's a woman out there for me
somewhere. I looked here. Looked there. Saw Rose and latched on to
her." I latched on to her and told her—I'm gonna tell you the truth—I
told her, "Baby, I don't wanna marry, I just wanna be your man."
Rose told me . . . tell him what you told me, Rose.

ROSE: I told him if he wasn't the marrying kind, then move out the way
so the marrying kind could find me.

TROY: That's what she told me. "Nigger, you in my way. You blocking
the view! Move out the way so I can find me a husband." I thought it
over two or three days. Come back—

ROSE: Ain't no two or three days nothing. You was back the same night.

TROY: Come back, told her . . . "Okay, baby . . . but I'm gonna buy me a
banty rooster and put him out there in the backyard . . . and when he
see a stranger come, he'll flap his wings and crow . . ." Look here,
Bono, I could watch the front door by myself . . . it was that back
door I was worried about.

50 **ROSE:** Troy, you ought not talk like that. Troy ain't doing nothing but
telling a lie.

TROY: Only thing is . . . when we first got married . . . forget the rooster
. . . we ain't had no yard!

BONO: I hear you tell it. Me and Lucille was staying down there on
Logan Street. Had two rooms with the outhouse in the back. I ain't
mind the outhouse none. But when that goddamn wind blow through
there in the winter . . . that's what I'm talking about! To this day I
wonder why in the hell I ever stayed down there for six long years.
But see, I didn't know I could do no better. I thought only white
folks had inside toilets and things.

ROSE: There's a lot of people don't know they can do no better than
they doing now. That's just something you got to learn. A lot of folks
still shop at Bella's.

TROY: Ain't nothing wrong with shopping at Bella's. She got fresh food.

55 **ROSE:** I ain't said nothing about if she got fresh food. I'm talking about
what she charge. She charge ten cents more than the A&P.

TROY: The A&P ain't never done nothing for me. I spends my money
where I'm treated right. I go down to Bella, say, "I need a loaf of
bread, I'll pay you Friday." She give it to me. What sense that make
when I got money to go and spend it somewhere else and ignore the
person who done right by me? That ain't in the Bible.

ROSE: We ain't talking about what's in the Bible. What sense it make to
shop there when she overcharge?

TROY: You shop where you want to. I'll do my shopping where the
people been good to me.

ROSE: Well, I don't think it's right for her to overcharge. That's all I
was saying.

60 **BONO:** Look here . . . I got to get on. Lucille going be raising all kind of hell.

TROY: Where you going, nigger? We ain't finished this pint. Come here, finish this pint.

BONO: Well, hell, I am . . . if you ever turn the bottle loose.

TROY: *(hands him the bottle)* The only thing I say about the A&P is I'm glad Cory got that job down there. Help him take care of his school clothes and things. Gabe done moved out and things getting tight around here. He got that job . . . He can start to look out for himself.

ROSE: Cory done went and got recruited by a college football team.

65 **TROY:** I told that boy about that football stuff. The white man ain't gonna let him get nowhere with that football. I told him when he first come to me with it. Now you come telling me he done went and got more tied up in it. He ought to go and get recruited in how to fix cars or something where he can make a living.

ROSE: He ain't talking about making no living playing football. It's just something the boys in school do. They gonna send a recruiter by to talk to you. He'll tell you he ain't talking about making no living playing football. It's a honor to be recruited.

TROY: It ain't gonna get him nowhere. Bono'll tell you that.

BONO: If he be like you in the sports . . . he's gonna be all right. Ain't but two men ever played baseball as good as you. That's Babe Ruth[2] and Josh Gibson.[3] Them's the only two men ever hit more home runs than you.

TROY: What it ever get me? Ain't got a pot to piss in or a window to throw it out of.

70 **ROSE:** Times have changed since you was playing baseball, Troy. That was before the war. Times have changed a lot since then.

TROY: How in hell they done changed?

ROSE: They got lots of colored boys playing ball now. Baseball and football.

BONO: You right about that, Rose. Times have changed, Troy. You just come along too early.

TROY: There ought not never have been no time called too early! Now you take that fellow . . . what's that fellow they had playing right field for the Yankees back then? You know who I'm talking about, Bono. Used to play right field for the Yankees.

75 **ROSE:** Selkirk?

---

2 George Herman Ruth (1895–1948) American baseball player most prominent as a New York Yankee during the 1910's and 20's; known for his homerun hitting and his flamboyant lifestyle.

3 (1911–1947) American baseball player in the Negro Leagues of the 1920's, 30's, and 40's; known as "the Negro Babe Ruth"; barred from Major League baseball by an unwritten rule against black players.

TROY: Selkirk! That's it! Man batting .269, understand? .269. What kind of sense that make? I was hitting .432 with thirty-seven home runs! Man batting .269 and playing right field for the Yankees! I saw Josh Gibson's daughter yesterday. She walking around with raggedy shoes on her feet. Now I bet you Selkirk's daughter ain't walking around with raggedy shoes on her feet! I bet you that!

ROSE: They got a lot of colored baseball players now. Jackie Robinson[4] was the first. Folks had to wait for Jackie Robinson.

TROY: I done seen a hundred niggers play baseball better than Jackie Robinson. Hell, I know some teams Jackie Robinson couldn't even make! What you talking about Jackie Robinson. Jackie Robinson wasn't nobody. I'm talking about if you could play ball then they ought to have let you play. Don't care what color you were. Come telling me I come along too early. If you could play . . . then they ought to have let you play.

Troy takes a long drink from the bottle.

ROSE: You gonna drink yourself to death. You don't need to be drinking like that.

80 **TROY:** Death ain't nothing. I done seen him. Done wrassled with him. You can't tell me nothing about death. Death ain't nothing but a fastball on the outside corner. And you know what I'll do to that! Lookee here, Bono . . . am I lying? You get one of them fastballs, about waist high, over the outside corner of the plate where you can get the meat of the bat on it . . . and good god! You can kiss it goodbye. Now, am I lying?

BONO: Naw, you telling the truth there. I seen you do it.

TROY: If I'm lying . . . that 450 feet worth of lying! *(Pause.)* That's all death is to me. A fastball on the outside corner.

ROSE: I don't know why you want to get on talking about death.

TROY: Ain't nothing wrong with talking about death. That's part of life. Everybody gonna die. You gonna die, I'm gonna die. Bono's gonna die. Hell, we all gonna die.

85 **ROSE:** But you ain't got to talk about it. I don't like to talk about it.

TROY: You the one brought it up. Me and Bono was talking about baseball . . . you tell me I'm gonna drink myself to death. Ain't that right, Bono? You know I don't drink this but one night out of the week. That's Friday night. I'm gonna drink just enough to where I can handle it. Then I cuts it loose. I leave it alone. So don't you worry about me drinking myself to death. 'Cause I ain't worried about Death. I done seen him. I done wrestled with him.

---

4 John Roosevelt Robinson (1919–1972), first black player to enter Major League baseball; joined the Brooklyn Dodgers in 1947.

Look here, Bono . . . I looked up one day and Death was marching straight at me. Like Soldiers on Parade! The Army of Death was marching straight at me. The middle of July, 1941. It got real cold just like it be winter. It seem like Death himself reached out and touched me on the shoulder. He touch me just like I touch you. I got cold as ice and Death standing there grinning at me.

ROSE: Troy, why don't you hush that talk.

TROY: I say . . . what you want, Mr. Death? You be wanting me? You done brought your army to be getting me? I looked him dead in the eye. I wasn't fearing nothing. I was ready to tangle. Just like I'm ready to tangle now. The Bible say be ever vigilant. That's why I don't get but so drunk. I got to keep watch.

ROSE: Troy was right down there in Mercy Hospital. You remember he had pneumonia? Laying there with a fever talking plumb out of his head.

90 TROY: Death standing there staring at me . . . carrying that sickle in his hand. Finally he say, "You want bound over for another year?" See, just like that . . . "You want bound over for another year?" I told him, "Bound over hell! Let's settle this now!"

It seem like he kinda fell back when I said that, and all the cold went out of me. I reached down and grabbed that sickle and threw it just as far as I could throw it . . . and me and him commenced to wrestling.

We wrestled for three days and three nights. I can't say where I found the strength from. Every time it seemed like he was gonna get the best of me, I'd reach way down deep inside myself and find the strength to do him one better.

ROSE: Every time Troy tell that story he find different ways to tell it. Different things to make up about it.

TROY: I ain't making up nothing. I'm telling you the facts of what happened. I wrestled with Death for three days and three nights and I'm standing here to tell you about it. *(Pause.)* All right. At the end of the third night we done weakened each other to where we can't hardly move. Death stood up, throwed on his robe . . . had him a white robe with a hood on it. He throwed on that robe and went off to look for his sickle. Say, "I'll be back." Just like that. "I'll be back." I told him, say, "Yeah, but . . . you gonna have to find me!" I wasn't no fool. I wan't going looking for him. Death ain't nothing to play with. And I know he's gonna get me. I know I got to join his army . . . his camp followers. But as long as I keep my strength and see him coming . . . as long as I keep up my vigilance . . . he's gonna have to fight to get me. I ain't going easy.

BONO: Well, look here, since you got to keep up your vigilance . . . let me have the bottle.

TROY: Aw hell, I shouldn't have told you that part. I should have left out that part.

95 **ROSE:**   Troy be talking that stuff and half the time don't even know
what he be talking about.

TROY: Bono know me better than that.

BONO: That's right. I know you. I know you got some Uncle Remus[5] in
your blood. You got more stories than the devil got sinners.

TROY: Aw hell, I done seen him too! Done talked with the devil.

ROSE: Troy, don't nobody wanna be hearing all that stuff.

*Lyons enters the yard from the street. Thirty-four years old, Troy's son by a pre-
vious marriage, he sports a neatly trimmed goatee, sport coat, white shirt, tieless
and buttoned at the collar. Though he fancies himself a musician, he is more
caught up in the rituals and "idea" of being a musician than in the actual practice of the music. He has come to borrow money from Troy, and while he knows
he will be successful, he is uncertain as to what extent his lifestyle will be held
up to scrutiny and ridicule.*

100 **LYONS:**   Hey, Pop.

TROY: What you come "Hey, Popping" me for?

LYONS: How you doing, Rose? *(He kisses her.)* Mr. Bono. How you doing?

BONO: Hey, Lyons . . . how you been?

TROY: He must have been doing all right. I ain't seen him around here
last week.

105 **ROSE:**   Troy, leave your boy alone. He come by to see you and you wanna
start all that nonsense.

TROY: I ain't bothering Lyons. *(Offers him the bottle.)* Here . . . get you a
drink. We got an understanding. I know why he come by to see me
and he know I know.

LYONS: Come on, Pop . . . I just stopped by to say hi . . . see how you
was doing.

TROY: You ain't stopped by yesterday.

ROSE: You gonna stay for supper, Lyons? I got some chicken cooking in
the oven.

110 **LYONS:**   No, Rose . . . thanks. I was just in the neighborhood and
thought I'd stop by for a minute.

TROY: You was in the neighborhood all right, nigger. You telling the
truth there. You was in the neighborhood cause it's my payday.

LYONS: Well, hell, since you mentioned it . . . let me have ten dollars.

TROY: I'll be damned! I'll die and go to hell and play blackjack with the
devil before I give you ten dollars.

BONO: That's what I wanna know about . . . that devil you done seen.

115 **LYONS:**   What . . . Pop done seen the devil? You too much, Pops.

TROY: Yeah, I done seen him. Talked to him too!

---

5 Narrator of *Uncle Remus: His Songs and His Sayings* (1880) and a number of sequels by
Joel Chandler Harris; tells tales about characters such as Brer Rabbit and the Tarbaby in
exaggerated dialect, now widely considered to be a derogatory representation of
African Americans.

ROSE: You ain't seen no devil. I done told you that man ain't had nothing to do with the devil. Anything you can't understand, you want to call it the devil.

TROY: Look here, Bono . . . I went down to see Hertzberger about some furniture. Got three rooms for two-ninety-eight. That what it say on the radio. "Three rooms . . . two-ninety-eight." Even made up a little song about it. Go down there . . . man tell me I can't get no credit. I'm working every day and can't get no credit. What to do? I got an empty house with some raggedy furniture in it. Cory ain't got no bed. He's sleeping on a pile of rags on the floor. Working every day and can't get no credit. Come back here—Rose'll tell you—madder than hell. Sit down . . . try to figure what I'm gonna do. Come a knock on the door. Ain't been living here but three days. Who know I'm here? Open the door . . . devil standing there bigger than life. White fellow . . . white fellow . . . got on good clothes and everything. Standing there with a clipboard in his hand. I ain't had to say nothing. First words come out of his mouth was . . . "I understand you need some furniture and can't get no credit." I liked to fell over. He say, "I'll give you all the credit you want, but you got to pay the interest on it." I told him, "Give me three rooms worth and charge whatever you want." Next day a truck pulled up here and two men unloaded them three rooms. Man what drove the truck give me a book. Say send ten dollars, first of every month to the address in the book and everything will be all right. Say if I miss a payment the devil was coming back and it'll be hell to pay. That was fifteen years ago. To this day . . . the first of the month I send my ten dollars, Rose'll tell you.

ROSE: Troy lying.

120 TROY: I ain't never seen that man since. Now you tell me who else that could have been but the devil? I ain't sold my soul or nothing like that, you understand. Naw, I wouldn't have truck with the devil about nothing like that. I got my furniture and pays my ten dollars the first of the month just like clockwork.

BONO: How long you say you been paying this ten dollars a month?

TROY: Fifteen years!

BONO: Hell, ain't you finished paying for it yet? How much the man done charged you?

TROY: Ah hell, I done paid for it. I done paid for it ten times over! The fact is I'm scared to stop paying it.

125 ROSE: Troy lying. We got that furniture from Mr. Glickman. He ain't paying no ten dollars a month to nobody.

TROY: Aw hell, woman. Bono know I ain't that big a fool.

LYONS: I was just getting ready to say . . . I know where there's a bridge for sale.

TROY: Look here, I'll tell you this . . . it don't matter to me if he was the devil. It don't matter if the devil give credit. Somebody has got to give it.

Rose: It ought to matter. You going around talking about having truck with the devil . . . God's the one you gonna have to answer to. He's the one gonna be at the Judgment.

130 **Lyons:**   Yeah, well, look here, Pop . . . let me have that ten dollars. I'll give it back to you. Bonnie got a job working at the hospital.

Troy: What I tell you, Bono? The only time I see this nigger is when he wants something. That's the only time I see him.

Lyons: Come on, Pop, Mr. Bono don't want to hear all that. Let me have the ten dollars. I told you Bonnie working.

Troy: What that mean to me? "Bonnie working." I don't care if she working. Go ask her for the ten dollars if she working. Talking about "Bonnie working." Why ain't you working?

Lyons: Aw, Pop, you know I can't find no decent job. Where am I gonna get a job at? You know I can't get no job.

135 **Troy:**   I told you I know some people down there. I can get you on the rubbish if you want to work. I told you that the last time you came by here asking me for something.

Lyons: Naw, Pop . . . thanks. That ain't for me. I don't wanna be carrying nobody's rubbish. I don't wanna be punching nobody's time clock.

Troy: What's the matter, you too good to carry people's rubbish? Where you think that ten dollars you talking about come from? I'm just supposed to haul people's rubbish and give my money to you cause you too lazy to work. You too lazy to work and wanna know why you ain't got what I got.

Rose: What hospital Bonnie working at? Mercy?

Lyons: She's down at Passavant working in the laundry.

140 **Troy:**   I ain't got nothing as it is. I give you that ten dollars and I got to eat beans the rest of the week. Naw . . . you ain't getting no ten dollars here.

Lyons: You ain't got to be eating no beans. I don't know why you wanna say that.

Troy: I ain't got no extra money. Gabe done moved over to Miss Pearl's paying her the rent and things done got tight around here. I can't afford to be giving you every payday.

Lyons: I ain't asked you to give me nothing. I asked you to loan me ten dollars. I know you got ten dollars.

Troy: Yeah, I got it. You know why I got it? Cause I don't throw my money away out there in the streets. You living the fast life . . . wanna be a musician . . . running around in them clubs and things . . . then, you learn to take care of yourself. You ain't gonna find me going and asking nobody for nothing. I done spent too many years without.

145 **Lyons:**   You and me is two different people, Pop.

Troy: I done learned my mistake and learned to do what's right by it. You still trying to get something for nothing. Life don't owe you nothing. You owe it to yourself. Ask Bono. He'll tell you I'm right.

LYONS: You got your way of dealing with the world . . . I got mine. The only thing that matters to me is the music.

TROY: Yeah, I can see that! It don't matter how you gonna eat . . . where your next dollar is coming from. You telling the truth there.

LYONS: I know I got to eat. But I got to live too. I need something that gonna help me to get out of the bed in the morning. Make me feel like I belong in the world. I don't bother nobody. I just stay with the music cause that's the only way I can find to live in the world. Otherwise there ain't no telling what I might do. Now I don't come criticizing you and how you live. I just come by to ask you for ten dollars. I don't wanna hear all that about how I live.

150   **TROY:**   Boy, your mama did a hell of a job raising you.

LYONS: You can't change me, Pop. I'm thirty-four years old. If you wanted to change me, you should have been there when I was growing up. I come by to see you . . . ask for ten dollars and you want to talk about how I was raised. You don't know nothing about how I was raised.

ROSE: Let the boy have ten dollars, Troy.

TROY: *(to Lyons)* What the hell you looking at me for? I ain't got no ten dollars. You know what I do with my money. *(To Rose.)* Give him ten dollars if you want him to have it.

ROSE: I will. Just as soon as you turn it loose.

155   **TROY:**   *(handing Rose the money)* There it is. Seventy-six dollars and forty-two cents. You see this, Bono? Now, I ain't gonna get but six of that back.

ROSE: You ought to stop telling that lie. Here, Lyons. *(She hands him the money.)*

LYONS: Thanks, Rose. Look . . . I got to run . . . I'll see you later.

TROY: Wait a minute. You gonna say "thanks, Rose" and ain't gonna look to see where she got that ten dollars from? See how they do me, Bono?

LYONS: I know she got it from you, Pop. Thanks. I'll give it back to you.

160   **TROY:**   There he go telling another lie. Time I see that ten dollars . . . he'll be owing me thirty more.

LYONS: See you, Mr. Bono.

BONO: Take care, Lyons!

LYONS: Thanks, Pop. I'll see you again.

Lyons exits the yard.

TROY: I don't know why he don't go and get him a decent job and take care of that woman he got.

165   **BONO:**   He'll be all right, Troy. The boy is still young.

TROY: The *boy* is thirty-four years old.

ROSE: Let's not get off into all that.

BONO: Look here . . . I got to be going. I got to be getting on. Lucille gonna be waiting.

TROY: *(puts his arm around Rose)* See this woman, Bono? I love this
woman. I love this woman so much it hurts. I love her so much . . . I
done run out of ways of loving her. So I got to go back to basics.
Don't you come by my house Monday morning talking about time to
go to work . . . 'cause I'm still gonna be stroking!

170 **ROSE:** Troy! Stop it now!

BONO: I ain't paying him no mind, Rose. That ain't nothing but gin-
talk. Go on, Troy. I'll see you Monday.

TROY: Don't you come by my house, nigger! I done told you what I'm
gonna be doing.

The lights go down to black.

SCENE II
‾‾‾‾‾‾‾‾‾‾

*The lights come up on Rose hanging up clothes. She hums and sings softly to
herself. It is the following morning.*

ROSE: *(sings)* Jesus, be a fence all around me every day
Jesus, I want you to protect me as I travel on my way.
Jesus, be a fence all around me every day.

Troy enters from the house.

Jesus, I want you to protect me
As I travel on my way.
(To Troy.) 'Morning, You ready for breakfast? I can fix it soon as I
finish hanging up these clothes?

TROY: I got the coffee on. That'll be all right. I'll just drink some of
that this morning.

175 **ROSE:** That 651 hit yesterday. That's the second time this month. Miss
Pearl hit for a dollar . . . seem like those that need the least always get
lucky. Poor folks can't get nothing.

TROY: Them numbers don't know nobody. I don't know why you fool
with them. You and Lyons both.

ROSE: It's something to do.

TROY: You ain't doing nothing but throwing your money away.

ROSE: Troy, you know I don't play foolishly. I just play a nickel here and
a nickel there.

180 **TROY:** That's two nickels you done thrown away.

ROSE: Now I hit sometimes . . . that makes up for it. It always comes in
handy when I do hit. I don't hear you complaining then.

TROY: I ain't complaining now. I just say it's foolish. Trying to guess
out of six hundred ways which way the number gonna come. If I had
all the money niggers, these Negroes, throw away on numbers for one
week—just one week—I'd be a rich man.

ROSE: Well, you wishing and calling it foolish ain't gonna stop folks
from playing numbers. That's one thing for sure. Besides . . . some
good things come from playing numbers. Look where Pope done
bought him that restaurant off of numbers.

TROY: I can't stand niggers like that. Man ain't had two dimes to
rub together. He walking around with his shoes all run over
bumming money for cigarettes. All right. Got lucky there and hit
the numbers . . .

185 ROSE: Troy, I know all about it.

TROY: Had good sense, I'll say that for him. He ain't throwing his
money away. I seen niggers hit the numbers and go through two
thousand dollars in four days. Man bought him that restaurant down
there . . . fixed it up real nice . . . and then didn't want nobody to
come in it! A Negro go in there and can't get no kind of service. I
seen a white fellow come in there and order a bowl of stew. Pope
picked all the meat out the pot for him. Man ain't had nothing but a
bowl of meat! Negro come behind him and ain't got nothing but the
potatoes and carrots. Talking about what numbers do for people, you
picked a wrong example. Ain't done nothing but make a worser fool
out of him than he was before.

ROSE: Troy, you ought to stop worrying about what happened at work
yesterday.

TROY: I ain't worried. Just told me to be down there at the
Commissioner's office on Friday. Everybody think they gonna fire
me. I ain't worried about them firing me. You ain't got to worry
about that. *(Pause.)* Where's Cory? Cory in the house? *(Calls.)* Cory?

ROSE: He gone out.

190 TROY: Out, huh? He gone out 'cause he know I want him to help me
with this fence. I know how he is. That boy scared of work.

*Gabriel enters. He comes halfway down the alley and, hearing Troy's voice,
stops.*

TROY: *(continues)* He ain't done a lick of work in his life.

ROSE: He had to go to football practice. Coach wanted them to get in a
little extra practice before the season start.

TROY: I got his practice . . . running out of here before he get his chores
done.

ROSE: Troy, what is wrong with you this morning? Don't nothing set
right with you. Go on back in there and go to bed . . . get up on the
other side.

195 TROY: Why something got to be wrong with me? I ain't said nothing
wrong with me.

ROSE: You got something to say about everything. First it's the numbers
. . . then it's the way the man runs his restaurant . . . then you done
got on Cory. What's it gonna be next? Take a look up there and see if
the weather suits you . . . or is it gonna be how you gonna put up the
fence with the clothes hanging in the yard.

TROY: You hit the nail on the head then.

ROSE: I know you like I know the back of my hand. Go on in there and get you some coffee . . . see if that straighten you up. 'Cause you ain't right this morning.

Troy starts into the house and sees Gabriel. Gabriel starts singing. Troy's brother, he is seven years younger than Troy. Injured in World War II, he has a metal plate in his head. He carries an old trumpet tied around his waist and believes with every fiber of his being that he is the Archangel Gabriel.[6] He carries a chipped basket with an assortment of discarded fruits and vegetables he has picked up in the strip district and which he attempts to sell.

GABRIEL: *(singing)* Yes, ma'am, I got plums
    You ask me how I sell them
    Oh ten cents apiece
    Three for a quarter
    Come and buy now
    'Cause I'm here today
    And tomorrow I'll be gone

Gabriel enters.

    Hey, Rose!
200 **ROSE:** How you doing, Gabe?

GABRIEL: There's Troy . . . Hey, Troy!

TROY: Hey, Gabe.

Exit into kitchen.

ROSE: *(to Gabriel)* What you got there?

GABRIEL: You know what I got, Rose. I got fruits and vegetables.

205 **ROSE:** *(looking in basket)* Where's all these plums you talking about?

GABRIEL: I ain't got no plums today, Rose. I was just singing that. Have some tomorrow. Put me in a big order for plums. Have enough plums tomorrow for St. Peter and everybody.

Troy reenters from kitchen, crosses to steps.

    (To Rose.) Troy's mad at me.

TROY: I ain't mad at you. What I got to be mad at you about? You ain't done nothing to me.

GABRIEL: I just moved over to Miss Pearl's to keep out from in your way. I ain't mean no harm by it.

TROY: Who said anything about that? I ain't said anything about that.

210 **GABRIEL:** You ain't mad at me, is you?

TROY: Naw . . . I ain't mad at you, Gabe. If I was mad at you I'd tell you about it.

---

6 The Archangel Gabriel, a messenger of God.

GABRIEL: Got me two rooms. In the basement. Got my own door too. Wanna see my key? *(He holds up a key.)* That's my own key! Ain't nobody else got a key like that. That's my key! My two rooms!

TROY: Well, that's good, Gabe. You got your own key . . . that's good.

ROSE: You hungry, Gabe? I was just fixing to cook Troy his breakfast.

215 **GABRIEL:** I'll take some biscuits. You got some biscuits? Did you know when I was in heaven . . . every morning me and St. Peter[7] would sit down by the gate and eat some big fat biscuits? Oh, yeah! We had us a good time. We'd sit there and eat us them biscuits and then St. Peter would go off to sleep and tell me to wake him up when it's time to open the gates for the judgment.

ROSE: Well, come on . . . I'll make up a batch of biscuits.

Rose exits into the house.

GABRIEL: Troy . . . St. Peter got your name in the book. I seen it. It say . . . Troy Maxson. I say . . . I know him! He got the same name like what I got. That's my brother!

TROY: How many times you gonna tell me that, Gabe?

GABRIEL: Ain't got my name in the book. Don't have to have my name. I done died and went to heaven. He got your name though. One morning St. Peter was looking at his book . . . marking it up for the judgment . . . and he let me see your name. Got it in there under M. Got Rose's name . . . I ain't seen it like I seen yours . . . but I know it's in there. He got a great big book. Got everybody's name what was ever been born. That's what he told me. But I seen your name. Seen it with my own eyes.

220 **TROY:** Go on in the house there. Rose going to fix you something to eat.

GABRIEL: Oh, I ain't hungry. I done had breakfast with Aunt Jemimah. She come by and cooked me up a whole mess of flapjacks. Remember how we used to eat them flapjacks?

TROY: Go on in the house and get you something to eat now.

GABRIEL: I got to sell my plums. I done sold some tomatoes. Got me two quarters. Wanna see? *(He shows Troy his quarters.)* I'm gonna save them and buy me a new horn so St. Peter can hear me when it's time to open the gates. *(Gabriel stops suddenly. Listens.)* Hear that? That's the hellhounds. I got to chase them out of here. Go on get out of here! Get out!

Gabriel exits singing.

> Better get ready for the judgment
> Better get ready for the judgment
> My Lord is coming down

Rose enters from the house.

---

[7] Disciple of Christ, believed to be the guard at the gates of heaven.

TROY: He's gone off somewhere.

225 **GABRIEL:**   *(offstage)* Better get ready for the judgment
Better get ready for the judgment morning
Better get ready for the judgment
My God is coming down

ROSE: He ain't eating right. Miss Pearl say she can't get him to eat nothing.

TROY: What you want me to do about it, Rose? I done did everything I can for the man. I can't make him get well. Man got half his head blown away . . . what you expect?

ROSE: Seem like something ought to be done to help him.

TROY: Man don't bother nobody. He just mixed up from that metal plate he got in his head. Ain't no sense for him to go back into the hospital.

230 **ROSE:**   Least he be eating right. They can help him take care of himself.

TROY: Don't nobody wanna be locked up, Rose. What you wanna lock him up for? Man go over there and fight the war . . . messin' around with them Japs, get half his head blown off . . . and they give him a lousy three thousand dollars. And I had to swoop down on that.

ROSE: Is you fixing to go into that again?

TROY: That's the only way I got a roof over my head . . . cause of that metal plate.

ROSE: Ain't no sense you blaming yourself for nothing. Gabe wasn't in no condition to manage that money. You done what was right by him. Can't nobody say you ain't done what was right by him. Look how long you took care of him . . . till he wanted to have his own place and moved over there with Miss Pearl.

235 **TROY:**   That ain't what I'm saying, woman! I'm just stating the facts. If my brother didn't have that metal plate in his head . . . I wouldn't have a pot to piss in or a window to throw it out of. And I'm fifty-three years old. Now see if you can understand that!

Troy gets up from the porch and starts to exit the yard.

ROSE: Where you going off to? You been running out of here every Saturday for weeks. I thought you was gonna work on this fence?

TROY: I'm gonna walk down to Taylors'. Listen to the ball game. I'll be back in a bit. I'll work on it when I get back.

He exits the yard. The lights go to black.

SCENE III

The lights come up on the yard. It is four hours later. Rose is taking down the clothes from the line. Cory enters carrying his football equipment.

ROSE: Your daddy like to had a fit with you running out of here this morning without doing your chores.

CORY: I told you I had to go to practice.

240 ROSE: He say you were supposed to help him with this fence.

CORY: He been saying that the last four or five Saturdays, and then he don't never do nothing, but go down to Taylors. Did you tell him about the recruiter?

ROSE: Yeah, I told him.

CORY: What he say?

ROSE: He ain't said nothing too much. You get in there and get started on your chores before he gets back. Go on and scrub down them steps before he gets back here hollering and carrying on.

245 CORY: I'm hungry. What you got to eat, Mama?

ROSE: Go on and get started on your chores. I got some meat loaf in there. Go on and make you a sandwich . . . and don't leave no mess in there.

Cory exits into the house. Rose continues to take down the clothes. Troy enters the yard and sneaks up and grabs her from behind.

Troy! Go on, now. You liked to scared me to death. What was the score of the game? Lucille had me on the phone and I couldn't keep up with it.

TROY: What I care about the game? Come here, woman. *(He tries to kiss her.)*

ROSE: I thought you went down Taylors' to listen to the game. Go on, Troy! You supposed to be putting up this fence.

TROY: *(attempting to kiss her again)* I'll put it up when I finish with what is at hand.

250 ROSE: Go on, Troy. I ain't studying you.

TROY: *(chasing after her)* I'm studying you . . . fixing to do my homework!

ROSE: Troy, you better leave me alone.

TROY: Where's Cory? That boy brought his butt home yet?

ROSE: He's in the house doing his chores.

255 TROY: *(calling)* Cory! Get your butt out here, boy!

Rose exits into the house with the laundry. Troy goes over to the pile of wood, picks up a board, and starts sawing. Cory enters from the house.

TROY: You just now coming in here from leaving this morning?

CORY: Yeah, I had to go to football practice.

TROY: Yeah, what?

CORY: Yessir.

260 TROY: I ain't but two seconds off you noway. The garbage sitting in there overflowing . . . you ain't done none of your chores . . . and you come in here talking about "Yeah."

CORY: I was just getting ready to do my chores now, Pop . . .

TROY: Your first chore is to help me with this fence on Saturday. Everything else come after that. Now get that saw and cut them boards.

Cory takes the saw and begins cutting the boards. Troy continues working. There is a long pause.

CORY: Hey, Pop . . . why don't you buy a TV?

TROY: What I want with a TV? What I want one of them for?

265 CORY: Everybody got one. Earl, Ba Bra . . . Jesse!

TROY: I ain't asked you who had one. I say what I want with one?

CORY: So you can watch it. They got lots of things on TV. Baseball games and everything. We could watch the World Series.

TROY: Yeah . . . and how much this TV cost?

CORY: I don't know. They got them on sale for around two hundred dollars.

270 TROY: Two hundred dollars, huh?

CORY: That ain't that much, Pop.

TROY: Naw, it's just two hundred dollars. See that roof you got over your head at night? Let me tell you something about that roof. It's been over ten years since that roof was last tarred. See now . . . the snow comes this winter and sit up there on that roof like it is . . . and it's gonna seep inside. It's just gonna be a little bit . . . ain't gonna hardly notice it. Then the next thing you know, it's gonna be leaking all over the house. Then the wood rot from all that water and you gonna need a whole new roof. Now, how much you think it cost to get that roof tarred?

CORY: I don't know.

TROY: Two hundred and sixty-four dollars . . . cash money. While you thinking about a TV, I got to be thinking about the roof . . . and whatever else go wrong here. Now if you had two hundred dollars, what would you do . . . fix the roof or buy a TV?

275 CORY: I'd buy a TV. Then when the roof started to leak . . . when it needed fixing . . . I'd fix it.

TROY: Where you gonna get the money from? You done spent it for a TV. You gonna sit up and watch the water run all over your brand new TV.

CORY: Aw, Pop. You got money. I know you do.

TROY: Where I got it at, huh?

CORY: You got it in the bank.

280 TROY: You wanna see my bankbook? You wanna see that seventy-three dollars and twenty-two cents I got sitting up in there.

CORY: You ain't got to pay for it all at one time. You can put a down payment on it and carry it on home with you.

TROY: Not me. I ain't gonna owe nobody nothing if I can help it. Miss a payment and they come and snatch it right out your house. Then what you got? Now, soon as I get two hundred dollars clear, then I'll buy a TV. Right now, as soon as I get two hundred and sixty-four dollars, I'm gonna have this roof tarred.

CORY: Aw . . . Pop!

TROY: You go on and get you two hundred and buy one if ya want it. I got better things to do with my money.

285 **CORY:** I can't get no two hundred dollars. I ain't never seen two hundred dollars.

TROY: I'll tell you what . . . you get you a hundred dollars and I'll put the other hundred with it.

CORY: All right, I'm gonna show you.

TROY: You gonna show me how you can cut them boards right now.

Cory begins to cut the boards. There is a long pause.

CORY: The Pirates won today. That makes five in a row.

290 **TROY:** I ain't thinking about the Pirates. Got an all-white team. Got that boy . . . that Puerto Rican boy . . . Clemente. Don't even half-play him. That boy could be something if they give him a chance. Play him one day and sit him on the bench the next.

CORY: He gets a lot of chances to play.

TROY: I'm talking about playing regular. Playing every day so you can get your timing. That's what I'm talking about.

CORY: They got some white guys on the team that don't play every day. You can't play everybody at the same time.

TROY: If they got a white fellow sitting on the bench . . . you can bet your last dollar he can't play! The colored guy got to be twice as good before he get on the team. That's why I don't want you to get all tied up in them sports. Man on the team and what it get him? They got colored on the team and don't use them. Same as not having them. All them teams the same.

295 **CORY:** The Braves got Hank Aaron and Wes Covington. Hank Aaron hit two home runs today. That makes forty-three.

TROY: Hank Aaron ain't nobody. That what you supposed to do. That's how you supposed to play the game. Ain't nothing to it. It's just a matter of timing . . . getting the right follow-through. Hell, I can hit forty-three home runs right now!

CORY: Not off no major-league pitching, you couldn't.

TROY: We had better pitching in the Negro leagues. I hit seven home runs off of Satchel Paige.[8] You can't get no better than that!

---

[8] Leroy Robert Paige (1906–1982) American baseball player in the Negro Leagues from the 1920's until 1948, when he joined the Cleveland Indians; reportedly pitched 55 no-hit games during his career; called by Joe DiMaggio "the best pitcher I have ever faced."

CORY: Sandy Koufax.[9] He's leading the league in strikeouts.

300 **TROY:**   I ain't thinking of no Sandy Koufax.

CORY: You got Warren Spahn[10] and Lew Burdette.[11] I bet you couldn't hit no home runs off of Warren Spahn.

TROY: I'm through with it now. You go on and cut them boards. *(Pause.)* Your mama tell me you done got recruited by a college football team? Is that right?

CORY: Yeah. Coach Zellman say the recruiter gonna be coming by to talk to you. Get you to sign the permission papers.

TROY: I thought you supposed to be working down there at the A&P. Ain't you suppose to be working down there after school?

305 **CORY:**   Mr. Stawicki say he gonna hold my job for me until after the football season. Say starting next week I can work weekends.

TROY: I thought we had an understanding about this football stuff? You suppose to keep up with your chores and hold that job down at the A&P. Ain't been around here all day on a Saturday. Ain't none of your chores done . . . and now you telling me you done quit your job.

CORY: I'm going to be working weekends.

TROY: You damn right you are! And ain't no need for nobody coming around here to talk to me about signing nothing.

CORY: Hey, Pop . . . you can't do that. He's coming all the way from North Carolina.

310 **TROY:**   I don't care where he coming from. The white man ain't gonna let you get nowhere with that football noway. You go on and get your book-learning so you can work yourself up in that A&P or learn how to fix cars or build houses or something, get you a trade. That way you have something can't nobody take away from you. You go on and learn how to put your hands to some good use. Besides hauling people's garbage.

CORY: I get good grades, Pop. That's why the recruiter wants to talk with you. You got to keep up your grades to get recruited. This way I'll be going to college. I'll get a chance . . .

TROY: First you gonna get your butt down there to the A&P and get your job back.

---

9   Sanford Koufax (1935–) left-handed pitcher who won 129 games and lost only 47 for the Los Angeles Dodgers in the six seasons between 1961 and 1966; won three Cy Young Awards; pitched four no-hit games, the last of which (1965) was a perfect game.

10   (1921–) left-handed pitcher who at the time of his retirement in 1966 held the National League record of 363 wins; won twenty or more games in four consecutive seasons (1947–1950) and in several other seasons during the 1950's.

11   Selva Lewis Burdette (1926–) American baseball player who pitched and won three games for the Milwaukee Braves against the New York Yankees in the 1957 World Series; ERA of .067 for that Series.

CORY: Mr. Stawicki done already hired somebody else 'cause I told him I was playing football.

TROY: You a bigger fool than I thought . . . to let somebody take away your job so you can play some football. Where you gonna get your money to take out your girlfriend and whatnot? What kind of foolishness is that to let somebody take away your job?

315 **CORY:** I'm still gonna be working weekends.

TROY: Naw . . . naw. You getting your butt out of here and finding you another job.

CORY: Come on, Pop! I got to practice. I can't work after school and play football too. The team needs me. That's what Coach Zellman say . . .

TROY: I don't care what nobody else say. I'm the boss . . . you understand? I'm the boss around here. I do the only saying what counts.

CORY: Come on, Pop!

320 **TROY:** I asked you . . . did you understand?

CORY: Yeah . . .

TROY: What?!

CORY: Yessir.

TROY: You go on down there to that A&P and see if you can get your job back. If you can't do both . . . then you quit the football team. You've got to take the crookeds with the straights.

325 **CORY:** Yessir. *(Pause.)* Can I ask you a question?

TROY: What the hell you wanna ask me? Mr. Stawicki the one you got the questions for.

CORY: How come you ain't never liked me?

TROY: Liked you? Who the hell say I got to like you? What law is there say I got to like you? Wanna stand up in my face and ask a damn fool-ass question like that. Talking about liking somebody. Come here, boy, when I talk to you.

Cory comes over to where Troy is working. He stands slouched over and Troy shoves him on his shoulder.

Straighten up, goddammit! I asked you a question . . . what law is there say I got to like you?

CORY: None.

330 **TROY:** Well, all right then! Don't you eat every day? *(Pause.)* Answer me when I talk to you! Don't you eat every day?

CORY: Yeah.

TROY: Nigger, as long as you in my house, you put that sir on the end of it when you talk to me!

CORY: Yes . . . sir.

TROY: You eat every day.

335 **CORY:** Yessir!

TROY: Got a roof over your head.

CORY: Yessir!

TROY: Got clothes on your back.

CORY: Yessir.

340 **TROY:**   Why you think that is?

CORY: Cause of you.

TROY: Ah, hell I know it's cause of me . . . but why do you think that is?

CORY: *(hesitant)* Cause you like me.

TROY: Like you? I go out of here every morning . . . bust my butt . . . putting up with them crackers[12] every day . . . cause I like you? You are the biggest fool I ever saw. *(Pause.)* It's my job. It's my responsibility! You understand that? A man got to take care of his family. You live in my house . . . sleep you behind on my bedclothes . . . fill you belly up with my food . . . cause you my son. You my flesh and blood. Not cause I like you! Cause it's my duty to take care of you. I owe a responsibility to you! Let's get this straight right here . . . before it go along any further . . . I ain't got to like you. Mr. Rand don't give me my money come payday cause he likes me. He give me cause he owe me. I done give you everything I had to give you. I gave you your life! Me and your mama worked that out between us. And liking your black ass wasn't part of the bargain. Don't you try and go through life worrying about if somebody like you or not. You best be making sure they doing right by you. You understand what I'm saying, boy?

345 **CORY:**   Yessir.

TROY: Then get the hell out of my face, and get on down to that A&P.

Rose has been standing behind the screen door for much of the scene. She enters as Cory exits.

ROSE: Why don't you let the boy go ahead and play football, Troy? Ain't no harm in that. He's just trying to be like you with the sports.

TROY: I don't want him to be like me! I want him to move as far away from my life as he can get. You the only decent thing that ever happened to me. I wish him that. But I don't wish him a thing else from my life. I decided seventeen years ago that boy wasn't getting involved in no sports. Not after what they did to me in the sports.

ROSE: Troy, why don't you admit you was too old to play in the major leagues? For once . . . why don't you admit that?

350 **TROY:**   What do you mean too old? Don't come telling me I was too old. I just wasn't the right color. Hell, I'm fifty-three years old and can do better than Selkirk's .269 right now!

ROSE: How's was you gonna play ball when you were over forty? Sometimes I can't go no sense out of you.

---

12 Derogatory term for white people, generally poor Southern whites.

TROY: I got good sense, woman. I got sense enough not to let my boy get hurt over playing no sports. You been mothering that boy too much. Worried about if people like him.

ROSE: Everything that boy do . . . he do for you. He wants you to say "Good job, son." That's all.

TROY: Rose, I ain't got time for that. He's alive. He's healthy. He's got to make his own way. I made mine. Ain't nobody gonna hold his hand when he get out there in that world.

355 **ROSE:** Times have changed from when you was young, Troy. People change. The world's changing around you and you can't even see it.

TROY: *(slow, methodical)* Woman . . . I do the best I can do. I come in here every Friday. I carry a sack of potatoes and a bucket of lard. You all line up at the door with your hands out. I give you the lint from my pockets. I give you my sweat and my blood. I ain't got no tears. I done spent them. We go upstairs in that room at night . . . and I fall down on you and try to blast a hole into forever. I get up Monday morning . . . find my lunch on the table. I go out. Make my way. Find my strength to carry me through to the next Friday. *(Pause.)* That's all I got, Rose. That's all I got to give. I can't give nothing else.

Troy exits into the house. The lights go down to black.

SCENE IV
....

It is Friday. Two weeks later. Cory starts out of the house with his football equipment. The phone rings.

CORY: *(calling)* I got it! *(He answers the phone and stands in the screen door talking.)* Hello? Hey, Jesse. Naw . . . I was just getting ready to leave now.

ROSE: *(calling)* Cory!

CORY: I told you, man, them spikes[13] is all tore up. You can use them if you want, but they ain't no good. Earl got some spikes.

360 **ROSE:** *(calling)* Cory!

CORY: *(calling to Rose)* Mam? I'm talking to Jesse. *(Into phone.)* When she say that? *(Pause.)* Aw, you lying, man. I'm gonna tell her you said that.

ROSE: *(calling)* Cory, don't you go nowhere!

CORY: I got to go to the game, Ma! *(Into the phone.)* Yeah, hey, look, I'll talk to you later. Yeah, I'll meet you over Earl's house. Later. Bye, Ma.

Cory exits the house and starts out the yard.

365 **ROSE:** Cory, where you going off to? You got that stuff all pulled out and thrown all over your room.

---

13 Athletic shoes with sharp metal grips set into the soles.

CORY: *(in the yard)* I was looking for my spikes. Jesse wanted to borrow my spikes.

ROSE: Get up there and get that cleaned up before your daddy get back in here.

CORY: I got to go to the game! I'll clean it up *when I get back.*

Cory exits.

ROSE: That's all he need to do is see that room all messed up.

Rose exits into the house. Troy and Bono enter the yard. Troy is dressed in clothes other than his work clothes.

370 **BONO:** He told him the same thing he told you. Take it to the union.

TROY: Brownie ain't got that much sense. Man wasn't thinking about nothing. He wait until I confront them on it . . . then he wanna come crying seniority. *(Calls.)* Hey, Rose!

BONO: I wish I could have seen Mr. Rand's face when he told you.

TROY: He couldn't get it out of his mouth! Liked to bit his tongue! When they called me down there to the Commissioner's office . . . he thought they was gonna fire me. Like everybody else.

BONO: I didn't think they was gonna fire you. I thought they was gonna put you on the warning paper.

375 **TROY:** Hey, Rose! *(To Bono.)* Yeah, Mr. Rand like to bit his tongue.

Troy breaks the seal on the bottle, takes a drink, and hands it to Bono.

BONO: I see you run right down to Taylors' and told that Alberta gal.

TROY: *(calling)* Hey Rose! *(To Bono.)* I told everybody. Hey, Rose! I went down there to cash my check.

ROSE: *(entering from the house)* Hush all that hollering, man! I know you out here. What they say down there at the Commissioner's office?

TROY: You supposed to come when I call you, woman. Bono'll tell you that. *(To Bono.)* Don't Lucille come when you call her?

380 **ROSE:** Man, hush your mouth, I ain't no dog . . . talk about "come when you call me."

TROY: *(puts his arm around Rose)* You hear this, Bono? I had me an old dog used to get uppity like that. You say, "C'mere, Blue!" . . . and he just lay there and look at you. End up getting a stick and chasing him away trying to make him come.

ROSE: I ain't studying you and your dog. I remember you used to sing that old song.

TROY: *(he sings)* Hear it ring! Hear it ring! I had a dog his name was Blue.

ROSE: Don't nobody wanna hear you sing that old song.

385 **TROY:** *(sings)* You know Blue was mighty true.

ROSE: Used to have Cory running around here singing that song.

BONO: Hell, I remember that song myself.

TROY: *(sings)* You know Blue was a good old dog.
Blue treed a possum in a hollow log.
That was my daddy's song. My daddy made up that song.

ROSE: I don't care who made it up. Don't nobody wanna hear you sing it.

390 **TROY:**   *(makes a song like calling a dog)* Come here, woman.

ROSE: You come in here carrying on, I reckon they ain't fired you. What they say down there at the Commissioner's office?

TROY: Look here, Rose . . . Mr. Rand called me into his office today when I got back from talking to them people down there . . . it come from up top . . . he called me in and told me they was making me a driver.

ROSE: Troy, you kidding!

TROY: No I ain't. Ask Bono.

395 **ROSE:**   Well, that's great, Troy. Now you don't have to hassle them people no more.

Lyons enters from the street.

TROY: Aw hell, I wasn't looking to see you today. I thought you was in jail. Got it all over the front page of the *Courier* about them raiding Sefus's place . . . where you be hanging out with all them thugs.

LYONS: Hey, Pop . . . that ain't got nothing to do with me. I don't go down there gambling. I go down there to sit in with the band. I ain't got nothing to do with the gambling part. They got some good music down there.

TROY: They got some rogues . . . is what they got.

LYONS: How you been, Mr. Bono? Hi, Rose.

400 **BONO:**   I see where you playing down at the Crawford Grill tonight.

ROSE: How come you ain't brought Bonnie like I told you? You should have brought Bonnie with you, she ain't been over in a month of Sundays.

LYONS: I was just in the neighborhood . . . thought I'd stop by.

TROY: Here he come . . .

BONO: Your daddy got a promotion on the rubbish. He's gonna be the first colored driver. Ain't got to do nothing but sit up there and read the paper like them white fellows.

405 **LYONS:**   Hey, Pop . . . if you knew how to read you'd be all right.

BONO: Naw . . . naw . . . you mean if the nigger knew how to *drive* he'd be all right. Been fighting with them people about driving and ain't even got a license. Mr. Rand know you ain't got no driver's license?

TROY: Driving ain't nothing. All you do is point the truck where you want it to go. Driving ain't nothing.

BONO: Do Mr. Rand know you ain't got no driver's license? That's what I'm talking about. I ain't asked if driving was easy. I asked if Mr. Rand know you ain't got no driver's license.

TROY: He ain't got to know. The man ain't got to know my business. Time he find out, I have two or three driver's licenses.

410 **Lyons:**   *(going into his pocket)* Say, look here, Pop . . .

Troy: I knew it was coming. Didn't I tell you, Bono? I know what kind of "Look here, Pop" that was. The nigger fixing to ask me for some money. It's Friday night. It's my payday. All them rogues down there on the avenue . . . the ones that ain't in jail . . . and Lyons is hopping in his shoes to get down there with them.

Lyons: See, Pop . . . if you give somebody else a chance to talk sometimes, you'd see that I was fixing to pay you back your ten dollars like I told you. Here . . . I told you I'd pay you when Bonnie got paid.

Troy: Naw . . . you go ahead and keep that ten dollars. Put it in the bank. The next time you feel like you wanna come by here and ask me for something . . . you go on down there and get that.

Lyons: Here's your ten dollars, Pop. I told you I don't want you to give me nothing. I just wanted to borrow ten dollars.

415 **Troy:**   Naw . . . you go on and keep that for the next time you want to ask me.

Lyons: Come on, Pop . . . here go your ten dollars.

Rose: Why don't you go on and let the boy pay you back, Troy?

Lyons: Here you go, Rose. If you don't take it I'm gonna have to hear about it for the next six months. *(He hands her the money.)*

Rose: You can hand yours over here too, Troy.

420 **Troy:**   You see this, Bono. You see how they do me.

Bono: Yeah, Lucille do me the same way.

Gabriel is heard singing offstage. He enters.

Gabriel: Better get ready for the Judgment! Better get ready for . . . Hey! . . . Hey! . . . There's Troy's boy!

Lyons: How are you doing, Uncle Gabe?

Gabriel: Lyons . . . The King of the Jungle! Rose . . . hey, Rose. Got a flower for you. *(He takes a rose from his pocket.)* Picked it myself. That's the same rose like you is!

425 **Rose:**   That's right nice of you, Gabe.

Lyons: What you been doing, Uncle Gabe?

Gabriel: Oh, I been chasing hellhounds and waiting on the time to tell St. Peter to open the gates.

Lyons: You been chasing hellhounds, huh? Well . . . you doing the right thing, Uncle Gabe. Somebody got to chase them.

Gabriel: Oh, yeah . . . I know it. The devil's strong. The devil ain't no pushover. Hellhounds snipping at everybody's heels. But I got my trumpet waiting on the judgment time.

430 **Lyons:**   Waiting on the Battle of Armageddon, huh?

Gabriel: Ain't gonna be too much of a battle when God get to waving that Judgment sword. But the people's gonna have a hell of a time trying to get into heaven if them gates ain't open.

Lyons: *(putting his arm around Gabriel)* You hear this, Pop. Uncle Gabe, you all right!

GABRIEL: *(laughing with Lyons)* Lyons! King of the Jungle.

ROSE: You gonna stay for supper, Gabe? Want me to fix you a plate?

435 **GABRIEL:**   I'll take a sandwich, Rose. Don't want no plate. Just wanna eat with my hands. I'll take a sandwich.

ROSE: How about you, Lyons? You staying? Got some short ribs cooking.

LYONS: Naw, I won't eat nothing till after we finished playing. *(Pause.)* You ought to come down and listen to me play, Pop.

TROY: I don't like that Chinese music. All that noise.

ROSE: Go on in the house and wash up, Gabe . . . I'll fix you a sandwich.

440 **GABRIEL:**   *(to Lyons, as he exits)* Troy's mad at me.

LYONS: What you mad at Uncle Gabe for, Pop?

ROSE: He thinks Troy's mad at him cause he moved over to Miss Pearl's.

TROY: I ain't mad at the man. He can live where he want to live at.

LYONS: What he move over there for? Miss Pearl don't like nobody.

445 **ROSE:**   She don't mind him none. She treats him real nice. She just don't allow all that singing.

TROY: She don't mind that rent he be paying . . . that's what she don't mind.

ROSE: Troy, I ain't going through that with you no more. He's over there cause he want to have his own place. He can come and go as he please.

TROY: Hell, he could come and go as he please here. I wasn't stopping him. I ain't put no rules on him.

ROSE: It ain't the same thing, Troy. And you know it.

Gabriel comes to the door.

Now, that's the last I wanna hear about that. I don't wanna hear nothing else about Gabe and Miss Pearl. And next week . . .

450 **GABRIEL:**   I'm ready for my sandwich, Rose.

ROSE: And next week . . . when that recruiter come from that school . . . I want you to sign that paper and go on and let Cory play football. Then that'll be the last I have to hear about that.

TROY: *(to Rose as she exits into the house)* I ain't thinking about Cory nothing.

LYONS: What . . . Cory got recruited? What school he going to?

TROY: That boy walking around here smelling his piss . . . thinking he's grown. Thinking he's gonna do what he want, irrespective of what I say. Look here, Bono . . . I left the Commissioner's office and went down to the A&P . . . that boy ain't working down there. He lying to me. Telling me he got his job back . . . telling me he working weekends . . . telling me he working after school . . . Mr. Stawicki tell me he ain't working down there at all!

455 **LYONS:**   Cory just growing up. He's just busting at the seams trying to fill out your shoes.

TROY: I don't care what he's doing. When he get to the point where he wanna disobey me . . . then it's time for him to move on. Bono'll tell you that. I bet he ain't never disobeyed his daddy without paying the consequences.

BONO: I ain't never had a chance. My daddy came on through . . . but I ain't never knew him to see him . . . or what he had on his mind or where he went. Just moving on through. Searching out the New Land. That's what the old folks used to call it. See a fellow moving around from place to place . . . woman to woman . . . called it searching out the New Land. I can't say if he ever found it. I come along, didn't want no kids. Didn't know if I was gonna be in one place long enough to fix on them right as their daddy. I figured I was going searching too. As it turned out I been hooked up with Lucille near about as long as your daddy been with Rose. Going on sixteen years.

TROY: Sometimes I wish I hadn't known my daddy. He ain't cared nothing about no kids. A kid to him wasn't nothing. All he wanted was for you to learn how to walk so he could start you to working. When it come time for eating . . . he ate first. If there was anything left over, that's what you got. Man would sit down and eat two chickens and give you the wing.

LYONS: You ought to stop that, Pop. Everybody feed their kids. No matter how hard times is . . . everybody care about their kids. Make sure they have something to eat.

460 **TROY:** The only thing my daddy cared about was getting them bales of cotton in to Mr. Lubin. That's the only thing that mattered to him. Sometimes I used to wonder why he was living. Wonder why the devil hadn't come and got him. "Get them bales of cotton in to Mr. Lubin" and find out he owe him money . . .

LYONS: He should have just went on and left when he saw he couldn't get nowhere. That's what I would have done.

TROY: How he gonna leave with eleven kids? And where he gonna go? He ain't knew how to do nothing but farm. No, he was trapped and I think he knew it. But I'll say this for him . . . he felt a responsibility toward us. Maybe he ain't treated us the way I felt he should have . . . but without that responsibility he could have walked off and left us . . . made his own way.

BONO: A lot of them did. Back in those days what you talking about . . . they walk out their front door and just take on down one road or another and keep on walking.

LYONS: There you go? That's what I'm talking about.

465 **BONO:** Just keep on walking till you come to something else. Ain't you never heard of nobody having the walking blues? Well, that's what you call it when you just take off like that.

TROY: My daddy ain't had them walking blues! What you talking about? He stayed right there with his family. But he was just as evil as he could be. My mama couldn't stand him. Couldn't stand that evilness. She run off when I was about eight. She sneaked off one night after he had gone to sleep. Told me she was coming back for me. I ain't never seen her no more. All his women run off and left him. He wasn't good for nobody.

When my turn come to head out, I was fourteen and got to sniffing around Joe Canewell's daughter. Had us an old mule we called Greyboy. My daddy sent me out to do some plowing and tied up Greyboy and went to fooling around with Joe Canewell's daughter. We done found us a nice little spot, got real cozy with each other. She about thirteen and we done figured we was grown anyway . . . so we down there enjoying ourselves . . . ain't thinking about nothing. We didn't know Greyboy had got loose and wandered back to the house and my daddy was looking for me. We down there by the creek enjoying ourselves when my daddy come up on us. Surprised us. He had them leather straps off the mule and commenced to whupping me like there was no tomorrow. I jumped up, mad and embarrassed. I was scared of my daddy. When he commenced to whupping on me . . . quite naturally I run to get out of the way. *(Pause.)* Now I thought he was mad cause I ain't done my work. But I see where he was chasing me off so he could have that gal for himself. When I see what the matter of it was, I lost all fear of my daddy. Right there is where I become a man . . . at fourteen years of age. *(Pause.)* Now it was my turn to run him off. I picked up them same reins that he had used on me. I picked up them reins and commenced to whupping on him. The gal jumped up and run off . . . and when my daddy turned to face me, I could see why the devil had never come to get him . . . cause he was the devil himself. I don't know what happened. When I woke up, I was laying right there by the creek, and Blue . . . this old dog we had . . . was licking my face. I thought I was blind. I couldn't see nothing. Both my eyes were swollen shut. I laid there and cried. I didn't know what I was gonna do. The only thing I knew was the time had come for me to leave my daddy's house. And right there the world suddenly got big. And it was a long time before I could cut it down to where I could handle it.

Part of that cutting down was when I got to the place where I could feel him kicking in my blood and knew that the only thing that separated us was the matter of a few years.

Gabriel enters from the house with a sandwich.

LYONS: What you got there, Uncle Gabe?

GABRIEL: Got me a ham sandwich. Rose gave me a ham sandwich.

TROY: I don't know what happened to him. I done lost touch with everybody except Gabriel. But I hope he's dead. I hope he found some peace.

470 **LYONS:** That's a heavy story, Pop. I didn't know you left home when you was fourteen.

TROY: And didn't know nothing. The only part of the world I knew was the forty-two acres of Mr. Lubin's land. That's all I knew about life.

Lyons: Fourteen's kinda young to be out on your own. *(Phone rings.)* I don't even think I was ready to be out on my own at fourteen. I don't know what I would have done.

Troy: I got up from the creek and walked on down to Mobile.[14] I was through with farming. Figured I could do better in the city. So I walked the two hundred miles to Mobile.

Lyons: Wait a minute . . . you ain't walked no two hundred miles, Pop. Ain't nobody gonna walk no two hundred miles. You talking about some walking there.

475 **Bono:**   That's the only way you got anywhere back in them days.

Lyons: Shhh. Damn if I wouldn't have hitched a ride with somebody!

Troy: Who you gonna hitch it with? They ain't got no cars and things like they got now. We talking about 1918.

Rose: *(entering)* What you all out here getting into?

Troy: *(to Rose)* I'm telling Lyons how good he got it. He don't know nothing about this I'm talking.

480 **Rose:**   Lyons, that was Bonnie on the phone. She say you supposed to pick her up.

Lyons: Yeah, okay, Rose.

Troy: I walked on down to Mobile and hitched up with some of them fellows that was heading this way. Got up here and found out . . . not only couldn't you get a job . . . you couldn't find no place to live. I thought I was in freedom. Shhh. Colored folks living down there on the riverbanks in whatever kind of shelter they could find for themselves. Right down there under the Brady Street Bridge. Living in shacks made of sticks and tarpaper. Messed around there and went from bad to worse. Started stealing. First it was food. Then I figured, hell, if I steal money I can buy me some food. Buy me some shoes too! One thing led to another. Met your mama. I was young and anxious to be a man. Met your mama and had you. What I do that for? Now I got to worry about feeding you and her. Got to steal three times as much. Went out one day looking for somebody to rob . . . that's what I was, a robber. I'll tell you the truth. I'm ashamed of it today. But it's the truth. Went to rob this fellow . . . pulled out my knife . . . and he pulled out a gun. Shot me in the chest. I felt just like somebody had taken a hot branding iron and laid it on me. When he shot me I jumped at him with my knife. They told me I killed him and they put me in the penitentiary and locked me up for fifteen years. That's where I met Bono. That's where I learned how to play baseball. Got out that place and your mama had taken you and went on to make life without me. Fifteen years was a long time for her to wait. But that fifteen years cured me of that robbing stuff.

---

14   City and seaport in southwestern Alabama.

Rose'll tell you. She asked me when I met her if I had gotten all that foolishness out of my system. And I told her, "Baby, it's you and baseball all what count with me." You hear me, Bono? I meant it too. She say, "Which one comes first?" I told her, "Baby, ain't no doubt it's baseball . . . but you stick and get old with me and we'll both outlive this baseball." Am I right, Rose? And it's true.

ROSE: Man, hush your mouth. You ain't said no such thing. Talking about "Baby, you know you'll always be number one with me." That's what you was talking.

TROY: You hear that, Bono. That's why I love her.

485 **BONO:** Rose'll keep you straight. You get off the track, she'll straighten you up.

ROSE: Lyons, you better get on up and get Bonnie. She waiting on you.

LYONS: *(gets up to go)* Hey, Pop, why don't you come on down to the Grill and hear me play?

TROY: I ain't going down there. I'm too old to be sitting around in them clubs.

BONO: You got to be good to play down at the Grill.

490 **LYONS:** Come on, Pop . . .

TROY: I got to get up in the morning.

LYONS: You ain't got to stay long.

TROY: Naw, I'm gonna get my supper and go on to bed.

LYONS: Well, I got to go. I'll see you again.

495 **TROY:** Don't you come around my house on my payday.

ROSE: Pick up the phone and let somebody know you coming. And bring Bonnie with you. You know I'm always glad to see her.

LYONS: Yeah, I'll do that, Rose. You take care now. See you, Pop. See you, Mr. Bono. See you, Uncle Gabe.

GABRIEL: Lyons! King of the Jungle!

Lyons exits.

TROY: Is supper ready, woman? Me and you got some business to take care of. I'm gonna tear it up too.

500 **ROSE:** Troy, I done told you now!

TROY: *(puts his arm around Bono)* Aw hell, woman . . . this is Bono. Bono like family. I done known this nigger since . . . how long I done know you?

BONO: It's been a long time.

TROY: I done know this nigger since Skippy was a pup. Me and him done been through some times.

BONO: You sure right about that.

505 **TROY:** Hell, I done know him longer than I known you. And we still standing shoulder to shoulder. Hey, look here, Bono . . . a man can't ask for no more than that. *(Drinks to him.)* I love you, nigger.

BONO: Hell, I love you too . . . I got to get home see my woman. You got yours in hand. I got to go get mine.

Bono starts to exit as Cory enters the yard, dressed in his football uniform. He gives Troy a hard, uncompromising look.

CORY: What you do that for, Pop?

He throws his helmet down in the direction of Troy.

ROSE: What's the matter? Cory . . . what's the matter?

CORY: Papa done went up to the school and told Coach Zellman I can't play football no more. Wouldn't even let me play the game. Told him to tell the recruiter not to come.

510 **ROSE:**   Troy . . .

TROY: What you Troying me for. Yeah, I did it. And the boy know why I did it.

CORY: Why you wanna do that to me? That was the one chance I had.

ROSE: Ain't nothing wrong with Cory playing football, Troy.

TROY: The boy lied to me. I told the nigger if he wanna play football . . . to keep up his chores and hold down that job at the A&P. That was the conditions. Stopped down there to see Mr. Stawicki . . .

515 **CORY:**   I can't work after school during the football season, Pop! I tried to tell you that Mr. Stawicki's holding my job for me. You don't never want to listen to nobody. And then you wanna go and do this to me!

TROY: I ain't done nothing to you. You done it to yourself.

CORY: Just cause you didn't have a chance! You just scared I'm gonna be better than you, that's all.

TROY: Come here.

ROSE: Troy . . .

Cory reluctantly crosses over to Troy.

520 **TROY:**   All right! See. You done made a mistake.

CORY: I didn't even do nothing!

TROY: I'm gonna tell you what your mistake was. See . . . you swung at the ball and didn't hit it. That's strike one. See, you in the batter's box now. You swung and you missed. That's strike one. Don't you strike out!

Lights fade to black.

ACT II

SCENE I

The following morning. Cory is at the tree hitting the ball with the bat. He tries to mimic Troy, but his swing is awkward, less sure. Rose enters from the house.

ROSE: Cory, I want you to help me with this cupboard.

CORY: I ain't quitting the team. I don't care what Poppa say.

ROSE: I'll talk to him when he gets back. He had to go see about your Uncle Gabe. The police done arrested him. Say he was disturbing the peace. He'll be back directly. Come on in here and help me clean out the top of this cupboard.

Cory exits into the house. Rose sees Troy and Bono coming down the alley.

Troy . . . what they say down there?

TROY: Ain't said nothing. I give them fifty dollars and they let him go. I'll talk to you about it. Where's Cory?

5 **ROSE:** He's in there helping me clean out these cupboards.

TROY: Tell him to get his butt out here.

Troy and Bono go over to the pile of wood. Bono picks up the saw and begins sawing.

TROY: *(to Bono)* All they want is the money. That makes six or seven times I done went down there and got him. See me coming they stick out their *hands.*

BONO: Yeah. I know what you mean. That's all they care about . . . that money. They don't care about what's right. *(Pause.)* Nigger, why you got to go and get some hard wood? You ain't doing nothing but building a little old fence. Get you some soft pine wood. That's all you need.

TROY: I know what I'm doing. This is outside wood. You put pine wood inside the house. Pine wood is inside wood. This here is outside wood. Now you tell me where the fence is gonna be?

10 **BONO:** You don't need this wood. You can put it up with pine wood and it'll stand as long as you gonna be here looking at it.

TROY: How you know how long I'm gonna be here, nigger? Hell, I might just live forever. Live longer than old man Horsely.

BONO: That's what Magee used to say.

TROY: Magee's a damn fool. Now you tell me who you ever heard of gonna pull their own teeth with a pair of rusty pliers.

BONO: The old folks . . . my granddaddy used to pull his teeth with pliers. They ain't had no dentists for the colored folks back then.

15 **TROY:** Get clean pliers! You understand? Clean pliers! Sterilize them! Besides we ain't living back then. All Magee had to do was walk over to Doc Goldblum's.

BONO: I see where you and that Tallahassee gal . . . that Alberta . . . I see where you all done got tight.

TROY: What you mean "got tight"?

BONO: I see where you be laughing and joking with her all the time.

TROY: I laughs and jokes with all of them, Bono. You know me.

20 **BONO:** That ain't the kind of laughing and joking I'm talking about.

Cory enters from the house.

CORY: How you doing, Mr. Bono?

TROY: Cory? Get that saw from Bono and cut some wood. He talking about the wood's too hard to cut. Stand back there, Jim, and let that young boy show you how it's done.

BONO: He's sure welcome to it.

Cory takes the saw and begins to cut the wood.

Whew-e-e! Look at that. Big old strong boy. Look like Joe Louis.[15] Hell, must be getting old the way I'm watching that boy whip through that wood.

CORY: I don't see why Mama want a fence around the yard noways.

25 **TROY:** Damn if I know either. What the hell she keeping out with it? She ain't got nothing nobody want.

BONO: Some people build fences to keep people out . . . and other people build fences to keep people in. Rose wants to hold on to you all. She loves you.

TROY: Hell, nigger, I don't need nobody to tell me my wife loves me. Cory . . . go on in the house and see if you can find that other saw.

CORY: Where's it at?

TROY: I said find it! Look for it till you find it!

Cory exits into the house.

What's that supposed to mean? Wanna keep us in?

30 **BONO:** Troy . . . I done known you seem like damn near my whole life. You and Rose both. I done know both of you all for a long time. I remember when you met Rose. When you was hitting them baseballs out the park. A lot of them gals was after you then. You had the pick of the litter. When you picked Rose, I was happy for you. That was the first time I knew you had any sense. I said . . . My man Troy knows what he's doing . . . I'm gonna follow this nigger . . . he might take me somewhere. I been following you too. I done learned a whole heap of things about life watching you. I done learned how to tell where the shit lies. How to tell it from the alfalfa. You done learned me a lot of things. You showed me how to not make the same mistakes . . . to take life as it comes along and keep putting one foot in front of the other. *(Pause.)* Rose a good woman, Troy.

TROY: Hell, nigger, I know she a good woman. I been married to her for eighteen years. What you got on your mind, Bono?

BONO: I just say she a good woman. Just like I say anything. I ain't got to have nothing on my mind.

TROY: You just gonna say she a good woman and leave it hanging out there like that? Why you telling me she a good woman?

---

15 Joseph Louis Barrow (1914–1981), known as "the Brown Bomber"; in 1937 became the youngest boxer ever to win the Heavyweight Championship, which he defended twenty-five times; retired undefeated in 1949.

BONO: She loves you, Troy. Rose loves you.

35 **TROY:** You saying I don't measure up. That's what you trying to say. I don't measure up cause I'm seeing this other gal. I know what you trying to say.

BONO: I know what Rose means to you, Troy. I'm just trying to say I don't want to see you mess up.

TROY: Yeah, I appreciate that, Bono. If you was messing around on Lucille I'd be telling you the same thing.

BONO: Well, that's all I got to say. I just say that because I love you both.

TROY: Hell, you know me . . . I wasn't out there looking for nothing. You can't find a better woman than Rose. I know that. But seems like this woman just stuck onto me where I can't shake her loose. I done wrestled with it, tried to throw her off me . . . but she just stuck on tighter. Now she's stuck on for good.

40 **BONO:** You's in control . . . that's what you tell me all the time. You responsible for what you do.

TROY: I ain't ducking the responsibility of it. As long as it sets right in my heart . . . then I'm okay. Cause that's all I listen to. It'll tell me right from wrong every time. And I ain't talking about doing Rose no bad turn. I love Rose. She done carried me a long ways and I love and respect her for that.

BONO: I know you do. That's why I don't want to see you hurt her. But what you gonna do when she find out? What you got then? If you try and juggle both of them . . . sooner or later you gonna drop one of them. That's common sense.

TROY: Yeah, I hear what you saying, Bono. I been trying to figure a way to work it out.

BONO: Work it out right, Troy. I don't want to be getting all up between you and Rose's business . . . but work it so it come out right.

45 **TROY:** Ah hell, I get all up between you and Lucille's business. When you gonna get that woman that refrigerator she been wanting? Don't tell me you ain't got no money now. I know who your banker is. Mellon don't need that money bad as Lucille want that refrigerator. I'll tell you that.

BONO: Tell you what I'll do . . . when you finish building this fence for Rose . . . I'll buy Lucille that refrigerator.

TROY: You done stuck your foot in your mouth now!

Troy grabs up a board and begins to saw. Bono starts to walk out the yard.

Hey, nigger . . . where you going?

BONO: I'm going home. I know you don't expect me to help you now. I'm protecting my money. I wanna see you put that fence up by yourself. That's what I want to see. You'll be here another six months without me.

TROY: Nigger, you ain't right.

50 **BONO:**   When it comes to my money . . . I'm right as fireworks on the
     Fourth of July.
  TROY: All right, we gonna see now. You better get out your bankbook.

Bono exits, and Troy continues to work. Rose enters from the house.

  ROSE: What they say down there? What's happening with Gabe?
  TROY: I went down there and got him out. Cost me fifty dollars. Say he
     was disturbing the peace. Judge set up a hearing for him in three
     weeks. Say to show cause why he shouldn't be recommitted.
  ROSE: What was he doing that cause them to arrest him?
55 **TROY:**   Some kids were teasing him and he run them off home. Say he
     was howling and carrying on. Some folks seen him and called the
     police. That's all it was.
  ROSE: Well, what's you say? What'd you tell the judge?
  TROY: Told him I'd look after him. It didn't make no sense to recommit
     the man. He stuck out his big greasy palm and told me to give him
     fifty dollars and take him on home.
  ROSE: Where's he at now? Where'd he go off to?
  TROY: He's gone about his business. He don't need nobody to hold his
     hand.
60 **ROSE:**   Well, I don't know. Seem like that would be the best place for
     him if they did put him into the hospital. I know what you're gonna
     say. But that's what I think would be best.
  TROY: The man done had his life ruined fighting for what? And they
     wanna take and lock him up. Let him be free. He don't bother
     nobody.
  ROSE: Well, everybody got their own way of looking at it I guess. Come
     on and get your lunch. I got a bowl of lima beans and some
     cornbread in the oven. Come and get something to eat. Ain't no sense
     you fretting over Gabe.

Rose turns to go into the house.

  TROY: Rose . . . got something to tell you.
  ROSE: Well, come on . . . wait till I get this food on the table.
65 **TROY:**   Rose!

She stops and turns around.

     I don't know how to say this. *(Pause.)* I can't explain it none. It just
     sort of grows on you till it gets out of hand. It starts out like a little
     bush . . . and the next thing you know it's a whole forest.
  ROSE: Troy . . . what is you talking about?
  TROY: I'm talking, woman, let me talk. I'm trying to find a way to tell
     you . . . I'm gonna be a daddy. I'm gonna be somebody's daddy.
  ROSE: Troy . . . you're not telling me this? You're gonna be . . . what?
  TROY: Rose . . . now . . . see . . .

70 **Rose:**   You telling me you gonna be somebody's daddy? You telling your
    wife this?

Gabriel enters from the street. He carries a rose in his hand.

Gabriel: Hey, Troy! Hey, Rose!
Rose: I have to wait eighteen years to hear something like this.
Gabriel: Hey, Rose . . . I got a flower for you. *(He hands it to her.)* That's
    a rose. Same rose like you is.
Rose: Thanks, Gabe.
75 **Gabriel:**   Troy, you ain't mad at me is you? Them bad mens come and
    put me away. You ain't mad at me is you?
Troy: Naw, Gabe, I ain't mad at you.
Rose: Eighteen years and you wanna come with this.
Gabriel: *(takes a quarter out of his pocket)* See what I got? Got a brand
    new quarter.
Troy: Rose . . . it's just . . .
80 **Rose:**   Ain't nothing you can say, Troy. Ain't no way of explaining that.
Gabriel: Fellow that give me this quarter had a whole mess of them.
    I'm gonna keep this quarter till it stop shining.
Rose: Gabe, go on in the house there. I got some watermelon in the
    Frigidaire. Go on and get you a piece.
Gabriel: Say, Rose . . . you know I was chasing hellhounds and them
    bad mens come and get me and take me away. Troy helped me. He
    come down there and told them they better let me go before he beat
    them up. Yeah, he did!
Rose: You go on and get you a piece of watermelon, Gabe. Them bad
    mens is gone now.
85 **Gabriel:**   Okay, Rose . . . gonna get me some watermelon. The kind
    with the stripes on it.

Gabriel exits into the house.

Rose: Why, Troy? Why? After all these years to come dragging this in
    to me now. It don't make no sense at your age. I could have expected
    this ten or fifteen years ago, but not now.
Troy: Age ain't got nothing to do with it, Rose.
Rose: I done tried to be everything a wife should be. Everything a wife
    could be. Been married eighteen years and I got to live to see the day
    you tell me you been seeing another woman and done fathered a
    child by her. And you know I ain't never wanted no half nothing in
    my family. My whole family is half. Everybody got different fathers
    and mothers . . . my two sisters and my brother. Can't hardly tell
    who's who. Can't never sit down and talk about Papa and Mama. It's
    your papa and your mama and my papa and my mama . . .
Troy: Rose . . . stop it now.
90 **Rose:**   I ain't never wanted that for none of my children. And now you
    wanna drag your behind in here and tell me something like this.

TROY: You ought to know. It's time for you to know.

ROSE: Well, I don't want to know, goddamn it!

TROY: I can't just make it go away. It's done now. I can't wish the circumstance of the thing away.

ROSE: And you don't want to either. Maybe you want to wish me and my boy away. Maybe that's what you want? Well, you can't wish us away. I've got eighteen years of my life invested in you. You ought to have stayed upstairs in my bed where you belong.

95 **TROY:** Rose . . . now listen to me . . . we can get a handle on this thing. We can talk this out . . . come to an understanding.

ROSE: All of a sudden it's "we." Where was "we" at when you was down there rolling around with some godforsaken woman? "We" should have come to an understanding before you started making a damn fool of yourself. You're a day late and a dollar short when it comes to an understanding with me.

TROY: It's just . . . She gives me a different idea . . . a different understanding about myself. I can step out of this house and get away from the pressures and problems . . . be a different man. I ain't got to wonder how I'm gonna pay the bills or get the roof fixed. I can just be a part of myself that I ain't never been.

ROSE: What I want to know . . . is do you plan to continue seeing her. That's all you can say to me.

TROY: I can sit up in her house and laugh. Do you understand what I'm saying. I can laugh out loud . . . and it feels good. It reaches all the way down to the bottom of my shoes. *(Pause.)* Rose, I can't give that up.

100 **ROSE:** Maybe you ought to go on and stay down there with her . . . if she's a better woman than me.

TROY: It ain't about nobody being a better woman or nothing. Rose, you ain't the blame. A man couldn't ask for no woman to be a better wife than you've been. I'm responsible for it. I done locked myself into a pattern trying to take care of you all that I forgot about myself.

ROSE: What the hell was I there for? That was my job, not somebody else's.

TROY: Rose, I done tried all my life to live decent . . . to live a clean . . . hard . . . useful life. I tried to be a good husband to you. In every way I knew how. Maybe I come into the world backwards, I don't know. But . . . you born with two strikes on you before you come to the plate. You got to guard it closely . . . always looking for the curve ball on the inside corner. You can't afford to let none get past you. You can't afford a call strike. If you going down . . . you going down swinging. Everything lined up against you. What you gonna do. I fooled them, Rose. I bunted. When I found you and Cory and a halfway decent job . . . I was safe. Couldn't nothing touch me. I wasn't gonna strike out no more. I wasn't going back to the penitentiary. I wasn't gonna lay in the streets with a bottle of wine.

I was safe. I had me a family. A job. I wasn't gonna get that last
strike. I was on first looking for one of them boys to knock me in. To
get me home.

ROSE: You should have stayed in my bed, Troy.

105 **TROY:** Then when I saw that gal . . . she firmed up my backbone. And I
got to thinking that if I tried . . . I just might be able to steal second.
Do you understand after eighteen years I wanted to steal second.

ROSE: You should have held me tight. You should have grabbed me and
held on.

TROY: I stood on first base for eighteen years and I thought . . . well,
goddamn it . . . go on for it!

ROSE: We're not talking about baseball! We're talking about you going
off to lay in bed with another woman . . . and then bring it home to
me. That's what we're talking about. We ain't talking about no
baseball.

TROY: Rose, you're not listening to me. I'm trying the best I can to
explain it to you. It's not easy for me to admit that I been standing
in the same place for eighteen years.

110 **ROSE:** I been standing with you! I been right here with you, Troy. I got
a life too. I gave eighteen years of my life to stand in the same spot
with you. Don't you think I ever wanted other things? Don't you
think I had dreams and hopes? What about my life? What about
me. Don't you think it ever crossed my mind to want to know other
men? That I wanted to lay up somewhere and forget about my
responsibilities? That I wanted someone to make me laugh so I could
feel good? You not the only one who's got wants and needs. But I
held on to you, Troy. I took all my feelings, my wants and needs, my
dreams . . . and I buried them inside you. I planted a seed and
watched and prayed over it. I planted myself inside you and waited to
bloom. And it didn't take me no eighteen years to find out the soil
was hard and rocky and it wasn't never gonna bloom.

But I held on to you, Troy. I held you tighter. You was my
husband. I owed you everything I had. Every part of me I could find
to give you. And upstairs in that room . . . with the darkness falling
in on me . . . I gave everything I had to try and erase the doubt
that you wasn't the finest man in the world. And wherever you was
going . . . I wanted to be there with you. Cause you was my husband.
Cause that's the only way I was gonna survive as your wife. You
always talking about what you give . . . and what you don't have to
give. But you take too. You take . . . and don't even know nobody's
giving!

Rose turns to exit into the house; Troy grabs her arm.

TROY: You say I take and don't give!

ROSE: Troy! You're hurting me!

TROY: You say I take and don't give!

Rose: Troy . . . you're hurting my arm! Let go!

115 **Troy:** I done give you everything I got. Don't you tell that lie on me.

Rose: Troy!

Troy: Don't you tell that lie on me!

Cory enters from the house.

Cory: Mama!

Rose: Troy. You're hurting me.

120 **Troy:** Don't you tell me about no taking and giving.

Cory comes up behind Troy and grabs him. Troy, surprised, is thrown off balance just as Cory throws a glancing blow that catches him on the chest and knocks him down. Troy is stunned, as is Cory.

Rose: Troy. Troy. No!

Troy gets to his feet and starts at Cory.

Troy . . . no. Please! Troy!

Rose pulls on Troy to hold him back. Troy stops himself.

Troy: *(to Cory)* All right. That's strike two. You stay away from around me, boy. Don't you strike out. You living with a full count. Don't you strike out.

Troy exits out the yard as the lights go down.

S C E N E I I

It is six months later, early afternoon. Troy enters from the house and starts to exit the yard. Rose enters from the house.

Rose: Troy, I want to talk to you.

Troy: All of a sudden, after all this time, you want to talk to me, huh? You ain't wanted to talk to me for months. You ain't wanted to talk to me last night. You ain't wanted no part of me then. What you wanna talk to me about now?

125 **Rose:** Tomorrow's Friday.

Troy: I know what day tomorrow is. You think I don't know tomorrow's Friday? My whole life I ain't done nothing but look to see Friday coming and you got to tell me it's Friday.

Rose: I want to know if you're coming home.

Troy: I always come home, Rose. You know that. There ain't never been a night I ain't come home.

Rose: That ain't what I mean . . . and you know it. I want to know if you're coming straight home after work.

130 **Troy:** I figure I'd cash my check . . . hang out at Taylors' with the boys . . . maybe play a game of checkers . . .

ROSE: Troy, I can't live like this. I won't live like this. You livin' on
borrowed time with me. It's been going on six months now you ain't
been coming home.

TROY: I be here every Friday. Every night of the year. That's 365 days.

ROSE: I want you to come home tomorrow after work.

TROY: Rose . . . I don't mess up my pay. You know that now. I take my
pay and I give it to you. I don't have no money but what you give me
back. I just want to have a little time to myself . . . a little time to
enjoy life.

135   **ROSE:**   What about me? When's my time to enjoy life?

TROY: I don't know what to tell you, Rose. I'm doing the best I can.

ROSE: You ain't been home from work but time enough to change your
clothes and run out . . . and you wanna call that the best you can do?

TROY: I'm going over to the hospital to see Alberta. She went into the
hospital this afternoon. Look like she might have the baby early. I
won't be gone long.

ROSE: Well, you ought to know. They went over to Miss Pearl's and got
Gabe today. She said you told them to go ahead and lock him up.

140   **TROY:**   I ain't said no such thing. Whoever told you that is telling a lie.
Pearl ain't doing nothing but telling a big fat lie.

ROSE: She ain't had to tell me. I read it on the papers.

TROY: I ain't told them nothing of the kind.

ROSE: I saw it right there on the papers.

TROY: What it say, huh?

145   **ROSE:**   It said you told them to take him.

TROY: Then they screwed that up, just the way they screw up
everything. I ain't worried about what they got on the paper.

ROSE: Say the government send part of his check to the hospital and the
other part to you.

TROY: I ain't got nothing to do with that if that's the way it works. I
ain't made up the rules about how it work.

ROSE: You did Gabe just like you did Cory. You wouldn't sign the paper
for Cory . . . but you signed for Gabe. You signed that paper.

The telephone is heard ringing inside the house.

150   **TROY:**   I told you I ain't signed nothing, woman! The only thing I signed
was the release form. Hell, I can't read. I don't know what they had
on that paper! I ain't signed nothing about sending Gabe away.

ROSE: I said sent him to the hospital . . . you said let him be free . . .
now you done went down there and signed him to the hospital for
half his money. You went back on yourself, Troy. You gonna have to
answer for that.

TROY: See now . . . you been over there talking to Miss Pearl. She done
got mad cause she ain't getting Gabe's rent money. That's all it is.
She's liable to say anything.

ROSE: Troy, I seen where you signed the paper.

TROY: You ain't seen nothing I signed. What she doing got papers on my brother anyway? Miss Pearl telling a big fat lie. And I'm gonna tell her about it too! You ain't seen nothing I signed. Say . . . you ain't seen nothing I signed.

Rose exits into the house to answer the telephone. Presently she returns.

155   **ROSE:**   Troy . . . that was the hospital. Alberta had the baby.
TROY: What she have? What is it?
ROSE: It's a girl.
TROY: I better get on down to the hospital to see her.
ROSE: Troy . . .
160   **TROY:**   Rose . . . I got to go see her now. That's only right . . . what's the matter . . . the baby's all right, ain't it?
ROSE: Alberta died having the baby.
TROY: Died . . . you say she's dead? Alberta's dead?
ROSE: They said they done all they could. They couldn't do nothing for her.
TROY: The baby? How's the baby?
165   **ROSE:**   They say it's healthy. I wonder who's gonna bury her.
TROY: She had family, Rose. She wasn't living in the world by herself.
ROSE: I know she wasn't living in the world by herself.
TROY: Next thing you gonna want to know if she had any insurance.
ROSE: Troy, you ain't got to talk like that.
170   **TROY:**   That's the first thing that jumped out your mouth. "Who's gonna bury her?" Like I'm fixing to take on that task for myself.
ROSE: I am your wife. Don't push me away.
TROY: I ain't pushing nobody away. Just give me some space. That's all. Just give me some room to breathe.

Rose exits into the house. Troy walks about the yard.

TROY: *(with a quiet rage that threatens to consume him)* All right . . . Mr. Death. See now . . . I'm gonna tell you what I'm gonna do. I'm gonna take and build me a fence around this yard. See? I'm gonna build me a fence around what belongs to me. And then I want you to stay on the other side. See? You stay over there until you're ready for me. Then you come on. Bring your army. Bring your sickle. Bring your wrestling clothes. I ain't gonna fall down on my vigilance this time. You ain't gonna sneak up on me no more. When you ready for me . . . when the top of your list say Troy Maxson . . . that's when you come around here. You come up and knock on the front door. Ain't nobody else got nothing to do with this. This is between you and me. Man to man. You stay on the other side of the fence until you ready for me. Then you come up and knock on the front door. Anytime you want. I'll be ready for you.

The lights go down to black.

SCENE III

The lights come up on the porch. It is late evening three days later. Rose sits listening to the ball game waiting for Troy. The final out of the game is made and Rose switches off the radio. Troy enters the yard carrying an infant wrapped in blankets. He stands back from the house and calls.

Rose enters and stands on the porch. There is a long, awkward silence, the weight of which grows heavier with each passing second.

TROY: Rose . . . I'm standing here with my daughter in my arms. She ain't but a wee bittie little old thing. She don't know nothing about grownups' business. She innocent . . . and she ain't got no mama.

175 **ROSE:**   What you telling me for, Troy?

She turns and exits into the house.

TROY: Well . . . I guess we'll just sit out here on the porch.

He sits down on the porch. There is an awkward indelicateness about the way he handles the baby. His largeness engulfs and seems to swallow it. He speaks loud enough for Rose to hear.

A man's got to do what's right for him. I ain't sorry for nothing I done. It felt right in my heart. *(To the baby.)* What you smiling at? Your daddy's a big man. Got these great big old hands. But sometimes he's scared. And right now your daddy's scared cause we sitting out here and ain't got no home. Oh, I been homeless before. I ain't had no little baby with me. But I been homeless. You just be out on the road by your lonesome and you see one of them trains coming and you just kinda go like this . . .

He sings a lullaby.

Please, Mr. Engineer let a man ride the line
Please, Mr. Engineer let a man ride the line
I ain't got no ticket please let me ride the blinds

Rose enters from the house. Troy, hearing her steps behind him, stands and faces her.

She's my daughter, Rose. My own flesh and blood. I can't deny her no more than I can deny them boys. *(Pause.)* You and them boys is my family. You and them and this child is all I got in the world. So I guess what I'm saying is . . . I'd appreciate it if you'd help me take care of her.

ROSE: Okay, Troy . . . you're right. I'll take care of your baby for you . . . cause . . . like you say . . . she's innocent . . . and you can't visit the sins of the father upon the child. A motherless child has got a hard time. *(She takes the baby from him.)* From right now . . . this child got a mother. But you a womanless man.

Rose turns and exits into the house with the baby. Lights go down to black.

SCENE IV
....

It is two months later. Lyons enters from the street. He knocks on the door and calls.

LYONS: Hey, Rose! *(Pause.)* Rose!

ROSE: *(from inside the house)* Stop that yelling. You gonna wake up Raynell. I just got her to sleep.

180 **LYONS:** I just stopped by to pay Papa this twenty dollars I owe him. Where's Papa at?

ROSE: He should be here in a minute. I'm getting ready to go down to the church. Sit down and wait on him.

LYONS: I got to go pick up Bonnie over her mother's house.

ROSE: Well, sit it down there on the table. He'll get it.

LYONS: *(enters the house and sets the money on the table)* Tell Papa I said thanks. I'll see you again.

185 **ROSE:** All right, Lyons. We'll see you.

Lyons starts to exit as Cory enters.

CORY: Hey, Lyons.

LYONS: What's happening, Cory? Say man, I'm sorry I missed your graduation. You know I had a gig and couldn't get away. Otherwise, I would have been there, man. So what you doing?

CORY: I'm trying to find a job.

LYONS: Yeah I know how that go, man. It's rough out there. Jobs are scarce.

190 **CORY:** Yeah, I know.

LYONS: Look here, I got to run. Talk to Papa . . . he know some people. He'll be able to help get you a job. Talk to him . . . see what he say.

CORY: Yeah . . . all right, Lyons.

LYONS: You take care. I'll talk to you soon. We'll find some time to talk.

Lyons exits the yard. Cory wanders over to the tree, picks up the bat, and assumes a batting stance. He studies an imaginary pitcher and swings. Dissatisfied with the result, he tries again. Troy enters. They eye each other for a beat. Cory puts the bat down and exits the yard. Troy starts into the house as Rose exits with Raynell. She is carrying a cake.

TROY: I'm coming in and everybody's going out.

195 **ROSE:** I'm taking this cake down to the church for the bake sale. Lyons was by to see you. He stopped by to pay you your twenty dollars. It's laying in there on the table.

TROY: *(going into his pocket)* Well . . . here go this money.

ROSE: Put it in there on the table, Troy. I'll get it.

TROY: What time you coming back?

ROSE: Ain't no use in you studying me. It don't matter what time I come back.

200 **TROY:** I just asked you a question, woman. What's the matter . . . can't I ask you a question?

ROSE: Troy, I don't want to go into it. Your dinner's in there on the stove. All you got to do is heat it up. And don't you be eating the rest of them cakes in there. I'm coming back for them. We having a bake sale at the church tomorrow.

Rose exits the yard. Troy sits down on the steps, takes a pint bottle from his pocket, opens it, and drinks. He begins to sing.

TROY: Hear it ring! Hear it ring!
    Had an old dog his name was Blue
    You know Blue was mighty true
    You know Blue was a good old dog
    Blue trees a possum in a hollow log
    You know from that he was a good old dog

Bono enters the yard.

BONO: Hey, Troy.
TROY: Hey, what's happening, Bono?
205 **BONO:**   I just thought I'd stop by to see you.
TROY: What you stop by and see me for? You ain't stopped by in a month of Sundays. Hell, I must owe you money or something.
BONO: Since you got your promotion I can't keep up with you. Used to see you every day. Now I don't even know what route you working.
TROY: They keep switching me around. Got me out in Greentree now . . . hauling white folks' garbage.
BONO: Greentree, huh? You lucky, at least you ain't got to be lifting them barrels. Damn if they ain't getting heavier. I'm gonna put in my two years and call it quits.
210 **TROY:**   I'm thinking about retiring myself.
BONO: You got it easy. You can *drive* for another five years.
TROY: It ain't the same, Bono. It ain't like working the back of the truck. Ain't got nobody to talk to . . . feel like you working by yourself. Naw, I'm thinking about retiring. How's Lucille?
BONO: She all right. Her arthritis get to acting up on her sometime. Saw Rose on my way in. She going down to the church, huh?
TROY: Yeah, she took up going down there. All them preachers looking for somebody to fatten their pockets. *(Pause.)* Got some gin here.
215 **BONO:**   Naw, thanks. I just stopped by to say hello.
TROY: Hell, nigger . . . you can take a drink. I ain't never known you to say no to a drink. You ain't got to work tomorrow.
BONO: I just stopped by. I'm fixing to go over to Skinner's. We got us a domino game going over his house every Friday.
TROY: Nigger, you can't play no dominoes. I used to whup you four games out of five.
BONO: Well, that learned me. I'm getting better.
220 **TROY:**   Yeah? Well, that's all right.
BONO: Look here . . . I got to be getting on. Stop by sometime, huh?

TROY: Yeah, I'll do that, Bono. Lucille told Rose you bought her a new refrigerator.

BONO: Yeah, Rose told Lucille you had finally built your fence . . . so I figured we'd call it even.

TROY: I knew you would.

225 **BONO:** Yeah . . . okay. I'll be talking to you.

TROY: Yeah, take care, Bono. Good to see you. I'm gonna stop over.

BONO: Yeah. Okay, Troy.

Bono exits. Troy drinks from the bottle.

TROY: Old Blue died and I dig his grave

Let him down with a golden chain
Every night when I hear old Blue bark
I know Blue treed a possum in Noah's Ark.
Hear it ring! Hear it ring!

Cory enters the yard. They eye each other for a beat. Troy is sitting in the middle of the steps. Cory walks over.

CORY: I got to get by.

230 **TROY:** Say what? What's you say?

CORY: You in my way. I got to get by.

TROY: You got to get by where? This is my house. Bought and paid for. In full. Took me fifteen years. And if you wanna go in my house and I'm sitting on the steps . . . you say excuse me. Like your mama taught you.

CORY: Come on, Pop . . . I got to get by.

Cory starts to maneuver his way past Troy. Troy grabs his leg and shoves him back.

TROY: You just gonna walk over top of me?

235 **CORY:** I live here too!

TROY: *(advancing toward him)* You just gonna walk over top of me in my own house?

CORY: I ain't scared of you.

TROY: I ain't asked if you was scared of me. I asked you if you was fixing to walk over top of me in my own house? That's the question. You ain't gonna say excuse me? You just gonna walk over top of me?

CORY: If you wanna put it like that.

240 **TROY:** How else am I gonna put it?

CORY: I was walking by you to go into the house cause you sitting on the steps drunk, singing to yourself. You can put it like that.

TROY: Without saying excuse me???

Cory doesn't respond.

I asked you a question. Without saying excuse me???

CORY: I ain't got to say excuse me to you. You don't count around here
no more.

TROY: Oh, I see . . . I don't count around here no more. You ain't got to
say excuse me to your daddy. All of a sudden you done got so grown
that your daddy don't count around here no more . . . Around here in
his own house and yard that he done paid for with the sweat of his
brow. You done got so grown to where you gonna take over. You
gonna take over my house. Is that right? You gonna wear my pants.
You gonna go in there and stretch out on my bed. You ain't got to say
excuse me cause I don't count around here no more. Is that right?

245   **CORY:**   That's right. You always talking this dumb stuff. Now, why don't
you just get out my way?

TROY: I guess you got someplace to sleep and something to put in your
belly. You got that, huh? You got that? That's what you need. You got
that, huh?

CORY: You don't know what I got. You ain't got to worry about what I
got.

TROY: You right! You one hundred percent right! I done spent the last
seventeen years worrying about what you got. Now it's your turn,
see? I'll tell you what to do. You grown . . . we done established that.
You a man. Now, let's see you act like one. Turn your behind around
and walk out this yard. And when you get out there in the alley . . .
you can forget about this house. See? Cause this is my house. You go
on and be a man and get your own house. You can forget about this.
Cause this is mine. You go on and get yours cause I'm through with
doing for you.

CORY: You talking about what you did for me . . . what'd you ever give
me?

250   **TROY:**   Them feet and bones! That pumping heart, nigger! I give you
more than anybody else is ever gonna give you.

CORY: You ain't never gave me nothing! You ain't never done nothing
but hold me back. Afraid I was gonna be better than you. All you ever
did was try and make me scared of you. I used to tremble every time
you called my name. Every time I heard your footsteps in the house.
Wondering all the time . . . what's Papa gonna say if I do this? . . .
What's he gonna say if I do that? . . . What's Papa gonna say if I turn
on the radio? And Mama, too . . . she tries . . . but she's scared of you.

TROY: You leave your mama out of this. She ain't got nothing to do
with this.

CORY: I don't know how she stand you . . . after what you did to her.

TROY: I told you to leave your mama out of this!

He advances toward Cory.

255   **CORY:**   What you gonna do . . . give me a whupping? You can't whup me
no more. You're too old. You just an old man.

TROY: *(shoves him on his shoulder)* Nigger! That's what you are. You just
another nigger on the street to me!

CORY: You crazy! You know that?

TROY: Go on now! You got the devil in you. Get on away from me!

CORY: You just a crazy old man . . . talking about I got the devil in me.

260 **TROY:** Yeah, I'm crazy! If you don't get on the other side of that yard . . . I'm gonna show you how crazy I am! Go on . . . get the hell out of my yard.

CORY: It ain't your yard. You took Uncle Gabe's money he got from the army to buy this house and then you put him out.

TROY: *(advances on Cory)* Get your black ass out of my yard!

Troy's advance backs Cory up against the tree. Cory grabs up the bat.

CORY: I ain't going nowhere! Come on . . . put me out! I ain't scared of you.

TROY: That's my bat!

265 **CORY:** Come on!

TROY: Put my bat down!

CORY: Come on, put me out.

Cory swings at Troy, who backs across the yard.

What's the matter? You so bad . . . put me out!

Troy advances toward Cory.

CORY: *(backing up)* Come on! Come on!

TROY: You're gonna have to use it! You wanna draw that bat back on me . . . you're gonna have to use it.

270 **CORY:** Come on! . . . Come on!

Cory swings the bat at Troy a second time. He misses. Troy continues to advance toward him.

TROY: You're gonna have to kill me! You wanna draw that bat back on me. You're gonna have to kill me.

Cory, backed up against the tree, can go no farther. Troy taunts him. He sticks out his head and offers him a target.

Come on! Come on!

Cory is unable to swing the bat. Troy grabs it.

TROY: Then I'll show you.

Cory and Troy struggle over the bat. The struggle is fierce and fully engaged. Troy ultimately is the stronger and takes the bat away from Cory and stands over him ready to swing. He stops himself.

Go on and get away from around my house.

Cory, stung by his defeat, picks himself up, walks slowly out of the yard and up the alley.

CORY: Tell Mama I'll be back for my things.

TROY: They'll be on the other side of that fence.

Cory exits.

275 **TROY:**   I can't taste nothing. Helluljah! I can't taste nothing no more.
(*Troy assumes a batting posture and begins to taunt Death, the fastball on
the outside corner.*) Come on! It's between you and me now! Come on!
Anytime you want! Come on! I be ready for you . . . but I ain't gonna
be easy.

The lights go down on the scene.

S C E N E   V

*The time is 1965. The lights come up in the yard. It is the morning of Troy's
funeral. A funeral plaque with a light hangs beside the door. There is a small
garden plot off to the side. There is noise and activity in the house as Rose,
Gabriel, and Bono have gathered. The door opens and Raynell, seven years old,
enters dressed in a flannel nightgown. She crosses to the garden and pokes
around with a stick. Rose calls from the house.*

ROSE: Raynell!
RAYNELL: Mam?
ROSE: What you doing out there?
RAYNELL: Nothing.

Rose comes to the door.

280 **ROSE:**   Girl, get in here and get dressed. What you doing?
RAYNELL: Seeing if my garden growed.
ROSE: I told you it ain't gonna grow overnight. You got to wait.
RAYNELL: It don't look like it never gonna grow. Dag!
ROSE: I told you a watched pot never boils. Get in here and get dressed.
285 **RAYNELL:**   This ain't even no pot, Mama.
ROSE: You just have to give it a chance. It'll grow. Now you come on
and do what I told you. We got to be getting ready. This ain't no
morning to be playing around. You hear me?
RAYNELL: Yes, mam.

*Rose exits into the house. Raynell continues to poke at her garden with a stick.
Cory enters. He is dressed in a Marine corporal's uniform, and carries a duffel
bag. His posture is that of a military man, and his speech has a clipped sternness.*

CORY: (*to Raynell*) Hi. (*Pause.*) I bet your name is Raynell.
RAYNELL: Uh huh.
290 **CORY:**   Is your mama home?

Raynell runs up on the porch and calls through the screen door.

RAYNELL: Mama . . . there's some man out here. Mama?

Rose comes to the door.

Rose: Cory? Lord have mercy! Look here, you all!

Rose and Cory embrace in a tearful reunion as Bono and Lyons enter from the house dressed in funeral clothes.

Bono: Aw, looka here . . .

Rose: Done got all grown up!

295 **Cory:** Don't cry, Mama. What you crying about?

Rose: I'm just so glad you made it.

Cory: Hey Lyons. How you doing, Mr. Bono.

Lyons goes to embrace Cory.

Lyons: Look at you, man. Look at you. Don't he look good, Rose. Got them Corporal stripes.

Rose: What took you so long?

300 **Cory:** You know how the Marines are, Mama. They got to get all their paperwork straight before they let you do anything.

Rose: Well, I'm sure glad you made it. They let Lyons come. Your Uncle Gabe's still in the hospital. They don't know if they gonna let him out or not. I just talked to them a little while ago.

Lyons: A Corporal in the United States Marines.

Bono: Your daddy knew you had it in you. He used to tell me all the time.

Lyons: Don't he look good, Mr. Bono?

305 **Bono:** Yeah, he remind me of Troy when I first met him. *(Pause.)* Say, Rose, Lucille's down at the church with the choir. I'm gonna go down and get the pallbearers lined up. I'll be back to get you all.

Rose: Thanks, Jim.

Cory: See you, Mr. Bono.

Lyons: *(with his arm around Raynell)* Cory . . . look at Raynell. Ain't she precious? She gonna break a whole lot of hearts.

Rose: Raynell, come and say hello to your brother. This is your brother, Cory. You remember Cory.

310 **Raynell:** No, Mam.

Cory: She don't remember me, Mama.

Rose: Well, we talk about you. She heard us talk about you. *(To Raynell.)* This is your brother, Cory. Come on and say hello.

Raynell: Hi.

Cory: Hi. So you're Raynell. Mama told me a lot about you.

315 **Rose:** You all come on into the house and let me fix you some breakfast. Keep up your strength.

Cory: I ain't hungry, Mama.

Lyons: You can fix me something, Rose. I'll be in there in a minute.

Rose: Cory, you sure you don't want nothing? I know they ain't feeding you right.

Cory: No, Mama . . . thanks. I don't feel like eating. I'll get something later.

320 **Rose:** Raynell . . . get on upstairs and get that dress on like I told you.

Rose and Raynell exit into the house.

LYONS: So . . . I hear you thinking about getting married.

CORY: Yeah, I done found the right one, Lyons. It's about time.

LYONS: Me and Bonnie been split up about four years now. About the time Papa retired. I guess she just got tired of all them changes I was putting her through. *(Pause.)* I always knew you was gonna make something out yourself. Your head was always in the right direction. So . . . you gonna stay in . . . make it a career . . . put in your twenty years?

CORY: I don't know. I got six already, I think that's enough.

325   **LYONS:** Stick with Uncle Sam and retire early. Ain't nothing out here. I guess Rose told you what happened with me. They got me down the workhouse. I thought I was being slick cashing other people's checks.

CORY: How much time you doing?

LYONS: They give me three years. I got that beat now. I ain't got but nine more months. It ain't so bad. You learn to deal with it like anything else. You got to take the crookeds with the straights. That's what Papa used to say. He used to say that when he struck out. I seen him strike out three times in a row . . . and the next time up he hit the ball over the grandstand. Right out there in Homestead Field. He wasn't satisfied hitting in the seats . . . he want to hit it over everything! After the game he had two hundred people standing around waiting to shake his hand. You got to take the crookeds with the straights. Yeah, Papa was something else.

CORY: You still playing?

LYONS: Cory . . . you know I'm gonna do that. There's some fellows down there we got us a band . . . we gonna try and stay together when we get out . . . but yeah, I'm still playing. It still helps me to get out of bed in the morning. As long as it do that I'm gonna be right there playing and trying to make some sense out of it.

330   **ROSE:** *(calling)* Lyons, I got these eggs in the pan.

LYONS: Let me go on and get these eggs, man. Get ready to go bury Papa. *(Pause.)* How you doing? You doing all right?

Cory nods. Lyons touches him on the shoulder and they share a moment of silent grief. Lyons exits into the house. Cory wanders about the yard. Raynell enters.

RAYNELL: Hi.

CORY: Hi.

RAYNELL: Did you used to sleep in my room?

335   **CORY:** Yeah . . . that used to be my room.

RAYNELL: That's what Papa call it. "Cory's room." It got your football in the closet.

Rose comes to the door.

ROSE: Raynell, get in there and get them good shoes on.

RAYNELL: Mama, can't I wear these? Them other ones hurt my feet.

ROSE: Well, they just gonna have to hurt your feet for a while. You ain't said they hurt your feet when you went down to the store and got them.

340 **RAYNELL:** They didn't hurt then. My feet done got bigger.

ROSE: Don't you give me no backtalk now. You get in there and get them shoes on.

Raynell exits into the house.

Ain't too much changed. He still got that piece of rag tied to that tree. He was out here swinging that bat. I was just ready to go back in the house. He swung that bat and then he just fell over. Seem like he swung it and stood there with this grin on his face . . . and then he just fell over. They carried him on down to the hospital, but I knew there wasn't no need . . . why don't you come on in the house?

CORY: Mama . . . I got something to tell you. I don't know how to tell you this . . . but I've got to tell you . . . I'm not going to Papa's funeral.

ROSE: Boy, hush your mouth. That's your daddy you talking about. I don't want hear that kind of talk this morning. I done raised you to come to this? You standing there all healthy and grown talking about you ain't going to your daddy's funeral?

CORY: Mama . . . listen . . .

345 **ROSE:** I don't want to hear it, Cory. You just get that thought out of your head.

CORY: I can't drag Papa with me everywhere I go. I've got to say no to him. One time in my life I've got to say no.

ROSE: Don't nobody have to listen to nothing like that. I know you and your daddy ain't seen eye to eye, but I ain't got to listen to that kind of talk this morning. Whatever was between you and your daddy . . . the time has come to put it aside. Just take it and set it over there on the shelf and forget about it. Disrespecting your daddy ain't gonna make you a man, Cory. You got to find a way to come to that on your own. Not going to your daddy's funeral ain't gonna make you a man.

CORY: The whole time I was growing up . . . living in his house . . . Papa was like a shadow that followed you everywhere. It weighed on you and sunk into your flesh. It would wrap around you and lay there until you couldn't tell which one was you anymore. That shadow digging in your flesh. Trying to crawl in. Trying to live through you. Everywhere I looked, Troy Maxson was staring back at me . . . hiding under the bed . . . in the closet. I'm just saying I've got to find a way to get rid of that shadow, Mama.

ROSE: You just like him. You got him in you good.

350 **CORY:** Don't tell me that, Mama.

ROSE: You Troy Maxson all over again.

CORY: I don't want to be Troy Maxson. I want to be me.

ROSE: You can't be nobody but who you are, Cory. That shadow wasn't nothing but you growing into yourself. You either got to grow into it or cut it down to fit you. But that's all you got to make life with. That's all you got to measure yourself against that world out there. Your daddy wanted you to be everything he wasn't . . . and at the same time he tried to make you into everything he was. I don't know if he was right or wrong . . . but I do know he meant to do more good than he meant to do harm. He wasn't always right. Sometimes when he touched he bruised. And sometimes when he took me in his arms he cut.

When I first met your daddy I thought . . . Here is a man I can lay down with and make a baby. That's the first thing I thought when I seen him. I was thirty years old and had done seen my share of men. But when he walked up to me and said, "I can dance a waltz that'll make you dizzy." I thought, Rose Lee, here is a man that you can open yourself up to and be filled to bursting. Here is a man that can fill all them empty spaces you been tipping around the edges of. One of them empty spaces was being somebody's mother.

I married your daddy and settled down to cooking his supper and keeping clean sheets on the bed. When your daddy walked through the house he was so big he filled it up. That was my first mistake. Not to make him leave some room for me. For my part in the matter. But at that time I wanted that. I wanted a house that I could sing in. And that's what your daddy gave me. I didn't know to keep up his strength I had to give up little pieces of mine. I did that. I took on his life as mine and mixed up the pieces so that you couldn't hardly tell which was which anymore. It was my choice. It was my life and I didn't have to live it like that. But that's what life offered me in the way of being a woman and I took it. I grabbed hold of it with both hands.

By the time Raynell came into the house, me and your daddy had done lost touch with one another. I didn't want to make my blessing off of nobody's misfortune . . . but I took on to Raynell like she was all them babies I had wanted and never had.

The phone rings.

Like I'd been blessed to relive a part of my life. And if the Lord see fit to keep up my strength . . . I'm gonna do her just like your daddy did you . . . I'm gonna give her the best of what's in me.

RAYNELL: *(entering, still with her old shoes)* Mama . . . Reverend Tollivier on the phone.

Rose exits into the house.

355 **RAYNELL:** Hi.

CORY: Hi.

RAYNELL: You in the Army or the Marines?

CORY: Marines.

RAYNELL: Papa said it was the Army. Did you know Blue?

360 **CORY:**   Blue? Who's Blue?

RAYNELL: Papa's dog what he sing about all the time.

CORY: *(singing)* Hear it ring! Hear it ring!
I had a dog his name was Blue
You know Blue was mighty true
You know Blue was a good old dog
Blue treed a possum in a hollow log
You know from that he was a good old dog.
Hear it ring! Hear it ring!

Raynell joins in singing.

CORY and **RAYNELL:**   Blue treed a possum out on a limb
Blue looked at me and I looked at him
Grabbed that possum and put him in a sack
Blue stayed there till I came back
Old Blue's feets was big and round
Never allowed a possum to touch the ground.

Old Blue died and I dug his grave
I dug his grave with a silver spade
Let him down with a golden chain
And every night I call his name
Go on Blue, you good dog you
Go on Blue, you good dog you

RAYNELL: Blue laid down and died like a man
Blue laid down and died . . .

365 **BOTH:**   Blue laid down and died like a man
Now he's treeing possums in the Promised Land
I'm gonna tell you this to let you know
Blue's gone where the good dogs go
When I hear old Blue bark
When I hear old Blue bark
Blue treed a possum in Noah's Ark[16]
Blue treed a possum in Noah's Ark.

Rose comes to the screen door.

ROSE: Cory, we gonna be ready to go in a minute.

CORY: *(to Raynell)* You go on in the house and change them shoes like
Mama told you so we can go to Papa's funeral.

RAYNELL: Okay, I'll be back.

*Raynell exits into the house. Cory gets up and crosses over to the tree. Rose
stands in the screen door watching him. Gabriel enters from the alley.*

GABRIEL: *(calling)* Hey, Rose!

---

16 See Genesis 6: 14–20.

370 **ROSE:** Gabe?

GABRIEL: I'm here, Rose. Hey Rose, I'm here!

Rose enters from the house.

ROSE: Lord . . . Look here, Lyons!

LYONS: See, I told you, Rose . . . I told you they'd let him come.

CORY: How you doing, Uncle Gabe?

375 **LYONS:** How you doing, Uncle Gabe?

GABRIEL: Hey, Rose. It's time. It's time to tell St. Peter to open the gates. Troy, you ready? You ready, Troy. I'm gonna tell St. Peter to open the gates. You get ready now.

Gabriel, with great fanfare, braces himself to blow. The trumpet is without a mouthpiece. He puts the end of it into his mouth and blows with great force, like a man who has been waiting some twenty-odd years for this single moment. No sound comes out of the trumpet. He braces himself and blows again with the same result. A third time he blows. There is a weight of impossible description that falls away and leaves him bare and exposed to a frightful realization. It is a trauma that a sane and normal mind would be unable to withstand. He begins to dance. A slow, strange dance, eerie and life-giving. A dance of atavistic signature and ritual. Lyons attempts to embrace him. Gabriel pushes Lyons away. He begins to howl in what is an attempt at song, or perhaps a song turning back into itself in an attempt at speech. He finishes his dance and the gates of heaven stand open as wide as God's closet.

That's the way that go!

READING AND REACTING

1. Obviously, fences are a central metaphor of the play. To what different kinds of fences does the play's title refer?

2. In what ways are the fathers and sons in the play alike? In what ways are they different? Does the play imply that sons must inevitably follow in their fathers' footsteps, or does it suggest that they can go their own way?

3. What purpose does the section of the stage directions entitled "the play" serve? How does it prepare readers for the events to follow?

4. What is the significance of the fact that the play is set in 1957? Given the racial climate of the country at that time, how realistic are Cory's ambitions? How reasonable are his father's criticisms?

5. What events in the play refer specifically to the African-American experience in the United States? In what ways has Troy's character been shaped by his contact with the white world?

6. Is Troy a tragic hero? If so, what is his flaw?

7. Which of the play's characters, if any, do you consider to be stereotypes? What comment do you think the play makes about stereotypes?

8. In what ways does the conflict between Troy and his son reflect conflicts within the contemporary African-American community? Does the play suggest any possibilities for compromise?

9. With which characters do you sympathize? Which do you dislike? Why?

10. Would you consider the primary message of this play to be optimistic or pessimistic? Explain your conclusion.

11. **JOURNAL ENTRY** How would the play be different if all the characters were white? What would be the same?

12. **CRITICAL PERSPECTIVE** Theater critic Robert Brustein has criticized Wilson on the ground that "his recurrent theme is the familiar American charge of victimization"; in *Fences,* he argues, "Wilson's larger purpose depends on his conviction that Troy's potential was stunted not [by] 'his own behavior' but by centuries of racist oppression." However, Lloyd Richards, the director of the original production, characterizes the theme of the play in less extreme terms: "Chance and the color of one's skin, chance again, can tip the balance. 'You've got to take the crooked with the straight.'"

   Do you think that Wilson intends Troy Maxson to be seen simply as a victim of racism? Or do you find greater complexity in the development of this character?

WRITING SUGGESTIONS: THEME

1. Both *Antigone* and *Another Antigone* deal with the theme of obedience to authority: Antigone is executed for defying Creon's orders, and Judy is punished for refusing to rewrite a term paper for a course. Write an essay in which you discuss your ideas about obedience to authority. Be specific, and use examples from your own experience as well as from at least one of the two plays to support your points.

2. In an interview John Tillinger, who directed *Another Antigone,* said that Gurney "worried that some theatergoers might . . . see the heroine as simply a stereotype of an aggressive young Jewish-American woman." Write an essay in which you discuss whether or not Gurney's concerns are justified.

3. Write an essay in which you analyze how baseball images are developed throughout *Fences.* Keep in mind that a bat and a rag ball hang in the yard and that Wilson mentions the 1957 Milwaukee Braves in his stage notes to the play. (If you wish, you can compare the role of sports in *Fences* and *Death of a Salesman.*)

4. Write an essay in which you discuss how Antigone and Creon change in *Antigone.* What does the change or lack of change in these characters contribute to the development of the theme of the play?

5. Although *Crimes of the Heart* examines some serious problems, it also contains a good deal of humor. Identify some of the humorous moments in the play, and write an essay in which you discuss how they help to communicate the play's major theme.

Drama Casebook

This section contains the play *The Glass Menagerie* by Tennessee Williams, a collection of source materials,* twelve questions to stimulate discussion and writing, and a student paper.

Source Materials

◆ Williams, Tennessee. "Author's Production Notes." *The Glass Menagerie.* New York: Random, 1945. The preface to the published edition of *The Glass Menagerie.* (p. 1947)

◆ Excerpts from Three Memoirs:

Williams, Edwina Dakin. *Remember Me to Tom.* New York: Putnam's, 1963. A memoir written by Tennessee Williams's mother. (p. 1949)

Williams, Tennessee. *Tennessee Williams: Memoirs.* New York: Doubleday, 1975. A memoir written by the playwright. (p. 1951)

Williams, Dakin, and Shepherd Meade. *Tennessee Williams: An Intimate Biography.* New York: Arbor House, 1983. A memoir written by the playwright's brother and a personal friend. (p. 1954)

◆ Excerpts from Two Interviews with Williams:

Evans, Jean. "Interview 1945." *New York PM* (1945). A magazine interview with Tennessee Williams conducted during the initial New York run of *The Glass Menagerie.* (p. 1955)

Wager, Walter. "Tennessee Williams." *The Playwrights Speak.* New York: Delacorte Press, 1967. A later interview with Tennessee Williams. (p. 1956)

◆ Boxill, Robert. "The Glass Menagerie." *Tennessee Williams.* New York: St. Martin's: 1987. A section of a book in which the author discusses the historical and political background of *The Glass Menagerie.* (p. 1956)

---

* Note that the Scanlan article does not use the parenthetical style recommended by the most recent guidelines set by the Modern Language Association and explained in Appendix A of this text.

♦ King, Thomas L. "Irony and Distance in *The Glass Menagerie.*" *Educational Theatre Journal* 25.2 (May 1973): 85–94. An article that discusses the importance of Tom's soliloquies.   (p. 1962)

♦ Scanlan, Tom. "Family, Drama, and American Dreams." *Reactions II: Tennessee Williams.* New York: Greenwood, 1978. A discussion of the portrayal of family life in *The Glass Menagerie.*   (p. 1970)

♦ Williams, Tennessee. "Portrait of a Girl in Glass." *Collected Stories.* New Directions, 1985. A 1943 short story that was later developed into *The Glass Menagerie.*   (p. 1978)

Each of the sources offers insights into *The Glass Menagerie* that can help you to understand, enjoy, and perhaps write about it. In preparation for writing an essay on a topic of your choice about *The Glass Menagerie,* read the play and the accompanying source materials. After doing so, explore— in your journal, in group discussions, or in brainstorming notes—the possibilities suggested by the questions on page 2015. Keep in mind the ideas expressed in the critical articles, memoirs, short story, and interviews as well as those in the play itself. Your goal is to decide on a topic you can develop in a three- to five-page essay. For guidelines on evaluating literary criticism, see page 14; for guidelines on using source materials, see page 34. Remember to document any words or ideas you borrow from the play or from any other source. See Appendix A for information about documentation style.

A complete student paper, "Laura's Gentleman Caller," based on the source materials in this casebook, begins on p. 2017.

TENNESSEE WILLIAMS (1911–1983) was born in Columbus, Mississippi, but moved to St. Louis, the setting of *The Glass Menagerie,* when he was eight. He became interested in playwriting while at college, eventually graduating from the University of Iowa in 1938. Christened Thomas Lanier Williams, he began to publish under the name Tennessee in 1939. His plays include *A Streetcar Named Desire* (1947), *Cat on a Hot Tin Roof* (1955), *Night of the Iguana* (1961), and *Sweet Bird of Youth* (1959).

The Glass Menagerie (1945) was his first major success, winning the New York Drama Critics Circle award and freeing him to write plays full-time. *The Glass Menagerie* was written partly at Provincetown,

Massachusetts, the site of Susan Glaspell's theater company, and partly while Williams was working as a Hollywood screenwriter. Williams saw the play as somewhat autobiographical: He said his sister Rose had a collection of glass animals in her room in St. Louis, and he gives his real first name to Tom, Laura's brother in the play. When the first movie version of the play was made, it was altered to include a second, more promising Gentleman Caller at its conclusion, giving it a happy ending; to the end of his life, Williams regretted the change.

TENNESSEE WILLIAMS

The Glass Menagerie

(1945)

Nobody, not even the rain, has such small hands.

E. E. CUMMINGS

CHARACTERS

AMANDA WINGFIELD, *the mother. A little woman of great but confused vitality clinging frantically to another time and place. Her characterization must be carefully created, not copied from type. She is not paranoiac, but her life is paranoia. There is much to admire in Amanda, and as much to love and pity as there is to laugh at. Certainly she has endurance and a kind of heroism, and though her foolishness makes her unwittingly cruel at times, there is tenderness in her slight person.*

LAURA WINGFIELD, *her daughter. Amanda, having failed to establish contact with reality, continues to live vitally in her illusions, but Laura's situation is even graver. A childhood illness has left her crippled, one leg slightly shorter than the other, and held in a brace. This defect need not be more than suggested on the stage. Stemming from this, Laura's separation increases till she is like a piece of her own glass collection, too exquisitely fragile to move from the shelf.*

TOM WINGFIELD, *her son. And the narrator of the play. A poet with a job in a warehouse. His nature is not remorseless, but to escape from a trap he has to act without pity.*

JIM O'CONNOR, *the gentleman caller. A nice, ordinary, young man.*

Scene.
An alley in St. Louis.

Part I.
Preparation for a Gentleman Caller.

Part II.
The Gentleman Calls.

Time.
Now and the Past.

SCENE I

The Wingfield apartment is in the rear of the building, one of those vast hive-like conglomerations of cellular living-units that flower as warty growths in over-crowded urban centers of lower middle-class population and are symptomatic of the impulse of this largest and fundamentally enslaved section of American society to avoid fluidity and differentiation and to exist and function as one interfused mass of automatism.

The apartment faces an alley and is entered by a fire-escape, a structure whose name is a touch of accidental poetic truth, for all of these huge buildings are always burning with the slow and implacable fires of human desperation. The fire-escape is included in the set—that is, the landing of it and steps descending from it.

The scene is memory and is therefore nonrealistic. Memory takes a lot of poetic license. It omits some details; others are exaggerated, according to the emotional value of the articles it touches, for memory is seated predominantly in the heart. The interior is therefore rather dim and poetic.

At the rise of the curtain, the audience is faced with the dark, grim rear wall of the Wingfield tenement. This building, which runs parallel to the footlights, is flanked on both sides by dark, narrow alleys which run into murky canyons of tangled clotheslines, garbage cans and the sinister latticework of neighboring fire-escapes. It is up and down these side alleys that exterior entrances and exits are made, during the play. At the end of Tom's opening commentary, the dark tenement wall slowly reveals (by means of a transparency) the interior of the ground floor Wingfield apartment.

Downstage is the living room, which also serves as a sleeping room for Laura, the sofa unfolding to make her bed. Upstage, center, and divided by a wide arch or second proscenium with transparent faded portieres (or second curtain), is the dining room. In an old-fashioned what-not in the living room are seen scores of transparent glass animals. A blown-up photograph of the father hangs on the wall of the living room, facing the audience, to the left of the archway. It is the face of a very handsome young man in a doughboy's First World War cap. He is gallantly smiling, ineluctably smiling, as if to say, "I will be smiling forever."

The audience hears and sees the opening scene in the dining room through both the transparent fourth wall of the building and the transparent gauze portieres of the dining-room arch. It is during this revealing scene that the fourth wall slowly ascends, out of sight. This transparent exterior wall is not brought down again until the very end of the play, during Tom's final speech.

The narrator is an undisguised convention of the play. He takes whatever license with dramatic convention as is convenient to his purposes.

Tom enters dressed as a merchant sailor from the alley, stage left, and strolls across the front of the stage to the fire-escape. There he stops and lights a cigarette. He addresses the audience.

Tom: Yes, I have tricks in my pocket, I have things up my sleeve. But I am the opposite of a stage magician. He gives you illusion that has the appearance of truth. I give you truth in the pleasant disguise of illusion. To begin with, I turn back time. I reverse it to that quaint period, the thirties, when the huge middle class of America was matriculating in a school for the blind. Their eyes had failed them, or they had failed their eyes, and so they were having their fingers pressed forcibly down on the fiery Braille alphabet of a dissolving economy. In Spain there was revolution.[1] Here there was only shouting and confusion. In Spain there was Guernica.[2] Here there were disturbances of labor, sometimes pretty violent, in otherwise peaceful cities such as Chicago, Cleveland, Saint Louis. . . . This is the social background of the play.

(Music.)

The play is memory. Being a memory play, it is dimly lighted, it is sentimental, it is not realistic. In memory everything seems to happen to music. That explains the fiddle in the wings. I am the narrator of the play, and also a character in it. The other characters are my mother, Amanda, my sister, Laura, and a gentleman caller who appears in the final scenes. He is the most realistic character in the play, being an emissary from a world of reality that we were somehow set apart from. But since I have a poet's weakness for symbols, I am using this character also as a symbol; he is the long delayed but always expected something that we live for. There is a fifth character in the play who doesn't appear except in this larger-than-life photograph over the mantel. This is our father who left us a long time ago. He was a telephone man who fell in love with long distances; he gave up his job with the telephone company and skipped the light fantastic out of town . . . The last we heard of him was a picture post-card from Mazatlan, on the Pacific coast of Mexico, containing a message of two words—"Hello—Good-bye!" and an address. I think the rest of the play will explain itself. . . .

Amanda's voice becomes audible through the portieres.

(Legend On Screen: "Où Sont Les Neiges.")[3]

He divides the portieres and enters the upstage area.

   Amanda and Laura are seated at a drop-leaf table. Eating is indicated by gestures without food or utensils. Amanda faces the audience. Tom and Laura are seated in profile.

---

[1]   The Spanish Civil War (1936–1939).

[2]   A Basque town in northern Spain, bombed and virtually destroyed on April 27, 1937 by German planes aiding fascist General Francisco Franco's Nationalists. The destruction is depicted in one of Pablo Picasso's most famous paintings, *Guernica* (1937).

[3]   "Where are the snows [of yesteryear]." A famous line by French poet François Villon (1431–1463?).

The interior has lit up softly and through the scrim we see Amanda and Laura seated at the table in the upstage area.

AMANDA: *(calling)* Tom?

TOM: Yes, Mother.

AMANDA: We can't say grace until you come to the table!

5 **TOM:**   Coming, Mother. *(He bows slightly and withdraws, reappearing a few moments later in his place at the table.)*

AMANDA: *(to her son)* Honey, don't *push* with your *fingers*. If you have to push with something, the thing to push with is a crust of bread. And chew—chew! Animals have sections in their stomachs which enable them to digest food without mastication, but human beings are supposed to chew their food before they swallow it down. Eat food leisurely, son, and really enjoy it. A well-cooked meal has lots of delicate flavors that have to be held in the mouth for appreciation. So chew your food and give your salivary glands a chance to function!

Tom deliberately lays his imaginary fork down and pushes his chair back from the table.

TOM: I haven't enjoyed one bite of this dinner because of your constant directions on how to eat it. It's you that makes me rush through meals with your hawk-like attention to every bite I take. Sickening—spoils my appetite—all this discussion of animals' secretion—salivary glands— mastication!

AMANDA: *(lightly)* Temperament like a Metropolitan star! *(He rises and crosses downstage.)* You're not excused from the table.

TOM: I am getting a cigarette.

10 **AMANDA:**   You smoke too much.

Laura rises.

LAURA: I'll bring in the blanc mange.

He remains standing with his cigarette by the portieres during the following.

AMANDA: *(rising)* No, sister, no, sister—you be the lady this time and I'll be the darky.

LAURA: I'm already up.

AMANDA: Resume your seat, little sister—I want you to stay fresh and pretty—for gentlemen callers!

15 **LAURA:**   I'm not expecting any gentlemen callers.

AMANDA: *(crossing out to kitchenette. Airily)* Sometimes they come when they are least expected! Why, I remember one Sunday afternoon in Blue Mountain—*(Enters kitchenette.)*

TOM: I know what's coming!

LAURA: Yes. But let her tell it.

TOM: Again?

20 **LAURA:**   She loves to tell it.

Amanda returns with bowl of dessert.

AMANDA: One Sunday afternoon in Blue Mountain—your mother received—
seventeen!—gentlemen callers! Why, sometimes there weren't chairs
enough to accommodate them all. We had to send the nigger over to
bring in folding chairs from the parish house.

TOM: *(remaining at portieres)* How did you entertain those gentlemen
callers?

AMANDA: I understood the art of conversation!

TOM: I bet you could talk.

25 **AMANDA:** Girls in those days *knew* how to talk, I can tell you.

TOM: Yes?

(Image: Amanda As A Girl On A Porch Greeting Callers.)

AMANDA: They knew how to entertain their gentlemen callers. It wasn't
enough for a girl to be possessed of a pretty face and a graceful figure—
although I wasn't slighted in either respect. She also needed to have a
nimble wit and a tongue to meet all occasions.

TOM: What did you talk about?

AMANDA: Things of importance going on in the world! Never anything
coarse or common or vulgar. *(She addresses Tom as though he were seated
in the vacant chair at the table though he remains by portieres. He plays this
scene as though he held the book.)* My callers were gentlemen—all! Among
my callers were some of the most prominent young planters of the
Mississippi Delta—planters and sons of planters!

*Tom motions for music and a spot of light on Amanda. Her eyes lift, her face glows,
her voice becomes rich and elegiac.*

(Screen Legend: "Où Sont Les Neiges.")

There was young Champ Laughlin who later became vice-president of the
Delta Planters Bank. Hadley Stevenson who was drowned in Moon Lake
and left his widow one hundred and fifty thousand in Government
bonds. There were the Cutrere brothers, Wesley and Bates. Bates was one
of my bright particular beaux! He got in a quarrel with that wild
Wainright boy. They shot it out on the floor of Moon Lake Casino. Bates
was shot through the stomach. Died in the ambulance on his way to
Memphis. His widow was also well-provided for, came into eight or ten
thousand acres, that's all. She married him on the rebound—never loved
her—carried my picture on him the night he died! And there was that
boy that every girl in the Delta had set her cap for! That beautiful,
brilliant young Fitzhugh boy from Green County!

30 **TOM:** What did he leave his widow?

AMANDA: He never married! Gracious, you talk as though all of my old
admirers had turned up their toes to the daisies!

TOM: Isn't this the first you mentioned that still survives?

AMANDA: That Fitzhugh boy went North and made a fortune—came to be
known as the Wolf of Wall Street! He had the Midas touch, whatever he

touched turned to gold! And I could have been Mrs. Duncan J. Fitzhugh,
mind you! But—I picked your *father!*

LAURA: *(rising)* Mother, let me clear the table.

35 **AMANDA:**   No dear, you go in front and study your typewriter chart. Or
practice your shorthand a little. Stay fresh and pretty!—It's almost time
for our gentlemen callers to start arriving. *(She flounces girlishly toward the
kitchenette.)* How many do you suppose we're going to entertain this
afternoon?

Tom throws down the paper and jumps up with a groan.

LAURA: *(alone in the dining room)* I don't believe we're going to receive any,
Mother.

AMANDA: *(reappearing, airily)* What? No one—not one? You must be
joking! *(Laura nervously echoes her laugh. She slips in a fugitive manner
through the half-open portieres and draws them gently behind her. A shaft
of very clear light is thrown on her face against the faded tapestry of the
curtains.) (Music: "The Glass Menagerie" under faintly.) (Lightly.)* Not one
gentleman caller? It can't be true! There must be a flood, there must
have been a tornado!

LAURA: It isn't a flood, it's not a tornado, Mother. I'm just not popular like
you were in Blue Mountain. . . . *(Tom utters another groan. Laura glances
at him with a faint, apologetic smile. Her voice catching a little.)* Mother's
afraid I'm going to be an old maid.

(The Scene Dims Out With "Glass Menagerie" Music.)

SCENE II
....

"Laura, Haven't You Ever Liked Some Boy?"
    On the dark stage the screen is lighted with the image of blue roses.
    Gradually Laura's figure becomes apparent and the screen goes out.
    The music subsides.
    Laura is seated in the delicate ivory chair at the small clawfoot table.
    *She wears a dress of soft violet material for a kimono—her hair tied back from
her forehead with a ribbon.*
    She is washing and polishing her collection of glass.
    *Amanda appears on the fire-escape steps. At the sound of her ascent, Laura
catches her breath, thrusts the bowl of ornaments away and seats herself stiffly
before the diagram of the typewriter keyboard as though it held her spellbound.
Something has happened to Amanda. It is written in her face as she climbs to the
landing: a look that is grim and hopeless and a little absurd.*
    *She has on one of those cheap or imitation velvety-looking cloth coats with
imitation fur collar. Her hat is five or six years old, one of those dreadful cloch
hats that were worn in the late twenties, and she is clasping an enormous black*

patent-leather pocketbook with nickel clasp and initials. This is her fulldress outfit, the one she usually wears to the D.A.R.[4]

Before entering she looks through the door.

She purses her lips, opens her eyes wide, rolls them upward and shakes her head.

Then she slowly lets herself in the door. Seeing her mother's expression Laura touches her lips with a nervous gesture.

LAURA: Hello, Mother, I was—*(She makes a nervous gesture toward the chart on the wall. Amanda leans against the shut door and stares at Laura with a martyred look.)*

AMANDA: Deception? Deception? *(She slowly removes her hat and gloves, continuing the swift suffering stare. She lets the hat and gloves fall on the floor—a bit of acting.)*

LAURA: *(shakily)* How was the D.A.R. meeting? *(Amanda slowly opens her purse and removes a dainty white handkerchief which she shakes out delicately and delicately touches to her lips and nostrils.)* Didn't you go to the D.A.R. meeting, Mother?

AMANDA: *(faintly, almost inaudibly)*—No.—No. *(Then more forcibly.)* I did not have the strength—to go the D.A.R. In fact, I did not have the courage! I wanted to find a hole in the ground and hide myself in it forever! *(She crosses slowly to the wall and removes the diagram of the typewriter keyboard. She holds it in front of her for a second, staring at it sweetly and sorrowfully—then bites her lips and tears it in two pieces.)*

5 **LAURA:** *(faintly)* Why did you do that, Mother? *(Amanda repeats the same procedure with the chart of the Gregg Alphabet.)* Why are you—

AMANDA: Why? Why? How old are you, Laura?

LAURA: Mother, you know my age.

AMANDA: I thought that you were an adult; it seems that I was mistaken. *(She crosses slowly to the sofa and sinks down and stares at Laura.)*

LAURA: Please don't stare at me, Mother.

Amanda closes her eyes and lowers her head. Count ten.

10 **AMANDA:** What are we going to do, what is going to become of us, what is the future?

Count ten.

LAURA: Has something happened, Mother? *(Amanda draws a long breath and takes out the handkerchief again. Dabbing process.)* Mother, has—something happened?

AMANDA: I'll be all right in a minute. I'm just bewildered—*(count five)*—by life. . . .

---

[4] The Daughters of the American Revolution, an organization for female descendants of participants in the American Revolution, founded in 1890. That Amanda is a member says much about her concern with the past, as well as about her pride and affectations.

LAURA: Mother, I wish that you would tell me what's happened.

AMANDA: As you know, I was supposed to be inducted into my office at the D.A.R. this afternoon. *(Image: A Swarm of Typewriters.)* But I stopped off at Rubicam's Business College to speak to your teachers about your having a cold and ask them what progress they thought you were making down there.

15 **LAURA:**   Oh. . . .

AMANDA: I went to the typing instructor and introduced myself as your mother. She didn't know who you were. Wingfield, she said. We don't have any such student enrolled at the school! I assured her she did, that you had been going to classes since early in January. "I wonder," she said, "if you could be talking about that terribly shy little girl who dropped out of school after only a few days' attendance?" "No," I said, "Laura, my daughter, has been going to school every day for the past six weeks!" "Excuse me," she said. She took the attendance book out and there was your name, unmistakably printed, and all the dates you were absent until they decided that you had dropped out of school. I still said, "No, there must have been some mistake! There must have been some mix-up in the records!" And she said, "No—I remember her perfectly now. Her hand shook so that she couldn't hit the right keys! The first time we gave a speed-test, she broke down completely—was sick at the stomach and almost had to be carried into the wash-room! After that morning she never showed up any more. We phoned the house but never got any answer"— while I was working at Famous and Barr, I suppose, demonstrating those— Oh! I felt so weak I could barely keep on my feet. I had to sit down while they got me a glass of water! Fifty dollars' tuition, all of our plans—my hopes and ambitions for you—just gone up the spout, just gone up the spout like that. *(Laura draws a long breath and gets awkwardly to her feet. She crosses to the Victrola and winds it up.)* What are you doing?

LAURA: Oh! *(She releases the handle and returns to her seat.)*

AMANDA: Laura, where have you been going when you've gone out pretending that you were going to business college?

LAURA: I've just been going out walking.

20 **AMANDA:**   That's not true.

LAURA: It is. I just went walking.

AMANDA: Walking? Walking? In winter? Deliberately courting pneumonia in that light coat? Where did you walk to, Laura?

LAURA: It was the lesser of two evils, Mother. *(Image: Winter Scene In Park.)* I couldn't go back up. I—threw up—on the floor!

AMANDA: From half past seven till after five every day you mean to tell me you walked around in the park, because you wanted to make me think that you were still going to Rubicam's Business College?

25 **LAURA:**   It wasn't as bad as it sounds. I went inside places to get warmed up.

AMANDA: Inside where?

LAURA: I went in the art museum and the bird-houses at the Zoo. I visited the penguins every day! Sometimes I did without lunch and went to the movies. Lately I've been spending most of my afternoons in the Jewel-box, that big glass house where they raise the tropical flowers.

AMANDA: You did all this to deceive me, just for the deception? *(Laura looks down.)* Why?

LAURA: Mother, when you're disappointed, you get that awful suffering look on your face, like the picture of Jesus' mother in the museum!

30 **AMANDA:** Hush!

LAURA: I couldn't face it.

Pause. A whisper of strings.

(Legend: "The Crust of Humility.")

AMANDA: *(hopelessly fingering the huge pocketbook)* So what are we going to do the rest of our lives? Stay home and watch the parades go by? Amuse ourselves with the glass menagerie, darling? Eternally play those worn-out phonograph records your father left as a painful reminder of him? We won't have a business career—we've given that up because it gave us nervous indigestion! *(Laughs wearily.)* What is there left but dependency all our lives? I know so well what becomes of unmarried women who aren't prepared to occupy a position. I've seen such pitiful cases in the South—barely tolerated spinsters living upon the grudging patronage of sister's husband or brother's wife!—stuck away in some little mouse-trap of a room—encouraged by one in-law to visit another—little birdlike women without any nest—eating the crust of humility all their life! Is that the future that we've mapped out for ourselves? I swear it's the only alternative I can think of! It isn't a very pleasant alternative, is it? Of course—some girls *do marry. (Laura twists her hands nervously.)* Haven't you ever liked some boy?

LAURA: Yes I liked one once. *(Rises.)* I came across his picture a while ago.

AMANDA: *(with some interest)* He gave you his picture?

35 **LAURA:** No, it's in the year-book.

AMANDA: *(disappointed)* Oh—a high-school boy.

(Screen Image: Jim As A High-School Hero Bearing A Silver Cup.)

LAURA: Yes. His name was Jim. *(Laura lifts the heavy annual from the clawfoot table.)* Here he is in *The Pirates of Penzance.*[5]

AMANDA: *(absently)* The what?

LAURA: The operetta the senior class put on. He had a wonderful voice and we sat across the aisle from each other Mondays, Wednesdays and Fridays in the Aud. Here he is with the silver cup for debating! See his grin?

40 **AMANDA:** *(absently)* He must have had a jolly disposition.

LAURA: He used to call me—Blue Roses.

(Image: Blue Roses.)

---

[5] A musical by Gilbert and Sullivan.

AMANDA: Why did he call you such a name as that?

LAURA: When I had that attack of pleurosis—he asked me what was the matter when I came back. I said pleurosis—he thought that I said Blue Roses! So that's what he always called me after that. Whenever he saw me, he'd holler, "Hello, Blue Roses!" I didn't care for the girl that he went out with. Emily Meisenbach. Emily was the best-dressed girl at Soldan. She never struck me, though, as being sincere . . . It says in the Personal Section—they're engaged. That's—six years ago! They must be married by now.

AMANDA: Girls that aren't cut out for business careers usually wind up married to some nice man. *(Gets up with a spark of revival.)* Sister, that's what you'll do!

Laura utters a startled, doubtful laugh. She reaches quickly for a piece of glass.

45   **LAURA:**   But, Mother—

AMANDA: Yes? *(Crossing to photograph.)*

LAURA: *(in a tone of frightened apology)* I'm—crippled!

(Image: Screen.)

AMANDA: Nonsense! Laura, I've told you never, never to use that word. Why, you're not crippled, you just have a little defect—hardly noticeable, even! When people have some slight disadvantage like that, they cultivate other things to make up for it—develop charm—and vivacity—and— charm! That's all you have to do! *(She turns again to the photograph.)* One thing your father had *plenty of*—was *charm!*

Tom motions to the fiddle in the wings.

(The Scene Fades Out With Music.)

SCENE III

(Legend On The Screen: "After The Fiasco—")

Tom speaks from the fire-escape landing.

TOM: After the fiasco at Rubicam's Business College, the idea of getting a gentleman caller for Laura began to play a more important part in Mother's calculations. It became an obsession. Like some archetype of the universal unconscious, the image of the gentleman caller haunted our small apartment. . . . *(Image: Young Man At Door With Flowers.)* An evening at home rarely passed without some allusion to this image, this spectre, this hope. . . . Even when he wasn't mentioned, his presence hung in Mother's preoccupied look and in my sister's frightened, apologetic manner—hung like a sentence passed upon the Wingfields! Mother was a woman of action as well as words. She began to take logical steps in the planned direction. Late that winter and in the early spring—realizing that extra money would be needed to properly feather the nest and plume the bird—she conducted a vigorous campaign on the telephone, roping in subscribers to one of those magazines for matrons called *The Home-maker's Companion,* the type of journal that features the serialized sublimations of ladies of letters who think in terms of delicate cup-like breasts, slim, tapering waists, rich, creamy thighs, eyes like wood-smoke in autumn, fingers that soothe and caress like strains of music, bodies as powerful as Etruscan sculpture.

(Screen Image: a glamour magazine cover.)

Amanda enters with phone on long extension cord. She is spotted in the dim stage.

AMANDA: Ida Scott? This is Amanda Wingfield! We *missed* you at the D.A.R. last Monday! I said to myself: She's probably suffering with that sinus condition! How is that sinus condition? Horrors! Heaven have mercy!— You're a Christian martyr, yes, that's what you are, a Christian martyr! Well, I just now happened to notice that your subscription to the *Companion's* about to expire! Yes, it expires with the next issue, honey!—just when that wonderful new serial by Bessie Mae Hopper is getting off to such an exciting start. Oh, honey, it's something that you can't miss! You remember how *Gone With the Wind* took everybody by storm? You simply couldn't go out if you hadn't read it. All everybody *talked* was Scarlett O'Hara. Well, this is a book that critics already compare to *Gone With the Wind*. It's the *Gone With the Wind* of the post-World War generation!—What?—Burning?—Oh, honey, don't let them burn, go take a look in the oven and I'll hold the wire! Heavens—I think she's hung up!

(Dim Out.)

(Legend On Screen: "You Think I'm In Love With Continental Shoemakers?")

Before the stage is lighted, the violent voices of Tom and Amanda are heard. They are quarreling behind the portieres. In front of them stands Laura with clenched hands and panicky expression.

   A clear pool of light on her figure throughout this scene.

TOM: What in Christ's name am I—
AMANDA: *(shrilly)* Don't you use that—
5 **TOM:**   Supposed to do!
AMANDA: Expression! Not in my—
TOM: Ohhh!
AMANDA: Presence! Have you gone out of your senses?
TOM: I have, that's true, *driven* out!
10 **AMANDA:**   What is the matter with you, you—big—big—IDIOT!
TOM: Look—I've got *no thing,* no single thing—
AMANDA: Lower your voice!

Tom: In my life here that I can call my OWN! Everything is—

Amanda: Stop that shouting!

15 **Tom:** Yesterday you confiscated my books! You had the nerve to—

Amanda: I took that horrible novel back to the library—yes! That hideous book by that insane Mr. Lawrence. *(Tom laughs wildly.)* I cannot control the output of diseased minds or people who cater to them—*(Tom laughs still more wildly.)* BUT I WON'T ALLOW SUCH FILTH BROUGHT INTO MY HOUSE! No, no, no, no, no!

Tom: House, house! Who pays rent on it, who makes a slave of himself to—

Amanda: *(fairly screeching)* Don't you DARE to—

Tom: No, no, I mustn't say things! *I've* got to just—

20 **Amanda:** Let me tell you—

Tom: I don't want to hear any more! *(He tears the portieres open. The upstage area is lit with a turgid smoky red glow.)*

Amanda's hair is in metal curlers and she wears a very old bathrobe, much too large for her slight figure, a relic of the faithless Mr. Wingfield.

An upright typewriter and a wild disarray of manuscripts are on the drop-leaf table. The quarrel was probably precipitated by Amanda's interruption of his creative labor. A chair lying overthrown on the floor.

Their gesticulating shadows are cast on the ceiling by the fiery glow.

Amanda: You *will* hear more, you—

Tom: No, I won't hear more, I'm going out!

Amanda: You come right back in—

25 **Tom:** Out, out out! Because I'm—

Amanda: Come back here, Tom Wingfield! I'm not through talking to you!

Tom: Oh, go—

Laura: *(desperately)* Tom!

Amanda: You're going to listen, and no more insolence from you! I'm at the end of my patience! *(He comes back toward her.)*

30 **Tom:** What do you think I'm at? Aren't I supposed to have any patience to reach the end of, Mother? I know, I know. It seems unimportant to you, what I'm *doing*—what I *want* to do—having a little *difference* between them! You don't think that—

Amanda: I think you've been doing things that you're ashamed of. That's why you act like this. I don't believe that you go every night to the movies. Nobody goes to the movies night after night. Nobody in their right mind goes to the movies as often as you pretend to. People don't go to the movies at nearly midnight, and movies don't let out at two A.M. Come in stumbling. Muttering to yourself like a maniac! You get three hours' sleep and then go to work. Oh, I can picture the way you're doing down there. Moping, doping, because you're in no condition.

Tom: *(wildly)* No, I'm in no condition!

Amanda: What right have you got to jeopardize your job? Jeopardize the security of us all? How do you think we'd manage if you were—

Tom: Listen! You think I'm crazy *about* the *warehouse? (He bends fiercely toward her slight figure.)* You think I'm in love with the Continental Shoemakers? You think I want to spend fifty-five *years* down there in that—*celotex interior!* with—*fluorescent—tubes!* Look! I'd rather somebody picked up a crowbar and battered out my brains—than go back mornings! I *go!* Every time you come in yelling that God damn *"Rise and Shine!" "Rise and Shine!"* I say to myself "How *lucky dead* people are!" But I get up. I *go!* For sixty-five dollars a month I give up all that I dream of doing and being *ever!* And you say self—*self's* all I ever think of. Why, listen, if self is what I thought of, Mother, I'd be where he is—GONE! *(Pointing to father's picture.)* As far as the system of transportation reaches! *(He starts past her. She grabs his arm.)* Don't grab at me, Mother!

35 **Amanda:** Where are you going?

Tom: I'm going to the *movies!*

Amanda: I don't believe that lie!

Tom: *(crouching toward her, overtowering her tiny figure. She backs away, gasping)* I'm going to opium dens! Yes, opium dens, dens of vice and criminals' hang-outs, Mother. I've joined the Hogan gang, I'm a hired assassin, I carry a tommy-gun in a violin case! I run a string of cat-houses in the Valley! They call me Killer, Killer Wingfield, I'm leading a double-life, a simple, honest warehouse worker by day, by night a dynamic *czar* of the *underworld, Mother.* I go to gambling casinos, I spin away fortunes on the roulette table! I wear a patch over one eye and a false mustache, sometimes I put on green whiskers. On those occasions they call me—*El Diablo!* Oh, I could tell you things to make you sleepless! My enemies plan to dynamite this place. They're going to blow us all sky-high some night! I'll be glad, very happy, and so will you! You'll go up, up on a broomstick, over Blue Mountain with seventeen gentlemen callers! You ugly—babbling old—*witch.* . . . *(He goes through a series of violent, clumsy movements, seizing his overcoat, lunging to the door, pulling it fiercely open. The women watch him, aghast. His arm catches in the sleeve of the coat as he struggles to pull it on. For a moment he is pinioned by the bulky garment. With an outraged groan he tears the coat off again, splitting the shoulders of it, and hurls it across the room. It strikes against the shelf of Laura's glass collection, there is a tinkle of shattering glass. Laura cries out as if wounded.)*

(Music Legend: "The Glass Menagerie.")

Laura: *My glass!*—menagerie. . . . *(She covers her face and turns away.)*

But Amanda is still stunned and stupefied by the "ugly witch" so that she barely notices this occurrence. Now she recovers her speech.

40 **Amanda:** *(in an awful voice)* I won't speak to you—until you apologize! *(She crosses through portieres and draws them together behind her. Tom is left with Laura. Laura clings weakly to the mantel with her face averted. Tom stares at her stupidly for a moment. Then he crosses to shelf. Drops*

awkwardly to his knees to collect the fallen glass, glancing at Laura as if he would speak but couldn't.)

"The Glass Menagerie" steals in as

(The Scene Dims Out.)

SCENE IV

The interior is dark. Faint in the alley.

    A deep-voiced bell in a church is tolling the hour of five as the scene commences.

    Tom appears at the top of the alley. After each solemn boom of the bell in the tower, he shakes a little noise-maker or rattle as if to express the tiny spasm of man in contrast to the sustained power and dignity of the Almighty. This and the unsteadiness of his advance make it evident that he has been drinking.

    As he climbs the few steps to the fire-escape landing light steals up inside. Laura appears in night-dress, observing Tom's empty bed in the front room.

    Tom fishes in his pockets for the door-key, removing a motley assortment of articles in the search, including a perfect shower of movie-ticket stubs and an empty bottle. At last he finds the key, but just as he is about to insert it, it slips from his fingers. He strikes a match and crouches below the door.

TOM: *(bitterly)* One crack—and it falls through!

Laura opens the door.

LAURA: Tom! Tom, what are you doing?
TOM: Looking for a door-key.
LAURA: Where have you been all this time?
5 **TOM:** I have been to the movies.
LAURA: All this time at the movies?
TOM: There was a very long program. There was a Garbo picture and a Mickey Mouse and a travelogue and a newsreel and a preview of coming attractions. And there was an organ solo and a collection for the milk-fund—simultaneously—which ended up in a terrible fight between a fat lady and an usher!
LAURA: *(innocently)* Did you have to stay through everything?
TOM: Of course! And, oh, I forgot! There was a big stage show! The headliner on this stage show was Malvolio the Magician. He performed wonderful tricks, many of them, such as pouring water back and forth between pitchers. First it turned to wine and then it turned to beer and then it turned to whiskey. I know it was whiskey it finally turned into because he needed somebody to come up out of the audience to help him, and I came up—both shows! It was Kentucky Straight Bourbon. A very generous fellow, he gave souvenirs. *(He pulls from his back pocket a shimmering rainbow-colored scarf.)* He gave me this. This is his magic scarf.

You can have it, Laura. You wave it over a canary cage and you get a bowl of gold-fish. You wave it over the gold-fish bowl and they fly away canaries. . . . But the wonderfullest trick of all was the coffin trick. We nailed him into a coffin and he got out of the coffin without removing one nail. *(He has come inside.)* There is a trick that would come in handy for me—get me out of this 2 by 4 situation! *(Flops onto bed and starts removing shoes.)*

10 **LAURA:**   Tom—Shhh!

TOM: What you shushing me for?

LAURA: You'll wake up Mother.

TOM: Goody, goody! Pay 'er back for all those "Rise an' Shines." *(Lies down, groaning.)* You know it don't take much intelligence to get yourself into a nailed-up coffin, Laura. But who in hell ever got himself out of one without removing one nail?

As if in answer, the father's grinning photograph lights up.

(Scene Dims Out.)

Immediately following: The church bell is heard striking six. At the sixth stroke the alarm clock goes off in Amanda's room, and after a few moments we hear her calling: "Rise and Shine! Rise and Shine! Laura, go tell your brother to rise and shine!"

TOM: *(sitting up slowly)* I'll rise—but I won't shine.

The light increases.

15 **AMANDA:**   Laura, tell your brother his coffee is ready.

Laura slips into front room.

LAURA: Tom! it's nearly seven. Don't make Mother nervous. *(He stares at her stupidly. Beseechingly.)* Tom, speak to Mother this morning. Make up with her, apologize, speak to her!

TOM: She won't to me. It's her that started not speaking.

LAURA: If you just say you're sorry she'll start speaking.

TOM: Her not speaking—is that such a tragedy?

20 **LAURA:**   Please—please!

AMANDA: *(calling from kitchenette)* Laura, are you going to do what I asked you to do, or do I have to get dressed and go out myself?

LAURA: Going, going—soon as I get on my coat! *(She pulls on a shapeless felt hat with nervous, jerky movement, pleadingly glancing at Tom. Rushes awkwardly for coat. The coat is one of Amanda's inaccurately made-over, the sleeves too short for Laura.)* Butter and what else?

AMANDA: *(entering upstage)* Just butter. Tell them to charge it.

LAURA: Mother, they make such faces when I do that.

25 **AMANDA:**   Sticks and stones may break my bones, but the expression on Mr. Garfinkel's face won't harm us! Tell your brother his coffee is getting cold.

LAURA: *(at door)* Do what I asked you, will you, will you, Tom?

He looks sullenly away.

AMANDA: Laura, go now or just don't go at all!

LAURA: *(rushing out)* Going—going! *(A second later she cries out. Tom springs up and crosses to the door. Amanda rushes anxiously in. Tom opens the door.)*

TOM: Laura?

30 **LAURA:**   I'm all right. I slipped, but I'm all right.

AMANDA: *(peering anxiously after her)* If anyone breaks a leg on those fire-escape steps, the landlord ought to be sued for every cent he possesses! *(She shuts door. Remembers she isn't speaking and returns to other room.)*

As Tom enters listlessly for his coffee, she turns her back to him and stands rigidly facing the window on the gloomy gray vault of the areaway. Its light on her face with its aged but childish features is cruelly sharp, satirical as a Daumier print.

(Music Under: "Ave Maria.")

Tom glances sheepishly but sullenly at her averted figure and slumps at the table. The coffee is scalding hot; he sips it and gasps and spits it back in the cup. At his gasp, Amanda catches her breath and half turns. Then catches herself and turns back to window.

Tom blows on his coffee, glancing sidewise at his mother. She clears her throat. Tom clears his. He starts to rise. Sinks back down again, scratches his head, clears his throat again. Amanda coughs. Tom raises his cup in both hands to blow on it, his eyes staring over the rim of it at his mother for several moments. Then he slowly sets the cup down and awkwardly and hesitantly rises from the chair.

TOM: *(hoarsely)* Mother. I—I apologize. Mother. *(Amanda draws a quick, shuddering breath. Her face works grotesquely. She breaks into childlike tears.)* I'm sorry for what I said, for everything that I said, I didn't mean it.

AMANDA: *(sobbingly)* My devotion has made me a witch and so I make myself hateful to my children!

TOM: No, you *don't.*

35 **AMANDA:**   I worry so much, don't sleep, it makes me nervous!

TOM: *(gently)* I understand that.

AMANDA: I've had to put up a solitary battle all these years. But you're my right-hand bower! Don't fall down, don't fail!

TOM: *(gently)* I try, Mother.

AMANDA: *(with great enthusiasm)* Try and you will SUCCEED! *(The notion makes her breathless.)* Why, you—you're just *full* of natural endowments! Both of my children—they're *unusual* children! Don't you think I know it? I'm so—*proud!* Happy and—feel I've—so much to be thankful for but— Promise me one thing, son!

40 **TOM:**   What, Mother?

AMANDA: Promise, son, you'll—never be a drunkard!

TOM: *(turns to her grinning)* I will never be a drunkard, Mother.

AMANDA: That's what frightened me so, that you'd be drinking! Eat a bowl of Purina!

TOM: Just coffee, Mother.

45 **AMANDA:**   Shredded wheat biscuit?

TOM: No. No, Mother, just coffee.

AMANDA: You can't put in a day's work on an empty stomach. You've got ten minutes—don't gulp! Drinking too-hot liquids makes cancer of the stomach. . . . Put cream in.

TOM: No, thank you.

AMANDA: To cool it.

50 **TOM:**   No! No, thank you, I want it black.

AMANDA: I know, but it's not good for you. We have to do all that we can to build ourselves up. In these trying times we live in, all that we have to cling to is—each other. . . . That's why it's so important to—Tom, I—I sent out your sister so I could discuss something with you. If you hadn't spoken I would have spoken to you. (*Sits down.*)

TOM: (*gently*) What is it, Mother, that you want to discuss?

AMANDA: Laura!

Tom puts his cup down slowly.

(*Legend On Screen: "Laura."*)

(*Music: "The Glass Menagerie."*)

TOM: —Oh.—Laura . . .

55 **AMANDA:**   (*touching his sleeve*) You know how Laura is. So quiet but—still water runs deep! She notices things and I think she—broods about them. (*Tom looks up.*) A few days ago I came in and she was crying.

TOM: What about?

AMANDA: You.

TOM: Me?

AMANDA: She has an idea that you're not happy here.

60 **TOM:**   What gave her that idea?

AMANDA: What gives her any idea? However, you do act strangely. I—I'm not criticizing, understand *that!* I know your ambitions do not lie in the warehouse, that like everybody in the whole wide world—you've had to—make sacrifices, but—Tom—Tom—life's not easy, it calls for—Spartan endurance! There's so many things in my heart that I cannot describe to you! I've never told you but I—*loved* your father. . . .

TOM: (*gently*) I know that, Mother.

AMANDA: And you—when I see you taking after his ways! Staying out late—and—well, you *had* been drinking the night you were in that—terrifying condition! Laura says that you hate the apartment and that you go out nights to get away from it! Is that true, Tom?

TOM: No. You say there's so much in your heart that you can't describe to me. That's true of me, too. There's so much in my heart that I can't describe to *you!* So let's respect each other's—

65 **AMANDA:** But, why—*why*, Tom—are you always so *restless?* Where do you
go to, nights?

TOM: I—go to the movies.

AMANDA: Why do you go to the movies so much, Tom?

TOM: I go to the movies because—I like adventure. Adventure is something
I don't have much of at work, so I go to the movies.

AMANDA: But, Tom, you go to the movies *entirely* too *much!*

70 **TOM:** I like a lot of adventure.

*Amanda looks baffled, then hurt. As the familiar inquisition resumes he becomes
hard and impatient again. Amanda slips back into her querulous attitude toward
him.*

(Image On Screen: Sailing Vessel With Jolly Roger.)

AMANDA: Most young men find adventure in their careers.

TOM: Then most young men are not employed in a warehouse.

AMANDA: The world is full of young men employed in warehouses and
offices and factories.

TOM: Do all of them find adventure in their careers?

75 **AMANDA:** They do or they do without it! Not everybody has a craze for
adventure.

TOM: Man is by instinct a lover, a hunter, a fighter, and none of those
instincts are given much play at the warehouse!

AMANDA: Man is by instinct! Don't quote instinct to me! Instinct is
something that people have got away from! It belongs to animals!
Christian adults don't want it!

TOM: What do Christian adults want, then, Mother?

AMANDA: Superior things! Things of the mind and the spirit! Only animals
have to satisfy instincts! Surely your aims are somewhat higher than
theirs! Than monkeys—pigs—

80 **TOM:** I reckon they're not.

AMANDA: You're joking. However, that isn't what I wanted to discuss.

TOM: *(rising)* I haven't much time.

AMANDA: *(pushing his shoulders)* Sit down.

TOM: You want me to punch in red at the warehouse, Mother?

85 **AMANDA:** You have five minutes. I want to talk about Laura.

(Legend: "Plans And Provisions.")

TOM: All right! What about Laura?

AMANDA: We have to be making plans and provisions for her. She's older
than you, two years, and nothing has happened. She just drifts along
doing nothing. It frightens me terribly how she just drifts along.

TOM: I guess she's the type that people call home girls.

AMANDA: There's no such type, and if there is, it's a pity! That is unless the
home is hers, with a husband!

90 **TOM:** What?

AMANDA: Oh, I can see the handwriting on the wall as plain as I see the nose in front of my face! It's terrifying! More and more you remind me of your father! He was out all hours without explanation—Then *left!* *Goodbye!* And me with the bag to hold. I saw that letter you got from the Merchant Marine. I know what you're dreaming of. I'm not standing here blindfolded. Very well, then. Then *do* it! But not till there's somebody to take your place.

TOM: What do you mean?

AMANDA: I mean that as soon as Laura has got somebody to take care of her, married, a home of her own, independent—why, then you'll be free to go wherever you please, on land, on sea, whichever way the wind blows! But until that time you've got to look out for your sister. I don't say me because I'm old and don't matter! I say for your sister because she's young and dependent. I put her in business college—a dismal failure! Frightened her so it made her sick to her stomach. I took her over to the Young People's League at the church. Another fiasco. She spoke to nobody, nobody spoke to her. Now all she does is fool with those pieces of glass and play those worn-out records. What kind of a life is that for a girl to lead!

TOM: What can I do about it?

95 **AMANDA:** Overcome selfishness! Self, self, self is all that you ever think of! *(Tom springs up and crosses to get his coat. It is ugly and bulky. He pulls on a cap with earmuffs.)* Where is your muffler? Put your wool muffler on! *(He snatches it angrily from the closet and tosses it around his neck and pulls both ends tight.)* Tom! I haven't said what I had in mind to ask you.

TOM: I'm too late to—

AMANDA: *(catching his arms—very importunately. Then shyly)* Down at the warehouse, aren't there some—nice young men?

TOM: No!

AMANDA: There *must* be—*some* . . .

100 **TOM:** Mother—

Gesture.

AMANDA: Find out one that's clean-living—doesn't drink and—ask him out for sister!

TOM: What?

AMANDA: For *sister!* To *meet!* Get *acquainted!*

TOM: *(stamping to door)* Oh, my *go-osh!*

105 **AMANDA:** Will you? *(He opens door. Imploringly.)* Will you? *(He starts down.)* Will you? *Will* you, dear?

TOM: *(calling back)* YES!

Amanda closes the door hesitantly and with a troubled but faintly hopeful expression.

(Screen Image: a glamour magazine cover.)

Spot Amanda at phone.

AMANDA: Ella Cartwright? This is Amanda Wingfield! How are you, honey? How is that kidney condition? *(Count five.)* Horrors! *(Count five.)* You're a Christian martyr, yes, honey, that's what you are, a Christian martyr! Well, I just happened to notice in my little red book that your subscription to the *Companion* has just run out! I knew that you wouldn't want to miss out on the wonderful serial starting in this new issue. It's by Bessie Mae Hopper, the first thing she's written since *Honeymoon for Three*. Wasn't that a strange and interesting story? Well, this one is even lovelier, I believe. It has a sophisticated society background. It's all about the horsey set on Long Island!

(Fade Out.)

SCENE V

(Legend On Screen: "Annunciation.") Fade with music.

It is early dusk of a spring evening. Supper has just been finished in the Wingfield apartment. Amanda and Laura in light colored dresses are removing dishes from the table, in the upstage area, which is shadowy, their movements formalized almost as a dance or ritual, their moving forms as pale and silent as moths.

Tom, in white shirt and trousers, rises from the table and crosses toward the fire-escape.

AMANDA: *(as he passes her)* Son, will you do me a favor?
TOM: What?
AMANDA: Comb your hair! You look so pretty when your hair is combed! *(Tom slouches on sofa with evening paper. Enormous caption "Franco Triumphs.")* There is only one respect in which I would like you to emulate your father.
TOM: What respect is that?
5 **AMANDA:** The care he always took of his appearance. He never allowed himself to look untidy. *(He throws down the paper and crosses to fire-escape.)* Where are you going?
TOM: I'm going out to smoke.
AMANDA: You smoke too much. A pack a day at fifteen cents a pack. How much would that amount to in a month? Thirty times fifteen is how much, Tom? Figure it out and you will be astounded at what you could save. Enough to give you a night-school course in accounting at Washington U! Just think what a wonderful thing that would be for you, son!

Tom is unmoved by the thought.

TOM: I'd rather smoke. *(He steps out on landing, letting the screen door slam.)*
AMANDA: *(sharply)* I know! That's the tragedy of it. . . . *(Alone, she turns to look at her husband's picture.)*

(Dance Music: "All The World Is Waiting For The Sunrise!")

10 **TOM:** *(to the audience)* Across the alley from us was the Paradise Dance Hall. On evenings in spring the windows and doors were open and the music came outdoors. Sometimes the lights were turned out except for a large glass sphere that hung from the ceiling. It would turn slowly about and filter the dusk with delicate rainbow colors. Then the orchestra played a waltz or a tango, something that had a slow and sensuous rhythm. Couples would come outside, to the relative privacy of the alley. You could see them kissing behind ash-pits and telephone poles. This was the compensation for lives that passed like mine, without any change or adventure. Adventure and change were imminent in this year. They were waiting around the corner for all these kids. Suspended in the mist over Berchtesgaden,[6] caught in the folds of Chamberlain's[7] umbrella—In Spain there was Guernica! But here there was only hot swing music and liquor, dance halls, bars, and movies, and sex that hung in the gloom like a chandelier and flooded the world with brief, deceptive rainbows. . . . All the world was waiting for bombardments!

Amanda turns from the picture and comes outside.

AMANDA: *(sighing)* A fire-escape landing's a poor excuse for a porch. *(She spreads a newspaper on a step and sits down, gracefully and demurely as if she were settling into a swing on a Mississippi veranda.)* What are you looking at?

TOM: The moon.

AMANDA: Is there a moon this evening?

TOM: It's rising over Garfinkel's Delicatessen.

15 **AMANDA:** So it is! A little silver slipper of a moon. Have you made a wish on it yet?

TOM: Um-hum.

AMANDA: What did you wish for?

TOM: That's a secret.

AMANDA: A secret, huh? Well, I won't tell mine either. I will be just as mysterious as you.

20 **TOM:** I bet I can guess what yours is.

AMANDA: Is my head so transparent?

TOM: You're not a sphinx.

AMANDA: No, I don't have secrets. I'll tell you what I wished for on the moon. Success and happiness for my precious children! I wish for that whenever there's a moon, and when there isn't a moon, I wish for it, too.

TOM: I thought perhaps you wished for a gentleman caller.

---

6 A resort in West Germany, in the Bavarian Alps, site of Hitler's fortified retreat, the Berghof.

7 (Arthur) Neville Chamberlain (1869–1940)—Conservative party Prime Minister of England (1937–1940) who advocated a policy of appeasement toward Hitler.

25 **AMANDA:**   Why do you say that?

TOM: Don't you remember asking me to fetch one?

AMANDA: I remember suggesting that it would be nice for your sister if you brought home some nice young man from the warehouse. I think I've made that suggestion more than once.

TOM: Yes, you have made it repeatedly.

AMANDA: Well?

30 **TOM:**   We are going to have one.

AMANDA: What?

TOM: A gentleman caller!

(The Annunciation Is Celebrated With Music.)

Amanda rises.

(Image On Screen: Caller With Bouquet.)

AMANDA: You mean you have asked some nice young man to come over?

TOM: Yep. I've asked him to dinner.

35 **AMANDA:**   You really did?

TOM: I did!

AMANDA: You did, and did he—*accept?*

TOM: He did!

AMANDA: Well, well—well, well! That's—lovely!

40 **TOM:**   I thought that you would be pleased.

AMANDA: It's definite, then?

TOM: Very definite.

AMANDA: Soon?

TOM: Very soon.

45 **AMANDA:**   For heaven's sake, stop putting on and tell me some things, will you?

TOM: What things do you want me to tell you?

AMANDA: Naturally I would like to know when he's *coming!*

TOM: He's coming tomorrow.

AMANDA: *Tomorrow?*

50 **TOM:**   Yep. Tomorrow.

AMANDA: But, Tom!

TOM: Yes, Mother?

AMANDA: Tomorrow gives me no time!

TOM: Time for what?

55 **AMANDA:**   Preparations! Why didn't you phone me at once, as soon as you asked him, the minute that he accepted? Then, don't you see, I could have been getting ready!

TOM: You don't have to make any fuss.

AMANDA: Oh, Tom, Tom, Tom, of course I have to make a fuss! I want things nice, not sloppy! Not thrown together. I'll certainly have to do some fast thinking, won't I?

TOM: I don't see why you have to think at all.

AMANDA: You just don't know. We can't have a gentleman caller in a pig-sty! All my wedding silver has to be polished, the monogrammed table linen ought to be laundered! The windows have to be washed and fresh curtains put up. And how about clothes? We have to *wear* something, don't we?

60 **TOM:** Mother, this boy is no one to make a fuss over!

AMANDA: Do you realize he's the first young man we've introduced to your sister? It's terrible, dreadful, disgraceful that poor little sister has never received a single gentleman caller! Tom, come inside! *(She opens the screen door.)*

TOM: What for?

AMANDA: I want to ask you some things.

TOM: If you're going to make such a fuss, I'll call it off, I'll tell him not to come.

65 **AMANDA:** You certainly won't do anything of the kind. Nothing offends people worse than broken engagements. It simply means I'll have to work like a Turk! We won't be brilliant, but we'll pass inspection. Come on inside. *(Tom follows, groaning.)* Sit down.

TOM: Any particular place you would like me to sit?

AMANDA: Thank heavens I've got that new sofa! I'm also making payments on a floor lamp I'll have sent out! And put the chintz covers on, they'll brighten things up! Of course I'd hoped to have these walls re-papered. . . . What is the young man's name?

TOM: His name is O'Connor.

AMANDA: That, of course, means fish—tomorrow is Friday! I'll have that salmon loaf—with Durkee's dressing! What does he do? He works at the warehouse?

70 **TOM:** Of course! How else would I—

AMANDA: Tom, he—doesn't drink?

TOM: Why do you ask me that?

AMANDA: Your father *did!*

TOM: Don't get started on that!

75 **AMANDA:** He *does* drink, then?

TOM: Not that I know of!

AMANDA: Make sure, be certain! The last thing I want for my daughter's a boy who drinks!

TOM: Aren't you being a little premature? Mr. O'Connor has not yet appeared on the scene!

AMANDA: But will tomorrow. To meet your sister, and what do I know about his character? Nothing! Old maids are better off than wives of drunkards!

80 **TOM:** Oh, my God!

AMANDA: Be still!

TOM: *(leaning forward to whisper)* Lots of fellows meet girls whom they don't marry!

AMANDA: Oh, talk sensibly, Tom—and don't be sarcastic! *(She has gotten a hairbrush.)*

Tom: What are you doing?

85 **Amanda:** I'm brushing that cow-lick down! What is this young man's position at the warehouse?

Tom: *(submitting grimly to the brush and the interrogation)* This young man's position is that of a shipping clerk, Mother.

Amanda: Sounds to me like a fairly responsible job, the sort of a job *you* would be in if you just had more *get-up*. What is his salary? Have you got any idea?

Tom: I would judge it to be approximately eighty-five dollars a month.

Amanda: Well—not princely, but—

90 **Tom:** Twenty more than I make.

Amanda: Yes, how well I know! But for a family man, eighty-five dollars a month is not much more than you can just get by on. . . .

Tom: Yes, but Mr. O'Connor is not a family man.

Amanda: He might be, mightn't he? Some time in the future?

Tom: I see. Plans and provisions.

95 **Amanda:** You are the only young man that I know of who ignores the fact that the future becomes the present, the present the past, and the past turns into everlasting regret if you don't plan for it!

Tom: I will think that over and see what I can make of it.

Amanda: Don't be supercilious with your mother! Tell me some more about this—what do you call him?

Tom: James D. O'Connor. The D. is for Delaney.

Amanda: Irish on *both* sides! *Gracious!* And doesn't drink?

100 **Tom:** Shall I call him up and ask him right this minute?

Amanda: The only way to find out about those things is to make discreet inquiries at the proper moment. When I was a girl in Blue Mountain and it was suspected that a young man drank, the girl whose attentions he had been receiving, if any girl *was,* would sometimes speak to the minister of his church, or rather her father would if her father was living, and sort of feel him out on the young man's character. That is the way such things are discreetly handled to keep a young woman from making a tragic mistake!

Tom: Then how did you happen to make a tragic mistake?

Amanda: That innocent look of your father's had everyone fooled! He *smiled*—the world was *enchanted!* No girl can do worse than put herself at the mercy of a handsome appearance! I hope that Mr. O'Connor is not too good-looking.

Tom: No, he's not too good-looking. He's covered with freckles and hasn't too much of a nose.

105 **Amanda:** He's not right-down homely, though?

Tom: Not right-down homely. Just medium homely, I'd say.

Amanda: Character's what to look for in a man.

Tom: That's what I've always said, Mother.

Amanda: You've never said anything of the kind and I suspect you would never give it a thought.

110 **Tom:**   Don't be suspicious of me.

Amanda: At least I hope he's the type that's up and coming.

Tom: I think he really goes in for self-improvement.

Amanda: What reason have you to think so?

Tom: He goes to night school.

115 **Amanda:**   *(beaming)* Splendid! What does he do, I mean study?

Tom: Radio engineering and public speaking!

Amanda: Then he has visions of being advanced in the world! Any young
man who studies public speaking is aiming to have an executive job some
day! And radio engineering? A thing for the future! Both of these facts are
very illuminating. Those are the sort of things that a mother should know
concerning any young man who comes to call on her daughter. Seriously
or—not.

Tom: One little warning. He doesn't know about Laura. I didn't let on that
we had dark ulterior motives. I just said, why don't you come have dinner
with us? He said okay and that was the whole conversation.

Amanda: I bet it was! You're eloquent as an oyster. However, he'll know
about Laura when he gets here. When he sees how lovely and sweet and
pretty she is, he'll thank his lucky stars he was asked to dinner.

120 **Tom:**   Mother, you mustn't expect too much of Laura.

Amanda: What do you mean?

Tom: Laura seems all those things to you and me because she's ours and we
love her. We don't even notice she's crippled any more.

Amanda: Don't say crippled! You know that I never allow that word to be
used!

Tom: But face facts, Mother. She is and—that's not all—

125 **Amanda:**   What do you mean "not all"?

Tom: Laura is very different from other girls.

Amanda: I think the difference is all to her advantage.

Tom: Not quite all—in the eyes of others—strangers—she's terribly shy and
lives in a world of her own and those things make her seem a little
peculiar to people outside the house.

Amanda: Don't say peculiar.

130 **Tom:**   Face the facts. She is.

*(The Dance-hall Music Changes To A Tango That Has A Minor And Somewhat
Ominous Tone.)*

Amanda: In what way is she peculiar—may I ask?

Tom: *(gently)* She lives in a world of her own—a world of—little glass
ornaments, Mother. . . . *(Gets up. Amanda remains holding brush, looking
at him, troubled.)* She plays old phonograph records and—that's about
all—*(He glances at himself in the mirror and crosses to door.)*

Amanda: *(sharply)* Where are you going?

Tom: I'm going to the movies. *(Out screen door.)*

135 **Amanda:**   Not to the movies, every night to the movies! *(Follows quickly to
screen door.)* I don't believe you always go to the movies! *(He is gone.*

Amanda looks worriedly after him for a moment. Then vitality and optimism return and she turns from the door. Crossing to portieres.) Laura! Laura! *(Laura answers from kitchenette.)*

LAURA: Yes, Mother.

AMANDA: Let those dishes go and come in front! *(Laura appears with dish towel. Gaily.)* Laura, come here and make a wish on the moon!

LAURA: *(entering)* Moon—moon?

AMANDA: A little silver slipper of a moon. Look over your left shoulder, Laura, and make a wish! *(Laura looks faintly puzzled as if called out of sleep. Amanda seizes her shoulders and turns her at an angle by the door.)* Now! Now, darling, *wish!*

140 **LAURA:**   What shall I wish for, Mother?

AMANDA: *(her voice trembling and her eyes suddenly filling with tears)* Happiness! Good Fortune!

The violin rises and the stage dims out.

SCENE VI

(Image: High-School Hero.)

TOM: And so the following evening I brought Jim home to dinner. I had known Jim slightly in high school. In high school Jim was a hero. He had tremendous Irish good nature and vitality with the scrubbed and polished look of white chinaware. He seemed to move in a continual spotlight. He was a star in basketball, captain of the debating club, president of the senior class and the glee club and he sang the male lead in the annual light operas. He was always running or bounding, never just walking. He seemed always at the point of defeating the law of gravity. He was shooting with such velocity through his adolescence that you would logically expect him to arrive at nothing short of the White House by the time he was thirty. But Jim apparently ran into more interference after his graduation from Soldan. His speed had definitely slowed. Six years after he left high school he was holding a job that wasn't much better than mine.

(Image: Clerk.)

He was the only one at the warehouse with whom I was on friendly terms. I was valuable to him as someone who could remember his former glory, who had seen him win basketball games and the silver cup in debating. He knew of my secret practice of retiring to a cabinet of the washroom to work on poems when business was slack in the warehouse. He called me Shakespeare. And while the other boys in the warehouse regarded me with suspicious hostility, Jim took a humorous attitude toward me. Gradually his attitude affected the others, their hostility wore off and they also began to smile at me as people smile at an oddly fashioned dog who trots across their path at some distance.

I knew that Jim and Laura had known each other at Soldan, and I had heard Laura speak admiringly of his voice. I didn't know if Jim remembered her or not. In high school Laura had been as unobtrusive as Jim had been astonishing. If he did remember Laura, it was not as my sister, for when I asked him to dinner, he grinned and said, "You know, Shakespeare, I never thought of you as having folks!"
He was about to discover that I did. . . .

(Light Up Stage.)

(Legend On Screen: "The Accent Of A Coming Foot.")

Friday evening. It is about five o'clock of a late spring evening which comes "scattering poems in the sky."
A delicate lemony light is in the Wingfield apartment.
Amanda has worked like a Turk in preparation for the gentleman caller. The results are astonishing. The new floor lamp with its rose-silk shade is in place, a colored paper lantern conceals the broken light fixture in the ceiling, new billowing white curtains are at the windows, chintz covers are on chairs and sofa, a pair of new sofa pillows make their initial appearance.
Open boxes and tissue paper are scattered on the floor.
Laura stands in the middle with lifted arms while Amanda crouches before her, adjusting the hem of the new dress, devout and ritualistic. The dress is colored and designed by memory. The arrangement of Laura's hair is changed; it is softer and more becoming. A fragile, unearthly prettiness has come out in Laura: she is like a piece of translucent glass touched by light, given a momentary radiance, not actual, not lasting.

AMANDA: *(impatiently)* Why are you trembling?
LAURA: Mother, you've made me so nervous!
AMANDA: How have I made you nervous?
5 **LAURA:** By all this fuss! You make it seem so important!
AMANDA: I don't understand you, Laura. You couldn't be satisfied with just sitting home, and yet whenever I try to arrange something for you, you seem to resist it. *(She gets up.)* Now take a look at yourself. No, wait! Wait just a moment—I have an idea!
LAURA: What is it now?

Amanda produces two powder puffs which she wraps in handkerchiefs and stuffs in Laura's bosom.

LAURA: Mother, what are you doing?
AMANDA: They call them "Gay Deceivers"!
10 **LAURA:** I won't wear them!
AMANDA: You will!
LAURA: Why should I?
AMANDA: Because, to be painfully honest, your chest is flat.
LAURA: You make it seem like we were setting a trap.

15 **AMANDA:**   All pretty girls are a trap, a pretty trap, and men expect them to
be. *(Legend: "A Pretty Trap.")* Now look at yourself, young lady. This is the
prettiest you will ever be! I've got to fix myself now! You're going to be
surprised by your mother's appearance! *(She crosses through portieres,
humming gaily.)*

Laura moves slowly to the long mirror and stares solemnly at herself.
*A wind blows the white curtains inward in a slow, graceful motion and with a
faint, sorrowful sighing.*

AMANDA: *(offstage)* It isn't dark enough yet. *(She turns slowly before the
mirror with a troubled look.)*

(Legend On Screen: "This Is My Sister: Celebrate Her With Strings!" Music.)

AMANDA: *(laughing, off)* I'm going to show you something. I'm going to
make a spectacular appearance!

LAURA: What is it, Mother?

AMANDA: Possess your soul in patience—you will see! Something I've
resurrected from that old trunk! Styles haven't changed so terribly much
after all. . . . *(She parts the portieres.)* Now just look at your mother! *(She
wears a girlish frock of yellowed voile with a blue silk sash. She carries a
bunch of jonquils—the legend of her youth is nearly revived. Feverishly.)* This
is the dress in which I led the cotillion. Won the cakewalk twice at Sunset
Hill, wore one spring to the Governor's ball in Jackson! See how I
sashayed around the ballroom, Laura? *(She raises her skirt and does a
mincing step around the room.)* I wore it on Sundays for my gentlemen
callers! I had it on the day I met your father—I had malaria fever all that
spring. The change of climate from East Tennessee to the Delta—
weakened resistance—I had a little temperature all the time—not enough
to be serious—just enough to make me restless and giddy! Invitations
poured in—parties all over the Delta!—"Stay in bed," said Mother, "you
have fever!"—but I just wouldn't.—I took quinine but kept on going,
going!—Evenings, dances!—Afternoons, long, long rides! Picnics—
lovely!—So lovely, that country in May.All lacy with dogwood, literally
flooded with jonquils!—That was the spring I had the craze for jonquils.
Jonquils became an absolute obsession. Mother said, "Honey, there's no
more room for jonquils." And still I kept bringing in more jonquils.
Whenever, wherever I saw them, I'd say, "Stop! Stop! I see jonquils!" I
made the young men help me gather the jonquils! It was a joke, Amanda
and her jonquils! Finally there were no more vases to hold them, every
available space was filled with jonquils. No vases to hold them? All right,
I'll hold them myself! And then I—*(She stops in front of the picture.)*
(Music) met your father! Malaria fever and jonquils and then—this—
boy. . . . *(She switches on the rose-colored lamp.)* I hope they get here
before it starts to rain. *(She crosses upstage and places the jonquils in bowl
on table.)* I gave your brother a little extra change so he and Mr.
O'Connor could take the service car home.

20 **LAURA:**   *(with altered look)* What did you say his name was?

AMANDA: O'Connor.

LAURA: What is his first name?

AMANDA: I don't remember. Oh, yes, I do. It was—Jim!

Laura sways slightly and catches hold of a chair.

(Legend On Screen: "Not Jim!")

LAURA: *(faintly)* Not—Jim!

25 **AMANDA:** Yes, that was it, it was Jim! I've never known a Jim that wasn't nice!

(Music: Ominous.)

LAURA: Are you sure his name is Jim O'Connor?

AMANDA: Yes. Why?

LAURA: Is he the one that Tom used to know in high school?

AMANDA: He didn't say so. I think he just got to know him at the warehouse.

30 **LAURA:** There was a Jim O'Connor we both knew in high school—*(Then, with effort.)* If that is the one that Tom is bringing to dinner—you'll have to excuse me, I won't come to the table.

AMANDA: What sort of nonsense is this?

LAURA: You asked me once if I'd ever liked a boy. Don't you remember I showed you this boy's picture?

AMANDA: You mean the boy you showed me in the year book?

LAURA: Yes, that boy.

35 **AMANDA:** Laura, Laura, were you in love with that boy?

LAURA: I don't know, Mother. All I know is I couldn't sit at the table if it was him!

AMANDA: It won't be him! It isn't the least bit likely. But whether it is or not, you will come to the table. You will not be excused.

LAURA: I'll have to be, Mother.

AMANDA: I don't intend to humor your silliness, Laura. I've had too much from you and your brother, both! So just sit down and compose yourself till they come. Tom has forgotten his key so you'll have to let them in, when they arrive.

40 **LAURA:** *(panicky)* Oh, Mother—*you* answer the door!

AMANDA: *(lightly)* I'll be in the kitchen—busy!

LAURA: Oh, Mother, please answer the door, don't make me do it!

AMANDA: *(crossing into kitchenette)* I've got to fix the dressing for the salmon. Fuss, fuss—silliness!—over a gentleman caller!

Door swings shut. Laura is left alone.

(Legend: "Terror!")

She utters a low moan and turns off the lamp—sits stiffly on the edge of the sofa, knotting her fingers together.

(Legend On Screen: "The Opening Of A Door!")

Tom and Jim appear on the fire-escape steps and climb to landing. Hearing their approach, Laura rises with a panicky gesture. She retreats to the portieres. The doorbell. Laura catches her breath and touches her throat. Low drums.

Amanda: *(calling)* Laura, sweetheart! The door!

Laura stares at it without moving.

45 **Jim:**   I think we just beat the rain.

 Tom: Uh-huh. *(He rings again, nervously. Jim whistles and fishes for a cigarette.)*

 Amanda: *(very, very gaily)* Laura, that is your brother and Mr. O'Connor! Will you let them in, darling?

Laura crosses toward kitchenette door.

 Laura: *(breathlessly)* Mother—you go to the door!

Amanda steps out of kitchenette and stares furiously at Laura. She points imperiously at the door.

 Laura: Please, please!

50 **Amanda:**   *(in a fierce whisper)* What is the matter with you, you silly thing?

 Laura: *(desperately)* Please, you answer it, *please!*

 Amanda: I told you I wasn't going to humor you, Laura. Why have you chosen this moment to lose your mind?

 Laura: Please, please, please, you go!

 Amanda: You'll have to go to the door because I can't!

55 **Laura:**   *(despairingly)* I can't either!

 Amanda: Why?

 Laura: I'm *sick!*

 Amanda: I'm sick, too—of your nonsense! Why can't you and your brother be normal people? Fantastic whims and behavior! *(Tom gives a long ring.)* Preposterous goings on! Can you give me one reason—*(Calls out lyrically.)* COMING! JUST ONE SECOND!—why should you be afraid to open a door? Now you answer it, Laura!

 Laura: Oh, oh, oh . . . *(She returns through the portieres. Darts to the Victrola and winds it frantically and turns it on.)*

60 **Amanda:**   Laura Wingfield, you march right to that door!

 Laura: Yes—yes, Mother!

A faraway, scratchy rendition of "Dardanella" softens the air and gives her strength to move through it. She slips to the door and draws it cautiously open. Tom enters with the caller, Jim O'Connor.

 Tom: Laura, this is Jim. Jim, this is my sister, Laura.

 Jim: *(stepping inside)* I didn't know that Shakespeare had a sister!

 Laura: *(retreating stiff and trembling from the door)* How—how do you do?

65 **Jim:**   *(heartily extending his hand)* Okay!

Laura touches it hesitantly with hers.

JIM: Your hand's *cold*, Laura!

LAURA: Yes, well—I've been playing the Victrola. . . .

JIM: Must have been playing classical music on it! You ought to play a little hot swing music to warm you up!

LAURA: Excuse me—I haven't finished playing the Victrola. . . .

She turns awkwardly and hurries into the front room. She pauses a second by the Victrola. Then catches her breath and darts through the portieres like a frightened deer.

70 **JIM:** *(grinning)* What was the matter?

TOM: Oh—with Laura? Laura is—terribly shy.

JIM: Shy, huh? It's unusual to meet a shy girl nowadays. I don't believe you ever mentioned you had a sister.

TOM: Well, now you know. I have one. Here is the *Post Dispatch.* You want a piece of it?

JIM: Uh-huh.

75 **TOM:** What piece? The comics?

JIM: Sports! *(Glances at it.)* Ole Dizzy Dean is on his bad behavior.

TOM: *(disinterested)* Yeah? *(Lights cigarette and crosses back to fire-escape door.)*

JIM: Where are *you* going?

TOM: I'm going out on the terrace.

80 **JIM:** *(goes after him)* You know, Shakespeare—I'm going to sell you a bill of goods!

TOM: What goods?

JIM: A course I'm taking.

TOM: Huh?

JIM: In public speaking! You and me, we're not the warehouse type.

85 **TOM:** Thanks—that's good news. But what has public speaking got to do with it?

JIM: It fits you for—executive positions!

TOM: Awww.

JIM: I tell you it's done a helluva lot for me.

(Image: Executive At Desk.)

TOM: In what respect?

90 **JIM:** In every! Ask yourself what is the difference between you an' me and men in the office down front? Brains?—No!—Ability?—No! Then what? Just one little thing—

TOM: What is that one little thing?

JIM: Primarily it amounts to—social poise! Being able to square up to people and hold your own on any social level!

AMANDA: *(offstage)* Tom?

TOM: Yes, Mother?

95 **AMANDA:** Is that you and Mr. O'Connor?

TOM: Yes, Mother.

AMANDA: Well, you just make yourselves comfortable in there.

TOM: Yes, Mother.

AMANDA: Ask Mr. O'Connor if he would like to wash his hands.

100 **JIM:**   Aw—no—thank you—I took care of that at the warehouse. Tom—

TOM: Yes?

JIM: Mr. Mendoza was speaking to me about you.

TOM: Favorably?

JIM: What do you think?

105 **TOM:**   Well—

JIM: You're going to be out of a job if you don't wake up.

TOM: I am waking up—

JIM: You show no signs.

TOM: The signs are interior.

(Image On Screen: The Sailing Vessel With Jolly Roger Again.)

110 **TOM:**   I'm planning to change. *(He leans over the rail speaking with quiet exhilaration. The incandescent marquees and signs of the first-run movie houses light his face from across the alley. He looks like a voyager.)* I'm right at the point of committing myself to a future that doesn't include the warehouse and Mr. Mendoza or even a night-school course in public speaking.

JIM: What are you gassing about?

TOM: I'm tired of the movies.

JIM: Movies!

TOM: Yes, movies! Look at them—*(A wave toward the marvels of Grand Avenue.)* All of those glamorous people—having adventures—hogging it all, gobbling the whole thing up! You know what happens? People go to the *movies* instead of *moving!* Hollywood characters are supposed to have all the adventures for everybody in America, while everybody in America sits in a dark room and watches them have them! Yes, until there's a war. That's when adventure becomes available to the masses! *Everyone's* dish, not only Gable's! Then the people in the dark room come out of the dark room to have some adventures themselves—Goody, goody—It's our turn now, to go to the South Sea Island—to make a safari—to be exotic, far-off—But I'm not patient. I don't want to wait till then. I'm tired of the *movies* and I am *about* to *move!*

115 **JIM:**   *(incredulously)* Move?

TOM: Yes.

JIM: When?

TOM: Soon!

JIM: Where? Where?

Theme three music seems to answer the question, while Tom thinks it over. He searches among his pockets.

120 **TOM:**   I'm starting to boil inside. I know I seem dreary, but insidewell, I'm boiling! Whenever I pick up a shoe, I shudder a little thinking how short

life is and what I am doing!—Whatever that means. I know it doesn't mean shoes—except as something to wear on a traveler's feet! *(Finds paper.)* Look—

Jim: What?

Tom: I'm a member.

Jim: *(reading)* The Union of Merchant Seamen.

Tom: I paid my dues this month, instead of the light bill.

125 **Jim:** You will regret it when they turn the lights off.

Tom: I won't be here.

Jim: How about your mother?

Tom: I'm like my father. The bastard son of a bastard! See how he grins? And he's been absent going on sixteen years!

Jim: You're just talking, you drip. How does your mother feel about it?

130 **Tom:** Shhh—Here comes Mother! Mother is not acquainted with my plans!

Amanda: *(enters portieres)* Where are you all?

Tom: On the terrace, Mother.

They start inside. She advances to them. Tom is distinctly shocked at her appearance. Even Jim blinks a little. He is making his first contact with girlish Southern vivacity and in spite of the night-school course in public speaking is somewhat thrown off the beam by the unexpected outlay of social charm.

Certain responses are attempted by Jim but are swept aside by Amanda's gay laughter and chatter. Tom is embarrassed but after the first shock Jim reacts very warmly. Grins and chuckles, is altogether won over.

(Image: Amanda As A Girl.)

Amanda: *(coyly smiling, shaking her girlish ringlets)* Well, well, well, so this is Mr. O'Connor. Introductions entirely unnecessary. I've heard so much about you from my boy. I finally said to him, Tom—good gracious!—why don't you bring this paragon to supper? I'd like to meet this nice young man at the warehouse!—Instead of just hearing him sing your praises so much! I don't know why my son is so stand-offishthat's not Southern behavior! Let's sit down and—I think we could stand a little more air in here! Tom, leave the door open. I felt a nice fresh breeze a moment ago. Where has it gone? Mmm, so warm already! And not quite summer, even. We're going to burn up when summer really gets started. However, we're having—we're having a very light supper. I think light things are better fo' this time of year. The same as light clothes are. Light clothes an' light food are what warm weather calls fo'. You know our blood gets so thick during th' winter—it takes a while fo' us to *adjust* ou'selves!— when the season changes . . . It's come so quick this year. I wasn't prepared. All of a sudden—heavens! Already summer!—I ran to the trunk an' pulled out this light dress—Terribly old! Historical almost! But feels so good—so good an' co-ol, y'know. . . .

Tom: Mother—

135 **Amanda:** Yes, honey?

Tom: How about—supper?

Amanda: Honey, you go ask Sister if supper is ready! You know that Sister is in full charge of supper! Tell her you hungry boys are waiting for it. *(To Jim.)* Have you met Laura?

Jim: She—

Amanda: Let you in? Oh, good, you've met already! It's rare for a girl as sweet an' pretty as Laura to be domestic! But Laura is, thank heavens, not only pretty but also very domestic. I'm not at all. I never was a bit. I never could make a thing but angel-food cake. Well, in the South we had so many servants. Gone, gone, gone. All vestiges of gracious living! Gone completely! I wasn't prepared for what the future brought me. All of my gentlemen callers were sons of planters and so of course I assumed that I would be married to one and raise my family on a large piece of land with plenty of servants. But man proposes—and woman accepts the proposal!—To vary that old, old saying a little bit—I married no planter! I married a man who worked for the telephone company!—that gallantly smiling gentleman over there! *(Points to the picture.)* A telephone man who—fell in love with long-distance!—Now he travels and I don't even know where!—But what am I going on for about my—tribulations? Tell me yours—I hope you don't have any! Tom?

140 **Tom:** *(returning)* Yes, Mother?

Amanda: Is supper nearly ready?

Tom: It looks to me like supper is on the table.

Amanda: Let me look—*(She rises prettily and looks through portieres.)* Oh, lovely—But where is Sister?

Tom: Laura is not feeling well and says that she thinks she'd better not come to the table.

145 **Amanda:** What?—Nonsense!—Laura? Oh, Laura!

Laura: *(offstage, faintly)* Yes, Mother.

Amanda: You really must come to the table. We won't be seated until you come to the table! Come in, Mr. O'Connor. You sit over there and I'll— Laura? Laura Wingfield! You're keeping us waiting, honey! We can't say grace until you come to the table!

The back door is pushed weakly open and Laura comes in. She is obviously quite faint, her lips trembling, her eyes wide and staring. She moves unsteadily toward the table.

(Legend: "Terror!")

Outside a summer storm is coming abruptly. The white curtains billow inward at the windows and there is a sorrowful murmur and deep blue dusk.
Laura suddenly stumbles—She catches at a chair with a faint moan.

Tom: Laura!

Amanda: Laura! *(There is a clap of thunder.)* *(Legend: "Ah!")* *(Despairingly.)* Why, Laura, you *are* sick, darling! Tom, help your sister into the living room, dear! Sit in the living room, Laura—rest on the sofa. Well! *(To the* *gentleman caller.)* Standing over the hot stove made her ill!—I told her that it was just too warm this evening, but—*(Tom comes back in. Laura is on the sofa.)* Is Laura all right now?

TOM: Yes.

AMANDA: What *is* that? Rain? A nice cool rain has come up! *(She gives the gentleman caller a frightened look.)* I think we may—have grace—now . . . *(Tom looks at her stupidly.)* Tom, honey—you say grace!

TOM: Oh . . . "For these and all thy mercies—" *(They bow their heads, Amanda stealing a nervous glance at Jim. In the living room Laura, stretched on the sofa, clenches her hand to her lips, to hold back a shuddering sob.)* God's Holy Name be praised—

(The Scene Dims Out.)

SCENE VII

(A Souvenir.)

Half an hour later. Dinner is just being finished in the upstage area which is concealed by the drawn portieres.

As the curtain rises Laura is still huddled upon the sofa, her feet drawn under her, her head resting on a pale blue pillow, her eyes wide and mysteriously watchful. The new floor lamp with its shade of rose-colored silk gives a soft, becoming light to her face, bringing out the fragile, unearthly prettiness which usually escapes attention. There is a steady murmur of rain, but it is slackening and stops soon after the scene begins; the air outside becomes pale and luminous as the moon breaks out.

A moment after the curtain rises, the lights in both rooms flicker and go out.

JIM: Hey, there, Mr. Light Bulb!

Amanda laughs nervously.

(Legend: "Suspension Of A Public Service.")

AMANDA: Where was Moses when the lights went out? Ha-ha. Do you know the answer to that one, Mr. O'Connor?

JIM: No, Ma'am, what's the answer?

AMANDA: In the dark! *(Jim laughs appreciatively.)* Everybody sit still. I'll light the candles. Isn't it lucky we have them on the table? Where's a match? Which of you gentlemen can provide a match?

5 **JIM:** Here.

AMANDA: Thank you, sir.

JIM: Not at all, Ma'am!

AMANDA: I guess the fuse has burnt out. Mr. O'Connor, can you tell a burnt-out fuse? I know I can't and Tom is a total loss when it comes to mechanics. *(Sound: Getting Up: Voices Recede A Little To Kitchenette.)* Oh, be careful you don't bump into something. We don't want our gentleman caller to break his neck. Now wouldn't that be a fine howdy-do?

Jim: Ha-ha! Where is the fuse-box?

10 **Amanda:**   Right here next to the stove. Can you see anything?

Jim: Just a minute.

Amanda: Isn't electricity a mysterious thing? Wasn't it Benjamin Franklin who tied a key to a kite? We live in such a mysterious universe, don't we? Some people say that science clears up all the mysteries for us. In my opinion it only creates more! Have you found it yet?

Jim: No, Ma'am. All these fuses look okay to me.

Amanda: Tom!

15 **Tom:**   Yes, Mother?

Amanda: That light bill I gave you several days ago. The one I told you we got the notices about?

Tom: Oh.—Yeah.

(Legend: "Ha!")

Amanda: You didn't neglect to pay it by any chance?

Tom: Why, I—

20 **Amanda:**   Didn't! I might have known it!

Jim: Shakespeare probably wrote a poem on that light bill, Mrs. Wingfield.

Amanda: I might have known better than to trust him with it! There's such a high price for negligence in this world!

Jim: Maybe the poem will win a ten-dollar prize.

Amanda: We'll just have to spend the remainder of the evening in the nineteenth century, before Mr. Edison made the Mazda lamp!

25 **Jim:**   Candlelight is my favorite kind of light.

Amanda: That shows you're romantic! But that's no excuse for Tom. Well, we got through dinner. Very considerate of them to let us get through dinner before they plunged us into everlasting darkness, wasn't it, Mr. O'Connor?

Jim: Ha-ha!

Amanda: Tom, as a penalty for your carelessness you can help me with the dishes.

Jim: Let me give you a hand.

30 **Amanda:**   Indeed you will not!

Jim: I ought to be good for something.

Amanda: Good for something? *(Her tone is rhapsodic.)* You? Why, Mr. O'Connor, nobody, *nobody's* given me this much entertainment in years—as you have!

Jim: Aw, now, Mrs. Wingfield!

Amanda: I'm not exaggerating, not one bit! But Sister is all by her lonesome. You go keep her company in the parlor! I'll give you this lovely old candelabrum that used to be on the altar at the church of the Heavenly Rest. It was melted a little out of shape when the church burnt down. Lightning struck it one spring. Gypsy Jones was holding a revival at the time and he intimated that the church was destroyed because the Episcopalians gave card parties.

35 **JIM:** Ha-ha.

AMANDA: And how about coaxing Sister to drink a little wine? I think it would be good for her! Can you carry both at once?

JIM: Sure. I'm Superman!

AMANDA: Now, Thomas, get into this apron!

The door of kitchenette swings closed on Amanda's gay laughter; the flickering light approaches the portieres.

Laura sits up nervously as he enters. Her speech at first is low and breathless from the almost intolerable strain of being alone with a stranger.

(The Legend: "I Don't Suppose You Remember Me At All!")

In her first speeches in this scene, before Jim's warmth overcomes her paralyzing shyness, Laura's voice is thin and breathless as though she has run up a steep flight of stairs.

Jim's attitude is gently humorous. In playing this scene it should be stressed that while the incident is apparently unimportant, it is to Laura the climax of her secret life.

JIM: Hello, there, Laura.

40 **LAURA:** *(faintly)* Hello. *(She clears her throat.)*

JIM: How are you feeling now? Better?

LAURA: Yes. Yes, thank you.

JIM: This is for you. A little dandelion wine. *(He extends it toward her with extravagant gallantry.)*

LAURA: Thank you.

45 **JIM:** Drink it—but don't get drunk! *(He laughs heartily. Laura takes the glass uncertainly; laughs shyly.)* Where shall I set the candles?

LAURA: Oh—oh, anywhere . . .

JIM: How about here on the floor? Any objections?

LAURA: No.

JIM: I'll spread a newspaper under to catch the drippings. I like to sit on the floor. Mind if I do?

50 **LAURA:** Oh, no.

JIM: Give me a pillow?

LAURA: What?

JIM: A pillow!

LAURA: Oh . . . *(Hands him one quickly.)*

55 **JIM:** How about you? Don't you like to sit on the floor?

LAURA: Oh—yes.

JIM: Why don't you, then?

LAURA: I—will.

JIM: Take a pillow! *(Laura does. Sits on the other side of the candelabrum. Jim crosses his legs and smiles engagingly at her.)* I can't hardly see you sitting way over there.

60 **LAURA:**   I can—see you.

JIM: I know, but that's not fair, I'm in the limelight. *(Laura moves her pillow closer.)* Good! Now I can see you! Comfortable?

LAURA: Yes.

JIM: So am I. Comfortable as a cow. Will you have some gum?

LAURA: No, thank you.

65 **JIM:**   I think that I will indulge, with your permission. *(Musingly unwraps it and holds it up.)* Think of the fortune made by the guy that invented the first piece of chewing gum. Amazing, huh? The Wrigley Building is one of the sights of Chicago.—I saw it summer before last when I went up to the Century of Progress. Did you take in the Century of Progress?

LAURA: No, I didn't.

JIM: Well, it was quite a wonderful exposition. What impressed me most was the Hall of Science. Gives you an idea of what the future will be in America, even more wonderful than the present time is! *(Pause. Smiling at her.)* Your brother tells me you're shy. Is that right, Laura?

LAURA: I—don't know.

JIM: I judge you to be an old-fashioned type of girl. Well, I think that's a pretty good type to be. Hope you don't think I'm being too personal— do you?

70 **LAURA:**   *(hastily, out of embarrassment)* I believe I *will* take a piece of gum, if you—don't mind. *(Clearing her throat.)* Mr. O'Connor, have you—kept up with your singing?

JIM: Singing? Me?

LAURA: Yes. I remember what a beautiful voice you had.

JIM: When did you hear me sing?

(Voice Offstage In The Pause.)

Voice (offstage):

O blow, ye winds, heigh-ho,
A-roving I will go!
I'm off to my love
With a boxing glove—
Ten thousand miles away!

JIM: You say you've heard me sing?

75 **LAURA:**   Oh, yes! Yes, very often . . . I—don't suppose you remember me—at all?

JIM: *(smiling doubtfully)* You know I have an idea I've seen you before. I had that idea soon as you opened the door. It seemed almost like I was about to remember your name. But the name that I started to call you—wasn't a name! And so I stopped myself before I said it.

LAURA: Wasn't it—Blue Roses?

JIM: *(springs up, grinning)* Blue Roses! My gosh, yes—Blue Roses! That's what I had on my tongue when you opened the door! Isn't it funny what tricks your memory plays? I didn't connect you with the high school

somehow or other. But that's where it was; it was high school. I didn't
even know you were Shakespeare's sister! Gosh, I'm sorry.

Laura: I didn't expect you to. You—barely knew me!

80 **Jim:** But we did have a speaking acquaintance, huh?

Laura: Yes, we—spoke to each other.

Jim: When did you recognize me?

Laura: Oh, right away!

Jim: Soon as I came in the door?

85 **Laura:** When I heard your name I thought it was probably you. I knew that
Tom used to know you a little in high school. So when you came in the
door—Well, then I was—sure.

Jim: Why didn't you *say* something, then?

Laura: *(breathlessly)* I didn't know what to say, I was—too surprised!

Jim: For goodness' sakes! You know, this sure is funny!

Laura: Yes! Yes, isn't it, though . . .

90 **Jim:** Didn't we have a class in something together?

Laura: Yes, we did.

Jim: What class was that?

Laura: It was—singing—Chorus!

Jim: Aw!

95 **Laura:** I sat across the aisle from you in the Aud.

Jim: Aw.

Laura: Mondays, Wednesdays and Fridays.

Jim: Now I remember—you always came in late.

Laura: Yes, it was so hard for me, getting upstairs. I had that brace on my
leg—it clumped so loud!

100 **Jim:** I never heard any clumping.

Laura: *(wincing at the recollection)* To me it sounded like—thunder!

Jim: Well, well, well. I never even noticed.

Laura: And everybody was seated before I came in. I had to walk in front
of all those people. My seat was in the back row. I had to go clumping all
the way up the aisle with everyone watching!

Jim: You shouldn't have been self-conscious.

105 **Laura:** I know, but I was. It was always such a relief when the singing
started.

Jim: Aw, yes, I've placed you now! I used to call you Blue Roses. How was it
that I got started calling you that?

Laura: I was out of school a little while with pleurosis. When I came back
you asked me what was the matter. I said I had pleurosis—you thought I
said Blue Roses. That's what you always called me after that!

Jim: I hope you didn't mind.

Laura: Oh, no—I liked it. You see, I wasn't acquainted with many—
people. . . .

110 **Jim:** As I remember you sort of stuck by yourself.

Laura: I—I—never had much luck at—making friends.

Jim: I don't see why you wouldn't.

Laura: Well, I—started out badly.

Jim: You mean being—

115 **Laura:**   Yes, it sort of—stood between me—

Jim: You shouldn't have let it!

Laura: I know, but it did, and—

Jim: You were shy with people!

Laura: I tried not to be but never could—

120 **Jim:**   Overcome it?

Laura: No, I—I never could!

Jim: I guess being shy is something you have to work out of kind of gradually.

Laura: *(sorrowfully)* Yes—I guess it—

Jim: Takes time!

125 **Laura:**   Yes—

Jim: People are not so dreadful when you know them. That's what you have to remember! And everybody has problems, not just you, but practically everybody has got some problems. You think of yourself as having the only problems, as being the only one who is disappointed. But just look around you and you will see lots of people as disappointed as you are. For instance, I hoped when I was going to high school that I would be further along at this time, six years later, than I am now—You remember that wonderful write-up I had in *The Torch?*

Laura: Yes! *(She rises and crosses to table.)*

Jim: It said I was bound to succeed in anything I went into! *(Laura returns with the annual.)* Holy Jeez! *The Torch!* (He accepts it reverently. They smile across it with mutual wonder. Laura crouches beside him and they begin to turn through it. Laura's shyness is dissolving in his warmth.)*

Laura: Here you are in *Pirates of Penzance!*

130 **Jim:**   *(wistfully)* I sang the baritone lead in that operetta.

Laura: *(rapidly)* So—*beautifully!*

Jim: *(protesting)* Aw—

Laura: Yes, yes—beautifully—beautifully!

Jim: You heard me?

135 **Laura:**   All three times!

Jim: No!

Laura: Yes!

Jim: All three performances?

Laura: *(looking down)* Yes.

140 **Jim:**   Why?

Laura: I—wanted to ask you to—autograph my program.

Jim: Why didn't you ask me to?

Laura: You were always surrounded by your own friends so much that I never had a chance to.

Jim: You should have just—

145 **Laura:**   Well, I—thought you might think I was—

Jim: Thought I might think you was—what?

LAURA: Oh—

JIM: *(with reflective relish)* I was beleaguered by females in those days.

LAURA: You were terribly popular!

150 **JIM:** Yeah—

LAURA: You had such a—friendly way—

JIM: I was spoiled in high school.

LAURA: Everybody—liked you!

JIM: Including you?

155 **LAURA:** I—yes, I—I did, too—*(She gently closes the book in her lap.)*

JIM: Well, well, well!—Give me that program, Laura. *(She hands it to him. He signs it with a flourish.)* There you are—better late than never!

LAURA: Oh, I—what a—surprise!

JIM: My signature isn't worth very much right now. But some day—maybe—it will increase in value! Being disappointed is one thing and being discouraged is something else. I am disappointed but I'm not discouraged. I'm twenty-three years old. How old are you?

LAURA: I'll be twenty-four in June.

160 **JIM:** That's not old age!

LAURA: No, but—

JIM: You finished high school?

LAURA: *(with difficulty)* I didn't go back.

JIM: You mean you dropped out?

165 **LAURA:** I made bad grades in my final examinations. *(She rises and replaces the book and the program. Her voice strained.)* How is—Emily Meisenbach getting along?

JIM: Oh, that kraut-head!

LAURA: Why do you call her that?

JIM: That's what she was.

LAURA: You're not still—going with her?

170 **JIM:** I never see her.

LAURA: It said in the Personal Section that you were—engaged!

JIM: I know, but I wasn't impressed by that—propaganda!

LAURA: It wasn't—the truth?

JIM: Only in Emily's optimistic opinion!

175 **LAURA:** Oh—

(Legend: "What Have You Done Since High School?")

Jim lights a cigarette and leans indolently back on his elbows smiling at Laura with a warmth and charm which light her inwardly with altar candles. She remains by the table and turns in her hands a piece of glass to cover her tumult.

JIM: *(after several reflective puffs on a cigarette)* What have you done since high school? *(She seems not to hear him.)* Huh? *(Laura looks up.)* I said what have you done since high school, Laura?

LAURA: Nothing much.

Jim: You must have been doing something these six long years.

Laura: Yes.

180   **Jim:**   Well, then, such as what?

Laura: I took a business course at business college—

Jim: How did that work out?

Laura: Well, not very—well—I had to drop out, it gave me—indigestion—

Jim laughs gently.

Jim: What are you doing now?

185   **Laura:**   I don't do anything—much. Oh, please don't think I sit around doing nothing! My glass collection takes up a good deal of my time. Glass is something you have to take good care of.

Jim: What did you say—about glass?

Laura: Collection I said—I have one—*(She clears her throat and turns away again, acutely shy.)*

Jim: *(abruptly)* You know what I judge to be the trouble with you? Inferiority complex! Know what that is? That's what they call it when someone low-rates himself! I understand it because I had it, too. Although my case was not so aggravated as yours seems to be. I had it until I took up public speaking, developed my voice, and learned that I had an aptitude for science. Before that time I never thought of myself as being outstanding in any way whatsoever! Now I've never made a regular study of it, but I have a friend who says I can analyze people better than doctors that make a profession of it. I don't claim that to be necessarily true, but I can sure guess a person's psychology, Laura! *(Takes out his gum.)* Excuse me, Laura. I always take it out when the flavor is gone. I'll use this scrap of paper to wrap it in. I know how it is to get it stuck on a shoe. Yep—that's what I judge to be your principal trouble. A lack of confidence in yourself as a person. You don't have the proper amount of faith in yourself. I'm basing that fact on a number of your remarks and also on certain observations I've made. For instance that clumping you thought was so awful in high school. You say that you even dreaded to walk into class. You see what you did? You dropped out of school, you gave up an education because of a clump, which as far as I know was practically non-existent! A little physical defect is what you have. Hardly noticeable even! Magnified thousands of times by imagination! You know what my strong advice to you is? Think of yourself as *superior* in some way!

Laura: In what way would I think?

190   **Jim:**   Why, man alive, Laura! Just look about you a little. What do you see? A world full of common people! All of 'em born and all of 'em going to die! Which of them has one-tenth of your good points! Or mine! Or anyone else's, as far as that goes—Gosh! Everybody excels in some one thing. Some in many! *(Unconsciously glances at himself in the mirror.)* All you've got to do is discover in *what!* Take me, for instance. *(He adjusts his tie at the mirror.)* My interest happens to lie in electro-dynamics. I'm taking a

course in radio engineering at night school, Laura, on top of a fairly responsible job at the warehouse. I'm taking that course and studying public speaking.

Laura: Ohhhh.

Jim: Because I believe in the future of television! *(Turning back to her.)* I wish to be ready to go up right along with it. Therefore I'm planning to get in on the ground floor. In fact, I've already made the right connections and all that remains is for the industry itself to get underway! Full steam—*(His eyes are starry.) Knowledge*—Zzzzzp! *Money*—Zzzzzzp!—*Power!* That's the cycle democracy is built on! *(His attitude is convincingly dynamic. Laura stares at him, even her shyness eclipsed in her absolute wonder. He suddenly grins.)* I guess you think I think a lot of myself!

Laura: No—o-o-o, I—

Jim: Now how about you? Isn't there something you take more interest in than anything else?

195 **Laura:** Well, I do—as I said—have my—glass collection—

A peal of girlish laughter from the kitchen.

Jim: I'm not right sure I know what you're talking about. What kind of glass is it?

Laura: Little articles of it, they're ornaments mostly! Most of them are little animals made out of glass, the tiniest little animals in the world. Mother calls them a glass menagerie! Here's an example of one, if you'd like to see it! This one is one of the oldest. It's nearly thirteen. *(He stretches out his hand.) (Music: "The Glass Menagerie.")* Oh, be careful—if you breathe, it breaks!

Jim: I'd better not take it. I'm pretty clumsy with things.

Laura: Go on, I trust you with him! *(Places it in his palm.)* There now— you're holding him gently! Hold him over the light, he loves the light! You see how the light shines through him?

200 **Jim:** It sure does shine!

Laura: I shouldn't be partial, but he is my favorite one.

Jim: What kind of a thing is this one supposed to be?

Laura: Haven't you noticed the single horn on his forehead?

Jim: A unicorn, huh?

205 **Laura:** Mmm-hmmm!

Jim: Unicorns, aren't they extinct in the modern world?

Laura: I know!

Jim: Poor little fellow, he must feel sort of lonesome.

Laura: *(smiling)* Well, if he does he doesn't complain about it. He stays on a shelf with some horses that don't have horns and all of them seem to get along nicely together.

210 **Jim:** How do you know?

Laura: *(lightly)* I haven't heard any arguments among them!

Jim: *(grinning)* No arguments, huh? Well, that's a pretty good sign! Where shall I set him?

LAURA: Put him on the table. They all like a change of scenery once in a while!

JIM: *(stretching)* Well, well, well, well—Look how big my shadow is when I stretch!

215 **LAURA:**   Oh, oh, yes—it stretches across the ceiling!

JIM: *(crossing to door)* I think it's stopped raining. *(Opens fire-escape door.)* Where does the music come from?

LAURA: From the Paradise Dance Hall across the alley.

JIM: How about cutting the rug a little, Miss Wingfield?

LAURA: Oh, I—

220 **JIM:**   Or is your program filled up? Let me have a look at it. *(Grasps imaginary card.)* Why, every dance is taken! I'll just have to scratch some out. *(Waltz Music: "La Golondrina.")* Ahhh, a waltz! *(He executes some sweeping turns by himself, then holds his arms toward Laura.)*

LAURA: *(breathlessly)* I—can't dance!

JIM: There you go, that inferiority stuff!

LAURA: I've never danced in my life!

JIM: Come on, try!

225 **LAURA:**   Oh, but I'd step on you!

JIM: I'm not made out of glass.

LAURA: How—how—how do we start?

JIM: Just leave it to me. You hold your arms out a little.

LAURA: Like this?

230 **JIM:**   A little bit higher. Right. Now don't tighten up, that's the main thing about it—relax.

LAURA: *(laughing breathlessly)* It's hard not to.

JIM: Okay.

LAURA: I'm afraid you can't budge me.

JIM: What do you bet I can't? *(He swings her into motion.)*

235 **LAURA:**   Goodness, yes, you can!

JIM: Let yourself go, now, Laura, just let yourself go.

LAURA: I'm—

JIM: Come on!

LAURA: Trying!

240 **JIM:**   Not so stiff—Easy does it!

LAURA: I know but I'm—

JIM: Loosen th' backbone! There now, that's a lot better.

LAURA: Am I?

JIM: Lots, lots better! *(He moves her about the room in a clumsy waltz.)*

245 **LAURA:**   Oh, my!

JIM: Ha-ha!

LAURA: Goodness, yes you can!

JIM: Ha-ha-ha! *(They suddenly bump into the table, Jim stops.)* What did we hit on?

LAURA: Table.

250 **JIM:**   Did something fall off it? I think—

Laura: Yes.

Jim: I hope that it wasn't the little glass horse with the horn!

Laura: Yes.

Jim: Aw, aw, aw. Is it broken?

255 **Laura:** Now it is just like all the other horses.

Jim: It's lost its—

Laura: Horn! It doesn't matter. Maybe it's a blessing in disguise.

Jim: You'll never forgive me. I bet that that was your favorite piece of glass.

Laura: I don't have favorites much. It's no tragedy, Freckles. Glass breaks so easily. No matter how careful you are. The traffic jars the shelves and things fall off them.

260 **Jim:** Still I'm awfully sorry that I was the cause.

Laura: *(smiling)* I'll just imagine he had an operation. The horn was removed to make him feel less—freakish! *(They both laugh.)* Now he will feel more at home with the other horses, the ones that don't have horns . . .

Jim: Ha-ha, that's very funny! *(Suddenly serious.)* I'm glad to see that you have a sense of humor. You know—you're—well—very different! Surprisingly different from anyone else I know! *(His voice becomes soft and hesitant with a genuine feeling.)* Do you mind me telling you that? *(Laura is abashed beyond speech.)* You make me feel sort of—I don't know how to put it! I'm usually pretty good at expressing things, but—This is something that I don't know how to say! *(Laura touches her throat and clears it—turns the broken unicorn in her hands.)* *(Even softer.)* Has anyone ever told you that you were pretty? *(Pause: Music.)* *(Laura looks up slowly, with wonder, and shakes her head.)* Well, you are! In a very different way from anyone else. And all the nicer because of the difference, too. *(His voice becomes low and husky. Laura turns away, nearly faint with the novelty of her emotions.)* I wish you were my sister. I'd teach you to have some confidence in yourself. The different people are not like other people, but being different is nothing to be ashamed of. Because other people are not such wonderful people. They're one hundred times one thousand. You're one times one! They walk all over the earth. You just stay here. They're common as—weeds, but—you—well, you're—*Blue Roses!*

(Image On Screen: Blue Roses.)

(Music Changes.)

Laura: But blue is wrong for—roses . . .

Jim: It's right for you—You're—pretty!

265 **Laura:** In what respect am I pretty?

Jim: In all respects—believe me! Your eyes—your hair—are pretty! Your hands are pretty! *(He catches hold of her hand.)* You think I'm making this up because I'm invited to dinner and have to be nice. Oh, I could do that! I could put on an act for you, Laura, and say lots of things without being very sincere. But this time I am. I'm talking to you sincerely. I happened to notice you had this inferiority complex that keeps you from feeling comfortable with people. Somebody needs to build your confidence up and make you proud instead of shy and turning away and—blushing—Somebody ought to—ought to—*kiss* you, Laura! *(His hand slips slowly up her arm to her shoulder.) (Music Swells Tumultuously.) (He suddenly turns her about and kisses her on the lips. When he releases her Laura sinks on the sofa with a bright, dazed look. Jim backs away and fishes in his pocket for a cigarette.) (Legend On Screen: "Souvenir.")* Stumble-john! *(He lights the cigarette, avoiding her look. There is a peal of girlish laughter from Amanda in the kitchen. Laura slowly raises and opens her hand. It still contains the little broken glass animal. She looks at it with a tender, bewildered expression.)* Stumble-john! I shouldn't have done that—That was way off the beam. You don't smoke, do you? *(She looks up, smiling, not hearing the question. He sits beside her a little gingerly. She looks at him speechlessly—waiting. He coughs decorously and moves a little farther aside as he considers the situation and senses her feelings, dimly, with perturbation. Gently.)* Would you—care for a—mint? *(She doesn't seem to hear him but her look grows brighter even.)* Peppermint—Life Saver? My pocket's a regular drug store—wherever I go . . . *(He pops a mint in his mouth. Then gulps and decides to make a clean breast of it. He speaks slowly and gingerly.)* Laura, you know, if I had a sister like you, I'd do the same thing as Tom, I'd bring out fellows—introduce her to them. The right type of boys of a type to—appreciate her. Only—well—he made a mistake about me. Maybe I've got no call to be saying this. That may not have been the idea in having me over. But what if it was? There's nothing wrong about that. The only trouble is that in my case—I'm not in a situation to do the right thing. I can't take down your number and say I'll phone. I can't call up next week and—ask for a date. I thought I had better explain the situation in case you misunderstood it and—hurt your feelings. . . . *(Pause. Slowly, very slowly, Laura's look changes, her eyes returning slowly from his to the ornament in her palm.)*

Amanda utters another gay laugh in the kitchen.

LAURA: *(faintly)* You—won't—call again?

JIM: No, Laura. I can't. *(He rises from the sofa.)* As I was just explaining, I've—got strings on me, Laura, I've—been going steady! I go out all the time with a girl named Betty. She's a home-girl like you, and Catholic, and Irish, and in a great many ways we—get along fine. I met her last summer on a moonlight boat trip up the river to Alton, on the *Majestic*. Well—right away from the start it was—love! *(Legend: Love!) (Laura sways slightly forward and grips the arm of the sofa. He fails to notice, now enrapt in his own comfortable being.)* Being in love has made a new man of me! *(Leaning stiffly forward, clutching the arm of the sofa, Laura struggles visibly with her storm. But Jim is oblivious, she is a long way off.)* The power of love is really pretty tremendous! Love is something that—changes the whole world, Laura! *(The storm abates a little and Laura leans back. He notices her again.)* It happened that Betty's aunt took sick, she got a wire and had to go to Centralia. So Tom—when he asked me to dinner—I naturally just accepted the invitation, not knowing that you—that he—that I—*(He stops awkwardly.)* Huh—I'm a stumble-john! *(He flops back on the sofa. The holy candles in the altar of Laura's face have been snuffed out! There is a look of almost infinite desolation. Jim glances at her uneasily.)* I wish that you would—say something. *(She bites her lip which was trembling and then bravely smiles. She opens her hand again on the broken glass ornament. Then she gently takes his hand and raises it level with her own. She carefully places the unicorn in the palm of his hand, then pushes his fingers closed upon it.)* What are you—doing that for? You want me to have him?—Laura? *(She nods.)* What for?

LAURA: A—souvenir . . .

She rises unsteadily and crouches beside the Victrola to wind it up.

(Legend On Screen: "Things Have A Way Of Turning Out So Badly.")

(Or Image: "Gentleman Caller Waving Good-bye!—Gaily.")

At this moment Amanda rushes brightly back in the front room. She bears a pitcher of fruit punch in an old-fashioned cut-glass pitcher and a plate of macaroons. The plate has a gold border and poppies painted on it.

270 **AMANDA:** Well, well, well! Isn't the air delightful after the shower? I've made you children a little liquid refreshment. *(Turns gaily to the gentleman caller.)* Jim, do you know that song about lemonade?

> "Lemonade, lemonade
> Made in the shade and stirred with a spade—
> Good enough for any old maid!"

JIM: *(uneasily)* Ha-ha! No—I never heard it.

AMANDA: Why, Laura! You look so serious!

JIM: We were having a serious conversation.

AMANDA: Good! Now you're better acquainted!

275 **JIM:** *(uncertainly)* Ha-ha! Yes.

AMANDA: You modern young people are much more serious-minded than my generation. I was so gay as a girl!

JIM: You haven't changed, Mrs. Wingfield.

AMANDA: Tonight I'm rejuvenated! The gaiety of the occasion, Mr. O'Connor! *(She tosses her head with a peal of laughter. Spills lemonade.)* Oooo! I'm baptizing myself!

JIM: Here—let me—

280 **AMANDA:** *(setting the pitcher down)* There now. I discovered we had some maraschino cherries. I dumped them in, juice and all!

JIM: You shouldn't have gone to that trouble. Mrs. Wingfield.

AMANDA: Trouble, trouble? Why it was loads of fun! Didn't you hear me cutting up in the kitchen? I bet your ears were burning! I told Tom how outdone with him I was for keeping you to himself so long a time! He should have brought you over much, much sooner! Well, now that you've found your way, I want you to be a very frequent caller! Not just occasional but all the time. Oh, we're going to have a lot of gay times together! I see them coming! Mmm, just breathe that air! So fresh, and the moon's so pretty! I'll skip back out—I know where my place is when young folks are having a—serious conversation!

JIM: Oh, don't go out, Mrs. Wingfield. The fact of the matter is I've got to be going.

AMANDA: Going, now? You're joking! Why, it's only the shank of the evening, Mr. O'Connor!

285   **JIM:**   Well, you know how it is.

AMANDA: You mean you're a young workingman and have to keep workingmen's hours. We'll let you off early tonight. But only on the condition that next time you stay later. What's the best night for you? Isn't Saturday night the best night for you workingmen?

JIM: I have a couple of time-clocks to punch, Mrs. Wingfield. One at morning, another one at night!

AMANDA: My, but you *are* ambitious! You work at night, too?

JIM: No, Ma'am, not work but—Betty! *(He crosses deliberately to pick up his hat. The band at the Paradise Dance Hall goes into a tender waltz.)*

290   **AMANDA:**   Betty? Betty? Who's Betty! *(There is an ominous cracking sound in the sky.)*

JIM: Oh, just a girl. The girl I go steady with! *(He smiles charmingly. The sky falls.)*

(Legend: "The Sky Falls.")

AMANDA: *(a long-drawn exhalation)* Ohhhh . . . Is it a serious romance, Mr. O'Connor?

JIM: We're going to be married the second Sunday in June.

AMANDA: Ohhhh—how nice! Tom didn't mention that you were engaged to be married.

295   **JIM:**   The cat's not out of the bag at the warehouse yet. You know how they are. They call you Romeo and stuff like that. *(He stops at the oval mirror to put on his hat. He carefully shapes the brim and the crown to give a discreetly dashing effect.)* It's been a wonderful evening, Mrs. Wingfield. I guess this is what they mean by Southern hospitality.

AMANDA: It really wasn't anything at all.

JIM: I hope it don't seem like I'm rushing off. But I promised Betty I'd pick her up at the Wabash depot, an' by the time I get my jalopy down there her train'll be in. Some women are pretty upset if you keep 'em waiting.

AMANDA: Yes, I know—The tyranny of women! *(Extends her hand.)* Goodbye, Mr. O'Connor. I wish you luck—and happiness—and success! All three of them, and so does Laura!—Don't you, Laura?

LAURA: Yes!

300   **JIM:**   *(taking her hand)* Goodbye, Laura. I'm certainly going to treasure that souvenir. And don't you forget the good advice I gave you. *(Raises his*

voice to a cheery shout.) So long, Shakespeare! Thanks again, ladies—
Good night!

He grins and ducks jauntily out.

    *Still bravely grimacing, Amanda closes the door on the gentleman caller. Then
she turns back to the room with a puzzled expression. She and Laura don't dare to
face each other. Laura crouches beside the Victrola to wind it.*

AMANDA: *(faintly)* Things have a way of turning out so badly. I don't believe
that I would play the Victrola. Well, well—well—Our gentleman caller
was engaged to be married! Tom!

TOM: *(from back)* Yes, Mother?

AMANDA: Come in here a minute. I want to tell you something awfully funny.

TOM: *(enters with macaroon and a glass of the lemonade)* Has the gentleman
caller gotten away already?

305 **AMANDA:**   The gentleman caller has made an early departure. What a
wonderful joke you played on us!

TOM: How do you mean?

AMANDA: You didn't mention that he was engaged to be married.

TOM: Jim? Engaged?

AMANDA: That's what he just informed us.

310 **TOM:**   I'll be jiggered! I didn't know about that.

AMANDA: That seems very peculiar.

TOM: What's peculiar about it?

AMANDA: Didn't you call him your best friend down at the warehouse?

TOM: He is, but how did I know?

315 **AMANDA:**   It seems extremely peculiar that you wouldn't know your best
friend was going to be married!

TOM: The warehouse is where I work, not where I know things about
people!

AMANDA: You don't know things anywhere! You live in a dream; you
manufacture illusions! *(He crosses to door.)* Where are you going?

TOM: I'm going to the movies.

AMANDA: That's right, now that you've had us make such fools of
ourselves. The effort, the preparations, all the expense! The new floor
lamp, the rug, the clothes for Laura! All for what? To entertain some
other girl's fiancé! Go to the movies, go! Don't think about us, a mother
deserted, an unmarried sister who's crippled and has no job! Don't let
anything interfere with your selfish pleasure! Just go, go, go—to the
movies!

320 **TOM:**   All right, I will! The more you shout about my selfishness to me the
quicker I'll go, and I won't go to the movies!

AMANDA: Go, then! Then go to the moon—you selfish dreamer!

*Tom smashes his glass on the floor. He plunges out on the fire-escape, slamming
the door. Laura screams—cut by door.*

    *Dance-hall music up. Tom goes to the rail and grips it desperately, lifting his
face in the chill white moonlight penetrating the narrow abyss of the alley.*

(Legend On Screen: "And So Good-bye . . .")

Tom's closing speech is timed with the interior pantomime. The interior scene is played as though viewed through sound-proof glass. Amanda appears to be making a comforting speech to Laura who is huddled upon the sofa. Now that we cannot hear the mother's speech, her silliness is gone and she has dignity and tragic beauty. Laura's dark hair hides her face until at the end of the speech she lifts it to smile at her mother. Amanda's gestures are slow and graceful, almost dancelike, as she comforts the daughter. At the end of her speech she glances a moment at the father's picture—then withdraws through the portieres. At close of Tom's speech, Laura blows out the candles, ending the play.

Tom: I didn't go to the moon, I went much further—for time is the longest distance between two places—Not long after that I was fired for writing a poem on the lid of a shoe-box. I left Saint Louis. I descended the steps of this fire-escape for a last time and followed, from then on, in my father's footsteps, attempting to find in motion what was lost in space—I traveled around a great deal. The cities swept about me like dead leaves, leaves that were brightly colored but torn away from the branches. I would have stopped, but was pursued by something. It always came upon me unawares, taking me altogether by surprise. Perhaps it was a familiar bit of music. Perhaps it was only a piece of transparent glass. Perhaps I am walking along a street at night, in some strange city, before I have found companions. I pass the lighted window of a shop where perfume is sold. The window is filled with pieces of colored glass, tiny transparent bottles in delicate colors, like bits of a shattered rainbow. Then all at once my sister touches my shoulder. I turn around and look into her eyes . . . Oh, Laura, Laura, I tried to leave you behind me, but I am more faithful than I intended to be! I reach for a cigarette, I cross the street, I run into the movies or a bar, I buy a drink, I speak to the nearest stranger—anything that can blow your candles out! *(Laura bends over the candles.)*—for nowadays the world is lit by lightning! Blow out your candles, Laura—and so goodbye . . .

She blows the candles out.

(The Scene Dissolves.)

Author's Production Notes
(Preface to Published Edition)

Being a "memory play," The Glass Menagerie can be presented with unusual freedom of convention. Because of its considerably delicate or tenuous material, atmospheric touches and subtleties of direction play a particularly important part. Expressionism and all other unconventional techniques in drama have only one valid aim, and that is a closer approach to truth. When a play employs unconventional techniques, it is not, or certainly shouldn't be, trying to escape its responsibility of dealing with reality, or interpreting experience, but is actually or should be attempting to find a closer approach, a more penetrating and vivid expression of things as they are. The straight realistic play with its genuine frigidaire and authentic ice-cubes, its characters that speak exactly as its audience speaks, corresponds to the academic landscape and has the same virtue of a photographic likeness. Everyone should know nowadays the unimportance of the photographic in art: that truth, life, or reality is an organic thing which the poetic imagination can represent or suggest, in essence, only through transformation, through changing into other forms than those which were merely present in appearance.

These remarks are not meant as a preface only to this particular play. They have to do with a conception of a new, plastic theatre which must take the place of the exhausted theater of realistic conventions if the theatre is to resume vitality as a part of our culture.

The Screen Device: There is *only one important difference between the original and acting version of the play* and that is the *omission* in the latter of the device which I tentatively included in my *original* script. This device was the use of a screen on which were projected magic-lantern slides bearing images or titles. I do not regret the omission of this device from the present Broadway production. The extraordinary power of Miss Taylor's performance made it suitable to have the utmost simplicity in the physical production. But I think it may be interesting to some readers to see how this device was conceived. So I am putting it into the published manuscript. These images and legends, projected from behind, were cast on a section of wall between the front-room and dining-room areas, which should be indistinguishable from the rest when not in use.

The purpose of this will probably be apparent. It is to give accent to certain values in each scene. Each scene contains a particular point (or several) which is structurally the most important. In an episodic play, such as this, the basic structure or narrative line may be obscured from the audience; the effect may seem fragmentary rather than architectural. This may not be the fault of the play so much as a lack of attention in the audience. The legend or image upon the screen will strengthen the effect of what is merely allusion in the writing and allow the primary point to be made more simply and lightly than if the entire responsibility were on the spoken lines. Aside from this structural value, I think the screen will have a definite emotional appeal, less definable but just as important. An imaginative producer or director may invent many other uses for this device than those indicated in the present script. In fact the possibilities of the device seem much larger to me than the instance of this play can possibly utilize.

The Music: Another extra-literary accent in this play is provided by the use of music. A single recurring tune, "The Glass Menagerie," is used to give emotional emphasis to suitable passages. This tune is like circus music, not when you are on the grounds or in the immediate vicinity of the parade, but when you are at some distance and very likely thinking of something else. It seems under those circumstances to continue almost interminably and it weaves in and out of the preoccupied consciousness; then it is the lightest, most delicate music in the world and perhaps the saddest. It expresses the surface vivacity of life with the underlying strain of immutable and inexpressible sorrow. When you look at a piece of delicately span glass you think of two things: how beautiful it is and how easily it can be broken. Both of those ideas should be woven into the recurring tune, which dips in and out of the play as if it were carried on a wind that changes. It serves as a thread of connection and allusion between the narrator with his separate point in time and space and the subject of his story. Between each episode it returns as reference to the emotion, nostalgia, which is the first condition of the play. It is primarily Laura's music and therefore comes out most clearly when the play focuses upon her and the lovely fragility of glass which is her image.

The Lighting: The lighting in the play is not realistic. In keeping with the atmosphere of memory, the stage is dim. Shafts of light are focused on selected areas or actors, sometimes in contradistinction to what is the apparent center. For instance, in the quarrel scene between Tom and Amanda, in which Laura has no active part, the clearest pool of light is on her figure. This is also true of the supper scene, when her silent figure on the sofa should remain the visual center. The light upon Laura should be distinct from the others, having a peculiar pristine clarity such as light used in early religious portraits of female saints or madonnas. A certain correspondence to light in religious paintings, such as El Greco's, where the figures are radiant in atmosphere that is relatively dusky, could be effectively used throughout the play. (It will also permit a more effective use of the screen.) A free, imaginative use of light can be of enormous value in giving a mobile, plastic quality to plays of a more or less static nature.

T. W.

Excerpts from Three Memoirs

(1) TENNESSEE WILLIAMS'S MOTHER
(EDWINA DAKIN WILLIAMS)

I had not read *Menageria*, knew nothing of its story except the snatches I glimpsed at rehearsals. After the curtain went up, I became lost in the magic of the words and the superb performance of its four players. You couldn't call Laurette or Julie pretty but they imbued their parts with a strong spiritual quality.

This was the first of Tom's plays I had seen, . . . and I was thrilled to think he had created a play without a wasted word and one in which every moment added drama. I don't think there's been a play like it, before or since.

The audience, too, seemed spellbound throughout and particularly when Mr. Dowling stood to one side of the stage and uttered the words, "I didn't go to the moon, I went much further—for time is the longest distance between two places. . . . Oh, Laura, Laura, I tried to leave you behind me, but I am more faithful than I intended to be! I reach for a cigarette, I cross the street, I run into the movies or a bar, I buy a drink, I speak to the nearest stranger—anything that can blow your candles out!"

At this moment, in the center of the stage behind a thin veil of a curtain, Julie bent low over the candles in her tenement home as Mr. Dowling said sadly, "—for nowadays the world is lit by lightning! Blow out your candles, Laura—and so goodbye. . . ."

And the curtain dropped slowly on the world premiere of *The Glass Menagerie*.

At first it was so quiet I thought the audience didn't like the play. A young woman behind me clapped wildly, as though to make up for the lack of applause, and I heard her remark indignantly, "These Chicago audiences make me mad! This is a beautiful play."

Then, all of a sudden, a tumultuous clapping of hands broke out. The audience had been recovering from the mood into which the play had plunged it. Gratefully I turned to the young woman, who I later found out was a student of English at the University of Chicago, and asked, "Would you like to meet the author? I'm his mother." When Tom arrived to take me backstage, I introduced the young woman, breathless with excitement, and we invited her to go behind the scenes with us.

I wanted to congratulate Laurette, who had brought down the house with her amazing performance as Amanda Wingfield, the faded, fretful, dominating mother lost in the dream world of her past, bullying her son into finding a gentleman caller for his abnormally shy sister.

I entered Laurette's dressing room, not knowing what to expect, for she was sometimes quite eccentric. She was sitting with her feet propped up on the radiator, trying to keep warm. Before I had a chance to get out a word, she greeted me.

"Well, how did you like you'seff, Miz' Williams?" she asked.

I was so shocked I didn't know what to say. It had not occurred to me as I watched Tom's play that *I* was Amanda. But I recovered quickly.

"You were magnificent," I said quietly to Laurette.

Someone mentioned to Tom the opposite receptions given *Angels* and *Menagerie* and he explained this by saying, "You can't mix sex and religion . . . but you can always write safely about mothers."

To which I say, "Ah, can you, Tom?"

Over the years both subtly and not so subtly, I have often been reminded that the character of Amanda was rooted in me, and this is not generally meant as a compliment. The critics have described Amanda in such inelegant words as "an old witch riding a broomstick," "a raddled belle of the old South, sunk deep in frustration," "the scuffed, rundown slipper that outlived the ball," "a simple, sanely insane, horrible Mother, pathetic and terribly human and terribly real" and "a bit of a scold, a bit of a snob."

Tom's own description of Amanda as stated in the play held that she was "a little woman of great but confused vitality clinging frantically to another time and place. Her characterization must be carefully created, not copied from type. She is not paranoiac, but her life is paranoia. There is much to admire in Amanda, and as much to love and pity as there is to laugh at. Certainly she has endurance and a kind of heroism, and though her foolishness makes her unwittingly cruel at times, there is tenderness in her slight person."

Tom has contradicted himself when asked if the play were based on his life. Once he told a reporter it was a "memory play," adding, "My mother and sister will never forgive me for that." Another time he said, "It was derived from years of living." Then again, he denied it was autobiographical, calling it "a dream or fantasy play. The gentleman caller is meant to be the symbol of the world and its attitude toward the unrealistic dreamers who are three characters of the play."

I think it is high time the ghost of Amanda was laid. I am *not* Amanda. I'm sure if Tom stops to think, he realizes I am not. The only resemblance I have to Amanda is that we both like jonquils.

(2) TENNESSEE WILLIAMS

Rose was a popular girl in high school but only for a brief while. Her beauty was mainly in her expressive green-gray eyes and in her curly auburn hair. She was too narrow-shouldered and her state of anxiety when in male company inclined her to hunch them so they looked even narrower; this made her strong-featured, very Williams head seem too large for her thin, small-breasted body. She also, when she was on a date, would talk with an almost hysterical animation which few young men knew how to take.

The first real breakdown occurred shortly after I had suffered the heart attack that ended my career as a clerk-errand boy at the shoe company.

My first night back from St. Vincent's, as I mentioned, Rose came walking like a somnambulist into my tiny bedroom and said, "We must all die together."

I can assure you that the idea did not offer to me an irresistible appeal. Being now released at last from my three years as a clerk-typist at Continental, God damn it I was in no mood to consider group suicide with the family, not even at Rose's suggestion—however appropriate the suggestion may have been.

For several days Rose was demented. One afternoon she put a kitchen knife in her purse and started to leave for her psychiatrist's office with apparent intent of murder.

The knife was noticed by Mother and snatched away.

Then a day or so later this first onset of dementia praecox passed off and Rose was, at least on the surface, her usual (now very quiet) self again.

A few days later I departed for Memphis to recuperate at my grandparents' little house on Snowden Avenue near Southwestern University in Memphis.

I think it was about this time that our wise old family doctor told Mother that Rose's physical and mental health depended upon what struck Miss Edwina as a monstrous thing—an arranged, a sort of "therapeutic" marriage. Obviously old Doc Alexander had hit upon the true seat of Rose's afflictions. She was a very normal—but highly sexed—girl who was tearing herself apart mentally and physically by those repressions imposed upon her by Miss Edwina's monolithic Puritanism.

I may have inadvertently omitted a good deal of material about the unusually close relations between Rose and me. Some perceptive critic of the theatre made the observation that the true theme of my work is "incest." My sister and I had a close relationship, quite unsullied by any carnal knowledge. As a matter of fact, we were rather shy of each other, physically, there was no casual physical intimacy of the sort that one observes among the Mediterranean people in their family relations. And yet our love was, and is, the deepest in our lives and was, perhaps, very pertinent to our withdrawal from extrafamilial attachments.

There were years when I was in the shoe company and summers when I was a student at the State University of Missouri when my sister and I spent nearly all our evenings together aside from those which I spent with Hazel.

What did we do those evenings, Rose and I? Well, we strolled about the business streets of University City. It was a sort of ritual with a pathos that I assure you was never caught in *Menagerie* nor in my story "Portrait of Girl in Glass," on which *Menagerie* was based.

I think it was Delmar—that long, long street which probably began near the Mississippi River in downtown St. Louis and continued through University City and on out into the country—that Rose and I strolled along in the evenings. There was a root-beer stand at which we always stopped. Rose was inordinately fond of root-beer, especially on warm summer evenings. And before

and after our root-beer stop, we would window-shop. Rose's passion, as well as Blanche's, was clothes. And all along that part of Delmar that cut through University City were little shops with lighted windows at night in which were displayed dresses and accessories for women. Rose did not have much of a wardrobe and so her window-shopping on Delmar was like a hungry child's gazing through the window-fronts of restaurants. Her taste in clothes was excellent.

"How about *that* dress, Rose?"

"Oh no, that's tacky. But this one here's very nice."

The evening excursions lasted about an hour and a half, and although, as I've noted, we had a physical shyness of each other, never even touching hands except when dancing together in the Enright apartment, I'd usually follow her into her bedroom when we came home, to continue our warmly desultory chats. I felt most at home in that room, which was furnished with the white ivory bedroom set that had been acquired with the family's "furnished apartment" on Westminster Place when we first moved to St. Louis in 1918.

It was the only attractive room in the apartment—or did it seem so because it was my sister's?

I have mentioned our dancing together.

Rose taught me to dance to the almost aboriginal standing (non-horned) Victrola that had been acquired in Mississippi and shipped to St. Louis at the time of the disastrous family move there.

◆ ◆ ◆

As I drifted away from my sister, during this period, she drew close to our little Boston terrier Jiggs. She was constantly holding and hugging him and now and then Miss Edwina would say:

"Miss Florence, I'm afraid that you forget we have neighbors and Mrs. Ebbs upstairs sometimes complains when Cornelius raises his voice."

Miss Florence would be likely to reply something to the effect that Mrs. Ebbs upstairs could go to hell, for all it mattered to her . . .

The last time I was in St. Louis, for a visit at Christmas, I had my brother Dakin drive me about all the old places where we had lived in my childhood. It was a melancholy tour. Westminster Place and Forest Park Boulevard had lost all semblance of their charm in the twenties. The big old residences had been converted into sleazy rooming-houses or torn down for nondescript duplexes and small apartment buildings.

The Kramer residence was gone: in fact, all of the family, including dear Hazel, were by then dead.

This can only serve as a preamble, in this "thing," to the story of my great love for Hazel, and not at all an adequate one at that . . .

In my adolescence in St. Louis, at the age of sixteen, several important events in my life occurred. It was in the sixteenth year that I wrote "The Vengeance of Nitocris" and received my first publication in a magazine and the magazine was *Weird Tales.* The story wasn't published till June of 1928. That same year my grandfather Dakin took me with him on a tour of Europe with a large party of Episcopalian ladies from the Mississippi Delta. . . . And, it was in my sixteenth year that my deep nervous problems approached what might

well have been a crisis as shattering as that which broke my sister's mind, lastingly, when she was in her twenties.

I was at sixteen a student at University City High School in St. Louis and the family was living in a cramped apartment at 6254 Enright Avenue.

University City was not a fashionable suburb of St. Louis and our neighborhood, while a cut better than that of the Wingfields in *Menagerie,* was only a little cut better: it was an ugly region of hive-like apartment buildings, for the most part, and fire escapes and pathetic little patches of green among concrete driveways.

My younger brother, Dakin, always an indomitable enthusiast at whatever he got into, had turned our little patch of green behind the apartment on Enright into quite an astonishing little vegetable garden. If there were flowers in it, they were, alas, obscured by the profuse growth of squash, pumpkins, and other edible flora.

I would, of course, have preempted all the space with rosebushes but I doubt they would have borne roses. The impracticalities, let's say the fantastic impracticalities, of my adolescence were not at all inclined to successful ends: and I can recall no roses in all the years that I spent in St. Louis and its environs except the two living Roses in my life, my grandmother, Rose O. Dakin, and, of course, my sister, Rose Isabel.

My adolescent problems took their most violent form in a shyness of a pathological degree. Few people realize, now, that I have always been and even remain in my years as a crocodile an extremely shy creature—in my crocodile years I compensate for this shyness by the typical Williams heartiness and bluster and sometimes explosive fury of behavior. In my high school days I had no disguise, no façade. And it was at University City High School that I developed the habit of blushing whenever anyone looked me in the eyes, as if I harbored behind them some quite dreadful or abominable secret.

(3) TENNESSEE WILLIAMS'S BROTHER AND A FRIEND
(DAKIN WILLIAMS AND SHEPHERD MEADE)

While they were at the Webster Groves house a minor episode occurred that Tom might have made into a one-act play. All the actors were strictly in character. Dakin remembers it well. It was a Saturday midnight in August and still very hot. Tom telephoned. He was in his old Scatterbolt jalopy out on Sappington Road, and had run out of gas. (Very much in character. Tom never did and never would remember to put either oil or gas in cars.) "What *can* we do?" cried Rose frantically. (And in character.)

"Well," said Edwina, organizing things (in character), "your father has the car—and it's Saturday, so *he* won't be home until dawn." (Cornelius in character, and Edwina in character for putting it that way.)

Edwina decided that Rose and Dakin should get a taxi, stop for a can of gas and find Tom. They followed his directions, and there he was, standing with Scatterbolt beside a closed gas station.

"Oh, where have you been, Tom?" said Rose.

Tom answered, "To the movies."

"Mother won't believe that," said Rose, who didn't believe it either, knowing that Tom always said that as a cover story when he'd been with anybody his mother didn't approve of, which was practically everybody.

And that was what happened. When they reached home, Edwina was wearing her standard look of advanced suffering, like Amanda's in *The Glass Menagerie.*

"I was at the movies, mother," Tom said.

"I don't believe that lie!" Edwina said, in character.

"Well, you can go to hell then!" said Tom, going a bit beyond his character.

And then, Dakin remembers, "Mother's eyes shot up in their sockets toward the ceiling. She staggered backward as if struck by a physical blow. Cunningly she glanced behind her to be sure there was an overstuffed chair in the correct position, and proceeded to fall backward in a well-planned and frequently performed faint."

"Oh, my God!" gasped Rose (in character). "Tom, look what you've done! You've killed our mother!"

But Dakin wasn't worried. He had seen his mother "pull this on a monthly basis when arguing with dad over bills." He was, however, impressed by the performance, which he thought was better than usual.

If there'd only been a gentleman caller around, the whole scene might have come right out of one of Tom's plays.

Excerpts from Two Interviews with Williams

(1) JEAN EVANS (1945)

I'd read four of Mr. Williams's one-act plays. All but one had been about poverty-stricken people whose situations seemed hopeless. I asked Mr. Williams if he always wrote about unhappy, trapped, hopeless people. He'd been half-reclining against a pillow on his bed, but he sat up now.

"I hadn't thought of them as being hopeless," he said. "That's not really what I was writing about. It's human valor that moves me. The one dominant theme in most of my writings, the most magnificent thing in all human nature, is valor—and endurance.

"The mother's valor is the core of *The Glass Menagerie*," he went on. "She's confused, pathetic, even stupid, but everything has *got* to be all right. She fights to make it that way in the only way she knows how."

We talked a little about his other plays and then, a trifle anxiously, he asked if I had found them without humor. I said no. There was a great deal of humor in them if he meant the wry kind that sprang out of incredibly miserable situations, the kind that made an audience want to cry while it was laughing. He nodded.

"George Jean Nathan, in his review of *Menagerie,* said I was *deficient* in humor," Williams remarked. [*New York Journal American,* 9 April 1945, 11—Editor] His manner was casual, but there was an edge of annoyance in his voice. "He said that all the humor had been embroidered into the play by Mr. Dowling." (Dowling is co-producer of the play, plays the narrator, and the son, Tom) "I'd love

for somebody who knows my other work to refute him."

He paused, and then went on defensively, "Not one line of *Glass Menagerie* was changed after the final draft came back from the typist. A scene was inserted, the drunk scene. That was Mr. Dowling's idea, but entirely of my authorship. And one line by Mr. Dowling, was added. The last line, where he says to the audience, 'Here's where memory stops and your imagination begins.'" He paused. "Mr. Dowling did a great job. A magnificent job. But there was humor *contained* in the play. I had that in mind, along with the rest, when I was writing it."

Mr. Nathan had also written that the play, as originally written, was *freakish.* I wanted to know if Mr. Williams liked writing plays unconventional in form.

"If you mean unconventional in that my plays are light on plot and heavy on characterization, yes. But not in structure. *Glass Menagerie* is not at all freakish in structure.

"Have you read Saroyan's *Get Away, Old Man?*" Williams gave a peal of gay, sudden laughter that rang through the room. "There's a play that would give Mr. Nathan pause. The curtain goes up and down, up and down, all through the play."

He said he liked Saroyan very much, "his short stories perhaps, more than his plays."

I said I'd like Saroyan better if he were able to admit there was evil under the sun. Mr. Williams smiled. "His point of view—his attitude—I suppose you could say, is childish," he said. "Saroyan's characters are all little Saroyans. He multiplies himself like rabbits. But he is himself so interesting, that he usually gets away with writing only about himself."

How did he think the human situation could be improved? I asked. He looked as though the question had startled him.

"It's a social and economic problem, of course," he said, "not something mystical. I don't think there will be any equity in American life until at least 90 percent of our population are living under different circumstances. The white collar worker, for instance. Most people consider him pretty well off. I think his situation is horrible.

"I'd like to see people getting a lot more for what they invest in the way of effort and time. It's insane for human beings to work their whole lives away at dull, stupid, routine, anesthetizing jobs for just a little more than the necessities of life. There should be time—and money—for development. For living."

(2) W A L T E R   W A G E R   (1 9 6 7)

Albee said to me that he writes a play when it becomes more painful not to write it than to write it.

WILLIAMS: That's a very good way of putting it, you know.

Then the subject literally forces itself out?

WILLIAMS: Yes, some people accuse you of being too personal, you know, in your writing. The truth of the matter is—I don't think you can escape being personal in your writing.

Impossible.

WILLIAMS: That doesn't mean that you are one of the characters in the play. What it means simply is that the dynamics of the characters in the play, the tensions correspond to something that you are personally going through—the concerns of the play and the tensions of the play and your own concerns and tensions at the time you wrote it. I have always found that to be true.

The Glass Menagerie

ROGER BOXILL

The play is cradled in the playwright's recall of the Depression years when he worked in the warehouse of the International Shoe Company by day and wrote by night. The faded belle as doting mother derives from Miss Edwina. The absent father who fell in love with long distance alludes to C. C. during his happy days as a Delta drummer. Rose Williams's short-lived business studies, disappointing relationships and withdrawal from life inform the character of Laura as the predestined spinster with a lost love. Even the title refers to the collection of little glass animals that Rose and Tom kept in her room in St Louis, tiny figurines that came to represent for him all the softest emotions that belong to the remembrance of things past.

The theme of this gentle confessional work is aspiration and disappointment. The action is contained in the dashing of Laura's hope for romance, anticipated in the break-up of Amanda's marriage, and echoed in the failure of Tom's effort to become a writer. The plot centres on Laura's non-Cinderella story. A shy, crippled girl encounters in the flesh the very man she loves, who leads her on and quickly lets her down. The exposition of Amanda's ideal girlhood in Blue Mountain and unfortunate middle age in St Louis is like an organ point that sounds the play's nostalgic note. She was once the belle of the ball, surrounded by suitors and is now a deserted housewife, struggling for survival. As the disillusioned narrator, Tom looks back to a time when adventure and success seemed possible. Even Jim, although not discouraged, finds life after adolescence disappointing.

The historical setting provides an enveloping action that ironically reflects the play's theme. The economic recovery following the Great Depression came with the Second World War. The optimistic phrases in which Jim forecasts his future—'Knowledge—Zzzzp! Money—Zzzzp!—Power!'—hint at the sounds of battle. The customers of the Paradise Dance Hall across the alley from the Wingfield apartment house find an end to boredom in a hell on earth. Tom gets his wish to live the life of a hero in an adventure movie through his role as a merchant seaman in a world lit by lightning.

The full historical background extends from the Second World War, in which Tom serves, to the First World War, in which his father served before him, and even to the American Civil War, which ended in the fall of the Old South, to whose vestiges of gracious living his mother still so desperately clings. Amanda Wingfield is an anachronism in the St Louis of the 1930s and may even have been one in the Blue Mountain of her girlhood. Besides the story of her failed marriage, she brings to the play the sense of a world that, like herself, has long since faded. Her expectation that she would marry a wealthy planter and settle down to raise her family on a large plantation with many servants is a *belle rêve* of Southern aristocratic life in antebellum times. Her reminiscences are a confusion of wish and reality consistent with the play's premise that memory is primarily seated in the heart.

The Glass Menagerie is a dramatic elegy that plays within three concentric spheres of time: the time of the Second World War, in which Tom speaks to the audience as a merchant seaman; the time of the Depression, in which Tom lived with his mother and his sister in St Louis; and the time that Amanda thinks of as a vanished golden age—her girlhood in the rural South before the Great War. Like Tom's, the memory of her cherished past is partly enacted when she appears for the evening of the dinner party with a bunch of jonquils on her arm and skips conquettishly around the living-room, dressed in the girlish frock of yellowed voile with blue silk sash in which she led the cotillion long ago, won the cakewalk twice at Sunset Hill, and went to the Governor's Ball in Jackson.

The primary conditions of Amanda's poignant resurrection of her youth—spring and courtship—conform to the conventions of pastoral romance. Invitations poured in from all over the Delta that enchanted season when she had her craze for jonquils. In the evenings there were dances, and in the afternoons picnics and long carriage rides through the countryside, lacy with dogwood in May, and flooded with the jonquils that she made her young men help gather for her. On a single Sunday afternoon in Blue Mountain, she had seventeen gentleman callers, and extra chairs had to be brought in from the parish house to accommodate them. She could have become the wife of the brilliant Duncan J. Fitzhugh or of the dashing Bates Cutrere, who married another after Amanda refused him but carried her picture on him until he died. Amanda's arias on the lost dreams of her youth echo spring rites and tall tales of princesses wooed by many suitors. Tom's memory of his mother's memory modulates easily into legend because it is twice removed from reality, recessed within the play's innermost sphere of time.

The Christian symbolism with which *Menagerie* is filled suggests that the time of Amanda's youth, the time of the Depression and the time of the Second World War are analogues, respectively, of Paradise, Purgatory and Hell. From the midst of global conflagration Tom looks back to the years of trial in St Louis that followed the disappearance of the Edenic South his mother remembers. The idea of the gentleman caller as saviour is clear from the 'Annunciation' to Amanda by her son that Jim is coming to dinner. One might

at the movies Tom sees a stage magician turn water into wine and escape from a coffin. Amanda exhorts her children to 'rise and shine' and calls her ailing magazine-subscribers 'Christian martyrs'. In an atmosphere that is relatively dusky, the light on Laura has a pristine clarity reminiscent of that on saints in medieval paintings. The qualities of intimacy and reverence combine in her scene with Jim, the only light for which is provided by a candelabrum that once stood on the alter of a church.

As the gentleman caller does not fulfil his role as redeemer, the altar candles in Laura's heart are soon extinguished. The play's central image—light playing on a broken surface—suggests the ephemeral nature of life, beauty and human feeling. Joyful moments flicker only for an instant within the surrounding darkness of eternity, as when Jim and Laura look at the little glass unicorn together by candlelight, Amanda wishes on the moon, or couples find brief comfort in fleeting intimacy at the nearby dance hall, whose glass sphere, revolving slowly at the ceiling, filters the surrounding shadows with delicate rainbow colours. In the dim poetic interior of the Wingfield living-room, the picture of the absent father with smiling doughboy face is intermittently illuminated, while outside, beyond the dark alleyways and murky canyons of tangled clotheslines, garbage cans, and neighbouring fire escapes, the running lights of movie marquees blink and beckon in the distance. The movies themselves are no more than images of light that pass quickly into oblivion like cut jonquils or spring showers. For even art in *The Glass Menagerie* is presented as a feeble consolation for the sorry transience of life—fragile glass, scratchy phonograph records, scraps of poetry scribbled on shoe boxes.

Like the spotty, shadowy lighting, other extra-literary effects, drawn principally from film, emphasise the first condition of the play, which is nostalgia, and help to project the sense of an insubstantial world, wispy as memory itself. Transparent gauze scrims, one representing the outside wall of the tenement, another the portieres in the archway or second proscenium between the living-room and dining-room upstage, not only make scene transitions cinematic in their fluidity but also create a stage within a stage within a stage—a use of space which relates to the idea of containing time within time within time. After Tom's introductory speech, the grim wall of the building before which he has stood fades out as the Wingfield living-room fades in behind it. In turn, the portieres upstage dissolve and separate like a second curtain or inner veil of memory as soft lighting slowly reveals the family seated at the dining-table. The first scene is played without food or utensils. The last is played without words. During Tom's closing speech, Amanda appears to comfort Laura as if behind sound proof glass, her studied gestures reminiscent of the silent screen.

Music from three sources weaves through the scenes, bridging the spheres of time. On the on-stage Victrola Laura plays the music of her parents' youth, records her father left behind. The dance hall mixes the hot swing of the thirties with the slow tangos of the twenties and the tender waltzes of Amanda's girlhood. The music to which Jim and Laura dance, 'La Golondrina', is the same Mexican waltz that Alma Winemiller sings on Independence Day 1916 in *Summer and Smoke*. Most prominent is the recurring theme that comes out of nowhere and fades away again in accordance with film convention, like the images in a reverie. It is primarily Laura's *Leitmotiv* and suggests her fragile beauty as does the spun glass with which she is also identified. Williams's idea of barely audible circus music is consistent with his central image of light glimmering sporadically in the void. The immutable sorrow of life persists under the superficial gaiety of the passing moment. The distant calliope, with its associations of sad clowns, trapeze acts and performing animals, is an invitation occasionally to escape into a garish, itinerant world of make-believe. Human creativity is once more presented in the most pathetic terms. Indeed the circus animals are continuous with the figurines of Laura's menagerie, whose tiny size on stage corresponds to the remoteness of the fairground.

In the course of this memory play, some forty projections of images, speeches or titles associate the graphic with the verbal in the sometimes whimsical manner of the mind when in the relatively free condition of sleep or reverie. Williams's explanation notwithstanding, the projections do not make structural points but instead spoof the sentiment of the scenes in which they appear. A pirate ship, a magazine cover, or the gentleman caller waving goodbye are pictures that undermine the pathos of the play like the farcical moments in Chekhov. Since the first production, directors have almost without exception cut the device as an expressionist intrusion upon an essentially naturalistic work. Perhaps they are right. Yet the projections are indebted less to the German theatre than to the silent screen. Such lines as 'Ah!' or 'Not Jim!' and such titles as 'The Annunciation', 'The Accent of a Coming Foot' or 'The Sky Falls' appear to derive, like so much else in *Menagerie,* from the playwright's frequent movie-going in childhood.

The call in Williams's production notes for 'a new, plastic theatre' to replace the outworn theatre of conventional realism is essentially a manifesto of the cinematic stage. The writer is to become more visual. He is to use lighting to suggest mood and assert relationships—such as the clear pool of light in which the fragile and unearthly Laura sits while Jim, Tom and Amanda are having supper upstage. He is to bring in music from out of the blue or flash images on a screen in order to give a plastic, mobile quality to plays that are relatively actionless. The lyric naturalism of the twentieth-century play of sensibility depends for its theatrical expression upon the writer's imaginative use of the methods and resources with which motion pictures have enriched theatrical art.

This explains why the American theatre became more of a director's medium, like film, in the time of Williams. When Elia Kazan founded the Actors Studio in 1947, three years after *Menagerie,* it was for the purpose of training actors to give film-size performances. His successor, Lee Strasberg, would later train them in the requisite docility. Actors were to become more compliant, more 'plastic', like the scenery and the lighting through which the all-powerful director would express his predetermined 'concept'. The neo-Stanislavskyan American Method repudiates 'projection consciousness' as leading to oversized mannerisms put out of date by the microphone and camera.

It is partly the convention of film, although chiefly that of the short story, from which the episodic structure of *Menagerie* derives. The play is an adaptation of a film script *(The Gentleman Caller)* based on a short story ('Portrait of a Girl in Glass'). The seven scenes mingle with allusive narrative speeches to convey a casual sense of order that accords with the nature of memory. In neither the story nor the play is the tiny plot the point. It is the revelation of characters locked in time. This explains why nothing much happens in *Menagerie.* Its lyrical, non-linear form is rooted in the gently exfoliative 'Portrait of a Girl in Glass'. It is also rooted in a particular character's point of view, a technique common enough in fiction but atypical of drama. Since that character happens to be an aspiring poet in both the story and the play, an inclination to lyricism is obligatory.

'Portrait' is essentially a character sketch of Laura, as its title from the static art of sculpture implies. Her brother, Tom, remembers her from the time they lived in St Louis with their mother and he worked in a warehouse. Their father had long ago deserted them. Laura was a frightened, reclusive girl who appeared to exist in a world of make-believe. While decorating the tree one Christmas, she picked up the star that went on top and asked Tom if stars really had five points. She spent most of the time listening to her father's old records, polishing her collection of glass figurines, and rereading Gene Stratton Porter's *Freckles,* with whose hero, a young one-armed lumberjack, she carried on an imaginary relationship. He would drop by her room for an occasional visit just as her brother habitually did. When she was twenty, she was unable to face the demands of secretarial school. When she turned twenty-three, her mother asked Tom to bring a friend home to dinner in order to meet her. He turned out to be a hearty and befreckled fellow employee (Jim Delaney), with whom Laura, much to her family's amazement, got along famously because she confused him in her mind with the hero of the much-read book. Unfortunately, he was already engaged. Not long after Jim's visit, Tom lost his job at the warehouse, left St Louis and took to wandering. He became independent and succeeded in forgetting his home, although from time to time he thinks of his sister.

The revelation that Jim is already engaged becomes more pathetic in the play because Williams makes the gentleman caller into Laura's real rather than her imaginary love. Her abnormality is less mental but more physical. Instead of the obsession to reread the same book, she has the more playable handicap of a slight limp. It is particularly effective when she and Jim dance together by candlelight (they are never alone in 'Portrait') and accidentally break the glass unicorn's horn—a piece of business, missing from the story, that uses the play's titular symbol and suggests, among other things, the sudden collapse of male ardour upon the removal of maidenly defence.

'Portrait' is a wistful memory, *Menagerie* a moving elegy. The play gains power from an intensification of theme and a strengthening of logic in the progression of events. The three years that pass in the story between the mother's discovery of her daughter's truancy and the appearance of the gentleman caller are reduced to three months in the play, long enough considering Amanda's determination to find Laura a husband if she is not to be a secretary. In the story, Tom's departure is peremptory because it is not preceded by a climactic quarrel with his mother. Jim Delaney makes no thematic contribution of his own because he is not a former high-school hero like Jim O'Connor. The mother is a minor character with neither reminiscences nor a name. Nor are the Wingfields specifically from the South.

The Glass Menagerie combines Williams's two archetypal actions. The climax of the outer play is the spoiled occasion, the climax of the inner play the eviction or loss of home. Laura does not sit at table with Jim. The gentleman caller, having declined his hostess's offer of lemonade, leaves early to meet his fiancée. After all the preparation, Amanda's party is ruined. Tom's curtain speech reminds us that everything has happened within his memory, and we may be sure that it will do so again and again. Whether the two belles, one faded, one never having bloomed, manage to keep their home after his departure we can only guess; but it is clear that the wanderer has none apart from them.

In the play's last moments, Tom's two roles, narrator and participant, coalesce. Dressed as a merchant seaman, the one who broke free to seek adventure stands before the audience and admits that he is a haunted fugitive. He calls out to Laura that he has tried but not been able to forget her. The many cities to which he has sailed seem to sweep about him like dead leaves torn loose from their branches. A strain of familiar music, a display of perfumes in a store window, or simply a fragment of transparent glass is enough to remind him of what he has lost. Up stage, behind the gauze scrim which marks the outside wall of the St Louis tenement that was once his home, the mother and sister he left behind enact a scene without words, like silent ghosts, visible only to the eye of memory. Still facing the audience, he tells Laura to blow out the candles which light the dim interior. She does so, he says goodbye, but on his exit the elusive, nostalgic music that has dipped in and out of the scenes from the beginning breaks off without resolution. Tom's climactic realisation that he will play out his 'memory play' for the rest of his days is like the 'epiphany' in a short story by Joyce. His confession throws all of the events that have preceded it into a different light; or, more precisely, it casts them into a greater elegiac darkness.

The problem of playing *The Glass Menagerie* arises from the fact that, whereas from a dramatic critic's point of view it is Tom's play, from an actor's it is Amanda's. . . .

In 1973 Thomas L. King published a valuable article arguing that *Menagerie* belongs to Tom, who tricks the audience into shouldering the pain he exorcises by creating his memory play. In 1975 Rip Torn, cast opposite Maureen Stapleton's second Amanda, made the only all-out effort to read the narrations from character. The curtain speech was the key to his portrait. The result was a wild, brooding, quirky, homosexual Tom who flung his words at the house like accusations. Torn's performance did not receive a unanimous welcome; but neither was it damned with faint praise. Those who attacked it were inclined to do so without reserve; others were as absolute in their esteem. Barnes of the *New York Times* was reminded of a Greek tragic hero, Kalem of *Time* thought it 'just right', and Watt of the *New York Daily News* made the telling observation that Torn was at his best in 'the beautifully written narrative sections'.

Irony and Distance in The Glass Menagerie

THOMAS L. KING

Tennessee Williams's *The Glass Menagerie*, though it has achieved a firmly established position in the canon of American plays, is often distorted, if not misunderstood, by readers, directors, and audiences. The distortion results from an overemphasis on the scenes involving Laura and Amanda and their plight, so that the play becomes a sentimental tract on the trapped misery of two women in St. Louis. This leads to the neglect of Tom's soliloquies—speeches that can be ignored or discounted only at great peril, since they occupy such a prominent position in the play.

When not largely ignored, they are in danger of being treated as nostalgic yearnings for a former time. But they are not sentimental excursions into the past, paralleling Amanda's, for while they contain sentiment and nostalgia, they also evince a pervasive humor and irony and, indeed, form and contain the entire play.

Judging from the reviews, the distortion of the play began with the original production. The reviews deal almost wholly with Laurette Taylor's performance, making Amanda seem to be the principal character, and nearly ignore the soliloquies. Even the passage of time has failed to correct this tendency, for many later writers also force the play out of focus by pushing Amanda forward. Among the original reviewers, Stark Young was one of the few who recognized that the play is Tom's when he said: "The story . . . all happens in the son's mind long afterward." He also recognized that the production and Laurette Taylor tended to obscure the script, for, after a lengthy discussion of Miss Taylor, he said, "But true as all this may be of Miss Taylor, we must not let that blind us to the case of the play itself and of the whole occasion." Young blamed on Eddie Dowling the failure of the narration noted by others: "He speaks his Narrator scenes plainly and serviceably by which, I think, they are made to seem to be a mistake on the playwright's part, a mistake to include them at all; for they seem extraneous and tiresome in the midst of the play's emotional current. If these speeches were spoken with variety, impulse and intensity . . . the whole thing would be another matter, truly a part of the story." Young indicates that while the reviewers tended to

neglect Tom and the soliloquies to concentrate on Laurette Taylor, they were encouraged to do so by a production which made the play Amanda's.

The play, however, is not Amanda's. Amanda is a striking and a powerful character, but the play is Tom's. Tom opens the play and he closes it; he also opens the second act and two further scenes in the first act—his is the first word and the last. Indeed, Amanda, Laura, and the Gentleman Caller do not appear in the play at all as separate characters. In a sense, as Stark Young noted, Tom is the only character in the play, for we see not the characters but Tom's memory of them— Amanda and the rest are merely aspects of Tom's consciousness. Tom's St. Louis is not an objective one, but a solipsist's created by Tom, the artist-magician, and containing Amanda, Laura, and the Gentleman Caller. Tom is the Prospero of *The Glass Menagerie,* and its world is the world of Tom's mind even more than *Death of a Salesman*'s is the world of Willy Loman's mind. The play is warped and distorted when any influence gives Amanda, Laura, or the glass menagerie any undue prominence. If Amanda looms large, she looms large in Tom's mind, not in her own right: though of course the image that finally dominates Tom's mind is that of Laura and the glass menagerie.

The full meaning of the scenes between the soliloquies lies not in themselves alone but also in the commentary provided by Tom standing outside the scenes and speaking with reasonable candor to the audience and reader. Moreover, the comment that the soliloquies makes is not a sentimental one; that is, they are not only expressions of a wistful nostalgia for the lost, doomed world of Amanda, Laura, and the glass menagerie but also contain a good deal of irony and humor which work in the opposite direction. They reveal Tom as an artist figure whose utterances show how the artist creates, using the raw material of his own life.

The nature of the narrator's role as artist figure is indicated by Tom's behavior in the scenes. He protects himself from the savage in-fighting in the apartment by maintaining distance between himself and the pain of the situation through irony. For example, when he gets into a fight with Amanda in the third scene and launches into a long, ironic, and even humorous tirade—about how he "runs a string of cat-houses in the valley," how they call him "Killer, Killer Wingfield," how, on some occasions, he wears green whiskers— the irony is heavy and propels him out of the painful situation, out of the argument, and ultimately to the movies. Significantly, this scene begins with Tom writing, Tom the artist, and in it we see how the artistic sensibility turns a painful situation into "art" by using distance. In his verbal assault on his mother, Tom "creates" Killer Wingfield. Tom's ability to distance his experience, to protect himself from the debilitating atmosphere of the apartment makes him different from Laura. Laura does not have this refuge; she is unable to detach herself completely from the situation and she is destroyed by it. She does, of course, retreat to the glass menagerie and the Victrola, but this is the behavior of a severely disturbed woman. Her method of dealing with the situation, retreating

into a "world of her own," does indeed, as Tom says, make her seem "just a little bit peculiar." Tom's method is more acceptable; he makes art.

The kind of contrast that exists between Laura and Tom is illustrated by a comment Jung made about James Joyce and his daughter, Lucia. Lucia had had a history of severe mental problems and, in 1934, she was put under the care of Jung. Discussing his patient and her famous father in a letter, Jung wrote: "His [Joyce's] 'psychological' style is definitely schizophrenic, with the difference, however, that the ordinary patient cannot help himself talking and thinking in such a way, while Joyce willed it and moreover developed it with all his creative forces, which incidentally explains why he himself did not go over the border. But his daughter did, because she was not a genius like her father, but merely a victim of her disease." On another occasion Jung said that the father and daughter "were like two people going to the bottom of a river, one falling and the other diving." We see here a psychoanalyst's perception of the problem of artist and non-artist which is much the same as the problem of Tom and Laura. Tennessee Williams's real-life sister, Rose, has also suffered from mental disturbances.

That an author's early play should contain a highly autobiographical character who shows the mechanism by which art is made out of the material of one's life is not particularly surprising, but it is a generally unnoted feature of *The Glass Menagerie* which is inextricably linked to the irony of the soliloquies. For the artist, irony is a device that protects him from the pain of his experience so that he may use it objectively in his art. We may suppose that Swift's irony shielded him from the dark view that he had of the world and that the failure of that irony brought on the madness that affected him at the end of his life. The artist needs his distance from the material of his art so that he may handle it objectively, and the soliloquies of *The Glass Menagerie,* in part, reveal the nature of that distance and how it is maintained.

Generally, each soliloquy oscillates between a sentimental memory of the past, which draws the narrator into it, and a wry irony which keeps him from being fully engulfed and controlled by it. This tension is found in all the soliloquies, though it is not always handled in the same way: sometimes the fond memory is predominant and sometimes the irony, but both are always present. At times, Tom seems almost deliberately to court disaster by creating for himself and the audience a memory so lovely and poignant that the pain of giving it up to return to reality is too much to bear, but return he does with mockery and a kind of wit that interrupts the witchery of memory just short of a withdrawn madness surrounded by soft music and a mind filled with "delicate rainbow colors." In short, Tom toys with the same madness in which his sister Laura is trapped but saves himself with irony.

The opening soliloquy begins on an ironic note. Tom says:

Yes, I have tricks in my pocket, I have things up my sleeve. But I am the opposite of a stage magician. He gives you illusion that has the appearance of truth. I give you truth in the pleasant disguise of illusion.

These opening lines have a cocky tone—"I will trick you," Tom says, "I'll tell you that I'm going to trick you and I'll still do it even after you've been warned. Besides," he says with perhaps just a touch of derision, "you prefer trickery to the naked truth." Tom begins in the attitude of Whitman on the facing page of the first edition of *Leaves of Grass*—head thrown back, mocking, insolent, but not cruel.

Tom continues in the same mode by saying:

To begin with, I turn back time. I reverse it to that quaint period, the thirties, when the huge middle class of America was matriculating in a school for the blind. Their eyes had failed them, or they had failed their eyes, and so they were having their fingers pressed forcibly down on the fiery Braille alphabet of a dissolving economy.

In Spain there was revolution. Here there was only shouting and confusion. In Spain there was Guernica. Here there were disturbances of labor, sometimes pretty violent, in otherwise peaceful cities such as Chicago, Cleveland, Saint Louis . . .

To this point in the speech, Tom's principal mode is ironic, but as he moves on, though the irony remains, a stronger element of sentiment, of poignant memory creeps in. He begins to speak of memory and to enumerate the characters in the play:

The play is memory. Being a memory play, it is dimly lighted, it is sentimental, it is not realistic. In memory everything seems to happen to music. That explains the fiddle in the wings.

I am the narrator of the play, and also a character in it. The other characters are my mother, Amanda, my sister, Laura, and a gentleman caller who appears in the final scenes.

The only break in this poignant mood is the phrase "that explains the fiddle in the wings"—an unfortunate phrase, but demonstrative of the tension, of the rhythmic swing back and forth between sweet nostalgia and bitter irony. The play may be sentimental rather than realistic, but "that explains the fiddle in the wings" breaks the sentiment.

Tom continues by saying:

> He [the gentleman caller] is the most realistic character in the play, being an emissary from a world of reality that we were somehow set apart from. But since I have a poet's weakness for symbols, I am using this character also as a symbol; he is the long delayed but always expected something that we live for.

With these words, the narrator drops his ironic detachment and enters into the mood of memory. The words can hardly be delivered but as in a reverie, in a deep reflection, the voice coming out of a man who, after frankly acknowledging the audience at the beginning of the speech, has now sunk far into himself so that the audience seems to overhear his thoughts. He then shakes off the mood with a return to irony and makes a kind of joke:

> There is a fifth character in the play who doesn't appear except in this larger-than-life-size photograph over the mantel. This is our father who left us a long time ago. He was a telephone man who fell in love with long distances; he gave up his job with the telephone company and skipped the light fantastic out of town . . .

The last we heard of him was a picture post-card from Mazatlan, on the Pacific coast of Mexico, containing a message of two words— "Hello—Good-bye!" and no address.

There is humor here—not sentiment and not sentimental humor. Tom speaks fondly of his mother and sister and remembers their lost lives and the gentleman caller who symbolizes the loss and the failure, and we can imagine that his gaze becomes distant and withdrawn as he allows himself to be carried away into the memory, but then he remembers another member of the family, the father, and that hurts too much to give in to so he shakes off the reverie and returns once more to irony. The irony is no longer the playful irony of the interlocutor before the audience, but an irony which protects him from the painful memories of the past, that allows him to rise superior to the "father who left us" and to get a laugh from the audience, for the audience should and will chuckle at the end of the opening soliloquy as the light fades on Tom and he leaves his seaman's post. The chuckle may be good-natured, but the humor is not; it is gallows humor in which the condemned man asserts himself before a crowd in relation to which he is horribly disadvantaged by making it laugh. Tom is in control of his memory and already he is beginning to endeavor to work his trick by manipulating the audience's mood.

The opening soliloquy, then, reveals a number of elements that are to be important in the play: it establishes a tension between sentimental nostalgia and detached irony as well as a narrator who is to function as stage magician. The narrator disavows this, but we cannot take him at his word. He says that he is the opposite of a stage magician, but only because his truth looks like illusion rather than the other way round; he is still the magician who creates the play. He says that the play is sentimental rather than realistic, but that is a half truth, for while it contains large doses of sentiment, for the narrator at least, irony sometimes quenches the sentiment. Indeed, Irving Babbit's phrase describing romantic irony is appropriate here: "Hot baths of sentiment . . . followed by sold douches of irony."

The dominant note of the second soliloquy, at the beginning of the third scene, is irony. In the first soliloquy, Tom has provided the audience with a poignant picture of Laura and Amanda cut off from the world "that we were somehow set apart from." In the second soliloquy, irony almost completely obliterates the poignance as we see Amanda at work trying to find a gentleman caller for Laura, a gentleman caller who is "like some archetype of the universal unconscious." Tom continues the irony as he says:

> She began to take logical steps in the planned direction.
>
> Late that winter and in the early spring—realizing that extra money would be needed to properly feather the nest and plume the bird—she conducted a vigorous campaign on the telephone, roping in subscribers to one of those magazines for matrons called *The Home-maker's Companion,* the type of journal that features the serialized sublimations of ladies of letters who think in terms of delicate cup-like breasts, slim, tapering waists, rich, creamy thighs, eyes like wood-smoke in autumn, fingers that soothe and caress like strains of music, bodies as powerful as Etruscan sculpture.

The mocking humor in this is revealed by the derisive alliteration, the hyperbolic language, and in the humorous, parodying evocation of all the clichés of these stories. The speech makes fun of the literary equivalents of Amanda's memories of gentleman callers in the mythical South. This is not to say that Amanda is savagely attacked with a kind of Swiftian irony; nevertheless, the attack is there, though the irony is balanced somewhat by one irruption of the nostalgic, pitying mode of discourse when Tom says that even when the gentleman caller was not mentioned "his presence hung in mother's preoccupied look and in my sister's frightened, apologetic manner." The irony is also humorous and gets a laugh from audiences if it is performed as irony—especially at the end of the speech where, just as the first soliloquy breaks into a mild humor at the end, Tom humorously parodies the magazine stories.

The first soliloquy strikes a balance between irony and nostalgia, the second is primarily ironic, and the third is primarily nostalgic. The third soliloquy begins with the Paradise Dance Hall:

> Across the alley from us was the Paradise Dance Hall. On evenings in spring the windows and doors were open and the music came outdoors. Sometimes the lights were turned out except for a large glass sphere that hung from the ceiling. It would turn slowly about and filter the dusk with delicate rainbow colors.

Rainbow colors, in fact, fill much of the play: in the scene with Laura, late at light, after Tom has returned from the movies, the magic scarf he produces is rainbow-colored—this is one of the few scenes in which Tom and Laura relate tenderly to one another; the Paradise Dance Hall filters the dusk with "delicate rainbow colors"; sex hangs "in the gloom like a chandelier" and floods the world with "brief, deceptive rainbows"; and, in the last soliloquy Tom says that he sometimes passes the window of a shop where perfume is sold—"The window is filled with pieces of colored glass, tiny transparent bottles in delicate colors like bits of a shattered rainbow." In the third soliloquy, the Paradise Dance Hall provides the rainbow colors that fill and transform the alley. The irony breaks through in only a few places: when Tom disrupts the mood of magic by pointing out that you could see the young couples "kissing behind ash-pits and telephone poles," and, as usual at the end when he says, "All the world was waiting for bombardments."

All three soliloquies in the first act work together to help define its movement. The first soliloquy is fairly well balanced between nostalgia and irony. The detached irony of the second soliloquy foreshadows Tom's struggle to detach himself from his situation; after it Tom fights with his mother and leaves to go to the movies. The third soliloquy asserts the nostalgic mode, and the scene following this, in which Tom and Amanda talk of the gentleman caller, is a tender, loving one. We see a playful, warm scene between Tom and his mother out on the fire escape which shows how, in spite of their quarrels, Tom and Amanda could also have their warm, understanding moments. By the end of the first act, the audience should be taken in by Tom's trick, drawn into the rainbow-colored world and the pleasant memory of past times. The

pain of Tom's memory has been repudiated in the second soliloquy with irony, and, after the fight, when Tom runs off to the movies, with the delicate nostalgia of the third soliloquy, flooding the stage with rainbow light. The trick is working—we begin to think that Tom and his mother will get along after all, that a gentleman caller will come to rescue them, but it remains a trick wrought by the magic of the rainbow which is broken, whose colors are "deceptive."

The second act begins with a soliloquy which, like the first, strikes something of a balance between irony and nostalgia. Tom begins with a description of Jim in language that indicates that he has a genuine kind of amazed liking for this Irish boy. Only gentle irony is present in the following words:

> In high school, Jim was a hero. He had tremendous Irish good nature and vitality with the scrubbed and polished look of white chinaware. He seemed to move in a continual spotlight. He was a star in basketball, captain of the debating club, president of the senior class and the glee club, and he sang the male lead in the annual light operas. He was always running or bounding, never just walking. He seemed always at the point of defeating the law of gravity.

Jim is made light of by the phrases "white chinaware" and "defeating the law of gravity," but the mockery is mild, though it becomes stronger as the speech continues:

> He was shooting with such velocity through his adolescence that you would logically expect him to arrive at nothing short of the White House by the time he was thirty.

But Jim apparently ran into more interference after his graduation from Soldan. His speed had definitely slowed. Six years after he left high school he was holding a job that wasn't much better than mine.

The irony begins to break through even more strongly after these words, for Tom was "valuable to him as someone who could remember his former glory, who had seen him win basketball games and the silver cup in debating. And the irony even cuts against Tom: "He knew of my secret practice of retiring to a cabinet of the wash-room to work on poems whenever business was slack in the warehouse." A degree of bitterness begins to emerge when Tom says that, with the example of Jim, the other boys began to smile at him too, "as people smile at some oddly fashioned dog that trots across their path at some distance." The bitterness is quickly moderated, however, when Tom sympathetically remembers his sister in high school: "In high school Laura was as unobtrusive as Jim was astonishing." Finally, as always in these soliloquies, the speech ends with an ironic barb that can often draw a laugh from the audience. Tom says that when he asked Jim home to dinner, "he grinned and said, 'You know, Shakespeare, I never thought of you as having folks!' He was about to discover that I did. . . .'"

The culmination of all the soliloquies and of the tension between irony and nostalgia that is carefully developed in them, is in the final one. Tom's last speech contains just two touches of ironic detachment, but these are critical and are the foci on which this speech and, indeed, for Tom, the whole play turns. The speech begins with a touch of ironic humor. In the preceding scene, Amanda has told Tom to go to the moon. He begins his final speech with "I didn't go to the moon." This is a decidedly humorous line, indicating that Tom still has access to his detachment, but the audience is not laughing anymore, its detachment has been broken down. The speech then quickly moves into a tone of lyric regret:

I didn't go to the moon, I went much further—for time is the longest distance between two places. Not long after that I was fired for writing a poem on the lid of a shoe-box. I left Saint Louis. I descended the steps of this fire-escape for a last time and followed, from then on, in my father's footsteps, attempting to find in motion what was lost in space. I traveled around a great deal. The cities swept about me like dead leaves, leaves that were brightly colored but torn away from the branches. I would have stopped, but I was pursued by something. It always came upon me unawares, taking me altogether by surprise. Perhaps it was a familiar bit of music. Perhaps it was only a piece of transparent glass. Perhaps I am walking along a street at night, in some strange city, before I have found companions. I pass the lighted window of a shop where perfume is sold. The window is filled with pieces of colored glass, tiny transparent bottles in delicate colors, like bits of a shattered rainbow. Then all at once my sister touches my shoulder. I turn around and look into her eyes. Oh, Laura, Laura, I tried to leave you behind me, but I am more faithful than I intended to be! I reach for a cigarette, I cross the street, I run into the movies or a bar, I buy a drink, I speak to the nearest stranger—anything that can blow your candles out!

For nowadays the world is lit by lightning! Blow out your candles, Laura—and so good-bye.

The irony in this passage is no longer humorous. When Tom says "I didn't go to the moon," no one is laughing, and the final, ironic "and so good-bye" is not even potentially humorous. Tom seems to have been captured by the memory and the audience has almost certainly been captured, but Tom, in the end, still has his detachment. Laura's candles go out and Tom is relieved of his burden, uttering a final, flip farewell, but the audience has been more faithful than it intended to be; they are left behind, tricked by Tom who is free for the moment while they must face their grief, their cruelty, for they are the world that the Wingfields were somehow set apart from, they are the ones who shattered the rainbow.

The soliloquies, then, are of a piece: they all alternate between sentiment and irony, between mockery and nostalgic regret, and they all end with an ironic tag, which, in most cases, is potentially humorous. They show us the artist manipulating his audience, seeming to be manipulated himself to draw them in, but in the end resuming once more his detached stance. When Tom departs, the audience is left with Laura and Amanda alone before the dead, smoking candles, and Tom escapes into his artist's detachment having exorcized the pain with the creation of the play. This is the trick that Tom has in his pocket.

Family, Drama, and American Dreams

TOM SCANLAN

The major dilemmas of family life are imbedded in the dramatic action of Williams's plays, and the ideal that haunts his characters is family-related. Moreover, those plays which have been most successful artistically have been those mostly about the family . . . .

In the earlier plays Williams dramatized the family world in a state of collapse; in later ones family collapse is antecedent to the action. These two situations are combined in *The Glass Menagerie*, Williams's first successful play (and probably his most popular one[1]). The play is a perfect fusion of the two subjects and so is a figure for Williams's entire career. In it the family is long lost and, also, we witness its struggle before it is lost. Williams captures the poignancy of family memories in a way all his own, without sacrificing the core of dramatic conflict which makes such memories less static.

The play is a prime example of Williams's artistry in establishing the relation between his own dramatic world and the conventions of realistic domestic drama to which his audience owes great allegiance, as he well knew. The play occurs in the mind of Tom Wingfield, who drifts in and out of the action both as narrator and participant in a peculiarly appropriate way. From the moment at the beginning when the scrim of the tenement wall dissolves and we enter the Wingfield's apartment, we are reminded of the household of so many family plays. The realistic convention of the fourth wall is evoked as Tom remembers his family.

Tom's evocation is self-conscious, for as "stage manager" he has control over the setting. But Tom is also at the mercy of his memories and irresistibly must relive them. The play keeps us poised between these two styles, these two times, throughout. This is, in fact, its strongest and most subtle conflict. Like Tom, we are continually tempted into the world of a realistic family struggle, but never allowed to enter it completely. The projections and lighting keep the effect slightly stylized during the scenes, the fragmented structure blocks us from too long an absorption in the action, and the reappearance of Tom as narrator forces us back to the present. It is Tom's final reappearance in this role, when the action of the memory play is completed, which releases the tension created between the two styles and dramatizes, in a final rush of emotion, the irretrievable loss of the family which Tom can never escape.

Tom cannot shake the memory of his family from his mind; the dissolution of time and space in the play—that is, in his consciousness— heightens the importance of what he is remembering to make it the most significant thing about his existence. What he remembers—the bulk of the play—centers around two lines of action. The first is his desire to escape from his family just as his father had done before him: "He was a telephone man who fell in love with long distances."[2] Tom, a would-

be writer, is caught between a domineering mother and a stultifying warehouse job. He escapes to the porch, to the movies, to the saloon. And finally, in the end, we learn that he has followed his father out into long distances. The second line of action, the principal one, concerns his mother, Amanda, and her attempts to establish some kind of life for Tom's crippled sister, Laura. Amanda pins her hopes on getting "sister" married, after Laura fails because of painful shyness to continue in business school. A "gentleman caller" is found, Jim O'Connor, "an emissary from the world of reality," but all of Amanda's hopes are crushed as he turns out to be already engaged.

The plot is slight stuff, as Williams himself knew.[3] The effect of the play derives in part from the contrast between its two lines of action. Amanda is given over to memories of her past life of happiness as a young southern debutante in Blue Mountain, Mississippi, where on one incredible Sunday she had seventeen gentlemen callers. She imitates the manners and graciousness of those days, a faintly ludicrous parody of southern gentility, the played-out tradition of the antebellum South and its family of security. But she has spirit, too, and responds to the problems of raising two children in a St. Louis tenement during the Depression. Her practicality is what gives her dignity; as she cares for Laura we realize how much Amanda herself needs to be cared for. Her refusal to give in to her nostalgia, even while she indulges in it, enhances her character and makes us susceptible to her longing.

Tom is smothered by such a woman. He fights with her, in part, because she continually tells him what to do: how to eat; how to sleep; how to get ahead. But he fights, also, because her standards represent the conventionality of family responsibility:

AMANDA: Where are you going?
TOM: I'm going to the *movies!*
AMANDA: I don't believe that lie!

(Tom crouches toward her, overtowering her tiny figure. She backs away, gasping.)

TOM: I'm going to opium dens! Yes, opium dens, dens of vice and criminals, hang-outs, Mother. I've joined the Hogan Gang, I'm a hired assassin, I carry a tommy-gun in a violin case! I run a string of cathouses in the Valley! They call me Killer, Killer Wingfield, I'm leading a double-life, a simple, honest warehouse worker by day, by night a dynamic *czar* of the *underworld,* *Mother.* I go to gambling casinos, I spin away fortunes on the roulette table! I wear a patch over one eye and a false mustache, sometimes I put on green whiskers. On those occasions they call me—*El Diablo!* Oh, I could tell you things to make you sleepless! My enemies plan to dynamite this place. They're going to blow us all sky-high some night! I'll be glad, very happy, and so will you! You'll go up, on a broomstick, over Blue Mountain with seventeen gentlemen callers! You ugly—babbling old—*witch. . . .*[4]

He can no more accept her memories of genteel home life in Blue Mountain than he can the spirit with which she has managed to carry on. Both suffocate him. The dead family world of the past is as stultifying as the present. Tom feels the need to escape both:

You know it don't take much intelligence to get yourself into a nailed-up coffin, Laura. But who in hell ever got himself out of one without removing one nail?

(As if in answer, the father's grinning photograph lights up. The scene dims out.)[5]

The absent father, who still represents the memory of romantic family love to Amanda, is the possibility of romantic escape from family to Tom.[6] He loves his sister Laura, yet he will not accept the responsibility for her which Amanda demands of him. The Wingfields are only a ghost of the family of security, but even this demand to be close-knit repels the restless Tom.

Tom's love for Laura needs to be emphasized, I think, not only because it is one part of the final image of the play—the moment of revelation toward which the action tends—but because it shows Williams's interest in the special qualities of those whom the world has hurt. They are the delicate and fragile people, too sensitive to be able to withstand the crude and harsh necessities by which life drives us along. They have an extraordinary awareness of hidden, almost mystical, qualities of spiritual beauty; and this openness dooms them to be crushed or perverted by the animal vigor of the world.

Laura's specialness is seen largely in contrast with Jim, her gentleman caller. He is, by all odds, the kindest of Williams's emissaries from reality, perhaps because his faith in the American dream of self-improvement and success is so complete as to be itself a touching illusion:

JIM: *(Going after him)* You know, Shakespeare—I'm going to sell you a bill of goods!
TOM: What goods?

JIM: A course I'm taking.
TOM: Huh?
JIM: In public speaking! You and me, we're not the warehouse type.
TOM: Thanks—that's good news. But what has public speaking got to do with it?
JIM: It fits you for—executive positions!
TOM: Awww.
JIM: I tell you it's done a helluva lot for me.

(Image on screen: Executive at his desk.)[7]

Williams mocks Jim just enough in the use of the slide projection so that we need not take him seriously, yet he makes Jim's naïveté spring from high spirits and an openheartedness which is endearing. He is healthy, happy, and full of hope, but set next to Laura and her needs he is crude, clumsy, and shallow:

You know what I judge to be the trouble with you? Inferiority complex! Know what that is? That's what they call it when someone low-rates himself![8]

So much for the intricacies of the human personality. To Jim, Laura's problems are easily solved and he sets about, in his well-intentioned way, to cure her. First, he persuades her to dance; and then, caught up himself in the romance of the moment, he kisses her. But Laura needs more than a kiss, more in fact than Jim could ever give her. She needs a tenderness and love that she will never find. Her needs are so great that to satisfy them would mean altering the real world to fit her, changing it into a world like that inhabited by her glass animals, full of delicacy, beauty, and tender harmony.

When this incompatible couple waltzes into the glass menagerie, they begin to destroy it. At first, Laura does not mind. She is too thrilled with the prospect of being normal to care whether her glass unicorn has lost its distinctive horn. But the accident warns us of what Jim awkwardly confesses after the kiss—that he has made a mistake and will see her no more:

I wish that you would—say something.

(She bites her lip which was trembling and then bravely smiles. She opens her hand again on the broken glass ornament. Then she gently takes his hand and raises it level with her own. She carefully places the unicorn in the palm of his hand, then pushes his fingers closed upon it.)

What are you—doing that for? You want me to have him?—Laura?

(She nods.)

What for?
LAURA: A—souvenir. . . .[9]

Laura now knows that she belongs to a different world from Jim. He wandered into a zoo of exotic animals, but that was on his day off and he must return to the workaday world.

There will be no normal love of marriage and family for Laura nor for any of the Wingfields. Laura is too tender, too special, too fragile like her glass menagerie. It is Tom's painful sensitivity to Laura's predicament which makes him love her and which drives him from her. But he cannot escape Laura. The necessity of leaving her and the guilt over doing so, haunt him:

Oh, Laura, Laura, I tried to leave you behind me, but I am more faithful than I intended to be! I reach for a cigarette, I cross the street, I run into the movies or a bar, I buy a drink, I speak to the nearest stranger—anything that can blow your candles out!

(Laura bends over the candles.)

For nowadays the world is lit by lightning! Blow out your candles, Laura—and so good-bye. . . .

(She blows the candles out.)[10]

Laura's painful encounter with the world's lightning represents all of the Wingfields. Amanda's last glance at her husband's picture reveals as much of her as does Tom's final speech of him. The family is the supreme case of love trying to struggle against the world, and the family fails. Fundamentally romantic, Williams evokes the beauty of failure, the beauty which must fail.

While family life is impossibly difficult, Williams does not actually reject it. Instead, he allows his characters—and his audience—the full "pleasures" of family nostalgia and suffering. It is Williams's peculiar ability to do so without bathos. We can savor the situation because, like Amanda, we are never lost in it uninterruptedly. Williams insures his family memories against outright sentimentality by a delightful (and convenient) comic touch. He does not really create a comic perspective, which would change the meaning of his vision and would suggest the sanity of compromise. Rather, he edges the serious matter of his plays with humor. For example, early in *Orpheus Descending* one of the minor characters declares that most people find hate in marriage and an outlet in money. Her laughter at this observation is a perfect Williams moment. It conveys his temporary emotional defense against the painful truth. *Streetcar* is framed in

the same way, with a dirty joke at the beginning and an ironic double entendre at the end: "This game is seven-card stud." Williams seldom maintains his comic view, however, since it is for him, and for his strongest characters, a temporary way of keeping the world at bay. When he waxes "true," his characters speak directly, often lyrically, and the ironic edge disappears. Maggie, in *Cat*, has this edge, this style as part of her character. For her, it is a defense against the suffocating world of her in-laws. At private moments she may drop this defense; the curtain parts, and we see the loneliness, the isolation, and the gentleness within her. The painful inner lives of his characters remain as desperate as ever, only we are given alternate moments of rest from the hurt.

The distancing in *The Glass Menagerie* is fully and artfully done. In Tom's opening speech, for example, the touch of social comment which appears mocks the world of the middle class as well as itself:

> In Spain there was revolution. Here there was only shouting and confusion. . . . This is the social background of the play.[11]

Later, when this motif reappears, it is directly associated with the dilemmas of the Wingfield family. Their private world looks out on the social world in the same way that their windows look out on the alley. Tom says to the audience:

> Couples would come outside, to the relative privacy of the alley. You could see them kissing behind ashpits and telephone poles. This was the compensation for lives that passed like mine, without any change or adventure. . . .
> In Spain there was Guernica![12]

And immediately Amanda unwittingly provides the mocking counterpoint:

A fire-escape landing's a poor excuse for a porch. *(She spreads a newspaper on a step and sits down, gracefully and demurely as if she were settling into a swing on a Mississippi veranda.)* What are you looking at?[13]

A more often used technique in *The Glass Menagerie* to provide a comic edge is the projection of legends or images onto a wall in the Wingfield apartment, an element which is frequently dropped in production.[14] The published editions of the play continue to retain them. Williams argues that their use is important to maintain a sense of the play's structure beneath its episodic surface.[15] A number of the projections do seem to have only this architectural function: legends such as "After the Fiasco," "You Think I'm in Love with Continental Shoemaker's?," "High School Hero;" images such as typewriters or a wintry scene in the park. But many are obviously funny, sardonic, or ironic as well. Amanda's memories of Blue Mountain are introduced with "Où Sont Les Neiges d'Antan?" Tom's desire for adventure brings forth the image of a sailing vessel with a Jolly Roger. Music, too, is used to evoke straightforward emotion. "Between each episode it [the theme tune] returns as a reference to the emotion, nostalgia, which is the first condition of the play."[16] But music also mocks the characters as when Amanda's self-pitying reproach to Tom's rudeness is introduced with "Ave Maria."

Perhaps the most complex use of these alternating effects is near the end of the play. Laura and Jim waltz to "La Golondrina." Their kiss is preceded by the symbol of Laura's freakish beauty—a projected image of blue roses—and swelling music. Then, having given us the emotional luxury of this melodrama, the legend becomes slightly ambiguous— "Souvenir" anticipates the broken glass figure Laura will give to Jim, and it also comes directly after the kiss and may refer to it as well. There is less doubt about the next legend. Jim's cliché explanation of his feelings for another girl brings forth the mock-enthusiastic "Love!" on the screen, and Laura's tender gesture with the broken unicorn ends with a choice of the legend "Things Have a Way of Turning Out So Badly" or the harsh image "Gentleman Caller Waving Good-bye—Gaily." Finally, when Jim tells Amanda he is engaged to another girl, we read the sardonic "The Sky Falls."

Williams tries to have his sentiment and mock it, too, using these devices both to intensify the family drama and to pull back from it. These "plastic" elements, then, are Williams's way of using the realistic situation while not being exclusively bound to it. The core of the play is the attempt by Amanda to find a family and the desire by Tom to escape from family. This surface action is alternately heightened and diminished by these nonrealistic devices. We are asked to embrace the characters and to laugh at them, to empathize and then to sympathize. Much of the same strategy can be seen in the dialogue, once we are alerted to it. Amanda's telephone campaign to sell subscriptions to the magazine *Companion* is filled with this juxtaposition of tears and laughter. More poignantly, her memories of her home life in Blue Mountain are made up of a dramatic alternation between vivid nostalgia and shrewd practicality:

> Finally there were no more vases to hold them, every available space was filled with jonquils. No vases to hold them? All right, I'll hold them myself! And then I—*[She stops in front of the picture. Music plays.]* met your father! Malaria fever and jonquils and then—this—boy. . . . *[She switches on the rose-colored lamp.]*
> I hope they get here before it starts to rain.[17]

Nearly lost in the intensity of her memory, Amanda begins to speak as though the past were the present, only to be brought up short by the reality of her situation. The rose-colored lamp is both a reprise of her vulnerability to charm and an instance of her coping, in the only way she knows how, with the situation in which that vulnerability has placed her: she puts a good light on harsh truths, and she dresses up the faded room to catch the gentleman caller for sister. And one might even say that all the Wingfields get caught out in the rain, away from the warm safety of home. Thus, the drama is embodied in the rhetoric and through its sequential movement each emotionally resonant element is followed by a flat deflation.

Williams uses a similar technique to add a more complex texture to the raw emotions of the Wingfields' family battles. Tom's angry speech denouncing his mother as a witch is slightly muted by his satiric, fanciful tone. But if the direct emotion is reduced in volume, it can also be said that the sense of calculation which Tom's imagery implies makes

the hurt Amanda receives all the keener for having been so carefully designed. And in the rare moments when mother and son can talk to, rather than at, each other, Williams manages this shift in tone with greatest delicacy:

> **AMANDA:** When I was a girl in Blue Mountain and it was suspected that a young man drank, the girl whose attentions he had been receiving, if any girl *was,* would sometimes speak to the minister of his church, or rather her father would if her father was living, and sort of feel him out on the young man's character. That is the way such things are discreetly handled to keep a young woman from making a tragic mistake!
> **TOM:** Then how did you happen to make a tragic mistake?
> **AMANDA:** That innocent look of your father's had everyone fooled! He *smiled*—the world was *enchanted!* No girl can do worse than put herself at the mercy of a handsome appearance! I hope that Mr. O'Connor is not too good-looking.
> **TOM:** No, he's not too good-looking. He's covered with freckles and hasn't too much of a nose.
> **AMANDA:** He's not right-down homely, though?
> **TOM:** Not right-down homely. Just medium homely, I'd say.[18]

The lines play first between Amanda's nostalgia and Tom's blunt irony, and then between her ecstatic memories (with the painful lesson they teach) and Tom's more gentle teasing. At moments such as these, the play's tone becomes a mode of encounter between characters, its surface ingenuity a way of revealing inner lives. The Wingfields exist most vividly when they appear to us caught between moments of direct revelation of their psyches and moments of indirect relief from that painful confrontation. In *The Glass Menagerie* the longing for the family of security is mocked but never abandoned, indulged even as it is shown up.

In *The Glass Menagerie* Williams consciously manipulated his subject matter and his tone, playing off the oppressiveness of the family of security against a teasing stylized realism. He did not grapple with the assumptions beneath the conflicting claims of personal freedom and security, nor did he construct a dramatic action which defined them. Rather, he relied on the evocative power of family strife, running the risk of being merely agitated and pathos-filled as in the soap opera. His family victims are at their most vivid at those points where they are both caught up in their lyrical self-indulgence and at the same time aware of the difficulty in communi-cating to those around them what they truly feel.

Williams does not test the family attitudes which are his subject. He has evoked family fears and frustra-tions without probing them. But it is important to recognize the genuine, if limited, appeal of Williams's strat-egy. He has asked us to see his plays as artifice and as reports on reality. And he has used the artificial, "plas-tic" elements both to intensify and to relieve the intensity of the family struggles. This paradox is a most in-triguing one. He has counted on our familiarity with the family drama, reminded us of it, and then eluded its more rigid restrictions. He has been a realist, if only in part, to re-fresh our response to the dilemmas of family life. His best plays remind us of our quest for relatedness and independence and so depend on, and contribute to, the very tradition of American domestic drama which he proposed to escape.

Notes

1 Jackson, *Broken World*, p. viii, note 1.

2 Williams, *Menagerie*, p. 145.

3 "A free, imaginative use of light can be of enormous value in giving a mobile, plastic quality to plays of a more or less static nature." Williams, "Production Notes," *Menagerie*, p. 134.

4 Ibid., pp. 163–164.

5 Ibid., pp. 167–168.

6 Tischler, *Williams*, p. 97.

7 Williams, *Menagerie*, p. 199.

8 Ibid., p. 220.

9 Ibid., pp. 230–231.

10 Ibid., p. 237.

11 Ibid., p. 145.

12 Ibid., p. 179.

13 Ibid., p. 180.

14 The original New York production and the recent revival both omitted the projections. Without them the play is moved even closer to the conventional realism of domestic drama, a tendency which can also be seen in the Broadway productions of *Streetcar,* which have deemphasized the expressionist elements in such scenes as those presenting symbolic images of Blanche's mental state.

15 Williams, "Production Notes," p. 132.

16 Ibid., p. 133.

17 Ibid., p. 194.

18 Ibid., p. 186.

Portrait of a Girl in Glass

TENNESSEE WILLIAMS

We lived in a third floor apartment on Maple Street in Saint Louis, on a block which also contained the Ever-ready Garage, a Chinese laundry, and a bookie shop disguised as a cigar store.

Mine was an anomalous character, one that appeared to be slated for radical change or disaster, for I was a poet who had a job in a warehouse. As for my sister Laura, she could be classified even less readily than I. She made no positive motion toward the world but stood at the edge of the water, so to speak, with feet that anticipated too much cold to move. She'd never have budged an inch, I'm pretty sure, if my mother who was a relatively aggressive sort of woman had not shoved her roughly forward, when Laura was twenty years old, by enrolling her as a student in a nearby business college. Out of her "magazine money" (she sold subscriptions to women's magazines), Mother had paid my sister's tuition for a term of six months. It did not work out. Laura tried to memorize the typewriter keyboard, she had a chart at home, she used to sit silently in front of it for hours, staring at it while she cleaned and polished her infinite number of little glass ornaments. She did this every evening after dinner. Mother would caution me to be very quiet. "Sister is looking at her typewriter chart!" I felt somehow that it would do her no good, and I was right. She would seem to know the positions of the keys until the weekly speed drill got underway, and then they would fly from her mind like a bunch of startled birds.

At last she couldn't bring herself to enter the school any more. She kept this failure a secret for a while. She left the house each morning as before and spent six hours walking around the park. This was in February, and all the walking outdoors regardless of weather brought on influenza. She was in bed for a couple of weeks with a curiously happy little smile on her face. Of course Mother phoned the business college to let them know she was ill. Whoever was talking on the other end of the line had some trouble, it seems, in remembering who Laura was, which annoyed my mother and she spoke up pretty sharply. "Laura has been attending that school of yours for two months, you certainly ought to recognize her name!" Then came the stunning disclosure. The person sharply retorted, after a moment or two, that now she *did* remember the Wingfield girl, and that she had not been at the business college *once* in about a month. Mother's voice became strident. Another person was brought to the phone to verify the statement of the first. Mother hung up and went to Laura's bedroom where she lay with a tense and frightened look in place of the faint little smile. Yes, admitted my sister, what they said was true. "I couldn't go any longer, it scared me too much, it made me sick at the stomach!"

After this fiasco, my sister stayed at home and kept in her bedroom mostly. This was a narrow room that had two windows on a dusky areaway between two wings of the building. We called this areaway Death Valley for a reason that seems worth telling. There were a great many alley cats in the neighborhood and one particularly vicious dirty white Chow who stalked them continually. In the open or on the fire escapes they could usually elude him but now and again he cleverly contrived to run some youngster among them into the cul-de-sac of this narrow areaway at the far end of which, directly beneath my sister's bedroom windows, they made the blinding discovery that what had appeared to be an avenue of escape was really a locked arena, a gloomy vault of concrete and brick with walls too high for any cat to spring, in which they must suddenly turn to spit at their death until it was hurled upon them. Hardly a week went by without a repetition of this violent drama. The areaway had grown to be hateful to Laura because she could not look out on it without recalling the screams and the snarls of killing. She kept the shades drawn down, and as Mother would not permit the use of electric current except when needed, her days were spent almost in perpetual twilight. There were three pieces of dingy ivory furniture in the room, a bed, a bureau, a chair. Over the bed was a remarkably bad religious painting, a very effeminate head of Christ with teardrops visible just below the eyes. The charm of the room was produced by my sister's collection of glass. She loved colored glass and had covered the walls with shelves of little glass articles, all of them light and delicate in color. These she washed and polished with endless care. When you entered the room there was always this soft, transparent radiance in it which came from the glass absorbing whatever faint light came through the shades on Death Valley. I have no idea how many articles there were of this delicate glass. There must have been hundreds of them. But Laura could tell you exactly. She loved each one.

She lived in a world of glass and also a world of music. The music came from a 1920 Victrola and a bunch of records that dated from about the same period, pieces such as "Whispering" or "The Love Nest" or "Dardanella." These records were souvenirs of our father, a man whom we barely remembered, whose name was spoken rarely. Before his sudden and unexplained disappearance from our lives, he had made this gift to the household, the phonograph and the records, whose music remained as a sort of apology for him. Once in a while, on payday at the warehouse, I would bring home a new record. But Laura seldom cared for these new records, maybe because they reminded her too much of the noisy tragedies in Death Valley or the speed drills at the business college. The tunes she loved were the ones she had always heard. Often she sang to herself at night in her bedroom. Her voice was thin, it usually wandered off-key. Yet it had a curious childlike sweetness. At eight o'clock in the evening I sat down to write in my own mousetrap of a room. Through the closed doors, through the walls, I would hear my sister singing to herself, a piece like "Whispering" or "I Love You" or "Sleepy Time Gal," losing the tune now and then but always preserving the minor atmosphere of the music. I think that was why I always wrote such strange and sorrowful poems in those days. Because I had in my ears the wispy sound of my sister serenading her pieces of colored glass, washing them while she sang or merely looking down at them with her vague blue eyes until the points of gem-like radiance in them gently drew the arching particles of reality from her mind and finally produced a state of hypnotic calm in which she even stopped singing or washing the glass and merely sat without motion until my mother knocked at the door and warned her against the waste of electric current.

I don't believe that my sister was actually foolish. I think the petals of her mind had simply closed through fear, and it's no telling how much they had closed upon in the way of secret wisdom. She never talked very much, not even to me, but once in a while she did pop out with something that took you by surprise.

After work at the warehouse or after I'd finished my writing in the evening, I'd drop in her room for a little visit because she had a restful and soothing effect on nerves that were worn rather thin from trying to ride two horses simultaneously in two opposite directions.

I usually found her seated in the straight-back ivory chair with a piece of glass cupped tenderly in her palm.

"What are you doing? Talking to it?" I asked.

"No," she answered gravely, "I was just looking at it."

On the bureau were two pieces of fiction which she had received as Christmas or birthday presents. One was a novel called the *Rose-Garden Husband* by someone whose name escapes me. The other was *Freckles* by Gene Stratton Porter. I never saw her reading the *Rose-Garden Husband,* but the other book was one that she actually lived with. It had probably never occurred to Laura that a book was something you read straight through and then laid aside as finished. The character Freckles, a one-armed orphan youth who worked in a lumber camp, was someone that she invited into her bedroom now and then for a friendly visit just as she did me. When I came in and found this novel open upon her lap, she would gravely remark that Freckles was having some trouble with the foreman of the lumber camp or that he had just received an injury to his spine when a tree fell on him. She frowned with genuine sorrow when she reported these misadventures of her story-book hero, possibly not recalling how successfully he came through them all, that the injury to the spine fortuitously resulted in the discovery of rich parents and that the bad-tempered foreman has a heart of gold at the end of the book. Freckles became involved in romance with a girl he called The Angel, but my sister usually stopped reading when this girl became too prominent in the story. She closed the book or turned back to the lonelier periods in the orphan's story. I only remember her making one reference to this heroine of the novel. "The Angel is nice," she said, "but seems to be kind of conceited about her looks."

Then one time at Christmas, while she was trimming the artificial tree, she picked up the Star of Bethlehem that went on the topmost branch and held it gravely toward the chandelier.

"Do stars have five points really?" she enquired.

This was the sort of thing that you didn't believe and that made you stare at Laura with sorrow and confusion.

"No," I told her, seeing she really meant it, "they're round like the earth and most of them much bigger."

She was gently surprised by this new information. She went to the window to look up at the sky which was, as usual during Saint Louis winters, completely shrouded by smoke.

"It's hard to tell," she said, and returned to the tree.

So time passed on till my sister was twenty-three. Old enough to be married, but the fact of the matter was she had never even had a date with a boy. I don't believe this seemed as awful to her as it did to Mother.

At breakfast one morning Mother said to me, "Why don't you cultivate some nice young friends? How about down at the warehouse? Aren't there some young men down there you could ask to dinner?"

This suggestion surprised me because there was seldom quite enough food on her table to satisfy three people. My mother was a terribly stringent housekeeper, God knows we were poor enough in actuality, but my mother had an almost obsessive dread of becoming even poorer. A not unreasonable fear since the man of the house was a poet who worked in a warehouse, but one which I thought played too important a part in all her calculations.

Almost immediately Mother explained herself.

"I think it might be nice," she said, "for your sister."

I brought Jim home to dinner a few nights later. Jim was a big red-haired Irishman who had the scrubbed and polished look of well-kept chinaware. His big square hands seemed to have a direct and very innocent hunger for touching his friends. He was always clapping them on your arms or shoulders and they burned through the cloth of your shirt like plates taken out of an oven. He was the best-liked man in the warehouse and oddly enough he was the only one that I was on good terms with. He found me agreeably ridiculous I think. He knew of my secret practice of retiring to a cabinet in the lavatory and working on rhyme schemes when work was slack in the warehouse, and of sneaking up on the roof now and then to smoke my cigarette with a view across the river at the undulant open country of Illinois. No doubt I was classified as screwy in Jim's mind as much as in the others', but while their attitude was suspicious and hostile when they first knew me, Jim's was warmly tolerant from the beginning. He called me Slim, and gradually his cordial acceptance drew the others around, and while he remained the only one who actually had anything to do with me, the others had now begun to smile when they saw me as people smile at an oddly fashioned dog who crosses their path at some distance.

Nevertheless it took some courage for me to invite Jim to dinner. I thought about it all week and delayed the action till Friday noon, the last possible moment, as the dinner was set for that evening.

"What are you doing tonight?" I finally asked him.

"Not a God damn thing," said Jim. "I had a date but her Aunt took sick and she's hauled her freight to Centralia!"

"Well," I said, "why don't you come over for dinner?"

"Sure!" said Jim. He grinned with astonishing brightness.

I went outside to phone the news to Mother.

Her voice that was never tired responded with an energy that made the wires crackle.

"I suppose he's Catholic?" she said

"Yes," I told her, remembering the tiny silver cross on his freckled chest.

"Good!" she said. "I'll bake a salmon loaf!"

And so we rode home together in his jalopy.

I had a curious feeling of guilt and apprehension as I led the lamb-like Irishman up three flights of cracked marble steps to the door of Apartment F, which was not thick enough to hold inside it the odor of baking salmon.

Never having a key, I pressed the bell.

"Laura!" came Mother's voice. "That's Tom and Mr. Delaney! Let them in!"

There was a long, long pause.

"Laura?" she called again. "I'm busy in the kitchen, you answer the door!"

Then at last I heard my sister's footsteps. They went right past the door at which we were standing and into the parlor. I heard the creaking noise of the phonograph crank. Music commenced. One of the oldest records, a march of Sousa's, put on to give her the courage to let in a stranger.

The door came timidly open and there she stood in a dress from Mother's wardrobe, a black chiffon ankle-length and high-heeled slippers on which she balanced uncertainly like a tipsy crane of melancholy plumage. Her eyes stared back at us with a glass brightness and her delicate wing-like shoulders were hunched with nervousness.

"Hello!" said Jim, before I could introduce him.

He stretched out his hand. My sister touched it only for a second.

"Excuse me!" she whispered, and turned with a breathless rustle back to her bedroom door, the sanctuary beyond it briefly revealing itself with the tinkling, muted radiance of glass before the door closed rapidly but gently on her wraithlike figure.

Jim seemed to be incapable of surprise.

"Your sister?" he asked.

"Yes, that was her," I admitted. "She's terribly shy with strangers."

"She looks like you," said Jim, "except she's pretty."

Laura did not reappear till called to dinner. Her place was next to Jim at the drop-leaf table and all through the meal her figure was slightly tilted away from his. Her face was feverishly bright and one eyelid, the one on the side toward Jim, had developed a nervous wink. Three times in the course of the dinner she dropped her fork on her plate with a terrible clatter and she was continually raising the water glass to her lips for hasty little gulps. She went on doing this even after the water was gone from the glass. And her handling of the silver became more awkward and hurried all the time.

I thought of nothing to say.

To Mother belonged the conversational honors, such as they were. She asked the caller about his home and family. She was delighted to learn that his father had a business of his own, a retail shoe store somewhere in Wyoming. The news that he went to night school to study accounting was still more edifying. What was his heart set on beside the warehouse? Radio-engineering? My, my, my! It was easy to see that here was a very up-and-coming young man who was certainly going to make his place in the world!

Then she started to talk about her children. Laura, she said, was not cut out for business. She was domestic, however, and making a home was really a girl's best bet.

Jim agreed with all this and seemed not to sense the ghost of an implication. I suffered through it dumbly, trying not to see Laura trembling more and more beneath the incredible unawareness of Mother.

And bad as it was, excruciating in fact, I thought with dread of the moment when dinner was going to be over, for then the diversion of food would be taken away, we would have to go into the little steam-heated parlor. I fancied the four of us having run out of talk, even Mother's seemingly endless store of questions about Jim's home and his job all used up finally—the four of us, then, just sitting there in the parlor, listening to the hiss of the radiator and nervously clearing our throats in the kind of self-consciousness that gets to be suffocating.

But when the blancmange was finished, a miracle happened.

Mother got up to clear the dishes away. Jim gave me a clap on the shoulders and said, "Hey, slim, let's go have a look at those old records in there!"

He sauntered carelessly into the front room and flopped down on the floor beside the Victrola. He began sorting through the collection of worn-out records and reading their titles aloud in a voice so hearty that it shot like beams of sunlight through the vapors of self-consciousness engulfing my sister and me.

He was sitting directly under the floor-lamp and all at once my sister jumped up and said to him, "Oh—you have freckles!"

Jim grinned. "Sure that's what my folks call me—Freckles!"

"Freckles?" Laura repeated. She looked toward me as if for the confirmation of some too wonderful hope. I looked away quickly, not knowing whether to feel relieved or alarmed at the turn that things were taking.

Jim had wound the Victrola and put on *Dardanella*.

He grinned at Laura.

"How about you an' me cutting the rug a little?"

"What?" said Laura breathlessly, smiling and smiling.

"Dance!" he said, drawing her into his arms.

As far as I knew she had never danced in her life. But to my everlasting wonder she slipped quite naturally into those huge arms of Jim's, and they danced round and around the small steam-heated parlor, bumping against the sofa and chairs and laughing loudly and happily together. Something opened up in my sister's face. To say it was love is not too hasty a judgment, for after all he had freckles and that was what his folks called him. Yes, he had un- doubtedly assumed the identity—for all practical purposes—of the one-armed orphan youth who lived in the Limberlost, that tall and misty region to which she retreated whenever the walls of Apartment F became too close to endure.

Mother came back in with some lemonade. She stopped short as she en- tered the portieres.

"Good heavens! Laura? Dancing?"

Her look was absurdly grateful as well as startled.

"But isn't she stepping all over you, Mr. Delaney?"

"What if she does?" said Jim, with bearish gallantry. "I'm not made of eggs!"

"Well, well, well!" said Mother, senselessly beaming.

"She's light as a feather!" said Jim. "With a little more practice she'd dance as good as Betty!"

There was a little pause of silence.

"Betty?" said Mother.

"The girl I go out with!" said Jim.

"Oh!" said Mother.

She set the pitcher of lemonade carefully down and with her back to the caller and her eyes on me, she asked him just how often he and the lucky young lady went out together.

"Steady!" said Jim.

Mother's look, remaining on my face, turned into a glare of fury.

"Tom didn't mention that you went out with a girl!"

"Nope," said Jim. "I didn't mean to let the cat out of the bag. The boys at the warehouse'll kid me to death when Slim gives the news away."

He laughed heartily but his laughter dropped heavily and awkwardly away as even his dull senses were gradually penetrated by the unpleasant sensation the news of Betty had made.

"Are you thinking of getting married?" said Mother.

"First of next month!" he told her.

It took her several moments to pull herself together. Then she said in a dis- mal tone, "How nice! If Tom had only told us we could have asked you *both!*"

Jim had picked up his coat.

"Must you be going?" said Mother.

"I hope it don't seem like I'm rushing off," said Jim, "but Betty's gonna get back on the eight o'clock train an' by the time I get my jalopy down to the Wabash depot—"

"Oh, then, we mustn't keep you."

Soon as he'd left, we all sat down, looking dazed.

Laura was the first to speak.

"Wasn't he nice?" she asked. "And all those freckles!"

"Yes," said Mother. Then she turned to me.

"You didn't mention that he was engaged to be married!"

"Well, how did I know that he was engaged to be married?"

"I thought you called him your best friend down at the warehouse?"

"Yes, but I didn't know he was going to be married!"

"How peculiar!" said Mother. "How very peculiar!"

"No," said Laura gently, getting up from the sofa. "There's nothing peculiar about it."

She picked up one of the records and blew on its surface a little as if it were dusty, then set it softly back down.

"People in love," she said, "take everything for granted."

What did she mean by that? I never knew.

She slipped quietly back to her room and closed the door.

Not very long after that I lost my job at the warehouse. I was fired for writing a poem on the lid of a shoe-box. I left Saint Louis and took to moving around. The cities swept about me like dead leaves, leaves that were brightly colored but torn away from the branches. My nature changed. I grew to be firm and sufficient.

In five years' time I had nearly forgotten home. I had to forget it, I couldn't carry it with me. But once in a while, usually in a strange town before I have found companions, the shell of deliberate hardness is broken through. A door comes softly and irresistibly open. I hear the tired old music my unknown father left in the place he abandoned as faithlessly as I. I see the faint and sorrowful radiance of the glass, hundreds of little transparent pieces of it in very delicate colors. I hold my breath, for if my sister's face appears among them— the night is hers!

June 1943 (*Published* 1948)

Questions

1. Who is this play really about—Tom, Laura, or Amanda?

2. What function does the absent father serve in the play?

3. Besides serving as a possible suitor for Laura, what other roles might Jim play?

4. The historical events that are occurring at the time of the play's action could be said to constitute a subplot. Identify references to these events, and discuss how they relate to the play's central plot.

5. Is Tom's primary role in the play actor, character, playwright, or director?

6. How do the music, the lighting and the words and pictures projected on slides—which Tennessee Williams called "extra-literary accents"— contribute to the play's action? Are they essential? (Note that at the urging of the director, Williams eliminated these "accents" when the play opened on Broadway.)

7. Tennessee Williams called *The Glass Menagerie* a "memory play." What events are presented as memories? How close are these to Williams's own memories?

8. Discuss how props help to develop the play's plot. For example, consider the picture of the father, the Victrola, the fire escape, the telephone, the alarm clock, the high school yearbook, the unicorn, the candles.

9. What events and dialogue foreshadow Tom's escape?

10. Do you think Tom's decision to leave his family is a sign of strength or weakness?

11. Do Amanda and Laura change as the play proceeds? What do you think will happen to them after the action of the play is over? What is the significance of Laura's blowing out the candles at the end of the play?

12. Find several examples of religious imagery in the play—for example, the Paradise Dance Hall. What is the significance of this imagery? In what way does it relate to the major theme of the play?

Jenkins 1

Heather Jenkins
English 202
Professor Spand
April 17, 1996

Laura's Gentleman Caller

One of the major points of debate about Tennessee Williams's play *The Glass Menagerie* centers on the character Jim O'Connor, "the gentleman caller." Jim is an outgoing young man who approaches life lightheartedly, and his friendliness and charm make him a good suitor for Laura. But beside being Laura's suitor, what role does Jim play in the drama? Is Jim merely another character lost in the world of illusion, or is he something more? The answers to these questions become clear when we examine Jim's behavior and his influence on the other characters.

One possible interpretation of Jim's role is that he is simply another character living in a world of illusion. Jim's vision of the future is a grand one. He dreams of becoming part of the newly formed television industry, and throughout his appearance on stage, he rambles on about himself and his plans for the future:

> Because I believe in the future of television! (Turning back to her.) I wish to be ready to go up right along with it. Therefore I'm planning to get in on the ground floor. In fact, I've already made the right connections and all that remains is for the industry to itself to get underway! Full steam—(His eyes are starry.) Knowledge— Zzzzzp! Money—Zzzzzp!—Power! That's the cycle

Jenkins 2

democracy is built on! (*His attitude is convincingly dynamic. Laura stares at him, even her
shyness eclipsed in her absolute wonder. He suddenly grins.*) I guess you think I think a lot of
myself! (1940)

Jim is so enthralled with his own self-importance that
when Amanda asks Jim to persuade Laura to drink some
wine, he refers to himself as "Superman." This reference
suggests that Jim believes his training in public speaking
has given him the strength to overcome any obstacle. Jim's
delusions define his view of reality to such an extent that
he considers his view of life to be the only appropriate one.
As a result, he continually compares his perspective to that
of others, expecting to convince them that his views and
his views alone are correct.

Because Jim believes that he has discovered the one
true path to success, he considers Tom's dream of being a
poet to be unrealistic. Likewise, Jim regards Tom's plan to
join the Merchant Marine, to live the glamorous and adventurous life depicted in the movies, as a delusion. To "save"
Tom, Jim tries to persuade him to take a public speaking
course that will make him fit for "executive positions." All
of Jim's prodding, however, only reinforces Tom's desire to
proceed with his plan to join the Merchant Marine. Indeed,
when Jim tells Tom that he had better wake up, Jim totally
misses the irony of Tom's reply, "I am waking up--" (1929).

Jim's fantasies about the future reinforce Amanda's
romantic fantasies. Amanda's plans to find Laura a husband surface long before Jim enters the Wingfield house. As

Jenkins 3

Tom observes early in the play, Amanda's desire to find a suitor for Laura is "an obsession"; according to Tom, "[T]he image of the gentleman caller haunted our small apartment" (1907). When Amanda learns that Jim will attend their dinner, her dream of entertaining gentlemen callers in the Southern tradition becomes a reality. As a result, she begins to have unrealistically high expectations for Jim's visit. When Jim charms Amanda and attempts to impress her with his dreams of success, he unknowingly fulfills her fantasy.

Another possible interpretation of Jim's role is that he acts as a savior. In his article *"The Glass Menagerie,"* Robert Boxill explains that Jim's role as savior is inherent in the play's Christian symbolism, which first appears when Tom announces Jim's plans to come to dinner. Boxill asserts that along with his "Annunciation" of Jim's visit, Tom is alluding to Transubstantiation and the Resurrection when he discusses a movie in which "a stage magician turns[s] water to wine and escape[s] from a coffin" (1958). In simpler terms, Jim's role as possible savior for the family is suggested by his ability to reach out to Laura and encourage her to enjoy the pleasures of the real world— dancing and romance.

Jim's role as Laura's savior can be seen in the short story "Portrait of a Girl in Glass," from which the play evolved, as well as in the play itself. In the story, Jim and Laura begin to dance almost immediately after they are left alone. Although their encounter in the story is less intimate than the one in the play, Laura responds to Jim with joy and hope. In the play, Laura's visit with Jim evokes a similar response: Laura enjoys the feeling of being valued and accepted. Thus, when Jim announces his departure and his engagement, Laura realizes what she has lost and is overwhelmed with emotion.

Ironically, just as Jim offers Laura a way to escape her world of illusions, he abandons her, leaving her trapped in her own world. For this reason, Jim fails as a savior. One might argue that he consciously rejects his role as a savior; but we must remember that Jim enters the play unaware of the family's expectations; he views the visit purely as an opportunity to pass the time and to meet his friend's family, not as a prelude to romance. Jim's perception of his visit is made clear in "Portrait of a Girl in Glass," where he agrees to visit the Wingfields only because he has nothing else to do:

> "What are you doing tonight?" I finally asked him.
>
> "Not a God damn thing," said Jim. "I had a date but her Aunt took sick and she's hauled her freight to Centralia!"
>
> "Well," I said, "why don't you come over for dinner?"
>
> "Sure!" said Jim. He grinned with astonishing brightness. (1982)

Although both these interpretations of Jim's role offer insights into the play, neither adequately explains Jim's function. Perhaps the best explanation of Jim's role comes from the play itself, where Jim is called "an emissary from a world of reality" (1900). In this sense, his solid presence in the play emphasizes the fragility of the other characters. As an emissary of reality, Jim lives in the real world and realizes the importance of striving for a better life. He attends public speaking and radio engineering classes so that he can advance beyond his low-level job at the warehouse. He scolds Tom for wanting to be a poet, an impractical goal for anyone living during the economic depression of the 1930s. Likewise, Jim challenges Laura to relinquish her feelings of deformity and difference; he does not understand why Laura has given up hope and isolated herself. The contrast between Jim and Laura emphasizes not only Laura's vulnerability, but also her family's consuming and ultimately debilitating delusions.

Because Jim lives in a world of reality, he is the only character who escapes the illusions that engulf the Wingfields. Jim's connection with reality allows him to continue to search for a better life, something that none of the Wingfields will even attain (King 1970). For even though Tom escapes the confines of the apartment, he is unable to leave behind the imaginary world his mother and his sister have created. Moreover, like his father, Tom leaves not to seek reality but to escape from one dream world into another, one that is little different from the movies in which he has lost himself. As the play ends, Tom delivers a monologue about how he has been unable to leave the memory of his sister behind. And we are reminded of Jim, the happy and healthy gentleman caller, who has moved on.

Although Jim is referred to as the gentleman caller, his role in the play is much more complex. In one sense, Jim is detached from reality, enchanted by his own egotistical vision of how people should behave. In another sense, he is a kind of savior who reaches out to Laura, conveying the warmth and compassion of a saint. But these two conflicting images are overshadowed by Jim's role as an emissary from the real world who journeys to the seductive world of fantasy and whose presence these emphasizes the destructive power of dreams that have become delusions. In this role, Jim is "the kindest of Williams's emissaries from reality, perhaps because his faith in the American dream of self-improvement and success is so complete as to be itself a touching illusion" (Scanlan 1972).

Jenkins 7

Works Cited

Boxill, Robert. *"The Glass Menagerie."* Kirszner and Mandell 1956–62.

King, Thomas L. "Irony and Distance in *The Glass Menagerie*." Kirszner and Mandell 1962–70.

Kirszner, Laurie G., and Stephen R. Mandell, eds. *Literature: Reading, Reacting, Writing*. 3rd ed. Fort Worth: Harcourt, 1997.

Scanlan, Tom. "Family, Drama, and American Dreams." Kirszner and Mandell 1970–78.

Williams, Tennessee. "Portrait of a Girl in Glass." Kirszner and Mandell 1978–85.

---. *The Glass Menagerie*. Kirszner and Mandell 1898–1947.

Documenting Sources

Documentation is the acknowledgment of information from an outside source that you use in a paper. In general, you should give credit to your sources whenever you quote, paraphrase, summarize, or in any other way incorporate borrowed information or ideas into your work. Not to do so—on purpose or by accident—is to commit **plagiarism,** to appropriate the intellectual property of others. By following accepted conventions of documentation, you not only help avoid plagiarism, but also show your readers that you write with care and precision. In addition, you enable them to distinguish your ideas from those of your sources and, if they wish, to locate and consult the sources you cite.

Not all ideas from your sources need to be documented. You can assume that certain information—facts from encyclopedias, textbooks, newspapers, magazines, and dictionaries, or even from television and radio—is common knowledge. Even if the information is new to you, it need not be documented as long as it is found in several reference sources and as long as you do not use the exact wording of your source. Information that is in dispute or that is the original contribution of a particular person, however, *must* be documented. You need not, for example, document the fact that Arthur Miller's *Death of a Salesman* was first performed in 1949 or that it won a Pulitzer Prize for drama. (You could find this information in any current encyclopedia.) You would, however, have to document a critic's interpretation of a performance or a scholar's analysis of an early draft of the play, even if you do not use your source's exact words.

Students of literature use the documentation style recommended by the Modern Language Association of America (MLA), a professional organization of more than 25,000 teachers and students of English and other languages. This method of documentation, the one that you should use any time you write a literature paper, has three components: *parenthetical references in the text, a list of works cited,* and *explanatory notes.*

Parenthetical References in the Text

MLA documentation uses references inserted in parentheses within the text that refer to an alphabetical list of works cited at the end of the paper.

A typical **parenthetical reference** consists of the author's last name and a page number.

> Gwendolyn Brooks uses the sonnet form to create poems that have a wide social and aesthetic range (Williams 972).

If you use more than one source by the same author, include a shortened title in the parenthetical reference. In the following entry, "Brooks's Way" is a shortened form of the complete title of the article "Gwendolyn Brooks's Way with the Sonnet."

> Brooks not only knows Shakespeare, Spenser, and Milton, she also knows the full range of African-American poetry (Williams, "Brooks's Way" 972).

If you mention the author's name or the title of the work in your paper, only a page reference is necessary.

> According to Gladys Margaret Williams in "Gwendolyn Brooks's Way with the Sonnet," Brooks combines a sensitivity to poetic forms with a depth of emotion appropriate for her subject matter (972–73).

Keep in mind that you use different punctuation for parenthetical references used with *paraphrases and summaries,* with *direct quotations run in with the text,* and with *quotations of more than four lines.*

Paraphrases and summaries

Place the parenthetical reference after the last word of the sentence and before the final punctuation:

> In her works Brooks combines the pessimism of Modernist poetry with the optimism of the Harlem Renaissance (Smith 978).

Direct quotations run in with the text

Place the parenthetical reference after the quotation marks and before the final punctuation:

> According to Gary Smith, Brooks's A Street in Bronzeville "conveys the primacy of suffering in the lives of poor Black women" (980).

> According to Gary Smith, the poems in A Street in Bronzeville, "served notice that Brooks had learned her craft . . ." (978).

> Along with Thompson we must ask, "Why did it take so long for critics to acknowledge that Gwendolyn Brooks is an important voice in twentieth-century American poetry?" (123)

Quotations set off from the text

Omit the quotation marks and place the parenthetical reference one space after the final punctuation.

> For Gary Smith, the identity of Brooks's African-American women is inextricably linked with their sense of race and poverty:
>> For Brooks, unlike the Renaissance poets, the victimization of poor Black women becomes not simply a minor chord but a predominant theme of <u>A Street in Bronzeville.</u> Few, if any, of her female characters are able to free themselves from a web of poverty that threatens to strangle their lives. (980)

[Quotations of more than four lines are indented ten spaces (or one inch) from the margin and are not enclosed within quotation marks. The first line of a single paragraph of quoted material is not indented further. If you quote two or more paragraphs, indent the first line of each paragraph three additional spaces (one-quarter inch).]

SAMPLE REFERENCES

The following formats are used for parenthetical references to various kinds of sources used in papers about literature. (Keep in mind that the parenthetical reference contains just enough information to enable readers to find the source in the list of works cited at the end of the paper.)

An entire work

> August Wilson's play <u>Fences</u> treats many themes frequently expressed in modern drama.

[When citing an entire work, state the name of the author in your paper instead of in a parenthetical reference.]

A work by two or three authors

> Myths cut across boundaries and cultural spheres and reappear in strikingly similar forms from country to country (Feldman and Richardson 124).

> The effect of a work of literature depends on the audience's predispositions that derive from membership in various social groups (Hovland, Janis, and Kelley 87).

A work by more than three authors

> Hawthorne's short stories frequently use a combination of allegorical and symbolic methods (Guerin et al. 91).

[The abbreviation *et al.* is Latin for "and others."]

A work in an anthology

> In his essay "Flat and Round Characters" E. M. Forster
> distinguishes between one-dimensional characters and those that
> are well developed (Stevick 223–31).

[The parenthetical reference cites the anthology (edited by Stevick) that
contains Forster's essay; full information about the anthology appears in
the list of works cited.]

A work with volume and page numbers

> In 1961 one of Albee's plays, The Zoo Story, was finally
> performed in America (Eagleton 2:17).

An indirect source

> Wagner observed that myth and history stood before him "with
> opposing claims" (qtd. in Winkler 10).

[The abbreviation *qtd. in* (quoted in) indicates that the quoted material
was not taken from the original source.]

A play or poem with numbered lines

> "Give thy thoughts no tongue," says Polonius, "Nor any
> unproportioned thought his act" (Ham. 1.3.59–60).

[The parentheses contain the act, scene, and line numbers, separated by
periods. When included in parenthetical references, titles of the books of
the Bible and well-known literary works are often abbreviated—*Gen.* for
Gensis and *Ado* for *Much Ado about Nothing,* for example.]

> "I muse my life-long hate, and without flinch / I bear it nobly as
> I live my part," says Claude McKay in his bitterly ironic poem
> "The White City" (3–4).

[Notice that a slash (/) is used to separate lines of poetry run in with the
text. The parenthetical reference cites the lines quoted.]

The List of Works Cited

Parenthetical references refer to a **list of works cited** that includes all
the sources you refer to in your paper. (If your list includes all the works
consulted, whether you cite them or not, use the title *Works Consulted.*)
Begin the works cited list on a new page, continuing the page numbers of
the paper. For example, if the text of the paper ends on page 6, the works
cited section will begin on page 7.

Center the title *Works Cited* one inch from the top of the page. Arrange entries alphabetically, according to the last name of each author (or the first word of the title if the author is unknown). Articles—*a, an,* and *the*—at the beginning of a title are not considered first words. Thus, *A Handbook of Critical Approaches to Literature* would be alphabetized under *H.* In order to conserve space, publishers' names are abbreviated—for example, *Harcourt* for Harcourt Brace College Publishers. Double-space the entire works cited list between and within entries. Begin typing each entry at the left margin, and indent subsequent lines five spaces or one-half inch. The entry itself generally has three divisions—author, title, and publishing information—separated by periods.*

A book by a single author

Kingston, Maxine Hong. The Woman Warrior: Memoirs of a Girlhood among Ghosts. New York: Knopf, 1976.

A book by two or three authors

Feldman, Burton, and Robert D. Richardson. The Rise of Modern Mythology. Bloomington: Indiana UP, 1972.

[Notice that only the *first* author's name is in reverse order.]

A book by more than three authors

Guerin, Wilfred, et al., eds. A Handbook of Critical Approaches to Literature. 3rd. ed. New York: Harper, 1992.

[Instead of using *et al.,* you may list all the authors' names in the order in which they appear on the title page.]

Two or more works by the same author

Novoa, Juan-Bruce. Chicano Authors: Inquiry by Interview. Austin, U of Texas P, 1980.

---. "Themes in Rudolfo Anaya's Work." Address given at New Mexico State University, Las Cruces. 11 Apr. 1987.

[List two or more works by the same author in alphabetical order by title. Include the author's full name in the first entry; use three unspaced hyphens followed by a period to take the place of the author's name in second and subsequent entries.]

---

* The fourth edition of the *MLA Handbook for Writers of Research Papers* (1995) shows a single space after all end punctuation.

An edited book

> Oosthuizen, Ann, ed. <u>Sometimes When it Rains: Writings
> by South African Women.</u> New York: Pandora, 1987.

[Note that the abbreviation *ed.* stands for *editor.*]

A book with a volume number

> Eagleton, T. Allston. <u>A History of the New York Stage.</u>
> Vol. 2. Englewood Cliffs: Prentice, 1987.

[All three volumes have the same title.]

> Durant, Will, and Ariel Durant. <u>The Age of Napoleon: A
> History of European Civilization from 1789 to 1815.</u>
> New York: Simon, 1975.

[Each volume has a different title. *The Age of Napoleon* is Volume II of *The
Story of Civilization.*]

A short story, poem, or play in a collection of the author's work

> Gordimer, Nadine. "Once upon a Time." <u>"Jump" and Other Stories.</u>
> New York: Farrar, 1991. 23–30.

A short story in an anthology

> Salinas, Marta. "The Scholarship Jacket." <u>Nosotros:
> Latina Literature Today.</u> Ed. Maria del Carmen Boza,
> Beverly Silva, and Carmen Valle. Binghamton:
> Bilingual, 1986. 68–70.

[The inclusive page numbers follow the year of publication. Note that here
the abbreviation *Ed.* stands for *Edited by.*]

A poem in an anthology

> Simmerman, Jim. "Child's Grave, Hale County,
> Alabama." <u>The Pushcart Prize, X: Best of the Small
> Presses.</u> Ed. Bill Henderson. New York: Penguin,
> 1986. 198–99.

A play in an anthology

> Hughes, Langston. <u>Mother and Child. Black Drama
> Anthology.</u> Ed. Woodie King and Ron Miller. New
> York: NAL, 1986. 399–406.

An article in an anthology

> Forster, E. M. "Flat and Round Characters." <u>The Theory</u>
> <u>of the Novel.</u> Ed. Philip Stevick. New York: Free,
> 1980. 223–31.

More than one selection from the same anthology

If you are using more than one selection from an anthology, cite the anthology in one entry. In addition, list each individual selection separately, including the author and title of the selection, the anthology editor's last name, and the inclusive page numbers.

> Kirszner, Laurie G., and Stephen R. Mandell, eds.
> <u>Literature: Reading, Reacting, Writing.</u> 3rd ed. Fort
> Worth: Harcourt, 1997.

> Rich, Adrienne. "Diving into the Wreck." Kirszner and
> Mandell. 874–76.

A translation

> Carpentier, Alejo. <u>Reasons of State.</u> Trans. Francis
> Partridge. New York: Norton, 1976.

An article in a journal with continuous pagination in each issue

> LeGuin, Ursula K. "American Science Fiction and the
> Other." <u>Science Fiction Studies</u> 2 (1975): 208–10.

An article with separate pagination in each issue

> Grossman, Robert. "The Grotesque in Faulkner's 'A Rose for
> Emily.'" <u>Mosaic</u> 20.3 (1987): 40–55.

[20.3 signifies volume 20, issue 3.]

An article in a magazine

> Milosz, Czeslaw. "A Lecture." <u>The New Yorker</u> 22 June
> 1992: 32.

> "Solzhenitsyn: An Artist Becomes an Exile." <u>Time</u> 25
> Feb. 1974: 34+.

[34+ indicates that the article appears on pages that are not consecutive; in this case the article begins on page 34 and then continues on page 37. An article with no listed author is entered by title on the works cited list.]

An article in a daily newspaper

> Oates, Joyce Carol. "When Characters from the Page Are
>   Made Flesh on the Screen." New York Times 23 Mar. 1986,
>   late ed.: C1+

[C1+ indicates that the article begins on page 1 of Section C and continues on a subsequent page.]

An article in a reference book

> "Dance Theatre of Harlem." The New Encyclopaedia Britannica:
>   Micropaedia. 15th ed. 1987.

[You do not need to include publication information for well-known reference books.]

> Grimstead, David. "Fuller, Margaret Sarah." Encyclopedia of
>   American Biography. Ed. John A. Garraty. New York:
>   Harper, 1974.

[You must include publication information when citing reference books
that are not well known.]

A CD-ROM: Entry with a print version

> Zurbach, Kate. "The Linguistic Roots of Three Terms." Linguistic
>   Quarterly 37 (1994): 12–47. Infotrac: Magazine Index Plus.
>   CD-ROM. Information Access. Jan. 1996.

[When you cite information with a print version from a CD-ROM, include
the publication information, the underlined title of the database (Infotrac:
Magazine Index Plus), the publication medium (CD-ROM), the name of
the company that produced the CD-ROM (Information Access), and the
electronic publication date.]

A CD-ROM: Entry with no print version

> "Surrealism." Encarta 1996. CD-ROM. Redmond: Microsoft, 1996.

[If you are citing a part of a work, include the title in quotation marks.]

> A Music Lover's Multimedia Guide to Beethoven's 5th. CD-ROM.
>   Spring Valley: Interactive, 1993.

[If you are citing an entire work, include the underlined title.]

An online source: Entry with a print version

> Dekoven, Marianne. "Utopias Limited: Post-sixties and
>   Postmodern American Fiction." Modern Fiction Studies 41.1
>   (Spring 1995): 121–34. Online. Internet. 17 Mar. 1996.

Available http://muse.jhu.edu/journals/MFS/v041/41.1
dekoven.html.

[When you cite information with a print version from an online source,
include the publication information for the printed source, the number of
pages (*n. pag.* if no pages are given), the publication medium (Online), the
name of the computer network (Internet), and the date of access. If you
wish, you may also include the electronic address, preceded by the word
Available. Information from a commercial computer service—America
Online, Prodigy, and CompuServe, for example—will not have an electronic address.]

O'Hara, Sandra. "Reexamining the Canon." <u>Time</u> 13 May 1994:
27. Online. America Online. 22 Aug. 1994.

An online source: Entry with no print version

"Romanticism." <u>Academic American Encyclopedia.</u> Online.
Prodigy. 6 Nov. 1995.

[This entry shows that the material was accessed on November 6, 1996.]

An online source: Public Posting

Peters, Olaf. "Studying English through German." 29 Feb. 1996.
Online Posting. Foreign Language Forum, Multi Language
Section. CompuServe. 15 Mar. 1996.

Gilford, Mary. "Dog Heroes in Children's Literature." 4 Oct.
1996. Newsgroup alt.animals.dogs. America Online. 23 Mar.
1996.

[**WARNING:** Using information from online forums and newsgroups is
risky. Contributors are not necessarily experts, and frequently they are incorrect and misinformed. Unless you can be certain that the information you
are receiving from these sources is reliable, do not use it in your papers.]

An online source: Electronic Text

Twain, Mark. <u>The Adventures of Huckleberry Finn.</u> From
<u>The Writing of Mark Twain.</u> Vol. 13. New York: Harper, 1970.
Online. Wiretap.spies. Internet. 13 Jan. 1996. Available
http://www.sci.dixie.edu/DixieCollege/Ebooks/huckfin.html.

[This electronic text was originally published by Harper. The name of the
repository for the electronic edition is Wiretap.spies.]

An online source: E-Mail

Adkins, Camille. E-Mail to the author. 8 June 1995.

An interview

> Brooks, Gwendolyn. "Interview." <u>Triquarterly</u> 60
>   (1984): 405–10.

A lecture or address

> Novoa, Juan-Bruce. "Themes in Rudolfo Anaya's Work."
>   New Mexico State University, Las Cruces,
>   11 Apr. 1987.

A film or videocassette

> "<u>A Worn Path.</u>" By Eudora Welty. Dir. John Reid and Claudia
> Velasco. Perf. Cora Lee Day and Conchita Ferrell. Videocassette.
> Harcourt, 1994.

[In addition to the title, the director, and the year, include other pertinent information such as the principal performers.]

Explanatory Notes

Explanatory notes, indicated by a superscript (a raised number) in the text, may be used to cite several sources at once or to provide commentary or explanations that do not fit smoothly into your paper. The full text of these notes appears on the first numbered page following the last page of the paper. (If your paper has no explanatory notes, the works cited page follows the last page of the paper.) Like works cited entries, explanatory notes are double-spaced within and between entries. However, the first line of each explanatory note is indented five spaces (or one-half inch), with subsequent lines flush with the left-hand margin.

To Cite Several Sources

In the paper

> Surprising as it may seem, there have been many attempts to
> define literature.[1]

In the note

> [1] For an overview of critical opinion, see Arnold 72; Eagleton
> 1–2; Howe 43–44; and Abrams 232–34.

To Provide Explanations

In the paper

>   In recent years gothic novels have achieved great popularity.[3]

In the note

>   [3]Gothic novels, works written in imitation of medieval romances, originally relied on supernatural occurrences. They flourished in the late eighteenth and early nineteenth centuries.

Sample Literature Papers with MLA Documentation

The following two research papers, written for introduction to literature courses, follow the conventions of MLA documentation style. Note that the second paper uses electronic sources.

Daniel Collins
English 201
Professor Smith
January 30, 1996

And Again She Makes the Journey: Character
and Act in Eudora Welty's "A Worn Path"

Over the past fifty years, Eudora Welty's "A Worn
Path," the tale of an elderly black woman, Phoenix Jackson,
traveling to the city to obtain medicine for her sick grandson, has been the subject of much critical interpretation.
Critics have speculated on the meaning of the many death
and rebirth symbols, including the scarecrow, which the old
woman perceives as a ghost; the buzzard who watches her
travel; the skeleton-like branches that reach out to slow her;
and her first name, Phoenix. From the study of these symbols, various critics have concluded that "A Worn Path" represents either a "heroic act of sacrifice," "a parable for the
journey of life," or "a religious pilgrimage" (Keys 354). It
is certainly true, as these interpretations imply, that during her journey Phoenix Jackson struggles through difficult
terrain and encounters many dangers, and that despite
these obstacles, she does not abandon her quest. However, it
is neither the quest itself nor the symbols associated with it
that is the story's primary focus; what is most important is
Phoenix Jackson's character and her act of making the
journey.

Eudora Welty discusses the characterization of Phoenix
Jackson in a videotaped interview. In it Welty acknowledges
that Jackson's first name refers to a mythical bird that dies

and is reborn every five hundred years. She explains, however, that despite her symbolic name, the character is a
complex being with human frailties and emotions (Henley).

Phoenix Jackson has a number of physical frailties
that challenge her ability to perform daily tasks. Because of
her age, she has failing eyesight, which distorts her perception of the objects she encounters during her journey. For
instance, Phoenix mistakes a patch of thorns for "a pretty
little green bush," and she believes a scarecrow is the ghost
of a man (Welty 372–73). Likewise, her ability to walk is
limited, so she must rely on a cane; at one point, she is unable to bend and tie her own shoes. Because of these physical disabilities, readers might expect her to fail in her
attempt to reach town, for "the journey is long; the path,
though worn, is difficult" (Keys 354). So what gives
Phoenix Jackson the energy and endurance for the journey?
The question can best be answered by looking at the inner
qualities of the woman: Although Jackson's body is weak,
she has great spiritual and emotional strength.

Phoenix Jackson's spiritual strength comes from her
oneness with nature and her belief in God. This oneness
with nature, claims James Saunders, helps her overcome
the environmental dangers that she encounters (67). Because Phoenix Jackson is "a child of nature," her impaired
vision, although it slows her journey, does not stop it, for as
Saunders explains, "mere human vision would not have
been sufficient for the journey" (67). Instead of allowing
her failing vision to restrict her actions, Phoenix Jackson
relies on her spiritual connection with nature; thus, she

warns various animals to "Keep out from under these feet" (Welty 371). Additionally, she exhibits her spiritual strength through her belief in God--a quality seen when she refers to God watching her steal the hunter's nickel.

Phoenix Jackson's spiritual strength is complemented by her emotional strength. Her love for her grandson compels her to endure any difficulty and to defy any personal danger. Thus, throughout her journey, she demonstrates fearlessness and selflessness. For example, when the hunter threatens her with his gun, she tells him that she has faced worse dangers. Even after stealing and accepting nickels, she does not consider replacing her own worn shoes, but instead remains intent upon buying something nice for her grandson--a paper windmill.

In her video interview, Eudora Welty explains how she came to create the paradoxical Phoenix Jackson--outwardly frail and inwardly strong. Welty tells how she noticed an "old lady" slowly making her way across a "silent horizon,"[1] driven by an overwhelming determination to reach her destination; as Welty says, "she had a purpose" (Henley). Welty created Phoenix Jackson in the image of this determined woman. In order to emphasize the character's strength, Welty had her make the journey to Natchez to retrieve medication for her grandson. Because the act had to be performed repeatedly, the journey became a ritual that had to be completed at all costs. Thus, as Welty explains in her interview, the act of making the journey is the most important element in the story (Henley).

In order to convey the significance of the journey, Welty

Collins 4

focuses her story on the process of the journey. For this reason, readers receive little information about the daily life of the boy and his grandmother, or about the illness for which the boy is being treated. Regardless of the boy's condition--or even whether he is alive or dead--Jackson must complete her journey (Henley). The nurse's statement--"The doctor said as long as you came to get it [the medicine], you could have it" (Welty 377)--reinforces the ritualistic nature of Jackson's journey, a journey that Bartel suggests is a "subconscious" act (289). Thus, Phoenix Jackson cannot answer the nurse's questions because she does not consciously know what compels her to make the journey. According to Welty, the character's silence and disorientation can also be attributed to her relief and disillusionment upon completing the ritualistic journey (Henley). Nevertheless, next Saturday, Phoenix Jackson will again walk "miles and miles, and will continue to do so, regardless of the difficulties facing her, along the worn path that leads through the wilderness of the Natchez Trace, cheerfully performing her labor of love" (Howard 84).

Clearly, the interaction of character (Phoenix Jackson) and act (the ritual journey in search of medication) are the most important aspects of Welty's story. By relying heavily on the characterization of Phoenix Jackson and by detailing her difficult encounters during her ritual journey to town, Welty emphasizes how spiritual and emotional strength can overcome physical frailty and how determination and fearlessness can thwart any danger. These moral messages become clear by the time Phoenix reaches the doctor's office. The image of the elderly woman determinedly walking across the horizon, the image that prompted Welty's writing of the story, remains in the minds of the readers, and significantly, it is the final image of the videotaped version of "A Worn Path."

Note

[1]Unlike the written version of "A Worn Path," the video of the short story ends not at the doctor's office but with a vision similar to the one that inspired Welty to write the story--the elderly black woman silently walking along the horizon at dusk.

Collins 7

Works Cited

Bartel, Roland. "Life and Death in Eudora Welty's 'A Worn Path.'" Studies in Short Fiction 14 (1977): 288–290.

Henley, Beth. Interview with Eudora Welty. Dir. John Reid and Claudia Velasco. Videocassette. Harcourt, 1994.

Howard, Zelma Turner. The Rhetoric of Eudora Welty's Short Stories. Jackson: UP of Mississippi, 1973.

Keys, Marilyn. "'A Worn Path': The Way of Dispossession" Studies in Short Fiction 16 (1979): 354–56.

Saunders, James Robert. "'A Worn Path': The Eternal Quest of Welty's Phoenix Jackson." Southern Literary Journal 25.1 (Fall 1992): 62–73.

Welty, Eudora. "A Worn Path." Literature: Reading, Reacting, Writing, 3rd ed. Ed. Laurie G. Kirszner and Stephen R. Mandell. Forth Worth: Harcourt, 1997. 371–77.

"A Worn Path." By Eudora Welty. Dir. John Reid and Claudia Velasco. Perf. Cora Lee Day and Conchita Ferrell. Videocassette. Harcourt, 1994.

Tim Westmoreland

Professor Adkins

Literature 2101

5 April 1997

"A & P": A Class Act

John Updike's "A & P," like many of his works, is a "profoundly American" story about social inequality and an attempt to bridge the gap between social classes (Steiner 105). The story is told from the perspective of an eighteen-year-old boy who is working as a check-out clerk in an A & P in a small New England town five miles from the beach. The narrative is told in a slangy, colloquial voice that captures a brief but powerful encounter with a "beautiful but inaccessible girl" from another social and economic level (Wells). Sammy, the narrator, is working his cash register on a slow Thursday afternoon when, as he says, "In walks these three girls in nothing but bathing suits" ("A & P" 105). Lengel, the store's manager--a Sunday school teacher and "self appointed moral policeman"--confronts the girls, telling them that they should be decently dressed (Wells). It is a moment of heightened embarrassment and insight for all parties concerned, and in an apparently impulsive act, Sammy quits his job. Although the plot is uncomplicated, what is at the heart of this story is more complex: a noble gesture that serves as a futile attempt to cross social and economic boundaries that are all but unbridgeable.

Through Sammy's eyes we see the class conflict that defines the story. The privileged young girls in bathing suits are set in sharp contrast to the few customers who are shopping in the store. Sammy refers to the customers as "sheep" and describes one of them as "a witch about fifty with rouge on her cheekbones and no eyebrows" ("A & P" 105). Other customers are characterized in equally mundane terms--for example, "houseslaves in pin curlers" ("A & P" 106) and "an old party in baggy gray pants" ("A & P" 107). Unlike the other customers, the leader of the three girls is described as a "queen": "She came down a little hard on her heels, as if she didn't walk in her bare feet that much, putting down her heels and then letting the weight move along to her toes as if she was testing the floor with every step, putting a little deliberate extra action to it" ("A & P" 105–106). The mere fact that "Queenie" does not seem to have walked barefoot much seems to hint at a social gap between the girls and the other customers. However, it seems clear that Sammy realizes that Queenie and her friends come from further away than just the beach. They have come to test the floors of the less well off and do it openly, in defiance of social rules. In a sense, they are "slumming."

Queenie, whose name suggests her superior status, clearly understands her position in social as well as sexual terms. She has come to the A & P to purchase "Kingfish Fancy Herring Snacks in Pure Sour Cream" for her parents, while Sammy has to spend the summer working. Even the choice of the exotic and expensive herring snacks hints at their different backgrounds. Regardless, the two act in ways that are not all that different. Both are self-consciously trying out new roles, with Sammy trying to rise above his station in life and Queenie trying to move below hers. As Queenie arrives at the register, Sammy observes, "Now her hands are empty, not a ring or a bracelet, bare as God made them, and I wonder where the money's coming from. Still with that prim look she lifts a folded dollar bill out of the hollow at the center of her nubbled pink top" ("A & P" 108). With this gesture, she not only tests her own sexual powers but also sinks to the level of the supermarket and its workers and customers. Despite her act, though, Sammy knows how different Queenie's world is from his:

> I slid down her voice into her living room. Her father and the other men were standing around in ice-cream coats and bow ties and women were in sandals picking up herring snacks on toothpicks off a big glass plate and they were holding drinks the color of water with olives and sprigs of mint in them. When my parents have somebody over they get lemonade and if its a real racy affair Schlitz in tall glasses with "They'll Do It Every Time" cartoons stenciled on. ("A & P" 108)

As Updike says in a 1996 interview, "[Sammy] is a blue-collar kid longing for a white-collar girl" (Murray).

At this point in the story, as Sammy says, "everybody's luck begins to run out" ("A & P" 108). Lengel, the store manager, who, according to Updike, was named after a strict boss for whom his mother once worked, hints at "the cruel and unethical" rules that govern matters of social etiquette (Murray, Interview). In the story he confronts the girls' breach of etiquette, telling them that they are indecently dressed. "'We *are* decent,' Queenie says suddenly, her lower lip pushing, getting sore now that she remembers her place, a place from which the crowd that runs the A & P must look pretty crummy. Fancy Herring Snacks flashed in her very blue eyes" ("A & P" 108). Suddenly, Sammy can no longer be a detached observer and, in a gesture of defiance, he quits. The real question here is *why* he quits. Updike himself muses, "I wonder to what extent his gesture of quitting has to do with the fact that she is rich and he is poor?" (Murray).

Sammy confronts social inequality, but is his response simply heroic posturing or an action that expresses his longstanding frustration? In other words, does Sammy quit because of what Updike calls a "simple misunderstanding of how the world is put together" (Murray, <u>Interview</u>) or because he is "a boy who's tried to reach out of his immediate environment towards something bigger and better" (Updike, "Still Afraid" 55)? Although his action may be the result of both--Sammy even states it would be fatal not to go through with his initial impulse--it seems likely that he is taking a deliberate stand against what he sees as social injustice. Unlike Queenie's act, Sammy's gesture will have long-term consequences. As Updike points out, in Sammy's small town everyone will find out what he has done, and he may be "known . . . as a quitter" (Murray, <u>Interview</u>). Sammy's understanding and acceptance of these consequences ("'You'll feel this for the rest of your life,' Lengel says, and I know that's true"), and of the limitations his social class impose upon him, constitute his initiation into adulthood

("A & P" 109). Whether quitting is Sammy's first step toward overcoming these limitations or a romantic gesture he will live to regret remains to be seen.[1] As Updike says, "How blind we are, as we awkwardly push outward into the world!" (Updike, "Still Afraid" 57).

Although it is true that both Queenie and Sammy attempt to cross social boundaries, the reasons for their actions are different. Queenie's provocative gesture is well thought out; she deliberately relinquishes her trappings, her clothes and jewelry, and it is her position that allows her this privilege. She concedes, only for a few minutes, her dignity and wealth in order to flaunt her sexuality and her power. In contrast, Sammy chooses impulsively, in what Updike calls a "hot flash," a "moment of manly decisiveness," to take action and, ultimately, gives up both his dignity and his power (Murray, Interview). He gains only a brief moment of glory before he finds himself alone in the parking lot. In this instant, he confronts the social inequality and the unspeakable frustration it represents. According to Updike, Sammy cannot win, though in a "noble surrender of his position," he gains an understanding of the weight he must bear (Murray, Interview).

Westmoreland 6

Note

[1]In a recent E-mail message, Donald Murray agrees that Sammy's quitting will have implications for him that it will not have for Queenie and her friends. He goes on to say, however, that it is also possible that the young women will remain "imprisoned in their class," while Sammy may have a chance of escaping the limitations of his.

Westmoreland 7

Works Cited

Murray, Donald. E-mail to the author. 2 April 1996.

---. Interview with John Updike. Dir. Bruce Schwartz. Videocassette. Harcourt, 1997.

Steiner, George. "Supreme Fiction: America is in the Details." The New Yorker 11 Mar. 1996: 2pp. Online.
America Online. 20 Mar. 1996.

Updike, John. "A & P." Literature: Reading, Reacting, Writing. Ed. Laurie G. Kirszner and Stephen R. Mandell.
Fort Worth: Harcourt, 1997. 105–110.

---. "Still Afraid of Being Caught." New York Times 8 Oct.
1995, late ed., sec. 6: 55+. New York Times Online.
Online. Nexis. 14 Jan. 1996.

Wells, Walter. "John Updike's 'A&P': A Return Visit to
Araby." Studies in Short Fiction 30.2 (Spring 1993):
7pp. Online. Infotrac. 26 Mar. 1996.

Literary History: Aristotle to the Twentieth Century

The standard literary *canon* (the works of authors commonly read and taught) has been, until very recently, mainly male, white, upper-class, and European—with some American influence. Most readers are not aware, however, that the fiction, drama, and poetry now designated "classics" represent a series of choices about literary worth made over a long period of time. During the past twenty-five years or so, many challenges to the traditional canon have been made. To understand both the development of the traditional canon and the challenges to that canon, it is important to understand the history of Western literary criticism.

BEGINNINGS: THE GREEKS AND ROMANS (C. 450 B.C.–A.D. 400)

The Western critical tradition begins with the Greeks. In the *Republic* Plato (427–347 B.C.) described the ideal state as well as the role of philosophers and poets. His pupil, Aristotle (384–322 B.C.), was by far the most significant classical influence on Europeans of the Middle Ages and the Renaissance. Even today drama critics and students pay careful attention to the theories presented in Aristotle's *Poetics* about how literature imitates life, how an audience responds with pity and fear to a tragedy, and how a well-written play is constructed.

The Romans contributed works on what would now be called "loftiness of style" (*On the Sublime,* Longinus, first century A.D.) and a treatise on the art of poetry (*Ars Poetica,* Horace, 65–8 B.C.). These writers were typically more interested in the craft of poetry—in how one might construct a poem that would have a pleasing effect on a reader—than in the power of the poet. In contrast to the Greek philosophical approach, Roman literary criticism was more like a practical handbook.

THE MIDDLE AGES (C. A.D. 400–1500)

After the fall of the Western Roman Empire in the fifth century A.D., Christianity became the unifying force of Western culture. The literature of the European Middle Ages was intended to demonstrate moral virtue in the hopes that people would follow the behavior patterns it praised. Much literature of this period took the form of morality and mystery plays, both of which had religious themes. Worldly art was discouraged because the clergy who kept learning alive during these hard times believed that the role of literature was to instruct people in the way to lead a virtuous life. Significant departures from moralistic literature appeared in the French romances, which depicted adventures undertaken in the cause of love, and in Chaucer's *Canterbury Tales*, which drew on English, French, and Italian sources. These served as antidotes to the traditional cautionary plays and tales. It is not surprising, given the strong moral purpose of most literature of the Middle Ages, that literary criticism was not a priority of the intellectual life of the period.

THE RENAISSANCE (C. 1500–1660)

During the fourteenth and fifteenth centuries, Europe emerged from the church-centered Middle Ages with a rebirth (*renaissance* is French for "rebirth") of learning. Renewed access to Greek and Roman writers led Renaissance humanists to a broad interest in intellectual considerations. Sir Philip Sidney's (1554–1586) *The Defense of Poesy* (c. 1580) is usually considered the most important work of literary criticism from this period. In his *Defense* Sidney argues that poetry must not simply give pleasure, but also contribute positively to the life of society. Unlike the writers of medieval allegories, however, Sidney believed that literature could—and should—have a moral impact without being didactic or prescriptive. Despite Sidney's contributions, Aristotle continued to be the undisputed arbiter of critical questions, although his role was complicated by the emergence of William Shakespeare (1564–1616) as a dramatist of exceptional talent.

Shakespeare's work posed a problem because many critics realized that he was a fine playwright despite his frequent disregard for Aristotle's rules governing well-constructed plays. As a result, a major concern of criticism up to the eighteenth century became the reconciling of Aristotle's standards with the challenges of contemporary playwriting.

THE ENLIGHTENMENT (1660–1798)

Samuel Johnson (1709–1784), who devoted much of the preface of his edition of Shakespeare's plays to the question of the bard's departures from Aristotle's rules, was a major critical figure of the Enlightenment, a period of neoclassicism characterized by a revitalized interest in the values and ideas of the classical world, particularly of the Romans. Along with Johnson, poets John Dryden (1631–1700) and Alexander Pope (1688–1744), as well as philosopher Edmund Burke (1729–1797), compared contemporary practice with the ideas of their Roman forebears.

Burke, for instance, addressed the subject of Longinus's *On the Sublime* in his own treatise, *The Origin of Our Ideas of the Sublime and the Beautiful* (1757). Eighteenth-century critics stressed the value of reason and what they called "common sense." Their architectural style, familiar to us in structures like the Capitol building in Washington, D.C., provides a visual example of what they sought in literature: clarity, symmetry, discipline. They demanded that a play or poem be tightly constructed and favored the heroic couplet (two lines of rhymed iambic pentameter) as the perfect building block with which to construct didactic poems such as Pope's famous *Essay on Criticism* (1711), a scathing statement of neoclassical literary principles.

Thomas Paine's *Common Sense: Addressed to the Inhabitants of America* (1776) inspired his fellow Americans to revolution, and his *Rights of Man* (1791, 1792) made a stirring case for freedom as the right of every individual. The literature of the American Revolutionary Age, when Paine, Thomas Jefferson, Alexander Hamilton, Philip Freneau, and Joel Barlow were writing, reflected the patriotic concerns of the infant democracy.

THE ROMANTIC PERIOD (1798–1837)

Perhaps as an inevitable counterreaction to the Enlightenment came the Romantics. They believed that poetry was *not* an objective construction like a building with a precise and unchanging meaning but, instead, a subjective creation whose meaning depends on the poet's emotional state and a reader's personal response. Romantic poet William Blake (1757–1827) illustrated the conflict between romanticism and neoclassicism through his criticism of the opinions of Enlightenment artist Joshua Reynolds. In his notes on Reynolds's views, Blake observed that the emphasis on materialism and on physical evidence (empiricism) impoverishes art. Blake believed that the neoclassicists denied both imagination and subjective experience their preeminent role in the creative process. He thought that the artist must begin from the most concrete and minute sensory experience in order to reach the truth. Unlike most eighteenth-century writers, Blake and his fellow Romantics believed in the importance of the individual example rather than the general principle.

Like Blake, Samuel Taylor Coleridge (1772–1834) and William Wordsworth (1770–1850) placed value on the mysterious and on the significance of the common person's experience. Wordsworth in particular stressed the importance of concrete, simple language and offered, in his preface to the second edition of *Lyrical Ballads* (1800), a definition of poetry that has since become famous. A poem, Wordsworth says, should originate in "the spontaneous overflow of powerful feelings" whose energy comes from "emotion recollected in tranquility." George Gordon, Lord Byron (1788–1824), who himself lived a flamboyant life of publicly expressed powerful emotions, created in his poetry the melancholy Romantic hero, defiant and haunted by secret guilt. Percy Bysshe Shelley

(1792–1822) makes perhaps the greatest claims for the poet's power and obligation to society in "A Defense of Poetry" (1821), where he argues that the "great instrument of moral good is the imagination."

The difference in attitude between neoclassicists and Romantics can also be seen through a comparison of the Shakespearean criticism of Samuel Johnson and Samuel Taylor Coleridge. In his *Preface to Shakespeare* (1765) Johnson argues that Shakespeare's faults include being much more concerned with pleasing an audience than with teaching it morals; he observes that often virtue is not rewarded, nor wickedness suitably punished. Additionally, Johnson notes, Shakespeare's diction is too elevated, and he lets the characters in the tragedies talk too much without advancing the action.

Coleridge, on the other hand, sees in the tragic character of Hamlet the prototype of the Romantic hero and argues in his lecture "Shakespeare's Judgment Equal to his Genius" (1836) that Shakespeare knew exactly what he was doing in describing how people actually behave rather than how they ought to behave.

John Keats (1795–1821), another Romantic poet, continued Coleridge's defense of Shakespeare. Keats believed that Shakespeare's intensity, particularly evident in the tragedies, moved his work onto another level altogether, where the work itself takes on life through its relationship with "beauty and truth" rather than with teaching proper patterns of behavior.

The Romantics in general, both in Britain and in the United States, saw the poet as particularly close to God and nature. The American philosopher Ralph Waldo Emerson (1803–1882) thought nature offered to the poet a mystical symbolism, while Henry David Thoreau (1817–1862) extolled the view that man should live close to nature and follow his personal conscience rather than the dictates of society. Mary Shelley (1797–1851) and Edgar Allan Poe (1809–1849) were influential in another strand of romanticism: the macabre, melancholy, and mysterious.

THE VICTORIAN PERIOD (1837–1901)

The literary problem facing the post-Romantic generation of critics was dealing with a world where sublime isolation and communing with nature were less and less possible, even as ideals. During the Victorian era rapid industrialization, poverty, population growth, and mass transportation contributed to a general sense that the world was changing rapidly, and people had difficulty coping with these changes. In England critics like poet Matthew Arnold (1822–1888) argued that literature could help anchor people to their world and that literary criticism, as an occupation, should be a "disinterested endeavor" whose responsibility was to minister to a modern society that had lost its faith in other things, particularly religion. Although Arnold differed in many ways from the Romantics, he too believed in the ability of poetry to help us live productive, satisfying lives.

Just before the turn of the nineteenth century, the pendulum swung back from the Arnoldian view that poetry has moral utility—and that the best of it is serious and elevating—to the view that art should exist for its own sake. The dichotomy seen by the Romantics between intellect and feeling became in the 1890s the split between art and science. Oscar Wilde (1854–1900), Stéphane Mallarmé (1842–1898), and Charles Baudelaire (1821–1867) all dealt with this dichotomy by retreating altogether into the world of art and denying connection with anything else. These members of the symbolist movement valued suggestion, private symbols, and evocative references in their poetry. They attempted to connect their writing with a spiritual world they believed existed but knew was not accessible by the rational methods of science.

Charles Darwin (1809–1882) presented his theory of natural selection in his landmark *Origin of Species* (1859), and his ideas influenced novels and poetry of the latter part of the century. Those who believed natural selection contradicted the Bible were outraged, and others interpreted his theories as evidence of latent bestiality in humans. The certainty that mankind was the center of the universe was undermined, as was the conviction that the universe had been intelligently planned for a good purpose.

American writers of the late nineteenth century, including William Dean Howells and Henry James, were noted for realism; others, including naturalists Frank Norris and Theodore Dreiser, built on Darwin's views, exploring the idea of individuals being at the mercy of their instinctual drives and of external sociological forces.

THE MODERN PERIOD (1901–PRESENT)

In the next major attempt to demonstrate some objective significance to poetry, T. S. Eliot (1888–1965) argued against the lingering Romantic idea that a poem is the original child of a poet's inspiration. Instead, he proposed in "Tradition and the Individual Talent" (1917) that the poem supersedes the poet, who is merely the agent of its creation. Eliot argues that Wordsworth is wrong to put the poet in the central role of life-experiencer and recreator. According to Eliot, the poem itself will join the tradition, and it will be up to the *critic* to make sense of that tradition. To continue with the example of Shakespeare, Eliot's analysis of *Hamlet* focuses neither on the character of Hamlet and his personal agony (as did the Romantics) nor on the moral tone of the play (as did the neoclassicists), but rather on the story of Hamlet as treated by dramatists before Shakespeare. Eliot concludes that the problems with Shakespeare's play come about because he cannot successfully balance the early source materials with his own desire to write a play about the effect of Gertrude's guilt on her son. Thus, Eliot judges Shakespeare within a literary and historical tradition rather than within a moral or personal context.

The twentieth century has produced many important critics and theo-reticians of literature who built upon the legacy of the past, though some only to the extent that they attempt to contradict earlier approaches. The dominant critical views, which are discussed more fully in Appendix C, can be divided into three categories: *formal,* those concerned with the structure or form of texts (formalism, structuralism, deconstruction); *social,* those concerned with texts in relation to social contexts (new histori-cism, feminism, Marxism); and *personal,* those concerned with the interaction of the individual (author or reader) and texts (reader-response criticism, psychoanalytic criticism). Each of these theoretical approaches can be traced to the writings of authors in the early part of the twentieth century or before.

Formalism, which acquired prominence in English and American crit-icism in the middle part of the century, actually began in the early part of the century in Moscow and Petrograd, and was initially a term used in a negative fashion because the techniques focused on patterns and devices in a work of literature and ignored the subject matter. Soon, however, for-malism's logical appeal took hold, and it was advocated by Victor Shklovsky, Boris Eichenbaum, and Roman Jakobson in the 1920s. Though many literary theorists since Aristotle have stressed the importance of structure, the roots of structuralist criticism can be traced more directly to Russian formalists and French anthropologist Claude Levi-Strauss (1908–   ), who posited that all cultural phenomena have an underlying structural system. Deconstruction both reacts against the tenets of struc-turalism and builds upon the theories of German philosophers Friedrich Nietzsche (1844–1900) and Martin Heidegger (1889–1976), who ques-tioned the validity and verifiability of "truth," "knowledge," and other basic philosophical concepts.

Social criticism also had precursors in pre–twentieth-century writing. For example, Mary Wollstonecraft's *A Vindication of the Rights of Women* (1792) was an early forerunner of feminism. Virginia Woolf's *A Room of One's Own* (1929) anticipated feminist criticism by addressing the effects upon women of the patriarchal Western society and identifying deeply en-trenched attitudes of male-oriented society that hindered women in the pursuit of their creative possibilities. Similarly, Marxist criticism is based on the writings of Karl Marx and Friedrich Engels; they borrowed their key term *ideology* from French philosophers of the late eighteenth century who used it to label the study of how sense perceptions develop into concepts. The term Marxism itself was used in the same period to mean a rigidly held set of political ideas. Marx and Engels adapted and changed the terms, in-vesting them with new meaning that built upon meanings already present in the culture. New historicism is an even more recent mode of literary study, beginning in the 1980s, that reacts to formalism, structuralism, and deconstruction, arguing that the historical context is an integral part of a literary work and that the text cannot be considered in isolation.

Personal criticism too has its origins in earlier writing. For instance, the roots of psychoanalytic criticism can be traced to the psychological criticism of the early nineteenth century. Thomas Carlyle suggested in 1827 that the best criticism of the day was psychological, deriving meaning from a poem by analyzing the mental state and personality structure of the author. Finally, reader-response criticism, a late-twentieth-century approach begun in the 1960s, focuses on the reader and the reader's process and experience, rather than on the text or the text and its historical context.

The theoretical positions and techniques of each of these approaches to the study of literature are considered in detail in Appendix C.

Twentieth-Century
Literary Theories

As you become aware of various schools of literary criticism, you see new ways to think about fiction, poetry, and drama. Just as you value the opinions of your peers and your professors, you will also find that the ideas of literary critics can enrich your own reactions and evaluations of literature. Keep in mind that no single literary theory offers the "right" way of approaching what you read; no single critic provides the definitive analysis of any short story, poem, or play. As you become aware of the richly varied possibilities of twentieth-century criticism, you will begin to ask new questions and discover new insights about the works you read.

Formalism

Formalism stresses the importance of literary form in determining the meaning of a work. Each work of literature is considered in isolation. Formalist scholars consider biographical, historical, and social questions to be irrelevant to the real meaning of a play, short story, novel, or poem. For example, a formalist would see the relationship between Adam and Eve in *Paradise Lost* as entirely unrelated to Milton's own marital concerns, and theological themes in the same work would be viewed as entirely separate from Milton's deep involvement with the Puritan religious and political cause in seventeenth-century England. Milton's intentions and readers' responses to the famous epic poem would also be regarded by formalists as irrelevant. Instead, formalists would read the text closely, paying attention to organization and structure, to verbal nuances (suggested by word choice and use of figurative language), and to multiple meanings (often created through the writer's use of paradox and irony). The formalist critic tries to reconcile the tensions and oppositions inherent in the text in order to develop a unified reading.

The formalist movement in English language criticism began in England with I. A. Richards's *Practical Criticism* (1929). To explain and introduce his theory, Richards asked students to interpret famous poems without telling them the poet's names. This strategy encouraged close reading of the text rather than reliance on a poet's reputation, biographical data, or historical context. The American formalist movement, called *new criticism,* was made popular largely by college instructors who realized that formalist criticism provided a useful way for students to work along with an instructor in interpreting a literary work rather than passively listening to a lecture on biographical, literary, and historical influences. In fact, the new critical theorists Cleanth Brooks and Robert Penn Warren put together a series of textbooks (*Understanding Poetry, Understanding Fiction,* and *Understanding Drama,* first published in the late 1930s) used in colleges for years. After the 1950s, many new critics began to reevaluate their theories and to broaden their approaches. Although few scholars currently maintain a strictly formalist approach, nearly every critical movement of this century, including feminist, Marxist, psychoanalytic, structuralist, and deconstructionist criticism, owes a debt to the close reading techniques introduced by the formalists.

A FORMALIST READING: KATE CHOPIN'S "THE STORM" (P. 146)

A formalist critic reading Chopin's "The Storm," might begin by noting the story's three distinctive sections. What relationship do the sections bear to one another? What do we learn from the word choice, the figures of speech, and the symbols in these sections? And, most important, how do these considerations lead readers to a unified view of the story?

In the first section of "The Storm," readers meet Bobinôt and his son Bibi. The description of the approaching clouds as "sombre," "sinister," and "sullen" suggests an atmosphere of foreboding, yet the alliteration of these words also introduces a poetic tone. The conversation between father and son in the final part of this section contrasts, yet does not conflict with, the rather formal language of the introduction. Both Bobinôt and Bibi speak in Cajun dialect, suggesting their humble origins, yet their words have a rhythm that echoes the poetic notes struck in the description of the storm. As the section closes, Bobinôt, thinking of his wife, Calixta, at home, buys a can of the shrimp he knows she likes and holds the treasure "stolidly," ironically suggesting the protection he cannot offer his wife in his separation from her during the coming storm.

The long second section brings readers to the story's central action. Calixta, as she watches the rain, sees her former lover, Alcée, riding up to seek shelter. Just as in the first section, the language of the narrator is somewhat formal and always poetic, filled with sensuous diction and images. For instance, we see Calixta "unfasten[ing] her white sacque at the throat" and, later, Alcée envisions her lips "as red and moist as pomegranate seed." Again, paralleling the first section, the conversation of the characters is carried on in dialect, suggesting their lack of sophistication and their connection to the powerful natural forces that surround them. The lovemaking that follows, then, seems both natural and poetic. There is nothing sordid about this interlude and, as the final sections of the story suggest through their rather ordinary, matter-of-fact language, nothing has been harmed by Calixta and Alcée's yielding to passion.

In Section 3, Bobinôt brings home the shrimp, symbol of his love for Calixta, and, although we recognize the tension between Bobinôt's shy, gentle approach and Alcée's passion, readers can accept the final sentence as literal rather than ironic. The "storms" (both the rain and the storm of passion) have passed, and no one has been hurt. The threat suggested in the opening sentences has been diffused; both the power and the danger evoked by the poetic diction of the first two sections have disappeared, to be replaced entirely by the rhythms of daily life and speech.

For Further Reading: Formalism

Brooks, Cleanth. *The Well Wrought Urn*. 1947.
Empson, William. *Seven Types of Ambiguity*. 1930.
Hartman, Geoffrey H. *Beyond Formalism*. 1970.
Stallman, Robert W. *Critiques and Essays in Criticism. 1920–1948*. 1949.
Wellek, René. *A History of Modern Criticism*. Vol. 6. 1986.
Wimsatt, W. K. *The Verbal Icon*. 1954.

Reader-Response Criticism

Reader-response criticism suggests a critical view that opposes formalism, seeing the reader's interaction with the text as central to interpretation. Unlike formalists, reader-response critics do not believe that a work of literature exists as a separate, closed entity. Instead, they consider the reader's contribution to the text as essential. A poem, short story, novel, or play is not a solid piece of fabric, but rather a series of threads separated by gaps that readers must fill in, drawing on their own experiences and knowledge.

As we read realistic fiction (where the world of the text closely resembles what we call reality), we may not notice that we are contributing our interpretation. As we read one sentence and then the next, we develop expectations; and, in realistic stories, these expectations are generally met. Nevertheless, nearly every reader supplies personal meanings and observations, making each reader's experience with a work unique and distinctive from every other reader's experience with the same work. For example, imagine Shakespeare's *Romeo and Juliet* as it might be read by a fourteen-year-old high school student and by her father. The young woman, whose age is the same as Juliet's, is almost certain to identify closely with the female protagonist and to "read" Lord Capulet, Juliet's father, as overbearing and rigid. The young reader's father, however, may be drawn to the poignant passage where Capulet talks with a prospective suitor, urging that he wait while Juliet has time to enjoy her youth. Capulet describes the loss of his other children and calls Juliet "the hopeful lady of my earth." Although the young woman reading this line may interpret it as yet another indication of Capulet's possessiveness, her father may see it as a sign of love and even generosity. The twentieth-century father may "read" Capulet as a man willing to risk offending a friend in order to keep his daughter safe from the rigors of early marriage (and early childbearing). Whose interpretation is correct? Reader-response theorists would say that both readings are entirely possible and, therefore, equally "right."

The differing interpretations produced by different readers can be seen as simply the effect of the different personalities (and personal histories) involved in constructing meaning from the same series of clues. Not only does the reader "create" the work of literature, in large part, but the literature itself may work on the reader as he or she reads, altering the reader's experience, and thus the reader's interpretation. For example, the father reading *Romeo and Juliet* may alter his sympathetic view of Capulet as he continues through the play and observes the old Lord's later, angry exchanges with Juliet.

Reader-response theorists believe in the importance of *recursive reading*—that is, reading and rereading with the idea that no interpretation is carved in stone. A second or third interaction with the text may well produce a new interpretation. This changing view is particularly likely when the rereading takes place significantly later than the initial reading. For example, if the young woman just described reread *Romeo and Juliet* when she was middle-aged and herself the mother of teenage children, her reaction to Capulet would quite likely be different from her reaction when she read the work at age fourteen.

In one particular application of reader-response theory, called *reception theory*, the idea of developing readings is applied to the general reading public rather than to individual readers. Reception theory, as proposed by Hans Robert Jauss ("Literary History as a Challenge to Literary Theory" in *New Literary History*," Vol. 2. 1970–71), suggests that each new generation reads the same works of literature differently. Because each generation of readers has experienced different historical events, read different books, and been aware of different critical theories, each generation will view the same works very differently from its predecessors. Certainly a quick look back at the summary of literary history in Appendix B will support this idea. (Consider, for example, the changing views toward Shakespeare from the seventeenth to the twentieth centuries.)

Reader-response criticism has received serious attention since the 1960s, with Norman Holland's *The Dynamics of Literary Response* (1968) formulating the theory. The German critic Wolfgang Iser (*The Implied Reader*, 1974) argued that in order to be an effective reader, one must be familiar with the conventions and "codes" of writing. This, then, is one reason for studying literature in a classroom, not to produce only approved interpretations, but to develop strategies and information that will make sense of a text. Stanley Fish, an American critic, goes even further, arguing that there may not be any "objective" text at all (*Is There a Text in This Class?*, 1980). Fish says that no two readers read the same book, though readers can be trained to have relatively similar responses to a text if they have had relatively similar experiences. For instance, if readers have gone to college and taken an introduction to literature course, where they have learned to respond to the various elements of literature such as character, theme, irony, and figurative language, they are likely to have similar responses to a text.

READER-RESPONSE READINGS: KATE CHOPIN'S "THE STORM" (P. 146)

To demonstrate possible reader-response readings, we can look at the same story previously considered from a formalist perspective. (Of course, if several formalist critics read the story, they too would each write a somewhat different interpretation.)

Written by a 25-year-old man; has studied American literature

In Kate Chopin's "The Storm," attention must be paid to the two adult male characters, Bobinôt and Alcée. Usually in a love triangle situation one man is portrayed more sympathetically than the other. But Chopin provides us with a dilemma. Alcée is not merely the cavalier seducer; he genuinely cares for Calixta. Neither is he the brooding hero. There is nothing gruff or angry about Alcée, and he returns to his family home with no apparent harm done following the passionate interlude. On the other hand, Bobinôt is not a cruel or abusive husband. We can see no clear reason for Calixta's affair except for her desire to fulfill a sexual longing for Alcée.

Written by an 18-year-old man; first-year literature course

Bibi doesn't seem to be a very important character in the story, but we should pay attention to him as a reflection of his father. At the beginning of the story, Bibi worries about his mother and he expresses his concern to his father. Bobinôt tries to reassure his son, but he gets up and buys a treat for Calixta as much to comfort himself as to get something for her. Then Bibi sits with his father, and it seems as if he has transferred all his worries to Bobinôt. In the third section of the story, after Calixta and Alcée have had their love affair, Bibi and Bobinôt come home. They both seem like children, worried about how Calixta will react. She, of course, is nice to them because she feels so guilty. At the end of Section 3, both father and son are happy and enjoying themselves. You can't help but feel great sympathy for them both because they are so loving and simple and because they have been betrayed by Calixta, who has not behaved the way a loving mother and wife should.

Written by a 45-year-old woman; has studied Kate Chopin's life and work

A decade after the controversial novel *The Awakening* was published in 1899, one critic protested, "To think of Kate Chopin, who once contented herself with mild yarns about genteel Creole life . . . blowing us a hot blast like that!" (qtd. in Gilbert and Gubar 981). This literary observer was shocked, as one might expect from an early-twentieth-century reader, by Chopin's frank picture of sexual relations, and particularly of the sexual feelings of the novel's heroine. One cannot help but wonder, however, whether the scandalized reader was really widely acquainted with Chopin.

Certainly he could not have read "The Storm." This short story is surprising for many reasons, but primarily because it defies the sexual mores of the late nineteenth century by showing a woman who is neither evil nor doomed enjoying, even glorying in, her sexuality. Calixta is presented as a good wife and loving mother, concerned about her husband and son who are away from home during the storm. Yet her connection to Bobinôt and Bibi does not keep her from passionately enjoying her interlude with Alcée. She goes to his arms unhesitatingly, with no false modesty or guilt (feigned or real) to hold her back. Somehow, this scenario does not seem to fit the definition of "a mild yarn about genteel Creole life."

For Further Reading: Reader-Response Criticism

Bleich, David. *Subjective Criticism*. 1978.
Fish, Stanley. *Is There a Text in This Class?* 1980.
Holland, Norman. *The Dynamics of Literary Response*. 1968.
Iser, Wolfgang. *The Implied Reader*. 1974; *The Act of Reading: A Theory of Aesthetic Response*. 1978.
Rosenblatt, Louise. *The Reader, the Text, the Poem*. 1978.
Sulleiman, Susan, and Inge Crosman, eds. *The Reader in the Text*. 1980.
Tomkins, Jane P., ed. *Reader-Response Criticism*. 1980.

Sociological Criticism

Like reader-response criticism, **sociological criticism** takes issue with formalism. Sociological theorists maintain that the literary work cannot be separated from the social context in which it was created, insisting that literature reflects society and derives its essential existence and significance from the social situations to which it responds. Sociological critics speculate about why a particular work might have been written and explore the ways in which it reacts to a specific situation.

For instance, a sociological literary scholar might note with interest that Shakespeare's history plays about Richard II, Henry IV, and Henry V deal with the consequences of uncertain royal succession and usurpation.

These dramas were written during the final reigning years of Queen Elizabeth I, a monarch who had not produced an heir and refused to designate one. Although the plays cited were set considerably before Elizabeth's time, a sociological critic might conclude that they reflect the English concern about the threat of monarchic chaos should Elizabeth die with no clear line of succession.

In the twentieth century two strong arms of sociological criticism have emerged as dominant: feminist criticism and Marxist criticism. They are particularly forceful theories because most of their practitioners have a strong commitment to these ideologies, which they apply as they read literature. Feminism and Marxism share a concern with segments of society that have been underrepresented and often ignored. These views are, of course, supported by modern critical theories such as the reader-response idea of gaps in the text that must be filled in through the reader's own experience and knowledge. In addition, the techniques of New Criticism (in particular, close reading of the text), psychoanalysis, and structuralism have allowed sociological critics to focus on what had been overlooked or skewed in traditional readings and to analyze how the experience of marginal and minority groups has been represented in literature.

FEMINIST CRITICISM

Throughout the nineteenth century, women such as the Brontë sisters, George Eliot (Mary Ann Evans), Elizabeth Barrett Browning, and Christina Rossetti struggled for the right to be taken as seriously as their male counterparts. In addition, in 1929 Virginia Woolf, an experimental novelist and literary critic, published *A Room of One's Own,* which described the difficulties that women writers faced and defined a tradition of literature written by women.

Feminist criticism emerged as a defined approach to literature in the late 1960s. Modern feminist criticism began with works such as Mary Ellman's *Thinking About Women* (1968), which focuses on the negative female stereotypes in books authored by men and points out alternative feminine characteristics suggested by women authors. Another pioneering feminist work was Kate Millet's *Sexual Politics* (1969), which analyzes the societal mechanisms that perpetuate male domination of women. Since that time feminist writings, though not unified in one theory or methodology, have appeared in ever growing numbers. Some feminist critics have adapted psychoanalytic, Marxist, or other post-structuralist theories, and others have broken new ground. In general, feminist critics take the view that our culture—and by extension our literature—is primarily patriarchal (controlled by males).

According to feminist critics, what is at issue is not anatomical sex, but gender. As Simone de Beauvoir explained, a person is not born feminine, as our society defines it, but rather becomes so because of cultural conditioning. According to feminist critics, paternalist Western culture has defined the feminine as "other" to the male, as passive and emotional in opposition to the masculine as dominating and rational.

Feminist critics claim that paternalist cultural stereotypes pervade works of literature in the canon. Feminists point out that, until very recently, the canon has consisted of works almost exclusively written by males and has focused on male experiences. Female characters, when they do appear, are often subordinate to male characters. A female reader of these works must either identify with the male protagonist or accept a marginalized role.

One response of feminist critics is to reinterpret works in the traditional canon. As Judith Fetterley explains in *The Resisting Reader* (1978), the reader "revisions" the text, focusing on the covert sexual bias in a literary work. For example, a feminist scholar might study Shakespeare's *Macbeth*, looking closely at the role played by Lady Macbeth and arguing that she was not, in fact, simply a cold-hearted villain. Instead, a feminist might see her as a victim of the circumstances of her time: Women were not permitted to follow their own ambitions but were relegated to supporting roles, living their lives through achievements of their husbands and sons.

A second focus of feminist scholars has been the redefinition of the canon. By seeking out, analyzing, and evaluating little-known works by women, feminist scholars have rediscovered women writers who were ignored or shunned by the reading public and by critics of their own times. Thus, writers such as Kate Chopin (whose short story "The Storm" has been discussed above) and Charlotte Perkins Gilman (see "The Yellow Wall-Paper," p. 160), who wrote during the late nineteenth and early twentieth centuries, are now recognized as worthy of study and consideration.

A FEMINIST READING: TILLIE OLSEN'S "I STAND HERE IRONING" (P. 152)

To approach Tillie Olsen's "I Stand Here Ironing," feminist scholars might focus on the passages in which the narrator describes her relationships and encounters with men.

Some readings of Tillie Olsen's "I Stand Here Ironing" suggest that the narrator makes choices that doom her older daughter to a life of confusion. If we look at the narrator's relationships with the men in her life, however, we can see that she herself is the story's primary victim.

At nineteen the narrator is a mother, abandoned by her husband who leaves her a note saying that he "could no longer endure sharing want" with his wife and infant daughter. This is the first desertion we hear about in the narrator's life, and although she agonizingly describes her painful decisions and the mistakes she makes with her daughter Emily, we cannot help but recognize that she is the one who stays and tries to make things right. Her actions contrast sharply with those of her husband, who runs away, implying that his wife and daughter are burdens too great for him to bear.

The second abandonment is more subtle than the first but no less devastating. After the narrator has remarried, she is once again left alone to cope with a growing family while her second husband goes off to war. True, this desertion comes for a "noble" purpose and is probably not voluntary, but the narrator must, nevertheless, seek one of the low-paying jobs available to women to supplement her allotment checks. This time she is again forced to leave her children because her husband must serve the needs of the male-dominated military establishment.

The narrator is alone at crucial points in Emily's life and must turn away from her daughter simply in order to survive. Although she has been brought up in a world that teaches women to depend on men, she learns that she is ultimately alone. Although the desertions she endures are not always intentional, she must bear the brunt of circumstances that are not her choice but are, rather, foisted on her by the patriarchal society in which she lives.

For Further Reading: Feminist Criticism

Benstock, Shari, ed. *Feminist Issues in Literary Scholarship.* 1987.
Eagleton, Mary, ed. *Feminist Issues in Literary Theory: A Reader.* 1986.
Gilbert, Sandra, and Susan Gubar. *The Madwoman in the Attic.* 1979.
———. *No Man's Land.* 3 vols. 1988, 1989, 1994.
———, eds. *The Norton Anthology of Literature by Women.* 1985.
Heilbrun, Carolyn G. *Hamlet's Mother and Other Women.* 1990.
Jacobus, Mary. *Reading Woman: Essays in Feminist Criticism.* 1986.
Miller, Nancy, K., ed. *The Poetics of Gender.* 1986.
———. *Subject to Change.* 1988.
Showalter, Elaine. *A Literature of Their Own.* 1977.
———. *Sisters Choice: Tradition and Change in American Women's Writing.*
    1991.

MARXIST CRITICISM

Scholars influenced by Marxist criticism base their readings of literature on the social and economic theories of Karl Marx (*Das Kapital,* 1867–94) and his colleague and coauthor Friedrich Engels (*The Communist Manifesto,* 1884). Marx and Engels believed that the dominant capitalist middle class would eventually be challenged and overthrown by the working class. In the meantime, however, middle-class capitalists exploit the working class, who produce excess products and profits yet do not share in the benefits of their labor. Marx and Engels further regarded all parts of the society in which they lived—religious, legal, educational, governmental—as tainted by what they saw as the corrupt values of middle-class capitalists.

Marxist critics apply these views to their readings of poetry, fiction, and drama. They tend to analyze the literary works of any historical era as products of the ideology, or network of concepts, that supports the interests of the cultural elite and suppresses those of the working class. Some Marxist critics see all Western literature as distorted by the privileged views of the elite class, but most believe that at least some creative writers reject the distorted views of their society and instead see clearly the wrongs to which working-class people have been subjected. For example, George Lukacs, a Hungarian Marxist critic, proposed that great works of literature create their own worlds, which reflect life with clarity. These great works, though not written by Marxists, can be studied for their revealing examples of class conflict and other Marxist concerns. A Marxist critic would certainly look with favor on Charles Dickens, who in nearly every novel pointed out inequities in the political, legal, and educational establishments of his time. Those who remember Oliver Twist's pitiful plea for "more" workhouse porridge (refused by evil Mr. Bumble, who skims money from funds intended to feed the impoverished inmates) cannot help but see fertile ground for the Marxist critic, who would certainly applaud Dickens's scathing criticism of Victorian social and economic inequality.

Although Marxist criticism developed in the 1920s and 1930s in Germany and the Soviet Union, British and American Marxism has received greatest attention since 1960 with works such as Raymond Williams's *Culture and Society, 1780–1950* (1960) and Terry Eagleton's *Criticism and Ideology* (1976).

A MARXIST READING: TILLIE OLSEN'S "I STAND HERE IRONING" (P. 152)

The Marxist theorist reading Tillie Olsen's "I Stand Here Ironing" might concentrate on the events that demonstrate how both the narrator's and Emily's fates have been directly affected by the capitalist society of the United States.

Tillie Olsen's "I Stand Here Ironing" stands as a powerful indictment of the capitalist system. The narrator and her daughter Emily are repeatedly exploited and defeated by the pressures of the economic system in which they live.

The narrator's first child, Emily, is born into the world of the 1930s depression—an economic disaster brought on by the excesses and greed of Wall Street. When the young mother is deserted by her husband, there are no government programs in place to help her. She says it was the "pre-relief, pre-WPA world of the depression" that forced her away from her child and into "a job hashing at night." Although she is willing to work, she is paid so poorly that she must finally send Emily to live with her husband's family. Raising the money to bring Emily back takes a long time, and after this incident Emily's health, both physical and emotional, is precarious.

When Emily gets the measles, we get a hard look at what the few social programs that existed during the Depression were like. The child is sent—at the urging of a government social worker—to a convalescent home. The narrator notes bitterly, "They still send children to that place. I see pictures on the society page of sleek young women planning affairs to raise money for it, or dancing at the affairs, or decorating Easter eggs or filling Christmas stockings for the children." The privileged class basks in the artificial glow of their charity work for the poor, yet the newspapers never show pictures of the hospitalized children who are kept isolated from anyone they loved and forced to eat "runny eggs . . . or mush with lumps." Here again the mother is separated from her daughter by a system that discriminates against the poor. Because the family cannot afford private treatment, Emily is forced to undergo treatment in a public institution that not only denies her any contact with her family, but also cruelly forbids her to save the letters she receives from home. Normal family relationships are severely disrupted by an uncaring economic structure that only grudgingly offers aid to the poor.

It is clear that the division between mother and daughter is created and exacerbated by the social conditions in which they live. Because they are poor, they are separated at crucial times and, therefore, never get to know each other fully. Thus, neither can truly understand the ordeals the other has been forced to endure.

For Further Reading: Marxist Criticism

Agger, Ben. *The Discourse of Domination.* 1992.

Bullock, Chris, and David Peck, eds. *Guide to Marxist Literary Criticism.* 1980.

Eagleton, Terry. *Marxism and Literary Criticism.* 1976.

Frow, John. *Marxism and Literary History.* 1986.

Holub, Renate and Antonio Gramsci. *Beyond Marxism and Postmodernism.* 1992.

Jameson, Fredric. *Marxism and Form.* 1971.

Lentricchia, Frank. *Criticism and Social Change.* 1983.

Ohmann, Richard M. *Politics of Letters.* 1987.

Strelka, Joseph P., ed., *Literary Criticism and Sociology.* 1973.

Williams, Raymond. *Culture and Society, 1780–1950.* 1960; *Marxism and Literature.* 1977.

New Historicism

New historicist critics focus on a text in relation to the historical and cultural contexts of the period in which it was created and the periods in which it was critically evaluated. These contexts are not considered simply as "background" but as integral parts of a text. According to new historicists, history is not an objective fact; rather, like literature, history is interpreted and reinterpreted depending on the power structure of a society.

Louis Althusser, for example, suggests that ideology intrudes in the discourse of an era, subjecting readers to the interests of the ruling establishment. Michel Foucault reflects that the discourse of an era defines the nature of "truth" and what behaviors are acceptable, sane, or criminal. "Truth," for Foucault, is produced by the interaction of power and the systems in which the power flows, and it changes as society changes. Mikhail Bakhtin suggests that all discourse is dialogic, containing within it many independent and sometimes conflicting voices.

Literature, in new historical criticism, does not exist outside time and place and cannot be interpreted without reference to the era in which it was written. Criticism likewise cannot be evaluated without reference to the time and place in which it was written. A fallacy of much criticism, according to new historicists, is to consider a literary text as an organic whole, ignoring the diversity of conflicting voices in a text or in the cultural context in which a text is embedded. Indeed, Stephen Greenblatt prefers the term "cultural poetics" to new historicism because it acknowledges the integral role literature and art play in the culture of any era of history. Works of art and literature, according to Greenblatt, actively foster subversive elements or voices but somehow "contain" those forces in ways that defuse challenges to the dominant culture.

New historicists also point out that readers, like texts, are influenced and shaped by the cultural context of their eras. A thoroughly objective "reading" of a text is, then, impossible. All readers to some degree "appropriate" a text. Acknowledging this problem, some new historicists present their criticism of texts as "negotiations" between past and present contexts. Thus, criticism of a particular work of literature would involve both the cultural contexts of the era in which the text was written and the critic's present cultural context; and the critic would acknowledge how the latter context influences the interpretation of the former.

Beginning in the early 1970s, feminist critics adopted some new historicist positions, focusing on male-female power conflicts. And critics interested in multicultural texts stressed the role of the dominant white culture in suppressing or marginalizing the texts of nonwhites. Marxist critics, including Raymond Williams, have adopted the term "cultural materialism" in discussing their mode of new historicism, which focuses on the political significance of a literary text.

A NEW HISTORICIST READING: CHARLOTTE PERKINS GILMAN'S "THE YELLOW WALL-PAPER" (P. 160)

A new historicist scholar might write an essay about "The Yellow Wall-Paper" as an illustration of the destructive effects of the patriarchical culture of the late nineteenth century upon women. This reading would be vastly different from that of most nineteenth-century critics, who interpreted the story as a harrowing case study of female mental illness. Even some earlier twentieth-century readings have considered the narrator's mental illness caused by her individual psychological problems. New historicist critics, however, might focus on the social conventions of the time, which produced conflicting discourses that drove the narrator to madness.

The female narrator of "The Yellow Wall-Paper," who is writing in her private journal (which is the text of the short story), explains that her husband, a physician, has diagnosed her as having a "temporary nervous depression—a slight hysterical tendency." She says she should believe such a "physician of high standing" and cooperate with his treatment, which is to confine her to a room in an isolated country estate and compel her to rest and have no visitors and not to write. The "cure" is intended to reduce her nervousness, she further explains. But as the story unfolds, the narrator reveals that she suspects the treatment will not cure her because it leaves her alone with her thoughts without even her writing to occupy her mind. Her husband's "cure" forces her into a passive role and eliminates any possibility of asserting her own personality. However, she guiltily suggests that her own lack of confidence in her husband's diagnosis may be what is preventing her cure.

The text of "The Yellow Wall-Paper" can, then, be divided into at least two conflicting discourses: 1) the husband, who has the authority both of a highly respected physician and of a husband, two positions reinforced by the patriarchical culture of the time; and 2) the narrator, whose own hesitant personal female voice contradicts the masculine voice or discourse but undermines itself because it keeps reminding her that women should obey their husbands and their physicians.

A third discourse underlies the two dominant ones—that of the gothic horror tale, a popular genre of the late nineteenth century. The narrator in "The Yellow Wall-Paper" is isolated against her will in a room with barred windows in an almost deserted palatial country mansion she describes as "the most beautiful place"; she is at the mercy of her captor, in this case her husband; she is not sure whether she is hallucinating and thinks the mansion may be haunted; she does not know whom to trust, not being sure whether her husband really wants to "cure" her or to punish her for expressing her rebellion.

The narrator learns to hide her awareness of the conflicting discourses. She avoids mentioning her thoughts and fears about her illness or her fancies about the house being haunted, and she hides her writing. She speaks reasonably and in "a very quiet voice." But this inability to speak freely to anyone is a kind of torture, and alone in her room with the barred windows, she takes up discourse with the wallpaper. At first she describes it as "one of those sprawling flamboyant patterns committing every artistic sin." But she is fascinated by the pattern, which has been distorted by mildew and by portions that have been torn away. The narrator begins to strip off the wallpaper to free a woman she thinks is trapped inside; and, eventually, she visualizes herself as that woman, trapped, yet freed by the destruction of the wallpaper. The narrator retreats, or escapes into madness, driven there by the multiple discourses she cannot resolve.

For Further Reading: New Historicist Criticism

Brook, Thomas. *The New Historicism and Other Old Fashioned Topics.* 1991.

Coates, Christopher. "What Was the new Historicism?" *Centennial Review* 32.2 (Spring 1993): 267–80.

Geertz, Clifford. "Thick Description: Toward an Interpretive Theory of Culture," in *The Interpretation of Cultures*. 1973.

Greenblatt, Stephen, ed. *Representing the English Renaissance*. 1988.

Levin, David. "American Historicism: Old and New." *American Literary History* 6.3 (Fall 1994): 527–38.

Rabinov, Paul, ed. *The Foucault Reader*. 1986.

Veeser, H. Aram, ed. *The New Historicism*. 1989.

Psychoanalytic Criticism

Psychoanalytic criticism focuses on a work of literature as an expression in fictional form of the inner workings of the human mind. The premises and procedures used in psychoanalytic criticism were developed by Sigmund Freud (1846–1939), though some critics disagree strongly with his conclusions and their therapeutic and literary applications. Feminists, for example, take issue with Freud's notion that women are inherently masochistic. Some of the major points of Freud's theories depend on the idea that much of what is most significant to us does not take place in our conscious life. Freud believed that we have been forced (mostly by the rigors of having to live in harmony with other people) to repress much of our experience and many of our desires in order to coexist peacefully with others.

Some of this repressed experience Freud saw as available to us through dreams and other unconscious structures. He believed that literature could often be interpreted as the reflection of our unconscious life. Freud himself was among the first psychoanalytic critics, often using the techniques developed for interpreting dreams to interpret literature. Among other analyses, he wrote an insightful study of Dostoevsky's *The Brothers Karamazov* as well as brief commentaries on several of Shakespeare's plays, including *A Midsummer Night's Dream, Macbeth, King Lear,* and *Hamlet.* The latter study may have inspired a classic of psychoanalytic criticism: Ernest Jones's *Hamlet and Oedipus* (1949), in which Jones explains Hamlet's strange reluctance to act against his Uncle Claudius as resulting from Hamlet's unresolved longings for his mother and subsequent drive to eliminate his father. Since Hamlet's own father is dead, Jones argues, Claudius becomes, in the young man's subconscious mind, a father substitute. Hamlet, then, cannot make up his mind to kill his uncle because he does not see a simple case of revenge (for Claudius's murder of his father) but rather a complex web that includes incestuous desire for his own mother (now wed to Claudius). Jones extends his analysis to include the suggestion that Shakespeare himself experienced such a conflict and reflected his own Oedipal feelings in *Hamlet.*

A French psychoanalyst, Jacques Lacan (1901–1981), combined Freudian theories with structuralist literary theories to argue that the essential alienating experience of the human psyche is the acquisition of language. Lacan believed that once you can name yourself and distinguish yourself from others, you have entered the difficult social world that requires you to repress your instincts. Like Lacan, who modified and adapted psychoanalytic criticism to connect it to structuralism, many twentieth-century literary scholars, including Marxists and feminists, have found useful approaches in psychoanalytic literary theory (see, for example, Mary Jacobus's *Reading Woman: Essays in Feminist Criticism,* 1986).

PSYCHOANALYTIC TERMS

To fully appreciate psychoanalytic criticism, you should understand the following terms:

- ◆ *id*—The part of the mind that determines sexual drives and other unconscious compulsions that urge individuals to unthinking gratification.

- ◆ *ego*—The conscious mind that strives to deal with the demands of the id and to balance its needs with messages from the superego.

- ◆ *superego*—The part of the unconscious that seeks to repress the demands of the id and to prevent gratification of basic physical appetites. The superego, then, is a sort of censor that represents the prohibitions of society, religion, family beliefs, and so on.

- ◆ *condensation*—A process that takes place in dreams (and in literature) when several elements from the repressed unconscious are linked together to form a new, yet disguised, whole.

- ◆ *symbolism*—Use of representative objects to stand for forbidden (often sexual) objects. This process takes place in dreams and in literature. For instance, a pole, knife, or gun may stand for the penis.

- ◆ *displacement*—Substitution of a socially acceptable desire for a desire that is not acceptable. Again, this process may take place in dreams or in literature. For example, a woman who experiences sexual desires for her son may instead dream of being intimate with a neighbor who has the same first name as (or who looks like) her son.

- ◆ *Oedipus complex*—Repressed desire of a son to unite sexually with his mother and kill his father. According to Freud, all young boys go through this stage, but most resolve these conflicts before puberty.

- ◆ *projection*—Defense mechanism in which people mistakenly see in others antisocial impulses they fail to recognize in themselves.

A PSYCHOANALYTIC READING: EDGAR ALLAN POE'S "THE CASK OF AMONTILLADO" (P. 209)

Since Edgar Allan Poe died in 1849, six years before Freud was born, Poe could not possibly have known Freud's work. Nevertheless, psychoanalytic critics argue that the principles discovered by Freud and those who followed are inherent in human nature. Therefore, they believe it is perfectly plausible to use modern psychiatric terms when analyzing a work that was written before their invention.

Montresor, the protagonist of Poe's "The Cask of Amontillado," has long fascinated readers who have puzzled over his motives for the story's climactic action when he imprisons his rival, Fortunato, and leaves him to die. Montresor claims that Fortunato has insulted him and has dealt him a "thousand injuries." Yet when we meet Fortunato, although he appears something of a pompous fool, none of his actions—or even his comments—seems powerful enough to motivate Montresor's thirst for revenge.

If, however, we consider a defense mechanism, first named "projection" and described by Sigmund Freud, we gain a clearer picture of Montresor. Those who employ projection are often people who experience antisocial impulses yet are not conscious of these impulses. It seems highly likely that Fortunato has not persecuted Montresor; rather, Montresor himself has experienced the impulse to act in a hostile manner toward Fortunato. We know, for instance, that Fortunato belongs to the exclusive order of masons because he gives Montresor the secret masonic sign. Montresor's failure to recognize the sign shows that he is only a mason in the grimmest literal sense. Montresor clearly resents Fortunato's high standing and projects onto Fortunato all of his own hostility toward those who (he thinks) have more or know more than he does. Thus he imagines that Fortunato's main business in life is to persecute and insult him.

Montresor's obsessive behavior further indicates his pathology. He plans Fortunato's punishment with the cunning one might ordinarily reserve for a major battle, cleverly figuring out a way to keep his servants from the house and to lure the ironically named Fortunato to his death. Each step of the revenge is carefully plotted. This is no sudden crime of passion, but rather the diabolically planned act of a deeply disturbed mind.

If we understand Montresor's need to take all of the hatred and anger that is inside himself and to rid himself of those socially unacceptable emotions by projecting them on to someone else, then we can see how he rationalizes a crime that seems otherwise nearly unmotivated. By killing Fortunato, Montresor symbolically kills the evil in himself. It is interesting to note that the final lines of the story support this reading. Montresor observes that "for half of a century no mortal has disturbed" the bones. In other words, these unacceptable emotions have not again been aroused. His last words, a Latin phrase from the mass for the dead meaning "rest in peace," suggest that only through his heinous crime has he found release from the torment of his own hatred.

For Further Reading: Psychoanalytic Criticism

Freud, Sigmund. *The Interpretation of Dreams.* 1900.

Gardner, Shirley N., ed. *The (M)other Tongue: Essays in Feminist Psychoanalytic Interpretation.* 1985.

Hartman, Geoffrey H., ed. *Psychoanalysis and the Question of the Text.* 1979.

Kris, Ernst. *Psychoanalytic Explorations in Art.* 1952.

Kristeva, Julia. *Desire in Language.* 1980.

Nelson, Benjamin, ed. *Sigmund Freud on Creativity and the Unconscious.* 1958.

Wright, Elizabeth. *Psychoanalytic Criticism: Theory in Practice.* 1984.

Structuralism

Structuralism is a literary movement with roots in linguistics and anthropology that concentrates on literature as a system of signs that have no inherent meaning except in their agreed-upon or conventional relation to one another. Structuralism is usually described by its proponents not as a new way to interpret literary works, but rather as a way to understand how works of literature come to have meaning for us. Because structuralism developed from linguistic theory, some structuralists use linguistic approaches to literature. That is, they talk about literary texts using terms employed by linguists (such as *morpheme* and *phoneme*) as they study the nature of language. Many structuralists, however, use the linguistic model as an analogy. To understand the analogy, then, you need to know a bit of linguistic theory.

The French linguist Ferdinand de Saussure (*Course in General Linguistics,* 1915) suggested that the relationship between an object and the name we use to designate it is purely arbitrary. What, for example, makes "C-A-T" signify a small, furry animal with pointed ears and whiskers? It is only our learned expectation that makes us associate "cat" with the family feline pet. Had we grown up in France, we would make the same association with *chat,* or in Mexico with *gato.* Therefore, the words we use to designate objects (linguists call these words *signs*) make sense only within the large context of our entire language system and would not be understood as meaningful by someone who did not know that language system. Further, Saussure pointed out, signs become truly useful only when we use them to designate difference. For instance, "cat" becomes useful when we want to differentiate a small furry animal that meows from a small furry animal that barks. Saussure was interested in how language, as a structure of conventions, worked. He asked intriguing questions about the underlying rules that allowed this made-up structure of signs to work, and, as a result, his pioneering study caught the interest of scholars in many fields.

Many literary scholars saw linguistic structuralism as analogous to the study of literary works. Literary structuralism leads readers to think of poems, short stories, novels, and plays not as self-contained and individual entities that have some kind of inherent meaning, but rather as part of a larger literary system. In order to fully appreciate and analyze the work, then, the reader must understand the system within which it operates.

Like linguistic structuralism, literary structuralism focuses on the importance of difference. We must, for example, understand the difference between the structure of poetry and the structure of prose before we can make sense of a sentence like this:

> *so much depends*
> *upon*
> *a red wheel*
> *barrow*

> (from William Carlos Williams, "Red Wheelbarrow," p. 747)

Readers unacquainted with the conventions of poetry would find these lines meaningless and confusing, although if they knew the conventions of prose they would readily understand this sentence:

> *So much depends upon a red wheelbarrow.*

The way we interpret any group of "signs," then, depends on how they are structured and on the way we understand the system that governs their structure.

Structuralists believe that literature is basically artificial because although it uses the same "signs" as our everyday language, whose purpose is to give information, the purpose of literature is *not* primarily to relay data. For example, a poem like Dylan Thomas's "Do Not Go Gentle into That Good Night" (p. 642) is written in the linguistic form of a series of commands, yet the poem goes much further than that. Its meaning is created not only by our understanding the lines as a series of commands, but also by our recognition of the poetic form, the rhyming conventions, and the figures of speech Thomas uses. We can only fully discuss the poem within the larger context of our literary knowledge.

A STRUCTURALIST READING: WILLIAM FAULKNER'S "BARN BURNING" (P. 216)

A structuralist reading tries to bring to light some of the assumptions about language and form that we are likely to take for granted. Looking at the opening paragraph of Faulkner's "Barn Burning," a structuralist critic might first look at an interpretation that reads the passage as a stream of Sarty's thoughts. The structuralist critic might then consider the assumptions a reader would have to make to see what Faulkner has written as the thoughts of an illiterate child. Next, the structuralist might look at evidence to suggest the language in this section operates outside the system of language that would be available to Sarty and that, therefore, "Barn Burning" opens not with a simple recounting of the main character's thoughts but rather with something far more complex.

The opening paragraph of William Faulkner's "Barn Burning" is often read as an excursion into the mind of Sarty, the story's young protagonist. When we read the passage closely, however, we note that a supposedly simple consciousness is represented in a highly complex way. For Sarty—uneducated and illiterate—the "scarlet devils" and "silver curve of fish" on the labels of food tins serve as direct signs appealing to his hunger. It is unlikely, however, that Sarty could consciously understand what he sees and express it as metaphor. We cannot, then, read this opening passage as a recounting of the thoughts that pass through Sarty's mind. Instead, these complex sentences and images offer possibilities that reach beyond the limits of Sarty's linguistic system.

Because our own knowledge is wider than Sarty's, the visual images the narrator describes take on meanings for us that are unavailable to the young boy. For example, like Sarty, we know that the "scarlet devils" stand for preserved ham. Yet the devils also carry another possible connotation. They may indicate evil and thus serve to emphasize the despair and grief Sarty feels are ever-present. So, then, we are given images that flash through the mind of an illiterate young boy, apparently intended to suggest his poverty and ignorance (he cannot read the words on the labels), yet we are led to see a highly complicated set of meanings. When we encounter later in the passage Sarty's articulated thought, "our enemy . . . ourn! mine and hisn both! . . . ," his down-to-earth dialect shows clearly the sharp distinction between the system of language the narrator uses to describe Sarty's view of the store shelves and the system of language Sarty uses to describe what he sees and feels.

For Further Reading: Structuralism

Barthes, Roland. *Critical Essays*. 1964.

Culler, Jonathan. *Structuralist Poetics*. 1975.

Greimas, A. J. *Structured Semantics: An Attempt at a Method*. Trans. McDowell, Schleifer, and Velie. 1983.

Hawkes, Terence. *Structuralism and Semiotics*. 1977.

Lentricchia, Frank. *After the New Criticism*. 1980.

Pettit, Philip. *The Concept of Structuralism: A Critical Analysis*. 1975.

Scholes, Robert. *Structuralism in Literature: An Introduction*. 1974.

Deconstruction

Deconstruction is a literary movement developed from structuralism. It argues that every text contains within it some ingredient undermining its purported system of meaning. In other words, the structure that seems to hold the text together is unstable because it depends on the conclusions of a particular ideology (for instance, the idea that women are inferior to men or that peasants are content with their lowly position in life), conclusions that are not really as natural or inevitable as the text may pretend. The practice of finding the point at which the text falls apart because of these internal inconsistencies is called deconstruction.

Deconstructive theorists share with formalists and structuralists a concern for the work itself rather than for biographical, historical, or ideological influences. Like formalists, deconstructionists focus on possibilities for multiple meanings within texts. However, while formalists seek to explain paradox by discovering tensions and ironies that can lead to a unified reading, deconstructionists insist on the primacy of multiple possibilities. Any given text is capable of yielding many divergent readings, all of which are equally valid and yet all of which may in some way undermine and oppose one another.

Like structuralists, deconstructionists see literary texts as part of larger systems of discourse. A key structuralist technique is identifying opposites in an attempt to show the structure of language used in a work. Having identified the opposites, the structuralist rests the case. Deconstructionists, however, go further. Jacques Derrida, a French philosopher, noticed that these oppositions do not simply reflect linguistic structures but are the linguistic response to the way people deal with their beliefs (their ideologies). For instance, if you believe strongly that democracy is the best possible form of government, you tend to lump other forms of government into the category of nondemocracies. If a government is nondemocratic, that—not its other distinguishing characteristics—would be significant to you. This typical ideological response operates in all kinds of areas of belief, even ones we are not aware of. Deconstructionists contend that texts tend to give away their ideological basis by means of this opposition.

Derrida called this distinction between "A" and "Not-A" (rather than "A" and "B") *différance*, a word he coined to suggest a concept represented by the French verb *différer*, which has two meanings: "to be different" and "to defer." (Note that in Derrida's new term an "a" is substituted for an "e"—a distinction that can be seen in writing, but not heard in speaking.) When a deconstructionist uncovers *différance* through careful examination of a text, he or she also finds an (often unwitting) ideological bias. Deconstructionists argue that the reader must transcend such ideological biases and must instead acknowledge contradictory possibilities as equally worthy of consideration. No one meaning can or should be designated as correct.

Deconstruction, then, is not really a system of criticism (and, in fact, deconstructionists resist being labeled as a school of criticism). Rather, deconstruction offers a way to take apart a literary text and thereby reveal its separate layers. Deconstructionists often focus on the metaphorical nature of language, claiming that all language is basically metaphoric because the sign we use to designate any given object or action stands apart from the object itself. In fact, deconstructionists believe that all writing is essentially literary and metaphorical because language, by its very nature, can only *stand for* what we call reality or truth; it cannot *be* reality or truth.

A major contribution of deconstructive critics lies in their playful approach to language and to literary criticism. They refuse to accept as absolute any one way of reading poetry, fiction, or drama, and they guard against what they see as the fixed conclusions and arbitrary operating assumptions of many schools of criticism.

A DECONSTRUCTIONIST READING: FLANNERY O'CONNOR'S "A GOOD MAN IS HARD TO FIND (P. 261)

A deconstructionist reading of Flannery O'Connor's "A Good Man Is Hard to Find" might challenge the essentially religious interpretations the author offered of her own stories in essays and letters. A deconstructionist critic might argue that the author's reading of the story is no more valid than anyone else's, and that the story can just as legitimately be read as an investigation of the functions of irony in language.

Flannery O'Connor has explained that the grotesque and violent aspects of her stories are intended to shock the reader into recognizing the inhospitable nature of the world and thereby the universal human need for divine grace. The last sentence of "A Good Man Is Hard to Find" is spoken by The Misfit, who has just murdered a family of travelers: "It's no real pleasure in life."

However, the language of O'Connor's stories is extremely ironic. That is, her narrators and characters often say one thing but mean another. So it is possible that their statements are not empirically true but are representations of a persona or elements of a story they have created using language.

The Grandmother, for example, lives almost entirely in fictions—newspaper clippings, stories for the grandchildren, her belief that The Misfit is a good man. On the other hand, The Misfit is more literal than the Grandmother in his perception of reality. He knows, for example, whether the car has turned over once or twice. But he too is posing, at first as the tough guy who rejects religious and societal norms by saying, "It's nothing for you to do but enjoy the few minutes you got left the best way you can—by killing somebody or burning down his house or doing some other meanness to him. No pleasure but meanness." Finally, he poses as the pessimist—or, according to O'Connor's reading, the Christian—who claims, "It's no real pleasure in life." The contradictions in The Misfit's language make it impossible to tell which of these façades is "real."

For Further Reading: Deconstruction

Abrams, M. H. "Rationality and the Imagination in Cultural History." *Critical Inquiry* 2 (1976): 447–64. (Abrams claims deconstructionists are parasites who depend on other critics to come up with interpretations that can be deconstructed.)

Arac, Jonathan, Wlad Godzich, and Wallace Martin, eds. *The Yale Critics: Deconstruction in America.* 1983.

Berman, Art. *From the New Criticism to Deconstruction.* 1988.

Culler, Jonathan. *On Deconstruction: Theory and Criticism After Structuralism.* 1982.

Jefferson, Ann. "Structuralism and Post-Structuralism." *Modern Literary Theory: A Comparative Introduction.* 1982.

Johnson, Barbara. *The Critical Difference: Essays in the Contemporary Rhetoric of Reading.* 1980.

Leitsch, Vincent B. *Deconstructive Theory and Practice.* 1982.

Lynn, Steven. "A Passage into Critical Theory." *College English* 52 (1990): 258–271.

Miller, J. Hillis. "The Critic as Host." *In Deconstruction and Criticism.* Ed. Harold Bloom, et al. 1979. (response to Abrams article above)

Norris, Christopher. *Deconstruction: Theory and Practice.* 1982.

Glossary of
Literary Terms

Action What happens in a drama.

Alexandrine Iambic hexameter, a common form in French poetry but relatively rare in English poetry.

Allegorical figure or framework See **Allegory.**

Allegory Story with two parallel and consistent levels of meaning, one literal and one figurative, in which the figurative level offers a moral or political lesson; John Bunyan's *The Pilgrim's Progress* and Nathaniel Hawthorne's "Young Goodman Brown" are examples of moral allegory. An **allegorical figure** has only one meaning (for instance, it may represent good or evil), as opposed to a **symbol,** which may suggest a complex network of meanings. An **allegorical framework** is the system of ideas that conveys the allegory's message.

Alliteration Repetition of initial sounds in a series of words, as in Blake's "The Chimney Sweeper": "So your chimneys I sweep, and in soot I sleep." Alliteration may be reinforced by repeated sounds within and at the ends of words.

Allusion Reference, often to literature, history, mythology, or the Bible, that is unacknowledged in the text but that the author expects a reader to recognize. An example of

allusion in a title is Charles Baxter's "Gryphon" (a mythical beast). Some modern writers, notably T.S. Eliot and James Joyce, use allusions drawn from their private reading, expecting few readers to understand them.

Ambiguity Device in which authors intentionally evoke a number of possible meanings of a word or grammatical structure by leaving unclear which meaning they intend.

Anapest See **Meter.**

Antagonist Character who is in conflict with or opposition to the protagonist; the villain. Sometimes the antagonist may be a force or situation (war or poverty) rather than a person.

Antihero Modern character who possesses the opposite attributes of a hero. Rather than being dignified and powerful, the antihero tends to be passive and ineffectual. Willy Loman, the main character in *Death of a Salesman,* is an antihero.

Apostrophe Figure of speech in which an absent character or a personified force or object is addressed directly, as if it were present or could comprehend: "O Rose, thou art sick!"

Archetype   Image or symbol that is so common or significant to a culture that it seems to have a universal importance. The psychologist Carl Jung believed that because archetypes are an inherent part of psyches, we recognize them subconsciously when we encounter them and therefore give them a greater meaning than they would otherwise possess. Many archetypes appear in classical myths (for example, a journey to the underworld).

Arena stage   Stage on which the actors are surrounded by the audience; also called *theater in the round*.

Aside   Brief comment spoken by the actor to the audience (such as, "Here she comes. I'll play a fine trick on her now!") and assumed not to be heard by the other characters. Chekhov's *The Brute* includes asides.

Assonance   Repetition of vowel sounds in a series of words: "creep three feet."

Atmosphere   Tone or mood of a literary work, often established by the setting and language. Atmosphere is the emotional aura that determines readers' expectations about a work— for example, the sense of doom established at the beginning of Shakespeare's *Macbeth*.

Aubade   Poem about morning, usually celebrating the dawn—for example, Philip Larkin's "Aubade."

Ballad   Narrative poem, rooted in an oral tradition, usually arranged in quatrains rhyming *abcb* and containing a refrain.

Ballad stanza   See **Stanza.**

Beast fable   Short tale, usually including a moral, in which animals assume human characteristics—for example, Aesop's "The Tortoise and the Hare."

Beginning rhyme   See **Rhyme.**

Black comedy   Comedy that relies on the morbid and absurd. Often black comedies are so satiric that they become ironic and tragic; examples are Joseph Heller's novel *Catch 22* and Edward Albee's play *The Sandbox*.

Blank verse   Lines of unrhymed iambic pentameter in no particular stanzaic form. Because iambic pentameter resembles the rhythms of ordinary English speech, blank verse is often unobtrusive; for instance, Shakespeare's noble characters usually use it, though they may seem to us at first reading to be speaking in prose. See **Meter.**

Blocking   Decisions about how characters move and where they stand on stage in a dramatic production.

Box set   A stage setting that gives the audience the illusion of looking into a room.

Cacophony   Harsh or unpleasant spoken sound created by clashing consonants: "squawking chipmunks."

Caesura   Strong or long pause in the middle of a poetic line, created by punctuation or by the sense of the poem, as in Yeats's "Leda and the Swan": "And Agamemnon dead. Being so caught up. . . ."

Carpe diem   "Seize the day"; the philosophy that gave its name to a kind of seventeenth-century poetry arguing that one should enjoy life today before it passes one by, as seen in Herrick's "To the Virgins, to Make Much of Time."

Catastrophe   Traditionally, the moment in a tragedy after the climax, when the rising action has ended and the falling action has begun, when the protagonist begins to understand the implications of events that will lead to his or her downfall, and when such events begin to occur.

Catharsis Aristotle's term for the emotional reaction or "purgation" that takes place in an audience watching a tragedy. Aristotle theorized that when we see a good tragedy, we feel both pity (and thus closeness to the protagonist) and fear (or revulsion from the actions taking place on stage) because we recognize in ourselves the potential for similar action. The purging of these emotions we experience by seeing the dramatic action unfold before us is **catharsis.**

Character Fictional representation of a person, usually but not necessarily in a psychologically realistic way. E. M. Forster classified characters as **round** (well developed, closely involved in the action and responsive to it) or **flat** (static, stereotypical, or operating as **foils** for the protagonist). Characters can also be classified as **dynamic** (growing and changing in the course of the action) or **static** (remaining unchanged). Also, a brief satirical sketch illustrating a type of personality, popular in eighteenth-century England.

Characterization Way in which writers develop their characters and reveal those characters' traits to readers.

Choragos See **Chorus.**

Chorus Group of actors in classical Greek drama who comment in unison on the action and the hero; they are led by the **Choragos.**

Classicism Attitude toward art that values symmetry, clarity, discipline, and objectivity. Neoclassicism, such as that practiced in eighteenth-century Europe, appreciated those qualities as found in Greek and Roman art and culture; Alexander

Pope's poetry follows neoclassical principles.

Cliché Overused phrase or expression.

Climax Point of greatest tension or importance, where the decisive action of a play or story takes place.

Closed form Type of poetic structure that has a recognizable rhyme scheme, meter, or stanzaic pattern; also called *fixed form.*

Closet drama Play meant to be read instead of performed—for example, Shelley's *Prometheus Unbound.*

Comedy Any literary work, but especially a play, in which events end happily, a character's fortunes are reversed for the better, and a community is drawn more closely together, often by the marriage of one or more protagonists at the end.

Comedy of humours Comedy that focuses on characters whose behavior is controlled by a characteristic trait, or humour, such as *Volpone* (1606) by Ben Jonson, who popularized the form.

Comedy of manners Satiric comedy that developed during the sixteenth century and achieved great popularity in the nineteenth century. This form focuses on the manners and customs of society and directs its satire against the characters who violate its social conventions and norms. *The Importance of Being Earnest* by Oscar Wilde is a comedy of manners.

Common measure See **Stanza.**

Conceit Extended or complicated metaphor, common in the Renaissance, that is impressive largely because it shows off an author's power to manipulate and sustain a striking comparison between two dissimilar items; John Donne's use of the compass metaphor in "A Valediction: Forbidding Mourning" is an example.

Concrete poem   Poem whose typographical appearance on the page reenforces its theme, as with George Herbert's "Easter Wings."

Conflict   Struggle between opposing forces (protagonist and antagonist) in a work of literature.

Connotation   Meaning that a word suggests beyond its literal, explicit meaning, carrying emotional associations, judgments, or opinions. Connotations can be positive, neutral, or negative. For example, *family* has a positive connotation when it describes a group of loving relatives; a neutral connotation when it describes a biological category; and a negative connotation when it describes an organization of criminals.

Convention   See **Literary convention.**

Conventional symbol   See **Symbol.**

Cosmic irony   See **Irony.**

Couplet   See **Stanza.**

Crisis   Peak or moment of tension in the action of a story; the point of greatest tension is the **climax.**

Dactyl   See **Meter.**

Denotation   Dictionary meaning of a word; its explicit, literal meaning.

Denouement   See **Resolution.**

Deus ex machina   "The god from the machine": any improbable resolution of plot involving the intervention of some force or agent hitherto extraneous to the story.

Dialect   Particular regional variety of language, which may differ from the more widely used standard or written language in its pronunciation,

grammar, or vocabulary. Eliza Doolittle's cockney dialect in the George Bernard Shaw play *Pygmalion* is an example.

Dialogue   Conversation between two or more characters.

Diction   Word choice of an author, which determines the level of language used in a piece of literature. **Formal diction** is lofty and elaborate (typical of Shakespearean nobility); **informal diction** is idiomatic and relaxed (like the dialogue in John Updike's "A&P"). **Jargon** is the specialized diction of a professional or occupational group (such as computer hackers). **Idioms** are the colloquial expressions, including slang, of a particular group or society.

Didactic poetry   Poetry whose purpose is to make a point or teach a lesson, particularly common in the eighteenth century.

Double entendre   Phrase or word with a deliberate double meaning, one of which is usually sexual.

Double plot   See **Plot.**

Drama   Literature written to be performed.

Dramatic irony   See **Irony.**

Dramatic monologue   Type of poem perfected by Robert Browning that consists of a single speaker talking to one or more listeners and often revealing much more about the speaker than he or she seems to intend; Browning's "My Last Duchess" is the best known example of this form.

Dramatis personae   Characters in a play.

Dynamic character   See **Character.**

Elegy   Poem commemorating someone's death, usually in a reflective or mournful tone, such as A. E. Housman's "To an Athlete Dying Young."

Elision   Leaving out an unstressed syllable or vowel, usually in order to keep a regular meter in a line of poetry ("o'er" instead of "over," for example).

End rhyme   See **Rhyme.**

End-stopped line   Line of poetry that has a full pause at the end, typically indicated by a period or semicolon.

Enjambment   See **Run-on line.**

Envoi   Three-line conclusion to a sestina that includes all six of the poem's key words, three placed at the ends of lines and three within the lines. See **Sestina.**

Epic   Long narrative poem, such as the *Iliad* or the *Aeneid*, recounting the adventures of heroes on whose actions depend the fate of a nation or race. Frequently the gods or other supernatural beings take active interest in the events presented in the epic.

Epigram   Short witty poem or phrase that makes a pointed statement—for example, Dorothy Parker's comment on an actress's performance, "She runs the gamut of emotions from A to B."

Epiphany   Term first applied to literature by James Joyce and now used generally to describe a sudden moment of revelation about the deep meaning inherent in common things, such as the boy's realization at the end of "Araby."

Euphemism   Word consciously chosen for its pleasant **Connotations;** often used for subjects like sex and death whose frank discussion is somewhat taboo in our society. For example, a euphemism for "to die" is "to pass away" or "to go to one's reward."

Euphony   Pleasant spoken sound created by smooth consonants such as "ripple" or "pleasure."

Exposition   First stage of a plot, where the author presents the information a reader or viewer will need to understand the characters and subsequent action.

Expressionism   Artistic and literary movement that attempts to portray inner experience. It moves away from realistic portrayals of life and is characterized by violent exaggeration of objective reality and extremes of mood and feeling. In drama, expressionistic stage sets mirror the inner states of the character.

Extended metaphor   See **Metaphor.**

Extended simile   See **Metaphor.** Also see **Conceit.**

Eye rhyme   See **Rhyme.**

Fable   Short didactic story, often involving animals or supernatural beings and stressing plot above character development, whose object is to teach a pragmatic or moral lesson. See **Beast fable.**

Fairy tale   See **Folktale.**

Falling action   Stage in a play's plot during which the intensity of the climax subsides.

Falling meter   Trochiac and dactylic meters, so called because they move from stressed to unstressed syllables. See **Rising meter.**

Fantasy   Nonrealistic piece of literature that depends on whimsical plot, supernatural or mythical characters, and implausible actions, usually with a happy ending.

Farce Comedy in which stereotypical characters engage in boisterous horseplay and slapstick humor, as in Chekhov's *The Brute*.

Feminine rhyme See **Rhyme.**

Fiction Form of narrative that is primarily imaginative, though its form may resemble that of factual writing like history and biography.

Figures of speech Expressions that describe one thing in terms of something else. The primary figures of speech are **hyperbole, metaphor, metonymy, personification, simile, synechdoche,** and **understatement.**

Flashback Variation on chronological order that presents an event or situation that occurred before the time in which the story's action takes place.

Flat character See **Character.**

Foil Minor character whose role is to highlight the main character by presenting a contrast with him or her. In a modern comedic team, the "straight man" can be seen as a foil for the other performer.

Folktale Contemporary version of an old, even ancient, oral tale that can be traced back centuries through many different cultures. Folktales include fairy tales, myths, and fables.

Foot See **Meter.**

Foreshadowing Presentation early in a story of situations, characters, or objects that seem to have no special importance but in fact are later revealed to have great significance. For example, a casual mention of a character's unusually accurate

memory for faces may become significant only when his or her fate turns out to hinge on recognizing a person from the distant past.

Form Structure or shape of a literary work; the way a work's parts fit together to form a whole. In poetry, form is described in terms of the presence (or absence) in a particular work of elements like rhyme, meter, and stanzaic pattern. See **Open form** and **Closed form.**

Formal diction See **Diction.**

Free verse See **Open form.**

Freytag's pyramid The five parts of classic dramatic plots: exposition, complication (the introduction of elements that will lead to conflict and ultimately crisis), climax, catastrophe, and resolution. In his *Technique of the Drama* (1863) Gustav Freytag suggested that this pattern resembles a pyramid, with rising action leading to the climax and giving way to falling action.

Genre Category of literature. Fiction, drama, and poetry are the three major genres; subgenres include the novel, the farce, and the lyric poem.

Haiku Seventeen-syllable, three-line form of Japanese verse that almost always uses concrete imagery and deals with the natural world.

Hamartia Aristotle's term for the "tragic flaw" in characters that eventually causes their downfall in Greek tragedy.

Hermeneutics Traditionally, the use of the Bible to interpret other historical or current events; in current critical theory, the principles and procedures followed to determine the meaning of a text.

Heroic couplet See **Stanza.**

High comedy Term introduced in 1877 by George Meredith to denote comedy that appeals to the intellect, such as Shakespeare's *As You Like It*. See **Low comedy.**

Hubris Tragic flaw of overwhelming pride that exists in the protagonist of a tragedy.

Hyperbole Figurative language that depends on intentional overstatement; Mark Twain often used it to create humor; Jonathan Swift used it for **satire.**

Iamb See **Meter.**

Imagery Words and phrases that describe the concrete experience of the five senses, most often sight. A **pattern of imagery** is a group of related images developed throughout a work. **Synesthesia** is a form of imagery that mixes the experience of the senses (hearing something visual, smelling something audible, and so on): "He smelled the blue fumes of her scent." **Static imagery** freezes the moment to give it the timeless quality of painting or sculpture. **Kinetic imagery** attempts to show motion or change.

Imagism Movement in modern poetry much influenced by **haiku,** stressing terseness and concrete imagery. Imagists were a group of American poets in the early twentieth century, such as Ezra Pound, William Carlos Williams, and Amy Lowell, who completely dispensed with traditional principles of English versification, creating new rhythms and meters.

Imperfect rhyme See **Rhyme.**

In medias res Latin phrase describing works like Homer's *Iliad* that begin in the middle of the action in order to catch a reader's interest.

Informal diction See **Diction.**

Internal rhyme See **Rhyme.**

Irony Literary device or situation that depends on the existence of at least two separate and contrasting levels of meaning or experience. **Dramatic** or **tragic irony,** such as that found in *Oedipus the King,* depends on the audience's knowing something the protagonist has not yet realized (and thus experiencing simultaneously its own interpretation of the events and that of the protagonist). **Situational irony** exists when what happens is at odds with what the story's situation leads readers to expect will happen, as in Browning's "Porphyria's Lover." **Cosmic irony** (or irony of fate) exists when fate frustrates any effort a character might make to control or reverse his or her destiny. **Verbal irony** occurs when what is said is in contrast with what is meant. It can be expressed as **understatement, hyperbole,** or **sarcasm.**

Jargon Specialized language associated with a particular trade or profession.

Kinetic imagery Imagery that attempts to show motion or change. See, for example, William Carlos Williams's "The Great Figure."

Literary canon Group of literary works generally acknowledged by critics and teachers to be the best and most significant to have emerged from our history. Until recently, the canon tended to be conservative (it was difficult to add to or remove works from it), and it reflected ideological positions that were not universally accepted. Many contemporary teachers and critics have attempted to expand the canon to include works by women and by writers of color.

Literary convention Something whose meaning is so widely understood within a society that authors can expect their audiences to accept and comprehend it unquestioningly—for example, the division of plays into acts or the fact that stepmothers in fairy tales are likely to be wicked.

Literary criticism   Descriptions, analyses, interpretations, or evaluations of works of literature by experts in the field.

Literary symbol   See **Symbol.**

Low comedy   Introduced by George Meredith, it refers to comedy with little or no intellectual appeal. Low comedy is used as comic relief in *Macbeth*. See **High comedy.**

Lyric   Form of poetry, usually brief and intense, that expresses a poet's subjective response to the world. In classical times, lyrics were set to music. The Romantic poets, particularly Keats, often wrote lyrics about love, death, and nature.

Masculine rhyme   See **Rhyme.**

Meditation   Lyric poem that focuses on a physical object—for example, Keats's "Ode on a Grecian Urn"—using this object as a vehicle for considering larger issues.

Melodrama   Sensational play that appeals shamelessly to the emotions, contains elements of tragedy but ends happily, and often relies on set plots and stock characters.

Metaphor   Concise form of comparison equating two things that may at first seem completely dissimilar, often an abstraction and a concrete image—for example, "My love's a fortress." Some people consider metaphor to be the essential element of poetry. An *extended metaphor*, or **conceit,** is a comparison used throughout a work; in Tillie

Olsen's "I Stand Here Ironing," the mother compares her daughter to a dress waiting to be ironed, thus conveying her daughter's passivity and vulnerability. See **Simile.**

Meter   Regular pattern of stressed and unstressed syllables, each repeated unit of which is called a **foot:** an **anapest** has three syllables, two unstressed and the third stressed; a **dactyl** has three syllables, the first stressed and the subsequent ones unstressed. An **iamb** has two syllables, unstressed followed by stressed; a **trochee** has a stressed syllable followed by an unstressed one; a **spondee** has two stressed syllables; and a **pyrrhic** has two unstressed syllables. A poem's meter is described in terms of the kind of foot (anapest, for example) and the number of feet found in each line. The number of feet is designated by the Greek prefix for the number, so one foot per line is called *monometer,* two feet is *dimeter,* followed by *trimeter,* tetrameter, pentameter, hexameter, and so on. The most common meter in English is *iambic pentameter.* See also **Rising meter** and **Falling meter.**

Metonymy   Figure of speech in which the term for one thing can be applied to another with which it is closely associated—for example, using "defend the flag" to mean "defend the nation."

Mimesis   Aristotle's term for the purpose of literature, which he felt was "imitation" of life; literature represents the essence of life and we are affected by it because we recognize (perhaps in another form) elements of our own experiences.

Monologue   Extended speech by one character.

Mood   Atmosphere created by the elements of a literary work (setting, characterization, imagery, tone, and so on).

Morality play Medieval Christian allegory.

Motivation Reasons behind a character's behavior that make us accept or believe that character.

Mystery play Medieval play depicting biblical scenes.

Myth Anonymous story reflecting the religious and social values of a culture or explaining natural phenomena, often involving gods and heroes.

Narrative The "storytelling" of a piece of fiction; the forward-moving recounting of episode and description. When an event that occurred earlier is told during a later sequence of events, it is called a **flashback;** suggesting earlier in a narration something that will occur later on is called **foreshadowing.**

Narrator Person who tells the story. See **Point of view.**

Naturalism Nineteenth-century movement whose followers believed that life should not be idealized when depicted in literature. Rather, literature should show that human experience is a continual (and for the most part losing) struggle against the natural world. Émile Zola, Jack London, and Stephen Crane are important practitioners of naturalism.

New Comedy Greek comedies of the fourth and third centuries B.C. that followed the Old Comedies. They were comedies of romance with stock characters and conventional settings. They lacked the satire, abusive language, and bawdiness of Old Comedies. New Comedy originated in the works of the Greek dramatist Meander and was further developed by the Roman dramatists Plautus and Terence. See **Old Comedy.**

Novel Fictional narrative, traditionally realistic, relating a series of events or following the history of a character or group of characters through a period of time.

Novella Extended short story, usually concentrated in episode and action (like a short story) but involving greater character development (like a novel); Franz Kafka's "The Metamorphosis" is a novella.

Octave See **Sonnet.**

Ode Relatively long lyric poem, common in antiquity and adapted by the Romantic poets, for whom it was a serious poem of formal diction, often addressed to some significant object (such as a nightingale or the west wind) that has stimulated the poet's imagination.

Old Comedy The first comedies, written in Greece in the fifth century B.C., which heavily satirized the religious and social issues of the day. The chief practitioner of Old Comedy was Aristophanes. See **New Comedy.**

Onomatopoeia Word whose sound resembles what it describes: "snap, crackle, pop." Lewis Carroll's "Jabberwocky" uses onomatopoeia.

Open form Sometimes called *free verse* or *vers libre*, open form poetry makes use of varying line lengths, abandoning stanzaic divisions, breaking lines in unexpected places, and even dispensing with any pretense of formal structure. See **Form.**

Ottava rima See **Stanza.**

Oxymoron Phrase combining two seemingly incompatible elements: "crashing silence."

Parable Story that uses analogy to make a moral point, such as the parable of the prodigal son in the New Testament.

Paradox Seemingly contradictory situation. Adrienne Rich's "A Woman Mourned by Daughters" uses paradox.

Parody "Take-off" or exaggerated imitation of a serious piece of literature for humorous effect. Shakespeare's "My Mistress' Eyes are Nothing Like the Sun" is a parody of traditional Renaissance love poetry.

Pastoral Literary work, such as Christopher Marlowe's lyric poem "The Passionate Shepherd to His Love," that deals nostalgically and usually unrealistically with a simple, preindustrial rural life; the name comes from the fact that traditionally pastorals feature shepherds.

Pastoral romance Prose tale set in an idealized rural world; popular in Renaissance England.

Pathos Suffering that exists simply to satisfy the sentimental or morbid sensibilities of the audience.

Pattern of imagery See **Imagery.**

Perfect rhyme See **Rhyme.**

Persona Narrator or speaker of a poem or story; in Greek tragedy, a persona was a mask worn by an actor.

Personification Endowing inanimate objects or abstract ideas with life or human characteristics: "the river wept."

Petrarchan sonnet See **Sonnet.**

Picaresque Episodic, often satirical work about a rogue or rascal—for example, Cervantes's *Don Quixote.* The form emerged in sixteenth-century Spain.

Picture-frame stage Stage that looks like a room with a missing fourth wall through which the audience views the play. The **proscenium arch** separates the audience from the play.

Plot Way in which the events of the story are arranged. When there are two stories of more or less equal importance, the work has a **double plot;** when there is more than one story but one string of events is clearly the most significant, the other stories are called **subplots.** Plot in fiction often follows the pattern of action in drama, rising to a **climax** and then falling to a resolution.

Poetic rhythm See **Rhythm.**

Point of view Perspective from which a story is told. The storyteller may be a character in the story (*first-person narrator*) or someone who does not figure in the action (*third-person narrator*), in which case he or she may know the actions and internal doings of everyone in the story (*omniscient narrator*) or some part of these (*limited omniscient narrator*). Rarely, there may be a *second-person narrator* who uses "you" and the imperative mood throughout the story.

The narrator may be an *observer* or a *participant.* If he or she is untrustworthy (stupid or bad, for instance), one has an *unreliable narrator;* narrators who are unreliable because they do not understand what they are reporting (children, for instance) are called *naive narrators.* If the perspective on the events is the same as one would get by simply watching the action unfold on stage, the point of view is *dramatic* or *objective.*

Popular fiction Works aimed at a mass audience.

Prologue First part of a play (originally of a Greek tragedy) in which the actor gives the background or explanations that the audience needs to follow the rest of the drama.

Props (short for properties) Pictures, furnishings, and so on that decorate the stage for a play.

Proscenium arch   Arch that surrounds the opening in a **picture-frame stage;** through this arch the audience views the performances.

Prose poem   Open form poem whose long lines appear to be prose set in paragraphs—for example, Walt Whitman's "Cavalry Crossing a Ford."

Protagonist   Principal character of a drama or fiction; the hero. The *tragic hero* is the noble protagonist in classical Greek drama who falls because of a tragic flaw.

Pyrrhic   See **Meter.**

Quatrain   See **Stanza.**

Realism   Writing that stresses careful description of setting and the trappings of daily life, psychological probability, and the lives of ordinary people. Its practitioners believe they are presenting life "as it really is"; Ibsen's *A Doll House* is an example.

Resolution   Also called the **denouement,** this is the final stage in the plot of a drama or work of fiction. Here the action comes to an end and remaining loose ends are tied up.

Rhetoric   Organization, strategy, and development of literary works, guided by an eye to how such elements will further the writer's intended effect on the reader.

Rhyme   Repetition of concluding sounds in different words, often intentionally used at the ends of poetic lines. In **masculine rhyme** (also called **rising rhyme**) single syllables correspond. In **feminine rhyme** (also called **double rhyme** or **falling rhyme**) two syllables correspond, the second of which is stressed. In **triple rhyme,** three syllables correspond. **Eye rhyme**

occurs when words look as though they should rhyme but are pronounced differently ("cough/tough"). In **perfect rhyme** the corresponding vowel and consonant sounds of accented syllables must be preceded by different consonants—for example, the *b* and *h* in "born" and "horn." **Imperfect rhyme,** also called *near rhyme, off rhyme,* or *slant rhyme,* occurs when consonants in two words are the same but intervening vowels are different—for example, "pick/pack," "lads/lids." The most common type of rhyme within a poem is **end rhyme,** where the rhyming syllables are placed at the end of a rhyme. **Internal rhyme** consists of rhyming words found within a line of poetry. **Beginning rhyme** occurs in the first syllable or syllables of the line.

Rhyme royal   See **Stanza.**

Rhythm   Regular recurrence of sounds in a poem. Ordinarily rhythm is determined by the arrangement of metrical feet in a line, but sometimes an alternate form of "sprung" rhythm, introduced by Gerard Manley Hopkins, is used. In this type of rhythm the number of strong stresses in a line determines the rhythm, regardless of how many weak stresses there might be.

Rising action   Stage in a play's plot during which the action builds in intensity. See **Freytag's pyramid.**

Romance   Type of narrative that deals with love and adventure in a nonrealistic way, most popular in the Middle Ages but sometimes used by more modern authors, such as Hawthorne, to separate themselves from the drabness of ordinary life.

Romantic comedy   Comedy such as Shakespeare's *Much Ado about Nothing* in which love is the main subject and idealized lovers endure great difficulties until the inevitable happy ending is reached.

Romanticism   Eighteenth- and nineteenth-century literary movement that valued subjectivity, individuality, the imagination, nature, excess, the exotic, and the mysterious.

Round character   See **Character.**

Run-on line   Line of poetry that ends with no punctuation or natural pause and consequently runs over into the next line; also called *enjambment.*

Sarcasm   Form of irony in which apparent praise is used to convey strong, bitter criticism.

Satire   Literary attack on folly or vanity by means of ridicule; usually intended to improve society.

Scansion   Process of determining the meter of a poem by analyzing the strong and weak stresses in a line to find the unit of **meter** (each recurring pattern of stresses) and the number of these units (or **feet**) in each line.

Scrim   Curtain that when illuminated from the front appears solid but when lit from the back becomes transparent.

Sentimental comedy   Reaction against the **comedy of manners.** This type of comedy relies on sentimental emotion rather than on wit or humor to move an audience and dwells on the virtues of life.

Sestet   See **Sonnet.**

Sestina   Poem composed of six six-line stanzas and a three-line conclusion called an **envoi.** Each line ends with one of six key words. The alternation of these six words in different positions—but always at the ends of lines—in the poem's six stanzas creates a rhythmic verbal pattern that unifies the poem.

Setting   Background against which the action of a piece of literature takes place: the historical time, locale, season, time of day, interior decoration, and so on. See **Context.**

Shakespearean sonnet   See **Sonnet.**

Short story   Fictional narrative centered on one climatic event and usually developing only a single character in depth; its scope is narrower than that of the **novel,** and it often uses setting and characterization more directly to make its theme clear.

Simile   Comparison of two seemingly unlike things using the words *like* or *as:* "My love is like an arrow through my heart." See **Metaphor.**

Situational irony   See **Irony.**

Soliloquy   Convention of drama in which a character speaks directly to the audience, revealing thoughts and feelings which other characters present on stage are assumed not to hear. By convention, a soliloquy is taken to reflect a character's sincere feelings and beliefs.

Sonnet   Fourteen-line poem, usually a **lyric** in *iambic pentameter* (see **Meter**). It has a strict rhyme scheme in one of two forms: the *Italian,* or **Petrarchan sonnet** (an octave rhymed *abba/abba* with a sestet rhymed *cdc/cdc* or a variation) and the *English,* or **Shakespearean sonnet** (three quatrains rhymed *abab/cdcd/efef* with a concluding couplet rhymed *gg*). The English sonnet developed partly because the Italian rhyme scheme was so difficult to achieve in English, where end rhymes are less frequent than they are in Italian. Modern poets often exploit the rigorous sonnet form by contrasting its restraints with violent content or imagery, as in Yeats's "Leda and the Swan."

Speaker   See **Persona.**

Spenserian stanza   See **Stanza.**

Spondee   See **Meter.**

Stage business   Actions or movements of an actor onstage—for example, lighting a cigarette, leaning on a mantel, straightening a picture.

Stage directions   Words in a play that describe an actor's role apart from the dialogue, dealing with movements, attitudes, and so on.

Stage setting (set)   In the production of a play, scenery and props. In *expressionist* stage settings, scenery and props are exaggerated and distorted to reflect the workings of a troubled, even abnormal mind. *Surrealistic* stage settings are designed to mirror the uncontrolled images of dreams or nightmares. See **Staging.**

Staging   Overall production of a play in performance: the sets, costumes, lighting, sound, music, and so on.

Stanza   Group of lines in a poem that forms a metrical or thematic unit. Each stanza is usually separated from others by a blank space on the page. Some common stanzaic forms are the **couplet** (two lines), **tercet** (three lines), **quatrain** (four lines), **sestet** (six lines), and **octave** (eight lines). The **heroic couplet,** first used by Chaucer and especially popular throughout the eighteenth century, as in Alexander Pope's poetry, consists of two rhymed lines of iambic pentameter, with a weak pause after the first line and a strong pause after the second. **Terza rima,** a form used

by Dante, has a rhyme scheme (*aba, bcb, ded*) that creates an interlocking series of stanzas. The **ballad stanza** alternates lines of eight and six syllables. Typically only the second and fourth lines rhyme. **Common measure** is a four-line stanzaic pattern closely related to the ballad stanza. It differs in that its rhyme scheme is *abab* rather than *abcb.* **Rhyme royal** is a seven-line stanza (*ababbcc*) set in iambic pentameter. **Ottava rima** is an eight-line stanza (*abababcc*) set in iambic pentameter. The **Spenserian stanza** is a nine-line form (*ababbcbcc*) with the first eight lines in iambic pentameter and the last line in iambic hexameter.

Static character   See **Character.**

Static imagery   Imagery that freezes a moment to give it the timeless quality of painting or sculpture. Much visual imagery is static.

Stock character   Stereotypical character who behaves consistently and whom the audience of a play can recognize and classify instantly: the town drunk, the nerd, and so on.

Stream of consciousness   Form of narration controlled not by external events but by the thoughts and subjective impressions of the narrator, commonly found in modern literature, such as the work of Virginia Woolf and James Joyce.

Stress   Accent or emphasis, either strong or weak, given to each syllable in a piece of writing, as determined by conventional pronunciation (cárpĕt, not cărpét) and intended emphasis ("going dówn, dówn, dówn tŏ thĕ bóttŏm ŏf thĕ óceăn"). Strong stresses are marked with a ´ and weak ones with a ˘; stress can be an important clue in helping to determine a poet's intended emphasis.

Structure Formal pattern or arrangement of elements to form a whole in a piece of literature.

Style Way an author selects and arranges words to express ideas and, ultimately, theme.

Subplot See **Plot.**

Surrealism Literary movement that allows unconventional use of syntax; chronology; juxtaposition; and bizarre, dreamlike images in prose and poetry.

Symbol Person, object, action, or idea whose meaning transcends its literal or denotative sense in a complex way. For instance, if someone wears a rose in a lapel to a dance, the rose may simply be a decoration, but in Blake's "The Sick Rose" it becomes a symbol because it takes on a range of paradoxical and complementary meanings. A symbol is invested with significance beyond what it could carry on its own: A swastika, for instance, is a powerful and frightening symbol as a result of Hitler's Nazism. **Universal symbols,** such as the grim reaper, may be called **archetypes; conventional symbols,** such as national flags, evoke a general and agreed-upon response from most people. There are also **private symbols,** such as the "gyre" created by Yeats, which the poet himself invested with extraordinary significance.

Synechdoche Figure of speech in which a part of something is used to represent the whole—for example, "hired hand" represents a laborer.

Synesthesia See **Imagery.**

Tale Short story often involving mysterious atmosphere and supernatural or inexplicable events,

such as "The Black Cat" by Edgar Allan Poe.

Tercet See **Stanza.**

Terza rima See **Stanza.**

Theater in the round See **Arena stage.**

Theater of the absurd Type of drama that discards conventions of plot, character, and motivation in order to depict a world in which nothing makes sense. Albee's *The Sandbox* is an example.

Theme Central or dominant idea of a piece of literature, made concrete by the details and emphasis in the work itself.

Thrust stage Stage that juts out into the audience so the action may be viewed from three sides.

Tone Attitude of the speaker or author of a work toward the subject itself or the audience, as can be determined from the word choice and arrangement of the piece.

Tragedy Literary work, especially a play, that recounts the downfall of an individual. Greek tragedy demanded a noble protagonist whose fall could be traced to a tragic personal flaw. Shakespearean tragedy also treats noble figures, but the reasons for their tragedies may be less clear-cut than in Greek drama. Domestic or modern tragedy tends to deal with the fates of ordinary people.

Tragic irony See **Irony.**

Tragicomedy Type of Elizabethan and Jacobean drama that uses elements of both tragedy and comedy.

Triple rhyme See **Rhyme.**

Trochee See **Meter.**

Understatement Intentional downplaying of a situation's

significance, often for ironic or humorous effect, as in Mark Twain's famous comment on reading his own obituary, "The reports of my death are greatly exaggerated."

Unities   Rules that require a dramatic work to be unified in terms of its time, place, and action. *Oedipus the King* illustrates the three unities.

Universal symbol   See **Symbol.**

Verbal irony   See **Irony.**

Villanelle   First introduced in France in the Middle Ages, a nineteen-line poem composed of five tercets and a concluding quatrain; its rhyme scheme is *aba aba aba aba aba abaa*. Two different lines are systematically repeated in the poem: line 1 appears again in lines 6, 12, and 18, and line 3 reappears as lines 9, 15, and 19. Thus each tercet concludes with an exact (or close) duplication of either line 1 or line 3, and the final quatrain concludes by repeating both line 1 and line 3.

Wagons   Sets mounted on wheels, which make possible rapid changes of scenery.

1964 by Geoffrey Bownas and Anthony Thwaite. Published by Penguin Books Limited. No portion of this text may be reproduced without permission of the publisher.

Charles Baxter, "Gryphon" from *Through the Safety Net* by Charles Baxter. Copyright © 1985 by Charles Baxter. All rights reserved. No portion of this text may be reproduced without written permission of Viking Penguin, a division of Penguin Books USA, Inc.

Suzanne E. Berger, "The Meal" from *Legacies* by Suzanne E. Berger. Originally published by Alice James Books, then again in *Tendrill*. Copyright © 1984 by and reprinted by permission of Suzanne E. Berger.

John Berryman, "Dream Song #14" from *The Dream Songs* by John Berryman. Copyright © 1959, 1962, 1964, 1966, 1969 by John Berryman. No portion of this text may be reproduced without the permission of Farrar, Straus & Giroux, Inc.

Elizabeth Bishop, "Sestina" from *The Complete Poems* by Elizabeth Bishop. Copyright © 1940, 1956, 1978 by Elizabeth Bishop. Copyright © 1979, 1983 by Alice Helen Meathfessel. No portion of this text may be reproduced without the permission of Farrar, Straus & Giroux, Inc.

Robert Bly, "Snowfall in the Afternoon" from *Silence in the Snowy Fields* by Robert Bly. Originally published by Wesleyan University Press, 1962. Copyright © 1962 by Robert Bly. Reprinted by permission of Robert Bly.

Louise Bogan, "The Dragonfly," copyright © 1941. No portion of this text may be reproduced without permission of Farrar, Straus, & Giroux, Inc. "Women" from *The Blue Estuaries* by Louise Bogan. Copyright © 1968 by Louise Bogan. No portion of this text may be reprinted without permission of Farrar, Straus, & Giroux, Inc.

Tadeusz Borowski, "Silence" from *This Way for the Gas, Ladies and Gentlemen, and Other Stories* by Tadeusz Borowski, selected and translated by Barbara Vedder. Copyright © 1959 by Maria Borowski. Translation copyright © 1967 by Penguin Books, Ltd. No portion of this text may be reprinted without permission of Viking Penguin, a division of Penguin Books USA, Inc.

Robert Boxill, "The Glass Menagerie" from *Tennessee Williams*. No portion of this text may be reprinted without permission of St. Martin's Press, Inc., New York, NY.

T. Coraghessan Boyle, "Greasy Lake" from *Greasy Lake and Other Stories* by T. Coraghessan Boyle. Copyright © 1982 by T. Coraghessan Boyle. No portion of this text may be reprinted without permission of Viking Penguin, a division of Penguin Books USA, Inc.

Richard Brautigan, "Widow's Lament" from *The Pill Versus the Springhill Mine Disaster* by Richard Brautigan. Copyright © 1968 by Richard Brautigan. Renewal copyright 1996 by Ianthe Brautigan Swensen. Reprinted by permission.

Gwendolyn Brooks, "A Song in the Front Yard," "We Real Cool," "What Shall I Give My Children?" "The Ballad of Chocolate Mabbie," "The Ballad of Rudolph Reed," "The Bean Eaters," "The Blackstone Rangers," "First Fight. Then Fiddle," "The Chicago Defender Sends a Man to Little Rock," "Medgar Evers," "People Who Have No Children Can Be Hard," and "Sadie and Maud" from *Blacks* by Gwendolyn Brooks. Copyright © 1991. Publisher, Third World Press. No portion of this text may be reprinted without permission of Gwendolyn Brooks. "Discussion of Your Poems: 'We Real Cool' and 'Ballad of Rudolph Reed'" by Gwendolyn Brooks, from *Report from Part One*, Broadside Press, 1972. No portion of this text may be reprinted without permission of the author. "The Boy Died in My Alley" from *Beckonings* by Gwendolyn Brooks. No portion of this text may be reprinted without permission of the author. "Interview with Gwendolyn Brooks" from *Tri-Quarterly*. Copyright © by and reprinted by permission of Gwendolyn Brooks. No portion of this text may be reprinted without permission of the author.

Audre Lorde, "Rooming Houses Are Old Women" from *Chosen Poems, Old and New* by Audre Lorde. Copyright © 1982, 1976, 1974, 1973, 1970, 1968 by Audre Lorde. No portion of this text may be reprinted without permission of W. W. Norton & Company, Inc.

Robert Lowell, "For the Union Dead" from *For the Union Dead* by Robert Lowell. Copyright © 1960, 1964 by Robert Lowell. No portion of this text may be reprinted without written permission of Farrar, Straus, & Giroux, Inc.

Archibald MacLeish, "Ars Poetica" from *Collected Poems 1917–1982* by Archibald MacLeish. Copyright © 1985 by The Estate of Archibald MacLeish. Reprinted by permission of Houghton Mifflin Company. All rights reserved.

Katherine Mansfield, "Miss Brill" from *The Short Stories of Katherine Mansfield* by Katherine Mansfield. Copyright © 1922 by Alfred A. Knopf, Inc. and renewed 1950 by John Middleton Murry. Reprinted by permission of the publisher.

Bob Marley, "Get Up, Stand Up." Copyright © Tuff Gong (New York, NY). No portion of this text may be reprinted without permission.

Gabriel García Márquez, "A Very Old Man with Enormous Wings: A Tale for Children" from *Leaf Storm and Other Stories* by Gabriel García Márquez, translated by Gregory Rabassa. Copyright © 1971 by Gabriel García Márquez. Reprinted by permission of HarperCollins Publishers, Inc.

Colleen J. McElroy, "My Father's Wars" from *Queen of the Ebony Isles* by Colleen McElroy. Copyright © 1984 by Colleen McElroy. No portion of this text may be reprinted without permission of the University Press of New England.

Claude McKay, "If We Must Die" and "The White City" from *Selected Poems of Claude McKay* by Claude McKay. Copyright © 1981 by Mrs. Hope McKay Virtue. Reprinted by permission of The Archives of Claude McKay, Carl Cowl, Administrator.

William Meredith, "In Memory of Donald A. Stauffer" and "Dreams of Suicide" from *Partial Accounts: New and Selected Poems* by William Meredith. Copyright © 1987 by William Meredith. No portion of this text may be reprinted without permission of Alfred A. Knopf, Inc.

Edna St. Vincent Millay, "Elegy before Death" and "What Lips My Lips Have Kissed" from *Collected Poems,* HarperCollins. Copyright © 1921, 1923, 1948, 1951 by Edna St. Vincent Millay and Norma Millay Ellis. Reprinted by permission of Elizabeth Barnett, Literary Executor.

Arthur Miller, *Death of a Salesman.* Copyright © 1949 , renewed © 1977 by Arthur Miller. No portion of this text may be reprinted without permission of Viking Penguin, a division of Penguin Books USA, Inc. From "Tragedy and the Common Man." No portion of this text may be reprinted without permission of Penguin Books USA, Inc.

Janice Mirikitani, "Suicide Note" and "Breaking Silence" from *Shredding Silence.* Copyright © 1987 by Janice Mirikitani. Reprinted by permission of Celestial Arts, Berkeley, CA.

N. Scott Momaday, "Comparatives." Copyright © 1976 by and reprinted by permission of N. Scott Momaday. "The Bear" from *In the Presence of the Sun* by N. Scott Momaday. Copyright © 1992 by N. Scott Momaday. Reprinted by permission of St. Martin's Press, Inc., New York, NY.

Lorrie Moore, "How to Talk to Your Mother (Notes)" from *Self-Help* by Lorrie Moore. Copyright © 1985 by M. L. Moore. Reprinted by permission of Alfred A. Knopf, Inc.

Marianne Moore, "Poetry" from *Collected Poems of Marianne Moore.* Copyright © 1935 by Marianne Moore, renewed 1963 by Marianne Moore and T. S. Eliot. No portion of this text may be reproduced without permission of Macmillan Publishing Company.

Maria K. Mootry, " 'Chocolate Mabbie' and 'Pearl May Lee': Gwendolyn Brooks and the Ballad Tradition" from *CLA Journal,* March 1987, Vol. 30:3, pp. 278–293. Reprinted by permission of College Language Association.

Alice Munro, "Boys and Girls" from *Dance of the Happy Shades* by Alice Munro.
Copyright © 1986 by Alice Munro. Originally published in *The Montrealer*.
No portion of this text may be reproduced without permission of Virginia
Barber Literary Agency, Inc. All rights reserved.

Ogden Nash, "The Lama" from *Verses from 1929 On* by Ogden Nash. Copyright © 1931
by Ogden Nash. Copyright © renewed 1985 by Frances Nash, Isabel Nash
Eberstadt, and Linel Nash Smith. By permission of Little, Brown and
Company.

Howard Nemerov, "Life Cycle of Common Man" from *Collected Poems of Howard
Nemerov,* 1977. Reprinted by permission of Mrs. Howard Nemerov.

Pablo Neruda, "The United Fruit Co." translated by Robert Bly. Copyright © 1950 and
reprinted by permission of Robert Bly.

Joyce Carol Oates, "When Characters from the Page Are Made Flesh on the Screen"
from *The New York Times,* March 23, 1986. Copyright © 1986 by The New
York Times Company. Reprinted by permission of Blanche C. Gregory, as
agent for the author. "Where Are You Going, Where Have You Been?" from
The Wheel of Love and Other Stories. Copyright © 1970 by Joyce Carol Oates.
Reprinted by permission of John Hawkins & Associates, Inc.

Tim O'Brien, "The Things They Carried" from *Esquire Magazine.* No portion of this text
may be reprinted without permission of International Creative Management,
Inc. Copyright © 1986 by Tim O'Brien.

Flannery O'Connor, "A Good Man Is Hard to Find" from *A Good Man Is Hard to Find and
Other Stories* by Flannery O'Connor. Copyright © 1953 by Flannery O'Connor
and renewed 1981 by Mrs. Regina O'Connor. Reprinted by permission of
Harcourt Brace Jovanovich, Inc.

Sharon Olds, "Rites of Passage" from *The Dead and the Living* by Sharon Olds. Copyright
© 1983 by Sharon Olds. Reprinted by permission of Alfred A. Knopf, Inc.

Tillie Olsen, "I Stand Here Ironing," copyright © 1956, 1957, 1960, 1961 by Tillie Olsen.
From *Tell Me a Riddle* by Tillie Olsen, introduction by John Leonard. Used by
permission of Delacorte Press/Seymour Lawrence, a division of Bantam
Doubleday Dell Publishing Group, Inc.

Simon J. Ortiz, "My Father's Song." Copyright © by Simon J. Ortiz. Reprinted by
permission of Simon J. Ortiz. "Speaking," originally published in *Woven
Stone,* University of Arizona Press, Tucson, AZ. Reprinted by permission of the
author, Simon J. Ortiz.

Wilfred Owen, "Anthem for Doomed Youth" and "Dulce et Decorum Est." No portion of
this text may be reprinted (except in the U. S.) without permission of Chatto
& Windus.

Linda Pastan, "Ethics" from *Waiting for My Life, Poems* by Linda Pastan. Copyright ©
1981 by Linda Pastan. No portion of this text may be reprinted without
written permission of W. W. Norton & Company, Inc.

Ann Petry, "Like a Winding Sheet" from *Miss Muriel and Other Stories,* copyright © 1971
by Ann Petry. Published by Houghton Mifflin. Reprinted by permission of
Russell & Volkening as agents for the author.

Marge Piercy, "A Work of Artifice" from *Circles on the Water* by Marge Piercy.
Copyright © 1982 by Marge Piercy. Reprinted by permission of Alfred A.
Knopf, Inc. "The Secretary Chant" from *Circles on the Water* by Marge
Piercy. Copyright © 1982 by Marge Piercy. Reprinted by permission of
Alfred A. Knopf, Inc.

Sylvia Plath, "Daddy" from *Ariel* by Sylvia Plath. Copyright © 1963 by Ted Hughes.
Copyright renewed. Reprinted by permission of HarperCollins Publishers, Inc.
Reprinted by permission of HarperCollins Publishers, Inc. For Canadian
rights, contact Faber & Faber Limited (London). "Metaphors" from *Crossing
the Water* by Sylvia Plath. Copyright © 1960 by Ted Hughes. Copyright
renewed. Reprinted by permission of HarperCollins Publishers, Inc. For

Canadian rights, contact Faber & Faber Limited. "Mirror" from *Crossing the Water* by Sylvia Plath. Copyright © 1963 by Ted Hughes. Originally appeared in the *New Yorker*. Reprinted by permission of HarperCollins Publishers, Inc. For Canadian rights, contact Faber & Faber Limited (London). "Morning Song" from *Ariel* by Sylvia Plath. Copyright © 1961 by Ted Hughes. Copyright renewed. Reprinted by permission of HarperCollins Publishers, Inc. For Canadian rights, contact Faber & Faber Limited (London).

Katherine Anne Porter, "The Jilting of Granny Weatherall" from *Flowering Judas and Other Stories* by Katherine Anne Porter. Copyright © 1930 and renewed 1958 by Katherine Anne Porter. Reprinted by permission of Harcourt Brace & Company.

Dick Pothier and Thomas J. Gibbons, Jr., "A Woman's Wintry Death Leads to a Long-Dead Friend" from *Philadelphia Inquirer,* January 30, 1987. No portion of this text may be reprinted without permission of the publisher.

Ezra Pound, "In a Station of the Metro," "Canto LXXVI," and "The River-Merchant's Wife: A Letter" from *Personae*. Copyright © 1926 by Ezra Pound. Reprinted by permission of New Directions Publishing Corp.

Anna Quindlen, "Error Stage Left" from *New York Times*. No portion of this text may be reprinted without permission.

Dudley Randall, "Ballad of Birmingham." Copyright © 1969 by and reprinted by permission of Dudley Randall.

John Crowe Ransom, "Bells for John Whiteside's Daughter" from *Selected Poems* by John Crowe Ransom. Copyright © 1924 by Alfred A. Knopf, Inc. and renewed 1952 by John Crowe Ransom. Reprinted by permission of the publisher.

Henry Reed, "Naming of Parts." Copyright © 1946 by Henry Reed. Reprinted by permission of Literary Executor of the Estate of Henry Reed, John Tydemann.

Adrienne Rich, "A Woman Mourned by Daughters," "Aunt Jennifer's Tigers," "Diving into the Wreck," "Living in Sin" and "The Roofwalker" reprinted from *The Fact of a Doorframe: Poems Selected and New, 1950–1984* by Adrienne Rich. Copyright © 1984 by Adrienne Rich. Copyright © 1975, 1978 by W. W. Norton & Company, Inc. Copyright © 1981 by Adrienne Rich. Reprinted by permission of the author and W. W. Norton & Company, Inc.

Alberto Alvaro Ríos, "The Secret Lion" from *The Uguana Killer: Twelve Stories of the Heart* by Alberto Alvaro Ríos. Copyright © 1984 by Alberto Alvaro Ríos. Reprinted by permission of Lewis & Clark College. "Nani" (1982) from *Whispering to Fool the Wind*. Reprinted by permission of the author.

Edward Arlington Robinson, "Miniver Cheevy," "Mr. Flood's Party" and "Richard Cory" from *Collected Poems of Edward Arlington Robinson*. Copyright © 1921 by Edward Arlington Robinson, renewed 1949 by Ruth Nivision. No portion of this text may be reprinted without permission of Macmillan Publishing Company.

Theodore Roethke, "I Knew a Woman," copyright © 1954 by Theodore Roethke. "My Papa's Waltz," copyright © 1942 by Hearst Magazines, Inc. "Night Crow," copyright © 1944 by Saturday Review Association, Inc. "The Waking," copyright © 1953 by Theodore Roethke. From *The Collected Poems of Theodore Roethke* by Theodore Roethke. Used by permission of Doubleday, a division of Bantam Doubleday Dell Publishing Group, Inc.

Jim Sagel, "Baca Grande" from *Hispanics in the U.S.: An Anthology of Creative Literature,* Vol. 2, 1982. Reprinted by permission of Bilingual Press/Editorial Bilingüe (Arizona State University, Tempe, AZ).

Sonia Sanchez, "On Passing thru Morgantown, Pa." from *Homegirls and Handgrenades* by Sonia Sanchez. Copyright © 1984 by and reprinted by permission of Sonia Sanchez. "right on: white america" from *We Are BadddDDD People* by Sonia Sanchez. Copyright © 1970 by Sonia Sanchez. Reprinted by permission. No

Stevie Smith, "Not Waving But Drowning" from *Collected Poems of Stevie Smith.* Copyright © 1972 by Stevie Smith. Reprinted by permission of New Directions Publishing Corp.

Gary Snyder, "Some Good Things to Be Said for the Iron Age." Copyright © 1970 by Gary Snyder. No portion of this text may be reprinted without permission of the author.

Cathy Song, "Lost Sister" from *Picture Bride* by Cathy Song. Copyright © 1983. Reprinted by permission of Yale University Press.

Sophocles, *Antigone,* from *The Antigone of Sophocles: An English Version* translated by Dudley Fitts and Robert Fitzgerald. Copyright © 1939 by Harcourt Brace Jovanovich, Inc. Reprinted by permission of the publisher. *Oedipus the King,* translated by Thomas Gould. Copyright © 1970 by Thomas Gould. Reprinted by permission of Thomas Gould.

Gary Soto, "History" from *The Elements of San Joaquin* by Gary Soto. Published by University of Pittsburgh Press. No portion of this text may be reprinted without permission of the author. "Black Hair" from *Black Hair* by Gary Soto. Copyright © 1985 by Gary Soto. Published by University of Pittsburgh Press. No portion of this text may be reprinted without permission of Gary Soto.

Wole Soyinka, "Telephone Conversation" and "Future Plans" from *A Shuttle in the Crypt.* No portion of this text may be reprinted without permission of Farrar, Straus, & Giroux, Inc.

Barry Spacks, "Finding a Yiddish Paper on the Riverside Line" from *Imaging a Unicorn* by Barry Spacks. Copyright © 1978 by and reprinted by permission of The University of Georgia Press.

Bruce Springsteen, "My Hometown" (1984). Reprinted by permission of John Landau Management. No portion of this text may be reproduced without also acquiring permission from Columbia Records, Inc.

William Stafford, "For the Grave of Daniel Boone" from *Stories That Could Be True: New and Collected Poems* by William Stafford. Copyright © 1947 and 1966 by William Stafford. Reprinted by permission of William Stafford. "Traveling through the Dark" from *Stories That Could Be True: New and Collected Poems* by William Stafford. Copyright © 1960 and 1977 by William Stafford. Reprinted by permission of William Stafford.

George Stavros, "An Interview with Gwendolyn Brooks" from *Contemporary Literature,* Volume 11, Number 1 (Winter 1970): 1–20. Reprinted by permission of the University of Wisconsin Press.

Dona Stein, "Putting Mother By" from *Ploughshares and Children of the Mafiosi,* 1977. Reprinted by permission of the author.

John Steinbeck, "The Chrysanthemums" from *The Long Valley* by John Steinbeck. Copyright © 1937, renewed © 1965 by John Steinbeck. No portion of this text may be reprinted without permission of Viking Penguin, a division of Penguin Books USA, Inc.

Wallace Stevens, "Anecdote of the Jar," "Disillusionment of Ten o'clock," and "The Emperor of Ice-Cream" from *The Collected Poems of Wallace Stevens* by Wallace Stevens. Copyright © 1923 and renewed 1951 by Wallace Stevens. No portion of this text may be reprinted without permission of Alfred A. Knopf, Inc.

Mark Strand, excerpt from "Pot Roast" from *Selected Poems* by Mark Strand. Copyright © 1979, 1980 by Mark Strand. No portion of this text may be reproduced without permission of Alfred A. Knopf, Inc.

Andrew Suknaski, "The Bitter Word" from *Wood Mountain Poems* by Andrew Suknaski. Copyright © 1976 by and reprinted by permission of Andrew Suknaski.

May Swenson, "Women" from *Iconographs,* copyright © 1970. Used with permission of the Literary Estate of May Swenson, C/O R. Knudson, Sea Cliffs, NY.

Amy Tan, "Two Kinds" from *The Joy Luck Club* by Amy Tan. Copyright © 1989 by Amy Tan. Reprinted by permission of the Putnam Publishing Group.

Dylan Thomas, "Do Not Go Gentle into That Good Night," "Fern Hill" and "The Hand That Signed the Paper" from *Poems of Dylan Thomas* by Dylan Thomas. Copyright © 1945 by the Trustees for the Copyrights of Dylan Thomas, 1952 by Dylan Thomas. Reprinted by permission of New Directions Publishing Corporation (in the U.S.). For Canadian rights, contact David Higham Associates.

James Thurber, "The Catbird Seat" from *The Thurber Carnival* by James Thurber. Copyright © 1945 by James Thurber. Copyright © 1973 by Helen W. Thurber and Rosemary Thurber. Reprinted by permission of Rosemary A. Thurber, Executrix.

Mike Tierce and John Michael Crafton, "Connie's Tambourine Man: A New Reading of Arnold Friend" from *Studies in Short Fiction,* 22 (1985): 219–224. Copyright © 1985 by Newberry College. Reprinted by permission.

Jean Toomer, "Reapers" from *Cane* by Jean Toomer. Copyright © 1923 by Boni & Liveright. Copyright © renewed 1921 by Jean Toomer. No portion of this text may be reprinted without permission of Liveright Publishing Corporation.

Anne Tyler, "Teenage Wasteland" from *Seventeen Magazine,* November 1983. Copyright © 1983 by Anne Tyler. Reprinted by permission of Russell & Volkening as agents for the author.

John Updike, "A & P" from *Pigeon Feathers and Other Stories* by John Updike. Copyright © 1962 by John Updike. Reprinted by permission of Alfred A. Knopf, Inc. Originally appeared in *The New Yorker.* "Ex-Basketball Player" from *The Carpentered Hen and Other Tame Creatures* by John Updike. Copyright © 1982 by John Updike. Reprinted by permission of Alfred A. Knopf, Inc.

Luisa Valenzuela, "All about Suicide," translated by Helen Lane. Copyright © 1967.

Ed Vega, "The Barbosa Express" from *Mendoza's Dream.* Reprinted by permission of the publisher (Houston: Arte Publico Press—University of Houston, 1987).

Diane Wakoski, "Sleep," copyright © 1966. No portion of this text may be reprinted without permission.

Derek Walcott, "Sea Grapes" from *Sea Grapes* by Derek Walcott. Copyright © 1976 by Derek Walcott. No portion of this text may be reprinted without permission of Farrar, Straus, & Giroux, Inc.

Alice Walker, "Everyday Use" from *In Love & Trouble: Stories of Black Women,* copyright © 1973 by Alice Walker, reprinted by permission of Harcourt Brace & Company. "Revolutionary Petunias" from *Revolutionary Petunias & Other Poems,* copyright © 1972 by Alice Walker, reprinted by permission of Harcourt Brace & Company.

Margaret Walker, "Lineage" from *This is My Sensory* by Margaret Walker. Copyright © 1942 by and reprinted by permission of Margaret Walker.

Joyce M. Wegs, "Don't You Know Who I Am? The Grotesque in Oates's 'Where Are You Going, Where Have You Been?'" from *The Journal of Narrative Techniques,* Vol. 5, 1975. Copyright © by and reprinted by permission of Joyce M. Wegs.

James Welch, "Going to Remake This World" and "The Man from Washington" from *Riding the Earthboy 40* by James Welch, 1976. No portion of this text may be reprinted without permission of the author, C/O Elaine Markson Agency.

Eudora Welty, "A Worn Path" from *A Curtain of Green and Other Stories* by Eudora Welty. Copyright © 1941 and renewed 1961 by Eudora Welty. Reprinted by permission of Harcourt Brace Jovanovich, Inc.

Richard Wilbur, "A Sketch" from *The Mind Reader* by Richard Wilbur. Copyright © 1975 by Richard Wilbur. Reprinted by permission of Harcourt Brace & Company. "For the Student Strikers" from *The Mind Reader.* Copyright © 1970 by Richard Wilbur. Reprinted by permission of Harcourt Brace & Company. "Sleepless at Crown Point" from *The Mind Reader* by Richard Wilbur. Copyright © 1973 by Richard Wilbur. Reprinted by permission of Harcourt Brace & Company. "Museum Piece" from *Ceremony and Other Poems* by

Richard Wilbur. Copyright © 1950 and renewed 1978 by Richard Wilbur. Reprinted by permission of Harcourt Brace & Company.

Dakin Williams and Shepherd Meade, excerpt from *Tennessee Williams: An Intimate Biography.* No portion of this text may be reprinted without permission of Arbor House (NY).

Edwina Dakin Williams, *Remember Me to Tom,* 1963. Published by the Putnam Publishing Group. No portion of this text may be reprinted without permission.

Tennessee Williams, *The Glass Menagerie.* Copyright © 1945 by Tennessee Williams and Edwina D. Williams and renewed 1973 by Tennessee Williams. Reprinted by permission of Random House, Inc. Excerpt from *Tennessee Williams: Memoirs.* Copyright © 1975. No portion of this text may be reprinted without permission of Doubleday, a division of Bantam Doubleday Dell Publishing Group, Inc. "Portrait of a Girl in Glass" from *Collected Stories,* 1985. No portion of this text may be reprinted without permission of New Directions Publishing Corp.

William Carlos Williams, "This Is Just to Say," "The Great Figure," "Red Wheelbarrow" and "Spring and All" from *Collected Poems: 1909–1939,* Volume I. Copyright © 1938 by New Directions Publishing Corp. Reprinted by permission of New Directions Publishing Corp. "The Dance" from *Collected Poems, 1909–1939,* Volume I. Copyright © 1944, 1945 by New Directions Publishing Corp. Reprinted by permission of New Directions Publishing Corp.

August Wilson, *Fences,* 1986. No portion of this text may be reprinted without permission of Penguin USA, Inc.

James Wright, "A Blessing" from *Collected Poems* by James Wright. Copyright © 1961 by James Wright. No portion of this text may be reprinted without permission of The University Press of New England. "Autumn Begins in Martins Ferry, Ohio" from *The Branch Will Not Break* by James Wright. Copyright © 1963 by James Wright. No portion of this text may be reprinted without permission of The University Press of New England.

Richard Wright, "Big Black Good Man." No portion of this text may be reprinted without permission of Chatto & Windus. "Hokku Poems" from *Richard Wright Reader,* edited by Ellen Wright and Michel Fabre. Copyright © 1978 by Ellen Wright and Michel Fabre. Reprinted by permission of HarperCollins Publishers, Inc.

Hisaye Yamamoto, "Seventeen Syllables" from *Seventeen Syllables and Other Stories* by Hisaye Yamamoto. Copyright © 1988. Reprinted by permission of the author and of Kitchen Table: Women of Color Press, Box 40–4920, Brooklyn, NY 11240.

William Butler Yeats, "Sailing to Byzantium" from *The Poems of W. B. Yeats: A New Edition,* edited by Richard J. Finneran. Copyright © 1928 by Macmillan Publishing Company, renewed 1956 by Bertha Georgie Yeats. Reprinted by permission of Macmillan Publishing Company. "The Second Coming" from *The Poems of W. B. Yeats: A New Edition,* edited by Richard J. Finneran. Copyright © 1924 by Macmillan Publishing Company, renewed 1952 by Bertha Georgie Yeats. Reprinted by permission of Macmillan Publishing Company. "Leda and the Swan" from *The Poems of W. B. Yeats: A New Edition,* edited by Richard J. Finneran. Copyright © 1928 by Macmillan Publishing Company, renewed © 1956 by Georgie Yeats. Reprinted with the permission of Simon & Schuster. For Canadian rights, contact A. P. Watt, Limited, London. "An Irish Airman Foresees His Death," "The Lake Isle of Innisfree" and "The Rose of Peace" from *The Poems of W. B. Yeats: A New Edition,* edited by Richard J. Finneran (New York: Macmillan, 1983). Reprinted with the permission of Simon & Schuster. "Crazy Jane Talks with the Bishop" from *The Poems of W. B. Yeats: A New Edition,* edited by Richard J. Finneran. Copyright

Photo Credits

Index of Authors, Titles, and First Lines of Poetry

INDEX OF KEY TERMS